California

PROBATE CODE

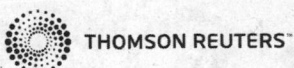
THOMSON REUTERS™

Mt #41769476

ISBN: 978–0–314–67949–9

This publication was created to provide you with accurate and authoritative information concerning the subject matter covered; however, this publication was not necessarily prepared by persons licensed to practice law in a particular jurisdiction. The publisher is not engaged in rendering legal or other professional advice and this publication is not a substitute for the advice of an attorney. If you require legal or other expert advice, you should seek the services of a competent attorney or other professional.

PREFACE

California Probate Code features the complete text of the California Probate Code, along with selected sections from other codes, in order to provide broad coverage of California statutory law as it relates to probate matters. It includes both cross references and Law Revision Commission Comments, to provide a better understanding of the subject matter. It also includes court rules and regulations related to probate law, to give an overview of the subject matter outside of statutory law.

WHAT'S NEW

Includes all laws through Ch. 893 of the 2016 portion of the 2015–2016 Regular Session, Ch. 8 of the 2015–2016 Second Extraordinary Session, and all propositions voted on at the June 7 and Nov. 8, 2016 elections.

Court rules reflect all amendments available through October 15, 2016.

Regulations reflect all changes through Register 2016, No. 43 (Oct. 21, 2016).

Election Results—June 7, 2016 Election

Propositions	Results
50. Suspension of Legislators. Legislative Constitutional Amendment	Approved

Election Results—November 8, 2016 Election

Semi-Official results pending count of unprocessed ballots.
Official results to be posted at www.sos.ca.gov.

Propositions	Results
51. School Bonds. Funding for K–12 School and Community College Facilities. Initiative Statute.	Approved
52. Medi–Cal Hospital Fee Program. Initiative Constitutional Amendment and Statute.	Approved
53. Revenue Bonds. Statewide Voter Approval. Initiative Constitutional Amendment.	Rejected
54. Legislature. Legislation and Proceedings. Initiative Constitutional Amendment and Statute.	Approved
55. Tax Extension to Fund Education and Healthcare. Initiative Constitutional Amendment.	Approved
56. Cigarette Tax to Fund Healthcare, Tobacco Use Prevention, Research, and Law Enforcement. Initiative Constitutional Amendment and Statute.	Approved
57. Criminal Sentences. Parole. Juvenile Criminal Proceedings and Sentencing. Initiative Constitutional Amendment and Statute.	Approved
58. English Proficiency. Multilingual Education. Initiative Statute.	Approved
59. Corporations. Political Spending. Federal Constitutional Protections. Legislative Advisory Question.	Approved
60. Adult Films. Condoms. Health Requirements. Initiative Statute.	Rejected
61. State Prescription Drug Purchases. Pricing Standards. Initiative Statute.	Rejected
62. Death Penalty. Initiative Statute.	Rejected
63. Firearms. Ammunition Sales. Initiative Statute.	Approved
64. Marijuana Legalization. Initiative Statute.	Approved
65. Carryout Bags. Charges. Initiative Statute.	Rejected
66. Death Penalty. Procedures. Initiative Statute.	Approved
67. Ban on Single-Use Plastic Bags. Referendum.	Approved

PREFACE

ADDITIONAL INFORMATION

All California legislative enactments in 2016 are effective January 1, 2017, unless indicated otherwise. Additions or changes affected by 2016 legislation are indicated by underlining; deletions are indicated by asterisks. In court rules, additions or changes are indicated by underlining; deletions are indicated by strikethroughs.

Codified legislation which is subject to a governor's veto is followed by an italicized note indicating that fact. For the text of the message, please consult the Historical and Statutory Notes for the provision in *West's Annotated California Codes* or the material pertaining to the legislation affecting the provision in *West's California Legislative Service*.

To facilitate the inclusion of applicable provisions in one portable volume, repealed regulations and court rules are omitted.

CONTACT US

For additional information or research assistance call the Reference Attorneys at 1-800-REF-ATTY (1-800-733-2889). Contact our U.S. legal editorial department directly with your question and suggestions by e-mail at editors.us-legal@tr.com.

Thank you for subscribing to this product. Should you have any questions regarding this product, please contact Customer Service at 1-800-328-4880 or by fax at 1-800-340-9378. If you would like to inquire about related publications, or to place an order, please contact us at 1-888-728-7677 or visit us at legalsolutions.thomsonreuters.com.

THE PUBLISHER

December 2016

TABLE OF SECTIONS AFFECTED

This table indicates sections affected by 2016 legislation

Probate Code

TABLE OF SECTIONS AFFECTED

TABLE OF CONTENTS

PROBATE CODE

IX

TABLE OF CONTENTS

TABLE OF CONTENTS

RELATED LAWS
SELECT PROVISIONS FROM
CODE OF CIVIL PROCEDURE

SELECT PROVISIONS FROM THE
REVENUE AND TAXATION CODE

SELECT PROVISIONS FROM
THE WELFARE AND INSTITUTIONS CODE

CALIFORNIA RULES OF COURT
TITLE 7
PROBATE RULES

TITLE 10
JUDICIAL ADMINISTRATION RULES

STANDARDS OF JUDICIAL ADMINISTRATION

CALIFORNIA CODE OF REGULATIONS

INDEX
(Page I–1)

PROBATE CODE

Division 1

PRELIMINARY PROVISIONS AND DEFINITIONS

Law Revision Commission Comments

1990 Enactment

This division supersedes Division 1 (commencing with Section 1) of the repealed Probate Code. Division 1 of the repealed Probate Code was enacted upon recommendation of the California Law Revision Commission. See Tentative Recommendation Relating to Wills and Intestate Succession, 16 Cal.L.Revision Comm'n Reports 2301 (1982). See also Report of Senate Committee on Judiciary on Assembly Bills 25 and 68, 17 Cal.L.Revision Comm'n Reports 867–68 (1984). Division 1 was thereafter revised upon recommendations of the California Law Revision Commission. See Recommendation Relating to Revision of Wills and Intestate Succession Law, 17 Cal.L.Revision Comm'n Reports 537 (1984); Communication of Law Revision Commission Concerning Assembly Bill 2290, 18 Cal.L.Revision Comm'n Reports 77, 78–79 (1986); Recommendation Relating to Preliminary Provisions and Definitions of the Probate Code, 18 Cal.L.Revision Comm'n Reports 1807 (1986); Recommendation Proposing the Trust Law, 18 Cal.L.Revision Comm'n Reports 501, 779–80 (1986); Communication from California Law Revision Commission Concerning Assembly Bill 2625, 18 Cal.L.Revision Comm'n Reports 1743, 1745 (1986); Communication from California Law Revision Commission Concerning Assembly Bill 2652, 18 Cal.L.Revision Comm'n Reports 1763, 1765–66 (1986); Comments to Conforming Revisions and Repeals, 19 Cal.L.Revision Comm'n Reports 391, 393–94 (1988); Comments to Conforming Revisions and Repeals, 19 Cal.L.Revision Comm'n Reports 1031, 1041 (1988); Communication from the California Law Revision Commission Concerning Assembly Bill 2841, 19 Cal.L.Revision Comm'n Reports 1201, 1207–09 (1988). [20 Cal.L.Rev.Comm.Reports 1001 (1990)].

Part 1

PRELIMINARY PROVISIONS

Cross References

Application of old and new law, see Probate Code § 3.

§ 1. Title of code

This code shall be known as the Probate Code. *(Stats. 1990, c. 79 (A.B.759), § 14, operative July 1, 1991.)*

Law Revision Commission Comments

1990 Enactment

Section 1 continues Section 1 of the repealed Probate Code without change.

Background on Section 1 of Repealed Code

Section 1 was added by 1983 Cal.Stat. ch. 842 § 21. The section continued former Probate Code Section 1 (repealed by 1983 Cal.Stat. ch. 842 § 17). For background on the provisions of this division, see the Comment to this division under the division heading. [20 Cal.L.Rev.Comm.Reports 1001 (1990)].

§ 2. Continuation of existing statutes; construction as provision of uniform act

(a) A provision of this code, insofar as it is substantially the same as a previously existing provision relating to the same subject matter, shall be construed as a restatement and continuation thereof and not as a new enactment.

(b) A provision of this code, insofar as it is the same in substance as a provision of a uniform act, shall be so construed as to effectuate the general purpose to make uniform the law in those states which enact that provision. *(Stats.1990, c. 79 (A.B.759), § 14, operative July 1, 1991.)*

Law Revision Commission Comments

1995 [Revised Comment]

Section 2 continues Section 2 of the repealed Probate Code without change. See also Gov't Code §§ 9604 (reference made in statute, charter, or ordinance to provisions of one statute carried into another statute under circumstances in which they are required to be construed as restatements and continuations and not as new enactments), 9605 (construction of amended statutory provision).

Some of the provisions of this code are the same as or similar to provisions of uniform acts. Subdivision (b) provides a rule for interpretation of these provisions. Many of the provisions of this code are drawn from the Uniform Probate Code (1987). Some provisions are drawn from other uniform acts:

Sections 220–224—Uniform Simultaneous Death Act (1953)

Sections 260–288—Uniform Disclaimer of Transfers by Will, Intestacy or Appointment Act (1978)

Sections 260–288—Uniform Disclaimer of Transfers Under Nontestamentary Instrument Act (1978)

Sections 3900–3925—Uniform Transfers to Minors Act (1983)

Sections 4001, 4124–4127, 4206, 4304–4305—Uniform Durable Power of Attorney Act

Sections 4400–4465—Uniform Statutory Form Power of Attorney Act

Sections 6300–6303—Uniform Testamentary Additions to Trusts Act (1960)

Sections 6380–6390—Uniform International Wills Act (1977). See also Section 6387 (need for uniform interpretation of Uniform International Wills Act)

Sections 16002(a), 16003, 16045–16054—Uniform Prudent Investor Act (1994)

Sections 16200–16249—Uniform Trustees' Powers Act (1964)

Sections 16300–16313—Revised Uniform Principal and Income Act (1962)

A number of terms and phrases are used in the Comments to the sections of the new Probate Code (including the "Background" portion of each Comment) to indicate the sources of the new provisions and to describe how they compare with prior law. The portion of the Comment giving the background on each section of the repealed code may also use terms and phrases to indicate the source or sources of the repealed section and to describe how the repealed section compared with the prior law.

The following discussion is intended to provide guidance in interpreting the terminology most commonly used in the Comments.

(1) *Continues without change.* A new provision "continues" a former provision "without change" if the two provisions are identical or nearly so. In some cases, there may be insignificant technical differences, such as where punctuation is changed without a change in meaning. Some Comments may describe the relationship by simply stating that a new provision "continues" or is "the same as" a former provision of the repealed Probate Code, or is "the same as" a provision of the Uniform Probate Code or another uniform act.

(2) *Continues without substantive change.* A new provision "continues" a former provision "without substantive change" if the substantive law remains the same but the language differs to an insignificant degree.

(3) *Restates without substantive change.* A new provision "restates" a former provision "without substantive change" if the substantive law remains the same but the language differs to a significant degree. Some Comments may describe the new provision as being the "same in substance."

(4) *Exceptions, additions, omissions.* If part of a former provision is "continued" or "restated," the Comment may say that the former provision is continued or restated but also note the specific differences as "exceptions to," "additions to," or "omissions from" the former provision.

(5) *Generalizes, broadens, restates in general terms.* A new provision may be described as "generalizing," "broadening," or "restating in general terms" a provision of prior law. This description means that a limited rule has been expanded to cover a broader class of cases.

(6) *Supersedes, replaces.* A provision "supersedes" or "replaces" a former provision if the new provision deals with the same subject as the former provision but treats it in a significantly different manner.

(7) *New.* A provision is described as "new" where it has no direct source in prior statutes.

(8) *Drawn from, similar to, consistent with.* A variety of terms is used to indicate a source for a new provision, typically a source other than California statutes. For example, a provision may be "drawn from" a uniform act, model code, Restatement, or the statutes of another state. In such cases, it may be useful to consult any available commentary or interpretation of the source from which the new provision is drawn for background information.

(9) *Codifies.* A Comment may state that a new provision "codifies" a case-law rule that has not previously been enacted into statutory law. A provision may also be described as codifying a Restatement rule, which may or may not represent previously existing common law in California.

(10) *Makes clear, clarifies.* A new provision may be described as "making clear" a particular rule or "clarifying" a rule as a way of emphasizing the rule, particularly if the situation under prior law was doubtful or contradictory.

(11) *Statement in Comment that section is "comparable" to another section.* A Comment may state that a provision is "comparable" to another provision. If the Comment to a section notes that another section is "comparable" that does not mean that the other section is the same or substantially the same. The statement is included in the Comment so that the statute user is alerted to the other section and can review the cases under that section for possible use in interpreting the section containing the statement in the Comment. [24 Cal.L.Rev.Comm. Reports 323 (1994); 25 Cal.L.Rev.Comm. Reports 673 (1995)].

1999 Revised Comment

Section 2 continues Section 2 of the repealed Probate Code without change. See also Gov't Code §§ 9604 (reference made in statute, charter, or ordinance to provisions of one statute carried into another statute under circumstances in which they are required to be construed as restatements and continuations and not as new enactments), 9605 (construction of amended statutory provision).

Some of the provisions of this code are the same as or similar to provisions of uniform acts. Subdivision (b) provides a rule for interpretation of these provisions. Many of the provisions of this code are drawn from the Uniform Probate Code (1987). Some provisions are drawn from other uniform acts:

Sections 220–224 C Uniform Simultaneous Death Act (1953)

Sections 260–288 C Uniform Disclaimer of Transfers by Will, Intestacy or Appointment Act (1978)

Sections 260–288 C Uniform Disclaimer of Transfers Under Nontestamentary Instrument Act (1978)

Sections 3900–3925 C Uniform Transfers to Minors Act (1983)

Sections 4001, 4124–4127, 4206, 4304–4305 C Uniform Durable Power of Attorney Act

Sections 4400–4465 C Uniform Statutory Form Power of Attorney Act

Sections 4670–4743 C Uniform Health–Care Decisions Act (1993)

Sections 6300–6303 C Uniform Testamentary Additions to Trusts Act (1960)

Sections 6380–6390 C Uniform International Wills Act (1977). See also Section 6387 (need for uniform interpretation of Uniform International Wills Act)

Sections 16002(a), 16003, 16045–16054 C Uniform Prudent Investor Act (1994)

Sections 16200–16249 C Uniform Trustees' Powers Act (1964)

Sections 16300–16313 C Revised Uniform Principal and Income Act (1962)

A number of terms and phrases are used in the Comments to the sections of the new Probate Code (including the "Background" portion of each Comment) to indicate the sources of the new provisions and to describe how they compare with prior law. The portion of the Comment giving the background on each section of the repealed code may also use terms and phrases to indicate the source or sources of the repealed section and to describe how the repealed section compared with the prior law.

The following discussion is intended to provide guidance in interpreting the terminology most commonly used in the Comments.

(1) *Continues without change.* A new provision "continues" a former provision "without change" if the two provisions are identical or nearly so. In some cases, there may be insignificant technical differences, such as where punctuation is changed without a change in meaning. Some Comments may describe the relationship by simply stating that a new provision "continues" or is "the same as" a former provision of the repealed Probate Code, or is "the same as" a provision of the Uniform Probate Code or another uniform act.

(2) *Continues without substantive change.* A new provision "continues" a former provision "without substantive change" if the substantive law remains the same but the language differs to an insignificant degree.

(3) *Restates without substantive change.* A new provision "restates" a former provision "without substantive change" if the substantive law remains the same but the language differs to a significant degree. Some Comments may describe the new provision as being the "same in substance."

(4) *Exceptions, additions, omissions.* If part of a former provision is "continued" or "restated," the Comment may say that the former provision is continued or restated but also note the specific differences as "exceptions to," "additions to," or "omissions from" the former provision.

(5) *Generalizes, broadens, restates in general terms.* A new provision may be described as "generalizing," "broadening," or "restating in general terms" a provision of prior law. This description means that a limited rule has been expanded to cover a broader class of cases.

(6) *Supersedes, replaces.* A provision "supersedes" or "replaces" a former provision if the new provision deals with the same subject as the former provision but treats it in a significantly different manner.

(7) *New.* A provision is described as "new" where it has no direct source in prior statutes.

(8) *Drawn from, similar to, consistent with.* A variety of terms is used to indicate a source for a new provision, typically a source other than California statutes. For example, a provision may be "drawn from" a uniform act, model code, Restatement, or the statutes of another state. In such cases, it may be useful to consult any available commentary or interpretation of the source from which the new provision is drawn for background information.

(9) *Codifies.* A Comment may state that a new provision "codifies" a case-law rule that has not previously been enacted into statutory law. A provision may also be described as codifying a Restatement rule, which may or may not represent previously existing common law in California.

(10) *Makes clear, clarifies.* A new provision may be described as "making clear" a particular rule or "clarifying" a rule as a way of emphasizing the rule, particularly if the situation under prior law was doubtful or contradictory.

(11) *Statement in Comment that section is "comparable" to another section.* A Comment may state that a provision is "comparable" to another provision. If the Comment to a section notes that another section is "comparable" that does not mean that the other section is the same or substantially the same. The statement is included in the Comment so that the statute user is alerted to the other section and can review the cases under that section for possible use in interpreting the section containing the statement in the Comment. [29 Cal.L.Rev.Comm. Reports 1 (1999)].

Background on Section 2 of Repealed Code

Section 2 was added by 1983 Cal.Stat. ch. 842 § 21 and was amended by 1987 Cal.Stat. ch. 923 § 3. Subdivision (a) of Section 2 as added in 1983 continued the substance of former Probate Code Section 2 (repealed by 1983 Cal.Stat. ch. 842 § 17). Subdivision (b) of Section 2 as added in 1983 was a new provision and recognized that some provisions of the Probate Code are the same in substance as the provisions of the Uniform Probate Code (1987). Section 2 was amended in 1987 to make nonsubstantive revisions in subdivision (a) and to revise subdivision (b) to broaden its scope to cover all uniform acts, not just the Uniform Probate Code. For background on the provisions of this division, see the Comment to this division under the division heading. [20 Cal.L.Rev.Comm.Report 1001 (1990)].

Cross References

California Uniform Transfers to Minors Act, see Probate Code § 3900.

General rules of construction, see Code of Civil Procedure §§ 1858, 1859; Government Code § 9603.

Liberal construction, see Civil Code § 4.

Preference accorded interpretation which gives effect, see Civil Code § 3541.

Reasonableness of interpretation, see Civil Code § 3542.

Repeal of prior laws on same subject, see Civil Code § 20.

Restatements and continuations of statutes, see Government Code § 9604.

Uniform Health Care Decisions Act, see Probate Code § 4670 et seq.

Uniform International Wills Act, see Probate Code § 6380 et seq.

Uniform Principal and Income Act, see Probate Code § 16320 et seq.

Uniform Simultaneous Death Act, see Probate Code § 220 et seq.

Uniform Testamentary Additions to Trusts Acts, see Probate Code § 6300 et seq.

Vested rights, effect of repeal of statutes relating to subjects covered by Code, see Code of Civil Procedure § 18.

§ 3. Change in code; operative date; application of new law; filings; orders; liability for action taken before operative date

(a) As used in this section:

(1) "New law" means either of the following, as the case may be:

(A) The act that enacted this code.

(B) The act that makes a change in this code, whether effectuated by amendment, addition, or repeal of any provision of this code.

(2) "Old law" means the applicable law in effect before the operative date of the new law.

(3) "Operative date" means the operative date of the new law.

(b) This section governs the application of a new law except to the extent otherwise expressly provided in the new law.

(c) Subject to the limitations provided in this section, a new law applies on the operative date to all matters governed by the new law, regardless of whether an event occurred or circumstance existed before, on, or after the operative date, including, but not limited to, creation of a fiduciary relationship, death of a person, commencement of a proceeding, making of an order, or taking of an action.

(d) If a petition, account, report, inventory, appraisal, or other document or paper is filed before the operative date, the contents, execution, and notice thereof are governed by the old law and not by the new law; but any subsequent proceedings taken after the operative date concerning the petition, account, report, inventory, appraisal, or other document or paper, including an objection or response, a hearing, an order, or other matter relating thereto is governed by the new law and not by the old law.

(e) If an order is made before the operative date, including an order appointing a personal representative, guardian, conservator, trustee, probate referee, or any other fiduciary or officer, or any action on an order is taken before the operative date, the validity of the order or action is governed by the old law and not by the new law. Nothing in this subdivision precludes proceedings after the operative date to modify an order made, or alter a course of action commenced, before the operative date to the extent proceedings for modification of an order or alteration of a course of action of that type are otherwise provided by statute.

(f) No personal representative, guardian, conservator, trustee, probate referee, or any other fiduciary, officer, or person is liable for any action taken before the operative date that was proper at the time the action was taken, even though the action would be improper if taken on or after the operative date, and such a person has no duty, as a result of the enactment of the new law, to take any step to alter the course of action or its consequences.

(g) If the new law does not apply to a matter that occurred before the operative date, the old law continues to govern the matter notwithstanding its amendment or repeal by the new law.

(h) If a party shows, and the court determines, that application of a particular provision of the new law or of the old law in the manner required by this section or by the new law would substantially interfere with the effective conduct of the proceedings or the rights of the parties or other interested persons in connection with an event that occurred or circumstance that existed before the operative date, the court may, notwithstanding this section or the new law, apply either the new law or the old law to the extent reasonably necessary to mitigate the substantial interference. *(Stats.1990, c. 79 (A.B.759), § 14, operative July 1, 1991.)*

Law Revision Commission Comments

1990 Enactment

Section 3 provides general transitional rules applicable to changes in the Probate Code. The section continues the substance of Section 3 of the repealed Probate Code with revisions that make clear that the section applies both to the act which enacted the new Probate Code and to any subsequent act which changes the new code, whether the change is effectuated by amendment, addition, or repeal of a provision of the new code.

The rules stated in Section 3 are general provisions that apply absent a special rule stated in the new law. Special rules may defer or accelerate application of the new law despite the general rules stated in Section 3. See subdivision (b).

The general rule prescribed in subdivision (c) is that a new law applies immediately on its operative date to all matters, including pending proceedings. The general rule is qualified by the exceptions listed in subdivision (d) (contents, execution, and notice of papers and documents are governed by the law applicable when the paper or document was filed), subdivision (e) (orders are governed by the law applicable when the order was made, subject to any applicable modification procedures), and subdivision (f) (acts are governed by the law applicable when the act was done).

Where a new law fails to address a matter that occurred before its operative date, subdivision (g) makes clear that old law continues to govern the matter.

Because it is impractical to attempt to deal with all the possible transitional problems that may arise in the application of the new law to various circumstances, subdivision (h) provides a safety-valve that permits the court to vary the application of the new law where there would otherwise be a substantial impairment of procedure or justice. This provision is intended to apply only in the extreme and unusual case, and is not intended to excuse compliance with the basic transitional provisions simply because of minor inconveniences or minor impacts on expectations or other interests.

In addition to governing other substantive provisions, Section 3 also governs itself. It therefore becomes operative on the date the new code becomes operative and applies to provisions enacted and operative before, on, or after that date.

Background on Section 3 of Repealed Code

Section 3 was a new provision added by 1988 Cal.Stat. ch. 1199 § 24.5. For background on the provisions of this division, see the Comment to this division under the division heading. Section 3 was amended by 1989 Cal.Stat. ch. 21 § 1 to make two technical, nonsubstantive corrections in the section: (1) Subdivision (d) was revised to correct an obvious inadvertent error in language, thereby stating more accurately the intent of the subdivision, and (2) subdivision (g) was amended to add "or amendment", thereby making the subdivision complete. See Communication from the California Law Revision Commission Concerning Assembly Bill 156, 20 Cal.L.Revision Comm'n Reports 227, 228 (1990). [20 Cal.L.Rev.Comm.Reports 1001 (1990)].

Cross References

Appointment of personal representative, generally, see Probate Code § 8400 et seq.
Probate referees, appointment and duties, see Probate Code § 400 et seq.

§ 4. Effect of headings

Division, part, chapter, article, and section headings do not in any manner affect the scope, meaning, or intent of the provisions of this code. *(Stats.1990, c. 79 (A.B.759), § 14, operative July 1, 1991.)*

Law Revision Commission Comments

1990 Enactment

Section 4 continues Section 4 of the repealed Probate Code without change.

Background on Section 4 of Repealed Code

Section 4 was added by 1983 Cal.Stat. ch. 842 § 21. The section continued the substance of former Probate Code Section 4 (repealed by 1983 Cal.Stat. ch. 842 § 17). For background on the provisions of this division, see the Comment to this division under the division heading. [20 Cal.L.Rev.Comm.Reports 1001 (1990)].

§ 5. Certified mail; compliance with mailing provisions

If a notice or other communication is required by this code to be mailed by registered mail, the mailing of the notice or other communication by certified mail is deemed to be sufficient compliance with the requirement. *(Stats.1990, c. 79 (A.B.759), § 14, operative July 1, 1991.)*

Law Revision Commission Comments

1990 Enactment

Section 5 continues Section 5 of the repealed Probate Code without substantive change. For general provisions relating to mailing, see Sections 1215–1217.

Background on Section 5 of Repealed Code

Section 5 was added by 1983 Cal.Stat. ch. 842 § 21. The section was the same in substance as former Probate Code Section 5 (repealed by 1983 Cal.Stat. ch. 842 § 17). For background on the provisions of this division, see the Comment to this division under the division heading. [20 Cal.L.Rev.Comm.Reports 1001 (1990)].

Cross References

Notice, mailing, see Probate Code § 1215 et seq.
Notice, posting, see Probate Code § 1230.
Notice, proof of giving notice, see Probate Code § 1260 et seq.
Notice, special notice, see Probate Code § 1250 et seq.
Notice, this code, generally, see Probate Code § 1200 et seq.
Notice mailed to or by State, see Government Code § 8311.
Service of process, generally, see Code of Civil Procedure § 413.10 et seq.
Service of process, mail, see Code of Civil Procedure §§ 415.30, 1012 et seq.
Service of process, personal delivery, see Code of Civil Procedure § 415.10.
Service of process, proof of service, see Code of Civil Procedure § 417.10 et seq.
Service of process, publication, see Code of Civil Procedure § 415.50.

§ 6. Construction of code

Unless the provision or context otherwise requires, the general provisions and rules of construction in this part govern the construction of this code. *(Stats.1990, c. 79 (A.B.759), § 14, operative July 1, 1991.)*

Law Revision Commission Comments

1990 Enactment

Section 6 continues Section 6 of the repealed Probate Code without substantive change. See also the Comment to Section 2.

Background on Section 6 of Repealed Code

Section 6 was added by 1983 Cal.Stat. ch. 842 § 21. The section continued former Probate Code Section 6 (repealed by 1983 Cal.Stat. ch. 842 § 17). For background on the provisions of this division, see the Comment to this division under the division heading. [20 Cal.L.Rev.Comm.Reports 1001 (1990)].

Cross References

General rules for construction to be as prescribed in preliminary provisions of codes, see Government Code § 9603.
Operation of statutes, see Government Code § 9600 et seq.

§ 7. Reference to statutes; amendments and additions

Whenever a reference is made to any portion of this code or to any other law, the reference applies to all amendments and additions heretofore or hereafter made. *(Stats.1990, c. 79 (A.B.759), § 14, operative July 1, 1991.)*

Law Revision Commission Comments

1990 Enactment

Section 7 continues Section 7 of the repealed Probate Code without change. The rule stated in Section 7 applies unless the provision or context otherwise requires. See Section 6. See also Gov't Code § 9604 (reference made in statute, charter, or ordinance to provisions of one statute carried into another statute under circumstances in which they are required to be construed as restatements and continuations and not as new enactments).

Background on Section 7 of Repealed Code

Section 7 was added by 1983 Cal.Stat. ch. 842 § 21. The section continued former Probate Code Section 7 (repealed by 1983 Cal.Stat. ch. 842 § 17). For background on the provisions of this division, see the Comment to this division under the division heading. [20 Cal.L.Rev.Comm.Reports 1001 (1990)].

§ 8. Definitions

Unless otherwise expressly stated:

(a) "Division" means a division of this code.

(b) "Part" means a part of the division in which that term occurs.

(c) "Chapter" means a chapter of the division or part, as the case may be, in which that term occurs.

(d) "Article" means an article of the chapter in which that term occurs.

(e) "Section" means a section of this code.

(f) "Subdivision" means a subdivision of the section in which that term occurs.

(g) "Paragraph" means a paragraph of the subdivision in which that term occurs.

(h) "Subparagraph" means a subparagraph of the paragraph in which that term occurs. *(Stats.1990, c. 79 (A.B.759), § 14, operative July 1, 1991.)*

Law Revision Commission Comments

1990 Enactment

Section 8 continues Section 8 of the repealed Probate Code without change.

Background on Section 8 of Repealed Code

Section 8 was added by 1983 Cal.Stat. ch. 842 § 21 and was amended by 1987 Cal.Stat. ch. 923 § 4. The section as added in 1983 continued former Probate Code Section 8 (repealed by 1983 Cal.Stat. ch. 842 § 17). The 1987 amendment added subdivision (h) defining "subparagraph." For background on the provisions of this division, see the Comment to this division under the division heading. [20 Cal.L.Rev.Comm.Reports 1001 (1990)].

§ 9. Tense

The present tense includes the past and future tenses, and the future, the present. *(Stats.1990, c. 79 (A.B.759), § 14, operative July 1, 1991.)*

Law Revision Commission Comments

1990 Enactment

Section 9 continues Section 9 of the repealed Probate Code without change.

Background on Section 9 of Repealed Code

Section 9 was added by 1983 Cal.Stat. ch. 842 § 21. The section continued former Probate Code Section 9 (repealed by 1983 Cal.Stat. ch. 842 § 17). For background on the provisions of this division, see the Comment to this division under the division heading. [20 Cal.L.Rev.Comm.Reports 1001 (1990)].

§ 10. Numbers; singular and plural

The singular number includes the plural, and the plural, the singular. *(Stats.1990, c. 79 (A.B.759), § 14, operative July 1, 1991.)*

Law Revision Commission Comments

1990 Enactment

Section 10 continues Section 10 of the repealed Probate Code without change.

Background on Section 10 of Repealed Code

Section 10 was added by 1983 Cal.Stat. ch. 842 § 21. The section continued former Probate Code Section 10 (repealed by 1983 Cal.Stat. ch. 842 § 17). For background on the provisions of this division, see the Comment to this division under the division heading. [20 Cal.L.Rev.Comm.Reports 1001 (1990)].

§ 11. Severability

If any provision or clause of this code or application thereof to any person or circumstances is held invalid, the invalidity does not affect other provisions or applications of the code which can be given effect without the invalid provision or application, and to this end the provisions of this code are severable. *(Stats.1990, c. 79 (A.B.759), § 14, operative July 1, 1991.)*

Law Revision Commission Comments

1990 Enactment

Section 11 continues Section 11 of the repealed Probate Code without change.

Background on Section 11 of Repealed Code

Section 11 was added by 1983 Cal.Stat. ch. 842 § 21. The section continued former Probate Code Section 11 (repealed by 1983 Cal.Stat. ch. 842 § 17). For background on the provisions of this division, see the Comment to this division under the division heading. [20 Cal.L.Rev.Comm.Reports 1001 (1990)].

§ 12. Meaning of "shall" and "may"

"Shall" is mandatory and "may" is permissive. *(Stats.1990, c. 79 (A.B.759), § 14, operative July 1, 1991.)*

Law Revision Commission Comments

1990 Enactment

Section 12 continues Section 12 of the repealed Probate Code without change.

Background on Section 12 of Repealed Code

Section 12 was a new provision added by 1983 Cal.Stat. ch. 842 § 21. For background on the provisions of this division, see the Comment to this division under the division heading. [20 Cal.L.Rev.Comm.Reports 1001 (1990)].

§ 13. Kinship; lineal and collateral; calculation of degree

(a) The degree of kinship or consanguinity between two persons is determined by counting the number of generations separating those persons, pursuant to subdivision (b) or (c). Each generation is called a degree.

(b) Lineal kinship or consanguinity is the relationship between two persons, one of whom is a direct descendant of the other. The degree of kinship between those persons is determined by counting the generations separating the first person from the second person. In counting the generations, the first person is excluded and the second person is included. For example, parent and child are related in the first degree of lineal kinship or consanguinity, grandchild and grandparent are related in the second degree, and great-grandchild and great-grandparent are related in the third degree.

(c) Collateral kinship or consanguinity is the relationship between two people who spring from a common ancestor, but neither person is the direct descendent of the other. The degree of kinship is determined by counting the generations from the first person up to the common ancestor and from the common ancestor down to the second person. In counting the generations, the first person is excluded, the second person is included, and the common ancestor is counted only once. For example, siblings are related in the second degree of collateral kinship or consanguinity, an aunt or uncle and a niece or nephew are related in the third degree, and first cousins are related in the fourth degree. *(Added by Stats.2009, c. 348 (S.B.308), § 4.)*

Law Revision Commission Comments

2009 Addition

Subdivision (a) of Section 13 restates the substance of former Section 251, as enacted by 1931 Cal. Stat. ch. 281.

Subdivision (b) restates the substance of former Section 252, as enacted by 1931 Cal. Stat. ch. 281.

Subdivision (c) restates the substance of former Section 253, as enacted by 1931 Cal. Stat. ch. 281. There is no first degree of collateral kinship or consanguinity. [38 Cal.L.Rev.Comm. Reports 107 (2008)].

Part 2

DEFINITIONS

Section
43. Repealed.
44. Heir.
45. Instrument.
46. Insured account in a financial institution.
48. Interested person.
50. Issue.
51. Repealed.
52. Letters.
53. Repealed.
54. Parent.
55. Pay-on-death account or P.O.D. account.
56. Person.
56.1 to 56.14. Repealed.
58. Personal representative; general personal representative.
59. Predeceased spouse.
60. Probate homestead.
60.1. Professional fiduciary; licensing requirement.
60.2 to 60.8. Repealed.
62. Property.
66. Quasi-community property.
68. Real property.
69. Revocable transfer on death deed or revocable TOD deed.
70. Security.
71. Repealed.
72. Spouse.
73. Repealed.
74. State.
75. Repealed.
76. Subscribing witness.
77. Repealed.
78. Surviving spouse.
79. Repealed.
80. Totten trust account.
81. Transferor.
81.5. Transferee.
82. Trust.
83. Trust company.
84. Trustee.
85. [Blank].
86. Undue influence.
87. [Blank].
88. Will.
90 to 92. Repealed.

Cross References

Application of old and new law, see Probate Code § 3.

§ 20. Applicability of part

Unless the provision or context otherwise requires, the definitions in this part govern the construction of this code. *(Stats.1990, c. 79 (A.B.759), § 14, operative July 1, 1991. Amended by Stats.1991, c. 82 (S.B.896), § 1, eff. June 30, 1991, operative July 1, 1991.)*

Law Revision Commission Comments
1990 Enactment

Section 20 broadens Section 20 of the repealed Probate Code to make the definitions in this part applicable to the entire Probate Code. Under Section 20 of the repealed Probate Code, those definitions did not apply to Division 4 (commencing with Section 1400).

The introductory portion of Section 20 recognizes that, in a particular context, the context may require that a word or phrase used in a particular section be given a meaning different from the definition provided in this part. The introductory clause also recognizes that special definitions may be used that differ from those provided in this part. See, e.g., Sections 20100 ("person interested in the estate," "property"), 20200 ("property," "trustee").

1991 Amendment

Section 20 is amended to delete "(a)." There is no other subdivision in the section.

Background on Section 20 of Repealed Code

Section 20 was added by 1983 Cal.Stat. ch. 842 § 21 and was amended by 1986 Cal.Stat. ch. 783 § 3, 1986 Cal.Stat. ch. 820 § 27.5, 1987 Cal.Stat. ch. 923 § 6, 1988 Cal.Stat. ch. 1199 § 25, and 1989 Cal.Stat. ch. 397 § 21.

Section 20 as added in 1983 was a new provision. The section was amended in 1986, 1987, 1988, and 1989 to make the definitions in this part applicable to additional portions of the Probate Code. See Communications from California Law Revision Commission Concerning Assembly Bill 2625, 18 Cal.L.Revision Comm'n Reports 1743, 1745 (1986) (discussing 1986 amendment); Recommendation Relating to Preliminary Provisions and Definitions of the Probate Code, 18 Cal.L.Revision Comm'n Reports 1807, 1816–17 (1986) (discussing 1987 amendment); Comments to Conforming Revisions and Repeals, 19 Cal.L.Revision Comm'n Reports 1031, 1041 (1988) (discussing 1988 amendment); Recommendation Relating to Multiple–Party Accounts in Financial Institutions, 20 Cal.L.Revision Comm'n Reports 95, 159 (1990) (discussing 1989 amendment). For additional background on the provisions of this division, see the Comment to this division under the division heading. [20 Cal.L.Rev.Comm.Reports 1001 (1990)].

§ 21. Account

"Account," when used to mean a contract of deposit of funds between a depositor and a financial institution, includes a checking account, savings account, certificate of deposit, share account, mutual capital certificate, and other like arrangements. *(Stats.1990, c. 79 (A.B.759), § 14, operative July 1, 1991.)*

Law Revision Commission Comments
1990 Enactment

Section 21 continues Section 21 of the repealed Probate Code without change. This section is comparable to Section 6–101(1) of the Uniform Probate Code (1987). As to the construction of provisions drawn from uniform acts, see Section 2. The context may require that a word or phrase used in a particular section be given a meaning different from the definition provided in this part. Also special definitions may be used for a particular portion of the code that differ from those provided in this part. See Section 20. For example, the term "account" is not used in the defined sense when it is used to refer to an accounting to the court. See, e.g., Sections 16062–16064 (trustee's duty to account).

Background on Section 21 of Repealed Code

Section 21 was a new provision added by 1983 Cal.Stat. ch. 842 § 21 and was amended by 1987 Cal.Stat. ch. 923 § 7. The 1987 amendment added a reference to a mutual capital certificate and made clear that the definition of "account" applied only to a contract of deposit of funds between a depositor and a financial institution. For background on the provisions of this division, see the Comment to this division under the division heading. [20 Cal.L.Rev.Comm.Reports 1001 (1990)].

§ 22. Account in an insured credit union

"Account in an insured credit union" means a share account in a credit union, either federally chartered or state licensed, that is insured under Title II of the Federal Credit Union Act (12 U.S.C. Sec. 1781, et seq.). *(Stats.1990, c. 79 (A.B.759), § 14, operative July 1, 1991.)*

Law Revision Commission Comments
1990 Enactment

Section 22 continues Section 22 of the repealed Probate Code without substantive change. The context may require that a word or phrase used in a particular section be given a meaning different from the definition provided in this part. Also special definitions may be used for a particular portion of the code that differ from those provided in this part. See Section 20. [20 Cal.L.Rev.Comm.Reports 1001 (1990)].

Background on Section 22 of Repealed Code

Section 22 was a new provision added by 1987 Cal.Stat. ch. 923 § 9. Section 22 did not include shares guaranteed by the California Credit Union Share Guaranty Corporation or comparable insurance or guaranty under Financial Code Section 14858. Compare Section 1443 of the repealed Probate Code (not continued in the new Probate Code). Section 22 referred to a share account in a credit union, rather than to shares issued by a credit union, and thus was consistent with Section 21 ("account" defined). See also Fin.Code § 14865 (shares owned by member of credit union may be referred to as a share account). For background on the provisions of this division, see the Comment to this division under the division heading. [20 Cal.L.Rev.Comm.Reports 1001 (1990)].

§ 22.1. Repealed by Stats.1983, c. 842, § 18, operative Jan. 1, 1985

§ 23. Account in an insured savings and loan association

(a) "Account in an insured savings and loan association" means a savings account or mutual capital certificate of either of the following:

(1) A federal association.

(2) A savings association doing business in this state which is an "insured institution" as defined in Title IV of the National Housing Act (12 U.S.C. Sec. 1724, et seq.).

(b) As used in this section:

(1) "Federal association" has the meaning given that term in subdivision (b) of Section 5102 of the Financial Code.

(2) "Mutual capital certificate" has the meaning given that term in Section 5111 of the Financial Code.

(3) "Savings account" has the meaning given that term in Section 5116 of the Financial Code.

(4) "Savings association" has the meaning given that term in subdivision (a) of Section 5102 of the Financial Code. *(Stats.1990, c. 79 (A.B.759), § 14, operative July 1, 1991.)*

Law Revision Commission Comments
1990 Enactment

Section 23 continues Section 23 of the repealed Probate Code without substantive change. The context may require that a word or phrase used in a particular section be given a meaning different from the definition provided in this part. Also special definitions may be used for a particular portion of the code that differ from those provided in this part. See Section 20.

Background on Section 23 of Repealed Code

Section 23 was a new provision added by 1987 Cal.Stat. ch. 923 § 10. See Recommendation Relating to Preliminary Provisions and Definitions of the Probate Code, 18 Cal.L.Revision Comm'n Reports

1807, 1818 (1986). For background on the provisions of this division, see the Comment to this division under the division heading. [20 Cal.L.Rev.Comm.Reports 1001 (1990)].

Cross References

Public employees' retirement system, death benefits, minors, see Government Code § 21502.
Credit unions,
 Generally, see Financial Code § 14000 et seq.
 Insuring share accounts, see Financial Code § 14858.
Savings associations, generally, see Financial Code § 5000.

§ 24. Beneficiary

"Beneficiary" means a person to whom a donative transfer of property is made or that person's successor in interest, and:

(a) As it relates to the intestate estate of a decedent, means an heir.

(b) As it relates to the testate estate of a decedent, means a devisee.

(c) As it relates to a trust, means a person who has any present or future interest, vested or contingent.

(d) As it relates to a charitable trust, includes any person entitled to enforce the trust. *(Stats.1990, c. 79 (A.B.759), § 14, operative July 1, 1991.)*

Law Revision Commission Comments
1990 Enactment

Section 24 continues Section 24 of the repealed Probate Code without substantive change. The context may require that a word or phrase used in a particular section be given a meaning different from the definition provided in this part. Also special definitions may be used for a particular portion of the code that differ from those provided in this part. See Section 20.

Section 24 is comparable to Section 1–201(2) of the Uniform Probate Code (1987). As to the construction of provisions drawn from uniform acts, see Section 2. Successors in interest include assignees and other transferees of an interest in a donative transfer of property. Cf. Section 45 ("instrument" means a will, trust, deed, or other writing that designates a beneficiary or makes a donative transfer of property).

Subdivisions (a) and (b) define "beneficiary" for the purposes of estate administration. If a decedent's estate is partly testate and partly intestate, "beneficiary" refers to a devisee as to property passing by will and to an heir as to property passing by intestate succession. Trust beneficiaries are not included within the term as used in subdivisions (a) and (b). See Section 34 ("devisee" in the case of a devise to a trust or trustee does not include trust beneficiaries). However, a particular section relating to estate administration may refer specifically to trust beneficiaries.

Subdivisions (c) and (d) define "beneficiary" for the purposes of the Trust Law. See Sections 15000–18201.

Background on Section 24 of Repealed Code

Section 24 was a new provision added by 1983 Cal.Stat. ch. 842 § 21 and amended by 1987 Cal.Stat. ch. 923 § 11. The 1987 amendment expanded the scope of this definition to cover other donative transfers, in addition to wills and trusts. See Recommendation Relating to Preliminary Provisions and Definitions of the Probate Code, 18 Cal.L.Revision Comm'n Reports 1807, 1812, 1818–19 (1986). For background on the provisions of this division, see the Comment to this division under the division heading. [20 Cal.L.Rev.Comm.Reports 1001 (1990)].

Cross References

Administration of estates of persons missing over five years, see Probate Code § 12401 et seq.

Trustees and beneficiaries, generally, see Probate Code § 15600 et seq.

§ 25. Repealed by Stats.1983, c. 842, § 18, operative Jan. 1, 1985

§ 26. Child

"Child" means any individual entitled to take as a child under this code by intestate succession from the parent whose relationship is involved. *(Stats.1990, c. 79 (A.B.759), § 14, operative July 1, 1991.)*

Law Revision Commission Comments

1990 Enactment

Section 26 continues Section 26 of the repealed Probate Code without change. The context may require that a word or phrase used in a particular section be given a meaning different from the definition provided in this part. Also special definitions may be used for a particular portion of the code that differ from those provided in this part. See Section 20.

Section 26 is comparable to Section 1–201(3) of the Uniform Probate Code (1987). As to the construction of provisions drawn from uniform acts, see Section 2. "Child" is limited to the persons who are entitled to take as a child by intestate succession. The definition of "child" in Section 26 applies unless the provision or context otherwise requires. See Section 20.

Although under Section 26 a stepchild or foster child is not included within the meaning of "child" only on the basis of that relationship, a stepchild or foster child may be included if the relationship began during the person's minority, continued throughout the parties' joint lifetimes, and it is established by clear and convincing evidence that the stepparent or foster parent would have adopted the person but for a legal barrier. See Section 6408. [Repealed, see now, Probate Code § 6454.] See also Sections 54 (definition of "parent"), 6152 (parent-child relationship for purposes of construing will).

Background on Section 26 of Repealed Code

Section 26 was a new provision added by 1983 Cal.Stat. ch. 842 § 21 and amended by 1984 Cal.Stat. ch. 892 § 4 and 1987 Cal.Stat. ch. 923 § 12. The 1984 amendment deleted the last clause of the section which excluded from the definition of "child" any person "who is only a stepchild, a foster child, a grandchild, or any more remote descendant." The amendment did not make a substantive change; the deleted language was omitted because it was unnecessary and was confusing. Deletion of the last clause from Section 26 made it clearer that a stepchild or foster child may be included within the definition of "child" when the requirements of Section 6408 are met. See Report of Senate Committee on Judiciary on Assembly Bills 25 and 68, 17 Cal.L.Revision Comm'n Reports 867 (1984); Communication of Law Revision Commission Concerning Assembly Bill 2290, 18 Cal.L.Revision Comm'n Reports 77, 78–79 (1986). The 1987 amendment replaced "includes" with "means." This made clear that "child" is limited to the persons who are entitled to take as a child by intestate succession. See Recommendation Relating to Preliminary Provisions and Definitions of the Probate Code, 18 Cal.L.Revision Comm'n Reports 1807, 1812–13, 1819 (1986). For background on the provisions of this division, see the Comment to this division under the division heading. [20 Cal.L.Rev.Comm.Reports 1001 (1990)].

Cross References

Succession of persons to decedent's separate property, generally, see Probate Code § 6400 et seq.

§ 27. Repealed by Stats.1983, c. 842, § 18, operative Jan. 1, 1985

§ 28. Community property

"Community property" means:

(a) Community property heretofore or hereafter acquired during marriage by a married person while domiciled in this state.

(b) All personal property wherever situated, and all real property situated in this state, heretofore or hereafter acquired during the marriage by a married person while domiciled elsewhere, that is community property, or a substantially equivalent type of marital property, under the laws of the place where the acquiring spouse was domiciled at the time of its acquisition.

(c) All personal property wherever situated, and all real property situated in this state, heretofore or hereafter acquired during the marriage by a married person in exchange for real or personal property, wherever situated, that is community property, or a substantially equivalent type of marital property, under the laws of the place where the acquiring spouse was domiciled at the time the property so exchanged was acquired. *(Stats.1990, c. 79 (A.B.759), § 14, operative July 1, 1991.)*

Law Revision Commission Comments

1990 Enactment

Section 28 continues Section 28 of the repealed Probate Code without substantive change. The context may require that a word or phrase used in a particular section be given a meaning different from the definition provided in this part. Also special definitions may be used for a particular portion of the code that differ from those provided in this part. See Section 20.

Subdivision (a) is consistent with Civil Code Sections 687 and 5110. Under subdivisions (b) and (c), community property acquired while domiciled in another community property jurisdiction is treated as community property in California even though the property might not have been community if acquired while domiciled in California. For example, property is community property under subdivision (b) if it is the income of separate property and the income of separate property is community property under the laws of the place where the spouse owning the separate property is domiciled at the time the income is earned. Thus, subdivisions (b) and (c) ensure generally comparable treatment of the property in California to that given it in the other community property jurisdiction and fills a gap in the quasi-community property law. See Section 66 ("quasi-community property" defined). Section 28 applies whether the property is acquired before or after the operative date of the section. The reference in subdivisions (b) and (c) to substantially equivalent types of marital property is intended to cover possible adoption in other jurisdictions of the Uniform Marital Property Act (1983) or other laws establishing a community property regime. See also Section 68 ("real property" defined).

Background on Section 28 of Repealed Code

Section 28 was a new provision added by 1983 Cal.Stat. ch. 842 § 21. See Report of Senate Committee on Judiciary on Assembly Bills 25 and 68, 17 Cal.L.Revision Comm'n Reports 867 (1984). For background on the provisions of this division, see the Comment to this division under the division heading. [20 Cal.L.Rev.Comm.Reports 1001 (1990)].

Cross References

Community property, see Family Code §§ 65, 760.
Effect of death of married person on community property, see Probate Code § 100.

§ 29. Conservatee

"Conservatee" includes a limited conservatee. *(Stats.1990, c. 79 (A.B.759), § 14, operative July 1, 1991.)*

Law Revision Commission Comments

1990 Enactment

Section 29 is a new provision, not found in the general definitions of the repealed Probate Code. The section continues Section 1411 of the repealed Probate Code, but expands the coverage of the definition which applied only to Division 4 (Guardianship–Conservatorship Law) to apply to the entire Probate Code. The context may require that a word or phrase used in a particular section be given a meaning different from the definition provided in this part. Also special definitions may be used for a particular portion of the code that differ from those provided in this part. See Section 20. [20 Cal.L.Rev.Comm.Reports 1001 (1990)].

§ 30. Conservator

"Conservator" includes a limited conservator. *(Stats.1990, c. 79 (A.B.759), § 14, operative July 1, 1991.)*

Law Revision Commission Comments

1990 Enactment

Section 30 is a new provision, not found in the general definitions of the repealed Probate Code. The section continues Section 1410 of the repealed Probate Code, but expands the coverage of the definition which applied only to Division 4 (Guardianship–Conservatorship Law) to apply to the entire Probate Code. The context may require that a word or phrase used in a particular section be given a meaning different from the definition provided in this part. Also special definitions may be used for a particular portion of the code that differ from those provided in this part. See Section 20. [20 Cal.L.Rev.Comm.Reports 1001 (1990)].

§ 32. Devise

"Devise," when used as a noun, means a disposition of real or personal property by will, and, when used as a verb, means to dispose of real or personal property by will. *(Stats.1990, c. 79 (A.B.759), § 14, operative July 1, 1991.)*

Law Revision Commission Comments

1990 Enactment

Section 32 continues Section 32 of the repealed Probate Code without change. This section is the same in substance as Section 1–201(7) of the Uniform Probate Code (1987). As to the construction of provisions drawn from uniform acts, see Section 2. The context may require that a word or phrase used in a particular section be given a meaning different from the definition provided in this part. Also special definitions may be used for a particular portion of the code that differ from those provided in this part. See Section 20. [20 Cal.L.Rev.Comm.Reports 1001 (1990)].

Background on Section 32 of Repealed Code

Section 32 was a new provision added by 1983 Cal.Stat. ch. 842 § 21. For background on the provisions of this division, see the Comment to this division under the division heading. [20 Cal.L.Rev.Comm.Reports 1001 (1990)].

§ 34. Devisee

(a) "Devisee" means any person designated in a will to receive a devise.

(b) In the case of a devise to an existing trust or trustee, or to a trustee on trust described by will, the trust or trustee is the devisee and the beneficiaries are not devisees. *(Stats. 1990, c. 79 (A.B.759), § 14, operative July 1, 1991.)*

Law Revision Commission Comments

1990 Enactment

Section 34 continues Section 34 of the repealed Probate Code without change. This section is the same in substance as Section 1–201(8) of the Uniform Probate Code (1987). As to the construction of provisions drawn from uniform acts, see Section 2. The context may require that a word or phrase used in a particular section be given a meaning different from the definition provided in this part. Also special definitions may be used for a particular portion of the code that differ from those provided in this part. See Section 20.

Background on Section 34 of Repealed Code

Section 34 was a new provision added by 1983 Cal.Stat. ch. 842 § 21. For background on the provisions of this division, see the Comment to this division under the division heading. [20 Cal.L.Rev.Comm.Reports 1001 (1990)].

Cross References

Estate defined for purposes of this Part, see Probate Code § 21601.

§ 36. Dissolution of marriage

"Dissolution of marriage" includes divorce. *(Stats.1990, c. 79 (A.B.759), § 14, operative July 1, 1991.)*

Law Revision Commission Comments

1990 Enactment

Section 36 continues Section 36 of the repealed Probate Code without change. "Dissolution of marriage" does not include an annulment of the marriage. See Section 78 ("surviving spouse") which makes a distinction between a dissolution of marriage and an annulment of marriage. The context may require that a word or phrase used in a particular section be given a meaning different from the definition provided in this part. Also special definitions may be used for a particular portion of the code that differ from those provided in this part. See Section 20.

Background on Section 36 of Repealed Code

Section 36 was a new provision added by 1983 Cal.Stat. ch. 842 § 21. For background on the provisions of this division, see the Comment to this division under the division heading. [20 Cal.L.Rev.Comm.Reports 1001 (1990)].

§ 37. Domestic partner

(a) "Domestic partner" means one of two persons who have filed a Declaration of Domestic Partnership with the Secretary of State pursuant to Division 2.5 (commencing with Section 297) of the Family Code, provided that the domestic partnership has not been terminated pursuant to Section 299 of the Family Code.

(b) Notwithstanding Section 299 of the Family Code, if a domestic partnership is terminated by the death of one of the parties and Notice of Termination was not filed by either party prior to the date of death of the decedent, the domestic partner who survives the deceased is a surviving domestic partner, and shall be entitled to the rights of a surviving domestic partner as provided in this code. *(Added by Stats.2001, c. 893 (A.B.25), § 13.)*

§ 38. Family allowance

"Family allowance" means an allowance provided for in Chapter 4 (commencing with Section 6540) of Part 3 of Division 6. *(Stats.1990, c. 79 (A.B.759), § 14, operative July 1, 1991.)*

Law Revision Commission Comments
1990 Enactment

Section 38 continues Section 38 of the repealed Probate Code without change. The context may require that a word or phrase used in a particular section be given a meaning different from the definition provided in this part. Also special definitions may be used for a particular portion of the code that differ from those provided in this part. See Section 20.

Background on Section 38 of Repealed Code

Section 38 was a new provision added by 1983 Cal.Stat. ch. 842 § 21. For background on the provisions of this division, see the Comment to this division under the division heading. [20 Cal.L.Rev.Comm.Reports 1001 (1990)].

§ 39. Fiduciary

"Fiduciary" means personal representative, trustee, guardian, conservator, attorney-in-fact under a power of attorney, custodian under the California Uniform Transfer To Minors Act (Part 9 (commencing with Section 3900) of Division 4), or other legal representative subject to this code. *(Stats. 1990, c. 79 (A.B.759), § 14, operative July 1, 1991. Amended by Stats.1997, c. 724 (A.B.1172), § 2.)*

Law Revision Commission Comments
1990 Enactment

Section 39 continues Section 39 of the repealed Probate Code without change. The context may require that a word or phrase used in a particular section be given a meaning different from the definition provided in this part. Also special definitions may be used for a particular portion of the code that differ from those provided in this part. See Section 20. For provisions using the defined term, see Sections 350–388 (Fiduciaries' Wartime Substitution Law), Division 11 (commencing with Section 21101) (construction of wills, trusts, and other instruments).

Background on Section 39 of Repealed Code

Section 39 was added by 1988 Cal.Stat. ch. 1199 § 25.2. The section continued former Probate Code Section 21100(a) (repealed by 1988 Cal.Stat. ch. 1199 § 107.8) without substantive change and restated former Code of Civil Procedure Section 1700.3 without substantive change but expanded the scope of the former provisions to apply to all parts of the Probate Code to which the general definitions applied. See Section 20 (application of definitions). See also Communication from the California Law Revision Commission Concerning Assembly Bill 2841, 19 Cal.L.Revision Comm'n Reports 1201, 1208 (1988). For background on the provisions of this division, see the Comment to this division under the division heading. [20 Cal.L.Rev.Comm.Reports 1001 (1990)].

Cross References
Powers of attorney, generally, see Probate Code § 4000 et seq.

§ 40. Financial institution

"Financial institution" means a state or national bank, state or federal savings and loan association or credit union, or like organization. *(Stats.1990, c. 79 (A.B.759), § 14, operative July 1, 1991.)*

Law Revision Commission Comments
1990 Enactment

Section 40 continues Section 40 of the repealed Probate Code without change. This section is the same as a portion of Code of Civil Procedure Section 680.200. The context may require that a word or phrase used in a particular section be given a meaning different from the definition provided in this part. Also special definitions may be used for a particular portion of the code that differ from those provided in this part. See Section 20.

Background on Section 40 of Repealed Code

Section 40 was a new provision added by 1983 Cal.Stat. ch. 842 § 21. For background on the provisions of this division, see the Comment to this division under the division heading. [20 Cal.L.Rev.Comm.Reports 1001 (1990)].

§ 41. Repealed by Stats.1971, c. 1395, § 1

§ 42. General personal representative

"General personal representative" is defined in subdivision (b) of Section 58. *(Stats.1990, c. 79 (A.B.759), § 14, operative July 1, 1991.)*

Law Revision Commission Comments
1990 Enactment

Section 42 is new and is intended for cross-referencing purposes. [20 Cal.L.Rev.Comm.Reports 1001 (1990)].

§ 43. Repealed by Stats.1971, c. 1395, § 1

§ 44. Heir

"Heir" means any person, including the surviving spouse, who is entitled to take property of the decedent by intestate succession under this code. *(Stats.1990, c. 79 (A.B.759), § 14, operative July 1, 1991.)*

Law Revision Commission Comments
1990 Enactment

Section 44 continues Section 44 of the repealed Probate Code without substantive change. The context may require that a word or phrase used in a particular section be given a meaning different from the definition provided in this part. Also, special definitions may be used for a particular portion of the code that differ from those provided in this part. See Section 20.

Section 44 is the same in substance as Section 1–201(17) of the Uniform Probate Code (1987). As to the construction of provisions drawn from uniform acts, see Section 2. See also Section 78 ("surviving spouse" defined). As to a surviving spouse's waiver of rights at death, see Sections 140–147.

Background on Section 44 of Repealed Code

Section 44 was a new provision added by 1983 Cal.Stat. ch. 842 § 21. For background on the provisions of this division, see the Comment to this division under the division heading. [20 Cal.L.Rev.Comm.Reports 1001 (1990)].

Cross References
Persons entitled to distribution, proceedings, pleadings, see Probate Code § 11700 et seq.

§ 45. Instrument

"Instrument" means a will, trust, deed, or other writing that designates a beneficiary or makes a donative transfer of property. *(Stats.1990, c. 79 (A.B.759), § 14, operative July 1, 1991.)*

Law Revision Commission Comments
1990 Enactment

Section 45 continues Section 45 of the repealed Probate Code without change. The context may require that a word or phrase used in a particular section be given a meaning different from the definition provided in this part. Also special definitions may be used for a particular portion of the code that differ from those provided in this part. See Section 20. For provisions using the defined word, see Sections 350–388 (Fiduciaries' Wartime Substitution Law), Division 11 (commencing with Section 21101) (construction of wills, trusts, and other instruments).

Background on Section 45 of Repealed Code

Section 45 was added by 1988 Cal.Stat. ch. 1199 § 25.4. The section continued former Probate Code Section 21100(b) (repealed by 1988 Cal.Stat. ch. 1199 § 107.8) without change but expanded the scope of the former provision to apply to all parts of the code to which the general definitions applied. See Section 20 (application of definitions). See also Communication from the California Law Revision Commission Concerning Assembly Bill 2841, 19 Cal.L.Revision Comm'n Reports 1201, 1208 (1988). For background on the provisions of this division, see the Comment to this division under the division heading. [20 Cal.L.Rev.Comm.Reports 1001 (1990)].

Cross References

Trusts, creation, validity, modification, and termination, see Probate Code § 15200 et seq.

§ 46. Insured account in a financial institution

"Insured account in a financial institution" means an account in a bank, an account in an insured credit union, and an account in an insured savings and loan association, to the extent that the account is insured. *(Stats.1990, c. 79 (A.B. 759), § 14, operative July 1, 1991.)*

Law Revision Commission Comments
1990 Enactment

Section 46 continues Section 46 of the repealed Probate Code without change. The context may require that a word or phrase used in a particular section be given a meaning different from the definition provided in this part. Also special definitions may be used for a particular portion of the code that differ from those provided in this part. See Section 20.

The final clause of Section 46 makes clear that the definition applies only to that part of an account that is insured. Thus, if a deposit in an insured account exceeds the limits of the insurance, the excess does not fall within this definition.

Background on Section 46 of Repealed Code

Section 46 was a new provision added by 1987 Cal.Stat. ch. 923 § 13. For background on the provisions of this division, see the Comment to this division under the division heading. [20 Cal.L.Rev.Comm.Reports 1001 (1990)].

§ 48. Interested person

(a) Subject to subdivision (b), "interested person" includes any of the following:

(1) An heir, devisee, child, spouse, creditor, beneficiary, and any other person having a property right in or claim against a trust estate or the estate of a decedent which may be affected by the proceeding.

(2) Any person having priority for appointment as personal representative.

(3) A fiduciary representing an interested person.

(b) The meaning of "interested person" as it relates to particular persons may vary from time to time and shall be determined according to the particular purposes of, and matter involved in, any proceeding. *(Stats.1990, c. 79 (A.B. 759), § 14, operative July 1, 1991.)*

Law Revision Commission Comments
1990 Enactment

Section 48 continues Section 48 of the repealed Probate Code without change. This section is the same in substance as Section 1–201(20) of the Uniform Probate Code (1987). As to the construction of provisions drawn from uniform acts, see Section 2. The context may require that a word or phrase used in a particular section be given a meaning different from the definition provided in this part. Also special definitions may be used for a particular portion of the code that differ from those provided in this part. See Section 20. See also Sections 354 (defining "interested person" for purposes of the Fiduciaries' Wartime Substitution Law), 1424 (defining "interested person" for purposes of guardianship and conservatorship law).

Background on Section 48 of Repealed Code

Section 48 was a new provision added by 1983 Cal.Stat. ch. 842 § 21. For background on the provisions of this division, see the Comment to this division under the division heading. [20 Cal.L.Rev.Comm.Reports 1001 (1990)].

Cross References

Civil actions for abuse of elderly or dependent adults, jurisdiction, right to maintain action, see Welfare and Institutions Code § 15657.3.
Trusts, judicial proceedings, generally, see Probate Code § 17000 et seq.

§ 50. Issue

"Issue" of a person means all his or her lineal descendants of all generations, with the relationship of parent and child at each generation being determined by the definitions of child and parent. *(Stats.1990, c. 79 (A.B.759), § 14, operative July 1, 1991.)*

Law Revision Commission Comments
1990 Enactment

Section 50 continues Section 50 of the repealed Probate Code without change. This section is the same in substance as Section 1–201(21) of the Uniform Probate Code (1987). As to the construction of provisions drawn from uniform acts, see Section 2. See also Section 6408 (parent-child relationship for determination of rights under intestate succession). The context may require that a word or phrase used in a particular section be given a meaning different from the definition provided in this part. Also, special definitions may be used for a particular portion of the code that differ from those provided in this part. See Section 20.

Background on Section 50 of Repealed Code

Section 50 was a new provision added by 1983 Cal.Stat. ch. 842 § 21. For background on the provisions of this division, see the Comment to this division under the division heading. [20 Cal.L.Rev.Comm.Reports 1001 (1990)].

§ 51. Repealed by Stats.1983, c. 842, § 18, operative Jan. 1, 1985

§ 52. Letters

"Letters":

(a) As it relates to a personal representative, means letters testamentary, letters of administration, letters of administration with the will annexed, or letters of special administration.

(b) As it relates to a guardian or conservator, means letters of guardianship or conservatorship or temporary guardianship or conservatorship. *(Stats.1990, c. 79 (A.B.759), § 14, operative July 1, 1991.)*

Law Revision Commission Comments

1990 Enactment

Section 52 continues Section 52 of the repealed Probate Code without substantive change except that the scope of subdivision (a) is expanded to cover "letters" "as it relates to a personal representative," this subdivision formerly being limited to "letters" as used in Division 7 (commencing with Section 7000).

Section 52 is drawn in part from Section 1–201(23) of the Uniform Probate Code (1987). As to the construction of provisions drawn from uniform acts, see Section 2. Special definitions may be used for a particular portion of the code that differ from those provided in this part. Also, the context may require that a word or phrase used in a particular section be given a meaning different from the definition provided in this part. See Section 20. Thus, the context of a particular section determines the types of letters included within the term as used in that section. For example, in a provision relating to exercise of a power that is not available to a special administrator, "letters" would not include letters of special administration.

Background on Section 52 of Repealed Code

Section 52 was a new provision added by 1987 Cal.Stat. ch. 923 § 14. See Recommendation Relating to Preliminary Provisions and Definitions of the Probate Code, 18 Cal.L.Revision Comm'n Reports 1807, 1813, 1820 (1986). Section 52 was amended by 1988 Cal.Stat. ch. 1199 § 26. The 1988 amendment added subdivision (b). See Communication from California Law Revision Commission Concerning Assembly Bill 2841, 19 Cal.L.Revision Comm'n Reports 1201, 1208 (1988). For background on the provisions of this division, see the Comment to this division under the division heading. [20 Cal.L.Rev.Comm.Reports 1001 (1990)].

Cross References

Temporary guardians and conservators, generally, see Probate Code § 2250 et seq.

§ 53. Repealed by Stats.1983, c. 842, § 18, operative Jan. 1, 1985

§ 54. Parent

"Parent" means any individual entitled to take as a parent under this code by intestate succession from the child whose relationship is involved. *(Stats.1990, c. 79 (A.B.759), § 14, operative July 1, 1991.)*

Law Revision Commission Comments

1990 Enactment

Section 54 continues Section 54 of the repealed Probate Code without change. The context may require that a word or phrase used in a particular section be given a meaning different from the definition provided in this part. Also special definitions may be used for a particular portion of the code that differ from those provided in this part. See Section 20.

Section 54 is comparable to Section 1–201(28) of the Uniform Probate Code (1987). As to the construction of provisions drawn from uniform acts, see Section 2. "Parent" is limited to the persons who are entitled to take as a parent by intestate succession. See also Section 26 ("child" defined).

A stepparent or foster parent is not included within the definition of "parent" on the basis of that relationship alone. A stepparent or foster parent may be included within the definition of "parent" when the requirements of Section 6408 are met. See also Section 6152 (parent-child relationship for purpose of construing will).

Background on Section 54 of Repealed Code

Section 54 was a new provision added by 1983 Cal.Stat. ch. 842 § 21 and amended by 1984 Cal.Stat. ch. 892 § 5 and 1987 Cal.Stat. ch. 923 § 15. For background on the provisions of this division, see the Comment to this division under the division heading. See also Communication of Law Revision Commission Concerning Assembly Bill 2290, 18 Cal.L.Revision Comm'n Reports 77, 79 (1986). [20 Cal.L.Rev.Comm.Reports 1001 (1990)].

Cross References

Succession of persons to decedent's separate property, generally, see Probate Code § 6400 et seq.

§ 55. Pay-on-death account or P.O.D. account

"Pay-on-death account" or "P.O.D. account" is defined in Section 5140. *(Stats.1990, c. 79 (A.B.759), § 14, operative July 1, 1991.)*

Law Revision Commission Comments

1990 Enactment

Section 55 is a new provision, not found in the general definitions of the repealed Probate Code. The section adopts the definition in Section 5140. See also Recommendation Relating to Multiple–Party Accounts in Financial Institutions, 20 Cal.L.Revision Comm'n Reports 95, 126–27 (1990). The context may require that a word or phrase used in a particular section be given a meaning different from the definition provided in this part. Also special definitions may be used for a particular portion of the code that differ from those provided in this part. See Section 20. [20 Cal.L.Rev.Comm.Reports 1001 (1990)].

§ 56. Person

"Person" means an individual, corporation, government or governmental subdivision or agency, business trust, estate, trust, partnership, limited liability company, association, or other entity. *(Stats.1990, c. 79 (A.B.759), § 14, operative July 1, 1991. Amended by Stats.1994, c. 1010 (S.B.2053), § 202.)*

Law Revision Commission Comments

1990 Enactment

Section 56 continues Section 56 of the repealed Probate Code without change. This section is drawn from paragraphs (27) and (29) of Section 1–201 of the Uniform Probate Code (1987). As to the construction of provisions drawn from uniform acts, see Section 2. The context may require that a word or phrase used in a particular section be given a meaning different from the definition provided in this part. Also special definitions may be used for a particular portion of the code that differ from those provided in this part. See Section 20.

Background on Section 56 of Repealed Code

Section 56 was a new provision added by 1983 Cal.Stat. ch. 842 § 21. For background on the provisions of this division, see the Comment to this division under the division heading. [20 Cal.L.Rev.Comm.Reports 1001 (1990)].

§§ 56.1 to 56.14. Repealed by Stats.1983, c. 842, § 18, operative Jan. 1, 1985

§ 58. Personal representative; general personal representative

(a) "Personal representative" means executor, administrator, administrator with the will annexed, special administrator, successor personal representative, public administrator acting pursuant to Section 7660, or a person who performs substantially the same function under the law of another jurisdiction governing the person's status.

(b) "General personal representative" excludes a special administrator unless the special administrator has the powers, duties, and obligations of a general personal representative under Section 8545. *(Stats.1990, c. 79 (A.B.759), § 14, operative July 1, 1991. Amended by Stats.2004, c. 888 (A.B.2687), § 1.)*

Law Revision Commission Comments

1990 Enactment

Section 58 continues Section 58 of the repealed Probate Code without change. The context may require that a word or phrase used in a particular section be given a meaning different from the definition provided in this part. Also special definitions may be used for a particular portion of the code that differ from those provided in this part. See Section 20.

Subdivision (a) is drawn from the first sentence of Section 1–201(30) of the Uniform Probate Code (1987). Subdivision (b) is drawn in part from the second sentence of Section 1–201(30) of the Uniform Probate Code (1987). As to the construction of provisions drawn from uniform acts, see Section 2. The term "general personal representative" is used in Sections 9050 (notice to creditors required), 9051 (time of notice to creditors), 9100 (claim period), 9103 (late claims), 9104 (amended or revised claim), 9154 (waiver of formal defects), 9202 (notice to Director of Health Services), and 11422 (payment of debts on court order).

Background on Section 58 of Repealed Code

Section 58 was a new provision added by 1987 Cal.Stat. ch. 923 § 17 and amended by 1988 Cal.Stat. ch. 1199 § 27. Subdivision (b) was drawn from former Probate Code Section 465 (repealed by 1988 Cal.Stat. ch. 1199 § 46) and former Probate Code Section 700 (repealed by 1987 Cal.Stat. ch. 923 § 37), and from the second sentence of Section 1–201(30) of the Uniform Probate Code (1987). As to the construction of provisions drawn from uniform acts, see Section 2. For background on the provisions of this division, see the Comment to this division under the division heading. See also Recommendation Relating to Preliminary Provisions and Definitions of the Probate Code, 18 Cal.L.Revision Comm'n Reports 1807, 1813, 1821 (1986). The 1988 amendment corrected terminology and a section reference. See Recommendation Relating to Creditor Claims Against Decedent's Estate, 19 Cal.L.Revision Comm'n Reports 299, 352 (1988); Comments to Conforming Revisions and Repeals, 19 Cal.L.Revision Comm'n Reports 391, 394 (1988); Communication from California Law Revision Commission Concerning Assembly Bill 708, 19 Cal.L.Revision Comm'n Reports 545, 546 (1988). [20 Cal.L.Rev.Comm.Reports 1001 (1990)].

Cross References

Appointment of personal representative, generally, see Probate Code § 8400 et seq.
Persons authorized to sue without joining beneficiary, see Code of Civil Procedure § 369.
Trusts, judicial proceedings,
   Generally, see Probate Code § 17000 et seq.

Transfer from another jurisdiction, see Probate Code § 17450 et seq.

§ 59. Predeceased spouse

"Predeceased spouse" means a person who died before the decedent while married to the decedent, except that the term does not include any of the following:

(a) A person who obtains or consents to a final decree or judgment of dissolution of marriage from the decedent or a final decree or judgment of annulment of their marriage, which decree or judgment is not recognized as valid in this state, unless they (1) subsequently participate in a marriage ceremony purporting to marry each to the other or (2) subsequently live together as * * * spouses.

(b) A person who, following a decree or judgment of dissolution or annulment of marriage obtained by the decedent, participates in a marriage ceremony to a third person.

(c) A person who was a party to a valid proceeding concluded by an order purporting to terminate all marital property rights. *(Stats.1990, c. 79 (A.B.759), § 14, operative July 1, 1991. Amended by Stats.2016, c. 50 (S.B.1005), § 76, eff. Jan. 1, 2017.)*

Law Revision Commission Comments

1990 Enactment

Section 59 continues Section 59 of the repealed Probate Code without change. The context may require that a word or phrase used in a particular section be given a meaning different from the definition provided in this part. Also special definitions may be used for a particular portion of the code that differ from those provided in this part. See Section 20.

Section 59 is consistent with Section 78 ("surviving spouse" defined). See the Comment to Section 78. Under Section 59, it is possible that the decedent may have more than one predeceased spouse. For California provisions relating to annulment of marriage, see Title 2 (commencing with Section 4400) of Part 5 of the Civil Code (judicial determination of void or voidable marriage). As to a surviving spouse's waiver of rights at death, see Sections 140–147.

Background on Section 59 of Repealed Code

Section 59 was a new provision added by 1984 Cal.Stat. ch. 892 § 6. See Recommendation Relating to Revision of Wills and Intestate Succession Law, 17 Cal.L.Revision Comm'n Reports 537, 546, 547–48 (1984). For background on the provisions of this division, see the Comment to this division under the division heading. [20 Cal.L.Rev.Comm.Reports 1001 (1990)].

§ 60. Probate homestead

"Probate homestead" means a homestead provided for in Chapter 3 (commencing with Section 6520) of Part 3 of Division 6. *(Stats.1990, c. 79 (A.B.759), § 14, operative July 1, 1991.)*

Law Revision Commission Comments

1990 Enactment

Section 60 continues Section 60 of the repealed Probate Code without change. The context may require that a word or phrase used in a particular section be given a meaning different from the definition provided in this part. Also special definitions may be used for a particular portion of the code that differ from those provided in this part. See Section 20.

Section 60 was a new provision added by 1983 Cal.Stat. ch. 842 § 21. For background on the provisions of this division, see the Comment to this division under the division heading. [20 Cal.L.Rev.Comm.Reports 1001 (1990)].

§ 60.1. Professional fiduciary; licensing requirement

(a) "Professional fiduciary" means a person who is a professional fiduciary as defined under subdivision (f) of Section 6501 of the Business and Professions Code.

(b) On and after January 1, 2009, no person shall act or hold himself or herself out to the public as a professional fiduciary unless he or she is licensed as a professional fiduciary under Chapter 6 (commencing with Section 6500) of Division 3 of the Business and Professions Code. *(Added by Stats.2006, c. 491 (S.B.1550), § 4. Amended by Stats.2007, c. 354 (S.B.1047), § 70.)*

Cross References

Professional Fiduciaries Act, see Business and Professions Code § 6500 et seq.

§§ 60.2 to 60.8. Repealed by Stats.1983, c. 842, § 18, operative Jan. 1, 1985

§ 62. Property

"Property" means anything that may be the subject of ownership and includes both real and personal property and any interest therein. *(Stats.1990, c. 79 (A.B.759), § 14, operative July 1, 1991.)*

Law Revision Commission Comments

1990 Enactment

Section 62 continues Section 62 of the repealed Probate Code without change. This section is the same in substance as Section 1–201(33) of the Uniform Probate Code (1987). As to the construction of provisions drawn from uniform acts, see Section 2. The context may require that a word or phrase used in a particular section be given a meaning different from the definition provided in this part. Also special definitions may be used for a particular portion of the code that differ from those provided in this part. See Section 20.

Background on Section 62 of Repealed Code

Section 62 was a new provision added by 1983 Cal.Stat. ch. 842 § 21 and amended by 1987 Cal.Stat. ch. 923 § 18. For background on the provisions of this division, see the Comment to this division under the division heading. [20 Cal.L.Rev.Comm.Reports 1001 (1990)].

Cross References

Actions for partition against personal representative, see Probate Code § 9823.
Guardians or conservators, partition actions, see Probate Code § 2463.
Partition, generally, see Code of Civil Procedure § 872.010 et seq.
Partition of decedent's estates before distribution, generally, see Probate Code § 11950.

§ 66. Quasi-community property

"Quasi-community property" means the following property, other than community property as defined in Section 28:

(a) All personal property wherever situated, and all real property situated in this state, heretofore or hereafter acquired by a decedent while domiciled elsewhere that would have been the community property of the decedent and the surviving spouse if the decedent had been domiciled in this state at the time of its acquisition.

(b) All personal property wherever situated, and all real property situated in this state, heretofore or hereafter acquired in exchange for real or personal property, wherever situated, that would have been the community property of the decedent and the surviving spouse if the decedent had been domiciled in this state at the time the property so exchanged was acquired. *(Stats.1990, c. 79 (A.B.759), § 14, operative July 1, 1991.)*

Law Revision Commission Comments

1990 Enactment

Section 66 continues Section 66 of the repealed Probate Code without substantive change. The context may require that a word or phrase used in a particular section be given a meaning different from the definition provided in this part. Also special definitions may be used for a particular portion of the code that differ from those provided in this part. See Section 20.

Community property under the laws of another jurisdiction is classified as community rather than quasi-community property. See Section 28 ("community property" defined) and the Comment thereto. See also Section 68 ("real property" defined). For background on the definition of "quasi-community property," see Recommendation and Study Relating to Rights of Surviving Spouse in Property Acquired by Decedent While Domiciled Elsewhere, 1 Cal.L.Revision Comm'n Reports E–1 (1957); Recommendation and Study Relating to Inter Vivos Marital Property Rights in Property Acquired While Domiciled Elsewhere, 3 Cal.L.Revision Comm'n Reports I–1 (1961); Recommendation Relating to Quasi–Community Property, 9 Cal.L.Revision Comm'n Reports 113 (1969).

Background on Section 66 of Repealed Code

Section 66 was added by 1983 Cal.Stat. ch. 842 § 21. The section continued the substance of portions of former Probate Code Section 201.5 (repealed by 1983 Cal.Stat. ch. 842 § 19), except that community property under the laws of another jurisdiction was classified by Sections 28 and 66 as community rather than quasi-community property. For background on the provisions of this division, see the Comment to this division under the division heading. [20 Cal.L.Rev.Comm.Reports 1001 (1990)].

Cross References

Effect of death of married person on quasi-community property, see Probate Code § 101.

§ 68. Real property

"Real property" includes a leasehold interest in real property. *(Stats.1990, c. 79 (A.B.759), § 14, operative July 1, 1991.)*

Law Revision Commission Comments

1990 Enactment

Section 68 continues Section 68 of the repealed Probate Code without change. This section is consistent with the last sentence of Civil Code Section 5110. The context may require that a word or phrase used in a particular section be given a meaning different from the definition provided in this part. Also special definitions may be used for a particular portion of the code that differ from those provided in this part. See Section 20.

Background on Section 68 of Repealed Code

Section 68 was a new provision added by 1983 Cal.Stat. ch. 842 § 21. For background on the provisions of this division, see the

Comment to this division under the division heading. [20 Cal.L.Rev.Comm.Reports 1001 (1990)].

Actions for partition against personal representative, see Probate Code § 9823.

Guardians or conservators, partition actions, see Probate Code § 2463.

Partition, generally, see Code of Civil Procedure § 872.010 et seq.

Partition of decedent's estates before distribution, generally, see Probate Code § 11950.

§ 69.   Revocable transfer on death deed or revocable TOD deed

"Revocable transfer on death deed" or "revocable TOD deed" means a revocable transfer on death deed as described in Section 5614. *(Added by Stats.2015, c. 293 (A.B.139), § 3, eff. Jan. 1, 2016.)*

§ 70.   Security

"Security" includes any note, stock, treasury stock, bond, debenture, evidence of indebtedness, certificate of interest or participation in an oil, gas, or mining title or lease or in payments out of production under such a title or lease, collateral trust certificate, transferable share, voting trust certificate or, in general, any interest or instrument commonly known as a security, or any certificate of interest or participation, any temporary or interim certificate, receipt, or certificate of deposit for, or any warrant or right to subscribe to or purchase, any of the foregoing. *(Stats.1990, c. 79 (A.B.759), § 14, operative July 1, 1991.)*

Law Revision Commission Comments

1990 Enactment

Section 70 continues Section 70 of the repealed Probate Code without change. This section is the same as Section 1–201(37) of the Uniform Probate Code (1987). As to the construction of provisions drawn from uniform acts, see Section 2. The context may require that a word or phrase used in a particular section be given a meaning different from the definition provided in this part. Also special definitions may be used for a particular portion of the code that differ from those provided in this part. See Section 20.

Background on Section 70 of Repealed Code

Section 70 was a new provision added by 1983 Cal.Stat. ch. 842 § 21. For background on the provisions of this division, see the Comment to this division under the division heading. [20 Cal.L.Rev.Comm.Reports 1001 (1990)].

§ 71.   Repealed by Stats.1983, c. 842, § 18, operative Jan. 1, 1985

§ 72.   Spouse

"Spouse" includes domestic partner, as defined in Section 37 of this code, as required by Section 297.5 of the Family Code. *(Added by Stats.2016, c. 50 (S.B.1005), § 77, eff. Jan. 1, 2017.)*

§ 73.   Repealed by Stats.1983, c. 842, § 18, operative Jan. 1, 1985

§ 74.   State

"State" includes any state of the United States, the District of Columbia, the Commonwealth of Puerto Rico, and any territory or possession subject to the legislative authority of the United States. *(Stats.1990, c. 79 (A.B.759), § 14, operative July 1, 1991.)*

Law Revision Commission Comments

1990 Enactment

Section 74 continues Section 74 of the repealed Probate Code without change. This section is the same as Section 1–201(40) of the Uniform Probate Code (1987). As to the construction of provisions drawn from uniform acts, see Section 2. The context may require that a word or phrase used in a particular section be given a meaning different from the definition provided in this part. Also special definitions may be used for a particular portion of the code that differ from those provided in this part. See Section 20.

Background on Section 74 of Repealed Code

Section 74 was a new provision added by 1983 Cal.Stat. ch. 842 § 21. For background on the provisions of this division, see the Comment to this division under the division heading. [20 Cal.L.Rev.Comm.Reports 1001 (1990)].

§ 75.   Repealed by Stats.1983, c. 842, § 18, operative Jan. 1, 1985

§ 76.   Subscribing witness

A "subscribing witness" to a will means a witness who signs the will as provided in Section 6110. *(Stats.1990, c. 79 (A.B.759), § 14, operative July 1, 1991.)*

Law Revision Commission Comments

1990 Enactment

Section 76 is a new provision, not found in the general definitions of the repealed Probate Code. The requirements for a person to be a subscribing witness are stated in Section 6110. The subscribing witnesses' signatures need not be "at the end" of the will. See discussion in "Background on Section 6110 of Repealed Code," following the Comment to Section 6110. [20 Cal.L.Rev.Comm.Reports 1001 (1990)].

§ 77.   Repealed by Stats.1983, c. 842, § 18, operative Jan. 1, 1985

§ 78.   Surviving spouse

"Surviving spouse" does not include any of the following:

(a) A person whose marriage to, or registered domestic partnership with, the decedent has been dissolved or annulled, unless, by virtue of a subsequent marriage or registered domestic partnership, the person is married to, or in a registered domestic partnership with, the decedent at the time of death.

(b) A person who obtains or consents to a final decree or judgment of dissolution of marriage or termination of registered domestic partnership from the decedent or a final decree or judgment of annulment of their marriage or termination of registered domestic partnership, which decree or judgment is not recognized as valid in this state, unless they (1) subsequently participate in a marriage ceremony purporting to marry each to the other or (2) subsequently live together as * * * spouses.

(c) A person who, following a decree or judgment of dissolution or annulment of marriage or registered domestic partnership obtained by the decedent, participates in a marriage ceremony with a third person.

(d) A person who was a party to a valid proceeding concluded by an order purporting to terminate all marital or registered domestic partnership property rights. *(Stats.1990, c. 79 (A.B.759), § 14, operative July 1, 1991. Amended by Stats.2016, c. 50 (S.B.1005), § 78, eff. Jan. 1, 2017.)*

Law Revision Commission Comments

1990 Enactment

Section 78 continues Section 78 of the repealed Probate Code without change. The context may require that a word or phrase used in a particular section be given a meaning different from the definition provided in this part. Also, special definitions may be used for a particular portion of the code that differ from those provided in this part. See Section 20.

Section 78 is drawn from Section 2–802 of the Uniform Probate Code (1987). As to the construction of provisions drawn from uniform acts, see Section 2. See also Section 40 ("heir" defined). Subdivisions (b) and (c) address the problem of a divorce or annulment which is not recognized in California, and apply an estoppel principle against the surviving spouse. These provisions are consistent with prior California law. See, e.g., Spellens v. Spellens, 49 Cal.2d 210, 317 P.2d 613 (1957) (estoppel to deny validity of marriage); Estate of Atherley, 44 Cal.App.3d 758, 764, 119 Cal.Rptr. 41 (1975) (recognizing principle but declining to apply it). See also Sections 36 ("dissolution of marriage" defined), 59 ("predeceased spouse" defined) and the Comments to those sections. As to a surviving spouse's waiver of rights at death, see Sections 140–147. For California provisions relating to annulment of marriage, see Title 2 (commencing with Section 4400) of Part 5 of the Civil Code (judicial determination of void or voidable marriage).

Background on Section 78 of Repealed Code

Section 78 was a new provision added by 1983 Cal.Stat. ch. 842 § 21. For background on the provisions of this division, see the Comment to this division under the division heading. [20 Cal.L.Rev.Comm.Reports 1001 (1990)].

Cross References

Nonprobate transfers, former spouse, failure, see Probate Code § 5600.

Nonprobate transfers, joint tenancy, severance, see Probate Code § 5601.

§ 79. Repealed by Stats.1983, c. 842, § 18, operative Jan. 1, 1985

§ 80. Totten trust account

"Totten trust account" means an account in the name of one or more parties as trustee for one or more beneficiaries where the relationship is established by the form of the account and the deposit agreement with the financial institution and there is no subject of the trust other than the sums on deposit in the account. In a Totten trust account, it is not essential that payment to the beneficiary be mentioned in the deposit agreement. A Totten trust account does not include (1) a regular trust account under a testamentary trust or a trust agreement which has significance apart from the account or (2) a fiduciary account arising from a fiduciary relation such as attorney-client. *(Stats.1990, c. 79 (A.B.759), § 14, operative July 1, 1991.)*

Law Revision Commission Comments

1990 Enactment

Section 80 continues Section 80 of the repealed Probate Code without change. This section is the same in substance as Section 6–101(14) of the Uniform Probate Code (1987). As to the construction of provisions drawn from uniform acts, see Section 2. See also Section 21 ("account" defined). See generally Recommendation Relating to Multiple–Party Accounts in Financial Institutions, 20 Cal.L.Revision Comm'n Reports 95 (1990).

The context may require that a word or phrase used in a particular section be given a meaning different from the definition provided in this part. Also special definitions may be used for a particular portion of the code that differ from those provided in this part. See Section 20.

Background on Section 80 of Repealed Code

Section 80 was a new provision added by 1983 Cal.Stat. ch. 842 § 21. For background on the provisions of this division, see the Comment to this division under the division heading. [20 Cal.L.Rev.Comm.Reports 1001 (1990)].

Cross References

Share accounts and certificates for funds, totten trust account, beneficiary addresses, see Financial Code § 14868.

§ 81. Transferor

"Transferor" means the testator, settlor, grantor, owner, or other person who executes an instrument. *(Stats.1990, c. 79 (A.B.759), § 14, operative July 1, 1991.)*

Law Revision Commission Comments

1990 Enactment

Section 81 continues Section 81 of the repealed Probate Code without change. The context may require that a word or phrase used in a particular section be given a meaning different from the definition provided in this part. Also, special definitions may be used for a particular portion of the code that differ from those provided in this part. See Section 20.

Background on Section 81 of Repealed Code

Section 81 was added by 1988 Cal.Stat. ch. 1199 § 27.5. The section continued former Probate Code Section 21100(c) (repealed by 1988 Cal.Stat. ch. 1199 § 107.8) without change but expanded the scope of the former provision to apply to all parts of the code to which the definitions apply. See Section 20 (application of definitions). For background on the provisions of this division, see the Comment to this division under the division heading. [20 Cal.L.Rev.Comm.Reports 1001 (1990)].

§ 81.5. Transferee

"Transferee" means the beneficiary, donee, or other recipient of an interest transferred by an instrument. *(Added by Stats.1994, c. 806 (A.B.3686), § 2.)*

§ 82. Trust

(a) "Trust" includes the following:

(1) An express trust, private or charitable, with additions thereto, wherever and however created.

(2) A trust created or determined by a judgment or decree under which the trust is to be administered in the manner of an express trust.

(b) "Trust" excludes the following:

(1) Constructive trusts, other than those described in paragraph (2) of subdivision (a), and resulting trusts.

(2) Guardianships and conservatorships.

(3) Personal representatives.

(4) Totten trust accounts.

(5) Custodial arrangements pursuant to the Uniform Gifts to Minors Act or the Uniform Transfers to Minors Act of any state.

(6) Business trusts that are taxed as partnerships or corporations.

(7) Investment trusts subject to regulation under the laws of this state or any other jurisdiction.

(8) Common trust funds.

(9) Voting trusts.

(10) Security arrangements.

(11) Transfers in trust for purpose of suit or enforcement of a claim or right.

(12) Liquidation trusts.

(13) Trusts for the primary purpose of paying debts, dividends, interest, salaries, wages, profits, pensions, or employee benefits of any kind.

(14) Any arrangement under which a person is nominee or escrowee for another. *(Stats.1990, c. 79 (A.B.759), § 14, operative July 1, 1991.)*

Law Revision Commission Comments
1990 Enactment

Section 82 continues Section 82 of the repealed Probate Code without change. This section is the same in substance as Section 1–201(45) of the Uniform Probate Code (1987). As to the construction of provisions drawn from uniform acts, see Section 2. See also Sections 80 ("Totten trust account" defined), 15003(c) (application of the Trust Law to entities and relationships that are excluded from the definition of "trust" in this section).

The context may require that a word or phrase used in a particular section be given a meaning different from the definition provided in this part. Also special definitions may be used for a particular portion of the code that differ from those provided in this part. See Section 20.

Background on Section 82 of Repealed Code

Section 82 was added by 1987 Cal.Stat. ch. 128 § 5. The section restated and reorganized the provisions of former Probate Code Section 82 (added to the Probate Code by 1983 Cal.Stat. ch. 842 § 21, amended by 1984 Cal.Stat. ch. 892 § 7 and 1986 Cal.Stat. ch. 820 § 28, and repealed by 1987 Cal.Stat. ch. 128 § 4).

Subdivision (a)(1) of Section 82 restated the first part of subdivision (a) of former Probate Code Section 82 without substantive change. The last part of subdivision (a) of former Section 82 relating to charitable trusts that are not subject to the jurisdiction of the Attorney General was omitted. For a provision concerning the application of Trust Law to charitable trusts, see Section 15004. Subdivision (a)(2) restated subdivision (b) of former Section 82 without substantive change.

Subdivision (b) restated subdivision (c) of former Section 82 without substantive change. This subdivision, like its predecessor, was drawn in part from Section 1–201(45) of the Uniform Probate Code (1987), but also included references to various entities that were listed in former Probate Code Section 1138 (repealed by 1986 Cal.Stat. ch. 820 § 31). As to the construction of provisions drawn from uniform acts, see Section 2. See also Section 15003(c)

(application of the Trust Law to entities and relationships that are excluded from the definition of "trust" in this section).

For background on the provisions of this division, see the Comment to this division under the division heading. See also Recommendation Relating to Technical Revisions in the Trust Law, 18 Cal.L.Revision Comm'n Reports 1823, 1832–34 (1986). [20 Cal.L.Rev.Comm.Reports 1001 (1990)].

Cross References

Administration of trust transferred from another jurisdiction, see Probate Code § 17457.

Application of trust statutes to entity or relationship excluded from definition in this section, see Probate Code § 15003.

California Uniform Transfers to Minors Act, see Probate Code § 3900.

Common trust funds, see Financial Code § 1564.

Conservatorship, generally, see Probate Code § 1800 et seq.

Enforcement of money judgment against interest in trust, see Code of Civil Procedure § 709.010.

Guardianship, generally, see Probate Code § 1500 et seq.

Mortgages, generally, see Civil Code § 2920 et seq.

Taking possession of an asset of the conservatee or ward at an institution or opening or changing ownership of an account of safe-deposit box in a financial institution, see California Rules of Court, Rule 7.1011.

Transfer of trust to another jurisdiction, see Probate Code § 17400 et seq.

Trust administration, see Probate Code § 16000 et seq.

Trustees and beneficiaries, generally, see Probate Code § 15600 et seq.

Trusts, judicial proceedings, rights of third persons, see Probate Code § 18000 et seq.

Trusts not subject to this article, proceedings to transfer jurisdiction, see Probate Code § 17000.

Uniform Principal and Income Act, see Probate Code § 16320 et seq.

§ 83. Trust company

"Trust company" means an entity that has qualified to engage in and conduct a trust business in this state. *(Stats. 1990, c. 79 (A.B.759), § 14, operative July 1, 1991.)*

Law Revision Commission Comments
1990 Enactment

Section 83 continues Section 83 of the repealed Probate Code without change. See also Section 15643 (vacancy in office of trustee), 17351–17353 (removal of trust from continuing court jurisdiction). The context may require that a word or phrase used in a particular section be given a meaning different from the definition provided in this part. Also special definitions may be used for a particular portion of the code that differ from those provided in this part. See Section 20.

Entities that may qualify to conduct a trust business in this state include state chartered commercial banks (see Fin.Code §§ 107, 1500.1) and national banking associations (see Fin.Code §§ 1502, 1503), corporations authorized to conduct a trust business (see Fin.Code § 107, trust departments of title insurance companies (see Fin.Code §§ 107, 1501; Ins.Code §§ 12392, 12393, 12395), and state and federal savings and loan associations (see Fin.Code §§ 5102, 6515). See also Fin.Code § 106 ("trust business" defined). Whether an entity has qualified to engage in and conduct a trust business in this state depends on other law. In order to fall within the definition of "trust company" in Section 83, a corporation, association, or other entity must satisfy the requirements of state or federal law that apply to the particular type of entity.

Background on Section 83 of Repealed Code

Section 83 was added by 1986 Cal.Stat. ch. 820 § 29. The section was drawn from parts of former Probate Code Sections 480 (repealed by 1988 Cal.Stat. ch. 1199 § 47) and 1120.1a (repealed by 1986 Cal.Stat. ch. 820 § 31). For background on the provisions of this division, see the Comment to this division under the division heading. [20 Cal.L.Rev.Comm.Reports 1001 (1990)].

Cross References

Bond of personal representatives, see Probate Code § 8480.
Estate management, interest on deposits in financial institutions, see Probate Code § 9705.
Professional Fiduciaries Act, see Business and Professions Code § 6500 et seq.
Trustees, generally, see Probate Code § 15600 et seq.

§ 84. Trustee

"Trustee" includes an original, additional, or successor trustee, whether or not appointed or confirmed by a court. *(Stats.1990, c. 79 (A.B.759), § 14, operative July 1, 1991.)*

Law Revision Commission Comments

1990 Enactment

Section 84 continues Section 84 of the repealed Probate Code without change. This section is the same as Section 1–201(46) of the Uniform Probate Code (1987). As to the construction of provisions drawn from uniform acts, see Section 2. The context may require that a word or phrase used in a particular section be given a meaning different from the definition provided in this part. Also special definitions may be used for a particular portion of the code that differ from those provided in this part. See Section 20.

Background on Section 84 of Repealed Code

Section 84 was a new provision added by 1983 Cal.Stat. ch. 842 § 21. For background on the provisions of this division, see the Comment to this division under the division heading. [20 Cal.L.Rev.Comm.Reports 1001 (1990)].

Cross References

Duties of trustees, see Probate Code § 16000 et seq.
Trustees, powers, see Probate Code § 16200 et seq.

§ 85. [Blank]

§ 86. Undue influence

"Undue influence" has the same meaning as defined in Section 15610.70 of the Welfare and Institutions Code. It is the intent of the Legislature that this section supplement the common law meaning of undue influence without superseding or interfering with the operation of that law. *(Added by Stats.2013, c. 668 (A.B.140), § 1.)*

§ 87. [Blank]

§ 88. Will

"Will" includes codicil and any testamentary instrument which merely appoints an executor or revokes or revises another will. *(Stats.1990, c. 79 (A.B.759), § 14, operative July 1, 1991.)*

Law Revision Commission Comments

1990 Enactment

Section 88 continues Section 88 of the repealed Probate Code without change. This section is the same as Section 1–201(48) of the Uniform Probate Code (1987). As to the construction of provisions drawn from uniform acts, see Section 2. The context may require that a word or phrase used in a particular section be given a meaning different from the definition provided in this part. Also special definitions may be used for a particular portion of the code that differ from those provided in this part. See Section 20.

Background on Section 88 of Repealed Code

Section 88 was a new provision added by 1983 Cal.Stat. ch. 842 § 21. For background on the provisions of this division, see the Comment to this division under the division heading. [20 Cal.L.Rev.Comm.Reports 1001 (1990)].

Cross References

California statutory will, see Probate Code § 6200 et seq.
Wills, generally, see Probate Code § 6100 et seq.
Wills, revocation and revival, see Probate Code § 6120.

§§ 90 to 92. Repealed by Stats.1983, c. 842, § 18, operative Jan. 1, 1985

Division 2

GENERAL PROVISIONS

Part 1

EFFECT OF DEATH OF MARRIED PERSON ON COMMUNITY AND QUASI–COMMUNITY PROPERTY

Application

Part 1 applies only where decedent died on or after Jan. 1, 1985, see Probate Code § 105.

Law Revision Commission Comments

1990 Enactment

This part supersedes Part 1 (commencing with Section 100) of Division 2 of the repealed Probate Code. The superseded part was enacted upon recommendation of the California Law Revision Commission. See Tentative Recommendation Relating to Wills and Intestate Succession, 16 Cal.L.Revision Comm'n Reports 2301 (1982). See also Report of Senate Committee on Judiciary on Assembly Bills 25 and 68, 17 Cal.L.Revision Comm'n Reports 867, 868–69 (1984). Technical and substantive revisions were made as a result of a subsequent recommendation. See Recommendation Relating to Revision of Wills and Intestate Succession Law, 17 Cal.L.Revision Comm'n Reports 537 (1984). See also Communication of Law Revision Commission Concerning Assembly Bill 2290, 18 Cal.L.Revision Comm'n Reports 77, 79–84 (1986). [20 Cal.L.Rev.Comm.Reports 1001 (1990)].

Cross References

Application of old and new law, see Probate Code § 3.
Community property, defined, see Probate Code § 28; Family Code §§ 65, 760.
Quasi-community property, defined, see Probate Code § 66.
Surviving spouse, defined, see Probate Code § 78.

§ 100. Community property

(a) Upon the death of a <u>person who is</u> married * * * <u>or in a registered domestic partnership</u>, one-half of the community property belongs to the surviving spouse and the other <u>one-half</u> belongs to the decedent.

(b) Notwithstanding subdivision (a), * * * <u>spouses</u> may agree in writing to divide their community property on the basis of a non pro rata division of the aggregate value of the community property or on the basis of a division of each individual item or asset of community property, or partly on each basis. Nothing in this subdivision shall be construed to require this written agreement in order to permit or recognize a non pro rata division of community property. *(Stats. 1990, c. 79 (A.B.759), § 14, operative July 1, 1991. Amended by Stats.1998, c. 682 (A.B.2069), § 2; Stats.2016, c. 50 (S.B.1005), § 79, eff. Jan. 1, 2017.)*

Law Revision Commission Comments

1990 Enactment

Section 100 continues Section 100 of the repealed Probate Code without change. The decedent's half of the community property is subject to the testamentary disposition of the decedent (Section 6101) and, in the absence of testamentary disposition, goes to the surviving spouse (Section 6401). But see Section 103 (effect on community property where married persons die simultaneously). As to the allocation of debts between the estate and the surviving spouse, see Sections 11440–11446. As to the liability of the surviving spouse for debts of the deceased spouse chargeable against community property, see Sections 13550–13554. See also Sections 28 ("community property" defined), 104 (community property held in revocable trust). This part applies only where the decedent died on or after January 1, 1985. See Section 105. As to the application of any amendments made after that date, see Section 3.

Background on Section 100 of Repealed Code

Section 100 was added by 1983 Cal.Stat. ch. 842 § 22. Section 100 restated a portion of former Probate Code Section 201 (repealed by 1983 Cal.Stat. ch. 842 § 19) without substantive change. For background on the provisions of this part, see the Comment to this part under the part heading. [20 Cal.L.Rev.Comm.Reports 1001 (1990)].

§ 101. Quasi-community property

(a) Upon the death of a <u>person who is</u> married * * * <u>or in a registered domestic partnership, and is</u> domiciled in this state, one-half of the decedent's quasi-community property belongs to the surviving spouse and the other <u>one-half</u> belongs to the decedent.

(b) Notwithstanding subdivision (a), * * * <u>spouses</u> may agree in writing to divide their quasi-community property on the basis of a non pro rata division of the aggregate value of the quasi-community property, or on the basis of a division of each individual item or asset of quasi-community property, or partly on each basis. Nothing in this subdivision shall be construed to require this written agreement in order to permit or recognize a non pro rata division of quasi-community property. *(Stats.1990, c. 79 (A.B.759), § 14, operative July 1, 1991. Amended by Stats.1998, c. 682 (A.B.2069), § 3; Stats.2016, c. 50 (S.B.1005), § 80, eff. Jan. 1, 2017.)*

surviving spouse for debts of the deceased spouse chargeable against quasi-community property, see Sections 13550–13554. This part applies only where the decedent died on or after January 1, 1985. See Section 105. As to the application of any amendments made after that date, see Section 3.

The California Law Revision Commission made a series of recommendations concerning the subject matter of this section. See Recommendation and Study Relating to Rights of Surviving Spouse in Property Acquired by Decedent While Domiciled Elsewhere, 1 Cal.L.Revision Comm'n Reports E–1 (1957); Recommendation and Study Relating to Inter Vivos Marital Property Rights in Property Acquired While Domiciled Elsewhere, 3 Cal.L.Revision Comm'n Reports I–1 (1961); Recommendation Relating to Quasi–Community Property, 9 Cal.L.Revision Comm'n Reports 113 (1969).

§ 102. Transfer of quasi-community property; restoration of decedent's estate; requirements

(a) The decedent's surviving spouse may require the transferee of property in which the surviving spouse had an expectancy under Section 101 at the time of the transfer to restore to the decedent's estate one-half of the property if the transferee retains the property or, if not, one-half of its proceeds or, if none, one-half of its value at the time of transfer, if all of the following requirements are satisfied:

(1) The decedent died domiciled in this state.

(2) The decedent made a transfer of the property to a person other than the surviving spouse without receiving in exchange a consideration of substantial value and without the written consent or joinder of the surviving spouse.

(3) The transfer is any of the following types:

(A) A transfer under which the decedent retained at the time of death the possession or enjoyment of, or the right to income from, the property.

(B) A transfer to the extent that the decedent retained at the time of death a power, either alone or in conjunction with any other person, to revoke or to consume, invade, or dispose of the principal for the decedent's own benefit.

(C) A transfer whereby property is held at the time of the decedent's death by the decedent and another with right of survivorship.

(b) Nothing in this section requires a transferee to restore to the decedent's estate any life insurance, accident insurance, joint annuity, or pension payable to a person other than the surviving spouse.

(c) All property restored to the decedent's estate under this section belongs to the surviving spouse pursuant to Section 101 as though the transfer had not been made. *(Stats.1990, c. 79 (A.B.759), § 14, operative July 1, 1991.)*

Law Revision Commission Comments

1990 Enactment

Section 102 continues Section 102 of the repealed Probate Code without change. This section provides that the property shall be restored to the decedent's estate rather than that the surviving spouse may recover it directly from the transferee. This is to make the property available to creditors of the decedent to the extent that it would have been available to them if no inter vivos transfer had been made.

The provision of Section 102 that only one-half of the property transferred is to be restored is applied when the decedent dies intestate as well as when the decedent dies testate. This is because the decedent has manifested an intention to deprive the surviving spouse of the property. The intent of the intestate decedent should be given effect to the extent he or she could have accomplished the same result by will.

Paragraph (2) of subdivision (a) provides that a transfer may be set aside only if the decedent made it without receiving in exchange a consideration of "substantial" value. Where the consideration is not substantial and the transfer is set aside, no provision is made for return of the insubstantial consideration given by the transferee when property transferred is required to be restored. It is not expected that a transfer will be set aside under the statute if the transferee gave a consideration equal to one-half or more of the value of the property received. Thus, in cases in which the transfer is set aside, the one-half which the transferee keeps will be at least equal in value to any consideration given. Paragraph (3) of subdivision (a) is drawn from Uniform Probate Code Section 2–202(1) (1987) and Idaho Code Section 15–2–202 (1979). Subdivision (b) is drawn from a portion of Uniform Probate Code Section 2–202 (1987). As to the construction of provisions drawn from uniform acts, see Section 2.

Subdivision (c) provides that all of the property restored to the estate belongs to the surviving spouse pursuant to Section 101. Such property is, in effect, the one-half which the surviving spouse could have claimed against the decedent's will. The one-half which the transferee is permitted to retain is, in effect, the one-half which the decedent could have given to the transferee by will. The surviving spouse is entitled to all of the first half.

Section 102 is limited in application to transfers made at a time when the surviving spouse has an expectancy under Section 101—i.e., at a time when the transferor is domiciled in California. This is to avoid the application of the statute to transfers made before the transferor moved here, when the transferor could not reasonably have anticipated that the transfer would later be subjected to California law.

This part applies only where the decedent died on or after January 1, 1985. See Section 105. As to the application of any amendments made after that date, see Section 3.

The California Law Revision Commission made a recommendation which resulted in the enactment of a statutory provision (former Probate Code Section 201.8) on the subject matter of this section. See Recommendation and Study Relating to Rights of Surviving Spouse in Property Acquired by Decedent While Domiciled Elsewhere, 1 Cal.L.Revision Comm'n Reports E–1 (1957). With respect to Section 201.8, see the discussion, infra, under "Background on Section 102 of Repealed Code."

Background on Section 102 of Repealed Code

Section 102 was added by 1983 Cal.Stat. ch. 842 § 22. Subdivisions (a) and (b) superseded the first sentence of former Probate Code Section 201.8 (repealed by 1983 Cal.Stat. ch. 842 § 19). Subdivision (c) restated the last sentence of former Section 201.8 without substantive change.

The second sentence of former Section 201.8 which required the surviving spouse to elect to take under or against the decedent's will was not continued. Under the law as revised in 1983, the rule for quasi-community property was the same as for community property: The surviving spouse no longer was forced to an election unless the decedent's will expressly so provides or unless such a requirement should be implied to avoid thwarting the testator's apparent intent. See 7 B. Witkin, Summary of California Law Wills and Probate §§ 21–22, at 5542–44 (8th ed. 1974).

Paragraph (3) of subdivision (a) of Section 102 replaced the provision of former Probate Code Section 201.8 that required as a condition of recapture that the decedent had a "substantial quantum of ownership or control of the property at death."

For background on the provisions of this part, see the Comment to this part under the part heading. [20 Cal.L.Rev.Comm.Reports 1001 (1990)].

Cross References

Estate administration, generally, see Probate Code § 7000 et seq.
Quasi-community property, defined, see Probate Code § 66.
Small estate set aside, see Probate Code § 6600 et seq.
Surviving spouse, defined, see Probate Code § 78.

§ 103. Simultaneous death; community or quasi-community property

Except as provided by Section 224, if * * * spouses die leaving community or quasi-community property and it cannot be established by clear and convincing evidence that one spouse survived the other:

(a) One-half of the community property and one-half of the quasi-community property shall be administered or distributed, or otherwise dealt with, as if one spouse had survived and as if that one-half belonged to that spouse.

(b) The other one-half of the community property and the other one-half of the quasi-community property shall be administered or distributed, or otherwise dealt with, as if the other spouse had survived and as if that one-half belonged to that spouse. *(Stats.1990, c. 79 (A.B.759), § 14, operative July 1, 1991. Amended by Stats.2016, c. 50 (S.B.1005), § 81, eff. Jan. 1, 2017.)*

Law Revision Commission Comments

1990 Enactment

Section 103 continues Section 103 of the repealed Probate Code without substantive change. The introductory clause recognizes that Section 224 governs the disposition of life or accident insurance benefits where one spouse is the insured and the other the beneficiary, even if the source of the insurance premiums was community property. This section, insofar as it is the same in substance as a provision of the Uniform Simultaneous Death Act (1953), is to be so construed and interpreted as to effectuate the general purpose to make uniform the law in those states which enact that act. See Section 2 (general provision relating to construction of provisions drawn from uniform acts). See also Sections 230–234 (proceeding to determine whether one spouse survived the other). This part applies only where the decedent died on or after January 1, 1985. See Section 105. As to the application of any amendments made after that date, see Section 3.

Background on Section 103 of Repealed Code

Section 103 was added by 1983 Cal.Stat. ch. 842 § 22. The section superseded the first paragraph of former Probate Code Section 296.4 (repealed by 1983 Cal.Stat. ch. 842 § 20) and extended to quasi-community property the rule formerly applicable only to community property. For background on the provisions of this part, see the Comment to this part under the part heading. [20 Cal.L.Rev.Comm.Reports 1001 (1990)].

Cross References

Community property, generally, see Family Code §§ 65, 760.
Community property, defined, see Probate Code § 28.
Quasi-community property, defined, see Probate Code § 66.

§ 104. Community property held in revocable trusts

Notwithstanding Section 100, community property held in a revocable trust described in Section 761 of the Family Code is governed by the provisions, if any, in the trust for disposition in the event of death. *(Stats.1990, c. 79 (A.B. 759), § 14, operative July 1, 1991. Amended by Stats.1992, c. 163 (A.B.2641), § 119, operative Jan. 1, 1994.)*

Law Revision Commission Comments

1990 Enactment

Section 104 continues Section 104 of the repealed Probate Code without change. This part applies only where the decedent died on or after January 1, 1985. See Section 105. As to the application of any amendments made after that date, see Section 3.

1992 Amendment

Section 104 is amended to substitute a reference to the Family Code provision that replaced former Civil Code Section 5110.150. [22 Cal.L.Rev.Comm.Reports 1 (1992)].

Background on Section 104 of Repealed Code

Section 104 was added by 1983 Cal.Stat. ch. 842 § 22 and amended by 1987 Cal.Stat. ch. 128 § 6. The section restated a portion of former Probate Code Section 206 (repealed by 1983 Cal.Stat. ch. 842 § 19) without substantive change. The 1987 amendment to Section 104 corrected a cross-reference. For background on the provisions of this part, see the Comment to this part under the part heading. [20 Cal.L.Rev.Comm.Reports 1001 (1990)].

Cross References

Community property, generally, see Family Code §§ 65, 760.
Community property, defined, see Probate Code § 28.

§ 104.5. Transfer of community property to revocable trust; presumption as to character of assets

Transfer of community and quasi-community property to a revocable trust shall be presumed to be an agreement, pursuant to Sections 100 and 101, that those assets retain their character in the aggregate for purposes of any division provided by the trust. This section shall apply to all transfers prior to, on, or after January 1, 2000. *(Added by Stats.1999, c. 263 (A.B.1051), § 1.)*

Cross References

Community property, generally, see Family Code §§ 65, 760.
Community property, defined, see Probate Code § 28.
Presumptions, see Evidence Code § 600 et seq.
Quasi-community property, defined, see Probate Code § 66.

Trusts, creation, validity, modification, and termination, see Probate Code § 15200 et seq.

§ 105. Application of part

This part does not apply where the decedent died before January 1, 1985, and the law applicable prior to January 1, 1985, continues to apply where the decedent died before January 1, 1985. *(Stats.1990, c. 79 (A.B.759), § 14, operative July 1, 1991.)*

Law Revision Commission Comments

1990 Enactment

Section 105 continues Section 105 of the repealed Probate Code without substantive change. This section limits the application of Sections 100–104 to cases where the decedent died on or after January 1, 1985 (the date this part of the repealed Probate Code first became operative). As to the application of any amendments made after that date, see Section 3.

Background on Section 105 of Repealed Code

Section 105 was a new provision added by 1984 Cal.Stat. ch. 892 § 7.5. For background on the provisions of this part, see the Comment to this part under the part heading. [20 Cal.L.Rev.Comm.Reports 1001 (1990)].

§§ 106 to 109. Repealed by Stats.1983, c. 842, § 18, operative Jan. 1, 1985

Part 2

SURVIVING SPOUSE'S RIGHT IN CALIFORNIA REAL PROPERTY OF NONDOMICILIARY DECEDENT

Section
120. Nondomiciliary decedent; real property within state; surviving spouse's right; effect of will.
121 to 126. Repealed.

Law Revision Commission Comments

1990 Enactment

This part supersedes Part 2 (commencing with Section 120) of Division 2 of the repealed Probate Code. The superseded part was enacted upon recommendation of the California Law Revision Commission. See Tentative Recommendation Relating to Wills and Intestate Succession, 16 Cal.L.Revision Comm'n Reports 2301 (1982). [20 Cal.L.Rev.Comm.Reports 1001 (1990)].

Cross References

Application of old and new law, see Probate Code § 3.
Surviving spouse, defined, see Probate Code § 78.

§ 120. Nondomiciliary decedent; real property within state; surviving spouse's right; effect of will

If a married person dies not domiciled in this state and leaves a valid will disposing of real property in this state which is not the community property of the decedent and the surviving spouse, the surviving spouse has the same right to elect to take a portion of or interest in such property against the will of the decedent as though the property were located in the decedent's domicile at death. *(Stats.1990, c. 79 (A.B.759), § 14, operative July 1, 1991.)*

Law Revision Commission Comments

1990 Enactment

Section 120 continues Section 120 of the repealed Probate Code without substantive change. This section gives the surviving spouse the same protected interest in California as the surviving spouse would have under the law of the decedent's domicile. See also Section 68 ("real property" defined).

The California Law Revision Commission made a recommendation which resulted in the enactment of a statutory provision (former Probate Code Section 201.6, repealed by 1983 Cal.Stat. ch. 842 § 19) on the subject matter of this section. See Recommendation and Study Relating to Rights of Surviving Spouse in Property Acquired by Decedent While Domiciled Elsewhere, 1 Cal.L.Revision Comm'n Reports E–1 (1957).

Background on Section 120 of Repealed Code

Section 120 was added by 1983 Cal.Stat. ch. 842 § 22. The section restated former Probate Code Section 201.6 (repealed by 1983 Cal.Stat. ch. 842 § 19) without substantive change. For background on the provisions of this part, see the Comment to this part under the part heading. [20 Cal.L.Rev.Comm.Reports 1001 (1990)].

Cross References

Community property, generally, see Family Code §§ 65, 760.
Community property, defined, see Probate Code § 28.
Estate administration, generally, see Probate Code § 7000 et seq.
Real property, defined, see Probate Code § 68.
Surviving spouse, defined, see Probate Code § 78.

§§ 121 to 126.   Repealed by Stats.1983, c. 842, § 18, operative Jan. 1, 1985

Part 3

CONTRACTUAL ARRANGEMENTS RELATING TO RIGHTS AT DEATH

Law Revision Commission Comments

1990 Enactment

This part supersedes Part 3 (commencing with Section 140) of Division 2 of the repealed Probate Code. The superseded part was enacted upon recommendation of the California Law Revision Commission. See Tentative Recommendation Relating to Wills and Intestate Succession, 16 Cal.L.Revision Comm'n Reports 2301, 2347–51, 2375–81 (1982). See also Report of Senate Committee on Judiciary on Assembly Bills 25 and 68, 17 Cal.L.Revision Comm'n Reports 867, 869–70 (1984); Communication of Law Revision Commission Concerning Assembly Bill 2290, 18 Cal.L.Revision Comm'n Reports 77, 79–82 (1986). [20 Cal.L.Rev.Comm.Reports 1001 (1990)].

CHAPTER 1.   SURVIVING SPOUSE'S WAIVER OF RIGHTS

Application

Limited applicability of Chapter 1 before Jan. 1, 1985, see Probate Code § 147.

Cross References

Application of old and new law, see Probate Code § 3.
Surviving spouse, defined, see Probate Code § 78.

§ 140.   Waiver

As used in this chapter, "waiver" means a waiver by the surviving spouse of any of the rights listed in subdivision (a) of Section 141, whether signed before or during marriage. *(Stats.1990, c. 79 (A.B.759), § 14, operative July 1, 1991.)*

Law Revision Commission Comments

1990 Enactment

Section 140 continues Section 140 of the repealed Probate Code without change. This chapter has no effect on waivers, agreements, or property settlements made prior to January 1, 1985 (the date this chapter of the repealed Probate Code first became operative). See Section 147. As to the application of any amendments made after that date, see Section 3. As to premarital property agreements, see Section 147 and the Comment thereto.

Background on Section 140 of Repealed Code

Section 140 was a new provision added by 1983 Cal.Stat. ch. 842 § 22 and amended by 1984 Cal.Stat. ch. 892 § 8. The 1984 amendment made a clarifying, nonsubstantive revision. For background on the provisions of this part, see the Comment to this part under the part heading. [20 Cal.L.Rev.Comm.Reports 1001 (1990)].

Cross References

Surviving spouse, defined, see Probate Code § 78.

§ 141.   Rights which may be waived

(a) The right of a surviving spouse to any of the following may be waived in whole or in part by a waiver under this chapter:

(1) Property that would pass from the decedent by intestate succession.

(2) Property that would pass from the decedent by testamentary disposition in a will executed before the waiver.

(3) A probate homestead.

(4) The right to have exempt property set aside.

(5) Family allowance.

(6) The right to have an estate set aside under Chapter 6 (commencing with Section 6600) of Part 3 of Division 6.

(7) The right to elect to take community or quasi-community property against the decedent's will.

(8) The right to take the statutory share of an omitted spouse.

(9) The right to be appointed as the personal representative of the decedent's estate.

(10) An interest in property that is the subject of a nonprobate transfer on death under Part 1 (commencing with Section 5000) of Division 5.

(b) Nothing in this chapter affects or limits the waiver or manner of waiver of rights other than those referred to in subdivision (a), including, but not limited to, the right to property that would pass from the decedent to the surviving spouse by nonprobate transfer upon the death of the decedent, such as the survivorship interest under a joint tenancy, a Totten trust account, or a pay-on-death account. *(Stats.1990, c. 79 (A.B.759), § 14, operative July 1, 1991. Amended by Stats.1992, c. 51 (A.B.1719), § 2.)*

Law Revision Commission Comments

1990 Enactment

Section 141 continues Section 141 of the repealed Probate Code without substantive change. This section is drawn in part from the first sentence of Section 2–204 of the Uniform Probate Code (1987). As to the construction of provisions drawn from uniform acts, see Section 2.

Paragraphs (1) and (2) of subdivision (a) permit waiver of property, interests, or benefits that would pass to the spouse making the waiver by intestate succession or by virtue of a will of the other spouse executed before the waiver.

Paragraphs (3), (4), and (5) are the same in substance as provisions found in Section 2–204 of the Uniform Probate Code (1987) and are consistent with prior California case law. See, e.g., Estate of Howe, 81 Cal.App.2d 95, 183 P.2d 329 (1947) (probate homestead); In re Estate of Fulton, 15 Cal.App.2d 202, 59 P.2d 508 (1936) (exempt property); Estate of Brooks, 28 Cal.2d 748, 171 P.2d 724 (1946) (family allowance). As to the construction of provisions drawn from uniform acts, see Section 2.

Paragraph (6) is consistent with prior California case law. See Soares v. Steidtmann, 130 Cal.App.2d 401, 278 P.2d 953 (1955).

Paragraph (7) is comparable to the provision in Section 2–204 of the Uniform Probate Code (1987) for waiver of the elective share under the Uniform Probate Code. As to the construction of provisions drawn from uniform acts, see Section 2. Paragraph (7) is consistent with prior California case law. See 7 B. Witkin, Summary of California Law Wills and Probate § 20, at 5541 (8th ed. 1974).

Paragraph (8) is included to make clear that a spouse may waive the right to claim as an omitted spouse under Section 6560. Paragraph (9) is consistent with Section 8440 (waiver of right to appointment by executor).

Subdivision (b) makes clear that this chapter applies only to the waiver of the rights listed in subdivision (a). The law applicable to the waiver of other rights is not affected by this chapter. See, e.g., Civil Code §§ 5200–5317. See also Section 80 ("Totten trust account" defined). As to pay-on-death accounts, see also Division 5 (commencing with Section 5100) (multiple-party accounts in financial institutions).

This chapter has no effect on waivers, agreements, or property settlements made prior to January 1, 1985 (the date this chapter of the repealed Probate Code first became operative). See Section 147. As to the application of any amendments made after that date, see Section 3. As to premarital property agreements, see Section 147 and the Comment thereto.

1992 Amendment

Paragraph (10) is added to Section 141(a) for purposes of cross-referencing the provisions on nonprobate transfers. See also Section 5013 (waiver or agreement that affects rights in community property). [21 Cal.L.Rev.Comm.Reports 163 (1991)].

Background on Section 141 of Repealed Code

Section 141 was a new provision added by 1983 Cal.Stat. ch. 842 § 22 and amended by 1987 Cal.Stat. ch. 923 § 19. The 1987 amendment revised a cross-reference to another statute and made other nonsubstantive revisions. For background on the provisions of this part, see the Comment to this part under the part heading. [20 Cal.L.Rev.Comm.Reports 1001 (1990)].

Cross References

Appointment of personal representative, generally, see Probate Code § 8400 et seq.
Community property, generally, see Family Code §§ 65, 760.
Community property, defined, see Probate Code § 28.
Disposition of estate without administration, passage of property to surviving spouse, see Probate Code § 13500 et seq.
Estate administration, generally, see Probate Code § 7000 et seq.
Family allowance, defined, see Probate Code § 38.
Intestate succession, generally, see Probate Code § 6400 et seq.
Pay-on-death account, defined, see Probate Code § 55.
Personal representative and general personal representative, defined, see Probate Code § 58.
Probate homestead, defined, see Probate Code § 60.
Quasi-community property, defined, see Probate Code § 66.
Surviving spouse, defined, see Probate Code § 78.
Totten trust account, defined, see Probate Code § 80.

§ 142. Requirement of writing; enforceability; defenses

(a) A waiver under this chapter shall be in writing and shall be signed by the surviving spouse.

(b) Subject to subdivision (c), a waiver under this chapter is enforceable only if it satisfies the requirements of subdivision (a) and is enforceable under either Section 143 or Section 144.

(c) Enforcement of the waiver against the surviving spouse is subject to the same defenses as enforcement of a contract, except that:

(1) Lack of consideration is not a defense to enforcement of the waiver.

(2) A minor intending to marry may make a waiver under this chapter as if married, but the waiver becomes effective only upon the marriage. *(Stats.1990, c. 79 (A.B.759), § 14, operative July 1, 1991.)*

Law Revision Commission Comments

1990 Enactment

Section 142 continues Section 142 of the repealed Probate Code without change. Subdivision (a) requires that a waiver be in writing and be signed by the surviving spouse in order to be effective under this chapter. See also Sections 143–145 (enforcement of waiver), 146 (alteration, amendment, or revocation of waiver).

Subdivisions (b) and (c) make clear that enforcement of the waiver is subject to the same defenses as enforcement of a contract, but lack of consideration is not a defense and a minor intending to marry is treated as an emancipated minor (Civil Code § 63). The surviving spouse can raise the defense of lack of capacity to contract. See Civil Code § 1556 (unsound mind or deprived of civil rights). The defense of lack of consent because of duress, menace, fraud, undue influence, or mistake (Civil Code §§ 1565–1579) also is available. But see the Comment to Section 143.

This chapter has no effect on waivers, agreements, or property settlements made prior to January 1, 1985 (the date this chapter of the repealed Probate Code first became operative). See Section 147. As to the application of any amendments made after that date, see

Section 3. As to premarital property agreements, see Section 147 and the Comment thereto.

Background on Section 142 of Repealed Code

Section 142 was a new provision added by 1983 Cal.Stat. ch. 842 § 22 and amended by 1984 Cal.Stat. ch. 892 § 9. Subdivision (a) was enacted in 1983; subdivisions (b) and (c) were added to Section 142 by the 1984 amendment. For background on the provisions of this part, see the Comment to this part under the part heading. [20 Cal.L.Rev.Comm.Reports 1001 (1990)].

Cross References

Minors, defined, see Family Code § 6500.
Surviving spouse, defined, see Probate Code § 78.

§ 143. Enforceability

(a) Subject to Section 142, a waiver is enforceable under this section unless the surviving spouse proves either of the following:

(1) A fair and reasonable disclosure of the property or financial obligations of the decedent was not provided to the surviving spouse prior to the signing of the waiver unless the surviving spouse waived such a fair and reasonable disclosure after advice by independent legal counsel.

(2) The surviving spouse was not represented by independent legal counsel at the time of signing of the waiver.

(b) Subdivision (b) of Section 721 of the Family Code does not apply if the waiver is enforceable under this section. *(Stats.1990, c. 79 (A.B.759), § 14, operative July 1, 1991. Amended by Stats.1992, c. 163 (A.B.2641), § 120, operative Jan. 1, 1994.)*

Law Revision Commission Comments
1990 Enactment

Section 143 continues Section 143 of the repealed Probate Code without change. This section establishes the basic standards of enforceability for a waiver.

The court shall enforce the waiver unless the surviving spouse proves either (or both) of the following:

(1) The surviving spouse was not provided a fair and reasonable disclosure of property (absent a waiver of such disclosure after advice by independent legal counsel).

(2) The surviving spouse was not represented by independent legal counsel at the time of execution.

By satisfying the conditions of disclosure and independent counsel, the parties can have certainty that their affairs will be governed in an agreed upon manner. If these conditions are not satisfied (for example, counsel may not have been sought at all or the surviving spouse may not have been separately represented), a waiver may still be enforceable under Section 144 (waiver enforceable in discretion of court).

The disclosure required under subdivision (a)(1) includes a disclosure both of the property and of the financial obligations of the decedent. Information concerning financial obligations may be important in determining whether the rights described in Section 141 should be waived.

The introductory clause of Section 143 makes clear that enforcement of a waiver under Section 143 is subject to the same defenses as enforcement of a contract. See Section 142(c). However, the requirement of representation by independent legal counsel and disclosure or waiver of disclosure on the advice of independent legal counsel should permit enforcement of the waiver against a claim of undue influence, duress, or mistake, except where the surviving spouse lacked sound mind or there was some type of duress, mistake,

or fraud that the independent counsel and disclosure requirements do not protect against. Thus, parties who want more assurance that the waiver is enforceable should obtain independent legal counsel despite the added expense. See Rothschild, Antenuptial and Post-nuptial Agreements, in 2 California Marital Dissolution Practice § 29.2, at 1174–75, § 29.4, at 1176–77 (Cal.Cont.Ed.Bar 1983); Wolfe & Hellman, Handling Surviving Spouse's Share of Marital Property, in California Will Drafting Practice §§ 5.31–5.33, at 205–07 (Cal.Cont.Ed.Bar 1982). However, even if the requirements of Section 143 are not satisfied, the waiver may be enforceable under Section 144.

Subdivision (b) makes clear that the fiduciary standards normally applicable to spouses pursuant to Civil Code Section 5103 do not apply if the waiver is enforceable under Section 143.

This chapter has no effect on waivers, agreements, or property settlements made prior to January 1, 1985 (the date this chapter of the repealed Probate Code first became operative). See Section 147. As to the application of any amendments made after that date, see Section 3. As to premarital property agreements, see Section 147 and the Comment thereto.

1992 Amendment

Subdivision (b) of Section 143 is amended to substitute a reference to the Family Code provision that replaced former Civil Code Section 5103. [22 Cal.L.Rev.Comm.Reports 1 (1992)].

Background on Section 143 of Repealed Code

Section 143 was a new provision added by 1983 Cal.Stat. ch. 842 § 22 and amended by 1984 Cal.Stat. ch. 892 § 10. The 1984 amendment made substantive and clarifying revisions. For background on the provisions of this part, see the Comment to this part under the part heading. [20 Cal.L.Rev.Comm.Reports 1001 (1990)].

Cross References

Rights and obligations during marriage, contracts with each other and third parties, see Family Code § 721.
Surviving spouse, defined, see Probate Code § 78.

§ 144. Enforceability under certain circumstances

(a) Except as provided in subdivision (b), subject to Section 142, a waiver is enforceable under this section if the court determines either of the following:

(1) The waiver at the time of signing made a fair and reasonable disposition of the rights of the surviving spouse.

(2) The surviving spouse had, or reasonably should have had, an adequate knowledge of the property and financial obligations of the decedent and the decedent did not violate the duty imposed by subdivision (b) of Section 721 of the Family Code.

(b) If, after considering all relevant facts and circumstances, the court finds that enforcement of the waiver pursuant to subdivision (a) would be unconscionable under the circumstances existing at the time enforcement is sought, the court may refuse to enforce the waiver, enforce the remainder of the waiver without the unconscionable provisions, or limit the application of the unconscionable provisions to avoid an unconscionable result.

(c) Except as provided in paragraph (2) of subdivision (a), subdivision (b) of Section 721 of the Family Code does not apply if the waiver is enforceable under this section. *(Stats. 1990, c. 79 (A.B.759), § 14, operative July 1, 1991. Amended by Stats.1992, c. 163 (A.B.2641), § 121, operative Jan. 1, 1994.)*

Law Revision Commission Comments
1990 Enactment

Section 144 continues Section 144 of the repealed Probate Code without change.

Under subdivision (a), a waiver that is not enforceable pursuant to Section 143 may be enforceable if it is shown that the waiver at the time of execution made a fair and reasonable disposition of the rights of the surviving spouse or the surviving spouse had, or reasonably should have had, an adequate knowledge of the property and the financial obligations of the other spouse.

Subdivision (b) provides a "safety valve" from the liberal standards of enforceability provided by subdivision (a). It permits the court to refuse to enforce all or a portion of the waiver if the court finds that enforcement would be "unconscionable" under the circumstances existing at the time enforcement is sought. Satisfaction of the standards of enforceability provided by subdivision (a) should insure in the vast majority of cases that the waiver was fairly made and properly enforceable. However, in the exceptional case, circumstances may have changed in a way that neither party may have contemplated and enforcement of the waiver in its entirety would now be unconscionable. In short, subdivision (b) provides a measure of flexibility. It should be emphasized, however, that this subdivision is not intended to apply in any but the extraordinary case and never applies where the conditions of Section 143 are met.

Subdivision (a)(2) and subdivision (c) of Section 144 make clear the extent to which the fiduciary standards normally applicable to spouses pursuant to Civil Code Section 5103 apply when the waiver is sought to be enforced under Section 144. See also Wolfe & Hellman, Handling Surviving Spouse's Share of Marital Property, in California Will Drafting Practice §§ 5.31–5.32, at 205–06 (Cal. Cont.Ed.Bar 1982).

The reference to Section 142 in the introductory clause of subdivision (a) makes clear that enforcement of the waiver against the surviving spouse is subject to the same defenses as enforcement of a contract. See the Comments to Sections 142 and 143.

This chapter has no effect on waivers, agreements, or property settlements made prior to January 1, 1985 (the date this chapter of the repealed Probate Code first became operative). See Section 147. As to the application of any amendments made after that date, see Section 3. As to premarital property agreements, see Section 147 and the Comment thereto.

1992 Amendment

Subdivisions (a)(2) and (c) of Section 144 are amended to substitute references to the Family Code provision that replaced former Civil Code Section 5103. [22 Cal.L.Rev.Comm.Reports 1 (1992)].

Background on Section 144 of Repealed Code

Section 144 was a new provision added by 1983 Cal.Stat. ch. 842 § 22 and amended by 1984 Cal.Stat. ch. 892 § 11. The 1984 amendment made substantive and clarifying revisions. For background on the provisions of this part, see the Comment to this part under the part heading. [20 Cal.L.Rev.Comm.Reports (1990)].

Cross References

Rights and obligations during marriage, contracts with each other and third parties, see Family Code § 721.
Surviving spouse, defined, see Probate Code § 78.

§ 145. Waiver of "all rights"

Unless the waiver or property settlement provides to the contrary, a waiver under this chapter of "all rights" (or equivalent language) in the property or estate of a present or prospective spouse, or a complete property settlement entered into after or in anticipation of separation or dissolution or annulment of marriage, is a waiver by the spouse of the rights described in subdivision (a) of Section 141. *(Stats. 1990, c. 79 (A.B.759), § 14, operative July 1, 1991.)*

Law Revision Commission Comments
1990 Enactment

Section 145 continues Section 145 of the repealed Probate Code without change. This section is drawn from the second sentence of Section 2–204 of the Uniform Probate Code (1987). As to the construction of provisions drawn from uniform acts, see Section 2. Nothing in Section 145 affects or limits the waiver or manner of waiver of rights other than those mentioned in subdivision (a) of Section 141. See Section 141(b) and the Comment thereto. This chapter has no effect on waivers, agreements, or property settlements made before January 1, 1985 (the date this chapter of the repealed Probate Code first became operative). See Section 147. As to the application of any amendments made after that date, see Section 3. As to the requirements for a property settlement made on or after January 1, 1985, insofar as the settlement affects rights listed in subdivision (a) of Section 141, see Section 147. As to premarital property agreements, see Section 147 and the Comment thereto.

Background on Section 145 of Repealed Code

Section 145 was added by 1983 Cal.Stat. ch. 842 § 22. The section superseded former Probate Code Section 80 (repealed by 1983 Cal.Stat. ch. 842 § 18). For background on the provisions of this part, see the Comment to this part under the part heading. [20 Cal.L.Rev.Comm.Reports 1001 (1990)].

§ 146. Agreement; requirements

(a) As used in this section, "agreement" means a written agreement signed by each spouse or prospective spouse altering, amending, or revoking a waiver under this chapter.

(b) Except as provided in subdivisions (c) and (d) of Section 147, unless the waiver specifically otherwise provides, a waiver under this chapter may not be altered, amended, or revoked except by a subsequent written agreement signed by each spouse or prospective spouse.

(c) Subject to subdivision (d), the agreement is enforceable only if it satisfies the requirements of subdivision (b) and is enforceable under either subdivision (e) or subdivision (f).

(d) Enforcement of the agreement against a party to the agreement is subject to the same defenses as enforcement of any other contract, except that:

(1) Lack of consideration is not a defense to enforcement of the agreement.

(2) A minor intending to marry may enter into the agreement as if married, but the agreement becomes effective only upon the marriage.

(e) Subject to subdivision (d), an agreement is enforceable under this subdivision unless the party to the agreement against whom enforcement is sought proves either of the following:

(1) A fair and reasonable disclosure of the property or financial obligations of the other spouse was not provided to the spouse against whom enforcement is sought prior to the signing of the agreement unless the spouse against whom enforcement is sought waived such a fair and reasonable disclosure after advice by independent legal counsel.

(2) The spouse against whom enforcement is sought was not represented by independent legal counsel at the time of signing of the agreement.

(f) Subject to subdivisions (d) and (g), an agreement is enforceable under this subdivision if the court determines that the agreement at the time of signing made a fair and reasonable disposition of the rights of the spouses.

(g) If, after considering all relevant facts and circumstances, the court finds that enforcement of the agreement pursuant to subdivision (f) would be unconscionable under the circumstances existing at the time enforcement is sought, the court may refuse to enforce the agreement, enforce the remainder of the agreement without the unconscionable provisions, or limit the application of the unconscionable provisions to avoid an unconscionable result.

(h) Subdivision (b) of Section 721 of the Family Code does not apply if the agreement is enforceable under this section. *(Stats.1990, c. 79 (A.B.759), § 14, operative July 1, 1991. Amended by Stats.1992, c. 163 (A.B.2641), § 122, operative Jan. 1, 1994.)*

Law Revision Commission Comments
1990 Enactment

Section 146 continues Section 146 of the repealed Probate Code without change. This section prescribes the conditions that must be satisfied if the agreement to alter, amend, or revoke the waiver is to be enforceable. The provisions of Section 146 are consistent with those provided by Sections 142–144 for a waiver. Under subdivision (b), a waiver expressly may provide, for example, that it is revocable during the lifetime of the other spouse. See also, e.g., Wolfe & Hellman, Handling Surviving Spouse's Share of Marital Property, in California Will Drafting Practice §§ 5.34, 5.36, at 207–09 (Cal. Cont.Ed.Bar 1982).

Nothing in this chapter limits any right one spouse otherwise has to revoke a consent or election to disposition of his or her half of the community or quasi-community property under the will of the other spouse. See Section 147(d). This chapter has no effect on waivers, agreements, or property settlements made prior to January 1, 1985 (the date this chapter of the repealed Probate Code first became operative). See Section 147. As to the application of any amendments made after that date, see Section 3. As to premarital property agreements, see Section 147 and the Comment thereto.

1992 Amendment

Subdivision (h) of Section 146 is amended to substitute a reference to the Family Code provision that replaced former Civil Code Section 5103. [22 Cal.L.Rev.Comm.Reports 1 (1992)].

Background on Section 146 of Repealed Code

Section 146 was added by 1983 Cal.Stat. ch. 842 § 22 and amended by 1984 Cal.Stat. ch. 892 § 12. The section was extensively revised by the 1984 amendment. For background on the provisions of this part, see the Comment to this part under the part heading. [20 Cal.L.Rev.Comm.Reports 1001 (1990)].

Cross References

Minors, defined, see Family Code § 6500.
Rights and obligations during marriage, contracts with each other and third parties, see Family Code § 721.

§ 147. Waiver, agreement or property settlement; validity; validity or effect of premarital property agreement; right to dispose of community or quasi-community property

(a) Subject to subdivisions (c) and (d), a waiver, agreement, or property settlement made after December 31, 1984, is invalid insofar as it affects the rights listed in subdivision (a) of Section 141 unless it satisfies the requirements of this chapter.

(b) Nothing in this chapter affects the validity or effect of any waiver, agreement, or property settlement made prior to January 1, 1985, and the validity and effect of such waiver, agreement, or property settlement shall continue to be determined by the law applicable to the waiver, agreement, or settlement prior to January 1, 1985.

(c) Nothing in this chapter affects the validity or effect of any premarital property agreement, whether made prior to, on, or after January 1, 1985, insofar as the premarital property agreement affects the rights listed in subdivision (a) of Section 141, and the validity and effect of such premarital property agreement shall be determined by the law otherwise applicable to the premarital property agreement. Nothing in this subdivision limits the enforceability under this chapter of a waiver made under this chapter by a person intending to marry that is otherwise enforceable under this chapter.

(d) Nothing in this chapter limits any right one spouse otherwise has to revoke a consent or election to disposition of his or her half of the community or quasi-community property under the will of the other spouse. *(Stats.1990, c. 79 (A.B.759), § 14, operative July 1, 1991.)*

Law Revision Commission Comments
1990 Enactment

Section 147 continues Section 147 of the repealed Probate Code without change. Subdivision (a) makes clear that, absent a valid premarital property agreement, interspousal agreements or waivers of rights on death must satisfy the requirements of this chapter. See also Civil Code §§ 5300–5317 (Uniform Premarital Agreement Act). Under the Uniform Premarital Agreement Act, the parties to a premarital agreement may contract with respect to the disposition of property upon death, the making of a will, trust, or other arrangement to carry out the provisions of the agreement, the disposition of the death benefit from a life insurance policy, and other matters. See Civil Code § 5312. As to the requirements for execution of a premarital agreement under the Uniform Act, see Civil Code §§ 5311, 5314, 5315.

Subdivision (b) makes clear that the provisions of this chapter have no effect on waivers, agreements, or property settlements made prior to January 1, 1985 (the date this chapter of the repealed Probate Code first became operative). As to the application of any amendments made after that date, see Section 3. See also Section 141(b) (nothing in chapter affects or limits the waiver or manner of waiver of rights other than those referred to in subdivision (a) of Section 141).

Subdivision (c) makes two things clear. First, an enforceable agreement affecting rights listed in subdivision (a) of Section 141 may be made in a valid premarital property agreement. Second, a premarital waiver of rights listed in subdivision (a) also is enforceable under this chapter if the requirements of this chapter are satisfied.

Subdivision (d) makes clear that this chapter does not limit the right of a spouse to revoke a consent or election to disposition of his or her half of the community or quasi-community property under the will of the other spouse. See Wolfe & Hellman, Handling Surviving Spouse's Share of Marital Property, in California Will Drafting Practice §§ 5.31–5.34, at 205–08 (Cal.Cont.Ed.Bar 1982). See also the Comment to Section 146.

Background on Section 147 of Repealed Code

Section 147 was a new provision added by 1983 Cal.Stat. ch. 842 § 22. The section was amended by 1984 Cal.Stat. ch. 892 § 13 to add subdivisions (c) and (d). For background on the provisions of this part, see the Comment to this part under the part heading. [20 Cal.L.Rev.Comm.Reports 1001 (1990)].

Cross References

Community property, generally, see Family Code §§ 65, 760.
Community property, defined, see Probate Code § 28.
Quasi-community property, defined, see Probate Code § 66.

CHAPTER 2. CONTRACTS CONCERNING WILL OR SUCCESSION [REPEALED]

§ 150. Repealed by Stats.2000, c. 17 (A.B.1491), § 2

§ 160. Repealed by Stats.1990, c. 79 (A.B.759), § 13, operative July 1, 1991

Law Revision Commission Comments

1990 Repeal

Section 160 of the repealed Probate Code is restated without substantive change in Section 5000 (nonprobate transfers at death). [20 Cal.L.Rev.Comm.Reports 1001 (1990)].

§§ 161 to 190.10. Repealed by Stats.1983, c. 842, § 18, operative Jan. 1, 1985

Part 4

ESTABLISHING AND REPORTING FACT OF DEATH

CHAPTER 1. PROCEEDINGS TO ESTABLISH DEATH

Law Revision Commission Comments

1990 Enactment

This chapter provides an expeditious procedure for establishing the fact of death for the purpose of clearing title to property. See Chapter 2 (commencing with Section 210) (recording evidence of death). Other proceedings to establish the fact of death for other purposes include Health and Safety Code Sections 10550–10558 (court proceedings to establish record of birth, death, or marriage) and Probate Code Sections 8000–8577 (opening estate administration), 12400–12408 (administration of estates of missing persons presumed dead).

This chapter supersedes Chapter 1 (commencing with Section 200) of Part 4 of Division 2 of the repealed Probate Code. The superseded chapter was enacted upon recommendation of the California Law Revision Commission. See Recommendation Relat-

ing to Recording Affidavit of Death, 17 Cal.L.Revision Comm'n Reports 493 (1984). [20 Cal.L.Rev.Comm.Reports 1001 (1990)].

Cross References

Application of old and new law, see Probate Code § 3.

§ 200. Commencement of proceedings

If title to or an interest in real or personal property is affected by the death of a person, another person who claims an interest in the property may commence proceedings pursuant to this chapter to establish the fact of the death. *(Stats.1990, c. 79 (A.B.759), § 14, operative July 1, 1991.)*

Law Revision Commission Comments

1990 Enactment

Section 200 continues Section 200 of the repealed Probate Code without change.

Background on Section 200 of Repealed Code

Section 200 was added by 1984 Cal.Stat. ch. 527 § 2. The section restated the first portion of former Probate Code Section 1170 (repealed by 1984 Cal.Stat. ch. 527 § 5) without substantive change. For background on the provisions of this chapter, see the Comment to this chapter under the chapter heading. [20 Cal.L.Rev.Comm.Reports 1001 (1990)].

Cross References

Fee for filing petition commencing or opposition papers concerning certain probate proceedings, see Government Code § 70655.
Missing persons presumed dead, see Probate Code § 12400 et seq.
Persons entitled to distribution, proceedings, pleadings, see Probate Code § 11700 et seq.
Persons purchasing property from killer, liability of killer, see Probate Code § 255.

§ 201. Venue; petition

(a) Proceedings under this chapter shall be commenced in the superior court of the county of which the decedent was a resident at the time of death or in the superior court of any county in which the property is located.

(b) Proceedings under this chapter shall be commenced by filing a petition that sets forth all of the following information:

(1) The jurisdictional facts.

(2) A particular description of the affected property and of the interest of the petitioner in the property. *(Stats.1990, c. 79 (A.B.759), § 14, operative July 1, 1991.)*

Law Revision Commission Comments

1990 Enactment

Section 201 continues Section 201 of the repealed Probate Code without substantive change. The requirement of the repealed Probate Code section that the petition be verified has been omitted because this requirement is generalized in Section 1021. See also Sections 1004 (notice of pendency of proceeding), 1020–1023 (signing and verifying petition).

Background on Section 201 of Repealed Code

Section 201 was added by 1984 Cal.Stat. ch. 527 § 2. The section restated the last portion of former Probate Code Section 1170 (repealed by 1984 Cal.Stat. ch. 527 § 5) without substantive change. For background on the provisions of this chapter, see the Comment to this chapter under the chapter heading. [20 Cal.L.Rev.Comm.Reports 1001 (1990)].

§§ 201.5 to 201.8. Repealed by Stats.1983, c. 842, § 19, operative Jan. 1, 1985

§ 202. Combining proceedings with administration of estate; manner

If proceedings for the administration of the decedent's estate are pending, proceedings under this chapter may be combined with the administration proceedings in the following manner:

(a) The petition shall be filed in the administration proceedings by the person affected or by the personal representative.

(b) The petition shall be filed at any time before the filing of a petition for final distribution. The petition may be included in a petition for probate of the will of the decedent or for letters.

(c) The petition shall be filed without any additional fee. *(Stats.1990, c. 79 (A.B.759), § 14, operative July 1, 1991.)*

Law Revision Commission Comments

1990 Enactment

Section 202 continues Section 202 of the repealed Probate Code without substantive change. The requirement of the repealed Probate Code section that the petition be verified has been omitted because this requirement is generalized in Section 1021. "Personal representative" has been substituted for "executor or administrator." See Section 58 (defining "personal representative"). See also Sections 1020–1023 (signing and verifying petition). A reference to "letters" has been substituted for "letters of administration." This is a nonsubstantive change. See Section 52 (defining "letters").

Background on Section 202 of Repealed Code

Section 202 was added by 1984 Cal.Stat. ch. 527 § 2. The section restated former Probate Code Section 1171 (repealed by 1984 Cal.Stat. ch. 527 § 5) without substantive change. For background on the provisions of this chapter, see the Comment to this chapter under the chapter heading. [20 Cal.L.Rev.Comm.Reports 1001 (1990)].

Cross References

Estate administration, generally, see Probate Code § 7000 et seq.
Letters, defined, see Probate Code § 52.
Missing persons presumed dead, administration of estate, see Probate Code § 12400 et seq.
Passage of property to surviving spouse without administration, see Probate Code § 13506.
Personal representative and general personal representative, defined, see Probate Code § 58.
Probate of will, generally, see Probate Code § 8200 et seq.

§ 203. Hearing; notice; ex parte proceedings

(a) Except as provided in subdivision (b), notice of the hearing shall be given as provided in Section 1220.

(b) If the person who commenced the proceedings files an affidavit with the petition stating that the person has no reason to believe there is any opposition to, or contest of, the petition, the court may act ex parte. *(Stats.1990, c. 79 (A.B.759), § 14, operative July 1, 1991.)*

Law Revision Commission Comments

1990 Enactment

Section 203 continues Section 203 of the repealed Probate Code without change. For general provisions relating to notice, see Sections 1200–1221. See also Sections 1250–1252 (request for special notice), 1260–1265 (proof of giving of notice). The notice provision of subdivision (a) does not apply to a particular notice where the notice was delivered, mailed, posted, or first published before July 1, 1991. In such a case, the applicable law in effect before July 1, 1991, continues to apply to the giving of the notice. See Section 1200(c). As to the application of any amendments made after that date, see Section 3.

Background on Section 203 of Repealed Code

Section 203 was added by 1984 Cal.Stat. ch. 527 § 2 and amended by 1987 Cal.Stat. ch. 923 § 21. The section restated former Probate Code Section 1172 (repealed by 1984 Cal.Stat. ch. 527 § 5) without substantive change. The 1987 amendment deleted the requirement that the clerk set the petition for hearing, this requirement having been generalized in former Probate Code Section 1285 (repealed by 1988 Cal.Stat. ch. 1199 § 64.5), which has been continued as Section 1041. The amendment also made the section consistent with the general notice provisions. For background on the provisions of this chapter, see the Comment to this chapter under the chapter heading. [20 Cal.L.Rev.Comm.Reports 1001 (1990)].

Cross References

Affidavits, see Code of Civil Procedure § 2009 et seq.
Passage of property to surviving spouse without administration, see Probate Code § 13506.

§ 204. Petition and affidavits as evidence; judgment as prima facie evidence

(a) The petition and supporting affidavits may be received in evidence and acted upon by the court with the same force and effect as if the petitioner and affiants were personally present and testified to the facts set forth.

(b) The court may render judgment establishing the fact of the death. The judgment is prima facie evidence of the fact of the death. The presumption established by this subdivision is a presumption affecting the burden of producing evidence. *(Stats.1990, c. 79 (A.B.759), § 14, operative July 1, 1991.)*

Law Revision Commission Comments

1990 Enactment

Section 204 continues Section 204 of the repealed Probate Code without change. The judgment establishing the fact of death does not establish the title of the person who commenced the proceedings. As to the effect of a presumption affecting the "burden of producing evidence," see Evid.Code § 604. For general provisions relating to hearings and orders, see Sections 1040–1050. The judgment may be recorded pursuant to Chapter 2 (commencing with Section 210).

Background on Section 204 of Repealed Code

Section 204 was added by 1984 Cal.Stat. ch. 527 § 2. The section restated former Probate Code Section 1174 (repealed by 1984 Cal.Stat. ch. 527 § 5) without substantive change. For background on the provisions of this chapter, see the Comment to this chapter under the chapter heading. [20 Cal.L.Rev.Comm.Reports 1001 (1990)].

Cross References

Affidavits, see Code of Civil Procedure § 2009 et seq.
Burden of proof, generally, see Evidence Code § 500 et seq.

Newspapers, publications and official advertising, see Government Code § 6000 et seq.

Official records and other official writings, see Evidence Code § 1280 et seq.

Passage of property to surviving spouse without administration, see Probate Code § 13506.

Petitions and other papers,
Generally, see Probate Code § 1020 et seq.
Contents, see Probate Code § 8002.

Presumptions, see Evidence Code § 600 et seq.

§§ 205, 206. Repealed by Stats.1984, c. 527, § 1

§ 207. Inoperative

CHAPTER 2. RECORDING EVIDENCE OF DEATH

Section

210. Authority to record documents establishing fact of death.
211. Documents subject to statutory requirements; index entry.
212. Document establishing fact of death as prima facie evidence.

Law Revision Commission Comments

1990 Enactment

This chapter supersedes Chapter 2 (commencing with Section 210) of Part 4 of Division 2 of the repealed Probate Code. The superseded chapter was enacted upon recommendation of the California Law Revision Commission. See Recommendation Relating to Recording Affidavit of Death, 17 Cal.L.Revision Comm'n Reports 493 (1984). [20 Cal.L.Rev.Comm.Reports 1001 (1990)].

§ 210. Authority to record documents establishing fact of death

If title to real property is affected by the death of a person, any person may record in the county in which the property is located any of the following documents establishing the fact of the death:

(a) An affidavit of death executed by a person having knowledge of the facts. The affidavit shall include a particular description of the real property and an attested or certified copy of a record of the death made and filed in a designated public office as required by law. For purposes of this subdivision, a certified copy issued in this state shall include any copy issued pursuant to Section 103525 of, subdivision (a) of Section 103526 of, or paragraph (1) of subdivision (b) of Section 103526 of, the Health and Safety Code.

(b) A certified copy of a court order that determines the fact of death made pursuant to Chapter 1 (commencing with Section 200) or pursuant to another statute that provides for a determination of the fact of death. (Stats.1990, c. 79 (A.B.759), § 14, operative July 1, 1991. Amended by Stats. 2013, c. 78 (A.B.464), § 4.)

Law Revision Commission Comments

1990 Enactment

Section 210 continues Section 210 of the repealed Probate Code without substantive change. This section makes clear that a document establishing the death of a person is entitled to recordation. Cf. Gov't Code §§ 27280 (recordation of instrument or judgment affecting title to property), 27322 (recordation of instrument required or permitted by law to be recorded).

Subdivision (a) codified the prior practice. See, e.g., 1 A. Bowman, Ogden's Revised California Real Property Law § 7.17, at 280–81 (Cal.Cont.Ed.Bar 1974); cf. Health & Safety Code § 8628 (affidavit of death of joint tenant of cemetery plot). It is comparable to authority found in a number of jurisdictions for affidavits as to death. See, e.g., P. Basye, Clearing Land Titles § 33, at 128 (2d ed. 1970). An affidavit must be made under oath or upon penalty of perjury. Code Civ.Proc. §§ 2003, 2015.5 (affidavits). Independent authority for recordation of a death certificate may be found in Health and Safety Code Sections 10060 and 10570.

Subdivision (b) permits recording of a certified copy of a court order that determines the fact of death. Other proceedings establishing the fact of death include Health and Safety Code Sections 10550–10558 (court proceedings to establish record of birth, death, or marriage) and Probate Code Sections 12400–12408 (administration of estates of missing persons presumed dead).

Background on Section 210 of Repealed Code

Section 210 was added by 1984 Cal.Stat. ch. 527 § 2. Subdivision (a) was new and codified the practice under prior law. Subdivision (b) continued the substance of former Probate Code Section 1175 (repealed by 1984 Cal.Stat. ch. 527 § 5) (recordation of decree establishing fact of death). For background on the provisions of this chapter, see the Comment to this chapter under the chapter heading. [20 Cal.L.Rev.Comm.Reports 1001 (1990)].

Cross References

Affidavits, see Code of Civil Procedure § 2009 et seq.

Inspection of public records, see Government Code § 6250 et seq.

Newspapers, publications and official advertising, see Government Code § 6000 et seq.

Official records and other official writings, see Evidence Code § 1280 et seq.

Real property, defined, see Probate Code § 68.

Recordation of orders affecting real estate, see Probate Code § 7263.

Recorded conveyance as constructive notice, see Civil Code § 1213.

§ 211. Documents subject to statutory requirements; index entry

(a) A document establishing the fact of death recorded pursuant to this chapter is subject to all statutory requirements for recorded documents.

(b) The county recorder shall index a document establishing the fact of death recorded pursuant to this chapter in the index of grantors and grantees. The index entry shall be for the grantor, and for the purpose of this index, the person whose death is established shall be deemed to be the grantor. (Stats.1990, c. 79 (A.B.759), § 14, operative July 1, 1991.)

Law Revision Commission Comments

1990 Enactment

Section 211 continues Section 211 of the repealed Probate Code without change. This section provides indexing only for the decedent and not for the person who records a document establishing the fact of death. Recordation gives notice only of the fact of death; it does not establish the claim of any person who claims an interest in the property. See Section 212 (effect of recording).

Background on Section 211 of Repealed Code

Section 211 was a new provision added by 1984 Cal.Stat. ch. 527 § 2. For background on the provisions of this chapter, see the Comment to this chapter under the chapter heading. [20 Cal.L.Rev.Comm.Reports 1001 (1990)].

§ 212. Document establishing fact of death as prima facie evidence

A document establishing the fact of the death of a person recorded pursuant to this chapter is prima facie evidence of the death insofar as the document identifies real property located in the county, title to which is affected by the death. The presumption established by this section is a presumption affecting the burden of producing evidence. *(Stats.1990, c. 79 (A.B.759), § 14, operative July 1, 1991.)*

Law Revision Commission Comments

1990 Enactment

Section 212 continues Section 212 of the repealed Probate Code without substantive change. This section is consistent with Section 204 (hearing and judgment) and Health and Safety Code Section 10577 (death certificate prima facie evidence of fact of death). This section is subject to express statutory provisions giving greater effect to a document that establishes the fact of the decedent's death. See, e.g., Sections 11605 (conclusive effect of order for distribution), 11705 (conclusive effect of determination of persons entitled to distribution). As to the effect of a presumption affecting the burden of producing evidence, see Evid.Code § 604.

Background on Section 212 of Repealed Code

Section 212 was a new provision added by 1984 Cal.Stat. ch. 527 § 2. For background on the provisions of this chapter, see the Comment to this chapter under the chapter heading. [20 Cal.L.Rev.Comm.Reports 1001 (1990)].

Cross References

Burden of proof, generally, see Evidence Code § 500 et seq.
Newspapers, publications and official advertising, see Government Code § 6000 et seq.
Official records and other official writings, see Evidence Code § 1280 et seq.
Presumptions, see Evidence Code § 600 et seq.
Real property, defined, see Probate Code § 68.

CHAPTER 3. REPORTING FACT OF DEATH

Section
215. Death of person or surviving spouse of person receiving public health care; notice to Director of Health Care Services.
216. Death of person with heir in correctional facility; notice to director of Victim Compensation Board; method and content of notice.
217. In-person cancellation of services not required.

Law Revision Commission Comments

1990 Enactment

This chapter supersedes Chapter 3 (commencing with Section 215) of Part 4 of Division 2 of the repealed Probate Code. The superseded chapter was enacted upon recommendation of the California Law Revision Commission. See Recommendation Relating to Creditor Claims Against Decedent's Estate, 19 Cal.L.Revision Comm'n Reports 299, 352 (1988). [20 Cal.L.Rev.Comm.Reports 1001 (1990)].

§ 215. Death of person or surviving spouse of person receiving public health care; notice to Director of Health Care Services

Where a deceased person has received or may have received health care under Chapter 7 (commencing with Section 14000) or Chapter 8 (commencing with Section 14200) of Part 3 of Division 9 of the Welfare and Institutions Code, or was the surviving spouse of a person who received that health care, the estate attorney, or if there is no estate attorney, the beneficiary, the personal representative, or the person in possession of property of the decedent shall give the Director of Health Care Services notice of the decedent's death not later than 90 days after the date of death. The notice shall include a copy of the decedent's death certificate. The notice shall be given as provided in Section 1215, addressed to the director at the Sacramento office of the director. *(Stats.1990, c. 79 (A.B.759), § 14, operative July 1, 1991. Amended by Stats.1993, c. 69 (S.B.35), § 4, eff. June 30, 1993; Stats.2014, c. 71 (S.B.1304), § 135, eff. Jan. 1, 2015.)*

Law Revision Commission Comments

1990 Enactment

Section 215 continues Section 215 of the repealed Probate Code without change. This section requires a beneficiary or a person in possession of property of the decedent to give notice of the decedent's death to the Director of Health Services if the decedent received health care and related services at public expense under a statute listed in the section. Section 9202 requires the personal representative to give notice of the decedent's death to the Director of Health Services if the decedent received health care under the same circumstances.

Background on Section 215 of Repealed Code

Section 215 was added by 1987 Cal.Stat. ch. 923 § 22. The section restated subdivision (b) and a portion of subdivision (a) of former Probate Code Section 700.1 (repealed by 1987 Cal.Stat. ch. 923 § 37). For background on the provisions of this chapter, see the Comment to this chapter under the chapter heading. [20 Cal.L.Rev.Comm.Reports 1001 (1990)].

Cross References

Beneficiary, defined, see Probate Code § 24
Personal representative and general personal representative, defined, see Probate Code § 58.
Surviving spouse, defined, see Probate Code § 78.

§ 216. Death of person with heir in correctional facility; notice to director of Victim Compensation Board; method and content of notice

(a) For the purposes of this section "confined" means to be confined in a prison or facility under the jurisdiction of the Department of Corrections and Rehabilitation, or its Division of Juvenile Facilities, or confined in any county or city jail, road camp, industrial farm, or other local correctional facility.

(b) The estate attorney, or if there is no estate attorney, the beneficiary, the personal representative, or the person in possession of property of the decedent shall give the Director of the California Victim Compensation * * * Board notice of a decedent's death not later than 90 days after the date of death in either of the following circumstances:

(1) The deceased person has an heir or beneficiary who is confined.

(2) The estate attorney, or if there is no estate attorney, the beneficiary, the personal representative, or the person in possession of property of the decedent, knows that an heir or beneficiary has previously been confined.

(c) The notice shall be given as provided in Section 1215 and shall include all of the following:

(1) The name, date of birth, and location of incarceration, or current address if no longer incarcerated, of the decedent's heir or beneficiary.

(2) The heir's or beneficiary's CDCR number if incarcerated in a Department of Corrections and Rehabilitation facility or booking number if incarcerated in a county facility.

(3) A copy of the decedent's death certificate.

(4) The probate case number, and the name of the superior court hearing the case.

(d) Nothing in this section shall be interpreted as requiring the estate attorney, the beneficiary, the personal representative, or the person in possession of property of the decedent to conduct an additional investigation to determine whether a decedent has an heir or beneficiary who has been confined in a prison or facility under the jurisdiction of the Department of Corrections and Rehabilitation, or its Division of Juvenile Facilities, or confined in any county or city jail, road camp, industrial farm, or other local correctional facility. *(Added by Stats.2005, c. 238 (S.B.972), § 3. Amended by Stats.2008, c. 582 (A.B.717), § 3; Stats.2014, c. 508 (A.B.2685), § 3, eff. Jan. 1, 2015; Stats.2016, c. 31 (S.B.836), § 260, eff. June 27, 2016.)*

Cross References

Death of person with heir in correctional facility, notice to director of Victim Compensation and Government Claims Board, see Probate Code § 9202.

§ 217. In-person cancellation of services not required

(a) A business that receives an oral or written request from a family member, attorney, or personal representative of a deceased person to cancel that person's services may not require an in-person cancellation.

(b) For purposes of this section, "services" include, but are not limited to, gas, electrical, water, sewage, cable, satellite, telephone, or cellular telephone service. *(Added by Stats. 2007, c. 14 (A.B.604), § 1.)*

Part 5

SIMULTANEOUS DEATH

Law Revision Commission Comments

1990 Enactment

This part supersedes Part 5 (commencing with Section 220) of Division 2 of the repealed Probate Code. The superseded part was enacted upon recommendation of the California Law Revision Commission. See Tentative Recommendation Relating to Wills and Intestate Succession, 16 Cal.L.Revision Comm'n Reports 2301, 2345–46, 2386–91, 2509–2510 (1982). See also Report of Senate Committee on Judiciary on Assembly Bills 25 and 68, 17 Cal.L.Revision Comm'n Reports 867, 870–71 (1984). [20 Cal.L.Rev.Comm.Reports 1001 (1990)].

Cross References

Public employees' retirement system, simultaneous death, see Government Code § 21509.

State teachers' retirement system, procedures concerning payment, simultaneous death, see Education Code § 24611.

State teachers' retirement system cash balance plan, distribution of lump-sum death benefit, application of Part 5 of Division 2 of Probate Code, see Education Code § 27102.

CHAPTER 1. GENERAL PROVISIONS

Application

Chapter 1 applicable to estates of decedents who died after Jan. 1, 1985, see Probate Code § 226.

§ 220. Disposition of property; insufficient evidence of survivorship

Except as otherwise provided in this chapter, if the title to property or the devolution of property depends upon priority of death and it cannot be established by clear and convincing evidence that one of the persons survived the other, the property of each person shall be administered or distributed, or otherwise dealt with, as if that person had survived the other. *(Stats.1990, c. 79 (A.B.759), § 14, operative July 1, 1991.)*

Law Revision Commission Comments

1990 Enactment

Section 220 continues Section 220 of the repealed Probate Code without substantive change. The introductory clause of Section 220 recognizes that other provisions of this chapter limit the application of Section 220. Section 221 provides that this chapter does not apply to cases covered by Sections 103 (community and quasi-community property), 6146 (wills), or 6403 (survival of heirs). Other provisions of this chapter provide rules that apply to particular cases. See Sections 222 (survival of beneficiaries), 223 (survival of joint tenants), 224 (survival of insurance beneficiaries). The rule provided by Section 220 may be varied by a provision in the governing instrument. See Section 221. See also Sections 230–234 (proceeding to determine whether one person survived another).

Section 226 limits the application of this chapter to cases where the person the priority of whose death is in issue died on or after January 1, 1985 (the date this chapter of the repealed Probate Code first became operative). As to the application of any amendments made after that date, see Section 3.

Background on Section 220 of Repealed Code

Section 220 was added by 1983 Cal.Stat. ch. 842 § 22. The section superseded former Probate Code Section 296 (repealed by 1983 Cal.Stat. ch. 842 § 20) and modified the prior rule to require proof of survival by clear and convincing evidence. For background on the provisions of this part, see the Comment to this part under the part heading. [20 Cal.L.Rev.Comm.Reports 1001 (1990)].

Cross References

Community or quasi-community property, simultaneous death, see Probate Code § 103.

§ 221. Application of chapter

(a) This chapter does not apply in any case where Section 103, 6211, or 6403 applies.

(b) This chapter does not apply in the case of a trust, deed, or contract of insurance, or any other situation, where (1) provision is made dealing explicitly with simultaneous deaths or deaths in a common disaster or otherwise providing for distribution of property different from the provisions of this chapter or (2) provision is made requiring one person to survive another for a stated period in order to take property or providing for a presumption as to survivorship that results in a distribution of property different from that provided by this chapter. *(Stats.1990, c. 79 (A.B.759), § 14, operative July 1, 1991. Amended by Stats.1990, c. 710 (S.B.1775), § 1, operative July 1, 1991; Stats.2002, c. 138 (A.B.1784), § 3.)*

Law Revision Commission Comments

1990 Enactment

Section 221 continues Section 221 of the repealed Probate Code without change. Subdivision (a) makes clear that the provisions of this chapter do not apply in cases where Section 103 (effect on community and quasi-community property where married person does not survive death of spouse), 6146 (wills), or 6403 (intestate succession) applies. Subdivision (b) provides that the distribution provision of a trust, deed, contract of insurance, or other instrument controls if it results in a different distribution of property than that provided in this chapter. Subdivision (b) uses language drawn from Section 2–601 of the Uniform Probate Code (1987) and includes the substance of the 1953 revision of Section 6 of the Uniform Simultaneous Death Act (1983). As to the construction of provisions drawn from uniform acts, see Section 2.

Section 226 limits the application of this chapter to cases where the person the priority of whose death is in issue died on or after January 1, 1985 (the date this chapter of the repealed Probate Code first became operative). As to the application of any amendments made after that date, see Section 3.

1990 Amendment

Section 221 (enacted as a part of the new Probate Code by 1990 Cal.Stat. ch. 79 § 14) was amended by 1990 Cal.Stat. ch. 710 § 1. The amendment added a reference to Section 6211 (120–hour survival requirement under California statutory will). For background on the 1990 amendment, see Recommendation Relating to Survival Requirement for Beneficiary of Statutory Will, 20 Cal.L.Revision Comm'n Reports 549 (1990). [20 Cal.L.Rev.Comm.Reports 1001 (1990)].

2002 Amendment

Section 221 is amended to delete the reference to former Section 6146, which has been repealed. The former section is superseded by Section 21109 (requirement that transferee survive transferor), which is amended to delete its special rules in reliance on this chapter. [31 Cal.L.Rev.Comm. Reports 218 (2001)].

Background on Section 221 of Repealed Code

Section 221 was added by 1983 Cal.Stat. ch. 842 § 22. Subdivision (a) was new. Subdivision (b) continued the substance of former Probate Code Section 296.6 (repealed by 1983 Cal.Stat. ch. 842 § 20) but omitted the reference to "wills" (will now being covered by Section 6146), substituted "trust" for "living trusts," added language drawn from Section 2–601 of the Uniform Probate Code (1987), and

included the substance of the 1953 revision of Section 6 of the Uniform Simultaneous Death Act (1983). As to the construction of provisions drawn from uniform acts, see Section 2. The 1953 revision, which had not previously been adopted in California, inserted the phrase "or any other situation" and added the clause which appeared as the last portion of clause (2) of subdivision (b) of Section 221. For background on the provisions of this part, see the Comment to this part under the part heading. [20 Cal.L.Rev.Comm.Reports 1001 (1990)].

Cross References

Death of person not heard from in five years, see Evidence Code § 667.

Finding of presumed death by authorized federal employee, see Evidence Code § 1282.

Income tax, inclusion and exclusion from gross income, see Revenue and Taxation Code § 17131 et seq.

Insurance,
  Causes of loss, see Insurance Code § 530 et seq.
  Computation of cash surrender value, see Insurance Code § 10161.
  Funeral expenses, see Insurance Code § 10114.
  Insurable interests, see Insurance Code § 280 et seq.
  Life insurance defined, see Insurance Code § 101.
  Notice and proofs of loss, see Insurance Code § 550 et seq.
  Payment of proceeds, see Insurance Code § 10170 et seq.

Trusts, judicial proceedings, generally, see Probate Code § 17000 et seq.

§ 222. Beneficiaries; right to succeed to interest conditional upon surviving another person; insufficient evidence

(a) If property is so disposed of that the right of a beneficiary to succeed to any interest in the property is conditional upon surviving another person and it cannot be established by clear and convincing evidence that the beneficiary survived the other person, the beneficiary is deemed not to have survived the other person.

(b) If property is so disposed of that one of two or more beneficiaries would have been entitled to the property if he or she had survived the others, and it cannot be established by clear and convincing evidence that any beneficiary survived any other beneficiary, the property shall be divided into as many equal portions as there are beneficiaries and the portion of each beneficiary shall be administered or distributed, or otherwise dealt with, as if that beneficiary had survived the other beneficiaries. *(Stats.1990, c. 79 (A.B.759), § 14, operative July 1, 1991.)*

Law Revision Commission Comments

1990 Enactment

Section 222 continues Section 222 of the repealed Probate Code without substantive change. Subdivision (a) is drawn from the first sentence of Section 2 of the Uniform Simultaneous Death Act (1983), as Section 2 was revised in 1953. As to the construction of provisions drawn from uniform acts, see Section 2. See also Sections 221 (provision of governing instrument prevails), 230–234 (proceeding to determine whether one person survived another). For the definition of "beneficiary," see Section 24.

Section 226 limits the application of this chapter to cases where the person the priority of whose death is in issue died on or after January 1, 1985 (the date this chapter of the repealed Probate Code first became operative). As to the application of any amendments made after that date, see Section 3.

Background on Section 222 of Repealed Code

Section 222 was added by 1983 Cal.Stat. ch. 842 § 22. Subdivision (a) was new. Subdivision (b) superseded former Probate Code Section 296.1 (repealed by 1983 Cal.Stat. ch. 842 § 20). For background on the provisions of this part, see the Comment to this part under the part heading. [20 Cal.L.Rev.Comm.Reports 1001 (1990)].

Cross References

Administration of property of person missing for seven years, see Probate Code § 280.

Beneficiary, defined, see Probate Code § 24

Death of person not heard from in five years, see Evidence Code § 667.

Finding of presumed death by authorized federal employee, see Evidence Code § 1282.

§ 223. Joint tenants

(a) As used in this section, "joint tenants" includes owners of property held under circumstances that entitled one or more to the whole of the property on the death of the other or others.

(b) If property is held by two joint tenants and both of them have died and it cannot be established by clear and convincing evidence that one survived the other, the property held in joint tenancy shall be administered or distributed, or otherwise dealt with, one-half as if one joint tenant had survived and one-half as if the other joint tenant had survived.

(c) If property is held by more than two joint tenants and all of them have died and it cannot be established by clear and convincing evidence that any of them survived the others, the property held in joint tenancy shall be divided into as many portions as there are joint tenants and the share of each joint tenant shall be administered or distributed, or otherwise dealt with, as if that joint tenant had survived the other joint tenants. *(Stats.1990, c. 79 (A.B.759), § 14, operative July 1, 1991.)*

Law Revision Commission Comments

1990 Enactment

Section 223 continues Section 223 of the repealed Probate Code without substantive change. The section is drawn from Section 3 of the Uniform Simultaneous Death Act (1953). As to the construction of provisions drawn from uniform acts, see Section 2. See also Sections 221 (provision of governing instrument prevails), 230–234 (proceeding to determine whether one person survived another). Section 226 limits the application of this chapter to cases where the person the priority of whose death is in issue died on or after January 1, 1985 (the date this chapter of the repealed Probate Code first became operative). As to the application of any amendments made after that date, see Section 3.

Background on Section 223 of Repealed Code

Section 223 was added by 1983 Cal.Stat. ch. 842 § 22. The section superseded former Probate Code Section 296.2 (repealed by 1983 Cal.Stat. ch. 842 § 20). The rule governing the dividing of the property was the same as under former law. For background on the provisions of this part, see the Comment to this part under the part heading. [20 Cal.L.Rev.Comm.Reports 1001 (1990)].

§ 224. Life or accident insurance; insured and beneficiary

If the insured and a beneficiary under a policy of life or accident insurance have died and it cannot be established by clear and convincing evidence that the beneficiary survived the insured, the proceeds of the policy shall be administered or distributed, or otherwise dealt with, as if the insured had survived the beneficiary, except if the policy is community or quasi-community property of the insured and the spouse of the insured and there is no alternative beneficiary except the estate or personal representative of the insured, the proceeds shall be distributed as community property under Section 103. *(Stats.1990, c. 79 (A.B.759), § 14, operative July 1, 1991.)*

Law Revision Commission Comments

1990 Enactment

Section 224 continues Section 224 of the repealed Probate Code without substantive change. The rule provided by this section is subject to contrary provisions in the insurance contract. See Section 221. See also Sections 230–234 (proceeding to determine whether one person survived another).

Section 224 adopts the special rule provided by the optional provision of Section 5 of the Uniform Simultaneous Death Act (1953). As to the construction of provisions drawn from uniform acts, see Section 2. This special rule applies where the insurance policy is community or quasi-community property and there is no alternative beneficiary except the estate or personal representative of the insured. In such a case, the proceeds are not paid to the estate or personal representative of the insured, but are distributed half as if one spouse had survived and as if that half belonged to that spouse, and half as if the other spouse had survived and as if that other half belonged to the other spouse. See Section 103.

Section 226 limits the application of this chapter to cases where the person the priority of whose death is in issue died on or after January 1, 1985 (the date this chapter of the repealed Probate Code first became operative). As to the application of any amendments made after that date, see Section 3.

Background on Section 224 of Repealed Code

Section 224 was added by 1983 Cal.Stat. ch. 842 § 22 and was amended by 1984 Cal.Stat. ch. 892 § 15. The section superseded former Probate Code Section 296.3 (repealed by 1983 Cal.Stat. ch. 842 § 20). The 1984 amendment substituted the special rule provided by the optional provision of Section 5 of the Uniform Simultaneous Death Act (1953) for former subdivision (b) of Section 224. For background on the provisions of this part, see the Comment to this part under the part heading. [20 Cal.L.Rev.Comm.Reports 1001 (1990)].

Cross References

Beneficiary, defined, see Probate Code § 24

Community property, defined, see Probate Code § 28; Family Code §§ 65, 760.

Effect of death of insured on policy, see Insurance Code § 303.

Insurance,

　　Causes of loss, see Insurance Code § 530 et seq.

　　Computation of cash surrender value, see Insurance Code § 10161.

　　Funeral expenses, see Insurance Code § 10114.

　　Insurable interests, see Insurance Code § 280 et seq.

　　Life insurance defined, see Insurance Code § 101.

　　Notice and proofs of loss, see Insurance Code § 550 et seq.

　　Payment of proceeds, see Insurance Code § 10170 et seq.

Personal representative and general personal representative, defined, see Probate Code § 58.

Quasi-community property, defined, see Probate Code § 66.

§ 225. Repealed by Stats.1990, c. 79 (A.B.759), § 13, operative July 1, 1991

Section 225 of the repealed Probate Code is omitted from the new Probate Code because it is unnecessary. See Section 2(b) (construction of uniform acts). [20 Cal.L.Rev.Comm.Reports 1001 (1990)].

§ 226. Application of chapter

This chapter does not apply where a person the priority of whose death is in issue died before January 1, 1985, and the law applicable prior to January 1, 1985, continues to apply where none of the persons the priority of whose death is in issue died on or after January 1, 1985. *(Stats.1990, c. 79 (A.B.759), § 14, operative July 1, 1991.)*

Section 226 continues Section 226 of the repealed Probate Code without substantive change. This section limits the application of Sections 220–224 to cases where the person the priority of whose death is in issue died on or after the date those sections of the repealed Probate Code first became operative. As to the application of any amendments made after that date, see Section 3.

Background on Section 226 of Repealed Code

Section 226 was a new provision added by 1984 Cal.Stat. ch. 892 § 15.2. For background on the provisions of this part, see the Comment to this part under the part heading. [20 Cal.L.Rev.Comm.Reports 1001 (1990)].

§ 227. Repealed by Stats.1983, c. 842, § 19, operative Jan. 1, 1985

§ 228. Repealed by Stats.1980, c. 136, p. 320, § 1

§ 229. Repealed by Stats.1983, c. 842, § 19, operative Jan. 1, 1985

CHAPTER 2. PROCEEDINGS TO DETERMINE SURVIVAL

§ 230. Petitions; purposes

A petition may be filed under this chapter for any one or more of the following purposes:

(a) To determine for the purposes of Section 103, 220, 222, 223, 224, 6211, 6242, 6243, 6403, 21109, 21110 or other provision of this code whether one person survived another.

(b) To determine for the purposes of Section 673 whether issue of an appointee survived the donee.

(c) To determine for the purposes of Section 24611 of the Education Code whether a person has survived in order to receive benefits payable under the system.

(d) To determine for the purposes of Section 21509 of the Government Code whether a person has survived in order to receive money payable under the system. *(Stats.1990, c. 79 (A.B.759), § 14, operative July 1, 1991. Amended by Stats. 1990, c. 710 (S.B.1775), § 2, operative July 1, 1991; Stats.2002, c. 138 (A.B.1784), § 4.)*

Section 230 continues Section 230 of the repealed Probate Code without substantive change. This section refers to various provisions that present an issue of survival. See also Sections 1020–1023 (signing and verifying petition).

1990 Amendment

Section 230 (enacted as a part of the new Probate Code by 1990 Cal.Stat. ch. 79 § 14) was amended by 1990 Cal.Stat. ch. 710 § 2. The amendment added a reference to Section 6211 (120–hour survival requirement under California statutory will). For background on the 1990 amendment, see Recommendation Relating to Survival Requirement for Beneficiary of Statutory Will, 20 Cal.L.Revision Comm'n Reports 549 (1990). [20 Cal.L.Rev.Comm.Reports 1001 (1990)].

2002 Amendment

Section 230 is amended to correct cross-references. References to former provisions that have been repealed are replaced by references to the provisions, if any, that have superseded them. Subdivision (e), relating to determinations under the former Uniform Simultaneous Death Act, is repealed as obsolete. [31 Cal.L.Rev.Comm. Reports 218 (2001)].

Background on Section 230 of Repealed Code

Section 230 was a new provision added by 1983 Cal.Stat. ch. 842 § 22. Sections 230–234 were drawn from former Sections 296.41 and 296.42 (repealed by 1983 Cal.Stat. ch. 842 § 20). For background on the provisions of this part, see the Comment to this part under the part heading. [20 Cal.L.Rev.Comm.Reports 1001 (1990)].

§ 231. Petitions; persons who may file

A petition may be filed under this chapter by any of the following:

(a) The personal representative of any person the priority of whose death is in issue under the applicable provision referred to in Section 230.

(b) Any other person interested in the estate of any such person. *(Stats.1990, c. 79 (A.B.759), § 14, operative July 1, 1991.)*

Section 231 continues Section 231 of the repealed Probate Code without substantive change. "Personal representative" has been substituted for "executor or administrator." See Section 58 (defining "personal representative"). See also Sections 1004 (notice of pendency of proceeding), 1020–1023 (signing and verifying petition).

Background on Section 231 of Repealed Code

Section 231 was added by 1983 Cal.Stat. ch. 842 § 22. The section restated a portion of the first sentence of former Probate Code Section 296.41 (repealed by 1983 Cal.Stat. ch. 842 § 20) without substantive change. For background on the provisions of this part, see the Comment to this part under the part heading. [20 Cal.L.Rev.Comm.Reports 1001 (1990)].

Cross References

Appointment of personal representative, generally, see Probate Code § 8400 et seq.
Interested person, defined, see Probate Code § 48.
Personal representative and general personal representative, defined, see Probate Code § 58.

§ 232. Petitions; proceedings in which filed; exclusive jurisdiction

(a) The petition shall be filed in the estate proceeding in which the person filing the petition received his or her appointment or in the estate proceeding for the estate in which the person filing the petition claims an interest.

(b) The court that first acquires jurisdiction under this section has exclusive jurisdiction for the purposes of this chapter. *(Stats.1990, c. 79 (A.B.759), § 14, operative July 1, 1991.)*

Law Revision Commission Comments

1990 Enactment

Section 232 continues Section 232 of the repealed Probate Code without change.

Background on Section 232 of Repealed Code

Section 232 was added by 1983 Cal.Stat. ch. 842 § 22. Subdivision (a) restated a portion of the first sentence of former Probate Code Section 296.41 (repealed by 1983 Cal.Stat. ch. 842 § 20) without substantive change. Subdivision (b) restated the last sentence of former Probate Code Section 296.42 (repealed by 1983 Cal.Stat. ch. 842 § 20) without substantive change. For background on the provisions of this part, see the Comment to this part under the part heading. [20 Cal.L.Rev.Comm.Reports 1001 (1990)].

Cross References

Trusts, judicial proceedings, generally, see Probate Code § 17000 et seq.

§ 233. Notice of hearing

Notice of the hearing on the petition shall be given as provided in Section 1220 to all of the following persons:

(a) The personal representative of each person the priority of whose death is in issue if there is a personal representative for the person.

(b) Each known devisee of each person the priority of whose death is in issue.

(c) Each known heir of each person the priority of whose death is in issue.

(d) All persons (or their attorneys if they have appeared by attorneys) who have requested special notice as provided in Section 1250 in the proceeding in which the petition is filed or who have given notice of appearance in person or by attorney in that proceeding. *(Stats.1990, c. 79 (A.B.759), § 14, operative July 1, 1991.)*

Law Revision Commission Comments

1990 Enactment

Section 233 continues Section 233 of the repealed Probate Code without substantive change. For general provisions relating to notice, see Sections 1200–1221. See also Sections 1250–1252 (request for special notice), 1260–1265 (proof of giving of notice). As to notice to known heirs or known devisees, see Section 1206.

The notice provisions referred to in Section 233 do not apply to a particular notice where the notice was delivered, mailed, posted, or first published before July 1, 1991. In such a case, the applicable law in effect before July 1, 1991, continues to apply to the giving of the notice. Section 1200(c). As to the application of any amendments made after that date, see Section 3.

Background on Section 233 of Repealed Code

Section 233 was added by 1983 Cal.Stat. ch. 842 § 22 and amended by 1987 Cal.Stat. ch. 923 § 23. Subdivision (a) restated the second sentence of former Probate Code Section 296.41 (repealed by 1983 Cal.Stat. ch. 842 § 20) without substantive change. Subdivision (b) superseded a portion of the second sentence and all of the third sentence of former Probate Code Section 296.41. Subdivision (c) was drawn from a portion of the first sentence of former Probate Code Section 296.42 (repealed by 1983 Cal.Stat. ch. 842 § 20). For background on the provisions of this part, see the Comment to this part under the part heading.

The 1987 amendment revised Section 233 to conform to the new general notice and procedural provisions. See Sections 1200–1299 of the 1987 Probate Code. The cross-reference to the section governing the mailing of notice of hearing was revised to substitute a reference to Section 1220 for the former reference to Probate Code Section 1200.5 (repealed by 1987 Cal.Stat. ch. 923 § 59). Fifteen days' notice is required under Section 1220, instead of ten days' notice as required under former Section 1200.5. The former provision that excused giving notice to a person who joins in the petition was omitted because this provision had been generalized in former Probate Code Section 1201 (repealed by 1988 Cal.Stat. ch. 1199 § 64.5), which was continued as Section 1041. Subdivision (b) was revised by adding the reference to "known" devisees. This revision conforms to Section 1206 (notice to known heirs or devisees). The cross-reference to the section relating to special notice was revised to refer to Section 1250. The former provision that required the clerk to set the petition for hearing was generalized in Section 1285 (repealed by 1988 Cal.Stat. ch. 1199 § 64.5), continued in Section 1041. Former subdivision (c) was deleted because it was unnecessary in light of the general provision in Section 1260 (proof of giving notice of hearing required). [20 Cal.L.Rev.Comm.Reports 1001 (1990)].

Cross References

Devisee, defined, see Probate Code § 34.
Heirs, defined, see Probate Code § 44.
Personal representative and general personal representative, defined, see Probate Code § 58.

§ 234. Order

If the court determines that the named persons are dead and that it has not been established by clear and convincing evidence that one person survived another, the court shall make an order to that effect. If the court determines that the named persons are dead and that there is clear and convincing evidence that one person survived another, the court shall make an order setting forth the order in which the persons died. The order, when it becomes final, is a binding determination of the facts set forth in the order and is conclusive as against the personal representatives of the deceased persons named in the order and against all persons claiming by, through, or under any of the deceased persons. *(Stats.1990, c. 79 (A.B.759), § 14, operative July 1, 1991.)*

Law Revision Commission Comments

1990 Enactment

Section 234 continues Section 234 of the repealed Probate Code with the first sentence of the former section omitted. The omitted sentence, which required the court to hear the petition and any objections to the petition, was unnecessary in view of the general provision found in Section 1046. For general provisions relating to hearings and orders, see Sections 1040–1050.

Background on Section 234 of Repealed Code

Section 234 was added by 1983 Cal.Stat. ch. 842 § 22. Section 234 restated a portion of former Probate Code Section 296.42 (repealed by 1983 Cal.Stat. ch. 842 § 20) with the addition of the "clear and convincing evidence" standard. For background on the provisions of this part, see the Comment to this part under the part heading. [20 Cal.L.Rev.Comm.Reports 1001 (1990)].

Cross References

Personal representative and general personal representative, defined, see Probate Code § 58.

§§ 235, 236. Repealed by Stats.1983, c. 842, § 19, operative Jan. 1, 1985

Part 6

DISTRIBUTION AMONG HEIRS OR BENEFICIARIES

Law Revision Commission Comments

1990 Enactment

This part supersedes Part 6 (commencing with Section 240) of Division 2 of the repealed Probate Code. The superseded part was enacted upon recommendation of the California Law Revision Commission. See Recommendation Relating to Distribution Under a Will or Trust, 18 Cal.L.Revision Comm'n Reports 269 (1986); Communication Concerning Assembly Bill 196, 18 Cal.L.Revision Comm'n Reports 367, 369–70 (1986). See also Recommendation Relating to Revision of Wills and Intestate Succession Law, 17 Cal.L.Revision Comm'n Reports 537, 542–44, 549–50 (1984); Communication of Law Revision Commission Concerning Assembly Bill 2290, 18 Cal.L.Revision Comm'n Reports 77, 83–84 (1986); Tentative Recommendation Relating to Wills and Intestate Succession, 16 Cal.L.Revision Comm'n Reports 2301, 2338–40 (1982); Report of Senate Committee on Judiciary on Assembly Bills 25 and 68, 17 Cal.L.Revision Comm'n Reports 867, 871 (1984). [20 Cal.L.Rev.Comm.Reports 1001 (1990)].

CHAPTER 1. INTESTATE DISTRIBUTION SYSTEM

§ 240. Division into equal shares

If a statute calls for property to be distributed or taken in the manner provided in this section, the property shall be divided into as many equal shares as there are living members of the nearest generation of issue then living and deceased members of that generation who leave issue then living, each living member of the nearest generation of issue then living receiving one share and the share of each deceased member of that generation who leaves issue then living being divided

in the same manner among his or her then living issue. *(Stats.1990, c. 79 (A.B.759), § 14, operative July 1, 1991.)*

Application

This section applicable to estates of decedents who died after Jan. 1, 1985, see Probate Code § 241.

Law Revision Commission Comments

1990 Enactment

Section 240 continues Section 240 of the repealed Probate Code without change. This section was drawn from Section 2–106 of the Uniform Probate Code (1987). As to the construction of provisions drawn from uniform acts, see Section 2. Under this section, the primary division of the estate takes place at the first generation having any living members. This changes the rule of Maud v. Catherwood, 67 Cal.App.2d 636, 155 P.2d 111 (1945). For sections applying Section 240, see Civil Code § 1389.4; Prob.Code §§ 6147, 6402, 6402.5. For an example of distribution under Section 240, see the Comment to Section 245. As to the effect of a disclaimer, see Section 282.

Section 240 applies only where the death of the decedent in the case of intestate succession or of the testator or trustor occurs on or after January 1, 1985; the law applicable prior to January 1, 1985, continues to apply where the death occurred before January 1, 1985. See Section 241. As to the application of any amendments made after that date, see Section 3.

Background on Section 240 of Repealed Code

Section 240 was a new provision added by 1983 Cal.Stat. ch. 842 § 22 and was amended by 1984 Cal.Stat. ch. 892 § 16 and 1985 Cal.Stat. ch. 982 § 6. The 1984 and 1985 amendments made substantive and clarifying revisions. For background on the provisions of this part, see the Comment to this part under the part heading. [20 Cal.L.Rev.Comm.Reports 1001 (1990)].

Cross References

Adopted child as heir, see Probate Code § 6451.
Deceased personality's name, voice, signature, photograph, or likeness, successors in interest or licensees, see Civil Code § 3344.1.
Defeat of certain future interests, birth of posthumous child, see Civil Code § 739.
Determination of heirship, see Probate Code § 21114.
Issue, defined, see Probate Code § 50.
Issue of deceased transferee, see Probate Code § 21110.
Kindred of the half blood as heirs, see Probate Code § 6406.
Posthumous children, future interests, see Civil Code § 698; Probate Code § 6407.
Transfer or encumbrance of utility property, transfer of interest in a water utility from a decedent, exclusion from prohibition, see Public Utilities Code § 853.
Unborn child deemed existing person, see Civil Code § 43.1

§ 241. Application of previous section

Section 240 does not apply where the death of the decedent in the case of intestate succession or of the testator, settlor, or other transferor occurred before January 1, 1985, and the law applicable prior to January 1, 1985, shall continue to apply where the death occurred before January 1, 1985. *(Stats.1990, c. 79 (A.B.759), § 14, operative July 1, 1991.)*

Law Revision Commission Comments

1990 Enactment

Section 241 continues Section 241 of the repealed Probate Code without substantive change. The reference to the death of the "testator or trustor" has been revised and expanded to include the death of the "testator, settlor, or other transferor." This section limits the application of Section 240 to cases where the decedent died on or after January 1, 1985 (the operative date of the 1984 amendment to Section 240 of the repealed Probate Code). As to the application of any amendments made after that date, see Section 3.

Background on Section 241 of Repealed Code

Section 241 was a new provision added by 1984 Cal.Stat. ch. 892 § 16.1. For background on the provisions of this part, see the Comment to this part under the part heading. [20 Cal.L.Rev.Comm.Reports 1001 (1990)].

CHAPTER 2. DISTRIBUTION UNDER A WILL, TRUST, OR OTHER INSTRUMENT

Section
245. Application of § 240; per capita and per stirpes; equally and by right of representation.
246. Distribution in manner provided in § 246; per stirpes, by representation, or by right of representation.
247. Distribution in manner provided in § 247; per capita at each generation.

Cross References

Application of old and new law, see Probate Code § 3.

§ 245. Application of § 240; per capita and per stirpes; equally and by right of representation

(a) Where a will, trust, or other instrument calls for property to be distributed or taken "in the manner provided in Section 240 of the Probate Code," or where a will, trust, or other instrument that expresses no contrary intention provides for issue or descendants to take without specifying the manner, the property to be distributed shall be distributed in the manner provided in Section 240.

(b) Use of the following words without more, as applied to issue or descendants, is not an expression of contrary intention:

(1) "Per capita" when living members of the designated class are not all of the same generation.

(2) Contradictory wording, such as "per capita and per stirpes" or "equally and by right of representation." *(Stats. 1990, c. 79 (A.B.759), § 14, operative July 1, 1991.)*

Law Revision Commission Comments
1990 Enactment

Section 245 continues Section 245 of the repealed Probate Code, but the section is expanded to cover not only a will or trust, but also any "other instrument." The addition of the words "other instrument" makes clear, for example, that the section would apply to an instrument exercising a power of appointment.

Section 245 gives one drafting a will, trust, or other instrument the option of selecting the distribution system provided in Section 240. Section 240 is the distribution system used in case of intestate succession. As to the effect of a disclaimer, see Section 282.

Under Section 240, if the first generation of issue of the deceased ancestor are themselves all deceased, the initial division of the property is not made at that generation, but is instead made at the first descending generation of issue having at least one living member. See generally Fellows, Simon & Rau, Public Attitudes About Property Distribution at Death and Intestate Succession Laws in the United States, 1978 Am.B.Found.Research J. 321, 380. For example, if there have been four generations of descendants of the deceased ancestor but all of the deceased ancestor's children are dead, distribution under Section 240 is made as follows (brackets indicate those who are dead when distribution is made):

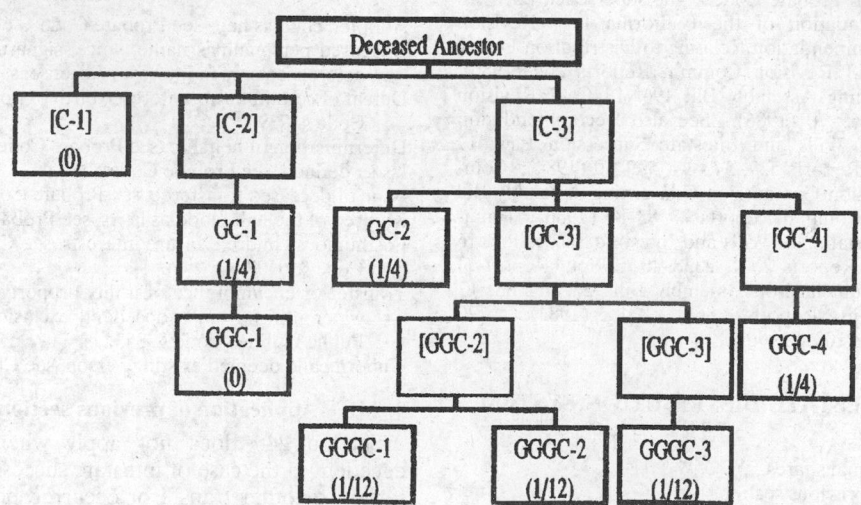

If GGGC–3 in the above example were deceased, leaving three surviving children, each of the surviving children would take a one-thirty-sixth share.

Subdivision (b) provides that certain language is not an expression of a contrary intention sufficient to negate application of Section 245. For example, if property in a testamentary trust is to be distributed when the trust terminates to "the descendants of the testator per capita" and at the time of distribution the testator's three children survive and one of the surviving children has five children, each of the surviving children takes a one-third share; the five grandchildren of the testator take nothing since their parent survives. This results from applying the distribution scheme of Section 240. Under paragraph (1) of subdivision (b) of Section 245, this scheme is not negated by use of the term "per capita," since the living members of the designated class ("descendants of the testator") are not all of the same generation. In this context, it is reasonable to assume that the use of the term "per capita" is not intended to provide a share for a class member whose parent or other ancestor is still living and takes a share, although the drafter of the instrument may provide for such a result by appropriately clear language. In order for the testator's grandchildren in the above example to take under Section 245, their parent (the testator's child) must be dead at the time of distribution. In such a case, the testator's two living children each take a one-third share and the five children of the deceased child share equally in the one-third share their deceased parent would have taken.

Background on Section 245 of Repealed Code

Section 245 was a new provision added by 1985 Cal.Stat. ch. 982 § 7. Language in subdivision (a) ("when a will or trust that expresses no contrary intention provides for issue or descendants to take without specifying the manner", it is governed by Section 240) continued a provision found in former Probate Code Section 240 before that section was amended by 1985 Cal.Stat. ch. 982 § 6. For background on the provisions of this part, see the Comment to this part under the part heading. [20 Cal.L.Rev.Comm.Reports 1001 (1990)].

Cross References

Instrument, defined, see Probate Code § 45.
Issue, defined, see Probate Code § 50.

§ 246. Distribution in manner provided in § 246; per stirpes, by representation, or by right of representation

(a) Where a will, trust, or other instrument calls for property to be distributed or taken "in the manner provided in Section 246 of the Probate Code," the property to be distributed shall be divided into as many equal shares as there are living children of the designated ancestor, if any, and deceased children who leave issue then living. Each living child of the designated ancestor is allocated one share, and the share of each deceased child who leaves issue then living is divided in the same manner.

(b) Unless the will, trust, or other instrument expressly provides otherwise, if an instrument executed on or after January 1, 1986, calls for property to be distributed or taken "per stirpes," "by representation," or "by right of representation," the property shall be distributed in the manner provided in subdivision (a).

(c) If a will, trust, or other instrument executed before January 1, 1986, calls for property to be distributed or taken "per stirpes," "by representation," or by "right of representation," the property shall be distributed in the manner provided in subdivision (a), absent a contrary intent of the transferor. *(Stats.1990, c. 79 (A.B.759), § 14, operative July 1, 1991.)*

Law Revision Commission Comments

1990 Enactment

Section 246 continues Section 246 of the repealed Probate Code, but the section is expanded to cover not only a will or trust, but also any "other instrument." This section gives one drafting a will, trust, or other instrument (such as an instrument exercising a power of appointment) the option of selecting a pure stirpital representation system. Under such a system, the roots or stocks are determined at the children's generation, whether or not any children are then living. See generally Fellows, Simon & Rau, Public Attitudes About Property Distribution at Death and Intestate Succession Laws in the United States, 1978 Am.B.Found.Research J. 321, 378–79. See also the discussion in Maud v. Catherwood, 67 Cal.App.2d 636, 155 P.2d 111 (1945).

For example, if there have been four generations of descendants of the deceased ancestor but all of the deceased ancestor's children are dead, distribution under Section 246 is made as follows (brackets indicate those who are dead when distribution is made):

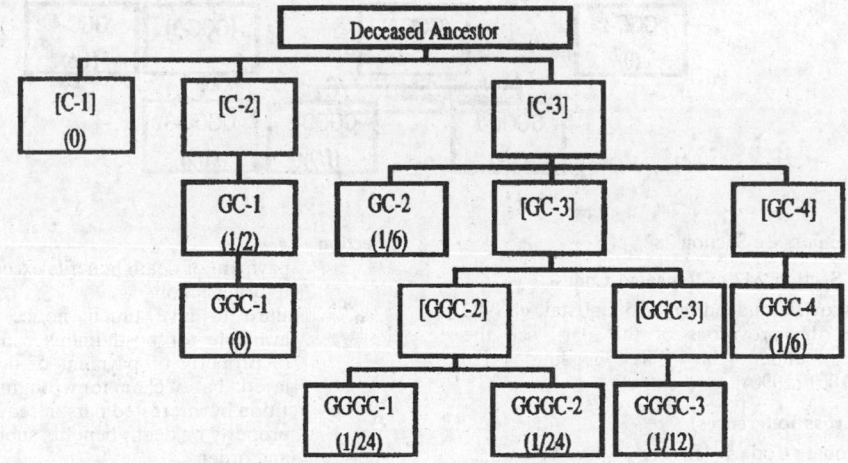

The terms defined in subdivision (b) are subject to some other definition which may be provided in the instrument. For example, a will may define "by right of representation" to refer to the distribution pattern for intestate succession, rather than to a pure stirpital distribution pattern as under subdivision (a). In such a case, the definition provided in the instrument will control. As to the effect of a disclaimer, see Section 282.

Background on Section 246 of Repealed Code

Section 246 was a new provision added by 1985 Cal.Stat. ch. 982 § 7. Subdivision (c) superseded a provision that was found in Section 240 of the repealed Probate Code before that section was amended by 1985 Cal.Stat. ch. 982 § 6. For background on the

provisions of this part, see the Comment to this part under the part heading. [20 Cal.L.Rev.Comm.Reports 1001 (1990)].

Cross References

Child, defined, see Probate Code § 26.
Instrument, defined, see Probate Code § 45.
Issue, defined, see Probate Code § 50.

§ 247. Distribution in manner provided in § 247; per capita at each generation

(a) Where a will, trust, or other instrument calls for property to be distributed or taken "in the manner provided in Section 247 of the Probate Code," the property to be distributed shall be divided into as many equal shares as there are living members of the nearest generation of issue then living and deceased members of that generation who leave issue then living. Each living member of the nearest generation of issue then living is allocated one share, and the remaining shares, if any, are combined and then divided and allocated in the same manner among the remaining issue as if the issue already allocated a share and their descendants were then deceased.

(b) Unless the will, trust, or other instrument expressly provides otherwise, if an instrument executed on or after January 1, 1986, calls for property to be distributed or taken "per capita at each generation," the property shall be distributed in the manner provided in subdivision (a).

(c) If a will, trust, or other instrument executed before January 1, 1986, calls for property to be distributed or taken "per capita at each generation," the property shall be distributed in the manner provided in subdivision (a), absent a contrary intent of the transferor. *(Stats.1990, c. 79 (A.B.759), § 14, operative July 1, 1991.)*

Law Revision Commission Comments

1990 Enactment

Section 247 continues Section 247 of the repealed Probate Code, but the section is expanded to cover not only a will or trust, but also any "other instrument." This section gives one drafting a will, trust, or other instrument (such as an instrument exercising a power of appointment) the option of selecting the system of per capita at each generation distribution. See generally Waggoner, A Proposed Alternative to the Uniform Probate Code's System for Intestate Distribution Among Descendants, 66 Nw.U.L.Rev. 626, 630–33 (1971); Fellows, Simon & Rau, Public Attitudes About Property Distribution at Death and Intestate Succession Laws in the United States, 1978 Am.B.Found.Research J. 321, 380–82.

For example, if there have been four generations of descendants of the deceased ancestor but all of the deceased ancestor's children are dead, distribution under Section 247 is made as follows (brackets indicate those who are dead when distribution is made):

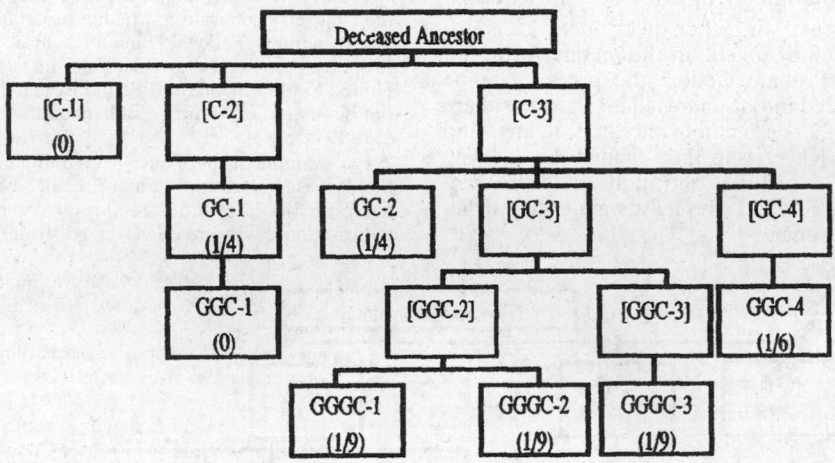

As to the effect of a disclaimer, see Section 282.

Background on Section 247 of Repealed Code

Section 247 was a new provision added by 1985 Cal.Stat. ch. 982 § 7. For background on the provisions of this part, see the Comment to this part under the part heading. [20 Cal.L.Rev.Comm.Reports 1001 (1990)].

Cross References

CHAPTER 3. IDENTITY OF HEIRS

§ 248. Petition; filing; contents

When title to real or personal property, or any interest therein, vests, other than by laws of succession, on the heirs, heirs of the body, issue, or children of any person, without other description, or means of identification of the persons embraced in the description, any person interested in the property as the heir, heir of the body, issue, or child, or his or her successor in interest, or the personal representative of any interested person or of his or her successor in interest, may file a verified petition in the superior court of the county in which the property or any part thereof is situated, setting forth briefly the deraignment of title of petitioner, a description of the property affected, and so far as known to the petitioner, the names, ages, and residences of the heirs, heirs of the body, issue or children whose identity is sought to be determined, and if any is dead or if the residence of any is unknown, stating the facts, and requesting that a decree be entered determining and establishing the identity of the persons embraced in the general description. *(Added by Stats.1992, c. 871 (A.B.2975), § 1.)*

Cross References

Child, defined, see Probate Code § 26.
Heir, defined, see Probate Code § 44.
Interested person, defined, see Probate Code § 48.
Issue, defined, see Probate Code § 50.
Personal representative and general personal representative, defined, see Probate Code § 58.

§ 248.5.   Notice of hearing

The clerk shall set the petition for hearing by the court and give notice thereof in the manner provided in Sections 1230 and 1260.   The petitioner shall cause notice of the hearing to be given in the manner specified in Sections 1220 and 1260. *(Added by Stats.1992, c. 871 (A.B.2975), § 1.)*

§ 249.   Answer; hearing; decree

At any time before the hearing any person interested in the property may answer the petition and deny any of the matters contained therein.   The court shall hear the proofs offered by the petitioner and by any person contesting and shall make a decree conformable to the proofs.   The decree shall be prima facie evidence of the facts determined thereby, and shall be conclusive in favor of anyone acting thereon in good faith without notice of any conflicting interest. *(Added by Stats. 1992, c. 871 (A.B.2975), § 1.)*

Cross References

Interested person, defined, see Probate Code § 48.
Newspapers, publications and official advertising, see Government Code § 6000 et seq.
Official records and other official writings, see Evidence Code § 1280 et seq.

§ 249.5.   Posthumous conception; child of decedent deemed born in decedent's lifetime; conditions

For purposes of determining rights to property to be distributed upon the death of a decedent, a child of the decedent conceived and born after the death of the decedent shall be deemed to have been born in the lifetime of the decedent, and after the execution of all of the decedent's testamentary instruments, if the child or his or her representative proves by clear and convincing evidence that all of the following conditions are satisfied:

(a) The decedent, in writing, specifies that his or her genetic material shall be used for the posthumous conception of a child of the decedent, subject to the following:

(1) The specification shall be signed by the decedent and dated.

(2) The specification may be revoked or amended only by a writing, signed by the decedent and dated.

(3) A person is designated by the decedent to control the use of the genetic material.

(b) The person designated by the decedent to control the use of the genetic material has given written notice by certified mail, return receipt requested, that the decedent's genetic material was available for the purpose of posthumous conception.   The notice shall have been given to a person who has the power to control the distribution of either the decedent's property or death benefits payable by reason of the decedent's death, within four months of the date of issuance of a certificate of the decedent's death or entry of a judgment determining the fact of the decedent's death, whichever event occurs first.

(c) The child was in utero using the decedent's genetic material and was in utero within two years of the date of issuance of a certificate of the decedent's death or entry of a judgment determining the fact of the decedent's death, whichever event occurs first.   This subdivision does not apply to a child who shares all of his or her nuclear genes with the person donating the implanted nucleus as a result of the application of somatic nuclear transfer technology commonly known as human cloning. *(Added by Stats.2004, c. 775 (A.B.1910), § 5.   Amended by Stats.2005, c. 285 (A.B.204), § 1.)*

Cross References

Determination of parent and child relationship,
Action to determine existence or nonexistence of mother and child relationship, woman presumed natural mother pursuant to this section, see Family Code § 7650.
Status as natural father presumed pursuant to this section, see Family Code § 7611.
Genetic depositories,
Form provided to depositor regarding decedent's intent for use of material pursuant to this section, contents, see Health and Safety Code § 1644.7.
Form provided to depositor regarding revocation of decedent's intent for use of material pursuant to this section, contents, see Health and Safety Code § 1644.8.
Intestate succession, natural parent and child relationship established under this section, see Probate Code § 6453.
Life and disability insurance, discharge of insurer by payment, see Insurance Code § 10172.

§ 249.6.   Notice of genetic material available for post-humous conception; delay of distribution of property or payment of death benefits exceptions; liability; time to bring action

(a) Upon timely receipt of the notice required by Section 249.5 or actual knowledge by a person who has the power to control the distribution of either the decedent's property or death benefits payable by reason of the decedent's death, that person may not make a distribution of property or pay death benefits payable by reason of the decedent's death before two years following the date of issuance of a certificate of the decedent's death or entry of a judgment determining the fact of decedent's death, whichever event occurs first.

(b) Subdivision (a) does not apply to, and the distribution of property or the payment of benefits may proceed in a timely manner as provided by law with respect to, any property if the birth of a child or children of the decedent conceived after the death of the decedent will not have an effect on any of the following:

(1) The proposed distribution of the decedent's property.

(2) The payment of death benefits payable by reason of the decedent's death.

(3) The determination of rights to property to be distributed upon the death of the decedent.

(4) The right of any person to claim a probate homestead or probate family allowance.

(c) Subdivision (a) does not apply to, and the distribution of property or the payment of benefits may proceed in a timely manner as provided by law with respect to, any property if the person named in subdivision (a) of Section 249.5 sends written notice by certified mail, return receipt requested, that the person does not intend to use the genetic material for the posthumous conception of a child of a decedent. This notice shall be signed by the person named in paragraph (3) of subdivision (a) of Section 249.5 and at least one competent witness, and dated.

(d) A person who has the power to control the distribution of either the decedent's property or death benefits payable by reason of the decedent's death, shall incur no liability for making a distribution of property or paying death benefits if that person made a distribution of property or paid death benefits prior to receiving notice or acquiring actual knowledge of the existence of genetic material available for posthumous conception purposes or the written notice required by subdivision (b) of Section 249.5.

(e) Each person to whom payment, delivery, or transfer of the decedent's property is made is personally liable to a person who, pursuant to Section 249.5, has a superior right to the payment, delivery, or transfer of the decedent's property. The aggregate of the personal liability of a person shall not exceed the fair market value, valued as of the time of the transfer, of the property paid, delivered, or transferred to the person under this section, less the amount of any liens and encumbrances on that property at that time.

(f) In addition to any other liability a person may have pursuant to this section, any person who fraudulently secures the payment, delivery, or transfer of the decedent's property pursuant to this section shall be liable to the person having a superior right for three times the fair market value of the property.

(g) An action to impose liability under this section shall be barred three years after the distribution to the holder of the decedent's property, or three years after the discovery of fraud, whichever is later. The three-year period specified in this subdivision may not be tolled for any reason. *(Added by Stats.2004, c. 775 (A.B.1910), § 6. Amended by Stats.2005, c. 285 (A.B.204), § 2.)*

§ 249.7. Failure to give timely notice of genetic material available for posthumous conception; distribution of property or payment of death benefits not delayed; bar of claim for wrongful distribution

If the written notice required pursuant to Section 249.5 is not given in a timely manner to any person who has the power to control the distribution of either the decedent's property or death benefits payable by reason of the decedent's death, that person may make the distribution in the manner provided by law as if any child of the decedent conceived after the death of the decedent had predeceased the decedent without heirs. Any child of a decedent conceived after the death of the decedent, or that child's representative, shall be barred from making a claim against either the person making the distribution or the recipient of the distribution when the claim is based on wrongful distribution and written notice has not been given in a timely manner pursuant to Section 249.5 to the person making that distribution. *(Added by Stats.2004, c. 775 (A.B.1910), § 7.)*

§ 249.8. Petition by interested person requesting distribution of property or death benefits subject to delay; hearing and order

Notwithstanding Section 249.6, any interested person may file a petition in the manner prescribed in Section 248 or 17200 requesting a distribution of property of the decedent or death benefits payable by reason of decedent's death that are subject to the delayed distribution provisions of Section 249.6. The court may order distribution of all, or a portion of, the property or death benefits, if at the hearing it appears that distribution can be made without any loss to any interested person, including any loss, either actual or contingent, to a decedent's child who is conceived after the death of the decedent. The order for distribution shall be stayed until any bond required by the court is filed. *(Added by Stats.2004, c. 775 (A.B.1910), § 8. Amended by Stats.2005, c. 285 (A.B. 204), § 3.)*

Part 7

EFFECT OF HOMICIDE OR ABUSE OF AN ELDER OR DEPENDENT ADULT

Law Revision Commission Comments

1990 Enactment

This part supersedes Part 7 (commencing with Section 250) of Division 2 of the repealed Probate Code. The superseded part was enacted upon recommendation of the California Law Revision Commission. See Tentative Recommendation Relating to Wills and Intestate Succession, 16 Cal.L.Revision Comm'n Reports 2301, 2346–47, 2382–85, 2509 (1982). See also Report of Senate Committee on Judiciary on Assembly Bills 25 and 68, 17 Cal.L.Revision Comm'n Reports 867, 870 (1984).

The Commission recommended legislation was originally enacted as Sections 200–206 of the repealed Probate Code (added by 1983 Cal.Stat. ch. 842 § 22). These provisions were repealed by 1984

Cal.Stat. ch. 527 § 1 and reenacted as Sections 250–256 of the repealed Probate Code by 1984 Cal.Stat. ch. 527 § 3. See Recommendation Relating to Recording Affidavit of Death, 17 Cal.L.Revision Comm'n Reports 493, 504–07 (1984). [20 Cal.L.Rev.Comm.Reports 1001 (1990)].

§ 250. Person feloniously and intentionally killing decedent; entitlement to decedent's property; effect on decedent's estate

(a) A person who feloniously and intentionally kills the decedent is not entitled to any of the following:

(1) Any property, interest, or benefit under a will of the decedent, or a trust created by or for the benefit of the decedent or in which the decedent has an interest, including any general or special power of appointment conferred by the will or trust on the killer and any nomination of the killer as executor, trustee, guardian, or conservator or custodian made by the will or trust.

(2) Any property of the decedent by intestate succession.

(3) Any of the decedent's quasi-community property the killer would otherwise acquire under Section 101 or 102 upon the death of the decedent.

(4) Any property of the decedent under Division 5 (commencing with Section 5000).

(5) Any property of the decedent under Part 3 (commencing with Section 6500) of Division 6.

(b) In the cases covered by subdivision (a):

(1) The property interest or benefit referred to in paragraph (1) of subdivision (a) passes as if the killer had predeceased the decedent and Section 21110 does not apply.

(2) Any property interest or benefit referred to in paragraph (1) of subdivision (a) which passes under a power of appointment and by reason of the death of the decedent passes as if the killer had predeceased the decedent, and Section 673 does not apply.

(3) Any nomination in a will or trust of the killer as executor, trustee, guardian, conservator, or custodian which becomes effective as a result of the death of the decedent shall be interpreted as if the killer had predeceased the decedent. *(Stats.1990, c. 79 (A.B.759), § 14, operative July 1, 1991. Amended by Stats.1991, c. 1055 (S.B.271), § 13; Stats.1992, c. 871 (A.B.2975), § 2; Stats.1997, c. 724 (A.B. 1172), § 3; Stats.2002, c. 138 (A.B.1784), § 5; Stats.2015, c. 293 (A.B.139), § 4, eff. Jan. 1, 2016.)*

Law Revision Commission Comments
1990 Enactment

Section 250 continues Section 250 of the repealed Probate Code with the addition of references to nomination of a "conservator." This section is consistent with Section 2–803(a) of the Uniform Probate Code (1987), except that language is added to Section 250 to cover various matters in more detail than the Uniform Probate Code section. As to the construction of provisions drawn from uniform acts, see Section 2.

Under paragraph (3) of subdivision (a), one who feloniously and intentionally kills a spouse is entitled to no share of the decedent's quasi-community property since, for most purposes, the decedent's quasi-community property is treated as the decedent's separate property during the decedent's lifetime. See 7 B. Witkin, Summary of California Law Community Property § 125, at 5219 (8th ed. 1974).

By way of contrast, under paragraph (2) of subdivision (a), the spousal killer is disqualified from taking the decedent's half of the community property by intestate succession, but the killer's one-half ownership interest in the community property (see Civil Code § 5105) is not affected. See also Prob.Code §§ 100, 103.

1991 Amendment

Section 250 is amended to add a reference in subdivision (a) to the provisions relating to gifts in view of impending death (Prob.Code §§ 5700–5705). This is consistent with Section 253. [20 Cal.L.Rev.Comm.Reports 2869 (1990)].

2002 Amendment

Section 250 is amended to correct a cross-reference. [31 Cal. L.Rev.Comm. Reports 219 (2001)].

Background on Section 250 of Repealed Code

Section 250 was added by 1984 Cal.Stat. ch. 527 § 3. The section restated without substantive change former Probate Code Section 200 (enacted by 1983 Cal.Stat. ch. 842 § 22 and repealed by 1984 Cal.Stat. ch. 527 § 1). Former Probate Code Sections 200–206 (repealed by 1984 Cal.Stat. ch. 527 § 1) superseded former Probate Code Section 258 (repealed by 1983 Cal.Stat. ch. 842 § 19). Under Section 250, the killer is disqualified from taking from the victim only if the killing is felonious and intentional. Under former Probate Code Section 258, the killer was disqualified if the killing was accidental but was within the felony murder rule. This part applies only where the decedent was killed on or after January 1, 1985. See Section 257. As to the application of any amendments made after that date, see Section 3. For background on the provisions of this part, see the Comment to this part under the part heading. [20 Cal.L.Rev.Comm.Reports 1001 (1990)].

2015 Amendment

Section 250 is amended to expand its express application to all forms of nonprobate transfer under Division 5, including a provision for transfer on death in a written instrument (Section 5000), a multiple party account (Section 5100), a TOD security registration (Section 5500), and a revocable TOD deed (Section 5600). This is consistent with Section 253 (no acquisition of property by killer). [36 Cal.L.Rev.Comm. Reports 103 (2006)].

Cross References

Intestate succession, generally, see Probate Code § 6400 et seq.
Murder defined, see Penal Code § 187.
Powers of appointment, general and special powers, see Probate Code § 610 et seq.
Quasi-community property, defined, see Probate Code § 66.
Voluntary manslaughter defined, see Penal Code § 192.

§ 251. Joint tenants; rights by survivorship

A joint tenant who feloniously and intentionally kills another joint tenant thereby effects a severance of the interest of the decedent so that the share of the decedent passes as the decedent's property and the killer has no rights by survivorship. This section applies to joint tenancies in real and personal property, joint and multiple-party accounts in financial institutions, and any other form of coownership with survivorship incidents. *(Stats.1990, c. 79 (A.B.759), § 14, operative July 1, 1991.)*

Law Revision Commission Comments
1990 Enactment

Section 251 continues Section 251 of the repealed Probate Code without change. This section is the same in substance as Section 2–803(b) of the Uniform Probate Code (1987) and is consistent with prior California law. See, e.g., Estate of Hart, 135 Cal.App.3d 684, 185 Cal.Rptr. 544 (1982); Johansen v. Pelton, 8 Cal.App.3d 625, 87 Cal.Rptr. 784 (1970). As to the construction of provisions drawn from uniform acts, see Section 2. This part applies only where the decedent was killed on or after January 1, 1985. See Section 257. As to the application of any amendments made after that date, see Section 3.

Background on Section 251 of Repealed Code

Section 251 was added by 1984 Cal.Stat. ch. 527 § 3. The section restated without substantive change former Probate Code Section 201 (enacted by 1983 Cal.Stat. ch. 842 § 22 and repealed by 1984 Cal.Stat. ch. 527 § 1). Former Probate Code Sections 200–206 (repealed by 1984 Cal.Stat. ch. 527 § 1) superseded former Probate Code Section 258 (repealed by 1983 Cal.Stat. ch. 842 § 19). For background on the provisions of this part, see the Comment to this part under the part heading. [20 Cal.L.Rev.Comm.Reports 1001 (1990)].

Cross References

Account, defined, see Probate Code § 21
Financial institution, defined, see Probate Code § 40.

§ 252. Named beneficiaries; felonious and intentional killing of decedent

A named beneficiary of a bond, life insurance policy, or other contractual arrangement who feloniously and intentionally kills the principal obligee or the person upon whose life the policy is issued is not entitled to any benefit under the bond, policy, or other contractual arrangement, and it becomes payable as though the killer had predeceased the decedent. *(Stats.1990, c. 79 (A.B.759), § 14, operative July 1, 1991.)*

Law Revision Commission Comments
1990 Enactment

Section 252 continues Section 252 of the repealed Probate Code without change. This section is the same in substance as Section 2–803(c) of the Uniform Probate Code (1987). As to the construction of provisions drawn from uniform acts, see Section 2.

Under Sections 252 and 253, if the killer is treated as having predeceased the decedent for the purpose of life insurance or other contractual benefits, the killer's heirs are similarly disqualified. See Meyer v. Johnson, 115 Cal.App. 646, 2 P.2d 456 (1931); cf. Estate of Jeffers, 134 Cal.App.3d 729, 182 Cal.Rptr. 300 (1982) (killer may not designate alternate beneficiary of insurance proceeds).

This part applies only where the decedent was killed on or after January 1, 1985. See Section 257. As to the application of any amendments made after that date, see Section 3.

Background on Section 252 of Repealed Code

Section 252 was added by 1984 Cal.Stat. ch. 527 § 3. The section continued without change former Probate Code Section 202 (enacted by 1983 Cal.Stat. ch. 842 § 22 and repealed by 1984 Cal.Stat. ch. 527 § 1). Former Probate Code Sections 200–206 (repealed by 1984 Cal.Stat. ch. 527 § 1) superseded former Probate Code Section 258 (repealed by 1983 Cal.Stat. ch. 842 § 19). For background on the provisions of this part, see the Comment to this part under the part heading. [20 Cal.L.Rev.Comm.Reports 1001 (1990)].

Cross References

Beneficiary, defined, see Probate Code § 24

§ 253. Acquisition of property, interest, or benefit right by killer as result of killing

In any case not described in Section 250, 251, or 252 in which one person feloniously and intentionally kills another,

any acquisition of property, interest, or benefit by the killer as a result of the killing of the decedent shall be treated in accordance with the principles of this part. *(Stats.1990, c. 79 (A.B.759), § 14, operative July 1, 1991.)*

Law Revision Commission Comments
1990 Enactment

Section 253 continues Section 253 of the repealed Probate Code without change. This section is the same in substance as Section 2–803(d) of the Uniform Probate Code (1987). As to the construction of provisions drawn from uniform acts, see Section 2. Section 253 makes clear that any other acquisition by the killer is treated in accordance with the principles of this part. See Estate of Jeffers, 134 Cal.App.3d 729, 182 Cal.Rptr. 300 (1982) (killer may not designate alternate beneficiary of insurance proceeds). See the Comment to Section 252. This part applies only where the decedent was killed on or after January 1, 1985. See Section 257. As to the application of any amendments made after that date, see Section 3.

Background on Section 253 of Repealed Code

Section 253 was added by 1984 Cal.Stat. ch. 527 § 3. The section continued without change former Probate Code Section 203 (enacted by 1983 Cal.Stat. ch. 842 § 22 and repealed by 1984 Cal.Stat. ch. 527 § 1). Former Probate Code Sections 200–206 (repealed by 1984 Cal.Stat. ch. 527 § 1) superseded former Probate Code Section 258 (repealed by 1983 Cal.Stat. ch. 842 § 19). For background on the provisions of this part, see the Comment to this part under the part heading. [20 Cal.L.Rev.Comm.Reports 1001 (1990)].

§ 254. Judgment of conviction as conclusive; preponderance of evidence

(a) A final judgment of conviction of felonious and intentional killing is conclusive for purposes of this part.

(b) In the absence of a final judgment of conviction of felonious and intentional killing, the court may determine by a preponderance of evidence whether the killing was felonious and intentional for purposes of this part. The burden of proof is on the party seeking to establish that the killing was felonious and intentional for the purposes of this part. *(Stats.1990, c. 79 (A.B.759), § 14, operative July 1, 1991.)*

Law Revision Commission Comments
1990 Enactment

Section 254 continues Section 254 of the repealed Probate Code without change. This section is the same in substance as Section 2–803(e) of the Uniform Probate Code (1987). An acquittal after a criminal trial has no effect in a subsequent civil proceeding to establish that the killing was felonious and intentional for the purposes of this part. The last sentence of Section 254 is not found in the Uniform Probate Code, but it is consistent with the Uniform Probate Code Section 2–803(e) (1987). This part applies only where the decedent was killed on or after January 1, 1985. See Section 257. As to the application of any amendments made after that date, see Section 3. As to the construction of provisions drawn from uniform acts, see Section 2.

Background on Section 254 of Repealed Code

Section 254 was added by 1984 Cal.Stat. ch. 527 § 3. The section continued without change former Probate Code Section 204 (enacted by 1983 Cal.Stat. ch. 842 § 22 and repealed by 1984 Cal.Stat. ch. 527 § 1). Former Probate Code Sections 200–206 (repealed by 1984 Cal.Stat. ch. 527 § 1) superseded former Probate Code Section 258 (repealed by 1983 Cal.Stat. ch. 842 § 19).

Section 254 was amended by 1989 Cal.Stat. ch. 21 § 2 to add the words "a final judgment of" in subdivision (b). This made clear that the civil court may determine the issue by the civil standard of proof during the pendency of an appeal from a criminal conviction of felonious and intentional killing.

Under Section 254, the civil standard of proof (preponderance of the evidence) is used in the civil proceeding to disqualify the killer from taking from the victim. Under prior law, the criminal burden of proof (beyond a reasonable doubt) was used in the civil proceeding. Estate of McGowan, 35 Cal.App.3d 611, 619, 111 Cal.Rptr. 39, 45 (1973). Under Section 254, an acquittal after a criminal trial has no effect in a subsequent civil proceeding. Under former Section 258, an acquittal was given conclusive effect in the later civil proceeding. See Communication from the California Law Revision Commission Concerning Assembly Bill 156, 20 Cal.L.Revision Comm'n Reports 227, 228 (1990). For background on the provisions of this part, see the Comment to this part under the part heading. [20 Cal.L.Rev.Comm.Reports 1001 (1990)].

Cross References

Appeals in criminal cases, rules on appeal in criminal cases, see California Rules of Court, Rules 8.300 and 8.700 et seq.
Definitions,
   Burden of proof, see Evidence Code § 115.
   Criminal action, see Evidence Code § 130.
Felonies, definition and penalties, see Penal Code §§ 17, 18.
Murder, burden of proving mitigation, justification or excuse, see Penal Code § 189.5.
Proof of guilt beyond reasonable doubt, see Penal Code § 1096.
Sanity, restoration, burden of proof, see Penal Code § 1026.2.
Unity of fact and intent, see Penal Code § 20.

§ 255. Persons purchasing property from killer; liability of killer

This part does not affect the rights of any person who, before rights under this part have been adjudicated, purchases from the killer for value and without notice property which the killer would have acquired except for this part, but the killer is liable for the amount of the proceeds or the value of the property. *(Stats.1990, c. 79 (A.B.759), § 14, operative July 1, 1991.)*

Law Revision Commission Comments
1990 Enactment

Section 255 continues Section 255 of the repealed Probate Code without change. This section is the same in substance as the first sentence of Section 2–803(f) of the Uniform Probate Code (1987). As to the construction of provisions drawn from uniform acts, see Section 2. This part applies only where the decedent was killed on or after January 1, 1985. See Section 257. As to the application of any amendments made after that date, see Section 3.

Background on Section 255 of Repealed Code

Section 255 was added by 1984 Cal.Stat. ch. 527 § 3. The section continued without change former Probate Code Section 205 (enacted by 1983 Cal.Stat. ch. 842 § 22 and repealed by 1984 Cal.Stat. ch. 527 § 1). Former Probate Code Sections 200–206 (repealed by 1984 Cal.Stat. ch. 527 § 1) superseded former Probate Code Section 258 (repealed by 1983 Cal.Stat. ch. 842 § 19). For background on the provisions of this part, see the Comment to this part under the part heading. [20 Cal.L.Rev.Comm.Reports 1001 (1990)].

§ 256. Liability of insurance company, financial institution, or other obligor

An insurance company, financial institution, or other obligor making payment according to the terms of its policy or obligation is not liable by reason of this part, unless prior to payment it has received at its home office or principal address written notice of a claim under this part. *(Stats.1990, c. 79 (A.B.759), § 14, operative July 1, 1991.)*

Law Revision Commission Comments
1990 Enactment

Section 256 continues Section 256 of the repealed Probate Code without change. This section is the same in substance as the second sentence of Section 2–803(f) of the Uniform Probate Code (1987). As to the construction of provisions drawn from uniform acts, see Section 2. This part applies only where the decedent was killed on or after January 1, 1985. See Section 257. As to the application of any amendments made after that date, see Section 3.

Background on Section 256 of Repealed Code

Section 256 was added by 1984 Cal.Stat. ch. 527 § 3. The section continued without change former Probate Code Section 206 (enacted by 1983 Cal.Stat. ch. 842 § 22 and repealed by 1984 Cal.Stat. ch. 527 § 1). Former Probate Code Sections 200–206 superseded former Probate Code Section 258 (repealed by 1983 Cal.Stat. ch. 842 § 19). For background on the provisions of this part, see the Comment to this part under the part heading. [20 Cal.L.Rev.Comm.Reports 1001 (1990)].

Cross References

Financial institution, defined, see Probate Code § 40.

§ 257. Application of part

This part does not apply where the decedent was killed before January 1, 1985; and the law applicable prior to January 1, 1985, continues to apply where the decedent was killed before January 1, 1985. *(Stats.1990, c. 79 (A.B.759), § 14, operative July 1, 1991.)*

Law Revision Commission Comments
1990 Enactment

Section 257 continues Section 257 of the repealed Probate Code without substantive change. This section limits the application of Sections 250–256 to cases where the decedent was killed on or after January 1, 1985 (the operative date of those sections of the repealed Probate Code). As to the application of any amendments made after that date, see Section 3.

Background on Section 257 of Repealed Code

Section 257 was a new provision added by 1984 Cal.Stat. ch. 892 § 16.5. For background on the provisions of this part, see the Comment to this part under the part heading. [20 Cal.L.Rev.Comm.Reports 1001 (1990)].

§ 258. Wrongful death actions

A person who feloniously and intentionally kills the decedent is not entitled to bring an action for wrongful death of the decedent or to benefit from the action brought by the decedent's personal representative. The persons who may bring an action for wrongful death of the decedent and to benefit from the action are determined as if the killer had predeceased the decedent. *(Added by Stats.1992, c. 178 (S.B.1496), § 29.5.)*

Law Revision Commission Comments
1992 Addition

Section 258 is a new section that changes the rule of Marks v. Lyerla, 1 Cal.App.4th 556, 2 Cal.Rptr.2d 63 (1991). See also Code Civ.Proc. § 377.60 (persons who may sue for wrongful death). [22 Cal.L.Rev.Comm.Reports 895 (1992)].

Personal representative and general personal representative, defined, see Probate Code § 58.

§ 259. Predeceasing a decedent

(a) Any person shall be deemed to have predeceased a decedent to the extent provided in subdivision (c) where all of the following apply:

(1) It has been proven by clear and convincing evidence that the person is liable for physical abuse, neglect, or financial abuse of the decedent, who was an elder or dependent adult.

(2) The person is found to have acted in bad faith.

(3) The person has been found to have been reckless, oppressive, fraudulent, or malicious in the commission of any of these acts upon the decedent.

(4) The decedent, at the time those acts occurred and thereafter until the time of his or her death, has been found to have been substantially unable to manage his or her financial resources or to resist fraud or undue influence.

(b) Any person shall be deemed to have predeceased a decedent to the extent provided in subdivision (c) if that person has been convicted of a violation of Section 236 of the Penal Code or any offense described in Section 368 of the Penal Code.

(c) Any person found liable under subdivision (a) or convicted under subdivision (b) shall not (1) receive any property, damages, or costs that are awarded to the decedent's estate in an action described in subdivision (a) or (b), whether that person's entitlement is under a will, a trust, or the laws of intestacy; or (2) serve as a fiduciary as defined in Section 39, if the instrument nominating or appointing that person was executed during the period when the decedent was substantially unable to manage his or her financial resources or resist fraud or undue influence. This section shall not apply to a decedent who, at any time following the act or acts described in paragraph (1) of subdivision (a), or the act or acts described in subdivision (b), was substantially able to manage his or her financial resources and to resist fraud or undue influence within the meaning of subdivision (b) of Section 1801 of the Probate Code and subdivision (b) of Section 39 of the Civil Code.

(d) For purposes of this section, the following definitions shall apply:

(1) "Physical abuse" as defined in Section 15610.63 of the Welfare and Institutions Code.

(2) "Neglect" as defined in Section 15610.57 of the Welfare and Institutions Code.

(3) "False imprisonment" as defined in Section 368 of the Penal Code.

(4) "Financial abuse" as defined in Section 15610.30 of the Welfare and Institutions Code.

(e) Nothing in this section shall be construed to prohibit the severance and transfer of an action or proceeding to a separate civil action pursuant to Section 801. *(Added by Stats.1998, c. 935 (S.B.1715), § 4. Amended by Stats.2011, c. 308 (S.B.647), § 9.)*

Fiduciary, defined, see Probate Code § 39.
Instrument, defined, see Probate Code § 45.

§§ 259.1 to 259.2. Repealed by Stats.1974, c. 425, p. 1025, § 1

Part 8

DISCLAIMER OF TESTAMENTARY AND OTHER INTERESTS

Application

Application of Part 8 to interests created on or after Jan. 1, 1984, see Probate Code §§ 287 and 288.

Law Revision Commission Comments

1990 Enactment

This part supersedes Part 8 (commencing with Section 260) of the repealed Probate Code. The superseded division was enacted upon recommendation of the California Law Revision Commission. See Recommendation Relating to Disclaimer of Testamentary and Other Interests, 16 Cal.L.Revision Comm'n Reports 207 (1982).

As to interests created before January 1, 1984, see Section 287. After December 31, 1983, an interest that would otherwise be taken by a beneficiary may be disclaimed only as provided in this part. See Section 288. As to the application of any amendments made after that date, see Section 3. A disclaimer effective under federal law is effective as a disclaimer under this part. See Section 295. [20 Cal.L.Rev.Comm.Reports 1001 (1990)].

Application of old and new law, see Probate Code § 3.
Orders in summons, temporary restraining orders, execution and filing of disclaimer pursuant to this part excluded, see Family Code § 2040.
Release of discretionary power of appointment, see Probate Code § 661.
Two or more donees, see Probate Code § 634.

CHAPTER 1. DEFINITIONS

Application

Application of Part 8 to interests created on or after Jan. 1, 1984, see Probate Code §§ 287 and 288.

Release of discretionary power of appointment, see Probate Code § 661.
Two or more donees, see Probate Code § 634.

§ 260. Definitions as governing construction

Unless the provision or context otherwise requires, the definitions in this chapter govern the construction of this part. *(Stats.1990, c. 79 (A.B.759), § 14, operative July 1, 1991.)*

Law Revision Commission Comments

1990 Enactment

Section 260 continues Section 260 of the repealed Probate Code without substantive change.

Background on Section 260 of Repealed Code

Section 260 was a new provision added by 1983 Cal.Stat. ch. 17 § 2 and amended by 1988 Cal.Stat. ch. 1199 § 29. The 1988 amendment made a nonsubstantive revision. See Comments to Conforming Revisions and Repeals, 19 Cal.L.Revision Comm'n Reports 1031, 1042 (1988). For background on the provisions of this part, see the Comment to this part under the part heading. [20 Cal.L.Rev.Comm.Reports 1001 (1990)].

Cross References

Gifts, generally, see Civil Code § 1146 et seq.
Powers of appointment, see Probate Code § 600 et seq.

§ 261. Repealed by Stats.1988, c. 1199, § 30, operative July 1, 1989

Law Revision Commission Comments

1988 Repeal

Former Section 261 duplicated Section 21 ("account" defined). See also Section 20 (application of definitions) [19 Cal.L.Rev.Comm. Reports 1042 (1988)].

§ 262. Beneficiary

"Beneficiary" means the person entitled, but for the person's disclaimer, to take an interest. *(Stats.1990, c. 79 (A.B.759), § 14, operative July 1, 1991.)*

Law Revision Commission Comments

1990 Enactment

Section 262 continues Section 262 of the repealed Probate Code without change. See also Section 56 ("person" defined).

Background on Section 262 of Repealed Code

Section 262 was added by 1983 Cal.Stat. ch. 17 § 2. The section restated the first portion of subdivision (a) of former Probate Code Section 190 (repealed by 1983 Cal.Stat. ch. 17 § 1) without substantive change. For background on the provisions of this part, see the Comment to this part under the part heading. [20 Cal.L.Rev.Comm.Reports 1001 (1990)].

§ 263. Creator of the interest

(a) "Creator of the interest" means a person who establishes, declares, creates, or otherwise brings into existence an interest.

(b) "Creator of the interest" includes, but is not limited to, the following:

(1) With respect to an interest created by intestate succession, the person dying intestate.

(2) With respect to an interest created under a will, the testator.

(3) With respect to an interest created under a trust, the settlor.

(4) With respect to an interest created by succession to a disclaimed interest, the disclaimant of the disclaimed interest.

(5) With respect to an interest created by virtue of an election to take against a will, the testator.

(6) With respect to an interest created by creation of a power of appointment, the donor.

(7) With respect to an interest created by exercise or nonexercise of a power of appointment, the donee.

(8) With respect to an interest created by an inter vivos gift, the donor.

(9) With respect to an interest created by surviving the death of a depositor of a Totten trust account or P.O.D. account, the deceased depositor.

(10) With respect to an interest created under an insurance or annuity contract, the owner, the insured, or the annuitant.

(11) With respect to an interest created by surviving the death of another joint tenant, the deceased joint tenant.

(12) With respect to an interest created under an employee benefit plan, the employee or other owner of an interest in the plan.

(13) With respect to an interest created under an individual retirement account, annuity, or bond, the owner. *(Stats. 1990, c. 79 (A.B.759), § 14, operative July 1, 1991.)*

Law Revision Commission Comments

1990 Enactment

Section 263 continues Section 263 of the repealed Probate Code without substantive change. The word "settlor" has been substituted for "trustor" in paragraph (3) of subdivision (a) to conform to the terminology in the Trust Law. See also Sections 55 ("P.O.D. account" defined), 56 ("person" defined), 80 ("Totten trust account" defined), 266 ("employee benefit plan" defined), 267 ("interest" defined).

Background on Section 263 of Repealed Code

Section 263 was a new provision added by 1983 Cal.Stat. ch. 17 § 2. For background on the provisions of this part, see the Comment to this part under the part heading. [20 Cal.L.Rev.Comm.Reports 1001 (1990)].

Cross References

Pay-on-death account, defined, see Probate Code § 55.
Totten trust account, defined, see Probate Code § 80.
Trustees and beneficiaries, generally, see Probate Code § 15600 et seq.

§ 264. Disclaimant

"Disclaimant" means a beneficiary who executes a disclaimer on his or her own behalf or a person who executes a disclaimer on behalf of a beneficiary. *(Stats.1990, c. 79 (A.B.759), § 14, operative July 1, 1991.)*

Law Revision Commission Comments

1988 Repeal

Former Section 268 duplicated Section 56 ("person" defined). See also Section 20 (application of definitions) [19 Cal.L.Rev.Comm. Reports 1042 (1988)].

§ 269. Repealed by Stats.1990, c. 79 (A.B.759), § 13, operative July 1, 1991

Law Revision Commission Comments

1990 Repeal

Section 269 of the repealed Probate Code is omitted from the new Probate Code because it is unnecessary. See Section 55 (applying the definition of "P.O.D. account" in Section 5140 to the new code). [20 Cal.L.Rev.Comm.Reports 1001 (1990)].

§ 270. Repealed by Stats.1988, c. 1199, § 32, operative July 1, 1989

Law Revision Commission Comments

1988 Repeal

Former Section 270 duplicated Section 80 ("Totten trust account" defined). See also Section 20 (application of definitions) [19 Cal.L.Rev.Comm. Reports 1042 (1988)].

§§ 271, 272. Repealed by Stats.1983, c. 201, § 3

CHAPTER 2. GENERAL PROVISIONS

Application

Application of Part 8 to interests created on or after Jan. 1, 1984, see Probate Code §§ 287 and 288.

Cross References

Application of old and new law, see Probate Code § 3.

§ 275. Beneficiary; filing disclaimer

A beneficiary may disclaim any interest, in whole or in part, by filing a disclaimer as provided in this part. *(Stats.1990, c. 79 (A.B.759), § 14, operative July 1, 1991.)*

Law Revision Commission Comments

1990 Enactment

Section 275 continues Section 275 of the repealed Probate Code without change. A disclaimer may be valid under this chapter but not meet the requirements of federal law. See I.R.C. § 2518 (1988); Jewett v. Commissioner, 455 U.S. 305 (1982). Hence, if a disclaimer is executed to avoid federal taxes, the requirements of federal law must be met. A disclaimer effective under federal law is effective as a disclaimer under this part. See Section 295. As to interests created before January 1, 1984, see Section 287. After December 31, 1983, an interest that would otherwise be taken by a beneficiary may be disclaimed only as provided in this part. As to the application of any amendments made after that date, see Section 3. See Section 288.

Background on Section 275 of Repealed Code

Section 275 was added by 1983 Cal.Stat. ch. 17 § 2 and amended by 1988 Cal.Stat. ch. 1199 § 33. The section continued the first sentence of former Probate Code Section 190.1 (repealed by 1983 Cal.Stat. ch. 17 § 1). The 1988 amendment made a nonsubstantive revision. See Comments to Conforming Revisions and Repeals, 19 Cal.L.Revision Comm'n Reports 1031, 1042 (1988). For background on the provisions of this part, see the Comment to this part under the part heading. [20 Cal.L.Rev.Comm.Reports 1001 (1990)].

§ 276. Conservatee; disclaimer by conservator

A disclaimer on behalf of a conservatee shall be made by the conservator of the estate of the conservatee pursuant to a court order obtained under Article 10 (commencing with Section 2580) of Chapter 6 of Part 4 of Division 4 authorizing or requiring the conservator to execute and file the disclaimer. *(Stats.1990, c. 79 (A.B.759), § 14, operative July 1, 1991.)*

Law Revision Commission Comments

1990 Enactment

Section 276 continues Section 276 of the repealed Probate Code without change. As to interests created before January 1, 1984, see Section 287. After December 31, 1983, an interest that would otherwise be taken by a beneficiary may be disclaimed only as provided in this part. As to the application of any amendments made after that date, see Section 3. See Section 288. A disclaimer effective under federal law is effective as a disclaimer under this part. See Section 295.

Background on Section 276 of Repealed Code

Section 276 was added by 1983 Cal.Stat. ch. 17 § 2. The section continued the substance of a portion of former Probate Code Section 190.2 (repealed by 1983 Cal.Stat. ch. 17 § 1) and added a reference to the substituted judgment provisions of the Guardianship–Conservatorship Law. This continued prior law which made the substituted judgment provisions specifically applicable to disclaimers. See Section 2580(b)(9). For background on the provisions of this part, see the Comment to this part under the part heading. [20 Cal.L.Rev.Comm.Reports 1001 (1990)].

§ 277. Minors or decedents; disclaimer by guardian or representative; petition for order; notice of hearing; order

(a) A disclaimer on behalf of a minor shall be made by the guardian of the estate of the minor if one has been appointed or, if none has been appointed, by a guardian ad litem of the minor. A disclaimer by a guardian is not effective unless made pursuant to a court order obtained under this section.

(b) A disclaimer on behalf of a decedent shall be made by the personal representative of the decedent. Except as provided in Part 6 (commencing with Section 10400) of Division 7, a disclaimer by a guardian or personal representative is not effective unless made pursuant to a court order obtained under this section.

(c) A petition for an order authorizing or requiring a guardian or personal representative to execute and file a disclaimer shall be filed in the superior court in the county in which the estate of the minor or decedent is administered or, if there is no administration, the superior court in any county in which administration would be proper. The petition may be filed by the guardian, personal representative, or other interested person.

(d) The petition shall:

(1) Identify the creator of the interest.

(2) Describe the interest to be disclaimed.

(3) State the extent of the disclaimer.

(4) Identify the person or persons the petitioner believes would take the interest in the event of the disclaimer.

(e) Notice of the hearing on the petition shall be given as follows:

(1) If the petition is for an order authorizing or requiring the guardian of the estate of a minor to execute and file the disclaimer, notice of the hearing on the petition shall be given for the period and in the manner provided in Chapter 3 (commencing with Section 1460) of Part 1 of Division 4 to all of the persons required to be given notice under that chapter.

(2) If the petition is for an order authorizing or requiring the personal representative of a decedent to execute and file the disclaimer, notice of the hearing on the petition shall be given as provided in Section 1220.

(3) If the petition is for an order authorizing or requiring a guardian ad litem of a minor to execute and file the disclaimer, notice of the hearing on the petition shall be given to the persons and in the manner that the court shall by order direct.

(f) After hearing, the court in its discretion may make an order authorizing or requiring the guardian or personal representative to execute and file the disclaimer if the court determines, taking into consideration all of the relevant circumstances, that the minor or decedent as a prudent person would disclaim the interest if he or she had the capacity to do so. *(Stats.1990, c. 79 (A.B.759), § 14, operative July 1, 1991.)*

Law Revision Commission Comments
1990 Enactment

Section 277 continues Section 277 of the repealed Probate Code without substantive change. The phrase "other than the petitioner or persons joining in the petition" has been omitted as unnecessary in view of Section 1201. See also Section 1003 (appointment of guardian ad litem).

Under subdivision (b), a disclaimer on behalf of a decedent may be made under the Independent Administration of Estates Act. A disclaimer may be made under that act only if the requirements of Chapter 4 (commencing with Section 10580) of Part 6 of Division 7 (notice of proposed action procedure) are satisfied. See Sections 10510, 10519.

Paragraph (1) of subdivision (e) is drawn from Civil Code Section 1388.3 (release of power of appointment on behalf of minor donee).

Subdivision (f) adopts the standard provided by Civil Code Section 1388.3 for release of a power of appointment on behalf of a minor donee.

The new notice provisions referred to in Section 277 do not apply to a particular notice where the notice was delivered, mailed, posted, or first published before July 1, 1991. In such a case, the applicable law in effect before July 1, 1991, continues to apply to the giving of the notice. Section 1200(c). As to interests created before January 1, 1984, see Section 287. After December 31, 1983, an interest that would otherwise be taken by a beneficiary may be disclaimed only as provided in this part. See Section 288. As to the application of any amendments made after those dates, see Section 3. A disclaimer effective under federal law is effective as a disclaimer under this part. See Section 295.

Background on Section 277 of Repealed Code

Section 277 was added by 1983 Cal.Stat. ch. 17 § 2 and was amended by 1987 Cal.Stat. ch. 923 § 24. Subdivision (a) continued the substance of a portion of former Probate Code Section 190.2 (repealed by 1983 Cal.Stat. ch. 17 § 1) but added a reference to a guardian ad litem and required court approval. Subdivision (b) continued the substance of a portion of former Probate Code Section 190.2 and required court approval unless the personal representative is acting under the Independent Administration of Estates Act. Subdivisions (c), (d), (e), and (f) were new.

The 1987 amendments made the following revisions in Section 277:

(1) In subdivision (b) the cross-reference to the Independent Administration of Estates Act was revised.

(2) In subdivision (e)(2) the cross-reference to notice of hearing was revised.

(3) Subdivision (e)(4) was deleted as an unnecessary duplication of the general provision in Section 1202 (additional notice on court order).

For background on the provisions of this part, see the Comment to this part under the part heading. See also Communication from California Law Revision Commission Concerning Assembly Bill 708, 19 Cal.L.Revision Comm'n Reports 545, 547 (1988). [20 Cal.L.Rev.Comm.Reports 1001 (1990)].

Cross References

Appointment of personal representative, generally, see Probate Code § 8400 et seq.
Guardianship, generally, see Probate Code § 1500 et seq.
Personal representative and general personal representative, defined, see Probate Code § 58.

§ 278. Disclaimer; writing; contents

The disclaimer shall be in writing, shall be signed by the disclaimant, and shall:

(a) Identify the creator of the interest.

(b) Describe the interest to be disclaimed.

(c) State the disclaimer and the extent of the disclaimer. *(Stats.1990, c. 79 (A.B.759), § 14, operative July 1, 1991.)*

Law Revision Commission Comments
1990 Enactment

Section 278 continues Section 278 of the repealed Probate Code without substantive change. As to interests created before January 1, 1984, see Section 287. After December 31, 1983, an interest that would otherwise be taken by a beneficiary may be disclaimed only as provided in this part. See Section 288. As to the application of any amendments made after that date, see Section 3. A disclaimer effective under federal law is effective as a disclaimer under this part. See Section 295.

Background on Section 278 of Repealed Code

Section 278 was added by 1983 Cal.Stat. ch. 17 § 2. The section restated the second sentence of former Probate Code Section 190.1 (repealed by 1983 Cal.Stat. ch. 17 § 1) without substantive change. For background on the provisions of this part, see the Comment to this part under the part heading. [20 Cal.L.Rev.Comm.Reports 1001 (1990)].

§ 279. Effectiveness of disclaimer; knowledge of disclaimant; presumptions of reasonable time; burden of proof

(a) A disclaimer to be effective shall be filed within a reasonable time after the person able to disclaim acquires knowledge of the interest.

(b) In the case of any of the following interests, a disclaimer is conclusively presumed to have been filed within a reasonable time if it is filed within nine months after the death of the creator of the interest or within nine months after the interest becomes indefeasibly vested, whichever occurs later:

(1) An interest created under a will.

(2) An interest created by intestate succession.

(3) An interest created pursuant to the exercise or nonexercise of a testamentary power of appointment.

(4) An interest created by surviving the death of a depositor of a Totten trust account or P.O.D. account.

(5) An interest created under a life insurance or annuity contract.

(6) An interest created by surviving the death of another joint tenant.

(7) An interest created under an employee benefit plan.

(8) An interest created under an individual retirement account, annuity, or bond.

(9) An interest created under a transfer on death beneficiary designation in a deed or other instrument.

(c) In the case of an interest created by a living trust, an interest created by the exercise of a presently exercisable power of appointment, an outright inter vivos gift, a power of appointment, or an interest created or increased by succession to a disclaimed interest, a disclaimer is conclusively presumed to have been filed within a reasonable time if it is filed within nine months after whichever of the following times occurs latest:

(1) The time of the creation of the trust, the exercise of the power of appointment, the making of the gift, the creation of the power of appointment, or the disclaimer of the disclaimed property.

(2) The time the first knowledge of the interest is acquired by the person able to disclaim.

(3) The time the interest becomes indefeasibly vested.

(d) In case of an interest not described in subdivision (b) or (c), a disclaimer is conclusively presumed to have been filed within a reasonable time if it is filed within nine months after whichever of the following times occurs later:

(1) The time the first knowledge of the interest is acquired by the person able to disclaim.

(2) The time the interest becomes indefeasibly vested.

(e) In the case of a future estate, a disclaimer is conclusively presumed to have been filed within a reasonable time if it is filed within whichever of the following times occurs later:

(1) Nine months after the time the interest becomes an estate in possession.

(2) The time specified in subdivision (b), (c), or (d), whichever is applicable.

(f) If the disclaimer is not filed within the time provided in subdivision (b), (c), (d), or (e), the disclaimant has the burden of establishing that the disclaimer was filed within a reasonable time after the disclaimant acquired knowledge of the interest. *(Stats.1990, c. 79 (A.B.759), § 14, operative July 1, 1991. Amended by Stats.2015, c. 293 (A.B.139), § 6, eff. Jan. 1, 2016.)*

Law Revision Commission Comments
1990 Enactment

Section 279 continues Section 279 of the repealed Probate Code without substantive change. The phrase "a living trust" has been substituted for "an inter vivos trust" to conform to the terminology of the Trust Law. This section provides a more liberal rule concerning time of filing than does federal law. See I.R.C. § 2518 (1988); Jewett v. Commissioner, 455 U.S. 305 (1982). Federal law should be consulted if the disclaimer is executed to avoid federal taxes. See also Sections 55 ("P.O.D. account" defined), 56 ("person" defined), 80 ("Totten trust account" defined), 263 ("creator of the interest" defined), 266 ("employee benefit plan" defined). As to interests created before January 1, 1984, see Section 287. After December 31, 1983, an interest that would otherwise be taken by a beneficiary may be disclaimed only as provided in this part. See Section 288. As to the application of any amendments made after that date, see Section 3. A disclaimer effective under federal law is effective as a disclaimer under this part. See Section 295.

Background on Section 279 of Repealed Code

Section 279 was added by 1983 Cal.Stat. ch. 17 § 2. The section superseded former Probate Code Section 190.3 (repealed by 1983 Cal.Stat. ch. 17 § 1). For background on the provisions of this part, see the Comment to this part under the part heading. [20 Cal.L.Rev.Comm.Reports 1001 (1990)].

2015 Amendment

Paragraph (9) is added to Section 279(b) in recognition of the establishment of the revocable TOD deed and other nonprobate transfer instruments. See Sections 5000 (nonprobate transfer), 5614 (revocable transfer on death deed). [36 Cal.L.Rev.Comm. Reports 103 (2006)].

Cross References

Intestate succession, generally, see Probate Code § 6400 et seq.
Pay-on-death account, defined, see Probate Code § 55.
Presumptions,
  Generally, see Evidence Code § 600 et seq.
  Conclusive presumptions, see Evidence Code § 620 et seq.
Totten trust account, defined, see Probate Code § 80.
Trusts, creation, validity, modification, and termination, see Probate Code § 15200 et seq.
Wills, generally, see Probate Code § 6100 et seq.

§ 280. Filing of disclaimers; place; disclaimers affecting realty

(a) A disclaimer shall be filed with any of the following:

(1) The superior court in the county in which the estate of the decedent is administered or, if there is no administration

of the decedent's estate, the superior court in any county in which administration of the estate of the decedent would be proper.

(2) The trustee, personal representative, other fiduciary, or person responsible for distributing the interest to the beneficiary.

(3) Any other person having custody or possession of or legal title to the interest.

(4) The creator of the interest.

(b) If a disclaimer made pursuant to this part affects real property or an obligation secured by real property and the disclaimer is acknowledged and proved in like manner as a grant of real property, the disclaimer may be recorded in like manner and with like effect as a grant of real property, and all statutory provisions relating to the recordation or nonrecordation of conveyances of real property and to the effect thereof apply to the disclaimer with like effect, without regard to the date when the disclaimer was filed pursuant to subdivision (a). Failure to file a disclaimer pursuant to subdivision (a) which is recorded pursuant to this subdivision does not affect the validity of any transaction with respect to the real property or the obligation secured thereby, and the general laws on recording and its effect govern any such transaction. *(Stats.1990, c. 79 (A.B.759), § 14, operative July 1, 1991.)*

Law Revision Commission Comments
1990 Enactment

Section 280 continues Section 280 of the repealed Probate Code without change. Acknowledgment of a disclaimer affecting real property is not a prerequisite to the effectiveness of the disclaimer. See Section 278 (disclaimer to be in writing and be signed by disclaimant). However, subdivision (b) of Section 280 makes clear that acknowledgment of a disclaimer affecting real property is permissible, and subdivision (b) requires acknowledgment as a prerequisite to recording the disclaimer. As to interests created before January 1, 1984, see Section 287. After December 31, 1983, an interest that would otherwise be taken by a beneficiary may be disclaimed only as provided in this part. See Section 288. As to the application of any amendments made after that date, see Section 3. A disclaimer effective under federal law is effective as a disclaimer under this part. See Section 295.

Background on Section 280 of Repealed Code

Section 280 was added by 1983 Cal.Stat. ch. 17 § 2 and amended by 1988 Cal.Stat. ch. 1199 § 34. Subdivision (a) superseded the first paragraph of former Probate Code Section 190.4 (repealed by 1983 Cal.Stat. ch. 17 § 1) and was less restrictive than the former law. Subdivision (b) superseded the last paragraph of former Probate Code Section 190.4. The 1988 amendment made a nonsubstantive revision. See Comments to Conforming Revisions and Repeals, 19 Cal.L.Revision Comm'n Reports 1031, 1042 (1988). For background on the provisions of this part, see the Comment to this part under the part heading. [20 Cal.L.Rev.Comm.Reports 1001 (1990)].

Cross References

Appraisal, generally, see Probate Code § 8900 et seq.
Estate administration, generally, see Probate Code § 7000 et seq.
Personal representative and general personal representative, defined, see Probate Code § 58.
Proof and acknowledgement of instruments, see Civil Code § 1180 et seq.
Real property, defined, see Probate Code § 68.
Recorder, see Government Code § 27201 et seq.

Recording, constructive notice, conveyances or real property or estate for years, see Civil Code § 1213.
Recording, instruments or judgments, documents to be recorded and manner of recording, see Government Code §§ 27320 et seq., 27280 et seq.
Recording, property transfers, place of recordation, see Civil Code § 1169.
Recording transfers, see Civil Code § 1169 et seq.
Transfer of real property, see Civil Code § 1091 et seq.

§ 281. Binding effect on beneficiaries and others

A disclaimer, when effective, is irrevocable and binding upon the beneficiary and all persons claiming by, through, or under the beneficiary, including creditors of the beneficiary. *(Stats.1990, c. 79 (A.B.759), § 14, operative July 1, 1991.)*

Law Revision Commission Comments
1990 Enactment [Revised Comment]

Section 281 continues Section 281 of the repealed Probate Code without change. This section makes clear the effect of a disclaimer on creditors of the beneficiary. See also Section 283 (disclaimer not a fraudulent transfer). The binding effect of a disclaimer has no effect on the passing of the disclaimed interest pursuant to Section 282. As to interests created before January 1, 1984, see Section 287. After December 31, 1983, an interest that would otherwise be taken by a beneficiary may be disclaimed only as provided in this part. See Section 288. As to the application of any amendments made after that date, see Section 3. A disclaimer effective under federal law is effective as a disclaimer under this part. See Section 295.

Background on Section 281 of Repealed Code

Section 281 was added by 1983 Cal.Stat. ch. 17 § 2. The section restated the first sentence of former Probate Code Section 190.5 (repealed by 1983 Cal.Stat. ch. 17 § 1) without substantive change. For background on the provisions of this part, see the Comment to this part under the part heading. [21 Cal.L.Rev.Comm.Reports 75 (1991)].

§ 282. Disclaimed interest; disposition; interest created by intestate succession

(a) Unless the creator of the interest provides for a specific disposition of the interest in the event of a disclaimer, the interest disclaimed shall descend, go, be distributed, or continue to be held (1) as to a present interest, as if the disclaimant had predeceased the creator of the interest or (2) as to a future interest, as if the disclaimant had died before the event determining that the taker of the interest had become finally ascertained and the taker's interest indefeasibly vested. A disclaimer relates back for all purposes to the date of the death of the creator of the disclaimed interest or the determinative event, as the case may be.

(b) Notwithstanding subdivision (a), where the disclaimer is filed on or after January 1, 1985:

(1) The beneficiary is not treated as having predeceased the decedent for the purpose of determining the generation at which the division of the estate is to be made under Part 6 (commencing with Section 240) or other provision of a will, trust, or other instrument.

(2) The beneficiary of a disclaimed interest is not treated as having predeceased the decedent for the purpose of applying subdivision (d) of Section 6409 or subdivision (b) of Section 6410. *(Stats.1990, c. 79 (A.B.759), § 14, operative July 1, 1991.)*

Law Revision Commission Comments

1990 Enactment [Revised Comment]

Section 282 continues Section 282 of the repealed Probate Code without substantive change, except that subdivision (b)(1) is revised to refer to other instruments for conformity with Part 6 (commencing with Section 240). The introductory clause of subdivision (b) continues the substance of 1984 Cal.Stat. ch. 892, § 50.

The introductory clause of subdivision (a) makes clear that a condition of survival is not a contingency otherwise provided in the will, disapproving dictum in Estate of Murphy, 92 Cal.App.3d 413, 426, 154 Cal.Rptr. 859 (1979).

Clause (2) of the first sentence of subdivision (a) makes clear that a disclaimer has the effect of accelerating the possession and enjoyment of subsequent interests. This provision is drawn from Section 3 of the Uniform Disclaimer of Transfers by Will, Intestacy or Appointment Act (1978) and Section 3 of the Uniform Disclaimer of Transfers Under Nontestamentary Instruments Act (1978). The pertinent portion of the Comment to Section 3 of the Uniform Disclaimer of Transfers by Will, Intestacy or Appointment Act explains the provision as follows:

"*Acceleration of Future Interests:* If a life estate or other future interest is disclaimed, the problem is raised of whether succeeding interests or estates accelerate in possession or enjoyment or whether the disclaimed interest must be marshalled to await the actual happening of the contingency. Section 3 provides that remainder interests are accelerated, the second clause specifically stating that any future interest which is to take effect in possession or enjoyment after the termination of the estate or interest disclaimed, takes effect as if the disclaimant had predeceased the event which determines that the taker has become finally ascertained and his interest indefeasibly vested. Thus, unless the decedent or donor of the power has otherwise provided, if T leaves his estate in trust to pay the income to his son S for life, remainder to his son's children who survive him, and S disclaims with two children then living, the remainder in the children accelerates; the trust terminates and the children receive possession and enjoyment, even though the son may subsequently have other children or one or more of the living children may die during their father's lifetime. The will or instrument of transfer may be drafted to avoid acceleration if desired."

Paragraph (1) of subdivision (b) is designed to prevent an heir from disclaiming property for the purpose of increasing the share of his or her line at the expense of other lines of the decedent's descendants. For example, suppose the decedent has two children: The disclaimant (C–1) is living and has two children (GC–1 and GC–2, the decedent's grandchildren). The decedent's other child (C–2) has predeceased the decedent leaving one child (GC–3). But for the disclaimer, C–1's share is one-half and GC–3 takes the other half. See Sections 240, 245. See also Section 6402. If the disclaimant (C–1) is treated as having predeceased the decedent as provided in subdivision (a) of Section 282 and the rule of Sections 240 and 245 is applied, the estate would be divided at the grandchildren's generation, with GC–1, GC–2, and GC–3 each taking one-third. Paragraph (1) of subdivision (b) precludes the disclaimer from reducing the estate to which GC–3 would otherwise be entitled were the disclaimer not exercised. Paragraph (1) of subdivision (b) changes the rule concerning manner of distribution to children of the disclaimant as enunciated in Estate of Bryant, 149 Cal.App.3d 323, 335, 196 Cal.Rptr. 856 (1983).

Paragraph (2) of subdivision (b) makes clear that the rule governing advancements and the rule governing charging a debt against an intestate share apply notwithstanding a disclaimer.

As to the construction of provisions drawn from uniform acts, see Section 2.

As to interests created before January 1, 1984, see Section 287. After December 31, 1983, an interest that would otherwise be taken by a beneficiary may be disclaimed only as provided in this part. See Section 288. As to the application of any amendments made after that date, see Section 3. A disclaimer effective under federal law is effective as a disclaimer under this part. See Section 295.

Background on Section 282 of Repealed Code

Section 282 was added by 1983 Cal.Stat. ch. 17 § 2 and amended by 1983 Cal.Stat. ch. 842 § 23, 1984 Cal.Stat. ch. 892 § 17, and 1987 Cal.Stat. ch. 923 § 25. The section superseded former Probate Code Section 190.6 (repealed by 1983 Cal.Stat. ch. 17 § 1). The 1983 amendment added subdivision (b). The 1984 amendment broadened paragraph (1) of subdivision (b) by deleting the former limitation in that paragraph to disclaimers of "an interest created by intestate succession" and by applying the paragraph to situations where the division is made under any "other provision of a will or trust." See *Communication of Law Revision Commission Concerning Assembly Bill 2290*, 18 Cal.L.Revision Comm'n Reports 77, 84 (1986). The 1987 amendment revised the cross-reference in subdivision (b)(1). For background on the provisions of this part, see the Comment to this part under the part heading. [21 Cal.L.Rev.Comm.Reports 75 (1991)].

Cross References

Trustees and beneficiaries, generally, see Probate Code § 15600 et seq.

§ 283. Disclaimer not a voidable transfer

A disclaimer is not a voidable transfer by the beneficiary under the Uniform Voidable Transactions Act (Chapter 1 (commencing with Section 3439) of Title 2 of Part 2 of Division 4 of the Civil Code). *(Stats.1990, c. 79 (A.B.759), § 14, operative July 1, 1991. Amended by Stats.2015, c. 44 (S.B.161), § 26, eff. Jan. 1, 2016.)*

Law Revision Commission Comments

1990 Enactment

Section 283 continues Section 283 of the repealed Probate Code without change. This section rejects the rule of Estate of Kalt, 16 Cal.2d 807, 108 P.2d 401 (1940), that the disclaimer of a legacy after the testator's death may be a fraudulent conveyance. See also Section 281 (binding effect of disclaimer). As to interests created before January 1, 1984, see Section 287. After December 31, 1983, an interest that would otherwise be taken by a beneficiary may be disclaimed only as provided in this part. See Section 288. As to the application of any amendments made after that date, see Section 3. A disclaimer effective under federal law is effective as a disclaimer under this part. See Section 295.

Background on Section 283 of Repealed Code

Section 283 was a new provision added by 1983 Cal.Stat. ch. 17 § 2 and amended by 1987 Cal.Stat. ch. 40 § 6. The 1987 amendment substituted "transfer" for "conveyance" to conform to the terminology of the Uniform Fraudulent Transfer Act (Civil Code Sections 3439–3439.12) and corrected a statutory cross-reference. For background on the provisions of this part, see the Comment to this part under the part heading. As to the construction of provisions drawn from uniform acts, see Section 2. [20 Cal.L.Rev.Comm.Reports 1001 (1990)].

§ 284. Waiver of right to disclaim; effect

A person who could file a disclaimer under this part may instead file a written waiver of the right to disclaim. The waiver shall specify the interest to which the waiver applies. Upon being filed as provided in Section 280, the waiver is irrevocable and is binding upon the beneficiary and all persons claiming by, through, or under the beneficiary. *(Stats.1990, c. 79 (A.B.759), § 14, operative July 1, 1991.)*

Section 284 continues Section 284 of the repealed Probate Code without change. As to interests created before January 1, 1984, see Section 287. After December 31, 1983, an interest that would otherwise be taken by a beneficiary may be disclaimed only as provided in this part. See Section 288. As to the application of any amendments made after that date, see Section 3. A disclaimer effective under federal law is effective as a disclaimer under this part. See Section 295.

Background on Section 284 of Repealed Code

Section 284 was added by 1983 Cal.Stat. ch. 17 § 2 and amended by 1988 Cal.Stat. ch. 1199 § 35. The section restated the second sentence of former Probate Code Section 190.5 (repealed by 1983 Cal.Stat. ch. 17 § 1) without substantive change. The 1988 amendment made a nonsubstantive revision. See Comments to Conforming Revisions and Repeals, 19 Cal.L.Revision Comm'n Reports 1031, 1042 (1988). For background on the provisions of this part, see the Comment to this part under the part heading. [20 Cal.L.Rev.Comm.Reports 1001 (1990)].

§ 285. Restriction on making disclaimer; acceptance by beneficiary; exception; joint tenancy

(a) A disclaimer may not be made after the beneficiary has accepted the interest sought to be disclaimed.

(b) For the purpose of this section, a beneficiary has accepted an interest if any of the following occurs before a disclaimer is filed with respect to that interest:

(1) The beneficiary, or someone acting on behalf of the beneficiary, makes a voluntary assignment, conveyance, encumbrance, pledge, or transfer of the interest or part thereof, or contracts to do so; provided, however, that a beneficiary will not have accepted an interest if the beneficiary makes a gratuitous conveyance or transfer of the beneficiary's entire interest in property to the person or persons who would have received the property had the beneficiary made an otherwise qualified disclaimer pursuant to this part.

(2) The beneficiary, or someone acting on behalf of the beneficiary, executes a written waiver under Section 284 of the right to disclaim the interest.

(3) The beneficiary, or someone acting on behalf of the beneficiary, accepts the interest or part thereof or benefit thereunder.

(4) The interest or part thereof is sold at a judicial sale.

(c) An acceptance does not preclude a beneficiary from thereafter disclaiming all or part of an interest if both of the following requirements are met:

(1) The beneficiary became entitled to the interest because another person disclaimed an interest.

(2) The beneficiary or other person acting on behalf of the beneficiary at the time of the acceptance had no knowledge of the interest to which the beneficiary so became entitled.

(d) The acceptance by a joint tenant of the joint tenancy interest created when the joint tenancy is created is not an acceptance by the joint tenant of the interest created when the joint tenant survives the death of another joint tenant. *(Stats.1990, c. 79 (A.B.759), § 14, operative July 1, 1991. Amended by Stats.1994, c. 806 (A.B.3686), § 3.)*

Section 285 continues Section 285 of the repealed Probate Code without change. Subdivision (b) is drawn in part from Section 4(a) of the Uniform Disclaimer of Transfers by Will, Intestacy or Appointment Act (1978).

Subdivision (d) makes clear that a joint tenant is not, during the life of the joint tenancy, to be considered as having accepted the interest that is taken by surviving the other joint tenant. This is consistent with Sections 263(b)(11) ("creator of the interest" defined with respect to joint tenancies) and 267(b)(11) ("interest" defined). Under this chapter there are two interests that may be disclaimed by a joint tenant—the interest created when the person becomes a joint tenant and the interest that is acquired by operation of the right of survivorship when the other joint tenant dies. A similar rule is provided in Section 2(d) of the Uniform Disclaimer of Property Interests Act (1978) and in Section 1 of the Uniform Disclaimer of Transfers Under Nontestamentary Instruments Act (1978).

As to the construction of provisions drawn from uniform acts, see Section 2.

As to interests created before January 1, 1984, see Section 287. After December 31, 1983, an interest that would otherwise be taken by a beneficiary may be disclaimed only as provided in this part. See Section 288. As to the application of any amendments made after that date, see Section 3. A disclaimer effective under federal law is effective as a disclaimer under this part. See Section 295.

Background on Section 285 of Repealed Code

Section 285 was added by 1983 Cal.Stat. ch. 17 § 2. The section superseded former Probate Code Section 190.7 (repealed by 1983 Cal.Stat. ch. 17 § 1). For background on the provisions of this part, see the Comment to this part under the part heading. [20 Cal.L.Rev.Comm.Reports 1001 (1990)].

§ 286. Right to disclaim not affected by spendthrift or other restrictions

The right to disclaim exists regardless of any limitation imposed on the interest of a beneficiary in the nature of an expressed or implied spendthrift provision or similar restriction. *(Stats.1990, c. 79 (A.B.759), § 14, operative July 1, 1991.)*

Section 286 continues Section 286 of the repealed Probate Code without change. As to the effect of a disclaimer, see Sections 281–283. As to interests created before January 1, 1984, see Section 287. After December 31, 1983, an interest that would otherwise be taken by a beneficiary may be disclaimed only as provided in this part. See Section 288. As to the application of any amendments made after that date, see Section 3. A disclaimer effective under federal law is effective as a disclaimer under this part. See Section 295.

Background on Section 286 of Repealed Code

Section 286 was added by 1983 Cal.Stat. ch. 17 § 2. The section continued former Probate Code Section 190.8 (repealed by 1983 Cal.Stat. ch. 17 § 1). For background on the provisions of this part, see the Comment to this part under the part heading. [20 Cal.L.Rev.Comm.Reports 1001 (1990)].

§ 287. Interests created after Jan. 1, 1984; effect of part

An interest created before January 1, 1984, that has not been accepted may be disclaimed after December 31, 1983, in the manner provided in this part, but no interest that arose before January 1, 1984, in a person other than the beneficiary may be destroyed or diminished by any action of the disclaimant taken pursuant to this part. *(Stats.1990, c. 79 (A.B.759), § 14, operative July 1, 1991.)*

Law Revision Commission Comments

1990 Enactment

Section 287 continues Section 287 of the repealed Probate Code without change. After December 31, 1983, an interest that would otherwise be taken by a beneficiary may be disclaimed only as provided in this part. See Section 288. As to the application of any amendments made after that date, see Section 3. A disclaimer effective under federal law is effective as a disclaimer under this part. See Section 295. Subdivision (b) of Section 282 (preventing heir from disclaiming property for purpose of increasing share of his or her line at the expense of other lines of the decedent's descendants) applies only to cases where the disclaimer is filed on or after January 1, 1985. See Section 282.

Background on Section 287 of Repealed Code

Section 287 was added by 1983 Cal.Stat. ch. 17 § 2 and amended by 1988 Cal.Stat. ch. 1199 § 36. The section was drawn from former Probate Code Section 190.9 (repealed by 1983 Cal.Stat. ch. 17 § 1) but provided a new operative date. The 1988 amendment made a nonsubstantive revision. See Comments to Conforming Revisions and Repeals, 19 Cal.L.Revision Comm'n Reports 1031, 1042 (1988). For background on the provisions of this part, see the Comment to this part under the part heading. [20 Cal.L.Rev.Comm.Reports 1001 (1990)].

§ 288.   Exclusive means of disclaimer

This part does not limit or abridge any right a person may have under any other law to assign, convey, or release any property or interest, but after December 31, 1983, an interest that would otherwise be taken by a beneficiary may be declined, refused, renounced, or disclaimed only as provided in this part. *(Stats.1990, c. 79 (A.B.759), § 14, operative July 1, 1991.)*

Law Revision Commission Comments

1990 Enactment

Section 288 continues Section 288 of the repealed Probate Code without change. A purported disclaimer made after December 31, 1983, must comply with the requirements of this part; if it does not, it is not recognized as valid as a common law disclaimer or renunciation. As to interests created before January 1, 1984, see Section 287. A disclaimer effective under federal law is effective as a disclaimer under this part. See Section 295.

Background on Section 288 of Repealed Code

Section 288 was added by 1983 Cal.Stat. ch. 17 § 2 and amended by 1988 Cal.Stat. ch. 1199 § 37. The section continued the substance of former Probate Code Section 190.10 (repealed by 1983 Cal.Stat. ch. 17 § 1) except that Section 288 made ineffective a common law renunciation or disclaimer that did not satisfy the requirements of this part. See also Section 295 (disclaimers effective under federal law are effective under this part). The 1988 amendment made a nonsubstantive revision. See Comments to Conforming Revisions and Repeals, 19 Cal.L.Revision Comm'n Reports 1031, 1042 (1988). For background on the provisions of this part, see the Comment to this part under the part heading. [20 Cal.L.Rev.Comm.Reports 1001 (1990)].

§§ 289 to 294.   Repealed by Stats.1983, c. 201, § 3

CHAPTER 3.   DISCLAIMERS EFFECTIVE UNDER FEDERAL LAW

Application

Application of Part 8 to interests created on or after Jan. 1, 1984, see Probate Code §§ 287 and 288.

Cross References

Application of old and new law, see Probate Code § 3.

§ 295.   Effect of federal law transfers or disclaimers

Notwithstanding any other provision of this part, if as a result of a disclaimer or transfer the disclaimed or transferred interest is treated pursuant to the provisions of Title 26 of the United States Code, as now or hereafter amended, or any successor statute thereto, and the regulations promulgated thereunder, as never having been transferred to the beneficiary, then the disclaimer or transfer is effective as a disclaimer under this part. *(Stats.1990, c. 79 (A.B.759), § 14, operative July 1, 1991.)*

Law Revision Commission Comments

1990 Enactment

Section 295 continues Section 295 of the repealed Probate Code without change. This section makes a disclaimer that is valid under federal law effective under California law even though the disclaimer would not otherwise be effective under this part. See I.R.C. § 2518 (qualified disclaimers for purposes of federal gift tax). Section 295 also makes clear that certain transfers qualifying as disclaimers under federal law are effective as disclaimers under California law. See I.R.C. § 2518(c)(3). As to interests created before January 1, 1984, see Section 287. After December 31, 1983, an interest that would otherwise be taken by a beneficiary may be disclaimed only as provided in this part. See Section 288. As to the application of any amendments made after that date, see Section 3.

Background on Section 295 of Repealed Code

Section 295 was a new provision added by 1983 Cal.Stat. ch. 17 § 2 and amended by 1988 Cal.Stat. ch. 1199 § 38. The 1988 amendment made a nonsubstantive revision. See Comments to Conforming Revisions and Repeals, 19 Cal.L.Revision Comm'n Reports 1031, 1043 (1988). For background on the provisions of this part, see the Comment to this part under the part heading. [20 Cal.L.Rev.Comm.Reports 1001 (1990)].

§§ 295.1 to 295.4.   Repealed by Stats.1983, c. 201, § 3

§§ 296 to 296.8.   Repealed by Stats.1983, c. 842, § 20, operative Jan. 1, 1985

Part 9

TRUST COMPANY AS FIDUCIARY

Application of old and new law, see Probate Code § 3.

§ 300. Appointment as personal representative, guardian or conservator, or trustee

A trust company may be appointed to act as a personal representative, guardian or conservator of an estate, or trustee, in the same manner as an individual. A trust company may not be appointed guardian or conservator of the person of a ward or conservatee. *(Stats.1990, c. 79 (A.B.759), § 14, operative July 1, 1991.)*

Law Revision Commission Comments

1990 Enactment

Section 300 continues Section 300 of the repealed Probate Code without change.

Background on Section 300 of Repealed Code

Section 300 was added by 1988 Cal.Stat. ch. 1199 § 41. The section restated former Probate Code Section 480 (repealed by 1988 Cal.Stat. ch. 1199 § 47) without substantive change. See Communication from the California Law Revision Commission Concerning Assembly Bill 2841, 19 Cal.L.Revision Comm'n Reports 1201, 1209 (1988). [20 Cal.L.Rev.Comm.Reports 1001 (1990)].

Cross References

Appointment of personal representative, generally, see Probate Code § 8400 et seq.
Duties of trustees, see Probate Code § 16000 et seq.
Personal representative and general personal representative, defined, see Probate Code § 58.
Trust company, defined, see Probate Code § 83.
Trustees, powers, see Probate Code § 16200 et seq.

§ 301. Bond; liability; oaths and affidavits

(a) A trust company appointed to act as a personal representative, or guardian or conservator of an estate, may not be required to give a bond.

(b) The liability of a trust company and the manner of its making of oaths and affidavits are governed by Article 3 (commencing with Section 1540) of Chapter 12 of Division 1 of, and Section 1587 of, the Financial Code. *(Stats.1990, c. 79 (A.B.759), § 14, operative July 1, 1991.)*

Law Revision Commission Comments

1990 Enactment

Section 301 continues Section 301 of the repealed Probate Code without change. As to a trust company acting as a trustee, see Section 15602 (Trust Law).

Background on Section 301 of Repealed Code

Section 301 was added by 1988 Cal.Stat. ch. 1199 § 41. The section restated former Probate Code Section 481 (repealed by 1988 Cal.Stat. ch. 1199 § 47) but Section 301 no longer applies to a trust company acting as a trustee. See Section 15602 (trust law). See also Communication from the California Law Revision Commission Concerning Assembly Bill 2841, 19 Cal.L.Revision Comm'n Reports 1201, 1209 (1988). [20 Cal.L.Rev.Comm.Reports 1001 (1990)].

Cross References

Duties of trustees, see Probate Code § 16000 et seq.
Oaths, affirmation in lieu of, see Code of Civil Procedure § 2015.6.
Oaths, letters, and bond, generally, see Probate Code § 2300 et seq.
Oaths, officers authorized to administer, see Government Code § 1225.
Personal representative and general personal representative, defined, see Probate Code § 58.
Trust company, defined, see Probate Code § 83.

Code of Regulations References

Inheritance tax, court jurisdiction-nonresident decedent, see 18 Cal. Code of Regs. § 14653.
Inheritance tax, court jurisdiction-resident decedent, see 18 Cal. Code of Regs. § 14651.

§§ 302 to 305. Repealed by Stats.1988, c. 1199, § 40, operative July 1, 1989

Law Revision Commission Comments

1988 Repeal

Former Section 302 is restated in Section 8007 (determination of jurisdiction conclusive), which extends it to cover probate of a will as well as appointment of a personal representative [19 Cal.L.Rev. Comm. Reports 1044 (1988)].

Subdivision (a) of former Section 303 is restated in Section 7060 (disqualification of judge) without substantive change.

Subdivision (b) is restated in Sections 7070 (grounds for transfer) and 7071 (place of transfer). See also Section 1000 (general rules of civil practice); Code Civ.Proc. § 399 (transmittal of papers; jurisdiction of receiving court).

Subdivision (c) is restated in Section 7060(c) (disqualification of judge) without substantive change [19 Cal.L.Rev.Comm. Reports 1209 (1988)].

Former Section 304 is omitted as unnecessary [19 Cal.L.Rev. Comm. Reports 1044 (1988)].

Former Section 305 is restated in Section 7072 (retransfer), which makes retransfer permissive rather than mandatory. See also Section 1000 (general rules of civil practice); Code Civ.Proc. § 399 (transmittal of papers) [19 Cal.L.Rev.Comm. Reports 1044 (1988)].

§§ 320 to 324. Repealed by Stats.1988, c. 1199, § 40, operative July 1, 1989

Law Revision Commission Comments

1988 Repeal

Former Section 320 is superseded by Section 8200 (delivery of will) [19 Cal.L.Rev.Comm. Reports 1044 (1988)].

Former Section 321 is restated in Sections 8201 (order for production of will), 7050 (authority of court or judge), and 1000 (general rules of practice) [19 Cal.L.Rev.Comm. Reports 1209 (1988)].

Former Section 322 is omitted. The section's major effect was to enable a title insurer to provide insurance in the occasional case in which title is insured in a purchaser from an heir without requiring administration proceedings, the insurance being predicated on the property's small value and satisfactory proof (usually by affidavit) of heirship. 2A. Bowman, Ogden's Revised California Real Property Law § 29.81, at 1498 (1975). For this purpose, Sections 13200–13209 (affidavit procedure for real property of small value) provide a more complete and detailed procedure [19 Cal.L.Rev.Comm. Reports 1209 (1988)].

Former Section 323 is restated in Section 8000 (petition) without substantive change [19 Cal.L.Rev.Comm. Reports 1045 (1988)].

Former Section 324 is restated in Section 8001 (failure of person named executor to petition) without substantive change [19 Cal. L.Rev.Comm. Reports 1045 (1988)].

§ 325. Repealed by Stats.1982, c. 187, p. 570, § 6

§§ 326 to 329. Repealed by Stats.1988, c. 1199, § 40, operative July 1, 1989

Law Revision Commission Comments

1988 Repeal

The first part of former Section 326 is restated in Section 8002 (contents of petition), which substitutes the address for the residence of heirs and devisees and adds an express requirement that a copy of the will be attached. The last part is restated in Section 8006(b) (court order) without substantive change [19 Cal.L.Rev.Comm. Reports 1045 (1988)].

Former Section 327 is restated in Section 8003 (setting and notice of hearing), except that the petitioner rather than the clerk has the duty of giving notice [19 Cal.L.Rev.Comm. Reports 1210 (1988)].

The first sentence of the first paragraph of former Section 328 is restated in Sections 8110 (persons on whom notice served), 1201 (notice not given to petitioner), 1215 (manner of mailing), 1217 (service by mail or personal delivery), with the addition of a provision limiting service to known heirs. The second sentence is restated in Section 8100 (form of notice).

The second paragraph is restated in Sections 8111 (service on Attorney General) and 1215 (manner of mailing) without substantive change [19 Cal.L.Rev.Comm. Reports 1210 (1988)].

Former Section 328.3 is restated in Section 6104 (will or revocation procured by duress, menace, fraud, or undue influence) without substantive change [19 Cal.L.Rev.Comm. Reports 1046 (1988)].

Former Section 328.7 is restated in Section 6105 (conditional will) without substantive change [19 Cal.L.Rev.Comm. Reports 1210 (1988)].

The first two sentences of former Section 329 are restated in Section 8220 (evidence of subscribing witness) without substantive change. The third sentence is not continued because it is unnecessary. See Comment to Section 8221 (proof where no subscribing witness available). See also Evid.Code § 240 ("unavailable as witness"). The fourth sentence is restated in Section 8221 (proof where no subscribing witness available), with the exception of the language relating to a writing "at the end" of the will. The signatures of subscribing witnesses no longer must appear at the end. Section 6110 (execution) [19 Cal.L.Rev.Comm. Reports 1046 (1988)].

Part 10

IMMEDIATE STEPS CONCERNING DECEDENT'S TANGIBLE PERSONAL PROPERTY AND SAFE DEPOSIT BOX

Section

330. Delivery to specified persons; undisputed right to possession; proof of identity; liability.
331. Safe deposit box.
332 to 334. Repealed.

§ 330. Delivery to specified persons; undisputed right to possession; proof of identity; liability

(a) Except as provided in subdivision (b), a public administrator, government official, law enforcement agency, the hospital or institution in which a decedent died, or the decedent's employer, may, without the need to wait 40 days after death, deliver the tangible personal property of the decedent in its possession, including keys to the decedent's residence, to the decedent's surviving spouse, relative, or conservator or guardian of the estate acting in that capacity at the time of death.

(b) A person shall not deliver property pursuant to this section if the person knows or has reason to believe that there is a dispute over the right to possession of the property.

(c) A person that delivers property pursuant to this section shall require reasonable proof of the status and identity of the person to whom the property is delivered, and may rely on any document described in subdivision (d) of Section 13104 as proof of identity.

(d) A person that delivers property pursuant to this section shall, for a period of three years after the date of delivery of the property, keep a record of the property delivered and the status and identity of the person to whom the property is delivered.

(e) Delivery of property pursuant to this section does not determine ownership of the property or confer any greater rights in the property than the recipient would otherwise have and does not preclude later proceedings for administration of the decedent's estate. If proceedings for administration of the decedent's estate are commenced, the person holding the property shall deliver it to the personal representative on request by the personal representative.

(f) A person that delivers property pursuant to this section is not liable for loss or damage to the property caused by the person to whom the property is delivered. *(Stats.1990, c. 79 (A.B.759), § 14, operative July 1, 1991.)*

Law Revision Commission Comments

1990 Enactment

Section 330 continues Section 330 of the repealed Probate Code without substantive change. Section 330 makes clear that the specified officials and agencies need not wait 40 days from the death of the decedent to deliver decedent's personal effects and other tangible personal property to decedent's spouse, relatives, conservator, or guardian. Cf. Section 13100 (40–day delay for use of affidavit procedure). If the official or agency relies on a document described in subdivision (d) of Section 13104 as reasonable proof of identity, the official or agency is not liable for so relying.

Background on Section 330 of Repealed Code

Section 330 was added by 1989 Cal.Stat. ch. 21 § 3. See Communication from the California Law Revision Commission Concerning Assembly Bill 156, 20 Cal.L.Revision Comm'n Reports 227, 228 (1990). [20 Cal.L.Rev.Comm.Reports 1001 (1990)].

Cross References

Estate management, generally, see Probate Code § 9600 et seq.
Personal representative and general personal representative, defined, see Probate Code § 58.
Public administrators, see Probate Code § 7600 et seq.
Surviving spouse, defined, see Probate Code § 78.

§ 331. Safe deposit box

(a) This section applies only to a safe deposit box in a financial institution held by the decedent in the decedent's sole name, or held by the decedent and others where all are deceased. Nothing in this section affects the rights of a surviving coholder.

(b) A person who has a key to the safe deposit box may, before letters have been issued, obtain access to the safe deposit box only for the purposes specified in this section by providing the financial institution with both of the following:

(1) Proof of the decedent's death. Proof shall be provided by a certified copy of the decedent's death certificate or by a written statement of death from the coroner, treating physician, or hospital or institution where the decedent died.

(2) Reasonable proof of the identity of the person seeking access. Reasonable proof of identity is provided for the purpose of this paragraph if the requirements of Section 13104 are satisfied.

(c) The financial institution has no duty to inquire into the truth of any statement, declaration, certificate, affidavit, or document offered as proof of the decedent's death or proof of identity of the person seeking access.

(d) When the person seeking access has satisfied the requirements of subdivision (b), the financial institution shall do all of the following:

(1) Keep a record of the identity of the person.

(2) Permit the person to open the safe deposit box under the supervision of an officer or employee of the financial institution, and to make an inventory of its contents.

(3) Make a photocopy of all wills and trust instruments removed from the safe deposit box, and keep the photocopy in the safe deposit box until the contents of the box are removed by the personal representative of the estate or other legally authorized person. The financial institution may charge the person given access a reasonable fee for photocopying.

(4) Permit the person given access to remove instructions for the disposition of the decedent's remains, and, after a photocopy is made, to remove the wills and trust instruments.

(e) The person given access shall deliver all wills found in the safe deposit box to the clerk of the superior court and mail or deliver a copy to the person named in the will as executor or beneficiary as provided in Section 8200.

(f) Except as provided in subdivision (d), the person given access shall not remove any of the contents of the decedent's safe deposit box. *(Added by Stats.1991, c. 1055 (S.B.271), § 15.)*

Law Revision Commission Comments
1991 Addition [Revised Comment]

Section 331 is new. It permits a person who has a key to a decedent's safe deposit box to gain immediate access in order to remove the decedent's wills, trust instruments, and instructions for disposition of the decedent's remains, and to inventory the contents of the box. If no other directions have been given by the decedent, the right to control the disposition of the decedent's remains devolves, in order, on the surviving spouse, children, parents, other kindred, and the public administrator. Health and Safety Code § 7100.

If the person seeking access does not have a key to the safe deposit box and is not the public administrator, the person must obtain letters from the court to gain access to the box. Concerning the authority of the public administrator, see Section 7603.

Subdivision (e) requires the person given access to deliver the wills to the clerk of the superior court and mail or deliver a copy to the person named in the will as executor or beneficiary "as provided in Section 8200." Section 8200 requires the custodian to deliver the will to the clerk of the superior court in the county in which the estate of the decedent may be administered, and to mail a copy of the will to the person named in the will as executor, if the person's whereabouts is known to the custodian, or if not, to a person named in the will as

beneficiary, if the person's whereabouts is known to the custodian. For the county in which the estate of the decedent may be administered, see Sections 7051 (for California domiciliary, county of domicile), 7052 (nondomiciliary). See also Sections 40 ("financial institution" defined), 52 ("letters" defined), 58 ("personal representative" defined), 88 ("will" includes a codicil). [21 Cal.L.Rev.Comm.Reports 71 (1991)].

Cross References
Beneficiary, defined, see Probate Code § 24
Establishing and reporting fact of death, generally, see Probate Code § 200 et seq.
Financial institution, defined, see Probate Code § 40.
Instrument, defined, see Probate Code § 45.
Letters, defined, see Probate Code § 52.
Personal representative and general personal representative, defined, see Probate Code § 58.

§§ 332 to 334. Repealed by Stats.1988, c. 1199, § 40, operative July 1, 1989
Law Revision Commission Comments
1988 Repeal

The first sentence of former Section 332 is superseded by Section 8225 (admission of will to probate). The second sentence is superseded by Section 8002(b) (contents of petition) [19 Cal.L.Rev. Comm. Reports 1047 (1988)].

Subdivision (a) of former Section 333 is restated in Section 8121 (publication of notice), but the posting provision is omitted because it is no longer necessary.

The introductory part of subdivision (b) is restated in Section 8123 (type size) without substantive change. The remainder of subdivision (b) is restated in Section 8100 (form of notice), except that reference to notice of the decedent's death is eliminated from the caption and a reference to the decedent's will is added to the notice.

Subdivision (c) is restated in Section 8124 (affidavit of publication) without substantive change.

Subdivision (d) is not continued because it is no longer necessary.

The substance of subdivision (e) is continued in Section 8100 (form of notice) [19 Cal.L.Rev.Comm. Reports 1210 (1988)].

Former Section 334 is restated in Section 8122 (good faith compliance with publication requirement) without substantive change [19 Cal.L.Rev.Comm. Reports 1047 (1988)].

Part 11
FIDUCIARIES' WARTIME SUBSTITUTION LAW

Application
Application of Part, see Probate Code §§ 360, 361.

Law Revision Commission Comments
1990 Enactment

This part supersedes Part 11 (commencing with Section 350) of Division 2 of the repealed Probate Code. The superseded part was enacted upon recommendation of the California Law Revision Commission. See Communication from the California Law Revision Commission Concerning Assembly Bill 2841, 19 Cal.L.Revision Comm'n Reports 1201, 1211–16 (1988). [20 Cal.L.Rev.Comm.Reports 1001 (1990)].

Cross References

Application of old and new law, see Probate Code § 3.
Fiduciary, defined, see Probate Code § 39.

CHAPTER 1. GENERAL PROVISIONS

Application

Application of Part, see Probate Code §§ 360, 361.

ARTICLE 1. SHORT TITLE AND DEFINITIONS

Application

Application of Part, see Probate Code §§ 360, 361.

§ 350. Short title

This part may be cited as the Fiduciaries' Wartime Substitution Law. *(Stats.1990, c. 79 (A.B.759), § 14, operative July 1, 1991.)*

Law Revision Commission Comments

1990 Enactment

Section 350 continues Section 350 of the repealed Probate Code without change.

Background on Section 350 of Repealed Code

Section 350 was added by 1988 Cal.Stat. ch. 1199 § 41.5. The section restated former Code of Civil Procedure Section 1700 without substantive change. For background on the provisions of this part, see the Comment to this part under the part heading. [20 Cal.L.Rev.Comm.Reports 1001 (1990)].

§ 351. Scope of article

Unless the provision or context otherwise requires, the definitions in this article govern the construction of this part. *(Stats.1990, c. 79 (A.B.759), § 14, operative July 1, 1991.)*

Law Revision Commission Comments

1990 Enactment

Section 351 continues Section 351 of the repealed Probate Code without change.

Background on Section 351 of Repealed Code

Section 351 was added by 1988 Cal.Stat. ch. 1199 § 41.5. The section restated part of former Code of Civil Procedure Section 1700.1 without substantive change. For background on the provisions of this part, see the Comment to this part under the part heading. [20 Cal.L.Rev.Comm.Reports 1001 (1990)].

§ 352. Consultant

"Consultant" means a person, other than a trustee, designated in a trust to advise or direct the trustee concerning the trust, or whose consent or approval is required for a purchase, sale, exchange, or other transaction by the trustee, and includes a settlor who reserves the power of a consultant. *(Stats.1990, c. 79 (A.B.759), § 14, operative July 1, 1991.)*

Law Revision Commission Comments

1990 Enactment

Section 352 continues Section 352 of the repealed Probate Code without change.

Background on Section 352 of Repealed Code

Section 352 was added by 1988 Cal.Stat. ch. 1199 § 41.5. The section restated former Code of Civil Procedure Section 1700.6 (consultant under a trust) without substantive change. For background on the provisions of this part, see the Comment to this part under the part heading. [20 Cal.L.Rev.Comm.Reports 1001 (1990)].

§ 353. Estate

"Estate" means a trust estate, a decedent's estate, a guardianship or conservatorship estate, or other property that is the subject of a donative transfer. *(Stats.1990, c. 79 (A.B.759), § 14, operative July 1, 1991.)*

Law Revision Commission Comments

1990 Enactment

Section 353 continues Section 353 of the repealed Probate Code without change.

Background on Section 353 of Repealed Code

Section 353 was a new provision added by 1988 Cal.Stat. ch. 1199 § 41.5. For background on the provisions of this part, see the Comment to this part under the part heading. [20 Cal.L.Rev.Comm.Reports 1001 (1990)].

Cross References

Conservatorship, generally, see Probate Code § 1800 et seq.
Guardianship, generally, see Probate Code § 1500 et seq.
Trusts, creation, validity, modification, and termination, see Probate Code § 15200 et seq.

§ 354. Interested person

"Interested person" means, in addition to the meaning given that term in Section 48, a person having a property right in or claim against a guardianship or conservatorship estate or other estate that may be affected by the proceeding. *(Stats.1990, c. 79 (A.B.759), § 14, operative July 1, 1991.)*

Law Revision Commission Comments

1990 Enactment

Section 354 continues Section 354 of the repealed Probate Code without change.

Background on Section 354 of Repealed Code

Section 354 was a new provision added by 1988 Cal.Stat. ch. 1199 § 41.5. For background on the provisions of this part, see the Comment to this part under the part heading. [20 Cal.L.Rev.Comm.Reports 1001 (1990)].

Cross References

Conservatorship, generally, see Probate Code § 1800 et seq.
Guardianship, generally, see Probate Code § 1500 et seq.

Interested person, defined, see Probate Code § 48.

§ 355. Original fiduciary

"Original fiduciary" means a fiduciary who is replaced by a substitute fiduciary or who makes a delegation of power under this part. *(Stats.1990, c. 79 (A.B.759), § 14, operative July 1, 1991.)*

Law Revision Commission Comments
1990 Enactment

Section 355 continues Section 355 of the repealed Probate Code without change.

Background on Section 355 of Repealed Code

Section 355 was a new provision added by 1988 Cal.Stat. ch. 1199 § 41.5. For background on the provisions of this part, see the Comment to this part under the part heading. [20 Cal.L.Rev.Comm.Report 1001 (1990)].

§ 356. War service

A fiduciary or consultant is engaged in war service for the purpose of this part in each of the following cases:

(a) Where the person is a member of the armed forces of the United States or like forces of any nation with which the United States is allied or associated in time of war, including all of the following:

(1) Members of the Army, Navy, Marine Corps, Air Force, and Coast Guard.

(2) Members of the Public Health Service detailed by proper authority for duty with the armed forces.

(3) Members of all other organizations or services recognized by the laws of the United States as a part of or auxiliary to the armed forces of the United States.

(b) Where the person has been accepted for and is awaiting induction into the armed forces, or is receiving training or education under government supervision preliminary to induction into any of these forces, in time of war.

(c) Where the person is engaged, outside the 50 states of the United States, in any work in connection with a governmental agency of the United States or with the American Red Cross or any other body with similar objects operating with the approval and sanction of the government of the United States or of any nation with which the United States is allied or associated in time of war.

(d) Where the person is engaged in time of war in service on any ship of United States registry.

(e) Where the person is interned or a prisoner of war in a foreign country or in the United States or any possession or dependency of the United States.

(f) Where the person is absent from the 50 states of the United States and, due to war conditions, is unable to return freely at his or her own volition.

(g) Where the person is engaged in any service in the United States or abroad arising out of or connected with a state of war that the court having jurisdiction of the estate finds prevents the person from giving proper attention to his or her duties. *(Stats.1990, c. 79 (A.B.759), § 14, operative July 1, 1991.)*

Law Revision Commission Comments
1990 Enactment

Section 356 continues Section 356 of the repealed Probate Code without substantive change.

Background on Section 356 of Repealed Code

Section 356 was added by 1988 Cal.Stat. ch. 1199 § 41.5. The section restated former Code of Civil Procedure Section 1700.7 without substantive change, except that the former reference to the part of the continental United States below the 49th parallel was replaced by a reference in subdivision (c) to the fifty states. In subdivision (a), the reference to the Air Force was new and the references to certain auxiliary organizations was omitted as unnecessary in light of the general language. In subdivision (b), the reference to time of war was new. For background on the provisions of this part, see the Comment to this part under the part heading. [20 Cal.L.Rev.Comm.Reports 1001 (1990)].

ARTICLE 2. SCOPE OF PART

Section
360. Application to fiduciaries and consultants.
361. Conflicting provisions.
362. Repealed.

§ 360. Application to fiduciaries and consultants

This part applies to all fiduciaries and consultants, whether appointed or acting before, on, or after July 1, 1989. *(Stats.1990, c. 79 (A.B.759), § 14, operative July 1, 1991.)*

Law Revision Commission Comments
1990 Enactment

Section 360 continues Section 360 of the repealed Probate Code with the addition of the reference to "consultants." This part applies to personal representatives, trustees, guardians, conservators, and other legal representatives. See Section 39 ("fiduciary" defined).

Background on Section 360 of Repealed Code

Section 360 was added by 1988 Cal.Stat. ch. 1199 § 41.5. The section superseded former Code of Civil Procedure Section 1706. For background on the provisions of this part, see the Comment to this part under the part heading. [20 Cal.L.Rev.Comm.Reports 1001 (1990)].

Cross References

Fiduciary, defined, see Probate Code § 39.

§ 361. Conflicting provisions

This part does not apply to the extent an otherwise valid provision in an instrument provides a different or contrary rule or is otherwise inconsistent with this part. *(Stats.1990, c. 79 (A.B.759), § 14, operative July 1, 1991.)*

Law Revision Commission Comments
1990 Enactment

Section 361 continues Section 361 of the repealed Probate Code without change.

Background on Section 361 of Repealed Code

Section 361 was added by 1988 Cal.Stat. ch. 1199 § 41.5. The section superseded former Code of Civil Procedure Section 1705. For background on the provisions of this part, see the Comment to this part under the part heading. [20 Cal.L.Rev.Comm.Reports 1001 (1990)].

Cross References

Instrument, defined, see Probate Code § 45.

§ 362. Repealed by Stats.1988, c. 1199, § 40, operative July 1, 1989

Law Revision Commission Comments

1988 Repeal

Former Section 362 is superseded by Sections 12522 (sister state proceedings) and 12523 (foreign nation proceedings). See the Comments to these sections. The provision relating to the validity of the will under the law of this state or other jurisdiction is omitted. In the case of sister state probate orders, it is contrary to full faith and credit principles to relitigate the validity of the will. See also Section 6113 (choice of law as to execution of will). In the case of foreign nation probate orders, the condition is automatically satisfied if probate has been granted and the order is to be given recognition [19 Cal.L.Rev.Comm. Reports 1048 (1988)].

ARTICLE 3. PROCEDURAL PROVISIONS

Section
365. Jurisdiction.
366. Notice of hearing.

Application

Application of Part, see Probate Code §§ 360, 361.

§ 365. Jurisdiction

Proceedings under this part are in the court having jurisdiction over the estate or, if none, any court in which jurisdiction of the estate is proper. *(Stats.1990, c. 79 (A.B.759), § 14, operative July 1, 1991.)*

Law Revision Commission Comments

1990 Enactment

Section 365 continues Section 365 of the repealed Probate Code without change. For the proper court in a decedent's estate, see Sections 7050–7052. For the proper court in a guardianship or conservatorship estate, see Sections 2200–2203. For the proper court in a trust estate, see Sections 17000–17005. For general provisions, see Sections 1000–1004 (rules of practice), 1020–1023 (petitions and other papers), 1040–1050 (hearings and orders).

Background on Section 365 of Repealed Code

Section 365 was added by 1988 Cal.Stat. ch. 1199 § 41.5. The section superseded the second sentence of former Code of Civil Procedure Section 1701, the third sentence of former Code of Civil Procedure Section 1702, and part of the first sentence of former Code of Civil Procedure Section 1702.1. For background on the provisions of this part, see the Comment to this part under the part heading. [20 Cal.L.Rev.Comm.Reports 1001 (1990)].

Cross References

Trusts, judicial proceedings, generally, see Probate Code § 17000 et seq.

§ 366. Notice of hearing

Notice of a hearing under this part shall be mailed at least 15 days before the hearing to each fiduciary and consultant and to the following persons:

(a) In the case of a trust, to each known beneficiary, subject to the provisions of Chapter 2 (commencing with Section 15800) of Part 3 of Division 9.

(b) In the case of a decedent's estate, as provided in Section 1220 to both of the following:

(1) Each known heir whose interest in the estate would be affected by the proceedings.

(2) Each known devisee whose interest in the estate would be affected by the proceedings.

(c) In the case of a guardianship or conservatorship estate, as provided in Section 1460.

(d) In other cases, to any additional interested persons required by the court to receive notice. *(Stats.1990, c. 79 (A.B.759), § 14, operative July 1, 1991.)*

Law Revision Commission Comments

1990 Enactment

Section 366 continues Section 366 of the repealed Probate Code without substantive change. Notice under this part is subject to general provisions governing notice under this code. For general provisions relating to notice, see 1200–1230 (notice of hearing), 1250–1252 (request for special notice), 1260–1265 (proof of giving of notice).

Background on Section 366 of Repealed Code

Section 366 was added by 1988 Cal.Stat. ch. 1199 § 41.5. The section superseded former Code of Civil Procedure Section 1701.1, part of the second sentence of former Code of Civil Procedure Section 1701.2, the second sentence of former Code of Civil Procedure Section 1702.1, the introductory part of former Code of Civil Procedure Section 1703.1, part of the first sentence of former Code of Civil Procedure Section 1703.2, and former Code of Civil Procedure Section 1704. For background on the provisions of this part, see the Comment to this part under the part heading. [20 Cal.L.Rev.Comm.Reports 1001 (1990)].

Cross References

Beneficiary, defined, see Probate Code § 24
Computation of time, see Code of Civil Procedure §§ 12 and 12a; Government Code § 6800 et seq.
Devisee, defined, see Probate Code § 34.
Heir, defined, see Probate Code § 44.
Trusts, beneficiaries, see Probate Code § 15800 et seq.

CHAPTER 2. APPOINTMENT OF SUBSTITUTE FIDUCIARY

Section
370. Petition; court order for substitute, suspension, or accounting.
371. Powers of substitute fiduciary.
372. Bond.
372.5. Repealed.
373. Reinstatement of original fiduciary.
374. Liability of reinstated fiduciary.

Application

Application of Part, see Probate Code §§ 360, 361.

§ 370. Petition; court order for substitute, suspension, or accounting

If a fiduciary is engaged in war service, on petition of the fiduciary, a cofiduciary, or an interested person, the court may do any one or more of the following:

(a) Appoint a substitute fiduciary. If there is a qualified and acting cofiduciary, the court is not required to appoint a substitute fiduciary but may vest in the cofiduciary the powers of the original fiduciary engaged in war service.

(b) Order a suspension of the powers and duties of the original fiduciary for the period the original fiduciary is engaged in war service and until further order of the court.

(c) Order an account by the original fiduciary. *(Stats. 1990, c. 79 (A.B.759), § 14, operative July 1, 1991.)*

Law Revision Commission Comments

1990 Enactment

Section 370 continues Section 370 of the repealed Probate Code without substantive change. Where there is a cofiduciary, appointment of a substitute fiduciary may be unnecessary, since the cofiduciary may be authorized to act. See, e.g., Sections 2105 (authority of joint guardian or conservator to act), 9630 (authority of joint personal representative to act), 15622 (temporary incapacity of cotrustee). This section does not apply to the extent the will, trust, or other instrument provides a different rule. See Section 361 (provision in instrument controls).

Background on Section 370 of Repealed Code

Section 370 was added by 1988 Cal.Stat. ch. 1199 § 41.5. Subdivision (a) restated the first sentence of former Code of Civil Procedure Section 1701 and former Code of Civil Procedure Section 1701.3 without substantive change. Subdivisions (b) and (c) superseded the first sentence of former Code of Civil Procedure 1701.2. For background on the provisions of this part, see the Comment to this part under the part heading. [20 Cal.L.Rev.Comm.Reports 1001 (1990)].

Cross References

Fiduciaries' Wartime Substitution Law, interested person, defined, see Probate Code § 366.
Fiduciary, defined, see Probate Code § 39.

§ 371. Powers of substitute fiduciary

A substitute fiduciary has all the powers, including discretionary powers, that the original fiduciary had, except powers that the court determines are purely personal to the original fiduciary, and is subject to the same duties as the original fiduciary. *(Stats.1990, c. 79 (A.B.759), § 14, operative July 1, 1991.)*

Law Revision Commission Comments

1990 Enactment

Section 371 continues Section 371 of the repealed Probate Code without change. This section does not apply to the extent the will, trust, or other instrument provides a different rule. See Section 361 (provision in instrument controls).

Background on Section 371 of Repealed Code

Section 371 was added by 1988 Cal.Stat. ch. 1199 § 41.5. The section restated former Code of Civil Procedure Section 1701.4 without substantive change. The reference to duties was new. For background on the provisions of this part, see the Comment to this part under the part heading. [20 Cal.L.Rev.Comm.Reports 1001 (1990)].

Cross References

Fiduciary, defined, see Probate Code § 39.

§ 372. Bond

Except as otherwise ordered by the court, a substitute fiduciary shall give a bond in the manner and to the extent provided by law for the original fiduciary. *(Stats.1990, c. 79 (A.B.759), § 14, operative July 1, 1991.)*

Law Revision Commission Comments

1990 Enactment

Section 372 continues Section 372 of the repealed Probate Code without change. This section gives the court authority to vary the bond requirement. This would be appropriate, for example, where the instrument has waived the bond for the original fiduciary and it would be inappropriate to waive bond for the substitute fiduciary. This section does not apply to the extent the will, trust, or other instrument provides a different rule. See Section 361 (provision in instrument controls).

Background on Section 372 of Repealed Code

Section 372 was added by 1988 Cal.Stat. ch. 1199 § 41.5. The section restated former Code of Civil Procedure Section 1701.6 without substantive change, except for the addition of court authority to vary the bond requirement. For background on the provisions of this part, see the Comment to this part under the part heading. [20 Cal.L.Rev.Comm.Reports 1001 (1990)].

Cross References

Fiduciary, defined, see Probate Code § 39.
Oaths, affirmation in lieu of, see Code of Civil Procedure § 2015.6.
Oaths, letters, and bond, generally, see Probate Code § 2300 et seq.
Oaths, officers authorized to administer, see Government Code § 1225.

§ 372.5. Repealed by Stats.1988, c. 1199, § 42, operative July 1, 1989

Law Revision Commission Comments

1988 Repeal

Former Section 372.5 is restated in Section 6112(d) without substantive change [19 Cal.L.Rev.Comm. Reports 1049 (1988)].

§ 373. Reinstatement of original fiduciary

After the expiration of an original fiduciary's war service, if the estate has not been closed, the original fiduciary, on petition, is entitled to reinstatement as fiduciary. On reinstatement, the substitute fiduciary may, in the discretion of the court, be removed and may be discharged on conditions prescribed by the court. *(Stats.1990, c. 79 (A.B.759), § 14, operative July 1, 1991.)*

Law Revision Commission Comments

1990 Enactment

Section 373 continues Section 373 of the repealed Probate Code without change. This section gives the court discretion not to remove the substitute fiduciary. In certain circumstances, the court may determine that it is advisable to retain the substitute as a cofiduciary upon reinstatement of the original fiduciary. This section does not apply to the extent the will, trust, or other instrument provides a different rule. See Section 361 (provision in instrument controls).

Background on Section 373 of Repealed Code

Section 373 was added by 1988 Cal.Stat. ch. 1199 § 41.5. The section restated the second and third sentences of former Code of Civil Procedure Section 1701.2 without substantive change, except that the court was given discretion not to remove the substitute fiduciary. For background on the provisions of this part, see the Comment to this part under the part heading. [20 Cal.L.Rev.Comm.Reports 1001 (1990)].

§ 374. Liability of reinstated fiduciary

A substitute fiduciary or an original fiduciary reinstated under Section 373 is not liable for the acts or omissions of the predecessor fiduciary. *(Stats.1990, c. 79 (A.B.759), § 14, operative July 1, 1991.)*

Law Revision Commission Comments

1990 Enactment

Section 374 continues Section 374 of the repealed Probate Code without change. This section does not apply to the extent the will, trust, or other instrument provides a different rule. See Section 361 (provision in instrument controls).

Background on Section 374 of Repealed Code

Section 374 was added by 1988 Cal.Stat. ch. 1199 § 41.5. The section restated part of former Code of Civil Procedure Section 1701.7 without substantive change. For background on the provisions of this part, see the Comment to this part under the part heading. [20 Cal.L.Rev.Comm.Reports 1001 (1990)].

CHAPTER 3. DELEGATION OF POWERS

Application

Application of Part, see Probate Code §§ 360, 361.

ARTICLE 1. DELEGATION BY FIDUCIARY

Application

Application of Part, see Probate Code §§ 360, 361.

§ 380. Delegation; period of delegation; petition and court approval

(a) A fiduciary who is or will be engaged in war service may delegate the fiduciary's powers, including discretionary powers, to a fiduciary who is not engaged in war service. Delegation may be made for the period during which the original fiduciary is engaged in war service and not to exceed six months following the expiration of that period.

(b) Approval of the court, on petition of the original fiduciary, the delegate, or an interested person, is required for delegation. *(Stats.1990, c. 79 (A.B.759), § 14, operative July 1, 1991.)*

Law Revision Commission Comments

1990 Enactment

Section 380 continues Section 380 of the repealed Probate Code without change. Where there is a cofiduciary, delegation of power may be unnecessary, since the cofiduciary may be authorized to act. See, e.g., Sections 15622 (temporary incapacity of cotrustee), 9630 (authority of joint personal representative to act), 2105 (authority of joint guardian or conservator to act). The authority to delegate powers to a cofiduciary under this chapter is an exception to the usual duty not to delegate. See Section 16012 (duty not to delegate to cotrustee). This section does not apply to the extent the will, trust, or other instrument provides a different rule. See Section 361 (provision in instrument controls).

Background on Section 380 of Repealed Code

Section 380 was added by 1988 Cal.Stat. ch. 1199 § 41.5. Subdivision (a) restated the first and second sentences of former Code of Civil Procedure Section 1702 without substantive change. Subdivision (b) superseded the first sentence of former Code of Civil Procedure Section 1702.1. For background on the provisions of this part, see the Comment to this part under the part heading. [20 Cal.L.Rev.Comm.Reports 1001 (1990)].

§ 381. Personal powers

The right of delegation does not exist to the extent the court determines that powers to be delegated are purely personal to the original fiduciary. *(Stats.1990, c. 79 (A.B. 759), § 14, operative July 1, 1991.)*

Law Revision Commission Comments

1990 Enactment

Section 381 continues Section 381 of the repealed Probate Code without change. Where there is a cofiduciary, delegation of power may be unnecessary, since the cofiduciary may be authorized to act. See, e.g., Sections 2105 (authority of joint guardian or conservator to act), 9630 (authority of joint personal representative to act), 15622 (temporary incapacity of cotrustee). This section does not apply to the extent the will, trust, or other instrument provides a different rule. See Section 361 (provision in instrument controls).

Background on Section 381 of Repealed Code

Section 381 was added by 1988 Cal.Stat. ch. 1199 § 41.5. The section restated the introductory clause and subdivision (a) of former Code of Civil Procedure Section 1702.2 without substantive change. For background on the provisions of this part, see the Comment to this part under the part heading. [20 Cal.L.Rev.Comm.Reports 1001 (1990)].

§ 382. Resumption of powers by original fiduciary

After the expiration of the original fiduciary's war service, the court may, on petition of the original fiduciary, authorize the original fiduciary to resume the exercise of the fiduciary functions, and the delegated powers cease. *(Stats.1990, c. 79 (A.B.759), § 14, operative July 1, 1991.)*

Law Revision Commission Comments

1990 Enactment

Section 382 continues Section 382 of the repealed Probate Code without change. This section does not apply to the extent the will, trust, or other instrument provides a different rule. See Section 361 (provision in instrument controls).

Background on Section 382 of Repealed Code

Section 382 was added by 1988 Cal.Stat. ch. 1199 § 41.5. The section restated the third sentence of former Code of Civil Procedure Section 1702.1 without substantive change. For background on the provisions of this part, see the Comment to this part under the part heading. [20 Cal.L.Rev.Comm.Reports 1001 (1990)].

Cross References

Fiduciary, defined, see Probate Code § 39.

§ 383. Liability of original fiduciary

The original fiduciary is not liable for the acts or omissions of the delegate. *(Stats.1990, c. 79 (A.B.759), § 14, operative July 1, 1991.)*

Law Revision Commission Comments

1990 Enactment

Section 383 continues Section 383 of the repealed Probate Code without change. This section does not apply to the extent the will, trust, or other instrument provides a different rule. See Section 361 (provision in instrument controls).

Background on Section 383 of Repealed Code

Section 383 was added by 1988 Cal.Stat. ch. 1199 § 41.5. The section restated former Code of Civil Procedure Section 1702.4 without substantive change. For background on the provisions of this part, see the Comment to this part under the part heading. [20 Cal.L.Rev.Comm.Reports 1001 (1990)].

Cross References

Fiduciary, defined, see Probate Code § 39.

§ 384. Repealed by Stats.1988, c. 1199, § 42, operative July 1, 1989

Law Revision Commission Comments

1988 Repeal

The first part of former Section 384 is restated in Section 8226(a) (effect of admission of will to probate) without substantive change. The last part is superseded by Section 8270(b) (petition for revocation) [19 Cal.L.Rev.Comm. Reports 1050 (1988)].

ARTICLE 2. DELEGATION BY CONSULTANT

Section

Application

Application of Part, see Probate Code §§ 360, 361.

§ 385. Delegation to coconsultant; procedure; personal powers

(a) A consultant who is or will be engaged in war service may delegate the powers of the consultant, including discretionary powers, to a coconsultant who is not engaged in war service, or to the trustee administering the trust. The procedure for delegation by a fiduciary governs delegation by a consultant.

(b) The right of delegation does not exist to the extent the court determines that powers to be delegated are purely personal to the consultant. These powers are suspended until their exercise is resumed pursuant to this article. *(Stats.1990, c. 79 (A.B.759), § 14, operative July 1, 1991.)*

Law Revision Commission Comments

1990 Enactment

Section 385 continues Section 385 of the repealed Probate Code without change. This section does not apply to the extent the will, trust, or other instrument provides a different rule. See Section 361 (provision in instrument controls).

Background on Section 385 of Repealed Code

Section 385 was added by 1988 Cal.Stat. ch. 1199 § 41.5. The section restated former Code of Civil Procedure Section 1703 without substantive change. For background on the provisions of this part, see the Comment to this part under the part heading. [20 Cal.L.Rev.Comm.Reports 1001 (1990)].

Cross References

Fiduciary, defined, see Probate Code § 39.

§ 386. Court orders where consultant does not delegate; suspension of powers; conferring powers upon coconsultant

If a consultant who is engaged in war service does not delegate the consultant's powers, the court, on petition of the trustee or an interested person, may do either of the following:

(a) Suspend the consultant's powers for the period of the consultant's war service and not to exceed six months following the expiration of that period.

(b) Confer the powers, except discretionary powers that the court determines are purely personal to the consultant, on a coconsultant designated in the trust, the trustee, or any other qualified person. *(Stats.1990, c. 79 (A.B.759), § 14, operative July 1, 1991.)*

Law Revision Commission Comments

1990 Enactment

Section 386 continues Section 386 of the repealed Probate Code without change. This section does not apply to the extent the will, trust, or other instrument provides a different rule. See Section 361 (provision in instrument controls).

Background on Section 386 of Repealed Code

Section 386 was added by 1988 Cal.Stat. ch. 1199 § 41.5. The section restated former Code of Civil Procedure Section 1703.1 without substantive change. For background on the provisions of this part, see the Comment to this part under the part heading. [20 Cal.L.Rev.Comm.Reports 1001 (1990)].

Fiduciaries' Wartime Substitution Law, interested person, defined, see Probate Code § 366.

§ 387. Resumption of powers by consultant

If a consultant has delegated or the court has suspended the powers of the consultant, the court may, on petition by the consultant within six months following the expiration of the period of the consultant's war service, authorize the consultant to resume the exercise of the consultant's functions. All powers delegated to or conferred on other persons thereupon cease. *(Stats.1990, c. 79 (A.B.759), § 14, operative July 1, 1991.)*

Law Revision Commission Comments

1990 Enactment

Section 387 continues Section 387 of the repealed Probate Code without change. This section does not apply to the extent the will, trust, or other instrument provides a different rule. See Section 361 (provision in instrument controls).

Background on Section 387 of Repealed Code

Section 387 was added by 1988 Cal.Stat. ch. 1199 § 41.5. The section restated former Code of Civil Procedure Section 1703.2 without substantive change. For background on the provisions of this part, see the Comment to this part under the part heading. [20 Cal.L.Rev.Comm.Reports 1001 (1990)].

§ 388. Liability of consultant

A consultant who delegates powers under this article is not liable for the acts or omissions of the delegate. *(Stats.1990, c. 79 (A.B.759), § 14, operative July 1, 1991.)*

Law Revision Commission Comments

1990 Enactment

Section 388 continues Section 388 of the repealed Probate Code without change. This section does not apply to the extent the will, trust, or other instrument provides a different rule. See Section 361 (provision in instrument controls).

Background on Section 388 of Repealed Code

Section 388 was added by 1988 Cal.Stat. ch. 1199 § 41.5. The section restated former Code of Civil Procedure Section 1703.3 without substantive change. For background on the provisions of this part, see the Comment to this part under the part heading. [20 Cal.L.Rev.Comm.Reports 1001 (1990)].

Part 12

PROBATE REFEREES

Law Revision Commission Comments

1990 Enactment

This part supersedes Part 12 (commencing with Section 400) of Division 2 of the repealed Probate Code. The superseded part was enacted upon recommendation of the California Law Revision Commission. See Recommendation Relating to Inventory and Appraisal, 19 Cal.L.Revision Comm'n Reports 741 (1988). See also Communication from the California Law Revision Commission

Concerning Assembly Bill 2841, 19 Cal.L.Revision Comm'n Reports 1201, 1215–17 (1988). [20 Cal.L.Rev.Comm.Reports 1001 (1990)].

Cross References

State and political subdivisions, filing and service fees, judgments for agencies, costs of court reporters, application to probate referees, see Government Code § 6103.

CHAPTER 1. APPOINTMENT AND REVOCATION

Application

Probate referees appointed before July 1, 1989, see Probate Code § 408.

§ 400. County referee appointment; lack of qualified applicants

(a) The Controller shall appoint at least one person in each county to act as a probate referee for the county.

(b) If there are fewer than three qualified applicants to serve in a county, the Controller may designate a probate referee from another county or make an interim appointment, to serve until the vacancy has been filled by a qualified applicant. *(Stats.1990, c. 79 (A.B.759), § 14, operative July 1, 1991.)*

Law Revision Commission Comments

1990 Enactment

Section 400 continues Section 400 of the repealed Probate Code without change. For qualification of an applicant, see Section 401. See also Section 402(c) (list of qualified applicants).

Background on Section 400 of Repealed Code

Section 400 was added by 1988 Cal.Stat. ch. 1199 § 44. Subdivision (a) continued a portion of the first sentence of the first paragraph of former Probate Code Section 1305 (repealed by 1988 Cal.Stat. ch. 1199 § 65) without change. Subdivision (b) superseded the third sentence of the first paragraph of former Probate Code Section 1305. For background on the provisions of this part, see the Comment to this part under the part heading. [20 Cal.L.Rev.Comm.Reports 1001 (1990)].

Cross References

Probate referees, authority and powers, see Probate Code § 450 et seq.

§ 401. Eligibility; nondiscriminatory merit appointment

(a) Appointment shall be from among persons passing a qualification examination. A person who passes the examination is eligible for appointment for a period of five years from the date of the examination.

(b) Appointment shall be on the basis of merit without regard to sex, race, religious creed, color, national origin, ancestry, marital status, or political affiliation. *(Stats.1990, c. 79 (A.B.759), § 14, operative July 1, 1991.)*

Law Revision Commission Comments
1990 Enactment

Section 401 continues Section 401 of the repealed Probate Code without change.

Background on Section 401 of Repealed Code

Section 401 was added by 1988 Cal.Stat. ch. 1199 § 44. Subdivision (a) restated a portion of the first sentence of the first paragraph and the fifth sentence of the second paragraph of former Probate Code Section 1305 (repealed by 1988 Cal.Stat. ch. 1199 § 65) without substantive change. Subdivision (b) continued the second sentence of the first paragraph of former Probate Code Section 1305 without change. The reference to the State Personnel Board was not continued. See "Background to Section 402 of Repealed Code." For background on the provisions of this part, see the Comment to this part under the part heading. [20 Cal.L.Rev.Comm.Reports 1001 (1990)].

Cross References

Probate referees, authority and powers, see Probate Code § 450 et seq.

§ 402. Qualification examination; administration; fee

(a) The qualification examination for applicants for appointment to act as a probate referee shall be held at times and places within the state determined by the Controller.

(b) The Controller may contract with another agency to administer the qualification examination. Administration of the examination shall include:

(1) Development of standards for passage of the examination.

(2) Preparation of examination questions.

(3) Giving the examination.

(4) Scoring the examination.

(c) Each applicant shall pay a fee for taking the qualification examination. The agency administering the examination shall transmit to the Controller a list of candidates who have received a passing score in the examination. The list is a public record. *(Stats.1990, c. 79 (A.B.759), § 14, operative July 1, 1991.)*

Law Revision Commission Comments
1990 Enactment

Section 402 continues Section 402 of the repealed Probate Code without change.

Background on Section 402 of Repealed Code

Section 402 was added by 1988 Cal.Stat. ch. 1199 § 44. The section restated former Probate Code Section 1306 (repealed by 1988 Cal.Stat. ch. 1199 § 65), deleting the references to the State Personnel Board. At the time former Section 1306 was repealed, the State Personnel Board no longer administered the examination. Instead, the Controller was contracting with Cooperative Personnel Services, an agency created through a joint powers agreement, for administration of the examination. For background on the provi-

sions of this part, see the Comment to this part under the part heading. [20 Cal.L.Rev.Comm.Reports 1001 (1990)].

Cross References

Inspection of public records, see Government Code § 6250 et seq. Probate referees, authority and powers, see Probate Code § 450 et seq.

§ 403. Term of office

(a) The term of office of a probate referee is four years, expiring June 30. A person may be appointed to complete the unexpired term of office of a probate referee whose appointment is revoked or is otherwise terminated. For a period of five years from the date of expiration of the term of office, a person who had been appointed to act as a probate referee is eligible for reappointment.

(b) If the Controller increases the number of probate referees in a county, the Controller shall stagger the terms of the new appointees so that one-quarter, or as close to one-quarter as possible, of the terms of the probate referees in that county expire on June 30 of each succeeding year. *(Stats.1990, c. 79 (A.B.759), § 14, operative July 1, 1991.)*

Law Revision Commission Comments
1990 Enactment

Section 403 continues Section 403 of the repealed Probate Code without change.

Background on Section 403 of Repealed Code

Section 403 was added by 1988 Cal.Stat. ch. 1199 § 44. The section restated the second, third, and sixth sentences of the second paragraph of former Probate Code Section 1305 (repealed by 1988 Cal.Stat. ch. 1199 § 65), with the addition that a probate referee's eligibility for reappointment lasts until five years after expiration of the referee's term of office. Section 403 also made clear that an appointment may be for a term less than four years in the case of an appointment for the purpose of completion of the term of another probate referee. For background on the provisions of this part, see the Comment to this part under the part heading. [20 Cal.L.Rev.Comm.Reports 1001 (1990)].

Cross References

Probate referees, authority and powers, see Probate Code § 450 et seq.

§ 404. Standards of training, performance, and ethics; revocation of appointment for noncompliance; review

(a) The Controller shall establish and may amend standards of training, performance, and ethics of probate referees. The standards are a public record.

(b) The Controller may revoke the appointment of a person to act as a probate referee for noncompliance with any standard of training, performance, or ethics established under subdivision (a). The Controller may revoke an appointment under this subdivision without notice or a hearing, but the revocation is subject to review by writ of mandate in a court of competent jurisdiction. *(Stats.1990, c. 79 (A.B.759), § 14, operative July 1, 1991.)*

Law Revision Commission Comments
1990 Enactment

Section 404 continues Section 404 of the repealed Probate Code without substantive change.

Background on Section 404 of Repealed Code

Section 404 was added by 1988 Cal.Stat. ch. 1199 § 44. Subdivision (a) restated former Probate Code Section 1307 (repealed by 1988 Cal.Stat. ch. 1199 § 65), but made the adoption of standards mandatory rather than permissive. Subdivision (b) restated subdivision (a) of former Probate Code Section 1308 (repealed by 1988 Cal.Stat. ch. 1199 § 65) without substantive change. For background on the provisions of this part, see the Comment to this part under the part heading. [20 Cal.L.Rev.Comm.Reports 1001 (1990)].

Cross References

Controller, powers and duties, see Government Code § 12410 et seq.
Inspection of public records, see Government Code § 6250 et seq.
Mandamus, generally, see Code of Civil Procedure § 1085.
Probate referees, authority and powers, see Probate Code § 450 et seq.

§ 405. Peremptory revocation; number of revocations

Notwithstanding Section 404, the Controller may, at the Controller's pleasure, revoke the appointment of a person to act as a probate referee. Under this section, the Controller may revoke the appointment of not more than 10 percent of the probate referees in each county in any one calendar year, but may revoke the appointment of at least one probate referee in each county in any one calendar year. *(Stats.1990, c. 79 (A.B.759), § 14, operative July 1, 1991.)*

Law Revision Commission Comments

1990 Enactment

Section 405 continues Section 405 of the repealed Probate Code without change. Revocation of appointment under Section 405 is independent of revocation under Section 404 (standards for probate referee).

Background on Section 405 of Repealed Code

Section 405 was added by 1988 Cal.Stat. ch. 1199 § 44. The section restated the first sentence of subdivision (b) of former Probate Code Section 1308 (repealed by 1988 Cal.Stat. ch. 1199 § 65) without substantive change. For background on the provisions of this part, see the Comment to this part under the part heading. [20 Cal.L.Rev.Comm.Reports 1001 (1990)].

Cross References

Probate referees, authority and powers, see Probate Code § 450 et seq.

§§ 405.1 to 405.6. Repealed by Stats.1988, c. 1199, § 43, operative July 1, 1989

Law Revision Commission Comments

1988 Repeal

Former Section 405.1 is restated in Section 8572 (Secretary of State as attorney) without substantive change [19 Cal.L.Rev.Comm.Reports 1051 (1988)].

Former Section 405.2 is restated in Section 8573 (statement of address) with the omission of the acknowledgment requirement [19 Cal.L.Rev.Comm.Reports 1051 (1988)].

Former Section 405.3 is restated in Section 8574 (manner of service) without substantive change [19 Cal.L.Rev.Comm.Reports 1051 (1988)].

Former Section 405.4 is restated in Section 8575 (proof of service) without substantive change [19 Cal.L.Rev.Comm.Reports 1051 (1988)].

Former Section 405.5 is restated in Section 8576 (effect of service) without substantive change [19 Cal.L.Rev.Comm.Reports 1051 (1988)].

Former Section 405.6 is restated in Section 8577 (noncompliance) without substantive change [19 Cal.L.Rev.Comm.Reports 1051 (1988)].

§ 406. Cessation of authority

(a) The authority of a person to act as a probate referee ceases immediately upon expiration of the person's term of office, revocation of the person's appointment, or other termination pursuant to law.

(b) Upon cessation of authority of a person to act as a probate referee, the Controller shall notify the superior court of the county for which the probate referee was appointed. Upon receipt of notice, or if it otherwise comes to the attention of the court that the authority of a person to act as a probate referee has ceased, the court shall reassign any estate for which the person had been designated as probate referee to another probate referee. *(Stats.1990, c. 79 (A.B.759), § 14, operative July 1, 1991.)*

Law Revision Commission Comments

1990 Enactment

Section 406 continues Section 406 of the repealed Probate Code without substantive change. Other termination pursuant to law includes resignation.

Background on Section 406 of Repealed Code

Section 406 was added by 1988 Cal.Stat. ch. 1199 § 44. Subdivision (a) restated former Probate Code Section 1309 (repealed by 1988 Cal.Stat. ch. 1199 § 65) without substantive change. Subdivision (b) codified existing practice. For background on the provisions of this part, see the Comment to this part under the part heading. [20 Cal.L.Rev.Comm.Reports 1001 (1990)].

Cross References

Probate referees, authority and powers, see Probate Code § 450 et seq.

§ 407. Prohibited political activities

(a) As used in this section, "prohibited political activity" means directly or indirectly soliciting, receiving, or contributing, or being in any manner involved in soliciting, receiving, or contributing, any of the following:

(1) An assessment, subscription, or contribution to any party, incumbent, committee, or candidate exceeding two hundred dollars ($200) in any one calendar year for any partisan public office of this state.

(2) An assessment, subscription, contribution, or political service in any amount for any campaign for the office of Controller.

(b) Upon a person's appointment and thereafter in January of each year during the person's tenure as a probate referee, the person shall file with the Controller a verified statement indicating whether the person has engaged in prohibited political activity during the preceding two calendar years.

(c) The Controller may not appoint or reappoint as a probate referee a person who within the preceding two calendar years has engaged in prohibited political activity, and any such appointment or reappointment is void and shall be revoked. The Controller shall revoke the appointment of a person who, during the person's tenure as a probate referee, engages in prohibited political activity. However, all acts not otherwise invalid, performed by the person before revocation of the person's appointment, are valid.

(d) A person shall not engage in prohibited political activity during the time the person is an applicant for appointment or reappointment, or during the person's tenure as a probate referee. A violation of this subdivision is a misdemeanor.

(e) Subdivisions (a), (c), and (d) do not apply to any prohibited political activity that occurred before July 1, 1989, and the applicable law in effect before July 1, 1989, continues to apply. Subdivision (b) applies on July 1, 1989, to persons who apply for appointment on or after July 1, 1989. A person who applied for appointment or who was appointed before July 1, 1989, shall file the first statement required by subdivision (b) on or before July 1, 1989, and thereafter as prescribed in subdivision (b). *(Stats.1990, c. 79 (A.B.759), § 14, operative July 1, 1991.)*

Law Revision Commission Comments

1990 Enactment

Section 407 continues Section 407 of the repealed Probate Code without substantive change. The two hundred dollar limitation of subdivision (a)(1) does not apply to the State Controller; solicitation, receipt, or contribution of any amount to a State Controller campaign is absolutely prohibited by subdivision (a)(2).

Background on Section 407 of Repealed Code

Section 407 was added by 1988 Cal.Stat. ch. 1199 § 44. Subdivisions (a) and (d) restated former Probate Code Section 1311 (repealed by 1988 Cal.Stat. ch. 1199 § 65), with the addition of references to incumbency, reappointment, and committees, and the deletion of references to campaigns (other than campaigns for Controller) and seeking appointment. The two hundred dollar limitation of subdivision (a)(1) of Section 407 was extended to apply during a person's tenure as probate referee as well as during the time a person is an applicant for appointment.

Subdivision (b) was a new provision designed to facilitate compliance with the other requirements of the section.

Subdivision (c) restated former Probate Code Section 1312 (repealed by 1988 Cal.Stat. ch. 1199 § 65), with the added requirement of removal from office.

The transitional provision in former Probate Code Section 1312 (repealed by 1988 Cal.Stat. ch. 1199 § 65) was replaced by a new transitional provision in subdivision (e) of Section 407.

For background on the provisions of this part, see the Comment to this part under the part heading. [20 Cal.L.Rev.Comm.Reports 1001 (1990)].

Cross References

Misdemeanors, definition and penalties, see Penal Code §§ 17, 19 and 19.2.
Probate referees, authority and powers, see Probate Code § 450 et seq.

§ 408. Transitional provisions

The appointment of a probate referee by the Controller before July 1, 1989, is not invalidated by the repeal of the law under which the appointment was made. Appointment of a probate referee before July 1, 1989, may be revoked under this chapter only if revocation would otherwise be proper

under this chapter. *(Stats.1990, c. 79 (A.B.759), § 14, operative July 1, 1991.)*

Law Revision Commission Comments

1990 Enactment

Section 408 continues Section 408 of the repealed Probate Code without change. This section is a transitional provision intended to save an appointment made under the old law that could not necessarily be made under the new law. Revocation of an appointment made under the old law is authorized only under the revocation provisions of the new law.

Background on Section 408 of Repealed Code

Section 408 was a new provision added by 1988 Cal.Stat. ch. 1199 § 44. For background on the provisions of this part, see the Comment to this part under the part heading. [20 Cal.L.Rev.Comm.Reports 1001 (1990)].

Cross References

Probate referees, authority and powers, see Probate Code § 450 et seq.

§§ 409, 410. Repealed by Stats.1988, c. 1199, § 43, operative July 1, 1989

Law Revision Commission Comments

1988 Repeal

The first sentence of former Section 409 is restated in Section 8442 (authority of administrator with will annexed), with the addition of court discretion to permit exercise of a discretionary power or authority. The second and third sentences are superseded by Section 8441 (priority for appointment) [19 Cal.L.Rev.Comm.Reports 1217 (1988)].

Former Section 410 is restated in Section 8480 (bond required) without substantive change [19 Cal.L.Rev.Comm.Reports 1052 (1988)].

§§ 420 to 443. Repealed by Stats.1988, c. 1199, § 45, operative July 1, 1989

Law Revision Commission Comments

1988 Repeal

Former Section 420 is restated in Section 8402 (qualifications) without substantive change [19 Cal.L.Rev.Comm.Reports 1052 (1988)].

Former Section 421 is restated in Section 8402 (qualifications) without substantive change [19 Cal.L.Rev.Comm.Reports 1053 (1988)].

Former Section 422 is restated in Sections 8460 (appointment of administrator), 8461 (priority for appointment), 8462 (priority of relatives), and 8463 (surviving spouse). The new provisions include language to reflect changes in the law governing intestate succession and to recognize the priority of relatives of a predeceased spouse. The new provisions are expanded to include any relative of the decedent who satisfies prescribed conditions [19 Cal.L.Rev.Comm.Reports 1217 (1988)].

Former Section 423 is restated in Section 8465 (nominee of person entitled to appointment) [19 Cal.L.Rev.Comm.Reports 1053 (1988)].

Former Section 424 is not continued. Wholeblood relatives are no longer preferred over halfblood relatives. Section 6406 [19 Cal.L.Rev.Comm.Reports 1053 (1988)].

The first clause of former Section 425 is restated in Section 8467 (equal priority) with the addition of authority to appoint a disinterested person where there is a conflict between persons of equal priority. The second clause is restated in Section 8466 (priority of creditor) but the requirement that there be a request of another creditor before the court may appoint another person is omitted [19 Cal.L.Rev.Comm.Reports 1053 (1988)].

Former Section 426 is restated in Section 8464 (minors and incompetent persons) without substantive change [19 Cal.L.Rev.Comm.Reports 1053 (1988)].

Former Section 427 is restated in Section 8468 (administration by any competent person) without substantive change [19 Cal.L.Rev.Comm.Reports 1053 (1988)].

The introductory portion of former Section 440 is superseded by Section 1020 (petitions, reports, accounts). The first paragraph is superseded by Section 8002(a) (contents of petition). The last paragraph is restated in Section 8006(b) (court order) without substantive change [19 Cal.L.Rev.Comm.Reports 1217 (1988)].

The first two sentences of former Section 441 are restated in Sections 8003 (setting and notice of hearing), 8110 (persons on whom notice served), and 1041 (clerk to set matters for hearing), except that the petitioner rather than the clerk has the duty of giving notice. See also Section 1215 (manner of mailing). The third sentence is restated in Section 8100 (form of notice) without substantive change [19 Cal.L.Rev.Comm.Reports 1217 (1988)].

Former Section 442 is restated in Sections 1043 (response or objection) and 8004 (opposition) without substantive change [19 Cal.L.Rev.Comm.Reports 1054 (1988)].

Former Section 443 is restated in Section 8005 (hearing) without substantive change [19 Cal.L.Rev.Comm.Reports 1054 (1988)].

CHAPTER 2. POWERS OF PROBATE REFEREE

Section

§ 450. Powers of superior court referee and enumerated powers

Upon designation by the court, the probate referee has all the powers of a referee of the superior court and all other powers provided in this chapter. *(Stats.1990, c. 79 (A.B.759), § 14, operative July 1, 1991.)*

Law Revision Commission Comments

1990 Enactment

Section 450 continues Section 450 of the repealed Probate Code without change. For provisions relating to decedents' estates, see Sections 8900–8980. For general provisions relating to referees of the court, see Code Civ.Proc. §§ 638–645.1.

Background on Section 450 of Repealed Code

Section 450 was added by 1988 Cal.Stat. ch. 1199 § 44. The section restated subdivision (b) of former Probate Code Section 1301 (repealed by 1988 Cal.Stat. ch. 1199 § 65) without substantive change. For background on the provisions of this part, see the Comment to this part under the part heading. [20 Cal.L.Rev.Comm.Reports 1001 (1990)].

Cross References

Probate referees, appointment and duties, see Probate Code § 400 et seq.

§ 451. Appraisal powers; subpoenas

(a) For the purpose of appraisal of property in the estate, the probate referee may require, and may issue a subpoena to compel, the appearance before the referee of the personal representative, guardian, conservator, or other fiduciary, an interested person, or any other person the referee has reason to believe has knowledge of the property.

(b) A subpoena issued under subdivision (a) is subject to the provisions of Chapter 6 (commencing with Section 2020.010) of Title 4 of Part 4 of the Code of Civil Procedure governing deposition subpoenas. *(Stats.1990, c. 79 (A.B. 759), § 14, operative July 1, 1991. Amended by Stats.2004, c. 182 (A.B.3081), § 52, operative July 1, 2005.)*

Law Revision Commission Comments

1990 Enactment

Section 451 continues Section 451 of the repealed Probate Code without change.

2004 Amendment

Subdivision (b) of Section 451 is amended to reflect nonsubstantive reorganization of the rules governing civil discovery. [33 Cal.L.Rev. Comm. Reports 1061 (2003)].

Background on Section 451 of Repealed Code

Section 451 was added by 1988 Cal.Stat. ch. 1199 § 44. Subdivision (a) restated subdivision (a) of former Probate Code Section 1301 and former Probate Code Section 1302 (provisions repealed by 1988 Cal.Stat. ch. 1199 § 65), with the addition of the reference to a guardian, conservator, or other fiduciary, since the probate referee may appraise estates other than decedents' estates. Subdivision (b) was new. For background on the provisions of this part, see the Comment to this part under the part heading. [20 Cal.L.Rev.Comm.Reports 1001 (1990)].

Cross References

Appraisal, generally, see Probate Code § 8900 et seq.
Interested person, defined, see Probate Code § 48.
Licensing and certification of real estate appraisers, definitions, see Business and Professions Code § 11302.
Personal representative and general personal representative, defined, see Probate Code § 58.
Probate referees, appointment and duties, see Probate Code § 400 et seq.

§ 452. Witnesses; examination and testimony; subpoenas to compel production

(a) The probate referee may:

(1) Examine and take the testimony under oath of a person appearing before the referee.

(2) Require, and issue a subpoena to compel, the person to produce any document in the person's possession or control, concerning the value of any property in the estate.

(b) A subpoena issued under subdivision (a) is subject to the provisions of Chapter 6 (commencing with Section 2020.010) of Title 4 of Part 4 of the Code of Civil Procedure governing deposition subpoenas. *(Stats.1990, c. 79 (A.B. 759), § 14, operative July 1, 1991. Amended by Stats.2004, c. 182 (A.B.3081), § 53, operative July 1, 2005.)*

Law Revision Commission Comments

1990 Enactment

Section 452 continues Section 452 of the repealed Probate Code without substantive change.

2004 Amendment

Subdivision (b) of Section 452 is amended to reflect nonsubstantive reorganization of the rules governing civil discovery. [33 Cal.L.Rev. Comm. Reports 1061 (2003)].

Background on Section 452 of Repealed Code

Section 452 was added by 1988 Cal.Stat. ch. 1199 § 44. Subdivision (a) restated former Probate Code Section 1303 (repealed by 1988 Cal.Stat. ch. 1199 § 65), with the addition of the reference to production of documents. See Section 453 (protective orders and enforcement). Subdivision (b) was new. For background on the provisions of this part, see the Comment to this part under the part heading. [20 Cal.L.Rev.Comm.Reports 1001 (1990)].

Cross References

Oaths, affirmation in lieu of, see Code of Civil Procedure § 2015.6.
Oaths, letters, and bond, generally, see Probate Code § 2300 et seq.
Oaths, officers authorized to administer, see Government Code § 1225.
Probate referees, appointment and duties, see Probate Code § 400 et seq.

§ 453. Protective orders; orders to show cause

(a) On petition of a person required to appear before the probate referee pursuant to this chapter, the court may make a protective order to protect the person from annoyance, embarrassment, or oppression. The petitioner shall mail notice of the hearing on the petition to the probate referee and to the personal representative, guardian, conservator, or other fiduciary at least 15 days before the date set for the hearing. Any subpoena issued by the probate referee is stayed during the pendency of the petition.

(b) On petition of the probate referee, the court may make an order to show cause why a person who is required, but fails, to appear before the probate referee pursuant to this chapter, should not be compelled to do so. The probate referee shall mail notice of the hearing on the petition to the person at least 15 days before the date set for the hearing. *(Stats.1990, c. 79 (A.B.759), § 14, operative July 1, 1991.)*

Law Revision Commission Comments

1990 Enactment

Section 453 continues Section 453 of the repealed Probate Code with the addition of the requirement that notice of the hearing be mailed not only to the probate referee and personal representative but also to the guardian, conservator, or other fiduciary. This conforms Section 453 to the scope of Section 451. For general provisions, see Sections 1000–1004 (rules of practice), 1020–1023 (petitions and other papers), 1040–1050 (hearings and orders), 1200–1230 (notice of hearing), 1250–1252 (request for special notice), 1260–1265 (proof of giving of notice).

Background on Section 453 of Repealed Code

Section 453 was added by 1988 Cal.Stat. ch. 1199 § 44. Subdivision (a) was drawn from Code of Civil Procedure Section 2037.8, with the addition of an automatic stay of enforcement during pendency of the petition. Subdivision (b) was new. For background on the provisions of this part, see the Comment to this part under the part heading. [20 Cal.L.Rev.Comm.Reports 1001 (1990)].

Cross References

Computation of time, see Code of Civil Procedure §§ 12 and 12a; Government Code § 6800 et seq.
Estate administration, generally, see Probate Code § 7000 et seq.
Estate administration, rules of procedure, see Probate Code § 7200 et seq.
Notice, mailing, see Probate Code § 1215 et seq.
Notice, posting, see Probate Code § 1230.
Notice, proof of giving notice, see Probate Code § 1260 et seq.
Notice, special notice, see Probate Code § 1250 et seq.
Notice, this code, generally, see Probate Code § 1200 et seq.
Personal representative and general personal representative, defined, see Probate Code § 58.
Service of process,
   Generally, see Code of Civil Procedure § 413.10 et seq.
   Mail, see Code of Civil Procedure §§ 415.30, 1012 et seq.
   Personal delivery, see Code of Civil Procedure § 415.10.
   Proof of service, see Code of Civil Procedure § 417.10 et seq.
   Publication, see Code of Civil Procedure § 415.50.

§§ 460 to 469. Repealed by Stats.1988, c. 1199, § 46, operative July 1, 1989

Law Revision Commission Comments

1988 Repeal

The first clause of former Section 460 is superseded by Sections 8540 (grounds for appointment) and 8544 (special powers, duties, and obligations). The last clause is restated in Section 8541 (procedure for appointment) without substantive change [19 Cal.L.Rev.Comm.Reports 1055 (1988)].

Former Section 461 is restated in Section 8541 (procedure for appointment) without substantive change. See also Section 7240 (appealable orders and refusals to make orders) [19 Cal.L.Rev.Comm.Reports 1055 (1988)].

Subdivisions (a) and (b) of former Section 462 are restated in Section 8542 (issuance of letters) without substantive change. Subdivision (c)(1) is restated in Section 8481 (waiver of bond) without substantive change. Subdivision (c)(2) is restated in Section 8543 (waiver of bond) without substantive change [19 Cal.L.Rev.Comm.Reports 1218 (1988)].

Former Section 463 is restated in Section 8544 (special powers, duties, and obligations) without substantive change [19 Cal.L.Rev.Comm.Reports 1055 (1988)].

Former Section 464 is restated in Section 8544(b)(2) (special powers, duties, and obligations) with the addition of a provision that the order remains in effect until appointment of a successor [19 Cal.L.Rev.Comm.Reports 1056 (1988)].

Former Section 465 is superseded by Section 8545 (general powers, duties, and obligations) [19 Cal.L.Rev.Comm.Reports 1056 (1988)].

Former Section 466 is restated in Sections 8546(a)–(b) (termination of authority) and 8524 (successor personal representative), with the addition of language expressly permitting court authorization of the special administrator to complete ongoing transactions [19 Cal.L.Rev.Comm.Reports 1056 (1988)].

The first sentence of former Section 467 is restated in Section 8546(c) (termination of authority), with the addition of language expressly permitting a consolidated account where the special administrator and general personal representative are the same person. The second sentence is restated in Section 8547(a)–(c) (fees and commissions), with the addition of provisions limiting payment of the special administrator until close of administration (except for extra allowances) and recognizing agreements of the special administrator, personal representative, and attorneys as to division of fees and commissions [19 Cal.L.Rev.Comm.Reports 1218 (1988)].

Former Section 468 is restated in Section 8547(b)–(c) (fees and commissions), with the addition of provisions limiting payment of the special administrator until close of administration (except for extra allowances) and recognizing agreements of the special administrator, personal representative, and attorneys as to division of fees and commissions [19 Cal.L.Rev.Comm.Reports 1218 (1988)].

Former Section 469 is superseded by Section 8547(d) (fees and commissions) [19 Cal.L.Rev.Comm.Reports 1057 (1988)].

§§ 480 to 526. Repealed by Stats.1988, c. 1199, § 47, operative July 1, 1989

Law Revision Commission Comments

1988 Repeal

Former Section 480 is restated in Sections 83 ("trust company" defined) and 300 (appointment of trust company) without substantive change [19 Cal.L.Rev.Comm.Reports 1057 (1988)].

Former Section 481 is restated in Sections 83 ("trust company" defined) and 301 (oath and bond of trust company) without substantive change [19 Cal.L.Rev.Comm.Reports 1057 (1988)].

Former Section 500 is superseded by Section 8405 (form of letters) [19 Cal.L.Rev.Comm.Reports 1057 (1988)].

Former Section 501 is superseded by Sections 8405 (form of letters) and 1001 (Judicial Council to prescribe forms) [19 Cal.L.Rev.Comm.Reports 1218 (1988)].

Former Section 502 is superseded by Sections 8405 (form of letters) and 1001 (Judicial Council to prescribe forms) [19 Cal.L.Rev.Comm.Reports 1219 (1988)].

The first sentence of former Section 510 is restated in Sections 8504 (subsequent probate of will) and 8525(b) (effect of vacancy) without substantive change. The second sentence is restated and broadened in Section 8524 (successor personal representative). [19 Cal.L.Rev.Comm.Reports 1057 (1988)].

Former Section 511 is restated in Section 8521 (vacancy where other personal representatives remain) without substantive change. [19 Cal.L.Rev.Comm.Reports 1058 (1988)].

Former Section 512 is restated in Section 8522 (vacancy where no personal representatives remain) without substantive change. [19 Cal.L.Rev.Comm.Reports 1058 (1988].

The first sentence of former Section 520 is restated in Sections 8520 (vacancy in office) and 8525(b) (effect of vacancy) without substantive change. The second sentence is superseded by Section 8523 (interim protection of estate). The third sentence is restated in Section 8525(b) (effect of vacancy) without substantive change. [19 Cal.L.Rev.Comm.Reports 1058 (1988)].

The substance of the first sentence of former Section 521 is restated in Sections 8500(b) (procedure for removal) and 8502 (grounds for removal), with the exception of the provision relating to permanent removal from the state, which is not continued. See Section 8570 *et seq.* (nonresident personal representative). The second sentence is not continued; it was impliedly repealed by former Section 1207 (service of citation), which is continued as Section 1242. [19 Cal.L.Rev.Comm.Reports 1058 (1988)].

Former Section 522 is restated in Section 8500(c) (procedure for removal) without substantive change. [19 Cal.L.Rev.Comm.Reports 1058 (1988)].

Former Section 523 is restated in Section 8500(c) (procedure for removal) without substantive change. [19 Cal.L.Rev.Comm.Reports 1058 (1988)].

Former Section 524 is restated in Section 8502 (grounds for removal) without substantive change. See also Section 8500 (procedure for removal). [19 Cal.L.Rev.Comm.Reports 1059 (1988)].

Former Section 525 is restated in Section 8525 (effect of vacancy) without substantive change. [19 Cal.L.Rev.Comm.Reports 1059 (1988)].

Former Section 526 is restated in Sections 8505 (contempt) and 8501 (revocation of letters), omitting the requirement of 30 days custody. [19 Cal.L.Rev.Comm.Reports 1059 (1988)].

§§ 530 to 530.1. Repealed, by Stats.1941, c. 1162, p. 2893, § 2

§§ 540 to 541.1. Repealed by Stats.1988, c. 1199, § 48, operative July 1, 1989

Law Revision Commission Comments

1988 Repeal

Former Section 540 is restated in Section 8403 (oath), with the addition of authority to sign the oath at the time the petition is signed. [19 Cal.L.Rev.Comm.Reports 1219 (1988)].

The first sentence of subdivision (a) of former Section 541 is restated in Sections 8480 (bond required) and 8481(a) (waiver of bond), and in Code of Civil Procedure Section 166 (actions in chambers), without substantive change. The second sentence is superseded by Section 8482(a)–(b) (amount of bond), which makes explicit the authority of the court to impose a fixed minimum bond.

Subdivision (b) is restated in Section 8481(a)(2) (waiver of bond) without substantive change. [19 Cal.L.Rev.Comm.Reports 1219 (1988)].

Former Section 541.1 is restated in Sections 8401 (deposit in controlled account) and 8483 (reduction of bond by deposit of assets) without substantive change. [19 Cal.L.Rev.Comm.Reports 1059 (1988)].

§ 541.3. Repealed by Stats.1982, c. 517, p. 2408, § 325

Law Revision Commission Comments

1982 Repeal

The substance of former Section 541.3 is continued in Code Civ.Proc. §§ 995.710 (deposit in lieu of bond), 995.730 (effect of deposit), and 995.770 (return of deposit). (16 Cal.L.Rev.Comm.Reports 501).

§§ 541.5 to 544. Repealed by Stats.1988, c. 1199, § 48, operative July 1, 1989

Law Revision Commission Comments

1988 Repeal

Former Section 541.5 is superseded by Section 8486 (cost of bond). [19 Cal.L.Rev.Comm.Reports 1059 (1988)].

Former Section 542 is superseded by Section 8482(c) (amount of bond). [19 Cal.L.Rev.Comm.Reports 1219 (1988)].

Former Section 543 is restated in Section 8481(b) (waiver of bond) without substantive change. [19 Cal.L.Rev.Comm.Reports 1219 (1988)].

Former Section 544 is restated in Section 8480 (bond required) without substantive change. [19 Cal.L.Rev.Comm.Reports 1060 (1988)].

§§ 545 to 548. Repealed by Stats.1982, c. 517, p. 2409, §§ 326 to 329

Law Revision Commission Comments

1982 Repeal

The substance of former Section 545 is continued in Code of Civil Procedure Sections 995.520 (affidavit of surety), 995.630 (authentication of bond), 995.840 (court approval of bond), 995.350 (entry in register of actions), and 995.260 (evidence of bond). (16 Cal.L.Rev.Comm.Reports 501).

Former Section 546 is superseded by Code of Civil Procedure Section 996.010 (insufficient bonds). (16 Cal.L.Rev.Comm.Reports 501).

Former Section 547 is superseded by Code of Civil Procedure Section 996.010 (insufficient bonds). (16 Cal.L.Rev.Comm.Reports 501).

Former Section 548 is superseded by Code of Civil Procedure Section 996.010 (insufficient bonds) and 995.030 (manner of service). See also Section 549 (failure to provide sufficient bond). (16 Cal.L.Rev.Comm.Reports 501).

§ 549. Repealed by Stats.1988, c. 1199, § 48, operative July 1, 1989

Law Revision Commission Comments

1988 Repeal

The effect of former Section 549 is continued in Sections 8480 (bond required) and 8501 (revocation of letters). See also Section 8520 *et seq.* (changes in administration). [19 Cal.L.Rev.Comm.Reports 1060 (1988)].

Part 13

LITIGATION INVOLVING DECEDENT

CHAPTER 1. LIABILITY OF DECEDENT COVERED BY INSURANCE

Application

Applicable to actions commenced on or after July 1, 1989. See Probate Code § 555.

Law Revision Commission Comments

1990 Enactment

This chapter supersedes Chapter 1 (commencing with Section 550) of Part 13 of Division 2 of the repealed Probate Code. The superseded chapter was enacted upon recommendation of the California Law Revision Commission. See Recommendation Relating to Litigation Involving Decedents, 19 Cal.L.Revision Comm'n Reports 899 (1988). See also Communication from the California Law Revision Commission Concerning Assembly Bill 2841, 19 Cal.L.Revision Comm'n Reports 1201, 1219 (1988).

This chapter made the following significant changes in prior law:

(1) This chapter applies uniformly to actions pending at the death of the decedent and actions commenced after the decedent's death.

(2) Court approval is not required before the plaintiff may commence an action against the estate for the insured amount.

(3) The estate of the decedent need not otherwise qualify for treatment under Sections 13100–13116 (affidavit procedure for collection or transfer of personal property).

(4) This chapter applies in any case where there is a claim for damages for which the decedent was insured, whether for injury to or death of a person caused by the wrongful act or neglect of the decedent, or otherwise.

(5) This chapter excuses a claim in probate only where the plaintiff is proceeding under this chapter, whether or not the insurer has otherwise accepted the defense of the cause or an appearance has been made on behalf of the decedent. [20 Cal.L.Rev.Comm.Reports 1001 (1990)].

Cross References

Allocation between estate and surviving spouse, see Probate Code § 11440 et seq.
Allowance and rejection of claims, see Probate Code § 9250 et seq.
Claims by public entities, priority, see Probate Code § 9204.
Claims established by judgment, see Probate Code § 9300 et seq.
Established claims, payment, see Probate Code § 9003.
Filing and payment of claims, see Probate Code § 9150 et seq.
Insurance protecting decedent from liability, claim, insurer reimbursement, see Probate Code § 9390.
Order of priority, payment of mortgages, see Probate Code § 11420.
Parties to civil actions, effect of death, commencement or continuance of action, see Code of Civil Procedure § 377.50.
Personal powers not subject to delegation, see Code of Civil Procedure §§ 381, 385.
Representation in actions and proceedings, see Probate Code §§ 2462, 2463.
Request for special notice, see Probate Code § 2700 et seq.
Review on settlement of accounts, see Probate Code § 2625.

§ 550. Commencement or continuation of action against estate; cumulative remedy

(a) Subject to the provisions of this chapter, an action to establish the decedent's liability for which the decedent was protected by insurance may be commenced or continued against the decedent's estate without the need to join as a party the decedent's personal representative or successor in interest.

(b) The remedy provided in this chapter is cumulative and may be pursued concurrently with other remedies. *(Stats. 1990, c. 79 (A.B.759), § 14, operative July 1, 1991.)*

Law Revision Commission Comments

1990 Enactment

Section 550 continues Section 550 of the repealed Probate Code without change. If the plaintiff seeks damages in excess of the insurance policy limits, the plaintiff must file a claim and establish the liability other than under this chapter. See Section 554 (damages). Subdivision (b) makes clear that this chapter does not preclude the establishment of liability by another procedure. See, e.g., Section 9000 et seq. (creditor claims). The time limited for bringing an action under this chapter is one year after expiration of the applicable statute of limitations, if it has not expired before the decedent's death. See Section 551 (statute of limitations).

Background on Section 550 of Repealed Code

Section 550 was added by 1988 Cal.Stat. ch. 1199 § 49. This chapter replaced former subdivision (b) of Section 385 of the Code of Civil Procedure, former Probate Code Sections 707, 709.1, and 721, and the third sentence of former Probate Code Section 709 (provisions of former Probate Code repealed by 1988 Cal.Stat. ch. 1199 § 53). For background on the provisions of this chapter, see the Comment to this chapter under the chapter heading. [20 Cal.L.Rev.Comm.Reports 1001 (1990)].

Cross References

Allocation between estate and surviving spouse, see Probate Code § 11440 et seq.
Allowance and rejection of claims, see Probate Code § 9250 et seq.
Claims by public entities, priority, see Probate Code § 9204.

Claims established by judgment, see Probate Code § 9300 et seq.
Creditor claims, generally, see Probate Code § 9000 et seq.
Established claims, payment, see Probate Code § 9003.
Filing and payment of claims, see Probate Code § 9150 et seq.
Insurance protecting decedent from liability, claim, insurer reimbursement, see Probate Code § 9390.
Order of priority, payment of mortgages, see Probate Code § 11420.
Parties to civil actions, effect of death, commencement or continuance of action, see Code of Civil Procedure § 377.50.
Personal powers not subject to delegation, see Code of Civil Procedure §§ 381, 385.
Personal representative and general personal representative, defined, see Probate Code § 58.
Representation in actions and proceedings, see Probate Code §§ 2462, 2463.
Request for special notice, see Probate Code § 2700 et seq.
Review on settlement of accounts, see Probate Code § 2625.

§ 551. Limitations

Notwithstanding Section 366.2 of the Code of Civil Procedure, if the limitations period otherwise applicable to the action has not expired at the time of the decedent's death, an action under this chapter may be commenced within one year after the expiration of the limitations period otherwise applicable. *(Stats.1990, c. 79 (A.B.759), § 14, operative July 1, 1991. Amended by Stats.1990, c. 140 (S.B.1855), § 3.1, operative July 1, 1991; Stats.1992, c. 178 (S.B.1496), § 30.)*

Law Revision Commission Comments
1992 Amendment

Section 551 is amended to revise a section reference. This revision is a technical, nonsubstantive change. [22 Cal.L.Rev.Comm.Reports 895 (1992)].

Background on Section 551 of Repealed Code

Section 551 was added by 1988 Cal.Stat. ch. 1199 § 49. This section restated the last part of Code of Civil Procedure Section 353(b) without substantive change. For background on the provisions of this chapter, see the Comment to this chapter under the chapter heading. [20 Cal.L.Rev.Comm.Reports 1001 (1990)].

§ 552. Parties; substitution; consolidation

(a) An action under this chapter shall name as the defendant, "Estate of (name of decedent), Deceased." Summons shall be served on a person designated in writing by the insurer or, if none, on the insurer. Further proceedings shall be in the name of the estate, but otherwise shall be conducted in the same manner as if the action were against the personal representative.

(b) On motion of an interested person, or on its own motion, the court in which the action is pending may, for good cause, order the appointment and substitution of a personal representative as the defendant.

(c) An action against the estate of the decedent under this chapter may be consolidated with an action against the personal representative. *(Stats.1990, c. 79 (A.B.759), § 14, operative July 1, 1991.)*

Law Revision Commission Comments
1990 Enactment

Section 552 continues Section 552 of the repealed Probate Code without change. Subdivision (c) makes clear that an action directed toward collecting from the insurance proceeds under this chapter may be consolidated with an action against the decedent's personal representative for the excess. Consolidation may be appropriate since the issues relating to liability are the same. See also Sections 550(b) (remedies cumulative), 553 (defenses).

Background on Section 552 of Repealed Code

Section 552 was added by 1988 Cal.Stat. ch. 1199 § 49. As to subdivisions (a) and (b) of Section 552, see the Comment to Section 550. Subdivision (c) was new. For background on the provisions of this chapter, see the Comment to this chapter under the chapter heading. [20 Cal.L.Rev.Comm.Reports 1001 (1990)].

Cross References

Estate administration, generally, see Probate Code § 7000 et seq.
Estate administration, rules of procedure, see Probate Code § 7200 et seq.
Interested person, defined, see Probate Code § 48.
Personal representative and general personal representative, defined, see Probate Code § 58.

§ 553. Contesting liability; res adjudicata

The insurer may deny or otherwise contest its liability in an action under this chapter or by an independent action. Unless the personal representative is joined as a party, a judgment in the action under this chapter or in the independent action does not adjudicate rights by or against the estate. *(Stats.1990, c. 79 (A.B.759), § 14, operative July 1, 1991.)*

Law Revision Commission Comments
1990 Enactment

Section 553 continues Section 553 of the repealed Probate Code without change.

Background on Section 553 of Repealed Code

Section 553 was added by 1988 Cal.Stat. ch. 1199 § 49. See the Comment to Section 550. For background on the provisions of this chapter, see the Comment to this chapter under the chapter heading. [20 Cal.L.Rev.Comm.Reports 1001 (1990)].

Cross References

Personal representative and general personal representative, defined, see Probate Code § 58.

§§ 553.3, 553.5. Repealed by Stats.1988, c. 1199, § 48, operative July 1, 1989

Law Revision Commission Comments
1988 Repeal

Former Section 553.3 is restated in Section 8484 (excessive bond) without substantive change [19 Cal.L.Rev.Comm. Reports 1060 (1988)].

Former Section 553.5 is restated in Section 8485 (substitution or release of sureties) without substantive change [19 Cal.L.Rev.Comm. Reports 1060 (1988)].

§ 553.6. Repealed by Stats.1982, c. 517, p. 2409, § 337

Law Revision Commission Comments
1982 Repeal

The substance of former Section 553.6 is continued in Section 553.5 and Code of Civil Procedure Sections 996.120–996.130 (substitution of sureties). (16 Cal.L.Rev.Comm.Reports 501).

§ 554. Damages; insurance coverage

(a) Except as provided in subdivision (b), either the damages sought in an action under this chapter shall be within the limits and coverage of the insurance, or recovery of damages outside the limits or coverage of the insurance shall be waived. A judgment in favor of the plaintiff in the action is enforceable only from the insurance coverage and not against property in the estate.

(b) Where the amount of damages sought in the action exceeds the coverage of the insurance, subdivision (a) does not apply if both of the following conditions are satisfied:

(1) The personal representative is joined as a party to the action.

(2) The plaintiff files a claim in compliance with Section 9390. *(Stats.1990, c. 79 (A.B.759), § 14, operative July 1, 1991. Amended by Stats.1990, c. 710 (S.B.1775), § 3, operative July 1, 1991.)*

Law Revision Commission Comments
1990 Enactment

Section 554 continues Section 554 of the repealed Probate Code without change.

1990 Amendment

Section 554 (enacted as a part of the new Probate Code by 1990 Cal.Stat. ch. 79 § 14) was amended by 1990 Cal.Stat. ch. 710 § 3. The 1990 amendment revised subdivision (b)(2) to make clear that the claim must comply with the requirements of Section 9390. This was a technical, nonsubstantive revision. [20 Cal.L.Rev.Comm.Reports 1001 (1990)].

Background on Section 554 of Repealed Code

Section 554 was added by 1988 Cal.Stat. ch. 1199 § 49. Subdivision (a) of Section 554 restated subdivision (a) of former Probate Code Section 721 (repealed by 1988 Cal.Stat. ch. 1199 § 53) without substantive change, but made clear that the rule limiting recovery is subject to the exception provided in subdivision (b) of Section 554. Subdivision (b) was generalized from the second sentence of former Probate Code Section 707 (repealed by 1988 Cal.Stat. ch. 1199 § 53). See also the Comment to Section 550. For background on the provisions of this chapter, see the Comment to this chapter under the chapter heading. [20 Cal.L.Rev.Comm.Reports 1001 (1990)].

Cross References

Personal representative and general personal representative, defined, see Probate Code § 58.

§ 555. Application of chapter; continuing application of repealed provision

(a) This chapter does not apply to an action commenced before July 1, 1989.

(b) The applicable law in effect before July 1, 1989, continues to apply to an action commenced before July 1, 1989, notwithstanding its repeal by Chapter 1199 of the Statutes of 1988. *(Stats.1990, c. 79 (A.B.759), § 14, operative July 1, 1991.)*

Law Revision Commission Comments
1990 Enactment

Section 555 continues Section 555 of the repealed Probate Code without substantive change.

Background on Section 555 of Repealed Code

Section 555 was added by 1988 Cal.Stat. ch. 1199 § 49. For background on the provisions of this chapter, see the Comment to this chapter under the chapter heading. [20 Cal.L.Rev.Comm.Reports 1001 (1990)].

§§ 570 to 572. Repealed by Stats.1987, c. 923, § 35, operative July 1, 1988

Law Revision Commission Comments
1987 Repeal

Former Section 570 is replaced by Section 9630. See the Comment to Section 9630. [19 Cal.L.Rev.Comm. Reports 398 (1988)].

Subdivision (a) of former Section 571 is restated in Section 9650(a)(1) without substantive change. See Section 58 ("personal representative" defined).

The duty of a surviving partner to wind up partnership affairs as provided in subdivision (b) of former Section 571 is omitted since this is a matter governed by the Uniform Partnership Act. See Corp. Code §§ 15024 (rights of partner), 15025(2)(d) (rights in specific property upon death of partner), 15037 (right to wind up partnership affairs), 15041 (creditor's rights against continued partnership), 15042 (rights of deceased partner where partnership continued). The provision in subdivision (b) of former Section 571 requiring the personal representative to include the partnership interest in the inventory and appraisal is unnecessary, because it is already covered by Section 600 (inventory shall include statement of decedent's interest in any partnership and be appraised as a single item).

The duties imposed on surviving partners by subdivision (b) of former Section 571 are omitted as unnecessary in light of the comprehensive rules in the Uniform Partnership Act. See, *e.g.,* Corp. Code §§ 15018 (rights and duties of partners), 15020 (disclosure of information on demand), 15022 (right to formal accounting), 15025 (rights in partnership property), 15031(4) (dissolution on death of partner unless otherwise provided), 15033 (effect of dissolution on partner's authority), 15034 (liability of partner on dissolution), 15037 (right of surviving partner to wind up partnership affairs), 15040 (rules for settling accounts between partners after dissolution), 15042 (right of personal representative of deceased partner against partners continuing business).

The first part of the last sentence of subdivision (b) is replaced by Section 9761. See the Comment to Section 9761. The last part of the last sentence is restated in Section 9763(a) without substantive change.

Subdivision (c) is restated in Section 9651 without substantive change. [19 Cal.L.Rev.Comm. Reports 398 (1988)].

The provisions in the first sentence of former Section 572 relating to a decedent's business other than a partnership are replaced by Section 9760(c)-(d). The remainder of former Section 572 relating to partnerships is replaced by Section 9762 and subdivision (b) of Section 9763. See the Comments to Sections 9762 and 9763(b). [19 Cal.L.Rev.Comm. Reports 399 (1988)].

CHAPTER 2.   SURVIVAL OF ACTIONS [REPEALED]

§ 573.   Repealed by Stats.1992, c. 178 (S.B.1496), § 31
Law Revision Commission Comments
1992 Repeal

Subdivision (a) of former Section 573 is restated without substantive change in Code of Civil Procedure Sections 377.20(a) (survival of cause of action), 377.30 (commencement of action decedent could have brought), and 377.40 (assertion of cause of action against decedent).

Subdivision (b) is restated and generalized in Code of Civil Procedure Section 377.42 (damages recoverable in action against decedent's personal representative).

Subdivision (c) is restated and generalized in Code of Civil Procedure Section 337.350 [sic; see C.C.P. § 377.34] (damages recoverable in action by decedent's personal representative or successor in interest.)

Subdivision (d) is restated in Code of Civil Procedure 377.20(b) survival of cause of action) without substantive change.

Subdivision (e) is restated in Code of Civil Procedure Section 377.22 (assignability of causes of action) without substantive change.

Subdivision (f) is omitted as unnecessary, since Section 13107.5 specifically incorporates the procedure that supersedes former Section 573. See Code Civ.Proc. §§ 377.30–377.35. [22 Cal.L.Rev.Comm.Reports 895 (1992)].

Background on Former Section 573 of Repealed Code

Former section 573 was added by 1987 Cal.Stat. ch. 923 § 35.5. The section restated former Section 573 (repealed by 1987 Cal.Stat. ch. 923 § 35) without substantive change. [20 Cal.L.Rev.Comm.Reports 1001 (1990)].

§ 574. Repealed by Stats.1961, c. 657, p. 1868, § 3

§§ 575 to 591.9. Repealed by Stats.1987, c. 923, § 35, operative July 1, 1988

Law Revision Commission Comments

1987 Repeal

Former Section 575 is restated in Section 9823 without substantive change. See also Section 58 ("personal representative" defined). [19 Cal.L.Rev.Comm. Reports 399 (1988)].

Former Section 576 is restated in Section 9822 without substantive change. See Sections 48 ("interested person" defined), 58 ("personal representative" defined). [19 Cal.L.Rev.Comm. Reports 399 (1988)].

Former Section 577 is omitted as unnecessary, because a person who has not qualified as executor is not an executor. See Section 400. [19 Cal.L.Rev.Comm. Reports 399 (1988)].

The first three sentences of former Section 578 are replaced by Section 9830. See the Comment to Section 9830. The fourth and fifth sentences of former Section 578 are replaced by Section 9837. The provision requiring the petition to be verified is generalized in Section 1284. The provision requiring the clerk to set the petition for hearing is generalized in Section 1285. Fifteen days' notice is required under Section 1220, instead of ten days' notice as required under former Section 1200.5. [19 Cal.L.Rev.Comm. Reports 404 (1988)].

The first paragraph of former Section 578a is restated in Sections 9835 and 9836 without substantive change. The second paragraph of former Section 578a is replaced by Section 9837. The provision requiring the petition to be verified is generalized in Section 1284. The provision requiring the clerk to set the petition for hearing is generalized in Section 1285. Fifteen days' notice is required under Section 1220, instead of ten days' notice as required under former Section 1200.5. See also Section 58 ("personal representative" defined). [19 Cal.L.Rev.Comm. Reports 400 (1988)].

Former Section 579 is restated in Section 9653(a) without substantive change, except that the provision that the personal representative must prosecute the action to final judgment is omitted as unnecessary. See also Section 58 ("personal representative" defined). [19 Cal.L.Rev.Comm. Reports 400 (1988)].

Former Section 580 is restated in subdivisions (b) and (c) of Section 9653, with the addition of authority for the court to require the creditor to pay the personal representative's attorney's fees, and for application of sale proceeds first to payment of costs and expenses of suit. See also Section 58 ("personal representative" defined). [19 Cal.L.Rev.Comm. Reports 400 (1988)].

The first, second, and third sentences of former Section 581 are replaced by Section 9650. See the Comment to Section 9650. The last sentence is restated in Section 9654 and is broadened to apply to both real and personal property. The phrase in the last sentence reading "but they are not required to do so" has been omitted as redundant, since it is clear from Section 9654 that the section is

permissive, not mandatory. See also Section 58 ("personal representative" defined). [19 Cal.L.Rev.Comm. Reports 401 (1988)].

Former Section 582 is replaced by Section 9650(c). See the Comment to Section 9650(c). See also Section 58 ("personal representative" defined). [19 Cal.L.Rev.Comm. Reports 401 (1988)].

The second half of the first paragraph of former Section 583 is restated in Section 9839 without substantive change. The remainder of former Section 583 is replaced by Sections 9880–9885. See the Comments to Sections 9880–9885. [19 Cal.L.Rev.Comm. Reports 401 (1988)].

Former Section 584 is replaced by Sections 9731 and 9733. See the Comments to Sections 9731 and 9733. The provision requiring the clerk to set the petition for hearing is generalized in Section 1285. Fifteen days' notice is required under Section 1220, instead of ten days' notice as required under former Section 1200.5. See also Section 58 ("personal representative" defined). [19 Cal.L.Rev.Comm. Reports 401 (1988)].

Former Section 584.1 is replaced by Section 9730(a)–(b). See the Comment to Section 9730. [19 Cal.L.Rev.Comm. Reports 401 (1988)].

Former Section 584.2 is restated in Section 9734 without substantive change, except that (1) the requirement that the option right be one that is nontransferable save only by testate or intestate succession from the decedent is omitted, (2) it must be shown that exercise of the option would be to the advantage of the estate, rather than in the best interest of the estate, and (3) 15 days' notice as required under Section 1220, instead of ten days' notice as required under former Section 1200.5. The former provision requiring the petition to be filed "with the clerk" is omitted as unnecessary. The provision requiring the clerk to set the petition for hearing is generalized in Section 1285. The provision for shortening the period of notice is generalized in Section 1203. The provision permitting the court to dispense with notice is generalized in Section 1220(e). See also Section 58 ("personal representative" defined). [19 Cal.L.Rev.Comm. Reports 402 (1988)].

The first paragraph of former Section 584.3 is restated in Section 9960 without substantive change.

Subdivision (a) is restated in Section 9961 without substantive change. The provision requiring the petition to be verified is generalized in Section 1284.

Subdivision (b) is restated in Section 9962, except that the appraisal is required to be made within one year before the hearing on the petition, rather than 90 days before the filing of the petition.

Subdivision (c) is replaced by Section 9963. The provision requiring the clerk to set the petition for hearing is generalized in Section 1285. The 10–day notice period is increased to 15 days to conform to the general notice period provided in Section 1220.

The proof of notice requirement in the first sentence of subdivision (d) is generalized in Section 1260(a). The requirement that the court is to hear the petition and any objection thereto is generalized in Section 1287. The requirement that the court is to examine into the advantage to the estate in granting the option is replaced by Section 9964(a)(1).

The second, third, and fourth sentences of subdivision (d) are restated in Section 9964 without substantive change.

The first sentence of subdivision (e) is restated in Section 1021.5 without substantive change. The last sentence of subdivision (e) is restated in Section 9965 without substantive change.

See also Section 58 ("personal representative" defined). [19 Cal.L.Rev.Comm. Reports 402 (1988)].

Former Section 584.5 is replaced by Section 9732. See the Comment to Section 9732. Fifteen days' notice is required under Section 1220, instead of ten days' notice as required under former Section 1200.5. The provision requiring the petition to be verified is generalized in Section 1284. The provision requiring the clerk to set the petition for hearing is generalized in Section 1285. [19 Cal. L.Rev.Comm. Reports 403 (1988)].

The first and second sentences of former Section 584.6 are restated in Section 9732(d) without substantive change. The last sentence is restated in Section 9732(c) without substantive change, except that 15 days' notice is required under Section 1220, instead of ten days' notice as required under former Section 1200.5. [19 Cal.L.Rev. Comm. Reports 403 (1988)].

Former Section 585 is replaced by Section 9700. See the Comment to Section 9700. See also Section 58 ("personal representative" defined). [19 Cal.L.Rev.Comm. Reports 403 (1988)].

Former Section 585.1 is restated in Section 9730(c) without substantive change. The provision that prior court authorization is not required is generalized in Section 9610. See also Section 58 ("personal representative" defined). [19 Cal.L.Rev.Comm. Reports 403 (1988)].

Former Section 586 is replaced by Section 9701. See the Comment to Section 9701. [19 Cal.L.Rev.Comm. Reports 403 (1988)].

Former Section 586.1 is restated in Section 9702(b) without substantive change. The references to the Financial Code licensing provisions are omitted because they are unnecessary in light of Financial Code Section 775, which is incorporated by Probate Code Section 9702. [19 Cal.L.Rev.Comm. Reports 404 (1988)].

Former Section 586.5 is restated in Section 9704 without substantive change and is expanded to apply to all types of financial institutions where money or property may be deposited. [19 Cal.L.Rev.Comm. Reports 404 (1988)].

Former Section 587 is restated in Sections 9900–9901 without substantive change, except that (1) it must be shown that exercise of the power would be to the advantage of the estate and in the best interest of the interested persons and (2) 15 days' notice is required under Section 1220, instead of ten days' notice as required under former Section 1200.5. See also Section 58 ("personal representative" defined). [19 Cal.L.Rev.Comm. Reports 404 (1988)].

Former Section 588 is restated in Section 9611 without substantive change, except that 15 days' notice is required under Section 1220, instead of ten days' notice as required under former Section 1200.5. See also Section 58 ("personal representative" defined). [19 Cal. L.Rev.Comm. Reports 404 (1988)].

Former Section 589 is restated in Section 9655 without substantive change, except that the former requirement that authorization by a personal representative of any action that could be taken by shareholders be "in writing" is omitted. Whether a writing is required in such cases is governed by the Corporations Code. See the Comment to Section 9655. See also Section 58 ("personal representative" defined). [19 Cal.L.Rev.Comm. Reports 404 (1988)].

Former Section 590 is restated in subdivisions (a) and (c) of Section 9702 without substantive change. The references to the Financial Code licensing provisions are omitted because they are unnecessary in light of Financial Code Section 775, which is incorporated by Probate Code Section 9702. [19 Cal.L.Rev.Comm. Reports 405 (1988)].

Former Section 591 is restated in Section 10400 without substantive change. [19 Cal.L.Rev.Comm. Reports 405 (1988)].

The first sentence of subdivision (a) of former Section 591.1 is restated in Section 10450(a) without substantive change. The second sentence is restated in Section 10404 without substantive change. The last sentence is replaced by Section 10405. See the Comment to Section 10405.

Subdivision (b) is replaced by Section 10450(b). See the Comment to Section 10450.

Subdivision (c) is restated in Section 10451(a) without substantive change.

Subdivision (d) is replaced by Section 10451(b). See the Comment to Section 10451. The provision in subdivision (d) requiring the clerk to set the petition for hearing is generalized in Section 1285.

Subdivision (e) is replaced by Section 10451(c). See the Comment to Section 10451.

Subdivision (f) is replaced by Section 10452(a).

The first part of subdivision (g) is restated in the first sentence of subdivision (b) of Section 10452 without substantive change.

The last part of subdivision (g) is replaced by Section 10452(c). See the Comment to Section 10452.

See also Section 58 ("personal representative" defined). [19 Cal.L.Rev.Comm. Reports 405 (1988)].

The first sentence and the first part of the second sentence of subdivision (a) of former Section 591.2 are restated in Section 10500(a) without substantive change. The part of the second sentence defining "court supervision" is restated in Section 10401 without substantive change. The part of subdivision (a) stating the matters that require court supervision is replaced by Section 10501. See the Comment to Section 10501.

The first sentence of subdivision (b) is restated in Section 10500(b) without substantive change. The second sentence of subdivision (b) is omitted as unnecessary. If the personal representative does not take the proposed action under independent administration authority, the action is taken under the procedures that apply where the personal representative does not have independent administration authority, and, except as provided in Sections 10301–10303, the requirement that notice of sale be published must be satisfied. See the Comment to Section 10500.

See also Section 58 ("personal representative" defined). [19 Cal.L.Rev.Comm. Reports 405 (1988)].

Paragraph (1) of subdivision (a) of former Section 591.3 is restated in the first sentence of Section 10580(a) without substantive change. See the Comment to Section 10580. The part of paragraph (2) of subdivision (a) defining "advice of proposed action" is omitted as unnecessary since the term "notice of proposed action" is uniformly used in the new statutory provisions. The remainder of paragraph (2) and the introductory clause of subdivision (a) are replaced by Section 10581. See the Comment to Section 10581.

The introductory clause of subdivision (b) is replaced by Sections 10510 and 10530. Paragraph (1) of subdivision (b) is restated in Section 10511 without substantive change. Paragraph (2) is restated in Section 10515 without substantive change. Paragraph (3) is replaced by Section 10537. See the Comment to Section 10537. Paragraph (4) is replaced by Section 10536(a)–(b). See the Comment to Section 10536. Paragraph (5) is replaced by Section 10532(a)–(b). See the Comment to Section 10532. The part of paragraph (6) relating to operation of a business is replaced by Section 10534. See the Comment to Section 10534. See also Section 9760(a) and the Comment thereto. The part of paragraph (6) relating to sale or incorporation is restated in Section 10512 without substantive change. See the Comment to Section 10512. Paragraph (7) is restated in Section 10535 without substantive change. Paragraph (8) is replaced by Section 10533. See the Comment to Section 10533. Paragraph (9) is restated in Section 10517 without substantive change. Paragraph (10) is replaced by Section 10514. See the Comment to Section 10514. Paragraph (11) is restated in Section 10518 without substantive change.

Subdivision (c) is restated in Section 10582 without substantive change. Subdivision (d) is restated in Section 10583(a) without substantive change.

See also Section 58 ("personal representative" defined). [19 Cal.L.Rev.Comm. Reports 406 (1988)].

The first and fourth sentences of subdivision (a) of former Section 591.4 are replaced by Section 10586. See the Comment to Section 10586. The second, third, and last sentences are replaced by Section 10585. See the Comment to Section 10585.

Subdivision (b) is restated in Section 10591 without substantive change.

See also Section 58 ("personal representative" defined). [19 Cal.L.Rev.Comm. Reports 407 (1988)].

Subdivision (a)(1) of former Section 591.5 is restated in Section 10588 without substantive change. See the Comment to Section 10588. Subdivision (a)(2) is restated in Section 10587 without substantive change, but the former provision is made applicable to any case where notice of proposed action is given, whether or not the proposed action is one for which notice is required. See the Comment to Section 10587.

The first sentence of subdivision (b) is restated in Section 10589(a) without substantive change. The last sentence of subdivision (b) is replaced by Section 10592. See the Comment to Section 10592.

Subdivision (c) is restated in Section 10591 without substantive change.

The substantive effect of the first sentence of subdivision (d) is continued in Section 10590(d). The remainder of subdivision (d) is replaced by Section 10590(a)–(c). See the Comment to Section 10590.

Subdivision (e) is restated in Section 10589(c) without substantive change.

See also Section 58 ("personal representative" defined). [19 Cal.L.Rev.Comm. Reports 407 (1988)].

The introductory clause of former Section 591.6 is replaced by Sections 10502 and 10551. See the Comments to Sections 10502 and 10551. See also Sections 10510, 10530, and 10550.

The part of subdivision (a) granting the power to manage and control property is restated in Section 10531 without substantive change. The part of subdivision (a) granting the power to "exchange" is replaced by Sections 10511 and 10537. The part of subdivision (a) granting the power to "convey" property is replaced by Section 10555. See the Comment to Section 10555; see also the Comments to Sections 10516 and 10531. The part of subdivision (a) granting the power to "divide" and "partition" is omitted. But see Section 10553 (power to commence, maintain, and defend actions and proceedings). See also the Comment to Section 10531. The phrase "for cash or credit" is continued in Section 10503. The part of subdivision (a) granting the power to lease is replaced by Section 10536. See the Comment to Section 10536. The part of subdivision (a) granting the power to grant options to purchase real property is restated in Section 10515 without substantive change.

Subdivision (b) is replaced by Section 10533. See the Comment to Section 10533.

Subdivision (c) is restated in Section 10514 without substantive change.

Subdivision (d) is replaced by Section 10513. See the Comment to Section 10513.

Subdivision (e) is restated in Section 10562 without substantive change.

Subdivision (f) has been omitted as unnecessary in view of Section 10551. See the Comment to Section 10551.

The substantive effect of subdivision (g) is continued in Sections 10537 and 10561, with the expansion of the scope of the provision to cover "securities" instead of "stock." See the Comments to Sections 10537 and 10561.

Subdivision (h) is restated without substantive change in Section 10560, except for the provision relating to liability. See the Comment to Section 10560.

Subdivision (i) has been omitted as unnecessary in view of Section 10551. See the Comment to Section 10551.

The part of subdivision (j) relating to claims against the estate is restated in Section 10552 without substantive change. See the Comment to Section 10552. The part relating to instituting and defending actions and proceedings is restated in Section 10553 without substantive change. See the Comment to Section 10553.

The part relating to compromises and releases is replaced by Section 10552. See the Comment to Section 10552.

Subdivision (k) is restated in Section 10556 without substantive change.

Subdivision (l) is replaced by Section 10534. See the Comment to Section 10534.

Subdivision (m) is restated in Section 10535(a) without substantive change.

Subdivision (n) is restated in Section 10519 without substantive change, except that notice of proposed action is required to make a disclaimer. See the Comment to Section 10519.

Subdivision (o) is restated in Section 10538(a)(1) without substantive change, except that the standard for exercising the power is omitted as unnecessary. See the Comment to Section 10538.

See also Section 58 ("personal representative" defined). [19 Cal.L.Rev.Comm. Reports 408 (1988)].

Former Section 591.7 is replaced by Section 10454. See the Comment to Section 10454. The provision requiring the clerk to set the petition for hearing is generalized in Section 1285. See also Section 58 ("personal representative" defined). [19 Cal.L.Rev. Comm. Reports 409 (1988)].

Former Section 591.8 is replaced by Section 10585 and by the last sentence of subdivision (b) of Section 10587. See the Comment to Section 10585. See also Section 58 ("personal representative" defined). [19 Cal.L.Rev.Comm. Reports 409 (1988)].

Subdivision (a) of former Section 591.9 is restated in Section 10503 without substantive change. The reference to "applicable fiduciary duties" is generalized in Section 10502. See also the Comment to Section 10502.

Subdivision (b) is replaced by Section 10453. See the Comment to Section 10453.

See also Section 58 ("personal representative" defined). [19 Cal.L.Rev.Comm. Reports 409 (1988)].

Part 14

POWERS OF APPOINTMENT

Law Revision Commission Comments

1992 Addition

This part supersedes Title 7 (commencing with Section 1380.1) of Part 4 of Division 2 of the Civil Code. The former power of appointment statute is continued in this part without change, except as noted in the Comments to the new sections. The former statute was originally enacted and later revised on recommendation of the California Law Revision Commission. See *Recommendation and a Study Relating to Powers of Appointment,* 9 Cal.L.Revision Comm'n Reports 301 (1969); *Background Statement Concerning Reasons for Amending Statute Relating to Powers of Appointment,* 14 Cal.L.Revision Comm'n Reports 257 (1978); *Recommendation Relating to Revision of the Powers of Appointment Statute,* 15 Cal.L.Revision Comm'n Reports 1667 (1980); see also *Tentative Recommendation Relating to Wills and Intestate Succession,* 16 Cal.L.Revision Comm'n

Reports 2301, 2484 (1982); *Recommendation Proposing the Trust Law,* 18 Cal.L.Revision Comm'n Reports 501, 755 (1986); *Recommendation Relating to Uniform Statutory Rule Against Perpetuities,* 20 Cal.L.Revision Comm'n Reports 2501, 2538–39 (1990).

This part does not codify all of the law relating to powers of appointment. Its provisions deal with the problems most likely to arise and afford positive statutory rules to govern these problems. Many minor matters are not covered by this part or other statutes; these are left to court decisions under the common law which remains in effect. See Section 600 & Comment. This approach was taken in other states. See Mich.Stat.Ann. § 26.155(119) (Callaghan 1984); Minn.Stat.Ann. § 502.62 (West 1990); N.Y.Est.Powers & Trusts Law § 10–1.1 (McKinney 1967); Wis.Stat.Ann. § 702.19 (West Supp.1990). [21 Cal.L.Rev.Comm.Reports 91 (1991)].

The powers of appointment statute in former Civil Code Sections 1380.1–1392.1 is continued without substantive change in Probate Code Sections 600–695, except as otherwise noted in the Comments to the new sections. The following table indicates the disposition of each of the former Civil Code sections in the Probate Code.

Civ. Code	Prob. Code
1380.1	600
1380.2	601
1381.1	610
1381.2	611
1381.3	612
1381.4	613
1382.1	620
1384.1	625
1385.1	630
1385.2	632
1385.3	633
1385.4	634
1385.5	635
1386.1	640
1386.2	641
1386.3	642
1387.1	650
1387.2	651
1387.3	652
1388.1	660
1388.2	661
1388.3	662
1389.1	670
1389.2	671
1389.3	672
1389.4	673
1389.5	674
1390.1	680
1390.2	681
1390.3	682
1390.4	683
1390.5	684
1391	690
1392.1	695

[21 Cal.L.Rev.Comm.Reports 91 (1991)].

Cross References

Disclaimer of interests created by power of appointment, effectiveness, see Probate Code § 279.

Dissolution or annulment of marriage, revocation of power of appointment, see Probate Code § 6122.

Homicide, effect on power of appointment, see Probate Code § 250.

CHAPTER 1. GENERAL PROVISIONS

Section
600. Common law rules as law of state.

Section
601. Law governing; validation of powers created prior to July 1, 1970.
602 to 609.5. Repealed.

§ 600. Common law rules as law of state

Except to the extent that the common law rules governing powers of appointment are modified by statute, the common law as to powers of appointment is the law of this state. *(Added by Stats.1992, c. 30 (A.B.1722), § 2.)*

Law Revision Commission Comments

1992 Addition

Section 600 continues former Civil Code Section 1380.1 without change. This section codifies the holding in *In re* Estate of Sloan, 7 Cal.App.2d 319, 46 P.2d 1007 (1935), that the common law of powers of appointment is in effect in California unless modified by statute. See also *In re* Estate of Elston, 32 Cal.App.2d 652, 90 P.2d 608 (1939); *In re* Estate of Davis, 13 Cal.App.2d 64, 56 P.2d 584 (1936). As used in this section, the "common law" does not refer to the common law as it existed in 1850 when the predecessor of Civil Code Section 22.2 was enacted. Rather, the reference is to the contemporary and evolving rules of decisions developed by the courts in exercise of their power to adapt the law to new situations and to changing conditions. See, e.g., Fletcher v. Los Angeles Trust & Sav. Bank, 182 Cal. 177, 187 P. 425 (1920). [21 Cal.L.Rev.Comm.Reports 91 (1991)].

§ 601. Law governing; validation of powers created prior to July 1, 1970

If the law existing at the time of the creation of a power of appointment and the law existing at the time of the release or exercise of the power of appointment or at the time of the assertion of a right given by this part differ, the law existing at the time of the release, exercise, or assertion of a right controls. Nothing in this section makes invalid a power of appointment created before July 1, 1970, that was valid under the law in existence at the time it was created. *(Added by Stats.1992, c. 30 (A.B.1722), § 2.)*

Law Revision Commission Comments

1992 Addition

Section 601 continues former Civil Code Section 1380.2 without substantive change. This section makes this part applicable where a release is executed, a power is exercised, or a right is asserted on or after July 1, 1970 (operative date of former Civil Code Sections 1380.1–1392.1), regardless of when the power was created. However, Section 601 deals only with the "release" or "exercise" of a power of appointment or the "assertion of a right" given by this part. The section does not deal with "creation" of powers of appointment, and nothing in the section makes invalid a power of appointment created before July 1, 1970, where the power was valid under the law in effect at the time it was created.

Under this section, the rights of creditors after July 1, 1970, with respect to a power of appointment—whether created before or after July 1, 1970—are controlled by Sections 680–683. Likewise, after July 1, 1970, such matters as the exercise of a power of appointment are governed by this part, even though the power of appointment was created before July 1, 1970.

Provisions similar to this section have been enacted in other states. See Mich.Stat.Ann. § 26.155(122) (Callaghan 1984); Wis.Stat.Ann. § 702.21 (West 1981). [21 Cal.L.Rev.Comm.Reports 91 (1991)].

§§ 602 to 609.5. Repealed by Stats.1988, c. 1199, § 51, operative July 1, 1989

Law Revision Commission Comments
1988 Repeal

Former Section 602 is continued in Section 9605 (claims against personal representative) without substantive change. See also Section 8851 (discharge or devise of claims) [19 Cal.L.Rev.Comm.Reports 1220 (1988)].

Former Section 603 is restated in Section 8851 (discharge or devise of claims) without substantive change [19 Cal.L.Rev.Comm.Reports 1061 (1988)].

Former Section 604 is restated in Section 8852 (oath of personal representative) without substantive change [19 Cal.L.Rev.Comm.Reports 1061 (1988)].

The introductory part of subdivision (a) of former Section 605 is superseded by Section 8900 (appraisal by personal representative, probate referee, and independent expert). Subdivision (a)(1) is superseded by Section 8901 (appraisal by personal representative). See also Sections 40 ("financial institution" defined) and 8800 (inventory and appraisal required).

Subdivision (a)(2) is restated in Sections 8902 (appraisal by probate referee), 8920 (designation by court), and Section 8903 (waiver of appraisal by probate referee) without substantive change.

Subdivision (a)(3) is restated in Section 8903(b)–(d) (waiver of appraisal by probate referee), with clarifying changes.

Subdivision (b) is superseded by Sections 450–453 (powers of probate referee). Subdivision (c) is restated in Section 8907 (fee for appraisal by personal representative) and expanded to preclude extra compensation not only for appraising cash items but also for appraising other property in the estate.

Subdivision (d) is omitted as unnecessary. See Section 6608. Subdivision (e) is omitted as unnecessary. See Sections 13103, 13152(b), 13200(c), and 13658 [19 Cal.L.Rev.Comm.Reports 1061 (1988)].

Former Section 606 is restated in Section 8923 (disqualification of probate referee) without substantive change [19 Cal.L.Rev.Comm.Reports 1062 (1988)].

Former Section 607 is omitted; the procedure provided in the section was ignored in practice [19 Cal.L.Rev.Comm.Reports 1062 (1988)].

Former Section 608 is restated in Section 8905 (verification of appraisal), with the addition of an independent appraisal expert [19 Cal.L.Rev.Comm.Reports 1062 (1988)].

Former Section 608.5 is restated in Section 8906 (objection to appraisal) without substantive change [19 Cal.L.Rev.Comm.Reports 1220 (1988)].

The first part of the first sentence of the first paragraph of former Section 609 is restated in Sections 8960 (payment of commission and expenses) and 8961 (amount of commission and expenses) without substantive change. The last part of the first sentence is restated in Section 8963 (maximum and minimum commissions) without substantive change. The second sentence is restated in Section 8961 (amount of commission and expenses) without substantive change. The third sentence is omitted because it was an obsolete relic from the inheritance tax function of probate referees.

The second paragraph is restated in Section 8961 (amount of commission and expenses) without substantive change. The third paragraph is restated in Section 8963 (maximum and minimum commissions), with the addition of a provision for notice [19 Cal.L.Rev.Comm.Reports 1062 (1988)].

Former Section 609.5 is restated in Section 8964 (division of commission between referees) without substantive change [19 Cal.L.Rev.Comm.Reports 1063 (1988)].

CHAPTER 2. DEFINITIONS; CLASSIFICATION OF POWERS OF APPOINTMENT

§ 610. Definitions

As used in this part:

(a) "Appointee" means the person in whose favor a power of appointment is exercised.

(b) "Appointive property" means the property or interest in property that is the subject of the power of appointment.

(c) "Creating instrument" means the deed, will, trust, or other writing or document that creates or reserves the power of appointment.

* * *

(d) "Donor" means the person who creates or reserves a power of appointment.

(e) "Permissible appointee" means a person in whose favor a power of appointment can be exercised.

(f) "Power of appointment" means a power that enables a powerholder acting in a nonfiduciary capacity to designate a recipient of an ownership interest in or another power of appointment over the appointive property. The term does not include a power of attorney.

(g) "Powerholder" means the person to whom a power of appointment is given or in whose favor a power of appointment is reserved. (Added by Stats.1992, c. 30 (A.B.1722), § 2. Amended by Stats.2016, c. 81 (A.B.2846), § 1, eff. Jan. 1, 2017.)

Law Revision Commission Comments
1992 Addition

Section 610 continues former Civil Code Section 1381.1 without substantive change. The definitions have been reorganized in alphabetical order. See also Sections 56 ("person" defined), 62 ("property" defined), 82 ("trust" defined), 88 ("will" defined).

The definitions of "appointee," "donee," and "donor" are substantially the same as provided in Restatement of Property Section 319 (1940). Accord Restatement (Second) of Property (Donative Transfers) § 11.2 (1986). The definition of "creating instrument" in subdivision (c) is similar to a Michigan provision. See Mich.Stat. Ann. § 26.155(102)(g) (Callaghan 1984). The definitions of "appointive property" and "permissible appointee" are different from the Restatement, but are substantially the same in meaning as Restatement of Property Section 319(3), (6) (1940). See also Restatement (Second) of Property (Donative Transfers) § 11.3 (1986). [21 Cal.L.Rev.Comm.Reports 91 (1991)].

Cross References
Instrument, defined, see Probate Code § 45.

§ 611. General and special powers

(a) A power of appointment is "general" only to the extent that it is exercisable in favor of the powerholder, the powerholder's estate, the powerholder's creditors, or creditors of the powerholder's estate, whether or not it is exercisable in favor of others.

(b) A power to consume, invade, or appropriate property for the benefit of a person in discharge of the powerholder's obligation of support that is limited by an ascertainable standard relating to the person's health, education, support, or maintenance is not a general power of appointment.

(c) A power exercisable by the powerholder only in conjunction with a person having a substantial interest in the appointive property that is adverse to the exercise of the power in favor of the powerholder, the powerholder's estate, the powerholder's creditors, or creditors of the powerholder's estate is not a general power of appointment.

(d) A power of appointment that is not "general" is "special."

(e) A power of appointment may be general as to some appointive property, or an interest in or a specific portion of appointive property, and be special as to other appointive property. *(Added by Stats.1992, c. 30 (A.B.1722), § 2. Amended by Stats.2016, c. 81 (A.B.2846), § 2, eff. Jan. 1, 2017.)*

Law Revision Commission Comments
1992 Addition

Section 611 continues former Civil Code Section 1381.2 without substantive change. The reference to "persons" in subdivision (b) has been omitted as surplus. See Section 10 (singular includes plural).

This part generally codifies the common law and adopts the prevailing professional usage, which is in accord with the definitions contained in the federal estate tax law and provisions in other states. See I.R.C. § 2041(b)(1); Mich.Stat.Ann. § 26.155(102)(h), (i) (Callaghan 1984); N.Y.Est.Powers & Trusts Law § 10–3.2(b), (c) (McKinney 1967); Wis.Stat.Ann. § 702.01(3) (West Supp.1990); Restatement (Second) of Property (Donative Transfers) § 11.4 (1986).

A power of appointment is "general" only to the extent that it is exercisable in favor of the donee, the donee's estate, the donee's creditors, or creditors of the donee's estate. Thus, for example, *A* places property in trust, and gives *B* a power to consume the income from the trust in such amounts as are necessary to support *B* in accordance with *B*'s accustomed manner of living whenever *B*'s annual income from all other sources is less than $15,000. *B*'s power is limited to consumption of the income from the trust; in no event can *B* (or *B*'s creditors under Section 682) reach the trust principal. Moreover, *B*'s power is limited by one of a variety of commonly used ascertainable standards and is therefore under this section a "general" power only to the extent that that standard is satisfied. Finally, *B*'s power is subject to the condition that *B*'s annual income from all other sources must be less than $15,000, and is not, therefore, presently exercisable until that condition is met.

A power is general so long as it can be exercised in favor of any one of the following: the donee, the donee's estate, the donee's creditors, or the creditors of the donee's estate. To be classified as general, the power does not have to give the donee a choice among all of this group; it is sufficient if the power enables the donee to appoint to any one of them. However, a power that is not otherwise considered to be a general power is not classified as general merely because a particular permissible appointee may, in fact, be a creditor of the donee or the donee's estate. A similar rule obtains under the federal estate tax and gift tax regulations. Treas.Reg. §§ 20.2041–1(c), 25.2514–1(c) (1991). Moreover, the mere fact that the donee has a power to appoint for the benefit of persons in discharge of an obligation of support does not make the power a general one if it is

limited by an ascertainable standard relating to their support. See subdivision (b). This exception is not found in the tax law definition.

Subdivision (c) sets forth the "adverse party" exception contained in both the federal and state tax laws.

A special power generally is one that permits the donee to appoint to a class that does not include the donee, the donee's estate, the donee's creditors, or the creditors of the donee's estate. If the class among whom the donee may appoint includes only specified persons but also includes the donee, the donee's estate, the donee's creditors, or the creditors of the donee's estate, the power to that extent is general rather than special.

Subdivision (e) is included to make clear that a power of appointment may be general as to part of the appointive property and special as to the rest. Thus, where *A* devises property to *B* for life and at *B*'s death to be distributed, one-half to any person *B* by will directs, and one-half to *C*, *D*, or *E* as *B* by will directs, *B* has a general testamentary power as to one-half the property and a special testamentary power as to the remaining one-half.

See also Sections 610(b) ("appointive property" defined), 610(d) ("donee" defined). [21 Cal.L.Rev.Comm.Reports 91 (1991)].

§ 612. Testamentary powers; presently exercisable; not presently exercisable; postponed powers

(a) A power of appointment is "testamentary" if it is exercisable only by a will.

(b) A power of appointment is "presently exercisable" at the time in question to the extent that an irrevocable appointment can be made.

(c) A power of appointment is "not presently exercisable" if it is "postponed." A power of appointment is "postponed" in either of the following circumstances:

(1) The creating instrument provides that the power of appointment may be exercised only after a specified act or event occurs or a specified condition is met, and the act or event has not occurred or the condition has not been met.

(2) The creating instrument provides that an exercise of the power of appointment is revocable until a specified act or event occurs or a specified condition is met, and the act or event has not occurred or the condition has not been met. *(Added by Stats.1992, c. 30 (A.B.1722), § 2.)*

Law Revision Commission Comments
1992 Addition

Section 612 continues former Civil Code Section 1381.3 without substantive change. This section differentiates among powers of appointment by focusing on the time at which the power may be effectively exercised. A power of appointment that can be exercised by inter vivos instrument as well as by will is not a power that can be exercised "only by a will," and hence is not a testamentary power under subdivision (a).

A power may be neither "testamentary" nor "presently exercisable" if it is "postponed," as provided in subdivision (c). When the term "power not presently exercisable" is used in this part, it includes both testamentary powers and powers that are otherwise postponed. The following is an example of a "postponed" power of appointment: The creating instrument provides that a wife's power of appointment over certain property held in trust by a bank is exercisable "only by a written instrument other than a will on file with the trustee at the death of my wife" and, to ensure that the wife retains unlimited discretion throughout her lifetime, the creating instrument further provides that any instrument of appointment shall be revocable during the donee's lifetime. Although the wife has filed a written instrument with the trustee designating the appointees, she is still alive.

See also Section 610(c) ("creating instrument" defined). [21 Cal.L.Rev.Comm.Reports 91 (1991)].

Instrument, defined, see Probate Code § 45.

§ 613. Imperative powers; discretionary powers

A power of appointment is "imperative" where the creating instrument manifests an intent that the permissible appointees be benefited even if the powerholder fails to exercise the power. An imperative power can exist even though the powerholder has the privilege of selecting some and excluding others of the designated permissible appointees. All other powers of appointment are "discretionary." The powerholder of a discretionary power is privileged to exercise, or not to exercise, the power as the powerholder chooses. *(Added by Stats.1992, c. 30 (A.B.1722), § 2. Amended by Stats.2016, c. 81 (A.B.2846), § 3, eff. Jan. 1, 2017.)*

Law Revision Commission Comments

1992 Addition

Section 613 continues former Civil Code Section 1381.4 without substantive change. A power of appointment is either imperative or discretionary. If a power is imperative, the donee must exercise it or the court will divide the appointive property among the potential appointees. See Section 671. The duty to make an appointment is normally considered unenforceable during the life of the donee. See Restatement of Property § 320 special note, at 1830 (1940). A discretionary power, on the other hand, may be exercised or not exercised as the donee chooses. Nonexercise will result in the property passing to the takers in default or returning to the donor's estate. See Section 672.

Section 613 does not state what constitutes a manifestation of intent that "the permissible appointees be benefited even if the donee fails to exercise the power." The common law determines when such an intent has been manifested. See Section 600 & Comment. See also O'Neil v. Ross, 98 Cal.App. 306, 277 P. 123 (1929) (discussion of "mandatory" powers but no holding concerning them).

Section 613 is similar to a New York provision. See N.Y.Est.Powers & Trusts Law § 10–3.4 (McKinney 1967).

See also Sections 610(a) ("appointee" defined), 610(c) ("creating instrument" defined), 610(d) ("donee" defined). [21 Cal.L.Rev.Comm.Reports 91 (1991)].

Cross References

Instrument, defined, see Probate Code § 45.

§§ 614, 615. Repealed by Stats.1988, c. 1199, § 51, operative July 1, 1989

Law Revision Commission Comments

1988 Repeal

The first sentence of former Section 614 is superseded by Section 8870(c) (citation to appear and be examined concerning decedent's property). The third sentence is restated in Section 8871 (interrogatories) without substantive change. The second and fourth sentences are restated in Section 8872 (examination) [19 Cal.L.Rev.Comm.Reports 1220 (1988)].

Former Section 615 is restated in Section 8873 (citation to appear and account), substituting a petition for a complaint [19 Cal.L.Rev.Comm.Reports 1221 (1988)].

CHAPTER 3. CREATION OF POWERS OF APPOINTMENT

Cross References

Prisoners' civil rights, creation of power of appointment, see Penal Code § 2601.

§ 620. Capacity of donor to transfer interest in property

A power of appointment can be created only by a donor having the capacity to transfer the interest in property to which the power relates. *(Added by Stats.1992, c. 30 (A.B. 1722), § 2.)*

Law Revision Commission Comments

1992 Addition

Section 620 continues former Civil Code Section 1382.1 without change. This section codifies case law. See Swart v. Security–First Nat'l Bank, 48 Cal.App.2d 824, 120 P.2d 697 (1942). See also Section 610(e) ("donor" defined); Code Civ.Proc. § 1971 (creation of power relating to real property). [21 Cal.L.Rev.Comm.Reports 91 (1991)].

§ 621. Requirements for creation of power of appointment

(a) A power of appointment is created only if all of the following are satisfied:

(1) There is a creating instrument.

(2) The creating instrument is valid under applicable law.

(3) Except as provided in subdivision (b), the creating instrument transfers the appointive property.

(4) The terms of the creating instrument manifest the donor's intent to create in a powerholder a power of appointment over the appointive property exercisable in favor of a permissible appointee.

(b) Paragraph (3) of subdivision (a) does not apply to the creation of a power of appointment by the exercise of a power of appointment. *(Added by Stats.2016, c. 81 (A.B. 2846), § 4, eff. Jan. 1, 2017.)*

CHAPTER 4. EXERCISE OF POWERS OF APPOINTMENT

ARTICLE 1. DONEE'S CAPACITY

§ 625. Capacity of powerholder to transfer interest in property; minors

(a) A power of appointment can be exercised only by a powerholder having the capacity to transfer the interest in property to which the power relates.

(b) Unless the creating instrument otherwise provides, a powerholder who is a minor may not exercise a power of appointment during minority. *(Added by Stats.1992, c. 30 (A.B.1722), § 2. Amended by Stats.2016, c. 81 (A.B.2846), § 5, eff. Jan. 1, 2017.)*

Law Revision Commission Comments

1992 Addition

Section 625 continues former Civil Code Section 1384.1 without change. Under this section, the normal rules for determining capacity govern the capacity of the donee to exercise a power of appointment. See Swart v. Security–First Nat'l Bank, 48 Cal.App.2d 824, 120 P.2d 697 (1942). Subdivision (a) states the common law rule embodied in Section 345 of the Restatement of Property (1940) and is substantially the same as provisions in Michigan and Wisconsin. See Mich.Stat.Ann. § 26.155(105)(1) (Callaghan 1984); Wis. Stat.Ann. § 702.05(1) (West 1981). *Accord* Restatement (Second) of Property (Donative Transfers) § 18.1(1) (1986).

Subdivision (b) states a requirement applicable to a donee who is a minor. This requirement is in addition to the general requirement stated in subdivision (a) (e.g., that the donee has not been judicially determined to be incapacitated) that a minor donee also must satisfy.

See also Sections 610(c) ("creating instrument" defined), 610(d) ("donee" defined). [21 Cal.L.Rev.Comm.Reports 91 (1991)].

Cross References

Instrument, defined, see Probate Code § 45.

ARTICLE 2. SCOPE OF DONEE'S AUTHORITY

Section

§ 630. Compliance with requirements of creating instrument for exercise of power; exercise by written will

(a) Except as otherwise provided in this part, if the creating instrument specifies requirements as to the manner, time, and conditions of the exercise of a power of appointment, the power can be exercised only by complying with those requirements.

(b) Unless expressly prohibited by the creating instrument, a power stated to be exercisable by an inter vivos instrument is also exercisable by a written will. *(Added by Stats.1992, c. 30 (A.B.1722), § 2.)*

Law Revision Commission Comments

1992 Addition

Section 630 continues former Civil Code Section 1385.1 without substantive change. Subdivision (a) codifies the common law rule embodied in Section 346 of the Restatement of Property (1940). *Accord* Restatement (Second) of Property (Donative Transfers) § 18.2 (1986); see also Restatement of Property § 324 (1940).

Subdivision (b) states an exception to the rule codified in subdivision (a). This exception is not found in the common law, but a similar exception is found in the law of other states. See Mich.Stat.Ann. § 26.155(105)(2) (Callaghan 1984); Minn.Stat.Ann. § 502.64 (West 1990); N.Y.Est.Powers & Trusts Law § 10–6.2(a)(3) (McKinney 1967). Often a directive in the creating instrument that a power be exercised by an inter vivos instrument places an inadvertent and overlooked limitation on the exercise of the power. If and when such a prescription is encountered, it is reasonable to say that, "All the purposes of substance which the donor would have had in mind are accomplished by a will of the donee." See Restatement of Property § 347 comment b (1940). However, if the donor expressly prohibits the testamentary exercise of the power, the donor's clear intent should be enforced. For example, if the creating instrument requires exercise of the power "only by an instrument other than a will," subdivision (b) is not applicable. See also Code Civ.Proc. § 1971 (power relating to real property).

See also Section 610(c) ("creating instrument" defined). [21 Cal.L.Rev.Comm.Reports 91 (1991)].

Cross References

California statutory will, see Probate Code § 6200 et seq.
California Uniform Transfers to Minors Act, see Probate Code § 3900.
Instrument, defined, see Probate Code § 45.
Wills, generally, see Probate Code § 6100 et seq.

§ 630.5. Repealed by Stats.1984, c. 451, § 10

Law Revision Commission Comments

1984 Repeal

Former Section 630.5 is superseded by Sections 630 and 632 which permit the surviving spouse to collect the decedent's personal property (including funds on deposit in a financial institution) in a small estate and Sections 649.1–649.4 and 650–656 which permit the surviving spouse to obtain an order confirming title to property without the need for a probate proceeding. [17 Cal.L.Rev.Comm.Reports 421 (1984)].

§ 631. Judicial relief from formalities specified in creating instrument

(a) Where an appointment does not satisfy the formal requirements specified in the creating instrument as provided in subdivision (a) of Section 630, the court may excuse compliance with the formal requirements and determine that exercise of the appointment was effective if both of the following requirements are satisfied:

(1) The appointment approximates the manner of appointment prescribed by the donor.

(2) The failure to satisfy the formal requirements does not defeat the accomplishment of a significant purpose of the donor.

(b) This section does not permit a court to excuse compliance with a specific reference requirement under Section 632. *(Added by Stats.1992, c. 30 (A.B.1722), § 2.)*

Law Revision Commission Comments

1992 Addition

Section 631 is new. Subdivision (a) is drawn from Section 18.3 of the Restatement (Second) of Property (Donative Transfers) (1986). See also Restatement of Property § 347 (1940). The general rule in subdivision (a) is consistent with Estate of Wood, 32 Cal.App.3d 862, 881–83, 108 Cal.Rptr. 522 (1973).

The formal requisites of an appointment described in subdivision (a) include both the formal requirements imposed by the donor that are significant and those that are of minor importance. For an exception, however, see subdivision (b). Unless some significant purpose is accomplished by an additional formal requirement imposed by the donor, equitable relief from the rigid enforcement of the additional formality is available. The rule stated in this subdivision arose in the English courts of Chancery and is still expressed as a rule that "equity will aid the defective execution of a power." Restatement (Second) of Property (Donative Transfers) § 18.3 comment *a* (1986).

Under subdivision (a), where the donor imposes formal requirements with respect to the instrument of appointment that exceed the requirements imposed by law for the instrument, the donor's purpose in imposing additional formal requirements must be determined. To the extent the failure to comply with the additional formal requirements will not undermine the accomplishment of a significant purpose, the court in applying equitable principles may save the appointment if the appointment approximates the formal requirements imposed by the donor. See Restatement (Second) of Property (Donative Transfers) § 18.3 comment *c* (1986). The rule in Section 631(a) is not limited to the favored class of appointees described in the Restatement rule.

Subdivision (b) makes clear that the donor's requirement that the donee specifically refer to the power of appointment or the instrument creating it, as provided in Section 632, is not subject to equitable relief under this section. [21 Cal.L.Rev.Comm.Reports 91 (1991)].

Cross References

Instrument, defined, see Probate Code § 45.

§ 631.1. Repealed by Stats.1986, c. 783, § 9, operative July 1, 1987

Law Revision Commission Comments

1986 Repeal

Section 631.1 is continued without substantive change in Section 13107. [18 Cal.L.Rev.Comm. Reports 1005 (1986)].

§ 632. Exercise of power by instrument making specific reference to power or instrument creating power

If the creating instrument expressly directs that a power of appointment be exercised by an instrument that makes a specific reference to the power or to the instrument that created the power, the power can be exercised only by an instrument containing the required reference. *(Added by Stats.1992, c. 30 (A.B.1722), § 2.)*

Law Revision Commission Comments

1992 Addition

Section 632 continues former Civil Code Section 1385.2 without substantive change. This section permits a donor to require an express reference to the power of appointment to ensure a conscious exercise by the donee. In such a case, the specific reference to the power is a condition to its exercise. This condition precludes the use of form wills with "blanket" clauses exercising all powers of appointment owned by the testator. The use of blanket clauses may result in passing property without knowledge of the tax consequences and may cause appointment to unintended beneficiaries. This section embodies the rule set out in Michigan and Wisconsin law. See Mich.Stat.Ann. § 26.155(104) (Callaghan 1984); Wis.Stat.Ann. § 702.03(1) (West 1981).

See also Section 610(c) ("creating instrument" defined). [21 Cal.L.Rev.Comm.Reports 91 (1991)].

Cross References

Instrument, defined, see Probate Code § 45.

§ 633. Consent of donor or other person to exercise of power

(a) If the creating instrument requires the consent of the donor or other person to exercise a power of appointment, the power can only be exercised when the required consent is contained in the instrument of exercise or in a separate written instrument, signed in each case by the person whose consent is required.

(b) Unless expressly prohibited by the creating instrument:

(1) If a person whose consent is required dies, the power may be exercised by the powerholder without the consent of that person.

(2) If a person whose consent is required becomes legally incapable of consenting, the person's guardian or conservator may consent to an exercise of the power.

(3) A consent may be given before or after the exercise of the power by the powerholder. *(Added by Stats.1992, c. 30 (A.B.1722), § 2. Amended by Stats.2016, c. 81 (A.B.2846), § 6, eff. Jan. 1, 2017.)*

Law Revision Commission Comments

1992 Addition

Section 633 continues former Civil Code Section 1385.3 without substantive change. The reference to "persons" in subdivision (a) has been omitted as surplus. See Section 10 (singular includes plural). Section 633 reflects a policy similar to provisions in other states. See Mich.Stat.Ann. § 26.155(105) (Callaghan 1984); Minn. Stat.Ann. § 502.68 (West 1990); N.Y.Est.Powers & Trusts Law § 10–6.4 (McKinney 1967); Wis.Stat.Ann. § 702.05(3) (West 1981). It is important to note that additional formalities may be necessary to entitle the instrument of exercise and the consent to be recorded. For example, under Government Code Section 27287, a consent apparently must be acknowledged to be recordable.

See also Sections 610(c) ("creating instrument" defined), 610(d) ("donee" defined), 610(e) ("donor" defined). [21 Cal.L.Rev.Comm.Reports 91 (1991)].

Cross References

Instrument, defined, see Probate Code § 45.

§ 634. Exercise of power by two or more powerholders

A power of appointment created in favor of two or more powerholders can only be exercised when all of the powerholders unite in its exercise. If one or more of the powerholders dies, becomes legally incapable of exercising the power, or releases the power, the power may be exercised by the others, unless expressly prohibited by the creating instrument. *(Added by Stats.1992, c. 30 (A.B.1722), § 2. Amended by Stats.2016, c. 81 (A.B.2846), § 7, eff. Jan. 1, 2017.)*

Section 634 continues former Civil Code Section 1385.4 without change. This section is consistent with the rule applicable to trustees under Section 15620 and the law of other states. See Mich.Stat.Ann. § 26.155(105)(5) (Callaghan 1984); Minn.Stat.Ann. § 502.67 (West 1990); N.Y.Est.Powers & Trusts Law § 10–6.7 (McKinney 1967); Wis.Stat.Ann. § 702.05(4) (West 1981).

See also Sections 610(c) ("creating instrument" defined), 610(d) ("donee" defined). [21 Cal.L.Rev.Comm.Reports 91 (1991)].

Cross References

Instrument, defined, see Probate Code § 45.

§ 635. Defective exercise of imperative power; remedy

Nothing in this chapter affects the power of a court of competent jurisdiction to remedy a defective exercise of an imperative power of appointment. *(Added by Stats.1992, c. 30 (A.B.1722), § 2.)*

Section 635 continues former Civil Code Section 1385.5 without change. This section is included to make clear that this chapter does not limit the power of a court under Section 671. The same provision is included in New York law. See N.Y.Est.Powers & Trusts Law § 10–6.2 (McKinney 1967).

See also Section 613 ("imperative" power defined). [21 Cal.L.Rev.Comm.Reports 91 (1991)].

ARTICLE 3. DONEE'S REQUIRED INTENT

§ 640. Manifestation of intent

(a) The exercise of a power of appointment requires a manifestation of the powerholder's intent to exercise the power.

(b) A manifestation of the powerholder's intent to exercise a power of appointment exists in any of the following circumstances:

(1) The powerholder declares, in substance, that the powerholder exercises specific powers or all the powers the powerholder has.

(2) The powerholder purports to transfer an interest in the appointive property that the powerholder would have no power to transfer except by virtue of the power.

(3) The powerholder makes a disposition that, when considered with reference to the property owned and the circumstances existing at the time of the disposition, manifests the powerholder's understanding that the powerholder was disposing of the appointive property.

(c) The circumstances described in subdivision (b) are illustrative, not exclusive. *(Added by Stats.1992, c. 30 (A.B. 1722), § 2. Amended by Stats.2016, c. 81 (A.B.2846), § 8, eff. Jan. 1, 2017.)*

Section 640 continues former Civil Code Section 1386.1 without substantive change. This section codifies case law and the common law generally. See Childs v. Gross, 41 Cal.App.2d 680, 107 P.2d 424 (1940); Reed v. Hollister, 44 Cal.App. 533, 186 P. 819 (1919); Restatement of Property §§ 342, 343 (1940).

Subdivision (b) gives examples of when the donee has sufficiently manifested the intent under this section to exercise the power. The list is not exclusive, as provided in subdivision (c), and is similar to New York law. See N.Y.Est.Powers & Trusts Law § 10–6.1(a)(1)–(3) (McKinney 1967); see also Mich.Stat.Ann. § 26.155(104) (Callaghan 1984).

See also Sections 610(b) ("appointive property" defined), 610(d) ("donee" defined). [21 Cal.L.Rev.Comm.Reports 91 (1991)].

§ 641. Exercise by general residuary clause in wills; wills making general disposition of all testator's property

(a) A general residuary clause in a will, or a will making general disposition of all the testator's property, does not exercise a power of appointment held by the testator unless specific reference is made to the power or there is some other indication of intent to exercise the power.

(b) This section applies in a case where the powerholder dies on or after July 1, 1982. *(Added by Stats.1992, c. 30 (A.B.1722), § 2. Amended by Stats.2016, c. 81 (A.B.2846), § 9, eff. Jan. 1, 2017.)*

Subdivision (a) of Section 641 continues former Civil Code Section 1386.2 without substantive change. The word "intention" has been changed to "intent" for conformity with Section 640(a). Subdivision (b) codifies the transitional provision in 1981 Cal.Stat. ch. 63, §§ 10(d) & 11.

Section 641 adopts the substance of Uniform Probate Code Section 2–610 (1989). Under this section, a power of appointment is not exercised unless there is some manifestation of intent to exercise the power. A general residuary clause or disposition of all of the testator's property, alone, is not such a manifestation of intent. This section recognizes that donees today may frequently intend that assets subject to a power of appointment pass to the takers in default, particularly assets held in a marital deduction trust. See Unif.Prob. Code § 2–610 comment (1989); French, *Exercise of Powers of Appointment: Should Intent to Exercise Be Inferred from a General Disposition of Property?*, 1979 Duke L.J. 747; *cf.* Unif.Prob.Code § 2–608 (1990) (revised rule).

Under Section 641, a general disposition of property in the donee's will may exercise a power of appointment if there is some other indication of intent to include the appointive property in the disposition made. Such other indication of intent to exercise the power may be found in the will or in other evidence apart from the will. Section 640 sets forth a nonexclusive list of types of evidence that indicate an intent to exercise a power of appointment. An exercise of a power of appointment may be found if a preponderance of the evidence indicates that the donee intended to exercise the power. See Bank of New York v. Black, 26 N.J. 276, 286–87, 139 A.2d 393, 398 (1958). Section 641 does not apply where the donor has conditioned the exercise of the power on a specific reference to the power or to the instrument that created the power or has specified a specific method of exercise of the power. See Sections 630, 632. [21 Cal.L.Rev.Comm.Reports 91 (1991)].

Cross References

California statutory will, see Probate Code § 6200 et seq.
Wills, generally, see Probate Code § 6100 et seq.

§ 642. Will executed before creation of power of appointment

If a power of appointment existing at the powerholder's death, but created after the execution of the powerholder's will, is exercised by the will, the appointment is effective except in either of the following cases:

(a) The creating instrument manifests an intent that the power may not be exercised by a will previously executed.

(b) The will manifests an intent not to exercise a power subsequently acquired. *(Added by Stats.1992, c. 30 (A.B. 1722), § 2. Amended by Stats.2016, c. 81 (A.B.2846), § 10, eff. Jan. 1, 2017.)*

Law Revision Commission Comments
1992 Addition

Section 642 continues former Civil Code Section 1386.3 without substantive change. This section codifies the rule of California Trust Co. v. Ott, 59 Cal.App.2d 715, 140 P.2d 79 (1943). It also states the rule in Section 344 of the Restatement of Property (1940). This section requires that a power of appointment be one "existing at the donee's death." Thus, where the donor executes a will creating a power exercisable by will, the donee executes a will purporting to exercise that power and thereafter dies, and later the donor dies without having changed his or her will, the attempted exercise by the donee is ineffective. This conclusion follows because the power of appointment was not one "existing at the donee's death" since the donor could have revoked or changed the will at any time before the donor died.

See also Section 610(d) ("donee" defined). [21 Cal.L.Rev.Comm.Reports 91 (1991)].

Cross References

Instrument, defined, see Probate Code § 45.

§ 643. Repealed by Stats.1986, c. 783, § 9, operative July 1, 1987

Law Revision Commission Comments
1986 Repeal

Subdivision (a) of former Section 643 is continued in a revised form in subdivision (a) of Section 6607. Subdivision (b) is continued in substance in subdivision (c) of Section 6607. [18 Cal.L.Rev. Comm. Reports 1101 (1986)].

§ 644. Repealed by Stats.1986, c. 783, § 9, operative July 1, 1987

Law Revision Commission Comments
1986 Repeal

Former Section 644 is superseded by Section 6608. [18 Cal.L.Rev. Comm. Reports 1101 (1986)].

§ 645. Repealed by Stats.1986, c. 783, § 9, operative July 1, 1987

Law Revision Commission Comments
1986 Repeal

Former Section 645 is superseded by Section 6609. See the Comment to Section 6609. See also the Comment to Section 6601. [18 Cal.L.Rev.Comm. Reports 1101 (1986)].

§ 645.1. Repealed by Stats.1986, c. 783, § 9, operative July 1, 1987

Law Revision Commission Comments
1986 Repeal

Former Section 645.1 is superseded by Section 6610. See the Comment to Section 6610. [18 Cal.L.Rev.Comm. Reports 1101 (1986)].

§ 645.3. Repealed by Stats.1986, c. 783, § 9, operative July 1, 1987

§ 646. Repealed by Stats.1986, c. 783, § 9, operative July 1, 1987

Law Revision Commission Comments
1986 Repeal

Former Section 646 is superseded by Section 6612. See the Comment to Section 6612. [18 Cal.L.Rev.Comm. Reports 1101 (1986)].

§ 647. Repealed by Stats.1986, c. 783, § 9, operative July 1, 1987

Law Revision Commission Comments
1986 Repeal

Former Section 647 is continued without substantive change in subdivision (b) of Section 6600. [18 Cal.L.Rev.Comm. Reports 1101 (1986)].

§ 647.5. Repealed by Stats.1986, c. 783, § 9, operative July 1, 1987

§ 649.1. Repealed by Stats.1986, c. 783, § 9, operative July 1, 1987

Law Revision Commission Comments
1986 Repeal

Former Section 649.1 is continued in substance by the following provisions of the Probate Code: Subdivision (a) is continued in Section 13500; subdivisions (b) and (c) are continued in Section 13502; subdivision (d) is continued in Section 13503. [18 Cal.L.Rev. Comm. Reports 1005 (1986)].

§ 649.2. Repealed by Stats.1986, c. 783, § 9, operative July 1, 1987

Law Revision Commission Comments
1986 Repeal

Former Section 649.2 is continued in substance by the following provisions of the Probate Code: The first sentence is continued in Sections 13540 and 13541, the second and third sentences are continued in Section 13541, and the fourth sentence is continued in Section 13540. [18 Cal.L.Rev.Comm. Reports 1005 (1986)].

§ 649.3. Repealed by Stats.1986, c. 783, § 9, operative July 1, 1987

Law Revision Commission Comments

1986 Repeal

Former Section 649.3 is continued without substantive change in Section 13501. [18 Cal.L.Rev.Comm. Reports 1005 (1986)].

§ 649.4. Repealed by Stats.1986, c. 783, § 9, operative July 1, 1987

Law Revision Commission Comments

1986 Repeal

Former Section 649.4 is continued in substance by the following provisions of the Probate Code: Subdivision (a) is continued in Section 13550; subdivision (b) is continued in Section 13551; subdivision (c) is continued in Section 13553; subdivision (d) is continued in Section 13552; subdivision (e) is continued in Section 13554. [18 Cal.L.Rev.Comm. Reports 1005 (1986)].

§ 649.5. Repealed by Stats.1986, c. 783, § 9, operative July 1, 1987

Law Revision Commission Comments

1986 Repeal

Former Section 649.5 is continued in substance in Section 13504. [18 Cal.L.Rev.Comm. Reports 1005 (1986)].

§ 649.6. Repealed by Stats.1986, c. 783, § 9, operative July 1, 1987

ARTICLE 4. TYPES OF APPOINTMENTS

Section
650. General power of appointment.
651. Special power of appointment.
652. Appointive share or amount; exclusive and nonexclusive powers.
653. Repealed.
654. Repealed.
655. Repealed.
656. Repealed.
657. Repealed.
658. Repealed.
659. Repealed.

§ 650. General power of appointment

(a) The powerholder of a general power of appointment may make an appointment:

(1) Of all of the appointive property at one time, or several partial appointments at different times, where the power is exercisable inter vivos.

(2) Of present or future interests or both.

(3) Subject to conditions or charges.

(4) Subject to otherwise lawful restraints on the alienation of the appointed interest.

(5) In trust.

(6) Creating a new power of appointment.

(b) The listing in subdivision (a) is illustrative, not exclusive. *(Added by Stats.1992, c. 30 (A.B.1722), § 2. Amended by Stats.2016, c. 81 (A.B.2846), § 11, eff. Jan. 1, 2017.)*

Law Revision Commission Comments

1992 Addition

Section 650 continues former Civil Code Section 1387.1 without change. This section embodies the common law rules found in Sections 356 and 357 of the Restatement of Property (1940). See also Restatement (Second) of Property (Donative Transfers) §§ 19.1, 19.2 (1986). It makes clear that, under a general power of appointment, the donee has the same freedom of disposition that the donee has with respect to property he or she owns. The types of appointment mentioned in subdivision (a) are those about which questions have most often arisen.

See also Sections 610(b) ("appointive property" defined), 610(d) ("donee" defined), 611 ("general" power of appointment defined). [21 Cal.L.Rev.Comm.Reports 91 (1991)].

§ 651. Special power of appointment

Subject to the limitations imposed by the creating instrument, the powerholder of a special power may make any of the types of appointment permissible for the powerholder of a general power under Section 650. *(Added by Stats.1992, c. 30 (A.B.1722), § 2. Amended by Stats.2016, c. 81 (A.B.2846), § 12, eff. Jan. 1, 2017.)*

Law Revision Commission Comments

1992 Addition

Section 651 continues former Civil Code Section 1387.2 without substantive change. This section embodies the rules stated in Sections 358 and 359 of the Restatement of Property (1940), except that this section authorizes the donee of a special power to exercise the power by creating a special power of appointment in a permissible appointee. Under Section 359 of the Restatement of Property, the donee could only exercise the power by creating a new special power under certain circumstances. Since the donee can appoint outright to one of the permissible appointees of the special power, it would be undesirable to refuse to allow the donee to give such a person a special power to appoint. See 3 R. Powell, Real Property ¶ 398 (1991); see also Restatement (Second) of Property (Donative Transfers) §§ 19.3, 19.4 (1986). A special power is not, of course, the substantial equivalent of outright ownership and the creation of a special power in a permissible appointee may fail therefore to constitute a valid exercise of an imperative power. For example, where each of the permissible appointees under an imperative power is to receive not less than 10 percent of the appointive property, the creation of a special power in a permissible appointee would not satisfy this 10–percent requirement.

The donee of a special power of appointment may not have the same freedom as to types of appointments that the donee of a general power has. Other rules of law may limit the donee's ability to appoint in a particular manner. For example, although the donee of a special power may create a new power or appoint a future interest under this section, the appointment may be subject to a different method of computing the applicable period under the rule against perpetuities than under a general power. See Section 690 & Comment. In addition, the common law rules against fraud on a special power by appointing to persons who are not permissible appointees are not affected by this section. See *In re* Estate of Carroll, 153 Misc. 649, 275 N.Y.S. 911 (1934), *modified sub.nom. In re* Content, 247 App.Div. 11, 286 N.Y.S. 307 (1936), *modified sub.nom. In re* Will of Carroll, 274 N.Y. 288, 8 N.E.2d 864 (1937).

See also Sections 610(c) ("creating instrument" defined), 611 ("general" and "special" powers of appointment defined). [21 Cal.L.Rev.Comm.Reports 91 (1991)].

Cross References

Instrument, defined, see Probate Code § 45.

Passage of property to surviving spouse without administration, see Probate Code § 13506.

§ 652. Appointive share or amount; exclusive and nonexclusive powers

(a) Except as provided in subdivision (b), the powerholder of a special power of appointment may appoint the whole or any part of the appointive property to any one or more of the permissible appointees and exclude others.

(b) If the donor specifies either a minimum or maximum share or amount to be appointed to one or more of the permissible appointees, the exercise of the power must conform to the specification. *(Added by Stats.1992, c. 30 (A.B.1722), § 2. Amended by Stats.2016, c. 81 (A.B.2846), § 13, eff. Jan. 1, 2017.)*

Law Revision Commission Comments
1992 Addition

Section 652 continues former Civil Code Section 1387.3 without substantive change. This section deals with the problem of whether the donee of a special power of appointment can appoint all of the property to one appointee and exclude others, or must appoint some of the property to each of the permissible appointees. For example, if the donee is given power "to appoint to his children," there is a question whether the donee must give each child a share or whether the donee can appoint all of the assets to one child. If the donee may appoint to one or more of the permissible appointees and exclude others, the power is "exclusive." If the donee must appoint a minimum share or amount specified in the creating instrument to each member of the class of permissible appointees, the power is "nonexclusive." This section provides, in effect, that all powers are construed to be exclusive except to the extent that the donor has specified a minimum or maximum amount. It embodies the constructional preference for exclusive powers contained in Section 360 of the Restatement of Property (1940). *Accord* Restatement (Second) of Property (Donative Transfers) § 21.1 (1986).

The rule in this section changed California law as developed in *In re* Estate of Sloan, 7 Cal.App.2d 319, 46 P.2d 1007 (1935), which was contrary to many common law decisions. See Annot., 69 A.L.R.2d 1285 (1960). Similar provisions have been adopted in other states. See Mich.Stat.Ann. § 26.155 (107) (Callaghan 1984); N.Y.Est.Powers & Trusts Law § 10–5.1 (McKinney Supp.1991); Wis.Stat.Ann. § 702.07 (West 1981).

See also Sections 610(a) ("appointee" defined), 610(b) ("appointive property" defined), 610(d) ("donee" defined), 610(e) ("donor" defined), 610(f) ("permissible appointee" defined), 611 ("special" power of appointment defined). [21 Cal.L.Rev.Comm.Reports 91 (1991)].

Cross References

Passage of property to surviving spouse without administration, see Probate Code § 13506.

§ 653. Repealed by Stats.1986, c. 783, § 9, operative July 1, 1987

Law Revision Commission Comments
1986 Repeal

Former Section 653 is superseded by subdivision (b) of Section 13655. See the Comment to Section 13655. [18 Cal.L.Rev.Comm. Reports 1005 (1986)].

§ 654. Repealed by Stats.1986, c. 783, § 9, operative July 1, 1987

Law Revision Commission Comments
1986 Repeal

Former Section 654 is superseded by subdivision (a) of Section 13655. See the Comment to Section 13655. [18 Cal.L.Rev.Comm. Reports 1005 (1986)].

§ 655. Repealed by Stats.1986, c. 783, § 9, operative July 1, 1987

Law Revision Commission Comments
1986 Repeal

Subdivisions (a) and (b) of former Section 655 are continued without substantive change in Section 13656. Subdivision (c) is continued in Section 13657 without substantive change. [18 Cal.L.Rev.Comm. Reports 1005 (1986)].

§ 656. Repealed by Stats.1986, c. 783, § 9, operative July 1, 1987

Law Revision Commission Comments
1986 Repeal

Former Section 656 is continued without substantive change in Section 13658 except that it is made clear that the provision is limited to creditors of an "unincorporated" business. See also the Comment to Section 13658. [18 Cal.L.Rev.Comm. Reports 1005 (1986)].

§ 657. Repealed by Stats.1986, c. 783, § 9, operative July 1, 1987

Law Revision Commission Comments
1986 Repeal

The first three sentences of former Section 657 are continued without substantive change in Section 13659. The last sentence is superseded by the first sentence of Section 13659 and the last portion of Section 13658. [18 Cal.L.Rev.Comm. Reports 1005 (1986)].

§ 658. Repealed by Stats.1986, c. 783, § 9, operative July 1, 1987

Law Revision Commission Comments
1986 Repeal

Former Section 658 is replaced by Section 13505. [18 Cal.L.Rev. Comm. Reports 1005 (1986)].

§ 659. Repealed by Stats.1975, c. 173, p. 320, § 6, eff. June 30, 1975

ARTICLE 5. CONTRACTS TO APPOINT; RELEASES

Section

§ 660. Authority to contract to make appointment

(a) The powerholder of a power of appointment that is presently exercisable, whether general or special, can contract to make an appointment to the same extent that the powerholder could make an effective appointment.

(b) The powerholder of a power of appointment cannot contract to make an appointment while the power of appointment is not presently exercisable. If a promise to make an appointment under such a power is not performed, the promisee cannot obtain either specific performance or damages, but the promisee is not prevented from obtaining restitution of the value given by the promisee for the promise.

(c) Unless the creating instrument expressly provides that the powerholder may not contract to make an appointment while the power of appointment is not presently exercisable, subdivision (b) does not apply to the case where the donor and the powerholder are the same person. In this case, the powerholder can contract to make an appointment to the same extent that the powerholder could make an effective appointment if the power of appointment were presently exercisable. *(Added by Stats.1992, c. 30 (A.B.1722), § 2. Amended by Stats.2016, c. 81 (A.B.2846), § 14, eff. Jan. 1, 2017.)*

Law Revision Commission Comments
1992 Addition

Section 660 continues former Civil Code Section 1388.1 without substantive change.

Section 660 is not intended to deal with the question of the extent to which an appointment is invalid when the donee of a special power appoints, either directly or indirectly to a person who is not a permissible appointee. This problem—fraud on special power—is left to the common law. See *In re* Estate of Carroll, 153 Misc. 649, 275 N.Y.S. 911 (1934), *modified sub.nom. In re* Content, 247 App.Div. 11, 286 N.Y.S. 307 (1936), *modified sub.nom. In re* Will of Carroll, 274 N.Y. 288, 8 N.E.2d 864 (1937).

Under subdivision (b), by giving a testamentary or postponed power to the donee, the donor expresses the desire that the donee's discretion be retained until the donee's death or such other time as is stipulated. To allow the donee to contract to appoint under such a power would permit the donor's intent to be defeated. The rule stated in subdivision (b) applies to all promises that are, in substance, promises to appoint. This would include, for example, a promise not to revoke an existing will that makes an appointment in favor of the promisee. The rule with respect to releases of testamentary and postponed powers is similar. See Section 661. Subdivision (b) states the common law rule. See Restatement of Property § 340 (1940); *accord* Restatement (Second) of Property (Donative Transfers) § 16.2 (1986); *cf.* Briggs v. Briggs, 122 Cal.App.2d 766, 265 P.2d 587 (1954); Childs v. Gross, 41 Cal.App.2d 680, 107 P.2d 424 (1940).

Subdivision (b) also provides that the promisee can obtain neither specific performance nor damages for the breach of a promise to appoint although the donee is not prevented from obtaining restitution of value given for the promise to appoint. Restitution generally will be available unless precluded by other factors. This is the common law rule. Restatement of Property § 340 (1940); *accord* Restatement (Second) of Property (Donative Transfers) § 16.2 (1986).

Subdivision (c) restricts the prohibition in subdivision (b) to cases where the donor and the donee are different persons. This follows a revision in New York law. See N.Y.Est.Powers & Trusts Law § 10–5.3 (McKinney Supp.1991); N.Y.Law Revision Comm'n, *Recommendation Relating to the Ability of a Donee of a Testamentary Power of Appointment to Contract to Appoint and to the Donee's Release of the Power, Under the Estates, Powers and Trusts Law,* N.Y.Leg.Doc. No. 65(C) (1977).

Under subdivision (a), a contract by a donee to make an appointment in the future that the donee could have made at the time the contract was executed does not conflict with any rule of the law of powers of appointment. The objection to such promises under a testamentary power—that if the promise is given full effect, the donee is accomplishing by contract what is forbidden by appointment—is inapplicable to a power of appointment that is presently exercisable. Subdivision (a) states the common law rule.

See Restatement of Property § 339 (1940). It is substantially the same as the law in Michigan and New York. See Mich.Stat.Ann. § 26.155(110)(1) (Callaghan 1984); N.Y. Est.Powers & Trusts Law § 10–5.2 (McKinney 1967).

The purpose of subdivision (b) is to prevent the donor's intent from being defeated by the donee contracting to appoint under a power of appointment that is not presently exercisable. By giving a testamentary or postponed power to the donee, the donor expresses the desire that the donee's discretion be retained until the donee's death or such other time as is stipulated. However, where the donor and the donee are the same person, the donor's intent is better protected by an exception permitting the option of dealing with the power during the donor-donee's lifetime. Subdivision (c) makes clear that the donee of a power of appointment may contract to make an appointment while the power of appointment is not presently exercisable if the donor and donee are the same person, unless the creating instrument expressly provides that the donor-donee may not make an appointment while the power of appointment is not presently exercisable.

Subdivision (c) reflects a policy consistent with Section 683 which makes an unexercised general power of appointment created by the donor in the donor's own favor, whether or not presently exercisable, subject to the claims of creditors of the donor or of the donor's estate and to the expenses of administration of the estate. A similar policy is reflected in Section 695(a) which permits the donor to revoke the creation of a power of appointment when the power is created in connection with a revocable trust.

See also Sections 610(c) ("creating instrument" defined), 610(d) ("donee" defined), 610(e) ("donor" defined), 611 ("general" and "special" powers of appointment defined), 612(b) ("presently exercisable" defined). [21 Cal.L.Rev.Comm.Reports 91 (1991)].

Cross References
Instrument, defined, see Probate Code § 45.

§ 661. Release of discretionary power

(a) Unless the creating instrument otherwise provides, a general or special power of appointment that is a discretionary power, whether testamentary or otherwise, may be released, either with or without consideration, by a written instrument signed by the powerholder and delivered as provided in subdivision (c).

(b) A releasable power may be released with respect to the whole or any part of the appointive property and may also be released in such manner as to reduce or limit the permissible appointees. No partial release of a power shall be deemed to make imperative the remaining power that was not imperative before the release unless the instrument of release expressly so provides. No release of a power that is not presently exercisable is permissible where the donor designated persons or a class to take in default of the powerholder's exercise of the power unless the release serves to benefit all persons designated as provided by the donor.

(c) A release shall be delivered as follows:

(1) If the creating instrument specifies a person to whom a release is to be delivered, the release shall be delivered to that person, but delivery need not be made as provided in this paragraph if the person cannot with due diligence be found.

(2) In a case where the property to which the power relates is held by a trustee, the release shall be delivered to the trustee.

(3) In a case not covered by paragraph (1) or (2), the release may be delivered to any of the following:

(A) A person, other than the <u>powerholder</u>, who could be adversely affected by the exercise of the power.

(B) The county recorder of the county in which the <u>powerholder</u> resides or in which the deed, will, or other instrument creating the power is filed.

(d) A release of a power of appointment that affects real property or obligations secured by real property shall be acknowledged and proved, and may be certified and recorded, in like manner and with like effect as grants of real property, and all statutory provisions relating to the recordation or nonrecordation of conveyances of real property and to the effect thereof apply to a release with like effect, without regard to the date when the release was delivered, if at all, pursuant to subdivision (c). Failure to deliver, pursuant to subdivision (c), a release that is recorded pursuant to this subdivision does not affect the validity of any transaction with respect to the real property or obligation secured thereby, and the general laws of this state on recording and its effect govern the transaction.

(e) This section does not impair the validity of a release made before July 1, 1970. *(Added by Stats.1992, c. 30 (A.B.1722), § 2. Amended by Stats.2016, c. 81 (A.B.2846), § 15, eff. Jan. 1, 2017.)*

Law Revision Commission Comments

1992 Addition

Section 661 continues former Civil Code Section 1388.2 without substantive change.

Subdivision (b) requires that, where the donor designated persons or a class to take in default of the donee's exercise of the power, a release of a power that is not presently exercisable must benefit all those so designated as provided by the donor. This requirement, added in 1981, substituted for the former rule that no release of a power was permissible when the result of the release was the present exercise of a power not presently exercisable. The language of the last sentence of subdivision (b) is taken from New York law. See N.Y.Est.Powers & Trusts Law § 10–5.3(b) (McKinney Supp.1991). This provision is necessary to ensure that the release of a power not presently exercisable does not defeat the donor's intent by benefiting some but not all of the takers in default.

Subdivision (c) deals only with "delivery" of the release. Nothing in subdivision (c) precludes the recording of a release delivered in accordance with paragraph (1), (2), or (3)(A) of subdivision (c). See Civ.Code §§ 1213–1215.

Subdivision (d) makes clear that a subsequent purchaser or encumbrancer, in good faith and for a valuable consideration, who first records is protected. See Civ.Code § 1214. The unrecorded instrument is valid as between the parties thereto and those who have notice thereof if the instrument is otherwise effective. See Civ.Code § 1217.

See also Sections 610(b) ("appointive property" defined), 610(c) ("creating instrument" defined), 610(d) ("donee" defined), 610(f) ("permissible appointee" defined), 611 ("general" and "special" powers of appointment defined), 612(a) ("testamentary" power of appointment defined), 612(c) ("not presently exercisable" power of appointment defined), 613 ("discretionary" power of appointment defined). [21 Cal.L.Rev.Comm.Reports 91 (1991)].

Cross References

Instrument, defined, see Probate Code § 45.

Real property, defined, see Probate Code § 68.

§ 662. Release on behalf of minor powerholder

(a) A release on behalf of a minor <u>powerholder</u> shall be made by the guardian of the estate of the minor pursuant to an order of court obtained under this section.

(b) The guardian or other interested person may file a petition with the court in which the guardianship of the estate proceeding is pending for an order of the court authorizing or requiring the guardian to release the ward's powers as a <u>powerholder</u> or a power of appointment in whole or in part.

(c) Notice of the hearing on the petition shall be given for the period and in the manner provided in Chapter 3 (commencing with Section 1460) of Part 1 of Division 4 to all of the following (other than the petitioner or persons joining in the petition):

(1) The persons required to be given notice under Chapter 3 (commencing with Section 1460) of Part 1 of Division 4.

(2) The donor of the power, if alive.

(3) The trustee, if the property to which the power relates is held by a trustee.

(4) Other persons as ordered by the court.

(d) After hearing, the court in its discretion may make an order authorizing or requiring the guardian to release on behalf of the ward a general or special power of appointment as permitted under Section 661, if the court determines, taking into consideration all the relevant circumstances, that the ward as a prudent person would make the release of the power of appointment if the ward had the capacity to do so.

(e) Nothing in this section imposes any duty on the guardian to file a petition under this section, and the guardian is not liable for failure to file a petition under this section. *(Added by Stats.1992, c. 30 (A.B.1722), § 2. Amended by Stats.2016, c. 81 (A.B.2846), § 16, eff. Jan. 1, 2017.)*

Law Revision Commission Comments

1992 Addition

Section 662 continues former Civil Code Section 1388.3 without substantive change. This section provides a procedure for the release of a general or special power of a minor donee. The extent to which a general or special power of a minor donee may be released is determined by Section 661. The court in which a conservatorship proceeding is pending has authority to make an order authorizing or requiring the conservator on behalf of the conservatee to exercise or release the conservatee's powers as donee of a power of appointment. See Sections §§ 2580–2586. Section 662 gives the court in which the guardianship proceeding is pending authority to make an order authorizing or requiring the guardian to release the ward's powers as donee of a power of appointment, but the court is not authorized to order an exercise of the power of appointment. Section 625 provides that a minor donee may not exercise a power of appointment during minority unless the creating instrument otherwise provides. The court may make an order authorizing or requiring the guardian to release the power of appointment only if the court determines, taking into consideration all the relevant circumstances, that the ward as a prudent person would release the power if the ward had the capacity to do so. For example, to avoid unfavorable tax consequences, it may be desirable that the power of appointment be disclaimed or released in whole or in part.

See also Section 610(d) ("donee" defined). [21 Cal.L.Rev.Comm.Reports 91 (1991)].

Cross References

Interested person, defined, see Probate Code § 48.

§§ 663 to 665. Repealed by Stats.1988, c. 1199, § 52, operative July 1, 1989

Law Revision Commission Comments

1988 Repeal

The provision of subdivision (a) of former Section 663 that interest on a general pecuniary legacy commences one year after death is restated in Section 12003 without substantive change. The provision of subdivision (a) that the rate of interest is that payable on a money judgment entered in this state is superseded by Section 12001.

Subdivision (b) is continued in Section 12004(a).

The part of subdivision (c) that related to interest on annuities is restated in Section 12004(b), the part that related to interest on a devise for maintenance is restated in Section 12005, the provision governing the interest rate is superseded by Section 12001, and the provision governing an income beneficiary of a trust is superseded by Section 16304(a) (when right to trust income arises) [19 Cal.L.Rev.Comm.Reports 1065 (1988)].

Subdivision (a) of former Section 664 is superseded by Sections 12000 (application of chapter) and 12006 (remaining income to residuary or intestate distributees).

Subdivision (b) is superseded by Section 16305(a) (income earned during administration of decedent's estate) [19 Cal.L.Rev.Comm.Reports 1065 (1988)].

Subdivision (a) of former Section 665 is generalized in Section 2(a). Subdivision (b) is omitted [19 Cal.L.Rev.Comm.Reports 1065 (1988)].

§§ 666, 667. Repealed by Stats.1983, c. 842, § 39, operative Jan. 1, 1985

§ 668. Repealed by Stats.1980, c. 119, p. 285, § 16

Law Revision Commission Comments

1980 Repeal

Section 668 is repealed in recognition of the elimination of the survivorship right in the declared homestead. See Comment to Civil Code § 1265.

CHAPTER 5. EFFECT OF FAILURE TO MAKE EFFECTIVE APPOINTMENT

Cross References

Unexecuted power of appointment, effect on estates in real property, see Civil Code § 781.

§ 670. Validity of exercise of power

An exercise of a power of appointment is not void solely because it is more extensive than authorized by the power, but is valid to the extent that the exercise was permissible under the terms of the power. *(Added by Stats.1992, c. 30 (A.B.1722), § 2.)*

Law Revision Commission Comments

1992 Addition

Section 670 continues former Civil Code Section 1389.1 without substantive change. This section is based on a New York rule. See N.Y.Est.Powers & Trusts Law § 10–6.6(a)(1) (McKinney 1967).

Section 670 makes clear that, when a power is exercised partly in favor of an unauthorized person, the exercise is valid to the extent that it is permissible under the terms of the power. However, if a fraud on a special power is involved, the appointment is not permissible under the terms of the power and the disposition of the property should be determined by common law principles. See *In re Estate of Carroll*, 153 Misc. 649, 275 N.Y.S. 911 (1934), *modified sub. nom. In re Content*, 247 App.Div. 11, 286 N.Y.S. 307 (1936), *modified sub. nom. In re Will of Carroll*, 274 N.Y. 288, 8 N.E.2d 864 (1937).

Section 670 also covers other types of nonpermissible exercises of the power. For example, if the donor of a power specifies that the donee is to appoint 20 percent or less of the corpus of a trust to each of six permissible appointees and the donee appoints 25 percent to one of the permissible appointees, this section permits the appointee to receive 20 percent of the assets. Thus, an appointment of an excess amount will not invalidate the appointment, but will instead be deemed to be an appointment of the maximum amount. [21 Cal.L.Rev.Comm.Reports 91 (1991)].

§ 671. Imperative powers

(a) Unless the creating instrument or the powerholder, in writing, manifests a contrary intent, where the powerholder dies without having exercised an imperative power of appointment either in whole or in part, the persons designated as permissible appointees take equally of the property not already appointed. Where the creating instrument establishes a minimum distribution requirement that is not satisfied by an equal division of the property not already appointed, the appointees who have received a partial appointment are required to return a pro rata portion of the property they would otherwise be entitled to receive in an amount sufficient to meet the minimum distribution requirement.

(b) Where an imperative power of appointment has been exercised defectively, either in whole or in part, its proper execution may be adjudged in favor of the person intended to be benefited by the defective exercise.

(c) Where an imperative power of appointment has been created so that it confers on a person a right to have the power exercised in the person's favor, the proper exercise of the power can be compelled in favor of the person, or the person's assigns, creditors, guardian, or conservator. *(Added by Stats.1992, c. 30 (A.B.1722), § 2. Amended by Stats.2016, c. 81 (A.B.2846), § 17, eff. Jan. 1, 2017.)*

Law Revision Commission Comments

1992 Addition

Section 671 continues former Civil Code Section 1389.2 without substantive change. The reference to "persons" in subdivision (b) has been omitted as surplus. See Section 10 (singular includes plural).

Section 671 states the consequences flowing from the imperative character of a power of appointment. Under subdivision (a), if an imperative power of appointment is created and the donee of the power dies without exercising it, the appointive assets go equally to the permissible objects of the power. Where there has been a partial appointment, unless the creating instrument or the donee has manifested a contrary intent, the assets already appointed are not thrown into a hotchpot and are considered only to the extent necessary to satisfy a requirement set by the donor that each of the permissible appointees receive a certain minimum amount. The following illustrates these rules. The donor of a power specifies that the donee is to appoint at least 25 percent of the corpus of a trust to each of three permissible appointees (*A, B,* and *C*). (1) Donee appoints 10 percent to *A*, but fails to appoint the remainder. *B* and *C* each take 30 percent and *A* takes 40 percent (30 plus 10). (2) Donee appoints 40 percent to *A*, but fails to appoint the remainder. Since 60 divided by 3 equals 20, the donee failed to satisfy the minimum distribution requirement set by the donor. *A* therefore must "return" a portion of the property received. The appointive property will be distributed 25 percent (20 plus 5) each to *B* and *C* and 50 percent (40 plus 20 minus 10) to *A*. (3) Donee appoints 60 percent to *A*, 40 percent to *B*. This again fails to satisfy the minimum distribution requirement. To obtain the 25 percent required, *A* and *B* must "return" on a pro rata basis and distribution is made accordingly—45 percent (60 minus 15) to *A*, 30 percent (40 minus 10) to *B*, and 25 percent to *C*. The arithmetic can become quite complex but the principle remains the same. Unless the creating instrument or the donee, in writing, manifests a contrary intent, a partial appointment is to be treated as reflecting an intended preference. The requirement of a writing by the donee is consistent with Sections 6174 and 6409 concerning advancements.

Under subdivision (b), if the donee exercises the power defectively (e.g., without proper formalities), the court may allow the intended appointment to pass the assets to the person whom the donee attempted to benefit. A similar rule obtains in California concerning the defective exercise of a power of attorney. Gerdes v. Moody, 41 Cal. 335 (1871).

Under subdivision (c), if the power creates a right in the permissible appointee to compel the exercise of the power (e.g., where the donee must appoint to the donee's children within ten years of the creation of the power and at the end of ten years the donee has only one child), that person may compel exercise of the power by the donee. In addition, the assignees or creditors of the appointee who possesses the right to compel exercise may also compel its exercise.

See also Sections 610(b) ("appointive property" defined), 610(c) ("creating instrument" defined), 610(d) ("donee" defined), 610(f) ("permissible appointee" defined), 613 ("imperative" power of appointment defined). [21 Cal.L.Rev.Comm.Reports 91 (1991)].

Cross References

Instrument, defined, see Probate Code § 45.

§ 672. Discretionary powers; general powers

(a) Except as provided in subdivision (b), if the powerholder of a discretionary power of appointment fails to appoint the property, releases the entire power, or makes an ineffective appointment, in whole or in part, the appointive property not effectively appointed passes to the person named by the donor as taker in default or, if there is none, reverts to the donor.

(b) If the powerholder of a general power of appointment makes an ineffective appointment, an implied alternative appointment to the powerholder's estate may be found if the powerholder has manifested an intent that the appointive property be disposed of as property of the powerholder rather than as in default of appointment. *(Added by Stats. 1992, c. 30 (A.B.1722), § 2. Amended by Stats.2016, c. 81 (A.B.2846), § 18, eff. Jan. 1, 2017.)*

Law Revision Commission Comments

1992 Addition

Section 672 continues former Civil Code Section 1389.3 without substantive change. The reference to "persons" in subdivision (a) has been omitted as surplus. See Section 10 (singular includes plural).

Section 672 states the rules determining to whom property passes that has not been effectively appointed. Subdivision (a) states the accepted common law rule. See Restatement of Property § 365(1) (1940); see also Restatement (Second) of Property (Donative Transfers) §§ 23.1, 23.2 (1986). It also accords with the established rule in California. Estate of Baird, 120 Cal.App.2d 219, 260 P.2d 1052 (1953); Estate of Baird, 135 Cal.App.2d 333, 287 P.2d 365 (1955) (later decision in same case on different point). Under this section, the property passes directly from the donor to the ultimate takers.

Subdivision (b) provides a uniform rule as to the application of the doctrine of capture in cases where the donee of a general power of appointment makes an ineffective appointment. The distinction formerly made between appointments upon a trust that fails and other ineffective appointments has not been continued. In other respects Section 672 is intended to adopt the substance of the common law doctrine of capture or implied alternative appointment to the donee's estate. See L. Simes, Handbook of the Law of Future Interests § 69 (2d ed. 1966); Restatement of Property § 365(2)–(3) (1940); see also Restatement (Second) of Property (Donative Transfers) § 23.2 (1986).

See also Sections 610(b) ("appointive property" defined), 613 ("discretionary" power of appointment defined), 610(d) ("donee" defined), 610(e) ("donor" defined), 611 ("general" power of appointment defined). [21 Cal.L.Rev.Comm.Reports 91 (1991)].

§ 673. Death of appointee before appointment becomes effective

(a) Except as provided in subdivision (b), if an appointment by will or by instrument effective only at the death of the powerholder is ineffective because of the death of an appointee before the appointment becomes effective and the appointee leaves issue surviving the powerholder, the surviving issue of the appointee take the appointed property in the same manner as the appointee would have taken had the appointee survived the powerholder, except that the property passes only to persons who are permissible appointees, including appointees permitted under Section 674. If the surviving issue are all of the same degree of kinship to the deceased appointee, they take equally, but if of unequal degree, then those of more remote degree take in the manner provided in Section 240.

(b) This section does not apply if either the donor or powerholder manifests an intent that some other disposition of the appointive property shall be made. *(Added by*

Stats.1992, c. 30 (A.B.1722), § 2. Amended by Stats.2016, c. 81 (A.B.2846), § 19, eff. Jan. 1, 2017.)

Law Revision Commission Comments

1992 Addition

Section 673 continues former Civil Code Section 1389.4 without substantive change.

Section 673 embodies the theory of Sections 349 and 350 of the Restatement of Property (1940). It is broadened to cover special powers by employing the language used by Michigan law. Mich.Stat. Ann. § 26.155(120) (Callaghan 1984). This section is necessary because the general anti-lapse provision in Section 6147 does not specifically deal with lapse of a testamentary appointment. This section is not intended to cover the attempt to appoint property inter vivos to a predeceased appointee, but does apply to an instrument other than a will effective only at the death of the donee. Such an instrument is for all practical purposes identical to a will and is accorded the same effect.

Section 673 permits issue of an appointee to take the appointed property where an appointee dies before the appointment becomes effective and leaves issue surviving the donee, whether or not the issue is related to the donee. Prior to the 1981 amendment of former Civil Code Section 1389.4, the section apparently permitted only issue of an appointee related to the donee to take the appointed property where the appointee died before the appointment becomes effective. See French, *Application of Antilapse Statutes to Appointments Made by Will,* 53 Wash.L.Rev. 405, 432 (1978).

Section 673 provides a more liberal antilapse provision than the general antilapse provision of Section 6147, because Section 673 does not require that the issue of the predeceased appointee be related either to the donor or donee. This section permits the children of the donee's spouse to take if the donee's spouse is the appointee and dies before the appointment becomes effective. Likewise, an appointment to a brother, sister, niece, or nephew of the donee's spouse will not lapse. A person may not take under Section 673 unless the person is a permissible appointee.

Section 673 adopts the general rule of representation provided by Section 240. See also Sections 230–234 (proceeding to determine whether issue of an appointee survived the donee).

As provided in subdivision (b), this section applies only in the absence of a manifestation of a contrary intent by the donor or donee. It is intended to fill the gap if there is no discernible intent of the donor or donee as to the desired disposition of the property when an intended taker dies before the effective date of the disposition.

See also Sections 610(a) ("appointee" defined), 610(b) ("appointive property" defined), 610(d) ("donee" defined), 610(e) ("donor" defined), 610(f) ("permissible appointee" defined). [21 Cal.L.Rev.Comm.Reports 91 (1991)].

Cross References

Effect of homicide or abuse of an elder or dependent adult, felonious and intentional killing, entitlement to decedent's property, see Probate Code § 250.
Instrument, defined, see Probate Code § 45.
Issue, defined, see Probate Code § 50.
Simultaneous death, determination of survival, petitions and purposes, see Probate Code § 230.

§ 674. Death of permissible appointee before exercise of special power

(a) Unless the creating instrument expressly provides otherwise, if a permissible appointee dies before the exercise of a special power of appointment, the <u>powerholder</u> has the power to appoint to the issue of the deceased permissible appointee, whether or not the issue was included within the description of the permissible appointees, if the deceased permissible appointee was alive at the time of the execution of the creating instrument or was born thereafter.

(b) This section applies whether the special power of appointment is exercisable by inter vivos instrument, by will, or otherwise.

(c) This section applies to a case where the power of appointment is exercised on or after July 1, 1982, but does not affect the validity of any exercise of a power of appointment made before July 1, 1982. *(Added by Stats.1992, c. 30 (A.B.1722), § 2. Amended by Stats.2016, c. 81 (A.B. 2846), § 20, eff. Jan. 1, 2017.)*

Law Revision Commission Comments

1992 Addition

Subdivisions (a) and (b) of Section 674 continue former Civil Code Section 1389.5 without substantive change. Subdivision (a) permits an appointment under a special power to the issue of a predeceased permissible appointee. A special power of appointment is usually designed to permit flexibility in the ultimate disposition of the property by permitting the donee to take into account changing family circumstances. Permitting the donee to select not only among the primary class members, but also among the issue of those who are deceased, is necessary to permit effectuation of the donor's purpose. Section 674 applies the principle of the antilapse statute to this situation without regard to whether the substitute takers are included within the permissible appointees. See generally French, *Application of Antilapse Statutes to Appointments Made by Will,* 53 Wash.L.Rev. 405 (1978).

As provided in subdivision (b), this section applies in the absence of an express contrary provision in the creating instrument. The section is designed to fill the gap if the creating instrument is silent as to the desired disposition of the property when a permissible appointee dies before the time of the exercise of the power.

Subdivision (c) codifies the operative date rule in 1981 Cal.Stat. ch. 63, §§ 10(c) & 11.

See also Sections 610(c) ("creating instrument" defined), 610(d) ("donee" defined), 611 ("special" power of appointment defined), 610(f) ("permissible appointee" defined). [21 Cal.L.Rev.Comm.Reports 91 (1991)].

Cross References

Instrument, defined, see Probate Code § 45.
Issue, defined, see Probate Code § 50.

§ 675. Disposition of powerholder's property in dispositive instrument; allocation of owned and appointive property

If a powerholder exercises a power of appointment in a disposition that also disposes of property the powerholder owns, the owned property and the appointive property shall be allocated in the permissible manner in accordance with the terms of the creating instrument and that best carries out the powerholder's intent. *(Added by Stats.2016, c. 81 (A.B.2846), § 21, eff. Jan. 1, 2017.)*

§ 676. Partial appointment to taker in default of appointment

Unless the terms of the instrument creating or exercising a power of appointment manifest a contrary intent, if the powerholder makes a valid partial appointment to a taker in default of appointment, the taker in default of appointment may share fully in unappointed property. *(Added by Stats. 2016, c. 81 (A.B.2846), § 22, eff. Jan. 1, 2017.)*

CHAPTER 6.   RIGHTS OF CREDITORS

§ 680. Authority of donor to nullify or alter rights of creditors of powerholder

The donor of a power of appointment cannot nullify or alter the rights given creditors of the powerholder by Sections 682, 683, and 684 by any language in the instrument creating the power. *(Added by Stats.1992, c. 30 (A.B.1722), § 2. Amended by Stats.2016, c. 81 (A.B.2846), § 23, eff. Jan. 1, 2017.)*

Law Revision Commission Comments

1992 Addition

Section 680 continues former Civil Code Section 1390.1 without substantive change. This section deals with a question that has not been considered by the California appellate courts. It is patterned after a provision adopted in New York. See N.Y.Est.Powers & Trusts Law § 10–4.1(4) (McKinney 1967). This section prevents instruments utilizing Treasury Regulations Section 20.2056(b)–5(f)(7) (allowing a marital deduction despite a spendthrift clause in the instrument creating the power) from nullifying the rights given creditors under Sections 682 and 683. The addition of the reference to Section 684 protects the dependents' support rights from being avoided by language in the creating instrument.

See also Sections 610(c) ("creating instrument" defined), 610(d) ("donee" defined), 610(e) ("donor" defined). [21 Cal.L.Rev.Comm.Reports 91 (1991)].

Cross References

Instrument, defined, see Probate Code § 45.

§ 681. Property covered by special power of appointment

* * * (a) Except as provided in subdivision (b), property covered by a special power of appointment is not subject to the claims of creditors of the powerholder or of the powerholder's estate or to the expenses of the administration of the powerholder's estate.

(b) Property subject to a special power of appointment shall be subject to the claims of creditors of the powerholder or of the powerholder's estate or the expenses of administration of the powerholder's estate under either of the following circumstances:

(1) To the extent that the powerholder owned the property and, reserving the special power, transferred the property in violation of the Uniform Voidable Transactions Act (Chapter 1 (commencing with Section 3439) of Title 2 of Part 2 of Division 4 of the Civil Code).

(2) If the initial gift in default of the exercise of the power is to the powerholder or the powerholder's estate. *(Added by Stats.1992, c. 30 (A.B.1722), § 2. Amended by Stats.2016, c. 81 (A.B.2846), § 24, eff. Jan. 1, 2017.)*

Law Revision Commission Comments

1992 Addition

Section 681 continues former Civil Code Section 1390.2 without substantive change. This section codifies the common law rule that bars creditors from reaching the property covered by a special power of appointment. See Restatement of Property § 326 (1940). The section is the same in substance as a New York provision. See N.Y.Est.Powers & Trusts Law § 10–7.1 (McKinney 1967).

See also Section 610(d) ("donee" defined). [21 Cal.L.Rev.Comm.Reports 91 (1991)].

§ 682. Property subject to general power of appointment or general testamentary power of appointment of powerholder

(a) To the extent that the property owned by the powerholder is inadequate to satisfy the claims of the powerholder's creditors, property subject to a general power of appointment that is presently exercisable is subject to the claims to the same extent that it would be subject to the claims if the property were owned by the powerholder.

(b) Upon the death of the powerholder, to the extent that the powerholder's estate is inadequate to satisfy the claims of creditors of the estate and the expenses of administration of the estate, property subject to a general testamentary power of appointment or to a general power of appointment that was presently exercisable at the time of the powerholder's death is subject to the claims and expenses to the same extent that it would be subject to the claims and expenses if the property had been owned by the powerholder.

(c) This section applies whether or not the power of appointment has been exercised. *(Added by Stats.1992, c. 30 (A.B.1722), § 2. Amended by Stats.2016, c. 81 (A.B.2846), § 25, eff. Jan. 1, 2017.)*

Law Revision Commission Comments

1992 Addition

Section 682 continues former Civil Code Section 1390.3 without substantive change. This section states the rule with respect to the availability of property subject to a general power of appointment to satisfy the donee's debts. It is intended to make appointive property available to satisfy creditors' claims where the donee has the equivalent of full ownership of the property. See Comment to Section 611.

Subdivision (a) provides that the creditors of a donee possessing a power of appointment that is both general and presently exercisable can reach the appointive property for the satisfaction of their claims. However, these creditors must first exhaust the remainder of the donee's assets before resorting to the appointive property. See Estate of Masson, 142 Cal.App.2d 510, 298 P.2d 619 (1956). Subject to this limitation, appointive property is treated just as property owned by the donee. Thus, where the property has been appointed by an inter vivos instrument, the property is liable if, had it been owned by the donee, the transfer would have been subject to the rules relating to fraudulent conveyances. See Restatement of Property § 330 (1940); see also Restatement (Second) of Property (Donative Transfers) § 13.5 (1986).

Subdivision (b) provides that the same rule applies to property covered by a general testamentary power (or equivalent) that has, in effect, become presently exercisable because of the donee's death. In this case, the appointive property has come under the power of disposition of the debtor-donee and hence is treated the same as other property of the decedent.

Subdivision (c) provides that the rights of creditors are not dependent on the exercise of the power. Unlike the common law rule, which requires the exercise of the power, the mere existence of the power is the operative fact essential to the rights of creditors. In addition, the nature of the donee's interest in the property is irrelevant. The property available to creditors can be either a present or a future interest.

See also Sections 610(d) ("donee" defined), 611 ("general" power of appointment defined), 612(a) ("testamentary" power of appointment defined), 612(b) ("presently exercisable" power of appointment defined). [21 Cal.L.Rev.Comm.Reports 91 (1991)].

§ 683. Property subject to unexercised general power of appointment created by donor in donor's favor

Property subject to * * * a general power of appointment created by the donor in the donor's favor, whether or not presently exercisable, is subject to the claims of the donor's creditors or the donor's estate and to the expenses of the administration of the donor's <u>estate, except to the extent the donor effectively irrevocably appointed the property subject to the general power of appointment in favor of a person other than the donor or the donor's estate.</u> *(Added by Stats.1992, c. 30 (A.B.1722), § 2. Amended by Stats.2016, c. 81 (A.B.2846), § 26, eff. Jan. 1, 2017.)*

Law Revision Commission Comments

1992 Addition

Section 683 continues former Civil Code Section 1390.4 without substantive change. This section provides that, when the donor of a general power of appointment is also its donee, creditors of the donor-donee can reach the appointive property even though it is in terms exercisable only at a future date (as, for example, by will of the donor-donee). This section codifies the common law rule. See Restatement of Property § 328 (1940); *accord* Restatement (Second) of Property (Donative Transfers) § 13.3 (1986).

See also Sections 610(e) ("donor" defined), 611 ("general" power of appointment defined), 612(b) ("presently exercisable" power of appointment defined). [21 Cal.L.Rev.Comm.Reports 91 (1991)].

§ 684. Support obligation; status as creditor of powerholder

For the purposes of Sections 682 and 683, a person to whom the <u>powerholder</u> owes an obligation of support shall be considered a creditor of the <u>powerholder</u> to the extent that a legal obligation exists for the <u>powerholder</u> to provide the support. *(Added by Stats.1992, c. 30 (A.B.1722), § 2. Amended by Stats.2016, c. 81 (A.B.2846), § 27, eff. Jan. 1, 2017.)*

Law Revision Commission Comments

1992 Addition

Section 684 continues former Civil Code Section 1390.5 without substantive change. This section makes clear that the donee's support obligations can be enforced against (1) property subject to a general power of appointment that is presently exercisable (Section 682), and (2) property subject to an unexercised general power of appointment created in the donor's own favor, whether or not presently exercisable (Section 683).

See also Section 610(d) ("donee" defined). [21 Cal.L.Rev.Comm.Reports 91 (1991)].

CHAPTER 7. RULE AGAINST PERPETUITIES

Section
690. Application of rule to powers of appointment.

§ 690. Application of rule to powers of appointment

The statutory rule against perpetuities provided by Part 2 (commencing with Section 21200) of Division 11 applies to powers of appointment governed by this part. *(Added by Stats.1992, c. 30 (A.B.1722), § 2.)*

Law Revision Commission Comments

1992 Addition

Section 690 continues former Civil Code Section 1391 without substantive change. See Sections 21206 (statutory rule against perpetuities as to general power of appointment not presently exercisable because of condition precedent), 21207 (statutory rule against perpetuities as to nongeneral power of appointment or general testamentary power of appointment), 21210 (when power of appointment created), 21211 (postponement of time of creation of power of appointment), 21212 (time of creation of power of appointment arising from transfer to trust or other arrangement). [21 Cal.L.Rev.Comm.Reports 91 (1991)].

CHAPTER 8. REVOCABILITY OF CREATION, EXERCISE, OR RELEASE OF POWER OF APPOINTMENT

Section
695. Authority to revoke or release.

§ 695. Authority to revoke or release

(a) Unless the power to revoke is in the creating instrument or exists pursuant to Section 15400, the creation of a power of appointment is irrevocable.

(b) Unless made expressly irrevocable by the creating instrument or the instrument of exercise, an exercise of a power of appointment is revocable if the power to revoke exists pursuant to Section 15400 or so long as the interest in the appointive property, whether present or future, has not been transferred or become distributable pursuant to the appointment.

(c) Unless the power to revoke is reserved in the instrument releasing the power, a release of a power of appointment is irrevocable. *(Added by Stats.1992, c. 30 (A.B.1722), § 2.)*

Law Revision Commission Comments

1992 Addition

Section 695 continues former Civil Code Section 1392.1 without substantive change. Under subdivision (a), the creation of a power of appointment is irrevocable unless the power to revoke is reserved in the instrument creating the power or unless the power is created in connection with a trust that is revocable under the presumption in Section 15400. In the latter case, to avoid a conflict between this section and Section 15400, the power of appointment is revocable to the same extent that the trust in connection with which it is created is revocable.

Under subdivision (b), an exercise of a power of appointment is revocable as long as the interest in the appointive property has not been transferred or become distributable, unless the creating instrument or instrument of exercise provides otherwise. This subdivision embodies a policy that the donee should be permitted to modify or revoke an exercise of the power as long as the appointive property has not been effectively transferred. A donee may exercise the power of appointment by creating a trust for the benefit of permissible appointees. To avoid conflict with Section 15400 (presumption of revocability of trusts), subdivision (b) permits the donee to revoke the exercise, even though there has been an effective transfer, if the power to revoke exists pursuant to Section 15400.

Under subdivision (c), the release of a power of appointment is irrevocable, unless the power to revoke is reserved in the instrument of release. The procedure necessary to effect a release is provided in Section 661.

See also Sections 610(b) ("appointive property" defined), 610(c) ("creating instrument" defined). [21 Cal.L.Rev.Comm.Reports 91 (1991)].

Cross References

Instrument, defined, see Probate Code § 45.

Part 15

DEPOSIT OF ESTATE PLANNING DOCUMENTS WITH ATTORNEY

Cross References

Conservator's authority to take actions authorized for depositor, see Probate Code § 2586.

CHAPTER 1. DEFINITIONS

§ 700. Applicability of chapter

Unless the provision or context otherwise requires, the definitions in this chapter govern the construction of this part. *(Added by Stats.1993, c. 519 (A.B.209), § 4.)*

Law Revision Commission Comments

1993 Addition

Section 700 is new. [23 Cal.L.Rev.Comm. Reports 901 (1993) (Annual Report, App. 7)].

Cross References

Court authority to order delivery of documents to appointed custodian for safekeeping, see Probate Code § 2586.

§ 700.1. Repealed by Stats.1987, c. 923, § 37, operative July 1, 1988

Law Revision Commission Comments

1987 Repeal

The first sentence of subdivision (a), subdivision (b), and the first sentence of subdivision (c) of former Section 700.1 are restated without substantive change in Sections 215 (report to Director of Health Services), 1215 (mailing), 9201 (claims governed by other statutes), and 9202 (claim by Director of Health Services).

The last two sentences of subdivision (c) and subdivision (d) are restated without substantive change in Section 9203 (distribution before claim) and generalized to apply to all public entities.

See also Section 58 ("personal representative" defined). [19 Cal.L.Rev.Comm.Reports 550 (1988)].

§ 701. Attorney

"Attorney" means an individual licensed to practice law in this state. *(Added by Stats.1993, c. 519 (A.B.209), § 4.)*

Law Revision Commission Comments

1993 Addition

Section 701 is new. Although the depositary is the individual attorney, liability for failing to maintain an adequate standard of care may be imposed on the attorney's law partnership or law corporation under traditional rules of vicarious liability. See 2 B. Witkin, Summary of California Law *Agency and Employment* § 115, at 109–111 (9th ed. 1987); 9 B. Witkin, Summary of California Law *Partnership* § 38, at 434–35 (9th ed. 1989). [23 Cal.L.Rev.Comm. Reports 901 (1993) (Annual Report, App. 7)].

Cross References

Attorneys, rules of professional conduct, see California Rules of Professional Conduct, Rule 1–100 et seq.
Attorneys, State Bar Act, see Business and Professions Code § 6000.

§ 702. Deposit

"Deposit" means delivery of a document by a depositor to an attorney for safekeeping or authorization by a depositor for an attorney to retain a document for safekeeping. *(Added by Stats.1993, c. 519 (A.B.209), § 4.)*

Law Revision Commission Comments

1993 Addition

Section 702 is new. [23 Cal.L.Rev.Comm. Reports 901 (1993) (Annual Report, App. 7)].

§ 703. Depositor

"Depositor" means a natural person who deposits the person's document with an attorney. *(Added by Stats.1993, c. 519 (A.B.209), § 4.)*

Law Revision Commission Comments

1993 Addition

Section 703 is new. The definition of "depositor" in Section 703 does not preclude the person whose document is deposited from using an agent, such as an attorney-in-fact, to make the deposit. [23 Cal.L.Rev.Comm. Reports 901 (1993) (Annual Report, App. 7)].

§ 704. Document

"Document" means any of the following:

(a) A signed original will, declaration of trust, trust amendment, or other document modifying a will or trust.

(b) A signed original power of attorney.

(c) A signed original nomination of conservator.

(d) Any other signed original instrument that the attorney and depositor agree in writing to make subject to this part. *(Added by Stats.1993, c. 519 (A.B.209), § 4.)*

Law Revision Commission Comments

1993 Addition

Section 704 is new. "Will" includes a codicil. Section 88. [23 Cal.L.Rev.Comm. Reports 901 (1993) (Annual Report, App. 7)].

Cross References

Instrument, defined, see Probate Code § 45.
Trusts, generally, see Probate Code § 15000 et seq.

§§ 704.2 to 706. Repealed by Stats.1987, c. 923, § 37, operative July 1, 1988

Law Revision Commission Comments

1987 Repeal

Part of the first sentence of former Section 704.2 is generalized in Section 9150(a) (how claim is filed). The remainder of this section is replaced by Sections 11440, 11441, and 11442 (allocation of debts between estate and surviving spouse). See the Comments to Sections 11440–11442. [19 Cal.L.Rev.Comm. Reports 411 (1988)].

Former Section 704.4 is replaced by Sections 11440, 11441, and 11442 (allocation of debts between estate and surviving spouse). See the Comments to Sections 11440–11442. [19 Cal.L.Rev.Comm. Reports 411 (1988)].

Former Section 705 is restated in Section 9151 (documentary support of claim) without substantive change. See also Section 58 ("personal representative" defined). [19 Cal.L.Rev.Comm. Reports 411 (1988)].

Former Section 706 is restated in Section 9152 (claim based on written instrument) without substantive change. See also Section 58 ("personal representative" defined). [19 Cal.L.Rev.Comm. Reports 411 (1988)].

§ 707. Repealed by Stats.1988, c. 1199, § 53, operative July 1, 1989

Law Revision Commission Comments

1988 Repeal

Former Section 707 is replaced by Sections 550–555 (liability of decedent covered by insurance) and 9390 (claim covered by insurance). [19 Cal.L.Rev.Comm. Reports 1221 (1988)].

§§ 707.5, 708. Repealed by Stats.1987, c. 923, § 37, operative July 1, 1988

Law Revision Commission Comments

1987 Repeal

Subdivision (a) of former Section 707.5 is restated in Section 9200 (claim by public entity required) without substantive change. Subdivision (b) is restated in Section 9201 (claims governed by other statutes) without substantive change. Subdivision (c) is restated in Section 9000(a)(2) ("claim" defined) with clarifying changes. See the Comment to Section 9000. Subdivision (d) is restated in Section 9204 (priority of claims not affected by chapter) without substantive change. Subdivision (e) is restated in Section 9205 (limitation on application of chapter) without substantive change. [19 Cal.L.Rev. Comm. Reports 412 (1988)].

The first sentence of former Section 708 is restated in Section 9253(b) (effect of statute of limitations) without substantive change. The second sentence is restated in Section 9251(b) (procedure by court) without substantive change. The last sentence is restated in Section 9253(c) (effect of statute of limitations) without substantive change. See also Section 58 ("personal representative" defined). [19 Cal.L.Rev.Comm. Reports 412 (1988)].

§§ 709, 709.1. Repealed by Stats.1988, c. 1199, § 53, operative July 1, 1989

Law Revision Commission Comments

1988 Repeal

The first two sentences of former Section 709 are restated in Section 9370 (claim prerequisite to continuing action) with the addition of a requirement that the plaintiff act to substitute the personal representative as a party within three months after rejection of the claim. The third sentence is replaced by Sections 550–555 (liability of decedent covered by insurance) and 9390 (claim covered by insurance).

The fourth sentence of the first paragraph and the second and third paragraphs of former Section 709 are restated in Section 9103 (late claim), with clarifying and generalizing changes made to combine it with former Section 720. [19 Cal.L.Rev.Comm. Reports 1221 (1988)].

Former Section 709.1 is replaced by Sections 550–555 (liability of decedent covered by insurance) and 9390 (claim covered by insurance). [19 Cal.L.Rev.Comm.Reports 1222 (1988)].

CHAPTER 2. DUTIES AND LIABILITIES OF ATTORNEY

Section

710.   Safekeeping of documents; duty of care for preservation.
711.   Lost or destroyed documents; notice.
712.   Liability for loss or destruction of documents; actual notice by depositor.
713.   Acceptance of documents by attorney; no duty imposed; validity of contents of documents; legal services to depositor.
713.5.   Repealed.
714.   Compensation and expenses charged by attorney for safekeeping of documents; lien.
715.   Written notice to depositor; acknowledgement; contents.
716.   Minimal duty of care by attorney; slight care for preservation of documents.
717 to 718.7.   Repealed.
719.   Repealed.

§ 710. Safekeeping of documents; duty of care for preservation

If a document is deposited with an attorney, the attorney, and a successor attorney that accepts transfer of the document, shall use ordinary care for preservation of the document on and after July 1, 1994, whether or not consideration is given, and shall hold the document in a safe, vault, safe deposit box, or other secure place where it will be reasonably protected against loss or destruction. *(Added by Stats.1993, c. 519 (A.B.209), § 4.)*

Law Revision Commission Comments

1993 Addition

Section 710 is new. Under Section 710, an attorney must use ordinary care for preservation of the document deposited. This applies the rule of Civil Code Section 1852 (deposit for hire) to the attorney-depositary, whether or not consideration is given. This is a departure from Civil Code Section 1846, under which a gratuitous depositary need only use slight care for preservation of the property deposited.

The duty imposed by Section 710 to hold the document in a safe, vault, safe deposit box, or other secure place is a reasonable one, and allows reasonable periods for the document to be out of safekeeping for the purpose of examination or delivery in appropriate circumstances. At all times the document should be reasonably protected against loss or destruction, although what is reasonable may vary with the circumstances.

Although Section 710 applies to attorneys who are holding documents on July 1, 1994, an attorney is not liable for action taken before that date that was proper when the action was taken. Section 3.

For an exception to the standard of care provided in Section 710, see Section 716 (slight care after specified steps taken). [23 Cal.L.Rev.Comm. Reports 901 (1993) (Annual Report, App. 7)].

§ 711. Lost or destroyed documents; notice

If a document deposited with an attorney is lost or destroyed, the attorney shall give notice of the loss or destruction to the depositor by one of the following methods:

(a) By mailing the notice to the depositor's last known address.

(b) By the method most likely to give the depositor actual notice. *(Added by Stats.1993, c. 519 (A.B.209), § 4.)*

Law Revision Commission Comments

1993 Addition

Section 711 is new. Even though a will is lost or destroyed, it still may be proven and admitted to probate. See Section 8223. [23 Cal.L.Rev.Comm. Reports 901 (1993) (Annual Report, App. 7)].

Cross References

Notice, mailing, see Probate Code § 1215 et seq.
Notice, this code, generally, see Probate Code § 1200 et seq.

§ 712. Liability for loss or destruction of documents; actual notice by depositor

Notwithstanding failure of an attorney to satisfy the standard of care required by Section 710 or 716, the attorney is not liable for loss or destruction of the document if the depositor has actual notice of the loss or destruction and a reasonable opportunity to replace the document, and the attorney offers without charge either to assist the depositor in replacing the document, or to prepare a substantially similar document and assist in its execution. *(Added by Stats.1993, c. 519 (A.B.209), § 4.)*

Law Revision Commission Comments

1993 Addition

Section 712 is new. Even though a will is lost or destroyed, it still may be proven and admitted to probate. See Section 8223. [23 Cal.L.Rev.Comm. Reports 901 (1993) (Annual Report, App. 7)].

§ 713. Acceptance of documents by attorney; no duty imposed; validity of contents of documents; legal services to depositor

The acceptance by an attorney of a document for deposit imposes no duty on the attorney to do either of the following:

(a) Inquire into the content, validity, invalidity, or completeness of the document, or the correctness of any information in the document.

(b) Provide continuing legal services to the depositor or to any beneficiary under the document. This subdivision does not affect the duty, if any, of the drafter of the document to provide continuing legal services to any person. *(Added by Stats.1993, c. 519 (A.B.209), § 4.)*

Law Revision Commission Comments

1993 Addition

Section 713 is new. Section 713 does not relieve the drafter of the document from the duty of drafting competently. [23 Cal.L.Rev. Comm. Reports 901 (1993) (Annual Report, App. 7)].

Cross References

Beneficiary, defined, see Probate Code § 24

§ 713.5. Repealed by Stats.1987, c. 923, § 37, operative July 1, 1988

Law Revision Commission Comments

1987 Repeal

Former Section 713.5 is replaced by Sections 11444 and 11445 (allocation of debts between estate and surviving spouse). [19 Cal.L.Rev.Comm.Reports 414 (1988)].

§ 714. Compensation and expenses charged by attorney for safekeeping of documents; lien

(a) If so provided in a written agreement signed by the depositor, an attorney may charge the depositor for compensation and expenses incurred in safekeeping or delivery of a document deposited with the attorney.

(b) No lien arises for the benefit of an attorney on a document deposited with the attorney, whether before or after its transfer, even if provided by agreement. *(Added by Stats.1993, c. 519 (A.B.209), § 4.)*

Law Revision Commission Comments

1993 Addition

Section 714 is new. Subdivision (b) is a departure from Civil Code Section 1856 (depositary's lien). [23 Cal.L.Rev.Comm. Reports 901 (1993) (Annual Report, App. 7)].

Cross References

Attorney's fees and costs, action on contract, see Civil Code § 1717.
Attorney's fees and costs, generally, see Code of Civil Procedure § 1021.
Estate attorney, compensation, amount, see Probate Code § 10810 et seq.

§ 715. Written notice to depositor; acknowledgement; contents

An attorney may give written notice to a depositor, and obtain written acknowledgment from the depositor, in the following form:

NOTICE AND ACKNOWLEDGMENT

To: _____
(Name of depositor)

_____
(Address)

_____
(City, state, and ZIP)

99

I have accepted your will or other estate planning document for safekeeping. I must use ordinary care for preservation of the document.

You must keep me advised of any change in your address shown above. If you do not and I cannot return this document to you when necessary, I will no longer be required to use ordinary care for preservation of the document, and I may transfer it to another attorney, or I may transfer it to the clerk of the superior court of the county of your last known domicile, and give notice of the transfer to the State Bar of California.

_____
(Signature of attorney)

_____
(Address of attorney)

_____
(City, state, ZIP)

My address shown above is correct. I understand that I must keep you advised of any change in this address.

Dated: _____

_____
(Signature of depositor)

(Added by Stats.1993, c. 519 (A.B.209), § 4.)

Law Revision Commission Comments

1993 Addition

Section 715 is new. By giving the notice and obtaining the acknowledgment provided by this section, the attorney's duty of care may reduced to slight care if the requirements of Section 716 are satisfied. See also Section 731 (mailing document to depositor's last known address). [23 Cal.L.Rev.Comm. Reports 901 (1993) (Annual Report, App. 7)].

§ 716. Minimal duty of care by attorney; slight care for preservation of documents

Notwithstanding Section 710, if an attorney has given written notice to the depositor, and has obtained written acknowledgment from the depositor, in substantially the form provided in Section 715, and the requirements of subdivision (a) of Section 732 are satisfied, the attorney, and a successor attorney that accepts transfer of a document, shall use at least slight care for preservation of a document deposited with the attorney. *(Added by Stats.1993, c. 519 (A.B.209), § 4.)*

Law Revision Commission Comments

1993 Addition

Section 716 is new. The "slight care" standard of Section 716 is the same as the standard of care of a gratuitous depositary under Civil Code Section 1846. [23 Cal.L.Rev.Comm. Reports 901 (1993) (Annual Report, App. 7)].

Cross References

Attorneys, rules of professional conduct, see California Rules of Professional Conduct, Rule 1–100 et seq.

§§ 717 to 718.7. Repealed by Stats.1987, c. 923, § 37, operative July 1, 1988

Law Revision Commission Comments

1987 Repeal

Former Section 717 is restated in Section 9255 (partial allowance) without substantive change. See also Section 58 ("personal representative" defined). [19 Cal.L.Rev.Comm. Reports 415 (1988)].

The introductory paragraph and paragraph (2) of former Section 718 are restated and generalized in Section 9620 (submission of dispute to temporary judge). See the Comment to Section 9620. Paragraph (1) is omitted as unnecessary, since the general provisions relating to reference are applicable to probate matters. See Code Civ.Proc. §§ 638–645.1. [19 Cal.L.Rev.Comm. Reports 415 (1988)].

Former Section 718.6 is restated in Section 9850 without substantive change, except that (1) Section 9850 requires the petitioner to show the advantage to the estate by clear and convincing evidence and (2) 15 days' notice is required under Section 1220, instead of ten days' notice as required under former Section 1200.5. See also Section 58 ("personal representative" defined). [19 Cal.L.Rev. Comm. Reports 416 (1988)].

Former Section 718.7 is restated in Section 9851 without substantive change, except that 15 days' notice is required under Section 1220, instead of ten days' notice as required under former Section 1200.5. [19 Cal.L.Rev.Comm. Reports 416 (1988)].

§§ 719. Repealed by Stats.1988, c. 1199, § 53, operative July 1, 1989

Law Revision Commission Comments

1988 Repeal

Former Section 719 is not continued. See Prob.Code § 1002 (costs under Probate Code); see also Code Civ.Proc. § 1026 (costs in actions by or against fiduciaries). [19 Cal.L.Rev.Comm. Reports 1066 (1988)].

Former Section 721 is replaced by Sections 550–555 (liability of decedent covered by insurance) and 9390 (claim covered by insurance) [19 Cal.L.Rev.Comm. Reports 1222 (1988)].

CHAPTER 3. TERMINATION OF DEPOSIT

Article	Section
1. Termination by Depositor	720
2. Termination by Attorney	730

ARTICLE 1. TERMINATION BY DEPOSITOR

Section
720. Termination of document deposits by depositor.
721. Repealed.

§ 720. Termination of document deposits by depositor

A depositor may terminate a deposit on demand, in which case the attorney shall deliver the document to the depositor. *(Added by Stats.1993, c. 519 (A.B.209), § 4.)*

Law Revision Commission Comments

1993 Addition

Section 720 is new, and is consistent with Civil Code Section 1822, except that under Section 714 no lien is permitted against the document deposited.

If the depositor has an attorney in fact acting under a statutory form power of attorney that confers general authority with respect to estate transactions, the attorney in fact may terminate the deposit. See Civ. Code § 2493.

If the depositor has a conservator of the estate, the court may order the attorney to deliver the document to the court for examination, and for good cause may order that the document be delivered to some other custodian for safekeeping. Section 2586. [23 Cal.L.Rev.Comm. Reports 901 (1993) (Annual Report, App. 7)].

§§ 721. Repealed by Stats.1988, c. 1199, § 53, operative July 1, 1989

Law Revision Commission Comments

1988 Repeal

Former Section 721 is replaced by Sections 550–555 (liability of decedent covered by insurance) and 9390 (claim covered by insurance) [19 Cal.L.Rev.Comm. Reports 1222 (1988)].

ARTICLE 2. TERMINATION BY ATTORNEY

§ 730. Termination of document deposits by attorney

An attorney with whom a document has been deposited, or to whom a document has been transferred pursuant to this article, may terminate the deposit only as provided in this article. *(Added by Stats.1993, c. 519 (A.B.209), § 4.)*

Law Revision Commission Comments

1993 Addition

Section 730 is new. The methods by which an attorney may terminate a deposit under this article are provided in Sections 731–735. [23 Cal.L.Rev.Comm. Reports 901 (1993) (Annual Report, App. 7)].

§ 731. Methods of termination of document deposits by attorney

An attorney may terminate the deposit by one of the following methods:

(a) Personal delivery of the document to the depositor.

(b) Mailing the document to the depositor's last known address, by registered or certified mail with return receipt requested, and receiving a signed receipt.

(c) The method agreed on by the depositor and attorney. *(Added by Stats.1993, c. 519 (A.B.209), § 4.)*

Law Revision Commission Comments

1993 Addition

Section 731 is new. The depositor's last known address may be shown in a notice and acknowledgment under Section 715, in the depositor's advice of change of address to the attorney, or otherwise.

Section 731 provides some of the ways an attorney may terminate a deposit. An attorney may also terminate a deposit as provided in Section 732 or, if applicable, Section 734. [23 Cal.L.Rev.Comm. Reports 901 (1993) (Annual Report, App. 7)].

Cross References

Mailing requirements, certified mail, see Probate Code § 5.

§ 732. Transfer of documents by attorney

(a) An attorney may terminate a deposit under this section if the attorney has mailed notice to reclaim the document to the depositor's last known address and the depositor has failed to reclaim the document within 90 days after the mailing.

(b) Subject to subdivision (f), an attorney may terminate a deposit under this section by transferring the document to another attorney. All documents transferred under this subdivision shall be transferred to the same attorney.

(c) Subject to subdivision (f), if an attorney is deceased, lacks legal capacity, or is no longer an active member of the State Bar, a deposit may be terminated under this section by transferring the document to the clerk of the superior court of the county of the depositor's last known domicile. The attorney shall advise the clerk that the document is being transferred pursuant to Section 732.

(d) An attorney may not accept a fee or compensation from a transferee for transferring a document under this section. An attorney may charge a fee for receiving a document under this section.

(e) Transfer of a document by an attorney under this section is not a waiver or breach of any privilege or confidentiality associated with the document, and is not a violation of the rules of professional conduct. If the document is privileged under Article 3 (commencing with Section 950) of Chapter 4 of Division 8 of the Evidence Code, the document remains privileged after the transfer.

(f) If the document is a will and the attorney has actual notice that the depositor has died, the attorney may terminate a deposit only as provided in Section 734. *(Added by Stats.1993, c. 519 (A.B.209), § 4.)*

Law Revision Commission Comments

1993 Addition [Revised Comment]

Section 732 is new. The depositor's last known address may be shown in a notice and acknowledgment under Section 715, in the depositor's advice of change of address to the attorney, or otherwise.

Section 732 provides one way an attorney may terminate a deposit. An attorney may also terminate a deposit as provided in Section 731 or, if applicable, Section 734.

By permitting an attorney to transfer a document to another depositary, Section 732 departs from the common law of bailments under which a depositary ordinarily has no authority to transfer the property to someone else. See 8 Am. Jur. 2d *Bailments* § 97 (1980).

Under Section 732, if an attorney transfers estate planning documents to another attorney, all documents must go to the same attorney. Presumably, the transferring attorney will use this procedure at the time the transferring attorney retires or ceases to practice in the estate planning area. See also Bus. & Prof. Code §§ 6180, 6180.1 (notice of cessation of law practice required when attorney goes out of practice).

For the fee to transfer an estate planning document to the superior court clerk under subdivision (c), see Gov't Code § 26827.6. See also Sections 1215–1217 (mailing of notice). [23 Cal.L.Rev.Comm. Reports 989 (1993)].

Cross References

Destruction of court records, notice, retention periods, see Government Code § 68152.

Estate attorney, compensation, amount, see Probate Code § 10810 et seq.

Estate planning documents, storage, and reduction or waiver of fees, see Government Code § 70660.

Transferred documents to the clerk of the superior court,
Reproduction, see Government Code § 26810.
Searching, fees, see Government Code § 26827.7.
Storage fees, see Government Code § 26827.6.

§ 732.5. Repealed by Stats.1982, c. 497, p. 2208, § 142, operative July 1, 1983

§ 733. Notice of transfer of documents; contents

(a) An attorney transferring one or more documents under Section 732 shall mail notice of the transfer to the State Bar of California. The notice shall contain all of the following information:

(1) The name of the depositor.

(2) The date of the transfer.

(3) The name, address, and State Bar number of the transferring attorney.

(4) Whether any documents are transferred to an attorney, and the name, address, and State Bar number of the attorney to whom the documents are transferred.

(5) Whether any documents are transferred to a superior court clerk.

(b) The State Bar shall record only one notice of transfer for each transferring attorney. The State Bar shall prescribe the form for the notice of transfer. On request by any person, the State Bar shall give that person information in the notice of transfer. At its sole election, the State Bar may give the information orally or in writing. *(Added by Stats.1993, c. 519 (A.B.209), § 4.)*

Law Revision Commission Comments

1993 Addition

Section 733 is new. [23 Cal.L.Rev.Comm. Reports 901 (1993) (Annual Report, App. 7)].

Cross References

Transferred documents to the clerk of the superior court,
Reproduction, see Government Code § 26810.
Searching, fees, see Government Code § 26827.7.
Storage fees, see Government Code § 26827.6.

§ 734. Death of depositor; termination of document deposits by attorney

(a) In cases not governed by subdivision (b) or (c), after the death of the depositor an attorney may terminate a deposit by personal delivery of the document to the depositor's personal representative.

(b) If the document is a will and the attorney has actual notice that the depositor has died but does not have actual notice that a personal representative has been appointed for the depositor, an attorney may terminate a deposit only as provided in Section 8200.

(c) If the document is a trust, after the death of the depositor an attorney may terminate a deposit by personal delivery of the document either to the depositor's personal representative or to the trustee named in the document. *(Added by Stats.1993, c. 519 (A.B.209), § 4.)*

Law Revision Commission Comments

1993 Addition

Section 734 is new. Subdivisions (a) and (c) are permissive, but subdivision (b) is mandatory. If subdivision (b) does not apply, an attorney may terminate a deposit, for example, by the method agreed on by the depositor and attorney. Section 731.

As used in Section 734, "personal representative" includes a successor personal representative and a personal representative appointed in another state. Section 58. "Trustee" includes a successor trustee (Section 84), and "will" includes a codicil (Section 88). [23 Cal.L.Rev.Comm. Reports 901 (1993) (Annual Report, App. 7)].

Cross References

Destruction of court records, notice, retention periods, see Government Code § 68152.

Personal representative and general personal representative, defined, see Probate Code § 58.

Transferred documents to the clerk of the superior court,
Reproduction, see Government Code § 26810.
Searching, fees, see Government Code § 26827.7.
Storage fees, see Government Code § 26827.6.

Trust administration, see Probate Code § 16000 et seq.

§ 735. Death or lack of legal capacity of attorney; termination of document deposits

(a) If the attorney is deceased or lacks legal capacity, a deposit may be terminated as provided in this article by the attorney's law partner, by a shareholder of the attorney's law corporation, or by a lawyer or nonlawyer employee of the attorney's firm, partnership, or corporation.

(b) If the attorney lacks legal capacity and there is no person to act under subdivision (a), a deposit may be terminated by the conservator of the attorney's estate or by an attorney in fact acting under a durable power of attorney. A conservator of the attorney's estate may act without court approval.

(c) If the attorney is deceased and there is no person to act under subdivision (a), a deposit may be terminated by the attorney's personal representative.

(d) If a person authorized under this section terminates a deposit as provided in Section 732, the person shall give the notice required by Section 733. *(Added by Stats.1993, c. 519 (A.B.209), § 4.)*

Law Revision Commission Comments

1993 Addition

Section 735 is new. [23 Cal.L.Rev.Comm. Reports 901 (1993) (Annual Report, App. 7)].

Cross References

Personal representative and general personal representative, defined, see Probate Code § 58.

Transferred documents to the clerk of the superior court,
Reproduction, see Government Code § 26810.
Searching, fees, see Government Code § 26827.7.
Storage fees, see Government Code § 26827.6.

§ 736. Repealed by Stats.1988, c. 1199, § 53, operative July 1, 1989

Law Revision Commission Comments

1988 Repeal

Former Section 736 is restated in Sections 21400 (abatement subject to transferor's intent) and 21404 (exoneration by abatement of specific gift), which generalize it to apply to exoneration of personal as well as real property and to apply to other gifts as well as devises [19 Cal.L.Rev.Comm. Reports 1067 (1988)].

§§ 737, 738. Repealed by Stats.1987, c. 923, § 37, operative July 1, 1988

Law Revision Commission Comments

1987 Repeal

Former Section 737 is restated in Section 9604 without substantive change. See also Section 58 ("personal representative" defined). [19 Cal.L.Rev.Comm.Reports 418 (1988)].

Former Section 738 is restated in Section 11428 (deposit for missing creditor) without substantive change. See also Section 58 ("personal representative" defined). [19 Cal.L.Rev.Comm.Reports 418 (1988)].

§ 739. Repealed by Stats.1953, c. 1758, p. 3517, § 2

§§ 750 to 753. Repealed by Stats.1988, c. 1199, § 53.5, operative July 1, 1989

Law Revision Commission Comments

1988 Repeal

The first sentence of former Section 750 is restated in Sections 21400 (abatement subject to transferor's intent) and 21401 (purposes for which abatement made), which generalize it to apply to other gifts as well as devises. The second sentence is restated in Sections 21400 (abatement subject to transferor's intent) and 21402 (order of abatement), which generalize it to apply to other gifts as well as devises [19 Cal.L.Rev.Comm. Reports 1067 (1988)].

Former Section 751 is restated in Sections 21401 (purposes for which abatement made) and 21402 (order of abatement), which generalize it to apply to other gifts as well as devises [19 Cal.L.Rev. Comm. Reports 1067 (1988)].

Former Section 752 is superseded by Sections 21400 (abatement subject to transferor's intent) and 21402 (order of abatement) [19 Cal.L.Rev.Comm. Reports 1067 (1988)].

The first part of former Section 753 (if preferred devise sold, all others must contribute) is superseded by subdivision (a) of Section 21403 (abatement within classes). The last part of former Section 753 (court to decree each person's contribution when distribution is made) is restated in subdivision (b) of Section 21405 (contribution in case of abatement) without substantive change [19 Cal.L.Rev.Comm. Reports 1067 (1988)].

§§ 754 to 789. Repealed by Stats.1987, c. 923, § 39, operative July 1, 1988

Law Revision Commission Comments

1987 Repeal

The first sentence of former Section 754 is restated in Section 10003(a) without substantive change. See the Comment to Section 10003. The second sentence is restated in Section 10000(a)–(b) and in Section 10003(a) and (c) without substantive change. See the Comment to Section 10000. The last sentence is restated in Section 10003(b) without substantive change. [19 Cal.L.Rev.Comm. Reports 419 (1988)].

Former Section 754.5 is restated in Section 10004 without substantive change, except that the property may be sold if it is to the advantage, rather than in the best interests, of the estate as provided in Section 10004(b). See also Section 58 ("personal representative" defined). [19 Cal.L.Rev.Comm. Reports 419 (1988)].

Former Section 754.6 is restated in Section 10203 without substantive change. [19 Cal.L.Rev.Comm. Reports 420 (1988)].

Former Section 755 is restated in Sections 10260 (personal property) and 10308 (real property) without substantive change, except that (1) the new sections give the purchaser the right to file the report of sale and petition for confirmation, if the personal representative fails to do so within 30 days after the sale, and (2) notice of hearing must be mailed and posted 15 days before the hearing pursuant to Sections 1220 and 1230 instead of 10 days as provided by former Sections 1200 and 1200.5. The provision requiring the petition to be verified is generalized in Section 1284. The provision requiring the clerk to set the petition for hearing is generalized in Section 1285. [19 Cal.L.Rev.Comm. Reports 420 (1988)].

The first sentence of former Section 756 is restated in Sections 10261(b) (personal property) and 10310(c) (real property) without substantive change. The last sentence is restated in Sections 10263 (personal property) and 10312 (real property) without substantive change. [19 Cal.L.Rev.Comm. Reports 420 (1988)].

Former Section 756.5 is restated in Section 10262 without substantive change, except that Section 10262 permits an overbid where the original bid is less than $100 and the overbid is not less than $100 more than the original bid. [19 Cal.L.Rev.Comm. Reports 420 (1988)].

The first sentence of former Section 757 is restated without substantive change in Sections 10000(c)–(d) and 10003(c), in Section 10303 (real property), and in the introductory clause and subdivisions (a) and (b) of Section 10252 (personal property).

The second sentence is restated without substantive change in Section 10260(a) and the second sentence of subdivision (a) of Section 10261 (personal property) and in Section 10308(a), the second sentence of subdivision (a) of Section 10310, and Section 10313(a)(1) (real property).

The last sentence is restated in Section 10002(a) without substantive change. See also Section 58 ("personal representative" defined). [19 Cal.L.Rev.Comm. Reports 420 (1988)].

Former Section 758 is replaced by Section 10001. See the Comment to Section 10001. The provision in the last sentence requiring the clerk to set the petition for hearing is generalized in Section 1285. See also Section 58 ("personal representative" defined). [19 Cal.L.Rev.Comm. Reports 421 (1988)].

Former Section 759 is restated in Section 10380 without substantive change. See the Comment to Section 10380.

See also Section 58 ("personal representative" defined). [19 Cal.L.Rev.Comm. Reports 421 (1988)].

The first, third, fourth, and last sentences of former Section 760 are restated in Sections 10150 and 10161(a) without substantive change, except that the reference in former Section 760 to a "multiple group of agents or brokers" is replaced by the last sentence of subdivision (a)(1) of Section 10150 (multiple listing service).

The second sentence is replaced by Section 10164(c). See the Comment to Section 10164.

See also Section 58 ("personal representative" defined). [19 Cal.L.Rev.Comm. Reports 421 (1988)].

The first sentence of former Section 760.5 is replaced by Section 10151(a). See the Comment to Section 10151. The second and third sentences are restated in Section 10151(c) without substantive change. The fourth, fifth, sixth, and last sentences are restated in Section 10151(d), but the reference to "tangible" personal property is omitted. See the Comment to Section 10151. See also Section 58 ("personal representative" defined). [19 Cal.L.Rev.Comm. Reports 421 (1988)].

The first part of the first sentence of former Section 761 (commission on full amount for which sale is confirmed) is restated in Section 10165(b) without substantive change. The last part of the first sentence (allocation of commission) is restated by Section 10165(b)–(c) without substantive change. The last sentence is restated in Section 10164(a)–(b) without substantive change. [19 Cal.L.Rev.Comm. Reports 422 (1988)].

Former Section 761.5 is restated in Sections 10161(a) and 10163 without substantive change. [19 Cal.L.Rev.Comm. Reports 422 (1988)].

Former Section 762 is restated in Section 10361 without substantive change, except as noted in the Comment to Section 10361. [19 Cal.L.Rev.Comm. Reports 422 (1988)].

Former Section 763 is restated in Section 10362 without substantive change. See also Section 58 ("personal representative" defined). [19 Cal.L.Rev.Comm. Reports 422 (1988)].

Former Section 764 is restated in Section 10363 without substantive change, except as noted in the Comment to Section 10363. See also section 58 ("personal representative" defined). [19 Cal.L.Rev. Comm. Reports 422 (1988)].

Former Section 770 is restated in the introductory clause and subdivisions (c) and (d) of Section 10252 and in Section 10259 without substantive change. See also Section 58 ("personal representative" defined). [19 Cal.L.Rev.Comm. Reports 422 (1988)].

Subdivisions (a) and (b) of former Section 771 are restated in Section 10200 without substantive change, except that notice of hearing must be mailed and posted 15 days before the hearing pursuant to Sections 1220 and 1230 instead of 10 days as provided by former Sections 1200 and 1200.5. The provision in the third sentence of subdivision (a) permitting the court to shorten the period of notice is generalized in Section 1203 and the provision permitting the court to dispense with notice is generalized in Section 1220(e). Subdivision (c) is restated in Section 10201 without substantive change. See also Section 58 ("personal representative" defined). [19 Cal.L.Rev.Comm. Reports 423 (1988)].

The first, third, and last sentences of former Section 771.3 are restated in Section 9735 without substantive change, except that 15 days' notice is required under Section 1220, instead of ten days' notice as required under former Section 1200.5. The provision in the second sentence requiring the clerk to set the petition for hearing is generalized in Section 1285. The provision in the third sentence of subdivision (a) permitting the court to shorten the period of notice is generalized in Section 1203 and the provision permitting the court to dispense with notice is generalized in Section 1220(e). See also Section 58 ("personal representative" defined). [19 Cal.L.Rev. Comm. Reports 423 (1988)].

Former Section 771.5 is restated in Section 10202 without substantive change, except that language is added in Section 10202 to make clear that notice of sale is not required and that confirmation of sale is not required. See also Sections 58 ("personal representative" defined), 70 ("security" defined). [19 Cal.L.Rev.Comm. Reports 423 (1988)].

The first sentence of former Section 772 is restated in Section 10250 without substantive change, except that the 10 day notice period is increased to 15 days. The second sentence is restated in Section 10251 without substantive change. The third sentence is restated in Section 10253(a) without substantive change. The fourth sentence is restated without substantive change in Sections 10253(a)(2) and 10255(a). The fifth, sixth, and seventh sentences are restated in Section 10254(c) without substantive change, except as noted in the Comment to Section 10254. The last sentence is restated in Section 10259 without substantive change. See also Section 58 ("personal representative" defined). [19 Cal.L.Rev. Comm. Reports 423 (1988)].

The first four sentences of former Section 773 are restated in Section 10257(a)–(c) without substantive change. See the Comment to Section 10257.

The fifth through the last sentences are restated in Section 10258 without substantive change, except that notice of hearing must be mailed and posted 15 days before the hearing pursuant to Sections 1220 and 1230 instead of 10 days as provided by former Sections 1200 and 1200.5. The provision requiring the clerk to set the petition for hearing is generalized in Section 1285.

See also Section 58 ("personal representative" defined). [19 Cal.L.Rev.Comm. Reports 424 (1988)].

The first sentence of former Section 774 is restated in Sections 10204 and 10205 without substantive change. The last sentence is restated in Section 10261(c) without substantive change, except as noted in the Comment to Section 10261(c). [19 Cal.L.Rev.Comm. Reports 424 (1988)].

The first sentence of former Section 775 is restated in Section 10350(a)–(b) without substantive change. The second and third sentences are replaced by Section 10350(c)–(d). The last sentence is replaced by Section 10350(e). See the Comment to Section 10350. See also Section 58 ("personal representative" defined). [19 Cal. L.Rev.Comm. Reports 424 (1988)].

Former Section 776 is restated in Section 10351 without substantive change. See also Section 10350(b). [19 Cal.L.Rev.Comm. Reports 424 (1988)].

The first sentence of former Section 780 is restated in Section 10300 without substantive change, except that the requirement that the notice state the "time and place of sale" is restated in Section 10304(a)(2) without substantive change. The second sentence is restated in Section 10301 without substantive change, except that (1) the maximum value of real property that may be sold without publication is increased from $1,000 to $5,000 and (2) the notice period is increased from 10 to 15 days. The third and last sentences are replaced by Section 10304(a)(3). See also Section 58 ("personal representative" defined). [19 Cal.L.Rev.Comm. Reports 425 (1988)].

The first sentence of former Section 781 is restated in Section 10305(a) without substantive change. The last sentence is restated in Section 10305(b) without substantive change, except that the closing time of the sale is changed from sunset to 9:00 p.m. [19 Cal.L.Rev. Comm. Reports 425 (1988)].

The first sentence of former Section 782 is restated in Sections 10302, 10304(a)(2), and 10306(a) without substantive change, except that the one-week period is changed to five days. The provision that notice should also be given "otherwise in accordance with Section 780 of this code" is omitted as unnecessary. The last sentence is restated in Section 10306(b) without substantive change, except that the authority for filing bids with the court clerk is omitted. See also Section 58 ("personal representative" defined). [19 Cal.L.Rev. Comm. Reports 425 (1988)].

Former Section 783 is restated in Section 10305(c) without substantive change. See also Section 58 ("personal representative" defined). [19 Cal.L.Rev.Comm. Reports 425 (1988)].

Former Section 784 is restated in Section 10309 without substantive change, except that Section 10309(1) requires the appraisal and valuation to be made within one year of the confirmation hearing rather than the date of sale and (2) permits appointment of a new probate referee if "there is other reason to appoint another probate referee" in place of the former language permitting appointment of a new probate referee "for just cause." [19 Cal.L.Rev.Comm. Reports 425 (1988)].

The first sentence of former Section 785 is replaced by Sections 10310(a)–(b) and 10313(a) and (c)–(d). See the Comments to Sections 10310 and 10313. The second and third sentences are restated without substantive change in Sections 10161, 10311(a)–(c), and 10313(a)–(b). The fourth sentence is replaced by Section 10162. See the Comment to Section 10162. The fifth sentence is restated in Section 10311(e) without substantive change. The sixth sentence is restated in Section 10166 and 10311(e) without substantive change. The last sentence is restated without substantive change in the introductory clause of subdivision (a) and subdivision (d) of Section

10311. See also Section 58 ("personal representative" defined). [19 Cal.L.Rev.Comm. Reports 426 (1988)].

Former Section 785.1 is restated in Section 10311(d) without substantive change. [19 Cal.L.Rev.Comm. Reports 426 (1988)].

The first sentence of former Section 786 is restated in Section 10314(a) without substantive change. The last sentence is restated in Section 10314(c) without substantive change. See the Comment to Section 10314(c). See also Section 58 ("personal representative" defined). [19 Cal.L.Rev.Comm. Reports 426 (1988)].

The first sentence of former Section 787 is restated in subdivision (a) of Section 10315 (real property) without substantive change. The second and last sentences are restated in subdivision (d) of Section 10257 (personal property) and in subdivision (b) of Section 10315 (real property). See also Section 58 ("personal representative" defined). [19 Cal.L.Rev.Comm. Reports 426 (1988)].

The first and second sentences of former Section 788 are restated in Section 10350(a)–(d) without substantive change, except that notice need not be given to a defaulting purchaser who has filed a written consent to vacation of the order confirming sale under Section 10350(b). The last sentence is replaced by Section 10350(e). See the Comment to Section 10350. See also Section 58 ("personal representative" defined). [19 Cal.L.Rev.Comm. Reports 427 (1988)].

Former Section 789 is restated in Section 10351 without substantive change. See also Section 10350(b). [19 Cal.L.Rev.Comm. Reports 427 (1988)].

§§ 790 to 791. Repealed by Stats.1935, c. 128, p. 479, § 4

§§ 792 to 794. Repealed by Stats.1987, c. 923, § 39, operative July 1, 1988

Law Revision Commission Comments

1987 Repeal

Former Section 792 is restated in Section 10381 without substantive change, except (1) damages are double the value of the "real property" sold rather than double the value of the "land" sold, (2) language is added to make clear that damages are computed using the value of the property on the date it was sold, and (3) the new section makes clear that the liquidated damages provided for in the section are in addition to any other recoverable damages. See also Section 58 ("personal representative" defined). [19 Cal.L.Rev. Comm. Reports 427 (1988)].

The first sentence of former Section 793 is restated in Section 10382(a) without substantive change. The last sentence providing for tolling for minors and others under legal disability is replaced by Section 10382(b) which provides that the limitations period is not tolled. See also Section 58 ("personal representative" defined). [19 Cal.L.Rev.Comm. Reports 427 (1988)].

Subdivision (a) of former Section 794 (finding and declaration of legislative purpose) is omitted as a codified provision, but may be found in 1978 Cal.Stat. ch. 40. Subdivision (b) is restated in Section 10207 without substantive change, except that 15 days' notice is required under Section 1220, instead of ten days, notice as required under former Section 1200.5. See also Section 58 ("personal representative" defined). [19 Cal.L.Rev.Comm. Reports 427 (1988)].

Part 16

JURISDICTION

Cross References

Trusts, judicial proceedings, generally, see Probate Code § 17000 et seq.

§ 800. General jurisdiction; power and authority

The court in proceedings under this code is a court of general jurisdiction and the court, or a judge of the court, has the same power and authority with respect to the proceedings as otherwise provided by law for a superior court, or a judge of the superior court, including, but not limited to, the matters authorized by Section 128 of the Code of Civil Procedure. *(Added by Stats.1994, c. 806 (A.B.3686), § 4.)*

Cross References

Trusts, judicial proceedings, generally, see Probate Code § 17000 et seq.

§ 801. Severed actions; determination by court; transfer

The court, on its own motion or on the motion of any interested party, may order that an action or proceeding not specifically provided in this code be determined in a separate civil action. Upon the payment of the appropriate filing fees, the court may order transfer of the severed action or proceeding to the separate civil action. *(Added by Stats.1996, c. 862 (A.B.2751), § 2.)*

Cross References

Interested person, defined, see Probate Code § 48.

§ 802. Repealed by Stats.1987, c. 923, § 39, operative July 1, 1988

Law Revision Commission Comments

1987 Repeal

Former Section 802 is restated in Section 10314(b) and (d) without substantive change. See also Section 58 ("personal representative" defined). [19 Cal.L.Rev.Comm. Reports 428 (1988)].

Part 17

LEGAL MENTAL CAPACITY

§ 810. Findings and declarations; capabilities of persons with mental or physical disorders; judicial determination; evidence

The Legislature finds and declares the following:

(a) For purposes of this part, there shall exist a rebuttable presumption affecting the burden of proof that all persons have the capacity to make decisions and to be responsible for their acts or decisions.

(b) A person who has a mental or physical disorder may still be capable of contracting, conveying, marrying, making medical decisions, executing wills or trusts, and performing other actions.

(c) A judicial determination that a person is totally without understanding, or is of unsound mind, or suffers from one or more mental deficits so substantial that, under the circumstances, the person should be deemed to lack the legal capacity to perform a specific act, should be based on evidence of a deficit in one or more of the person's mental functions rather than on a diagnosis of a person's mental or physical disorder. *(Added by Stats.1995, c. 842 (S.B.730), § 2. Amended by Stats.1998, c. 581 (A.B.2801), § 19.)*

Cross References

Burden of proof, generally, see Evidence Code § 500 et seq.
Presumptions, see Evidence Code § 600 et seq.
Statutes, construction and legislative intent, see Code of Civil Procedure §§ 1858 and 1859.

§ 811. Deficits in mental functions

(a) A determination that a person is of unsound mind or lacks the capacity to make a decision or do a certain act, including, but not limited to, the incapacity to contract, to make a conveyance, to marry, to make medical decisions, to execute wills, or to execute trusts, shall be supported by evidence of a deficit in at least one of the following mental functions, subject to subdivision (b), and evidence of a correlation between the deficit or deficits and the decision or acts in question:

(1) Alertness and attention, including, but not limited to, the following:

(A) Level of arousal or consciousness.

(B) Orientation to time, place, person, and situation.

(C) Ability to attend and concentrate.

(2) Information processing, including, but not limited to, the following:

(A) Short- and long-term memory, including immediate recall.

(B) Ability to understand or communicate with others, either verbally or otherwise.

(C) Recognition of familiar objects and familiar persons.

(D) Ability to understand and appreciate quantities.

(E) Ability to reason using abstract concepts.

(F) Ability to plan, organize, and carry out actions in one's own rational self-interest.

(G) Ability to reason logically.

(3) Thought processes. Deficits in these functions may be demonstrated by the presence of the following:

(A) Severely disorganized thinking.

(B) Hallucinations.

(C) Delusions.

(D) Uncontrollable, repetitive, or intrusive thoughts.

(4) Ability to modulate mood and affect. Deficits in this ability may be demonstrated by the presence of a pervasive and persistent or recurrent state of euphoria, anger, anxiety, fear, panic, depression, hopelessness or despair, helplessness, apathy or indifference, that is inappropriate in degree to the individual's circumstances.

(b) A deficit in the mental functions listed above may be considered only if the deficit, by itself or in combination with one or more other mental function deficits, significantly impairs the person's ability to understand and appreciate the consequences of his or her actions with regard to the type of act or decision in question.

(c) In determining whether a person suffers from a deficit in mental function so substantial that the person lacks the capacity to do a certain act, the court may take into consideration the frequency, severity, and duration of periods of impairment.

(d) The mere diagnosis of a mental or physical disorder shall not be sufficient in and of itself to support a determination that a person is of unsound mind or lacks the capacity to do a certain act.

(e) This part applies only to the evidence that is presented to, and the findings that are made by, a court determining the capacity of a person to do a certain act or make a decision, including, but not limited to, making medical decisions. Nothing in this part shall affect the decisionmaking process set forth in Section 1418.8 of the Health and Safety Code, nor increase or decrease the burdens of documentation on, or potential liability of, health care providers who, outside the judicial context, determine the capacity of patients to make a medical decision. *(Added by Stats.1996, c. 178 (S.B.1650), § 3. Amended by Stats.1998, c. 581 (A.B.2801), § 20.)*

Cross References

Capacity determinations, generally, see Probate Code § 3200 et seq.
Powers and duties of guardian or conservator of the person, dementia, placement in secured facility, see Probate Code § 2356.5.

§ 812. Capacity to make decisions

Except where otherwise provided by law, including, but not limited to, Section 813 and the statutory and decisional law of testamentary capacity, a person lacks the capacity to make a decision unless the person has the ability to communicate verbally, or by any other means, the decision, and to understand and appreciate, to the extent relevant, all of the following:

(a) The rights, duties, and responsibilities created by, or affected by the decision.

(b) The probable consequences for the decisionmaker and, where appropriate, the persons affected by the decision.

(c) The significant risks, benefits, and reasonable alternatives involved in the decision. *(Added by Stats.1996, c. 178 (S.B.1650), § 5.)*

Cross References

Capacity determinations, generally, see Probate Code § 3200 et seq.
Estates of persons with a disability, orders or judgments with respect to adults who have capacity to consent, see Probate Code § 3613.

§ 813. Capacity to give informed consent to proposed medical treatment; judicial determination

(a) For purposes of a judicial determination, a person has the capacity to give informed consent to a proposed medical treatment if the person is able to do all of the following:

(1) Respond knowingly and intelligently to queries about that medical treatment.

(2) Participate in that treatment decision by means of a rational thought process.

(3) Understand all of the following items of minimum basic medical treatment information with respect to that treatment:

(A) The nature and seriousness of the illness, disorder, or defect that the person has.

(B) The nature of the medical treatment that is being recommended by the person's health care providers.

(C) The probable degree and duration of any benefits and risks of any medical intervention that is being recommended by the person's health care providers, and the consequences of lack of treatment.

(D) The nature, risks, and benefits of any reasonable alternatives.

(b) A person who has the capacity to give informed consent to a proposed medical treatment also has the capacity to refuse consent to that treatment. *(Added by Stats.1995, c. 842 (S.B.730), § 5. Amended by Stats.1996, c. 178 (S.B.1650), § 6.)*

Cross References

Capacity determinations, generally, see Probate Code § 3200 et seq.
Health care decisions, generally, see Probate Code § 4600 et seq.

§ 814. Repealed by Stats.1996, c. 178 (S.B.1650), § 7

Part 18

RIGHT TO TRIAL

§ 825. No general right to jury trial

Except as otherwise expressly provided in this code, there is no right to a jury trial in proceedings under this code. *(Added by Stats.1999, c. 175 (A.B.239), § 1.)*

Cross References

Jury trial,
Contests of wills, see Probate Code §§ 8252, 8271, 8272.
Determination of persons entitled to distribution, see Probate Code §§ 11704, 11705.

§§ 830 to 845. Repealed by Stats.1987, c. 923, § 41, operative July 1, 1988

Law Revision Commission Comments

1987 Repeal

The first sentence of former Section 830 is restated in Sections 9800(a) and 9804(a). The provision that the court may make an order "as often as occasion therefor shall arise in the administration of the estate" is omitted as unnecessary. There is no limit on the number of times that the court may be petitioned.

The second sentence is restated in Section 9801 without substantive change. The last sentence is restated in Section 9800(a) without substantive change. See also Section 58 ("personal representative" defined). [19 Cal.L.Rev.Comm. Reports 429 (1988)].

The first sentence of former Section 831 is restated in Section 9802 without substantive change. The provision requiring the petition to be verified is generalized in Section 1284. The first part of the last sentence requiring the clerk to set the petition for hearing is generalized in Section 1285. The last part of the last sentence is restated in Section 9803 without substantive change, except that 15 days' notice is required under Section 1220, instead of ten days' notice as required under former Section 1200.5. See also Section 58 ("personal representative" defined). [19 Cal.L.Rev.Comm. Reports 429 (1988)].

The first and second sentences of former Section 832 are restated in Section 9804 without substantive change, except that the former provision that the court "may direct in what coin or currency" the loan shall be paid has been omitted as obsolete. This omission is consistent with the 1982 amendment to Section 667 of the Code of Civil Procedure. See 1982 Cal.Stat. ch. 497, § 7. See also Code Civ.Proc. § 577.5 (judgment stated in dollars and cents). The provision in the first sentence relating to proof of notice is generalized in Section 1260. See also Section 58 ("personal representative" defined).

The last sentence of former Section 832 (recording required of certified copy of order) is restated in Section 1292 without substantive change. [19 Cal.L.Rev.Comm. Reports 430 (1988)].

Former Section 833 is restated in Section 9805 without substantive change, except that Section 9805 is broadened to apply to an instrument creating a security interest in personal property as well as to a mortgage or deed of trust of real property. See also Section 58 ("personal representative" defined). [19 Cal.L.Rev.Comm. Reports 430 (1988)].

The first and second sentences and the first part of the last sentence of former Section 834 are restated in Section 9806 without substantive change. The last part of the last sentence is restated in Section 9807 without substantive change. [19 Cal.L.Rev.Comm. Reports 430 (1988)].

Former Section 840 is restated in Section 9942(a) without substantive change. The provision that the court may make an order "as often as occasion therefor shall arise in the administration of the estate" is omitted as unnecessary. There is no limit on the number of times that the court may be petitioned. See also Section 58 ("personal representative" defined). [19 Cal.L.Rev.Comm. Reports 430 (1988)].

The first sentence of former Section 841 is restated in Section 9943(a) without substantive change. The provision in the first sentence requiring the petition to be verified is generalized in Section 1284. The first part of the second sentence requiring the clerk to set the petition for hearing is generalized in Section 1285. The last part of the second sentence and all of the last sentence are replaced by Section 9944(a)–(b). See the Comment to Section 9944. Fifteen days' notice is required under Sections 1220 and 1230, instead of ten days' notice as required under former Sections 1200 and 1200.5. See also Section 58 ("personal representative" defined). [19 Cal.L.Rev. Comm. Reports 431 (1988)].

The first sentence of former Section 842 is restated in Section 9945 without substantive change. The second sentence is restated in Sections 9946(a) and 9947(b) without substantive change, except that the former provision permitting the court to authorize a lease longer than 10 years for the growing of asparagus is replaced by Section 9946(a) (no lease longer than 10 years if heir or devisee having interest in property objects). The third sentence is restated in Section 9946(b) without substantive change. The fourth sentence is restated in Section 9946(c) without substantive change. The fifth sentence is restated in Section 9947(c) without substantive change. The last sentence is restated in Section 1292 without substantive change. See also Section 58 ("personal representative" defined). [19 Cal.L.Rev.Comm. Reports 431 (1988)].

The first sentence of former Section 842.1 is restated in Sections 9943(b) and 9945(b) without substantive change. The provision in the first sentence requiring the petition to be verified is generalized in Section 1284.

The second sentence is restated in Section 9944(c) without substantive change. The 20–day notice period in the second sentence is changed to 15 days to conform to the general notice period provided in Section 1220. The authority in the second sentence for the court to require additional notice is continued in the general authority for the court to require additional notice in Section 1202.

The last sentence is restated in Section 9947(b) without substantive change. See also Section 34 ("devisee" defined). [19 Cal.L.Rev. Comm. Reports 431 (1988)].

Former Section 843 is restated in Section 9948 without substantive change. See also Section 58 ("personal representative" defined). [19 Cal.L.Rev.Comm. Reports 432 (1988)].

Former Section 844 is replaced by Section 9941. See the Comment to Section 9941. [19 Cal.L.Rev.Comm. Reports 434 (1988)].

The first part of former Section 845 is restated in Section 9940(a) without substantive change. The last part is restated in Section 9942(b) without substantive change. [19 Cal.L.Rev.Comm. Reports 434 (1988)].

Part 19

CONVEYANCE OR TRANSFER OF PROPERTY CLAIMED TO BELONG TO DECEDENT OR OTHER PERSON

Cross References

Appeals, grounds for appeal, adjudicating merits of claim made under this part, see Probate Code § 1300.

Distribution of estate, partition or allotment of property, objection to jurisdiction to be made in manner prescribed in this Part, see Probate Code § 11952.

Inventory and appraisal, disagreement among personal representatives as to inventory, specified determinations to be made pursuant to this Part, see Probate Code § 8852.

Purchase of claims or estate property by personal representative or personal representative's attorney, purchases pursuant to contract, see Probate Code § 9884.

Trusts, judicial proceedings concerning trusts, see Probate Code § 17200 et seq.

§ 850. Petitions for court orders

(a) The following persons may file a petition requesting that the court make an order under this part:

(1) A guardian, conservator, or any claimant, in the following cases:

(A) Where the conservatee is bound by a contract in writing to convey real property or to transfer personal property, executed by the conservatee while competent or executed by the conservatee's predecessor in interest, and the contract is one that can be specifically enforced.

(B) Where the minor has succeeded to the interest of a person bound by a contract in writing to convey real property or to transfer personal property, and the contract is one that can be specifically enforced.

(C) Where the guardian or conservator or the minor or conservatee is in possession of, or holds title to, real or personal property, and the property or some interest therein is claimed to belong to another.

(D) Where the minor or conservatee has a claim to real or personal property title to or possession of which is held by another.

(2) The personal representative or any interested person in any of the following cases:

(A) Where the decedent while living is bound by a contract in writing to convey real property or to transfer personal property and dies before making the conveyance or transfer and the decedent, if living, could have been compelled to make the conveyance or transfer.

(B) Where the decedent while living binds himself or herself or his or her personal representative by a contract in writing to convey real property or to transfer personal property upon or after his or her death and the contract is one which can be specifically enforced.

(C) Where the decedent died in possession of, or holding title to, real or personal property, and the property or some interest therein is claimed to belong to another.

(D) Where the decedent died having a claim to real or personal property, title to or possession of which is held by another.

(3) The trustee or any interested person in any of the following cases:

(A) Where the trustee is in possession of, or holds title to, real or personal property, and the property, or some interest, is claimed to belong to another.

(B) Where the trustee has a claim to real or personal property, title to or possession of which is held by another.

(C) Where the property of the trust is claimed to be subject to a creditor of the settlor of the trust.

(b) The petition shall set forth facts upon which the claim is based. *(Added by Stats.2001, c. 49 (S.B.669), § 1.)*

Cross References

Construction of wills, trusts, and other instruments, see Probate Code § 21101 et seq.

Contracts,
　Generally, see Civil Code § 1549 et seq.
　Necessity of writing, see Civil Code §§ 1091, 1624.
Fraudulent instruments and transfers, see Civil Code § 3439 et seq.
Interested person, defined, see Probate Code § 48.
Interests in property, see Civil Code § 678 et seq.
No-contest clause, see Probate Code § 21300 et seq.
Orders with respect to real estate, see Probate Code § 7263.
Ownership of property, see Civil Code §§ 654, 669 et seq.
Personal representative and general personal representative, defined, see Probate Code § 58.
Possession of real or personal property, see Civil Code §§ 3375, 3379, 3380.
Real property, defined, see Probate Code § 68.
Recovery of real or personal property, see Civil Code § 3375 et seq.
Sale of contract to purchase, generally, see Probate Code §§ 10206, 10314.
Sale of real property by executor or administrator, see Probate Code § 10300 et seq.
Specific performance, generally, see Civil Code § 3384 et seq.
Transfers,
　Generally, see Civil Code § 1039 et seq.
　Defined, see Civil Code § 3439.01.
　Personal property, see Commercial Code §§ 2101 et seq., 2401 et seq.
　Real property, see Civil Code § 1091 et seq.
Trusts, judicial proceedings, generally, see Probate Code § 17000 et seq.
Trusts, judicial proceedings, rights of third persons, see Probate Code § 18000 et seq.

§ 851.　Notice of hearing

(a) At least 30 days prior to the day of the hearing, the petitioner shall cause notice of the hearing and a copy of the petition to be served in the manner provided in Chapter 4 (commencing with Section 413.10) of Title 5 of Part 2 of the Code of Civil Procedure on all of the following persons where applicable:

(1) The personal representative, conservator, guardian, or trustee as appropriate.

(2) Each person claiming an interest in, or having title to or possession of, the property.

(b) Except for those persons given notice pursuant to subdivision (a), notice of the hearing, together with a copy of the petition, shall be given as provided in Section 1220 if the matter concerns a decedent estate, as provided in Section 1460 if the matter concerns a conservatorship or guardianship, or as provided in Section 17203 if the matter concerns a trust to all of the following persons:

(1) Each person listed in Section 1220 along with any heir or devisee whose interest in the property may be affected by the petition if the matter concerns a decedent estate.

(2) Each person listed in Section 1460 if the matter concerns a conservatorship or guardianship.

(3) Each person listed in Section 17203 if the matter concerns a trust.

(c) The court may not shorten the time for giving the notice of hearing under this section. *(Added by Stats.2001, c. 49 (S.B.669), § 1.)*

Cross References

Computation of time, see Code of Civil Procedure §§ 12 and 12a; Government Code § 6800 et seq.

Devisee, defined, see Probate Code § 34.
Estate administration, generally, see Probate Code § 7000 et seq.
Estate administration, sales, see Probate Code § 10000 et seq.
Heir, defined, see Probate Code § 44.
Personal representative and general personal representative, defined, see Probate Code § 58.
Request for special notice, see Probate Code § 2700 et seq.
Trusts, judicial proceedings, generally, see Probate Code § 17000 et seq.

§ 851.5.　Repealed by Stats.1987, c. 923, § 41, operative July 1, 1988

Law Revision Commission Comments

1987 Repeal

The second sentence requiring the clerk to set the petition for hearing is generalized in Section 1285.

The third sentence is replaced by Section 9861(b). Fifteen days' notice is required under Section 1220, instead of ten days' notice as required under former Section 1200.5.

The fourth sentence is restated in Section 9861(a) without substantive change. The fifth sentence is continued in Section 9862 without change. The sixth sentence is restated in Section 9863 without substantive change. The seventh sentence is restated in Section 9864 without substantive change. The last sentence is restated in Section 9865(a) without substantive change.

See also Section 58 ("personal representative" defined). [19 Cal.L.Rev.Comm. Reports 432 (1988)].

§ 852.　Continuances

An interested person may request time for filing a response to the petition for discovery proceedings, or for other preparation for the hearing, and the court shall grant a continuance for a reasonable time for any of these purposes. *(Added by Stats.2001, c. 49 (S.B.669), § 1.)*

Cross References

Civil actions, postponement, see Code of Civil Procedure §§ 473, 594a, 1054.
Discovery proceedings, see Code of Civil Procedure § 2016 et seq.
Estate administration, generally, see Probate Code § 7000 et seq.
Estate administration, rules of procedure, see Probate Code § 7200 et seq.
Interested person, defined, see Probate Code § 48.
Interested person, guardianship or conservatorship, defined, see Probate Code § 1424.

§ 853.　Objections to hearing petition

A person having or claiming title to or an interest in the property which is the subject of the petition may, at or prior to the hearing, object to the hearing of the petition if the petition is filed in a court which is not the proper court under any other provision of law for the trial of a civil action seeking the same relief and, if the objection is established, the court shall not grant the petition. *(Added by Stats.2001, c. 49 (S.B.669), § 1.)*

Cross References

Proper court,
　Civil actions, see Code of Civil Procedure § 395.
　Real property actions, see Code of Civil Procedure § 392.

§ 854.　Abatement of petition

If a civil action is pending with respect to the subject matter of a petition filed pursuant to this chapter and jurisdiction has been obtained in the court where the civil action is pending prior to the filing of the petition, upon request of any party to the civil action, the court shall abate the petition until the conclusion of the civil action. This section shall not apply if the court finds that the civil action was filed for the purpose of delay. *(Added by Stats.2001, c. 49 (S.B.669), § 1.)*

§ 855. Scope of action; matters normally raised in civil actions

An action brought under this part may include claims, causes of action, or matters that are normally raised in a civil action to the extent that the matters are related factually to the subject matter of a petition filed under this part. *(Added by Stats.2001, c. 49 (S.B.669), § 1.)*

§ 856. Order authorizing conveyance or transfer

Except as provided in Sections 853 and 854, if the court is satisfied that a conveyance, transfer, or other order should be made, the court shall make an order authorizing and directing the personal representative or other fiduciary, or the person having title to or possession of the property, to execute a conveyance or transfer to the person entitled thereto, or granting other appropriate relief. *(Added by Stats.2001, c. 49 (S.B.669), § 1.)*

§ 856.5. Authority of court to grant petition; civil action

The court may not grant a petition under this chapter if the court determines that the matter should be determined by a civil action. *(Added by Stats.2001, c. 417 (A.B.873), § 3.)*

§ 857. Nature and effect of order

(a) The order is prima facie evidence of the correctness of the proceedings and of the authority of the personal representative or other fiduciary or other person to make the conveyance or transfer.

(b) After entry of an order that the personal representative, other fiduciary, or other person execute a conveyance or transfer, the person entitled thereunder has the right to the possession of the property, and the right to hold the property,

according to the terms of the order as if the property had been conveyed or transferred in accordance with the terms of the order. *(Added by Stats.2001, c. 49 (S.B.669), § 1.)*

§ 858. Death of conservatee or minor during pendency of proceeding

If a proceeding has been brought under this part by a conservator on behalf of a conservatee, or by a guardian on behalf of a minor, and the conservatee or minor dies during the pendency of the proceeding, the personal representative of the conservatee or minor's estate or other successor in interest may proceed with the matter and the existing proceeding shall not be dismissed on account of the death of the conservatee or minor. *(Added by Stats.2001, c. 49 (S.B.669), § 1. Amended by Stats.2004, c. 183 (A.B.3082), § 278.)*

§ 859. Wrongful taking, concealment or disposition of property; liability; remedies

If a court finds that a person has in bad faith wrongfully taken, concealed, or disposed of property belonging to a conservatee, a minor, an elder, a dependent adult, a trust, or the estate of a decedent, or has taken, concealed, or disposed of the property by the use of undue influence in bad faith or through the commission of elder or dependent adult financial abuse, as defined in Section 15610.30 of the Welfare and Institutions Code, the person shall be liable for twice the value of the property recovered by an action under this part. In addition, except as otherwise required by law, including Section 15657.5 of the Welfare and Institutions Code, the person may, in the court's discretion, be liable for reasonable attorney's fees and costs. The remedies provided in this section shall be in addition to any other remedies available in law to a person authorized to bring an action pursuant to this part. *(Added by Stats.2001, c. 49 (S.B.669), § 1. Amended by Stats.2011, c. 55 (A.B.354), § 1; Stats.2013, c. 99 (A.B.381), § 1.)*

Cross References

Personal representative and general personal representative, defined, see Probate Code § 58.

§ 860. Repealed by Stats.1987, c. 923, § 41, operative July 1, 1988

Law Revision Commission Comments

1987 Repeal

The first part of the first sentence of former Section 860 is restated in Sections 9920 and 9921 without substantive change, except that the alternative standard for issuance of the order based on the best interests of the estate is omitted. The last part of the first sentence (notice by posting) and all of the second sentence (notice by mail) of former Section 860 are replaced by Section 9922(a). Notice of hearing must be mailed and posted 15 days before the hearing pursuant to Sections 1220 and 1230, instead of 10 days as provided by former Sections 1200 and 1200.5. The last sentence of former Section 860 is restated in Section 9922(b) without substantive change. See also Section 58 ("personal representative" defined). [19 Cal. L.Rev.Comm. Reports 434 (1988)].

Part 20

REVISED UNIFORM FIDUCIARY ACCESS TO DIGITAL ASSETS ACT

§ 870. Short title

This part shall be known, and may be cited, as the Revised Uniform Fiduciary Access to Digital Assets Act. *(Added by Stats.2016, c. 551 (A.B.691), § 1, eff. Jan. 1, 2017.)*

§ 871. Definitions

As used in this part, the following terms shall have the following meanings:

(a) "Account" means an arrangement under a terms-of-service agreement in which the custodian carries, maintains, processes, receives, or stores a digital asset of the user or provides goods or services to the user.

(b) "Carries" means engages in the transmission of electronic communications.

(c) "Catalogue of electronic communications" means information that identifies each person with which a user has had an electronic communication, the time and date of the communication, and the electronic address of the person.

(d) "Content of an electronic communication" means information concerning the substance or meaning of the communication, which meets all of the following requirements:

(1) Has been sent or received by a user.

(2) Is in electronic storage by a custodian providing an electronic communication service to the public or is carried or maintained by a custodian providing a remote-computing service to the public.

(3) Is not readily accessible to the public.

(e) "Court" means the superior court presiding over the judicial proceedings which have been initiated under this code to administer the estate of the deceased user, or, if none, the superior court sitting in the exercise of jurisdiction under this code in the county of the user's domicile, and the court, as defined in this section, shall have exclusive jurisdiction over proceedings brought under this part.

(f) "Custodian" means a person that carries, maintains, processes, receives, or stores a digital asset of a user.

(g) "Designated recipient" means a person chosen by a user using an online tool to administer digital assets of the user.

(h) "Digital asset" means an electronic record in which an individual has a right or interest. The term "digital asset" does not include an underlying asset or liability, unless the asset or liability is itself an electronic record.

(i) "Electronic" means relating to technology having electrical, digital, magnetic, wireless, optical, electromagnetic, or similar capabilities.

(j) "Electronic communication" has the same meaning as the definition in Section 2510(12) of Title 18 of the United States Code.

(k) "Electronic communication service" means a custodian that provides to a user the ability to send or receive an electronic communication.

(*l*) "Fiduciary" means an original, additional, or successor personal representative or trustee.

(m) "Information" means data, text, images, videos, sounds, codes, computer programs, software, databases, or other items with like characteristics.

(n) "Online tool" means an electronic service provided by a custodian that allows the user, in an agreement distinct from the terms-of-service agreement between the custodian and user, to provide directions for disclosure or nondisclosure of digital assets to a third person.

(*o*) "Person" means an individual, estate, business or nonprofit entity, public corporation, government or governmental subdivision, agency, or instrumentality, or other legal entity.

(p) "Personal representative" means an executor, administrator, special administrator, or person that performs substantially the same function under any other law.

(q) "Power of attorney" means a record that grants an agent authority to act in the place of the principal.

(r) "Record" means information that is inscribed on a tangible medium or that is stored in an electronic or other medium and is retrievable in a perceivable form.

(s) "Remote-computing service" means a custodian that provides to a user computer processing services or the storage of digital assets by means of an electronic communications system, as defined in Section 2510(14) of Title 18 of the United States Code.

(t) "Terms-of-service agreement" means an agreement that controls the relationship between a user and a custodian.

(u) "Trustee" means a fiduciary with legal title to property under an agreement or declaration that creates a beneficial interest in another. The term includes a successor trustee.

(v) "User" means a person that has an account with a custodian.

(w) "Will" includes a codicil, a testamentary instrument that only appoints an executor, or an instrument that revokes or revises a testamentary instrument. *(Added by Stats.2016, c. 551 (A.B.691), § 1, eff. Jan. 1, 2017.)*

§ 872.   Application of part

(a) This part shall apply to any of the following:

(1) A fiduciary acting under a will executed before, on, or after January 1, 2017.

(2) A personal representative acting for a decedent who died before, on, or after January 1, 2017.

(3) A trustee acting under a trust created before, on, or after January 1, 2017.

(4) A custodian of digital assets for a user if the user resides in this state or resided in this state at the time of the user's death.

(b) This part shall not apply to a digital asset of an employer used by an employee in the ordinary course of the employer's business. *(Added by Stats.2016, c. 551 (A.B.691), § 1, eff. Jan. 1, 2017.)*

§ 873.   User direction for disclosure of digital assets

(a) A user may use an online tool to direct the custodian to disclose to a designated recipient or not disclose some or all of the user's digital assets, including the content of electronic communications. If the online tool allows the user to modify or delete a direction at all times, a direction regarding disclosure using an online tool overrides a contrary direction by the user in a will, trust, power of attorney, or other record.

(b) If a user has not used an online tool to give direction under subdivision (a) or if a custodian has not provided an online tool, a user may allow or prohibit in a will, trust, power of attorney, or other record the disclosure to a fiduciary of some or all of the user's digital assets, including the contents of electronic communications sent or received by the user.

(c) A user's direction under subdivision (a) or (b) overrides a contrary provision in a terms-of-service agreement. *(Added by Stats.2016, c. 551 (A.B.691), § 1, eff. Jan. 1, 2017.)*

§ 874.   Terms-of-service agreement

(a) This part does not change or impair a right of a custodian or a user under a terms-of-service agreement to access and use digital assets of a user.

(b) This part does not give a fiduciary or designated recipient any new or expanded rights other than those held by the user for whom, or for whose estate or trust, the fiduciary or designated recipient acts or represents.

(c) A fiduciary's or designated recipient's access to digital assets may be modified or eliminated by a user, by federal law, or by a terms-of-service agreement when the user has not provided any direction that is recognized in Section 873. *(Added by Stats.2016, c. 551 (A.B.691), § 1, eff. Jan. 1, 2017.)*

§ 875.   Procedure for disclosing digital assets

(a) When disclosing the digital assets of a user under this part, the custodian may, in its sole discretion, do any of the following:

(1) Grant the fiduciary or designated recipient full access to the user's account.

(2) Grant the fiduciary or designated recipient partial access to the user's account sufficient to perform the tasks with which the fiduciary or designated recipient is charged.

(3) Provide the fiduciary or designated recipient with a copy in a record of any digital asset that, on the date the custodian received the request for disclosure, the user could have accessed if the user were alive and had full capacity and access to the account.

(b) A custodian may assess a reasonable administrative charge for the cost of disclosing digital assets under this part.

(c) A custodian need not disclose under this part a digital asset deleted by a user.

(d) If a user directs or a fiduciary or designated recipient requests a custodian to disclose under this part some, but not all, of the user's digital assets, the custodian need not disclose the assets if segregation of the assets would impose an undue burden on the custodian. If the custodian believes the direction or request imposes an undue burden, the custodian, fiduciary, or designated recipient may petition the court for an order to do any of the following:

(1) Disclose a subset limited by date of the user's digital assets.

(2) Disclose all of the user's digital assets to the fiduciary or designated recipient.

(3) Disclose none of the user's digital assets.

(4) Disclose all of the user's digital assets to the court for review in camera. *(Added by Stats.2016, c. 551 (A.B.691), § 1, eff. Jan. 1, 2017.)*

§ 876. Disclosure of content of electronic communications of deceased user

If a deceased user consented to or a court directs disclosure of the content of electronic communications of the user, the custodian shall disclose to the personal representative of the estate of the user the content of an electronic communication sent or received by the user if the personal representative gives to the custodian all of the following:

(a) A written request for disclosure in physical or electronic form.

(b) A certified copy of the death certificate of the user.

(c) A certified copy of the letter of appointment of the representative, a small-estate affidavit under Section 13101, or court order.

(d) Unless the user provided direction using an online tool, a copy of the user's will, trust, power of attorney, or other record evidencing the user's consent to disclosure of the content of electronic communications.

(e) If requested by the custodian, any of the following:

(1) A number, username, address, or other unique subscriber or account identifier assigned by the custodian to identify the user's account.

(2) Evidence linking the account to the user.

(3) An order of the court finding any of the following:

(A) That the user had a specific account with the custodian, identifiable by the information specified in paragraph (1).

(B) That disclosure of the content of the user's electronic communications would not violate Chapter 121 (commencing with Section 2701) of Part 1 of Title 18 of, and Section 222 of Title 47 of, the United States Code, or other applicable law.

(C) Unless the user provided direction using an online tool, that the user consented to disclosure of the content of electronic communications.

(D) That disclosure of the content of electronic communications of a user is reasonably necessary for estate administration. *(Added by Stats.2016, c. 551 (A.B.691), § 1, eff. Jan. 1, 2017.)*

§ 877. Disclosure of other digital assets of deceased user

Unless the user prohibited disclosure of digital assets or the court directs otherwise, a custodian shall disclose to the personal representative of the estate of a deceased user a catalogue of electronic communications sent or received by the user and digital assets, other than the content of electronic communications, of the user, if the personal representative gives to the custodian all of the following:

(a) A written request for disclosure in physical or electronic form.

(b) A certified copy of the death certificate of the user.

(c) A certified copy of the letter of appointment of the representative, a small-estate affidavit under Section 13101, or court order.

(d) If requested by the custodian, any of the following:

(1) A number, username, address, or other unique subscriber or account identifier assigned by the custodian to identify the user's account.

(2) Evidence linking the account to the user.

(3) An affidavit stating that disclosure of the user's digital assets is reasonably necessary for estate administration.

(4) An order of the court finding either of the following:

(A) That the user had a specific account with the custodian, identifiable by the information specified in paragraph (1).

(B) That disclosure of the user's digital assets is reasonably necessary for estate administration. *(Added by Stats.2016, c. 551 (A.B.691), § 1, eff. Jan. 1, 2017.)*

§ 878. Disclosure of contents of electronic communications held in trust when trustee not original user

Unless otherwise ordered by the court, directed by the user, or provided in a trust, a custodian shall disclose to a trustee that is not an original user of an account the content of an electronic communication sent or received by an original or successor user and carried, maintained, processed, received, or stored by the custodian in the account of the trust if the trustee gives to the custodian all of the following:

(a) A written request for disclosure in physical or electronic form.

(b) A certified copy of the death certificate of the settlor.

(c) A certified copy of the trust instrument, or a certification of trust under Section 18100.5, evidencing the settlor's consent to disclosure of the content of electronic communications to the trustee.

(d) A certification by the trustee, under penalty of perjury, that the trust exists and that the trustee is a currently acting trustee of the trust.

(e) If requested by the custodian, any of the following:

(1) A number, username, address, or other unique subscriber or account identifier assigned by the custodian to identify the trust's account.

(2) Evidence linking the account to the trust. *(Added by Stats.2016, c. 551 (A.B.691), § 1, eff. Jan. 1, 2017.)*

§ 879. Disclosure of other digital assets held in trust when trustee not original user

Unless otherwise ordered by the court, directed by the user, or provided in a trust, a custodian shall disclose, to a trustee that is not an original user of an account, the catalogue of electronic communications sent or received by an original or successor user and stored, carried, or maintained by the custodian in an account of the trust and any digital assets, other than the content of electronic communications, in which the trust has a right or interest if the settlor of the trust is deceased and the trustee gives the custodian all of the following:

(a) A written request for disclosure in physical or electronic form.

(b) A certified copy of the death certificate of the settlor.

(c) A certified copy of the trust instrument or a certification of trust under Section 18100.5.

(d) A certification by the trustee, under penalty of perjury, that the trust exists and that the trustee is a currently acting trustee of the trust.

(e) If requested by the custodian, any of the following:

(1) A number, username, address, or other unique subscriber or account identifier assigned by the custodian to identify the trust's account.

(2) Evidence linking the account to the trust. *(Added by Stats.2016, c. 551 (A.B.691), § 1, eff. Jan. 1, 2017.)*

§ 880. Fiduciary duties and authority

(a) The legal duties imposed on a fiduciary charged with managing tangible property apply to the management of digital assets, including all of the following:

(1) The duty of care.

(2) The duty of loyalty.

(3) The duty of confidentiality.

(b) All of the following shall apply to a fiduciary's or designated recipient's authority with respect to a digital asset of a user:

(1) Except as otherwise provided in Section 873, a fiduciary's or designated recipient's authority is subject to the applicable terms-of-service agreement.

(2) A fiduciary's or designated recipient's authority is subject to other applicable law, including copyright law.

(3) In the case of a fiduciary, a fiduciary's authority is limited by the scope of the fiduciary's duties.

(4) A fiduciary's or designated recipient's authority may not be used to impersonate the user.

(c) A fiduciary with authority over the property of a decedent or settlor has the right of access to any digital asset in which the decedent or settlor had a right or interest and that is not held by a custodian or subject to a terms-of-service agreement. Nothing in this subdivision requires a custodian to share passwords or decrypt protected devices.

(d) A fiduciary acting within the scope of the fiduciary's duties is an authorized user of the property of the decedent or settlor for the purpose of applicable computer-fraud and unauthorized-computer-access laws.

(e) The following shall apply to a fiduciary with authority over the tangible, personal property of a decedent or settlor:

(1) The fiduciary has the right to access the property and any digital asset stored in it. Nothing in this subdivision requires a custodian to share passwords or decrypt protected devices.

(2) The fiduciary is an authorized user for purposes of any applicable computer-fraud and unauthorized-computer-access laws.

(f) A custodian may disclose information in an account to a fiduciary of the decedent or settlor when the information is required to terminate an account used to access digital assets licensed to the user.

(g) A fiduciary of a decedent or settlor may request a custodian to terminate the user's account. A request for termination shall be in writing, in either physical or electronic form, and accompanied by all of the following:

(1) If the user is deceased, a certified copy of the death certificate of the user.

(2) A certified copy of the letter of appointment of the representative, a small-estate affidavit under Section 13101, a court order, a certified copy of the trust instrument, or a certification of the trust under Section 18100.5 giving the fiduciary authority over the account.

(3) If requested by the custodian, any of the following:

(A) A number, username, address, or other unique subscriber or account identifier assigned by the custodian to identify the user's account.

(B) Evidence linking the account to the user.

(C) A finding by the court that the user had a specific account with the custodian, identifiable by the information specified in subparagraph (A). *(Added by Stats.2016, c. 551 (A.B.691), § 1, eff. Jan. 1, 2017.)*

§ 881. Custodian compliance and immunity

(a) Not later than 60 days after receipt of the information required under Sections 876 to 879, inclusive, a custodian shall comply with a request under this part from a fiduciary or designated recipient to disclose digital assets or terminate an account. If the custodian fails to comply with a request, the fiduciary or designated recipient may apply to the court for an order directing compliance.

(b) An order under subdivision (a) directing compliance shall contain a finding that compliance is not in violation of Section 2702 of Title 18 of the United States Code.

(c) A custodian may notify a user that a request for disclosure of digital assets or to terminate an account was made pursuant to this part.

(d) A custodian may deny a request under this part from a fiduciary or designated recipient for disclosure of digital assets or to terminate an account if the custodian is aware of any lawful access to the account following the date of death of the user.

(e) This part does not limit a custodian's ability to obtain or to require a fiduciary or designated recipient requesting disclosure or account termination under this part to obtain a court order that makes all of the following findings:

(1) The account belongs to the decedent, principal, or trustee.

(2) There is sufficient consent from the decedent, principal, or settlor to support the requested disclosure.

(3) Any specific factual finding required by any other applicable law in effect at that time, including, but not limited to, a finding that disclosure is not in violation of Section 2702 of Title 18 of the United States Code.

(f)(1) A custodian and its officers, employees, and agents are immune from liability for an act or omission done in good faith <u>and</u> in compliance with this part.

(2) The protections specified in paragraph (1) shall not apply in a case of gross negligence or willful or wanton misconduct of the custodian or its officers, employees, or agents. *(Added by Stats.2016, c. 551 (A.B.691), § 1, eff. Jan. 1, 2017. Amended by Stats.2016, c. 585 (S.B.873), § 2, eff. Jan. 1, 2017.)*

§ 882. Relation to federal Electronic Signatures in Global and National Commerce Act

This part modifies, limits, or supersedes the federal Electronic Signatures in Global and National Commerce Act (15 U.S.C. Sec. 7001 et seq.), but does not modify, limit, or supersede Section 101(c) of that act (15 U.S.C. Sec. 7001(c)) or authorize electronic delivery of any of the notices described in Section 103(b) of that act (15 U.S.C. Sec. 7003(b)). *(Added by Stats.2016, c. 551 (A.B.691), § 1, eff. Jan. 1, 2017.)*

§ 883. Application of same license, restrictions, terms of service, and legal obligations that applied to deceased user or settlor

Disclosure of the contents of the deceased user's or settlor's account to a fiduciary of the deceased user or settlor is subject to the same license, restrictions, terms of service, and legal obligations, including copyright law, that applied to the deceased user or settlor. *(Added by Stats.2016, c. 551 (A.B.691), § 1, eff. Jan. 1, 2017.)*

§ 884. Severability

If any provision of this part or its application to any person or circumstance is held invalid, the invalidity does not affect other provisions or applications of this part that can be given effect without the invalid provision or application, and, to this end, the provisions of this part are severable. *(Added by Stats.2016, c. 551 (A.B.691), § 1, eff. Jan. 1, 2017.)*

§ 900. Repealed by Stats.1991, c. 82 (S.B.896), § 2, eff. June 30, 1991, operative July 1, 1991

Law Revision Commission Comments

1991 Repeal

Former Section 900 is repealed as unnecessary in view of Section 10850 (application of provisions of this part). [20 Cal.L.Rev.Comm.Reports 2909 (1990)].

§§ 901 to 911. Repealed by Stats.1990, c. 79 (A.B.759), § 13, operative July 1, 1991

§§ 920, 920.3. Repealed by Stats.1988, c. 1199, § 54.5, operative July 1, 1989

Law Revision Commission Comments

1988 Repeal

Former Section 920 is a general provision that is omitted as unnecessary; the duty to account, the contents of accounts, and the settlement of accounts are governed by specific statutory provisions. [19 Cal.L.Rev.Comm. Reports 1068 (1988)].

Former Section 920.3 is superseded by Section 10900 (contents of account). See the Comment to Section 10900. [19 Cal.L.Rev. Comm. Reports 1068 (1988)].

§ 920.5. Repealed by Stats.1987, c. 923, § 46, operative July 1, 1988

Law Revision Commission Comments

1987 Repeal

Former Section 920.5 is restated in Section 9705 without substantive change. See also Section 58 ("personal representative" defined). [19 Cal.L.Rev. Comm. Reports 435 (1988)].

§§ 921 to 930. Repealed by Stats.1988, c. 1199, § 54.5, operative July 1, 1989

Law Revision Commission Comments

1988 Repeal

The first sentence of former Section 921 is restated in Sections 10950 (court ordered account) and 10900 (contents of account), and in Code of Civil Procedure Section 166 (actions in chambers). The last sentence is restated in Section 11052 (punishment for contempt) without substantive change. [19 Cal.L.Rev.Comm. Reports 1068 (1988)].

The first sentence of former Section 922 is restated in Sections 10950 (court ordered account) and 10900 (contents of account). The second sentence is superseded by Section 10951 (final account). The third sentence is restated in Section 11050 (sanction for failure to account) without substantive change. The last sentence is restated in Section 11051(a) (citation) without substantive change. [19 Cal. L.Rev.Comm. Reports 1068 (1988)].

Former Section 923 is superseded by Section 10952 (account after authority terminated). [19 Cal.L.Rev.Comm. Reports 1068 (1988)].

Former Section 924 is restated in Sections 11051(b) (citation) and 11052 (punishment for contempt) without substantive change. [19 Cal.L.Rev.Comm. Reports 1068 (1988)].

Former Section 925 is superseded by Section 10901 (production of supporting documents), which extends the voucher procedure to supporting documents generally. [19 Cal.L.Rev.Comm. Reports 1069 (1988)].

The first sentence of subdivision (a) of former Section 926 is restated in Section 1041 (clerk to set matter for hearing). The second sentence is restated in Sections 11000(d) (notice of hearing), 11641 (distribution under court order). Subdivisions (b) and (c) are restated in Section 11000 (notice of hearing) without substantive change. [19 Cal.L.Rev.Comm. Reports 1222 (1988)].

The first sentence of former Section 927 is restated in Sections 11001 (contest of account) and 1043 (response or objection) without substantive change. The second sentence is superseded by Section 11003 (litigation expenses). The third and fifth sentences are restated in Section 11002(a) (hearing on account) without substantive change. The fourth sentence is restated in Section 11001 (contest of account) without substantive change. The last sentence is not continued because it is no longer necessary. [19 Cal.L.Rev.Comm. Reports 1222 (1988)].

Section 928 is not continued. See Section 7200 (trial by jury). [19 Cal.L.Rev.Comm. Reports 1069 (1988)].

Former Section 929 is restated in Section 11005 (settlement of claim not properly filed) without substantive change. [19 Cal.L.Rev. Comm. Reports 1069 (1988)].

Former Section 930 is not continued. The voucher procedure was generally not used. [19 Cal.L.Rev.Comm. Reports 1069 (1988)].

§ 930.5. Repealed by Stats.1939, c. 761, p. 2293, § 6

§§ 931 to 933. Repealed by Stats.1988, c. 1199, § 54.5, operative July 1, 1989

Law Revision Commission Comments

1988 Repeal

Former Section 931 is restated in Section 11006 (effect of order settling account) without substantive change. [19 Cal.L.Rev.Comm. Reports 1069 (1988)].

Former Section 932 is restated in Section 10953 (account where personal representative dies or becomes incompetent) with changes for internal consistency. [19 Cal.L.Rev.Comm) Reports 1070 (1988)].

Former Section 933 is restated in Section 10954 (when account is not required). [19 Cal.L.Rev.Comm. Reports 1223 (1988)].

§§ 950 to 955. Repealed by Stats.1987, c. 923, § 48, operative July 1, 1988

Law Revision Commission Comments

1987 Repeal

Former Section 950 is replaced by Sections 11401 ("debt" defined), 11402 ("wage claim" defined), and 11420 (priority for payment). See the Comments to these sections. [19 Cal.L.Rev.Comm.Reports 436 (1988)].

Former Section 951 is restated without substantive change in Sections 11402 ("wage claim" defined), 11421 (immediate payment of priority debts), and 11422(a) (payment of debts on court order). See also Section 58 ("personal representative" defined). [19 Cal.L.Rev.Comm.Reports 436 (1988)].

Former Section 951.1 is restated without substantive change in Section 11446 (funeral expenses and last illness expenses), which also recognizes state and federal priorities. [19 Cal.L.Rev.Comm.Reports 436 (1988)].

The first, second, and fourth sentences of former Section 952 are restated in Section 11422(b)–(c) (payment of debts on court order) without substantive change. The third sentence is restated in Section 11420(b) (priority for payment) without substantive change. See also Section 58 ("personal representative" defined). [19 Cal.L.Rev.Comm.Reports 436 (1988)].

The first sentence of former Section 953 is restated in Section 11427 (disputed and contingent claims) without substantive change. The second sentence is restated in Section 11425 (payment of debt not due) without substantive change. The last sentence is replaced by Section 11420(b) (priority for payment). [19 Cal.L.Rev.Comm.Reports 436 (1988)].

The first paragraph of former Section 953.1 is restated in Section 11426 (trust for installment or contingent debt) without substantive change. The transitional provision in the second paragraph is omitted as no longer necessary. [19 Cal.L.Rev.Comm. Reports 436 (1988)].

Former Section 954 is restated in Section 11424 (enforcement of order for payment) without substantive change. See also Section 58 ("personal representative" defined). [19 Cal.L.Rev.Comm. Reports 437 (1988)].

Former Section 955 is replaced by Section 11429 (unpaid creditor). See also Section 58 ("personal representative" defined). [19 Cal. L.Rev.Comm. Reports 437 (1988)].

§ 956. Repealed by Stats.1988, c. 1199, § 55, operative July 1, 1989

Law Revision Commission Comments

1988 Repeal

The first clause of former Section 956 is restated in Section 11640 (petition and order for final distribution) without substantive change. The last clause is superseded by Section 12201 (report of status of administration). [19 Cal.L.Rev.Comm. Reports 1070 (1988)].

§§ 970 to 973. Repealed by Stats.1986, c. 783, § 16, operative July 1, 1987

Law Revision Commission Comments

1986 Repeal

Sections 970–977 are superseded by Sections 20100–20125 (proration of estate taxes). Comparable provisions of the old and new law are listed below.

OLD LAW	NEW LAW
970	20110
971	20111
972	20112
973	20113
975	20116
976	20123
977	20100

§ 974. Repealed by Stats.1984, c. 1711, § 3, eff. Sept. 30, 1984

§§ 975 to 977. Repealed by Stats.1986, c. 783, § 16, operative July 1, 1987

Law Revision Commission Comments

1986 Repeal

Sections 970–977 are superseded by Sections 20100–20125 (proration of estate taxes). Comparable provisions of the old and new law are listed below.

OLD LAW	NEW LAW
970	20110
971	20111
972	20112
973	20113
975	20116
976	20123
977	20100

§ 980. Repealed by Stats.1987, c. 923, § 48.6, operative July 1, 1988

Law Revision Commission Comments

1987 Repeal

Subdivision (a) of former Section 980 is combined with portions of former Sections 704.2 and 704.4 in Section 11440 (when allocation may be made), which allows petition at any time before the order for final distribution is made.

Subdivision (b) is combined with portions of former Sections 704.2 and 704.4 in Section 11441 (petition for allocation).

Subdivision (c) is restated in Section 11442 (inventory of property of surviving spouse) without substantive change.

Subdivision (d) is replaced by Section 11443 (notice of hearing), which incorporates general service of notice procedures. Fifteen days' notice is required under Section 1220, instead of ten days' notice as required under former law.

Subdivision (e) is combined with a part of former Section 713.5 in Section 11444 (allocation), making clear that allocation of liability is to be based on rules applicable to liability of marital property for debts during marriage.

Subdivision (f) is combined with a part of former Section 713.5 in Section 11445 (order implementing allocation).

See also Section 58 ("personal representative" defined). [19 Cal.L.Rev.Comm. Reports 437 (1988)].

Division 3

GENERAL PROVISIONS OF A PROCEDURAL NATURE

Part 1

GENERAL PROVISIONS

Law Revision Commission Comments

1990 Enactment

This part supersedes Part 1 (commencing with Section 1000) of Division 3 of the repealed Probate Code. The superseded part was enacted upon recommendation of the California Law Revision Commission. See Recommendation Relating to Rules of Procedure in Probate, 19 Cal.L.Revision Comm'n Reports 917–39, 951 (1988). See also Communication from California Law Revision Commission Concerning Assembly Bill 2841, 19 Cal.L.Revision Comm'n Reports 1201, 1223–26 (1988); Comments to Conforming Revisions and Repeals, 19 Cal.L.Revision Comm'n Reports 1031, 1082–84 (1988). For an earlier Law Revision Commission recommendation that included probate procedural provisions, see Recommendation Relating to Notice in Probate Proceedings, 19 Cal.L.Revision Comm'n Reports 357, 365–66, 383–90 (1988). [20 Cal.L.Rev.Comm.Reports 1001 (1990)].

CHAPTER 1. RULES OF PRACTICE

Cross References

Application of old and new law, see Probate Code § 3.
Compelling attendance of witnesses,
   Power of courts, see Code of Civil Procedure § 128.
   Power of judicial officers, see Code of Civil Procedure § 177.
   Referees, see Code of Civil Procedure § 708.140.
   Residency requirements, see Code of Civil Procedure § 1989.
Conduct of trial, generally, see Code of Civil Procedure § 607 et seq.
Contempt for disobedience of subpoena, see Code of Civil Procedure §§ 1209, 1991.
Entry and enforcement of orders, see Probate Code §§ 1048, 1049.
General and special verdicts, see Code of Civil Procedure § 624 et seq.
Hearings and orders, generally, see Probate Code § 1040 et seq.
Judicial authorization or approval, effect of, see Probate Code § 7250.

Manner of giving and entering judgment, generally, see Code of Civil Procedure § 664 et seq.
Means of production of evidence, see Code of Civil Procedure § 1985 et seq.
Necessary recitals in orders, see Probate Code § 1047.
Notices, see Probate Code § 1200 et seq.
Orders for production of will, see Probate Code § 8201.
Parties in probate proceedings, see Probate Code § 1044.
Power of judges to hear motions for new trial, see Code of Civil Procedure § 166.
Probate proceedings, new trials, see Probate Code § 7220.
Real estate, orders and transactions affecting, see Probate Code § 7260 et seq.
Trial by jury, see Probate Code §§ 825 and 1452.

§ 1000. Civil action rules applicable

Except to the extent that this code provides applicable rules, the rules of practice applicable to civil actions, including discovery proceedings and proceedings under Title 3a (commencing with Section 391) of Part 2 of the Code of Civil Procedure, apply to, and constitute the rules of practice in, proceedings under this code. All issues of fact joined in probate proceedings shall be tried in conformity with the rules of practice in civil actions. *(Stats.1990, c. 79 (A.B.759), § 14, operative July 1, 1991. Amended by Stats.1994, c. 806 (A.B.3686), § 5; Stats.1997, c. 724 (A.B.1172), § 4; Stats. 2002, c. 1118 (A.B.1938), § 5.)*

Law Revision Commission Comments

1990 Enactment

Section 1000 continues Section 1000 of the repealed Probate Code without change. This section provides a default rule that applies in circumstances where there is no special rule applicable in probate proceedings. For example, the general rules of practice apply to discovery, trials, new trials, appeals, and other matters of procedure. General rules of the Code of Civil Procedure do not apply, however, where this code provides a special rule. For example, jury trials are strictly limited in proceedings under this code. See Sections 1452 (guardianship and conservatorship proceedings), 7200 (estate administration), 17006 (trust administration). The right to make a motion for a new trial in proceedings for administration of a decedent's estate is limited in Section 7220. The right to appeal in decedent estate administration is limited to the orders set out in Section 7240. Many other limitations are provided in this chapter and in other provisions throughout this code. This general rule is also subject to the rulemaking power of the courts. See Section 1001.

Background on Section 1000 of Repealed Code

Section 1000 was added by 1988 Cal.Stat. ch. 1199 § 56. The section replaced the first, third, and fourth sentences of former Probate Code Section 1280 (repealed by 1988 Cal.Stat. ch. 1199 § 64.5) and the first sentence of former Probate Code Section 1283 (repealed by 1988 Cal.Stat. ch. 1199 § 64.5). For background on the provisions of this part, see the Comment to this part under the part heading. [20 Cal.L.Rev.Comm.Reports 1001 (1990)].

Cross References

Civil action defined, see Code of Civil Procedure § 30.
Depositions and discovery, see Code of Civil Procedure § 2016 et seq.

Execution of judgment in civil actions, generally, see Code of Civil Procedure § 683.010 et seq.

Filing decisions in writing in civil actions, see Code of Civil Procedure § 632.

Judicial Council rules, see California Rules of Court, Rule 10.1 et seq.

Jury trial, see Probate Code §§ 825 and 1452.

Rules of practice in civil actions,
    Generally, see Code of Civil Procedure § 307 et seq.
    Court rules, see California Rules of Court, Rule 3.1 et seq.

Trial by court, see Code of Civil Procedure § 631 et seq.

§ 1001. Judicial Council and local court rules; forms

(a) The Judicial Council may provide by rule for the practice and procedure under this code. Unless disapproved by the Judicial Council, a court may provide by local rule for the practice and procedure under this code. Judicial Council and local court rules shall be consistent with the applicable statutes.

(b) The Judicial Council may prescribe the form of the applications, notices, orders, and other documents required by this code. Any form prescribed by the Judicial Council is deemed to comply with this code. *(Stats.1990, c. 79 (A.B. 759), § 14, operative July 1, 1991.)*

Law Revision Commission Comments

1990 Enactment

Section 1001 continues Section 1001 of the repealed Probate Code without change. This section is consistent with the fourth paragraph of Section 6 of Article VI of the California Constitution and with Government Code Section 68511.

Background on Section 1001 of Repealed Code

Section 1001 was a new provision added by 1988 Cal.Stat. ch. 1199 § 56. For background on the provisions of this part, see the Comment to this part under the part heading. [20 Cal.L.Rev.Comm.Reports 1001 (1990)].

§ 1002. Costs

Unless it is otherwise provided by this code or by rules adopted by the Judicial Council, either the superior court or the court on appeal may, in its discretion, order costs to be paid by any party to the proceedings, or out of the assets of the estate, as justice may require. *(Stats.1990, c. 79 (A.B. 759), § 14, operative July 1, 1991.)*

Law Revision Commission Comments

1990 Enactment

Section 1002 continues Section 1002 of the repealed Probate Code without change. For special provisions relating to costs, see, e.g., Sections 6544 (costs of proceedings for family allowance), 9255 (costs where creditor contests amount of allowed claim), 9653 (costs in action to recover fraudulently conveyed property), 11624 (costs on preliminary distribution). See also Code Civ.Proc. § 1026 (costs in actions involving fiduciary estate).

Background on Section 1002 of Repealed Code

Section 1002 was added by 1988 Cal.Stat. ch. 1199 § 56. The section restated former Probate Code Section 1282 (repealed by 1988 Cal.Stat. ch. 1199 § 64.5) without substantive change. For background on the provisions of this part, see the Comment to this part under the part heading. [20 Cal.L.Rev.Comm.Reports 1001 (1990)].

Cross References

Costs,
    Generally, see Code of Civil Procedure § 1021 et seq.
    As expenses of administration in proceedings for family allowance, see Probate Code § 6544.
    Claims of personal representative or attorney of personal representative, see Probate Code § 9252.
    Denial to creditor in subsequent action to recover claims, see Probate Code § 9255.
    Proceedings for preliminary distribution, see Probate Code § 11624.
    Recovery of fraudulently conveyed property, see Probate Code § 9653.

Costs on appeal,
    Generally, see California Rules of Court, Rule 8.276; Code of Civil Procedure § 1034.
    Multiple appeals, apportionment, see California Rules of Court, Rule 8.147.
    Reporter's transcript, see California Rules of Court, Rule 8.130.
    Transcript, clerk's charges, see California Rules of Court, Rule 8.120.

§ 1003. Guardian ad litem

(a) The court may, on its own motion or on request of a personal representative, guardian, conservator, trustee, or other interested person, appoint a guardian ad litem at any stage of a proceeding under this code to represent the interest of any of the following persons, if the court determines that representation of the interest otherwise would be inadequate:

(1) A minor.

(2) An incapacitated person.

(3) An unborn person.

(4) An unascertained person.

(5) A person whose identity or address is unknown.

(6) A designated class of persons who are not ascertained or are not in being.

(b) If not precluded by a conflict of interest, a guardian ad litem may be appointed to represent several persons or interests.

(c) The reasonable expenses of the guardian ad litem, including compensation and attorney's fees, shall be determined by the court and paid as the court orders, either out of the property of the estate involved or by the petitioner or from such other source as the court orders. *(Stats.1990, c. 79 (A.B.759), § 14, operative July 1, 1991.)*

Law Revision Commission Comments

1990 Enactment

Section 1003 continues Section 1003 of the repealed Probate Code without substantive change. Language has been added to make clear that the section applies in any proceeding under this code. Section 1003 is comparable to Section 1–403(4) of the Uniform Probate Code (1987). As to the construction of provisions drawn from uniform acts, see Section 2. The general provisions for appointment of a guardian ad litem in Code of Civil Procedure Sections 372–373.5 do not apply to the appointment of a guardian ad litem under this code. See Section 1000 (general rules of civil practice apply unless this code provides a different rule). See also Sections 3112, 3140 (appointment of guardian ad litem to represent interest of spouse whose legal capacity for a proposed transaction is to be determined or who lacks legal capacity for a proposed transaction). Section 1003 is not intended to limit any power the court may have to appoint an attorney to represent the interests of an incapacitated person. If a beneficiary has an interest in only part of an estate, the court may not charge expenses to the whole estate, but only to the beneficiary's interest. See Estate of Corotto, 125 Cal.App.2d 314, 325, 270 P.2d 498 (1954).

Background on Section 1003 of Repealed Code

Section 1003 was a new provision added by 1988 Cal.Stat. ch. 1199 § 56. The section generalized former Probate Code Section 17208 (repealed by 1988 Cal.Stat. ch. 1199 § 107.5) (guardian ad litem in trust proceedings). For background on the provisions of this part, see the Comment to this part under the part heading. [20 Cal.L.Rev.Comm.Reports 1001 (1990)].

Cross References

Attorney's fees and costs, generally, see Code of Civil Procedure § 1021.
Capacity determinations, generally, see Probate Code § 3200 et seq.
Estate attorney, compensation, amount, see Probate Code § 10810 et seq.
Interested person, defined, see Probate Code § 48.
Personal representative and general personal representative, defined, see Probate Code § 58.
Power to make compromise, see Code of Civil Procedure § 372; Probate Code § 3500.

§ 1003.5. Public guardian; appointment as guardian ad litem

The public guardian shall not be appointed as a guardian ad litem pursuant to Section 1003 unless the court, after reasonable notice and inquiry, finds that no other qualified person is willing to act as a guardian ad litem. *(Added by Stats.1994, c. 472 (A.B.2725), § 1.)*

Cross References

Public guardian, generally, see Probate Code § 2900 et seq.

§ 1004. Proceeding affecting real property; notice

If a proceeding under this code affects the title to or the right of possession of real property, notice of the pendency of the proceeding may be filed pursuant to Title 4.5 (commencing with Section 405) of Part 2 of the Code of Civil Procedure. *(Stats.1990, c. 79 (A.B.759), § 14, operative July 1, 1991. Amended by Stats.2003, c. 32 (A.B.167), § 1.)*

Law Revision Commission Comments

1990 Enactment

Section 1004 continues Section 1004 of the repealed Probate Code without substantive change. Language has been added to make clear that the section applies in any proceeding under this code. This section does not refer to proceedings that "concern" title or the right of possession of real property, as does Code of Civil Procedure Section 409, and thus provides a more restrictive rule than would otherwise apply through the incorporation provision of Section 1000. Other provisions of the Code of Civil Procedure applicable to lis pendens apply under this code by virtue of Section 1000 (general rules of practice). See, e.g., Code Civ.Proc. § 409.1 (expunging lis pendens).

2003 Amendment

Section 1004 is amended to reflect relocation of the lis pendens statutes from former Code of Civil Procedure Section 409 to Code of Civil Procedure Section 405 *et seq.* See 1992 Cal. Stat. ch. 883, §§ 1, 2. [33 Cal.L.Rev.Comm. Reports 151 (2003)].

Background on Section 1004 of Repealed Code

Section 1004 was a new provision added by 1988 Cal.Stat. ch. 1199 § 56. Section 1004 generalized former Probate Code Sections 2523 (repealed by 1988 Cal.Stat. ch. 1199 § 69.5) (Guardianship–Conservatorship Law) and 9863 (repealed by 1988 Cal.Stat. ch. 1199 § 88.5) (claims of title in estate administration). For background on the provisions of this part, see the Comment to this part under the part heading. [20 Cal.L.Rev.Comm.Reports 1001 (1990)].

Cross References

Actions concerning real estate, see Code of Civil Procedure § 760.010 et seq.
Pending action, defined, see Code of Civil Procedure § 1049.
Real property, defined, see Probate Code § 68.
Recovery of property, termination of right during pendency of civil action, see Code of Civil Procedure § 740.

§§ 1010 to 1013. Repealed by Stats.1953, c. 417, p. 1666, § 1

CHAPTER 2. PETITIONS AND OTHER PAPERS

Section
1020. Signatures; filing; verification.
1020.1, 1020.5. Repealed.
1021. Verification of documents.
1021.5. Repealed.
1022. Affidavits and verified petitions; evidence.
1023. Signature or verification by attorney.
1024 to 1028. Repealed.
1029. Repealed.
1030 to 1039. Repealed.

Cross References

Application of old and new law, see Probate Code § 3.

§ 1020. Signatures; filing; verification

Except as provided in Section 1023, a petition, objection, response, report, or account filed pursuant to this code shall be in writing, signed by all of the petitioners, objectors, or respondents or by all of the persons making the report or account, and filed with the court clerk. Verification of a document shall constitute signature of that document, unless expressly provided to the contrary. *(Stats.1990, c. 79 (A.B. 759), § 14, operative July 1, 1991. Amended by Stats.1992, c. 871 (A.B.2975), § 3.)*

Law Revision Commission Comments

1990 Enactment

Section 1020 continues Section 1020 of the repealed Probate Code without substantive change. Language has been added to make clear that the section applies to any of the described documents "filed pursuant to this code." The introductory clause recognizes that the attorney for a nonfiduciary may sign a petition, objection, or response under certain circumstances. See Section 1023. See also Section 9630 (authority of joint personal representatives to act).

Background on Section 1020 of Repealed Code

Section 1020 was a new provision added by 1988 Cal.Stat. ch. 1199 § 56. Section 1020 generalized several former provisions. See, e.g., former Prob.Code §§ 380 (repealed by 1988 Cal.Stat. ch. 1199 § 42) (will contest after probate), 440 (repealed by 1988 Cal.Stat. ch. 1199 § 45) (petition for letters of administration), 522 (repealed by 1988 Cal.Stat. ch. 1199 § 47) (removal of personal representative), 921 (repealed by 1988 Cal.Stat. ch. 1199 § 54.5) (filing of verified account), 1025.5 (repealed by 1988 Cal.Stat. ch. 1199 § 55.5) (report of status of administration). For background on the provisions of this part, see the Comment to this part under the part heading. [20 Cal.L.Rev.Comm.Reports 1001 (1990)].

§§ 1020.1, 1020.5. Repealed by Stats.1988, c. 1199, § 55.5, operative July 1, 1989

Law Revision Commission Comments

1988 Repeal

Former Section 1020.1 is restated in Section 11604 (distribution to person other than beneficiary), standardizing the manner of notice with other provisions in the code [19 Cal.L.Rev.Comm. Reports 1224 (1988)].

Former Section 1020.5 is not continued; it is superseded by Sections 11750 (responsibility for distribution), 11753 (filing receipts and discharge), and 11642 (after-acquired or after-discovered property) [19 Cal.L.Rev.Comm. Reports 1071 (1988)].

§ 1021. Verification of documents

(a) All of the following shall be verified:

(1) A petition, report, or account filed pursuant to this code.

(2) An objection or response filed pursuant to this code to a petition, report, or account.

(b) Except as provided in Section 1023, the verification shall be made as follows:

(1) A petition shall be verified by the petitioner or, if there are two or more parties joining in the petition, by any of them.

(2) A report or account shall be verified by the person who has the duty to make the report or account or, if there are two or more persons having a duty to make the report or account, by any of them.

(3) An objection or response shall be verified by the objector or respondent or, if there are two or more parties joining in the objection or response, by any of them. *(Stats.1990, c. 79 (A.B.759), § 14, operative July 1, 1991. Amended by Stats.1992, c. 871 (A.B.2975), § 4; Stats.1996, c. 862 (A.B.2751), § 3.)*

Law Revision Commission Comments

1990 Enactment

Section 1021 continues Section 1021 of the repealed Probate Code without change. In the case of a corporate fiduciary, a responsible person, such as a corporate officer, should verify a report or account. See also Section 10953 (verification of account prepared for dead or incapacitated personal representative upon information and belief).

Background on Section 1021 of Repealed Code

Section 1021 was added by 1988 Cal.Stat. ch. 1199 § 56. The section restated former Probate Code Section 1284 (repealed by 1988 Cal.Stat. ch. 1199 § 64.5) without substantive change. Former Section 1284 had earlier been enacted upon recommendation of the Law Revision Commission by 1987 Cal.Stat. ch. 923 § 60.5. Subdivision (a) of former Section 1284 generalized and superseded provisions formerly found in the repealed Probate Code. Subdivision (b) was new. For background on the provisions of this part, see the Comment to this part under the part heading. [20 Cal.L.Rev.Comm.Reports 1001 (1990)].

§ 1021.5. Repealed by Stats.1988, c. 1199, § 55.5, operative July 1, 1989

Law Revision Commission Comments

1988 Repeal

Former Section 1021.5 is restated in Section 11603 (hearing and order for distribution) without substantive change [19 Cal.L.Rev. Comm. Reports 1072 (1988)].

§ 1022. Affidavits and verified petitions; evidence

An affidavit or verified petition shall be received as evidence when offered in an uncontested proceeding under this code. *(Stats.1990, c. 79 (A.B.759), § 14, operative July 1, 1991.)*

Law Revision Commission Comments

1990 Enactment

Section 1022 continues Section 1022 of the repealed Probate Code without change. The declaration of an attorney is admissible as an affidavit under this section. Proceedings under this code include proceedings relating to the administration of estates of decedents and proceedings relating to the administration of estates of persons for whom a guardian or conservator has been appointed. For other provisions, see Section 204 (use of petition and affidavit in proceeding to establish fact of death). See also Code Civ.Proc. § 2009 (affidavit may be used to establish record of birth).

Background on Section 1022 of Repealed Code

Section 1022 was a new provision added by 1988 Cal.Stat. ch. 1199 § 56. The section generalized the first sentence of the second paragraph of former Probate Code Section 1283 (repealed by 1988 Cal.Stat. ch. 1199 § 64.5). For background on the provisions of this part, see the Comment to this part under the part heading. [20 Cal.L.Rev.Comm.Reports 1001 (1990)].

Cross References

Affidavits, see Code of Civil Procedure § 2009 et seq.

§ 1023. Signature or verification by attorney

If a petitioner, objector, or respondent is absent from the county or for some other cause is unable to sign or verify a petition, objection, or response filed pursuant to this code, the person's attorney may sign or verify the petition, objection, or response unless the person is a fiduciary appointed in the proceeding. *(Stats.1990, c. 79 (A.B.759), § 14, operative July 1, 1991.)*

Law Revision Commission Comments

1990 Enactment

Section 1023 continues Section 1023 of the repealed Probate Code without substantive change. Language has been added to make clear the section applies when a petition, objection, or response is "filed pursuant to this code."

Section 1023 provides exceptions to the general rules applicable to signing and verification under Sections 1020 and 1021. Under Section 1023, an attorney may sign or verify papers for a person other than a fiduciary appointed in the particular proceeding to which the papers relate. Thus, for example, a petition filed by the personal representative in a probate proceeding would be covered by the prohibition, but an objection or response to such a petition by the trustee of an inter vivos trust or by the conservator of an heir would not be covered, since neither the trustee nor the conservator is a fiduciary appointed in the probate proceeding.

Section 1023 is drawn in part from Code of Civil Procedure Section 446, but provides a different rule governing the situations where an attorney may make a verification in place of a party. The manner of verification, however, is governed by Code of Civil Procedure Section 446.

Background on Section 1023 of Repealed Code

Section 1023 was a new provision added by 1988 Cal.Stat. ch. 1199 § 56. It was amended by 1989 Cal.Stat. ch. 21 § 4 to prohibit a fiduciary's attorney from verifying papers for the fiduciary. See Communication from the California Law Revision Commission Concerning Assembly Bill 156, 20 Cal.L.Revision Comm'n Reports 227, 228–29 (1990). For background on the provisions of this part, see the Comment to this part under the part heading. [20 Cal.L.Rev.Comm.Reports 1001 (1990)].

Cross References

Fiduciary, defined, see Probate Code § 39.

§§ 1024 to 1028. Repealed by Stats.1988, c. 1199, § 55.5, operative July 1, 1989

Law Revision Commission Comments

1988 Repeal

Former Section 1024 is not continued, because it is unnecessary. Payment of taxes is an obligation of the personal representative (Section 9650), and the estate may not be distributed unless obligations of the estate are accommodated (Section 11621 (order for distribution)) [19 Cal.L.Rev.Comm. Reports 1072 (1988)].

Former Section 1025 is restated without substantive change in Section 12206 (testamentary limitation of time for administration) [19 Cal.L.Rev.Comm. Reports 1072 (1988)].

The first sentence of the first paragraph of former Section 1025.5 is restated without substantive change in Sections 12200 (time required for closing or status report), 1284 (verification required), and 12201 (report of status of administration). The second, third, and fourth sentences are restated without substantive change in Section 12201 (report of status of administration).

The second paragraph is restated without substantive change in Section 12202 (failure to petition or make report). The third paragraph is restated without substantive change in Section 12204 (failure of personal representative to comply with order). The fourth paragraph is restated without substantive change in Section 12205 (sanction for failure to timely close estate) [19 Cal.L.Rev. Comm. Reports 1072 (1988)].

Former Section 1026 is continued without substantive change in Section 12203 (continuation of administration to pay family allowance) [19 Cal.L.Rev.Comm. Reports 1073 (1988)].

The first sentence of subdivision (a) of former Section 1027 is restated without substantive change in Section 11640 (petition and order). The remainder of subdivision (a) is restated without substantive change in Section 11900 (distribution to State of California).

Subdivision (b) is continued without change in Section 11601(a) (notice of hearing). Subdivision (c) is continued without change in Section 11601(b) (notice of hearing).

Subdivision (d) is restated without substantive change in Section 11601 (notice of hearing), except that the provision for 30 days notice is not continued. Subdivision (e) is restated without substantive change in Section 11901 (distribution in trust for a class).

Subdivisions (f) and (g) are restated without substantive change in Section 11902 (disposition of property distributed to state). Subdivision (h) is restated without substantive change in Sections 11904 (no deposit in county treasury) and 7622 (general rules governing administration of estates apply to public administrator). Subdivisions (i) and (j) are restated without substantive change in Section 11903 (claims against property distributed to state) [19 Cal.L.Rev. Comm. Reports 1225 (1988)].

Former Section 1028 is restated without substantive change in Section 11902 (disposition of property distributed to state) [19 Cal.L.Rev.Comm. Reports 1073 (1988)].

§ 1029. Repealed by Stats.1982, c. 41, p. 91, § 2

§§ 1030 to 1039. Repealed by Stats.1987, c. 923, § 54.5, operative Jan. 1, 1988

Law Revision Commission Comments

1987 Repeal

Subdivision (a) of former Section 1030 is restated in Section 21120(b) (satisfaction of a pecuniary gift) without substantive change. Subdivisions (b) and (d) are restated in Section 21520 (definitions) and expanded to apply to the gift tax as well as the estate tax. Subdivision (c) is restated by general language in Section 21523 (maximum marital deduction for instrument dated September 12, 1981, or earlier). Subdivision (e) is restated in Section 88 ("will" defined) without substantive change. Subdivision (f) is restated in Sections 21100 (definitions, and 10 (singular and plural) without substantive change. Subdivision (g) is restated in Section 21500 ("Internal Revenue Code" defined) without substantive change. Subdivision (h) is superseded by general language in the provisions to which it related. [19 Cal.L.Rev.Comm. Reports 635 (1988)].

The effect of the first sentence of subdivision (a) of former Section 1031 is preserved in subdivision (b) of Section 21501. The second sentence of subdivision (a) is restated in subdivision (a) of Section 21502.

Subdivision (b) of former Section 1031 is restated in subdivision (b) of Section 21502. [19 Cal.L.Rev.Comm. Reports 635 (1988)].

The first three sentences of subdivision (a) of former Section 1032 are restated in Section 21522(a)–(b) (marital deduction gifts) without substantive change. The fourth sentence is restated in Section 21521 (chapter inapplicable to estate trust) without substantive change. The fifth sentence is superseded by Section 21526 (QTIP election).

Subdivision (b) is restated in Section 21540 (charitable remainder unitrusts and annuity trusts), which applies it to inter vivos as well as testamentary gifts. [19 Cal.L.Rev.Comm. Reports 635 (1988)].

Subdivision (a) of former Section 1033 is restated in Section 21120(a) (satisfaction of a pecuniary gift) without substantive change. Subdivision (b) is restated in Section 21522(c) (marital deduction gifts) without substantive change. [19 Cal.L.Rev.Comm. Reports 635 (1988)].

Subdivisions (a) and (c) of former Section 1034 are restated in Section 21523 (maximum marital deduction for instrument dated September 12, 1981, or earlier), with the addition of a provision to make it possible to make a "QTIP" trust election in a pre-September 13, 1981, instrument under Internal Revenue Code Section 2056(b)(7) without thereby reducing the formula marital deduction bequest on a dollar-for-dollar basis. Subdivision (b) is omitted in conformity with the change in the generation-skipping transfer tax made by the Tax Reform Act of 1986 (H.R. 3838). [19 Cal.L.Rev. Comm. Reports 635 (1988)].

Former Section 1035 is restated in Section 21524 (marital deduction gift in trust), with provision for qualification of a QTIP trust that is silent about the payment of income between the last distribution date of the trust and the date of the spouse's death and, beyond that, with provision for qualification of a QTIP trust that mandates payment of income to the remaindermen. [19 Cal.L.Rev.Comm. Reports 635 (1988)].

Former Section 1036 is restated in Section 21524 (survival requirement for marital deduction gift) without substantive change. [19 Cal.L.Rev.Comm. Reports 635 (1988)].

Former Section 1037 is not continued. It was a transitional provision that is no longer necessary. [19 Cal.L.Rev.Comm. Reports 635 (1988)].

GENERAL PROVISIONS OF A PROCEDURAL NATURE

Former Section 1038 is not continued. It duplicated Section 11 (severability clause). [19 Cal.L.Rev.Comm. Reports 635 (1988)].

Former Section 1039 is not continued. The provision did not serve a useful purpose. [19 Cal.L.Rev.Comm. Reports 635 (1988)].

CHAPTER 3. HEARINGS AND ORDERS

Section

Cross References

Application of old and new law, see Probate Code § 3.

§ 1040. Scope of chapter

This chapter governs the hearing of all matters under this code, except where the statute that provides for the hearing of the matter prescribes a different procedure. *(Stats.1990, c. 79 (A.B.759), § 14, operative July 1, 1991.)*

Law Revision Commission Comments
1990 Enactment

Section 1040 continues Section 1040 of the repealed Probate Code without change.

Background on Section 1040 of Repealed Code

Section 1040 was a new provision added by 1988 Cal.Stat. ch. 1199 § 56. For background on the provisions of this part, see the Comment to this part under the part heading. [20 Cal.L.Rev.Comm.Reports 1001 (1990)].

§ 1041. Court clerk; filing and setting matters for hearing

When a petition, report, account, or other matter that requires a hearing is filed with the court clerk, the clerk shall set the matter for hearing. *(Stats.1990, c. 79 (A.B.759), § 14, operative July 1, 1991.)*

Law Revision Commission Comments
1990 Enactment

Section 1041 continues Section 1041 of the repealed Probate Code without change.

Background on Section 1041 of Repealed Code

Section 1041 was added by 1988 Cal.Stat. ch. 1199 § 56. The section restated former Probate Code Section 1285 (repealed by 1988 Cal.Stat. ch. 1199 § 64.5) without substantive change. Former Section 1285 was earlier enacted upon recommendation of the Law Revision Commission by 1987 Cal.Stat. ch. 923 § 60.5. The section generalized and superseded provisions found in sections of the repealed Probate Code. For background on the provisions of this part, see the Comment to this part under the part heading. [20 Cal.L.Rev.Comm.Reports 1001 (1990)].

§ 1042. Notice of hearing

A hearing under this code shall be on notice unless the statute that provides for the hearing dispenses with notice. *(Stats.1990, c. 79 (A.B.759), § 14, operative July 1, 1991.)*

Law Revision Commission Comments
1990 Enactment

Section 1042 continues Section 1042 of the repealed Probate Code without change. For provisions permitting ex parte hearings, see, e.g., Sections 203 (proceedings to establish fact of death), 8541 (procedure for appointment of special administrator), 9735 (purchase of securities or commodities sold short), 10200 (sale or surrender for redemption or conversion of securities). See also Section 1220(c) (mailed notice dispensed with for good cause). For general provisions relating to notice, see Sections 1200–1265.

Background on Section 1042 of Repealed Code

Section 1042 was a new provision added by 1988 Cal.Stat. ch. 1199 § 56. For background on the provisions of this part, see the Comment to this part under the part heading. [20 Cal.L.Rev.Comm.Reports 1001 (1990)].

Cross References

Notice, mailing, see Probate Code § 1215 et seq.
Notice, posting, see Probate Code § 1230.
Notice, proof of giving notice, see Probate Code § 1260 et seq.
Notice, special notice, see Probate Code § 1250 et seq.
Notice, this code, generally, see Probate Code § 1200 et seq.
Service of process, generally, see Code of Civil Procedure § 413.10 et seq.
Service of process, mail, see Code of Civil Procedure §§ 415.30, 1012 et seq.
Service of process, personal delivery, see Code of Civil Procedure § 415.10.
Service of process, proof of service, see Code of Civil Procedure § 417.10 et seq.
Service of process, publication, see Code of Civil Procedure § 415.50.

§ 1043. Appearances and responses or objections; interested persons

(a) An interested person may appear and make a response or objection in writing at or before the hearing.

(b) An interested person may appear and make a response or objection orally at the hearing. The court in its discretion shall either hear and determine the response or objection at the hearing, or grant a continuance for the purpose of allowing a response or objection to be made in writing.

(c) A request for a continuance for the purpose of making a written response or objection shall not itself be considered as a response or objection, nor shall the failure to make a response or objection during the time allowed be considered as a response or objection. *(Stats.1990, c. 79 (A.B.759), § 14, operative July 1, 1991.)*

Law Revision Commission Comments
1990 Enactment

Section 1043 continues Section 1043 of the repealed Probate Code without change. This section does not apply where a particular statute provides a different procedure. See Section 1040. In the context of a will contest, subdivision (c) means that a potential contestant is not deemed to have contested the will merely because of a request for a continuance for the purpose of determining whether to contest the will.

Background on Section 1043 of Repealed Code

Section 1043 was added by 1988 Cal.Stat. ch. 1199 § 56. Section 1043 superseded a number of former provisions. See, e.g., former Prob.Code §§ 370 (repealed by 1988 Cal.Stat. ch. 1199 § 42) (written grounds of opposition to probate of will), 442 (repealed by 1988 Cal.Stat. ch. 1199 § 45) (opposition to petition for administration), 927 (repealed by 1988 Cal.Stat. ch. 1199 § 54.5) (written exceptions to account), 1041 (repealed by 1988 Cal.Stat. ch. 1199 § 55.5) (written objection to delivery of estate of nonresident). Subdivision (c) was a new provision. For background on the provisions of this part, see the Comment to this part under the part heading.

Cross References

Interested person, defined, see Probate Code § 48.

§ 1043a. Repealed by Stats.1988, c. 1199, § 55.5, operative July 1, 1989

Law Revision Commission Comments

1988 Repeal

Former Section 1043a is superseded by Sections 12570–12572 (collection of personal property of small estate without ancillary administration) [19 Cal.L.Rev. Comm. Reports 1074 (1988)].

§ 1044. Parties plaintiff and defendant

The petitioner or other party affirming is the plaintiff and the party objecting or responding is the defendant. *(Stats. 1990, c. 79 (A.B.759), § 14, operative July 1, 1991.)*

Law Revision Commission Comments

1990 Enactment

Section 1044 continues Section 1044 of the repealed Probate Code without change.

Background on Section 1044 of Repealed Code

Section 1044 was added by 1988 Cal.Stat. ch. 1199 § 56. The section restated the second sentence of former Probate Code Section 1280 (repealed by 1988 Cal.Stat. ch. 1199 § 64.5) without substantive change. For background on the provisions of this part, see the Comment to this part under the part heading. [20 Cal.L.Rev.Comm.Reports 1001 (1990)].

§ 1045. Continuances and postponements

The court may continue or postpone any hearing, from time to time, in the interest of justice. *(Stats.1990, c. 79 (A.B.759), § 14, operative July 1, 1991.)*

Law Revision Commission Comments

1990 Enactment

Section 1045 continues Section 1045 of the repealed Probate Code without change.

Background on Section 1045 of Repealed Code

Section 1045 was added by 1988 Cal.Stat. ch. 1199 § 56. The section continued former Probate Code Section 1286 (repealed by 1988 Cal.Stat. ch. 1199 § 64.5) without change. For background on the provisions of this part, see the Comment to this part under the part heading. [20 Cal.L.Rev.Comm.Reports 1001 (1990)].

Cross References

Adjournments deemed recesses, see Code of Civil Procedure § 74.
Postponement of trial, see Code of Civil Procedure § 594a et seq.

Powers in conducting proceedings, see Code of Civil Procedure §§ 128, 177.

§ 1046. Hearing and determination; court orders

The court shall hear and determine any matter at issue and any response or objection presented, consider evidence presented, and make appropriate orders. *(Stats.1990, c. 79 (A.B.759), § 14, operative July 1, 1991.)*

Law Revision Commission Comments

1990 Enactment

Section 1046 continues Section 1046 of the repealed Probate Code without change.

Background on Section 1046 of Repealed Code

Section 1046 was added by 1988 Cal.Stat. ch. 1199 § 56. The section restated former Probate Code Section 1287 (repealed by 1988 Cal.Stat. ch. 1199 § 64.5) without substantive change. The reference to consideration of evidence generalized part of former Probate Code Section 1103 (repealed by 1988 Cal.Stat. ch. 1199 § 57). Former Section 1287 was earlier enacted upon recommendation of the Law Revision Commission by 1987 Cal.Stat. ch. 923 § 60.5. Section 1287 generalized and superseded a number of former provisions. For background on the provisions of this part, see the Comment to this part under the part heading. [20 Cal.L.Rev.Comm.Reports 1001 (1990)].

Cross References

Appealable orders, see Probate Code § 1300 et seq.
Stay of judgment or order, see Probate Code § 1310

§ 1047. Contents of orders

Except as otherwise provided in this code, an order made in a proceeding under this code need not recite the existence of facts, or the performance of acts, upon which jurisdiction depends, but need only contain the matters ordered. *(Stats. 1990, c. 79 (A.B.759), § 14, operative July 1, 1991.)*

Law Revision Commission Comments

1990 Enactment

Section 1047 continues Section 1047 of the repealed Probate Code without change. For an exception to this section, see Section 8006 (jurisdictional facts in court order opening probate). See also Sections 1260 (order finding that notice of hearing was given), 1962 (order authorizing sterilization to be accompanied by a written statement of decision).

Background on Section 1047 of Repealed Code

Section 1047 was added by 1988 Cal.Stat. ch. 1199 § 56. The section restated former Probate Code Section 1290 (repealed by 1988 Cal.Stat. ch. 1199 § 64.5) without substantive change. For background on the provisions of this part, see the Comment to this part under the part heading. [20 Cal.L.Rev.Comm.Reports 1001 (1990)].

§ 1048. Entering or signing of orders

(a) Except as provided in subdivision (b), orders shall be either entered at length in the minute book of the court or signed by the judge and filed.

(b) An order for distribution shall be entered at length in a judgment book or other permanent record of the court. *(Stats.1990, c. 79 (A.B.759), § 14, operative July 1, 1991.)*

Section 1048 continues Section 1048 of the repealed Probate Code without change.

Background on Section 1048 of Repealed Code

Section 1048 was added by 1988 Cal.Stat. ch. 1199 § 56. The section restated former Probate Code Section 1291 (repealed by 1988 Cal.Stat. ch. 1199 § 64.5) and part of the fourth sentence of former Probate Code Section 1280 (repealed by 1988 Cal.Stat. ch. 1199 § 64.5) without substantive change. For background on the provisions of this part, see the Comment to this part under the part heading. [20 Cal.L.Rev. Comm. Reports 1001 (1990)].

Cross References

Final distribution decree, see Probate Code §§ 11603, 11605, 11641.
Judgment books, see Code of Civil Procedure § 668.
Preliminary distribution, order, see Probate Code § 11621 et seq.

§ 1049. Enforcement of orders

An order may be enforced as provided in Title 9 (commencing with Section 680.010) of Part 2 of the Code of Civil Procedure. *(Stats.1990, c. 79 (A.B.759), § 14, operative July 1, 1991.)*

Law Revision Commission Comments

1990 Enactment

Section 1049 continues Section 1049 of the repealed Probate Code without change. This section elaborates one aspect of Section 1000 (general rules of practice govern). A personal representative may be removed from office if the personal representative is found in contempt for disobeying an order of the court. See Section 8505. See also Sections 20123 (enforcement of estate tax proration order), 20223 (enforcement of order prorating taxes on generation-skipping transfer).

Background on Section 1049 of Repealed Code

Section 1049 was added by 1988 Cal.Stat. ch. 1199 § 56. The section restated part of the last sentence of former Probate Code Section 1280 (repealed by 1988 Cal.Stat. ch. 1199 § 64.5) without substantive change. For background on the provisions of this part, see the Comment to this part under the part heading. [20 Cal.L.Rev.Comm.Reports 1001 (1990)].

§ 1050. Judgment roll; contents

The judgment roll in a proceeding under this code consists of the following papers, where applicable:

(a) In all cases:

(1) The petition, application, report, or account that initiates a particular proceeding.

(2) Any order directing notice of the hearing to be given.

(3) Any notice of the hearing, and any order to show cause made in the proceeding, with the affidavits showing publication, posting, mailing, or personal delivery of the notice or order as may be required by law or court order.

(4) Any citation, in case no answer or written opposition is filed by a party entitled, by law or court order, to notice of the proceeding by citation, with the affidavit or proof of service and, if service of the citation is made by publication, the affidavit of publication and the order directing publication.

(5) Any finding of the court or referee in the proceeding.

(6) The order or statement of decision made in the proceeding.

(7) Any letters (as defined in Section 52).

(b) If an answer, demurrer, written opposition, or counter petition is filed in a proceeding:

(1) Pleadings and papers in the nature of pleadings.

(2) Any orders striking out a pleading in whole or in part.

(3) Any order made on demurrer, or relating to a change of parties, in the proceeding.

(4) The verdict of the jury, if any.

(c) If the proceeding is for the probate of a will, the will.

(d) If the proceeding is a contest of a will, for the revocation of the probate of a will, or for a preliminary or final distribution of the estate under a will:

(1) The will.

(2) The order admitting the will to probate.

(e) If the proceeding is for the settlement of the final account of a personal representative or for the final distribution of an estate, the affidavit showing publication of notice to creditors. *(Stats.1990, c. 79 (A.B.759), § 14, operative July 1, 1991.)*

Law Revision Commission Comments

1990 Enactment

Section 1050 continues Section 1050 of the repealed Probate Code without substantive change. A number of revisions have been made to conform to the terminology of the new Probate Code.

Background on Section 1050 of Repealed Code

Section 1050 was added by 1988 Cal.Stat. ch. 1199 § 56. The section restated former Probate Code Section 1299 (repealed by 1988 Cal.Stat. ch. 1199 § 64.5) without substantive change. However, the former provision stating that the papers constituting the judgment roll need not be attached together was omitted as unnecessary. The reference to the statement of decision in subdivision (a)(6) was new. The reference in subdivision (c) of former Section 1299 to partial and ratable distributions was replaced by a reference to preliminary distributions. For background on the provisions of this part, see the Comment to this part under the part heading. [20 Cal.L.Rev.Comm.Reports 1001 (1990)].

Cross References

Affidavits, see Code of Civil Procedure § 2009 et seq.
Estate administration, generally, see Probate Code § 7000 et seq.
Estate administration, rules of procedure, see Probate Code § 7200 et seq.
Judgment roll, generally, contents, see Code of Civil Procedure § 670.
Notice, mailing, see Probate Code § 1215 et seq.
Notice, posting, see Probate Code § 1230.
Notice, proof of giving notice, see Probate Code § 1260 et seq.
Notice, special notice, see Probate Code § 1250 et seq.
Notice, this code, generally, see Probate Code § 1200 et seq.
Personal representative, compensation, amount, see Probate Code § 10800 et seq.
Personal representative and general personal representative, defined, see Probate Code § 58.
Probate of will, generally, see Probate Code § 8200 et seq.
Probate referees, authority and powers, see Probate Code § 450 et seq.
Proof of service, see Code of Civil Procedure § 417.10 et seq.

Record on appeal, clerk's transcript, see California Rules of Court, Rule 8.120.

Service of process,
  Generally, see Code of Civil Procedure § 413.10 et seq.
  Mail, see Code of Civil Procedure §§ 415.30, 1012 et seq.
  Personal delivery, see Code of Civil Procedure § 415.10.
  Proof of service, see Code of Civil Procedure § 417.10 et seq.
  Publication, see Code of Civil Procedure § 415.50.

Will contest, see Probate Code § 8250 et seq.

Wills,
  Generally, see Probate Code § 6100 et seq.
  Revocation and revival, see Probate Code § 6120.

§ 1051. Ex parte communications; prohibitions upon; exceptions

(a) In the absence of a stipulation to the contrary between parties who have filed pleadings in a proceeding under this code, there shall be no ex parte communications between any party, or attorney for the party, and the court concerning a subject raised in those pleadings, except as permitted or required by law.

(b) Notwithstanding subdivision (a), in any case upon which the court has exercised its jurisdiction, the court may refer to the court investigator or take other appropriate action in response to an ex parte communication regarding either or both of the following: (1) a fiduciary, as defined in Section 39, about the fiduciary's performance of his or her duties and responsibilities, and (2) a person who is the subject of a conservatorship or guardianship proceeding under Division 4 (commencing with Section 1400). Any action by the court pursuant to this subdivision shall be consistent with due process and the requirements of this code. The court shall disclose the ex parte communication to all parties and counsel. The court may, for good cause, dispense with the disclosure if necessary to protect the ward or conservatee from harm.

(c) The Judicial Council shall, on or before January 1, 2008, adopt a rule of court to implement this section.

(d) Subdivisions (a) and (b) of this section shall become operative on January 1, 2008.

(e) A superior court shall not be required to perform any duties imposed by this section until the Legislature makes an appropriation identified for this purpose. *(Added by Stats. 2006, c. 492 (S.B.1716), § 2. Amended by Stats.2011, c. 10 (S.B.78), § 11, eff. March 24, 2011.)*

§§ 1052, 1053. Repealed by Stats.1983, c. 842, §§ 46 to 47, operative Jan. 1, 1985

§§ 1054, 1055. Repealed by Stats.1988, c. 1199, § 55.5, operative July 1, 1989

Law Revision Commission Comments

1988 Repeal

Former Section 1054 is restated without substantive change in Sections 11640 (petition and order) and 11605 (conclusiveness of order and distribution) [19 Cal.L.Rev.Comm. Reports 1074 (1988)].

Former Section 1055 is restated in Section 6179 without substantive change [19 Cal.L.Rev.Comm. Reports 1074 (1988)].

CHAPTER 4. ACCOUNTS

§ 1060. Governance of chapter; additional information required

This chapter governs all accounts to be filed with the court. Except as specifically provided elsewhere in this code, or unless good cause is shown therefore, no information in addition to that required in this chapter need be in an account. *(Added by Stats.1996, c. 862 (A.B.2751), § 4, operative July 1, 1997. Amended by Stats.1997, c. 724 (A.B.1172), § 5.)*

Cross References

Trusts funded by court order, required provisions in trust instruments, see California Rules of Court, Rule 7.903.

§ 1060.1. Repealed by Stats.1988, c. 1199, § 55.5, operative July 1, 1989

Law Revision Commission Comments

1988 Repeal

Former Section 1060.1 is restated without substantive change in Section 11853 (copy of order for distribution) [19 Cal.L.Rev.Comm.Reports 1075 (1988)].

§ 1060.5. Operative date of chapter

This chapter shall be operative on and after July 1, 1997. *(Added by Stats.1996, c. 862 (A.B.2751), § 4, operative July 1, 1997.)*

§ 1061. Summary; contents; format

(a) All accounts shall state the period covered by the account and contain a summary showing all of the following, to the extent applicable:

(1) The property on hand at the beginning of the period covered by the account, which shall be the value of the property initially received by the fiduciary if this is the first account, and shall be the property on hand at the end of the prior account if this is a subsequent account.

(2) The value of any assets received during the period of the accounting which are not assets on hand as of the commencement of the administration of an estate.

(3) The amount of any receipts of income or principal, excluding items listed under paragraphs (1) and (2) or receipts from a trade or business.

(4) Net income from a trade or business.

(5) Gains on sales.

(6) The amount of disbursements, excluding disbursements for a trade or business or distributions.

(7) Loss on sales.

(8) Net loss from trade or business.

(9) Distributions to beneficiaries, the ward or conservatee.

(10) Property on hand at the end of the accounting period, stated at its carry value.

(b) The summary shall be in a format substantially the same as the following, except that inapplicable categories need not be shown:

SUMMARY OF ACCOUNT

CHARGES:

Property on hand at beginning of account (or Inventories)	$ _____
Additional property received (or Supplemental Inventories)	_____
Receipts (Schedule _____)	_____
Gains on Sale or Other Disposition (Schedule _____)	_____
Net income from trade or business (Schedule _____)	_____
Total Charges:	$ _____

CREDITS:

Disbursements (Schedule _____)	$ _____
Losses on Sale or Other Disposition (Schedule _____)	_____
Net loss from trade or business (Schedule _____)	_____
Distributions (Schedule _____)	_____
Property on hand at close of account (Schedule _____)	_____
Total Credits:	$ _____

(c) Total charges shall equal total credits.

(d) For purposes of this section, the terms "net income" and "net loss" shall be utilized in accordance with general accounting principles. Nothing in this section is intended to require that the preparation of the summary must include "net income" and "net loss" as reflected in the tax returns governing the period of the account. *(Added by Stats.1996, c. 862 (A.B.2751), § 4, operative July 1, 1997. Amended by Stats.1997, c. 724 (A.B.1172), § 6.)*

Cross References

Beneficiary defined, see Probate Code § 24

Fiduciary defined, see Probate Code § 39.

Real property located in foreign jurisdiction, guardian or conservator use of ordinary care and diligence in determination of ownership, see Probate Code § 2401.1.

§ 1062. Support of summary; schedules

The summary shall be supported by detailed schedules showing the following:

(a) Receipts, showing the nature or purpose of each item, the source of the receipt, and the date thereof.

(b) Disbursement, including the nature or purpose of each item, the name of the payee, and the date thereof.

(c) Net income or loss from a trade or business, which shall be sufficient if it provides the information disclosed on Schedule C or F of the federal income tax return.

(d) Calculation of gains or losses on sale or other disposition.

(e) Distributions of cash or property to beneficiaries, ward or conservatee, showing the date and amount of each, with the distribution of property shown at its carry value.

(f) Itemized list of property on hand, describing each item at its carry value. *(Added by Stats.1996, c. 862 (A.B.2751), § 4, operative July 1, 1997.)*

Cross References

Beneficiary, defined, see Probate Code § 24

Real property located in foreign jurisdiction, guardian or conservator use of ordinary care and diligence in determination of ownership, see Probate Code § 2401.1.

§ 1063. Additional schedule; estimated market value of assets; changes during accounting period; income; disbursements; interest; distributions; liabilities; real property in foreign jurisdiction

(a) In all accounts, there shall be an additional schedule showing the estimated market value of the assets on hand as of the end of the accounting period, and a schedule of the estimated market value of the assets on hand as of the beginning of the accounting period for all accounts subsequent to the initial account. The requirement of an estimated value of real estate, a closely held business, or other assets without a ready market, may be satisfied by a good faith estimate by the fiduciary.

(b) If there were purchases or other changes in the form of assets occurring during the period of the account, there shall be a schedule showing these transactions. However, no reporting is required for transfers between cash or accounts in a financial institution or money market mutual funds as defined in subdivision (d) of Section 8901.

(c) If an estate of a decedent or a trust will be distributed to an income beneficiary, there shall be a schedule showing an allocation of receipts and disbursements between principal and income.

(d) If there is specifically devised property, there shall be an additional schedule accounting for income, disbursements, and proceeds of sale pursuant to Section 12002 and subdivision (a) of Section 16340.

(e) If any interest has been paid or is to be paid under Section 12003, 12004, or 12005, or subdivision (b) of Section

16340, there shall be a schedule showing the calculation of the interest.

(f) If the accounting contemplates a proposed distribution, there shall be a schedule setting forth the proposed distribution, including the allocation of income required under Section 12006. If the distribution requires an allocation between trusts, the allocation shall be set forth on the schedule, unless the allocation is to be made by a trustee after receipt of the assets. If the distribution requires valuation of assets as of the date of distribution, the schedule shall set forth the fair market value of those assets.

(g) If, at the end of the accounting period, there are liabilities of the estate or trust, except current or future periodic payments, including rent, salaries, utilities, or other recurring expenses, there shall be a schedule showing all of the following:

(1) All liabilities which are a lien on estate or trust assets.

(2) Taxes due but unpaid as shown on filed returns or assessments received subsequent to filing of returns.

(3) All notes payable.

(4) Any judgments for which the estate or trust is liable.

(5) Any other material liability.

(h) If the guardian or conservator has knowledge of any real property of the conservatee or ward located in a foreign jurisdiction, the guardian or conservator shall include an additional schedule that identifies the real property, provides a good faith estimate of the fair market value of the real property, and states what action, if any, will or has been taken to preserve and protect the real property, including a recommendation whether an ancillary proceeding is necessary to preserve and protect the real property. *(Added by Stats.1996, c. 862 (A.B.2751), § 4, operative July 1, 1997. Amended by Stats.1997, c. 724 (A.B.1172), § 7; Stats.1999, c. 145 (A.B.846), § 2; Stats.2008, c. 52 (A.B.2014), § 1.)*

Law Revision Commission Comments

1999 Amendment

Subdivisions (d) and (e) of Section 1063 are amended to revise cross-references to former Section 16314. See Section 16340 Comment. [29 Cal.L.Rev.Comm. Reports 245 (1999)].

Cross References

Account, defined, see Probate Code § 21.
Duties of trustees, see Probate Code § 16000 et seq.
Fiduciary, defined, see Probate Code § 39.
Financial institution, defined, see Probate Code § 40.
Independent administration of estates, see Probate Code § 10400 et seq.
Inventory and appraisal, generally, see Probate Code § 8800 et seq.
Mechanics liens, see Civil Code § 8400.
Trustees, liability to beneficiaries, see Probate Code § 16400 et seq.

§ 1064. Petition for approval of account; contents; additional petitions

(a) The petition for approval of the account or a report accompanying the petition shall contain all of the following:

(1) A description of all sales, purchases, changes in the form of assets, or other transactions occurring during the period of the account that are not otherwise readily understandable from the schedule.

(2) An explanation of any unusual items appearing in the account.

(3) A statement of all compensation paid from the assets subject to the account to the fiduciary or to the attorneys for the fiduciary other than pursuant to a prior court order.

(4) A statement disclosing any family or affiliate relationship between the fiduciary and any agent hired by the fiduciary during the accounting period.

(5) An allegation disclosing whether all of the cash has been invested and maintained in interest bearing accounts or in investments authorized by law or the governing instrument, except for an amount of cash that is reasonably necessary for the orderly administration of the estate.

(b) The filing of an account shall be deemed to include a petition requesting its approval, and may include additional petitions for authorization, instruction or confirmation authorized by the code, including, but not limited to, a request for an order for compensation of the fiduciary and the attorney for the fiduciary.

(c) For purposes of this section, "family" means a relationship created by blood or marriage. For purposes of this section, "affiliate" means an entity that directly or indirectly through one or more intermediaries controls, is controlled by, or is under common control with, the fiduciary. *(Added by Stats.1996, c. 862 (A.B.2751), § 4, operative July 1, 1997. Amended by Stats.1997, c. 724 (A.B.1172), § 8.)*

Cross References

Civil actions for abuse of elderly or dependent adults, jurisdiction, right to maintain action, see Welfare and Institutions Code § 15657.3.
Estate attorney, compensation, amount, see Probate Code § 10810 et seq.
Fiduciary, defined, see Probate Code § 39.
Instrument, defined, see Probate Code § 45.

§§ 1065 to 1068. Repealed by Stats.1988, c. 1199, § 55.5, operative July 1, 1989

Law Revision Commission Comments

1988 Repeal

Former Section 1065 is not continued. For the receipt of the distributee, see Section 11751 (receipt for distributed property) [19 Cal.L.Rev.Comm.Reports 1076 (1988)].

Former Section 1066 is restated without substantive change in Section 12250 (order of discharge), except that the provision for production of vouchers is not continued and the petition is made ex parte [19 Cal.L.Rev.Comm.Reports 1076 (1988)].

Former Section 1067 is restated without substantive change in Section 12252 (administration after discharge) [19 Cal.L.Rev.Comm.Reports 1076 (1988)].

Former Section 1068 is restated without substantive change in Sections 12251 (discharge without administration), 1021 (verification required), and 1041 (clerk to set matter for hearing) [19 Cal.L.Rev.Comm.Reports 1226 (1988)].

§§ 1080 to 1082. Repealed by Stats.1988, c. 1199, § 56.5, operative July 1, 1989

Law Revision Commission Comments

1988 Repeal

The first sentence of former Section 1080 is restated without substantive change in Section 11700 (petition). The second and third sentences are superseded by Section 11701 (notice of hearing). The fourth and fifth sentences are restated without substantive change in Section 11702 (responsive pleading). The last sentence is restated without substantive change in Section 11703 (Attorney General as party) [19 Cal.L.Rev.Comm.Reports 1076 (1988)].

The first sentence of the first paragraph of former Section 1081, providing for jury trial, is not continued. *Cf.* Section 7200 (trial by jury). The second and third sentences are restated without substantive change in Sections 11704 (hearing) and 11705 (court order). The second paragraph is superseded by Section 1000 (general rules of practice govern) [19 Cal.L.Rev.Comm.Reports 1226 (1988)].

Former Section 1082 is restated without substantive change in Section 11705(b) (court order) [19 Cal.L.Rev.Comm.Reports 1077 (1988)].

§§ 1100 to 1106. Repealed by Stats.1988, c. 1199, § 57, operative July 1, 1989

Law Revision Commission Comments

1988 Repeal

Former Section 1100 is restated without substantive change in Sections 11950 (right to partition or allotment) and 62 ("property" defined) [19 Cal.L.Rev.Comm.Reports 1077 (1988)].

The first and second sentences of Section 1101 are restated in Section 11951 (petition). The third, fourth, and fifth sentences are superseded by subdivision (a) of Section 11952 (parties and notice) [19 Cal.L.Rev.Comm.Reports 1226 (1988)].

Former Section 1102 is superseded by Section 11952 (parties and notice) [19 Cal.L.Rev.Comm.Reports 1077 (1988)].

Former Section 1103 is restated without substantive change in Section 11953 (disposition of property) [19 Cal.L.Rev.Comm.Reports 1077 (1988)].

Former Section 1104 is restated without substantive change in Section 11954 (referees) [19 Cal.L.Rev.Comm.Reports 1077 (1988)].

Former Section 1105 is restated without substantive change in Section 11955 (costs) [19 Cal.L.Rev.Comm.Reports 1077 (1988)].

Former Section 1106 is restated without substantive change in Section 11956 (effect of division) [19 Cal.L.Rev.Comm.Reports 1077 (1988)].

§§ 1120 to 1133. Repealed by Stats.1986, c. 820, § 31, operative July 1, 1987

Law Revision Commission Comments

1986 Repeal

Former Section 1120 is restated in Article 1 (commencing with Section 17300) of Chapter 4 of Part 5 of Division 9 with minor changes. See Sections 17300–17302. Trusts not subject to continuing court jurisdiction under Sections 17300–17302 are subject to the intermittent jurisdiction of the courts when invoked pursuant to Section 17200. The new law contains provisions comparable to parts of former Section 1120 and other sections in former Article 1. See Sections 17000 (jurisdiction in superior court), 17200(b)(5) (petition to settle accounts), 17200(b)(6) (petition for instructions), 17200(b)(15) (amending trust for charitable estate tax deduction), 17203 (notice of hearing on petition), 16200–16249 (trustees' powers); see also 17100–17107 (notice), 17201(b) (clerk to set petition for hearing), 17208 (appointment of guardian ad litem). The provision for accepting additions to trusts is superseded by Section 16221 (power to accept additions to trust). [18 Cal.L.Rev.Comm. Reports 501 (1986)].

Former Section 1120.1 is superseded by Section 82 which defines "trust" to include additions to a trust. [18 Cal.L.Rev.Comm. Reports 501 (1986)].

Former Section 1120.1a is restated in Sections 17350–17354 (removal of trusts from continuing court supervision) with some technical changes. See the Comments to Sections 17350–17354.

See also Sections 16060–16062 and 16064 (trustee's duty to report information and account to beneficiaries), 16063 (contents of annual account), 17201(b) (clerk to set petition for hearing). References to "remaindermen" are omitted since they are unnecessary in light of the definition of "beneficiary" in Section 24. [18 Cal.L.Rev.Comm. Reports 501 (1986)].

Former Section 1120.2 is superseded by Sections 16200–16249 (trustees' powers). The provision in the first paragraph of former Section 1120.2 requiring a petition in order to exercise powers not expressed in the trust instrument or otherwise conferred is superseded by Section 16200 which grants extensive powers notwithstanding the silence of the trust instrument. See also Section 16201 (power of court to relieve trustee from restrictions on powers).

The first clause of subdivision (1) of former Section 1120.2 is restated in Sections 16226 (acquisition and disposition of property) and 16227 (management of property) without substantive change. The second and third clauses of subdivision (1) are restated in Sections 16231 (leases) and 16232 (mineral leases) without substantive change.

Parts of subdivision (2) are restated in Sections 16220 (retaining trust property) and 16223 (investments) without substantive change. The reference to reinvesting, stock of the trustee, and common trust funds are omitted as unnecessary. The power to invest under Section 16223 applies to any type of property. See also Section 62 ("property" defined); Fin.Code § 1564 (common trust funds).

The first clause of subdivision (3) is superseded by Section 16241 (borrowing money). The remainder of subdivision (3) is superseded by Section 16228 (encumbrances).

Subdivision (4) is continued in Section 16237 (consent to change in form of business, voting trusts) without substantive change.

The first clause of subdivision (5) is restated in Section 16226 (acquisition and disposition of property) without substantive change. The second clause is continued in Section 16227 (management of property) without change, except that "property" is used in place of "asset."

Subdivision (6) is continued in Section 16229 (repairs and alterations) without substantive change.

Subdivision (7) is continued in Section 16230 (development of land) without substantive change.

Subdivision (8) is restated in Section 16233 (options) without substantive change, except that Section 16233 makes clear that an option may be exercisable beyond the term of the trust.

Subdivision (9) is restated in Section 16234 (voting rights with respect to corporate shares, memberships, or property) without substantive change.

Subdivision (10) is continued in Section 16235 (payment of calls and assessments) without substantive change.

Subdivision (11) is continued in Section 16236 (stock subscriptions and conversions) without substantive change.

Subdivision (12) is continued in Section 16238 (holding securities in name of nominee) without substantive change.

Subdivision (13) is restated in Section 16240 (insurance) without substantive change.

The first part of subdivision (14) is superseded by Section 16243 (payment of expenses in administration of the trust). No power is needed for the trustee to advance its own funds since in doing so it is not acting as trustee. However, if a trustee does advance its own funds in protection of the trust, the trustee's right of reimbursement may arise under Section 15684 or the trustee may have a lien on trust property. The part of subdivision (14) relating to the trustee's lien for advances of the trustee's funds is restated in Section 15685 without substantive change, but Section 15685 makes clear that the lien is an equitable lien.

The first two clauses of subdivision (15) are continued in Section 16242(a) and (b) (payment and settlement of claims) without substantive change. The third clause is continued in Section 16242(c) except that the reference to releasing claims to the "extent that the claim is uncollectible" is not continued. The last clause is superseded by Section 16249 (actions and proceedings).

Subdivision (16) is continued in Section 16243 (payment of taxes, trustee's compensation, and other expenses) without substantive change, except that the power to pay compensation is limited to "reasonable" compensation.

Subdivision (17) is continued in Section 16222(a) (participation in business; change in form of business) without substantive change, but Section 16222(a) makes clear that the trustee has power to participate only in a business that is part of trust property. See also Section 16222(b) (limitation on power to continue operation of business).

Subdivision (18) is superseded by Sections 16200 (general powers without court authorization) and 16201 (power of court to relieve trustee from restrictions on powers). See the Comment to Section 16200.

The second paragraph is superseded by Section 15001 (application of Trust Law).

The last paragraph is omitted as unnecessary in light of Section 11 (severability). [18 Cal.L.Rev.Comm. Reports 501 (1986)].

Former Section 1120.5 is superseded by Section 17204 (request for notice). See also Section 17105(a) (additional notice). [18 Cal. L.Rev.Comm. Reports 501 (1986)].

Subdivisions (a) and (d) of former Section 1120.6 are restated in Section 15408(a) and (c) (modification or termination of trust with uneconomically low principal) without substantive change. The first clause of subdivision (b) is restated in Section 15410(c) (disposition of property upon termination of trust) without substantive change. The last clause of subdivision (b) is superseded by Section 17206 (authority to make necessary orders). Subdivision (c) is superseded by Probate Code Section 15002 (common law as law of state). [18 Cal.L.Rev.Comm. Reports 501 (1986)].

Former Section 1121 is superseded by Sections 17200(b)(7) (petition to compel account) and Sections 16060–16062 and 16064 (trustee's duty to report information and account to beneficiary). See also Section 15800 (limitation on rights of beneficiary of revocable trust). [18 Cal.L.Rev.Comm. Reports 501 (1986)].

The first and second sentences of former Section 1122 are restated in Section 15680(a) and (b) (trustee's compensation as provided under trust instrument) without substantive change, but Section 15680 permits the court to decrease the trustee's compensation as well as increase it. The reference to the decree of distribution is not continued since the new law applies to both living and testamentary trusts. The first part of the third sentence is restated in Section 15681 (trustee's compensation where trust silent) without substantive change. The remainder of the third sentence is superseded by Sections 15682 (court determination of prospective compensation) and 17200(b)(9) (petition to fix or allow compensation). The fourth sentence is restated in Section 15683 (compensation of cotrustees) without substantive change. The last sentence is superseded by Sections 15684 (repayment of trustee for expenditures) and 17200(b)(5) (petition to settle accounts). See also Section 16243 (trustee's power to pay compensation and expenses). [18 Cal.L.Rev. Comm. Reports 501 (1986)].

Former Section 1123 is superseded by Section 17104(b). [18 Cal.L.Rev.Comm. Reports 501 (1986)].

Former Section 1123.5 is superseded by Section 15642 (removal of trustee). See also Sections 16420(a)(5) (removal of trustee for breach of trust), 17000 et seq. (judicial proceedings concerning trusts), 17201(b) (clerk to set petition for hearing). [18 Cal.L.Rev. Comm. Reports 501 (1986)].

Former Section 1123.6 is restated in Section 15642(c) without substantive change. See also Section 17206 (general authority to appoint temporary trustee). [18 Cal.L.Rev.Comm. Reports 501 (1986)].

Former Section 1123.7 is superseded by Section 17000 (subject-matter jurisdiction). [18 Cal.L.Rev.Comm. Reports 501 (1986)].

Former Section 1124 is superseded by Section 15601 (rejection of trust). See also Sections 15600 (acceptance of trust by trustee), 15640 (resignation of trustee), 16000 (duty to administer trust upon acceptance). [18 Cal.L.Rev.Comm. Reports 501 (1986)].

Former Section 1125 is superseded by Sections 15660 (appointment of trustee to fill vacancy) and 17200(a), (b)(10) (petition to appoint trustee). [18 Cal.L.Rev.Comm. Reports 501 (1986)].

The first paragraph of former Section 1125.1 is superseded by Sections 15640 (resignation of trustee), 17101 (form of notice), 17102 (manner of mailing notice), 17200(a), (b)(11) (petition to accept resignation), 17201(b) (clerk to set matter for hearing), 17203 (notice).

The first part of the second paragraph is restated in Section 15641 (liability of resigning trustee) without substantive change. The remainder of the second paragraph is restated in Section 15644 (delivery of property by former trustee upon occurrence of vacancy) without substantive change. [18 Cal.L.Rev.Comm. Reports 501 (1986)].

Former Section 1126 is superseded by Sections 15660 (appointment of trustee to fill vacancy), 17101 (form of notice), 17102 (manner of mailing notice), 17203 (notice), and 17200(a), (b)(10) (petition to appoint trustee). See also Sections 15601 (rejection of trust by writing or inaction), 15642 (removal of trustee), 15643 (vacancy in office of trustee), 17204 (request for special notice). [18 Cal.L.Rev.Comm. Reports 501 (1986)].

Former Section 1127 is superseded by Section 15602 (trustee's bond). The requirement that an individual successor trustee who is not named in the trust must give bond is restated in Section 15602(a)(3) without substantive change. [18 Cal.L.Rev.Comm. Reports 501 (1986)].

Former Section 1127.5 is superseded by Section 15602(e) (bond not required of trustees who are not individuals). [18 Cal.L.Rev. Comm. Reports 501 (1986)].

Former Section 1128 is restated in Sections 17304(a)–(b) (transfer of jurisdiction of trust to different county) and 17201(a) (petition to be verified). [18 Cal.L.Rev.Comm.Reports 501 (1986)].

The first three sentences of the first paragraph of former Section 1129 are superseded by Sections 17102 (manner of mailing), 17201(b) (clerk to set matter for hearing), and 17203 (notice). The fourth and fifth sentences are continued in Sections 17304(c) (transfer of jurisdiction over trust to different county) without substantive change. The sixth sentence is continued in Section 17304(d) without substantive change.

The second paragraph is continued in Section 17304(e) without substantive change.

The third paragraph is superseded by Section 17302 (applicable procedures). [18 Cal.L.Rev.Comm. Reports 501 (1986)].

Former Section 1130 is omitted. Vouchers in support of an account are not required under the Trust Law. [18 Cal.L.Rev. Comm. Reports 501 (1986)].

Former Section 1130.1 is restated in Section 15603 (certificate of trustee) without substantive change, but Section 15603 also applies to living trusts. See also Section 10 (singular includes plural). [18 Cal.L.Rev.Comm. Reports 501 (1986)].

Former Section 1132 is superseded by Section 17401 (transfer of trust from California). See also Sections 82 ("trust" defined), 17400 (application of transfer provisions). [18 Cal.L.Rev.Comm. Reports 501 (1986)].

Former Section 1133 is superseded by Section 15411 (combination of similar trusts). [18 Cal.L.Rev.Comm. Reports 501 (1986)].

§§ 1134 to 1136. Repealed by Stats.1971, c. 958, p. 1868, §§ 5 to 7

§§ 1137 to 1137.14. Repealed by Stats.1970, c. 849, p. 1582, § 1, eff. Sept. 3, 1970

§§ 1138 to 1139.19.   Repealed by Stats.1986, c. 820, § 31, operative July 1, 1987

Law Revision Commission Comments

1986 Repeal

Subdivision (a) of former Section 1138 is restated in Section 82(a) ("trust" defined) without substantive change, except that the procedure relating to internal trust affairs under the new law is not limited to written trusts and the reference to "voluntary" trusts is omitted because it is unnecessary. See the Comment to former Civil Code § 2215. See also Section 17200 (proceedings concerning trusts). The language in subdivision (a) concerning trusts "entirely administered or to be entirely administered in this state" is superseded by Section 17002 which delineates the principal place of administration of the trust.

Subdivision (b) of former Section 1138 is continued in Section 82(c) without substantive change except as noted. The former exclusion of trusts subject to court supervision is superseded by Section 17302 (general procedures applicable). See also the Comment to former Section 1120. The former exclusion of deeds of trust is continued in Section 82 by the reference to security arrangements. The former exclusion of charitable trusts subject to supervision of the Attorney General is omitted. See Section 82(a) ("trust" defined); see also Section 15004 (application of Trust Law to certain charitable trusts). [18 Cal.L.Rev.Comm. Reports 501 (1986)].

Subdivision (a) of former Section 1138.1 is restated in Section 17200 (petitioners; grounds for petition) with the following changes: Paragraph (3) is omitted since Section 16221 permits additions to trusts without the need for court approval. Paragraph (6) is superseded by Section 17200(b)(8) which is drafted in recognition of the automatic powers available under Sections 16200–16249. See Section 16201 (power of court to relieve trustee from restrictions on powers); see also Sections 16060–16062 & 16064 (duty to report information and account to beneficiaries). Paragraph (14) is superseded by Section 15412 (division of trusts). See also Section 15640(b) (acceptance of trustee's resignation by court).

Subdivision (b) is omitted; the trust instrument may not limit the availability of proceedings under Section 17200 et seq. [18 Cal. L.Rev.Comm. Reports 501 (1986)].

Former Section 1138.2 is continued in Section 17206 without change. [18 Cal.L.Rev.Comm. Reports 501 (1986)].

The first sentence of subdivision (a) of former Section 1138.3 is restated in Section 17005(a) (venue) without substantive change. See also Section 17000(a) (subject-matter jurisdiction of superior court). The second and third sentences of subdivision (a) are superseded by Section 17002 (principal place of administration of trust).

Subdivision (b) is restated in Section 17005(a)(2) (alternative venue for testamentary trusts) without substantive change. [18 Cal.L.Rev.Comm. Reports 501 (1986)].

The first sentence of former Section 1138.4 is restated in Section 17201(a) (commencement of proceeding) without substantive change, except that the provision relating to authorization by the terms of the trust is omitted since the trust can not prevent resort to the statutory procedure. The second sentence is omitted. [18 Cal.L.Rev.Comm. Reports 501 (1986)].

Subdivision (a) of former Section 1138.5 is restated in Section 17202 (dismissal of petition) without substantive change. See also Section 24 ("beneficiary" defined to include remaindermen). Subdivision (b) is omitted. [18 Cal.L.Rev.Comm. Reports 501 (1986)].

The first paragraph of subdivision (a) of former Section 1138.6 is restated in Section 17201(b) (clerk to set petition for hearing) without substantive change. The second paragraph is restated in Sections 17203 (notice of hearing on petition) and 17102 (manner of notice; notice in manner directed by court) without substantive change. The third paragraph is restated in Section 17205 (request for and service of copy of petition) without substantive change. The

fourth paragraph is restated in Section 17103 (personal delivery) without substantive change. The fifth paragraph is restated in Section 17104 (proof of notice) without substantive change. See also Section 24 ("beneficiary" defined to include remaindermen).

Subdivision (b) is omitted. Trust proceedings are governed by the new Trust Law, Division 9 (commencing with Section 15000), not by the provisions on administration of decedents' estates.

Subdivision (c) is restated in Section 17106 (shortening time for notice) without substantive change.

Subdivision (d) is superseded by Section 17203(c) (notice to Attorney General). [18 Cal.L.Rev.Comm. Reports 501 (1986)].

Subdivision (a) of former Section 1138.7 is restated in Section 17208(a)–(b) (appointment of guardian ad litem) without substantive change.

Subdivision (b) is superseded by Sections 17200 (petition), 17201(a) (grounds for petition), and 17203 (notice). See also Section 17100 et seq. (general notice provisions), 17208 (appointment of guardian ad litem).

Subdivision (c) is continued in Section 17208(c) without substantive change. [18 Cal.L.Rev.Comm. Reports 501 (1986)].

The first three sentences of former Section 1138.8 are superseded by Section 15640 (resignation of trustee). The first part of the last sentence is restated in Section 15641 (liability of resigning trustee) without substantive change. The remainder of the last sentence is superseded by Section 15644 (delivery of property by resigning trustee). [18 Cal.L.Rev.Comm. Reports 501 (1986)].

Former Section 1138.9 is superseded by Sections 15642(b)(5) (removal of trustee for other cause), 15643 (vacancy in office of trustee), 15660 (appointment of trustee to fill vacancy), and 17200(a), (b)(10) (petition for appointment of trustee to fill vacancy). [18 Cal.L.Rev.Comm. Reports 501 (1986)].

Former Section 1138.10 is superseded by Section 17207 (appeal). See the Comment to Section 17207. [18 Cal.L.Rev.Comm. Reports 501 (1986)].

The provision of former Section 1138.11 relating to the cumulative nature of remedies is restated in Section 16420(b) without substantive change. The provision relating to nonexclusive remedies, to the extent it related to jurisdiction, is superseded by Section 17000(a) (exclusive jurisdiction over internal affairs of trusts). See also Sections 16420–16421 (remedies for breach of trust), 17001 (court as full-power court), 17206 (authority to make necessary orders). [18 Cal.L.Rev.Comm. Reports 501 (1986)].

Former Section 1138.12 is restated in Section 17209 (intermittent judicial intervention in trust administration) without substantive change. [18 Cal.L.Rev.Comm. Reports 501 (1986)].

The first sentence of former Section 1138.13 is restated in Section 15001(a) (application of Trust Law) without substantive change. The second sentence is omitted; the right to petition under Section 17200 cannot be restricted by the trust instrument under the Trust Law. See also Section 82 ("trust" defined). [18 Cal.L.Rev.Comm. Reports 501 (1986)].

Former Section 1138.14 is continued in Section 15005 (law applicable to marital deduction gifts in trust) without substantive change. [18 Cal.L.Rev.Comm. Reports 501 (1986)].

Subdivision (a) of former Section 1139 is restated in Section 17400(a) (application of chapter) without substantive change, except that the limitation to written trusts is omitted. Subdivision (b) is superseded by Section 17400(b) (availability of other means of transfer). Subdivision (c) is omitted because it is no longer needed. [18 Cal.L.Rev.Comm. Reports 501 (1986)].

The introductory clause of Section 1139.1 is restated in Section 17401(a) (authority of court) without substantive change. See also Sections 17000 (subject-matter jurisdiction of superior court), 17200(a), (b)(16) (petition for transfer). Clause (a) pertaining to trusts under continuing jurisdiction of the court is superseded by the more general language of Section 17401(a). Clause (b) is superseded by Sections 17200(a) (who may petition) and 17404(b) (order granting transfer if not violative of terms of trust). [18 Cal.L.Rev. Comm. Reports 501 (1986)].

The first sentence of former Section 1139.2 is restated in Section 17200(a) (who may petition) without substantive change. The remainder of former Section 1139.2 is restated in Sections 17402 (contents of petition) and 17201(a) (petition to be verified) without substantive change, except that a statement of the age of a trustee is required only for an individual and the statement relating to civil actions is limited to actions arising out of administration of the trust. [18 Cal.L.Rev.Comm. Reports 501 (1986)].

The provision of former Section 1139.3 requiring the clerk to set the petition for hearing is continued in Section 17201(b) without substantive change. The remainder of the first sentence is omitted; notice is given by the petitioner. See Section 17403(a). The last three sentences are restated in Sections 17203(c) (notice to Attorney General regarding charitable trust) and 17403 (notice and hearing) without substantive change, except that 30 rather than 20 days' notice must be given the Attorney General. See also Sections 17102 (manner of mailing notice). [18 Cal.L.Rev.Comm. Reports 501 (1986)].

The introductory clause and subdivisions (1), (3), and (4) of former Section 1139.4 are restated in Section 17404 (order granting transfer) without substantive change, except that the court is required to take into account the interest in economical and convenient administration rather than to find that it would necessarily result from the transfer. Subdivision (2) is omitted. [18 Cal.L.Rev.Comm. Reports 501 (1986)].

Former Section 1139.5 is continued in Section 17405 (manner and effect of transfer) without substantive change. [18 Cal.L.Rev.Comm. Reports 501 (1986)].

Former Section 1139.6 is omitted. See Sections 17000 (subject-matter jurisdiction in superior court), 17002 (principal place of administration), 17005 (venue), 17400 (application of transfer procedure). [18 Cal.L.Rev.Comm. Reports 501 (1986)].

Former Section 1139.7 is restated in Sections 24 ("beneficiary" defined) and 17402(b) (notice of petition to living beneficiaries) without substantive change. [18 Cal.L.Rev.Comm. Reports 501 (1986)].

Subdivision (a) of former Section 1139.10 is restated in Section 17450(a) (application of chapter) without substantive change, except that the limitation to written trusts is omitted. Subdivision (b) is superseded by Section 17450(b) (nonexclusive procedure). [18 Cal.L.Rev.Comm. Reports 501 (1986)].

Former Section 1139.11 is restated in Section 17451(a) (authority of court) without substantive change. See also Section 17200(a), (b)(16) (petition for transfer). [18 Cal.L.Rev.Comm. Reports 501 (1986)].

Former Section 1139.12 is restated in Section 17200(a) (petition) without substantive change. [18 Cal.L.Rev.Comm. Reports 501 (1986)].

Former Section 1139.13 is continued in Sections 17452 (venue) and 17000(a) (subject-matter jurisdiction in superior court) without substantive change. [18 Cal.L.Rev.Comm. Reports 501 (1986)].

Former Section 1139.14 is continued in Sections 17453 (contents of petition) and 17201(a) (petition to be verified) without substantive change, except that a statement of the age of a trustee is required only for an individual. [18 Cal.L.Rev.Comm. Reports 501 (1986)].

The part of subdivision (a) of former Section 1139.15 requiring the clerk to set the petition for hearing is continued in Section 17201(b). The remainder of the first sentence of subdivision (a) is omitted. The second sentence of subdivision (a) is continued in Section 17454 (notice) without substantive change. Subdivision (b) is continued in Section 17454 (notice and hearing) without change. See also Section 17102 (manner of mailing notice). [18 Cal.L.Rev.Comm. Reports 501 (1986)].

Former Section 1139.16 is restated in Section 17455 (order accepting transfer and appointing trustee) without substantive

change, except as follows: (1) the court is required to take into account the interest in economical and convenient administration rather than to find that it would necessarily result from the transfer, (2) the discretion of the court to require bond is governed by the general provisions in Section 15602, and (3) a bond is required only if the law of the other jurisdiction or California so provides. [18 Cal.L.Rev.Comm. Reports 501 (1986)].

Former Section 1139.17 is continued in Section 17456 (conditional order accepting transfer) without change. [18 Cal.L.Rev.Comm. Reports 501 (1986)].

Former Section 1139.18 is superseded by Section 17457 (administration of transferred trust). See the Comment to Section 17457. [18 Cal.L.Rev.Comm. Reports 501 (1986)].

Section 1139.19 is restated in Sections 24 ("beneficiary" defined) and 17453(b) (notice of petition to living beneficiaries) without substantive change. [18 Cal.L.Rev.Comm. Reports 501 (1986)].

§§ 1140 to 1150. Repealed by Stats.1988, c. 1199, § 57.5, operative July 1, 1989

Law Revision Commission Comments

1988 Repeal

The first sentence of subdivision (a) of former Section 1140 is restated in Section 7601 (duty of public administrator), with the addition of misappropriation as a ground for taking possession or control of property. The court may also appoint the public administrator as special administrator. Section 8541 (procedure for appointment). The second sentence of subdivision (a) is restated in Section 7620 (authority of public administrator).

Subdivision (b) is restated without substantive change in Section 7621 (appointment of public administrator), with the addition of provisions for appointment of a public administrator on the court's own motion and for county recoupment from the estate of a bond fee [19 Cal.L.Rev.Comm.Reports 1078 (1988)].

Former Section 1140.5 is omitted. The county may not return alien indigents to their native land [19 Cal.L.Rev.Comm.Reports 1078 (1988)].

Former Section 1141 is restated without substantive change in Sections 7602 (search for property, will, and instructions for disposition of remains) and 7603 (providing information and access to public administrator), with the elimination of the requirement that there be reasonable grounds to believe the public administrator may be appointed personal representative [19 Cal.L.Rev.Comm.Reports 1078 (1988)].

Former Section 1142 is restated without substantive change in Section 7622 (general rules governing administration of estates apply) [19 Cal.L.Rev.Comm.Reports 1078 (1988)].

Former Section 1142.3 is restated without substantive change in Section 7623 (additional compensation) [19 Cal.L.Rev.Comm.Reports 1078 (1988)].

Former Section 1142.5 is omitted as unnecessary. See, e.g., Gov't Code §§ 1190–1195 & 24100–24155, governing deputies and assistants [19 Cal.L.Rev.Comm.Reports 1079 (1988)].

Former Section 1143 is superseded by Sections 7660–7666 (summary disposition of small estates) [19 Cal.L.Rev.Comm.Reports 1079 (1988)].

Former Section 1144 is superseded by Sections 7660–7666 (summary disposition of small estates) [19 Cal.L.Rev.Comm.Reports 1079 (1988)].

Former Section 1144.5 is restated in Section 7604 (costs and fees for taking possession or control of property) [19 Cal.L.Rev.Comm.Reports 1079 (1988)].

Former Section 1145 is superseded by Sections 7600 (report of public officer or employee) and 7600.5 (notice of death of patient) [19 Cal.L.Rev.Comm.Reports 1079 (1988)].

Former Section 1146 is restated without substantive change in Section 7600 (report of public officer or employee) [19 Cal.L.Rev.Comm.Reports 1079 (1988)].

The first sentence of the first paragraph of former Section 1147 is restated without substantive change in Section 7640 (deposit by public administrator). The second sentence is restated without substantive change in Section 7641 (withdrawal of amounts deposited). The second paragraph is restated in Section 7642 (interest on money deposited) [19 Cal.L.Rev.Comm.Reports 1080 (1988)].

Former Section 1147.5 is restated without substantive change in Section 7644 (deposit unclaimed in financial institution) [19 Cal.L.Rev.Comm.Reports 1080 (1988)].

Former Section 1148 is restated without substantive change in Section 7643 (deposit with county treasurer) [19 Cal.L.Rev.Comm. Reports 1080 (1988)].

Former Section 1149 is omitted. Payment of fees is controlled by general rules governing payment of the expenses of administration. See e.g., Sections 7622 (general rules governing administration of estates apply) and 7662 (payment of demands). [19 Cal.L.Rev. Comm. Reports 1080 (1988)].

Former Section 1150 is omitted. General rules governing fiduciary obligations of the personal representative apply to the public administrator. Government Code Section 27443 provides an additional sanction [19 Cal.L.Rev.Comm. Reports 1080 (1988)].

§ 1151. Repealed by Stats.1981, c. 607, p. 2335, § 2

§ 1152. Repealed by Stats.1988, c. 1199, § 57.5, operative July 1, 1989

Law Revision Commission Comments

1988 Repeal

Former Section 1152 is superseded by Government Code Section 27444 (expiration of term of office), which reverses the rule that a public administrator whose tenure is terminated may complete the administration of pending estates. [19 Cal.L.Rev.Comm. Reports 1080 (1988)].

§ 1153. Repealed by Stats.1981, c. 108, § 1

§§ 1154, 1155. Repealed by Stats.1988, c. 1199, § 57.5, operative July 1, 1989

Law Revision Commission Comments

1988 Repeal

Former Section 1154 is restated in Section 7624 (payment of unclaimed funds), which allows 60 days instead of 10 days for making payment. [19 Cal.L.Rev.Comm. Reports 1081 (1988)].

Former Section 1155 is omitted. Special sanctions are unnecessary in view of applicable general sanctions. [19 Cal.L.Rev.Comm. Reports 1081 (1988)].

§§ 1170 to 1172. Repealed by Stats.1984, c. 527, § 5

Law Revision Commission Comments

1984 Repeal

The substance of former Article 1, consisting of Sections 1170 to 1175 (establishment of fact of death), is continued in Part 4 of Division 2 as Sections 200–204 (proceedings to establish death) and Section 210 (recording authorized). [17 Cal.L.Rev.Comm. Reports 493 (1984)].

§ 1173. Repealed by Stats.1970, c. 952, p. 1974, § 3

§§ 1174, 1175. Repealed by Stats.1984, c. 527, § 5

§§ 1180 to 1183. Repealed by Stats.1937, c. 374, p. 1185

§§ 1190 to 1192. Repealed by Stats.1988, c. 1199, § 58, operative July 1, 1989

Law Revision Commission Comments

1988 Repeal

The procedure provided by former Sections 1190–1192 for determining membership in certain classes entitled to property other than by succession is omitted as unnecessary. Where proceedings for administration of a decedent's estate are pending, this issue is determined in proceedings for distribution. If proceedings for administration are not pending, an action to quiet title may be appropriate. [19 Cal.L.Rev.Comm. Reports 1081 (1988)].

Part 2

NOTICES AND CITATIONS

Application

Application of Part 2, see Probate Code § 1200.

Law Revision Commission Comments

1990 Enactment

This part supersedes Part 2 (commencing with Section 1200) of Division 3 of the repealed Probate Code. The superseded part was enacted upon recommendation of the Law Revision Commission. See Recommendation Relating to Notice in Probate Proceedings, 19 Cal.L. Revision Comm'n Reports 357–83 (1988); Communication from California Law Revision Commission Concerning Assembly Bill 708, 19 Cal.L.Revision Comm'n Reports 545, 555–58 (1988). See also Comments to Conforming Revisions and Repeals, 19 Cal.L. Revision Comm'n Reports 1031, 1081–82 (1988); Communication from California Law Revision Commission Concerning Assembly Bill 2841, 19 Cal.L. Revision Comm'n Reports 1201, 1226 (1988). [20 Cal.L.Rev.Comm. Reports 1001 (1990)].

Cross References

Service of process,
Generally, see Code of Civil Procedure § 413.10 et seq.
Mail, see Code of Civil Procedure §§ 415.30, 1012 et seq.
Personal delivery, see Code of Civil Procedure § 415.10.
Proof of service, see Code of Civil Procedure § 417.10 et seq.
Publication, see Code of Civil Procedure § 415.50.

CHAPTER 1. GENERAL NOTICE PROVISIONS

Application

Application of part, see Probate Code § 1200.

Cross References

Application of old and new law, see Probate Code § 3.

§ 1200. Applicability

(a) Except as otherwise provided in this code, this part governs notice required or permitted under this code.

(b) This part does not apply to notice under a particular provision to the extent that the particular provision is inconsistent with this part.

(c) This part does not apply to the giving of a particular notice where the notice was delivered, mailed, posted, or first published before July 1, 1991. The applicable law in effect before July 1, 1991, continues to apply to the giving of that notice, notwithstanding its repeal. *(Stats.1990, c. 79 (A.B. 759), § 14, operative July 1, 1991.)*

Law Revision Commission Comments

1990 Enactment

Section 1200 continues the substance of Section 1200 of the repealed Probate Code, but does not continue the former provision that this part (with some specific exceptions) did not apply to proceedings under Division 4 (Guardianship–Conservatorship Law) or Division 9 (Trust Law). Except as otherwise provided in this code, this part applies to the entire Probate Code. A noticed hearing is required unless the statute that provides for the hearing dispenses with notice. See Section 1042. Subdivision (b) makes clear that this part does not apply to the extent that a particular notice provision is inconsistent with this part. See, e.g., Sections 8100–8125 (petition for administration of a decedent's estate). Subdivision (c) is a transitional provision continued from the repealed Probate Code section, but the date has been changed to July 1, 1991, so that under subdivision (c) the former law now applies to notices that are first given before July 1, 1991. As to the application of any amendments made after that date, see Section 3.

Background on Section 1200 of Repealed Code

Section 1200 was added by 1987 Cal.Stat. ch. 923 § 60. Subdivision (b) superseded subdivisions (c) and (d) of former Probate Code Section 1200 (repealed by 1987 Cal.Stat. ch. 923 § 59) and subdivisions (d) and (e) of former Probate Code Section 1200.5 (repealed by 1987 Cal.Stat. ch. 923 § 59). The remainder of the section was new. The section was amended by 1989 Cal.Stat. ch. 21 § 5 to make technical changes. See Communication from the California Law Revision Commission Concerning Assembly Bill 156, 20 Cal.L. Revision Comm'n Reports 227, 229 (1990). For background on the provisions of this part, see the Comment to this part under the part heading. [20 Cal.L.Rev.Comm. Reports 1001 (1990)].

Cross References

Service of process,
Generally, see Code of Civil Procedure § 413.10 et seq.
Mail, see Code of Civil Procedure §§ 415.30, 1012 et seq.
Personal delivery, see Code of Civil Procedure § 415.10.
Proof of service, see Code of Civil Procedure § 417.10 et seq.
Publication, see Code of Civil Procedure § 415.50.

§§ 1200.1, 1200.5. Repealed by Stats.1987, c. 923, § 59, operative July 1, 1988

Law Revision Commission Comments

1987 Repeal

Former Section 1200.1 is omitted. The statutory form has been replaced by Judicial Council forms. [19 Cal.L.Rev.Comm. Reports 440 (1988)].

§ 1201. Giving of notice to oneself or joining party

If a person is required to give notice, the person required to give the notice need not give the notice to himself or herself or to any other person who joins in the petition. *(Stats.1990, c. 79 (A.B.759), § 14, operative July 1, 1991.)*

Application

Application of part, see Probate Code § 1200.

Law Revision Commission Comments

1990 Enactment

Section 1201 continues Section 1201 of the repealed Probate Code without change. See also Section 1208 (notice where personal representative and trustee are same person). This part does not apply to the giving of a particular notice where the notice was delivered, mailed, posted, or first published before July 1, 1991. See Section 1200(c). As to the application of any amendments made after that date, see Section 3.

Background on Section 1201 of Repealed Code

Section 1201 was a new provision added by 1987 Cal.Stat. ch. 923 § 60. The part of Section 1201 relating to giving notice to oneself was drawn from other provisions in the repealed Probate Code. The part relating to giving notice to another person who joins in a petition was drawn from subdivision (b) of former Probate Code Section 1200.5 (repealed by 1987 Cal.Stat. ch. 923 § 59) (notice to coexecutor or coadministrator not petitioning). For background on the provisions of this part, see the Comment to this part under the part heading. [20 Cal.L.Rev.Comm. Reports 1001 (1990)].

§ 1201a. Repealed by Stats.1941, c. 1162, p. 2893, § 2

§ 1202. Determination of insufficient notice

Where the court determines that the notice otherwise required is insufficient in the particular circumstances, the court may require that further or additional notice, including a longer period of notice, be given. *(Stats.1990, c. 79 (A.B.759), § 14, operative July 1, 1991.)*

Application

Application of part, see Probate Code § 1200.

Law Revision Commission Comments

1990 Enactment

Section 1202 continues Section 1202 of the repealed Probate Code without change. This part does not apply to the giving of a particular notice where the notice was delivered, mailed, posted, or first published before July 1, 1991. See Section 1200(c). As to the application of any amendments made after that date, see Section 3.

Background on Section 1202 of Repealed Code

Section 1202 was added by 1987 Cal.Stat. ch. 923 § 60. The section restated former Probate Code Section 1204 (repealed by 1987 Cal.Stat. ch. 923 § 59) without substantive change, using language drawn from subdivision (b) of Section 1462 (Guardianship–Conservatorship Law) of the repealed Probate Code. The section also generalized a provision found in paragraph (4) of subdivision (e) of Section 277 of the repealed Probate Code prior to its amendment by 1987 Cal.Stat. ch. 923 § 24. For background on the provisions of this part, see the Comment to this part under the part heading. [20 Cal.L.Rev.Comm. Reports 1001 (1990)].

§ 1202.5. Repealed by Stats.1987, c. 923, § 59, operative July 1, 1988

Law Revision Commission Comments

1987 Repeal

Former Section 1202.5 is replaced by Sections 1250 (request for special notice), 1252 (notice to be given to person requesting special notice), and 1260 (proof of notice required). The reference to legatee is unneeded because of the definition of "devisee' in Section 32. See also Sections 52 ("letters" defined), 58 ("personal representative" defined). [19 Cal.L.Rev.Comm. Reports 441 (1988)].

§ 1203. Shortening of time for giving notice of hearing; exceptions

(a) Subject to subdivision (b), unless the particular provision governing the notice of hearing provides that the time for giving notice may not be shortened, the court may, for good cause, shorten the time for giving a notice of hearing.

(b) Unless the particular provision governing the publication of notice of hearing otherwise provides, the court may not shorten the time for publication of notice of hearing. *(Stats.1990, c. 79 (A.B.759), § 14, operative July 1, 1991. Amended by Stats.1991, c. 82 (S.B.896), § 2.5, eff. June 1, 1991, operative July 1, 1991.)*

Application

Application of part, see Probate Code § 1200.

Law Revision Commission Comments

1991 Amendment [Revised Comment]

Subdivision (a) of Section 1203 is amended to make clear that the general rule permitting shortening of time applies unless the general rule is made inapplicable by a provision to that effect in a particular statute. This is a technical, nonsubstantive change. [21 L.Rev.Comm.Reports 67 (1991)].

Background on Section 1203 of Repealed Code

Section 1203 was added by 1987 Cal.Stat. ch. 923 § 60 and was amended by 1988 Cal.Stat. ch. 1199 § 59.5. The section was drawn from Sections 1462(a) (Guardianship–Conservatorship Law) and 17106 (Trust Law) of the repealed Probate Code and generalized former provisions. The 1988 amendment corrected cross-references to other sections. For background on the provisions of this part, see the Comment to this part under the part heading. [20 Cal.L.Rev. Comm. Reports 1001 (1990)].

Cross References

Service of process,
  Generally, see Code of Civil Procedure § 413.10 et seq.
  Mail, see Code of Civil Procedure §§ 415.30, 1012 et seq.

Personal delivery, see Code of Civil Procedure § 415.10.
Proof of service, see Code of Civil Procedure § 417.10 et seq.
Publication, see Code of Civil Procedure § 415.50.

§ 1204. Waiver

A person, including a guardian ad litem, guardian, conservator, trustee, or other fiduciary, may waive notice by a writing signed by the person or the person's attorney and filed in the proceeding. *(Stats.1990, c. 79 (A.B.759), § 14, operative July 1, 1991.)*

Application

Application of part, see Probate Code § 1200.

Law Revision Commission Comments

1990 Enactment

Section 1204 continues Section 1204 of the repealed Probate Code without change. This section is drawn from Section 1–402 of the Uniform Probate Code (1987). As to the construction of provisions drawn from uniform acts, see Section 2. As to the power of a guardian or conservator to waive any process, notice, or order to show cause on behalf of the ward or conservatee, see Section 1210. This part does not apply to the giving of a particular notice where the notice was delivered, mailed, posted, or first published before July 1, 1991. See Section 1200(c). As to the application of any amendments made after that date, see Section 3. Nothing in this section creates any implication as to the power of an attorney to act with respect to matters other than waiver of notice. See also Section 1023 (verification by attorney of petition, objection, or response).

Background on Section 1204 of Repealed Code

Section 1204 was added by 1987 Cal.Stat. ch. 923 § 60. For background on the provisions of this part, see the Comment to this part under the part heading. [20 Cal.L.Rev.Comm. Reports 1001 (1990)].

Cross References

Fiduciary, defined, see Probate Code § 39.

§ 1205. Continuance or postponement of hearing

If a hearing is continued or postponed, no further notice of the continued or postponed hearing is required unless ordered by the court. *(Stats.1990, c. 79 (A.B.759), § 14, operative July 1, 1991.)*

Application

Application of part, see Probate Code § 1200.

Law Revision Commission Comments

1990 Enactment

Section 1205 continues Section 1205 of the repealed Probate Code without change. As to the court's authority to continue or postpone a hearing, see Section 1045. This part does not apply to the giving of a particular notice where the notice was delivered, mailed, posted, or first published before July 1, 1991. See Section 1200(c). As to the application of any amendments made after that date, see Section 3.

Background on Section 1205 of Repealed Code

Section 1205 was added by 1987 Cal.Stat. ch. 923 § 60. The section was drawn from part of former Probate Code Section 1205 (repealed by 1987 Cal.Stat. ch. 923 § 59). For background on the provisions of this part, see the Comment to this part under the part heading. [20 Cal.L.Rev.Comm. Reports 1001 (1990)].

Postponement of trial, see Code of Civil Procedure § 594a et seq.

§ 1206. Persons entitled to notice

(a) Subject to subdivision (b), where notice is required to be given to known heirs or known devisees, notice shall be given to the following persons:

(1) If the estate is an intestate estate, to the heirs named in the petition for letters of administration and to any additional heirs who become known to the person giving the notice prior to the giving of the notice.

(2) If the estate is a testate estate, to the devisees named in the petition for probate of the will and to any additional devisees who become known to the person giving the notice prior to the giving of the notice.

(b) Notice need not be given to a person under subdivision (a) if the person's interest has been satisfied pursuant to court order or as evidenced by the person's written receipt. *(Stats.1990, c. 79 (A.B.759), § 14, operative July 1, 1991.)*

Application

Application of part, see Probate Code § 1200.

Law Revision Commission Comments

1990 Enactment

Section 1206 continues Section 1206 of the repealed Probate Code without substantive change. This section governs who must be given notice when the statute requires that notice be given to known heirs or known devisees. Where the estate is partially testate and partially intestate and notice is required to be given to known heirs or known devisees, notice must be given both to known heirs and to known devisees. The court may require additional notice. See Section 1202. The period and manner of notice are governed (1) by the provision that incorporates this section or (2) by Section 1217 and either Section 1220 or Section 1221.

Subdivision (b) is amended to delete the reference to a distributee's written acceptance, which is not implemented in the distribution statutes. The requirement that a receipt be in writing is subject to exceptions in certain cases. See, e.g., Sections 11751, 11753.

This part does not apply to the giving of a particular notice where the notice was delivered, mailed, posted, or first published before July 1, 1991. See Section 1200(c). As to the application of any amendments made after that date, see Section 3.

Background on Section 1206 of Repealed Code

Section 1206 was a new provision added by 1987 Cal.Stat. ch. 923 § 60. This section codified prior practice as to the giving of notice. For background on the provisions of this part, see the Comment to this part under the part heading. [20 Cal.L.Rev.Comm. Reports 1001 (1990)].

Cross References

Devisee, defined, see Probate Code § 34.
Heir, defined, see Probate Code § 44.

§ 1207. Persons not entitled to notice

(a) Subject to subdivision (b), where notice is required to be given to a decedent's beneficiaries, devisees, or heirs, notice need not be given to a person who, because of a possible parent-child relationship between a stepchild and a stepparent or between a foster child and a foster parent, may be (1) an heir of the decedent or (2) a member of a class to which a devise is made.

(b) Subdivision (a) does not apply where the person required to give the notice has actual knowledge of facts that a person would reasonably believe give rise under Section 6454 to the parent-child relationship between the stepchild and the stepparent or between the foster child and the foster parent. *(Stats.1990, c. 79 (A.B.759), § 14, operative July 1, 1991. Amended by Stats.1993, c. 529 (A.B.1137), § 1.)*

Application

Application of part, see Probate Code § 1200.

Law Revision Commission Comments

1993 Amendment

Section 1207 is amended to revise a cross-reference. [23 Cal. L.Rev.Comm. Reports 901 (1993) (Annual Report, App. 9)].

Background on Section 1207 of Repealed Code

Section 1207 was added by 1987 Cal.Stat. ch. 923 § 60. The section restated former Probate Code Section 1201 (repealed by 1987 Cal.Stat. ch. 923 § 59) without substantive change. For background on the provisions of this part, see the Comment to this part under the part heading. [20 Cal.L.Rev.Comm. Reports 1001 (1990)].

Cross References

Beneficiary, defined, see Probate Code § 24.
Devise, defined, see Probate Code § 32.
Heir, defined, see Probate Code § 44.

§ 1208. Notice given to trust or trustee

(a) Except as provided in subdivision (b), if notice is required to be given to a trust or trustee, notice to trust beneficiaries is not required.

(b) Subject to subdivision (c), where the personal representative and the trustee are the same person, or where no trustee has been appointed, notice shall be given to (1) each person to whom income or principal would be required or authorized in the trustee's discretion to be currently distributed if the trust were in effect, or (2) if there are no such persons, to each person who, under the terms of the trust, would be entitled to any distribution if the trust were terminated at the time the notice is required to be given.

(c) Notice to trust beneficiaries is not required under subdivision (b) where the trust has more than one trustee and notice is given to a cotrustee who is not a personal representative. *(Stats.1990, c. 79 (A.B.759), § 14, operative July 1, 1991. Amended by Stats.1992, c. 871 (A.B.2975), § 5; Stats. 1995, c. 730 (A.B.1466), § 2.)*

Application

Application of part, see Probate Code § 1200.

Law Revision Commission Comments

1990 Enactment

Section 1208 continues Section 1208 of the repealed Probate Code without change. Subdivision (a) recognizes the general rule that notice is given to the trustee and not to the beneficiaries of the trust where notice is required to be given to devisees and a trust or trustee is a devisee. See Section 34 (trust beneficiaries are not devisees).

Subdivision (b) provides an exception to the general rule provided in subdivision (a). This exception recognizes that notice given by the personal representative to himself or herself as trustee would be meaningless and that, in some cases, the issue involved may present a conflict of interest between the interests of the personal representative and the interests of the trust beneficiaries.

Subdivision (c) makes clear that notice to trust beneficiaries under subdivision (b) is not required if there is a cotrustee who is independent of the estate administration.

This part does not apply to the giving of a particular notice where the notice was delivered, mailed, posted, or first published before July 1, 1991. See Section 1200(c). As to the application of any amendments made after that date, see Section 3.

Background on Section 1208 of Repealed Code

Section 1208 was a new provision added by 1987 Cal.Stat. ch. 923 § 60. For background on the provisions of this part, see the Comment to this part under the part heading. [20 Cal.L.Rev.Comm. Reports 1001 (1990)].

Cross References

Beneficiary, defined, see Probate Code § 24.
Personal representative and general personal representative, defined, see Probate Code § 58.
Trusts, judicial proceedings, generally, see Probate Code § 17000 et seq.

§ 1209. Notice given to State of California

(a) Where notice is required to be given to the State of California, the notice shall be given to the Attorney General.

(b) Where notice is required to be given to the Attorney General, the notice shall be mailed to the Attorney General at the office of the Attorney General at Sacramento, California. *(Stats.1990, c. 79 (A.B.759), § 14, operative July 1, 1991.)*

Application

Application of part, see Probate Code § 1200.

Law Revision Commission Comments

1990 Enactment

Section 1209 continues Section 1209 of the repealed Probate Code without change. This section applies, for example, in a case where notice is required to be given to devisees under a will and the state is a devisee. In this case, the Attorney General is the proper recipient of the notice. This provision does not apply in a case where a specific provision requires notice to be given to some other officer. See, e.g., Section 215 (notice of death to Director of Health Services).

This part does not apply to the giving of a particular notice where the notice was delivered, mailed, posted, or first published before July 1, 1991. See Section 1200(c). As to the application of any amendments made after that date, see Section 3.

Background on Section 1209 of Repealed Code

Section 1209 was added by 1987 Cal.Stat. ch. 923 § 60. Subdivision (a) was new. Subdivision (b) generalized a provision found in the second paragraph of former Probate Code Section 328 before that section was amended by 1987 Cal.Stat. ch. 923 § 29. For background on the provisions of this part, see the Comment to this part under the part heading. [20 Cal.L.Rev.Comm. Reports 1001 (1990)].

Cross References

Attorney General, powers and duties, see Government Code § 12510.

§ 1210. Guardians and conservators; service; waivers

If an interested person has a guardian or conservator of the estate who resides in this state, personal service on the guardian or conservator of any process, notice, or court order concerning a decedent's estate is equivalent to service on the ward or conservatee, and it is the duty of the guardian or conservator to attend to the interests of the ward or conservatee in the matter. The guardian or conservator may appear for the ward or conservatee and waive any process, notice, or order to show cause that a person not under legal disability might waive. *(Stats.1990, c. 79 (A.B.759), § 14, operative July 1, 1991.)*

Application

Application of part, see Probate Code § 1200.

Law Revision Commission Comments

1990 Enactment

Section 1210 continues Section 1210 of the repealed Probate Code without change. See Section 48 ("interested person" defined).

Background on Section 1210 of Repealed Code

Section 1210 was added by 1988 Cal.Stat. ch. 1199 § 60. Section 1210 restated former Probate Code Section 1289 (repealed by 1988 Cal.Stat. ch. 1199 § 64.5) without substantive change. Former Section 1289 had earlier been enacted upon recommendation of the Law Revision Commission by 1987 Cal.Stat. ch. 923 § 60.5. Former Section 1289 restated former Probate Code Section 1208 (repealed by 1987 Cal.Stat. ch. 923 § 59) without substantive change. For background on the provisions of this part, see the Comment to this part under the part heading. [20 Cal.L.Rev.Comm. Reports 1001 (1990)].

Cross References

Estate,
  Generally, see Probate Code § 7000 et seq.
  Rules of procedure, see Probate Code § 7220 et seq.
Interested person, defined, see Probate Code § 48.
Service of notice of hearing, probate rules, see California Rules of Court, Rule 7.51.
Service of process,
  Generally, see Code of Civil Procedure § 413.10 et seq.
  Mail, see Code of Civil Procedure §§ 415.30, 1012 et seq.
  Personal delivery, see Code of Civil Procedure § 415.10.
  Proof of service, see Code of Civil Procedure § 417.10 et seq.
  Publication, see Code of Civil Procedure § 415.50.

§ 1211. Notice where type of notice not otherwise prescribed

If a notice is required by this code and no other type of notice is prescribed by law, by the Judicial Council, or by the court or judge, the notice shall be in substantially the following form:

SUPERIOR COURT OF THE STATE OF CALIFORNIA
FOR THE (CITY AND) COUNTY OF _____

Estate of _____ No. _____

NOTICE OF HEARING

(If to be published, describe purport or character of the notice to be given.)

Notice is hereby given that (name of petitioner and representative capacity, if any) has filed herein a (nature of petition, application, report, or account), reference to which is made for further particulars, and that the time and place of hearing the same has been set for _____ (date)

_____, at ___.m., in the courtroom (of Department No. _____, if any) of said court, at (the courthouse, or state other location of the court), in the City of _____, California.

Dated _____

_____

Clerk

By _____, Deputy Clerk

(Stats.1990, c. 79 (A.B.759), § 14, operative July 1, 1991.)

Application

Application of part, see Probate Code § 1200.

Law Revision Commission Comments
1990 Enactment

Section 1211 continues Section 1211 of the repealed Probate Code without change.

Background on Section 1211 of Repealed Code

Section 1211 was added by 1988 Cal.Stat. ch. 113 § 13.3. The section restated the general provisions of former Probate Code Section 1200.1 (repealed by 1987 Cal.Stat. ch. 923 § 59) without substantive change. For background on the provisions of this part, see the Comment to this part under the part heading. [20 Cal.L.Rev.Comm. Reports 1001 (1990)].

Cross References

Service of process,
  Generally, see Code of Civil Procedure § 413.10 et seq.
  Mail, see Code of Civil Procedure §§ 415.30, 1012 et seq.
  Personal delivery, see Code of Civil Procedure § 415.10.
  Proof of service, see Code of Civil Procedure § 417.10 et seq.
  Publication, see Code of Civil Procedure § 415.50.

§ 1212. Notice or other paper; requisite mailing or delivery; unknown address

Unless the court dispenses with the notice, if the address of the person to whom a notice or other paper is required to be mailed or delivered is not known, notice shall be given as the court may require in the manner provided in Section 413.30 of the Code of Civil Procedure. *(Added by Stats.1990, c. 710 (S.B.1775), § 4, operative July 1, 1991.)*

Application

Application of part, see Probate Code § 1200.

Law Revision Commission Comments
1990 Addition

Section 1212 (added by 1990 Cal.Stat. ch. 710 § 4) generalizes former Section 17102 (enacted by 1990 Cal.Stat. ch. 79 and repealed by 1990 Cal.Stat. ch. 710 § 45) (manner of giving notice under Trust Law where address is unknown). For background on this section, see Recommendation Relating to Notice in Probate Where Address Unknown, 20 Cal.L.Revision Comm'n Reports 2245 (1990). [20 Cal.L.Rev.Comm. Reports 1001 (1990)].

Cross References

Service of process,
  Generally, see Code of Civil Procedure § 413.10 et seq.
  Mail, see Code of Civil Procedure §§ 415.30, 1012 et seq.
  Personal delivery, see Code of Civil Procedure § 415.10.

Proof of service, see Code of Civil Procedure § 417.10 et seq.
Publication, see Code of Civil Procedure § 415.50.

§ 1213. Notice mailed to surety who has filed court bond; specified persons

(a) The following persons shall mail a notice, as described in Section 1211, to a surety who has filed a court bond in a proceeding:

(1) A person who files a petition to surcharge.

(2) A person who files an objection to an account.

(3) A person who files a petition to suspend or remove a guardian, conservator, or personal representative.

(4) An attorney who files a motion to withdraw from representation of a guardian, conservator, or personal representative.

(b) Within five days after entry of an order to suspend or remove a guardian, conservator, or personal representative, the person who filed a petition to suspend or remove a guardian or, if the order to suspend or remove a guardian, conservator, or personal representative was issued upon a motion by the court, the court, shall notify the surety who has filed a court bond of the order by first-class mail, postage prepaid.

(c) The notice required by this section shall be mailed to the address listed on the surety bond.

(d) Notwithstanding subdivisions (a) and (b), notice is not required to a surety pursuant to this section if the surety bond is for a guardian, conservator, or personal representative who is not the subject of the petition, motion, or order described in this section. *(Added by Stats.1997, c. 198 (S.B.792), § 1.)*

Application

Application of part, see Probate Code § 1200.

Cross References

Computation of time, see Code of Civil Procedure §§ 12 and 12a; Government Code § 6800 et seq.
Guardians and conservators, removal or resignation, see Probate Code § 2650 et seq.
Personal representative and general personal representative, defined, see Probate Code § 58.
Service of process,
  Generally, see Code of Civil Procedure § 413.10 et seq.
  Mail, see Code of Civil Procedure §§ 415.30, 1012 et seq.
  Personal delivery, see Code of Civil Procedure § 415.10.
  Proof of service, see Code of Civil Procedure § 417.10 et seq.
  Publication, see Code of Civil Procedure § 415.50.
Suretyship, see Civil Code § 2787 et seq.

§ 1214. Notice or service of other paper; mailing to attorney

If a notice or other paper is required or permitted to be mailed, delivered, served, or otherwise given to a person who is represented by an attorney of record, the notice or other paper shall also be mailed to this attorney, unless otherwise specified in a request for special notice. *(Added by Stats. 1999, c. 263 (A.B.1051), § 2.)*

Application

Application of part, see Probate Code § 1200.

Service of process,
    Generally, see Code of Civil Procedure § 413.10 et seq.
    Mail, see Code of Civil Procedure §§ 415.30, 1012 et seq.
    Personal delivery, see Code of Civil Procedure § 415.10.
    Proof of service, see Code of Civil Procedure § 417.10 et seq.
    Publication, see Code of Civil Procedure § 415.50.

CHAPTER 2. MAILING IN GENERAL

Section

Application

Application of part, see Probate Code § 1200.

Cross References

Application of old and new law, see Probate Code § 3.

§ 1215. Mailing of notice

Unless otherwise expressly provided:

(a) If a notice or other paper is required or permitted to be mailed to a person, the notice or other paper shall be mailed as provided in this section or personally delivered as provided in Section 1216.

(b) The notice or other paper shall be sent by:

(1) First-class mail if the person's address is within the United States. First-class mail includes certified, registered, and express mail.

(2) Airmail if the person's address is not within the United States.

(c) The notice or other paper shall be deposited for collection in the United States mail, in a sealed envelope, with postage paid, addressed to the person to whom it is mailed.

(d) Subject to Section 1212, the notice or other paper shall be addressed to the person at the person's place of business or place of residence.

(e) When the notice or other paper is deposited in the mail, mailing is complete and the period of notice is not extended. *(Stats.1990, c. 79 (A.B.759), § 14, operative July 1, 1991. Amended by Stats.1990, c. 710 (S.B.1775), § 5, operative July 1, 1991.)*

Application

Application of part, see Probate Code § 1200.

Law Revision Commission Comments
1990 Enactment and Amendment

Section 1215 (enacted as a part of the new Probate Code by 1990 Cal.Stat. ch. 79 § 14) was amended by 1990 Cal.Stat. ch. 710 § 5.

As enacted, Section 1215 continued Section 1215 of the repealed Probate Code without substantive change, but subdivision (d) made clear that the rule provided by that subdivision is limited to proceedings under this code concerning the administration of a decedent's estate. The 1990 amendment revised subdivision (d) to delete the authority to mail notice to the person at the county seat where the proceedings are pending and to provide a cross reference to Section 1212 governing the manner of giving notice to a person whose address is unknown. For background on the 1990 amendment, see Recommendation Relating to Notice in Probate Where Address Unknown, 20 Cal.L.Revision Comm'n Reports 2245 (1990).

Deposit for collection in the United States mail includes deposit in a post office, mailbox, subpost office, substation, mail chute, or other like facility regularly maintained by the United States Postal Service.

The introductory clause makes clear that this section does not apply to the extent that the applicable mailing provision expressly provides a different rule. This section does not apply where service is required to be made by mail in the manner authorized in Section 415.30 of the Code of Civil Procedure. See Section 1467 and the Comment thereto. This section does not apply where service is made out-of-state in the manner provided in Section 415.40 of the Code of Civil Procedure. For special notice provisions relating to guardianships and conservatorships, see Sections 1460–1467. See also Section 5 (certified mail sufficient compliance with requirement of use of registered mail).

Subdivision (e) makes clear that the applicable period of notice is not extended where a notice or other paper is mailed.

This part does not apply to the giving of a particular notice where the notice was delivered, mailed, posted, or first published before July 1, 1991. See Section 1200(c). As to the application of any amendments made after that date, see Section 3.

Background on Section 1215 of Repealed Code

Section 1215 was a new provision added by 1987 Cal.Stat. ch. 923 § 60. The section was amended by 1988 Cal.Stat. ch. 1199 § 60.7. The section was drawn in part from Section 1465 (Guardianship–Conservatorship Law) of the repealed Probate Code and also generalized part of former Probate Code Section 328 (repealed by 1988 Cal.Stat. ch. 1199 § 40). [20 Cal.L.Rev.Comm. Reports 1001 (1990)].

Cross References

Death of person with heir in correctional facility, notice to board director, see Probate Code § 216.
Mailing of notices, franchise tax board of the administration of estate, see Probate Code § 9202.
Service of process,
    Generally, see Code of Civil Procedure § 413.10 et seq.
    Mail, see Code of Civil Procedure §§ 415.30, 1012 et seq.
    Personal delivery, see Code of Civil Procedure § 415.10.
    Proof of service, see Code of Civil Procedure § 417.10 et seq.
    Publication, see Code of Civil Procedure § 415.50.

§§ 1215.1 to 1215.4. Repealed by Stats.1986, c. 820, § 35, operative July 1, 1987

Law Revision Commission Comments
1986 Repeal

Former Section 1215.1 is restated in Section 15804(a) (notice in cases involving future interests) without substantive change. [18 Cal.L.Rev.Comm. Reports 501 (1986)].

Former Section 1215.2 is restated in Section 15804(b) (notice where conflict of interest) without substantive change. [18 Cal. L.Rev.Comm. Reports 501 (1986)].

Former Section 1215.3 is restated in Sections 17208 (appointment of guardian ad litem) and 17105(a) (court-ordered additional notice) without substantive change. [18 Cal.L.Rev.Comm. Reports 501 (1986)].

The first sentence of former Section 1215.4 is restated in Section 15804(c) (effect on other notice requirements) without substantive change. The second sentence is restated in Section 17105(b) (additional notice by party) without substantive change. [18 Cal. L.Rev.Comm. Reports 501 (1986)].

§ 1216. Personal delivery

(a) If a notice or other paper is required or permitted to be mailed to a person, it may be delivered personally to that person. Personal delivery as provided in this section satisfies a provision that requires or permits a notice or other paper to be mailed.

(b) Personal delivery pursuant to this section is complete when the notice or other paper is delivered personally to the person who is to receive it. *(Stats.1990, c. 79 (A.B.759), § 14, operative July 1, 1991.)*

Application

Application of part, see Probate Code § 1200.

Law Revision Commission Comments

1990 Enactment

Section 1216 continues Section 1216 of the repealed Probate Code without change.

This part does not apply to the giving of a particular notice where the notice was delivered, mailed, posted, or first published before July 1, 1991. See Section 1200(c). As to the application of any amendments made after that date, see Section 3.

Background on Section 1216 of Repealed Code

Section 1216 was a new provision added by 1987 Cal.Stat. ch. 923 § 60. Subdivision (a) was drawn from Section 1466 (Guardianship–Conservatorship Law) of the repealed Probate Code. For background on the provisions of this part, see the Comment to this part under the part heading. [20 Cal.L.Rev.Comm. Reports 1001 (1990)].

Cross References

Service of process,
  Generally, see Code of Civil Procedure § 413.10 et seq.
  Mail, see Code of Civil Procedure §§ 415.30, 1012 et seq.
  Personal delivery, see Code of Civil Procedure § 415.10.
  Proof of service, see Code of Civil Procedure § 417.10 et seq.
  Publication, see Code of Civil Procedure § 415.50.

§ 1217. Manner of notice not statutorily specified

If a notice or other paper is required to be served or otherwise given and no other manner of giving the notice or other paper is specified by statute, the notice or other paper shall be mailed or personally delivered as provided in this chapter. *(Stats.1990, c. 79 (A.B.759), § 14, operative July 1, 1991.)*

Application

Application of part, see Probate Code § 1200.

Law Revision Commission Comments

1990 Enactment

Section 1217 continues Section 1217 of the repealed Probate Code without change. Where notice of a hearing is required but no other manner of giving notice is prescribed by statute, notice shall be given as provided in Section 1217 and either Section 1220 or Section 1221.

This part does not apply to the giving of a particular notice where the notice was delivered, mailed, posted, or first published before July 1, 1991. See Section 1200(c). As to the application of any amendments made after that date, see Section 3.

Background on Section 1217 of Repealed Code

Section 1217 was a new provision added by 1987 Cal.Stat. ch. 923 § 60. The section was amended by 1989 Cal.Stat. ch. 21 § 6 to make a technical change. See Communication from the California Law Revision Commission Concerning Assembly Bill 156, 20 Cal.L.Revision Comm'n Reports 227, 229 (1990). For background on the provisions of this part, see the Comment to this part under the part heading. [20 Cal.L.Rev.Comm. Reports 1001 (1990)].

Cross References

Notice to attorney general, amending or conforming trust instrument to qualify estate for charitable estate tax deduction, see Probate Code § 17203.
Service of process,
  Generally, see Code of Civil Procedure § 413.10 et seq.
  Mail, see Code of Civil Procedure §§ 415.30, 1012 et seq.
  Personal delivery, see Code of Civil Procedure § 415.10.
  Proof of service, see Code of Civil Procedure § 417.10 et seq.
  Publication, see Code of Civil Procedure § 415.50.

§ 1218. Repealed by Stats.1999, c. 263 (A.B.1051), § 3

CHAPTER 3. MAILING NOTICE OF HEARING

Section
1220. Requirements.
1221. Giving of notice absent specific provisions.
1222. Repealed.
1223. Repealed.
1224. Repealed.

Application

Application of part, see Probate Code § 1200.

Cross References

Application of old and new law, see Probate Code § 3.

§ 1220. Requirements

(a) When notice of hearing is required to be given as provided in this section:

(1) At least 15 days before the time set for the hearing, the petitioner or the person filing the report, account, or other paper shall cause notice of the time and place of the hearing to be mailed to the persons required to be given notice.

(2) Unless the statute requiring notice specifies the persons to be given notice, notice shall be mailed to all of the following:

(A) The personal representative.

(B) All persons who have requested special notice in the estate proceeding pursuant to Section 1250.

(3) Subject to Section 1212, the notice shall be addressed to the person required to be given notice at the person's place of business or place of residence.

(b) Subject to subdivision (c), nothing in this section excuses compliance with the requirements for notice to a person who has requested special notice pursuant to Chapter 6 (commencing with Section 1250).

(c) The court for good cause may dispense with the notice otherwise required to be given to a person as provided in this section. *(Stats.1990, c. 79 (A.B.759), § 14, operative July 1, 1991. Amended by Stats.1990, c. 710 (S.B.1775), § 6, operative July 1, 1991; Stats.1994, c. 806 (A.B.3686), § 7.)*

Application

Application of part, see Probate Code § 1200.

Law Revision Commission Comments

1990 Enactment

Section 1220 continues subdivisions (a)(1) and (b)–(f) of Section 1220 of the repealed Probate Code without substantive change. As revised, Section 1220 applies only where another statute requires notice of hearing to be given as provided in Section 1220. The substance of the remainder of Section 1220 of the repealed Probate Code (governing the giving of notice where notice of hearing is required but no other period or manner is prescribed by statute) is continued in Section 1221. For general provisions relating to notice, see Sections 1200–1211. For provisions relating to mailing, see Sections 1215–1217.

Subdivision (b) makes clear that notice must be given to persons who have requested special notice, but language has been added to subdivision (b) to recognize that subdivision (c) permits the court to dispense with notice to a person who has requested special notice. See Section 1252 (notice required to be given to person requesting special notice).

Under subdivision (c), the court may dispense with notice to a person listed in this section or to a person who has requested special notice. However, another statutory provision may limit the extent to which the court may dispense with notice in proceedings under that provision. See, e.g., Section 11623 (petition for order for preliminary distribution).

The person required to give notice by mail as provided in this section can satisfy that requirement by personal delivery of the notice to the person required to be given the notice. See Section 1216. As to shortening the time of notice, see Section 1203. The court may order additional notice. See Section 1202.

This part does not apply to the giving of a particular notice where the notice was delivered, mailed, posted, or first published before July 1, 1991. See Section 1200(c). As to the application of any amendments made after that date, see Section 3.

1990 Amendment

Section 1220 (enacted as a part of the new Probate Code by 1990 Cal.Stat. ch. 79 § 14) was amended by 1990 Cal.Stat. ch. 710 § 6. The 1990 amendment revised subdivision (a)(3) to adopt the general rule applicable where notice is required to be mailed to a person whose address is unknown. See the Comment to Section 1212. For background on the 1990 amendment, see Recommendation Relating to Notice in Probate Where Address Unknown, 20 Cal.L.Revision Comm'n Reports 2245 (1990). [20 Cal.L.Rev.Comm. Reports 1001 (1990)].

Background on Section 1220 of Repealed Code

Section 1220 was added by 1987 Cal.Stat. ch. 923 § 60 and was amended by 1988 Cal.Stat. ch. 1199 § 61.3. The section superseded subdivisions (a) and (b) of former Probate Code Section 1200.5 (repealed by 1987 Cal.Stat. ch. 923 § 59). The list of petitions found in subdivision (a) of former Section 1200.5 was omitted as unnecessary; the provision that relates to the particular petition was revised to include a specific requirement in that provision that notice of hearing be given as provided in new Section 1220.

Subdivisions (b) and (c) continued a portion of subdivision (b) of former Probate Code Section 1200.5, but the time for mailing the notice was increased from 10 to 15 days before the time set for the hearing. In addition, the requirement of subdivision (b) of former Section 1200.5 that notice be given to all persons who have requested notice was omitted from subdivision (b) of Section 1220 as unnecessary.

Subdivision (d) restated part of subdivision (b) of former Probate Code Section 1200.5 without substantive change. Subdivisions (e) and (f) were new provisions drawn from Section 1460 (Guardianship–Conservatorship Law) of the repealed Probate Code. Subdivision (f) generalized provisions of former Probate Code Sections 584.2 (repealed by 1987 Cal.Stat. ch. 923 § 35) and 860 (repealed by 1987 Cal.Stat. ch. 923 § 41).

The 1988 amendment revised subdivision (d) of Section 1220 to conform to Section 1215(d).

The section was amended by 1989 Cal.Stat. ch. 21 § 7 to make a technical change. See Communication from the California Law Revision Commission Concerning Assembly Bill 156, 20 Cal.L. Revision Comm'n Reports 227, 229 (1990).

For background on the provisions of this part, see the Comment to this part under the part heading. [20 Cal.L.Rev.Comm. Reports 1001 (1990)].

Cross References

Computation of time, see Code of Civil Procedure §§ 12 and 12a; Government Code § 6800 et seq.
Discretion to order costs paid by parties or estate, see Probate Code § 1002.
Distribution of estate, personal representative petition to participate, notice, see Probate Code § 11704.
Personal representative and general personal representative, defined, see Probate Code § 58.
Service of process,
Generally, see Code of Civil Procedure § 413.10 et seq.
Mail, see Code of Civil Procedure §§ 415.30, 1012 et seq.
Personal delivery, see Code of Civil Procedure § 415.10.
Proof of service, see Code of Civil Procedure § 417.10 et seq.
Publication, see Code of Civil Procedure § 415.50.

§ 1221. Giving of notice absent specific provisions

Where notice of hearing is required but no other period or manner is prescribed by statute, unless the period or manner of giving the notice is ordered by the court or judge, the notice of hearing shall be given for the period and in the manner provided in Section 1220. *(Stats.1990, c. 79 (A.B. 759), § 14, operative July 1, 1991.)*

Application

Application of part, see Probate Code § 1200.

Law Revision Commission Comments

1990 Enactment

Section 1221 is a new provision that continues the substance of paragraph (2) of subdivision (a) of Section 1220 of the repealed Probate Code. This part does not apply to the giving of a particular notice where the notice was delivered, mailed, posted, or first published before July 1, 1991. See Section 1200(c). As to the application of any amendments made after that date, see Section 3. [20 Cal.L.Rev.Comm. Reports 1001 (1990)].

§ 1222. Repealed by Stats.1987, c. 923, § 59, operative July 1, 1988

Law Revision Commission Comments

1987 Repeal

Former Section 1222 is continued in Section 1292 without change. [19 Cal.L.Rev.Comm. Reports 443 (1988)].

§ 1223. Repealed by Stats.1967, c. 384, p. 1607, § 1

§ 1224. Repealed by Stats.1987, c. 923, § 59, operative July 1, 1988

1987 Repeal

The first paragraph of former Section 1224 is restated in Section 1293 without substantive change. See also Section 58 ("personal representative" defined). The second paragraph is omitted; it was a transitional provision that is no longer necessary. [19 Cal.L.Rev. Comm. Reports 443 (1988)].

CHAPTER 4. POSTING NOTICE OF HEARING

Section
1230. Posting of notice.
1231 to 1233. Repealed.

Application

Application of part, see Probate Code § 1200.

Cross References

Application of old and new law, see Probate Code § 3.

§ 1230. Posting of notice

Where notice of hearing is required to be posted as provided in this section:

(a) At least 15 days before the time set for the hearing, the court clerk shall cause a notice of the time and place of the hearing to be posted at the courthouse of the county where the proceedings are pending. If court is held at a place other than the county seat, the notice may be posted either at the courthouse of the county where the proceedings are pending or at the building where the court is held.

(b) The posted notice of hearing shall state all of the following:

(1) The name of the estate.

(2) The name of the petitioner.

(3) The nature of the petition, referring to the petition for further particulars.

(4) The time and place of the hearing of the petition. *(Stats.1990, c. 79 (A.B.759), § 14, operative July 1, 1991.)*

Application

Application of part, see Probate Code § 1200.

Law Revision Commission Comments

1990 Enactment

Section 1230 continues Section 1230 of the repealed Probate Code without change. This part does not apply to the giving of a particular notice where the notice was delivered, mailed, posted, or first published before July 1, 1991. See Section 1200(c). As to the application of any amendments made after that date, see Section 3.

Background on Section 1230 of Repealed Code

Section 1230 was added by 1987 Cal.Stat. ch. 923 § 60. The section restated subdivision (a) of former Probate Code Section 1200 and all of former Probate Code Section 1210 (provisions repealed by 1987 Cal.Stat. ch. 923 § 59) with the following significant revisions:

(1) Former Section 1200 listed the petitions to which the posting requirement applied. This list was not continued in Section 1230. Instead, a reference to Section 1230 was included in each provision that provided for notice by posting.

(2) Former Section 1200 required posting at least 10 days before the hearing. The 15-day posting requirement conformed to the

requirement that notice be mailed 15 days before the hearing. See Section 1220.

(3) The portion of former Section 1200 requiring the clerk to set the petition for hearing by the court was omitted as unnecessary in view of the general provision imposing this requirement. See Section 1041 (clerk to set petitions for hearing). [20 Cal.L.Rev. Comm. Reports 1001 (1990)].

Cross References

Civil action defined, see Code of Civil Procedure § 30.
Computation of time, see Code of Civil Procedure §§ 12 and 12a;
    Government Code § 6800 et seq.
Jury trial, see Probate Code § 825.
Probate proceedings, transfer, see Probate Code § 7070 et seq.
Rules of practice in civil actions,
    Generally, see Code of Civil Procedure § 307 et seq.
    Court rules, see California Rules of Court, Rule 3.1 et seq.
    Probate proceedings, generally, see Probate Code § 1000 et seq.
Service of process,
    Generally, see Code of Civil Procedure § 413.10 et seq.
    Mail, see Code of Civil Procedure §§ 415.30, 1012 et seq.
    Personal delivery, see Code of Civil Procedure § 415.10.
    Proof of service, see Code of Civil Procedure § 417.10 et seq.
    Publication, see Code of Civil Procedure § 415.50.
Trial by court, see Code of Civil Procedure § 631 et seq.

§§ 1231 to 1233. Repealed by Stats.1987, c. 923, § 59, operative July 1, 1988

Law Revision Commission Comments

1987 Repeal

Former Section 1231 is continued in Section 1281 without change. [19 Cal.L.Rev.Comm. Reports 443 (1988)].

Former Section 1232 is continued in Section 1282 without change. [19 Cal.L.Rev.Comm. Reports 443 (1988)].

Former Section 1233 is continued in Section 1283 without change. [19 Cal.L.Rev.Comm. Reports 443 (1988)].

CHAPTER 5. CITATIONS

Section
1240. Issuance of citation.
1241. Requirements.
1242. Service.

Application

Application of part, see Probate Code § 1200.

Cross References

Application of old and new law, see Probate Code § 3.

§ 1240. Issuance of citation

Where use of a citation is authorized or required by statute, a citation may be issued by the court clerk on the application of any party, without a court order, except in cases where an order is expressly required by law. *(Stats. 1990, c. 79 (A.B.759), § 14, operative July 1, 1991.)*

Application

Application of part, see Probate Code § 1200.

Law Revision Commission Comments

1990 Enactment

Section 1240 continues Section 1240 of the repealed Probate Code without substantive change. The section has been revised to make clear that a citation may be issued by the court clerk without a court order only where use of a citation is authorized or required by statute.

Background on Section 1240 of Repealed Code

Section 1240 was added by 1987 Cal.Stat. ch. 923 § 60. The section restated the first sentence of former Probate Code Section 1207 (repealed by 1987 Cal.Stat. ch. 923 § 59) without substantive change. For background on the provisions of this part, see the Comment to this part under the part heading. [20 Cal.L.Rev.Comm. Reports 1001 (1990)].

Cross References

Citation to proposed conservatee, contents, see Probate Code § 1823.

§ 1241. Requirements

The citation shall be directed to the person to be cited, signed by the court clerk, and issued under the seal of the court. The citation shall contain the title of the proceeding, a brief statement of the nature of the proceeding, and a direction that the person cited appear at a time and place specified. *(Stats.1990, c. 79 (A.B.759), § 14, operative July 1, 1991.)*

Application

Application of part, see Probate Code § 1200.

Law Revision Commission Comments

1990 Enactment

Section 1241 continues Section 1241 of the repealed Probate Code without change.

Background on Section 1241 of Repealed Code

Section 1241 was added by 1987 Cal.Stat. ch. 923 § 60. The section restated the second sentence of former Probate Code Section 1206 (repealed by 1987 Cal.Stat. ch. 923 § 59) without substantive change. For background on the provisions of this part, see the Comment to this part under the part heading. [20 Cal.L.Rev.Comm. Reports 1001 (1990)].

§ 1242. Service

The citation shall be served on the person cited in the manner provided in Chapter 4 (commencing with Section 413.10) of Title 5 of Part 2 of the Code of Civil Procedure. Except as otherwise provided by statute, the citation shall be served at least five days before its return day. *(Stats.1990, c. 79 (A.B.759), § 14, operative July 1, 1991.)*

Application

Application of part, see Probate Code § 1200.

Law Revision Commission Comments

1990 Enactment

Section 1242 continues Section 1242 of the repealed Probate Code without substantive change.

Background on Section 1242 of Repealed Code

Section 1242 was added by 1987 Cal.Stat. ch. 923 § 60. The section restated the second sentence of former Probate Code Section 1207 (repealed by 1987 Cal.Stat. ch. 923 § 59) without substantive change. For background on the provisions of this part, see the Comment to this part under the part heading. [20 Cal.L.Rev.Comm. Reports 1001 (1990)].

Cross References

Computation of time, see Code of Civil Procedure §§ 12 and 12a; Government Code § 6800 et seq.

CHAPTER 6. REQUEST FOR SPECIAL NOTICE

Section
1250. Request for special notice.
1251. Modification or withdrawal.
1252. Requirement of written notice.

Application

Application of part, see Probate Code § 1200.

Cross References

Application of old and new law, see Probate Code § 3.

§ 1250. Request for special notice

(a) At any time after the issuance of letters in a proceeding under this code for the administration of a decedent's estate, any person interested in the estate, whether as devisee, heir, creditor, beneficiary under a trust, or as otherwise interested, may in person or by attorney, file with the court clerk a written request for special notice.

(b) The request for special notice shall be so entitled and shall set forth the name of the person and the address to which notices shall be sent.

(c) Special notice may be requested of one or more of the following matters:

(1) Petitions filed in the administration proceeding.

(2) Inventories and appraisals of property in the estate, including any supplemental inventories and appraisals.

(3) Objections to an appraisal.

(4) Accounts of a personal representative.

(5) Reports of status of administration.

(d) Special notice may be requested of any matter in subdivision (c) by describing it, or of all the matters in subdivision (c) by referring generally to "the matters described in subdivision (c) of Section 1250 of the Probate Code" or by using words of similar meaning.

(e) A copy of the request shall be personally delivered or mailed to the personal representative or to the attorney for the personal representative. If personally delivered, the request is effective when it is delivered. If mailed, the request is effective when it is received.

(f) When the original of the request is filed with the court clerk, it shall be accompanied by a written admission or proof of service. *(Stats.1990, c. 79 (A.B.759), § 14, operative July 1, 1991.)*

Application of part, see Probate Code § 1200.

Law Revision Commission Comments

1990 Enactment

Section 1250 continues Section 1250 of the repealed Probate Code without substantive change. Language has been added to the first sentence of subdivision (a) to make clear that the section applies only in a proceeding under this code for the administration of a decedent's estate. This chapter does not apply to proceedings under Division 4 (commencing with Section 1400) (Guardianship–Conservatorship Law) or Division 9 (commencing with Section 15000) (Trust Law).

If a request for special notice is made as provided in this section, notice is required to be given as provided in Section 1252. Subdivision (c) permits the person requesting special notice to request notice of the matters described in that subdivision. The described matters include all petitions and specified additional matters. Subdivision (d) gives the person requesting special notice the option to describe specifically those matters of which special notice is requested if the person does not wish to receive special notice of all matters.

Where the State Controller has an interest in the estate, the State Controller would be included within the persons who can request special notice as a person "otherwise interested." As to the right of a federal agency to request special notice, see Section 7280.

Subdivision (e) requires that the request for special notice be given to the personal representative or the personal representative's attorney. As to the manner of giving notice, see Sections 1220, 1221. As to proof of giving notice, see Section 1260.

This part does not apply to the giving of a particular notice where the notice was delivered, mailed, posted, or first published before July 1, 1991. See Section 1200(c). As to the application of any amendments made after that date, see Section 3.

Background on Section 1250 of Repealed Code

Section 1250 was added by 1987 Cal.Stat. ch. 923 § 60 and was amended by 1988 Cal.Stat. ch. 1199 § 63. The section replaced parts of former Probate Code Sections 1202 and 1202.5 (both repealed by 1987 Cal.Stat. ch. 923 § 59).

Section 1250 corrected a defect in former Probate Code Section 1202. Former Section 1202 provided for special notice of only those petitions mentioned in former Section 1200. But in 1980, provisions in former Section 1200 applying to notice by mail were split out of that section and added to the then newly-enacted Section 1200.5. See 1980 Cal.Stat. ch. 955 § 31. Many sections containing cross-references to the mailed notice provisions of former Section 1200 were revised to refer to Section 1200.5, but not all cross-references were corrected. Former Section 1202 was not amended to reflect the fact that, after the 1980 revision, giving notice of most petitions by mail was made under Section 1200.5, rather than under Section 1200. As a result, former Section 1202 (which provided for special notice of only those petitions mentioned in Section 1200) did not on its face require special notice of the petitions mentioned in former Section 1200.5 but not mentioned in former Section 1200. Therefore, by its terms, former Section 1202 provided for special notice only by posting, and only for petitions that were still mentioned in former Section 1200.

Subdivision (a) omitted as unnecessary the specific reference to the State Controller that was found in former Probate Code Section 1202. See the Comment to Section 1250.

The 1988 amendment to Section 1250 made technical, nonsubstantive revisions.

For background on the provisions of this part, see the Comment to this part under the part heading. [20 Cal.L.Rev.Comm. Reports 1001 (1990)].

Cross References

Beneficiary, defined, see Probate Code § 24.
Devisee, defined, see Probate Code § 34.
Estate administration, rules of procedure, see Probate Code § 825 et seq.
Heir, defined, see Probate Code § 44.
Interested person, defined, see Probate Code § 48.
Letters, defined, see Probate Code § 52.
Personal representative, compensation, amount, see Probate Code § 10800 et seq.
Personal representative and general personal representative, defined, see Probate Code § 58.
Request for special notice pursuant to this section, superior court filing fees, see Government Code § 70662.
Service of process,
  Generally, see Code of Civil Procedure § 413.10 et seq.
  Mail, see Code of Civil Procedure §§ 415.30, 1012 et seq.
  Personal delivery, see Code of Civil Procedure § 415.10.
  Proof of service, see Code of Civil Procedure § 417.10 et seq.
  Publication, see Code of Civil Procedure § 415.50.
Trusts, judicial proceedings, special notice requests, see Probate Code § 17204 et seq.

§ 1251. Modification or withdrawal

A request for special notice under this chapter may be modified or withdrawn in the same manner as provided for the making of the initial request. *(Stats.1990, c. 79 (A.B.759), § 14, operative July 1, 1991.)*

Application

Application of part, see Probate Code § 1200.

Law Revision Commission Comments

1990 Enactment

Section 1251 continues Section 1251 of the repealed Probate Code without substantive change. This section is comparable to part of subdivision (a) of Section 2701 (Guardianship–Conservatorship Law).

This section does not apply to proceedings under Division 4 (commencing with Section 1400) (Guardianship–Conservatorship Law) or Division 9 (commencing with Section 15000) (Trust Law). See Section 1250 (chapter applies in a proceeding under this code for the administration of a decedent's estate). This part does not apply to the giving of a particular notice where the notice was delivered, mailed, posted, or first published before July 1, 1991. See Section 1200(c). As to the application of any amendments made after that date, see Section 3.

Background on Section 1251 of Repealed Code

Section 1251 was a new provision added by 1987 Cal.Stat. ch. 923 § 60. For background on the provisions of this part, see the Comment to this part under the part heading. [20 Cal.L.Rev.Comm. Reports 1001 (1990)].

§ 1252. Requirement of written notice

(a) Unless the court makes an order dispensing with the notice, if a request has been made pursuant to Section 1250 for special notice of a hearing, the person filing the petition, report, account, or other paper shall give written notice of the filing, together with a copy of the petition, report, account, or other paper, and the time and place set for the hearing, by mail to the person named in the request at the address set forth in the request, at least 15 days before the time set for the hearing.

(b) If a request has been made pursuant to Section 1250 for special notice of the filing of an inventory and appraisal of the estate or of the filing of any other paper that does not require a hearing, the inventory and appraisal or other paper shall be mailed not later than 15 days after the inventory and appraisal or other paper is filed with the court. *(Stats.1990, c. 79 (A.B.759), § 14, operative July 1, 1991.)*

Application

Application of part, see Probate Code § 1200.

Law Revision Commission Comments

1990 Enactment

Section 1252 continues Section 1252 of the repealed Probate Code without substantive change. The introductory clause is added to subdivision (a) to recognize the authority of the court to dispense with notice in certain cases. See, e.g., Section 1220(b)–(c). This section is comparable to Section 2702 (Guardianship–Conservatorship Law). The 15–day period for special notice is consistent with the general period of notice provided in Section 1220 (notice of hearing by mail). The 15–day period may be reduced by an order shortening time. See Section 1203. See also Section 1204 (waiver of notice).

This section does not apply to proceedings under Division 4 (commencing with Section 1400) (Guardianship–Conservatorship Law) or Division 9 (commencing with Section 15000) (Trust Law). See the introductory clause of subdivision (a) of Section 1250. This part does not apply to the giving of a particular notice where the notice was delivered, mailed, posted, or first published before July 1, 1991. See Section 1200(c). As to the application of any amendments made after that date, see Section 3.

Background on Section 1252 of Repealed Code

Section 1252 was added by 1987 Cal.Stat. ch. 923 § 60 and was amended by 1988 Cal.Stat. ch. 1199 § 63.5. The section replaced the last sentence of former Probate Code Section 1202 and the second sentence of former Probate Code Section 1202.5 (both provisions repealed by 1987 Cal.Stat. ch. 923 § 59). The requirement that a copy of the appropriate papers be served was new. The 10–day notice period of former Section 1202.5 was replaced by a 15–day period. The 1988 amendment to Section 1252 made technical, nonsubstantive revisions. For background on the provisions of this part, see the Comment to this part under the part heading. [20 Cal.L.Rev.Comm. Reports 1001 (1990)].

Cross References

Computation of time, see Code of Civil Procedure §§ 12 and 12a; Government Code § 6800 et seq.
Failure to file inventory and appraisal, compelled filing pursuant to this chapter, see Probate Code § 8804.
Inventory and appraisal of partnership interest of decedent, generally, see Probate Code § 8850.

CHAPTER 7. PROOF OF GIVING NOTICE

Application

Application of part, see Probate Code § 1200.

Cross References

Application of old and new law, see Probate Code § 3.

§ 1260.   Proof of giving notice

(a) If notice of a hearing is required, proof of giving notice of the hearing shall be made to the satisfaction of the court at or before the hearing.

(b) If it appears to the satisfaction of the court that notice has been regularly given or that the party entitled to notice has waived it, the court shall so find in its order.

(c) The finding described in subdivision (b), when the order becomes final, is conclusive on all persons. *(Stats.1990, c. 79 (A.B.759), § 14, operative July 1, 1991.)*

Application

Application of part, see Probate Code § 1200.

Law Revision Commission Comments
1990 Enactment

Section 1260 continues Section 1260 of the repealed Probate Code without change. This part does not apply to the giving of a particular notice where the notice was delivered, mailed, posted, or first published before July 1, 1991. See Section 1200(c). As to the application of any amendments made after that date, see Section 3.

Background on Section 1260 of Repealed Code

Section 1260 was added by 1987 Cal.Stat. ch. 923 § 60. Section 1260 was drawn from subdivision (b) of former Probate Code Section 1200 and subdivision (c) of former Probate Code Section 1200.5 (both provisions repealed by 1987 Cal.Stat. ch. 923 § 59).

Subdivision (a) superseded provisions formerly found in various sections of the Probate Code. See, e.g., former Prob.Code §§ 333(c) (repealed by 1988 Cal.Stat. ch. 1199 § 40), 584.3(d) (repealed by 1987 Cal.Stat. ch. 923 § 35), 852 (repealed by 1987 Cal.Stat. ch. 923 § 41), and 1202.5 (repealed by 1987 Cal.Stat. ch. 923 § 59). Subdivision (a) added the requirement that proof of notice be made either at or before the hearing. This was consistent with existing practice.

Subdivision (b) of Section 1260 restated without substantive change parts of former Probate Code Sections 1200(b) and 1200.5(c) (both provisions repealed by 1987 Cal.Stat. ch. 923 § 59). The provision for waiver of notice was drawn from case law. See In re Poder's Estate, 274 Cal.App.2d 786, 791–92, 79 Cal.Rptr. 484 (1969); Estate of Pailhe, 114 Cal.App.2d 658, 662, 251 P.2d 76 (1952); Estate of Palm, 68 Cal.App.2d 204, 213–14, 156 P.2d 62 (1945); In re Estate of Pierce, 28 Cal.App.2d 8, 11–12, 81 P.2d 1037 (1938). See also Section 1204 (waiver of notice).

Subdivision (c) restated the rule of conclusiveness of the finding by the court concerning the giving of notice, which was found in former Sections 1200(b) and 1200.5(c) (both provisions repealed by 1987 Cal.Stat. ch. 923 § 59), without substantive change.

For background on the provisions of this part, see the Comment to this part under the part heading. [20 Cal.L.Rev.Comm. Reports 1001 (1990)].

Cross References

Proof of service, see Code of Civil Procedure § 417.10 et seq.

§ 1261.   Proof of mailing

Proof of mailing may be made in the manner prescribed in Section 1013a of the Code of Civil Procedure. *(Stats.1990, c. 79 (A.B.759), § 14, operative July 1, 1991.)*

Application

Application of part, see Probate Code § 1200.

Law Revision Commission Comments

1990 Enactment

Section 1261 continues Section 1261 of the repealed Probate Code without change. This part does not apply to the giving of a particular notice where the notice was delivered, mailed, posted, or first published before July 1, 1991. See Section 1200(c). As to the application of any amendments made after that date, see Section 3.

Background on Section 1261 of Repealed Code

Section 1261 was a new provision added by 1987 Cal.Stat. ch. 923 § 60. [20 Cal.L.Rev.Comm. Reports 1001 (1990)].

§ 1262. Proof of publication

Proof of publication may be made by the affidavit of the publisher or printer, or the foreman or principal clerk of the publisher or printer, showing the time and place of publication. *(Stats.1990, c. 79 (A.B.759), § 14, operative July 1, 1991.)*

Application

Application of part, see Probate Code § 1200.

Law Revision Commission Comments

1990 Enactment

Section 1262 continues Section 1262 of the repealed Probate Code without change. A declaration under penalty of perjury may be used instead of an affidavit. See Code Civ.Proc. § 2015.5; see also Code Civ.Proc. § 2015.6 (affirmation instead of oath). This part does not apply to the giving of a particular notice where the notice was delivered, mailed, posted, or first published before July 1, 1991. See Section 1200(c). As to the application of any amendments made after that date, see Section 3.

Background on Section 1262 of Repealed Code

Section 1262 was a new provision added by 1987 Cal.Stat. ch. 923 § 60. For background on the provisions of this part, see the Comment to this part under the part heading. [20 Cal.L.Rev.Comm. Reports 1001 (1990)].

Cross References

Affidavits, see Code of Civil Procedure § 2009 et seq.

§ 1263. Proof of posting

Proof of posting may be made by the affidavit of the person who posted the notice. *(Stats.1990, c. 79 (A.B.759), § 14, operative July 1, 1991.)*

Application

Application of part, see Probate Code § 1200.

Law Revision Commission Comments

1990 Enactment

Section 1263 continues Section 1263 of the repealed Probate Code without change. A declaration under penalty of perjury may be used instead of an affidavit. See Code Civ.Proc. § 2015.5; see also Code Civ.Proc. § 2015.6 (affirmation instead of oath). This part does not apply to the giving of a particular notice where the notice was delivered, mailed, posted, or first published before July 1, 1991. See Section 1200(c). As to the application of any amendments made after that date, see Section 3.

Background on Section 1263 of Repealed Code

Section 1263 was a new provision added by 1987 Cal.Stat. ch. 923 § 60. For background on the provisions of this part, see the Comment to this part under the part heading. [20 Cal.L.Rev.Comm. Reports 1001 (1990)].

Cross References

Affidavits, see Code of Civil Procedure § 2009 et seq.
Service of process,
   Generally, see Code of Civil Procedure § 413.10 et seq.
   Mail, see Code of Civil Procedure §§ 415.30, 1012 et seq.
   Personal delivery, see Code of Civil Procedure § 415.10.
   Proof of service, see Code of Civil Procedure § 417.10 et seq.
   Publication, see Code of Civil Procedure § 415.50.

§ 1264. Proof of personal delivery

Proof of notice by personal delivery may be made by the affidavit of the person making the delivery showing the time and place of delivery and the name of the person to whom delivery was made. *(Stats.1990, c. 79 (A.B.759), § 14, operative July 1, 1991.)*

Application

Application of part, see Probate Code § 1200.

Law Revision Commission Comments

1990 Enactment

Section 1264 continues Section 1264 of the repealed Probate Code without change. A declaration under penalty of perjury may be used instead of an affidavit. See Code Civ.Proc. § 2015.5; see also Code Civ.Proc. § 2015.6 (affirmation instead of oath). This part does not apply to the giving of a particular notice where the notice was delivered, mailed, posted, or first published before July 1, 1991. See Section 1200(c). As to the application of any amendments made after that date, see Section 3.

Background on Section 1264 of Repealed Code

Section 1264 was a new provision added by 1987 Cal.Stat. ch. 923 § 60. For background on the provisions of this part, see the Comment to this part under the part heading. [20 Cal.L.Rev.Comm. Reports 1001 (1990)].

Cross References

Affidavits, see Code of Civil Procedure § 2009 et seq.
Service of process,
   Generally, see Code of Civil Procedure § 413.10 et seq.
   Mail, see Code of Civil Procedure §§ 415.30, 1012 et seq.
   Personal delivery, see Code of Civil Procedure § 415.10.
   Proof of service, see Code of Civil Procedure § 417.10 et seq.
   Publication, see Code of Civil Procedure § 415.50.

§ 1265. Evidence presented at hearing

Proof of notice, however given, may be made by evidence presented at the hearing. *(Stats.1990, c. 79 (A.B.759), § 14, operative July 1, 1991.)*

Application

Application of part, see Probate Code § 1200.

Law Revision Commission Comments

1990 Enactment

Section 1265 continues Section 1265 of the repealed Probate Code without change. This part does not apply to the giving of a particular notice where the notice was delivered, mailed, posted, or first published before July 1, 1991. See Section 1200(c). As to the application of any amendments made after that date, see Section 3.

Background on Section 1265 of Repealed Code

Section 1265 was a new provision added by 1987 Cal.Stat. ch. 923 § 60. For background on the provisions of this part, see the Comment to this part under the part heading. [20 Cal.L.Rev.Comm. Reports 1001 (1990)].

§§ 1280 to 1299. Repealed by Stats.1988, c. 1199, § 64.5, operative July 1, 1989

Law Revision Commission Comments

1988 Repeal

The first sentence of former Section 1280 is superseded by Section 1000 (general rules of practice). See the Comment to Section 1000. The second sentence is restated in Section 1044 (plaintiff and defendant) without substantive change.

The third and fourth sentences are superseded by Sections 1000 (general rules of practice), 1452 (jury trial under guardianship and conservatorship law), 7200 (jury trial in estate administration), and 17006 (jury trial under Trust Law). See also Code Civ. Proc. §§ 309 (court may submit issue to jury not defined by pleadings), 631 (jury trial waived if not demanded).

The last sentence is restated in Sections 1048 (entry and filing and 1049 (enforcement of order). [19 Cal.L.Rev.Comm. Reports 1227 (1988)].

Former Section 1281 is restated in Section 7220 without substantive change. The provision for new trial in proceedings to determine heirship and interests in estates is omitted because this procedure is not continued. [19 Cal.L.Rev.Comm. Reports 1082 (1988)].

Former Section 1282 is restated in Section 1002 without substantive change. [19 Cal.L.Rev.Comm. Reports 1082 (1988)].

The first paragraph of former Section 1283 is superseded by Section 1000 (general rules of practice govern). See the Comment to Section 1000; see also Code Civ.Proc. § 2009 (affidavit may be used to establish record of birth). The first sentence of the second paragraph is superseded by Section 1022 (affidavit or verified petition as evidence) and Code of Civil Procedure Section 2009 (affidavit in uncontested proceedings to establish record of birth). The second sentence is restated in Section 8220 (evidence of subscribing witness) without substantive change. [19 Cal.L.Rev. Comm. Reports 1082 (1988)].

Former Section 1284 is restated in Section 1021 without substantive change. [19 Cal.L.Rev.Comm. Reports 1083 (1988)].

Former Section 1285 is restated in Section 1041 without substantive change. [19 Cal.L.Rev.Comm. Reports 1083 (1988)].

Former Section 1286 is continued in Section 1045 without change. [19 Cal.L.Rev.Comm. Reports 1083 (1988)].

Former Section 1287 is restated in Section 1046 without substantive change. [19 Cal.L.Rev.Comm. Reports 1083 (1988)].

Former Section 1288 is restated in Section 7280 without substantive change. [19 Cal.L.Rev.Comm. Reports 1083 (1988)].

Former Section 1289 is restated in Section 1210 without substantive change. [19 Cal.L.Rev.Comm. Reports 1083 (1988)].

Former Section 1290 is restated in Section 1047 without substantive change. [19 Cal.L.Rev.Comm. Reports 1083 (1988)].

Former Section 1291 is restated in Section 1048 without substantive change. [19 Cal.L.Rev.Comm. Reports 1083 (1988)].

Former Section 1292 is restated in Section 7263 (recordation of order affecting real property) without substantive change, except that the last clause relating to the effect of recording is omitted as unnecessary. See also Section 7262 (transfer or conveyance of property pursuant to court order). [19 Cal.L.Rev.Comm. Reports 1084 (1988)].

Former Section 1293 is superseded by Section 11853. [19 Cal. L.Rev.Comm. Reports 1084 (1988)].

Former Section 1297 is restated in Section 7240 without substantive change, except that the part of subdivision (m) relating to determination of heirship is omitted since this procedure is not continued. [19 Cal.L.Rev.Comm. Reports 1084 (1988)].

Former Section 1298 is replaced by Section 8406 (effect of reversal of appointment of personal representative). See the Comment to Section 8406. [19 Cal.L.Rev.Comm. Reports 1084 (1988)].

Former Section 1299 is restated in Section 1050 without substantive change. However, the former provision to the effect that the papers constituting the judgment roll need not be attached together is omitted as unnecessary [19 Cal.L.Rev.Comm. Reports 1084 (1988)].

Part 3

APPEALS

Cross References

Nonprobate transfer to trustee named in decedent's will, appealable orders, see Probate Code § 6327.

CHAPTER 1.   GENERAL

§ 1300.   Grounds for appeal; all proceedings governed by this code

In all proceedings governed by this code, an appeal may be taken from the making of, or the refusal to make, any of the following orders:

(a) Directing, authorizing, approving, or confirming the sale, lease, encumbrance, grant of an option, purchase, conveyance, or exchange of property.

(b) Settling an account of a fiduciary.

(c) Authorizing, instructing, or directing a fiduciary, or approving or confirming the acts of a fiduciary.

(d) Directing or allowing payment of a debt, claim, or cost.

(e) Fixing, authorizing, allowing, or directing payment of compensation or expenses of an attorney.

(f) Fixing, directing, authorizing, or allowing payment of the compensation or expenses of a fiduciary.

(g) Surcharging, removing, or discharging a fiduciary.

(h) Transferring the property of the estate to a fiduciary in another jurisdiction.

(i) Allowing or denying a petition of the fiduciary to resign.

(j) Discharging a surety on the bond of a fiduciary.

(k) Adjudicating the merits of a claim made under Part 19 (commencing with Section 850) of Division 2. *(Added by Stats.1997, c. 724 (A.B.1172), § 11. Amended by Stats.2001, c. 417 (A.B.873), § 4.)*

Cross References

Appeals in civil actions, generally, see Code of Civil Procedure § 901 et seq.

Appeals in civil actions, rules on appeal in civil cases, see California Rules of Court, Rule 8.1 et seq.

Attorney's fees and costs, generally, see Code of Civil Procedure § 1021.

Estate attorney, compensation, amount, see Probate Code § 10810 et seq.

Fee for filing petition or opposition paper concerning appealable order filed after issuance of letters in probate court, see Government Code § 70658.

Fiduciary, defined, see Probate Code § 39.

Mandamus, generally, see Code of Civil Procedure § 1085.

Trusts, judicial proceedings,

Generally, see Probate Code § 17000 et seq.

Transfer to another jurisdiction, see Probate Code § 17400 et seq.

§ 1301. Guardianships, conservatorships, and other protective proceedings; grounds for appeal

With respect to guardianships, conservatorships, and other protective proceedings, the grant or refusal to grant the following orders is appealable:

(a) Granting or revoking of letters of guardianship or conservatorship, except letters of temporary guardianship or temporary conservatorship.

(b) Granting permission to the guardian or conservator to fix the residence of the ward or conservatee at a place not within this state.

(c) Directing, authorizing, approving, or modifying payments, whether for support, maintenance, or education of the ward or conservatee or for a person legally entitled to support, maintenance, or education from the ward or conservatee.

(d) Granting or denying a petition under Section 2423 or under Article 10 (commencing with Section 2580) of Chapter 6 of Part 4 of Division 4.

(e) Affecting the legal capacity of the conservatee pursuant to Chapter 4 (commencing with Section 1870) of Part 3 of Division 4.

(f) Adjudicating the merits of a claim under Article 5 (commencing with Section 2500) of Chapter 6 of Part 4 of Division 4.

(g) Granting or denying a petition under Chapter 3 (commencing with Section 3100) of Part 6 of Division 4. *(Added by Stats.1997, c. 724 (A.B.1172), § 11. Amended by Stats.2001, c. 417 (A.B.873), § 5.)*

Cross References

Conservatorship, generally, see Probate Code § 1800 et seq.

Fee for filing petition or opposition paper concerning appealable order filed after issuance of letters in probate court, see Government Code § 70658.

Guardianship, generally, see Probate Code § 1500 et seq.

Temporary guardians and conservators, generally, see Probate Code § 2250 et seq.

§ 1301.5. Conservatorships; appealable orders

The following rules apply with respect to the California Conservatorship Jurisdiction Act (Chapter 8 (commencing with Section 1980) of Part 3 of Division 4):

(a)(1) An appeal may be taken from an order assessing expenses against a party under Section 1997 if the amount exceeds five thousand dollars ($5,000).

(2) An order under Section 1997 assessing expenses of five thousand dollars ($5,000) or less against a party may be reviewed on an appeal by that party after entry of a final judgment or an appealable order in the conservatorship proceeding. At the discretion of the court of appeal, that type of order may also be reviewed upon petition for an extraordinary writ.

(b) An appeal may be taken from an order under Section 2001 denying a petition to transfer a conservatorship to another state.

(c) An appeal may be taken from a final order under Section 2002 accepting a transfer and appointing a conservator in this state.

(d) Notwithstanding any other law, an appeal may not be taken from either of the following until the court enters a final order under Section 2002 accepting the proposed transfer and appointing a conservator in this state:

(1) An order under Section 2002 determining whether or how to conform a conservatorship to the law of this state.

(2) An order that is made pursuant to a court review under Sections 1851.1 and 2002. *(Added by Stats.2014, c. 553 (S.B.940), § 3, eff. Jan. 1, 2015, operative Jan. 1, 2016.)*

Law Revision Commission Comments

2014 Addition

Section 1301.5 is added to reflect the enactment of the California Conservatorship Jurisdiction Act (Section 1980 *et seq.*).

Paragraph (1) of subdivision (a) is modeled on Code of Civil Procedure Section 904.1(a)(12). Paragraph (2) is modeled on Code of Civil Procedure Section 904.1(b).

Subdivision (b) makes clear that an order *denying* a petition to transfer a conservatorship to another state is appealable. An order *provisionally granting* such a petition is not appealable. If a court issues a *final* order granting a transfer to another state, the court will terminate the conservatorship and enter a final judgment, which will be appealable. See Code Civ. Proc. § 904.1.

Subdivision (c) makes clear that a *final* order accepting a transfer of a conservatorship is appealable. See also Section 1301(a) (order granting letters of conservatorship is appealable). In contrast, an order *provisionally granting* a petition to transfer a conservatorship to California is not appealable. If a court *denies* such a petition, the California proceeding will be over and the court will enter an order of dismissal, which will be appealable. See Code Civ. Proc. §§ 581d, 904.1.

Subdivision (d) makes clear that a conformity determination under Section 2002 is not appealable until the court issues a final order accepting the transfer and appointing a California conservator. The same is true of an order that is made pursuant to a court review under Sections 1851.1 and 2002. [43 Cal.L.Rev.Comm. Reports 93 (2013)].

§ 1302. Power of attorney; grounds for appeal

With respect to a power of attorney governed by the Power of Attorney Law (Division 4.5 (commencing with Section 4000)), an appeal may be taken from any of the following:

(a) Any final order under Section 4541, except an order pursuant to subdivision (c) of Section 4541.

(b) An order dismissing the petition or denying a motion to dismiss under Section 4543. *(Added by Stats.1997, c. 724 (A.B.1172), § 11. Amended by Stats.1999, c. 658 (A.B.891), § 9, operative July 1, 2000.)*

Law Revision Commission Comments
1999 Amendment

Section 1302 is amended to reflect the renumbering of former Sections 4900–4947 and to refer to powers of attorney governed by the Power of Attorney Law. Appeals relating to powers of attorney governed by the Health Care Decisions Law are governed by Section 1302.5. The introductory clause is also revised to correct erroneous language. [29 Cal.L.Rev.Comm. Reports 1 (1999)].

Cross References

Appeals in civil actions, generally, see Code of Civil Procedure § 901 et seq.
Appeals in civil actions, rules on appeal in civil cases, see California Rules of Court, Rule 8.1 et seq.
Powers of attorney, generally, see Probate Code § 4000 et seq.

§ 1302.5. Advance health care directive; grounds for appeal

With respect to an advance health care directive governed by the Health Care Decisions Law (Division 4.7 (commencing with Section 4600)), an appeal may be taken from any of the following:

(a) Any final order under Section 4766.

(b) An order dismissing the petition or denying a motion to dismiss under Section 4768. *(Added by Stats.1999, c. 658 (A.B.891), § 10, operative July 1, 2000.)*

Law Revision Commission Comments
1999 Addition

Section 1302.5 is added to reflect enactment of the Health Care Decisions Law (Section 4600 *et seq.*) and the removal of health care powers of attorney from the Power of Attorney Law (Section 4000 *et seq.*) [29 Cal.L.Rev.Comm. Reports 1 (1999)].

Cross References

Appeals in civil actions, generally, see Code of Civil Procedure § 901 et seq.
Appeals in civil actions, rules on appeal in civil cases, see California Rules of Court, Rule 8.1 et seq.
Health care decisions, generally, see Probate Code § 4600 et seq.

§ 1303. Decedent's estate; grounds for appeal

With respect to a decedent's estate, the grant or refusal to grant the following orders is appealable:

(a) Granting or revoking letters to a personal representative, except letters of special administration or letters of special administration with general powers.

(b) Admitting a will to probate or revoking the probate of a will.

(c) Setting aside a small estate under Section 6609.

(d) Setting apart a probate homestead or property claimed to be exempt from enforcement of a money judgment.

(e) Granting, modifying, or terminating a family allowance.

(f) Determining heirship, succession, entitlement, or the persons to whom distribution should be made.

(g) Directing distribution of property.

(h) Determining that property passes to, or confirming that property belongs to, the surviving spouse under Section 13656.

(i) Authorizing a personal representative to invest or reinvest surplus money under Section 9732.

(j) Determining whether an action constitutes a contest under former Chapter 2 (commencing with Section 21320) of Part 3 of Division 11, as that chapter read prior to its repeal by Chapter 174 of the Statutes of 2008.

(k) Determining the priority of debts under Chapter 3 (commencing with Section 11440) of Part 9 of Division 7.

(*l*) Any final order under Chapter 1 (commencing with Section 20100) or Chapter 2 (commencing with Section 20200) of Division 10. *(Added by Stats.1997, c. 724 (A.B. 1172), § 11. Amended by Stats.2001, c. 417 (A.B.873), § 6; Stats.2001, c. 699 (A.B.232), § 1; Stats.2009, c. 348 (S.B.308), § 5.)*

Law Revision Commission Comments
2009 Amendment

Section 1303 is amended to reflect the repeal of former Chapter 2 (commencing with Section 21320) of Part 3 of Division 11. See 2008 Cal. Stat. ch. 174. The reference to the former law is retained because the former law continues to apply to the enforcement of a no contest clause in an instrument that became irrevocable prior to January 1, 2001, notwithstanding the repeal of the former law. See Sections 3(g) ("If the new law does not apply to a matter that occurred before the operative date, the old law continues to govern the matter notwithstanding its amendment or repeal by the new law."), 21315(b) (new law does not apply to instrument that became irrevocable prior to January 1, 2001). [38 Cal.L.Rev.Comm. Reports 203 (2008)].

Cross References

Disposition of estate without administration, passage of property to surviving spouse, see Probate Code § 13500 et seq.
Family allowance, defined, see Probate Code § 38.
Personal representative and general personal representative, defined, see Probate Code § 58.
Probate homestead, defined, see Probate Code § 60.
Probate of will, generally, see Probate Code § 8200 et seq.
Surviving spouse, defined, see Probate Code § 78.
Will contest, see Probate Code § 8250 et seq.

§ 1304. Trusts; grounds for appeal

With respect to a trust, the grant or denial of the following orders is appealable:

(a) Any final order under Chapter 3 (commencing with Section 17200) of Part 5 of Division 9, except the following:

(1) Compelling the trustee to submit an account or report acts as trustee.

(2) Accepting the resignation of the trustee.

(b) Any final order under Chapter 2 (commencing with Section 19020) of Part 8 of Division 9.

(c) Any final order under Part 1 (commencing with Section 20100) and Part 2 (commencing with Section 20200) of Division 10.

(d) Determining whether an action constitutes a contest under former Chapter 2 (commencing with Section 21320) of Part 3 of Division 11, as that chapter read prior to its repeal by Chapter 174 of the Statutes of 2008. *(Added by Stats.1997, c. 724 (A.B.1172), § 11. Amended by Stats.2009, c. 348 (S.B.308), § 6.)*

Law Revision Commission Comments
2009 Amendment

Section 1304 is amended to reflect the repeal of former Chapter 2 (commencing with Section 21320) of Part 3 of Division 11. See 2008 Cal. Stat. ch. 174. The reference to the former law is retained because the former law continues to apply to the enforcement of a no contest clause in an instrument that became irrevocable prior to January 1, 2001, notwithstanding the repeal of the former law. See Sections 3(g) ("If the new law does not apply to a matter that occurred before the operative date, the old law continues to govern the matter notwithstanding its amendment or repeal by the new law."), 21315(b) (new law does not apply to instrument that became irrevocable prior to January 1, 2001). [38 Cal.L.Rev.Comm. Reports 203 (2008)].

Cross References

Nonprobate transfer to trustee named in decedent's will, appealable orders, see Probate Code § 6327.

§§ 1305 to 1309. Repealed by Stats.1988, c. 1199, § 65, operative July 1, 1989

Validity of appointment of a probate referee under these sections before July 1, 1989, see Probate Code § 408.

Law Revision Commission Comments
1988 Repeal

The first sentence of the first paragraph of former Section 1305 is restated in Section 400(a) (appointment by Controller) and the first sentence of Section 401(a) (qualifications for appointment) without substantive change. The second sentence is restated in Section 401(b) (qualifications for appointment) without change. The third sentence is superseded by Section 400(b) (appointment by Controller).

The first sentence of the second paragraph is omitted; it is a transitional provision that no longer serves a function. The second sentence is restated in the first sentence of Section 403(a) (term of office of probate referee) without substantive change. The third sentence is restated in Section 403(b) (term of office of probate referee) without substantive change. The fourth sentence is omitted; it is a transitional provision that no longer serves a function. The fifth sentence is restated in the second sentence of Section 401(a) (qualifications for appointment) without substantive change. The sixth sentence is restated in the second sentence of Section 403(a) (term of office of probate referee) without substantive change. [19 Cal.L.Rev.Comm. Reports 1085 (1988)].

Former Section 1306 is restated in Section 402 (qualification examination), deleting the references to the State Personnel Board. The State Personnel Board no longer administers the examination. The Controller currently contracts with Cooperative Personnel Services, an agency created through a joint powers agreement, for

administration of the examination. [19 Cal.L.Rev.Comm. Reports 1227 (1988)].

Former Section 1307 is restated in Section 404(a) (standards for probate referee), making adoption of standards mandatory rather than permissive. This codifies existing practice. [19 Cal.L.Rev. Comm. Reports 1086 (1988)].

Subdivision (a) of former Section 1308 is restated in Section 404(b) (standards for probate referee) without substantive change. Subdivision (b) is restated in Section 405 (revocation of appointment of probate referee) without substantive change. [19 Cal.L.Rev.Comm. Reports 1227 (1988)].

Former Section 1309 is restated in Section 406 (termination of authority) without substantive change. [19 Cal.L.Rev.Comm. Reports 1227 (1988)].

CHAPTER 2. EFFECT OF AN APPEAL

§ 1310. Stay of judgment or order; acts of fiduciaries directed by court; guardianship proceedings; undertaking required by court

(a) Except as provided in subdivisions (b), (c), (d), and (e), an appeal pursuant to Chapter 1 (commencing with Section 1300) stays the operation and effect of the judgment or order.

(b) Notwithstanding that an appeal is taken from the judgment or order, for the purpose of preventing injury or loss to a person or property, the trial court may direct the exercise of the powers of the fiduciary, or may appoint a temporary guardian or conservator of the person or estate, or both, or a special administrator or temporary trustee, to exercise the powers, from time to time, as if no appeal were pending. All acts of the fiduciary pursuant to the directions of the court made under this subdivision are valid, irrespective of the result of the appeal. An appeal of the directions made by the court under this subdivision shall not stay these directions.

(c) In proceedings for guardianship of the person, Section 917.7 of the Code of Civil Procedure shall apply.

(d) An appeal shall not stay the operation and effect of the judgment or order if the court requires an undertaking, as provided in Section 917.9 of the Code of Civil Procedure, and the undertaking is not given.

(e) An appeal shall not stay the operation and effect of a judgment for money or an order directing payment of money, unless one of the following applies:

(1) A bond is posted as provided in Section 917.1 of the Code of Civil Procedure.

(2) The payment is to be made from a decedent's estate being administered under Division 7 (commencing with Section 7000) or from the estate of a person who is subject to a guardianship or conservatorship of the estate under Division 4 (commencing with Section 1400). However, a court

may require a bond as provided in subdivision (d). *(Added by Stats.1997, c. 724 (A.B.1172), § 11. Amended by Stats.2000, c. 688 (A.B.1669), § 20; Stats.2010, c. 94 (A.B.2271), § 1.)*

Cross References

Appeals,
  Generally, see Code of Civil Procedure § 901 et seq.
  Rules on appeal in civil cases, see California Rules of Court, Rule 8.1 et seq.
Conservatorship, generally, see Probate Code § 1800 et seq.
Estate administration, generally, see Probate Code § 7000 et seq.
Estate administration, payment of debts, see Probate Code § 11400 et seq.
Fiduciary, defined, see Probate Code § 39.
Guardianship, generally, see Probate Code § 1500 et seq.
Temporary guardians and conservators, generally, see Probate Code § 2250 et seq.

§ 1311. Appointment of fiduciary; reversal for error; validity of fiduciary acts; liability

If an order appointing a fiduciary is reversed on appeal for error, all acts of the fiduciary performed after issuance of letters and prior to the reversal are as valid as though the order were affirmed and the person appointed is not liable for any otherwise proper act done in good faith before the reversal, nor is any transaction void by reason of the reversal if entered into with a third person dealing in good faith and for value. *(Added by Stats.1997, c. 724 (A.B.1172), § 11.)*

Cross References

Fiduciary, defined, see Probate Code § 39.
Letters, defined, see Probate Code § 52.

§ 1312. Inheritance tax; orders fixing, refusing to fix, or determining none due

Notwithstanding the repeal of former Section 1297 by Chapter 1199 of the Statutes of 1988, an appeal may be taken from an order or the refusal to make an order fixing an inheritance tax or determining that none is due. *(Added by Stats.1997, c. 724 (A.B.1172), § 11.)*

§ 1313. Repealed by Stats.1988, c. 1199, § 65, operative July 1, 1989

§§ 1350 to 1359. Repealed by Stats.1987, c. 923, § 60.7, operative July 1, 1988

Law Revision Commission Comments

1987 Repeal

Former Section 1350 is restated in Section 12400 ("missing person" defined) without substantive change. [19 Cal.L.Rev.Comm. Reports 389 (1988)].

Former Section 1351 is restated in Section 12401 (presumption of death for purposes of administration) without substantive change. [19 Cal.L.Rev.Comm. Reports 389 (1988)].

Former Section 1352 is restated without substantive change in Section 12402 (manner of administration and distribution of missing person's estate), except that the one-year delay of distribution is not continued. Under Section 12402, the general limitations on distribution of estates apply. The reference to distribution of the estate is also omitted; distribution is included in the process of administration under Section 12402. [19 Cal.L.Rev.Comm. Reports 389 (1988)].

Former Section 1353 is restated in Section 12403 (jurisdiction of court) without substantive change. [19 Cal.L.Rev.Comm. Reports 389 (1988)].

Subdivisions (a)–(c) of former Section 1354 are restated in Section 12404 (petition for administration) without substantive change, except as noted in the Comment to Section 12404. Subdivision (d) is restated and generalized in Section 1284 (verification required). [19 Cal.L.Rev.Comm. Reports 389 (1988)].

Former Section 1355 is replaced by Section 12405 (notice of hearing). Section 12405 no longer delays the hearing for three months nor requires publication 90 days before hearing. See the Comment to Section 12405. [19 Cal.L.Rev.Comm. Reports 389 (1988)].

Subdivisions (a) and (b) of former Section 1356 are restated in Section 12406(a) and (b) (determination whether person is person presumed to be dead and search for missing person) without substantive change. Subdivision (c) is replaced by Section 12406(c). [19 Cal.L.Rev.Comm. Reports 389 (1988)].

Former Section 1357 is restated in Section 12407 (appointment of personal representative and determination of date of disappearance) without substantive change. [19 Cal.L.Rev.Comm. Reports 389 (1988)].

Former Section 1358 is restated in Section 12408 (recovery of property by missing person upon reappearance) without substantive change, except that the five-year period runs from the time of distribution rather than the time of the petition and the term "beneficiaries" is substituted for "heirs and devisees." [19 Cal.L.Rev.Comm. Reports 389 (1988)].

Former Section 1359 is restated in Section 12409 (application of part) without substantive change. [19 Cal.L.Rev.Comm. Reports 389 (1988)].

Division 4

GUARDIANSHIP, CONSERVATORSHIP, AND OTHER PROTECTIVE PROCEEDINGS

Cross References

Application of guardianship and conservatorship law, see Health and Safety Code § 416.1.

Cancellation and voter file maintenance, mentally incompetent persons, review under Probate Code of capability to complete affidavit, see Elections Code § 2209.

Conservatorship and guardianship for developmentally disabled, Evaluation report, see Health and Safety Code § 416.8.

Fiduciary powers and duties, see Health and Safety Code § 416.16.

Conservatorship for gravely disabled persons, appointment, procedure, see Welfare and Institutions Code § 5350.

Enforcement of money judgments, property in guardianship or conservatorship estate, see Code of Civil Procedure § 709.030.

Human experimentation, informed consent, see Health and Safety Code § 24175.

Judicial determination of incapacity, conservatorship, see Civil Code § 40.

Mentally incompetent persons, disqualification from voting, see Elections Code § 2208.

Persons with intellectual disabilities, cost of determining fitness of person for admission to home, see Welfare and Institutions Code § 6717.

Public defender, duties, probate proceedings, see Government Code § 27706.

Part 1

DEFINITIONS AND GENERAL PROVISIONS

Law Revision Commission Comments

1990 Enactment

This part supersedes Part 1 (commencing with Section 1400) of Division 4 of the repealed Probate Code. The superseded part was enacted upon recommendation of the California Law Revision Commission. See Recommendation Relating to Guardianship–Conservatorship Law, 14 Cal.L.Revision Comm'n Reports 501

(1978). For the Guardianship–Conservatorship Law as enacted in 1979 (Chapter 726 of the Statutes of 1979) with the revisions made by Chapters 89 and 246 of the Statutes of 1980, see Guardianship–Conservatorship Law, 15 Cal.L.Revision Comm'n Reports 451 (1980). [20 Cal.L.Rev.Comm. Reports 1001 (1990)].

Cross References

Freedom from parental custody and control, stay of proceedings and effect upon jurisdiction under these provisions, see Family Code § 7807.

Termination of parental rights of father, filing of petition, stay of proceedings affecting a child pending final determination of parental rights, see Family Code § 7662.

CHAPTER 1. SHORT TITLE AND DEFINITIONS

Cross References

Application of division to guardianship and conservatorship appointments for developmentally disabled persons, see Health and Safety Code § 416.1.

Application of old and new law, see Probate Code § 3.

Inapplicability of certain notice provisions, see Probate Code § 1200.

Public defender, duty to represent persons not financially able to employ counsel in proceedings under this division, see Government Code § 27706.

Public guardians, see Government Code § 27430 et seq.

Statutory construction, generally, see Cal. Const. Art. 4, § 19; Code of Civil Procedure §§ 1858, 1859; Government Code § 9603 et seq.

§ 1400. Guardianship–Conservatorship Law

The portion of this division consisting of Part 1 (commencing with Section 1400), Part 2 (commencing with Section 1500), Part 3 (commencing with Section 1800), and Part 4 (commencing with Section 2100) may be cited as the Guardianship-Conservatorship Law. *(Stats.1990, c. 79 (A.B.759), § 14, operative July 1, 1991.)*

Law Revision Commission Comments

1990 Enactment

Section 1400 is a new provision, not found in the repealed Probate Code. For background on the provisions of this part, see the Comment to this part under the part heading. [20 Cal.L.Rev.Comm. Reports 1001 (1990)].

Cross References

Professional fiduciaries, suspension, revocation or other adverse action, see Business and Professions Code § 6584.

Property in guardianship or conservatorship, see Code of Civil Procedure § 709.030.

§ 1401. Application of definitions

Unless the provision or context otherwise requires, the definitions in this chapter govern the construction of this division. *(Stats.1990, c. 79 (A.B.759), § 14, operative July 1, 1991.)*

Law Revision Commission Comments

1990 Enactment

Section 1401 restates Section 1400 of the repealed Probate Code without substantive change. For background on the provisions of this part, see the Comment to this part under the part heading. [20 Cal.L.Rev.Comm. Reports 1001 (1990)].

§ 1402. Repealed by Stats.1979, c. 726, p. 2334, § 1, operative Jan. 1, 1981

§ 1403. Absentee

"Absentee" means either of the following:

(a) A member of a uniformed service covered by United States Code, Title 37, Chapter 10, who is determined thereunder by the secretary concerned, or by the authorized delegate thereof, to be in missing status as missing status is defined therein.

(b) An employee of the United States government or an agency thereof covered by United States Code, Title 5, Chapter 55, Subchapter VII, who is determined thereunder by the head of the department or agency concerned, or by the authorized delegate thereof, to be in missing status as missing status is defined therein. *(Stats.1990, c. 79 (A.B.759), § 14, operative July 1, 1991.)*

Law Revision Commission Comments

1990 Enactment

Section 1403 continues Section 1403 of the repealed Probate Code without change. "Secretary concerned" is defined in Section 1440. For background on the provisions of this part, see the Comment to this part under the part heading. [20 Cal.L.Rev.Comm. Reports 1001 (1990)].

Cross References

Absentee principal, application of this section, see Civil Code § 2357.

Conservator of estate of absentee, appointment, see Probate Code § 1803.

Personal property of absentees, see Probate Code § 3700 et seq.

Review of conservatorship, inapplicability of chapter to absentees, see Probate Code § 1850.

Secretary concerned, defined, see Probate Code § 1440.

Special provisions applicable where proposed conservatee is an absentee, see Probate Code § 1840 et seq.

Spouse of absentee, appointment as conservator of the estate, see Probate Code § 1813.

§§ 1404 to 1405.1. Repealed by Stats.1979, c. 726, p. 2334, § 1, operative Jan. 1, 1981

§ 1406. Repealed by Stats.1990, c. 79 (A.B.759), § 13, operative July 1, 1991

Law Revision Commission Comments

1990 Repeal

Section 1406 of the repealed Probate Code is omitted from the new Probate Code because it is unnecessary. See Section 23 ("account in an insured savings and loan association" defined for new code). [20 Cal.L.Rev.Comm. Reports 1001 (1990)].

§ 1406.5. Repealed by Stats.1979, c. 726, p. 2334, § 1, operative Jan. 1, 1981

§§ 1407 to 1409. Repealed by Stats.1979, c. 726, p. 2334, § 1, operative Jan. 1, 1981

§§ 1410, 1411. Repealed by Stats.1990, c. 79 (A.B.759), § 13, operative July 1, 1991

Law Revision Commission Comments

1990 Repeal

Section 1410 of the repealed Probate Code is omitted from the new Probate Code because it is unnecessary. See Section 30 ("conservator" defined for new code). [20 Cal.L.Rev.Comm. Reports 1001 (1990)].

Section 1411 of the repealed Probate Code is omitted from the new Probate Code because it is unnecessary. See Section 29 ("conservatee" defined for new code). [20 Cal.L.Rev.Comm. Reports 1001 (1990)].

§ 1418. Court

"Court," when used in connection with matters in the guardianship or conservatorship proceeding, means the court in which such proceeding is pending. *(Stats.1990, c. 79 (A.B.759), § 14, operative July 1, 1991.)*

Law Revision Commission Comments

1990 Enactment

Section 1418 continues Section 1418 of the repealed Probate Code without change. This definition does not apply where the context otherwise requires. See Section 1401. For examples of where the context otherwise requires, see Sections 2216, 2803. For background on the provisions of this part, see the Comment to this part under the part heading. [20 Cal.L.Rev.Comm. Reports 1001 (1990)].

§ 1419. Court investigator

"Court investigator" means the person referred to in Section 1454. *(Stats.1990, c. 79 (A.B.759), § 14, operative July 1, 1991.)*

Law Revision Commission Comments

1990 Enactment

Section 1419 continues Section 1419 of the repealed Probate Code without change. For background on the provisions of this part, see the Comment to this part under the part heading. [20 Cal.L.Rev. Comm. Reports 1001 (1990)].

§ 1419.5. Custodial parent

"Custodial parent" means the parent who either (a) has been awarded sole legal and physical custody of the child in another proceeding, or (b) with whom the child resides if there is currently no operative custody order. If the child resides with both parents, then they are jointly the custodial parent. *(Added by Stats.1993, c. 978 (S.B.305), § 1.)*

Cross References

Child, defined, see Probate Code § 26.

§ 1420. Developmental disability

"Developmental disability" means a disability that originates before an individual attains 18 years of age, continues, or can be expected to continue, indefinitely, and constitutes a substantial handicap for the individual. As defined by the Director of Developmental Services, in consultation with the Superintendent of Public Instruction, this term includes intellectual disability, cerebral palsy, epilepsy, and autism. This term also includes handicapping conditions found to be closely related to intellectual disability or to require treatment similar to that required for individuals with an intellectual disability, but does not include other handicapping conditions that are solely physical in nature. *(Stats.1990, c. 79 (A.B.759), § 14, operative July 1, 1991. Amended by Stats.2012, c. 448 (A.B.2370), § 44; Stats.2012, c. 457 (S.B. 1381), § 44.)*

Law Revision Commission Comments

1990 Enactment

Section 1420 continues Section 1420 of the repealed Probate Code without substantive change. For background on the provisions of this part, see the Comment to this part under the part heading. [20 Cal.L.Rev.Comm. Reports 1001 (1990)].

Cross References

Conservatorship and guardianship for developmentally disabled persons, see Health and Safety Code § 416 et seq.
Services for the developmentally disabled, see Welfare and Institutions Code § 4500 et seq.
Sterilization of adults with developmental disabilities, petition by limited conservator, see Probate Code § 1952.

§ 1424. Interested person

"Interested person" includes, but is not limited to:

(a) Any interested state, local, or federal entity or agency.

(b) Any interested public officer or employee of this state or of a local public entity of this state or of the federal government. *(Stats.1990, c. 79 (A.B.759), § 14, operative July 1, 1991.)*

Law Revision Commission Comments

1990 Enactment

Section 1424 continues Section 1424 of the repealed Probate Code without change. This section makes clear that a public officer or employee or a public entity may be an interested person for the purposes of this division. See also Section 1461 (notice to Director of Mental Health or Director of Developmental Services) and the Comment thereto. For background on the provisions of this part, see the Comment to this part under the part heading. [20 Cal.L.Rev.Comm. Reports 1001 (1990)].

Recommendations relating to revision of the guardianship-conservatorship law, 15 Cal.L.Rev.Comm. Reports 1463 (1980).

Cross References

Interested person, defined, see Probate Code § 48.

§ 1430. Petition

"Petition" includes an application or request in the nature of a petition. *(Stats.1990, c. 79 (A.B.759), § 14, operative July 1, 1991.)*

Law Revision Commission Comments

1990 Enactment

Section 1430 continues Section 1430 of the repealed Probate Code without change. For background on the provisions of this part, see the Comment to this part under the part heading. For general provisions relating to petitions and other papers, see Sections 1020–1023. [20 Cal.L.Rev.Comm. Reports 1001 (1990)].

§ 1430.5. Repealed by Stats.1979, c. 726, p. 2334, § 1, operative Jan. 1, 1981

§ 1431. Proceedings to establish a limited conservatorship

"Proceedings to establish a limited conservatorship" include proceedings to modify or revoke the powers or duties of a limited conservator. *(Stats.1990, c. 79 (A.B.759), § 14, operative July 1, 1991.)*

Law Revision Commission Comments

1990 Enactment

Section 1431 continues Section 1431 of the repealed Probate Code without change. For background on the provisions of this part, see the Comment to this part under the part heading. [20 Cal.L.Rev. Comm. Reports 1001 (1990)].

§§ 1432 to 1435.18. Repealed by Stats.1979, c. 726, § 1, operative Jan. 1, 1981

§ 1435.19. Repealed by Stats.1959, c. 125, § 1

§§ 1435.20, 1435.21. Renumbered §§ 1435.6, 1435.7 and amended by Stats.1959, c. 125, §§ 7, 8

§ 1435.22. Repealed by Stats.1959, c. 125, § 1

§ 1435.23. Renumbered § 1435.8 and amended by Stats. 1959, c. 125, § 9

§§ 1435.24 to 1435.31. Repealed by Stats.1959, c. 125, § 1

§ 1435.32. Renumbered § 1435.10 and amended by Stats. 1959, c. 125, § 11

§ 1435.33. Repealed by Stats.1959, c. 125, § 1

§§ 1435.34 to 1435.36. Renumbered §§ 1435.11 to 1435.13 and amended by Stats.1959, c. 125, §§ 12 to 14

§ 1435.37. Repealed by Stats.1959, c. 125, § 1

§ 1435.38. Renumbered § 1435.14 and amended by Stats. 1959, c. 125, § 15

§ 1435.39. Repealed by Stats.1959, c. 125, § 1

§ 1440. Secretary concerned

"Secretary concerned" has the same meaning as provided in United States Code, Title 37, Section 101. *(Stats.1990, c. 79 (A.B.759), § 14, operative July 1, 1991.)*

Law Revision Commission Comments

1990 Enactment

Section 1440 continues Section 1440 of the repealed Probate Code without substantive change. For background on the provisions of this part, see the Comment to this part under the part heading. [20 Cal.L.Rev.Comm. Reports 1001 (1990)].

§§ 1440.1 to 1442. Repealed by Stats.1979, c. 726, p. 2334, § 1, operative Jan. 1, 1981

§ 1443. Repealed by Stats.1990, c. 79 (A.B.759), § 13, operative July 1, 1991

Law Revision Commission Comments

1990 Repeal

Section 1443 of the repealed Probate Code is superseded by Section 23 ("account in an insured credit union" defined for new code). [20 Cal.L.Rev.Comm. Reports 1001 (1990)].

§ 1444. Repealed by Stats.1979, c. 726, p. 2334, § 1, operative Jan. 1, 1981

§ 1446. Single-premium deferred annuity

"Single-premium deferred annuity" means an annuity offered by an admitted life insurer for the payment of a one-time lump-sum premium and for which the insurer neither assesses any initial charges or administrative fees against the premium paid nor exacts or assesses any penalty for withdrawal of any funds by the annuitant after a period of five years. *(Stats.1990, c. 79 (A.B.759), § 14, operative July 1, 1991.)*

Law Revision Commission Comments

1990 Enactment

Section 1446 continues Section 1446 of the repealed Probate Code without change. For background on the provisions of this part, see the Comment to this part under the part heading. [20 Cal.L.Rev. Comm. Reports 1001 (1990)].

§ 1449. Indian child custody proceedings; definitions; membership in more than one tribe

(a) As used in this division, unless the context otherwise requires, the terms "Indian," "Indian child," "Indian child's tribe," "Indian custodian," "Indian tribe," "reservation," and "tribal court" shall be defined as provided in Section 1903 of the Indian Child Welfare Act (25 U.S.C. Sec. 1901 et seq.).

(b) When used in connection with an Indian child custody proceeding, the terms "extended family member" and "parent" shall be defined as provided in Section 1903 of the Indian Child Welfare Act (25 U.S.C. Sec. 1901 et seq.).

(c) "Indian child custody proceeding" means a "child custody proceeding" within the meaning of Section 1903 of the Indian Child Welfare Act (25 U.S.C. Sec. 1901 et seq.), including a voluntary or involuntary proceeding that may result in an Indian child's temporary or long-term foster care or guardianship placement if the parent or Indian custodian cannot have the child returned upon demand, termination of parental rights or adoptive placement.

(d) When an Indian child is a member of more than one tribe or is eligible for membership in more than one tribe, the court shall make a determination, in writing together with the reasons for it, as to which tribe is the Indian child's tribe for purposes of the Indian child custody proceeding. The court shall make that determination as follows:

(1) If the Indian child is or becomes a member of only one tribe, that tribe shall be designated as the Indian child's tribe, even though the child is eligible for membership in another tribe.

(2) If an Indian child is or becomes a member of more than one tribe, or is not a member of any tribe but is eligible for membership in more than one tribe, the tribe with which the child has the more significant contacts shall be designated as the Indian child's tribe. In determining which tribe the child has the more significant contacts with, the court shall consider, among other things, the following factors:

(A) The length of residence on or near the reservation of each tribe and frequency of contact with each tribe.

(B) The child's participation in activities of each tribe.

(C) The child's fluency in the language of each tribe.

(D) Whether there has been a previous adjudication with respect to the child by a court of one of the tribes.

(E) The residence on or near one of the tribes' reservations by the child parents, Indian custodian, or extended family members.

(F) Tribal membership of custodial parent or Indian custodian.

(G) Interest asserted by each tribe in response to the notice specified in Section 1460.2.

(H) The child's self-identification.

(3) If an Indian child becomes a member of a tribe other than the one designated by the court as the Indian child's tribe under paragraph (2), actions taken based on the court's determination prior to the child's becoming a tribal member shall continue to be valid. *(Added by Stats.2006, c. 838 (S.B.678), § 16.)*

§§ 1450, 1451. Repealed by Stats.1990, c. 79 (A.B.759), § 13, operative July 1, 1991

1990 Repeal

Section 1450 of the repealed Probate Code is omitted from the new Probate Code because it is unnecessary. See Section 1021(a) (verification required). [20 Cal.L.Rev.Comm. Reports 1001 (1990)].

Section 1451 of the repealed Probate Code is omitted from the new Probate Code because it is unnecessary. See Section 1041 (clerk to set matters for hearing). [20 Cal.L.Rev.Comm. Reports 1001 (1990)].

CHAPTER 2. GENERAL PROVISIONS

§ 1452. Trial by jury

Except as otherwise specifically provided in this division, there is no right to trial by jury in proceedings under this division. *(Stats.1990, c. 79 (A.B.759), § 14, operative July 1, 1991.)*

Law Revision Commission Comments

1990 Enactment

Section 1452 continues Section 1452 of the repealed Probate Code without change. There is a right to a jury trial in a hearing on a petition for establishment of a conservatorship (see Section 1827), for termination of conservatorship (see Section 1863), and for modification of the powers of a limited conservator (Section 2351.5(c)). For background on the provisions of this part, see the Comment to this part under the part heading. [20 Cal.L.Rev.Comm. Reports 1001 (1990)].

Cross References

Establishment of conservatorship, trial by jury, see Probate Code § 1827.
Jury trial, generally, see Code of Civil Procedure § 592; Cal. Const. Art. 1, § 16.
Termination of conservatorship, trial by jury, see Probate Code § 1863.

§ 1453. Motion for new trial

A motion for a new trial may be made only in cases in which, under the provisions of this division, a right to jury trial is expressly granted, whether or not the case was tried by a jury. *(Stats.1990, c. 79 (A.B.759), § 14, operative July 1, 1991.)*

Law Revision Commission Comments

1990 Enactment

Section 1453 continues Section 1453 of the repealed Probate Code without change. For background on the provisions of this part, see the Comment to this part under the part heading. [20 Cal.L.Rev. Comm. Reports 1001 (1990)].

Cross References

Appeals, see Probate Code § 1300 et seq.
Jury trial, conservatorship,
Establishment, see Probate Code § 1827.
Termination, see Probate Code § 1863.
New trials, generally, see Code of Civil Procedure § 656 et seq.

§ 1454. Court investigator; appointment; qualifications

(a) The court shall appoint a court investigator when one is required for the purposes of a proceeding under this division. The person appointed as the court investigator shall be an officer or special appointee of the court with no personal or other beneficial interest in the proceeding.

(b) The person appointed as the court investigator shall have the following qualifications:

(1) The training or experience, or both, necessary (i) to make the investigations required under this division, (ii) to communicate with, assess, and deal with persons who are or may be the subject of proceedings under this division, and (iii) to perform the other duties required of a court investigator.

(2) A demonstrated sufficient knowledge of law so as to be able to inform conservatees and proposed conservatees of the nature and effect of a conservatorship proceeding and of their rights, to answer their questions, and to inform conservators concerning their powers and duties. *(Stats.1990, c. 79 (A.B.759), § 14, operative July 1, 1991.)*

Law Revision Commission Comments

1990 Enactment

Section 1454 continues Section 1454 of the repealed Probate Code without change. For background on the provisions of this part, see the Comment to this part under the part heading. See also Report of Assembly Committee on Judiciary on Assembly Bills Nos. 261 and 167, reprinted in 15 Cal.L.Revision Comm'n Reports 1061–67 (1980). [20 Cal.L.Rev.Comm. Reports 1001 (1990)].

§ 1455. Petitions for instructions, or grant of power or authority; persons authorized to file

Any petition for instructions or to grant a guardian or a conservator any power or authority under this division, which may be filed by a guardian or conservator, may also be filed by a person who petitions for the appointment of a guardian or conservator, including, but not limited to, a person who petitions under Section 2002 for transfer of conservatorship. *(Added by Stats.1996, c. 563 (S.B.392), § 5. Amended by Stats.2014, c. 553 (S.B.940), § 4, eff. Jan. 1, 2015, operative Jan. 1, 2016.)*

Law Revision Commission Comments

2014 Amendment

Section 1455 is amended to reflect the enactment of the California Conservatorship Jurisdiction Act (Section 1980 et seq.). [43 Cal. L.Rev.Comm. Reports 93 (2013)].

§ 1456. Court-appointed attorneys, examiners and investigators; educational requirements

(a) In addition to any other requirements that are part of the judicial branch education program, on or before January 1, 2008, the Judicial Council shall adopt a rule of court that shall do all of the following:

(1) Specifies the qualifications of a court-employed staff attorney, examiner, and investigator, and any attorney appointed pursuant to Sections 1470 and 1471.

(2) Specifies the number of hours of education in classes related to conservatorships or guardianships that a judge who is regularly assigned to hear probate matters shall complete, upon assuming the probate assignment, and then over a three-year period on an ongoing basis.

(3) Specifies the number of hours of education in classes related to conservatorships or guardianships that a court-employed staff attorney, examiner, and investigator, and any attorney appointed pursuant to Sections 1470 and 1471 shall complete each year.

(4) Specifies the particular subject matter that shall be included in the education required each year.

(5) Specifies reporting requirements to ensure compliance with this section.

(b) In formulating the rule required by this section, the Judicial Council shall consult with interested parties, including, but not limited to, the California Judges Association, the California Association of Superior Court Investigators, the California Public Defenders Association, the County Counsels' Association of California, the State Bar of California, the National Guardianship Association, the Professional Fiduciary Association of California, the California Association of Public Administrators, Public Guardians and Public Conservators, a disability rights organization, and the Association of Professional Geriatric Care Managers. *(Added by Stats.2006, c. 493 (A.B.1363), § 3. Amended by Stats.2007, c. 553 (A.B.1727), § 2.)*

§ 1456.2. Continuing education requirements; compliance by public conservator

On or before January 1, 2010, the public conservator shall comply with the continuing education requirements that are established by the California State Association of Public Administrators, Public Guardians, and Public Conservators. *(Added by Stats.2008, c. 237 (A.B.2343), § 2.)*

§ 1456.5. Compliance with filing requirements

Each court shall ensure compliance with the requirements of filing the inventory and appraisal and the accountings required by this division. Courts may comply with this section in either of the following ways:

(a) By placing on the court's calendar, at the time of the appointment of the guardian or conservator and at the time of approval of each accounting, a future hearing date to enable the court to confirm timely compliance with these requirements.

(b) By establishing and maintaining internal procedures to generate an order for appearance and consideration of appropriate sanctions or other actions if the guardian or conservator fails to comply with the requirements of this section. *(Added by Stats.2007, c. 553 (A.B.1727), § 3.)*

§ 1457. Nonprofessional conservators and guardians; educational program and training

In order to assist relatives and friends who may seek appointment as a nonprofessional conservator or guardian the Judicial Council shall, on or before January 1, 2008, develop a short educational program of no more than three hours that is user-friendly and shall make that program available free of charge to each proposed conservator and guardian and each court-appointed conservator and guardian who is not required to be licensed as a professional conservator or guardian pursuant to Chapter 6 (commencing with Section 6500) of Division 3 of the Business and Professions Code. The program may be available by video presentation or Internet access. *(Added by Stats.2006, c. 493 (A.B.1363), § 4. Amended by Stats.2007, c. 553 (A.B.1727), § 4.)*

§ 1458. Repealed by Stats.2007, c. 553 (A.B.1727), § 5, operative Jan. 1, 2009

§ 1459. Legislative findings and declarations; children of Indian ancestry

(a) The Legislature finds and declares the following:

(1) There is no resource that is more vital to the continued existence and integrity of recognized Indian tribes than their children, and the State of California has an interest in protecting Indian children who are members of, or are eligible for membership in, an Indian tribe. The state is committed to protecting the essential tribal relations and best interest of an Indian child by promoting practices, in accordance with the Indian Child Welfare Act (25 U.S.C. Sec. 1901 et seq.) and other applicable law, designed to prevent the child's involuntary out-of-home placement and, whenever such placement is necessary or ordered, by placing the child, whenever possible, in a placement that reflects the unique values of the child's tribal culture and is best able to assist the child in establishing, developing, and maintaining a political, cultural, and social relationship with the child's tribe and tribal community.

(2) It is in the interest of an Indian child that the child's membership in the child's Indian tribe and connection to the tribal community be encouraged and protected, regardless of whether or not the child is in the physical custody of an Indian parent or Indian custodian at the commencement of a child custody proceeding, the parental rights of the child's parents have been terminated, or where the child has resided or been domiciled.

(b) In all Indian child custody proceedings, as defined in the federal Indian Child Welfare Act, the court shall consider all of the findings contained in subdivision (a), strive to promote the stability and security of Indian tribes and families, comply with the federal Indian Child Welfare Act, and seek to protect the best interest of the child. Whenever an Indian child is removed from a foster care home or institution, guardianship, or adoptive placement for the purpose of further foster care, guardianship, or adoptive placement, placement of the child shall be in accordance with the Indian Child Welfare Act.

(c) A determination by an Indian tribe that an unmarried person, who is under the age of 18 years, is either (1) a member of an Indian tribe or (2) eligible for membership in an Indian tribe and a biological child of a member of an Indian tribe shall constitute a significant political affiliation with the tribe and shall require the application of the federal Indian Child Welfare Act to the proceedings.

(d) In any case in which this code or other applicable state or federal law provides a higher standard of protection to the rights of the parent or Indian custodian of an Indian child, or the Indian child's tribe, than the rights provided under the Indian Child Welfare Act, the court shall apply the higher state or federal standard.

(e) Any Indian child, the Indian child's tribe, or the parent or Indian custodian from whose custody the child has been removed, may petition the court to invalidate an action in an Indian child custody proceeding for foster care or guardianship placement or termination of parental rights if the action violated Sections 1911, 1912, and 1913 of the Indian Child Welfare Act. *(Added by Stats.2006, c. 838 (S.B.678), § 17.)*

§ 1459.5. Application of federal law to proceedings involving children of Indian ancestry

(a) The Indian Child Welfare Act (25 U.S.C. Sec. 1901 et seq.) shall apply to the following guardianship or conservatorship proceedings under this division when the proposed ward or conservatee is an Indian child:

(1) In any case in which the petition is a petition for guardianship of the person and the proposed guardian is not the natural parent or Indian custodian of the proposed ward, unless the proposed guardian has been nominated by the natural parents pursuant to Section 1500 and the parents retain the right to have custody of the child returned to them upon demand.

(2) To a proceeding to have an Indian child declared free from the custody and control of one or both parents brought in a guardianship proceeding.

(3) In any case in which the petition is a petition for conservatorship of the person of a minor whose marriage has been dissolved, the proposed conservator is seeking physical custody of the minor, the proposed conservator is not the natural parent or Indian custodian of the proposed conservatee and the natural parent or Indian custodian does not retain the right to have custody of the child returned to them upon demand.

(b) When the Indian Child Welfare Act applies to a proceeding under this division, the court shall apply Sections 224.3 to 224.6, inclusive, and Sections 305.5, 361.31, and 361.7 of the Welfare and Institutions Code, and the following rules from the California Rules of Court, as they read on January 1, 2005:

(1) Paragraph (7) of subdivision (b) of Rule 1410.

(2) Subdivision (i) of Rule 1412.

(c) In the provisions cited in subdivision (b), references to social workers, probation officers, county welfare department, or probation department shall be construed as meaning the party seeking a foster care placement, guardianship, or adoption. *(Added by Stats.2006, c. 838 (S.B.678), § 18.)*

CHAPTER 3. NOTICES

Cross References

Notice of hearing on the petition, conservatorships, modification or vacation of orders for application of community property for support and maintenance, see Probate Code § 3088.

§ 1460. Notice of time and place; mailing; posting; special notice; dispensation

(a) Subject to Sections 1202 and 1203, if notice of hearing is required under this division but the applicable provision does not fix the manner of giving notice of hearing, the notice of the time and place of the hearing shall be given at least 15 days before the day of the hearing as provided in this section.

(b) Subject to subdivision (e), the petitioner, who includes for the purposes of this section a person filing a petition, report, or account, shall cause the notice of hearing to be mailed to each of the following persons:

(1) The guardian or conservator.

(2) The ward or the conservatee.

(3) The spouse of the ward or conservatee, if the ward or conservatee has a spouse, or the domestic partner of the conservatee, if the conservatee has a domestic partner.

(4) Any person who has requested special notice of the matter, as provided in Section 2700.

(5) For any hearing on a petition to terminate a guardianship, to accept the resignation of, or to remove the guardian, the persons described in subdivision (c) of Section 1510.

(6) For any hearing on a petition to terminate a conservatorship, to accept the resignation of, or to remove the conservator, the persons described in subdivision (b) of Section 1821.

(c) The clerk of the court shall cause the notice of the hearing to be posted as provided in Section 1230 if the posting is required by subdivision (c) of Section 2543.

(d) Except as provided in subdivision (e), nothing in this section excuses compliance with the requirements for notice to a person who has requested special notice pursuant to Chapter 10 (commencing with Section 2700) of Part 4.

(e) The court for good cause may dispense with the notice otherwise required to be given to a person as provided in this section. *(Stats.1990, c. 79 (A.B.759), § 14, operative July 1, 1991. Amended by Stats.1994, c. 806 (A.B.3686), § 8; Stats. 1996, c. 862 (A.B.2751), § 5; Stats.2001, c. 893 (A.B.25), § 14.)*

Law Revision Commission Comments

1990 Enactment

Section 1460 continues Section 1460 of the repealed Probate Code with revisions that permit the court for good cause to dispense with notice to a person who has requested special notice. A reference to Sections 1202 and 1203 has been substituted for the reference to Section 1462, the substance of former Section 1462 now being found in Sections 1202 and 1203. The phrase "other than the petitioner or persons joining in the petition" has been omitted from subdivision (b), this phrase being unnecessary in view of Section 1201. The reference in subdivision (c) to the courthouse of the county of the court where the proceedings are pending has been omitted as unnecessary in view of comparable provision in subdivision (a) of Section 1230.

For general provisions relating to notice of hearing, see Sections 1200–1221. Where the court determines that the notice otherwise required is insufficient under the particular circumstances, the court may require that further or additional notice be given. See Section 1202. The court may for good cause shorten or lengthen the 15–day notice required by this section. See Sections 1202, 1203. A petitioner need not give notice of himself or herself or to persons joining in the petition. See Section 1201.

The court may dispense with the required notice where good cause is shown. See subdivision (e). This authority permits the court to dispense with notice, for example, where the person specified to receive the notice is in such mental or physical condition that giving the person notice would be useless or detrimental to the person or where, after the exercise of reasonable diligence, the whereabouts of the person is unknown.

Any interested person may receive notice of hearing on all petitions or notice of hearing of certain specified matters by filing and serving a request for special notice under Section 2700. Subdivision (d) makes clear that the provisions of this section have no effect on the requirements for notice to a person who has requested special notice. See Section 2700 and the Comment thereto. However, subdivision (e) permits the court for good cause to dispense with notice to a person who has requested special notice.

Section 1460 does not deal with the effect of giving notice or the failure to receive notice. See Section 1260(c) (conclusiveness of order concerning notice) and the Comment thereto. Proof of the giving of notice must be made at or before the hearing as provided in Sections 1260–1265. For background on the provisions of this part, see the Comment to this part under the part heading. See also Report of Senate Committee on Judiciary on Assembly Bill No. 261, reprinted in 15 Cal.L.Revision Comm'n Reports 1097–99 (1980). [20 Cal.L.Rev.Comm. Reports 1001 (1990)].

Cross References

Account of guardian or conservator, notice of hearing, see Probate Code § 2621.
Computation of time, see Code of Civil Procedure §§ 12 and 12a; Government Code § 6800 et seq.
Definitions,
    Court, see Probate Code § 1418.
    Domestic partner, see Probate Code § 37.
    Interested person, see Probate Code § 1424.
    Petition, see Probate Code § 1430.

Guardians and conservators, removal or resignation, see Probate Code § 2650 et seq.
Notice,
    Mailing, see Probate Code § 1215 et seq.
    Posting, see Probate Code § 1230.
    Proof of giving notice, see Probate Code § 1260 et seq.
    Special notice, see Probate Code § 1250 et seq.
    This code, generally, see Probate Code § 1200 et seq.
Notice of conservatee's death, see Probate Code § 2361.
Notice of hearing on the petition,
    Borrowing money and giving security, see Probate Code § 2551.
    Change of venue, see Probate Code § 2214.
    Compelling guardian or conservator to pay support or debts, see Probate Code § 2404.
    Compensation of guardian, conservator, and attorney, see Probate Code § 2640 et seq.
    Compromise of claims and actions, extension, renewal or modification of obligations, see Probate Code § 2500.
    Contingent fee contract with attorney, see Probate Code § 2644.
    Conveyance or transfer of property claimed to belong to ward or conservatee or other person, see Probate Code § 851.
    Court ordered medical treatment, see Probate Code § 2357.
    Dedication or conveyance of real property or easement with or without consideration, see Probate Code § 2556.
    Determination of capacity of conservatee to marry, see Probate Code § 1901.
    Disposition of remaining balance of money or property paid or delivered pursuant to compromise or judgment for minor or incompetent person, see Probate Code § 3602.
    Estate management, limitation of powers of guardian or conservator, see Probate Code § 2450.
    Exchange of property, see Probate Code § 2557.
    Guardianship or conservatorship of the estate, instructions from or confirmation by court, see Probate Code § 2403.
    Guardianship or conservatorship of the person, instructions from or confirmation by court, see Probate Code § 2359.
    Guardianship or conservatorship of the person, order for care, custody, control and education of ward or conservatee, see Probate Code § 2351.
    Independent exercise of powers, order granting, see Probate Code § 2592.
    Independent exercise of powers, withdrawal or subsequent limitation of powers, see Probate Code § 2593.
    Investments of proceeds of sale and other money of the estate, see Probate Code § 2570.
    Leases, see Probate Code § 2553.
    Reduction in amount of bond of guardian or conservator, see Probate Code § 2329.
    Residence of ward or conservatee, notice according to this section, see Probate Code § 2352.
    Resignation of guardian or conservator, see Probate Code § 2660.
    Substituted judgment, see Probate Code § 2581.
    Support and maintenance of ward or conservatee and dependents by guardian or conservator of the estate, see Probate Code § 2421 et seq.
    Termination of guardianship, see Probate Code § 1601.
Notice to specified persons,
    Director of Developmental Services, see Probate Code §§ 1461, 2611, 2621.
    Director of Social Services, see Probate Code § 1542.
    Director of State Hospitals, see Probate Code §§ 1461, 2611, 2621.
Professional fiduciary as guardian or conservator, court authorization of periodic payments, contents of petition, see Probate Code § 2643.1.
Service of copy of final account on termination of guardianship, probate rules, see California Rules of Court, Rule 7.1006.
Service of copy of final account or report after resignation or removal of guardian, probate rules, see California Rules of Court, Rule 7.1005.

Service of process,
  Generally, see Code of Civil Procedure § 413.10 et seq.
  Mail, see Code of Civil Procedure §§ 415.30, 1012 et seq.
  Personal delivery, see Code of Civil Procedure § 415.10.
  Proof of service, see Code of Civil Procedure § 417.10 et seq.
  Publication, see Code of Civil Procedure § 415.50.
Vacancy in office of guardian or conservator, appointment of
  successor, notice and hearing, see Probate Code § 2670.

§ 1460.1. Children under 12 years of age; exceptions to notice requirements

Notwithstanding any other provision of this division, no notice is required to be given to any child under the age of 12 years if the court determines either of the following:

(a) Notice was properly given to a parent, guardian, or other person having legal custody of the minor, with whom the minor resides.

(b) The petition is brought by a parent, guardian, or other person having legal custody of the minor, with whom the minor resides. *(Added by Stats.1997, c. 724 (A.B.1172), § 9.)*

Cross References

Child, defined, see Probate Code § 26.

§ 1460.2. Knowledge that proposed ward or conservatee may be a child of Indian ancestry; notice to interested parties; requirements; time; proof

(a) If the court or petitioner knows or has reason to know that the proposed ward or conservatee may be an Indian child, notice shall comply with subdivision (b) in any case in which the Indian Child Welfare Act (25 U.S.C. Sec. 1901 et seq.) applies, as specified in Section 1459.5.

(b) Any notice sent under this section shall be sent to the minor's parent or legal guardian, Indian custodian, if any, and the Indian child's tribe, and shall comply with all of the following requirements:

(1) Notice shall be sent by registered or certified mail with return receipt requested. Additional notice by first-class mail is recommended, but not required.

(2) Notice to the tribe shall be to the tribal chairperson, unless the tribe has designated another agent for service.

(3) Notice shall be sent to all tribes of which the child may be a member or eligible for membership until the court makes a determination as to which tribe is the Indian child's tribe in accordance with subdivision (d) of Section 1449, after which notice need only be sent to the tribe determined to be the Indian child's tribe.

(4) Notice, to the extent required by federal law, shall be sent to the Secretary of the Interior's designated agent, the Sacramento Area Director, Bureau of Indian Affairs. If the identity or location of the Indian child's tribe is known, a copy of the notice shall also be sent directly to the Secretary of the Interior, unless the Secretary of the Interior has waived the notice in writing and the person responsible for giving notice under this section has filed proof of the waiver with the court.

(5) The notice shall include all of the following information:

(A) The name, birthdate, and birthplace of the Indian child, if known.

(B) The name of any Indian tribe in which the child is a member or may be eligible for membership, if known.

(C) All names known of the Indian child's biological parents, grandparents and great-grandparents or Indian custodians, including maiden, married, and former names or aliases, as well as their current and former addresses, birthdates, places of birth and death, tribal enrollment numbers, and any other identifying information, if known.

(D) A copy of the petition.

(E) A copy of the child's birth certificate, if available.

(F) The location, mailing address, and telephone number of the court and all parties notified pursuant to this section.

(G) A statement of the following:

(i) The absolute right of the child's parents, Indian custodians, and tribe to intervene in the proceeding.

(ii) The right of the child's parents, Indian custodians, and tribe to petition the court to transfer the proceeding to the tribal court of the Indian child's tribe, absent objection by either parent and subject to declination by the tribal court.

(iii) The right of the child's parents, Indian custodians, and tribe to, upon request, be granted up to an additional 20 days from the receipt of the notice to prepare for the proceeding.

(iv) The potential legal consequences of the proceedings on the future custodial rights of the child's parents or Indian custodians.

(v) That if the parents or Indian custodians are unable to afford counsel, counsel shall be appointed to represent the parents or Indian custodians pursuant to Section 1912 of the Indian Child Welfare Act (25 U.S.C. Sec. 1901 et seq.).

(vi) That the information contained in the notice, petition, pleading, and other court documents is confidential, so any person or entity notified shall maintain the confidentiality of the information contained in the notice concerning the particular proceeding and not reveal it to anyone who does not need the information in order to exercise the tribe's rights under the Indian Child Welfare Act (25 U.S.C. Sec. 1901 et seq.).

(c) Notice shall be sent whenever it is known or there is reason to know that an Indian child is involved, and for every hearing thereafter, including, but not limited to, the hearing at which a final adoption order is to be granted. After a tribe acknowledges that the child is a member or eligible for membership in the tribe, or after the Indian child's tribe intervenes in a proceeding, the information set out in subparagraphs (C), (D), (E), and (G) of paragraph (5) of subdivision (b) need not be included with the notice.

(d) Proof of the notice, including copies of notices sent and all return receipts and responses received, shall be filed with the court in advance of the hearing except as permitted under subdivision (e).

(e) No proceeding shall be held until at least 10 days after receipt of notice by the parent, Indian custodian, the tribe or the Bureau of Indian Affairs. The parent, Indian custodian, or the tribe shall, upon request, be granted up to 20 additional days to prepare for the proceeding. Nothing herein shall be construed as limiting the rights of the parent, Indian custodian, or tribe to 10 days' notice when a lengthier notice period is required by statute.

(f) With respect to giving notice to Indian tribes, a party shall be subject to court sanctions if that person knowingly and willfully falsifies or conceals a material fact concerning whether the child is an Indian child, or counsels a party to do so.

(g) The inclusion of contact information of any adult or child that would otherwise be required to be included in the notification pursuant to this section, shall not be required if that person is at risk of harm as a result of domestic violence, child abuse, sexual abuse, or stalking. *(Added by Stats.2006, c. 838 (S.B.678), § 19.)*

§ 1461. Notice to director; conditions; certificate; limitations

(a) As used in this section, "director" means:

(1) The Director of State Hospitals when the state hospital referred to in subdivision (b) is under the jurisdiction of the State Department of State Hospitals.

(2) The Director of Developmental Services when the state hospital referred to in subdivision (b) is under the jurisdiction of the State Department of Developmental Services.

(b) Notice of the time and place of hearing on the petition, report, or account, and a copy of the petition, report, or account, shall be mailed to the director at the director's office in Sacramento at least 15 days before the hearing if both of the following conditions exist:

(1) The ward or conservatee is or has been during the guardianship or conservatorship proceeding a patient in, or on leave from, a state hospital under the jurisdiction of the State Department of State Hospitals or the State Department of Developmental Services.

(2) The petition, report, or account is filed under any one or more of the following provisions: Section 1510, 1820, 1861, 2212, 2403, 2421, 2422, or 2423; Article 7 (commencing with Section 2540) of Chapter 6 of Part 4; Section 2580, 2592, or 2620; Chapter 9.5 (commencing with Section 2670) of Part 4; Section 3080 or 3088; or Chapter 3 (commencing with Section 3100) of Part 6. Notice under this section is not required in the case of an account pursuant to Section 2620 if the total guardianship or conservatorship assets are less than one thousand five hundred dollars ($1,500) and the gross annual income, exclusive of any public assistance income, is less than six thousand dollars ($6,000), and the ward or conservatee is not a patient in, or on leave or on outpatient status from, a state hospital at the time of the filing of the petition.

(c) If the ward or conservatee has been discharged from the state hospital, the director, upon ascertaining the facts, may file with the court a certificate stating that the ward or conservatee is not indebted to the state and waive the giving of further notices under this section. Upon the filing of the certificate of the director, compliance with this section thereafter is not required unless the certificate is revoked by the director and notice of the revocation is filed with the court.

(d) The statute of limitations does not run against any claim of the State Department of State Hospitals or the State Department of Developmental Services against the estate of the ward or conservatee for board, care, maintenance, or transportation with respect to an account that is settled without giving the notice required by this section. *(Stats. 1990, c. 79 (A.B.759), § 14, operative July 1, 1991. Amended by Stats.2012, c. 440 (A.B.1488), § 39, eff. Sept. 22, 2012.)*

Law Revision Commission Comments

1990 Enactment

Section 1461 continues Section 1461 of the repealed Probate Code without substantive change. The exception for a petition, report, or account filed by the director in the introductory clause of subdivision (b) has been omitted as unnecessary in view of Section 1201.

The following provisions, listed in paragraph (2) of subdivision (b), require a notice in cases where the condition in paragraph (1) of subdivision (b) exists:

Section 1510 (petition for appointment of guardian)
Section 1820 (petition for appointment of conservator)
Section 1861 (petition for termination of conservatorship)
Section 2212 (petition for change of venue)
Section 2403 (authorization and instructions or approval and confirmation by court for guardian or conservator of estate)
Section 2421 (petition for allowance for ward or conservatee)
Section 2422 (petition for support of ward or conservatee out of the estate notwithstanding existence of person legally obligated to provide support)
Section 2423 (petition for payment of surplus income to relatives of conservatee)
Article 7 (commencing with Section 2540) of Chapter 6 of Part 4 (petitions for sales)
Section 2580 (substituted judgment)
Section 2592 (independent exercise of powers)
Section 2620 (presentation of account for settlement and allowance)
Chapter 9.5 (commencing with Section 2670) (appointment of successor guardian or conservator)
Sections 3080 and 3088 (enforcement of support for spouse who has conservator)
Chapter 3 (commencing with Section 3100) of Part 6 (special proceeding to authorize transaction involving community property)

For other provisions concerning notice to the Director of Mental Health or the Director of Developmental Services, see Sections 2611 (inventory and appraisal), 2621 (hearing on accounts). See also Section 1542 (notice of petition for nonrelative guardianship to Director of Social Services). Where the Director of Mental Health or the Director of Developmental Services is an interested person (Section 1424), a request for special notice may be filed under Section 2700. For general provisions relating to notice, see Sections 1200–1230. See also Sections 1260–1265 (proof of giving notice). For background on the provisions of this part, see the Comment to this part under the part heading. See also Recommendation Relating to Revision of the Guardianship–Conservatorship Law, 15 Cal.L.Revision Comm'n Reports 1463, 1473–74 (1980); Report of Assembly Committee on Judiciary on Assembly Bills Nos. 261 and 167, reprinted in 15 Cal.L.Revision Comm'n Reports 1061–67 (1980). [20 Cal.L.Rev.Comm. Reports 1001 (1990)].

Cross References

Appointment of guardian, notice of hearing, see Probate Code § 1511.
Computation of time, see Code of Civil Procedure §§ 12 and 12a; Government Code § 6800 et seq.
Definitions,
  Court, see Probate Code § 1418.
  Petition, see Probate Code § 1430.

Establishment of conservatorship, mailing of notice of hearing, see Probate Code § 1822.

Inventory and appraisement procedures when unrevoked certificate is on file with court, see Probate Code § 2611.

Notice,
Mailing, see Probate Code § 1215 et seq.
Posting, see Probate Code § 1230.
Proof of giving notice, see Probate Code § 1260 et seq.
Special notice, see Probate Code § 1250 et seq.
This code, generally, see Probate Code § 1200 et seq.

Notice to,
Director of Social Services, see Probate Code § 1542.
Director of State Hospitals, see Probate Code §§ 2611, 2621.
Interested persons, request for special notice, see Probate Code § 2700.

Service of process,
Generally, see Code of Civil Procedure § 413.10 et seq.
Mail, see Code of Civil Procedure §§ 415.30, 1012 et seq.
Personal delivery, see Code of Civil Procedure § 415.10.
Proof of service, see Code of Civil Procedure § 417.10 et seq.
Publication, see Code of Civil Procedure § 415.50.

§§ 1461.1, 1461.3. Repealed by Stats.1979, c. 726, p. 2335, § 1, operative Jan. 1, 1981

§ 1461.4. Regional center for developmentally disabled; notice of hearing and copy of petition; report and recommendation

(a) The petitioner shall mail or personally serve a notice of the hearing and a copy of the petition to the director of the regional center for the developmentally disabled at least 30 days before the day of the hearing on a petition for appointment in any case in which all of the following conditions exist:

(1) The proposed ward or conservatee has developmental disabilities.

(2) The proposed guardian or conservator is not the natural parent of the proposed ward or conservatee.

(3) The proposed guardian or conservator is a provider of board and care, treatment, habilitation, or other services to persons with developmental disabilities or is a spouse or employee of a provider.

(4) The proposed guardian or conservator is not a public entity.

(b) The regional center shall file a written report and recommendation with the court regarding the suitability of the petitioners to meet the needs of the proposed ward or conservatee in any case described in subdivision (a). *(Stats. 1990, c. 79 (A.B.759), § 14, operative July 1, 1991.)*

Law Revision Commission Comments

1990 Enactment

Section 1461.4 continues Section 1461.4 of the repealed Probate Code without change. For background on the provisions of this part, see the Comment to this part under the part heading. [20 Cal.L.Rev.Comm. Reports 1001 (1990)].

Cross References

Computation of time, see Code of Civil Procedure §§ 12 and 12a; Government Code § 6800 et seq.
Notice,
Mailing, see Probate Code § 1215 et seq.
Posting, see Probate Code § 1230.

Proof of giving notice, see Probate Code § 1260 et seq.
Special notice, see Probate Code § 1250 et seq.
This code, generally, see Probate Code § 1200 et seq.
Service of process,
Generally, see Code of Civil Procedure § 413.10 et seq.
Mail, see Code of Civil Procedure §§ 415.30, 1012 et seq.
Personal delivery, see Code of Civil Procedure § 415.10.
Proof of service, see Code of Civil Procedure § 417.10 et seq.
Publication, see Code of Civil Procedure § 415.50.

§ 1461.5. Veterans Administration; notice of hearing on petition, report, account or inventory; time; conditions

Notice of the time and place of hearing on a petition, report, or account, and a notice of the filing of an inventory, together with a copy of the petition, report, inventory, or account, shall be mailed to the office of the Veterans Administration having jurisdiction over the area in which the court is located at least 15 days before the hearing, or within 15 days after the inventory is filed, if both of the following conditions exist:

(a) The guardianship or conservatorship estate consists or will consist wholly or in part of any of the following:

(1) Money received from the Veterans Administration.

(2) Revenue or profit from such money or from property acquired wholly or in part from such money.

(3) Property acquired wholly or in part with such money or from such property.

(b) The petition, report, inventory, or account is filed under any one or more of the following provisions: Section 1510, 1601, 1820, 1861, 1874, 2422, or 2423; Article 7 (commencing with Section 2540) of Chapter 6 of Part 4; Section 2570, 2571, 2580, 2592, 2610, 2613, or 2620; Chapter 8 (commencing with Section 2640) of Part 4; Chapter 9.5 (commencing with Section 2670) of Part 4; Section 3080 or 3088; or Chapter 3 (commencing with Section 3100) of Part 6. *(Stats.1990, c. 79 (A.B.759), § 14, operative July 1, 1991.)*

Law Revision Commission Comments

1990 Enactment

Section 1461.5 continues Section 1461.5 of the repealed Probate Code without substantive change. The exception for a petition filed by the Veterans Administration in the introductory clause of the section has been omitted as unnecessary in view of Section 1201. For general provisions relating to notice, see Sections 1200–1230. See also Sections 1260–1265 (proof of giving notice). For the recommendation of the California Law Revision Commission that resulted in the repeal of the Uniform Veterans Guardianship Act and the enactment of this section of the repealed Probate Code, see Recommendation Relating to Uniform Veterans Guardianship Act, 15 Cal.L.Revision Comm'n Reports 1289 (1980). For additional background on the provisions of this part, see the Comment to this part under the part heading. See also Recommendation Relating to Revision of the Guardianship–Conservatorship Law, 15 Cal.L.Revision Comm'n Reports 1463, 1474 (1980). [20 Cal.L.Rev.Comm. Reports 1001 (1990)].

Cross References

Appointment of guardian, notice of hearing, see Probate Code § 1511.
Computation of time, see Code of Civil Procedure §§ 12 and 12a; Government Code § 6800 et seq.

Establishment of conservatorship, notice of hearing, mailing, see Probate Code § 1822.

§ 1461.7.   Time and place of hearing on petition, report, or account; copies

Unless the court for good cause dispenses with such notice, notice of the time and place of the hearing on a petition, report, or account, together with a copy of the petition, report, or account, shall be given to the same persons who are required to be given notice under Section 2581 for the period and in the manner provided in this chapter if both of the following conditions exist:

(a) A conservator of the estate has been appointed under Article 5 (commencing with Section 1845) of Chapter 1 of Part 3 for a person who is missing and whose whereabouts is unknown.

(b) The petition, report, or account is filed in the conservatorship proceeding under any one or more of the following provisions:

(1) Section 1861 or 2423.

(2) Article 7 (commencing with Section 2540) of Chapter 6 of Part 4.

(3) Section 2570, 2571, 2580, 2592, or 2620.

(4) Chapter 8 (commencing with Section 2640) of Part 4.

(5) Chapter 9.5 (commencing with Section 2670) of Part 4.

(6) Chapter 3 (commencing with Section 3100) of Part 6. *(Stats.1990, c. 79 (A.B.759), § 14, operative July 1, 1991.)*

Law Revision Commission Comments

1990 Enactment

Section 1461.7 continues Section 1461.7 of the repealed Probate Code without change. For the recommendation of the California Law Revision Commission that resulted in the enactment of this section of the repealed Probate Code, see Recommendation Relating to Missing Persons, 16 Cal.L.Revision Comm'n Reports 105 (1982). For additional background on the provisions of this part, see the Comment to this part under the part heading. [20 Cal.L.Rev.Comm. Reports 1001 (1990)].

§§ 1462 to 1466.   Repealed by Stats.1990, c. 79 (A.B.759), § 13, operative July 1, 1991

Law Revision Commission Comments

1990 Repeal

Section 1462 of the repealed Probate Code is omitted from the new Probate Code because it is unnecessary. See Sections 1202 (additional notice on court order), 1203(a) (order shortening time). [20 Cal.L.Rev.Comm. Reports 1001 (1990)].

Section 1463 of the repealed Probate Code is omitted from the new Probate Code because it is unnecessary. See Section 1045 (continuance and postponement of hearings), 1205 (notice of continued or postponed hearings). [20 Cal.L.Rev.Comm. Reports 1001 (1990)].

Section 1464 of the repealed Probate Code is superseded by Section 1001(b) (Judicial Council forms). [20 Cal.L.Rev.Comm. Reports 1001 (1990)].

Section 1465 of the repealed Probate Code is omitted from the new Probate Code because it is unnecessary. See Section 1215 (manner of mailing; when mailing complete). [20 Cal.L.Rev.Comm. Reports 1001 (1990)].

Section 1466 of the repealed Probate Code is omitted from the new Probate Code because it is unnecessary. See Section 1216(a)

(personal delivery instead of mailing). [20 Cal.L.Rev.Comm. Reports 1001 (1990)].

§ 1467.   Service by mail deemed complete

If service is made by mail pursuant to this division in the manner authorized in Section 415.30 of the Code of Civil Procedure, the service is complete on the date a written acknowledgment of receipt is executed. *(Stats.1990, c. 79 (A.B.759), § 14, operative July 1, 1991.)*

Law Revision Commission Comments

1990 Enactment

Section 1467 continues Section 1467 of the repealed Probate Code without change. This section makes clear that, when service is made under this division in the manner authorized in Section 415.30 of the Code of Civil Procedure, the service is complete on the date the acknowledgment of receipt is executed. This section does not include the requirement found in Section 415.30 that the acknowledgment be returned "to the sender." It is sufficient if proof is made that the person served (or a person authorized to acknowledge service on behalf of such person) did execute a written acknowledgment of receipt. For example, service is complete under Section 1467 if the written acknowledgment is returned to a person other than the sender.

This section applies only where service is made by mail in the manner authorized in Section 415.30. This section does not apply where a provision of this division merely requires that a notice or other paper be mailed. In the latter case, the applicable provision ordinarily is satisfied when the notice or other paper is deposited in the mail. See Section 1215.

For background on the provisions of this part, see the Comment to this part under the part heading. [20 Cal.L.Rev.Comm. Reports 1001 (1990)].

Cross References

Notice,
  Mailing, see Probate Code § 1215 et seq.
  Posting, see Probate Code § 1230.
  Proof of giving notice, see Probate Code § 1260 et seq.
  Special notice, see Probate Code § 1250 et seq.
  This code, generally, see Probate Code § 1200 et seq.
Service of process, mail, see Code of Civil Procedure §§ 415.30, 1012 et seq.
Service of process, proof of service, see Code of Civil Procedure § 417.10 et seq.

§ 1468.   Repealed by Stats.1990, c. 79 (A.B.759), § 13, operative July 1, 1991

Law Revision Commission Comments

1990 Repeal

Section 1468 of the repealed Probate Code is omitted from the new Probate Code because it is unnecessary. See Sections 1260–1265 (proof of giving notice). [20 Cal.L.Rev.Comm. Reports 1001 (1990)].

§ 1469.   References to § 1220 deemed references to this chapter

Where a provision of this division applies the provisions of this code applicable to personal representatives to proceedings under this division, a reference to Section 1220 in the provisions applicable to personal representatives shall be deemed to be a reference to this chapter. *(Stats.1990, c. 79 (A.B.759), § 14, operative July 1, 1991.)*

Law Revision Commission Comments
1990 Enactment

Section 1469 continues Section 1469 of the repealed Probate Code with the omission of the reference to Section 1230. The reference to Section 1230 has been omitted as unnecessary in view of the revision of Section 1460(c). Section 1469 ensures that the notice provisions contained in this chapter will be used in all proceedings under this division. Section 2543 adopts the procedures applicable to personal representatives for manner of sale for sales under this division. The manner of sale procedures applicable to the personal representative require giving of notice as provided in Section 1220 (notice provision applicable to proceedings with respect to estates of decedents). However, Section 1469 provides that notice is to be given under this chapter rather than as provided in that section. See also Section 2100 (law governing where no specific provision of this division applicable). For background on the provisions of this part, see the Comment to this part under the part heading. See also Report of Assembly Committee on Judiciary on Assembly Bills Nos. 261 and 167, reprinted in 15 Cal.L.Revision Comm'n Reports 1061, 1063–64 (1980); Comments to Conforming Revisions and Repeals, 19 Cal.L.Revision Comm'n Reports 391, 444 (1988). [20 Cal.L.Rev. Comm. Reports 1001 (1990)].

Cross References

Appointment of personal representative, generally, see Probate Code § 8400 et seq.
Personal representative and general personal representative, defined, see Probate Code § 58.

CHAPTER 4. APPOINTMENT OF LEGAL COUNSEL

Section

§ 1470. Discretionary appointment; compensation and expenses; source for payment

(a) The court may appoint private legal counsel for a ward, a proposed ward, a conservatee, or a proposed conservatee in any proceeding under this division if the court determines the person is not otherwise represented by legal counsel and that the appointment would be helpful to the resolution of the matter or is necessary to protect the person's interests.

(b) If a person is furnished legal counsel under this section, the court shall, upon conclusion of the matter, fix a reasonable sum for compensation and expenses of counsel. The sum may, in the discretion of the court, include compensation for services rendered, and expenses incurred, before the date of the order appointing counsel.

(c) The court shall order the sum fixed under subdivision (b) to be paid:

(1) If the person for whom legal counsel is appointed is an adult, from the estate of that person.

(2) If the person for whom legal counsel is appointed is a minor, by a parent or the parents of the minor or from the minor's estate, or any combination thereof, in any proportions the court deems just.

(3) If a ward or proposed ward is furnished legal counsel for a guardianship proceeding, upon its own motion or that of a party, the court shall determine whether a parent or parents of the ward or proposed ward or the estate of the ward or proposed ward is financially unable to pay all or a portion of the cost of counsel appointed pursuant to this section. Any portion of the cost of that counsel that the court finds the parent or parents or the estate of the ward or proposed ward is unable to pay shall be paid by the county. The Judicial Council shall adopt guidelines to assist in determining financial eligibility for county payment of counsel appointed by the court pursuant to this chapter.

(d) The court may make an order under subdivision (c) requiring payment by a parent or parents of the minor only after the parent or parents, as the case may be, have been given notice and the opportunity to be heard on whether the order would be just under the circumstances of the particular case. *(Stats.1990, c. 79 (A.B.759), § 14, operative July 1, 1991. Amended by Stats.1992, c. 572 (S.B.1455), § 1.5; Stats.2007, c. 719 (S.B.241), § 1.)*

Law Revision Commission Comments
1992 Amendment

Subdivision (b) of section 1470 is amended to make clear that, when legal counsel is appointed under this section, the court is not precluded from awarding compensation for legal services rendered, and expenses incurred, before the date of appointment.

Although Section 1470(b) provides that the court shall fix compensation of counsel "upon conclusion of the matter," this does not prevent the court from later making an award of compensation. See 1 W. Johnstone & S. House, California Conservatorships and Guardianships § 7.68, at 374–75 (Cal.Cont.Ed.Bar 1990). The "matter" to which Section 1470 refers is the particular matter for which counsel was appointed. See Section 1471.

Subdivision (b) deals with compensation of appointed counsel for a ward or conservatee. Section 1470 does not affect the right to compensation in cases not covered by the section. *Cf.* Estate of Moore, 258 Cal.App.2d 458, 65 Cal.Rptr. 831 (1968) (payment of attorney's fees of petitioner for conservatorship where another person appointed as conservator); *In re* Guardianship of Bundy, 44 Cal.App. 466, 186 P. 811 (1919) (payment of attorney's fees of petitioner for adult guardianship where proposed ward contested petition). [21 Cal.L.Rev.Comm. Reports 227 (1991)].

Cross References

Child custody, private counsel, see Family Code § 3150 et seq.
Conservatorships and other protective proceedings, educational requirements for court-appointed attorneys and other staff members, see Probate Code § 1456.
Minors, see Family Code § 6500.
Parent, defined, see Probate Code § 54.
Public defender, duty to represent persons not financially able to employ counsel, see Government Code § 27706.

§ 1471. Mandatory appointment; proceedings

(a) If a conservatee, proposed conservatee, or person alleged to lack legal capacity is unable to retain legal counsel and requests the appointment of counsel to assist in the particular matter, whether or not that person lacks or appears to lack legal capacity, the court shall, at or before the time of the hearing, appoint the public defender or private counsel to represent the interest of that person in the following proceedings under this division:

(1) A proceeding to establish or transfer a conservatorship or to appoint a proposed conservator.

(2) A proceeding to terminate the conservatorship.

(3) A proceeding to remove the conservator.

(4) A proceeding for a court order affecting the legal capacity of the conservatee.

(5) A proceeding to obtain an order authorizing removal of a temporary conservatee from the temporary conservatee's place of residence.

(b) If a conservatee or proposed conservatee does not plan to retain legal counsel and has not requested the court to appoint legal counsel, whether or not that person lacks or appears to lack legal capacity, the court shall, at or before the time of the hearing, appoint the public defender or private counsel to represent the interests of that person in any proceeding listed in subdivision (a) if, based on information contained in the court investigator's report or obtained from any other source, the court determines that the appointment would be helpful to the resolution of the matter or is necessary to protect the interests of the conservatee or proposed conservatee.

(c) In any proceeding to establish a limited conservatorship, if the proposed limited conservatee has not retained legal counsel and does not plan to retain legal counsel, the court shall immediately appoint the public defender or private counsel to represent the proposed limited conservatee. The proposed limited conservatee shall pay the cost for that legal service if he or she is able. This subdivision applies irrespective of any medical or psychological inability to attend the hearing on the part of the proposed limited conservatee as allowed in Section 1825. *(Stats.1990, c. 79 (A.B.759), § 14, operative July 1, 1991. Amended by Stats.2014, c. 553 (S.B.940), § 5, eff. Jan. 1, 2015, operative Jan. 1, 2016.)*

Law Revision Commission Comments

1990 Enactment

Section 1471 continues Section 1471 of the repealed Probate Code without substantive change. This section specifies those instances where appointment of counsel is required under this division. Compensation of counsel appointed under Section 1471 is governed by Section 1472.

Subdivision (b) requires appointment of legal counsel in the cases listed in subdivision (a) where the conservatee or proposed conservatee does not request the appointment but the court determines that the appointment would be helpful to the resolution of the matter or is necessary to protect the interests of the conservatee or proposed conservatee. Although the court is given discretionary authority under Section 1470 to appoint legal counsel where the court determines that the appointment would be helpful to the resolution of the matter or is necessary to protect a person's interests, the appointment under Section 1471(b) is mandatory and makes Section 1472 applicable. Sections 1471–1472 permit appointment of the public defender, compensation of legal counsel by the county in cases where the person furnished counsel is determined by the court to lack the ability to pay, and installment payments. These provisions are not found in Section 1470 which provides for discretionary appointment of private legal counsel.

Appointment of the public defender or private counsel under Sections 1471–1472 is also required under some circumstances in a proceeding under Section 1852 (removal of conservator, restoration of conservatee's right to register to vote, making, modification, or revocation of order affecting conservatee's legal capacity, termination of conservatorship), 2357 (authorization of medical treatment for ward or conservatee), Chapter 3 (commencing with Section 3100) of Part 6 (transaction involving community property—Section 3140), or Part 7 (commencing with Section 3200) (authorization of medical treatment of an adult who does not have conservator of the person—Section 3205). See also Gov't Code § 27706 (duty of public defender to represent indigent person). For background on the provisions of this part, see the Comment to this part under the part heading. See also Report of Assembly Committee on Judiciary on Assembly Bills Nos. 261 and 167, reprinted in 15 Cal.L.Revision Comm'n Reports 1061, 1064–65 (1980). [20 Cal.L.Rev.Comm. Reports 1001 (1990)].

2014 Amendment

Section 1471 is amended to make clear that it applies when a conservatorship is transferred under the California Conservatorship Jurisdiction Act (Sections 1980–2024).

The section is also amended to replace "such" with "that," in conformity with California drafting practices. [43 Cal.L.Rev.Comm. Reports 93 (2013)].

Cross References

Authorization of medical treatment for adult without conservator, appointment of counsel, see Probate Code § 3205.

Community property, transactions, representation of counsel, see Probate Code § 3140.

Conservatorships and other protective proceedings, educational requirements for court-appointed attorneys and other staff members, see Probate Code § 1456.

Counsel, right to, see Cal. Const. Art. 1, § 15.

Court investigator,
Appointment and qualifications, see Probate Code § 1454.
Defined, see Probate Code § 1419.
Duties and report, see Probate Code §§ 1826, 1894.

Court ordered medical treatment, duty of attorney, see Probate Code § 2357.

Duty of public defender to represent persons not financially able to employ counsel, see Government Code § 27706.

Establishment of conservatorship, see Probate Code § 1800 et seq.

Guardians and conservators, removal or resignation, see Probate Code § 2650 et seq.

Legal capacity of conservatee, see Probate Code § 1870 et seq.

Limited conservatorship,
Establishment, developmentally disabled adults, see Probate Code §§ 1801, 1828.5, 1830.
Proceedings to establish, defined, see Probate Code § 1431.

Periodic review of conservatorship, notification of counsel, see Probate Code § 1852.

Referral of conservatee for assessment to determine if conservatee has treatable mental illness and is unwilling or unable to accept voluntary treatment, counsel, see Welfare and Institutions Code § 5350.5.

Removal of temporary conservatee from place of residence, see Probate Code §§ 2253, 2254.

Termination of conservatorship, see Probate Code § 1860 et seq.

§ 1472. Mandatory appointment; compensation and expenses; determination by court; source for payment

(a) If a person is furnished legal counsel under Section 1471:

(1) The court shall, upon conclusion of the matter, fix a reasonable sum for compensation and expenses of counsel

and shall make a determination of the person's ability to pay all or a portion of that sum. The sum may, in the discretion of the court, include compensation for services rendered, and expenses incurred, before the date of the order appointing counsel.

(2) If the court determines that the person has the ability to pay all or a portion of the sum, the court shall order the conservator of the estate or, if none, the person, to pay in any installments and in any manner the court determines to be reasonable and compatible with the person's financial ability.

(3) In a proceeding under Chapter 3 (commencing with Section 3100) of Part 6 for court authorization of a proposed transaction involving community property, the court may order payment out of the proceeds of the transaction.

(4) If a conservator is not appointed for the person furnished legal counsel, the order for payment may be enforced in the same manner as a money judgment.

(b) If the court determines that a person furnished private counsel under Section 1471 lacks the ability to pay all or a portion of the sum determined under paragraph (1) of subdivision (a), the county shall pay the sum to the private counsel to the extent the court determines the person is unable to pay.

(c) The payment ordered by the court under subdivision (a) shall be made to the county if the public defender has been appointed or if private counsel has been appointed to perform the duties of the public defender and the county has compensated that counsel. In the case of other court-appointed counsel, the payment shall be made to that counsel. *(Stats.1990, c. 79 (A.B.759), § 14, operative July 1, 1991. Amended by Stats.1992, c. 572 (S.B.1455), § 2.)*

Law Revision Commission Comments

1992 Amendment

Paragraph (1) of subdivision (a) of Section 1472 is amended to make clear that, when legal counsel is appointed under Section 1471, the court is not precluded from awarding compensation for legal services rendered, and expenses incurred, before the date of appointment.

Although Section 1472(a)(1) provides that the court shall fix compensation of counsel "upon conclusion of the matter," this does not prevent the court from later making an award of compensation. See 1 W. Johnstone & S. House, California Conservatorships and Guardianships § 6.57, at 291–92 (Cal.Cont.Ed.Bar 1990). The "matter" to which Section 1472 refers is the particular matter for which counsel was appointed. See Section 1471.

Section 1472 deals with compensation of counsel appointed under Section 1471. The section does not affect the right to compensation in cases not covered by the section. *Cf.* Estate of Moore, 258 Cal.App.2d 458, 65 Cal.Rptr. 831 (1968) (payment of attorney's fees of petitioner for conservatorship where another person appointed as conservator); *In re* Guardianship of Bundy, 44 Cal.App. 466, 186 P. 811 (1919) (payment of attorney's fees of petitioner for adult guardianship where proposed ward contested petition). [21 Cal. L.Rev.Comm. Reports 227 (1991)].

Cross References

Authorization of medical treatment for adult without conservator, application of this section, see Probate Code § 3205.
Community property, see Family Code §§ 65, 760.
Community property, defined, see Probate Code § 28.
Counsel, right to, see Cal. Const. Art. 1, § 15.

Court ordered medical treatment, duty of attorney, see Probate Code § 2357.
Enforcement of judgment in civil actions, see Code of Civil Procedure § 683.010 et seq.
Periodic review of conservatorship, see Probate Code § 1852.
Transaction involving community property, compensation of appointed legal counsel, see Probate Code § 3140.

§ 1474. Matters involving children of Indian ancestry

If an Indian custodian or biological parent of an Indian child lacks the financial ability to retain counsel and requests the appointment of counsel in proceedings described in Section 1459.5, the provisions of subsection (b) of Section 1912 of the Indian Child Welfare Act (25 U.S.C. Sec. 1901 et seq.) and Section 23.13 of Title 25 of the Code of Federal Regulations are applicable. *(Added by Stats.2006, c. 838 (S.B.678), § 20.)*

§ 1480. Repealed by Stats.1990, c. 79 (A.B.759), § 13, operative July 1, 1991

Law Revision Commission Comments

1990 Repeal

Section 1480 of the repealed Probate Code is omitted from the new Probate Code because it is no longer necessary. [20 Cal.L.Rev. Comm. Reports 1001 (1990)].

§§ 1480.3 to 1480.6. Repealed by Stats.1979, c. 726, p. 2334, § 1, operative Jan. 1, 1981

§§ 1481 to 1483. Repealed by Stats.1990, c. 79 (A.B.759), § 13, operative July 1, 1991

Law Revision Commission Comments

1990 Repeal

Section 1481 of the repealed Probate Code is omitted from the new Probate Code because it is no longer necessary. See Sections 2, 3. [20 Cal.L.Rev.Comm. Reports 1001 (1990)].

Section 1482 of the repealed Probate Code is omitted from the new Probate Code because it is no longer necessary. See Sections 2, 3. [20 Cal.L.Rev.Comm. Reports 1001 (1990)].

Section 1483 of the repealed Probate Code is omitted from the new Probate Code because it is no longer necessary. See Sections 2, 3. [20 Cal.L.Rev.Comm. Reports 1001 (1990)].

§§ 1483.1 to 1483.3. Repealed by Stats.1979, c. 726, p. 2334, § 1, operative Jan. 1, 1981

§§ 1484, 1485. Repealed by Stats.1990, c. 79 (A.B.759), § 13, operative July 1, 1991

Law Revision Commission Comments

1990 Repeal

Section 1484 of the repealed Probate Code is omitted from the new Probate Code because it is no longer necessary. See Sections 2, 3. [20 Cal.L.Rev.Comm. Reports 1001 (1990)].

Section 1485 of the repealed Probate Code is omitted from the new Probate Code because it is no longer necessary. See Sections 2, 3. [20 Cal.L.Rev.Comm. Reports 1001 (1990)].

§ 1486. Repealed by Stats.1979, c. 726, p. 2334, § 1, operative Jan. 1, 1981

§ 1487. Repealed by Stats.1990, c. 79 (A.B.759), § 13, operative July 1, 1991

Section 1487 of the repealed Probate Code is omitted from the new Probate Code because it is no longer necessary. See Sections 2, 3. [20 Cal.L.Rev.Comm. Reports 1001 (1990)].

CHAPTER 5. TRANSITIONAL PROVISIONS

§ 1488. Nomination by adult of guardian for such adult deemed nomination of conservator

If before January 1, 1981, an adult has in a signed writing nominated a person to serve as guardian if a guardian is in the future appointed for such adult, such nomination shall be deemed to be a nomination of a conservator. This section applies whether or not the signed writing was executed in the same manner as a witnessed will so long as the person signing the writing had at the time the writing was signed sufficient capacity to form an intelligent preference. *(Stats.1990, c. 79 (A.B.759), § 14, operative July 1, 1991.)*

Section 1488 continues Section 1488 of the repealed Probate Code without substantive change. This section ensures that a nomination of a guardian made under former Probate Code Section 1463 (repealed by 1979 Cal.Stat. ch. 726, § 1) will be given effect under Section 1810. Under Section 1810, a conservator may be nominated in a signed writing whether or not the writing is executed in the same manner as a witnessed will. The second sentence of Section 1488 applies the same standard to a signed writing made under pre–1979 law and purporting to nominate a guardian, even though the writing may not have met the stricter requirement of former Probate Code Section 1463. For background on the provisions of this part, see the Comment to this part under the part heading.

§ 1489. Appointment of guardian by parent or other person for a minor; effect

If, before January 1, 1981, a parent or other person has in a signed writing appointed a person to serve as the guardian of the person or estate or both of a minor, or as the guardian of the property the minor receives from or by designation of the person making the appointment, such appointment shall be deemed to be a nomination of a guardian if the requirements of Section 1500 or 1501 are satisfied and, in such case, shall be given the same effect it would have under Section 1500 or 1501, as the case may be, if made on or after January 1, 1981. This section applies whether or not the signed writing is a will or deed so long as the person signing the writing had at the time the writing was signed sufficient capacity to form an intelligent preference. *(Stats.1990, c. 79 (A.B.759), § 14, operative July 1, 1991.)*

Section 1489 continues Section 1489 of the repealed Probate Code without substantive change. This section ensures that appointment of a testamentary guardian made under former Section 1402 or 1403 (provisions repealed by 1979 Cal.Stat. ch. 726, § 1) will be given effect as a nomination of a guardian under Sections 1500 and 1501. See also Section 1514(c)–(d); Civil Code § 4600.

Under Sections 1500 and 1501, a guardian may be nominated in a signed writing whether or not the writing is a will or deed. See Section 1502 and the Comment thereto. The second sentence of Section 1489 applies the same standard to a signed writing made prior to January 1, 1981, and purporting to appoint a guardian, even though the writing may not have met the stricter requirements of former Section 1402 or 1403 (provisions repealed by 1979 Cal.Stat. ch. 726, § 1). As to the application of any amendments made after that date, see Section 3. For background on the provisions of this part, see the Comment to this part under the part heading. [20 Cal.L.Rev.Comm. Reports 1001 (1990)].

§ 1490. References in statutes

Except as set forth in Section 1510.1, when used in any statute of this state with reference to an adult or to the person of a married minor, "guardian" means the conservator of that adult or the conservator of the person in the case of the married minor. *(Stats.1990, c. 79 (A.B.759), § 14, operative July 1, 1991. Amended by Stats.2015, c. 694 (A.B.900), § 2, eff. Jan. 1, 2016; Stats.2016, c. 86 (S.B.1171), § 244, eff. Jan. 1, 2017.)*

Section 1490 continues subdivision (a) of Section 1490 of the repealed Probate Code without change. This section recognizes that through inadvertence some conforming changes may not have been made in sections containing references made obsolete by enactment of this division in 1979. Subdivisions (b) and (c) of Section 1490 of the repealed Probate Code are omitted as unnecessary. See Sections 22 (defining "account in an insured credit union"), 23 (defining "account in an insured savings and loan association"), 1403 (defining "absentee"), 1440 (defining "secretary concerned"), 1446 (defining "single-premium deferred annuity"). For background on the provisions of this part, see the Comment to this part under the part heading. [20 Cal.L.Rev. Comm. Reports 1001 (1990)].

§ 1491. Repealed by Stats.1990, c. 79 (A.B.759), § 13, operative July 1, 1991

Section 1491 of the repealed Probate Code is superseded by Section 1001(a) (Judicial Council rules). See also Section 3 (general transitional provision). [20 Cal.L.Rev.Comm. Reports 1001 (1990)].

Part 2

GUARDIANSHIP

Law Revision Commission Comments
1990 Enactment

This part supersedes Part 2 (commencing with Section 1500) of Division 4 of the repealed Probate Code. The superseded part was enacted upon recommendation of the California Law Revision Commission. See Recommendation Relating to Guardianship–Conservatorship Law, 14 Cal.L.Revision Comm'n Reports 501 (1978). For the Guardianship–Conservatorship Law as enacted in 1979 (Chapter 726 of the Statutes of 1979) with the revisions made by Chapters 89 and 246 of the Statutes of 1980, see Guardianship–Conservatorship Law, 15 Cal.L.Revision Comm'n Reports 451 (1980). [20 Cal.L.Rev.Comm. Reports 1001 (1990)].

Cross References

Delinquents and wards of the juvenile court, custody of child, see Welfare and Institutions Code § 304.

Freedom from parental custody and control, stay of proceedings and effect upon jurisdiction under these provisions, see Family Code § 7807.

Juvenile case file inspection, confidentiality, release, probation reports, destruction of records, and liability, see Welfare and Institutions Code § 827.

Juvenile court law, guardianships resulting from selection or implementation of a permanent plan, see Welfare and Institutions Code § 366.4.

Termination of parental rights of father, filing of petition, stay of proceedings affecting a child pending final determination of parental rights, see Family Code § 7662.

CHAPTER 1. ESTABLISHMENT OF GUARDIANSHIP

ARTICLE 1. NOMINATION OF GUARDIAN

Cross References

Right to custody of minor child, nomination of guardian by parent, see Family Code § 3043.

§ 1500. Nomination of guardian of person or estate or both by parent

Subject to Section 1502, a parent may nominate a guardian of the person or estate, or both, of a minor child in either of the following cases:

(a) Where the other parent nominates, or consents in writing to the nomination of, the same guardian for the same child.

(b) Where, at the time the petition for appointment of the guardian is filed, either (1) the other parent is dead or lacks legal capacity to consent to the nomination or (2) the consent of the other parent would not be required for an adoption of the child. *(Stats.1990, c. 79 (A.B.759), § 14, operative July 1, 1991.)*

Law Revision Commission Comments
1990 Enactment

Section 1500 continues Section 1500 of the repealed Probate Code without substantive change. As to the effect to be given to a nomination under this section, see Section 1514. See also Civil Code Section 4600 (consideration in proceeding where there is at issue the custody of a minor child of a nomination of a guardian of the person of the child by a parent). As to providing in the nomination for the powers of the guardian, see Section 2108. See also Sections 300–301 (trust company as guardian of estate), 2104 (nonprofit charitable corporation as guardian).

A nomination under Section 1500 is subject to Section 1502, which requires that the nomination be made in the petition for appointment of the guardian or at the hearing on the petition or in a writing signed either before or after the petition is filed. See Section 1502 and the Comment thereto.

An appointment of a guardian for a minor under the law before January 1, 1981, is deemed to be a nomination of a guardian. Section 1489.

For background on the provisions of this part, see the Comment to this part under the part heading. [20 Cal.L.Rev.Comm. Reports 1001 (1990)].

Cross References

Additional powers of guardian nominated by will, see Probate Code § 2108.

Appointment of guardian, see Probate Code § 1514.

Bond of nominated guardian, see Probate Code § 2324.

Capacity of trust company to act as guardian or conservator of estate, see Probate Code § 300.

Child, defined, see Probate Code § 26.

Consent of parent to adoption of child, see Family Code § 8604 et seq.

Joint guardians for one ward, see Probate Code § 2105.

Manner of nomination, see Probate Code § 1502.

Nonrelative guardianships, see Probate Code § 1540 et seq.

Notice of hearing, see Probate Code § 1511.

One guardian for several wards, see Probate Code § 2106.

Parent, defined, see Probate Code § 54.

Petition for appointment, contents, see Probate Code § 1510.

Powers and duties,
  Guardian of estate, see Probate Code § 2400 et seq.
  Guardian of person, see Probate Code § 2350 et seq.

Transitional provision, appointment of guardian deemed to be nomination of guardian, see Probate Code § 1489.

§ 1500.1. Consent by Indian child's parent; requirements

(a) Notwithstanding any other section in this part, and in accordance with Section 1913 of the Indian Child Welfare Act (25 U.S.C. Sec. 1901 et seq.), consent to nomination of a guardian of the person or of a guardian of the person and the estate given by an Indian child's parent is not valid unless both of the following occur:

(1) The consent is executed in writing at least 10 days after the child's birth and recorded before a judge.

(2) The judge certifies that the terms and consequences of the consent were fully explained in detail in English and were fully understood by the parent or that they were interpreted into a language that the parent understood.

(b) The parent of an Indian child may withdraw his or her consent to guardianship for any reason at any time prior to the issuance of letters of guardianship and the child shall be returned to the parent. *(Added by Stats.2006, c. 838 (S.B. 678), § 21.)*

§ 1500.2. Repealed by Stats.1979, c. 76, p. 2334, § 1, operative Jan. 1, 1981

§ 1501. Nomination of guardian for property received by minor

Subject to Section 1502, a parent or any other person may nominate a guardian for property that a minor receives from or by designation of the nominator (whether before, at the time of, or after the nomination) including, but not limited to, property received by the minor by virtue of a gift, deed, trust, will, succession, insurance, or benefits of any kind. *(Stats. 1990, c. 79 (A.B.759), § 14, operative July 1, 1991.)*

Law Revision Commission Comments
1990 Enactment

Section 1501 continues Section 1501 of the repealed Probate Code without change. As to the effect to be given to a nomination under this section, see Section 1514. As to the powers and duties of the guardian, see Section 2109. See also Sections 300–301 (trust company as guardian of estate), 2104 (nonprofit charitable corporation as guardian).

A nomination under Section 1501 is subject to Section 1502, which requires that the nomination be made in the petition for appointment of the guardian or at the hearing on the petition or in a writing signed either before or after the petition is filed. See Section 1502 and the Comment thereto.

Section 1501 covers all property received from or by designation of the person making the nomination, and includes such property as proceeds from an insurance policy. This changes the rule of Estate of Welfer, 110 Cal.App.2d 262, 242 P.2d 655 (1952). Under Section 1501, a person may nominate a guardian for the proceeds of a life insurance policy owned by the nominator on the life of the nominator or on the life of a person surviving the nominator.

Where a parent attempts to nominate a general guardian of the estate of a child as authorized by Section 1500, but the nomination does not satisfy the requirements of Section 1500 because written consent of the other parent is required but not obtained, the nomination may nevertheless satisfy the requirements of Section 1501 and permit appointment of a guardian with respect to the property of the nominating parent that the child takes from that parent. See Guardianship of Joaquin, 168 Cal.App.2d 99, 335 P.2d 507 (1959).

For background on the provisions of this part, see the Comment to this part under the part heading. [20 Cal.L.Rev.Comm. Reports 1001 (1990)].

Cross References
Appointment of guardian, see Probate Code § 1514.
Bond of nominated guardian, see Probate Code § 2324.
California Uniform Transfers to Minors Act, see Probate Code § 3900.
Duties of trustees, see Probate Code § 16000 et seq.
Guardian, powers and duties,
    Nominated in will, see Probate Code § 2108.
    Particular property appointed, see Probate Code § 2109.
Notice of hearing, see Probate Code § 1511.
Petition for appointment, contents, see Probate Code § 1510.
Transitional provision, appointment of guardian deemed to be nomination of guardian, see Probate Code § 1489.

Trustees, powers, see Probate Code § 16200 et seq.

§ 1501a. Repealed by Stats.1979, c. 726, p. 2334, § 1, operative Jan. 1, 1981

§ 1502. Manner of nomination; time effective; subsequent legal incapacity or death of nominator

(a) A nomination of a guardian under this article may be made in the petition for the appointment of the guardian or at the hearing on the petition or in a writing signed either before or after the petition for the appointment of the guardian is filed.

(b) The nomination of a guardian under this article is effective when made except that a writing nominating a guardian under this article may provide that the nomination becomes effective only upon the occurrence of such specified condition or conditions as are stated in the writing, including but not limited to such conditions as the subsequent legal incapacity or death of the person making the nomination.

(c) Unless the writing making the nomination expressly otherwise provides, a nomination made under this article remains effective notwithstanding the subsequent legal incapacity or death of the person making the nomination. *(Stats.1990, c. 79 (A.B.759), § 14, operative July 1, 1991.)*

Law Revision Commission Comments
1990 Enactment

Section 1502 continues Section 1502 of the repealed Probate Code without change. Subdivision (b) makes clear that a writing making a nomination under this article may specify one or more conditions the occurrence of which makes the nomination become effective. Absent such specification, the nomination is effective, unless revoked, when made. Subdivision (c) makes clear that death or subsequent lack of legal capacity does not make the nomination ineffective unless the writing making the nomination expressly otherwise provides. For background on the provisions of this part, see the Comment to this part under the part heading. [20 Cal.L.Rev.Comm. Reports 1001 (1990)].

Cross References
Petition for appointment, see Probate Code § 1510.

§§ 1503 to 1509. Repealed by Stats.1979, c. 726, p. 2334, § 1, operative Jan. 1, 1981

ARTICLE 2. APPOINTMENT OF GUARDIAN GENERALLY

Cross References

Aid to Families with Dependent Children—Foster Care, child whose
nonrelated guardianship was ordered in probate court pursuant
to this Article, eligibility of nonminor for continued benefits, see
Welfare and Institutions Code § 11405.

§ 1510. Petition for appointment; contents

(a) A relative or other person on behalf of the minor, or
the minor if 12 years of age or older, may file a petition for
the appointment of a guardian of the minor. A relative may
file a petition for the appointment of a guardian under this
section regardless of the relative's immigration status.

(b) The petition shall request that a guardian of the person
or estate of the minor, or both, be appointed, shall specify the
name and address of the proposed guardian and the name
and date of birth of the proposed ward, and shall state that
the appointment is necessary or convenient.

(c) The petition shall set forth, so far as is known to the
petitioner, the names and addresses of all of the following:

(1) The parents of the proposed ward.

(2) The person having legal custody of the proposed ward
and, if that person does not have the care of the proposed
ward, the person having the care of the proposed ward.

(3) The relatives of the proposed ward within the second
degree.

(4) In the case of a guardianship of the estate, the spouse
of the proposed ward.

(5) Any person nominated as guardian for the proposed
ward under Section 1500 or 1501.

(6) In the case of a guardianship of the person involving an
Indian child, any Indian custodian and the Indian child's
tribe.

(d) If the petitioner or proposed guardian is a professional
fiduciary, as described in Section 2340, who is required to be
licensed under the Professional Fiduciaries Act (Chapter 6
(commencing with Section 6500) of Division 3 of the Business
and Professions Code), the petition shall include the following:

(1) The petitioner's or proposed guardian's proposed
hourly fee schedule or another statement of his or her
proposed compensation from the estate of the proposed ward
for services performed as a guardian. The petitioner's or
proposed guardian's provision of a proposed hourly fee

schedule or another statement of his or her proposed
compensation, as required by this paragraph, shall not
preclude a court from later reducing the petitioner's or
proposed guardian's fees or other compensation.

(2) Unless a petition for appointment of a temporary
guardian that contains the statements required by this
paragraph is filed together with a petition for appointment of
a guardian, both of the following:

(A) A statement of the petitioner's or proposed guardian's
license information.

(B) A statement explaining who engaged the petitioner or
proposed guardian or how the petitioner or proposed guardian was engaged to file the petition for appointment of a
guardian or to agree to accept the appointment as guardian
and what prior relationship the petitioner or proposed
guardian had with the proposed ward or the proposed ward's
family or friends.

(e) If the proposed ward is a patient in or on leave of
absence from a state institution under the jurisdiction of the
State Department of State Hospitals or the State Department
of Developmental Services and that fact is known to the
petitioner or proposed guardian, the petition shall state that
fact and name the institution.

(f) The petition shall state, so far as is known to the
petitioner or proposed guardian, whether or not the proposed
ward is receiving or is entitled to receive benefits from the
Veterans Administration and the estimated amount of the
monthly benefit payable by the Veterans Administration for
the proposed ward.

(g) If the petitioner or proposed guardian has knowledge
of any pending adoption, juvenile court, marriage dissolution,
domestic relations, custody, or other similar proceeding
affecting the proposed ward, the petition shall disclose the
pending proceeding.

(h) If the petitioners or proposed guardians have accepted
or intend to accept physical care or custody of the child with
intent to adopt, whether formed at the time of placement or
formed subsequent to placement, the petitioners or proposed
guardians shall so state in the guardianship petition, whether
or not an adoption petition has been filed.

(i) If the proposed ward is or becomes the subject of an
adoption petition, the court shall order the guardianship
petition consolidated with the adoption petition, and the
consolidated case shall be heard and decided in the court in
which the adoption is pending.

(j) If the proposed ward is or may be an Indian child, the
petition shall state that fact. *(Stats.1990, c. 79 (A.B.759),
§ 14, operative July 1, 1991. Amended by Stats.1992, c. 1064
(S.B.1445), § 1; Stats.2006, c. 838 (S.B.678), § 22; Stats.
2008, c. 534 (S.B.1726), § 12; Stats.2012, c. 440 (A.B.1488),
§ 40, eff. Sept. 22, 2012; Stats.2012, c. 845 (S.B.1064), § 2;
Stats.2013, c. 248 (A.B.1339), § 1.)*

Law Revision Commission Comments

1990 Enactment

Section 1510 continues Section 1510 of the repealed Probate Code
without change. For general provisions relating to petitions and
other papers, see Sections 1020–1023. See also Sections 1021
(petition to be verified), 1041 (clerk to set petition for hearing), 1512

(amendment of petition to disclose newly discovered proceeding affecting custody). For background on the provisions of this part, see the Comment to this part under the part heading. See also Recommendation Relating to the Uniform Veterans Guardianship Act, 15 Cal.L.Revision Comm'n Reports 1289, 1299 (1980). [20 Cal.L.Rev.Comm. Reports 1001 (1990)].

Cross References

Adoption, see Family Code § 8500 et seq.
Appointment of guardian to fill vacancy, see Probate Code § 2670 et seq.
Appointment of legal counsel for proposed ward, see Probate Code § 1470.
Child, defined, see Probate Code § 26.
Custody of children, see Family Code § 3000 et seq.
Guardianship proceedings, exclusive jurisdiction, consolidation of guardianship and adoption proceedings, see Probate Code § 2205.
Independent exercise of powers, see Probate Code § 2592.
Joint guardians for one ward, see Probate Code § 2105.
Jurisdiction and venue, see Probate Code § 2200 et seq.
Juvenile court law, see Welfare and Institutions Code § 200 et seq.
Marriage dissolution, see Family Code § 2300 et seq.
Nonprofit charitable corporation as guardian, see Probate Code § 2104.
Notice to directors, see Probate Code §§ 1461, 1542.
Notice to Veterans Administration, see Probate Code § 1461.5.
One guardian for several wards, see Probate Code § 2106.
Parent, defined, see Probate Code § 54.
Petition,
    Clerk to set petition for hearing, see Probate Code § 1041.
    Nonrelative guardianships, see Probate Code §§ 1541, 1542.
Petitions and other papers, see Probate Code § 1020 et seq.
Professional fiduciary as guardian or conservator, submission of new proposed hourly fee schedule or statement of compensation on or after one year from original submission, see Probate Code § 2614.8.
Service of summons on minors, wards and conservatees, see Code of Civil Procedure §§ 416.60, 416.70.
Temporary guardian or conservator, see Probate Code § 2250 et seq.

§ 1510.1. Appointment of guardian for unmarried individual between 18 and 21 years of age; findings regarding special immigrant juvenile status; rights as an adult; adoption of rules and forms for implementation

(a)(1) With the consent of the proposed ward, the court may appoint a guardian of the person for an unmarried individual who is 18 years of age or older, but who has not yet attained 21 years of age, in connection with a petition to make the necessary findings regarding special immigrant juvenile status pursuant to subdivision (b) of Section 155 of the Code of Civil Procedure.

(2) A petition for guardianship of the person of a proposed ward who is 18 years of age or older, but who has not yet attained 21 years of age, may be filed by a relative or any other person on behalf of the proposed ward, or the proposed ward.

(b)(1) At the request of, or with the consent of, the ward, the court may extend an existing guardianship of the person for a ward past 18 years of age, for purposes of allowing the ward to complete the application process with the United States Citizenship and Immigration Services for classification as a special immigrant juvenile pursuant to Section 1101(a)(27)(J) of Title 8 of the United States Code.

(2) A relative or any other person on behalf of a ward, or the ward, may file a petition to extend the guardianship of the person for a period of time not to extend beyond the ward reaching 21 years of age.

(c) This section does not authorize the guardian to abrogate any of the rights that a person who has attained 18 years of age may have as an adult under state law, including, but not limited to, decisions regarding the ward's medical treatment, education, or residence, without the ward's express consent.

(d) For purposes of this division, the terms "child," "minor," and "ward" include an unmarried individual who is younger than 21 years of age and who, pursuant to this section, consents to the appointment of a guardian or extension of a guardianship after he or she attains 18 years of age.

(e) The Judicial Council shall, by July 1, 2016, adopt any rules and forms needed to implement this section. *(Added by Stats.2015, c. 694 (A.B.900), § 3, eff. Jan. 1, 2016. Amended by Stats.2016, c. 86 (S.B.1171), § 245, eff. Jan. 1, 2017.)*

§ 1511. Notice of hearing

(a) Except as provided in subdivisions (f) and (g), at least 15 days before the hearing on the petition for the appointment of a guardian, notice of the time and place of the hearing shall be given as provided in subdivisions (b), (c), (d), and (e) of this section. The notice shall be accompanied by a copy of the petition. The court may not shorten the time for giving the notice of hearing under this section.

(b) Notice shall be served in the manner provided in Section 415.10 or 415.30 of the Code of Civil Procedure, or in any manner authorized by the court, on all of the following persons:

(1) The proposed ward if 12 years of age or older.

(2) Any person having legal custody of the proposed ward, or serving as guardian of the estate of the proposed ward.

(3) The parents of the proposed ward.

(4) Any person nominated as a guardian for the proposed ward under Section 1500 or 1501.

(c) Notice shall be given by mail sent to their addresses stated in the petition, or in any manner authorized by the court, to all of the following:

(1) The spouse named in the petition.

(2) The relatives named in the petition, except that if the petition is for the appointment of a guardian of the estate only the court may dispense with the giving of notice to any one or more or all of the relatives.

(3) The person having the care of the proposed ward if other than the person having legal custody of the proposed ward.

(d) If notice is required by Section 1461 or Section 1542 to be given to the Director of State Hospitals or the Director of Developmental Services or the Director of Social Services, notice shall be mailed as so required.

(e) If the petition states that the proposed ward is receiving or is entitled to receive benefits from the Veterans Administration, notice shall be mailed to the office of the Veterans Administration referred to in Section 1461.5.

(f) Unless the court orders otherwise, notice shall not be given to any of the following:

(1) The parents or other relatives of a proposed ward who has been relinquished to a licensed adoption agency.

(2) The parents of a proposed ward who has been judicially declared free from their custody and control.

(g) Notice need not be given to any person if the court so orders upon a determination of either of the following:

(1) The person cannot with reasonable diligence be given the notice.

(2) The giving of the notice would be contrary to the interest of justice.

(h) Before the appointment of a guardian is made, proof shall be made to the court that each person entitled to notice under this section either:

(1) Has been given notice as required by this section.

(2) Has not been given notice as required by this section because the person cannot with reasonable diligence be given the notice or because the giving of notice to that person would be contrary to the interest of justice.

(i) If notice is required by Section 1460.2 to be given to an Indian custodian or tribe, notice shall be mailed as so required. *(Stats.1990, c. 79 (A.B.759), § 14, operative July 1, 1991. Amended by Stats.1992, c. 1064 (S.B.1445), § 2; Stats.1996, c. 563 (S.B.392), § 6; Stats.2006, c. 838 (S.B.678), § 23; Stats.2012, c. 440 (A.B.1488), § 41, eff. Sept. 22, 2012.)*

Law Revision Commission Comments

1990 Enactment

Section 1511 continues Section 1511 of the repealed Probate Code without substantive change. The provision that the court may not shorten the time for giving the notice of hearing has been added to Section 1511, but this provision continues a provision formerly found in the introductory clause of subdivision (a) of Section 1462 of the repealed Probate Code. The phrase "other than the petitioner or persons joining in the petition" has been omitted from two places in the section. This phrase is unnecessary in view of Section 1201.

Subdivision (a) requires that notice be given at least 15 days before the hearing, and this time may not be shortened by the court. If there is urgency, a temporary guardian may be appointed under Section 2250. For general provisions relating to notice of hearing, see Sections 1200–1221, 1460–1469. See also Sections 1260–1265 (proof of giving notice). For general provisions relating to hearings and orders, see Sections 1040–1050. For background on the provisions of this part, see the Comment to this part under the part heading. See also Recommendation Relating to the Uniform Veterans Guardianship Act, 15 Cal.L.Revision Comm'n Reports 1289, 1299–300 (1980); Report of Assembly Committee on Judiciary on Assembly Bills Nos. 261 and 167, reprinted in 15 Cal.L.Revision Comm'n Reports 1061, 1067 (1980). [20 Cal.L.Rev.Comm. Reports 1001 (1990)].

Cross References

Computation of time, see Code of Civil Procedure §§ 12 and 12a; Government Code § 6800 et seq.
Developmental services, director, see Welfare and Institutions Code § 4404 et seq.
Freedom from parental custody and control,
    Generally, see Family Code § 7800 et seq.
    Appointment of guardian, see Family Code § 7893.
Hearings and orders, see Probate Code § 1040 et seq.

Juvenile court rules,
    Orders after filing of petition under section 601 or 602, see California Rules of Court, Rule 5.625.
    Restraining orders, custody orders, and guardianships, see California Rules of Court, Rule 5.620.
Mailing, completion of service, see Probate Code § 1467.
Mental health, director, see Welfare and Institutions Code §§ 4004, 4005.
Notices,
    Generally, see Probate Code § 1200 et seq.
    Filing and service of papers, see Code of Civil Procedure § 1010 et seq.
    Mailing, see Probate Code § 1215 et seq.
    Petition for removal of guardian or conservator, see Probate Code § 2652.
    Posting, see Probate Code § 1230.
    Residence of ward or conservatee, notice according to this section, see Probate Code § 2352.
    Special notice, see Probate Code § 1250 et seq.
Parent, defined, see Probate Code § 54.
Proof of giving of notice, see Probate Code § 1260 et seq.
Relinquishment of child to licensed adoption agency, see Family Code § 8700 et seq.
Request for special notice of proceedings by guardian, see Probate Code § 2700.
Service of process,
    Generally, see Code of Civil Procedure § 413.10 et seq.
    Mail, see Code of Civil Procedure §§ 415.30, 1012 et seq.
    Personal delivery, see Code of Civil Procedure § 415.10.
    Proof of service, see Code of Civil Procedure § 417.10 et seq.
    Publication, see Code of Civil Procedure § 415.50.
Social services, director, see Welfare and Institutions Code § 10552.
Termination or modification of guardianship under the Probate Code, see Welfare and Institutions Code § 728.

§ 1512. Amendment of petition to disclose newly discovered proceeding affecting custody

Within 10 days after the petitioner in the guardianship proceeding becomes aware of any proceeding not disclosed in the guardianship petition affecting the custody of the proposed ward (including any adoption, juvenile court, marriage dissolution, domestic relations, or other similar proceeding affecting the proposed ward), the petitioner shall amend the guardianship petition to disclose the other proceeding. *(Stats.1990, c. 79 (A.B.759), § 14, operative July 1, 1991.)*

Law Revision Commission Comments

1990 Enactment

Section 1512 continues Section 1512 of the repealed Probate Code without change. The purpose of this section is to alert the court to any other proceeding affecting custody of the proposed ward that was not disclosed in the initial guardianship petition. See also Section 1510(h) (consolidation of guardianship petition with adoption petition). For background on the provisions of this part, see the Comment to this part under the part heading. [20 Cal.L.Rev.Comm. Reports 1001 (1990)].

Cross References

Adoption, see Family Code § 8500 et seq.
Computation of time, see Code of Civil Procedure §§ 12 and 12a; Government Code § 6800 et seq.
Custody of children, see Family Code § 3000 et seq.
Juvenile court law, see Welfare and Institutions Code § 200 et seq.

Marriage dissolution, see Family Code § 2300 et seq.

§ 1513. Investigation; filing of report and recommendation concerning proposed guardianship; contents of report; confidentiality; application of section

(a) Unless waived by the court, a court investigator, probation officer, or domestic relations investigator shall make an investigation and file with the court a report and recommendation concerning each proposed guardianship of the person or guardianship of the estate. Investigations where the proposed guardian is a relative shall be made by a court investigator. Investigations where the proposed guardian is a nonrelative shall be made by the county agency designated to investigate potential dependency. The report for the guardianship of the person shall include, but need not be limited to, an investigation and discussion of all of the following:

(1) A social history of the guardian.

(2) A social history of the proposed ward, including, to the extent feasible, an assessment of any identified developmental, emotional, psychological, or educational needs of the proposed ward and the capability of the petitioner to meet those needs.

(3) The relationship of the proposed ward to the guardian, including the duration and character of the relationship, where applicable, the circumstances whereby physical custody of the proposed ward was acquired by the guardian, and a statement of the proposed ward's attitude concerning the proposed guardianship, unless the statement of the attitude is affected by the proposed ward's developmental, physical, or emotional condition.

(4) The anticipated duration of the guardianship and the plans of both natural parents and the proposed guardian for the stable and permanent home for the child. The court may waive this requirement for cases involving relative guardians.

(b) If the proposed ward is or may be described by Section 300 of the Welfare and Institutions Code, the court may refer the matter to the local child welfare services agency to initiate an investigation of the referral pursuant to Sections 328 and 329 of the Welfare and Institutions Code and to report the findings of that investigation to the court. Pending completion of the investigation, the court may take any reasonable steps it deems appropriate to protect the child's safety, including, but not limited to, appointment of a temporary guardian or issuance of a temporary restraining order. If dependency proceedings are initiated, the guardianship proceedings shall be stayed in accordance with Section 304 of the Welfare and Institutions Code. Nothing in this section shall affect the applicability of Section 16504 or 16506 of the Welfare and Institutions Code. If a dependency proceeding is not initiated, the probate court shall retain jurisdiction to hear the guardianship matter.

(c) Prior to ruling on the petition for guardianship, the court shall read and consider all reports submitted pursuant to this section, which shall be reflected in the minutes or stated on the record. Any person who reports to the court pursuant to this section may be called and examined by any party to the proceeding.

(d) All reports authorized by this section are confidential and shall only be made available to persons who have been served in the proceedings or their attorneys. The clerk of the court shall make provisions to limit access to the reports exclusively to persons entitled to receipt. The reports shall be made available to all parties entitled to receipt no less than three court days before the hearing on the guardianship petition.

(e) For the purpose of writing either report authorized by this section, the person making the investigation and report shall have access to the proposed ward's school records, probation records, and public and private social services records, and to an oral or written summary of the proposed ward's medical records and psychological records prepared by any physician, psychologist, or psychiatrist who made or who is maintaining those records. The physician, psychologist, or psychiatrist shall be available to clarify information regarding these records pursuant to the investigator's responsibility to gather and provide information for the court.

(f) This section does not apply to guardianships resulting from a permanency plan for a dependent child pursuant to Section 366.26 of the Welfare and Institutions Code.

(g) For purposes of this section, a "relative" means a person who is a spouse, parent, stepparent, brother, sister, stepbrother, stepsister, half-brother, half-sister, uncle, aunt, niece, nephew, first cousin, or any person denoted by the prefix "grand" or "great," or the spouse of any of these persons, even after the marriage has been terminated by death or dissolution.

(h) In an Indian child custody proceeding, any person making an investigation and report shall consult with the Indian child's tribe and include in the report information provided by the tribe. *(Stats.1990, c. 79 (A.B.759), § 14, operative July 1, 1991. Amended by Stats.1992, c. 572 (S.B.1455), § 3; Stats.1993, c. 59 (S.B.443), § 16, eff. June 30, 1993; Stats.1996, c. 563 (S.B.392), § 7; Stats.2002, c. 784 (S.B.1316), § 576; Stats.2006, c. 838 (S.B.678), § 24; Stats. 2012, c. 638 (A.B.1757), § 14.)*

Law Revision Commission Comments
1990 Enactment

Section 1513 continues Section 1513 of the repealed Probate Code without substantive change. See also Section 1454 (court investigator), 1543 (report on suitability of guardian). For background on the provisions of this part, see the Comment to this part under the part heading. [20 Cal.L.Rev.Comm. Reports 1001 (1990)].

2002 Amendment

Subdivision (d) of Section 1513 is amended to reflect elimination of the county clerk's role as ex officio clerk of the superior court. See former Gov't Code § 26800 (county clerk acting as clerk of superior court). The powers, duties, and responsibilities formerly exercised by the county clerk as ex officio clerk of the court are delegated to the court administrative or executive officer, and the county clerk is relieved of those powers, duties, and responsibilities. See Gov't Code §§ 69840 (powers, duties, and responsibilities of clerk of court and deputy clerk of court), 71620 (trial court personnel). [32 Cal.L.Rev. Comm. Reports 516 (2002)].

Cross References

Appointment of legal counsel for proposed ward, see Probate Code § 1470 et seq.

Child Abuse and Neglect Reporting Act, notice to child protection agencies or district attorneys, see Penal Code § 11170.

Court investigator,
    Appointment, see Probate Code § 1454.
    Defined, see Probate Code § 1419.
Custody investigation and report, court appointed investigator, see
    Family Code § 3111.
Inspection of public records, exemptions from disclosure, "guardian"
    to "guardianship", see Government Code § 6276.22.
Parent, defined, see Probate Code § 54.
Report in case of certain nonrelative guardianships, see Probate
    Code § 1543.
Waiver of court fees and costs, initial fee waiver, see Government
    Code § 68631.

§ 1513.1. Assessments

(a) Each court or county shall assess (1) the parent, parents, or other person charged with the support and maintenance of the ward or proposed ward, and (2) the guardian, proposed guardian, or the estate of the ward or proposed ward, for court or county expenses incurred for any investigation or review conducted by the court investigator, probation officer, or domestic relations investigator. Subject to Section 68631 of the Government Code, the court may order reimbursement to the court or to the county in the amount of the assessment, unless the court finds that all or any part of the assessment would impose a hardship on the ward or the ward's estate. A county may waive any or all of an assessment against the guardianship on the basis of hardship. There shall be a rebuttable presumption that the assessment would impose a hardship if the ward is receiving Medi–Cal benefits.

(b) Any amount chargeable as state-mandated local costs incurred by a county for the cost of the investigation or review shall be reduced by any assessments actually collected by the county pursuant to subdivision (a) during that fiscal year. *(Stats.1990, c. 79 (A.B.759), § 14, operative July 1, 1991. Amended by Stats.1991, c. 82 (S.B.896), § 4, eff. June 30, 1991, operative July 1, 1991; Stats.1996, c. 563 (S.B.392), § 8; Stats.2002, c. 1008 (A.B.3028), § 27; Stats.2003, c. 62 (S.B. 600), § 242; Stats.2014, c. 913 (A.B.2747), § 27.5, eff. Jan. 1, 2015.)*

Law Revision Commission Comments

1990 Enactment

Section 1513.1 continues Section 1513.1 of the repealed Probate Code without substantive change. For background on the provisions of this part, see the Comment to this part under the part heading.

1991 Amendment

Section 1513.1 is amended to delete subdivision (a) and language in subdivision (b) relating to determination by the Controller of the statewide average cost per investigation or review by the court investigator, probation officer, or domestic relations officer incurred by each county. This requirement was deleted from Section 1513.1 of the repealed Probate Code by 1990 Cal.Stat. ch. 1208. This amendment preserves the effect of that legislation. [20 Cal.L.Rev. Comm. Reports 1001 (1990)].

Cross References

Organization and government of courts, collection of fees and fines pursuant to this section, deposits, see Government Code § 68085.1.
Parent, defined, see Probate Code § 54.

Presumptions, see Evidence Code § 600 et seq.

§ 1513.2. Status report; form; contents; confidentiality

(a) To the extent resources are available, the court shall implement procedures, as described in this section, to ensure that every guardian annually completes and returns to the court a status report, including the statement described in subdivision (b). A guardian who willfully submits any material information required by the form which he or she knows to be false shall be guilty of a misdemeanor. Not later than one month prior to the date the status report is required to be returned, the clerk of the court shall mail to the guardian by first-class mail a notice informing the guardian that he or she is required to complete and return the status report to the court. The clerk shall enclose with the letter a blank status report form for the guardian to complete and return by mail. If the status report is not completed and returned as required, or if the court finds, after a status report has been completed and returned, that further information is needed, the court shall attempt to obtain the information required in the report from the guardian or other sources. If the court is unable to obtain this information within 30 days after the date the status report is due, the court shall either order the guardian to make himself or herself available to the investigator for purposes of investigation of the guardianship, or to show cause why the guardian should not be removed.

(b) The Judicial Council shall develop a form for the status report. The form shall include the following statement: "A guardian who willfully submits any material information required by this form which he or she knows to be false is guilty of a misdemeanor." The form shall request information the Judicial Council deems necessary to determine the status of the guardianship, including, but not limited to, the following:

(1) The guardian's present address.

(2) The name and birth date of the child under guardianship.

(3) The name of the school in which the child is enrolled, if any.

(4) If the child is not in the guardian's home, the name, relationship, address, and telephone number of the person or persons with whom the child resides.

(5) If the child is not in the guardian's home, why the child was moved.

(c) The report authorized by this section is confidential and shall only be made available to persons who have been served in the proceedings or their attorneys. The clerk of the court shall implement procedures for the limitation of the report exclusively to persons entitled to its receipt.

(d) The Judicial Council shall report to the Legislature no later than December 31, 2004, regarding the costs and benefits of utilizing the annual status report. *(Added by Stats.2002, c. 1115 (A.B.3036), § 2.)*

Cross References

Confidential guardianship status report form, probate rules, see California Rules of Court, Rule 7.1003.

§ 1514. Appointment of guardian

(a) Upon hearing of the petition, if it appears necessary or convenient, the court may appoint a guardian of the person or estate of the proposed ward or both.

(b)(1) In appointing a guardian of the person, the court is governed by Chapter 1 (commencing with Section 3020) and Chapter 2 (commencing with Section 3040) of Part 2 of Division 8 of the Family Code, relating to custody of a minor.

(2) Except as provided in Section 2105, a minor's parent may not be appointed as a guardian of the person of the minor.

(c) The court shall appoint a guardian nominated under Section 1500 insofar as the nomination relates to the guardianship of the estate unless the court determines that the nominee is unsuitable. If the nominee is a relative, the nominee's immigration status alone shall not constitute unsuitability.

(d) The court shall appoint the person nominated under Section 1501 as guardian of the property covered by the nomination unless the court determines that the nominee is unsuitable. If the person so appointed is appointed only as guardian of the property covered by the nomination, the letters of guardianship shall so indicate.

(e) Subject to subdivisions (c) and (d), in appointing a guardian of the estate:

(1) The court is to be guided by what appears to be in the best interest of the proposed ward, taking into account the proposed guardian's ability to manage and to preserve the estate as well as the proposed guardian's concern for and interest in the welfare of the proposed ward.

(2) If the proposed ward is of sufficient age to form an intelligent preference as to the person to be appointed as guardian, the court shall give consideration to that preference in determining the person to be so appointed. *(Stats.1990, c. 79 (A.B.759), § 14, operative July 1, 1991. Amended by Stats.1992, c. 163 (A.B.2641), § 123, operative Jan. 1, 1994; Stats.2011, c. 102 (A.B.458), § 1; Stats.2012, c. 845 (S.B. 1064), § 3.)*

Law Revision Commission Comments

1992 Amendment

Subdivision (b) of Section 1514 is amended to substitute references to the Family Code provisions that replaced the former Civil Code provision. [22 Cal.L.Rev.Comm. Reports 1 (1992)].

Cross References

Action, guardian or conservator bringing and defending, see Probate Code § 2462.
Action for exclusive custody of children, see Family Code § 3120.
Appealable orders, see Probate Code § 1300 et seq.
Appointment of guardian to fill vacancy, see Probate Code § 2670.
Appointment of legal counsel for proposed ward, see Probate Code § 1470.
Authority of guardian does not extend beyond jurisdiction of Government under which that person was invested with authority, see Code of Civil Procedure § 1913.
Capacity of trust company to act as guardian or conservator of estate, see Probate Code §§ 300, 301.
Child custody, order of preference, see Family Code § 3040.
Conservatorship and guardianship for developmentally disabled persons, see Health and Safety Code § 416 et seq.
Conservatorship for gravely disabled persons, see Welfare and Institutions Code § 5350 et seq.
Enforcement of minor's rights by guardian, see Family Code § 6601.
Hearings and orders, generally, see Probate Code § 1040 et seq.

Nonprofit charitable corporation as guardian, see Probate Code § 2104.
Powers and duties of guardian or conservator,
 Generally, see Probate Code § 2350 et seq.
 Guardian for particular property, see Probate Code § 2109.
 Guardian nominated by will, see Probate Code § 2108.
Public guardian, see Government Code § 27430 et seq.
Removal of guardian for insolvency or bankruptcy, see Probate Code § 2650.
Temporary guardians, appointment, see Probate Code § 2250.

§ 1514.5. Information available for probate guardianship proceeding and guardianship investigator regarding best interest of child; confidentiality

Notwithstanding any other provision of law, except provisions of law governing the retention and storage of data, a family law court shall, upon request from the court in any county hearing a probate guardianship matter proceeding before the court pursuant to this part, provide to the court all available information the court deems necessary to make a determination regarding the best interest of a child, as described in Section 3011 of the Family Code, who is the subject of the proceeding. The information shall also be released to a guardianship investigator, as provided in subdivision (a) of Section 1513, acting within the scope of his or her duties in that proceeding. Any information released pursuant to this section that is confidential pursuant to any other provision of law shall remain confidential and may not be released, except to the extent necessary to comply with this section. No records shared pursuant to this section may be disclosed to any party in a case unless the party requests the agency or court that originates the record to release these records and the request is granted. In counties that provide confidential family law mediation, or confidential dependency mediation, those mediations are not covered by this section. *(Added by Stats.2004, c. 574 (A.B.2228), § 2.)*

Cross References

Child custody evaluations, availability of report, see Family Code § 3111.
Information available for juvenile court proceedings regarding best interest of child, see Welfare and Institutions Code § 204.

§ 1515. No guardian of person for married minor

Notwithstanding any other provision of this part, no guardian of the person may be appointed for a minor who is married or whose marriage has been dissolved. This section does not apply in the case of a minor whose marriage has been adjudged a nullity. *(Stats.1990, c. 79 (A.B.759), § 14, operative July 1, 1991.)*

Law Revision Commission Comments

1990 Enactment

Section 1515 continues Section 1515 of the repealed Probate Code without substantive change. A conservator of the person may be appointed where necessary for a minor who is married or whose marriage has been dissolved. See Section 1800.3(b). Nothing in Section 1515 precludes appointment of a guardian of the estate of a married minor. For background on the provisions of this part, see the Comment to this part under the part heading. [20 Cal.L.Rev. Comm. Reports 1001 (1990)].

Cross References

Action to test validity of marriage, see Family Code § 309.

Dissolution of marriage, defined, see Probate Code § 36.

Minors, see Family Code § 6500.

Termination of guardianship by majority, death, adoption or marriage of ward, see Probate Code § 1600.

§ 1515.5. Repealed by Stats.1979, c. 726, p. 2334, § 1, operative Jan. 1, 1981

§ 1516. Petitions for guardianship of the person; mailing of notice of hearing and copy of petition; screening of guardians; application of section

(a) In each case involving a petition for guardianship of the person, the petitioner shall mail a notice of the hearing and a copy of the petition, at least 15 days prior to the hearing, to the local agency designated by the board of supervisors to investigate guardianships for the court. The local social services agency providing child protection services shall screen the name of the guardian for prior referrals of neglect or abuse of minors. The results of this screening shall be provided to the court.

(b) This section does not apply to guardianships resulting from a permanency plan for a dependent child pursuant to Section 366.25 of the Welfare and Institutions Code. *(Stats. 1990, c. 79 (A.B.759), § 14, operative July 1, 1991.)*

Law Revision Commission Comments

1990 Enactment

Section 1516 continues Section 1516 of the repealed Probate Code without substantive change. The phrase "having jurisdiction over the case" is omitted as unnecessary in view of the definition of "court" found in Section 1418. For background on the provisions of this part, see the Comment to this part under the part heading. [20 Cal.L.Rev.Comm. Reports 1001 (1990)].

Cross References

Computation of time, see Code of Civil Procedure §§ 12 and 12a; Government Code § 6800 et seq.

Notice,
  Mailing, see Probate Code § 1215 et seq.
  Posting, see Probate Code § 1230.
  Proof of giving notice, see Probate Code § 1260 et seq.
  Special notice, see Probate Code § 1250 et seq.
  This code, generally, see Probate Code § 1200 et seq.

Service of process,
  Generally, see Code of Civil Procedure § 413.10 et seq.
  Mail, see Code of Civil Procedure §§ 415.30, 1012 et seq.
  Personal delivery, see Code of Civil Procedure § 415.10.
  Proof of service, see Code of Civil Procedure § 417.10 et seq.
  Publication, see Code of Civil Procedure § 415.50.

§ 1516.5. Proceeding to have child declared free from custody and control of one or both parents

(a) A proceeding to have a child declared free from the custody and control of one or both parents may be brought in accordance with the procedures specified in Part 4 (commencing with Section 7800) of Division 12 of the Family Code within an existing guardianship proceeding, in an adoption action, or in a separate action filed for that purpose, if all of the following requirements are satisfied:

(1) One or both parents do not have the legal custody of the child.

(2) The child has been in the physical custody of the guardian for a period of not less than two years.

(3) The court finds that the child would benefit from being adopted by his or her guardian. In making this determination, the court shall consider all factors relating to the best interest of the child, including, but not limited to, the nature and extent of the relationship between all of the following:

(A) The child and the birth parent.

(B) The child and the guardian, including family members of the guardian.

(C) The child and any siblings or half siblings.

(b) The court shall appoint a court investigator or other qualified professional to investigate all factors enumerated in subdivision (a). The findings of the investigator or professional regarding those issues shall be included in the written report required pursuant to Section 7851 of the Family Code.

(c) The rights of the parent, including the rights to notice and counsel provided in Part 4 (commencing with Section 7800) of Division 12 of the Family Code, shall apply to actions brought pursuant to this section.

(d) This section does not apply to any child who is a dependent of the juvenile court or to any Indian child. *(Added by Stats.2003, c. 251 (S.B.182), § 11. Amended by Stats.2006, c. 838 (S.B.678), § 25; Stats.2010, c. 588 (A.B. 2020), § 9.)*

§ 1517. Guardianships resulting from selection and implementation of a permanent plan; application of part; administration of funds for benefit of child

(a) This part does not apply to guardianships resulting from the selection and implementation of a permanent plan pursuant to Section 366.26 of the Welfare and Institutions Code. For those minors, Section 366.26 of the Welfare and Institutions Code and Division 3 (commencing with Rule 5.500) of Title Five of the California Rules of Court specify the exclusive procedures for establishing, modifying, and terminating legal guardianships. If no specific provision of the Welfare and Institutions Code or the California Rules of Court is applicable, the provisions applicable to the administration of estates under Part 4 (commencing with Section 2100) govern so far as they are applicable to like situations.

(b) This chapter shall not be construed to prevent a court that assumes jurisdiction of a minor child pursuant to Section 300 of the Welfare and Institutions Code, or a probate court, as appropriate, from issuing orders or making appointments, on motion of the child's counsel, consistent with Division 2 of the Welfare and Institutions Code or Divisions 4 to 6, inclusive, of the Probate Code necessary to ensure the appropriate administration of funds for the benefit of the child. Orders or appointments regarding those funds may continue after the court's jurisdiction is terminated pursuant to Section 391 of the Welfare and Institutions Code. *(Added by Stats.1991, c. 82 (S.B.896), § 6, eff. June 30, 1991, operative July 1, 1991. Amended by Stats.2008, c. 166 (A.B.3051), § 2.)*

Law Revision Commission Comments

1991 Addition

Section 1517 continues former Section 1517 which was added to the repealed Probate Code by 1990 Cal.Stat. ch. 1530. [20 Cal. L.Rev.Comm. Reports 2909 (1990)].

§§ 1518 to 1530a.   Repealed by Stats.1979, c. 726, p. 2334, § 1, operative Jan. 1, 1981

§ 1531.   Repealed by Stats.1943, c. 97, p. 802, § 2

§§ 1532 to 1539.   Repealed by Stats.1979, c. 726, p. 2334, § 1, operative Jan. 1, 1981

ARTICLE 3.   NONRELATIVE GUARDIANSHIPS

Cross References

Child Abuse and Neglect Reporting Act, notice to child protection agencies or district attorneys, see Penal Code § 11170.

§ 1540.   Application of article

This article does not apply in any of the following cases:

(a) Where the petition is for guardianship of the estate exclusively.

(b) Where the proposed guardian is a relative of the proposed ward.

(c) Where the Director of Developmental Services is appointed guardian pursuant to Article 7.5 (commencing with Section 416) of Chapter 2 of Part 1 of Division 1 of the Health and Safety Code.

(d) Where the director of the department designated by the board of supervisors to provide social services is appointed guardian.

(e) Where the public guardian is appointed guardian.

(f) Where the guardianship results from a permanency plan for a dependent child pursuant to Section 366.25 of the Welfare and Institutions Code. *(Stats.1990, c. 79 (A.B.759), § 14, operative July 1, 1991.)*

Law Revision Commission Comments

1990 Enactment

Section 1540 continues Section 1540 of the repealed Probate Code without substantive change. For background on the provisions of this part, see the Comment to this part under the part heading. [20 Cal.L.Rev.Comm. Reports 1001 (1990)].

Cross References

Director of Developmental Services, see Welfare and Institutions Code § 4404 et seq.
Public guardian, see Government Code § 27430 et seq.
Public guardian, generally, see Probate Code § 2900 et seq.

§ 1541.   Petition for guardianship; additional contents

In addition to the other required contents of the petition for appointment of a guardian, the petition shall include both of the following:

(a) A statement by the proposed guardian that, upon request by an agency referred to in Section 1543 for information relating to the investigation referred to in that section, the proposed guardian will promptly submit the information required.

(b) A disclosure of any petition for adoption by the proposed guardian of the minor who is the subject of the guardianship petition regardless of when or where filed.

(c) A statement whether or not the home of the proposed guardian is a licensed * * * foster family home, a certified family home of a licensed foster family agency, or a resource family home approved by a county or a licensed foster family agency. *(Stats.1990, c. 79 (A.B.759), § 14, operative July 1, 1991. Amended by Stats.2016, c. 612 (A.B.1997), § 58, eff. Jan. 1, 2017.)*

Law Revision Commission Comments

1990 Enactment

Section 1541 continues Section 1541 of the repealed Probate Code without change. For cases in which this article does not apply, see Section 1540. For general provisions relating to petitions and other papers, see Sections 1020–1023. For background on the provisions of this part, see the Comment to this part under the part heading. [20 Cal.L.Rev.Comm. Reports 1001 (1990)].

Cross References

Disclosure of proceedings affecting custody, see Probate Code §§ 1510, 1512.

§ 1542.   Notice of hearing and copy of petition to director and local agency

In each case involving a petition for guardianship of the person, the petitioner shall mail a notice of the hearing and a copy of the petition, at least 15 days prior to the hearing, to the Director of Social Services at the director's office in Sacramento and to the local agency designated by the board of supervisors to investigate guardianships for the court. *(Stats.1990, c. 79 (A.B.759), § 14, operative July 1, 1991.)*

Law Revision Commission Comments

1990 Enactment

Section 1542 continues Section 1542 of the repealed Probate Code without change. For cases in which this article does not apply, see Section 1540. For general provisions relating to notice of hearing, see Sections 1200–1221, 1460–1469. See also Sections 1260–1265 (proof of giving notice). For background on the provisions of this part, see the Comment to this part under the part heading. [20 Cal.L.Rev.Comm. Reports 1001 (1990)].

Cross References

Completion of mailing, see Probate Code § 1467.
Computation of time, see Code of Civil Procedure §§ 12 and 12a; Government Code § 6800 et seq.
Director of Social Services, see Welfare and Institutions Code § 10552.
Notice,
  Mailing, see Probate Code § 1215 et seq.
  Posting, see Probate Code § 1230.
  Proof of giving notice, see Probate Code § 1260 et seq.
  Special notice, see Probate Code § 1250 et seq.
  This code, generally, see Probate Code § 1200 et seq.
Service of process,
  Generally, see Code of Civil Procedure § 413.10 et seq.
  Mail, see Code of Civil Procedure §§ 415.30, 1012 et seq.
  Personal delivery, see Code of Civil Procedure § 415.10.

Proof of service, see Code of Civil Procedure § 417.10 et seq.
Publication, see Code of Civil Procedure § 415.50.

§ 1543. Suitability of proposed guardian for guardianship; report; confidentiality

(a) If the petition as filed or as amended states that an adoption petition has been filed, a report with respect to the suitability of the proposed guardian for guardianship shall be filed with the court by the agency investigating the adoption. In other cases, the local agency designated by the board of supervisors to provide public social services shall file a report with the court with respect to the proposed guardian of the same character required to be made with regard to an applicant for foster family home licensure, or, on and after January 1, 2020, resource family approval, as described in Section 16519.5 of the Welfare and Institutions Code.

(b) The report filed with the court pursuant to this section is confidential. The report may be considered by the court and shall be made available only to the persons who have been served in the proceeding and the persons who have appeared in the proceeding or their attorneys. The report may be received in evidence upon stipulation of counsel for all * * * of those persons who are present at the hearing or, if a person is present at the hearing but is not represented by counsel, upon consent of that person. *(Stats.1990, c. 79 (A.B.759), § 14, operative July 1, 1991. Amended by Stats. 2016, c. 612 (A.B.1997), § 59, eff. Jan. 1, 2017.)*

Law Revision Commission Comments

1990 Enactment

Section 1543 continues Section 1543 of the repealed Probate Code without change. See also Section 1513 (investigation by court investigator, probation officer, or domestic relations investigator). For cases in which this article does not apply, see Section 1540. For background on the provisions of this part, see the Comment to this part under the part heading. [20 Cal.L.Rev.Comm. Reports 1001 (1990)].

Cross References

Appointment of legal counsel, see Probate Code § 1470.
Inspection of public records, exemptions from disclosure, "guardian" to "guardianship", see Government Code § 6276.22.
Investigation and report, see Probate Code § 1513.
Licensure foster family home, see Health and Safety Code § 1502 et seq.

§§ 1550 to 1593. Repealed by Stats.1979, c. 726, p. 2334, § 1, operative Jan. 1, 1981

CHAPTER 2. TERMINATION

Section

§ 1600. Majority, death, adoption, or emancipation of ward

(a) A guardianship of the person or estate or both terminates when the ward attains majority unless, pursuant to Section 1510.1, the ward requests the extension of, or consents to the extension of, the guardianship of the person until the ward attains 21 years of age.

(b) A guardianship of the person terminates upon the death of the ward, the adoption of the ward, or upon the emancipation of the ward under Section 7002 of the Family Code. *(Stats.1990, c. 79 (A.B.759), § 14, operative July 1, 1991. Amended by Stats.1996, c. 862 (A.B.2751), § 6; Stats. 2015, c. 694 (A.B.900), § 4, eff. Jan. 1, 2016.)*

Law Revision Commission Comments

1990 Enactment

Section 1600 continues Section 1600 of the repealed Probate Code without change. The court retains jurisdiction of the guardianship proceeding despite the termination of the guardianship. See Section 2630. If a married minor needs protective supervision of the person, a petition for conservatorship of the person may be filed. See Section 1800.3. See also Section 1820(b) (filing petition for appointment of conservator during proposed conservatee's minority so appointment may be effective immediately upon minor becoming 18) and Section 2467 (powers and duties after death of ward). For background on the provisions of this part, see the Comment to this part under the part heading. [20 Cal.L.Rev.Comm. Reports 1001 (1990)].

Cross References

Age of majority, see Family Code § 6500 et seq.
Allowance of disbursements after termination of guardianship, allowance of expenses for care of estate after death of ward, see Probate Code § 2623.
Care of estate after death of ward, see Probate Code § 2467.
Conservatorship,
 Comparable provisions, see Probate Code § 1860.
 Filing petition during minority to become effective upon attaining age of majority, see Probate Code § 1820.
Disposition of assets after death of ward, see Probate Code § 2631.
Marriage of ward, consent of guardian of ward under age of 18, see Family Code § 302.
Married minors, conservatorships, see Probate Code § 1800.3.
Restriction on appointment of guardian of married minor, see Probate Code § 1515.
Service of final account after termination of conservatorship, probate rules, see California Rules of Court, Rule 7.1054.
Settlement of accounts with guardian, ward reaching majority, see Probate Code § 2627.
Termination of guardianship, probate rules, see California Rules of Court, Rule 7.1004.

§ 1601. Court order; notice

Upon petition of the guardian, a parent, the minor ward, or, in the case of an Indian child custody proceeding, an Indian custodian or the ward's tribe, the court may make an order terminating the guardianship if the court determines that it is in the ward's best interest to terminate the guardianship. Upon petition of a ward who is 18 years of age or older, the court shall make an order terminating the guardianship. Notice of the hearing on the petition shall be given for the period and in the manner provided in Chapter 3 (commencing with Section 1460) of Part 1. *(Stats.1990, c. 79 (A.B.759), § 14, operative July 1, 1991. Amended by Stats. 2002, c. 1118 (A.B.1938), § 6; Stats.2006, c. 838 (S.B.678), § 26; Stats.2015, c. 694 (A.B.900), § 5, eff. Jan. 1, 2016.)*

Law Revision Commission Comments

1990 Enactment

Section 1601 continues Section 1601 of the repealed Probate Code without change. The court retains jurisdiction of the guardianship proceeding despite termination of the guardianship. See Section 2630. For general provisions, see Sections 1000–1004 (rules of practice), 1020–1023 (petitions and other papers), 1040–1050 (hearings and orders), 2103 (effect of final order). For general provisions relating to notice of hearing, see Sections 1200–1221, 1460–1469. See also Sections 1260–1265 (proof of giving notice), 2700–2702 (notice to persons who request special notice). For background on the provisions of this part, see the Comment to this part under the part heading. See also Report of Assembly Committee on Judiciary on Assembly Bills Nos. 261 and 167, reprinted in 15 Cal.L.Revision Comm'n Reports 1061, 1068 (1980). [20 Cal.L.Rev.Comm. Reports 1001 (1990)].

Cross References

Allowance of disbursements after termination, see Probate Code § 2623.
Appealable orders, see Probate Code § 1300 et seq.
Notice to Veterans Administration, see Probate Code § 1461.5.
Order for permanent plan of adoption or legal guardianship, termination of guardianship, see Welfare and Institutions Code § 366.3.
Parent, defined, see Probate Code § 54.
Request for special notice, see Probate Code § 2700.
Termination of proceedings upon,
  Exhaustion of estate, see Probate Code § 2626.
  Transfer of all assets to foreign guardian, see Probate Code § 2808.
Termination or modification of guardianship under the Probate Code, see Welfare and Institutions Code § 728.

§ 1602. Visitation

(a) The Legislature hereby finds and declares that guardians perform a critical and important role in the lives of minors, frequently assuming a parental role and caring for a child when the child's parent or parents are unable or unwilling to do so.

(b) Upon making a determination that a guardianship should be terminated pursuant to Section 1601, the court may consider whether continued visitation between the ward and the guardian is in the ward's best interest. As part of the order of termination, the court shall have jurisdiction to issue an order providing for ongoing visitation between a former guardian and his or her former minor ward after the termination of the guardianship. The order granting or denying visitation may not be modified unless the court determines, based upon evidence presented, that there has been a significant change of circumstances since the court issued the order and that modification of the order is in the best interest of the child.

(c) A copy of the visitation order shall be filed in any court proceeding relating to custody of the minor. If a prior order has not been filed, and a proceeding is not pending relating to the custody of the minor in the court of any county, the visitation order may be used as the sole basis for opening a file in the court of the county in which the custodial parent resides. While a parent of the child has custody of the child, proceedings for modification of the visitation order shall be determined in a proceeding under the Family Code. (Added by Stats.2004, c. 301 (A.B.2292), § 2.)

§ 1603. Repealed by Stats.1979, c. 726, p. 2334, § 1, operative Jan. 1, 1981

§ 1604. Repealed by Stats.1969, c. 293, § 6

§ 1605. Repealed by Stats.1951, c. 888, p. 2409, § 2

§§ 1606 to 1607. Repealed by Stats.1979, c. 726, p. 2334, §§ 1, 2, operative Jan. 1, 1981

CHAPTER 3. PERMANENT AND STABLE HOME

§ 1610. Legislative findings and declarations

(a) The Legislature finds and declares that it is in the best interests of children to be raised in a permanent, safe, stable, and loving environment.

(b) Unwarranted petitions, applications, or motions other than discovery motions after the guardianship has been established create an environment that can be harmful to children and are inconsistent with the goals of permanency, safety, and stability. (Added by Stats.2002, c. 1118 (A.B. 1938), § 7. Amended by Stats.2006, c. 493 (A.B.1363), § 6.)

§ 1611. Petitions without merit or intended to harass or annoy guardian

If a person files a petition for visitation, termination of the guardianship, or instruction to the guardian that is unmeritorious, or intended to harass or annoy the guardian, and the person has previously filed pleadings in the guardianship proceedings that were unmeritorious, or intended to harass or annoy the guardian, this petition shall be grounds for the court to determine that the person is a vexatious litigant for the purposes of Title 3a (commencing with Section 391) of Part 2 of the Code of Civil Procedure. For these purposes, the term "new litigation" shall include petitions for visitation, termination of the guardianship, or instruction to the guardian. (Added by Stats.2002, c. 1118 (A.B.1938), § 7.)

§§ 1630 to 1783. Repealed by Stats.1979, c. 726, p. 2334, §§ 1, 2, operative Jan. 1, 1981

Part 3

CONSERVATORSHIP

This part supersedes Part 3 (commencing with Section 1800) of Division 4 of the repealed Probate Code. The superseded part was enacted upon recommendation of the California Law Revision Commission. See Recommendation Relating to Guardianship–Conservatorship Law, 14 Cal.L.Revision Comm'n Reports 501 (1978). For the Guardianship–Conservatorship Law as enacted in 1979 (Chapter 726 of the Statutes of 1979) with the revisions made by Chapters 89 and 246 of the Statutes of 1980, see Guardianship–Conservatorship Law, 15 Cal.L.Revision Comm'n Reports 451 (1980). [20 Cal.L.Rev.Comm. Reports 1001 (1990)].

Cross References

California Community Care Facilities Act, placement agencies, see Health and Safety Code § 1536.1.
Residential care facilities for the elderly, placement agencies, see Health and Safety Code § 1569.47.

CHAPTER 1. ESTABLISHMENT OF CONSERVATORSHIP

ARTICLE 1. PERSONS FOR WHOM CONSERVATOR MAY BE APPOINTED

Cross References

Application of old and new law, see Probate Code § 3.
Placement agency defined to include conservator,
Community care facilities, see Health and Safety Code § 1536.1.
Residential care facilities for the elderly, see Health and Safety Code § 1569.47.

§ 1800. Purpose of chapter

It is the intent of the Legislature in enacting this chapter to do the following:

(a) Protect the rights of persons who are placed under conservatorship.

(b) Provide that an assessment of the needs of the person is performed in order to determine the appropriateness and extent of a conservatorship and to set goals for increasing the conservatee's functional abilities to whatever extent possible.

(c) Provide that the health and psychosocial needs of the proposed conservatee are met.

(d) Provide that community-based services are used to the greatest extent in order to allow the conservatee to remain as independent and in the least restrictive setting as possible.

(e) Provide that the periodic review of the conservatorship by the court investigator shall consider the best interests of the conservatee.

(f) Ensure that the conservatee's basic needs for physical health, food, clothing, and shelter are met.

(g) Provide for the proper management and protection of the conservatee's real and personal property. *(Stats.1990, c. 79 (A.B.759), § 14, operative July 1, 1991.)*

Section 1800 continues Section 1800 of the repealed Probate Code without change. [20 Cal.L.Rev.Comm. Reports 1001 (1990)].

Cross References

Conservatorship and guardianship for developmentally disabled persons, see Health and Safety Code § 416 et seq.
Conservatorship for gravely disabled persons, see Welfare and Institutions Code § 5350 et seq.
Legislative intent, construction of statutes, see Code of Civil Procedure § 1859.
Public guardian, see Probate Code § 2900 et seq.; Government Code § 27430 et seq.
Residential care facilities for the elderly, definitions, see 22 Cal. Code of Regs. § 87101.
Temporary guardians, appointment, see Probate Code § 2250.

§ 1800.3. Conservatorship for adults and married minors

(a) If the need therefor is established to the satisfaction of the court and the other requirements of this chapter are satisfied, the court may appoint:

(1) A conservator of the person or estate of an adult, or both.

(2) A conservator of the person of a minor who is married or whose marriage has been dissolved.

(b) No conservatorship of the person or of the estate shall be granted by the court unless the court makes an express finding that the granting of the conservatorship is the least restrictive alternative needed for the protection of the conservatee. *(Stats.1990, c. 79 (A.B.759), § 14, operative July 1, 1991. Amended by Stats.1997, c. 663 (S.B.628), § 1; Stats.2007, c. 553 (A.B.1727), § 6.)*

Section 1800.3 continues Section 1800.3 of the repealed Probate Code without change. This section makes clear that a conservatorship may be established only for (1) adults and (2) minors who are married or whose marriage has been dissolved. In case of a minor who is married or whose marriage has been dissolved, a conservator of the person may be appointed if the requirements of this chapter are satisfied. A guardian of the estate of the minor may be appointed where necessary or convenient. See Sections 1514, 1515. In case of a minor whose marriage has been adjudged a nullity, guardianship and not conservatorship is the appropriate protective proceeding of the person. See Section 1515. However, if a conservatorship is established for a married minor and the marriage is later adjudged a nullity, the conservatorship does not terminate. See Section 1860 and the Comment thereto. For background on the provisions of this part, see the Comment to this part under the part heading. [20 Cal.L.Rev.Comm. Reports 1001 (1990)].

Cross References

Capacity of conservatee to marry, see Probate Code §§ 1900, 1901.
Dissolution of marriage, defined, see Probate Code § 36.

§ 1801. Conservator of person or estate or person and estate; limited conservator; appointment; standard of proof

Subject to Section 1800.3:

(a) A conservator of the person may be appointed for a person who is unable to provide properly for his or her personal needs for physical health, food, clothing, or shelter, except as provided for the person as described in subdivision (b) or (c) of Section 1828.5.

(b) A conservator of the estate may be appointed for a person who is substantially unable to manage his or her own financial resources or resist fraud or undue influence, except as provided for that person as described in subdivision (b) or (c) of Section 1828.5. Substantial inability may not be proved solely by isolated incidents of negligence or improvidence.

(c) A conservator of the person and estate may be appointed for a person described in subdivisions (a) and (b).

(d) A limited conservator of the person or of the estate, or both, may be appointed for a developmentally disabled adult. A limited conservatorship may be utilized only as necessary to promote and protect the well-being of the individual, shall be designed to encourage the development of maximum self-reliance and independence of the individual, and shall be ordered only to the extent necessitated by the individual's proven mental and adaptive limitations. The conservatee of the limited conservator shall not be presumed to be incompetent and shall retain all legal and civil rights except those which by court order have been designated as legal disabilities and have been specifically granted to the limited conservator. The intent of the Legislature, as expressed in Section 4501 of the Welfare and Institutions Code, that developmentally disabled citizens of this state receive services resulting in more independent, productive, and normal lives is the underlying mandate of this division in its application to adults alleged to be developmentally disabled.

(e) The standard of proof for the appointment of a conservator pursuant to this section shall be clear and convincing evidence. *(Stats.1990, c. 79 (A.B.759), § 14, operative July 1, 1991. Amended by Stats.1995, c. 842 (S.B.730), § 7.)*

Law Revision Commission Comments

1990 Enactment

Section 1801 continues Section 1801 of the repealed Probate Code without substantive change. For background on the provisions of this part, see the Comment to this part under the part heading. [20 Cal.L.Rev.Comm. Reports 1001 (1990)].

Cross References

Conservatorship for gravely disabled persons, see Welfare and Institutions Code § 5350 et seq.
Contracts, fraud, see Civil Code §§ 1571 to 1574.
Developmental disability, defined, see Probate Code § 1420.
Developmentally disabled adult,
Contents of order appointing conservator or limited conservator, see Probate Code § 1830.
Duties of court at hearing to appoint limited conservator, see Probate Code § 1828.5.
Developmentally disabled persons, guardianship and conservatorship, see Health and Safety Code § 416 et seq.; Welfare and Institutions Code § 4825.
Legal capacity of conservatee, see Probate Code § 1870 et seq.
Statutes, construction and legislative intent, see Code of Civil Procedure §§ 1858 and 1859.
Termination of limited conservatorship, see Probate Code § 1860.5.

§ 1802. Appointment upon request of proposed conservatee; good cause

Subject to Section 1800.3, a conservator of the person or estate, or both, may be appointed for a person who voluntarily requests the appointment and who, to the satisfaction of the court, establishes good cause for the appointment. *(Stats.1990, c. 79 (A.B.759), § 14, operative July 1, 1991.)*

Law Revision Commission Comments

1990 Enactment

Section 1802 continues Section 1802 of the repealed Probate Code without substantive change. For background on the provisions of this part, see the Comment to this part under the part heading. [20 Cal.L.Rev.Comm. Reports 1001 (1990)].

§ 1802.5. Repealed by Stats.1979, c. 726, p. 2334, § 2, operative Jan. 1, 1981

§ 1803. Conservator of estate of absentee; appointment

A conservator of the estate may be appointed for a person who is an absentee as defined in Section 1403. *(Stats.1990, c. 79 (A.B.759), § 14, operative July 1, 1991.)*

Law Revision Commission Comments

1990 Enactment

Section 1803 continues Section 1803 of the repealed Probate Code without substantive change. For special provisions applicable where the proposed conservatee is an absentee, see Article 4 (commencing with Section 1840). For background on the provisions of this part, see the Comment to this part under the part heading. [20 Cal.L.Rev.Comm. Reports 1001 (1990)].

Cross References

Special provisions applicable where proposed conservatee is an absentee, see Probate Code § 1840 et seq.

§ 1803.5. Repealed by Stats.1979, c. 726, p. 2334, § 2, operative Jan. 1, 1981

§ 1804. Missing persons; appointment of conservator of estate

Subject to Section 1800.3, a conservator of the estate may be appointed for a person who is missing and whose whereabouts is unknown. *(Stats.1990, c. 79 (A.B.759), § 14, operative July 1, 1991.)*

1990 Enactment

Section 1804 continues Section 1804 of the repealed Probate Code without substantive change. For special provisions applicable where the proposed conservatee is a missing person, see Article 5 (commencing with Section 1845). See also Section 1461.7 (notice of hearing on petition, report, or account). If a minor is a missing person, a guardianship of the estate may be established for the minor. See Section 1514 (guardian may be appointed if it appears necessary or convenient). For the recommendation of the California Law Revision Commission that resulted in the enactment of this section of the repealed Probate Code, see Recommendation Relating to Missing Persons, 16 Cal.L.Revision Comm'n Reports 105 (1982). For background on the provisions of this part, see the Comment to this part under the part heading. [20 Cal.L.Rev.Comm. Reports 1001 (1990)].

Cross References

Administration of estates of missing persons presumed dead, see Probate Code § 12400 et seq.

Death of persons not heard from in five years, presumption, see Evidence Code § 667.

Federal Missing Persons Act, findings under, see Evidence Code §§ 1282, 1283.

Property of absent federal personnel, see Probate Code § 3700 et seq.

Special conservatorship provisions where proposed conservatee is a missing person, see Probate Code § 1845 et seq.

§§ 1805, 1806. Repealed by Stats.1979, c. 726, p. 2334, § 2, operative Jan. 1, 1981

ARTICLE 2. ORDER OF PREFERENCE FOR APPOINTMENT OF CONSERVATOR

Section
1810. Nomination by proposed conservatee.
1811. Nomination by spouse or relative of proposed conservatee.
1812. Order of preference for appointment as conservator.
1813. Appointment of spouse; conditions; consultation with counsel and report by counsel; disclosure of specified matters.
1813.1. Domestic partner of proposed conservatee.

§ 1810. Nomination by proposed conservatee

If the proposed conservatee has sufficient capacity at the time to form an intelligent preference, the proposed conservatee may nominate a conservator in the petition or in a writing signed either before or after the petition is filed. The court shall appoint the nominee as conservator unless the court finds that the appointment of the nominee is not in the best interests of the proposed conservatee. *(Stats.1990, c. 79 (A.B.759), § 14, operative July 1, 1991.)*

1990 Enactment

Section 1810 continues Section 1810 of the repealed Probate Code without change. This section does not require that the writing containing the nomination be executed in the same manner as a witnessed will. The only formal requirements for a nomination under this section are that the nomination be in writing and be signed by the proposed conservatee. The nomination may be made in a writing made long before conservatorship proceedings are commenced. But, whenever made, the proposed conservatee must have

had at the time the writing was executed sufficient capacity to form an intelligent preference. A nomination of a guardian made by an adult before January 1, 1981, is deemed to be a nomination of a conservator. See Section 1488. The proposed conservatee—whether or not the petitioner—may waive bond and, in such a case, the court may in its discretion dispense with bond or reduce its amount. See Section 2321. See also Sections 300–301 (trust company as guardian of estate), 2104 (nonprofit charitable corporation as guardian). For background on the provisions of this part, see the Comment to this part under the part heading. See also Report of Assembly Committee on Judiciary on Assembly Bills Nos. 261 and 167, reprinted in 15 Cal.L.Revision Comm'n Reports 1061, 1068 (1980). [20 Cal.L.Rev.Comm. Reports 1001 (1990)].

Cross References

Nomination by means of durable power of attorney, see Probate Code § 4126.
Petition,
  Contents, see Probate Code § 1821.
  Defined, see Probate Code § 1430.

§ 1811. Nomination by spouse or relative of proposed conservatee

(a) Subject to Sections 1813 and 1813.1, the spouse, domestic partner, or an adult child, parent, brother, or sister of the proposed conservatee may nominate a conservator in the petition or at the hearing on the petition.

(b) Subject to Sections 1813 and 1813.1, the spouse, domestic partner, or a parent of the proposed conservatee may nominate a conservator in a writing signed either before or after the petition is filed and that nomination remains effective notwithstanding the subsequent legal incapacity or death of the spouse, domestic partner, or parent. *(Stats. 1990, c. 79 (A.B.759), § 14, operative July 1, 1991. Amended by Stats.2000, c. 17 (A.B.1491), § 3; Stats.2001, c. 893 (A.B.25), § 15; Stats.2014, c. 913 (A.B.2747), § 28, eff. Jan. 1, 2015.)*

1990 Enactment

Section 1811 continues Section 1811 of the repealed Probate Code without change. Unlike a nominated guardian of the estate which the court must appoint unless the nominee is "unsuitable" (Section 1514), or the nominee of the proposed conservatee which the court must appoint unless it is not in the best interests of the proposed conservatee (Section 1810), a nomination made under Section 1811 merely entitles the nominee to some preference for appointment. See Section 1812. See also Sections 300–301 (trust company as guardian of estate), 2104 (nonprofit charitable corporation as guardian). For background on the provisions of this part, see the Comment to this part under the part heading. [20 Cal.L.Rev.Comm. Reports 1001 (1990)].

2014 Amendment

Section 1811 is amended to reflect the addition of Section 1813.1 (specifying conditions for appointment of domestic partner as conservator), which is similar to Section 1813 (specifying conditions for appointment of spouse as conservator). [43 Cal.L.Rev.Comm. Reports 35 (2013)].

Cross References

Dissolution of marriage,
  Generally, see Family Code § 2300 et seq.
  Methods, see Family Code § 310.
Domestic partner, defined, see Probate Code § 37.

Guardianship, subsequent legal incapacity or death of nominator, see Probate Code § 1502.

Parent, defined, see Probate Code § 54.

§ 1812. Order of preference for appointment as conservator

(a) Subject to Sections 1810, 1813, and 1813.1, the selection of a conservator of the person or estate, or both, is solely in the discretion of the court and, in making the selection, the court is to be guided by what appears to be for the best interests of the proposed conservatee.

(b) Subject to Sections 1810, 1813, and 1813.1, of persons equally qualified in the opinion of the court to appointment as conservator of the person or estate or both, preference is to be given in the following order:

(1) The spouse or domestic partner of the proposed conservatee or the person nominated by the spouse or domestic partner pursuant to Section 1811.

(2) An adult child of the proposed conservatee or the person nominated by the child pursuant to Section 1811.

(3) A parent of the proposed conservatee or the person nominated by the parent pursuant to Section 1811.

(4) A brother or sister of the proposed conservatee or the person nominated by the brother or sister pursuant to Section 1811.

(5) Any other person or entity eligible for appointment as a conservator under this code or, if there is no person or entity willing to act as a conservator, under the Welfare and Institutions Code.

(c) The preference for any nominee for appointment under paragraphs (2), (3), and (4) of subdivision (b) is subordinate to the preference for any other parent, child, brother, or sister in that class. *(Stats.1990, c. 79 (A.B.759), § 14, operative July 1, 1991. Amended by Stats.2001, c. 893 (A.B.25), § 16; Stats.2014, c. 913 (A.B.2747), § 29, eff. Jan. 1, 2015.)*

Law Revision Commission Comments
1990 Enactment

Section 1812 continues Section 1812 of the repealed Probate Code without change. For background on the provisions of this part, see the Comment to this part under the part heading. [20 Cal.L.Rev. Comm. Reports 1001 (1990)].

2014 Amendment

Section 1812 is amended to reflect the addition of Section 1813.1 (specifying conditions for appointment of domestic partner as conservator), which is similar to Section 1813 (specifying conditions for appointment of spouse as conservator). [43 Cal.L.Rev.Comm. Reports 35 (2013)].

Cross References

Appointment of conservator to fill vacancy, see Probate Code § 2680 et seq.

Appointment of director as guardian or conservator, request for adjudication of incompetency, see Health and Safety Code § 416.9.

Child, defined, see Probate Code § 26.

Conservatorship for gravely disabled persons, appointment, procedure, see Welfare and Institutions Code § 5350 et seq.

Domestic partner, defined, see Probate Code § 37.

Nonprofit charitable corporation as guardian, see Probate Code § 2104.

Parent, defined, see Probate Code § 54.

Public guardian, see Probate Code § 2900 et seq.; Government Code § 27430 et seq.

Temporary guardians, appointment, see Probate Code § 2250.

§ 1813. Appointment of spouse; conditions; consultation with counsel and report by counsel; disclosure of specified matters

(a)(1) The spouse of a proposed conservatee may not petition for the appointment of a conservator for a spouse or be appointed as conservator of the person or estate of the proposed conservatee unless the petitioner alleges in the petition for appointment as conservator, and the court finds, that the spouse is not a party to any action or proceeding against the proposed conservatee for legal separation of the parties, dissolution of marriage, or adjudication of nullity of their marriage. However, if the court finds by clear and convincing evidence that the appointment of the spouse, who is a party to an action or proceeding against the proposed conservatee for legal separation of the parties, dissolution of marriage, or adjudication of nullity of their marriage, or has obtained a judgment in any of these proceedings, is in the best interests of the proposed conservatee, the court may appoint the spouse.

(2) Prior to making this appointment, the court shall appoint counsel to consult with and advise the conservatee, and to report to the court his or her findings concerning the suitability of appointing the spouse as conservator.

(b) The spouse of a conservatee shall disclose to the conservator, or if the spouse is the conservator, shall disclose to the court, the filing of any action or proceeding against the conservatee for legal separation of the parties, dissolution of marriage, or adjudication of nullity of the marriage, within 10 days of the filing of the action or proceeding by filing a notice with the court and serving the notice according to the notice procedures under this title. The court may, upon receipt of the notice, set the matter for hearing on an order to show cause why the appointment of the spouse as conservator, if the spouse is the conservator, should not be terminated and a new conservator appointed by the court. *(Stats.1990, c. 79 (A.B.759), § 14, operative July 1, 1991. Amended by Stats.2000, c. 17 (A.B.1491), § 4; Stats.2001, c. 159 (S.B.662), § 165; Stats.2014, c. 913 (A.B.2747), § 30, eff. Jan. 1, 2015.)*

Law Revision Commission Comments
1990 Enactment

Section 1813 continues Section 1813 of the repealed Probate Code without substantive change. The reference to "divorce" is omitted as unnecessary in view of Section 36 ("dissolution of marriage" includes divorce). For background on the provisions of this part, see the Comment to this part under the part heading. [20 Cal.L.Rev.Comm. Reports 1001 (1990)].

2014 Amendment

Subdivision (a) of Section 1813 is amended to move the paragraph break and label paragraphs. [43 Cal.L.Rev.Comm. Reports 35 (2013)].

§ 1813.1. Domestic partner of proposed conservatee

(a)(1) The domestic partner of a proposed conservatee may not petition for the appointment of a conservator for a domestic partner or be appointed as conservator of the person or estate of the proposed conservatee unless the petitioner alleges in the petition for appointment as conservator, and the court finds, that the domestic partner has not terminated and is not intending to terminate the domestic partnership as provided in Section 299 of the Family Code. However, if the court finds by clear and convincing evidence that the appointment of a domestic partner who has terminated or is intending to terminate the domestic partnership is in the best interests of the proposed conservatee, the court may appoint the domestic partner.

(2) Prior to making this appointment, the court shall appoint counsel to consult with and advise the conservatee, and to report to the court his or her findings concerning the suitability of appointing the domestic partner as conservator.

(b) The domestic partner of a conservatee shall disclose to the conservator, or if the domestic partner is the conservator, shall notify the court, of the termination of a domestic partnership as provided in Section 299 of the Family Code within 10 days of its occurrence. The court may, upon receipt of the notice, set the matter for hearing on an order to show cause why the appointment of the domestic partner as conservator, if the domestic partner is the conservator, should not be terminated and a new conservator appointed by the court. *(Added by Stats.2001, c. 893 (A.B.25), § 16.5.)*

ARTICLE 3. ESTABLISHMENT OF CONSERVATORSHIP

§ 1820. Petition; filing; persons authorized

(a) A petition for the appointment of a conservator may be filed by any of the following:

(1) The proposed conservatee.

(2) The spouse or domestic partner of the proposed conservatee.

(3) A relative of the proposed conservatee.

(4) Any interested state or local entity or agency of this state or any interested public officer or employee of this state or of a local public entity of this state.

(5) Any other interested person or friend of the proposed conservatee.

(b) If the proposed conservatee is a minor, the petition may be filed during his or her minority so that the appointment of a conservator may be made effective immediately upon the minor's attaining the age of majority. An existing guardian of the minor may be appointed as conservator under this part upon the minor's attaining the age of majority, whether or not the guardian's accounts have been settled.

(c) A creditor of the proposed conservatee may not file a petition for appointment of a conservator unless the creditor is a person described in paragraph (2), (3), or (4) of subdivision (a). *(Stats.1990, c. 79 (A.B.759), § 14, operative July 1, 1991. Amended by Stats.2001, c. 893 (A.B.25), § 17.)*

Law Revision Commission Comments
1990 Enactment

Section 1820 continues Section 1820 of the repealed Probate Code without change. Subdivision (b) permits uninterrupted continuation of protective proceedings for a minor under guardianship who is approaching majority and will need a conservator. For general provisions relating to petitions and other papers, see Sections 1020–1023. For background on the provisions of this part, see the Comment to this part under the part heading. See also Report of Assembly Committee on Judiciary on Assembly Bills Nos. 261 and 167, reprinted in 15 Cal.L.Revision Comm'n Reports 1061, 1069 (1980). [20 Cal.L.Rev.Comm. Reports 1001 (1990)].

Cross References

Age of majority, see Family Code § 6500 et seq.
Appointment of legal counsel for proposed conservatee, see Probate Code § 1471.
Domestic partner, defined, see Probate Code § 37.
Interested person, defined, see Probate Code § 1424.
Notice to Veterans Administration, see Probate Code § 1461.5.

§ 1821. Contents of petition; supplemental information; form

(a) The petition shall request that a conservator be appointed for the person or estate, or both, shall specify the name, address, and telephone number of the proposed conservator and the name, address, and telephone number of the proposed conservatee, and state the reasons why a conservatorship is necessary. Unless the petitioner or proposed conservator is a bank or other entity authorized to conduct the business of a trust company, the petitioner or proposed conservator shall also file supplemental information as to why the appointment of a conservator is required. The supplemental information to be submitted shall include a brief statement of facts addressed to each of the following categories:

(1) The inability of the proposed conservatee to properly provide for his or her needs for physical health, food, clothing, and shelter.

(2) The location of the proposed conservatee's residence and the ability of the proposed conservatee to live in the residence while under conservatorship.

(3) Alternatives to conservatorship considered by the petitioner or proposed conservator and reasons why those alternatives are not available.

(4) Health or social services provided to the proposed conservatee during the year preceding the filing of the petition, when the petitioner or proposed conservator has information as to those services.

(5) The inability of the proposed conservatee to substantially manage his or her own financial resources, or to resist fraud or undue influence.

The facts required to address the categories set forth in paragraphs (1) to (5), inclusive, shall be set forth by the petitioner or proposed conservator if he or she has knowledge of the facts or by the declarations or affidavits of other persons having knowledge of those facts.

If any of the categories set forth in paragraphs (1) to (5), inclusive, are not applicable to the proposed conservatorship, the petitioner or proposed conservator shall so indicate and state on the supplemental information form the reasons therefor.

The Judicial Council shall develop a supplemental information form for the information required pursuant to paragraphs (1) to (5), inclusive, after consultation with individuals or organizations approved by the Judicial Council, who

represent public conservators, court investigators, the State Bar, specialists with experience in performing assessments and coordinating community-based services, and legal services for the elderly and disabled.

The supplemental information form shall be separate and distinct from the form for the petition. The supplemental information shall be confidential and shall be made available only to parties, persons given notice of the petition who have requested this supplemental information or who have appeared in the proceedings, their attorneys, and the court. The court shall have discretion at any other time to release the supplemental information to other persons if it would serve the interests of the conservatee. The clerk of the court shall make provision for limiting disclosure of the supplemental information exclusively to persons entitled thereto under this section.

(b) The petition shall set forth, so far as they are known to the petitioner or proposed conservator, the names and addresses of the spouse or domestic partner, and of the relatives of the proposed conservatee within the second degree. If no spouse or domestic partner of the proposed conservatee or relatives of the proposed conservatee within the second degree are known to the petitioner or proposed conservator, the petition shall set forth, so far as they are known to the petitioner or proposed conservator, the names and addresses of the following persons who, for the purposes of Section 1822, shall all be deemed to be relatives:

(1) A spouse or domestic partner of a predeceased parent of a proposed conservatee.

(2) The children of a predeceased spouse or domestic partner of a proposed conservatee.

(3) The siblings of the proposed conservatee's parents, if any, but if none, then the natural and adoptive children of the proposed conservatee's parents' siblings.

(4) The natural and adoptive children of the proposed conservatee's siblings.

(c) If the petitioner or proposed conservator is a professional fiduciary, as described in Section 2340, who is required to be licensed under the Professional Fiduciaries Act (Chapter 6 (commencing with Section 6500) of Division 3 of the Business and Professions Code), the petition shall include the following:

(1) The petitioner's or proposed conservator's proposed hourly fee schedule or another statement of his or her proposed compensation from the estate of the proposed conservatee for services performed as a conservator. The petitioner's or proposed conservator's provision of a proposed hourly fee schedule or another statement of his or her proposed compensation, as required by this paragraph, shall not preclude a court from later reducing the petitioner's or proposed conservator's fees or other compensation.

(2) Unless a petition for appointment of a temporary conservator that contains the statements required by this paragraph is filed together with a petition for appointment of a conservator, both of the following:

(A) A statement of the petitioner's or proposed conservator's license information.

(B) A statement explaining who engaged the petitioner or proposed conservator or how the petitioner or proposed conservator was engaged to file the petition for appointment of a conservator or to agree to accept the appointment as conservator and what prior relationship the petitioner or proposed conservator had with the proposed conservatee or the proposed conservatee's family or friends.

(d) If the petition is filed by a person other than the proposed conservatee, the petition shall include a declaration of due diligence showing both of the following:

(1) Either the efforts to find the proposed conservatee's relatives or why it was not feasible to contact any of them.

(2) Either the preferences of the proposed conservatee concerning the appointment of a conservator and the appointment of the proposed conservator or why it was not feasible to ascertain those preferences.

(e) If the petition is filed by a person other than the proposed conservatee, the petition shall state whether or not the petitioner is a creditor or debtor, or the agent of a creditor or debtor, of the proposed conservatee.

(f) If the proposed conservatee is a patient in or on leave of absence from a state institution under the jurisdiction of the State Department of State Hospitals or the State Department of Developmental Services and that fact is known to the petitioner or proposed conservator, the petition shall state that fact and name the institution.

(g) The petition shall state, so far as is known to the petitioner or proposed conservator, whether or not the proposed conservatee is receiving or is entitled to receive benefits from the Veterans Administration and the estimated amount of the monthly benefit payable by the Veterans Administration for the proposed conservatee.

(h) The petition may include an application for any order or orders authorized under this division, including, but not limited to, orders under Chapter 4 (commencing with Section 1870).

(i) The petition may include a further statement that the proposed conservatee is not willing to attend the hearing on the petition, does not wish to contest the establishment of the conservatorship, and does not object to the proposed conservator or prefer that another person act as conservator.

(j) In the case of an allegedly developmentally disabled adult, the petition shall set forth the following:

(1) The nature and degree of the alleged disability, the specific duties and powers requested by or for the limited conservator, and the limitations of civil and legal rights requested to be included in the court's order of appointment.

(2) Whether or not the proposed limited conservatee is or is alleged to be developmentally disabled.

Reports submitted pursuant to Section 416.8 of the Health and Safety Code meet the requirements of this section, and conservatorships filed pursuant to Article 7.5 (commencing with Section 416) of Chapter 2 of Part 1 of Division 1 of the Health and Safety Code are exempt from providing the supplemental information required by this section, so long as the guidelines adopted by the State Department of Developmental Services for regional centers require the same information that is required pursuant to this section.

(k) The petition shall state, so far as is known to the petitioner, whether or not the proposed conservatee is a member of a federally recognized Indian tribe. If so, the petition shall state the name of the tribe, the state in which the tribe is located, whether the proposed conservatee resides on tribal land, and whether the proposed conservatee is known to own property on tribal land. For the purposes of this subdivision, "tribal land" means land that is, with respect to a specific Indian tribe and the members of that tribe, "Indian country" as defined in Section 1151 of Title 18 of the United States Code. *(Stats.1990, c. 79 (A.B.759), § 14, operative July 1, 1991. Amended by Stats.1991, c. 82 (S.B.896), § 8, eff. June 30, 1991, operative July 1, 1991; Stats.2001, c. 893 (A.B.25), § 18; Stats.2002, c. 784 (S.B.1316), § 577; Stats.2008, c. 293 (A.B.1340), § 1; Stats.2012, c. 440 (A.B. 1488), § 42, eff. Sept. 22, 2012; Stats.2013, c. 248 (A.B.1339), § 2; Stats.2014, c. 553 (S.B.940), § 6, eff. Jan. 1, 2015, operative Jan. 1, 2016.)*

Law Revision Commission Comments
1990 Addition

Section 1821 continues Section 1821 of the repealed Probate Code without substantive change. An application under subdivision (f) may include a request for an order authorizing independent exercise of powers (Section 2592) or an order relating to the legal capacity of the proposed conservatee (Sections 1870–1901). If the allegation provided for in subdivision (g) is made, it triggers an investigation and report by the court investigator (Section 1826) which may result in a determination by the court that the proposed conservatee need not attend the hearing (Section 1825). For general provisions relating to petitions and other papers, see Sections 1020–1023. For background on the provisions of this part, see the Comment to this part under the part heading. See also *Report of Assembly Committee on Judiciary on Assembly Bills Nos. 261 and 167*, reprinted in 15 Cal.L. Revision Comm'n Reports 1061, 1069 (1980); *Recommendation Relating to the Uniform Veterans Guardianship Act*, 15 Cal.L. Revision Comm'n Reports 1289, 1301 (1980).

1991 Amendment

Section 1821 is amended to conform it to amendments made to Section 1821 of the repealed Probate Code by 1990 Cal.Stat. ch. 1208. Subdivision (i), which is deleted from Section 1821, is continued in substance in Section 1831. [20 Cal.L.Rev. Comm. Reports 1001 (1990)].

2002 Amendment

Subdivision (a)(5) of Section 1821 is amended to reflect elimination of the county clerk's role as ex officio clerk of the superior court. See former Gov't Code § 26800 (county clerk acting as clerk of superior court). The powers, duties, and responsibilities formerly exercised by the county clerk as ex officio clerk of the court are delegated to the court administrative or executive officer, and the county clerk is relieved of those powers, duties, and responsibilities. See Gov't Code §§ 69840 (powers, duties, and responsibilities of clerk of court and deputy clerk of court), 71620 (trial court personnel). [32 Cal.L.Rev.Comm. Reports 518 (2002)].

2014 Amendment

Section 1821 is amended to provide that the petition include specified information about a proposed conservatee who is known to be a member of a federally recognized Indian tribe. Subdivision (k) does not impose a duty of inquiry on the petitioner.

Section 1821 is also amended to correct an incomplete cross-reference in subdivision (j). [43 Cal.L.Rev.Comm. Reports 93 (2013)].

Cross References

Additional contents of petition for conservatorship of absentee, see Probate Code §§ 1813, 1841.

Attendance of proposed conservatee at hearing, see Probate Code § 1825.

Child, defined, see Probate Code § 26.

Conservators for gravely disabled persons, petition, see Welfare and Institutions Code § 5352.

Contracts, fraud, see Civil Code §§ 1571 to 1574.

Department of Developmental Services, see Welfare and Institutions Code § 4400 et seq.

Department of State Hospitals, see Welfare and Institutions Code § 4000 et seq.

Developmental disability, defined, see Probate Code § 1420.

Developmentally disabled adult,
  Contents of order appointing conservator or limited conservator, see Probate Code § 1830.
  Duties of court at hearing to appoint limited conservator, see Probate Code § 1828.5.

Developmentally disabled persons, guardianship and conservatorship, see Health and Safety Code § 416 et seq.; Welfare and Institutions Code § 4825.

Domestic partner, defined, see Probate Code § 37.

Independent exercise of powers, guardians and conservators,
  Order granting, see Probate Code § 2592.
  Withdrawal or subsequent limitation of powers, see Probate Code § 2593.

Inspection of public records, exemptions from disclosure, "conservatee" to "conservatorship", see Government Code § 6276.12.

Jurisdiction and venue, see Probate Code § 2200 et seq.

Legal capacity of conservatee, see Probate Code § 1870 et seq.

Parent, defined, see Probate Code § 54.

Predeceased spouse, defined, see Probate Code § 59.

Professional fiduciary as guardian or conservator, submission of new proposed hourly fee schedule or statement of compensation on or after one year from original submission, see Probate Code § 2614.8.

Termination of limited conservatorship, see Probate Code § 1860.5.

Transfer of conservatorship to state, investigation and report, duties of investigator, see Probate Code § 1851.1.

Trust company, defined, see Probate Code § 83.

§ 1822. Notice of hearing; mailing

(a) At least 15 days before the hearing on the petition for appointment of a conservator, notice of the time and place of the hearing shall be given as provided in this section. The notice shall be accompanied by a copy of the petition. The court may not shorten the time for giving the notice of hearing under this section.

(b) Notice shall be mailed to the following persons:

(1) The spouse, if any, or registered domestic partner, if any, of the proposed conservatee at the address stated in the petition.

(2) The relatives named in the petition at their addresses stated in the petition.

(c) If notice is required by Section 1461 to be given to the Director of State Hospitals or the Director of Developmental Services, notice shall be mailed as so required.

(d) If the petition states that the proposed conservatee is receiving or is entitled to receive benefits from the Veterans Administration, notice shall be mailed to the Office of the Veterans Administration referred to in Section 1461.5.

(e) If the proposed conservatee is a person with developmental disabilities, at least 30 days before the day of the hearing on the petition, the petitioner shall mail a notice of the hearing and a copy of the petition to the regional center identified in Section 1827.5.

(f) If the petition states that the petitioner and the proposed conservator have no prior relationship with the proposed conservatee and are not nominated by a family member, friend, or other person with a relationship to the proposed conservatee, notice shall be mailed to the public guardian of the county in which the petition is filed. *(Stats.1990, c. 79 (A.B.759), § 14, operative July 1, 1991. Amended by Stats.1991, c. 82 (S.B.896), § 10, eff. June 30, 1991, operative July 1, 1991; Stats.2001, c. 893 (A.B.25), § 19; Stats.2006, c. 493 (A.B.1363), § 7; Stats.2008, c. 293 (A.B.1340), § 2; Stats.2012, c. 440 (A.B.1488), § 43, eff. Sept. 22, 2012.)*

Law Revision Commission Comments

1990 Enactment

Section 1822 restates Section 1822 of the repealed Probate Code without substantive change. The provision that the court may not shorten the time for giving the notice of hearing has been added to subdivision (a) of Section 1822, but this provision continues a provision formerly found in the introductory clause of subdivision (a) of Section 1462 of the repealed Probate Code. The phrase "other than the petitioner or persons joining in the petition" has been omitted from two places in the section, this phrase being unnecessary in view of Section 1201. The requirement of subdivision (f) that the notice be accompanied by a copy of the petition has been omitted as unnecessary since subdivision (a) already imposes this requirement in all cases where notice of hearing is given as provided in the section. Subdivision (f) has been revised to require that the notice of hearing be mailed at least 30 days before the day of the hearing on the petition. This conforms subdivision (f) to Section 1461.4. For general provisions relating to notice of hearing, see Sections 1200–1221, 1460–1469. See also Sections 1260–1265 (proof of giving notice), 2700–2702 (notice to persons who request special notice). For background on the provisions of this part, see the Comment to this part under the part heading. See also *Recommendation Relating to the Uniform Veterans Guardianship Act*, 15 Cal. L. Revision Comm'n Reports 1289, 1302 (1980).

1991 Amendment

Section 1822 is amended to preserve the substance of amendments made to Section 1822 of the repealed Probate Code by 1990 Cal.Stat. ch. 1598. The language in former subdivision (f), redesignated as new subdivision (e), requiring notice to the regional center if "the petition is for the appointment of a limited conservator" is revised to require the notice if "the proposed conservatee is a person with developmental disabilities." This revision is necessary because, under Section 1827.5 as revised, the regional center must make an assessment of a person with developmental disabilities if the proceeding is for limited conservatorship, and may do so if the proceeding is for general conservatorship. [20 Cal.L.Rev.Comm. Reports 1001 1990)].

Cross References

Computation of time, see Code of Civil Procedure §§ 12 and 12a; Government Code § 6800 et seq.

Domestic partner, defined, see Probate Code § 37.

Limited conservator for developmentally disabled adult, appointment, see Probate Code § 1828.5.

Mailing, completion, see Probate Code § 1467.

Notice,
  Mailing, see Probate Code § 1215 et seq.

Missing persons, petition for appointment of conservator, see Probate Code § 1847.

Posting, see Probate Code § 1230.

Proof of giving notice, see Probate Code § 1260 et seq.

Special notice, see Probate Code § 1250 et seq.

This code, generally, see Probate Code § 1200 et seq.

This division, generally, see Probate Code § 1460 et seq.

Residence of ward or conservatee, notice according to this section, see Probate Code § 2352.

Service of process,

Generally, see Code of Civil Procedure § 413.10 et seq.

Mail, see Code of Civil Procedure §§ 415.30, 1012 et seq.

Personal delivery, see Code of Civil Procedure § 415.10.

Proof of service, see Code of Civil Procedure § 417.10 et seq.

Publication, see Code of Civil Procedure § 415.50.

Termination of conservatorship, notice of hearing, see Probate Code § 1862.

§ 1823. Citation to proposed conservatee; contents

(a) If the petition is filed by a person other than the proposed conservatee, the clerk shall issue a citation directed to the proposed conservatee setting forth the time and place of hearing.

(b) The citation shall state the legal standards by which the need for a conservatorship is adjudged as stated in Section 1801 and shall state the substance of all of the following:

(1) The proposed conservatee may be adjudged unable to provide for personal needs or to manage financial resources and, by reason thereof, a conservator may be appointed for the person or estate, or both.

(2) Such adjudication may affect or transfer to the conservator the proposed conservatee's right to contract, in whole or in part, to manage and control property, to give informed consent for medical treatment, and to fix a residence.

(3)(A) The proposed conservatee may be disqualified from voting pursuant to Section 2208 of the Elections Code if he or she is incapable of communicating, with or without reasonable accommodations, a desire to participate in the voting process.

(B) The proposed conservatee shall not be disqualified from voting on the basis that he or she does, or would need to do, any of the following to complete an affidavit of voter registration:

(i) Signs the affidavit of voter registration with a mark or a cross pursuant to subdivision (b) of Section 2150 of the Elections Code.

(ii) Signs the affidavit of voter registration by means of a signature stamp pursuant to Section 354.5 of the Elections Code.

(iii) Completes the affidavit of voter registration with the assistance of another person pursuant to subdivision (d) of Section 2150 of the Elections Code.

(iv) Completes the affidavit of voter registration with reasonable accommodations.

(4) The court or a court investigator will explain the nature, purpose, and effect of the proceeding to the proposed conservatee and will answer questions concerning the explanation.

(5) The proposed conservatee has the right to appear at the hearing and to oppose the petition, and in the case of an alleged developmentally disabled adult, to oppose the petition in part, by objecting to any or all of the requested duties or powers of the limited conservator.

(6) The proposed conservatee has the right to choose and be represented by legal counsel and has the right to have legal counsel appointed by the court if unable to retain legal counsel.

(7) The proposed conservatee has the right to a jury trial if desired. *(Stats.1990, c. 79 (A.B.759), § 14, operative July 1, 1991. Amended by Stats.2014, c. 591 (A.B.1311), § 4, eff. Jan. 1, 2015; Stats.2015, c. 736 (S.B.589), § 8, eff. Jan. 1, 2016.)*

Law Revision Commission Comments
1990 Enactment

Section 1823 continues Section 1823 of the repealed Probate Code without change. A citation is not required if the proposed conservatee is an "absentee." Section 1843. For a general provision relating to citations, see Sections 1240–1241. For background on the provisions of this part, see the Comment to this part under the part heading. [20 Cal.L.Rev.Comm. Reports 1001 (1990)].

Cross References

Appointment of legal counsel for proposed conservatee, see Probate Code § 1470 et seq.

Counsel, right to, see Cal. Const. Art. 1, § 15.

Court investigator, see Probate Code § 1419.

Developmental disability, defined, see Probate Code § 1420.

Disqualification from voting, see Elections Code § 2208 et seq.

Informed consent for medical treatment, capacity of conservatee to give, see Probate Code § 1880 et seq.

Jury trial, see Cal. Const. Art. 1, § 16.

Legal capacity of conservatee, see Probate Code § 1870 et seq.

Limited conservator, powers and duties, see Probate Code § 2351.5.

§ 1824. Service of citation and petition upon proposed conservatee

The citation and a copy of the petition shall be served on the proposed conservatee at least 15 days before the hearing. Service shall be made in the manner provided in Section 415.10 or 415.30 of the Code of Civil Procedure or in such manner as may be authorized by the court. If the proposed conservatee is outside this state, service may also be made in the manner provided in Section 415.40 of the Code of Civil Procedure. *(Stats.1990, c. 79 (A.B.759), § 14, operative July 1, 1991.)*

Law Revision Commission Comments
1990 Enactment

Section 1824 continues Section 1824 of the repealed Probate Code without change. No citation is required if the proposed conservatee is the petitioner. See Section 1823(a). If the proposed conservatee is an "absentee," no citation is required. Section 1843. For background on the provisions of this part, see the Comment to this part under the part heading. [20 Cal.L.Rev.Comm. Reports 1001 (1990)].

Cross References

Citation not required to proposed conservatee who is an absentee, see Probate Code § 1843.

Computation of time, see Code of Civil Procedure §§ 12 and 12a; Government Code § 6800 et seq.

Notice,

Mailing, see Probate Code § 1215 et seq.

Posting, see Probate Code § 1230.

Proof of giving notice, see Probate Code § 1260 et seq.
Special notice, see Probate Code § 1250 et seq.
This code, generally, see Probate Code § 1200 et seq.
This division, generally, see Probate Code § 1460 et seq.
Service of process,
Generally, see Code of Civil Procedure § 413.10 et seq.
Mail, see Code of Civil Procedure §§ 415.30, 1012 et seq.
Personal delivery, see Code of Civil Procedure § 415.10.
Proof of service, see Code of Civil Procedure § 417.10 et seq.
Publication, see Code of Civil Procedure § 415.50.

§ 1825. Attendance of proposed conservatee at hearing; exceptions; inability to attend; affidavit

(a) The proposed conservatee shall be produced at the hearing except in the following cases:

(1) Where the proposed conservatee is out of the state when served and is not the petitioner.

(2) Where the proposed conservatee is unable to attend the hearing by reason of medical inability.

(3) Where the court investigator has reported to the court that the proposed conservatee has expressly communicated that the proposed conservatee (i) is not willing to attend the hearing, (ii) does not wish to contest the establishment of the conservatorship, and (iii) does not object to the proposed conservator or prefer that another person act as conservator, and the court makes an order that the proposed conservatee need not attend the hearing.

(b) If the proposed conservatee is unable to attend the hearing because of medical inability, such inability shall be established (1) by the affidavit or certificate of a licensed medical practitioner or (2) if the proposed conservatee is an adherent of a religion whose tenets and practices call for reliance on prayer alone for healing and is under treatment by an accredited practitioner of that religion, by the affidavit of the practitioner. The affidavit or certificate is evidence only of the proposed conservatee's inability to attend the hearing and shall not be considered in determining the issue of need for the establishment of a conservatorship.

(c) Emotional or psychological instability is not good cause for the absence of the proposed conservatee from the hearing unless, by reason of such instability, attendance at the hearing is likely to cause serious and immediate physiological damage to the proposed conservatee. *(Stats.1990, c. 79 (A.B.759), § 14, operative July 1, 1991.)*

Law Revision Commission Comments
1990 Enactment

Section 1825 continues Section 1825 of the repealed Probate Code without change. An "absentee," as defined in Section 1403, need not attend the hearing. See Section 1844. For general provisions relating to hearings and orders, see Sections 1040–1050. For background on the provisions of this part, see the Comment to this part under the part heading. [20 Cal.L.Rev.Comm. Reports 1001 (1990)].

Cross References

Absentees, proof of status of proposed conservatee, attendance at hearing not required, see Probate Code § 1844.
Affidavits, see Code of Civil Procedure §§ 2003, 2009 et seq.
Conservatorship and guardianship for developmentally disabled persons, affidavit or certificate, see Health and Safety Code § 416.7.

Court investigator, defined, see Probate Code § 1419.
Transfer of conservatorship to state, investigation and report, duties of investigator, see Probate Code § 1851.1.

§ 1826. Court investigator; duties; report; distribution; confidentiality

(a) Regardless of whether the proposed conservatee attends the hearing, the court investigator shall do all of the following:

(1) Conduct the following interviews:

(A) The proposed conservatee personally.

(B) All petitioners and all proposed conservators who are not petitioners.

(C) The proposed conservatee's spouse or registered domestic partner and relatives within the first degree. If the proposed conservatee does not have a spouse, registered domestic partner, or relatives within the first degree, to the greatest extent possible, the proposed conservatee's relatives within the second degree.

(D) To the greatest extent practical and taking into account the proposed conservatee's wishes, the proposed conservatee's relatives within the second degree not required to be interviewed under subparagraph (C), neighbors, and, if known, close friends.

(2) Inform the proposed conservatee of the contents of the citation, of the nature, purpose, and effect of the proceeding, and of the right of the proposed conservatee to oppose the proceeding, to attend the hearing, to have the matter of the establishment of the conservatorship tried by jury, to be represented by legal counsel if the proposed conservatee so chooses, and to have legal counsel appointed by the court if unable to retain legal counsel.

(3) Determine if it appears that the proposed conservatee is unable to attend the hearing and, if able to attend, whether the proposed conservatee is willing to attend the hearing.

(4) Review the allegations of the petition as to why the appointment of the conservator is required and, in making his or her determination, do the following:

(A) Refer to the supplemental information form submitted by the petitioner and consider the facts set forth in the form that address each of the categories specified in paragraphs (1) to (5), inclusive, of subdivision (a) of Section 1821.

(B) Consider, to the extent practicable, whether he or she believes the proposed conservatee suffers from any of the mental function deficits listed in subdivision (a) of Section 811 that significantly impairs the proposed conservatee's ability to understand and appreciate the consequences of his or her actions in connection with any of the functions described in subdivision (a) or (b) of Section 1801 and identify the observations that support that belief.

(5) Determine if the proposed conservatee wishes to contest the establishment of the conservatorship.

(6) Determine if the proposed conservatee objects to the proposed conservator or prefers another person to act as conservator.

(7) Determine if the proposed conservatee wishes to be represented by legal counsel and, if so, whether the proposed

conservatee has retained legal counsel and, if not, the name of an attorney the proposed conservatee wishes to retain.

(8)(A) Determine if the proposed conservatee is incapable of communicating, with or without reasonable accommodations, a desire to participate in the voting process, and may be disqualified from voting pursuant to Section 2208 of the Elections Code.

(B) The proposed conservatee shall not be disqualified from voting on the basis that he or she does, or would need to do, any of the following to complete an affidavit of voter registration:

(i) Signs the affidavit of voter registration with a mark or a cross pursuant to subdivision (b) of Section 2150 of the Elections Code.

(ii) Signs the affidavit of voter registration by means of a signature stamp pursuant to Section 354.5 of the Elections Code.

(iii) Completes the affidavit of voter registration with the assistance of another person pursuant to subdivision (d) of Section 2150 of the Elections Code.

(iv) Completes the affidavit of voter registration with reasonable accommodations.

(9) If the proposed conservatee has not retained legal counsel, determine if the proposed conservatee desires the court to appoint legal counsel.

(10) Determine if the appointment of legal counsel would be helpful to the resolution of the matter or is necessary to protect the interests of the proposed conservatee in a case where the proposed conservatee does not plan to retain legal counsel and has not requested the appointment of legal counsel by the court.

(11) Report to the court in writing, at least five days before the hearing, concerning all of the foregoing, including the proposed conservatee's express communications concerning both of the following:

(A) Representation by legal counsel.

(B) If the proposed conservatee is not willing to attend the hearing, does not wish to contest the establishment of the conservatorship, and does not object to the proposed conservator or prefers that another person act as conservator.

(12) Mail, at least five days before the hearing, a copy of the report referred to in paragraph (11) to all of the following:

(A) The attorney, if any, for the petitioner.

(B) The attorney, if any, for the proposed conservatee.

(C) The proposed conservatee.

(D) The spouse, registered domestic partner, and relatives within the first degree of the proposed conservatee who are required to be named in the petition for appointment of the conservator, unless the court determines that the mailing will harm the conservatee.

(E) Any other persons as the court orders.

(b) The court investigator has discretion to release the report required by this section to the public conservator, interested public agencies, and the long-term care ombudsman.

(c) The report required by this section is confidential and shall be made available only to parties, persons described in paragraph (12) of subdivision (a), persons given notice of the petition who have requested this report or who have appeared in the proceedings, their attorneys, and the court. The court has discretion at any other time to release the report, if it would serve the interests of the conservatee. The clerk of the court shall provide for the limitation of the report exclusively to persons entitled to its receipt.

(d) This section does not apply to a proposed conservatee who has personally executed the petition for conservatorship, or a proposed conservatee who has nominated his or her own conservator, if he or she attends the hearing.

(e) If the court investigator has performed an investigation within the preceding six months and furnished a report thereon to the court, the court may order, upon good cause shown, that another investigation is not necessary or that a more limited investigation may be performed.

(f) An investigation by the court investigator related to a temporary conservatorship also may be a part of the investigation for the general petition for conservatorship, but the court investigator shall make a second visit to the proposed conservatee and the report required by this section shall include the effect of the temporary conservatorship on the proposed conservatee.

(g) The Judicial Council shall, on or before January 1, 2009, adopt rules of court and Judicial Council forms as necessary to implement an expedited procedure to authorize, by court order, a proposed conservatee's health care provider to disclose confidential medical information about the proposed conservatee to a court investigator pursuant to federal medical information privacy regulations promulgated under the federal Health Insurance Portability and Accountability Act of 1996 (Public Law 104–191).

(h) A superior court shall not be required to perform any duties imposed pursuant to the amendments to this section enacted by Chapter 493 of the Statutes of 2006 until the Legislature makes an appropriation identified for this purpose. *(Stats.1990, c. 79 (A.B.759), § 14, operative July 1, 1991. Amended by Stats.1998, c. 581 (A.B.2801), § 21; Stats.2002, c. 784 (S.B.1316), § 578; Stats.2006, c. 493 (A.B.1363), § 8, operative July 1, 2007; Stats.2007, c. 553 (A.B.1727), § 7; Stats.2011, c. 10 (S.B.78), § 12, eff. March 24, 2011; Stats.2014, c. 591 (A.B.1311), § 5, eff. Jan. 1, 2015; Stats.2015, c. 736 (S.B.589), § 9, eff. Jan. 1, 2016.)*

Law Revision Commission Comments

1990 Enactment

Section 1826 continues Section 1826 of the repealed Probate Code without change. The determinations referred to in subdivisions (c), (e), and (f) are relevant to whether the proposed conservatee must attend the hearing. See Section 1825(a)(2)–(3). See also Section 1851.5 (assessment of estate for investigation expense). For background on the provisions of this part, see the Comment to this part under the part heading. See also Report of Assembly Committee on Judiciary on Assembly Bills Nos. 261 and 167, reprinted in 15 Cal.L.Revision Comm'n Reports 1061, 1070–71 (1980); Report of Senate Committee on Judiciary on Assembly Bill No. 261, reprinted in 15 Cal.L.Revision Comm'n Reports 1097, 1099 (1980). [20 Cal.L.Rev.Comm. Reports 1001 (1990)].

2002 Amendment

Subdivision (n) of Section 1826 is amended to reflect elimination of the county clerk's role as ex officio clerk of the superior court. See former Gov't Code § 26800 (county clerk acting as clerk of superior court). The powers, duties, and responsibilities formerly exercised by the county clerk as ex officio clerk of the court are delegated to the court administrative or executive officer, and the county clerk is relieved of those powers, duties, and responsibilities. See Gov't Code §§ 69840 (powers, duties, and responsibilities of clerk of court and deputy clerk of court), 71620 (trial court personnel). [32 Cal.L.Rev. Comm. Reports 521 (2002)].

Cross References

Appointment of legal counsel, see Probate Code § 1470 et seq.

Citation, contents, see Probate Code § 1823.

Conservatorship for gravely disabled persons, appointment, procedure, see Welfare and Institutions Code § 5350.

Court investigator,
Appointment, see Probate Code § 1454.
Defined, see Probate Code § 1419.

Guardianship and conservatorship, interested person, defined, see Probate Code § 1424.

Inspection of public records, exemptions from disclosure, "conservatee" to "conservatorship", see Government Code § 6276.12.

Waiver of court fees and costs, initial fee waiver, see Government Code § 68631.

§ 1827. Law and procedure applicable to hearing

The court shall hear and determine the matter of the establishment of the conservatorship according to the law and procedure relating to the trial of civil actions, including trial by jury if demanded by the proposed conservatee. *(Stats. 1990, c. 79 (A.B.759), § 14, operative July 1, 1991. Amended by Stats.2000, c. 17 (A.B.1491), § 4.2.)*

Law Revision Commission Comments

1990 Enactment

Section 1827 continues Section 1827 of the repealed Probate Code without change. Under Section 1827, the proposed conservatee is entitled to a jury trial on the question of the establishment of the conservatorship. However, the question of who is to be appointed as conservator is a matter to be determined by the court. See Sections 1452, 1810–1813. Likewise, there is no right to a jury trial in connection with an order relating to the legal capacity of the conservatee. See Sections 1452, 1873, 1890, 1901, 1910. For general provisions relating to hearings and orders, see Sections 1040–1050. See also Section 2103 (effect of final order). For background on the provisions of this part, see the Comment to this part under the part heading. [20 Cal.L.Rev.Comm. Reports 1001 (1990)].

Cross References

Civil action defined, see Code of Civil Procedure § 30.

Counsel, right to, see Cal. Const. Art. 1, § 15.

Depositions and discovery, see Code of Civil Procedure § 2016 et seq.

Execution of judgment in civil actions, generally, see Code of Civil Procedure § 683.010 et seq.

Filing decisions in writing in civil actions, see Code of Civil Procedure § 632.

Judicial Council rules, see California Rules of Court, Rule 10.1 et seq.

Jury trial, see Cal. Const. Art. 1, § 16; Probate Code § 825.

Rules of practice in civil actions,
Generally, see Code of Civil Procedure § 307 et seq.; Probate Code § 1000 et seq.
Court rules, see California Rules of Court, Rule 3.1 et seq.

Trial by court, see Code of Civil Procedure § 631 et seq.

§ 1827.5. Assessment of proposed limited or general conservatee

(a) In the case of any proceeding to establish a limited conservatorship for a person with developmental disabilities, within 30 days after the filing of a petition for limited conservatorship, a proposed limited conservatee, with his or her consent, shall be assessed at a regional center as provided in Chapter 5 (commencing with Section 4620) of Division 4.5 of the Welfare and Institutions Code. The regional center shall submit a written report of its findings and recommendations to the court.

(b) In the case of any proceeding to establish a general conservatorship for a person with developmental disabilities, the regional center, with the consent of the proposed conservatee, may prepare an assessment as provided in Chapter 5 (commencing with Section 4620) of Division 4.5 of the Welfare and Institutions Code. If an assessment is prepared, the regional center shall submit its findings and recommendations to the court.

(c) A report prepared under subdivision (a) or (b) shall include a description of the specific areas, nature, and degree of disability of the proposed conservatee or proposed limited conservatee. The findings and recommendations of the regional center are not binding upon the court.

In a proceeding where the petitioner is a provider of board and care, treatment, habilitation, or other services to persons with developmental disabilities or a spouse or employee of a provider, is not the natural parent of the proposed conservatee or proposed limited conservatee, and is not a public entity, the regional center shall include a recommendation in its report concerning the suitability of the petitioners to meet the needs of the proposed conservatee or proposed limited conservatee.

(d) At least five days before the hearing on the petition, the regional center shall mail a copy of the report referred to in subdivision (a) to all of the following:

(1) The proposed limited conservatee.

(2) The attorney, if any, for the proposed limited conservatee.

(3) If the petitioner is not the proposed limited conservatee, the attorney for the petitioner or the petitioner if the petitioner does not have an attorney.

(4) Such other persons as the court orders.

(e) The report referred to in subdivisions (a) and (b) shall be confidential and shall be made available only to parties listed in subdivision (d) unless the court, in its discretion, determines that the release of the report would serve the interests of the conservatee who is developmentally disabled. The clerk of the court shall make provision for limiting disclosure of the report exclusively to persons entitled thereto under this section. *(Stats.1990, c. 79 (A.B.759), § 14, operative July 1, 1991. Amended by Stats.1991, c. 82 (S.B.896), § 12, eff. June 30, 1991, operative July 1, 1991; Stats.2002, c. 784 (S.B.1316), § 579.)*

1990 Enactment

Section 1827.5 continues Section 1827.5 of the repealed Probate Code without substantive change. For the recommendation of the California Law Revision Commission that resulted in the amendment of this section of the repealed Probate Code, see *Recommendation Relating to Notice in Limited Conservatorship Proceedings*, 16 Cal. L. Revision Comm'n Reports 199 (1982). For background on the provisions of this part, see the Comment to this part under the part heading.

1991 Amendment

Section 1827.5 is amended to conform to amendments made to Section 1827.5 of the repealed Probate Code by 1990 Cal.Stat. ch. 1598. [20 Cal.L.Rev. Comm. Reports 1001 (1990)].

2002 Amendment

Subdivision (e) of Section 1827.5 is amended to reflect elimination of the county clerk's role as ex officio clerk of the superior court. See former Gov't Code § 26800 (county clerk acting as clerk of superior court). The powers, duties, and responsibilities formerly exercised by the county clerk as ex officio clerk of the court are delegated to the court administrative or executive officer, and the county clerk is relieved of those powers, duties, and responsibilities. See Gov't Code §§ 69840 (powers, duties, and responsibilities of clerk of court and deputy clerk of court), 71620 (trial court personnel). [32 Cal.L.Rev. Comm. Reports 523 (2002)].

Cross References

Computation of time, see Code of Civil Procedure §§ 12 and 12a; Government Code § 6800 et seq.
Developmentally disabled persons, evaluation report, see Health and Safety Code § 416.8.
Inspection of public records, exemptions from disclosure, "conservatee" to "conservatorship", see Government Code § 6276.12.
Notice of hearing to regional center, see Probate Code § 1822.
Services for the developmentally disabled, confidential information and records, disclosure, see Welfare and Institutions Code § 4514.

§ 1828. Information to proposed conservatee by court

(a) Except as provided in subdivision (c), before the establishment of a conservatorship of the person or estate, or both, the court shall inform the proposed conservatee of all of the following:

(1) The nature and purpose of the proceeding.

(2) The establishment of a conservatorship is a legal adjudication of the <u>proposed</u> conservatee's inability to properly provide for * * * his or her personal needs or to manage the conservatee's own financial resources, or both, depending on the allegations made and the determinations requested in the petition, and the effect of such an adjudication on the <u>proposed</u> conservatee's basic rights.

(3)(A) The proposed conservatee may be disqualified from voting pursuant to Section 2208 of the Elections Code if he or she is incapable of communicating, with or without reasonable accommodations, a desire to participate in the voting process.

(B) The proposed conservatee shall not be disqualified from voting on the basis that he or she does, or would need to do, any of the following to complete an affidavit of voter registration:

(i) Signs the affidavit of voter registration with a mark or a cross pursuant to subdivision (b) of Section 2150 of the Elections Code.

(ii) Signs the affidavit of voter registration by means of a signature stamp pursuant to Section 354.5 of the Elections Code.

(iii) Completes the affidavit of voter registration with the assistance of another person pursuant to subdivision (d) of Section 2150 of the Elections Code.

(iv) Completes the affidavit of voter registration with reasonable accommodations.

(4) The identity of the proposed conservator.

(5) The nature and effect on the <u>proposed</u> conservatee's basic rights of any order requested under Chapter 4 (commencing with Section 1870), and in the case of an allegedly developmentally disabled adult, the specific effects of each limitation requested in such order.

(6) The proposed conservatee has the right to oppose the proceeding, to have the matter of the establishment of the conservatorship tried by jury, to be represented by legal counsel if the proposed conservatee so chooses, and to have legal counsel appointed by the court if unable to retain legal counsel.

(b) After the court so informs the proposed conservatee and before the establishment of the conservatorship, the court shall consult the proposed conservatee to determine the proposed conservatee's opinion concerning all of the following:

(1) The establishment of the conservatorship.

(2) The appointment of the proposed conservator.

(3) Any order requested under Chapter 4 (commencing with Section 1870), and in the case of an allegedly developmentally disabled adult, of each limitation requested in such order.

(c) This section does not apply where both of the following conditions are satisfied:

(1) The proposed conservatee is absent from the hearing and is not required to attend the hearing under subdivision (a) of Section 1825.

(2) Any showing required by Section 1825 has been made. *(Stats.1990, c. 79 (A.B.759), § 14, operative July 1, 1991. Amended by Stats.2014, c. 591 (A.B.1311), § 6, eff. Jan. 1, 2015; Stats.2015, c. 736 (S.B.589), § 10, eff. Jan. 1, 2016; Stats.2016, c. 86 (S.B.1171), § 246, eff. Jan. 1, 2017.)*

1990 Enactment

Section 1828 continues Section 1828 of the repealed Probate Code without change. For background on the provisions of this part, see the Comment to this part under the part heading. [20 Cal.L.Rev. Comm. Reports 1001 (1990)].

Cross References

Appointment of legal counsel for proposed conservatee, see Probate Code § 1471.
Counsel, right to, see Cal. Const. Art. 1, § 15.

Disqualification from voting, see Probate Code § 1910; Elections Code § 2208 et seq.

§ 1828.5. Limited conservator for developmentally disabled adult; appointment; hearing

(a) At the hearing on the petition for appointment of a limited conservator for an allegedly developmentally disabled adult, the court shall do each of the following:

(1) Inquire into the nature and extent of the general intellectual functioning of the individual alleged to be developmentally disabled.

(2) Evaluate the extent of the impairment of his or her adaptive behavior.

(3) Ascertain his or her capacity to care for himself or herself and his or her property.

(4) Inquire into the qualifications, abilities, and capabilities of the person seeking appointment as limited conservator.

(5) If a report by the regional center, in accordance with Section 1827.5, has not been filed in court because the proposed limited conservatee withheld his or her consent to assessment by the regional center, the court shall determine the reason for withholding such consent.

(b) If the court finds that the proposed limited conservatee possesses the capacity to care for himself or herself and to manage his or her property as a reasonably prudent person, the court shall dismiss the petition for appointment of a limited conservator.

(c) If the court finds that the proposed limited conservatee lacks the capacity to perform some, but not all, of the tasks necessary to provide properly for his or her own personal needs for physical health, food, clothing, or shelter, or to manage his or her own financial resources, the court shall appoint a limited conservator for the person or the estate or the person and the estate.

(d) If the court finds that the proposed limited conservatee lacks the capacity to perform all of the tasks necessary to provide properly for his or her own personal needs for physical health, food, clothing, or shelter, or to manage his or her own financial resources, the court shall appoint either a conservator or a limited conservator for the person or the estate, or the person and the estate.

(e) The court shall define the powers and duties of the limited conservator so as to permit the developmentally disabled adult to care for himself or herself or to manage his or her financial resources commensurate with his or her ability to do so.

(f) Prior to the appointment of a limited conservator for the person or estate or person and estate of a developmentally disabled adult, the court shall inform the proposed limited conservatee of the nature and purpose of the limited conservatorship proceeding, that the appointment of a limited conservator for his or her person or estate or person and estate will result in the transfer of certain rights set forth in the petition and the effect of such transfer, the identity of the person who has been nominated as his or her limited conservator, that he or she has a right to oppose such proceeding, and that he or she has a right to have the matter tried by jury. After communicating such information to the person and prior to the appointment of a limited conservator, the court shall consult the person to determine his or her opinion concerning the appointment. *(Stats.1990, c. 79 (A.B.759), § 14, operative July 1, 1991.)*

Law Revision Commission Comments
1990 Enactment

Section 1828.5 continues Section 1828.5 of the repealed Probate Code without change. For background on the provisions of this part, see the Comment to this part under the part heading. [20 Cal.L.Rev.Comm. Reports 1001 (1990)].

Cross References

Developmental disability, defined, see Probate Code § 1420.
Developmentally disabled adult,
    Authorization for appointment of limited conservator, see Probate Code § 1801.
    Contents of order appointing conservator or limited conservator, see Probate Code § 1830.
Developmentally disabled persons,
    Application of this division, see Health and Safety Code § 416.1 et seq.
    Guardianships and conservatorships for those in state hospitals, see Welfare and Institutions Code § 4825.
Limited conservator, powers and duties, see Probate Code § 2351.5.
Regional centers for persons with developmental disabilities, see Welfare and Institutions Code § 4620 et seq.

§ 1829. Persons who may support or oppose petition

Any of the following persons may appear at the hearing to support or oppose the petition:

(a) The proposed conservatee.

(b) The spouse or registered domestic partner of the proposed conservatee.

(c) A relative of the proposed conservatee.

(d) Any interested person or friend of the proposed conservatee. *(Stats.1990, c. 79 (A.B.759), § 14, operative July 1, 1991. Amended by Stats.2001, c. 893 (A.B.25), § 20; Stats.2006, c. 493 (A.B.1363), § 9.)*

Law Revision Commission Comments
1990 Enactment

Section 1829 restates Section 1829 of the repealed Probate Code without substantive change. The reference to "any officer or agency of this state, or of the United States, or any authorized representative thereof" has been omitted as unnecessary in view of Section 1424 (defining "interested person"). See also Section 1043 (response or objection by interested person). For background on the provisions of this part, see the Comment to this part under the part heading. [20 Cal.L.Rev.Comm. Reports 1001 (1990)].

Cross References

Domestic partner, defined, see Probate Code § 37.
Interested person, defined, see Probate Code § 1424.

§ 1830. Order appointing conservator or limited conservator for developmentally disabled adult; contents

(a) The order appointing the conservator shall contain, among other things, the names, addresses, and telephone numbers of:

(1) The conservator.

(2) The conservatee's attorney, if any.

(3) The court investigator, if any.

(b) In the case of a limited conservator for a developmentally disabled adult, any order the court may make shall include the findings of the court specified in Section 1828.5. The order shall specify the powers granted to and duties imposed upon the limited conservator, which powers and duties may not exceed the powers and duties applicable to a conservator under this code. The order shall also specify the following:

(1) The properties of the limited conservatee to which the limited conservator is entitled to possession and management, giving a description of the properties that will be sufficient to identify them.

(2) The debts, rentals, wages, or other claims due to the limited conservatee which the limited conservator is entitled to collect, or file suit with respect to, if necessary, and thereafter to possess and manage.

(3) The contractual or other obligations which the limited conservator may incur on behalf of the limited conservatee.

(4) The claims against the limited conservatee which the limited conservator may pay, compromise, or defend, if necessary.

(5) Any other powers, limitations, or duties with respect to the care of the limited conservatee or the management of the property specified in this subdivision by the limited conservator which the court shall specifically and expressly grant.

(c) An information notice of the rights of conservatees shall be attached to the order. The conservator shall mail the order and the attached information notice to the conservatee and the conservatee's relatives, as set forth in subdivision (b) of Section 1821, within 30 days of the issuance of the order. By January 1, 2008, the Judicial Council shall develop the notice required by this subdivision. *(Stats.1990, c. 79 (A.B.759), § 14, operative July 1, 1991. Amended by Stats. 2006, c. 493 (A.B.1363), § 10; Stats.2007, c. 553 (A.B.1727), § 8.)*

Law Revision Commission Comments
1990 Enactment

Section 1830 continues Section 1830 of the repealed Probate Code without substantive change. For general provisions relating to hearings and orders, see Sections 1040–1050. See also Sections 300–301 (trust company as guardian of estate), 2104 (nonprofit charitable corporation as guardian). As to the effect of final order, see Section 2103. See also Section 2650 (grounds of removal of conservator include incapacity to perform duties suitably, conviction of felony, gross immorality, and conflict of interest). Insolvency or bankruptcy of conservator also is a cause for removal. See Section 2650. See also Section 2750 (granting letters, other than temporary letters, an appealable order). As to the effect of reversal on appeal of order appointing conservator, see Section 2752. For background on the provisions of this part, see the Comment to this part under the part heading. [20 Cal.L.Rev.Comm. Reports 1001 (1990)].

Cross References
Appealable orders, see Probate Code § 1300 et seq.
Contracts,
  Generally, see Civil Code § 1549 et seq.
  Interpretation, see Civil Code § 1635 et seq.
Court investigator, defined, see Probate Code § 1419.
Developmental disability, defined, see Probate Code § 1420.

Limited conservator, powers and duties, see Probate Code § 2351.5.
Order of appointment, additional conditions, see Probate Code §§ 2358, 2402.
Powers and duties of conservators, see Probate Code §§ 2350 et seq., 2400 et seq.

§ 1831. Repealed by Stats.1993, c. 70 (S.B.86), § 9, eff. June 30, 1993

§ 1834. Acknowledgment of receipt by conservator; statement of duties and liabilities; conservatorship information

(a) Before letters are issued in a conservatorship that originates in this state or a conservatorship that is transferred to this state under Chapter 8 (commencing with Section 1980), the conservator (other than a trust company or a public conservator) shall file an acknowledgment of receipt of (1) a statement of duties and liabilities of the office of conservator, and (2) a copy of the conservatorship information required under Section 1835. The acknowledgment and the statement shall be in the form prescribed by the Judicial Council.

(b) The court may by local rules require the acknowledgment of receipt to include the conservator's birth date and driver's license number, if any, provided that the court ensures their confidentiality.

(c) The statement of duties and liabilities prescribed by the Judicial Council shall not supersede the law on which the statement is based. *(Added by Stats.1991, c. 1019 (S.B.1022), § 1. Amended by Stats.1994, c. 806 (A.B.3686), § 9; Stats. 2014, c. 553 (S.B.940), § 7, eff. Jan. 1, 2015, operative Jan. 1, 2016.)*

Law Revision Commission Comments
2014 Amendment

Section 1834 is amended to make clear that it applies to a conservatorship that is transferred to California under the California Conservatorship Jurisdiction Act (Section 1980 *et seq.*), as well as one that originates in California. [43 Cal.L.Rev.Comm. Reports 93 (2013)].

Cross References
Inspection of public records, exemptions from disclosure, "conservatee" to "conservatorship", see Government Code § 6276.12.
Letters, defined, see Probate Code § 52.

§ 1835. Conservator's rights, duties, limitations and responsibilities; dissemination of information by Superior Court; failure to provide information

(a) Every superior court shall provide all private conservators with written information concerning a conservator's rights, duties, limitations, and responsibilities under this division.

(b) The information to be provided shall include, but need not be limited to, the following:

(1) The rights, duties, limitations, and responsibilities of a conservator.

(2) The rights of a conservatee.

(3) How to assess the needs of the conservatee.

(4) How to use community-based services to meet the needs of the conservatee.

(5) How to ensure that the conservatee is provided with the least restrictive possible environment.

(6) The court procedures and processes relevant to conservatorships.

(7) The procedures for inventory and appraisal, and the filing of accounts.

(c) An information package shall be developed by the Judicial Council, after consultation with the following organizations or individuals:

(1) The California State Association of Public Administrators, Public Guardians, and Public Conservators, or other comparable organizations.

(2) The State Bar.

(3) Individuals or organizations, approved by the Judicial Council, who represent court investigators, specialists with experience in performing assessments and coordinating community-based services, and legal services programs for the elderly.

(d) The failure of any court or any employee or agent thereof, to provide information to a conservator as required by this section does not:

(1) Relieve the conservator of any of the conservator's duties as required by this division.

(2) Make the court or the employee or agent thereof, liable, in either a personal or official capacity, for damages to a conservatee, conservator, the conservatorship of a person or an estate, or any other person or entity.

(e) The information package shall be made available to individual courts. The Judicial Council shall periodically update the information package when changes in the law warrant revision. The revisions shall be provided to individual courts.

(f) To cover the costs of providing the written information required by this section, a court may charge each private conservator a fee of twenty dollars ($20) which shall be distributed to the court in which it was collected. *(Stats.1990, c. 79 (A.B.759), § 14, operative July 1, 1991. Amended by Stats.1991, c. 1019 (S.B.1022), § 2; Stats.2005, c. 75 (A.B. 145), § 147, eff. July 19, 2005, operative Jan. 1, 2006.)*

Law Revision Commission Comments

1990 Enactment

Section 1835 continues Section 1835 of the repealed Probate Code but substitutes "under this division" for "under this part" to recognize that the conservator's rights, duties, limitations, and responsibilities are stated in this division, not just in this part. The section also is revised to make other conforming and nonsubstantive revisions. [20 Cal.L.Rev.Comm. Reports 1001 (1990)].

Cross References

Deposit of fees or fines collected pursuant to this section in the Trial Court Trust Fund, effect of prior agreements or practices, long-term revenue allocation schedule proposal, see Government Code § 68085.5.

Organization and government of courts, collection of fees and fines pursuant to this section, deposits, see Government Code § 68085.1.

Public guardian, generally, see Probate Code § 2900 et seq.

ARTICLE 4. SPECIAL PROVISIONS APPLICABLE WHERE PROPOSED CONSERVATEE IS AN ABSENTEE

Cross References

Application of old and new law, see Probate Code § 3.

§ 1840. Appointment of conservator for absentee; procedure

Except as otherwise provided in this article, a conservator for an absentee (Section 1403) shall be appointed as provided in Article 3 (commencing with Section 1820) of this chapter or Article 3 (commencing with Section 2001) of Chapter 8. *(Stats.1990, c. 79 (A.B.759), § 14, operative July 1, 1991. Amended by Stats.2014, c. 553 (S.B.940), § 8, eff. Jan. 1, 2015, operative Jan. 1, 2016.)*

Law Revision Commission Comments

1990 Enactment

Section 1840 continues Section 1840 of the repealed Probate Code without change. For background on the provisions of this part, see the Comment to this part under the part heading. [20 Cal.L.Rev. Comm. Reports 1001 (1990)].

2014 Amendment

Section 1840 is amended to reflect the enactment of the California Conservatorship Jurisdiction Act (Section 1980 *et seq.*). [43 Cal. L.Rev.Comm. Reports 93 (2013)].

Cross References

Absentee, defined, see Probate Code § 1403.

Condition for appointment of spouse of absentee as conservator, see Probate Code § 1813.

Conservator of estate, appointment for absentee, see Probate Code § 1803.

Termination of conservatorship of absentee, see Probate Code § 1864.

§ 1841. Petition; additional contents

In addition to the other required contents of the petition, if the proposed conservatee is an absentee:

(a) The petition, and any notice required by Section 1822 or 2002, or any other law, shall set forth the last known military rank or grade and the social security account number of the proposed conservatee.

(b) The petition shall state whether the absentee's spouse has commenced any action or proceeding against the absentee for judicial or legal separation, dissolution of marriage, annulment, or adjudication of nullity of their marriage. *(Stats.1990, c. 79 (A.B.759), § 14, operative July 1, 1991. Amended by Stats.2014, c. 553 (S.B.940), § 9, eff. Jan. 1, 2015, operative Jan. 1, 2016.)*

Law Revision Commission Comments
1990 Enactment

Section 1841 continues Section 1841 of the repealed Probate Code without substantive change. The reference to "divorce" is omitted as unnecessary in view of the definition provided by Section 36 ("dissolution of marriage" includes divorce). For general provisions relating to petitions and other papers, see Sections 1020–1023. "Absentee" is defined in Section 1403. For background on the provisions of this part, see the Comment to this part under the part heading. [20 Cal.L.Rev.Comm. Reports 1001 (1990)].

2014 Amendment

Section 1841 is amended to reflect the enactment of the California Conservatorship Jurisdiction Act (Section 1980 *et seq.*). [43 Cal. L.Rev.Comm. Reports 93 (2013)].

Cross References

Absentee, defined, see Probate Code § 1403
Condition for appointment of spouse of absentee as conservator, see Probate Code § 1813.
Contents of petition, see Probate Code § 1821.
Dissolution of marriage, defined, see Probate Code § 36.

§ 1842. Notice of hearing

In addition to the persons and entities to whom notice of hearing is required under Section 1822 or 2002, if the proposed conservatee is an absentee, a copy of the petition and notice of the time and place of the hearing shall be mailed at least 15 days before the hearing to the secretary concerned or to the head of the United States department or agency concerned, as the case may be. In such case, notice shall also be published pursuant to Section 6061 of the Government Code in a newspaper of general circulation in the county in which the hearing will be held. *(Stats.1990, c. 79 (A.B.759), § 14, operative July 1, 1991. Amended by Stats.2014, c. 553 (S.B.940), § 10, eff. Jan. 1, 2015, operative Jan. 1, 2016.)*

Law Revision Commission Comments
1990 Enactment

Section 1842 continues Section 1842 of the repealed Probate Code without change. See also Section 1440 ("secretary concerned" defined). For general provisions relating to notice of hearing, see Sections 1200–1221, 1460–1469. See also Sections 1260–1265 (proof of giving notice), 2700–2702 (notice to persons who request special notice). For background on the provisions of this part, see the Comment to this part under the part heading. [20 Cal.L.Rev.Comm. Reports 1001 (1990)].

2014 Amendment

Section 1842 is amended to reflect the enactment of the California Conservatorship Jurisdiction Act (Section 1980 *et seq.*). [43 Cal. L.Rev.Comm. Reports 93 (2013)].

Cross References

Computation of time, see Code of Civil Procedure §§ 12 and 12a; Government Code § 6800 et seq.
Definitions,
  Absentee, see Probate Code § 1403.
  Secretary concerned, see Probate Code § 1440.
Mailing, completion, see Probate Code § 1467.
Newspaper of general circulation, establishment of standing, see Government Code § 6020 et seq.
Notice,
  Mailing, see Probate Code § 1215 et seq.

Posting, see Probate Code § 1230.
Proof of giving notice, see Probate Code § 1260 et seq.
Special notice, see Probate Code § 1250 et seq.
This code, generally, see Probate Code § 1200 et seq.
This division, generally, see Probate Code § 1460 et seq.
Service of process,
  Generally, see Code of Civil Procedure § 413.10 et seq.
  Mail, see Code of Civil Procedure §§ 415.30, 1012 et seq.
  Personal delivery, see Code of Civil Procedure § 415.10.
  Proof of service, see Code of Civil Procedure § 417.10 et seq.
  Publication, see Code of Civil Procedure § 415.50.

§ 1843. Citation to proposed conservatee not required; notice to absentee conservatee not required

(a) No citation is required under Section 1823 to the proposed conservatee if the proposed conservatee is an absentee.

(b) No notice is required under Section 2002 to the proposed conservatee if the proposed conservatee is an absentee. *(Stats.1990, c. 79 (A.B.759), § 14, operative July 1, 1991. Amended by Stats.2014, c. 553 (S.B.940), § 11, eff. Jan. 1, 2015, operative Jan. 1, 2016.)*

Law Revision Commission Comments
1990 Enactment

Section 1843 continues Section 1843 of the repealed Probate Code without change. For background on the provisions of this part, see the Comment to this part under the part heading. [20 Cal.L.Rev. Comm. Reports 1001 (1990)].

2014 Amendment

Section 1843 is amended to reflect the enactment of the California Conservatorship Jurisdiction Act (Section 1980 *et seq.*). [43 Cal. L.Rev.Comm. Reports 93 (2013)].

§ 1844. Proof of status of proposed conservatee; attendance at hearing not required

(a) In a proceeding to appoint a conservator for an absentee under Article 3 (commencing with Section 1820) of this chapter or Article 3 (commencing with Section 2001) of Chapter 8, an official written report or record complying with Section 1283 of the Evidence Code that a proposed conservatee is an absentee shall be received as evidence of that fact and the court shall not determine the status of the proposed conservatee inconsistent with the status determined as shown by the written report or record.

(b) The inability of the proposed conservatee to attend the hearing is established by the official written report or record referred to in subdivision (a). *(Stats.1990, c. 79 (A.B.759), § 14, operative July 1, 1991. Amended by Stats.2014, c. 553 (S.B.940), § 12, eff. Jan. 1, 2015, operative Jan. 1, 2016.)*

Law Revision Commission Comments
1990 Enactment

Section 1844 continues Section 1844 of the repealed Probate Code without change. For background on the provisions of this part, see the Comment to this part under the part heading. [20 Cal.L.Rev. Comm. Reports 1001 (1990)].

2014 Amendment

Section 1844 is amended to reflect the enactment of the California Conservatorship Jurisdiction Act (Section 1980 *et seq.*). [43 Cal. L.Rev.Comm. Reports 93 (2013)].

Absentee, defined, see Probate Code § 1403.

Attendance of proposed conservatee at hearing, generally, see Probate Code § 1825.

ARTICLE 5. SPECIAL PROVISIONS APPLICABLE WHERE PROPOSED CONSERVATEE IS A MISSING PERSON

Law Revision Commission Comments

1990 Enactment

For the recommendation of the California Law Revision Commission that resulted in the enactment of this article of the repealed Probate Code, see Recommendation Relating to Missing Persons, 16 Cal.L.Revision Comm'n Reports 105 (1982). [20 Cal.L.Rev.Comm. Reports 1001 (1990)].

Cross References

Application of old and new law, see Probate Code § 3.

Appointment of conservator authorized, see Probate Code § 1804.

Death of persons not heard from in five years, presumption, see Evidence Code § 667.

Personal property of absent federal personnel, see Probate Code § 3700 et seq.

Persons to whom notice of time and place of hearing on petition, report or account if conservator of estate appointed under this article, see Probate Code § 1461.7.

§ 1845. Appointment of conservator

(a) Except as otherwise provided in this article, a conservator of the estate of a person who is missing and whose whereabouts is unknown shall be appointed as provided in Article 3 (commencing with Section 1820) of this chapter or Article 3 (commencing with Section 2001) of Chapter 8.

(b) This article does not apply where the proposed conservatee is an absentee as defined in Section 1403. *(Stats.1990, c. 79 (A.B.759), § 14, operative July 1, 1991. Amended by Stats.2014, c. 553 (S.B.940), § 13, eff. Jan. 1, 2015, operative Jan. 1, 2016.)*

Law Revision Commission Comments

1990 Enactment

Section 1845 continues Section 1845 of the repealed Probate Code without change. Subdivision (a) is comparable to Section 1840 (conservatee who is an "absentee"). The appointment of a conservator is governed by other provisions where the proposed conservatee is an absentee as defined in Section 1403. See Article 4 (commencing with Section 1840). For background on the provisions of this article, see the Comment to this article under the article heading. [20 Cal.L.Rev.Comm. Reports 1001 (1990)].

2014 Amendment

Section 1845 is amended to reflect the enactment of the California Conservatorship Jurisdiction Act (Section 1980 *et seq.*). [43 Cal. L.Rev.Comm. Reports 93 (2013)].

§ 1846. Contents of petition for conservatorship of missing person's estate

In addition to the other required contents of the petition, if the proposed conservatee is a person who is missing and whose whereabouts is unknown, the petition shall state all of the following:

(a) The proposed conservatee owns or is entitled to the possession of real or personal property located in this state. In a proceeding to transfer a conservatorship of a missing person to this state under Article 3 (commencing with Section 2001) of Chapter 8, this requirement is also satisfied if the petition states that the proposed conservatee owns or is entitled to the possession of personal property that is to be relocated to this state upon approval of the transfer.

(b) The time and circumstance of the person's disappearance and that the missing person has not been heard from by the persons most likely to hear (naming them and their relationship to the missing person) since the time of disappearance and that the whereabouts of the missing person is unknown to those persons and to the petitioner.

(c) The last known residence of the missing person.

(d) A description of any search or inquiry made concerning the whereabouts of the missing person.

(e) A description of the estate of the proposed conservatee which requires attention, supervision, and care. *(Stats.1990, c. 79 (A.B.759), § 14, operative July 1, 1991. Amended by Stats.2014, c. 553 (S.B.940), § 14, eff. Jan. 1, 2015, operative Jan. 1, 2016.)*

Law Revision Commission Comments

1990 Enactment

Section 1846 continues Section 1846 of the repealed Probate Code without substantive change. Under some circumstances, the court may decline to appoint a permanent conservator pending further developments, but may appoint a temporary conservator. See Section 2250 (petition for appointment of temporary conservator pending court's final determination of petition for appointment of conservator). See also Section 2252 (powers and duties of temporary conservator). In other circumstances, the court may determine that a permanent conservator should be appointed without delay. For general provisions relating to petitions and other papers, see Sections 1020–1023. For background on the provisions of this article, see the Comment to this article under the article heading. [20 Cal.L.Rev.Comm. Reports 1001 (1990)].

2014 Amendment

Section 1846 is amended to reflect the enactment of the California Conservatorship Jurisdiction Act (Section 1980 *et seq.*). [43 Cal. L.Rev.Comm. Reports 93 (2013)].

Cross References

Missing persons presumed dead, estate administration, see Probate Code § 12400 et seq.

§ 1847. Notice; petition for appointment of conservator

In addition to the persons and entities to whom notice of hearing is required under Section 1822 or 2002, if the proposed conservatee is a person who is missing and whose whereabouts is unknown:

(a) A copy of the petition for appointment of a conservator and notice of the time and place of the hearing on the petition shall be mailed at least 15 days before the hearing to the proposed conservatee at the last known address of the proposed conservatee.

(b) Notice of the time and place of the hearing shall also be published pursuant to Section 6061 of the Government Code in a newspaper of general circulation in the county in which the proposed conservatee was last known to reside if the proposed conservatee's last known address is in this state.

(c) Pursuant to Section 1202, the court may require that further or additional notice of the hearing be given. *(Stats. 1990, c. 79 (A.B.759), § 14, operative July 1, 1991. Amended by Stats.2014, c. 553 (S.B.940), § 15, eff. Jan. 1, 2015, operative Jan. 1, 2016.)*

Law Revision Commission Comments

1990 Enactment

Section 1847 continues Section 1847 of the repealed Probate Code without substantive change. A reference to Section 1202 has been substituted for a reference to Section 1462, Section 1202 having superseded Section 1462.

Unlike Section 1842, which requires notice to be published in the county where the hearing will be held, Section 1847 requires notice to be published in the county where the proposed conservatee was last known to reside if his or her last known address is in this state. Publishing notice in this county is more likely to give actual notice to the proposed conservatee. If the last known address is not in this state, Section 1847 does not require publication of notice, but, in such a case, the court may require publication within or without this state pursuant to subdivision (c). For general provisions relating to notice of hearing, see Sections 1200–1221, 1460–1469. See also Sections 1260–1265 (proof of giving notice), 2700–2702 (notice to persons who request special notice).

Nothing in this section limits the authority of the court in determining the need for conservatorship to require that a search be made for the missing person before a conservator is appointed. Whether to require such a search and the type of search to be required is left to the court's discretion. In exercising this discretion, the court may consider all the circumstances, including the nature of the disappearance, the character and amount of the estate, and the circumstances of persons who have an interest in the proceeding. For example, the court may dispense with a search if the missing person's estate is nominal, there are dependents entitled to support, and the funds necessary for support would be significantly reduced by the cost of the search. In other cases, no purpose would be served by a court-ordered search, such as where the proposed conservatee is lost at sea.

For background on the provisions of this article, see the Comment to this article under the article heading. [20 Cal.L.Rev.Comm. Reports 1001 (1990)].

2014 Amendment

Section 1847 is amended to reflect the enactment of the California Conservatorship Jurisdiction Act (Section 1980 *et seq.*). [43 Cal. L.Rev.Comm. Reports 93 (2013)].

Cross References

Computation of time, see Code of Civil Procedure §§ 12 and 12a; Government Code § 6800 et seq.

Publication, generally, see Government Code § 6000 et seq.

§ 1848. Appointment of conservator; acts not required

(a) In a proceeding under Article 3 (commencing with Section 1820) to appoint a conservator of the estate of a person who is missing and whose whereabouts is unknown, the following acts are not required:

(1) Issuance of a citation to the proposed conservatee pursuant to Section 1823.

(2) Service of a citation and petition pursuant to Section 1824.

(3) Production of the proposed conservatee at the hearing pursuant to Section 1825.

(4) Performance of the duties of the court investigator pursuant to Section 1826.

(5) Performance of any other act that depends upon knowledge of the location of the proposed conservatee.

(b) In a proceeding to transfer a conservatorship of a missing person to this state under Article 3 (commencing with Section 2001) of Chapter 8, the following acts are not required:

(1) Notice to the proposed conservatee pursuant to Section 2002.

(2) Production of the proposed conservatee at the hearings pursuant to Section 2002.

(3) Performance of the duties of the court investigator pursuant to Section 1851.1.

(4) Performance of any other act that depends upon knowledge of the location of the proposed conservatee. *(Stats.1990, c. 79 (A.B.759), § 14, operative July 1, 1991. Amended by Stats.2014, c. 553 (S.B.940), § 16, eff. Jan. 1, 2015, operative Jan. 1, 2016.)*

Law Revision Commission Comments

1990 Enactment

Section 1848 continues Section 1848 of the repealed Probate Code without change. This section excuses performance of any duty under the general provisions that depends upon knowledge of the whereabouts of the missing person. The section does not limit the authority of the court to require that an attempt be made to locate the missing person. See the Comment to Section 1847. For background on the provisions of this article, see the Comment to this article under the article heading. [20 Cal.L.Rev.Comm. Reports 1001 (1990)].

2014 Amendment

Section 1848 is amended to reflect the enactment of the California Conservatorship Jurisdiction Act (Section 1980 *et seq.*). [43 Cal. L.Rev.Comm. Reports 93 (2013)].

Cross References

Notice,
  Mailing, see Probate Code § 1215 et seq.
  Posting, see Probate Code § 1230.
  Proof of giving notice, see Probate Code § 1260 et seq.
  Special notice, see Probate Code § 1250 et seq.
  This code, generally, see Probate Code § 1200 et seq.
  This division, generally, see Probate Code § 1460 et seq.
Service of process,
  Generally, see Code of Civil Procedure § 413.10 et seq.
  Mail, see Code of Civil Procedure §§ 415.30, 1012 et seq.
  Personal delivery, see Code of Civil Procedure § 415.10.
  Proof of service, see Code of Civil Procedure § 417.10 et seq.
  Publication, see Code of Civil Procedure § 415.50.

§ 1849. Appointment of conservator; conditions

A conservator of the estate of a person who is missing and whose whereabouts is unknown may be appointed only if the court finds all of the following:

(a) The proposed conservatee owns or is entitled to the possession of real or personal property located in this state. In a proceeding to transfer a conservatorship of a missing person to this state under Article 3 (commencing with Section 2001) of Chapter 8, this requirement is also satisfied if the court finds that the proposed conservatee owns or is entitled to the possession of personal property that is to be relocated to this state upon approval of the transfer.

(b) The proposed conservatee remains missing and his or her whereabouts remains unknown.

(c) The estate of the proposed conservatee requires attention, supervision, and care. *(Stats.1990, c. 79 (A.B.759), § 14, operative July 1, 1991. Amended by Stats.2014, c. 553 (S.B.940), § 17, eff. Jan. 1, 2015, operative Jan. 1, 2016.)*

Law Revision Commission Comments

1990 Enactment

Section 1849 continues Section 1849 of the repealed Probate Code without substantive change. For a special provision relating to notice of hearing on a petition, report, or account, see Section 1461.7. For general provisions, see Sections 1000–1004 (rules of practice), 1020–1023 (petitions and other papers), 1040–1050 (hearings and orders). As to the effect of final order, see Section 2103. For background on the provisions of this article, see the Comment to this article under the article heading. [20 Cal.L.Rev.Comm. Reports 1001 (1990)].

2014 Amendment

Section 1849 is amended to reflect the enactment of the California Conservatorship Jurisdiction Act (Section 1980 *et seq.*). [43 Cal. L.Rev.Comm. Reports 93 (2013)].

§ 1849.5. Application of article

(a) A petition may be filed under this article regardless of when the proposed conservatee became missing or how long the proposed conservatee has been missing.

(b) If a trustee was appointed pursuant to former Section 262, repealed by Chapter 201 of the Statutes of 1983, the provisions of former Sections 260 to 272, inclusive, repealed by Chapter 201 of the Statutes of 1983, continue to apply to the case after December 31, 1983, unless, upon a petition filed under this article after December 31, 1983, the trustee is replaced by a conservator. *(Stats.1990, c. 79 (A.B.759), § 14, operative July 1, 1991.)*

Law Revision Commission Comments

1990 Enactment

Section 1849.5 continues Section 1849.5 of the repealed Probate Code without substantive change. Subdivision (a) permits a petition to be filed under this article, without regard to when the missing person disappeared. Subdivision (b) makes clear that a trusteeship created under former law continues under that law, but may be changed to a conservatorship under this article on petition. For background on the provisions of this article, see the Comment to this article under the article heading. [20 Cal.L.Rev.Comm. Reports 1001 (1990)].

CHAPTER 2. PERIODIC REVIEW OF CONSERVATORSHIP

Cross References

Application of old and new law, see Probate Code § 3.
Cancellation and voter file maintenance, mentally incompetent persons, review under Probate Code of capability to complete affidavit, see Elections Code § 2209.
Conservatorship for gravely disabled persons, appointment, procedure, see Welfare and Institutions Code § 5350.

§ 1850. Review of conservatorship; application

(a) Except as provided in subdivision (b), each conservatorship initiated pursuant to this part shall be reviewed by the court as follows:

(1) At the expiration of six months after the initial appointment of the conservator, the court investigator shall visit the conservatee, conduct an investigation in accordance with the provisions of subdivision (a) of Section 1851, and report to the court regarding the appropriateness of the conservatorship and whether the conservator is acting in the best interests of the conservatee regarding the conservatee's placement, quality of care, including physical and mental treatment, and finances. The court may, in response to the investigator's report, take appropriate action including, but not limited to:

(A) Ordering a review of the conservatorship pursuant to subdivision (b).

(B) Ordering the conservator to submit an accounting pursuant to subdivision (a) of Section 2620.

(2) One year after the appointment of the conservator and annually thereafter. However, at the review that occurs one year after the appointment of the conservator, and every subsequent review conducted pursuant to this paragraph, the court may set the next review in two years if the court determines that the conservator is acting in the best interest interests of the conservatee. In these cases, the court shall require the investigator to conduct an investigation pursuant to subdivision (a) of Section 1851 one year before the next review and file a status report in the conservatee's court file regarding whether the conservatorship still appears to be warranted and whether the conservator is acting in the best interests of the conservatee. If the investigator determines pursuant to this investigation that the conservatorship still appears to be warranted and that the conservator is acting in the best interests of the conservatee regarding the conserva-

tee's placement, quality of care, including physical and mental treatment, and finances, no hearing or court action in response to the investigator's report is required.

(b) The court may, on its own motion or upon request by any interested person, take appropriate action including, but not limited to, ordering a review of the conservatorship, including at a noticed hearing, and ordering the conservator to present an accounting of the assets of the estate pursuant to Section 2620.

(c) Notice of a hearing pursuant to subdivision (b) shall be provided to all persons listed in subdivision (b) of Section 1822.

(d) This chapter does not apply to either of the following:

(1) A conservatorship for an absentee as defined in Section 1403.

(2) A conservatorship of the estate for a nonresident of this state where the conservatee is not present in this state.

(e) The amendments made to this section by the act [1] adding this subdivision shall become operative on July 1, 2007.

(f) A superior court shall not be required to perform any duties imposed pursuant to the amendments to this section enacted by Chapter 493 of the Statutes 2006 until the Legislature makes an appropriation identified for this purpose. *(Stats.1990, c. 79 (A.B.759), § 14, operative July 1, 1991. Amended by Stats.2006, c. 492 (S.B.1716), § 3; Stats. 2006, c. 493 (A.B.1363), § 11.5, operative July 1, 2007; Stats.2011, c. 10 (S.B.78), § 13, eff. March 24, 2011.)*

[1] Stats.2006, c. 493 (A.B.1363).

Law Revision Commission Comments
1990 Enactment

Section 1850 continues Section 1850 of the repealed Probate Code without change. Subdivision (b) provides two exceptions to application of the chapter. The first exception recognizes that the chapter as a practical matter cannot apply where the conservatee is an absentee. The second exception is consistent with Section 1825(a)(1). See also Section 1851.5 (assessment of estate for investigation expense). For background on the provisions of this part, see the Comment to this part under the part heading. [20 Cal.L.Rev.Comm. Reports 1001 (1990)].

§ 1850.5. Limited conservatorship for developmentally disabled adult; judicial review

(a) Notwithstanding Section 1850, each limited conservatorship for a developmentally disabled adult, as defined in subdivision (d) of Section 1801, shall be reviewed by the court one year after the appointment of the conservator and biennially thereafter.

(b) The court may, on its own motion or upon request by any interested person, take appropriate action, including, but not limited to, ordering a review of the limited conservatorship, including at a noticed hearing, at any time.

(c) A superior court shall not be required to perform any duties imposed by this section until the Legislature makes an appropriation identified for this purpose. *(Added by Stats. 2006, c. 493 (A.B.1363), § 11.7, operative July 1, 2007. Amended by Stats.2011, c. 10 (S.B.78), § 14, eff. March 24, 2011.)*

§ 1851. Court investigator; visitation of conservatee, conservator, or others; findings; recommendation

(a)(1) If court review is required pursuant to Section 1850, the court investigator shall, without prior notice to the conservator except as ordered by the court for necessity or to prevent harm to the conservatee, visit the conservatee. The court investigator shall inform the conservatee personally that the conservatee is under a conservatorship and shall give the name of the conservator to the conservatee. The court investigator shall determine all of the following:

(A) If the conservatee wishes to petition the court for termination of the conservatorship.

(B) If the conservatee is still in need of the conservatorship.

(C) If the * * * conservator is acting in the best interests of the conservatee. In determining if the conservator is acting in the best interests of the conservatee, the court investigator's evaluation shall include an examination of the conservatee's placement, the quality of care, including physical and mental treatment, and the conservatee's finances. To the extent practicable, the investigator shall review the accounting with a conservatee who has sufficient capacity. To the greatest extent possible, the court investigator shall interview individuals set forth in paragraph (1) of subdivision (a) of Section 1826, in order to determine if the conservator is acting in the best interests of the conservatee.

(D)(i) If the conservatee is incapable of communicating, with or without reasonable accommodations, a desire to participate in the voting process and may be disqualified from voting pursuant to Section 2208 or 2209 of the Elections Code.

(ii) The conservatee shall not be disqualified from voting on the basis that he or she does, or would need to do, any of the following to complete an affidavit of voter registration:

(I) Signs the affidavit of voter registration with a mark or a cross pursuant to subdivision (b) of Section 2150 of the Elections Code.

(II) Signs the affidavit of voter registration by means of a signature stamp pursuant to Section 354.5 of the Elections Code.

(III) Completes the affidavit of voter registration with the assistance of another person pursuant to subdivision (d) of Section 2150 of the Elections Code.

(IV) Completes the affidavit of voter registration with reasonable accommodations.

(2) If the court has made an order under Chapter 4 (commencing with Section 1870), the court investigator shall determine if the present condition of the conservatee is such that the terms of the order should be modified or the order revoked.

(3) Upon request of the court investigator, the conservator shall make available to the court investigator during the investigation for inspection and copying all books and records, including receipts and any expenditures, of the conservatorship.

(b)(1) The findings of the court investigator, including the facts upon which the findings are based, shall be certified in writing to the court not less than 15 days before the date of review. A copy of the report shall be mailed to the conservator and to the attorneys of record for the conservator and conservatee at the same time it is certified to the court. A copy of the report, modified as set forth in paragraph (2), also shall be mailed to the conservatee's spouse or registered domestic partner, the conservatee's relatives in the first degree, and if there are no such relatives, to the next closest relative, unless the court determines that the mailing will harm the conservatee.

(2) Confidential medical information and confidential information from the California Law Enforcement Telecommunications System shall be in a separate attachment to the report and shall not be provided in copies sent to the conservatee's spouse or registered domestic partner, the conservatee's relatives in the first degree, and if there are no such relatives, to the next closest relative.

(c) In the case of a limited conservatee, the court investigator shall recommend continuing or terminating the limited conservatorship.

(d) The court investigator may personally visit the conservator and other persons as may be necessary to determine if the * * * conservator is acting in the best interests of the conservatee.

(e) The report required by this section shall be confidential and shall be made available only to parties, persons described in subdivision (b), persons given notice of the petition who have requested the report or who have appeared in the proceeding, their attorneys, and the court. The court shall have discretion at any other time to release the report if it would serve the interests of the conservatee. The clerk of the court shall limit disclosure of the report exclusively to persons entitled to the report under this section.

(f) A superior court is not * * * required to perform any duties imposed pursuant to the amendments to this section enacted by Chapter 493 of the Statutes of 2006 until the Legislature makes an appropriation identified for this purpose. *(Stats.1990, c. 79 (A.B.759), § 14, operative July 1, 1991. Amended by Stats.1991, c. 82 (S.B.896), § 16, eff. June 30, 1991, operative July 1, 1991; Stats.2002, c. 784 (S.B.1316), § 580; Stats.2002, c. 1008 (A.B.3028), § 28; Stats.2006, c. 492 (S.B.1716), § 4; Stats.2006, c. 493 (A.B.1363), § 12.5, operative July 1, 2007; Stats.2007, c. 553 (A.B.1727), § 9; Stats. 2011, c. 10 (S.B.78), § 15, eff. March 24, 2011; Stats.2014, c. 591 (A.B.1311), § 7, eff. Jan. 1, 2015; Stats.2015, c. 736 (S.B.589), § 11, eff. Jan. 1, 2016; Stats.2016, c. 86 (S.B.1171), § 247, eff. Jan. 1, 2017.)*

Law Revision Commission Comments

1990 Enactment

Section 1851 continues Section 1851 of the repealed Probate Code without change. See also Section 1851.5 (assessment of estate for investigation expense). For background on the provisions of this part, see the Comment to this part under the part heading.

1991 Amendment

Section 1851 is amended to add subdivisions (d) and (e). These subdivisions were added to Section 1851 of the repealed Probate Code by 1990 Cal.Stat. ch. 1208. This amendment preserves the effect of that legislation. [20 Cal. L. Rev. Comm. Reports 1001 (1990)].

2002 Amendment

[By Stats.2002, c. 784 (S.B.1316)] [s]ubdivision (e) of Section 1851 is amended to reflect elimination of the county clerk's role as ex officio clerk of the superior court. See former Gov't Code § 26800 (county clerk acting as clerk of superior court). The powers, duties, and responsibilities formerly exercised by the county clerk as ex officio clerk of the court are delegated to the court administrative or executive officer, and the county clerk is relieved of those powers, duties, and responsibilities. See Gov't Code §§ 69840 (powers, duties, and responsibilities of clerk of court and deputy clerk of court), 71620 (trial court personnel). [32 Cal.L.Rev.Comm. Reports 524 (2002)].

Cross References

Affidavit of voter registration, see Elections Code §§ 2102, 2150 et seq., 3400 et seq.
Completion of affidavit of voter registration, report concerning capability of conservatee, see Elections Code § 2209.
Court investigator,
   Defined, see Probate Code § 1419.
   Qualifications, see Probate Code § 1454.
Disqualification from voting, see Elections Code § 2208.
Inspection of public records, exemptions from disclosure, "conservatee" to "conservatorship", see Government Code § 6276.12.
Termination of conservatorship, see Probate Code § 1860 et seq.
Waiver of court fees and costs, initial fee waiver, see Government Code § 68631.

§ 1851.1. Transfer of conservatorship to state; investigation and report; duties of investigator

(a) When a court issues an order provisionally granting a petition under Section 2002, the investigator appointed under Section 2002 shall promptly commence an investigation under this section.

(b) In conducting an investigation and preparing a report under this section, the court investigator shall do all of the following:

(1) Comply with the requirements of Section 1851.

(2) Conduct an interview of the conservator.

(3) Conduct an interview of the conservatee's spouse or registered domestic partner, if any.

(4) Inform the conservatee of the nature, purpose, and effect of the conservatorship.

(5) Inform the conservatee and all other persons entitled to notice under subdivision (b) of Section 2002 of the right to seek termination of the conservatorship.

(6) Determine whether the conservatee objects to the conservator or prefers another person to act as conservator.

(7) Inform the conservatee of the right to attend the hearing under subdivision (c).

(8) Determine whether it appears that the conservatee is unable to attend the hearing and, if able to attend, whether the conservatee is willing to attend the hearing.

(9) Inform the conservatee of the right to be represented by legal counsel if the conservatee so chooses, and to have legal counsel appointed by the court if the conservatee is unable to retain legal counsel.

(10) Determine whether the conservatee wishes to be represented by legal counsel and, if so, whether the conservatee has retained legal counsel and, if not, the name of an attorney the conservatee wishes to retain.

(11) If the conservatee has not retained legal counsel, determine whether the conservatee desires the court to appoint legal counsel.

(12) Determine whether the appointment of legal counsel would be helpful to the resolution of the matter or is necessary to protect the interests of the conservatee in any case where the conservatee does not plan to retain legal counsel and has not requested the appointment of legal counsel by the court.

(13) Consider each of the categories specified in paragraphs (1) to (5), inclusive, of subdivision (a) of Section 1821.

(14) Consider, to the extent practicable, whether the investigator believes the conservatee suffers from any of the mental function deficits listed in subdivision (a) of Section 811 that significantly impairs the conservatee's ability to understand and appreciate the consequences of the conservatee's actions in connection with any of the functions described in subdivision (a) or (b) of Section 1801 and identify the observations that support that belief.

(c) The court shall review the conservatorship as provided in Section 2002. The conservatee shall attend the hearing unless the conservatee's attendance is excused under Section 1825. The court may take appropriate action in response to the court investigator's report under this section.

(d) The court investigator's report under this section shall be confidential as provided in Section 1851.

(e) Except as provided in paragraph (2) of subdivision (a) of Section 1850, the court shall review the conservatorship again one year after the review conducted pursuant to subdivision (c), and annually thereafter, in the manner specified in Section 1850.

(f) The first time that the need for a conservatorship is challenged by any interested person or raised on the court's own motion after a transfer under Section 2002, whether in a review pursuant to this section or in a petition to terminate the conservatorship under Chapter 3 (commencing with Section 1860), the court shall presume that there is no need for a conservatorship. This presumption is rebuttable, but can only be overcome by clear and convincing evidence. The court shall make an express finding on whether continuation of the conservatorship is the least restrictive alternative needed for the protection of the conservatee.

(g) If a duty described in this section is the same as a duty imposed pursuant to the amendments to Sections 1826, 1850, 1851, 2250, 2253, and 2620 and the addition of Sections 2250.4 and 2250.6 enacted by Chapter 493 of the Statutes of 2006, and the addition of Section 1051 enacted by Chapter 492 of the Statutes of 2006, a superior court shall not be required to perform that duty until the Legislature makes an appropriation identified for this purpose. *(Added by Stats. 2014, c. 553 (S.B.940), § 18, eff. Jan. 1, 2015, operative Jan. 1, 2016.)*

Law Revision Commission Comments

2014 Addition

Section 1851.1 is added to provide guidance on the nature of the investigation and review that is required when a conservatorship is transferred to California from another state under the California Conservatorship Jurisdiction Act (Section 1980 *et seq.*). In conducting

a review under this section, the court investigator might be able to use some evidence or other resources from the proceeding that was transferred to California, particularly if the transferring court recently conducted a review of that proceeding.

The court investigator's fee for conducting an investigation under this section is to be paid in the same manner as if the conservatorship was originally established in California. See Section 1851.5 (assessment of conservatee for cost of conducting court investigation). [43 Cal.L.Rev.Comm. Reports 93 (2013)].

Cross References

Conservatorships, appealable orders, see Probate Code § 1301.5.

§ 1851.2. Coordination

Each court shall coordinate investigations with the filing of accountings, so that investigators may review accountings before visiting conservatees, if feasible. *(Added by Stats.2007, c. 553 (A.B.1727), § 10.)*

§ 1851.5. Court investigators; assessments

Each court shall assess each conservatee in the county for any investigation or review conducted by a court investigator with respect to that person. Subject to Section 68631 of the Government Code, the court may order reimbursement to the court for the amount of the assessment, unless the court finds that all or any part of the assessment would impose a hardship on conservatee or the conservatee's estate. There shall be a rebuttable presumption that the assessment would impose a hardship if the conservatee is receiving Medi–Cal benefits. *(Stats.1990, c. 79 (A.B.759), § 14, operative July 1, 1991. Amended by Stats.1991, c. 82 (S.B.896), § 18, eff. June 30, 1991, operative July 1, 1991; Stats.1996, c. 563 (S.B.392), § 9; Stats.2002, c. 1008 (A.B.3028), § 29; Stats.2014, c. 913 (A.B.2747), § 30.5, eff. Jan. 1, 2015.)*

Law Revision Commission Comments

1990 Enactment

Section 1851.5 restates Section 1851.5 of the repealed Probate Code without substantive change, except that subdivision (b) is revised to give the court discretion to order reimbursement from the estate and subdivision (c) is revised to substitute a reference to Government Code Sections 17561 and 17565 in place of the reference to Revenue and Taxation Code Sections 2231 and 2234. The Revenue and Taxation Code sections were repealed (1986 Cal.Stat. ch. 879) and were superseded by the Government Code sections. For background on the provisions of this part, see the Comment to this part under the part heading.

1991 Amendment

Section 1851.5 is amended to delete subdivision (a) and language in subdivision (b) relating to determination by the Controller of the statewide average cost per investigation or review by a court investigator. This requirement was deleted from Section 1851.5 of the repealed Probate Code by 1990 Cal.Stat. ch. 1208. This amendment preserves the effect of that legislation. [20 Cal.L.Rev. Comm. Reports 1001 (1990)].

Cross References

Medi–Cal Act, see Welfare and Institutions Code § 14000 et seq. Organization and government of courts, collection of fees and fines pursuant to this section, deposits, see Government Code § 68085.1.

§ 1852. Notification of counsel; representation of conservatee at hearing

If the conservatee wishes to petition the court for termination of the conservatorship or for removal of the existing conservator or for the making, modification, or revocation of a court order under Chapter 4 (commencing with Section 1870) or for restoration of the right to register to vote, or if, based on information contained in the court investigator's report or obtained from any other source, the court determines that a trial or hearing for termination of the conservatorship or removal of the existing conservator is in the best interests of the conservatee, the court shall notify the attorney of record for the conservatee, if any, or shall appoint the public defender or private counsel under Section 1471, to file the petition and represent the conservatee at the trial or hearing and, if such appointment is made, Section 1472 applies. *(Stats.1990, c. 79 (A.B.759), § 14, operative July 1, 1991.)*

Law Revision Commission Comments
1990 Enactment

Section 1852 continues Section 1852 of the repealed Probate Code without change. This section supplements subdivisions (a) and (b) of Section 1471. For general provisions, see Sections 1000–1004 (rules of practice), 1020–1023 (petitions and other papers), 1040–1050 (hearings and orders). As to the effect of final order, see Section 2103. For background on the provisions of this part, see the Comment to this part under the part heading. [20 Cal.L.Rev.Comm. Reports 1001 (1990)].

Cross References

Counsel, right to, see Cal. Const. Art. 1, § 15.
Guardians and conservators, removal or resignation, see Probate Code § 2650 et seq.
Removal of guardian or conservator, petition, see Probate Code § 2651.
Representation of persons not financially able to employ counsel, by public defender, see Government Code § 27706.
Restoration of right to register to vote, see Probate Code § 1865.
Termination of conservatorship, petition, see Probate Code § 1861.

§ 1853. Failure to locate conservatee; termination of conservatorship; discharge of conservator; petition to appoint new conservator

(a) If the court investigator is unable to locate the conservatee, the court shall order the court investigator to serve notice upon the conservator of the person, or upon the conservator of the estate if there is no conservator of the person, in the manner provided in Section 415.10 or 415.30 of the Code of Civil Procedure or in such other manner as is ordered by the court, to make the conservatee available for the purposes of Section 1851 to the court investigator within 15 days of the receipt of such notice or to show cause why the conservatorship should not be terminated.

(b) If the conservatee is not made available within the time prescribed, unless good cause is shown for not doing so, the court shall make such a finding and shall enter judgment terminating the conservatorship and, in case of a conservatorship of the estate, shall order the conservator to file an account and to surrender the estate to the person legally entitled thereto. At the hearing, or thereafter on further notice and hearing, the conservator may be discharged and the bond given by the conservator may be exonerated upon the settlement and approval of the conservator's final account by the court.

(c) Termination of the conservatorship under this section does not preclude institution of new proceedings for the appointment of a conservator. Nothing in this section limits the power of a court to appoint a temporary conservator under Chapter 3 (commencing with Section 2250) of Part 4. *(Stats.1990, c. 79 (A.B.759), § 14, operative July 1, 1991.)*

Law Revision Commission Comments
1990 Enactment

Section 1853 continues Section 1853 of the repealed Probate Code without substantive change. The conservatorship is to be terminated only if the conservator fails to show good cause for not making the conservatee available. What constitutes good cause depends on the circumstances. For example, good cause is shown (1) where it is established that the conservatee disappeared from his or her place of residence and a diligent search was made to find the conservatee or (2) where the conservatee is out of state to receive necessary medical treatment. Section 1853 provides for the manner of service and provides that the conservatee is to be made available to the court investigator for the purposes of Section 1851. Under Section 1853, the conservator of the person, if there is one, has the duty to make the conservatee available. If there is no conservator of the person, the duty falls on the conservator of the estate. For general provisions, see Sections 1000–1004 (rules of practice), 1020–1023 (petitions and other papers), 1040–1050 (hearings and orders). See also Section 2750 (order removing conservator an appealable order). As to the effect of final order, see Section 2103. For background on the provisions of this part, see the Comment to this part under the part heading. See also Report of Assembly Committee on Judiciary on Assembly Bills Nos. 261 and 167, reprinted in 15 Cal.L.Revision Comm'n Reports 1061, 1071 (1980). [20 Cal.L.Rev.Comm. Reports 1001 (1990)].

Cross References

Accounts on termination of conservatorship, see Probate Code § 2630 et seq.
Appointment to fill vacancy, see Probate Code § 2670.
Computation of time, see Code of Civil Procedure §§ 12 and 12a; Government Code § 6800 et seq.
Court investigator, defined, see Probate Code § 1419.
Notice,
  Mailing, see Probate Code § 1215 et seq.
  Posting, see Probate Code § 1230.
  Proof of giving notice, see Probate Code § 1260 et seq.
  Special notice, see Probate Code § 1250 et seq.
  This code, generally, see Probate Code § 1200 et seq.
  This division, generally, see Probate Code § 1460 et seq.
Representation of persons not financially able to employ counsel by public defender, see Government Code § 27706.
Service of process,
  Generally, see Code of Civil Procedure § 413.10 et seq.
  Mail, see Code of Civil Procedure §§ 415.30, 1012 et seq.
  Personal delivery, see Code of Civil Procedure § 415.10.
  Proof of service, see Code of Civil Procedure § 417.10 et seq.
  Publication, see Code of Civil Procedure § 415.50.
Temporary guardians and conservators, generally, see Probate Code § 2250 et seq.

§§ 1854 to 1859. Repealed by Stats.1979, c. 726, p. 2334, § 2, operative Jan. 1, 1981

Cross References

Application of old and new law, see Probate Code § 3.

§ 1860.   Death of conservatee or order of court; continuation of conservatorship of married minor upon marriage dissolution or nullity

(a) A conservatorship continues until terminated by the death of the conservatee or by order of the court.

(b) If a conservatorship is established for the person of a married minor, the conservatorship does not terminate if the marriage is dissolved or is adjudged a nullity.

(c) This section does not apply to limited conservatorships. *(Stats.1990, c. 79 (A.B.759), § 14, operative July 1, 1991.)*

Law Revision Commission Comments
1990 Enactment

Section 1860 continues Section 1860 of the repealed Probate Code without substantive change. As to limited conservatorships, see Section 1860.5.

Subdivision (b) provides that a conservatorship of the person does not terminate if the marriage of a minor is dissolved or adjudged a nullity. Although a conservatorship cannot be established under Section 1800.3 for a minor whose marriage has been adjudged a nullity (Section 1515 permits creation of a guardianship in such a case), subdivision (b) of Section 1860 permits a conservatorship of the person to continue if the minor's marriage is adjudged a nullity after the conservatorship is established. Subdivision (b) avoids the need to establish a guardianship for the person of a married minor whose marriage is adjudged a nullity and then to reestablish a conservatorship of the person when the minor reaches majority. Subdivision (b) makes no reference to a conservatorship of the estate, since guardianship is the appropriate protective proceeding for the estate of a minor, whether married or unmarried. See the Comment to Section 1515.

Death of the conservator merely terminates the relationship of conservator and conservatee, but does not terminate the conservatorship proceeding. The court retains jurisdiction of the conservatorship proceeding despite termination of the relationship of conservator and conservatee. See Section 2630. Cf. Estate of Mims, 202 Cal.App.2d 332, 20 Cal.Rptr. 667 (1962) (guardianship). See also Section 2467 (powers and duties after death of conservatee).

For background on the provisions of this part, see the Comment to this part under the part heading. [20 Cal.L.Rev.Comm. Reports 1001 (1990)].

Cross References

Allowance for, care of estate after conservatee's death, disbursements after termination of conservatorship, see Probate Code § 2623.
Disposition of assets after death of conservatee, see Probate Code § 2631.

Dissolution,
  Generally, see Family Code § 2300 et seq.
  Defined, see Probate Code § 36.
No guardian of person for married minor, see Probate Code § 1515.
Termination of conservatorship, probate rules, see California Rules of Court, Rule 7.1052.
Termination of proceeding upon,
  Exhaustion of estate, see Probate Code § 2626.
  Transfer of all assets to foreign guardian or conservator, see Probate Code § 2808.

§ 1860.5.   Limited conservatorship

(a) A limited conservatorship continues until the authority of the conservator is terminated by one of the following:

(1) The death of the limited conservator.

(2) The death of the limited conservatee.

(3) By an order appointing a conservator of the former limited conservatee.

(4) By an order of the court stating that the limited conservatorship is no longer necessary for the limited conservatee and terminating the limited conservatorship.

(b) A petition for the termination of a limited conservatorship may be filed by any of the following:

(1) The limited conservator.

(2) The limited conservatee.

(3) Any relative or friend of the limited conservatee.

(c) The petition shall state facts showing that the limited conservatorship is no longer required.

(d) The petition shall be set for hearing and notice thereof shall be given to the persons in the same manner as provided for a petition for the appointment of a limited conservator. The limited conservator in such case, if he or she is not the petitioner or has not joined in the petition, shall be served with a notice of the time and place of the hearing accompanied by a copy of the petition at least five days prior to the hearing. Such service shall be made in the same manner provided for in Section 415.10 or 415.30 of the Code of Civil Procedure or in such other manner as may be authorized by the court. If the limited conservator cannot, with reasonable diligence, be so served with notice, the court may dispense with notice.

(e) The limited conservator or any relative or friend of the limited conservatee may appear and oppose the petition. The court shall hear and determine the matter according to the laws and procedures relating to the trial of civil actions, including trial by jury if demanded. If it is determined that the limited conservatorship is no longer required, the limited conservatorship shall cease. If the petition alleges and if it is determined that the limited conservatee is able to properly care for himself or herself and for his or her property, the court shall make such finding and enter judgment accordingly. The limited conservator may at the hearing, or thereafter on further notice and hearing, be discharged and his or her bond exonerated upon the settlement and approval of the final account by the court. *(Stats.1990, c. 79 (A.B.759), § 14, operative July 1, 1991.)*

1990 Enactment

Section 1860.5 continues Section 1860.5 of the repealed Probate Code with the omission of some unnecessary provisions. The reference to the duty of the limited conservator to see to the custody and conservation of the estate pending delivery to person or representative of the limited conservatee's estate has been omitted as unnecessary in view of Section 2467 (care of estate pending delivery to personal representative). See also Sections 2630–2631 (accounts on termination of relationship). The requirement that the petition be verified has been omitted as unnecessary in view of Section 1021. The portion of the section relating to the revoking of specific powers and duties of the limited conservatorship has been omitted because the procedure provided in this chapter deals with termination of the conservatorship and the omitted portion is unnecessary in view of subdivisions (c) and (d) of Section 2351.5. As to the effect of final order, see Section 2103. For background on the provisions of this part, see the Comment to this part under the part heading. [20 Cal.L.Rev.Comm. Reports 1001 (1990)].

Cross References

Accounts, see Probate Code § 2620 et seq.
Bonds of guardians and conservators, see Probate Code § 2320 et seq.
Jury trial, see Cal. Const. Art. 1, § 16.
Notice,
  Mailing, see Probate Code § 1215 et seq.
  Posting, see Probate Code § 1230.
  Proof of giving notice, see Probate Code § 1260 et seq.
  Special notice, see Probate Code § 1250 et seq.
  This code, generally, see Probate Code § 1200 et seq.
  This division, generally, see Probate Code § 1460 et seq.
Powers and duties of limited conservator, see Probate Code § 2351.5.
Service of process,
  Generally, see Code of Civil Procedure § 413.10 et seq.
  Mail, see Code of Civil Procedure §§ 415.30, 1012 et seq.
  Personal delivery, see Code of Civil Procedure § 415.10.
  Proof of service, see Code of Civil Procedure § 417.10 et seq.
  Publication, see Code of Civil Procedure § 415.50.

§ 1861. Petition; persons authorized to file; contents

(a) A petition for the termination of the conservatorship may be filed by any of the following:

(1) The conservator.

(2) The conservatee.

(3) The spouse, or domestic partner, or any relative or friend of the conservatee or other interested person.

(b) The petition shall state facts showing that the conservatorship is no longer required. *(Stats.1990, c. 79 (A.B.759), § 14, operative July 1, 1991. Amended by Stats.2001, c. 893 (A.B.25), § 21.)*

1990 Enactment

Section 1861 continues Section 1861 of the repealed Probate Code without change. For general provisions relating to petitions and other papers, see Sections 1020–1023. For background on the provisions of this part, see the Comment to this part under the part heading. [20 Cal.L.Rev.Comm. Reports 1001 (1990)].

Cross References

Domestic partner, defined, see Probate Code § 37.
Interested person, defined, see Probate Code § 1424.

Persons who may petition where conservatee is an absentee, see Probate Code § 1864.

§ 1862. Notice of hearing

Notice of the hearing on the petition shall be given for the period and in the manner provided in Chapter 3 (commencing with Section 1460) of Part 1. *(Stats.1990, c. 79 (A.B.759), § 14, operative July 1, 1991.)*

1990 Enactment

Section 1862 continues Section 1862 of the repealed Probate Code without change. For general provisions relating to notice of hearing, see Sections 1200–1221, 1460–1469. See also Sections 1260–1265 (proof of giving notice), 2700–2702 (notice to persons who request special notice). For background on the provisions of this part, see the Comment to this part under the part heading. [20 Cal.L.Rev. Comm. Reports 1001 (1990)].

Cross References

Notice to,
  Director of State Hospitals or Director of Developmental Services, see Probate Code § 1461.
  Persons requesting special notice, see Probate Code § 2700 et seq.
Service by mail, completion, see Probate Code § 1467.

§ 1863. Hearing and judgment

(a) The court shall hear and determine the matter according to the law and procedure relating to the trial of civil actions, including trial by jury if demanded by the conservatee. The conservator, the conservatee, or the spouse, or domestic partner, or any relative or friend of the conservatee or other interested person may appear and support or oppose the petition.

(b) If the court determines that the conservatorship is no longer required or that grounds for establishment of a conservatorship of the person or estate, or both, no longer exist, the court shall make this finding and shall enter judgment terminating the conservatorship accordingly.

(c) At the hearing, or thereafter on further notice and hearing, the conservator may be discharged and the bond given by the conservator may be exonerated upon the settlement and approval of the conservator's final account by the court.

(d) Termination of conservatorship does not preclude a new proceeding for appointment of a conservator on the same or other grounds. *(Stats.1990, c. 79 (A.B.759), § 14, operative July 1, 1991. Amended by Stats.2000, c. 17 (A.B. 1491), § 4.4; Stats.2001, c. 893 (A.B.25), § 22.)*

1990 Enactment

Section 1863 continues Section 1863 of the repealed Probate Code without substantive change. For general provisions, see Sections 1000–1004 (rules of practice), 1020–1023 (petitions and other papers), 1040–1050 (hearings and orders). As to the effect of final order, see Section 2103. For background on the provisions of this part, see the Comment to this part under the part heading. [20 Cal.L.Rev.Comm. Reports 1001 (1990)].

Cross References

Bonds of conservators, see Probate Code § 2320 et seq.

Domestic partner, defined, see Probate Code § 37.
Establishment of conservatorship, see Probate Code § 1820 et seq.
Interested person, defined, see Probate Code § 1424.
Jurisdiction of court after termination of conservatorship, see Probate Code § 2630.
Termination of court order affecting legal capacity, see Probate Code § 1896.

§ 1864. Conservatorship of absentee; petition; filing; order

(a) In the case of the conservatorship of an absentee as defined in Section 1403, the petition to terminate the conservatorship may also be filed by any officer or agency of this state or of the United States or the authorized delegate thereof.

(b) If the petition states and the court determines that the absentee has returned to the controllable jurisdiction of the military department or civilian department or agency concerned, or is deceased, as determined under 37 United States Code, Section 556, or 5 United States Code, Section 5566, as the case may be, the court shall order the conservatorship terminated. An official written report or record of such military department or civilian department or agency that the absentee has returned to such controllable jurisdiction or is deceased shall be received as evidence of such fact. *(Stats. 1990, c. 79 (A.B.759), § 14, operative July 1, 1991.)*

Law Revision Commission Comments

1990 Enactment

Section 1864 continues Section 1864 of the repealed Probate Code without change. For general provisions, see Sections 1000–1004 (rules of practice), 1020–1023 (petitions and other papers), 1040–1050 (hearings and orders). As to the effect of final order, see Section 2103. For background on the provisions of this part, see the Comment to this part under the part heading. [20 Cal.L.Rev.Comm. Reports 1001 (1990)].

Cross References

Newspapers, publications and official advertising, see Government Code § 6000 et seq.
Official records and other official writings, see Evidence Code § 1280 et seq.
Record by federal employee as evidence, see Evidence Code § 1283.

§ 1865. Restoration of right to register to vote; notice to county elections official

If the conservatee has been disqualified from voting pursuant to Section 2208 or 2209 of the Elections Code, upon termination of the conservatorship, the court shall notify the county elections official of the county of residence of the former conservatee that the former conservatee's right to register to vote is restored. *(Stats.1990, c. 79 (A.B.759), § 14, operative July 1, 1991. Amended by Stats.1994, c. 923 (S.B.1546), § 160; Stats.2002, c. 221 (S.B.1019), § 80.)*

Law Revision Commission Comments

1990 Enactment

Section 1865 continues Section 1865 of the repealed Probate Code without substantive change. For background on the provisions of this part, see the Comment to this part under the part heading. [20 Cal.L.Rev.Comm. Reports 1001 (1990)].

Cross References

Disqualification from voting, see Probate Code § 1910.

CHAPTER 4. LEGAL CAPACITY OF CONSERVATEE

Cross References

Modification or revocation of court order, petition by conservatee, periodic review of conservatorship, see Probate Code § 1852.
Periodic review of conservatorship, court investigator's findings, modification or revocation of order, see Probate Code § 1851.
Request for special notice, see Probate Code § 2700.

ARTICLE 1. CAPACITY TO BIND OR OBLIGATE CONSERVATORSHIP ESTATE

Cross References

Application of old and new law, see Probate Code § 3.

§ 1870. Transaction

As used in this article, unless the context otherwise requires, "transaction" includes, but is not limited to, making a contract, sale, transfer, or conveyance, incurring a debt or encumbering property, making a gift, delegating a power, and waiving a right. *(Stats.1990, c. 79 (A.B.759), § 14, operative July 1, 1991.)*

Law Revision Commission Comments

1990 Enactment

Section 1870 continues Section 1870 of the repealed Probate Code without change. The right to make a will may not be limited under this article. Section 1871(c). As to other rights not denied to the conservatee, see Section 1871. For background on the provisions of this part, see the Comment to this part under the part heading. [20 Cal.L.Rev.Comm. Reports 1001 (1990)].

Cross References

Transaction, provisions common to guardianships and conservators, see Probate Code § 2111.

§ 1871. Rights not limited by this article

Nothing in this article shall be construed to deny a conservatee any of the following:

(a) The right to control an allowance provided under Section 2421.

(b) The right to control wages or salary to the extent provided in Section 2601.

(c) The right to make a will.

(d) The right to enter into transactions to the extent reasonable to provide the necessaries of life to the conservatee and the spouse and minor children of the conservatee and to provide the basic living expenses, as defined in Section 297 of the Family Code, to the domestic partner of the conservatee. *(Stats.1990, c. 79 (A.B.759), § 14, operative July 1, 1991. Amended by Stats.2001, c. 893 (A.B.25), § 23.)*

Law Revision Commission Comments

1990 Enactment

Section 1871 continues Section 1871 of the repealed Probate Code without change. This section lists certain rights of the conservatee that are not affected by Section 1872.

Subdivision (a) recognizes that the conservatee has sole control of an allowance provided under Section 2421. Section 2421(c).

Subdivision (b) recognizes that wages or salary of the conservatee are subject to the conservatee's control unless the court otherwise orders. Section 2601.

Subdivision (c) codifies Estate of Powers, 81 Cal.App.2d 480, 184 P.2d 319 (1947). Appointment of a conservator is not a determination that the conservatee lacks testamentary capacity. Testamentary capacity is determined by a different standard, which depends on soundness of mind. Section 6100.

Subdivision (d) makes clear that this article does not limit the right of the conservatee to obtain (for reasonable value) necessaries of life for the conservatee and the conservatee's spouse and minor children. The subdivision is consistent with the requirement that the conservator must pay debts incurred by the conservatee during the conservatorship for necessaries of life for the conservatee and the conservatee's spouse and minor children, to the extent the debt is reasonable. Section 2430(a)(2). See also Civil Code § 38 ("person entirely without understanding" is liable for "the reasonable value of things furnished to him necessary for his support or the support of his family").

For background on the provisions of this part, see the Comment to this part under the part heading. See also Report of Assembly Committee on Judiciary on Assembly Bills Nos. 261 and 167, reprinted in 15 Cal.L.Revision Comm'n Reports 1061, 1071–72 (1980); Tentative Recommendation Relating to Wills and Intestate Succession, 16 Cal.L.Revision Comm'n Reports 2301, 2496–97 (1982). [20 Cal.L.Rev.Comm. Reports 1001 (1990)].

Cross References

Domestic partner, defined, see Probate Code § 37.
Judicial determination of incapacity, conservatorship, see Civil Code § 40.

§ 1872. Effect of conservatorship or limited conservatorship

(a) Except as otherwise provided in this article, the appointment of a conservator of the estate is an adjudication that the conservatee lacks the legal capacity to enter into or make any transaction that binds or obligates the conservatorship estate.

(b) Except as otherwise provided in the order of the court appointing a limited conservator, the appointment does not limit the legal capacity of the limited conservatee to enter into transactions or types of transactions. *(Stats.1990, c. 79 (A.B.759), § 14, operative July 1, 1991.)*

Law Revision Commission Comments

1990 Enactment

Section 1872 continues Section 1872 of the repealed Probate Code with the omission of subdivision (b) which was inconsistent with and unnecessary in view of subdivision (c), now subdivision (b). See also Civil Code § 40. Section 1872 governs any type of transaction including, but not limited to, debts, gifts, sales, encumbrances, conveyances, delegations of powers, and waivers of rights. See Section 1870 (defining "transaction"). Making a will is not covered by Section 1872. See Section 1871(c). As to contracts and debts incurred for necessaries, see Section 1871(d). As to capacity of a conservatee concerning community property, see Section 3012. As to the effect of final order, see Section 2103. For background on the provisions of this part, see the Comment to this part under the part heading.

Other consequences of appointing a conservator are that (1) court proceedings must be conducted through the conservator or a guardian ad litem (Code Civ.Proc. §§ 372, 416.70; see also Prob. Code § 1003), (2) the office of trustee held by a conservatee is vacated (Prob.Code § 15643(e)), and (3) many rights may be exercised by the conservator rather than by the conservatee, such as (i) the right to vote shares of stock (Corp.Code § 702), and (ii) the right to disclaim testamentary and other interests (Prob.Code § 276). This listing is illustrative and not exclusive.

The limitation of Section 1872 does not apply to the extent that the court has so ordered under Section 1873. Section 1873 gives the court flexibility to make an order authorizing the conservatee to enter into such transactions as may be appropriate for the particular conservatee and conservatorship estate.

For background on the provisions of this part, see the Comment to this part under the part heading. See also Report of Assembly Committee on Judiciary on Assembly Bills Nos. 261 and 167, reprinted in 15 Cal.L.Revision Comm'n Reports 1061, 1072–73 (1980). [20 Cal.L.Rev.Comm. Reports 1001 (1990)].

Cross References

Legal capacity with respect to community property, see Probate Code § 3012.

§ 1873. Court order; authority of conservatee; limitations and conditions; termination; continuation

(a) In the order appointing the conservator or upon a petition filed under Section 1874, the court may, by order, authorize the conservatee, subject to Section 1876, to enter into transactions or types of transactions as may be appropriate in the circumstances of the particular conservatee and conservatorship estate. The court, by order, may modify the legal capacity a conservatee would otherwise have under Section 1872 by broadening or restricting the power of the conservatee to enter into transactions or types of transactions as may be appropriate in the circumstances of the particular conservatee and conservatorship estate.

(b) In an order made under this section, the court may include limitations or conditions on the exercise of the authority granted to the conservatee as the court determines to be appropriate including, but not limited to, the following:

(1) A requirement that for specific types of transactions or for all transactions authorized by the order, the conservatee obtain prior approval of the transaction by the court or conservator before exercising the authority granted by the order.

(2) A provision that the conservator has the right to avoid any transaction made by the conservatee pursuant to the

authority of the order if the transaction is not one into which a reasonably prudent person might enter.

(c) The court, in its discretion, may provide in the order that, unless extended by subsequent order of the court, the order or specific provisions of the order terminate at a time specified in the order.

(d) An order under this section continues in effect until the earliest of the following times:

(1) The time specified in the order, if any.

(2) The time the order is modified or revoked.

(3) The time the conservatorship of the estate is terminated.

(e) An order under this section may be modified or revoked upon petition filed by the conservator, conservatee, the spouse or domestic partner of the conservatee, or any relative or friend of the conservatee, or any interested person. Notice of the hearing on the petition shall be given for the period and in the manner provided in Chapter 3 (commencing with Section 1460) of Part 1. *(Stats.1990, c. 79 (A.B.759), § 14, operative July 1, 1991. Amended by Stats.2001, c. 893 (A.B.25), § 24.)*

Law Revision Commission Comments
1990 Enactment

Section 1873 continues Section 1873 of the repealed Probate Code without change. This section permits the court to give the conservatee the right to enter into transactions affecting the conservatorship estate which, but for the order, the conservatee would not have under Section 1872. The court might, for example, permit the conservatee to enter into specified types of transactions or transactions not exceeding specified amounts (such as contracts not in excess of $500). Compare Welf. & Inst. Code § 5357 (similar court authority in Lanterman–Petris–Short Act conservatorships). See also Section 1876 (conservatee's transactions subject to general principles of law).

Any rights given to the conservatee under Section 1873 do not affect powers and duties of the conservator, other than the duty to carry out a transaction validly executed by the conservatee. See, e.g., Section 2430. See also Section 2404 (court order for payment of debt, expense, or charge lawfully due and payable). The conservator has the management and control of the conservatorship estate, including the duty to marshal, take possession of, and inventory the conservatee's assets. See Section 2401 and the Comment thereto. A person seeking to enforce a transaction under Section 1873 will ordinarily seek compliance by the conservator, who decides in the first instance whether the transaction satisfies the requirements of this section. The conservator, conservatee, or third person may obtain a court determination and instructions to the conservator if necessary. Section 2403.

In determining whether a transaction is one "into which a reasonably prudent person might enter" under paragraph (2) of subdivision (b), the conservator and the court should consider all the circumstances of the conservatee and conservatorship estate. One important circumstance to be considered is whether the transaction might impair the ability to provide for support, maintenance, and education of the conservatee and of persons the conservatee is legally obligated to support, maintain, or educate. See Section 2430(b) (payment of debts).

For general provisions, see Sections 1000–1004 (rules of practice), 1020–1023 (petitions and other papers), 1040–1050 (hearings and orders). For general provisions relating to notice of hearing, see Sections 1200–1221, 1460–1469. See also Sections 1260–1265 (proof of giving notice), 2700–2702 (notice to persons who request special notice). See also Section 2750 (order affecting legal capacity of

conservatee pursuant to this chapter an appealable order). As to the effect of final order, see Section 2103. For background on the provisions of this part, see the Comment to this part under the part heading. See also Report of Assembly Committee on Judiciary on Assembly Bills Nos. 261 and 167, reprinted in 15 Cal.L.Revision Comm'n Reports 1061, 1073–74 (1980). [20 Cal.L.Rev.Comm. Reports 1001 (1990)].

Cross References
Definitions,
  Interested person, see Probate Code § 1424.
  Transaction, see Probate Code § 1870.
Domestic partner, defined, see Probate Code § 37.
Judicial determination of incapacity, conservatorship, see Civil Code § 40.
Termination, see Probate Code § 1860 et seq.

§ 1874. Petition for order; person authorized to file

(a) After a conservator has been appointed, a petition requesting an order under Section 1873 may be filed by any of the following:

(1) The conservator.

(2) The conservatee.

(3) The spouse, domestic partner, or any relative or friend of the conservatee.

(b) Notice of the hearing on the petition shall be given for the period and in the manner provided in Chapter 3 (commencing with Section 1460) of Part 1. *(Stats.1990, c. 79 (A.B.759), § 14, operative July 1, 1991. Amended by Stats. 2001, c. 893 (A.B.25), § 25.)*

Law Revision Commission Comments
1990 Enactment

Section 1874 continues Section 1874 of the repealed Probate Code without change. For general provisions relating to petitions and other papers, see Sections 1020–1023. For general provisions relating to notice of hearing, see Sections 1200–1221, 1460–1469. See also Sections 1260–1265 (proof of giving notice), 2700–2702 (notice to persons who request special notice). For background on the provisions of this part, see the Comment to this part under the part heading. See also Report of Assembly Committee on Judiciary on Assembly Bills Nos. 261 and 167, reprinted in 15 Cal.L.Revision Comm'n Reports 1061, 1074 (1980). [20 Cal.L.Rev.Comm. Reports 1001 (1990)].

Cross References
Domestic partner, defined, see Probate Code § 37.
Judicial determination of incapacity, conservatorship, see Civil Code § 40.

§ 1875. Transactions affecting real property; persons acting in good faith

A transaction that affects real property of the conservatorship estate, entered into by a person acting in good faith and for a valuable consideration and without knowledge of the establishment of the conservatorship, is not affected by any provision of this article or any order made under this article unless a notice of the establishment of the conservatorship or temporary conservatorship has been recorded prior to the transaction in the county in which the property is located. *(Stats.1990, c. 79 (A.B.759), § 14, operative July 1, 1991. Amended by Stats.1991, c. 82 (S.B.896), § 20, eff. June 30, 1991, operative July 1, 1991.)*

Law Revision Commission Comments

1990 Enactment

Section 1875 revises Section 1875 of the repealed Probate Code to extend to any person who enters into a transaction in good faith and for a valuable consideration, not only purchasers and encumbrancers. The purpose of this section is to protect innocent third parties who do not have notice of the conservatorship and the resulting incapacity of the conservatee. Nothing in Section 1875 validates a transaction that is invalid under Section 38 of the Civil Code, or prevents rescission of a transaction under Section 39 of the Civil Code, if the conservatee would lack legal capacity for the transaction absent the establishment of the conservatorship. See Section 1876 and the Comment thereto. The sole effect of Section 1875 is to make the limitations on the conservatee's capacity under Section 1872 or under an order made under Section 1873 inapplicable to the transaction if notice of establishment of the conservatorship has not been recorded. For a comparable provision applicable to community property, see Section 3074. For general provisions relating to hearings and orders, see Sections 1040–1050. For background on the provisions of this part, see the Comment to this part under the part heading. See also *Report of Assembly Committee on Judiciary on Assembly Bills Nos. 261 and 167*, reprinted in 15 Cal. L. Revision Comm'n Reports 1061, 1074 (1980).

1991 Amendment

Section 1875 is amended to add a reference to temporary conservatorship. This reference was added to Section 1875 of the repealed Probate Code by 1990 Cal.Stat. ch. 1208. This amendment preserves the effect of that legislation. [20 Cal. Law Rev. Comm. Reports 1001 (1990)].

Cross References

Comparable provision, real property, see Probate Code § 3074.
Judicial determination of incapacity, conservatorship, see Civil Code § 40.
Mode of recording, see Civil Code § 1169 et seq.
Real property, defined, see Probate Code § 68.

§ 1876. Applicability of other law

The provisions of this article relating to the legal capacity of a conservatee to bind or obligate the conservatorship estate, and the provisions of any order of the court broadening such capacity, do not displace but are supplemented by general principles of law and equity relating to transactions including, but not limited to, capacity to contract, joinder or consent requirements, estoppel, fraud, misrepresentation, duress, coercion, mistake, or other validating or invalidating cause. *(Stats.1990, c. 79 (A.B.759), § 14, operative July 1, 1991.)*

Law Revision Commission Comments

1990 Enactment

Section 1876 continues Section 1876 of the repealed Probate Code without change. The purpose of this section is to ensure that the provisions of this article relating to the power of the conservatee to affect the conservatorship estate are not construed as the exclusive rules by which the validity of any transaction entered into by the conservatee is measured. For a comparable provision, see Com. Code § 1103 (supplementary general principles of law applicable). For example, the power of the conservatee to bind the estate by a transaction authorized by the court under Section 1873 is subject to the limitation that the transaction may still be void or voidable because the conservatee lacks contractual capacity under Civil Code Section 38 or 39. For background on the provisions of this part, see the Comment to this part under the part heading. See also Report

of Assembly Committee on Judiciary on Assembly Bills Nos. 261 and 167, reprinted in 15 Cal.L.Revision Comm'n Reports 1061, 1074 (1980). [20 Cal.L.Rev.Comm. Reports 1001 (1990)].

Cross References

Consent, see Civil Code § 1565 et seq.
Contracts, generally, see Civil Code § 1549 et seq.
Contracts, fraud, see Civil Code §§ 1571 to 1574.
Duress, see Civil Code § 1569.
Judicial determination of incapacity, conservatorship, see Civil Code § 40.
Mistake, see Civil Code § 1576 et seq.
Persons capable of contracting, see Civil Code §§ 1556, 1557.

ARTICLE 2. CAPACITY TO GIVE INFORMED CONSENT FOR MEDICAL TREATMENT

Section

Cross References

Application of old and new law, see Probate Code § 3.

§ 1880. Determination by court; order

If the court determines that there is no form of medical treatment for which the conservatee has the capacity to give an informed consent, the court shall (1) adjudge that the conservatee lacks the capacity to give informed consent for medical treatment and (2) by order give the conservator of the person the powers specified in Section 2355. If an order is made under this section, the letters shall include a statement that the conservator has the powers specified in Section 2355. *(Stats.1990, c. 79 (A.B.759), § 14, operative July 1, 1991.)*

Law Revision Commission Comments

1990 Enactment

Section 1880 continues Section 1880 of the repealed Probate Code without substantive change. The word "letters" has been substituted for the phrase "letters of conservatorship." See Section 52(b) (defining "letters").

Section 1880 applies only where the court determines that the conservatee lacks capacity to give informed consent to any form of medical treatment. See also Section 2355 and the Comment thereto. If the conservatee has capacity to give informed consent to some forms of medical treatment but lacks capacity to give informed consent to other forms of medical treatment, an order under Section 1880 is not appropriate. In such a case, if medical treatment is required and the conservatee lacks capacity to give informed consent to that treatment, a court order authorizing the treatment must be obtained under Section 2357. For general provisions, see Sections 1000–1004 (rules of practice), 1020–1023 (petitions and other papers), 1040–1050 (hearings and orders). See also Section 2750 (order affecting the legal capacity of conservatee pursuant to this chapter an appealable order). As to the effect of final order, see Section 2103. For background on the provisions of this part, see the Comment to this part under the part heading. [20 Cal.L.Rev.Comm. Reports 1001 (1990)].

Court ordered medical treatment, see Probate Code § 2357.
Duration of order, see Probate Code § 1897.
Legal and civil rights of persons involuntarily detained under Lanterman–Petris–Short Act, see Welfare and Institutions Code § 5325 et seq.
Letters, defined, see Probate Code § 52.
Letters of conservatorship, see Probate Code § 2310 et seq.
Modification or revocation of order, see Probate Code § 1898.
Petition for order, modification or revocation of order, see Probate Code § 1891.
Termination of order, see Probate Code § 1896.

§ 1881. Inability of conservatee to give informed medical consent; judicial determination; factors

(a) A conservatee shall be deemed unable to give informed consent to any form of medical treatment pursuant to Section 1880 if, for all medical treatments, the conservatee is unable to respond knowingly and intelligently to queries about medical treatment or is unable to participate in a treatment decision by means of a rational thought process.

(b) In order for a court to determine that a conservatee is unable to respond knowingly and intelligently to queries about his or her medical treatment or is unable to participate in treatment decisions by means of a rational thought process, a court shall do both of the following:

(1) Determine that, for all medical treatments, the conservatee is unable to understand at least one of the following items of minimum basic medical treatment information:

(A) The nature and seriousness of any illness, disorder, or defect that the conservatee has or may develop.

(B) The nature of any medical treatment that is being or may be recommended by the conservatee's health care providers.

(C) The probable degree and duration of any benefits and risks of any medical intervention that is being or may be recommended by the conservatee's health care providers, and the consequences of lack of treatment.

(D) The nature, risks, and benefits of any reasonable alternatives.

(2) Determine that one or more of the mental functions of the conservatee described in subdivision (a) of Section 811 is impaired and that there is a link between the deficit or deficits and the conservatee's inability to give informed consent.

(c) A deficit in the mental functions listed in subdivision (a) of Section 811 may be considered only if the deficit by itself, or in combination with one or more other mental function deficits, significantly impairs the conservatee's ability to understand the consequences of his or her decisions regarding medical care.

(d) In determining whether a conservatee's mental functioning is so severely impaired that the conservatee lacks the capacity to give informed consent to any form of medical

treatment, the court may take into consideration the frequency, severity, and duration of periods of impairment.

(e) In the interest of minimizing unnecessary expense to the parties to a proceeding, paragraph (2) of subdivision (b) shall not apply to a petition pursuant to Section 1880 wherein the conservatee, after notice by the court of his or her right to object which, at least, shall include an interview by a court investigator pursuant to Section 1826 prior to the hearing on the petition, does not object to the proposed finding of incapacity, or waives any objections. *(Added by Stats.1995, c. 842 (S.B.730), § 8. Amended by Stats.1996, c. 178 (S.B.1650), § 8.)*

Health care decisions, generally, see Probate Code § 4600 et seq.

§ 1890. Order; inclusion in order appointing conservator; limited conservatee; physician's declaration

(a) An order of the court under Section 1880 may be included in the order of appointment of the conservator if the order was requested in the petition for the appointment of the conservator or the transfer petition under Section 2002 or, except in the case of a limited conservator, may be made subsequently upon a petition made, noticed, and heard by the court in the manner provided in this article.

(b) In the case of a petition filed under this chapter requesting that the court make an order under this chapter or that the court modify or revoke an order made under this chapter, when the order applies to a limited conservatee, the order may only be made upon a petition made, noticed, and heard by the court in the manner provided by Article 3 (commencing with Section 1820) of Chapter 1.

(c) No court order under Section 1880, whether issued as part of an order granting the original petition for appointment of a conservator or issued subsequent thereto, may be granted unless supported by a declaration, filed at or before the hearing on the request, executed by a licensed physician, or a licensed psychologist within the scope of his or her licensure, and stating that the proposed conservatee or the conservatee, as the case may be, lacks the capacity to give an informed consent for any form of medical treatment and the reasons therefor. Nothing in this section shall be construed to expand the scope of practice of psychologists as set forth in the Business and Professions Code. *(Stats.1990, c. 79 (A.B.759), § 14, operative July 1, 1991. Amended by Stats. 1992, c. 572 (S.B.1455), § 4; Stats.1996, c. 563 (S.B.392), § 10; Stats.1997, c. 724 (A.B.1172), § 10; Stats.2014, c. 553 (S.B.940), § 19, eff. Jan. 1, 2015, operative Jan. 1, 2016.)*

Law Revision Commission Comments
1990 Enactment

Section 1890 continues Section 1890 of the repealed Probate Code without change.

Section 1890 permits an order under Section 1880 to be made when the conservatorship is established or later. There is no right to jury trial in a proceeding under this article. See Section 1452. For general provisions, see Sections 1000–1004 (rules of practice), 1020–1023 (petitions and other papers), 1040–1050 (hearings and orders). For general provisions relating to notice of hearing, see Sections 1200–1221, 1460–1469. See also Sections 1260–1265 (proof of giving notice), 2700–2702 (notice to persons who request special notice). As to the effect of final order, see Section 2103. For background on the provisions of this part, see the Comment to this part under the part heading. See also Report of Assembly Committee on Judiciary on Assembly Bills Nos. 261 and 167, reprinted in 15 Cal.L.Revision Comm'n Reports 1061, 1075 (1980). [20 Cal.L.Rev.Comm. Reports 1001 (1990)].

2014 Amendment

Subdivision (a) of Section 1890 is amended to reflect the enactment of the California Conservatorship Jurisdiction Act (Section 1980 *et seq.*). [43 Cal.L.Rev.Comm. Reports 93 (2013)].

§ 1891. Petition for order; modification or revocation; contents

(a) A petition may be filed under this article requesting that the court make an order under Section 1880 or that the court modify or revoke an order made under Section 1880. The petition shall state facts showing that the order requested is appropriate.

(b) The petition may be filed by any of the following:

(1) The conservator.

(2) The conservatee.

(3) The spouse, domestic partner, or any relative or friend of the conservatee.

(c) The petition shall set forth, so far as they are known to the petitioner, the names and addresses of the spouse or domestic partner and of the relatives of the conservatee within the second degree. *(Stats.1990, c. 79 (A.B.759), § 14, operative July 1, 1991. Amended by Stats.2001, c. 893 (A.B.25), § 26.)*

Law Revision Commission Comments
1990 Enactment

Section 1891 continues Section 1891 of the repealed Probate Code without change. Sections 1891 to 1896 adapt the procedure for appointment of a conservator to the situation where an order affecting the capacity of the conservatee to give informed consent to medical treatment is sought apart from appointment of a conservator. Sections 1891–1896 do not, however, grant the right to a jury trial on the issue. See Section 1452. For general provisions relating to petitions and other papers, see Sections 1020–1023. For background on the provisions of this part, see the Comment to this part under the part heading. See also Report of Assembly Committee on Judiciary on Assembly Bills Nos. 261 and 167, reprinted in 15 Cal.L.Revision Comm'n Reports 1061, 1075 (1980). [20 Cal.L.Rev. Comm. Reports 1001 (1990)].

Cross References
Domestic partner, defined, see Probate Code § 37.

§ 1892. Notice of hearing

Notice of the hearing on the petition shall be given for the period and in the manner provided in Chapter 3 (commencing with Section 1460) of Part 1. *(Stats.1990, c. 79 (A.B.759), § 14, operative July 1, 1991.)*

Law Revision Commission Comments
1990 Enactment

Section 1892 continues Section 1892 of the repealed Probate Code without change. For general provisions relating to notice of hearing, see Sections 1200–1221, 1460–1469. See also Sections 1260–1265 (proof of giving notice), 2700–2702 (notice to persons who request special notice). For background on the provisions of this part, see

the Comment to this part under the part heading. See also Recommendation Relating to Notice in Guardianship and Conservatorship Proceedings, 18 Cal.L.Revision Comm'n Reports 1793, 1802–03 (1985). [20 Cal.L.Rev.Comm. Reports 1001 (1990)].

Cross References
Mailing, completion, see Probate Code § 1467.

§ 1893. Attendance of conservatee at hearing

The conservatee shall be produced at the hearing except in the following cases:

(a) Where the conservatee is out of state when served and is not the petitioner.

(b) Where the conservatee is unable to attend the hearing by reason of medical inability established (1) by the affidavit or certificate of a licensed medical practitioner or (2) if the conservatee is an adherent of a religion whose tenets and practices call for reliance on prayer alone for healing and is under treatment by an accredited practitioner of that religion, by the affidavit of the practitioner. The affidavit or certificate is evidence only of the conservatee's inability to attend the hearing and shall not be considered in determining the issue of the legal capacity of the conservatee. Emotional or psychological instability is not good cause for the absence of the conservatee from the hearing unless, by reason of such instability, attendance at the hearing is likely to cause serious and immediate physiological damage to the conservatee.

(c) Where the court investigator has reported to the court that the conservatee has expressly communicated that the conservatee (1) is not willing to attend the hearing and (2) does not wish to contest the petition, and the court makes an order that the conservatee need not attend the hearing. *(Stats.1990, c. 79 (A.B.759), § 14, operative July 1, 1991.)*

Law Revision Commission Comments
1990 Enactment

Section 1893 continues Section 1893 of the repealed Probate Code without change. For background on the provisions of this part, see the Comment to this part under the part heading. [20 Cal.L.Rev. Comm. Reports 1001 (1990)].

Cross References
Affidavits, see Code of Civil Procedure §§ 2003, 2009 et seq.
Capacity determinations, generally, see Probate Code § 3200 et seq.
Court investigator, see Probate Code §§ 1419, 1454.
Information given to conservatee prior to granting petition, see Probate Code § 1895.

§ 1894. Court investigator; duties; report

If the petition alleges that the conservatee is not willing to attend the hearing or upon receipt of an affidavit or certificate attesting to the medical inability of the conservatee to attend the hearing, the court investigator shall do all of the following:

(a) Interview the conservatee personally.

(b) Inform the conservatee of the contents of the petition, of the nature, purpose, and effect of the proceeding, and of the right of the conservatee to oppose the petition, attend the hearing, and be represented by legal counsel.

(c) Determine whether it appears that the conservatee is unable to attend the hearing and, if able to attend, whether the conservatee is willing to attend the hearing.

(d) Determine whether the conservatee wishes to contest the petition.

(e) Determine whether the conservatee wishes to be represented by legal counsel and, if so, whether the conservatee has retained legal counsel and, if not, the name of an attorney the conservatee wishes to retain.

(f) If the conservatee has not retained counsel, determine whether the conservatee desires the court to appoint legal counsel.

(g) Determine whether the appointment of legal counsel would be helpful to the resolution of the matter or is necessary to protect the interests of the conservatee in any case where the conservatee does not plan to retain legal counsel and has not requested the court to appoint legal counsel.

(h) Report to the court in writing, at least five days before the hearing, concerning all of the foregoing, including the conservatee's express communications concerning both (1) representation by legal counsel and (2) whether the conservatee is not willing to attend the hearing and does not wish to contest the petition. *(Stats.1990, c. 79 (A.B.759), § 14, operative July 1, 1991.)*

Law Revision Commission Comments

1990 Enactment

Section 1894 continues Section 1894 of the repealed Probate Code without change. For background on the provisions of this part, see the Comment to this part under the part heading. [20 Cal.L.Rev. Comm. Reports 1001 (1990)].

Cross References

Court investigator, see Probate Code §§ 1419, 1454.

§ 1895. Hearing, appearances; information to conservatee

(a) The conservatee, the spouse, the domestic partner, any relative, or any friend of the conservatee, the conservator, or any other interested person may appear at the hearing to support or oppose the petition.

(b) Except where the conservatee is absent from the hearing and is not required to attend the hearing under the provisions of Section 1893 and any showing required by Section 1893 has been made, the court shall, prior to granting the petition, inform the conservatee of all of the following:

(1) The nature and purpose of the proceeding.

(2) The nature and effect on the conservatee's basic rights of the order requested.

(3) The conservatee has the right to oppose the petition, to be represented by legal counsel if the conservatee so chooses, and to have legal counsel appointed by the court if unable to retain legal counsel.

(c) After the court informs the conservatee of the matters listed in subdivision (b) and prior to granting the petition, the court shall consult the conservatee to determine the conservatee's opinion concerning the order requested in the petition. *(Stats.1990, c. 79 (A.B.759), § 14, operative July 1, 1991. Amended by Stats.2001, c. 893 (A.B.25), § 27.)*

Law Revision Commission Comments

1990 Enactment

Section 1895 continues Section 1895 of the repealed Probate Code without change. For general provisions relating to hearings and orders, see Sections 1040–1050. For background on the provisions of this part, see the Comment to this part under the part heading. [20 Cal.L.Rev.Comm. Reports 1001 (1990)].

Cross References

Appointment of legal counsel, see Probate Code § 1470 et seq.
Domestic partner, defined, see Probate Code § 37.
Interested person, see Probate Code § 1424.

§ 1896. Order; termination

(a) If the court determines that the order requested in the petition is proper, the court shall make the order.

(b) The court, in its discretion, may provide in the order that, unless extended by subsequent order of the court, the order or specific provisions of the order terminate at a time specified in the order. *(Stats.1990, c. 79 (A.B.759), § 14, operative July 1, 1991.)*

Law Revision Commission Comments

1990 Enactment

Section 1896 continues Section 1896 of the repealed Probate Code without change. For general provisions relating to hearings and orders, see Sections 1040–1050. See also Section 2750 (order affecting legal capacity of conservatee pursuant to this chapter an appealable order). As to the effect of final order, see Section 2103. For background on the provisions of this part, see the Comment to this part under the part heading. [20 Cal.L.Rev.Comm. Reports 1001 (1990)].

§ 1897. Duration of order

An order of the court under Section 1880 continues in effect until the earliest of the following times:

(1) The time specified in the order, if any.

(2) The time the order is modified or revoked.

(3) The time the conservatorship is terminated. *(Stats. 1990, c. 79 (A.B.759), § 14, operative July 1, 1991.)*

Law Revision Commission Comments

1990 Enactment

Section 1897 continues Section 1897 of the repealed Probate Code without change. For authority to make an order limited in duration, see Section 1896. For modification or revocation of the order, see Section 1898. As to the effect of final order, see Section 2103. For termination of conservatorship, see Chapter 3 (commencing with Section 1860). For background on the provisions of this part, see the Comment to this part under the part heading. See also Report of Assembly Committee on Judiciary on Assembly Bills Nos. 261 and 167, reprinted in 15 Cal.L.Revision Comm'n Reports 1061, 1075 (1980). [20 Cal.L.Rev.Comm. Reports 1001 (1990)].

Cross References

Termination of conservatorship, see Probate Code § 1860 et seq.

§ 1898. Modification or revocation of order

An order of the court under Section 1880 may be modified or revoked upon a petition made, noticed, and heard by the court in the manner provided in this article. *(Stats.1990, c. 79 (A.B.759), § 14, operative July 1, 1991.)*

1990 Enactment

Section 1898 continues Section 1898 of the repealed Probate Code without change. This section makes clear that the court may modify or revoke an order relating to capacity of the conservatee to give informed consent to medical treatment. For general provisions, see Sections 1000–1004 (rules of practice), 1020–1023 (petitions and other papers), 1040–1050 (hearings and orders). For general provisions relating to notice of hearing, see Sections 1200–1221, 1460–1469. See also Sections 1260–1265 (proof of giving notice), 2700–2702 (notice to persons who request special notice). See also Section 2750 (order pursuant to this chapter affecting legal capacity of conservatee an appealable order). As to the effect of final order, see Section 2103. For background on the provisions of this part, see the Comment to this part under the part heading. See also Report of Assembly Committee on Judiciary on Assembly Bills Nos. 261 and 167, reprinted in 15 Cal.L.Revision Comm'n Reports 1061, 1075 (1980). [20 Cal.L.Rev.Comm. Reports 1001 (1990)].

ARTICLE 3. CAPACITY OF CONSERVATEE TO MARRY

Section
1900. Appointment of conservator; effect.
1901. Determination of capacity; order; law governing; filing of petition; notice of hearing.
1901.5 to 1909. Repealed.

§ 1900. Appointment of conservator; effect

The appointment of a conservator of the person or estate or both does not affect the capacity of the conservatee to marry or to enter into a registered domestic partnership. *(Stats.1990, c. 79 (A.B.759), § 14, operative July 1, 1991. Amended by Stats.2005, c. 418 (S.B.973), § 26.)*

Law Revision Commission Comments
1990 Enactment

Section 1900 continues Section 1900 of the repealed Probate Code without change. This section makes clear that appointment of a conservator under the Probate Code does not deprive the conservatee of capacity to marry. Cf. Conservatorship of Roulet, 23 Cal.3d 219, 228, 590 P.2d 1, 152 Cal.Rptr. 425 (1979) (one found to be gravely disabled under Lanterman–Petris–Short Act faces "possible loss" of right to marry). Whether the conservatee has capacity to marry is determined by the law that would be applicable had no conservatorship been established. See also Section 1901 (court determination of conservatee's capacity to marry). For background on the provisions of this part, see the Comment to this part under the part heading. See also Report of Assembly Committee on Judiciary on Assembly Bills Nos. 261 and 167, reprinted in 15 Cal.L.Revision Comm'n Reports 1061, 1075–76 (1980). [20 Cal.L.Rev.Comm. Reports 1001 (1990)].

Cross References
Capacity to consent to marry, see Family Code § 301.

§ 1901. Determination of capacity; order; law governing; filing of petition; notice of hearing

(a) The court may by order determine whether the conservatee has the capacity to enter into a valid marriage, as provided in Part 1 (commencing with Section 300) of Division 3 of the Family Code, or to enter into a registered domestic partnership, as provided in Section 297 of the Family Code, at the time the order is made.

(b) A petition for an order under this section may be filed by the conservator of the person or estate or both, the conservatee, any relative or friend of the conservatee, or any interested person.

(c) Notice of the hearing on the petition shall be given for the period and in the manner provided in Chapter 3 (commencing with Section 1460) of Part 1. *(Stats.1990, c. 79 (A.B.759), § 14, operative July 1, 1991. Amended by Stats. 1992, c. 163 (A.B.2641), § 124, operative Jan. 1, 1994; Stats.2005, c. 418 (S.B.973), § 27.)*

Law Revision Commission Comments
1992 Amendment

Subdivision (a) of Section 1901 is amended to substitute references to the Family Code provisions that replaced the former Civil Code provisions. [22 Cal.L.Rev.Comm. Reports 1 (1992)].

Cross References
Action to test validity of marriage, see Family Code § 309.
Authorization of conservator to commence annulment proceedings, see Family Code § 2211.
Capacity determinations, generally, see Probate Code § 3200 et seq.
Hearings and orders, see Probate Code § 1040 et seq.
Interested person, defined, see Probate Code § 1424.
Petitions and other papers, see Probate Code § 1020 et seq.
Proceeding to have marriage adjudged a nullity, see Family Code § 2210 et seq.
Rules of practice, see Probate Code § 1000 et seq.

§§ 1901.5 to 1909. Repealed by Stats.1979, c. 726, p. 2334, § 2, operative Jan. 1, 1981

CHAPTER 5. DISQUALIFICATION FROM VOTING

Section
1910. Disqualification by order of court; exceptions.
1911, 1912. Repealed.

§ 1910. Disqualification by order of court; exceptions

(a) If the court determines the conservatee is incapable of communicating, with or without reasonable accommodations, a desire to participate in the voting process, the court shall by order disqualify the conservatee from voting pursuant to Section 2208 or 2209 of the Elections Code.

(b) The conservatee shall not be disqualified from voting on the basis that he or she does, or would need to do, any of the following to complete an affidavit of voter registration:

(1) Signs the affidavit of voter registration with a mark or a cross pursuant to subdivision (b) of Section 2150 of the Elections Code.

(2) Signs the affidavit of voter registration by means of a signature stamp pursuant to Section 354.5 of the Elections Code.

(3) Completes the affidavit of voter registration with the assistance of another person pursuant to subdivision (d) of Section 2150 of the Elections Code.

(4) Completes the affidavit of voter registration with reasonable accommodations. *(Stats.1990, c. 79 (A.B.759), § 14, operative July 1, 1991. Amended by Stats.1994, c. 923 (S.B.1546), § 161; Stats.2014, c. 591 (A.B.1311), § 8, eff. Jan. 1, 2015; Stats.2015, c. 736 (S.B.589), § 12, eff. Jan. 1, 2016.)*

Law Revision Commission Comments
1990 Enactment

Section 1910 continues Section 1910 of the repealed Probate Code without change. See also Section 1865 (restoration of right to vote. For general provisions, see Sections 1000–1004 (rules of practice), 1020–1023 (petitions and other papers), 1040–1050 (hearings and orders). As to the effect of final order, see Section 2103. For background on the provisions of this part, see the Comment to this part under the part heading. See also Report of Assembly Committee on Judiciary on Assembly Bills Nos. 261 and 167, reprinted in 15 Cal.L.Revision Comm'n Reports 1061, 1076 (1980). [20 Cal.L.Rev. Comm. Reports 1001 (1990)].

Cross References

Final judgment or order, see Probate Code § 2103.
Hearings and orders, see Probate Code § 1040 et seq.
Petitions and other papers, see Probate Code § 1020 et seq.
Restoration of right to vote, see Probate Code § 1865.

§§ 1911, 1912. Repealed by Stats.1979, c. 726, p. 2334, § 2, operative Jan. 1, 1981

CHAPTER 6. STERILIZATION

§ 1950. Persons with developmental disabilities; legislative intent

The Legislature recognizes that the right to exercise choice over matters of procreation is fundamental and may not be denied to an individual on the basis of disability. This chapter is enacted for the benefit of those persons with developmental disabilities who, despite those disabilities, are capable of engaging in sexual activity yet who, because of those disabilities, are unable to give the informed, voluntary consent necessary to their fully exercising the right to procreative choice, which includes the right to choose sterilization.

However, the Legislature further recognizes that the power to sterilize is subject to abuse and, historically, has been abused. It is the intent of the Legislature that no individual shall be sterilized solely by reason of a developmental disability and that no individual who knowingly opposes sterilization be sterilized involuntarily. It is further the intent of the Legislature that this chapter shall be applied in accord with the overall intent of Division 4.5 (commencing with Section 4500) of the Welfare and Institutions Code that persons with developmental disabilities be provided with those services needed to enable them to live more normal, independent, and productive lives, including assistance and training that might obviate the need for sterilization. *(Stats. 1990, c. 79 (A.B.759), § 14, operative July 1, 1991.)*

Law Revision Commission Comments
1990 Enactment

Section 1950 continues Section 1950 of the repealed Probate Code without change. [20 Cal.L.Rev.Comm. Reports 1001 (1990)].

Cross References

Statutes, construction and legislative intent, see Code of Civil Procedure §§ 1858 and 1859.

§ 1951. Persons with ability to consent to sterilization; definitions

(a) No person who has the ability to consent to his or her sterilization shall be sterilized pursuant to this chapter.

(b) For the purposes of this chapter, the following terms have the meanings given:

(1) "Consent to sterilization" means making a voluntary decision to undergo sterilization after being fully informed about, and after fully understanding the nature and consequences of, sterilization.

(2) "Voluntary" means performed while competent to make the decision, and as a matter of free choice and will and not in response to coercion, duress, or undue influence.

(3) "Fully understanding the nature and consequences of sterilization," includes, but is not limited to, the ability to understand each of the following:

(A) That the individual is free to withhold or withdraw consent to the procedure at any time before the sterilization without affecting the right to future care or treatment and

213

without loss or withdrawal of any publicly funded program benefits to which the individual might be otherwise entitled.

(B) Available alternative methods of family planning and birth control.

(C) That the sterilization procedure is considered to be irreversible.

(D) The specific sterilization procedure to be performed.

(E) The discomforts and risks that may accompany or follow the performing of the procedure, including an explanation of the type and possible effects of any anesthetic to be used.

(F) The benefits or advantages that may be expected as a result of the sterilization.

(G) The approximate length of the hospital stay.

(H) The approximate length of time for recovery.

(c) The court shall appoint a facilitator or interpreter if such a person's assistance would enable the person named in the petition to understand any of these factors. *(Stats.1990, c. 79 (A.B.759), § 14, operative July 1, 1991.)*

Law Revision Commission Comments

1990 Enactment

Section 1951 continues Section 1951 of the repealed Probate Code without change. [20 Cal.L.Rev.Comm. Reports 1001 (1990)].

§ 1952. Appointment of limited conservator to consent to sterilization of developmentally disabled adults; petition; contents

The conservator of an adult, or any person authorized to file a petition for the appointment of a conservator under paragraphs (2) to (5), inclusive, of subdivision (a) of Section 1820, may file a petition under this chapter for appointment of a limited conservator authorized to consent to the sterilization of an adult with a developmental disability. The content of the petition under this chapter shall conform to the provisions of Section 1821 and in addition allege that the person for whom sterilization is proposed has a developmental disability as defined in Section 1420 and shall allege specific reasons why court-authorized sterilization is deemed necessary. A petition under this chapter shall be considered separately from any contemporaneous petition for appointment of a conservator under this division. *(Stats.1990, c. 79 (A.B.759), § 14, operative July 1, 1991.)*

Law Revision Commission Comments

1990 Enactment

Section 1952 continues Section 1952 of the repealed Probate Code without change. See also Section 2356(d) (no minor may be sterilized under this division). For general provisions relating to petitions and other papers, see Sections 1020–1023. [20 Cal.L.Rev. Comm. Reports 1001 (1990)].

§ 1953. Hearing on petition; service of notice and copy of petition

At least 90 days before the hearing on the petition under this chapter, notice of the time and place of the hearing and a copy of the petition shall be served on the person named in the petition and, if the petitioner is not the conservator of the person, on the conservator, if any. Service shall be made in the manner provided in Section 415.10 or Section 415.30 of the Code of Civil Procedure or in such manner as may be authorized by the court. *(Stats.1990, c. 79 (A.B.759), § 14, operative July 1, 1991.)*

Law Revision Commission Comments

1990 Enactment

Section 1953 continues Section 1953 of the repealed Probate Code without change. For general provisions relating to notice of hearing, see Sections 1200–1221, 1460–1469. See also Sections 1260–1265 (proof of giving notice), 2700–2702 (notice to persons who request special notice). [20 Cal.L.Rev.Comm. Reports 1001 (1990)].

Cross References

Computation of time, see Code of Civil Procedure §§ 12 and 12a; Government Code § 6800 et seq.
Notice of hearing,
  Generally, see Probate Code §§ 1200 et seq., 1460 et seq.
  Mailing, see Probate Code § 1215 et seq.
  Posting, see Probate Code § 1230.
  Proof of giving notice, see Probate Code § 1260 et seq.
  Special notice, see Probate Code §§ 1250 and 2700 et seq.
Service of process,
  Generally, see Code of Civil Procedure § 413.10 et seq.
  Mail, see Code of Civil Procedure §§ 415.30, 1012 et seq.
  Personal delivery, see Code of Civil Procedure § 415.10.
  Proof of service, see Code of Civil Procedure § 417.10 et seq.
  Publication, see Code of Civil Procedure § 415.50.

§ 1954. Appointment of counsel; presumption

In any proceeding under this chapter, if the person named in the petition for court authorization to consent to sterilization has not retained legal counsel and does not plan to retain legal counsel, the court shall immediately appoint the public defender or private counsel to represent the individual for whom sterilization is proposed. Counsel shall undertake the representation with the presumption that the individual opposes the petition. *(Stats.1990, c. 79 (A.B.759), § 14, operative July 1, 1991.)*

Law Revision Commission Comments

1990 Enactment

Section 1954 continues Section 1954 of the repealed Probate Code without change. [20 Cal.L.Rev.Comm. Reports 1001 (1990)].

Cross References

Counsel, right to, see Cal. Const. Art. 1, § 15.
Presumptions, see Evidence Code § 600 et seq.

§ 1954.5. Appointment of facilitator; duties; considerations

(a) The court shall appoint a facilitator for the person named in the petition, who shall assist the person named in the petition to do all of the following:

(1) Understand the nature of the proceedings.

(2) Understand the evaluation process required by Section 1955.

(3) Communicate his or her views.

(4) Participate as fully as possible in the proceedings.

(b) All of the following factors shall be considered by the court in appointing a facilitator:

(1) The preference of the person named in the petition.

(2) The proposed facilitator's personal knowledge of the person named in the petition.

(3) The proposed facilitator's ability to communicate with the person named in the petition, when that person is nonverbal, has limited verbal skills, or relies on alternative modes of communication.

(4) The proposed facilitator's knowledge of the developmental disabilities service system.

(c) The petitioner may not be appointed as the facilitator. *(Stats.1990, c. 79 (A.B.759), § 14, operative July 1, 1991.)*

Law Revision Commission Comments

1990 Enactment

Section 1954.5 continues Section 1954.5 of the repealed Probate Code without substantive change. [20 Cal.L.Rev.Comm. Reports 1001 (1990)].

§ **1955. Investigation; preparation of written report by appropriate regional center; examination of person named in petition; reports; confidentiality; use of examiners as expert witnesses**

(a) The court shall request the director of the appropriate regional center for the developmentally disabled to coordinate an investigation and prepare and file a written report thereon. The appropriate regional center for purposes of this section is (1) the regional center of which the person named in the petition is a client, (2) if the individual named in the petition is not a client of any regional center, the regional center responsible for the area in which the individual is then living, or (3) such other regional center as may be in the best interests of the individual. The report shall be based upon comprehensive medical, psychological, and sociosexual evaluations of the individual conducted pursuant to subdivisions (b) and (c), and shall address, but shall not be limited to, each of the factors listed in Section 1958. A copy of the report shall be provided to each of the parties at least 15 days prior to the hearing.

(b) Prior to the hearing on the issue of sterilization, the person who is proposed to be sterilized shall be personally examined by two physicians, one of whom shall be a surgeon competent to perform the procedure, and one psychologist or clinical social worker, each of whom has been mutually agreed to by the petitioner and counsel for the person named in the petition or, if agreement is not reached, appointed by the court from a panel of qualified professionals. At the request of counsel for the person named in the petition, the court shall appoint one additional psychologist, clinical social worker, or physician named by counsel. Any psychologist or clinical social worker and, to the extent feasible, any physicians conducting an examination shall have had experience with persons who have developmental disabilities. To the extent feasible, each of the examiners shall also have knowledge and experience relating to sociosexual skills and behavior. The examinations shall be at county expense subject to Section 1963.

(c) The examiners shall consider all available alternatives to sterilization and shall recommend sterilization only if no suitable alternative is available. Each examiner shall prepare a written, comprehensive report containing all relevant aspects of the person's medical, psychological, family, and sociosexual conditions. Each examiner shall address those factors specified in Section 1958 related to his or her particular area of expertise. In considering the factors in subdivision (a) of, and paragraph (1) of subdivision (d) of, Section 1958, each examiner shall include information regarding the intensity, extent, and recentness of the person's education and training, if any, regarding human sexuality, including birth control methods and parenting skills, and in addition, shall consider whether the individual would benefit from training provided by persons competent in education and training of persons with comparable intellectual impairments. If an examiner recommends against sterilization, the examiner shall set forth in his or her report available alternatives, including, as warranted, recommendations for sex education, parent training, or training in the use of alternative methods of contraception. Copies of each report shall be furnished at least 30 days prior to the hearing on the petition to the person or persons who filed the petition, the conservator, if any, and counsel for the person proposed to be sterilized, the regional center responsible for the investigation and report required under this section, and such other persons as the court may direct. The court may receive these reports in evidence.

(d) The contents of the reports prepared pursuant to this section shall be confidential. Upon judgment in the action or the proceeding becoming final, the court shall order the contents of the reports sealed.

(e) Regional centers for the developmentally disabled shall compile and maintain lists of persons competent to perform the examinations required by this section. These lists shall be provided to the court. If the person named in the petition resides at a state hospital or other residential care facility, no person conducting an examination pursuant to subdivision (b) shall be an employee of the facility.

(f) Any party to the proceedings has the right to submit additional reports from qualified experts.

(g) Any person who has written a report received in evidence may be subpoenaed and questioned by any party to the proceedings or by the court and when so called is subject to all rules of evidence including those of legal objections as to the qualification of expert witnesses.

(h) No regional center or person acting in his or her capacity as a regional center employee may file a petition under Section 1952. *(Stats.1990, c. 79 (A.B.759), § 14, operative July 1, 1991.)*

Law Revision Commission Comments

1990 Enactment

Section 1955 continues Section 1955 of the repealed Probate Code without substantive change. For general provisions relating to hearings and orders, see Sections 1040–1050. [20 Cal.L.Rev.Comm. Reports 1001 (1990)].

Cross References

Sterilization of disabled, confidentiality of evaluation report, see Government Code § 6276.42.

§ **1956. Presence of person named in petition at hearing**

The person to whom the petition applies shall be present at the hearing except for reason of medical inability. Emotional or psychological instability is not good cause for the absence of the proposed conservatee from the hearing unless, by reason of the instability, attendance at the hearing is likely to cause serious and immediate physiological damage to the proposed conservatee. *(Stats.1990, c. 79 (A.B.759), § 14, operative July 1, 1991.)*

Section 1956 continues Section 1956 of the repealed Probate Code without change. [20 Cal.L.Rev.Comm. Reports 1001 (1990)].

§ 1957. Consideration of views of person for whom sterilization is proposed

To the greatest extent possible, the court shall elicit and take into account the views of the individual for whom sterilization is proposed in determining whether sterilization is to be authorized. *(Stats.1990, c. 79 (A.B.759), § 14, operative July 1, 1991.)*

Section 1957 continues Section 1957 of the repealed Probate Code without change. [20 Cal.L.Rev.Comm. Reports 1001 (1990)].

§ 1958. Authorization for conservator to consent to sterilization of person named in petition; findings required by court beyond a reasonable doubt

The court may authorize the conservator of a person proposed to be sterilized to consent to the sterilization of that person only if the court finds that the petitioner has established all of the following beyond a reasonable doubt:

(a) The person named in the petition is incapable of giving consent to sterilization, as defined in Section 1951, and the incapacity is in all likelihood permanent.

(b) Based on reasonable medical evidence, the individual is fertile and capable of procreation.

(c) The individual is capable of engaging in, and is likely to engage in sexual activity at the present or in the near future under circumstances likely to result in pregnancy.

(d) Either of the following:

(1) The nature and extent of the individual's disability as determined by empirical evidence and not solely on the basis of any standardized test, renders him or her permanently incapable of caring for a child, even with appropriate training and reasonable assistance.

(2) Due to a medical condition, pregnancy or childbirth would pose a substantially elevated risk to the life of the individual to such a degree that, in the absence of other appropriate methods of contraception, sterilization would be deemed medically necessary for an otherwise nondisabled woman under similar circumstances.

(e) All less invasive contraceptive methods including supervision are unworkable even with training and assistance, inapplicable, or medically contraindicated. Isolation and segregation shall not be considered as less invasive means of contraception.

(f) The proposed method of sterilization entails the least invasion of the body of the individual.

(g) The current state of scientific and medical knowledge does not suggest either (1) that a reversible sterilization procedure or other less drastic contraceptive method will shortly be available, or (2) that science is on the threshold of an advance in the treatment of the individual's disability.

(h) The person named in the petition has not made a knowing objection to his or her sterilization. For purposes of this subdivision, an individual may be found to have knowingly objected to his or her sterilization notwithstanding his or her inability to give consent to sterilization as defined in Section 1951. In the case of persons who are nonverbal, have limited verbal ability to communicate, or who rely on alternative modes of communication, the court shall ensure that adequate effort has been made to elicit the actual views of the individual by the facilitator appointed pursuant to Section 1954.5, or by any other person with experience in communicating with developmentally disabled persons who communicate using similar means. *(Stats.1990, c. 79 (A.B. 759), § 14, operative July 1, 1991.)*

Section 1958 continues Section 1958 of the repealed Probate Code without change. For general provisions, see Sections 1000–1004 (rules of practice), 1020–1023 (petitions and other papers), 1040–1050 (hearings and orders). [20 Cal.L.Rev.Comm. Reports 1001 (1990)].

Capacity determinations, generally, see Probate Code § 3200 et seq.
Hearings and orders, see Probate Code § 1040 et seq.
Petitions and other papers, see Probate Code § 1020 et seq.
Rules of practice, see Probate Code § 1000 et seq.

§ 1959. Vulnerability of developmentally disabled person to unlawful sexual conduct by others; not a consideration in sterilization determination

The fact that, due to the nature or severity of his or her disability, a person for whom an authorization to consent to sterilization is sought may be vulnerable to sexual conduct by others that would be deemed unlawful, shall not be considered by the court in determining whether sterilization is to be authorized under this chapter. *(Stats.1990, c. 79 (A.B.759), § 14, operative July 1, 1991.)*

Section 1959 continues Section 1959 of the repealed Probate Code without change. [20 Cal.L.Rev.Comm. Reports 1001 (1990)].

§ 1960. Assurance by court of adequate representation by existing conservator or appointment of limited conservator

If the person named in the petition already has a conservator, the court may authorize that person to consent to sterilization or may appoint another person as limited conservator under the provisions of this chapter. The court shall ensure that the person or agency designated as conservator under this chapter is capable of adequately representing and safeguarding the interests of the conservatee. *(Stats. 1990, c. 79 (A.B.759), § 14, operative July 1, 1991.)*

Section 1960 continues Section 1960 of the repealed Probate Code without change. [20 Cal.L.Rev.Comm. Reports 1001 (1990)].

§ 1961. Sterilization procedure not to include hysterectomy or castration unless medically indicated

A sterilization procedure authorized under this chapter shall not include hysterectomy or castration. However, if the report prepared under Section 1955 indicates that hysterectomy or castration is a medically necessary treatment, regardless of the need for sterilization, the court shall proceed pursuant to Section 2357. *(Stats.1990, c. 79 (A.B.759), § 14, operative July 1, 1991.)*

Section 1961 continues Section 1961 of the repealed Probate Code without change. [20 Cal.L.Rev.Comm. Reports 1001 (1990)].

§ 1962. Court order granting petition; written statement of findings; appeal

(a) Any court order granting a petition under this chapter shall be accompanied by a written statement of decision pursuant to Section 632 of the Code of Civil Procedure detailing the factual and legal bases for the court's determination on each of the findings required under Section 1958.

(b) When a judgment authorizing the conservator of a person to consent to the sterilization is rendered, an appeal is automatically taken by the person proposed to be sterilized without any action by that person, or by his or her counsel. The Judicial Council shall provide by rule for notice of and procedure for the appeal. The appeal shall have precedence over other cases in the court in which the appeal is pending. *(Stats.1990, c. 79 (A.B.759), § 14, operative July 1, 1991.)*

Section 1962 continues Section 1962 of the repealed Probate Code without change. For general provisions, see Sections 1000–1004 (rules of practice), 1020–1023 (petitions and other papers), 1040–1050 (hearings and orders). As to the effect of final order, see Section 2103. [20 Cal.L.Rev.Comm. Reports 1001 (1990)].

Appeals,
Generally, see Code of Civil Procedure § 901 et seq.
Rules on appeal in civil cases, see California Rules of Court, Rule 8.1 et seq.
Appellate rules, appeals from judgment authorizing conservator to consent to sterilization of conservatee, see California Rules of Court, Rule 8.482.
Effect of final orders, see Probate Code § 2103.
Hearings and orders, see Probate Code § 1040 et seq.
Petitions and other papers, see Probate Code § 1020 et seq.
Rules of practice, see Probate Code § 1000 et seq.

§ 1963. Payment of costs and fees

(a) At the conclusion of the hearing, the court, after inquiring into financial ability, may make an order based upon their ability that any one or more of the following persons pay court costs and fees in whole or in part as in the opinion of the court is proper and in any installments and manner which is both reasonable and compatible with ability to pay:

(1) The person to whom the petition applies.

(2) The petitioner.

(3) Any person liable for the support and maintenance of the person to whom the petition applies.

(b) An order under subdivision (a) may be enforced in the same manner as a money judgment.

(c) For the purposes of this section, court costs and fees include the costs of any examination or investigation ordered by the court, expert witnesses' fees, and the costs and fees of the court-appointed public defender or private counsel representing the person to whom the petition applies.

(d) Any fees and costs not ordered to be paid by persons under subdivision (a) are a charge against and paid out of the treasury of the county on order of the court. *(Stats.1990, c. 79 (A.B.759), § 14, operative July 1, 1991.)*

Section 1963 continues Section 1963 of the repealed Probate Code without substantive change. For general provisions, see Sections 1000–1004 (rules of practice), 1020–1023 (petitions and other papers), 1040–1050 (hearings and orders). As to the effect of final order, see Section 2103. See also Section 1049 (enforcement of order). [20 Cal.L.Rev.Comm. Reports 1001 (1990)].

Appellate rules, appeals from judgment authorizing conservator to consent to sterilization of conservatee, see California Rules of Court, Rule 8.482.
Costs, see Probate Code § 1002.
Effect of final orders, see Probate Code § 2103.
Enforcement of orders, see Probate Code § 1049.
Hearings and orders, see Probate Code §' 1040 et seq.
Petitions and other papers, see Probate Code § 1020 et seq.
Rules of practice, see Probate Code § 1000 et seq.

§ 1964. Expiration of consent to sterilization; termination of conservatorship upon completion of sterilization

An order of the court authorizing a conservator to consent to sterilization which is upheld on appeal automatically expires in one year from the final determination on appeal unless earlier terminated by the court. A conservatorship established for the sole purpose of authorizing a conservator to consent to sterilization under this chapter shall automatically terminate upon completion of the sterilization procedure or upon expiration of the court's order authorizing the conservator to consent to sterilization, whichever occurs first. If, upon the expiration of the court's order under this chapter, the person named as conservator determines that the conservatorship is still required for the purpose of this chapter, he or she may petition the court for reappointment as conservator for a succeeding six-month period upon a showing of good cause as to why any sterilization authorized by the court has not been completed. *(Stats.1990, c. 79 (A.B.759), § 14, operative July 1, 1991.)*

Law Revision Commission Comments

1990 Enactment

Section 1964 continues Section 1964 of the repealed Probate Code without change. For general provisions, see Sections 1000–1004 (rules of practice), 1020–1023 (petitions and other papers), 1040–1050 (hearings and orders). [20 Cal.L.Rev.Comm. Reports 1001 (1990)].

§ 1965. Stay of court order pending appeal

Any court order made pursuant to this chapter granting authority to consent to sterilization shall be stayed pending a final determination on appeal. *(Stats.1990, c. 79 (A.B.759), § 14, operative July 1, 1991.)*

Law Revision Commission Comments

1990 Enactment

Section 1965 continues Section 1965 of the repealed Probate Code without change. [20 Cal.L.Rev.Comm. Reports 1001 (1990)].

Cross References

Appeals,
Generally, see Code of Civil Procedure § 901 et seq.
Rules on appeal in civil cases, see California Rules of Court, Rule 8.1 et seq.

§ 1966. Denial of first petition; filing of subsequent petitions on showing of material change in circumstances

After the filing of a first petition for sterilization pursuant to this chapter and a determination by the court that any one or more of the conditions required in Section 1958 has not been proven beyond a reasonable doubt, and that therefore authorization for the proposed sterilization should not be given by the court, a subsequent petition may be filed only on the showing of a material change in circumstances. *(Stats. 1990, c. 79 (A.B.759), § 14, operative July 1, 1991.)*

Law Revision Commission Comments

1990 Enactment

Section 1966 continues Section 1966 of the repealed Probate Code without change. [20 Cal.L.Rev.Comm. Reports 1001 (1990)].

§ 1967. Immunity from liability; exception; civil liability for petitioner who seeks sterilization when person named in petition is capable of consent

(a) The sterilization of a person in accordance with this chapter does not render the petitioner or any person participating in the conservatorship proceedings or sterilization liable, either civilly or criminally, except for any injury caused by negligent or willful misconduct in the performance of the sterilization.

(b) Notwithstanding the provisions of subdivision (a), any individual who petitions for authorization to consent to sterilization knowing that the person to whom the petition relates is capable of giving consent to sterilization as defined in Section 1951 is guilty of a misdemeanor, and may be civilly liable to the person concerning whom sterilization was sought. *(Stats.1990, c. 79 (A.B.759), § 14, operative July 1, 1991.)*

Law Revision Commission Comments

1990 Enactment

Section 1967 continues Section 1967 of the repealed Probate Code without substantive change. [20 Cal.L.Rev.Comm. Reports 1001 (1990)].

Cross References

Misdemeanors, definition and penalties, see Penal Code §§ 17, 19 and 19.2.

§ 1968. Unavoidable sterilization as part of other medical treatment

This chapter does not prohibit medical treatment or surgery required for other medical reasons and in which sterilization is an unavoidable or medically probable consequence, but is not the object of the treatment or surgery. *(Stats.1990, c. 79 (A.B.759), § 14, operative July 1, 1991.)*

Law Revision Commission Comments

1990 Enactment

Section 1968 continues Section 1968 of the repealed Probate Code without change. [20 Cal.L.Rev.Comm. Reports 1001 (1990)].

§ 1969. Right of persons with developmental disabilities to consent to sterilization without court order

Nothing in this chapter shall infringe on the right of persons with developmental disabilities who are capable of giving consent to sterilization to give that consent without the necessity of a court order or substitute decisionmaker. *(Stats.1990, c. 79 (A.B.759), § 14, operative July 1, 1991.)*

Law Revision Commission Comments

1990 Enactment

Section 1969 continues Section 1969 of the repealed Probate Code without change. [20 Cal.L.Rev.Comm. Reports 1001 (1990)].

CHAPTER 7. UNWARRANTED PETITIONS

Section

§ 1970. Legislative findings; vexatious litigants

(a) The Legislature finds that unwarranted petitions, applications, or motions other than discovery motions after a conservatorship has been established create an environment that can be harmful to the conservatee and are inconsistent with the goal of protecting the conservatee.

(b) Notwithstanding Section 391 of the Code of Civil Procedure, if a person other than the conservatee files a petition for termination of the conservatorship, or instruction to the conservator, that is unmeritorious or intended to harass or annoy the conservator, and the person has previously filed pleadings in the conservatorship proceedings that were unmeritorious or intended to harass or annoy the conservator, the petition shall be grounds for the court to determine that the person is a vexatious litigant for the purposes of Title 3A (commencing with Section 391) of Part 2 of the Code of Civil Procedure. For these purposes, the term "new litigation" shall include petitions for visitation, termination of the conservatorship, or instruction to the conservator. *(Added by Stats.2008, c. 293 (A.B.1340), § 3.)*

CHAPTER 8. INTERSTATE JURISDICTION, TRANSFER, AND RECOGNITION: CALIFORNIA CONSERVATORSHIP JURISDICTION ACT

Law Revision Commission Comments

2014 Addition

The Uniform Law Commission approved the Uniform Adult Guardianship and Protective Proceedings Jurisdiction Act ("UAGPPJA") in 2007. This chapter contains the California version of that Act, which may be referred to as the California Conservatorship Jurisdiction Act. See Section 1980 & Comment. Many provisions in this chapter are the same as or are drawn from UAGPPJA. In Comments to sections in this chapter, a reference to the "uniform act" or "UAGPPJA" means the official text of the uniform act approved by the Uniform Law Commission. Variations from the official text of the uniform act are noted in the Comments to sections in this chapter. [43 Cal.L.Rev.Comm. Reports 93 (2013)].

Cross References

Acknowledgment of receipt by conservator, statement of duties and liabilities, conservatorship information, see Probate Code § 1834.
Jurisdiction and venue, determination of state jurisdiction, see Probate Code § 2200.

ARTICLE 1.   GENERAL PROVISIONS

Section
1980. Legislative intent; short title.
1981. Application of chapter.
1982. Definitions.
1983. International application of chapter.
1984. Communication between courts.
1985. Cooperation between courts.
1986. Taking testimony in another state.

Law Revision Commission Comments

2014 Addition

Background from Uniform Act. Article 1 contains definitions and general provisions used throughout the Act. Definitions applicable only to Article 2 are found in Section [1991]. Section [1980] is the title, Section [1982] contains the definitions, and Sections [1983–1986] the general provisions. Section [1983] provides that a court of an enacting state may treat a foreign country as a state for the purpose of applying all portions of the Act other than Article 4.... Section [1984] addresses communication between courts, Section [1985] requests by a court to a court in another state for assistance, and Section [1986] the taking of testimony in other states. These Article 1 provisions relating to court communication and assistance are essential tools to assure the effectiveness of the provisions of Article 2 determining jurisdiction and in facilitating transfer of a proceeding to another state as authorized in Article 3. [Adapted from the Uniform Law Commission's General Comment to Article 1 of UAGPPJA.] [43 Cal.L.Rev.Comm. Reports 93 (2013)].

§ 1980. Legislative intent; short title

(a) By enacting this chapter, it is the Legislature's intent to enact a modified version of the Uniform Adult Guardianship and Protective Proceedings Jurisdiction Act.

(b) This chapter may be cited as the "California Conservatorship Jurisdiction Act." *(Added by Stats.2014, c. 553 (S.B.940), § 20, eff. Jan. 1, 2015, operative Jan. 1, 2016.)*

Law Revision Commission Comments

2014 Addition

Section 1980 is similar to Section 101 of the Uniform Adult Guardianship and Protective Proceedings Jurisdiction Act (2007) ("UAGPPJA"). The section provides a shorthand means of referring to the content of this chapter.

Due to differences between California terminology and that of the Uniform Law Commission, the short title provided in the uniform act ("Uniform Adult Guardianship and Protective Proceedings Jurisdiction Act") could cause confusion within this state. See Sections 1500–1502 ("guardian" may only be nominated for minor, not for adult); see also Sections 1301, 4126 & 4672 (using term "protective proceeding" differently than in uniform act); Cal. R. Ct. 7.51(d), 10.478(a) & 10.776(a) (same); Welf. & Inst. Code § 15703 (same). The alternative title provided in this section ("California Conservatorship Jurisdiction Act") is consistent with California terminology for the types of proceedings covered by UAGPPJA.

For guidance on interpretation of a uniform act enacted in this state, see Section 2(b) ("A provision of this code, insofar as it is the same in substance as a provision of a uniform act, shall be so construed as to effectuate the general purpose to make uniform the law in those states which enact that provision."); see also Section 2021 (uniformity of application and construction of California Conservatorship Jurisdiction Act).

Background from Uniform Act. The title to the Act succinctly describes the Act's scope. The Act applies only to court jurisdiction and related topics for adults for whom the appointment of a [conservator] is being sought or has been issued.

The drafting committee elected to limit the Act to adults for two reasons. First, jurisdictional issues concerning guardians for minors are subsumed by the Uniform Child Custody Jurisdiction and Enforcement Act (1997). Second, while the UCCJEA does not address ... issues involving the property of minors, all of the problems and concerns that led the Uniform Law Commission to appoint a drafting committee involved adults. [Adapted from the Uniform Law Commission's Comment to UAGPPJA § 101.] [43 Cal.L.Rev. Comm. Reports 93 (2013)].

§ 1981. Application of chapter

(a)(1) This chapter does not apply to a minor, regardless of whether the minor is or was married.

(2) This chapter does not apply to any proceeding in which a person is appointed to provide personal care or property administration for a minor, including, but not limited to, a guardianship under Part 2 (commencing with Section 1500).

(b) This chapter does not apply to any proceeding in which a person is involuntarily committed to a mental health facility or subjected to other involuntary mental health care, including, but not limited to, any of the following proceedings or any proceeding that is similar in substance:

(1) A proceeding under Sections 1026 to 1027, inclusive, of the Penal Code.

(2) A proceeding under Chapter 6 (commencing with Section 1367) of Title 10 of Part 2 of the Penal Code.

(3) A proceeding under Article 4 (commencing with Section 2960) of Chapter 7 of Title 1 of Part 3 of the Penal Code.

(4) A proceeding under Article 6 (commencing with Section 1800) of Chapter 1 of Division 2.5 of the Welfare and Institutions Code.

(5) A proceeding under Article 2 (commencing with Section 3050) of Chapter 1 of Division 3 of the Welfare and Institutions Code.

(6) A proceeding under Article 3 (commencing with Section 3100) of Chapter 1 of Division 3 of the Welfare and Institutions Code.

(7) A proceeding under Part 1 (commencing with Section 5000) of Division 5 of the Welfare and Institutions Code, which is also known as the Lanterman–Petris–Short Act.

(8) A proceeding under Article 2 (commencing with Section 6500) of Chapter 2 of Part 2 of Division 6 of the Welfare and Institutions Code.

(9) A proceeding under Article 4 (commencing with Section 6600) of Chapter 2 of Part 2 of Division 6 of the Welfare and Institutions Code.

(c) Article 3 (commencing with Section 2001) does not apply to an adult with a developmental disability, or to any proceeding in which a person is appointed to provide personal care or property administration for an adult with a developmental disability, including, but not limited to, the following types of proceedings:

(1) A proceeding under Article 7.5 (commencing with Section 416) of Chapter 2 of Part 1 of Division 1 of the Health and Safety Code.

(2) A limited conservatorship under subdivision (d) of Section 1801.

(3) A proceeding under Section 4825 of the Welfare and Institutions Code.

(4) A proceeding under Article 2 (commencing with Section 6500) of Chapter 2 of Part 2 of Division 6 of the Welfare and Institutions Code.

(d) Application of this chapter to a conservatee with dementia is subject to the express limitations of Sections 2002 and 2016, as well as the other requirements of this chapter. *(Added by Stats.2014, c. 553 (S.B.940), § 20, eff. Jan. 1, 2015, operative Jan. 1, 2016.)*

Law Revision Commission Comments
2014 Addition

Section 1981 restricts the scope of this chapter.

Paragraph (1) of subdivision (a) makes explicit that this chapter does not apply to a minor, even if the minor is married or has had a marriage dissolved. Paragraph (2) states a corollary rule: The chapter does not apply to any proceeding in which a person is appointed to provide personal care or property administration for a minor. Those limitations are consistent with the scope of the Uniform Adult Guardianship and Protective Proceedings Jurisdiction Act (2007) ("UAGPPJA"). See UAGPPJA § 102(1) (defining "adult" as "an individual who has attained [18] years of age"). The uniform act does, however, recognize that some states may wish to modify that scope because their conservatorship law encompasses certain minors. See UAGPPJA § 102 Comment. Under California law, a minor who is or was married is treated as an adult for some but not all purposes. See,

e.g., Sections 1515 & Comment (guardian of estate may be appointed for minor who is married or has had marriage dissolved, but not guardian of person), 1800.3 & Comment (conservator of person may be appointed for minor who is married or has had marriage dissolved, but not conservator of estate), 1860 & Comment (dissolution of minor's marriage does not terminate conservatorship of person established for that minor). Different treatment of such minors may apply in other states. To prevent confusion and avoid complications that might arise due to differential treatment of such minors across state lines, they are expressly excluded from the scope of this chapter and the chapter is strictly limited to adults. For definitions consistent with this limitation, see Section 1982 (defining "adult," "conservatee" & other terms).

Subdivision (b) makes clear that this chapter is inapplicable to any proceeding in which an individual is involuntarily committed to a mental health facility or subjected to other involuntary mental health care. This encompasses, but is not limited to, a conservatorship under the Lanterman–Petris–Short Act (Welf. & Inst. Code §§ 5000–5550), a civil commitment of a person found not guilty by reason of insanity (Penal Code §§ 1026–1027), a civil commitment of a person found incompetent to stand trial (Penal Code §§ 1367–1376), a civil commitment of a mentally disordered offender (Penal Code §§ 2960–2981), a civil commitment of a person who would otherwise be discharged from the Youth Authority (Welf. & Inst. Code §§ 1800–1803), a civil commitment of a narcotics addict (Welf. & Inst. Code §§ 3050–3555, 3100–3111), a civil commitment of a person with a developmental disability who is dangerous to others or to self (Welf. & Inst. Code §§ 6500–6513), and a civil commitment of a sexually violent predator (Welf. & Inst. Code §§ 6600–6609.3).

Authority to involuntarily commit a person in California, or to subject a person to other involuntary mental health treatment here, cannot be obtained merely by transferring an out-of-state conservatorship pursuant to Article 3, or by registering an out-of-state conservatorship pursuant to Article 4. To obtain such authority, it is necessary to follow the procedures provided by California law.

Subdivision (c) makes clear that the transfer procedure provided in Article 3 of this chapter (Sections 2001–2002) does not apply to an adult with a developmental disability. Consistent with that rule, subdivision (c) also states that the transfer procedure is inapplicable to several types of proceedings specifically designed for such an adult.

Under California law, an adult with a developmental disability is entitled to be evaluated by a regional center and to receive a broad range of services pursuant to an individualized plan. See Welf. & Inst. Code § 4646; see also Sanchez v. Johnson, 416 F.3d 1051, 1064–68 (9th Cir. 2001). The intent is to "enable persons with developmental disabilities to approximate the pattern of everyday living available to people without disabilities of the same age." Welf. & Inst. Code § 4501; see also Welf. & Inst. Code §§ 4500–4868 ("Services for the Developmentally Disabled"). To further that intent, California provides a variety of conservatorship possibilities for an adult with a developmental disability, including the option of a limited conservatorship in which the adult "retain[s] all legal and civil rights except those which by court order have been designated as legal disabilities and have been specifically granted to the limited conservator." Section 1801(d); cf. Section 1801(a)-(c) (regular Probate Code conservatorship); Health & Safety Code §§ 416–416.23 (Director of Developmental Services as conservator for developmentally disabled person); Welf. & Inst. Code §§ 6500–6513 (judicial commitment of person with developmental disability who is dangerous to others or to self).

By precluding use of Article 3's streamlined transfer procedure, subdivision (c) serves to ensure that when an adult with a developmental disability is relocated to California, that adult will receive the benefit of California's procedures for such adults, and full recognition of the rights to which the adult is entitled under California law. Likewise, subdivision (c) helps assure that when such an adult is relocated from California to another jurisdiction, that jurisdiction will have to evaluate the adult's needs and the available resources using its normal processes, not an abbreviated transfer procedure.

Subdivision (d) serves to highlight the rules applicable to a conservatee with dementia. [43 Cal.L.Rev.Comm. Reports 93 (2013)].

§ 1982. Definitions

In this chapter:

(a) "Adult" means an individual who has attained 18 years of age.

(b) "Conservatee" means an adult for whom a conservator of the estate, a conservator of the person, or a conservator of the person and estate has been appointed.

(c) "Conservator" means a person appointed by the court to serve as a conservator of the estate, a conservator of the person, or a conservator of the person and estate.

(d) "Conservator of the estate" means a person appointed by the court to administer the property of an adult, including, but not limited to, a person appointed for that purpose under subdivision (b) of Section 1801.

(e) "Conservator of the person" means a person appointed by the court to make decisions regarding the person of an adult, including, but not limited to, a person appointed for that purpose under subdivision (a) of Section 1801.

(f) "Conservator of the person and estate" means a person appointed by the court to make decisions regarding the person of an adult and to administer the property of that adult, including, but not limited to, a person appointed for those purposes under subdivision (c) of Section 1801.

(g) "Conservatorship order" means an order appointing a conservator of the estate, a conservator of the person, or a conservator of the person and estate in a conservatorship proceeding.

(h) "Conservatorship proceeding" means a judicial proceeding in which an order for the appointment of a conservator of the estate, a conservator of the person, or a conservator of the person and estate is sought or has been issued.

(i) "Party" means the conservatee, proposed conservatee, petitioner, conservator, proposed conservator, or any other person allowed by the court to participate in a conservatorship proceeding.

(j) "Person" means an individual, corporation, business trust, estate, trust, partnership, limited liability company, association, joint venture, public corporation, government or governmental subdivision, agency, or instrumentality, or any other legal or commercial entity.

(k) "Proposed conservatee" means an adult for whom a conservatorship order is sought.

(l) "Record" means information that is inscribed on a tangible medium or that is stored in an electronic or other medium and is retrievable in perceivable form.

(m) Notwithstanding Section 74, "state" means a state of the United States, the District of Columbia, Puerto Rico, the United States Virgin Islands, a federally recognized Indian tribe, or any territory or insular possession subject to the jurisdiction of the United States. *(Added by Stats.2014, c. 553 (S.B.940), § 20, eff. Jan. 1, 2015, operative Jan. 1, 2016.)*

Law Revision Commission Comments
2014 Addition

Section 1982 defines terms used in this chapter. To prevent confusion, the definitions generally conform to usage elsewhere in this code and throughout this state, instead of the conflicting usage employed by the Uniform Law Commission in the Uniform Adult Guardianship and Protective Proceedings Jurisdiction Act (2007) ("UAGPPJA").

Subdivision (a) (defining "adult") is the same as Section 102(1) of UAGPPJA. This chapter only applies to a conservatorship for an adult. The chapter does not apply to a minor, even if the minor is married or has had a marriage dissolved. See Section 1981(a) & Comment (scope of chapter).

Subdivision (b) (defining "conservatee") is similar to Section 102(6) & (9) of UAGPPJA (defining "incapacitated person" and "protected person").

Subdivision (c) (defining "conservator") is included for drafting convenience.

Subdivision (d) (defining "conservator of the estate") is similar to Section 102(2) of UAGPPJA (defining "conservator"). See Section 1801(b) (standard for appointment of conservator of estate).

Subdivision (e) (defining "conservator of the person") is similar to Section 102(3) of UAGPPJA (defining "guardian"). See Section 1801(a) (standard for appointment of conservator of person).

Subdivision (f) (defining "conservator of the person and estate") is included for the sake of completeness. See Section 1801(c) (standard for appointment of conservator of person and estate).

Subdivision (g) (defining "conservatorship order") is similar to Section 102(4) & (10) of UAGPPJA (defining "guardianship order" and "protective order").

Subdivision (h) (defining "conservatorship proceeding") is similar to Section 102(5) & (11) of UAGPPJA (defining "guardianship proceeding" and "protective proceeding").

Subdivision (i) (defining "party") is similar to Section 102(7) of UAGPPJA (defining "party").

Subdivision (j) (defining "person") is similar to Section 102(8) of UAGPPJA (defining "person"). See also Section 56 ("person").

Subdivision (k) (defining "proposed conservatee") is similar to Section 102(13) of UAGPPJA (defining "respondent").

Subdivision (l) (defining "record") is the same as Section 102(12) of UAGPPJA.

Subdivision (m) (defining "State") is the same as Section 102(14) of UAGPPJA.

Background from Uniform Act. Section [1982] is not the sole definitional section in the Act. Section [1991] contains definitions of important terms used only in Article 2. These are the definitions of "emergency" [Section [1991(a)(1)], "home state" [Section 1991(a)(2)], and "significant-connection state" [Section 1991(a)(3)]. [Adapted from the Uniform Law Commission's Comment to UAGPPJA § 102.] [43 Cal.L.Rev.Comm. Reports 93 (2013)].

§ 1983. International application of chapter

A court of this state may treat a foreign country as if it were a state for the purpose of applying this article and Articles 2, 3, and 5. *(Added by Stats.2014, c. 553 (S.B.940), § 20, eff. Jan. 1, 2015, operative Jan. 1, 2016.)*

Law Revision Commission Comments
2014 Addition

Section 1983 is the same as Section 103 of the Uniform Adult Guardianship and Protective Proceedings Jurisdiction Act (2007) ("UAGPPJA"). In determining whether to treat a foreign country as if it were a state pursuant to this section, the court should consider all relevant factors, including, but not limited to, evidence showing any of the following:

(1) The judicial system in the foreign country does not regularly provide impartial tribunals.

(2) The judicial system in the foreign country does not regularly provide procedures compatible with the requirements of due process of law.

(3) The specific proceeding in the foreign court was not conducted in an impartial tribunal.

(4) The specific proceeding in the foreign court was not compatible with the requirements of due process of law.

(5) An aspect of the foreign proceeding is repugnant to the public policy of this state or of the United States.

(6) The circumstances of the foreign proceeding raise substantial doubt about the integrity of the foreign judicial system.

See generally Code Civ. Proc. § 1716; Uniform Foreign–Country Money Judgments Recognition Act § 4 (2005).

Background from Uniform Act. This section addresses application of the Act to [conservatorship orders] issued in other countries. A foreign order is not enforceable pursuant to the registration procedures of Article 4, but a court in this country may otherwise apply this Act to a foreign proceeding if the foreign country were an American state. Consequently, a court may conclude that the court in the foreign country has jurisdiction because it constitutes the [proposed conservatee's] "home state" or "significant-connection state" and may therefore decline to exercise jurisdiction on the ground that the court of the foreign country has a higher priority under Section [1993]. Or the court may treat the foreign country as if it were a state of the United States for purposes of applying the transfer provisions of Article 3.

This section addresses similar issues to but differs in result from Section 105 of the Uniform Child Custody Jurisdiction and Enforcement Act (1997). Under the UCCJEA, the United States court must honor a custody order issued by the court of a foreign country if the order was issued under factual circumstances in substantial conformity with the jurisdictional standards of the UCCJEA. Only if the child custody law violates fundamental principles of human rights is enforcement excused. Because [conservatorship] regimes vary so greatly around the world, particularly in civil law countries, it was concluded that under this Act a more flexible approach was needed. Under this Act, a court may but is not required to recognize the foreign order.

The fact that a [conservatorship] order of a foreign country cannot be enforced pursuant to the registration procedures of Article 4 does not preclude enforcement by the court under some other provision or rule of law. [Adapted from the Uniform Law Commission's Comment to UAGPPJA § 103.] [43 Cal.L.Rev.Comm. Reports 93 (2013)].

§ 1984. Communication between courts

(a) A court of this state may communicate with a court in another state concerning a proceeding arising under this chapter. The court may allow the parties to participate in the communication. Except as otherwise provided in subdivision (b), the court shall make a record of the communication. The record may be limited to the fact that the communication occurred.

(b) Courts may communicate concerning schedules, calendars, court records, and other administrative matters without making a record. *(Added by Stats.2014, c. 553 (S.B.940), § 20, eff. Jan. 1, 2015, operative Jan. 1, 2016.)*

Law Revision Commission Comments
2014 Addition

Section 1984 is the same as Section 104 of the Uniform Adult Guardianship and Protective Proceedings Jurisdiction Act (2007) ("UAGPPJA"). For another provision on communication between courts, see Family Code Section 3410 (communication between courts regarding child custody jurisdiction), which is similar to Section 110 of the Uniform Child Custody Jurisdiction and Enforcement Act (1997). See also Section 2204 (communication between courts regarding venue of guardianship and child custody or visitation matters); Cal. R. Ct. 7.1014 (same).

Although this section authorizes communication between courts, it does not authorize ex parte communication between a party (or attorney for a party) and a court. For guidance on ex parte communication, see Section 1051 and Rule 7.10 of the California Rules of Court.

Background from Uniform Act This section emphasizes the importance of communications among courts with an interest in a particular matter. Most commonly, this would include communication between courts of different states to resolve an issue of which court has jurisdiction to proceed under Article 2. It would also include communication between courts of different states to facilitate the transfer of a ... conservatorship to a different state under Article 3. Communication can occur in a variety of ways, including by electronic means. This section does not prescribe the use of any particular means of communication.

The court may authorize the parties to participate in the communication. But the Act does not mandate participation or require that the court give the parties notice of any communication. Communication between courts is often difficult to schedule and participation by the parties may be impractical. Phone calls or electronic communications often have to be made after-hours or whenever the schedules of judges allow. When issuing a jurisdictional or transfer order, the court should set forth the extent to which a communication with another court may have been a factor in the decision.

....

This section does not prescribe the extent of the record that the court must make, leaving that issue to the court. A record might include notes or transcripts of a court reporter who listened to a conference call between the courts, an electronic recording of a telephone call, a memorandum summarizing a conversation, and email communications. No record need be made of relatively inconsequential matters such as scheduling, calendars, and court records.

Section 110 of the Uniform Child Custody Jurisdiction and Enforcement Act (1997) addresses similar issues as this section but is more detailed. As is the case with several other provisions of this Act, the drafters of this Act concluded that the more varied circumstances of [conservatorship] proceedings suggested a greater need for flexibility. [Adapted from the Uniform Law Commission's Comment to UAGPPJA § 104.] [43 Cal.L.Rev.Comm. Reports 93 (2013)].

§ 1985. Cooperation between courts

(a) In a conservatorship proceeding in this state, a court of this state may request the appropriate court of another state to do any of the following:

(1) Hold an evidentiary hearing.

(2) Order a person in that state to produce evidence or give testimony pursuant to procedures of that state.

(3) Order that an evaluation or assessment be made of the proposed conservatee.

(4) Order any appropriate investigation of a person involved in a proceeding.

(5) Forward to the court of this state a certified copy of the transcript or other record of a hearing under paragraph (1) or any other proceeding, any evidence otherwise produced under paragraph (2), and any evaluation or assessment prepared in compliance with an order under paragraph (3) or (4).

(6) Issue any order necessary to ensure the appearance in the proceeding of a person whose presence is necessary for the court to make a determination, including the conservatee or the proposed conservatee.

(7) Issue an order authorizing the release of medical, financial, criminal, or other relevant information in that state, including protected health information as defined in Section 160.103 of Title 45 of the Code of Federal Regulations.

(b) If a court of another state in which a conservatorship proceeding is pending requests assistance of the kind provided in subdivision (a), a court of this state has jurisdiction for the limited purpose of granting the request or making reasonable efforts to comply with the request.

(c) Travel and other necessary and reasonable expenses incurred under subdivisions (a) and (b) may be assessed against the parties according to the law of this state. *(Added by Stats.2014, c. 553 (S.B.940), § 20, eff. Jan. 1, 2015, operative Jan. 1, 2016.)*

Law Revision Commission Comments

2014 Addition

Subdivisions (a) and (b) of Section 1985 are similar to Section 105 of the Uniform Adult Guardianship and Protective Proceedings Jurisdiction Act (2007) ("UAGPPJA"). Revisions have been made to conform to California terminology for the proceedings in question. See Section 1982 & Comment (definitions); see also Section 1980 Comment.

Subdivision (c) provides guidance on assessment of expenses under this section. For a similar provision, see Family Code Section 3412(c).

For limitations on the scope of this chapter, see Section 1981 & Comment. For another provision on cooperation between courts, see Family Code Section 3412 (cooperation between courts regarding child custody jurisdiction), which is similar to Section 112 of the Uniform Child Custody Jurisdiction and Enforcement Act (1997).

Background from Uniform Act [Subdivision (a)] of this section is similar to Section 112(a) of the Uniform Child Custody Jurisdiction and Enforcement Act (1997), although modified to address issues of concern in [conservatorship] proceedings and with the addition of [paragraph (a)(7)], which addresses the release of health information protected under HIPAA. [Subdivision (b)], which clarifies that a court has jurisdiction to respond to requests for assistance from courts in other states even though it might otherwise not have jurisdiction over the proceeding, is not found in although probably implicit in the UCCJEA.

Court cooperation is essential to the success of this Act. This section is designed to facilitate such court cooperation. It provides mechanisms for courts to cooperate with each other in order to decide cases in an efficient manner without causing undue expense to the parties. Courts may request assistance from courts of other states and may assist courts of other states. Typically, such assistance will be requested to resolve a jurisdictional issue arising under Article 2 or an issue concerning a transfer proceeding under Article 3.

This section [of the Act] does not address assessment of costs and expenses, leaving that issue to local law. Should a court have acquired jurisdiction because of a party's unjustifiable conduct, Section [1997(b)] authorizes the court to assess against the party all costs and expenses, including attorney's fees. [Adapted from the Uniform Law Commission's Comment to UAGPPJA § 105.] [43 Cal.L.Rev. Comm. Reports 93 (2013)].

§ 1986. Taking testimony in another state

(a) In a conservatorship proceeding, in addition to other procedures that may be available, testimony of a witness who is located in another state may be offered by deposition or other means allowable in this state for testimony taken in another state. The court on its own motion may order that the testimony of a witness be taken in another state and may prescribe the manner in which and the terms upon which the testimony is to be taken.

(b) In a conservatorship proceeding, a court in this state may permit a witness located in another state to be deposed or to testify by telephone or audiovisual or other electronic means. A court of this state shall cooperate with the court of the other state in designating an appropriate location for the deposition or testimony. *(Added by Stats.2014, c. 553 (S.B. 940), § 20, eff. Jan. 1, 2015, operative Jan. 1, 2016.)*

Law Revision Commission Comments

2014 Addition

Section 1986 is similar to Section 106(a)-(b) of the Uniform Adult Guardianship and Protective Proceedings Jurisdiction Act (2007) ("UAGPPJA"). Revisions have been made to conform to California terminology for the proceedings in question. See Section 1982 & Comment (definitions); see also Section 1980 Comment. For limitations on the scope of this chapter, see Section 1981 & Comment. For a child custody provision like Section 1986, see Family Code Section 3411 (evidence from another state in child custody case), which is similar to Section 111 of the Uniform Child Custody Jurisdiction and Enforcement Act (1997).

For further guidance on taking a deposition in another state for purposes of a proceeding pending in this state, see Code Civ. Proc. § 2026.010; Gov't Code § 70626. For further guidance on telephone depositions, see Code Civ. Proc. § 2025.310. For further guidance on audio or video recording of a deposition, see Code Civ. Proc. §§ 2020.310(c), 2025.220(a), 2025.330(c), 2025.340, 2025.510(f), 2025.530, 2025.560. For the admissibility of secondary evidence (including secondary evidence of a deposition), see Evid. Code §§ 1520–1523 (proof of content of writing). For guidance on taking a deposition in this state for purposes of a proceeding pending in another state, see Code Civ. Proc. §§ 2029.100–2029.900 (Interstate and International Depositions and Discovery Act); Gov't Code § 70626; *Deposition in Out-of-State Litigation*, 37 Cal.L.Rev.Comm. Reports 99 (2007).

Background from Uniform Act This section is similar to Section 111 of the Uniform Child Custody Jurisdiction and Enforcement Act (1997). That section was in turn derived from Section 316 of the Uniform Interstate Family Support Act (1992) and the much earlier and now otherwise obsolete Uniform Interstate and International Procedure Act (1962).

This section is designed to fill the vacuum that often exists in cases involving an adult with interstate contacts when much of the essential information about the individual is located in another state.

[Subdivision (a)] empowers the court to initiate the gathering of out-of-state evidence, including depositions, written interrogatories and other discovery devices. The authority granted to the court in no way precludes the gathering of out-of-state evidence by a party, including the taking of depositions out-of-state.

[Subdivision (b) clarifies] that modern modes of communication are permissible for the taking of depositions and receipt of documents into evidence....

This section is consistent with and complementary to the Uniform Interstate Depositions and Discovery Act (2007), which specifies the procedure for taking depositions in other states. [Adapted from the Uniform Law Commission's Comment to UAGPPJA § 106.] [43 Cal.L.Rev.Comm. Reports 93 (2013)].

ARTICLE 2. JURISDICTION

Law Revision Commission Comments
2014 Addition

Background from Uniform Act The jurisdictional rules in Article 2 will determine which state's courts may appoint a ... conservator. Section [1991] contains definitions of "emergency," "home state," and "significant connection-state," terms used only in Article 2 that are key to understanding the jurisdictional rules under the Act. Section [1992] provides that Article 2 is the exclusive jurisdictional basis for a court of the enacting state to appoint a [conservator]. Consequently, Article 2 is applicable even if all of the [proposed conservatee's] significant contacts are in-state. Section [1993] is the principal provision governing jurisdiction, creating a three-level priority; the home state, followed by a significant-connection state, followed by other jurisdictions. But there are circumstances under Section [1993] where a significant-connection state may have jurisdiction even if the [proposed conservatee] also has a home state, or a state that is neither a home or significant-connection state may be able to assume jurisdiction even though the particular [proposed conservatee] has both a home state and one or more significant-connection states. One of these situations is if a state declines to exercise jurisdiction under Section [1996] because a court of that state concludes that a court of another state is a more appropriate forum. Another is Section [1997], which authorizes a court to decline jurisdiction or fashion another appropriate remedy if jurisdiction was acquired because of unjustifiable conduct. Section [1995] provides that once an appointment is made or order issued, the court's jurisdiction continues until the proceeding is terminated or the appointment order expires by its own terms.

Section [1994] addresses special cases. Regardless of whether it has jurisdiction under the general principles stated in Section [1993], a court in the state where the individual is currently physically present has jurisdiction to appoint a [conservator of the person] in an emergency, and a court in a state where an individual's real or tangible personal property is located has jurisdiction to appoint a [conservator of the estate]. In addition, a court not otherwise having jurisdiction under Section [1993] has jurisdiction to consider a petition to accept the transfer of an already existing ... conservatorship from another state as provided in Article 3.

The remainder of Article 2 address[es] procedural issues. Section [1998] prescribes additional notice requirements if a proceeding is brought in a state other than the [proposed conservatee's] home state. Section [1999] specifies a procedure for resolving jurisdictional issues if petitions are pending in more than one state. [Adapted from the Uniform Law Commission's General Comment to Article 2 of UAGPPJA.] [43 Cal.L.Rev.Comm. Reports 93 (2013)].

§ 1991. Definitions; significant connection factors

(a) In this article:

(1) "Emergency" means a circumstance that likely will result in substantial harm to a proposed conservatee's health, safety, or welfare, and for which the appointment of a conservator of the person is necessary because no other person has authority and is willing to act on behalf of the proposed conservatee.

(2) "Home state" means the state in which the proposed conservatee was physically present, including any period of temporary absence, for at least six consecutive months immediately before the filing of a petition for a conservatorship order, or, if none, the state in which the proposed conservatee was physically present, including any period of temporary absence, for at least six consecutive months ending within the six months prior to the filing of the petition.

(3) "Significant–connection state" means a state, other than the home state, with which a proposed conservatee has a significant connection other than mere physical presence and in which substantial evidence concerning the proposed conservatee is available.

(b) In determining under Section 1993 and subdivision (e) of Section 2001 whether a proposed conservatee has a significant connection with a particular state, the court shall consider all of the following:

(1) The location of the proposed conservatee's family and other persons required to be notified of the conservatorship proceeding.

(2) The length of time the proposed conservatee at any time was physically present in the state and the duration of any absence.

(3) The location of the proposed conservatee's property.

(4) The extent to which the proposed conservatee has ties to the state such as voting registration, state or local tax return filing, vehicle registration, driver's license, social relationship, and receipt of services. *(Added by Stats.2014, c. 553 (S.B.940), § 20, eff. Jan. 1, 2015, operative Jan. 1, 2016.)*

Law Revision Commission Comments
2014 Addition

Subdivision (a) of Section 1991 is similar to Section 201(a) of the Uniform Adult Guardianship and Protective Proceedings Jurisdiction Act (2007) ("UAGPPJA"). Revisions have been made to conform to California terminology for the proceedings in question. See Section 1982 & Comment (definitions); see also Section 1980 Comment.

Subdivision (b) is similar to Section 201(b) of UAGPPJA. Revisions have been made to conform to California terminology for the proceedings in question. See Section 1982 & Comment (definitions); see also Section 1980 Comment.

For limitations on the scope of this chapter, see Section 1981 & Comment.

Background from Uniform Act. The terms "emergency," "home state," and "significant-connection state" are defined in this section and not in Section [1982] because they are used only in Article 2.

The definition of "emergency" [paragraph (a)(1)] is taken from the emergency guardianship provision of the Uniform Guardianship and Protective Proceedings Act (1997), Section 312.

Pursuant to Section [1994], a court has jurisdiction to appoint a [temporary conservator] in an emergency for a [limited] period ... even though it does not otherwise have jurisdiction. However, the emergency appointment is subject to the direction of the court in the [proposed conservatee's] home state. Pursuant to Section [1994(b)], the emergency proceeding must be dismissed at the request of the court in the [proposed conservatee's] home state.

Appointing a [conservator of the person] in an emergency should be an unusual event. Although most states have emergency [conservatorship] statutes, not all states do, and in those states that do have such statutes, there is great variation on whether and how an emergency is defined. To provide some uniformity on when a court acquires emergency jurisdiction, the drafters of this Act concluded that adding a definition of emergency was essential. The definition does not preclude an enacting jurisdiction from appointing a [conservator] under an emergency [conservatorship] statute with a different or broader test of emergency if the court otherwise has jurisdiction to make an appointment under Section [1993].

Pursuant to Section [1993], a court in the [proposed conservatee's] home state has primary jurisdiction to appoint a [conservator]. A court in a significant-connection state has jurisdiction if the [proposed conservatee] does not have a home state and in other circumstances specified in Section [1993]. The definitions of "home state" and "significant-connection state" are therefore important to an understanding of the Act.

The definition of "home state" [paragraph (a)(2)] is derived from but differs in a couple of respects from the definition of the same term in Section 102 of the Uniform Child Custody Jurisdiction and Enforcement Act (1997). First, unlike the definition in the UCCJEA, the definition in this Act clarifies that actual physical presence is necessary. The UCCJEA definition instead focuses on where the child has "lived" for the prior six months. Basing the test on where someone has "lived" may imply that the term "home state" is similar to the concept of domicile. Domicile, in [a conservatorship] context, is a vague concept that can easily lead to claims of jurisdiction by courts in more than one state. Second, under the UCCJEA, home state jurisdiction continues for six months following physical removal from the state and the state has ceased to be the actual home. Under this Act, the six-month tail is incorporated directly into the definition of home state. The place where the [proposed conservatee] was last physically present for six months continues as the home state for six months following physical removal from the state. This modification of the UCCJEA definition eliminates the need to refer to the six-month tail each time home state jurisdiction is mentioned in the Act.

The definition of "significant-connection state" [paragraph (a)(3)] is similar to Section 201(a)(2) of the Uniform Child Custody Jurisdiction and Enforcement Act (1997). However, [subdivision (b)] of this Section adds a list of factors relevant to [conservatorship] proceedings to aid the court in deciding whether a particular place is a significant-connection state. Under Section [2001(e)(1)], the significant connection factors listed in the definition are to be taken into account in determining whether a conservatorship may be transferred to another state. [Adapted from the Uniform Law Commission's Comment to UAGPPJA § 201.] [43 Cal.L.Rev.Comm. Reports 93 (2013)].

§ 1992. Exclusive basis

For a conservatorship proceeding governed by this article, this article provides the exclusive basis for determining whether the courts of this state, as opposed to the courts of another state, have jurisdiction to appoint a conservator of the person, a conservator of the estate, or a conservator of the person and estate. *(Added by Stats.2014, c. 553 (S.B.940), § 20, eff. Jan. 1, 2015, operative Jan. 1, 2016.)*

Law Revision Commission Comments
2014 Addition

Section 1992 is similar to Section 202 of the Uniform Adult Guardianship and Protective Proceedings Jurisdiction Act (2007) ("UAGPPJA"). Revisions have been made to:

(1) Conform to California terminology for the proceedings in question. See Section 1982 & Comment (definitions); see also Section 1980 Comment.

(2) Make clear that this article only focuses on which state's courts have jurisdiction to appoint a conservator. The article does not address other jurisdictional issues, such as whether an appellate court may make such an appointment.

For limitations on the scope of this chapter, see Section 1981 & Comment.

Background from Uniform Act. Similar to Section 201(b) of the Uniform Child Custody Jurisdiction and Enforcement Act (1997), which provides that the UCCJEA is the exclusive basis for determining jurisdiction to issue a child custody order, this section provides that this article is the exclusive jurisdictional basis for determining jurisdiction to appoint a [conservator]. An enacting jurisdiction will therefore need to repeal any existing provisions addressing jurisdiction in [conservatorship proceedings]. The drafters of this Act concluded that limiting the Act to "interstate" cases was unworkable. Such cases are hard to define, but even if they could be defined, overlaying this Act onto a state's existing jurisdictional rules would leave too many gaps and inconsistencies. In addition, if the particular case is truly local, the local court would likely have jurisdiction under both this Act as well as under prior law. [Adapted from the Uniform Law Commission's Comment to UAGPPJA § 202.] [43 Cal.L.Rev. Comm. Reports 93 (2013)].

§ 1993. Jurisdiction

(a) A court of this state has jurisdiction to appoint a conservator for a proposed conservatee if this state is the proposed conservatee's home state.

(b) A court of this state has jurisdiction to appoint a conservator for a proposed conservatee if, on the date the petition is filed, this state is a significant-connection state and the respondent does not have a home state.

(c) A court of this state has jurisdiction to appoint a conservator for a proposed conservatee if, on the date the petition is filed, this state is a significant-connection state and a court of the proposed conservatee's home state has expressly declined to exercise jurisdiction because this state is a more appropriate forum.

(d) A court of this state has jurisdiction to appoint a conservator for a proposed conservatee if both of the following conditions are satisfied:

(1) On the date the petition is filed, this state is a significant-connection state, the proposed conservatee has a home state, and a conservatorship petition is not pending in a court of the home state or another significant-connection state.

(2) Before the court makes the appointment, no conservatorship petition is filed in the proposed conservatee's home state, no objection to the court's jurisdiction is filed by a person required to be notified of the proceeding, and the court in this state concludes that it is an appropriate forum under the factors set forth in Section 1996.

(e) A court of this state has jurisdiction to appoint a conservator for a proposed conservatee if all of the following conditions are satisfied:

(1) This state does not have jurisdiction under subdivision (a), (b), (c), or (d).

(2) The proposed conservatee's home state and all significant-connection states have expressly declined to exercise jurisdiction because this state is the more appropriate forum.

(3) Jurisdiction in this state is consistent with the constitutions of this state and the United States.

(f) A court of this state has jurisdiction to appoint a conservator for a proposed conservatee if the requirements for special jurisdiction under Section 1994 are met. *(Added by Stats.2014, c. 553 (S.B.940), § 20, eff. Jan. 1, 2015, operative Jan. 1, 2016.)*

Law Revision Commission Comments

2014 Addition

Section 1993 is similar to Section 203 of the Uniform Adult Guardianship and Protective Proceedings Jurisdiction Act (2007) ("UAGPPJA"). Revisions have been made to follow local drafting practices and conform to California terminology for the proceedings in question. See Section 1982 & Comment (definitions); see also Section 1980 Comment.

Subdivision (a), relating to jurisdiction in the proposed conservatee's home state, corresponds to Section 203(1) of UAGPPJA.

Subdivisions (b) and (c), relating to jurisdiction in a significant-connection state, correspond to Section 203(2)(A) of UAGPPJA. Revisions have been made to emphasize that a court may not be deemed to have "declined jurisdiction" unless the court has expressly taken that step.

Subdivision (d), providing another basis for jurisdiction in a significant-connection state, corresponds to Section 203(2)(B) of UAGPPJA.

Subdivision (e), relating to jurisdiction in a state that is neither the home state nor a significant-connection state, corresponds to Section 203(3) of UAGPPJA. Revisions have been made to emphasize that a court may not be deemed to have "declined jurisdiction" unless the court has expressly taken that step.

Subdivision (f), relating to special jurisdiction, corresponds to Section 203(4) of UAGPPJA.

See Section 1991(a) (defining "home state" & "significant-connection state"). For limitations on the scope of this chapter, see Section 1981 & Comment.

Background from Uniform Act. Similar to the Uniform Child [Custody] Jurisdiction and Enforcement Act (1997), this Act creates a three-level priority for determining which state has jurisdiction to appoint a [conservator]; the home state (defined in Section [1991(a)(2)]), followed by a significant-connection state (defined in Section [1991(a)(3)]), followed by other jurisdictions. The principal objective of this section is to eliminate the possibility of dual appointments or orders except for the special circumstances specified in Section [1994].

While this section is the principal provision for determining whether a particular court has jurisdiction to appoint a [conservator], it is not the only provision. As indicated in the cross-reference in Section [1993(f)], a court that does not otherwise have jurisdiction under Section [1993] may have jurisdiction under the special circumstances specified in Section [1994].

Pursuant to Section [1993(a)], the home state has primary jurisdiction to appoint a ... conservator .... This jurisdiction terminates if the state ceases to be the home state, if a court of the home state declines to exercise jurisdiction under Section [1996] on the basis that another state is a more appropriate forum, or, as provided in Section [1995], a court of another state has appointed a [conservator] consistent with this Act. The standards by which a home state that has enacted the Act may decline jurisdiction on the basis that another state is a more appropriate forum are specified in Section [1996]. Should the home state not have enacted the Act, Section [1993(a)] does not require that the declination meet the standards of Section [1996].

Once a petition is filed in a court of the [proposed conservatee's] home state, that state does not cease to be the [proposed conservatee's] home state upon the passage of time even though it may be many months before an appointment is made or order issued and during that period the [proposed conservatee] is physically located [elsewhere]. Only upon dismissal of the petition can the court cease to be the home state due to the passage of time. Under the definition of "home state," the six-month physical presence requirement is fulfilled or not on the date the petition is filed. See Section [1991(a)(2)].

A significant-connection state has jurisdiction under [these] possible bases: Section [1993(b), (c), and (d)]. Under Section [1993(b)], a significant-connection state has jurisdiction if the individual does not

have a home state .... [Under Section 1993(c), a significant-connection state has jurisdiction] if the home state has declined jurisdiction on the basis that the significant-connection state is a more appropriate forum.

Section [1993(d)] is designed to facilitate consideration of cases where jurisdiction is not in dispute. Section [1993(d)] allows a court in a significant-connection state to exercise jurisdiction even though the [proposed conservatee] has a home state and the home state has not declined jurisdiction. The significant-connection state may assume jurisdiction under these circumstances, however, only in situations where the parties are not in disagreement concerning which court should hear the case. Jurisdiction may not be exercised by a significant-connection state under Section [1993(d)] if (1) a petition has already been filed and is still pending in the home state or other significant-connection state; or (2) prior to making the appointment ..., a petition is filed in the [proposed conservatee's] home state or an objection to the court's jurisdiction is filed by a person required to be notified of the proceeding. Additionally, the court in the significant-connection state must conclude that it is an appropriate forum applying the factors listed in Section [1996].

There is nothing comparable to Section [1993(d)] in the Uniform Child Custody Jurisdiction and Enforcement Act (1997). Under Section 201 of the UCCJEA a court in a significant-connection state acquires jurisdiction only if the child does not have a home state or the court of that state has declined jurisdiction. The drafters of this Act concluded that cases involving adults differed sufficiently from child custody matters that a different rule is appropriate for adult proceedings in situations where jurisdiction is uncontested.

Pursuant to Section [1993(e)], a court in a state that is neither the home state or a significant-connection state has jurisdiction if the home state and all significant-connection states have declined jurisdiction or the [proposed conservatee] does not have a home state or significant-connection state. The state must have some connection with the proceeding, however. As Section [1993(e)] clarifies, jurisdiction in the state must be consistent with the state and United States constitutions. [Adapted from the Uniform Law Commission's Comment to UAGPPJA § 203.] [43 Cal.L.Rev.Comm. Reports 93 (2013)].

§ 1994. Special jurisdiction

(a) A court of this state lacking jurisdiction under subdivisions (a) to (e), inclusive, of Section 1993 has special jurisdiction to do any of the following:

(1) Appoint a temporary conservator of the person in an emergency for a proposed conservatee who is physically present in this state. In making an appointment under this paragraph, a court shall follow the procedures specified in Chapter 3 (commencing with Section 2250) of Part 4. The temporary conservatorship shall terminate in accordance with Section 2257.

(2) Appoint a conservator of the estate with respect to real or tangible personal property located in this state.

(3) Appoint a conservator of the person, conservator of the estate, or conservator of the person and estate for a proposed conservatee for whom a provisional order to transfer a proceeding from another state has been issued under procedures similar to Section 2001. In making an appointment under this paragraph, a court shall follow the procedures specified in Chapter 3 (commencing with Section 2250) of Part 4. The temporary conservatorship shall terminate in accordance with Section 2257.

(b) If a petition for the appointment of a conservator of the person in an emergency is brought in this state and this state was not the home state of the proposed conservatee on

---

the date the petition was filed, the court shall dismiss the proceeding at the request of the court of the home state, if any, whether dismissal is requested before or after the emergency appointment of a temporary conservator of the person. *(Added by Stats.2014, c. 553 (S.B.940), § 20, eff. Jan. 1, 2015, operative Jan. 1, 2016.)*

Law Revision Commission Comments
2014 Addition

Section 1994 is similar to Section 204 of the Uniform Adult Guardianship and Protective Proceedings Jurisdiction Act (2007) ("UAGPPJA"). Revisions have been made to conform to California terminology for the proceedings in question. See Section 1982 & Comment (definitions); see also Section 1980 Comment. Revisions have also been made to specify the procedure for making an emergency appointment under paragraph (a)(1) or an appointment under paragraph (a)(3) while a transfer petition is pending.

See Section 1991(a) (defining "emergency" & "home state"). For limitations on the scope of this chapter, see Section 1981 & Comment.

Background from Uniform Act. This section lists the special circumstances where a court without jurisdiction under the general rule of Section [1993] has jurisdiction for limited purposes. The three purposes are (1) the appointment of a [conservator of the person] in an emergency for a [limited] term ... for a [proposed conservatee] who is physically located in the state ([paragraph] (a)(1)); (2) the [appointment of a conservator of the estate] for a [proposed conservatee] who owns an interest in real or tangible personal property located in the state ([paragraph] (a)(2)); and (3) the grant of jurisdiction to consider a petition requesting the transfer of a ... conservatorship proceeding from another state ([paragraph] (a)(3)). If the court has jurisdiction under Section [1993], reference to Section [1994] is unnecessary. The general jurisdiction granted under Section [1993] includes within it all of the special circumstances specified in this section.

When an emergency arises, action must often be taken on the spot in the place where the [proposed conservatee] happens to be physically located at the time. This place may not necessarily be located in the [proposed conservatee's] home state or even a significant-connection state. [Paragraph] (a)(1) assures that the court where the [proposed conservatee] happens to be physically located at the time has jurisdiction to appoint a [conservator of the person] in an emergency but only for a limited period .... As provided in [paragraph] (b), the emergency jurisdiction is also subject to the authority of the court in the [proposed conservatee's] home state to request that the emergency proceeding be dismissed. The theory here is that the emergency appointment in the temporary location should not be converted into a de facto permanent appointment through repeated temporary appointments.

"Emergency" is specifically defined in Section [1991(a)(1)]. Because of the great variation among the states on how an emergency is defined and its important role in conferring jurisdiction, the drafters of this Act concluded that adding a uniform definition of emergency was essential. The definition does not preclude an enacting jurisdiction from appointing a guardian under an emergency [conservatorship] statute with a different or broader test of emergency if the court otherwise has jurisdiction to make an appointment under Section [1993].

[Paragraph] (a)(2) grants a court jurisdiction to [appoint a conservator of the estate] with respect to real and tangible personal property located in the state even though the court does not otherwise have jurisdiction. Such orders are most commonly issued when a conservator has been appointed but the [conservatee] owns real property located in another state. The drafters specifically rejected using a general reference to any property located in the state because of the tendency of some courts to issue protective orders with respect to intangible personal property such as a bank account

where the technical situs of the asset may have little relationship to the protected person.

[Paragraph] (a)(3) is closely related to and is necessary for the effectiveness of Article 3, which addresses transfer of a ... conservatorship to another state. A "Catch–22" arises frequently in such cases. The court in the transferring state will not allow the [conservatee] to move and will not terminate the case until the court in the transferee state has accepted the matter. But the court in the transferee state will not accept the case until the [conservatee] has physically moved and presumably become a resident of the transferee state. [Paragraph] (a)(3), which grants the court in the transferee state limited jurisdiction to consider a petition requesting transfer of a proceeding [from] another state, is intended to unlock the stalemate.

Not included in this section but a provision also conferring special jurisdiction on the court is Section [1985(b)], which grants the court jurisdiction to respond to a request for assistance from a court of another state. [Adapted from the Uniform Law Commission's Comment to UAGPPJA § 204.] [43 Cal.L.Rev.Comm. Reports 93 (2013)].

§ 1995. Exclusive and continuing jurisdiction

Except as otherwise provided in Section 1994, a court that has appointed a conservator consistent with this chapter has exclusive and continuing jurisdiction over the proceeding until it is terminated by the court or the appointment expires by its own terms. *(Added by Stats.2014, c. 553 (S.B.940), § 20, eff. Jan. 1, 2015, operative Jan. 1, 2016.)*

Law Revision Commission Comments
2014 Addition

Section 1995 is similar to Section 205 of the Uniform Adult Guardianship and Protective Proceedings Jurisdiction Act (2007) ("UAGPPJA"). Revisions have been made to conform to California terminology for the proceedings in question. See Section 1982 & Comment (definitions); see also Section 1980 Comment.

For limitations on the scope of this chapter, see Section 1981 & Comment.

Background from Uniform Act. While this Act relies heavily on the Uniform Child [Custody] Jurisdiction and Enforcement Act (1997) for many basic concepts, the identity is not absolute. Section 202 of the UCCJEA specifies a variety of circumstances whereby a court can lose jurisdiction based on loss of physical presence by the child and others, loss of a significant connection, or unavailability of substantial evidence. Section 203 of the UCCJEA addresses the jurisdiction of the court to modify a custody determination made in another state. Nothing comparable to either UCCJEA section is found in this Act. Under this Act, a [conservatorship] may be modified only upon request to the court that made the appointment ..., which retains exclusive and continuing jurisdiction over the proceeding. Unlike child custody matters, [conservatorships] are ordinarily subject to continuing court supervision. Allowing the court's jurisdiction to terminate other than by its own order would open the possibility of competing ... conservatorship appointments in different states for the same person at the same time, the problem under current law that enactment of this Act is designed to avoid. Should the [conservatee] and others with an interest in the proceeding relocate to a different state, the appropriate remedy is to seek transfer of the proceeding to the other state as provided in Article 3.

The exclusive and continuing jurisdiction conferred by this section only applies to [conservatorship] orders made ... under Section [1993]. Orders made under the special jurisdiction conferred by Section [1994] are not exclusive. And as provided in Section [1994(b)], the jurisdiction of a court in a state other than the home state to appoint a [conservator] in an emergency is subject to the right of a court in the home state to request that the proceeding be dismissed and any appointment terminated.

Article 3 authorizes a ... conservator to petition to transfer the proceeding to another state. Upon the conclusion of the transfer, the court in the accepting state will appoint the ... conservator as ... conservator in the accepting state and the court in the transferring [state] will terminate the local proceeding, whereupon the jurisdiction of the transferring court terminates and the court in the accepting state acquires exclusive and continuing jurisdiction as provided in Section [1995]. [Adapted from the Uniform Law Commission's Comment to UAGPPJA § 205.] [43 Cal.L.Rev. Comm. Reports 93 (2013)].

§ 1996.   Appropriate forum

(a)(1) A court of this state having jurisdiction under Section 1993 to appoint a conservator may decline to exercise its jurisdiction if it determines at any time that a court of another state is a more appropriate forum.

(2) The issue of appropriate forum may be raised upon petition of any interested person, the court's own motion, or the request of another court.

(3) The petitioner, or, if there is no petitioner, the court in this state, shall give notice of the petition, motion, or request to the same persons and in the same manner as for a petition for a conservatorship under Section 1801. The notice shall state the basis for the petition, motion, or request, and shall inform the recipients of the date, time, and place of the hearing under paragraph (4). The notice shall also advise the recipients that they have a right to object to the petition, motion, or request. The notice to the potential conservatee shall inform the potential conservatee of the right to be represented by legal counsel if the potential conservatee so chooses, and to have legal counsel appointed by the court if the potential conservatee is unable to retain legal counsel.

(4) The court shall hold a hearing on the petition, motion, or request.

(b) If a court of this state declines to exercise its jurisdiction under subdivision (a), it shall grant the petition, motion, or request, and either dismiss or stay any conservatorship proceeding pending in this state. The court's order shall be based on evidence presented to the court. The order shall be in a record and shall expressly state that the court declines to exercise its jurisdiction because a court of another state is a more appropriate forum. The court may impose any condition the court considers just and proper, including the condition that a petition for the appointment of a conservator of the person, conservator of the estate, or conservator of the person and estate be filed promptly in another state.

(c) In determining whether it is an appropriate forum, the court shall consider all relevant factors, including all of the following:

(1) Any expressed preference of the proposed conservatee.

(2) Whether abuse, neglect, or exploitation of the proposed conservatee has occurred or is likely to occur and which state could best protect the proposed conservatee from the abuse, neglect, or exploitation.

(3) The length of time the proposed conservatee was physically present in or was a legal resident of this or another state.

(4) The location of the proposed conservatee's family, friends, and other persons required to be notified of the conservatorship proceeding.

(5) The distance of the proposed conservatee from the court in each state.

(6) The financial circumstances of the estate of the proposed conservatee.

(7) The nature and location of the evidence.

(8) The ability of the court in each state to decide the issue expeditiously and the procedures necessary to present evidence.

(9) The familiarity of the court of each state with the facts and issues in the proceeding.

(10) If an appointment were made, the court's ability to monitor the conduct of the conservator. *(Added by Stats. 2014, c. 553 (S.B.940), § 20, eff. Jan. 1, 2015, operative Jan. 1, 2016.)*

Law Revision Commission Comments

2014 Addition

Section 1996 is similar to Section 206 of the Uniform Adult Guardianship and Protective Proceedings Jurisdiction Act (2007) ("UAGPPJA"). Revisions have been made to conform to California terminology for the proceedings in question. See Section 1982 & Comment (definitions); see also Section 1980 Comment.

Revisions have also been made to:

(1) Permit an interested person, a court of this state, or a court of another state to raise the issue of appropriate forum by a petition, motion, or request specifically directed to that issue, without filing a conservatorship proceeding in this state.

(2) Specify procedural requirements applicable to such a petition, motion, or request. Among other things, a hearing on the petition, motion, or request is mandatory in every case. If there is no opposition, the court may place the matter on the consent calendar.

(3) Require a court to prepare a record when it declines to exercise its jurisdiction, which expressly states that the court is taking that step. A person can present that record when seeking jurisdiction in another state.

(4) Emphasize that in determining whether it is an appropriate forum, a court must consider the location of the proposed conservatee's family, friends, and other persons required to be notified of the conservatorship proceeding.

For limitations on the scope of this chapter, see Section 1981 & Comment.

Background from Uniform Act. This section authorizes a court otherwise having jurisdiction to decline jurisdiction on the basis that a court in another state is in a better position to make a [conservatorship] determination. The effect of a declination of jurisdiction under this section is to rearrange the priorities specified in Section [1993]. A court of the home state may decline in favor of a court of a significant-connection or other state and a court in a significant-connection state may decline in favor of a court in another significant-connection or other state. The court declining jurisdiction may either dismiss or stay the proceeding. The court may also impose any condition the court considers just and proper, including the condition that a petition for the appointment of a [conservator] be filed promptly in another state.

This section is similar to Section 207 of the Uniform Child Custody Jurisdiction and Enforcement Act (1997) except that the factors in [subdivision (c) of this section] have been adapted to address issues most commonly encountered in [conservatorship] proceedings as opposed to child custody determinations.

Under Section [1993(d)], the factors specified in [subdivision] (c) of this section are to be employed in determining whether a court of a significant-connection state may assume jurisdiction when a petition has not been filed in the [proposed conservatee's] home state or in another significant-connection state. Under Section [1997(a)(3)(B)], the court is to consider these factors in deciding whether it will retain jurisdiction when unjustifiable conduct has occurred. [Adapted from the Uniform Law Commission's Comment to UAGPPJA § 206.] [43 Cal.L.Rev.Comm. Reports 93 (2013)].

§ 1997. Jurisdiction declined by reason of conduct

(a) If at any time a court of this state determines that it acquired jurisdiction to appoint a conservator because of unjustifiable conduct, the court may do any of the following:

(1) Decline to exercise jurisdiction.

(2) Exercise jurisdiction for the limited purpose of fashioning an appropriate remedy to ensure the health, safety, and welfare of the conservatee or proposed conservatee or the protection of the property of the conservatee or proposed conservatee or to prevent a repetition of the unjustifiable conduct, including staying the proceeding until a petition for the appointment of a conservator of the person, conservator of the estate, or conservator of the person and estate is filed in a court of another state having jurisdiction.

(3) Continue to exercise jurisdiction after considering all of the following:

(A) The extent to which the conservatee or proposed conservatee and all persons required to be notified of the proceedings have acquiesced in the exercise of the court's jurisdiction.

(B) Whether it is a more appropriate forum than the court of any other state under the factors set forth in subdivision (c) of Section 1996.

(C) Whether the court of any other state would have jurisdiction under factual circumstances in substantial conformity with the jurisdictional standards of Section 1993.

(b) If a court of this state determines that it acquired jurisdiction to appoint a conservator because a party seeking to invoke its jurisdiction engaged in unjustifiable conduct, it may assess against that party necessary and reasonable expenses, including attorney's fees, investigative fees, court costs, communication expenses, medical examination expenses, witness fees and expenses, and travel expenses. The court may not assess fees, costs, or expenses of any kind against this state or a governmental subdivision, agency, or instrumentality of this state unless authorized by law other than this chapter. *(Added by Stats.2014, c. 553 (S.B.940), § 20, eff. Jan. 1, 2015, operative Jan. 1, 2016.)*

Law Revision Commission Comments
2014 Addition

Section 1997 is similar to Section 207 of the Uniform Adult Guardianship and Protective Proceedings Jurisdiction Act (2007) ("UAGPPJA"). Revisions have been made to conform to California terminology for the proceedings in question. See Section 1982 & Comment (definitions); see also Section 1980 Comment.

In subdivision (b), revisions have also been made to expressly authorize recovery of medical examination expenses. For a similar provision, see Conn. Gen. Stat. Ann. § 45–667m(b).

For limitations on the scope of this chapter, see Section 1981 & Comment.

Background from Uniform Act. This section is similar to ... Section 208 of the Uniform Child Custody Jurisdiction and Enforcement Act (1997). Like the UCCJEA, this Act does not attempt to define "unjustifiable conduct," concluding that this issue is best left to the courts. However, a common example could include the unauthorized removal of an adult to another state, with that state acquiring emergency jurisdiction under Section [1994] immediately upon the move and home state jurisdiction under Section [1993] six months following the move if a [conservatorship petition] is not filed during the interim in the soon-to-be former home state. Although child custody cases frequently raise different issues than [conservatorships], the element of unauthorized removal is encountered in both types of proceedings. For the caselaw on unjustifiable conduct under the predecessor Uniform Child Custody Jurisdiction Act (1968), see David Carl Minneman, *Parties' Misconduct as Grounds for Declining Jurisdiction Under § 8 of the Uniform Child Custody Jurisdiction Act (UCCJA)*, 16 A.L.R. 5th 650 (1993).

[Subdivision] (a) gives the court authority to fashion an appropriate remedy when it has acquired jurisdiction because of unjustifiable conduct. The court may decline to exercise jurisdiction; exercise jurisdiction for the limited purpose of fashioning an appropriate remedy to ensure the health, safety, and welfare of the [conservatee or proposed conservatee] or the protection of the ... property [of the conservatee or proposed conservatee] or [to] prevent a repetition of the unjustifiable conduct; or continue to exercise jurisdiction after considering several specified factors. Under [subdivision] (a), the unjustifiable conduct need not have been committed by a party.

[Subdivision] (b) authorizes a court to assess costs and expenses, including attorney's fees, against a party whose unjustifiable conduct caused the court to acquire jurisdiction. [Subdivision] (b) applies only if the unjustifiable conduct was committed by a party and allows for costs and expenses to be assessed only against that party. Similar to Section 208 of the UCCJEA, the court may not assess fees, costs, or expenses of any kind against this state or a governmental subdivision, agency, or instrumentality of the state unless authorized by other law. [Adapted from the Uniform Law Commission's Comment to UAGPPJA § 207.] [43 Cal.L.Rev.Comm. Reports 93 (2013)].

Cross References

Conservatorships, appealable orders, see Probate Code § 1301.5.

§ 1998. Notice of proceeding

If a petition for the appointment of a conservator of the person, conservator of the estate, or conservator of the person and estate is brought in this state and this state was not the home state of the proposed conservatee on the date the petition was filed, in addition to complying with the notice requirements of this state, the petitioner shall give notice of the petition or of a hearing on the petition to those persons who would be entitled to notice of the petition or of a hearing on the petition if a proceeding were brought in the home state of the proposed conservatee. The notice shall be given in the same manner as notice is required to be given in this state. *(Added by Stats.2014, c. 553 (S.B.940), § 20, eff. Jan. 1, 2015, operative Jan. 1, 2016.)*

Law Revision Commission Comments
2014 Addition

Section 1998 is similar to Section 208 of the Uniform Adult Guardianship and Protective Proceedings Jurisdiction Act (2007) ("UAGPPJA"). Revisions have been made to conform to California drafting practices and terminology for the proceedings in question. See Section 1982 & Comment (definitions); see also Section 1980 Comment. Revisions have also been made to:

(1) Reflect that some states require notice of a hearing on a petition, as opposed to notice of a petition.

(2) Make clear that the petitioner is responsible for giving the required notice. For a similar provision, see Ohio Rev. Code Ann. § 2112.26.

See Section 1991(a) (defining home state). For limitations on the scope of this chapter, see Section 1981 & Comment.

Background from Uniform Act. While this Act tries not to interfere with a state's underlying substantive law on [conservatorship] proceedings, the issue of notice is fundamental. Under this section, when a proceeding is brought other than in the [proposed conservatee's] home state, the petitioner must give notice in the method provided under local law not only to those entitled to notice under local law but also to the persons required to be notified were the proceeding brought in the [proposed conservatee's] home state. Frequently, the respective lists of persons to be notified will be the same. But where the lists are different, notice under this section will assure that someone with a right to assert that the home state has a primary right to jurisdiction will have the opportunity to make that assertion. [Adapted from the Uniform Law Commission's Comment to UAGPPJA § 208.] [43 Cal.L.Rev.Comm. Reports 93 (2013)].

§ 1999. Proceedings in more than one state

Except for a petition for the appointment of a conservator under paragraph (1) or paragraph (2) of subdivision (a) of Section 1994, if a petition for the appointment of a conservator is filed in this state and in another state and neither petition has been dismissed or withdrawn, the following rules apply:

(a) If the court in this state has jurisdiction under Section 1993, it may proceed with the case unless a court in another state acquires jurisdiction under provisions similar to Section 1993 before the appointment.

(b) If the court in this state does not have jurisdiction under Section 1993, whether at the time the petition is filed or at any time before the appointment, the court shall stay the proceeding and communicate with the court in the other state. If the court in the other state has jurisdiction, the court in this state shall dismiss the petition unless the court in the other state determines that the court in this state is a more appropriate forum. *(Added by Stats.2014, c. 553 (S.B.940), § 20, eff. Jan. 1, 2015, operative Jan. 1, 2016.)*

Law Revision Commission Comments
2014 Addition

Section 1999 is similar to Section 209 of the Uniform Adult Guardianship and Protective Proceedings Jurisdiction Act (2007) ("UAGPPJA"). Revisions have been made to conform to California terminology for the proceedings in question. See Section 1982 & Comment (definitions); see also Section 1980 Comment. For limitations on the scope of this chapter, see Section 1981 & Comment.

Background from Uniform Act. Similar to Section 206 of the Uniform Child Custody Jurisdiction and Enforcement Act (1997), this section addresses the issue of which court has the right to proceed when proceedings for the same [proposed conservatee] are brought in more than one state. The provisions of this section, however, have been tailored to the needs of [conservatorship] proceedings and the particular jurisdictional provisions of this Act. Emergency [conservatorship] appointments [Section 1994(a)(1)] and [conservatorships] with respect to property in other states [Section 1994(a)(2)] are excluded from this section because the need for dual appointments is frequent in these cases; for example, a petition will be brought in the [proposed conservatee's] home state but emergency action will be necessary in the place where the [proposed conservatee] is temporarily located, or a petition for the appointment of a [conservator of the estate] will be brought in the [proposed conserva-

tee's] home state but real estate located in some other state needs to be brought under management.

Under the Act only one court in which a petition is pending will have jurisdiction under Section [1993]. If a petition is brought in the [proposed conservatee's] home state, that court has jurisdiction over that of any significant-connection or other state. If the petition is first brought in a significant-connection state, that jurisdiction will be lost if a petition is later brought in the home state prior to an appointment .... Jurisdiction will also be lost in the significant-connection state if the [proposed conservatee] has a home state and an objection is filed in the significant-connection state that jurisdiction is properly in the home state. If petitions are brought in two significant-connection states, the first state has a right to proceed over that of the second state, and if a petition is brought in any other state, any claim to jurisdiction of that state is subordinate to that of the home state and all significant-connection states.

Under this section, if the court has jurisdiction under Section [1993], it has the right to proceed unless a court of another state acquires jurisdiction prior to the first court making an appointment .... If the court does not have jurisdiction under Section [1993], it must defer to the court with jurisdiction unless that court determines that the court in this state is the more appropriate forum and it thereby acquires jurisdiction. While the rules are straightforward, factual issues can arise as to which state is the home state or significant-connection state. Consequently, while under Section [1993] there will almost always be a court having jurisdiction to proceed, reliance on the communication, court cooperation, and evidence gathering provisions of Sections [1984–1986] will sometimes be necessary to determine which court that might be. [Adapted from the Uniform Law Commission's Comment to UAGPPJA § 209.] [43 Cal.L.Rev.Comm. Reports 93 (2013)].

ARTICLE 3. TRANSFER OF CONSERVATORSHIP

Law Revision Commission Comments
2014 Addition

Background from Uniform Act. While this article consists of two separate sections, they are part of one integrated procedure. Article 3 authorizes a ... conservator to petition the court to transfer the ... conservatorship proceeding to a court of another state. Such a transfer is often appropriate when the [conservatee] has moved or has been placed in a facility in another state, making it impossible for the original court to adequately monitor the proceeding. Article 3 authorizes a transfer of a [conservatorship of the person, a conservatorship of the estate], or both. There is no requirement that both categories of proceeding be administered in the same state.

Section [2001] addresses procedures in the transferring state. Section [2002] addresses procedures in the accepting state.

A transfer begins with the filing of a petition by the conservator as provided in Section [2001(a)].... Assuming the court in the transferring state is satisfied that the grounds for transfer stated in Section [2001(d) (conservatorship of the person)] or [2001(e) (conservatorship of the estate)] have been met, one of which is that the court is satisfied that the court in the other state will accept the case, the court must issue a provisional order approving the transfer. The transferring court will not issue a final order dismissing the case until, as provided in Section [2001(f)], it receives a copy of the provisional order from the accepting court accepting the transferred proceeding.

Following issuance of the provisional order by the transferring court, a petition must be filed in the accepting court as provided in

Section [2002(a)].... The court [may not issue] a provisional order accepting the case [if] it is established that the transfer would be contrary to the ... conservatee's interests .... Section [2002(f)]. The term "interests" as opposed to "best interests" was chosen because of the strong autonomy values in modern [conservatorship] law. Should the court decline the transfer petition, it may consider a separately brought petition for the appointment of a [conservator] only if the court has a basis for jurisdiction under Sections [1993 or 1994] other than by reason of the provisional order of transfer. Section [2002(k)].

.... Pursuant to Section [2001(g)], the provisional order from the accepting court must be filed in the transferring court. The transferring court will then issue a final order terminating the proceeding, subject to local requirements such as filing of a final report or account and the release of any bond. Pursuant to Section [2002(i)], the final order terminating the proceeding in the transferring court must then be filed in the accepting court, which will then convert its provisional order accepting the case into a final order appointing the petitioning ... conservator as ... conservator in the accepting state.

Because ... conservatorship law and practice will likely differ between the two states, the court in the accepting state must ... determine whether the ... conservatorship needs to be modified to conform to the law of the accepting state. Section [2002(h)].... [The conformity review] in the accepting state is also an appropriate time to change the ... conservator if there is a more appropriate person to act as ... conservator in the accepting state. The drafters specifically did not try to design the procedures in Article 3 for the difficult problems that can arise in connection with a transfer when the ... conservator is ineligible to act in the second state, a circumstance that can occur when a financial institution is acting as [conservator of the estate] or a government agency is acting as [conservator of the person]. Rather, the procedures in Article 3 are designed for the typical case where the ... conservator is legally eligible to act in the second state. Should that particular ... conservator not be the best person to act in the accepting state, a change of ... conservator can be initiated ....

The transfer procedure in this article responds to numerous problems that have arisen in connection with attempted transfers under the existing law of most states. Sometimes a court will dismiss a case on the assumption a proceeding will be brought in another state, but such proceeding is never filed. Sometimes a court will refuse to dismiss a case until the court in the other state accepts the matter, but the court in the other state refuses to consider the petition until the already existing ... conservatorship has been terminated. Oftentimes the court will conclude that it is without jurisdiction to make an appointment until the [conservatee] is physically present in the state, a problem which Section [1994(a)(3)] addresses by granting a court special jurisdiction to consider a petition to accept a proceeding from another state. But the most serious problem is the need to prove the case in the second state from scratch, including proving the [conservatee's] incapacity and the choice of ... conservator. Article 3 eliminates this problem.... [Adapted from the Uniform Law Commission's General Comment to Article 3 of UAGPPJA.] [43 Cal.L.Rev.Comm. Reports 93 (2013)].

Cross References

Appointment of conservator for absentee, procedure, see Probate Code § 1840.
Powers and duties of guardian or conservator of the person, residence of ward or conservatee, see Probate Code § 2352.
Proof of status of proposed conservatee, attendance at hearing not required, see Probate Code § 1844.
Removal of property of nonresident, petition not required for conservatorship transferred pursuant to this Article, see Probate Code § 3800.
Special provisions applicable where proposed conservatee is a missing person,
Appointment of conservator, see Probate Code § 1845.

Appointment of conservator, acts not required, see Probate Code § 1848.
Appointment of conservator, conditions, see Probate Code § 1849.
Contents of petition for conservatorship of missing person's estate, see Probate Code § 1846.

§ 2001. Transfer of conservatorship to another state

(a) A conservator appointed in this state may petition the court to transfer the conservatorship to another state.

(b) The petitioner shall give notice of a hearing on a petition under subdivision (a) to the persons that would be entitled to notice of a hearing on a petition in this state for the appointment of a conservator.

(c) The court shall hold a hearing on a petition filed pursuant to subdivision (a).

(d) The court shall issue an order provisionally granting a petition to transfer a conservatorship of the person, and shall direct the conservator of the person to petition for acceptance of the conservatorship in the other state, if the court is satisfied that the conservatorship will be accepted by the court in the other state and the court finds all of the following:

(1) The conservatee is physically present in or is reasonably expected to move permanently to the other state.

(2) An objection to the transfer has not been made or, if an objection has been made, the court determines that the transfer would not be contrary to the interests of the conservatee.

(3) Plans for care and services for the conservatee in the other state are reasonable and sufficient.

(e) The court shall issue a provisional order granting a petition to transfer a conservatorship of the estate, and shall direct the conservator of the estate to petition for acceptance of the conservatorship in the other state, if the court is satisfied that the conservatorship will be accepted by the court of the other state and the court finds all of the following:

(1) The conservatee is physically present in or is reasonably expected to move permanently to the other state, or the conservatee has a significant connection to the other state considering the factors in subdivision (b) of Section 1991.

(2) An objection to the transfer has not been made or, if an objection has been made, the court determines that the transfer would not be contrary to the interests of the conservatee.

(3) Adequate arrangements will be made for management of the conservatee's property.

(f) The court shall issue a provisional order granting a petition to transfer a conservatorship of the person and estate, and shall direct the conservator to petition for acceptance of the conservatorship in the other state, if the requirements of subdivision (d) and the requirements of subdivision (e) are both satisfied.

(g) The court shall issue a final order confirming the transfer and terminating the conservatorship upon its receipt of both of the following:

(1) A provisional order accepting the proceeding from the court to which the proceeding is to be transferred which is issued under provisions similar to Section 2002.

(2) The documents required to terminate a conservatorship in this state, including, but not limited to, any required accounting. *(Added by Stats.2014, c. 553 (S.B.940), § 20, eff. Jan. 1, 2015, operative Jan. 1, 2016.)*

Law Revision Commission Comments
2014 Addition

Section 2001 is similar to Section 301 of the Uniform Adult Guardianship and Protective Proceedings Jurisdiction Act (2007) ("UAGPPJA"). Revisions have been made to conform to California drafting practices and terminology for the proceedings in question. See Section 1982 & Comment (definitions); see also Section 1980 Comment.

Revisions have also been made to more clearly coordinate this section with Section 2002 (corresponding to UAGPPJA Section 302), which requires the conservator to file a petition "to accept the conservatorship" (not a petition "for a conservatorship") in the state to which the conservatorship would be transferred.

Subdivision (a) corresponds to Section 301(a) of UAGPPJA.

Subdivision (b) corresponds to Section 301(b) of UAGPPJA. Revisions have been made to specify that the petitioner is responsible for giving the notice (*cf.* Ohio Rev. Code Ann. § 2112.31(b)), and to conform to California practice, under which a party is required to give notice *of a hearing* on a motion or petition, not just notice *of a petition*.

Subdivision (c) corresponds to Section 301(c) of UAGPPJA, but a hearing under subdivision (c) is mandatory in every case. If there is no opposition to a transfer petition, the court may place the matter on the consent calendar. A similar requirement applies when a conservator seeks to establish an out-of-state residence for a conservatee without petitioning for a transfer of the conservatorship. See Section 2253(c); Cal. R. Ct. 7.1063(f).

Subdivision (d) corresponds to Section 301(d) of UAGPPJA, but modifies the procedure that applies if a person objects to transfer of a conservatorship of the person. To prevent such a transfer, the UAGPPJA provision would require an objector to establish that the transfer would be contrary to the interests of the subject of the proceeding. If there was no objection, or the objector failed to meet that burden, the transfer would go forward. In contrast, under subdivision (d) of this section, a transfer from California to another state would go forward over an objection only if the court affirmatively determines that the transfer would not be contrary to the interests of the conservatee.

Subdivision (e) corresponds to Section 301(e) of UAGPPJA, but modifies the procedure that applies if a person objects to transfer of a conservatorship of the estate. To prevent such a transfer, the UAGPPJA provision would require an objector to establish that the transfer would be contrary to the interests of the subject of the proceeding. If there was no objection, or the objector failed to meet that burden, the transfer would go forward. In contrast, under subdivision (e) of this section, a transfer from California to another state would go forward over an objection only if the court affirmatively determines that the transfer would not be contrary to the interests of the conservatee.

Subdivision (f) provides guidance on the transfer requirements applicable to a conservatorship of the person and estate.

Subdivision (g) corresponds to Section 301(f) of UAGPPJA. If a conservatorship is transferred from California to another state, the conservator must continue to comply with California law until the court issues a final order confirming the transfer and terminating the conservatorship. See Section 2300 (oath & bond).

For limitations on the scope of this chapter, see Section 1981 & Comment. For guidance regarding the fee for filing a petition under this section, see Gov't Code § 70655. [43 Cal.L.Rev.Comm. Reports 93 (2013)].

Cross References
Conservatorships, appealable orders, see Probate Code § 1301.5.
Oath and bond, necessity before appointment, see Probate Code § 2300.

§ 2002. Accepting conservatorship transferred from another state

(a)(1) To confirm transfer of a conservatorship transferred to this state under provisions similar to Section 2001, the conservator shall petition the court in this state to accept the conservatorship.

(2) The petition shall include a certified copy of the other state's provisional order of transfer.

(3) On the first page of the petition, the petitioner shall state that the conservatorship does not fall within the limitations of Section 1981. The body of the petition shall allege facts showing that this chapter applies and the requirements for transfer of the conservatorship are satisfied.

(4) The petition shall specify any modifications necessary to conform the conservatorship to the law of this state, and the terms of a proposed final order accepting the conservatorship.

(5) A petition for the appointment of a temporary conservator under Section 1994 and Chapter 3 (commencing with Section 2250) of Part 4 may be filed while a petition under this section is pending. The petition for the appointment of a temporary conservator shall request the appointment of a temporary conservator eligible for appointment in this state, and shall be limited to powers authorized for a temporary conservator in this state. For purposes of Chapter 3 (commencing with Section 2250) of Part 4, the court shall treat a petition under this section as the equivalent of a petition for a general conservatorship.

(b) The petitioner shall give notice of a hearing on a petition under subdivision (a) to those persons that would be entitled to notice if the petition were a petition for the appointment of a conservator in both the transferring state and this state. The petitioner shall also give notice to any attorney of record for the conservatee in the transferring state and to any attorney appointed or appearing for the conservatee in this state. The petitioner shall give the notice in the same manner that notice of a petition for the appointment of a conservator is required to be given in this state, except that notice to the conservatee shall be given by mailing the petition instead of by personal service of a citation.

(c) Any person entitled to notice under subdivision (b) may object to the petition on one or more of the following grounds:

(1) Transfer of the proceeding would be contrary to the interests of the conservatee.

(2) Under the law of the transferring state, the conservator is ineligible for appointment in this state.

(3) Under the law of this state, the conservator is ineligible for appointment in this state, and the transfer petition does not identify a replacement who is willing and eligible to serve in this state.

(4) This chapter is inapplicable under Section 1981.

(d) Promptly after the filing of a petition under subdivision (a), the court shall appoint an investigator under Section 1454. The investigator shall promptly commence a preliminary investigation of the conservatorship, which focuses on the matters described in subdivision (f).

(e) The court shall hold a hearing on a petition filed pursuant to subdivision (a).

(f) The court shall issue an order provisionally granting a petition filed under subdivision (a) unless any of the following occurs:

(1) The court determines that transfer of the proceeding would be contrary to the interests of the conservatee.

(2) The court determines that, under the law of the transferring state, the conservator is ineligible for appointment in this state.

(3) The court determines that, under the law of this state, the conservator is ineligible for appointment in this state, and the transfer petition does not identify a replacement who is willing and eligible to serve in this state.

(4) The court determines that this chapter is inapplicable under Section 1981.

(g) If the court issues an order provisionally granting the petition, the investigator shall promptly commence an investigation under Section 1851.1.

(h)(1) Not later than 60 days after issuance of an order provisionally granting the petition, the court shall determine whether the conservatorship needs to be modified to conform to the law of this state. The court may take any action necessary to achieve compliance with the law of this state, including, but not limited to, striking or modifying any conservator powers that are not permitted under the law of this state.

(2) At the same time that it makes the determination required by paragraph (1), the court shall review the conservatorship as provided in Section 1851.1.

(3) The conformity determination and the review required by this subdivision shall occur at a hearing, which shall be noticed as provided in subdivision (b).

(i)(1) The court shall issue a final order accepting the proceeding and appointing the conservator in this state upon completion of the conformity determination and review required by subdivision (h), or upon its receipt from the court from which the proceeding is being transferred of a final order issued under provisions similar to Section 2001 transferring the proceeding to this state, whichever occurs later. In appointing a conservator under this paragraph, the court shall comply with Section 1830.

(2) A transfer to this state does not become effective unless and until the court issues a final order under paragraph (1). A conservator may not take action in this state pursuant to a transfer petition unless and until the transfer becomes effective and all of the following steps have occurred:

(A) The conservator has taken an oath in accordance with Section 2300.

(B) The conservator has filed the required bond, if any.

(C) The court has provided the information required by Section 1835 to the conservator.

(D) The conservator has filed an acknowledgment of receipt as required by Section 1834.

(E) The clerk of the court has issued the letters of conservatorship.

(3) Paragraph (2) does not preclude a person who has been appointed as a temporary conservator pursuant to Chapter 3 (commencing with Section 2250) from taking action in this state pursuant to the order establishing the temporary conservatorship.

(4) When a transfer to this state becomes effective, the conservatorship is subject to the law of this state and shall thereafter be treated as a conservatorship under the law of this state. If a law of this state, including, but not limited to, Section 2356.5, mandates compliance with special requirements to exercise a particular conservatorship power or take a particular step, the conservator of a transferred conservatorship may not exercise that power or take that step without first complying with those special requirements.

(j) Except as otherwise provided by Section 1851.1, Chapter 3 (commencing with Section 1860), Chapter 9 (commencing with Section 2650) of Part 4, and other law, when the court grants a petition under this section, the court shall recognize a conservatorship order from the other state, including the determination of the conservatee's incapacity and the appointment of the conservator.

(k) The denial by a court of this state of a petition to accept a conservatorship transferred from another state does not affect the ability of the conservator to seek appointment as conservator in this state under Chapter 1 (commencing with Section 1800) of Part 3 if the court has jurisdiction to make an appointment other than by reason of the provisional order of transfer. *(Added by Stats.2014, c. 553 (S.B.940), § 20, eff. Jan. 1, 2015, operative Jan. 1, 2016.)*

Law Revision Commission Comments
2014 Addition

Section 2002 is similar to Section 302 of the Uniform Adult Guardianship and Protective Proceedings Jurisdiction Act (2007) ("UAGPPJA"). Revisions have been made to conform to California drafting practices and terminology for the proceedings in question. See Section 1982 & Comment (definitions); see also Section 1980 Comment. For limitations on the scope of this chapter, see Section 1981 & Comment. For guidance regarding the fee for filing a petition under this section, see Gov't Code § 70655. For rules governing appointment of counsel, see Sections 1470–1472; see also Section 1851.1(b)(9)-(12).

Paragraphs (1) and (2) of subdivision (a) correspond to Section 302(a) of UAGPPJA. Paragraphs (3) and (4) of that subdivision provide guidance on the content of a petition under this section. The first sentence of paragraph (3) serves to facilitate compliance with Section 1981 (scope of chapter). Paragraph (5) of subdivision (a) makes clear that an out-of-state conservator may simultaneously seek a transfer under this section and a temporary conservatorship under Sections 1994 and 2250–2258.

Subdivision (b) corresponds to Section 302(b) of UAGPPJA. Revisions have been made to specify that the petitioner is responsible for giving the notice, and to conform to California practice, under which a party is required to give notice *of a hearing* on a motion or petition, not just notice *of a petition*. Revisions have also been made to eliminate the necessity for personal service of a citation on the conservatee, and make clear that all attorneys for the conservatee must receive notice.

Subdivision (c) specifies the permissible grounds for objecting to a petition under this section.

Subdivision (d) directs the court to appoint an investigator, to help it determine whether to provisionally accept the transfer.

Subdivision (e) corresponds to Section 302(c) of UAGPPJA, but a hearing under subdivision (e) is mandatory in every case. If there is no opposition to a transfer petition, the court may place the matter on the consent calendar.

Paragraph (1) of subdivision (f) corresponds to Section 302(d)(1) of UAGPPJA. Revisions have been made to eliminate the necessity of an objection and the corollary requirement of having "the objector establis[h]" that transfer would be contrary to the conservatee's interests. Under paragraph (f)(1), it is sufficient if the court makes the required determination on its own motion, on the basis of any evidence it has at hand.

Paragraphs (2) and (3) of subdivision (f) correspond to Section 302(d)(2) of UAGPPJA. Revisions have been made to differentiate between: (1) a conservator who is ineligible, *under the law of the transferring state,* to serve in California (e.g., a public guardian who, under the law of another jurisdiction, is only authorized to act in that jurisdiction) and (2) a conservator who is ineligible, *under California law,* to serve in California. In the former situation, paragraph (f)(2) precludes the California court from provisionally granting the transfer. If the proceeding is to be transferred to California, the transferring court must first replace the existing conservator with one who would be authorized to act beyond the boundaries of the transferring state. In contrast, if the existing conservator is ineligible due to California law, the transfer can proceed so long as the transfer petition identifies a replacement who is willing and eligible to serve in California. See paragraph (f)(3).

Paragraph (4) of subdivision (f) is necessary to reflect the limitations on the scope of this chapter. See Section 1981 & Comment (scope of chapter).

Subdivision (g) directs the court-appointed investigator to further investigate the conservatorship if the court provisionally accepts the transfer. For details of this investigative process, see Section 1851.1 (investigation & review of out-of-state conservatorship).

Paragraph (1) of subdivision (h) corresponds to Section 302(f) of UAGPPJA, but the court is to undertake the conformity determination before it issues a final order accepting a transfer, rather than afterwards. In addition, the paragraph expressly authorizes the court to take any action necessary to conform a conservatorship to California law, including elimination or reduction of the conservator's powers.

Paragraph (2) of subdivision (h) directs the court to review the conservatorship at the same time that it determines whether the conservatorship "needs to be modified to conform to the law of this state" under paragraph (1) of subdivision (h). For details of this review process, see Section 1851.1 (investigation & review of out-of-state conservatorship).

Paragraph (3) of subdivision (h) makes clear that the required conformity determination and review must occur at a hearing. If there is no opposition to a transfer petition, the court may place the matter on the consent calendar.

Paragraph (1) of subdivision (i) corresponds to Section 302(e) of UAGPPJA, but the court investigation, court review, and determination of how to conform the transferred conservatorship to California law must be complete before the court issues a final order accepting a proceeding and appointing the conservator to serve in California. The second sentence makes clear that such an order must meet the same requirements as an order appointing a conservator in a proceeding that originates in California.

Paragraph (2) of subdivision (i) makes clear that a transfer to California does not become effective until the California court enters a final order accepting the conservatorship and appointing the

conservator in California. Absent some other source of authority (e.g., registration of the conservatorship under Article 4), the conservator cannot begin to function here as such until the transfer becomes effective *and* all five of the enumerated follow-up steps have occurred.

Paragraph (3) of subdivision (i) makes clear that a person who has been appointed as a temporary conservator in California can begin to function in the state even though a transfer petition is pending.

Paragraph (4) of subdivision (i) underscores that once a conservatorship is transferred to California, it is henceforth subject to California law and will be treated as a California conservatorship. For example, if a conservatorship is transferred to California and the conservator wishes to exercise the powers specified in Section 2356.5 (conservatee with dementia), the requirements of that section must be satisfied.

Subdivision (j) corresponds to Section 302(g) of UAGPPJA, but there are limitations on the comity accorded to the transferring court's determination of capacity and choice of conservator. See Sections 1851.1 (investigation & review of transferred conservatorship), 1860–1865 (termination of conservatorship), 2650–2655 (removal of guardian or conservator).

Subdivision (k) corresponds to Section 302(h) of UAGPPJA. [43 Cal.L.Rev.Comm. Reports 93 (2013)].

Cross References

Capacity to give informed consent for medical treatment, inclusion in transfer petition, see Probate Code § 1890.

Citation to proposed conservatee not required, notice to absentee conservatee not required, see Probate Code § 1843.

Conservatorships, appealable orders, see Probate Code § 1301.5.

Establishment of conservatorship,

  Notice of hearing, see Probate Code § 1842.

  Petition, additional contents, see Probate Code § 1841.

Oath and bond, necessity before appointment, see Probate Code § 2300.

Petitions for instructions, or grant of power or authority, persons authorized to file, see Probate Code § 1455.

Special provisions applicable where proposed conservatee is a missing person,

  Appointment of conservator, acts not required, see Probate Code § 1848.

  Notice, petition for appointment of conservator, see Probate Code § 1847.

Transfer of conservatorship to state, investigation and report, duties of investigator, see Probate Code § 1851.1.

§ 2003. Transfer involving court of California tribe

If a conservatorship is transferred under this article from a court of this state to the court of a California tribe or from the court of a California tribe to a court of this state, the order that provisionally grants the transfer may expressly provide that specified powers of the conservator will not be transferred. Jurisdiction over the specified powers will be retained by the transferring state and will not be included in the powers that are granted to the conservator in the state that accepts the transfer. *(Added by Stats.2014, c. 553 (S.B.940), § 20, eff. Jan. 1, 2015, operative Jan. 1, 2016.)*

Law Revision Commission Comments
2014 Addition

Section 2003 is new. See Section 2031(a) ("California tribe" defined). [43 Cal.L.Rev.Comm. Reports 93 (2013)].

§§ 2004 to 2007. Repealed by Stats.1979, c. 726, § 2, operative Jan. 1, 1981

ARTICLE 4. REGISTRATION AND RECOGNITION OF ORDERS FROM OTHER STATES

Section
2011. Registration of order of conservatorship of person.
2012. Registration of order of conservatorship of estate.
2013. Registration of order of conservatorship of person and estate.
2014. Notice of intent to register conservatorship.
2015. Court to provide written information to conservator regarding rights, duties, etc.
2016. Effect of registration.
2017. Third parties; actions in good faith reliance on conservatorship order.
2018. Recording copies of registration documents; reasonable fee.
2019. Registration of California tribal orders.

Law Revision Commission Comments

2014 Addition

Background from Uniform Act. Article 4 is designed to facilitate the enforcement of [conservatorship] orders in other states. This article does not make distinctions among the types of orders that can be enforced.... While some states have expedited procedures for sales of real estate by [a conservator of the estate] appointed in [another state], few states have enacted statutes dealing with enforcement of [an order appointing a conservator of the person], such as when a care facility questions the authority of a [conservator of the person] appointed in another state. Sometimes, these sorts of refusals necessitate that the proceeding be transferred to the other state or that an entirely new petition be filed, problems that could often be avoided if [conservatorship] orders were entitled to recognition in other states.

Article 4 provides for such recognition. The key concept is registration. Section [2011] provides for registration of [an order appointing a conservator of the person], and Section [2012] for registration of [an order appointing a conservator of the estate]. Following registration of the order in the appropriate county of the other state, and after giving notice to the [supervising] court of the intent to register the order in the other state, Section [2016] authorizes the ... conservator to thereafter exercise all powers authorized in the order of appointment except as prohibited under the laws of the registering state.

The drafters of the Act concluded that the registration of certified copies provides sufficient protection and that it was not necessary to mandate the filing of authenticated copies. [Adapted from the Uniform Law Commission's General Comment to Article 4 of UAGPPJA.] [44 Cal.L.Rev.Comm. Reports 77 [Appendix 4] (2014)].

Cross References

Conservatorships, appealable orders, see Probate Code § 1301.5.
Fee for registering conservatorship, see Government Code § 70663.
Powers and duties of guardian or conservator of the person, court approval of transaction or matter, provisions inapplicable to this Article, see Probate Code § 2505.

§ 2011. Registration of order of conservatorship of person

If a conservator of the person has been appointed in another state and a petition for the appointment of a conservator of the person is not pending in this state, the conservator of the person appointed in the other state, after providing notice pursuant to Section 2014, may register the conservatorship order in this state by filing certified copies of the order and letters of office, and proof of notice as required herein, together with a cover sheet approved by the Judicial

Council, in the superior court of any appropriate county of this state. *(Added by Stats.2014, c. 553 (S.B.940), § 20, eff. Jan. 1, 2015, operative Jan. 1, 2016.)*

Law Revision Commission Comments

2014 Addition

Section 2011 is similar to Section 401 of the Uniform Adult Guardianship and Protective Proceedings Jurisdiction Act (2007) ("UAGPPJA"). Revisions have been made to conform to California terminology for the proceedings in question. See Section 1982 & Comment (definitions); see also Section 1980 Comment. Revisions have also been made to clarify the proper filing procedure under California law.

For further information on the effect of a registration under this article, see Section 2016 (effect of registration). For the applicable filing fee, see Gov't Code § 70663 (fee for registration under California Conservatorship Jurisdiction Act). For recordation with a county recorder, see Section 2018 (recordation of registration documents). For guidance regarding third party reliance on a conservatorship order registered under this section, see Section 2017 (good faith reliance on registration). For a special rule applicable to a California tribe, see Section 2019 (California tribal court conservatorship order). For limitations on the scope of this chapter, see Section 1981 & Comment. [44 Cal.L.Rev.Comm. Reports 77 [Appendix 4] (2014)].

§ 2012. Registration of order of conservatorship of estate

If a conservator of the estate has been appointed in another state and a petition for a conservatorship of the estate is not pending in this state, the conservator appointed in the other state, after providing notice pursuant to Section 2014, may register the conservatorship order in this state by filing certified copies of the order and letters of office and of any bond, and proof of notice as required herein, together with a cover sheet approved by the Judicial Council, in the superior court of any county of this state in which property belonging to the conservatee is located. *(Added by Stats. 2014, c. 553 (S.B.940), § 20, eff. Jan. 1, 2015, operative Jan. 1, 2016.)*

Law Revision Commission Comments

2014 Addition

Section 2012 is similar to Section 402 of the Uniform Adult Guardianship and Protective Proceedings Jurisdiction Act (2007) ("UAGPPJA"). Revisions have been made to conform to California terminology for the proceedings in question. See Section 1982 & Comment (definitions); see also Section 1980 Comment. Revisions have also been made to clarify the proper filing procedure under California law.

For further information on the effect of a registration under this article, see Section 2016 (effect of registration). For the applicable filing fee, see Gov't Code § 70663 (fee for registration under California Conservatorship Jurisdiction Act). For recordation with a county recorder, see Section 2018 (recordation of registration documents). For guidance regarding third party reliance on a conservatorship order registered under this section, see Section 2017 (good faith reliance on registration). For a special rule applicable to a California tribe, see Section 2019 (California tribal court conservatorship order). For limitations on the scope of this chapter, see Section 1981 & Comment. [44 Cal.L.Rev.Comm. Reports 77 [Appendix 4] (2014)].

§ 2013. Registration of order of conservatorship of person and estate

If a conservator of the person and estate has been appointed in another state and a petition for a conservatorship of the person, conservatorship of the estate, or conservatorship of the person and estate is not pending in this state, the conservator appointed in the other state, after providing notice pursuant to Section 2014, may register the conservatorship order in this state by filing certified copies of the order and letters of office and of any bond, and proof of notice as required herein, together with a cover sheet approved by the Judicial Council, in the superior court of any appropriate county of this state. *(Added by Stats.2014, c. 553 (S.B.940), § 20, eff. Jan. 1, 2015, operative Jan. 1, 2016.)*

Law Revision Commission Comments

2014 Addition

Section 2013 is included for the sake of completeness. It serves to clarify the registration procedure applicable to a conservatorship of the person and estate.

For further information on the effect of a registration under this article, see Section 2016 (effect of registration). For the applicable filing fee, see Gov't Code § 70663 (fee for registration under California Conservatorship Jurisdiction Act). For recordation with a county recorder, see Section 2018 (recordation of registration documents). For guidance regarding third party reliance on a conservatorship order registered under this section, see Section 2017 (good faith reliance on registration). For a special rule applicable to a California tribe, see Section 2019 (California tribal court conservatorship order). For limitations on the scope of this chapter, see Section 1981 & Comment.

See Section 1982 (definitions). [44 Cal.L.Rev.Comm. Reports 77 [Appendix 4] (2014)].

§ 2014. Notice of intent to register conservatorship

(a) At least 15 days before registering a conservatorship in this state, the conservator shall provide notice of an intent to register to all of the following:

(1) The court supervising the conservatorship.

(2) Every person who would be entitled to notice of a petition for the appointment of a conservator in the state where the conservatorship is being supervised.

(3) Every person who would be entitled to notice of a petition for the appointment of a conservator in this state.

(b) Each notice provided pursuant to subdivision (a) shall comply with all of the following:

(1) The notice shall prominently state that when a conservator acts pursuant to this article, the conservator is subject to the law of this state governing the action, including, but not limited to, all applicable procedures, and is not authorized to take any action prohibited by the law of this state.

(2) The notice shall explain that if a conservatorship is registered pursuant to this article, and the conservator later proposes to take a specific action pursuant to this article, which, under the law of this state, requires court approval or other action in court, the conservator will be required to notify the recipient of the request for court approval or other court action, and the recipient will have an opportunity to object or otherwise participate at that time, in the same manner as other persons are entitled to object or otherwise participate under the law of this state.

(3) The notice shall advise the recipient that information about a conservator's rights, duties, limitations, and responsibilities under the law of this state is available, free of charge, on an Internet Web site maintained by the Judicial Council. The notice shall explain specifically how to locate that information on the Judicial Council's Internet Web site.

(c) Except as provided in subdivision (c) of Section 2023, each notice provided pursuant to subdivision (a) shall also prominently state that the registration is effective only while the conservatee resides in another jurisdiction and does not authorize the conservator to take any action while the conservatee is residing in this state. *(Added by Stats.2014, c. 553 (S.B.940), § 20, eff. Jan. 1, 2015, operative Jan. 1, 2016.)*

Law Revision Commission Comments

2014 Addition

Section 2014 requires notice to specified persons as a prerequisite to registration under this article.

Paragraph (1) of subdivision (a) is similar to the notice requirements in UAGPPJA Sections 401 and 402. The reference to the "appointing court" has been replaced with a reference to the "court supervising the conservatorship," because the court currently supervising a conservatorship might not be the same court that originally appointed the conservator. See Article 3 (transfer of conservatorship).

Paragraphs (2) and (3) of subdivision (a) provide for additional notice, so as to alert interested persons that the conservatorship is being registered in California and the conservator might take action in California. If a person has concerns about such action, the person can either challenge a proposed action directly in a California court, or seek redress in the court supervising the conservatorship.

Under subdivisions (b) and (c), a notice under this section must prominently inform the recipient about key limitations on the effect of registering a conservatorship in this state. The notice must also provide other information on the applicable law and procedures. [44 Cal.L.Rev.Comm. Reports 77 [Appendix 4] (2014)].

§ 2015. Court to provide written information to conservator regarding rights, duties, etc.

Upon registration of a conservatorship pursuant to this article, the court shall provide the conservator with written information concerning a conservator's rights, duties, limitations, and responsibilities in this state, as specified in Section 1835. To cover the costs of providing that information, a court may charge the conservator the fee specified in Section 1835, which shall be distributed as specified in that section. The conservator shall file an acknowledgment of receipt of the written information, on a form prescribed by the Judicial Council. *(Added by Stats.2014, c. 553 (S.B.940), § 20, eff. Jan. 1, 2015, operative Jan. 1, 2016.)*

Law Revision Commission Comments

2014 Addition

Section 2015 requires that specified information be provided to a conservator as a prerequisite to registration under this article. [44 Cal.L.Rev.Comm. Reports 77 [Appendix 4] (2014)].

§ 2016. Effect of registration

(a) Upon registration of a conservatorship order from another state and the filing by the conservator of an acknowledgment of receipt of the written information required by Section 2015, the conservator may, while the conservatee resides out of this state, exercise in any county of this state all powers authorized in the order of appointment except as prohibited under the laws of this state, including maintaining actions and proceedings in this state and, if the conservator is not a resident of this state, subject to any conditions imposed upon nonresident parties. When acting pursuant to registration, the conservator is subject to the law of this state governing the action, including, but not limited to, all applicable procedures, and is not authorized to take any action prohibited by the law of this state. If a law of this state, including, but not limited to, Section 2352, 2352.5, 2355, 2356.5, 2540, 2543, 2545, or 2591.5, or Article 2 (commencing with Section 1880) of Chapter 4 of Part 4, mandates compliance with special requirements to exercise a particular conservatorship power or take a particular step, the conservator of a registered conservatorship may not exercise that power or take that step without first complying with those special requirements.

(b)(1) When subdivision (a) requires a conservator to comply with a law of this state that makes it necessary to obtain court approval or take other action in court, the conservator shall seek that approval or proceed as needed in an appropriate court of this state. In handling the matter, that court shall communicate and cooperate with the court that is supervising the conservatorship, in accordance with Sections 1984 and 1985.

(2) In addition to providing any other notice required by law, the conservator shall provide notice of a court proceeding under paragraph (1) to all of the following:

(A) The court supervising the conservatorship.

(B) Every person who would be entitled to notice of a petition for the appointment of a conservator in the state where the conservatorship is being supervised.

(C) Every person who would be entitled to notice of a petition for the appointment of a conservator in this state.

(3) Any person entitled to notice under paragraph (2) may raise an objection or otherwise participate in the proceeding in the same manner as other persons are allowed to do under the law of this state.

(c) Subdivision (a) applies only when the conservatee resides out of this state. When the conservatee resides in this state, a conservator may not exercise any powers pursuant to a registration under this article.

(d) A court of this state may grant any relief available under this chapter and other law of this state to enforce a registered order. *(Added by Stats.2014, c. 553 (S.B.940), § 20, eff. Jan. 1, 2015, operative Jan. 1, 2016.)*

Law Revision Commission Comments
2014 Addition

Subdivision (a) of Section 2016 is similar to Section 403(a) of the Uniform Adult Guardianship and Protective Proceedings Jurisdiction Act (2007) ("UAGPPJA"). Revisions have been made to conform to California terminology for the proceedings in question. See Section 1982 & Comment (definitions); see also Section 1980 Comment. Revisions have also been made to:

(1) Underscore that any conservatorship registered in California is fully subject to California law while the conservator is acting in the state. For example, if a conservatorship is registered in California and the conservator seeks to exercise a power specified in Section 2356.5 (conservatee with dementia) within the state, the requirements of

that section must be satisfied. Similarly, if the conservator of a registered conservatorship wishes to sell the conservatee's personal residence located in California, the transaction must comply with California's special requirements for such a sale (see, e.g., Sections 2540(b), 2543, 2591.5).

(2) Emphasize that registration of an out-of-state conservatorship in one county is sufficient; it is not necessary to register in every county in which the conservator seeks to act.

(3) Make clear that a registration is only effective if the conservator files an acknowledgment of receipt of the written information required by Section 2015.

(4) Make clear that a registration is only effective while the conservatee resides in another state. If the conservatee becomes a California resident, the conservator cannot act pursuant to a registration under this article, but can petition for transfer of the conservatorship to California under Article 3. For an exception to the rule that a registration is only effective while the conservatee resides in another state, see Section 2019 (California tribal court conservatorship order).

Paragraph (1) of subdivision (b) provides guidance on which court is the appropriate forum for purposes of complying with California procedures as required under subdivision (a). Paragraphs (2) and (3) make clear that those entitled to notice under Section 2014 are also entitled to notice and an opportunity to be heard in the proceedings specified in paragraph (1).

Subdivision (c) further underscores that a registration is only effective while the conservatee resides in another jurisdiction. For an exception to this rule, see Section 2019 (California tribal court conservatorship order).

Subdivision (d) is the same as Section 403(b) of UAGPPJA.

For limitations on the scope of this chapter, see Section 1981 & Comment. [44 Cal.L.Rev.Comm. Reports 77 [Appendix 4] (2014)].

§ 2017. Third parties; actions in good faith reliance on conservatorship order

(a) A third person who acts in good faith reliance on a conservatorship order registered under this article is not liable to any person for so acting if all of the following requirements are satisfied:

(1) The conservator presents to the third person a file-stamped copy of the registration documents required by Section 2011, 2012, or 2013, including, but not limited to, the certified copy of the conservatorship order.

(2) Each of the registration documents, including, but not limited to, the conservatorship order and the file-stamped cover sheet, appears on its face to be valid.

(3) The conservator presents to the third person a form approved by the Judicial Council, in which the conservator attests that the conservatee does not reside in this state and the conservator promises to promptly notify the third person if the conservatee becomes a resident of this state. The form shall also prominently state that the registration is effective only while the conservatee resides in another jurisdiction and does not authorize the conservator to take any action while the conservatee is residing in this state.

(4) The third person has not received any actual notice that the conservatee is residing in this state.

(b) Nothing in this section is intended to create an implication that a third person is liable for acting in reliance on a conservatorship order registered under this article under circumstances where the requirements of subdivision (a) are not satisfied. Nothing in this section affects any immunity that may otherwise exist apart from this section. *(Added by*

Stats.2014, c. 553 (S.B.940), § 20, eff. Jan. 1, 2015, operative Jan. 1, 2016.)

Law Revision Commission Comments

2014 Addition

Section 2017 is modeled on Section 4303 (good faith reliance on power of attorney).

For the effect of registration under this article, see Section 2016 & Comment. For a special rule applicable to a conservatorship order of a court of a California tribe, see Section 2019 & Comment. [44 Cal.L.Rev.Comm. Reports 77 [Appendix 4] (2014)].

§ 2018. Recording copies of registration documents; reasonable fee

(a) A file-stamped copy of the registration documents required by Section 2011, 2012, or 2013 may be recorded in the office of any county recorder in this state.

(b) A county recorder may charge a reasonable fee for recordation under subdivision (a). *(Added by Stats.2014, c. 553 (S.B.940), § 20, eff. Jan. 1, 2015, operative Jan. 1, 2016.)*

Law Revision Commission Comments

2014 Addition

Section 2018 makes clear that registration documents under this chapter are recordable in county property records. [44 Cal.L.Rev. Comm. Reports 77 [Appendix 4] (2014)].

§ 2019. Registration of California tribal orders

Notwithstanding any other provision of this article:

(a) A conservatorship order of a court of a California tribe can be registered under Section 2011, 2012, or 2013, regardless of whether the conservatee resides in California.

(b) The effect of a conservatorship order of a court of a California tribe that is registered under Section 2011, 2012, or 2013 is not contingent on whether the conservatee resides in California.

(c) Paragraphs (3) and (4) of subdivision (a) of Section 2017 do not apply to a conservatorship order of a court of a California tribe. *(Added by Stats.2014, c. 553 (S.B.940), § 20, eff. Jan. 1, 2015, operative Jan. 1, 2016.)*

Law Revision Commission Comments

2014 Addition

Section 2019 provides that the residence-based limitations on registration of a conservatorship order, in Sections 2014 and 2017, do not apply to a conservatorship order of a court of a California tribe. See Section 2031(a) ("California tribe" defined). [44 Cal.L.Rev. Comm. Reports 77 [Appendix 4] (2014)].

ARTICLE 5. MISCELLANEOUS PROVISIONS

§ 2021. Uniformity of application and construction

In applying and construing this uniform act, consideration shall be given to the need to promote uniformity of the law with respect to its subject matter among states that enact it, consistent with the need to protect individual civil rights and in accordance with due process. *(Added by Stats.2014, c. 553 (S.B.940), § 20, eff. Jan. 1, 2015, operative Jan. 1, 2016.)*

Law Revision Commission Comments

2014 Addition

Section 2021 is similar to Section 501 of the Uniform Adult Guardianship and Protective Proceedings Jurisdiction Act (2007) ("UAGPPJA"). A clause has been added to underscore the importance of protecting a conservatee's civil rights, particularly the constitutional right of due process, which is deeply implicated in conservatorship proceedings. See U.S. Const. amend. XIV; Cal. Const. art. I, §§ 7, 15; see also 2012 Conn. Pub. Act No. 12–22, § 22. The provision has also been revised to replace "must" with "shall," in conformity with California drafting practices. [43 Cal.L.Rev.Comm. Reports 93 (2013)].

§ 2022. Relation to Electronic Signatures in Global and National Commerce Act

This chapter modifies, limits, and supersedes the federal Electronic Signatures in Global and National Commerce Act (Title 15 (commencing with Section 7001) of the United States Code), but does not modify, limit, or supersede subdivision (c) of Section 101 of that act, which is codified as subdivision (c) of Section 7001 of Title 15 of the United States Code, or authorize electronic delivery of any of the notices described in subdivision (b) of Section 103 of that act, which is codified as subdivision (b) of Section 7003 of Title 15 of the United States Code. *(Added by Stats.2014, c. 553 (S.B.940), § 20, eff. Jan. 1, 2015, operative Jan. 1, 2016.)*

Law Revision Commission Comments

2014 Addition

Section 2022 is similar to Section 502 of the Uniform Adult Guardianship and Protective Proceedings Jurisdiction Act (2007) ("UAGPPJA"). Revisions have been made to conform to local drafting practices. [43 Cal.L.Rev.Comm. Reports 93 (2013)].

§ 2023. Development of court rules and forms

(a) On or before January 1, 2016, the Judicial Council shall develop court rules and forms as necessary for the implementation of this chapter.

(b) The materials developed pursuant to this section shall include, but not be limited to, all of the following:

(1) A cover sheet for registration of a conservatorship under Section 2011, 2012, or 2013. The cover sheet shall explain that a proceeding may not be registered under Section 2011, 2012, or 2013 if the proceeding relates to a minor. The cover sheet shall further explain that a proceeding in which a person is subjected to involuntary mental health care may not be registered under Section 2011, 2012, or 2013. The cover sheet shall require the conservator to initial each of these explanations. The cover sheet shall also prominently state that when a conservator acts pursuant to registration, the conservator is subject to the law of this state governing the action, including, but not limited to, all applicable procedures, and is not authorized to take any action prohibited by the law of this state. Except as provided in subdivision (c), the cover sheet shall also prominently state that the registration is effective only while the conservatee resides in another jurisdiction and does not authorize the conservator to take any action while the conservatee is

residing in this state. Directly beneath these statements, the cover sheet shall include a signature box in which the conservator attests to these matters.

(2) The form required by paragraph (3) of subdivision (a) of Section 2017. If the Judicial Council deems it advisable, this form may be included in the civil cover sheet developed under paragraph (1).

(3) A form for providing notice of intent to register a proceeding under Section 2011, 2012, or 2013.

(4) A form for a conservator to acknowledge receipt of the written information required by Section 2015.

(c) The materials prepared pursuant to this section shall be consistent with Section 2019. *(Added by Stats.2014, c. 553 (S.B.940), § 20, eff. Jan. 1, 2015, operative Jan. 1, 2015.)*

Law Revision Commission Comments

2014 Addition

Section 2023 directs the Judicial Council to prepare any court rules and forms that are necessary to implement this chapter before it becomes operative.

Subdivision (c) requires that the materials prepared by the Judicial Council be consistent with Section 2019, relating to the registration of a conservatorship order of a court of a California tribe. [44 Cal.L.Rev.Comm. Reports 77 [Appendix 4] (2014)].

§ 2024. Transitional provisions

(a) This chapter applies to conservatorship proceedings begun on or after January 1, 2016.

(b) Articles 1, 3, and 4 and Sections 2021 and 2022 apply to proceedings begun before January 1, 2016, regardless of whether a conservatorship order has been issued. *(Added by Stats.2014, c. 553 (S.B.940), § 20, eff. Jan. 1, 2015, operative Jan. 1, 2016.)*

Law Revision Commission Comments

2014 Addition

Section 2024 is similar to Section 504 of the Uniform Adult Guardianship and Protective Proceedings Jurisdiction Act (2007) ("UAGPPJA"). Revisions have been made to conform to California terminology for the proceedings in question. See Section 1982 & Comment (definitions); see also Section 1980 Comment. For limitations on the scope of this chapter, see Section 1981 & Comment.

Background from Uniform Act. This Act applies retroactively to ... conservatorships in existence on the effective date. The ... conservator appointed prior to the [operative] date of the Act may petition to transfer the proceeding to another state under Article 3 and register and enforce the order in other states pursuant to Article 4. The jurisdictional provisions of Article 2 also apply to proceedings begun on or after the [operative] date. What the Act does not do is change the jurisdictional rules midstream for petitions filed prior to the effective date for which an appointment has not been made ... as of the effective date. Jurisdiction in such cases is governed by prior law. Nor does the Act affect the validity of already existing appointments even though the court might not have had jurisdiction had this Act been [operative] at the time the appointment was made. [Adapted from the Uniform Law Commission's Comment to UAGPPJA § 504.] [43 Cal.L.Rev.Comm. Reports 93 (2013)].

ARTICLE 6. FEDERALLY RECOGNIZED INDIAN TRIBE

§ 2031. Definitions

For the purposes of this chapter:

(a) "California tribe" means an Indian tribe with jurisdiction that has tribal land located in California.

(b) "Indian tribe with jurisdiction" means a federally recognized Indian tribe that has a court system that exercises jurisdiction over proceedings that are substantially equivalent to conservatorship proceedings.

(c) "Tribal land" means land that is, with respect to a specific Indian tribe and the members of that tribe, "Indian country" as defined in Section 1151 of Title 18 of the United States Code. *(Added by Stats.2014, c. 553 (S.B.940), § 20, eff. Jan. 1, 2015, operative Jan. 1, 2016.)*

Law Revision Commission Comments

2014 Addition

Section 2031 is new. [43 Cal.L.Rev.Comm. Reports 93 (2013)].

§ 2032. Application of Article 2

Article 2 (commencing with Section 1991) does not apply to a proposed conservatee who is a member of an Indian tribe with jurisdiction. *(Added by Stats.2014, c. 553 (S.B.940), § 20, eff. Jan. 1, 2015, operative Jan. 1, 2016.)*

Law Revision Commission Comments

2014 Addition

Section 2032 is new. [43 Cal.L.Rev.Comm. Reports 93 (2013)].

§ 2033. Proposed conservatees who are tribal members; dismissal of petition; factors considered

(a) If a petition for the appointment of a conservator has been filed in a court of this state and a conservator has not yet been appointed, any person entitled to notice of a hearing on the petition may move to dismiss the petition on the grounds that the proposed conservatee is a member of an Indian tribe with jurisdiction. The petition shall state the name of the Indian tribe.

(b) If, after communicating with the named tribe, the court of this state finds that the proposed conservatee is a member of an Indian tribe with jurisdiction, it may grant the motion to dismiss if it finds that there is good cause to do so. If the motion is granted, the court may impose any condition the court considers just and proper, including the condition that a petition for the appointment of a conservator be filed promptly in the tribal court.

(c) In determining whether there is good cause to grant the motion, the court may consider all relevant factors, including, but not limited to, the following:

(1) Any expressed preference of the proposed conservatee.

(2) Whether abuse, neglect, or exploitation of the proposed conservatee has occurred or is likely to occur and which state could best protect the proposed conservatee from the abuse, neglect, or exploitation.

(3) The length of time the proposed conservatee was physically present in or was a legal resident of this or another state.

(4) The location of the proposed conservatee's family, friends, and other persons required to be notified of the conservatorship proceeding.

(5) The distance of the proposed conservatee from the court in each state.

(6) The financial circumstances of the estate of the proposed conservatee.

(7) The nature and location of the evidence.

(8) The ability of the court in each state to decide the issue expeditiously and the procedures necessary to present evidence.

(9) The familiarity of the court of each state with the facts and issues in the proceeding.

(10) If an appointment were made, the court's ability to monitor the conduct of the conservator.

(11) The timing of the motion, taking into account the parties' and court's expenditure of time and resources.

(d) Notwithstanding subdivision (b), the court shall not grant a motion to dismiss pursuant to this section if the tribal court expressly declines to exercise its jurisdiction with regard to the proposed conservatee. *(Added by Stats.2014, c. 553 (S.B.940), § 20, eff. Jan. 1, 2015, operative Jan. 1, 2016.)*

Law Revision Commission Comments

2014 Addition

Section 2033 is new.

The second sentence of subdivision (b) is similar to the fourth sentence of Section 1996(b).

The factors listed in paragraphs (c)(1)-(10) are drawn from Section 1996(c). Paragraph (c)(11) is similar to a factor considered in determining whether to transfer a child custody case to tribal court under 25 U.S.C. § 1911(b). See also Welf. & Inst. Code § 305.5(c)(2)(B). [43 Cal.L.Rev.Comm. Reports 93 (2013)].

§§ 2051 to 2055. Repealed by Stats.1979, c. 726, § 2, operative Jan. 1, 1981

Part 4

PROVISIONS COMMON TO GUARDIANSHIP AND CONSERVATORSHIP

Law Revision Commission Comments

1990 Enactment

This part supersedes Part 4 (commencing with Section 2100) of Division 4 of the repealed Probate Code. The superseded part was enacted upon recommendation of the California Law Revision Commission. See Recommendation Relating to Guardianship–Conservatorship Law, 14 Cal.L.Revision Comm'n Reports 501 (1978). See also Report of Assembly Committee on Judiciary on Assembly Bills Nos. 261 and 167, republished in 15 Cal.L.Revision Comm'n Reports 1061, 1076–89 (1980); Report of Senate Committee on Judiciary on Assembly Bill No. 261, republished in 15 Cal.L.Revision Comm'n Reports 1097, 1099 (1980); Communication from the California Law Revision Commission concerning Assembly Bill 158, 20 Cal.L.Revision Comm'n Reports 235 (1990). For the Guardianship–Conservatorship Law as enacted in 1979 (Chapter 726 of the Statutes of 1979) with the revisions made by Chapters 89 and 246 of the Statutes of 1980, see Guardianship–Conservatorship Law, 15 Cal.L.Revision Comm'n Reports 451 (1980). [20 Cal.L.Rev. Comm. Reports 1001 (1990)].

Cross References

Freedom from parental custody and control, stay of proceedings and effect upon jurisdiction under these provisions, see Family Code § 7807.

Juvenile court law, guardianships resulting from selection or implementation of a permanent plan, see Welfare and Institutions Code § 366.4.

Termination of parental rights of father, filing of petition, stay of proceedings affecting a child pending final determination of parental rights, see Family Code § 7662.

CHAPTER 1.   GENERAL PROVISIONS

§ 2100. Law governing

Guardianships and conservatorships are governed by Division 3 (commencing with Section 1000), except to the extent otherwise expressly provided by statute, and by this division. If no specific provision of this division is applicable, the provisions applicable to administration of estates of decedents govern so far as they are applicable to like situations. *(Stats.1990, c. 79 (A.B.759), § 14, operative July 1, 1991.)*

Law Revision Commission Comments

1990 Enactment

Section 2100 continues Section 2100 of the repealed Probate Code without substantive change and also makes applicable the general provisions relating to notice in Part 2 (commencing with Section 1200) of Division 3. Section 1452 establishes a specific rule concerning when the right to jury trial exists under this division. See the Comment to Section 1452. For general provisions, see Sections 1000–1004 (rules of practice), 1020–1023 (petitions and other papers), 1040–1050 (hearings and orders), 1200–1221 & 1460–1469 (notice of hearing), 1260–1265 (proof of giving notice), 2700–2702 (notice to persons who request special notice). See also Section 2103 (effect of final order). For background on the provisions of this part, see the Comment to this part under the part heading. [20 Cal.L.Rev.Comm. Reports 1001 (1990)].

Cross References

Estate administration, generally, see Probate Code § 7000 et seq.
Final orders, effect of, see Probate Code § 2103.
Notice, general provisions, see Probate Code § 1200 et seq.
Notice of hearing, see Probate Code § 1460 et seq.
Petitions and other papers, see Probate Code § 1020 et seq.
Special notice to persons requesting, see Probate Code § 2700 et seq.
Trial by jury, see Probate Code § 1452.

§ 2101. Fiduciary relationship; trust law

The relationship of guardian and ward and of conservator and conservatee is a fiduciary relationship that is governed by the law of trusts, except as provided in this division. *(Stats. 1990, c. 79 (A.B.759), § 14, operative July 1, 1991. Amended by Stats.1993, c. 293 (A.B.21), § 2.)*

Law Revision Commission Comments

1990 Enactment

Section 2101 restates Section 2101 of the repealed Probate Code without substantive change. A statement that the relationship is a fiduciary relationship has been substituted for the reference to the law relating to trusts. This change is not intended to make any substantive change in the law. The change reflects the repeal of the general provisions relating to confidential relationships in former Civil Code Sections 2215–2244 (repealed by 1986 Cal.Stat. ch. 820, § 7). See also Section 15003(b) (repeal of Civil Code provisions not intended to alter rules applied to fiduciary and confidential relationships). As to the duty to use ordinary care and diligence in managing the estate, see Section 2401 and the Comment thereto. The guardian or conservator may be removed for having such an interest adverse to the faithful performance of duties that there is an unreasonable risk that he or she will fail faithfully to perform duties. Section 2650(f). For background on the provisions of this part, see the Comment to this part under the part heading. [20 Cal.L.Rev. Comm. Reports 1001 (1990)].

Cross References

Duties of trustees, see Probate Code § 16000 et seq.
Fiduciary, defined, see Probate Code § 39.

§ 2102. Control by court

A guardian or conservator is subject to the regulation and control of the court in the performance of the duties of the office. *(Stats.1990, c. 79 (A.B.759), § 14, operative July 1, 1991.)*

Law Revision Commission Comments

1990 Enactment

Section 2102 continues Section 2102 of the repealed Probate Code without change. For background on the provisions of this part, see the Comment to this part under the part heading. [20 Cal.L.Rev. Comm. Reports 1001 (1990)].

Cross References

Court, defined, see Probate Code § 1418.
Instructions from or confirmation by court, see Probate Code §§ 2359, 2403.

§ 2103. Final judgment or order

(a) When a judgment or order made pursuant to this division becomes final, it releases the guardian or conservator and the sureties from all claims of the ward or conservatee and of any persons affected thereby based upon any act or omission directly authorized, approved, or confirmed in the judgment or order. For the purposes of this section, "order" includes an order settling an account of the guardian or conservator, whether an intermediate or final account.

(b) This section does not apply where the judgment or order is obtained by fraud or conspiracy or by misrepresentation contained in the petition or account or in the judgment or order as to any material fact. For the purposes of this subdivision, misrepresentation includes, but is not limited to, the omission of a material fact. *(Stats.1990, c. 79 (A.B.759), § 14, operative July 1, 1991.)*

Law Revision Commission Comments

1990 Enactment

Subdivision (a) of Section 2103 restates subdivision (a) of Section 2103 of the repealed Probate Code using language consistent with the language used in Section 7250, the comparable provision relating to estates of decedents. Subdivision (b) restates subdivision (b) of Section 2103 of the repealed Probate Code without substantive change. See also Conservatorship of Harvey, 3 Cal.3d 646, 651, 477 P.2d 742, 91 Cal.Rptr. 510 (1970) (protection extended to conservator's attorney). Under subdivision (b), the guardian or conservator is not released from liability for transactions which are not fully disclosed to the court. See also Section 1049 (enforcement of orders). For related provisions, see Sections 2545 (protection of good faith purchaser of personal property sold without court authorization), 2551(e) & 2552(c) (effect of proceedings for borrowing money and giving security therefor), 2553(d) (effect of proceedings authorizing the giving of lease), 2557 (effect of proceedings authorizing exchange of property). See also Section 2750 (appealable orders). For background on the provisions of this part, see the Comment to this part under the part heading. [20 Cal.L.Rev.Comm. Reports 1001 (1990)].

Cross References

Appealable orders, see Probate Code § 1300 et seq.
Claims of heirs or devisees, release, see Probate Code § 7250.

Fraud, see Civil Code § 1571 et seq.
Reversal of order appointing guardian or conservator, see Probate Code § 1311.

§ 2104. Nonprofit charitable corporation; appointment

(a) A nonprofit charitable corporation may be appointed as a guardian or conservator of the person or estate, or both, if all of the following requirements are met:

(1) The corporation is incorporated in this state.

(2) The articles of incorporation specifically authorize the corporation to accept appointments as guardian or conservator, as the case may be.

(3) The corporation has been providing, at the time of appointment, care, counseling, or financial assistance to the proposed ward or conservatee under the supervision of a registered social worker certified by the Board of Behavioral Science Examiners of this state.

(b) The petition for appointment of a nonprofit charitable corporation described in this section as a guardian or conservator shall include in the caption the name of a responsible corporate officer who shall act for the corporation for the purposes of this division. If, for any reason, the officer so named ceases to act as the responsible corporate officer for the purposes of this division, the corporation shall file with the court a notice containing (1) the name of the successor responsible corporate officer and (2) the date the successor becomes the responsible corporate officer.

(c) If a nonprofit charitable corporation described in this section is appointed as a guardian or conservator:

(1) The corporation's compensation as guardian or conservator shall be allowed only for services actually rendered.

(2) Any fee allowed for an attorney for the corporation shall be for services actually rendered. *(Stats.1990, c. 79 (A.B.759), § 14, operative July 1, 1991. Amended by Stats. 2001, c. 351 (A.B.479), § 1.)*

Law Revision Commission Comments
1990 Enactment

Section 2104 continues Section 2104 of the repealed Probate Code without change. For background on the provisions of this part, see the Comment to this part under the part heading. [20 Cal.L.Rev. Comm. Reports 1001 (1990)].

Cross References

Attorney's fees and costs, generally, see Code of Civil Procedure § 1021.
Board of Behavioral Sciences, see Business and Professions Code § 4990.
Compensation of guardian, conservator, and attorney, see Probate Code § 2640 et seq.

§ 2105. Joint guardians or conservators; appointment

(a) The court, in its discretion, may appoint for a ward or conservatee:

(1) Two or more joint guardians or conservators of the person.

(2) Two or more joint guardians or conservators of the estate.

(3) Two or more joint guardians or conservators of the person and estate.

(b) When joint guardians or conservators are appointed, each shall qualify in the same manner as a sole guardian or conservator.

(c) Subject to subdivisions (d) and (e):

(1) Where there are two guardians or conservators, both must concur to exercise a power.

(2) Where there are more than two guardians or conservators, a majority must concur to exercise a power.

(d) If one of the joint guardians or conservators dies or is removed or resigns, the powers and duties continue in the remaining joint guardians or conservators until further appointment is made by the court.

(e) Where joint guardians or conservators have been appointed and one or more are (1) absent from the state and unable to act, (2) otherwise unable to act, or (3) legally disqualified from serving, the court may, by order made with or without notice, authorize the remaining joint guardians or conservators to act as to all matters embraced within its order.

(f) If a custodial parent has been diagnosed as having a terminal condition, as evidenced by a declaration executed by a licensed physician, the court, in its discretion, may appoint the custodial parent and a person nominated by the custodial parent as joint guardians of the person of the minor. However, this appointment shall not be made over the objection of a noncustodial parent without a finding that the noncustodial parent's custody would be detrimental to the minor, as provided in Section 3041 of the Family Code. It is the intent of the Legislature in enacting the amendments to this subdivision adopted during the 1995–96 Regular Session for a parent with a terminal condition to be able to make arrangements for the joint care, custody, and control of his or her minor children so as to minimize the emotional stress of, and disruption for, the minor children whenever the parent is incapacitated or upon the parent's death, and to avoid the need to provide a temporary guardian or place the minor children in foster care, pending appointment of a guardian, as might otherwise be required.

"Terminal condition," for purposes of this subdivision, means an incurable and irreversible condition that, without the administration of life-sustaining treatment, will, within reasonable medical judgment, result in death. *(Stats.1990, c. 79 (A.B.759), § 14, operative July 1, 1991. Amended by Stats.1993, c. 978 (S.B.305), § 2; Stats.1995, c. 278 (A.B. 1104), § 1; Stats.1999, c. 658 (A.B.891), § 11, operative July 1, 2000.)*

Law Revision Commission Comments
1990 Enactment

Section 2105 continues Section 2105 of the repealed Probate Code without change. Under subdivision (e), the absence of a guardian or conservator from California does not of itself suspend the power to act or participate in joint decision-making. This is the same as the rule for joint personal representatives. See Section 9630(c) and the Comment thereto. For background on the provisions of this part, see the Comment to this part under the part heading. [20 Cal.L.Rev.Comm. Reports 1001 (1990)].

1999 Amendment

The last paragraph of Section 2105 is deleted because the definition to which it referred is repealed. See former Health and Safety Code § 7186 Comment. [29 Cal.L.Rev.Comm. Reports 1 (1999)].

Cross References

Appointment of guardian, parent not to be appointed as guardian of minor except as provided in this section, see Probate Code § 1514.
Guardians and conservators, removal or resignation, see Probate Code § 2650 et seq.
Joint personal representatives, death or disqualification of one or all, see Probate Code §§ 8521, 8522, 9630.
Parent, defined, see Probate Code § 54.
Personal representatives, breach of fiduciary duty committed by another representative, see Probate Code § 9631.
Powers and duties, see Probate Code § 2350 et seq.
Removal or resignation, see Probate Code § 2650 et seq.
Temporary guardians and conservators, generally, see Probate Code § 2250 et seq.
Termination of guardianship as affected by death of guardian, see Probate Code § 2632.
Vacancy in office of cotrustee, see Probate Code § 15621.

§ 2105.5. Multiple guardians or conservators; liability for breach of another guardian or conservator

(a) Except as provided in subdivision (b), where there is more than one guardian or conservator of the estate, one guardian or conservator is not liable for a breach of fiduciary duty committed by another guardian or conservator.

(b) Where there is more than one guardian or conservator of the estate, one guardian or conservator is liable for a breach of fiduciary duty committed by another guardian or conservator of the same estate under any of the following circumstances:

(1) Where the guardian or conservator participates in a breach of fiduciary duty committed by the other guardian or conservator.

(2) Where the guardian or conservator improperly delegates the administration of the estate to the other guardian or conservator.

(3) Where the guardian or conservator approves, knowingly acquiesces in, or conceals a breach of fiduciary duty committed by the other guardian or conservator.

(4) Where the guardian or conservator negligently enables the other guardian or conservator to commit a breach of fiduciary duty.

(5) Where the guardian or conservator knows or has information from which the guardian or conservator reasonably should have known of the breach of fiduciary duty by the other guardian or conservator and fails to take reasonable steps to compel the other guardian or conservator to redress the breach.

(c) The liability of a guardian or conservator for a breach of fiduciary duty committed by another guardian or conservator that occurred before July 1, 1988, is governed by prior law and not by this section. *(Stats.1990, c. 79 (A.B.759), § 14, operative July 1, 1991.)*

Law Revision Commission Comments
1990 Enactment

Section 2105.5 continues Section 2105.5 of the repealed Probate Code without change. This section is comparable to the joint liability provision for personal representatives and applies prospectively only. See Section 9631. For background on the provisions of this part, see the Comment to this part under the part heading. [20 Cal.L.Rev.Comm. Reports 1001 (1990)].

Cross References
Fiduciary, defined, see Probate Code § 39.

§ 2106. One guardian or conservator for several wards or conservatees; appointment

(a) The court, in its discretion, may appoint one guardian or conservator for several wards or conservatees.

(b) The appointment of one guardian or conservator for several wards or conservatees may be requested in the initial petition filed in the proceeding or may be requested subsequently upon a petition filed in the same proceeding and noticed and heard with respect to the newly proposed ward or conservatee in the same manner as an initial petition for appointment of a guardian or conservator. *(Stats.1990, c. 79 (A.B.759), § 14, operative July 1, 1991.)*

Law Revision Commission Comments
1990 Enactment

Section 2106 continues Section 2106 of the repealed Probate Code without change. For general provisions, see Sections 1000–1004 (rules of practice), 1020–1023 (petitions and other papers), 1040–1050 (hearings and orders). For general provisions relating to notice of hearing, see Sections 1200–1221, 1460–1469. See also Sections 1260–1265 (proof of giving notice), 2700–2702 (notice to persons who request special notice). For background on the provisions of this part, see the Comment to this part under the part heading. [20 Cal.L.Rev.Comm. Reports 1001 (1990)].

§ 2107. Person or estate of nonresident; guardian or conservator; powers and duties

(a) Unless limited by court order, when a court of this state appoints a guardian or conservator of the person of a nonresident, the appointee has the same powers and duties as a guardian or conservator of the person of a resident while the nonresident is in this state.

(b) When a court of this state appoints a guardian or conservator of the estate of a nonresident, the appointee has, with respect to the property of the nonresident within this state, the same powers and duties as a guardian or conservator of the estate of a resident. The responsibility of such a guardian or conservator with regard to inventory, accounting, and disposal of the estate is confined to the property that comes into the hands of the guardian or conservator in this state. *(Stats.1990, c. 79 (A.B.759), § 14, operative July 1, 1991. Amended by Stats.2014, c. 553 (S.B.940), § 21, eff. Jan. 1, 2015, operative Jan. 1, 2016.)*

Law Revision Commission Comments
1990 Enactment

Section 2107 continues Section 2107 of the repealed Probate Code without substantive change. This section prescribes powers and duties of a guardian or conservator appointed in California for a nonresident. The court may limit the powers and duties of a guardian or conservator of the person of a nonresident. For example, if a guardian or conservator of the person is appointed for a nonresident for a limited purpose such as to consent to medical treatment, the court may limit the powers and duties of the guardian or conservator to accomplishment of that purpose. Subdivision (a) states only the powers and duties while the ward or conservatee is in this state. Section 2107 does not deal with the powers of the California guardian or conservator of the person when the nonresident ward or conservatee is not in California. See generally Mayer v. Willing, 196 Cal.App.2d 379, 16 Cal.Rptr. 476 (1961); 39 Am.Jur.2d Guardian and Ward §§ 26, 219 (1968 & Supp.1989). For background on the provisions of this part, see the Comment to this part under the part heading. [20 Cal.L.Rev.Comm. Reports 1001 (1990)].

2014 Amendment

Section 2107 is amended to prevent confusion regarding its application, which might otherwise arise due to the enactment of the California Conservatorship Jurisdiction Act (Section 1980 *et seq.*). This clarification is not a substantive change. See Section 2107 Comment (1990 enactment), which explains that "[t]his section prescribes powers and duties of a guardian or conservator *appointed in California* for a nonresident." (Emphasis added.) [43 Cal.L.Rev. Comm. Reports 93 (2013)].

Cross References

Inventory and accounts, see Probate Code § 2600 et seq.
Powers and duties of guardian or conservator, see Probate Code § 2350 et seq.

§ 2108. Powers granted guardian nominated by will

(a) Except to the extent the court for good cause determines otherwise, if a guardian of the person is nominated as provided in Article 1 (commencing with Section 1500) of Chapter 1 of Part 2 and is appointed by the court, the guardian shall be granted in the order of appointment, to the extent provided in the nomination, the same authority with respect to the person of the ward as a parent having legal custody of a child and may exercise such authority without notice, hearing, or court authorization, instructions, approval, or confirmation in the same manner as if such authority were exercised by a parent having legal custody of a child.

(b) Except to the extent the court for good cause determines otherwise and subject to Sections 2593, 2594, and 2595, if a guardian of the estate is nominated under Section 1500 or a guardian for property is nominated under Section 1501 and the guardian is appointed by the court, the guardian shall be granted in the order of appointment, to the extent provided in the nomination, the right to exercise any one or more of the powers listed in Section 2591 without notice, hearing, or court authorization, instructions, approval, or confirmation in the same manner as if such authority were granted by order of the court under Section 2590. In the case of a guardian nominated under Section 1501, such additional authority shall be limited to the property covered by the nomination.

(c) The terms of any order made under this section shall be included in the letters. *(Stats.1990, c. 79 (A.B.759), § 14, operative July 1, 1991.)*

Law Revision Commission Comments
1990 Enactment

Section 2108 continues Section 2108 of the repealed Probate Code except that the application of the section covers any nomination in writing and is not restricted to nomination made "by will." The word "letters" is substituted for "letters of guardianship" in subdivision (c). See Section 52(b) (defining "letters").

Subdivision (a) permits the person making the nomination to give the nominated guardian of the person the same authority as a parent, unless the court for good cause determines otherwise. Appointment of a nominated guardian of the person is subject to Section 4600 of the Civil Code relating to custody of a minor. See Section 1514(b). But, if the nominated person is appointed by the court, subdivision (a) of Section 2108 applies.

Subdivision (b) permits the person making the nomination to give a guardian of the estate, or of particular property, authority to act without court authorization as provided in provisions listed in subdivision (b) relating to independent exercise of powers. The court must appoint the person nominated as guardian of the estate (Section 1500) or of particular property (Section 1501) unless the court determines that the nominee is "unsuitable." See Section 1514(c)–(d). If the nominated person is appointed by the court, subdivision (b) of Section 2108 applies.

Where good cause is shown, the court may decline to give the guardian the powers provided in the nominating instrument.

Under Section 2108, the court may grant additional powers to the guardian only "to the extent provided in the nomination." The nominating instrument may grant only one or a few of the specific additional powers permissible under Section 2108, or may provide the broadest grant of additional powers possible under the section. Nothing in Section 2108 precludes the court from granting a nominated guardian additional powers listed in Section 2591 under the independent exercise of powers provisions, even though these additional powers were not granted in the instrument that nominated the guardian.

For background on the provisions of this part, see the Comment to this part under the part heading. [20 Cal.L.Rev.Comm. Reports 1001 (1990)].

Cross References

Bond of nominated guardian, see Probate Code § 2324.
Child, defined, see Probate Code § 26.
Custody of minors, see Family Code § 3020 et seq.
Letters, defined, see Probate Code § 52.

§ 2109. Guardian for particular property; powers and duties

(a) Subject to Section 2108, a guardian appointed under subdivision (d) of Section 1514 for particular property upon a nomination made under Section 1501 has, with respect to that property, the same powers and duties as a guardian of the estate. The responsibility of such a guardian with regard to inventory, accounting, and disposal of the estate is confined to the property covered by the nomination.

(b) When a guardian is appointed under subdivision (d) of Section 1514 for particular property upon a nomination made under Section 1501 and there is a guardian of the estate appointed under any other provision of Part 2 (commencing with Section 1500):

(1) The guardian appointed for the property covered by the nomination manages and controls that property and the guardian of the estate manages and controls the balance of the guardianship estate.

(2) Either guardian may petition under Section 2403 to the court in which the guardianship of the estate proceeding is pending for instructions concerning how the duties that are imposed by law upon the guardian of the estate are to be allocated between the two guardians. *(Stats.1990, c. 79 (A.B.759), § 14, operative July 1, 1991.)*

Law Revision Commission Comments
1990 Enactment

Section 2109 continues Section 2109 of the repealed Probate Code without change. Subdivision (a) is analogous to subdivision (b) of Section 2107 (guardian of estate of nonresident). Paragraph (1) of subdivision (b) codified Guardianship of Joaquin, 168 Cal.App.2d 99, 335 P.2d 507 (1959). Paragraph (2) of subdivision (b) authorizes the court in which the general guardianship of the estate is pending to allocate between the two guardians the duties of a guardian of the estate. This permits the court to determine, for example, which guardian will pay particular debts or how much each will contribute to the support of the ward. For general provisions, see Sections 1000–1004 (rules of practice), 1020–1023 (petitions and other papers), 1040–1050 (hearings and orders). For background on the provisions of this part, see the Comment to this part under the part heading. [20 Cal.L.Rev.Comm. Reports 1001 (1990)].

Cross References

Inventory and accounts, see Probate Code § 2600 et seq.
Powers and duties of guardian of the estate, see Probate Code § 2400 et seq.

§ 2110. Personal liability

Unless otherwise provided in the instrument or in this division, a guardian or conservator is not personally liable on an instrument, including but not limited to a note, mortgage, deed of trust, or other contract, properly entered into in the guardian's or conservator's fiduciary capacity in the course of the guardianship or conservatorship unless the guardian or conservator fails to reveal the guardian's or conservator's representative capacity or identify the guardianship or conservatorship estate in the instrument. *(Stats.1990, c. 79 (A.B.759), § 14, operative July 1, 1991.)*

Law Revision Commission Comments
1990 Enactment

Section 2110 is new. It generalizes provisions formerly found in Section 2551(d) and is comparable to Sections 18000 (trust law) and 9606 (decedent estate administration). [20 Cal.L.Rev.Comm. Reports 1001 (1990)].

Cross References

Instrument, defined, see Probate Code § 45.
Trustees, liability to beneficiaries, see Probate Code § 16400 et seq.

§ 2111. Transaction

(a) As used in this section, "transaction" means any of the following:

(1) A conveyance or lease of real property of the guardianship or conservatorship estate.

(2) The creation of a mortgage or deed of trust on real property of the guardianship or conservatorship estate.

(3) A transfer of personal property of the guardianship or conservatorship estate.

(4) The creation of a security interest or other lien in personal property of the guardianship or conservatorship estate.

(b) Whenever the court authorizes or directs a transaction, the transaction shall be carried out by the guardian or conservator of the estate in accordance with the terms of the order.

(c) A conveyance, lease, or mortgage of, or deed of trust on, real property executed by a guardian or conservator shall set forth therein that it is made by authority of the order authorizing or directing the transaction and shall give the date of the order. A certified copy of the order shall be recorded in the office of the county recorder in each county in which any portion of the real property is located.

(d) A transaction carried out by a guardian or conservator in accordance with an order authorizing or directing the transaction has the same effect as if the ward or conservatee had carried out the transaction while having legal capacity to do so. *(Stats.1990, c. 79 (A.B.759), § 14, operative July 1, 1991.)*

Law Revision Commission Comments
1990 Enactment

Section 2111 continues Section 2111 of the repealed Probate Code without change. For comparable provisions relating to decedents' estates, see Sections 7260–7263.

Subdivision (d) permits the guardian or conservator to convey or transfer the title, right, or interest to the same extent as it might have been conveyed or transferred by a person having legal capacity for the transaction. Thus, for example, in a proceeding under Sections 2520–2528, the court might order the guardian or conservator to execute a quitclaim deed to remove a cloud on petitioner's property. Or the court might direct a conveyance of real property to complete a contract and order the guardian or conservator to execute a grant deed that will pass after-acquired title. See Civil Code § 1106; 4 B. Witkin, Summary of California Law Real Property § 136 at 351–52, § 212 at 417–18 (9th ed. 1987). For general provisions, see Sections 1046–1049 (orders), Section 2103 (effect of final order), 2750 (appealable orders). See also Sections 1875 (effect of failure to record order limiting capacity of conservatee), 2550–2557 (notes, mortgages, leases, conveyances, and exchanges). For background on the provisions of this part, see the Comment to this part under the part heading. [20 Cal.L.Rev.Comm. Reports 1001 (1990)].

Cross References

Borrowing money and mortgaging property by personal representative, see Probate Code § 9800 et seq.
Contracts, interpretation, see Civil Code § 1635 et seq.
Exchange of property, see Probate Code § 2557.
Execution of conveyance or transfer, effective order, see Probate Code § 857.
Leases, see Probate Code § 2553 et seq.; Civil Code § 1940 et seq.
Liens, see Civil Code § 2872 et seq.
Mechanics liens, see Civil Code § 8400.
Mortgages, see Civil Code § 2920 et seq.
Orders, see Probate Code § 1047 et seq.
Real property, defined, see Probate Code § 68.
Transaction, legal capacity of conservatee, see Probate Code § 1870.
Transfer, defined, see Civil Code § 3439.01.
Transfer of interest by death of insured, see Insurance Code § 303.
Transfer of personal property, generally, see Commercial Code §§ 2101 et seq., 2401 et seq.
Transfer of real property,
  Effect, see Civil Code § 1104 et seq.
  Method, see Civil Code § 1091 et seq.
  Recording, see Civil Code § 1169 et seq.

§ 2111.5. Court official's or employee's with responsibilities related to guardians or conservators; prohibitions against purchasing, leasing, or renting property from estate

(a) Except as provided in subdivision (b), every court official or employee who has duties or responsibilities related to the appointment of a guardian or conservator, or the processing of any document related to a guardian or conservator, and every person who is related by blood or marriage to a court official or employee who has these duties, is prohibited from purchasing, leasing, or renting any real or personal property from the estate of the ward or conservatee whom the guardian or conservator represents. For purposes of this subdivision, a "person related by blood or marriage" means any of the following:

(1) A person's spouse or domestic partner.

(2) Relatives within the second degree of lineal or collateral consanguinity of a person or a person's spouse.

(b) A person described in subdivision (a) is not prohibited from purchasing real or personal property from the estate of the ward or conservatee whom the guardian or conservator represents where the purchase is made under terms and conditions of a public sale of the property.

(c) A violation of this section shall result in the rescission of the purchase, lease, or rental of the property. Any losses incurred by the estate of the ward or conservatee because the property was sold or leased at less than fair market value shall be deemed as charges against the guardian or conservator under the provisions of Sections 2401.3 and 2401.5. The court shall assess a civil penalty equal to three times the charges against the guardian, conservator, or other person in violation of this section, and may assess punitive damages as it deems proper. If the estate does not incur losses as a result of the violation, the court shall order the guardian, conservator, or other person in violation of this section to pay a fine of up to five thousand dollars ($5,000) for each violation. The fines and penalties provided in this section are in addition to any other rights and remedies provided by law. *(Added by Stats.2000, c. 565 (A.B.1950), § 3. Amended by Stats.2001, c. 893 (A.B.25), § 28.)*

Cross References

Domestic partner, defined, see Probate Code § 37.

§ 2112. Repealed by Stats.2006, c. 838 (S.B.678), § 27

§ 2113. Balance of conflicting interests

A conservator shall accommodate the desires of the conservatee, except to the extent that doing so would violate the conservator's fiduciary duties to the conservatee or impose an unreasonable expense on the conservatorship estate. *(Added by Stats.2006, c. 493 (A.B.1363), § 13.)*

§ 2151. Repealed by Stats.1979, c. 726, p. 2334, § 2, operative Jan. 1, 1981

CHAPTER 2. JURISDICTION AND VENUE

ARTICLE 1. JURISDICTION AND VENUE

Cross References

Application of old and new law, see Probate Code § 3.
Trusts, judicial proceedings, generally, see Probate Code § 17000 et seq.

§ 2200. Superior court jurisdiction; determination of state jurisdiction

(a) The superior court has jurisdiction of guardianship and conservatorship proceedings.

(b) Chapter 8 (commencing with Section 1980) of Part 3 governs which state has jurisdiction of a conservatorship proceeding. *(Stats.1990, c. 79 (A.B.759), § 14, operative July 1, 1991. Amended by Stats.2014, c. 553 (S.B.940), § 22, eff. Jan. 1, 2015, operative Jan. 1, 2016.)*

Law Revision Commission Comments

1990 Enactment

Section 2200 continues Section 2200 of the repealed Probate Code without change. For a comparable provision relating to decedents' estates, see Section 7050. For background on the provisions of this part, see the Comment to this part under the part heading. [20 Cal.L.Rev.Comm. Reports 1001 (1990)].

2014 Amendment

Section 2200 is amended to direct attention to the jurisdictional provisions in the California Conservatorship Jurisdiction Act (Section 1980 *et seq.*). [43 Cal.L.Rev.Comm. Reports 93 (2013)].

Cross References

Jurisdiction necessary for judgment, see Code of Civil Procedure § 1917.
Jurisdictional limitation on guardian's or conservator's authority, see Code of Civil Procedure § 1913.
Superior courts,
    Generally, see Cal. Const. Art. 6, § 4.
    Jurisdiction, see Cal. Const. Art. 6, §§ 10, 11.
Trusts, judicial proceedings, generally, see Probate Code § 17000 et seq.

§ 2201. Residents; venue

The proper county for the commencement of a guardianship or conservatorship proceeding for a resident of this state is either of the following:

(a) The county in which the proposed ward or proposed conservatee resides.

(b) Such other county as may be in the best interests of the proposed ward or proposed conservatee. *(Stats.1990, c. 79 (A.B.759), § 14, operative July 1, 1991.)*

1990 Enactment

Section 2201 continues Section 2201 of the repealed Probate Code without change. Subdivision (b) permits the court to determine that venue is proper, even though the place of residence is in dispute. See Hillman v. Stults, 263 Cal.App.2d 848, 871–72, 70 Cal.Rptr. 295, 309 (1968); Guardianship of Smith, 147 Cal.App.2d 686, 306 P.2d 86 (1957). This avoids the need to litigate the issue of residence if the court determines that continuance of the proceeding in the county where filed is in the best interests of the ward or conservatee. For background on the provisions of this part, see the Comment to this part under the part heading. [20 Cal.L.Rev.Comm. Reports 1001 (1990)].

Cross References

Change of venue, see Probate Code § 2210 et seq.
Place of trial, see Code of Civil Procedure § 395 et seq.
Probate proceedings, jurisdiction and venue, see Probate Code § 7050 et seq.
Residence,
   Determination of place of residence, see Government Code § 244.
   Effect of absence from state on official business, see Government Code § 245.
   Voting residence, see Cal. Const. Art. 2, § 3; Elections Code § 349.

§ 2201.5. Repealed by Stats.1979, c. 726, p. 2334, § 2, operative Jan. 1, 1981

§ 2202. Nonresidents; venue

(a) The proper county for the commencement of a proceeding for the guardianship or conservatorship of the person of a nonresident of this state is either of the following:

(1) The county in which the proposed ward or conservatee is temporarily living.

(2) Such other county as may be in the best interests of the proposed ward or proposed conservatee.

(b) The proper county for the commencement of a proceeding for the guardianship or conservatorship of the estate for a nonresident of this state is any of the following:

(1) The county in which the proposed ward or proposed conservatee is temporarily living.

(2) Any county in which the proposed ward or proposed conservatee has property.

(3) Such other county as may be in the best interests of the proposed ward or proposed conservatee. *(Stats.1990, c. 79 (A.B.759), § 14, operative July 1, 1991.)*

1990 Enactment

Section 2202 continues Section 2202 of the repealed Probate Code without substantive change. The provision in subdivisions (a) and (b) that venue is proper in "such other county as may be in the best interests of the proposed ward or proposed conservatee" enables the court of the county where the property is located to determine that venue is proper with respect to the person as well as the estate where a guardianship or conservatorship of the person is necessary in California. For background on the provisions of this part, see the Comment to this part under the part heading. [20 Cal.L.Rev.Comm. Reports 1001 (1990)].

Cross References

Change of venue, see Probate Code § 2210 et seq.
Place of trial, see Code of Civil Procedure § 395 et seq.

§ 2203. Priority of court; proceedings instituted in several counties

(a) If proceedings for the guardianship or conservatorship of the estate are commenced in more than one county, the guardianship or conservatorship of the estate first granted, including a temporary guardianship or conservatorship of the estate, governs and extends to all the property of the ward or conservatee within this state and the other proceeding shall be dismissed.

(b) If proceedings for the guardianship or conservatorship of the person are commenced in more than one county, the guardianship or conservatorship of the person first granted, including a temporary guardianship or conservatorship of the person, governs and the other proceeding shall be dismissed.

(c) If a proceeding for the guardianship or conservatorship of the person is commenced in one county and a proceeding for the guardianship or conservatorship of the estate is commenced in a different county, the court first granting the guardianship or conservatorship, whether of the person or of the estate, may find that it is in the best interests of the ward or conservatee that the guardianship or conservatorship of both the person and the estate be maintained in that county or in such other county as the court shall determine. Thereupon, the guardianship or conservatorship proceeding in the court of the county found by the court to be in the best interests of the ward or conservatee shall govern and shall extend to all property of the ward or conservatee within this state, and the other proceeding shall be dismissed. *(Stats. 1990, c. 79 (A.B.759), § 14, operative July 1, 1991.)*

1990 Enactment

Section 2203 continues Section 2203 of the repealed Probate Code without substantive change. For background on the provisions of this part, see the Comment to this part under the part heading. [20 Cal.L.Rev.Comm. Reports 1001 (1990)].

Cross References

Jurisdictional limitation on guardian's or conservator's authority, see Code of Civil Procedure § 1913.
Temporary guardians and conservators, generally, see Probate Code § 2250 et seq.
Trusts, judicial proceedings, generally, see Probate Code § 17000 et seq.

§ 2204. Custody or visitation proceedings pending in more than one court; determination of venue; communications between the courts

(a) If a proceeding for the guardianship of the person of the minor is filed in one county and a custody or visitation proceeding has already been filed in one or more other counties, the following shall apply:

(1) If the guardianship proceeding is filed in a county where the proposed ward and the proposed guardian have resided for six or more consecutive months immediately prior to the commencement of the proceeding, or, in the case of a minor less than six months of age, since the minor's birth, the court in that county is the proper court to hear and determine

the guardianship proceeding, unless that court determines that the best interests of the minor require that the proceeding be transferred to one of the other courts. A period of temporary absence no longer than 30 days from the county of the minor or the proposed guardian shall not be considered an interruption of the six-month period.

(2) If the guardianship proceeding is filed in a county where the proposed ward and the proposed guardian have resided for less than six consecutive months immediately prior to the commencement of the proceeding, or, in the case of a minor less than six months of age, a period less than the minor's life, the court shall transfer the case to one of the other courts, unless the court determines that the best interests of the minor require that the guardianship proceeding be maintained in the court where it was filed.

(3) If a petitioner or respondent in a custody or visitation proceeding who is an authorized petitioner under Section 2212 petitions the court where the guardianship proceeding is filed for transfer of the guardianship proceeding to the court where the custody or visitation proceeding is on file at any time before the appointment of a guardian, including a temporary guardian, the provisions of this subdivision shall apply to the court's determination of the petition for transfer. Except as provided in this paragraph, the petition for transfer shall be determined as provided in Sections 2212 to 2217, inclusive.

(b) The following shall apply concerning communications between the courts:

(1) The court where the guardianship proceeding is commenced shall communicate concerning the proceedings with each court where a custody or visitation proceeding is on file prior to making a determination authorized in subdivision (a), including a determination of a petition to transfer.

(2) If a petitioner or respondent, who is authorized to petition to transfer under Section 2212, petitions the court where the guardianship proceeding is filed for transfer of the guardianship after the appointment of a guardian, including a temporary guardian, the court in the guardianship proceeding may communicate with each court where a custody or visitation proceeding is on file before determining the petition for transfer.

(3) If the court in the guardianship proceeding appoints a guardian of the person of the minor, including a temporary guardian, the court shall transmit a copy of the order appointing a guardian to each court where a custody or visitation proceeding is on file, and each of those courts shall file the order in the case file for its custody or visitation proceeding.

(4) The provisions of subdivisions (b) to (e), inclusive, of Section 3410 of the Family Code shall apply to communications between courts under this subdivision.

(5) The Judicial Council shall, on or before January 1, 2013, adopt rules of court to implement the provisions of this subdivision.

(c) For purposes of this section, "custody or visitation proceeding" means a proceeding described in Section 3021 of the Family Code that relates to the rights to custody or visitation of the minor under Part 2 (commencing with Section 3020) of Division 8 of the Family Code. (Added by

Stats.2011, c. 102 (A.B.458), § 2. Amended by Stats.2012, c. 207 (A.B.2683), § 1.)

§ 2205. Exclusive jurisdiction; consolidation of guardianship and adoption proceedings

(a) Except as provided in Section 304 of the Welfare and Institutions Code, and subject to the provisions specified in subdivision (b), upon the filing of an order appointing a guardian of the person of a minor in a guardianship proceeding, including an order appointing a temporary guardian of the person of the minor, the court in the guardianship proceeding shall have exclusive jurisdiction to determine all issues of custody or visitation of the minor until the guardianship proceeding is terminated.

(b) This section is subject to the provisions of Sections 1510 of this code, and 8714, 8714.5, and 8802 of the Family Code, relating to consolidation of guardianship and adoption proceedings and the court where the consolidated case is to be heard and decided. *(Added by Stats.2011, c. 102 (A.B. 458), § 3.)*

§ 2206, 2207. Repealed by Stats.1979, c. 726, p. 2334, § 2, operative Jan. 1, 1981

ARTICLE 2. CHANGE OF VENUE

§ 2210. Definitions

As used in this article:

(a) "Guardian or conservator" includes a proposed guardian or proposed conservator.

(b) "Ward or conservatee" includes a proposed ward or proposed conservatee. *(Stats.1990, c. 79 (A.B.759), § 14, operative July 1, 1991.)*

Law Revision Commission Comments

1990 Enactment

Section 2210 continues Section 2210 of the repealed Probate Code without change. For background on the provisions of this part, see the Comment to this part under the part heading. [20 Cal.L.Rev. Comm. Reports 1001 (1990)].

§ 2211. Transfer of proceedings

The court in which a guardianship or conservatorship proceeding is pending may, upon petition therefor, transfer the proceeding to another county within this state. *(Stats. 1990, c. 79 (A.B.759), § 14, operative July 1, 1991.)*

Law Revision Commission Comments

1990 Enactment

Section 2211 continues Section 2211 of the repealed Probate Code without change. For general provisions, see Sections 1000–1004 (rules of practice), 1020–1023 (petitions and other papers), 1040–1050 (hearings and orders), 2103 (effect of final order). For background on the provisions of this part, see the Comment to this part under the part heading. [20 Cal.L.Rev.Comm. Reports 1001 (1990)].

Cross References

Civil actions, change of place of trial, generally, see Code of Civil Procedure § 397 et seq.

Probate proceedings, transfer to another county, see Probate Code § 7070 et seq.

§ 2212. Petition for transfer; persons authorized to file

The petition for transfer may be filed only by one or more of the following:

(a) The guardian or conservator.

(b) The ward or conservatee.

(c) The spouse of the ward or the spouse or domestic partner of the conservatee.

(d) A relative or friend of the ward or conservatee.

(e) Any other interested person. *(Stats.1990, c. 79 (A.B. 759), § 14, operative July 1, 1991. Amended by Stats.2001, c. 893 (A.B.25), § 29.)*

Law Revision Commission Comments

1990 Enactment

Section 2212 continues Section 2212 of the repealed Probate Code without change. For background on the provisions of this part, see the Comment to this part under the part heading. [20 Cal.L.Rev. Comm. Reports 1001 (1990)].

Cross References

Domestic partner, defined, see Probate Code § 37.
Guardian or conservator, defined, see Probate Code § 2210.
Interested person, see Probate Code § 1424.
Ward or conservatee, defined, see Probate Code § 2210.

§ 2213. Petition for transfer; contents

The petition for transfer shall set forth all of the following:

(a) The county to which the proceeding is to be transferred.

(b) The name and address of the ward or conservatee.

(c) A brief description of the character, value, and location of the property of the ward or conservatee.

(d) The reasons for the transfer.

(e) The names and addresses, so far as they are known to the petitioner, of the spouse and of the relatives of the ward within the second degree, or of the spouse or domestic partner and of the relatives of the conservatee within the second degree.

(f) The name and address of the guardian or conservator if other than the petitioner. *(Stats.1990, c. 79 (A.B.759), § 14, operative July 1, 1991. Amended by Stats.2001, c. 893 (A.B.25), § 30.)*

Law Revision Commission Comments

1990 Enactment

Section 2213 continues Section 2213 of the repealed Probate Code without change. For general provisions relating to petitions and other papers, see Sections 1020–1023. For background on the provisions of this part, see the Comment to this part under the part heading. [20 Cal.L.Rev.Comm. Reports 1001 (1990)].

Cross References

Domestic partner, defined, see Probate Code § 37.

§ 2214. Notice of hearing

Notice of the hearing shall be given for the period and in the manner provided in Chapter 3 (commencing with Section 1460) of Part 1. In addition, the petitioner shall mail a notice of the time and place of the hearing and a copy of the petition to all persons required to be listed in the petition at least 15 days before the date set for the hearing. *(Stats.1990, c. 79 (A.B.759), § 14, operative July 1, 1991.)*

Law Revision Commission Comments

1990 Enactment

Section 2214 continues Section 2214 of the repealed Probate Code without change. For general provisions relating to notice of hearing, see Sections 1200–1221, 1460–1469. See also Sections 1260–1265 (proof of giving notice), 2700–2702 (notice to persons who request special notice). For background on the provisions of this part, see the Comment to this part under the part heading. [20 Cal.L.Rev. Comm. Reports 1001 (1990)].

Cross References

Computation of time, see Code of Civil Procedure §§ 12 and 12a; Government Code § 6800 et seq.
Mailing, completion, see Probate Code § 1467.
Notice,
    Mailing, see Probate Code § 1215 et seq.
    Posting, see Probate Code § 1230.
    Proof of giving notice, see Probate Code § 1260 et seq.
    Special notice, see Probate Code § 1250 et seq.
    This code, generally, see Probate Code § 1200 et seq.
    This division, generally, see Probate Code § 1460 et seq.
    To directors, see Probate Code § 1461.
Request for special notice, see Probate Code § 2700 et seq.
Service of process,
    Generally, see Code of Civil Procedure § 413.10 et seq.
    Mail, see Code of Civil Procedure §§ 415.30, 1012 et seq.
    Personal delivery, see Code of Civil Procedure § 415.10.
    Proof of service, see Code of Civil Procedure § 417.10 et seq.
    Publication, see Code of Civil Procedure § 415.50.

§ 2215. Hearing and order

(a) Any of the following persons may appear at the hearing to support or oppose the petition and may file written objections to the petition:

(1) Any person required to be listed in the petition.

(2) Any creditor of the ward or conservatee or of the estate.

(3) Any other interested person.

(b)(1) If the court determines that the transfer requested in the petition will be for the best interests of the ward or conservatee, it shall make an order transferring the proceeding to the other county.

(2) In those cases in which the court has approved a change of residence of the conservatee, it shall be presumed to be in the best interests of the conservatee to transfer the proceedings if the ward or conservatee has moved his or her residence to another county within the state in which any person set forth in subdivision (b) of Section 1821 also resides. The presumption that the transfer is in the best interests of the ward or conservatee, may be rebutted by clear and convincing evidence that the transfer will harm the ward or conservatee. *(Stats.1990, c. 79 (A.B.759), § 14, operative July 1, 1991. Amended by Stats.2006, c. 493 (A.B.1363), § 14.)*

Law Revision Commission Comments

1990 Enactment

Section 2215 continues Section 2215 of the repealed Probate Code without change. Subdivision (a) permits any person required to be listed in the petition to support or oppose the petition. These persons are listed in Section 2213. For general provisions, see Sections 1000–1004 (rules of practice), 1020–1023 (petitions and other papers), 1040–1050 (hearings and orders), 2103 (effect of final order). For background on the provisions of this part, see the Comment to this part under the part heading. [20 Cal.L.Rev.Comm. Reports 1001 (1990)].

Cross References

Interested person, defined, see Probate Code § 1424.

§ 2216.　Transfer of proceedings; fees

(a) Upon the order of transfer, the clerk shall transmit to the clerk of the court to which the proceeding is transferred a certified or exemplified copy of the order, together with all papers in the proceeding on file with the clerk.

(b) The clerk of the court from which the removal is made shall receive no fee therefor but shall be paid out of the estate all expenses incurred by the clerk in the removal. The clerk of the court to which the proceeding is transferred is entitled to such fees as are payable on the filing of a like original proceeding. *(Stats.1990, c. 79 (A.B.759), § 14, operative July 1, 1991.)*

Law Revision Commission Comments

1990 Enactment

Section 2216 continues Section 2216 of the repealed Probate Code without substantive change. For background on the provisions of this part, see the Comment to this part under the part heading. [20 Cal.L.Rev.Comm. Reports 1001 (1990)].

Cross References

Civil actions, transfer of cases, transmission of papers, fees and costs, see Code of Civil Procedure § 399.

§ 2217.　Transferred guardianship or conservatorship; notice of receipt; compliance; review; hearing by transferring court

(a) When an order has been made transferring venue to another county, the court transferring the matter shall set a hearing within two months to confirm receipt of the notification described in subdivision (b). If the notification has not been made, the transferring court shall make reasonable inquiry into the status of the matter.

(b) When a court receives the file of a transferred guardianship or conservatorship, the court:

(1) Shall send written notification of the receipt to the court that transferred the matter.

(2) Shall take proper action pursuant to ensure compliance by the guardian or conservator with the matters provided in Section 1456.5.

(3) If the case is a conservatorship, may conduct a review, including an investigation, as described in Sections 1851 to 1853, inclusive. *(Added by Stats.2007, c. 553 (A.B.1727), § 11.)*

CHAPTER 3.　TEMPORARY GUARDIANS AND CONSERVATORS

Cross References

Application of old and new law, see Probate Code § 3.

§ 2250.　Petition for appointment

(a) On or after the filing of a petition for appointment of a guardian or conservator, any person entitled to petition for appointment of the guardian or conservator may file a petition for appointment of:

(1) A temporary guardian of the person or estate, or both.

(2) A temporary conservator of the person or estate, or both.

(b) The petition shall state facts which establish good cause for appointment of the temporary guardian or temporary conservator. The court, upon that petition or other showing as it may require, may appoint a temporary guardian of the person or estate, or both, or a temporary conservator of the person or estate, or both, to serve pending the final determination of the court upon the petition for the appointment of the guardian or conservator.

(c) If the petitioner, proposed guardian, or proposed conservator is a professional fiduciary, as described in Section 2340, who is required to be licensed under the Professional Fiduciaries Act (Chapter 6 (commencing with Section 6500) of Division 3 of the Business and Professions Code), the petition for appointment of a temporary guardian or temporary conservator shall include the following:

(1) The petitioner's, proposed guardian's, or proposed conservator's proposed hourly fee schedule or another statement of his or her proposed compensation from the estate of the proposed ward or proposed conservatee for services performed as a guardian or conservator. The petitioner's, proposed guardian's, or proposed conservator's provision of a proposed hourly fee schedule or another statement of his or her proposed compensation, as required by this paragraph, shall not preclude a court from later reducing the petitioner's, proposed guardian's, or proposed conservator's fees or other compensation.

(2) Unless a petition for appointment of a guardian or conservator that contains the statements required by this paragraph is filed together with a petition for appointment of a temporary guardian or temporary conservator, both of the following:

(A) A statement of the petitioner's, proposed guardian's, or proposed conservator's registration or license information.

(B) A statement explaining who engaged the petitioner, proposed guardian, or proposed conservator or how the petitioner, proposed guardian, or proposed conservator was engaged to file the petition for appointment of a temporary guardian or temporary conservator or to agree to accept the appointment as temporary guardian or temporary conservator and what prior relationship the petitioner, proposed guardian, or proposed conservator had with the proposed ward or proposed conservatee or the proposed ward's or proposed conservatee's family or friends.

(d) If the petition is filed by a party other than the proposed conservatee, the petition shall include a declaration of due diligence showing both of the following:

(1) Either the efforts to find the proposed conservatee's relatives named in the petition for appointment of a general conservator or why it was not feasible to contact any of them.

(2) Either the preferences of the proposed conservatee concerning the appointment of a temporary conservator and the appointment of the proposed temporary conservator or why it was not feasible to ascertain those preferences.

(e) Unless the court for good cause otherwise orders, at least five court days before the hearing on the petition, notice of the hearing shall be given as follows:

(1) Notice of the hearing shall be personally delivered to the proposed ward if he or she is 12 years of age or older, to the parent or parents of the proposed ward, and to any person having a valid visitation order with the proposed ward that was effective at the time of the filing of the petition. Notice of the hearing shall not be delivered to the proposed ward if he or she is under 12 years of age. In a proceeding for temporary guardianship of the person, evidence that a custodial parent has died or become incapacitated, and that the petitioner or proposed guardian is the nominee of the custodial parent, may constitute good cause for the court to order that this notice not be delivered.

(2) Notice of the hearing shall be personally delivered to the proposed conservatee, and notice of the hearing shall be served on the persons required to be named in the petition for appointment of conservator. If the petition states that the petitioner and the proposed conservator have no prior relationship with the proposed conservatee and has not been nominated by a family member, friend, or other person with a relationship to the proposed conservatee, notice of hearing shall be served on the public guardian of the county in which the petition is filed.

(3) A copy of the petition for temporary appointment shall be served with the notice of hearing.

(f) If a temporary guardianship is granted ex parte and the hearing on the general guardianship petition is not to be held within 30 days of the granting of the temporary guardianship, the court shall set a hearing within 30 days to reconsider the temporary guardianship. Notice of the hearing for reconsideration of the temporary guardianship shall be provided pursuant to Section 1511, except that the court may for good cause shorten the time for the notice of the hearing.

(g) Visitation orders with the proposed ward granted prior to the filing of a petition for temporary guardianship shall remain in effect, unless for good cause the court orders otherwise.

(h)(1) If a temporary conservatorship is granted ex parte, and a petition to terminate the temporary conservatorship is filed more than 15 days before the first hearing on the general petition for appointment of conservator, the court shall set a hearing within 15 days of the filing of the petition for termination of the temporary conservatorship to reconsider the temporary conservatorship. Unless the court otherwise orders, notice of the hearing on the petition to terminate the temporary conservatorship shall be given at least 10 days prior to the hearing.

(2) If a petition to terminate the temporary conservatorship is filed within 15 days before the first hearing on the general petition for appointment of conservator, the court shall set the hearing at the same time that the hearing on the general petition is set. Unless the court otherwise orders, notice of the hearing on the petition to terminate the temporary conservatorship pursuant to this section shall be given at least five court days prior to the hearing.

(i) If the court suspends powers of the guardian or conservator under Section 2334 or 2654 or under any other provision of this division, the court may appoint a temporary guardian or conservator to exercise those powers until the powers are restored to the guardian or conservator or a new guardian or conservator is appointed.

(j) If for any reason a vacancy occurs in the office of guardian or conservator, the court, on a petition filed under subdivision (a) or on its own motion, may appoint a temporary guardian or conservator to exercise the powers of the guardian or conservator until a new guardian or conservator is appointed.

(k) On or before January 1, 2008, the Judicial Council shall adopt a rule of court that establishes uniform standards for good cause exceptions to the notice required by subdivision (e), limiting those exceptions to only cases when waiver of the notice is essential to protect the proposed conservatee or ward, or the estate of the proposed conservatee or ward, from substantial harm.

(*l*) A superior court shall not be required to perform any duties imposed pursuant to the amendments to this section enacted by Chapter 493 of the Statutes 2006 until the Legislature makes an appropriation identified for this purpose. *(Stats.1990, c. 79 (A.B.759), § 14, operative July 1, 1991. Amended by Stats.1993, c. 978 (S.B.305), § 3; Stats. 1995, c. 730 (A.B.1466), § 3; Stats.2006, c. 493 (A.B.1363), § 15, operative July 1, 2007; Stats.2007, c. 553 (A.B.1727), § 12; Stats.2008, c. 293 (A.B.1340), § 4; Stats.2011, c. 10 (S.B.78), § 16, eff. March 24, 2011; Stats.2013, c. 248 (A.B.1339), § 3.)*

Law Revision Commission Comments

1990 Enactment

Section 2250 continues Section 2250 of the repealed Probate Code with the substitution of "parent" for "natural parent" in subdivision (c). This substitution requires notice to all parents, including natural parents. For general provisions, see Sections 1000–1004 (rules of practice), 1020–1023 (petitions and other papers), 1040–1050 (hearings and orders), 2103 (effect of final order). See also Section 2751 (appointment of temporary guardian or conservator to exercise power which appeal pending). For background on the provisions of this part, see the Comment to this part under the part heading. [20 Cal.L.Rev.Comm. Reports 1001 (1990)].

Cross References

Action for exclusive custody of children, see Family Code § 3120.
Computation of time, see Code of Civil Procedure §§ 12 and 12a; Government Code § 6800 et seq.
Elder Abuse and Dependent Adult Civil Protection Act, victim's refusal or withdrawal of consent, see Welfare and Institutions Code § 15636.
Elder or dependent adults as abuse victims, appointment of conservator or guardian, see Welfare and Institutions Code § 15650.
Parent, defined, see Probate Code § 54.
Petition for appointment,
  Conservator, see Probate Code § 1820.
  Guardian, see Probate Code § 1510.
Professional fiduciary as guardian or conservator, submission of new proposed hourly fee schedule or statement of compensation on or after one year from original submission, see Probate Code § 2614.8.
Relationship of guardian and ward, generally, see Probate Code § 2101.
Temporary guardian or conservator pending appeal, see Probate Code § 1310.

§ 2250.2. Petition for appointment of a temporary conservator

(a) On or after the filing of a petition for appointment of a conservator, any person entitled to petition for appointment of the conservator may file a petition for appointment of a temporary conservator of the person or estate or both.

(b) The petition shall state facts that establish good cause for appointment of the temporary conservator. The court, upon that petition or any other showing as it may require, may appoint a temporary conservator of the person or estate or both, to serve pending the final determination of the court upon the petition for the appointment of the conservator.

(c) Unless the court for good cause otherwise orders, not less than five days before the appointment of the temporary conservator, notice of the proposed appointment shall be personally delivered to the proposed conservatee.

(d) If the court suspends powers of the conservator under Section 2334 or 2654 or under any other provision of this division, the court may appoint a temporary conservator to exercise those powers until the powers are restored to the conservator or a new conservator is appointed.

(e) If for any reason a vacancy occurs in the office of conservator, the court, on a petition filed under subdivision (a) or on its own motion, may appoint a temporary conservator to exercise the powers of the conservator until a new conservator is appointed.

(f) This section shall only apply to proceedings under Chapter 3 (commencing with Section 5350) of Part 1 of Division 5 of the Welfare and Institutions Code. *(Added by Stats.2006, c. 493 (A.B.1363), § 15.5, operative July 1, 2007. Amended by Stats.2007, c. 553 (A.B.1727), § 12.5.)*

§ 2250.4. Hearing on appointment of temporary conservatee

The proposed temporary conservatee shall attend the hearing except in the following cases:

(a) If the proposed temporary conservatee is out of the state when served and is not the petitioner.

(b) If the proposed temporary conservatee is unable to attend the hearing by reason of medical inability.

(c) If the court investigator has visited the proposed conservatee prior to the hearing and the court investigator has reported to the court that the proposed temporary conservatee has expressly communicated that all of the following apply:

(1) The proposed conservatee is not willing to attend the hearing.

(2) The proposed conservatee does not wish to contest the establishment of the temporary conservatorship.

(3) The proposed conservatee does not object to the proposed temporary conservator or prefer that another person act as temporary conservator.

(d) If the court determines that the proposed conservatee is unable or unwilling to attend the hearing, and holding the hearing in the absence of the proposed conservatee is necessary to protect the conservatee from substantial harm.

(e) A superior court shall not be required to perform any duties imposed by this section until the Legislature makes an appropriation identified for this purpose. *(Added by Stats. 2006, c. 493 (A.B.1363), § 16, operative July 1, 2007. Amended by Stats.2011, c. 10 (S.B.78), § 17, eff. March 24, 2011.)*

§ 2250.6. Investigation and interview relative to proposed temporary conservatee

(a) Regardless of whether the proposed temporary conservatee attends the hearing, the court investigator shall do all of the following prior to the hearing, unless it is not feasible to do so, in which case the court investigator shall comply with the requirements set forth in subdivision (b):

(1) Interview the proposed conservatee personally. The court investigator also shall do all of the following:

(A) Interview the petitioner and the proposed conservator, if different from the petitioner.

(B) To the greatest extent possible, interview the proposed conservatee's spouse or registered domestic partner, relatives within the first degree, neighbors and, if known, close friends.

(C) To the extent possible, interview the proposed conservatee's relatives within the second degree as set forth in subdivision (b) of Section 1821 before the hearing.

(2) Inform the proposed conservatee of the contents of the citation, of the nature, purpose, and effect of the temporary conservatorship, and of the right of the proposed conservatee to oppose the proceeding, to attend the hearing, to have the matter of the establishment of the conservatorship tried by jury, to be represented by legal counsel if the proposed conservatee so chooses, and to have legal counsel appointed by the court if unable to retain legal counsel.

(3) Determine whether it appears that the proposed conservatee is unable to attend the hearing and, if able to attend, whether the proposed conservatee is willing to attend the hearing.

(4) Determine whether the proposed conservatee wishes to contest the establishment of the conservatorship.

(5) Determine whether the proposed conservatee objects to the proposed conservator or prefers another person to act as conservator.

(6) Report to the court, in writing, concerning all of the foregoing.

(b) If not feasible before the hearing, the court investigator shall do all of the following within two court days after the hearing:

(1) Interview the conservatee personally. The court investigator also shall do all of the following:

(A) Interview the petitioner and the proposed conservator, if different from the petitioner.

(B) To the greatest extent possible, interview the proposed conservatee's spouse or registered domestic partner, relatives within the first degree, neighbors and, if known, close friends.

(C) To the extent possible, interview the proposed conservatee's relatives within the second degree as set forth in subdivision (b) of Section 1821.

(2) Inform the conservatee of the nature, purpose, and effect of the temporary conservatorship, as well as the right of the conservatee to oppose the proposed general conservatorship, to attend the hearing, to have the matter of the establishment of the conservatorship tried by jury, to be represented by legal counsel if the proposed conservatee so chooses, and to have legal counsel appointed by the court if unable to retain legal counsel.

(c) If the investigator does not visit the conservatee until after the hearing at which a temporary conservator was appointed, and the conservatee objects to the appointment of the temporary conservator, or requests an attorney, the court investigator shall report this information promptly, and in no event more than three court days later, to the court. Upon receipt of that information, the court may proceed with appointment of an attorney as provided in Chapter 4 (commencing with Section 1470) of Part 1.

(d) If it appears to the court investigator that the temporary conservatorship is inappropriate, the court investigator shall immediately, and in no event more than two court days later, provide a written report to the court so the court can consider taking appropriate action on its own motion.

(e) A superior court shall not be required to perform any duties imposed by this section until the Legislature makes an appropriation identified for this purpose. (Added by Stats. 2006, c. 493 (A.B.1363), § 17, operative July 1, 2007. Amend-ed by Stats.2007, c. 553 (A.B.1727), § 13; Stats.2011, c. 10 (S.B.78), § 18, eff. March 24, 2011.)

§ 2250.8. Appointment of temporary conservatorship in instances of gravely disabled persons

Sections 2250, 2250.4, and 2250.6 shall not apply to proceedings under Chapter 3 (commencing with Section 5350) of Part 1 of Division 5 of the Welfare and Institutions Code. (Added by Stats.2006, c. 493 (A.B.1363), § 17.5.)

§ 2251. Issuance of letters

A temporary guardian or temporary conservator shall be issued letters of temporary guardianship or conservatorship upon taking the oath and filing the bond as in the case of a guardian or conservator. The letters shall indicate the termination date of the temporary appointment. (Stats.1990, c. 79 (A.B.759), § 14, operative July 1, 1991.)

Law Revision Commission Comments

1990 Enactment

Section 2251 continues Section 2251 of the repealed Probate Code without change. See also Section 2257 (termination of powers of temporary guardian or temporary conservator). Order granting or revoking temporary letters is not an appealable order. See Section 2750. For background on the provisions of this part, see the Comment to this part under the part heading. [20 Cal.L.Rev.Comm. Reports 1001 (1990)].

Cross References

Letters of conservatorship or guardianship, generally, see Probate Code § 2310 et seq.
Oaths, affirmation in lieu of, see Code of Civil Procedure § 2015.6.
Oaths, letters, and bond, generally, see Probate Code § 2300 et seq.
Oaths, officers authorized to administer, see Government Code § 1225.
Termination date, see Probate Code § 2257.

§ 2252. Powers and duties

(a) Except as otherwise provided in subdivisions (b) and (c), a temporary guardian or temporary conservator has only those powers and duties of a guardian or conservator that are necessary to provide for the temporary care, maintenance, and support of the ward or conservatee and that are necessary to conserve and protect the property of the ward or conservatee from loss or injury.

(b) Unless the court otherwise orders:

(1) A temporary guardian of the person has the powers and duties specified in Section 2353 (medical treatment).

(2) A temporary conservator of the person has the powers and duties specified in Section 2354 (medical treatment).

(3) A temporary guardian of the estate or temporary conservator of the estate may marshal assets and establish accounts at financial institutions.

(c) The temporary guardian or temporary conservator has the additional powers and duties as may be ordered by the court (1) in the order of appointment or (2) by subsequent order made with or without notice as the court may require. Notwithstanding subdivision (e), those additional powers and duties may include relief granted pursuant to Article 10 (commencing with Section 2580) of Chapter 6 if this relief is not requested in a petition for the appointment of a temporary conservator but is requested in a separate petition.

(d) The terms of any order made under subdivision (b) or (c) shall be included in the letters of temporary guardianship or conservatorship.

(e) A temporary conservator is not permitted to sell or relinquish, on the conservatee's behalf, any lease or estate in real or personal property used as or within the conservatee's place of residence without the specific approval of the court. This approval may be granted only if the conservatee has been served with notice of the hearing, the notice to be personally delivered to the temporary conservatee unless the court for good cause otherwise orders, and only if the court finds that the conservatee will be unable to return to the residence and exercise dominion over it and that the action is necessary to avert irreparable harm to the conservatee. The temporary conservator is not permitted to sell or relinquish on the conservatee's behalf any estate or interest in other real or personal property without specific approval of the court, which may be granted only upon a finding that the action is necessary to avert irreparable harm to the conservatee. A finding of irreparable harm as to real property may be based upon a reasonable showing that the real property is vacant, that it cannot reasonably be rented, and that it is impossible or impractical to obtain fire or liability insurance on the property. *(Stats.1990, c. 79 (A.B.759), § 14, operative July 1, 1991. Amended by Stats.1994, c. 806 (A.B.3686), § 10; Stats.1996, c. 563 (S.B.392), § 11.)*

Law Revision Commission Comments
1990 Enactment

Section 2252 continues Section 2252 of the repealed Probate Code without substantive change. Under subdivision (b), a temporary guardian or conservator has limited authority with respect to medical treatment for the ward or conservatee unless the court by order limits or expands the authority given by Section 2353 (guardian) or 2354 (conservator). The court might, for example, give a temporary conservator the powers and duties of a conservator under Section 2355 (medical treatment of conservatee adjudicated to lack capacity to give informed consent) where the circumstances require such an order. See also Section 2357 (petition by temporary guardian or conservator for court authorization of medical treatment for ward or conservatee). For background on the provisions of this part, see the Comment to this part under the part heading. [20 Cal.L.Rev.Comm. Reports 1001 (1990)].

Cross References

Account, defined, see Probate Code § 21
Court ordered medical treatment, see Probate Code § 2357.
Custody, services and earnings of minors, see Family Code §§ 7500, 7503.
Determination of place of residence, see Government Code § 244.
Financial institution, defined, see Probate Code § 40.
Notice,
　Mailing, see Probate Code § 1215 et seq.
　Posting, see Probate Code § 1230.
　Proof of giving notice, see Probate Code § 1260 et seq.
　Special notice, see Probate Code § 1250 et seq.
　This code, generally, see Probate Code § 1200 et seq.
　This division, generally, see Probate Code § 1460 et seq.
Real property, defined, see Probate Code § 68.
Service of process,
　Generally, see Code of Civil Procedure § 413.10 et seq.
　Mail, see Code of Civil Procedure §§ 415.30, 1012 et seq.

Personal delivery, see Code of Civil Procedure § 415.10.
Proof of service, see Code of Civil Procedure § 417.10 et seq.
Publication, see Code of Civil Procedure § 415.50.

§ 2253. Change of residence of conservatee; request; duties of court investigator

(a) If a temporary conservator of the person proposes to fix the residence of the conservatee at a place other than that where the conservatee resided prior to the commencement of the proceedings, that power shall be requested of the court in writing, unless the change of residence is required of the conservatee by a prior court order. The request shall be filed with the petition for temporary conservatorship or, if a temporary conservatorship has already been established, separately. The request shall specify in particular the place to which the temporary conservator proposes to move the conservatee, and the precise reasons why it is believed that the conservatee will suffer irreparable harm if the change of residence is not permitted, and why no means less restrictive of the conservatee's liberty will suffice to prevent that harm.

(b) Unless the court for good cause orders otherwise, the court investigator shall do all of the following:

(1) Interview the conservatee personally.

(2) Inform the conservatee of the nature, purpose, and effect of the request made under subdivision (a), and of the right of the conservatee to oppose the request, attend the hearing, be represented by legal counsel if the conservatee so chooses, and to have legal counsel appointed by the court if unable to obtain legal counsel.

(3) Determine whether the conservatee is unable to attend the hearing because of medical inability and, if able to attend, whether the conservatee is willing to attend the hearing.

(4) Determine whether the conservatee wishes to oppose the request.

(5) Determine whether the conservatee wishes to be represented by legal counsel at the hearing and, if so, whether the conservatee has retained legal counsel and, if not, the name of an attorney the proposed conservatee wishes to retain or whether the conservatee desires the court to appoint legal counsel.

(6) If the conservatee does not plan to retain legal counsel and has not requested the appointment of legal counsel by the court, determine whether the appointment of legal counsel would be helpful to the resolution of the matter or is necessary to protect the interests of the conservatee.

(7) Determine whether the proposed change of place of residence is required to prevent irreparable harm to the conservatee and whether no means less restrictive of the conservatee's liberty will suffice to prevent that harm.

(8) Report to the court in writing, at least two days before the hearing, concerning all of the foregoing, including the conservatee's express communications concerning representation by legal counsel and whether the conservatee is not willing to attend the hearing and does not wish to oppose the request.

(c) Within seven days of the date of filing of a temporary conservator's request to remove the conservatee from his or her previous place of residence, the court shall hold a hearing on the request.

(d) The conservatee shall be present at the hearing except in the following cases:

(1) Where the conservatee is unable to attend the hearing by reason of medical inability. Emotional or psychological instability is not good cause for the absence of the conservatee from the hearing unless, by reason of that instability, attendance at the hearing is likely to cause serious and immediate physiological damage to the conservatee.

(2) Where the court investigator has reported to the court that the conservatee has expressly communicated that the conservatee is not willing to attend the hearing and does not wish to oppose the request, and the court makes an order that the conservatee need not attend the hearing.

(e) If the conservatee is unable to attend the hearing because of medical inability, that inability shall be established (1) by the affidavit or certificate of a licensed medical practitioner or (2) if the conservatee is an adherent of a religion whose tenets and practices call for reliance on prayer alone for healing and is under treatment by an accredited practitioner of that religion, by the affidavit of the practitioner. The affidavit or certificate is evidence only of the conservatee's inability to attend the hearing and shall not be considered in determining the issue of need for the establishment of a conservatorship.

(f) At the hearing, the conservatee has the right to be represented by counsel and the right to confront and cross-examine any witness presented by or on behalf of the temporary conservator and to present evidence on his or her own behalf.

(g) The court may approve the request to remove the conservatee from the previous place of residence only if the court finds (1) that change of residence is required to prevent irreparable harm to the conservatee and (2) that no means less restrictive of the conservatee's liberty will suffice to prevent that harm. If an order is made authorizing the temporary conservator to remove the conservatee from the previous place of residence, the order shall specify the specific place wherein the temporary conservator is authorized to place the conservatee. The temporary conservator may not be authorized to remove the conservatee from this state unless it is additionally shown that such removal is required to permit the performance of specified nonpsychiatric medical treatment, consented to by the conservatee, which is essential to the conservatee's physical survival. A temporary conservator who willfully removes a temporary conservatee from this state without authorization of the court is guilty of a felony.

(h) Subject to subdivision (e) of Section 2252, the court shall also order the temporary conservator to take all reasonable steps to preserve the status quo concerning the conservatee's previous place of residence.

(i) A superior court shall not be required to perform any duties imposed pursuant to the amendments to this section enacted by Chapter 493 of the Statutes 2006 until the Legislature makes an appropriation identified for this purpose. *(Stats.1990, c. 79 (A.B.759), § 14, operative July 1, 1991. Amended by Stats.2006, c. 493 (A.B.1363), § 18, operative July 1, 2007; Stats.2011, c. 10 (S.B.78), § 19, eff. March 24, 2011.)*

§ 2254. Removal of conservatee from residence in emergency; medical treatment; removal to health facility with consent of conservatee

(a) Notwithstanding Section 2253, a temporary conservator may remove a temporary conservatee from the temporary conservatee's place of residence without court authorization if an emergency exists. For the purposes of this section, an emergency exists if the temporary conservatee's place of residence is unfit for habitation or if the temporary conservator determines in good faith based upon medical advice that the case is an emergency case in which removal from the place of residence is required (1) to provide medical treatment needed to alleviate severe pain or (2) to diagnose or treat a medical condition which, if not immediately diagnosed and treated, will lead to serious disability or death.

(b) No later than one judicial day after the emergency removal of the temporary conservatee, the temporary conservator shall file a written request pursuant to Section 2253 for authorization to fix the residence of the temporary conservatee at a place other than the temporary conservatee's previous place of residence.

(c) Nothing in this chapter prevents a temporary conservator from removing a temporary conservatee from the place of residence to a health facility for treatment without court authorization when the temporary conservatee has given informed consent to the removal.

(d) Nothing in this chapter prevents a temporary conservator from removing a temporary conservatee without court authorization from one health facility where the conservatee is receiving medical care to another health facility where the conservatee will receive medical care. *(Stats.1990, c. 79 (A.B.759), § 14, operative July 1, 1991.)*

this part, see the Comment to this part under the part heading. [20 Cal.L.Rev.Comm. Reports 1001 (1990)].

§ 2255. Inventory and appraisement of estate

(a) Except as provided in subdivision (b), an inventory and appraisal of the estate shall be filed by the temporary guardian or temporary conservator of the estate as required by Article 2 (commencing with Section 2610) of Chapter 7.

(b) A temporary guardian or temporary conservator of the estate may inventory the estate in the final account, without the necessity for an appraisal of the estate, if the final account is filed within 90 days after the appointment of the temporary guardian or temporary conservator. *(Stats.1990, c. 79 (A.B. 759), § 14, operative July 1, 1991.)*

Law Revision Commission Comments

1990 Enactment

Section 2255 continues Section 2255 of the repealed Probate Code without substantive change. See also Section 2633 (termination before filing of inventory). For background on the provisions of this part, see the Comment to this part under the part heading. [20 Cal.L.Rev.Comm. Reports 1001 (1990)].

§ 2256. Settlement and allowance of accounts

(a) Except as provided in subdivision (b), the temporary guardian or temporary conservator of the estate shall present his or her account to the court for settlement and allowance within 90 days after the appointment of a guardian or conservator of the estate or within such other time as the court may fix.

(b) If the temporary guardian or temporary conservator of the estate is appointed guardian or conservator of the estate, the guardian or conservator may account for the administration as temporary guardian or temporary conservator in his or her first regular account.

(c) Accounts are subject to Sections 2621 to 2626, inclusive, Sections 2630 to 2633, inclusive, and Sections 2640 to 2642, inclusive. *(Stats.1990, c. 79 (A.B.759), § 14, operative July 1, 1991.)*

Law Revision Commission Comments

1990 Enactment

Section 2256 continues Section 2256 of the repealed Probate Code without change. For background on the provisions of this part, see the Comment to this part under the part heading. [20 Cal.L.Rev. Comm. Reports 1001 (1990)].

§ 2257. Termination of powers; time

(a) Except as provided in subdivision (b), the powers of a temporary guardian or temporary conservator terminate,

except for the rendering of the account, at the earliest of the following times:

(1) The time the temporary guardian or conservator acquires notice that a guardian or conservator is appointed and qualified.

(2) Thirty days after the appointment of the temporary guardian or temporary conservator or such earlier time as the court may specify in the order of appointment.

(b) With or without notice as the court may require, the court may for good cause order that the time for the termination of the powers of the temporary guardian or temporary conservator be extended or shortened pending final determination by the court of the petition for appointment of a guardian or conservator or pending the final decision on appeal therefrom or for other cause. The order which extends the time for termination shall fix the time when the powers of the temporary guardian or temporary conservator terminate except for the rendering of the account. *(Stats.1990, c. 79 (A.B.759), § 14, operative July 1, 1991. Amended by Stats.2007, c. 553 (A.B.1727), § 14.)*

Law Revision Commission Comments

1990 Enactment

Section 2257 continues Section 2257 of the repealed Probate Code without change. For background on the provisions of this part, see the Comment to this part under the part heading. [20 Cal.L.Rev. Comm. Reports 1001 (1990)].

§ 2258. Suspension, removal, resignation and discharge

A temporary guardian or temporary conservator is subject to the provisions of this division governing the suspension, removal, resignation, and discharge of a guardian or conservator. *(Stats.1990, c. 79 (A.B.759), § 14, operative July 1, 1991.)*

Law Revision Commission Comments

1990 Enactment

Section 2258 continues Section 2258 of the repealed Probate Code without change. For background on the provisions of this part, see the Comment to this part under the part heading. [20 Cal.L.Rev. Comm. Reports 1001 (1990)].

CHAPTER 4. OATH, LETTERS, AND BOND

Oaths,
  Affirmation in lieu of, see Code of Civil Procedure § 2015.6.
  Officers authorized to administer, see Government Code § 1225.
Sureties on bond, see Code of Civil Procedure § 995.520.
Trust company acting as guardian or conservator, oath, see Financial Code § 1607.

ARTICLE 1. REQUIREMENT OF OATH AND BOND

Section
  2300. Oath and bond; necessity before appointment.

Cross References

Application of old and new law, see Probate Code § 3.
Oaths,
  Affirmation in lieu of, see Code of Civil Procedure § 2015.6.
  Officers authorized to administer, see Government Code § 1225.

§ 2300. Oath and bond; necessity before appointment

Before the appointment of a guardian or conservator is effective, including, but not limited to, the appointment of a conservator under Section 2002, the guardian or conservator shall:

(a) Take an oath to perform the duties of the office according to law. The oath obligates the guardian or conservator to comply with the law of this state, as well as other applicable law, at all times, in any location within or without the state. If the conservator petitions for transfer of the conservatorship to another state pursuant to Section 2001, the conservator shall continue to comply with the law of this state until the court issues a final order confirming the transfer and terminating the conservatorship pursuant to Section 2001. The oath shall be attached to or endorsed upon the letters.

(b) File the required bond if a bond is required. *(Stats. 1990, c. 79 (A.B.759), § 14, operative July 1, 1991. Amended by Stats.2014, c. 553 (S.B.940), § 23, eff. Jan. 1, 2015, operative Jan. 1, 2016.)*

Law Revision Commission Comments

1990 Enactment

Section 2300 continues Section 2300 of the repealed Probate Code without substantive change. See Section 52(b) (defining "letters"). See also Sections 300–301 (trust company as guardian or conservator of estate), 2922 (bond and oath of public guardian). For background on the provisions of this part, see the Comment to this part under the part heading. [20 Cal.L.Rev.Comm. Reports 1001 (1990)].

2014 Amendment

Section 2300 is amended to reflect the enactment of the California Conservatorship Jurisdiction Act (Section 1980 *et seq.*), particularly Article 3 (transfer of conservatorship) and Article 4 (registration and recognition of orders from other states). [43 Cal.L.Rev.Comm. Reports 93 (2013)].

Cross References

Additional bond when required, see Probate Code § 2330.
Filing bond with clerk, see Code of Civil Procedure § 995.340.
Letters, defined, see Probate Code § 52.
Oath and bond,
  Personal representative, see Probate Code § 8403.
  Temporary guardian or conservator, see Probate Code § 2251.

Oath as including affirmation or declaration, see Code of Civil Procedure § 17.
Oaths, affirmation in lieu of, see Code of Civil Procedure § 2015.6.
Oaths, officers authorized to administer, see Government Code § 1225.
Principal and sureties, liability on bond, see Code of Civil Procedure § 996.460 et seq.

ARTICLE 2. LETTERS

Section
  2310. Issuance; evidence of appointment; warning.
  2311. Form.
  2312. Repealed.
  2313. Recording of letters.

Cross References

Application of old and new law, see Probate Code § 3.

§ 2310. Issuance; evidence of appointment; warning

(a) The appointment, the taking of the oath, and the filing of the bond, if required, shall thereafter be evidenced by the issuance of letters by the clerk of the court.

(b) The order appointing a guardian or conservator shall state in capital letters on the first page of the order, in at least 12–point type, the following: "WARNING: THIS APPOINTMENT IS NOT EFFECTIVE UNTIL LETTERS HAVE ISSUED." *(Stats.1990, c. 79 (A.B.759), § 14, operative July 1, 1991. Amended by Stats.1996, c. 862 (A.B.2751), § 7.)*

Law Revision Commission Comments

1990 Enactment

Section 2310 continues Section 2310 of the repealed Probate Code without substantive change. See Section 52(b) (defining "letters"). For background on the provisions of this part, see the Comment to this part under the part heading. [20 Cal.L.Rev.Comm. Reports 1001 (1990)].

Cross References

Additional conditions in order of appointment, inclusion in letters, see Probate Code § 2358.
Filing bond with court, see Code of Civil Procedure § 995.340.
Letters, defined, see Probate Code § 52.
Letters of temporary guardianship or conservatorship, see Probate Code §§ 2251, 2252.
Oaths, affirmation in lieu of, see Code of Civil Procedure § 2015.6.
Oaths, officers authorized to administer, see Government Code § 1225.

§ 2311. Form

Except as otherwise required by the order of appointment, the letters of guardianship or conservatorship shall be in substantially the same form as letters of administration. *(Stats.1990, c. 79 (A.B.759), § 14, operative July 1, 1991.)*

Law Revision Commission Comments

1990 Enactment

Section 2311 continues Section 2311 of the repealed Probate Code without substantive change. See Section 52(b) (defining "letters"). See also Sections 1880 (order granting conservator exclusive authority to make medical decisions), 2108 (terms of order under Section 2108, concerning powers of nominated guardian, to be included in letters of guardianship), 2251 (termination date of temporary guardianship or conservatorship), 2252 (powers of temporary guardian or conservator concerning medical treatment), 2300 (oath to be attached to or endorsed upon letters), 2351.5 (change in powers of limited conservator), 2358 (conditions concerning care, treatment, education, and welfare of ward or conservatee), 2402 (conditions concerning care and custody of property of the ward or conservatee), 2594 (powers that may be independently exercised), 2922 (issuance of letters to "the public guardian" of the county without naming the public guardian). See also Gov't Code § 27433 (letters issued to "the public guardian" are sufficient to authorize action by the successor and new letters need not be issued). For background on the provisions of this part, see the Comment to this part under the part heading. [20 Cal.L.Rev.Comm. Reports 1001 (1990)].

Cross References

Letters of administration, see Probate Code § 8405.
Letters of temporary guardianship or conservatorship, see Probate Code §§ 2251, 2252.
Oath, attachment to or endorsement upon letters, see Probate Code § 2300.

§ 2312. Repealed by Stats.1997, c. 724 (A.B.1172), § 12

§ 2313. Recording of letters

Except in temporary conservatorships, a conservator of the estate shall record a certified copy of the letters with the county recorder's office in each county in which the conservatee owns an interest in real property, including a security interest. The conservator shall record the letters as soon as practicable after they are issued, but no later than 90 days after the conservator is appointed. A temporary conservator of the estate may record the letters if the conservator deems it appropriate. *(Added by Stats.1991, c. 1019 (S.B.1022), § 3.)*

Cross References

Letters, defined, see Probate Code § 52.
Real property, defined, see Probate Code § 68.

ARTICLE 3. BONDS OF GUARDIANS AND CONSERVATORS

Section

Cross References

Application of old and new law, see Probate Code § 3.
Bond and Undertaking Law, see Code of Civil Procedure § 995.010 et seq.

§ 2320. Necessity; amount

(a) Except as otherwise provided by statute, every person appointed as guardian or conservator shall, before letters are issued, give a bond approved by the court.

(b) The bond shall be for the benefit of the ward or conservatee and all persons interested in the guardianship or conservatorship estate and shall be conditioned upon the faithful execution of the duties of the office, according to law, by the guardian or conservator.

(c) Except as otherwise provided by statute, unless the court increases or decreases the amount upon a showing of good cause, the amount of a bond given by an admitted surety insurer shall be the sum of all of the following:

(1) The value of the personal property of the estate.

(2) The probable annual gross income of all of the property of the estate.

(3) The sum of the probable annual gross payments from the following:

(A) Part 3 (commencing with Section 11000) of, Part 4 (commencing with Section 16000) of, or Part 5 (commencing with Section 17000) of, Division 9 of the Welfare and Institutions Code.

(B) Subchapter II (commencing with Section 401) of, or Part A of Subchapter XVI (commencing with Section 1382) of, Chapter 7 of Title 42 of the United States Code.

(C) Any other public entitlements of the ward or conservatee.

(4) On or after January 1, 2008, a reasonable amount for the cost of recovery to collect on the bond, including attorney's fees and costs. The attorney's fees and costs incurred in a successful action for surcharge against a conservator or guardian for breach of his or her duty under this code shall be a surcharge against the conservator or guardian and, if unpaid, shall be recovered against the surety on the bond. The Judicial Council shall, on or before January 1, 2008, adopt a rule of court to implement this paragraph.

(d) If the bond is given by personal sureties, the amount of the bond shall be twice the amount required for a bond given by an admitted surety insurer.

(e) The Bond and Undertaking Law (Chapter 2 (commencing with Section 995.010) of Title 14 of Part 2 of the Code of Civil Procedure) applies to a bond given under this article, except to the extent inconsistent with this article. *(Stats.1990, c. 79 (A.B.759), § 14, operative July 1, 1991. Amended by Stats.2006, c. 493 (A.B.1363), § 19; Stats.2007, c. 553 (A.B.1727), § 15.)*

Law Revision Commission Comments
1990 Enactment

Section 2320 continues Section 2320 of the repealed Probate Code with revisions that conform the section to comparable provisions relating to decedents' estates. Section 2320 is comparable to Sections 8480, 8482, and 8487 (bond of personal representative), with the addition of a provision to make clear that the amount of the bond of a guardian or conservator is to be sufficient to cover public entitlements of the ward or conservatee. The cost of a surety bond is an allowable expense of the guardian or conservator. See Section 2623(a). Section 2328 qualifies Section 2320 by permitting the amount of bond to be reduced when personal property is delivered to a trust company, or money is invested in an insured account in a financial institution, subject to withdrawal only with court authorization. See also Sections 300–301 (trust company as guardian or conservator of estate). As to bond of the public guardian, see Gov't Code § 27434. See also Section 2941(c) (bond fee of public guardian). For background on the provisions of this part, see the Comment to this part under the part heading. [20 Cal.L.Rev.Comm. Reports 1001 (1990)].

Cross References

Additional bond on real property transactions, see Probate Code § 2330.

Additional conditions in order of appointment, liability of surety, see Probate Code §§ 2358, 2402.

Bond, approval of individual sureties, see Code of Civil Procedure § 996.010.

Bond of nominated guardian, see Probate Code § 2324.

Cost of surety bond as an allowable expense of guardian or conservator, see Probate Code § 2623.

Estate consisting solely of public benefits, bond, see Probate Code § 2323.

Guardian or conservator of person only, bond, see Probate Code § 2322.

Letters, defined, see Probate Code § 52.

Limitation of actions against sureties upon bond, see Probate Code § 2333.

Principal and sureties, liability on bond, see Code of Civil Procedure § 996.470.

Reduction in amount of bond,
  Generally, see Probate Code § 2329.
  Deposit of money or other property subject to court control, see Probate Code § 2328.

Separate bonds, single bond or combination, several wards or conservatees, see Probate Code § 2327.

Sureties on bond, see Code of Civil Procedure § 995.520.

Suretyship, generally, see Civil Code § 2787 et seq.

Trust company acting as guardian or conservator, oath, see Probate Code § 301; Financial Code § 1607.

Trusts funded by court order, required provisions in trust instruments, see California Rules of Court, Rule 7.903.

§ 2320.1. Bond in lesser amount than required; ex parte applications for order increasing the amount of the bond

When the conservator or guardian has knowledge of facts from which the guardian or conservator knows or should know that the bond posted is less than the amount required under Section 2320, the conservator or guardian, and the attorney, if any, shall make an ex parte application for an order increasing the bond to the amount required under Section 2320. *(Added by Stats.2001, c. 359 (S.B.140), § 1.)*

§ 2320.2. Additional bond required by court

If additional bond is required by the court when the account is heard, the order approving the account and related matters, including fees, is not effective and the court shall not file the order until the additional bond is filed. *(Added by Stats.2001, c. 359 (S.B.140), § 2.)*

§ 2321. Waiver of bond

(a) Notwithstanding any other provision of law, the court in a conservatorship proceeding may not waive the filing of a bond or reduce the amount of bond required, without a good cause determination by the court which shall include a determination by the court that the conservatee will not suffer harm as a result of the waiver or reduction of the bond. Good cause may not be established merely by the conservator having filed a bond in another or prior proceeding.

(b) In a conservatorship proceeding, where the conservatee, having sufficient capacity to do so, has waived the filing of a bond, the court in its discretion may permit the filing of a bond in an amount less than would otherwise be required under Section 2320. *(Added by Stats.1979, c. 726, p. 2335, § 3, operative Jan. 1, 1981. Amended by Stats.2001, c. 563 (A.B.1286), § 4; Stats.2006, c. 493 (A.B.1363), § 20.)*

Law Revision Commission Comments

1990 Enactment

Section 2321 continues Section 2321 of the repealed Probate Code without change. For background on the provisions of this part, see the Comment to this part under the part heading. [20 Cal.L.Rev. Comm. Reports 1001 (1990)].

Cross References

Legal capacity of conservatee, see Probate Code § 1870 et seq.

§ 2322. Guardian or conservator of person; necessity of court order

One appointed only as guardian of the person or conservator of the person need not file a bond unless required by the court. *(Stats.1990, c. 79 (A.B.759), § 14, operative July 1, 1991.)*

Law Revision Commission Comments

1990 Enactment

Section 2322 continues Section 2322 of the repealed Probate Code without change. For background on the provisions of this part, see the Comment to this part under the part heading. [20 Cal.L.Rev. Comm. Reports 1001 (1990)].

§ 2323. Estate consisting solely of public benefits

(a) The court may dispense with the requirement of a bond if it appears likely that the estate will satisfy the conditions of subdivision (a) of Section 2628 for its duration.

(b) If at any time it appears that the estate does not satisfy the conditions of subdivision (a) of Section 2628, the court shall require the filing of a bond unless the court determines that good cause exists, as provided in Section 2321. *(Stats. 1990, c. 79 (A.B.759), § 14, operative July 1, 1991. Amended by Stats.2008, c. 293 (A.B.1340), § 5.)*

Law Revision Commission Comments

1990 Enactment

Section 2323 continues Section 2323 of the repealed Probate Code without change. For background on the provisions of this part, see the Comment to this part under the part heading. [20 Cal.L.Rev. Comm. Reports 1001 (1990)].

§ 2324. Nominated guardian

If the person making the nomination has waived the filing of the bond, a guardian nominated under Section 1500 or 1501 need not file a bond unless required by the court. *(Stats.1990, c. 79 (A.B.759), § 14, operative July 1, 1991.)*

Law Revision Commission Comments

1990 Enactment

Section 2324 continues Section 2324 of the repealed Probate Code without change. For background on the provisions of this part, see the Comment to this part under the part heading. [20 Cal.L.Rev. Comm. Reports 1001 (1990)].

Cross References

Nomination of guardian, see Probate Code § 1500 et seq.

§ 2325. Bond of nonprofit charitable corporation

The surety on the bond of a nonprofit charitable corporation described in Section 2104 shall be an admitted surety insurer. *(Stats.1990, c. 79 (A.B.759), § 14, operative July 1, 1991.)*

Law Revision Commission Comments

1990 Enactment

Section 2325 continues Section 2325 of the repealed Probate Code without change. The cost of the bond is an allowable expense. See Section 2623(a). For background on the provisions of this part, see the Comment to this part under the part heading. [20 Cal.L.Rev. Comm. Reports 1001 (1990)].

Cross References

Cost of surety bond as an allowable expense, see Probate Code § 2623.
Suretyship, see Civil Code § 2787 et seq.

§ 2326. Joint guardians or conservators

(a) If joint guardians or conservators are appointed, the court may order that separate bonds or a joint bond or a combination thereof be furnished.

(b) If a joint bond is furnished, the liability on the bond is joint and several. *(Stats.1990, c. 79 (A.B.759), § 14, operative July 1, 1991.)*

Law Revision Commission Comments

1990 Enactment

Section 2326 continues Section 2326 of the repealed Probate Code without change. This section is consistent with Section 8480 (bond of personal representative). For background on the provisions of this part, see the Comment to this part under the part heading. [20 Cal.L.Rev.Comm. Reports 1001 (1990)].

Cross References

Bonds by several personal representatives, see Probate Code § 8480.
Joint guardians or conservators, see Probate Code § 2105.
Joint or several obligations, see Civil Code § 1430 et seq.

§ 2327. Separate bond for each ward or conservatee

(a) In a conservatorship proceeding, the court shall order a separate bond for each conservatee, except where the assets of the conservatees are commingled in which case a combined bond that covers all assets may be provided.

(b) If a guardianship proceeding involves more than one ward, the court may order separate bonds, or a single bond which is for the benefit of two or more wards in that proceeding, or a combination thereof. *(Added by Stats.1990, c. 79 (A.B.759), § 14, operative July 1, 1991. Amended by Stats.2001, c. 563 (A.B.1286), § 5.)*

Law Revision Commission Comments

1990 Enactment

Section 2327 continues Section 2327 of the repealed Probate Code without change. For background on the provisions of this part, see the Comment to this part under the part heading. [20 Cal.L.Rev. Comm. Reports 1001 (1990)].

Cross References

One guardian or conservator for several wards or conservatees, see Probate Code § 2106.

§ 2328. Deposit of property subject to court control

(a) In any proceeding to determine the amount of the bond of the guardian or conservator (whether at the time of appointment or subsequently), if the estate includes property which has been or will be deposited with a trust company or financial institution pursuant to Sections 2453 to 2456, inclusive, upon the condition that the property, including any earnings thereon, will not be withdrawn except on authorization of the court, the court, in its discretion, with or without notice, may so order and may do either of the following:

(1) Exclude the property deposited in determining the amount of the required bond or reduce the amount of the bond to be required in respect to the property deposited to such an amount as the court determines is reasonable.

(2) If a bond has already been furnished or the amount fixed, reduce the amount to such an amount as the court determines is reasonable.

(b) The petitioner for letters, or the proposed guardian or conservator in advance of appointment of a guardian or conservator, may do any one or more of the following:

(1) Deliver personal property in the person's possession to a trust company.

(2) Deliver money in the person's possession for deposit in an insured account in a financial institution in this state.

(3) Allow a trust company to retain personal property already in its possession.

(4) Allow a financial institution in this state to retain money already invested in an insured account in a financial institution.

(c) In the cases described in subdivision (b), the petitioner or proposed guardian or conservator shall obtain and file with the court a written receipt including the agreement of the trust company or financial institution that the property deposited, including any earnings thereon, shall not be allowed to be withdrawn except upon authorization of the court.

(d) In receiving and retaining property on deposit pursuant to subdivisions (b) and (c), the trust company or financial institution is protected to the same extent as though it received the property on deposit from a person to whom letters had been issued. *(Stats.1990, c. 79 (A.B.759), § 14, operative July 1, 1991.)*

Law Revision Commission Comments
1990 Enactment

Section 2328 restates Section 2328 of the repealed Probate Code revisions to conform Section 2328 to Sections 2453 to 2456. Under Section 2328, a guardian or conservator may deposit jewelry or other personal property of the ward or conservatee with a trust company, subject to withdrawal only on order of court, and have the bond reduced accordingly. For related sections, see Fin.Code §§ 764, 765, 1586. See also Sections 2453 (insured account in financial institution), 2454 (deposit of personal property with trust company), 2456 (deposits withdrawable only on court order). Securities deposited with a trust company under Section 2328 may be deposited in a securities depository. See Section 2455(b). For definitions, see Section 40 ("financial institution"), 46 ("insured account in a financial institution"), 83 ("trust company"). For background on the provisions of this part, see the Comment to this part under the part heading. [20 Cal.L.Rev.Comm. Reports 1001 (1990)].

Cross References

Account, defined, see Probate Code § 21
Banks, see Financial Code § 99 et seq.
Capacity of trust company to act as guardian of estate of ward, see Probate Code § 300.
Court ordered deposits, see Financial Code §§ 1586, 7000.
Deposits in bank and savings accounts, see Probate Code § 2453.
Deposits withdrawable only on court order, see Probate Code § 2456.
Financial institution, defined, see Probate Code § 40.
Letters, defined, see Probate Code § 52.
Management or disposition of community property where spouse lacks legal capacity, bond of petitioner, see Probate Code § 3150.
Personal property, deposit with trust company, see Probate Code § 2454.
Savings associations, see Financial Code § 5000.
Trust companies, see Financial Code § 1550 et seq.
Trust company, defined, see Probate Code § 83.

§ 2329. Reduction in the amount of bond

(a) If a guardian or conservator moves the court for reduction in the amount of the bond, the motion shall include an affidavit setting forth the condition of the estate.

(b) Except upon a showing of good cause, the amount of the bond shall not be reduced below the amount determined pursuant to Section 2320.

(c) Nothing in this section limits the authority of the court to reduce the amount of the bond with or without notice under Section 2328. *(Stats.1990, c. 79 (A.B.759), § 14, operative July 1, 1991.)*

Law Revision Commission Comments
1990 Enactment

Section 2329 continues Section 2329 of the repealed Probate Code without change. See also Code of Civil Procedure Section 996.030 (determination that amount of bond is excessive). For background on the provisions of this part, see the Comment to this part under the part heading. [20 Cal.L.Rev.Comm. Reports 1001 (1990)].

Cross References

Affidavits, see Code of Civil Procedure § 2009 et seq.

Bond in excessive amount, recover on, see Code of Civil Procedure § 996.470.

§ 2330. Additional bond on real property transactions

Upon the confirmation of the sale of any real property of the estate, or upon the authorization of the borrowing of money secured by a mortgage or deed of trust on real property of the estate, the guardian or conservator shall furnish an additional bond as is required by the court in order to make the sum of the bonds furnished by the guardian or conservator equal to the amount determined pursuant to Section 2320, taking into account the proceeds of the sale or mortgage or deed of trust, unless the court makes an express finding stating the reason why the bond should not be increased. If a bond or additional bond is required under this section, the order confirming the sale of real property of the estate or authorizing the borrowing of money secured by a mortgage or deed of trust on real property of the estate is not effective and the court shall not file the order until the additional bond is filed. *(Stats.1990, c. 79 (A.B.759), § 14, operative July 1, 1991. Amended by Stats.2001, c. 359 (S.B.140), § 3.)*

Law Revision Commission Comments
1990 Enactment

Section 2330 restates Section 2330 of the repealed Probate Code without substantive change. For background on the provisions of this part, see the Comment to this part under the part heading. [20 Cal.L.Rev.Comm. Reports 1001 (1990)].

Cross References

Additional bond on realty sales by administrator, see Probate Code § 8482.
Cost of bond, see Probate Code § 2623.
Filing of bonds, see Code of Civil Procedure § 995.340.
Limitation of actions on bonds, see Probate Code § 2333.
Mortgages, generally, see Civil Code § 2920 et seq.
Real property, defined, see Probate Code § 68.
Sales of real or personal property, see Probate Code § 2540 et seq.

§§ 2331, 2332. Repealed by Stats.1982, c. 517, p. 2410, §§ 343, 344

Law Revision Commission Comments
1982 Repeal

The substance of former Section 2331 is continued in Code of Civil Procedure Sections 995.710 (deposit in lieu of bond), 995.730 (effect of deposit), and 995.770 (return of deposit). (16 Cal.L.Rev.Comm. Reports 501).

The substance of former Section 2332 is continued in Code of Civil Procedure Section 995.340 (filing required). (16 Cal.L.Rev.Comm. Reports 501).

§ 2333. Suit against sureties on bond; limitation period

(a) In case of a breach of a condition of the bond, an action may be brought against the sureties on the bond for the use and benefit of the ward or conservatee or of any person interested in the estate.

(b) No action may be maintained against the sureties on the bond unless commenced within four years from the discharge or removal of the guardian or conservator or within four years from the date the order surcharging the guardian or conservator becomes final, whichever is later.

(c) In any case, and notwithstanding subdivision (b) of Section 2103, no action may be maintained against the sureties on the bond unless the action commences within six years from the date the judgment under Section 2103 or the later of the orders under subdivision (b) of this section becomes final. *(Stats.1990, c. 79 (A.B.759), § 14, operative July 1, 1991. Amended by Stats.1990, c. 710 (S.B.1775), § 7, operative July 1, 1991; Stats.1993, c. 794 (A.B.516), § 1; Stats.1994, c. 806 (A.B.3686), § 11.)*

Law Revision Commission Comments
1990 Enactment

Section 2333 continues Section 2333 of the repealed Probate Code without change. See also Sections 2358 (performance of conditions concerning care, treatment, education, and welfare of ward or conservatee), 2402 (performance of conditions concerning care and custody of the property of the ward or conservatee). For a comparable provision relating to decedents' estates, see Section 8488. For background on the provisions of this part, see the Comment to this part under the part heading. [20 Cal.L.Rev.Comm. Reports 1001 (1990)].

1990 Amendment

Section 2333 (enacted as a part of the new Probate Code by 1990 Cal.Stat. ch. 79 § 14) was amended by 1990 Cal.Stat. ch. 710 § 7. The amendment deleted subdivision (c) to make the rule under Section 2333 consistent with the rule for decedents' estates. See Section 8488. For background on the 1990 amendment, see Recommendation Relating to Limitation Period for Action Against Surety in Guardianship or Conservatorship Proceeding, 20 Cal.L.Revision Comm'n Reports 565 (1990). [20 Cal.L.Rev.Comm. Reports 1001 (1990)].

Cross References

Actions on bonds, see Code of Civil Procedure § 996.460 et seq.; Probate Code § 9822.
Guardianship and conservatorship, interested person, defined, see Probate Code § 1424.
Nature of surety's liability, see Code of Civil Procedure § 996.460 et seq.
Periods of limitation, generally, see Code of Civil Procedure § 335 et seq.
Removal of guardian or conservator, see Probate Code § 2650 et seq.
Suretyship, see Civil Code § 2787 et seq.

§ 2334.   Petition to require bond or objection to sufficiency of bond; suspension of powers

Where a petition is filed requesting an order that a guardian or conservator be required to give a bond where no bond was originally required, or an objection is made to the sufficiency of the bond, and the petition or affidavit supporting the objection alleges facts showing that the guardian or conservator is failing to use ordinary care and diligence in the management of the estate, the court, by order, may suspend the powers of the guardian or conservator until the matter can be heard and determined. *(Stats.1990, c. 79 (A.B.759), § 14, operative July 1, 1991.)*

Law Revision Commission Comments
1990 Enactment

Section 2334 continues Section 2334 of the repealed Probate Code without substantive change. For general provisions, see Sections 1000–1004 (rules of practice), 1020–1023 (petitions and other pa-

pers), 1040–1050 (hearings and orders). See also Section 2250(e) (appointment of temporary guardian or conservator where court suspends powers of guardian or conservator under Section 2334). For background on the provisions of this part, see the Comment to this part under the part heading. [20 Cal.L.Rev.Comm. Reports 1001 (1990)].

Cross References

Accounts on removal of guardian or conservator, see Probate Code § 2630.
Executors and administrators, insufficiency of sureties, see Code of Civil Procedure § 996.010.
Removal of guardian or conservator, see Probate Code § 2650 et seq.
Suspension of powers of guardian or conservator upon petition for removal, see Probate Code § 2654.
Temporary guardian or conservator, appointment by court upon suspension of powers of the guardian or conservator, see Probate Code § 2250.

§ 2335.   Substitution of surety

A guardian or conservator who applies for a substitution and release of a surety shall file an account with the application. The court shall not order a substitution unless the account is approved. *(Stats.1990, c. 79 (A.B.759), § 14, operative July 1, 1991.)*

Law Revision Commission Comments
1990 Enactment

Section 2335 continues Section 2335 of the repealed Probate Code without substantive change. See also Section 2750 (order discharging surety an appealable order). For background on the provisions of this part, see the Comment to this part under the part heading. [20 Cal.L.Rev.Comm. Reports 1001 (1990)].

Cross References

Accounts, see Probate Code § 2620 et seq.
Application for release of surety, see Code of Civil Procedure §§ 996.110, 996.130.

§ 2336.   Repealed by Stats.1982, c. 517, p. 2410, § 347
Law Revision Commission Comments
1982 Repeal

The substance of former Section 2336 is continued in Code of Civil Procedure Sections 996.110–996.150 (substitution and release of sureties). (16 Cal.L.Rev.Comm. Reports 501).

ARTICLE 4.   PROFESSIONAL FIDUCIARIES

§ 2340.   Appointment of professional fiduciaries; licensing requirements

A superior court may not appoint a person to carry out the duties of a professional fiduciary, or permit a person to continue those duties, unless he or she holds a valid, unexpired, unsuspended license as a professional fiduciary under Chapter 6 (commencing with Section 6500) of Division 3 of the Business and Professions Code, is exempt from the definition of "professional fiduciary" under Section 6501 of the Business and Professions Code, or is exempt from the licensing requirements of Section 6530 of the Business and Professions Code. *(Added by Stats.2006, c. 491 (S.B.1550), § 5, operative July 1, 2008. Amended by Stats.2008, c. 293 (A.B.1340), § 6.)*

Cross References

Petition for appointment as guardian, contents of petition, see Probate Code § 1510.
Petition for temporary guardian or conservator, contents of petition, see Probate Code § 2250.
Petition to appoint a conservator, contents of petition, see Probate Code § 1821.
Professional fiduciary as guardian or conservator, court authorization of periodic payments, contents of petition, see Probate Code § 2643.1.
Professional fiduciary as guardian or conservator, proposed hourly fee schedule or proposed compensation filing requirement, see Probate Code § 2614.7.

§ 2341. Operative date

This article shall become operative on July 1, 2008. *(Added by Stats.2006, c. 491 (S.B.1550), § 5, operative July 1, 2008.)*

§§ 2342 to 2345. Repealed by Stats.2006, c. 491 (S.B.1550), § 6, operative Jan. 1, 2009

CHAPTER 5. POWERS AND DUTIES OF GUARDIAN OR CONSERVATOR OF THE PERSON

Cross References

Application of old and new law, see Probate Code § 3.

§ 2350. Definitions

As used in this chapter:

(a) "Conservator" means the conservator of the person.

(b) "Guardian" means the guardian of the person.

(c) "Residence" does not include a regional center established pursuant to Chapter 5 (commencing with Section 4620) of Division 4.5 of the Welfare and Institutions Code. *(Stats.1990, c. 79 (A.B.759), § 14, operative July 1, 1991. Amended by Stats.2008, c. 293 (A.B.1340), § 7.)*

Law Revision Commission Comments
1990 Enactment

Section 2350 continues Section 2350 of the repealed Probate Code without change. This chapter deals with powers and duties of a guardian or conservator of the person. The definitions in Section 2350 permit shorthand reference to such a guardian or conservator in this chapter. If one person is appointed conservator of the person and estate, or guardian of the person and estate, that person has the powers and duties conferred by this chapter. For background on the provisions of this part, see the Comment to this part under the part heading. [20 Cal.L.Rev.Comm. Reports 1001 (1990)].

Cross References

Nonresident ward or conservatee, powers and duties of guardian or conservator, see Probate Code § 2107.

§ 2351. Care, custody, control and education

(a) Subject to subdivision (b), the guardian or conservator, but not a limited conservator, has the care, custody, and control of, and has charge of the education of, the ward or conservatee. This control shall not extend to personal rights retained by the conservatee, including, but not limited to, the right to receive visitors, telephone calls, and personal mail, unless specifically limited by court order. The court may issue an order that specifically grants the conservator the power to enforce the conservatee's rights to receive visitors, telephone calls, and personal mail, or that directs the conservator to allow those visitors, telephone calls, and personal mail.

(b) Where the court determines that it is appropriate in the circumstances of the particular conservatee, the court, in its discretion, may limit the powers and duties that the conservator would otherwise have under subdivision (a) by an order stating either of the following:

(1) The specific powers that the conservator does not have with respect to the conservatee's person and reserving the powers so specified to the conservatee.

(2) The specific powers and duties the conservator has with respect to the conservatee's person and reserving to the conservatee all other rights with respect to the conservatee's person that the conservator otherwise would have under subdivision (a).

(c) An order under this section (1) may be included in the order appointing a conservator of the person or (2) may be made, modified, or revoked upon a petition subsequently filed, notice of the hearing on the petition having been given for the period and in the manner provided in Chapter 3 (commencing with Section 1460) of Part 1.

(d) The guardian or conservator, in exercising his or her powers, may not hire or refer any business to an entity in which he or she has a financial interest except upon authorization of the court. Prior to authorization from the court, the guardian or conservator shall disclose to the court in writing his or her financial interest in the entity. For the purposes of this subdivision, "financial interest" shall mean

(1) an ownership interest in a sole proprietorship, a partnership, or a closely held corporation, or (2) an ownership interest of greater than 1 percent of the outstanding shares in a publicly traded corporation, or (3) being an officer or a director of a corporation. This subdivision shall apply only to conservators and guardians required to register with the Statewide Registry under Chapter 13 (commencing with Section 2850). *(Stats.1990, c. 79 (A.B.759), § 14, operative July 1, 1991. Amended by Stats.2000, c. 565 (A.B.1950), § 4; Stats.2013, c. 127 (A.B.937), § 1; Stats.2015, c. 92 (A.B.1085), § 2, eff. Jan. 1, 2016.)*

Law Revision Commission Comments

1990 Enactment

Section 2351 continues Section 2351 of the repealed Probate Code without substantive change. Subdivisions (b) and (c) give the court flexibility to make an order appropriate to the particular conservatee. Subdivision (b) is useful because the broad power given the conservator under subdivision (a) may be more than is needed if the conservator is appointed on voluntary petition of a developmentally disabled adult. Subdivision (b) gives the court authority that may be useful in other types of cases where a voluntary or involuntary conservatorship is established. Under subdivision (b), for example, the court has discretion to make an order allowing the conservatee to fix his or her own residence or to make decisions concerning his or her own education. See also Section 2650 (continued failure to perform duties or incapacity to perform duties suitably is grounds for removal of guardian or conservator). For general provisions, see Sections 1000–1004 (rules of practice), 1020–1023 (petitions and other papers), 1040–1050 (hearings and orders), 2103 (effect of final order). See also Sections 1021 (petition to be verified), 1041 (clerk to set petition for hearing). For general provisions relating to notice of hearing, see Sections 1200–1221, 1460–1469. See also Sections 1260–1265 (proof of giving notice), 2700–2702 (notice to persons who request special notice). For background on the provisions of this part, see the Comment to this part under the part heading. [20 Cal.L.Rev.Comm. Reports 1001 (1990)].

Cross References

Additional powers of guardian nominated by will, see Probate Code § 2108.

§ 2351.5. Limited conservator; modification of powers; notice; hearing

(a) Subject to subdivision (b):

(1) The limited conservator has the care, custody, and control of the limited conservatee.

(2) The limited conservator shall secure for the limited conservatee those habilitation or treatment, training, education, medical and psychological services, and social and vocational opportunity as appropriate and as will assist the limited conservatee in the development of maximum self-reliance and independence.

(b) A limited conservator does not have any of the following powers or controls over the limited conservatee unless those powers or controls are specifically requested in the petition for appointment of a limited conservator and granted by the court in its order appointing the limited conservator:

(1) To fix the residence or specific dwelling of the limited conservatee.

(2) Access to the confidential records and papers of the limited conservatee.

(3) To consent or withhold consent to the marriage of, or the entrance into a registered domestic partnership by, the limited conservatee.

(4) The right of the limited conservatee to contract.

(5) The power of the limited conservatee to give or withhold medical consent.

(6) The limited conservatee's right to control his or her own social and sexual contacts and relationships.

(7) Decisions concerning the education of the limited conservatee.

(c) Any limited conservator, the limited conservatee, or any relative or friend of the limited conservatee may apply by petition to the superior court of the county in which the proceedings are pending to have the limited conservatorship modified by the elimination or addition of any of the powers which must be specifically granted to the limited conservator pursuant to subdivision (b). The petition shall state the facts alleged to establish that the limited conservatorship should be modified. The granting or elimination of those powers is discretionary with the court. Notice of the hearing on the petition shall be given for the period and in the manner provided in Chapter 3 (commencing with Section 1460) of Part 1.

(d) The limited conservator or any relative or friend of the limited conservatee may appear and oppose the petition. The court shall hear and determine the matter according to the laws and procedures relating to the trial of civil actions, including trial by jury if demanded. If any of the powers which must be specifically granted to the limited conservator pursuant to subdivision (b) are granted or eliminated, new letters of limited conservatorship shall be issued reflecting the change in the limited conservator's powers. *(Stats.1990, c. 79 (A.B.759), § 14, operative July 1, 1991. Amended by Stats. 2005, c. 418 (S.B.973), § 28.)*

Law Revision Commission Comments

1990 Enactment

Section 2351.5 restates Section 2351.5 of the repealed Probate Code without substantive change. For general provisions, see Sections 1000–1004 (rules of practice), 1020–1023 (petitions and other papers), 1040–1050 (hearings and orders), 2103 (effect of final order). See also Sections 1021 (petition to be verified), 1041 (clerk to set petition for hearing). For general provisions relating to notice of hearing, see Sections 1200–1221, 1460–1469. See also Sections 1260–1265 (proof of giving notice), 2700–2702 (notice to persons who request special notice). See also Section 2650 (continued failure to perform duties or incapacity to perform duties suitably is grounds for removal of guardian or conservator). For background on the provisions of this part, see the Comment to this part under the part heading. [20 Cal.L.Rev.Comm. Reports 1001 (1990)].

Cross References

Capacity of conservatee to give informed consent for medical treatment, see Probate Code § 1880 et seq.
Capacity of conservatee to marry, see Probate Code §§ 1900, 1901.
Determination of place of residence, see Government Code § 244.
Letters, generally, see Probate Code § 2310 et seq.
Marriage, generally, see Family Code § 300 et seq.

Persons capable of contracting, see Civil Code §§ 1556, 1557.

§ 2352. Residence of ward or conservatee

(a) The guardian may establish the residence of the ward at any place within this state without the permission of the court. The guardian shall select the least restrictive appropriate residence that is available and necessary to meet the needs of the ward, and that is in the best interests of the ward.

(b) The conservator may establish the residence of the conservatee at any place within this state without the permission of the court. The conservator shall select the least restrictive appropriate residence, as described in Section 2352.5, that is available and necessary to meet the needs of the conservatee, and that is in the best interests of the conservatee.

(c) If permission of the court is first obtained, a guardian or conservator may establish the residence of a ward or conservatee at a place not within this state. Notice of the hearing on the petition to establish the residence of the ward or conservatee out of state, together with a copy of the petition, shall be given in the manner required by subdivision (a) of Section 1460 to all persons entitled to notice under subdivision (b) of Section 1511 or subdivision (b) of Section 1822.

(d)(1) An order under subdivision (c) relating to a ward shall require the guardian either to return the ward to this state, or to cause a guardianship proceeding or its equivalent to be commenced in the place of the new residence, when the ward has resided in the place of new residence for a period of four months or a longer or shorter period specified in the order.

(2) An order under subdivision (c) relating to a conservatee shall require the conservator to do one of the following when the conservatee has resided in the other state for a period of four months or a longer or shorter period specified in the order:

(A) Return the conservatee to this state.

(B) Petition for transfer of the conservatorship to the other state under Article 3 (commencing with Section 2001) of Chapter 8 of Part 3 and corresponding law of the other state.

(C) Cause a conservatorship proceeding or its equivalent to be commenced in the other state.

(e)(1) The guardian or conservator shall file a notice of change of residence with the court within 30 days of the date of the change. The guardian or conservator shall include in the notice of change of residence a declaration stating that the ward's or conservatee's change of residence is consistent with the standard described in subdivision (b).

(2) The guardian or conservator shall mail a copy of the notice to all persons entitled to notice under subdivision (b) of Section 1511 or subdivision (b) of Section 1822 and shall file proof of service of the notice with the court. The court may, for good cause, waive the mailing requirement pursuant to this paragraph in order to prevent harm to the conservatee or ward.

(3) If the guardian or conservator proposes to remove the ward or conservatee from his or her personal residence, except as provided by subdivision (c), the guardian or conservator shall mail a notice of his or her intention to change the residence of the ward or conservatee to all persons entitled to notice under subdivision (b) of Section 1511 and subdivision (b) of Section 1822. In the absence of an emergency, that notice shall be mailed at least 15 days before the proposed removal of the ward or conservatee from his or her personal residence. If the notice is served less than 15 days prior to the proposed removal of the ward or conservatee, the guardian or conservator shall set forth the basis for the emergency in the notice. The guardian or conservator shall file proof of service of that notice with the court.

(f) This section does not apply where the court has made an order under Section 2351 pursuant to which the conservatee retains the right to establish his or her own residence.

(g) As used in this section, "guardian" or "conservator" includes a proposed guardian or proposed conservator and "ward" or "conservatee" includes a proposed ward or proposed conservatee.

(h) This section does not apply to a person with developmental disabilities for whom the Director of Developmental Services or a regional center, established pursuant to Chapter 5 (commencing with Section 4620) of Division 4.5 of the Welfare and Institutions Code, acts as the conservator. *(Stats.1990, c. 79 (A.B.759), § 14, operative July 1, 1991. Amended by Stats.2006, c. 490 (S.B.1116), § 1; Stats.2008, c. 293 (A.B.1340), § 8; Stats.2014, c. 553 (S.B.940), § 24, eff. Jan. 1, 2015, operative Jan. 1, 2016.)*

Law Revision Commission Comments

1990 Enactment

Section 2352 continues Section 2352 of the repealed Probate Code without change. See also Section 2750 (order granting permission to fix residence at a place not within this state an appealable order). For background on the provisions of this part, see the Comment to this part under the part heading. [20 Cal.L.Rev.Comm. Reports 1001 (1990)].

2014 Amendment

Subdivision (d) of Section 2352 is amended to reflect the enactment of the California Conservatorship Jurisdiction Act (Section 1980 *et seq.*).

Subdivision (e) is amended to replace an erroneous reference to "conservatee" with a reference to "conservator." [44 Cal.L.Rev. Comm. Reports 77 [Appendix 4] (2014)].

Cross References

Determination of place of residence, see Government Code § 244.
Notice,
   Mailing, see Probate Code § 1215 et seq.
   Posting, see Probate Code § 1230.
   Proof of giving notice, see Probate Code § 1260 et seq.
   Special notice, see Probate Code § 1250 et seq.
   This code, generally, see Probate Code § 1200 et seq.
   This division, generally, see Probate Code § 1460 et seq.
Request for special notice, see Probate Code § 2700 et seq.
Service of process,
   Generally, see Code of Civil Procedure § 413.10 et seq.
   Mail, see Code of Civil Procedure §§ 415.30, 1012 et seq.
   Personal delivery, see Code of Civil Procedure § 415.10.
   Proof of service, see Code of Civil Procedure § 417.10 et seq.
   Publication, see Code of Civil Procedure § 415.50.

§ 2352.5. Presumption relating to residence of conservatee; level of care determination; conservatees with developmental disabilities

(a) It shall be presumed that the personal residence of the conservatee at the time of commencement of the proceeding is the least restrictive appropriate residence for the conservatee. In any hearing to determine if removal of the conservatee from his or her personal residence is appropriate, that presumption may be overcome by a preponderance of the evidence.

(b) Upon appointment, the conservator shall determine the appropriate level of care for the conservatee.

(1) That determination shall include an evaluation of the level of care existing at the time of commencement of the proceeding and the measures that would be necessary to keep the conservatee in his or her personal residence.

(2) If the conservatee is living at a location other than his or her personal residence at the commencement of the proceeding, that determination shall either include a plan to return the conservatee to his or her personal residence or an explanation of the limitations or restrictions on a return of the conservatee to his or her personal residence in the foreseeable future.

(c) The determination made by the conservator pursuant to subdivision (b) shall be in writing, signed under penalty of perjury, and submitted to the court within 60 days of appointment as conservator.

(d) The conservator shall evaluate the conservatee's placement and level of care if there is a material change in circumstances affecting the conservatee's needs for placement and care.

(e)(1) This section shall not apply to a conservatee with developmental disabilities for whom the Director of Developmental Services or a regional center for the developmentally disabled, established pursuant to Chapter 5 (commencing with Section 4620) of Division 4.5 of the Welfare and Institutions Code, acts as the conservator and who receives services from a regional center pursuant to the Lanterman Developmental Disabilities Act (Division 4.5 (commencing with Section 4500) of the Welfare and Institutions Code).

(2) Services, including residential placement, for a conservatee described in paragraph (1) who is a consumer, as defined in Section 4512 of the Welfare and Institutions Code, shall be identified, delivered, and evaluated consistent with the individual program plan process described in Article 2 (commencing with Section 4640) of Chapter 5 of Division 4.5 of the Welfare and Institutions Code. *(Added by Stats.2006, c. 490 (S.B.1116), § 2. Amended by Stats.2007, c. 130 (A.B.299), § 195.)*

§ 2353. Medical treatment of ward

(a) Subject to subdivision (b), the guardian has the same right as a parent having legal custody of a child to give consent to medical treatment performed upon the ward and to require the ward to receive medical treatment.

(b) Except as provided in subdivision (c), if the ward is 14 years of age or older, no surgery may be performed upon the ward without either (1) the consent of both the ward and the

guardian or (2) a court order obtained pursuant to Section 2357 specifically authorizing such treatment.

(c) The guardian may consent to surgery to be performed upon the ward, and may require the ward to receive the surgery, in any case where the guardian determines in good faith based upon medical advice that the case is an emergency case in which the ward faces loss of life or serious bodily injury if the surgery is not performed. In such a case, the consent of the guardian alone is sufficient and no person is liable because the surgery is performed upon the ward without the ward's consent.

(d) Nothing in this section requires the consent of the guardian for medical or surgical treatment for the ward in any case where the ward alone may consent to such treatment under other provisions of law. *(Stats.1990, c. 79 (A.B.759), § 14, operative July 1, 1991.)*

Law Revision Commission Comments
1990 Enactment

Section 2353 continues Section 2353 of the repealed Probate Code without substantive change.

Subdivisions (b) and (c) are similar to subdivision (b) of Section 5358 of the Welfare and Institutions Code (Lanterman–Petris–Short Act). See also In re Roger S., 19 Cal.3d 921, 931, 569 P.2d 1286, 1292, 141 Cal.Rptr. 298, 304 (1977) (minor over 14 has independent right to assert protections of due process clause).

The immunity from liability provided by the second sentence of subdivision (c) does not extend to malpractice. The immunity is only for failure to obtain consent of the patient (the ward) to the surgery.

Subdivision (d) makes clear that Section 2353 does not override such provisions as Civil Code Sections 25.5 (blood donation by minor), 25.7 (minor on active duty with armed services), 34.5 (surgical care related to prevention or treatment of pregnancy), 34.6 (minor living apart from parent or guardian), 34.7 (surgical care related to diagnosis or treatment of contagious disease), 34.8 (surgical care related to diagnosis or treatment of rape victim), 34.9 (surgical care related to diagnosis and treatment of victim of sexual assault). See also Health & Safety Code § 25958 (abortion in case of unemancipated minor). Also, nothing in Section 2353 or elsewhere in this chapter overrides state quarantine regulations. See, e.g., Health & Safety Code §§ 3050–3053.

Section 2353 does not deal with the question of what constitutes informed consent for the purpose of medical treatment. Concerning informed consent, see the Comment to Section 2354.

Unless the court otherwise orders, a temporary guardian of the person has the powers and duties conferred by Section 2353. Section 2252.

For background on the provisions of this part, see the Comment to this part under the part heading. [20 Cal.L.Rev.Comm. Reports 1001 (1990)].

Cross References

Additional powers of guardian nominated by will, see Probate Code § 2108.
Caregiver, authorization for medical or dental care of minor, see Family Code § 6550.
Consent by,
    Director of regional center, see Welfare and Institutions Code § 4655.
    Medical director of state hospital, see Welfare and Institutions Code § 7518.
Medical treatment for adult without conservator, authorization, see Probate Code § 3200 et seq.

Minors, caregivers, authorization affidavits, see Family Code § 6550.

§ 2354. Medical treatment of conservatee not adjudicated to lack capacity to give informed consent

(a) If the conservatee has not been adjudicated to lack the capacity to give informed consent for medical treatment, the conservatee may consent to his or her medical treatment. The conservator may also give consent to the medical treatment, but the consent of the conservator is not required if the conservatee has the capacity to give informed consent to the medical treatment, and the consent of the conservator alone is not sufficient under this subdivision if the conservatee objects to the medical treatment.

(b) The conservator may require the conservatee to receive medical treatment, whether or not the conservatee consents to the treatment, if a court order specifically authorizing the medical treatment has been obtained pursuant to Section 2357.

(c) The conservator may consent to medical treatment to be performed upon the conservatee, and may require the conservatee to receive the medical treatment, in any case where the conservator determines in good faith based upon medical advice that the case is an emergency case in which the medical treatment is required because (1) the treatment is required for the alleviation of severe pain or (2) the conservatee has a medical condition which, if not immediately diagnosed and treated, will lead to serious disability or death. In such a case, the consent of the conservator alone is sufficient and no person is liable because the medical treatment is performed upon the conservatee without the conservatee's consent. (Stats.1990, c. 79 (A.B.759), § 14, operative July 1, 1991.)

Law Revision Commission Comments
1990 Enactment

Section 2354 continues Section 2354 of the repealed Probate Code without substantive change. This section provides clear guidelines where the conservatee has not been adjudicated to lack capacity to give informed consent for medical treatment. See Section 1880 (adjudication of lack of capacity to give informed consent for medical treatment).

Under subdivision (a), if the conservatee consents to the medical treatment (which includes surgery), there is no restriction imposed by this division on providing the medical treatment to the conservatee. Accordingly, medical personnel may safely rely on the conservatee's informed consent as long as the conservatee has not been adjudicated to lack capacity to give informed consent for medical treatment. This section does not deal with the question of what constitutes informed consent for the purpose of medical treatment. In connection with what constitutes informed consent, see Cobbs v. Grant, 8 Cal.3d 229, 502 P.2d 1, 104 Cal.Rptr. 505 (1972).

If the medical practitioner is unwilling to rely on consent of the conservatee, the practitioner may also require consent of the conservator. If the medical practitioner is willing to rely on consent of the conservatee alone, a conservator who wishes to forestall the treatment must seek an adjudication under Section 1880 that the conservatee lacks capacity to give informed consent for medical treatment. If the medical practitioner also requires consent of the conservator but the conservator refuses to consent, the conservatee or other interested person may petition the court for an order requiring the conservator to consent. See Section 2357(i).

Consent of the conservator alone is sufficient consent for medical treatment if the conservatee does not object to the treatment.

Accordingly, if the conservatee is in such condition that he or she is unable to give consent, consent of the conservator is sufficient since consent of the conservatee is not required under subdivision (a)—all that is required is that the conservatee not object.

Subdivisions (b) and (c) are drawn from Section 5358 of the Welfare and Institutions Code (Lanterman–Petris–Short Act). The immunity from liability provided by the second sentence of subdivision (c) does not extend to malpractice; the immunity goes only to failure to obtain consent of the patient (the conservatee).

Unless the court otherwise orders, a temporary conservator of the person has the powers and duties conferred by Section 2354. See Section 2252.

Section 2354 does not deal with payment of expenses of medical treatment; determining the reasonableness of such expenses and paying them is the responsibility of the conservator of the estate. See Section 2430.

Where involuntary civil mental health treatment is involved, proceedings may be had only under the Lanterman–Petris–Short Act, and not under this division. See Section 2356(a). See also Section 2356(b)–(e) (experimental drugs, convulsive treatment, sterilization, Natural Death Act, durable power of attorney for health care).

For background on the provisions of this part, see the Comment to this part under the part heading. [20 Cal.L.Rev.Comm. Reports 1001 (1990)].

Cross References

Adjudication of lack of capacity to give informed consent for medical treatment, see Probate Code § 1880.
Consent by,
  Director of regional center, see Welfare and Institutions Code § 4655.
  Medical director of state hospital, see Welfare and Institutions Code § 7518.
Gravely disabled persons, medical treatment of conservatee, see Welfare and Institutions Code § 5358.2.
Human experimentation, informed consent, see Health and Safety Code § 24175.
Medical treatment for adult without conservator, authorization, see Probate Code § 3200 et seq.

§ 2355. Medical treatment of conservatee adjudicated to lack capacity to make health care decisions

(a) If the conservatee has been adjudicated to lack the capacity to make health care decisions, the conservator has the exclusive authority to make health care decisions for the conservatee that the conservator in good faith based on medical advice determines to be necessary. The conservator shall make health care decisions for the conservatee in accordance with the conservatee's individual health care instructions, if any, and other wishes to the extent known to the conservator. Otherwise, the conservator shall make the decision in accordance with the conservator's determination of the conservatee's best interest. In determining the conservatee's best interest, the conservator shall consider the conservatee's personal values to the extent known to the conservator. The conservator may require the conservatee to receive the health care, whether or not the conservatee objects. In this case, the health care decision of the conservator alone is sufficient and no person is liable because the health care is administered to the conservatee without the conservatee's consent. For the purposes of this subdivision, "health care" and "health care decision" have the meanings provided in Sections 4615 and 4617, respectively.

(b) If prior to the establishment of the conservatorship the conservatee was an adherent of a religion whose tenets and practices call for reliance on prayer alone for healing, the treatment required by the conservator under the provisions of this section shall be by an accredited practitioner of that religion. *(Stats.1990, c. 79 (A.B.759), § 14, operative July 1, 1991. Amended by Stats.1999, c. 658 (A.B.891), § 12, operative July 1, 2000.)*

Law Revision Commission Comments

1990 Enactment

Section 2355 continues Section 2355 of the repealed Probate Code without change. Subdivision (a) makes clear that, when the conservatee has been adjudicated to lack capacity to give informed consent to medical treatment (Section 1880), the power to give consent rests exclusively with the conservator. The adjudication of lack of capacity referred to in Section 2355 may be included in the order of appointment of the conservator or may be made upon a subsequently filed petition. See Section 1890.

The immunity provided by the last sentence of subdivision (a) does not extend to malpractice; the immunity goes only to failure to obtain consent of the patient (the conservatee). Section 2355 does not deal with the question of what constitutes informed consent. Concerning informed consent, see the Comment to Section 2354. If the conservator fails to consent to or to obtain medical treatment for the conservatee, the court, upon petition of the conservatee or an interested person, may order the conservator to consent to or to obtain such treatment. See Section 2357(i).

Subdivision (b) provides recognition of the religious beliefs of the conservatee prior to conservatorship insofar as those beliefs relate to medical treatment. The subdivision does not limit the authority of the court under Section 2357.

Where involuntary civil mental health treatment is involved, proceedings may be had only under the Lanterman–Petris–Short Act, and not under this division. See Section 2536(a). See also Section 2536(b)–(e) (experimental drugs, convulsive treatment, sterilization, Natural Death Act). As to sterilization of an adult, see Sections 1950–1969.

For background on the provisions of this part, see the Comment to this part under the part heading. [20 Cal.L.Rev.Comm. Reports 1001 (1990)].

1999 Amendment

Subdivision (a) of Section 2355 is amended to add the second sentence providing a standard for making health care decisions. This standard is the same in substance as the standard applicable to other surrogate health care decisionmakers under the Health Care Decisions Law of Division 4.7 (commencing with Section 4600). See Sections 4684 (standard governing agent's health care decisions under power of attorney for health care), 4714 (standard governing statutory surrogate's health care decisions). Under this standard, the surrogate has both the right and fiduciary duty ("shall make health care decisions") to make a decision based on the individual circumstances of the conservatee. As amended, subdivision (a) is consistent with Conservatorship of Drabick, 200 Cal.App.3d 185, 245 Cal.Rptr. 840 (1988):

Incapacitated patients retain the right to have appropriate medical decisions made on their behalf. An appropriate medical decision is one that is made in the patient's best interests, as opposed to the interests of the hospital, the physicians, the legal system, or someone else. To summarize, California law gives persons a right to determine the scope of their own medical treatment, this right survives incompetence in the sense that incompetent patients retain the right to have appropriate decisions made on their behalf, and Probate Code section 2355 delegates to conservators the right and duty to make such decisions.

Id. at 205. Use of the terms "health care" and "health care decision" from the Health Care Decisions Law make clear that the scope of health care decisions that can be made by a conservator under this section is the same as provided in the Health Care Decisions Law.

The importance of the statutory language concerning the exclusive authority of the conservator and the duty this places on the conservator was also emphasized in *Drabick*:

The statute gives the conservator the exclusive authority to exercise the conservatee's rights, and it is the conservator who must make the final treatment decision regardless of how much or how little information about the conservatee's preferences is available. There is no necessity or authority for adopting a rule to the effect that the conservatee's desire to have medical treatment withdrawn must be proved by clear and convincing evidence or another standard. Acknowledging that the patient's expressed preferences are relevant, it is enough for the conservator, who must act in the conservatee's best interests, to consider them in good faith.

Id. at 211–12. The intent of the rule in subdivision (a) is to protect and further the patient's interest in making a health care decision in accordance with the patient's expressed desires, where known, and if not, to make a decision in the patient's best interest, taking personal values into account. The necessary determinations are to be made by the conservator, whether private or public, in accordance with the statutory standard. Court control or intervention in this process is neither required by statute, nor desired by the courts. See, e.g., Conservatorship of Morrison, 206 Cal.App.3d 304, 312, 253 Cal.Rptr. 530 (1988). *Drabick*, 200 Cal.App.3d at 198–200. See also Sections 4650(c) (legislative findings), 4750 (judicial intervention disfavored).

This section does not specify any special evidentiary standard for the determination of the conservatee's wishes or best interest. Consequently, the general rule applies: the standard is by preponderance of the evidence. Proof is not required by clear and convincing evidence. [29 Cal.L.Rev.Comm. Reports App. 6 (1999)].

2001–2002 Annual Report

In Conservatorship of Wendland, 26 Cal.4th 519, 28 P.3d 151, 110 Cal.Rptr.2d 412 (2001), the court held that, while constitutional on its face, Probate Code Section 2355 (medical treatment of conservatee who lacks capacity to give informed consent) should be construed to minimize the possibility of its unconstitutional application by requiring clear and convincing evidence to support withholding life-sustaining treatment from a conscious conservatee. [31 Cal.L.Rev. Comm. Reports 29 (2001)].

Cross References

Adjudication of lack of capacity to give informed consent for medical treatment, see Probate Code § 1880.
Consent by,
  Director of regional center, see Welfare and Institutions Code § 4655.
  Medical director of state hospital, see Welfare and Institutions Code § 7518.
Court ordered medical treatment, see Probate Code § 2357.
Gravely disabled persons, medical treatment of conservatee, see Welfare and Institutions Code § 5358.2.
Health care decisions, generally, see Probate Code § 4600 et seq.
Human experimentation, informed consent, see Health and Safety Code § 24175.

§ 2356. Limitations on application of chapter

(a) A ward or conservatee shall not be placed in a mental health treatment facility under this division against his or her will. Involuntary civil placement of a ward or conservatee in a mental health treatment facility may be obtained only pursuant to Chapter 2 (commencing with Section 5150) or Chapter 3 (commencing with Section 5350) of Part 1 of Division 5 of the Welfare and Institutions Code. Nothing in this subdivision precludes the placing of a ward in a state hospital under Section 6000 of the Welfare and Institutions Code upon application of the guardian as provided in that section.

(b) An experimental drug as defined in Section 111515 of the Health and Safety Code shall not be prescribed for or administered to a ward or conservatee under this division. An experimental drug may be prescribed for or administered to a ward or conservatee only as provided in Article 4 (commencing with Section 111515) of Chapter 6 of Part 5 of Division 104 of the Health and Safety Code.

(c) Convulsive treatment as defined in Section 5325 of the Welfare and Institutions Code shall not be performed on a ward or conservatee under this division. Convulsive treatment may be performed on a ward or conservatee only as provided in Article 7 (commencing with Section 5325) of Chapter 2 of Part 1 of Division 5 of the Welfare and Institutions Code.

(d) A minor shall not be sterilized under this division.

(e) This chapter is subject to a valid and effective advance health care directive under the Health Care Decisions Law (Division 4.7 (commencing with Section 4600)). *(Stats.1990, c. 79 (A.B.759), § 14, operative July 1, 1991. Amended by Stats.1990, c. 710 (S.B.1775), § 8, operative July 1, 1991; Stats.1996, c. 1023 (S.B.1497), § 398, eff. Sept. 29, 1996; Stats.1999, c. 658 (A.B.891), § 13, operative July 1, 2000; Stats.2014, c. 442 (S.B.1465), § 12, eff. Sept. 18, 2014; Stats.2015, c. 117 (A.B.468), § 1, eff. Jan. 1, 2016.)*

Law Revision Commission Comments

1990 Enactment

Section 2356 continues Section 2356 of the repealed Probate Code with nonsubstantive revisions and with the addition of paragraph (2) to subdivision (e). See also In re Roger S., 19 Cal.3d 921, 569 P.2d 1286, 141 Cal.Rptr. 298 (1977) (minor over 14 has independent right to assert protections of due process clause).

Subdivisions (b)–(d) make clear that provisions of other statutes relating to highly intrusive forms of medical treatment are the only provisions under which such treatment may be authorized for a ward or conservatee, thus assuring that procedural safeguards in those provisions will be applied. Subdivision (d) is consistent with Guardianship of Tulley, 83 Cal.App.3d 698, 146 Cal.Rptr. 266 (1978), and Guardianship of Kemp, 43 Cal.App.3d 758, 118 Cal.Rptr. 64 (1974). As to sterilization of an adult, see Sections 1950–1969. A guardian or conservator who violates any provision of Section 2356 may be removed. See Section 2650.

For background on the provisions of this part, see the Comment to this part under the part heading. [20 Cal.L.Rev.Comm. Reports 1001 (1990)].

1990 Amendment

Section 2356 (enacted as a part of the new Probate Code by 1990 Cal.Stat. ch. 79 § 14) was amended by 1990 Cal.Stat. ch. 710 § 8. The 1990 amendment revised subdivision (a) to resolve an inconsistency in language between the first and second sentences. This amendment recognizes that the provisions of the Welfare and Institutions Code (part of the Lanterman–Petris–Short Act) cited in the second sentence govern situations where a person may be involuntarily placed (e.g., Welf. & Inst.Code §§ 5150, 5350.1), detained (e.g., Welf. & Inst.Code § 5151), confined (e.g., Welf. & Inst.Code § 5260), or committed (e.g., Welf. & Inst.Code § 5300). The language as revised is also consistent with Section 3211(a). The 1990 amendment also recognizes the court's power under Section 2357 to authorize treatment in the case of a serious threat to the mental health of the ward or conservatee. See Section 2357. For background on the 1990 amendment, see Recommendation Relating to Court–Authorized Medical Treatment, 20 Cal.L.Revision Comm'n Reports 537 (1990). [20 Cal.L.Rev.Comm. Reports 1001 (1990)].

1999 Amendment

Subdivision (e) of Section 2356 is amended to refer to the provisions of the Health Care Decisions Law that replace the former Natural Death Act and the former durable power of attorney for health care provisions. This is a technical, nonsubstantive change that preserves the supremacy of the individual's advance directive over the rules concerning conservatorships. [29 Cal.L.Rev.Comm. Reports 1 (1999)].

Cross References

Health care decisions, generally, see Probate Code § 4600 et seq.
Medical experiments, informed consent, see Health and Safety Code § 24175.
Minors, caregivers, authorization affidavits, see Family Code § 6550.

§ 2356.5. Dementia; placement in secured facility; administration of medication; procedures

(a) The Legislature hereby finds and declares:

(1) That people with dementia, as defined in the last published edition of the "Diagnostic and Statistical Manual of Mental Disorders," should have a conservatorship to serve their unique and special needs.

(2) That, by adding powers to the probate conservatorship for people with dementia, their unique and special needs can be met. This will reduce costs to the conservatee and the family of the conservatee, reduce costly administration by state and county government, and safeguard the basic dignity and rights of the conservatee.

(3) That it is the intent of the Legislature to recognize that the administration of psychotropic medications has been, and can be, abused by caregivers and, therefore, granting powers to a conservator to authorize these medications for the treatment of dementia requires the protections specified in this section.

(b) Notwithstanding any other law, a conservator may authorize the placement of a conservatee in a secured perimeter residential care facility for the elderly operated pursuant to Section 1569.698 of the Health and Safety Code, and which has a care plan that meets the requirements of Section 87705 of Title 22 of the California Code of Regulations, upon a court's finding, by clear and convincing evidence, of all of the following:

(1) The conservatee has dementia, as defined in the last published edition of the "Diagnostic and Statistical Manual of Mental Disorders."

(2) The conservatee lacks the capacity to give informed consent to this placement and has at least one mental function deficit pursuant to subdivision (a) of Section 811, and this deficit significantly impairs the person's ability to understand and appreciate the consequences of his or her actions pursuant to subdivision (b) of Section 811.

(3) The conservatee needs or would benefit from a restricted and secure environment, as demonstrated by evidence presented by the physician or psychologist referred to in paragraph (3) of subdivision (f).

(4) The court finds that the proposed placement in a locked facility is the least restrictive placement appropriate to the needs of the conservatee.

(c) Notwithstanding any other law, a conservator of a person may authorize the administration of medications appropriate for the care and treatment of dementia, upon a court's finding, by clear and convincing evidence, of all of the following:

(1) The conservatee has dementia, as defined in the last published edition of the "Diagnostic and Statistical Manual of Mental Disorders."

(2) The conservatee lacks the capacity to give informed consent to the administration of medications appropriate to the care of dementia, and has at least one mental function deficit pursuant to subdivision (a) of Section 811, and this deficit or deficits significantly impairs the person's ability to understand and appreciate the consequences of his or her actions pursuant to subdivision (b) of Section 811.

(3) The conservatee needs or would benefit from appropriate medication as demonstrated by evidence presented by the physician or psychologist referred to in paragraph (3) of subdivision (f).

(d) Pursuant to subdivision (b) of Section 2355, in the case of a person who is an adherent of a religion whose tenets and practices call for a reliance on prayer alone for healing, the treatment required by the conservator under subdivision (c) shall be by an accredited practitioner of that religion in lieu of the administration of medications.

(e) A conservatee who is to be placed in a facility pursuant to this section shall not be placed in a mental health rehabilitation center as described in Section 5675 of the Welfare and Institutions Code, or in an institution for mental disease as described in Section 5900 of the Welfare and Institutions Code.

(f) A petition for authority to act under this section is governed by Section 2357, except:

(1) The conservatee shall be represented by an attorney pursuant to Chapter 4 (commencing with Section 1470) of Part 1. Upon granting or denying authority to a conservator under this section, the court shall discharge the attorney or order the continuation of the legal representation, consistent with the standard set forth in subdivision (a) of Section 1470.

(2) The conservatee shall be produced at the hearing, unless excused pursuant to Section 1893.

(3) The petition shall be supported by a declaration of a licensed physician, or a licensed psychologist within the scope of his or her licensure, regarding each of the findings required to be made under this section for any power requested, except that the psychologist has at least two years of experience in diagnosing dementia.

(4) The petition may be filed by any of the persons designated in Section 1891.

(g) The court investigator shall annually investigate and report to the court every two years pursuant to Sections 1850 and 1851 if the conservator is authorized to act under this section. In addition to the other matters provided in Section 1851, the conservatee shall be specifically advised by the investigator that the conservatee has the right to object to the conservator's powers granted under this section, and the report shall also include whether powers granted under this section are warranted. If the conservatee objects to the conservator's powers granted under this section, or the investigator determines that some change in the powers granted under this section is warranted, the court shall provide a copy of the report to the attorney of record for the conservatee. If no attorney has been appointed for the conservatee, one shall be appointed pursuant to Chapter 4 (commencing with Section 1470) of Part 1. The attorney shall, within 30 days after receiving this report, do one of the following:

(1) File a petition with the court regarding the status of the conservatee.

(2) File a written report with the court stating that the attorney has met with the conservatee and determined that the petition would be inappropriate.

(h) A petition to terminate authority granted under this section shall be governed by Section 2359.

(i) Nothing in this section shall be construed to affect a conservatorship of the estate of a person who has dementia.

(j) Nothing in this section shall affect the laws that would otherwise apply in emergency situations.

(k) Nothing in this section shall affect current law regarding the power of a probate court to fix the residence of a conservatee or to authorize medical treatment for any conservatee who has not been determined to have dementia. *(Added by Stats.1996, c. 910 (S.B.1481), § 1. Amended by Stats.1997, c. 724 (A.B.1172), § 13; Stats.2003, c. 32 (A.B. 167), § 2; Stats.2014, c. 913 (A.B.2747), § 31, eff. Jan. 1, 2015; Stats.2015, c. 197 (A.B.436), § 1, eff. Jan. 1, 2016.)*

Law Revision Commission Comments

2003 Amendment

Section 2356.5 is amended to correct incorrect section references. [33 Cal.L.Rev.Comm. Reports 155 (2003)].

2014 Amendment

Subdivision (b) of Section 2356.5 is amended to delete an obsolete reference to "a locked and secured nursing facility which specializes in the care and treatment of people with dementia pursuant to subdivision (c) of Section 1569.691 of the Health and Safety Code." Former Health and Safety Code Section 1569.691, relating to a pilot program, was repealed by its own terms on January 1, 1998. See 1995 Cal. Stat. ch. 550, § 1.

Subdivision (b) is also amended to update a cross-reference to the California Code of Regulations. The cross-reference is to care plan requirements for a residential care facility for the elderly that houses dementia patients. Those requirements were moved from Section 87724 to Section 87705 of Title 22 of the California Code of Regulations. See Regulatory Notice Register 2008, No. 11–Z, p. 387 (Mar. 14, 2008).

Subdivision (*l*), a transitional provision, is deleted as obsolete. [43 Cal.L.Rev.Comm. Reports 35 (2013)].

Cross References

Capacity determinations, generally, see Probate Code § 3200 et seq.
Counsel, right to, see Cal. Const. Art. 1, § 15.
Due process, generally, see Cal. Const. Art. 1, § 7.
Health care decisions, generally, see Probate Code § 4600 et seq.

Legislative intent, construction of statutes, see Code of Civil Procedure § 1859.

§ 2357. Court ordered medical treatment

(a) As used in this section:

(1) "Guardian or conservator" includes a temporary guardian of the person or a temporary conservator of the person.

(2) "Ward or conservatee" includes a person for whom a temporary guardian of the person or temporary conservator of the person has been appointed.

(b) If the ward or conservatee requires medical treatment for an existing or continuing medical condition which is not authorized to be performed upon the ward or conservatee under Section 2252, 2353, 2354, or 2355, and the ward or conservatee is unable to give an informed consent to this medical treatment, the guardian or conservator may petition the court under this section for an order authorizing the medical treatment and authorizing the guardian or conservator to consent on behalf of the ward or conservatee to the medical treatment.

(c) The petition shall state, or set forth by medical affidavit attached thereto, all of the following so far as is known to the petitioner at the time the petition is filed:

(1) The nature of the medical condition of the ward or conservatee which requires treatment.

(2) The recommended course of medical treatment which is considered to be medically appropriate.

(3) The threat to the health of the ward or conservatee if authorization to consent to the recommended course of treatment is delayed or denied by the court.

(4) The predictable or probable outcome of the recommended course of treatment.

(5) The medically available alternatives, if any, to the course of treatment recommended.

(6) The efforts made to obtain an informed consent from the ward or conservatee.

(7) The name and addresses, so far as they are known to the petitioner, of the persons specified in subdivision (c) of Section 1510 in a guardianship proceeding or subdivision (b) of Section 1821 in a conservatorship proceeding.

(d) Upon the filing of the petition, unless an attorney is already appointed the court shall appoint the public defender or private counsel under Section 1471, to consult with and represent the ward or conservatee at the hearing on the petition and, if that appointment is made, Section 1472 applies.

(e) Notice of the petition shall be given as follows:

(1) Not less than 15 days before the hearing, notice of the time and place of the hearing, and a copy of the petition shall be personally served on the ward, if 12 years of age or older, or the conservatee, and on the attorney for the ward or conservatee.

(2) Not less than 15 days before the hearing, notice of the time and place of the hearing, and a copy of the petition shall be mailed to the following persons:

(A) The spouse or domestic partner, if any, of the proposed conservatee at the address stated in the petition.

(B) The relatives named in the petition at their addresses stated in the petition.

(f) For good cause, the court may shorten or waive notice of the hearing as provided by this section. In determining the period of notice to be required, the court shall take into account both of the following:

(1) The existing medical facts and circumstances set forth in the petition or in a medical affidavit attached to the petition or in a medical affidavit presented to the court.

(2) The desirability, where the condition of the ward or conservatee permits, of giving adequate notice to all interested persons.

(g) Notwithstanding subdivisions (e) and (f), the matter may be submitted for the determination of the court upon proper and sufficient medical affidavits or declarations if the attorney for the petitioner and the attorney for the ward or conservatee so stipulate and further stipulate that there remains no issue of fact to be determined.

(h) The court may make an order authorizing the recommended course of medical treatment of the ward or conservatee and authorizing the guardian or conservator to consent on behalf of the ward or conservatee to the recommended course of medical treatment for the ward or conservatee if the court determines from the evidence all of the following:

(1) The existing or continuing medical condition of the ward or conservatee requires the recommended course of medical treatment.

(2) If untreated, there is a probability that the condition will become life-endangering or result in a serious threat to the physical or mental health of the ward or conservatee.

(3) The ward or conservatee is unable to give an informed consent to the recommended course of treatment.

(i) Upon petition of the ward or conservatee or other interested person, the court may order that the guardian or conservator obtain or consent to, or obtain and consent to, specified medical treatment to be performed upon the ward or conservatee. Notice of the hearing on the petition under this subdivision shall be given for the period and in the manner provided in Chapter 3 (commencing with Section 1460) of Part 1. *(Stats.1990, c. 79 (A.B.759), § 14, operative July 1, 1991. Amended by Stats.1990, c. 710 (S.B.1775), § 9, operative July 1, 1991; Stats.1999, c. 175 (A.B.239), § 2; Stats.2000, c. 135 (A.B.2539), § 143; Stats.2001, c. 893 (A.B.25), § 31.)*

Law Revision Commission Comments
1990 Enactment

Section 2357 continues Section 2357 of the repealed Probate Code without change. For general provisions, see Sections 1000–1004 (rules of practice), 1020–1023 (petitions and other papers), 1040–1050 (hearings and orders), 2103 (effect of final order). See also Sections 1021 (petition to be verified), 1041 (clerk to set petition for hearing). For general provisions relating to notice of hearing, see Sections 1200–1221, 1460–1469. See also Sections 1260–1265 (proof of giving notice), 2700–2702 (notice to persons who request special notice).

Section 2357 serves the same purpose as Section 5358.2 of the Welfare and Institutions Code (Lanterman–Petris–Short Act). But Section 2357 provides for notice to interested persons, for appointment of counsel to represent the ward or conservatee where necessary, for presentation to the court of medical affidavits showing the need for medical treatment, and for findings by the court before an order authorizing treatment is made.

Subdivision (i) has no counterpart in the Welfare and Institutions Code section. This subdivision covers the situation where the ward or conservatee or an interested person believes the ward or conservatee needs medical treatment which the guardian or conservator is unwilling to obtain or has failed to obtain.

As to powers and duties concerning medical treatment generally, see Sections 2252 (temporary guardian or conservator), 2353 (guardian), 2354–2355 (conservator). See also Section 2356 (limitations on application of chapter). For background on the provisions of this part, see the Comment to this part under the part heading. [20 Cal.L.Rev.Comm. Reports 1001 (1990)].

1990 Amendment

Section 2357 (enacted as a part of the new Probate Code by 1990 Cal.Stat. ch. 79 § 14) was amended by 1990 Cal.Stat. ch. 710 § 9. The amendment expanded subdivision (h)(2) to include a serious threat to mental health as a condition that justifies court authorization of medical treatment. See also Section 3208. For background on the 1990 amendment, see Recommendation Relating to Court-Authorized Medical Treatment, 20 Cal.L.Revision Comm'n Reports 537 (1990). [20 Cal.L.Rev.Comm. Reports 1001 (1990)].

Cross References

Adjudication of lack of capacity to give informed consent for medical treatment, see Probate Code § 1880.
Affidavits, see Code of Civil Procedure §§ 2003, 2009 et seq.
Computation of time, see Code of Civil Procedure §§ 12 and 12a; Government Code § 6800 et seq.
Counsel, right to, see Cal. Const. Art. 1, § 15, Cl. 3.
Domestic partner, defined, see Probate Code § 37.
Effect of court authorization, see Probate Code § 2103.
Interested person, defined, see Probate Code § 1424.
Medical treatment,
  Conservatee not adjudicated to lack capacity to give informed consent, see Probate Code § 2354.
  Ward, see Probate Code § 2353.
Temporary guardians and conservators, generally, see Probate Code § 2250 et seq.

§ 2358. Additional conditions in order of appointment

When a guardian or conservator is appointed, the court may, with the consent of the guardian or conservator, insert in the order of appointment conditions not otherwise obligatory providing for the care, treatment, education, and welfare of the ward or conservatee. Any such conditions shall be included in the letters. The performance of such conditions is a part of the duties of the guardian or conservator for the faithful performance of which the guardian or conservator and the sureties on the bond are responsible. *(Stats.1990, c. 79 (A.B.759), § 14, operative July 1, 1991.)*

Law Revision Commission Comments
1990 Enactment

Section 2358 continues Section 2358 of the repealed Probate Code without substantive change. See Section 52 (defining "letters"). For background on the provisions of this part, see the Comment to this part under the part heading. [20 Cal.L.Rev.Comm. Reports 1001 (1990)].

Cross References

Additional powers of guardian nominated by will, see Probate Code § 2108.
Guardian or conservator, liability not limited to amount of bond, see Code of Civil Procedure § 996.470.
Letters, defined, see Probate Code § 52.
Nature of surety's liability, see Code of Civil Procedure § 996.470.
Suit against sureties on bond, see Probate Code § 2333.

§ 2359. Petitions of guardian, conservator, ward or conservatee; approval of purchase, lease, or rental of property from estate; violations of section

(a) Upon petition of the guardian or conservator or ward or conservatee or other interested person, the court may authorize and instruct the guardian or conservator or approve and confirm the acts of the guardian or conservator.

(b) Notice of the hearing on the petition shall be given for the period and in the manner provided in Chapter 3 (commencing with Section 1460) of Part 1.

(c)(1) When a guardian or conservator petitions for the approval of a purchase, lease, or rental of real or personal property from the estate of a ward or conservatee, the guardian or conservator shall provide a statement disclosing the family or affiliate relationship between the guardian and conservator and the purchaser, lessee, or renter of the property, and the family or affiliate relationship between the guardian or conservator and any agent hired by the guardian or conservator.

(2) For the purposes of this subdivision, "family" means a person's spouse, domestic partner, or relatives within the second degree of lineal or collateral consanguinity of a person or a person's spouse. For the purposes of this subdivision, "affiliate" means an entity that is under the direct control, indirect control, or common control of the guardian or conservator.

(3) A violation of this section shall result in the rescission of the purchase, lease, or rental of the property. Any losses incurred by the estate of the ward or conservatee because the property was sold or leased at less than fair market value shall be deemed as charges against the guardian or conservator under the provisions of Sections 2401.3 and 2401.5. The court shall assess a civil penalty equal to three times the charges against the guardian, conservator, or other person in violation of this section, and may assess punitive damages as it deems proper. If the estate does not incur losses as a result of the violation, the court shall order the guardian, conservator, or other person in violation of this section to pay a fine of up to five thousand dollars ($5,000) for each violation. The fines and penalties provided in this section are in addition to any other rights and remedies provided by law. *(Stats.1990, c. 79 (A.B.759), § 14, operative July 1, 1991. Amended by Stats.2000, c. 565 (A.B.1950), § 5; Stats.2001, c. 893 (A.B.25), § 32.)*

Law Revision Commission Comments
1990 Enactment

Section 2359 continues Section 2359 of the repealed Probate Code without change. For general provisions, see Sections 1000–1004 (rules of practice), 1020–1023 (petitions and other papers), 1040–1050 (hearings and orders), 2103 (effect of final order). See also Sections 1021 (petition to be verified), 1041 (clerk to set petition for hearing). For general provisions relating to notice of hearing, see Sections 1200–1221, 1460–1469. See also Sections 1260–1265 (proof of giving notice), 2700–2702 (notice to persons who request special notice). For background on the provisions of this part, see the Comment to this part under the part heading. [20 Cal.L.Rev.Comm. Reports 1001 (1990)].

Cross References

Domestic partner, defined, see Probate Code § 37.

Effect of court authorization, approval or confirmation, see Probate Code § 2103.

Guardianship and conservatorship, interested person, defined, see Probate Code § 1424.

§ 2360.   Photograph of conservatee

Upon the establishment of a conservatorship by the court and annually thereafter, the conservator shall ensure that a clear photograph of the conservatee is taken and preserved for the purpose of identifying the conservatee if he or she becomes missing. *(Added by Stats.2010, c. 97 (A.B.2493), § 1.)*

§ 2361.   Notice of conservatee's death

A conservator shall provide notice of a conservatee's death by mailing a copy of the notice to all persons entitled to notice under Section 1460 and by filing a proof of service with the court, unless otherwise ordered by the court. *(Added by Stats.2015, c. 92 (A.B.1085), § 3, eff. Jan. 1, 2016.)*

CHAPTER 6.   POWERS AND DUTIES OF GUARDIAN OR CONSERVATOR OF THE ESTATE

Cross References

Conservatorship for gravely disabled persons, general and special powers, see Welfare and Institutions Code § 5357.

Court-ordered termination of guardianship over minor's estate where sole asset is money, deposit of funds with county treasurer, see Probate Code § 3412.

Court-orders relating to minors and persons with a disability who are paid money or property but lack guardianship or conservatorship over the estate, order to deposit with county treasurer the remaining balances of money paid or to be paid, see Probate Code § 3611.

Court-orders relating to minors having monetary estates but no guardian, order to deposit funds with county treasurer, see Probate Code § 3413.

ARTICLE 1.   DEFINITIONS AND GENERAL PROVISIONS

Cross References

Application of old and new law, see Probate Code § 3.

§ 2400.   Definitions

As used in this chapter:

(a) "Conservator" means the conservator of the estate, or the limited conservator of the estate to the extent that the powers and duties of the limited conservator are specifically and expressly provided by the order appointing the limited conservator.

(b) "Estate" means all of the conservatee's or ward's personal property, wherever located, and real property located in this state.

(c) "Guardian" means the guardian of the estate. *(Stats. 1990, c. 79 (A.B.759), § 14, operative July 1, 1991. Amended by Stats.2008, c. 52 (A.B.2014), § 2.)*

Law Revision Commission Comments

1990 Enactment

Section 2400 continues Section 2400 of the repealed Probate Code without change. This chapter deals with powers and duties of a guardian or conservator of the estate. The definitions provided by Section 2400 permit shorthand reference in this chapter to such a guardian or conservator. If one person is appointed as conservator of the person and estate or as guardian of the person and estate, that person has the powers and duties conferred by this chapter. For background on the provisions of this part, see the Comment to this part under the part heading. [20 Cal.L.Rev.Comm. Reports 1001 (1990)].

Cross References

Appointment of limited conservator, see Probate Code §§ 1801, 1828.5.

Order appointing limited conservator for developmentally disabled adult, see Probate Code § 1830.

§ 2401. Management and control of estate; ordinary care and diligence

(a) The guardian or conservator, or limited conservator to the extent specifically and expressly provided in the appointing court's order, has the management and control of the estate and, in managing and controlling the estate, shall use ordinary care and diligence. What constitutes use of ordinary care and diligence is determined by all the circumstances of the particular estate.

(b) The guardian or conservator:

(1) Shall exercise a power to the extent that ordinary care and diligence requires that the power be exercised.

(2) Shall not exercise a power to the extent that ordinary care and diligence requires that the power not be exercised.

(c) Notwithstanding any other law, a guardian or conservator who is not a trust company, in exercising his or her powers, may not hire or refer any business to an entity in which he or she has a financial interest except upon authorization of the court. Prior to authorization from the court, the guardian or conservator shall disclose to the court in writing his or her financial interest in the entity. For the purposes of this subdivision, "financial interest" shall mean (1) an ownership interest in a sole proprietorship, a partnership, or a closely held corporation, or (2) an ownership interest of greater than 1 percent of the outstanding shares in a publicly held corporation, or (3) being an officer or a director of a corporation.

(d) Notwithstanding any other law, a guardian or conservator who is a trust company, in exercising its powers may not, except upon authorization of the court, invest in securities of the trust company or an affiliate or subsidiary, or other securities from which the trust company or affiliate or subsidiary receives a financial benefit or in a mutual fund, other than a mutual fund authorized in paragraph (5) of subdivision (a) of Section 2574, registered under the Investment Company Act of 1940 (Subchapter 1 (commencing with Sec. 80a–1) of Chapter 2D of Title 15 of the United States Code), to which the trust company or its affiliate provides services, including, but not limited to, services as an investment adviser, sponsor, distributor, custodian, agent, registrar, administrator, servicer, or manager, and for which the trust company or its affiliate receives compensation.

Prior to authorization from the court, the guardian or conservator shall disclose to the court in writing the trust company's financial interest. *(Stats.1990, c. 79 (A.B.759), § 14, operative July 1, 1991. Amended by Stats.2000, c. 565 (A.B.1950), § 6; Stats.2006, c. 493 (A.B.1363), § 21.)*

Law Revision Commission Comments
1990 Enactment

Section 2401 continues Section 2401 of the repealed Probate Code without change. Section 2401 supplements Section 2101 (relationship of guardian and ward and conservator and conservatee is a fiduciary relationship). The standard in subdivision (a) of Section 2401 is consistent with trust principles (see Section 16040), but recognizes that what is ordinary care and diligence varies with the circumstances of each case. In determining what constitutes ordinary care and diligence, a professional guardian or conservator (such

as a trust company or the trust department of a bank) will be held to a greater standard of care based on its presumed expertise than a lay guardian or conservator. Cf. Estate of Beach, 15 Cal.3d 623, 542 P.2d 994, 125 Cal.Rptr. 570 (1975) (executor). Section 2401 applies to all powers and duties of the guardian or conservator, whether or not prior court authorization is required. But see Section 2103 (effect of court authorization or approval). See also Section 2650 (failure to use ordinary case and diligence in management of estate, or continued failure to perform duties or incapacity to perform duties suitably, or having adverse interest, among causes for removal of guardian or conservator).

The duty of management and control stated in subdivision (a) requires that the conservator act diligently in marshaling, taking possession of, and making an inventory of the conservatee's assets. This obligation is imposed on the conservator whether or not the court makes an order under Section 1873 authorizing the conservatee to enter into certain kinds of transactions. As to community property, see Section 3051.

Subdivision (b) of Section 2401 makes clear that ordinary care and diligence may require that the guardian or conservator exercise a power. For example, the guardian or conservator may fail to exercise ordinary care and diligence under the circumstances of the particular estate if the guardian or conservator fails to secure insurance to cover the risk of loss of property of the estate. Subdivision (b) also makes clear that the extent to which a power should be exercised is limited to what is required by the exercise of ordinary care and diligence under all circumstances. Thus, for example, in purchasing insurance covering the estate property, the guardian or conservator should not purchase an amount in excess of the amount that would be purchased using ordinary care and diligence in the management and control of the estate. See also the Comment to Section 2451 (collection of debts). See also Sections 2403 (court may authorize and instruct guardian or conservator or approve and confirm acts of guardian or conservator), 2625 (review of sales, purchases and other transactions not previously authorized or approved at time of accounting).

For a comparable provision for decedents' estates, see Section 9600. For background on the provisions of this part, see the Comment to this part under the part heading. [20 Cal.L.Rev.Comm. Reports 1001 (1990)].

Cross References

Community property, management and control, see Probate Code § 3051.

Inventory and accounting by guardian or conservator, generally, see Probate Code § 2600 et seq.

Review of sales, purchases and other transactions upon accounting, see Probate Code § 2625.

§ 2401.1. Real property located in foreign jurisdiction; guardian or conservator use of ordinary care and diligence in determination of ownership

The guardian or conservator shall use ordinary care and diligence to determine whether the ward or conservatee owns real property in a foreign jurisdiction and to preserve and protect that property. What constitutes use of ordinary care and diligence shall be determined by all the facts and circumstances known, or that become known, to the guardian or conservator, the value of the real property located in the foreign jurisdiction, and the needs of the ward or conservatee. The guardian or conservator, except as provided in subdivision (a) of Section 1061 and in Section 1062, is not charged with, and shall have no duty to inventory or account for the real property located in a foreign jurisdiction, but the guardian or conservator shall, when presenting the inventory and appraisal and accounting to the court, include the schedule set forth in subdivision (h) of Section 1063. *(Added by Stats.2008, c. 52 (A.B.2014), § 3.)*

§ 2401.3. Breach of fiduciary duty; liability

(a) If the guardian or conservator breaches a fiduciary duty, the guardian or conservator is chargeable with any of the following that is appropriate under the circumstances:

(1) Any loss or depreciation in value of the estate resulting from the breach of duty, with interest.

(2) Any profit made by the guardian or conservator through the breach of duty, with interest.

(3) Any profit that would have accrued to the estate if the loss of profit is the result of the breach of duty.

(b) If the guardian or conservator has acted reasonably and in good faith under the circumstances as known to the guardian or conservator, the court, in its discretion, may excuse the guardian or conservator in whole or in part from liability under subdivision (a) if it would be equitable to do so. *(Stats.1990, c. 79 (A.B.759), § 14, operative July 1, 1991.)*

Law Revision Commission Comments

1990 Enactment

Section 2401.3 is a new provision that is comparable to Sections 9601 (decedents' estates) and 16440 (trusts). See the Comments to those sections. See also Section 2401.7 (other remedies not affected). [20 Cal.L.Rev.Comm. Reports 1001 (1990)].

Cross References

Fiduciary, defined, see Probate Code § 39.

§ 2401.5. Breach of fiduciary duty; interest liability calculation; excuse from liability

(a) If the guardian or conservator is liable for interest pursuant to Section 2401.3, the guardian or conservator is liable for the greater of the following amounts:

(1) The amount of interest that accrues at the legal rate on judgments.

(2) The amount of interest actually received.

(b) If the guardian or conservator has acted reasonably and in good faith under the circumstances as known to the guardian or conservator, the court, in its discretion, may excuse the guardian or conservator in whole or in part from liability under subdivision (a) if it would be equitable to do so. *(Stats.1990, c. 79 (A.B.759), § 14, operative July 1, 1991. Amended by Stats.1998, c. 77 (S.B.1841), § 2.)*

Law Revision Commission Comments

1990 Enactment

Section 2401.5 is a new provision that is comparable to Sections 9602 (decedents' estates) and 16441 (trusts). See the Comments to those sections. [20 Cal.L.Rev.Comm. Reports 1001 (1990)].

Cross References

Personal representatives, duties and liabilities, interest and excuse, see Probate Code § 9602.

Trustees, measure of liability, interest and excuse, see Probate Code § 16441.

§ 2401.6. Surcharge; offset against future fees prohibited

Any surcharge that a guardian or conservator incurs under the provisions of Sections 2401.3 or 2401.5 may not be paid by or offset against future fees or wages to be provided by the estate to the guardian or conservator. *(Added by Stats.2000, c. 565 (A.B.1950), § 7.)*

§ 2401.7. Breach of fiduciary duty; additional remedies

The provisions of Sections 2401.3 and 2401.5 for liability of a guardian or conservator for breach of a fiduciary duty do not prevent resort to any other remedy available against the guardian or conservator under the statutory or common law. *(Stats.1990, c. 79 (A.B.759), § 14, operative July 1, 1991.)*

Law Revision Commission Comments

1990 Enactment

Section 2401.7 is a new provision that is comparable to Sections 9603 (decedents' estates) and 16443 (trusts). See the Comments to those sections. [20 Cal.L.Rev.Comm. Reports 1001 (1990)].

§ 2402. Additional conditions in order of appointment

When a guardian or conservator is appointed, the court may, with the consent of the guardian or conservator, insert in the order of appointment conditions not otherwise obligatory providing for the care and custody of the property of the ward or conservatee. Any such conditions shall be included in the letters. The performance of such conditions is a part of the duties of the guardian or conservator for the faithful performance of which the guardian or conservator and the sureties on the bond are responsible. *(Stats.1990, c. 79 (A.B.759), § 14, operative July 1, 1991.)*

Law Revision Commission Comments

1990 Enactment

Section 2402 continues Section 2402 of the repealed Probate Code without substantive change. See Section 52 ("letters" defined). For background on the provisions of this part, see the Comment to this part under the part heading. [20 Cal.L.Rev.Comm. Reports 1001 (1990)].

Cross References

Bonds of guardians or conservators, see Probate Code § 2320 et seq.
Letters, generally, see Probate Code § 2310 et seq.
Letters, defined, see Probate Code § 52.
Nature of surety's liability, see Code of Civil Procedure § 996.470.

§ 2403. Instructions from or confirmation by court; petitions for approval or purchase, lease, or rental of property from estate

(a) Upon petition of the guardian or conservator, the ward or conservatee, a creditor, or other interested person, the court may authorize and instruct the guardian or conservator, or approve and confirm the acts of the guardian or conservator, in the administration, management, investment, disposition, care, protection, operation, or preservation of the estate, or the incurring or payment of costs, fees, or expenses in connection therewith.

(b) Notice of the hearing on the petition shall be given for the period and in the manner provided in Chapter 3 (commencing with Section 1460) of Part 1.

(c)(1) When a guardian or conservator petitions for the approval of a purchase, lease, or rental of real or personal property from the estate of a ward or conservatee, the guardian or conservator shall provide a statement disclosing the family or affiliate relationship between the guardian and conservator and the purchaser, lessee, or renter of the property, and the family or affiliate relationship between the guardian or conservator and any agent hired by the guardian or conservator.

(2) For the purposes of this subdivision, "family" means a person's spouse, domestic partner, or relatives within the second degree of lineal or collateral consanguinity of a person or a person's spouse. For the purposes of this subdivision, "affiliate" means an entity that is under the direct control, indirect control, or common control of the guardian or conservator.

(3) A violation of this section shall result in the rescission of the purchase, lease, or rental of the property. Any losses incurred by the estate of the ward or conservatee because the property was sold or leased at less than fair market value shall be deemed as charges against the guardian or conservator under the provisions of Sections 2401.3 and 2401.5. The court shall assess a civil penalty equal to three times the charges against the guardian, conservator, or other person in violation of this section, and may assess punitive damages as it deems proper. If the estate does not incur losses as a result of the violation, the court shall order the guardian, conservator, or other person in violation of this section to pay a fine of up to five thousand dollars ($5,000) for each violation. The fines and penalties provided in this section are in addition to any other rights and remedies provided by law. *(Stats.1990, c. 79 (A.B.759), § 14, operative July 1, 1991. Amended by Stats.2000, c. 565 (A.B.1950), § 8; Stats.2001, c. 893 (A.B.25), § 33.)*

Law Revision Commission Comments

1990 Enactment

Section 2403 continues Section 2403 of the repealed Probate Code without change. This section authorizes the court not only to instruct the conservator in advance but also to confirm actions already taken. See *Place v. Trent,* 27 Cal.App.3d 526, 103 Cal.Rptr. 841 (1972). See also Sections 2625 (review of sales, purchases, and other transactions at time of accounting), 2750 (order authorizing or instructing or approving and confirming acts an appealable order). As to the compensation of the guardian or conservator and attorney in connection with obtaining authorization or instructions on a matter not requiring court authorization, see the Comment to Section 2640. For a comparable provision relating to decedents' estates, see Section 9611. For general provisions, see Sections 1000–1004 (rules of practice), 1020–1023 (petitions and other papers), 1040–1050 (hearings and orders), 2103 (effect of final order). See also Sections 1021 (petition to be verified), 1041 (clerk to set petition for hearing). For general provisions relating to notice of hearing, see Sections 1200–1221, 1460–1469. See also Sections 1260–1265 (proof of giving notice), 2700–2702 (notice to persons who request special notice). For background on the provisions of this part, see the Comment to this part under the part heading. [20 Cal.L.Rev. Comm. Reports 1001 (1990)].

Cross References

Compensation of guardian, conservator, and attorney, see Probate Code § 2640 et seq.

Domestic partner, defined, see Probate Code § 37.

Guardian for particular property and guardian of the estate, allocation of powers and duties, see Probate Code § 2109.

Interested person, defined, see Probate Code § 1424.

Payment of debts and expenses, guardian or conservator of the estate, petition for instructions, see Probate Code §§ 2430, 2431, 2500.

Support, maintenance and education of ward or conservatee, see Probate Code § 2420.

§ 2404. Order compelling guardian or conservator to pay support or debts

(a) If the guardian or conservator fails, neglects, or refuses to furnish comfortable and suitable support, maintenance, or education for the ward or conservatee as required by this division, or to pay a debt, expense, or charge lawfully due and payable by the ward or conservatee or the estate as provided in this division, the court shall, upon petition or upon its own motion, order the guardian or conservator to do so from the estate.

(b) The petition may be filed by the ward or conservatee or by the creditor or any other interested person. Notice of the hearing on the petition shall be given for the period and in the manner provided in Chapter 3 (commencing with Section 1460) of Part 1. *(Stats.1990, c. 79 (A.B.759), § 14, operative July 1, 1991.)*

Law Revision Commission Comments

1990 Enactment

Section 2404 continues Section 2404 of the repealed Probate Code without change. For general provisions relating to notice of hearing, see Sections 1200–1221, 1460–1469. See also Sections 1260–1265 (proof of giving notice), 2700–2702 (notice to persons who request special notice). For general provisions, see Sections 1000–1004 (rules of practice), 1020–1023 (petitions and other papers), 1040–1050 (hearings and orders), 2103 (effect of final order), 2750 (appealable orders). See also Sections 1021 (petition to be verified), 1041 (clerk to set petition for hearing). For background on the provisions of this part, see the Comment to this part under the part heading. [20 Cal.L.Rev.Comm. Reports 1001 (1990)].

Cross References

Guardianship and conservatorship, interested person, defined, see Probate Code § 1424.

§ 2405. Summary determination of disputes

If there is a dispute relating to the estate between the guardian or conservator and a third person, the guardian or conservator, or the limited conservator to the extent specifically and expressly provided in the order appointing the limited conservator, may do either of the following:

(a) Enter into an agreement in writing with the third person to refer the dispute to a temporary judge designated in the agreement. The agreement shall be filed with the clerk, who shall thereupon, with the approval of the court, enter an order referring the matter to the designated person. The temporary judge shall proceed promptly to hear and determine the matter in controversy by summary procedure, without any pleadings, discovery, or jury trial. The decision of the temporary judge is subject to Section 632 of the Code of Civil Procedure. Judgment shall be entered on the decision and is as valid and effective as if rendered by a judge of the court in an action against the guardian or conservator or the third person commenced by ordinary process.

(b) Enter into an agreement in writing with the third person that a judge of the court, pursuant to the agreement and with the written consent of the judge, both filed with the clerk within the time for bringing an independent action on the matter in dispute, may hear and determine the dispute pursuant to the procedure provided in subdivision (a). *(Stats.1990, c. 79 (A.B.759), § 14, operative July 1, 1991.)*

Law Revision Commission Comments
1990 Enactment

Section 2405 continues Section 2405 of the repealed Probate Code with nonsubstantive revisions. See also Section 2750 (appealable orders). For a comparable provision applicable to decedents' estates, see Section 9620.

Section 2405 is designed to reduce the cost of administration of estates and to ease the court's workload by encouraging settlement of disputes relating to the estate by summary proceedings rather than by litigation. See Review of Selected 1968 Code Legislation 226–27 (Cal.Cont.Ed.Bar 1968). Because of the binding effect of a decision under Section 2405, an agreement to submit a dispute for summary determination under the section requires approval of the court in which the guardianship or conservatorship proceeding is pending. See Section 1418 (defining "court").

Under Section 2405, any member of the State Bar (including a court commissioner or referee) may be appointed as a temporary judge. See also Code Civ.Proc. § 259(5) (power of court commissioner to act as temporary judge). Section 2405 does not require that the temporary judge try the matter in a regular courtroom; the temporary judge may try the matter at his or her office or other place.

Nothing in Section 2405 limits the alternative of reference and trial by a referee under Code of Civil Procedure Sections 638–645.1, and those provisions remain applicable to guardianship and conservatorship proceedings.

For background on the provisions of this part, see the Comment to this part under the part heading. [20 Cal.L.Rev.Comm. Reports 1001 (1990)].

§ 2406. Submission of dispute to arbitration

If there is a dispute relating to the estate between the guardian or conservator and a third person, the guardian or conservator may enter into an agreement in writing with the third person to submit the dispute to arbitration under Title 9 (commencing with Section 1280) of Part 3 of the Code of Civil Procedure. The agreement is not effective unless it has first been approved by the court and a copy of the approved agreement is filed with the court. *(Stats.1990, c. 79 (A.B. 759), § 14, operative July 1, 1991.)*

Law Revision Commission Comments
1990 Enactment

Section 2406 continues Section 2406 of the repealed Probate Code without change. This section makes clear that the guardian or conservator may use arbitration to resolve a dispute. Because of the binding effect of a decision under Section 2406, an agreement to submit a controversy to arbitration under the section requires approval of the court in which the guardianship or conservatorship proceeding is pending. See Section 1418 (defining "court").

Section 2406 has the same scope as the rule applicable to decedents' estates. See Section 9621 and the Comment thereto.

For background on the provisions of this part, see the Comment to this part under the part heading. [20 Cal.L.Rev.Comm. Reports 1001 (1990)].

Cross References

Appeals from order in arbitration, see Code of Civil Procedure §§ 1294, 1294.2.
Arbitration, generally, see Code of Civil Procedure § 1281 et seq.

§ 2407. Application of chapter to community property

This chapter applies to property owned by * * * spouses as community property only to the extent authorized by Part 6 (commencing with Section 3000). *(Stats.1990, c. 79 (A.B. 759), § 14, operative July 1, 1991. Amended by Stats.2016, c. 50 (S.B.1005), § 82, eff. Jan. 1, 2017.)*

Law Revision Commission Comments
1990 Enactment

Section 2407 continues Section 2407 of the repealed Probate Code without change. For background on the provisions of this part, see the Comment to this part under the part heading. [20 Cal.L.Rev. Comm. Reports 1001 (1990)].

Cross References

Community property, generally, see Family Code §§ 65, 760.
Community property, succession as to, see Probate Code §§ 100, 6101, 6401.
Definitions, community property, see Probate Code §§ 28 and 3002; Civil Code § 687.

§ 2408. Construction with other laws

Nothing in this chapter limits or restricts any authority granted to a guardian or conservator pursuant to Article 11 (commencing with Section 2590) to administer the estate under that article. *(Stats.1990, c. 79 (A.B.759), § 14, operative July 1, 1991.)*

Law Revision Commission Comments
1990 Enactment

Section 2408 is a new provision, not found in the repealed Probate Code, that is drawn from Section 9640 (decedents' estates). The section makes clear that this chapter does not limit the authority of the guardian or conservator under the independent exercise of powers provisions. [20 Cal.L.Rev.Comm. Reports 1001 (1990)].

§ 2410. Uniform standards of conduct

On or before January 1, 2008, the Judicial Council, in consultation with the California Judges Association, the California Association of Superior Court Investigators, the California State Association of Public Administrators, Public Guardians, and Public Conservators, the State Bar of California, the National Guardianship Association, and the Association of Professional Geriatric Care Managers, shall adopt a rule of court that shall require uniform standards of conduct for actions that conservators and guardians may take under this chapter on behalf of conservatees and wards to ensure that the estate of conservatees or wards are maintained and conserved as appropriate and to prevent risk of loss or harm to the conservatees or wards. This rule shall include at a minimum standards for determining the fees that may be charged to conservatees or wards and standards for asset management. *(Added by Stats.2006, c. 493 (A.B.1363), § 22.)*

ARTICLE 2. SUPPORT AND MAINTENANCE OF WARD OR CONSERVATEE AND DEPENDENTS

Section

Cross References

Application of old and new law, see Probate Code § 3.

§ 2420. Support, maintenance and education

(a) Subject to Section 2422, the guardian or conservator shall apply the income from the estate, so far as necessary, to the comfortable and suitable support, maintenance, and education of the ward or conservatee (including care, treatment, and support of a ward or conservatee who is a patient in a state hospital under the jurisdiction of the State Department of State Hospitals or the State Department of Developmental Services) and of those legally entitled to support, maintenance, or education from the ward or conservatee, taking into account the value of the estate and the condition of life of the persons required to be furnished such support, maintenance, or education.

(b) If the income from the estate is insufficient for the purpose described in subdivision (a), the guardian or conservator may sell or give a security interest in or other lien on any personal property of the estate, or sell or mortgage or give a deed of trust on any real property of the estate, as provided in this part.

(c) When the amount paid by the guardian or conservator for the purpose described in subdivision (a) satisfies the standard set out in that subdivision, and the payments are supported by proper vouchers or other proof satisfactory to the court, the guardian or conservator shall be allowed credit for such payments when the accounts of the guardian or conservator are settled.

(d) Nothing in this section requires the guardian or conservator to obtain court authorization before making the payments authorized by this section, but nothing in this section dispenses with the need to obtain any court authorization otherwise required for a particular transaction.

(e) Nothing in this section precludes the guardian or conservator from seeking court authorization or instructions or approval and confirmation pursuant to Section 2403. *(Stats.1990, c. 79 (A.B.759), § 14, operative July 1, 1991. Amended by Stats.2012, c. 440 (A.B.1488), § 44, eff. Sept. 22, 2012.)*

Law Revision Commission Comments

1990 Enactment

Section 2420 continues Section 2420 of the repealed Probate Code without change. As to subdivision (b), see Sections 2541, 2551 (sale or encumbrance of property).

Section 2420 does not require that the guardian or conservator obtain court authorization to make payments for the purposes specified in subdivision (a). See subdivision (d). However many guardians and conservators seek court authorization in advance (as authorized under Section 2403) for providing a monthly sum for support and maintenance of the ward or conservatee and dependents. See W. Johnstone, G. Zillgitt, & S. House, California Conservatorships § 6.40, at 331 (Cal.Cont.Ed.Bar 2d ed. 1983 & Supp.1989). See also Sections 2111 (orders for sale or encumbrance of property), 2750 (appealable orders).

Subdivision (e) makes clear that the guardian or conservator may obtain advance authority for payments, and may seek any other court authorizations, instructions, approvals, or confirmations that the circumstances require.

For background on the provisions of this part, see the Comment to this part under the part heading. [20 Cal.L.Rev.Comm. Reports 1001 (1990)].

Cross References

Authority to exchange property, see Probate Code § 2557.
Borrowing money and giving security, see Probate Code § 2551.
Duty to support and maintain ward or conservatee in state hospital, see Welfare and Institutions Code §§ 7275, 7279.
Instructions from or confirmation by court, see Probate Code § 2403.
Mentally disordered in state institutions, care and maintenance by guardian or conservator, see Welfare and Institutions Code §§ 7275, 7278, 7281, 7282.
Order authorizing support from estate where third party liable for support, see Probate Code § 2422.
Payment or settlement of debts by guardian or conservator, see Probate Code §§ 2430, 2500.
Powers and duties of guardians or conservators of the person generally, see Probate Code § 2350 et seq.
Review on settlement of accounts, see Probate Code § 2625.
Sale of estate property, see Probate Code § 2541.

§ 2421. Allowance for ward or conservatee

(a) Upon petition of the guardian or conservator or the ward or conservatee, the court may authorize the guardian or conservator to pay to the ward or conservatee out of the estate a reasonable allowance for the personal use of the ward or conservatee. The allowance shall be in such amount as the court may determine to be for the best interests of the ward or conservatee.

(b) Notice of the hearing on the petition shall be given for the period and in the manner provided in Chapter 3 (commencing with Section 1460) of Part 1.

(c) The guardian or conservator is not required to account for such allowance other than to establish that it has been paid to the ward or conservatee. The funds so paid are subject to the sole control of the ward or conservatee. *(Stats.1990, c. 79 (A.B.759), § 14, operative July 1, 1991.)*

Law Revision Commission Comments

1990 Enactment

Section 2421 continues Section 2421 of the repealed Probate Code without change. If the court makes an order under Section 2421, the allowance paid to the ward or conservatee is subject to the sole control of the ward or conservatee. See generally W. Johnstone, G. Zillgitt, & S. House, California Conservatorships § 6.49, at 342–43 (Cal.Cont.Ed.Bar 2d ed. 1983 & Supp.1989). For general provisions, see Sections 1000–1004 (rules of practice), 1020–1023 (petitions and other papers), 1040–1050 (hearings and orders), 2103 (effect of final order). See also Sections 1021 (petition to be verified), 1041 (clerk to set petition for hearing). For general provisions relating to notice of hearing, see Sections 1200–1221, 1460–1469. See also Sections 1260–1265 (proof of giving notice), 2700–2702 (notice to persons who request special notice). For background on the provisions of this part, see the Comment to this part under the part heading. [20 Cal.L.Rev.Comm. Reports 1001 (1990)].

Cross References

Right of conservatee to control allowance, legal capacity, see Probate Code § 1871.

Wages of ward or conservatee, see Probate Code § 2601.

§ 2422. Order authorizing support notwithstanding third party liability

(a) Upon petition of the guardian or conservator, the ward or conservatee, or any other interested person, the court may for good cause order the ward or conservatee to be wholly or partially supported, maintained, or educated out of the estate notwithstanding the existence of a third party legally obligated to provide such support, maintenance, or education. Such order may be made for a limited period of time. If not so limited, it continues in effect until modified or revoked.

(b) Notice of the hearing on the petition shall be given for the period and in the manner provided in Chapter 3 (commencing with Section 1460) of Part 1. *(Stats.1990, c. 79 (A.B.759), § 14, operative July 1, 1991.)*

Law Revision Commission Comments

1990 Enactment

Section 2422 continues Section 2422 of the repealed Probate Code without change. To accomplish the purposes of this section, the guardian or conservator may use income of the estate and, if necessary, may sell or encumber estate property. See Sections 2420, 2541, 2551. For general provisions, see Sections 1000–1004 (rules of practice), 1020–1023 (petitions and other papers), 1040–1050 (hearings and orders), 2103 (effect of final order), 2750 (appealable orders). See also Sections 1021 (petition to be verified), 1041 (clerk to set petition for hearing). For general provisions relating to notice of hearing, see Sections 1200–1221, 1460–1469. See also Sections 1260–1265 (proof of giving notice), 2700–2702 (notice to persons who request special notice). For background on the provisions of this part, see the Comment to this part under the part heading. [20 Cal.L.Rev.Comm. Reports 1001 (1990)].

Cross References

Guardianship and conservatorship, interested person, defined, see Probate Code § 1424.
Notice to,
 Director of State Hospitals or Director of Developmental Services, see Probate Code § 1461.
 Veterans Administration, see Probate Code § 1461.5.
Use of income from the estate for support, see Probate Code § 2420.

§ 2423. Payment of surplus income to relatives of conservatee

(a) Upon petition of the conservator, the conservatee, the spouse or domestic partner of the conservatee, or a relative within the second degree of the conservatee, the court may by order authorize or direct the conservator to pay and distribute surplus income of the estate or any part of the surplus income (not used for the support, maintenance, and education of the conservatee and of those legally entitled to support, maintenance, or education from the conservatee) to the spouse or domestic partner of the conservatee and to relatives within the second degree of the conservatee whom the conservatee would, in the judgment of the court, have aided but for the existence of the conservatorship. The court in ordering payments under this section may impose conditions if the court determines that the conservatee would have imposed the conditions if the conservatee had the capacity to act.

(b) The granting of the order and the amounts and proportions of the payments are discretionary with the court, but the court shall consider all of the following:

(1) The amount of surplus income available after adequate provision has been made for the comfortable and suitable support, maintenance, and education of the conservatee and of those legally entitled to support, maintenance, or education from the conservatee.

(2) The circumstances and condition of life to which the conservatee and the spouse or domestic partner and relatives have been accustomed.

(3) The amount that the conservatee would in the judgment of the court have allowed the spouse or domestic partner and relatives but for the existence of the conservatorship.

(c) Notice of the hearing on the petition shall be given for the period and in the manner provided in Chapter 3 (commencing with Section 1460) of Part 1. *(Stats.1990, c. 79 (A.B.759), § 14, operative July 1, 1991. Amended by Stats. 2001, c. 893 (A.B.25), § 34.)*

Law Revision Commission Comments

1990 Enactment

Section 2423 continues Section 2423 of the repealed Probate Code without substantive change. "Suitable" is substituted for "proper" in subdivision (b(1) to conform to Sections 2420(a) and 2541(a). Section 2423 makes clear that income is not "surplus" if needed for those legally entitled to support from the conservatee. An order granting or denying a petition under this section is an appealable order. See Section 2750. See also Sections 2580–2585 (substituted judgment) which permit gifts to persons other than the spouse and relatives, and gifts of principal as well as income. Unlike other powers and duties in this chapter, Section 2423 applies only to conservatorships and not to guardianships. For general provisions, see Sections 1000–1004 (rules of practice), 1020–1023 (petitions and other papers), 1040–1050 (hearings and orders), 2103 (effect of final order). See also Sections 1021 (petition to be verified), 1041 (clerk to set petition for hearing). For general provisions relating to notice of hearing, see Sections 1200–1221, 1460–1469. See also Sections 1260–1265 (proof of giving notice), 2700–2702 (notice to persons who request special notice). For background on the provisions of this part, see the Comment to this part under the part heading. [20 Cal.L.Rev.Comm. Reports 1001 (1990)].

Cross References

Domestic partner, defined, see Probate Code § 37.
Notice to,
 Directors, see Probate Code § 1461.
 Veterans Administration, see Probate Code § 1461.5.
Support of ward's dependents, see Probate Code §§ 2420, 2541.

ARTICLE 3. PAYMENT OF DEBTS AND EXPENSES

Cross References
Application of old and new law, see Probate Code § 3.

§ 2430. Payments from principal and income; debts and expenses

(a) Subject to subdivisions (b) and (c), the guardian or conservator shall pay the following from any principal and income of the estate:

(1) The debts incurred by the ward or conservatee before creation of the guardianship or conservatorship, giving priority to the debts described in Section 2431 to the extent required by that section.

(2) The debts incurred by the ward or conservatee during the guardianship or conservatorship to provide the necessaries of life to the ward or conservatee, and to the spouse and minor children of the ward or conservatee, to the extent the debt is reasonable. Also, the debts reasonably incurred by the conservatee during the conservatorship to provide the basic living expenses, as defined in Section 297 of the Family Code, to the domestic partner of the conservatee. The guardian or conservator may deduct the amount of any payments for these debts from any allowance otherwise payable to the ward or conservatee.

(3) In the case of a conservatorship, any other debt incurred by the conservatee during the conservatorship only if the debt satisfies the requirements of any order made under Chapter 4 (commencing with Section 1870) of Part 3.

(4) The reasonable expenses incurred in the collection, care, and administration of the estate, but court authorization is required for payment of compensation to any of the following:

(A) The guardian or conservator of the person or estate or both.

(B) An attorney for the guardian or conservator of the person or estate or both.

(C) An attorney for the ward or conservatee.

(D) An attorney for the estate.

(E) The public guardian for the costs and fee under Section 2902.

(b) The payments provided for by paragraph (3) of subdivision (a) are not required to be made to the extent the payments would impair the ability to provide the necessaries of life to the conservatee and the spouse and minor children of the conservatee and to provide the basic living expenses, as defined in Section 297 of the Family Code, of the domestic partner of the conservatee.

(c) The guardian or conservator may petition the court under Section 2403 for instructions when there is doubt whether a debt should be paid under this section. *(Stats. 1990, c. 79 (A.B.759), § 14, operative July 1, 1991. Amended by Stats.2001, c. 893 (A.B.25), § 35.)*

Law Revision Commission Comments

1990 Enactment

Section 2430 continues Section 2430 of the repealed Probate Code without change. An order directing or allowing payment of a debt or claim is an appealable order. See Section 2750. As to compensation of the guardian or conservator and the attorney when court instructions are sought, see the Comment to Section 2640. See also Section 2902 (right of public guardian to recover reasonable costs incurred for protection of property and reasonable compensation for services when another person subsequently appointed as guardian or conservator of the estate). For background on the provisions of this part, see the Comment to this part under the part heading. [20 Cal.L.Rev.Comm. Reports 1001 (1990)].

Cross References
Allowance for ward or conservatee, see Probate Code § 2421.
Attorney's fees and costs, generally, see Code of Civil Procedure § 1021.
Capacity of conservatee to bind or obligate conservatorship estate, see Probate Code § 1870 et seq.
Compensation and expenses of guardian or conservator or attorney, see Probate Code §§ 2623, 2640 et seq.
Compromise and settlement of claims, see Probate Code § 2500.
Domestic partner, defined, see Probate Code § 37.
Order compelling payment of debts, see Probate Code § 2404.
Review on settlement of accounts, see Probate Code § 2625.

§ 2431. Wage claims; priority

(a) Subject to subdivision (d), the guardian or conservator may petition the court under Section 2403 for instructions when there is doubt whether a wage claim should be paid under this section.

(b) The guardian or conservator shall promptly pay wage claims for work done or services rendered for the ward or conservatee within 30 days prior to the date the petition for appointment of the guardian or conservator was filed. The payments made pursuant to this subdivision shall not exceed nine hundred dollars ($900) to each claimant. If there is insufficient money to pay all the claims described in this subdivision up to nine hundred dollars ($900), the money available shall be distributed among such claimants in proportion to the amount of their respective claims.

(c) After the payments referred to in subdivision (b) have been made, the guardian or conservator shall pay wage claims for work done or services rendered for the ward or conservatee within 90 days prior to the date the petition for appointment of the guardian or conservator was filed, excluding the claims described in subdivision (b). The payments made pursuant to this subdivision shall not exceed one thousand one hundred dollars ($1,100) to each claimant. If there is insufficient money to pay all the claims described in this subdivision up to one thousand one hundred dollars ($1,100), the money available shall be distributed among such claimants in proportion to the amounts of their respective claims.

(d) The guardian or conservator may require sworn claims to be presented. If there is reasonable cause to believe that the claim is not valid, the guardian or conservator may refuse to pay the claim in whole or in part but shall pay any part thereof that is not disputed without prejudice to the claimant's rights as to the balance of the claim. The guardian or conservator shall withhold sufficient money to cover the disputed portion until the claimant has had a reasonable opportunity to establish the validity of the claim by bringing an action, either in the claimant's own name or through an assignee, against the guardian or conservator.

(e) If the guardian or conservator neglects or refuses to pay all or any portion of a claim which is not in dispute, the court shall order the guardian or conservator to do so upon the informal application of any wage claimant or the assignee or legal representative of such claimant. *(Stats.1990, c. 79 (A.B.759), § 14, operative July 1, 1991.)*

Law Revision Commission Comments

1990 Enactment

Section 2431 continues Section 2431 of the repealed Probate Code with an increase in the dollar amount of the priority wage claims, making a total of $2,000 that is given priority. This increase conforms the amount of the priority wage claims under Section 2431 to the amount given priority as a wage claim for decedents' estates. See Sections 11402, 11420, 11421 (decedents' estates). The balance of the wage claim not given priority under Section 2431 is payable under subdivision (a)(1) of Section 2430. Nothing in Section 2431 requires the guardian or conservator to obtain court authorization before making the payments required by the section. For general provisions, see Sections 1000–1004 (rules of practice), 1020–1023 (petitions and other papers), 1040–1050 (hearings and orders), 2103 (effect of final order). An order directing or allowing payment of a debt or claim is an appealable order. See Section 2750. For background on the provisions of this part, see the Comment to this part under the part heading. [20 Cal.L.Rev.Comm. Reports 1001 (1990)].

Cross References

Assignment of wages by minor, written consent of guardian required, see Labor Code § 300.
Instructions from or confirmation by court, see Probate Code § 2403.
Order compelling payment of debts, see Probate Code § 2404.
Payment of wages or debts,
　Generally, see Labor Code § 200 et seq.
　Claims in decedent's estates, see Probate Code § 11401 et seq.

ARTICLE 4. ESTATE MANAGEMENT POWERS GENERALLY

Section
2450. Extent of court supervision.
2451. Collection of debts and benefits.
2451.5. Powers of guardian or conservator.
2452. Checks, warrants and drafts.
2453. Financial institution insured account.
2453.5. Deposit of estate money in trust company department; interest rate.
2454. Deposit of personal property with trust company.
2455. Deposit of securities in securities depository.
2456. Deposits withdrawable only upon court authorization.
2457. Maintenance of home of ward or conservatee and dependents.
2458. Voting rights with respect to corporate shares, memberships or property.
2459. Life insurance, medical, retirement and other plans and benefits.
2460. Liability and casualty insurance.
2461. Taxes and tax returns.
2462. Representation in actions and proceedings.
2463. Partition actions.
2464. Acceptance of deed in lieu of foreclosure or trustee's sale.
2465. Abandonment of valueless property.
2466. Advances by guardian or conservator.
2467. Care of estate pending delivery to personal representative.
2468. Disabled attorney; petition for appointment; notice and hearing; contents; compensation; termination.

Cross References

Application of old and new law, see Probate Code § 3.

§ 2450. Extent of court supervision

(a) Unless this article specifically provides a proceeding to obtain court authorization or requires court authorization, the powers and duties set forth in this article may be exercised or performed by the guardian or conservator without court authorization, instruction, approval, or confirmation. Nothing in this subdivision precludes the guardian or conservator from seeking court authorization, instructions, approval, or confirmation pursuant to Section 2403.

(b) Upon petition of the ward or conservatee, a creditor, or any other interested person, or upon the court's own motion, the court may limit the authority of the guardian or conservator under subdivision (a) as to a particular power or duty or as to particular powers or duties. Notice of the hearing on a petition under this subdivision shall be given for the period and in the manner provided in Chapter 3 (commencing with Section 1460) of Part 1. *(Stats.1990, c. 79 (A.B.759), § 14, operative July 1, 1991.)*

Law Revision Commission Comments

1990 Enactment

Section 2450 continues Section 2450 of the repealed Probate Code without change. The exercise of all the powers in this article and the performance of all the duties in this article remain subject to the duty of the guardian or conservator to exercise ordinary care and diligence in the management of the estate. See Section 2401 and the Comment thereto. Subdivision (b) permits the court to impose other restrictions and conditions on the exercise of powers and duties under this article. See also Section 2403 (permitting the guardian or conservator to seek court authorization, instructions, approval, or confirmation for particular transactions), 2625 (review at time of accounting of sales, purchases, and other transactions not previously authorized or approved), 2750 (appealable orders).

The second sentence of subdivision (a) makes clear that a guardian or conservator may seek court authorization and instructions even though court authorization is not required before exercising a power. Examples of cases where such instructions might be sought can be found in the Comments to Sections 2451 and 2457. If the guardian or conservator is doubtful as to the proper action to take, the guardian or conservator may wish to obtain authorization under Section 2403 before acting or failing to act rather than risk that the court will find on settlement of the accounts that the guardian or conservator failed to use ordinary care and diligence in managing the estate. As to compensation of the guardian or conservator and the attorney in connection with obtaining instructions concerning the exercise of a power where court authorization is not required by statute, see the Comment to Section 2640. See also Section 2103 (effect of court authorization or approval).

The court may add to the list of powers exercisable by the guardian or conservator without court authorization. See Section 2408 and Article 11 (commencing with Section 2590) (independent exercise of powers).

Some powers prescribed in other articles of this chapter are also exercisable without prior court authorization. See, e.g., Sections 2420 (support, maintenance, and education of ward or conservatee and dependents), 2430 (payment of debts), 2431 (wage claims), 2500 (compromises), 2544 (sale of listed stocks and bonds), 2545 (certain sales of tangible personal property), 2555 (certain leases), 2574 (investing in listed securities).

For a comparable provision relating to decedents' estates, see Section 9610. For general provisions, see Sections 1000–1004 (rules of practice), 1020–1023 (petitions and other papers), 1040–1050 (hearings and orders), 2103 (effect of final order). For general provisions relating to notice of hearing, see Sections 1200–1221, 1460–1469. See also Sections 1260–1265 (proof of giving notice), 2700–2702 (notice to persons who request special notice). For background on the provisions of this part, see the Comment to this part under the part heading. [20 Cal.L.Rev.Comm. Reports 1001 (1990)].

Cross References

Administration of decedent's estate, extent of court supervision, see Probate Code §§ 10500, 10501.
Extension, renewal or modifications of obligations, see Probate Code § 2500 et seq.
Guardianship and conservatorship, interested person, defined, see Probate Code § 1424.
Request for special notice, see Probate Code § 2700 et seq.

§ 2451. Collection of debts and benefits

The guardian or conservator may collect debts and benefits due to the ward or conservatee and the estate. *(Stats.1990, c. 79 (A.B.759), § 14, operative July 1, 1991.)*

Law Revision Commission Comments

1990 Enactment

Section 2451 continues Section 2451 of the repealed Probate Code without change. The guardian or conservator must use ordinary care and diligence in managing the estate (Section 2401). This duty ordinarily will require that the guardian or conservator take appropriate action to collect a debt or benefit. But if the potential recovery is less than the cost of taking action that might result in recovery of a debt, Section 2451 does not require the guardian or conservator to act. If there is a question about the propriety of initiating a lawsuit to collect the debt, the guardian or conservator should obtain instructions from the court under Section 2403 before commencing the action. The power granted by Section 2451 may be exercised without court authorization. See Section 2450. See also Section 2750 (appealable orders). For a comparable provision relating to decedents' estates, see Section 9650. For background on the provisions of this part, see the Comment to this part under the part heading. [20 Cal.L.Rev.Comm. Reports 1001 (1990)].

Cross References

Review on settlement of accounts, see Probate Code § 2625.

§ 2451.5. Powers of guardian or conservator

The guardian or conservator may do any of the following:

(a) Contract for the guardianship or conservatorship, perform outstanding contracts, and, thereby, bind the estate.

(b) Purchase tangible personal property.

(c) Subject to the provisions of Chapter 8 (commencing with Section 2640), employ an attorney to advise and represent the guardian or conservator in all matters, including the conservatorship proceeding and all other actions or proceedings.

(d) Employ and pay the expense of accountants, investment advisers, agents, depositaries, and employees.

(e) Operate for a period of 45 days after the issuance of the letters of guardianship or conservatorship, at the risk of the estate, a business, farm, or enterprise constituting an asset of the estate. *(Added by Stats.2007, c. 553 (A.B.1727), § 16.)*

§ 2452. Checks, warrants and drafts

(a) The guardian or conservator may endorse and cash or deposit any checks, warrants, or drafts payable to the ward or conservatee which constitute property of the estate.

(b) If it appears likely that the estate will satisfy the conditions of subdivision (b) of Section 2628, the court may order that the guardian or conservator be the designated payee for public assistance payments received pursuant to Part 3 (commencing with Section 11000) or Part 4 (commencing with Section 16000) of Division 9 of the Welfare and Institutions Code. *(Stats.1990, c. 79 (A.B.759), § 14, operative July 1, 1991.)*

Law Revision Commission Comments

1990 Enactment

Section 2452 continues Section 2452 of the repealed Probate Code without change. In some instances, the check may not be property of the estate and hence will not be covered by the power granted by this section. See, e.g., Sections 2421 (allowance for ward or conservatee), 2601 (wages of ward or conservatee). The power granted by Section 2452 may be exercised without court authorization. See Section 2450. For background on the provisions of this part, see the Comment to this part under the part heading. [20 Cal.L.Rev.Comm. Reports 1001 (1990)].

Cross References

Draft or check, defined, see Commercial Code § 3104.
Indorsements, see Commercial Code § 3204 et seq.

§ 2453. Financial institution insured account

The guardian or conservator may deposit money belonging to the estate in an insured account in a financial institution in this state. Unless otherwise provided by court order, the money deposited under this section may be withdrawn without order of court. *(Stats.1990, c. 79 (A.B.759), § 14, operative July 1, 1991.)*

Law Revision Commission Comments

1990 Enactment

Section 2453 continues Section 2453 of the repealed Probate Code without substantive change. See Section 46 (defining "insured account in a financial institution"). Section 2453 provides independent authority for the deposit or investment of money without court authorization. See Section 2450 (prior court authorization not required). See also Sections 2456 (money or other property withdrawable only on court order), 2328 (effect of deposit of money or property subject to court control in determining amount of bond), and sections referred to in the Comment to Section 2328. For a comparable section relating to decedents' estates, see Section 9700. For background on the provisions of this part, see the Comment to this part under the part heading. [20 Cal.L.Rev.Comm. Reports 1001 (1990)].

Cross References

Account, defined, see Probate Code § 21.
Deposit of estate funds and assets with trust company, see Financial Code § 1586.
Deposits of money or property subject to court control, use in determining amount of bond, see Probate Code § 2328.
Deposits withdrawable only upon court order, see Probate Code § 2456.
Financial institution, defined, see Probate Code § 40.
Investments requiring court authorization, see Probate Code § 2570.

Prior court authorization not required, see Probate Code § 2450.

§ 2453.5. Deposit of estate money in trust company department; interest rate

(a) Subject to subdivision (b), where a trust company is a guardian or conservator and in the exercise of reasonable judgment deposits money of the estate in an account in any department of the corporation or association of which it is a part, it is chargeable with interest thereon at the rate of interest prevailing among banks of the locality on such deposits.

(b) Where it is to the advantage of the estate, the amount of cash that is reasonably necessary for orderly administration of the estate may be deposited in a checking account that does not bear interest which is maintained in a department of the corporation or association of which the trust company is a party. *(Stats.1990, c. 79 (A.B.759), § 14, operative July 1, 1991.)*

Law Revision Commission Comments

1990 Enactment

Section 2453.5 continues Section 2453.5 of the repealed Probate Code with the addition of subdivision (b) which is comparable to Section 9705(b) (decedents' estates). Cf. Section 16225 (trusts). See also Section 2401 (duty of guardian or conservator to manage estate using ordinary care and diligence). For a comparable section relating to decedents' estates, see Section 9705. For background on the provisions of this part, see the Comment to this part under the part heading. [20 Cal.L.Rev.Comm. Reports 1001 (1990)].

Cross References

Trust company, defined, see Probate Code § 83.

§ 2454. Deposit of personal property with trust company

The guardian or conservator may deposit personal property of the estate with a trust company for safekeeping. Unless otherwise provided by court order, the personal property may be withdrawn without order of court. *(Stats.1990, c. 79 (A.B.759), § 14, operative July 1, 1991.)*

Law Revision Commission Comments

1990 Enactment

Section 2454 continues Section 2454 of the repealed Probate Code without substantive change. See Section 83 (defining "trust company"). The procedure to be followed by the guardian or conservator in exercising the power under Section 2454 is provided in the statutory provisions to which reference is made in the section. See the Comment to Section 2328. See also Section 2456 (deposits withdrawable only on court order). For a comparable section relating to decedents' estates, see Section 9701. For background on the provisions of this part, see the Comment to this part under the part heading. [20 Cal.L.Rev.Comm. Reports 1001 (1990)].

Cross References

Deposits,
   Estate funds and assets in trust company by guardian, reduction of bond, see Financial Code § 1586.
   Withdrawable only upon court order, see Probate Code § 2456.
Trust companies,
   Generally, see Financial Code § 1550 et seq.
   Capacity to act as guardian, see Probate Code § 300.
   Definitions, see Financial Code §§ 107, 109; Probate Code § 83.

§ 2455. Deposit of securities in securities depository

(a) A trust company serving as guardian or conservator may deposit securities that constitute all or part of the estate in a securities depository as provided in Section 775 of the Financial Code.

(b) If the securities have been deposited with a trust company pursuant to Section 2328 or Section 2454, the trust company may deposit the securities in a securities depository as provided in Section 775 of the Financial Code.

(c) The securities depository may hold securities deposited with it in the manner authorized by Section 775 of the Financial Code. *(Stats.1990, c. 79 (A.B.759), § 14, operative July 1, 1991.)*

Law Revision Commission Comments

1990 Enactment

Section 2455 continues Section 2455 of the repealed Probate Code without change. The power granted by Section 2455 may be exercised without court authorization. See Section 2450. For a comparable section relating to decedents' estates, see Section 9702. For background on the provisions of this part, see the Comment to this part under the part heading. [20 Cal.L.Rev.Comm. Reports 1001 (1990)].

Cross References

Security, defined, see Probate Code § 70.
Trust company,
   Definition, see Probate Code § 83.
   Deposit of securities held under court order in securities depository, see Financial Code § 1606.

§ 2456. Deposits withdrawable only upon court authorization

(a) Upon application of the guardian or conservator, the court may, with or without notice, order that money or other personal property be deposited pursuant to Section 2453 or 2454, and be subject to withdrawal only upon authorization of the court.

(b) The guardian or conservator shall deliver a copy of the court order to the financial institution or trust company at the time the deposit is made.

(c) No financial institution or trust company accepting a deposit pursuant to Section 2453 or 2454 is on notice of the existence of an order that the money or other property is subject to withdrawal only upon authorization of the court unless it has actual notice of the order. *(Stats.1990, c. 79 (A.B.759), § 14, operative July 1, 1991.)*

Law Revision Commission Comments

1990 Enactment

Section 2456 continues Section 2456 of the repealed Probate Code with the addition of a specific reference to "trust company" in subdivisions (b) and (c). This addition conforms Section 2456 to Section 9703, the comparable section relating to decedents' estates. For background on the provisions of this part, see the Comment to this part under the part heading. [20 Cal.L.Rev.Comm. Reports 1001 (1990)].

Cross References

Deposit of estate funds with trust company, see Financial Code § 1586.
Deposit of money, generally, see Probate Code § 2453.

Deposit of personal property, generally, see Probate Code § 2454.

Financial institution, defined, see Probate Code § 40.

Money or property paid or delivered pursuant to compromise or judgment for minor or incompetent person, disposition of remaining balance, see Probate Code § 3602.

Request for special notice, see Probate Code § 2700 et seq.

Trust company, defined, see Probate Code § 83.

§ 2457. Maintenance of home of ward or conservatee and dependents

The guardian or conservator may maintain in good condition and repair the home or other dwelling of either or both of the following:

(a) The ward or conservatee.

(b) The persons legally entitled to such maintenance and repair from the ward or conservatee. *(Stats.1990, c. 79 (A.B.759), § 14, operative July 1, 1991.)*

Law Revision Commission Comments

1990 Enactment

Section 2457 continues Section 2457 of the repealed Probate Code without change. The power given by Section 2457 may be exercised without court authorization. See Section 2450. The power to add improvements is not included under this section. If there is doubt as to whether the particular project is permitted under this section, the guardian or conservator should seek court authorization under Section 2403. As to when a power should or should not be exercised, see Section 2401(b) and the Comment thereto. For background on the provisions of this part, see the Comment to this part under the part heading. [20 Cal.L.Rev.Comm. Reports 1001 (1990)].

Cross References

Order compelling guardian or conservator to furnish support and maintenance, see Probate Code § 2404.

§ 2458. Voting rights with respect to corporate shares, memberships or property

With respect to a share of stock of a domestic or foreign corporation held in the estate, a membership in a nonprofit corporation held in the estate, or other property held in the estate, a guardian or conservator may do any one or more of the following:

(a) Vote in person, and give proxies to exercise, any voting rights with respect to the share, membership, or other property.

(b) Waive notice of a meeting or give consent to the holding of a meeting.

(c) Authorize, ratify, approve, or confirm any action which could be taken by shareholders, members, or property owners. *(Stats.1990, c. 79 (A.B.759), § 14, operative July 1, 1991.)*

Law Revision Commission Comments

1990 Enactment

Section 2458 continues Section 2458 of the repealed Probate Code without substantive change. The nonsubstantive revisions conform the language of Section 2458 to that used in Section 9655, the comparable section relating to decedents' estates. See also Corp. Code §§ 702(a) (guardian or conservator may vote shares), 705(a) (person entitled to vote shares may give proxy). The word "meeting" in subdivision (b) includes a meeting of shareholders, members, or property owners, but is not so limited. Subdivision (c) permits

authorization of action taken at a defectively noticed meeting by approval of the minutes of the meeting if such approval satisfies the requirements of the Corporations Code or other applicable law. The powers under Section 2458 may be exercised without court authorization. See Section 2450. As to when a power should or should not be exercised, see Section 2401(b) and the Comment thereto.

The court may grant the right to exercise additional powers without prior court authorization under Article 11 (commencing with Section 2590) (independent exercise of powers). These additional powers include the power to exercise stock rights and stock options and the power to participate in and become subject to and to consent to provisions of a voting trust and of a reorganization, consolidation, merger, dissolution, liquidation, or other modification or adjustment affecting estate property. See Section 2591. If authority for independent exercise of such powers has not been granted, the guardian or conservator should obtain court authorization under an applicable provision or under Section 2403 (instructions) before exercising the powers. See also Sections 2544 (sale of listed stocks, bonds, and securities and United States obligations), 2557 (exchange of stocks, bonds, or securities for different stocks, bonds, or securities), 2574 (investment in United States or California obligations and listed stocks, bonds, and securities). For background on the provisions of this part, see the Comment to this part under the part heading. [20 Cal.L.Rev.Comm. Reports 1001 (1990)].

Cross References

By-law provisions governing use of proxies, see Corporations Code § 212.

Persons entitled to vote, record date, see Corporations Code § 701.

Proxies, revocation, see Corporations Code § 705.

Shareholders' meetings, notice, see Corporations Code § 601.

§ 2459. Life insurance, medical, retirement and other plans and benefits

(a) The guardian or conservator may obtain, continue, renew, modify, terminate, or otherwise deal in any of the following for the purpose of providing protection to the ward or conservatee or a person legally entitled to support from the ward or conservatee:

(1) Medical, hospital, and other health care policies, plans, or benefits.

(2) Disability policies, plans, or benefits.

(b) The conservator may continue in force any of the following in which the conservatee, or a person legally entitled to support, maintenance, or education from the conservatee, has or will have an interest:

(1) Life insurance policies, plans, or benefits.

(2) Annuity policies, plans, or benefits.

(3) Mutual fund and other dividend reinvestment plans.

(4) Retirement, profit-sharing, and employee welfare plans or benefits.

(c) The right to elect benefit or payment options, to terminate, to change beneficiaries or ownership, to assign rights, to borrow, or to receive cash value in return for a surrender of rights, or to take similar actions under any of the policies, plans, or benefits described in subdivision (b) may be exercised by the conservator only after authorization or direction by order of the court, except as permitted in Section 2544.5. To obtain such an order, the conservator or other interested person shall petition under Article 10 (commencing with Section 2580).

(d) Notwithstanding subdivision (c), unless the court otherwise orders, the conservator without authorization of the court may borrow on the loan value of an insurance policy to pay the current premiums to keep the policy in force if the conservatee followed that practice prior to the establishment of the conservatorship.

(e) The guardian may give the consent provided in Section 10112 of the Insurance Code without authorization of the court, but the guardian may use funds of the guardianship estate to effect or maintain in force a contract entered into by the ward under Section 10112 of the Insurance Code only after authorization by order of the court. To obtain such an order, the guardian, the ward, or any other interested person shall file a petition showing that it is in the best interest of the ward or of the guardianship estate to do so. Notice of the hearing on the petition shall be given for the period and in the manner provided in Chapter 3 (commencing with Section 1460) of Part 1.

(f) Nothing in this section limits the power of the guardian or conservator to make investments as otherwise authorized by this division. *(Stats.1990, c. 79 (A.B.759), § 14, operative July 1, 1991. Amended by Stats.1996, c. 86 (A.B.2146), § 1.)*

Law Revision Commission Comments

1990 Enactment

Section 2459 continues Section 2459 of the repealed Probate Code without change. Subdivision (a) gives the guardian or conservator authority to deal with medical, hospital, and other health care policies, plans, or benefits and with disability policies, plans, or benefits. These policies, plans, and benefits are an alternative method of meeting expenses that may be charged against the estate. The authority under this subdivision may be exercised without court authorization. See Section 2450.

Subdivision (b) gives the conservator more limited power with respect to life insurance, annuity policies, mutual funds, retirement and employee welfare plans, and the like. The authority under subdivision (b), which may be exercised without court authorization (Section 2450), is limited to continuing the plans in force.

Subdivision (d) permits the conservator to borrow on the loan value of an insurance policy to pay current premiums on the policy to keep the policy in force without court authorization if the conservatee followed that practice prior to establishment of the conservatorship. However, absent a showing of such past practice, court authorization is required to borrow on the loan value of the insurance policy to pay current premiums. See subdivision (c).

Under Section 10112 of the Insurance Code, a minor may, with written consent of a parent or guardian, contract for a life, disability, or annuity policy for the benefit of a limited class of persons.

The authority of the guardian or conservator under Section 2459 may be limited by court order (Section 2450), and subdivision (c) requires court authorization under the provisions relating to substituted judgment for actions that affect expectations of beneficiaries of insurance policies or other benefit plans.

As to when a power should or should not be exercised, see Section 2401(b) and the Comment thereto. For general provisions, see Sections 1000–1004 (rules of practice), 1020–1023 (petitions and other papers), 1040–1050 (hearings and orders), 2103 (effect of final order). For general provisions relating to notice of hearing, see Sections 1200–1221, 1460–1469. See also Sections 1260–1265 (proof of giving notice), 2700–2702 (notice to persons who request special notice). For background on the provisions of this part, see the Comment to this part under the part heading. [20 Cal.L.Comm.Reports 1001 (1990)].

Cross References

Guardianship and conservatorship, interested person, defined, see Probate Code § 1424.
Investments, see Probate Code § 2570 et seq.
Life and disability insurance for minors, see Insurance Code § 10112.
Request for special notice, see Probate Code § 2700 et seq.

§ 2460. Liability and casualty insurance

The guardian or conservator may insure:

(a) Property of the estate against loss or damage.

(b) The ward or conservatee, the guardian or conservator, and all or any part of the estate against liability to third persons. *(Stats.1990, c. 79 (A.B.759), § 14, operative July 1, 1991.)*

Law Revision Commission Comments

1990 Enactment

Section 2460 continues Section 2460 of the repealed Probate Code without change. This section states the power of the guardian or conservator to secure liability and casualty insurance without first obtaining authorization from the court. See Section 2450 (authorization of court not required). As to when a power should or should not be exercised, see Section 2401(b) and the Comment thereto. For a comparable provision relating to decedents' estates, see Section 9656. For background on the provisions of this part, see the Comment to this part under the part heading. [20 Cal.L.Rev.Comm. Reports 1001 (1990)].

Cross References

Liability insurance, see Insurance Code §§ 108, 11550 et seq.

§ 2461. Taxes and tax returns

(a) The guardian or conservator may prepare, execute, and file tax returns for the ward or conservatee and for the estate and may exercise options and elections and claim exemptions for the ward or conservatee and for the estate under the applicable tax laws.

(b) Notwithstanding Section 2502, the guardian or conservator may pay, contest, and compromise taxes, penalties, and assessments upon the property of the estate and income and other taxes payable or claimed to be payable by the ward or conservatee or the estate. *(Stats.1990, c. 79 (A.B.759), § 14, operative July 1, 1991.)*

Law Revision Commission Comments

1990 Enactment

Section 2461 continues Section 2461 of the repealed Probate Code without change. Court authorization or approval is not required to exercise the powers under Section 2461. See Section 2450. As to when a power should or should not be exercised, see Section 2401(b) and the Comment thereto. Subdivision (b) is not subject to the limitation on compromises in Section 2502 (compromise in excess of $25,000 requires court approval). Under subdivision (b), the guardian or conservator may, without court authorization, compromise taxes, penalties, and assessments, whether or not in excess of $25,000, and pay to taxing authorities the amount required to be paid under the compromise. For background on the provisions of this part, see the Comment to this part under the part heading. [20 Cal.L.Rev. Comm. Reports 1001 (1990)].

Property tax refund, action to recover, see Revenue and Taxation Code § 5140.

§ 2462.   Representation in actions and proceedings

Subject to Section 2463, unless another person is appointed for that purpose, the guardian or conservator may:

(a) Commence and maintain actions and proceedings for the benefit of the ward or conservatee or the estate.

(b) Defend actions and proceedings against the ward or conservatee, the guardian or conservator, or the estate.

(c) File a petition commencing a case under Title 11 of the United States Code (Bankruptcy) on behalf of the ward or conservatee. *(Stats.1990, c. 79 (A.B.759), § 14, operative July 1, 1991.)*

Law Revision Commission Comments
1990 Enactment

Section 2462 continues Section 2462 of the repealed Probate Code with the addition of the reference to guardian or conservator in subdivision (b). This addition makes Section 2462 consistent with Section 9820, the comparable provision relating to decedents' estates. Court authorization is not required to exercise the powers under Section 2462. See Section 2450.

Section 2462 states the general principle that the conservator is authorized to bring or defend actions on behalf of the conservatee. See also Code Civ.Proc. § 372; In re Marriage of Higgason, 10 Cal.3d 476, 484, 516 P.2d 289, 110 Cal.Rptr. 897, (1973) (minor or conservatee must appear by representative). See also Sections 1210 (duty of guardian or conservator to represent ward or conservatee in estate proceeding), 2463 (partition actions). As to when a power should or should not be exercised, see Section 2401(b) and the Comment thereto. See also the Comment to Section 2451.

For background on the provisions of this part, see the Comment to this part under the part heading. [20 Cal.L.Rev.Comm. Reports 1001 (1990)].

Cross References

Compromise of claims and actions, see Probate Code § 2500 et seq.
Election of guardian or conservator of surviving spouse to have property administered in probate, see Probate Code § 13502 et seq.

§ 2463.   Partition actions

(a) The guardian or conservator may bring an action against the other cotenants for partition of any property in which the ward or conservatee has an undivided interest if the court has first made an order authorizing the guardian or conservator to do so. The court may make such an order ex parte on a petition filed by the guardian or conservator.

(b) The guardian or conservator may consent and agree, without an action, to a partition of the property and to the part to be set off to the estate, and may execute deeds or conveyances to the owners of the remaining interests of the parts to which they may be respectively entitled, if the court has made an order under Article 5 (commencing with Section 2500) authorizing the guardian or conservator to do so.

(c) If the ward or conservatee, or the guardian or conservator as such, is made a defendant in a partition action, the guardian or conservator may defend the action without authorization of the court. *(Stats.1990, c. 79 (A.B.759), § 14, operative July 1, 1991.)*

Law Revision Commission Comments
1990 Enactment

Section 2463 continues Section 2463 of the repealed Probate Code without substantive change. Subdivision (a) has been restated using language drawn from Section 9823(b), the comparable provision relating to decedents' estates. For general provisions, see Sections 1000–1004 (rules of practice), 1020–1023 (petitions and other papers), 1040–1050 (hearings and orders), 2103 (effect of final order). See also Sections 1021 (petition to be verified), 1041 (clerk to set petition for hearing). For general provisions relating to notice of hearing, see Sections 1200–1221, 1460–1469. See also Sections 1260–1265 (proof of giving notice), 2111 (orders affecting real property), 2700–2702 (notice to persons who request special notice). For background on the provisions of this part, see the Comment to this part under the part heading. [20 Cal.L.Rev.Comm. Reports 1001 (1990)].

Cross References

Actions for partition against personal representative, see Probate Code § 9823.
Consent to appointment of referee in partition action, see Code of Civil Procedure § 873.040.
Conveyance or transfer of property, generally, see Probate Code § 2111.
Instructions from or confirmation by court, see Probate Code § 2403.
Partition, generally, see Code of Civil Procedure § 872.010 et seq.
Partition of decedents' estates before distribution, generally, see Probate Code § 11950.
Recording,
    Constructive notice, conveyances of real property or estate for years, see Civil Code § 1213.
    Instruments or judgments, documents to be recorded and manner of recording, see Government Code § 27320 et seq., 27280 et seq.
Property transfers, place of recordation, see Civil Code § 1169.

§ 2464.   Acceptance of deed in lieu of foreclosure or trustee's sale

(a) If it is to the advantage of the estate to accept a deed to property which is subject to a mortgage or deed of trust in lieu of foreclosure of the mortgage or sale under the deed of trust, the guardian or conservator may, after authorization by order of the court and upon such terms and conditions as may be imposed by the court, accept a deed conveying the property to the ward or conservatee.

(b) To obtain an order under this section, the guardian or conservator shall file a petition showing the advantage to the estate of accepting the deed. Notice of the hearing on the petition shall be given for the period and in the manner provided in Chapter 3 (commencing with Section 1460) of Part 1.

(c) The court shall make an order under this section only if the advantage to the estate of accepting the deed is shown by clear and convincing evidence. *(Stats.1990, c. 79 (A.B.759), § 14, operative July 1, 1991.)*

Law Revision Commission Comments
1990 Enactment

Section 2464 continues Section 2464 of the repealed Probate Code with the addition of subdivision (c). This addition makes Section 2464 consistent with Section 9850(c), the comparable provision relating to decedents' estates. For general provisions, see Sections 1000–1004 (rules of practice), 1020–1023 (petitions and other papers), 1040–1050 (hearings and orders), 2103 (effect of final order),

2750 (appealable orders). For general provisions relating to notice of hearing, see Sections 1200–1221, 1460–1469. See also Sections 1260–1265 (proof of giving notice), 2700–2702 (notice to persons who request special notice). For background on the provisions of this part, see the Comment to this part under the part heading. [20 Cal.L.Rev.Comm. Reports 1001 (1990)].

Cross References

Appealable orders, see Probate Code § 1300 et seq.
Mortgages, generally, see Civil Code § 2920 et seq.
Trustees, powers, see Probate Code § 16200 et seq.

§ 2465. Abandonment of valueless property

The guardian or conservator may dispose of or abandon valueless property. *(Stats.1990, c. 79 (A.B.759), § 14, operative July 1, 1991.)*

Law Revision Commission Comments

1990 Enactment

Section 2465 continues Section 2465 of the repealed Probate Code without change. The power under Section 2465 may be exercised without authorization of the court. See Section 2450. As to when a power should or should not be exercised, see Section 2401(b) and the Comment thereto.

If the property has value, its disposition without court authorization is not permitted under Section 2465. Court authorization is required for its sale or other disposition unless the disposition falls within some other provision—such as Section 2545—permitting disposition without court authorization.

For comparable provisions relating to decedents' estates, see Sections 9780–9788. For background on the provisions of this part, see the Comment to this part under the part heading. [20 Cal.L.Rev.Comm. Reports 1001 (1990)].

§ 2466. Advances by guardian or conservator

The guardian or conservator may advance the guardian's or conservator's own funds for the benefit of the ward or conservatee or the estate and may reimburse the advance out of the income and principal of the estate first available. With court authorization or approval, interest on the amount advanced may be allowed at the legal rate payable on judgments. *(Stats.1990, c. 79 (A.B.759), § 14, operative July 1, 1991.)*

Law Revision Commission Comments

1990 Enactment

Section 2466 continues Section 2466 of the repealed Probate Code without substantive change. Except for allowance of interest, court authorization is not required under Section 2466. See Section 2450. For background on the provisions of this part, see the Comment to this part under the part heading. [20 Cal.L.Rev.Comm. Reports 1001 (1990)].

Cross References

Instructions from or confirmation by court, see Probate Code § 2403.
Legal rate of interest, see Cal. Const. Art. 15, § 1; Civil Code § 1916–1 et seq.

§ 2467. Care of estate pending delivery to personal representative

(a) The guardian or conservator continues to have the duty of custody and conservation of the estate after the death of the ward or conservatee pending the delivery thereof to the personal representative of the ward's or conservatee's estate or other disposition according to law.

(b) The guardian or conservator has such powers as are granted to a guardian or conservator under this division as are necessary for the performance of the duty imposed by subdivision (a). *(Stats.1990, c. 79 (A.B.759), § 14, operative July 1, 1991.)*

Law Revision Commission Comments

1990 Enactment

Section 2467 continues Section 2467 of the repealed Probate Code without change. See also Section 2623(e) (allowance of reasonable expenses in care, preservation, and disposition of the estate after death of ward or conservatee). For background on the provisions of this part, see the Comment to this part under the part heading. [20 Cal.L.Rev.Comm. Reports 1001 (1990)].

Cross References

Disposition of assets upon death of ward or conservatee, see Probate Code § 2631.
Personal representative and general personal representative, defined, see Probate Code § 58.
Review on settlement of accounts, see Probate Code § 2625.
Termination of conservatorship upon death of conservatee or by order of the court, see Probate Code § 1860.
Termination of guardianship upon majority, death, adoption or emancipation of ward, see Probate Code § 1600.

§ 2468. Disabled attorney; petition for appointment; notice and hearing; contents; compensation; termination

(a) The conservator of the estate of a disabled attorney who was engaged in the practice of law at the time of his or her disability, or other person interested in the estate, may bring a petition seeking the appointment of an active member of the State Bar of California to take control of the files and assets of the practice of the disabled member.

(b) The petition may be filed and heard on such notice that the court determines is in the best interests of the persons interested in the estate of the disabled member. If the petition alleges that the immediate appointment of a practice administrator is required to safeguard the interests of the estate, the court may dispense with notice provided that the conservator is the petitioner or has joined in the petition or has otherwise waived notice of hearing on the petition.

(c) The petition shall indicate the powers sought for the practice administrator from the list of powers set forth in Section 6185 of the Business and Professions Code. These powers shall be specifically listed in the order appointing the practice administrator.

(d) The petition shall allege the value of the assets that are to come under the control of the practice administrator, including but not limited by the amount of funds in all accounts used by the disabled member. The court shall require the filing of a surety bond in the amount of the value of the personal property to be filed with the court by the practice administrator. No action may be taken by the practice administrator unless a bond has been duly filed with the court.

(e) The practice administrator shall not be the attorney representing the conservator.

(f) The court shall appoint the attorney nominated by the disabled member in a writing, including but not limited to the disabled member's will, unless the court concludes that the appointment of the nominated person would be contrary to the best interests of the estate or would create a conflict of interest with any of the clients of the disabled member.

(g) The practice administrator shall be compensated only upon order of the court making the appointment for his or her reasonable and necessary services. The law practice shall be the source of the compensation for the practice administrator unless the assets are insufficient, in which case, the compensation of the practice administrator shall be charged against the assets of the estate as a cost of administration. The practice administrator shall also be entitled to reimbursement of his or her costs.

(h) Upon conclusion of the services of the practice administrator, the practice administrator shall render an accounting and petition for its approval by the superior court making the appointment. Upon settlement of the accounting, the practice administrator shall be discharged and the surety on his or her bond exonerated.

(i) If the court appointing the practice administrator determines upon petition that the disabled attorney has recovered his or her capacity to resume his or her law practice, the appointment of a practice administrator shall forthwith terminate and the disabled attorney shall be restored to his or her practice.

(j) For purposes of this section, the person appointed to take control of the practice of the disabled member shall be referred to as the "practice administrator" and the conservatee shall be referred to as the "disabled member." *(Added by Stats.1998, c. 682 (A.B.2069), § 4.)*

Cross References

Guardianship and conservatorship, interested person, defined, see Probate Code § 1424.
Incapacity to attend to law practice, jurisdiction of courts, see Business and Professions Code § 6185.

ARTICLE 5. COMPROMISE OF CLAIMS AND ACTIONS; EXTENSION, RENEWAL, OR MODIFICATION OF OBLIGATIONS

Cross References

Application of old and new law, see Probate Code § 3.

§ 2500. Authority

(a) Unless this article or some other applicable statute requires court authorization or approval, if it is to the advantage of the estate, the guardian or conservator may do any of the following without court authorization, instruction, approval, or confirmation:

(1) Compromise or settle a claim, action, or proceeding by or for the benefit of, or against, the ward or conservatee, the guardian or conservator, or the estate, including the giving of a covenant not to sue.

(2) Extend, renew, or in any manner modify the terms of an obligation owing to or running in favor of the ward or conservatee or the estate.

(b) Nothing in this section precludes the guardian or conservator from seeking court authorization, instructions, approval, or confirmation pursuant to Section 2403.

(c) Upon petition of the ward or conservatee, a creditor, or any interested person, or upon the court's own motion, the court may limit the authority of the guardian or conservator under subdivision (a). Notice of the hearing on the petition shall be given for the period and in the manner provided in Chapter 3 (commencing with Section 1460) of Part 1. *(Stats.1990, c. 79 (A.B.759), § 14, operative July 1, 1991.)*

Law Revision Commission Comments
1990 Enactment

Section 2500 restates Section 2500 of the repealed Probate Code without substantive change. The requirement that the power may be exercised "if it is to the advantage of the estate" and the reference to the giving of a covenant not to sue have been added. These additions make Section 2500 more consistent with Section 9830 (decedents' estates). Court approval is required for a compromise, extension, renewal, or modification relating to real property (Section 2501), a compromise in excess of a specified amount (Section 2502), a compromise of a claim of the ward or conservatee against the guardian or conservator (Section 2503), support, wrongful death, and personal injury claims (Section 2504). However, the court may add to the list of powers exercisable by the guardian or conservator without court authorization. See Article 11 (commencing with Section 2590) (independent exercise of powers). See also Code Civ.Proc. § 372 (court approval required for compromise or settlement of pending action or proceeding). Subdivisions (b) and (c) of Section 2500 are comparable to Section 2450 (powers of estate management generally). As to when a power should or should not be exercised, see Section 2401(b) and the Comment thereto. See also Section 2101 and the Comment thereto. See also Section 2403 (permitting the guardian or conservator to seek court authorization, instructions, approval, or confirmation for particular transactions), 2625 (review at time of accounting of sales, purchases, and other transactions not previously authorized or approved). Adjudicating the merits of any claim under this article is an appealable judgment or order. See Section 2750. For a comparable provision relating to decedents' estates, see Section 9830. For general provisions, see Sections 1000–1004 (rules of practice), 1020–1023 (petitions and other papers), 1040–1050 (hearings and orders), 2103 (effect of final order). For general provisions relating to notice of hearing, see Sections 1200–1221, 1460–1469. See also Sections 1260–1265 (proof of giving notice), 2700–2702 (notice to persons who request special notice). For background on the provisions of this part, see the Comment to this part under the part heading. [20 Cal.L.Rev.Comm. Reports 1001 (1990)].

Cross References

Filing and payment of claims, see Probate Code § 9150 et seq.
Guardianship and conservatorship, interested person, defined, see Probate Code § 1424.

Representation in actions and proceedings, see Probate Code §§ 2462, 2463.

Request for special notice, see Probate Code § 2700 et seq.

Review on settlement of accounts, see Probate Code § 2625.

§ 2501. Matters relating to real property

(a) Except as provided in subdivision (b), court approval is required for a compromise, settlement, extension, renewal, or modification which affects any of the following:

(1) Title to real property.

(2) An interest in real property or a lien or encumbrance on real property.

(3) An option to purchase real property or an interest in real property.

(b) If it is to the advantage of the estate, the guardian or conservator without prior court approval may extend, renew, or modify a lease of real property in either of the following cases:

(1) Where under the lease as extended, renewed, or modified the rental does not exceed five thousand dollars ($5,000) a month and the term does not exceed two years.

(2) Where the lease is from month to month, regardless of the amount of the rental.

(c) For the purposes of subdivision (b), if the lease as extended, renewed, or modified gives the lessee the right to extend the term of the lease, the length of the term shall be considered as though the right to extend had been exercised. *(Stats.1990, c. 79 (A.B.759), § 14, operative July 1, 1991. Amended by Stats.1990, c. 710 (S.B.1775), § 10, operative July 1, 1991.)*

Law Revision Commission Comments

1990 Enactment

Section 2501 restates Section 2501 of the repealed Probate Code with the addition of the provision concerning the effect of a right to extend the term of a lease. This revision conforms subdivision (b) to Sections 2552.5 and 2555 (leases permitted without authorization of court).

As a general rule, Section 2501 requires court approval because title to real property is involved and a court order approving the transaction may be needed for title insurance. See also Section 2111 (recording certified copy of court order authorizing transaction with respect to real property). Adjudicating the merits of any claim under this article is an appealable judgment or order. See Section 2750. Subdivision (b) provides an exception to the requirement of court approval. The subdivision is consistent with Section 2555 (leases permitted without court authorization). For a comparable provision relating to decedents' estates, see Section 9832. For background on the provisions of this part, see the Comment to this part under the part heading.

The court may add to the list of powers exercisable by the guardian or conservator without court authorization. See Article 11 (commencing with Section 2590) (independent exercise of powers). [20 Cal.L.Rev.Comm. Reports 1001 (1990)].

1990 Amendment

Section 2501 (enacted as a part of the new Probate Code by 1990 Cal.Stat. ch. 79 § 14) was amended by 1990 Cal.Stat. ch. 710 § 10. The amendment revised subdivision (b) to increase the limit on extending, renewing, or modifying a lease without court approval from $1,500 to $5,000. See also Section 2555 (execution of lease by guardian or conservator). For a comparable provision relating to personal representatives, see Section 9832. For background on the 1990 amendment, see Recommendation Relating to Execution or Modification of Lease Without Court Order, 20 Cal.L. Revision Comm'n Reports 557 (1990). [20 Cal.L.Rev.Comm. Reports 1001 (1990)].

Cross References

Acceptance of deed in lieu of foreclosure, see Probate Code § 2464.

Court authorized to approve transaction or matter, see Probate Code § 2505.

Leases authorized without court permission, see Probate Code § 2555.

Life and disability insurance, insurance of minors, see Insurance Code § 10112.

Real property, defined, see Probate Code § 68.

§ 2502. Compromise in excess of specified amount

Court approval is required for a compromise or settlement of a matter when the transaction requires the transfer or encumbrance of property of the estate, or the creation of an unsecured liability of the estate, or both, in an amount or value in excess of twenty-five thousand dollars ($25,000). *(Stats.1990, c. 79 (A.B.759), § 14, operative July 1, 1991.)*

Law Revision Commission Comments

1990 Enactment

Section 2502 continues Section 2502 of the repealed Probate Code without substantive change. This section permits compromises and settlements without court approval where the amount to be paid or charged against the estate is not more than $25,000, unless court approval is otherwise required, as, for example, under Section 2501 (matter affecting real property) or under Code of Civil Procedure Section 372 (pending actions and proceedings). Section 2502 does not apply to a claim by the estate. Nor does the section apply to compromises of tax matters. See Section 2461. Adjudicating the merits of any claim under this article is an appealable judgment or order. See Section 2750. For a comparable provision relating to decedents' estates, see Section 9833. For background on the provisions of this part, see the Comment to this part under the part heading.

The court may add to the list of powers exercisable by the guardian or conservator without court authorization. See Article 11 (commencing with Section 2590) (independent exercise of powers). [20 Cal.L.Rev.Comm. Reports 1001 (1990)].

Cross References

Court authorized to approve transaction or matter, see Probate Code § 2505.

Life and disability insurance, insurance of minors, see Insurance Code § 10112.

§ 2503. Compromise of claim of ward or conservatee against guardian or conservator

Court approval is required for any of the following:

(a) A compromise or settlement of a claim by the ward or conservatee against the guardian or conservator or against the attorney for the guardian or conservator, whether or not the claim arises out of the administration of the estate.

(b) An extension, renewal, or modification of the terms of a debt or similar obligation of the guardian or conservator, or of the attorney for the guardian or conservator, owing to or running in favor of the ward or conservatee or the estate. *(Stats.1990, c. 79 (A.B.759), § 14, operative July 1, 1991.)*

Law Revision Commission Comments

1990 Enactment

Section 2503 continues Section 2503 of the repealed Probate Code with the extension of the section to cover transactions with respect to the attorney for the guardian or conservator. This extension makes the coverage of Section 2503 consistent with the coverage of Section 9834 (decedents' estates). Section 2503 requires court approval because it involves matters where there may be a conflict of interest for the guardian or conservator. Adjudicating the merits of any claim under this article is an appealable judgment or order. See Section 2750. See also Section 2101 (relationship is a fiduciary relationship) and the Comment thereto; Section 16004(a) (transaction in which trustee has interest adverse to beneficiary). See also the Comment to Section 9834, the comparable provision for decedents' estates. For background on the provisions of this part, see the Comment to this part under the part heading. [20 Cal.L.Rev.Comm. Reports 1001 (1990)].

Cross References

Appealable orders, see Probate Code § 1300 et seq.
Court authorized to approve transaction or matter, see Probate Code § 2505.
Life and disability insurance, insurance of minors, see Insurance Code § 10112.

§ 2504. Support, wrongful death and personal injury claims

Court approval is required for the compromise or settlement of any of the following:

(a) A claim for the support, maintenance, or education of (1) the ward or conservatee, or (2) a person whom the ward or conservatee is legally obligated to support, maintain, or educate, against any other person (including, but not limited to, the spouse or parent of the ward or the spouse, domestic partner, parent, or adult child of the conservatee).

(b) A claim of the ward or conservatee for wrongful death.

(c) A claim of the ward or conservatee for physical or nonphysical harm to the person. *(Stats.1990, c. 79 (A.B.759), § 14, operative July 1, 1991. Amended by Stats.2001, c. 893 (A.B.25), § 36.)*

Law Revision Commission Comments

1990 Enactment

Section 2504 continues Section 2504 of the repealed Probate Code without change. This section requires court approval because a claim of the type covered by the section may be a major asset of the estate. Adjudicating the merits of any claim under this article is an appealable judgment or order. See Section 2750. For a comparable provision relating to decedents' estates, see Section 9835. For background on the provisions of this part, see the Comment to this part under the part heading.

The court may add to the list of powers exercisable by the guardian or conservator without court authorization. See Article 11 (commencing with Section 2590) (independent exercise of powers). [20 Cal.L.Rev.Comm. Reports 1001 (1990)].

Cross References

Appealable orders, see Probate Code § 1300 et seq.
Domestic partner, defined, see Probate Code § 37.
Life and disability insurance, insurance of minors, see Insurance Code § 10112.
Parent, defined, see Probate Code § 54.
Pending actions and proceedings, compromise, see Code of Civil Procedure § 372.

Support and maintenance of ward or conservatee and dependents, see Probate Code § 2420 et seq.
Wrongful death, see Code of Civil Procedure § 377.60 et seq.

§ 2505. Court approval of transaction or matter; exemptions

(a) Subject to subdivision (c), where the claim or matter is the subject of a pending action or proceeding, the court approval required by this article shall be obtained from the court in which the action or proceeding is pending.

(b) Where the claim or matter is not the subject of a pending action or proceeding, the court approval required by this article shall be obtained from one of the following:

(1) The court in which the guardianship or conservatorship proceeding is pending.

(2) The superior court of the county where the ward or conservatee or guardian or conservator resides at the time the petition for approval is filed.

(3) The superior court of any county where a suit on the claim or matter properly could be brought.

(c) Where the claim or matter is the subject of a pending action or proceeding that is not brought in a court of this state, court approval required by this article shall be obtained from either of the following:

(1) The court in which the action or proceeding is pending.

(2) The court in which the guardianship or conservatorship proceeding is pending.

(d)(1) Subdivisions (a), (b), and (c) do not apply to a conservatorship that is registered in this state pursuant to Article 4 (commencing with Section 2011) of Chapter 8 of Part 3.

(2) Except as provided in paragraph (3), when a conservatorship is registered in this state pursuant to Article 4 (commencing with Section 2011) of Chapter 8 of Part 3, the court approval required by this article shall be obtained in accordance with Section 2016.

(3) Notwithstanding Section 2016, when a conservatorship is registered in this state pursuant to Article 4 (commencing with Section 2011) of Chapter 8 of Part 3, and the claim or matter in question is the subject of a pending action or proceeding that is not brought in a court of this state, the court approval required by this article may be obtained from the court in which the action or proceeding is pending. *(Stats.1990, c. 79 (A.B.759), § 14, operative July 1, 1991. Amended by Stats.2014, c. 553 (S.B.940), § 25, eff. Jan. 1, 2015, operative Jan. 1, 2016.)*

Law Revision Commission Comments

1990 Enactment

Section 2505 continues Section 2505 of the repealed Probate Code without substantive change. Subdivision (c) applies to cases in federal court and in sister state courts or courts outside the United States. For a comparable provision relating to decedents' estates, see Section 9836. For background on the provisions of this part, see the Comment to this part under the part heading. [20 Cal.L.Rev. Comm. Reports 1001 (1990)].

2014 Amendment

Section 2505 is amended to reflect the enactment of the California Conservatorship Jurisdiction Act (Section 1980 *et seq.*). [43 Cal. L.Rev.Comm. Reports 93 (2013)].

Cross References

Life and disability insurance, insurance of minors, see Insurance Code § 10112.

§ 2506. Petition for approval of court in guardianship or conservatorship proceeding

Where approval of the court in which the guardianship or conservatorship proceeding is pending is required under this article, the guardian or conservator shall file a petition with the court showing the advantage of the compromise, settlement, extension, renewal, or modification to the ward or conservatee and the estate. Notice of the hearing on the petition shall be given for the period and in the manner provided in Chapter 3 (commencing with Section 1460) of Part 1. *(Stats.1990, c. 79 (A.B.759), § 14, operative July 1, 1991.)*

Law Revision Commission Comments

1990 Enactment

Section 2506 continues Section 2506 of the repealed Probate Code without change. For a comparable provision relating to decedents' estates, see Section 9837. For general provisions, see Sections 1000–1004 (rules of practice), 1020–1023 (petitions and other papers), 1040–1050 (hearings and orders), 2103 (effect of final order). For general provisions relating to notice of hearing, see Sections 1200–1221, 1460–1469. See also Sections 1260–1265 (proof of giving notice), 2700–2702 (notice to persons who request special notice). For background on the provisions of this part, see the Comment to this part under the part heading. [20 Cal.L.Rev.Comm. Reports 1001 (1990)].

§ 2507. Application of another statute to the compromise, settlement, etc.

Notwithstanding Sections 2500 to 2506, inclusive:

(a) Whenever another statute requires, provides a procedure for, or dispenses with court approval of a compromise, settlement, extension, renewal, or modification, the provisions of that statute govern any case to which that statute applies.

(b) Whenever another statute provides that a compromise or settlement of an administrative proceeding is not valid unless approved in such proceeding, the approval is governed by that statute, and approval in the guardianship or conservatorship proceeding is not required. *(Stats.1990, c. 79 (A.B. 759), § 14, operative July 1, 1991.)*

Law Revision Commission Comments

1990 Enactment

Section 2507 continues Section 2507 of the repealed Probate Code without substantive change. Subdivision (a) makes clear that this article has no effect on Code of Civil Procedure Section 372 (compromise of pending action or proceeding) or any other applicable statute. Where approval of a compromise or settlement of an administrative proceeding is required in such proceeding for the compromise or settlement to be valid (see, e.g., Labor Code Section 5001 concerning compromise of a worker's compensation proceeding), subdivision (b) requires that approval of the compromise or settlement be obtained in the administrative proceeding rather than

in the guardianship or conservatorship proceeding. For background on the provisions of this part, see the Comment to this part under the part heading. [20 Cal.L.Rev.Comm. Reports 1001 (1990)].

Cross References

Life and disability insurance, insurance of minors, see Insurance Code § 10112.

ARTICLE 6. CONVEYANCE OR TRANSFER OF PROPERTY CLAIMED TO BELONG TO WARD OR CONSERVATEE OR OTHER PERSON [REPEALED]

§§ 2520 to 2522. Repealed by Stats.2001, c. 49 (S.B.669), § 2

§ 2523. Repealed by Stats.1988, c. 1199, § 69.5, operative July 1, 1989.

Law Revision Commission Comments

1988 Repeal

Former Section 2523 is generalized in Section 1004 [19 Cal.L.Rev. Comm. Reports 1088 (1988)].

§§ 2524 to 2529. Repealed by Stats.2001, c. 49 (S.B.669), § 2

ARTICLE 7. SALES

Cross References

Application of old and new law, see Probate Code § 3.

§ 2540. Court supervision; exceptions; personal residence

(a) Except as otherwise provided in Sections 2544 and 2545, and except for the sale of a conservatee's present or former personal residence as set forth in subdivision (b), sales of real or personal property of the estate under this article are subject to authorization, confirmation, or direction of the court, as provided in this article.

(b) In seeking authorization to sell a conservatee's present or former personal residence, the conservator shall notify the court that the present or former personal residence is proposed to be sold and that the conservator has discussed the proposed sale with the conservatee. The conservator shall inform the court whether the conservatee supports or is opposed to the proposed sale and shall describe the circumstances that necessitate the proposed sale, including whether the conservatee has the ability to live in the personal residence and why other alternatives, including, but not limited to, in-home care services, are not available. The court, in its discretion, may require the court investigator to discuss the proposed sale with the conservatee. This subdivision shall not apply when the conservator is granted the power to sell real property of the estate pursuant to Article 11 (commencing with Section 2590). *(Stats.1990, c. 79 (A.B. 759), § 14, operative July 1, 1991. Amended by Stats.2006, c. 490 (S.B.1116), § 3.)*

Section 2540 continues Section 2540 of the repealed Probate Code without change. The court may authorize the guardian or conservator to sell property without court authorization. See Article 11 (commencing with Section 2590 (independent exercise of powers). See also Section 2408. See also Section 2625 (review at time of accounting of sales not previously authorized or approved), 2750 (appealable orders). For background on the provisions of this part, see the Comment to this part under the part heading. [20 Cal.L.Rev.Comm. Reports 1001 (1990)].

Cross References

Exchanges of property, see Probate Code § 2557.

§ 2541. Purpose

The guardian or conservator may sell real or personal property of the estate in any of the following cases:

(a) If the income of the estate is insufficient for the comfortable and suitable support, maintenance, and education of the ward or conservatee (including care, treatment, and support of the ward or conservatee if a patient in a state hospital under the jurisdiction of the State Department of State Hospitals or the State Department of Developmental Services) or of those legally entitled to support, maintenance, or education from the ward or conservatee.

(b) If the sale is necessary to pay the debts referred to in Sections 2430 and 2431.

(c) If the sale is for the advantage, benefit, and best interest of (1) the ward or conservatee, (2) the estate, or (3) the ward or conservatee and those legally entitled to support, maintenance, or education from the ward or conservatee. *(Stats.1990, c. 79 (A.B.759), § 14, operative July 1, 1991. Amended by Stats.2012, c. 440 (A.B.1488), § 45, eff. Sept. 22, 2012.)*

Law Revision Commission Comments

1990 Enactment

Section 2541 restates Section 2541 of the repealed Probate Code without substantive change. As to the duty to provide comfortable and suitable support, maintenance, and education, see Section 2420. Subdivision (b) is revised to eliminate the preference for sale of personal property before real property is sold. This conforms Section 2541 to subdivision (a) of Section 2543 (mode of sale) and to Section 10000(a), the comparable provisions relating to decedents' estates. For background on the provisions of this part, see the Comment to this part under the part heading. [20 Cal.L.Rev.Comm. Reports 1001 (1990)].

Cross References

Borrowing money and giving security, see Probate Code § 2551.
County aid and relief to indigents, termination and recovery of assistance, see Welfare and Institutions Code § 17403.
Disposition of proceeds of sale, see Probate Code § 2547.

Sale or encumbrance of property when income is insufficient for support, see Probate Code § 2420.
State Department of Developmental Services, see Welfare and Institutions Code § 4400 et seq.
State Department of State Hospitals, see Welfare and Institutions Code § 4000 et seq.
Tangible personal property, sale or other disposition, see Probate Code § 2545.

§ 2542. Terms of sales

(a) All sales shall be for cash or for part cash and part deferred payments. Except as otherwise provided in Sections 2544 and 2545, the terms of sale are subject to the approval of the court.

(b) If real property is sold for part deferred payments, the guardian or conservator shall take the note of the purchaser for the unpaid portion of the purchase money, with a mortgage or deed of trust on the property to secure payment of the note. The mortgage or deed of trust shall be subject only to encumbrances existing at the date of sale and such other encumbrances as the court may approve.

(c) If real or personal property of the estate sold for part deferred payments consists of an undivided interest, a joint tenancy interest, or any other interest less than the entire ownership, and the owner or owners of the remaining interests in the property join in the sale, the note and deed of trust or mortgage may be made to the ward or conservatee and the other owner or owners. *(Stats.1990, c. 79 (A.B.759), § 14, operative July 1, 1991.)*

Law Revision Commission Comments

1990 Enactment

Section 2542 continues Section 2542 of the repealed Probate Code without substantive change. Subdivision (b) has been revised to conform to Section 10315(a) (decedents' estates). The court may add to the list of powers exercisable by the guardian or conservator without court authorization. See Article 11 (commencing with Section 2590) (independent exercise of powers). See also Section 2570 (appealable orders). For background on the provisions of this part, see the Comment to this part under the part heading. [20 Cal.L.Rev.Comm. Reports 1001 (1990)].

Cross References

Interests in property, see Civil Code § 678 et seq.
Joint tenancy, see Civil Code § 683.
Mortgages, see Civil Code § 2920 et seq.
Real property, defined, see Probate Code § 68.
Sales by personal representatives, see Probate Code §§ 10257, 10315.
Transfers of real property, see Civil Code § 1091 et seq.

§ 2543. Manner of sale

(a) If estate property is required or permitted to be sold, the guardian or conservator may:

(1) Use discretion as to which property to sell first.

(2) Sell the entire interest of the estate in the property or any lesser interest therein.

(3) Sell the property either at public auction or private sale.

(b) Subject to Section 1469, unless otherwise specifically provided in this article, all proceedings concerning sales by guardians or conservators, publishing and posting notice of sale, reappraisal for sale, minimum offer price for the property, reselling the property, report of sale and petition for confirmation of sale, and notice and hearing of that petition, making orders authorizing sales, rejecting or confirming sales and reports of sales, ordering and making conveyances of property sold, and allowance of commissions, shall conform, as nearly as may be, to the provisions of this code concerning sales by a personal representative, including, but not limited to, Articles 6 (commencing with Section 10300), 7 (commencing with Section 10350), 8 (commencing with Section 10360), and 9 (commencing with Section 10380) of Chapter 18 of Part 5 of Division 7. The provisions concerning sales by a personal representative as described in the Independent Administration of Estates Act, Part 6 (commencing with Section 10400) of Division 7 shall not apply to this subdivision.

(c) Notwithstanding Section 10309, if the last appraisal of the conservatee's personal residence was conducted more than six months prior to the confirmation hearing, a new appraisal shall be required prior to the confirmation hearing, unless the court finds that it is in the best interests of the conservatee to rely on an appraisal of the personal residence that was conducted not more than one year prior to the confirmation hearing.

(d) The clerk of the court shall cause notice to be posted pursuant to subdivision (b) only in the following cases:

(1) If posting of notice of hearing is required on a petition for the confirmation of a sale of real or personal property of the estate.

(2) If posting of notice of a sale governed by Section 10250 (sales of personal property) is required or authorized.

(3) If posting of notice is ordered by the court. *(Stats. 1990, c. 79 (A.B.759), § 14, operative July 1, 1991. Amended by Stats.2006, c. 490 (S.B.1116), § 4; Stats.2007, c. 553 (A.B.1727), § 17.)*

Law Revision Commission Comments

1990 Enactment

Section 2543 supersedes Section 2543 of the repealed Probate Code. Subdivision (a) is revised to conform to Section 10003 (decedents' estates). Under subdivision (a) there is no priority between personal and real property in selling property, whatever the reason that causes the property to be sold.

Subdivision (b) continues subdivision (b) of Section 2543 of the repealed Probate Code without substantive change. Subdivision (b) does not apply to sales under Section 2544 (listed securities and certain over-the-counter securities) or 2545 (certain tangible personal property).

Subdivision (c) continues subdivision (c) of Section 2543 of the repealed Probate Code, but the statement that the notice be posted at the courthouse of the county where the proceedings described are pending has omitted as unnecessary, this matter being governed by the provisions incorporated by subdivision (b).

The court may add to the list of powers exercisable by the guardian or conservator without court authorization. See Article 11 (commencing with Section 2590) (independent exercise of powers). See also Section 2570 (appealable orders). For general provisions, see Sections 1000–1004 (rules of practice), 1020–1023 (petitions and other papers), 1040–1050 (hearings and orders), 2103 (effect of final order), 2111 (orders for sale or encumbrance of property). See also Sections 1021 (petition to be verified), 1041 (clerk to set petition for hearing). For general provisions relating to notice of hearing, see Sections 1200–1221, 1460–1469. See also Sections 1260–1265 (proof

of giving notice), 2700–2702 (notice to persons who request special notice). For a provision relating to decedents' estates that is comparable to subdivision (a), see Section 10003. For background on the provisions of this part, see the Comment to this part under the part heading. [20 Cal.L.Rev.Comm. Reports 1001 (1990)].

Cross References

Administration of decedents' estates, abatement, see Probate Code § 21400 et seq.
Conveyance by guardian or conservator, see Probate Code § 2111.
Notice,
  Mailing, see Probate Code § 1215 et seq.
  Posting, see Probate Code § 1230.
  Proof of giving notice, see Probate Code § 1260 et seq.
  Special notice, see Probate Code § 1250 et seq.
  This code, generally, see Probate Code § 1200 et seq.
  This division, generally, see Probate Code § 1460 et seq.
Notice to,
  Directors, see Probate Code § 1461.
  Veterans Administration, see Probate Code § 1461.5.
Personal representative and general personal representative, defined, see Probate Code § 58.
Service of process,
  Generally, see Code of Civil Procedure § 413.10 et seq.
  Mail, see Code of Civil Procedure §§ 415.30, 1012 et seq.
  Personal delivery, see Code of Civil Procedure § 415.10.
  Proof of service, see Code of Civil Procedure § 417.10 et seq.
  Publication, see Code of Civil Procedure § 415.50.

§ 2544. Sale of securities

(a) Except as specifically limited by order of the court, subject to Section 2541, the guardian or conservator may sell securities without authorization, confirmation, or direction of the court if any of the following conditions is satisfied:

(1) The securities are to be sold on an established stock or bond exchange.

(2) The securities to be sold are securities designated as a national market system security on an interdealer quotation system or subsystem thereof, by the National Association of Securities Dealers, Inc., sold through a broker-dealer registered under the Securities Exchange Act of 1934 during the regular course of business of the broker-dealer.

(3) The securities are to be directly redeemed by the issuer thereof.

(b) Section 2543 does not apply to sales under this section. *(Stats.1990, c. 79 (A.B.759), § 14, operative July 1, 1991. Amended by Stats.1996, c. 86 (A.B.2146), § 2.)*

Law Revision Commission Comments

1990 Enactment

Section 2544 continues Section 2544 of the repealed Probate Code with the addition of paragraph (2) of subdivision (a). This section permits sales of securities to be sold on an established stock or bond exchange and certain over-the-counter securities without court authorization, confirmation, or direction. Compare Section 10200(e)(2), (3) (decedents' estates). As to the authority to invest in securities, see Section 2574. As to when a power should or should not be exercised, see Section 2401(b) and the Comment thereto. A sale under Section 2544 is subject to review on settlement of the accounts of the guardian or conservator. See Section 2625. For a comparable provision relating to decedents' estates, see Section 10200. For background on the provisions of this part, see the Comment to this part under the part heading. [20 Cal.L.Rev.Comm. Reports 1001 (1990)].

Court supervision, see Probate Code § 2540.
Investment in government obligations, stocks, bonds and securities, see Probate Code § 2574.
Security, defined, see Probate Code § 70.

§ 2544.5. Sale of mutual funds held without beneficiary designation

Except as specifically limited by the court, subject to Section 2541, the guardian or conservator may sell mutual funds held without designation of a beneficiary without authorization, confirmation, or direction of the court. Section 2543 does not apply to sales under this section. *(Added by Stats.1996, c. 86 (A.B.2146), § 2.5.)*

§ 2545. Sale or other disposition of tangible personal property

(a) Subject to subdivisions (b) and (c) and to Section 2541, the guardian or conservator may sell or exchange tangible personal property of the estate without authorization, confirmation, or direction of the court.

(b) The aggregate of the sales or exchanges made during any calendar year under this section may not exceed five thousand dollars ($5,000).

(c) A sale or exchange of personal effects or of furniture or furnishings used for personal, family, or household purposes may be made under this section only if:

(1) In the case of a guardianship, the ward is under the age of 14 or, if 14 years of age or over, consents to the sale or exchange.

(2) In the case of a conservatorship, the conservatee either (i) consents to the sale or exchange or (ii) the conservatee does not have legal capacity to give such consent.

(d) Failure of the guardian or conservator to observe the limitations of subdivision (b) or (c) does not invalidate the title of, or impose any liability upon, a third person who acts in good faith and without actual notice of the lack of authority of the guardian or conservator.

(e) Subdivision (b) of Section 2543 does not apply to sales under this section. *(Stats.1990, c. 79 (A.B.759), § 14, operative July 1, 1991.)*

Law Revision Commission Comments
1990 Enactment

Section 2545 continues Section 2545 of the repealed Probate Code without change. This section gives the guardian or conservator broader authority than exists in the case of a probate estate. The section applies whether or not the property is perishable or is property which may be disposed of without court order in a probate estate (see Sections 10252, 10259).

The reference in subdivision (c) to furniture and furnishings does not include property in commercial use. Hence, consent is not required to sell furniture or furnishings in commercial use. Subdivision (d) protects innocent third persons if the guardian or conservator acts in excess of the authority granted by the section. Subdivision (e) permits sale in such manner as the guardian or conservator considers best under the circumstances.

Sales of tangible personal property that do not fall within Section 2545 are made under the general provisions of this article (Sections 2541–2543). Exchanges of tangible personal property that do not fall within Section 2545 are made under Section 2557. Sales made under

Section 2545 are subject to review on settlement of the accounts of the guardian or conservator. See Section 2625.

For background on the provisions of this part, see the Comment to this part under the part heading. [20 Cal.L.Rev.Comm. Reports 1001 (1990)].

Court supervision, see Probate Code § 2540.
Legal capacity of conservatee, see Probate Code § 1870 et seq.

§ 2546. Repealed by Stats.1987, c. 923, § 78, operative July 1, 1988

Law Revision Commission Comments
1987 Repeal

Former Section 2546 is omitted for consistency with the sale provisions applicable to decedents' estates which no longer provide special rules governing sales of mines or mining claims. See Sections 2543 (sales under guardianship and conservatorship law governed by law concerning sales by administrators), 10000 et seq. (sales in decedents' estates). [19 Cal.L.Rev.Comm. Reports 448 (1988)].

§ 2547. Disposition of proceeds of sale

The guardian or conservator shall apply the proceeds of the sale to the purposes for which it was made, as far as necessary, and the residue, if any, shall be managed as the other property of the estate. *(Stats.1990, c. 79 (A.B.759), § 14, operative July 1, 1991.)*

Law Revision Commission Comments
1990 Enactment

Section 2547 continues Section 2547 of the repealed Probate Code without substantive change. For background on the provisions of this part, see the Comment to this part under the part heading. [20 Cal.L.Rev.Comm. Reports 1001 (1990)].

Investment of proceeds of sales, see Probate Code § 2570.
Purposes for which sale can be made, see Probate Code § 2541.

§ 2548. Recovery of property sold; limitation of action

No action for the recovery of any property sold by a guardian or conservator may be maintained by the ward or conservatee or by any person claiming under the ward or conservatee unless commenced within the later of the following times:

(a) Three years after the termination of the guardianship or conservatorship.

(b) When a legal disability to sue exists by reason of minority or otherwise at the time the cause of action accrues, within three years after the removal thereof. *(Stats.1990, c. 79 (A.B.759), § 14, operative July 1, 1991.)*

Law Revision Commission Comments
1990 Enactment

Section 2548 continues Section 2548 of the repealed Probate Code without change. For background on the provisions of this part, see the Comment to this part under the part heading. [20 Cal.L.Rev.Comm. Reports 1001 (1990)].

Administration of decedents' estates, limitation of actions, see Probate Code § 10382.

Disabilities as affecting computation of time, generally, see Code of
    Civil Procedure §§ 328, 352, 357, 358.
Limitations on actions, generally, see Code of Civil Procedure § 312
    et seq.
Minors defined, see Family Code § 6500.
Three year statute of limitations, see Code of Civil Procedure § 338.

ARTICLE 8. NOTES, MORTGAGES, LEASES, CONVEYANCES, AND EXCHANGES

Cross References

Application of old and new law, see Probate Code § 3.
Mortgages in administration of estates, see Probate Code § 9800 et
    seq.

§ 2550. Court supervision

Except as otherwise provided by statute, a guardian or conservator may borrow money, lend money, give security, lease, convey, or exchange property of the estate, or engage in any other transaction under this article only after authorization by order of the court. Such an order may be obtained in the manner provided in this article. *(Stats.1990, c. 79 (A.B.759), § 14, operative July 1, 1991. Amended by Stats. 1992, c. 572 (S.B.1455), § 5.)*

Law Revision Commission Comments
1990 Enactment

Section 2550 continues Section 2550 of the repealed Probate Code without change. A court order authorizing the transaction may be obtained under this article or under another applicable provision such as Section 2403 (authorization and instructions from court). See also Section 2625 (review at time of accounting of transactions not previously authorized or approved by the court). For a provision permitting exchanges of certain tangible personal property without authorization of the court, see Section 2545. The court may add to the list of powers the guardian or conservator may exercise without court authorization. See Article 11 (commencing with Section 2590) (independent exercise of powers). See also Sections 2111 (order for sale or encumbrance of property), 2750 (appealable orders). For background on the provisions of this part, see the Comment to this part under the part heading. [20 Cal.L.Rev.Comm. Reports 1001 (1990)].

Cross References

Exchanges of certain tangible personal property without court
    authorization, see Probate Code § 2545.

§ 2551. Borrowing money and giving security

(a) In any case described in Section 2541 or Section 2552, the guardian or conservator, after authorization by order of the court, may borrow money upon a note, either unsecured or to be secured by a security interest or other lien on the personal property of the estate or any part thereof or to be secured by a mortgage or deed of trust on the real property of the estate or any part thereof. The guardian or conservator shall apply the money to the purpose specified in the order.

(b) To obtain an order under this section, the guardian or conservator, the ward or conservatee, or any other interested person may file a petition with the court. The petition shall state the purpose for which the order is sought, the necessity for or advantage to accrue from the order, the amount of money proposed to be borrowed, the rate of interest to be paid, the length of time the note is to run, and a general description of the property proposed to be mortgaged or subjected to a deed of trust or other lien. Notice of the hearing on the petition shall be given for the period and in the manner provided in Chapter 3 (commencing with Section 1460) of Part 1.

(c) The court may require such additional proof of the fairness and feasibility of the transaction as the court determines is necessary. If the required showing is made, the court may make an order authorizing the transaction.

The court in its order may do any one or more of the following:

(1) Order that the amount specified in the petition, or a lesser amount, be borrowed.

(2) Prescribe the maximum rate of interest and the period of the loan.

(3) Require that the interest and the whole or any part of the principal be paid from time to time out of the estate or any part thereof.

(4) Require that the personal property used as security or any buildings on real property to be mortgaged or subjected to the deed of trust be insured for the further security of the lender and that the premiums be paid out of the estate.

(5) Specify the purpose for which the money to be borrowed is to be applied.

(6) Prescribe such other terms and conditions concerning the transaction as the court determines to be to the advantage of the estate.

(d) The note and the mortgage or deed of trust, if any, shall be signed by the guardian or conservator.

(e) Jurisdiction of the court to administer the estate of the ward or conservatee is effectual to vest the court with jurisdiction to make the order for the note and for the security interest, lien, mortgage, or deed of trust. This jurisdiction shall conclusively inure to the benefit of the owner of the security interest or lien, mortgagee named in the mortgage, or the trustee and beneficiary named in the deed of trust, and their heirs and assigns. No omission, error, or irregularity in the proceedings shall impair or invalidate the proceedings or the note, security interest, lien, mortgage, or deed of trust given pursuant to an order under this section.

(f) Upon any foreclosure or sale under a security interest, lien, mortgage, or deed of trust described in subdivision (a), if the proceeds of the sale of the encumbered property are insufficient to pay the note, the security interest, lien, mortgage, or deed of trust, and the costs or expenses of sale, no judgment or claim for any deficiency may be had or allowed against the ward or conservatee or the estate. *(Stats.1990, c. 79 (A.B.759), § 14, operative July 1, 1991.)*

Law Revision Commission Comments
1990 Enactment

Section 2551 restates Section 2551 of the repealed Probate Code without substantive change. The reference to hearing petitions and objections thereto has been omitted from the introductory clause of subdivision (c). This reference is unnecessary in light of Section 1046. The remainder of subdivision (c) has been restated without substantive change to conform to Section 9804(b) (decedents' estates). Subdivision (d) is revised to delete the provision relating the personal liability of the guardian or conservator. This matter is governed by Section 2110 (liability of guardian or conservator who signs instrument. For general provisions, see Sections 1000–1004 (rules of practice), 1020–1023 (petitions and other papers), 1040–1050 (hearings and orders), 2103 (effect of final order), 2111 (orders and transactions affecting property), 2750 (appealable orders). For general provisions relating to notice of hearing, see Sections 1200–1221, 1460–1469. See also Sections 1260–1265 (proof of giving notice), 2700–2702 (notice to persons who request special notice). The second sentence of subdivision (a) is comparable to Section 2547 (sales). For comparable provisions relating to decedents' estates, see Sections 9800, 9802–9806. For background on the provisions of this part, see the Comment to this part under the part heading. [20 Cal.L.Rev.Comm. Reports 1001 (1990)].

Cross References

Borrowing money or mortgaging property, see Probate Code § 9800 et seq.
Deficiency judgment, see Code of Civil Procedure §§ 580a, 726.
Foreclosure,
    Actions for foreclosure of trust deeds and mortgages, see Code of Civil Procedure § 725a et seq.
    Authority for, see Civil Code § 2931.
Interested person, defined, see Probate Code § 1424.
Liens,
    Generally, see Civil Code § 2872 et seq.
    Mortgages, generally, see Civil Code § 2920 et seq.
Mortgage not a personal obligation, see Civil Code § 2928.
Real property, defined, see Probate Code § 68.

§ 2552. Refinancing, improving or repairing property

(a) The guardian or conservator may give a security interest or other lien upon the personal property of the estate or any part thereof or a mortgage or deed of trust upon the real property of the estate or any part thereof, after authorization by order of the court as provided in Section 2551, for any of the following purposes:

(1) To pay, reduce, extend, or renew a security interest, lien, mortgage, or deed of trust already existing on property of the estate.

(2) To improve, use, operate, or preserve the property proposed to be mortgaged or subjected to a deed of trust, or some part thereof.

(b) If property of the estate consists of an undivided interest in real or personal property, or any other interest therein less than the entire ownership, upon a showing that it would be to the advantage of the estate to borrow money to improve, use, operate, or preserve the property jointly with the owners of the other interests therein, or to pay, reduce, extend, or renew a security interest, lien, mortgage, or deed of trust already existing on all of the property, the guardian or conservator, after authorization by order of the court as provided in Section 2551, may join with the owners of the other interests in the borrowing of money and the execution of a joint and several note and such security interest, lien,

mortgage, or deed of trust as may be required to secure the payment of the note. The note may be for such sum as is required for the purpose.

(c) No omission, error, or irregularity in the proceedings under this section shall impair or invalidate the proceedings or the note, security interest, lien, mortgage, or deed of trust given pursuant to an order made under this section. *(Stats. 1990, c. 79 (A.B.759), § 14, operative July 1, 1991.)*

Law Revision Commission Comments
1990 Enactment

Section 2552 continues the substance of Section 2552 of the repealed Probate Code with the addition of subdivision (c). This addition is drawn from subdivision (c) of Section 9806, the comparable provision relating to decedents' estates. See also Sections 2103 (effect of final order), 2111 (orders and transactions affecting property), 2750 (appealable orders). For comparable provisions relating to decedents' estates, see Sections 9800–9801. For background on the provisions of this part, see the Comment to this part under the part heading. [20 Cal.L.Rev.Comm. Reports 1001 (1990)].

Cross References

Instructions from or confirmation by court, see Probate Code § 2403.
Interests in property, see Civil Code § 678 et seq.
Liens,
    Generally, see Civil Code § 2872 et seq.
    Mortgages, generally, see Civil Code § 2920 et seq.
Mechanics liens, see Civil Code § 8400.
Real property, defined, see Probate Code § 68.

§ 2552.5. Leases; length of term

For the purpose of this article, if a lease gives the lessee the right to extend the term of the lease, the length of the term shall be considered as though the right to extend had been exercised. *(Stats.1990, c. 79 (A.B.759), § 14, operative July 1, 1991.)*

Law Revision Commission Comments
1990 Enactment

Section 2552.5 is a new provision drawn from subdivision (b) of Section 9940 (decedents' estates). [20 Cal.L.Rev.Comm. Reports 1001 (1990)].

§ 2553. Leases; necessity for court order

(a) Except as provided in Section 2555, leases may be executed by the guardian or conservator with respect to the property of the estate only after authorization by order of the court.

(b) To obtain an order under this section, the guardian or conservator or any interested person may file a petition with the court. The petition shall state (1) a general description of the property proposed to be leased, (2) the term, rental, and general conditions of the proposed lease, and (3) the advantage to the estate to accrue from giving the lease. If the lease is proposed to be for a term longer than 10 years, the petition shall also state facts showing the need for the longer lease and its advantage to the estate. Notice of the hearing on the petition shall be given for the period and in the manner provided in Chapter 3 (commencing with Section 1460) of Part 1.

(c) At the hearing, the court shall entertain and consider any other offer made in good faith at the hearing to lease the same property on more favorable terms. If the court is satisfied that it will be to the advantage of the estate, the court shall make an order authorizing the guardian or conservator to make the lease to the person and on the terms and conditions stated in the order. The court shall not make an order authorizing the guardian or conservator to make the lease to any person other than the lessee named in the petition unless the offer made at the hearing is acceptable to the guardian or conservator.

(d) Jurisdiction of the court to administer the estate of the ward or conservatee is effectual to vest the court with jurisdiction to make the order for the lease. This jurisdiction shall conclusively inure to the benefit of the lessee and the lessee's heirs and assigns. No omission, error, or irregularity in the proceedings shall impair or invalidate the proceedings or the lease made pursuant to an order made under this article. *(Stats.1990, c. 79 (A.B.759), § 14, operative July 1, 1991.)*

Law Revision Commission Comments
1990 Enactment

Section 2553 continues Section 2553 of the repealed Probate Code without substantive change. The portion relating to hearing the petition and any objection has been omitted as unnecessary in view of Section 1046. For general provisions, see Sections 1000–1004 (rules of practice), 1020–1023 (petitions and other papers), 1040–1050 (hearings and orders), 2103 (effect of final order), 2111 (orders and transactions affecting property), 2750 (appealable orders). For general provisions relating to notice of hearing, see Sections 1200–1221, 1460–1469. See also Sections 1260–1265 (proof of giving notice), 2700–2702 (notice to persons who request special notice). For comparable provisions relating to decedents' estates, see Sections 9942–9945. For background on the provisions of this part, see the Comment to this part under the part heading. [20 Cal.L.Rev.Comm. Reports 1001 (1990)].

Cross References
Interested person, defined, see Probate Code § 1424.
Leases by personal representatives, see Probate Code § 9942.
Orders, see Probate Code § 1047 et seq.

§ 2554. Leases; terms and conditions

(a) An order authorizing the execution of a lease shall set forth the minimum rental or royalty or both and the period of the lease, which shall be for such time as the court may authorize.

(b) The order may authorize other terms and conditions, including, with respect to a lease for the purpose of exploration for or production or removal of minerals, oil, gas, or other hydrocarbon substances, or geothermal energy, any one or more of the following:

(1) A provision for the payment of rental and royalty to a depositary.

(2) A provision for the appointment of a common agent to represent the interests of all the lessors.

(3) A provision for the payment of a compensatory royalty in lieu of rental and in lieu of drilling and producing operations on the land covered by the lease.

(4) A provision empowering the lessee to enter into any agreement authorized by Section 3301 of the Public Resources Code with respect to the land covered by the lease.

(5) A provision for a community oil lease or pooling or unitization by the lessee.

(c) If the lease covers additional property owned by other persons or an undivided or other interest of the ward or conservatee less than the entire ownership in the property, the order may authorize the lease to provide for division of rental and royalty in the proportion that the land or interest of each owner bears to the total area of the land or total interests covered by such lease.

(d) If the lease is for the purpose of exploration for or production or removal of minerals, oil, gas, or other hydrocarbon substances, or geothermal energy, the court may authorize that the lease be for a fixed period and any of the following:

(1) So long thereafter as minerals, oil, gas, or other hydrocarbon substances or geothermal energy are produced in paying quantities from the property leased or mining or drilling operations are conducted thereon.

(2) If the lease provides for the payment of a compensatory royalty, so long thereafter as such compensatory royalty is paid.

(3) If the land covered by the lease is included in an agreement authorized by Section 3301 of the Public Resources Code, so long thereafter as oil, gas, or other hydrocarbon substances are produced in paying quantities from any of the lands included in any such agreement or drilling operations are conducted thereon. *(Stats.1990, c. 79 (A.B.759), § 14, operative July 1, 1991.)*

Law Revision Commission Comments
1990 Enactment

Section 2554 continues Section 2554 of the repealed Probate Code with revisions to conform the section to Section 9946 and subdivision (c) of Section 9947, the comparable provisions relating to decedents' estates. These conforming revisions add references to geothermal energy and a community oil lease to Section 2554. See also Sections 2103 (effect of final order), 2111 (orders affecting property), 2750 (appealable orders). For background on the provisions of this part, see the Comment to this part under the part heading. [20 Cal.L.Rev.Comm. Reports 1001 (1990)].

Cross References
Lease of property in administration of estates, see Probate Code § 9945.
Oil, gas and mineral leases,
  Generally, see Public Resources Code § 6801 et seq.
  Duration, see Civil Code § 718.
Recordation and constructive notice, oil and gas leases, see Civil Code § 1219.

§ 2555. Leases; authorized without court permission

If it is to the advantage of the estate, the guardian or conservator may lease, as lessor, real property of the estate without authorization of the court in either of the following cases:

(a) Where the rental does not exceed five thousand dollars ($5,000) a month and the term does not exceed two years.

(b) Where the lease is from month to month, regardless of the amount of the rental. *(Stats.1990, c. 79 (A.B.759), § 14, operative July 1, 1991. Amended by Stats.1990, c. 710 (S.B.1775), § 11, operative July 1, 1991.)*

1990 Enactment

Section 2555 restates Section 2555 of the repealed Probate Code without substantive change. For a comparable provision relating to decedents' estates, see Section 9941. For background on the provisions of this part, see the Comment to this part under the part heading. [20 Cal.L.Rev.Comm. Reports 1001 (1990)].

1990 Amendment

Section 2555 (enacted as a part of the new Probate Code by 1990 Cal.Stat. ch. 79 § 14) was amended by 1990 Cal.Stat. ch. 710 § 11. The amendment increased the limit on executing a lease without court approval from $1,500 to $5,000. See also Section 2501 (extension, renewal, or modification of lease by guardian or conservator). For a comparable provision relating to personal representatives, see Section 9941. For background on the 1990 amendment, see Recommendation Relating to Execution or Modification of Lease Without Court Order, 20 Cal.L.Revision Comm'n Reports 557 (1990). [20 Cal.L.Rev.Comm. Reports 1001 (1990)].

Cross References

Effect of court authorization or approval, see Probate Code § 2103.
Hiring of real property, see Civil Code § 1940 et seq.
Instructions from or confirmation by court, see Probate Code § 2403.
Modification, extension, or renewal of leases, see Probate Code § 2501.
Real property, defined, see Probate Code § 68.

§ 2556. Dedication or conveyance of real property or easement with or without consideration

(a) If it is for the advantage, benefit, and best interests of the estate and those interested therein, the guardian or conservator, after authorization by order of the court, may do any of the following either with or without consideration:

(1) Dedicate or convey real property of the estate for any purpose to any of the following:

(A) This state or any public entity in this state.

(B) The United States or any agency or instrumentality of the United States.

(2) Dedicate or convey an easement over any real property of the estate to any person for any purpose.

(3) Convey, release, or relinquish to this state or any public entity in this state any access rights to any street, highway, or freeway from any real property of the estate.

(4) Consent as a lienholder to a dedication, conveyance, release, or relinquishment under paragraph (1), (2), or (3) by the owner of property subject to the lien.

(b) To obtain an order under this section, the guardian or conservator or any other interested person shall file a petition with the court. Notice of the hearing on the petition shall be given for the period and in the manner provided in Chapter 3 (commencing with Section 1460) of Part 1. *(Stats.1990, c. 79 (A.B.759), § 14, operative July 1, 1991.)*

1990 Enactment

Section 2556 restates the substance of Section 2556 of the repealed Probate Code using language drawn from Section 9900, the comparable provision relating to decedents' estates. For general provisions, see Sections 1000–1004 (rules of practice), 1020–1023 (petitions and other papers), 1040–1050 (hearings and orders), 2103 (effect of final order), 2111 (orders and transactions affecting property), 2750 (appealable orders). For general provisions relating to notice of hearing, see Sections 1200–1221, 1460–1469. See also Sections 1260–1265 (proof of giving notice), 2700–2702 (notice to persons who request special notice). For background on the provisions of this part, see the Comment to this part under the part heading. [20 Cal.L.Rev.Comm. Reports 1001 (1990)].

Cross References

Community property, court authorization, see Probate Code §§ 3101, 3102.
Dedication of real property for public purposes, see Government Code § 7050.
Easements, generally, see Civil Code § 801 et seq.
Interested person, defined, see Probate Code § 1424.
Liens, generally, see Civil Code § 2872 et seq.
Personal representatives, similar provisions relating to, see Probate Code § 9900.
Power of legislative body to acquire easements for public interest, see Streets and Highways Code § 10102.
Real property, defined, see Probate Code § 68.

§ 2557. Exchange of property

(a) Whenever it is for the advantage, benefit, and best interests of the ward or conservatee and those legally entitled to support, maintenance, or education from the ward or conservatee, the guardian or conservator, after authorization by order of the court, may exchange any property of the estate for other property upon such terms and conditions as may be prescribed by the court. The terms and conditions prescribed by the court may include the payment or receipt of part cash by the guardian or conservator.

(b) To obtain an order under this section, the guardian or conservator or any interested person shall file a petition containing all of the following:

(1) A description of the property.

(2) The terms and conditions of the proposed exchange.

(3) A showing that the proposed exchange is for the advantage, benefit, and best interests of the ward or conservatee and those legally entitled to support, maintenance, or education from the ward or conservatee.

(c) Except as provided in subdivision (d), notice of the hearing on the petition shall be given for the period and in the manner provided in Chapter 3 (commencing with Section 1460) of Part 1.

(d) If the petition is for authorization to exchange stocks, bonds, or other securities as defined in Section 10200 for different stocks, bonds, or other securities, the court, upon a showing of good cause, may order that the notice be given for a shorter period or be dispensed with.

(e) After authorization by order of the court, the guardian or conservator may execute the conveyance or transfer to the person with whom the exchange is made to effectuate the exchange.

(f) No omission, error, or irregularity in the proceedings under this section shall impair or invalidate the proceedings or the exchange made pursuant to an order made under this section. *(Stats.1990, c. 79 (A.B.759), § 14, operative July 1, 1991.)*

Law Revision Commission Comments

1990 Enactment

Section 2557 restates Section 2557 of the repealed Probate Code without substantive change, with the addition of provisions in subdivision (b) stating the contents of the petition and the addition of subdivision (f). The provision stating the contents of the petition has been drawn from Section 9921, the comparable provision relating to decedents' estates. Subdivision (f) is comparable to Section 9923 (decedents' estates). Subdivision (d) has been revised to recognize that the court may order that notice be given for a shorter period as an alternative to dispensing with notice. For general provisions, see Sections 1000–1004 (rules of practice), 1020–1023 (petitions and other papers), 1040–1050 (hearings and orders), 2103 (effect of final order), 2111 (orders and transactions affecting property), 2750 (appealable orders). For general provisions relating to notice of hearing, see Sections 1200–1221, 1460–1469. See also Sections 1260–1265 (proof of giving notice), 2700–2702 (notice to persons who request special notice). For comparable provisions relating to decedents' estates, see Sections 9920–9922. See also Section 10200 (sale or surrender for redemption or conversion of securities). For background on the provisions of this part, see the Comment to this part under the part heading. [20 Cal.L.Rev.Comm. Reports 1001 (1990)].

Cross References

Conveyance by guardian or conservator, see Probate Code § 2111.
Disposition or sale of tangible personal property, see Probate Code § 2545.
Exchange of property by personal representative, see Probate Code § 9920.
Interested person, defined, see Probate Code § 1424.
Security, defined, see Probate Code § 70.

ARTICLE 9. INVESTMENTS AND PURCHASE OF PROPERTY

Section
2570. Authority; petition; hearing; order.
2571. Purchase of home for ward, conservatee or dependents.
2572. Purchase of real property; order.
2573. Investment in governmental bonds; order.
2574. Investment of funds; federal and state obligations; stocks, bonds and securities.
2575. Repealed.

Cross References

Application of old and new law, see Probate Code § 3.

§ 2570. Authority; petition; hearing; order

(a) The guardian or conservator, after authorization by order of the court, may invest the proceeds of sales and any other money of the estate as provided in the order.

(b) To obtain an order of the court authorizing a transaction under subdivision (a) of this section, the guardian or conservator, the ward or conservatee, or any other interested person may file a petition with the court.

(c) Notice of the hearing on the petition shall be given for the period and in the manner provided in Chapter 3 (commencing with Section 1460) of Part 1. The court may order that the notice be dispensed with.

(d) The court may require such proof of the fairness and feasibility of the transaction as the court determines is necessary.

(e) If the required showing is made, the court may make an order authorizing the transaction and may prescribe in the order the terms and conditions upon which the transaction shall be made. *(Stats.1990, c. 79 (A.B.759), § 14, operative July 1, 1991.)*

Law Revision Commission Comments

1990 Enactment

Section 2570 continues Section 2570 of the repealed Probate Code without substantive change. The provision that the court shall hear the petition and any objections has been omitted as unnecessary in view of Section 1046. Subdivision (a) provides general authority for the investment of surplus funds of the estate in real property or tangible or intangible personal property. An investment made under Section 2570 requires court authorization. Other provisions in this article and elsewhere permit specific types of investments without the need for court authorization. For example, see Sections 2453 (account in financial institution), 2574 (United States and State of California obligations and listed stocks, bonds, and other securities). For general provisions, see Sections 1000–1004 (rules of practice), 1020–1023 (petitions and other papers), 1040–1050 (hearings and orders), 2103 (effect of final order). For general provisions relating to notice of hearing, see Sections 1200–1221, 1460–1469. See also Sections 1260–1265 (proof of giving notice), 2700–2702 (notice to persons who request special notice). See also Section 2403 (permitting the guardian or conservator to seek court authorization, instructions, approval, or confirmation for particular transactions), 2625 (review at time of accounting of sales, purchases, and other transactions not previously authorized or approved). For background on the provisions of this part, see the Comment to this part under the part heading. [20 Cal.L.Rev.Comm. Reports 1001 (1990)].

Cross References

Deposits in bank and savings accounts, see Probate Code § 2453.
Disposition of proceeds of sale, see Probate Code § 2547.
Interested persons, defined, see Probate Code § 1424.

§ 2571. Purchase of home for ward, conservatee or dependents

When authorized by order of the court under Section 2570, the guardian or conservator may purchase:

(a) Real property in this state as a home for the ward or conservatee if such purchase is for the advantage, benefit, and best interest of the ward or conservatee.

(b) Real property as a home for those legally entitled to support and maintenance from the ward or conservatee if such purchase is for the advantage, benefit, and best interest of the ward or conservatee and of those legally entitled to support and maintenance from the ward or conservatee. *(Stats.1990, c. 79 (A.B.759), § 14, operative July 1, 1991.)*

Law Revision Commission Comments

1990 Enactment

Section 2571 continues Section 2571 of the repealed Probate Code without change. A purchase under this section requires court authorization under Section 2570. For general provisions, see Sections 1000–1004 (rules of practice), 1020–1023 (petitions and other papers), 1040–1050 (hearings and orders), 2103 (effect of final order). For background on the provisions of this part, see the Comment to this part under the part heading. [20 Cal.L.Rev.Comm. Reports 1001 (1990)].

Cross References

Order authorizing purchase of real property, see Probate Code § 2572.

Real property, defined, see Probate Code § 68.

§ 2572. Purchase of real property; order

An order authorizing the guardian or conservator to purchase real property may authorize the guardian or conservator to join with the spouse of the ward or the spouse or domestic partner of the conservatee or with any other person or persons in the purchase of the real property, or an interest, equity, or estate therein, in severalty, in common, in community, or in joint tenancy, for cash or upon a credit or for part cash and part credit. When the court authorizes the purchase of real property, the court may order the guardian or conservator to execute all necessary instruments and commitments to complete the transaction. *(Stats.1990, c. 79 (A.B.759), § 14, operative July 1, 1991. Amended by Stats. 2001, c. 893 (A.B.25), § 37.)*

Law Revision Commission Comments

1990 Enactment

Section 2572 continues Section 2572 of the repealed Probate Code without change. As to community property, see Sections 3020, 3023. For general provisions, see Sections 1000–1004 (rules of practice), 1020–1023 (petitions and other papers), 1040–1050 (hearings and orders), 2103 (effect of final order), 2111 (orders and transactions affecting property), 2750 (appealable orders). For background on the provisions of this part, see the Comment to this part under the part heading. [20 Cal.L.Rev.Comm. Reports 1001 (1990)].

Cross References

Community property, see Probate Code § 3020 et seq.

Domestic partner, defined, see Probate Code § 37.

Instrument, defined, see Probate Code § 45.

Interests in property, see Civil Code § 678 et seq.

Real property, defined, see Probate Code § 68.

§ 2573. Investment in governmental bonds; order

An order authorizing investment in bonds issued by any state or of any city, county, city and county, political subdivision, public corporation, district, or special district of any state may authorize the guardian or conservator to select from among bonds issued by any such issuer, without specifying any particular issuer or issue of bonds, if the type of issuer is designated in general terms and the order specifies as to such bonds a minimum quality rating as shown in a recognized investment service, a minimum interest coupon rate, a minimum yield to maturity, and the date of maturity within a five-year range. *(Stats.1990, c. A.B. 759), § 14, operative July 1, 1991.)*

Law Revision Commission Comments

1990 Enactment

Section 2573 continues Section 2573 of the repealed Probate Code without substantive change. For background on the provisions of this part, see the Comment to this part under the part heading. [20 Cal.L.Rev.Comm. Reports 1001 (1990)].

Cross References

Sales of stocks, bonds and securities, see Probate Code § 2544.

§ 2574. Investment of funds; federal and state obligations; stocks, bonds and securities

(a) Subject to subdivision (b), the guardian or conservator, without authorization of the court, may invest funds of the estate pursuant to this section in:

(1) Direct obligations of the United States, or of the State of California, maturing not later than five years from the date of making the investment.

(2) United States Treasury bonds redeemable at par value on the death of the holder for payment of federal estate taxes, regardless of maturity date.

(3) Securities listed on an established stock or bond exchange in the United States which are purchased on such exchange.

(4) Eligible securities for the investment of surplus state moneys as provided for in Section 16430 of the Government Code.

(5) An interest in a money market mutual fund registered under the Investment Company Act of 1940 (15 U.S.C. Sec. 80a–1, et seq.) or an investment vehicle authorized for the collective investment of trust funds pursuant to Section 9.18 of Part 9 of Title 12 of the Code of Federal Regulations, the portfolios of which are limited to United States government obligations maturing not later than five years from the date of investment and to repurchase agreements fully collateralized by United States government obligations.

(6) Units of a common trust fund described in Section 1585 of the Financial Code. The common trust fund shall have as its objective investment primarily in short-term fixed income obligations and shall be permitted to value investments at cost pursuant to regulations of the appropriate regulatory authority.

(b) In making and retaining investments made under this section, the guardian or conservator shall take into consideration the circumstances of the estate, indicated cash needs, and, if reasonably ascertainable, the date of the prospective termination of the guardianship or conservatorship.

(c) This section shall not limit the authority of the guardian or conservator to seek court authorization for any investment, or to make other investments with court authorization, as provided in this division. *(Stats.1990, c. 79 (A.B.759), § 14, operative July 1, 1991. Amended by Stats. 2014, c. 71 (S.B.1304), § 136, eff. Jan. 1, 2015.)*

Law Revision Commission Comments

1990 Enactment

Section 2574 continues Section 2574 of the repealed Probate Code without substantive change. Subdivision (a)(1) is revised using language drawn from Section 9730(a), the comparable provision relating to decedents' estates. Subdivision (a) eliminates the need to apply in advance for a court order to invest or reinvest as described. Subdivision (b) requires consideration of the circumstances of the estate and the time when protective proceedings will likely terminate.

Section 2574 is consistent with scheme of Section 2544 which permits sale of listed securities and certain over-the-counter securities without court authorization, but departs from comparable provisions relating to probate estates which require a court order for sale of securities (Section 10200).

An investment in a government obligation, stock, bond, or security that is not one described in Section 2574 may be made only if court authorization is obtained under Section 2570. An investment made under Section 2574 is subject to court review on settlement of the accounts of the guardian or conservator. See Section 2625.

For a comparable provision relating to decedents' estates, see Section 9730. For background on the provisions of this part, see the Comment to this part under the part heading. [20 Cal.L.Rev.Comm. Reports 1001 (1990)].

Cross References

Administration of decedents' estates, court order for sale of securities, see Probate Code § 10200.
Court authorization, see Probate Code § 2570.
Effect of court authorization or approval, see Probate Code § 2103.
Sales of stocks, bonds and securities, see Probate Code § 2544.
Security, defined, see Probate Code § 70.
Trusts funded by court order, required provisions in trust instruments, see California Rules of Court, Rule 7.903.

§ 2575. Repealed by Stats.1990, c. 79 (A.B.759), § 13, operative July 1, 1991

Law Revision Commission Comments

1990 Repeal

Section 2575 of the repealed Probate Code is omitted from the new Probate Code because it is unnecessary. The authority provided by former Section 2575 is duplicated in Section 2574(a)(6). [20 Cal.L.Rev.Comm. Reports 1001 (1990)].

ARTICLE 10. SUBSTITUTED JUDGMENT

Section
2580. Petition to authorize proposed action.
2581. Notice of hearing of petition.
2582. Consent or lack of capacity of conservatee; adequate provision for conservatee and dependents.
2583. Proposed actions by court; relevant circumstances.
2584. Determination and order.
2585. No duty to propose action.
2586. Production of conservatee's will and other relevant estate plan documents; safekeeping of documents by custodian appointed by the court.

Law Revision Commission Comments

1990 Enactment

This article (commencing with Section 2580) codifies the court-recognized doctrine of substituted judgment. See Estate of Christiansen, 248 Cal.App.2d 398, 56 Cal.Rptr. 505 (1967); Conservatorship of Wemyss, 20 Cal.App.3d 877, 98 Cal.Rptr. 85 (1971). For prior cases discussing gifts of surplus income for religious or charitable purposes to carry out the presumed wishes of an incompetent ward, see Harris v. Harris, 57 Cal.2d 367, 369 P.2d 481, 19 Cal.Rptr. 793 (1962); Guardianship of Hall, 31 Cal.2d 157, 187 P.2d 396 (1947).

For gifts of income from the conservatorship estate, this article supplements Section 2423 which authorizes payments of surplus income to the spouse and to relatives within the second degree of the conservatee under certain circumstances. Gifts of surplus income under this article are not limited to the spouse and such relatives.

For background on the provisions of this part, see Comment to this part under the part heading. [20 Cal.L.Rev.Comm. Reports 1001 (1990)].

Cross References

Application of old and new law, see Probate Code § 3.
Fee for filing petition and opposition papers concerning internal affairs of certain trusts or first accounts of trustees of certain testamentary trusts, see Government Code § 70652.
Powers of appointment, generally, see Probate Code § 600 et seq.
Trusts funded by court order, see California Rules of Court, Rule 7.903.

§ 2580. Petition to authorize proposed action

(a) The conservator or other interested person may file a petition under this article for an order of the court authorizing or requiring the conservator to take a proposed action for any one or more of the following purposes:

(1) Benefiting the conservatee or the estate.

(2) Minimizing current or prospective taxes or expenses of administration of the conservatorship estate or of the estate upon the death of the conservatee.

(3) Providing gifts for any purposes, and to any charities, relatives (including the other spouse or domestic partner), friends, or other objects of bounty, as would be likely beneficiaries of gifts from the conservatee.

(b) The action proposed in the petition may include, but is not limited to, the following:

(1) Making gifts of principal or income, or both, of the estate, outright or in trust.

(2) Conveying or releasing the conservatee's contingent and expectant interests in property, including marital property rights and any right of survivorship incident to joint tenancy or tenancy by the entirety.

(3) Exercising or releasing the conservatee's powers as donee of a power of appointment.

(4) Entering into contracts.

(5) Creating for the benefit of the conservatee or others, revocable or irrevocable trusts of the property of the estate, which trusts may extend beyond the conservatee's disability or life. A special needs trust for money paid pursuant to a compromise or judgment for a conservatee may be established only under Chapter 4 (commencing with Section 3600) of Part 8, and not under this article.

(6) Transferring to a trust created by the conservator or conservatee any property unintentionally omitted from the trust.

(7) Exercising options of the conservatee to purchase or exchange securities or other property.

(8) Exercising the rights of the conservatee to elect benefit or payment options, to terminate, to change beneficiaries or ownership, to assign rights, to borrow, or to receive cash value in return for a surrender of rights under any of the following:

(A) Life insurance policies, plans, or benefits.

(B) Annuity policies, plans, or benefits.

(C) Mutual fund and other dividend investment plans.

(D) Retirement, profit sharing, and employee welfare plans and benefits.

(9) Exercising the right of the conservatee to elect to take under or against a will.

(10) Exercising the right of the conservatee to disclaim any interest that may be disclaimed under Part 8 (commencing with Section 260) of Division 2.

(11) Exercising the right of the conservatee (A) to revoke or modify a revocable trust or (B) to surrender the right to revoke or modify a revocable trust, but the court shall not authorize or require the conservator to exercise the right to revoke or modify a revocable trust if the instrument governing the trust (A) evidences an intent to reserve the right of revocation or modification exclusively to the conservatee, (B) provides expressly that a conservator may not revoke or modify the trust, or (C) otherwise evidences an intent that would be inconsistent with authorizing or requiring the conservator to exercise the right to revoke or modify the trust.

(12) Making an election referred to in Section 13502 or an election and agreement referred to in Section 13503.

(13) Making a will.

(14) Making or revoking a revocable transfer on death deed. *(Stats.1990, c. 79 (A.B.759), § 14, operative July 1, 1991. Amended by Stats.1992, c. 355 (A.B.3328), § 1; Stats. 1992, c. 572 (S.B.1455), § 6.5; Stats.1995, c. 730 (A.B.1466), § 4; Stats.1999, c; 175 (A.B.239), § 3; Stats.2001, c. 893 (A.B.25), § 38; Stats.2015, c. 293 (A.B.139), § 7, eff. Jan. 1, 2016.)*

Law Revision Commission Comments

1990 Enactment

Section 2580 continues Section 2580 of the repealed Probate Code without change. Section 2580 is drawn in part from Mass.Ann.Laws ch. 201, § 38 (West 1958 & Supp.1989). See also 20 Pa.Cons.Stat. Ann. § 5536(b) (Purdon 1975 & Supp.1989); Uniform Probate Code § 5–408 (1987).

For general provisions relating to petitions and other papers, see Sections 1020–1023.

Subdivision (a) indicates three situations where substituted judgment may be exercised:

(1) Where the action proposed to be taken by the conservator is for the benefit of the conservatee or the estate.

(2) Where the proposed action is designed to minimize taxes (such as federal, state, or local income taxes or estate taxes) or expenses of administration during the lifetime and on death of the conservatee.

(3) Where there is a person to whom the conservatee probably would have made gifts or provided support from excess funds or assets, or where there are charities or other objects of bounty which the conservatee showed an inclination to support.

The nonexclusive listing in subdivision (b) of the types of actions which may be proposed in the petition is drawn in part from the Massachusetts and Pennsylvania statutes and from Uniform Probate Code Section 5–408(3) (1987). As to transactions involving community property, see Section 3102(f).

For general provisions, see Sections 1000–1004 (rules of practice), 1020–1023 (petitions and other papers), 1040–1050 (hearings and orders), 2103 (effect of final order). See also Sections 1021 (petition to be verified), 1041 (clerk to set petition for hearing). For background on the provisions of this article, see the Comment to this article under the article heading. See also Recommendation Relating to Disclaimer of Testamentary and Other Interests, 16 Cal.L.Revision Comm'n Reports 207, 229–31 (1982). [20 Cal.L.Rev.Comm. Reports 1001 (1990)].

1992 Amendment [Revised Comment]

Paragraph (5) of subdivision (b) of Section 2580 is amended to make clear that a special needs trust for money paid pursuant to a compromise or judgment for a conservatee may only be established under Chapter 4 (commencing with Section 3600) of Part 8. See Sections 3602–3605.

Section 2580 is also amended to add paragraph (6) to subdivision (b). If property is discovered after the conservatee's death that has been unintentionally omitted from a trust created by the conservator or conservatee, the conservator has control of the property pending its disposition according to law. Prob.Code § 2467. See also Prob.Code § 2630 (continuing jurisdiction of court). [22 Cal.L.Rev. Comm. Reports 983 (1992)].

Cross References

Contracts, generally, see Civil Code § 1549 et seq.
Destruction of court records, notice, retention periods, see Government Code § 68152.
Disclaimer of testamentary and other interests on behalf of ward or conservatee, see Probate Code § 276.
Domestic partner, defined, see Probate Code § 37.
Election of benefit or payment options, etc., of certain policies or plans, authority of guardian or conservator, see Probate Code § 2459.
Election of guardian or conservator of surviving spouse to have property administered in probate, see Probate Code § 13502 et seq.
Exchange of securities, see Probate Code § 2557.
Gifts, generally, see Civil Code § 1146 et seq.
Instrument, defined, see Probate Code § 45.
Interested person, defined, see Probate Code § 1424.
Interests in property, see Civil Code § 678 et seq.
Joint tenancy, see Civil Code § 683.
Payment of surplus income to relatives of conservatee, see Probate Code § 2423.
Proration of estate taxes, see Probate Code § 20100 et seq.
Proration of generation-skipping transfer tax, see Probate Code § 20200 et seq.
Security, defined, see Probate Code § 70.
Transfers of property, generally, see Civil Code § 1039 et seq.
Trusts, creation, validity, modification, and termination, see Probate Code § 15200 et seq.

§ 2581. Notice of hearing of petition

Notice of the hearing of the petition shall be given, regardless of age, for the period and in the manner provided in Chapter 3 (commencing with Section 1460) or Part 1 to all of the following:

(a) The persons required to be given notice under Chapter 3 (commencing with Section 1460) of Part 1.

(b) The persons required to be named in a petition for the appointment of a conservator.

(c) So far as is known to the petitioner, beneficiaries under any document executed by the conservatee which may have testamentary effect unless the court for good cause dispenses with such notice.

(d) So far as is known to the petitioner, the persons who, if the conservatee were to die immediately, would be the conservatee's heirs under the laws of intestate succession unless the court for good cause dispenses with such notice.

(e) Such other persons as the court may order. *(Stats. 1990, c. 79 (A.B.759), § 14, operative July 1, 1991. Amended by Stats.1996, c. 862 (A.B.2751), § 8.)*

Section 2581 continues Section 2581 of the repealed Probate Code without substantive change. The phrase "other than the petitioner or persons joining in the petition" has been omitted as unnecessary in view of Section 1201. For general provisions relating to notice of hearing, see Sections 1200–1221, 1460–1469. See also Sections 1260–1265 (proof of giving notice), 2700–2702 (notice to persons who request special notice). For background on the provisions of this article, see the Comment to this article under the article heading. [20 Cal.L.Rev.Comm. Reports 1001 (1990)].

Beneficiary, defined, see Probate Code § 24
Contents of petition for appointment of conservator, see Probate Code § 1821.
Notice to directors, see Probate Code § 1461.
Request for special notice, see Probate Code § 2700 et seq.
Succession, generally, see Probate Code § 250.

§ 2582. Consent or lack of capacity of conservatee; adequate provision for conservatee and dependents

The court may make an order authorizing or requiring the proposed action under this article only if the court determines all of the following:

(a) The conservatee either (1) is not opposed to the proposed action or (2) if opposed to the proposed action, lacks legal capacity for the proposed action.

(b) Either the proposed action will have no adverse effect on the estate or the estate remaining after the proposed action is taken will be adequate to provide for the needs of the conservatee and for the support of those legally entitled to support, maintenance, and education from the conservatee, taking into account the age, physical condition, standards of living, and all other relevant circumstances of the conservatee and those legally entitled to support, maintenance, and education from the conservatee. *(Stats.1990, c. 79 (A.B.759), § 14, operative July 1, 1991.)*

Section 2582 continues Section 2582 of the repealed Probate Code without change. Subdivision (a) precludes an order under this article if the conservatee has legal capacity for the proposed action and is opposed to it. This is consistent with Estate of Christiansen, 248 Cal.App.2d 398, 56 Cal.Rptr. 505 (1967), permitting exercise of substituted judgment for a conservatee who is "insane" or "incompetent." Subdivision (b) recognizes that the conservatee and those legally entitled to support, maintenance, and education from the conservatee have first claim on the income and assets of the estate. For general provisions relating to hearings and orders, see Sections 1040–1050. See also Section 2750 (appealable orders). For background on the provisions of this article, see the Comment to this article under the article heading. [20 Cal.L.Rev.Comm. Reports 1001 (1990)].

Legal capacity of conservatee, see Probate Code § 1870 et seq.

§ 2583. Proposed actions by court; relevant circumstances

In determining whether to authorize or require a proposed action under this article, the court shall take into consideration all the relevant circumstances, which may include, but are not limited to, the following:

(a) Whether the conservatee has legal capacity for the proposed transaction and, if not, the probability of the conservatee's recovery of legal capacity.

(b) The past donative declarations, practices, and conduct of the conservatee.

(c) The traits of the conservatee.

(d) The relationship and intimacy of the prospective donees with the conservatee, their standards of living, and the extent to which they would be natural objects of the conservatee's bounty by any objective test based on such relationship, intimacy, and standards of living.

(e) The wishes of the conservatee.

(f) Any known estate plan of the conservatee (including, but not limited to, the conservatee's will, any trust of which the conservatee is the settlor or beneficiary, any power of appointment created by or exercisable by the conservatee, and any contract, transfer, or joint ownership arrangement with provisions for payment or transfer of benefits or interests at the conservatee's death to another or others which the conservatee may have originated).

(g) The manner in which the estate would devolve upon the conservatee's death, giving consideration to the age and the mental and physical condition of the conservatee, the prospective devisees or heirs of the conservatee, and the prospective donees.

(h) The value, liquidity, and productiveness of the estate.

(i) The minimization of current or prospective income, estate, inheritance, or other taxes or expenses of administration.

(j) Changes of tax laws and other laws which would likely have motivated the conservatee to alter the conservatee's estate plan.

(k) The likelihood from all the circumstances that the conservatee as a reasonably prudent person would take the proposed action if the conservatee had the capacity to do so.

(*l*) Whether any beneficiary is the spouse or domestic partner of the conservatee.

(m) Whether a beneficiary has committed physical abuse, neglect, false imprisonment, or financial abuse against the conservatee after the conservatee was substantially unable to manage his or her financial resources, or resist fraud or undue influence, and the conservatee's disability persisted throughout the time of the hearing on the proposed substituted judgment. *(Stats.1990, c. 79 (A.B.759), § 14, operative July 1, 1991. Amended by Stats.1992, c. 871 (A.B.2975), § 6; Stats.1993, c. 293 (A.B.21), § 3; Stats.1998, c. 935 (S.B.1715), § 5; Stats.2010, c. 620 (S.B.105), § 2; Stats.2011, c. 308 (S.B.647), § 10.)*

Section 2583 continues Section 2583 of the repealed Probate Code without substantive change.

This section gives the court discretion and flexibility in applying the doctrine of substituted judgment under the circumstances of the case. The listing in Section 2583 is not exclusive, and the weight to be given to any particular matter listed depends on the circumstances of the case. Subdivision (k) lists a relevant consideration absent a showing of contrary intent. See Estate of Christiansen, 248 Cal.App.2d 398, 414, 424, 56 Cal.Rptr. 505, 516, 522–23 (1967) (court will not assume conservatee is abnormally selfish unless that trait is established). A matter not listed may be significant in a particular case. For example, the conservatee may have received property from a parent with the understanding that the conservatee would leave the property to the descendants of that parent. Such an understanding would be a circumstance the court should consider with other relevant circumstances. For general provisions relating to hearings and orders, see Sections 1040–1050. For background on the provisions of this article, see the Comment to this article under the article heading. [20 Cal.L.Rev.Comm. Reports 1001 (1990)].

2010 Amendment

Section 2583(*l*) is amended to replace a reference to former Section 21350(b)(1) with the substance of that former provision. [38 Cal.L.Rev.Comm. Reports 107 (2008)].

Cross References

Beneficiary, defined, see Probate Code § 24
Devisee, defined, see Probate Code § 34.
Legal capacity of conservatee, see Probate Code § 1870 et seq.
Powers of appointment, generally, see Probate Code § 600 et seq.
Presumption of fraud or undue influence with respect to wills and trusts, enumeration of certain donative transfers subject to the presumption, see Probate Code § 21380.
Production of conservatee's will and other relevant estate plan documents, see Probate Code § 2586.
Proration of estate taxes, see Probate Code § 20100 et seq.
Proration of generation-skipping transfer tax, see Probate Code § 20200 et seq.

§ 2584. Determination and order

After hearing, the court, in its discretion, may approve, modify and approve, or disapprove the proposed action and may authorize or direct the conservator to transfer or dispose of assets or take other action as provided in the court's order. *(Stats.1990, c. 79 (A.B.759), § 14, operative July 1, 1991.)*

Law Revision Commission Comments
1990 Enactment

Section 2584 continues Section 2584 of the repealed Probate Code without change. For general provisions, see Sections 1000–1004 (rules of practice), 1020–1023 (petitions and other papers), 1040–1050 (hearings and orders), 2103 (effect of final order), 2111 (orders and transactions affecting property). See also Section 2750 (granting or denying petition under this chapter is an appealable order). For background on the provisions of this article, see the Comment to this article under the article heading. [20 Cal.L.Rev.Comm. Reports 1001 (1990)].

Cross References

Appealable orders, see Probate Code § 1300 et seq.

§ 2585. No duty to propose action

Nothing in this article imposes any duty on the conservator to propose any action under this article, and the conservator is not liable for failure to propose any action under this article. *(Stats.1990, c. 79 (A.B.759), § 14, operative July 1, 1991.)*

Law Revision Commission Comments
1990 Enactment

Section 2585 continues Section 2585 of the repealed Probate Code without change. This section makes clear that a conservator is not liable for failure to propose an estate plan or other action under this article even though the conservatee, if competent and acting as a reasonably prudent person, would have developed an estate plan or would have taken other action to minimize taxes or expenses of administration. The remedy for a person who believes that some action should be taken by the conservator under this article is to petition under Section 2580 for an order requiring the conservator to take such action with respect to estate planning or making gifts as is set out in the petition. For background on the provisions of this article, see the Comment to this article under the article heading. [20 Cal.L.Rev.Comm. Reports 1001 (1990)].

§ 2586. Production of conservatee's will and other relevant estate plan documents; safekeeping of documents by custodian appointed by the court

(a) As used in this section, "estate plan of the conservatee" includes, but is not limited to, the conservatee's will, any trust of which the conservatee is the settlor or beneficiary, any power of appointment created by or exercisable by the conservatee, and any contract, transfer, or joint ownership arrangement with provisions for payment or transfer of benefits or interests at the conservatee's death to another or others which the conservatee may have originated.

(b) Notwithstanding Article 3 (commencing with Section 950) of Chapter 4 of Division 8 of the Evidence Code (lawyer-client privilege), the court, in its discretion, may order that any person having possession of any document constituting all or part of the estate plan of the conservatee shall deliver the document to the court for examination by the court, and, in the discretion of the court, by the attorneys for the persons who have appeared in the proceedings under this article, in connection with the petition filed under this article.

(c) Unless the court otherwise orders, no person who examines any document produced pursuant to an order under this section shall disclose the contents of the document to any other person. If that disclosure is made, the court may adjudge the person making the disclosure to be in contempt of court.

(d) For good cause, the court may order that a document constituting all or part of the estate plan of the conservatee, whether or not produced pursuant to an order under this section, shall be delivered for safekeeping to the custodian designated by the court. The court may impose those conditions it determines are appropriate for holding and safeguarding the document. The court may authorize the conservator to take any action a depositor may take under Part 15 (commencing with Section 700) of Division 2. *(Stats.1990, c. 79 (A.B.759), § 14, operative July 1, 1991. Amended by Stats.1993, c. 519 (A.B.209), § 5.)*

Law Revision Commission Comments
1993 Amendment

Section 2586 is amended to add subdivision (d) to permit the court to order that the conservatee's estate planning documents be delivered to some other custodian for safekeeping. Under subdivision (d), "good cause" for ordering a transfer to some other custodian might include, for example, the case where the previous custodian has not used ordinary care for preservation of the document.   See Section 710.   See generally Sections 700–735 (deposit of estate planning documents with attorney).   [23 Cal. L.Rev.Comm. Reports 901 (1993) (Annual Report, App. 7)].

Cross References

Appealable orders, see Probate Code § 1300 et seq.

Appointment of legal counsel, see Probate Code § 1470 et seq.

Attorneys, rules of professional conduct, see California Rules of Professional Conduct, Rule 1–100 et seq.

Contempt of court, generally, see Code of Civil Procedure § 1209 et seq.

Contracts, generally, see Civil Code § 1549 et seq.

Inspection of public records, exemptions from disclosure, "conservatee" to "conservatorship", see Government Code § 6276.12.

Interests in property, generally, see Civil Code § 678 et seq.

Powers of appointment, generally, see Probate Code § 600 et seq.

Transfers of property, generally, see Civil Code § 1039 et seq.

Wills, generally, see Probate Code § 6100 et seq.

ARTICLE 11.   INDEPENDENT EXERCISE OF POWERS

Law Revision Commission Comments
1990 Enactment

Article 11 (commencing with Section 2590) permits the court to authorize an experienced and qualified guardian or conservator to exercise one or more powers to which the article applies without the need to petition for court authorization in each instance a power is to be exercised.   In appropriate cases, use of the authority under this article will save time and expense in managing the estate while preserving adequate safeguards through the requirement of accounting.   For background on the provisions of this part, see the Comment to this part under the part heading.   [20 Cal.L.Rev.Comm. Reports 1001 (1990)].

Cross References

Application of old and new law, see Probate Code § 3.

Conservatorship for gravely disabled persons, general and special powers, see Welfare and Institutions Code § 5357.

§ 2590.   Independent exercise of powers; order granting authority

(a) The court may, in its discretion, make an order granting the guardian or conservator any one or more or all of the powers specified in Section 2591 if the court determines that, under the circumstances of the particular guardianship or conservatorship, it would be to the advantage, benefit, and best interest of the estate to do so.   Subject only to the requirements, conditions, or limitations as are specifically and expressly provided, either directly or by reference, in the order granting the power or powers, and if consistent with Section 2591, the guardian or conservator may exercise the granted power or powers without notice, hearing, or court authorization, instructions, approval, or confirmation in the same manner as the ward or conservatee could do if possessed of legal capacity.

(b) The guardian or conservator does not have a power specified in Section 2591 without authorization by a court under this article or other express provisions of this code. *(Stats.1990, c. 79 (A.B.759), § 14, operative July 1, 1991. Amended by Stats.2006, c. 490 (S.B.1116), § 5; Stats.2007, c. 553 (A.B.1727), § 18.)*

Law Revision Commission Comments
1990 Enactment

Section 2590 continues Section 2590 of the repealed Probate Code without change.   For general provisions, see Sections 1000–1004 (rules of practice), 1020–1023 (petitions and other papers), 1040–1050 (hearings and orders), 2103 (effect of final order), 2111 (orders and transactions affecting property).   In determining whether to make an order under this article, the court shall consider the circumstances of the case, the need to grant the power or powers, the qualifications of the guardian or conservator, and the expense of obtaining court authorization for each exercise of the power or powers requested if the petition were to be denied.

If sale of real property is authorized, it is not necessary to comply with Article 7 of this chapter, since the ward or conservatee would not have to do so if competent.   However, the guardian or conservator must use ordinary care and diligence in the management of the estate.   See Section 2401.   The court may withdraw or limit a power previously granted under this article.   See Section 2593.

Although, if so ordered, powers may be exercised under this article without notice, hearing, authorization, instruction, approval, or confirmation, a transaction not previously authorized, approved, or confirmed by the court is subject to review by the court on the next accounting of the guardian or conservator.   See Section 2625.

For background on the provisions of this article, see the Comment to this article under the article heading.   [20 Cal.L.Rev.Comm. Reports 1001 (1990)].

Cross References

Additional powers of guardian nominated by will, see Probate Code § 2108.

Appointment of legal counsel, see Probate Code § 1470 et seq.

Request for special notice, see Probate Code § 2700 et seq.

§ 2591.   Powers that may be granted

The powers referred to in Section 2590 are:

(a) The power to operate, for a period longer than 45 days, at the risk of the estate a business, farm, or enterprise constituting an asset of the estate.

(b) The power to grant and take options.

(c)(1) The power to sell at public or private sale real or personal property of the estate without confirmation of the court of the sale, other than the personal residence of a conservatee.

(2) The power to sell at public or private sale the personal residence of the conservatee as described in Section 2591.5 without confirmation of the court of the sale.   The power granted pursuant to this paragraph is subject to the requirements of Sections 2352.5 and 2541.

(3) For purposes of this subdivision, authority to sell property includes authority to contract for the sale and fulfill the terms and conditions of the contract, including conveyance of the property.

(d) The power to create by grant or otherwise easements and servitudes.

(e) The power to borrow money.

(f) The power to give security for the repayment of a loan.

(g) The power to purchase real or personal property.

(h) The power to alter, improve, raze, replace, and rebuild property of the estate.

(i) The power to let or lease property of the estate, or extend, renew, or modify a lease of real property, for which the monthly rental or lease term exceeds the maximum specified in Sections 2501 and 2555 for any purpose (including exploration for and removal of gas, oil, and other minerals and natural resources) and for any period, including a term commencing at a future time.

(j) The power to lend money on adequate security.

(k) The power to exchange property of the estate.

(l) The power to sell property of the estate on credit if any unpaid portion of the selling price is adequately secured.

(m) The power to commence and maintain an action for partition.

(n) The power to exercise stock rights and stock options.

(o) The power to participate in and become subject to and to consent to the provisions of a voting trust and of a reorganization, consolidation, merger, dissolution, liquidation, or other modification or adjustment affecting estate property.

(p) The power to pay, collect, compromise, or otherwise adjust claims, debts, or demands upon the guardianship or conservatorship described in subdivision (a) of Section 2501, Section 2502 or 2504, or to arbitrate any dispute described in Section 2406. *(Stats.1990, c. 79 (A.B.759), § 14, operative July 1, 1991. Amended by Stats.2006, c. 490 (S.B.1116), § 6; Stats.2007, c. 553 (A.B.1727), § 19.)*

Law Revision Commission Comments

1990 Enactment

Section 2591 continues Section 2591 of the repealed Probate Code without change. Except to the extent the court for good cause otherwise orders, a nominated guardian may, to the extent provided in the nomination, exercise any one or more of the powers listed in Section 2591 without notice, hearing, or court authorization, instructions, approval, or confirmation. See Section 2108.

The listing of a power in this section does not require the guardian or conservator to obtain an order under this article to exercise the power. See Section 2595(b). In some instances, a power listed in this section may be exercised by the guardian or conservator without court authorization under another provision of this division. See, e.g., Section 2555 (certain leases permitted without court authorization). However, the power is listed in this section because, in other instances, exercise of the same power requires authorization, and an order under this article may permit exercise of the power without such court authorization. See, e.g., Sections 2553 (leases generally), 2457 (repair and maintenance of home of ward or conservatee and dependents), 2500–2507 (compromise of claims and actions).

For background on the provisions of this article, see the Comment to this article under the article heading. [20 Cal.L.Rev.Comm. Reports 1001 (1990)].

Cross References

Conservatorship for gravely disabled persons, recommendations of officer providing conservatorship investigation, see Welfare and Institutions Code § 5360.

Easements and servitudes, see Civil Code § 801 et seq.

Voting of corporate shares, see Corporations Code § 700 et seq.

§ 2591.5. Sale of personal residence; best interests of conservatee

(a) Notwithstanding any other provisions of this article, a conservator seeking an order under Section 2590 authorizing a sale of the conservatee's personal residence shall demonstrate to the court that the terms of sale, including the price for which the property is to be sold and the commissions to be paid from the estate, are in all respects in the best interests of the conservatee.

(b) A conservator authorized to sell the conservatee's personal residence pursuant to Section 2590 shall comply with the provisions of Section 10309 concerning appraisal or new appraisal of the property for sale and sale at a minimum offer price. Notwithstanding Section 10309, if the last appraisal of the conservatee's personal residence was conducted more than six months prior to the proposed sale of the property, a new appraisal shall be required prior to the sale of the property, unless the court finds that it is in the best interests of the conservatee to rely on an appraisal of the personal residence that was conducted not more than one year prior to the proposed sale of the property. For purposes of this section, the date of sale is the date of the contract for sale of the property.

(c) Within 15 days of the close of escrow, the conservator shall serve a copy of the final escrow settlement statement on all persons entitled to notice of the petition for appointment for a conservator and all persons who have filed and served a request for special notice and shall file a copy of the final escrow statement along with a proof of service with the court.

(d) The court may, for good cause, waive any of the requirements of this section. *(Added by Stats.2006, c. 490 (S.B.1116), § 7. Amended by Stats.2007, c. 553 (A.B.1727), § 20.)*

§ 2592. Petition

(a) The guardian or conservator may apply by petition for an order under Section 2590.

(b) The application for the order may be included in the petition for the appointment of the guardian or conservator. In such case, the notice of hearing on the petition shall include a statement that the petition includes an application for the grant of one or more powers under this article and shall list the specific power or powers applied for.

(c) If the application for the order is made by petition filed after the filing of the petition for the appointment of the guardian or conservator, notice of the hearing on the petition shall be given for the period and in the manner provided in Chapter 3 (commencing with Section 1460) of Part 1. *(Stats.1990, c. 79 (A.B.759), § 14, operative July 1, 1991.)*

Law Revision Commission Comments

1990 Enactment

Section 2592 continues Section 2592 of the repealed Probate Code without change. For general provisions, see Sections 1000–1004 (rules of practice), 1020–1023 (petitions and other papers), 1040–1050 (hearings and orders), 2103 (effect of final order). For general provisions relating to notice of hearing, see Sections 1200–1221, 1460–1469. See also Sections 1260–1265 (proof of giving notice), 2700–2702 (notice to persons who request special notice). For background on the provisions of this article, see the Comment to this article under the article heading. [20 Cal.L.Rev.Comm. Reports 1001 (1990)].

Cross References

Notice to,
Directors, see Probate Code § 1461.
Veterans Administration, see Probate Code § 1461.5.

§ 2593. Withdrawal or subsequent limitation of powers

(a) The court, on its own motion or on petition of any interested person, when it appears to be for the best interests of the ward or conservatee or the estate, may withdraw any or all of the powers previously granted pursuant to this article or may impose restrictions, conditions, and limitations on the exercise of such powers by the guardian or conservator.

(b) Notice of the hearing on a petition under this section shall be given for the period and in the manner provided in Chapter 3 (commencing with Section 1460) of Part 1. *(Stats.1990, c. 79 (A.B.759), § 14, operative July 1, 1991.)*

Law Revision Commission Comments

1990 Enactment

Section 2593 continues Section 2593 of the repealed Probate Code without change. For general provisions, see Sections 1000–1004 (rules of practice), 1020–1023 (petitions and other papers), 1040–1050 (hearings and orders), 2103 (effect of final order). For general provisions relating to notice of hearing, see Sections 1200–1221, 1460–1469. See also Sections 1260–1265 (proof of giving notice), 2700–2702 (notice to persons who request special notice). For background on the provisions of this article, see the Comment to this article under the article heading. [20 Cal.L.Rev.Comm. Reports 1001 (1990)].

Cross References

Interested person, defined, see Probate Code § 1424.
Powers granted guardian nominated by will, see Probate Code § 2108.

§ 2594. Letters; contents; requirements for new letters

(a) When a power or powers are granted pursuant to this article, the letters of guardianship or conservatorship shall state the power or powers so granted and the restrictions, conditions, or limitations, if any, prescribed in the order and shall refer to this article.

(b) When a power or powers are granted by a subsequent order, new letters shall be issued in the form described in subdivision (a).

(c) If the powers are withdrawn, or if the powers are restricted, conditioned, or limited by a subsequent order after they are granted, new letters shall be issued accordingly. *(Stats.1990, c. 79 (A.B.759), § 14, operative July 1, 1991.)*

Law Revision Commission Comments

1990 Enactment

Section 2594 continues Section 2594 of the repealed Probate Code without change. For background on the provisions of this article, see the Comment to this article under the article heading. [20 Cal. L.Rev.Comm. Reports 1001 (1990)].

Cross References

Letters of guardianship or conservatorship, see Probate Code § 2310 et seq.
Powers granted guardian nominated by will, see Probate Code § 2108.

§ 2595. Effect of article

(a) The grant of a power or powers pursuant to this article does not affect the right of the guardian or conservator to petition the court as provided in Section 2403 or to petition the court under other provisions of this code, as to a particular transaction or matter, in the same manner as if the power or powers had not been granted pursuant to this article.

(b) Where authority exists under other provisions of law, either general or specific, for the guardian or conservator to do any act or to enter into any transaction described in Section 2591, the guardian or conservator may proceed under such other provisions of law and is not required to obtain authority under this article. *(Stats.1990, c. 79 (A.B.759), § 14, operative July 1, 1991.)*

Law Revision Commission Comments

1990 Enactment

Section 2595 continues Section 2595 of the repealed Probate Code without change. Subdivision (b) makes clear that this article does not preclude the exercise of powers under other provisions of law. See the Comment to Section 2591 (last paragraph). As to compensation of the guardian or conservator and attorney in connection with obtaining court instructions on exercise of powers granted under this article, see the Comment to Section 2640. For background on the provisions of this article, see the Comment to this article under the article heading. [20 Cal.L.Rev.Comm. Reports 1001 (1990)].

CHAPTER 7. INVENTORY AND ACCOUNTS

ARTICLE 1. DEFINITIONS AND GENERAL PROVISIONS

Cross References

Application of old and new law, see Probate Code § 3.

§ 2600. Definitions

As used in this chapter, unless the context otherwise requires:

(a) "Conservator" means (1) the conservator of the estate or (2) the limited conservator of the estate to the extent that the powers and duties of the limited conservator are specifically and expressly provided by the order appointing the limited conservator.

(b) "Estate" means all of the conservatee's or ward's personal property, wherever located, and real property located in this state.

(c) "Guardian" means the guardian of the estate. *(Stats. 1990, c. 79 (A.B.759), § 14, operative July 1, 1991. Amended by Stats.2008, c. 52 (A.B.2014), § 4.)*

Law Revision Commission Comments

1990 Enactment

Section 2600 continues Section 2600 of the repealed Probate Code without substantive change. If one person is appointed conservator of the person and estate or guardian of the person and estate, that person has the powers and duties provided in this chapter. For background on the provisions of this part, see the Comment to this part under the part heading. [20 Cal.L.Rev.Comm. Reports 1001 (1990)].

Cross References

Order appointing limited conservator for developmentally disabled adult, see Probate Code § 1830.

§ 2601. Wages of ward or conservatee

(a) Unless otherwise ordered by the court, if the ward or conservatee is employed at any time during the continuance of the guardianship or conservatorship:

(1) The wages or salaries for such employment are not a part of the estate and the guardian or conservator is not accountable for such wages or salaries.

(2) The wages or salaries for such employment shall be paid to the ward or conservatee and are subject to his or her control to the same extent as if the guardianship or conservatorship did not exist.

(b) Any court order referred to in subdivision (a) is binding upon the employer only after notice of the order has been received by the employer. *(Stats.1990, c. 79 (A.B.759), § 14, operative July 1, 1991.)*

Law Revision Commission Comments

1990 Enactment

Section 2601 continues Section 2601 of the repealed Probate Code without substantive change. For background on the provisions of this part, see the Comment to this part under the part heading. [20 Cal.L.Rev.Comm. Reports 1001 (1990)].

Cross References

Allowance for ward or conservatee, see Probate Code § 2421.
Payment of earnings to minor, see Family Code § 7503.
Payment of wages, generally, see Labor Code § 200 et seq.
Right of conservatee to control wages or salary, legal capacity, see Probate Code § 1871.

§ 2602. Repealed by Stats.1990, c. 79 (A.B.759), § 13, operative July 1, 1991

Law Revision Commission Comments

1990 Repeal

Section 2602 of the repealed Probate Code is continued without substantive change in Section 2614.5 insofar as Section 2602 related to failure to file the inventory and appraisal. Insofar as former Section 2602 related to failure to render an account, it is superseded by Section 2629. [20 Cal.L.Rev.Comm. Reports 1001 (1990)].

ARTICLE 2. INVENTORY AND APPRAISAL OF ESTATE

Cross References

Application of old and new law, see Probate Code § 3.

§ 2610. Filing inventory and appraisal

(a) Within 90 days after appointment, or within any further time as the court for reasonable cause upon ex parte petition of the guardian or conservator may allow, the guardian or conservator shall file with the clerk of the court and mail to the conservatee and to the attorneys of record for the ward or conservatee, along with notice of how to file an objection, an inventory and appraisal of the estate, made as of the date of the appointment of the guardian or conservator. A copy of this inventory and appraisal, along with notice of how to file an objection, also shall be mailed to the conservatee's spouse or registered domestic partner, the conservatee's relatives in the first degree, and, if there are no such relatives, to the next closest relative, unless the court determines that the mailing will result in harm to the conservatee.

(b) The guardian or conservator shall take and subscribe to an oath that the inventory contains a true statement of all of the estate of the ward or conservatee of which the guardian or conservator has possession or knowledge. The oath shall be endorsed upon or annexed to the inventory.

(c) The property described in the inventory shall be appraised in the manner provided for the inventory and appraisal of estates of decedents. The guardian or conservator may appraise the assets that a personal representative could appraise under Section 8901.

(d) If a conservatorship is initiated pursuant to the Lanterman–Petris–Short Act (Part 1 (commencing with Section 5000) of Division 5 of the Welfare and Institutions Code), and no sale of the estate will occur:

(1) The inventory and appraisal required by subdivision (a) shall be filed within 90 days after appointment of the conservator.

(2) The property described in the inventory may be appraised by the conservator and need not be appraised by a probate referee.

(e) By January 1, 2008, the Judicial Council shall develop a form to effectuate the notice required in subdivision (a). *(Stats.1990, c. 79 (A.B.759), § 14, operative July 1, 1991. Amended by Stats.2006, c. 493 (A.B.1363), § 23.)*

Law Revision Commission Comments

1990 Enactment

Section 2610 continues Section 2610 of the repealed Probate Code without change. For comparable provisions relating to decedents' estates, see Sections 8800, 8852(a). See also Sections 2614.5 (court order requiring filing inventory and appraisal and removal of guardian or conservator who fails to comply with order), 2650 (removal of guardian or conservator who fails to comply with order), 2633 (order dispensing with need to file inventory and appraisal where guardianship or conservatorship terminates before inventory has been filed), 2700(c)(2) (request for special notice of inventories and appraisals), 2943 (appraisal of small estate by public guardian). For background on the provisions of this part, see the Comment to this part under the part heading. See also Report of Senate Committee on Judiciary on Assembly Bill No. 261, 15 Cal.L.Revision Comm'n Reports 1097, 1099 (1980). [20 Cal.L.Rev.Comm. Reports 1001 (1990)].

Cross References

Affirmation in lieu of oath, see Code of Civil Procedure § 2015.6.
Appraisement of decedent's estates, manner of, see Probate Code § 8901.
Declaration under penalty of perjury, see Code of Civil Procedure § 2015.5.
Inventory and appraisal, generally, see Probate Code § 8800 et seq.
Inventory and appraisement by,
  Guardian for particular property, see Probate Code § 2109.
  Guardian or conservator for nonresident, see Probate Code § 2107.
  Temporary guardian or conservator, see Probate Code § 2255.
Oaths,
  Affirmation in lieu of, see Code of Civil Procedure § 2015.6.
  Letters and bond, generally, see Probate Code § 2300 et seq.
  Officers authorized to administer, see Government Code § 1225.
Personal representative and general personal representative, defined, see Probate Code § 58.
Professional fiduciary as guardian or conservator, proposed hourly fee schedule or proposed compensation filing requirement, see Probate Code § 2614.7.

§ 2611. Copy to directors of state hospitals or developmental services

If the ward or conservatee is or has been during the guardianship or conservatorship a patient in a state hospital under the jurisdiction of the State Department of State Hospitals or the State Department of Developmental Services, the guardian or conservator shall mail a copy of the inventory and appraisal filed under Section 2610 to the director of the appropriate department at the director's office in Sacramento not later than 15 days after the inventory and appraisal is filed with the court. Compliance with this section is not required if an unrevoked certificate described in subdivision (c) of Section 1461 is on file with the court with respect to the ward or conservatee. *(Stats.1990, c. 79 (A.B.759), § 14, operative July 1, 1991. Amended by Stats. 2012, c. 440 (A.B.1488), § 46, eff. Sept. 22, 2012.)*

Law Revision Commission Comments

1990 Enactment

Section 2611 continues Section 2611 of the repealed Probate Code without substantive change. See also Section 1216 (personal delivery in lieu of mailing). For background on the provisions of this part, see the Comment to this part under the part heading. [20 Cal.L.Rev.Comm. Reports 1001 (1990)].

Cross References

Department of Developmental Services, see Welfare and Institutions Code § 4400 et seq.
Department of State Hospitals, see Welfare and Institutions Code § 4000 et seq.
Mailing, completion, see Probate Code § 1467.

§ 2612. Copy to county assessor

If a timely request is made, the clerk of court shall mail a copy of the inventory and appraisal filed under Section 2610 to the county assessor. *(Stats.1990, c. 79 (A.B.759), § 14, operative July 1, 1991.)*

Law Revision Commission Comments

1990 Enactment

Section 2612 continues Section 2612 of the repealed Probate Code without substantive change. See also Section 1216 (personal delivery in lieu of mailing). For background on the provisions of this part, see the Comment to this part under the part heading. [20 Cal.L.Rev.Comm. Reports 1001 (1990)].

Cross References

County assessor, see Government Code § 24000.

§ 2613. Subsequently discovered or acquired property; supplemental inventory and appraisement

Whenever any property of the ward or conservatee is discovered that was not included in the inventory, or whenever any other property is received by the ward or conservatee or by the guardian or conservator on behalf of the ward or conservatee (other than by the actions of the guardian or conservator in the investment and management of the estate), the guardian or conservator shall file a supplemental inventory and appraisal for that property and like proceedings shall be followed with respect thereto as in the case of an original inventory, but the appraisal shall be made as of the date the property was so discovered or received. *(Stats.1990, c. 79 (A.B.759), § 14, operative July 1, 1991.)*

Law Revision Commission Comments

1990 Enactment

Section 2613 continues Section 2613 of the repealed Probate Code without substantive change. Wages or salaries of the ward or conservatee from employment during the guardianship or conservatorship are not part of the estate unless ordered by the court. See Section 2601. For a comparable provision relating to decedents' estates, see Section 8801. For background on the provisions of this part, see the Comment to this part under the part heading. [20 Cal.L.Rev.Comm. Reports 1001 (1990)].

§ 2614. Objections to appraisals

(a) Within 30 days after the inventory and appraisal is filed, the guardian or conservator or any creditor or other interested person may file written objections to any or all appraisals. The clerk shall set the objections for hearing not less than 15 days after their filing.

(b) Notice of the hearing, together with a copy of the objections, shall be given for the period and in the manner provided in Chapter 3 (commencing with Section 1460) of Part 1. If the appraisal was made by a probate referee, the person objecting shall also mail notice of the hearing and a copy of the objection to the probate referee at least 15 days before the time set for the hearing.

(c) The court shall determine the objections and may fix the true value of any asset to which objection has been filed. For the purpose of this subdivision, the court may cause an independent appraisal or appraisals to be made by at least one additional appraiser at the expense of the estate or, if the objecting party is not the guardian or conservator and the objection is rejected by the court, the court may assess the cost of any such additional appraisal or appraisals against the objecting party. *(Stats.1990, c. 79 (A.B.759), § 14, operative July 1, 1991.)*

Law Revision Commission Comments
1990 Enactment

Section 2614 continues Section 2614 of the repealed Probate Code without substantive change. For general provisions, see Sections 1000–1004 (rules of practice), 1020–1023 (petitions and other papers), 1040–1050 (hearings and orders), 2103 (effect of final order). For general provisions relating to notice of hearing, see Sections 1200–1221, 1460–1469. See also Sections 1260–1265 (proof of giving notice), 2700–2702 (notice to persons who request special notice). For a comparable provision relating to decedents' estates, see Section 8906. For background on the provisions of this part, see the Comment to this part under the part heading. [20 Cal.L.Rev.Comm. Reports 1001 (1990)].

Cross References

Computation of time, see Code of Civil Procedure §§ 12 and 12a; Government Code § 6800 et seq.
Interested person, defined, see Probate Code § 1424.
Mailing, completion, see Probate Code § 1467.
Notice,
  Mailing, see Probate Code § 1215 et seq.
  Posting, see Probate Code § 1230.
  Proof of giving notice, see Probate Code § 1260 et seq.
  Special notice, see Probate Code § 1250 et seq.
  This code, generally, see Probate Code § 1200 et seq.
  This division, generally, see Probate Code § 1460 et seq.
Probate referees,
  Appointment and duties, see Probate Code § 400 et seq.
  Authority and powers, see Probate Code § 450 et seq.
Service of process,
  Generally, see Code of Civil Procedure § 413.10 et seq.
  Mail, see Code of Civil Procedure §§ 415.30, 1012 et seq.
  Personal delivery, see Code of Civil Procedure § 415.10.
  Proof of service, see Code of Civil Procedure § 417.10 et seq.
  Publication, see Code of Civil Procedure § 415.50.

§ 2614.5. Failure to file inventory and appraisal; removal of guardian or conservator

(a) If the guardian or conservator fails to file an inventory and appraisal within the time allowed by law or by court order, upon request of the ward or conservatee, the spouse of the ward or the spouse or domestic partner of the conservatee, any relative or friend of the ward or conservatee, or any interested person, the court shall order the guardian or conservator to file the inventory and appraisal within the time prescribed in the order or to show cause why the guardian or conservator should not be removed. The person who requested the order shall serve it upon the guardian or conservator in the manner provided in Section 415.10 or 415.30 of the Code of Civil Procedure or in a manner as is ordered by the court.

(b) If the guardian or conservator fails to file the inventory and appraisal as required by the order within the time prescribed in the order, unless good cause is shown for not doing so, the court, on its own motion or on petition, may remove the guardian or conservator, revoke the letters of guardianship or conservatorship, and enter judgment accordingly, and order the guardian or conservator to file an account and to surrender the estate to the person legally entitled thereto.

(c) The procedure provided in this section is optional and does not preclude the use of any other remedy or sanction when an inventory and appraisal is not timely filed. *(Stats. 1990, c. 79 (A.B.759), § 14, operative July 1, 1991. Amended by Stats.2001, c. 893 (A.B.25), § 39.)*

Law Revision Commission Comments
1990 Enactment

Section 2614.5 continues Section 2602 of the repealed Probate Code without substantive change insofar as that section dealt with failure to file an inventory and appraisal. This section provides a procedure for requiring an inventory and appraisal short of removing the guardian or conservator. See also Section 2650 (removal of guardian or conservator for failure to file inventory or render account). For general provisions, see Sections 1000–1004 (rules of practice), 1020–1023 (petitions and other papers), 1040–1050 (hearings and orders), 2103 (effect of final order). For general provisions relating to notice of hearing, see Sections 1200–1221, 1460–1469. See also Sections 1260–1265 (proof of giving notice), 2700–2702 (notice to persons who request special notice). For a comparable provision relating to decedents' estates, see Section 8804. For background on the provisions of this part, see the Comment to this part under the part heading. [20 Cal.L.Rev.Comm. Reports 1001 (1990)].

Cross References

Domestic partner, defined, see Probate Code § 37.
Guardians and conservators, removal or resignation, see Probate Code § 2650 et seq.
Interested person, defined, see Probate Code § 1424.

§ 2614.7. Professional fiduciary as guardian or conservator; proposed hourly fee schedule or proposed compensation filing requirement

If a guardian or conservator of the person or estate, or both, is a professional fiduciary, as described in Section 2340, who is required to be licensed under the Professional Fiduciaries Act (Chapter 6 (commencing with Section 6500) of Division 3 of the Business and Professions Code), the guardian or conservator shall file, concurrently with the inventory and appraisal required by Section 2610, a proposed hourly fee schedule or another statement of his or her proposed compensation from the estate of the ward or conservatee for services performed as a guardian or conservator. The filing of a proposed hourly fee schedule or another statement of the guardian's or conservator's proposed compensation, as required by this section, shall not preclude a court from later reducing the guardian's, conservator's, or his or her attorney's fees or other compensation. *(Added by Stats.2013, c. 248 (A.B.1339), § 4.)*

Cross References

Professional fiduciary as guardian or conservator, court authorization of periodic payments, contents of petition, see Probate Code § 2643.1.

§ 2614.8. Professional fiduciary as guardian or conservator; submission of new proposed hourly fee schedule or statement of compensation on or after one year from original submission

At any time on or after one year from the submission of an hourly fee schedule or another statement of proposed compensation under this section or under Section 1510, 1821, 2250, or 2614.7, a guardian or conservator who is a professional fiduciary may submit a new proposed hourly fee schedule or another statement of his or her proposed compensation from the estate of the proposed ward or proposed conservatee. The submittal of a new hourly fee schedule or another statement of the guardian's or conservator's proposed compensation, as authorized by this section, shall not preclude a court from later reducing the guardian's or conservator's hourly fees or other compensation, or his or her attorney's fees or other compensation. *(Added by Stats.2013, c. 248 (A.B.1339), § 5.)*

§ 2615. Failure to file inventory; liability; damages; bond

If a guardian or conservator fails to file any inventory required by this article within the time prescribed by law or by court order, the guardian or conservator is liable for damages for any injury to the estate, or to any interested person, directly resulting from the failure timely to file the inventory. Damages awarded pursuant to this section are a personal liability of the guardian or conservator and a liability on the bond, if any. *(Stats.1990, c. 79 (A.B.759), § 14, operative July 1, 1991.)*

Law Revision Commission Comments
1990 Enactment

Section 2615 restates Section 2615 of the repealed Probate Code without substantive change. For a comparable provision relating to decedents' estates, see Section 8804. For background on the provisions of this part, see the Comment to this part under the part heading. [20 Cal.L.Rev.Comm. Reports 1001 (1990)].

Cross References

Bonds of guardians and conservators, see Probate Code § 2320 et seq.
Interested person, defined, see Probate Code § 1424.
Principal and sureties, liability on bond, see Code of Civil Procedure § 996.460.
Removal of guardian or conservator for failure to file inventory, see Probate Code § 2650.

ARTICLE 2.5. EXAMINATION CONCERNING ASSETS OF ESTATE

Section
2616.   Examination concerning assets of estate.

Section
2617.   Interrogatories; answers.
2618.   Witnesses; truth or falsity of allegations; disclosure of personal knowledge; payment of person's expenses.
2619.   Account of property and guardian's or conservator's actions; citation.
2619.5. Repealed.

Cross References

Conveyances or transfers of property claimed to belong to decedent or other person, see Probate Code § 850 et seq.

§ 2616. Examination concerning assets of estate

(a) A petition may be filed under this article by any one or more of the following:

(1) The guardian or conservator.

(2) The ward or conservatee.

(3) A creditor or other interested person, including persons having only an expectancy or prospective interest in the estate.

(b) Upon the filing of a petition under this article, the court may order that a citation be issued to a person to answer interrogatories, or to appear before the court and be examined under oath, or both, concerning any of the following allegations made in the petition:

(1) The person has wrongfully taken, concealed, or disposed of property of the ward or conservatee.

(2) The person has knowledge or possession of any of the following:

(A) A deed, conveyance, bond, contract, or other writing that contains evidence of or tends to disclose the right, title, interest, or claim of the ward or conservatee to property.

(B) An instrument in writing belonging to the ward or conservatee.

(3) The person asserts a claim against the ward or conservatee or the estate.

(4) The estate asserts a claim against the person.

(c) If the citation requires the person to appear before the court, the court and the petitioner may examine the person under oath upon the matters recited in the petition. The citation may include a requirement for this person to produce documents and other personal property specified in the citation.

(d) Disobedience of a citation issued pursuant to this section may be punished as a contempt of the court issuing the citation. *(Stats.1990, c. 79 (A.B.759), § 14, operative July 1, 1991. Amended by Stats.1994, c. 806 (A.B.3686), § 18.)*

Law Revision Commission Comments
1990 Enactment

Section 2616 restates Section 2616 of the repealed Probate Code with the following changes. Some of the language of the revised section is drawn from Section 8870(a) (decedents' estates). Subdivision (b) has been revised to conform it more closely to Section 8870(a) (decedents' estates). The last sentence of subdivision (c), which incorporated by reference Sections 8871–8874 (decedents' estates), has been deleted. In its place, provisions drawn from Sections 8871–8874 have been added to this article. See Sections 2617–2619.5. Subdivision (d) is new and continues Section 8870(c) as that section was applied to guardianship and conservatorship proceedings by former subdivision (c) of Section 2616. For general provisions, see Sections 1000–1004 (rules of practice), 1020–1023 (petitions and other papers), 1040–1050 (hearings and orders), 1240–1242 (citations). [20 Cal.L.Rev.Comm. Reports 1001 (1990)].

Cross References

Examination or interrogatories in court, see Probate Code § 8870 et seq.

Instrument, defined, see Probate Code § 45.

Newspapers, publications and official advertising, see Government Code § 6000 et seq.

Oaths,

  Affirmation in lieu of, see Code of Civil Procedure § 2015.6.

  Letters and bond, generally, see Probate Code § 2300 et seq.

  Officers authorized to administer, see Government Code § 1225.

Official records and other official writings, see Evidence Code § 1280 et seq.

Production of conservatee's will or other document, see Probate Code § 2586.

Recording,

  Constructive notice, conveyance of real property or estate for years, see Civil Code § 1213.

  Instruments or judgments, documents to be recorded and manner of recording, see Government Code §§ 27280 et seq., 27320 et seq.

Property transfers, place of recordation, see Civil Code § 1169.

§ 2617. Interrogatories; answers

Interrogatories may be put to a person cited to answer interrogatories under Section 2616. The interrogatories and answers shall be in writing. The answers shall be signed under penalty of perjury by the person cited. The interrogatories and answers shall be filed with the court. *(Stats.1990, c. 79 (A.B.759), § 14, operative July 1, 1991.)*

Law Revision Commission Comments

1990 Enactment

Section 2617 is new and continues Section 8871 as that section was applied to guardianship and conservatorship proceedings by former subdivision (c) of Section 2616. [20 Cal.L.Rev.Comm. Reports 1001 (1990)].

§ 2618. Witnesses; truth or falsity of allegations; disclosure of personal knowledge; payment of person's expenses

(a) At an examination, witnesses may be produced and examined on either side.

(b) If upon the examination it appears that the allegations of the petition are true, the court may order the person to disclose the person's knowledge of the facts.

(c) If upon the examination it appears that the allegations of the petition are not true, the person's necessary expenses, including reasonable attorney's fees, shall be charged against the petitioner or allowed out of the estate, in the discretion of the court. *(Stats.1990, c. 79 (A.B.759), § 14, operative July 1, 1991.)*

Law Revision Commission Comments

1990 Enactment

Section 2618 is new and continues Section 8872 as that section was applied to guardianship and conservatorship proceedings by former subdivision (c) of Section 2616. [20 Cal.L.Rev.Comm. Reports 1001 (1990)].

Cross References

Attorney's fees and costs, generally, see Code of Civil Procedure § 1021.

Estate attorney, compensation, amount, see Probate Code § 10810 et seq.

§ 2619. Account of property and guardian's or conservator's actions; citation

(a) On petition of the guardian or conservator, the court may issue a citation to a person who has possession or control of property in the estate of the ward or conservatee to appear before the court and make an account under oath of the property and the person's actions with respect to the property.

(b) Disobedience of a citation issued pursuant to this section may be punished as a contempt of the court issuing the citation. *(Stats.1990, c. 79 (A.B.759), § 14, operative July 1, 1991.)*

Law Revision Commission Comments

1990 Enactment

Section 2619 is new and is drawn from Section 8873 (decedents' estates). [20 Cal.L.Rev.Comm. Reports 1001 (1990)].

Cross References

Oaths,

  Affirmation in lieu of, see Code of Civil Procedure § 2015.6.

  Letters and bond, generally, see Probate Code § 2300 et seq.

  Officers authorized to administer, see Government Code § 1225.

§ 2619.5. Repealed by Stats.2001, c. 49 (S.B.669), § 3

ARTICLE 3. ACCOUNTS

Cross References

Application of old and new law, see Probate Code § 3.

§ 2620. Periodic accounting of guardian or conservator; final court accounting; filing of original account statements

(a) At the expiration of one year from the time of appointment and thereafter not less frequently than biennially, unless otherwise ordered by the court to be more frequent, the guardian or conservator shall present the accounting of the assets of the estate of the ward or conservatee to the court for settlement and allowance in the manner provided in Chapter 4 (commencing with Section 1060) of Part 1 of Division 3. By January 1, 2008, the Judicial Council, in consultation with the California Judges Association, the California Association of Superior Court Investigators, the California State Association of Public Administrators, Public Guardians, and Public Conservators, the State Bar of California, and the California Society of Certified Public Accountants, shall develop a standard accounting form, a simplified accounting form, and rules for when the simplified accounting form may be used. After January 1, 2008, all accountings submitted pursuant to this section shall be submitted on the Judicial Council form.

(b) The final court accounting of the guardian or conservator following the death of the ward or conservatee shall include a court accounting for the period that ended on the date of death and a separate accounting for the period subsequent to the date of death.

(c) Along with each court accounting, the guardian or conservator shall file supporting documents, as provided in this section.

(1) For purposes of this subdivision, the term "account statement" shall include any original account statement from any institution, as defined in Section 2890, or any financial institution, as defined in Section 2892, in which money or other assets of the estate are held or deposited.

(2) The filing shall include all account statements showing the account balance as of the closing date of the accounting period of the court accounting. If the court accounting is the first court accounting of the guardianship or conservatorship, the guardian or conservator shall provide to the court all account statements showing the account balance immediately preceding the date the conservator or guardian was appointed and all account statements showing the account balance as of the closing date of the first court accounting.

(3) If the guardian or conservator is a private professional or licensed guardian or conservator, the guardian or conservator shall also file all original account statements, as described above, showing the balance as of all periods covered by the accounting.

(4) The filing shall include the original closing escrow statement received showing the charges and credits for any sale of real property of the estate.

(5) If the ward or conservatee is in a residential care facility or a long-term care facility, the filing shall include the original bill statements for the facility.

(6) This subdivision shall not apply to the public guardian if the money belonging to the estate is pooled with money belonging to other estates pursuant to Section 2940 and Article 3 (commencing with Section 7640) of Chapter 4 of Part 1 of Division 7. Nothing in this section shall affect any other duty or responsibility of the public guardian with regard to managing money belonging to the estate or filing accountings with the court.

(7) If any document to be filed or lodged with the court under this section contains the ward's or conservatee's social security number or any other personal information regarding the ward or conservatee that would not ordinarily be disclosed in a court accounting, an inventory and appraisal, or other nonconfidential pleadings filed in the action, the account statement or other document shall be attached to a separate affidavit describing the character of the document, captioned "CONFIDENTIAL FINANCIAL STATEMENT" in capital letters. Except as otherwise ordered by the court, the clerk of the court shall keep the document confidential except to the court and subject to disclosure only upon an order of the court. The guardian or conservator may redact the ward's or conservatee's social security number from any document lodged with the court under this section.

(8) Courts may provide by local rule that the court shall retain all documents lodged with it under this subdivision until the court's determination of the guardian's or conservator's account has become final, at which time the supporting documents shall be returned to the depositing guardian or conservator or delivered to any successor appointed by the court.

(d) Each accounting is subject to random or discretionary, full or partial review by the court. The review may include consideration of any information necessary to determine the accuracy of the accounting. If the accounting has any material error, the court shall make an express finding as to the severity of the error and what further action is appropriate in response to the error, if any. Among the actions available to the court is immediate suspension of the guardian or conservator without further notice or proceedings and appointment of a temporary guardian or conservator or removal of the guardian or conservator pursuant to Section 2650 and appointment of a temporary guardian or conservator.

(e) The guardian or conservator shall make available for inspection and copying, upon reasonable notice, to any person designated by the court to verify the accuracy of the accounting, all books and records, including receipts for any expenditures, of the guardianship or conservatorship.

(f) A superior court shall not be required to perform any duties imposed pursuant to the amendments to this section enacted by Chapter 493 of the Statutes 2006 until the Legislature makes an appropriation identified for this purpose. *(Added by Stats.1996, c. 862 (A.B.2751), § 10, operative July 1, 1997. Amended by Stats.1998, c. 581 (A.B.2801), § 22; Stats.2000, c. 565 (A.B.1950), § 9; Stats.2001, c. 232 (A.B.1517), § 1; Stats.2001, c. 563 (A.B.1286), § 6; Stats. 2006, c. 493 (A.B.1363), § 24, operative July 1, 2007; Stats. 2008, c. 293 (A.B.1340), § 9; Stats.2009, c. 54 (S.B.544), § 8; Stats.2011, c. 10 (S.B.78), § 20, eff. March 24, 2011.)*

Law Revision Commission Comments

1990 Enactment

Section 2620 continues Section 2620 of the repealed Probate Code without substantive change. See also Sections 1021 (verification of account), 2420 (payments for support, maintenance, and education), 2421 (personal allowance for ward or conservatee), 2614.5 (court order requiring account upon removal of guardian or conservator for failure to file inventory and appraisal), 2629 (court order requiring filing of account and removal of guardian or conservator who fails to comply with order), 2633 (account where guardianship or conservatorship terminates before inventory of estate has been filed), 2650 (removal of guardian or conservator for failure to file account within time allowed by law or by court order), 2750 (order settling account is an appealable order).

Subdivision (e) makes clear that the petition for approval of the account may include such additional requests as requests for compensation for the guardian or conservator of the person or estate or for the attorney, monthly allowance for support of the conservatee and dependents, periodic payments to the guardian or conservator or attorney, or distribution of excess income to relatives of the conservatee. The courts generally prefer to determine these kinds of matters when an account is being settled. W. Johnstone, G. Zillgitt, & S. House, California Conservatorships § 12.1, at 698–99, § 12.9, at 703–04 (Cal.Cont.Ed.Bar 2d ed. 1983 & Supp.1989).

For comparable provisions relating to decedents' estates, see Sections 10900 (contents of account), 10950 (when account required). For background on the provisions of this part, see the Comment to this part under the part heading. [20 Cal.L.Rev.Comm. Reports 1001 (1990)].

Cross References

Account, defined, see Probate Code § 21
Accounting for deceased or incapacitated personal representative, see Probate Code § 10953.
Accounting upon removal of guardian or conservator, see Probate Code § 2653.
Appointment of legal counsel, see Probate Code § 1470 et seq.
Compensation of guardian, conservator, and attorney, see Probate Code § 2640 et seq.
Financial institution, defined, see Probate Code § 40.
Joint guardians or conservators, see Probate Code § 2105.
Professional fiduciary as guardian or conservator, court authorization of periodic payments, contents of petition, see Probate Code § 2643.1.
Public guardian, generally, see Probate Code § 2900 et seq.
Settlement of accounts upon, termination of guardianship or conservatorship, see Probate Code § 2630.

§ 2620.1. Guidelines to be developed

The Judicial Council shall, by January 1, 2009, develop guidelines to assist investigators and examiners in reviewing accountings and detecting fraud. *(Added by Stats.2007, c. 553 (A.B.1727), § 21.)*

§ 2620.2. Failure to file account; notice; citation; contempt; removal

(a) Whenever the conservator or guardian has failed to file an accounting as required by Section 2620, the court shall require that written notice be given to the conservator or guardian and the attorney of record for the conservatorship or guardianship directing the conservator or guardian to file an accounting and to set the accounting for hearing before the court within 30 days of the date of the notice or, if the conservator or guardian is a public agency, within 45 days of the date of the notice. The court may, upon cause shown, grant an additional 30 days to file the accounting.

(b) Failure to file the accounting within the time specified under subdivision (a), or within 45 days of actual receipt of the notice, whichever is later, shall constitute a contempt of the authority of the court as described in Section 1209 of the Code of Civil Procedure.

(c) If the conservator or guardian does not file an accounting with all appropriate supporting documentation and set the accounting for hearing as required by Section 2620, the court shall do one or more of the following and shall report that action to the bureau established pursuant to Section 6510 of the Business and Professions Code:

(1) Remove the conservator or guardian as provided under Article 1 (commencing with Section 2650) of Chapter 9 of Part 4 of Division 4.

(2) Issue and serve a citation requiring a guardian or conservator who does not file a required accounting to appear and show cause why the guardian or conservator should not be punished for contempt. If the guardian or conservator purposely evades personal service of the citation, the guardian or conservator shall be immediately removed from office.

(3) Suspend the powers of the conservator or guardian and appoint a temporary conservator or guardian, who shall take possession of the assets of the conservatorship or guardianship, investigate the actions of the conservator or guardian, and petition for surcharge if this is in the best interests of the ward or conservatee. Compensation for the temporary conservator or guardian, and counsel for the temporary conservator or guardian, shall be treated as a surcharge against the conservator or guardian, and if unpaid shall be considered a breach of condition of the bond.

(4)(A) Appoint legal counsel to represent the ward or conservatee if the court has not suspended the powers of the conservator or guardian and appoint a temporary conservator or guardian pursuant to paragraph (3). Compensation for the counsel appointed for the ward or conservatee shall be treated as a surcharge against the conservator or guardian, and if unpaid shall be considered a breach of a condition on the bond, unless for good cause shown the court finds that counsel for the ward or conservatee shall be compensated according to Section 1470. The court shall order the legal counsel to do one or more of the following:

(i) Investigate the actions of the conservator or guardian, and petition for surcharge if this is in the best interests of the ward or conservatee.

(ii) Recommend to the court whether the conservator or guardian should be removed.

(iii) Recommend to the court whether money or other property in the estate should be deposited pursuant to Section 2453, 2453.5, 2454, or 2455, to be subject to withdrawal only upon authorization of the court.

(B) After resolution of the matters for which legal counsel was appointed in subparagraph (A), the court shall terminate the appointment of legal counsel, unless the court determines that continued representation of the ward or conservatee and the estate is necessary and reasonable.

(5) If the conservator or guardian is exempt from the licensure requirements of Chapter 6 (commencing with Section 6500) of Division 3 of the Business and Professions Code, upon ex parte application or any notice as the court may require, extend the time to file the accounting, not to exceed an additional 30 days after the expiration of the deadline described in subdivision (a), where the court finds there is good cause and that the estate is adequately bonded. After expiration of any extensions, if the accounting has not been filed, the court shall take action as described in paragraphs (1) to (3), inclusive.

(d) Subdivision (c) does not preclude the court from additionally taking any other appropriate action in response to a failure to file a proper accounting in a timely manner. *(Stats.1990, c. 79 (A.B.759), § 14, operative July 1, 1991. Amended by Stats.1991, c. 1019 (S.B.1022), § 6; Stats.1992, c. 572 (S.B.1455), § 7; Stats.2001, c. 359 (S.B.140), § 4; Stats. 2002, c. 664 (A.B.3034), § 178.5; Stats.2006, c. 493 (A.B. 1363), § 25; Stats.2007, c. 553 (A.B.1727), § 22.)*

Law Revision Commission Comments

1990 Enactment

Section 2620.2 continues Section 2620.2 of the repealed Probate Code without change. [20 Cal.L.Rev.Comm. Reports 1001 (1990)].

Cross References

Guardians and conservators, removal or resignation, see Probate Code § 2650 et seq.
Notice,
    Mailing, see Probate Code § 1215 et seq.
    Posting, see Probate Code § 1230.
    Proof of giving notice, see Probate Code § 1260 et seq.
    Special notice, see Probate Code § 1250 et seq.
    This code, generally, see Probate Code § 1200 et seq.
Service of process,
    Generally, see Code of Civil Procedure § 413.10 et seq.
    Mail, see Code of Civil Procedure §§ 415.30, 1012 et seq.
    Personal delivery, see Code of Civil Procedure § 415.10.
    Proof of service, see Code of Civil Procedure § 417.10 et seq.
    Publication, see Code of Civil Procedure § 415.50.
Temporary guardians and conservators, generally, see Probate Code § 2250 et seq.

§ 2621. Notice of hearing

Notice of the hearing on the account of the guardian or conservator shall be given for the period and in the manner provided in Chapter 3 (commencing with Section 1460) of Part 1. If notice is required to be given to the Director of State Hospitals or the Director of Developmental Services under Section 1461, the account shall not be settled or allowed unless notice has been given as provided in Section 1461. *(Stats.1990, c. 79 (A.B.759), § 14, operative July 1, 1991. Amended by Stats.2012, c. 440 (A.B.1488), § 47, eff. Sept. 22, 2012.)*

Law Revision Commission Comments

1990 Enactment

Section 2621 continues Section 2621 of the repealed Probate Code without change. Unless notice is given or waived as provided in Section 1461, if the account is settled without giving notice to the Director of Mental Health or the Director of Developmental Services in cases where notice is required under Section 1461, the statute of limitations does not run against any claim of the State Department of Mental Health or the State Department of Developmental Services against the estate for board, care, maintenance, or transportation. See Section 1461(d). For general provisions relating to notice of hearing, see Sections 1200–1221, 1460–1469. See also Sections 1260–1265 (proof of giving notice), 2700–2702 (notice to persons who request special notice). For background on the provisions of this part, see the Comment to this part under the part heading. [20 Cal.L.Rev.Comm. Reports 1001 (1990)].

Cross References

Director of Developmental Services, see Welfare and Institutions Code § 4401 et seq.

Director of State Hospitals, see Welfare and Institutions Code §§ 4001, 4004.
Request for special notice, see Probate Code § 2700 et seq.

§ 2622. Objections to account

The ward or conservatee, the spouse of the ward or the spouse or domestic partner of the conservatee, any relative or friend of the ward or conservatee, or any creditor or other interested person may file written objections to the account of the guardian or conservator, stating the items of the account to which objection is made and the basis for the objection. *(Stats.1990, c. 79 (A.B.759), § 14, operative July 1, 1991. Amended by Stats.2001, c. 893 (A.B.25), § 40.)*

Law Revision Commission Comments

1990 Enactment

Section 2622 continues Section 2622 of the repealed Probate Code without change. See Section 1043 (handling of objections). For background on the provisions of this part, see the Comment to this part under the part heading. [20 Cal.L.Rev.Comm. Reports 1001 (1990)].

Cross References

Domestic partner, defined, see Probate Code § 37.
Interested person, defined, see Probate Code § 1424.

§ 2622.5. Objections or opposition to objections without reasonable cause or in bad faith; payment of costs and expenses; personal liability

(a) If the court determines that the objections were without reasonable cause and in bad faith, the court may order the objector to pay the compensation and costs of the conservator or guardian and other expenses and costs of litigation, including attorney's fees, incurred to defend the account. The objector shall be personally liable to the guardianship or conservatorship estate for the amount ordered.

(b) If the court determines that the opposition to the objections was without reasonable cause and in bad faith, the court may award the objector the costs of the objector and other expenses and costs of litigation, including attorney's fees, incurred to contest the account. The amount awarded is a charge against the compensation of the guardian or conservator, and the guardian or conservator is liable personally and on the bond, if any, for any amount that remains unsatisfied. *(Added by Stats.1996, c. 563 (S.B.392), § 12.)*

Cross References

Attorney's fees and costs, generally, see Code of Civil Procedure § 1021.
Costs, see Probate Code § 1002.

§ 2623. Compensation and expenses of guardian or conservator

(a) Except as provided in subdivision (b) of this section, the guardian or conservator shall be allowed all of the following:

(1) The amount of the reasonable expenses incurred in the exercise of the powers and the performance of the duties of the guardian or conservator (including, but not limited to, the cost of any surety bond furnished, reasonable attorney's fees, and such compensation for services rendered by the guardian

or conservator of the person as the court determines is just and reasonable).

(2) Such compensation for services rendered by the guardian or conservator as the court determines is just and reasonable.

(3) All reasonable disbursements made before appointment as guardian or conservator.

(4) In the case of termination other than by the death of the ward or conservatee, all reasonable disbursements made after the termination of the guardianship or conservatorship but prior to the discharge of the guardian or conservator by the court.

(5) In the case of termination by the death of the ward or conservatee, all reasonable expenses ,incurred prior to the discharge of the guardian or conservator by the court for the custody and conservation of the estate and its delivery to the personal representative of the estate of the deceased ward or conservatee or in making other disposition of the estate as provided for by law.

(b) The guardian or conservator shall not be compensated from the estate for any costs or fees that the guardian or conservator incurred in unsuccessfully opposing a petition, or other request or action, made by or on behalf of the ward or conservatee, unless the court determines that the opposition was made in good faith, based on the best interests of the ward or conservatee. *(Stats.1990, c. 79 (A.B.759), § 14, operative July 1, 1991. Amended by Stats.2006, c. 493 (A.B.1363), § 26.)*

Law Revision Commission Comments
1990 Enactment

Section 2623 continues Section 2623 of the repealed Probate Code without substantive change. See also Section 2750 (order fixing, directing, authorizing, or allowing payment of compensation or expenses of guardian or conservator or fixing, directing, authorizing, or allowing payment of the compensation of the attorney is an appealable order). The amount incurred in the performance of the duties of the guardian or conservator includes amounts paid for support, maintenance, or education of the ward or conservatee and of persons legally entitled to support, maintenance or education from the ward or conservatee. See Sections 2420 (support, maintenance, and education), 2421 (personal allowance for ward or conservatee), 2430–2431 (payment of debts). For background on the provisions of this part, see the Comment to this part under the part heading. [20 Cal.L.Rev.Comm. Reports 1001 (1990)].

Cross References

Attorney's fees and costs, generally, see Code of Civil Procedure § 1021.
Compensation of guardian, conservator, and attorney, see Probate Code § 2640 et seq.
Independent exercise of powers, see Probate Code § 2590 et seq.
Personal representative and general personal representative, defined, see Probate Code § 58.
Termination,
 Conservatorship, see Probate Code § 1860 et seq.
 Guardianship, see Probate Code §§ 1600, 1601.

§ 2624.   Repealed by Stats.1996, c. 862 (A.B.2751), § 12

§ 2625.   Review of sales, purchases and other transactions

Any sale or purchase of property or other transaction not previously authorized, approved, or confirmed by the court is subject to review by the court upon the next succeeding account of the guardian or conservator occurring after the transaction. Upon such account and review, the court may hold the guardian or conservator liable for any violation of duties in connection with the sale, purchase, or other transaction. Nothing in this section shall be construed to affect the validity of any sale or purchase or other transaction. *(Stats.1990, c. 79 (A.B.759), § 14, operative July 1, 1991.)*

Law Revision Commission Comments
1990 Enactment

Section 2625 continues Section 2625 of the repealed Probate Code without substantive change.

Section 2620 requires disclosure of transactions occurring during the period covered by the account: Subdivision (c) of Section 2620 requires that the account contain itemized schedules showing the transactions, and subdivision (d)(1) requires a description of all sales, purchases, changes in the form of assets, or other transactions that are not readily understandable from the schedules. If the transactions have been previously authorized, approved, or confirmed by the court, they need not again be reviewed under Section 2625. See Section 2103 (effect of court authorization, approval, or confirmation). However, other transactions—those that did not require court authorization and those that did require court authorization but were made without it—are subject to review under Section 2625 at the time of the accounting. See also Section 2750 (appealable orders).

The fact that a transaction required prior court authorization which was not obtained does not preclude the court from approving and confirming the transaction at the time of the accounting or on a petition for approval and confirmation under Section 2403. See Place v. Trent, 27 Cal.App.3d 526, 103 Cal.Rptr. 841 (1972). However, if the transaction required court authorization which was not obtained, when it is reviewed under Section 2625 the guardian or conservator must justify the transaction in the same manner that would have been required had authorization been sought before the transaction was made. And the guardian or conservator runs a risk that the court will not approve and confirm the transaction at the time of the accounting. A guardian or conservator may be surcharged for improper payments or other wrongful acts or omissions that cause pecuniary damage to the estate. W. Johnstone, G. Zillgitt, & S. House, California Conservatorships § 12.45, at 727 (Cal.Cont.Ed.Bar 2d ed. 1983 & Supp.1989). Nevertheless, unless the court determines that the transaction was improper because the guardian or conservator failed to use ordinary care and diligence (Section 2401) or for some other reason, the court should approve and confirm the transaction when it reviews the current account. But if the court determines that there was loss from failure to use ordinary care and diligence, the court may surcharge the guardian or conservator. Cf. Estate of Hilde, 112 Cal.App.2d 189, 246 P.2d 79 (1952) (administrator surcharged where estate property sold below appraised value without required court authorization).

For background on the provisions of this part, see the Comment to this part under the part heading. [20 Cal.L.Rev.Comm. Reports 1001 (1990)].

Cross References

Review of periodic payments of compensation to guardian, conservator or attorney, see Probate Code § 2643.

§ 2626.   Termination of proceeding upon exhaustion of estate

If it appears upon the settlement of any account that the estate has been entirely exhausted through expenditures or disbursements which are approved by the court, the court, upon settlement of the account, shall order the proceeding terminated and the guardian or conservator forthwith discharged unless the court determines that there is reason to continue the proceeding. *(Stats.1990, c. 79 (A.B.759), § 14, operative July 1, 1991.)*

Section 2626 continues Section 2626 of the repealed Probate Code without change. If it appears that the guardianship or conservatorship estate will be replenished by new assets, this section does not require termination of the proceeding. See also Section 2750 (order discharging guardian or conservator is an appealable order). For background on the provisions of this part, see the Comment to this part under the part heading. [20 Cal.L.Rev.Comm. Reports 1001 (1990)].

Cross References

Termination of guardianship by emancipation, majority, death or adoption, see Probate Code §§ 1600, 1601.
Termination of proceeding upon transfer of all assets out of state, see Probate Code § 2808.

§ 2627. Settlement of accounts and release by ward; discharge of guardian

(a) After a ward has reached majority, the ward may settle accounts with the guardian and give the guardian a release which is valid if obtained fairly and without undue influence.

(b) Except as otherwise provided by this code, a guardian is not entitled to a discharge until one year after the ward has attained majority. *(Stats.1990, c. 79 (A.B.759), § 14, operative July 1, 1991.)*

Law Revision Commission Comments

1990 Enactment

Section 2627 continues Section 2627 of the repealed Probate Code without change. A former guardian has the burden of showing that a release given by the ward pursuant to subdivision (a) is just and fair. Smith v. Fidelity & Deposit Co., 130 Cal.App. 45, 56–57, 19 P.2d 1018, 1023 (1933). Such a release does not discharge the guardian, however, since the discharge must be granted by the court. See also Section 2630 (ward's majority does not cause court to lose jurisdiction to settle accounts). For background on the provisions of this part, see the Comment to this part under the part heading. [20 Cal.L.Rev.Comm. Reports 1001 (1990)].

Cross References

Age of majority, see Family Code § 6500 et seq.
Removal of property of nonresident from state, discharge of personal representative, see Probate Code § 3803.

§ 2628. Public benefit payments; procedure; conditions

(a) The court may make an order that the guardian or conservator need not present the accounts otherwise required by this chapter so long as all of the following conditions are satisfied:

(1) The estate at the beginning and end of the accounting period for which an account is otherwise required consisted of property, exclusive of the residence of the ward or conservatee, of a total net value of less than fifteen thousand dollars ($15,000).

(2) The income of the estate for each month of the accounting period, exclusive of public benefit payments, was less than two thousand dollars ($2,000).

(3) All income of the estate during the accounting period, if not retained, was spent for the benefit of the ward or conservatee.

(b) Notwithstanding that the court has made an order under subdivision (a), the ward or conservatee or any interested person may petition the court for an order requiring the guardian or conservator to present an account as otherwise required by this chapter or the court on its own motion may make that an order. An order under this subdivision may be made ex parte or on such notice of hearing as the court in its discretion requires.

(c) For any accounting period during which all of the conditions of subdivision (a) are not satisfied, the guardian or conservator shall present the account as otherwise required by this chapter. *(Stats.1990, c. 79 (A.B.759), § 14, operative July 1, 1991. Amended by Stats.1991, c. 1019 (S.B.1022), § 7; Stats.1998, c. 103 (S.B.1487), § 1; Stats.2007, c. 553 (A.B. 1727), § 23.)*

Law Revision Commission Comments

1990 Enactment

Section 2628 continues Section 2628 of the repealed Probate Code without change. The purpose of this section is to reduce the expense of administration of small estates. In determining whether the monthly income of the estate satisfies the small estate requirements, income from public benefit payments is excluded. These payments are: (1) state aid and medical assistance (Welf. & Inst.Code §§ 11000–15754), (2) services for the care of children (Welf. & Inst.Code §§ 16100–16515), (3) county aid and relief to indigents (Welf. & Inst.Code §§ 17000–17410), (4) federal old age, survivors, and disability insurance benefits (42 U.S.C.A. §§ 401–431 (West 1983 & Supp.1989)), and (5) federal supplemental security income for the aged, blind, and disabled (42 U.S.C.A. §§ 1381–1383c (West 1983 & Supp.1989)). For general provisions, see Sections 1000–1004 (rules of practice), 1020–1023 (petitions and other papers), 1040–1050 (hearings and orders). See also Sections 1021 (petition to be verified), 1041 (clerk to set petition for hearing). For general provisions relating to notice of hearing, see Sections 1200–1221, 1460–1469. See also Sections 1260–1265 (proof of giving notice), 2700–2702 (notice to persons who request special notice). For background on the provisions of this part, see the Comment to this part under the part heading. [20 Cal.L.Rev.Comm. Reports 1001 (1990)].

Cross References

Designation of guardian or conservator as payee for public assistance payments, see Probate Code § 2452.
Guardianship and conservatorship, interested person, defined, see Probate Code § 1424.

§ 2629. Repealed by Stats.2001, c. 359 (S.B.140), § 5

ARTICLE 4. ACCOUNTS ON TERMINATION OF RELATIONSHIP

Cross References

Application of old and new law, see Probate Code § 3.

§ 2630. Continuing jurisdiction of the court

The termination of the relationship of guardian and ward or conservator and conservatee by the death of either, by the ward attaining majority, by the determination of the court that the guardianship or conservatorship is no longer necessary, by the removal or resignation of the guardian or conservator, or for any other reason, does not cause the court to lose jurisdiction of the proceeding for the purpose of settling the accounts of the guardian or conservator or for any other purpose incident to the enforcement of the judgments and orders of the court upon such accounts or upon the termination of the relationship. *(Stats.1990, c. 79 (A.B.759), § 14, operative July 1, 1991.)*

Law Revision Commission Comments
1990 Enactment

Section 2630 continues Section 2630 of the repealed Probate Code without change. For background on the provisions of this part, see the Comment to this part under the part heading. [20 Cal.L.Rev. Comm. Reports 1001 (1990)].

Cross References

Age of majority, see Family Code § 6500 et seq.
Removal or resignation of guardian or conservator, see Probate Code § 2650 et seq.
Termination,
 Conservatorship, see Probate Code § 1860 et seq.
 Guardianship, see Probate Code §§ 1600, 1601.
Trusts, judicial proceedings,
 Generally, see Probate Code § 17000 et seq.
 Continuing jurisdiction, see Probate Code § 17300 et seq.

§ 2631. Death of ward or conservatee; disposition of assets

(a) Upon the death of the ward or conservatee, the guardian or conservator may contract for and pay a reasonable sum for the expenses of the last illness and the disposition of the remains of the deceased ward or conservatee, and for unpaid court-approved attorney's fees, and may pay the unpaid expenses of the guardianship or conservatorship accruing before or after the death of the ward or conservatee, in full or in part, to the extent reasonable, from any personal property of the deceased ward or conservatee which is under the control of the guardian or conservator.

(b) If after payment of expenses under subdivision (a), the total market value of the remaining estate of the decedent does not exceed the amount determined under Section 13100, the guardian or conservator may petition the court for an order permitting the guardian or conservator to liquidate the decedent's estate. The guardian or conservator may petition even though there is a will of the decedent in existence if the will does not appoint an executor or if the named executor refuses to act. No notice of the petition need be given. If the order is granted, the guardian or conservator may sell personal property of the decedent, withdraw money of the decedent in an account in a financial institution, and collect a debt, claim, or insurance proceeds owed to the decedent or the decedent's estate, and a person having possession or control shall pay or deliver the money or property to the guardian or conservator.

(c) After payment of expenses, the guardian or conservator may transfer any remaining property as provided in Division 8 (commencing with Section 13000). For this purpose, the value of the property of the deceased ward or conservatee shall be determined after the deduction of the expenses so paid. *(Stats.1990, c. 79 (A.B.759), § 14, operative July 1, 1991. Amended by Stats.1996, c. 563 (S.B.392), § 13.)*

Law Revision Commission Comments
1990 Enactment

Section 2631 continues Section 2631 of the repealed Probate Code without substantive change, except that subdivision (b) is revised to substitute a reference to Section 13100 ($60,000 limit, excluding property described in Section 13050, for use of affidavit procedure for collection or transfer of personal property without probate) for the $10,000 limit found in Section 2631 of the repealed Probate Code. Subdivision (b) also authorizes a court order for liquidation of the decedent ward's or conservatee's estate whether or not required for payment of expenses. This generalizes a provision of former Welfare and Institutions Code Section 8012 (disposition of property by public guardian). If the guardian or conservator pays expenses from assets of the ward or conservatee which are the subject of a specific gift by will, the rules of abatement set forth in Sections 21400–21406 apply. Cf. Estate of Mason, 62 Cal.2d 213, 397 P.2d 1005, 42 Cal.Rptr. 13 (1965). For background on the provisions of this part, see the Comment to this part under the part heading. [20 Cal.L.Rev.Comm. Reports 1001 (1990)].

Cross References

Account, defined, see Probate Code § 21
Attorney's fees and costs, generally, see Code of Civil Procedure § 1021.
Care of estate after death of ward or conservatee, see Probate Code § 2467.
Estate administration,
 Generally, see Probate Code § 7000 et seq.
 Payment of debts, see Probate Code § 11400 et seq.
Estate attorney, compensation, amount, see Probate Code § 10810 et seq.
Financial institution, defined, see Probate Code § 40.
Inventory and appraisal, generally, see Probate Code § 8800 et seq.
Termination of estate upon death of conservatee, see Probate Code § 1860.
Termination of guardianship upon majority, death, adoption or emancipation of ward, see Probate Code § 1600.

§ 2632. Account of deceased; incapacitated or absconding guardian or conservator

(a) As used in this section:

(1) "Incapacitated" means lack of capacity to serve as guardian or conservator.

(2) "Legal representative" means the personal representative of a deceased guardian or conservator or the conservator of the estate of an incapacitated guardian or conservator.

(b) If a guardian or conservator dies or becomes incapacitated and a legal representative is appointed for the deceased or incapacitated guardian or conservator, the legal representative shall, not later than 60 days after appointment unless the court extends the time, file an account of the administration of the deceased or incapacitated guardian or conservator.

(c) If a guardian or conservator dies or becomes incapacitated and no legal representative is appointed for the deceased or incapacitated guardian or conservator, or if the guardian or conservator absconds, the court may compel the attorney for the deceased, incapacitated, or absconding guardian or conservator or the attorney of record in the guardianship or conservatorship proceeding to file an account of the administration of the deceased, incapacitated, or absconding guardian or conservator.

(d) The legal representative or attorney shall exercise reasonable diligence in preparing an account under this section. Verification of the account may be made on information and belief. The court shall settle the account as in other cases. The court shall allow reasonable compensation to the legal representative or the attorney for preparing the account. The amount allowed shall be a charge against the estate that was being administered by the deceased, incapacitated, or absconding guardian or conservator. Legal services for which compensation shall be allowed to the attorney under this subdivision include those services rendered by any paralegal performing the services under the direction and supervision of an attorney. The petition or application for compensation shall set forth the hours spent and services performed by the paralegal. *(Stats.1990, c. 79 (A.B.759), § 14, operative July 1, 1991.)*

Law Revision Commission Comments

1990 Enactment

Section 2632 supersedes Section 2632 of the repealed Probate Code. Section 2632 uses language drawn from Section 10953 (decedents' estates). The court referred to in this section is the court in which the guardianship or conservatorship proceeding is pending. See also Section 2642 (attorney's petition for payment for services provided by attorney). For background on the provisions of this part, see the Comment to this part under the part heading. [20 Cal.L.Rev.Comm. Reports 1001 (1990)].

Cross References

Appointment of personal representative, generally, see Probate Code § 8400 et seq.
Attorney's fees and costs, generally, see Code of Civil Procedure § 1021.
Capacity determinations, generally, see Probate Code § 3200 et seq.
Personal representative and attorney, compensation, generally, see Probate Code § 10800 et seq.
Personal representative and general personal representative, defined, see Probate Code § 58.
Petition by attorney for compensation, see Probate Code § 2642.
Removal of guardian or conservator in case of incapacity, see Probate Code § 2650.

§ 2633. Order that inventory and appraisement need not be filed; account of assets in possession and control

Subject to Section 2630, where the guardianship or conservatorship terminates before the inventory of the estate has been filed, the court, in its discretion and upon such notice as the court may require, may make an order that the guardian or conservator need not file the inventory and appraisal and that the guardian or conservator shall file an account covering only those assets of the estate of which the guardian or conservator has possession or control. *(Stats.1990, c. 79 (A.B.759), § 14, operative July 1, 1991.)*

Law Revision Commission Comments

1990 Enactment

Section 2633 continues Section 2633 of the repealed Probate Code without substantive change. This section authorizes the court to dispense with the inventory and appraisal where the conservatee dies a few days after appointment of a conservator. This will permit the court, in its discretion, to waive the inventory and permit an accounting of assets actually marshalled, thereby avoiding (1) the need to inventory estate assets—such as stocks, oil rights, or real property—where the conservator has not yet taken possession or control of the assets and (2) the resulting additional fees for the conservator and needless delay in turning the estate over to the personal representative of the deceased conservatee. For general provisions, see Sections 1000–1004 (rules of practice), 1020–1023 (petitions and other papers), 1040–1050 (hearings and orders), 2103 (effect of final order). For background on the provisions of this part, see the Comment to this part under the part heading. [20 Cal.L.Rev.Comm. Reports 1001 (1990)].

CHAPTER 8. COMPENSATION OF GUARDIAN, CONSERVATOR, AND ATTORNEY

Cross References

Application of old and new law, see Probate Code § 3.

§ 2640. Petition by guardian or conservator of estate

(a) At any time after the filing of the inventory and appraisal, but not before the expiration of 90 days from the issuance of letters or any other period of time as the court for good cause orders, the guardian or conservator of the estate may petition the court for an order fixing and allowing compensation to any one or more of the following:

(1) The guardian or conservator of the estate for services rendered to that time.

(2) The guardian or conservator of the person for services rendered to that time.

(3) The attorney for services rendered to that time by the attorney to the guardian or conservator of the person or estate or both.

(b) Notice of the hearing shall be given for the period and in the manner provided for in Chapter 3 (commencing with Section 1460) of Part 1.

(c) Upon the hearing, the court shall make an order allowing (1) any compensation requested in the petition the court determines is just and reasonable to the guardian or conservator of the estate for services rendered or to the guardian or conservator of the person for services rendered, or to both, and (2) any compensation requested in the petition the court determines is reasonable to the attorney for services rendered to the guardian or conservator of the person or estate or both. The compensation allowed to the guardian or conservator of the person, the guardian or conservator of the estate, and to the attorney may, in the discretion of the court, include compensation for services rendered before the date of the order appointing the guardian or conservator. The compensation allowed shall thereupon be charged to the estate. Legal services for which the attorney may be compensated include those services rendered by any paralegal performing legal services under the direction and supervision of an attorney. The petition or application for compensation shall set forth the hours spent and services performed by the paralegal.

(d) Notwithstanding the provisions of subdivision (c), the guardian or conservator shall not be compensated from the estate for any costs or fees that the guardian or conservator incurred in unsuccessfully opposing a petition, or other request or action, made by or on behalf of the ward or conservatee, unless the court determines that the opposition was made in good faith, based on the best interests of the ward or conservatee. *(Stats.1990, c. 79 (A.B.759), § 14, operative July 1, 1991. Amended by Stats.1992, c. 572 (S.B.1455), § 8; Stats.1998, c. 581 (A.B.2801), § 23; Stats. 2006, c. 493 (A.B.1363), § 27.)*

Law Revision Commission Comments

1992 Amendment

Subdivisions (a) and (c) of Section 2640 are amended to make clear the court is not precluded from awarding compensation for services rendered before the date of appointment. See also Sections 1470 (compensation of counsel), 1472 (compensation of counsel), 2623(c) (guardian or conservator allowed all reasonable disbursements made before appointment as guardian or conservator), 2641 (compensation of guardian or conservator of person).

Subdivision (c) is also amended to delete the former reference to compensation for which the attorney may "apply to the court." Under Section 2640, the application to the court for the attorney's compensation is made by the guardian or conservator of the estate, not by the attorney. [21 Cal.L.Rev.Comm. Reports 227 (1991)].

Cross References

Appointment of legal counsel, see Probate Code § 1470 et seq.
Attorney's fees and costs, generally, see Code of Civil Procedure § 1021.
Compensation for attorney rendering account for dead, incapacitated or absconding guardian or conservator, see Probate Code § 2632.
Filing inventory and appraisement, see Probate Code § 2610.
Independent exercise of powers, see Probate Code § 2590 et seq.
Issuance of letters, see Probate Code § 2310.
Letters, defined, see Probate Code § 52.
Personal representative and attorney, compensation, generally, see Probate Code § 10800 et seq.

Presentation of account for settlement and allowance, see Probate Code § 2620.

§ 2640.1. Person who has petitioned for appointment of conservator but was not appointed; petition for compensation and reimbursement; notice of hearing; order for compensation and costs; retroactive effect

(a) If a person has petitioned for the appointment of a particular conservator and another conservator was appointed while the petition was pending, but not before the expiration of 90 days from the issuance of letters, the person who petitioned for the appointment of a conservator but was not appointed and that person's attorney may petition the court for an order fixing and allowing compensation and reimbursement of costs, provided that the court determines that the petition was filed in the best interests of the conservatee.

(b) Notice of the hearing shall be given for the period and in the manner provided in Chapter 3 (commencing with Section 1460) of Part 1.

(c) Upon the hearing, the court shall make an order to allow both of the following:

(1) Any compensation or costs requested in the petition the court determines is just and reasonable to the person who petitioned for the appointment of a conservator but was not appointed, for his or her services rendered in connection with and to facilitate the appointment of a conservator, and costs incurred in connection therewith.

(2) Any compensation or costs requested in the petition the court determines is just and reasonable to the attorney for that person, for his or her services rendered in connection with and to facilitate the appointment of a conservator, and costs incurred in connection therewith.

Any compensation and costs allowed shall be charged to the estate of the conservatee. If a conservator of the estate is not appointed, but a conservator of the person is appointed, the compensation and costs allowed shall be ordered by the court to be paid from property belonging to the conservatee, whether held outright, in trust, or otherwise.

(d) It is the intent of the Legislature for this section to have retroactive effect. *(Added by Stats.1995, c. 730 (A.B. 1466), § 5. Amended by Stats.2006, c. 493 (A.B.1363), § 28.)*

Cross References

Attorney's fees and costs, generally, see Code of Civil Procedure § 1021.
Legislative intent, construction of statutes, see Code of Civil Procedure § 1859.
Letters, defined, see Probate Code § 52.

§ 2641. Petition by guardian or conservator of person

(a) At any time permitted by Section 2640 and upon the notice therein prescribed, the guardian or conservator of the person may petition the court for an order fixing and allowing compensation for services rendered to that time.

(b) Upon the hearing, the court shall make an order allowing any compensation the court determines is just and reasonable to the guardian or conservator of the person for services rendered. The compensation allowed to the guardian or conservator of the person may, in the discretion of the court, include compensation for services rendered before the date of the order appointing the guardian or conservator. The compensation allowed shall thereupon be charged against the estate.

(c) The guardian or conservator shall not be compensated from the estate for any costs or fees that the guardian or conservator incurred in unsuccessfully opposing a petition, or other request or action, made by or on behalf of the ward or conservatee, unless the court determines that the opposition was made in good faith, based on the best interests of the ward or conservatee. *(Stats.1990, c. 79 (A.B.759), § 14, operative July 1, 1991. Amended by Stats.1992, c. 572 (S.B.1455), § 9; Stats.2006, c. 493 (A.B.1363), § 29.)*

Law Revision Commission Comments

1992 Amendment

Section 2641 is amended to make clear the court is not precluded from awarding compensation for services rendered before the date of appointment. See also Sections 1470 (compensation of counsel), 1472 (compensation of counsel), 2623(c) (guardian or conservator allowed all reasonable disbursements made before appointment as guardian or conservator), 2640 (compensation of guardian or conservator of estate). [21 Cal.L.Rev.Comm. Reports 227 (1991)].

Cross References

Accounting, compensation for guardian of person, see Probate Code § 2623.

§ 2642. Petition by attorney

(a) At any time permitted by Section 2640 and upon the notice therein prescribed, an attorney who has rendered legal services to the guardian or conservator of the person or estate or both, including services rendered under Section 2632, may petition the court for an order fixing and allowing compensation for such services rendered to that time. Legal services for which the attorney may petition the court for an order fixing and allowing compensation under this subdivision include those services rendered by any paralegal performing the legal services under the direction and supervision of an attorney. The petition or application for compensation shall set forth the hours spent and services performed by the paralegal.

(b) Upon the hearing, the court shall make an order allowing such compensation as the court determines reasonable to the attorney for services rendered to the guardian or conservator. The compensation so allowed shall thereupon be charged against the estate. *(Stats.1990, c. 79 (A.B.759), § 14, operative July 1, 1991.)*

Law Revision Commission Comments

1990 Enactment

Section 2642 continues Section 2642 of the repealed Probate Code without change. For general provisions, see Sections 1000–1004 (rules of practice), 1020–1023 (petitions and other papers), 1040–1050 (hearings and orders), 2103 (effect of final order), 2750 (appealable orders). For general provisions relating to notice of hearing, see Sections 1200–1221, 1460–1469. See also Sections 1260–1265 (proof of giving notice), 2700–2702 (notice to persons who request special notice). See also the Comment to Section 2640. [20 Cal.L.Rev.Comm. Reports 1001 (1990)].

Cross References

Accounting, allowance for attorney's fees, see Probate Code § 2623.
Appointment of legal counsel, see Probate Code § 1470 et seq.
Attorney's fees and costs, generally, see Code of Civil Procedure § 1021.
Estate attorney, compensation, amount, see Probate Code § 10810 et seq.

§ 2643. Periodic payments of compensation to guardian, conservator or attorney; order

(a) Except as provided in Section 2643.1, on petition by the guardian or conservator of the person or estate, or both, the court may by order authorize periodic payments on account to any one or more of the following persons for the services rendered by that person during the period covered by each payment:

(1) The guardian of the person.

(2) The guardian of the estate.

(3) The conservator of the person.

(4) The conservator of the estate.

(5) The attorney for the guardian or conservator of the person or estate, or both.

(b) Notice of the hearing on the petition shall be given for the period and in the manner provided in Chapter 3 (commencing with Section 1460) of Part 1.

(c) The petition shall describe the services to be rendered on a periodic basis and the reason why authority to make periodic payments is requested. In fixing the amount of the periodic payment, the court shall take into account the services to be rendered on a periodic basis and the reasonable value of those services. The guardian or conservator of the estate may make the periodic payments authorized by the order only if the services described in the petition are actually rendered. The payments made pursuant to the order are subject to review by the court upon the next succeeding account of the guardian or conservator of the estate to determine that the services were actually rendered and that the amount paid on account was not unreasonable, and the court shall make an appropriate order if the court determines that the amount paid on account was either excessive or inadequate in view of the services actually rendered. *(Stats. 1990, c. 79 (A.B.759), § 14, operative July 1, 1991. Amended by Stats.2013, c. 248 (A.B.1339), § 6.)*

Law Revision Commission Comments

1990 Enactment

Section 2643 continues Section 2643 of the repealed Probate Code without substantive change. This section makes clear that the court, in its discretion, may authorize periodic payments of compensation. Similar authority to authorize periodic payments of compensation to a trustee is found in Section 15682. Section 2643 permits the court, for example, to authorize the guardian or conservator of the estate to make a payment each month on account to the attorney for services rendered during the immediately preceding month.

An order under Section 2643 may be useful for a large estate where there may be tax advantages from making periodic payments of compensation. Where a guardian or conservator of the person is compensated and devotes substantial time to the care of the ward or conservatee, periodic payments may be needed. Periodic payments also avoid problems that may exist when payment is delayed: The payments provide funds on a current basis to cover out-of-pocket expenses, avoid the need to determine questions that turn on the value of loss of use of money caused by delay in payment, and protect against variations in the value of money which may be significant in an inflationary period. Where services are rendered on a periodic basis, Section 2643 avoids the need for frequent accountings or petitions for compensation.

The periodic payments are "on account." Actual compensation is determined when the court reviews the account of the guardian or conservator. At that time, payments are reviewed by the court in light of services actually rendered. If the total of periodic payments is too low to be just and reasonable compensation for the guardian or conservator or attorney, the court should allow additional compensation for services actually rendered. If the amount paid is unreasonably high for services actually rendered, the court should make an appropriate order. Such an order might require the guardian or conservator to credit the excess paid against amounts to be paid for future services.

For general provisions, see Sections 1000–1004 (rules of practice), 1020–1023 (petitions and other papers), 1040–1050 (hearings and orders), 2103 (effect of final order), 2750 (appealable orders). For general provisions relating to notice of hearing, see Sections 1200–1221, 1460–1469. See also Sections 1260–1265 (proof of giving notice), 2700–2702 (notice to persons who request special notice). For background on the provisions of this part, see the Comment to this part under the part heading. [20 Cal.L.Rev.Comm. Reports 1001 (1990)].

Cross References

Attorney's fees and costs, generally, see Code of Civil Procedure § 1021.

Compensation and expenses of guardian or conservator or attorney, see Probate Code § 2623.

Trust administration, periodic payments of compensation to trustee, see Probate Code § 15682.

Trusts funded by court order, required provisions in trust instruments, see California Rules of Court, Rule 7.903.

§ 2643.1. Professional fiduciary as guardian or conservator; court authorization of periodic payments; contents of petition; notice; objections; payments; termination of authorization

(a) On petition by a guardian or conservator of the person or estate, or both, who is a professional fiduciary, as described in Section 2340 and who is required to be licensed under the Professional Fiduciaries Act (Chapter 6 (commencing with Section 6500) of Division 3 of the Business and Professions Code), the court may by order authorize periodic payments on account to a person described in subdivision (a) of Section 2643 for the services rendered by that person during the period covered by each payment only if that person has filed a proposed hourly fee schedule or another statement of his or her proposed compensation from the estate of the ward or conservatee for services performed as a guardian or conservator, as required by Section 2614.7, and only after the court has addressed any objections filed pursuant to subdivision (d).

(b) The petition shall describe the services to be rendered on a periodic basis, the reason why authority to make periodic payments is requested, and a good faith estimate of the fees to be charged by the professional fiduciary from the date the petition is filed up to, and including, the date of the next succeeding account required by Section 2620 or, if the next succeeding account required by Section 2620 is due in less than one year, a good faith estimate of the fees to be charged by the professional fiduciary from the date the

petition is filed through the next succeeding 12 months, inclusive. Prior to ordering periodic payments or fixing the amount of the periodic payment, the court shall determine whether making periodic payments is in the best interest of the ward or conservatee, taking into consideration the needs of the ward or conservatee and the need to preserve and protect the estate. If the court determines that making periodic payments is not in the best interest of the ward or conservatee, the court shall deny the petition to authorize periodic payments. If the court determines that making periodic payments is in the best interest of the ward or conservatee, the court shall fix the amount of the periodic payment. In fixing the amount of the periodic payment, the court shall take into account the services to be rendered on a periodic basis and the reasonable value of those services.

(c)(1) Notice of the hearing on the petition and notice of how to file an objection to the petition shall be given for the period and in the manner provided in Chapter 3 (commencing with Section 1460) of Part 1.

(2) The notices required by paragraph (1) shall be made to the court investigator for the period and in the manner provided in Chapter 3 (commencing with Section 1460) of Part 1.

(d)(1) Any person entitled to notice under paragraph (1) of subdivision (c) may file with the court a written objection to the authorization of periodic payments on account. The court clerk shall set any objections for a hearing no fewer than 15 days after the date the objections are filed.

(2) If an objection is filed pursuant to paragraph (1), the guardian or conservator shall have the burden of establishing the necessity for and amount, if any, of periodic payments.

(e) The guardian or conservator of the estate may make the periodic payments authorized by the order only if the services described in the petition are actually rendered. The payments made pursuant to the order shall be reviewed by the court upon the next succeeding account of the guardian or conservator of the estate to determine that the services were actually rendered and that the amount paid on account was reasonable and in the best interest of the ward or conservatee, taking into consideration the needs of the ward or conservatee and the need to preserve and protect the estate. The court shall make an appropriate order reducing the guardian or conservator's compensation if the court determines that the amount paid on account was either unreasonable or not in the best interest of the ward or conservatee in view of the services actually rendered.

(f) The authorization for periodic payments granted pursuant to this section shall terminate on a date determined by the court, but not later than the due date of the next succeeding account required by Section 2620. Nothing in this section shall preclude a guardian or conservator from filing a subsequent petition to receive periodic payments pursuant to this section. *(Added by Stats.2013, c. 248 (A.B.1339), § 7.)*

§ 2644. Contingent fee contract with attorney

(a) Where it is to the advantage, benefit, and best interest of the ward or conservatee or the estate, the guardian or conservator of the estate may contract with an attorney for a contingent fee for the attorney's services in representing the ward or conservatee or the estate in connection with a matter that is of a type that is customarily the subject of a contingent fee contract, but such a contract is valid only if (1) the contract is made pursuant to an order of the court authorizing the guardian or conservator to execute the contract or (2) the contract is approved by order of the court.

(b) To obtain an order under this section, the guardian or conservator shall file a petition with the court showing the advantage, benefit, and best interest to the ward or conservatee or the estate of the contingent fee contract. A copy of the contingent fee contract shall be attached to the petition.

(c) Notice of the hearing on the petition shall be given for the period and in the manner provided in Chapter 3 (commencing with Section 1460) of Part 1.

(d) As used in this section, "court" includes either of the following:

(1) The court in which the guardianship or conservatorship proceeding is pending.

(2) Where the contract is in connection with a matter in litigation, the court in which the litigation is pending. *(Stats.1990, c. 79 (A.B.759), § 14, operative July 1, 1991.)*

Law Revision Commission Comments
1990 Enactment

Section 2644 continues Section 2644 of the repealed Probate Code without substantive change. This section makes clear that the guardian or conservator may, with court authorization or approval, make a contingent fee contract with an attorney. The contract may, but need not, be made prior to the rendering of any services by the attorney. For general provisions, see Sections 1000–1004 (rules of practice), 1020–1023 (petitions and other papers), 1040–1050 (hearings and orders), 2103 (effect of final order). For general provisions relating to notice of hearing, see Sections 1200–1221, 1460–1469. See also Sections 1260–1265 (proof of giving notice), 2700–2702 (notice to persons who request special notice). For background on the provisions of this part, see the Comment to this part under the part heading. [20 Cal.L.Rev.Comm. Reports 1001 (1990)].

Cross References

Attorneys' fees and costs,
 Generally, see Code of Civil Procedure § 1021.
 Action on contract, see Civil Code § 1717.

§ 2645. Estate funds to compensate guardian or conservator for legal services; court approval; disclosure of relationships

(a) No attorney who is a guardian or conservator shall receive any compensation from the guardianship or conservatorship estate for legal services performed for the guardian or conservator unless the court specifically approves the right to the compensation and finds that it is to the advantage, benefit, and best interests of the ward or conservatee.

(b) No parent, child, sibling, or spouse of a person who is a guardian or conservator, and no law partnership or corporation whose partner, shareholder, or employee is serving as a guardian or conservator shall receive any compensation for legal services performed for the guardian or conservator unless the court specifically approves the right to the compensation and finds that it is to the advantage, benefit, and best interests of the ward or conservatee.

(c) This section shall not apply if the guardian or conservator is related by blood or marriage to, or is a cohabitant with, the ward or conservatee.

(d) After full disclosure of the relationships of all persons to receive compensation for legal services under this section, the court may, in its discretion and at any time, approve the right to that compensation, including any time during the pendency of any of the following orders:

(1) An order appointing the guardian or conservator.

(2) An order approving the general plan under Section 1831.

(3) An order settling any account of the guardian or conservator.

(4) An order approving a separate petition, with notice given under Section 2581. *(Added by Stats.1993, c. 293 (A.B.21), § 4.)*

§ 2646. Proceedings; determinations allowed

In proceedings under this chapter, the court shall only determine fees that are payable from the estate of the ward or conservatee and not limit fees payable from other sources. *(Added by Stats.1995, c. 730 (A.B.1466), § 6.)*

§ 2647. Attorney fees

No attorney fees may be paid from the estate of the ward or conservatee without prior court order. The estate of the ward or conservatee is not obligated to pay attorney fees established by any engagement agreement or other contract until it has been approved by the court. This does not preclude an award of fees by the court pursuant to this chapter even if the contractual obligations are unenforceable pursuant to this section. *(Added by Stats.2007, c. 553 (A.B.1727), § 24.)*

CHAPTER 9. REMOVAL OR RESIGNATION

ARTICLE 1. REMOVAL OF GUARDIAN OR CONSERVATOR

Cross References

Application of old and new law, see Probate Code § 3.

§ 2650. Causes for removal

A guardian or conservator may be removed for any of the following causes:

(a) Failure to use ordinary care and diligence in the management of the estate.

(b) Failure to file an inventory or an account within the time allowed by law or by court order.

(c) Continued failure to perform duties or incapacity to perform duties suitably.

(d) Conviction of a felony, whether before or after appointment as guardian or conservator.

(e) Gross immorality.

(f) Having such an interest adverse to the faithful performance of duties that there is an unreasonable risk that the guardian or conservator will fail faithfully to perform duties.

(g) In the case of a guardian of the person or a conservator of the person, acting in violation of any provision of Section 2356.

(h) In the case of a guardian of the estate or a conservator of the estate, insolvency or bankruptcy of the guardian or conservator.

(i) In the case of a conservator appointed by a court in another jurisdiction, removal because that person would not have been appointed in this state despite being eligible to serve under the law of this state.

(j) In any other case in which the court in its discretion determines that removal is in the best interests of the ward or conservatee; but, in considering the best interests of the ward, if the guardian was nominated under Section 1500 or 1501, the court shall take that fact into consideration. *(Stats.1990, c. 79 (A.B.759), § 14, operative July 1, 1991. Amended by Stats.2014, c. 553 (S.B.940), § 26, eff. Jan. 1, 2015, operative Jan. 1, 2016.)*

Law Revision Commission Comments
1990 Enactment

Section 2650 continues Section 2650 of the repealed Probate Code without substantive change. The procedure for removal is specified in Sections 2651–2654. The duty to use ordinary care and diligence is imposed by Section 2401. See also Sections 2614.5 (removal for failure to file inventory and appraisal as required by order), 2629 (removal for failure to account). For a comparable provision relating to decedents' estates, see Section 8502. For background on the provisions of this part, see the Comment to this part under the part heading. [20 Cal.L.Rev.Comm. Reports 1001 (1990)].

2014 Amendment

Section 2650 is amended to reflect the enactment of the California Conservatorship Jurisdiction Act (Section 1980 *et seq.*). [43 Cal. L.Rev.Comm. Reports 93 (2013)].

Cross References

Duty to use ordinary care and diligence in management and control of estate, see Probate Code § 2401.
Inventory and accounts, see Probate Code § 2600 et seq.
Removal for failure to,
   Furnish sufficient or additional surety, see Code of Civil Procedure § 996.010.
   Produce conservatee for court investigator, see Probate Code § 1853.

§ 2651. Petition for removal

The ward or conservatee, the spouse of the ward or the spouse or domestic partner of the conservatee, any relative or friend of the ward or conservatee, or any interested person may apply by petition to the court to have the guardian or conservator removed. The petition shall state facts showing cause for removal. *(Stats.1990, c. 79 (A.B.759), § 14, operative July 1, 1991. Amended by Stats.2001, c. 893 (A.B.25), § 41.)*

Law Revision Commission Comments
1990 Enactment

Section 2651 continues Section 2651 of the repealed Probate Code without change. For general provisions relating to petitions and other papers, see Sections 1020–1023. This section is comparable to Section 1861 (termination of conservatorship) and Section 8500(a) (decedents' estates). For general provisions, see Sections 1000–1004 (rules of practice), 1020–1023 (petitions and other papers), 1040–1050 (hearings and orders), 2103 (effect of final order). See also Sections 1021 (petition to be verified), 1041 (clerk to set petition for hearing). For background on the provisions of this part, see the Comment to this part under the part heading. [20 Cal.L.Rev.Comm. Reports 1001 (1990)].

Cross References

Domestic partner, defined, see Probate Code § 37.
Interested person, defined, see Probate Code § 1424.

§ 2652. Notice of hearing

Notice of the hearing on the petition shall be given for the period and in the manner provided in Chapter 3 (commencing with Section 1460) of Part 1. *(Stats.1990, c. 79 (A.B.759), § 14, operative July 1, 1991.)*

Law Revision Commission Comments
1990 Enactment

Section 2652 continues Section 2652 of the repealed Probate Code without change. This section is comparable to Section 1862 (termination of conservatorship). Under Section 2654, the court may suspend the powers of the guardian or conservator pending notice and hearing. For general provisions relating to notice of hearing, see Sections 1200–1221, 1460–1469. See also Sections 1260–1265 (proof of giving notice), 2700–2702 (notice to persons who request special notice). For background on the provisions of this part, see the Comment to this part under the part heading. [20 Cal.L.Rev.Comm. Reports 1001 (1990)].

§ 2653. Hearing and judgment

(a) The guardian or conservator, the ward or conservatee, the spouse of the ward or the spouse or registered domestic partner of the conservatee, any relative or friend of the ward or conservatee, and any interested person may appear at the hearing and support or oppose the petition.

(b) If the court determines that cause for removal of the guardian or conservator exists, the court may remove the guardian or conservator, revoke the letters of guardianship or conservatorship, and enter judgment accordingly and, in the case of a guardianship or conservatorship of the estate, order the guardian or conservator to file an accounting and to surrender the estate to the person legally entitled thereto. If the guardian or conservator fails to file the accounting as ordered, the court may compel the accounting pursuant to Section 2620.2.

(c) If the court removes the guardian or conservator for cause, as described in subdivisions (a) to (g), inclusive, of Section 2650 or Section 2655, both of the following shall apply:

(1) The court shall award the petitioner the costs of the petition and other expenses and costs of litigation, including attorney's fees, incurred under this article, unless the court determines that the guardian or conservator has acted in good faith, based on the best interests of the ward or conservatee.

(2) The guardian or conservator may not deduct from, or charge to, the estate his or her costs of litigation, and is personally liable for those costs and expenses. *(Stats.1990, c. 79 (A.B.759), § 14, operative July 1, 1991. Amended by Stats.2001, c. 893 (A.B.25), § 42; Stats.2006, c. 493 (A.B. 1363), § 30.)*

Law Revision Commission Comments

1990 Enactment

Section 2653 continues Section 2653 of the repealed Probate Code with the addition of the last sentence in subdivision (b) which is drawn from Section 10952 (decedents' estates). For general provisions, see Sections 1000–1004 (rules of practice), 1020–1023 (petitions and other papers), 1040–1050 (hearings and orders), 2103 (effect of final order). See also Section 2750 (revoking letters, other than temporary letters, an appealable order). This section is comparable to subdivisions (a) and (b) of Section 1863 (termination of conservatorship). For comparable provisions relating to decedents' estates, see Sections 8500(c), 8501. For background on the provisions of this part, see the Comment to this part under the part heading.

There is no right to jury trial in removal proceedings. See Section 1452. Despite the removal, the court retains jurisdiction to settle the accounts of the guardian or conservator. See Section 2630. As to the account of an incapacitated or absconding guardian or conservator, see Section 2632. [20 Cal.L.Rev.Comm. Reports 1001 (1990)].

Cross References

Domestic partner, defined, see Probate Code § 37.
Interested person, defined, see Probate Code § 1424.
Revoking letters for failure to furnish additional or sufficient surety, see Code of Civil Procedure § 996.010.

§ 2654. Suspension of powers and surrender of estate pending hearing

Whenever it appears that the ward or conservatee or the estate may suffer loss or injury during the time required for notice and hearing under this article, the court, on its own motion or on petition, may do either or both of the following:

(a) Suspend the powers of the guardian or conservator pending notice and hearing to such extent as the court deems necessary.

(b) Compel the guardian or conservator to surrender the estate to a custodian designated by the court. *(Stats.1990, c. 79 (A.B.759), § 14, operative July 1, 1991.)*

Law Revision Commission Comments

1990 Enactment

Section 2654 continues Section 2654 of the repealed Probate Code without change. See also Section 2250(e) (appointment of temporary guardian or conservator where powers of guardian or conservator are suspended under Section 2654). For a comparable provision relating to decedents' estates, see the second sentence of Section 8500(b). For background on the provisions of this part, see the Comment to this part under the part heading. [20 Cal.L.Rev.Comm. Reports 1001 (1990)].

Cross References

Suspension of powers of guardians, see Code of Civil Procedure § 166.
Suspension of powers when petition for further surety or bond filed, see Probate Code § 2334.

§ 2655. Contempt; disobeying order of court

(a) A guardian or conservator may be removed from office if the guardian or conservator is found in contempt for disobeying an order of the court.

(b) Notwithstanding any other provision of this article, a guardian or conservator may be removed from office under subdivision (a) by a court order reciting the facts and without further showing or notice. *(Stats.1990, c. 79 (A.B.759), § 14, operative July 1, 1991.)*

Law Revision Commission Comments

1990 Enactment

Section 2655 is a new provision drawn from Section 8505 (decedents' estates). See also Sections 2653 (revocation of letters), 2680 (successor personal representative). [20 Cal.L.Rev.Comm. Reports 1001 (1990)].

ARTICLE 2. RESIGNATION OF GUARDIAN OR CONSERVATOR

Section
2660. Resignation of guardian or conservator.
2662. Removal or limitation on power of guardian or conservator; appointment of responsible adult to make educational decisions for minor; conflicts of interest.

Cross References

Application of old and new law, see Probate Code § 3.

§ 2660. Resignation of guardian or conservator

A guardian or conservator may at any time file with the court a petition tendering the resignation of the guardian or conservator. Notice of the hearing on the petition shall be given for the period and in the manner provided in Chapter 3 (commencing with Section 1460) of Part 1. The court shall allow such resignation when it appears proper, to take effect at such time as the court shall fix, and may make any order as may be necessary to deal with the guardianship or conservatorship during the period prior to the appointment of a new guardian or conservator and the settlement of the accounts of the resigning guardian or conservator. *(Stats.1990, c. 79 (A.B.759), § 14, operative July 1, 1991.)*

Law Revision Commission Comments

1990 Enactment

Section 2660 continues Section 2660 of the repealed Probate Code without change. This section is comparable to Section 15640 (resignation of trustee). See also Section 8520 (vacancy caused by resignation of personal representative). For general provisions, see Sections 1000–1004 (rules of practice), 1020–1023 (petitions and other papers), 1040–1050 (hearings and orders), 2103 (effect of final order), 2750 (appealable orders). For general provisions relating to notice of hearing, see Sections 1200–1221, 1460–1469. See also Sections 1260–1265 (proof of giving notice), 2700–2702 (notice to persons who request special notice). For background on the provisions of this part, see the Comment to this part under the part heading.

The court may appoint a successor to the resigning guardian or conservator after notice and hearing. See Sections 2670, 2680. The court may appoint a temporary guardian or conservator if necessary. See Section 2250. Despite the resignation, the court retains jurisdiction to settle the accounts of the guardian or conservator. See Section 2630. [20 Cal.L.Rev.Comm. Reports 1001 (1990)].

Cross References

Appointment of successor, see Probate Code § 2670.
Continuing jurisdiction of court, settling of accounts, see Probate Code § 2630.
Resignation of temporary guardian or conservator, see Probate Code § 2258.
Resignation of trustee, see Probate Code § 15640.
Temporary guardian or conservator, appointment by court, see Probate Code § 2250.

§ 2662. Removal or limitation on power of guardian or conservator; appointment of responsible adult to make educational decisions for minor; conflicts of interest

Whenever the court grants a petition removing the guardian or conservator of a minor ward or conservatee or tendering the resignation of the guardian or conservator of a minor ward or conservatee, if the court does not immediately appoint a successor guardian or conservator, the court shall at the same time appoint a responsible adult to make educational decisions for the minor until a successor guardian or conservator is appointed. Whenever the court suspends or limits the powers of the guardian or conservator to make educational decisions for a minor ward or conservatee, the court shall at the same time appoint a responsible adult to make educational decisions for the minor ward or conservatee until the guardian or conservator is again authorized to make educational decisions for the minor ward or conservatee. An individual who would have a conflict of interest in representing the child may not be appointed to make educational decisions. For purposes of this section, "an individual who would have a conflict of interest," means a person having any interests that might restrict or bias his or her ability to make educational decisions, including, but not limited to, those conflicts of interest prohibited by Section 1126 of the Government Code, and the receipt of compensation or attorneys' fees for the provision of services pursuant to this section. A foster parent may not be deemed to have a conflict of interest solely because he or she receives compensation for the provision of services pursuant to this section. *(Added by Stats.2002, c. 180 (A.B.886), § 1.)*

Cross References

Dependent children, persons appointed to make educational decisions for, see Welfare and Institutions Code § 361.
Wards of court, persons appointed to make educational decisions for, see Welfare and Institutions Code § 726.

CHAPTER 9.5. APPOINTMENT OF SUCCESSOR GUARDIAN OR CONSERVATOR

Law Revision Commission Comments
1990 Enactment

This chapter supersedes Chapter 9.5 (commencing with Section 2670) of Part 4 of Division 4 of the repealed Probate Code. The superseded chapter was enacted upon recommendation of the California Law Revision Commission. See Recommendation Relating to Revision of the Guardianship–Conservatorship Law, 15 Cal.L.Revision Comm'n Reports 1463 (1980). [20 Cal.L.Rev.Comm. Reports 1001 (1990)].

ARTICLE 1. APPOINTMENT OF SUCCESSOR GUARDIAN

Section
2670. Vacancy; appointment of successor.

Cross References

Application of old and new law, see Probate Code § 3.

§ 2670. Vacancy; appointment of successor

When for any reason a vacancy occurs in the office of guardian, the court may appoint a successor guardian, after notice and hearing as in the case of an original appointment of a guardian. *(Stats.1990, c. 79 (A.B.759), § 14, operative July 1, 1991.)*

Law Revision Commission Comments
1990 Enactment

Section 2670 continues Section 2670 of the repealed Probate Code without change. For general provisions, see Sections 1000–1004 (rules of practice), 1020–1023 (petitions and other papers), 1040–1050 (hearings and orders), 2103 (effect of final order). For general provisions relating to notice of hearing, see Sections 1200–1221, 1460–1469. See also Sections 1260–1265 (proof of giving notice), 2700–2702 (notice to persons who request special notice). For a comparable provision relating to decedents' estates, see Section 8522. For background on the provisions of this chapter, see the Comment to this chapter under the chapter heading. [20 Cal.L.Rev.Comm. Reports 1001 (1990)].

Cross References

Conservator of person, estate or person and estate, original appointment, see Probate Code § 1801.
Original appointment of guardian, see Probate Code § 1514.

ARTICLE 2. APPOINTMENT OF SUCCESSOR CONSERVATOR

Section
2680. Vacancy; appointment of successor.
2681. Petition; filing; persons or entities authorized.
2682. Petition; contents.
2683. Notice of hearing; time and place; mailing.
2684. Court investigator; duties.
2685. Presence of conservatee at hearing; duty of court.
2686. Absence of conservatee from hearing; continuance; duties of court investigator.
2687. Persons authorized to support or oppose petition.
2688. Appointment; determination; law governing.
2689. Absentee conservatee; applicable provisions.

§ 2680. Vacancy; appointment of successor

When for any reason a vacancy occurs in the office of conservator, the court may appoint a successor conservator in the manner provided in this article. *(Stats.1990, c. 79 (A.B.759), § 14, operative July 1, 1991.)*

Law Revision Commission Comments

1990 Enactment

Section 2680 continues Section 2680 of the repealed Probate Code without change. For a comparable provision relating to decedents' estates, see Section 8522. For background on the provisions of this chapter, see the Comment to this chapter under the chapter heading. [20 Cal.L.Rev.Comm. Reports 1001 (1990)].

§ 2681. Petition; filing; persons or entities authorized

A petition for appointment of a successor conservator may be filed by any of the following:

(a) The conservatee.

(b) The spouse or domestic partner of the conservatee.

(c) A relative of the conservatee.

(d) Any interested state or local entity or agency of this state or any interested public officer or employee of this state or of a local public entity of this state.

(e) Any other interested person or friend of the conservatee. *(Stats.1990, c. 79 (A.B.759), § 14, operative July 1, 1991. Amended by Stats.2001, c. 893 (A.B.25), § 43.)*

Law Revision Commission Comments

1990 Enactment

Section 2681 continues Section 2681 of the repealed Probate Code without change. For general provisions relating to petitions and other papers, see Sections 1020–1023. This section is comparable to subdivision (a) of Section 1820 (petition for initial appointment of conservator). For background on the provisions of this chapter, see the Comment to this chapter under the chapter heading. [20 Cal.L.Rev.Comm. Reports 1001 (1990)].

Cross References

Domestic partner, defined, see Probate Code § 37.
Guardianship and conservatorship, interested person, defined, see Probate Code § 1424.
Petitions and other papers, see Probate Code § 1020 et seq.

§ 2682. Petition; contents

(a) The petition shall request that a successor conservator be appointed for the person or estate, or both, and shall specify the name and address of the proposed successor conservator and the name and address of the conservatee.

(b) The petition shall set forth, so far as they are known to the petitioner, the names and addresses of the spouse or domestic partner and of the relatives of the conservatee within the second degree.

(c) If the petition is filed by one other than the conservatee, the petition shall state whether or not the petitioner is a creditor or debtor of the conservatee.

(d) If the conservatee is a patient in or on leave of absence from a state institution under the jurisdiction of the State Department of State Hospitals or the State Department of Developmental Services and that fact is known to the petitioner, the petition shall state that fact and name the institution.

(e) The petition shall state, so far as is known to the petitioner, whether or not the conservatee is receiving or is entitled to receive benefits from the Veterans Administration and the estimated amount of the monthly benefit payable by the Veterans Administration for the conservatee.

(f) The petition shall state whether or not the conservatee will be present at the hearing. *(Stats.1990, c. 79 (A.B.759), § 14, operative July 1, 1991. Amended by Stats.2001, c. 893 (A.B.25), § 44; Stats.2012, c. 440 (A.B.1488), § 48, eff. Sept. 22, 2012.)*

Law Revision Commission Comments

1990 Enactment

Section 2682 continues Section 2682 of the repealed Probate Code without change. For general provisions relating to petitions and other papers, see Sections 1020–1023. This section is comparable to Section 1821 (petition for initial appointment of conservator). For background on the provisions of this chapter, see the Comment to this chapter under the chapter heading. [20 Cal.L.Rev.Comm. Reports 1001 (1990)].

Cross References

Domestic partner, defined, see Probate Code § 37.
Petitions and other papers, see Probate Code § 1020 et seq.

§ 2683. Notice of hearing; time and place; mailing

(a) At least 15 days before the hearing on the petition for appointment of a successor conservator, notice of the time and place of the hearing shall be given as provided in this section. The notice shall be accompanied by a copy of the petition.

(b) Notice shall be mailed to the persons designated in Section 1460 and to the relatives named in the petition.

(c) If notice is required by Section 1461 to be given to the Director of State Hospitals or the Director of Developmental Services, notice shall be mailed as so required.

(d) If notice is required by Section 1461.5 to be given to the Veterans Administration, notice shall be mailed as so required. *(Stats.1990, c. 79 (A.B.759), § 14, operative July 1, 1991. Amended by Stats.1994, c. 806 (A.B.3686), § 19; Stats.2012, c. 440 (A.B.1488), § 49, eff. Sept. 22, 2012.)*

Law Revision Commission Comments

1990 Enactment

Section 2683 continues Section 2683 of the repealed Probate Code without substantive change. The phrase "other than the petitioner or persons joining in the petition" has been omitted as unnecessary in view of Section 1201. Section 2683 is comparable to Section 1822 (notice on initial appointment of conservator). Notice may be personally delivered instead of being mailed. See Section 1216. For general provisions relating to notice of hearing, see Sections 1200–1221, 1460–1469. See also Sections 1260–1265 (proof of giving notice), 2700–2702 (notice to persons who request special notice). If the conservatee is an "absentee" as defined in Section 1403, notice must be given as provided in Sections 1842 and 2683, except that notice need not be given to the conservatee. See Section 2689. For background on the provisions of this chapter, see the Comment to this chapter under the chapter heading. [20 Cal.L.Rev.Comm. Reports 1001 (1990)].

Cross References

Absentee conservatees,
  Defined, see Probate Code § 1403
  Notice, see Probate Code §§ 1842, 2689.

Computation of time, see Code of Civil Procedure §§ 12 and 12a; Government Code § 6800 et seq.

Notice of hearing,
    Generally, see Probate Code §§ 1200 et seq., 1460 et seq.
    Delivery of notice instead of mailing, see Probate Code § 1216.
    Mailing, see Probate Code § 1215 et seq.
    Posting, see Probate Code § 1230.
    Proof of giving notice, see Probate Code § 1260 et seq.
    Special notice provisions, see Probate Code §§ 1250 et seq., 2700 et seq.

Service of process,
    Generally, see Code of Civil Procedure § 413.10 et seq.
    Mail, see Code of Civil Procedure §§ 415.30, 1012 et seq.
    Personal delivery, see Code of Civil Procedure § 415.10.
    Proof of service, see Code of Civil Procedure § 417.10 et seq.
    Publication, see Code of Civil Procedure § 415.50.

§ 2684. Court investigator; duties

Unless the petition states that the conservatee will be present at the hearing, the court investigator shall do all of the following:

(a) Interview the conservatee personally.

(b) Inform the conservatee of the nature of the proceeding to appoint a successor conservator, the name of the person proposed as successor conservator, and the conservatee's right to appear personally at the hearing, to object to the person proposed as successor conservator, to nominate a person to be appointed as successor conservator, to be represented by legal counsel if the conservatee so chooses, and to have legal counsel appointed by the court if unable to retain legal counsel.

(c) Determine whether the conservatee objects to the person proposed as successor conservator or prefers another person to be appointed.

(d) If the conservatee is not represented by legal counsel, determine whether the conservatee wishes to be represented by legal counsel and, if so, determine the name of an attorney the conservatee wishes to retain or whether the conservatee desires the court to appoint legal counsel.

(e) Determine whether the appointment of legal counsel would be helpful to the resolution of the matter or is necessary to protect the interests of the conservatee in any case where the conservatee does not plan to retain legal counsel and has not requested the appointment of legal counsel by the court.

(f) Report to the court in writing, at least five days before the hearing, concerning all of the foregoing, including the conservatee's express communications concerning representation by legal counsel and whether the conservatee objects to the person proposed as successor conservator or prefers that some other person be appointed.

(g) Mail, at least five days before the hearing, a copy of the report referred to in subdivision (f) to all of the following:

(1) The attorney, if any, for the petitioner.

(2) The attorney, if any, for the conservatee.

(3) Such other persons as the court orders. *(Stats.1990, c. 79 (A.B.759), § 14, operative July 1, 1991.)*

Law Revision Commission Comments
1990 Enactment

Section 2684 continues Section 2684 of the repealed Probate Code without change. This section is comparable to Section 1826 (interview and report of court investigator on initial appointment of conservator). If the conservatee is unable to retain legal counsel and requests the court to appoint counsel, or if the court determines that appointment of counsel would be helpful to the resolution of the matter or is necessary to protect the interests of the conservatee, the court must appoint the public defender or private counsel to represent the conservatee in proceedings under this article. See Section 1471. An interview and report by the court investigator is not required under Section 2684 if the conservatee is an "absentee" as defined in Section 1403. See Section 2689. For background on the provisions of this chapter, see the Comment to this chapter under the chapter heading. [20 Cal.L.Rev.Comm. Reports 1001 (1990)].

Cross References

Absentee conservatee,
    Applicable provisions, see Probate Code § 2689.
    Defined, see Probate Code § 1403.
Appointment of legal counsel, see Probate Code § 1471.

§ 2685. Presence of conservatee at hearing; duty of court

If the conservatee is present at the hearing, prior to making an order appointing a successor conservator the court shall do all of the following:

(a) Inform the conservatee of the nature and purpose of the proceeding.

(b) Inform the conservatee that the conservatee has the right to object to the person proposed as successor conservator, to nominate a person to be appointed as successor conservator, and, if not represented by legal counsel, to be represented by legal counsel if the conservatee so chooses and to have legal counsel appointed by the court if unable to retain legal counsel.

(c) After the court so informs the conservatee, the court shall consult the conservatee to determine the conservatee's opinion concerning the question of who should be appointed as successor conservator. *(Stats.1990, c. 79 (A.B.759), § 14, operative July 1, 1991.)*

Law Revision Commission Comments
1990 Enactment

Section 2685 continues Section 2685 of the repealed Probate Code without change. This section is comparable to Section 1828 (information to proposed conservatee by court on initial appointment of conservator). If the conservatee is unable to retain legal counsel and requests the court to appoint counsel, or if the court determines that appointment of counsel would be helpful to the resolution of the matter or is necessary to protect the interests of the conservatee, the court must appoint the public defender or private counsel to represent the conservatee in proceedings under this article. See Section 1471. For background on the provisions of this chapter, see the Comment to this chapter under the chapter heading. [20 Cal.L.Rev.Comm. Reports 1001 (1990)].

Cross References

Appointment of legal counsel, see Probate Code § 1471.

§ 2686. Absence of conservatee from hearing; continuance; duties of court investigator

If the petition states that the conservatee will be present at the hearing and the conservatee fails to appear at the hearing, the court shall continue the hearing and direct the court investigator to perform the duties set forth in Section 2684. *(Stats.1990, c. 79 (A.B.759), § 14, operative July 1, 1991.)*

Law Revision Commission Comments

1990 Enactment

Section 2686 continues Section 2686 of the repealed Probate Code without change. This section ensures that the conservatee is informed of his or her rights before a successor conservator is appointed. For background on the provisions of this chapter, see the Comment to this chapter under the chapter heading. [20 Cal.L.Rev. Comm. Reports 1001 (1990)].

§ 2687. Persons authorized to support or oppose petition

The conservatee, the spouse, the domestic partner, or any relative or friend of the conservatee, or any other interested person may appear at the hearing to support or oppose the petition. *(Stats.1990, c. 79 (A.B.759), § 14, operative July 1, 1991. Amended by Stats.2001, c. 893 (A.B.25), § 45.)*

Law Revision Commission Comments

1990 Enactment

Section 2687 continues Section 2687 of the repealed Probate Code without change. See also Section 1043 (objections to petition). This section is comparable to Section 1829 (persons who may support or oppose petition for initial appointment of conservator). "Interested person" includes state, local, or federal entities and employees. See Section 1424. For background on the provisions of this chapter, see the Comment to this chapter under the chapter heading. [20 Cal.L.Rev.Comm. Reports 1001 (1990)].

Cross References

Domestic partner, defined, see Probate Code § 37.
Interested persons, see Probate Code § 1424.
Objections to petition, see Probate Code § 1043.

§ 2688. Appointment; determination; law governing

(a) The court shall determine the question of who should be appointed as successor conservator according to the provisions of Article 2 (commencing with Section 1810) of Chapter 1 of Part 3.

(b) The order appointing the successor conservator shall contain, among other things, the names, addresses and telephone numbers of the successor conservator, the conservatee's attorney, if any, and the court investigator, if any. *(Stats.1990, c. 79 (A.B.759), § 14, operative July 1, 1991.)*

Law Revision Commission Comments

1990 Enactment

Section 2688 continues Section 2688 of the repealed Probate Code without change. Subdivision (a) makes clear that the order of preference for appointment as conservator in Section 1812 applies to selection of a successor conservator, and that a nomination made under Section 1810 or 1811 will be given the same weight as on initial appointment of a conservator. Subdivision (b) is comparable to Section 1830 (order for initial appointment of conservator).

There is no right to trial by jury on appointment of a successor conservator. See Section 1452. This is consistent with the rule applicable to initial appointment of a conservator (as distinguished from establishment of conservatorship), where there is no right to trial by jury. See the Comment to Section 1827.

For general provisions, see Sections 1000–1004 (rules of practice), 1020–1023 (petitions and other papers), 1040–1050 (hearings and

orders), 2103 (effect of final order), 2750 (appealable orders). For background on the provisions of this chapter, see the Comment to this chapter under the chapter heading. [20 Cal.L.Rev.Comm. Reports 1001 (1990)].

Cross References

Final order, effect, see Probate Code § 2103.
Hearings and orders, generally, see Probate Code § 1040 et seq.
Jury trial, right to, see Probate Code § 1452.
Petitions and other papers, generally, see Probate Code § 1020 et seq.
Rules of practice, see Probate Code § 1000 et seq.

§ 2689. Absentee conservatee; applicable provisions

If the conservatee is an "absentee" as defined in Section 1403:

(a) The petition for appointment of a successor conservator shall contain the matters required by Section 1841 in addition to the matters required by Section 2682.

(b) Notice of the hearing shall be given as provided by Section 1842 in addition to the requirements of Section 2683, except that notice need not be given to the conservatee.

(c) An interview and report by the court investigator is not required. *(Stats.1990, c. 79 (A.B.759), § 14, operative July 1, 1991.)*

Law Revision Commission Comments

1990 Enactment

Section 2689 continues Section 2689 of the repealed Probate Code without change. This section requires additional allegations in the petition and additional notice and dispenses with the interview and report by the court investigator where the conservatee is in missing status as determined under federal law. For general provisions relating to notice of hearing, see Sections 1200–1221, 1460–1469. See also Sections 1260–1265 (proof of giving notice), 2700–2702 (notice to persons who request special notice). For background on the provisions of this chapter, see the Comment to this chapter under the chapter heading. [20 Cal.L.Rev.Comm. Reports 1001 (1990)].

Cross References

Notice provisions,
  Generally, see Probate Code §§ 1200 et seq., 1460 et seq.
  Proof of giving notice, see Probate Code § 1260 et seq.
  Special notice provisions, see Probate Code § 2700 et seq.

CHAPTER 10. REQUESTS FOR SPECIAL NOTICE

Section
2700. Written request; persons authorized.
2701. Modification or withdrawal of request; new request.
2702. Petitioner required to give special notice.
2703. Repealed.

§ 2700. Written request; persons authorized

(a) At any time after the issuance of letters of guardianship or conservatorship, the ward, if over 14 years of age or the conservatee, the spouse of the ward or the spouse or domestic partner of the conservatee, any relative or creditor of the ward or conservatee, or any other interested person, in person or by attorney, may file with the court clerk a written request for special notice.

(b) The request for special notice shall be so entitled and shall set forth the name of the person and the address to which notices shall be sent.

(c) Special notice may be requested of any one or more of the following matters:

(1) Petitions filed in the guardianship or conservatorship proceeding.

(2) Inventories and appraisals of property in the estate, including any supplemental inventories and appraisals.

(3) Accounts of the guardian or conservator.

(4) Proceedings for the final termination of the guardianship or conservatorship proceeding.

(d) Special notice may be requested of:

(1) Any one or more of the matters in subdivision (c) by describing the matter or matters.

(2) All the matters in subdivision (c) by referring generally to "the matters described in subdivision (c) of Section 2700 of the Probate Code" or by using words of similar meaning.

(e) A copy of the request shall be personally delivered or mailed to the guardian or conservator or to the attorney for the guardian or conservator. If personally delivered, the request is effective when it is delivered. If mailed, the request is effective when it is received.

(f) When the original of the request is filed with the court clerk, it shall be accompanied by a written admission or proof of service. *(Stats.1990, c. 79 (A.B.759), § 14, operative July 1, 1991. Amended by Stats.2001, c. 893 (A.B.25), § 46.)*

Law Revision Commission Comments
1990 Enactment

Section 2700 supersedes Section 2700 of the repealed Probate Code. Rather than listing the various petitions for which special notice may be requested, Section 2700 permit a request for special notice of any petition filed in the guardianship or conservatorship proceeding. This revision makes Section 2700 consistent with Section 1250 (decedents' estates).

If a request for special notice is made as provided in this section, notice is required to be given as provided in Section 2702. Subdivision (c) permits the person requesting special notice to request notice of the matters described in subdivision (c), which includes all petitions and specified additional matters. Subdivision (d) gives the person requesting special notice the option to describe specifically those matters of which special notice is requested if the person does not wish to receive special notice of all matters.

Subdivision (e) makes clear that the request for special notice must be given to the guardian or conservator or the attorney for the guardian or conservator. As to the manner of giving notice, see Sections 1220–1221. As to proof of giving notice, see Section 1260.

Special notice must be given under this chapter even though the provision under which the petition is filed permits ex parte petition. See, e.g., Section 2463 (authorization to commence partition action). However, if the action is taken without court authorization, no notice is required. See Sections 2544–2545 (sales permitted without court authorization).

The ward, if over 14 years of age, or the conservatee may request special notice under Section 2700 and must be given such notice if requested, whether or not the court has dispensed with notice to the ward or conservatee under Section 1460.

For a comparable provision relating to decedents' estates, see Section 1250. For background on the provisions of this part, see the Comment to this part under the part heading. [20 Cal.L.Rev.Comm. Reports 1001 (1990)].

Cross References
Accounts, see Probate Code § 2620 et seq.
Conveyance or transfer of property, see Probate Code § 850.
Domestic partner, defined, see Probate Code § 37.
Guardianship and conservatorship, interested person, defined, see Probate Code § 1424.
Inventory and appraisement of estate, see Probate Code § 2610 et seq.
Notice requirements,
  Generally, see Probate Code § 1460.
  Mailing, see Probate Code § 1215 et seq.
  Posting, see Probate Code § 1230.
  Proof of notice, see Probate Code § 1260.
  Special notice, administration of estates of decedents, see Probate Code § 1250.
  This code, generally, see Probate Code § 1200 et seq.
Removal or resignation of guardian or conservator, see Probate Code § 2650 et seq.
Request for special notice pursuant to this section, superior court filing fees, see Government Code § 70662.
Service of process,
  Generally, see Code of Civil Procedure § 413.10 et seq.
  Mail, see Code of Civil Procedure §§ 415.30, 1012 et seq.
  Personal delivery, see Code of Civil Procedure § 415.10.
  Proof of service, see Code of Civil Procedure § 417.10 et seq.
  Publication, see Code of Civil Procedure § 415.50.

§ 2701. Modification or withdrawal of request; new request

(a) A request for special notice may be modified or withdrawn in the same manner as provided for the making of the initial request.

(b) A new request for special notice may be served and filed at any time as provided in the case of an initial request. *(Stats.1990, c. 79 (A.B.759), § 14, operative July 1, 1991. Amended by Stats.2006, c. 493 (A.B.1363), § 31.)*

Law Revision Commission Comments
1990 Enactment

Section 2701 continues Section 2701 of the repealed Probate Code without substantive change. For a comparable provision relating to decedents' estates, see Section 1251. For background on the provisions of this part, see the Comment to this part under the part heading. [20 Cal.L.Rev.Comm. Reports 1001 (1990)].

Cross References
Notice,
  Mailing, see Probate Code § 1215 et seq.
  Posting, see Probate Code § 1230.
  Proof of giving notice, see Probate Code § 1260 et seq.
  Special notice, see Probate Code § 1250 et seq.
  This code, generally, see Probate Code § 1200 et seq.
  This division, generally, see Probate Code § 1460 et seq.
Service of process,
  Generally, see Code of Civil Procedure § 413.10 et seq.
  Mail, see Code of Civil Procedure §§ 415.30, 1012 et seq.
  Personal delivery, see Code of Civil Procedure § 415.10.
  Proof of service, see Code of Civil Procedure § 417.10 et seq.
  Publication, see Code of Civil Procedure § 415.50.

§ 2702. Petitioner required to give special notice

(a) Unless the court makes an order dispensing with the notice, if a request has been made pursuant to this chapter for special notice of a hearing, the person filing the petition, account, or other paper shall give written notice of the filing, together with a copy of the petition, account, or other paper, and the time and place set for the hearing, by mail to the person named in the request at the address set forth in the request, at least 15 days before the time set for the hearing.

(b) If a request has been made pursuant to this chapter for special notice of the filing of an inventory and appraisal of the estate or of the filing of any other paper that does not require a hearing, the inventory and appraisal or other paper shall be mailed not later than 15 days after the inventory and appraisal or other paper is filed with the court. *(Stats.1990, c. 79 (A.B.759), § 14, operative July 1, 1991.)*

Law Revision Commission Comments

1990 Enactment

Section 2702 supersedes Section 2702 of the repealed Probate Code. The section uses language drawn from Section 1252, the comparable provision relating to decedents' estates. For general provisions relating to notice, see Section 1200 et seq. For background on the provisions of this part, see the Comment to this part under the part heading. [20 Cal.L.Rev.Comm. Reports 1001 (1990)].

Cross References

Computation of time, see Code of Civil Procedure §§ 12 and 12a; Government Code § 6800 et seq.
Inventory and appraisement of the estate, see Probate Code § 2610 et seq.
Mailing, completion, see Probate Code § 1467.

§ 2703. Repealed by Stats.1990, c. 79 (A.B.759), § 13, operative July 1, 1991

Law Revision Commission Comments

1990 Repeal

Section 2703 of the repealed Probate Code is omitted from the new Probate Code because it is unnecessary. See Section 1260 (proof of giving notice). [20 Cal.L.Rev.Comm. Reports 1001 (1990)].

CHAPTER 11. APPEALS [REPEALED]

§§ 2750 to 2752. Repealed by Stats.1997, c. 724 (A.B.1172), § 15

CHAPTER 12. TRANSFER OF PERSONAL PROPERTY OUT OF STATE

§ 2800. Foreign guardian or conservator

As used in this chapter, "foreign guardian or conservator" means a guardian, conservator, committee, or comparable fiduciary in another jurisdiction. *(Stats.1990, c. 79 (A.B.759), § 14, operative July 1, 1991.)*

Law Revision Commission Comments

1990 Enactment

Section 2800 continues Section 2800 of the repealed Probate Code without change. For background on the provisions of this part, see the Comment to this part under the part heading. [20 Cal.L.Rev. Comm. Reports 1001 (1990)].

Cross References

Fiduciary, defined, see Probate Code § 39.
Trusts, judicial proceedings,
   Generally, see Probate Code § 17000 et seq.
   Transfer from another jurisdiction, see Probate Code § 17450 et seq.

§ 2801. Order for transfer of assets out of state

Subject to the limitations and requirements of this chapter, the court in which the guardianship of the estate or conservatorship of the estate is pending may order the transfer of some or all of the personal property of the estate to a foreign guardian or conservator in another jurisdiction outside this state where the ward or conservatee resides at the time the petition for the order authorizing the transfer is filed. *(Stats.1990, c. 79 (A.B.759), § 14, operative July 1, 1991.)*

Law Revision Commission Comments

1990 Enactment

Section 2801 continues Section 2801 of the repealed Probate Code without substantive change. This section permits transfer of assets to a foreign country as well as to another state, consistent with the trust law. See Sections 17400–17405. See also Section 2750 (order transferring assets of guardianship or conservatorship estate to a fiduciary in another jurisdiction is an appealable order). For a procedure for removal of assets to another jurisdiction by a nonresident guardian or conservator or similar fiduciary where there is no California guardian or conservator, see Sections 3800–3803. For a comparable provision in trust law, see Section 17401. For background on the provisions of this part, see the Comment to this part under the part heading. [20 Cal.L.Rev.Comm. Reports 1001 (1990)].

Cross References

Administration of trusts, transfer of assets to another jurisdiction, see Probate Code § 17400 et seq.

§ 2802. Petition; persons authorized to file

A petition for an order authorizing a transfer may be filed by any of the following:

(a) The guardian of the estate or the conservator of the estate.

(b) The ward or conservatee.

(c) A foreign guardian or conservator. *(Stats.1990, c. 79 (A.B.759), § 14, operative July 1, 1991.)*

Law Revision Commission Comments

1990 Enactment

Section 2802 continues Section 2802 of the repealed Probate Code without change. For background on the provisions of this part, see the Comment to this part under the part heading. [20 Cal.L.Rev. Comm. Reports 1001 (1990)].

§ 2803. Petition; contents

The petition shall set forth all of the following:

(a) The name and address of:

(1) The foreign guardian or conservator, who may but need not be the guardian or conservator appointed in this state.

(2) The ward or conservatee.

(3) The guardian or conservator, so far as is known to the petitioner.

(b) The names, ages, and addresses, so far as they are known to the petitioner, of the spouse of the ward or the spouse or domestic partner of the conservatee and of relatives of the ward or conservatee within the second degree.

(c) A brief description of the character, condition, value, and location of the personal property sought to be transferred.

(d) A statement whether the foreign guardian or conservator has agreed to accept the transfer of the property. If the foreign guardian or conservator has so agreed, the acceptance shall be attached as an exhibit to the petition or otherwise filed with the court.

(e) A statement of the manner in which and by whom the foreign guardian or conservator was appointed.

(f) A general statement of the qualifications of the foreign guardian or conservator.

(g) The amount of bond, if any, of the foreign guardian or conservator.

(h) A general statement of the nature and value of the property of the ward or conservatee already under the management or control of the foreign guardian or conservator.

(i) The name of the court having jurisdiction of the foreign guardian or conservator or of the accounts of the foreign guardian or conservator or, if none, the court in which a proceeding may be had with respect to the guardianship or conservatorship if the property is transferred.

(j) Whether there is any pending civil action in this state against the guardian or conservator, the ward or conservatee, or the estate.

(k) A statement of the reasons for the transfer. *(Stats. 1990, c. 79 (A.B.759), § 14, operative July 1, 1991. Amended by Stats.2001, c. 893 (A.B.25), § 47.)*

Law Revision Commission Comments

1990 Enactment

Section 2803 continues Section 2803 of the repealed Probate Code without substantive change. For general provisions relating to petitions and other papers, see Sections 1020–1023. This section is comparable to Section 17402 (transfer of trust assets out of state). The information required to be included in the petition is needed so the court can decide whether the requirements of Section 2806 are satisfied. For background on the provisions of this part, see the Comment to this part under the part heading. [20 Cal.L.Rev.Comm. Reports 1001 (1990)].

Cross References

Domestic partner, defined, see Probate Code § 37.

Trusts, judicial proceedings,
  Generally, see Probate Code § 1700 et seq.
  Transfer from another jurisdiction, see Probate Code § 17450 et seq.

§ 2804. Notice of hearing

At least 30 days before the hearing, the petitioner shall mail a notice of the time and place of the hearing and a copy of the petition to each person required to be listed in the petition at the address stated in the petition. *(Stats.1990, c. 79 (A.B.759), § 14, operative July 1, 1991.)*

Law Revision Commission Comments

1990 Enactment

Section 2804 continues Section 2804 of the repealed Probate Code without substantive change. The phrase "other than the petitioner" has been omitted as unnecessary in view of Section 1201. Section 2804 is comparable to Section 17403 (transfer of trust assets out of state). For general provisions relating to notice of hearing, see Sections 1200–1221, 1460–1469. See also Sections 1260–1265 (proof of giving notice), 2700–2702 (notice to persons who request special notice). For background on the provisions of this part, see the Comment to this part under the part heading. [20 Cal.L.Rev.Comm. Reports 1001 (1990)].

Cross References

Computation of time, see Code of Civil Procedure §§ 12 and 12a; Government Code § 6800 et seq.
Mailing, completion, see Probate Code § 1467.
Notice,
  Mailing, see Probate Code § 1215 et seq.
  Posting, see Probate Code § 1230.
  Proof of giving notice, see Probate Code § 1260 et seq.
  Special notice, see Probate Code § 1250 et seq.
  This code, generally, see Probate Code § 1200 et seq.
  This division, generally, see Probate Code § 1460 et seq.
Service of process,
  Generally, see Code of Civil Procedure § 413.10 et seq.
  Mail, see Code of Civil Procedure §§ 415.30, 1012 et seq.
  Personal delivery, see Code of Civil Procedure § 415.10.
  Proof of service, see Code of Civil Procedure § 417.10 et seq.
  Publication, see Code of Civil Procedure § 415.50.

§ 2805. Objections to petition

Any of the following may appear and file written objections to the petition:

(a) Any person required to be listed in the petition.

(b) Any creditor of the ward or conservatee or of the estate.

(c) The spouse of the ward or the spouse or domestic partner of the conservatee or any relative or friend of the ward or conservatee.

(d) Any other interested person. *(Stats.1990, c. 79 (A.B. 759), § 14, operative July 1, 1991. Amended by Stats.2001, c. 893 (A.B.25), § 48.)*

Law Revision Commission Comments

1990 Enactment

Section 2805 continues Section 2805 of the repealed Probate Code without change. For general provisions relating to hearings and orders, see Sections 1040–1050. See also Section 1043 (manner of handling objections). For background on the provisions of this part, see the Comment to this part under the part heading. [20 Cal.L.Rev.Comm. Reports 1001 (1990)].

§ 2806. Order for transfer

The court may grant the petition and order the guardian or conservator to transfer some or all of the personal property of the estate to the foreign guardian or conservator if the court determines all of the following:

(a) The transfer will promote the best interests of the ward or conservatee and the estate.

(b) The substantial rights of creditors or claimants in this state will not be materially impaired by the transfer.

(c) The foreign guardian or conservator is qualified, willing, and able to administer the property to be transferred. *(Stats.1990, c. 79 (A.B.759), § 14, operative July 1, 1991.)*

Law Revision Commission Comments

1990 Enactment

Section 2806 continues Section 2806 of the repealed Probate Code without substantive change. This section is comparable to Section 17404 (transfer of trust assets out of state). Important elements in determining whether the "transfer will promote the best interests of the ward or conservatee and the estate" are whether the transfer will facilitate the economical and convenient administration of the estate and whether the guardianship or conservatorship estate will be administered by a capable fiduciary in the other jurisdiction. For general provisions, see Sections 1000–1004 (rules of practice), 1020–1023 (petitions and other papers), 1040–1050 (hearings and orders), 2103 (effect of final order), 2750 (appealable orders). For background on the provisions of this part, see the Comment to this part under the part heading.

§ 2807. Manner of transfer; terms and conditions

If a transfer is ordered, the court may direct the manner of transfer and impose such terms and conditions as may be just. *(Stats.1990, c. 79 (A.B.759), § 14, operative July 1, 1991.)*

Law Revision Commission Comments

1990 Enactment

Section 2807 continues Section 2807 of the repealed Probate Code without change. This section is comparable to the first sentence of Section 17405 (transfer of trust assets out of state). See also Section 2111 (order directing transfer). For background on the provisions of this part, see the Comment to this part under the part heading. [20 Cal.L.Rev.Comm. Reports 1001 (1990)].

§ 2808. Termination of guardianship or conservatorship

(a) If the court's order provides for the transfer of all of the property of the estate to the foreign guardian or conservator, the court, upon settlement of the final account, shall order the guardianship of the estate or the conservatorship of the estate terminated upon the filing with the clerk of the court of a receipt for the property executed by the foreign guardian or conservator.

(b) Unless notice is waived, a copy of the final account of the guardian or conservator and of the petition for discharge, together with a notice of the hearing thereon, shall be mailed at least 30 days before the date of the hearing to all persons required to be listed in the petition for transfer, including the foreign guardian or conservator. *(Stats.1990, c. 79 (A.B.759), § 14, operative July 1, 1991.)*

Law Revision Commission Comments

1990 Enactment

Section 2808 continues Section 2808 of the repealed Probate Code without substantive change. As to termination of the proceeding and discharge of the guardian or conservator when the estate is exhausted, see Section 2626. If there is California real property being administered in the California proceeding, it may be necessary to continue the California proceeding for the purpose of administering such property. W. Johnstone, G. Zillgitt, & S. House, California Conservatorships § 3.61, at 138, § 3.68, at 145 (Cal.Cont.Ed.Bar 2d ed. 1983 & Supp.1989). For background on the provisions of this part, see the Comment to this part under the part heading. [20 Cal.L.Rev.Comm. Reports 1001 (1990)].

CHAPTER 13. STATEWIDE REGISTRY [REPEALED]

§§ 2850 to 2856. Repealed by Stats.2006, c. 491 (S.B.1550), § 7, operative Jan. 1, 2009

CHAPTER 14. NOTIFICATION TO COURT BY INSTITUTIONS

§ 2890. Guardian or conservator taking possession or control of asset; filing of statement by institution; contents of statement

(a) When a guardian or conservator, pursuant to letters of guardianship or conservatorship of the estate, takes possession or control of any asset of the ward or conservatee held by an institution, as defined in subdivision (c), the institution shall file with the court having jurisdiction of the guardianship or conservatorship a statement containing the following information:

(1) The name of the ward or conservatee.

(2) The name of the guardian or joint guardians or conservator or joint conservators.

(3) The court case number.

(4) The name of the institution.

(5) The address of the institution.

(6) The account number of the account, if any, in which the asset was held by the ward or conservatee.

(7) A description of the asset or assets held by the institution. If an asset is a life insurance policy or annuity, the description shall include the policy number, if available. If the asset is a security listed on a public exchange, the description shall include the name and reference number, if available.

(8) The value, if known, or the estimated value otherwise, of the asset on the date the letters were issued by the court to the guardian or conservator, to the extent this value is routinely provided in the statements from the institution to the owner.

(b) Taking possession or control of an asset includes, for purposes of this chapter, changing title to the asset, withdrawing all or any portion of the asset, or transferring all or any portion of an asset from the institution.

(c) For purposes of this chapter, "institution" means an insurance company, insurance broker, insurance agent, investment company, investment bank, securities broker-dealer, investment adviser, financial planner, financial adviser, or any other person who takes, holds, or controls an asset subject to a conservatorship or guardianship that is not a "financial institution" as defined in Section 2892. *(Added by Stats.2001, c. 563 (A.B.1286), § 7.)*

Cross References

Security, defined, see Probate Code § 70.

§ 2891. Affidavit; application of chapter; fee

(a) The statement filed pursuant to Section 2890 shall be an affidavit by a person having authority to make the statement on behalf of the institution, as defined in Section 2890, and shall include that fact in the statement.

(b) If the affidavit and any accompanying information to be filed pursuant to this section also contains the ward or conservatee's social security number or any other personal information, including financial information regarding the ward or conservatee which would not be disclosed in an accounting, an inventory and appraisal, or any other nonconfidential pleading filed in the action, the information shall be kept confidential and subject to disclosure to any person only upon order of the court.

(c) This chapter does not apply to any trust arrangement described in subdivision (b) of Section 82 except paragraph (4) of that subdivision relating to assets held in Totten trust.

(d) No fee shall be charged by the court for the filing of the affidavit or related information as required by this section.

(e) The affidavit required by Section 2890 is not required to be filed in a proceeding more than once for each asset. However, all assets held by institutions may be listed in a single affidavit filed with the court.

(f) When a guardian or conservator takes possession or control of an asset in an institution, as defined in Section 2890, the institution may then file with the court the statement required by Section 2890 as to any or all other assets of the ward or conservatee held in the institution. *(Added by Stats.2001, c. 563 (A.B.1286), § 7.)*

Cross References

Affidavits, see Code of Civil Procedure § 2009 et seq.
Totten trust account, defined, see Probate Code § 80.

§ 2892. Guardian or conservator changing name of account of safe-deposit box; filing of statement by financial institution; contents of statement

(a) When a guardian or conservator, pursuant to letters of guardianship or conservatorship of the estate, opens or changes the name to an account or safe-deposit box in a financial institution, as defined in subdivision (b), the financial institution shall send to the court identified in the letters of guardianship or conservatorship a statement containing the following information:

(1) The name of the person with whom the account or safe-deposit box is opened or changed.

(2) The account number or reference number.

(3) The date the account or safe-deposit box was opened or changed ownership pursuant to letters of guardianship or conservatorship.

(4) If the asset is held in an account in a financial institution, the balance as of the date the account was opened or changed.

(5) If the asset is held in a safe-deposit box, and the financial institution has been given access to the safe-deposit box, a list of the contents, including, for example, currency, coins, jewelry, tableware, insurance policies or certificates, stock certificates, bonds, deeds, and wills.

(6) The name and address of the financial institution in which the asset is maintained.

(b) For purposes of this chapter, "financial institution" means a bank, trust, savings and loan association, savings bank, industrial bank, or credit union. *(Added by Stats.2001, c. 563 (A.B.1286), § 7. Amended by Stats.2003, c. 888 (A.B.394), § 7.)*

Cross References

Account, defined, see Probate Code § 21

Governmental access to financial records, authorized acts, see Government Code § 7480.

§ 2893. Affidavit; disclosure

(a) The written statement provided pursuant to Section 2892 by the financial institution shall be in the form of an affidavit signed by an officer of the financial institution and the officer shall provide his or her name and title in the affidavit.

(b) The affidavit required by this section is subject to disclosure under the circumstances described in subdivision (*l*) of Section 7480 of the Government Code under the California Right to Financial Privacy Act (Chapter 20 (commencing with Section 7460) of Division 7 of Title 1 of the Government Code).

(c) This chapter does not apply to any trust arrangement described in subdivision (b) of Section 82 except paragraph (4) of that subdivision relating to assets held in a Totten trust.

(d) The affidavit described in Section 2892 is not required to be filed in a proceeding more than once for each asset. However, all assets held by the financial institution may be listed in a single affidavit filed with the court.

(e) If the affidavit and any accompanying information to be filed pursuant to this section also contains the ward or conservatee's social security number or any other personal information, including financial information regarding the ward or conservatee which would not be disclosed in an accounting, an inventory and appraisal, or other nonconfidential pleading filed in the action, the information shall be kept confidential and subject to disclosure to any person only upon order of the court. *(Added by Stats.2001, c. 563 (A.B.1286), § 7.)*

Cross References

Affidavits, see Code of Civil Procedure § 2009 et seq.
Governmental access to financial records, authorized acts, see Government Code § 7480.
Totten trust account, defined, see Probate Code § 80.

Part 5

PUBLIC GUARDIAN

Law Revision Commission Comments

1990 Enactment

This part supersedes Part 5 (commencing with Section 2900) of Division 4 of the repealed Probate Code. The superseded part was enacted upon recommendation of the California Law Revision Commission. See Recommendation Relating to Public Guardians and Administrators, 19 Cal.L.Revision Comm'n Reports 707 (1988). See also Communication from the California Law Revision Commission Concerning Assembly Bill 2841, 19 Cal.L.Revision Comm'n Reports 1201, 1228 (1988). For general provisions governing the

office of the public guardian, formerly found in Welfare and Institutions Code Sections 8000–8005, 8008, and 8015, see Government Code Sections 27430–27436. [20 Cal.L.Rev.Comm.Reports 1001 (1990)].

CHAPTER 1. TAKING TEMPORARY POSSESSION OR CONTROL OF PROPERTY

Application

Application to possession or control of property by a public guardian on or after July 1, 1989, see Probate Code § 2903.

§ 2900. Loss, injury, waste or misappropriation of property; control or possession of property; restraint of persons from disposal of property held in trust; removal of occupants; hearing

(a)(1) If the public guardian or public conservator determines that the requirements for appointment of a guardian or conservator of the estate are satisfied and the public guardian or public conservator intends to apply for appointment, the public guardian or public conservator may take possession or control of real or personal property of a person domiciled in the county that is subject to loss, injury, waste, or misappropriation, and, subject to subdivision (b), may deny use of, access to, or prohibit residency in, the real or personal property, by anyone who does not have a written rental agreement or other legal right to the use of, or access to, the property.

(2)(A) Except as provided in subparagraph (C), if the public guardian or public conservator determines that the requirements for appointment of a guardian or conservator of the estate are satisfied and the public guardian or public conservator intends to apply for appointment as the guardian or conservator of a person domiciled in the county, the public guardian or public conservator may restrain any person from transferring, encumbering, or in any way disposing of any real or personal property held in a trust, provided all of the following requirements are met:

(i) The real or personal property held in the trust is subject to loss, injury, waste, or misappropriation.

(ii) The proposed ward or conservatee is a settlor of the trust.

(iii) The proposed ward or conservatee has a beneficial interest in the trust to currently receive income or principal from the trust.

(iv) The proposed ward or conservatee holds a power to revoke the trust.

(B) During the period of any restraint under this paragraph, the property subject to the restraint shall continue to be retained as property of the trust pending termination of the restraint or further court order. The public guardian or public conservator shall provide notice of any action taken under this paragraph to all of the persons required to be noticed pursuant to Section 17203, to the extent the public guardian or public conservator has access to the trust documents or is otherwise able to determine the persons entitled to receive notice. Any settlor, trustee, or beneficiary may petition the court for relief from any action taken by the public guardian or public conservator under this paragraph.

(C) This paragraph shall not apply if a current trustee or cotrustee is a spouse of the proposed ward or conservatee and that spouse is also a settlor of the trust, unless the public guardian or public conservator determines that the real or personal property held in the trust is subject to substantial loss, injury, waste, or misappropriation.

(b) The authority provided to the public guardian and public conservator in subdivision (a) includes the authority to terminate immediately the occupancy of anyone living in the home of an intended ward or conservatee, other than the intended ward or conservatee, and the authority to remove any such occupant residing therein, subject to the following requirements:

(1) The public guardian or public conservator shall first determine that the person whose occupancy is to be terminated has no written rental agreement or other legal right to occupancy, and has caused, contributed to, enabled, or threatened loss, injury, waste, or misappropriation of the home or its contents. In making this determination, the public guardian or public conservator shall contact the intended ward or conservatee and the occupant, advise them of the proposed removal and the grounds therefor, and consider whatever information they provide.

(2) At the time of the removal, the public guardian or public conservator shall advise the intended ward or conservatee and the occupant that a hearing will be held as provided in paragraph (3).

(3) The public guardian or public conservator shall file a petition regarding removal, showing the grounds therefor, to be set for hearing within 10 days of the filing of the petition and within 15 days of the removal. The person removed and the intended ward or conservatee shall be personally served with a notice of hearing and a copy of the petition at least five days prior to the hearing, subject to Part 2 (commencing with Section 1200) of Division 3. The right of the public guardian or public conservator to deny occupancy by the removed person to the premises shall terminate 15 days after removal, unless extended by the court at the hearing on the petition. The court shall not grant an extension unless the public guardian or public conservator has filed a petition for appointment as guardian or conservator of the estate.

(c) If the public guardian or public conservator takes possession of the residence of an intended ward or conservatee under this section, then for purposes of Section 602.3 of the Penal Code, the public guardian or public conservator shall be the owner's representative. *(Added by Stats.1992, c. 572 (S.B.1455), § 11. Amended by Stats.2011, c. 370 (A.B. 1288), § 1.)*

Law Revision Commission Comments
1990 Enactment

Section 2900 continues Section 2900 of the repealed Probate Code without change.

Background on Section 2900 of Repealed Code

Section 2900 was added by 1988 Cal.Stat. ch. 1199 § 72. The section superseded the fifth sentence of former Welfare and Institutions Code Section 8006. It replaced the concept of "referral" to the public guardian with a scheme based on the propriety of public guardian control. It also added misappropriation as grounds for taking possession or control. For background on the provisions of this part, see the Comment to this part under the part heading. [20 Cal.L.Rev.Comm.Reports 1001 (1990)].

§ 2901. Certificate of authority; standardized form; effect; surrender of property; discharge of liability

(a) A public guardian who is authorized to take possession or control of property under this chapter may issue a written certification of that fact. The written certification is effective for 30 days after the date of issuance.

(b) The written recordable certification shall substantially comply with the following form:

"CERTIFICATE OF AUTHORITY

THIS IS AN OFFICIAL CERTIFICATE ENTITLING THE PUBLIC GUARDIAN TO TAKE POSSESSION OF ANY AND ALL PROPERTY BELONGING TO THE FOLLOWING INDIVIDUAL:

(Name of Individual) _____

This Certificate of Authority has been issued by the Public Guardian pursuant to and in compliance with Chapter 1 (commencing with Section 2900) of Part 5 of Division 4 of the California Probate Code. Under California law, this Certificate of Authority authorizes the Public Guardian to take possession or control of property belonging to the above-named individual.

SPECIAL NOTE TO FINANCIAL INSTITUTIONS:
State law requires that upon receiving a copy of this Certificate of Authority, financial institutions shall provide the public guardian with information concerning property held by the above-named individual and surrender the property to the Public Guardian if requested.

This Certificate of Authority shall only be valid when signed and dated by the Public Guardian or a deputy Public Guardian of the County of _____ and affixed with the official seal of the Public Guardian below.

This Certificate of Authority expires 30 days after the date of issuance.

Signature of Public Guardian:
Date:
Official Seal"

(c) The public guardian may record a copy of the written certification in any county in which is located real property of which the public guardian is authorized to take possession or control under this chapter.

(d) A financial institution or other person shall, without the necessity of inquiring into the truth of the written certification and without court order or letters being issued:

(1) Provide the public guardian information concerning property held in the sole name of the proposed ward or conservatee.

(2) Surrender to the public guardian property of the proposed ward or conservatee that is subject to loss, injury, waste, or misappropriation.

(e) Receipt of the written certification:

(1) Constitutes sufficient acquittance for providing information and for surrendering property of the proposed ward or conservatee.

(2) Fully discharges the financial institution or other person from any liability for any act or omission of the public guardian with respect to the property. *(Stats.1990, c. 79 (A.B.759), § 14, operative July 1, 1991. Amended by Stats. 2001, c. 232 (A.B.1517), § 2; Stats.2011, c. 370 (A.B.1288), § 2.)*

Law Revision Commission Comments
1990 Enactment

Section 2901 continues Section 2901 of the repealed Probate Code without substantive change. The reference to the county recorder has been omitted from subdivision (d)(2) as unnecessary since the county recorder's only involvement is to record the written certification of the public guardian in the county real property records. Section 2901 is comparable to Section 7603 (providing information, access, or property to public administrator).

Background on Section 2901 of Repealed Code

Section 2901 was added by 1988 Cal.Stat. ch. 1199 § 72. The section was drawn from Section 7603 of the repealed Probate Code. See the Comment to Section 7603 of the new Probate Code for the source of Section 7603 of the repealed Probate Code. For background on the provisions of this part, see the Comment to this part under the part heading. [20 Cal.L.Rev.Comm.Reports 1001 (1990)].

§ 2901.5. Restraint of disposal of real or personal property held in trust; written certificate of authority

(a) A public guardian or public conservator, who is authorized to restrain any person from transferring, encumbering, or in any way disposing of any real or personal property held in a trust in accordance with paragraph (2) of subdivision (a) of Section 2900, may issue a written certification of that fact. The written certification is effective for 30 days after the date of issuance.

(b) The written recordable certification shall substantially comply with the following form:

"CERTIFICATE OF AUTHORITY

THIS IS AN OFFICIAL CERTIFICATE ENTITLING THE PUBLIC GUARDIAN/PUBLIC CONSERVATOR TO RESTRAIN ANY PERSON FROM TRANSFERRING, ENCUMBERING, OR IN ANY WAY DISPOSING OF ANY REAL OR PERSONAL PROPERTY HELD IN THE FOLLOWING TRUST:

(Name of Trust) _____

THE PUBLIC GUARDIAN/PUBLIC CONSERVATOR HAS DETERMINED THAT IT HAS AUTHORITY TO ISSUE THIS CERTIFICATE WITH RESPECT TO THE ABOVE–NAMED TRUST AND IN CONNECTION WITH PROCEEDINGS THAT ARE OR WILL BE PENDING RELATED TO THE FOLLOWING INDIVIDUAL:

(Name of Individual) _____

This Certificate of Authority has been issued by the Public Guardian/ Public Conservator pursuant to and in compliance with Chapter 1 (commencing with Section 2900) of Part 5 of Division 4 of the California Probate Code. Under California law, this Certificate of Authority authorizes the Public Guardian/Public Conservator to restrain any person from transferring, encumbering, or in any way disposing of any real or personal property held in the above-named trust.

SPECIAL NOTE TO FINANCIAL INSTITUTIONS:
State law requires that, upon receiving a copy of this Certificate of Authority, financial institutions shall provide the public guardian/public conservator with information concerning property held in the above-named trust and shall restrain any person from transferring, encumbering, or in any way disposing of any real or personal property held in the above-named trust.

This Certificate of Authority shall only be valid when signed and dated by the Public Guardian/Public Conservator or a deputy Public Guardian/Public Conservator of the County of _____ and affixed with the official seal of the Public Guardian/Public Conservator below.

This Certificate of Authority expires 30 days after the date of issuance.

Signature of Public Guardian/Public Conservator:
Date:
Official Seal"

(c) The public guardian or public conservator may record a copy of the written certification in any county in which is located real property held in a trust as to which the public guardian or public conservator has determined it has authority to issue the written certification.

(d) A financial institution or other person who is provided with the written certification by the public guardian or public conservator shall, without the necessity of inquiring into the truth of the written certification and without court order or letters being issued:

(1) Provide the public guardian or public conservator information concerning any real or personal property held in the trust identified in the written certification.

(2) Restrain any person from transferring, encumbering, or in any way disposing of any real or personal property, held in the trust identified in the written certification.

(e) Receipt of the written certification:

(1) Constitutes sufficient acquittance for providing information and for restraining any person from transferring, encumbering, or in any way disposing of any real or personal property held in the trust identified in the written certification.

(2) Fully discharges the financial institution or other person from any liability for any act or omission of the public guardian or public conservator with respect to the property. *(Added by Stats.2011, c. 370 (A.B.1288), § 3.)*

§ 2902. Costs and fees

A public guardian who takes possession or control of property pursuant to this chapter is entitled to reasonable costs incurred for the preservation of the property, together with reasonable compensation for services, in case of the subsequent appointment of another person as guardian or conservator of the estate. The costs and compensation are a proper and legal charge against the estate of the ward or conservatee. *(Stats.1990, c. 79 (A.B.759), § 14, operative July 1, 1991.)*

Law Revision Commission Comments

1990 Enactment

Section 2902 continues Section 2902 of the repealed Probate Code without substantive change. The costs and compensation provided by this section are subject to court approval under Section 2430. Where the public guardian is ultimately appointed guardian or conservator, the costs and compensation provided by this section are part of the public guardian's compensation. See Section 2942 (expenses and compensation of public guardian). For a comparable provision relating to the public administrator, see Section 7604.

Background on Section 2902 of Repealed Code

Section 2902 was added by 1988 Cal.Stat. ch. 1199 § 72. Section 2902 restated former Welfare and Institutions Code Section 8006.5, but eliminated the maximum and minimum fees. For background on the provisions of this part, see the Comment to this part under the part heading. [20 Cal.L.Rev.Comm.Reports 1001 (1990)].

§ 2903. Application of chapter; continuing application of repealed provisions

This chapter applies only to possession or control of property by a public guardian on or after July 1, 1989. Possession or control of property by a public guardian before July 1, 1989, is governed by the applicable law in effect before July 1, 1989, notwithstanding its repeal by Chapter 1199 of

the Statutes of 1988. *(Stats.1990, c. 79 (A.B.759), § 14, operative July 1, 1991.)*

Law Revision Commission Comments

1990 Enactment

Section 2903 continues Section 2903 of the repealed Probate Code without substantive change. A reference to Chapter 1199 of the Statutes of 1988 has been substituted for "the act that enacted this chapter." Section 2903 is a specific application of portions of the general operative date and transitional provision. See Section 3.

Background on Section 2903 of Repealed Code

Section 2903 was a new provision added by 1988 Cal.Stat. ch. 1199 § 72. For background on the provisions of this part, see the Comment to this part under the part heading. [20 Cal.L.Rev.Comm.Reports 1001 (1990)].

§§ 2904 to 2909. Repealed by Stats.1980, c. 89, § 7, operative Jan. 1, 1981

Law Revision Commission Comments

1980 Repeal

The Uniform Veterans' Guardianship Act (Prob.Code §§ 2900 to 2918) is repealed as a separate statute. Pertinent portions of the Uniform Veterans' Guardianship Act are continued elsewhere in Division 4 of the Probate Code and in the Government Code. The portions that are not continued are either obsolete or are superseded by existing provisions of general guardianship-conservatorship law. The disposition of each repealed section of the Uniform Veterans' Guardianship Act is indicated in the Comment to the repealed section set out below.

Former Section 2900 is not continued.

The terms in which "income" and "estate" were defined in former Section 2901 are continued in the substantive provisions of Section 1461.5 (notice to Veterans Administration). The terms in which "benefits" was defined in former Section 2901 are continued in the substantive provisions of Sections 1510 and 1821 (contents of petition). The remaining definitions of former Section 2901 are not continued.

Subdivision (a) of former Section 2902 is superseded by the requirement in Section 1514 that the court may appoint a guardian if it appears "necessary or convenient," and by the requirement in Section 1800 that the court may appoint a conservator if satisfied of the "need therefor." Subdivision (b) of former Section 2902 is superseded by the provision of Section 1510 that a guardian may be appointed only for a minor. An adult in need of protective supervision may have a conservator appointed. See Section 1800.

Subdivision (a) of former Section 2903 is superseded by Sections 1510 (guardianship), 1820 (conservatorship), and 2201 (venue). Subdivision (b) is superseded by Sections 1510 (guardianship) and 1821 (conservatorship). The requirement that the petition set forth the age of the proposed ward or conservatee is continued with respect to minor wards in Section 1510, but is not continued with respect to conservatees (see Section 1821). The substance of the requirement of subdivision (b) of allegations concerning Veterans Administration benefits is continued in Sections 1510 and 1821.

The first sentence of subdivision (c) is superseded with respect to minors by Section 1510; the requirement that the petition show the age, relationship, if any, and occupation of the proposed guardian is not continued. With respect to adults, the first sentence of subdivision (c) is not continued. The second sentence of subdivision (c) is superseded by Sections 1514 (guardianship) and 1810 to 1813 (conservatorship). Subdivision (d) is not continued.

Former Section 2904 is not continued.

Former Section 2905 is not continued.

Former Section 2906 is continued in Section 1461.5, except that the former requirement that the copy of the petition be a signed duplicate or be certified is not continued.

Subdivision (a) of former Section 2907 is superseded by Sections 1514 (guardianship) and 1810 to 1813 (conservatorship). Subdivision (b) is superseded by Sections 2300 and 2320 to 2336.

Former Section 2908 is superseded by Sections 2620 to 2633. The requirement of notice to the Veterans Administration is continued in Section 1461.5.

Former Section 2909 is superseded by Sections 2602 and 2650.

Former Section 2910 is superseded by Sections 2640 and 2643. The limitation on compensation contained in former Section 2910 is not continued; under Section 2640, the compensation must be "just and reasonable." The requirement of notice to the Veterans Administration is continued in Section 1461.5.

Former Section 2911 is superseded by Sections 2401 (duty to use ordinary care and diligence in management of estate), 2453 (deposit in bank or other financial institution), 2570 to 2574 (investments and purchase of property), and 2590 to 2595 (independent exercise of powers). The requirement of notice to the Veterans Administration is continued in Section 1461.5.

Former Section 2912 is superseded by Section 2423. The requirement of notice to the Veterans Administration is continued in Section 1461.5, except that the requirement that the copy of the petition be a signed duplicate or be certified is not continued.

Subdivision (a) of former Section 2913 is superseded by Section 2571. The limitation of subdivision (a) that real property may be purchased "only as a home" for the ward is not continued. The requirement of notice to the Veterans Administration is continued in Section 1461.5. Subdivision (b) is not continued. Notwithstanding the omission of the second sentence of subdivision (b) (which required that title be taken in the name of the ward), it is the accepted practice in guardianship and conservatorship proceedings to take title to real property in the name of the ward or conservatee. See W. Johnstone & G. Zillgitt, California Conservatorships § 4.17, at 116 (Cal.Cont.Ed.Bar 1968).

Subdivision (c) is superseded by Sections 2463 (partition), 2500–2501 (compromises affecting real property), and 2590–2591 (independent exercise of powers).

Former Section 2914 is continued in Government Code Section 6107.

The first sentence of former Section 2915 is not continued. The second and third sentences are superseded by Sections 1600–1601 (guardianship), 1860 to 1863 (conservatorship), 2627 (discharge of guardian), and 2630 (accounts on termination of relationship).

Former Section 2916 is not continued.

Former Section 2917 is not continued.

Former Section 2918 is not continued.

CHAPTER 2. PREFILING INVESTIGATION BY PUBLIC GUARDIAN

§ 2910. Petition for appointment of public guardian as conservator; investigation; notice and service of process

(a) Upon a showing of probable cause to believe that a person is in substantial danger of abuse or neglect and needs a conservator of the person, the estate, or the person and estate for his or her own protection, the public guardian or the county's adult protective services agency may petition for either or both of the orders of the court provided in subdivision (b) in connection with his or her investigation to determine whether a petition for the appointment of the public guardian as conservator of the person, estate, or the person and estate of the person would be necessary or appropriate.

(b) The petition may request either or both of the following orders for the limited purposes of the investigation concerning a person:

(1) An order authorizing identified health care providers or organizations to provide private medical information about the person to the public guardian's authorized representatives.

(2) An order authorizing identified financial institutions or advisers, accountants, and others with financial information about the person to provide the information to the public guardian's authorized representatives.

(c) Notice of the hearing and a copy of the petition shall be served on the person who is the subject of the investigation in the manner and for the period required by Section 1460 or, on application of the public guardian contained in or accompanying the petition, on an expedited basis in the manner and for the period ordered by the court. The court may dispense with notice of the hearing only on a showing of facts demonstrating an immediate threat of substantial harm to the person if notice is given. *(Added by Stats.2007, c. 553 (A.B.1727), § 25.)*

§ 2911. Contents of order issued in response to petition

A court order issued in response to a public guardian's petition pursuant to Section 2910 shall do all of the following:

(a) Authorize health care providers to disclose a person's confidential medical information as permitted under California law, and also authorize disclosure of the information under federal medical privacy regulations enacted pursuant to the Health Insurance Portability and Accountability Act of 1996.

(b) Direct the public guardian or the adult protective services agency to keep the information acquired under the order confidential, except as disclosed in a judicial proceeding or as required by law enforcement or an authorized regulatory agency.

(c) Direct the public guardian or the adult protective services agency to destroy all copies of written information obtained under the order or give them to the person who was the subject of the investigation if a conservatorship proceeding is not commenced within 60 days after the date of the order. The court may extend this time period as the court finds to be in the subject's best interest. *(Added by Stats. 2007, c. 553 (A.B.1727), § 25.)*

§§ 2912 to 2918. Repealed by Stats.1980, c. 89, § 7, operative Jan. 1, 1981

CHAPTER 3. APPOINTMENT OF PUBLIC GUARDIAN

Section

2921. Persons under jurisdiction of Department of State Hospitals or Department of Developmental Services; consent to application.

2922. Letters; bond and oath.

2923. Continuing education requirements.

§ 2920. Application for appointment; court order; notice and hearing

(a) If any person domiciled in the county requires a guardian or conservator and there is no one else who is qualified and willing to act and whose appointment as guardian or conservator would be in the best interests of the person, then either of the following shall apply:

(1) The public guardian shall apply for appointment as guardian or conservator of the person, the estate, or the person and estate, if there is an imminent threat to the person's health or safety or the person's estate.

(2) The public guardian may apply for appointment as guardian or conservator of the person, the estate, or the person and estate in all other cases.

(b) The public guardian shall apply for appointment as guardian or conservator of the person, the estate, or the person and estate, if the court so orders. The court may make an order under this subdivision on motion of an interested person or on the court's own motion in a pending proceeding or in a proceeding commenced for that purpose. The court shall order the public guardian to apply for appointment as guardian or conservator of the person, the estate, or the person and estate, on behalf of any person domiciled in the county who appears to require a guardian or conservator, if it appears that there is no one else who is qualified and willing to act, and if that appointment as guardian or conservator appears to be in the best interests of the person. However, if prior to the filing of the petition for appointment it is discovered that there is someone else who is qualified and willing to act as guardian or conservator, the public guardian shall be relieved of the duty under the order. The court shall not make an order under this subdivision except after notice to the public guardian for the period and in the manner provided for in Chapter 3 (commencing with Section 1460) of Part 1, consideration of the alternatives, and a determination by the court that the appointment is necessary. The notice and hearing under this subdivision may be combined with the notice and hearing required for appointment of a guardian or conservator.

(c) The public guardian shall begin an investigation within two business days of receiving a referral for conservatorship or guardianship. *(Stats.1990, c. 79 (A.B.759), § 14, operative July 1, 1991. Amended by Stats.2006, c. 493 (A.B.1363), § 32.)*

Law Revision Commission Comments

1990 Enactment

Section 2920 continues Section 2920 of the repealed Probate Code without change. For general provisions, see Sections 1000–1004 (rules of practice), 1020–1023 (petitions and other papers), 1040–1050 (hearings and orders), 2103 (effect of final order). For general provisions relating to notice of hearing, see Sections 1200–1221, 1460–1469. See also Sections 1260–1265 (proof of giving notice).

Section 2920 applies even though a person may be institutionalized in a facility in another county if the person is domiciled in the county of the public guardian. Even though there may be other persons qualified and willing to act, their appointment may not be in the best interest of the ward or conservatee. This could occur, for example, where a neutral party is needed because of family disputes. In such a situation, a public guardian is not liable for failure to take possession or control of property that is beyond the public guardian's ability to possess or control. See Section 2944 (immunity of public guardian).

The court may order appointment of the public guardian only after notice to the public guardian and a determination that the appointment is necessary. The determination of necessity may require the court to ascertain whether there is any other alternative to public guardianship, and whether the public guardianship is simply being sought as a convenience or as a strategic litigation device by the parties involved. Alternative means of resolving the situation, besides appointment of the public guardian, could include such options as use of a private guardian or appointment of a guardian ad litem, in an appropriate case.

Subdivision (b) permits the special notice to the public guardian and hearing under this subdivision to be combined with a general notice and hearing for appointment of a guardian or conservator, in the interest of procedural efficiency.

Background on Section 2920 of Repealed Code

Section 2920 was added by 1988 Cal.Stat. ch. 1199 § 72. The section superseded the first, second, and a portion of the third sentences of former Welfare and Institutions Code Section 8006. For background on the provisions of this part, see the Comment to this part under the part heading. [20 Cal.L.Rev.Comm.Reports 1001 (1990)].

§ 2920.5. Repealed by Stats.2002, c. 644 (A.B.1957), § 1, operative Jan. 1, 2007

§ 2921. Persons under jurisdiction of Department of State Hospitals or Department of Developmental Services; consent to application

An application of the public guardian for guardianship or conservatorship of the person, the estate, or the person and estate, of a person who is under the jurisdiction of the State Department of State Hospitals or the State Department of Developmental Services shall not be granted without the written consent of the department having jurisdiction of the person. *(Stats.1990, c. 79 (A.B.759), § 14, operative July 1, 1991. Amended by Stats.2012, c. 440 (A.B.1488), § 50, eff. Sept. 22, 2012.)*

Law Revision Commission Comments

1990 Enactment

Section 2921 continues Section 2921 of the repealed Probate Code without change.

Background on Section 2921 of Repealed Code

Section 2921 was added by 1988 Cal.Stat. ch. 1199 § 72. The section restated former Welfare and Institutions Code Section 8007 without substantive change. For background on the provisions of this part, see the Comment to this part under the part heading. [20 Cal.L.Rev.Comm.Reports 1001 (1990)].

Cross References

Department of Developmental Services, see Welfare and Institutions Code § 4400 et seq.

§ 2922. Letters; bond and oath

If the public guardian is appointed as guardian or conservator:

(a) Letters shall be issued in the same manner and by the same proceedings as letters are issued to other persons. Letters may be issued to "the public guardian" of the county without naming the public guardian.

(b) The official bond and oath of the public guardian are in lieu of the guardian or conservator's bond and oath on the grant of letters. *(Stats.1990, c. 79 (A.B.759), § 14, operative July 1, 1991.)*

Law Revision Commission Comments

1990 Enactment

Section 2922 continues Section 2922 of the repealed Probate Code without change. Letters issued to "the public guardian" are sufficient to enable a successor public guardian to act without issuance of new letters. Gov't Code § 27433 (termination of authority of public guardian). See also Section 52 ("letters" defined). The public guardian is allowed a share of the cost of the bond as an expense of administration. See Section 2942(c).

Background on Section 2922 of Repealed Code

Section 2922 was added by 1988 Cal.Stat. ch. 1199 § 72. The section restated the third and fourth sentences of former Welfare and Institutions Code Section 8006 with the addition of authority to issue letters to "the public guardian." For background on the provisions of this part, see the Comment to this part under the part heading. [20 Cal.L.Rev.Comm.Reports 1001 (1990)].

§ 2923. Continuing education requirements

On or before January 1, 2008, the public guardian shall comply with the continuing education requirements that are established by the California State Association of Public Administrators, Public Guardians, and Public Conservators. *(Added by Stats.2006, c. 493 (A.B.1363), § 33.)*

CHAPTER 4. ADMINISTRATION BY PUBLIC GUARDIAN

§ 2940. Funds; deposit or investment

All funds coming into the custody of the public guardian shall be deposited or invested in the same manner and subject to the same terms and conditions as deposit or investment by the public administrator of money in an estate pursuant to Article 3 (commencing with Section 7640) of Chapter 4 of Part 1 of Division 7. *(Stats.1990, c. 79 (A.B.759), § 14, operative July 1, 1991.)*

Law Revision Commission Comments

1990 Enactment

Section 2940 continues Section 2940 of the repealed Probate Code without change. This section cross-refers to comparable provisions of the public administrator statute.

Background on Section 2940 of Repealed Code

Section 2940 was added by 1988 Cal.Stat. ch. 1199 § 72. The section superseded former Welfare and Institutions Code Section 8009. For background on the provisions of this part, see the

Comment to this part under the part heading. [20 Cal.L.Rev.Comm.Reports 1001 (1990)].

§ 2941. Private attorneys; cost of employment

The public guardian may, if necessary and in the public guardian's discretion, employ private attorneys where the cost of employment can be defrayed out of estate funds or where satisfactory pro bono or contingency fee arrangements can be made. *(Stats.1990, c. 79 (A.B.759), § 14, operative July 1, 1991.)*

Law Revision Commission Comments

1990 Enactment

Section 2941 continues Section 2941 of the repealed Probate Code without change.

Background on Section 2941 of Repealed Code

Section 2941 was added by 1988 Cal.Stat. ch. 1199 § 72. The section restated former Welfare and Institutions Code Section 8010 with the addition of reference to satisfactory pro bono or contingency fee arrangements. For background on the provisions of this part, see the Comment to this part under the part heading. [20 Cal.L.Rev.Comm.Reports 1001 (1990)].

§ 2942. Payments from estate

The public guardian shall be paid from the estate of the ward or conservatee for all of the following:

(a) Reasonable expenses incurred in the execution of the guardianship or conservatorship.

(b) Compensation for services of the public guardian and the attorney of the public guardian, and for the filing and processing services of the county clerk or the clerk of the superior court, in the amount the court determines is just and reasonable. In determining what constitutes just and reasonable compensation, the court shall, among other factors, take into consideration the actual costs of the services provided, the amount of the estate involved, the special value of services provided in relation to the estate, and whether the compensation requested might impose an economic hardship on the estate. Nothing in this section shall require a public guardian to base a request for compensation upon an hourly rate of service.

(c) An annual bond fee in the amount of twenty-five dollars ($25) plus one-fourth of 1 percent of the amount of an estate greater than ten thousand dollars ($10,000). The amount charged shall be deposited in the county treasury. This subdivision does not apply if the ward or conservatee is eligible for Social Security Supplemental Income benefits. *(Stats.1990, c. 79 (A.B.759), § 14, operative July 1, 1991. Amended by Stats.1994, c. 472 (A.B.2725), § 2; Stats.1998, c. 103 (S.B.1487), § 2; Stats.1999, c. 866 (A.B.1152), § 1.)*

Law Revision Commission Comments

1990 Enactment

Section 2942 continues Section 2942 of the repealed Probate Code without change. Subdivision (c) is comparable to Section 7621(d) (public administrator).

Background on Section 2942 of Repealed Code

Section 2942 was added by 1988 Cal.Stat. ch. 1199 § 72. Subdivisions (a) and (b) of Section 2942 restated former Welfare and Institutions Code Section 8013 without substantive change. Subdivision (c) was new. For background on the provisions of this part, see the Comment to this part under the part heading. [20 Cal.L.Rev.Comm.Reports 1001 (1990)].

§ 2943. Appraisal of inventory property; sale of residence

(a) Notwithstanding subdivision (c) of Section 2610, the property described in the inventory may be appraised by the public guardian and need not be appraised by a probate referee if the public guardian files with the inventory an appraisal showing that the estimated value of the property in the estate does not exceed the amount prescribed in Section 13100.

(b) If the conservator seeks authority pursuant to subdivision (b) of Section 2540 to sell the conservatee's personal residence, whether or not it is real property, or if the conservator seeks authority pursuant to Section 2590 to sell the conservatee's real property, valued in excess of ten thousand dollars ($10,000), or an item of personal property valued in excess of ten thousand dollars ($10,000) that is not a security sold pursuant to subdivision (a) of Section 2544, that property shall be appraised by a probate referee. *(Stats.1990, c. 79 (A.B.759), § 14, operative July 1, 1991. Amended by Stats.1996, c. 86 (A.B.2146), § 3.)*

Law Revision Commission Comments

1990 Enactment

Section 2943 continues Section 2943 of the repealed Probate Code without change.

Background on Section 2943 of Repealed Code

Section 2943 was added by 1988 Cal.Stat. ch. 1199 § 72. The section superseded former Welfare and Institutions Code Section 8011. For background on the provisions of this part, see the Comment to this part under the part heading. [20 Cal.L.Rev.Comm.Reports 1001 (1990)].

§ 2944. Liability for failure to take possession

The public guardian is not liable for failing to take possession or control of property that is beyond the ability of the public guardian to possess or control. *(Stats.1990, c. 79 (A.B.759), § 14, operative July 1, 1991.)*

Law Revision Commission Comments

1990 Enactment

Section 2944 continues Section 2944 of the repealed Probate Code without change. Cf. Section 7601(b) (duty of public administrator).

Background on Section 2944 of Repealed Code

Section 2944 was a new provision added by 1988 Cal.Stat. ch. 1199 § 72. For background on the provisions of this part, see the Comment to this part under the part heading. [20 Cal.L.Rev.Comm.Reports 1001 (1990)].

CHAPTER 5. FINANCIAL ABUSE OF MENTALLY IMPAIRED ELDERS

ARTICLE 1. GENERAL

§ 2950. Legislative intent; coordination with existing programs

(a) It is the intent of the Legislature to do all of the following:

(1) Reduce the incidence of financial abuse perpetrated against mentally impaired elder adults.

(2) Minimize monetary losses to mentally impaired elder adults as a result of financial abuse.

(3) Facilitate timely intervention by law enforcement, in collaboration with the public guardian, to effectively protect mentally impaired elder adult victims of financial abuse, and to recover their assets.

(b) Any peace officer or public guardian of a county that has both of the following, as determined by the public guardian of that county, may take the actions authorized by this chapter:

(1) The existence of sufficient law enforcement personnel with expertise in the assessment of competence.

(2) The existence of a law enforcement unit devoted to investigating elder financial abuse and the enforcement of laws applicable to elder abuse.

(c) This chapter shall be coordinated with existing mandated programs affecting financial abuse of mentally impaired elders that are administered by the adult protective services agency of the county. *(Added by Stats.2000, c. 813 (S.B. 1742), § 1.)*

Cross References

Financial abuse defined for purposes of this Chapter, see Probate Code § 2951.

§ 2951. Definitions

The definitions contained in this section shall govern the construction of this chapter, unless the context requires otherwise.

(a) "Declaration" means a document that substantially complies with the requirements of Section 2954, and is signed by both a peace officer and a supervisor from the county's adult protective services agency and provided to the public guardian in accordance with subdivision (b) of Section 2952.

(b) "Elder person" means any person residing in this state, 65 years of age or older.

(c) "Financial abuse" means a situation described in Section 15610.30 of the Welfare and Institutions Code.

(d) "Financial abuse POST training" means an elder financial abuse training course certified by the Commission on Peace Officer Standards and Training.

(e) "Financial institution" means any bank, savings and loan, thrift, industrial loan company, credit union, or any branch of any of these institutions doing business in the state, as defined by provisions of the Financial Code.

(f) "Peace officer" means a sheriff, deputy sheriff, municipal police officer, or a peace officer authorized under subdivision (b) of Section 830.1 of the Penal Code, duly sworn under the requirements of state law, who satisfies any of the following requirements:

(1) The sheriff, deputy sheriff, municipal police officer, or peace officer authorized under subdivision (b) of Section 830.1 of the Penal Code has completed or participated as a lecturer in a financial abuse POST training program within the last 36 months. The completion of the course may be satisfied by telecourse, video training tape, or other instruction. The training shall, at a minimum, address relevant elder abuse laws, recognition of financial abuse and fraud, assessment of mental competence in accordance with the standards set forth in Part 17 (commencing with Section 810) of the Probate Code, reporting requirements and procedures for the investigation of financial abuse and related crimes, including neglect, and civil and criminal procedures for the protection of victims. The course may be presented as part of a training program that includes other subjects or courses.

(2) The sheriff, deputy sheriff, municipal police officer, or peace officer authorized under subdivision (b) of Section 830.1 of the Penal Code, has consulted with a sheriff, deputy sheriff, municipal police officer, or peace officer authorized under subdivision (b) of Section 830.1 of the Penal Code, who satisfies the requirements of paragraph (1) concerning the declaration defined in subdivision (a) and obtained the signature of that sheriff, deputy sheriff, municipal police officer, or peace officer authorized under subdivision (b) of Section 830.1 of the Penal Code on a declaration that substantially complies with the form described in Section 2954.

(g) "Property" means all personal property and real property of every kind belonging to, or alleged to belong to, the elder. *(Added by Stats.2000, c. 813 (S.B.1742), § 1.)*

ARTICLE 2.   ESTATE PROTECTION

§ 2952.   Issuance of declaration by peace officer; certificate of authority; standardized form; authority and responsibility; liabilities for actions under certificate; expiration; investigation by county adult protective services agency

(a) A peace officer may issue a declaration, as provided in Section 2954, concerning an elder person if all of the following conditions are satisfied:

(1) There is probable cause to believe that the elder person is substantially unable to manage his or her financial resources or to resist fraud or undue influence.

(2) There exists a significant danger that the elder person will lose all or a portion of his or her property as a result of

fraud or misrepresentations or the mental incapacity of the elder person.

(3) There is probable cause to believe that a crime is being committed against the elder person.

(4) The crime is connected to the inability of the elder person to manage his or her financial resources or to resist fraud or undue influence, and that inability is the result of deficits in the elder person's mental functions.

(5) The peace officer has consulted with an individual qualified to perform a mental status examination.

(b) If the requirements of subdivision (a) are satisfied, the peace officer may provide a signed declaration to the public guardian of the county. The declaration provided by the peace officer under this subdivision shall be signed by both the peace officer and a supervisor from the county's adult protective services agency. The declaration shall be transmitted to the public guardian within 24 hours of its being signed, and may be transmitted by facsimile.

(c)(1) Upon receiving a signed declaration from a peace officer, the public guardian is authorized to rely on the information contained in the declaration to take immediate possession or control of any real or personal property belonging to the elder person referred to in the declaration, including any property that is held jointly between the elder person and a third party that is subject to loss, injury, waste, or misappropriation, and may issue a written recordable certification of that fact pursuant to this section. The written recordable certification shall substantially comply with the following form:

"CERTIFICATE OF AUTHORITY

THIS IS AN OFFICIAL CERTIFICATE ENTITLING THE PUBLIC GUARDIAN TO TAKE POSSESSION OF ANY AND ALL PROPERTY BELONGING TO THE FOLLOWING INDIVIDUAL:

(Name of Victim) _____

This Certificate of Authority has been issued by the Public Guardian pursuant to and in compliance with the Financial Abuse of Mentally Impaired Elders statute, Chapter 4 (commencing with Section 2950) of Part 5 of Division 4 of the California Probate Code. Under California law, this Certificate of Authority authorizes the Public Guardian to take possession or control of property belonging to the above-named individual.

SPECIAL NOTE TO FINANCIAL INSTITUTIONS:

State law requires that upon receiving a copy of this Certificate of Authority, financial institutions shall provide the public guardian with information concerning property held by the above-named individual and surrender the property to the Public Guardian if requested.

This Certificate of Authority shall only be valid when signed and dated by the Public Guardian or a deputy Public Guardian of the County of _____ and affixed with the official seal of the Public Guardian below.

Signature of Public Guardian:

Date:

Official Seal"

(2) The mere issuance of the declaration provided by this section shall not require the public guardian to take possession or control of property and shall not require the public guardian to make a determination that the requirements for the appointment of a conservator are satisfied.

(3) The authority provided to the public guardian in paragraph (1) includes the authority to deny use of, access to, or prohibit residency in the home of the elder, by anyone who does not have a written rental agreement or other legal right to the use of, or access to, the residence, and, subject to the requirements of subdivision (b) of Section 2900, the authority to terminate the occupancy of anyone living in the home of the elder person, and the authority to remove that occupant residing therein.

(4) The public guardian shall serve, or cause to be served, a copy of the certification issued pursuant to this section on the elder person by mail within 24 hours of the execution of the certification, or as soon thereafter as is practical, in the manner provided in Chapter 4 (commencing with Section 413.10) of Title 5 of Part 2 of the Code of Civil Procedure.

(5) Receipt of a certification issued under this section constitutes sufficient acquittance to financial institutions and others in possession of an elder person's property to provide information and surrender property of the elder person to the public guardian. Any financial institution or other person who provides information or surrenders property pursuant to this section shall be discharged from any liability for any act or omission of the public guardian with respect to the property.

(6) A public guardian acting in good faith is not liable when taking possession or control of property pursuant to this section.

(7) A certification issued pursuant to this section is valid for 15 days after the date of issuance. Upon ex parte petition to the superior court, the public guardian may seek additional 15-day certifications. The court shall grant that petition only if it determines that the additional certification is necessary to protect the elder from financial abuse and the elder's property from loss, injury, waste, or misappropriation.

(d)(1) If the public guardian takes possession of an elder person's property pursuant to this section, the public guardian shall attempt to find agents pursuant to the use of durable powers of attorney or successor trustees nominated in trust instruments, or other persons having legal authority under existing legal instruments, to manage the elder person's estate.

(2) If the public guardian is unable to find any appropriate person to manage the elder person's estate pursuant to paragraph (1), the public guardian shall attempt to find appropriate family members willing to manage the elder person's estate. If no documents exist appointing appropriate fiduciaries, the public guardian shall follow the priorities set forth in Article 2 (commencing with Section 1810) of Chapter 1 of Part 3.

(3) The public guardian shall take the steps described in paragraphs (1) and (2) within 15 days of taking possession of an elder person's property pursuant to this section.

(e) Nothing in this section prevents the county's adult protective services agency from conducting an investigation regarding the elder person named in the declaration and providing appropriate services, in coordination with any actions taken with the public guardian under this section or an investigation conducted by law enforcement regarding the elder person. *(Added by Stats.2000, c. 813 (S.B.1742), § 1. Amended by Stats.2001, c. 232 (A.B.1517), § 3.)*

Cross References

Declaration defined for purposes of this Chapter, see Probate Code § 2951.
Elder person defined for purposes of this Chapter, see Probate Code § 2951.
Financial abuse defined for purposes of this Chapter, see Probate Code § 2951.
Peace officer defined for purposes of this Chapter, see Probate Code § 2951.
Property defined for purposes of this Chapter, see Probate Code § 2951.

§ 2953. Petition for costs and fees; duties of public guardian; petition for order to quash certification

(a)(1) A public guardian who has taken possession or control of the property of an elder person pursuant to this chapter is entitled to petition a court of competent jurisdiction for the reasonable costs incurred by the public guardian for the protection of the person or the property, together with reasonable fees for services, including, but not limited to, reasonable attorneys' fees. These fees shall be payable from the estate of the elder person if the person is not deemed competent by the court and if any of the following apply:

(A) The public guardian or someone else is appointed as the temporary or general conservator of the estate.

(B) An attorney-in-fact, under a durable power of attorney, or a trustee, takes steps, or is notified of the need to take steps, to protect the estate of the elder person.

(C) An action is brought against the alleged financial abuser by the elder person, his or her conservator, a trustee, a fiduciary, or a successor in interest of the elder person, arising from a harm that the public guardian taking charge was intended to prevent or minimize.

(2) Any costs incurred by the public guardian pursuant to paragraph (1) shall be compensable as provided in Section 2902. Fees collected by the public guardian pursuant to this chapter shall be used for the activities described in this chapter.

(b) When a public guardian has taken possession or control of the property of an elder person pursuant to this chapter, the public guardian shall exercise reasonable care to ensure that the reasonable living expenses and legitimate debts of the elder person are addressed as well as is practical under the circumstances.

(c) Any person identified as a victim in a declaration described in Section 2954 may bring an ex parte petition in the superior court for an order quashing the certification issued by the public guardian as provided in subdivision (c) of Section 2952.

(1) Upon request by the petitioner, the court may defer filing fees related to the petition, and order the public guardian to authorize the release of funds from a financial institution to reimburse the petitioner the filing fees from assets belonging to the petitioner, but shall waive filing fees if

the petitioner meets the standards of eligibility established by subparagraph (A) or (B) of paragraph (6) of subdivision (a) of Section 68511.3 of the Government Code for the waiver of a filing fee.

(2) The court shall quash the certification if the court determines that there is insufficient evidence to justify the imposition on the alleged victim's civil liberties caused by the certification.

(3) If the court determines that there is sufficient evidence to justify the imposition on the alleged victim's civil liberties caused by the certification, the court may, in its discretion, do one or more of the following:

(A) Order disbursements from the alleged victim's assets, as are reasonably needed to address the alleged victim's needs.

(B) Appoint a temporary conservator of the alleged victim's estate, where the facts before the court would be sufficient for the appointment of a temporary conservator under Section 2250.

(C) Deny the petition.

(D) Award reasonable attorney's fees to the respondent's attorney from the victim's estate. *(Added by Stats.2000, c. 813 (S.B.1742), § 1. Amended by Stats.2001, c. 232 (A.B. 1517), § 4.)*

Cross References

Declaration defined for purposes of this Chapter, see Probate Code § 2951.

Elder person defined for purposes of this Chapter, see Probate Code § 2951.

Peace officer defined for purposes of this Chapter, see Probate Code § 2951.

Property defined for purposes of this Chapter, see Probate Code § 2951.

§ 2954. Form of declaration

A declaration issued by a peace officer under this chapter shall not be valid unless it substantially complies with the following form:

DECLARATION

PRINT OR TYPE

1. My name is: _____.
   My badge number is: _____.
   My office address and telephone number are:
   _____
   _____
   _____

2. I am a duly sworn peace officer presently employed by
   _____
   _____, in the County of
   _____, in the State of California.

3. On _____ (date) I personally interviewed
   _____ (victim) at _____ a.m./p.m. at
   _____ (address). The victim resides at
   _____ (address, telephone number, and name of facility, if applicable).

4. There is probable cause to believe that:
   (a) _____ (Victim) is substantially unable to manage his or her financial resources or to resist fraud or undue influence, and

(b) There exists a significant danger the victim will lose all or a portion of his or her property as a result of fraud or misrepresentations or the mental incapacity of the victim, and

(c) There is probable cause to believe that a crime is being committed against the victim, and

(d) The crime is connected to the victim's inability to manage his or her financial resources or to resist fraud or undue influence, and

(e) The victim suffers from that inability as a result of deficits in one or more of the following mental functions:

INSTRUCTIONS TO PEACE OFFICER: CHECK ALL BOXES THAT APPLY:

[A] ALERTNESS AND ATTENTION

☐ 1. Levels of arousal. (Lethargic, responds only to vigorous and persistent stimulation, stupor.)

☐ 2. Orientation. Person _____ Time _____ (day, date, month, season, year), Place _____ (address, town, state), Situation _____ (why am I here?).

☐ 3. Ability to attend and concentrate. (Give detailed answers from memory, mental ability required to thread a needle.)

[B] INFORMATION PROCESSING
Ability to:

☐ 1. Remember, i.e., short- and long-term memory, immediate recall. (Deficits reflected by: forgets question before answering, cannot recall names, relatives, past presidents, events of past 24 hours.)

☐ 2. Understand and communicate either verbally or otherwise. (Deficits reflected by: inability to comprehend questions, follow instructions, use words correctly or name objects; nonsense words.)

☐ 3. Recognize familiar objects and persons. (Deficits reflected by: inability to recognize familiar faces, objects, etc.)

☐ 4. Understand and appreciate quantities. (Perform simple calculations.)

☐ 5. Reason using abstract concepts. (Grasp abstract aspects of his or her situation; interpret idiomatic expressions or proverbs.)

☐ 6. Plan, organize, and carry out actions (assuming physical ability) in one's own rational self-interest. (Break complex tasks down into simple steps and carry them out.)

☐ 7. Reason logically.

[C] THOUGHT DISORDERS

☐ 1. Severely disorganized thinking. (Rambling, nonsensical, incoherent, or nonlinear thinking.)

☐ 2. Hallucinations. (Auditory, visual, olfactory.)

☐ 3. Delusions. (Demonstrably false belief maintained without or against reason or evidence.)

☐ 4. Uncontrollable or intrusive thoughts. (Unwanted compulsive thoughts, compulsive behavior.)

[D] ABILITY TO MODULATE MOOD AND AFFECT
Pervasive and persistent or recurrent emotional state which appears severely inappropriate in degree to the patient's circumstances. Encircle the inappropriate mood(s):

Anger	Euphoria	Helplessness
Anxiety	Depression	Apathy

Fear	Hopelessness	Indifference
Panic	Despair	

5. The property at risk is identified as, but not limited to, the following:
   Bank account located at: _____

   (name, telephone number, and
address of the bank branch)

   Account number(s):_____

   Securities/other funds located at: _____

   (name, telephone number,
and address of
financial institution)

   Account number(s): _____

   Real property located at: _____

   (address)

   Automobile described as: _____

   (make, model/color)

   _____

   (license plate number and state)

   Other property described as: _____
   Other property located at: _____
6. A criminal investigation will ☐ will not ☐ be commenced
   against: _____

   (name, address, and telephone number)

   for alleged financial abuse.
   BLOCKS 1, 2, AND 3 MUST BE CHECKED IN
   ORDER FOR THIS DECLARATION TO BE VALID:

   ☐ 1. I am a peace officer in the county identified above.

   ☐ 2. I have consulted concerning this case with a supervisor in the county's adult protective services agency who has signed below, indicating that he or she concurs that, based on the information I provided to him or her, or based on information he or she obtained independently, this declaration is warranted under the circumstances.

   ☐ 3. I have consulted concerning this case with an individual qualified to perform a mental status examination.

   _____

   Signature of Declarant Peace Officer

   _____

   Date

   _____

   Signature of Concurring Adult Protective Services Supervisor

(Added by Stats.2000, c. 813 (S.B.1742), § 1.)

Cross References

Declaration defined for purposes of this Chapter, see Probate Code § 2951.
Financial abuse defined for purposes of this Chapter, see Probate Code § 2951.
Peace officer defined for purposes of this Chapter, see Probate Code § 2951.
Property defined for purposes of this Chapter, see Probate Code § 2951.

§ 2955. Powers of public guardian to undertake other proceedings

Nothing in this chapter shall prohibit or restrict a public guardian from undertaking any other proceeding authorized by law. *(Added by Stats.2000, c. 813 (S.B.1742), § 1.)*

Part 6

MANAGEMENT OR DISPOSITION OF COMMUNITY PROPERTY WHERE SPOUSE LACKS LEGAL CAPACITY

Law Revision Commission Comments

1990 Enactment

This part supersedes Part 6 (commencing with Section 3000) of Division 4 of the repealed Probate Code. The superseded part was enacted upon recommendation of the California Law Revision Commission. See Recommendation Relating to Guardianship–Conservatorship Law, 14 Cal.L. Revision Comm'n Reports 501 (1978). See also Report of Assembly Committee on Judiciary on Assembly Bills Nos. 261 and 167, republished in 15 Cal.L. Revision Comm'n Reports 1061, 1089–91 (1980). For the Guardianship–Conservatorship Law as enacted in 1979 (Chapter 726 of the Statutes of 1979) with the revisions made by Chapters 89 and 246 of the Statutes of 1980, see Guardianship–Conservatorship Law, 15 Cal.L. Revision Comm'n Reports 451 (1980). [20 Cal.L.Rev.Comm.Reports 1001 (1990)].

Cross References

Management and control of community property, one or both spouses having conservator of estate or lacking legal capacity, see Family Code § 1103.

CHAPTER 1. DEFINITIONS AND
GENERAL PROVISIONS

ARTICLE 1. DEFINITIONS

§ 3000. Application of definitions

Unless the provision or context otherwise requires, the definitions contained in this article govern the construction of this part. *(Stats.1990, c. 79 (A.B.759), § 14, operative July 1, 1991.)*

Law Revision Commission Comments

1990 Enactment

Section 3000 continues Section 3000 of the repealed Probate Code without change. For background on the provisions of this part, see the Comment to this part under the part heading. [20 Cal.L.Rev.Comm.Reports 1001 (1990)].

Cross References

Application of chapter regarding powers and duties of guardians or conservators of the estate, see Probate Code § 2407.

§ 3002. Community property

"Community property" means community real property and community personal property, including, but not limited to, a community property business that is or was under the primary management and control of one of the spouses. *(Stats.1990, c. 79 (A.B.759), § 14, operative July 1, 1991. Amended by Stats.1992, c. 163 (A.B.2641), § 125, operative Jan. 1, 1994; Stats.1996, c. 877 (A.B.1467), § 1.)*

Law Revision Commission Comments

1990 Enactment

Section 3002 continues Section 3002 of the repealed Probate Code without substantive change. The phrase "primary management and control" has been substituted for "sole management and control" to conform to the language used in Civil Code Section 5125(d).

Community property includes business property notwithstanding the fact that a spouse now lacking legal capacity formerly had primary management and control of the business. See Civil Code § 5125(d). The property may be community property notwithstanding that title is held in some other form. W. Johnstone, G. Zillgitt, & S. House, California Conservatorships § 11.11, at 653 (Cal. Cont.Ed.Bar 2d ed. 1983); see also 7 B. Witkin, Summary of California Law Community Property §§ 49–50, at 5140–42 (8th ed. 1974). Even though community property in a revocable trust described in Section 5110.150 of the Civil Code remains community property, it is excluded from the provisions of this part because the trust property is administered pursuant to the trust.

For background on the provisions of this part, see the Comment to this part under the part heading. [20 Cal.L.Rev.Comm.Reports 1001 (1990)].

1992 Amendment

Section 3002 is amended to substitute a reference to the Family Code provision that replaced former Civil Code Section 5110.150. [22 Cal.L.Rev.Comm.Reports 1 (1992)].

Cross References

Community property business under the sole management and control of one of the spouses, see Family Code § 1100.

§ 3004. Conservator

"Conservator" means conservator of the estate, or limited conservator of the estate to the extent that the powers and duties of the limited conservator are specifically and expressly provided by the order appointing the limited conservator, and includes the guardian of the estate of a married minor. *(Stats.1990, c. 79 (A.B.759), § 14, operative July 1, 1991.)*

Law Revision Commission Comments

1990 Enactment

Section 3004 continues Section 3004 of the repealed Probate Code without change. Conservator of the estate includes a person appointed as conservator of the person and estate. For background on the provisions of this part, see the Comment to this part under the part heading. [20 Cal.L.Rev.Comm.Reports 1001 (1990)].

Cross References

Limited conservator, appointment, see Probate Code §§ 1801, 1828.5.

Order appointing limited conservator, contents, see Probate Code § 1830.

§ 3006. Conservatorship estate

"Conservatorship estate" includes the guardianship estate of a married minor. *(Stats.1990, c. 79 (A.B.759), § 14, operative July 1, 1991.)*

Law Revision Commission Comments

1990 Enactment

Section 3006 continues Section 3006 of the repealed Probate Code without change. For background on the provisions of this part, see the Comment to this part under the part heading. [20 Cal.L.Rev.Comm.Reports 1001 (1990)].

§ 3008. Conservatorship proceeding

"Conservatorship proceeding" means conservatorship of the estate proceeding and includes a guardianship of the estate proceeding of a married minor. *(Stats.1990, c. 79 (A.B.759), § 14, operative July 1, 1991.)*

Law Revision Commission Comments

1990 Enactment

Section 3008 continues Section 3008 of the repealed Probate Code without change. For background on the provisions of this part, see the Comment to this part under the part heading. [20 Cal.L.Rev.Comm.Reports 1001 (1990)].

§ 3010. Repealed by Stats.1982, c. 497, p. 2209, § 147, operative July 1, 1983

§ 3012. Legal capacity with respect to community property

(a) Unless the spouse lacks legal capacity under the applicable standard prescribed in subdivision (b), a spouse has legal capacity to:

(1) Manage and control community property, including legal capacity to dispose of community property.

(2) Join in or consent to a transaction involving community property.

(b) A spouse lacks legal capacity to:

(1) Manage and control, including legal capacity to dispose of, community property if the spouse is substantially unable to manage or control the community property.

(2) Join in or consent to a transaction involving community property if the spouse does not have legal capacity for the particular transaction measured by principles of law otherwise applicable to the particular transaction.

(3) Do any act, or engage in any activity, described in paragraph (1) or (2) if the spouse has a conservator.

(c) Nothing in this section shall be construed to deny a spouse, whether or not lacking legal capacity, any of the following:

(1) The right to control an allowance provided under Section 2421.

(2) The right to control wages or salary to the extent provided in Section 2601.

(3) The right to make a will.

(4) The right to enter into transactions to the extent reasonable to provide the necessities of life to the spouse, the

other spouse, and the minor children of the spouses. *(Stats. 1990, c. 79 (A.B.759), § 14, operative July 1, 1991.)*

Law Revision Commission Comments

1990 Enactment

Section 3012 continues Section 3012 of the repealed Probate Code without change. This section governs the construction of this part. See Section 3000. The legal capacity of a conservatee for other purposes is governed by Sections 1870–1910 (legal capacity of conservatee).

Subdivision (a) is based on the presumption that a spouse has legal capacity, and its effect is to impose the burden of proof on a person seeking to show lack of legal capacity.

Subdivision (b)(3) implements the policy that a conservator of the estate acts for the conservatee under this part. See Section 3004 (defining "conservator"). This rule is consistent with the duty of the conservator to manage and control the conservatorship estate and provides needed certainty for property transactions.

Subdivision (b)(1) recognizes that a spouse not having a conservator may lack legal capacity to manage, control, and dispose of community property and adopts the rule that such a spouse lacks such legal capacity if the spouse is substantially unable to manage or control the community property. The standard of substantial inability is consistent with the grounds for appointment of a conservator. See Section 1801(b) (person substantially unable to manage his or her own financial resources).

Subdivision (b)(2) recognizes that a spouse not having a conservator may lack legal capacity to join in or consent to a particular transaction under principles of law otherwise applicable. See, e.g., Civil Code §§ 38, 39. Whether the spouse lacks legal capacity for the particular purpose depends on the act involved and the standards otherwise applicable to determine capacity for that act.

Subdivision (c) is comparable to Section 1871. See the Comment to Section 1871.

For background on the provisions of this part, see the Comment to this part under the part heading. [20 Cal.L.Rev.Comm.Reports 1001 (1990)].

Cross References

Community property defined for purposes of this Part, see Probate Code § 3002.

Conservator defined for purposes of this Part, see Probate Code § 3004.

Legal capacity of conservatee for other purposes, see Probate Code § 1870 et seq.

ARTICLE 2.   GENERAL PROVISIONS

§ 3020.   Preservation of community property interests

(a) The proceeds, rents, issues, and profits of community property dealt with or disposed of under this division, and any property taken in exchange for the community property or acquired with the proceeds, are community property.

(b) Except as provided in this part for the management, control, and disposition of community property, nothing in this division alters the rights of the spouses in community property or in the proceeds, rents, issues, or profits of community property. *(Stats.1990, c. 79 (A.B.759), § 14, operative July 1, 1991.)*

Law Revision Commission Comments

1990 Enactment

Section 3020 continues Section 3020 of the repealed Probate Code without change. For background on the provisions of this part, see the Comment to this part under the part heading. [20 Cal.L.Rev.Comm.Reports 1001 (1990)].

Cross References

Community property defined for purposes of this Part, see Probate Code § 3002.

Management, control, and disposition of community property, see Probate Code § 3051.

§§ 3021, 3022.   Repealed by Stats.1982, c. 497, p. 2210, §§ 149, 150, operative July 1, 1983

§ 3023.   Determination of character of property

(a) Except as provided in subdivisions (b) and (c), where one or both of the spouses has a conservator, the court in which any of the conservatorship proceedings is pending may hear and determine whether property is community property or the separate property of either spouse when the issue is raised in any proceeding under this division.

(b) Any person having or claiming title to or an interest in the property, at or prior to the hearing on the issue, may object to the hearing if the court is not the proper court under any other provision of law for the trial of an action to determine the issue. If the objection is established, the court shall not hear and determine the issue.

(c) Except as provided in subdivision (d), if a civil action is pending with respect to the issue and jurisdiction has been obtained in the court in which the civil action is pending, upon request of any party to the civil action, the court shall abate the hearing until the conclusion of the civil action.

(d) The court need not abate the hearing if the court determines that the civil action was filed for the purpose of delay. *(Stats.1990, c. 79 (A.B.759), § 14, operative July 1, 1991.)*

Law Revision Commission Comments

1990 Enactment

Section 3023 continues Section 3023 of the repealed Probate Code with the addition of subdivision (d) which is comparable to subdivision (b) of Section 2525 (conveyance or transfer of property claimed to belong to ward or conservatee or other person). Subdivision (c) has been modified to reflect the addition of subdivision (d).

Section 3023 applies to all proceedings under this division where an issue is raised whether property is community or separate property. The section is consistent with the holding in In re Baglione's Estate, 65 Cal.2d 192, 417 P.2d 683, 53 Cal.Rptr. 139 (1966) (probate court has jurisdiction in decedent's estate proceeding to determine interest of each spouse in community property). For background on the provisions of this part, see the Comment to this part under the part heading. [20 Cal.L.Rev.Comm.Reports 1001 (1990)].

Cross References

Community property defined for purposes of this Part, see Probate Code § 3002.

Conservator defined for purposes of this Part, see Probate Code § 3004.

Conservatorship proceeding defined for purposes of this Part, see Probate Code § 3008.

Nature of property in proceeding for particular transaction, determination, see Probate Code § 3101.

Title to property of decedent, see Probate Code § 9860.

§ 3024. Repealed by Stats.1997, c. 724 (A.B.1172), § 14

CHAPTER 2. MANAGEMENT, CONTROL, AND DISPOSITION

ARTICLE 1. MANAGEMENT, CONTROL, AND DISPOSITION GENERALLY

§ 3051. Community property

(a) Subject to Section 3071, the right of a spouse to manage and control community property, including the right to dispose of community property, is not affected by the lack or alleged lack of legal capacity of the other spouse.

(b) Except as provided in subdivision (c), if one spouse has legal capacity and the other has a conservator:

(1) The spouse who has legal capacity has the exclusive management and control of the community property including, subject to Section 3071, the exclusive power to dispose of the community property.

(2) The community property is not part of the conservatorship estate.

(c) If one spouse has legal capacity and the other has a conservator, the spouse having legal capacity may consent, by a writing filed in the proceeding, that all or part of the community property be included in and, subject to Section 3071, be managed, controlled, and disposed of as a part of the conservatorship estate.

(d) Except as provided in subdivision (e), if both spouses have conservators, an undivided one-half interest in the community property shall be included in and, subject to Section 3071, be managed, controlled, and disposed of as a part of the conservatorship estate of each spouse.

(e) If both spouses have conservators, when authorized by order of the court in which any of the conservatorship proceedings is pending, the conservators may agree in writing that all or specific parts of the community property shall be included in the conservatorship estate of one or the other of the spouses and, subject to Section 3071, be managed, controlled, and disposed of as a part of the conservatorship estate of that spouse. *(Stats.1990, c. 79 (A.B.759), § 14, operative July 1, 1991.)*

Law Revision Commission Comments
1990 Enactment

Section 3051 continues Section 3051 of the repealed Probate Code without change. Subdivisions (a) and (b) make clear that the lack of legal capacity of one spouse does not affect the right of the spouse having legal capacity to manage and control community property or to dispose of the property, whether or not the other spouse has a conservator. As to when a spouse lacks legal capacity, see Section 3012. The authority given the spouse having legal capacity is limited by Section 3071 which applies in any case where joinder or consent would be required for a transaction if both spouses had legal capacity. The spouse having legal capacity has the duty of good faith in managing and controlling the property. See Section 3057; Civil Code § 5125(e).

Community property is defined in Section 3002 to include both real and personal property, and to include a community property business. Such a business, even if formerly managed by a spouse now lacking legal capacity, is included in the management, control, and disposition provisions of this section.

If both spouses have conservators, the approval of only one of the courts in which the conservatorship proceedings are pending is required under subdivision (e). However, if the other conservatorship proceeding is pending in another court, that court may order that the community property not be included in that conservatorship estate (Section 3054) and, if the court so orders, subdivision (d) of Section 3051 applies. Similarly, if a spouse having legal capacity consents as provided in subdivision (c) to inclusion of property in the conservatorship estate of the other spouse, the court in which the conservatorship proceeding is pending may nevertheless order that the property not be included in the conservatorship estate. See Section 3054.

Section 3051 applies only where one spouse has legal capacity or both spouses have conservators. The section does not cover the situation where both spouses lack legal capacity and neither or only one has a conservator. In these situations, since Section 3051 applies only if both spouses lacking legal capacity have conservators, a conservator or conservators will need to be appointed in order to make the section applicable.

For background on the provisions of this part, see the Comment to this part under the part heading. [20 Cal.L.Rev.Comm.Reports 1001 (1990)].

Cross References

Community property, succession, see Probate Code § 100 et seq.

Community property defined for purposes of this Part, see Probate Code § 3002.

Community property interests, extent to which affected, see Probate Code § 3020.

Conservator defined for purposes of this Part, see Probate Code § 3004.

Conservatorship estate defined for purposes of this Part, see Probate Code § 3006.

Conservatorship proceeding defined for purposes of this Part, see Probate Code § 3008.

Determination whether property community or separate, see Probate Code § 3023.

Duty of good faith in managing and controlling property, see Family Code § 1100.

Legal capacity of spouse, see Probate Code § 3012.

Protection of rights of spouse lacking legal capacity, see Probate Code § 3057.

§§ 3052, 3053. Repealed by Stats.1982, c. 497, p. 2210, §§ 152, 153, operative July 1, 1983

§ 3054. Authority of court

When community property is included or proposed to be included in the conservatorship estate of a spouse, the court in which the conservatorship proceeding is pending, upon its own motion or upon petition of a spouse having legal capacity or the conservator of either spouse and upon such notice to such persons as the court prescribes, may do any of the following:

(a) Determine that the inclusion of some or all of the community property that is proposed to be included in the conservatorship estate would not be in the best interest of the spouses or their estates and order that such property not be included.

(b) Permit revocation of a written consent for inclusion of property in the conservatorship estate, with or without terms or conditions.

(c) Determine that the continued inclusion of some or all of the community property in the conservatorship estate is not in the best interest of the spouses or their estates and order that the inclusion of such property in the conservatorship estate be terminated, with or without terms or conditions.

(d) Make such other orders as may be appropriate for the orderly administration of the conservatorship estate or to protect the interests of the spouses. *(Stats.1990, c. 79 (A.B.759), § 14, operative July 1, 1991.)*

Law Revision Commission Comments

1990 Enactment

Section 3054 continues Section 3054 of the repealed Probate Code without change. This section states the powers of the court as to receipt and handling of additional assets under this chapter, and recognizes the right to revoke consent to administration in one of the conservatorship estates. For general provisions, see Sections 1000–1004 (rules of practice), 1020–1023 (petitions and other papers), 1040–1050 (hearings and orders). For general provisions relating to notice of hearing, see Sections 1200–1221. See also Sections 1260–1265 (proof of giving notice).

For background on the provisions of this part, see the Comment to this part under the part heading. [20 Cal.L.Rev.Comm.Reports 1001 (1990)].

Cross References

Community property defined for purposes of this Part, see Probate Code § 3002.
Community property interests, extent to which affected, see Probate Code § 3020.
Conservator defined for purposes of this Part, see Probate Code § 3004.
Conservatorship estate defined for purposes of this Part, see Probate Code § 3006.
Conservatorship proceeding defined for purposes of this Part, see Probate Code § 3008.
Determination whether property is community or separate, see Probate Code § 3023.
Legal capacity defined, see Probate Code § 3012.

§ 3055. Effect on consent of death or subsequent lack of legal capacity

(a) If consent is given under this article that community property be included in the conservatorship estate of a spouse, the death of either spouse terminates the consent.

(b) If a spouse consents under this article that community property be included in the conservatorship estate of the other spouse:

(1) Subject to paragraph (2), the subsequent lack of legal capacity of the spouse giving the consent has no effect on the inclusion of the property in the conservatorship estate of the other spouse.

(2) The appointment of a conservator for the spouse giving the consent terminates the consent. *(Stats.1990, c. 79 (A.B.759), § 14, operative July 1, 1991.)*

Law Revision Commission Comments

1990 Enactment

Section 3055 continues Section 3055 of the repealed Probate Code without change. If a conservator is appointed for a spouse that has given consent to inclusion of community property in the conservatorship estate of the other spouse, the appointment terminates the consent. But the two conservators may, when authorized by order of court, consent that the property continue to be included in the same conservatorship estate, or they may work out some other arrangement for administration of the property as part of a plan for administration of the community property of the two spouses. See Section 3051(d)–(e). As to revocation of consent or termination of inclusion of property in a conservatorship estate, see Section 3054. For background on the provisions of this part, see the Comment to this part under the part heading. [20 Cal.L.Rev.Comm.Reports 1001 (1990)].

Cross References

Community property defined for purposes of this Part, see Probate Code § 3002.
Conservator defined for purposes of this Part, see Probate Code § 3004.
Conservatorship estate defined for purposes of this Part, see Probate Code § 3006.
Legal capacity defined, see Probate Code § 3012.

§ 3056. Manner of management, control and disposition of property or a part of conservatorship estate

Except as otherwise provided in this part and subject to Section 3071, when community property is included in a conservatorship estate under this article for the purpose of management, control, and disposition, the conservator has the same powers and duties with respect to such property as the conservator has with respect to other property of the conservatorship estate. *(Stats.1990, c. 79 (A.B.759), § 14, operative July 1, 1991.)*

Law Revision Commission Comments

1990 Enactment

Section 3056 continues Section 3056 of the repealed Probate Code without change. It makes applicable to the property included in a conservatorship estate under this article the provisions of Part 4 (commencing with Section 2100) and any other applicable provisions. The introductory clause of Section 3056 recognizes the limitations on disposition imposed by Section 3071 (substitute for joinder or consent requirement) and by other provisions such as Sections 3020 (community property interests not affected), 3054 (authority of court), and 3055 (effect on consent of death or subsequent lack of legal capacity). See also Section 3057 (protection of rights of spouse who lacks legal capacity). For background on the provisions of this part, see the Comment to this part under the part heading. [20 Cal.L.Rev.Comm.Reports 1001 (1990)].

COMMUNITY PROPERTY MANAGEMENT

Cross References

Community property defined for purposes of this Part, see Probate Code § 3002.

Conservator defined for purposes of this Part, see Probate Code § 3004.

Conservatorship estate defined for purposes of this Part, see Probate Code § 3006.

§ 3057. Protection of rights of spouse lacking legal capacity

(a) Where a spouse lacks legal capacity and does not have a conservator, any interested person who has knowledge or reason to believe that the rights of such spouse in the community property are being prejudiced may bring an action on behalf of such spouse to enforce the duty imposed by Sections 721 and 1100 of the Family Code with respect to the management and control of the community property and to obtain such relief as may be appropriate.

(b) If one spouse has a conservator and the other spouse is managing or controlling community property, the conservator has the duty to keep reasonably informed concerning the management and control, including the disposition, of the community property. If the conservator has knowledge or reason to believe that the rights of the conservatee in the community property are being prejudiced, the conservator may bring an action on behalf of the conservatee to enforce the duty imposed by Sections 721 and 1100 of the Family Code with respect to the management and control of the community property and to obtain such relief as may be appropriate. *(Stats.1990, c. 79 (A.B.759), § 14, operative July 1, 1991. Amended by Stats.1992, c. 163 (A.B.2641), § 126, operative Jan. 1, 1994.)*

Law Revision Commission Comments

1990 Enactment

Section 3057 continues Section 3057 of the repealed Probate Code without change. As to the duty or good faith in managing and controlling community property, see Civil Code Section 5125(e). For background on the provisions of this part, see the Comment to this part under the part heading. [20 Cal.L.Rev.Comm.Reports 1001 (1990)].

1992 Amendment

Section 3057 is amended to substitute a reference to the relevant Family Code provisions in place of the former reference to the "duty of good faith." The relevant provisions of the Civil Code, now compiled in the Family Code, were amended in 1991 to replace the "duty of good faith" with "the general rules governing fiduciary relationships which control the actions of persons having relationships of personal confidence as specified in Section 721" of the Family Code. See Section 1100(e) of the Family Code. [22 Cal.L.Rev.Comm.Reports 1 (1992)].

Cross References

Community property defined for purposes of this Part, see Probate Code § 3002.

Conservator defined for purposes of this Part, see Probate Code § 3004.

Definitions,
Interested person, see Probate Code § 1424.
Legal capacity, see Probate Code § 3012.

Duty of good faith in managing and controlling community property, see Family Code § 1100.

ARTICLE 2. SUBSTITUTE FOR JOINDER OR CONSENT REQUIREMENTS

Section
3070. Satisfaction or requirements of this article; effect on other statutes.
3071. Satisfaction of joinder or consent requirements.
3072. Joinder or consent by conservator; authority; court order.
3073. Manner of joinder or consent.
3074. Good faith purchaser or encumbrancer for value.

§ 3070. Satisfaction or requirements of this article; effect on other statutes

If the requirements of this article are satisfied with respect to a transaction described in Section 3071, the transaction is deemed to satisfy the joinder or consent requirements of the statute referred to in that section. *(Stats.1990, c. 79 (A.B. 759), § 14, operative July 1, 1991.)*

Law Revision Commission Comments

1990 Enactment

Section 3070 continues Section 3070 of the repealed Probate Code without change. This section makes clear that a transaction that satisfies the provisions of this article is deemed to satisfy the joinder or consent requirement of the Civil Code sections or other statutory provision referred to in Section 3071. For background on the provisions of this part, see the Comment to this part under the part heading. [20 Cal.L.Rev.Comm.Reports 1001 (1990)].

§ 3071. Satisfaction of joinder or consent requirements

(a) In case of a transaction for which the joinder or consent of both spouses is required by Section 1100 or 1102 of the Family Code or by any other statute, if one or both spouses lacks legal capacity for the transaction, the requirement of joinder or consent shall be satisfied as provided in this section.

(b) Where one spouse has legal capacity for the transaction and the other spouse has a conservator, the requirement of joinder or consent is satisfied if both of the following are obtained:

(1) The joinder or consent of the spouse having legal capacity.

(2) The joinder or consent of the conservator of the other spouse given in compliance with Section 3072.

(c) Where both spouses have conservators, the joinder or consent requirement is satisfied by the joinder or consent of each such conservator given in compliance with Section 3072.

(d) In any case, the requirement of joinder or consent is satisfied if the transaction is authorized by an order of court obtained in a proceeding pursuant to Chapter 3 (commencing with Section 3100). *(Stats.1990, c. 79 (A.B.759), § 14, operative July 1, 1991. Amended by Stats.1992, c. 163 (A.B.2641), § 127, operative Jan. 1, 1994.)*

Law Revision Commission Comments
1990 Enactment

Section 3071 continues Section 3071 of the repealed Probate Code without change. Civil Code Section 5127 requires joint action by spouses with regard to disposition of community real property (lease for a longer period than one year or sale, conveyance, or encumbrance). The reference to Civil Code Section 5125, which requires joint action of spouses for certain community personal property transactions, applies to such matters as gifts of personal property and disposition of furniture and furnishings where consent is required by Civil Code Section 5125(b) and (c). For the manner in which joinder in or consent to the transaction under Section 3071 is to be given, see Section 3073. For background on the provisions of this part, see the Comment to this part under the part heading.

A spouse having a conservator of the estate is deemed to lack legal capacity for the purposes of this section. Section 3012(b)(3). However, a third person acting in good faith and for a valuable consideration is protected unless notice of establishment of the conservatorship is recorded. Section 3074.

If a spouse lacks legal capacity and does not have a conservator, either:

(1) A conservator must be appointed for that spouse so the conservator can join in or consent to the transaction in order to satisfy subdivision (b) or (c); or

(2) A proceeding may be brought under Chapter 3 (commencing with Section 3100) to authorize the transaction, thereby avoiding the need to appoint a conservator, if the other spouse has legal capacity for the transaction or has a conservator. [20 Cal.L.Rev.Comm.Reports 1001 (1990)].

1992 Amendment

Subdivision (a) of Section 3071 is amended to substitute a reference to the Family Code provisions that replaced former Civil Code Sections 5125 and 5127. [22 Cal.L.Rev.Comm.Reports 1 (1992)].

Cross References

Community property, succession, see Probate Code § 100 et seq.
Conservator defined for purposes of this Part, see Probate Code § 3004.
Legal capacity, see Probate Code § 3012.
Management, control, and disposition of community property, see Probate Code § 3051.
Manner of management, control and disposition of property or a part of conservatorship estate, see Probate Code § 3056.

§ 3072. Joinder or consent by conservator; authority; court order

(a) Except as provided in subdivision (b), a conservator may join in or consent to a transaction under Section 3071 only after authorization by either of the following:

(1) An order of the court obtained in the conservatorship proceeding upon a petition filed pursuant to Section 2403 or under Article 7 (commencing with Section 2540) or 10 (commencing with Section 2580) of Chapter 6 of Part 4.

(2) An order of the court made in a proceeding pursuant to Chapter 3 (commencing with Section 3100).

(b) A conservator may consent without court authorization to a sale, conveyance, or encumbrance of community personal property requiring consent under subdivision (c) of Section 1100 of the Family Code if the conservator could sell or transfer the property under Section 2545 without court authorization if the property were a part of the conservatorship estate. *(Stats.1990, c. 79 (A.B.759), § 14, operative July*

1, 1991. Amended by Stats.1992, c. 163 (A.B.2641), § 128, operative Jan. 1, 1994; Stats.1993, c. 219 (A.B.1500), § 223.)

Law Revision Commission Comments
1990 Enactment

Section 3072 continues Section 3072 of the repealed Probate Code without change. Subdivision (b) provides an exception to the requirement of a court order in certain cases where consent for a transaction involving community personal property is required. See Civil Code § 5125(c); Prob.Code § 2545. Subdivision (b) does not, however, dispense with the need for court authorization for the conservator to join in or consent to a gift of community personal property or a disposition of community personal property without valuable consideration under subdivision (b) of Civil Code Section 5125. See also Sections 3122(d)(4), 3144(b). For background on the provisions of this part, see the Comment to this part under the part heading. [20 Cal.L.Rev.Comm.Reports 1001 (1990)].

1992 Amendment

Subdivision (b) of Section 3072 is amended to substitute a reference to the Family Code provision that replaced former Civil Code Section 5125. [22 Cal.L.Rev.Comm.Reports 1 (1992)].

1993 Amendment

Subdivision (b) of Section 3072 is amended to correct a cross-reference. [23 Cal.L.Rev.Comm. Reports 1 (1993)].

Cross References

Conservator defined for purposes of this Part, see Probate Code § 3004.
Conservatorship estate defined for purposes of this Part, see Probate Code § 3006.
Conservatorship proceeding defined for purposes of this Part, see Probate Code § 3008.
Protection of rights of spouse who lacks legal capacity, see Probate Code § 3057.

§ 3073. Manner of joinder or consent

(a) The joinder or consent under Section 3071 of a spouse having legal capacity shall be in a manner that complies with Section 1100 or 1102 of the Family Code or other statute that applies to the transaction.

(b) The joinder or consent under Section 3071 of a conservator shall be in the same manner as a spouse would join in or consent to the transaction under the statute that applies to the transaction except that the joinder or consent shall be executed by the conservator and shall refer to the court order, if one is required, authorizing the conservator to join in or consent to the transaction. *(Stats.1990, c. 79 (A.B.759), § 14, operative July 1, 1991. Amended by Stats. 1992, c. 163 (A.B.2641), § 129, operative Jan. 1, 1994; Stats.1993, c. 219 (A.B.1500), § 224.)*

Law Revision Commission Comments
1990 Enactment

Section 3073 continues Section 3073 of the repealed Probate Code without change. This section requires that the joinder or consent satisfy the requirements of the statute applicable to the transaction. Civil Code Section 5125 requires written consent of a spouse for certain dispositions of community personal property. Civil Code Section 5127 requires that "both spouses either personally or by duly authorized agent, must join in executing any instrument by which such community real property or any interest therein is leased for a longer period than one year, or is sold, conveyed, or encumbered."

Under Section 3073, a spouse having legal capacity must satisfy the requirements of the statute that applies to the transaction just as if both spouses had legal capacity. If one or both spouses has a conservator, the conservator or conservators must satisfy the requirements of the statute that applies to the transaction and, in addition, subdivision (b) of Section 3073 requires that the joinder or consent refer to the court order (if one is required by Section 3072) authorizing the conservator to join in or consent to the transaction. As to requirements in connection with a conveyance of real property by a conservator and the effect of the conveyance, see Section 2111. For background on the provisions of this part, see the Comment to this part under the part heading. [20 Cal.L.Rev.Comm.Reports 1001 (1990)].

1992 Amendment

Subdivision (a) of Section 3073 is amended to substitute a reference to the Family Code provisions that replaced former Civil Code Sections 5125 and 5127. [22 Cal.L.Rev.Comm.Reports 1 (1992)].

1993 Amendment

Subdivision (a) of Section 3073 is amended to correct cross-references. [23 Cal.L.Rev.Comm. Reports 1 (1993)].

Cross References

Conservator defined for purposes of this Part, see Probate Code § 3004.
Legal capacity, see Probate Code § 3012.

§ 3074. Good faith purchaser or encumbrancer for value

Notwithstanding any other provision of this article, a transaction that affects real property, entered into by a person acting in good faith and for a valuable consideration, is not affected by the fact that one or both spouses have conservators unless a notice of the establishment of the conservatorship or conservatorships, as the case may be, has been recorded prior to the transaction in the county in which the property is located. *(Stats.1990, c. 79 (A.B.759), § 14, operative July 1, 1991.)*

Law Revision Commission Comments

1990 Enactment

Section 3074 continues Section 3074 of the repealed Probate Code without change, except that the section is revised to extend to any person who enters into a transaction in good faith and for a valuable consideration, not only purchasers or encumbrancers. This section protects innocent third parties who do not have knowledge of the existence of the conservatorship. The section is comparable to Section 1875. See the Comment to Section 1875. Nothing in Section 3074 validates a transaction that is invalid under Civil Code Section 38, nor prevents rescission of a transaction under Civil Code Section 39 if the conservatee would lack sufficient capacity to join in or consent to the transaction absent the conservatorship. For background on the provisions of this part, see the Comment to this part under the part heading. [20 Cal.L.Rev.Comm.Reports 1001 (1990)].

Cross References

Conservator defined for purposes of this Part, see Probate Code § 3004.
Mode of recording, see Civil Code § 1169 et seq.

ARTICLE 3. ENFORCEMENT OF SUPPORT OF SPOUSE WHO HAS CONSERVATOR

Section
3080. Petition for order.

Section
3081. Notice of hearing.
3082. Citation to and examination of spouse managing or controlling community property.
3083. Support pendente lite, effect of order; modification or revocation.
3084. Current income, expense and property declarations; service and filing; forms.
3085. Ex parte protective orders.
3086. Continuance; preparation for hearing.
3087. Character of property; determination.
3088. Application of income and principal for support and maintenance; circumstances; periodic payments; jurisdiction to modify or vacate; orders.
3089. Division of community property; transfer of property to conservator of estate; after-acquired property.
3090. Enforcement of orders.
3091. Rules for practice and procedure.
3092. Use of other procedures for enforcement of support obligation; authority.

Law Revision Commission Comments

1990 Enactment

This article supersedes Article 3 (commencing with Section 3080) of Chapter 2 of Part 6 of Division 4 of the repealed Probate Code. The superseded article was enacted upon recommendation of the California Law Revision Commission. See Recommendation Relating to Revision of the Guardianship–Conservatorship Law, 15 Cal.L. Revision Comm'n Reports 1463, 1469–73, 1486–94 (1980). [20 Cal.L.Rev.Comm.Reports 1001 (1990)].

§ 3080. Petition for order

If one spouse has a conservator and the other spouse has the management or control of community property, the conservator or conservatee, a relative or friend of the conservatee, or any interested person may file a petition under this article in the court in which the conservatorship proceeding is pending for an order requiring the spouse who has the management or control of community property to apply the income or principal, or both, of the community property to the support and maintenance of the conservatee as ordered by the court. *(Stats.1990, c. 79 (A.B.759), § 14, operative July 1, 1991.)*

Law Revision Commission Comments

1990 Enactment

Section 3080 continues Section 3080 of the repealed Probate Code without change. Sections 3080–3092 provide a procedure for obtaining an order requiring a spouse managing and controlling community property to apply the property to the support of the spouse having a conservator. A public officer or employee or a public entity may file a petition under this article. See Section 1424 (defining "interested person"). The procedure provided by this article is supplemental to other procedures to enforce the duty of support. Section 3092.

Where an issue is raised in a proceeding under this article whether property is community property or the separate property of either spouse, the court may hear and determine the issue in the proceeding. Section 3087.

For general provisions, see Sections 1000–1004 (rules of practice), 1020–1023 (petitions and other papers), 1040–1050 (hearings and orders). For background on the provisions of this article, see the Comment to this article under the article heading. [20 Cal.L.Rev.Comm.Reports 1001 (1990)].

Cross References

Community property defined for purposes of this Part, see Probate Code § 3002.

Conservator defined for purposes of this Part, see Probate Code § 3004.

Conservatorship proceeding defined for purposes of this Part, see Probate Code § 3008.

§ 3081.   Notice of hearing

(a) Notice of the hearing on the petition shall be given for the period and in the manner provided in Chapter 3 (commencing with Section 1460) of Part 1.

(b) If the spouse who has the management or control of community property is not the conservator, the petitioner shall also cause notice of the hearing and a copy of the petition to be served on that spouse in accordance with Title 5 (commencing with Section 410.10) of Part 2 of the Code of Civil Procedure. *(Stats.1990, c. 79 (A.B.759), § 14, operative July 1, 1991.)*

Law Revision Commission Comments

1990 Enactment

Section 3081 continues Section 3081 of the repealed Probate Code without change. This section is comparable to Section 2521 (property claimed to belong to ward or conservatee). For general provisions relating to notice of hearing, see Sections 1200–1221. See also Sections 1260–1265 (proof of giving notice). For background on the provisions of this article, see the Comment to this article under the article heading. [20 Cal.L.Rev.Comm.Reports 1001 (1990)].

Cross References

Community property defined for purposes of this Part, see Probate Code § 3002.

Conservator defined for purposes of this Part, see Probate Code § 3004.

§ 3082.   Citation to and examination of spouse managing or controlling community property

Upon the filing of a petition under this article, the court may cite the spouse who has the management or control of community property to appear before the court, and the court and the petitioner may examine the spouse under oath concerning the community property and other matters relevant to the petition filed under this article. If the person so cited refuses to appear and submit to an examination, the court may proceed against the person as provided in Article 2 (commencing with Section 8870) of Chapter 2 of Part 3 of Division 7. Upon such examination, the court may make an order requiring the person cited to disclose his or her knowledge of the community property and other matters relevant to the petition filed under this article, and if the order is not complied with the court may proceed against the person as provided in Article 2 (commencing with Section 8870) of Chapter 2 of Part 3 of Division 7. *(Stats.1990, c. 79 (A.B.759), § 14, operative July 1, 1991.)*

Law Revision Commission Comments

1990 Enactment

Section 3082 continues Section 3082 of the repealed Probate Code without change. This section is comparable to Section 2616 (examination concerning assets of guardianship or conservatorship estate). See also Sections 1240–1242 (citations). For background on the

provisions of this article, see the Comment to this article under the article heading. [20 Cal.L.Rev.Comm.Reports 1001 (1990)].

Cross References

Community property defined for purposes of this Part, see Probate Code § 3002.

§ 3083.   Support pendente lite, effect of order; modification or revocation

In any proceeding under this article, the court may, after notice and hearing, order the spouse who has the management or control of community property to pay from the community property such amount as the court determines is necessary to the support and maintenance of the conservatee spouse pending the determination of the petition under this article. An order made pursuant to this section does not prejudice the rights of the spouses or other interested parties with respect to any subsequent order which may be made under this article. Any order made under this section may be modified or revoked at any time except as to any amount that may have accrued prior to the date of filing of the petition to modify or revoke the order. *(Stats.1990, c. 79 (A.B.759), § 14, operative July 1, 1991.)*

Law Revision Commission Comments

1990 Enactment

Section 3083 continues Section 3083 of the repealed Probate Code without substantive change. This section is the same in substance as Civil Code Section 4357 (Family Law Act). The section permits the court to make a temporary order for support if necessary pending determination of the petition. For general provisions, see Sections 1000–1004 (rules of practice), 1040–1050 (hearings and orders). For background on the provisions of this article, see the Comment to this article under the article heading. [20 Cal.L.Rev.Comm.Reports 1001 (1990)].

Cross References

Community property defined for purposes of this Part, see Probate Code § 3002.

§ 3084.   Current income, expense and property declarations; service and filing; forms

When a petition is filed under this article, the spouse having the management or control of community property shall serve and file a current income and expense declaration and a current property declaration on the forms prescribed by the Judicial Council for use in family law proceedings. *(Stats.1990, c. 79 (A.B.759), § 14, operative July 1, 1991.)*

Law Revision Commission Comments

1990 Enactment

Section 3084 continues Section 3084 of the repealed Probate Code without change. The time for serving and filing the financial declarations may be prescribed by Judicial Council rule. Section 3091. For background on the provisions of this article, see the Comment to this article under the article heading. [20 Cal.L.Rev.Comm.Reports 1001 (1990)].

Cross References

Community property defined for purposes of this Part, see Probate Code § 3002.

§ 3085.   Ex parte protective orders

During the pendency of any proceeding under this article, the court, upon the application of the petitioner, may issue ex parte orders:

(a) Restraining the spouse having the management or control of community property from transferring, encumbering, hypothecating, concealing, or in any way disposing of any property, real or personal, whether community, quasi-community, or separate, except in the usual course of business or for the necessities of life.

(b) Requiring the spouse having the management or control of the community property to notify the petitioner of any proposed extraordinary expenditures and to account to the court for all such extraordinary expenditures. *(Stats. 1990, c. 79 (A.B.759), § 14, operative July 1, 1991.)*

Law Revision Commission Comments
1990 Enactment

Section 3085 continues Section 3085 of the repealed Probate Code without change. This section is the same in substance as subdivision (a)(1) of Civil Code Section 4359 (Family Law Act). For background on the provisions of this article, see the Comment to this article under the article heading. [20 Cal.L.Rev.Comm.Reports 1001 (1990)].

Cross References

Community property defined for purposes of this Part, see Probate Code § 3002.

§ 3086. Continuance; preparation for hearing

Any person interested in the proceeding under this article may request time for filing a response to the petition, for discovery proceedings, or for other preparation for the hearing, and the court shall grant a continuance for a reasonable time for any of such purposes. *(Stats.1990, c. 79 (A.B.759), § 14, operative July 1, 1991.)*

Law Revision Commission Comments
1990 Enactment

Section 3086 continues Section 3086 of the repealed Probate Code without change. This section is the same in substance as Section 2522 (property claimed to belong to ward or conservatee). For background on the provisions of this article, see the Comment to this article under the article heading. [20 Cal.L.Rev.Comm.Reports 1001 (1990)].

§ 3087. Character of property; determination

In a proceeding under this article, the court may hear and determine whether property is community property or the separate property of either spouse if that issue is raised in the proceeding. *(Stats.1990, c. 79 (A.B.759), § 14, operative July 1, 1991.)*

Law Revision Commission Comments
1990 Enactment

Section 3087 continues Section 3087 of the repealed Probate Code without change. This section makes clear that the court has jurisdiction to determine whether property is community or separate in a proceeding under this article. The section is consistent with Section 3023 which applies generally to proceedings under this division; but, unlike Section 3023, Section 3087 does not deprive the court of jurisdiction where an objection based on improper venue is raised. Also unlike Section 3023, Section 3087 does not contain an express provision requiring the court to abate a proceeding under this article when another action is pending. However, the general rules of civil procedure with respect to abatement when another action is pending apply to proceedings under this article. See Section 1000.

See generally 5 B. Witkin, California Procedure Pleading §§ 1060–71, at 473–84 (3d ed. 1985). For background on the provisions of this article, see the Comment to this article under the article heading.

Cross References

Community property defined for purposes of this Part, see Probate Code § 3002.

§ 3088. Application of income and principal for support and maintenance; circumstances; periodic payments; jurisdiction to modify or vacate; orders

(a) The court may order the spouse who has the management or control of community property to apply the income or principal, or both, of the community property to the support and maintenance of the conservatee, including care, treatment, and support of a conservatee who is a patient in a state hospital under the jurisdiction of the State Department of State Hospitals or the State Department of Developmental Services, as ordered by the court.

(b) In determining the amount ordered for support and maintenance, the court shall consider the following circumstances of the spouses:

(1) The earning capacity and needs of each spouse.

(2) The obligations and assets, including the separate property, of each spouse.

(3) The duration of the marriage.

(4) The age and health of the spouses.

(5) The standard of living of the spouses.

(6) Any other relevant factors which it considers just and equitable.

(c) At the request of any interested person, the court shall make appropriate findings with respect to the circumstances.

(d) The court may order the spouse who has the management or control of community property to make a specified monthly or other periodic payment to the conservator of the person of the conservatee or to any other person designated in the order. The court may order the spouse required to make the periodic payments to give reasonable security therefor.

(e)(1) The court may order the spouse required to make the periodic payments to assign, to the person designated in the order to receive the payments, that portion of the earnings of the spouse due or to be due in the future as will be sufficient to pay the amount ordered by the court for the support and maintenance of the conservatee. The order operates as an assignment and is binding upon any existing or future employer upon whom a copy of the order is served. The order shall be in the form of an earnings assignment order for support prescribed by the Judicial Council for use in family law proceedings. The employer may deduct the sum of one dollar and fifty cents ($1.50) for each payment made pursuant to the order. Any such assignment made pursuant to court order shall have priority as against any execution or other assignment unless otherwise ordered by the court or unless the other assignment is made pursuant to Chapter 8 (commencing with Section 5200) of Part 5 of Division 9 of the Family Code. No employer shall use any assignment authorized by this subdivision as grounds for the dismissal of that employee.

(2) As used in this subdivision, "employer" includes the United States government and any public entity as defined in Section 811.2 of the Government Code. This subdivision applies to the money and benefits described in Sections 704.110 and 704.113 of the Code of Civil Procedure to the extent that those moneys and benefits are subject to a wage assignment for support under Chapter 4 (commencing with Section 703.010) of Division 2 of Title 9 of Part 2 of the Code of Civil Procedure.

(f) The court retains jurisdiction to modify or to vacate an order made under this section where justice requires, except as to any amount that may have accrued prior to the date of the filing of the petition to modify or revoke the order. At the request of any interested person, the order of modification or revocation shall include findings of fact and may be made retroactive to the date of the filing of the petition to revoke or modify, or to any date subsequent thereto. At least 15 days before the hearing on the petition to modify or vacate the order, the petitioner shall mail a notice of the time and place of the hearing on the petition, accompanied by a copy of the petition, to the spouse who has the management or control of the community property. Notice shall be given for the period and in the manner provided in Chapter 3 (commencing with Section 1460) of Part 1 to any other persons entitled to notice of the hearing under that chapter.

(g) In a proceeding for dissolution of the marriage or for legal separation, the court has jurisdiction to modify or vacate an order made under this section to the same extent as it may modify or vacate an order made in the proceeding for dissolution of the marriage or for legal separation. *(Stats. 1990, c. 79 (A.B.759), § 14, operative July 1, 1991. Amended by Stats.1992, c. 163 (A.B.2641), § 130, operative Jan. 1, 1994; Stats.2004, c. 520 (A.B.2530), § 7; Stats.2012, c. 440 (A.B. 1488), § 51, eff. Sept. 22, 2012.)*

Law Revision Commission Comments

1990 Enactment

Section 3088 continues Section 3088 of the repealed Probate Code without substantive change. Subdivision (a) is comparable to subdivision (a) of Section 2420 (support, maintenance, and education of ward or conservatee). Subdivision (b) is comparable to Civil Code Section 246 (Uniform Civil Liability for Support Act). Subdivision (c) is comparable to the first sentence of the last paragraph of subdivision (a) of Civil Code Section 4801 (Family Law Act).

Subdivision (d) provides for periodic payments, which are to be made to the conservator of the person or other person designated in the order (such as the State Department of Mental Health or the State Department of Developmental Services). The second sentence of subdivision (d) is comparable to the second sentence of the last paragraph of subdivision (a) of Civil Code Section 4801.

Subdivision (e) is comparable to Civil Code Sections 4701 and 4801.6. The first two sentences of subdivision (f) are comparable to Civil Code Section 247 (Uniform Civil Liability of Support Act) and the last paragraph of subdivision (a) of Civil Code Section 4801.

For general provisions, see Sections 1000–1004 (rules of practice), 1040–1050 (hearings and orders). For general provisions relating to notice of hearing, see Sections 1200–1221. See also Sections 1260–1265 (proof of giving notice). For background on the provisions of this article, see the Comment to this article under the article heading. [20 Cal.L.Rev.Comm.Reports 1001 (1990)].

1992 Amendment

Subdivisions (e) of Section 3088 is amended to substitute a reference to the Family Code provisions that replaced the former Civil Code provision. Former Civil Code Section 4701 was repealed by 1989 Cal.Stat. ch. 1359, which enacted Civil Code Sections 4390–4390.19. Civil Code Sections 4390–4390.19 were replaced by Family Code Section 5200 *et seq*.

Other amendments are made in subdivisions (e) and (g) to conform to the terminology of the Family Code. [22 Cal.L.Rev.Comm.Reports 1 (1992)].

Cross References

Assignment of wages, validity and exceptions, see Labor Code § 300.
Community property defined for purposes of this Part, see Probate Code § 3002.
Conservator defined for purposes of this Part, see Probate Code § 3004.
Department of Developmental Services, see Welfare and Institutions Code § 4400 et seq.
Wage garnishment, definitions, see Code of Civil Procedure § 706.011.

§ 3089. Division of community property; transfer of property to conservator of estate; after-acquired property

If the spouse who has the management or control of the community property refuses to comply with any order made under this article or an order made in a separate action to provide support for the conservatee spouse, upon request of the petitioner or other interested person, the court may, in its discretion, divide the community property and the quasi-community property of the spouses, as it exists at the time of division, equally in the same manner as where a marriage is dissolved. If the property is so divided, the property awarded to each spouse is the separate property of that spouse and the court shall order that the property awarded to the conservatee spouse be transferred or paid over to the conservator of the estate of that spouse to be included in the conservatorship estate and be managed, controlled, and disposed of as a part of the conservatorship estate. The fact that property has been divided pursuant to this section has no effect on the nature of property thereafter acquired by the spouses, and the determination whether the thereafter-acquired property is community or separate property shall be made without regard to the fact that property has been divided pursuant to this section. *(Stats.1990, c. 79 (A.B.759), § 14, operative July 1, 1991.)*

Law Revision Commission Comments

1990 Enactment

Section 3089 continues Section 3089 of the repealed Probate Code without change. This section gives the court in which the conservatorship proceeding is pending authority to make an equal division of community and quasi-community property as in a marriage dissolution proceeding. The court has discretion whether to make such a division. The spouse having management or control of community property may consent to all or part of such property being administered in the conservatorship estate. Section 3051(c). Such consent may avoid the need for a division under Section 3089.

The authority to divide community property may not be exercised unless the competent spouse refuses to comply with an order made under this article or in a separate action for support of the conservatee spouse.

The authority granted by Section 3089 is useful, for example, where property awarded to the conservatee spouse is sufficient to provide for support and maintenance of that spouse. Division in such a case will avoid the need for further proceedings to enforce the support obligation from community property. Division of community property does not, however, necessarily eliminate the support obligation of the competent spouse. If community property is acquired by the competent spouse after division of the property, that community property may be ordered applied to support the conservatee under this article or by other procedures. However, a separate action is necessary to obtain future support from separate property of the competent spouse. See Section 3092 and the Comment thereto.

For general provisions, see Sections 1000–1004 (rules of practice), 1020–1023 (petitions and other papers), 1040–1050 (hearings and orders). For general provisions relating to notice of hearing, see Sections 1200–1221. See also Sections 1260–1265 (proof of giving notice). For background on the provisions of this article, see the Comment to this article under the article heading. [20 Cal.L.Rev.Comm.Reports 1001 (1990)].

Cross References

Community property defined for purposes of this Part, see Probate Code § 3002.

Conservator defined for purposes of this Part, see Probate Code § 3004.

Conservatorship estate defined for purposes of this Part, see Probate Code § 3006.

§ 3090. Enforcement of orders

Any order of the court made under this article may be enforced by the court by execution, the appointment of a receiver, contempt, or by such other order or orders as the court in its discretion may from time to time deem necessary. *(Stats.1990, c. 79 (A.B.759), § 14, operative July 1, 1991.)*

Law Revision Commission Comments

1990 Enactment

Section 3090 continues Section 3090 of the repealed Probate Code without change. This section is the same in substance as Section 4380 of the Civil Code (Family Law Act). The section adds to the methods of enforcement (such as wage assignment under Section 3088 or division of community property under Section 3089) that are specifically provided for elsewhere in this article. For background on the provisions of this article, see the Comment to this article under the article heading. [20 Cal.L.Rev.Comm.Reports 1001 (1990)].

§ 3091. Rules for practice and procedure

Notwithstanding any other provision of law, the Judicial Council may provide by rule for the practice and procedure in proceedings under this article. *(Stats.1990, c. 79 (A.B.759), § 14, operative July 1, 1991.)*

Law Revision Commission Comments

1990 Enactment

3091 continues Section 3091 of the repealed Probate Code without change. This section is the same in substance as Civil Code Section 4001 (Family Law Act). For background on the provisions of this article, see the Comment to this article under the article heading.

§ 3092. Use of other procedures for enforcement of support obligation; authority

Nothing in this article affects or limits the right of the conservator or any interested person to institute an action against any person to enforce the duty otherwise imposed by law to support the spouse having a conservator. This article is permissive and in addition to any other procedure other-

wise available to enforce the obligation of support. *(Stats. 1990, c. 79 (A.B.759), § 14, operative July 1, 1991.)*

Law Revision Commission Comments

1990 Enactment

Section 3092 continues Section 3092 of the repealed Probate Code without change. This section makes clear that this article may be used as an alternative to other procedures for enforcement of a support obligation, by a separate action for support against the spouse managing or controlling the community property. If a separate action is pending at the time a proceeding is brought under this article, the general rules of civil procedure relating to abatement apply. See the Comment to Section 3087. The procedure provided in this article cannot be used if support is sought from separate property of the spouse managing and controlling the community property or from some other person; a separate action is necessary. As to enforcement of support generally, see Civil Code §§ 241–254 (Uniform Civil Liability for Support Act). See also Code Civ.Proc. §§ 1650–1699.4 (Revised Uniform Reciprocal Enforcement of Support Act). For background on the provisions of this article, see the Comment to this article under the article heading. [20 Cal.L.Rev.Comm.Reports 1001 (1990)].

Cross References

Conservator defined for purposes of this Part, see Probate Code § 3004.

CHAPTER 3. PROCEEDING FOR PARTICULAR TRANSACTION

Cross References

Trusts funded by court order, see California Rules of Court, Rule 7.903.

ARTICLE 1. GENERAL PROVISIONS

Cross References

Fee for filing petition and opposition papers concerning internal affairs of certain trusts or first accounts of trustees of certain testamentary trusts, see Government Code § 70652.

§ 3100. Transaction

(a) As used in this chapter, "transaction" means a transaction that involves community real or personal property, tangible or intangible, or an interest therein or a lien or encumbrance thereon, including, but not limited to, those transactions with respect thereto as are listed in Section 3102.

(b) However, if a proposed transaction involves property in which a spouse also has a separate property interest, for good cause the court may include that separate property in the transaction. *(Stats.1990, c. 79 (A.B.759), § 14, operative July 1, 1991. Amended by Stats.1996, c. 877 (A.B.1467), § 2.)*

Law Revision Commission Comments

1990 Enactment

Section 3100 continues Section 3100 of the repealed Probate Code without change. For background on the provisions of this part, see the Comment to this part under the part heading. [20 Cal.L.Rev.Comm.Reports 1001 (1990)].

Cross References

Community property,
  Defined, see Probate Code § 3002.
  Succession, see Probate Code § 100 et seq.
Fee for filing petition commencing or opposition papers concerning certain probate proceedings, see Government Code § 70655.
Joinder or consent by conservator, see Probate Code § 3072.
Satisfaction of joinder or consent requirements, see Probate Code § 3071.

§ 3101. Nature of proceeding

(a) A proceeding may be brought under this chapter for a court order authorizing a proposed transaction, whether or not the proposed transaction is one that otherwise would require the joinder or consent of both spouses, if both of the following conditions are satisfied:

(1) One of the spouses is alleged to lack legal capacity for the proposed transaction, whether or not that spouse has a conservator.

(2) The other spouse either has legal capacity for the proposed transaction or has a conservator.

(b) A proceeding may be brought under this chapter for a court order declaring that one or both spouses has legal capacity for a proposed transaction.

(c) One proceeding may be brought under this chapter under both subdivision (a) and subdivision (b).

(d) In a proceeding under this chapter, the court may determine whether the property that is the subject of the proposed transaction is community property or the separate property of either spouse, but such determination shall not be made in the proceeding under this chapter if the court determines that the interest of justice requires that the determination be made in a civil action.

(e) This chapter is permissive and cumulative for the transactions to which it applies. *(Stats.1990, c. 79 (A.B.759), § 14, operative July 1, 1991.)*

Law Revision Commission Comments

1990 Enactment

Section 3101 continues Section 3101 of the repealed Probate Code without change. For the purposes of this chapter, a spouse lacks legal capacity for a transaction if a conservator of the estate has been appointed for the spouse. See Sections 3004 (defining "conservator"), 3012(b)(3) (legal capacity). This is consistent with Section 3071 which requires joinder or consent of the conservator rather than the spouse to a transaction requiring joinder or consent of both spouses. For background on the provisions of this part, see the Comment to this part under the part heading.

Section 3012 (legal capacity) also covers the case where, applying the principles of law otherwise applicable, a spouse not having a conservator of the estate lacks capacity for the particular proposed

transaction that is the subject of the proceeding. See generally Civil Code §§ 38, 39.

The proposed transaction must be one that involves community real or personal property, tangible or intangible, or an interest therein or a lien or encumbrance thereon, including, but not limited to, those transactions with respect thereto as are listed in Section 3102. See Section 3100 (defining "transaction"). See also Section 3002 (defining "community property"). Court authorization may be sought under this chapter in order to satisfy the requirements of Section 3071 (substitute for joinder or consent), or may be sought so that a transaction not requiring joinder or consent of both spouses cannot later be rescinded by someone acting on behalf of a spouse who lacks legal capacity for the transaction.

Approval of a proposed transaction in a proceeding under this chapter avoids the need to establish a conservatorship for a spouse lacking legal capacity merely to accomplish that transaction. Thus, where one spouse has a conservator of the estate and the other spouse lacks legal capacity for the transaction but does not have a conservator, a proceeding may be brought under this chapter to obtain authorization of the transaction, and the need to establish a conservatorship for the other spouse is avoided. See Section 3071. However, in order to bring a proceeding under subdivision (a), there must be at least one spouse having legal capacity for the transaction or there must be a conservator of the estate for one of the spouses. See also Section 3111 and the Comment thereto. Where both spouses have conservators of the estate, the procedure provided in this chapter is available to obtain court authorization as an alternative to the other methods provided in Section 3072.

Subdivision (b) covers the case where a spouse does not have a conservator and it is uncertain whether the spouse has legal capacity for the proposed transaction. The court is requested to determine that the spouse has legal capacity for the transaction. If the court determines the spouse has legal capacity for the transaction and if the other spouse has legal capacity for the transaction, the two spouses can proceed with the transaction without further court authorization as any other married persons having legal capacity. If the other spouse does not have legal capacity for the transaction, the transaction may be authorized under this chapter only if the spouse found to have legal capacity for the transaction is willing to join in or consent to the proposed transaction. See Section 3144.

Subdivision (c) enables a proceeding to be brought under this chapter, for example, to have one spouse declared to have legal capacity for a proposed transaction, to have the other spouse determined to lack legal capacity for the proposed transaction, and to authorize the proposed transaction.

Under subdivision (d), the court has broader authority than under Section 3023 (determination of character of property) because subdivision (d) has no limitations comparable to subdivisions (b) and (c) of Section 3023.

Subdivision (e) makes clear that the procedure provided in this part is not exclusive of other remedies. [20 Cal.L.Rev.Comm.Reports 1001 (1990)].

Cross References

Appointment of conservator for other spouse not required, see Probate Code § 3113.
Community property, succession, see Probate Code § 100 et seq.
Community property defined for purposes of this Part, see Probate Code § 3002.
Conservator defined for purposes of this Part, see Probate Code § 3004.
Determination of validity of character of property, see Probate Code § 3023.
Inconsistent allegations and alternative relief, see Probate Code § 3120.
Legal capacity defined, see Probate Code § 3012.
Order authorizing transaction, see Probate Code § 3144.
Persons who may file or join in petition, see Probate Code § 3111.

Protection of rights of spouse who lacks legal capacity, see Probate Code § 3057.

Satisfaction of joinder or consent requirements, see Probate Code § 3071.

Several proposed transactions may be included in one proceeding, see Probate Code § 3120.

Transaction defined for purposes of this Chapter, see Probate Code § 3100.

§ 3102. Transaction as subject of proceeding

The transactions that may be the subject of a proceeding under this chapter include, but are not limited to:

(a) Sale, conveyance, assignment, transfer, exchange, conveyance pursuant to a preexisting contract, encumbrance by security interest, deed of trust, mortgage, or otherwise, lease, including but not limited to a lease for the exploration for and production of oil, gas, minerals, or other substances, or unitization or pooling with other property for or in connection with such exploration and production.

(b) Assignment, transfer, or conveyance, in whole or in part, in compromise or settlement of an indebtedness, demand, or proceeding to which the property may be subject.

(c) Dedication or conveyance, with or without consideration, of any of the following:

(1) The property to this state or any public entity in this state, or to the United States or any agency or instrumentality of the United States, for any purpose.

(2) An easement over the property to any person for any purpose.

(d) Conveyance, release, or relinquishment to this state or any public entity in this state, with or without consideration, of any access rights to a street, highway, or freeway from the property.

(e) Consent as a lienholder to a dedication, conveyance, release, or relinquishment under subdivision (c) or (d) by the owner of property subject to the lien.

(f) Conveyance or transfer, without consideration, to provide gifts for such purposes, and to such charities, relatives (including one of the spouses), friends, or other objects of bounty, as would be likely beneficiaries of gifts from the spouses. *(Stats.1990, c. 79 (A.B.759), § 14, operative July 1, 1991.)*

Law Revision Commission Comments
1990 Enactment

Section 3102 continues Section 3102 of the repealed Probate Code without substantive change. Subdivisions (c), (d), and (e) are comparable to Section 2556 (power of conservator to dedicate or convey real property or easement).

Subdivision (f) is derived from Section 2580 (substituted judgment). A transaction proposed under subdivision (f) must satisfy the requirements of Sections 2582 and 2583. See Section 3144(b).

For background on the provisions of this part, see the Comment to this part under the part heading. [20 Cal.L.Rev.Comm.Reports 1001 (1990)].

Cross References

Community property, succession, see Probate Code § 100 et seq.
Dedication of real property for public purposes, see Government Code § 7050.
Easements, generally, see Civil Code § 801 et seq.

Lease of property in administration of estates, see Probate Code § 9945.

Liens, generally, see Civil Code § 2872 et seq.

Oil, gas and mineral leases,
Generally, see Public Resources Code § 6801 et seq.
Duration, see Civil Code § 718.

Order authorizing transaction, see Probate Code § 3144.

Power of legislative body to acquire easements for public interest, see Streets and Highways Code § 10102.

Transaction defined for purposes of this Chapter, see Probate Code § 3100.

ARTICLE 2. COMMENCEMENT OF PROCEEDING

Section
3110. Jurisdiction and venue.
3111. Persons authorized to file or join in petition.
3112. Legal capacity of petitioning spouse; determination; authority of court.
3113. Appointment of conservator for other spouse not required.

§ 3110. Jurisdiction and venue

(a) A proceeding under this chapter shall be brought by a petition filed in the superior court.

(b) The proper county for commencement of the proceeding is the county in which a conservatorship proceeding of one of the spouses is pending. If a conservatorship proceeding is not pending, then in either of the following:

(1) The county in which one or both of the spouses resides.

(2) Any other county as may be in the best interests of the spouses. *(Stats.1990, c. 79 (A.B.759), § 14, operative July 1, 1991. Amended by Stats.1994, c. 806 (A.B.3686), § 20.)*

Law Revision Commission Comments
1990 Enactment

Section 3110 continues Section 3110 of the repealed Probate Code without substantive change. Paragraph (3) of subdivision (c) is comparable to a portion of Sections 2201 and 2202 (venue for conservatorship proceeding).

Subdivision (d) requires the proceeding to be commenced in the county where the conservatorship proceedings of both spouses are pending if both spouses have conservators. Since that court will be settling the accounts of the two conservators and otherwise acting on petitions in connection with the conservatorship estates, it is the appropriate court to commence a proceeding under this chapter, even where the proceeding involves real property located in another county. For background on the provisions of this part, see the Comment to this part under the part heading. [20 Cal.L.Rev.Comm.Reports 1001 (1990)].

Cross References

Conservatorship proceeding defined for purposes of this Part, see Probate Code § 3008.
Venue for conservatorship proceeding, see Probate Code §§ 2201, 2202.

§ 3111. Persons authorized to file or join in petition

(a) Except as provided in subdivision (b), any of the following persons may file, or join in, a petition under this chapter:

(1) Either spouse, whether or not the spouse has legal capacity.

(2) The conservator of either spouse.

(b) If the petition requests approval of a proposed transaction, at least one of the petitioners shall be either a conservator or a spouse having legal capacity for the transaction. *(Stats.1990, c. 79 (A.B.759), § 14, operative July 1, 1991.)*

Law Revision Commission Comments

1990 Enactment

Section 3111 continues Section 3111 of the repealed Probate Code without change. Subdivision (b) ensures that, if the proposed transaction is approved, the petitioner will have legal capacity to carry out the court's orders concerning the transaction. Subdivision (b) does not apply where the only relief requested in the petition is a declaration that one or both spouses has legal capacity for a proposed transaction. For general provisions, see Sections 1020–1023 (petitions and other papers). For general provisions relating to notice of hearing, see Sections 1200–1221. See also Sections 1260–1265 (proof of giving notice). For background on the provisions of this part, see the Comment to this part under the part heading. [20 Cal.L.Rev.Comm.Reports 1001 (1990)].

Cross References

Conservator defined for purposes of this Part, see Probate Code § 3004.
Legal capacity defined, see Probate Code § 3012.
Nature of proceeding, see Probate Code § 3101.
Transaction defined for purposes of this Chapter, see Probate Code § 3100.

§ 3112. Legal capacity of petitioning spouse; determination; authority of court

(a) If a petitioning spouse is one whose legal capacity for the proposed transaction is to be determined in the proceeding, the court may do any of the following:

(1) Permit the spouse to appear without a representative.

(2) Appoint a guardian ad litem for the spouse.

(3) Take such other action as the circumstances warrant.

(b) If a petitioning spouse lacks legal capacity for the proposed transaction, the court may do either of the following:

(1) Require the spouse to be represented by the conservator of the spouse.

(2) Appoint a guardian ad litem for the spouse. *(Stats. 1990, c. 79 (A.B.759), § 14, operative July 1, 1991.)*

Law Revision Commission Comments

1990 Enactment

Section 3112 continues Section 3112 of the repealed Probate Code without change. Subdivision (a) supplements subdivisions (a) and (b) of Section 3101 and paragraph (1) of subdivision (a) of Section 3111 (who may petition). Subdivision (b) is consistent with Section 2462 and Code of Civil Procedure Section 372. As to appointment of a guardian ad litem, see Section 1003. For background on the provisions of this part, see the Comment to this part under the part heading. [20 Cal.L.Rev.Comm.Reports 1001 (1990)].

Cross References

Conservator as representative in actions and proceedings, see Probate Code § 2462.
Conservator defined for purposes of this Part, see Probate Code § 3004.

Parties to civil actions,
    Guardian ad litem, appointment procedure, see Code of Civil Procedure § 373.
    Minors, incompetent persons or persons for whom conservator appointed, see Code of Civil Procedure § 372.
Protection of rights of spouse who lacks legal capacity, see Probate Code § 3057.
Representation of spouse alleged to lack legal capacity, see Probate Code § 3140.
Transaction defined for purposes of this Chapter, see Probate Code § 3100.

§ 3113. Appointment of conservator for other spouse not required

A proceeding may be brought under this chapter by the conservator of a spouse, or by a spouse having legal capacity for the proposed transaction, without the necessity of appointing a conservator for the other spouse. *(Stats.1990, c. 79 (A.B.759), § 14, operative July 1, 1991.)*

Law Revision Commission Comments

1990 Enactment

Section 3113 continues Section 3113 of the repealed Probate Code without change. For background on the provisions of this part, see the Comment to this part under the part heading. [20 Cal.L.Rev.Comm.Reports 1001 (1990)].

Cross References

Conservator defined for purposes of this Part, see Probate Code § 3004.
Legal capacity, see Probate Code § 3012.
Transaction defined for purposes of this Chapter, see Probate Code § 3100.

ARTICLE 3. PETITION

§ 3120. Permissible allegations

(a) Several proposed transactions may be included in one petition and proceeding under this chapter.

(b) The petition may contain inconsistent allegations and may request relief in the alternative. *(Stats.1990, c. 79 (A.B.759), § 14, operative July 1, 1991.)*

Law Revision Commission Comments

1990 Enactment

Section 3120 continues Section 3120 of the repealed Probate Code without change. This section recognizes that a petition under this chapter may request the court to authorize a proposed transaction, to make a declaration of legal capacity for the proposed transaction, or both. See Section 3101. See also Sections 1020–1023 (petitions and other papers). For background on the provisions of this part, see the Comment to this part under the part heading. [20 Cal.L.Rev.Comm.Reports 1001 (1990)].

Cross References

Petitions and other papers, generally, see Probate Code § 1020 et seq.

Transaction defined for purposes of this Chapter, see Probate Code § 3100.

§ 3121. Required contents

The petition shall set forth all of the following information:

(a) The name, age, and residence of each spouse.

(b) If one or both spouses is alleged to lack legal capacity for the proposed transaction, a statement that the spouse has a conservator or a statement of the facts upon which the allegation is based.

(c) If there is a conservator of a spouse, the name and address of the conservator, the county in which the conservatorship proceeding is pending, and the court number of the proceeding.

(d) If a spouse alleged to lack legal capacity for the proposed transaction is a patient in or on leave of absence from a state institution under the jurisdiction of the State Department of State Hospitals or the State Department of Developmental Services, the name and address of the institution.

(e) The names and addresses of all of the following persons:

(1) Relatives within the second degree of each spouse alleged to lack legal capacity for the proposed transaction.

(2) If the petition is to provide gifts or otherwise affect estate planning of the spouse who is alleged to lack capacity, as would be properly the subject of a petition under Article 10 (commencing with Section 2580) of Chapter 6 of Part 4 (substituted judgment) in the case of a conservatorship, the names and addresses of the persons identified in Section 2581.

(f) A sufficient description of the property that is the subject of the proposed transaction.

(g) An allegation that the property is community property, and, if the proposed transaction involves property in which a spouse also has a separate property interest, an allegation of good cause to include that separate property in the transaction.

(h) The estimated value of the property.

(i) The terms and conditions of the proposed transaction, including the names of all parties thereto.

(j) The relief requested. *(Stats.1990, c. 79 (A.B.759), § 14, operative July 1, 1991. Amended by Stats.1996, c. 877 (A.B.1467), § 3; Stats.2003, c. 32 (A.B.167), § 3; Stats.2012, c. 440 (A.B.1488), § 52, eff. Sept. 22, 2012.)*

Law Revision Commission Comments

1990 Enactment

Section 3121 continues Section 3121 of the repealed Probate Code without change. The relief requested under subdivision (j) may be in the alternative. Sections 3101, 3120. Section 3121 states the required contents of a petition under this chapter regardless of the relief sought. For special allegations that depend upon the relief sought, see Sections 3122–3123. See also Sections 1020–1023 (petitions and other papers). For background on the provisions of this part, see the Comment to this part under the part heading. [20 Cal.L.Rev.Comm.Reports 1001 (1990)].

2003 Amendment

Section 3121 is amended to implement Section 3100(b) (transaction involving separate property interest). [33 Cal.L.Rev.Comm. Reports 156 (2003)].

Cross References

Community property defined for purposes of this Part, see Probate Code § 3002.
Conservator defined for purposes of this Part, see Probate Code § 3004.
Conservatorship proceeding defined for purposes of this Part, see Probate Code § 3008.
Department of Developmental Services, see Welfare and Institutions Code § 4400 et seq.
Legal capacity defined, see Probate Code § 3012.
Petitions and other papers, see Probate Code § 1020 et seq.
Transaction defined for purposes of this Chapter, see Probate Code § 3100.

§ 3122. Petition for court order authorizing transaction

If the proceeding is brought for a court order authorizing a proposed transaction, the petition shall set forth, in addition to the information required by Section 3121, all of the following:

(a) An allegation that one of the spouses has a conservator or facts establishing lack of legal capacity of the spouse for the proposed transaction.

(b) An allegation that the other spouse has legal capacity for the proposed transaction or has a conservator.

(c) An allegation that each spouse either: (1) joins in or consents to the proposed transaction, (2) has a conservator, or (3) is substantially unable to manage his or her financial resources or resist fraud or undue influence.

(d) Facts that may be relied upon to show that the authorization sought is for one or more of the following purposes:

(1) The advantage, benefit, or best interests of the spouses or their estates.

(2) The care and support of either spouse or of such persons as either spouse may be legally obligated to support.

(3) The payment of taxes, interest, or other encumbrances or charges for the protection and preservation of the community property.

(4) The providing of gifts for such purposes, and to such charities, relatives (including one of the spouses), friends, or other objects of bounty, as would be likely beneficiaries of gifts from the spouses. *(Stats.1990, c. 79 (A.B.759), § 14, operative July 1, 1991.)*

Law Revision Commission Comments

1990 Enactment

Section 3122 continues Section 3122 of the repealed Probate Code without change. Subdivisions (a) and (b) include the situation where each of the spouses has a conservator.

Subdivision (c) conforms to Section 3144(a)(4). It implements the policy of Section 3144 that the court may not authorize a transaction without the consent of a spouse alleged to lack legal capacity unless the spouse has a conservator or is a person for whom a conservator could be appointed.

Subdivision (d)(4) conforms to subdivision (f) of Section 3102. See also Section 3144(b).

For background on the provisions of this part, see the Comment to this part under the part heading. [20 Cal.L.Rev.Comm.Reports 1001 (1990)].

Community property defined for purposes of this Part, see Probate Code § 3002.
Conservator defined for purposes of this Part, see Probate Code § 3004.
Satisfaction of joinder or consent requirements, see Probate Code § 3071.
Transaction defined for purposes of this Chapter, see Probate Code § 3100.

§ 3123. Petition for court order declaring legal capacity for transaction

If the proceeding is brought for a court order declaring that one or both spouses has legal capacity for a proposed transaction, the petition shall set forth, in addition to the information required by Section 3121, an allegation of the legal capacity of such spouse or spouses for the proposed transaction. *(Stats.1990, c. 79 (A.B.759), § 14, operative July 1, 1991.)*

Law Revision Commission Comments

1990 Enactment

Section 3123 continues Section 3123 of the repealed Probate Code without change. This section implements the policy of Section 3101 to permit a proceeding for a judicial declaration of legal capacity for a transaction. For background on the provisions of this part, see the Comment to this part under the part heading. [20 Cal.L.Rev.Comm.Reports 1001 (1990)].

Cross References

Authorization of proceeding, lack of legal capacity, see Probate Code § 3101.
Legal capacity, see Probate Code § 3012.
Transaction defined for purposes of this Chapter, see Probate Code § 3100.

ARTICLE 4.   CITATION AND NOTICE OF HEARING

Section

§ 3130. Citation for nonpetitioning spouse alleged to lack legal capacity; notice to conservator in lieu of citation

(a) Except as provided in subdivision (b), upon the filing of the petition, the clerk shall issue a citation to each nonpetitioning spouse alleged to lack legal capacity for the proposed transaction, setting forth the time and place of hearing. The citation and a copy of the petition shall be served upon the spouse at least 15 days before the hearing.

(b) Unless the court otherwise orders, if a spouse alleged to lack legal capacity for the proposed transaction has a conservator, no citation to the spouse need be issued, and the petitioner shall cause a notice of the time and place of the hearing on the petition, accompanied by a copy of the petition, to be served on the conservator at least 15 days before the hearing.

(c) Service under this section shall be made in the manner provided in Section 415.10 or 415.30 of the Code of Civil Procedure or in such other manner as may be authorized by the court. If the person to be served is outside this state, service may also be made in the manner provided in Section 415.40 of the Code of Civil Procedure. *(Stats.1990, c. 79 (A.B.759), § 14, operative July 1, 1991.)*

Law Revision Commission Comments

1990 Enactment

Section 3130 continues Section 3130 of the repealed Probate Code without change. See also Sections 1240–1242 (citations). For general provisions relating to notice of hearing, see Sections 1200–1221. See also Sections 1260–1265 (proof of giving notice). For background on the provisions of this part, see the Comment to this part under the part heading. [20 Cal.L.Rev.Comm.Reports 1001 (1990)].

Cross References

Citations, see Probate Code § 1240 et seq.
Conservator defined for purposes of this Part, see Probate Code § 3004.
Duty of conservator to appear and represent spouse, see Probate Code § 3140.
Mailing, completion, see Probate Code § 1467.
Notice of hearing,
    Generally, see Probate Code § 1200 et seq.
    Proof of giving notice, see Probate Code § 1260 et seq.
Notice to,
    Directors, see Probate Code § 1461.
    Veterans Administration, see Probate Code § 1461.5.
Transaction defined for purposes of this Chapter, see Probate Code § 3100.

§ 3131. Notice to nonpetitioning spouse and other persons

(a) At least 15 days before the hearing on the petition, the petitioner shall cause a notice of the time and place of the hearing and a copy of the petition to be served upon any nonpetitioning spouse not alleged to lack legal capacity for the proposed transaction.

(b) Service under subdivision (a) shall be made in the manner provided in Section 415.10 or 415.30 of the Code of Civil Procedure or in such other manner as may be authorized by the court. If the person to be served is outside this state, service may also be made in the manner provided in Section 415.40 of the Code of Civil Procedure.

(c) At least 15 days before the hearing on the petition, the petitioner shall mail a notice of the time and place of the hearing on the petition to those persons required to be named in the petition at the addresses set forth in the petition. *(Stats.1990, c. 79 (A.B.759), § 14, operative July 1, 1991. Amended by Stats.1996, c. 877 (A.B.1467), § 4.)*

Law Revision Commission Comments

1990 Enactment

Section 3131 continues Section 3131 of the repealed Probate Code without change, except that subdivision (c) is revised to delete the requirement that a copy of the petition be mailed with the notice of the hearing to relatives of the spouse alleged to lack legal capacity. This change is made to afford greater privacy to the spouses.

Subdivisions (a) and (b) take into account that the nonpetitioning spouse may have legal capacity, making unnecessary the issuance and service of a citation. See also Section 1822 (notice of hearing on appointment of conservator). For general provisions relating to notice of hearing, see Sections 1200–1221. See also Sections 1260–1265 (proof of giving notice). For background on the provisions of this part, see the Comment to this part under the part heading. [20 Cal.L.Rev.Comm.Reports 1001 (1990)].

Cross References

Mailing, completion, see Probate Code § 1467.
Notice of hearing,
   Generally, see Probate Code § 1200 et seq.
   Appointment of conservator, see Probate Code § 1822.
   Proof of giving notice, see Probate Code § 1260 et seq.
Notice to,
   Directors, see Probate Code § 1461.
   Veterans Administration, see Probate Code § 1461.5.
Transaction defined for purposes of this Chapter, see Probate Code § 3100.

ARTICLE 5. HEARING AND ORDER

Section
3140. Representation of spouse alleged to lack legal capacity; appointment of investigator, guardian, or legal counsel; fees and costs.
3141. Presence of spouse at hearing.
3142. Information to be given spouse by court.
3143. Order declaring legal capacity.
3144. Order authorizing transaction.
3145. Effect of determination of lack of legal capacity.

§ 3140. Representation of spouse alleged to lack legal capacity; appointment of investigator, guardian, or legal counsel; fees and costs

(a) A conservator served pursuant to this article shall, and the Director of State Hospitals or the Director of Developmental Services given notice pursuant to Section 1461 may, appear at the hearing and represent a spouse alleged to lack legal capacity for the proposed transaction.

(b) The court may, in its discretion and if necessary, appoint an investigator to review the proposed transaction and report to the court regarding its advisability.

(c) If the court determines that a spouse alleged to lack legal capacity has not competently retained independent counsel, the court may in its discretion appoint the public guardian, public administrator, or a guardian ad litem to represent the interests of the spouse.

(d)(1) If a spouse alleged to lack legal capacity is unable to retain legal counsel, upon request of the spouse, the court shall appoint the public defender or private counsel under Section 1471 to represent the spouse and, if that appointment is made, Section 1472 applies.

(2) If the petition proposes a transfer of substantial assets to the petitioner from the other spouse and the court determines that the spouse has not competently retained independent counsel for the proceeding, the court may, in its discretion, appoint counsel for the other spouse if the court determines that appointment would be helpful to resolve the matter or necessary to protect the interests of the other spouse.

(e) Except as provided in paragraph (1) of subdivision (d), the court may fix a reasonable fee, to be paid out of the proceeds of the transaction or otherwise as the court may

direct, for all services rendered by privately engaged counsel, the public guardian, public administrator, or guardian ad litem, and by counsel for such persons.

(f) The court may order the cost of the review and report by a court investigator pursuant to subdivision (b) to be paid out of the proceeds of the transaction or otherwise as the court may direct, if the court determines that its order would not cause a hardship. *(Stats.1990, c. 79 (A.B.759), § 14, operative July 1, 1991. Amended by Stats.2008, c. 293 (A.B.1340), § 10; Stats.2009, c. 140 (A.B.1164), § 153; Stats. 2009, c. 596 (S.B.556), § 2; Stats.2012, c. 440 (A.B.1488), § 53, eff. Sept. 22, 2012.)*

Law Revision Commission Comments

1990 Enactment

Section 3140 continues Section 3140 of the repealed Probate Code without change. Subdivision (c) ensures that counsel will be appointed if requested by a spouse unable to retain legal counsel. Section 1472 relates to compensation for counsel appointed under subdivision (c). See also Code Civ.Proc. § 372. As to appointment of a guardian ad litem, see Section 1003. For background on the provisions of this part, see the Comment to this part under the part heading. [20 Cal.L.Rev.Comm.Reports 1001 (1990)].

Cross References

Conservator defined for purposes of this Part, see Probate Code § 3004.
Public administrators, see Probate Code § 7601 et seq.
Representation of petitioning spouse, see Probate Code § 3112.
Transaction defined for purposes of this Chapter, see Probate Code § 3100.

§ 3141. Presence of spouse at hearing

(a) If a spouse is alleged to lack legal capacity for the proposed transaction and has no conservator, the spouse shall be produced at the hearing unless unable to attend the hearing.

(b) If the spouse is not able to attend the hearing because of medical inability, such inability shall be established (1) by the affidavit or certificate of a licensed medical practitioner or (2) if the spouse is an adherent of a religion whose tenets and practices call for reliance upon prayer alone for healing and is under treatment by an accredited practitioner of the religion, by the affidavit of the practitioner.

(c) Emotional or psychological instability is not good cause for absence of the spouse from the hearing unless, by reason of such instability, attendance at the hearing is likely to cause serious and immediate physiological damage. *(Stats.1990, c. 79 (A.B.759), § 14, operative July 1, 1991.)*

Law Revision Commission Comments

1990 Enactment

Section 3141 continues Section 3141 of the repealed Probate Code without change. Subdivisions (b) and (c) are comparable to subdivisions (b) and (c) of Section 1825 (attendance of proposed conservatee). [20 Cal.L.Rev.Comm.Reports 1001 (1990)].

Cross References

Conservator defined for purposes of this Part, see Probate Code § 3004.
Representation of petitioning spouse, see Probate Code § 3112.

Transaction defined for purposes of this Chapter, see Probate Code § 3100.

§ 3142. Information to be given spouse by court

(a) If a spouse is alleged to lack legal capacity for the proposed transaction and has no conservator, the court, before commencement of the hearing on the merits, shall inform the spouse of all of the following:

(1) A determination of lack of legal capacity for the proposed transaction may result in approval of the proposed transaction.

(2) The spouse has the right to legal counsel of the spouse's own choosing, including the right to have legal counsel appointed by the court if unable to retain legal counsel.

(b) This section does not apply if the spouse is absent from the hearing and is not required to attend the hearing under the provisions of subdivision (a) of Section 3141 and any showing required by Section 3141 has been made. *(Stats. 1990, c. 79 (A.B.759), § 14, operative July 1, 1991.)*

Law Revision Commission Comments

1990 Enactment

Section 3142 continues Section 3142 of the repealed Probate Code without change. This section is comparable to Sections 1823 and 1828 (information to proposed conservatee). For background on the provisions of this part, see the Comment to this part under the part heading. [20 Cal.L.Rev.Comm.Reports 1001 (1990)].

Cross References

Appointment legal of counsel, see Probate Code §§ 1470 et seq., 3140.
Conservator defined for purposes of this Part, see Probate Code § 3004.
Establishment of conservatorship,
  Information to proposed conservatee by court, see Probate Code § 1828.
  Petition, supplemental information, see Probate Code § 1821.
Transaction defined for purposes of this Chapter, see Probate Code § 3100.

§ 3143. Order declaring legal capacity

(a) If the petition requests that the court make an order declaring a spouse to have legal capacity for the proposed transaction and the court determines that the spouse has legal capacity for the proposed transaction, the court shall so order.

(b) If the petition alleges that a spouse having no conservator lacks legal capacity for the proposed transaction and the court determines that the spouse has legal capacity for the transaction, the court shall make an order so declaring. *(Stats.1990, c. 79 (A.B.759), § 14, operative July 1, 1991.)*

Law Revision Commission Comments

1990 Enactment

Section 3143 continues Section 3143 of the repealed Probate Code without change. This section implements the policy of Section 3101 to permit a proceeding under this chapter for a declaration of legal capacity for a transaction. For general provisions relating to hearings and orders, see Sections 1040–1050. For background on the provisions of this part, see the Comment to this part under the part heading. [20 Cal.L.Rev.Comm.Reports 1001 (1990)].

Cross References

Authorization of proceedings, see Probate Code § 3101.
Conservator defined for purposes of this Part, see Probate Code § 3004.
Hearings and orders, see Probate Code § 1040 et seq.
Legal capacity, see Probate Code § 3012.
Transaction defined for purposes of this Chapter, see Probate Code § 3100.

§ 3144. Order authorizing transaction

(a) The court may authorize the proposed transaction if the court determines all of the following:

(1) The property that is the subject of the proposed transaction is community property of the spouses, and, if the proposed transaction involves property in which a spouse also has a separate property interest, that there is good cause to include that separate property in the transaction.

(2) One of the spouses then has a conservator or otherwise lacks legal capacity for the proposed transaction.

(3) The other spouse either has legal capacity for the proposed transaction or has a conservator.

(4) Each of the spouses either (i) joins in or consents to the proposed transaction, (ii) has a conservator, or (iii) is substantially unable to manage his or her own financial resources or resist fraud or undue influence. Substantial inability may not be proved by isolated incidents of negligence or improvidence.

(5) The proposed transaction is one that should be authorized under this chapter.

(b) If the proposed transaction is to provide gifts or otherwise affect estate planning of the spouse who is alleged to lack capacity, as would be properly the subject of a petition under Article 10 (commencing with Section 2580) of Chapter 6 of Part 4 (substituted judgment) in the case of a conservatorship, the court may authorize the transaction under this chapter only if the transaction is one that the court would authorize under that article.

(c) If the court determines under subdivision (a) that the transaction should be authorized, the court shall so order and may authorize the petitioner to do and perform all acts and to execute and deliver all papers, documents, and instruments necessary to effectuate the order.

(d) In an order authorizing a transaction, the court may prescribe any terms and conditions as the court in its discretion determines appropriate, including, but not limited to, requiring joinder or consent of another person. *(Stats. 1990, c. 79 (A.B.759), § 14, operative July 1, 1991. Amended by Stats.1996, c. 877 (A.B.1467), § 5; Stats.2003, c. 32 (A.B.167), § 4.)*

Law Revision Commission Comments

1990 Enactment

Section 3144 continues Section 3144 of the repealed Probate Code without change. For general provisions relating to hearings and orders, see Sections 1040–1050. For background on the provisions of this part, see the Comment to this part under the part heading. [20 Cal.L.Rev.Comm.Reports 1001 (1990)].

2003 Amendment

Section 3144 is amended to implement Section 3100(b) (transaction involving separate property interest). [33 Cal.L.Rev.Comm. Reports 158 (2003)].

Cross References

Community property defined for purposes of this Part, see Probate Code § 3002.
Conclusiveness of judgment, see Code of Civil Procedure § 1908.
Conservator defined for purposes of this Part, see Probate Code § 3004.
Determination of character of property, see Probate Code § 3101.
Fraud, see Civil Code § 1571 et seq.
Hearings and orders, generally, see Probate Code § 1040 et seq.
Negligence, see Civil Code § 1714.
Protection of rights of spouse who lacks legal capacity, see Probate Code § 3057.
Rights of spouses in proceeds of transaction, see Probate Code § 3020.
Satisfaction of joinder or consent requirements, see Probate Code § 3071.
Transaction defined for purposes of this Chapter, see Probate Code § 3100.
Undue influence, see Civil Code § 1575.

§ 3145. Effect of determination of lack of legal capacity

A court determination pursuant to this chapter that a spouse lacks legal capacity for the proposed transaction affects the legal capacity of the spouse for that transaction alone and has no effect on the legal capacity of the spouse for any other purpose. *(Stats.1990, c. 79 (A.B.759), § 14, operative July 1, 1991.)*

Law Revision Commission Comments

1990 Enactment

Section 3145 continues Section 3145 of the repealed Probate Code without change. This section makes clear that a determination of lack of legal capacity under this chapter is limited in scope. See also Section 3012 (legal capacity). For background on the provisions of this part, see the Comment to this part under the part heading. [20 Cal.L.Rev.Comm.Reports 1001 (1990)].

Cross References

Conclusiveness of judgment, see Code of Civil Procedure § 1908.
Legal capacity, see Probate Code § 3012.
Transaction defined for purposes of this Chapter, see Probate Code § 3100.

ARTICLE 6. CONSUMMATION OF TRANSACTION

Section
3150. Bond.
3151. Execution, delivery and recordation of documents.
3152. Validity of conveyance or other disposition.
3153. Liability of conservator.
3154. Further proceedings if transaction not consummated.

§ 3150. Bond

(a) Unless the court for good cause dispenses with the bond, the court shall require the petitioner to give a bond, in the amount fixed by the court, conditioned on the duty of the petitioner to account for and apply the proceeds of the transaction to be received by the petitioner only as the court may by order direct.

(b) Unless the court for good cause fixes the amount of the bond in a lesser amount, if given by an admitted surety insurer, the bond shall be in an amount not less than the value of the personal property (including cash and any notes) to be received by the petitioner, as determined by the court.

(c) If the sureties on the bond are personal sureties, the bond shall be approved by the court and shall be for twice the amount required for a bond given by an admitted surety insurer.

(d) Section 2328 is applicable to the bond of the petitioner under this chapter. *(Stats.1990, c. 79 (A.B.759), § 14, operative July 1, 1991.)*

Law Revision Commission Comments

1990 Enactment

Section 3150 continues Section 3150 of the repealed Probate Code without substantive change. For background on the provisions of this part, see the Comment to this part under the part heading. [20 Cal.L.Rev.Comm.Reports 1001 (1990)].

Cross References

Bond and Undertaking Law, see Code of Civil Procedure § 995.010 et seq.
Transaction defined for purposes of this Chapter, see Probate Code § 3100.

§ 3151. Execution, delivery and recordation of documents

(a) The petitioner shall, upon receipt of the consideration therefor, execute, acknowledge, and deliver any necessary instruments or documents as directed by the court, setting forth therein that they are made by authority of the order.

(b) The petitioner shall cause a certified copy of the order to be recorded in the office of the recorder of each county in which is located any real property affected by the order or any real property upon which there is a lien or encumbrance affected by the order.

(c) If a sale is made upon a credit pursuant to the order, the petitioner shall take the note of the person to whom the sale is made for the amount of the unpaid balance of the purchase money, with such security for the payment thereof as the court shall by order approve. The note shall be made payable to the petitioner or, if the petition was made by a conservator, to the petitioner as conservator. *(Stats.1990, c. 79 (A.B.759), § 14, operative July 1, 1991.)*

Law Revision Commission Comments

1990 Enactment

Section 3151 continues Section 3151 of the repealed Probate Code without substantive change. For background on the provisions of this part, see the Comment to this part under the part heading. [20 Cal.L.Rev.Comm.Reports 1001 (1990)].

Cross References

Acknowledgment of instruments, see Civil Code § 1180 et seq.
Conservator defined for purposes of this Part, see Probate Code § 3004.
Documents to be recorded, see Government Code § 27280 et seq.
Recording transfers, see Civil Code § 1169 et seq.

§ 3152. Validity of conveyance or other disposition

A sale, conveyance, assignment, transfer, exchange, encumbrance, security interest, mortgage, deed of trust, lease, dedication, release, or relinquishment, and any instrument or document, made pursuant to the court's order, is as valid and effectual as if the property affected thereby were the sole and absolute property of the person making it. *(Stats.1990, c. 79 (A.B.759), § 14, operative July 1, 1991.)*

Law Revision Commission Comments

1990 Enactment

Section 3152 continues Section 3152 of the repealed Probate Code without change. For background on the provisions of this part, see the Comment to this part under the part heading. [20 Cal.L.Rev.Comm.Reports 1001 (1990)].

§ 3153. Liability of conservator

Notes, encumbrances, security interests, mortgages, leases, or deeds of trust, executed as provided in this chapter by a petitioning conservator create no personal liability against the conservator so executing, unless the conservator is one of the spouses and then only to the extent that personal liability would have resulted had both spouses had legal capacity for the transaction and joined in the execution. *(Stats.1990, c. 79 (A.B.759), § 14, operative July 1, 1991.)*

Law Revision Commission Comments

1990 Enactment

Section 3153 continues Section 3153 of the repealed Probate Code without change. For background on the provisions of this part, see the Comment to this part under the part heading. [20 Cal.L.Rev.Comm.Reports 1001 (1990)].

Cross References

Conservator defined for purposes of this Part, see Probate Code § 3004.
Legal capacity defined, see Probate Code § 3012.
Transaction defined for purposes of this Chapter, see Probate Code § 3100.

§ 3154. Further proceedings if transaction not consummated

(a) If any party to the transaction, other than the petitioner, does not consummate a transaction authorized by the court, the court, on application of the petitioner, after such notice to the parties to the transaction as the court directs, may vacate the order authorizing the transaction.

(b) If the order authorized the sale or encumbrance of property, the petitioner may by supplemental petition apply to the court for an order authorizing any other sale or encumbrance of the property to the advantage, benefit, or best interests of the spouses or their estates. The supplemental petition and a notice of the time and place of the hearing shall be served and mailed as provided in Article 4 (commencing with Section 3130) except that (1) no further citation shall be issued and (2) a copy of the supplemental petition and a notice of the time and place of the hearing shall be served upon any person who has appeared as representative of a nonpetitioning spouse or upon counsel of record for a nonpetitioning spouse or as the court may otherwise direct.

(c) If it appears to the court that the other sale or encumbrance is to the advantage, benefit, or best interests of the spouses or their estates and that the request in the supplemental petition that the transaction be authorized

should be granted, the court may so order and may authorize the petitioner to do and perform acts and to execute and deliver all papers, documents, and instruments necessary to effectuate the order. *(Stats.1990, c. 79 (A.B.759), § 14, operative July 1, 1991.)*

Law Revision Commission Comments

1990 Enactment

Section 3154 continues Section 3154 of the repealed Probate Code without change. For general provisions relating to notice of hearing, see Sections 1200–1221. See also Sections 1260–1265 (proof of giving notice). For background on the provisions of this part, see the Comment to this part under the part heading. [20 Cal.L.Rev.Comm.Reports 1001 (1990)].

Cross References

Notice of hearing, generally, see Probate Code § 1200 et seq.
Proof of giving notice, see Probate Code § 1260 et seq.
Transaction defined for purposes of this Chapter, see Probate Code § 3100.

Part 7

CAPACITY DETERMINATIONS AND HEALTH CARE DECISIONS FOR ADULT WITHOUT CONSERVATOR

Section
3200. Definitions.
3201. Petition.
3202. Jurisdiction and venue.
3203. Persons authorized to file petition.
3204. Contents of petition.
3205. Appointment of legal counsel.
3206. Notice of hearing and copy of petition; service; exceptions; considerations by court.
3207. Submission for determination on medical declarations.
3208. Order authorizing health care.
3208.5. Patient with capacity to consent; court findings and orders.
3209. Continuing jurisdiction of court.
3210. Procedure supplemental and alternative.
3211. Prohibition against placement in mental health treatment facility; restrictions on treatment.
3212. Treatment by spiritual means.

Law Revision Commission Comments

1990 Revised Comment

This part supersedes Part 7 (commencing with Section 3200) of Division 4 of the repealed Probate Code. The superseded part was enacted on recommendation of the California Law Revision Commission. See *Recommendation Relating to Guardianship–Conservatorship Law*, 14 Cal. L. Revision Comm'n Reports 501 (1978). See also *Report of Assembly Committee on Judiciary on Assembly Bills Nos. 261 and 167*, republished in 15 Cal. L. Revision Comm'n Reports 1061, 1091 (1980). For the Guardianship–Conservatorship Law as enacted in 1979 (Chapter 726 of the Statutes of 1979) with the revisions made by Chapters 89 and 246 of the Statutes of 1980, see *Guardianship-Conservatorship Law*, 15 Cal. L. Revision Comm'n Reports 451 (1980).

The provisions of this part afford an alternative to establishing a conservatorship of the person where there is no ongoing need for a conservatorship. The procedural rules of this part provide an expeditious means of obtaining authorization for medical treatment while safeguarding basic rights of the patient: The patient has a right to counsel. Section 3205. The hearing is held after notice to the patient, the patient's attorney, and such other persons as the court orders. Section 3206. The court may determine the issue on medical declarations alone if the attorney for the petitioner and the attorney for the patient so stipulate. Section 3207. The court may not order medical treatment under this part if the patient has capacity to give informed consent to the treatment but refuses to do so. Section 3208.5. [29 Cal.L.Rev.Comm. Reports 1 (1999)].

1999 Revised Comment

The part heading is amended to reflect the expanded scope of this part. See 1995 Cal. Stat. ch. 842, § 9 (adding determination of capacity to consent to specified medical treatment as independent ground for petition under Section 3201). [29 Cal.L.Rev.Comm. Reports 1 (1999)].

§ 3200. Definitions

As used in this part:

(a) "Health care" means any care, treatment, service, or procedure to maintain, diagnose, or otherwise affect a patient's physical or mental condition.

(b) "Health care decision" means a decision regarding the patient's health care, including the following:

(1) Selection and discharge of health care providers and institutions.

(2) Approval or disapproval of diagnostic tests, surgical procedures, programs of medication.

(3) Directions to provide, withhold, or withdraw artificial nutrition and hydration and all other forms of health care, including cardiopulmonary resuscitation.

(c) "Health care institution" means an institution, facility, or agency licensed, certified, or otherwise authorized or permitted by law to provide health care in the ordinary course of business.

(d) "Patient" means an adult who does not have a conservator of the person and for whom a health care decision needs to be made. *(Stats.1990, c. 79 (A.B.759), § 14, operative July 1, 1991. Amended by Stats.1999, c. 658 (A.B.891), § 15, operative July 1, 2000.)*

Law Revision Commission Comments

1990 Enactment

Section 3200 continues Section 3200 of the repealed Probate Code without change. For background on the provisions of this part, see the Comment to this part under the part heading. [20 Cal.L.Rev.Comm.Reports 1001 (1990)].

1999 Amendment

Section 3200 is amended to adopt definitions that are consistent with the Health Care Decisions Law. See Section 4500 *et seq.* The definition of "health care decision" in subdivision (b) makes clear, as used in other provisions in this part, that court-authorized health care decisions include end-of-life decisions. See Section 3208(c). This is consistent with the scope of the Health Care Decisions Law. [29 Cal.L.Rev.Comm. Reports 1 (1999)].

Cross References

Fee for filing petition commencing or opposition papers concerning certain probate proceedings, see Government Code § 70655.
Medical treatment of ward or conservatee, consent, see Probate Code § 2353 et seq.

Powers and duties of guardian or conservator of the person, see Probate Code § 2350 et seq.

§ 3201. Petition

(a) A petition may be filed to determine that a patient has the capacity to make a health care decision concerning an existing or continuing condition.

(b) A petition may be filed to determine that a patient lacks the capacity to make a health care decision concerning specified treatment for an existing or continuing condition, and further for an order authorizing a designated person to make a health care decision on behalf of the patient.

(c) One proceeding may be brought under this part under both subdivisions (a) and (b). *(Stats.1990, c. 79 (A.B.759), § 14, operative July 1, 1991. Amended by Stats.1995, c. 842 (S.B.730), § 9; Stats.1996, c. 178 (S.B.1650), § 9; Stats.1999, c. 658 (A.B.891), § 16, operative July 1, 2000.)*

Law Revision Commission Comments

1990 Enactment

Section 3201 continues Section 3201 of the repealed Probate Code without change. This section is similar to a portion of subdivision (b) of Section 2357. For background on the provisions of this part, see the Comment to this part under the part heading.

In the ordinary, nonemergency case, medical treatment may be given to a person only with the person's informed consent. See Cobbs v. Grant, 8 Cal.3d 229, 502 P.2d 1, 104 Cal.Rptr. 505 (1972). If the person is incompetent or is otherwise unable to give informed consent and has no conservator, the physician may be willing to proceed with the consent of the person's nearest relative. See id. at 244, 502 P.2d at 10, 104 Cal.Rptr. at 514. However, if treatment is not available because of a question of the validity of the consent, court intervention may be needed to authorize the treatment and to protect medical personnel and facilities from later legal action based upon asserted lack of consent. [20 Cal.L.Rev.Comm.Reports 1001 (1990)].

1999 Amendment

Subdivisions (a) and (b) of Section 3201 are amended to use the terminology of Section 3200 and make the language internally consistent. See Section 3200 Comment. Other technical, nonsubstantive changes are also made.

Subdivision (d) is continued in Section 3208(b) (order authorizing treatment) without substantive change. See Section 3208 Comment.

Subdivision (e) is continued in Section 3210(c) (supplemental, alternative procedure) without substantive change. Subdivision (f) is continued in Section 3210(a) without substantive change. See Section 3210 Comment.

Subdivision (g) is continued in Section 3212 (choice of treatment by spiritual means) without substantive change. See Section 3212 Comment. [29 Cal.L.Rev.Comm. Reports 1 (1999)].

Cross References

Health care decision defined for purposes of this Part, see Probate Code § 3200.
Health care defined for purposes of this Part, see Probate Code § 3200.
Medical treatment of ward, see Probate Code § 2353 et seq.
Order authorizing treatment, see Probate Code § 3208.
Patient defined for purposes of this Part, see Probate Code § 3200.

Petitions and other papers, generally, see Probate Code § 1020 et seq.

§ 3202. Jurisdiction and venue

The petition may be filed in the superior court of any of the following counties:

(a) The county in which the patient resides.

(b) The county in which the patient is temporarily living.

(c) Such other county as may be in the best interests of the patient. *(Stats.1990, c. 79 (A.B.759), § 14, operative July 1, 1991.)*

Law Revision Commission Comments

1990 Enactment

Section 3202 continues Section 3202 of the repealed Probate Code without change. This section provides liberal venue rules for determining the county in which the petition is to be filed. See also the Comment to Section 2201. For background on the provisions of this part, see the Comment to this part under the part heading. [20 Cal.L.Rev.Comm.Reports 1001 (1990)].

Cross References

Guardianship and conservatorship proceedings, jurisdiction and venue, see Probate Code § 2200 et seq.
Patient defined for purposes of this Part, see Probate Code § 3200.

§ 3203. Persons authorized to file petition

A petition may be filed by any of the following:

(a) The patient.

(b) The patient's spouse.

(c) A relative or friend of the patient, or other interested person, including the patient's agent under a power of attorney for health care.

(d) The patient's physician.

(e) A person acting on behalf of the health care institution in which the patient is located if the patient is in a health care institution.

(f) The public guardian or other county officer designated by the board of supervisors of the county in which the patient is located or resides or is temporarily living. *(Stats.1990, c. 79 (A.B.759), § 14, operative July 1, 1991. Amended by Stats. 1999, c. 658 (A.B.891), § 17, operative July 1, 2000.)*

Law Revision Commission Comments

1990 Enactment

Section 3203 continues Section 3203 of the repealed Probate Code without change. This section permits any interested person to file a petition under this part, including a person acting on behalf of the medical facility if the patient is in a medical facility. For background on the provisions of this part, see the Comment to this part under the part heading. [20 Cal.L.Rev.Comm.Reports 1001 (1990)].

1999 Amendment

Section 3203 is amended to use the terminology of Section 3200. See Section 3200 Comment. Other technical, nonsubstantive changes are also made. Subdivision (c) is amended to make clear that an agent under a power of attorney for health care is an interested person. See Section 4607 ("agent" defined under Health Care Decisions Law). [29 Cal.L.Rev.Comm. Reports 1 (1999)].

Cross References

Health care defined for purposes of this Part, see Probate Code § 3200.
Health care institution defined for purposes of this Part, see Probate Code § 3200.
Interested person defined, see Probate Code § 1424.
Patient defined for purposes of this Part, see Probate Code § 3200.
Public guardian, generally, see Probate Code § 2900 et seq.

§ 3204. Contents of petition

The petition shall state, or set forth by a medical declaration attached to the petition, all of the following known to the petitioner at the time the petition is filed:

(a) The condition of the patient's health that requires treatment.

(b) The recommended health care that is considered to be medically appropriate.

(c) The threat to the patient's condition if authorization for the recommended health care is delayed or denied by the court.

(d) The predictable or probable outcome of the recommended health care.

(e) The medically available alternatives, if any, to the recommended health care.

(f) The efforts made to obtain consent from the patient.

(g) If the petition is filed by a person on behalf of a health care institution, the name of the person to be designated to give consent to the recommended health care on behalf of the patient.

(h) The deficit or deficits in the patient's mental functions listed in subdivision (a) of Section 811 that are impaired, and an identification of a link between the deficit or deficits and the patient's inability to respond knowingly and intelligently to queries about the recommended health care or inability to participate in a decision about the recommended health care by means of a rational thought process.

(i) The names and addresses, so far as they are known to the petitioner, of the persons specified in subdivision (b) of Section 1821. *(Stats.1990, c. 79 (A.B.759), § 14, operative July 1, 1991. Amended by Stats.1995, c. 842 (S.B.730), § 10; Stats.1996, c. 178 (S.B.1650), § 10; Stats.1996, c. 563 (S.B. 392), § 15; Stats.1999, c. 658 (A.B.891), § 18, operative July 1, 2000.)*

Law Revision Commission Comments

1990 Enactment

Section 3204 continues Section 3204 of the repealed Probate Code without change. This section is comparable to subdivision (c) of Section 2357. See also Sections 1020–1023 (petitions and other papers). For background on the provisions of this part, see the Comment to this part under the part heading. [20 Cal.L.Rev.Comm.Reports 1001 (1990)].

1999 Amendment

Section 3204 is amended to use the terminology of Section 3200. See Section 3200 Comment. Other technical, nonsubstantive changes are also made. The reference to "informed" consent is omitted as unnecessary. See Section 3208.5 Comment. [29 Cal.L.Rev.Comm. Reports 1 (1999)].

Affidavits, see Code of Civil Procedure §§ 2003, 2009 et seq.

Court ordered medical treatment of ward or conservatee, see Probate Code § 2353 et seq.

Health care defined for purposes of this Part, see Probate Code § 3200.

Health care institution defined for purposes of this Part, see Probate Code § 3200.

Patient defined for purposes of this Part, see Probate Code § 3200.

Petitions and other papers, generally, see Probate Code § 1020 et seq.

§ 3205. Appointment of legal counsel

Upon the filing of the petition, the court shall determine the name of the attorney the patient has retained to represent the patient in the proceeding under this part or the name of the attorney the patient plans to retain for that purpose. If the patient has not retained an attorney and does not plan to retain one, the court shall appoint the public defender or private counsel under Section 1471 to consult with and represent the patient at the hearing on the petition and, if such appointment is made, Section 1472 applies. *(Stats.1990, c. 79 (A.B.759), § 14, operative July 1, 1991.)*

Law Revision Commission Comments

1990 Enactment

Section 3205 continues Section 3205 of the repealed Probate Code without change. For background on the provisions of this part, see the Comment to this part under the part heading. [20 Cal.L.Rev.Comm.Reports 1001 (1990)].

Cross References

Appointment legal of counsel, see Probate Code § 1470 et seq.

Patient defined for purposes of this Part, see Probate Code § 3200.

Public defender, duty to represent persons not financially able to employ counsel, see Government Code § 27706.

§ 3206. Notice of hearing and copy of petition; service; exceptions; considerations by court

(a) Not less than 15 days before the hearing, notice of the time and place of the hearing and a copy of the petition shall be personally served on the patient, the patient's attorney, and the agent under the patient's power of attorney for health care, if any.

(b) Not less than 15 days before the hearing, notice of the time and place of the hearing and a copy of the petition shall be mailed to the following persons:

(1) The patient's spouse, if any, at the address stated in the petition.

(2) The patient's relatives named in the petition at their addresses stated in the petition.

(c) For good cause, the court may shorten or waive notice of the hearing as provided by this section. In determining the period of notice to be required, the court shall take into account both of the following:

(1) The existing medical facts and circumstances set forth in the petition or in a medical declaration attached to the petition or in a medical declaration presented to the court.

(2) The desirability, where the condition of the patient permits, of giving adequate notice to all interested persons.

(Added by Stats.1996, c. 563 (S.B.392), § 17. Amended by Stats.1999, c. 658 (A.B.891), § 19, operative July 1, 2000.)

Law Revision Commission Comments

1999 Amendment

Subdivision (b) of Section 3206 is amended to correct the reference to a "proposed conservatee." See Section 3200(d) ("patient" defined).

Subdivision (c) is amended to replace the references to "affidavit," in conformity with Section 3204. [29 Cal.L.Rev.Comm. Reports 1 (1999)].

Cross References

Affidavits, see Code of Civil Procedure §§ 2003, 2009 et seq.

Health care defined for purposes of this Part, see Probate Code § 3200.

Notices,
Generally, see Probate Code § 1460 et seq.
Proof of giving notice, see Probate Code § 1260 et seq.

Patient defined for purposes of this Part, see Probate Code § 3200.

§ 3207. Submission for determination on medical declarations

Notwithstanding Section 3206, the matter presented by the petition may be submitted for the determination of the court upon proper and sufficient medical declarations if the attorney for the petitioner and the attorney for the patient so stipulate and further stipulate that there remains no issue of fact to be determined. *(Stats.1990, c. 79 (A.B.759), § 14, operative July 1, 1991. Amended by Stats.1999, c. 658 (A.B.891), § 20, operative July 1, 2000.)*

Law Revision Commission Comments

1990 Enactment

Section 3207 continues Section 3207 of the repealed Probate Code without change. This section is comparable to subdivision (g) of Section 2357. For background on the provisions of this part, see the Comment to this part under the part heading. [20 Cal.L.Rev.Comm.Reports 1001 (1990)].

1999 Amendment

Section 3207 is amended to eliminate the reference to "affidavits," in conformity with Section 3204. [29 Cal.L.Rev.Comm. Reports 1 (1999)].

Cross References

Notice of hearing generally, see Probate Code § 1200 et seq.

Patient defined for purposes of this Part, see Probate Code § 3200.

§ 3208. Order authorizing health care

(a) Except as provided in subdivision (b), the court may make an order authorizing the recommended health care for the patient and designating a person to give consent to the recommended health care on behalf of the patient if the court determines from the evidence all of the following:

(1) The existing or continuing condition of the patient's health requires the recommended health care.

(2) If untreated, there is a probability that the condition will become life-endangering or result in a serious threat to the physical or mental health of the patient.

(3) The patient is unable to consent to the recommended health care.

(b) In determining whether the patient's mental functioning is so severely impaired that the patient lacks the capacity to make any health care decision, the court may take into consideration the frequency, severity, and duration of periods of impairment.

(c) The court may make an order authorizing withholding or withdrawing artificial nutrition and hydration and all other forms of health care and designating a person to give or withhold consent to the recommended health care on behalf of the patient if the court determines from the evidence all of the following:

(1) The recommended health care is in accordance with the patient's best interest, taking into consideration the patient's personal values to the extent known to the petitioner.

(2) The patient is unable to consent to the recommended health care. *(Stats.1990, c. 79 (A.B.759), § 14, operative July 1, 1991. Amended by Stats.1990, c. 710 (S.B.1775), § 12, operative July 1, 1991; Stats.1995, c. 842 (S.B.730), § 11; Stats.1999, c. 658 (A.B.891), § 21, operative July 1, 2000.)*

Law Revision Commission Comments

1990 Enactment

Section 3028 continues Section 3208 of the repealed Probate Code without change. Subdivision (a) is comparable to subdivision (h) of Section 2357. The person designated to give consent may be called upon to make decisions on particular matters that arise within the authorized course of medical treatment. Subdivision (b) makes clear that this part applies only to the case where the patient either lacks capacity to give informed consent or is in such condition that the patient is unable to give consent. For background on the provisions of this part, see the Comment to this part under the part heading. [20 Cal.L.Rev.Comm.Reports 1001 (1990)].

1990 Amendment

Section 3208 (enacted as a part of the new Probate Code by 1990 Cal.Stat. ch. 79 § 14) was amended by 1990 Cal.Stat. ch. 710 § 12. The amendment expanded subdivision (a)(2) to include a serious threat to mental health as a condition that justifies court authorization of medical treatment. See also Section 2357. For background on the 1990 amendment, see Recommendation Relating to Court–Authorized Medical Treatment, 20 Cal.L.Revision Comm'n Reports 537 (1990). [20 Cal.L.Rev.Comm. Reports 1001 (1990)].

1999 Amendment

Subdivision (a) of Section 3208 is amended to use the terminology of Section 3200. See Section 3200 Comment. Other technical, nonsubstantive changes are also made. The reference to "informed" consent has been omitted as surplus. See Section 3805 Comment.

New subdivision (b) continues former subdivision (d) of Section 3201 without substantive change.

A new subdivision (c) is added to permit withholding or withdrawal of health care, including artificial nutrition and hydration. This amendment extends the authority of the court to authorize health care decisions to the same extent as surrogates and subject to the same standards as provided in the Health Care Decisions Law. See, e.g., Sections 4684 (standard governing agent's health care decisions under power of attorney for health care), 4714 (standard governing surrogate's health care decisions).

Former subdivisions (b)-(d) are continued in Section 3208.5 without substantive change. See Section 3208.5 Comment. [29 Cal.L.Rev.Comm. Reports App. 6 (1999)].

Cross References

Health care decision defined for purposes of this Part, see Probate Code § 3200.
Health care defined for purposes of this Part, see Probate Code § 3200.
Patient defined for purposes of this Part, see Probate Code § 3200.

§ 3208.5. Patient with capacity to consent; court findings and orders

In a proceeding under this part:

(a) Where the patient has the capacity to consent to the recommended health care, the court shall so find in its order.

(b) Where the court has determined that the patient has the capacity to consent to the recommended health care, the court shall, if requested, determine whether the patient has accepted or refused the recommended health care, and whether the patient's consent to the recommended health care is an informed consent.

(c) Where the court finds that the patient has the capacity to consent to the recommended health care, but that the patient refuses consent, the court shall not make an order authorizing the recommended health care or designating a person to give consent to the recommended health care. If an order has been made authorizing the recommended health care and designating a person to give consent to the recommended health care, the order shall be revoked if the court determines that the patient has recovered the capacity to consent to the recommended health care. Until revoked or modified, the order is effective authorization for the recommended health care. *(Added by Stats.1999, c. 658 (A.B.891), § 22, operative July 1, 2000.)*

Law Revision Commission Comments

1999 Addition

Section 3208.5 continues former subdivisions (b)-(d) of Section 3208 without substantive change. The subdivisions have been placed in a different order. Terminology has been conformed to the definitions in Section 3200. Thus, for example, "health care" replaces "medical treatment" appearing in the former provision. Except in subdivision (b), references to "informed" consent have been omitted as surplus and for consistency with other provisions in this part and in the Health Care Decisions Law (Section 4600 *et seq.*). To be effective, the patient's consent must satisfy the law of informed consent. [29 Cal.L.Rev.Comm. Reports 1 (1999)].

Cross References

Health care defined for purposes of this Part, see Probate Code § 3200.
Patient defined for purposes of this Part, see Probate Code § 3200.

§ 3209. Continuing jurisdiction of court

The court in which the petition is filed has continuing jurisdiction to revoke or modify an order made under this part upon a petition filed, noticed, and heard in the same manner as an original petition filed under this part. *(Stats. 1990, c. 79 (A.B.759), § 14, operative July 1, 1991.)*

Law Revision Commission Comments

1990 Enactment

Section 3209 continues Section 3209 of the repealed Probate Code without change. This section gives the court continuing jurisdiction to make such further orders as are necessary concerning medical treatment of the patient. If the court determines that the patient has recovered capacity to give informed consent, the order under this part must be revoked. Section 3208(b). The patient can then determine whether to consent or to refuse to consent to continuation of treatment. For background on the provisions of this part, see the Comment to this part under the part heading. [20 Cal.L.Rev.Comm.Reports 1001 (1990)].

§ 3210. Procedure supplemental and alternative

(a) This part is supplemental and alternative to other procedures or methods for obtaining consent to health care or making health care decisions, and is permissive and cumulative for the relief to which it applies.

(b) Nothing in this part limits the providing of health care in an emergency case in which the health care is required because (1) the health care is required for the alleviation of severe pain or (2) the patient has a medical condition that, if not immediately diagnosed and treated, will lead to serious disability or death.

(c) Nothing in this part supersedes the right that any person may have under existing law to make health care decisions on behalf of a patient, or affects the decisionmaking process of a health care institution. *(Stats.1990, c. 79 (A.B.759), § 14, operative July 1, 1991. Amended by Stats. 1999, c. 658 (A.B.891), § 23, operative July 1, 2000.)*

Law Revision Commission Comments

1990 Enactment

Section 3210 continues Section 3210 of the repealed Probate Code without change. Subdivision (a) makes clear that this part does not limit other methods for obtaining medical consent. See the Comment to Section 3201.

Subdivision (b) makes clear that this part does not require informed consent of the patient in emergency cases where consent cannot reasonably be obtained. Such cases are governed by other law. See generally Cobbs v. Grant, 8 Cal.3d 229, 502 P.2d 1, 104 Cal.Rptr. 505 (1972).

For background on the provisions of this part, see the Comment to this part under the part heading. [20 Cal.L.Rev.Comm.Reports 1001 (1990)].

1999 Amendment

Subdivisions (a) and (b) of Section 3210 are amended to use the terminology of Section 3200. See Section 3200 Comment. Other technical, nonsubstantive changes are also made. The second clause added to subdivision (a) continues former subdivision (f) of Section 3201 without substantive change. The erroneous reference to "this chapter" in the former provision is corrected.

Subdivision (c) continues and generalizes former subdivision (e) of Section 3201. Subdivision (c) applies to all health care institutions, as defined in Section 3200(c), not just long-term health care facilities, as defined in Health and Safety Code Section 1418.8(b). Other technical, nonsubstantive changes are also made. [29 Cal.L.Rev.Comm. Reports App. 6 (1999)].

Cross References

Health care decision defined for purposes of this Part, see Probate Code § 3200.
Health care defined for purposes of this Part, see Probate Code § 3200.
Health care institution defined for purposes of this Part, see Probate Code § 3200.

Patient defined for purposes of this Part, see Probate Code § 3200.

§ 3211. Prohibition against placement in mental health treatment facility; restrictions on treatment

(a) No person may be placed in a mental health treatment facility under the provisions of this part.

(b) No experimental drug as defined in Section 111515 of the Health and Safety Code may be prescribed for or administered to any person under this part.

(c) No convulsive treatment as defined in Section 5325 of the Welfare and Institutions Code may be performed on any person under this part.

(d) No person may be sterilized under this part.

(e) The provisions of this part are subject to a valid advance health care directive under the Health Care Decisions Law, Division 4.7 (commencing with Section 4600). *(Stats.1990, c. 79 (A.B.759), § 14, operative July 1, 1991. Amended by Stats.1996, c. 1023 (S.B.1497), § 399, eff. Sept. 29, 1996; Stats.1999, c. 658 (A.B.891), § 24, operative July 1, 2000.)*

Law Revision Commission Comments

1990 Enactment

Section 3211 continues Section 3211 of the repealed Probate Code with the addition of the reference to a power of attorney for health care. This section is comparable to Section 2356 (Guardianship–Conservatorship Law). See the Comment to Section 2356. For background on the provisions of this part, see the Comment to this part under the part heading. [20 Cal.L.Rev.Comm.Reports 1001 (1990)].

1999 Amendment

Subdivision (e) of Section 3211 is amended to use the inclusive term "advance health care directive" used in the Health Care Decisions Law. This continues the substance of former law, since declarations under the former Natural Death Act and powers of attorney for health care are types of advance directives. See Section 4605 & Comment. Also covered by this language are "individual health care instructions." See Section 4623 & Comment. [29 Cal.L.Rev.Comm. Reports 1 (1999)].

Cross References

Health care decision defined for purposes of this Part, see Probate Code § 3200.
Health care defined for purposes of this Part, see Probate Code § 3200.
Wards or conservatees, involuntary placement in mental health treatment facility, see Probate Code § 2356.

§ 3212. Treatment by spiritual means

Nothing in this part shall be construed to supersede or impair the right of any individual to choose treatment by spiritual means in lieu of medical treatment, nor shall any individual choosing treatment by spiritual means, in accordance with the tenets and practices of that individual's established religious tradition, be required to submit to medical testing of any kind pursuant to a determination of capacity. *(Added by Stats.1999, c. 658 (A.B.891), § 25, operative July 1, 2000.)*

1999 Addition

Section 3212 continues former subdivision (g) of Section 3201 without substantive change. The former reference to "competency" has been changed to "capacity" to conform to the terminology of this part and related statutes. See, e.g., Section 3201 (capacity determination). [29 Cal.L.Rev.Comm. Reports 1 (1999)].

Part 8

OTHER PROTECTIVE PROCEEDINGS

1990 Enactment

This part supersedes Part 8 (commencing with Section 3300) of Division 4 of the repealed Probate Code. The superseded part was enacted upon recommendation of the California Law Revision Commission. See Recommendation Relating to Guardianship–Conservatorship Law, 14 Cal.L.Revision Comm'n Reports 501 (1978). For the Guardianship–Conservatorship Law as enacted in 1979 with the revisions made by Chapters 89 and 246 of the Statutes of 1980, see Guardianship–Conservatorship Law, 15 Cal.L.Revision Comm'n Reports 451 (1980). [20 Cal.L.Rev.Comm.Reports 1001 (1990)].

Cross References

Recovery by minor under uninsured motorists' coverage, see Insurance Code § 11580.3.

CHAPTER 1. GENERAL PROVISIONS

Section
3300. Accounting by parent to minor for money received.
3301. Repealed.
3302. Repealed.
3303. Effect on Uniform Transfers to Minors Act.

§ 3300. Accounting by parent to minor for money received

A parent who receives any money or property belonging to a minor under any provision of this part shall account to the minor for the money or other property when the minor reaches the age of majority. *(Stats.1990, c. 79 (A.B.759), § 14, operative July 1, 1991.)*

1990 Enactment

Section 3300 continues Section 3300 of the repealed Probate Code without change. For background on the provisions of this part, see the Comment to this part under the part heading. [20 Cal.L.Rev.Comm.Reports 1001 (1990)].

Cross References

Age of majority, see Family Code § 6500 et seq.

Money or property belonging to minor, see Probate Code § 3400 et seq.
Transfers to minors, accounts and accounting, see Probate Code §§ 3912, 3919.
Uniform Transfers to Minors Act, see Probate Code § 3900 et seq.

§ 3301. Repealed by Stats.1992, c. 162 (A.B.2650), § 11, operative Jan. 1, 1994

§ 3302. Repealed by Stats.1992, c. 162 (A.B.2650), § 12, operative Jan. 1, 1994

§ 3303. Effect on Uniform Transfers to Minors Act

Nothing in this part limits the provisions of the California Uniform Transfers to Minors Act, Part 9 (commencing with Section 3900). *(Stats.1990, c. 79 (A.B.759), § 14, operative July 1, 1991.)*

1990 Enactment

Section 3303 continues Section 3303 of the repealed Probate Code without change. Although this part does not limit the California Uniform Transfers to Minors Act, some provisions of this part supplement that act. See Sections 3412(b), 3413(b), 3602(c)(2), 3611(e). For background on this section, see Recommendation Relating to Uniform Transfers to Minors Act, 17 Cal.L.Revision Comm'n Reports 601 (1984). For background on the provisions of this part, see the Comment to this part under the part heading. [20 Cal.L.Rev.Comm.Reports 1001 (1990)].

CHAPTER 2. MONEY OR PROPERTY BELONGING TO MINOR

ARTICLE 1. TOTAL ESTATE NOT IN EXCESS OF $5,000

Section
3400. Total estate of minor; deductions.
3401. Delivery of money or property to parent.
3402. Written receipt of parent; effect.

§ 3400. Total estate of minor; deductions

(a) As used in this article, "total estate of the minor" includes both the money and other property belonging to the minor and the money and other property belonging to the guardianship estate, if any, of the minor.

(b) In computing the "total estate of the minor" for the purposes of this article, all of the following shall be deducted:

(1) "Custodial property" held pursuant to the California Uniform Transfers to Minors Act, Part 9 (commencing with Section 3900).

(2) Any money or property subject to court order pursuant to subdivision (c) of Section 3602 or Article 2 (commencing with Section 3610) of Chapter 4. *(Stats.1990, c. 79 (A.B.759), § 14, operative July 1, 1991.)*

Termination of guardianship by court, see Probate Code § 2626.

Law Revision Commission Comments
1990 Enactment

Section 3400 continues Section 3400 of the repealed Probate Code without change. For background on the provisions of this part, see the Comment to this part under the part heading. [20 Cal.L.Rev.Comm.Reports 1001 (1990)].

Cross References
Custody, services and earnings of minors, see Family Code §§ 7500, 7503.

§ 3401. Delivery of money or property to parent

(a) Where a minor does not have a guardian of the estate, money or other property belonging to the minor may be paid or delivered to a parent of the minor entitled to the custody of the minor to be held in trust for the minor until the minor reaches majority if the requirements of subdivision (c) are satisfied.

(b) Where the minor has a guardian of the estate, all the money and other property belonging to the guardianship estate may be paid or delivered to a parent entitled to the custody of the minor to be held in trust for the minor until the minor reaches majority if the requirements of subdivision (c) are satisfied.

(c) This section applies only if both of the following requirements are satisfied:

(1) The total estate of the minor, including the money and other property to be paid or delivered to the parent, does not exceed five thousand dollars ($5,000) in value.

(2) The parent to whom the money or other property is to be paid or delivered gives the person making the payment or delivery written assurance, verified by the oath of such parent, that the total estate of the minor, including the money or other property to be paid or delivered to the parent, does not exceed five thousand dollars ($5,000) in value. *(Stats. 1990, c. 79 (A.B.759), § 14, operative July 1, 1991.)*

Law Revision Commission Comments
1990 Enactment

Section 3401 continues Section 3401 of the repealed Probate Code without change. For background on the provisions of this part, see the Comment to this part under the part heading.

Subdivision (a) applies only where the minor has no guardian of the estate. If the minor has a guardian of the estate, the money is paid to the guardian, not to a parent. However, subdivision (b) permits the entire guardianship estate to be paid over to a parent without the need for a court order when the requirements of subdivision (c) are satisfied. Such payment does not avoid the need for termination of the guardianship by the court. See Section 2626. [20 Cal.L.Rev.Comm.Reports 1001 (1990)].

Cross References
Cities and counties, unclaimed money, see Government Code § 50052.5.
Duty of parent to account to minor, see Probate Code § 3300.
Payment of money belonging to minor, see Probate Code §§ 3412, 3413.
Payment of wages of minors, see Family Code § 7503.
Payment or delivery of proceeds of judgment, see Probate Code § 3611.
Right of parent to child's earnings, see Family Code § 7500.

§ 3402. Written receipt of parent; effect

The written receipt of the parent giving the written assurance under Section 3401 shall be an acquittance of the person making the payment of money or delivery of other property pursuant to this article. *(Stats.1990, c. 79 (A.B.759), § 14, operative July 1, 1991.)*

Law Revision Commission Comments
1990 Enactment

Section 3402 continues Section 3402 of the repealed Probate Code without change. For background on the provisions of this part, see the Comment to this part under the part heading. [20 Cal.L.Rev.Comm.Reports 1001 (1990)].

Cross References
Custody, services and earnings of minors, see Family Code §§ 7500, 7503.

ARTICLE 2. PROPERTY IN THE FORM OF MONEY

§ 3410. Application of article; computation of money belonging to minor

(a) This article applies to both of the following cases:

(1) Where the minor has a guardian of the estate and the sole asset of the guardianship estate is money.

(2) Where the minor has no guardian of the estate and there is money belonging to the minor.

(b) This article does not apply to, and there shall be excluded in computing "money belonging to the minor" for the purpose of this article, all of the following:

(1) Money or property which is or will be held as "custodial property" pursuant to the California Uniform Transfers to Minors Act, Part 9 (commencing with Section 3900).

(2) Any money or property subject to court order pursuant to subdivision (c) of Section 3602 or Article 2 (commencing with Section 3610) of Chapter 4. *(Stats.1990, c. 79 (A.B.759), § 14, operative July 1, 1991.)*

Law Revision Commission Comments
1990 Enactment

Section 3410 continues Section 3410 of the repealed Probate Code without change. For background on the provisions of this part, see the Comment to this part under the part heading. [20 Cal.L.Rev.Comm.Reports 1001 (1990)].

§ 3411. Filing of petition; venue

(a) A parent of a minor entitled to custody of the minor, the guardian of the estate of the minor, or the person holding the money belonging to the minor may file a petition requesting that the court make an order under this article.

(b) The petition shall be filed in the superior court of:

(1) The county where the minor resides if the minor has no guardian of the estate.

(2) The county having jurisdiction of the guardianship estate if the minor has a guardian of the estate. *(Stats.1990, c. 79 (A.B.759), § 14, operative July 1, 1991.)*

Law Revision Commission Comments

1990 Enactment

Section 3411 continues Section 3411 of the repealed Probate Code without change. For general provisions, see 1020–1023 (petitions and other papers). For background on the provisions of this part, see the Comment to this part under the part heading. [20 Cal.L.Rev.Comm.Reports 1001 (1990)].

§ 3412. Court-ordered termination of guardianship where sole asset of guardianship estate is money; additional orders within court's discretion

If the minor has a guardian of the estate and the sole asset of the guardianship estate is money, the court may order that the guardianship of the estate be terminated and, if the court so orders, the court in its discretion shall also order any one or more of the following:

(a) That the money be deposited in an insured account in a financial institution in this state, or in a single-premium deferred annuity, subject to withdrawal only upon authorization of the court.

(b) That all or any part of the money be transferred to a custodian for the benefit of the minor under the California Uniform Transfers to Minors Act, Part 9 (commencing with Section 3900).

(c) If the money of the guardianship estate does not exceed twenty thousand dollars ($20,000), that the money be held on any other condition that the court in its discretion determines to be in the best interests of the minor.

(d) If the money of the guardianship estate does not exceed five thousand dollars ($5,000), that all or any part of the money be paid to a parent of the minor, without bond, upon the terms and under the conditions specified in Article 1 (commencing with Section 3400).

(e) That the remaining balance of any money paid or to be paid be deposited with the county treasurer, if all of the following conditions are met:

(1) The county treasurer has been authorized by the county board of supervisors to handle the deposits.

(2) The county treasurer shall receive and safely keep all money deposited with the county treasurer pursuant to this subdivision, shall pay the money out only upon the order of the court, and shall credit each estate with the interest earned by the funds deposited less the county treasurer's actual cost authorized to be recovered under Section 27013 of the Government Code.

(3) The county treasurer and sureties on the official bond of the county treasurer are responsible for the safekeeping and payment of the money.

(4) The county treasurer shall ensure that the money deposited is to earn interest or dividends, or both, at the highest rate which the county can reasonably obtain as a prudent investor.

(5) Funds so deposited with the county treasurer shall only be invested or deposited in compliance with the provisions governing the investment or deposit of state funds set forth in Chapter 5 (commencing with Section 16640) of Part 2 of Division 4 of Title 2 of the Government Code, the investment or deposit of county funds set forth in Chapter 4 (commencing with Section 53600) of Part 1 of Division 2 of Title 5 of the Government Code, or as authorized under Chapter 6 (commencing with Section 2400) of Part 4. *(Stats.1990, c. 79 (A.B.759), § 14, operative July 1, 1991. Amended by Stats. 1991, c. 413 (A.B.934), § 1; Stats.2004, c. 67 (A.B.1851), § 1.)*

Law Revision Commission Comments

1990 Enactment

Section 3412 continues Section 3412 of the repealed Probate Code with the substitution of language that requires money to be deposited in an insured account in a financial institution in this state for the former language listing various financial institution accounts. This section applies only where the minor has a guardian of the estate. Where the minor has no guardian of the estate, Section 3413 applies. Section 3412 is comparable to Section 3611 (money received pursuant to compromise or judgment). For general provisions relating to hearings and orders, see Sections 1040–1050. For background on the provisions of this part, see the Comment to this part under the part heading.

Where the money of the guardianship estate does not exceed $5,000, the court, in its discretion, may make an order under subdivision (a), (b), (c), or (d). Where the money exceeds $5,000 but does not exceed $20,000, the court has discretion to make an order under subdivision (a), (b), or (c). Where the money exceeds $20,000, the court may make an order only under subdivision (a) or (b).

Where the total estate of the minor (as defined in Section 3400) does not exceed $5,000, money of the guardianship estate may be paid directly to a parent under Section 3401 without obtaining a court order under this article, or a petition may be filed under this article to obtain a court order under Section 3412. This article provides a guardian who is reluctant to turn over the money to a parent to hold in trust for the minor with the alternative of requesting that the court order the amount be deposited or invested under subdivision (a) of Section 3412. [20 Cal.L.Rev.Comm.Reports 1001 (1990)].

Cross References

Cities, and other agencies, deposit of funds, local agency fund audit reports, see Government Code § 53686.
Definitions, single-premium deferred annuity, see Probate Code § 1446.

§ 3413. Order of court if no guardianship exists

If the minor has no guardian of the estate and there is money belonging to the minor, the court may order that a guardian of the estate be appointed and that the money be paid to the guardian or the court may order any one or more of the following:

(a) That the money be deposited in an insured account in a financial institution in this state, or in a single-premium deferred annuity, subject to withdrawal only upon authorization of the court.

(b) That all or any part of the money be transferred to a custodian for the benefit of the minor under the California

Uniform Transfers to Minors Act, Part 9 (commencing with Section 3900).

(c) If the money belonging to the minor does not exceed twenty thousand dollars ($20,000), that the money be held on any other condition that the court in its discretion determines to be in the best interests of the minor.

(d) If the money belonging to the minor does not exceed five thousand dollars ($5,000), that all or any part of the money be paid to a parent of the minor, without bond, upon the terms and under the conditions specified in Article 1 (commencing with Section 3400).

(e) That the remaining balance of any money paid or to be paid be deposited with the county treasurer, if all of the following conditions are met:

(1) The county treasurer has been authorized by the county board of supervisors to handle the deposits.

(2) The county treasurer shall receive and safely keep all money deposited with the county treasurer pursuant to this subdivision, shall pay the money out only upon the order of the court, and shall credit each estate with the interest earned by the funds deposited less the county treasurer's actual cost authorized to be recovered under Section 27013 of the Government Code.

(3) The county treasurer and sureties on the official bond of the county treasurer are responsible for the safekeeping and payment of the money.

(4) The county treasurer shall ensure that the money deposited is to earn interest or dividends, or both, at the highest rate which the county can reasonably obtain as a prudent investor.

(5) Funds so deposited with the county treasurer shall only be invested or deposited in compliance with the provisions governing the investment or deposit of state funds set forth in Chapter 5 (commencing with Section 16640) of Part 2 of Division 4 of Title 2 of the Government Code, the investment or deposit of county funds set forth in Chapter 4 (commencing with Section 53600) of Part 1 of Division 2 of Title 5 of the Government Code, or as authorized under Chapter 6 (commencing with Section 2400) of Part 4. *(Stats.1990, c. 79 (A.B.759), § 14, operative July 1, 1991. Amended by Stats. 1991, c. 413 (A.B.934), § 2; Stats.2004, c. 67 (A.B.1851), § 2.)*

Definitions,
Money belonging to the minor, see Probate Code § 3410.
Single-premium deferred annuity, see Probate Code § 1446.

CHAPTER 3. COMPROMISE BY PARENT OF MINOR'S DISPUTED CLAIM

Section
3500. Parental right to compromise minor's claim.

§ 3500. Parental right to compromise minor's claim

(a) When a minor has a disputed claim for damages, money, or other property and does not have a guardian of the estate, the following persons have the right to compromise, or to execute a covenant not to sue on or a covenant not to enforce judgment on, the claim, unless the claim is against such person or persons:

(1) Either parent if the parents of the minor are not living separate and apart.

(2) The parent having the care, custody, or control of the minor if the parents of the minor are living separate and apart.

(b) The compromise or covenant is valid only after it has been approved, upon the filing of a petition, by the superior court of either of the following counties:

(1) The county where the minor resides when the petition is filed.

(2) Any county where suit on the claim or matter properly could be brought.

(c) Any money or other property to be paid or delivered for the benefit of the minor pursuant to the compromise or covenant shall be paid and delivered in the manner and upon the terms and conditions specified in Chapter 4 (commencing with Section 3600).

(d) A parent having the right to compromise the disputed claim of the minor under this section may execute a full release and satisfaction, or execute a covenant not to sue on or a covenant not to enforce judgment on the disputed claim, after the money or other property to be paid or delivered has been paid or delivered as provided in subdivision (c). If the court orders that all or any part of the money to be paid under the compromise or covenant be deposited in an insured account in a financial institution in this state, or in a single-premium deferred annuity, the release and satisfaction or covenant is not effective for any purpose until the money has been deposited as directed in the order of the court. *(Stats.1990, c. 79 (A.B.759), § 14, operative July 1, 1991.)*

Where the minor has a guardian of the estate, the guardian (rather than the parent) has authority to compromise the claim. See Sections 2500–2507. If the claim is the subject of pending litigation, the minor must appear in the action either by a guardian of the estate or by a guardian ad litem, and in such case Section 372 of the Code of Civil Procedure provides for compromise of the claim. [20 Cal.L.Rev.Comm.Reports 1001 (1990)].

Cross References

Bank accounts by or in name of minors, see Financial Code § 850.
Definitions, single-premium preferred annuity, see Probate Code § 1446.
Deposit of funds and assets in trust company, see Financial Code § 1586.
Insured savings associations, legal investment, see Financial Code § 7000 et seq.
Life and disability insurance, insurance of minors, see Insurance Code § 10112.
Money or property as delivered pursuant to compromise or judgment, see Code of Civil Procedure § 372.

CHAPTER 4. MONEY OR PROPERTY PAID OR DELIVERED PURSUANT TO COMPROMISE OR JUDGMENT FOR MINOR OR DISABLED PERSON

Application

For application of this chapter, see Probate Code § 3600.

Cross References

Destruction of court records, notice, retention periods, see Government Code § 68152.
Expedited petition for court approval of the compromise of, or a covenant on, a disputed claim, a compromise or settlement of a pending action, or the disposition of the proceeds of a judgment, see California Rules of Court, Rule 7.955.
Life and disability insurance, insurance of minors, see Insurance Code § 10112.
Petition for court approval of the compromise of, or a covenant on, a disputed claim, a compromised or settlement of a pending action, or the disposition of the proceeds of a judgment, see California Rules of Court, Rule 7.950.

ARTICLE 1.   GENERAL PROVISIONS

Application

For application of this chapter, see Probate Code § 3600.

Cross References

Fee for filing petition and opposition papers concerning internal affairs of certain trusts or first accounts of trustees of certain testamentary trusts, see Government Code § 70652.

§ 3600.   Application of chapter

This chapter applies whenever both of the following conditions exist:

(a) A court (1) approves a compromise of, or the execution of a covenant not to sue on or a covenant not to enforce judgment on, a minor's disputed claim, (2) approves a compromise of a pending action or proceeding to which a minor or person with a disability is a party, or (3) gives judgment for a minor or person with a disability.

(b) The compromise, covenant, or judgment provides for the payment or delivery of money or other property for the benefit of the minor or person with a disability. *(Stats.1990, c. 79 (A.B.759), § 14, operative July 1, 1991. Amended by Stats.2004, c. 67 (A.B.1851), § 3.)*

Law Revision Commission Comments

1990 Enactment

Section 3600 continues Section 3600 of the repealed Probate Code without change. The reference in this section to "incompetent person" includes "a person for whom a conservator may be appointed." See Section 3603. For background on the provisions of this part, see the Comment to this part under the part heading. [20 Cal.L.Rev.Comm.Reports 1001 (1990)].

Cross References

Attorney's fees for services to a minor or a person with a disability, see California Rules of Court, Rule 7.955.
Fee for filing petition commencing or opposition papers concerning certain probate proceedings, see Government Code § 70655.
Money or property as delivered pursuant to compromise or judgment, see Code of Civil Procedure § 372.
Payment of wages to minors until notice by guardian to employer, see Family Code § 7503.
References to "person with a disability" within this Chapter, see Probate Code § 3603.
Settlements or judgments in certain civil cases involving minors or persons with disabilities, see California Rules of Court, Standards of Judicial Administration, Standard 7.10.
Trusts funded by court order, review of certain trusts by probate department or judge, see California Rules of Court, Rule 7.903.

§ 3601.   Order directing payment of expenses, costs and fees

(a) The court making the order or giving the judgment referred to in Section 3600, as a part thereof, shall make a further order authorizing and directing that reasonable expenses, medical or otherwise and including reimbursement to a parent, guardian, or conservator, costs, and attorney's fees, as the court shall approve and allow therein, shall be paid from the money or other property to be paid or delivered for the benefit of the minor or person with a disability.

(b) The order required by subdivision (a) may be directed to the following:

(1) A parent of the minor, the guardian ad litem, or the guardian of the estate of the minor or the conservator of the estate of the person with a disability.

(2) The payer of any money to be paid pursuant to the compromise, covenant, or judgment for the benefit of the minor or person with a disability. *(Stats.1990, c. 79 (A.B. 759), § 14, operative July 1, 1991. Amended by Stats.2004, c. 67 (A.B.1851), § 4.)*

Application

For application of this chapter, see Probate Code § 3600.

Law Revision Commission Comments
1990 Enactment

Section 3601 continues Section 3601 of the repealed Probate Code without change. The reference in this section to "incompetent person" includes "a person for whom a conservator may be appointed." See Section 3603. For background on the provisions of this part, see the Comment to this part under the part heading.

Under subdivision (b)(2), the court may order the payer of the money to pay the expenses, costs, and fees approved and allowed by the court directly to the persons entitled thereto. For example, under subdivision (b), the court may either:

(1) Order pursuant to paragraph (1) that the money be paid to the guardian or conservator of the estate who is further ordered to pay the expenses, costs, and fees approved and allowed by the court to the persons entitled thereto; or

(2) Order pursuant to paragraph (2) that the payer of the money pay such expenses, costs, and fees directly to the persons entitled thereto and the remaining balance to the guardian or conservator of the estate or as otherwise provided in Article 2 (commencing with Section 3610). [20 Cal.L.Rev.Comm.Reports 1001 (1990)].

Cross References

Attorney's fees for services to a minor or a person with a disability, see California Rules of Court, Rule 7.955.
Contingent fee contract with attorney, see Probate Code § 2644.
Disposition of remaining balance where no guardianship or conservatorship, see Probate Code § 3610.
References to "person with a disability" within this Chapter, see Probate Code § 3603.

§ 3602. Disposition of remaining balance

(a) If there is no guardianship of the estate of the minor or conservatorship of the estate of the person with a disability, the remaining balance of the money and other property, after payment of all expenses, costs, and fees as approved and allowed by the court under Section 3601, shall be paid, delivered, deposited, or invested as provided in Article 2 (commencing with Section 3610).

(b) Except as provided in subdivisions (c) and (d), if there is a guardianship of the estate of the minor or conservatorship of the estate of the person with a disability, the remaining balance of the money and other property, after payment of all expenses, costs, and fees as approved and allowed by the court under Section 3601, shall be paid or delivered to the guardian or conservator of the estate. Upon application of the guardian or conservator, the court making the order or giving the judgment referred to in Section 3600 or the court in which the guardianship or conservatorship proceeding is pending may, with or without notice, make an order that all or part of the money paid or to be paid to the guardian or conservator under this subdivision be deposited or invested as provided in Section 2456.

(c) Upon ex parte petition of the guardian or conservator or upon petition of any person interested in the guardianship or conservatorship estate, the court making the order or giving the judgment referred to in Section 3600 may for good cause shown order one or more of the following:

(1) That all or part of the remaining balance of money not become a part of the guardianship or conservatorship estate and instead be deposited in an insured account in a financial institution in this state, or in a single-premium deferred annuity, subject to withdrawal only upon authorization of the court.

(2) If there is a guardianship of the estate of the minor, that all or part of the remaining balance of money and other property not become a part of the guardianship estate and instead be transferred to a custodian for the benefit of the minor under the California Uniform Transfers to Minors Act, Part 9 (commencing with Section 3900).

(3) That all or part of the remaining balance of money and other property not become a part of the guardianship estate and, instead, be transferred to the trustee of a trust which is either created by, or approved of, in the order or judgment described in Section 3600. This trust shall be revocable by the minor upon attaining 18 years of age, and shall contain other terms and conditions, including, but not limited to, terms and conditions concerning trustee's accounts and trustee's bond, as the court determines to be necessary to protect the minor's interests.

(d) Upon petition of the guardian, conservator, or any person interested in the guardianship or conservatorship estate, the court making the order or giving the judgment referred to in Section 3600 may order that all or part of the remaining balance of money not become a part of the guardianship or conservatorship estate and instead be paid to a special needs trust established under Section 3604 for the benefit of the minor or person with a disability.

(e) If the petition is by a person other than the guardian or conservator, notice of hearing on a petition under subdivision (c) shall be given for the period and in the manner provided in Chapter 3 (commencing with Section 1460) of Part 1.

(f) Notice of the time and place of hearing on a petition under subdivision (d), and a copy of the petition, shall be mailed to the State Director of Health Care Services, the Director of State Hospitals, and the Director of Developmental Services at the office of each director in Sacramento at least 15 days before the hearing. *(Stats.1990, c. 79 (A.B.759), § 14, operative July 1, 1991. Amended by Stats.1992, c. 355 (A.B.3328), § 2; Stats.1996, c. 563 (S.B.392), § 18; Stats. 2004, c. 67 (A.B.1851), § 5; Stats.2012, c. 440 (A.B.1488), § 54, eff. Sept. 22, 2012.)*

Application

For application of this chapter, see Probate Code § 3600.

Law Revision Commission Comments
1990 Enactment

Section 3602 continues Section 3602 of the repealed Probate Code with the substitution of language that requires money to be deposited in an insured account in a financial institution in this state for the former language listing various financial institution accounts. The reference in this section to "incompetent person" includes "a person for whom a conservator may be appointed." See Section 3603. For general provisions relating to notice of hearing, see Sections 1200–

1221. See also Sections 1260–1265 (proof of giving notice). For background on the provisions of this part, see the Comment to this part under the part heading.

Paragraph (2) of subdivision (c) gives the court the alternative of ordering that all or any part of the money and other property be transferred to a custodian to be subject to the California Uniform Transfers to Minors Act. This alternative gives the custodian more flexibility in handling money (by avoiding the need for court authorization for any withdrawal) and permits a custodian to handle other property (rather than requiring it in every case to become a part of the guardianship estate).

Nothing in the California Uniform Transfers to Minors Act gives a custodian under that act any authority to settle or release a claim of the minor against a third party. Only a guardian of the estate (Prob.Code §§ 2500–2507) or guardian ad litem or other person authorized under another law (see, e.g., Code Civ.Proc. § 372; Prob.Code § 3500) to act for the minor may settle or release such a claim. See Uniform Transfers to Minors Act § 8 comment (1986). [20 Cal.L.Rev.Comm.Reports 1001 (1990)].

1992 Amendment

Section 3602 is amended to add authority for the court to order that money of a minor or incompetent person be paid to a special needs trust established under Section 3604. As provided in Section 3604(d), before payment to the trustee, liens authorized by the Welfare and Institutions Code must first be satisfied. See, e.g., Welf. & Inst.Code §§ 7282.1, 14124.71–14124.76, 17109, 17403. [22 Cal.L.Rev.Comm.Reports 989 (1992)].

Cross References

Computation of money belonging to the minor, see Probate Code § 3410.
References to "person with a disability" within this Chapter, see Probate Code § 3603.
Single-premium deferred annuity, see Probate Code § 1446.
Total estate of minor, deductions, see Probate Code § 3400.

§ 3603. Reference to "person with a disability"

Where reference is made in this chapter to a "person with a disability," the reference shall be deemed to include the following:

(a) A person for whom a conservator may be appointed.

(b) Any of the following persons, subject to the provisions of Section 3613:

(1) A person who meets the definition of disability as defined in Section 1382c(a)(3) of Title 42 of the United States Code, or as defined in Section 416(i)(1) of Title II of the federal Social Security Act (42 U.S.C. Sec. 401 et seq.) and regulations implementing that act, as set forth in Part 416.905 of Title 20 of the Federal Code of Regulations.

(2) A person who meets the definition of disability as defined in paragraphs (1), (2), and (3) of subsection (d) of Section 423 of Title II of the federal Social Security Act (42 U.S.C. Sec. 401 et seq.) and regulations implementing that act, as set forth in Part 404.1505 of Title 20 of the Federal Code of Regulations.

(3) A minor who meets the definition of disability, as set forth in Part 416.906 of Title 20 of the Federal Code of Regulations.

(4) A person with a developmental disability, as defined in Section 4512 of the Welfare and Institutions Code. *(Stats. 1990, c. 79 (A.B.759), § 14, operative July 1, 1991. Amended by Stats.2004, c. 67 (A.B.1851), § 6.)*

Application

For application of this chapter, see Probate Code § 3600.

Law Revision Commission Comments
1990 Enactment

Section 3603 continues Section 3603 of the repealed Probate Code without substantive change. For background on the provisions of this part, see the Comment to this part under the part heading. [20 Cal.L.Rev.Comm.Reports 1001 (1990)].

Cross References

Continuing jurisdiction of court over trusts of persons with a disability who have reached the age of majority, see Probate Code § 3613.

§ 3604. Payment to special needs trust; petition for order; trust requirements; jurisdiction of court; court orders

(a)(1) If a court makes an order under Section 3602 or 3611 that money of a minor or person with a disability be paid to a special needs trust, the terms of the trust shall be reviewed and approved by the court and shall satisfy the requirements of this section. The trust is subject to continuing jurisdiction of the court, and is subject to court supervision to the extent determined by the court. The court may transfer jurisdiction to the court in the proper county for commencement of a proceeding as determined under Section 17005.

(2) If the court referred to in subdivision (a) could have made an order under Section 3602 or 3611 to place that money into a special needs trust, but that order was not requested, a parent, guardian, conservator, or other interested person may petition a court that exercises jurisdiction pursuant to Section 800 for that order. In doing so, notice shall be provided pursuant to subdivisions (e) and (f) of Section 3602, or subdivision (c) of Section 3611, and that notice shall be given at least 15 days before the hearing.

(b) A special needs trust may be established and continued under this section only if the court determines all of the following:

(1) That the minor or person with a disability has a disability that substantially impairs the individual's ability to provide for the individual's own care or custody and constitutes a substantial handicap.

(2) That the minor or person with a disability is likely to have special needs that will not be met without the trust.

(3) That money to be paid to the trust does not exceed the amount that appears reasonably necessary to meet the special needs of the minor or person with a disability.

(c) If at any time it appears (1) that any of the requirements of subdivision (b) are not satisfied or the trustee refuses without good cause to make payments from the trust for the special needs of the beneficiary, and (2) that the State Department of Health Care Services, the State Department of State Hospitals, the State Department of Developmental Services, or a county or city and county in this state has a claim against trust property, that department, county, or city and county may petition the court for an order terminating the trust.

(d) A court order under Section 3602 or 3611 for payment of money to a special needs trust shall include a provision that all statutory liens in favor of the State Department of Health Care Services, the State Department of State Hospitals, the State Department of Developmental Services, and any county or city and county in this state shall first be satisfied. *(Added by Stats.1992, c. 355 (A.B.3328), § 3. Amended by Stats.2004, c. 67 (A.B.1851), § 7; Stats.2012, c. 440 (A.B.1488), § 55, eff. Sept. 22, 2012.)*

Application

For application of this chapter, see Probate Code § 3600.

Law Revision Commission Comments

1992 Addition

Section 3604 is new. The section permits personal injury damages or settlement proceeds for a disabled minor or incompetent person to be delivered to a trustee of a special needs trust. In approving the terms of the trust, the court may, for example, require periodic accountings, court approval for certain kinds of investments, or the giving of a surety bond.

If the personal injury case is concluded in another jurisdiction, e.g., in federal court, a petition for supervision of the trust may be filed in the proper superior court as provided in Section 17200. [22 Cal.L.Rev.Comm.Reports 989 (1992)].

Cross References

Department of Developmental Services, see Welfare and Institutions Code § 4400 et seq.
Department of Health Care Services, generally, see Health and Safety Code § 100100 et seq.
Probate Rules, minors' claims, petition for the approval of the compromise of a claim, see California Rules of Court, Rule 7.950.
References to "person with a disability" within this Chapter, see Probate Code § 3603.
Trusts funded by court order, review of certain trusts by probate department or judge, see California Rules of Court, Rule 7.903.

§ 3605. Statutes of limitation; death of beneficiary; notice of death; payment of claims; application of section

(a) This section applies only to a special needs trust established under Section 3604 on or after January 1, 1993.

(b) While the special needs trust is in existence, the statute of limitations otherwise applicable to claims of the State Department of Health Care Services, the State Department of State Hospitals, the State Department of Developmental Services, and any county or city and county in this state is tolled. Notwithstanding any provision in the trust instrument, at the death of the special needs trust beneficiary or on termination of the trust, the trust property is subject to claims of the State Department of Health Care Services, the State Department of State Hospitals, the State Department of Developmental Services, and any county or city and county in this state to the extent authorized by law as if the trust property is owned by the beneficiary or is part of the beneficiary's estate.

(c) At the death of the special needs trust beneficiary or on termination of the trust, the trustee shall give notice of the beneficiary's death or the trust termination, in the manner provided in Section 1215, to all of the following:

(1) The State Department of Health Care Services, the State Department of State Hospitals, and the State Depart-

ment of Developmental Services, addressed to the director of that department at the Sacramento office of the director.

(2) Any county or city and county in this state that has made a written request to the trustee for notice, addressed to that county or city and county at the address specified in the request.

(d) Failure to give the notice required by subdivision (c) prevents the running of the statute of limitations against the claim of the department, county, or city and county not given the notice.

(e) The department, county, or city and county has four months after notice is given in which to make a claim with the trustee. If the trustee rejects the claim, the department, county, or city and county making the claim may petition the court for an order under Chapter 3 (commencing with Section 17200) of Part 5 of Division 9, directing the trustee to pay the claim. A claim made under this subdivision shall be paid as a preferred claim prior to any other distribution. If trust property is insufficient to pay all claims under this subdivision, the trustee shall petition the court for instructions and the claims shall be paid from trust property as the court deems just.

(f) If trust property is distributed before expiration of four months after notice is given without payment of the claim, the department, county, or city and county has a claim against the distributees to the full extent of the claim, or each distributee's share of trust property, whichever is less. The claim against distributees includes interest at a rate equal to that earned in the Pooled Money Investment Account, Article 4.5 (commencing with Section 16480) of Chapter 3 of Part 2 of Division 4 of Title 2 of the Government Code, from the date of distribution or the date of filing the claim, whichever is later, plus other accruing costs as in the case of enforcement of a money judgment. *(Added by Stats.1992, c. 355 (A.B. 3328), § 4. Amended by Stats.2012, c. 440 (A.B.1488), § 56, eff. Sept. 22, 2012.)*

Application

For application of this chapter, see Probate Code § 3600.

Law Revision Commission Comments

1992 Addition

Section 3605 is new. Section 3605 permits reimbursement from special needs trusts established under Section 3604, but only on termination of the trust. Section 3605 does not affect other trusts, including special needs trusts to receive damages or settlement proceeds established pursuant to court order before the operative date of this section.

A court order under subdivision (e) directing the trustee to pay the claim or denying the claim is appealable. Section 17207.

Except for statutory liens ordered paid under subdivision (d) of Section 3604, all reimbursement rights of public agencies are deferred while the special needs trust is in existence. On the death of the special needs trust beneficiary or on termination of the trust, trust property may become subject to reimbursement claims under federal or state law. See, e.g., 42 U.S.C. § 1396p(b)(1)(B) (Medicaid); Welf. & Inst.Code §§ 7276, 7513–7513.2 (state hospital costs), 14009.5 (Medi–Cal), 17109, 17403 (counties). For this purpose and only this purpose, the trust property is treated as the beneficiary's property or as property of the beneficiary's estate.

On termination of a special needs trust, the normal rules governing distribution of property are applicable, subject to the claims reimbursement provisions of this section. See Section 15410 (disposition of property on trust termination). [22 Cal.L.Rev.Comm.Reports 989 (1992)].

Cross References

Department of Developmental Services, see Welfare and Institutions Code § 4400 et seq.

Department of Health Care Services, generally, see Health and Safety Code § 100100 et seq.

ARTICLE 2. DISPOSITION OF MONEY OR OTHER PROPERTY WHERE NO GUARDIANSHIP OR CONSERVATORSHIP

Section
3610. Disposition of remaining balance.
3611. Order of court.
3612. Continuing jurisdiction until minor reaches majority; continuing jurisdiction over trust of person with a disability who reaches majority.
3613. Orders or judgments with respect to adults who have capacity to consent.

Application

For application of this chapter, see Probate Code § 3600.

§ 3610. Disposition of remaining balance

When money or other property is to be paid or delivered for the benefit of a minor or person with a disability under a compromise, covenant, order or judgment, and there is no guardianship of the estate of the minor or conservatorship of the estate of the person with a disability, the remaining balance of the money and other property (after payment of all expenses, costs, and fees as approved and allowed by the court under Section 3601) shall be paid, delivered, deposited, or invested as provided in this article. *(Stats.1990, c. 79 (A.B.759), § 14, operative July 1, 1991. Amended by Stats. 2004, c. 67 (A.B.1851), § 8.)*

Application

For application of this chapter, see Probate Code § 3600.

Law Revision Commission Comments

1990 Enactment

Section 3610 continues Section 3610 of the repealed Probate Code without change. This section makes clear that this article applies only where there is not an existing guardianship or conservatorship of the estate. The section is consistent with subdivision (a) of Section 3602. For provisions relating to the authority of a parent, guardian, conservator, or guardian ad litem to compromise claims and actions, see Sections 2500–2507 and 3500 and Code of Civil Procedure Sections 372 and 373.5. The reference in Section 3610 to "incompetent person" includes "a person for whom a conservator may be appointed." See Section 3603. For background on the provisions of this part, see the Comment to this part under the part heading. [20 Cal.L.Rev.Comm.Reports 1001 (1990)].

Cross References

Authority of parent, guardian, conservator to compromise claims and actions, see Code of Civil Procedure § 372; Probate Code §§ 2500 et seq., 3500.

Computation of money belonging to the minor, see Probate Code § 3410.

Payment of wages to minors until notice by guardian to employer, see Family Code § 7503.

References to "person with a disability" within this Chapter, see Probate Code § 3603.

Total estate of minor, deductions, see Probate Code § 3400.

Trustee's standard of care, see Probate Code § 16040 et seq.

§ 3611. Order of court

In any case described in Section 3610, the court making the order or giving the judgment referred to in Section 3600 shall, upon application of counsel for the minor or person with a disability, order any one or more of the following:

(a) That a guardian of the estate or conservator of the estate be appointed and that the remaining balance of the money and other property be paid or delivered to the person so appointed.

(b) That the remaining balance of any money paid or to be paid be deposited in an insured account in a financial institution in this state, or in a single-premium deferred annuity, subject to withdrawal only upon the authorization of the court, and that the remaining balance of any other property delivered or to be delivered be held on conditions the court determines to be in the best interest of the minor or person with a disability.

(c) After a hearing by the court, that the remaining balance of any money and other property be paid to a special needs trust established under Section 3604 for the benefit of the minor or person with a disability. Notice of the time and place of the hearing and a copy of the petition shall be mailed to the State Director of Health Care Services, the Director of State Hospitals, and the Director of Developmental Services at the office of each director in Sacramento at least 15 days before the hearing.

(d) If the remaining balance of the money to be paid or delivered does not exceed twenty thousand dollars ($20,000), that all or any part of the money be held on any other conditions the court in its discretion determines to be in the best interest of the minor or person with a disability.

(e) If the remaining balance of the money and other property to be paid or delivered does not exceed five thousand dollars ($5,000) in value and is to be paid or delivered for the benefit of a minor, that all or any part of the money and the other property be paid or delivered to a parent of the minor, without bond, upon the terms and under the conditions specified in Article 1 (commencing with Section 3400) of Chapter 2.

(f) If the remaining balance of the money and other property to be paid or delivered is to be paid or delivered for the benefit of the minor, that all or any part of the money and other property be transferred to a custodian for the benefit of the minor under the California Uniform Transfers to Minors Act, Part 9 (commencing with Section 3900).

(g) That the remaining balance of the money and other property be paid or delivered to the trustee of a trust which is created by, or approved of, in the order or judgment referred to in Section 3600. This trust shall be revocable by the minor upon attaining the age of 18 years, and shall contain other terms and conditions, including, but not limited to, terms and conditions concerning trustee's accounts and trustee's bond, as the court determines to be necessary to protect the minor's interests.

(h) That the remaining balance of any money paid or to be paid be deposited with the county treasurer, if all of the following conditions are met:

(1) The county treasurer has been authorized by the county board of supervisors to handle the deposits.

(2) The county treasurer shall receive and safely keep all money deposited with the county treasurer pursuant to this subdivision, shall pay the money out only upon the order of the court, and shall credit each estate with the interest earned by the funds deposited less the county treasurer's actual cost authorized to be recovered under Section 27013 of the Government Code.

(3) The county treasurer and sureties on the official bond of the county treasurer are responsible for the safekeeping and payment of the money.

(4) The county treasurer shall ensure that the money deposited is to earn interest or dividends, or both, at the highest rate which the county can reasonably obtain as a prudent investor.

(5) Funds so deposited with the county treasurer shall only be invested or deposited in compliance with the provisions governing the investment or deposit of state funds set forth in Chapter 5 (commencing with Section 16640) of Part 2 of Division 4 of Title 2 of the Government Code, the investment or deposit of county funds set forth in Chapter 4 (commencing with Section 53600) of Part 1 of Division 2 of Title 5 of the Government Code, or as authorized under Chapter 6 (commencing with Section 2400) of Part 4.

(i) That the remaining balance of the money and other property be paid or delivered to the person with a disability. *(Stats.1990, c. 79 (A.B.759), § 14, operative July 1, 1991. Amended by Stats.1991, c. 413 (A.B.934), § 3; Stats.1992, c. 355 (A.B.3328), § 5; Stats.1993, c. 978 (S.B.305), § 4; Stats. 1996, c. 563 (S.B.392), § 19; Stats.2004, c. 67 (A.B.1851), § 9; Stats.2012, c. 440 (A.B.1488), § 57, eff. Sept. 22, 2012.)*

Application

For application of this chapter, see Probate Code § 3600.

Law Revision Commission Comments
1990 Enactment

Section 3611 continues Section 3611 of the repealed Probate Code with the substitution of language that requires money to be deposited in an insured account in a financial institution in this state for the former language listing various financial institution accounts. Where the money and other property to be paid or delivered does not exceed $5,000 and is for the benefit of a minor, the court, in its discretion, may make an order under subdivision (a), (b), (c), (d), or (e). Where the amount exceeds $5,000 but does not exceed $20,000, the court has discretion to make an order under subdivision (a), (b), (c), or (e), but not under subdivision (d). Where the amount exceeds $20,000, the court may make an order under subdivision (a), (b), or (e). See also Section 3401 (direct payment to parent without court order). The reference in Section 3611 to "incompetent person" includes "a person for whom a conservator may be appointed." See Section 3603. For background on the provisions of this part, see the Comment to this part under the part heading. [20 Cal.L.Rev.Comm.Reports 1001 (1990)].

1992 Amendment

Section 3611 is amended to add subdivision (c) to permit money of a minor or incompetent person to be paid to the trustee of a special needs trust established under Section 3604. Before payment or delivery to the trust, all statutory liens in favor of the Department of Health Services, Department of Mental Health. Department of Developmental Services, and any county or city and county in this state must first be satisfied. See Section 3604(d); Welf. & Inst.Code §§ 7282.1, 14124.71–14124.76, 17109, 17403. [22 Cal.L.Rev.Comm.Reports 989 (1992)].

1993 Amendment

Subdivision (c) of Section 3611 is amended to require a hearing before the court may order money to be paid to a special needs trust under this section, and to require notice to affected state agencies. This amendment conforms Section 3611(c) to Section 3602(f). [23 Cal.L.Rev.Comm. Reports 901 (1993) (Annual Report, App. 4)].

Cross References

Accounting by parent to minor for money received, see Probate Code § 3300.
Cities, and other agencies, deposit of funds, local agency fund audit reports, see Government Code § 53686.
Delivery of money or property to parent, see Probate Code § 3401.
Payment of wages to minors until notice by guardian to employer, see Family Code § 7503.
References to "person with a disability" within this Chapter, see Probate Code § 3603.
Special needs trusts, requirements, see Probate Code § 3604.

§ 3612. Continuing jurisdiction until minor reaches majority; continuing jurisdiction over trust of person with a disability who reaches majority

(a) Notwithstanding any other provision of law and except to the extent the court orders otherwise, the court making the order under Section 3611 shall have continuing jurisdiction of the money and other property paid, delivered, deposited, or invested under this article until the minor reaches 18 years of age.

(b) Notwithstanding subdivision (a), the trust of an individual who meets the definition of a person with a disability under paragraph (3) of subdivision (b) of Section 3603 and who reaches 18 years of age, shall continue and be under continuing court jurisdiction until terminated by the court. *(Stats.1990, c. 79 (A.B.759), § 14, operative July 1, 1991. Amended by Stats.2004, c. 67 (A.B.1851), § 10.)*

Application

For application of this chapter, see Probate Code § 3600.

Law Revision Commission Comments
1990 Enactment

Section 3612 continues Section 3612 of the repealed Probate Code without change. For background on the provisions of this part, see the Comment to this part under the part heading. [20 Cal.L.Rev.Comm.Reports 1001 (1990)].

Cross References

References to "person with a disability" within this Chapter, see Probate Code § 3603.

§ 3613. Orders or judgments with respect to adults who have capacity to consent

Notwithstanding any other provision of this chapter, a court may not make an order or give a judgment pursuant to

Section 3600, 3601, 3602, 3610, or 3611 with respect to an adult who has the capacity within the meaning of Section 812 to consent to the order and who has no conservator of the estate with authority to make that decision, without the express consent of that person. *(Added by Stats.2004, c. 67 (A.B.1851), § 11.)*

Application

For application of this chapter, see Probate Code § 3600.

CHAPTER 5.　PROPERTY OF ABSENT FEDERAL PERSONNEL

Law Revision Commission Comments

1994 Amendment

The chapter heading is amended since the power of attorney provisions in Article 4 (commencing with Section 3720) are not restricted to personal property. [24 Cal.L.Rev.Comm.Reports 323 (1994)].

ARTICLE 1.　DEFINITIONS

Section
3700.　Meaning of terms used in chapter.

Cross References

Conservator of estate of missing persons, see Probate Code § 1804.
Death of persons not heard from in five years, presumption, see Evidence Code § 667.
Special conservatorship provisions where proposed conservatee is a missing person, see Probate Code § 1845 et seq.

§ 3700.　Meaning of terms used in chapter

As used in this chapter:

(a) "Absentee" is defined in Section 1403.

(b) "Certificate of missing status" means the official written report complying with Section 1283 of the Evidence Code and showing the determination of the secretary of the military department or the head of the department or agency concerned or the delegate of the secretary or head that the absentee is in missing status.

(c) "Eligible spouse" means the spouse of an absentee who has not commenced an action or proceeding for judicial or legal separation, annulment, adjudication of nullity, or dissolution of the marriage of the spouse and the absentee.

(d) "Family of an absentee" means an eligible spouse, if any, or if no eligible spouse, the child or children of an absentee, equally, or if no child or children, the parent or parents of an absentee, equally, provided these persons are dependents of the absentee as defined in Section 401 of Title 37 of the United States Code, and the guardian of the estate or conservator of the estate of any person bearing such relationship to the absentee.

(e) "Secretary concerned" is defined in Section 1440. *(Stats.1990, c. 79 (A.B.759), § 14, operative July 1, 1991.)*

Law Revision Commission Comments

1990 Enactment

Section 3700 continues Section 3700 of the repealed Probate Code without substantive change. The reference to "divorce" is omitted as unnecessary in view of Section 36 ("dissolution of marriage" includes divorce). For background on this section, see Recommendation Relating to Missing Persons, 16 Cal.L.Revision Comm'n Reports 105, 124–25 (1982). [20 Cal.L.Rev.Comm.Reports 1001 (1990)].

Cross References

Dissolution of marriage, see Family Code §§ 310, 2300 et seq.
Judicial determination of void or voidable marriage, see Family Code § 2200 et seq.

ARTICLE 2.　COURT PROCEEDING TO SET ASIDE PERSONAL PROPERTY OF ABSENTEE

§ 3701.　Setting aside personal property of absentee

Upon petition as provided in this chapter, the court may set aside to the family of an absentee personal property of the absentee situated in this state for the purpose of managing, controlling, encumbering, selling, or conveying, or otherwise engaging in any transaction with respect to the property, if the court determines that to do so will be in the best interest of the absentee, including the interest of the absentee in providing for shelter, food, health care, education, transportation, or the maintenance of a reasonable and adequate standard of living for the family of the absentee. The absentee's interest in the property set aside shall not exceed twenty thousand dollars ($20,000). *(Stats.1990, c. 79 (A.B. 759), § 14, operative July 1, 1991.)*

Law Revision Commission Comments

1990 Enactment

Section 3701 continues Section 3701 of the repealed Probate Code without change. The authority for the court to provide support for the absentee's family is consistent with the original purpose of the legislation, which was not only to avoid "prejudice to the estates of such missing persons," but also to avoid "difficulty and hardship to their families [caused] by their inability to consummate transactions, such as to sell property, withdraw funds, cash checks, transfer securities and the like, upon which the families are dependent." 1972 Cal.Stat. ch. 988 § 9. [20 Cal.L.Rev.Comm.Reports 1001 (1990)].

Cross References

Absentee defined, see Probate Code §§ 1403, 3700.
Contents of petition, see Probate Code § 3703.

Family of an absentee defined for purposes of this Chapter, see Probate Code § 3700.

§ 3702. Persons authorized to petition

A petition that personal property of an absentee be set aside as provided in this chapter may be filed by any of the following persons:

(a) A person in whose favor the personal property of the absentee may be set aside.

(b) A person to whom the absentee has issued a general power of attorney while serving in the armed forces of the United States or while an employee of any agency or department of the United States, provided the power of attorney was valid and effective at the time issued, regardless whether it has expired or terminated. *(Stats.1990, c. 79 (A.B.759), § 14, operative July 1, 1991.)*

Law Revision Commission Comments
1990 Enactment

Section 3702 continues Section 3702 of the repealed Probate Code without change. [20 Cal.L.Rev.Comm.Reports 1001 (1990)].

Cross References

Absentee defined, see Probate Code §§ 1403, 3700.

§ 3703. Contents of petition

(a) The petition shall contain all of the following:

(1) A statement that the petition is filed under this chapter.

(2) In its caption, the last known military rank or grade and the social security account number of the absentee.

(3) A specific description and estimate of the value of all of the absentee's property, wherever situated (including all sums due the absentee from the United States).

(4) A designation of the property to be set aside, and the facts establishing that setting aside the property is necessary and in the best interest of the absentee.

(5) If the property is to be set aside for the benefit of the spouse of the absentee, an allegation that the spouse is an eligible spouse.

(6) So far as known to the petitioner, the names and addresses of all persons comprising the family of the absentee, and an allegation whether a guardian of the estate or a conservator of the estate of any member of the family of the absentee has been appointed.

(b) There shall be attached to the petition a certificate of missing status. The certificate of missing status shall be received as evidence of that fact and the court shall not determine the status of the absentee inconsistent with the status shown in the certificate. *(Stats.1990, c. 79 (A.B.759), § 14, operative July 1, 1991.)*

Law Revision Commission Comments
1990 Enactment

Section 3703 continues Section 3703 of the repealed Probate Code without substantive change. For general provisions relating to petitions and other papers, see Sections 1020–1023. For background on this section, see Recommendation Relating to Missing Persons, 16

Cal.L.Revision Comm'n Reports 105, 125–26 (1982). [20 Cal.L.Rev.Comm.Reports 1001 (1990)].

Cross References

Absentee defined, see Probate Code §§ 1403, 3700.
Eligible spouse defined, see Probate Code § 3700.
Family of an absentee defined for purposes of this Chapter, see Probate Code § 3700.

§ 3704. Notice of hearing

(a) Notice of the nature of the proceedings and the time and place of the hearing shall be given by the petitioner at least 15 days before the hearing date by all of the following means:

(1) By mail, together with a copy of the petition, to all persons comprising the family of the absentee.

(2) By delivery by a method that would be sufficient for service of summons in a civil action, together with a copy of the petition, to the secretary concerned or to the head of the United States department or agency concerned.

(3) By publication pursuant to Section 6061 of the Government Code in a newspaper of general circulation in the county in which the proceedings will be held.

(b) Whenever notice to an officer or agency of this state or of the United States would be required under Section 1461 or Section 1822 upon petition for appointment of a conservator, like notice shall be given of the petition under this chapter. *(Stats.1990, c. 79 (A.B.759), § 14, operative July 1, 1991.)*

Law Revision Commission Comments
1990 Enactment

Section 3704 continues Section 3704 of the repealed Probate Code without change. For general provisions relating to notice of hearing, see Sections 1200–1221. See also Sections 1260–1265 (proof of giving notice). [20 Cal.L.Rev.Comm.Reports 1001 (1990)].

Cross References

Absentee defined, see Probate Code §§ 1403, 3700.
Family of an absentee defined for purposes of this Chapter, see Probate Code § 3700.
Secretary concerned defined, see Probate Code § 1440.
Service of summons, civil actions, see Code of Civil Procedure § 413.10 et seq.

§ 3705. Hearing and order

(a) Upon the hearing of the petition, any officer or agency of this state or the United States or the authorized delegate of the officer or agency, or any relative or friend of the absentee, may appear and support or oppose the petition.

(b) If the court determines that the allegations of the petition are true and correct, the court may order set aside to the family of the absentee personal property of the absentee situated in this state (excluding any sums due the absentee from the United States) in which the absentee's interest does not exceed twenty thousand dollars ($20,000). The property set aside shall be specified in the order.

(c) No bond shall be required of any person to whom property of the absentee has been set aside by order of the court pursuant to this chapter. *(Stats.1990, c. 79 (A.B.759), § 14, operative July 1, 1991.)*

Section 3705 continues Section 3705 of the repealed Probate Code without substantive change. For general provisions, see Sections 1000–1004 (rules of practice), 1040–1050 (hearings and orders). [20 Cal.L.Rev.Comm.Reports 1001 (1990)].

Cross References

Absentee defined, see Probate Code §§ 1403, 3700.
Family of an absentee defined for purposes of this Chapter, see
　Probate Code § 3700.

§ 3706. Jurisdiction of court; amount

A determination by the court that the value of all of the absentee's property, wherever situated, exceeds twenty thousand dollars ($20,000) or that the absentee owns or has an interest in real property, wherever situated, does not deprive the court of jurisdiction to set aside to the family of the absentee personal property of the absentee situated in this state in which the absentee's interest does not exceed twenty thousand dollars ($20,000), and the court shall order set aside such personal property to the family of the absentee if the court finds that all of the other provisions of this chapter have been complied with. The property set aside shall be specified in the order. *(Stats.1990, c. 79 (A.B.759), § 14, operative July 1, 1991.)*

Section 3706 continues Section 3706 of the repealed Probate Code without substantive change. [20 Cal.L.Rev.Comm.Reports 1001 (1990)].

Cross References

Absentee defined, see Probate Code §§ 1403, 3700.
Family of an absentee defined for purposes of this Chapter, see
　Probate Code § 3700.

§ 3707. Joint tenancy property

For the purposes of this chapter, any property or interest therein or lien thereon that the absentee holds as joint tenant shall be included in determining the property of the absentee and its value. The joint tenancy interest may be set aside to the family of the absentee as provided in this chapter but may only be set aside to a member of the absentee's family who was a joint tenant with the absentee in the property. *(Stats.1990, c. 79 (A.B.759), § 14, operative July 1, 1991.)*

Section 3707 continues Section 3707 of the repealed Probate Code without change. [20 Cal.L.Rev.Comm.Reports 1001 (1990)].

Cross References

Absentee defined, see Probate Code §§ 1403, 3700.
Family of an absentee defined for purposes of this Chapter, see
　Probate Code § 3700.
Joint tenancy, definition, method of creation, see Civil Code § 683.

§ 3708. Accounting

(a) Within six months after the absentee has returned to the controllable jurisdiction of the military department or civilian agency or department concerned, or within six months after the determination of death of the absentee by the secretary concerned or the head of the department or agency concerned or the delegate of the secretary or head, the former absentee or the personal representative of the deceased absentee may, by motion in the same proceeding, require the person or persons to whom the property of the absentee was set aside to account for the property and the proceeds, if any. The time of return to the controllable jurisdiction of the military department or civilian department or agency concerned or the determination of the time of death of the absentee shall be determined by the court under 37 United States Code, Section 556, or 5 United States Code, Section 5566. An official written report or record of the military department or civilian department or agency that the absentee has returned to its controllable jurisdiction or is deceased shall be received as evidence of that fact.

(b) This section does not in any manner derogate the finality and conclusiveness of any order, judgment, or decree previously entered in the proceeding. *(Stats.1990, c. 79 (A.B.759), § 14, operative July 1, 1991.)*

Section 3708 continues Section 3708 of the repealed Probate Code without change. [20 Cal.L.Rev.Comm.Reports 1001 (1990)].

Cross References

Absentee defined, see Probate Code §§ 1403, 3700.
Secretary concerned defined, see Probate Code § 1440.

ARTICLE 3. MANAGEMENT AND DISPOSITION OF PERSONAL PROPERTY OF ABSENTEE WITHOUT COURT PROCEEDING

Section

This article supersedes Article 3 (commencing with Section 3710) of Chapter 5 of Part 8 of Division 4 of the repealed Probate Code. The superseded article was enacted upon recommendation of the California Law Revision Commission. See Recommendation Relating to Missing Persons, 16 Cal.L.Revision Comm'n Reports 105, 126–28 (1982). [20 Cal.L.Rev.Comm.Reports 1001 (1990)].

§ 3710. Transactions relating to absentee's personal property

The family of an absentee may collect, receive, dispose of, or engage in any transaction relating to the absentee's personal property situated in this state without any judicial proceeding if all the following conditions are satisfied:

(a) The absentee owns no real property situated in this state.

(b) The aggregate value of all of the absentee's personal property situated in this state is five thousand dollars ($5,000) or less, excluding any money owed the absentee by the United States.

(c) The family of the absentee needs to dispose of such personal property to provide for shelter, food, health care, education, transportation, or the maintenance of a reasonable and adequate standard of living for the family of the absentee. *(Stats.1990, c. 79 (A.B.759), § 14, operative July 1, 1991.)*

§ 3711. Transfer of property; certificate; affidavit

(a) If the conditions set forth in Section 3710 are satisfied, the family of the absentee may have any evidence of interest, indebtedness, or right attributable to the absentee's personal property transferred to the family of the absentee, or transferred to the person to whom the property is to be sold or transferred by the family of the absentee, upon furnishing the person (including any governmental body) having custody of the property both of the following:

(1) A certificate of missing status.

(2) An affidavit stating under oath that the provisions of this article are applicable and that the aggregate value of all property received pursuant to this affidavit, together with all other property previously received under this article, does not exceed five thousand dollars ($5,000).

(b) The receipt of a certificate of missing status and affidavit under subdivision (a) constitutes sufficient acquittance for any payment of money or delivery of property made pursuant to this article and fully discharges the recipient from any further liability concerning the money or property without the necessity of inquiring into the truth of any of the facts stated in the affidavit. *(Stats.1990, c. 79 (A.B.759), § 14, operative July 1, 1991.)*

§ 3712. Limitation of actions

The time within which an absentee may commence an action against any person who executes an affidavit and receives property pursuant to this article commences to run on the earlier of the following dates:

(a) Ninety days after the absentee returns to the United States after the termination of the condition that caused the classification of an absentee.

(b) Two years after the termination of the condition that caused the classification of an absentee. *(Stats.1990, c. 79 (A.B.759), § 14, operative July 1, 1991.)*

ARTICLE 4. ABSENTEE'S POWER OF ATTORNEY

Section
3720. Termination of power; liability for relying or acting on power.
3721. Actual knowledge of principal's death or incapacity while absent; revocation by absent principal.
3722. Dissolution of marriage, annulment or legal separation; absentee's spouse acting as attorney-in-fact.

§ 3720. Termination of power; liability for relying or acting on power

If an absentee executed a power of attorney that expires during the period that occasions absentee status, the power of attorney continues in full force and effect until 30 days after the absentee status is terminated. Any person who acts in reliance upon the power of attorney when accompanied by a copy of a certificate of missing status is not liable for relying and acting upon the power of attorney. *(Stats.1990, c. 79 (A.B.759), § 14, operative July 1, 1991.)*

§ 3721. Actual knowledge of principal's death or incapacity while absent; revocation by absent principal

For the purposes of Chapter 5 (commencing with Section 4300) of Part 2 of Division 4.5, in the case of a principal who is an absentee, an attorney-in-fact or third person shall be deemed to be without actual knowledge of the following:

(a) The principal's death or incapacity while the absentee continues in missing status and until the attorney-in-fact or third person receives notice of the determination of the absentee's death by the secretary concerned or the head of the department or agency concerned or the delegate of the secretary or head.

(b) Revocation by the principal during the period described in subdivision (a). *(Added by Stats.1994, c. 307 (S.B.1907), § 14.)*

Law Revision Commission Comments

1994 Addition

Section 3721 continues without substantive change the part of Civil Code Section 2357 that related to powers of attorney involving federal absentees. References to "attorney-in-fact or third person" have been substituted for the former references to "person" for clarity and conformity with the language of the Power of Attorney Law.

See also Sections 1403 ("absentee" defined), 1440 ("secretary concerned" defined), 4014 ("attorney-in-fact" defined), 4026 ("principal" defined), 4034 ("third person" defined). [24 Cal.L.Rev.Comm.Reports 323 (1994)].

Cross References

Absentee defined, see Probate Code §§ 1403, 3700.

§ 3722. Dissolution of marriage, annulment or legal separation; absentee's spouse acting as attorney-in-fact

If after the absentee executes a power of attorney, the principal's spouse who is the attorney-in-fact commences a proceeding for dissolution, annulment, or legal separation, or a legal separation is ordered, the attorney-in-fact's authority is revoked. This section is in addition to the provisions of Sections 4154 and 4697. *(Added by Stats.1994, c. 307 (S.B.1907), § 15. Amended by Stats.1999, c. 658 (A.B.891), § 26, operative July 1, 2000.)*

Law Revision Commission Comments

1994 Addition

Section 3722 continues the part of former subdivision (f) of Civil Code Section 2355 relating to the effect of a legal separation and the filing of a petition for dissolution, nullity, or legal separation in the case of federal absentees. The reference in former law to contrary provisions "in writing" is omitted because it is unnecessary; powers of attorney are required to be in writing and the Power of Attorney Law permits variation of default rules in the power of attorney. See Sections 4022 ("power of attorney" defined), 4101 (priority of provisions of power of attorney).

See also Sections 1403 ("absentee" defined), 4014 ("attorney-in-fact" defined), 4022 ("power of attorney" defined). [24 Cal.L.Rev.Comm.Reports 323 (1994)].

1999 Amendment

Section 3722 is amended to refer to a corresponding section concerning advance health care directives.

See also Sections 1403 ("absentee" defined), 4014 ("attorney-in-fact" defined), 4022 ("power of attorney" defined). [29 Cal.L.Rev. Comm. Reports 1 (1999)].

Cross References

Absentee defined, see Probate Code §§ 1403, 3700.

CHAPTER 6. REMOVAL OF PROPERTY OF NONRESIDENT

§ 3800. Petition; filing; conservatorship transferred to another state

(a) If a nonresident has a duly appointed, qualified, and acting guardian, conservator, committee, or comparable fiduciary in the place of residence and if no proceeding for guardianship or conservatorship of the nonresident is pending or contemplated in this state, the nonresident fiduciary may petition to have property owned by the nonresident removed to the place of residence.

(b) The petition for removal of property of the nonresident shall be filed in the superior court of the county in which the nonresident is or has been temporarily present or in which the property of the nonresident, or the principal part thereof, is located.

(c) If a conservatorship was transferred from this state to another state pursuant to Article 3 (commencing with Section 2001) of Chapter 8 of Part 3, the foreign conservator may remove the conservatee's personal property from this state without seeking a petition under this chapter. *(Stats.1990, c. 79 (A.B.759), § 14, operative July 1, 1991. Amended by Stats.2014, c. 553 (S.B.940), § 27, eff. Jan. 1, 2015, operative Jan. 1, 2016.)*

Law Revision Commission Comments

1990 Enactment

Section 3800 continues Section 3800 of the repealed Probate Code without substantive change. For general provisions relating to petitions and other papers, see Sections 1020–1023. See also Sections 1260–1265 (proof of giving notice). [20 Cal.L.Rev.Comm.Reports 1001 (1990)].

2014 Amendment

Section 3800 is amended to reflect the enactment of the California Conservatorship Jurisdiction Act (Section 1980 *et seq.*). [43 Cal. L.Rev.Comm. Reports 93 (2013)].

Cross References

Transfer of assets of pending guardianship to another jurisdiction, see Probate Code § 2800 et seq.

§ 3801. Notice

(a) The petition shall be made upon 15 days' notice, by mail or personal delivery, to all of the following persons:

(1) The personal representative or other person in whose possession the property may be.

(2) Persons in this state, known to the petitioner, who are obligated to pay a debt, perform an obligation, or issue a security to the nonresident or the estate of the nonresident.

(b) The petition shall be made upon such additional notice, if any, as the court may order. *(Stats.1990, c. 79 (A.B.759), § 14, operative July 1, 1991.)*

Law Revision Commission Comments

1990 Enactment

Section 3801 continues Section 3801 of the repealed Probate Code without substantive change. For general provisions relating to notice of hearing, see Sections 1200–1221. See also Sections 1260–1265 (proof of giving notice). [20 Cal.L.Rev.Comm.Reports 1001 (1990)].

Request for special notice, see Probate Code § 2700 et seq.

§ 3802. Certificate of nonresident fiduciary

(a) The nonresident fiduciary shall produce and file one of the following certificates:

(1) A certificate that the fiduciary is entitled, by the laws of the place of appointment of the fiduciary, to the possession of the estate of the nonresident. The certificate shall be under the hand of the clerk and seal of the court from which the appointment of the fiduciary was derived and shall show a transcript of the record of appointment and that the fiduciary has entered upon the discharge of the duties of the fiduciary.

(2) A certificate that the fiduciary is entitled, by the laws of the place of residence, to custody of the estate of the nonresident, without the appointment of any court. The certificate shall be under the hand of the clerk and seal of either (i) the court in the place of residence having jurisdiction of estates of persons that have a guardian, conservator, committee, or comparable fiduciary or (ii) the highest court in the place of residence.

(b) In the case of a foreign country, the certificate shall be accompanied by a final statement certifying the genuineness of the signature and official position of (1) the court clerk making the original certificate or (2) any foreign official who has certified either the genuineness of the signature and official position of the court clerk making the original certificate or the genuineness of the signature and official position of another foreign official who has executed a similar certificate in a chain of such certificates beginning with a certificate of the genuineness of the signature and official position of the clerk making the original certificate. The final statement may be made only by a secretary of an embassy or legation, consul general, consul, vice consul, or consular agent of the United States, or a diplomatic or consular official of the foreign country assigned or accredited to the United States. *(Stats.1990, c. 79 (A.B.759), § 14, operative July 1, 1991.)*

Law Revision Commission Comments

1990 Enactment

Section 3802 continues Section 3802 of the repealed Probate Code without change. Subdivision (b) (persons who may attest certificate in foreign country) is consistent with Evidence Code Section 1530 (statement certifying genuineness of attestation to accuracy of copy of a writing). [20 Cal.L.Rev.Comm.Reports 1001 (1990)].

Cross References

Statements certifying genuineness of attestation to accuracy of copy of a writing, see Evidence Code § 1530.

§ 3803. Order for removal

(a) Upon the petition, if the court determines that removal of the property will not conflict with any restriction or limitation on the property or impair the right of the nonresident to the property or the rights of creditors or claimants in this state, the court shall make an order granting to the nonresident fiduciary leave to remove the property of the nonresident to the place of residence unless good cause to the contrary is shown.

(b) The order is authority to the fiduciary to sue for and receive the property in his or her own name for the use and benefit of the nonresident.

(c) The order is a discharge of the personal representative or other person in whose possession the property may be at the time the order is made and of the person obligated to pay a debt, perform an obligation, or issue a security to the nonresident or the estate of the nonresident, upon filing with the clerk of the court the receipt of the nonresident fiduciary for the property and transmitting a duplicate receipt, or a certified copy of the receipt, to the court, if any, from which the nonresident fiduciary received his or her appointment. *(Stats.1990, c. 79 (A.B.759), § 14, operative July 1, 1991.)*

Law Revision Commission Comments

1990 Enactment

Section 3803 continues Section 3803 of the repealed Probate Code without substantive change. For general provisions, see Sections 1000–1004 (rules of practice), 1040–1050 (hearings and orders). [20 Cal.L.Rev.Comm.Reports 1001 (1990)].

Part 9

CALIFORNIA UNIFORM TRANSFERS TO MINORS ACT

Application

Application of part to transfers made on or after January 1, 1985, see Probate Code §§ 3922, 3923.

Law Revision Commission Comments

1990 Enactment

This part supersedes Part 9 (commencing with Section 3900) of Division 4 of the repealed Probate Code. The superseded part was enacted upon recommendation of the California Law Revision Commission. See Recommendation Relating to Uniform Transfers to Minors Act, 17 Cal.L.Revision Comm'n Reports 601 (1984). See also Report of Senate Committee on Judiciary on Assembly Bill 2492, 18 Cal.L.Revision Comm'n Reports 105 (1986). As to the construction of provisions drawn from uniform acts, see Section 2. See also the Comments of the Uniform Law Commissioners to the Uniform Transfers to Minors Act (1986). [20 Cal.L.Rev.Comm.Reports 1001 (1990)].

Cross References

Devises subject to this act, see Probate Code § 6341 et seq.
Golden State Scholarshare Trust,
  Definitions, see Education Code § 69980.
  Ownership rights under participation agreements, see Education Code § 69986.

§ 3900. Short title

This part may be cited as the "California Uniform Transfers to Minors Act." *(Stats.1990, c. 79 (A.B.759), § 14, operative July 1, 1991.)*

Law Revision Commission Comments

1990 Enactment

Section 3900 continues Section 3900 of the repealed Probate Code without change. This section is the same as Section 24 of the Uniform Transfers to Minors Act (1986).

Background on Section 3900 of Repealed Code

Section 3900 was a new provision added by 1984 Cal.Stat. ch. 243 § 9. For background on the provisions of this part, see the Comment to this part under the part heading. [20 Cal.L.Rev.Comm.Reports 1001 (1990)].

Cross References

Minor defined for purposes of this Part, see Probate Code § 3901.
Transfer defined for purposes of this Part, see Probate Code § 3901.

§ 3901. Definitions

In this part:

(a) "Adult" means an individual who has attained the age of 18 years.

(b) "Benefit plan" means an employer's plan for the benefit of an employee or partner.

(c) "Broker" means a person lawfully engaged in the business of effecting transactions in securities or commodities for the person's own account or for the account of others.

(d) "Conservator" means a person appointed or qualified by a court to act as general, limited, or temporary guardian of a minor's property or a person legally authorized to perform substantially the same functions.

(e) "Court" means the superior court.

(f) "Custodial property" means (1) any interest in property transferred to a custodian under this part and (2) the income from and proceeds of that interest in property.

(g) "Custodian" means a person so designated under Section 3909 or a successor or substitute custodian designated under Section 3918.

(h) "Financial institution" means a bank, trust company, savings institution, or credit union, chartered and supervised under state or federal law or an industrial loan company licensed and supervised under the laws of this state.

(i) "Legal representative" means an individual's personal representative or conservator.

(j) "Member of the minor's family" means the minor's parent, stepparent, spouse, grandparent, brother, sister, uncle, or aunt, whether of the whole or half blood or by adoption.

(k) "Minor" means:

(1) Except as provided in paragraph (2), an individual who has not attained the age of 18 years.

(2) When used with reference to the beneficiary for whose benefit custodial property is held or is to be held, an individual who has not attained the age at which the custodian is required under Sections 3920 and 3920.5 to transfer the custodial property to the beneficiary.

(*l*) "Person" means an individual, corporation, organization, or other legal entity.

(m) "Personal representative" means an executor, administrator, successor personal representative, or special administrator of a decedent's estate or a person legally authorized to perform substantially the same functions.

(n) "State" includes any state of the United States, the District of Columbia, the Commonwealth of Puerto Rico, and any territory or possession subject to the legislative authority of the United States.

(*o*) "Transfer" means a transaction that creates custodial property under Section 3909.

(p) "Transferor" means a person who makes a transfer under this part.

(q) "Trust company" means a financial institution, corporation, or other legal entity, authorized to exercise general trust powers. *(Stats.1990, c. 79 (A.B.759), § 14, operative July 1, 1991.)*

Law Revision Commission Comments

1990 Enactment

Section 3901 continues Section 3901 of the repealed Probate Code without change. This section is the same in substance as Section 1 of the Uniform Transfers to Minors Act (1986), except as indicated below.

Section 3901 differs from the Uniform Transfers to Minors Act in the following respects:

(1) Definition of "adult." "Adult" is defined in subdivision (a) to mean an individual who has attained the age of 18 years. This is consistent with Civil Code Sections 25 and 27. One effect of this definition is that an individual custodian (other than a transferor-custodian) must be 18 years of age or older. See Section 3909. This minimum age requirement does not apply where the transferor is the custodian (see Section 3909); a transferor may be a custodian without regard to age so long as the transferor has the capacity to

make the transfer. Accordingly, if the minor can make an effective transfer of the property under the law relating to emancipation or competence to make a will, gift, or other transfer, a minor may transfer the property to a custodian for his or her own benefit or for the benefit of another minor. For example, Civil Code Section 63 permits an emancipated minor to make a will, gift, or other transfer. This authorizes an emancipated minor to make a transfer to a custodian for the minor's own benefit or for the benefit of another minor and also to serve as the custodian for custodial property the minor transfers under this part for the benefit of another minor.

The definition of "adult" is also used to determine persons who may file petitions under this part. See Section 3918, subdivision (d) ("adult member of the minor's family" may petition the court to designate a successor custodian), subdivision (f) ("adult member of the minor's family" may petition the court to remove the custodian for cause and to designate a successor custodian or to require the custodian to give appropriate bond), Section 3919(a) ("adult member of minor's family" may petition for accounting or determination of custodian's liability).

(2) Definition of "court." "Court" is defined in subdivision (e) to mean "the superior court."

(3) Definition of "financial institution." Subdivision (h) expands the Uniform Act definition of "financial institution" to include "an industrial loan company licensed and supervised under the laws of this state."

(4) Definition of "minor." "Minor" is defined in subdivision (k) to mean an individual who has not attained the age of 18 years (consistent with Civil Code § 25), except that the term "minor" may include an older individual under some circumstances when the term is used with reference to the beneficiary for whose benefit custodial property is held or is to be held. See Sections 3920, 3920.5. When used with reference to a beneficiary for whose benefit custodial property is held or is to be held, "minor" is defined in subdivision (k)(2) as an individual who has not attained the age at which the custodial property is to be transferred to the beneficiary. This age depends upon the type of transfer and whether the transfer specifically provides for the custodianship to continue until the minor attains an age older than 18 years of age. See Sections 3920 and 3920.5 and the Comments thereto. Where a custodianship may continue until a specified age older than 18, the custodianship may be established after the beneficiary has attained the age of 18 and may continue for so long as is specifically provided but not longer than the maximum duration permitted for a custodianship created by that type of transfer.

The definition of "benefit plan" in subdivision (b) is intentionally very broad and is meant to cover any contract, plan, system, account, or trust, such as a pension plan, retirement plan, death benefit plan, deferred compensation plan, employment agency arrangement, or stock bonus, option, or profit sharing plan.

The definition of "conservator" in subdivision (d) conforms to the Uniform Transfers to Minors Act. For California purposes, the term means the guardian of the estate of the minor, if the minor has not attained the age of 18 years (Prob.Code § 1600) and the conservator of the estate if the "minor" has attained the age of 18 years (Prob.Code § 1800.3).

The definition of "custodial property" in subdivision (f) encompasses every conceivable legal or equitable interest in property of any kind, including real property and tangible or intangible personal property. The term is intended, for example, to include joint interests with right of survivorship and beneficial interests in land trusts, as well as all other intangible interests in property. Contingent or expectancy interests such as the designation as a beneficiary under insurance policies or benefit plans become "custodial property" only if the designation is irrevocable, or when it becomes so, but this part specifically authorizes the "nomination" of a future custodian as beneficiary of such interests (see Section 3903). Proceeds of custodial property, both immediate and remote, are themselves custodial property.

Custodial property is defined without reference to the physical location of the property, even if it has one. No useful purpose would be served by restricting the application of this part to, for example, real estate "located in this state," since a conveyance recorded in the state of the property's location, if done with proper formalities, should be effective even if that state has not enacted the Uniform Transfers to Minors Act. The rights, duties and powers of the custodian should be determined by reference to the law of the state under which the custodianship is created, assuming there is sufficient nexus under Section 3902 between that state and the transferor, the minor, or the custodian.

The definition of "transfer" in subdivision (o) reflects the application of this part not only to gifts, but also to distributions from trusts and estates, obligors of the minor, and transfers of the minor's own assets to a custodianship by the legal representative of a minor, all of which are permitted by this part.

"Transferor" as defined in subdivision (p) includes not only the maker of a gift (i.e., a donor in the usual sense), but also fiduciaries and obligors who control or own property that is the subject of the transfer. Nothing requires that a transferor be an "adult." See discussion, supra, this Comment.

Only entities authorized to exercise "general" trust powers qualify as "trust companies" under subdivision (q); the authority to exercise only limited fiduciary responsibilities, such as the authority to accept Individual Retirement Account deposits, is not sufficient.

Background on Section 3901 of Repealed Code

Section 3901 was added by 1984 Cal.Stat. ch. 243 § 9. Section 3901 superseded former Civil Code Section 1155 (repealed by 1984 Cal.Stat. ch. 243 § 1) which provided definitions for the former California Uniform Gifts to Minors Act. To reflect the broader scope and the unlimited types of property to which the new California Uniform Transfers to Minors Act applies, a number of definitional changes were from the old California Uniform Gifts to Minors Act. For background on the provisions of this part, see the Comment to this part under the part heading.

Several definitions in the old Uniform Act specifically applicable to limited types of property (cash, securities, and insurance policies) covered before the expansion of the scope of the Uniform Act were omitted as unnecessary. These omitted definitions included the definitions of "bank," "issuer," "life or endowment insurance policies and annuity contracts," "savings and loan association," "security," and "transfer agent." No change in the meaning or construction of those terms as used in this part was intended by such omissions. See Uniform Transfers to Minors Act § 1 comment (1986). The substantive effect of the definition of "[l]ife or endowment insurance policies and annuity contracts" in the old Act was superseded by Section 3901(f) and subdivision (b)(2) of Section 3912 (right to retain property transferred to custodian) and subdivision (c) of Section 3912 (right to invest in or pay premiums on insurance or endowment policies). The definition of "insured financial institution" was omitted because the prudent person rule of Section 3912(b) may dictate the use of insured institutions or depositories, without having the Act so specify. See Uniform Transfers to Minors Act § 1 comment (1986).

The principal changes or additions to the remaining definitions contained in former Civil Code Section 1155 are discussed below.

Subdivision (a). Subdivision (a), defining "adult," continued subdivision (a) of former Section 1155 of the Civil Code. The requirement of former law—Civil Code Section 1156(a) (repealed by 1984 Cal.Stat. ch. 243 § 1)—that the donor be an "adult" was not continued.

Subdivision (b). The definition of "benefit plan" was new and drawn from the Uniform Transfers to Minors Act § 1(2).

Subdivision (d). The term "conservator" was defined instead of "guardian" to conform to the Uniform Transfers to Minors Act § 1(4).

Subdivision (e). The definition of "court" continued the definition of former Civil Code § 1155(d).

Subdivision (f). The definition of "custodial property" was generalized to conform to the Uniform Transfers to Minors Act § 1(6).

Subdivision (h). The definition of "financial institution" continued a provision of the definition of former Civil Code § 1155(g).

Subdivision (j). The definition of "member of the minor's family" expanded the definition under former Civil Code Section 1155 to include the minor's stepparent and spouse.

Subdivision (k). When used with reference to a beneficiary for whose benefit custodial property is held or is to be held, "minor" was defined as an individual who has not attained the age at which the custodial property is to be transferred to the beneficiary. Under former Civil Code Section 1155(m), the age of termination of the custodianship had been lowered from 21 to 18 (1972 Cal.Stat. ch. 579 § 11) to conform to the lowering of the age of majority from 21 to 18 (1971 Cal.Stat. ch. 1748 § 23).

Subdivision (m). The new definition of "personal representative" was based upon that definition in Section 1–201(30) of the Uniform Probate Code (1987). This definition was the same in substance as the Uniform Transfers to Minors Act § 1(13).

Subdivision (o). The new definition of "transfer" was necessary to reflect the application of the Act not only to gifts, but also to distributions from trusts and estates, obligors of the minor, and transfers of the minor's own assets to a custodianship by the legal representative of a minor, all of which are permitted by the Uniform Transfers to Minors Act and under this part.

Subdivision (p). The new definition of "transferor" was required because the term includes not only the maker of a gift, i.e., a donor in the usual sense, but also fiduciaries and obligors who control or own property that is the subject of the transfer.

Subdivision (q). The new definition of "trust company" replaced the definition of former Civil Code Section 1155 (which defined a trust company by reference to Financial Code Sections 107 and 109). [20 Cal.L.Rev.Comm.Reports 1001 (1990)].

§ 3902. Application of part

(a) This part applies to a transfer that refers to this part in the designation under subdivision (a) of Section 3909 by which the transfer is made if at the time of the transfer, the transferor, the minor, or the custodian is a resident of this state or the custodial property is located in this state. The custodianship so created remains subject to this part despite a subsequent change in residence of a transferor, the minor, or the custodian, or the removal of custodial property from this state.

(b) A person designated as custodian under this part is subject to personal jurisdiction in this state with respect to any matter relating to the custodianship.

(c) A transfer that purports to be made and which is valid under the Uniform Transfers to Minors Act, the Uniform Gifts to Minors Act, or a substantially similar act, of another state is governed by the law of the designated state and may be executed and is enforceable in this state if at the time of the transfer, the transferor, the minor, or the custodian is a resident of the designated state or the custodial property is located in the designated state. *(Stats.1990, c. 79 (A.B.759), § 14, operative July 1, 1991.)*

Law Revision Commission Comments
1990 Enactment

Section 3902 continues Section 3902 of the repealed Probate Code without change. This section is the same as Section 2 of the Uniform Transfers to Minors Act (1986). The section attempts to resolve

uncertainties and conflicts-of-law questions that have frequently arisen because of the former non-uniformity of Uniform Gifts to Minors Act (1966) in the various states and which may continue to arise during the transition from the Uniform Gifts to Minors Act to the Uniform Transfers to Minors Act.

The creation of a custodianship must invoke the law of a particular state because of the form of the transfer required under subdivision (a) of Section 3909. Section 3902 provides that a choice of the California Uniform Transfers to Minors Act is appropriate and effective if any of the nexus factors specified in subdivision (a) exists at the time of the transfer. The California Uniform Transfers to Minors Act continues to govern, and subdivision (b) makes the custodian subject to personal jurisdiction in the courts of this state for the duration of the custodianship, despite subsequent relocation of the parties or the property.

Subdivision (c) recognizes that residents of California may elect to have the law of another state apply to a transfer. That choice is valid if a nexus with the chosen state exists at the time of the transfer. If personal jurisdiction can be obtained in California under other law apart from the California Uniform Transfers to Minors Act, the custodianship may be enforced in a California court, which is directed to apply the law of the state elected by the transferor.

If the choice of law under subdivision (a) or (c) is ineffective because of the absence of the required nexus, the transfer may still be effective under the Uniform Transfers to Minors Act of another state with which a nexus does exist. See Uniform Transfers to Minors Act § 21 (1986) (Prob.Code § 3922).

Background on Section 3902 of Repealed Code

Section 3902 was a new provision added by 1984 Cal.Stat. ch. 243 § 9. For background on the provisions of this part, see the Comment to this part under the part heading. [20 Cal.L.Rev.Comm.Report 1001 (1990)].

Cross References

Custodial property defined for purposes of this Part, see Probate Code § 3901.
Custodian defined for purposes of this Part, see Probate Code § 3901.
Minor defined for purposes of this Part, see Probate Code § 3901.
Person defined for purposes of this Part, see Probate Code § 3901.
State defined for purposes of this Part, see Probate Code § 3901.
Transfer defined for purposes of this Part, see Probate Code § 3901.
Transferor defined for purposes of this Part, see Probate Code § 3901.

§ 3903. Nomination of custodian; creation of custodial property

(a) A person having the right to designate the recipient of property transferable upon the occurrence of a future event may revocably nominate a custodian to receive the property for a minor beneficiary upon the occurrence of the event by naming the custodian followed in substance by the words:

"as custodian for _____
                        (Name of Minor)
under the California Uniform Transfers to Minors Act."

The nomination may name one or more persons as substitute custodians to whom the property must be transferred, in the order named, if the first nominated custodian dies before the transfer or is unable, declines, or is ineligible to serve. The nomination may be made in a will, a trust, a deed, an instrument exercising a power of appointment, or in a writing designating a beneficiary of contractual rights which is registered with or delivered to the payor, issuer, or other obligor of the contractual rights.

(b) A custodian nominated under this section must be a person to whom a transfer of property of that kind may be made under subdivision (a) of Section 3909.

(c) The nomination of a custodian under this section does not create custodial property until the nominating instrument becomes irrevocable or a transfer to the nominated custodian is completed under Section 3909. Unless the nomination of a custodian has been revoked, upon the occurrence of the future event, the custodianship becomes effective, and the custodian shall enforce a transfer of the custodial property pursuant to Section 3909. *(Stats.1990, c. 79 (A.B.759), § 14, operative July 1, 1991.)*

Law Revision Commission Comments

1990 Enactment

Section 3903 continues Section 3903 of the repealed Probate Code without change. This section is the same as Section 3 of the Uniform Transfers to Minors Act (1986).

Section 3903 permits a future custodian for a minor to be nominated to receive a distribution under a will or trust, or as a beneficiary of a power of appointment, or of contractual rights such as a life or endowment insurance policy, annuity contract, P.O.D. account, benefit plan, or similar future payment right. Nomination of a future custodian does not constitute a "transfer" under this Act and does not create custodial property. If it did, the nomination and beneficiary designation would have to be permanent, since a "transfer" is irrevocable and indefeasibly vests ownership of the interest in the minor under subdivision (b) of Section 3911. Instead, Section 3903 permits a revocable beneficiary designation that takes effect only when the donor dies or when a lifetime transfer to the custodian for the minor beneficiary occurs, such as a distribution under an inter vivos trust. However, an unrevoked nomination under Section 3903 is binding on a personal representative or trustee (see subdivision (b) of Section 3905) and on insurance companies and other obligors who contract to pay in the future (see subdivision (b) of Section 3907).

The person making the nomination may name contingent or successive future custodians to serve, in the order named, in the event that the person first nominated dies, or is unable, declines, or is ineligible to serve. Such a substitute future custodian is a custodian "nominated . . . under Section 3903" to whom the transfer must be made under subdivision (b) of Section 3905 and subdivision (b) of Section 3907.

Any person nominated as future custodian may decline to serve before the transfer occurs and may resign at any time after the transfer. See Section 3918.

The transferor may designate one or more persons as successor custodians to serve, in the designated order of priority, in case the custodian originally designated or a prior successor custodian is unable, declines, or is ineligible to serve or resigns, dies, becomes incapacitated, or is removed. See Section 3918(b).

Background on Section 3903 of Repealed Code

Section 3903 was a new provision added by 1984 Cal.Stat. ch. 243 § 9. No provision like Section 3903 was included in the former California statute. But see former Probate Code Section 6340 (repealed by 1984 Cal.Stat. ch. 243 § 10) which permitted a person to designate in his or her will the custodian to receive property devised under the will to a minor to be transferred to a designated custodian for the benefit of a minor. For background on the provisions of this part, see the Comment to this part under the part heading. [20 Cal.L.Rev.Comm.Reports 1001 (1990)].

Cross References

Custodial property defined for purposes of this Part, see Probate Code § 3901.

Custodian defined for purposes of this Part, see Probate Code § 3901.
Minor defined for purposes of this Part, see Probate Code § 3901.
Person defined for purposes of this Part, see Probate Code § 3901.
Powers of appointment, generally, see Probate Code § 600 et seq.
Transfer defined for purposes of this Part, see Probate Code § 3901.

§ 3904. Transfer by gift or exercise of power of appointment

A person may make a transfer by irrevocable gift to, or the irrevocable exercise of a power of appointment in favor of, a custodian for the benefit of a minor pursuant to Section 3909. *(Stats.1990, c. 79 (A.B.759), § 14, operative July 1, 1991.)*

Law Revision Commission Comments

1990 Enactment

Section 3904 continues Section 3904 of the repealed Probate Code without change. This section is the same as Section 4 of the Uniform Transfers to Minors Act (1986).

To emphasize the different kinds of transfers that create presently effective custodianships under this Act, they are separately described in Sections 3904, 3905, 3906, and 3907. Section 3904 covers not only the traditional lifetime gift but also an irrevocable exercise of a power of appointment in favor of a custodian, as distinguished from the exercise of a power in a revocable instrument that results only in the nomination of a future custodian under Section 3903.

A custodianship created under this section will terminate upon the minor's attainment of the age of 18 unless the transfer specifies a later time. In the case of the traditional lifetime transfer, the custodianship cannot be continued after the time the beneficiary attains 21 years of age. This limitation satisfies the requirements of Section 2503(c) of the Internal Revenue Code which permits "minority trusts" to continue in effect until age 21. In the case of an irrevocable exercise of a power of appointment in favor of a custodian, the custodianship cannot be continued after the time the beneficiary attains 25 years of age. See Section 3920 and 3920.5 and the Comments thereto. A custodianship created under this section may be created for a beneficiary who has already attained the age of 18 if the transfer provides that the custodianship is to continue until the beneficiary attains a specified age older than 18. See Section 3901(k).

Background on Section 3904 of Repealed Code

Section 3904 was added by 1984 Cal.Stat. ch. 243 § 9. Section 3904 in part corresponded to subdivision (a) of former Civil Code Section 1156 (repealed by 1984 Cal.Stat. ch. 243 § 1) but was broader than that provision which covered only the traditional lifetime gift. Section 3904 did not continue the requirement of former Civil Code Section 1156 that the donor be an "adult person." See the Comment to subdivision (a) of Section 3901. See also Report of Senate Committee on Judiciary on Assembly Bill 2492, 18 Cal.L.Revision Comm'n Reports 105, 108 (1986). For background on the provisions of this part, see the Comment to this part under the part heading. [20 Cal.L.Rev.Comm.Reports 1001 (1990)].

Cross References

Custodian defined for purposes of this Part, see Probate Code § 3901.
Minor defined for purposes of this Part, see Probate Code § 3901.
Person defined for purposes of this Part, see Probate Code § 3901.
Powers of appointment,
 Generally, see Probate Code § 600 et seq.
 Revocability, see Probate Code § 695.

Transfer defined for purposes of this Part, see Probate Code § 3901.

§ 3905. Transfer authorized by will or trust

(a) A personal representative or trustee may make an irrevocable transfer pursuant to Section 3909 to a custodian for the benefit of a minor as authorized in the governing will or trust.

(b) If the testator or settlor has nominated a custodian under Section 3903 to receive the custodial property, the transfer shall be made to that person.

(c) If the testator or settlor has not nominated a custodian under Section 3903, or all persons so nominated as custodian die before the transfer or are unable, decline, or are ineligible to serve, the personal representative or the trustee, as the case may be, shall designate the custodian from among those eligible to serve as custodian for property of that kind under subdivision (a) of Section 3909. *(Stats.1990, c. 79 (A.B.759), § 14, operative July 1, 1991.)*

Law Revision Commission Comments

1990 Enactment

Section 3905 continues Section 3905 of the repealed Probate Code without change. This section is the same as Section 5 of the Uniform Transfers to Minors Act (1986). The section includes not only a testamentary disposition but also makes clear that a trustee may make a transfer to a custodian for the benefit of a minor as authorized in the governing trust. Section 3905 also authorizes the personal representative or trustee to designate the custodian whenever the settlor or testator fails to make a nomination or whenever a future custodian nominated under Section 3903 (and any alternate named) fails to qualify. See also Section 3918.

A custodianship created under this section will terminate upon the minor's attainment of the age of 18 unless a later time is specified in the will or trust and in the transfer, but in no event does the custodianship continue after the time the minor attains 25 years of age. See Section 3920 and 3920.5 and the Comments thereto. A custodianship created under this section may be created for a beneficiary who has already attained age 18 if the will or trust provides that the custodianship is to continue until the beneficiary attains a specified age older than 18. See Section 3901(k).

Background on Section 3905 of Repealed Code

Section 3905 was added by 1984 Cal.Stat. ch. 243 § 9. Former Probate Code Section 6340 (repealed by 1984 Cal.Stat. ch. 243 § 10) permitted a testator to devise any kind of property to a custodian subject to the California Uniform Gifts to Minors Act. Section 3905 expanded the authorization of former Probate Code Section 6340 to include not only a testamentary disposition but also to make clear that a trustee may make a transfer to a custodian for the benefit of a minor as authorized in the governing trust. See also Report of Senate Committee on Judiciary on Assembly Bill 2492, 18 Cal.L.Revision Comm'n Reports 105, 108 (1986). For background on the provisions of this part, see the Comment to this part under the part heading. [20 Cal.L.Rev.Comm.Reports 1001 (1990)].

Cross References

Custodial property defined for purposes of this Part, see Probate Code § 3901.

Custodian defined for purposes of this Part, see Probate Code § 3901.

Minor defined for purposes of this Part, see Probate Code § 3901.

Person defined for purposes of this Part, see Probate Code § 3901.

Personal representative defined for purposes of this Part, see Probate Code § 3901.

Transfer defined for purposes of this Part, see Probate Code § 3901.

§ 3906. Other transfer by fiduciary

(a) Subject to subdivision (c), a personal representative or trustee may make an irrevocable transfer to another adult or trust company as custodian for the benefit of a minor pursuant to Section 3909, in the absence of a will or under a will or trust that does not contain an authorization to do so.

(b) Subject to subdivision (c), a conservator may make an irrevocable transfer to another adult or trust company as custodian for the benefit of the minor pursuant to Section 3909.

(c) A transfer under subdivision (a) or (b) may be made only if all of the following requirements are satisfied:

(1) The personal representative, trustee, or conservator considers the transfer to be in the best interest of the minor.

(2) The transfer is not prohibited by or inconsistent with provisions of the applicable will, trust agreement, or other governing instrument. For the purposes of this subdivision, a spendthrift provision (such as that described in Section 15300) shall not prohibit or be inconsistent with the transfer.

(3) The transfer is authorized by the court if it exceeds ten thousand dollars ($10,000) in value; provided, however, that such court authorization shall not be required when the transfer is to a custodian who is either (A) a trust company or (B) an individual designated as a trustee by the terms of a trust instrument which does not require a bond. *(Stats.1990, c. 79 (A.B.759), § 14, operative July 1, 1991. Amended by Stats.1996, c. 862 (A.B.2751), § 13.)*

Law Revision Commission Comments

1990 Enactment

Section 3906 continues Section 3906 of the repealed Probate Code without change. This section is the same as Section 6 of the Uniform Transfers to Minors Act (1986).

Section 3906 permits custodianships to be used as guardianship substitutes, even though not specifically authorized by the person whose property is the subject of the transfer. Subdivision (a) permits the personal representative of a decedent's estate or a trustee to transfer estate property to a custodian for the benefit of a minor in the absence of a will or under a will or trust that does not contain an authorization to do so. Subdivision (b) permits the guardian of the estate of a minor to transfer the minor's own property to a new or existing custodianship for the purpose of convenience or economies of administration.

A custodianship may be created under this section even though not specifically authorized by the transferor, the testator, or the settlor of the trust if three tests are satisfied. First, the fiduciary making the transfer must determine in good faith and in his or her fiduciary capacity that a custodianship will be in the best interest of the minor. Second, a custodianship may not be prohibited by, or inconsistent with, the terms of any governing instrument. Inconsistent terms would include, for example, a spendthrift clause in a governing trust, provisions terminating a governing trust for the minor's benefit at a time other than the time of the minor's age of majority, and provisions for mandatory distributions of income or principal at specific times or periodic intervals. Provisions for other outright distributions or bequests would not be inconsistent with the creation of a custodianship under this section. Third, the amount of property transferred (as measured by its value) must be of such relatively small amount ($10,000 or less in value) that the lack of court supervision and the typically stricter investment standards that would apply to a guardianship will not be important. However, if the property is of greater value, transfer to a custodian may still be made if the court approves and if the other two tests are met.

The custodianship created under this section without express authority in the governing instrument will terminate upon the minor's attainment of the age of 18, the same age at which a guardianship of the estate would end. See Section 3920 and the Comment thereto.

Background on Section 3906 of Repealed Code

Section 3906 was a new provision added by 1984 Cal.Stat. ch. 243 § 9. See also Report of Senate Committee on Judiciary on Assembly Bill 2492, 18 Cal.L.Revision Comm'n Reports 105, 108 (1986). For background on the provisions of this part, see the Comment to this part under the part heading. [20 Cal.L.Rev.Comm.Reports 1001 (1990)].

Cross References

Adult defined for purposes of this Part, see Probate Code § 3901.
Conservator defined for purposes of this Part, see Probate Code § 3901.
Court defined for purposes of this Part, see Probate Code § 3901.
Custodian defined for purposes of this Part, see Probate Code § 3901.
Minor defined for purposes of this Part, see Probate Code § 3901.
Personal representative defined for purposes of this Part, see Probate Code § 3901.
Transfer defined for purposes of this Part, see Probate Code § 3901.
Trust company defined for purposes of this Part, see Probate Code § 3901.

§ 3907. Transfer by obligor

(a) Subject to subdivisions (b) and (c), a person not subject to Section 3905 or 3906 who holds property of, or owes a liquidated debt to, a minor not having a conservator may make an irrevocable transfer to a custodian for the benefit of the minor pursuant to Section 3909.

(b) If a person having the right to do so under Section 3903 has nominated a custodian under that section to receive the custodial property, the transfer shall be made to that person.

(c) If no custodian has been nominated under Section 3903, or all persons so nominated as custodian die before the transfer or are unable, decline, or are ineligible to serve, a transfer under this section may be made to an adult member of the minor's family or to a trust company unless the property exceeds ten thousand dollars ($10,000) in value. *(Stats.1990, c. 79 (A.B.759), § 14, operative July 1, 1991.)*

Law Revision Commission Comments

1990 Enactment

Section 3907 continues Section 3907 of the repealed Probate Code without change. This section is the same as Section 7 of the Uniform Transfers to Minors Act (1986).

Like Section 3906, Section 3907 permits a custodianship to be established as a substitute for a guardianship to receive payments due a minor from sources other than estates, trusts, and existing guardianships covered by Sections 3905 and 3906. For example, a tort judgment debtor of a minor, a bank holding a joint or P.O.D. account of which a minor is the surviving payee, or an insurance company holding life insurance policy or benefit plan proceeds payable to a minor may create a custodianship under this section.

Use of this section is mandatory when a future custodian has been nominated under Section 3903 as a named beneficiary of an insurance policy, benefit plan, deposit account, or the like, because the original owner of the property specified a custodianship (and a future custodian) to receive the property. If that custodian (or any

alternate named) is not available, if none was nominated, or none could have been nominated (as in the case of a tort judgment payable to the minor), this section is permissive and does not preclude the obligor from requiring the establishment of a guardianship of the estate to receive payment. The section merely allows the obligor to transfer to a custodian unless the property exceeds the stated value in which case a guardian of the estate must be appointed to receive it or some other procedure used (See Sections 3410–3413, 3600–3612).

Background on Section 3907 of Repealed Code

Section 3907 was a new provision added by 1984 Cal.Stat. ch. 243 § 9. For background on the provisions of this part, see the Comment to this part under the part heading. [20 Cal.L.Rev.Comm.Reports 1001 (1990)].

Cross References

Adult defined for purposes of this Part, see Probate Code § 3901.
Conservator defined for purposes of this Part, see Probate Code § 3901.
Custodial property defined for purposes of this Part, see Probate Code § 3901.
Custodian defined for purposes of this Part, see Probate Code § 3901.
Member of the minor's family defined for purposes of this Part, see Probate Code § 3901.
Minor defined for purposes of this Part, see Probate Code § 3901.
Person defined for purposes of this Part, see Probate Code § 3901.
Transfer defined for purposes of this Part, see Probate Code § 3901.
Trust company defined for purposes of this Part, see Probate Code § 3901.

§ 3908. Acknowledgment of delivery

A written acknowledgment of delivery by a custodian constitutes a sufficient receipt and discharge for custodial property transferred to the custodian pursuant to this part. *(Stats.1990, c. 79 (A.B.759), § 14, operative July 1, 1991.)*

Law Revision Commission Comments

1990 Enactment

Section 3908 continues Section 3908 of the repealed Probate Code without change. This section is the same as Section 8 of the Uniform Transfers to Minors Act (1986).

Section 3908 discharges transferors from further responsibility for custodial property delivered to and receipted for by the custodian. See also Section 3916 which protects transferors and other third parties dealing with custodians. A discharge or release for a donative transfer is not necessary. But see Section 3402 (effect of written receipt of parent).

Section 3908 does not authorize an existing custodian, or a custodian to whom an obligor makes a transfer under Section 3907, to settle or release a claim of the minor against a third party. Only a guardian, guardian ad litem or other person authorized under other law to act for the minor may release such a claim. See the Comment to Section 3602.

Background on Section 3908 of Repealed Code

Section 3908 was a new provision added by 1984 Cal.Stat. ch. 243 § 9. For background on the provisions of this part, see the Comment to this part under the part heading. [20 Cal.L.Rev.Comm.Reports 1001 (1990)].

Cross References

Custodial property defined for purposes of this Part, see Probate Code § 3901.

Custodian defined for purposes of this Part, see Probate Code § 3901.

§ 3909. Creation of custodial property; designation of initial custodian; control

(a) Custodial property is created and a transfer is made whenever any of the following occurs:

(1) An uncertificated security or a certificated security in registered form is either:

(A) Registered in the name of the transferor, an adult other than the transferor, or a trust company, followed in substance by the words:

"as custodian for _____
(Name of Minor)
under the California Uniform Transfers to Minors Act."

(B) Delivered if in certificated form, or any document necessary for the transfer of an uncertificated security is delivered, together with any necessary endorsement to an adult other than the transferor or to a trust company as custodian, accompanied by an instrument in substantially the form set forth in subdivision (b).

(2) Money is paid or delivered, or a security held in the name of a broker, financial institution, or its nominee is transferred, to a broker or financial institution for credit to an account in the name of the transferor, an adult other than the transferor, or a trust company, followed in substance by the words:

"as custodian for _____
(Name of Minor)
under the California Uniform Transfers to Minors Act."

(3) The ownership of a life or endowment insurance policy or annuity contract is either:

(A) Registered with the issuer in the name of the transferor, an adult other than the transferor, or a trust company, followed in substance by the words:

"as custodian for _____
(Name of Minor)
under the California Uniform Transfers to Minors Act."

(B) Assigned in a writing delivered to an adult other than the transferor or to a trust company whose name in the assignment is followed in substance by the words:

"as custodian for _____
(Name of Minor)
under the California Uniform Transfers to Minors Act."

(4) An irrevocable exercise of a power of appointment or an irrevocable present right to future payment under a contract is the subject of a written notification delivered to the payor, issuer, or other obligor that the right is transferred to the transferor, an adult other than the transferor, or a trust company, whose name in the notification is followed in substance by the words:

"as custodian for _____
(Name of Minor)
under the California Uniform Transfers to Minors Act."

(5) An interest in real property is recorded in the name of the transferor, an adult other than the transferor, or a trust company, followed in substance by the words:

"as custodian for _____
(Name of Minor)
under the California Uniform Transfers to Minors Act."

(6) A certificate of title issued by a department or agency of a state or of the United States which evidences title to tangible personal property is either:

(A) Issued in the name of the transferor, an adult other than the transferor, or a trust company, followed in substance by the words:

"as custodian for _____
(Name of Minor)
under the California Uniform Transfers to Minors Act."

(B) Delivered to an adult other than the transferor or to a trust company, endorsed to that person followed in substance by the words:

"as custodian for _____
(Name of Minor)
under the California Uniform Transfers to Minors Act."

(7) An interest in any property not described in paragraphs (1) through (6) is transferred to an adult other than the transferor or to a trust company by a written instrument in substantially the form set forth in subdivision (b).

(b) An instrument in the following form satisfies the requirements of subparagraph (B) of paragraph (1) and paragraph (7) of subdivision (a):

"TRANSFER UNDER THE CALIFORNIA UNIFORM TRANSFERS TO MINORS ACT

I, _____
(Name of Transferor or Name and Representative Capacity if a Fiduciary)
hereby transfer to _____,
(Name of Custodian)
as custodian for _____
(Name of Minor)
under the California Uniform Transfers to Minors Act, the following:

(insert a description of the custodial property sufficient to identify it).

Dated: _____

_____
(Signature)

_____ acknowledges receipt of the
(Name of Custodian)
property described above as custodian for the minor named above under the California Uniform Transfers to Minors Act.

Dated: _____

_____,
(Signature of Custodian)

(c) A transferor shall place the custodian in control of the custodial property as soon as practicable. *(Stats.1990, c. 79 (A.B.759), § 14, operative July 1, 1991. Amended by Stats. 1991, c. 1055 (S.B.271), § 17.)*

Law Revision Commission Comments

1990 Enactment

Section 3909 continues Section 3909 of the repealed Probate Code without change. It is the same in substance as Section 9 of the Uniform Transfers to Minors Act (1986).

Subdivision (a) describes how the property is to be transferred and persons eligible to serve as custodian:

Paragraph (1) of subdivision (a) permits a transfer of securities in registered form to be accomplished without registering the transfer in the name of the custodian. This permits securities to be held by custodians in street names. Although the transferor may serve as the custodian when the security is registered in the name of the custodian under subparagraph (A) of paragraph (1), the transferor may not serve as a custodian if the security is transferred in the manner provided in subparagraph (B) of paragraph (1).

Paragraph (3) of subdivision (a) covers the irrevocable transfer of ownership of life and endowment insurance policies and annuity contracts. It provides for registration with the issuer in the name of the custodian (in which case the transferor is eligible to serve as custodian) or for an assignment in writing delivered to the custodian (in which case the transferor is not eligible to serve as custodian).

Paragraph (4) of subdivision (a) covers the irrevocable exercise of a power of appointment and the irrevocable present assignment of future payments rights (such as royalties, interest and principal payments under a promissory note, or beneficial interests under life or endowment or annuity insurance contracts or benefit plans). The payor, issuer, or obligor may require additional formalities such as completion of a specific assignment form and an endorsement, but the transfer is effective upon delivery of the notification to the payor, issuer, or other obligor that the right is transferred to the custodian. Compare Section 3903 and the Comment thereto for the procedure for revocably "nominating" a future custodian as a beneficiary of a power of appointment or such payment rights.

Paragraph (5) of subdivision (a) provides the exclusive method for the transfer of real property, including a disposition made by a will. The transfer of an interest in real property must be recorded in the name of the custodian in order that the transfer be an effective transfer.

Paragraph (6) of subdivision (a) covers the transfer of tangible personal property (such as automobiles and aircraft) subject to registration of ownership with a state or federal agency. Either registration of the transfer in the name of the custodian (in which case the transferor is eligible to serve as custodian) or delivery of the endorsed certificate in registerable form (in which case the transferor is not eligible to serve as custodian) makes the transfer effective.

Paragraph (7) of subdivision (a) is a residual classification, covering all property not otherwise covered in the preceding paragraphs. Examples would include partnership interests and tangible personal property not subject to title certificates. The transferor is not eligible to be a custodian of property transferred under paragraph (7).

Execution of the acceptance by the custodian on the form of transfer document set forth in subdivision (b) is sufficient to satisfy the requirements of subparagraph (B) of paragraph (1) and paragraph (7) of subdivision (a). While such a form of written acceptance is not specifically required in the case of registered securities under subdivision (a)(1), money under subdivision (a)(2), insurance contracts or interests under subdivision (a)(3) or (4), real estate under subdivision (a)(5), or titled personal property under subdivision (a)(6), it is certainly the better and recommended practice to obtain the acknowledgment, consent, and acceptance of the designated custodian on the instrument of transfer or otherwise.

Failure of the transferor to comply with subdivision (c) does not affect the validity of a transfer. See Section 3911(a).

1991 Amendment

Subdivision (a)(2) of Section 3909 is amended to make a technical revision to fill a gap in the statute. The amendment covers the situation where a security held in the name of a broker, financial institution, or its nominee is to be transferred to a broker or financial institution for credit to an account in the name of the transferor, an adult other than the transferor, or a trust company, as custodian for a designated minor. [20 Cal.L.Rev.Comm.Reports 2907 (1990)].

Background on Section 3909 of Repealed Code

Section 3909 was added by 1984 Cal.Stat. ch. 243 § 9 and was amended by 1989 Cal.Stat. ch. 544 § 3. Section 3909 provided more detailed rules than former Civil Code Section 1156 (repealed by 1984 Cal.Stat. ch. 243 § 1) concerning the manner of creating custodial property and effecting the transfer. The 1989 amendment revised the former reference in the introductory clause of subdivision (b) to refer to "subparagraph (B)" rather than "subparagraph (A)"; this corrected an obvious error and made the provision conform to the Uniform Transfers to Minors Act (1986). See also Communication from the California Law Revision Commission Concerning Assembly Bill 158, 20 Cal.L.Revision Comm'n Reports 235 (1990). For background on the provisions of this part, see the Comment to this part under the part heading.

Subdivision (a) of Section 3909 superseded subdivision (a) of former Civil Code Section 1156. Paragraph (1) of subdivision (a) continued the substance of paragraphs (1) and (2) of subdivision (a) of former Section 1156 relating to securities and also permitted a transfer of securities in registered form to be accomplished without registering the transfer in the name of the custodian. Paragraph (2) of subdivision (a) continued the substance of paragraph (3) of subdivision (a) of former Civil Code Section 1156 relating to money credited to a custodial account. Paragraph (3) of subdivision (a) superseded paragraph (4) of subdivision (a) of former Civil Code Section 1156. Paragraph (4) of subdivision (a) was a new provision. Paragraph (5) of subdivision (a) changed the former law which required that the transfer be made "by executing and delivering in the appropriate manner a deed, assignment, or similar instrument" to the custodian. Former Civil Code § 1156(a)(5). Paragraph (6) of subdivision (a) was a new provision. Paragraph (7) of subdivision (a) was comparable to paragraph (6) of subdivision (a) of former Civil Code Section 1156; but, unlike the former California law, the transferor was not eligible to be a custodian of property transferred under paragraph (7) of subdivision (a) of Section 3909.

Former California law did not provide for the form for a transfer document such as is provided in subdivision (b) of Section 3909 except for the gift of a security not in registered form under former Civil Code Section 1156(a)(2). [20 Cal.L.Rev.Comm.Reports 1001 (1990)].

Cross References

Adult defined for purposes of this Part, see Probate Code § 3901.
Broker defined for purposes of this Part, see Probate Code § 3901.
Custodial property defined for purposes of this Part, see Probate Code § 3901.
Custodian defined for purposes of this Part, see Probate Code § 3901.
Financial institution defined for purposes of this Part, see Probate Code § 3901.
Minor defined for purposes of this Part, see Probate Code § 3901.
Person defined for purposes of this Part, see Probate Code § 3901.
State defined for purposes of this Part, see Probate Code § 3901.
Transfer defined for purposes of this Part, see Probate Code § 3901.
Transferor defined for purposes of this Part, see Probate Code § 3901.

Trust company defined for purposes of this Part, see Probate Code § 3901.

§ 3910. Single custodianship

A transfer may be made only for one minor, and only one person may be the custodian. All custodial property held under this part by the same custodian for the benefit of the same minor constitutes a single custodianship. *(Stats.1990, c. 79 (A.B.759), § 14, operative July 1, 1991.)*

Law Revision Commission Comments

1990 Enactment

Section 3910 continues Section 3910 of the repealed Probate Code without change. This section is the same in substance as Section 10 of the Uniform Transfers to Minors Act (1986).

Under Section 3910, additional transfers at different times and from different sources may be made to an existing custodian for the minor and do not create multiple custodianships. For the purpose of consolidating assets in a single custodianship, an existing custodian may be named as successor custodian by another custodian for the same minor who resigns under Section 3918. Note, however, that these results are limited to transfers made "under this part." Gifts previously made under the California Uniform Gifts to Minors Act or under the Uniform Gifts to Minors Act or Uniform Transfers to Minors Act of another state must be treated as separate custodianships, even though the same custodian and minor are involved, because of possible differences in the age of distribution and custodian's powers under those other Acts. But see Section 3923 (transfers made before January 1, 1985).

Even when all transfers to a single custodian are made "under this part" and a single custodianship results, custodial property transferred under Sections 3906 and 3907 or under Section 3412, 3413, 3602, or 3611 may have to be accounted for separately from property transferred under or pursuant to Section 3903, 3904, or 3905 because the custodianship may terminate sooner with respect to the former property. See Sections 3920 and 3920.5 and the Comments thereto.

Background on Section 3910 of Repealed Code

Section 3910 was added by 1984 Cal.Stat. ch. 243 § 9. The first sentence of Section 3910 continued subdivision (b) of former Civil Code Section 1156 (repealed by 1984 Cal.Stat. ch. 243 § 1). The second sentence of Section 3910 stated what was implicit in the former law. See Report of Senate Committee on Judiciary on Assembly Bill 2942, 18 Cal.L.Revision Comm'n Reports 105, 110 (1986). For background on the provisions of this part, see the Comment to this part under the part heading. [20 Cal.L.Rev.Comm.Reports 1001 (1990)].

Cross References

Custodial property defined for purposes of this Part, see Probate Code § 3901.
Custodian defined for purposes of this Part, see Probate Code § 3901.
Minor defined for purposes of this Part, see Probate Code § 3901.
Person defined for purposes of this Part, see Probate Code § 3901.
Transfer defined for purposes of this Part, see Probate Code § 3901.

§ 3911. Validity and effect of transfer

(a) The validity of a transfer made in a manner prescribed in this part is not affected by any of the following:

(1) Failure of the transferor to comply with subdivision (c) of Section 3909.

(2) Designation of an ineligible custodian, except designation of the transferor in the case of property for which the transferor is ineligible to serve as custodian under subdivision (a) of Section 3909.

(3) Death or incapacity of a person nominated under Section 3903 or designated under Section 3909 as custodian, or the disclaimer of the office by that person.

(b) A transfer made pursuant to Section 3909 is irrevocable, and the custodial property is indefeasibly vested in the minor, but the custodian has all the rights, powers, duties, and authority provided in this part, and neither the minor nor the minor's legal representative has any right, power, duty, or authority with respect to the custodial property except as provided in this part.

(c) By making a transfer, the transferor incorporates in the disposition all the provisions of this part and grants to the custodian, and to any third person dealing with a person designated as custodian, the respective powers, rights, and immunities provided in this part.

(d) A person is not precluded from being a custodian for a minor under this part with respect to some property because the person is a conservator of the minor with respect to other property.

(e) A person who is the conservator of the minor is not precluded from being a custodian for a minor under this part because the custodial property has or will be transferred to the custodian from the guardianship estate of the minor. In such case, for the purposes of Section 3909, the custodian shall be deemed to be "an adult other than the transferor."

(f) In the cases described in subdivisions (d) and (e), with respect to the property transferred to the custodian, this part applies to the extent it would apply if the person to whom the custodial property is transferred were not and had not been a conservator of the minor. *(Stats.1990, c. 79 (A.B.759), § 14, operative July 1, 1991.)*

Law Revision Commission Comments

1990 Enactment

Section 3911 continues Section 3911 of the repealed Probate Code without change. Subdivisions (a), (b), and (c) are the same as Section 11 of the Uniform Transfers to Minors Act (1986). The transferor's designation of himself or herself as custodian of property for which the transferor is not eligible to serve as custodian under subdivision (a) of Section 3909 makes the transfer ineffective. See the Comment to Section 3909. For a list of the immunities enjoyed by third persons under subdivision (c), see Section 3916 and the Comment thereto.

Subdivisions (d), (e), and (f) are not included in the Uniform Transfers to Minors Act. These subdivisions are included in Section 3911 to make clear that (1) a person serving as guardian of the estate of the minor may also serve as custodian under this part and in this case the custodial property does not become a part of the guardianship estate and (2) property may be transferred from a guardianship estate to the person who serves as guardian to be held by that person as custodian under this part and in such case the property is no longer a part of the guardianship estate but instead is governed solely by this part.

Background on Section 3911 of Repealed Code

Section 3911 was added by 1984 Cal.Stat. ch. 243 § 9. Subdivision (a) of Section 3911 generally continued the substance of the last portion of subdivision (c) of former Civil Code Section 1156 (repealed by 1984 Cal.Stat. ch. 243 § 1). The balance of Section 3911 generally continued former Civil Code Section 1157 (repealed by 1984 Cal.Stat. ch. 243 § 1) with a number of necessary, and perhaps significant, changes required by the new kinds of property subject to custodianship. Former Civil Code Section 1157 provided that a transfer made in accordance with its terms "conveys to the minor indefeasibly vested legal title to the custodial property." Because equitable interests in property may be the subject of a transfer under this Act, the reference to "legal title" was deleted, but no change concerning the effect or finality of the transfer was intended. However, subdivision (b) of Section 3911 qualified the rights of the minor in the property by making them subject to "the rights, powers, duties, and authority" of the custodian under this part, a concept that may have been implicit and intended in former Civil Code Section 1157, but was not expressed. For background on the provisions of this part, see the Comment to this part under the part heading. [20 Cal.L.Rev.Comm.Reports 1001 (1990)].

Cross References

Adult defined for purposes of this Part, see Probate Code § 3901.
Conservator defined for purposes of this Part, see Probate Code § 3901.
Custodial property defined for purposes of this Part, see Probate Code § 3901.
Custodian defined for purposes of this Part, see Probate Code § 3901.
Legal representative defined for purposes of this Part, see probate Code § 3901.
Minor defined for purposes of this Part, see Probate Code § 3901.
Person defined for purposes of this Part, see Probate Code § 3901.
Transfer defined for purposes of this Part, see Probate Code § 3901.
Transferor defined for purposes of this Part, see Probate Code § 3901.

§ 3912. Duties of custodians; standard of care; records

(a) A custodian shall do all of the following:

(1) Take control of custodial property.

(2) Register or record title to custodial property if appropriate.

(3) Collect, hold, manage, invest, and reinvest custodial property.

(b) In dealing with custodial property, a custodian shall observe the standard of care that would be observed by a prudent person dealing with property of another and is not limited by any other statute restricting investments by fiduciaries except that:

(1) If a custodian is not compensated for his or her services, the custodian is not liable for losses to custodial property unless they result from the custodian's bad faith, intentional wrongdoing, or gross negligence, or from the custodian's failure to maintain the standard of prudence in investing the custodial property provided in this section.

(2) A custodian, in the custodian's discretion and without liability to the minor or the minor's estate, may retain any custodial property received from a transferor.

(c) A custodian may invest in or pay premiums on life insurance or endowment policies on (1) the life of the minor only if the minor or the minor's estate is the sole beneficiary or (2) the life of another person in whom the minor has an insurable interest only to the extent that the minor, the minor's estate, or the custodian in the capacity of custodian, is the irrevocable beneficiary.

(d) A custodian at all times shall keep custodial property separate and distinct from all other property in a manner

sufficient to identify it clearly as custodial property of the minor. Custodial property consisting of an undivided interest is so identified if the minor's interest is held as a tenant in common and is fixed. Custodial property subject to recordation is so identified if it is recorded, and custodial property subject to registration is so identified if it is either registered, or held in an account designated, in the name of the custodian, followed in substance by the words:

"as a custodian for _____

(Name of Minor)

under the California Uniform Transfers to Minors Act."

(e) A custodian shall keep records of all transactions with respect to custodial property, including information necessary for the preparation of the minor's tax returns, and shall make them available for inspection at reasonable intervals by a parent or legal representative of the minor or by the minor if the minor has attained the age of 14 years. *(Stats.1990, c. 79 (A.B.759), § 14, operative July 1, 1991.)*

Law Revision Commission Comments

1990 Enactment

Section 3912 continues Section 3912 of the repealed Probate Code without change. This section is the same in substance as Section 12 of the Uniform Transfers to Minors Act (1986) except as indicated below.

Subdivision (b) does not include the provision of the Uniform Transfers to Minors Act which specifically provides a slightly higher standard for professional fiduciaries. However, in determining what constitutes "the standard of care that would be observed by a prudent person dealing with the property of another" under subdivision (b), a professional custodian (such as a trust company or the trust department of a bank) is held to a greater standard of care based on its presumed expertise than a lay custodian. Cf. Estate of Beach, 15 Cal.3d 623, 542 P.2d 994, 125 Cal.Rptr. 570 (1975) (executor). See also the Comments to Sections 2401 (guardian or conservator) and 16040 (trustee).

No provision comparable to subdivision (b)(1) is found in the Uniform Transfers to Minors Act. This provision is included because it is likely to reflect the desires of the transferor who makes a transfer to a custodian who serves without compensation.

Subdivision (d) includes a provision of the Uniform Transfers to Minors Act requiring that custodial property consisting of an undivided interest be held as a tenant in common. This provision permits the custodian to invest custodial property in common trust funds, mutual funds, or in a proportional interest in a "jumbo" certificate of deposit. Investment in property held in joint tenancy with right of survivorship is not permitted, but this does not preclude a transfer of such an interest to a custodian, and the custodian is authorized under subdivision (b) to retain a joint tenancy interest so received.

Subdivision (e) includes the requirement of the Uniform Transfers to Minors Act that income tax information be maintained and made available for preparation of the minor's tax returns. Because the custodianship is not a separate legal entity or taxpayer, the minor's tax identification number should be used to identify all custodial property accounts.

Background on Section 3912 of Repealed Code

Section 3912 was added by 1984 Cal.Stat. ch. 243 § 9. For background on the provisions of this part, see the Comment to this part under the part heading. See also Report of Senate Committee on Judiciary on Assembly Bill 2492, 18 Cal.L.Revision Comm'n Reports 105, 110–11 (1986).

Subdivision (a) expanded subdivision (a) of former Civil Code Section 1158 (repealed by 1984 Cal.Stat. ch. 243 § 1) to include the duties to take control and appropriately register or record custodial property in the name of the custodian.

Subdivision (b) restated and made somewhat stricter the prudent man fiduciary standard for the custodian, since Section 3912 cast the standard in terms of a prudent person "dealing with property of another" rather than one "who is seeking a reasonable income and preservation of his capital," as under subdivision (e) of former Civil Code Section 1158. Subdivision (b)(1) of Section 3912 continued subdivision (e) of former Civil Code Section 1159 (repealed by 1984 Cal.Stat. ch. 243 § 1)—a special immunity from liability for the custodian for losses to custodial property where the custodian is not compensated.

Subdivision (e) of former Civil Code Section 1158 permitted a custodian to retain any security received, without the obligation to diversify investment. Subdivision (b)(2) of Section 3912 extended that rule to any property received.

Subdivision (c) of Section 3912 was a new provision.

Subdivision (d) generally continued subdivision (g) of former Civil Code Section 1158, but added the provision requiring that custodial property consisting of an undivided interest be held as a tenant in common.

Subdivision (e) continued subdivision (h) of former Civil Code Section 1158, but added the requirement that income tax information be maintained and made available for preparation of the minor's tax returns. [20 Cal.L.Rev.Comm.Reports 1001 (1990)].

Cross References

Custodial property defined for purposes of this Part, see Probate Code § 3901.
Custodian defined for purposes of this Part, see Probate Code § 3901.
Legal representative defined for purposes of this Part, see Probate Code § 3901.
Minor defined for purposes of this Part, see Probate Code § 3901.
Person defined for purposes of this Part, see Probate Code § 3901.
Transfer defined for purposes of this Part, see Probate Code § 3901.
Transferor defined for purposes of this Part, see Probate Code § 3901.

§ 3913. Rights, powers, and authority of custodians over custodial property; liability

(a) A custodian, acting in a custodial capacity, has all the rights, powers, and authority over custodial property that unmarried adult owners have over their own property, but a custodian may exercise those rights, powers, and authority in that capacity only.

(b) This section does not relieve a custodian from liability for breach of Section 3912. *(Stats.1990, c. 79 (A.B.759), § 14, operative July 1, 1991.)*

Law Revision Commission Comments
1990 Enactment

Section 3913 continues Section 3913 of the repealed Probate Code without change. This section is the same in substance as Section 13 of the Uniform Transfers to Minors Act (1986).

Subdivision (a) replaces the specific list of custodian's powers contained in the former Uniform Gifts to Minors Act. The Uniform Law Commissioners decided not to expand that list to try to deal with all forms of property now covered by the Uniform Transfers to Minors Act and not to specify all powers that might be appropriate for each kind of property, nor to refer to an existing body of state law, such as a statutory provision stating powers of a trustee, since such powers would not be uniform. Instead, this provision grants the custodian the very broad and general powers of an unmarried adult owner of the property, subject to the prudent person rule and to the

duties of segregation and record keeping specified in Section 3912. (See subdivision (b) of Section 3913). This approach permits the Uniform Transfers to Minors Act to be self-contained and more readily understandable by volunteer, non-professional fiduciaries, who most often serve as custodians. It is intended that the authority granted includes the powers most often suggested for custodians, such as the power to borrow, whether at interest or interest free, the power to invest in common trust funds, and the power to enter contracts that extend beyond the termination of the custodianship.

Subdivision (a) further specifies that the custodian's power or incidents of ownership in custodial property such as insurance policies may be exercised only in the capacity as custodian. This provision is intended to prevent the exercise of those powers for the direct or indirect benefit of the custodian, so as to avoid as nearly as possible the result that a custodian who dies while holding an insurance policy on his or her own life for the benefit of a minor will have the policy taxed in his estate. See I.R.C. § 2042. But compare Terriberry v. United States, 517 F.2d 286 (5th Cir.1975) cert. denied, 424 U.S. 977 (1976); Rose v. United States, 511 F.2d 259 (5th Cir.1975).

Background on Section 3913 of Repealed Code

Section 3913 was added by 1984 Cal.Stat. ch. 243 § 9. Subdivision (a) replaced the specific list of custodian's powers contained in subdivisions (f), (i), and (j) of former Civil Code Section 1158 (repealed by 1984 Cal.Stat. ch. 243 § 1). For background on the provisions of this part, see the Comment to this part under the part heading. [20 Cal.L.Rev.Comm.Reports 1001 (1990)].

Cross References

Adult defined for purposes of this Part, see Probate Code § 3901.
Custodial property defined for purposes of this Part, see Probate Code § 3901.
Custodian defined for purposes of this Part, see Probate Code § 3901.

§ 3914. Use of custodial property

(a) A custodian may deliver or pay to the minor or expend for the minor's benefit as much of the custodial property as the custodian considers advisable for the use and benefit of the minor, without court order and without regard to (1) the duty or ability of the custodian personally, or of any other person, to support the minor or (2) any other income or property of the minor which may be applicable or available for that purpose.

(b) On petition of an interested person or the minor if the minor has attained the age of 14 years, the court may order the custodian to deliver or pay to the minor or expend for the minor's benefit so much of the custodial property as the court considers advisable for the use and benefit of the minor.

(c) A delivery, payment, or expenditure under this section is in addition to, not in substitution for, and does not affect, any obligation of a person to support the minor.

(d) In lieu of the powers and duties described in subdivision (a), a transferor who is also the custodian may elect to govern his or her custodial powers and duties under this subdivision. If such election is made, the custodian shall not pay over to the minor for expenditure by the minor, and shall not expend for the minor's use or benefit, any part of the custodial property for any purpose prior to the time specified in Section 3920, except by order of the court upon a showing that the expenditure is necessary for the support, maintenance, or education of the minor. When the powers and duties of the custodian are governed by this subdivision, the transferor-custodian shall file with the clerk of the court a declaration in substantially the following form:

Declaration Under the California Uniform Transfers to Minors Act

I, _____,

(Name of Transferor-Custodian)

as custodian for _____

(Name of Minor)

under the California Uniform Transfers to Minors Act, hereby irrevocably elect to be governed under subdivision (d) of Section 3914 of the Probate Code in my custodial capacity over the following described property

_____

_____.

(Description of Custodial Property)

I declare under penalty of perjury that the foregoing is true and correct.

Dated: _____, 19____

_____

(Signature of Transferor-Custodian)

(Stats.1990, c. 79 (A.B.759), § 14, operative July 1, 1991.)

Law Revision Commission Comments

1990 Enactment

Section 3914 continues Section 3914 of the repealed Probate Code without change. Subdivisions (a), (b), and (c) are the same as Section 14 of the Uniform Transfers to Minors Act (1986). Subdivision (d) is not included in the Uniform Act.

The "use and benefit" standard in subdivisions (a) and (b) is intended to avoid the implication that the custodial property can be used only for the required support of the minor. The "use and benefit" standard permits, for example, payment of the minor's legally enforceable obligations such as tax or child support obligations or tort claims. Custodial property can be reached by levy of a judgment creditor in any event, so there is no reason not to permit custodian or court-ordered expenditures for enforceable claims.

An "interested person" authorized to file a petition under subdivision (b) includes not only the parent or conservator or guardian of the minor and a transferor or a transferor's legal representative, but also a public agency or official with custody of the minor and a third party to whom the minor owes legally enforceable debts.

The Internal Revenue Service has taken the position that the income from custodial property, to the extent it is used for the support of the minor-donee, is includable in the gross income of any person who is legally obligated to support the minor-donee, whether or not that person or parent is serving as the custodian. Rev.Rul. 56–484, 1956–2 C.B. 23; Rev.Rul. 59–357, 1959–2 C.B. 212. However, Treasury Regulation § 1.662(a)–4 (1980) provides that the term "legal obligation" includes a legal obligation to support another person if, and only if, the obligation is not affected by the adequacy of the dependent's own resources. Thus, if under local law a parent may use the resources of a child for the child's support in lieu of supporting the child himself or herself, no obligation of support exists, whether or not income is actually used for support, at least if the child's resources are adequate. See 3 B. Bittker, Federal Taxation of Income, Estates and Gifts § 80.4.4 (1981). For this reason, subdivision (c) specifies that distributions or expenditures may be made for the minor without regard to the duty or ability of any other person to support the minor and that distributions or expenditures are not in substitution for, and shall not affect, the obligation of any person to support the minor.

Subdivision (d) of Section 3914 is a provision not found in the Uniform Transfers to Minors Act. This provision permits a transferor who is also a custodian to elect to eliminate the authority of the custodian to distribute property for the minor's use or benefit except pursuant to a court order. The section was added to the California statute in an effort to solve the tax problems that may arise when the transferor makes a transfer to a minor under the Act and designates himself or herself as custodian. For a discussion of the provision, see Review of Selected 1965 Code Legislation 52–53 (Cal.Cont.Ed.Bar 1965).

Background on Section 3914 of Repealed Code

Section 3914 was added by 1984 Cal.Stat. ch. 243 § 9. For background on the provisions of this part, see the Comment to this part under the part heading.

Subdivisions (a) and (b) continued subdivisions (b) and (c) of former Civil Code Section 1158 (repealed by 1984 Cal.Stat. ch. 243 § 1), with two changes. The standard for expenditure of custodial property was revised to substitute "for the use and benefit of the minor" for the language "for the support, maintenance, education, and benefit of the minor" used in former Section 1158. Subdivision (b) expanded the authority to file a petition under former Civil Code Section 1158 to permit a petition to be filed by "an interested person."

Subdivision (c) was a new provision. Subdivision (d) continued the substance of former Civil Code Section 1158.5 (repealed by 1984 Cal.Stat. ch. 243 § 1). [20 Cal.L.Rev.Comm.Reports 1001 (1990)].

Cross References

Court defined for purposes of this Part, see Probate Code § 3901.
Custodial property defined for purposes of this Part, see Probate Code § 3901.
Custodian defined for purposes of this Part, see Probate Code § 3901.
Minor defined for purposes of this Part, see Probate Code § 3901.
Person defined for purposes of this Part, see Probate Code § 3901.
Transfer defined for purposes of this Part, see Probate Code § 3901.
Transferor defined for purposes of this Part, see Probate Code § 3901.

§ 3915. Custodian's expenses, compensation and bond

(a) A custodian is entitled to reimbursement from custodial property for reasonable expenses incurred in the performance of the custodian's duties.

(b) Except for one who is a transferor under Section 3904, a custodian has a noncumulative election during each calendar year to charge reasonable compensation for services performed during that year.

(c) Except as provided in subdivision (f) of Section 3918, a custodian need not give a bond. *(Stats.1990, c. 79 (A.B.759), § 14, operative July 1, 1991.)*

Law Revision Commission Comments

1990 Enactment

Section 3915 continues Section 3915 of the repealed Probate Code without change. This section is the same as Section 15 of the Uniform Transfers to Minors Act (1986). Compensation may be determined by agreement, by a provision in a will (see Section 6345), by reference to a statute, or by a court order. To prevent abuse, the provision for permissive compensation is denied to a custodian who is also the donor of the custodial property.

The custodian's election to charge compensation must be exercised (although the compensation need not be actually paid) at least annually or it lapses and may not be exercised later. This provision is intended to avoid imputed income to the custodian who waives compensation, and also to avoid the accumulation of a large unanticipated claim for compensation exercisable at termination of the custodianship.

Background on Section 3915 of Repealed Code

Section 3915 was added by 1984 Cal.Stat. ch. 243 § 9. Section 3915 superseded former Civil Code Section 1159 (repealed by 1984 Cal.Stat. ch. 243 § 1). For background on the provisions of this part, see the Comment to this part under the part heading.

Section 3915 did not continue the statement in the former section that a custodian may act without compensation for services, since that concept is implied in the provision in Section 3915 that a custodian has an "election" to be compensated.

Section 3915 omits as surplusage the standard contained in subdivision (c) of former Civil Code Section 1159 for determining "reasonable compensation" which included, "in the order stated," a direction by the donor, statutes governing compensation of custodians or guardians, or court order. This was an optional provision of the Uniform Gifts to Minors Act (1966) and was not continued in the Uniform Transfers to Minors Act (1986). While compensation of custodians became a more likely occurrence and a more important issue under the Uniform Transfers to Minors Act because property requiring increased management may be subject to custodianship under the Act, compensation can still be determined by agreement, by a provision in a will (see Section 6345), by reference to a statute or by court order, without the need to so state in the Uniform Transfers to Minors Act. [20 Cal.L.Rev.Comm.Reports 1001 (1990)].

Cross References

Custodial property defined for purposes of this Part, see Probate Code § 3901.
Custodian defined for purposes of this Part, see Probate Code § 3901.
Transferor defined for purposes of this Part, see Probate Code § 3901.

§ 3916. Exemption of third person from liability

A third person in good faith and without court order may act on the instructions of, or otherwise deal with, any person purporting to make a transfer or purporting to act in the capacity of a custodian and, in the absence of knowledge, is not responsible for determining any of the following:

(a) The validity of the purported custodian's designation.

(b) The propriety of, or the authority under this part for, any act of the purported custodian.

(c) The validity or propriety under this part of any instrument or instructions executed or given either by the person purporting to make a transfer or by the purported custodian.

(d) The propriety of the application of any property of the minor delivered to the purported custodian. *(Stats.1990, c. 79 (A.B.759), § 14, operative July 1, 1991.)*

Law Revision Commission Comments
1990 Enactment

Section 3916 continues Section 3916 of the repealed Probate Code without change. This section is the same as Section 16 of the Uniform Transfers to Minors Act (1986).

Because Section 3916 refers to any custodian, and "custodian" is defined to include successor custodians (subdivision (g) of Section 3901), a successor custodian appointed by the minor is included among those upon whom third persons may rely. Similarly, because Section 3916 protects any "third person," it is not necessary to specify in Section 3916 or in subdivision (c) of Section 3911 that the

protection extends to any "issuer, transfer agent, bank, life insurance company, broker, or other person or financial institution," as did former Civil Code Section 1160. See the definition of "person" in Section 3901(*l*).

Section 3916 does not alter the requirements for bona fide purchaser or holder in due course status under other law for persons who acquire from a custodial property subject to recordation or registration.

Background on Section 3916 of Repealed Code

Section 3916 was added by 1984 Cal.Stat. ch. 243 § 9. For background on the provisions of this part, see the Comment to this part under the part heading.

Section 3916 carried forward, but shortened and simplified, former Civil Code Section 1160 (repealed by 1984 Cal.Stat. ch. 243 § 1), with no substantive change intended. The former section permitted a 14–year old minor to appoint a successor custodian and specifically provided that third parties were entitled to rely on the appointment. Because Section 3916 referred to any custodian, and "custodian" was defined to include successor custodians (subdivision (g) of Section 3901), a successor custodian appointed by the minor was included among those upon whom third parties may rely.

Section 3916 excluded from its protection persons with "knowledge" of the irregularity of a transaction, a concept not expressed but probably implied in former Civil Code Section 1160. See, e.g., State ex rel. Paden v. Carrel, 597 S.W.2d 167 (Mo.App.1980), disapproving the pledge of custodial property to secure a personal loan to the custodian. [20 Cal.L.Rev.Comm.Reports 1001 (1990)].

Cross References

Court defined for purposes of this Part, see Probate Code § 3901.
Custodian defined for purposes of this Part, see Probate Code § 3901.
Minor defined for purposes of this Part, see Probate Code § 3901.
Person defined for purposes of this Part, see Probate Code § 3901.
Transfer defined for purposes of this Part, see Probate Code § 3901.

§ 3917. Liability to third persons

(a) A claim based on (1) a contract entered into by a custodian acting in a custodial capacity, (2) an obligation arising from the ownership or control of custodial property, or (3) a tort committed during the custodianship, may be asserted against the custodial property by proceeding against the custodian in the custodial capacity, whether or not the custodian or the minor is personally liable therefor.

(b) A custodian is not personally liable for either of the following:

(1) On a contract properly entered into in the custodial capacity unless the custodian fails to reveal that capacity and to identify the custodianship in the contract.

(2) For an obligation arising from control of custodial property or for a tort committed during the custodianship unless the custodian is personally at fault.

(c) A minor is not personally liable for an obligation arising from ownership of custodial property or for a tort committed during the custodianship unless the minor is personally at fault. *(Stats.1990, c. 79 (A.B.759), § 14, operative July 1, 1991.)*

Law Revision Commission Comments
1990 Enactment

Section 3917 continues Section 3917 of the repealed Probate Code without change. This section is the same as Section 17 of the Uniform Transfers to Minors Act (1986) and is based upon Section

5–428 of the Uniform Probate Code (1987), relating to limitations on the liability of conservators.

Some forms of custodial property can give rise to liabilities as well as benefits (e.g., general partnership interests, interests in real estate or business proprietorships, automobiles, etc.). Section 3917 is included to protect the minor and other assets the minor might have or acquire from such liabilities, since the minor is unable to disclaim a transfer to a custodian for the minor's benefit. Similar protection for the custodian is necessary so as not to discourage nonprofessional or uncompensated persons from accepting the office. Therefore, this section generally limits the claims of third parties to recourse against the custodial property, as third parties dealing with a trust are generally limited to recourse against the trust corpus.

The custodian incurs personal liability only as provided in subdivision (b) for actual fault or for failure to disclose the custodial capacity "in the contract" when contracting with third parties. In oral contracts, oral disclosure of the custodial capacity is sufficient. The minor, on the other hand, incurs personal liability under subdivision (c) only for actual fault.

When custodial property is subjected to claims of third parties under this section, the minor or the minor's legal representative, if not a party to the action by which the claim is successfully established, may seek to recover the loss from the custodian in a separate action. See Section 3919 and the Comment thereto.

Background on Section 3917 of Repealed Code

Section 3917 was a new provision added by 1984 Cal.Stat. ch. 243 § 9. For background on the provisions of this part, see the Comment to this part under the part heading. Section 3917 appears to have been consistent with prior California law concerning the tort liability of a guardian. See Campbell v. Bradbury, 179 Cal. 364, 176 P. 685 (1918). But the provision may have restricted the liability under prior law of the custodian who makes a contract in the custodial capacity. See Hall v. Jameson, 151 Cal. 606, 91 P. 518 (1907) (trustee personally liable on contract unless contract stipulates trustee not liable). But see Prob. Code § 18000 (unless contract otherwise provides, trustee not personally liable on contract properly entered into in the trustee's fiduciary capacity in the course of administration of the trust unless the trustee fails to reveal the trustee's representative capacity or identify the trust in the contract). [20 Cal.L.Rev.Comm.Reports 1001 (1990)].

Cross References

Custodial property defined for purposes of this Part, see Probate Code § 3901.
Custodian defined for purposes of this Part, see Probate Code § 3901.
Minor defined for purposes of this Part, see Probate Code § 3901.

§ 3918. Substitute and successor custodians

(a) A person nominated under Section 3903 or designated under Section 3909 as custodian may decline to serve by delivering a valid disclaimer under Part 8 (commencing with Section 260) of Division 2 to the person who made the nomination or to the transferor or the transferor's legal representative. If the event giving rise to a transfer has not occurred and no substitute custodian able, willing, and eligible to serve was nominated under Section 3903, the person who made the nomination may nominate a substitute custodian under Section 3903; otherwise the transferor or the transferor's legal representative shall designate a substitute custodian at the time of the transfer, in either case from among the persons eligible to serve as custodian for that kind of property under subdivision (a) of Section 3909. The custodian so designated has the rights of a successor custodian.

(b) A custodian at any time may designate a trust company or an adult other than a transferor under Section 3904 as successor custodian by executing and dating an instrument of designation before a subscribing witness other than the successor. If the instrument of designation does not contain or is not accompanied by the resignation of the custodian, the designation of the successor does not take effect until the custodian resigns, dies, becomes incapacitated, or is removed. The transferor may designate one or more persons as successor custodians to serve, in the designated order of priority, in case the custodian originally designated or a prior successor custodian is unable, declines, or is ineligible to serve or resigns, dies, becomes incapacitated, or is removed. The designation either (1) shall be made in the same transaction and by the same document by which the transfer is made or (2) shall be made by executing and dating a separate instrument of designation before a subscribing witness other than a successor as a part of the same transaction and contemporaneously with the execution of the document by which the transfer is made. The designation is made by setting forth the successor custodian's name, followed in substance by the words: "is designated (first, second, etc., where applicable) successor custodian." A successor custodian designated by the transferor may be a trust company or an adult other than a transferor under Section 3904. A successor custodian effectively designated by the transferor has priority over a successor custodian designated by a custodian.

(c) A custodian may resign at any time by delivering written notice to the minor if the minor has attained the age of 14 years and to the successor custodian and by delivering the custodial property to the successor custodian.

(d) If the transferor has not effectively designated a successor custodian, and a custodian is ineligible, dies, or becomes incapacitated without having effectively designated a successor and the minor has attained the age of 14 years, the minor may designate as successor custodian, in the manner prescribed in subdivision (b), an adult member of the minor's family, a conservator of the minor, or a trust company. If the minor has not attained the age of 14 years or fails to act within 60 days after the ineligibility, death, or incapacity, the conservator of the minor becomes successor custodian. If the minor has no conservator or the conservator declines to act, the transferor, the legal representative of the transferor or of the custodian, an adult member of the minor's family, or any other interested person may petition the court to designate a successor custodian.

(e) A custodian who declines to serve under subdivision (a) or resigns under subdivision (c), or the legal representative of a deceased or incapacitated custodian, as soon as practicable, shall put the custodial property and records in the possession and control of the successor custodian. The successor custodian by action may enforce the obligation to deliver custodial property and records and becomes responsible for each item as received.

(f) A transferor, the legal representative of a transferor, an adult member of the minor's family, a guardian of the person of the minor, the conservator of the minor, or the minor if the minor has attained the age of 14 years, may petition the court to remove the custodian for cause and to designate a successor custodian other than a transferor under Section 3904 or to require the custodian to give appropriate bond.

(g) At least 15 days before the hearing on a petition under subdivision (d) or (f), the petitioner shall serve notice by mail or personal delivery on each of the following persons:

(1) The minor.

(2) The parent or parents of the minor.

(3) The transferor.

(h) Upon consideration of the petition under subdivision (d) or (f), the court may grant the relief that the court finds to be in the best interests of the minor. *(Stats.1990, c. 79 (A.B.759), § 14, operative July 1, 1991. Amended by Stats. 1992, c. 871 (A.B.2975), § 7.)*

Law Revision Commission Comments

1990 Enactment

Section 3918 continues Section 3918 of the repealed Probate Code without change. This section is the same in substance as Section 18 of the Uniform Transfers to Minors Act (1986) with the addition of subdivision (g) and the addition of provisions authorizing the transferor to designate a successor custodian. See also Section 3901(d) ("conservator" includes a guardian).

Background on Section 3918 of Repealed Code

Section 3918 was added by 1984 Cal.Stat. ch. 243 § 9 and was amended by 1985 Cal.Stat. ch. 90 § 1 and 1988 Cal.Stat. ch. 1199 § 73.5. For background on the provisions of this part, see the Comment to this part under the part heading. Section 3918 tracked but condensed former Civil Code Section 1161 (repealed by 1984 Cal.Stat. ch. 243 § 1).

Enactment of the Uniform Transfers to Minors Act broadened the category of persons the initial custodian may designate as successor custodian from an adult member of the minor's family, the guardian of the minor, or a trust company to include any adult other than the donor. However, the minor's designation remained limited to an adult member of the minor's family (expanded to include a spouse and a stepparent, see subdivision (j) of Section 3901), the guardian of the minor's estate, or a trust company. Subdivision (g) of Section 3918 continued subdivision (h) of former Civil Code Section 1161 (repealed by 1984 Cal.Stat. ch. 243 § 1). See also Sections 3905(c), 3907(c).

The 1985 amendment added provisions authorizing the transferor to designate a successor custodian. The language of the 1985 amendment was drawn in part from portions of former Civil Code Section 1161. For background on this amendment, see 18 Cal.L.Revision Comm'n Reports at 218 (1986).

The 1988 amendment substituted a reference in subdivision (a) to Part 8 of Division 2 in place of the former reference to Division 2.5, to reflect a change in the numbering of the provisions to which reference was made. [20 Cal.L.Rev.Comm.Reports 1001 (1990)].

Cross References

Adult defined for purposes of this Part, see Probate Code § 3901.
Conservator defined for purposes of this Part, see Probate Code § 3901.
Court defined for purposes of this Part, see Probate Code § 3901.
Custodial property defined for purposes of this Part, see Probate Code § 3901.
Custodian defined for purposes of this Part, see Probate Code § 3901.
Legal representative defined for purposes of this Part, see Probate Code § 3901.
Member of the minor's family defined for purposes of this Part, see Probate Code § 3901.

Minor defined for purposes of this Part, see Probate Code § 3901.
Person defined for purposes of this Part, see Probate Code § 3901.
Transfer defined for purposes of this Part, see Probate Code § 3901.
Transferor defined for purposes of this Part, see Probate Code § 3901.
Trust company defined for purposes of this Part, see Probate Code § 3901.

§ 3919. Petition for accounting; determination of liability of custodian; removal of custodian

(a) A minor who has attained the age of 14 years, the minor's guardian of the person or legal representative, an adult member of the minor's family, a transferor, or a transferor's legal representative may petition the court for any of the following:

(1) An accounting by the custodian or the custodian's legal representative.

(2) A determination of responsibility, as between the custodial property and the custodian personally, for claims against the custodial property unless the responsibility has been adjudicated in an action under Section 3917 to which the minor or the minor's legal representative was a party.

(b) A successor custodian may petition the court for an accounting by the predecessor custodian.

(c) The court, in a proceeding under this part or in any other proceeding, may require or permit the custodian or the custodian's legal representative to account.

(d) If a custodian is removed under subdivision (f) of Section 3918, the court shall require an accounting and order delivery of the custodial property and records to the successor custodian and the execution of all instruments required for transfer of the custodial property.

(e) The right to petition for an accounting shall continue for one year after the filing of a final accounting by the custodian or the custodian's legal representative and delivery of the custodial property to the minor or the minor's estate. *(Stats.1990, c. 79 (A.B.759), § 14, operative July 1, 1991.)*

Law Revision Commission Comments

1990 Enactment

Section 3919 continues Section 3919 of the repealed Probate Code without change. This section is the same as Section 19 of the Uniform Transfers to Minors Act (1986) with the addition of subdivision (e). The introductory clause of subdivision (a) states the persons who may require an accounting by the custodian. Subdivision (a) also gives the same parties (other than a successor custodian) the right to seek recovery from the custodian for loss or diminution of custodial property resulting from successful claims by third persons under Section 3917, unless that issue has already been adjudicated in an action under that section to which the minor was a party.

Subdivision (b) authorizes but does not obligate a successor custodian to seek an accounting by the predecessor custodian. Since the minor and other persons mentioned in subdivision (a) may also seek an accounting from the predecessor at any time, it is anticipated that the exercise of this right by the successor should be rare.

Property in a single custodianship may be distributable at different times, so separate accounting for custodial property (depending on the time of distribution) may be required. See the Comment to Section 3910.

Background on Section 3919 of Repealed Code

Section 3919 was added by 1984 Cal.Stat. ch. 243 § 9. The section carried forward former Civil Code Section 1162 (repealed by 1984 Cal.Stat. ch. 243 § 1), but expanded the class of parties who could require an accounting by the custodian. Subdivisions (c) and (d) continued the substance of subdivision (b) of former Civil Code Section 1162. Subdivision (e) continued the second sentence of subdivision (a) of former Civil Code Section 1162. For background on the provisions of this part, see the Comment to this part under the part heading. [20 Cal.L.Rev.Comm.Reports 1001 (1990)].

Cross References

Adult defined for purposes of this Part, see Probate Code § 3901.
Court defined for purposes of this Part, see Probate Code § 3901.
Custodial property defined for purposes of this Part, see Probate Code § 3901.
Custodian defined for purposes of this Part, see Probate Code § 3901.
Legal representative defined for purposes of this Part, see Probate Code § 3901.
Member of the minor's family defined for purposes of this Part, see Probate Code § 3901.
Minor defined for purposes of this Part, see Probate Code § 3901.
Person defined for purposes of this Part, see Probate Code § 3901.
Transfer defined for purposes of this Part, see Probate Code § 3901.
Transferor defined for purposes of this Part, see Probate Code § 3901.

§ 3920. Termination of custodianship

The custodian shall transfer in an appropriate manner the custodial property to the minor or to the minor's estate upon the earlier of the following:

(a) The minor's attainment of 18 years of age unless the time of transfer of the custodial property to the minor is delayed under Section 3920.5 to a time after the time the minor attains the age of 18 years.

(b) The time specified in the transfer pursuant to Section 3909 if the time of transfer of the custodial property to the minor is delayed under Section 3920.5 to a time after the time the minor attains the age of 18 years.

(c) The minor's death. *(Stats.1990, c. 79 (A.B.759), § 14, operative July 1, 1991.)*

Law Revision Commission Comments

1990 Enactment

Section 3920 continues Section 3920 of the repealed Probate Code without change. This section is drawn from Section 20 of the Uniform Transfers to Minors Act (1986). Subdivision (a) establishes the age of termination as 18 years unless the time of transfer of custodial property to the minor is delayed under Section 3920.5.

Background on Section 3920 of Repealed Code

Section 3920 was added by 1984 Cal.Stat. ch. 243 § 9. Sections 3920 and 3920.5 superseded subdivision (d) of former Civil Code Section 1158 (repealed by 1984 Cal.Stat. ch. 243 § 1). See Report of Senate Committee on Judiciary on Assembly Bill 2492, 18 Cal.L.Revision Comm'n Reports 105, 111 (1986). For background on the provisions of this part, see the Comment to this part under the part heading. [20 Cal.L.Rev.Comm.Reports 1001 (1990)].

Cross References

Custodial property defined for purposes of this Part, see Probate Code § 3901.

Custodian defined for purposes of this Part, see Probate Code § 3901.
Minor defined for purposes of this Part, see Probate Code § 3901.
Transfer defined for purposes of this Part, see Probate Code § 3901.

§ 3920.5. Delay in transfer of custodial property until after minor attains age eighteen; transfers not specifying age

(a) Subject to the requirements and limitations of this section, the time for transfer to the minor of custodial property transferred under or pursuant to Section 3903, 3904, 3905, or 3906, may be delayed until a specified time after the time the minor attains the age of 18 years, which time shall be specified in the transfer pursuant to Section 3909.

(b) To specify a delayed time for transfer to the minor of the custodial property, the words

"as custodian for _____
(Name of Minor)
until age _____
(Age for Delivery of Property to Minor)
under the California Uniform Transfers to Minors Act" shall be substituted in substance for the words
"as custodian for _____
(Name of Minor)
under the California Uniform Transfers to Minors Act" in making the transfer pursuant to Section 3909.

(c) The time for transfer to the minor of custodial property transferred under or pursuant to Section 3903 or 3905 may be delayed under this section only if the governing will or trust or nomination provides in substance that the custodianship is to continue until the time the minor attains a specified age, which time may not be later than the time the minor attains 25 years of age, and in that case the governing will or trust or nomination shall determine the time to be specified in the transfer pursuant to Section 3909.

(d) The time for transfer to the minor of custodial property transferred by the irrevocable exercise of a power of appointment under Section 3904 may be delayed under this section only if the transfer pursuant to Section 3909 provides in substance that the custodianship is to continue until the time the minor attains a specified age, which time may not be later than the time the minor attains 25 years of age.

(e) The time for transfer to the minor of custodial property transferred by irrevocable gift under Section 3904 may be delayed under this section only if the transfer pursuant to Section 3909 provides in substance that the custodianship is to continue until the time the minor attains a specified age, which time may not be later than the time the minor attains 21 years of age.

(f) The time for transfer to the minor of custodial property transferred by a trustee under Section 3906 may be delayed under this section only if the transfer pursuant to Section 3909 provides that the custodianship is to continue until a specified time not later than the time the minor attains 25 years of age or the time of termination of all present beneficial interests of the minor in the trust from which the custodial property was transferred, whichever is to occur first.

(g) If the transfer pursuant to Section 3909 does not specify any age, the time for the transfer of the custodial property to the minor under Section 3920 is the time when the minor attains 18 years of age.

(h) If the transfer pursuant to Section 3909 provides in substance that the duration of the custodianship is for a time longer than the maximum time permitted by this section for the duration of a custodianship created by that type of transfer, the custodianship shall be deemed to continue only until the time the minor attains the maximum age permitted by this section for the duration of a custodianship created by that type of transfer. *(Stats.1990, c. 79 (A.B.759), § 14, operative July 1, 1991. Amended by Stats.1996, c. 862 (A.B.2751), § 14.)*

Law Revision Commission Comments
1990 Enactment

Section 3920.5 continues Section 3920.5 of the repealed Probate Code without change. There is no provision under the Uniform Transfers to Minors Act (1986) for choice as to the age at which custodial property shall be transferred to the minor. Likewise, there was no such provision under prior California law. Section 3920.5 gives this choice since many transferors who specifically authorize a custodianship wish to preserve the custodianship as long as possible. This is most likely to be the case, for example, where the custodial property is intended to be preserved and used to finance a college education. Continuing the custodianship past the age of 18 permits the donor to avoid the expense of preparing a trust instrument to create a trust that otherwise would be required in order to retain the property under custodial management until the young person reaches the specified age.

The custodian is required to transfer the property to the minor when the minor attains the age of 18 years unless the transfer pursuant to Section 3909 specifies a later time. See Section 3920.

Subdivision (c) permits the custodianship to continue until not later than the time the minor attains the age of 25 years where the transfer is made pursuant to a provision in a will or trust that provides that the custodianship is to continue until the specified age, not later than the time the beneficiary attains the age of 25. A custodianship may be established pursuant to a provision in a will or trust that provides that the custodianship is to continue until a specified age after age 18 even though the beneficiary has attained an age older than 18 but younger than the specified age at which the custodianship is to terminate. See Section 3901(k).

Subdivision (d) permits the custodianship to continue until not later than the time the minor attains the age of 25 years where the custodial property is transferred by the irrevocable exercise of a power of appointment under Section 3904 if the transfer specifies that the custodianship is to continue until the specified age.

Subdivision (e) permits the custodianship to continue until not later than the time the minor attains the age of 21 years where the custodial property is transferred by a lifetime gift. The 21–year maximum duration of the custodianship is consistent with the Internal Revenue Code which permits "minority trusts" under Section 2503(c) of the Internal Revenue Code to continue in effect until age 21.

Section 3920.5 does not provide for continuance beyond age 18 of a custodianship created under or pursuant to Sections 3412, 3413, 3602, 3611, 3906, or 3907. These custodianships terminate at age 18 because they are substitutes for a guardianship that otherwise would terminate at that time (see Section 1600). And, in the cases where Section 3920.5 permits the custodianship to continue after the minor attains the age of 18 years, if the transfer pursuant to Section 3909 does not specify any age, the custodianship terminates when the minor attains 18 years of age. See subdivision (f) of Section 3920.5.

Subdivision (g) validates a transfer that specifies a maximum time for the duration of the custodianship that is longer than permitted by Section 3920.5 by reducing the duration of the custodianship to the maximum duration permitted for a custodianship created by that type of transfer.

Because property in a single custodianship may be distributable at different times, separate accounting for custodial property by source may be required. See the Comment to Section 3910.

Background on Section 3920.5 of Repealed Code

Section 3920.5 was a new provision added by 1984 Cal.Stat. ch. 243 § 9. See Report of Senate Committee on Judiciary on Assembly Bill 2492, 18 Cal.L.Revision Comm'n Reports 105, 111–13 (1986). For background on the provisions of this part, see the Comment to this part under the part heading. [20 Cal.L.Rev.Comm.Reports 1001 (1990)].

Cross References

Custodial property defined for purposes of this Part, see Probate Code § 3901.
Custodian defined for purposes of this Part, see Probate Code § 3901.
Minor defined for purposes of this Part, see Probate Code § 3901.
Transfer defined for purposes of this Part, see Probate Code § 3901.

§ 3921. Proceedings on petition; place

Subject to the power of the court to transfer actions and proceedings as provided in the Code of Civil Procedure, a petition filed under this part shall be heard and proceedings thereon held in the superior court in the proper county, which shall be determined as follows:

(a) If the minor resides in this state, in either of the following counties:

(1) Where the minor resides.

(2) Where the custodian resides.

(b) If the minor does not reside within this state, in any of the following counties:

(1) Where the transferor resides.

(2) Where the custodian resides.

(3) Where the estate of a deceased or legally incapacitated custodian is being administered.

(4) Where a parent of the minor resides.

(c) If neither the minor, nor the transferor, nor any parent resides within this state, and no estate of a deceased or legally incapacitated custodian is being administered within this state, in any county. *(Stats.1990, c. 79 (A.B.759), § 14, operative July 1, 1991.)*

Law Revision Commission Comments
1990 Enactment

Section 3921 continues Section 3921 of the repealed Probate Code without change. No comparable provision is included in the Uniform Transfers to Minors Act (1986). Even where the custodian resides in this state, the venue is proper in any county if neither the minor, nor the transferor, nor any parent reside in this state, and no estate of a deceased or legally incapacitated custodian is being administered in this state.

Background on Section 3921 of Repealed Code

Section 3921 was added by 1984 Cal.Stat. ch. 243 § 9. The section continued and expanded the venue provision of former Civil Code Section 1162.5 (repealed by 1984 Cal.Stat. ch. 243 § 1). The former provision was liberalized to add the county where the custodian resides as a proper county, whether or not the minor resides in this state. For background on the provisions of this part, see the Comment to this part under the part heading. [20 Cal.L.Rev.Comm.Reports 1001 (1990)].

Court defined for purposes of this Part, see Probate Code § 3901.
Custodian defined for purposes of this Part, see Probate Code § 3901.
Minor defined for purposes of this Part, see Probate Code § 3901.
State defined for purposes of this Part, see Probate Code § 3901.
Transfer defined for purposes of this Part, see Probate Code § 3901.
Transferor defined for purposes of this Part, see Probate Code § 3901.

§ 3922. Transfers made under Uniform Gifts to Minors Act or Uniform Transfers to Minors Act of other state

This part applies to a transfer within the scope of Section 3902 made on or after January 1, 1985, if either of the following requirements is satisfied:

(a) The transfer purports to have been made under the California Uniform Gifts to Minors Act.

(b) The instrument by which the transfer purports to have been made uses in substance the designation "as custodian under the Uniform Gifts to Minors Act" or "as custodian under the Uniform Transfers to Minors Act" of any other state, and the application of this part is necessary to validate the transfer. (Stats.1990, c. 79 (A.B.759), § 14, operative July 1, 1991.)

Law Revision Commission Comments
1990 Enactment

Section 3922 continues Section 3922 of the repealed Probate Code without change. This section is the same as Section 21 of the Uniform Transfers to Minors Act (1986). The section has two purposes. First, it operates as a "savings clause" to validate transfers made on or after January 1, 1985 (the effective date of the California Uniform Transfers to Minors Act) which mistakenly refer to the California Uniform Gifts to Minors Act rather than to the California Uniform Transfers to Minors Act. Second, it validates transfers attempted under the Uniform Gifts to Minors Act (1966) of another state which would not permit transfers from that source or of property of that kind or under the Uniform Transfers to Minors Act of another state with no nexus to the transaction, provided in each case that California has a sufficient nexus to the transaction under Section 3902.

Background on Section 3922 of Repealed Code

Section 3922 was a new provision added by 1984 Cal.Stat. ch. 243 § 9. For background on the provisions of this part, see the Comment to this part under the part heading. [20 Cal.L.Rev.Comm.Reports 1001 (1990)].

Cross References

Custodian defined for purposes of this Part, see Probate Code § 3901.
Minor defined for purposes of this Part, see Probate Code § 3901.
State defined for purposes of this Part, see Probate Code § 3901.
Transfer defined for purposes of this Part, see Probate Code § 3901.

§ 3923. Effect on existing custodianships

(a) As used in this section, "California Uniform Gifts to Minors Act" means former Article 4 (commencing with Section 1154) of Chapter 3 of Title 4 of Part 4 of Division 2 of the Civil Code.

(b) Any transfer of custodial property, as now defined in this part, made before January 1, 1985, is validated, notwithstanding that there was no specific authority in the California Uniform Gifts to Minors Act for the coverage of custodial property of that kind or for a transfer from that source at the time the transfer was made.

(c) This part applies to all transfers made before January 1, 1985, in a manner and form prescribed in the California Uniform Gifts to Minors Act, except insofar as the application impairs constitutionally vested rights.

(d) To the extent that this part, by virtue of subdivision (c), does not apply to transfers made in a manner prescribed in the California Uniform Gifts to Minors Act or to the powers, duties, and immunities conferred by transfers in that manner upon custodians and persons dealing with custodians, the repeal of the California Uniform Gifts to Minors Act does not affect those transfers or those powers, duties, and immunities. (Stats.1990, c. 79 (A.B.759), § 14, operative July 1, 1991.)

Law Revision Commission Comments
1990 Enactment

Section 3923 continues Section 3923 of the repealed Probate Code without change. Subdivision (b) is the same as subsection (a) of Section 22 of the Uniform Transfers to Minors Act (1986). This subdivision attempts to validate any transfer of custodial property made before the effective date of enactment of this part of the repealed Probate Code, notwithstanding that there was no specific authority in California law for the coverage of custodial property of that kind or for a transfer from that source at the time the transfer was made. The subdivision would, for example, validate a transfer from an intervivos trust by a trustee to a custodianship pursuant to an express provision in the trust instrument giving the trustee that authority. It was not clear under prior law that such a transfer created a valid custodianship.

Subdivision (c) is the same as subsection (b) of Section 22 of the Uniform Transfers to Minors Act (1986), except that subdivision (c) does not contain the language of Section 22(b) relating to extending the duration of custodianships in existence on the operative date. The omitted language is unnecessary because custodianships created under the California Uniform Gifts to Minors Act will still terminate at age 18 under this part. See Sections 3920, 3920.5. Subdivision (c) makes this part apply to all transfers made before January 1, 1985, in the manner and form prescribed in the California Uniform Gifts to Minors Act, except insofar as the application impairs constitutionally vested rights. This provision avoids having two bodies of law in force—one applicable to prior custodianships and the other to custodianships created under this part—for 18 more years until all custodianships created under the California Uniform Gifts to Minors Act have terminated. As to the application of any amendments made after that date, see Section 3.

Subdivision (d) is the same as the second sentence of Section 27 of the Uniform Transfers to Minors Act (1986). It preserves prior law for matters not governed by this part.

Background on Section 3923 of Repealed Code

Section 3923 was a new provision added by 1984 Cal.Stat. ch. 243 § 9. See Report of Senate Committee on Judiciary on Assembly Bill 2492, 18 Cal.L. Revision Comm'n Reports 105, 113 (1986). For background on the provisions of this part, see the Comment to this part under the part heading. [20 Cal.L.Rev.Comm.Reports 1001 (1990)].

Cross References

Custodial property defined for purposes of this Part, see Probate Code § 3901.
Custodian defined for purposes of this Part, see Probate Code § 3901.
Minor defined for purposes of this Part, see Probate Code § 3901.

Person defined for purposes of this Part, see Probate Code § 3901.
Transfer defined for purposes of this Part, see Probate Code § 3901.

§ 3924. Repealed by Stats.1990, c. 79 (A.B.759), § 13, operative July 1, 1991

Law Revision Commission Comments

1990 Repeal

Section 3924 of the repealed Probate Code is omitted from the new Probate Code because it is unnecessary. See Section 2(b) (construction of uniform acts). [20 Cal.L.Rev.Comm.Reports 1001 (1990)].

§ 3925. Part not exclusive

This part shall not be construed as providing an exclusive method for making gifts or other transfers to minors. *(Stats.1990, c. 79 (A.B.759), § 14, operative July 1, 1991.)*

Law Revision Commission Comments

1990 Enactment

Section 3925 continues Section 3925 of the repealed Probate Code without change. No comparable provision is found in the Uniform Transfers to Minors Act (1986).

Background on Section 3925 of Repealed Code

Section 3925 was added by 1984 Cal.Stat. ch. 243 § 9. The section continued the substance of subdivision (b) of former Civil Code Section 1163 (repealed by 1984 Cal.Stat. ch. 243 § 1). For background on the provisions of this part, see the Comment to this part under the part heading. [20 Cal.L.Rev.Comm.Reports 1001 (1990)].

Cross References

Minor defined for purposes of this Part, see Probate Code § 3901.
Transfer defined for purposes of this Part, see Probate Code § 3901.

Division 4.5

POWERS OF ATTORNEY

Cross References

Authorized attorney-in-fact, revocation, see Financial Code § 6725.
Powers of attorney, application of this Division, see Civil Code § 2400.
Professional fiduciaries, suspension, revocation or other adverse action, see Business and Professions Code § 6584.

Part 1

DEFINITIONS AND GENERAL PROVISIONS

CHAPTER 1. SHORT TITLE AND DEFINITIONS

§ 4000. Short title; Power of Attorney Law

This division may be cited as the Power of Attorney Law. *(Added by Stats.1994, c. 307 (S.B.1907), § 16.)*

Law Revision Commission Comments

1994 Addition

Section 4000 is new and provides a convenient means of referring to this division. The Power of Attorney Law is largely self-contained, but the general agency statutes are applicable as provided in Section 4051. See also Section 20 *et seq.* (general definitions applicable in Probate Code depending on context). [24 Cal.L.Rev.Comm.Reports 323 (1994)].

Cross References

Power of attorney defined for purposes of this Division, see Probate Code § 4022.

§ 4001. Short title; uniform durable power of attorney act

Sections 4124, 4125, 4126, 4127, 4206, 4304, and 4305 may be cited as the Uniform Durable Power of Attorney Act. *(Added by Stats.1994, c. 307 (S.B.1907), § 16.)*

Law Revision Commission Comments

1994 Addition

Section 4001 restates former Civil Code Section 2406 without substantive change. This section has the same purpose as the official text of Section 7 of the Uniform Durable Power of Attorney Act (1969). See also Sections 2(b) (construction of provisions drawn from uniform acts), 11 (severability). [24 Cal.L.Rev.Comm.Reports 323 (1994)].

Cross References

Durable power of attorney defined for purposes of this Division, see Probate Code § 4018.

§ 4010. Definitions

Unless the provision or context otherwise requires, the definitions in this chapter govern the construction of this division. *(Added by Stats.1994, c. 307 (S.B.1907), § 16.)*

Law Revision Commission Comments

1994 Addition

Section 4010 restates and generalizes the substance of the introductory clause of former Civil Code Section 2410. [24 Cal.L.Rev.Comm.Reports 323 (1994)].

§ 4014. Attorney-in-fact

(a) "Attorney-in-fact" means a person granted authority to act for the principal in a power of attorney, regardless of whether the person is known as an attorney-in-fact or agent, or by some other term.

(b) "Attorney-in-fact" includes a successor or alternate attorney-in-fact and a person delegated authority by an attorney-in-fact. *(Added by Stats.1994, c. 307 (S.B.1907), § 16.)*

Law Revision Commission Comments

1994 Addition [Revised Comment]

Subdivision (a) of Section 4014 supersedes part of former Civil Code Section 2400 and former Civil Code Section 2410(a), and is comparable to the first sentence of Civil Code Section 2295.

Subdivision (b) is comparable to Section 84 ("trustee" includes successor trustee). See Sections 4202 (multiple attorneys-in-fact), 4203 (successor attorneys-in-fact), 4205 (delegation of attorney-in-fact's authority). The purpose of subdivision (b) is to make clear that the rules applicable to attorneys-in-fact under the Power of Attorney Law apply as well to successors and alternates of the original attorney-in-fact, and to other persons who act in place of the attorney-in-fact.

See also Sections 4022 ("power of attorney" defined), 4026 ("principal" defined). [29 Cal.L.Rev.Comm. Reports 1 (1999)].

Cross References

Power of attorney defined for purposes of this Division, see Probate Code § 4022.

Principal defined for purposes of this Division, see Probate Code § 4026.

§ 4018. Durable power of attorney

"Durable power of attorney" means a power of attorney that satisfies the requirements for durability provided in Section 4124. *(Added by Stats.1994, c. 307 (S.B.1907), § 16.)*

Law Revision Commission Comments

1994 Addition

Section 4018 is a new section included for drafting convenience. [24 Cal.L.Rev.Comm.Reports 323 (1994)].

Cross References

Power of attorney defined for purposes of this Division, see Probate Code § 4022.

§ 4022. Power of attorney

"Power of attorney" means a written instrument, however denominated, that is executed by a natural person having the capacity to contract and that grants authority to an attorney-in-fact. A power of attorney may be durable or nondurable. *(Added by Stats.1994, c. 307 (S.B.1907), § 16.)*

Law Revision Commission Comments

1994 Addition

Section 4022 restates the first sentence of former Civil Code Section 2410(c) without substantive change. See Sections 4120 (who may execute a power of attorney), 4121 (formalities for executing power of attorney), 4123 (permissible purposes). See also Sections 4014 ("attorney-in-fact" defined), 4018 ("durable power of attorney" defined), 4609 ("health care" defined). [24 Cal.L.Rev.Comm.Reports 323 (1994)].

Cross References

Attorney-in-fact defined for purposes of this Division, see Probate Code § 4014.

§ 4026. Principal

"Principal" means a natural person who executes a power of attorney. *(Added by Stats.1994, c. 307 (S.B.1907), § 16.)*

Law Revision Commission Comments

1994 Addition

Section 4026 restates and generalizes former Civil Code Section 2410(d). See Section 4022 ("power of attorney" defined). [24 Cal.L.Rev.Comm.Reports 323 (1994)].

Cross References

Power of attorney defined for purposes of this Division, see Probate Code § 4022.

§ 4030. Springing power of attorney

"Springing power of attorney" means a power of attorney that by its terms becomes effective at a specified future time or on the occurrence of a specified future event or contingency, including, but not limited to, the subsequent incapacity of the principal. A springing power of attorney may be a durable power of attorney or a nondurable power of attorney. *(Added by Stats.1994, c. 307 (S.B.1907), § 16.)*

Law Revision Commission Comments

1994 Addition

Section 4030 continues former Civil Code Section 2514(a)(2) without substantive change. See Section 4129 (springing power of attorney). See also Sections 4018 ("durable power of attorney" defined), 4022 ("power of attorney" defined), 4026 ("principal" defined). [24 Cal.L.Rev.Comm.Reports 323 (1994)].

Cross References

Durable power of attorney defined for purposes of this Division, see Probate Code § 4018.
Power of attorney defined for purposes of this Division, see Probate Code § 4022.
Principal defined for purposes of this Division, see Probate Code § 4026.

§ 4034. Third person

"Third person" means any person other than the principal or attorney-in-fact. *(Added by Stats.1994, c. 307 (S.B.1907), § 16.)*

Law Revision Commission Comments

1994 Addition

Section 4034 is a new provision. For the purposes of this statute, a third person is a person who acts on a request from, contracts with, relies on, or otherwise deals with the attorney-in-fact. The Uniform Statutory Form Power of Attorney uses the equivalent term "third party." See Sections 4401–4402.

See also Sections 4014 ("attorney-in-fact" defined), 4026 ("principal" defined). [24 Cal.L.Rev.Comm.Reports 323 (1994)].

Cross References

Attorney-in-fact defined for purposes of this Division, see Probate Code § 4014.
Principal defined for purposes of this Division, see Probate Code § 4026.

CHAPTER 2. GENERAL PROVISIONS

§ 4050. Application of division

(a) This division applies to the following:

(1) Durable powers of attorney, other than powers of attorney for health care governed by Division 4.7 (commencing with Section 4600).

(2) Statutory form powers of attorney under Part 3 (commencing with Section 4400).

(3) Any other power of attorney that incorporates or refers to this division or the provisions of this division.

(b) This division does not apply to the following:

(1) A power of attorney to the extent that the authority of the attorney-in-fact is coupled with an interest in the subject of the power of attorney.

(2) Reciprocal or interinsurance exchanges and their contracts, subscribers, attorneys-in-fact, agents, and representatives.

(3) A proxy given by an attorney-in-fact to another person to exercise voting rights.

(c) This division is not intended to affect the validity of any instrument or arrangement that is not described in subdivision (a). *(Added by Stats.1994, c. 307 (S.B.1907), § 16. Amended by Stats.1999, c. 658 (A.B.891), § 27, operative July 1, 2000.)*

Law Revision Commission Comments
1994 Addition [Revised Comment]

Section 4050 describes the types of instruments that are subject to the Power of Attorney Law. If a section in this division refers to a "power of attorney," it generally refers to a durable power of attorney, but may, under certain circumstances, also apply to a nondurable power of attorney. For example, a statutory form power of attorney may be durable or nondurable. See Sections 4401, 4404. A nondurable power may incorporate provisions of this division, thereby becoming subject to its provisions as provided in Section 4050(a)(4).

Subdivision (b) makes clear that certain specialized types of power of attorney are not subject to the Power of Attorney Law. This list is not intended to be exclusive. See subdivision (c). Subdivision (b)(1) recognizes the special rule applicable to a power coupled with an interest in the subject of a power of attorney provided in Civil Code Section 2356(a). Subdivision (b)(2) continues the substance of the limitation in former Civil Code Section 2420(b) and broadens it to apply to the entire Power of Attorney Law. See Ins. Code § 1280 *et seq.* For the rules applicable to proxy voting in business corporations, see Corp. Code § 705. For other statutes dealing with proxies, see Corp. Code §§ 178, 702, 5069, 5613, 7613, 9417, 12405, 13242; Fin. Code §§ 5701, 5702, 5710, 6005. See also Civ. Code § 2356(e) (proxy under general agency rules).

Subdivision (c) makes clear that this division does not affect the validity of other agencies and powers of attorney. The Power of Attorney Law thus does not apply to other specialized agencies, such as real estate agents under Civil Code Sections 2373–2382. As a corollary, an instrument denominated a power of attorney that does not satisfy the execution requirements for a power of attorney under this division may be valid under general agency law or other principles.

See also Sections 4014 ("attorney-in-fact" defined), 4018 ("durable power of attorney" defined), 4022 ("power of attorney" defined). [29 Cal.L.Rev.Comm. Reports 1 (1999)].

1999 Amendment

Section 4050 is amended to reflect the revision of the law relating to powers of attorney for health care. See Section 4600 *et seq.* (Health Care Decisions Law). Division 4.5 no longer governs powers of attorney for health care. [29 Cal.L.Rev.Comm. Reports 1 (1999)].

Cross References
Attorney-in-fact defined for purposes of this Division, see Probate Code § 4014.
Durable power of attorney defined for purposes of this Division, see Probate Code § 4018.
Power of attorney defined for purposes of this Division, see Probate Code § 4022.

§ 4051. Agency law; application

Except where this division provides a specific rule, the general law of agency, including Article 2 (commencing with Section 2019) of Chapter 2 of Title 6 of, and Title 9

(commencing with Section 2295) of, Part 4 of Division 3 of the Civil Code, applies to powers of attorney. *(Added by Stats.1994, c. 307 (S.B.1907), § 16.)*

Law Revision Commission Comments
1994 Addition

Section 4051 is new. This section makes clear that the general agency statutes and the common law of agency apply to powers of attorney under this division, except where this division provides a specific rule. See also Section 4022 ("power of attorney" defined). [24 Cal.L.Rev.Comm.Reports 323 (1994)].

Cross References
Power of attorney defined for purposes of this Division, see Probate Code § 4022.

§ 4052. Application of Power of Attorney Law; conditions; change in domicile; removal of property

(a) If a power of attorney provides that the Power of Attorney Law of this state governs the power of attorney or otherwise indicates the principal's intention that the Power of Attorney Law of this state governs the power of attorney, this division governs the power of attorney and applies to acts and transactions of the attorney-in-fact in this state or outside this state where any of the following conditions is satisfied:

(1) The principal or attorney-in-fact was domiciled in this state when the principal executed the power of attorney.

(2) The authority conferred on the attorney-in-fact relates to property, acts, or transactions in this state.

(3) The acts or transactions of the attorney-in-fact occurred or were intended to occur in this state.

(4) The principal executed the power of attorney in this state.

(5) There is otherwise a reasonable relationship between this state and the subject matter of the power of attorney.

(b) If subdivision (a) does not apply to the power of attorney, this division governs the power of attorney and applies to the acts and transactions of the attorney-in-fact in this state where either of the following conditions is satisfied:

(1) The principal was domiciled in this state when the principal executed the power of attorney.

(2) The principal executed the power of attorney in this state.

(c) A power of attorney described in this section remains subject to this division despite a change in domicile of the principal or the attorney-in-fact, or the removal from this state of property that was the subject of the power of attorney. *(Added by Stats.1994, c. 307 (S.B.1907), § 16.)*

Law Revision Commission Comments
1994 Addition

Section 4052 is drawn from the Missouri Durable Power of Attorney Law. See Mo. Ann. Stat. § 404.730(1) (Vernon 1990). In part, this section is comparable to a provision of the Uniform Transfers to Minors Act. See Section 3902 & Comment. The power of attorney may also specify choice of law. Nothing in this section limits the jurisdiction exercisable under Code of Civil Procedure Section 410.10.

The rules in this section are subject to the general rules concerning the scope of the Power of Attorney Law set forth in Section 4050.

See also Sections 4014 ("attorney-in-fact" defined), 4022 ("power of attorney" defined), 4026 ("principal" defined), 4920–4923 (jurisdiction and venue). [24 Cal.L.Rev.Comm.Reports 323 (1994)].

Cross References

Attorney-in-fact defined for purposes of this Division, see Probate Code § 4014.

Power of attorney defined for purposes of this Division, see Probate Code § 4022.

Principal defined for purposes of this Division, see Probate Code § 4026.

§ 4053. Durable power of attorney executed in another state; validity

A durable power of attorney executed in another state or jurisdiction in compliance with the law of that state or jurisdiction or the law of this state is valid and enforceable in this state to the same extent as a durable power of attorney executed in this state, regardless of whether the principal is a domiciliary of this state. *(Added by Stats.1994, c. 307 (S.B.1907), § 16.)*

Law Revision Commission Comments

1994 Addition [Revised Comment]

Section 4053 is new. This section promotes use and enforceability of durable powers of attorney executed in other states. See also Section 4018 ("durable power of attorney" defined). [29 Cal.L.Rev. Comm. Reports 1 (1999)].

Cross References

Durable power of attorney defined for purposes of this Division, see Probate Code § 4018.

Power of attorney defined for purposes of this Division, see Probate Code § 4022.

Principal defined for purposes of this Division, see Probate Code § 4026.

§ 4054. Execution date; application of division; proceedings; validity of previously executed power

Except as otherwise provided by statute:

(a) On and after January 1, 1995, this division applies to all powers of attorney regardless of whether they were executed before, on, or after January 1, 1995.

(b) This division applies to all proceedings concerning powers of attorney commenced on or after January 1, 1995.

(c) This division applies to all proceedings concerning powers of attorney commenced before January 1, 1995, unless the court determines that application of a particular provision of this division would substantially interfere with the effective conduct of the proceedings or the rights of the parties and other interested persons, in which case the particular provision of this division does not apply and prior law applies.

(d) Nothing in this division affects the validity of a power of attorney executed before January 1, 1995, that was valid under prior law. *(Added by Stats.1994, c. 307 (S.B.1907), § 16. Amended by Stats.1995, c. 300 (S.B.984), § 3, eff. Aug. 3, 1995.)*

Law Revision Commission Comments

1994 Addition [Revised Comment]

Section 4054 is comparable to Section 15001 (application of Trust Law). Subdivision (a) provides the general rule that this division applies to all powers of attorney, regardless of when created.

Subdivision (b) is a specific application of the general rule in subdivision (a). See Section 4900 *et seq.* (judicial proceedings concerning powers of attorney). Subdivision (c) provides discretion to the court to resolve problems arising in proceedings commenced before the operative date.

For special transitional provisions, see Sections 4102 (durable power of attorney form); see also Section 4129(c) (springing powers).

See also Section 4022 ("power of attorney" defined). [29 Cal. L.Rev.Comm. Reports 1 (1999)].

1995 Amendment

Subdivision (d) is added to Section 4054 to make clear that enactment of the Power of Attorney Law is not intended to affect the validity of a pre-existing power of attorney. See Section 4050 (types of powers governed by Power of Attorney Law). Thus, for example, a durable power of attorney for property matters executed before January 1, 1995, that is neither notarized nor witnessed, is not made invalid by the new execution formalities provided by Section 4121. Subdivision (d) is declaratory of, and not a change in, the law. [25 Cal.L.Rev.Comm. Reports 709 (1995)].

Cross References

Power of attorney defined for purposes of this Division, see Probate Code § 4022.

Part 2

POWERS OF ATTORNEY GENERALLY

CHAPTER 1. GENERAL PROVISIONS

§ 4100. Application of part

This part applies to all powers of attorney under this division, subject to any special rules applicable to statutory form powers of attorney under Part 3 (commencing with Section 4400). *(Added by Stats.1994, c. 307 (S.B.1907), § 16. Amended by Stats.1999, c. 658 (A.B.891), § 28, operative July 1, 2000.)*

Law Revision Commission Comments

1994 Addition

Section 4100 provides the scope of this part and makes clear that these general rules are subject to exceptions and qualifications in the case of certain special types of powers of attorney. See also Sections

4022 ("power of attorney" defined), 4606 ("durable power of attorney for health care" defined). [24 Cal.L.Rev.Comm.Reports 323 (1994)].

1999 Amendment

Section 4100 is amended to delete a reference to powers of attorney for health care, which are governed by Division 4.7 (commencing with Section 4600) (Health Care Decisions Law). See also Section 4050 (types of powers of attorney governed by this division). [29 Cal.L.Rev.Comm. Reports 1 (1999)].

Cross References

Power of attorney defined for purposes of this Division, see Probate Code § 4022.

§ 4101. Principal's power to limit application of statute; express statements; inconsistent rules; exclusions

(a) Except as provided in subdivision (b), the principal may limit the application of any provision of this division by an express statement in the power of attorney or by providing an inconsistent rule in the power of attorney.

(b) A power of attorney may not limit either the application of a statute specifically providing that it is not subject to limitation in the power of attorney or a statute concerning any of the following:

(1) Warnings or notices required to be included in a power of attorney.

(2) Operative dates of statutory enactments or amendments.

(3) Execution formalities.

(4) Qualifications of witnesses.

(5) Qualifications of attorneys-in-fact.

(6) Protection of third persons from liability. *(Added by Stats.1994, c. 307 (S.B.1907), § 16.)*

Law Revision Commission Comments
1994 Addition [Revised Comment]

Section 4101 is new. This section makes clear that many of the statutory rules provided in this division are subject to express or implicit limitations in the power of attorney. If a statutory rule is not subject to control by the power of attorney, this is stated explicitly, either in a particular section or as to a group of sections. See, e.g., Sections 4130 (inconsistent authority), 4151(a)(2) (revocation of power of attorney by writing), 4153(a)(2)-(3) (revocation of attorney-in-fact's authority), 4155 (termination of authority under nondurable power of attorney on principal's incapacity), 4206 (relation of attorney-in-fact to court-appointed fiduciary), 4207 (resignation of attorney-in-fact), 4232 (duty of loyalty), 4233 (duty to keep principal's property separate and identified), 4234(b) (authority to disobey instructions with court approval), 4236 (duty to keep records and account; availability of records to other persons), 4502 (effect of provision in power of attorney attempting to limit right to petition), 4503 (limitations on right to petition).

See also Sections 4014 ("attorney-in-fact" defined), 4022 ("power of attorney" defined), 4026 ("principal" defined). [29 Cal.L.Rev. Comm. Reports 1 (1999)].

Cross References

Attorney-in-fact defined for purposes of this Division, see Probate Code § 4014.
Power of attorney defined for purposes of this Division, see Probate Code § 4022.

Principal defined for purposes of this Division, see Probate Code § 4026.
Third person defined for purposes of this Division, see Probate Code § 4034.

§ 4102. Printed form of durable power of attorney; sale or distribution; advice of legal counsel; validity

Notwithstanding Section 4128:

(a) Except as provided in subdivision (b), on and after January 1, 1995, a printed form of a durable power of attorney may be sold or otherwise distributed if it satisfies the requirements of former Section 2510.5 of the Civil Code.

(b) A printed form of a durable power of attorney printed on or after January 1, 1986, that is sold or otherwise distributed in this state for use by a person who does not have the advice of legal counsel shall comply with former Section 2510 of the Civil Code or with Section 4128 of this code.

(c) A durable power of attorney executed on or after January 1, 1995, using a printed form that complies with subdivision (b) of former Section 2400 of the Civil Code, as enacted by Chapter 511 of the Statutes of 1981, or with former Section 2510 of the Civil Code, is as valid as if it had been executed using a printed form that complies with Section 4128 of this code. *(Added by Stats.1994, c. 307 (S.B.1907), § 16.)*

Law Revision Commission Comments
1994 Addition

Section 4102 supersedes former Civil Code Section 2510.5. This section permits continued use of printed forms that comply with former law, specifically former Civil Code Section 2400 (as enacted by 1981 Cal. Stat. ch. 511, § 4) and former Civil Code Section 2510 (as enacted by 1985 Cal. Stat. ch. 403, § 12). Subdivision (c) permits use of the earlier forms after January 1, 1995, the operative date of Section 4128. This section, like its predecessor, former Civil Code Section 2510.5, avoids the need to discard existing printed forms on the operative date of this division. However, pursuant to subdivision (b), a form printed on or after January 1, 1986, may be sold or distributed in this state for use by a person who does not have the advice of legal counsel only if the form satisfies the requirements of former Civil Code Section 2510 or of Probate Code Section 4128. See also Section 4018 ("durable power of attorney" defined). [24 Cal.L.Rev.Comm.Reports 323 (1994)].

Cross References

Durable power of attorney defined for purposes of this Division, see Probate Code § 4018.

CHAPTER 2. CREATION AND EFFECT OF POWERS OF ATTORNEY

§ 4120. Execution; capacity

A natural person having the capacity to contract may execute a power of attorney. *(Added by Stats.1994, c. 307 (S.B.1907), § 16.)*

Law Revision Commission Comments

1994 Addition

Section 4120 states a requirement of general agency law, consistent with Civil Code Section 2296. See also Section 4022 ("power of attorney" defined). [24 Cal.L.Rev.Comm.Reports 323 (1994)].

Cross References

Power of attorney defined for purposes of this Division, see Probate Code § 4022.

§ 4121. Legal sufficiency; conditions

A power of attorney is legally sufficient if all of the following requirements are satisfied:

(a) The power of attorney contains the date of its execution.

(b) The power of attorney is signed either (1) by the principal or (2) in the principal's name by another adult in the principal's presence and at the principal's direction.

(c) The power of attorney is either (1) acknowledged before a notary public or (2) signed by at least two witnesses who satisfy the requirements of Section 4122. *(Added by Stats.1994, c. 307 (S.B.1907), § 16. Amended by Stats.1999, c. 658 (A.B.891), § 29, operative July 1, 2000.)*

Law Revision Commission Comments

1994 Addition [Revised Comment]

Section 4121 provides the general execution formalities for a power of attorney under this division. A power of attorney that complies with this section is legally sufficient as a grant of authority to an attorney-in-fact. Special rules apply to a statutory form power of attorney. See Section 4402.

The dating requirement in subdivision (a) generalizes the rule applicable to durable powers of attorney for health care under former Civil Code Section 2432(a)(2). This rule is also consistent with the statutory forms. See Sections 4401 (statutory form power of attorney).

In subdivision (b), the requirement that a power of attorney be signed by the principal or at the principal's direction continues a rule implicit in former law. See former Civ. Code §§ 2400, 2410(c). In addition, it generalizes the rule applicable to durable powers of attorney for health care under former Civil Code Section 2432.

The requirement that the power of attorney be either acknowledged or signed by two witnesses, in subdivision (c), generalizes part of the rule applicable to durable powers of attorney for health care under former Civil Code Section 2432(a)(3). Former general rules did not require either acknowledgment or witnessing. However, the statutory form power of attorney provided for acknowledgment. See former Civ. Code § 2475 (now Prob. Code § 4401). This rule still applies to the statutory form power of attorney; witnessing does not satisfy Section 4402. Subdivision (c) provides the general rule as to witnessing; specific qualifications for witnesses are provided in Section 4122.

Nothing in this section affects the requirements concerning recordable instruments. A power of attorney legally sufficient as a grant of authority under this division must satisfy the general rules concerning recordation in Civil Code Sections 1169–1231. To facilitate recordation of a power of attorney granting authority concerning real property, the power of attorney should be acknowledged before a notary, whether or not it is witnessed.

See also Sections 4022 ("power of attorney" defined), 4026 ("principal" defined). [29 Cal.L.Rev.Comm. Reports App. 6 (1999)].

1999 Amendment

Subdivision (b) of Section 4121 is amended to make clear that the person signing at the principal's direction must be an adult. This is consistent with the language of Section 4673 (formalities for executing written advance health care directive). [29 Cal.L.Rev.Comm. Reports App. 6 (1999)].

Cross References

Power of attorney defined for purposes of this Division, see Probate Code § 4022.

Principal defined for purposes of this Division, see Probate Code § 4026.

§ 4122. Witnesses; qualifications; duties

If the power of attorney is signed by witnesses, as provided in Section 4121, the following requirements shall be satisfied:

(a) The witnesses shall be adults.

(b) The attorney-in-fact may not act as a witness.

(c) Each witness signing the power of attorney shall witness either the signing of the instrument by the principal or the principal's acknowledgment of the signature or the power of attorney. *(Added by Stats.1994, c. 307 (S.B.1907), § 16. Amended by Stats.1999, c. 658 (A.B.891), § 30, operative July 1, 2000.)*

Law Revision Commission Comments

1994 Addition

Section 4122 generalizes witness qualifications from former Civil Code Section 2432(a)(3)(A) (first sentence) and (d)(3) (durable power of attorney for health care). Additional qualifications apply to witnesses for a durable power of attorney for health care, as recognized in subdivision (d). See also Section 4771 (statutory form durable power of attorney for health care). This section is not subject to limitation in the power of attorney. See Section 4101.

See also Sections 4014 ("attorney-in-fact" defined), 4022 ("power of attorney" defined), 4026 ("principal" defined), 4606 ("durable power of attorney for health care" defined). [24 Cal.L.Rev.Comm.Reports 323 (1994)].

1999 Amendment

Section 4122 is amended to delete a reference to powers of attorney for health care, which are governed by Division 4.7 (commencing with Section 4600) (Health Care Decisions Law). Witnessing requirements of this section, to the extent they applied to health care powers, are continued in Section 4674(a)-(c) without substantive change.

This section is not subject to limitation in the power of attorney. See Section 4101. See also Sections 4014 ("attorney-in-fact" defined), 4022 ("power of attorney" defined), 4026 ("principal" defined). [29 Cal.L.Rev.Comm. Reports App. 6 (1999)].

Cross References

Attorney-in-fact defined for purposes of this Division, see Probate Code § 4014.

Power of attorney defined for purposes of this Division, see Probate Code § 4022.

Principal defined for purposes of this Division, see Probate Code § 4026.

§ 4123. Authority granted to attorney-in-fact; lawful subjects and purposes; property; personal care

(a) In a power of attorney under this division, a principal may grant authority to an attorney-in-fact to act on the principal's behalf with respect to all lawful subjects and purposes or with respect to one or more express subjects or purposes. The attorney-in-fact may be granted authority with regard to the principal's property, personal care, or any other matter.

(b) With regard to property matters, a power of attorney may grant authority to make decisions concerning all or part of the principal's real and personal property, whether owned by the principal at the time of the execution of the power of attorney or thereafter acquired or whether located in this state or elsewhere, without the need for a description of each item or parcel of property.

(c) With regard to personal care, a power of attorney may grant authority to make decisions relating to the personal care of the principal, including, but not limited to, determining where the principal will live, providing meals, hiring household employees, providing transportation, handling mail, and arranging recreation and entertainment. *(Added by Stats.1994, c. 307 (S.B.1907), § 16. Amended by Stats.1999, c. 658 (A.B.891), § 31, operative July 1, 2000; Stats.2001, c. 230 (A.B.1278), § 2.)*

Law Revision Commission Comments
1994 Addition [Revised Comment]

Subdivision (a) of Section 4123 is new and is consistent with the general agency rules in Civil Code Sections 2304 and 2305. For provisions concerning the duties and powers of an attorney-in-fact, see Sections 4230–4266. See also Sections 4014 ("attorney-in-fact" defined), 4022 ("power of attorney" defined), 4026 ("principal" defined).

Subdivision (b) continues former Civil Code Section 2513 without substantive change. This subdivision makes clear that a power of attorney may by its terms apply to all real property of the principal, including after-acquired property, without the need for a specific description of the real property to which the power applies. This section is consistent with Section 4464 (after-acquired property under statutory form power of attorney).

Subdivision (c) is new and acknowledges the existing practice of providing authority to make personal care decisions in durable powers of attorney. For a comparable provision in the Health Care Decisions Law, see Section 4671. [29 Cal.L.Rev.Comm. Reports 1 (1999)].

1999 Amendment

Section 4123 is amended to delete subdivision (d), which referred to powers of attorney for health care that are now governed by Division 4.7 (commencing with Section 4600) (Health Care Decisions Law). See Section 4050 (types of powers of attorney governed by this division). [29 Cal.L.Rev.Comm. Reports 1 (1999)].

2001 Amendment

Subdivision (a) of Section 4123 is amended to recognize the limitations on the scope of this division. Powers of attorney for health care are governed by the Health Care Decisions Law, Division 4.7 (commencing with Section 4600). This division—the Power of Attorney Law, Division 4.5 (commencing with Section 4000)—does not apply to powers of attorney for health care. See Section 4050 (types of powers of attorney governed by this division). [30 Cal.L.Rev.Comm. Reports 621 (2000)].

Cross References

Attorney-in-fact defined for purposes of this Division, see Probate Code § 4014.

Power of attorney defined for purposes of this Division, see Probate Code § 4022.

Principal defined for purposes of this Division, see Probate Code § 4026.

§ 4124. Durable power of attorney; required language

A durable power of attorney is a power of attorney by which a principal designates another person as attorney-in-fact in writing and the power of attorney contains any of the following statements:

(a) "This power of attorney shall not be affected by subsequent incapacity of the principal."

(b) "This power of attorney shall become effective upon the incapacity of the principal."

(c) Similar words showing the intent of the principal that the authority conferred shall be exercisable notwithstanding the principal's subsequent incapacity. *(Added by Stats.1994, c. 307 (S.B.1907), § 16.)*

Law Revision Commission Comments
1994 Addition [Revised Comment]

Section 4124 restates former Civil Code Section 2400 without substantive change. For special rules applicable to statutory form powers of attorney, see Sections 4401, 4402. See also Section 4050 (powers subject to this division).

Section 4124 is similar to the official text of Section 1 of the Uniform Durable Power of Attorney Act (1984), Uniform Probate Code Section 5–501 (1991). See Section 2(b) (construction of provisions drawn from uniform acts). The reference in the uniform act to the principal's "disability" is omitted. Under Section 4155, it is the principal's incapacity to contract which would otherwise terminate the power of attorney. In addition, the phrase "or lapse of time" has not been included in the language set forth in subdivision (a) of Section 4124 because it is unnecessary. As a matter of law, unless a durable power of attorney states an earlier termination date, it remains valid regardless of any lapse of time since its creation. See, e.g., Sections 4127 (lapse of time), 4152(a)(1) (termination of attorney-in-fact's authority pursuant to terms of power of attorney).

See also Sections 4014 ("attorney-in-fact" defined), 4018 ("durable power of attorney" defined), 4022 ("power of attorney" defined), 4026 ("principal" defined). [29 Cal.L.Rev.Comm. Reports 1 (1999)].

Cross References

Attorney-in-fact defined for purposes of this Division, see Probate Code § 4014.

Durable power of attorney defined for purposes of this Division, see Probate Code § 4018.

Power of attorney defined for purposes of this Division, see Probate Code § 4022.

Principal defined for purposes of this Division, see Probate Code § 4026.

§ 4125. Incapacity of principal; acts of attorney-in-fact

All acts done by an attorney-in-fact pursuant to a durable power of attorney during any period of incapacity of the principal have the same effect and inure to the benefit of and bind the principal and the principal's successors in interest as if the principal had capacity. *(Added by Stats.1994, c. 307 (S.B.1907), § 16.)*

Law Revision Commission Comments

1994 Addition

Section 4125 continues former Civil Code Section 2401 without substantive change. This section is similar to the first sentence of the official text of Section 2 of the Uniform Durable Power of Attorney Act (1987), Uniform Probate Code Section 5–502 (1991). See Section 2(b) (construction of provisions drawn from uniform acts). This section omits the reference to the principal's "disability" found in the uniform act. Under Section 4155, it is the principal's incapacity to contract which would otherwise terminate the power of attorney.

See also Sections 4014 ("attorney-in-fact" defined), 4018 ("durable power of attorney" defined), 4026 ("principal" defined). [24 Cal.L.Rev.Comm.Reports 323 (1994)].

Cross References

Attorney-in-fact defined for purposes of this Division, see Probate Code § 4014.
Durable power of attorney defined for purposes of this Division, see Probate Code § 4018.
Principal defined for purposes of this Division, see Probate Code § 4026.

§ 4126. Nomination of conservator or guardian; protective proceedings

(a) A principal may nominate, by a durable power of attorney, a conservator of the person or estate or both, or a guardian of the person or estate or both, for consideration by the court if protective proceedings for the principal's person or estate are thereafter commenced.

(b) If the protective proceedings are conservatorship proceedings in this state, the nomination has the effect provided in Section 1810 and the court shall give effect to the most recent writing executed in accordance with Section 1810, whether or not the writing is a durable power of attorney. *(Added by Stats.1994, c. 307 (S.B.1907), § 16.)*

Law Revision Commission Comments

1994 Addition

Section 4126 continues former Civil Code Section 2402(b) without substantive change. This section is drawn from Section 3(b) of the Uniform Durable Power of Attorney Act (1979), Uniform Probate Code Section 5–503 (1991), but has been revised to make it consistent with the general provision for nomination of a conservator in Section 1810. See Section 2(b) (construction of provisions drawn from uniform acts). The second sentence of Section 3(b) of the Uniform Durable Power of Attorney Act (most recent nomination in a durable power shall be given effect) is not adopted in California. Thus, the principal may make a later nomination in a writing that is not a durable power of attorney and, if at that time the principal has sufficient capacity to form an intelligent preference (Section 1810), the later nomination will supersede an earlier nomination made in a durable power. This is consistent with the purpose and effect of Section 1810.

See also Section 4018 ("durable power of attorney" defined), 4026 ("principal" defined). [24 Cal.L.Rev.Comm.Reports 323 (1994)].

Cross References

Durable power of attorney defined for purposes of this Division, see Probate Code § 4018.

Principal defined for purposes of this Division, see Probate Code § 4026.

§ 4127. Termination of power of attorney; lapses of time

Unless a power of attorney states a time of termination, the authority of the attorney-in-fact is exercisable notwithstanding any lapse of time since execution of the power of attorney. *(Added by Stats.1994, c. 307 (S.B.1907), § 16.)*

Law Revision Commission Comments

1994 Addition

Section 4127 is the same in substance as the second sentence of the official text of Section 2 of the Uniform Durable Power of Attorney Act (1987), Uniform Probate Code Section 5–502 (1991). See Section 2(b) (construction of provisions drawn from uniform acts). See also Sections 4125 (effect of attorney-in-fact's acts under durable power of attorney during principal's incapacity), 4152 (termination of authority of attorney-in-fact).

See also Sections 4014 ("attorney-in-fact" defined), 4022 ("power of attorney" defined). [24 Cal.L.Rev.Comm.Reports 323 (1994)].

Cross References

Attorney-in-fact defined for purposes of this Division, see Probate Code § 4014.
Power of attorney defined for purposes of this Division, see Probate Code § 4022.

§ 4128. Warning statement; notice to person executing durable power of attorney

(a) Subject to subdivision (b), a printed form of a durable power of attorney that is sold or otherwise distributed in this state for use by a person who does not have the advice of legal counsel shall contain, in not less than 10–point boldface type or a reasonable equivalent thereof, the following warning statements:

Notice to Person Executing Durable Power of Attorney

A durable power of attorney is an important legal document. By signing the durable power of attorney, you are authorizing another person to act for you, the principal. Before you sign this durable power of attorney, you should know these important facts:

Your agent (attorney–in–fact) has no duty to act unless you and your agent agree otherwise in writing.

This document gives your agent the powers to manage, dispose of, sell, and convey your real and personal property, and to use your property as security if your agent borrows money on your behalf. This document does not give your agent the power to accept or receive any of your property, in trust or otherwise, as a gift, unless you specifically authorize the agent to accept or receive a gift.

Your agent will have the right to receive reasonable payment for services provided under this durable power of attorney unless you provide otherwise in this power of attorney.

The powers you give your agent will continue to exist for your entire lifetime, unless you state that the durable power of attorney will last for a shorter period of time or unless you otherwise terminate the durable power of attorney. The powers you give your agent in this durable power of attorney will continue to exist even if you can no longer make your own decisions respecting the management of your property.

You can amend or change this durable power of attorney only by executing a new durable power of attorney or by executing an amendment through the same formalities as an original. You have the right to revoke or terminate this durable power of attorney at any time, so long as you are competent.

This durable power of attorney must be dated and must be acknowledged before a notary public or signed by two witnesses. If it is signed by two witnesses, they must witness either (1) the signing of the power of attorney or (2) the principal's signing or acknowledgment of his or her signature. A durable power of attorney that may affect real property should be acknowledged before a notary public so that it may easily be recorded.

You should read this durable power of attorney carefully. When effective, this durable power of attorney will give your agent the right to deal with property that you now have or might acquire in the future. The durable power of attorney is important to you. If you do not understand the durable power of attorney, or any provision of it, then you should obtain the assistance of an attorney or other qualified person.

Notice to Person Accepting the Appointment as Attorney-in-Fact

By acting or agreeing to act as the agent (attorney–in–fact) under this power of attorney you assume the fiduciary and other legal responsibilities of an agent. These responsibilities include:

1. The legal duty to act solely in the interest of the principal and to avoid conflicts of interest.

2. The legal duty to keep the principal's property separate and distinct from any other property owned or controlled by you.

You may not transfer the principal's property to yourself without full and adequate consideration or accept a gift of the principal's property unless this power of attorney specifically authorizes you to transfer property to yourself or accept a gift of the principal's property. If you transfer the principal's property to yourself without specific authorization in the power of attorney, you may be prosecuted for fraud and/or embezzlement. If the principal is 65 years of age or older at the time that the property is transferred to you without authority, you may also be prosecuted for elder abuse under Penal Code Section 368. In addition to criminal prosecution, you may also be sued in civil court.

I have read the foregoing notice and I understand the legal and fiduciary duties that I assume by acting or agreeing to act as the agent (attorney–in–fact) under the terms of this power of attorney.

Date:

_____
(Signature of agent)

_____
(Print name of agent)

(b) Nothing in subdivision (a) invalidates any transaction in which a third person relied in good faith on the authority created by the durable power of attorney.

(c) This section does not apply to a statutory form power of attorney under Part 3 (commencing with Section 4400). *(Added by Stats.1994, c. 307 (S.B.1907), § 16. Amended by Stats.1999, c. 658 (A.B.891), § 32, operative July 1, 2000; Stats.2000, c. 999 (S.B.1869), § 1.)*

Law Revision Commission Comments
1994 Addition [Revised Comment]

The warning statement in subdivision (a) of Section 4128 replaces the statement provided in former Civil Code Section 2510(b). Subdivision (b) restates former Civil Code Section 2510(c) without substantive change. Subdivision (c) restates former Civil Code Section 2510(a) without substantive change, but the reference to statutory short form powers of attorney under former Civil Code Section 2450 is omitted as obsolete. This section is not subject to limitation in the power of attorney. See Section 4101(b).

Other provisions prescribe the contents of the warning statements for particular types of durable powers of attorney. See Section 4401 (statutory form power of attorney).

Section 4102 permits a printed form to be used after January 1, 1995, if the form complies with prior law. A form printed after January 1, 1986, may be sold or otherwise distributed in this state only if it complies with the requirements of Section 4128 (or its predecessor, former Civil Code Section 2510). See Section 4102(b).

See also Sections 4014 ("attorney-in-fact" defined), 4018 ("durable power of attorney" defined), 4026 ("principal" defined), 4034 ("third person" defined). [29 Cal.L.Rev.Comm. Reports 1 (1999)].

1999 Amendment

Subdivision (c) of Section 4128 is amended to delete a reference to powers of attorney for health care, which are governed by Division 4.7 (commencing with Section 4600) (Health Care Decisions Law). This is a technical, nonsubstantive change. [29 Cal.L.Rev.Comm. Reports 1 (1999)].

Cross References

City council, defined for purposes of this part, see Streets and Highways Code § 18313.
Construction of part, see Streets and Highways Code § 18301.
Contracts,
   Generally, see Civil Code § 1549 et seq.
   Impairment of, see Cal. Const. Art. 1, § 9.
   Interpretation, see Civil Code § 1635 et seq.
Contract year, defined for purposes of this part, see Streets and Highways Code § 18308.
Improvement, defined for purposes of this part, see Streets and Highways Code § 18307.
Installment assessment, defined for purposes of this part, see Streets and Highways Code § 18309.
Levy of tax, see Revenue and Taxation Code § 2151 et seq.
Special assessment, see Cal. Const. Art. 16, § 19.
Street lighting system or system, defined for purposes of this part, see Streets and Highways Code § 18304.

§ 4129. Springing power of attorney

(a) In a springing power of attorney, the principal may designate one or more persons who, by a written declaration under penalty of perjury, have the power to determine conclusively that the specified event or contingency has occurred. The principal may designate the attorney-in-fact or another person to perform this function, either alone or jointly with other persons.

(b) A springing power of attorney containing the designation described in subdivision (a) becomes effective when the person or persons designated in the power of attorney execute a written declaration under penalty of perjury that the specified event or contingency has occurred, and any person may act in reliance on the written declaration without liability to the principal or to any other person, regardless of whether the specified event or contingency has actually occurred.

(c) This section applies to a power of attorney whether executed before, on, or after January 1, 1991, if the power of attorney contains the designation described in subdivision (a).

(d) This section does not provide the exclusive method by which a power of attorney may be limited to take effect on the occurrence of a specified event or contingency. *(Added by Stats.1994, c. 307 (S.B.1907), § 16.)*

Law Revision Commission Comments

1994 Addition

Section 4129 continues former Civil Code Section 2514(b)-(e) without substantive change. This section is intended to make springing powers of attorney more effective by providing a mechanism for conclusively determining that the triggering event or contingency has occurred. See Section 4030 ("springing power of attorney" defined). Subdivision (a) makes clear that the principal may give the agent (or one or more other persons) the power to determine by written declaration under penalty of perjury that the event or contingency specified in the springing power of attorney has occurred so that the power of attorney is effective. This section does not apply to or affect springing powers of attorney containing different procedures for determining whether the triggering event or contingency has occurred. This section applies only where the terms of subdivision (a) are satisfied.

Subdivision (b) makes clear that the written declaration of the persons designated in the power of attorney is conclusive, even though it may turn out that the event or contingency did not occur, or that circumstances have returned to normal. The purpose of the conclusive written declaration is to permit other persons to act in reliance on the written declaration without liability.

A springing power of attorney may or may not be a durable power of attorney. A springing power that takes effect on the occurrence of a contingency other than the incapacity of the principal (such as, for example, the principal's failure to return from a vacation or business trip by a certain date) need not be a durable power of attorney. However, a springing power of attorney that takes effect upon the incapacity of the principal is necessarily a durable power of attorney, and the other rules concerning durable powers of attorney are applicable.

Subdivision (c) makes clear that this section applies to powers of attorney executed before the operative date of this section if they contain the designation provided in subdivision (a).

See also Sections 4014 ("attorney-in-fact" defined), 4022 ("power of attorney" defined), 4026 ("principal" defined). [24 Cal.L.Rev.Comm.Reports 323 (1994)].

Cross References

Attorney-in-fact defined for purposes of this Division, see Probate Code § 4014.
Power of attorney defined for purposes of this Division, see Probate Code § 4022.

Principal defined for purposes of this Division, see Probate Code § 4026.
Springing power of attorney defined for purposes of this Division, see Probate Code § 4030.

§ 4130. Multiple powers of attorney; inconsistencies

(a) If a principal grants inconsistent authority to one or more attorneys-in-fact in two or more powers of attorney, the authority granted last controls to the extent of the inconsistency.

(b) This section is not subject to limitation in the power of attorney. *(Added by Stats.1994, c. 307 (S.B.1907), § 16.)*

Law Revision Commission Comments

1999 Revised Comment

Section 4130 is new. See also Sections 4014 ("attorney-in-fact" defined), 4022 ("power of attorney" defined), 4026 ("principal" defined). [29 Cal.L.Rev.Comm. Reports 1 (1999)].

Cross References

Attorney-in-fact defined for purposes of this Division, see Probate Code § 4014.
Power of attorney defined for purposes of this Division, see Probate Code § 4022.
Principal defined for purposes of this Division, see Probate Code § 4026.

CHAPTER 3. MODIFICATION AND REVOCATION OF POWERS OF ATTORNEY

§ 4150. Modifications; notice

(a) A principal may modify a power of attorney as follows:

(1) In accordance with the terms of the power of attorney.

(2) By an instrument executed in the same manner as a power of attorney may be executed.

(b) An attorney-in-fact or third person who does not have notice of the modification is protected from liability as provided in Chapter 5 (commencing with Section 4300). *(Added by Stats.1994, c. 307 (S.B.1907), § 16. Amended by Stats.1995, c. 300 (S.B.984), § 4, eff. Aug. 3, 1995.)*

Law Revision Commission Comments

1994 Addition

Section 4150 is new. The manner of modifying a power of attorney as provided in subdivision (a)(2) is more formal than the manner of revoking the attorney-in-fact's authority provided by Section 4153(a). Subdivision (a)(2) is subject to limitation in the power of attorney. See Section 4101 (priority of provisions of power of attorney).

See also Sections 4014 ("attorney-in-fact" defined), 4022 ("power of attorney" defined), 4026 ("principal" defined), 4034 ("third person" defined). [24 Cal.L.Rev.Comm.Reports 323 (1994)].

Attorney-in-fact defined for purposes of this Division, see Probate Code § 4014.

Power of attorney defined for purposes of this Division, see Probate Code § 4022.

Principal defined for purposes of this Division, see Probate Code § 4026.

Third person defined for purposes of this Division, see Probate Code § 4034.

§ 4151. Revocation; notice

(a) A principal may revoke a power of attorney as follows:

(1) In accordance with the terms of the power of attorney.

(2) By a writing. This paragraph is not subject to limitation in the power of attorney.

(b) An attorney-in-fact or third person who does not have notice of the revocation is protected from liability as provided in Chapter 5 (commencing with Section 4300). *(Added by Stats.1994, c. 307 (S.B.1907), § 16. Amended by Stats.1995, c. 300 (S.B.984), § 5, eff. Aug. 3, 1995.)*

Law Revision Commission Comments

1994 Addition

Section 4151 is new. This section provides for revocation of the power of attorney in its entirety, as distinct from revocation or termination of the authority of the attorney-in-fact pursuant to Section 4152 or 4153. This section recognizes that a power of attorney may, for example, contain expressions of wishes, may nominate a conservator, or name a successor attorney-in-fact. These provisions may exist independent from the provisions granting authority to the attorney-in-fact. Revocation under this section revokes all provisions stated in the instrument, rather than modifying or terminating the authority of the attorney-in-fact. The rule in subdivision (a)(2) permitting revocation of a power of attorney by a writing executed by the principal acts as an escape hatch and is not subject to limitation in the power of attorney. See Section 4101(b) (exception to priority of provisions of power of attorney).

See also Sections 4014 ("attorney-in-fact" defined), 4022 ("power of attorney" defined), 4026 ("principal" defined), 4034 ("third person" defined); Civ. Code § 1216 (recordation of revocation of recorded instruments). [24 Cal.L.Rev.Comm.Reports 323 (1994)].

Cross References

Attorney-in-fact defined for purposes of this Division, see Probate Code § 4014.

Power of attorney defined for purposes of this Division, see Probate Code § 4022.

Principal defined for purposes of this Division, see Probate Code § 4026.

Third person defined for purposes of this Division, see Probate Code § 4034.

§ 4152. Termination of authority; triggering events; notice

(a) Subject to subdivision (b), the authority of an attorney-in-fact under a power of attorney is terminated by any of the following events:

(1) In accordance with the terms of the power of attorney.

(2) Extinction of the subject or fulfillment of the purpose of the power of attorney.

(3) Revocation of the attorney-in-fact's authority, as provided in Section 4153.

(4) Death of the principal, except as to specific authority permitted by statute to be exercised after the principal's death.

(5) Removal of the attorney-in-fact.

(6) Resignation of the attorney-in-fact.

(7) Incapacity of the attorney-in-fact, except that a temporary incapacity suspends the attorney-in-fact's authority only during the period of the incapacity.

(8) Dissolution or annulment of the marriage of the attorney-in-fact and principal, as provided in Section 4154.

(9) Death of the attorney-in-fact.

(b) An attorney-in-fact or third person who does not have notice of an event that terminates the power of attorney or the authority of an attorney-in-fact is protected from liability as provided in Chapter 5 (commencing with Section 4300). *(Added by Stats.1994, c. 307 (S.B.1907), § 16. Amended by Stats.1995, c. 300 (S.B.984), § 6, eff. Aug. 3, 1995.)*

Law Revision Commission Comments

1994 Addition [Revised Comment]

Section 4152 is drawn from the general agency rules provided in Civil Code Sections 2355 and 2356. This section continues the substance of former law as to termination of the authority of an attorney-in-fact under a power of attorney. For a special rule as to termination of nondurable powers of attorney on principal's incapacity, see Section 4155.

Subdivision (a)(1) is the same as Civil Code Section 2355(a). Subdivision (a)(2) is the same as Civil Code Section 2355(b), but the reference to fulfillment of the purpose of the power of attorney is new. Subdivision (a)(3) is the same as Civil Code Section 2356(a)(1). These subdivisions recognize that the authority of an attorney-in-fact necessarily ceases when the underlying power of attorney is terminated.

Subdivision (a)(4) is the same as Civil Code Section 2356(a)(2), but recognizes that certain tasks may remain to be performed after death. See, e.g., Sections 4238 (attorney-in-fact's duties on termination of authority).

Subdivision (a)(5) is generalized from Civil Code Section 2355(c)-(f). Subdivision (a)(6) is similar to Civil Code Section 2355(d) (renunciation by agent). For the manner of resignation, see Section 4207. Subdivision (a)(7) is similar to Civil Code Section 2355(e). Subdivision (a)(8) cross-refers to the rules governing the effect of dissolution and annulment of marriage. Subdivision (a)(9) is the same as Civil Code Section 2355(c).

Subdivision (b) preserves the substance of the introductory clause of Civil Code Section 2355 and Civil Code Section 2356(b), which protect persons without notice of events that terminate an agency.

See also Sections 4014 ("attorney-in-fact" defined), 4022 ("power of attorney" defined), 4026 ("principal" defined), 4034 ("third person" defined); Civ. Code § 1216 (recordation of revocation of recorded instruments). [29 Cal.L.Rev.Comm. Reports 1 (1999)].

Cross References

Attorney-in-fact defined for purposes of this Division, see Probate Code § 4014.

Power of attorney defined for purposes of this Division, see Probate Code § 4022.

Principal defined for purposes of this Division, see Probate Code § 4026.

Third person defined for purposes of this Division, see Probate Code § 4034.

§ 4153. Revocation of authority; methods; notice

(a) The authority of an attorney-in-fact under a power of attorney may be revoked as follows:

(1) In accordance with the terms of the power of attorney.

(2) Where the principal informs the attorney-in-fact orally or in writing that the attorney-in-fact's authority is revoked or when and under what circumstances it is revoked. This paragraph is not subject to limitation in the power of attorney.

(3) Where the principal's legal representative, with approval of the court as provided in Section 4206, informs the attorney-in-fact in writing that the attorney-in-fact's authority is revoked or when and under what circumstances it is revoked. This paragraph is not subject to limitation in the power of attorney.

(b) An attorney-in-fact or third person who does not have notice of the revocation is protected from liability as provided in Chapter 5 (commencing with Section 4300). *(Added by Stats.1994, c. 307 (S.B.1907), § 16. Amended by Stats.1995, c. 300 (S.B.984), § 7, eff. Aug. 3, 1995.)*

Law Revision Commission Comments

1994 Addition

Section 4153 is new. The rules concerning revocation of the attorney-in-fact's authority by the principal are not as strict as the rules on modification of the power of attorney. Compare subdivision (a)(2) with Section 4150(a)(2). No writing is required to revoke the attorney-in-fact's authority, and if a writing is used, it need not be witnessed or notarized to be effective between the principal and attorney-in-fact.

See also Sections 4014 ("attorney-in-fact" defined), 4022 ("power of attorney" defined), 4026 ("principal" defined), 4034 ("third person" defined); Civ. Code § 1216 (recordation of revocation of recorded instruments). [24 Cal.L.Rev.Comm.Reports 323 (1994)].

Cross References

Attorney-in-fact defined for purposes of this Division, see Probate Code § 4014.
Power of attorney defined for purposes of this Division, see Probate Code § 4022.
Principal defined for purposes of this Division, see Probate Code § 4026.
Third person defined for purposes of this Division, see Probate Code § 4034.

§ 4154. Dissolution or annulment of principal's marriage to attorney-in-fact; revocation; revival

(a) If after executing a power of attorney the principal's marriage to the attorney-in-fact is dissolved or annulled, the principal's designation of the former spouse as an attorney-in-fact is revoked.

(b) If the attorney-in-fact's authority is revoked solely by subdivision (a), it is revived by the principal's remarriage to the attorney-in-fact. *(Added by Stats.1994, c. 307 (S.B.1907), § 16.)*

Law Revision Commission Comments

1994 Addition

Section 4154 is generalized from former Civil Code Section 2437(e) (revocation of durable power of attorney for health care on dissolution or annulment) and part of former subdivision (f) of Civil Code Section 2355 (revocation in case of federal absentee principal). This section is also comparable to Section 6122(a)-(b) (revocation of provisions in will after dissolution or annulment). For special rules applicable to a federal "absentee" (as defined in Section 1403), see Section 3722.

This section is subject to limitation by the power of attorney. See Section 4101 (priority of provisions of power of attorney).

See also Sections 4014 ("attorney-in-fact" defined), 4022 ("power of attorney" defined), 4026 ("principal" defined); Civ. Code § 1216 (recordation of revocation of recorded instruments). [24 Cal.L.Rev.Comm.Reports 323 (1994)].

Cross References

Attorney-in-fact defined for purposes of this Division, see Probate Code § 4014.
Power of attorney defined for purposes of this Division, see Probate Code § 4022.
Principal defined for purposes of this Division, see Probate Code § 4026.

§ 4155. Incapacity of principal under a nondurable power of attorney; notice

(a) Subject to subdivision (b), the authority of an attorney-in-fact under a nondurable power of attorney is terminated by the incapacity of the principal to contract.

(b) An attorney-in-fact or third person who does not have notice of the incapacity of the principal is protected from liability as provided in Chapter 5 (commencing with Section 4300).

(c) This section is not subject to limitation in the power of attorney. *(Added by Stats.1994, c. 307 (S.B.1907), § 16. Amended by Stats.1995, c. 300 (S.B.984), § 8, eff. Aug. 3, 1995.)*

Law Revision Commission Comments

1994 Addition

Subdivision (a) of Section 4155 restates the general agency rule in Civil Code Section 2356(a)(3) without substantive change.

Subdivision (b) preserves the substance of the introductory clause of Civil Code Section 2355 and Civil Code Section 2356(b) protecting persons without notice of events that terminate an agency.

See also Sections 4014 ("attorney-in-fact" defined), 4018 ("durable power of attorney" defined), 4022 ("power of attorney" defined), 4026 ("principal" defined), 4034 ("third person" defined); Civ. Code § 1216 (recordation of revocation of recorded instruments). [24 Cal.L.Rev.Comm.Reports 323 (1994)].

Cross References

Attorney-in-fact defined for purposes of this Division, see Probate Code § 4014.
Power of attorney defined for purposes of this Division, see Probate Code § 4022.
Principal defined for purposes of this Division, see Probate Code § 4026.

Third person defined for purposes of this Division, see Probate Code § 4034.

ARTICLE 1. QUALIFICATIONS AND AUTHORITY OF ATTORNEYS–IN–FACT

§ 4200. Capacity to contract

Only a person having the capacity to contract is qualified to act as an attorney-in-fact. *(Added by Stats.1994, c. 307 (S.B.1907), § 16.)*

Law Revision Commission Comments

1994 Addition [Revised Comment]

Section 4200 supersedes the last part of Civil Code Section 2296 ("any person may be an agent") to the extent that it applied to attorneys-in-fact under powers of attorney.

See also Sections 56 ("person" defined), 4014 ("attorney-in-fact" defined). [29 Cal.L.Rev.Comm. Reports 1 (1999)].

Cross References

Attorney-in-fact defined for purposes of this Division, see Probate Code § 4014.

§ 4201. Designation of unqualified person; immunities of third persons; duties

Designating an unqualified person as an attorney-in-fact does not affect the immunities of third persons nor relieve the unqualified person of any applicable duties to the principal or the principal's successors. *(Added by Stats.1994, c. 307 (S.B.1907), § 16.)*

Law Revision Commission Comments

1994 Addition

Section 4201 is drawn from the Missouri Durable Power of Attorney Law. See Mo. Ann. Stat. § 404.707(4) (Vernon 1990). For provisions governing immunities of third persons, see Section 4300 *et seq.*

See also Sections 4014 ("attorney-in-fact" defined), 4026 ("principal" defined), 4034 ("third person" defined). [24 Cal.L.Rev.Comm.Reports 323 (1994)].

Cross References

Attorney-in-fact defined for purposes of this Division, see Probate Code § 4014.
Principal defined for purposes of this Division, see Probate Code § 4026.
Third person defined for purposes of this Division, see Probate Code § 4034.

§ 4202. Multiple attorneys-in-fact; action; vacancy; absence, illness or incapacity; liability

(a) A principal may designate more than one attorney-in-fact in one or more powers of attorney.

(b) Authority granted to two or more attorneys-in-fact is exercisable only by their unanimous action.

(c) If a vacancy occurs, the remaining attorneys-in-fact may exercise the authority conferred as if they are the only attorneys-in-fact.

(d) If an attorney-in-fact is unavailable because of absence, illness, or other temporary incapacity, the other attorneys-in-fact may exercise the authority under the power of attorney as if they are the only attorneys-in-fact, where necessary to accomplish the purposes of the power of attorney or to avoid irreparable injury to the principal's interests.

(e) An attorney-in-fact is not liable for the actions of other attorneys-in-fact, unless the attorney-in-fact participates in, knowingly acquiesces in, or conceals a breach of fiduciary duty committed by another attorney-in-fact. *(Added by Stats.1994, c. 307 (S.B.1907), § 16.)*

Law Revision Commission Comments

1994 Addition

Subdivision (a) of Section 4202 is drawn from the Missouri Durable Power of Attorney Law. See Mo. Ann. Stat. § 404.707(1) (Vernon 1990). This section is subject to limitation in the power of attorney. See Section 4101 (priority of provisions of power of attorney). The power of attorney may provide that the authority conferred on two or more attorneys-in-fact shall or may be exercised either jointly or severally or in a manner, with the priority, and with respect to particular subjects, provided in the power of attorney.

The default rule requiring unanimous action in subdivision (b) is the same in substance as the rule applicable under the statutory form power of attorney. See Section 4401.

Subdivisions (b)-(d) are comparable to the rules applicable to multiple trustees under Sections 15620–15622.

Subdivision (e) is comparable to the general rule as to cotrustees in Section 16402(a).

See also Sections 4014 ("attorney-in-fact" defined), 4022 ("power of attorney" defined), 4026 ("principal" defined). [24 Cal.L.Rev.Comm.Reports 323 (1994)].

Cross References

Attorney-in-fact defined for purposes of this Division, see Probate Code § 4014.
Power of attorney defined for purposes of this Division, see Probate Code § 4022.
Principal defined for purposes of this Division, see Probate Code § 4026.

§ 4203. Successor attorneys-in-fact; liability

(a) A principal may designate one or more successor attorneys-in-fact to act if the authority of a predecessor attorney-in-fact terminates.

(b) The principal may grant authority to another person, designated by name, by office, or by function, including the initial and any successor attorneys-in-fact, to designate at any time one or more successor attorneys-in-fact.

(c) A successor attorney-in-fact is not liable for the actions of the predecessor attorney-in-fact. *(Added by Stats.1994, c. 307 (S.B.1907), § 16. Amended by Stats.1999, c. 658 (A.B. 891), § 33, operative July 1, 2000.)*

Law Revision Commission Comments

1994 Addition

Section 4203 is drawn in part from the Missouri Durable Power of Attorney Law. See Mo. Ann. Stat. § 404.723(2)-(3) (Vernon 1990). For events that terminate the authority of an attorney-in-fact, see Section 4152.

Subdivision (c) is drawn from the general rule as to successor trustees in Section 16403(a).

A successor attorney-in-fact is the same as an original attorney-in-fact under this division. See Section 4014(b) ("attorney-in-fact" includes successor or alternate attorney-in-fact). See also Sections 4018 ("durable power of attorney" defined), 4022 ("power of attorney" defined), 4026 ("principal" defined). [24 Cal.L.Rev.Comm.Reports 323 (1994)].

1999 Amendment

Section 4203 is amended to delete a reference to powers of attorney for health care, which are governed by Division 4.7 (commencing with Section 4600) (Health Care Decisions Law). This is a technical, nonsubstantive change. [29 Cal.L.Rev.Comm. Reports 1 (1999)].

Cross References

Attorney-in-fact defined for purposes of this Division, see Probate Code § 4014.
Principal defined for purposes of this Division, see Probate Code § 4026.

§ 4204. Compensation

An attorney-in-fact is entitled to reasonable compensation for services rendered to the principal as attorney-in-fact and to reimbursement for reasonable expenses incurred as a result of acting as attorney-in-fact. *(Added by Stats.1994, c. 307 (S.B.1907), § 16.)*

Law Revision Commission Comments

1994 Addition

Section 4204 is drawn from the Missouri Durable Power of Attorney Law. See Mo. Ann. Stat. § 404.725 (Vernon 1990). This section is comparable to Sections 15681 (trustee's compensation) and 15684(a) (reimbursement for trustee's expenses). In many situations, a relative acting as an attorney-in-fact under a durable power of attorney expects to act for the principal as an accommodation. Normally, while the principal is not disabled, such service will be infrequent and will not involve substantial time. However, with the prospect that if the principal becomes disabled or incapacitated, substantial time, effort, and expense may be required of the attorney-in-fact and any successor attorneys-in-fact extending over a long period of time, compensation may be important. A definite understanding regarding compensation may be included in the power of attorney or in a separate agreement. Reimbursement of expenses would be expected to include the cost of bookkeeping, tax, and legal services incurred by the attorney-in-fact in performing duties on the principal's behalf. It would also include the cost of preparing an accounting and any travel or personal expense incurred by the attorney-in-fact. This section is subject to limitation in the power of

attorney. See Section 4101 (priority of provisions of power of attorney).
See Section 4231(b) (effect of compensation on standard of care). See also Sections 4014 ("attorney-in-fact" defined), 4026 ("principal" defined). [24 Cal.L.Rev.Comm.Reports 323 (1994)].

Cross References

Attorney-in-fact defined for purposes of this Division, see Probate Code § 4014.
Principal defined for purposes of this Division, see Probate Code § 4026.

§ 4205. Delegated authority

(a) An attorney-in-fact may revocably delegate authority to perform mechanical acts to one or more persons qualified to exercise the authority delegated.

(b) The attorney-in-fact making a delegation remains responsible to the principal for the exercise or nonexercise of the delegated authority. *(Added by Stats.1994, c. 307 (S.B. 1907), § 16.)*

Law Revision Commission Comments

1994 Addition

Subdivision (a) of Section 4205 is drawn from Civil Code Section 2349. As provided in subdivision (b), delegation does not relieve the attorney-in-fact of responsibility for the acts of subagents. This section is subject to limitation in the power of attorney. See Section 4101 (priority of provisions of power of attorney).

See also Sections 4014 ("attorney-in-fact" defined), 4026 ("principal" defined). [24 Cal.L.Rev.Comm.Reports 323 (1994)].

Cross References

Attorney-in-fact defined for purposes of this Division, see Probate Code § 4014.
Principal defined for purposes of this Division, see Probate Code § 4026.

§ 4206. Court-appointed fiduciary; management of principal's property; accountability of attorney-in-fact; modification or revocation by conservator

(a) If, following execution of a durable power of attorney, a court of the principal's domicile appoints a conservator of the estate, guardian of the estate, or other fiduciary charged with the management of all of the principal's property or all of the principal's property except specified exclusions, the attorney-in-fact is accountable to the fiduciary as well as to the principal. Except as provided in subdivision (b), the fiduciary has the same power to revoke or amend the durable power of attorney that the principal would have had if not incapacitated, subject to any required court approval.

(b) If a conservator of the estate is appointed by a court of this state, the conservator can revoke or amend the durable power of attorney only if the court in which the conservatorship proceeding is pending has first made an order authorizing or requiring the fiduciary to modify or revoke the durable power of attorney and the modification or revocation is in accord with the order.

(c) This section is not subject to limitation in the power of attorney. *(Added by Stats.1994, c. 307 (S.B.1907), § 16. Amended by Stats.1999, c. 658 (A.B.891), § 34, operative July 1, 2000.)*

Law Revision Commission Comments

1994 Addition

Section 4206 continues former Civil Code Section 2402(a) without substantive change. Subdivision (a) is substantially the same as the official text of Section 3(a) of the Uniform Durable Power of Attorney Act (1979), Uniform Probate Code Section 5–503(a) (1991), with several clarifying changes. "Conservator of the estate" has been substituted for "conservator." This change is consistent with the concept of the uniform act that the fiduciary to whom the attorney-in-fact under a durable power is accountable and who may revoke or amend the durable power includes only a fiduciary charged with the management of the principal's estate and does not include a person appointed only to exercise protective supervision over the person of the principal. See Unif. Durable Power of Attorney Act § 3 comment (1979); Unif. Prob. Code § 5–503 comment (1991). The reference in the uniform act to the principal's "disability" is omitted to conform with other provisions of this division. The authority of the fiduciary to revoke or amend is the same as in the official text of Section 3(a) of the Uniform Durable Power of Attorney Act, except that the possibility of a requirement of court approval is recognized, as in subdivision (b) which applies to California conservators.

For provisions concerning the powers of conservators, see, e.g., Sections 2252 (powers of temporary conservator), 2403 (petition for instructions), 2580 (petition for proposed action). See also Sections 2(b) (construction of provisions drawn from uniform acts), 4014 ("attorney-in-fact" defined), 4018 ("durable power of attorney" defined), 4026 ("principal" defined). [24 Cal.L.Rev.Comm.Reports 323 (1994)].

1999 Amendment

Section 4206 is amended to delete a reference to powers of attorney for health care, which are governed by Division 4.7 (commencing with Section 4600) (Health Care Decisions Law). This is a technical, nonsubstantive change. [29 Cal.L.Rev.Comm. Reports 1 (1999)].

Cross References

Attorney-in-fact defined for purposes of this Division, see Probate Code § 4014.
Durable power of attorney defined for purposes of this Division, see Probate Code § 4018.
Power of attorney defined for purposes of this Division, see Probate Code § 4022.
Principal defined for purposes of this Division, see Probate Code § 4026.

§ 4207. Resignation

(a) An attorney-in-fact may resign by any of the following means:

(1) If the principal is competent, by giving notice to the principal.

(2) If a conservator has been appointed, by giving notice to the conservator.

(3) On written agreement of a successor who is designated in the power of attorney or pursuant to the terms of the power of attorney to serve as attorney-in-fact.

(4) Pursuant to a court order.

(b) This section is not subject to limitation in the power of attorney. *(Added by Stats.1994, c. 307 (S.B.1907), § 16.)*

Law Revision Commission Comments

1994 Addition [Revised Comment]

Section 4207 is new. For judicial procedures for approving the attorney-in-fact's resignation, see Section 4541(e) (petition as to power of attorney other than durable power of attorney for health care).

See also Sections 4014 ("attorney-in-fact" defined), 4022 ("power of attorney" defined), 4026 ("principal" defined). [29 Cal.L.Rev. Comm. Reports 1 (1999)].

Cross References

Attorney-in-fact defined for purposes of this Division, see Probate Code § 4014.
Power of attorney defined for purposes of this Division, see Probate Code § 4022.
Principal defined for purposes of this Division, see Probate Code § 4026.

ARTICLE 2. DUTIES OF ATTORNEYS–IN–FACT

Section
4230. Duty to exercise authority; completing transaction; written agreements; consideration.
4231. Principal's property; standard of care; special skills or expertise.
4231.5. Breach of duty; chargeability; excuse; additional remedies for bad faith.
4232. Principal's interests; conflicts.
4233. Principal's property kept separate and distinct from other property.
4234. Regular contact and communication with principal; instruction; disobedience.
4235. Principal's incapacity; consultation and disclosures from third persons; privileges.
4236. Records; account of transactions; examination of records.
4237. Special skills; standard of care.
4238. Delivery of property upon termination of authority; records; accounting.

§ 4230. Duty to exercise authority; completing transaction; written agreements; consideration

(a) Except as provided in subdivisions (b) and (c), a person who is designated as an attorney-in-fact has no duty to exercise the authority granted in the power of attorney and is not subject to the other duties of an attorney-in-fact, regardless of whether the principal has become incapacitated, is missing, or is otherwise unable to act.

(b) Acting for the principal in one or more transactions does not obligate an attorney-in-fact to act for the principal in a subsequent transaction, but the attorney-in-fact has a duty to complete a transaction that the attorney-in-fact has commenced.

(c) If an attorney-in-fact has expressly agreed in writing to act for the principal, the attorney-in-fact has a duty to act pursuant to the terms of the agreement. The agreement to act on behalf of the principal is enforceable against the attorney-in-fact as a fiduciary regardless of whether there is any consideration to support a contractual obligation. *(Added by Stats.1994, c. 307 (S.B.1907), § 16.)*

Law Revision Commission Comments

1994 Addition

Section 4230 is drawn in part from the Missouri Durable Power of Attorney Law. See Mo. Ann. Stat. § 404.705(4) (Vernon 1990). Subdivision (a) makes clear that being named as an attorney-in-fact under a durable or nondurable power of attorney imposes no duty on the named person to act. This is true even if the attorney-in-fact knows of the designation and has received the power of attorney. A duty to act under this part arises only by reason of an express agreement in writing, as provided in subdivision (c). Reliance is not sufficient to impose a legal duty to act, as provided in subdivision (b). However, if the attorney-in-fact commences a particular transaction, it must be completed.

This section recognizes that many powers of attorney are given and accepted as a gratuitous accommodation by the attorney-in-fact. The principal wants someone to have the ability to act if something needs to be done, but rarely would the principal expect to impose a duty to act on a friend or family member if the attorney-in-fact chooses not to do so. Consequently, unless the attorney-in-fact has agreed to act, accepting a power of attorney designation imposes no duty to act and the named person may even renounce the designation. The person named as attorney-in-fact may also merely wait until the situation arises and then determine whether to act. The person may refuse to act because of personal inconvenience at the time of becoming involved, or for any other reason, and is not required to justify a decision not to act. The person named as attorney-in-fact may believe that there are others in a better position to act for the principal or that the situation really warrants appointment of a court-supervised guardian or conservator. However, once the attorney-in-fact agrees in writing to act under the power of attorney, the transaction is governed by the duties imposed in the law to act as a fiduciary. See subdivision (c).

See also Sections 4014 ("attorney-in-fact" defined), 4022 ("power of attorney" defined), 4026 ("principal" defined). [24 Cal.L.Rev.Comm.Reports 323 (1994)].

Cross References

Attorney-in-fact defined for purposes of this Division, see Probate Code § 4014.
Power of attorney defined for purposes of this Division, see Probate Code § 4022.
Principal defined for purposes of this Division, see Probate Code § 4026.

§ 4231. Principal's property; standard of care; special skills or expertise

(a) Except as provided in subdivision (b), in dealing with property of the principal, an attorney-in-fact shall observe the standard of care that would be observed by a prudent person dealing with property of another and is not limited by any other statute restricting investments by fiduciaries.

(b) An attorney-in-fact who has special skills or expertise or was designated as an attorney-in-fact on the basis of representations of special skills or expertise shall observe the standard of care that would be observed by others with similar skills or expertise. *(Added by Stats.1994, c. 307 (S.B.1907), § 16. Amended by Stats.2010, c. 48 (S.B.1038), § 1.)*

Law Revision Commission Comments

1994 Addition

Subdivisions (a) and (b) of Section 4231 are drawn from the standard applicable to custodians under Section 3912(b) (California Uniform Transfers to Minors Act). See also Section 4204 (compensation of attorneys-in-fact). The prudent person standard in subdivision (a) is generally consistent with the standard applicable under general agency law. See Restatement (Second) of Agency § 379 (1957).

Subdivision (c) is consistent with the general rule concerning expert fiduciaries stated in the cases. See the discussions in Estate of Beach, 15 Cal.3d 623, 635, 542 P.2d 994, 125 Cal.Rptr. 570 (1975) (bank as executor); Estate of Collins, 72 Cal.App.3d 663, 673, 139 Cal.Rptr. 644 (1977); Coberly v. Superior Court, 231 Cal.App.2d 685, 689, 42 Cal.Rptr. 64 (1965); see also Section 4237 (attorney-in-fact's duty to use special skills); Section 2401 Comment (standard of care applicable to professional guardian or conservator of estate); Section 3912 Comment (standard of care applicable to professional fiduciary acting as custodian under California Uniform Transfers to Minors Act); Section 16040 Comment (standard of care applicable to expert trustee).

This section is subject to limitation in the power of attorney. See Section 4101 (priority of provisions of power of attorney).

See also Sections 4014 ("attorney-in-fact" defined), 4026 ("principal" defined). [24 Cal.L.Rev.Comm.Reports 323 (1994)].

Cross References

Attorney-in-fact defined for purposes of this Division, see Probate Code § 4014.
Principal defined for purposes of this Division, see Probate Code § 4026.

§ 4231.5. Breach of duty; chargeability; excuse; additional remedies for bad faith

(a) If the attorney-in-fact breaches a duty pursuant to this division, the attorney-in-fact is chargeable with any of the following, as appropriate under the circumstances:

(1) Any loss or depreciation in value of the principal's property resulting from the breach of duty, with interest.

(2) Any profit made by the attorney-in-fact through the breach of duty, with interest.

(3) Any profit that would have accrued to the principal if the loss of profit is the result of the breach of duty.

(b) If the attorney-in-fact has acted reasonably and in good faith under the circumstances as known to the attorney-in-fact, the court, in its discretion, may excuse the attorney-in-fact in whole or in part from liability under subdivision (a) if it would be equitable to do so.

(c) If a court finds that a person has in bad faith wrongfully taken, concealed, or disposed of property that belongs to a principal under a power of attorney, or has taken, concealed, or disposed of property that belongs to a principal under a power of attorney by the use of undue influence in bad faith or through the commission of elder or dependent adult financial abuse, as defined in Section 15610.30 of the Welfare and Institutions Code, the person shall be liable for twice the value of the property recovered by an action to recover the property or for surcharge. In addition, except as otherwise required by law, including Section 15657.5 of the Welfare and Institutions Code, the person may, in the court's discretion, be liable for reasonable attorney's fees and costs to the prevailing party. The remedies provided in this section shall be in addition to any other remedies available in law to the principal or any successor in interest of the principal. *(Added by Stats.2010, c. 48 (S.B.1038), § 2. Amended by Stats.2013, c. 99 (A.B.381), § 2.)*

§4232. Principal's interests; conflicts

(a) An attorney-in-fact has a duty to act solely in the interest of the principal and to avoid conflicts of interest.

(b) An attorney-in-fact is not in violation of the duty provided in subdivision (a) solely because the attorney-in-fact also benefits from acting for the principal, has conflicting interests in relation to the property, care, or affairs of the principal, or acts in an inconsistent manner regarding the respective interests of the principal and the attorney-in-fact. *(Added by Stats.1994, c. 307 (S.B.1907), § 16.)*

Law Revision Commission Comments

1994 Addition

The first sentence of Section 4232 restates the substance of part of Civil Code Section 2322(c) in the general agency rules. The duty of loyalty is also consistent with Civil Code Section 2306 (agent not to defraud principal). Unlike Civil Code Section 2322(c), Section 4232 is stated as an affirmative duty, rather than a prohibition against violation of duties applicable to trustees under Sections 16002 and 16004. The duty of loyalty of an attorney-in-fact to the principal is subject to the limitations in Section 4230 relating to commencement of the duties of an attorney-in-fact under a power of attorney.

See also Sections 4014 ("attorney-in-fact" defined), 4022 ("power of attorney" defined), 4026 ("principal" defined). [24 Cal.L.Rev.Comm.Reports 323 (1994)].

Cross References

Attorney-in-fact defined for purposes of this Division, see Probate Code § 4014.
Principal defined for purposes of this Division, see Probate Code § 4026.

§4233. Principal's property kept separate and distinct from other property

(a) The attorney-in-fact shall keep the principal's property separate and distinct from other property in a manner adequate to identify the property clearly as belonging to the principal.

(b) An attorney-in-fact holding property for a principal complies with subdivision (a) if the property is held in the name of the principal or in the name of the attorney-in-fact as attorney-in-fact for the principal. *(Added by Stats.1994, c. 307 (S.B.1907), § 16.)*

Law Revision Commission Comments

1994 Addition

Section 4233 is drawn from the Missouri Durable Power of Attorney Law. See Mo. Ann. Stat. § 404.712 (Vernon 1990). This section is consistent with the general agency rule in Civil Code Section 2322(c) which formerly applied to powers of attorney. Unlike Civil Code Section 2322(c), Section 4233 is stated as an affirmative duty, rather than a prohibition against violation of a duty applicable to trustees under Section 16009.

See also Sections 4014 ("attorney-in-fact" defined), 4022 ("power of attorney" defined), 4026 ("principal" defined). [24 Cal.L.Rev.Comm.Reports 323 (1994)].

Cross References

Attorney-in-fact defined for purposes of this Division, see Probate Code § 4014.

Principal defined for purposes of this Division, see Probate Code § 4026.

§4234. Regular contact and communication with principal; instruction; disobedience

(a) To the extent reasonably practicable under the circumstances, an attorney-in-fact has a duty to keep in regular contact with the principal, to communicate with the principal, and to follow the instructions of the principal.

(b) With court approval, the attorney-in-fact may disobey instructions of the principal. *(Added by Stats.1994, c. 307 (S.B.1907), § 16.)*

Law Revision Commission Comments

1994 Addition [Revised Comment]

Section 4234 is drawn from general agency rules. The duty to follow the principal's instructions is consistent with the general agency rule in Civil Code Section 2309. See also Civ. Code § 2019 (agent not to exceed limits of actual authority). The duty to communicate with the principal is consistent with the general agency rule in Civil Code Sections 2020 and 2332.

Subdivision (b) is a limitation on the general agency rule in Civil Code Section 2320 (power to disobey instructions). For provisions relating to judicial proceedings, see Section 4500 *et seq.*

See also Sections 4014 ("attorney-in-fact" defined), 4022 ("power of attorney" defined), 4026 ("principal" defined). [29 Cal.L.Rev. Comm. Reports 1 (1999)].

Cross References

Attorney-in-fact defined for purposes of this Division, see Probate Code § 4014.
Principal defined for purposes of this Division, see Probate Code § 4026.

§4235. Principal's incapacity; consultation and disclosures from third persons; privileges

If the principal becomes wholly or partially incapacitated, or if there is a question concerning the capacity of the principal to give instructions to and supervise the attorney-in-fact, the attorney-in-fact may consult with a person previously designated by the principal for this purpose, and may also consult with and obtain information needed to carry out the attorney-in-fact's duties from the principal's spouse, physician, attorney, accountant, a member of the principal's family, or other person, business entity, or government agency with respect to matters to be undertaken on the principal's behalf and affecting the principal's personal affairs, welfare, family, property, and business interests. A person from whom information is requested shall disclose relevant information to the attorney-in-fact. Disclosure under this section is not a waiver of any privilege that may apply to the information disclosed. *(Added by Stats.1994, c. 307 (S.B.1907), § 16.)*

Law Revision Commission Comments

1994 Addition [Revised Comment]

Section 4235 is drawn from the Missouri Durable Power of Attorney Law. See Mo. Ann. Stat. § 404.714(4) (Vernon 1990). This section does not provide anything inconsistent with permissible practice under former law, but is intended to recognize the desirability of consultation in appropriate circumstances and provide assurance to third persons that consultation with the attorney-in-fact is proper and does not contravene privacy rights. See also Section 4455(f) (receipt of bank statements, etc., under statutory form powers of attorney). The right to obtain information may be enforced pursuant to Section 4541(f).

See also Sections 4014 ("attorney-in-fact" defined), 4026 ("principal" defined).   [29 Cal.L.Rev.Comm. Reports 1 (1999)].

Cross References

Attorney-in-fact defined for purposes of this Division, see Probate Code § 4014.

Principal defined for purposes of this Division, see Probate Code § 4026.

§ 4236.   Records; account of transactions; examination of records

(a) The attorney-in-fact shall keep records of all transactions entered into by the attorney-in-fact on behalf of the principal.

(b) The attorney-in-fact does not have a duty to make an account of transactions entered into on behalf of the principal, except in the following circumstances:

(1) At any time requested by the principal.

(2) Where the power of attorney requires the attorney-in-fact to account and specifies to whom the account is to be made.

(3) On request by the conservator of the estate of the principal while the principal is living.

(4) On request by the principal's personal representative or successor in interest after the death of the principal.

(5) Pursuant to court order.

(c) The following persons are entitled to examine and copy the records kept by the attorney-in-fact:

(1) The principal.

(2) The conservator of the estate of the principal while the principal is living.

(3) The principal's personal representative or successor in interest after the death of the principal.

(4) Any other person, pursuant to court order.

(d) This section is not subject to limitation in the power of attorney.   *(Added by Stats.1994, c. 307 (S.B.1907), § 16.)*

Law Revision Commission Comments
1994 Addition [Revised Comment]

Section 4236 is drawn in part from Minnesota law. See Minn. Stat. Ann. § 523.21 (West Supp. 1994). For provisions relating to judicial proceedings, see Section 4500 *et seq.*

See also Sections 4014 ("attorney-in-fact" defined), 4022 ("power of attorney" defined), 4026 ("principal" defined).   [29 Cal.L.Rev. Comm. Reports 1 (1999)].

Cross References

Attorney-in-fact defined for purposes of this Division, see Probate Code § 4014.

Power of attorney defined for purposes of this Division, see Probate Code § 4022.

Principal defined for purposes of this Division, see Probate Code § 4026.

§ 4237.   Special skills; standard of care

An attorney-in-fact with special skills has a duty to apply the full extent of those skills.   *(Added by Stats.1994, c. 307 (S.B.1907), § 16.)*

Law Revision Commission Comments
1994 Addition

Section 4237 is comparable to Section 16014(a) applicable to trustees.   See also Section 4231(c) (expert standard of care). This section is subject to limitation in the power of attorney. See Section 4101 (priority of provisions of power of attorney).

See also Section 4014 ("attorney-in-fact" defined).   [24 Cal.L.Rev.Comm.Reports 323 (1994)].

Cross References

Attorney-in-fact defined for purposes of this Division, see Probate Code § 4014.

§ 4238.   Delivery of property upon termination of authority; records; accounting

(a) On termination of an attorney-in-fact's authority, the attorney-in-fact shall promptly deliver possession or control of the principal's property as follows:

(1) If the principal is not incapacitated, to the principal or as directed by the principal.

(2) If the principal is incapacitated, to the following persons with the following priority:

(A) To a qualified successor attorney-in-fact.

(B) As to any community property, to the principal's spouse.

(C) To the principal's conservator of the estate or guardian of the estate.

(3) In the case of the death of the principal, to the principal's personal representative, if any, or the principal's successors.

(b) On termination of an attorney-in-fact's authority, the attorney-in-fact shall deliver copies of any records relating to transactions undertaken on the principal's behalf that are requested by the person to whom possession or control of the property is delivered.

(c) Termination of an attorney-in-fact's authority does not relieve the attorney-in-fact of any duty to render an account of actions taken as attorney-in-fact.

(d) The attorney-in-fact has the powers reasonably necessary under the circumstances to perform the duties provided by this section.   *(Added by Stats.1994, c. 307 (S.B.1907), § 16.)*

Law Revision Commission Comments
1994 Addition

Section 4238 is new.   The rules concerning duties on termination of the attorney-in-fact's authority are drawn in part from Section 15644 (delivery of property by former trustee upon occurrence of vacancy). This section is subject to limitation in the power of attorney.   See Section 4101 (priority of provisions of power of attorney).   For other rules concerning the attorney-in-fact's relation with court-appointed fiduciaries under a durable power of attorney, see Section 4206.

See also Sections 4014 ("attorney-in-fact" defined), 4026 ("principal" defined).   [24 Cal.L.Rev.Comm.Reports 323 (1994)].

Cross References

Attorney-in-fact defined for purposes of this Division, see Probate Code § 4014.

Principal defined for purposes of this Division, see Probate Code § 4026.

ARTICLE 3. AUTHORITY OF ATTORNEYS–IN–FACT

Section
4260. Application of article.
4261. General authority granted.
4262. Limited authority granted.
4263. Powers incorporated by reference to other statutes.
4264. Acts requiring express authorization in power of attorney.
4265. Acts that power of attorney may not authorize.
4266. Exercise of authority; fiduciary duties.

§ 4260. Application of article

(a) Except as specified in subdivision (b), this article applies to all powers of attorney under this division.

(b) Sections 4261 and 4263 do not apply to the provisions of Part 3 (commencing with Section 4400). *(Added by Stats.1994, c. 307 (S.B.1907), § 16. Amended by Stats.1999, c. 658 (A.B.891), § 35, operative July 1, 2000; Stats.2011, c. 113 (A.B.1082), § 1.)*

Law Revision Commission Comments

1994 Addition

Section 4260 limits the application of this article. Statutory form powers of attorney and durable power of attorney for health care have special rules concerning the authority of attorneys-in-fact. [24 Cal.L.Rev.Comm.Reports 323 (1994)].

1999 Amendment

Section 4260 is amended to delete a reference to powers of attorney for health care, which are governed by Division 4.7 (commencing with Section 4600) (Health Care Decisions Law). This is a technical, nonsubstantive change. [29 Cal.L.Rev.Comm. Reports 1 (1999)].

Cross References

Power of attorney defined for purposes of this Division, see Probate Code § 4022.

§ 4261. General authority granted

If a power of attorney grants general authority to an attorney-in-fact and is not limited to one or more express actions, subjects, or purposes for which general authority is conferred, the attorney-in-fact has all the authority to act that a person having the capacity to contract may carry out through an attorney-in-fact specifically authorized to take the action. *(Added by Stats.1994, c. 307 (S.B.1907), § 16.)*

Law Revision Commission Comments

1994 Addition

Section 4261 is new and provides for the broadest possible authority in a general power of attorney. For specific limitations applicable to this section, see Sections 4264 (authority that must be specifically granted), 4265 (actions that may not be taken by an attorney-in-fact).

See also Sections 4014 ("attorney-in-fact" defined), 4022 ("power of attorney" defined). [24 Cal.L.Rev.Comm.Reports 323 (1994)].

Cross References

Attorney-in-fact defined for purposes of this Division, see Probate Code § 4014.
Power of attorney defined for purposes of this Division, see Probate Code § 4022.

§ 4262. Limited authority granted

Subject to this article, if a power of attorney grants limited authority to an attorney-in-fact, the attorney-in-fact has the following authority:

(a) The authority granted in the power of attorney, as limited with respect to permissible actions, subjects, or purposes.

(b) The authority incidental, necessary, or proper to carry out the granted authority. *(Added by Stats.1994, c. 307 (S.B.1907), § 16.)*

Law Revision Commission Comments

1994 Addition

Section 4262 is drawn from Section 16200 governing the general powers of a trustee. The introductory clause recognizes that there are specific limitations on the general powers granted by this section. See Sections 4264 (authority that must be specifically granted), 4265 (excluded authority), 4266 (exercise of authority subject to duties). Subdivision (a) is consistent with the general agency rules in Civil Code Sections 2315 and 2318. Subdivision (b) is comparable to an agent's authority to do "everything necessary or proper and usual, in the ordinary course of business, for effecting the purpose of his agency," which is provided as to agents generally in Civil Code Section 2319(1).

See also Sections 4014 ("attorney-in-fact" defined), 4022 ("power of attorney" defined). [24 Cal.L.Rev.Comm.Reports 323 (1994)].

Cross References

Attorney-in-fact defined for purposes of this Division, see Probate Code § 4014.
Power of attorney defined for purposes of this Division, see Probate Code § 4022.

§ 4263. Powers incorporated by reference to other statutes

(a) A power of attorney may grant authority to the attorney-in-fact by incorporating powers by reference to another statute, including, but not limited to, the following:

(1) Powers of attorneys-in-fact provided by the Uniform Statutory Form Power of Attorney Act (Part 3 (commencing with Section 4400)).

(2) Powers of guardians and conservators provided by Chapter 5 (commencing with Section 2350) and Chapter 6 (commencing with Section 2400) of Part 4 of Division 4.

(3) Powers of trustees provided by Chapter 2 (commencing with Section 16200) of Part 4 of Division 9.

(b) Incorporation by reference to another statute includes any amendments made to the incorporated provisions after the date of execution of the power of attorney. *(Added by Stats.1994, c. 307 (S.B.1907), § 16.)*

Law Revision Commission Comments

1994 Addition

Section 4263 is new. Subdivision (b) is subject to limitation in the power of attorney. See Section 4101 (priority of provisions of power of attorney).

See also Sections 4014 ("attorney-in-fact" defined), 4022 ("power of attorney" defined). [24 Cal.L.Rev.Comm.Reports 323 (1994)].

Cross References

Attorney-in-fact defined for purposes of this Division, see Probate Code § 4014.

Power of attorney defined for purposes of this Division, see Probate Code § 4022.

§ 4264. Acts requiring express authorization in power of attorney

An attorney-in-fact under a power of attorney may perform any of the following acts on behalf of the principal or with the property of the principal only if the power of attorney expressly grants that authority to the attorney-in-fact:

(a) Create, modify, revoke, or terminate a trust, in whole or in part. If a power of attorney under this division empowers the attorney-in-fact to modify or revoke a trust created by the principal, the trust may be modified or revoked by the attorney-in-fact only as provided in the trust instrument.

(b) Fund with the principal's property a trust not created by the principal or a person authorized to create a trust on behalf of the principal.

(c) Make or revoke a gift of the principal's property in trust or otherwise.

(d) Exercise the right to reject, disclaim, release, or consent to a reduction in, or modification of, a share in, or payment from, an estate, trust, or other fund on behalf of the principal. This subdivision does not limit the attorney-in-fact's authority to disclaim a detrimental transfer to the principal with the approval of the court.

(e) Create or change survivorship interests in the principal's property or in property in which the principal may have an interest.

(f) Designate or change the designation of beneficiaries to receive any property, benefit, or contract right on the principal's death.

(g) Make a loan to the attorney-in-fact. *(Added by Stats.1994, c. 307 (S.B.1907), § 16. Amended by Stats.2011, c. 113 (A.B.1082), § 2.)*

Law Revision Commission Comments

1994 Addition

Section 4264 is drawn in part from the Missouri Durable Power of Attorney Law. See Mo. Ann. Stat. § 404.710(6) (Vernon 1990). This section is consistent with the general agency rule in Civil Code Section 2304. Subdivision (d) is intended to permit the attorney-in-fact to make a disclaimer of a donative transfer of property where, for example, acceptance of the property would make the principal liable for the cleanup of hazardous or toxic materials.

See also Sections 4014 ("attorney-in-fact" defined), 4022 ("power of attorney" defined), 4026 ("principal" defined). [24 Cal.L.Rev.Comm.Reports 323 (1994)].

Cross References

Attorney-in-fact defined for purposes of this Division, see Probate Code § 4014.

Power of attorney defined for purposes of this Division, see Probate Code § 4022.

Principal defined for purposes of this Division, see Probate Code § 4026.

§ 4265. Acts that power of attorney may not authorize

A power of attorney may not authorize an attorney-in-fact to make, publish, declare, amend, or revoke the principal's will. *(Added by Stats.1994, c. 307 (S.B.1907), § 16. Amended by Stats.1999, c. 658 (A.B.891), § 36, operative July 1, 2000.)*

Law Revision Commission Comments

1994 Addition

Section 4265 is consistent with the general agency rule in Civil Code Section 2304. See also Sections 4014 ("attorney-in-fact" defined), 4022 ("power of attorney" defined), 4026 ("principal" defined), 4606 ("durable power of attorney for health care" defined). [24 Cal.L.Rev.Comm.Reports 323 (1994)].

1999 Amendment

Section 4265 is amended to delete a reference to powers of attorney for health care, which are governed by Division 4.7 (commencing with Section 4600) (Health Care Decisions Law). See Section 4050 (scope of division).

Section 4265 is consistent with the general agency rule in Civil Code Section 2304. See also Sections 4014 ("attorney-in-fact" defined), 4022 ("power of attorney" defined), 4026 ("principal" defined). [29 Cal.L.Rev.Comm. Reports 1 (1999)].

Cross References

Attorney-in-fact defined for purposes of this Division, see Probate Code § 4014.

Power of attorney defined for purposes of this Division, see Probate Code § 4022.

Principal defined for purposes of this Division, see Probate Code § 4026.

§ 4266. Exercise of authority; fiduciary duties

The grant of authority to an attorney-in-fact, whether by the power of attorney, by statute, or by the court, does not in itself require or permit the exercise of the power. The exercise of authority by an attorney-in-fact is subject to the attorney-in-fact's fiduciary duties. *(Added by Stats.1994, c. 307 (S.B.1907), § 16.)*

Law Revision Commission Comments

1994 Addition

Section 4266 is drawn from Section 16202 (exercise of trustee's powers). See Sections 4230–4238 (duties of attorneys-in-fact). See also 4014 ("attorney-in-fact" defined), 4022 ("power of attorney" defined). [24 Cal.L.Rev.Comm.Reports 323 (1994)].

Cross References

Attorney-in-fact defined for purposes of this Division, see Probate Code § 4014.

Power of attorney defined for purposes of this Division, see Probate Code § 4022.

CHAPTER 5. RELATIONS WITH THIRD PERSONS

§ 4300. Rights and privileges of attorney-in-fact

A third person shall accord an attorney-in-fact acting pursuant to the provisions of a power of attorney the same rights and privileges that would be accorded the principal if the principal were personally present and seeking to act. However, a third person is not required to honor the attorney-in-fact's authority or conduct business with the attorney-in-fact if the principal cannot require the third person to act or conduct business in the same circumstances. *(Added by Stats.1994, c. 307 (S.B.1907), § 16.)*

Law Revision Commission Comments

1994 Addition [Revised Comment]

Section 4300 is new. This section provides the basic rule concerning the position of an attorney-in-fact: that the attorney-in-fact acts in place of the principal, within the scope of the power of attorney, and is to be treated as if the principal were acting. The second sentence generalizes a rule in former Civil Code Section 2480.5, which was applicable only to the Uniform Statutory Form Power of Attorney. Under this rule, a third person may be compelled to honor a power of attorney only to the extent that the principal, disregarding any legal disability, could bring an action to compel the third person to act. A third person who could not be forced to do business with the principal consequently may not be forced to deal with the attorney-in-fact. However, a third person who holds property of the principal, who owes a debt to the principal, or who is obligated by contract to the principal may be compelled to accept the attorney-in-fact's authority.

This general rule is subject to some specific exceptions. See, e.g., Sections 4309 (prior breach by attorney-in-fact), 4310 (transactions relating to accounts and loans in financial institution).

See also Sections 4014 ("attorney-in-fact" defined), 4022 ("power of attorney" defined), 4026 ("principal" defined), 4034 ("third person" defined). [29 Cal.L.Rev.Comm. Reports 1 (1999)].

Cross References

Attorney-in-fact defined for purposes of this Division, see Probate Code § 4014.

Power of attorney defined for purposes of this Division, see Probate Code § 4022.

Principal defined for purposes of this Division, see Probate Code § 4026.

Third person defined for purposes of this Division, see Probate Code § 4034.

§ 4301. Reliance on attorney-in-fact's acts, transactions or decisions

A third person may rely on, contract with, and deal with an attorney-in-fact with respect to the subjects and purposes encompassed or expressed in the power of attorney without regard to whether the power of attorney expressly authorizes the specific act, transaction, or decision by the attorney-in-fact. *(Added by Stats.1994, c. 307 (S.B.1907), § 16.)*

Law Revision Commission Comments

1994 Addition [Revised Comment]

Section 4301 is drawn from the Missouri Durable Power of Attorney Law. See Mo. Ann. Stat. § 404.710(8) (Vernon 1990). This general rule is subject to specific limitations provided elsewhere. See, e.g., Sections 4264 (authority that must be specifically granted).

See also Sections 4014 ("attorney-in-fact" defined), 4022 ("power of attorney" defined), 4034 ("third person" defined). [29 Cal.L.Rev. Comm. Reports 1 (1999)].

Cross References

Attorney-in-fact defined for purposes of this Division, see Probate Code § 4014.

Power of attorney defined for purposes of this Division, see Probate Code § 4022.

Third person defined for purposes of this Division, see Probate Code § 4034.

§ 4302. Identification, signature specimens and other information

When requested to engage in transactions with an attorney-in-fact, a third person, before incurring any duty to comply with the power of attorney, may require the attorney-in-fact to provide identification, specimens of the signatures of the principal and the attorney-in-fact, and any other information reasonably necessary or appropriate to identify the principal and the attorney-in-fact and to facilitate the actions of the third person in transacting business with the attorney-in-fact. A third person may require an attorney-in-fact to provide the current and permanent residence addresses of the principal before agreeing to engage in a transaction with the attorney-in-fact. *(Added by Stats.1994, c. 307 (S.B.1907), § 16.)*

Law Revision Commission Comments

1994 Addition [Revised Comment]

Section 4302 is drawn in part from the Missouri Durable Power of Attorney Law. See Mo. Ann. Stat. § 404.719(4) (Vernon 1990). See also former Civ. Code § 2512(a)(1) (presentation by attorney-in-fact named in power of attorney) & Comment.

See also Sections 4014 ("attorney-in-fact" defined), 4022 ("power of attorney" defined), 4026 ("principal" defined), 4034 ("third person" defined). [29 Cal.L.Rev.Comm. Reports 1 (1999)].

Cross References

Attorney-in-fact defined for purposes of this Division, see Probate Code § 4014.

Power of attorney defined for purposes of this Division, see Probate Code § 4022.

Principal defined for purposes of this Division, see Probate Code § 4026.

Third person defined for purposes of this Division, see Probate Code § 4034.

§ 4303. Good faith reliance on power of attorney; third person's liability

(a) A third person who acts in good faith reliance on a power of attorney is not liable to the principal or to any other person for so acting if all of the following requirements are satisfied:

(1) The power of attorney is presented to the third person by the attorney-in-fact designated in the power of attorney.

(2) The power of attorney appears on its face to be valid.

(3) The power of attorney includes a notary public's certificate of acknowledgment or is signed by two witnesses.

(b) Nothing in this section is intended to create an implication that a third person is liable for acting in reliance on a power of attorney under circumstances where the requirements of subdivision (a) are not satisfied. Nothing in this section affects any immunity that may otherwise exist apart from this section. *(Added by Stats.1994, c. 307 (S.B. 1907), § 16.)*

Law Revision Commission Comments

1994 Addition [Revised Comment]

Section 4303 continues former Civil Code Section 2512 without substantive change, with the addition of the witnessing rule in subdivision (a)(3). This section is intended to ensure that a power of attorney, whether durable or nondurable, will be accepted and relied on by third persons. The person presenting the power of attorney must actually be the attorney-in-fact designated in the power of attorney. If the person purporting to be the attorney-in-fact is an impostor, the immunity does not apply. The third person can rely in good faith on the notary public's certificate of acknowledgment or the signatures of the witnesses that the person who executed the power of attorney is the principal.

Subdivision (b) makes clear that this section provides an immunity from liability where the requirements of the section are satisfied. This section has no relevance in determining whether or not a third person who acts in reliance on a power of attorney is liable under the circumstances where, for example, the power of attorney does not include a notary public's certificate of acknowledgment.

For other immunity provisions not affected by Section 4303, see, e.g., Sections 4128(b) (reliance in good faith on durable power of attorney not containing "warning" statement required by Section 4128), 4301 (reliance by third person on general authority), 4304 (lack of knowledge of death or incapacity of principal). See also Section 3720 ("Any person who acts in reliance upon the power of attorney [of an absentee as defined in Section 1403] when accompanied by a copy of a certificate of missing status is not liable for relying and acting upon the power of attorney.").

See also Sections 4014 ("attorney-in-fact" defined), 4018 ("durable power of attorney" defined), 4022 ("power of attorney" defined), 4026 ("principal" defined), 4034 ("third person" defined). [29 Cal.L.Rev.Comm. Reports 1 (1999)].

Cross References

Attorney-in-fact defined for purposes of this Division, see Probate Code § 4014.
Power of attorney defined for purposes of this Division, see Probate Code § 4022.
Principal defined for purposes of this Division, see Probate Code § 4026.

Third person defined for purposes of this Division, see Probate Code § 4034.

§ 4304. Death or incapacity of principal; knowledge; good faith acts

(a) The death of a principal who has executed a power of attorney, whether durable or nondurable, does not revoke or terminate the agency as to the attorney-in-fact or a third person who, without actual knowledge of the principal's death, acts in good faith under the power of attorney. Any action so taken, unless otherwise invalid or unenforceable, binds the principal's successors in interest.

(b) The incapacity of a principal who has previously executed a nondurable power of attorney does not revoke or terminate the agency as to the attorney-in-fact or a third person who, without actual knowledge of the incapacity of the principal, acts in good faith under the power of attorney. Any action so taken, unless otherwise invalid or unenforceable, binds the principal and the principal's successors in interest. *(Added by Stats.1994, c. 307 (S.B.1907), § 16.)*

Law Revision Commission Comments

1994 Addition

Section 4304 continues former Civil Code Section 2403 without substantive change. This section is the same in substance as the official text of Section 4 of the Uniform Durable Power of Attorney Act (1979), Uniform Probate Code Section 5–504 (1990), except that the reference to the principal's "disability" is omitted. See Section 2(b) (construction of provisions drawn from uniform acts). Under Section 4155, it is the principal's incapacity to contract which would otherwise terminate the power of attorney.

See also Sections 4014 ("attorney-in-fact" defined), 4018 ("durable power of attorney" defined), 4022 ("power of attorney" defined), 4026 ("principal" defined), 4034 ("third person" defined). [24 Cal.L.Rev.Comm.Reports 323 (1994)].

Cross References

Attorney-in-fact defined for purposes of this Division, see Probate Code § 4014.
Power of attorney defined for purposes of this Division, see Probate Code § 4022.
Principal defined for purposes of this Division, see Probate Code § 4026.
Third person defined for purposes of this Division, see Probate Code § 4034.

§ 4305. Acts undertaken without knowledge of revoked power or principal's death or incapacity; affidavit; recordation

(a) As to acts undertaken in good faith reliance thereon, an affidavit executed by the attorney-in-fact under a power of attorney, whether durable or nondurable, stating that, at the time of the exercise of the power, the attorney-in-fact did not have actual knowledge of the termination of the power of attorney or the attorney-in-fact's authority by revocation or of the principal's death or incapacity is conclusive proof of the nonrevocation or nontermination of the power at that time. If the exercise of the power of attorney requires execution and delivery of any instrument that is recordable, the affidavit when authenticated for record is likewise recordable.

(b) This section does not affect any provision in a power of attorney for its termination by expiration of time or occurrence of an event other than express revocation or a change in the principal's capacity. *(Added by Stats.1994, c. 307 (S.B.1907), § 16.)*

Section 4305 continues former Civil Code Section 2404 without substantive change. A reference to termination of the attorney-in-fact's authority by revocation has also been added in subdivision (a) for consistency with other provisions in this part. See, e.g., Section 4152 (termination of attorney-in-fact's authority). This section is the same as the official text of Section 5 of the Uniform Durable Power of Attorney Act (1979), Uniform Probate Code Section 5–505 (1990), except that the reference to the principal's "disability" is omitted. See Section 2(b) (construction of provisions drawn from uniform acts). Under Section 4155, it is the principal's incapacity to contract which would otherwise terminate the power of attorney.

See also Sections 4014 ("attorney-in-fact" defined), 4018 ("durable power of attorney" defined), 4022 ("power of attorney" defined), 4026 ("principal" defined). [24 Cal.L.Rev.Comm.Reports 323 (1994)].

Attorney-in-fact defined for purposes of this Division, see Probate Code § 4014.
Power of attorney defined for purposes of this Division, see Probate Code § 4022.
Principal defined for purposes of this Division, see Probate Code § 4026.

§ 4306. Refusal to accept attorney-in-fact's authority referred to in affidavit; confirmation; attorney's fees; good faith actions

(a) If an attorney-in-fact furnishes an affidavit pursuant to Section 4305, whether voluntarily or on demand, a third person dealing with the attorney-in-fact who refuses to accept the exercise of the attorney-in-fact's authority referred to in the affidavit is liable for attorney's fees incurred in an action or proceeding necessary to confirm the attorney-in-fact's qualifications or authority, unless the court determines that the third person believed in good faith that the attorney-in-fact was not qualified or was attempting to exceed or improperly exercise the attorney-in-fact's authority.

(b) The failure of a third person to demand an affidavit pursuant to Section 4305 does not affect the protection provided the third person by this chapter, and no inference as to whether a third person has acted in good faith may be drawn from the failure to demand an affidavit from the attorney-in-fact. *(Added by Stats.1994, c. 307 (S.B.1907), § 16.)*

Section 4306 is analogous to the rule applicable to third persons dealing with trustees. See Section 18100.5(g)-(h) (reliance on trustee's certificate, liability for attorney's fees). For a special rule applicable to statutory form powers of attorney, see Section 4406. Unless the court determines that the third person refused in good faith to rely on the attorney-in-fact's affidavit, subdivision (a) imposes liability on the third person for attorney's fees in a proceeding needed to confirm exercise of a power. This provision is intended to make powers of attorney more effective and avoid the need to seek judicial confirmation of the existence of a power. The liability under subdivision (a) applies only where the attorney-in-fact executes an affidavit, whether voluntarily or on demand. If the attorney-in-fact

has not executed an affidavit, a third person may refuse to recognize the attorney-in-fact's authority even though the third person would be fully protected under this chapter.

Subdivision (b) makes clear that the failure to require the attorney-in-fact to execute an affidavit does not affect the protection provided to the third person by this chapter, and no inference as to whether a third person has acted in good faith should be drawn from the failure to request an affidavit. Consequently, a third person who satisfies the requirements of this chapter is fully protected. The availability of the affidavit is not intended to detract from the general protection provided in this chapter.

See also Sections 4014 ("attorney-in-fact" defined), 4034 ("third person" defined). [24 Cal.L.Rev.Comm.Reports 323 (1994)].

Attorney-in-fact defined for purposes of this Division, see Probate Code § 4014.
Third person defined for purposes of this Division, see Probate Code § 4034.

§ 4307. Certified copies of power of attorney

(a) A copy of a power of attorney certified under this section has the same force and effect as the original power of attorney.

(b) A copy of a power of attorney may be certified by any of the following:

(1) An attorney authorized to practice law in this state.

(2) A notary public in this state.

(3) An official of a state or of a political subdivision who is authorized to make certifications.

(c) The certification shall state that the certifying person has examined the original power of attorney and the copy and that the copy is a true and correct copy of the original power of attorney.

(d) Nothing in this section is intended to create an implication that a third person may be liable for acting in good faith reliance on a copy of a power of attorney that has not been certified under this section. *(Added by Stats.1994, c. 307 (S.B.1907), § 16. Amended by Stats.1995, c. 300 (S.B. 984), § 9, eff. Aug. 3, 1995.)*

Section 4307 is new. This section facilitates use of a power of attorney executed in this state as well as powers of attorney executed in other states. Subdivision (d) makes clear that certification under this section is not a requirement for use of copies of powers of attorney. This recognizes, for example, the existing practice of good faith reliance on copies of durable powers of attorney for health care. See former Section 4750 (immunities of health care provider); new Section 4740.

See also Section 4022 ("power of attorney" defined). [29 Cal. L.Rev.Comm. Reports 1 (1999)].

Notaries public,
Duties, see Government Code § 8205.
Fees, see Government Code § 8211.
Power of attorney defined for purposes of this Division, see Probate Code § 4022.

Third person defined for purposes of this Division, see Probate Code § 4034.

§ 4308. Actual knowledge; third persons conducting activities through employees; branches or multiple offices

(a) A third person who conducts activities through employees is not charged under this chapter with actual knowledge of any fact relating to a power of attorney, nor of a change in the authority of an attorney-in-fact, unless both of the following requirements are satisfied:

(1) The information is received at a home office or a place where there is an employee with responsibility to act on the information.

(2) The employee has a reasonable time in which to act on the information using the procedure and facilities that are available to the third person in the regular course of its operations.

(b) Knowledge of an employee in one branch or office of an entity that conducts business through branches or multiple offices is not attributable to an employee in another branch or office. *(Added by Stats.1994, c. 307 (S.B.1907), § 16.)*

Law Revision Commission Comments
1994 Addition

Section 4308 is new. Subdivision (a) is drawn from the Missouri Durable Power of Attorney Law. See Mo. Ann. Stat. § 404.719(3) (Vernon 1990).

See also Sections 4014 ("attorney-in-fact" defined), 4022 ("power of attorney" defined), 4034 ("third person" defined). [24 Cal.L.Rev.Comm.Reports 323 (1994)].

Cross References

Attorney-in-fact defined for purposes of this Division, see Probate Code § 4014.
Power of attorney defined for purposes of this Division, see Probate Code § 4022.
Third person defined for purposes of this Division, see Probate Code § 4034.

§ 4309. Agreements breached by attorney-in-fact; future transactions

Nothing in this chapter requires a third person to engage in any transaction with an attorney-in-fact if the attorney-in-fact has previously breached any agreement with the third person. *(Added by Stats.1994, c. 307 (S.B.1907), § 16.)*

Law Revision Commission Comments
1994 Addition

Section 4309 is new. See also Sections 4014 ("attorney-in-fact" defined), 4034 ("third person" defined). [24 Cal.L.Rev.Comm.Reports 323 (1994)].

Cross References

Attorney-in-fact defined for purposes of this Division, see Probate Code § 4014.
Third person defined for purposes of this Division, see Probate Code § 4034.

§ 4310. Deposit accounts or loans at financial institutions; principal not currently a depositor or borrower

Without limiting the generality of Section 4300, nothing in this chapter requires a financial institution to open a deposit account for a principal at the request of an attorney-in-fact if the principal is not currently a depositor of the financial institution or to make a loan to the attorney-in-fact on the principal's behalf if the principal is not currently a borrower of the financial institution. *(Added by Stats.1994, c. 307 (S.B.1907), § 16.)*

Law Revision Commission Comments
1994 Addition

Section 4310 is new. See also Sections 21 ("account" defined), 40 ("financial institution" defined), 4014 ("attorney-in-fact" defined), 4026 ("principal" defined). [24 Cal.L.Rev.Comm.Reports 323 (1994)].

Cross References

Attorney-in-fact defined for purposes of this Division, see Probate Code § 4014.
Principal defined for purposes of this Division, see Probate Code § 4026.

Part 3

UNIFORM STATUTORY FORM POWER OF ATTORNEY

CHAPTER 1. GENERAL PROVISIONS

§ 4400. Short title

This part may be cited as the Uniform Statutory Form Power of Attorney Act. *(Added by Stats.1994, c. 307 (S.B.1907), § 16.)*

Law Revision Commission Comments
1994 Addition

Section 4400 continues former Civil Code Section 2482 without change. This part is substantially the same as the Uniform Statutory Form Power of Attorney Act (1988). Section 4400 is the same as Section 19 of the uniform act. See Section 2(b) (construction of provisions drawn from uniform acts). See also Section 11 (severability of provisions). [24 Cal.L.Rev.Comm.Reports 323 (1994)].

Power of attorney defined for purposes of this Division, see Probate Code § 4022.

Power of Attorney form, see Probate Code § 4401.

§ 4401. Form

The following statutory form power of attorney is legally sufficient when the requirements of Section 4402 are satisfied:

UNIFORM STATUTORY FORM POWER OF AT-TORNEY

(California Probate Code Section 4401)

NOTICE: THE POWERS GRANTED BY THIS DOCUMENT ARE BROAD AND SWEEPING. THEY ARE EXPLAINED IN THE UNIFORM STATUTORY FORM POWER OF ATTORNEY ACT (CALIFORNIA PROBATE CODE SECTIONS 4400–4465). THE POWERS LISTED IN THIS DOCUMENT DO NOT INCLUDE ALL POWERS THAT ARE AVAILABLE UNDER THE PROBATE CODE. ADDITIONAL POWERS AVAILABLE UNDER THE PROBATE CODE MAY BE ADDED BY SPECIFICALLY LISTING THEM UNDER THE SPECIAL INSTRUCTIONS SECTION OF THIS DOCUMENT. IF YOU HAVE ANY QUESTIONS ABOUT THESE POWERS, OBTAIN COMPETENT LEGAL ADVICE. THIS DOCUMENT DOES NOT AUTHORIZE ANYONE TO MAKE MEDICAL AND OTHER HEALTH–CARE DECISIONS FOR YOU. YOU MAY REVOKE THIS POWER OF ATTORNEY IF YOU LATER WISH TO DO SO.

I _____
(your name and address)

appoint _____
(name and address of the person appointed, or of each person appointed if you want to designate more than one)

as my agent (attorney–in–fact) to act for me in any lawful way with respect to the following initialed subjects:

TO GRANT ALL OF THE FOLLOWING POWERS, INITIAL THE LINE IN FRONT OF (N) AND IGNORE THE LINES IN FRONT OF THE OTHER POWERS.

TO GRANT ONE OR MORE, BUT FEWER THAN ALL, OF THE FOLLOWING POWERS, INITIAL THE LINE IN FRONT OF EACH POWER YOU ARE GRANTING.

TO WITHHOLD A POWER, DO NOT INITIAL THE LINE IN FRONT OF IT. YOU MAY, BUT NEED NOT, CROSS OUT EACH POWER WITHHELD.

INITIAL

_____ (A) Real property transactions.
_____ (B) Tangible personal property transactions.
_____ (C) Stock and bond transactions.
_____ (D) Commodity and option transactions.
_____ (E) Banking and other financial institution transactions.
_____ (F) Business operating transactions.
_____ (G) Insurance and annuity transactions.
_____ (H) Estate, trust, and other beneficiary transactions.
_____ (I) Claims and litigation.
_____ (J) Personal and family maintenance.
_____ (K) Benefits from social security, medicare, medicaid, or other governmental programs, or civil or military service.
_____ (L) Retirement plan transactions.
_____ (M) Tax matters.
_____ (N) ALL OF THE POWERS LISTED ABOVE.

YOU NEED NOT INITIAL ANY OTHER LINES IF YOU INITIAL LINE (N).

SPECIAL INSTRUCTIONS:

ON THE FOLLOWING LINES YOU MAY GIVE SPECIAL INSTRUCTIONS LIMITING OR EXTENDING THE POWERS GRANTED TO YOUR AGENT.

_____
_____
_____
_____
_____
_____
_____
_____
_____

UNLESS YOU DIRECT OTHERWISE ABOVE, THIS POWER OF ATTORNEY IS EFFECTIVE IMMEDIATELY AND WILL CONTINUE UNTIL IT IS REVOKED.

This power of attorney will continue to be effective even though I become incapacitated.

STRIKE THE PRECEDING SENTENCE IF YOU DO NOT WANT THIS POWER OF ATTORNEY TO CONTINUE IF YOU BECOME INCAPACITATED.

EXERCISE OF POWER OF ATTORNEY WHERE MORE THAN ONE AGENT DESIGNATED

If I have designated more than one agent, the agents are to act

_____

IF YOU APPOINTED MORE THAN ONE AGENT AND YOU WANT EACH AGENT TO BE ABLE TO ACT ALONE WITHOUT THE OTHER AGENT JOINING, WRITE THE WORD "SEPARATELY" IN THE BLANK SPACE ABOVE. IF YOU DO NOT INSERT ANY WORD IN THE BLANK SPACE, OR IF YOU INSERT THE WORD "JOINTLY", THEN ALL OF YOUR AGENTS MUST ACT OR SIGN TOGETHER.

I agree that any third party who receives a copy of this document may act under it. A third party may seek identification. Revocation of the power of attorney is not effective as to a third party until the third party has actual knowledge of the revocation. I agree to indemnify the third party for any claims that arise against the third party because of reliance on this power of attorney.

Signed this _____ day of _____, 20_____

_____
(your signature)

State of _____ County of _____

BY ACCEPTING OR ACTING UNDER THE APPOINTMENT, THE AGENT ASSUMES THE FIDUCIARY AND OTHER LEGAL RESPONSIBILITIES OF AN AGENT.

[Include certificate of acknowledgment of notary public in compliance with Section 1189 of the Civil Code or other applicable law.]
(Added by Stats.1994, c. 307 (S.B.1907), § 16. Amended by Stats.2005, c. 251 (S.B.158), § 1; Stats.2011, c. 113 (A.B. 1082), § 3.)

Law Revision Commission Comments
1994 Addition [Revised Comment]

Section 4401 continues former Civil Code Section 2475 without change, except for the revision of cross-references to other provisions, the restoration of language erroneously omitted in 1993, and inclusion of a general reference to the law governing the notary's certificate of acknowledgment. Section 4401 is the same in substance as Section 1(a) of the Uniform Statutory Form Power of Attorney Act (1988), with the addition of provisions to permit designation of co-agents. See Section 2(b) (construction of provisions drawn from uniform acts).

The provisions added by former Civil Code Section 2475 were drawn from the former Statutory Short Form Power of Attorney statute. See former Civ. Code § 2450 (repealed by 1990 Cal. Stat. ch. 986, § 1). The acknowledgment portion of the form was revised to be consistent with the form used under California law. The word "incapacitated" was substituted for the words "disabled, incapacitated, or incompetent" used in the uniform act. This substitution conforms the statutory form to the California version of the Uniform Durable Power of Attorney Act. See Section 4018 (requirements for creation of durable power of attorney).

Section 4401 provides the text of the form that is sufficient and necessary to bring this part into operation. The statutory form can be used in whole or part instead of individually drafted forms or forms adapted from a form book.

A form used to create a power of attorney subject to this part should use the language provided in Section 4401. Minor variances in wording will not take it out of the scope of the part. For example, the use of the language of the official text of the uniform act in the last paragraph of the text of the statutory form (protection of third party who receives a copy of the statutory form power of attorney and acts in reliance on it) instead of the language provided in Section 4401 does not take the form out of the scope of this part. See Section 4402(a). Nor does the omission of the provisions relating to designation of co-agents take the form out of the scope of this part. See Section 4402(a).

After the introductory phrase, the term "agent" is used throughout the uniform act in place of the longer and less familiar "attorney-in-fact." Special effort is made throughout the uniform act to make the language as informal as possible without impairing its effectiveness.

The statutory form contains a list of powers. The powers listed relate to various separate classes of activities, except the last, which includes all the others. Health care matters are not included. For a power of attorney form for health care, see Section 4701.

Space is provided in the statutory form for "Special Instructions." In this space, the principal can add specially drafted provisions limiting or extending the powers granted to the agent. (If the space provided is not sufficient, a reference can be made in this space to an attached sheet or sheets, and the special provisions can be included on the attached sheet or sheets.)

The statutory form contains only a limited list of powers. If it is desired to give the agent the broadest possible powers, language similar to the following can be added under the "Special Instructions" portion of the form:

In addition to all of the powers listed in lines (A) to (M) above, I grant to my agent full power and authority to act for me, in any way which I myself could act if I were personally present and able to act, with respect to all other matters and affairs not listed in lines (A) to (M) above, but this authority does not include authority to make health care decisions.

Neither the form in this section, nor the constructional provisions in Sections 4450–4465, attempt to allow the grant of the power to make a will or to give the agent extensive estate planning authority, although several of the powers, especially lines (G), (H), and (L) of the statutory form, may be useful in planning the disposition of an estate. An individually tailored power of attorney can be used if the principal wants to give the agent extensive estate planning authority, or additional estate planning powers can be granted to the agent by stating those additional powers in the space provided in the form for "Special Instructions." For example, provisions like the following might be included under the special instructions portion of the statutory form:

In addition to the powers listed in lines (A) to (M) above, the agent is empowered to do all of the following:

(1) Establish a trust with property of the principal for the benefit of the principal and the spouse and descendants of the principal, or any one or more of them, upon such terms as the agent determines are necessary or proper, and transfer any property in which the principal has an interest to the trust.

(2) Exercise in whole or in part, release, or let lapse any power the principal may have under any trust whether or not created by the principal, including any power of appointment, revocation, or withdrawal, but a trust created by the principal may only be modified or revoked by the agent as provided in the trust instrument.

(3) Make a gift, grant, or other transfer without consideration to or for the benefit of the spouse or descendants of the principal or a charitable organization, or more than one or all of them, either outright or in trust, including the forgiveness of indebtedness and the completion of any charitable pledges the principal may have made; consent to the splitting of gifts under Internal Revenue Code Section 2513, or successor sections, if the spouse of the principal makes gifts to any one or more of the descendants of the principal or to a charitable institution; pay any gift tax that may arise by reason of those gifts.

(4) Loan any of the property of the principal to the spouse or descendants of the principal, or their personal representatives or a

trustee for their benefit, the loan bearing such interest, and to be secured or unsecured, as the agent determines advisable.

(5) In general, and in addition to all the specific acts enumerated, do any other act which the principal can do through an agent for the welfare of the spouse, children, or dependents of the principal or for the preservation and maintenance of other personal relationships of the principal to parents, relatives, friends, and organizations.

It should be noted that a trust may not be modified or revoked by an agent under a statutory form power of attorney unless it is expressly permitted by the instrument granting the power and by the trust instrument. See Section 15401(b).

Section 4404 and the statutory form itself make the power of attorney a durable power of attorney, remaining in effect after the incapacity of the principal, unless the person executing the form strikes out the language in the form that makes the instrument a durable power of attorney. See also Section 4018 ("durable power of attorney" defined).

The last paragraph of the text of the statutory form protects a third party who receives a copy of the statutory form power of attorney and acts in reliance on it. See also Section 4034 ("third person" defined). The statement in the statutory form—that revocation of the power of attorney is not effective as to a third party until the third party has actual knowledge of the revocation—is consistent with Sections 4304 (good faith reliance on power of attorney without actual knowledge of death or incapacity of principal), 4305 (affidavit of lack of knowledge of termination of power). See also Sections 4300 (third persons required to respect agent's authority), 4301 (immunities of third person), 4303 (protection of person who acts in good faith reliance upon power of attorney where specified requirements are satisfied). The protection provided by these sections and other immunities that may protect persons who rely on a power of attorney (see Section 4303(b)) apply to a statutory form power of attorney. See Sections 4100 (application of division to statutory form power of attorney), 4407 (general provisions applicable to statutory form power of attorney).

The language of the last portion of the text of the statutory form set forth in Section 4401 substitutes the phrase "has actual knowledge of the revocation" for the phrase "learns of the revocation" which is used in the uniform act form. This substitution does not preclude use of a form including the uniform act language. See Section 4402(a) (third sentence).

Neither this section, nor the part as a whole, attempts to provide an exclusive method for creating a power of attorney. Other forms may be used and other law employed to create powers of attorney. See Section 4408. However, this part should be sufficient for most purposes.

For provisions relating to court enforcement of the duties of the agent, see Sections 4500–4545.

The form provided by Section 4401 supersedes the former statutory short form power of attorney under former Civil Code Sections 2450–2473 (repealed by 1990 Cal. Stat. ch. 986, § 1). But older forms consistent with former Civil Code Sections 2450–2473 are still effective. See Section 4409 & Comment.

See also Sections 4014 ("attorney-in-fact" defined to include agent), 4026 ("principal" defined), 4034 ("third person" defined). [29 Cal.L.Rev.Comm. Reports 1 (1999)].

Cross References

Attorney-in-fact defined for purposes of this Division, see Probate Code § 4014.
Power of attorney defined for purposes of this Division, see Probate Code § 4022.

§ 4402. Legal sufficiency of form; conditions

A statutory form power of attorney under this part is legally sufficient if all of the following requirements are satisfied:

(a) The wording of the form complies substantially with Section 4401. A form does not fail to comply substantially with Section 4401 merely because the form does not include the provisions of Section 4401 relating to designation of co-agents. A form does not fail to comply substantially with Section 4401 merely because the form uses the sentence "Revocation of the power of attorney is not effective as to a third party until the third party learns of the revocation" in place of the sentence "Revocation of the power of attorney is not effective as to a third party until the third party has actual knowledge of the revocation," in which case the form shall be interpreted as if it contained the sentence "Revocation of the power of attorney is not effective as to a third party until the third party has actual knowledge of the revocation."

(b) The form is properly completed.

(c) The signature of the principal is acknowledged. *(Added by Stats.1994, c. 307 (S.B.1907), § 16. Amended by Stats.1995, c. 300 (S.B.984), § 10, eff. Aug. 3, 1995.)*

Law Revision Commission Comments

1994 Addition

Section 4402 continues former Civil Code Section 2476 without change, except for the revision of cross-references to other provisions and the deletion of language made obsolete by 1993 legislation. See 1993 Cal. Stat. ch. 141, § 2. Section 4402 is the same in substance as Section 1(b) of the Uniform Statutory Form Power of Attorney Act (1988), with the addition of the second and third sentences of subdivision (a). See Section 2(b) (construction of provisions drawn from uniform acts). The added sentences make clear that use of a form that complies with the requirements of the official text of the uniform act satisfies the requirements of this section, even though the form used does not include the provisions included in Section 4401 for designation of co-agents and even though the form uses the language "learns of the revocation."

See also Sections 4014 ("attorney-in-fact" defined to include agent), 4026 ("principal" defined), 4034 ("third person" defined). [24 Cal.L.Rev.Comm.Reports 323 (1994)].

Cross References

Power of attorney defined for purposes of this Division, see Probate Code § 4022.
Principal defined for purposes of this Division, see Probate Code § 4026.

§ 4403. Initialed lines on form; limitation of powers

If the line in front of (N) of the statutory form under Section 4401 is initialed, an initial on the line in front of any other power does not limit the powers granted by line (N). *(Added by Stats.1994, c. 307 (S.B.1907), § 16.)*

Law Revision Commission Comments

1994 Addition

Section 4403 continues former Civil Code Section 2477 without change, except for the revision of a cross-reference to another provision. Section 4403 is the same in substance as Section 1(c) of the Uniform Statutory Form Power of Attorney Act (1988). See Section 2(b) (construction of provisions drawn from uniform acts). [24 Cal.L.Rev.Comm.Reports 323 (1994)].

§ 4404. Durable power of attorney; language showing principal's intent

A statutory form power of attorney legally sufficient under this part is durable to the extent that the power of attorney contains language, such as "This power of attorney will continue to be effective even though I become incapacitated," showing the intent of the principal that the power granted may be exercised notwithstanding later incapacity. *(Added by Stats.1994, c. 307 (S.B.1907), § 16.)*

Law Revision Commission Comments

1994 Addition

Section 4404 continues former Civil Code Section 2478 without substantive change. Section 4404 is the same in substance as Section 2 of the Uniform Statutory Form Power of Attorney Act (1988). See Section 2(b) (construction of provisions drawn from uniform acts). The phrase "to the extent that durable powers are permitted by other law of this State," found in the uniform act, has been omitted as unnecessary. Durable powers of attorney are specifically authorized by Section 4124. The words "incapacitated" and "incapacity" are used in Section 4404 for consistency with the form used in Section 4401 and with Section 4124 (California version of the Uniform Durable Power of Attorney Act).

A durable power of attorney under this part continues in effect when the principal becomes incapacitated. The form in Section 4401 includes a provision for continuance under those circumstances. That provision may be used or stricken at the discretion of the principal. The provision is consistent with Section 4124 (Uniform Durable Power of Attorney Act). See also Sections 4125 (effect of acts by agent during incapacity of principal), 4304 (good faith reliance upon power of attorney after death or incapacity of principal). As to the effect of appointment of a conservator of the estate, guardian of the estate, or other fiduciary charged with the management of the principal's property, see Section 4206.

See also Sections 4018 ("durable power of attorney" defined), 4026 ("principal" defined). [24 Cal.L.Rev.Comm.Reports 323 (1994)].

Cross References

Power of attorney defined for purposes of this Division, see Probate Code § 4022.

Principal defined for purposes of this Division, see Probate Code § 4026.

§ 4405. Power dependent on occurrence of event or contingency; determination that event has occurred; written declaration; liability

(a) A statutory form power of attorney under this part that limits the power to take effect upon the occurrence of a specified event or contingency, including, but not limited to, the incapacity of the principal, may contain a provision designating one or more persons who, by a written declaration under penalty of perjury, have the power to determine conclusively that the specified event or contingency has occurred.

(b) A statutory form power of attorney that contains the provision described in subdivision (a) becomes effective when the person or persons designated in the power of attorney execute a written declaration under penalty of perjury that the specified event or contingency has occurred, and any person may act in reliance on the written declaration without liability to the principal or to any other person, regardless whether the specified event or contingency has actually occurred.

(c) The provision described in subdivision (a) may be included in the "Special Instructions" portion of the form set forth in Section 4401.

(d) Subdivisions (a) and (b) do not provide the exclusive method by which a statutory form power of attorney under this part may be limited to take effect upon the occurrence of a specified event or contingency. *(Added by Stats.1994, c. 307 (S.B.1907), § 16.)*

Law Revision Commission Comments

1994 Addition [Revised Comment]

Section 4405 continues former Civil Code Section 2479 without substantive change. Section 4405 is not found in the Uniform Statutory Form Power of Attorney Act (1988). This section is drawn from Section 5–1602 of the New York General Obligations Law. A provision described in subdivision (a) protects a third person who relies on the declaration under penalty of perjury of the person or persons designated in the power of attorney that the specified event or contingency has occurred. The principal may designate the agent or another person, or several persons, to make this declaration.

Subdivision (d) makes clear that subdivisions (a) and (b) are not the exclusive method for creating a "springing power" (a power of attorney that goes into effect upon the occurrence of a specified event or contingency). The principal is free to set forth in a power of attorney under this part any provision the principal desires to provide for the method of determining whether the specified event or contingency has occurred. For example, the principal may provide that his or her "incapacity" be determined by a court under Part 4 (commencing with Section 4500). See Section 4541(a). If the power of attorney provides only that it shall become effective "upon the incapacity of the principal," the determination whether the power of attorney is in effect also may be made under Part 4 (commencing with Section 4500).

See also Sections 4026 ("principal" defined), 4030 ("springing power of attorney" defined). [29 Cal.L.Rev.Comm. Reports 1 (1999)].

Cross References

Power of attorney defined for purposes of this Division, see Probate Code § 4022.

Principal defined for purposes of this Division, see Probate Code § 4026.

§ 4406. Third person's refusal to honor agent's authority under power of attorney; action to compel honor; remedies

(a) If a third person to whom a properly executed statutory form power of attorney under this part is presented refuses to honor the agent's authority under the power of attorney within a reasonable time, the third person may be compelled to honor the agent's authority under the power of attorney in an action brought against the third person for this purpose, except that the third person may not be compelled to honor the agent's authority if the principal could not compel the third person to act in the same circumstances.

(b) If an action is brought under this section, the court shall award attorney's fees to the agent if the court finds that the third person acted unreasonably in refusing to accept the agent's authority under the statutory form power of attorney.

(c) For the purpose of subdivision (b), and without limiting any other grounds that may constitute a reasonable refusal to accept an agent's authority under a statutory form power of attorney, a third person shall not be deemed to have acted unreasonably in refusing to accept an agent's authority if the refusal is authorized or required by state or federal statute or regulation.

(d) Notwithstanding subdivision (c), a third person's refusal to accept an agent's authority under a statutory form power of attorney under this part shall be deemed unreasonable if the only reason for the refusal is that the power of attorney is not on a form prescribed by the third person to whom the power of attorney is presented.

(e) The remedy provided in this section is cumulative and nonexclusive. *(Added by Stats.1994, c. 307 (S.B.1907), § 16.)*

Law Revision Commission Comments

1994 Addition

Section 4406 continues former Civil Code Section 2480.5 without substantive change. Section 4406 is not found in the Uniform Statutory Form Power of Attorney Act (1988). Subdivisions (a) and (b) are drawn in part from Section 13105(b) (compelling payment or delivery under affidavit procedure for collection or transfer of personal property of small estate). See also Section 4305 (affidavit of lack of knowledge of termination of power of attorney).

Subdivision (a) permits an agent to bring an action to compel a third person to honor a statutory form power of attorney only to the extent that the principal, disregarding any legal disability, could bring an action to compel the third person to act. Under this rule, a third person who could not be forced to do business with the principal consequently may not be forced to deal with the agent. However, a third person who holds property of the principal, who owes a debt to the principal, or who is obligated by contract to the principal may be compelled to accept the agent's authority. This rule has also been generalized in Section 4300.

In addition, as provided in subdivision (b), if the refusal to deal with the agent is found to be unreasonable, the third person will also be liable for attorney's fees incurred in the action to compel compliance. The determination of reasonableness depends on the particular circumstances of each case. A person to whom the power of attorney is presented may, for example, act reasonably in refusing to accept the agent's authority where it is not clear that the power of attorney grants the agent authority with respect to the particular transaction. Likewise, a third person may reasonably refuse to honor the power of attorney if, for example, the person is not reasonably satisfied as to the identity of the agent or has information that would lead a reasonable person to question the validity of the power of attorney. See also Section 4303 (protection of person relying in good faith).

Subdivision (c) provides some specific guidelines as to the meaning of the reasonableness rule in subdivision (b) as it relates to the liability for attorney's fees. However, subdivision (d) makes clear that an institution's preference for its own power of attorney form is never a reasonable ground for refusing to accept the authority of an agent under a properly executed and effective statutory form power of attorney.

See also Sections 4014 ("attorney-in-fact" defined to include agent), 4026 ("principal" defined), 4034 ("third person" defined). [24 Cal.L.Rev.Comm.Reports 323 (1994)].

Cross References

Power of attorney defined for purposes of this Division, see Probate Code § 4022.
Principal defined for purposes of this Division, see Probate Code § 4026.
Third person defined for purposes of this Division, see Probate Code § 4034.

§ 4407. Application of division to statutory form power of attorney; conflicting provisions

The provisions of this division apply to a statutory form power of attorney except when there is a conflicting provision in this part, in which case the provision of this part governs, or when a provision of this division is expressly made inapplicable to a statutory form power of attorney. *(Added by Stats.1994, c. 307 (S.B.1907), § 16. Amended by Stats. 2011, c. 113 (A.B.1082), § 4.)*

Law Revision Commission Comments

1994 Addition [Revised Comment]

Section 4407 restates the substance of former Civil Code Section 2480. Section 4407 makes clear that the general provisions that apply to powers of attorney generally apply to statutory form powers of attorney under this part. Thus, for example, the following provisions apply to a power of attorney under this part:

Section 4123(b) (application of power of attorney to all or part of principal's property; unnecessary to describe items or parcels of property).

Section 4124 (requirements for durable power of attorney). The statutory form set forth in Section 4401 satisfies the requirements for creation of a durable power of attorney, unless the provision making the power of attorney durable is struck out on the form.

Section 4125 (effect of acts by attorney-in-fact during incapacity of principal).

Section 4206 (relation of attorney-in-fact to court-appointed fiduciary).

Section 4303 (protection of person relying in good faith on power of attorney).

Section 4304 (good faith reliance on power of attorney after death or incapacity of principal).

Section 4306 (good faith reliance on attorney-in-fact's affidavit as conclusive proof of the nonrevocation or nontermination of the power).

Sections 4500–4545 (judicial proceedings). [29 Cal.L.Rev.Comm. Reports 1 (1999)].

Cross References

Power of attorney defined for purposes of this Division, see Probate Code § 4022.

§ 4408. Other forms; application of this part

Nothing in this part affects or limits the use of any other form for a power of attorney. A form that complies with the requirements of any law other than the provisions of this part may be used instead of the form set forth in Section 4401, and none of the provisions of this part apply if the other form is used. *(Added by Stats.1994, c. 307 (S.B.1907), § 16.)*

Law Revision Commission Comments

1994 Addition

Section 4408 continues former Civil Code Section 2481 without substantive change. See also Section 4022 ("power of attorney" defined). [24 Cal.L.Rev.Comm.Reports 323 (1994)].

Cross References

Power of attorney defined for purposes of this Division, see Probate Code § 4022.

§ 4409. Statutory short form powers of attorney executed under prior law; validity

(a) A statutory short form power of attorney executed before, on, or after the repeal of Chapter 3 (commencing with Section 2450) of Title 9 of Part 4 of Division 3 of the Civil Code by Chapter 986 of the Statutes of 1990, using a form that complied with former Section 2450 of the Civil Code, as originally enacted by Chapter 602 of the Statutes of

1984, or as amended by Chapter 403 of the Statutes of 1985, is as valid as if Chapter 3 (commencing with Section 2450) of Title 9 of Part 4 of Division 3 of the Civil Code had not been repealed by, and former Section 2511 of the Civil Code amended by, Chapter 986 of the Statutes of 1990.

(b) A statutory form power of attorney executed before, on, or after the repeal of Chapter 3.5 (commencing with Section 2475) of Title 9 of Part 4 of Division 3 of the Civil Code by the act that enacted this section, using a form that complied with the repealed chapter of the Civil Code is as valid as if that chapter had not been repealed. *(Added by Stats.1994, c. 307 (S.B.1907), § 16. Amended by Stats.1995, c. 300 (S.B.984), § 11, eff. Aug. 3, 1995.)*

Law Revision Commission Comments
1994 Addition

Subdivision (a) of Section 4409 restates former Civil Code Section 2450 without substantive change. The "statutory short form power of attorney" provided by former Civil Code Section 2450 was superseded by the Uniform Statutory Form Power of Attorney. See Sections 4400–4465 (continuing former Civ. Code §§ 2475–2499.5). This section permits use of the earlier forms after January 1, 1991, when the "statutory short form" was repealed. This avoids the need to discard existing printed forms and protects the unwary person who uses a printed form prepared pursuant to the former provisions. However, the new form provided by Sections 4400–4465 (and former Civ. Code §§ 2475–2499.5) should soon replace the older forms. [24 Cal.L.Rev.Comm.Reports 323 (1994)].

Cross References

Power of attorney defined for purposes of this Division, see Probate Code § 4022.

CHAPTER 2. CONSTRUCTION OF POWERS

Section
4450.   Subjects covered by statutory form power of attorney; general powers.
4451.   Real property transactions; powers granted.
4452.   Tangible personal property transactions; powers granted.
4453.   Stock and bond transactions; powers granted.
4454.   Commodity and option transactions; powers granted.
4455.   Banking and other financial institution transactions; powers granted.
4456.   Business operating transactions; powers granted.
4457.   Insurance and annuity transactions; powers granted.
4458.   Estate, trust and other beneficiary transactions; powers granted.
4459.   Claims and litigation; powers granted.
4460.   Personal and family maintenance; powers granted.
4461.   Social security or other governmental program; civil or military benefit; powers granted.
4462.   Retirement plan transactions; powers granted.
4463.   Tax matters; powers granted.
4464.   After-acquired property; state where property is located or where power is executed.
4465.   Empowerment of agent to take actions specified in Section 4264.

Law Revision Commission Comments
1994 Addition

This chapter (commencing with Section 4450) explains the powers listed in the statutory form in Section 4401. Section 4450 provides general powers that apply to all of the defined classes of authority listed in lines (A) through (M) of the statutory form, subject to any conditions set by the principal.

The language in Sections 4451–4463 makes explicit reference to authority that would be appropriate for each class of transaction. The language in those sections identifies activities that are typical responsibilities for the particular class of transaction.

Any of Sections 4451–4463, together with the general authority in Section 4450, gives the agent complete power for the class of transactions. The recitation of particular powers in each section explains the scope of the individual section and assures the user of this part and the form provided by this part that the matters that are the user's particular concern are covered by the part. As to use of a power executed outside this state, after-acquired property, use of the power with respect to property located outside this state, and exercise of the power outside this state, see Section 4464.

A general effect of this chapter is that the agent can exercise authority subject to the same conditions and limitations as the principal. In a few instances the limiting conditions are made explicit. For example, in Section 4456 it is stated that partnership powers are subject to the terms of the partnership agreement. But all authority is subject to conditions of fact and law that exist outside the part. For example, a collection agency could not escape regulation by acting under this power of attorney. See also Section 15401 (modifying or revoking trust).

Provisions of this chapter grant the agent authority to enforce rights of the principal "by litigation or otherwise" or to initiate litigation or to bring an action. These grants of authority do not affect the requirement of Code of Civil Procedure Section 367 that an action be prosecuted in the name of the real party in interest. [24 Cal.L.Rev.Comm.Reports 323 (1994)].

§ 4450. Subjects covered by statutory form power of attorney; general powers

By executing a statutory form power of attorney with respect to a subject listed in Section 4401, the principal, except as limited or extended by the principal in the power of attorney, empowers the agent, for that subject, to do all of the following:

(a) Demand, receive, and obtain by litigation or otherwise, money or other thing of value to which the principal is, may become, or claims to be entitled, and conserve, invest, disburse, or use anything so received for the purposes intended.

(b) Contract in any manner with any person, on terms agreeable to the agent, to accomplish a purpose of a transaction, and perform, rescind, reform, release, or modify the contract or another contract made by or on behalf of the principal.

(c) Execute, acknowledge, seal, and deliver a deed, revocation, mortgage, lease, notice, check, release, or other instrument the agent considers desirable to accomplish a purpose of a transaction.

(d) Prosecute, defend, submit to arbitration, settle, and propose or accept a compromise with respect to, a claim existing in favor of or against the principal or intervene in litigation relating to the claim.

(e) Seek on the principal's behalf the assistance of a court to carry out an act authorized by the power of attorney.

(f) Engage, compensate, and discharge an attorney, accountant, expert witness, or other assistant.

(g) Keep appropriate records of each transaction, including an accounting of receipts and disbursements.

(h) Prepare, execute, and file a record, report, or other document the agent considers desirable to safeguard or promote the principal's interest under a statute or governmental regulation.

(i) Reimburse the agent for expenditures properly made by the agent in exercising the powers granted by the power of attorney.

(j) In general, do any other lawful act with respect to the subject. *(Added by Stats.1994, c. 307 (S.B.1907), § 16.)*

Law Revision Commission Comments
1994 Addition [Revised Comment]

Section 4450 continues former Civil Code Section 2485 without change, except for the revision of a cross-reference to another provision. Section 4450 is the same in substance as Section 3 of the Uniform Statutory Form Power of Attorney Act (1988). See Section 2(b) (construction of provisions drawn from uniform acts). See the Comment to this chapter under the chapter heading. See also Sections 4500–4545 (court enforcement of agent's duties).

See also Sections 4014 ("attorney-in-fact" defined to include agent), 4022 ("power of attorney" defined), 4026 ("principal" defined). [29 Cal.L.Rev.Comm. Reports 1 (1999)].

Cross References

Power of attorney defined for purposes of this Division, see Probate Code § 4022.
Principal defined for purposes of this Division, see Probate Code § 4026.

§ 4451. Real property transactions; powers granted

In a statutory form power of attorney, the language granting power with respect to real property transactions empowers the agent to do all of the following:

(a) Accept as a gift or as security for a loan, reject, demand, buy, lease, receive, or otherwise acquire, an interest in real property or a right incident to real property.

(b) Sell, exchange, convey with or without covenants, quitclaim, release, surrender, mortgage, encumber, partition, consent to partitioning, subdivide, apply for zoning, rezoning, or other governmental permits, plat or consent to platting, develop, grant options concerning, lease, sublease, or otherwise dispose of, an interest in real property or a right incident to real property.

(c) Release, assign, satisfy, and enforce by litigation or otherwise, a mortgage, deed of trust, encumbrance, lien, or other claim to real property which exists or is asserted.

(d) Do any act of management or of conservation with respect to an interest in real property, or a right incident to real property, owned, or claimed to be owned, by the principal, including all of the following:

(1) Insuring against a casualty, liability, or loss.

(2) Obtaining or regaining possession, or protecting the interest or right, by litigation or otherwise.

(3) Paying, compromising, or contesting taxes or assessments, or applying for and receiving refunds in connection with them.

(4) Purchasing supplies, hiring assistance or labor, and making repairs or alterations in the real property.

(e) Use, develop, alter, replace, remove, erect, or install structures or other improvements upon real property in or incident to which the principal has, or claims to have, an interest or right.

(f) Participate in a reorganization with respect to real property or a legal entity that owns an interest in or right incident to real property and receive and hold shares of stock or obligations received in a plan of reorganization, and act with respect to them, including all of the following:

(1) Selling or otherwise disposing of them.

(2) Exercising or selling an option, conversion, or similar right with respect to them.

(3) Voting them in person or by proxy.

(g) Change the form of title of an interest in or right incident to real property.

(h) Dedicate to public use, with or without consideration, easements or other real property in which the principal has, or claims to have, an interest or right. *(Added by Stats.1994, c. 307 (S.B.1907), § 16.)*

Law Revision Commission Comments
1994 Addition

Section 4451 continues former Civil Code Section 2486 without change. Section 4451 is the same in substance as Section 4 of the Uniform Statutory Form Power of Attorney Act (1988). See Section 2(b) (construction of provisions drawn from uniform acts). See the Comment to this chapter under the chapter heading. See also Section 4450 (construction of powers generally).

See also Sections 4014 ("attorney-in-fact" defined to include agent), 4026 ("principal" defined). [24 Cal.L.Rev.Comm.Reports 323 (1994)].

Cross References

Power of attorney defined for purposes of this Division, see Probate Code § 4022.
Principal defined for purposes of this Division, see Probate Code § 4026.

§ 4452. Tangible personal property transactions; powers granted

In a statutory form power of attorney, the language granting power with respect to tangible personal property transactions empowers the agent to do all of the following:

(a) Accept as a gift or as security for a loan, reject, demand, buy, receive, or otherwise acquire ownership or possession of tangible personal property or an interest in tangible personal property.

(b) Sell, exchange, convey with or without covenants, release, surrender, mortgage, encumber, pledge, hypothecate, create a security interest in, pawn, grant options concerning, lease, sublease to others, or otherwise dispose of tangible personal property or an interest in tangible personal property.

(c) Release, assign, satisfy, or enforce by litigation or otherwise, a mortgage, security interest, encumbrance, lien, or other claim on behalf of the principal, with respect to tangible personal property or an interest in tangible personal property.

(d) Do an act of management or conservation with respect to tangible personal property or an interest in tangible personal property on behalf of the principal, including all of the following:

(1) Insuring against casualty, liability, or loss.

(2) Obtaining or regaining possession, or protecting the property or interest, by litigation or otherwise.

(3) Paying, compromising, or contesting taxes or assessments or applying for and receiving refunds in connection with taxes or assessments.

(4) Moving from place to place.

(5) Storing for hire or on a gratuitous bailment.

(6) Using, altering, and making repairs or alterations. *(Added by Stats.1994, c. 307 (S.B.1907), § 16.)*

Law Revision Commission Comments

1994 Addition

Section 4452 continues former Civil Code Section 2487 without change. Section 4452 is the same in substance as Section 5 of the Uniform Statutory Form Power of Attorney Act (1988). See Section 2(b) (construction of provisions drawn from uniform acts). See the Comment to this chapter under the chapter heading. See also Section 4450 (construction of powers generally).

See also Sections 4014 ("attorney-in-fact" defined to include agent), 4026 ("principal" defined). [24 Cal.L.Rev.Comm.Reports 323 (1994)].

Cross References

Power of attorney defined for purposes of this Division, see Probate Code § 4022.
Principal defined for purposes of this Division, see Probate Code § 4026.

§ 4453. Stock and bond transactions; powers granted

In a statutory form power of attorney, the language granting power with respect to stock and bond transactions empowers the agent to do all of the following:

(a) Buy, sell, and exchange stocks, bonds, mutual funds, and all other types of securities and financial instruments except commodity futures contracts and call and put options on stocks and stock indexes.

(b) Receive certificates and other evidences of ownership with respect to securities.

(c) Exercise voting rights with respect to securities in person or by proxy, enter into voting trusts, and consent to limitations on the right to vote. *(Added by Stats.1994, c. 307 (S.B.1907), § 16.)*

Law Revision Commission Comments

1994 Addition

Section 4453 continues former Civil Code Section 2488 without change. Section 4453 is the same in substance as Section 6 of the Uniform Statutory Form Power of Attorney Act (1988). See Section 2(b) (construction of provisions drawn from uniform acts). See the Comment to this chapter under the chapter heading. See also Sections 4050(b)(3) (proxies given by agent to exercise voting rights), 4450 (construction of powers generally).

See also Section 4014 ("attorney-in-fact" defined to include agent). [24 Cal.L.Rev.Comm.Reports 323 (1994)].

Cross References

Power of attorney defined for purposes of this Division, see Probate Code § 4022.

§ 4454. Commodity and option transactions; powers granted

In a statutory form power of attorney, the language granting power with respect to commodity and option transactions empowers the agent to do all of the following:

(a) Buy, sell, exchange, assign, settle, and exercise commodity futures contracts and call and put options on stocks and stock indexes traded on a regulated option exchange.

(b) Establish, continue, modify, and terminate option accounts with a broker. *(Added by Stats.1994, c. 307 (S.B. 1907), § 16.)*

Law Revision Commission Comments

1994 Addition

Section 4454 continues former Civil Code Section 2489 without change. Section 4454 is the same in substance as Section 7 of the Uniform Statutory Form Power of Attorney Act (1988). See Section 2(b) (construction of provisions drawn from uniform acts). See the Comment to this chapter under the chapter heading. See also Section 4450 (construction of powers generally).

See also Sections 4014 ("attorney-in-fact" defined to include agent). [24 Cal.L.Rev.Comm.Reports 323 (1994)].

Cross References

Power of attorney defined for purposes of this Division, see Probate Code § 4022.

§ 4455. Banking and other financial institution transactions; powers granted

In a statutory form power of attorney, the language granting power with respect to banking and other financial institution transactions empowers the agent to do all of the following:

(a) Continue, modify, and terminate an account or other banking arrangement made by or on behalf of the principal.

(b) Establish, modify, and terminate an account or other banking arrangement with a bank, trust company, savings and loan association, credit union, thrift company, industrial loan company, brokerage firm, or other financial institution selected by the agent.

(c) Hire or close a safe deposit box or space in a vault.

(d) Contract to procure other services available from a financial institution as the agent considers desirable.

(e) Withdraw by check, order, or otherwise money or property of the principal deposited with or left in the custody of a financial institution.

(f) Receive bank statements, vouchers, notices, and similar documents from a financial institution and act with respect to them.

(g) Enter a safe deposit box or vault and withdraw or add to the contents.

(h) Borrow money at an interest rate agreeable to the agent and pledge as security personal property of the principal necessary in order to borrow, pay, renew, or extend the time of payment of a debt of the principal.

(i) Make, assign, draw, endorse, discount, guarantee, and negotiate promissory notes, checks, drafts, and other negotiable or nonnegotiable paper of the principal, or payable to the principal or the principal's order, receive the cash or other proceeds of those transactions, and accept a draft drawn by a person upon the principal and pay it when due.

(j) Receive for the principal and act upon a sight draft, warehouse receipt, or other negotiable or nonnegotiable instrument.

(k) Apply for and receive letters of credit, credit cards, and traveler's checks from a financial institution, and give an indemnity or other agreement in connection with letters of credit.

(*l*) Consent to an extension of the time of payment with respect to commercial paper or a financial transaction with a financial institution. *(Added by Stats.1994, c. 307 (S.B.1907), § 16.)*

Law Revision Commission Comments
1994 Addition

Section 4455 continues former Civil Code Section 2490 without change. Section 4455 is the same in substance as Section 8 of the Uniform Statutory Form Power of Attorney Act (1988). See Section 2(b) (construction of provisions drawn from uniform acts). See the Comment to this chapter under the chapter heading. See also Section 4450 (construction of powers generally).

See also Sections 4014 ("attorney-in-fact" defined to include agent), 4026 ("principal" defined). [24 Cal.L.Rev.Comm.Reports 323 (1994)].

Cross References

Power of attorney defined for purposes of this Division, see Probate Code § 4022.
Principal defined for purposes of this Division, see Probate Code § 4026.

§ 4456. Business operating transactions; powers granted

In a statutory form power of attorney, the language granting power with respect to business operating transactions empowers the agent to do all of the following:

(a) Operate, buy, sell, enlarge, reduce, and terminate a business interest.

(b) To the extent that an agent is permitted by law to act for a principal and subject to the terms of the partnership agreement:

(1) Perform a duty or discharge a liability and exercise a right, power, privilege, or option that the principal has, may have, or claims to have, under a partnership agreement, whether or not the principal is a partner.

(2) Enforce the terms of a partnership agreement by litigation or otherwise.

(3) Defend, submit to arbitration, settle, or compromise litigation to which the principal is a party because of membership in the partnership.

(c) Exercise in person or by proxy, or enforce by litigation or otherwise, a right, power, privilege, or option the principal has or claims to have as the holder of a bond, share, or other instrument of similar character, and defend, submit to arbitration, settle, or compromise litigation to which the principal is a party because of a bond, share, or similar instrument.

(d) With respect to a business owned solely by the principal:

(1) Continue, modify, renegotiate, extend, and terminate a contract made with an individual or a legal entity, firm, association, or corporation by or on behalf of the principal with respect to the business before execution of the power of attorney.

(2) Determine the policy of the business as to (A) the location of its operation, (B) the nature and extent of its business, (C) the methods of manufacturing, selling, merchandising, financing, accounting, and advertising employed in its operation, (D) the amount and types of insurance carried, and (E) the mode of engaging, compensating, and dealing with its accountants, attorneys, and other agents and employees.

(3) Change the name or form of organization under which the business is operated and enter into a partnership agreement with other persons or organize a corporation to take over all or part of the operation of the business.

(4) Demand and receive money due or claimed by the principal or on the principal's behalf in the operation of the business, and control and disburse the money in the operation of the business.

(e) Put additional capital into a business in which the principal has an interest.

(f) Join in a plan of reorganization, consolidation, or merger of the business.

(g) Sell or liquidate a business or part of it at the time and upon the terms the agent considers desirable.

(h) Represent the principal in establishing the value of a business under a buy-out agreement to which the principal is a party.

(i) Prepare, sign, file, and deliver reports, compilations of information, returns, or other papers with respect to a business which are required by a governmental agency or instrumentality or which the agent considers desirable, and make related payments.

(j) Pay, compromise, or contest taxes or assessments and do any other act which the agent considers desirable to protect the principal from illegal or unnecessary taxation, fines, penalties, or assessments with respect to a business, including attempts to recover, in any manner permitted by law, money paid before or after the execution of the power of attorney. *(Added by Stats.1994, c. 307 (S.B.1907), § 16.)*

Law Revision Commission Comments
1994 Addition

Section 4456 continues former Civil Code Section 2491 without change. Section 4456 is the same in substance as Section 9 of the Uniform Statutory Form Power of Attorney Act (1988). See Section 2(b) (construction of provisions drawn from uniform acts). See the Comment to this chapter under the chapter heading. See also Section 4450 (construction of powers generally).

See also Sections 4014 ("attorney-in-fact" defined to include agent), 4026 ("principal" defined). [24 Cal.L.Rev.Comm.Reports 323 (1994)].

Power of attorney defined for purposes of this Division, see Probate Code § 4022.

Principal defined for purposes of this Division, see Probate Code § 4026.

§ 4457. Insurance and annuity transactions; powers granted

In a statutory form power of attorney, the language granting power with respect to insurance and annuity transactions empowers the agent to do all of the following:

(a) Continue, pay the premium or assessment on, modify, rescind, release, or terminate a contract procured by or on behalf of the principal that insures or provides an annuity to either the principal or another person, whether or not the principal is a beneficiary under the contract.

(b) Procure new, different, and additional contracts of insurance and annuities for the principal and the principal's spouse, children, and other dependents, and select the amount, type of insurance or annuity, and mode of payment.

(c) Pay the premium or assessment on, modify, rescind, release, or terminate a contract of insurance or annuity procured by the agent.

(d) Apply for and receive a loan on the security of the contract of insurance or annuity.

(e) Surrender and receive the cash surrender value.

(f) Exercise an election.

(g) Change the manner of paying premiums.

(h) Change or convert the type of insurance contract or annuity as to any insurance contract or annuity with respect to which the principal has or claims to have a power described in this section.

(i) Apply for and procure government aid to guarantee or pay premiums of a contract of insurance on the life of the principal.

(j) Collect, sell, assign, hypothecate, borrow upon, or pledge the interest of the principal in a contract of insurance or annuity.

(k) Pay from proceeds or otherwise, compromise or contest, and apply for refunds in connection with, a tax or assessment levied by a taxing authority with respect to a contract of insurance or annuity or its proceeds or liability accruing by reason of the tax or assessment. *(Added by Stats.1994, c. 307 (S.B.1907), § 16. Amended by Stats.2011, c. 113 (A.B.1082), § 5.)*

Law Revision Commission Comments

1994 Addition

Section 4457 continues former Civil Code Section 2492 without change. Section 4457 is the same in substance as Section 10 of the Uniform Statutory Form Power of Attorney Act (1988). See Section 2(b) (construction of provisions drawn from uniform acts). See the Comment to this chapter under the chapter heading. See also Section 4450 (construction of powers generally). Section 4457 covers, but is not limited to, life, accident, health, disability, or liability insurance and fire, marine, burglary, compensation, disability, liability, hurricane, earthquake, and casualty insurance.

See also Sections 4014 ("attorney-in-fact" defined to include agent), 4026 ("principal" defined). [24 Cal.L.Rev.Comm.Reports 323 (1994)].

Power of attorney defined for purposes of this Division, see Probate Code § 4022.

Principal defined for purposes of this Division, see Probate Code § 4026.

§ 4458. Estate, trust and other beneficiary transactions; powers granted

In a statutory form power of attorney, the language granting power with respect to estate, trust, and other beneficiary transactions, empowers the agent to act for the principal in all matters that affect a trust, probate estate, guardianship, conservatorship, escrow, custodianship, or other fund from which the principal is, may become, or claims to be entitled, as a beneficiary, to a share or payment, including the power to do all of the following:

(a) Accept, receive, receipt for, sell, assign, pledge, or exchange, a share in, or payment from, the fund.

(b) Demand or obtain by litigation or otherwise money or other thing of value to which the principal is, may become, or claims to be entitled by reason of the fund.

(c) Initiate, participate in, and oppose litigation to ascertain the meaning, validity, or effect of a deed, will, declaration of trust, or other instrument or transaction affecting the interest of the principal.

(d) Initiate, participate in, and oppose litigation to remove, substitute, or surcharge a fiduciary.

(e) Conserve, invest, disburse, and use anything received for an authorized purpose.

(f) Transfer an interest of the principal in real property, stocks, bonds, accounts with financial institutions, insurance, and other property, to the trustee of a revocable trust created by the principal as settlor.

(g) Disclaim a detrimental transfer to the principal with the approval of the court. *(Added by Stats.1994, c. 307 (S.B.1907), § 16. Amended by Stats.2011, c. 113 (A.B.1082), § 6.)*

Law Revision Commission Comments

1994 Addition

Section 4458 continues former Civil Code Section 2493 without change. Section 4458 is the same in substance as Section 11 of the Uniform Statutory Form Power of Attorney Act (1988). See Section 2(b) (construction of provisions drawn from uniform acts). See the Comment to this chapter under the chapter heading. See also Section 4450 (construction of powers generally).

See also Sections 82 ("trust" defined), 4014 ("attorney-in-fact" defined to include agent), 4026 ("principal" defined). [24 Cal.L.Rev.Comm.Reports 323 (1994)].

Power of attorney defined for purposes of this Division, see Probate Code § 4022.

Principal defined for purposes of this Division, see Probate Code § 4026.

§ 4459.   Claims and litigation; powers granted

In a statutory form power of attorney, the language with respect to claims and litigation empowers the agent to do all of the following:

(a) Assert and prosecute before a court or administrative agency a claim, claim for relief, cause of action, counterclaim, cross-complaint, or offset, and defend against an individual, a legal entity, or government, including suits to recover property or other thing of value, to recover damages sustained by the principal, to eliminate or modify tax liability, or to seek an injunction, specific performance, or other relief.

(b) Bring an action to determine adverse claims, intervene in litigation, and act as amicus curiae.

(c) In connection with litigation:

(1) Procure an attachment, garnishment, libel, order of arrest, or other preliminary, provisional, or intermediate relief and use any available procedure to effect, enforce, or satisfy a judgment, order, or decree.

(2) Perform any lawful act, including acceptance of tender, offer of judgment, admission of facts, submission of a controversy on an agreed statement of facts, consent to examination before trial, and binding the principal in litigation.

(d) Submit to arbitration, settle, and propose or accept a compromise with respect to a claim or litigation.

(e) Waive the issuance and service of process upon the principal, accept service of process, appear for the principal, designate persons upon whom process directed to the principal may be served, execute and file or deliver stipulations on the principal's behalf, verify pleadings, seek appellate review, procure and give surety and indemnity bonds, contract and pay for the preparation and printing of records and briefs, receive and execute and file or deliver a consent, waiver, release, confession of judgment, satisfaction of judgment, notice, agreement, or other instrument in connection with the prosecution, settlement, or defense of a claim or litigation.

(f) Act for the principal with respect to bankruptcy or insolvency proceedings, whether voluntary or involuntary, concerning the principal or some other person, or with respect to a reorganization proceeding, or with respect to an assignment for the benefit of creditors, receivership, or application for the appointment of a receiver or trustee which affects an interest of the principal in property or other thing of value.

(g) Pay a judgment against the principal or a settlement made in connection with litigation and receive and conserve money or other thing of value paid in settlement of or as proceeds of a claim or litigation. *(Added by Stats.1994, c. 307 (S.B.1907), § 16.)*

Law Revision Commission Comments

1994 Addition

Section 4459 continues former Civil Code Section 2494 without change. Section 4459 is the same in substance as Section 12 of the Uniform Statutory Form Power of Attorney Act (1988). See Section 2(b) (construction of provisions drawn from uniform acts). Subdivi-

sion (f) is clarified by adding a reference to an assignment for the benefit of creditors. See the Comment to this chapter under the chapter heading. See also Section 4450 (construction of powers generally).

See also Sections 4014 ("attorney-in-fact" defined to include agent), 4026 ("principal" defined). [24 Cal.L.Rev.Comm.Reports 323 (1994)].

Cross References

Power of attorney defined for purposes of this Division, see Probate Code § 4022.
Principal defined for purposes of this Division, see Probate Code § 4026.

§ 4460.   Personal and family maintenance; powers granted

(a) In a statutory form power of attorney, the language granting power with respect to personal and family maintenance empowers the agent to do all of the following:

(1) Do the acts necessary to maintain the customary standard of living of the principal, the principal's spouse, children, and other individuals customarily or legally entitled to be supported by the principal, including providing living quarters by purchase, lease, or other contract, or paying the operating costs, including interest, amortization payments, repairs, and taxes on premises owned by the principal and occupied by those individuals.

(2) Provide for the individuals described in paragraph (1) all of the following:

(A) Normal domestic help.

(B) Usual vacations and travel expenses.

(C) Funds for shelter, clothing, food, appropriate education, and other current living costs.

(3) Pay for the individuals described in paragraph (1) necessary medical, dental, and surgical care, hospitalization, and custodial care.

(4) Continue any provision made by the principal, for the individuals described in paragraph (1), for automobiles or other means of transportation, including registering, licensing, insuring, and replacing them.

(5) Maintain or open charge accounts for the convenience of the individuals described in paragraph (1) and open new accounts the agent considers desirable to accomplish a lawful purpose.

(6) Continue payments incidental to the membership or affiliation of the principal in a church, club, society, order, or other organization and continue contributions to those organizations.

(b) The authority of an agent with respect to personal and family maintenance under this section is not dependent on any other grant of authority to the agent to make gifts on the principal's behalf and is not limited by any limitation that otherwise applies to the authority of the agent to make gifts on the principal's behalf. *(Added by Stats.1994, c. 307 (S.B.1907), § 16. Amended by Stats.2011, c. 113 (A.B.1082), § 7.)*

Law Revision Commission Comments

1994 Addition

Section 4460 continues former Civil Code Section 2495 without change. Section 4460 is the same in substance as Section 13 of the

Uniform Statutory Form Power of Attorney Act (1988). See Section 2(b) (construction of provisions drawn from uniform acts). See the Comment to this chapter under the chapter heading. See also Section 4450 (construction of powers generally).

See also Sections 4014 ("attorney-in-fact" defined to include agent), 4026 ("principal" defined). [24 Cal.L.Rev.Comm.Reports 323 (1994)].

Cross References

Power of attorney defined for purposes of this Division, see Probate Code § 4022.
Principal defined for purposes of this Division, see Probate Code § 4026.

§ 4461. Social security or other governmental program; civil or military benefit; powers granted

In a statutory form power of attorney, the language granting power with respect to benefits from social security, Medicare, Medicaid, or other governmental programs, or civil or military service, empowers the agent to do all of the following:

(a) Execute vouchers in the name of the principal for allowances and reimbursements payable by the United States or a foreign government or by a state or subdivision of a state to the principal, including allowances and reimbursements for transportation of the individuals described in paragraph (1) of subdivision (a) of Section 4460, and for shipment of their household effects.

(b) Take possession and order the removal and shipment of property of the principal from a post, warehouse, depot, dock, or other place of storage or safekeeping, either governmental or private, and execute and deliver a release, voucher, receipt, bill of lading, shipping ticket, certificate, or other instrument for that purpose.

(c) Prepare, file, and prosecute a claim of the principal to a benefit or assistance, financial or otherwise, to which the principal claims to be entitled, under a statute or governmental regulation.

(d) Prosecute, defend, submit to arbitration, settle, and propose or accept a compromise with respect to any benefits the principal may be entitled to receive.

(e) Receive the financial proceeds of a claim of the type described in this section, conserve, invest, disburse, or use anything received for a lawful purpose. *(Added by Stats.1994, c. 307 (S.B.1907), § 16. Amended by Stats.2011, c. 113 (A.B.1082), § 8; Stats.2012, c. 162 (S.B.1171), § 138.)*

Law Revision Commission Comments

1994 Addition

Section 4461 continues former Civil Code Section 2496 without change, except for the revision of a cross-reference to another provision. Section 4461 is the same in substance as Section 14 of the Uniform Statutory Form Power of Attorney Act (1988). See Section 2(b) (construction of provisions drawn from uniform acts). See the Comment to this chapter under the chapter heading. See also Section 4450 (construction of powers generally).

See also Sections 4014 ("attorney-in-fact" defined to include agent), 4026 ("principal" defined). [24 Cal.L.Rev.Comm.Reports 323 (1994)].

Cross References

Power of attorney defined for purposes of this Division, see Probate Code § 4022.
Principal defined for purposes of this Division, see Probate Code § 4026.

§ 4462. Retirement plan transactions; powers granted

In a statutory form power of attorney, the language granting power with respect to retirement plan transactions empowers the agent to do all of the following:

(a) Select payment options under any retirement plan in which the principal participates, including plans for self-employed individuals.

(b) Make voluntary contributions to those plans.

(c) Exercise the investment powers available under any self-directed retirement plan.

(d) Make rollovers of plan benefits into other retirement plans.

(e) If authorized by the plan, borrow from, sell assets to, and purchase assets from the plan.

(f) Waive the right of the principal to be a beneficiary of a joint or survivor annuity if the principal is a spouse who is not employed. *(Added by Stats.1994, c. 307 (S.B.1907), § 16. Amended by Stats.2011, c. 113 (A.B.1082), § 9.)*

Law Revision Commission Comments

1994 Addition

Section 4462 continues former Civil Code Section 2497 without change. Section 4462 is the same in substance as Section 15 of the Uniform Statutory Form Power of Attorney Act (1988). See Section 2(b) (construction of provisions drawn from uniform acts). See the Comment to this chapter under the chapter heading. See also Section 4450 (construction of powers generally).

See also Sections 4014 ("attorney-in-fact" defined to include agent), 4026 ("principal" defined). [24 Cal.L.Rev.Comm.Reports 323 (1994)].

Cross References

Power of attorney defined for purposes of this Division, see Probate Code § 4022.
Principal defined for purposes of this Division, see Probate Code § 4026.

§ 4463. Tax matters; powers granted

In a statutory form power of attorney, the language granting power with respect to tax matters empowers the agent to do all of the following:

(a) Prepare, sign, and file federal, state, local, and foreign income, gift, payroll, Federal Insurance Contributions Act returns, and other tax returns, claims for refunds, requests for extension of time, petitions regarding tax matters, and any other tax-related documents, including receipts, offers, waivers, consents (including consents and agreements under Internal Revenue Code Section 2032A or any successor section), closing agreements, and any power of attorney required by the Internal Revenue Service or other taxing authority with respect to a tax year upon which the statute of limitations has not run and to the tax year in which the power of attorney was executed and any subsequent tax year.

(b) Pay taxes due, collect refunds, post bonds, receive confidential information, and contest deficiencies determined by the Internal Revenue Service or other taxing authority.

(c) Exercise any election available to the principal under federal, state, local, or foreign tax law.

(d) Act for the principal in all tax matters for all periods before the Internal Revenue Service and any other taxing authority. *(Added by Stats.1994, c. 307 (S.B.1907), § 16.)*

Law Revision Commission Comments

1994 Addition

Section 4463 continues former Civil Code Section 2498 without change. Section 4463 is the same in substance as Section 16 of the Uniform Statutory Form Power of Attorney Act (1988). See Section 2(b) (construction of provisions drawn from uniform acts). At the end of subdivision (a), reference is made to "a tax year upon which the statute of limitations has not run and to the tax year in which the power of attorney was executed and any subsequent tax year." This replaces the reference in the uniform act to "a tax year upon which the statute of limitations has not run and the following 25 tax years." This substitution is consistent with the power granted by subdivision (d) which extends to "all tax matters for all periods" and is not limited to particular tax years. See also the Comment to this chapter under the chapter heading. See also Section 4450 (construction of powers generally).

See also Sections 4014 ("attorney-in-fact" defined to include agent), 4026 ("principal" defined). [24 Cal.L.Rev.Comm.Reports 323 (1994)].

Cross References

Power of attorney defined for purposes of this Division, see Probate Code § 4022.
Principal defined for purposes of this Division, see Probate Code § 4026.

§ 4464. After-acquired property; state where property is located or where power is executed

The powers described in this chapter are exercisable equally with respect to an interest the principal has when the statutory form power of attorney is executed or acquires later, whether or not the property is located in this state, and whether or not the powers are exercised or the power of attorney is executed in this state. *(Added by Stats.1994, c. 307 (S.B.1907), § 16.)*

Law Revision Commission Comments

1994 Addition

Section 4464 continues former Civil Code Section 2499 without change. Section 4464 makes the power of attorney explicitly effective for property acquired at times and in places that might otherwise be subject to dispute. The section is the same in substance as Section 17 of the Uniform Statutory Form Power of Attorney Act (1988). See Section 2(b) (construction of provisions drawn from uniform acts). See also Section 4123(b) (no need to describe each item or parcel of property).

See also Section 4026 ("principal" defined). [24 Cal.L.Rev.Comm.Reports 323 (1994)].

Cross References

Power of attorney defined for purposes of this Division, see Probate Code § 4022.

Principal defined for purposes of this Division, see Probate Code § 4026.

§ 4465. Empowerment of agent to take actions specified in Section 4264

A statutory form power of attorney under this part does not empower the agent to take any of the actions specified in Section 4264 unless the statutory form power of attorney expressly grants that authority to the attorney-in-fact. *(Added by Stats.2011, c. 113 (A.B.1082), § 11.)*

Cross References

Power of attorney defined for purposes of this Division, see Probate Code § 4022.
Power of Attorney form, see Probate Code § 4401.
Principal defined for purposes of this Division, see Probate Code § 4026.

Part 4

JUDICIAL PROCEEDINGS CONCERNING POWERS OF ATTORNEY

CHAPTER 1. GENERAL PROVISIONS

§ 4500. Judicial intervention

A power of attorney is exercisable free of judicial intervention, subject to this part. *(Added by Stats.1999, c. 658 (A.B.891), § 37, operative July 1, 2000.)*

Law Revision Commission Comments

1999 Addition

Section 4500 continues former Section 4900 without change. See also Section 4022 ("power of attorney" defined). [29 Cal.L.Rev. Comm. Reports 1 (1999)].

Cross References

Power of attorney defined for purposes of this Division, see Probate Code § 4022.

§ 4501. Other remedies

The remedies provided in this part are cumulative and not exclusive of any other remedies provided by law. *(Added by Stats.1999, c. 658 (A.B.891), § 37, operative July 1, 2000.)*

Law Revision Commission Comments

1999 Addition

Section 4501 continues former Section 4901 without change. [29 Cal.L.Rev.Comm. Reports 1 (1999)].

§ 4502. Limitation in the power of attorney

Except as provided in Section 4503, this part is not subject to limitation in the power of attorney. *(Added by Stats.1999, c. 658 (A.B.891), § 37, operative July 1, 2000.)*

Law Revision Commission Comments

1999 Addition

Section 4502 continues former Section 4902 without change. See also Sections 4022 ("power of attorney" defined), 4101(b) (general rule on limitations provided in power of attorney). [29 Cal.L.Rev. Comm. Reports 1 (1999)].

Cross References

Power of attorney defined for purposes of this Division, see Probate Code § 4022.

§ 4503. Elimination of authority to petition court

(a) Subject to subdivision (b), a power of attorney may expressly eliminate the authority of a person listed in Section 4540 to petition the court for any one or more of the purposes enumerated in Section 4541 if both of the following requirements are satisfied:

(1) The power of attorney is executed by the principal at a time when the principal has the advice of a lawyer authorized to practice law in the state where the power of attorney is executed.

(2) The principal's lawyer signs a certificate stating in substance:

"I am a lawyer authorized to practice law in the state where this power of attorney was executed, and the principal was my client at the time this power of attorney was executed. I have advised my client concerning his or her rights in connection with this power of attorney and the applicable law and the consequences of signing or not signing this power of attorney, and my client, after being so advised, has executed this power of attorney."

(b) A power of attorney may not limit the authority of the attorney-in-fact, the principal, the conservator of the person or estate of the principal, or the public guardian to petition under this part. *(Added by Stats.1999, c. 658 (A.B.891), § 37, operative July 1, 2000.)*

Law Revision Commission Comments

1999 Addition

Subdivision (a) of Section 4503 continues former Section 4903(a) without change, except that the reference to the section governing petitions relating to powers of attorney for health care (former Section 4942) is omitted. Powers of attorney for health care are governed by Division 4.7 (commencing with Section 4600).

Subdivision (a) makes clear that a power of attorney may limit the applicability of this part only if it is executed with the advice and approval of the principal's counsel. This limitation is designed to ensure that the execution of a power of attorney that restricts the remedies of this part is accomplished knowingly by the principal. The inclusion of a provision in the power of attorney making this part inapplicable does not affect the right to resort to any judicial remedies that may otherwise be available. See Section 4501.

Subdivision (b) continues the part of former Section 4903(b) relating to non-health care powers of attorney without substantive change, except that the reference to the conservator of the person of the principal is added for consistency with Section 4540(e).

See also Sections 4014 ("attorney-in-fact" defined), 4022 ("power of attorney" defined), 4026 ("principal" defined). [29 Cal.L.Rev. Comm. Reports 1 (1999)].

Cross References

Attorney-in-fact defined for purposes of this Division, see Probate Code § 4014.
Power of attorney defined for purposes of this Division, see Probate Code § 4022.
Principal defined for purposes of this Division, see Probate Code § 4026.

§ 4504. Jury trial

There is no right to a jury trial in proceedings under this division. *(Added by Stats.1999, c. 658 (A.B.891), § 37, operative July 1, 2000.)*

Law Revision Commission Comments

1999 Addition

Section 4504 continues former Section 4904 without change. This section is consistent with the rule applicable to other fiduciaries. See Prob. Code §§ 1452 (guardianships and conservatorships), 7200 (decedents' estates), 17006 (trusts). [29 Cal.L.Rev.Comm. Reports 1 (1999)].

§ 4505. Application of Division 3

Except as otherwise provided in this division, the general provisions in Division 3 (commencing with Section 1000) apply to proceedings under this division. *(Added by Stats. 1999, c. 658 (A.B.891), § 37, operative July 1, 2000.)*

Law Revision Commission Comments

1999 Addition

Section 4505 continues former Section 4905 without change, and provides a cross reference to the general procedural rules that apply to this division. See, e.g., Sections 1003 (guardian ad litem), 1021 (verification required), 1041 (clerk to set matters for hearing), 1046 (hearing and orders), 1203 (order shortening time for notice), 1215–1216 (service), 1260 (proof of service). [29 Cal.L.Rev.Comm. Reports 1 (1999)].

CHAPTER 2. JURISDICTION AND VENUE

§ 4520. Superior court jurisdiction

(a) The superior court has jurisdiction in proceedings under this division.

(b) The court in proceedings under this division is a court of general jurisdiction and the court, or a judge of the court, has the same power and authority with respect to the proceedings as otherwise provided by law for a superior court, or a judge of the superior court, including, but not limited to, the matters authorized by Section 128 of the Code of Civil Procedure. *(Added by Stats.1999, c. 658 (A.B.891), § 37, operative July 1, 2000.)*

Principal defined for purposes of this Division, see Probate Code § 4026.

Law Revision Commission Comments

1999 Addition

Section 4520 continues former Section 4920 without change, and is comparable to Section 7050 governing the jurisdiction and authority of the court in proceedings concerning administration of decedents' estates. See Section 7050 Comment. [29 Cal.L.Rev.Comm. Reports 1 (1999)].

§ 4521. Exercise of jurisdiction

The court may exercise jurisdiction in proceedings under this division on any basis permitted by Section 410.10 of the Code of Civil Procedure. *(Added by Stats.1999, c. 658 (A.B.891), § 37, operative July 1, 2000.)*

Law Revision Commission Comments

1999 Addition

Section 4521 continues former Section 4921 without change, and is comparable to Section 17004 (jurisdiction under Trust Law). This section recognizes that the court, in proceedings relating to powers of attorney under this division, may exercise jurisdiction on any basis that is not inconsistent with the California or United States Constitutions, as provided in Code of Civil Procedure Section 410.10. See generally Judicial Council Comment to Code Civ. Proc. § 410.10; Prob. Code § 17004 Comment (basis of jurisdiction under Trust Law). [29 Cal.L.Rev.Comm. Reports 1 (1999)].

§ 4522. Attorney-in-fact subject to personal jurisdiction in this state

Without limiting Section 4521, a person who acts as an attorney-in-fact under a power of attorney governed by this division is subject to personal jurisdiction in this state with respect to matters relating to acts and transactions of the attorney-in-fact performed in this state or affecting property or a principal in this state. *(Added by Stats.1999, c. 658 (A.B.891), § 37, operative July 1, 2000.)*

Law Revision Commission Comments

1999 Addition

Section 4522 continues former Section 4922 without change, and is comparable to Sections 3902(b) (jurisdiction over custodian under Uniform Transfers to Minors Act) and 17003(a) (jurisdiction over trustee). This section is intended to facilitate exercise of the court's power under this part when the court's jurisdiction is properly invoked. As recognized by the introductory clause, constitutional limitations on assertion of jurisdiction apply to the exercise of jurisdiction under this section. Consequently, appropriate notice must be given to an attorney-in-fact as a condition of personal jurisdiction. Cf. Mullane v. Central Hanover Bank & Trust Co., 339 U.S. 306 (1950).

See also Sections 4014 ("attorney-in-fact" defined), 4022 ("power of attorney" defined), 4026 ("principal" defined). [29 Cal.L.Rev. Comm. Reports 1 (1999)].

Cross References

Attorney-in-fact defined for purposes of this Division, see Probate Code § 4014.
Power of attorney defined for purposes of this Division, see Probate Code § 4022.

§ 4523. Venue

The proper county for commencement of a proceeding under this division shall be determined in the following order of priority:

(a) The county in which the principal resides.

(b) The county in which the attorney-in-fact resides.

(c) A county in which property subject to the power of attorney is located.

(d) Any other county that is in the principal's best interest. *(Added by Stats.1999, c. 658 (A.B.891), § 37, operative July 1, 2000.)*

Law Revision Commission Comments

1999 Addition

Section 4523 continues former Section 4923 without change. This section is drawn from the rules applicable to guardianships and conservatorships. See Sections 2201–2202. See also Section 4053 (durable powers of attorney under law of another jurisdiction). [29 Cal.L.Rev.Comm. Reports 1 (1999)].

Cross References

Attorney-in-fact defined for purposes of this Division, see Probate Code § 4014.
Power of attorney defined for purposes of this Division, see Probate Code § 4022.
Principal defined for purposes of this Division, see Probate Code § 4026.

CHAPTER 3. PETITIONS, ORDERS, APPEALS

§ 4540. Persons authorized to file petition

Subject to Section 4503, a petition may be filed under this part by any of the following persons:

(a) The attorney-in-fact.

(b) The principal.

(c) The spouse of the principal.

(d) A relative of the principal.

(e) The conservator of the person or estate of the principal.

(f) The court investigator, described in Section 1454, of the county where the power of attorney was executed or where the principal resides.

(g) The public guardian of the county where the power of attorney was executed or where the principal resides.

(h) The personal representative or trustee of the principal's estate.

(i) The principal's successor in interest.

(j) A person who is requested in writing by an attorney-in-fact to take action.

(k) Any other interested person or friend of the principal. *(Added by Stats.1999, c. 658 (A.B.891), § 37, operative July 1, 2000.)*

Law Revision Commission Comments

1999 Addition

Section 4540 continues former Section 4940 without change, except that the reference to the treating health care provider in former subdivision (h) is omitted. Powers of attorney for health care are governed by Division 4.7 (commencing with Section 4600). The purposes for which a person may file a petition under this part are limited by other rules. See Sections 4502 (effect of provision in power of attorney attempting to limit right to petition), 4503 (limitations on right to petition); see also Section 4501 (other remedies not affected). See also the comparable rules governing petitioners for appointment of a conservator under Section 1820.

See also Sections 4014 ("attorney-in-fact" defined), 4022 ("power of attorney" defined), 4026 ("principal" defined). [29 Cal.L.Rev. Comm. Reports 1 (1999)].

Cross References

Attorney-in-fact defined for purposes of this Division, see Probate Code § 4014.

Power of attorney defined for purposes of this Division, see Probate Code § 4022.

Principal defined for purposes of this Division, see Probate Code § 4026.

§ 4541. Purposes for filing petition

A petition may be filed under this part for any one or more of the following purposes:

(a) Determining whether the power of attorney is in effect or has terminated.

(b) Passing on the acts or proposed acts of the attorney-in-fact, including approval of authority to disobey the principal's instructions pursuant to subdivision (b) of Section 4234.

(c) Compelling the attorney-in-fact to submit the attorney-in-fact's accounts or report the attorney-in-fact's acts as attorney-in-fact to the principal, the spouse of the principal, the conservator of the person or the estate of the principal, or to any other person required by the court in its discretion, if the attorney-in-fact has failed to submit an accounting or report within 60 days after written request from the person filing the petition.

(d) Declaring that the authority of the attorney-in-fact is revoked on a determination by the court of all of the following:

(1) The attorney-in-fact has violated or is unfit to perform the fiduciary duties under the power of attorney.

(2) At the time of the determination by the court, the principal lacks the capacity to give or to revoke a power of attorney.

(3) The revocation of the attorney-in-fact's authority is in the best interest of the principal or the principal's estate.

(e) Approving the resignation of the attorney–in–fact:

(1) If the attorney-in-fact is subject to a duty to act under Section 4230, the court may approve the resignation, subject

to any orders the court determines are necessary to protect the principal's interests.

(2) If the attorney-in-fact is not subject to a duty to act under Section 4230, the court shall approve the resignation, subject to the court's discretion to require the attorney-in-fact to give notice to other interested persons.

(f) Compelling a third person to honor the authority of an attorney-in-fact. *(Added by Stats.1999, c. 658 (A.B.891), § 37, operative July 1, 2000.)*

Law Revision Commission Comments

1999 Addition

Section 4541 continues former Section 4941 without change, except that the reference to powers of attorney for health care in the introductory paragraph of former law is omitted. Powers of attorney for health care are governed by Division 4.7 (commencing with Section 4600). This section applies to petitions concerning both durable and nondurable powers of attorney. See Sections 4022 ("power of attorney" defined), 4050 (scope of division).

Subdivision (a) makes clear that a petition may be filed to determine whether the power of attorney was ever effective, thus permitting, for example, a determination that the power of attorney was invalid when executed because its execution was induced by fraud. See also Section 4201 (unqualified attorney-in-fact).

The authority to petition to disobey the principal's instructions in subdivision (b) is new. This is a limitation on the general agency rule in Civil Code Section 2320. See Section 4234 (duty to follow instructions) & Comment.

Subdivision (d) requires a court determination that the principal has become incapacitated before the court is authorized to declare the power of attorney terminated because the attorney-in-fact has violated or is unfit to perform the fiduciary duties under the power of attorney.

Subdivision (e) provides a procedure for accepting the attorney-in-fact's resignation. The court's discretion in this type of case depends on whether the attorney-in-fact is subject to any duty to act under Section 4230, as in the situation where the attorney-in-fact has agreed in writing to act or is involved in an ongoing transaction. Under subdivision (e)(1) the court may make any necessary protective order. Under subdivision (e)(2), the court's discretion is limited to requiring that notice be given to others who may be expected to look out for the principal's interests, such as a public guardian or a relative. In addition, the attorney-in-fact is required to comply with the statutory duties on termination of authority. See Section 4238. The availability of this procedure is not intended to imply that an attorney-in-fact must or should petition for judicial acceptance of a resignation where the attorney-in-fact is not subject to a duty to act.

Subdivision (f) provides a remedy to achieve compliance with the power of attorney through recognition of the attorney-in-fact's authority. This remedy is also available to compel disclosure of information under Section 4235 (consultation and disclosure). See Section 4300 *et seq.* (relations with third persons).

A power of attorney may limit the authority to petition under this part. See Sections 4502 (effect of provision in power of attorney attempting to limit right to petition), 4503 (limitations on right to petition).

See also Sections 4014 ("attorney-in-fact" defined), 4022 ("power of attorney" defined), 4026 ("principal" defined). [29 Cal.L.Rev. Comm. Reports 1 (1999)].

Cross References

Attorney-in-fact defined for purposes of this Division, see Probate Code § 4014.

Fee for filing petition commencing or opposition papers concerning certain probate proceedings, see Government Code § 70655.

Power of attorney defined for purposes of this Division, see Probate Code § 4022.

Principal defined for purposes of this Division, see Probate Code § 4026.

Third person defined for purposes of this Division, see Probate Code § 4034.

§ 4542. Commencement of proceeding

A proceeding under this part is commenced by filing a petition stating facts showing that the petition is authorized under this part, the grounds of the petition, and, if known to the petitioner, the terms of the power of attorney. *(Added by Stats.1999, c. 658 (A.B.891), § 37, operative July 1, 2000.)*

Law Revision Commission Comments

1999 Addition

Section 4542 continues former Section 4943 without change For a comparable provision, see Section 17201 (commencement of proceeding under Trust Law). A petition is required to be verified. See Section 1021.

See also Section 4022 ("power of attorney" defined). [29 Cal. L.Rev.Comm. Reports 1 (1999)].

Cross References

Power of attorney defined for purposes of this Division, see Probate Code § 4022.

§ 4543. Dismissal of petition not reasonably necessary

The court may dismiss a petition if it appears that the proceeding is not reasonably necessary for the protection of the interests of the principal or the principal's estate and shall stay or dismiss the proceeding in whole or in part when required by Section 410.30 of the Code of Civil Procedure. *(Added by Stats.1999, c. 658 (A.B.891), § 37, operative July 1, 2000.)*

Law Revision Commission Comments

1999 Addition

Section 4543 continues former Section 4944 without change. Under former Section 4944, the dismissal standard was revised to permit dismissal when the proceeding is not "reasonably necessary," rather than "necessary" as under the prior section (Civil Code Section 2416). Under this section, the court has authority to stay or dismiss a proceeding in this state if, in the interest of substantial justice, the proceeding should be heard in a forum outside this state. See Code Civ. Proc. § 410.30.

See also Section 4026 ("principal" defined). [29 Cal.L.Rev. Comm. Reports 1 (1999)].

Cross References

Principal defined for purposes of this Division, see Probate Code § 4026.

§ 4544. Notice of time and place of hearing

(a) Subject to subdivision (b), at least 15 days before the time set for hearing, the petitioner shall serve notice of the time and place of the hearing, together with a copy of the petition, on the following:

(1) The attorney-in-fact if not the petitioner.

(2) The principal if not the petitioner.

(b) In the case of a petition to compel a third person to honor the authority of an attorney-in-fact, notice of the time and place of the hearing, together with a copy of the petition, shall be served on the third person in the manner provided in Chapter 4 (commencing with Section 413.10) of Title 5 of Part 2 of the Code of Civil Procedure. *(Added by Stats.1999, c. 658 (A.B.891), § 37, operative July 1, 2000.)*

Law Revision Commission Comments

1999 Addition

Subdivision (a) of Section 4544, pertaining to internal affairs of the power of attorney, continues former Section 4945(a) without change.

Subdivision (b) continues former Section 4945(b) without change, and provides a special rule applicable to service of notice in proceedings involving third persons, i.e., not internal affairs of the power of attorney. See Section 4541(f) (petition to compel third person to honor attorney-in-fact's authority).

See also Sections 4014 ("attorney-in-fact" defined), 4026 ("principal" defined). [29 Cal.L.Rev.Comm. Reports 1 (1999)].

Cross References

Attorney-in-fact defined for purposes of this Division, see Probate Code § 4014.

Principal defined for purposes of this Division, see Probate Code § 4026.

Third person defined for purposes of this Division, see Probate Code § 4034.

§ 4545. Attorney's fees

In a proceeding under this part commenced by the filing of a petition by a person other than the attorney-in-fact, the court may in its discretion award reasonable attorney's fees to one of the following:

(a) The attorney-in-fact, if the court determines that the proceeding was commenced without any reasonable cause.

(b) The person commencing the proceeding, if the court determines that the attorney-in-fact has clearly violated the fiduciary duties under the power of attorney or has failed without any reasonable cause or justification to submit accounts or report acts to the principal or conservator of the estate or of the person, as the case may be, after written request from the principal or conservator. *(Added by Stats. 1999, c. 658 (A.B.891), § 37, operative July 1, 2000.)*

Law Revision Commission Comments

1999 Addition

Section 4545 continues former Section 4947 without change.

See also Sections 4014 ("attorney-in-fact" defined), 4022 ("power of attorney" defined), 4026 ("principal" defined). [29 Cal.L.Rev. Comm. Reports 1 (1999)].

Cross References

Attorney-in-fact defined for purposes of this Division, see Probate Code § 4014.

Power of attorney defined for purposes of this Division, see Probate Code § 4022.

Principal defined for purposes of this Division, see Probate Code § 4026.

Part 5

JUDICIAL PROCEEDINGS CONCERNING POWERS OF ATTORNEY [REPEALED]

Division 4.7

HEALTH CARE DECISIONS

Cross References

Agent under health care power of attorney, liability for costs, see Health and Safety Code § 7100.

Professional fiduciaries, suspension, revocation or other adverse action, see Business and Professions Code § 6584.

Part 1

DEFINITIONS AND GENERAL

CHAPTER 1. SHORT TITLE AND DEFINITIONS

§ 4600. Short title

This division may be cited as the Health Care Decisions Law. *(Added by Stats.1999, c. 658 (A.B.891), § 39, operative July 1, 2000.)*

Law Revision Commission Comments

1999 Addition

Section 4600 is new and provides a convenient means of referring to this division. The Health Care Decisions Law is essentially self-contained, but other agency statutes may be applied as provided in Section 4688. See also Sections 20 *et seq.* (general definitions applicable in Probate Code depending on context), 4755 (application of general procedural rules). For the scope of this division, see Section 4651.

Many provisions in Parts 1, 2, and 3 are the same as or drawn from the Uniform Health–Care Decisions Act (1993). Several general provisions included in the Uniform Health–Care Decisions Act (1993) are generalized elsewhere in this code. See Sections 2(b) (construction of provisions drawn from uniform acts) (*cf.* UHCDA § 15), 11 (severability) (*cf.* UHCDA § 17). In Comments to sections in this title, a reference to the "Uniform Health–Care Decisions Act (1993)" or the "uniform act" (in context) means the official text of the uniform act approved by the National Conference of Commissioners on Uniform State Laws. [29 Cal.L.Rev.Comm. Reports 1 (1999)].

Cross References

Health care decision defined for purposes of this Division, see Probate Code § 4617.

Health care defined for purposes of this Division, see Probate Code § 4615.

§ 4603. Definitions governing construction of this division

Unless the provision or context otherwise requires, the definitions in this chapter govern the construction of this division. *(Added by Stats.1999, c. 658 (A.B.891), § 39, operative July 1, 2000.)*

Law Revision Commission Comments

1999 Addition

Section 4603 serves the same purpose as former Section 4600 and is comparable to Section 4010 (Power of Attorney Law).

Some definitions included in the Uniform Health–Care Decisions Act (1993) are generalized elsewhere in this code. See Sections 56 ("person" defined) (*cf.* uniform act Section 1(10)), 74 ("state" defined) (*cf.* uniform act Section 1(15)). [29 Cal.L.Rev.Comm. Reports 1 (1999)].

§ 4605. Advance health care directive

"Advance health care directive" or "advance directive" means either an individual health care instruction or a power of attorney for health care. *(Added by Stats.1999, c. 658 (A.B.891), § 39, operative July 1, 2000.)*

Law Revision Commission Comments

1999 Addition

Section 4605 is new. The first sentence is the same as Section 1(1) of the Uniform Health–Care Decisions Act (1993), except that the term "advance directive" is defined for convenience. "Advance directive" is commonly used in practice as a shorthand. Statutory language also may use the shorter term. See, e.g., Section 4698. A declaration or directive under the repealed Natural Death Act (former Health and Safety Code § 7185 *et seq.*) is a type of advance directive. See Section 4623 Comment.

See also Sections 4623 ("individual health care instruction" defined), 4629 ("power of attorney for health care" defined).

Background from Uniform Act. The term "advance health-care directive" appears in the federal Patient Self–Determination Act enacted as Sections 4206 and 4751 of the Omnibus Budget Reconciliation Act of 1990 and has gained widespread usage among health-care professionals. [Adapted from Unif. Health–Care Decisions Act § 1(1) comment (1993)] [29 Cal.L.Rev.Comm. Reports 1 (1999)].

Cross References

Health care defined for purposes of this Division, see Probate Code § 4615.

Individual health care instruction defined for purposes of this Division, see Probate Code § 4623.

Personal health care, written materials for patients, clarity and legibility requirement, see Health and Safety Code § 123222.1.

Power of attorney for health care defined for purposes of this Division, see Probate Code § 4629.

Residential care facilities for the elderly,

　Advance directives relating to provision of health care, see Health and Safety Code § 1569.156.

　Requests to forego resuscitative measures, policies to honor requests, see Health and Safety Code § 1569.74.

　Terminally ill residents or terminally ill persons to be accepted as a resident, see Health and Safety Code § 1569.73.

　Terminally ill individuals, waivers to remain in or become a resident at residential facilities, see Health and Safety Code § 1507.3.

§ 4606. Repealed by Stats.1999, c. 658, § 38, operative July 1, 2000

Law Revision Commission Comments

1999 Repeal

Former Section 4606 is superseded by Section 4629 ("power of attorney for health care" defined). See Section 4629 Comment. The durability of powers of attorney for health care is implicit, so the term has been shortened in the new law to "power of attorney for health care." [29 Cal.L.Rev.Comm. Reports 1 (1999)].

§ 4607. Agent

(a) "Agent" means an individual designated in a power of attorney for health care to make a health care decision for the principal, regardless of whether the person is known as an agent or attorney-in-fact, or by some other term.

(b) "Agent" includes a successor or alternate agent. *(Added by Stats.1999, c. 658 (A.B.891), § 39, operative July 1, 2000.)*

Law Revision Commission Comments

1999 Addition

Section 4607 is consistent with the definition of attorney-in-fact in the Power of Attorney Law. See Section 4014. The first part of subdivision (a) is the same as Section 1(2) of the Uniform Health–Care Decisions Act (1993). For limitations on who may act as a health care agent, see Section 4659.

See also Sections 4629 ("power of attorney for health care" defined), 4633 ("principal" defined).

Background from Uniform Act. The definition of "agent" is not limited to a single individual. The Act permits the appointment of co-agents and alternate agents. [Adapted from Unif. Health–Care Decisions Act § 1(2) comment (1993)] [29 Cal.L.Rev.Comm. Reports 1 (1999)].

Cross References

Health care decision defined for purposes of this Division, see Probate Code § 4617.

Health care defined for purposes of this Division, see Probate Code § 4615.

Power of attorney for health care defined for purposes of this Division, see Probate Code § 4629.

Principal defined for purposes of this Division, see Probate Code § 4633.

§ 4609. Capacity

"Capacity" means a person's ability to understand the nature and consequences of a decision and to make and communicate a decision, and includes in the case of proposed health care, the ability to understand its significant benefits, risks, and alternatives. *(Added by Stats.1999, c. 658 (A.B. 891), § 39, operative July 1, 2000. Amended by Stats.2001, c. 230 (A.B.1278), § 3.)*

Law Revision Commission Comments

1999 Addition

Section 4609 is a new provision drawn from Health and Safety Code Section 1418.8(b) and Section 1(3) of the Uniform Health–Care Decisions Act (1993). This standard replaces the capacity to contract standard that was formerly applicable to durable powers of attorney for health care under Section 4120 in the Power of Attorney Law.

For provisions in this division relating to capacity, see Sections 4651 (authority of person having capacity not affected), 4657 (presumption of capacity), 4658 (determination of capacity and other medical conditions), 4682 (when agent's authority effective), 4670 (authority to give individual health care instruction), 4671 (authority to execute power of attorney for health care), 4683 (scope of agent's authority), 4695 (revocation of power of attorney for health care), 4715 (disqualification of surrogate), 4732 (duty of primary physician to record relevant information), 4733 (obligations of health care provider), 4766 (petition as to durable power of attorney for health care).

See also Sections 4615 ("health care" defined), 4617 ("health care decision" defined). [29 Cal.L.Rev.Comm. Reports App. 6 (1999)].

2001 Amendment

Section 4609 is amended to generalize the capacity definition to avoid the implication that the definition would only apply in situations where there is proposed health care. Thus, the definition applies to an individual's capacity to make or revoke an advance health care directive, as well as to the making of a health care decision. In the latter case, the final clause provides additional guidance on the application of the capacity standard.

For provisions invoking capacity definition, see Sections 4651 (authority of person having capacity not affected), 4658 (determination of capacity and other medical conditions), 4670 (authority to give individual health care instruction), 4671 (authority to execute power of attorney for health care), 4682 (when agent's authority effective), 4683 (scope of agent's authority), 4695 (revocation of power of attorney for health care), 4715 (disqualification of surrogate).

See also Sections 4657 (presumption of capacity), 4732 (duty of primary physician to record relevant information), 4733 (obligations of health care provider), 4766 (petition as to durable power of attorney for health care). [30 Cal.L.Rev.Comm. Reports 621 (2000)].

Health care defined for purposes of this Division, see Probate Code § 4615.

§ 4611. Community care facility

"Community care facility" means a "community care facility" as defined in Section 1502 of the Health and Safety Code. *(Added by Stats.1999, c. 658 (A.B.891), § 39, operative July 1, 2000.)*

Law Revision Commission Comments

1999 Addition

Section 4611 continues former Section 4603 without substantive change.

For provisions in this division using this term, see Sections 4659 (limitations on who may act as agent or surrogate), 4673 (witnessing requirements in skilled nursing facility). [29 Cal.L.Rev.Comm. Reports 1 (1999)].

§ 4612. Repealed by Stats.1999, c. 658 (A.B.891), § 38, operative July 1, 2000

Law Revision Commission Comments

1999 Repeal

Former Section 4612 is superseded by Section 4617. See Section 4617 Comment. [29 Cal.L.Rev.Comm. Reports 1 (1999)].

§ 4613. Conservator

"Conservator" means a court-appointed conservator having authority to make a health care decision for a patient. *(Added by Stats.1999, c. 658 (A.B.891), § 39, operative July 1, 2000.)*

Law Revision Commission Comments

1999 Addition

Section 4613 is a new provision and serves the same purpose as Section 1(4) of the Uniform Health–Care Decisions Act (1993) (definition of "guardian"). Terminology in other states may vary, but the law applies the same rules regardless of terminology.

For provisions in this division concerning conservators, see Sections 4617 ("health care decision" defined), 4631 ("primary physician" defined), 4643 ("surrogate" defined), 4659 (limitations on who may act as agent or surrogate), 4672 (nomination of conservator in written advance health care directive), 4696 (duty to communicate revocation), 4732 (duty of primary physician to record relevant information), 4753 (limitations on right to petition), 4765 (petitioners), 4770 (temporary health care order).

See also Section 4617 ("health care decision" defined), 4625 ("patient" defined). [29 Cal.L.Rev.Comm. Reports App. 6 (1999)].

Cross References

Health care decision defined for purposes of this Division, see Probate Code § 4617.

Health care defined for purposes of this Division, see Probate Code § 4615.

Patient defined for purposes of this Division, see Probate Code § 4625.

§ 4615. Health care

"Health care" means any care, treatment, service, or procedure to maintain, diagnose, or otherwise affect a patient's physical or mental condition. *(Added by Stats.1999, c. 658 (A.B.891), § 39, operative July 1, 2000.)*

Law Revision Commission Comments

1999 Addition

Section 4615 continues the first part of former Section 4609 without substantive change and is the same in substance as Section 1(5) of the Uniform Health–Care Decisions Act (1993).

See also Section 4625 ("patient" defined).

Background from Uniform Act. The definition of "health care" is to be given the broadest possible construction. It includes the types of care referred to in the definition of "health-care decision" [Prob. Code§ 4617], and to care, including custodial care, provided at a "health-care institution" [Prob. Code § 4619]. It also includes non-medical remedial treatment. [Adapted from Unif. Health–Care Decisions Act § 1(5) comment (1993)] [29 Cal.L.Rev.Comm. Reports 1 (1999)].

Cross References

Patient defined for purposes of this Division, see Probate Code § 4625.

§ 4617. Health care decision

"Health care decision" means a decision made by a patient or the patient's agent, conservator, or surrogate, regarding the patient's health care, including the following:

(a) Selection and discharge of health care providers and institutions.

(b) Approval or disapproval of diagnostic tests, surgical procedures, and programs of medication.

(c) Directions to provide, withhold, or withdraw artificial nutrition and hydration and all other forms of health care, including cardiopulmonary resuscitation. *(Added by Stats. 1999, c. 658 (A.B.891), § 39, operative July 1, 2000.)*

Law Revision Commission Comments

1999 Addition

Section 4617 supersedes former Section 4612 and is the same in substance as Section 1(6) of the Uniform Health–Care Decisions Act (1993), with the substitution of the reference to cardiopulmonary resuscitation in subdivision (c) for the uniform act reference to orders not to resuscitate. Adoption of the uniform act formulation is not intended to limit the scope of health care decisions applicable under former law. Thus, like former law, this section encompasses consent, refusal of consent, or withdrawal of consent to health care, or a decision to begin, continue, increase, limit, discontinue, or not to begin any health care. Depending on the circumstances, a health care decision may range from a decision concerning one specific treatment through an extended course of treatment, as determined by applicable standards of medical practice.

An effective health care decision must be made with informed consent. See, e.g., Cobbs v. Grant, 8 Cal.3d 229, 242, 502 P.2d 1, 104 Cal.Rptr. 505 (1972); Barber v. Superior Court, 147 Cal.App.3d 1006, 1015, 195 Cal.Rptr. 484 (1983). While this division does not use the phrase "informed consent," it is assumed that the statute will be read in light of this well-established doctrine.

See also Sections 4607 ("agent" defined), 4613 ("conservator" defined), 4615 ("health care" defined), 4625 ("patient" defined), 4643 ("surrogate" defined). [29 Cal.L.Rev.Comm. Reports 1 (1999)].

Cross References

Agent defined for purposes of this Division, see Probate Code § 4607.

Conservator defined for purposes of this Division, see Probate Code § 4613.

Health care defined for purposes of this Division, see Probate Code § 4615.

Health care provider defined for purposes of this Division, see Probate Code § 4621.

Patient defined for purposes of this Division, see Probate Code § 4625.

Surrogate defined for purposes of this Division, see Probate Code § 4643.

§ 4618. Repealed by Stats.1999, c. 658 (A.B.891), § 38, operative July 1, 2000

Law Revision Commission Comments

1999 Repeal

Former Section 4618 is continued in Section 4637 without substantive change. [29 Cal.L.Rev.Comm. Reports 1 (1999)].

§ 4619. Health care institution

"Health care institution" means an institution, facility, or agency licensed, certified, or otherwise authorized or permitted by law to provide health care in the ordinary course of business. *(Added by Stats.1999, c. 658 (A.B.891), § 39, operative July 1, 2000.)*

Law Revision Commission Comments

1999 Addition

Section 4619 is a new provision and is the same as Section 1(7) of the Uniform Health–Care Decisions Act (1993).

For provisions in this division using this term, see Sections 4654 (compliance with generally accepted health care standards), 4659 (limitations on who may act as agent or surrogate), 4677 (restriction on requiring or prohibiting advance directive), 4696 (duty to communicate revocation), 4701 (optional form of advance health care directive), 4711 (patient's designation of surrogate), 4733 (obligations of health care institution), 4734 (right to decline for reasons of conscience or institutional policy), 4735 (health care institution's right to decline ineffective care), 4736 (obligations of declining health care institution), 4740 (immunities of health care provider or institution), 4742 (statutory damages), 4765 (petitioners), 4785 (application of request to forgo resuscitative measures).

See also Section 4615 ("health care" defined).

Background from Uniform Act. The term "health-care institution" includes a hospital, nursing home, residential-care facility, home health agency, or hospice. [Adapted from Unif. Health–Care Decisions Act § 1(7) comment (1993)] [29 Cal.L.Rev.Comm. Reports App. 6 (1999)].

Cross References

Health care defined for purposes of this Division, see Probate Code § 4615.

§ 4621. Health care provider

"Health care provider" means an individual licensed, certified, or otherwise authorized or permitted by the law of this state to provide health care in the ordinary course of business or practice of a profession. *(Added by Stats.1999, c. 658 (A.B.891), § 39, operative July 1, 2000.)*

Law Revision Commission Comments

1999 Addition

Section 4621 continues former Section 4615 without substantive change and is the same as Section 1(8) of the Uniform Health–Care Decisions Act (1993). This section also continues former Health and Safety Code Section 7186(c) (Natural Death Act) without substantive change.

For provisions in this division using this term, see Sections 4617 ("health care decision" defined), 4641 ("supervising health care provider" defined), 4654 (compliance with generally accepted health care standards), 4659 (limitations on who may act as agent or surrogate), 4673 (witnessing requirements in skilled nursing facility), 4676 (validity of written advance directive executed in another jurisdiction), 4677 (restriction on requiring or prohibiting advance directive), 4685 (agent's priority), 4696 (duty to communicate revocation), 4701 (optional form of advance health care directive), 4733 (obligations of health care provider), 4734 (health care provider's right to decline for reasons of conscience), 4735 (health care provider's right to decline ineffective care), 4736 (obligations of declining health care provider), 4740 (immunities of health care provider), 4742 (statutory damages).

See also Section 4615 ("health care" defined). [29 Cal.L.Rev. Comm. Reports App. 6 (1999)].

Cross References

Health care defined for purposes of this Division, see Probate Code § 4615.

Residential care facilities for the elderly, requests to forego resuscitative measures, policies to honor requests, see Health and Safety Code § 1569.74.

§ 4623. Individual health care instruction

"Individual health care instruction" or "individual instruction" means a patient's written or oral direction concerning a health care decision for the patient. *(Added by Stats.1999, c. 658 (A.B.891), § 39, operative July 1, 2000.)*

Law Revision Commission Comments

1999 Addition

Section 4623 is a new provision and is the same in substance as Section 1(9) of the Uniform Health–Care Decisions Act (1993). The term "individual health care instruction" is included to provide more clarity. A declaration or directive under the repealed Natural Death Act (former Health and Safety Code § 7185 *et seq.*) is an individual health care instruction.

For provisions in this division using this term, see Sections 4605 ("advance health care directive" defined), 4625 ("patient" defined), 4658 (determination of capacity and other medical conditions), 4670 (individual health care instruction recognized), 4671 (power of attorney for health care may include individual instruction), 4684 (standard governing agent's health care decisions), 4714 (standard governing surrogate's health care decisions), 4732 (duty of primary physician to record relevant information), 4733 (obligations of health care provider or institution), 4734 (health care provider's or institution's right to decline), 4735 (right to decline to provide ineffective care), 4736 (obligations of declining health care provider or institution).

See also Section 4617 ("health care decision" defined), 4625 ("patient" defined).

Background from Uniform Act. The term "individual instruction" includes any type of written or oral direction concerning health-care treatment. The direction may range from a written document which is intended to be effective at a future time if certain specified conditions arise and for which a form is provided in Section 4 [Prob. Code § 4701], to the written consent required before surgery is performed, to oral directions concerning care recorded in the health-care record. The instruction may relate to a particular health-care decision or to health care in general. [Adapted from Unif. Health–Care Decisions Act § 1(9) comment (1993)] [29 Cal.L.Rev.Comm. Reports App. 6 (1999)].

Health care decision defined for purposes of this Division, see Probate Code § 4617.
Health care defined for purposes of this Division, see Probate Code § 4615.
Patient defined for purposes of this Division, see Probate Code § 4625.
Request regarding resuscitative measures, conflict with health care instruction, see Probate Code § 4781.4.

§ 4625. Patient

"Patient" means an adult whose health care is under consideration, and includes a principal under a power of attorney for health care and an adult who has given an individual health care instruction or designated a surrogate. *(Added by Stats.1999, c. 658 (A.B.891), § 39, operative July 1, 2000.)*

Law Revision Commission Comments

1999 Addition

Section 4625 is a new provision added for drafting convenience. "Adult" includes an emancipated minor. See Fam. Code §§ 7002 (emancipation), 7050 (emancipated minor considered as adult for consent to medical, dental, or psychiatric care). For provisions governing surrogates, see Section 4711 *et seq.*

See also Sections 4615 ("health care" defined), 4623 ("individual health care instruction" defined), 4629 ("power of attorney for health care" defined), 4633 ("principal" defined), 4643 ("surrogate" defined). Compare Section 3200 ("patient" defined for purposes of court-authorized medical treatment procedure). [29 Cal.L.Rev. Comm. Reports App. 6 (1999)].

Cross References

Health care defined for purposes of this Division, see Probate Code § 4615.
Individual health care instruction defined for purposes of this Division, see Probate Code § 4623.
Power of attorney for health care defined for purposes of this Division, see Probate Code § 4629.
Principal defined for purposes of this Division, see Probate Code § 4633.
Surrogate defined for purposes of this Division, see Probate Code § 4643.

§ 4627. Physician

"Physician" means a physician and surgeon licensed by the Medical Board of California or the Osteopathic Medical Board of California. *(Added by Stats.1999, c. 658 (A.B.891), § 39, operative July 1, 2000.)*

Law Revision Commission Comments

1999 Addition

Section 4627 continues and generalizes former Health and Safety Code Section 7186(g) (Natural Death Act) and is the same in substance as Section 1(11) of the Uniform Health–Care Decisions Act (1993). [29 Cal.L.Rev.Comm. Reports 1 (1999)].

§ 4629. Power of attorney for health care

"Power of attorney for health care" means a written instrument designating an agent to make health care decisions for the principal. *(Added by Stats.1999, c. 658 (A.B. 891), § 39, operative July 1, 2000.)*

Law Revision Commission Comments

1999 Addition

Section 4629 supersedes former Section 4606 (defining "durable power of attorney for health care") and is the same in substance as Section 1(12) of the Uniform Health–Care Decisions Act (1993). The writing requirement continues part of Section 4022 (defining "power of attorney" generally) as it applied to powers of attorney for health care under former law, and is consistent with part of the second sentence of Section 2(b) of the Uniform Health–Care Decisions Act (1993).

See also Sections 4607 ("agent" defined), 4617 ("health care decision" defined). [29 Cal.L.Rev.Comm. Reports 1 (1999)].

Cross References

Agent defined for purposes of this Division, see Probate Code § 4607.
Health care decision defined for purposes of this Division, see Probate Code § 4617.
Health care defined for purposes of this Division, see Probate Code § 4615.
Principal defined for purposes of this Division, see Probate Code § 4633.

§ 4631. Primary physician

"Primary physician" means a physician designated by a patient or the patient's agent, conservator, or surrogate, to have primary responsibility for the patient's health care or, in the absence of a designation or if the designated physician is not reasonably available or declines to act as primary physician, a physician who undertakes the responsibility. *(Added by Stats.1999, c. 658 (A.B.891), § 39, operative July 1, 2000.)*

Law Revision Commission Comments

1999 Addition

Section 4631 supersedes former Health and Safety Code Section 7186(a) ("attending physician" defined) and is the same in substance as Section 1(13) of the Uniform Health–Care Decisions Act (1993), with the addition of the reference to the ability to decline to act as primary physician. To be a "primary physician" under this division, the substantive rules in this section must be complied with. The institutional designation of a person is not relevant. Hence, a "primary care physician" or a "hospitalist" may or may not be a "primary physician," depending on the circumstances.

For provisions in this division using this term, see Sections 4641 ("supervising health care provider" defined), 4658 (determination of capacity and other medical conditions), 4701 (optional form of advance health care directive), 4732 (duty of primary physician to record relevant information).

See also Sections 4607 ("agent" defined), 4613 ("conservator" defined), 4615 ("health care" defined), 4627 ("physician" defined), 4635 ("reasonably available" defined), 4643 ("surrogate" defined).

Background from Uniform Act. The Act employs the term "primary physician" instead of "attending physician." The term "attending physician" could be understood to refer to any physician providing treatment to the individual, and not to the physician whom the individual, or agent, guardian, or surrogate, has designated or, in the absence of a designation, the physician who has undertaken primary responsibility for the individual's health care. [Adapted from Unif. Health–Care Decisions Act § 1(13) comment (1993)] [29 Cal.L.Rev.Comm. Reports App. 6 (1999)].

Cross References

Agent defined for purposes of this Division, see Probate Code § 4607.

Conservator defined for purposes of this Division, see Probate Code § 4613.
Health care defined for purposes of this Division, see Probate Code § 4615.
Patient defined for purposes of this Division, see Probate Code § 4625.
Physician defined for purposes of this Division, see Probate Code § 4627.
Reasonably available defined for purposes of this Division, see Probate Code § 4635.
Surrogate defined for purposes of this Division, see Probate Code § 4643.

§ 4633. Principal

"Principal" means an adult who executes a power of attorney for health care. *(Added by Stats.1999, c. 658 (A.B.891), § 39, operative July 1, 2000.)*

Law Revision Commission Comments

1999 Addition

Section 4633 is the same in substance as Section 4026 in the Power of Attorney Law. "Adult" includes an emancipated minor. See Fam. Code §§ 7002 (emancipation), 7050 (emancipated minor considered as adult for consent to medical, dental, or psychiatric care).

See also Section 4629 ("power of attorney for health care" defined). [29 Cal.L.Rev.Comm. Reports 1 (1999)].

Cross References

Health care defined for purposes of this Division, see Probate Code § 4615.
Power of attorney for health care defined for purposes of this Division, see Probate Code § 4629.

§ 4635. Reasonably available

"Reasonably available" means readily able to be contacted without undue effort and willing and able to act in a timely manner considering the urgency of the patient's health care needs. *(Added by Stats.1999, c. 658 (A.B.891), § 39, operative July 1, 2000.)*

Law Revision Commission Comments

1999 Addition

Section 4635 is the same as Section 1(14) of the Uniform Health–Care Decisions Act (1993).

For provisions in this division using this term, see Sections 4631 ("primary physician" defined), 4641 ("supervising health care provider" defined), 4685 (agent's priority), 4701 (optional form of advance health care directive).

See also Section 4615 ("health care" defined), 4625 ("patient" defined).

Background from Uniform Act. The term "reasonably available" is used in the Act to accommodate the reality that individuals will sometimes not be timely available. The term is incorporated into the definition of "supervising health-care provider" [Prob. Code § 4641]. It appears in the optional statutory form (Section 4) [Prob. Code § 4701] to indicate when an alternate agent may act. [Adapted from Unif. Health–Care Decisions Act § 1(14) comment (1993)] [29 Cal.L.Rev.Comm. Reports App. 6 (1999)].

Cross References

Health care defined for purposes of this Division, see Probate Code § 4615.

Patient defined for purposes of this Division, see Probate Code § 4625.

§ 4637. Residential care facility for the elderly

"Residential care facility for the elderly" means a "residential care facility for the elderly" as defined in Section 1569.2 of the Health and Safety Code. *(Added by Stats.1999, c. 658 (A.B.891), § 39, operative July 1, 2000.)*

Law Revision Commission Comments

1999 Addition

Section 4637 continues former Section 4618 without substantive change.

For provisions in this division using this term, see Sections 4659 (limitations on who may act as agent or surrogate), 4673 (witnessing requirements in skilled nursing facility), 4701 (optional form of advance health care directive). [29 Cal.L.Rev.Comm. Reports 1 (1999)].

§ 4639. Skilled nursing facility

"Skilled nursing facility" means a "skilled nursing facility" as defined in Section 1250 of the Health and Safety Code. *(Added by Stats.1999, c. 658 (A.B.891), § 39, operative July 1, 2000.)*

Law Revision Commission Comments

1999 Addition

Section 4639 is a new provision that incorporates the relevant definition from the Health and Safety Code.

For provisions in this division using this term, see Sections 4673 (witnessing requirements in skilled nursing facility), 4701 (optional form of advance health care directive). [29 Cal.L.Rev.Comm. Reports 1 (1999)].

§ 4641. Supervising health care provider

"Supervising health care provider" means the primary physician or, if there is no primary physician or the primary physician is not reasonably available, the health care provider who has undertaken primary responsibility for a patient's health care. *(Added by Stats.1999, c. 658 (A.B.891), § 39, operative July 1, 2000.)*

Law Revision Commission Comments

1999 Addition

Section 4641 is a new provision and is the same in substance as Section 1(16) of the Uniform Health–Care Decisions Act (1993).

For provisions in this division using this term, see Sections 4659 (limitations on who may act as agent or surrogate), 4695 (revocation of power of attorney for health care), 4696 (duty to communicate revocation), 4701 (optional form of advance health care directive), 4711 (patient's designation of surrogate), 4715 (disqualification of surrogate), 4730 (duty of health care provider to communicate), 4731 (duty of supervising health care provider to record relevant information), 4765 (petitioners).

See also Sections 4607 ("agent" defined), 4615 ("health care" defined), 4621 ("health care provider" defined), 4625 ("patient" defined), 4631 ("primary physician" defined), 4635 ("reasonably available" defined).

Background from Uniform Act. The definition of "supervising health-care provider" accommodates the circumstance that frequently arises where care or supervision by a physician may not be readily available. The individual's primary physician is to assume the role, however, if reasonably available. [Adapted from Unif. Health–Care

Decisions Act § 1(16) comment (1993)] [29 Cal.L.Rev.Comm. Reports 1 (1999)].

Cross References

Health care defined for purposes of this Division, see Probate Code § 4615.

Health care provider defined for purposes of this Division, see Probate Code § 4621.

Patient defined for purposes of this Division, see Probate Code § 4625.

Physician defined for purposes of this Division, see Probate Code § 4627.

Primary physician defined for purposes of this Division, see Probate Code § 4631.

Reasonably available defined for purposes of this Division, see Probate Code § 4635.

§ 4643. Surrogate

"Surrogate" means an adult, other than a patient's agent or conservator, authorized under this division to make a health care decision for the patient. *(Added by Stats.1999, c. 658 (A.B.891), § 39, operative July 1, 2000.)*

Law Revision Commission Comments

1999 Addition

Section 4643 is a new provision and is the same in substance as Section 1(17) of the Uniform Health–Care Decisions Act (1993), except that this section refers to "conservator" instead of "guardian" and to "adult" instead of "individual." "Adult" includes an emancipated minor. See Fam. Code § 7002 (emancipation). For other provisions concerning surrogates, see Section 4711 *et seq.*

For provisions in this division using this term, see Sections 4617 ("health care decision" defined), 4625 ("patient" defined), 4631 ("primary physician" defined), 4653 (mercy killing, assisted suicide, euthanasia not approved), 4657 (presumption of capacity), 4658 (determination of capacity and other medical conditions), 4659 (limitations on who may act as agent or surrogate), 4660 (use of copies), 4696 (duty to communicate revocation), 4711–4715 (health care surrogates), 4731 (duty of supervising health care provider to record relevant information), 4732 (duty of primary physician to record relevant information), 4741 (immunities of agent and surrogate), 4750 (judicial intervention disfavored), 4762 (jurisdiction over agent or surrogate), 4763 (venue), 4765 (petitioners), 4766 (purposes of petition), 4769 (notice of hearing), 4771 (award of attorney's fees). See also 4780 (request to forgo resuscitative measures), 4783 (forms for requests to forgo resuscitative measures).

See also Section 4607 ("agent" defined).

Background from Uniform Act. The definition of "surrogate" refers to the individual having present authority under Section 5 [see Prob. Code § 4711 *et seq.*] to make a health-care decision for a patient. It does not include an individual who might have such authority under a given set of circumstances which have not occurred. [Adapted from Unif. Health–Care Decisions Act § 1(17) comment (1993)] [29 Cal.L.Rev.Comm. Reports App. 6 (1999)].

Cross References

Agent defined for purposes of this Division, see Probate Code § 4607.

Conservator defined for purposes of this Division, see Probate Code § 4613.

Health care decision defined for purposes of this Division, see Probate Code § 4617.

Health care defined for purposes of this Division, see Probate Code § 4615.

Patient defined for purposes of this Division, see Probate Code § 4625.

CHAPTER 2. GENERAL PROVISIONS

Section
4650. Legislative findings.
4651. Application; exemptions.
4652. Scope.
4653. Mercy killing, assisted suicide, or euthanasia.
4654. Health care contrary to generally accepted health care standards.
4655. Intention of patient.
4656. Effect of death resulting from withholding or withdrawing health care.
4657. Presumption of capacity.
4658. Determination regarding patient's capacity to be made by primary physician.
4659. Persons excluded from making decisions under this division.
4660. Copy of directive; effect.

Cross References

Assisted outpatient treatment, written treatment plan, see Welfare and Institutions Code § 5346.

§ 4650. Legislative findings

The Legislature finds the following:

(a) In recognition of the dignity and privacy a person has a right to expect, the law recognizes that an adult has the fundamental right to control the decisions relating to his or her own health care, including the decision to have life-sustaining treatment withheld or withdrawn.

(b) Modern medical technology has made possible the artificial prolongation of human life beyond natural limits. In the interest of protecting individual autonomy, this prolongation of the process of dying for a person for whom continued health care does not improve the prognosis for recovery may violate patient dignity and cause unnecessary pain and suffering, while providing nothing medically necessary or beneficial to the person.

(c) In the absence of controversy, a court is normally not the proper forum in which to make health care decisions, including decisions regarding life-sustaining treatment. *(Added by Stats.1999, c. 658 (A.B.891), § 39, operative July 1, 2000.)*

Law Revision Commission Comments

1999 Addition

Section 4650 preserves and continues the substance of the legislative findings set out in former Health and Safety Code Section 7185.5 (Natural Death Act). These findings, in an earlier form, have been relied upon by the courts. Conservatorship of Drabick, 200 Cal. App.3d 185, 206, 245 Cal.Rptr. 840, 853 (1988); Bouvia v. Superior Court, 179 Cal.App.3d 1127, 1137, 225 Cal.Rptr. 297, 302 (1986); Bartling v. Superior Court, 163 Cal.App.3d 186, 194–95, 209 Cal. Rptr. 220, 224–25 (1984); Barber v. Superior Court, 147 Cal.App.3d 1006, 1015–16, 195 Cal.Rptr. 484, 489–90 (1983). The earlier legislative findings were limited to persons with a terminal condition or permanent unconscious condition. This restriction is not continued here in recognition of the broader scope of this division and the development of case law since enactment of the original Natural Death Act in 1976. References to "medical care" in former law have been changed to "health care" for consistency with the language of this division. See Section 4615 ("health care" defined). This is not intended as a substantive change. "Adult" includes an emancipated minor. See Fam. Code §§ 7002 (emancipation), 7050 (emancipated minor considered as adult for consent to medical, dental, or psychiatric care).

Parts of former Health and Safety Code Section 7185.5 that are more appropriately stated as substantive provisions are not continued here. See also Section 4750 (judicial intervention disfavored). [29 Cal.L.Rev.Comm. Reports 1 (1999)].

Cross References

Health care decision defined for purposes of this Division, see Probate Code § 4617.

Health care defined for purposes of this Division, see Probate Code § 4615.

Patient defined for purposes of this Division, see Probate Code § 4625.

§ 4651. Application; exemptions

(a) Except as otherwise provided, this division applies to health care decisions for adults who lack capacity to make health care decisions for themselves.

(b) This division does not affect any of the following:

(1) The right of an individual to make health care decisions while having the capacity to do so.

(2) The law governing health care in an emergency.

(3) The law governing health care for unemancipated minors. *(Added by Stats.1999, c. 658 (A.B.891), § 39, operative July 1, 2000.)*

Law Revision Commission Comments

1999 Addition

Subdivision (a) of Section 4651 is a new provision.

Subdivision (b)(1) is the same in substance as Section 11(a) of the Uniform Health–Care Decisions Act (1993) and replaces former Health and Safety Code Sections 7189.5(a) and 7191.5(e) & (h) (Natural Death Act).

Subdivision (b)(2) continues the substance of former Section 4652(b).

Subdivision (b)(3) is new. This division applies to emancipated minors to the same extent as adults. See Fam. Code §§ 7002 (emancipation), 7050 (emancipated minor considered as adult for consent to medical, dental, or psychiatric care).

See also Sections 4605 ("advance health care directive" defined), 4615 ("health care" defined), 4617 ("health care decision" defined), 4687 (other authority of person named as agent not affected). [29 Cal.L.Rev.Comm. Reports App. 6 (1999)].

Cross References

Capacity defined for purposes of this Division, see Probate Code § 4609.

Health care decision defined for purposes of this Division, see Probate Code § 4617.

Health care defined for purposes of this Division, see Probate Code § 4615.

§ 4652. Scope

This division does not authorize consent to any of the following on behalf of a patient:

(a) Commitment to or placement in a mental health treatment facility.

(b) Convulsive treatment (as defined in Section 5325 of the Welfare and Institutions Code).

(c) Psychosurgery (as defined in Section 5325 of the Welfare and Institutions Code).

(d) Sterilization.

(e) Abortion. *(Added by Stats.1999, c. 658 (A.B.891), § 39, operative July 1, 2000.)*

Law Revision Commission Comments

1999 Addition

Section 4652 continues former Section 4722 without substantive change and revises language for consistency with the broader scope of this division. A power of attorney may not vary the limitations of this section. See also Section 4653 (mercy killing, assisted suicide, euthanasia not approved). [29 Cal.L.Rev.Comm. Reports 1 (1999)].

Cross References

Patient defined for purposes of this Division, see Probate Code § 4625.

§ 4653. Mercy killing, assisted suicide, or euthanasia

Nothing in this division shall be construed to condone, authorize, or approve mercy killing, assisted suicide, or euthanasia. This division is not intended to permit any affirmative or deliberate act or omission to end life other than withholding or withdrawing health care pursuant to an advance health care directive, by a surrogate, or as otherwise provided, so as to permit the natural process of dying. *(Added by Stats.1999, c. 658 (A.B.891), § 39, operative July 1, 2000.)*

Law Revision Commission Comments

1999 Addition

Section 4653 continues the first sentence of former Section 4723 without substantive change, and is consistent with Section 13(c) of the Uniform Health–Care Decisions Act (1993). This section also continues the substance of former Health and Safety Code Section 7191.5(g) (Natural Death Act). Language has been revised to conform to the broader scope of this division. This section provides a rule governing the interpretation of this division. It is not intended as a general statement beyond the scope of this division nor is it intended to affect any other authority that may exist.

See Sections 4670 *et seq.* (advance health care directives), 4711 *et seq.* (health care surrogates). See also Sections 4605 ("advance health care directive" defined), 4615 ("health care" defined), 4643 ("surrogate" defined). [29 Cal.L.Rev.Comm. Reports App. 6 (1999)].

Cross References

Advance health care directive defined for purposes of this Division, see Probate Code § 4605.

Health care defined for purposes of this Division, see Probate Code § 4615.

Surrogate defined for purposes of this Division, see Probate Code § 4643.

§ 4654. Health care contrary to generally accepted health care standards

This division does not authorize or require a health care provider or health care institution to provide health care contrary to generally accepted health care standards applicable to the health care provider or health care institution. *(Added by Stats.1999, c. 658 (A.B.891), § 39, operative July 1, 2000.)*

Section 4654 is the same as Section 13(d) of the Uniform Health–Care Decisions Act (1993). For a special application of this general rule, see Section 4735 (right to decline to provide ineffective care). This section continues the substance of former Health and Safety Code Section 7191.5(f) (Natural Death Act) and subsumes the specific duty under former Health and Safety Code Section 7189.5(b) concerning providing comfort care and alleviation of pain.

See also Sections 4615 ("health care" defined), 4619 ("health care institution" defined), 4621 ("health care provider" defined). [29 Cal.L.Rev.Comm. Reports 1 (1999)].

Cross References

Health care defined for purposes of this Division, see Probate Code § 4615.
Health care institution defined for purposes of this Division, see Probate Code § 4619.
Health care provider defined for purposes of this Division, see Probate Code § 4621.

§ 4655. Intention of patient

(a) This division does not create a presumption concerning the intention of a patient who has not made or who has revoked an advance health care directive.

(b) In making health care decisions under this division, a patient's attempted suicide shall not be construed to indicate a desire of the patient that health care be restricted or inhibited. *(Added by Stats.1999, c. 658 (A.B.891), § 39, operative July 1, 2000.)*

Subdivision (a) of Section 4655 continues and generalizes former Health and Safety Code Section 7191.5(d) (Natural Death Act), and is the same in substance as Section 13(a) of the Uniform Health–Care Decisions Act (1993).

Subdivision (b) continues the second sentence of former Section 4723 without substantive change and with wording changes to reflect the broader scope of this division.

See also Sections 4605 ("advance health care directive" defined), 4615 ("health care" defined), 4617 ("health care decision" defined), 4625 ("patient" defined). [29 Cal.L.Rev.Comm. Reports App. 6 (1999)].

Cross References

Advance health care directive defined for purposes of this Division, see Probate Code § 4605.
Health care decision defined for purposes of this Division, see Probate Code § 4617.
Health care defined for purposes of this Division, see Probate Code § 4615.
Patient defined for purposes of this Division, see Probate Code § 4625.

§ 4656. Effect of death resulting from withholding or withdrawing health care

Death resulting from withholding or withdrawing health care in accordance with this division does not for any purpose constitute a suicide or homicide or legally impair or invalidate a policy of insurance or an annuity providing a death benefit, notwithstanding any term of the policy or annuity to the contrary. *(Added by Stats.1999, c. 658 (A.B.891), § 39, operative July 1, 2000.)*

Section 4656 continues and generalizes former Health and Safety Code Section 7191.5(a)-(b) (Natural Death Act), and is the same in substance as Section 13(b) of the Uniform Health–Care Decisions Act (1993).

See also Section 4615 ("health care" defined). [29 Cal.L.Rev. Comm. Reports 1 (1999)].

Cross References

Health care defined for purposes of this Division, see Probate Code § 4615.

§ 4657. Presumption of capacity

A patient is presumed to have the capacity to make a health care decision, to give or revoke an advance health care directive, and to designate or disqualify a surrogate. This presumption is a presumption affecting the burden of proof. *(Added by Stats.1999, c. 658 (A.B.891), § 39, operative July 1, 2000.)*

Section 4657 is the same in substance as Section 11(b) of the Uniform Health–Care Decisions Act (1993). The presumption of capacity with regard to revocation continues the substance of former Section 4727(c), and is consistent with former Health and Safety Code Section 7189.5(a) (Natural Death Act). See also Section 4766(a) (petition to review capacity determinations). The burden of proof is on the person who seeks to establish that the principal did not have capacity. This section is also consistent with the rule applicable under Section 810 (due process in capacity determinations).

See also Sections 4605 ("advance health care directive" defined), 4609 ("capacity" defined), 4617 ("health care decision" defined), 4625 ("patient" defined), 4643 ("surrogate" defined).

Background from Uniform Act. Section 11 reinforces the principle of patient autonomy by providing a rebuttable presumption that an individual has capacity for all decisions relating to health care referred to in the Act. [Adapted from Unif. Health–Care Decisions Act § 11 comment (1993)] [29 Cal.L.Rev.Comm. Reports 1 (1999)].

Cross References

Advance health care directive defined for purposes of this Division, see Probate Code § 4605.
Burden of proof, generally, see Evidence Code § 500 et seq.
Capacity defined for purposes of this Division, see Probate Code § 4609.
Health care decision defined for purposes of this Division, see Probate Code § 4617.
Health care defined for purposes of this Division, see Probate Code § 4615.
Patient defined for purposes of this Division, see Probate Code § 4625.
Surrogate defined for purposes of this Division, see Probate Code § 4643.

§ 4658. Determination regarding patient's capacity to be made by primary physician

Unless otherwise specified in a written advance health care directive, for the purposes of this division, a determination that a patient lacks or has recovered capacity, or that another condition exists that affects an individual health care instruction or the authority of an agent or surrogate, shall be made by the primary physician. *(Added by Stats.1999, c. 658 (A.B.891), § 39, operative July 1, 2000.)*

Law Revision Commission Comments

1999 Addition

Section 4658 is drawn from Section 2(d) (advance directives) and part of Section 5(a) (surrogates) of the Uniform Health–Care Decisions Act (1993). This section also supersedes parts of the Natural Death Act relating to physician certification of the patient's condition. See former Health and Safety Code §§ 7187.5, 7189. This section makes clear that capacity determinations need not be made by the courts. For provisions governing judicial determinations of capacity, see Sections 810–813 (Due Process in Capacity Determinations Act). See also Section 4766 (petitions concerning advance directives). For the primary physician's duty to record capacity determinations, see Section 4732. See also Section 4766(a) (petition to review capacity determinations).

See also Sections 4605 ("advance health care directive" defined), 4607 ("agent" defined), 4609 ("capacity" defined), 4623 ("individual health care instruction" defined), 4625 ("patient" defined), 4631 ("primary physician" defined), 4643 ("surrogate" defined).

Background from Uniform Act. Section 2(d) provides that unless otherwise specified in a written advance health-care directive, a determination that a principal has lost or recovered capacity to make health-care decisions must be made by the primary physician. For example, a principal might specify that the determination of capacity is to be made by the agent in consultation with the primary physician. Or a principal, such as a member of the Christian Science faith who relies on a religious method of healing and who has no primary physician, might specify that capacity be determined by other means. In the event that multiple decision makers are specified and they cannot agree, it may be necessary to seek court instruction as authorized by Section 14 [see Prob. Code § 4766].

Section 2(d) also provides that unless otherwise specified in a written advance health-care directive, the existence of other conditions which affect an individual instruction or the authority of an agent must be determined by the primary physician. For example, an individual might specify that an agent may withdraw or withhold treatment that keeps the individual alive only if the individual has an incurable and irreversible condition that will result in the individual's death within a relatively short time. In that event, unless otherwise specified in the advance health-care directive, the determination that the individual has that condition must be made by the primary physician.

[Adapted from Unif. Health–Care Decisions Act § 2(d) comment (1993)] [29 Cal.L.Rev.Comm. Reports App. 6 (1999)].

Cross References

Advance health care directive defined for purposes of this Division, see Probate Code § 4605.
Agent defined for purposes of this Division, see Probate Code § 4607.
Capacity defined for purposes of this Division, see Probate Code § 4609.
Health care defined for purposes of this Division, see Probate Code § 4615.
Individual health care instruction defined for purposes of this Division, see Probate Code § 4623.
Patient defined for purposes of this Division, see Probate Code § 4625.
Physician defined for purposes of this Division, see Probate Code § 4627.
Primary physician defined for purposes of this Division, see Probate Code § 4631.

Surrogate defined for purposes of this Division, see Probate Code § 4643.

§ 4659. Persons excluded from making decisions under this division

(a) Except as provided in subdivision (b), none of the following persons may make health care decisions as an agent under a power of attorney for health care or a surrogate under this division:

(1) The supervising health care provider or an employee of the health care institution where the patient is receiving care.

(2) An operator or employee of a community care facility or residential care facility where the patient is receiving care.

(b) The prohibition in subdivision (a) does not apply to the following persons:

(1) An employee, other than the supervising health care provider, who is related to the patient by blood, marriage, or adoption, or is a registered domestic partner of the patient.

(2) An employee, other than the supervising health care provider, who is employed by the same health care institution, community care facility, or residential care facility for the elderly as the patient.

(c) A conservator under the Lanterman–Petris–Short Act (Part 1 (commencing with Section 5000) of Division 5 of the Welfare and Institutions Code) may not be designated as an agent or surrogate to make health care decisions by the conservatee, unless all of the following are satisfied:

(1) The advance health care directive is otherwise valid.

(2) The conservatee is represented by legal counsel.

(3) The lawyer representing the conservatee signs a certificate stating in substance:

"I am a lawyer authorized to practice law in the state where this advance health care directive was executed, and the principal or patient was my client at the time this advance directive was executed. I have advised my client concerning his or her rights in connection with this advance directive and the applicable law and the consequences of signing or not signing this advance directive, and my client, after being so advised, has executed this advance directive." *(Added by Stats.1999, c. 658 (A.B.891), § 39, operative July 1, 2000. Amended by Stats.2001, c. 230 (A.B.1278), § 4.)*

Law Revision Commission Comments

1999 Addition

Section 4659 restates former Section 4702 without substantive change, and extends its principles to cover surrogates. The terms "supervising health care provider" and "health care institution" have been substituted for "treating health care provider" as appropriate, for consistency with the terms used in this division. See Section 4641 ("supervising health care provider" defined).

Subdivisions (a) and (b) serve the same purpose as Section 2(b) (fourth sentence) and Section 5(i) of the Uniform Health–Care Decisions Act (1993). Subdivision (a) does not preclude a person from appointing, for example, a friend who is a physician as the agent under the person's power of attorney for health care, but if the physician becomes the person's "supervising health care provider," the physician is precluded from acting as the agent under the power of attorney. See also Section 4675 (witnessing requirements in skilled nursing facilities).

Subdivision (b) provides a special exception to subdivision (a). This will, for example, permit a nurse to serve as agent for the nurse's spouse when the spouse is being treated at the hospital where the nurse is employed.

Subdivision (c) prescribes conditions that must be satisfied if a conservator is to be designated as the agent or surrogate for a conservatee under the Lanterman–Petris–Short Act. This subdivision has no application where a person other than the conservator is so designated.

See also Sections 4605 ("advance health care directive" defined), 4607 ("agent" defined), 4611 ("community care facility" defined), 4613 ("conservator" defined), 4617 ("health care decision" defined), 4619 ("health care institution" defined), 4625 ("patient" defined), 4629 ("power of attorney for health care" defined), 4637 ("residential care facility for the elderly" defined), 4641 ("supervising health care provider" defined), 4643 ("surrogate" defined). [29 Cal.L.Rev. Comm. Reports App. 6 (1999)].

2001 Amendment

Section 4659 is amended to clarify an ambiguity that existed in prior law. See former Section 4702. As amended, the exception in subdivision (b) does not apply to supervising health care providers. Consequently, the bar on supervising health care providers acting as agents or surrogates for their patients, as provided in subdivision (a), is absolute. If a supervising health care provider is the spouse of a patient, he or she would need to cease acting as the patient's primary physician or other supervising health care provider in order to undertake responsibilities as an agent under a power of attorney for health care or as a surrogate health care decisionmaker. The extension of the relationship exception in subdivision (b)(1) to include registered domestic partners is new. See Fam. Code 297 *et seq.* (domestic partner registration). [30 Cal.L.Rev.Comm. Reports 621 (2000)].

Cross References

Advance health care directive defined for purposes of this Division, see Probate Code § 4605.
Agent defined for purposes of this Division, see Probate Code § 4607.
Community care facility defined for purposes of this Division, see Probate Code § 4611.
Conservator defined for purposes of this Division, see Probate Code § 4613.
Health care decision defined for purposes of this Division, see Probate Code § 4617.
Health care defined for purposes of this Division, see Probate Code § 4615.
Health care institution defined for purposes of this Division, see Probate Code § 4619.
Health care provider defined for purposes of this Division, see Probate Code § 4621.
Patient defined for purposes of this Division, see Probate Code § 4625.
Power of attorney for health care defined for purposes of this Division, see Probate Code § 4629.
Principal defined for purposes of this Division, see Probate Code § 4633.
Residential care facility for the elderly defined for purposes of this Division, see Probate Code § 4637.
Supervising health care provider defined for purposes of this Division, see Probate Code § 4641.
Surrogate defined for purposes of this Division, see Probate Code § 4643.

§ 4660. Copy of directive; effect

A copy of a written advance health care directive, revocation of an advance directive, or designation or disqualification of a surrogate has the same effect as the original. *(Added by Stats.1999, c. 658 (A.B.891), § 39, operative July 1, 2000.)*

Law Revision Commission Comments
1999 Addition

Section 4660 provides a special rule permitting the use of copies under this division. It is the same as Section 12 of the Uniform Health–Care Decisions Act (1993). The rule under this section for powers of attorney for health care differs from the rule under the Power of Attorney Law. See Section 4307 (certified copy of power of attorney).

See also Sections 4605 ("advance health care directive" defined), 4643 ("surrogate" defined).

Background from Uniform Act. The need to rely on an advance health-care directive may arise at times when the original is inaccessible. For example, an individual may be receiving care from several health-care providers or may be receiving care at a location distant from that where the original is kept. To facilitate prompt and informed decision making, this section provides that a copy of a valid written advance health-care directive, revocation of an advance health-care directive, or designation or disqualification of a surrogate has the same effect as the original. [Adapted from Unif. Health–Care Decisions Act § 12 comment (1993)] [29 Cal.L.Rev.Comm. Reports 1 (1999)].

Cross References

Advance health care directive defined for purposes of this Division, see Probate Code § 4605.
Surrogate defined for purposes of this Division, see Probate Code § 4643.

CHAPTER 3. TRANSITIONAL PROVISIONS

Section
4665. Application of division.

§ 4665. Application of division

Except as otherwise provided by statute:

(a) On and after July 1, 2000, this division applies to all advance health care directives, including, but not limited to, durable powers of attorney for health care and declarations under the Natural Death Act (former Chapter 3.9 (commencing with Section 7185) of Part 1 of Division 7 of the Health and Safety Code), regardless of whether they were given or executed before, on, or after July 1, 2000.

(b) This division applies to all proceedings concerning advance health care directives commenced on or after July 1, 2000.

(c) This division applies to all proceedings concerning written advance health care directives commenced before July 1, 2000, unless the court determines that application of a particular provision of this division would substantially interfere with the effective conduct of the proceedings or the rights of the parties and other interested persons, in which case the particular provision of this division does not apply and prior law applies.

(d) Nothing in this division affects the validity of an advance health care directive executed before July 1, 2000, that was valid under prior law.

(e) Nothing in this division affects the validity of a durable power of attorney for health care executed on a printed form that was valid under prior law, regardless of whether execution occurred before, on, or after July 1, 2000. *(Added by Stats.1999, c. 658 (A.B.891), § 39, operative July 1, 2000.)*

Law Revision Commission Comments

1999 Addition

Section 4665 serves the same purpose as Section 4054 in the Power of Attorney Law, but covers all advance health care directives, including powers of attorney, written or oral individual health care instructions, and surrogate designations.

Subdivision (a) provides the general rule that this division applies to all advance health care directives, regardless of when a written advance directive was executed or an oral individual instruction was made. As provided in subdivision (d), however, nothing in this division invalidates any advance directive that was validly executed under prior law, and subdivision (e) protects individuals who happen to use an outdated printed form.

Subdivision (b) is a specific application of the general rule in subdivision (a). See Section 4750 *et seq.* (judicial proceedings). Subdivision (c) provides discretion to the court to resolve problems arising in proceedings commenced before the operative date.

See also Sections 4605 ("advance health care directive" defined), 4629 ("power of attorney for health care" defined). [29 Cal.L.Rev. Comm. Reports 1 (1999)].

Cross References

Advance health care directive defined for purposes of this Division, see Probate Code § 4605.

Health care defined for purposes of this Division, see Probate Code § 4615.

Power of attorney for health care defined for purposes of this Division, see Probate Code § 4629.

Part 2

UNIFORM HEALTH CARE DECISIONS ACT

CHAPTER 1.   ADVANCE HEALTH CARE DIRECTIVES

ARTICLE 1.   GENERAL PROVISIONS

§ 4670.   Persons entitled to give individual health care instruction; method; conditions

An adult having capacity may give an individual health care instruction. The individual instruction may be oral or written. The individual instruction may be limited to take effect only if a specified condition arises. *(Added by Stats. 1999, c. 658 (A.B.891), § 39, operative July 1, 2000.)*

Law Revision Commission Comments

1999 Addition

Section 4670 is drawn from Section 2(a) of the Uniform Health–Care Decisions Act (1993). This section supersedes part of former Health and Safety Code Section 7186.5 (Natural Death Act). "Adult" includes an emancipated minor. See Fam. Code §§ 7002 (emancipation), 7050 (emancipated minor considered as adult for consent to medical, dental, or psychiatric care).

See also Sections 4615 ("health care" defined), 4623 ("individual health care instruction" defined).

Background from Uniform Act. The individual instruction authorized in Section 2(a) may but need not be limited to take effect in specified circumstances, such as if the individual is dying. An individual instruction may be either written or oral. [Adapted from Unif. Health–Care Decisions Act § 2(a) comment (1993)] [29 Cal.L.Rev.Comm. Reports 1 (1999)].

Cross References

Capacity defined for purposes of this Division, see Probate Code § 4609.

Health care defined for purposes of this Division, see Probate Code § 4615.

Individual health care instruction defined for purposes of this Division, see Probate Code § 4623.

Terminal illness diagnosis, end-of-life information and counseling options, see Health and Safety Code § 442.5.

§ 4671.   Persons entitled to execute power of attorney for health care; scope authority granted

(a) An adult having capacity may execute a power of attorney for health care, as provided in Article 2 (commencing with Section 4680). The power of attorney for health care may authorize the agent to make health care decisions and may also include individual health care instructions.

(b) The principal in a power of attorney for health care may grant authority to make decisions relating to the personal care of the principal, including, but not limited to, determining where the principal will live, providing meals, hiring household employees, providing transportation, handling mail, and arranging recreation and entertainment. *(Added by Stats.1999, c. 658 (A.B.891), § 39, operative July 1, 2000.)*

Law Revision Commission Comments

1999 Addition

Subdivision (a) of Section 4671 is drawn from the first and third sentences of the Uniform Health–Care Decisions Act (1993). The first sentence supersedes Section 4120 (who may execute power of attorney) to the extent it applied to powers of attorney for health care. "Adult" includes an emancipated minor. See Fam. Code §§ 7002 (emancipation), 7050 (emancipated minor considered as adult for consent to medical, dental, or psychiatric care).

Subdivision (b), relating to personal care authority, is parallel to Section 4123(c) (personal care authority permissible in non-health care power of attorney). For powers of attorney generally, see the

Power of Attorney Law, Section 4000 *et seq*. Personal care powers are not automatic. Under subdivision (b), the agent does not have personal care powers except to the extent that they are granted by the principal.

See also Sections 4607 ("agent" defined), 4617 ("health care decision" defined), 4623 ("individual health care instruction" defined), 4629 ("power of attorney for health care" defined).

Background from Uniform Act. Section 2(b) authorizes a power of attorney for health care to include instructions regarding the principal's health care. This provision has been included in order to validate the practice of designating an agent and giving individual instructions in one document instead of two. The authority of an agent falls within the discretion of the principal as expressed in the instrument creating the power and may extend to any health-care decision the principal could have made while having capacity.

Section 2(b) excludes the oral designation of an agent. Section 5(b) [Prob. Code § 4711] authorizes an individual to orally designate a surrogate by personally informing the supervising health-care provider. A power of attorney for health care, however, must be in writing and signed by the principal, although it need not be witnessed or acknowledged [except in certain circumstances].

[Adapted from Unif. Health–Care Decisions Act § 2(b) comment (1993)] [29 Cal.L.Rev.Comm. Reports 1 (1999)].

Cross References

Agent defined for purposes of this Division, see Probate Code § 4607.

Capacity defined for purposes of this Division, see Probate Code § 4609.

Health care decision defined for purposes of this Division, see Probate Code § 4617.

Health care defined for purposes of this Division, see Probate Code § 4615.

Individual health care instruction defined for purposes of this Division, see Probate Code § 4623.

Power of attorney for health care defined for purposes of this Division, see Probate Code § 4629.

Principal defined for purposes of this Division, see Probate Code § 4633.

§ 4672. Nomination of conservator

(a) A written advance health care directive may include the individual's nomination of a conservator of the person or estate or both, or a guardian of the person or estate or both, for consideration by the court if protective proceedings for the individual's person or estate are thereafter commenced.

(b) If the protective proceedings are conservatorship proceedings in this state, the nomination has the effect provided in Section 1810 and the court shall give effect to the most recent writing executed in accordance with Section 1810, whether or not the writing is a written advance health care directive. *(Added by Stats.1999, c. 658 (A.B.891), § 39, operative July 1, 2000.)*

Law Revision Commission Comments

1999 Addition

Section 4672 continues Section 4126 without substantive change, insofar as that section applied to powers of attorney for health care, and expands the scope of the rule to apply to other written advance health care directives. Subdivision (a) is the same in substance as Section 2(g) of the Uniform Health–Care Decisions Act (1993).

See also Sections 4605 ("advance health care directive" defined), 4613 ("conservator" defined). [29 Cal.L.Rev.Comm. Reports 1 (1999)].

Cross References

Advance health care directive defined for purposes of this Division, see Probate Code § 4605.

Conservator defined for purposes of this Division, see Probate Code § 4613.

§ 4673. Sufficiency of written or electronic directive

(a) A written advance health care directive is legally sufficient if all of the following requirements are satisfied:

(1) The advance directive contains the date of its execution.

(2) The advance directive is signed either by the patient or in the patient's name by another adult in the patient's presence and at the patient's direction.

(3) The advance directive is either acknowledged before a notary public or signed by at least two witnesses who satisfy the requirements of Sections 4674 and 4675.

(b) An electronic advance health care directive or power of attorney for health care is legally sufficient if the requirements in subdivision (a) are satisfied, except that for the purposes of paragraph (3) of subdivision (a), an acknowledgment before a notary public shall be required, and if a digital signature is used, it meets all of the following requirements:

(1) The digital signature either meets the requirements of Section 16.5 of the Government Code and Chapter 10 (commencing with Section 22000) of Division 7 of Title 2 of the California Code of Regulations or the digital signature uses an algorithm approved by the National Institute of Standards and Technology.

(2) The digital signature is unique to the person using it.

(3) The digital signature is capable of verification.

(4) The digital signature is under the sole control of the person using it.

(5) The digital signature is linked to data in such a manner that if the data are changed, the digital signature is invalidated.

(6) The digital signature persists with the document and not by association in separate files.

(7) The digital signature is bound to a digital certificate. *(Added by Stats.1999, c. 658 (A.B.891), § 39, operative July 1, 2000. Amended by Stats.2006, c. 579 (A.B.2805), § 1, eff. Sept. 28, 2006.)*

Law Revision Commission Comments

1999 Addition

Section 4673 continues the execution requirements in Section 4121 in the Power of Attorney Law to the extent it applied to powers of attorney for health care, and expands the execution requirements under former law to cover all written advance directives, not just powers of attorney. "Adult" has been substituted for "person" in subdivision (b). "Adult" includes an emancipated minor. See Fam. Code §§ 7002 (emancipation), 7050 (emancipated minor considered as adult for consent to medical, dental, or psychiatric care). Sections 4674 and 4675 provide additional requirements applicable where the written advance directive is signed by witnesses, instead of being notarized.

See also Sections 4605 ("advance health care directive" defined), 4625 ("patient" defined). [29 Cal.L.Rev.Comm. Reports App. 6 (1999)].

Advance health care directive defined for purposes of this Division, see Probate Code § 4605.

Health care defined for purposes of this Division, see Probate Code § 4615.

Patient defined for purposes of this Division, see Probate Code § 4625.

Power of attorney for health care defined for purposes of this Division, see Probate Code § 4629.

§ 4674. Requirements

If the written advance health care directive is signed by witnesses, as provided in Section 4673, the following requirements shall be satisfied:

(a) The witnesses shall be adults.

(b) Each witness signing the advance directive shall witness either the signing of the advance directive by the patient or the patient's acknowledgment of the signature or the advance directive.

(c) None of the following persons may act as a witness:

(1) The patient's health care provider or an employee of the patient's health care provider.

(2) The operator or an employee of a community care facility.

(3) The operator or an employee of a residential care facility for the elderly.

(4) The agent, where the advance directive is a power of attorney for health care.

(d) Each witness shall make the following declaration in substance:

"I declare under penalty of perjury under the laws of California (1) that the individual who signed or acknowledged this advance health care directive is personally known to me, or that the individual's identity was proven to me by convincing evidence, (2) that the individual signed or acknowledged this advance directive in my presence, (3) that the individual appears to be of sound mind and under no duress, fraud, or undue influence, (4) that I am not a person appointed as agent by this advance directive, and (5) that I am not the individual's health care provider, an employee of the individual's health care provider, the operator of a community care facility, an employee of an operator of a community care facility, the operator of a residential care facility for the elderly, nor an employee of an operator of a residential care facility for the elderly."

(e) At least one of the witnesses shall be an individual who is neither related to the patient by blood, marriage, or adoption, nor entitled to any portion of the patient's estate upon the patient's death under a will existing when the advance directive is executed or by operation of law then existing.

(f) The witness satisfying the requirement of subdivision (e) shall also sign the following declaration in substance:

"I further declare under penalty of perjury under the laws of California that I am not related to the individual executing this advance health care directive by blood, marriage, or adoption, and, to the best of my knowledge, I am not entitled to any part of the individual's estate upon his or her death under a will now existing or by operation of law."

(g) The provisions of this section applicable to witnesses do not apply to a notary public before whom an advance health care directive is acknowledged. *(Added by Stats.1999, c. 658 (A.B.891), § 39, operative July 1, 2000.)*

1999 Addition

The introductory clause and subdivisions (a) and (b) of Section 4674 continue the witnessing requirements in Section 4122(a) and (c) in the Power of Attorney Law to the extent they applied to powers of attorney for health care, and expands these rules to cover all written advance directives, not just powers of attorney.

Subdivision (c)(1)-(3) continues former Section 4701(a) without substantive change. Subdivision (c)(4) continues Section 4122(b) to the extent it applied to powers of attorney for health care.

Subdivisions (d)-(f) continue former Section 4701(b)-(d) without substantive change and expands the rules to cover all written advance directives.

Subdivision (g) is a new provision making clear that the special rules and restrictions applicable to witnesses are not applicable to notaries. Notaries are subject to obligations under other law by virtue of office. See Gov't Code § 8200 *et seq.*

See also Sections 4605 ("advance health care directive" defined), 4611 ("community care facility" defined), 4621 ("health care provider" defined), 4625 ("patient" defined), 4637 ("residential care facility for the elderly" defined). [29 Cal.L.Rev.Comm. Reports App. 6 (1999)].

Advance health care directive defined for purposes of this Division, see Probate Code § 4605.

Agent defined for purposes of this Division, see Probate Code § 4607.

Community care facility defined for purposes of this Division, see Probate Code § 4611.

Health care defined for purposes of this Division, see Probate Code § 4615.

Health care provider defined for purposes of this Division, see Probate Code § 4621.

Patient defined for purposes of this Division, see Probate Code § 4625.

Power of attorney for health care defined for purposes of this Division, see Probate Code § 4629.

Residential care facility for the elderly defined for purposes of this Division, see Probate Code § 4637.

§ 4675. Patients in skilled nursing facilities; witnesses

(a) If an individual is a patient in a skilled nursing facility when a written advance health care directive is executed, the advance directive is not effective unless a patient advocate or ombudsman, as may be designated by the Department of Aging for this purpose pursuant to any other applicable provision of law, signs the advance directive as a witness, either as one of two witnesses or in addition to notarization. The patient advocate or ombudsman shall declare that he or she is serving as a witness as required by this subdivision. It is the intent of this subdivision to recognize that some patients in skilled nursing facilities are insulated from a voluntary decisionmaking role, by virtue of the custodial nature of their care, so as to require special assurance that they are capable of willfully and voluntarily executing an advance directive.

(b) A witness who is a patient advocate or ombudsman may rely on the representations of the administrators or staff of the skilled nursing facility, or of family members, as convincing evidence of the identity of the patient if the patient advocate or ombudsman believes that the representations provide a reasonable basis for determining the identity of the patient. *(Added by Stats.1999, c. 658 (A.B.891), § 39, operative July 1, 2000.)*

Law Revision Commission Comments

1999 Addition

Subdivision (a) of Section 4675 continues former Section 4701(e) without substantive change. This section expands the witnessing rules under former law to cover all written advance directives executed in nursing homes, not just powers of attorney.

Subdivision (b) continues the substance of former Section 4751(c) (identity of patient in skilled nursing facility) and applies to all written advance directives covered by this section, not just powers of attorney for health care as under former law.

See also Sections 4605 ("advance health care directive" defined), 4621 ("health care provider" defined), 4625 ("patient" defined), 4639 ("skilled nursing facility" defined). [29 Cal.L.Rev.Comm. Reports App. 6 (1999)].

Cross References

Advance health care directive defined for purposes of this Division, see Probate Code § 4605.
Advance Health Care Directive form, see Probate Code § 4701.
Patient defined for purposes of this Division, see Probate Code § 4625.
Skilled nursing facility defined for purposes of this Division, see Probate Code § 4639.

§ 4676. Instruments from another state or jurisdiction; validity

(a) A written advance health care directive or similar instrument executed in another state or jurisdiction in compliance with the laws of that state or jurisdiction or of this state, is valid and enforceable in this state to the same extent as a written advance directive validly executed in this state.

(b) In the absence of knowledge to the contrary, a physician or other health care provider may presume that a written advance health care directive or similar instrument, whether executed in another state or jurisdiction or in this state, is valid. *(Added by Stats.1999, c. 658 (A.B.891), § 39, operative July 1, 2000.)*

Law Revision Commission Comments

1999 Addition

Subdivision (a) of Section 4676 continues former Section 4653 without substantive change, and extends its principles to apply to all written advance health care directives, which include both powers of attorney for health care and written individual instructions. This subdivision also continues and generalizes former Health and Safety Code Section 7192.5 (Natural Death Act). This subdivision is consistent with Section 2(h) of the Uniform Health–Care Decisions Act (1993), as applied to instruments.

Subdivision (b) continues former Section 4752 without substantive change, and broadens the former rule for consistency with the scope of this division. This subdivision also continues and generalizes former Health and Safety Code Section 7192 (Natural Death Act).

See also Section 4605 ("advance health care directive" defined), 4621 ("health care provider" defined), 4627 ("physician" defined). For the rule applicable under the Power of Attorney Law, see Section 4053.

Background from Uniform Act. Section 2(h) validates advance health-care directives which conform to the Act, regardless of when or where executed or communicated. This includes an advance health-care directive which would be valid under the Act but which was made prior to the date of its enactment and failed to comply with the execution requirements then in effect. It also includes an advance health-care directive which was made in another jurisdiction but which does not comply with that jurisdiction's execution or other requirements. [Adapted from Unif. Health–Care Decisions Act § 2(h) comment (1993)] [29 Cal.L.Rev.Comm. Reports App. 6 (1999)].

Cross References

Advance health care directive defined for purposes of this Division, see Probate Code § 4605.
Health care defined for purposes of this Division, see Probate Code § 4615.
Health care provider defined for purposes of this Division, see Probate Code § 4621.
Physician defined for purposes of this Division, see Probate Code § 4627.

§ 4677. Requiring execution or revocation of directive as condition for providing health care

A health care provider, health care service plan, health care institution, disability insurer, self-insured employee welfare plan, or nonprofit hospital plan or a similar insurance plan may not require or prohibit the execution or revocation of an advance health care directive as a condition for providing health care, admission to a facility, or furnishing insurance. *(Added by Stats.1999, c. 658 (A.B.891), § 39, operative July 1, 2000.)*

Law Revision Commission Comments

1999 Addition

Section 4677 continues and generalizes former Section 4725, and contains the substance of Section 7(h) of the Uniform Health–Care Decisions Act (1993). The former provision applied only to powers of attorney for health care. This section supersedes former Health and Safety Code Sections 7191(e)-(f) and 7191.5(c) (Natural Death Act). This section is intended to eliminate the possibility that duress might be used by a health care provider, insurer, plan, or other entity to cause the patient to execute or revoke an advance directive. The reference to a "health care service plan" is drawn from Health and Safety Code Section 1345(f) in the Knox–Keene Health Care Service Plan Act of 1975.

See also Sections 4605 ("advance health care directive" defined), 4615 ("health care" defined), 4619 ("health care institution" defined), 4621 ("health care provider" defined).

Background from Uniform Act. Section 7(h), forbidding a health-care provider or institution to condition provision of health care on execution, non-execution, or revocation of an advance health-care directive, tracks the provisions of the federal Patient Self-Determination Act. 42 U.S.C. §§ 1395cc(f)(1)(C) (Medicare), 1396a(w)(1)(C) (Medicaid). [Adapted from Unif. Health–Care Decisions Act § 7(h) comment (1993)] [29 Cal.L.Rev.Comm. Reports App. 6 (1999)].

Cross References

Advance health care directive defined for purposes of this Division, see Probate Code § 4605.
Health care defined for purposes of this Division, see Probate Code § 4615.
Health care institution defined for purposes of this Division, see Probate Code § 4619.

Health care provider defined for purposes of this Division, see Probate Code § 4621.

§ 4678. Examination and disclosure of medical information

Unless otherwise specified in an advance health care directive, a person then authorized to make health care decisions for a patient has the same rights as the patient to request, receive, examine, copy, and consent to the disclosure of medical or any other health care information. *(Added by Stats.1999, c. 658 (A.B.891), § 39, operative July 1, 2000.)*

Law Revision Commission Comments

1999 Addition

Section 4678 is drawn from Section 8 of the Uniform Health–Care Decisions Act (1993). This section continues former Section 4721 without substantive change, but is broader in scope since it covers all persons authorized to make health care decisions for a patient, not just agents. A power of attorney may limit the right of the agent, for example, by precluding examination of specified medical records or by providing that the examination of medical records is authorized only if the principal lacks the capacity to give informed consent. The right of the agent is subject to any limitations on the right of the patient to reach medical records. See Health and Safety Code §§ 1795.14 (denial of right to inspect mental health records), 1795.20 (providing summary of record rather than allowing access to entire record).

See also Sections 4605 ("advance health care directive" defined), 4617 ("health care decision" defined), 4625 ("patient" defined). **Background from Uniform Act.** An agent, conservator, [guardian,] or surrogate stands in the shoes of the patient when making health-care decisions. To assure fully informed decisionmaking, this section provides that a person who is then authorized to make health-care decisions for a patient has the same right of access to health-care information as does the patient unless otherwise specified in the patient's advance health-care directive. [Adapted from Unif. Health–Care Decisions Act § 8 comment (1993)] [29 Cal.L.Rev.Comm. Reports App. 6 (1999)].

Cross References

Advance health care directive defined for purposes of this Division, see Probate Code § 4605.

Health care decision defined for purposes of this Division, see Probate Code § 4617.

Health care defined for purposes of this Division, see Probate Code § 4615.

Patient defined for purposes of this Division, see Probate Code § 4625.

ARTICLE 2. POWERS OF ATTORNEY FOR HEALTH CARE

§ 4680. Sufficiency of power of attorney

A power of attorney for health care is legally sufficient if it satisfies the requirements of Section 4673. *(Added by Stats.1999, c. 658 (A.B.891), § 39, operative July 1, 2000.)*

Law Revision Commission Comments

1999 Addition

Section 4680 continues the general substance of former Section 4700(b)-(c). A power of attorney must be in writing. See Section 4629 ("power of attorney for health care" defined). A power of attorney that complies with this section and incorporated rules is legally sufficient as a grant of authority to an agent.

See also Section 4629 ("power of attorney for health care" defined). [29 Cal.L.Rev.Comm. Reports App. 6 (1999)].

Cross References

Health care defined for purposes of this Division, see Probate Code § 4615.

Power of attorney for health care defined for purposes of this Division, see Probate Code § 4629.

§ 4681. Limitations on statutory authority

(a) Except as provided in subdivision (b), the principal may limit the application of any provision of this division by an express statement in the power of attorney for health care or by providing an inconsistent rule in the power of attorney.

(b) A power of attorney for health care may not limit either the application of a statute specifically providing that it is not subject to limitation in the power of attorney or a statute concerning any of the following:

(1) Statements required to be included in a power of attorney.

(2) Operative dates of statutory enactments or amendments.

(3) Formalities for execution of a power of attorney for health care.

(4) Qualifications of witnesses.

(5) Qualifications of agents.

(6) Protection of third persons from liability. *(Added by Stats.1999, c. 658 (A.B.891), § 39, operative July 1, 2000.)*

Law Revision Commission Comments

1999 Addition

Section 4681 continues Section 4101, insofar as it applied to powers of attorney for health care, without substantive change. This section makes clear that many of the statutory rules provided in this division are subject to express or implicit limitations in the power of attorney. If a statutory rule is not subject to control by the power of attorney, this is stated explicitly, either in a particular section or as to a group of sections.

See also Sections 4607 ("agent" defined), 4629 ("power of attorney for health care" defined), 4633 ("principal" defined). [29 Cal.L.Rev. Comm. Reports 1 (1999)].

Cross References

Agent defined for purposes of this Division, see Probate Code § 4607.
Health care defined for purposes of this Division, see Probate Code § 4615.
Power of attorney for health care defined for purposes of this Division, see Probate Code § 4629.
Principal defined for purposes of this Division, see Probate Code § 4633.

§ 4682. Authority of agent

Unless otherwise provided in a power of attorney for health care, the authority of an agent becomes effective only on a determination that the principal lacks capacity, and ceases to be effective on a determination that the principal has recovered capacity. *(Added by Stats.1999, c. 658 (A.B. 891), § 39, operative July 1, 2000.)*

Law Revision Commission Comments

1999 Addition

Section 4682 is drawn from Section 2(c) of the Uniform Health–Care Decisions Act (1993) and continues the substance of the last part of former Section 4720(a). See Sections 4657 (presumption of capacity), 4658 (determination of capacity and other medical conditions) & Comment. As under former law, the default rule is that the agent is not authorized to make health care decisions if the principal has the capacity to make health care decisions. The power of attorney may, however, give the agent authority to make health care decisions for the principal even though the principal does have capacity, but the power of attorney is always subject to Section 4695 (revocation of advance directive).

See also Sections 4607 ("agent" defined), 4609 ("capacity" defined), 4629 ("power of attorney for health care" defined), 4633 ("principal" defined).

Background from Uniform Act. Section 2(c) provides that the authority of the agent to make health-care decisions ordinarily does not become effective until the principal is determined to lack capacity and ceases to be effective should the principal recover capacity. A principal may provide, however, that the authority of the agent becomes effective immediately or upon the happening of some event other than the loss of capacity but may do so only by an express provision in the power of attorney. For example, a mother who does not want to make her own health-care decisions but prefers that her daughter make them for her may specify that the daughter as agent is to have authority to make health-care decisions immediately. The mother in that circumstance retains the right to later revoke the power of attorney as provided in Section 3 [Prob. Code § 4696]. [Adapted from Unif. Health–Care Decisions Act § 2(c) comment (1993)] [29 Cal.L.Rev.Comm. Reports 1 (1999)].

Cross References

Agent defined for purposes of this Division, see Probate Code § 4607.
Capacity defined for purposes of this Division, see Probate Code § 4609.
Health care defined for purposes of this Division, see Probate Code § 4615.
Physicians Orders for Life Sustaining Treatment form, execution by health care decisionmaker, see Probate Code § 4780.
Power of attorney for health care defined for purposes of this Division, see Probate Code § 4629.

Principal defined for purposes of this Division, see Probate Code § 4633.

§ 4683. Scope of agent's authority

Subject to any limitations in the power of attorney for health care:

(a) An agent designated in the power of attorney may make health care decisions for the principal to the same extent the principal could make health care decisions if the principal had the capacity to do so.

(b) The agent may also make decisions that may be effective after the principal's death, including the following:

(1) Making a disposition under the Uniform Anatomical Gift Act (Chapter 3.5 (commencing with Section 7150) of Part 1 of Division 7 of the Health and Safety Code).

(2) Authorizing an autopsy under Section 7113 of the Health and Safety Code.

(3) Directing the disposition of remains under Section 7100 of the Health and Safety Code.

(4) Authorizing the release of the records of the principal to the extent necessary for the agent to fulfill his or her duties as set forth in this division. *(Added by Stats.1999, c. 658 (A.B.891), § 39, operative July 1, 2000. Amended by Stats. 2006, c. 249 (S.B.1307), § 2.)*

Law Revision Commission Comments

1999 Addition

Section 4683 continues former Section 4720(b) without substantive change. Subdivision (a) is consistent with the last part of the first sentence of Section 2(b) of the Uniform Health–Care Decisions Act (1993). Technical revisions have made to conform to the language of this division. See Section 4658 (determination of capacity and other medical conditions). The agent's authority is subject to Section 4652 which precludes consent to certain specified types of treatment. See also Section 4653 (impermissible acts and constructions). The principal is free to provide any limitations on types of treatment in the durable power of attorney that are desired. See also Section 4750 *et seq.* (judicial proceedings).

The description of certain post-death decisions in subdivision (b) is not intended to limit the authority to make such decisions under the governing statutes in the Health and Safety Code.

See also Sections 4607 ("agent" defined), 4609 ("capacity" defined), 4615 ("health care" defined), 4617 ("health care decision" defined), 4629 ("power of attorney for health care" defined), 4635 ("reasonably available" defined). [29 Cal.L.Rev.Comm. Reports 1 (1999)].

Cross References

Agent defined for purposes of this Division, see Probate Code § 4607.
Capacity defined for purposes of this Division, see Probate Code § 4609.
Health care decision defined for purposes of this Division, see Probate Code § 4617.
Health care defined for purposes of this Division, see Probate Code § 4615.
Power of attorney for health care defined for purposes of this Division, see Probate Code § 4629.

Principal defined for purposes of this Division, see Probate Code § 4633.

§ 4684. Decisions to be made in principal's best interests

An agent shall make a health care decision in accordance with the principal's individual health care instructions, if any, and other wishes to the extent known to the agent. Otherwise, the agent shall make the decision in accordance with the agent's determination of the principal's best interest. In determining the principal's best interest, the agent shall consider the principal's personal values to the extent known to the agent. *(Added by Stats.1999, c. 658 (A.B.891), § 39, operative July 1, 2000.)*

Law Revision Commission Comments
1999 Addition

Section 4684 continues the substance of former Section 4720(c) and is the same as Section 2(e) of the Uniform Health–Care Decisions Act (1993). Although the new wording of this fundamental rule is different, Section 4684 continues the principle of former law that, in exercising authority, the agent has the duty to act consistent with the principal's desires if known or, if the principal's desires are unknown, to act in the best interest of the principal. The agent's authority is subject to Section 4652, which precludes consent to certain specified types of treatment. See also Section 4653 (mercy killing, assisted suicide, euthanasia not approved). The principal is free to provide any limitations on types of treatment in the power of attorney that are desired. See also Section 4750 *et seq.* (judicial proceedings).

See also Sections 4607 ("agent" defined), 4623 ("individual health care instruction" defined), 4633 ("principal" defined).

Background from Uniform Act. Section 2(e) requires the agent to follow the principal's individual instructions and other expressed wishes to the extent known to the agent. To the extent such instructions or other wishes are unknown, the agent must act in the principal's best interest. In determining the principal's best interest, the agent is to consider the principal's personal values to the extent known to the agent. The Act does not prescribe a detailed list of factors for determining the principal's best interest but instead grants the agent discretion to ascertain and weigh the factors likely to be of importance to the principal. [Adapted from Unif. Health–Care Decisions Act § 2(e) comment (1993)] [29 Cal.L.Rev.Comm. Reports App. 6 (1999)].

Cross References

Agent defined for purposes of this Division, see Probate Code § 4607.
Health care decision defined for purposes of this Division, see Probate Code § 4617.
Health care decisionmaker, see Probate Code § 4781.5.
Health care defined for purposes of this Division, see Probate Code § 4615.
Individual health care instruction defined for purposes of this Division, see Probate Code § 4623.
Principal defined for purposes of this Division, see Probate Code § 4633.

§ 4685. Agent; priority in making health care decisions

Unless the power of attorney for health care provides otherwise, the agent designated in the power of attorney who is known to the health care provider to be reasonably available and willing to make health care decisions has priority over any other person in making health care decisions for the principal. *(Added by Stats.1999, c. 658 (A.B.891), § 39, operative July 1, 2000.)*

Law Revision Commission Comments
1999 Addition

Section 4685 continues without substantive change the first part of former Section 4720(a) and part of former Section 4652(a) relating to availability, willingness, and ability of agents. This section gives the agent priority over others, including a conservator or statutory surrogate, to make health care decisions if the agent is known to the health care provider to be available and willing to act. The power of attorney may vary this priority, as recognized in the introductory clause, and the rule of this section is subject to a contrary court order. See Section 4766. In part, this section serves the same purpose as Section 6(b) of the Uniform Health–Care Decisions Act (1993).

See also Sections 4607 ("agent" defined), 4617 ("health care decision" defined), 4621 ("health care provider" defined), 4629 ("power of attorney for health care" defined), 4633 ("principal" defined), 4635 ("reasonably available" defined). [29 Cal.L.Rev. Comm. Reports App. 6 (1999)].

Cross References

Agent defined for purposes of this Division, see Probate Code § 4607.
Health care decision defined for purposes of this Division, see Probate Code § 4617.
Health care defined for purposes of this Division, see Probate Code § 4615.
Health care provider defined for purposes of this Division, see Probate Code § 4621.
Power of attorney for health care defined for purposes of this Division, see Probate Code § 4629.
Principal defined for purposes of this Division, see Probate Code § 4633.
Reasonably available defined for purposes of this Division, see Probate Code § 4635.

§ 4686. Lapse of time since execution of power of attorney; effect

Unless the power of attorney for health care provides a time of termination, the authority of the agent is exercisable notwithstanding any lapse of time since execution of the power of attorney. *(Added by Stats.1999, c. 658 (A.B.891), § 39, operative July 1, 2000.)*

Law Revision Commission Comments
1999 Addition

Section 4686 continues Section 4127, insofar as it applied to powers of attorney for health care, without substantive change. This rule is the same in substance as the second sentence of the official text of Section 2 of the Uniform Durable Power of Attorney Act (1987), Uniform Probate Code Section 5–502 (1991). See Section 2(b) (construction of provisions drawn from uniform acts).

See also Sections 4607 ("agent" defined), 4629 ("power of attorney for health care" defined). [29 Cal.L.Rev.Comm. Reports 1 (1999)].

Cross References

Agent defined for purposes of this Division, see Probate Code § 4607.
Health care defined for purposes of this Division, see Probate Code § 4615.
Power of attorney for health care defined for purposes of this Division, see Probate Code § 4629.

§ 4687. Rights of agent apart from power of attorney

Nothing in this division affects any right the person designated as an agent under a power of attorney for health care may have, apart from the power of attorney, to make or participate in making health care decisions for the principal. *(Added by Stats.1999, c. 658 (A.B.891), § 39, operative July 1, 2000.)*

Law Revision Commission Comments

1999 Addition

Section 4687 continues former Section 4720(d) without substantive change, and supersedes part of former Section 4652(a). An agent may, without liability, decline to act under the power of attorney. For example, the agent may not be willing to follow the desires of the principal as stated in the power of attorney because of changed circumstances. This section makes clear that, in such a case, the person may make or participate in making health care decisions for the principal without being bound by the stated desires of the principal to the extent that the person designated as the agent has the right under the applicable law apart from the power of attorney.

See also Sections 4607 ("agent" defined), 4617 ("health care decision" defined), 4629 ("power of attorney for health care" defined), 4633 ("principal" defined). [29 Cal.L.Rev.Comm. Reports App. 6 (1999)].

Cross References

Agent defined for purposes of this Division, see Probate Code § 4607.
Health care decision defined for purposes of this Division, see Probate Code § 4617.
Health care defined for purposes of this Division, see Probate Code § 4615.
Power of attorney for health care defined for purposes of this Division, see Probate Code § 4629.
Principal defined for purposes of this Division, see Probate Code § 4633.

§ 4688. Law of agency; application

Where this division does not provide a rule governing agents under powers of attorney, the law of agency applies. *(Added by Stats.1999, c. 658 (A.B.891), § 39, operative July 1, 2000.)*

Law Revision Commission Comments

1999 Addition

Section 4688 is analogous to Section 4051 in the Power of Attorney Law. Under this section, reference may be made to relevant agency principles set forth in case law and statutes. See, e.g., Civ. Code §§ 2019 *et seq.*, 2295 *et seq.*; Prob. Code § 4000 *et seq.* (Power of Attorney Law). [29 Cal.L.Rev.Comm. Reports 1 (1999)].

Cross References

Agent defined for purposes of this Division, see Probate Code § 4607.

§ 4689. Objection to agent's health care decision by principal; effect

Nothing in this division authorizes an agent under a power of attorney for health care to make a health care decision if the principal objects to the decision. If the principal objects to the health care decision of the agent under a power of attorney, the matter shall be governed by the law that would apply if there were no power of attorney for health care. *(Added by Stats.1999, c. 658 (A.B.891), § 39, operative July 1, 2000.)*

Law Revision Commission Comments

1999 Addition

Section 4689 continues former Section 4724 without substantive change. Terminology has been revised for consistency with the language of the Health Care Decisions Law. See Sections 4607 ("agent" defined), 4629 ("power of attorney for health care" defined), 4617 ("health care decision" defined), 4633 ("principal" defined). As under the former section, this section does not limit any right the agent may have apart from the authority under the power of attorney for health care. See Section 4687. [29 Cal.L.Rev.Comm. Reports App. 6 (1999)].

Cross References

Agent defined for purposes of this Division, see Probate Code § 4607.
Health care decision defined for purposes of this Division, see Probate Code § 4617.
Health care defined for purposes of this Division, see Probate Code § 4615.
Power of attorney for health care defined for purposes of this Division, see Probate Code § 4629.
Principal defined for purposes of this Division, see Probate Code § 4633.

§ 4690. Incapacity of principal; determination; disclosure of information agent requires to carry out his or her duties

(a) If the principal becomes wholly or partially incapacitated, or if there is a question concerning the capacity of the principal, the agent may consult with a person previously designated by the principal for this purpose, and may also consult with and obtain information needed to carry out the agent's duties from the principal's spouse, physician, supervising health care provider, attorney, a member of the principal's family, or other person, including a business entity or government agency, with respect to matters covered by the power of attorney for health care.

(b) A person described in subdivision (a) from whom information is requested shall disclose information that the agent requires to carry out his or her duties. Disclosure under this section is not a waiver of any privilege that may apply to the information disclosed. *(Added by Stats.1999, c. 658 (A.B.891), § 39, operative July 1, 2000. Amended by Stats.2006, c. 249 (S.B.1307), § 3; Stats.2007, c. 130 (A.B. 299), § 196.)*

Law Revision Commission Comments

1999 Addition

Section 4690 is drawn from Section 4235 in the Power of Attorney Law, and continues the substance of former law as applied to durable powers of attorney for health care under former law. As with Section 4235, this section does not provide anything inconsistent with permissible practice under former law, but is intended to recognize the desirability of consultation in appropriate circumstances and provide assurance to third persons that consultation with the agent is proper and does not contravene privacy rights.

See also Sections 4607 ("agent" defined), 4629 ("power of attorney for health care" defined), 4633 ("principal" defined). [29 Cal.L.Rev. Comm. Reports App. 6 (1999)].

Cross References

Agent defined for purposes of this Division, see Probate Code § 4607.

Capacity defined for purposes of this Division, see Probate Code § 4609.

Health care defined for purposes of this Division, see Probate Code § 4615.

Health care provider defined for purposes of this Division, see Probate Code § 4621.

Physician defined for purposes of this Division, see Probate Code § 4627.

Power of attorney for health care defined for purposes of this Division, see Probate Code § 4629.

Principal defined for purposes of this Division, see Probate Code § 4633.

Supervising health care provider defined for purposes of this Division, see Probate Code § 4641.

§ 4691. Informing of individuals after death of principal

If directed by the principal in a power of attorney for health care, an attorney-in-fact shall, upon the death of the principal, inform those individuals whose names are provided by the principal to the attorney-in-fact for that purpose. *(Added by Stats.2015, c. 92 (A.B.1085), § 4, eff. Jan. 1, 2016.)*

ARTICLE 3. REVOCATION OF ADVANCE DIRECTIVES

Section
4695. Persons entitled to revoke advance directives; method.
4696. Communication of fact of revocation.
4697. Dissolution of marriage; effect.
4698. Conflicting directives.

§ 4695. Persons entitled to revoke advance directives; method

(a) A patient having capacity may revoke the designation of an agent only by a signed writing or by personally informing the supervising health care provider.

(b) A patient having capacity may revoke all or part of an advance health care directive, other than the designation of an agent, at any time and in any manner that communicates an intent to revoke. *(Added by Stats.1999, c. 658 (A.B.891), § 39, operative July 1, 2000.)*

Law Revision Commission Comments

1999 Addition

Section 4695 is drawn from Section 3(a)-(b) of the Uniform Health–Care Decisions Act (1993). This section replaces former Section 4727(a) (revocation rules applicable to durable power of attorney for health care) and former Health and Safety Code Section 7188(a) (revocation under former Natural Death Act). This section also supersedes Sections 4150 and 4151 in the Power of Attorney Law to the extent they applied to powers of attorney for health care. The principal may revoke the designation or authority only if, at the time of revocation, the principal has sufficient capacity to make a power of attorney for health care. The burden of proof is on the person who seeks to establish that the principal did not have capacity to revoke the designation or authority. See Section 4657 (presumption of capacity). "Personally informing," as used in subdivision (a), includes both oral and written communications.

See also Sections 4605 ("advance health care directive" defined), 4625 ("patient" defined), 4629 ("power of attorney for health care" defined), 4641 ("supervising health care provider" defined).

Background from Uniform Act. Section 3(b) provides that an individual may revoke any portion of an advance health-care directive at any time and in any manner that communicates an intent to revoke. However, a more restrictive standard applies to the

revocation of the portion of a power of attorney for health care relating to the designation of an agent. Section 3(a) provides that an individual may revoke the designation of an agent only by a signed writing or by personally informing the supervising health-care provider. This higher standard is justified by the risk of a false revocation of an agent's designation or of a misinterpretation or miscommunication of a principal's statement communicated through a third party. For example, without this higher standard, an individual motivated by a desire to gain control over a patient might be able to assume authority to act as agent by falsely informing a health-care provider that the principal no longer wishes the previously designated agent to act but instead wishes to appoint the individual.

The section does not specifically address amendment of an advance health-care directive because such reference is not necessary. Section 3(b) specifically authorizes partial revocation, and Section 3(e) [Prob. Code § 4698] recognizes that an advance health-care directive may be modified by a later directive.

[Adapted from Unif. Health–Care Decisions Act § 3(a)-(b), (e) comment (1993)] [29 Cal.L.Rev.Comm. Reports 1 (1999)].

Cross References

Advance health care directive defined for purposes of this Division, see Probate Code § 4605.

Agent defined for purposes of this Division, see Probate Code § 4607.

Capacity defined for purposes of this Division, see Probate Code § 4609.

Health care defined for purposes of this Division, see Probate Code § 4615.

Health care provider defined for purposes of this Division, see Probate Code § 4621.

Patient defined for purposes of this Division, see Probate Code § 4625.

Physicians Orders for Life Sustaining Treatment form, revocation by individual, see Probate Code § 4780.

Supervising health care provider defined for purposes of this Division, see Probate Code § 4641.

Surrogate for health care decisions, priority of agent under power of attorney, see Probate Code § 4711.

§ 4696. Communication of fact of revocation

A health care provider, agent, conservator, or surrogate who is informed of a revocation of an advance health care directive shall promptly communicate the fact of the revocation to the supervising health care provider and to any health care institution where the patient is receiving care. *(Added by Stats.1999, c. 658 (A.B.891), § 39, operative July 1, 2000.)*

Law Revision Commission Comments

1999 Addition

Section 4696 is the same as Section 3(c) of the Uniform Health–Care Decisions Act (1993).

See also Sections 4605 ("advance health care directive" defined), 4607 ("agent" defined), 4613 ("conservator" defined), 4619 ("health care institution" defined), 4621 ("health care provider" defined), 4625 ("patient" defined), 4641 ("supervising health care provider" defined), 4643 ("surrogate" defined).

Background from Uniform Act. Section 3(c) requires any health-care provider, agent, [conservator] or surrogate who is informed of a revocation to promptly communicate that fact to the supervising health-care provider and to any health-care institution at which the patient is receiving care. The communication triggers the Section 7(b) [Prob. Code § 4731] obligation of the supervising health-care provider to record the revocation in the patient's health-care record and reduces the risk that a health-care provider or agent, [conservator] or surrogate will rely on a health-care directive that is no longer valid. [Adapted from Unif. Health–Care Decisions Act § 3(c) comment (1993)] [29 Cal.L.Rev.Comm. Reports 1 (1999)].

Cross References

Advance health care directive defined for purposes of this Division, see Probate Code § 4605.

Agent defined for purposes of this Division, see Probate Code § 4607.

Conservator defined for purposes of this Division, see Probate Code § 4613.

Health care defined for purposes of this Division, see Probate Code § 4615.

Health care institution defined for purposes of this Division, see Probate Code § 4619.

Health care provider defined for purposes of this Division, see Probate Code § 4621.

Patient defined for purposes of this Division, see Probate Code § 4625.

Supervising health care provider defined for purposes of this Division, see Probate Code § 4641.

Surrogate defined for purposes of this Division, see Probate Code § 4643.

§ 4697. Dissolution of marriage; effect

(a) If after executing a power of attorney for health care the principal's marriage to the agent is dissolved or annulled, the principal's designation of the former spouse as an agent to make health care decisions for the principal is revoked.

(b) If the agent's authority is revoked solely by subdivision (a), it is revived by the principal's remarriage to the agent. *(Added by Stats.1999, c. 658 (A.B.891), § 39, operative July 1, 2000.)*

Law Revision Commission Comments

1999 Addition

Section 4697 continues former Section 4727(e) without substantive change. Subdivision (a) is comparable to Section 3(d) of the Uniform Health–Care Decisions Act (1993), but does not revoke the designation of an agent on legal separation. For special rules applicable to a federal "absentee" (as defined in Section 1403), see Section 3722.

This section is subject to limitation by the power of attorney. See Section 4681 (limitations expressed in power of attorney for health care). See also Sections 4607 ("agent" defined), 4617 ("health care decision" defined), 4629 ("power of attorney for health care" defined), 4633 ("principal" defined). [29 Cal.L.Rev.Comm. Reports 1 (1999)].

Cross References

Agent defined for purposes of this Division, see Probate Code § 4607.

Health care decision defined for purposes of this Division, see Probate Code § 4617.

Health care defined for purposes of this Division, see Probate Code § 4615.

Power of attorney for health care defined for purposes of this Division, see Probate Code § 4629.

Principal defined for purposes of this Division, see Probate Code § 4633.

§ 4698. Conflicting directives

An advance health care directive that conflicts with an earlier advance directive revokes the earlier advance directive to the extent of the conflict. *(Added by Stats.1999, c. 658 (A.B.891), § 39, operative July 1, 2000.)*

Law Revision Commission Comments

1999 Addition

Section 4698 is the same as Section 3(e) of the Uniform Health–Care Decisions Act (1993) and supersedes former Section 4727(d). This section is also consistent with former Health and Safety Code Section 7193 (Natural Death Act).

See also Section 4605 ("advance health care directive" defined).

Background from Uniform Act. Section 3(e) establishes a rule of construction permitting multiple advance health-care directives to be construed together in order to determine the individual's intent, with the later advance health-care directive superseding the former to the extent of any inconsistency. [Adapted from Unif. Health–Care Decisions Act § 3(e) comment (1993)] [29 Cal.L.Rev.Comm. Reports 1 (1999)].

Cross References

Advance health care directive defined for purposes of this Division, see Probate Code § 4605.

CHAPTER 2. ADVANCE HEALTH CARE DIRECTIVE FORMS

Section
4700. Use of particular form not required; effect of form or other writing.
4701. Statutory form.
4702 to 4704. Repealed.

§ 4700. Use of particular form not required; effect of form or other writing

The form provided in Section 4701 may, but need not, be used to create an advance health care directive. The other sections of this division govern the effect of the form or any other writing used to create an advance health care directive. An individual may complete or modify all or any part of the form in Section 4701. *(Added by Stats.1999, c. 658 (A.B.891), § 39, operative July 1, 2000.)*

Law Revision Commission Comments

1999 Addition

Section 4700 is drawn from the introductory paragraph of Section 4 of the Uniform Health–Care Decisions Act (1993). This section supersedes former Section 4779 (use of other forms).

See also Section 4605 ("advance health care directive" defined). [29 Cal.L.Rev.Comm. Reports 1 (1999)].

Cross References

Advance health care directive defined for purposes of this Division, see Probate Code § 4605.

§ 4701. Statutory form

The statutory advance health care directive form is as follows:

ADVANCE HEALTH CARE DIRECTIVE

(California Probate Code Section 4701)

Explanation

You have the right to give instructions about your own health care. You also have the right to name someone else to make health care decisions for you. This form lets you do either or both of these things. It also lets you express your wishes regarding donation of organs and the designation of your primary physician. If you use this form, you may complete or modify all or any part of it. You are free to use a different form.

Part 1 of this form is a power of attorney for health care. Part 1 lets you name another individual as agent to make health care decisions for you if you become incapable of making your own decisions or if you want someone else to make those decisions for you now even though you are still capable. You may also name an alternate agent to act for you if your first choice is not willing, able, or reasonably available to make decisions for you. (Your agent may not be an operator or employee of a community care facility or a residential care facility where you are receiving care, or your supervising health care provider or employee of the health care institution where you are receiving care, unless your agent is related to you or is a coworker.)

Unless the form you sign limits the authority of your agent, your agent may make all health care decisions for you. This form has a place for you to limit the authority of your agent. You need not limit the authority of your agent if you wish to rely on your agent for all health care decisions that may have to be made. If you choose not to limit the authority of your agent, your agent will have the right to:

(a) Consent or refuse consent to any care, treatment, service, or procedure to maintain, diagnose, or otherwise affect a physical or mental condition.

(b) Select or discharge health care providers and institutions.

(c) Approve or disapprove diagnostic tests, surgical procedures, and programs of medication.

(d) Direct the provision, withholding, or withdrawal of artificial nutrition and hydration and all other forms of health care, including cardiopulmonary resuscitation.

(e) Make anatomical gifts, authorize an autopsy, and direct disposition of remains.

Part 2 of this form lets you give specific instructions about any aspect of your health care, whether or not you appoint an agent. Choices are provided for you to express your wishes regarding the provision, withholding, or withdrawal of treatment to keep you alive, as well as the provision of pain relief. Space is also provided for you to add to the choices you have made or for you to write out any additional wishes. If you are satisfied to allow your agent to determine what is best for you in making end-of-life decisions, you need not fill out Part 2 of this form.

Part 3 of this form lets you express an intention to donate your bodily organs and tissues following your death.

Part 4 of this form lets you designate a physician to have primary responsibility for your health care.

After completing this form, sign and date the form at the end. The form must be signed by two qualified witnesses or acknowledged before a notary public. Give a copy of the signed and completed form to your physician, to any other health care providers you may have, to any health care institution at which you are receiving care, and to any health care agents you have named. You should talk to the person you have named as agent to make sure that he or she understands your wishes and is willing to take the responsibility.

You have the right to revoke this advance health care directive or replace this form at any time.

* * * * * * * * * * * * * * * * *

PART 1
POWER OF ATTORNEY FOR HEALTH CARE

(1.1) DESIGNATION OF AGENT: I designate the following individual as my agent to make health care decisions for me:

_____
(name of individual you choose as agent)

_____
(address)   (city)   (state)   (ZIP Code)

_____
(home phone)   (work phone)

OPTIONAL: If I revoke my agent's authority or if my agent is not willing, able, or reasonably available to make a health care decision for me, I designate as my first alternate agent:

_____
(name of individual you choose as first alternate agent)

_____
(address)   (city)   (state)   (ZIP Code)

_____
(home phone)   (work phone)

OPTIONAL: If I revoke the authority of my agent and first alternate agent or if neither is willing, able, or reasonably available to make a health care decision for me, I designate as my second alternate agent:

_____

(name of individual you choose as second alternate agent)

_____

| (address) | (city) | (state) | (ZIP Code) |

_____

(home phone)   (work phone)

(1.2) AGENT'S AUTHORITY: My agent is authorized to make all health care decisions for me, including decisions to provide, withhold, or withdraw artificial nutrition and hydration and all other forms of health care to keep me alive, except as I state here:

_____
_____
_____

(Add additional sheets if needed.)

(1.3) WHEN AGENT'S AUTHORITY BECOMES EFFECTIVE: My agent's authority becomes effective when my primary physician determines that I am unable to make my own health care decisions unless I mark the following box. If I mark this box ☐, my agent's authority to make health care decisions for me takes effect immediately.

(1.4) AGENT'S OBLIGATION: My agent shall make health care decisions for me in accordance with this power of attorney for health care, any instructions I give in Part 2 of this form, and my other wishes to the extent known to my agent. To the extent my wishes are unknown, my agent shall make health care decisions for me in accordance with what my agent determines to be in my best interest. In determining my best interest, my agent shall consider my personal values to the extent known to my agent.

(1.5) AGENT'S POSTDEATH AUTHORITY: My agent is authorized to make anatomical gifts, authorize an autopsy, and direct disposition of my remains, except as I state here or in Part 3 of this form:

_____
_____
_____

(Add additional sheets if needed.)

(1.6) NOMINATION OF CONSERVATOR: If a conservator of my person needs to be appointed for me by a court, I nominate the agent designated in this form. If that agent is not willing, able, or reasonably available to act as conservator, I nominate the alternate agents whom I have named, in the order designated.

PART 2
INSTRUCTIONS FOR HEALTH CARE

If you fill out this part of the form, you may strike any wording you do not want.

(2.1) END–OF–LIFE DECISIONS: I direct that my health care providers and others involved in my care provide, withhold, or withdraw treatment in accordance with the choice I have marked below:

☐ (a) Choice Not To Prolong Life

I do not want my life to be prolonged if (1) I have an incurable and irreversible condition that will result in my death within a relatively short time, (2) I become unconscious and, to a reasonable degree of medical certainty, I will not regain consciousness, or (3) the likely risks and burdens of treatment would outweigh the expected benefits, OR

☐ (b) Choice To Prolong Life

I want my life to be prolonged as long as possible within the limits of generally accepted health care standards.

(2.2) RELIEF FROM PAIN: Except as I state in the following space, I direct that treatment for alleviation of pain or discomfort be provided at all times, even if it hastens my death:

_____
_____

(Add additional sheets if needed.)

(2.3) OTHER WISHES: (If you do not agree with any of the optional choices above and wish to write your own, or if you wish to add to the instructions you have given above, you may do so here.) I direct that:

_____

_____

(Add additional sheets if needed.)

PART 3
DONATION OF ORGANS AT DEATH
(OPTIONAL)

(3.1) Upon my death (mark applicable box):

☐ (a) I give any needed organs, tissues, or parts, OR
☐ (b) I give the following organs, tissues, or parts only.
_____

(c) My gift is for the following purposes (strike any of the following you do not want):
(1) Transplant
(2) Therapy
(3) Research
(4) Education

PART 4
PRIMARY PHYSICIAN
(OPTIONAL)

(4.1) I designate the following physician as my primary physician:

_____
(name of physician)

_____
(address)   (city)   (state)   (ZIP Code)

_____
(phone)

OPTIONAL: If the physician I have designated above is not willing, able, or reasonably available to act as my primary physician, I designate the following physician as my primary physician:

_____
(name of physician)

_____
(address)   (city)   (state)   (ZIP Code)

_____
(phone)

* * * * * * * * * * * * * * * *

PART 5

(5.1) EFFECT OF COPY: A copy of this form has the same effect as the original.

(5.2) SIGNATURE: Sign and date the form here:

_____   _____
(date)   (sign your name)

_____   _____
(address)   (print your name)

_____
(city)   (state)

(5.3) STATEMENT OF WITNESSES: I declare under penalty of perjury under the laws of California (1) that the individual who signed or acknowledged this advance health care directive is personally known to me, or that the individual's identity was proven to me by convincing evidence, (2) that the individual signed or

472

acknowledged this advance directive in my presence, (3) that the individual appears to be of sound mind and under no duress, fraud, or undue influence, (4) that I am not a person appointed as agent by this advance directive, and (5) that I am not the individual's health care provider, an employee of the individual's health care provider, the operator of a community care facility, an employee of an operator of a community care facility, the operator of a residential care facility for the elderly, nor an employee of an operator of a residential care facility for the elderly.

First witness	Second witness
_____	_____
(print name)	(print name)
_____	_____
(address)	(address)
_____	_____
(city)　　　　(state)	(city)　　　　(state)
_____	_____
(signature of witness)	(signature of witness)
_____	_____
(date)	(date)

(5.4) ADDITIONAL STATEMENT OF WITNESSES: At least one of the above witnesses must also sign the following declaration:

I further declare under penalty of perjury under the laws of California that I am not related to the individual executing this advance health care directive by blood, marriage, or adoption, and to the best of my knowledge, I am not entitled to any part of the individual's estate upon his or her death under a will now existing or by operation of law.

_____	_____
(signature of witness)	(signature of witness)

PART 6
SPECIAL WITNESS REQUIREMENT

(6.1) The following statement is required only if you are a patient in a skilled nursing facility--a health care facility that provides the following basic services: skilled nursing care and supportive care to patients whose primary need is for availability of skilled nursing care on an extended basis. The patient advocate or ombudsman must sign the following statement:

STATEMENT OF PATIENT ADVOCATE OR OMBUDSMAN

I declare under penalty of perjury under the laws of California that I am a patient advocate or ombudsman as designated by the State Department of Aging and that I am serving as a witness as required by Section 4675 of the Probate Code.

_____	_____
(date)	(sign your name)
_____	_____
(address)	(print your name)
_____	
(city)　　　　(state)	

(Added by Stats.1999, c. 658 (A.B.891), § 39, operative July 1, 2000.)

Law Revision Commission Comments

1999 Addition

Section 4701 provides the contents of the optional statutory form for the Advance Health Care Directive. Parts 1–5 of this form are largely drawn from Section 4 of the Uniform Health–Care Decisions Act (1993). This form supersedes the Statutory Form Durable Power of Attorney for Health Care in former Section 4771 and the related rules in former Sections 4772–4774, 4776–4778. Part 6 of this form continues a portion of the former statutory form applicable to patients in skilled nursing facilities.

Background from Uniform Act. The optional form set forth in this section incorporates the Section 2 [Prob. Code § 4670 *et seq.*] requirements applicable to advance health-care directives.... An individual may complete all or any [of the first four] parts of the form. Any part of the form left blank is not to be given effect. For example, an individual may complete the instructions for health care part of the form alone. Or an individual may complete the power of attorney for health care part of the form alone. Or an individual may complete both the instructions and power of attorney for health care parts of the form. An individual may also, but need not, complete the parts of the form pertaining to donation of bodily organs and tissue and the designation of a primary physician.

Part 1, the power of attorney for health care, appears first on the form in order to ensure to the extent possible that it will come to the attention of a casual reader. This reflects the reality that the appointment of an agent is a more comprehensive approach to the making of health-care decisions than is the giving of an individual instruction, which cannot possibly anticipate all future circumstances which might arise.

Part [1.1] of the power of attorney for health care form requires only the designation of a single agent, but with opportunity given to designate a single first alternate and a single second alternate, if the individual chooses. No provision is made in the form for the designation of co-agents in order not to encourage the practice. Designation of co-agents is discouraged because of the difficulties likely to be encountered if the co-agents are not all readily available or do not agree. If co-agents are appointed, the instrument should specify that either is authorized to act if the other is not reasonably available. It should also specify a method for resolving disagreements.

Part [1.2] of the power of attorney for health care form grants the agent authority to make all health-care decisions for the individual subject to any limitations which the individual may state in the form. Reference is made to artificial nutrition and hydration and other forms of treatment to keep an individual alive in order to ensure that the individual is aware that those are forms of health care that the agent would have the authority to withdraw or withhold absent specific limitation.

Part [1.3] of the power of attorney for health care form provides that the agent's authority becomes effective upon a determination that the individual lacks capacity, but as authorized by Section 2(c) [Prob. Code § 4682] a box is provided for the individual to indicate that the authority of the agent takes effect immediately.

Part [1.4] of the power of attorney for health care form directs the agent to make health-care decisions in accordance with the power of attorney, any instructions given by the individual in Part 2 of the form, and the individual's other wishes to the extent known to the agent. To the extent the individual's wishes in the matter are not known, the agent is to make health-care decisions based on what the agent determines to be in the individual's best interest. In determining the individual's best interest, the agent is to consider the individual's personal values to the extent known to the agent. Section 2(e) [Prob. Code § 4684] imposes this standard, whether or not it is included in the form, but its inclusion in the form will bring it to the attention of the individual granting the power, to the agent, to any [conservator] or surrogate, and to the individual's health-care providers.

[Part 1.5 implements Probate Code Section 4683.]

Part [1.6] of the power of attorney for health care form nominates the agent, if available, able, and willing to act, otherwise the alternate agents in order of priority stated, as [conservators] of the person for the individual. This provision is included in the form for two reasons. First, if an appointment of a [conservator] becomes necessary the agent is the one whom the individual would most likely want to serve in that role. Second, the nomination of the agent as [conservator] will reduce the possibility that someone other than the agent will be appointed as [conservator] who could use the position to thwart the agent's authority.

Because the variety of treatment decisions to which health-care instructions may relate is virtually unlimited, Part 2 of the form does not attempt to be comprehensive, but is directed at the types of treatment for which an individual is most likely to have special wishes. Part [2.1] of the form, entitled "End-of-Life Decisions," provides two alternative choices for the expression of wishes concern-

ing the provision, withholding, or withdrawal of treatment. Under the first choice, the individual's life is not to be prolonged if the individual has an incurable and irreversible condition that will result in death within a relatively short time, if the individual becomes unconscious and, to a reasonable degree of medical certainty, will not regain consciousness, or if the likely risks and burdens of treatment would outweigh the expected benefits. Under the second choice, the individual's life is to be prolonged within the limits of generally accepted health-care standards.... Part [2.2] of the form provides space for an individual to specify any circumstance when the individual would prefer not to receive pain relief. Because the choices provided in Parts [2.1–2.2] do not cover all possible situations, Part [2.3] of the form provides space for the individual to write out his or her own instructions or to supplement the instructions given in the previous subparts of the form. Should the space be insufficient, the individual is free to add additional pages.

The health-care instructions given in Part 2 of the form are binding on the agent, any [conservator], any surrogate, and, subject to exceptions specified in Section 7(e)-(f) [Prob. Code §§ 4734–4735], on the individual's health-care providers. Pursuant to Section 7(d) [Prob. Code § 4733], a health-care provider must also comply with a reasonable interpretation of those instructions made by an authorized agent, [conservator], or surrogate.

Part 3 of the form provides the individual an opportunity to express an intention to donate bodily organs and tissues at death. The options provided are derived from a suggested form in the Comment to Section 2 of the Uniform Anatomical Gift Act (1987). [See Health and Safety Code § 7150 *et seq.*]

Part 4 of the form provides space for the individual to designate a primary physician should the individual choose to do so. Space is also provided for the designation of an alternate primary physician should the first designated physician not be available, able, or willing to act.

[Part 5.1] of the form conforms with the provisions of Section 12 [Prob. Code § 4660] by providing that a copy of the form has the same effect as the original....

The form does not require formal acceptance by an agent. Formal acceptance by an agent has been omitted not because it is an undesirable practice but because it would add another stage to executing an advance health-care directive, thereby further reducing the number of individuals who will follow through and create directives. However, practitioners who wish to adapt this form for use by their clients are strongly encouraged to add a formal acceptance. Designated agents have no duty to act until they accept the office either expressly or through their conduct. Consequently, requiring formal acceptance reduces the risk that a designated agent will decline to act when the need arises. Formal acceptance also makes it more likely that the agent will become familiar with the principal's personal values and views on health care. While the form does not require formal acceptance, the explanation to the form does encourage principals to talk to the person they have named as agent to make certain that the designated agent understands their wishes and is willing to take the responsibility.

[Adapted from Unif. Health–Care Decisions Act § 4 comment (1993)] [29 Cal.L.Rev.Comm. Reports App. 6 (1999)].

Cross References

Advance health care directive defined for purposes of this Division, see Probate Code § 4605.

Agent defined for purposes of this Division, see Probate Code § 4607.

Community care facility defined for purposes of this Division, see Probate Code § 4611.

Conservator defined for purposes of this Division, see Probate Code § 4613.

Health care decision defined for purposes of this Division, see Probate Code § 4617.

Health care defined for purposes of this Division, see Probate Code § 4615.

Health care institution defined for purposes of this Division, see Probate Code § 4619.

Health care provider defined for purposes of this Division, see Probate Code § 4621.

Patient defined for purposes of this Division, see Probate Code § 4625.

Physician defined for purposes of this Division, see Probate Code § 4627.

Power of attorney for health care defined for purposes of this Division, see Probate Code § 4629.

Primary physician defined for purposes of this Division, see Probate Code § 4631.

Reasonably available defined for purposes of this Division, see Probate Code § 4635.

Residential care facility for the elderly defined for purposes of this Division, see Probate Code § 4637.

Skilled nursing facility defined for purposes of this Division, see Probate Code § 4639.

Supervising health care provider defined for purposes of this Division, see Probate Code § 4641.

§§ 4702 to 4704.   Repealed by Stats.1999, c. 658 (A.B.891), § 38, operative July 1, 2000

Law Revision Commission Comments

1999 Repeal

Former Section 4702 is continued in Section 4659(a)-(c) without substantive change. See Section 4659 Comment. [29 Cal.L.Rev. Comm. Reports 1 (1999)].

Former Section 4703 is not continued. See Section 4701 (optional form of advance health care directive). [29 Cal.L.Rev.Comm. Reports 1 (1999)].

Former Section 4704 is not continued. See Section 4701 (optional form of advance health care directive). [29 Cal.L.Rev.Comm. Reports 1 (1999)].

CHAPTER 3.   HEALTH CARE SURROGATES

§ 4711.   Designation of surrogate for health care decisions; expiration; priority and revocation

(a) A patient may designate an adult as a surrogate to make health care decisions by personally informing the supervising health care provider. The designation of a surrogate shall be promptly recorded in the patient's health care record.

(b) Unless the patient specifies a shorter period, a surrogate designation under subdivision (a) is effective only during the course of treatment or illness or during the stay in the health care institution when the surrogate designation is made, or for 60 days, whichever period is shorter.

(c) The expiration of a surrogate designation under subdivision (b) does not affect any role the person designated under subdivision (a) may have in making health care decisions for the patient under any other law or standards of practice.

(d) If the patient has designated an agent under a power of attorney for health care, the surrogate designated under subdivision (a) has priority over the agent for the period provided in subdivision (b), but the designation of a surrogate does not revoke the designation of an agent unless the patient communicates the intention to revoke in compliance with subdivision (a) of Section 4695. *(Added by Stats.1999, c. 658 (A.B.891), § 39, operative July 1, 2000. Amended by Stats. 2001, c. 230 (A.B.1278), § 5.)*

Law Revision Commission Comments

1999 Addition

The first sentence of Section 4711 is drawn from Section 5(b) of the Uniform Health–Care Decisions Act (1993). Both the patient and the surrogate must be adults. See Sections 4625 ("patient" defined), 4643 ("surrogate" defined). "Adult" includes an emancipated minor. See Fam. Code § 7002 (emancipation). "Personally informing," as used in this section, includes both oral and written communications. The second sentence is intended to guard against the possibility of giving effect to obsolete oral statements entered in the patient's record.

See also Sections 4617 ("health care decision" defined), 4619 ("health care institution" defined), 4625 ("patient" defined), 4635 ("reasonably available" defined), 4641 ("supervising health care provider" defined), 4643 ("surrogate" defined).

Background from Uniform Act. While a designation of an agent in a written power of attorney for health care is preferred, situations may arise where an individual will not be in a position to execute a power of attorney for health care. In that event, subsection (b) affirms the principle of patient autonomy by allowing an individual to designate a surrogate by personally informing the supervising health-care provider. The supervising health-care provider would then, in accordance with Section 7(b) [Prob. Code § 4731], be obligated to promptly record the designation in the individual's health-care record. An oral designation of a surrogate made by a patient directly to the supervising health-care provider revokes a previous designation of an agent. See Section 3(a) [Prob. Code § 4695(a)]. [Adapted from Unif. Health–Care Decisions Act § 5(b) comments (1993)] [29 Cal.L.Rev.Comm. Reports App. 6 (1999)].

2001 Amendment

Section 4711 is amended to clarify the relation between a surrogate designation under this section and a formal agent designation in a power of attorney for health care under Section 4671 and related provisions, and to provide additional qualifications on surrogacy designations. Both the patient and the surrogate must be adults. See Sections 4625 ("patient" defined), 4643 ("surrogate" defined). "Adult" includes an emancipated minor. See Fam. Code 7002 (emancipation). "Personally informing," as used in this section, includes both oral and written communications.

Consistent with the statutory purpose of effectuating patient intent, subdivision (a) recognizes the patient's ability to name a person to act as surrogate health care decisionmaker. As amended, this section no longer distinguishes between surrogates named orally and surrogates named in a written communication to the supervising health care provider. Whether it is communicated to the supervising health care provider orally or in writing, the surrogate designation must be promptly recorded in the patient's health care record. See also Section 4731 (supervising health care provider's duty to record relevant information).

Subdivision (b) provides a maximum limit of 60 days on the duration of surrogate designations under this section. If the patient has an agent under a power of attorney for health care, the agent's authority is suspended during the time the surrogacy is in effect. See subdivision (d). If the patient names an agent in a power of attorney for health care executed after making a surrogate designation, the agent would have priority over the surrogate as provided in Section 4685 (agent's priority). As recognized in the introductory clause, the patient may specify a shorter period for the surrogate designation, by personally informing the supervising health care provider. A limitation might be phrased in terms of a period of time or as a condition, such as until the agent designated in the patient's power of attorney for health care becomes available.

Subdivision (c) makes clear that the limits on the duration of a surrogacy designation affect only the special surrogate rules in this section, and not the ability of the person who had been designated as surrogate to make or participate in making health care decisions for the patient under other principles. *Cf.* Section 4654 (compliance with generally accepted health care standards). After expiration of the period specified in subdivision (b), this section does not affect who may make health care decisions for adults lacking capacity.

Subdivision (d) makes clear that designation of a surrogate under this section suspends, but does not revoke, the appointment of an agent under a power of attorney for health care, unless the patient expresses the intent to revoke the agent's appointment, under the terms of the general rule in Section 4695(a). Subdivision (d) reverses the implication in background material that a surrogate designation made directly to the supervising health care provider revoked a previous designation of an agent. See Background from Uniform Act in Comment to Section 4711 as enacted, 1999 Cal. Stat. ch. 658, 39 (operative July 1, 2000).

See also Sections 4617 ("health care decision" defined), 4619 ("health care institution" defined), 4635 ("reasonably available" defined), 4639 ("skilled nursing facility" defined), 4641 ("supervising health care provider" defined). [30 Cal.L.Rev.Comm. Reports 621 (2000)].

Cross References

Agent defined for purposes of this Division, see Probate Code § 4607.
Health care decision defined for purposes of this Division, see Probate Code § 4617.
Health care defined for purposes of this Division, see Probate Code § 4615.
Health care institution defined for purposes of this Division, see Probate Code § 4619.
Health care provider defined for purposes of this Division, see Probate Code § 4621.
Patient defined for purposes of this Division, see Probate Code § 4625.
Power of attorney for health care defined for purposes of this Division, see Probate Code § 4629.
Supervising health care provider defined for purposes of this Division, see Probate Code § 4641.
Surrogate defined for purposes of this Division, see Probate Code § 4643.

§ 4714. Decisions based on patient's best interests

A surrogate, including a person acting as a surrogate, shall make a health care decision in accordance with the patient's individual health care instructions, if any, and other wishes to the extent known to the surrogate. Otherwise, the surrogate shall make the decision in accordance with the surrogate's determination of the patient's best interest. In determining the patient's best interest, the surrogate shall consider the patient's personal values to the extent known to the surrogate. *(Added by Stats.1999, c. 658 (A.B.891), § 39, operative July 1, 2000.)*

Law Revision Commission Comments

1999 Addition

Section 4714 is drawn from Section 5(f) of the Uniform Health–Care Decisions Act (1993). This standard is consistent with the health care decisionmaking standard applicable to agents. See Section 4684.

See also Sections 4617 ("health care decision" defined), 4623 ("individual health care instruction" defined), 4625 ("patient" defined), 4643 ("surrogate" defined).

Background from Uniform Act. Section 5(f) imposes on surrogates the same standard for health-care decision making as is prescribed for agents in Section 2(e) [Prob. Code § 4684]. The surrogate must follow the patient's individual instructions and other expressed wishes to the extent known to the surrogate. To the extent such instructions or other wishes are unknown, the surrogate must act in the patient's best interest. In determining the patient's best interest, the surrogate is to consider the patient's personal values to the extent known to the surrogate. [Adapted from Unif. Health–Care Decisions Act § 5(f) comment (1993)] [29 Cal.L.Rev.Comm. Reports App. 6 (1999)].

Cross References

Health care decision defined for purposes of this Division, see Probate Code § 4617.
Health care decisionmaker, see Probate Code § 4781.5.
Health care defined for purposes of this Division, see Probate Code § 4615.
Individual health care instruction defined for purposes of this Division, see Probate Code § 4623.
Patient defined for purposes of this Division, see Probate Code § 4625.
Surrogate defined for purposes of this Division, see Probate Code § 4643.

§ 4715. Disqualification of person from acting as surrogate

A patient having capacity at any time may disqualify another person, including a member of the patient's family, from acting as the patient's surrogate by a signed writing or by personally informing the supervising health care provider of the disqualification. *(Added by Stats.1999, c. 658 (A.B. 891), § 39, operative July 1, 2000.)*

Law Revision Commission Comments

1999 Addition

Section 4715 is drawn from Section 5(h) of the Uniform Health–Care Decisions Act (1993). See Section 4731 (duty to record surrogate's disqualification). "Personally informing," as used in this section, includes both oral and written communications.

See also Sections 4625 ("patient" defined), 4641 ("supervising health care provider" defined), 4643 ("surrogate" defined).

Background from Uniform Act. Section 5(h) permits an individual to disqualify any family member or other individual from acting as the individual's surrogate, including disqualification of a surrogate who was orally designated. [Adapted from Unif. Health–Care Decisions Act § 5(h) comment (1993)] [29 Cal.L.Rev.Comm. Reports 1 (1999)].

Cross References

Capacity defined for purposes of this Division, see Probate Code § 4609.
Health care defined for purposes of this Division, see Probate Code § 4615.
Health care provider defined for purposes of this Division, see Probate Code § 4621.
Patient defined for purposes of this Division, see Probate Code § 4625.

Supervising health care provider defined for purposes of this Division, see Probate Code § 4641.

Surrogate defined for purposes of this Division, see Probate Code § 4643.

§ 4716. Domestic partner of patient

(a) If a patient lacks the capacity to make a health care decision, the patient's domestic partner shall have the same authority as a spouse has to make a health care decision for his or her incapacitated spouse. This section may not be construed to expand or restrict the ability of a spouse to make a health care decision for an incapacitated spouse.

(b) For the purposes of this section, the following definitions shall apply:

(1) "Capacity" has the same meaning as defined in Section 4609.

(2) "Health care" has the same meaning as defined in Section 4615.

(3) "Health care decision" has the same meaning as defined in Section 4617.

(4) "Domestic partner" has the same meaning as that term is used in Section 297 of the Family Code. *(Added by Stats.2001, c. 893 (A.B.25), § 49.)*

Cross References

Capacity defined for purposes of this Division, see Probate Code § 4609.

Health care decision defined for purposes of this Division, see Probate Code § 4617.

Health care defined for purposes of this Division, see Probate Code § 4615.

Patient defined for purposes of this Division, see Probate Code § 4625.

§ 4717. Authority to make health care decisions on behalf of patient who is unconscious or incapable of communication; duty of hospital to make reasonable efforts to contact patient's agent, surrogate or family member; exceptions

(a) Notwithstanding any other provision of law, within 24 hours of the arrival in the emergency department of a general acute care hospital of a patient who is unconscious or otherwise incapable of communication, the hospital shall make reasonable efforts to contact the patient's agent, surrogate, or a family member or other person the hospital reasonably believes has the authority to make health care decisions on behalf of the patient. A hospital shall be deemed to have made reasonable efforts, and to have discharged its duty under this section, if it does all of the following:

(1) Examines the personal effects, if any, accompanying the patient and any medical records regarding the patient in its possession, and reviews any verbal or written report made by emergency medical technicians or the police, to identify the name of any agent, surrogate, or a family member or other person the hospital reasonably believes has the authority to make health care decisions on behalf of the patient.

(2) Contacts or attempts to contact any agent, surrogate, or a family member or other person the hospital reasonably believes has the authority to make health care decisions on behalf of the patient, as identified in paragraph (1).

(3) Contacts the Secretary of State directly or indirectly, including by voice mail or facsimile, to inquire whether the patient has registered an advance health care directive with the Advance Health Care Directive Registry, if the hospital finds evidence of the patient's Advance Health Care Directive Registry identification card either from the patient or from the patient's family or authorized agent.

(b) The hospital shall document in the patient's medical record all efforts made to contact any agent, surrogate, or a family member or other person the hospital reasonably believes has the authority to make health care decisions on behalf of the patient.

(c) Application of this section shall be suspended during any period in which the hospital implements its disaster and mass casualty program, or its fire and internal disaster program. *(Formerly § 4716, added by Stats.2001, c. 329 (S.B.751), § 1. Renumbered § 4717 and amended by Stats. 2004, c. 882 (A.B.2445), § 2.)*

Cross References

Advance health care directive defined for purposes of this Division, see Probate Code § 4605.

Advanced Health Care Directive Registry, establishment and procedures, see Probate Code § 4800 et seq.

Agent defined for purposes of this Division, see Probate Code § 4607.

Health care decision defined for purposes of this Division, see Probate Code § 4617.

Health care defined for purposes of this Division, see Probate Code § 4615.

Patient defined for purposes of this Division, see Probate Code § 4625.

Surrogate defined for purposes of this Division, see Probate Code § 4643.

§§ 4720 to 4727. Repealed by Stats.1999, c. 658 (A.B.891), § 38, operative July 1, 2000

Law Revision Commission Comments

1999 Repeal

Former Section 4721 is continued in Section 4678 without substantive change. [29 Cal.L.Rev.Comm. Reports App. 6 (1999)].

Former Section 4722 is continued in Section 4652 without substantive change. [29 Cal.L.Rev.Comm. Reports 1 (1999)].

The first sentence of former Section 4723 is continued in Section 4653 (mercy killing, assisted suicide, euthanasia not approved) without substantive change. The second sentence is continued in Section 4655(b) (impermissible constructions) without substantive change. [29 Cal.L.Rev.Comm. Reports App. 6 (1999)].

Former Section 4724 is continued in Section 4689 without substantive change. See also Section 4695 (revocation of advance directive). [29 Cal.L.Rev.Comm. Reports App. 6 (1999)].

Former Section 4725 is continued in Section 4677 without substantive change. [29 Cal.L.Rev.Comm. Reports App. 6 (1999)].

Former Section 4726 is continued in Section 4743 without substantive change. [29 Cal.L.Rev.Comm. Reports 1 (1999)].

Subdivision (a) of former Section 4727 is superseded by Section 4695(a) (revocation of advance health care directive).

Subdivision (b) is continued in Section 4731 (duty of supervising health care provider to record relevant information) without substantive change.

Subdivision (c) is continued in Section 4657 (presumption of capacity) without substantive change.

Subdivision (d) is superseded by Section 4698 (effect of later advance directive on earlier advance directive).

Subdivision (e) is continued in Section 4697 (effect of dissolution or annulment) without substantive change.

Subdivision (f) is superseded by Section 4740 (immunities of health care provider and institution). See Section 4740 Comment. [29 Cal.L.Rev.Comm. Reports 1 (1999)].

CHAPTER 4.   DUTIES OF HEALTH CARE PROVIDERS

§ 4730.   Communication to patient

Before implementing a health care decision made for a patient, a supervising health care provider, if possible, shall promptly communicate to the patient the decision made and the identity of the person making the decision. *(Added by Stats.1999, c. 658 (A.B.891), § 39, operative July 1, 2000.)*

Law Revision Commission Comments

1999 Addition

Section 4730 is drawn from Section 7(a) of the Uniform Health–Care Decisions Act (1993).

See also Sections 4617 ("health care decision" defined), 4625 ("patient" defined), 4641 ("supervising health care provider" defined).

Background from Uniform Act. Section 7(a) further reinforces the Act's respect for patient autonomy by requiring a supervising health-care provider, if possible, to promptly communicate to a patient, prior to implementation, a health-care decision made for the patient and the identity of the person making the decision. [Adapted from Unif. Health–Care Decisions Act § 7(a) comment (1993)] [29 Cal.L.Rev.Comm. Reports App. 6 (1999)].

Cross References

Health care decision defined for purposes of this Division, see Probate Code § 4617.
Health care defined for purposes of this Division, see Probate Code § 4615.
Health care provider defined for purposes of this Division, see Probate Code § 4621.
Patient defined for purposes of this Division, see Probate Code § 4625.
Supervising health care provider defined for purposes of this Division, see Probate Code § 4641.

§ 4731.   Recording of information in patient's health care record; notification to agent or surrogate regarding revocation or disqualification

(a) A supervising health care provider who knows of the existence of an advance health care directive, a revocation of an advance health care directive, or a designation or disqualification of a surrogate, shall promptly record its existence in the patient's health care record and, if it is in writing, shall request a copy. If a copy is furnished, the supervising health care provider shall arrange for its maintenance in the patient's health care record.

(b) A supervising health care provider who knows of a revocation of a power of attorney for health care or a disqualification of a surrogate shall make a reasonable effort to notify the agent or surrogate of the revocation or disqualification. *(Added by Stats.1999, c. 658 (A.B.891), § 39, operative July 1, 2000.)*

Law Revision Commission Comments

1999 Addition

Subdivision (a) of Section 4731 is drawn from Section 7(b) of the Uniform Health–Care Decisions Act (1993). With respect to recording notice of revocation of a power of attorney for health care, this section continues the substance of part of former Section 4727(b). The recordkeeping duty continues part of former Health and Safety Code Sections 7186.5(c) and 7188 (Natural Death Act).

Subdivision (b) continues the substance of part of former Section 4727(b) and applies the same duty to surrogate disqualification.

See also Sections 4605 ("advance health care directive" defined), 4625 ("patient" defined), 4629 ("power of attorney for health care" defined), 4641 ("supervising health care provider" defined), 4643 ("surrogate" defined).

Background from Uniform Act. The recording requirement in Section 7(b) reduces the risk that a health-care provider or institution, or agent, [conservator] or surrogate, will rely on an outdated individual instruction or the decision of an individual whose authority has been revoked. [Adapted from Unif. Health–Care Decisions Act § 7(b) comment (1993)] [29 Cal.L.Rev.Comm. Reports App. 6 (1999)].

Cross References

Advance health care directive defined for purposes of this Division, see Probate Code § 4605.
Agent defined for purposes of this Division, see Probate Code § 4607.
Health care defined for purposes of this Division, see Probate Code § 4615.
Health care provider defined for purposes of this Division, see Probate Code § 4621.
Patient defined for purposes of this Division, see Probate Code § 4625.
Power of attorney for health care defined for purposes of this Division, see Probate Code § 4629.
Supervising health care provider defined for purposes of this Division, see Probate Code § 4641.
Surrogate defined for purposes of this Division, see Probate Code § 4643.

§ 4732.   Primary physician; duty to record information regarding patient's capacity

A primary physician who makes or is informed of a determination that a patient lacks or has recovered capacity, or that another condition exists affecting an individual health care instruction or the authority of an agent, conservator of the person, or surrogate, shall promptly record the determination in the patient's health care record and communicate the determination to the patient, if possible, and to a person then authorized to make health care decisions for the patient.

(Added by Stats.1999, c. 658 (A.B.891), § 39, operative July 1, 2000.)

Law Revision Commission Comments

1999 Addition

Section 4732 is drawn from Section 7(c) of the Uniform Health–Care Decisions Act (1993). This duty generally continues record-keeping duties in former Health and Safety Code Sections 7186.5(c), 7188, and 7189 (Natural Death Act).

See also Sections 4607 ("agent" defined), 4609 ("capacity" defined), 4613 ("conservator" defined), 4617 ("health care decision" defined), 4623 ("individual health care instruction" defined), 4625 ("patient" defined), 4631 ("primary physician" defined).

Background from Uniform Act. Section 7(c) imposes recording and communication requirements relating to determinations that may trigger the authority of an agent, [conservator] or surrogate to make health-care decisions on an individual's behalf. The determinations covered by these requirements are those specified in Section 2(c)-(d) [Prob. Code §§ 4658 & 4682 respectively]. [Adapted from Unif. Health–Care Decisions Act § 7(c) comment (1993)] [29 Cal.L.Rev.Comm. Reports App. 6 (1999)].

Cross References

Agent defined for purposes of this Division, see Probate Code § 4607.
Capacity defined for purposes of this Division, see Probate Code § 4609.
Conservator defined for purposes of this Division, see Probate Code § 4613.
Health care decision defined for purposes of this Division, see Probate Code § 4617.
Health care defined for purposes of this Division, see Probate Code § 4615.
Individual health care instruction defined for purposes of this Division, see Probate Code § 4623.
Patient defined for purposes of this Division, see Probate Code § 4625.
Physician defined for purposes of this Division, see Probate Code § 4627.
Primary physician defined for purposes of this Division, see Probate Code § 4631.
Surrogate defined for purposes of this Division, see Probate Code § 4643.

§ 4733. Compliance with health care instructions and health care decisions

Except as provided in Sections 4734 and 4735, a health care provider or health care institution providing care to a patient shall do the following:

(a) Comply with an individual health care instruction of the patient and with a reasonable interpretation of that instruction made by a person then authorized to make health care decisions for the patient.

(b) Comply with a health care decision for the patient made by a person then authorized to make health care decisions for the patient to the same extent as if the decision had been made by the patient while having capacity. *(Added by Stats.1999, c. 658 (A.B.891), § 39, operative July 1, 2000.)*

Law Revision Commission Comments

1999 Addition

Section 4733 is drawn from Section 7(d) of the Uniform Health–Care Decisions Act (1993). This section generalizes a duty to comply

provided in former Health and Safety Code Section 7187.5 (2d sentence) (Natural Death Act).

See also Sections 4609 ("capacity" defined), 4617 ("health care decision" defined), 4619 ("health care institution" defined), 4621 ("health care provider" defined), 4623 ("individual health care instruction" defined), 4625 ("patient" defined).

Background from Uniform Act. Section 7(d) requires health-care providers and institutions to comply with a patient's individual instruction and with a reasonable interpretation of that instruction made by a person then authorized to make health-care decisions for the patient. A health-care provider or institution must also comply with a health-care decision made by a person then authorized to make health-care decisions for the patient to the same extent as if the decision had been made by the patient while having capacity. These requirements help to protect the patient's rights to autonomy and self-determination and validate and seek to effectuate the substitute decision making authorized by the Act. [Adapted from Unif. Health–Care Decisions Act § 7(d) comment (1993)] [29 Cal.L.Rev.Comm. Reports 1 (1999)].

Cross References

Capacity defined for purposes of this Division, see Probate Code § 4609.
Health care decision defined for purposes of this Division, see Probate Code § 4617.
Health care defined for purposes of this Division, see Probate Code § 4615.
Health care institution defined for purposes of this Division, see Probate Code § 4619.
Health care provider defined for purposes of this Division, see Probate Code § 4621.
Individual health care instruction defined for purposes of this Division, see Probate Code § 4623.
Patient defined for purposes of this Division, see Probate Code § 4625.

§ 4734. Declining to comply with health care instruction or decision due to reasons of conscience

(a) A health care provider may decline to comply with an individual health care instruction or health care decision for reasons of conscience.

(b) A health care institution may decline to comply with an individual health care instruction or health care decision if the instruction or decision is contrary to a policy of the institution that is expressly based on reasons of conscience and if the policy was timely communicated to the patient or to a person then authorized to make health care decisions for the patient. *(Added by Stats.1999, c. 658 (A.B.891), § 39, operative July 1, 2000.)*

Law Revision Commission Comments

1999 Addition

Section 4734 is drawn from Section 7(e) of the Uniform Health–Care Decisions Act (1993).

See also Sections 4615 ("health care" defined), 4619 ("health care institution" defined), 4621 ("health care provider" defined), 4623 ("individual health care instruction" defined), 4625 ("patient" defined).

Background from Uniform Act. Not all instructions or decisions must be honored, however. Section 7(e) [Prob. Code § 4734(a)] authorizes a health-care provider to decline to comply with an individual instruction or health-care decision for reasons of conscience. Section 7(e) also allows a health-care institution to decline to comply with a health-care instruction or decision if the instruction or decision is contrary to a policy of the institution which is expressly based on reasons of conscience and if the policy was timely communicated to the patient or to an individual then authorized to make health-care decisions for the patient. [Adapted from Unif. Health–Care Decisions Act § 7(e) comment (1993)] [29 Cal.L.Rev. Comm. Reports 1 (1999)].

Cross References

Health care decision defined for purposes of this Division, see Probate Code § 4617.

Health care defined for purposes of this Division, see Probate Code § 4615.

Health care institution defined for purposes of this Division, see Probate Code § 4619.

Health care provider defined for purposes of this Division, see Probate Code § 4621.

Individual health care instruction defined for purposes of this Division, see Probate Code § 4623.

Patient defined for purposes of this Division, see Probate Code § 4625.

§ 4735. Declining to comply with health care instruction or decision that is medically ineffective

A health care provider or health care institution may decline to comply with an individual health care instruction or health care decision that requires medically ineffective health care or health care contrary to generally accepted health care standards applicable to the health care provider or institution. *(Added by Stats.1999, c. 658 (A.B.891), § 39, operative July 1, 2000.)*

Law Revision Commission Comments
1999 Addition

Section 4735 is drawn from Section 7(f) of the Uniform Health–Care Decisions Act (1993). This section is a special application of the general rule in Section 4654.

See also Sections 4615 ("health care" defined), 4619 ("health care institution" defined), 4621 ("health care provider" defined), 4623 ("individual health care instruction" defined), 4625 ("patient" defined).

Background from Uniform Act. Section 7(f) [Prob. Code § 4734(b)] further authorizes a health-care provider or institution to decline to comply with an instruction or decision that requires the provision of care which would be medically ineffective or contrary to generally accepted health-care standards applicable to the provider or institution. "Medically ineffective health care," as used in this section, means treatment which would not offer the patient any significant benefit. [Adapted from Unif. Health–Care Decisions Act § 7(f) comment (1993)] [29 Cal.L.Rev.Comm. Reports 1 (1999)].

Cross References

Health care decision defined for purposes of this Division, see Probate Code § 4617.

Health care defined for purposes of this Division, see Probate Code § 4615.

Health care institution defined for purposes of this Division, see Probate Code § 4619.

Health care provider defined for purposes of this Division, see Probate Code § 4621.

Individual health care instruction defined for purposes of this Division, see Probate Code § 4623.

§ 4736. Duties upon declining to comply with health care instruction or decision

A health care provider or health care institution that declines to comply with an individual health care instruction or health care decision shall do all of the following:

(a) Promptly so inform the patient, if possible, and any person then authorized to make health care decisions for the patient.

(b) Unless the patient or person then authorized to make health care decisions for the patient refuses assistance, immediately make all reasonable efforts to assist in the transfer of the patient to another health care provider or institution that is willing to comply with the instruction or decision.

(c) Provide continuing care to the patient until a transfer can be accomplished or until it appears that a transfer cannot be accomplished. In all cases, appropriate pain relief and other palliative care shall be continued. *(Added by Stats. 1999, c. 658 (A.B.891), § 39, operative July 1, 2000.)*

Law Revision Commission Comments
1999 Addition

Section 4736 is drawn in part from Section 7(g) of the Uniform Health–Care Decisions Act (1993). This section applies to situations where the health care provider or institution declines to comply under Section 4734 or 4735. This section continues the duty to transfer provided in former Health and Safety Code Sections 7187.5 (2d sentence) and 7190 (Natural Death Act). Subdivision (c) continues statutory recognition of a duty to provide pain relief in former Health and Safety Code Section 7189.5(b). Nothing in this section requires administration of ineffective care. See Sections 4654, 4735.

See also Sections 4617 ("health care decision" defined), 4619 ("health care institution" defined), 4621 ("health care provider" defined), 4623 ("individual health care instruction" defined), 4625 ("patient" defined).

Background from Uniform Act. Section 7(g) requires a health-care provider or institution that declines to comply with an individual instruction or health-care decision to promptly communicate the refusal to the patient, if possible, and to any person then authorized to make health-care decisions for the patient. The provider or institution also must provide continuing care to the patient until a transfer can be effected. In addition, unless the patient or person then authorized to make health-care decisions for the patient refuses assistance, the health-care provider or institution must immediately make all reasonable efforts to assist in the transfer of the patient to another health-care provider or institution that is willing to comply with the instruction or decision. [Adapted from Unif. Health–Care Decisions Act § 7(g) comment (1993)] [29 Cal.L.Rev.Comm. Reports App. 6 (1999)].

Cross References

Health care decision defined for purposes of this Division, see Probate Code § 4617.

Health care defined for purposes of this Division, see Probate Code § 4615.

Health care institution defined for purposes of this Division, see Probate Code § 4619.

Health care provider defined for purposes of this Division, see Probate Code § 4621.

Individual health care instruction defined for purposes of this Division, see Probate Code § 4623.

Patient defined for purposes of this Division, see Probate Code § 4625.

CHAPTER 5. IMMUNITIES AND LIABILITIES

Section
4740. Health care provider or institution; immunity from civil or criminal liability.

Section

4741. Agent or surrogate; immunity from civil or criminal liability.
4742. Intentional violations and acts; liability; damages.
4743. Altering or forging health care directive; criminal liability.

§ 4740. Health care provider or institution; immunity from civil or criminal liability

A health care provider or health care institution acting in good faith and in accordance with generally accepted health care standards applicable to the health care provider or institution is not subject to civil or criminal liability or to discipline for unprofessional conduct for any actions in compliance with this division, including, but not limited to, any of the following conduct:

(a) Complying with a health care decision of a person that the health care provider or health care institution believes in good faith has the authority to make a health care decision for a patient, including a decision to withhold or withdraw health care.

(b) Declining to comply with a health care decision of a person based on a belief that the person then lacked authority.

(c) Complying with an advance health care directive and assuming that the directive was valid when made and has not been revoked or terminated.

(d) Declining to comply with an individual health care instruction or health care decision, in accordance with Sections 4734 to 4736, inclusive. *(Added by Stats.1999, c. 658 (A.B.891), § 39, operative July 1, 2000.)*

Law Revision Commission Comments

1999 Addition

Section 4740 is drawn in part from Section 9(a) of the Uniform Health–Care Decisions Act (1993) and supersedes former Sections 4727(f) and 4750 (durable power of attorney for health care). This section also supersedes former Health and Safety Code Section 7190.5 (Natural Death Act). The major categories of actions listed in subdivisions (a)-(d) are given as examples and not by way of limitation on the general rule stated in the introductory paragraph.

The good faith standard of former law is continued in this section. Like former law, this section protects the health care provider who acts in good faith reliance on a health care decision made by an agent pursuant to this division. The reference to acting in accordance with generally accepted health care standards makes clear that a health care provider is not protected from liability for malpractice. The specific qualifications built into the rules provided in former Section 4750(a) are superseded by the good faith rule in this section and by the affirmative requirements of other provisions. See, e. g., Sections 4683(a) (scope of agent's authority) (compare to second part of introductory language of former Section 4750(a)), 4684 (standard governing agent's health care decisions) (compare to former Section 4750(a)(1)-(2)). See also Section 4733 (duty of health care provider or institution to comply with health care instructions and decisions), 4734 (health care provider's or institution's right to decline), 4736 (duty of declining health care provider or institution).

See also Sections 4605 ("advance health care directive" defined), 4617 ("health care decision" defined), 4619 ("health care institution" defined), 4621 ("health care provider" defined), 4625 ("patient" defined).

Background from Uniform Act. Section 9 [Prob. Code §§ 4740–4741] grants broad protection from liability for actions taken in good faith. Section 9(a) permits a health-care provider or institution to comply with a health-care decision made by a person appearing to have authority to make health-care decisions for a patient; to decline to comply with a health-care decision made by a person believed to be without authority; and to assume the validity of and to comply with an advance health-care directive. Absent bad faith or actions taken that are not in accord with generally accepted health-care standards, a health-care provider or institution has no duty to investigate a claim of authority or the validity of an advance health-care directive. [Adapted from Unif. Health–Care Decisions Act § 9(a) comment (1993)] [29 Cal.L.Rev.Comm. Reports App. 6 (1999)].

Cross References

Advance health care directive defined for purposes of this Division, see Probate Code § 4605.
Health care decision defined for purposes of this Division, see Probate Code § 4617.
Health care defined for purposes of this Division, see Probate Code § 4615.
Health care institution defined for purposes of this Division, see Probate Code § 4619.
Health care provider defined for purposes of this Division, see Probate Code § 4621.
Individual health care instruction defined for purposes of this Division, see Probate Code § 4623.
Patient defined for purposes of this Division, see Probate Code § 4625.

§ 4741. Agent or surrogate; immunity from civil or criminal liability

A person acting as agent or surrogate under this part is not subject to civil or criminal liability or to discipline for unprofessional conduct for health care decisions made in good faith. *(Added by Stats.1999, c. 658 (A.B.891), § 39, operative July 1, 2000.)*

Law Revision Commission Comments

1999 Addition

Section 4741 is drawn from Section 9(b) of the Uniform Health–Care Decisions Act (1993).

See also Sections 4607 ("agent" defined), 4617 ("health care decision" defined), 4643 ("surrogate" defined).

Background from Uniform Act. Section 9(b) protects agents and surrogates acting in good faith from liability for making a health-care decision for a patient. Also protected from liability are individuals who mistakenly but in good faith believe they have the authority to make a health-care decision for a patient. For example, an individual who has been designated as agent in a power of attorney for health care might assume authority unaware that the power has been revoked. Or a family member might assume authority to act as surrogate unaware that a family member having a higher priority was reasonably available and authorized to act. [Adapted from Unif. Health–Care Decisions Act § 9(b) comment (1993)] [29 Cal.L.Rev. Comm. Reports App. 6 (1999)].

Cross References

Agent defined for purposes of this Division, see Probate Code § 4607.
Health care decision defined for purposes of this Division, see Probate Code § 4617.
Health care defined for purposes of this Division, see Probate Code § 4615.

Surrogate defined for purposes of this Division, see Probate Code § 4643.

§ 4742. Intentional violations and acts; liability; damages

(a) A health care provider or health care institution that intentionally violates this part is subject to liability to the aggrieved individual for damages of two thousand five hundred dollars ($2,500) or actual damages resulting from the violation, whichever is greater, plus reasonable attorney's fees.

(b) A person who intentionally falsifies, forges, conceals, defaces, or obliterates an individual's advance health care directive or a revocation of an advance health care directive without the individual's consent, or who coerces or fraudulently induces an individual to give, revoke, or not to give an advance health care directive, is subject to liability to that individual for damages of ten thousand dollars ($10,000) or actual damages resulting from the action, whichever is greater, plus reasonable attorney's fees.

(c) The damages provided in this section are cumulative and not exclusive of any other remedies provided by law. *(Added by Stats.1999, c. 658 (A.B.891), § 39, operative July 1, 2000.)*

Law Revision Commission Comments

1999 Addition

Subdivisions (a) and (b) of Section 4742 are drawn from Section 10 of the Uniform Health–Care Decisions Act (1993) and supersede former Health and Safety Code Section 7191(a)-(b) (Natural Death Act).

Subdivision (c) continues the rule of former Health and Safety Code Section 7191(g) (Natural Death Act) and is consistent with the uniform act. See Unif. Health–Care Decisions Act § 10 comment (1993).

See also Sections 4605 ("advance health care directive" defined), 4619 ("health care institution" defined), 4621 ("health care provider" defined).

Background from Uniform Act. Conduct which intentionally violates the Act and which interferes with an individual's autonomy to make health-care decisions, either personally or through others as provided under the Act, is subject to civil damages rather than criminal penalties out of a recognition that prosecutions are unlikely to occur. The legislature of an enacting state will have to determine the amount of damages which needs to be authorized in order to encourage the level of potential private enforcement actions necessary to effect compliance with the obligations and responsibilities imposed by the Act. The damages provided by this section do not supersede but are in addition to remedies available under other law. [Adapted from Unif. Health–Care Decisions Act § 10 comment (1993)] [29 Cal.L.Rev.Comm. Reports 1 (1999)].

Cross References

Advance health care directive defined for purposes of this Division, see Probate Code § 4605.
Health care defined for purposes of this Division, see Probate Code § 4615.
Health care institution defined for purposes of this Division, see Probate Code § 4619.
Health care provider defined for purposes of this Division, see Probate Code § 4621.

§ 4743. Altering or forging health care directive; criminal liability

Any person who alters or forges a written advance health care directive of another, or willfully conceals or withholds personal knowledge of a revocation of an advance directive, with the intent to cause a withholding or withdrawal of health care necessary to keep the patient alive contrary to the desires of the patient, and thereby directly causes health care necessary to keep the patient alive to be withheld or withdrawn and the death of the patient thereby to be hastened, is subject to prosecution for unlawful homicide as provided in Chapter 1 (commencing with Section 187) of Title 8 of Part 1 of the Penal Code. *(Added by Stats.1999, c. 658 (A.B.891), § 39, operative July 1, 2000.)*

Law Revision Commission Comments

1999 Addition

Section 4743 continues former Section 4726 without substantive change and supersedes former Health and Safety Code Section 7191(c)-(d) (Natural Death Act). References to "principal" have been changed to "patient" to reflect the broader scope of this division, and some surplus language has been omitted. The former incorrect cross-reference to "Title 4" has been corrected.

See also Sections 4605 ("advance health care directive" defined), 4615 ("health care" defined), 4625 ("patient" defined). [29 Cal. L.Rev.Comm. Reports 1 (1999)].

Cross References

Advance health care directive defined for purposes of this Division, see Probate Code § 4605.
Health care defined for purposes of this Division, see Probate Code § 4615.
Patient defined for purposes of this Division, see Probate Code § 4625.

Part 3

JUDICIAL PROCEEDINGS

CHAPTER 1.   GENERAL PROVISIONS

§ 4750.   Necessity of judicial intervention or approval

Subject to this division:

(a) An advance health care directive is effective and exercisable free of judicial intervention.

(b) A health care decision made by an agent for a principal is effective without judicial approval.

(c) A health care decision made by a surrogate for a patient is effective without judicial approval. *(Added by Stats.1999, c. 658 (A.B.891), § 39, operative July 1, 2000.)*

Law Revision Commission Comments

1999 Addition

This section makes clear that judicial involvement in health care decisionmaking is disfavored. See Section 4650(c) (legislative findings). Subdivision (a) of Section 4750 continues former Section 4900 to the extent it applied to powers of attorney for health care.

Subdivision (b) is drawn from Section 2(f) of the Uniform Health–Care Decisions Act (1993).

Subdivision (c) is drawn from Sections 2(f) and 5(g) of the Uniform Health–Care Decisions Act (1993).

See also Sections 4605 ("advance health care directive" defined), 4607 ("agent" defined), 4617 ("health care decision" defined), 4625 ("patient" defined), 4633 ("principal" defined), 4643 ("surrogate" defined). [29 Cal.L.Rev.Comm. Reports App. 6 (1999)].

Cross References

Advance health care directive" defined for purposes of this Division, see Probate Code § 4605.

Agent defined for purposes of this Division, see Probate Code § 4607.

Health care decision defined for purposes of this Division, see Probate Code § 4617.

Health care defined for purposes of this Division, see Probate Code § 4615.

Patient defined for purposes of this Division, see Probate Code § 4625.

Principal defined for purposes of this Division, see Probate Code § 4633.

Surrogate defined for purposes of this Division, see Probate Code § 4643.

§ 4751. Cumulative nature of remedies

The remedies provided in this part are cumulative and not exclusive of any other remedies provided by law. *(Added by Stats.1999, c. 658 (A.B.891), § 39, operative July 1, 2000.)*

Law Revision Commission Comments

1999 Addition

Section 4751 continues former Section 4901 to the extent it applied to powers of attorney for health care and supersedes Health and Safety Code Section 7191.5(h) (Natural Death Act) to the extent it applied to remedies. [29 Cal.L.Rev.Comm. Reports App. 6 (1999)].

§ 4752. Ability to limit judicial intervention or authority

Except as provided in Section 4753, this part is not subject to limitation in an advance health care directive. *(Added by Stats.1999, c. 658 (A.B.891), § 39, operative July 1, 2000.)*

Law Revision Commission Comments

1999 Addition

Section 4752 continues former Section 4902 to the extent it applied to powers of attorney for health care.

See also Sections 4605 ("advance health care directive" defined), 4681 (general rule on limitations provided in power of attorney). [29 Cal.L.Rev.Comm. Reports 1 (1999)].

Cross References

Advance health care directive defined for purposes of this Division, see Probate Code § 4605.

§ 4753. Limitation on ability of person to petition court; requirements; restrictions

(a) Subject to subdivision (b), an advance health care directive may expressly eliminate the authority of a person listed in Section 4765 to petition the court for any one or more of the purposes enumerated in Section 4766, if both of the following requirements are satisfied:

(1) The advance directive is executed by an individual having the advice of a lawyer authorized to practice law in the state where the advance directive is executed.

(2) The individual's lawyer signs a certificate stating in substance:

"I am a lawyer authorized to practice law in the state where this advance health care directive was executed, and _____ [insert name] was my client at the time this advance directive was executed. I have advised my client concerning his or her rights in connection with this advance directive and the applicable law and the consequences of signing or not signing this advance directive, and my client, after being so advised, has executed this advance directive."

(b) An advance health care directive may not limit the authority of the following persons to petition under this part:

(1) The conservator of the person, with respect to a petition relating to an advance directive, for a purpose specified in subdivision (b) or (d) of Section 4766.

(2) The agent, with respect to a petition relating to a power of attorney for health care, for a purpose specified in subdivision (b) or (c) of Section 4766. *(Added by Stats.1999, c. 658 (A.B.891), § 39, operative July 1, 2000.)*

Law Revision Commission Comments

1999 Addition

Section 4753 continues former Section 4903 to the extent it applied to powers of attorney for health care. Subdivision (a) makes clear that a power of attorney may limit the applicability of this part only if it is executed with the advice and approval of the principal's counsel. This limitation is designed to ensure that the execution of a power of attorney that restricts the remedies of this part is accomplished knowingly by the principal. The inclusion of a provision in the power of attorney making this part inapplicable does not affect the right to resort to any judicial remedies that may otherwise be available.

Subdivision (b) specifies the purposes for which a conservator of the person or an agent may petition the court under this part with respect to a power of attorney for health care. The rights provided in these paragraphs cannot be limited by a provision in an advance directive, but the advance directive may restrict or eliminate the right of any other persons to petition the court under this part if the individual executing the advance directive has the advice of legal counsel and the other requirements of subdivision (a) are met. See Section 4681 (effect of provision in power of attorney attempting to limit right to petition).

Under subdivision (b)(1), despite a contrary provision in the advance directive, the conservator of the person may obtain a determination of whether an advance directive is in effect or has terminated (Section 4766(b)) or whether the authority of an agent or surrogate is terminated (Section 4766(d)). See also Section 4766 Comment.

Under subdivision (b)(2), despite a contrary provision in the power of attorney, the agent may obtain a determination of whether the power of attorney for health care is in effect or has terminated (Section 4766(b)), or an order passing on the acts or proposed acts of the agent under the power of attorney (Section 4766(c)).

See also Sections 4605 ("advance health care directive" defined), 4607 ("agent" defined), 4613 ("conservator" defined), 4629 ("power of attorney for health care" defined). [29 Cal.L.Rev.Comm. Reports 1 (1999)].

Cross References

Advance health care directive defined for purposes of this Division, see Probate Code § 4605.

Agent defined for purposes of this Division, see Probate Code § 4607.

Conservator defined for purposes of this Division, see Probate Code § 4613.

Health care defined for purposes of this Division, see Probate Code § 4615.

Power of attorney for health care defined for purposes of this Division, see Probate Code § 4629.

§ 4754. Jury trial

There is no right to a jury trial in proceedings under this division. *(Added by Stats.1999, c. 658 (A.B.891), § 39, operative July 1, 2000.)*

Law Revision Commission Comments

1999 Addition

Section 4754 continues former Section 4904 to the extent it applied to powers of attorney for health care. This section is consistent with the rule applicable to other fiduciaries. See Sections 1452 (guardianships and conservatorships), 4504 (powers of attorney generally), 7200 (decedents' estates), 17006 (trusts). [29 Cal.L.Rev.Comm. Reports 1 (1999)].

§ 4755. Application of Division 3

Except as otherwise provided in this division, the general provisions in Division 3 (commencing with Section 1000) apply to proceedings under this division. *(Added by Stats. 1999, c. 658 (A.B.891), § 39, operative July 1, 2000.)*

Law Revision Commission Comments

1999 Addition

Section 4755 continues former Section 4905 to the extent it applied to powers of attorney for health care. Like Section 4505, this section provides a cross-reference to the general procedural rules that apply to this division. See, e.g., Sections 1003 (guardian ad litem), 1021 (verification required), 1041 (clerk to set matters for hearing), 1046 (hearing and orders), 1203 (order shortening time for notice), 1215–1216 (service), 1260 (proof of service). [29 Cal.L.Rev.Comm. Reports 1 (1999)].

CHAPTER 2.   JURISDICTION AND VENUE

Section
4760. Superior court jurisdiction.
4761. Exercise of jurisdiction.
4762. Agent or surrogate subject to personal jurisdiction.
4763. Venue.

§ 4760. Superior court jurisdiction

(a) The superior court has jurisdiction in proceedings under this division.

(b) The court in proceedings under this division is a court of general jurisdiction and the court, or a judge of the court, has the same power and authority with respect to the proceedings as otherwise provided by law for a superior court, or a judge of the superior court, including, but not limited to, the matters authorized by Section 128 of the Code of Civil Procedure. *(Added by Stats.1999, c. 658 (A.B.891), § 39, operative July 1, 2000.)*

§ 4761.   Exercise of jurisdiction

The court may exercise jurisdiction in proceedings under this division on any basis permitted by Section 410.10 of the Code of Civil Procedure. *(Added by Stats.1999, c. 658 (A.B.891), § 39, operative July 1, 2000.)*

§ 4762.   Agent or surrogate subject to personal jurisdiction

Without limiting Section 4761, a person who acts as an agent under a power of attorney for health care or as a surrogate under this division is subject to personal jurisdiction in this state with respect to matters relating to acts and transactions of the agent or surrogate performed in this state or affecting a patient in this state. *(Added by Stats.1999, c. 658 (A.B.891), § 39, operative July 1, 2000.)*

Law Revision Commission Comments

1999 Addition

Section 4762 continues former Section 4922 to the extent it applied to powers of attorney for health care, and extends its principles to cover surrogates. Like Section 4522, this section is comparable to Sections 3902(b) (jurisdiction over custodian under Uniform Transfers to Minors Act) and 17003(a) (jurisdiction over trustee). This section is intended to facilitate exercise of the court's power under this part when the court's jurisdiction is properly invoked. As recognized by the introductory clause, constitutional limitations on assertion of jurisdiction apply to the exercise of jurisdiction under this section. Consequently, appropriate notice must be given to an agent or surrogate as a condition of personal jurisdiction. *Cf.* Mullane v. Central Hanover Bank & Trust Co., 339 U.S. 306 (1950).

See also Sections 4607 ("agent" defined), 4625 ("patient" defined), 4629 ("power of attorney for health care" defined), 4643 ("surrogate" defined). [29 Cal.L.Rev.Comm. Reports 1 (1999)].

Cross References

Agent defined for purposes of this Division, see Probate Code § 4607.

Health care defined for purposes of this Division, see Probate Code § 4615.

Patient defined for purposes of this Division, see Probate Code § 4625.

Power of attorney for health care defined for purposes of this Division, see Probate Code § 4629.

Surrogate defined for purposes of this Division, see Probate Code § 4643.

§ 4763.   Venue

The proper county for commencement of a proceeding under this division shall be determined in the following order of priority:

(a) The county in which the patient resides.

(b) The county in which the agent or surrogate resides.

(c) Any other county that is in the patient's best interest. *(Added by Stats.1999, c. 658 (A.B.891), § 39, operative July 1, 2000.)*

Cross References

Agent defined for purposes of this Division, see Probate Code § 4607.

Patient defined for purposes of this Division, see Probate Code § 4625.

Surrogate defined for purposes of this Division, see Probate Code § 4643.

Law Revision Commission Comments

2001 Amendment

The chapter heading is amended to accurately reflect the contents of the chapter. Appeals under the Probate Code are governed generally by Part 3 (commencing with Section 1300) of Division 3. See Section 1302.5 (grounds for appeal under Health Care Decisions Law). [30 Cal.L.Rev.Comm. Reports 621 (2000)].

§ 4765. Persons entitled to file petition

Subject to Section 4753, a petition may be filed under this part by any of the following persons:

(a) The patient.

(b) The patient's spouse, unless legally separated.

(c) A relative of the patient.

(d) The patient's agent or surrogate.

(e) The conservator of the person of the patient.

(f) The court investigator, described in Section 1454, of the county where the patient resides.

(g) The public guardian of the county where the patient resides.

(h) The supervising health care provider or health care institution involved with the patient's care.

(i) Any other interested person or friend of the patient. (*Added by Stats.1999, c. 658 (A.B.891), § 39, operative July 1, 2000.*)

Law Revision Commission Comments

1999 Addition

Section 4765 continues former Section 4940 to the extent it applied to powers of attorney for health care, with some omissions and clarifications appropriate for the scope of this division. The purposes for which a person may file a petition under this part are limited by other rules. See Sections 4752 (effect of provision in advance directive attempting to limit right to petition), 4753 (limitations on right to petition), 4766 (petition with respect to advance directive). See also Section 4751 (other remedies not affected).

See also Sections 4607 ("agent" defined), 4613 ("conservator" defined), 4619 ("health care institution" defined), 4625 ("patient" defined), 4641 ("supervising health care provider" defined), 4643 ("surrogate" defined). [29 Cal.L.Rev.Comm. Reports App. 6 (1999)].

Cross References

Agent defined for purposes of this Division, see Probate Code § 4607.

Conservator defined for purposes of this Division, see Probate Code § 4613.

Health care defined for purposes of this Division, see Probate Code § 4615.

Health care institution defined for purposes of this Division, see Probate Code § 4619.

Health care provider defined for purposes of this Division, see Probate Code § 4621.

Patient defined for purposes of this Division, see Probate Code § 4625.

Supervising health care provider defined for purposes of this Division, see Probate Code § 4641.

Surrogate defined for purposes of this Division, see Probate Code § 4643.

§ 4766. Purposes for filing petition

A petition may be filed under this part for any one or more of the following purposes:

(a) Determining whether or not the patient has capacity to make health care decisions.

(b) Determining whether an advance health care directive is in effect or has terminated.

(c) Determining whether the acts or proposed acts of an agent or surrogate are consistent with the patient's desires as expressed in an advance health care directive or otherwise made known to the court or, where the patient's desires are unknown or unclear, whether the acts or proposed acts of the agent or surrogate are in the patient's best interest.

(d) Declaring that the authority of an agent or surrogate is terminated, upon a determination by the court that the agent or surrogate has made a health care decision for the patient that authorized anything illegal or upon a determination by the court of both of the following:

(1) The agent or surrogate has violated, has failed to perform, or is unfit to perform, the duty under an advance health care directive to act consistent with the patient's desires or, where the patient's desires are unknown or unclear, is acting (by action or inaction) in a manner that is clearly contrary to the patient's best interest.

(2) At the time of the determination by the court, the patient lacks the capacity to execute or to revoke an advance health care directive or disqualify a surrogate.

(e) Compelling a third person to honor individual health care instructions or the authority of an agent or surrogate. (*Added by Stats.1999, c. 658 (A.B.891), § 39, operative July 1, 2000. Amended by Stats.2001, c. 230 (A.B.1278), § 7.*)

Law Revision Commission Comments

1999 Addition

Section 4766 continues the substance of former Section 4942 to the extent it applied to powers of attorney for health care, and adds language relating to advance directives and surrogates for consistency with the scope of this division.

A determination of capacity under subdivision (a) is subject to the Due Process in Competency Determinations Act. See Sections 810–813.

Under subdivision (c), the patient's desires as expressed in the power of attorney for health care, individual health care instructions, or otherwise made known to the court provide the standard for judging the acts of the agent or surrogate. See Section 4714 (standard governing surrogate's health care decisions). Where it is not possible to use a standard based on the patient's desires because they are not stated in an advance directive or otherwise known or are unclear, subdivision (c) provides that the "patient's best interest" standard be used.

Subdivision (d) permits the court to terminate health care decisionmaking authority where an agent or surrogate is not complying with the duty to carry out the patient's desires or act in the patient's best interest. See Section 4714 (standard governing surrogate's health care decisions). Subdivision (d) permits termination of authority under an advance health care directive not only where an agent, for example, is acting illegally or failing to perform the duties under a power of attorney or is acting contrary to the known desires of the principal, but also where the desires of the principal are unknown or unclear and the agent is acting in a manner that is clearly contrary to the patient's best interest. The patient's desires may become unclear as a result of developments in medical treatment techniques that have occurred since the patient's desires were expressed, such developments having changed the nature or consequences of the treatment.

An advance health care directive may limit the authority to petition under this part. See Sections 4752 (effect of provision in advance directive attempting to limit right to petition), 4753 (limitations on right to petition).

See also Sections 4605 ("advance health care directive" defined), 4607 ("agent" defined), 4609 ("capacity" defined), 4613 ("conservator" defined), 4629 ("power of attorney for health care" defined), 4633 ("principal" defined), 4643 ("surrogate" defined). [29 Cal. L.Rev.Comm. Reports App. 6 (1999)].

2001 Amendment

Section 4766 is amended to add the grounds for a petition specified in subdivision (e). This subdivision is consistent with the provision applicable to compel compliance with powers of attorney for property matters in Section 4541(f). The remedy provided by this subdivision would be appropriate where the third person has a duty to honor the authority of an agent or surrogate. See, e.g., Sections 4685 (agent's priority), 4733 (duty of health care provider or institution to comply with health care instructions and decisions).

The extent to which a third person may be compelled to comply with decisions of an agent or surrogate is subject to other limitations in this division. See, e.g., Sections 4652 (excluded acts), 4653 (mercy killing, assisted suicide, euthanasia not approved), 4654 (compliance with generally accepted health care standards), 4734 (right to decline for reasons of conscience or institutional policy), 4735 (right to decline to provide ineffective care).

An advance health care directive may limit the authority to petition under this part. See Sections 4752 (effect of provision in advance directive attempting to limit right to petition), 4753 (limitations on right to petition).

See also Sections 4605 ("advance health care directive" defined), 4607 ("agent" defined), 4609 ("capacity" defined), 4613 ("conservator" defined), 4623 ("individual health care instructions" defined), 4629 ("power of attorney for health care" defined), 4633 ("principal" defined), 4643 ("surrogate" defined). [30 Cal.L.Rev.Comm. Reports 621 (2000)].

Cross References

Advance health care directive defined for purposes of this Division, see Probate Code § 4605.
Agent defined for purposes of this Division, see Probate Code § 4607.
Capacity defined for purposes of this Division, see Probate Code § 4609.
Fee for filing petition commencing or opposition papers concerning certain probate proceedings, see Government Code § 70655.
Health care decision defined for purposes of this Division, see Probate Code § 4617.

Health care defined for purposes of this Division, see Probate Code § 4615.
Individual health care instruction defined for purposes of this Division, see Probate Code § 4623.
Patient defined for purposes of this Division, see Probate Code § 4625.
Surrogate defined for purposes of this Division, see Probate Code § 4643.

§ 4767. Commencement of proceeding

A proceeding under this part is commenced by filing a petition stating facts showing that the petition is authorized under this part, the grounds of the petition, and, if known to the petitioner, the terms of any advance health care directive in question. *(Added by Stats.1999, c. 658 (A.B.891), § 39, operative July 1, 2000.)*

Law Revision Commission Comments

1999 Addition

Section 4767 continues former Section 4943 to the extent it applied to powers of attorney for health care.

See also Section 4605 ("advance health care directive" defined). [29 Cal.L.Rev.Comm. Reports 1 (1999)].

Cross References

Advance health care directive defined for purposes of this Division, see Probate Code § 4605.

§ 4768. Dismissal of petition

The court may dismiss a petition if it appears that the proceeding is not reasonably necessary for the protection of the interests of the patient and shall stay or dismiss the proceeding in whole or in part when required by Section 410.30 of the Code of Civil Procedure. *(Added by Stats.1999, c. 658 (A.B.891), § 39, operative July 1, 2000.)*

Law Revision Commission Comments

1999 Addition

Section 4768 is similar to Section 4944 in the Power of Attorney Law. Under this section, the court has authority to stay or dismiss a proceeding in this state if, in the interest of substantial justice, the proceeding should be heard in a forum outside this state. See Code Civ. Proc. § 410.30.

See also Section 4625 ("patient" defined). [29 Cal.L.Rev.Comm. Reports 1 (1999)].

Cross References

Patient defined for purposes of this Division, see Probate Code § 4625.

§ 4769. Notice of time and place of hearing

(a) Subject to subdivision (b), at least 15 days before the time set for hearing, the petitioner shall serve notice of the time and place of the hearing, together with a copy of the petition, on the following:

(1) The agent or surrogate, if not the petitioner.

(2) The patient, if not the petitioner.

(b) In the case of a petition to compel a third person to honor individual health care instructions or the authority of an agent or surrogate, notice of the time and place of the hearing, together with a copy of the petition, shall be served on the third person in the manner provided in Chapter 4 (commencing with Section 413.10) of Title 5 of Part 2 of the Code of Civil Procedure. *(Added by Stats.1999, c. 658 (A.B.891), § 39, operative July 1, 2000. Amended by Stats. 2001, c. 230 (A.B.1278), § 8.)*

Law Revision Commission Comments

1999 Addition

Section 4769 continues former Section 4945 to the extent it applied to powers of attorney for health care and extends its principles to apply to surrogates. Subdivision (b) is generalized from former Section 4945(b) applicable to property powers of attorney.

See also Sections 4607 ("agent" defined), 4625 ("patient" defined), 4633 ("principal" defined), 4643 ("surrogate" defined). [29 Cal. L.Rev.Comm. Reports 1 (1999)].

2001 Amendment

Subdivision (b) of Section 4769 is amended for consistency with Section 4766(e) (petition to compel third person to honor health care instructions or authority of agent or surrogate).

See also Sections 4607 ("agent" defined), 4623 ("individual health care instructions" defined), 4625 ("patient" defined), 4633 ("principal" defined), 4643 ("surrogate" defined). [30 Cal.L.Rev.Comm. Reports 621 (2000)].

Cross References

Agent defined for purposes of this Division, see Probate Code § 4607.

Health care defined for purposes of this Division, see Probate Code § 4615.

Individual health care instruction defined for purposes of this Division, see Probate Code § 4623.

Patient defined for purposes of this Division, see Probate Code § 4625.

Surrogate defined for purposes of this Division, see Probate Code § 4643.

§ 4770. Temporary order prescribing health care

The court in its discretion, on a showing of good cause, may issue a temporary order prescribing the health care of the patient until the disposition of the petition filed under Section 4766. If a power of attorney for health care is in effect and a conservator (including a temporary conservator) of the person is appointed for the principal, the court that appoints the conservator in its discretion, on a showing of good cause, may issue a temporary order prescribing the health care of the principal, the order to continue in effect for the period ordered by the court but in no case longer than the period necessary to permit the filing and determination of a petition filed under Section 4766. *(Added by Stats.1999, c. 658 (A.B.891), § 39, operative July 1, 2000.)*

Law Revision Commission Comments

1999 Addition

Section 4770 continues former Section 4946 to the extent it applied to powers of attorney for health care. This section is intended to make clear that the court has authority to provide, for example, for the continuance of treatment necessary to keep the patient alive pending the court's action on the petition. See also Section 1046 (court authority to make appropriate orders).

See also Sections 4605 ("advance health care directive" defined), 4613 ("conservator" defined), 4615 ("health care" defined), 4625 ("patient" defined), 4633 ("principal" defined). [29 Cal.L.Rev. Comm. Reports 1 (1999)].

Cross References

Conservator defined for purposes of this Division, see Probate Code § 4613.

Health care defined for purposes of this Division, see Probate Code § 4615.

Patient defined for purposes of this Division, see Probate Code § 4625.

Power of attorney for health care defined for purposes of this Division, see Probate Code § 4629.

Principal defined for purposes of this Division, see Probate Code § 4633.

§ 4771. Attorney's fees

In a proceeding under this part commenced by the filing of a petition by a person other than the agent or surrogate, the court may in its discretion award reasonable attorney's fees to one of the following:

(a) The agent or surrogate, if the court determines that the proceeding was commenced without any reasonable cause.

(b) The person commencing the proceeding, if the court determines that the agent or surrogate has clearly violated the duties under the advance health care directive. *(Added by Stats.1999, c. 658 (A.B.891), § 39, operative July 1, 2000.)*

Law Revision Commission Comments

1999 Addition

Section 4771 continues part of former Section 4947 to the extent it applied to powers of attorney for health care.

See also Sections 4605 ("advance health care directive" defined), 4607 ("agent" defined), 4633 ("principal" defined), 4643 ("surrogate" defined). [29 Cal.L.Rev.Comm. Reports 1 (1999)].

Cross References

Advance health care directive defined for purposes of this Division, see Probate Code § 4605.

Agent defined for purposes of this Division, see Probate Code § 4607.

Surrogate defined for purposes of this Division, see Probate Code § 4643.

§§ 4772 to 4779. Repealed by Stats.1999, c. 658 (A.B.891), § 38, operative July 1, 2000

Law Revision Commission Comments

1999 Repeal

Former Section 4772 is not continued. See Section 4701 (optional advance directive form) & Comment. [29 Cal.L.Rev.Comm. Reports 1 (1999)].

Former Section 4773 is not continued. For execution requirements, see Section 4680. See also Sections 4700 (substantive rules applicable to form), 4701 (optional advance directive form) & Comment. [29 Cal.L.Rev.Comm. Reports 1 (1999)].

Former Section 4774 is not continued. For execution requirements, see Section 4680. See also Sections 4700 (substantive rules applicable to form), 4701 (optional advance directive form) & Comment. [29 Cal.L.Rev.Comm. Reports 1 (1999)].

Former Section 4775 is not continued. See Section 4665 (application of Health Care Decisions Law to existing advance directives). [29 Cal.L.Rev.Comm. Reports 1 (1999)].

Former Section 4776 is not continued. See Section 4701 (optional advance directive form) & Comment. [29 Cal.L.Rev.Comm. Reports 1 (1999)].

Former Section 4777 is not continued. See Sections 4683 (scope of agent's authority), 4701 (optional advance directive form) & Comment. [29 Cal.L.Rev.Comm. Reports 1 (1999)].

Former Section 4778 is not continued. See Section 4701 (optional advance directive form) & Comment. [29 Cal.L.Rev.Comm. Reports 1 (1999)].

Former Section 4779 is superseded by Section 4700. [29 Cal. L.Rev.Comm. Reports 1 (1999)].

Part 4

REQUEST REGARDING RESUSCITATIVE MEASURES

§ 4780. Definitions

(a) As used in this part:

(1) "Request regarding resuscitative measures" means a written document, signed by (A) an individual with capacity, or a legally recognized health care decisionmaker, and (B) the individual's physician, that directs a health care provider regarding resuscitative measures. A request regarding resuscitative measures is not an advance health care directive.

(2) "Request regarding resuscitative measures" includes one, or both of, the following:

(A) A prehospital "do not resuscitate" form as developed by the Emergency Medical Services Authority or other substantially similar form.

(B) A Physician Orders for Life Sustaining Treatment form, as approved by the Emergency Medical Services Authority.

(3) "Physician Orders for Life Sustaining Treatment form" means a request regarding resuscitative measures that directs a health care provider regarding resuscitative and life-sustaining measures.

(b) A legally recognized health care decisionmaker may execute the Physician Orders for Life Sustaining Treatment form only if the individual lacks capacity, or the individual has designated that the decisionmaker's authority is effective pursuant to Section 4682.

(c) The Physician Orders for Life Sustaining Treatment form and medical intervention and procedures offered by the form shall be explained by a health care provider, as defined in Section 4621. The form shall be completed by a health care provider based on patient preferences and medical

indications, and signed by a physician, or a nurse practitioner or a physician assistant acting under the supervision of the physician and within the scope of practice authorized by law, and the patient or his or her legally recognized health care decisionmaker. The health care provider, during the process of completing the Physician Orders for Life Sustaining Treatment form, should inform the patient about the difference between an advance health care directive and the Physician Orders for Life Sustaining Treatment form.

(d) An individual having capacity may revoke a Physician Orders for Life Sustaining Treatment form at any time and in any manner that communicates an intent to revoke, consistent with Section 4695.

(e) A request regarding resuscitative measures may also be evidenced by a medallion engraved with the words "do not resuscitate" or the letters "DNR," a patient identification number, and a 24–hour toll-free telephone number, issued by a person pursuant to an agreement with the Emergency Medical Services Authority. *(Added by Stats.1999, c. 658 (A.B.891), § 39, operative July 1, 2000. Amended by Stats. 2008, c. 266 (A.B.3000), § 3; Stats.2015, c. 217 (A.B.637), § 1, eff. Jan. 1, 2016.)*

Law Revision Commission Comments
1999 Addition

Section 4780 continues former Section 4753(b) without substantive change. The phrase "for the individual" has been added at the end of subdivision (a)(1) for clarity. The former reference to "physician and surgeon" has been changed to "physician" for clarity. See Section 4627 ("physician" defined). For rules governing "legally recognized surrogate health care decisionmakers," see Part 2 (commencing with Section 4670) (Uniform Health Care Decisions Act).

See also Section 4781 ("health care provider" defined), 4625 ("patient" defined). [29 Cal.L.Rev.Comm. Reports 1 (1999)].

Cross References

Advance health care directive defined for purposes of this Division, see Probate Code § 4605.

Capacity defined for purposes of this Division, see Probate Code § 4609.

Health care defined for purposes of this Division, see Probate Code § 4615.

Health care provider defined for purposes of this Division, see Probate Code § 4621.

Health care provider defined for purposes of this Part, see Probate Code § 4781.

Patient defined for purposes of this Division, see Probate Code § 4625.

Physician defined for purposes of this Division, see Probate Code § 4627.

Requests to forego resuscitative measures, facilities without established policies, see Health and Safety Code § 1569.74.

§ 4781. "Health care provider"

As used in this part, "health care provider" includes, but is not limited to, the following:

(a) Persons described in Section 4621.

(b) Emergency response employees, including, but not limited to, firefighters, law enforcement officers, emergency medical technicians I and II, paramedics, and employees and volunteer members of legally organized and recognized volunteer organizations, who are trained in accordance with standards adopted as regulations by the Emergency Medical

Services Authority pursuant to Sections 1797.170, 1797.171, 1797.172, 1797.182, and 1797.183 of the Health and Safety Code to respond to medical emergencies in the course of performing their volunteer or employee duties with the organization. *(Added by Stats.1999, c. 658 (A.B.891), § 39, operative July 1, 2000.)*

Law Revision Commission Comments

1999 Addition

Section 4781 continues former Section 4753(g) without substantive change. [29 Cal.L.Rev.Comm. Reports 1 (1999)].

Cross References

Health care defined for purposes of this Division, see Probate Code § 4615.
Health care provider defined for purposes of this Division, see Probate Code § 4621.

§ 4781.2. Physician Orders for Life Sustaining Treatment form; treatment

(a) A health care provider shall treat an individual in accordance with a Physician Orders for Life Sustaining Treatment form.

(b) Subdivision (a) does not apply if the Physician Orders for Life Sustaining Treatment form requires medically ineffective health care or health care contrary to generally accepted health care standards applicable to the health care provider or institution.

(c) A physician may conduct an evaluation of the individual and, if possible, in consultation with the individual, or the individual's legally recognized health care decisionmaker, issue a new order consistent with the most current information available about the individual's health status and goals of care.

(d) The legally recognized health care decisionmaker of an individual without capacity shall consult with the physician who is, at that time, the individual's treating physician prior to making a request to modify that individual's Physician Orders for Life Sustaining Treatment form.

(e) An individual with capacity may, at any time, request alternative treatment to that treatment that was ordered on the form. *(Added by Stats.2008, c. 266 (A.B.3000), § 4.)*

Cross References

Capacity defined for purposes of this Division, see Probate Code § 4609.
Health care defined for purposes of this Division, see Probate Code § 4615.
Health care provider defined for purposes of this Division, see Probate Code § 4621.
Physician defined for purposes of this Division, see Probate Code § 4627.

§ 4781.4. Conflict of orders

If the orders in an individual's request regarding resuscitative measures directly conflict with his or her individual health care instruction, as defined in Section 4623, then, to the extent of the conflict, the most recent order or instruction is effective. *(Added by Stats.2008, c. 266 (A.B.3000), § 5.)*

Cross References

Health care defined for purposes of this Division, see Probate Code § 4615.
Individual health care instruction defined for purposes of this Division, see Probate Code § 4623.
Request regarding resuscitative measures defined for purposes of this Part, see Probate Code § 4780.

§ 4781.5. Health care decisionmaker

The legally recognized health care decisionmaker shall make health care decisions pursuant to this part in accordance with Sections 4684 and 4714. *(Added by Stats.2008, c. 266 (A.B.3000), § 6.)*

Cross References

Health care decision defined for purposes of this Division, see Probate Code § 4617.
Health care defined for purposes of this Division, see Probate Code § 4615.

§ 4782. Immunity from criminal or civil liability or other sanction

A health care provider who honors a request regarding resuscitative measures is not subject to criminal prosecution, civil liability, discipline for unprofessional conduct, administrative sanction, or any other sanction, as a result of his or her reliance on the request, if the health care provider (a) believes in good faith that the action or decision is consistent with this part, and (b) has no knowledge that the action or decision would be inconsistent with a health care decision that the individual signing the request would have made on his or her own behalf under like circumstances. *(Added by Stats.1999, c. 658 (A.B.891), § 39, operative July 1, 2000. Amended by Stats.2008, c. 266 (A.B.3000), § 7.)*

Law Revision Commission Comments

1999 Addition

Section 4782 continues former Section 4753(a) without substantive change.
See also Sections 4617 ("health care decision" defined), 4780 ("request to forgo resuscitative measures" defined), 4781 ("health care provider" defined). [29 Cal.L.Rev.Comm. Reports 1 (1999)].

Cross References

Health care decision defined for purposes of this Division, see Probate Code § 4617.
Health care defined for purposes of this Division, see Probate Code § 4615.
Health care provider defined for purposes of this Division, see Probate Code § 4621.
Health care provider defined for purposes of this Part, see Probate Code § 4781.
Request regarding resuscitative measures defined for purposes of this Part, see Probate Code § 4780.

§ 4783. Forms; contents

(a) Forms for requests regarding resuscitative measures printed after January 1, 1995, shall contain the following:
"By signing this form, the legally recognized health care decisionmaker acknowledges that this request regarding resuscitative measures is consistent with the known desires of, and with the best interest of, the individual who is the subject of the form."

(b) A printed form substantially similar to that described in subparagraph (A) of paragraph (2) of subdivision (a) of Section 4780 is valid and enforceable if all of the following conditions are met:

(1) The form is signed by the individual, or the individual's legally recognized health care decisionmaker, and a physician.

(2) The form directs health care providers regarding resuscitative measures.

(3) The form contains all other information required by this section. *(Added by Stats.1999, c. 658 (A.B.891), § 39, operative July 1, 2000. Amended by Stats.2008, c. 266 (A.B.3000), § 8.)*

Law Revision Commission Comments

1999 Addition

Section 4783 continues former Section 4753(c)-(d) without substantive change. For rules governing "legally recognized surrogate health care decisionmakers," see Part 2 (commencing with Section 4670) (Uniform Health Care Decisions Act).

See also Sections 4627 ("physician" defined), 4780 ("request to forgo resuscitative measures" defined), 4781 ("health care provider" defined). [29 Cal.L.Rev.Comm. Reports 1 (1999)].

Cross References

Health care defined for purposes of this Division, see Probate Code § 4615.
Health care provider defined for purposes of this Division, see Probate Code § 4621.
Health care provider defined for purposes of this Part, see Probate Code § 4781.
Physician defined for purposes of this Division, see Probate Code § 4627.
Request regarding resuscitative measures defined for purposes of this Part, see Probate Code § 4780.

§ 4784. Presumption of validity or request

In the absence of knowledge to the contrary, a health care provider may presume that a request regarding resuscitative measures is valid and unrevoked. *(Added by Stats.1999, c. 658 (A.B.891), § 39, operative July 1, 2000. Amended by Stats.2008, c. 266 (A.B.3000), § 9.)*

Law Revision Commission Comments

1999 Addition

Section 4784 continues former Section 4753(e) without change.

See also Sections 4780 ("request to forgo resuscitative measures" defined), 4781 ("health care provider" defined). [29 Cal.L.Rev. Comm. Reports 1 (1999)].

Cross References

Health care defined for purposes of this Division, see Probate Code § 4615.
Health care provider defined for purposes of this Division, see Probate Code § 4621.
Health care provider defined for purposes of this Part, see Probate Code § 4781.

Request regarding resuscitative measures defined for purposes of this Part, see Probate Code § 4780.

§ 4785. Persons within or outside of hospital; application of part

This part applies regardless of whether the individual executing a request regarding resuscitative measures is within or outside a hospital or other health care institution. *(Added by Stats.1999, c. 658 (A.B.891), § 39, operative July 1, 2000. Amended by Stats.2008, c. 266 (A.B.3000), § 10.)*

Law Revision Commission Comments

1999 Addition

Section 4785 continues former Section 4753(f) without substantive change.

See also Section 4619 ("health care institution" defined), 4780 ("request to forgo resuscitative measures" defined). [29 Cal.L.Rev. Comm. Reports 1 (1999)].

Cross References

Health care defined for purposes of this Division, see Probate Code § 4615.
Health care institution defined for purposes of this Division, see Probate Code § 4619.
Request regarding resuscitative measures defined for purposes of this Part, see Probate Code § 4780.

§ 4786. Effect on other laws

This part does not repeal or narrow laws relating to health care decisionmaking. *(Added by Stats.1999, c. 658 (A.B.891), § 39, operative July 1, 2000.)*

Law Revision Commission Comments

1999 Addition

Section 4786 restates former Section 4753(h) without substantive change. The references to the Durable Power of Attorney for Health Care and the Natural Death Act have been omitted as unnecessary. The reference to "current" laws had been eliminated as obsolete. [29 Cal.L.Rev.Comm. Reports 1 (1999)].

Cross References

Health care defined for purposes of this Division, see Probate Code § 4615.

§ 4788. POLST (Physician Orders for Life Sustaining Treatment) eRegistry Pilot

(a) For purposes of this section:

(1) "Authority" means the Emergency Medical Services Authority.

(2) "Authorized user" means a person authorized by the authority to submit information to, or to receive information from, the POLST eRegistry Pilot, including health care providers, as defined in Section 4781, and their designees.

(3) "POLST" means a Physician Orders for Life Sustaining Treatment that fulfills the requirements, in any format, of Section 4780.

(4) "POLST eRegistry Pilot" means the California POLST eRegistry Pilot program established pursuant to this section to make electronic, in addition to other modes of submission and transmission, POLST information available to authorized users.

(b)(1) The authority shall establish a pilot project, in consultation with stakeholders, to operate an electronic registry system on a pilot basis, to be known as the California POLST eRegistry Pilot, for the purpose of collecting a patient's POLST information received from a physician or physician's designee and disseminating the information to an authorized user.

(2) The authority shall implement this section only after determining that sufficient nonstate funds are available to allow for the development of the POLST eRegistry Pilot, any related startup costs, and an evaluation of the POLST eRegistry Pilot.

(3) The authority shall coordinate the POLST eRegistry Pilot, which shall be operated by, and as a part of, the health information exchange networks, or by an independent contractor, or by a combination thereof. The POLST eRegistry Pilot may operate in a single geographic area or multiple geographic areas and may test various methods of making POLST information available electronically. The design of the POLST eRegistry Pilot shall be sufficiently robust, based on the success of the pilot, to inform the permanent, statewide operation of a POLST eRegistry.

(4) The authority shall adopt guidelines necessary for the operation of the POLST eRegistry Pilot. In developing these guidelines, the authority shall seek input from interested parties and hold at least one public meeting. The adoption, amendment, or repeal of the guidelines authorized by this paragraph is hereby exempted from the Administrative Procedure Act (Chapter 3.5 (commencing with Section 11340) of Part 1 of Division 3 of Title 2 of the Government Code). The guidelines shall include, but not be limited to, the following:

(A) The means by which initial or subsequent POLST information may be submitted to, or withdrawn from, the POLST eRegistry Pilot, which shall include a method for electronic delivery of this information and the use of legally sufficient electronic signatures.

(B) Appropriate and timely methods by which the information in the POLST eRegistry Pilot may be disseminated to an authorized user.

(C) Procedures for verifying the identity of an authorized user.

(D) Procedures to ensure the accuracy of, and to appropriately protect the confidentiality of, POLST information submitted to the POLST eRegistry Pilot.

(E) The requirement that a patient, or, when appropriate, his or her legally recognized health care decisionmaker, receive a confirmation or a receipt that the patient's POLST information has been received by the POLST eRegistry Pilot.

(F) The ability of a patient, or, when appropriate, his or her legally recognized health care decisionmaker, with * * * the patient's health care provider, as defined in Section 4621, to modify or withdraw POLST information on the POLST eRegistry Pilot.

(5)(A) Prior to implementation of the POLST eRegistry Pilot, the authority shall submit a detailed plan to the Legislature that explains how the POLST eRegistry Pilot will operate.

(B) The plan to be submitted pursuant to subparagraph (A) shall be submitted in compliance with Section 9795 of the Government Code.

(c) The operation of the POLST eRegistry Pilot, for all users, shall comply with state and federal privacy and security laws and regulations, including, but not limited to, compliance with the Confidentiality of Medical Information Act (Part 2.6 (commencing with Section 56) of Division 1 of the Civil Code) and the regulations promulgated pursuant to the federal Health Insurance Portability and Accountability Act of 1996 (Public Law 104–191),[1] found at Parts 160 and 164 of Title 45 of the Code of Federal Regulations.

(d) When the POLST eRegistry Pilot is operable in the geographic area in which he or she practices or operates, a physician or physician's designee who completes POLST information with a patient or his or her legally recognized health care decisionmaker shall include the POLST information in the patient's official medical record and shall submit a copy of the POLST form to, or enter the POLST information into, the POLST eRegistry Pilot, unless the patient or the legally recognized health care decisionmaker chooses not to participate in the POLST eRegistry Pilot.

(e) When the POLST eRegistry Pilot is operable in the geographic area in which they practice or operate, physicians, hospitals, and health information exchange networks shall make electronic POLST information available, for use during emergencies, through the POLST eRegistry Pilot to health care providers, as defined in Section 4781, that also practice or operate in a geographic area where the POLST eRegistry Pilot is operable, but that are outside of their health information exchange networks.

(f) In accordance with Section 4782, a health care provider, as defined in Section 4781, who honors a patient's request regarding resuscitative measures obtained from the POLST eRegistry Pilot shall not be subject to criminal prosecution, civil liability, discipline for unprofessional conduct, administrative sanction, or any other sanction, if the health care provider (1) believes in good faith that the action or decision is consistent with this part, and (2) has no knowledge that the action or decision would be inconsistent with a health care decision that the individual signing the request would have made on his or her own behalf under like circumstances.

(g) An independent contractor approved by the authority shall perform an evaluation of the POLST eRegistry Pilot.

(h) This section shall remain in effect only until January 1, 2020, and as of that date is repealed, unless a later enacted statute, that is enacted before January 1, 2020, deletes or extends that date. *(Added by Stats.2015, c. 504 (S.B.19), § 2, eff. Jan. 1, 2016. Amended by Stats.2016, c. 86 (S.B.1171), § 248, eff. Jan. 1, 2017.)*

[1] For public law sections classified to the U.S.C.A., see USCA–Tables.

Repeal

For repeal of this section, see its terms.

Part 5

ADVANCE HEALTH CARE DIRECTIVE REGISTRY

Cross References

Inspection of public records, exemptions, procedures regarding release of registry records, see Government Code § 6254.

§ 4800. Registry system; establishment

(a) The Secretary of State shall establish a registry system through which a person who has executed a written advance health care directive may register in a central information center, information regarding the advance directive, making that information available upon request to any health care provider, the public guardian, or the legal representative of the registrant. A request for information pursuant to this section shall state the need for the information.

(b) The Secretary of State shall respond by the close of business on the next business day to a request for information made pursuant to Section 4717 by the emergency department of a general acute care hospital.

(c) Information that may be received is limited to the registrant's name, social security number, driver's license number, or other individual identifying number established by law, if any, address, date and place of birth, the registrant's advance health care directive, an intended place of deposit or safekeeping of a written advance health care directive, and the name and telephone number of the agent and any alternative agent. Information that may be released upon request may not include the registrant's social security number except when necessary to verify the identity of the registrant.

(d) When the Secretary of State receives information from a registrant, the secretary shall issue the registrant an Advance Health Care Directive Registry identification card indicating that an advance health care directive, or information regarding an advance health care directive, has been deposited with the registry. Costs associated with issuance of the card shall be offset by the fee charged by the Secretary of State to receive and register information at the registry.

(e) The Secretary of State, at the request of the registrant or his or her legal representative, shall transmit the information received regarding the written advance health care directive to the registry system of another jurisdiction as identified by the registrant, or his or her legal representative.

(f) The Secretary of State shall charge a fee to each registrant in an amount such that, when all fees charged to registrants are aggregated, the aggregated fees do not exceed the actual cost of establishing and maintaining the registry.

(Added by Stats.1999, c. 658 (A.B.891), § 39, operative July 1, 2000. Amended by Stats.2004, c. 882 (A.B.2445), § 3.)

Law Revision Commission Comments

1999 Addition

Section 4800 continues former Section 4800 without substantive change as applied to powers of attorney for health care, and generalizes the former provision to apply to all written advance health care directives. Hence, in addition to powers of attorney for health care, this section as revised permits registration of individual health care instructions.

See Section 4605 ("advance health care directive" defined), 4607 ("agent" defined), 4621 ("health care provider" defined). [29 Cal.L.Rev.Comm. Reports 1 (1999)].

Cross References

Advance health care directive defined for purposes of this Division, see Probate Code § 4605.
Agent defined for purposes of this Division, see Probate Code § 4607.
Health care defined for purposes of this Division, see Probate Code § 4615.
Health care provider defined for purposes of this Division, see Probate Code § 4621.

§ 4801. Procedures to verify identities; fees

The Secretary of State shall establish procedures to verify the identities of health care providers, the public guardian, and other authorized persons requesting information pursuant to Section 4800. No fee shall be charged to any health care provider, the public guardian, or other authorized person requesting information pursuant to Section 4800. *(Added by Stats.1999, c. 658 (A.B.891), § 39, operative July 1, 2000.)*

Law Revision Commission Comments

1999 Addition

Section 4801 continues former Section 4801 without change.

See also Section 4621 ("health care provider" defined). [29 Cal.L.Rev.Comm. Reports 1 (1999)].

Cross References

Health care defined for purposes of this Division, see Probate Code § 4615.
Health care provider defined for purposes of this Division, see Probate Code § 4621.

§ 4802. Procedures to advise registrants of certain matters

The Secretary of State shall establish procedures to advise each registrant of the following:

(a) A health care provider may not honor a written advance health care directive until it receives a copy from the registrant.

(b) Each registrant must notify the registry upon revocation of the advance directive.

(c) Each registrant must reregister upon execution of a subsequent advance directive. *(Added by Stats.1999, c. 658 (A.B.891), § 39, operative July 1, 2000.)*

Law Revision Commission Comments

1999 Addition

Section 4802 continues former Section 4802 without substantive change as applied to powers of attorney for health care, and generalizes it to apply to all written advance health care directives. Hence, in addition to powers of attorney for health care, this section as revised permits registration of individual health care instructions.

See also Section 4605 ("advance health care directive" defined), 4621 ("health care provider" defined). [29 Cal.L.Rev.Comm. Reports 1 (1999)].

Cross References

Advance health care directive defined for purposes of this Division, see Probate Code § 4605.
Health care defined for purposes of this Division, see Probate Code § 4615.
Health care provider defined for purposes of this Division, see Probate Code § 4621.

§ 4803. Failure to register; effect on validity of directive

Failure to register with the Secretary of State does not affect the validity of any advance health care directive. *(Added by Stats.1999, c. 658 (A.B.891), § 39, operative July 1, 2000.)*

Law Revision Commission Comments

1999 Addition

Section 4803 continues former Section 4804 without substantive change as applied to powers of attorney for health care, and generalizes it to apply to all written advance health care directives instead of the more limited class of durable powers of attorney for health care.

See also Section 4605 ("advance health care directive" defined). [29 Cal.L.Rev.Comm. Reports 1 (1999)].

Cross References

Advance health care directive defined for purposes of this Division, see Probate Code § 4605.

§ 4804. Effect of registration on ability to revoke directive

Registration with the Secretary of State does not affect the ability of the registrant to revoke the registrant's advance health care directive or a later executed advance directive, nor does registration raise any presumption of validity or superiority among any competing advance directives or revocations. *(Added by Stats.1999, c. 658 (A.B.891), § 39, operative July 1, 2000.)*

Law Revision Commission Comments

1999 Addition

Section 4804 continues former Section 4805 without substantive change as applied to powers of attorney for health care, and generalizes it to apply to all written advance health care directives. Hence, in addition to powers of attorney for health care, this section as revised permits registration of individual health care instructions.

See also Section 4605 ("advance health care directive" defined). [29 Cal.L.Rev.Comm. Reports 1 (1999)].

Cross References

Advance health care directive defined for purposes of this Division, see Probate Code § 4605.

§ 4805. Duties of health care providers; effect of part

Nothing in this part shall be construed to affect the duty of a health care provider to provide information to a patient regarding advance health care directives pursuant to any provision of federal law. *(Added by Stats.1999, c. 658 (A.B.891), § 39, operative July 1, 2000. Amended by Stats. 2004, c. 882 (A.B.2445), § 4.)*

Law Revision Commission Comments

1999 Addition

Section 4805 continues former Section 4806 without substantive change as applied to powers of attorney for health care, and generalizes it to apply to all written advance health care directives. Hence, in addition to powers of attorney for health care, this section as revised permits registration of individual health care instructions.

See also Section 4605 ("advance health care directive" defined), 4621 ("health care provider" defined), 4625 ("patient" defined). [29 Cal.L.Rev.Comm. Reports 1 (1999)].

Cross References

Advance health care directive defined for purposes of this Division, see Probate Code § 4605.
Health care defined for purposes of this Division, see Probate Code § 4615.
Health care provider defined for purposes of this Division, see Probate Code § 4621.
Patient defined for purposes of this Division, see Probate Code § 4625.

§ 4806. Advance Directives and Terminal Illness Decisions Program

(a) The Secretary of State shall work with the State Department of Health Services and the office of the Attorney General to develop information about end of life care, advance health care directives, and registration of the advance health care directives at the registry established pursuant to subdivision (a) of Section 4800. This information shall be developed utilizing existing information developed by the office of the Attorney General.

(b) Links to the information specified in subdivision (a) and to the registry shall be available on the Web sites of the Secretary of State, the State Department of Health Services, the office of the Attorney General, the Department of Managed Health Care, the Department of Insurance, the Board of Registered Nursing, and the Medical Board of California. *(Added by Stats.2005, c. 434 (A.B.1676), § 3.)*

Cross References

Advance health care directive defined for purposes of this Division, see Probate Code § 4605.
Attorney General, generally, see Government Code § 12500 et seq.
Department of Health Care Services, generally, see Health and Safety Code § 100100 et seq.
Department of Managed Health Care, generally, see Health and Safety Code § 1341 et seq.
Transfer of statutory duties, powers, purposes, responsibilities, and jurisdiction to State Department of Public Health, see Health and Safety Code § 131052.

§§ 4900 to 4947.   Repealed by Stats.1999, c. 658 (A.B.891), § 41, operative July 1, 2000

Law Revision Commission Comments

1999 Repeal

Former Section 4900 is continued in Sections 4500 (property powers) and 4750 (health care powers) without substantive change. [29 Cal.L.Rev.Comm. Reports 1 (1999)].

Former Section 4901 is continued in Sections 4501 (property powers) and 4751 (health care powers) without substantive change. [29 Cal.L.Rev.Comm. Reports 1 (1999)].

Former Section 4902 is continued in Sections 4502 (property powers) and 4752 (health care powers) without substantive change. [29 Cal.L.Rev.Comm. Reports 1 (1999)].

Former Section 4903 is continued in Sections 4503 (property powers) and 4753 (health care powers) without substantive change. [29 Cal.L.Rev.Comm. Reports 1 (1999)].

Former Section 4904 is continued in Sections 4504 (property powers) and 4754 (health care powers) without substantive change. [29 Cal.L.Rev.Comm. Reports 1 (1999)].

Former Section 4905 is continued in Sections 4505 (property powers) and 4755 (health care powers) without substantive change. [29 Cal.L.Rev.Comm. Reports 1 (1999)].

Former Section 4920 is continued in Sections 4520 (property powers) and 4760 (health care powers) without substantive change. [29 Cal.L.Rev.Comm. Reports 1 (1999)].

Former Section 4921 is continued in Sections 4521 (property powers) and 4761 (health care powers) without substantive change. [29 Cal.L.Rev.Comm. Reports 1 (1999)].

Former Section 4922 is continued in Sections 4522 (property powers) and 4762 (health care powers) without substantive change. [29 Cal.L.Rev.Comm. Reports 1 (1999)].

Former Section 4923 is continued in Sections 4523 (property powers) and 4763 (health care powers) without substantive change. [29 Cal.L.Rev.Comm. Reports 1 (1999)].

Former Section 4940 is continued in Section 4540 without change, except that the reference to the treating health care provider in subdivision (h) is omitted. Powers of attorney for health care are governed by Division 4.7 (commencing with Section 4600). As to health care powers, the former section is continued in Section 4765, with several changes. See Section 4765 Comment.   [29 Cal.L.Rev. Comm. Reports 1 (1999)].

As to property powers, former Section 4941 is continued in Section 4541 without change, except that the reference to powers of attorney for health care in the introductory paragraph is omitted. Powers of attorney for health care are governed by Division 4.7 (commencing with Section 4600).   [29 Cal.L.Rev.Comm. Reports 1 (1999)].

Former Section 4942 is continued in Section 4766 with several changes. See Section 4766 & Comment.   [29 Cal.L.Rev.Comm. Reports 1 (1999)].

Former Section 4943 is continued in Sections 4542 (property powers) and 4767 (health care powers) without substantive change. [29 Cal.L.Rev.Comm. Reports 1 (1999)].

Former Section 4944 is continued in Sections 4543 (property powers) and 4768 (health care powers) without substantive change. [29 Cal.L.Rev.Comm. Reports 1 (1999)].

Former Section 4945 is continued in Sections 4544 (property powers) and 4769 (health care powers) without substantive change. [29 Cal.L.Rev.Comm. Reports 1 (1999)].

Former Section 4946 is continued in Section 4770 without several changes. See Section 4770 Comment.   [29 Cal.L.Rev.Comm. Reports 1 (1999)].

Former Section 4947 is continued in Sections 4545 (property powers) and 4771 (health care powers) without substantive change. [29 Cal.L.Rev.Comm. Reports 1 (1999)].

§ 4948.   Repealed by Stats.1997, c. 724 (A.B.1172), § 16

Division 5

NONPROBATE TRANSFERS

Cross References

Professional fiduciaries, suspension, revocation or other adverse action, see Business and Professions Code § 6584.

Part 1

PROVISIONS RELATING TO EFFECT OF DEATH

Cross References

Community property of husband and wife, subject to express declaration in transfer documents, see Civil Code § 682.1.

CHAPTER 1. GENERAL PROVISIONS

Section
5000. Written instruments; compliance with requirements for execution of will; rights of creditors.
5002. Restrictions imposed by terms of the instrument.
5003. Protection of property; exceptions; notice.

§ 5000. Written instruments; compliance with requirements for execution of will; rights of creditors

(a) A provision for a nonprobate transfer on death in an insurance policy, contract of employment, bond, mortgage, promissory note, certificated or uncertificated security, account agreement, custodial agreement, deposit agreement, compensation plan, pension plan, individual retirement plan, employee benefit plan, trust, conveyance, deed of gift, revocable transfer on death deed, marital property agreement, or other written instrument of a similar nature is not invalid because the instrument does not comply with the requirements for execution of a will, and this code does not invalidate the instrument.

(b) Included within subdivision (a) are the following:

(1) A written provision that moneys or other benefits due to, controlled by, or owned by a decedent before death shall be paid after the decedent's death to a person whom the decedent designates either in the instrument or in a separate writing, including a will, executed either before or at the same time as the instrument, or later.

(2) A written provision that moneys due or to become due under the instrument shall cease to be payable in the event of the death of the promisee or the promisor before payment or demand.

(3) A written provision that any property controlled by or owned by the decedent before death that is the subject of the instrument shall pass to a person whom the decedent designates either in the instrument or in a separate writing, including a will, executed either before or at the same time as the instrument, or later.

(c) Nothing in this section limits the rights of creditors under any other law. *(Stats.1990, c. 79 (A.B.759), § 14, operative July 1, 1991. Amended by Stats.2015, c. 293 (A.B.139), § 8, eff. Jan. 1, 2016.)*

Law Revision Commission Comments

1990 Enactment

Section 5000 is a new provision that restates Section 160 of the repealed Probate Code without substantive change. Section 160 was a new provision added by 1983 Cal.Stat. ch. 842, § 22. Section 160 was enacted upon recommendation of the California Law Revision Commission. See Tentative Recommendation Relating to Wills and Intestate Succession, 16 Cal.L. Revision Comm'n Reports 2301, 2350–51, 2381–82 (1982). Section 5000 adopts the substance of Section 6–201 of the Uniform Probate Code (1987). As to the construction of provisions drawn from uniform acts, see Section 2.

Section 5000 differs from Section 160 of the repealed Probate Code in several respects:

(1) References to a certificated or uncertificated security, account agreement, custodial agreement, compensation plan, individual retirement plan, employee benefit plan, deed of gift, and marital property agreement have been added in Section 5000. The reference to a "marital property agreement" includes an agreement made during marriage as well as a premarital contract. The reference to profit-sharing plans is omitted for conformity with Section 6–201 of the Uniform Probate Code (1987).

(2) The examples in subdivision (b) of Section 5000 have been revised to include a separate writing executed before the instrument containing the written transfer provision.

(3) The phrase "or other written instrument of a similar nature" has been substituted in subdivision (a) of Section 5000 for the language "or any other written instrument effective as a contract, gift, conveyance, or trust" (which was found in the introductory portion of subdivision (a) of Section 160 of the repealed Probate Code). The Supreme Court of Washington read the replaced language to relieve against the delivery requirement of the law of deeds. See In re Estate of O'Brien, 109 Wash.2d 913, 749 P.2d 154 (1988). The substitution of the language in subdivision (a) makes clear that Section 5000 does not have this effect. See First Nat'l Bank of Minot v. Bloom, 264 N.W.2d 208, 212 (N.D.1978), in which the Supreme Court of North Dakota held that "nothing in ... the Uniform Probate Code [provision] eliminates the necessity of delivery of a deed to effectuate a conveyance from one living person to another."

An instrument making a transfer under this section does not have to be executed in compliance with the formalities for a will; nor does the instrument have to be probated, nor does the personal representative have any power or duty with respect to the property transferred. See also Section 6321 (designation of trustee named or to be named in will as primary or contingent beneficiary, payee, or owner of insurance or employee benefits need not comply with the formalities for execution of a will). The Uniform Probate Code language that any provision referred to in this section is "deemed to be nontestamentary" has been replaced by the language making the provision "not invalid because the instrument does not comply with the requirements for execution of a will." This change is nonsubstantive.

The sole purpose of this section is to prevent the transfers covered by the section from being treated as testamentary. This section does not invalidate other arrangements by negative implication. Thus, this section does not affect an oral trust to hold personal property at death for named persons, an arrangement given specific recognition by Section 15207. [20 Cal.L.Rev.Comm.Reports 1001 (1990)].

1992 Supplementary Comment

Section 5000 is intended broadly to validate written instruments that provide for nonprobate transfers on death. The listing in the section of types of written instruments is not exclusive, and the section also would validate, for example, a nonprobate transfer provision in a partnership agreement, stock redemption plan, buy-sell agreement, power of appointment, and the like.

Note. Section 5000 is unchanged. It is set out here for convenience of reference, together with a supplementary comment. [21 Cal.L.Rev.Comm.Reports 163 (1991)].

2015 Amendment

Section 5000 is revised to make explicit its application to a revocable TOD deed. See Section 5614 (revocable transfer on death deed). This is a specific instance of the general principle stated in the section. [36 Cal.L.Rev.Comm. Reports 103 (2006)].

Cross References

Dissolution of marriage and legal separation, effect of party's death, see Family Code § 2337.
Nonprobate transfers, former spouse, failure, see Probate Code § 5600.
Temporary restraining orders, nonprobate transfers, see Family Code § 2040.

§ 5002. Restrictions imposed by terms of the instrument

Notwithstanding any other provision of this part, a holder of property under an instrument of a type described in Section 5000 is not required to receive, hold, or transfer the property in compliance with a provision for a nonprobate transfer on death executed by a person who has an interest in the property if either (1) the person is not authorized by the terms of the instrument to execute a provision for transfer of the property, or (2) the provision for transfer of the property does not otherwise satisfy the terms of the instrument. *(Added by Stats.1992, c. 51 (A.B.1719), § 4.)*

Law Revision Commission Comments

1992 Addition

Section 5002 is added to make clear that this part is not a substantive grant of authority for a person to enforce a nonprobate transfer of the person's interest in property where such a transfer is not authorized by the terms of the instrument under which the property is held. Thus, for example, a nonemployee spouse under an employee benefit plan, or a nonowner spouse under an insurance policy, is not authorized by this part to direct a nonprobate transfer of the spouse's community property interest, if any, in the plan or policy. Although this chapter does not authorize execution of a provision for such a nonprobate transfer, the holder of the property may be required by federal law, by other state law, or by the terms of the instrument itself to recognize the property interest of a spouse. [21 Cal.L.Rev.Comm.Reports 163 (1991)].

§ 5003. Protection of property; exceptions; notice

(a) A holder of property under an instrument of a type described in Section 5000 may transfer the property in compliance with a provision for a nonprobate transfer on death that satisfies the terms of the instrument, whether or not the transfer is consistent with the beneficial ownership of the property as between the person who executed the provision for transfer of the property and other persons having an interest in the property or their successors, and whether or not the transfer is consistent with the rights of the person named as beneficiary.

(b) Except as provided in this subdivision, no notice or other information shown to have been available to the holder of the property affects the right of the holder to the protection provided by subdivision (a). The protection provided by subdivision (a) does not extend to a transfer made after either of the following events:

(1) The holder of the property has been served with a contrary court order.

(2) The holder of the property has been served with a written notice of a person claiming an adverse interest in the property. However, this paragraph does not apply to a pension plan to the extent the transfer is a periodic payment pursuant to the plan.

(c) The protection provided by this section does not affect the rights of the person who executed the provision for transfer of the property and other persons having an interest in the property or their successors in disputes among themselves concerning the beneficial ownership of the property.

(d) The protection provided by this section is not exclusive of any protection provided the holder of the property by any other provision of law.

(e) A person shall not serve notice under paragraph (2) of subdivision (b) in bad faith. If the court in an action or proceeding relating to the rights of the parties determines that a person has served notice under paragraph (2) of subdivision (b) in bad faith, the court shall award against the person the cost of the action or proceeding, including a reasonable attorney's fee, and the damages caused by the service. *(Added by Stats.1992, c. 51 (A.B.1719), § 5. Amended by Stats.2001, c. 417 (A.B.873), § 7.)*

Law Revision Commission Comments

1992 Addition

Section 5003 is drawn from portions of Section 5405 (protection of financial institution under California Multiple–Party Accounts Law). A holder of property that is the subject of a nonprobate transfer is not obligated to ascertain the respective separate, community, and quasi-community property interests in the property of participant and nonparticipant, or employee and nonemployee, or covered and noncovered, or insured and noninsured, spouses. Unless the holder of property has been served with a contrary court order or notice of an adverse claim, the holder may transfer the property in accordance with the terms of the instrument, and any adverse rights of a spouse or beneficiaries must be asserted against the estate of the person who executed the instrument or against the beneficiary, not against the holder of the property. See Sections 5012 (community property rights independent of transfer obligation), 5021 (transfer without consent)

For the manner and proof of service, see Part 2 (commencing with Section 1200) of Division 3. [21 Cal.L.Rev.Comm.Reports 163 (1991)].

2001 Amendment

Subdivision (a) of Section 5003 is amended to make clear that the section applies where a nonprobate transfer has been caused to fail by operation of Section 5600.

Subdivision (e) provides for compensation where a person serves a bad faith notice of a contrary claim to property held for the purpose of a nonprobate transfer. This provision is similar to Section 13541(d) (compensation where notice slanders title to community property after spouse's death). [28 Cal.L.Rev.Comm. Reports 599 (1998)].

CHAPTER 2.   NONPROBATE TRANSFERS OF COMMUNITY PROPERTY

Cross References

Transmutation of property, characterization of property in will, see Family Code § 853.

ARTICLE 1.   GENERAL PROVISIONS

§ 5010.   Written consent

As used in this chapter, "written consent" to a provision for a nonprobate transfer of community property on death includes a written joinder in such a provision. *(Added by Stats.1992, c. 51 (A.B.1719), § 6.)*

Law Revision Commission Comments

1992 Addition [Revised Comment]

Section 5010 is intended for drafting convenience. Written joinder in a provision for a nonprobate transfer includes joint action by both spouses in writing. A written consent, to be effective, need not satisfy the statutory requirements for a transmutation. See Section 5022 (written consent not a transmutation). A written consent becomes irrevocable on death of either spouse. Section 5030 (revocability of written consent).

It should be noted that the validity of a purported written consent is subject to relevant common law and statutory defenses, including but not limited to fraud, undue influence, misrepresentation, and violation of the special fiduciary duty applicable in transactions between spouses. See, e.g., Civ.Code § 5103. [22 Cal.L.Rev.Comm.Reports 985 (1992)].

§ 5011.   Rights of parties in nonprobate transfers; application of chapter

Notwithstanding any other provision of this part, the rights of the parties in a nonprobate transfer of community property on death are subject to all of the following:

(a) The terms of the instrument under which the nonprobate transfer is made.

(b) A contrary state statute specifically applicable to the instrument under which the nonprobate transfer is made.

(c) A written expression of intent of a party in the provision for transfer of the property or in a written consent to the provision. *(Added by Stats.1992, c. 51 (A.B.1719), § 6.)*

Law Revision Commission Comments

1992 Addition

Section 5011 establishes the principle that the rules in this chapter only apply in the absence of other governing provisions

Subdivision (a) recognizes that the terms of the instrument may define the rights of the parties. See also Section 5012 (community property rights independent of transfer obligation).

Subdivision (b) makes clear that the general rules set out in this chapter are not intended to override other state statutes that are narrowly drawn to govern rights under specific named instruments. It should also be noted that this chapter cannot override preempting federal law. See, e.g., Ablamis v. Roper, 937 F.2d 1450 (9th Cir.1991) (ERISA precludes testamentary disposition of community property interest of nonparticipant spouse).

Subdivision (c) makes clear that an expression of intent of the spouses in directing a nonprobate transfer of their interests in community property prevails over the default rules in this chapter. [21 Cal.L.Rev.Comm.Reports 163 (1991)].

Cross References

Written consent defined for purposes of this Chapter, see Probate Code § 5010.

§ 5012.   Holders of § 5000 instruments; application of chapter

A provision of this chapter concerning rights between a married person and the person's spouse in community property is relevant only to controversies between the person and spouse and their successors and does not affect the obligation of a holder of community property under an instrument of a type described in Section 5000 to hold, receive, or transfer the property in compliance with a provision for a nonprobate transfer on death, or the protection provided the holder by Section 5003. *(Added by Stats.1992, c. 51 (A.B.1719), § 6.)*

Law Revision Commission Comments

1992 Addition

Section 5012 is drawn from Section 5201 (multiple-party accounts). [21 Cal.L.Rev.Comm.Reports 163 (1991)].

§ 5013.   Waivers or other instruments or agreements affecting rights in community property

Nothing in this chapter limits the effect of a surviving spouse's waiver of rights in community property under Chapter 1 (commencing with Section 140) of Part 3 of Division 2 or other instrument or agreement that affects a married person's interest in community property. *(Added by Stats.1992, c. 51 (A.B.1719), § 6.)*

Law Revision Commission Comments

1992 Addition

Section 5013 recognizes alternate procedures for releasing rights of a surviving spouse in community property.

Waiver of a joint and survivor annuity or survivor's benefits under the federal Retirement Equity Act of 1984 is not a transmutation. Civ.Code § 5110.740 (estate planning instruments). [21 Cal.L.Rev.Comm.Reports 163 (1991)].

§ 5014. Application of chapter; transitional rules

(a) Except as provided in subdivision (b), this chapter applies to a provision for a nonprobate transfer of community property on the death of a married person, regardless of whether the provision for transfer of the property was executed by the person, or written consent to the provision for transfer of the property was given by the person's spouse, before, on, or after January 1, 1993.

(b) Subdivision (c) of Section 5030 does not apply, and the applicable law in effect on the date of death does apply, to revocation of a written consent given by a spouse who died before January 1, 1993. *(Added by Stats.1992, c. 51 (A.B. 1719), § 6.)*

Law Revision Commission Comments

1992 Addition

Section 5014 is an exception to the rule stated in Section 3 (general transitional provision). To the extent this chapter changes the law governing the rights of successors of a person who gives written consent to a nonprobate transfer by the person's spouse, this chapter does not seek to apply the change in law to rights that vested as a result of a death that occurred before the operative date of the chapter. [21 Cal.L.Rev.Comm.Reports 163 (1991)].

Cross References

Written consent defined for purposes of this Chapter, see Probate Code § 5010.

§ 5015. Fraud, undue influence, duress, mistake, or other invalidating causes

Nothing in this chapter limits the application of principles of fraud, undue influence, duress, mistake, or other invalidating cause to a written consent to a provision for a nonprobate transfer of community property on death. *(Added by Stats. 1992, c. 51 (A.B.1719), § 6.)*

Cross References

Written consent defined for purposes of this Chapter, see Probate Code § 5010.

ARTICLE 2. CONSENT TO NONPROBATE TRANSFER

§ 5020. Written consent requirement

A provision for a nonprobate transfer of community property on death executed by a married person without the written consent of the person's spouse (1) is not effective as to the nonconsenting spouse's interest in the property and (2) does not affect the nonconsenting spouse's disposition on death of the nonconsenting spouse's interest in the community property by will, intestate succession, or nonprobate transfer. *(Added by Stats.1992, c. 51 (A.B.1719), § 6.)*

Law Revision Commission Comments

1992 Addition

Section 5020 is comparable to Civil Code Section 5125(b). It codifies the case law rule that the statutory community property gift limitations apply to nonprobate transfers such as beneficiary designations in trusts and accounts. See, e.g., Tyre v. Aetna Life Ins. Co., 54 Cal.2d 399, 353 P.2d 725, 6 Cal.Rptr. 13 (1960) (beneficiary designation in life insurance policy); Yiatchos v. Yiatchos, 376 U.S. 306 (1964) (beneficiary designation for United States Savings Bonds).

It should be noted that while Section 5020 makes clear that a nonconsenting spouse retains full dispositional rights over the spouse's community property interest (subject to overriding governing principles as provided in Section 5011), this does not imply that a consenting spouse loses these rights. A written consent is revocable during the spouse's lifetime, and a revocation and contrary disposition may be made by will. See Section 5031 (form and service of revocation).

Section 5020 does not affect the principle that a holder of property may transfer the property as specified in the instrument. Section 5003 (protection of holder of property). But the actions of the holder do not affect rights between the spouses and their successors. See Section 5012 (community property rights independent of transfer obligation). [21 Cal.L.Rev.Comm.Reports 163 (1991)].

Cross References

Written consent defined for purposes of this Chapter, see Probate Code § 5010.

§ 5021. Transfers without written consent

(a) In a proceeding to set aside a nonprobate transfer of community property on death made pursuant to a provision for transfer of the property executed by a married person without the written consent of the person's spouse, the court shall set aside the transfer as to the nonconsenting spouse's interest in the property, subject to terms and conditions or other remedies that appear equitable under the circumstances of the case, taking into account the rights of all interested persons.

(b) Nothing in subdivision (a) affects any additional remedy the nonconsenting spouse may have against the person's estate for a nonprobate transfer of community property on death without the spouse's written consent. *(Added by Stats.1992, c. 51 (A.B.1719), § 6.)*

Law Revision Commission Comments

1992 Addition

Subdivision (a) of Section 5021 is consistent with the rule applicable to present gifts of community property at termination of the marriage by dissolution or death. See, e.g., Ballinger v. Ballinger, 9 Cal.2d 330, 70 P.2d 629 (1937); In re Marriage of Stephenson, 162 Cal.App.3d 1057, 209 Cal.Rptr. 383 (1984). It implements the concept that a nonprobate transfer is a will substitute, and that a person has the right to direct a transfer of the person's one-half interest in the community property at death, with or without the spouse's consent. See, e.g., Sections 100–102 (effect of death of married person on community and quasi-community property), 6101 (property which may be disposed of by will).

Under subdivision (a) the court has discretion to fashion an appropriate order, depending on the circumstances of the case. The order may, for example, provide for recovery of the value of the property rather than the particular item, or aggregate property received by a beneficiary instead of imposing a division by item.

Subdivision (b) makes clear that this section does not provide the exclusive remedy where a person has directed a nonprobate transfer of community property without the written consent of the other spouse. It may be proper, for example and without limitation, simply to allow the surviving spouse, instead of or in addition to proceeding against the beneficiary of the nonprobate asset, to proceed against the decedent's estate for an offset for the value of the property transferred out of the share of the decedent, or to give the surviving spouse a right of reimbursement. [21 Cal.L.Rev.Comm.Reports 163 (1991)].

Cross References

Written consent defined for purposes of this Chapter, see Probate Code § 5010.

§ 5022. Written consent not a transmutation; exception

(a) Except as provided in subdivision (b), a spouse's written consent to a provision for a nonprobate transfer of community property on death is not a transmutation of the consenting spouse's interest in the property.

(b) This chapter does not apply to a spouse's written consent to a provision for a nonprobate transfer of community property on death that satisfies Section 852 of the Family Code. Such a consent is a transmutation and is governed by the law applicable to transmutations. *(Added by Stats.1992, c. 51 (A.B.1719), § 6. Amended by Stats.1993, c. 219 (A.B.1500), § 224.3.)*

Law Revision Commission Comments

1992 Addition

Section 5022 is consistent with the result in Estate of MacDonald, 51 Cal.3d 262, 794 P.2d 911, 272 Cal.Rptr. 153 (1990). A consent to a nonprobate transfer is in effect a consent to a future gift of the person's interest in community property, and is subject to the legal incidents provided in this chapter. Until the gift is complete, however, it remains community property and is part of the community estate for purposes of division of property at dissolution of marriage until the consent becomes irrevocable by the death of either spouse. See Section 5030 (revocability of written consent). However, if the consent specifies a clear intent to transmute the property, the expression of intent controls over this section.

See Section 5011(c) (governing provision of consent). [21 Cal.L.Rev.Comm.Reports 163 (1991)].

1993 Amendment

Subdivision (b) of Section 5022 is amended to substitute the reference to the Family Code section that replaced the former Civil Code section. [23 Cal.L.Rev.Comm. Reports 1 (1993)].

Cross References

Written consent defined for purposes of this Chapter, see Probate Code § 5010.

§ 5023. Modifications

(a) As used in this section "modification" means revocation of a provision for a nonprobate transfer on death in whole or part, designation of a different beneficiary, or election of a different benefit or payment option. As used in this section, "modification" does not mean, and this section does not apply to, the exercise of a power of appointment under a trust.

(b) If a married person executes a provision for a nonprobate transfer of community property on death with the written consent of the person's spouse and thereafter executes a modification of the provision for transfer of the property without written consent of the spouse, the modification is effective as to the person's interest in the community property and has the following effect on the spouse's interest in the community property:

(1) If the person executes the modification during the spouse's lifetime, the modification revokes the spouse's previous written consent to the provision for transfer of the property.

(2) If the person executes the modification after the spouse's death, the modification does not affect the spouse's previous written consent to the provision for transfer of the property, and the spouse's interest in the community property is subject to the nonprobate transfer on death as consented to by the spouse.

(3) If a written expression of intent of a party in the provision for transfer of the property or in the written consent to the provision for transfer of the property authorizes the person to execute a modification after the spouse's death, the spouse's interest in the community property is deemed transferred to the married person on the spouse's death, and the modification is effective as to both the person's and the spouse's interests in the community property. *(Added by Stats.1992, c. 51 (A.B.1719), § 6. Amended by Stats.1993, c. 527 (A.B.908), § 3.)*

Law Revision Commission Comments

1992 Addition

Subdivision (a) of Section 5023 includes election of a different benefit or payment option among the types of modification covered by the section because the choice of benefit or payment options can substantially affect the rights of the parties. For example, rights can be substantially altered by selection of a life expectancy as opposed to term payout on a pension plan, or by selection of a cash benefit, annuity, or reinvestment option in a life insurance policy.

Subdivision (b)(1) treats a modification of a nonprobate transfer during the lifetimes of the spouses as a new nonprobate transfer, as to which the living spouse may consent if so desired. If the spouse does not have legal capacity to consent at the time, consent may be obtained through substituted judgment procedures. See Section 2580 (substituted judgment). Failure of consent to the changed terms during the spouse's lifetime revokes the original consent to the nonprobate transfer, and the spouse's interest ultimately passes with the spouse's estate or as otherwise disposed of by the spouse. See Section 5032 (effect of revocation). It should be noted that a modification is subject to the right of the decedent to make a contrary disposition by will. Section 5031 (form and service of revocation).

Under subdivision (b)(2), a modification by the surviving spouse after the death of the other spouse does not affect the nonprobate transfer of the community property interest of the deceased spouse as consented to by the deceased spouse. In effect, the consent is itself a nonprobate transfer which becomes irrevocable on the death of the spouse. See Section 5030 (revocability of consent). The deceased spouse's interest in the community property is transferred as consented to by the deceased spouse, unless by the terms of the consent the deceased spouse has authorized the surviving spouse to make modifications in the nonprobate transfer. See subdivision (b)(3). This is a special instance of the rule stated in Section 5011 that a nonprobate transfer of community property on death is governed by overriding principles, including a written expression of intent. [21 Cal.L.Rev.Comm.Reports 163 (1991)].

Cross References

Written consent defined for purposes of this Chapter, see Probate Code § 5010.

ARTICLE 3.   REVOCATION OF CONSENT

Section
5030.   Revocability of written consent.
5031.   Form and service of revocation.
5032.   Revocations; effect on transfers.

§ 5030.   Revocability of written consent

(a) A spouse's written consent to a provision for a nonprobate transfer of community property on death is revocable during the marriage.

(b) On termination of the marriage by dissolution or on legal separation, the written consent is revocable and the community property is subject to division under Division 7 (commencing with Section 2500) of the Family Code or other disposition on order within the jurisdiction of the court.

(c) On the death of either spouse, the written consent is irrevocable. *(Added by Stats.1992, c. 51 (A.B.1719), § 6. Amended by Stats.1993, c. 219 (A.B.1500), § 224.5.)*

Law Revision Commission Comments

1992 Addition

Section 5030 is subject to express terms to the contrary. See Section 5011 (governing provision of instrument, law, or consent). If the consent is part of a mutual estate plan, nothing in this section precludes enforcement of the mutual estate plan by appropriate remedies, including an injunction affecting revocation.

Subdivision (c), to the extent it relates to the death of the consenting spouse, overrules the effect of Estate of MacDonald, 51 Cal.3d 262, 794 P.2d 911, 272 Cal.Rptr. 153 (1990). The consent of a spouse to disposition of the spouse's one-half interest in the community property is subject to a contrary disposition in the spouse's will. Section 5031. The spouse's personal representative may not revoke the consent to a nonprobate transfer and impose a different estate plan on the spouse's property.

The surviving spouse may modify a provision for a nonprobate transfer of community property previously consented to by the deceased spouse to the extent provided in Section 5023.

It should be noted that these changes in the law are subject to Section 5014 (transitional provision). [21 Cal.L.Rev.Comm.Reports 163 (1991)].

1993 Amendment

Subdivision (b) of Section 5030 is amended to substitute the reference to the Family Code sections that replaced the former Civil Code section. [23 Cal.L.Rev.Comm. Reports 1 (1993)].

Cross References

Written consent defined for purposes of this Chapter, see Probate Code § 5010.

§ 5031.   Form and service of revocation

(a) If a married person executes a provision for a nonprobate transfer of community property on death with the written consent of the person's spouse, the consenting spouse may revoke the consent by a writing, including a will, that identifies the provision for transfer of the property being revoked, and that is served on the married person before the married person's death.

(b) Revocation of a spouse's written consent to a provision for a nonprobate transfer of community property on death does not affect the authority of the holder of the property to transfer the property in compliance with the provision for transfer of the property to the extent provided in Section 5003. *(Added by Stats.1992, c. 51 (A.B.1719), § 6.)*

Law Revision Commission Comments

1992 Addition

Section 5031 is consistent with subdivision (c) of Section 5030 (written consent irrevocable on death). Under this section any specific and served writing is sufficient, including a document purporting to be a will, whether or not admitted to probate. The will provision would change existing law as to life insurance by allowing the beneficiary designation to be overridden by an express provision in a will.

For the manner and proof of service, see Part 2 (commencing with Section 1200) of Division 3. This section is subject to a contrary provision in the instrument, and the instrument may include terms that specify the manner of revocation of consent. Section 5011 (governing provision of instrument, law, or consent). [21 Cal.L.Rev.Comm.Reports 163 (1991)].

Cross References

Written consent defined for purposes of this Chapter, see Probate Code § 5010.

§ 5032.   Revocations; effect on transfers

On revocation of a spouse's written consent to a nonprobate transfer of community property on death, the property passes in the same manner as if the consent had not been given. *(Added by Stats.1992, c. 51 (A.B.1719), § 6.)*

Law Revision Commission Comments

1992 Addition

Section 5032 governs the substantive rights of the spouses in the community property notwithstanding overriding contractual and legal requirements that bind a holder of the community property. See Sections 5003 (protection of holder of property), 5012 (community property rights independent of transfer obligation). However, this section is subject to contrary terms of the instrument and to overriding law governing the obligation of a holder of community property to deal with the property under the particular type of instrument. See Section 5011 (governing provision of instrument, law, or consent).

For rights of a spouse who has not given written consent, see Section 5020 (written consent required). [21 Cal.L.Rev.Comm.Reports 163 (1991)].

Operative Effect

For operative effect and application of Chapter 3, see Probate Code § 5048.

§ 5040. Nonprobate transfer to former spouse executed before or during marriage or registered domestic partnership; failure of transfer due to dissolution or annulment of marriage or termination of registered domestic partnership; situations that do not cause a nonprobate transfer to fail; rights of subsequent purchaser

(a) Except as provided in subdivision (b), a nonprobate transfer to the transferor's former spouse, in an instrument executed by the transferor before or during the marriage or registered domestic partnership, fails if, at the time of the transferor's death, the former spouse is not the transferor's surviving spouse as defined in Section 78, as a result of the dissolution or annulment of the marriage or termination of registered domestic partnership. A judgment of legal separation that does not terminate the status of * * * spouses is not a dissolution for purposes of this section.

(b) Subdivision (a) does not cause a nonprobate transfer to fail in any of the following cases:

(1) The nonprobate transfer is not subject to revocation by the transferor at the time of the transferor's death.

(2) There is clear and convincing evidence that the transferor intended to preserve the nonprobate transfer to the former spouse.

(3) A court order that the nonprobate transfer be maintained on behalf of the former spouse is in effect at the time of the transferor's death.

(c) Where a nonprobate transfer fails by operation of this section, the instrument making the nonprobate transfer shall be treated as it would if the former spouse failed to survive the transferor.

(d) Nothing in this section affects the rights of a subsequent purchaser or encumbrancer for value in good faith who relies on the apparent failure of a nonprobate transfer under this section or who lacks knowledge of the failure of a nonprobate transfer under this section.

(e) As used in this section, "nonprobate transfer" means a provision, other than a provision of a life insurance policy, of either of the following types:

(1) A provision of a type described in Section 5000.

(2) A provision in an instrument that operates on death, other than a will, conferring a power of appointment or naming a trustee. *(Formerly § 5600, added by Stats.2001, c. 417 (A.B.873), § 9, operative Jan. 1, 2002. Renumbered § 5040 and amended by Stats.2015, c. 293 (A.B.139), § 12, eff. Jan. 1, 2016. Amended by Stats.2016, c. 50 (S.B.1005), § 83, eff. Jan. 1, 2017.)*

Operative Effect

For operative effect and application of Chapter 3, see Probate Code § 5048.

Law Revision Commission Comments

2001 Addition

Subdivision (a) of Section 5600 establishes the general rule that a nonprobate transfer to a former spouse fails if, at the time of the transferor's death, the former spouse is not the transferor's surviving spouse, due to the dissolution or annulment of their marriage. "Dissolution or annulment" does not include legal separation. This is consistent with the law governing wills. See Sections 6122(d), 6227. "Surviving spouse" is defined in Section 78. "Nonprobate transfer" does not include life insurance. See subdivision (e).

Paragraph (1) of subdivision (b) provides that a nonprobate transfer to a former spouse does not fail by operation of subdivision (a) if, at the time of the transferor's death, the nonprobate transfer is not subject to revocation by the transferor. This precludes operation of subdivision (a) where a nonprobate transfer is irrevocable on execution, or later becomes irrevocable by the transferor (for reasons other than the death or incapacity of the transferor). The irrevocability of a trust can be established by certification of the trust's contents. See Section 18100.5.

Paragraph (2) of subdivision (b) provides that a nonprobate transfer to a former spouse does not fail on the transferor's death if there is clear and convincing evidence that the transferor intended to preserve the nonprobate transfer. For example, if after divorcing, the transferor modified the beneficiary terms of a trust without changing the designation of the former spouse as primary beneficiary, this might be sufficiently clear and convincing evidence of the transferor's intent to preserve the nonprobate transfer to the former spouse so as to prevent the operation of subdivision (a).

Subdivision (c) governs the effect of failure of a nonprobate transfer under this section. For the effect of a failed nonprobate transfer of property, see Section 21111. For the effect of a failure of a trustee designation, see Section 15660.

Subdivision (d) makes clear that nothing in this section affects the rights of a good faith purchaser or encumbrancer for value who relies on the apparent failure of a nonprobate transfer under this section or who lacks knowledge of the failure of a nonprobate transfer under this section. For the purpose of this subdivision, "knowledge" of the failure of a nonprobate transfer includes both actual knowledge and constructive knowledge through recordation of a judgment of dissolution or annulment or other relevant document. See Civ. Code 1213 (recordation as constructive notice to subsequent purchasers and mortgagees). The rights of a subsequent purchaser or encumbrancer are also protected if the purchaser or encumbrancer relies on an affidavit or declaration executed under Section 5602. The remedy for a person injured by a transaction with a subsequent purchaser or encumbrancer for value is against the transacting former spouse and not against the purchaser or encumbrancer.

In general, Section 5003 protects a property holder from liability for transferring the property according to the terms of the instrument making the nonprobate transfer, even if the nonprobate transfer has failed by operation of subdivision (a).

This section may be preempted by federal laws with respect to employer-provided benefits. See Egelhoff v. Egelhoff, 532 U.S. 141, 121 S. Ct. 1322 (2001) (ERISA preempts state law revoking spouse's rights as beneficiary of employer-provided life insurance). It is therefore especially important on dissolution or annulment of marriage to review beneficiary designations for employer-provided benefits. [31 Cal.L.Rev.Comm. Reports 76 (2001)].

2015 Addition

Section 5040 continues former Section 5600 without change. [36 Cal.L.Rev.Comm. Reports 103 (2006)].

Cross References

Dissolution of Marriage and Legal Separation, effect of party's death, see Family Code § 2337.

Nonprobate transfers, applicability and operative date, see Probate Code § 5604.

Nonprobate transfers, multiple-party accounts, sums remaining upon death of party, see Probate Code § 5302.

§ 5042. Joint tenancy created before or during marriage or registered domestic partnership severed if former spouse not decedent's surviving spouse; situations where joint tenancy is not severed

(a) Except as provided in subdivision (b), a joint tenancy between the decedent and the decedent's former spouse, created before or during the marriage or registered domestic partnership, is severed as to the decedent's interest if, at the time of the decedent's death, the former spouse is not the decedent's surviving spouse as defined in Section 78, as a result of the dissolution or annulment of the marriage or registered domestic partnership. A judgment of legal separation that does not terminate the status of * * * spouses is not a dissolution for purposes of this section.

(b) Subdivision (a) does not sever a joint tenancy in either of the following cases:

(1) The joint tenancy is not subject to severance by the decedent at the time of the decedent's death.

(2) There is clear and convincing evidence that the decedent intended to preserve the joint tenancy in favor of the former spouse.

(c) Nothing in this section affects the rights of a subsequent purchaser or encumbrancer for value in good faith who relies on an apparent severance under this section or who lacks knowledge of a severance under this section.

(d) For purposes of this section, property held in "joint tenancy" includes property held as community property with right of survivorship, as described in Section 682.1 of the Civil Code. *(Formerly § 5601, added by Stats.2001, c. 417 (A.B. 873), § 9, operative Jan. 1, 2002. Renumbered § 5042 and amended by Stats.2015, c. 293 (A.B.139), § 13, eff. Jan. 1, 2016. Amended by Stats.2016, c. 50 (S.B.1005), § 84, eff. Jan. 1, 2017.)*

Operative Effect

For operative effect and application of Chapter 3, see Probate Code § 5048.

Law Revision Commission Comments

2001 Addition

Subdivision (a) of Section 5601 establishes the general rule that a joint tenancy between a decedent and the decedent's former spouse is severed if, at the time of the decedent's death, the former spouse is not the decedent's surviving spouse, due to the dissolution or annulment of their marriage. "Dissolution or annulment" does not include legal separation. This is consistent with the law governing wills. See Sections 6122(d), 6227. "Surviving spouse" is defined in Section 78. This effectively reverses the common law rule that dissolution or annulment of marriage does not sever a joint tenancy between spouses. See, e.g., Estate of Layton, 44 Cal.App.4th 1337, 52 Cal.Rptr.2d 251 (1996).

Note that property acquired during marriage in joint tenancy form is presumed to be community property on dissolution of marriage or legal separation. See Fam. Code 2581. See also *In re* Marriage of Hilke, 4 Cal.4th 215, 841 P.2d 891, 14 Cal.Rptr.2d 371 (1992) (community property presumption applies after death of former spouse if court has entered judgment dissolving marriage and reserved jurisdiction over property matters). This section does not affect the community property presumption and does not affect property characterized as community property under that presumption.

This section applies to both real and personal property joint tenancies, and affects property rights that depend on the law of joint tenancy. See, e.g., Veh. Code 4150.5, 5600.5 (property passes as though in joint tenancy). This section does not affect United States Savings Bonds, which are subject to federal regulation. See Conrad v. Conrad, 66 Cal.App.2d 280, 284–85, 152 P.2d 221, 223 (1944) (federal law controls).

The method provided in this section for severing a joint tenancy is not exclusive. See, e.g., Civ. Code 683.2.

Where a joint tenancy involves three or more joint tenants, severance by operation of this section converts the decedent's interest into a tenancy in common, but does not sever the joint tenancy as between the other joint tenants. For example, husband, wife, and a third person create a joint tenancy during husband and wife's marriage to each other. On husband's death, wife is not husband's surviving spouse and the joint tenancy is severed by operation of this section. Husband's one third interest becomes a tenancy in common and does not pass by survivorship. The remaining two thirds remain in joint tenancy as between the third person and the former wife.

Paragraph (1) of subdivision (b) provides that a joint tenancy is not severed by operation of subdivision (a) if the joint tenancy is not subject to severance by the decedent (for reasons other than the decedent's death). For example, if the decedent is subject to a court order or binding agreement prohibiting severance of the joint tenancy by the decedent, then the joint tenancy is not severed by operation of subdivision (a).

Subdivision (c) makes clear that nothing in this section affects the rights of a good faith purchaser or encumbrancer who relies on an apparent severance by operation of this section or who lacks knowledge of a severance by operation of this section. For the purpose of this subdivision, "knowledge" of a severance of joint tenancy includes both actual knowledge and constructive knowledge through recordation of a judgment of dissolution or annulment or other relevant document. See Civ. Code 1213 (recordation as constructive notice to subsequent purchasers and mortgagees). The rights of a subsequent purchaser or encumbrancer are also protected if the purchaser or encumbrancer relies on an affidavit or declaration executed under Section 5602. The remedy for a person injured by a transaction with a subsequent purchaser or encumbrancer is against the transacting joint tenant and not against the purchaser or encumbrancer. [31 Cal.L.Rev.Comm. Reports 78 (2001)].

2015 Addition

Section 5042 continues former Section 5601 without change. [36 Cal.L.Rev.Comm. Reports 103 (2006)].

Cross References

Nonprobate transfers, applicability and operative date, see Probate Code § 5604.

§ 5044. Rights of purchaser or encumbrancer of real property who relies on affidavit or declaration

(a) Nothing in this chapter affects the rights of a purchaser or encumbrancer of real property for value who in good faith relies on an affidavit or a declaration under penalty of perjury under the laws of this state that states all of the following:

(1) The name of the decedent.

(2) The date and place of the decedent's death.

(3) A description of the real property transferred to the affiant or declarant by an instrument making a nonprobate transfer or by operation of joint tenancy survivorship.

(4) Either of the following, as appropriate:

(A) The affiant or declarant is the surviving spouse of the decedent.

(B) The affiant or declarant is not the surviving spouse of the decedent, but the rights of the affiant or declarant to the described property are not affected by Section 5040 or 5042.

(b) A person relying on an affidavit or declaration made pursuant to subdivision (a) has no duty to inquire into the truth of the matters stated in the affidavit or declaration.

(c) An affidavit or declaration made pursuant to subdivision (a) may be recorded. *(Formerly § 5602, added by Stats.2001, c. 417 (A.B.873), § 9, operative Jan. 1, 2002. Renumbered § 5044 and amended by Stats.2015, c. 293 (A.B.139), § 14, eff. Jan. 1, 2016.)*

Operative Effect

For operative effect and application of Chapter 3, see Probate Code § 5048.

Law Revision Commission Comments

2001 Addition

Section 5602 provides a procedure for certifying that a person's rights to real property transferred on the death of a spouse or former spouse, by an instrument making a nonprobate transfer or by operation of joint tenancy survivorship, are not affected by this part. See also Code Civ. Proc. 2015.5 (certification or declaration under penalty of perjury); Prob. Code 210–212 (recording evidence of death affecting title to real property). [28 Cal.L.Rev.Comm. Reports 599 (1998)].

2015 Addition

Section 5044 continues former Section 5602 without change. [36 Cal.L.Rev.Comm. Reports 103 (2006)].

§ 5046. Court authority to order dissolution or annulment of marriage to maintain former spouse as beneficiary or preserve joint tenancy

Nothing in this chapter is intended to limit the court's authority to order a party to a dissolution or annulment of marriage to maintain the former spouse as a beneficiary on any nonprobate transfer described in this chapter, or to preserve a joint tenancy in favor of the former spouse. *(Formerly § 5603, added by Stats.2001, c. 417 (A.B.873), § 9, operative Jan. 1, 2002. Renumbered § 5046 and amended by Stats.2015, c. 293 (A.B.139), § 15, eff. Jan. 1, 2016.)*

Operative Effect

For operative effect and application of Chapter 3, see Probate Code § 5048.

Law Revision Commission Comments

2001 Addition

Section 5603 clarifies the effect of this part. [31 Cal.L.Rev.Comm. Reports 79 (2001)].

2015 Addition

Section 5046 continues former Section 5603 without change. [36 Cal.L.Rev.Comm. Reports 103 (2006)].

§ 5048. Operative date and application

(a) This chapter, formerly Part 4 (commencing with Section 5600), is operative on January 1, 2002.

(b) Except as provided in subdivision (c), this chapter applies to an instrument making a nonprobate transfer or creating a joint tenancy whether executed before, on, or after the operative date of this chapter.

(c) Sections 5040 and 5042 do not apply, and the applicable law in effect before the operative date of this chapter applies, to an instrument making a nonprobate transfer or creating a joint tenancy in either of the following circumstances:

(1) The person making the nonprobate transfer or creating the joint tenancy dies before the operative date of this chapter.

(2) The dissolution of marriage or other event that terminates the status of the nonprobate transfer beneficiary or joint tenant as a surviving spouse occurs before the operative date of this chapter. *(Formerly § 5604, added by Stats.2001, c. 417 (A.B.873), § 9, operative Jan. 1, 2002. Renumbered § 5048 and amended by Stats.2015, c. 293 (A.B.139), § 16, eff. Jan. 1, 2016.)*

Law Revision Commission Comments

2001 Addition

Section 5604 governs the application of this part.

Under subdivision (c), where a dissolution of marriage, or other event terminating a person's status as a decedent's surviving spouse occurs before January 1, 2000, that person's rights as a nonprobate transfer beneficiary or joint tenant of the decedent are not affected by Section 5600 or 5601. See Section 78 ("surviving spouse" defined). [31 Cal.L.Rev.Comm. Reports 79 (2001)].

2015 Addition

Section 5048 continues former Section 5604 without change. [36 Cal.L.Rev.Comm. Reports 103 (2006)].

Part 2

MULTIPLE–PARTY ACCOUNTS

Application

Application of Part 2 to accounts in existence on or established after July 1, 1990, see Probate Code § 5205.

Law Revision Commission Comments

1990 Enactment

This part supersedes Part 1 (commencing with Section 5100) of Division 5 the repealed Probate Code. The superseded part was enacted upon recommendation of the California Law Revision Commission. See Recommendation Relating to Multiple–Party Accounts in Financial Institutions, 20 Cal.L.Revision Comm'n Reports 95 (1990). See also Communication from the California Law Revision Commission Concerning Senate Bill 985, 20 Cal.L.Revision Comm'n Reports 247 (1990).

For an earlier Commission recommendation which resulted in enactment of a statute covering credit unions and industrial loan companies, see Recommendation Relating to Nonprobate Transfers, 16 Cal.L.Revision Comm'n Reports 129 (1982). See also 17 Cal.L.Revision Comm'n Reports 823 (1984) (legislative history). For an earlier recommendation, see Recommendation Relating to Non–Probate Transfers, 15 Cal.L.Revision Comm'n Reports 1605 (1980). See also 16 Cal.L.Revision Comm'n Reports 2026 (1982) (legislative history). [20 Cal.L.Rev.Comm.Reports 1001 (1990)].

Cross References

Accounts of administrators, executors, guardians, custodians, trustees, and other fiduciaries, taxes and liability of association, see Financial Code § 6855.
Banks withdrawals and collections, adverse claims, see Financial Code § 952.
Community property of husband and wife, subject to express declaration in transfer documents, see Civil Code § 682.1.
Joint tenancy, method of creation, see Civil Code § 683.
Multiple-party account investment or thrift certificate, governing provisions, see Financial Code § 18318.5.
Multiple-party accounts, generally, see Financial Code §§ 852, 14854.
Savings operations,
Accounts governed by probate code, see Financial Code § 6800.
Adverse claims, see Financial Code § 6661.
Liability for taxes, see Financial Code § 6804.
Trust powers, see Financial Code § 14860.

CHAPTER 1. SHORT TITLE AND DEFINITIONS

Application

Application of Part 2 to accounts in existence on or established after July 1, 1990, see Probate Code § 5205.

Cross References

Adverse claim to bank deposit, effect of this part, see Financial Code § 952.
Adverse claim to savings account or personal property held for account, effect of this part, see Financial Code § 6661.
Bank accounts governed by this part, see Financial Code § 852.
Industrial loan company investment or thrift certificates governed by this part, see Financial Code § 18318.5.
Savings association accounts governed by this part, see Financial Code § 6800.
Savings association liability for estate, inheritance, or succession taxes because of payment of person in accordance with this part, see Financial Code §§ 6804, 6855.

ARTICLE 1. SHORT TITLE

Cross References

Uniform TOD Security Registration Act, definitions, see Probate Code § 5501.

§ 5100. Short title

This part may be cited as the California Multiple-Party Accounts Law. *(Stats.1990, c. 79 (A.B.759), § 14, operative July 1, 1991.)*

Law Revision Commission Comments

1990 Enactment

Section 5100 continues Section 5100 of the repealed Probate Code without change.

Background on Section 5100 of Repealed Code

Section 5100 was a new provision added by 1983 Cal.Stat. ch. 92 § 5. For background on the provisions of this part, see the Comment to this part under the part heading. [20 Cal.L.Rev.Comm.Reports 1001 (1990)].

Cross References

Multiple-party account defined for purposes of this Part, see Probate Code § 5132.
Party defined for purposes of this Part, see Probate Code § 5136.

§ 5101. Repealed by Stats.1989, c. 397, § 24, operative July 1, 1990

Law Revision Commission Comments

1989 Repeal

The introductory portion of former Section 5101 is restated without substantive change in Section 5120 (application of definitions). Subdivision (a) is restated without substantive change in Section 5122 ("account" defined). Subdivision (b) is restated in Section 5126 ("beneficiary" defined) without substantive change. Subdivision (c) is superseded by Section 5128. Subdivision (c) defined "financial institution" to mean a credit union or industrial loan company. Under new Section 5128, "financial institution" also includes a bank, savings and loan association, and other like organization. See the Comment to Section 5128. Subdivision (d) is continued without change in Section 5130. The first sentence of subdivision (e) is restated in Section 5132 without substantive change. The second sentence of subdivision (e) is restated without substantive change in subdivision (b) of Section 5122. Subdivision (f) is restated in Section 5134 without substantive change. Subdivision (g) is restated without substantive change in

Section 5136 except that the second sentence is not continued, this sentence being superseded by Section 5122(b)(4) ("account" does not include an account established for the deposit of funds of the estate of a ward, conservatee, or decedent). Subdivision (h) is restated in Section 5138 without substantive change. Subdivision (i) is continued without change in Section 5140. Subdivision (j) is continued without change in Section 5142. Subdivision (k) is continued without change in Section 5144. Subdivision (l) is continued without change in Section 5146. Subdivision (m) is restated in Section 5148 without substantive change. Subdivision (n) is restated in Section 5150 without substantive change. The first, second, and fourth sentences of subdivision (o) are omitted as unnecessary in view of the general definition of "Totten trust account" in Section 80 and the substitution of "Totten trust account" for "trust account" where appropriate in this part. The substance of the third sentence of subdivision (o) (added by 1987 Cal.Stat. ch. 1045) is continued in Section 14868 of the Financial Code. Subdivision (p) is restated in Section 5152 without substantive change. [20 Cal.L.Rev.Comm. Reports 119 (1990)].

ARTICLE 2. DEFINITIONS

Section
5120. Application of definitions.
5122. Account.
5124. Agent.
5126. Beneficiary.
5128. Financial institution.
5130. Joint account.
5132. Multiple-party account.
5134. Net contribution.
5136. Party.
5138. Payment.
5139. P.O.D.
5140. P.O.D. account.
5142. P.O.D. payee.
5144. Proof of death.
5146. Receives (order or notice received by institution).
5148. Request.
5150. Sums on deposit.
5152. Withdrawal.

§ 5120. Application of definitions

Unless the provision or context otherwise requires, the definitions in this article govern the construction of this part. *(Stats.1990, c. 79 (A.B.759), § 14, operative July 1, 1991.)*

Law Revision Commission Comments

1990 Enactment

Section 5120 continues Section 5120 of the repealed Probate Code without change. Section 5120 is consistent with the introductory clause of Uniform Probate Code Section 6–101 (1987). As to the construction of provisions drawn from uniform acts, see Section 2.

Background on Section 5120 of Repealed Code

Section 5120 was added by 1989 Cal.Stat. ch. 397 § 25. The section restated without substantive change the introductory portion of former Probate Code Section 5101 (repealed by 1989 Cal.Stat. ch. 397 § 24). For background on the provisions of this part, see the Comment to this part under the part heading. [20 Cal.L.Rev.Comm.Reports 1001 (1990)].

§ 5122. Account

(a) "Account" means a contract of deposit of funds between a depositor and a financial institution, and includes a checking account, savings account, certificate of deposit, share account, and other like arrangement.

(b) "Account" does not include:

(1) An account established for deposit of funds of a partnership, joint venture, or other association for business purposes.

(2) An account controlled by one or more persons as the duly authorized agent or trustee for a corporation, unincorporated association, or charitable or civic organization.

(3) A regular fiduciary or trust account where the relationship is established other than by deposit agreement.

(4) An account established for the deposit of funds of the estate of a ward, conservatee, or decedent. *(Stats.1990, c. 79 (A.B.759), § 14, operative July 1, 1991.)*

Law Revision Commission Comments

1990 Enactment

Section 5122 continues Section 5122 of the repealed Probate Code without change. Subdivision (a) is the same in substance as subsection (1) of Section 6–101 of the Uniform Probate Code (1987). Paragraphs (1)–(3) of subdivision (b) are the same in substance as the second sentence of subsection (5) of Section 6–101 of the Uniform Probate Code (1987). As to the construction of provisions drawn from uniform acts, see Section 2.

Background on Section 5122 of Repealed Code

Section 5122 was added by 1989 Cal.Stat. ch. 397 § 25. Subdivision (a) restated subdivision (a) of former Probate Code Section 5101 (repealed by 1989 Cal.Stat. ch. 397 § 24) without change. Paragraphs (1)–(3) of subdivision (b) restated the second sentence of subdivision (e) of former Section 5101 without substantive change. Paragraph (4) of subdivision (b) was new and superseded the third sentence of subdivision (g) of former Section 5101. The new paragraph made clear that the rules applicable to an account established for funds of a guardianship, conservatorship, or decedent's estate are not affected by this part. For background on the provisions of this part, see the Comment to this part under the part heading. [20 Cal.L.Rev.Comm.Reports 1001 (1990)].

Cross References

Agent defined for purposes of this Part, see Probate Code § 5124. Financial institution defined for purposes of this Part, see Probate Code § 5128.

§ 5124. Agent

"Agent" means a person who has a present right, subject to request, to payment from an account as an attorney in fact under a power of attorney. *(Stats.1990, c. 79 (A.B.759), § 14, operative July 1, 1991.)*

Law Revision Commission Comments

1990 Enactment

Section 5124 continues Section 5124 of the repealed Probate Code without change. See also Section 5204 (special power of attorney with respect to accounts at financial institutions).

Background on Section 5124 of Repealed Code

Section 5124 was a new provision added by 1989 Cal.Stat. ch. 397 § 25. For background on the provisions of this part, see the Comment to this part under the part heading. [20 Cal.L.Rev.Comm.Reports 1001 (1990)].

§ 5126. Beneficiary

"Beneficiary" means a person named in a Totten trust account as one for whom a party to the account is named as trustee. *(Stats.1990, c. 79 (A.B.759), § 14, operative July 1, 1991.)*

Law Revision Commission Comments
1990 Enactment

Section 5126 continues Section 5126 of the repealed Probate Code without change. The section is the same in substance as subsection (2) of Section 6–101 of the Uniform Probate Code (1987). As to the construction of provisions drawn from uniform acts, see Section 2. See also Section 80 (defining "Totten trust account"). As used in this part, "trustee" means the trustee of a Totten trust account.

Background on Section 5126 of Repealed Code

Section 5126 was added by 1989 Cal.Stat. ch. 397 § 25. The section restated subdivision (b) of former Probate Code Section 5101 (repealed by 1989 Cal.Stat. ch. 397 § 24) without substantive change. For background on the provisions of this part, see the Comment to this part under the part heading. [20 Cal.L.Rev.Comm.Reports 1001 (1990)].

§ 5128. Financial institution

"Financial institution" includes:

(a) A financial institution as defined in Section 40.

(b) An industrial loan company as defined in Section 18003 of the Financial Code. *(Stats.1990, c. 79 (A.B.759), § 14, operative July 1, 1991.)*

Law Revision Commission Comments
1990 Enactment

Section 5128 continues Section 5128 of the repealed Probate Code without change. Subdivision (a), read with the definition of "financial institution" in Section 40, is comparable to subsection (3) of Section 6–101 of the Uniform Probate Code (1987). As to the construction of provisions drawn from uniform acts, see Section 2.

Background on Section 5128 of Repealed Code

Section 5128 was added by 1989 Cal.Stat. ch. 397 § 25. The section superseded subdivision (c) of former Probate Code Section 5101 (repealed by 1989 Cal.Stat. ch. 397 § 24). The term "financial institution" as defined in subdivision (c) of former Section 5101 was limited to credit unions and industrial loan companies. The new definition in Section 5128 applied as well to banks, savings and loan associations, and other like organizations, by force of Section 40 defining "financial institution." For background on the provisions of this part, see the Comment to this part under the part heading. [20 Cal.L.Rev.Comm.Reports 1001 (1990)].

§ 5130. Joint account

"Joint account" means an account payable on request to one or more of two or more parties whether or not mention is made of any right of survivorship. *(Stats.1990, c. 79 (A.B. 759), § 14, operative July 1, 1991.)*

Law Revision Commission Comments
1990 Enactment

Section 5130 continues Section 5130 of the repealed Probate Code without change. The section is the same in substance as subsection (4) of Section 6–101 of the Uniform Probate Code (1987). As to the construction of provisions drawn from uniform acts, see Section 2.

The definition of "joint account" embraces all of the following:

(1) *Joint account with right of survivorship.* See Sections 5301(a), 5302(a).

(2) *Joint account without right of survivorship.* This is a special type of joint account where there is clear and convincing evidence of an intent not to have survivorship. The terms of the account may include an express statement making clear that there is no survivorship right (see subdivision (a) of Section 5302) or the account may be designated as a "tenancy in common" account (see Section 5306).

(3) *Joint account held by a husband and wife with right of survivorship that cannot be changed by will.* This is a joint account held by a husband and wife that is not specifically designated in the account agreement as a "community property" account and there is no clear and convincing evidence of an intent that there be no survivorship right. The statute creates a presumption that if the parties to an account are married to each other, whether or not they are so described in the deposit agreement, their net contribution to the account is presumed to be and remain their community property. See Section 5305. The rules stated in Sections 5301(a) and 5302(a) apply to this type of joint account, including a rule that the right of survivorship of the surviving spouse cannot be changed by will. However, if the deposit agreement or the terms of the account *clearly indicates an intent that there be no survivorship right,* either spouse can designate one or more P.O.D. payees (or Totten trust beneficiaries) to take that spouse's share of the account upon the death of that spouse and, absent such a designation, the share of the deceased spouse becomes a part of the estate of the deceased spouse.

(4) *Joint account held by husband and wife that is specifically designated as a "community property" account.* This is a joint account held by a husband and wife that is specifically designated in the account agreement as a "community property" account. Section 5307 provides that this type of account is governed by the rules that apply to community property generally. Accordingly, unless the parties have agreed otherwise, the right of survivorship of the surviving spouse can be changed by will (deceased spouse by will devises his or her one-half share of the account to a person other than the surviving spouse). Also, the deposit agreement or the terms of the account can include, for example, a provision that the one-half share of a spouse will pass on the death of that spouse to one or more P.O.D. payees (or Totten trust beneficiaries) upon the death of that spouse. On the other hand, absent a contrary agreement or a contrary disposition, the surviving spouse will take the one-half share of the deceased spouse as community property.

Background on Section 5130 of Repealed Code

Section 5130 was added by 1989 Cal.Stat. ch. 397 § 25. The section continued subdivision (d) of former Probate Code Section 5101 (repealed by 1989 Cal.Stat. ch. 397 § 24) without change. For background on the provisions of this part, see the Comment to this part under the part heading. [20 Cal.L.Rev.Comm.Reports 1001 (1990)].

No limitation in actions to recover money or property deposited with bank, see Code of Civil Procedure § 348.

Party defined for purposes of this Part, see Probate Code § 5136.

Request defined for purposes of this Part, see Probate Code § 5148.

Savings associations, multi-party accounts, see Financial Code § 6800.

§ 5132. Multiple-party account

A "multiple-party account" is any of the following types of account:

(a) A joint account.

(b) A P.O.D. account.

(c) A Totten trust account. *(Stats.1990, c. 79 (A.B.759), § 14, operative July 1, 1991.)*

Law Revision Commission Comments
1990 Enactment

Section 5132 continues Section 5132 of the repealed Probate Code without change. The section is the same in substance as the first sentence of subsection (5) of Section 6–101 of the Uniform Probate Code (1987). As to the construction of provisions drawn from uniform acts, see Section 2. See also Section 5204 (special power of attorney with respect to accounts at financial institutions). As to types of joint accounts, see the Comment to Section 5130.

Background on Section 5132 of Repealed Code

Section 5132 was added by 1989 Cal.Stat. ch. 397 § 25. The section restated the first sentence of subdivision (e) of former Probate Code Section 5101 (repealed by 1989 Cal.Stat. ch. 397 § 24) without substantive change. For background on the provisions of this part, see the Comment to this part under the part heading. [20 Cal.L.Rev.Comm.Reports 1001 (1990)].

Cross References

Account defined for purposes of this Part, see Probate Code § 5122.

Joint account defined for purposes of this Part, see Probate Code § 5130.

Multiple-party account investment or thrift certificate, governing provisions, see Financial Code § 18318.5.

Multiple-party accounts, generally, see Financial Code §§ 852, 14854.

Multiple-party accounts, pledge or hypothecation to association, see Financial Code § 6805.

Party defined for purposes of this Part, see Probate Code § 5136.

P.O.D. account defined for purposes of this Part, see Probate Code § 5140.

P.O.D. defined for purposes of this Division, see Probate Code § 5139.

Savings operations, accounts governed by probate code, see Financial Code § 6800.

§ 5134. Net contribution

(a) "Net contribution" of a party to an account as of any given time is the sum of all of the following:

(1) All deposits thereto made by or for the party, less all withdrawals made by or for the party that have not been paid to or applied to the use of any other party.

(2) A pro rata share of any interest or dividends earned, whether or not included in the current balance.

(3) Any proceeds of deposit life insurance added to the account by reason of the death of the party whose net contribution is in question.

(b) In the absence of proof otherwise:

(1) Only parties who have a present right of withdrawal shall be considered as having a net contribution.

(2) The net contribution of each of the parties having a present right of withdrawal is deemed to be an equal amount.

(c) It is the intent of the Legislature in enacting this section to provide a definition for the purpose of determining ownership interests in an account as between the parties to the account, and not as between the parties and the financial institution. *(Stats.1990, c. 79 (A.B.759), § 14, operative July 1, 1991.)*

Law Revision Commission Comments
1990 Enactment

Section 5134 continues Section 5134 of the repealed Probate Code without change.

Subdivision (a) is the same in substance as subsection (6) of Section 6–101 of the Uniform Probate Code (1987). As to the construction of provisions drawn from uniform acts, see Section 2. As may be seen from an examination of the provisions of this part, "net contribution" as defined in subdivision (a) has no application to the financial institution-depositor relationship. Rather, it is relevant only to controversies that may arise between parties to a multiple-party account. Subdivision (c), which is not found in the Uniform Probate Code (1987), makes this clear.

Subdivision (b) is not found in the Uniform Probate Code (1987). This subdivision provides a clear rule concerning the amount of "net contribution" in the absence of proof of a different amount.

Background on Section 5134 of Repealed Code

Section 5134 was added by 1989 Cal.Stat. ch. 397 § 25. The section restated the substance of subdivision (f) of former Probate Code Section 5101 (repealed by 1989 Cal.Stat. ch. 397 § 24) with the substitution of "whether or not included in the current balance" for the former phrase "included in the current balance" and with the addition of subdivision (c). For background on the provisions of this part, see the Comment to this part under the part heading. [20 Cal.L.Rev.Comm.Reports 1001 (1990)].

Cross References

Account defined for purposes of this Part, see Probate Code § 5122.

Financial institution defined for purposes of this Part, see Probate Code § 5128.

Party defined for purposes of this Part, see Probate Code § 5136.

Withdrawal defined for purposes of this Part, see Probate Code § 5152.

§ 5136. Party

(a) "Party" means a person who, by the terms of the account, has a present right, subject to request, to payment from a multiple-party account other than as an agent.

(b) A P.O.D. payee is a party, by reason of being a P.O.D. payee, only after the account becomes payable to the payee by reason of surviving all persons named as original payees.

(c) A beneficiary of a Totten trust account is a party, by reason of being a beneficiary, only after the account becomes payable to the beneficiary by reason of surviving all persons named as trustees. *(Stats.1990, c. 79 (A.B.759), § 14, operative July 1, 1991.)*

Law Revision Commission Comments
1990 Enactment

Section 5136 continues Section 5136 of the repealed Probate Code without change. This section is similar to subsection (7) of Section

6–101 of the Uniform Probate Code (1987). As to the construction of provisions drawn from uniform acts, see Section 2.

The phrase "other than as an agent" in subdivision (a) makes clear that the person named as an agent (attorney in fact under a power of attorney) is not a "party" for the purposes of this part. See Section 5124 (defining "agent"). A P.O.D. payee or a Totten trust beneficiary is a party under subdivision (a) if the payee or beneficiary has, by the terms of the account, a present right, subject to request, to payment from the account other than as an agent.

Background on Section 5136 of Repealed Code

Section 5136 was added by 1989 Cal.Stat. ch. 397 § 25. The section restated the substance of subdivision (g) of former Probate Code Section 5101 (repealed by 1989 Cal.Stat. ch. 397 § 24) with the following revisions:

(1) Section 5136 omitted the third sentence of former subdivision (g) (defining "party" to include a guardian, conservator, personal representative, or assignee, including a levying creditor, of a party). This part does not apply to an account established for the deposit of funds of the estate of a ward, conservatee, or decedent. See Section 5122(b)(4).

(2) Section 5136 omitted the portion of the last sentence of former subdivision (g) relating to "a person identified as a trustee of an account for another whether or not a beneficiary is named," this portion being unnecessary. Insofar as this language applied to the trustee of a Totten trust account, it was unnecessary in view of subdivision (a) of Section 5136 which applied to any person, including a trustee of a Totten trust, who has a present right to payment. Insofar as this language applied to a regular trust account under a testamentary trust or a trust agreement that has significance apart from the account, it was unnecessary because this statute does not apply to such a trustee. See Section 5122(b)(3). See also Section 80 (defining "Totten trust account").

(3) Section 5136 revised the remaining portion of the last sentence of former subdivision (g) to conform to the language used in subdivision (b) of Section 5136.

For background on the provisions of this part, see the Comment to this part under the part heading. [20 Cal.L.Rev.Comm.Reports 1001 (1990)].

Cross References

Account defined for purposes of this Part, see Probate Code § 5122.
Agent defined for purposes of this Part, see Probate Code § 5124.
Beneficiary defined for purposes of this Part, see Probate Code § 5136.
Multiple-party account defined for purposes of this Part, see Probate Code § 5132.
Payment defined for purposes of this Part, see Probate Code § 5138.
P.O.D. defined for purposes of this Division, see Probate Code § 5139.
P.O.D. payee defined for purposes of this Part, see Probate Code § 5142.
Request defined for purposes of this Part, see Probate Code § 5148.

§ 5138. Payment

"Payment" of sums on deposit includes all of the following:

(a) A withdrawal, including payment on check or other directive of a party.

(b) A pledge of sums of deposit.

(c) A setoff, reduction, or other disposition of all or part of an account pursuant to a pledge. *(Stats.1990, c. 79 (A.B.759), § 14, operative July 1, 1991.)*

Law Revision Commission Comments
1990 Enactment

Section 5138 continues Section 5138 of the repealed Probate Code without change. The section is the same in substance as subsection (8) of Section 6–101 of the Uniform Probate Code (1987). As to the construction of provisions drawn from uniform acts, see Section 2.

Background on Section 5138 of Repealed Code

Section 5138 was added by 1989 Cal.Stat. ch. 397 § 25. The section continued subdivision (h) of former Probate Code Section 5101 (repealed by 1989 Cal.Stat. ch. 397 § 24) without substantive change. For background on the provisions of this part, see the Comment to this part under the part heading. [20 Cal.L.Rev.Comm.Reports 1001 (1990)].

Cross References

Account defined for purposes of this Part, see Probate Code § 5122.
Party defined for purposes of this Part, see Probate Code § 5136.
Sums on deposit defined for purposes of this Part, see Probate Code § 5150.
Withdrawal defined for purposes of this Part, see Probate Code § 5152.

§ 5139. P.O.D.

"P.O.D." means pay on death. *(Stats.1990, c. 79 (A.B. 759), § 14, operative July 1, 1991.)*

Law Revision Commission Comments
1990 Enactment

Section 5139 continues Section 5139 of the repealed Probate Code without change. See also Sections 5140 ("P.O.D. account"), 5142 ("P.O.D. payee"). No comparable provision is found in the Uniform Probate Code (1987).

Background on Section 5139 of Repealed Code

Section 5139 was a new provision added by 1989 Cal.Stat. ch. 397 § 25. For background on the provisions of this part, see the Comment to this part under the part heading. [20 Cal.L.Rev.Comm.Reports 1001 (1990)].

§ 5140. P.O.D. account

"P.O.D. account" means any of the following:

(a) An account payable on request to one person during the person's lifetime and on the person's death to one or more P.O.D. payees.

(b) An account payable on request to one or more persons during their lifetimes and on the death of all of them to one or more P.O.D. payees. *(Stats.1990, c. 79 (A.B.759), § 14, operative July 1, 1991.)*

Law Revision Commission Comments
1990 Enactment

Section 5140 continues Section 5140 of the repealed Probate Code without change. The section is the same in substance as subsection (10) of Section 6–101 of the Uniform Probate Code (1987). As to the construction of provisions drawn from uniform acts, see Section 2.

Background on Section 5140 of Repealed Code

Section 5140 was added by 1989 Cal.Stat. ch. 397 § 25. The section continued subdivision (i) of former Probate Code Section 5101 (repealed by 1989 Cal.Stat. ch. 397 § 24) without substantive change. For background on the provisions of this part, see the

Comment to this part under the part heading. [20 Cal.L.Rev.Comm.Reports 1001 (1990)].

Cross References

Account defined for purposes of this Part, see Probate Code § 5122.
Deposit accounts, execution lien, liability of financial institutions, see Code of Civil Procedure § 700.140.
Deposit accounts, pay-on-death provisions, see Code of Civil Procedure § 488.455.
P.O.D. defined for purposes of this Division, see Probate Code § 5139.
P.O.D. payee defined for purposes of this Part, see Probate Code § 5142.
Request defined for purposes of this Part, see Probate Code § 5148.

§ 5142. P.O.D. payee

"P.O.D. payee" means a person designated on a P.O.D. account as one to whom the account is payable on request after the death of one or more persons. *(Stats.1990, c. 79 (A.B.759), § 14, operative July 1, 1991.)*

Law Revision Commission Comments

1990 Enactment

Section 5142 continues Section 5142 of the repealed Probate Code without change. The section is the same as subsection (11) of Section 6–101 of the Uniform Probate Code (1987). As to the construction of provisions drawn from uniform acts, see Section 2.

Background on Section 5142 of Repealed Code

Section 5142 was added by 1989 Cal.Stat. ch. 397 § 25. The section continued subdivision (j) of former Probate Code Section 5101 (repealed by 1989 Cal.Stat. ch. 397 § 24) without change. For background on the provisions of this part, see the Comment to this part under the part heading. [20 Cal.L.Rev.Comm.Reports 1001 (1990)].

Cross References

Account defined for purposes of this Part, see Probate Code § 5122.
P.O.D. account defined for purposes of this Part, see Probate Code § 5140.
P.O.D. defined for purposes of this Division, see Probate Code § 5139.
Request defined for purposes of this Part, see Probate Code § 5148.

§ 5144. Proof of death

"Proof of death" includes any of the following:

(a) An original or attested or certified copy of a death certificate.

(b) A record or report that is prima facie evidence of death under Section 103550 of the Health and Safety Code, Sections 1530 to 1532, inclusive, of the Evidence Code, or another statute of this state. *(Stats.1990, c. 79 (A.B.759), § 14, operative July 1, 1991. Amended by Stats.1996, c. 1023 (S.B.1497), § 400, eff. Sept. 29, 1996.)*

Law Revision Commission Comments

1990 Enactment

Section 5144 continues Section 5144 of the repealed Probate Code without change. The section is consistent with subsection (9) of Section 6–101 of the Uniform Probate Code (1987). As to the construction of provisions drawn from uniform acts, see Section 2.

Background on Section 5144 of Repealed Code

Section 5144 was added by 1989 Cal.Stat. ch. 397 § 25. The section continued subdivision (k) of former Probate Code Section 5101 (repealed by 1989 Cal.Stat. ch. 397 § 24) without substantive change. For background on the provisions of this part, see the Comment to this part under the part heading. [20 Cal.L.Rev.Comm.Reports 1001 (1990)].

Cross References

Prima facie evidence, see Evidence Code § 602.

§ 5146. Receives (order or notice received by institution)

Except to the extent the terms of the account or deposit agreement expressly provide otherwise, a financial institution "receives" an order or notice under this part when it is received by the particular office or branch office of the financial institution where the account is carried. *(Stats. 1990, c. 79 (A.B.759), § 14, operative July 1, 1991.)*

Law Revision Commission Comments

1990 Enactment

Section 5146 continues Section 5146 of the repealed Probate Code without change. No comparable provision is found in the Uniform Probate Code (1987).

Background on Section 5146 of Repealed Code

Section 5146 was added by 1989 Cal.Stat. ch. 397 § 25. The section continued subdivision (l) of former Probate Code Section 5101 (repealed by 1989 Cal.Stat. ch. 397 § 24) with the addition of the introductory clause to make clear that the terms of the account or deposit agreement may expressly provide when an order or notice is "received." For background on the provisions of this part, see the Comment to this part under the part heading. [20 Cal.L.Rev.Comm.Reports 1001 (1990)].

Cross References

Account defined for purposes of this Part, see Probate Code § 5122.
Financial institution defined for purposes of this Part, see Probate Code § 5128.

§ 5148. Request

"Request" means a proper request for withdrawal, including a check or order for payment, that complies with all conditions of the account (including special requirements concerning necessary signatures) and regulations of the financial institution; but, if the financial institution conditions withdrawal or payment on advance notice, for purposes of this part the request for withdrawal or payment is treated as immediately effective and a notice of intent to withdraw is treated as a request for withdrawal. *(Stats.1990, c. 79 (A.B.759), § 14, operative July 1, 1991.)*

Law Revision Commission Comments

1990 Enactment

Section 5148 continues Section 5148 of the repealed Probate Code without change. The section is the same in substance as subsection (12) of Section 6–101 of the Uniform Probate Code (1987). As to the construction of provisions drawn from uniform acts, see Section 2. Various signature requirements may be involved in order to meet the withdrawal requirements of the account. A "request" involves compliance with these requirements. A "party" is one (other than an agent) to whom an account is presently payable without regard for whose signature may be required for a "request." See Section 5136.

Background on Section 5148 of Repealed Code

Section 5148 was added by 1989 Cal.Stat. ch. 397 § 25. The section restated subdivision (m) of former Probate Code Section 5101 (repealed by 1989 Cal.Stat. ch. 397 § 24) without substantive change. For background on the provisions of this part, see the Comment to this part under the part heading. [20 Cal.L.Rev.Comm.Reports 1001 (1990)].

Cross References

Account defined for purposes of this Part, see Probate Code § 5122.
Financial institution defined for purposes of this Part, see Probate Code § 5128.
Payment defined for purposes of this Part, see Probate Code § 5138.
Withdrawal defined for purposes of this Part, see Probate Code § 5152.

§ 5150. Sums on deposit

"Sums on deposit" means both of the following:

(a) The balance payable on an account, including interest and dividends earned, whether or not included in the current balance.

(b) Any life insurance proceeds added to the account by reason of the death of a party. *(Stats.1990, c. 79 (A.B.759), § 14, operative July 1, 1991.)*

Law Revision Commission Comments

1990 Enactment

Section 5150 continues Section 5150 of the repealed Probate Code without change. The section is the same in substance as subsection (13) of Section 6–101 of the Uniform Probate Code (1987). As to the construction of provisions drawn from uniform acts, see Section 2.

Background on Section 5150 of Repealed Code

Section 5150 was added by 1989 Cal.Stat. ch. 397 § 25. The section continued subdivision (n) of former Probate Code Section 5101 (repealed by 1989 Cal.Stat. ch. 397 § 24) without substantive change. The language "whether or not included in the current balance" was added to cover the situation where interest or dividends have been earned but have not yet been credited to the account. For background on the provisions of this part, see the Comment to this part under the part heading. [20 Cal.L.Rev.Comm.Reports 1001 (1990)].

Cross References

Account defined for purposes of this Part, see Probate Code § 5122.
Party defined for purposes of this Part, see Probate Code § 5136.

§ 5152. Withdrawal

"Withdrawal" includes payment to a third person pursuant to a check or other directive of a party or an agent. *(Stats.1990, c. 79 (A.B.759), § 14, operative July 1, 1991.)*

Law Revision Commission Comments

1990 Enactment

Section 5152 continues Section 5152 of the repealed Probate Code without change. See Section 5124 (defining "agent"). See also Section 5204 (special power of attorney with respect to accounts at financial institutions). Section 5152 is the same in substance as subsection (15) of Section 6–101 of the Uniform Probate Code (1987), except that the UPC provision does not include the reference to payment to "an agent." As to the construction of provisions drawn from uniform acts, see Section 2.

Background on Section 5152 of Repealed Code

Section 5152 was added by 1989 Cal.Stat. ch. 397 § 25. The section continued subdivision (p) of former Probate Code Section 5101 (repealed by 1989 Cal.Stat. ch. 397 § 24) with the addition of the reference to payment to "an agent." For background on the provisions of this part, see the Comment to this part under the part heading. [20 Cal.L.Rev.Comm.Reports 1001 (1990)].

Cross References

Agent defined for purposes of this Part, see Probate Code § 5124.
Party defined for purposes of this Part, see Probate Code § 5136.
Payment defined for purposes of this Part, see Probate Code § 5138.

CHAPTER 2. GENERAL PROVISIONS

Section
5201. Application of provisions concerning beneficial ownership and liability of financial institutions.
5202. Fraudulent transfers.
5203. Words used to create accounts; effect of different wording.
5204. Special power of attorney; institution liability upon reliance on validity; records for accounting; attorney liability; application of other laws.
5205. Application; accounts in existence on July 1, 1990.

Application

Application of Part 2 to accounts in existence on or established after July 1, 1990, see Probate Code § 5205.

Cross References

Application of old and new law, see Probate Code § 3.

§ 5201. Application of provisions concerning beneficial ownership and liability of financial institutions

(a) The provisions of Chapter 3 (commencing with Section 5301) concerning beneficial ownership as between parties, or as between parties and P.O.D. payees or beneficiaries of multiple-party accounts, are relevant only to controversies between these persons and their creditors and other successors, and have no bearing on the power of withdrawal of these persons as determined by the terms of account contracts.

(b) The provisions of Chapter 4 (commencing with Section 5401) govern the liability of financial institutions who make payments pursuant to that chapter. *(Stats.1990, c. 79 (A.B. 759), § 14, operative July 1, 1991.)*

Law Revision Commission Comments

1990 Enactment

Section 5201 continues Section 5201 of the repealed Probate Code without change. The section is the same in substance as Section 6–102 of the Uniform Probate Code (1987). As to the construction of provisions drawn from uniform acts, see Section 2. Nothing in this part affects set off rights of financial institutions. See generally Kruger v. Wells Fargo Bank, 11 Cal.3d 352, 357, 521 P.2d 441, 113 Cal.Rptr. 449 (1974) (right of setoff is "based upon general principles of equity").

Background on Section 5201 of Repealed Code

Section 5201 was added by 1983 Cal.Stat. ch. 92 § 5. For background on the provisions of this part, see the Comment to this part under the part heading. [20 Cal.L.Rev.Comm.Reports 1001 (1990)].

Cross References

Account defined for purposes of this Part, see Probate Code § 5122.
Beneficiary defined for purposes of this Part, see Probate Code § 5136.
Financial institution defined for purposes of this Part, see Probate Code § 5128.
Multiple-party account defined for purposes of this Part, see Probate Code § 5132.
Party defined for purposes of this Part, see Probate Code § 5136.
Payment defined for purposes of this Part, see Probate Code § 5138.
P.O.D. defined for purposes of this Division, see Probate Code § 5139.
P.O.D. payee defined for purposes of this Part, see Probate Code § 5142.
Withdrawal defined for purposes of this Part, see Probate Code § 5152.

§ 5202. Fraudulent transfers

Nothing in this part affects the law relating to transfers in fraud of creditors. *(Stats.1990, c. 79 (A.B.759), § 14, operative July 1, 1991.)*

Law Revision Commission Comments

1990 Enactment

Section 5202 continues Section 5202 of the repealed Probate Code without change. No comparable provision is found in the Uniform Probate Code (1987).

Background on Section 5202 of Repealed Code

Section 5202 was added by 1983 Cal.Stat. ch. 92 § 5. For background on the provisions of this part, see the Comment to this part under the part heading. [20 Cal.L.Rev.Comm.Reports 1001 (1990)].

§ 5203. Words used to create accounts; effect of different wording

(a) Words in substantially the following form in a signature card, passbook, contract, or instrument evidencing an account, or words to the same effect, executed before, on, or after July 1, 1990, create the following accounts:

(1) Joint account: "This account or certificate is owned by the named parties. Upon the death of any of them, ownership passes to the survivor(s)."

(2) P.O.D. account with single party: "This account or certificate is owned by the named party. Upon the death of that party, ownership passes to the named pay-on-death payee(s)."

(3) P.O.D. account with multiple parties: "This account or certificate is owned by the named parties. Upon the death of any of them, ownership passes to the survivor(s). Upon the death of all of them, ownership passes to the named pay-on-death payee(s)."

(4) Joint account of * * * spouses with right of survivorship: "This account or certificate is owned by the named parties, who are * * * spouses, and is presumed to be their community property. Upon the death of either of them, ownership passes to the survivor."

(5) Community property account of * * * spouses: "This account or certificate is the community property of the named parties who are * * * spouses. The ownership during lifetime and after the death of a spouse is determined by the law applicable to community property generally and may be affected by a will."

(6) Tenancy in common account: "This account or certificate is owned by the named parties as tenants in common. Upon the death of any party, the ownership interest of that party passes to the named pay-on-death payee(s) of that party or, if none, to the estate of that party."

(b) Use of the form language provided in this section is not necessary to create an account that is governed by this part. If the contract of deposit creates substantially the same relationship between the parties as an account created using the form language provided in this section, this part applies to the same extent as if the form language had been used. *(Stats.1990, c. 79 (A.B.759), § 14, operative July 1, 1991. Amended by Stats.2016, c. 86 (S.B.1171), § 249, eff. Jan. 1, 2017; Stats.2016, c. 50 (S.B.1005), § 85, eff. Jan. 1, 2017.)*

Law Revision Commission Comments

1990 Enactment

Section 5203 continues Section 5203 of the repealed Probate Code without change. The section provides form language for multiple-party accounts, but does not require use of the form language. Accordingly, the account agreement for existing accounts need not be changed to conform to the form language provided in this section. Also, accounts may be established after this section becomes operative using forms that were used under the law in effect before this section was enacted. For the form language to establish a special power of attorney for account transactions, see Section 5204(c). Section 5203 is drawn in part from a Wisconsin statute. See Wis.Stat.Ann. § 705.02 (West 1981 & Supp.1988).

A contract of deposit that does not use the form language for a particular kind of account is nevertheless governed by this part if the contract of deposit provides for substantially the same relationship between the parties. For example, an account held by two persons as "joint tenants with right of survivorship" is treated as a joint account under this part. Likewise, an account payable on request to one or more of two or more parties is treated as a joint account under this part even though no mention is made of any right of survivorship unless the terms of the account or deposit agreement otherwise provide. See Section 5130 ("joint account" defined). An account treated as a joint account belongs to the parties in proportion to their net contributions and passes to the survivors unless there is clear and convincing evidence of a different intent. See Sections 5301 (ownership during lifetime), 5302 (right of survivorship). But see Sections 5306 (tenancy in common accounts), 5307 (account expressly described as "community property" account).

A party to a "tenancy in common" account can designate a P.O.D. beneficiary to receive that tenant's share of the account upon the tenant's death, and the provisions of this part are applicable with respect to the P.O.D. designation. Likewise, although the rights during lifetime and upon death of the parties to an account expressly described as a "community property" account are governed by the law applicable to community property generally, either spouse on the "community property" account can designate a P.O.D. beneficiary to receive that spouse's one-half share of the account upon the death of that spouse, and the provisions of this part are applicable with respect to the P.O.D. designation. See also the discussion in the Comment to Section 5130.

Section 5203 does not provide form language for a Totten trust account (as defined in Section 80), since the P.O.D. account serves the same function. However, a Totten trust account is authorized and is governed by the provisions of this part that apply to Totten trust accounts.

Background on Section 5203 of Repealed Code

Section 5203 was added by 1989 Cal.Stat. ch. 397 § 26. For background on the provisions of this part, see the Comment to this part under the part heading. [20 Cal.L.Rev.Comm.Reports 1001 (1990)].

Cross References

Account defined for purposes of this Part, see Probate Code § 5122.
Joint account defined for purposes of this Part, see Probate Code § 5130.
Party defined for purposes of this Part, see Probate Code § 5136.
P.O.D. account defined for purposes of this Part, see Probate Code § 5140.
P.O.D. defined for purposes of this Division, see Probate Code § 5139.

§ 5204. Special power of attorney; institution liability upon reliance on validity; records for accounting; attorney liability; application of other laws

(a) In addition to a power of attorney otherwise authorized by law, a special power of attorney is authorized under this section to apply to one or more accounts at a financial institution or to one or more contracts with a financial institution concerning safe deposit services. For the purposes of this section, "account" includes checking accounts, savings accounts, certificates of deposit, savings certificates, and any other depository relationship with the financial institution.

(b) The special power of attorney under this section shall:

(1) Be in writing.

(2) Be signed by the person or persons giving the power of attorney.

(3) Explicitly identify the attorney-in-fact or attorneys-in-fact, the financial institution, and the accounts or contracts subject to the power.

(c) The special power of attorney shall contain language in substantially the following form:

"WARNING TO PERSON EXECUTING THIS DOCUMENT: This is an important legal document. It creates a power of attorney that provides the person you designate as your attorney-in-fact with the broad powers it sets forth. You have the right to terminate this power of attorney. If there is anything about this form that you do not understand, you should ask a lawyer to explain it to you."

(d) In addition to the language required by subdivision (c), special powers of attorney that are or may be durable shall also contain substantially the following language:

"These powers of attorney shall continue even if you later become disabled or incapacitated."

(e) The power of attorney granted under this section shall endure as between the grantor and grantee of the power until the earliest of the following occurs:

(1) Revocation by the grantor of the power.

(2) Termination of the account.

(3) Death of the grantor of the power.

(4) In the case of a nondurable power of attorney, appointment of a guardian or conservator of the estate of the grantor of the power.

(f) A financial institution may rely in good faith upon the validity of the power of attorney granted under this section and is not liable to the principal or any other person for doing so if (1) the power of attorney is on file with the financial institution and the transaction is made by the attorney-in-fact named in the power of attorney, (2) the power of attorney appears on its face to be valid, and (3) the financial institution has convincing evidence of the identity of the person signing the power of attorney as principal.

(g) For the purposes of subdivision (f), "convincing evidence" requires both of the following:

(1) Reasonable reliance on a document that satisfies the requirement of Section 4751.

(2) The absence of any information, evidence, or other circumstances that would lead a reasonable person to believe that the person signing the power of attorney as principal is not the individual he or she claims to be.

(h) The protection provided by subdivision (f) does not extend to payments made after written notice is received by the financial institution as to any of the events of termination of the power under subdivision (e) if the financial institution has had a reasonable time to act on the notice. No other notice or any other information shown to have been available to the financial institution shall affect its right to the protection provided by this subdivision.

(i) The attorney-in-fact acting under the power of attorney granted under this section shall maintain books or records to permit an accounting of the acts of the attorney-in-fact if an accounting is requested by a legal representative of the grantor of the power.

(j) The attorney-in-fact acting under a power of attorney granted under this section is liable for any disbursement other than a disbursement to or for the benefit of the grantor of the power, unless the grantor has authorized the disbursement in writing.

(k) Nothing in this section limits the use or effect of any other form of power of attorney for transactions with a financial institution. Nothing in this section creates an implication that a financial institution is liable for acting in reliance upon a power of attorney under circumstances where the requirements of subdivision (f) are not satisfied. Nothing in this section affects any immunity that may otherwise exist apart from this section.

(*l*) Nothing in this section prevents the attorney-in-fact from also being designated as a P.O.D. payee.

(m) Except as otherwise provided in this section, the Power of Attorney Law, Division 4.5 (commencing with Section 4000) shall not apply to a special power of attorney under this section. Section 4130 and Part 5 (commencing with Section 4900) of Division 4.5 shall apply to a special power of attorney under this section. *(Stats.1990, c. 79 (A.B.759), § 14, operative July 1, 1991. Amended by Stats. 1994, c. 307 (S.B.1907), § 17; Stats.1995, c. 300 (S.B.984), § 15, eff. Aug. 3, 1995.)*

Law Revision Commission Comments
1990 Enactment

Section 5204 continues Section 5204 of the repealed Probate Code without substantive change. Naming a person as agent—technically giving the person named as agent a power of attorney with respect to account transactions—is commonly used for convenience and permits the agent to make withdrawals from the account. Even though the account is presently payable to the agent, the account belongs to the parties to the account, and the power of attorney gives the agent no ownership or survivorship right in the account.

1994 Amendment

Subdivision (f)(1) of Section 5204 is amended to substitute a reference to the provision of the Power of Attorney Law that replaced the former Civil Code section. [24 Cal.L.Rev.Comm.Reports 323 (1994)].

Background on Section 5204 of Repealed Code

Section 5204 was a new provision added by 1989 Cal.Stat. ch. 397 § 27. For background on the provisions of this part, see the Comment to this part under the part heading. [20 Cal.L.Rev.Comm.Reports 1001 (1990)].

Cross References

Account defined for purposes of this Part, see Probate Code § 5122.
Financial institution defined for purposes of this Part, see Probate Code § 5128.
Payment defined for purposes of this Part, see Probate Code § 5138.
P.O.D. defined for purposes of this Division, see Probate Code § 5139.
P.O.D. payee defined for purposes of this Part, see Probate Code § 5142.

§ 5205. Application; accounts in existence on July 1, 1990

This part applies to accounts in existence on July 1, 1990, and accounts thereafter established. *(Stats.1990, c. 79 (A.B. 759), § 14, operative July 1, 1991.)*

Law Revision Commission Comments

1990 Enactment

Section 5205 is a new provision that continues the substance of 1989 Cal.Stat. ch. 397, § 41. [20 Cal.L.Rev.Comm.Reports 1001 (1990)].

Cross References

Account defined for purposes of this Part, see Probate Code § 5122.

CHAPTER 3. OWNERSHIP BETWEEN PARTIES AND THEIR CREDITORS AND SUCCESSORS

Section
5301. Lifetime ownership; excess withdrawal; claim to recover ownership interest in excess withdrawal; P.O.D. accounts; Totten trusts.
5302. Sums remaining upon death of party.
5303. Survivorship determined by form of account at death; methods for change of terms; effect of withdrawals.
5304. Transfers not testamentary; necessity of writing.
5305. Married parties; community property; presumption; rebuttal; change of survivorship right, beneficiary, or payee by will.
5306. Tenancy in common; right of survivorship.
5307. Community property account.

Application

Application of Part 2 to accounts in existence on or established after July 1, 1990, see Probate Code § 5205.

§ 5301. Lifetime ownership; excess withdrawal; claim to recover ownership interest in excess withdrawal; P.O.D. accounts; Totten trusts

(a) An account belongs, during the lifetime of all parties, to the parties in proportion to the net contributions by each, unless there is clear and convincing evidence of a different intent.

(b) If a party makes an excess withdrawal from an account, the other parties to the account shall have an ownership interest in the excess withdrawal in proportion to the net contributions of each to the amount on deposit in the account immediately following the excess withdrawal, unless there is clear and convincing evidence of a contrary agreement between the parties.

(c) Only a living party, or a conservator, guardian, or agent acting on behalf of a living party, shall be permitted to make a claim to recover the living party's ownership interest in an excess withdrawal, pursuant to subdivision (b). A court may, at its discretion, and in the interest of justice, reduce any recovery under this section to reflect funds withdrawn and applied for the benefit of the claiming party.

(d) In the case of a P.O.D. account, the P.O.D. payee has no rights to the sums on deposit during the lifetime of any party, unless there is clear and convincing evidence of a different intent.

(e) In the case of a Totten trust account, the beneficiary has no rights to the sums on deposit during the lifetime of any party, unless there is clear and convincing evidence of a different intent. If there is an irrevocable trust, the account belongs beneficially to the beneficiary.

(f) For purposes of this section, "excess withdrawal" means the amount of a party's withdrawal that exceeds that party's net contribution on deposit in the account immediately preceding the withdrawal. *(Stats.1990, c. 79 (A.B.759), § 14, operative July 1, 1991. Amended by Stats.2012, c. 235 (A.B.1624), § 1.)*

Law Revision Commission Comments

1990 Enactment

Section 5301 continues Section 5301 of the repealed Probate Code without substantive change. Section 5301 is the same in substance as Section 6–103 of the Uniform Probate Code (1987). As to the construction of provisions drawn from uniform acts, see Section 2. The presumption under subdivision (a) that an account belongs to the parties during their lifetimes in proportion to the net contributions by each changed the rule under former law. Under former law, if the joint account provided for rights of survivorship, the account was presumed to be a joint tenancy and each joint tenant was presumed to have an equal interest in the account. Wallace v. Riley, 23 Cal.App.2d 654, 667, 74 P.2d 807 (1937).

Where there are several parties to an account and the account is one where there is no survivorship right among the parties (as where the terms of the account specifically provide that there is no survivorship right among the parties or the account is expressly designated as a "tenancy in common" account), any party may designate a P.O.D. payee (or Totten trust beneficiary) to take that party's share of the account upon the death of that party. The language "unless there is clear and convincing evidence of a different intent" in subdivisions (b) and (c) makes this clear. See also Sections 5305 (presumption that sum on deposit in joint account of married persons is community property), 5307 (account expressly described as "community property" account).

A party to a "community property" account may designate a P.O.D. payee to take that spouse's one-half interest in the account when that spouse dies. Under Section 5301, unless there is clear and convincing evidence of a different intent, the P.O.D. payee has no rights to the sums on deposit during the lifetime of the spouse naming the P.O.D. beneficiary.

Background on Section 5301 of Repealed Code

Section 5301 was added by 1983 Cal.Stat. ch. 92 § 5 and was amended by 1989 Cal.Stat. ch. 397 § 28. The 1989 amendment made no substantive change; it merely simplified the language of the section. For background on the provisions of this part, see the Comment to this part under the part heading. [20 Cal.L.Rev.Comm.Reports 1001 (1990)].

2012 Amendment

Subdivision (a) of Section 5301 is amended to avoid the implication that the net contribution rule is used only to determine the ownership interests of the parties in sums remaining on deposit. See Section 5150 ("sums on deposit" defined). The net contribution rule is used also to determine whether a party has withdrawn from the account an amount in excess of the party's ownership interest. The amendment reverses the holding of *Lee v. Yang*, 111 Cal. App. 4th 481, 3 Cal. Rptr. 3d 819 (2003) (withdrawing party owns funds withdrawn from joint account regardless of source of funds). In the absence of proof otherwise, the net contribution to an account of each of the parties having a present right of withdrawal is deemed to be an equal amount. Section 5134 ("net contribution" defined). [42 Cal.L.Rev.Comm. Reports 411 (2012)].

Cross References

Account defined for purposes of this Part, see Probate Code § 5122.
Beneficiary defined for purposes of this Part, see Probate Code § 5136.
Multiple-party accounts, required signatures, requirements regarding net contributions of party, see Probate Code § 5401.
Party defined for purposes of this Part, see Probate Code § 5136.
P.O.D. account defined for purposes of this Part, see Probate Code § 5140.
P.O.D. defined for purposes of this Division, see Probate Code § 5139.
P.O.D. payee defined for purposes of this Part, see Probate Code § 5142.
Sums on deposit defined for purposes of this Part, see Probate Code § 5150.

§ 5302. Sums remaining upon death of party

Subject to Section 5040:

(a) Sums remaining on deposit at the death of a party to a joint account belong to the surviving party or parties as against the estate of the decedent unless there is clear and convincing evidence of a different intent. If there are two or more surviving parties, their respective ownerships during lifetime are in proportion to their previous ownership interests under Section 5301 augmented by an equal share for each survivor of any interest the decedent may have owned in the account immediately before the decedent's death; and the right of survivorship continues between the surviving parties.

(b) If the account is a P.O.D. account:

(1) On death of one of two or more parties, the rights to any sums remaining on deposit are governed by subdivision (a).

(2) On death of the sole party or of the survivor of two or more parties, (A) any sums remaining on deposit belong to the P.O.D. payee or payees if surviving, or to the survivor of them if one or more die before the party, (B) if two or more P.O.D. payees survive, any sums remaining on deposit belong to them in equal and undivided shares unless the terms of the account or deposit agreement expressly provide for different shares, and (C) if two or more P.O.D. payees survive, there is no right of survivorship in the event of death of a P.O.D. payee thereafter unless the terms of the account or deposit agreement expressly provide for survivorship between them.

(c) If the account is a Totten trust account:

(1) On death of one of two or more trustees, the rights to any sums remaining on deposit are governed by subdivision (a).

(2) On death of the sole trustee or the survivor of two or more trustees, (A) any sums remaining on deposit belong to the person or persons named as beneficiaries, if surviving, or to the survivor of them if one or more die before the trustee, unless there is clear and convincing evidence of a different intent, (B) if two or more beneficiaries survive, any sums remaining on deposit belong to them in equal and undivided shares unless the terms of the account or deposit agreement expressly provide for different shares, and (C) if two or more beneficiaries survive, there is no right of survivorship in event of death of any beneficiary thereafter unless the terms of the account or deposit agreement expressly provide for survivorship between them.

(d) In other cases, the death of any party to a multiparty account has no effect on beneficial ownership of the account other than to transfer the rights of the decedent as part of the decedent's estate.

(e) A right of survivorship arising from the express terms of the account or under this section, a beneficiary designation in a Totten trust account, or a P.O.D. payee designation, cannot be changed by will. *(Stats.1990, c. 79 (A.B.759), § 14, operative July 1, 1991. Amended by Stats.2001, c. 417 (A.B.873), § 8; Stats.2015, c. 293 (A.B.139), § 9, eff. Jan. 1, 2016.)*

Law Revision Commission Comments
1990 Enactment

Section 5302 continues Section 5302 of the repealed Probate Code without change. The section is the same in substance as Section 6–104 of the Uniform Probate Code (1987), except that Section 5302 omits the UPC requirement that the intent that there be no rights of survivorship exist "at the time the account is created." Thus, under Section 5302, the intention to negate survivorship may be shown to have existed after the time of creation of the account, although the evidence must be clear and convincing. This is consistent with the rule under subdivision (a) of Section 5303 that rights of survivorship are determined by the form of the account at the death of a party. Under Section 5303, a party having the right of withdrawal can eliminate survivorship rights, for example, by closing out the account having the survivorship rights and opening a new account without survivorship rights. See the Comment to Section 5303. As to the construction of provisions drawn from uniform acts, see Section 2.

Subdivision (a) creates a right of survivorship in a joint account whether or not the account is described as a "joint tenancy" or mentions any right of survivorship. See Section 5130. The right of survivorship created by subdivision (a) may be rebutted by clear and convincing evidence of a different intent. This strengthens survivorship rights, since under prior law the presumption of survivorship arising from the joint tenancy form of the account could be overcome by a preponderance of the evidence. See Schmedding v. Schmedding, 240 Cal.App.2d 312, 315–16, 49 Cal.Rptr. 523 (1966) (presumption rebuttable); Evid.Code § 115 (except as otherwise provided by law, burden of proof requires preponderance of evidence); Comment to Evid.Code § 606 (ordinarily party against whom a rebuttable presumption operates must overcome the presumption by a preponderance of the evidence). To rebut the right of survivorship where no right of survivorship is desired, the parties to a joint account may, for example, establish a "JOINT ACCOUNT—NO SURVIVOR-SHIP."

Rights of survivorship are determined by the form of the account at the death of a party. See subdivision (a) of Section 5303. Under that subdivision, a party having the right of withdrawal can eliminate survivorship rights, for example, by closing out the account having the survivorship rights and opening a new account without survivorship rights. See the Comment to Section 5303.

Paragraph (2)(B) of subdivision (b), and paragraph (2)(B) of subdivision (c), are clarifying provisions not found in the Uniform Probate Code (1987). These provisions are drawn from the law of Maine. See Me.Rev.Stat.Ann. tit. 18–A, § 6–104 (West 1981).

Community funds may be deposited in an account held jointly by one of the spouses and a third person, with the other spouse not being a party to the account. Also community funds may be deposited in an account by one spouse as a trustee for a beneficiary who is not the other spouse or in a P.O.D. account where the P.O.D. payee is not the other spouse. In any of these cases, upon the death of the spouse who is a party to the account, the non-party spouse may recover his or her half interest in the community funds in preference to the survivorship rights of the third person. See Section 100. See also Section 6101 (formerly Section 201); Mazman v. Brown, 12 Cal.App.2d 272, 55 P.2d 539 (1936) (Former Probate Code Section 201 applied to nonprobate transfers with testamentary effect such as life insurance).

Even though the funds in a multiple-party account may be community funds under Section 5305, the financial institution may rely on the form of the account as a joint account, P.O.D. account, or Totten trust account and may make payment pursuant to Chapter 4 (commencing with Section 5401), and is protected from liability in so doing. See Section 5405. The nature of the property rights in such funds is to be determined among the competing claimants, and the financial institution has no interest in this controversy. See Section 5201.

Subdivision (c) codifies the judicially-recognized rule that, in the case of a tentative or "Totten" trust, the sums on deposit vest in the designated beneficiary on the death of the trustee. See 7 B. Witkin, Summary of California Law Trusts § 17, at 5379 (8th ed. 1974). However, subdivision (c) strengthens the rights of the beneficiary by permitting the trust to be attacked only by "clear and convincing" evidence that survivorship was not intended. Under prior California law, a tentative or "Totten" trust could be defeated by circumstantial and often flimsy evidence, making its use unreliable. Id. § 18, at 5380–82.

The rule stated in subdivision (d) applies to an account where there is clear and convincing evidence of an intent not to have a right of survivorship and the decedent has not designated a P.O.D. payee, such as a case where the terms of the account expressly provide that there is no right of survivorship or where the account is expressly described in the deposit agreement as a "tenancy in common" account (Section 5306). In a case where the rule stated in subdivision (d) applies, only the decedent's interest in the account becomes a part of the decedent's estate. A party to a "tenancy in common" account may, of course, designate a P.O.D. payee for the party's interest in the account, in which case upon the party's death the party's interest in the account is paid to the P.O.D. payee rather than to the party's estate. In the case of an account expressly designated in the deposit agreement as a "community property" account, either spouse may designate a P.O.D. payee for that spouse's interest, thereby making clear that the other spouse has no survivorship right to that interest, or may provide expressly in the

deposit agreement that there is no survivorship right or may make a disposition of the interest in his or her will, in which case the rule in subdivision (d) applies.

Subdivision (e) changes the rule applicable to a tentative or "Totten" trust under prior California law by preventing revocation or modification of the trust by will. See Brucks v. Home Fed. Sav. & Loan Ass'n, 36 Cal.2d 845, 852–53, 228 P.2d 545 (1951) (testamentary plan wholly inconsistent with terms of tentative trust revokes the trust).

Nothing in Section 5302 prevents the court, for example, from enforcing a promise by the surviving beneficiary to share the account funds with someone else. Cf. Jarkieh v. Badagliacco, 75 Cal.App.2d 505, 170 P.2d 994 (1946).

2001 Amendment

Section 5302 is amended to make clear that the transfer on death of funds in a multiple party account is subject to Section 5600, which causes a nonprobate transfer to a former spouse to fail if the former spouse is not the transferor's surviving spouse. See Section 5600 (effect of dissolution of marriage on nonprobate transfer). [28 Cal.L.Rev.Comm. Reports 599 (1998)].

Background on Section 5302 of Repealed Code

Section 5302 was added by 1983 Cal.Stat. ch. 92 § 5 and was amended by 1989 Cal.Stat. ch. 397 § 29. The 1989 amendment made technical, nonsubstantive revisions to conform to language used in other provisions of this part. For background on the provisions of this part, see the Comment to this part under the part heading. [20 Cal.L.Rev.Comm.Reports 1001 (1990)].

2015 Amendment

Section 5302 is amended to reflect the renumbering of former Section 5600 as Section 5040. [36 Cal.L.Rev.Comm. Reports 103 (2006)].

Cross References

Account defined for purposes of this Part, see Probate Code § 5122.
Beneficiary defined for purposes of this Part, see Probate Code § 5136.
Joint account defined for purposes of this Part, see Probate Code § 5130.
Multiple-party account defined for purposes of this Part, see Probate Code § 5132.
Party defined for purposes of this Part, see Probate Code § 5136.
P.O.D. account defined for purposes of this Part, see Probate Code § 5140.
P.O.D. defined for purposes of this Division, see Probate Code § 5139.
P.O.D. payee defined for purposes of this Part, see Probate Code § 5142.

§ 5303. Survivorship determined by form of account at death; methods for change of terms; effect of withdrawals

(a) The provisions of Section 5302 as to rights of survivorship are determined by the form of the account at the death of a party.

(b) Once established, the terms of a multiple-party account can be changed only by any of the following methods:

(1) Closing the account and reopening it under different terms.

(2) Presenting to the financial institution a modification agreement that is signed by all parties with a present right of withdrawal. If the financial institution has a form for this purpose, it may require use of the form.

(3) If the provisions of the terms of the account or deposit agreement provide a method of modification of the terms of the account, complying with those provisions.

(4) As provided in subdivision (c) of Section 5405.

(c) During the lifetime of a party, the terms of the account may be changed as provided in subdivision (b) to eliminate or to add rights of survivorship. Withdrawal of funds from the account by a party also eliminates rights of survivorship with respect to the funds withdrawn to the extent of the withdrawing party's net contribution to the account. *(Stats.1990, c. 79 (A.B.759), § 14, operative July 1, 1991. Amended by Stats. 2012, c. 235 (A.B.1624), § 2.)*

Law Revision Commission Comments

1990 Enactment

Section 5303 continues Section 5303 of the repealed Probate Code without change.

Subdivision (a) is the same as the first sentence of Section 6–105 of the Uniform Probate Code (1987). As to the construction of provisions drawn from uniform acts, see Section 2.

Subdivision (b) is substituted for the remainder of the Uniform Probate Code section and is drawn from Georgia law. See Ga.Code Ann. § 7–1–814 (1989). Paragraph (3) of subdivision (b) permits a change in the terms of a multiple-party account by complying with a method of modification provided in the terms of the account or deposit agreement. Accordingly, for example, if the terms of the account or deposit agreement permit a party to the account to change a P.O.D. beneficiary or to substitute a new party to a joint account for an original party to the account, the change would be effective to give the right of survivorship to the new beneficiary or new party to the joint account. The requirement of paragraph (1) that the account be closed and reopened under different terms would not apply where the modification is made under paragraph (2) or (3) of subdivision (b).

Under subdivision (a), rights of survivorship are determined by the form of the account at the death of a party. Subdivision (c) makes clear that the terms of the account that can be changed include terms relating to rights of survivorship. For example, under subdivision (b), a party having the right of withdrawal can eliminate survivorship rights by closing out the account having the survivorship rights and opening a new account without survivorship rights. Withdrawal of the funds from the account will not, however, change the other rights of the parties to the moneys withdrawn. See Sections 5301 (ownership during lifetime), 5305 (presumption of community property). See also the Comment to Section 5305.

Merely changing the terms of the account to eliminate survivorship rights does not affect the right of the financial institution to make payments in accordance with the terms of the account in effect at the time payment is made. See also Section 5405.

Section 5303 does not affect the presumption established by Section 5305 (funds of married persons who are parties to joint account presumed to be community property). See also Section 5405 (notice to financial institution from party that withdrawals should not be permitted).

Background on Section 5303 of Repealed Code

Section 5303 was added by 1983 Cal.Stat. ch. 92 § 5 and amended by 1984 Cal.Stat. ch. 452 § 7 and 1989 Cal.Stat. ch. 397 § 30. The 1984 amendment added subdivision (b)(4). The 1989 amendment added subdivision (c), a clarifying, nonsubstantive provision. For background on the provisions of this part, see the Comment to this part under the part heading. [20 Cal.L.Rev.Comm.Reports 1001 (1990)].

2012 Amendment

Section 5303 is amended to make clear that, although a party may sever the right of survivorship in a joint account by withdrawal of funds, the severance is limited in the case of an overwithdrawal. A party's ownership interest in an account, and the concomitant power to terminate a right of survivorship by withdrawing funds from the account, is determined by the party's net contribution to the account. See Section 5301 (ownership during lifetime). This codifies the rule in *Estate of Propst*, 50 Cal. 3d 448, 461–62, 268 Cal. Rptr. 114, 788 P.2d 628 (1990) ("Accordingly, we hold that in the absence of prior agreement, a joint tenant of personal property may unilaterally sever his or her own interest from the joint tenancy and thereby nullify the right of survivorship, as to that interest, of the other joint tenant or tenants without their consent."). [34 Cal.L.Rev.Comm. Reports 199 (2004)].

Cross References

Account defined for purposes of this Part, see Probate Code § 5122.
Financial institution defined for purposes of this Part, see Probate Code § 5128.
Multiple-party account defined for purposes of this Part, see Probate Code § 5132.
Multiple-party accounts, required signatures, requirements regarding net contributions of party, see Probate Code § 5401.
Party defined for purposes of this Part, see Probate Code § 5136.
Withdrawal defined for purposes of this Part, see Probate Code § 5152.

§ 5304. Transfers not testamentary; necessity of writing

Any transfers resulting from the application of Section 5302 are effective by reason of the account contracts involved and this part and are not to be considered as testamentary. The right under this part of a surviving party to a joint account, or of a beneficiary, or of a P.O.D. payee, to the sums on deposit on the death of a party to a multiple-party account shall not be denied, abridged, or affected because such right has not been created by a writing executed in accordance with the laws of this state prescribing the requirements to effect a valid testamentary disposition of property. *(Stats.1990, c. 79 (A.B.759), § 14, operative July 1, 1991.)*

Law Revision Commission Comments

1990 Enactment

Section 5304 continues Section 5304 of the repealed Probate Code without change. The first sentence is the same as the first portion of Section 6–106 of the Uniform Probate Code (1987). As to the construction of provisions drawn from uniform acts, see Section 2. The remainder of the Uniform Probate Code section is omitted. The second sentence of Section 5304 is comparable to New Jersey law. See N.J.Stat.Ann. § 17:16I–14 (West 1984). The purpose of Section 5304 is to make clear that the effectiveness of transfers under this part is not to be determined by the requirements for a will.

A transfer under this part is effective by reason of the provisions of this part and the terms of the account or deposit agreement. This transfer avoids the need for a probate proceeding to accomplish a transfer. However, the transfer does not affect rights otherwise provided by law. Also, for example, Section 5304 has no effect on a surviving spouse's right to his or her share of community funds deposited in a multiple-party account under which a third person has a survivorship right upon the death of the other spouse. See the Comment to Section 5302.

Background on Section 5304 of Repealed Code

Section 5304 was added by 1983 Cal.Stat. ch. 92 § 5. The section was drawn from portions of then-existing Financial Code Sections 852.5, 7604.5, 11203.5, 14854.5, and 18318.5 (pay-on-death transfers nontestamentary). For background on the provisions of this part, see the Comment to this part under the part heading. [20 Cal.L.Rev.Comm.Reports 1001 (1990)].

§ 5305. Married parties; community property; presumption; rebuttal; change of survivorship right, beneficiary, or payee by will

(a) Notwithstanding Sections 5301 to 5303, inclusive, if parties to an account are married to each other, whether or not they are so described in the deposit agreement, their net contribution to the account is presumed to be and remain their community property.

(b) Notwithstanding Sections 2581 and 2640 of the Family Code, the presumption established by this section is a presumption affecting the burden of proof and may be rebutted by proof of either of the following:

(1) The sums on deposit that are claimed to be separate property can be traced from separate property unless it is proved that the married persons made a written agreement that expressed their clear intent that the sums be their community property.

(2) The married persons made a written agreement, separate from the deposit agreement, that expressly provided that the sums on deposit, claimed not to be community property, were not to be community property.

(c) Except as provided in Section 5307, a right of survivorship arising from the express terms of the account or under Section 5302, a beneficiary designation in a Totten trust account, or a P.O.D. payee designation, may not be changed by will.

(d) Except as provided in subdivisions (b) and (c), a multiple-party account created with community property funds does not in any way alter community property rights.
(Stats.1990, c. 79 (A.B.759), § 14, operative July 1, 1991. Amended by Stats.1992, c. 163 (A.B.2641), § 131, operative Jan. 1, 1994; Stats.1993, c. 219 (A.B.1500), § 224.7.)

Law Revision Commission Comments
1990 Enactment

The introductory clause of subdivision (b) makes clear that the rule stated in subdivision (b) prevails over the rules stated in Civil Code Sections 4800.1 and 4800.2 with respect to the division of a joint account upon dissolution of marriage or legal separation as well as for all other purposes. Compare Section 5307 (account expressly described as "community property" account).

Paragraph (1) of subdivision (b) specifies one of the two methods of rebutting the presumption—the source-of-funds or tracing rule. If the person having the burden of proof can trace separate funds into a joint account, the presumption of community property is overcome and the funds retain their separate character. If separate funds have been commingled with community funds but remain ascertainable or traceable into a proportionate share of the account, the funds retain their separate character. On the other hand, if separate and community funds are so commingled that the party having the burden of proving that the funds are separate cannot meet that burden, then the entire account is treated as community property. See generally 7 B. Witkin, Summary of California Law Community Property §§ 33–34, at 5126–28 (8th ed. 1974). Even though the separate funds can still be traced, nothing prevents the married persons from making an agreement that expresses their clear intent that the funds be community property. If the person claiming that such an agreement was made proves that fact by a preponderance of the evidence, the agreement is given effect as provided in the last clause of paragraph (1).

Section 5305 continues Section 5305 of the repealed Probate Code without change. There is no comparable provision in the Uniform Probate Code (1987).

Section 5305 applies to "accounts" (defined in Section 5122), not just "multiple-party accounts" (defined in Section 5132). Thus, the presumption of community property applies, for example, to a husband and wife who have funds on deposit in a partnership account.

Section 5305 does not affect or limit the right of the financial institution to make payments pursuant to Sections 5401–5407 and the deposit agreement. See Section 5201. For this reason, Section 5305 does not affect the definiteness and certainty that the financial institution must have in order to be induced to make payments from the account and, at the same time, the section preserves the rights of the parties, creditors, and successors that arise out of the nature of the funds—community or separate—in the account.

The presumption created by Section 5305 is one affecting the burden of proof. See also Evid.Code § 606 ("The effect of a presumption affecting the burden of proof is to impose upon the party against whom it operates the burden of proof as to the nonexistence of the presumed fact"). This requires proof that the funds of married persons in a joint account are not community property. Subdivision (b) of Section 5305 specifies the proof that must be made to rebut the presumption that the property is community property.

Paragraph (2) of subdivision (b) specifies the other method by which the presumption may be rebutted: The spouses may expressly agree that the sums on deposit are not community property. But lay persons often do not understand the detailed provisions of the deposit agreement, and those provisions may not reflect the intent of the spouses as to the character of the property in the joint account. For this reason, paragraph (2) provides that the character of the property as community property is not changed unless there is an agreement—separate from the deposit agreement—expressly providing, for example, that the sums on deposit are not community property or that such sums are the separate property of one or both of the spouses. This scheme gives the spouses the necessary flexibility to change the character of the property where that is their intention but, at the same time, protects the spouses against unintentionally changing community property into separate property merely by signing a deposit agreement that would have that unintended effect.

The presumption created by Section 5305 does not affect the provisions of Sections 5302, 5402, and 5405 that permit prompt payment of the sums on deposit in a joint account to the surviving spouse. The prompt payment provisions are most useful where the estate is small and payment to the surviving spouse will avoid the expense and delay of probate. Yet, because the presumption created by Section 5305 governs the rights between the spouses and their successors, claimants who wish to show that the funds are community funds will find it easier to do so.

During the lifetimes of the married persons, the terms of the contract of deposit may be changed as provided in Section 5303 to eliminate or to add rights of survivorship. If there is a survivorship right in the surviving spouse at the time of the other spouse's death, the surviving spouse takes the share of the deceased spouse in the joint account by right of survivorship. See subdivision (c) of Section 5305. If there is no survivorship right in the surviving spouse at the time of the other spouse's death and the joint account consists of community property, the will of the deceased spouse may dispose of the deceased spouse's share of the account. See also Section 5307 (account expressly described in account agreement as a "community property" account is governed by law governing community property generally).

If a spouse has the unilateral right to withdraw funds from the joint account, that spouse may terminate all rights of survivorship by withdrawing the funds from the account and depositing them in another account that does not give the spouses rights of survivorship. Either spouse could then dispose of his or her share of the funds in the new account by will. One spouse may not, however, deprive the other spouse of community property rights by unilateral action with respect to funds in a joint account created with community property funds. For example, if a spouse withdraws community property funds from a joint account and deposits the funds withdrawn in an account in his or her name, this does not change the community property interest of the other spouse in the funds so deposited. See subdivision (d). See also Section 5307 (account expressly described in account agreement as a "community property" account is governed by law governing community property generally).

Likewise, for example, if the funds in a joint account of a married couple have their source in the separate property of the wife, the husband can eliminate survivorship rights by closing out the account and opening another account in his own name, but absent an agreement of the husband and wife this would not change the ownership interest of the wife in the funds withdrawn. See Section 5301 (joint account belongs, during the lifetime of all parties, to the parties in proportion to the net contributions of each to the sums on deposit, unless there is clear and convincing evidence of a different intent).

Community property funds on deposit in a multiple-party account are not subject to testamentary disposition by the deceased depositor. See subdivision (c). This is consistent with the general Uniform Probate Code rule stated in subdivision (e) of Section 5302. If a right to dispose of community property in a multiple-party account by will is desired to be retained, that objective can be accomplished by the two spouses establishing a joint account with the express provision that no right of survivorship arises upon the death of one of the spouses.

1992 Amendment [Revised Comment]

Subdivision (b) of Section 5305 is amended to substitute references to the Family Code provisions that replaced the former Civil Code provisions. [23 Cal.L.Rev.Comm. Reports 1 (1993)].

Background on Section 5305 of Repealed Code

Section 5305 was added by 1983 Cal.Stat. ch. 92 § 5 and amended by 1989 Cal.Stat. ch. 397 § 31. The 1989 amendment made the following revisions:

(1) References to Civil Code Sections 4800.1 and 4800.2 were added to the introductory clause of subdivision (b).

(2) Paragraph (1) of subdivision (b) was revised to require that the community property agreement be in writing. This is consistent with paragraph (2) of subdivision (b) and with Civil Code Section 5110.730.

With respect to the spouses and those claiming under them, Section 5305 reversed the presumption under former law that community funds deposited into a joint account with right of

survivorship are presumed to be converted into true joint tenancy funds and to lose their character as community property. See In re Estate of McCoin, 9 Cal.App.2d 480, 50 P.2d 114 (1935). See also Griffith, Community Property in Joint Tenancy Form, 14 Stan. L. Rev 87, 91–93 (1961). The former presumption was inconsistent with the general belief of married persons. Married persons generally believe that community funds deposited in a joint tenancy account remain community property. See Griffith, supra at 90, 95, 106–109. The presumption created by Section 5305 is consistent with this general belief.

For background on the provisions of this part, see the Comment to this part under the part heading. [20 Cal.L.Rev.Comm.Reports 1001 (1990)].

Cross References

Account defined for purposes of this Part, see Probate Code § 5122.
Beneficiary defined for purposes of this Part, see Probate Code § 5136.
Burden of proof, generally, see Evidence Code § 500 et seq.
Multiple-party account defined for purposes of this Part, see Probate Code § 5132.
Party defined for purposes of this Part, see Probate Code § 5136.
P.O.D. defined for purposes of this Division, see Probate Code § 5139.
P.O.D. payee defined for purposes of this Part, see Probate Code § 5142.
Sums on deposit defined for purposes of this Part, see Probate Code § 5150.

§ 5306. Tenancy in common; right of survivorship

For the purposes of this chapter, if an account is expressly described in the deposit agreement as a "tenancy in common" account, no right of survivorship arises from the terms of the account or under Section 5302 unless the terms of the account or deposit agreement expressly provide for survivorship. *(Stats.1990, c. 79 (A.B.759), § 14, operative July 1, 1991.)*

Law Revision Commission Comments
1990 Enactment

Section 5306 continues Section 5306 of the repealed Probate Code without change. There is no comparable provision in the Uniform Probate Code (1987). The purpose of Section 5306 is to preserve the effect of a tenancy in common account. A right of survivorship may exist in a "tenancy in common" account, for example, where a party to the account designates a P.O.D. beneficiary to receive that tenant's share of the account upon the tenant's death.

Background on Section 5306 of Repealed Code

Section 5306 was added by 1983 Cal.Stat. ch. 92 § 5 and amended by 1989 Cal.Stat. ch. 397 § 32. The 1989 amendment made the section applicable to all tenancy in common accounts, whenever established, and added an exception where the terms of the account or deposit agreement expressly provide for survivorship. For background on the provisions of this part, see the Comment to this part under the part heading. [20 Cal.L.Rev.Comm.Reports 1001 (1990)].

Cross References

Account defined for purposes of this Part, see Probate Code § 5122.

§ 5307. Community property account

For the purposes of this chapter, except to the extent the terms of the account or deposit agreement expressly provide otherwise, if the parties to an account are married to each other and the account is expressly described in the account agreement as a "community property" account, the ownership of the account during lifetime and after the death of a spouse is governed by the law governing community property generally. *(Stats.1990, c. 79 (A.B.759), § 14, operative July 1, 1991.)*

Law Revision Commission Comments

1990 Enactment

Section 5307 continues Section 5307 of the repealed Probate Code without change. The section deals with the situation where a joint account held by a husband and wife is specifically designated in the account agreement as a "community property" account. Section 5307 makes clear that this type of account is governed by the rules that apply to community property generally. Accordingly, unless the parties have agreed otherwise, the right of survivorship of the surviving spouse can be changed by will (deceased spouse by will devises his or her one-half share of the account to a person other than the surviving spouse). Also, the deposit agreement or the terms of the account can include, for example, a provision that the one-half share of a spouse will pass on the death of that spouse to one or more P.O.D. payees (or Totten trust beneficiaries) upon the death of that spouse. On the other hand, absent a contrary agreement or a contrary disposition, the surviving spouse will take the one-half share of the deceased spouse as community property.

Background on Section 5307 of Repealed Code

Section 5307 was a new provision added by 1989 Cal.Stat. ch. 397 § 33. For background on the provisions of this part, see the Comment to this part under the part heading. [20 Cal.L.Rev.Comm.Reports 1001 (1990)].

Cross References

Account defined for purposes of this Part, see Probate Code § 5122.
Party defined for purposes of this Part, see Probate Code § 5136.

CHAPTER 4. PROTECTION OF FINANCIAL INSTITUTION

Section
5401. Entry; payment; multiple signatures for transactions; requirements regarding net contributions of party; liens, etc.
5402. Payment of sums in joint account; personal representative or heir of deceased party.
5403. Payment of P.O.D. account; personal representative or heir of deceased payee.
5404. Totten trust account; payment; deceased trustee.
5405. Payment as discharge of financial institution from claims.
5406. Trust account; payment same as Totten trust account in absence of notice to contrary.
5407. Payment to minor.

Application

Application of Part 2 to accounts in existence on or established after July 1, 1990, see Probate Code § 5205.

§ 5401. Entry; payment; multiple signatures for transactions; requirements regarding net contributions of party; liens, etc.

(a) Financial institutions may enter into multiple-party accounts to the same extent that they may enter into single-party accounts. Any multiple-party account may be paid, on request and according to its terms, to any one or more of the parties or agents.

(b) The terms of the account or deposit agreement may require the signatures of more than one of the parties to a multiple-party account during their lifetimes or of more than one of the survivors after the death of any one of them on any check, check endorsement, receipt, notice of withdrawal, request for withdrawal, or withdrawal order. In such case, the financial institution shall pay the sums on deposit only in accordance with such terms, but those terms do not limit the right of the sole survivor or of all of the survivors to receive the sums on deposit.

(c) A financial institution is not required to do any of the following pursuant to Section 5301, 5303, or any other provision of this part:

(1) Inquire as to the source of funds received for deposit to a multiple-party account, or inquire as to the proposed application of any sum withdrawn from an account, for purposes of establishing net contributions.

(2) Determine any party's net contribution.

(3) Limit withdrawals or any other use of an account based on the net contribution of any party, whether or not the financial institution has actual knowledge of each party's contribution.

(d) All funds in an account, unless otherwise agreed in writing by the financial institution and the parties to the account, remain subject to liens, security interests, rights of setoff, and charges, notwithstanding the determination or allocation of net contributions with respect to the parties. *(Stats.1990, c. 79 (A.B.759), § 14, operative July 1, 1991. Amended by Stats.2012, c. 235 (A.B.1624), § 3.)*

Law Revision Commission Comments

1990 Enactment

Section 5401 continues Section 5401 of the repealed Probate Code without change. Subdivision (a) is the same as the first two sentences of Section 6–108 of the Uniform Probate Code (1987) with the addition of the clarifying phrase "and according to its terms." Paragraph (1) of subdivision (c) is the same in substance as the last sentence of Section 6–108 of the Uniform Probate Code (1987). As to the construction of provisions drawn from uniform acts, see Section 2.

Background on Section 5401 of Repealed Code

Section 5401 was added by 1983 Cal.Stat. ch. 92 § 5 and was amended by 1989 Cal.Stat. ch. 397 § 34. Subdivision (a) was a new provision. Subdivision (b) was drawn from portions of then-existing Financial Code Sections 852, 7603, 11204, and 14854 (second sentence). The 1989 amendment added the reference to agents in subdivision (a). See Section 5124 (defining "agent"). See also Section 5204 (special power of attorney with respect to accounts at financial institutions). The 1989 amendment also added paragraphs (2) and (3) to subdivision (c) and added subdivision (d). For background on the provisions of this part, see the Comment to this part under the part heading. [20 Cal.L.Rev.Comm.Reports 1001 (1990)].

2012 Amendment

Subdivision (c) of Section 5401 is amended to state expressly that a financial institution has no duty with respect to tracing net contributions of a party under either Section 5301 (ownership during lifetime) or 5303 (right of survivorship and terms of account). This is not a change in, but is declarative of, existing law.   [34 Cal.L.Rev.Comm. Reports 199 (2004)].

Cross References

Account defined for purposes of this Part, see Probate Code § 5122.
Agent defined for purposes of this Part, see Probate Code § 5124.
Financial institution defined for purposes of this Part, see Probate Code § 5128.
Multiple-party account defined for purposes of this Part, see Probate Code § 5132.
Party defined for purposes of this Part, see Probate Code § 5136.
Request defined for purposes of this Part, see Probate Code § 5148.
Sums on deposit defined for purposes of this Part, see Probate Code § 5150.
Withdrawal defined for purposes of this Part, see Probate Code § 5152.

§ 5402.   Payment of sums in joint account; personal representative or heir of deceased party

Any sums in a joint account may be paid, on request and according to its terms, to any party without regard to whether any other party is incapacitated or deceased at the time the payment is demanded; but payment may not be made to the personal representative or heirs of a deceased party unless proof of death is presented to the financial institution showing that the decedent was the last surviving party or unless there is no right of survivorship under Section 5302. *(Stats.1990, c. 79 (A.B.759), § 14, operative July 1, 1991.)*

Law Revision Commission Comments
1990 Enactment

Section 5402 continues Section 5402 of the repealed Probate Code without change. The section is the same in substance as Section 6–109 of the Uniform Probate Code (1987). As to the construction of provisions drawn from uniform acts, see Section 2.

Background on Section 5402 of Repealed Code

Section 5402 was a new provision added by 1983 Cal.Stat. ch. 92 § 5. For background on the provisions of this part, see the Comment to this part under the part heading. [20 Cal.L.Rev.Comm.Reports 1001 (1990)].

Cross References

Account defined for purposes of this Part, see Probate Code § 5122.
Financial institution defined for purposes of this Part, see Probate Code § 5128.
Joint account defined for purposes of this Part, see Probate Code § 5130.
Party defined for purposes of this Part, see Probate Code § 5136.
Payment defined for purposes of this Part, see Probate Code § 5138.
Proof of death defined for purposes of this Part, see Probate Code § 5144.
Request defined for purposes of this Part, see Probate Code § 5148.

§ 5403.   Payment of P.O.D. account; personal representative or heir of deceased payee

Any P.O.D. account may be paid, on request and according to its terms, to any original party to the account. Payment may be made, on request, to the P.O.D. payee or to the personal representative or heirs of a deceased P.O.D. payee upon presentation to the financial institution of proof of death showing that the P.O.D. payee survived all persons named as original payees. Payment may be made to the personal representative or heirs of a deceased original payee if proof of death is presented to the financial institution showing that the deceased original payee was the survivor of all other persons named on the account either as an original payee or as P.O.D. payee. *(Stats.1990, c. 79 (A.B.759), § 14, operative July 1, 1991.)*

Law Revision Commission Comments
1990 Enactment

Section 5403 continues Section 5403 of the repealed Probate Code without change. The section is the same in substance as Section 6–110 of the Uniform Probate Code (1987). As to the construction of provisions drawn from uniform acts, see Section 2.

Background on Section 5403 of Repealed Code

Section 5403 was a new provision added by 1983 Cal.Stat. ch. 92 § 5. For background on the provisions of this part, see the Comment to this part under the part heading. [20 Cal.L.Rev.Comm.Reports 1001 (1990)].

Cross References

Account defined for purposes of this Part, see Probate Code § 5122.
Financial institution defined for purposes of this Part, see Probate Code § 5128.
Party defined for purposes of this Part, see Probate Code § 5136.
Payment defined for purposes of this Part, see Probate Code § 5138.
P.O.D. account defined for purposes of this Part, see Probate Code § 5140.
P.O.D. defined for purposes of this Division, see Probate Code § 5139.
P.O.D. payee defined for purposes of this Part, see Probate Code § 5142.
Proof of death defined for purposes of this Part, see Probate Code § 5144.
Request defined for purposes of this Part, see Probate Code § 5148.

§ 5404.   Totten trust account; payment; deceased trustee

Any Totten trust account may be paid, on request and according to its terms, to any trustee. Unless the financial institution has received written notice that the beneficiary has a vested interest not dependent upon surviving the trustee, payment may be made to the personal representative or heirs of a deceased trustee if proof of death is presented to the financial institution showing that the deceased trustee was the survivor of all other persons named on the account either as trustee or beneficiary. A Totten trust account may be paid to a beneficiary or beneficiaries or the personal representative or heirs of a beneficiary or beneficiaries if proof of death is presented to the financial institution showing that the beneficiary or beneficiaries survived all persons named as trustees. *(Stats.1990, c. 79 (A.B.759), § 14, operative July 1, 1991.)*

Law Revision Commission Comments
1990 Enactment

Section 5404 continues Section 5404 of the repealed Probate Code without change. The section is the same in substance as Section 6–111 of the Uniform Probate Code (1987). As to the construction of provisions drawn from uniform acts, see Section 2.

Background on Section 5404 of Repealed Code

Section 5404 was a new provision added by 1983 Cal.Stat. ch. 92 § 5 and amended by 1989 Cal.Stat. ch. 397 § 35. The 1989 amendment substituted "Totten trust account" in place of "trust account." See Section 80 (defining "Totten trust account"). For background on the provisions of this part, see the Comment to this part under the part heading. [20 Cal.L.Rev.Comm.Reports 1001 (1990)].

§ 5405. Payment as discharge of financial institution from claims

(a) Payment made pursuant to Section 5401, 5402, 5403, or 5404 discharges the financial institution from all claims for amounts so paid whether or not the payment is consistent with the beneficial ownership of the account as between parties, P.O.D. payees, or beneficiaries, or their successors.

(b) The protection provided by subdivision (a) does not extend to payments made after the financial institution has been served with a court order restraining payment. No other notice or any other information shown to have been available to a financial institution shall affect its right to the protection provided by subdivision (a).

(c) Unless the notice is withdrawn by a subsequent writing, after receipt of a written notice from any party that withdrawals in accordance with the terms of the account, other than a checking account, share draft account, or other similar third-party payment instrument, should not be permitted, except with the signatures of more than one of the parties during their lifetimes or of more than one of the survivors after the death of any one of the parties, the financial institution may only pay the sums on deposit in accordance with the written instructions pending determination of the rights of the parties or their successors. No liability shall attach to the financial institution for complying with the terms of any written notice provided pursuant to this subdivision.

(d) The protection provided by this section has no bearing on the rights of parties in disputes between themselves or their successors concerning the beneficial ownership of funds in, or withdrawn from, multiple-party accounts and is in addition to, and not exclusive of, any protection provided the financial institution by any other provision of law. *(Stats. 1990, c. 79 (A.B.759), § 14, operative July 1, 1991.)*

Law Revision Commission Comments

1990 Enactment

Section 5405 continues Section 5405 of the repealed Probate Code without change. The section is drawn in part from Section 6–112 of the Uniform Probate Code (1987). Subdivision (a) is the same in substance as a portion of the Uniform Probate Code section. Subdivision (b) is substituted for the comparable portion of the Uniform Probate Code section. Subdivision (d) is the same in substance as the comparable portion of the Uniform Probate Code section. Receipt of notice under this section must be at the particular office or branch office where the account is carried unless the terms of the account or deposit agreement expressly provide otherwise. See Section 5146. As to the construction of provisions drawn from uniform acts, see Section 2.

Background on Section 5405 of Repealed Code

Section 5405 was added by 1983 Cal.Stat. ch. 92 § 5 and amended by 1984 Cal.Stat. ch. 452 § 8. Subdivision (a) was new. Subdivision (b) was drawn from then-existing Financial Code Sections 852.5, 7604.5, 11203.5, 14854.5, and 18318.5 relating to service of a court order restraining payment. Subdivision (c) was drawn from portions of Financial Code Sections 852 and 7603. Subdivision (d) was new. The 1984 amendment rewrote subdivision (c). For background on the provisions of this part, see the Comment to this part under the part heading. [20 Cal.L.Rev.Comm.Reports 1001 (1990)].

§ 5406. Trust account; payment same as Totten trust account in absence of notice to contrary

The provisions of this chapter that apply to the payment of a Totten trust account apply to an account in the name of one or more parties as trustee for one or more other persons if the financial institution has no other or further notice in writing that the account is not a Totten trust account as defined in Section 80. *(Stats.1990, c. 79 (A.B.759), § 14, operative July 1, 1991.)*

Law Revision Commission Comments

1990 Enactment

Section 5406 continues Section 5406 of the repealed Probate Code without change. The section permits a financial institution to treat an account in trust form as a Totten trust account (defined in Section 80) if it is unknown to the financial institution that the funds on deposit are subject to a trust created other than by the deposit of the funds in the account in trust form. If the financial institution does not have the additional information, the financial institution is protected from liability if it pays the account as provided in this chapter. See Section 5405. However, Section 5406 does not affect the rights as between the parties to the account, the beneficiary, or their successors. See Sections 5201, 5301(c), 5302(c).

Background on Section 5406 of Repealed Code

Section 5406 was added by 1983 Cal.Stat. ch. 92 § 5 and was amended by 1989 Cal.Stat. ch. 397 § 36. The section was drawn from a portion of Financial Code Section 853. The 1989 amendment substituted a reference to Section 80 (defining "Totten trust account") in place of the former reference to Section 5101. The 1989 amendment also required the notice that the account is not a Totten trust account to be in writing. This was consistent with a requirement also found in Financial Code Sections 853 and 6853. For background on the provisions of this part, see the Comment to this part under the part heading. [20 Cal.L.Rev.Comm.Reports 1001 (1990)].

Financial institution defined for purposes of this Part, see Probate Code § 5128.

Party defined for purposes of this Part, see Probate Code § 5136.

Payment defined for purposes of this Part, see Probate Code § 5138.

§ 5407. Payment to minor

If a financial institution is required or permitted to make payment pursuant to this chapter to a person who is a minor:

(a) If the minor is a party to a multiple-party account, payment may be made to the minor or to the minor's order, and payment so made is a valid release and discharge of the financial institution, but this subdivision does not apply if the account is to be paid to the minor because the minor was designated as a P.O.D. payee or as a beneficiary of a Totten trust account.

(b) In cases where subdivision (a) does not apply, payment shall be made pursuant to the California Uniform Transfers to Minors Act (Part 9 (commencing with Section 3900) of Division 4), or as provided in Chapter 2 (commencing with Section 3400) of Part 8 of Division 4. *(Stats.1990, c. 79 (A.B.759), § 14, operative July 1, 1991.)*

Law Revision Commission Comments
1990 Enactment

Section 5407 continues Section 5407 of the repealed Probate Code without change. Under the Uniform Transfers to Minors Act, if there has been no nomination of a custodian, $10,000 or less may be transferred to an adult member of the minor's family or to a trust company without the need for a court order. See Section 3907. In addition, the court may order that all or part of the money be paid to a custodian under the Uniform Act for the benefit of the minor. See Section 3413.

Background on Section 5407 of Repealed Code

Section 5407 was added by 1983 Cal.Stat. ch. 92 § 5 and amended by 1989 Cal.Stat. ch. 397 § 37. Subdivision (a) was consistent with Section 850 of the Financial Code. Subdivision (b) was new. The 1989 amendment authorized payment pursuant to the Uniform Transfers to Minors Act. For background on the provisions of this part, see the Comment to this part under the part heading. [20 Cal.L.Rev.Comm.Reports 1001 (1990)].

Cross References

Account defined for purposes of this Part, see Probate Code § 5122.

Beneficiary defined for purposes of this Part, see Probate Code § 5136.

Financial institution defined for purposes of this Part, see Probate Code § 5128.

Multiple-party account defined for purposes of this Part, see Probate Code § 5132.

Party defined for purposes of this Part, see Probate Code § 5136.

Payment defined for purposes of this Part, see Probate Code § 5138.

P.O.D. defined for purposes of this Division, see Probate Code § 5139.

P.O.D. payee defined for purposes of this Part, see Probate Code § 5142.

Part 3

UNIFORM TOD SECURITY REGISTRATION ACT

§ 5500. Short title; construction and application

(a) This part shall be known as and may be cited as the Uniform TOD Security Registration Act.

(b) This part shall be liberally construed and applied to promote its underlying purposes and policy.

(c) The underlying purposes and policy of this act are to (1) encourage development of a title form for use by individuals that is effective, without probate and estate administration, for transferring property at death in accordance with directions of a deceased owner of a security as included in the title form in which the security is held and (2) protect issuers offering and implementing the new title form.

(d) Unless displaced by the particular provisions of this part, the principles of law and equity supplement its provisions. *(Added by Stats.1998, c. 242 (A.B.1683), § 2.)*

Law Revision Commission Comments
1998 Addition

Section 5500 is the same in substance as Section 11 of the Uniform TOD Security Registration Act (1989). As to construing provisions drawn from uniform acts, see Section 2(b). Paragraphs (1) and (2) of subdivision (c) are not in the uniform act, but are included as a useful statement of the underlying purposes and policy of this part. For a severability provision, see Section 11. [28 Cal.L.Rev.Comm. Reports App. 6 (1998)].

Cross References

Security defined for purposes of this Part, see Probate Code § 5501.

§ 5501. Definitions

For purposes of this part:

(a) "Beneficiary form" means a registration of a security that indicates the present owner of the security and the intention of the owner regarding the person who will become the owner of the security upon the death of the owner.

(b) "Register," including its derivatives, means to issue a certificate showing the ownership of a certificated security or, in the case of an uncertificated security, to initiate or transfer an account showing ownership of securities.

(c) "Registering entity" means a person who originates or transfers a security title by registration, and includes a broker maintaining security accounts for customers and a transfer agent or other person acting for or as an issuer of securities.

(d) "Security" means a share, participation, or other interest in property, in a business, or in an obligation of an enterprise or other issuer, and includes a certificated security, an uncertificated security, and a security account.

(e)(1) "Security account" means any of the following:

(A) A reinvestment account associated with a security, a securities account with a broker, a cash balance in a brokerage account, cash, cash equivalents, interest, earnings, or dividends earned or declared on a security in an account, a reinvestment account, or a brokerage account, whether or not credited to the account before the owner's death.

(B) An investment management or custody account with a trust company or a trust department of a bank with trust powers, including the securities in the account, the cash balance in the account, and cash equivalents, and interest, earnings, or dividends earned or declared on a security in the account, whether or not credited to the account before the owner's death.

(C) A cash balance or other property held for or due to the owner of a security as a replacement for or product of an account security, whether or not credited to the account before the owner's death.

(2) For the purposes of this subdivision, "cash equivalent" means an investment that is easily converted into cash, including, treasury bills, treasury notes, money market funds, savings bonds, short-term instruments, and short-term obligations.

(f) This section may not be construed to govern cash equivalents in multiple-party accounts that are governed by the California Multiple–Party Accounts Law, Part 2 (commencing with Section 5100). *(Added by Stats.1998, c. 242 (A.B.1683), § 2. Amended by Stats.2002, c. 67 (S.B.1271), § 1; Stats.2002, c. 809 (S.B.1504), § 3.)*

Law Revision Commission Comments
1998 Addition

Section 5501 is the same as paragraphs (1), (7), (8), (9), and (10) of Section 1 of the Uniform TOD Security Registration Act (1989). Definitions in Section 1 of the Uniform TOD Security Registration Act that are not included here are in other provisions of this code. See Sections 34 ("devisee"), 44 ("heir"), 56 ("person"), 58 ("personal representative"), 62 ("property"), 74 ("state").

The definition of "security" includes shares of mutual funds and other investment companies. *Cf.* Com. Code § 8102 (definitions). The defined term "security account" is not intended to include securities held in the name of a bank or similar institution as nominee for the benefit of a trust.

"Survive" is not defined. No effort is made in this part to define survival as it is for purposes of intestate succession in Section 6403, which requires survival by an heir of the ancestor for 120 hours. For purposes of this part, "survive" is used in its common law sense of outliving another for any time interval, no matter how brief. The

drafters of the uniform act sought to avoid imposition of a new and unfamiliar meaning of the term on intermediaries familiar with the meaning of "survive" in joint tenancy registrations. [28 Cal.L.Rev. Comm. Reports 577 (1998)].

Cross References

Investment Securities, effective endorsement, instruction or entitlement, see Commercial Code § 8107.

§ 5502. Registration of securities; sole ownership by one individual or multiple ownership by two or more individuals with right of survivorship

Only individuals whose registration of a security shows sole ownership by one individual or multiple ownership by two or more individuals with right of survivorship, rather than as tenants in common, may obtain registration in beneficiary form. Multiple owners of a security registered in beneficiary form hold as joint tenants with right of survivorship, as tenants by the entireties, or as owners of community property held in survivorship form, and not as tenants in common. *(Added by Stats.1998, c. 242 (A.B.1683), § 2.)*

Law Revision Commission Comments
1998 Addition

Section 5502 is the same as Section 2 of the Uniform TOD Security Registration Act (1989). Section 5502 is designed to prevent co-owners from designating any death beneficiary other than one who is to take only upon survival of *all* co-owners. It coerces co-owning registrants to signal whether they hold as joint tenants with right of survivorship (JT TEN), as tenants by the entireties (T ENT), or as owners of community property. Also, it imposes survivorship on co-owners holding in a beneficiary form that fails to specify a survivorship form of holding. Nothing in Section 5502 authorizes a California married couple to register a security as "tenants by the entireties," since California does not recognize that form of ownership. See Civ. Code § 682. However, a California corporation may register a security to be held as tenants by the entireties if the shareholders are residents of another state which recognizes that form of ownership. Similarly, California does not permit property to be held as community property with a right of survivorship. However, this title form is recognized in Nevada and Arizona. See Nevada Rev. Stat. Ann. ch. 111.064 (Michie 1993); Ariz. Rev. Stat. Ann. 33–431 (Supp. 1997).

Tenancy in common and community property otherwise than in a survivorship setting are negated for registration in beneficiary form because persons desiring to signal independent death beneficiaries for each individual's fractional interest in a co-owned security normally will split their holdings into separate registrations of the number of units previously constituting their fractional share. Once divided, each can name his or her own choice of death beneficiary.

The term "individual," as used in this section, limits those who may register as owner or co-owner of a security in beneficiary form to natural persons. However, the section does not restrict an individual using this ownership form as to the choice of death beneficiary. The definition of "beneficiary form" in Section 5501 indicates that any "person" may be designated beneficiary in a registration in beneficiary form. "Person" is defined in Section 56 so that a church, trust company, family corporation, or other entity, as well as an individual, may be designated as a beneficiary. [28 Cal.L.Rev.Comm. Reports 577 (1998)].

Cross References

Beneficiary form defined for purposes of this Part, see Probate Code § 5501.

Security defined for purposes of this Part, see Probate Code § 5501.

§ 5503. Registration of securities in beneficiary form; authorized form; governing law

A security may be registered in beneficiary form if the form is authorized by this or a similar statute of the state of organization of the issuer or registering entity, the location of the registering entity's principal office, the office of its transfer agent or its office making the registration, or by this or a similar statute of the law of the state listed as the owner's address at the time of registration. A registration governed by the law of a jurisdiction in which this or similar legislation is not in force or was not in force when a registration in beneficiary form was made is nevertheless presumed to be valid and authorized as a matter of contract law. *(Added by Stats.1998, c. 242 (A.B.1683), § 2.)*

Law Revision Commission Comments

1998 Addition

Section 5503 is the same as Section 3 of the Uniform TOD Security Registration Act (1989). The section encourages registrations in beneficiary form to be made whenever a state with which either of the parties to a registration has contact has enacted this or a similar statute. Thus, a registration in beneficiary form of *X* Company shares might rely on the enactment of the uniform act in *X* Company's state of incorporation, or in the state of incorporation of *X* Company's transfer agent. Or, an enactment by the state of the issuer's principal office, of the transfer agent's principal office, or of the issuer's office making the registration also would validate the registration. An enactment of the state of the registered owner's address at the time of registration also might be used for validation purposes. The last sentence of Section 5503 is designed to establish a statutory presumption that a general principle of law is available to achieve a result like that made possible by this part. [28 Cal.L.Rev.Comm. Reports 577 (1998)].

Cross References

Beneficiary form defined for purposes of this Part, see Probate Code § 5501.
Registering entity defined for purposes of this Part, see Probate Code § 5501.
Security defined for purposes of this Part, see Probate Code § 5501.

§ 5504. Proof of registration of security in beneficiary form

A security, whether evidenced by certificate or account, is registered in beneficiary form when the registration includes a designation of a beneficiary to take the ownership at the death of the owner or the deaths of all multiple owners. *(Added by Stats.1998, c. 242 (A.B.1683), § 2.)*

Law Revision Commission Comments

1998 Addition

Section 5504 is the same as Section 4 of the Uniform TOD Security Registration Act (1989). As noted in the Comment to Section 5502, this part places no restriction on who may be designated beneficiary in a registration in beneficiary form. Any legal entity may be designated beneficiary in a registration in beneficiary form. [28 Cal.L.Rev.Comm. Reports 577 (1998)].

Cross References

Beneficiary form defined for purposes of this Part, see Probate Code § 5501.

Security defined for purposes of this Part, see Probate Code § 5501.

§ 5505. Form wording; transfer on death; pay on death; abbreviations

Registration in beneficiary form may be shown by the words "transfer on death" or the abbreviation "TOD," or by the words "pay on death" or the abbreviation "POD," after the name of the registered owner and before the name of a beneficiary. *(Added by Stats.1998, c. 242 (A.B.1683), § 2.)*

Law Revision Commission Comments

1998 Addition

Section 5505 is the same as Section 5 of the Uniform TOD Security Registration Act (1989). The abbreviation "POD" is included for use without regard to whether the subject is a money claim against an issuer, such as its own note or bond for money loaned, or is a claim to securities evidenced by conventional title documentation. The use of "POD" in a registration in beneficiary form of shares in an investment company should not be taken as a signal that the investment is to be sold or redeemed on the owner's death so that the sums realized may be "paid" to the death beneficiary. Rather, only a transfer on death, not a liquidation on death, is indicated. The drafters of the uniform act would have used only the abbreviation "TOD" except for the familiarity, rooted in experience with certificates of deposit and other deposit accounts in banks, with the abbreviation "POD" as signaling a valid nonprobate death benefit or transfer on death. [28 Cal.L.Rev.Comm. Reports 577 (1998)].

Cross References

Beneficiary form defined for purposes of this Part, see Probate Code § 5501.

§ 5506. Designation of a transfer on death beneficiary; effect on ownership; cancellation or change of registration

The designation of a TOD beneficiary on a registration in beneficiary form has no effect on ownership until the owner's death. A registration of a security in beneficiary form may be canceled or changed at any time by the sole owner or all then surviving owners without the consent of the beneficiary. *(Added by Stats.1998, c. 242 (A.B.1683), § 2.)*

Law Revision Commission Comments

1998 Addition

Section 5506 is the same as Section 6 of the Uniform TOD Security Registration Act (1989). The section simply affirms the right of a sole owner, or the right of all multiple owners, to end a TOD beneficiary registration without the assent of the beneficiary. The section says nothing about how a TOD beneficiary designation may be canceled, meaning that the registering entity's terms and conditions, if any, may be relevant. See Section 5510. If the terms and conditions have nothing on the point, cancellation of a beneficiary designation presumably would be effected by a reregistration showing a different beneficiary or omitting reference to a TOD beneficiary. [28 Cal.L.Rev.Comm. Reports 577 (1998)].

Cross References

Beneficiary form defined for purposes of this Part, see Probate Code § 5501.

Security defined for purposes of this Part, see Probate Code § 5501.

§ 5507. Action upon death of sole owner or last to die of all multiple owners; proof of death; reregistration of security

On death of a sole owner or the last to die of all multiple owners, ownership of securities registered in beneficiary form passes to the beneficiary or beneficiaries who survive all owners. On proof of death of all owners and compliance with any applicable requirements of the registering entity, a security registered in beneficiary form may be reregistered in the name of the beneficiary or beneficiaries who survive the death of all owners. Until division of the security after the death of all owners, multiple beneficiaries surviving the death of all owners hold their interests as tenants in common. If no beneficiary survives the death of all owners, the security belongs to the estate of the deceased sole owner or the estate of the last to die of all multiple owners. *(Added by Stats.1998, c. 242 (A.B.1683), § 2.)*

Law Revision Commission Comments

1998 Addition

Section 5507 is the same as Section 7 of the Uniform TOD Security Registration Act (1989). Even though multiple owners of a security registered in beneficiary form hold with right of survivorship, no survivorship rights attend the positions of multiple beneficiaries who become entitled to securities by reason of having survived the sole owner or the last to die of multiple owners. Issuers (and registering entities) who decide to accept registrations in beneficiary form involving more than one primary beneficiary should provide by rule whether fractional shares will be registered in the names of surviving beneficiaries where the number of shares held by the deceased owner does not divide without remnant among the survivors. If fractional shares are not desired, the issuer may wish to provide for sale of odd shares and division of proceeds, for an uneven distribution with the first or last named to receive the odd share, or for other resolution. Section 5508 deals with whether intermediaries have any obligation to offer beneficiary designations of any sort. Section 5510 enables issuers to adopt terms and conditions controlling the details of applications for registrations they decide to accept and procedures for implementing such registrations after an owner's death.

The statement that a security registered in beneficiary form is in the deceased owner's estate when no beneficiary survives the owner is not intended to prevent application of any antilapse statute that might direct a nonprobate transfer on death to the surviving issue of a beneficiary who failed to survive the owner. See, e.g., Section 21110 (antilapse). Rather, the statement is intended only to indicate that the registering entity involved should transfer or reregister the security as directed by the decedent's personal representative.

See also the Comment to Section 5501 on the meaning of "survive" for purposes of this part. [28 Cal.L.Rev.Comm. Reports 577 (1998)].

Cross References

Beneficiary form defined for purposes of this Part, see Probate Code § 5501.
Registering entity defined for purposes of this Part, see Probate Code § 5501.
Security defined for purposes of this Part, see Probate Code § 5501.

§ 5508. Registering entity; requests for security registration in beneficiary form; discharge from claims; protections

(a) A registering entity is not required to offer or to accept requests for security registration in beneficiary form. If a registration in beneficiary form is offered by a registering entity, the owner requesting registration in beneficiary form assents to the protections given to the registering entity by this part.

(b) By accepting a request for registration of a security in beneficiary form, the registering entity agrees that the registration will be implemented as provided in this part.

(c) A registering entity is discharged from all claims to a security by the estate, creditors, heirs, or devisees of a deceased owner if it registers a transfer of the security in accordance with Section 5507 and does so in good faith reliance (1) on the registration, (2) on this part, and (3) on information provided to it by affidavit of the personal representative of the deceased owner, or by the surviving beneficiary or the surviving beneficiary's representatives, or other information available to the registering entity. The protections of this part do not extend to a reregistration or payment made after a registering entity has received written notice from any claimant to any interest in the security objecting to implementation of a registration in beneficiary form. No other notice or other information available to the registering entity shall affect its right to protection under this part.

(d) The protection provided by this part to the registering entity of a security does not affect the rights of beneficiaries in disputes between themselves and other claimants to ownership of the security transferred or its value or proceeds. *(Added by Stats.1998, c. 242 (A.B.1683), § 2.)*

Law Revision Commission Comments

1998 Addition

Section 5508 is the same as Section 8 of the Uniform TOD Security Registration Act (1989), except for substitution of "part" for "act," substitution of "Section 5507" for "Section 7," and omission in subdivision (b) of language providing that the registering entity agrees that the registration will be implemented "on death of the deceased owner" as provided in this part. The omission from subdivision (b) is nonsubstantive, since subdivision (b) provides that the registering entity agrees to implement the registration as provided in this part, whether before or after the death of the deceased owner.

A "request" for registration in beneficiary form may be in any form chosen by a registering entity. This part does not prescribe a particular form and does not impose record-keeping requirements. Registering entities' business practices, including any industry standards or rules of transfer agent associations, will control.

The written notice referred to in subdivision (c) would qualify as a notice under Section 8403 of the Uniform Commercial Code.

"Good faith" as used in subdivision (c) is intended to mean "honesty in fact and the observance of reasonable commercial standards of fair dealing in the trade," as specified in Section 2103(1)(b) of the Uniform Commercial Code.

The protections described in this section are designed to meet any questions regarding registering entity protection that may not be foreclosed by issuer protections provided in the Uniform Commercial Code. For a discussion of the relevant Uniform Commercial Code provisions, see Wellman, *Transfer-on-Death Securities Registration: A New Title Form*, 21 Ga. L. Rev. 789, 823 n.90 (1987). [28 Cal.L.Rev.Comm. Reports App. 6 (1998)].

Cross References

Beneficiary form defined for purposes of this Part, see Probate Code § 5501.
Register defined for purposes of this Part, see Probate Code § 5501.

Registering entity defined for purposes of this Part, see Probate Code
   § 5501.
Security defined for purposes of this Part, see Probate Code § 5501.

§ 5509. Effectuation of transfer on death resulting from registration in beneficiary form; rights of surviving spouse or creditors of security owners

(a) Any transfer on death resulting from a registration in beneficiary form is effective by reason of the contract regarding the registration between the owner and the registering entity and this part and is not testamentary.

(b) This part does not limit the rights of a surviving spouse or creditors of security owners against beneficiaries and other transferees under other laws of this state. *(Added by Stats.1998, c. 242 (A.B.1683), § 2.)*

Law Revision Commission Comments

1998 Addition

Section 5509 is the same as Section 9 of the Uniform TOD Security Registration Act (1989), except for substitution of "part" for "act," and the addition of the language in subdivision (b) that this part does not limit the rights of a surviving spouse against beneficiaries and other transferees under other laws of this state. This language is consistent with Section 5511 (nothing in this part alters rights in community property). [28 Cal.L.Rev.Comm. Reports App. 6 (1998)].

Cross References

Beneficiary form defined for purposes of this Part, see Probate Code
   § 5501.
Registering entity defined for purposes of this Part, see Probate Code
   § 5501.
Security defined for purposes of this Part, see Probate Code § 5501.

§ 5510. Acceptance of registration in beneficiary form; terms and conditions

(a) A registering entity offering to accept registrations in beneficiary form may establish the terms and conditions under which it will receive requests for (1) registrations in beneficiary form, and (2) implementation of registrations in beneficiary form, including requests for cancellation of previously registered TOD beneficiary designations and requests for reregistration to effect a change of beneficiary.

(b) The terms and conditions established pursuant to subdivision (a) may provide for (1) proving death, (2) avoiding or resolving any problems concerning fractional shares, (3) designating primary and contingent beneficiaries, and (4) substituting a named beneficiary's descendants to take in the place of the named beneficiary in the event of the beneficiary's death. Substitution may be indicated by appending to the name of the primary beneficiary the letters LDPS, standing for "lineal descendants per stirpes." This designation substitutes a deceased beneficiary's descendants who survive the owner for a beneficiary who fails to so survive, the descendants to be identified and to share in accordance with the law of the beneficiary's domicile at the owner's death governing inheritance by descendants of an intestate. Other forms of identifying beneficiaries who are to take on one or more contingencies, and rules for providing proofs and assurances needed to satisfy reasonable concerns by registering entities regarding conditions and identities relevant to accurate implementation of registrations in bene-

ficiary form, may be contained in a registering entity's terms and conditions.

(c) The following are illustrations of registrations in beneficiary form that a registering entity may authorize:

(1) Sole owner-sole beneficiary: John S. Brown TOD (or POD) John S. Brown, Jr.

(2) Multiple owners-sole beneficiary: John S. Brown Mary B. Brown, JT TEN TOD John S. Brown, Jr.

(3) Multiple owners-primary and secondary (substituted) beneficiaries: John S. Brown Mary B. Brown, JT TEN TOD John S. Brown, Jr. SUB BENE Peter Q. Brown , or John S. Brown Mary B. Brown JT TEN TOD John S. Brown Jr. LDPS. *(Added by Stats.1998, c. 242 (A.B.1683), § 2.)*

Law Revision Commission Comments

1998 Addition

Section 5510 is the same as Section 10 of the Uniform TOD Security Registration Act (1989). Use of "and" or "or" between the names of persons registered as co-owners is unnecessary under this part and should be discouraged. If used, the two words should have the same meaning insofar as concerns a title form, i.e., that of "and" to indicate that both named persons own the asset.

Descendants of a named beneficiary who take by virtue of an "LDPS" designation appended to a beneficiary's name take as TOD beneficiaries rather than as intestate successors. For distributions to lineal descendants per stirpes, see Section 246. If no descendant of a predeceased primary beneficiary survives the owner, the security passes as part of the owner's estate as provided in Section 5507. [28 Cal.L.Rev.Comm. Reports 577 (1998)].

Cross References

Beneficiary form defined for purposes of this Part, see Probate Code
   § 5501.
Registering entity defined for purposes of this Part, see Probate Code
   § 5501.

§ 5511. Effect of Part on community character of community property or community rights in community property

Nothing in this part alters the community character of community property or community rights in community property. This part is subject to Chapter 2 (commencing with Section 5010) of Part 1 of Division 5. *(Added by Stats.1998, c. 242 (A.B.1683), § 2.)*

Law Revision Commission Comments

1998 Addition

Section 5511 makes clear that rights granted by this part are subject to Sections 5010–5032 (community property rights of nonconsenting spouse in nonprobate transfers).

Property rights under this part may be subject to other statutory qualifications than those noted in Section 5511. See, e.g., Sections 220–226 (simultaneous death), 250–258 (effect of homicide), 260–288 (disclaimer). Property received under this part may be subject to apportionment of estate taxes. See Sections 20100–20225. If a TOD beneficiary fails to survive the owner, the beneficiary's interest may be subject to the antilapse statute. See Section 21110. [28 Cal.L.Rev. Comm. Reports 577 (1998)].

§ 5512. Application of Part

This part applies to registrations of securities in beneficiary form made before, on, or after January 1, 1999, by decedents dying on or after January 1, 1999. *(Added by Stats.1998, c. 242 (A.B.1683), § 2.)*

Law Revision Commission Comments

1998 Addition

Section 5512 is the same as Section 12 of the Uniform TOD Security Registration Act (1989), except that it applies this "part" to registrations made before, "on," or after the operative date. [28 Cal.L.Rev.Comm. Reports App. 6 (1998)].

Cross References

Beneficiary form defined for purposes of this Part, see Probate Code § 5501.

Security defined for purposes of this Part, see Probate Code § 5501.

Part 4

REVOCABLE TRANSFER ON DEATH DEED

Repeal

For repeal of Part 4, see Probate Code § 5600.

Law Revision Commission Comments

2015 Repeal

Former Sections 5600–5604 are continued without change, other than renumbering, in Chapter 3 (commencing with Section 5040) of Part 1. The sections are relocated to make room for new Part 4 (commencing with Section 5600), relating to the revocable TOD deed. [36 Cal.L.Rev.Comm. Reports 103 (2006)].

CHAPTER 1. GENERAL PROVISIONS

Repeal

For repeal of Part 4, see Probate Code § 5600.

ARTICLE 1. PRELIMINARY PROVISIONS

Repeal

For repeal of Part 4, see Probate Code § 5600.

§ 5600. Application; duration of part

(a) This part applies to a revocable transfer on death deed made by a transferor who dies on or after January 1, 2016,

whether the deed was executed or recorded before, on, or after January 1, 2016.

(b) Nothing in this part invalidates an otherwise valid transfer under Section 5602.

(c) This part shall remain in effect only until January 1, 2021, and as of that date is repealed, unless a later enacted statute, that is enacted before January 1, 2021, deletes or extends that date. The repeal of this part pursuant to this subdivision shall not affect the validity or effect of a revocable transfer on death deed that is executed before January 1, 2021, and shall not affect the authority of the transferor to revoke a transfer on death deed by recording a signed and notarized instrument that is substantially in the form specified in Section 5644. *(Added by Stats.2015, c. 293 (A.B.139), § 17, eff. Jan. 1, 2016.)*

Law Revision Commission Comments

2015 Addition

Section 5600 implements the general rule that a new provision of the Probate Code applies retroactively. See Section 3. However, this part does not interfere with rights of a decedent's successors acquired by reason of the decedent's death before the operative date of this part. An instrument of a decedent who dies before the operative date of this part, or an instrument of a decedent who dies after the operative date of this part that was not executed in compliance with this part, is governed by other law. See Sections 3(g) (application of old law), 5602 (effect on other forms of transfer).

Former Sections 5600–5604, relating to a nonprobate transfer to a former spouse, are continued without change, other than renumbering, in Chapter 3 (commencing with Section 5040) of Part 1. The sections are relocated to make room for new Part 4 (commencing with Section 5600), relating to the revocable TOD deed. [36 Cal.L.Rev.Comm. Reports 103 (2006)].

§ 5601. Renumbered § 5042 and amended by Stats.2015, c. 293 (A.B.139), § 13, eff. Jan. 1, 2016

§ 5602. Use of other methods of conveying real property

This part does not preclude use of any other method of conveying real property that is permitted by law and that has the effect of postponing enjoyment of the property until the death of the owner. *(Added by Stats.2015, c. 293 (A.B.139), § 17, eff. Jan. 1, 2016.)*

Repeal

For repeal of Part 4, see Probate Code § 5600.

Law Revision Commission Comments

2015 Addition

Section 5602 recognizes the possibility of other devices that may achieve an effect similar to the revocable TOD deed, such as a revocable deed under *Tennant v. John Tennant Memorial Home*, 167 Cal. 570, 140 P. 242 (1914), or another instrument under Section 5000 (nonprobate transfer). [44 Cal.L.Rev.Comm. Reports 573 (2015) [2015–16 AR Appx. 5]]

§ 5603. Renumbered § 5046 and amended by Stats.2015, c. 293 (A.B.139), § 15, eff. Jan. 1, 2016

§ 5604. Application of other provisions relating to revocable transfer on death deeds

(a) Except as provided in subdivision (b), nothing in this part affects the application to a revocable transfer on death deed of any other statute governing a nonprobate transfer on death, including, but not limited to, any of the following provisions that by its terms or intent would apply to a nonprobate transfer on death:

(1) Division 2 (commencing with Section 100).

(2) Part 1 (commencing with Section 5000) of this division.

(3) Division 10 (commencing with Section 20100).

(4) Division 11 (commencing with Section 21101).

(b) Notwithstanding subdivision (a), a provision of another statute governing a nonprobate transfer on death does not apply to a revocable transfer on death deed to the extent this part provides a contrary rule. *(Added by Stats.2015, c. 293 (A.B.139), § 17, eff. Jan. 1, 2016.)*

Repeal

For repeal of Part 4, see Probate Code § 5600.

Law Revision Commission Comments

2015 Addition

Section 5604 makes clear that the revocable TOD deed law is supplemented by general statutory provisions governing a nonprobate transfer. The specific cross-references in this section are illustrative and not exclusive. General provisions referenced in this section include effect of death on community property, establishing and reporting fact of death, simultaneous death, effect of homicide or abuse, disclaimer, provisions relating to effect of death, nonprobate transfers of community property, nonprobate transfer to former spouse, proration of taxes, rules for interpretation of instruments, and limitations on transfers to drafters.

This part may in some instances limit the effect of a provision otherwise applicable to a nonprobate transfer on death. [44 Cal. L.Rev.Comm. Reports 573 (2015) [2015–16 AR Appx. 5]]

ARTICLE 2. DEFINITIONS

Section
5606. Construction of part.
5608. "Beneficiary" defined.
5610. "Real property" defined.
5612. "Recorded" defined.
5614. "Revocable transfer on death deed" defined.
5616. "Transferor" defined.

Repeal

For repeal of Part 4, see Probate Code § 5600.

§ 5606. Construction of part

Unless the provision or context otherwise requires, the definitions in this article govern the construction of this part. *(Added by Stats.2015, c. 293 (A.B.139), § 17, eff. Jan. 1, 2016.)*

Repeal

For repeal of Part 4, see Probate Code § 5600.

Law Revision Commission Comments

2015 Addition

Although Section 5606 limits the application of these definitions, a defined term may also be used in another statute in its defined sense. See, e.g., Section 5000(a) (nonprobate transfer includes revocable TOD deed).

The definitions in this article are supplemented by those in Part 2 (commencing with Section 20) of Division 1. See, e.g., Sections 24 (beneficiary), 28 (community property), 39 (fiduciary), 45 (instrument), 48 (interested person), 56 (person), 58 (personal representative), 62 (property), 68 (real property), 81 (transferor), 81.5 (transferee), 82 (trust), 84 (trustee), 88 (will). [36 Cal.L.Rev.Comm. Reports 103 (2006)].

§ 5608. "Beneficiary" defined

"Beneficiary" means a person named in a revocable transfer on death deed as transferee of the property. *(Added by Stats.2015, c. 293 (A.B.139), § 17, eff. Jan. 1, 2016.)*

Repeal

For repeal of Part 4, see Probate Code § 5600.

Law Revision Commission Comments

2015 Addition

Section 5608 is a specific application of Section 24 ("beneficiary" defined). The beneficiary must be identified by name. Section 5622 (beneficiary). [36 Cal.L.Rev.Comm. Reports 103 (2006)].

§ 5610. "Real property" defined

"Real property" means any of the following:

(a) Real property improved with not less than one nor more than four residential dwelling units.

(b) A condominium unit, including the limited common elements allocated to the exclusive use thereof that form an integral part of the condominium unit.

(c) A single tract of agricultural real estate consisting of 40 acres or less that is improved with a single-family residence. *(Added by Stats.2015, c. 293 (A.B.139), § 17, eff. Jan. 1, 2016.)*

Repeal

For repeal of Part 4, see Probate Code § 5600.

Law Revision Commission Comments

2015 Addition

Section 5610 supplements the definition of real property found in Section 68 ("real property" includes leasehold). [44 Cal.L.Rev. Comm. Reports 573 (2015) [2015–16 AR Appx. 5]]

§ 5612. "Recorded" defined

"Recorded" has the meaning provided in Section 1170 of the Civil Code. *(Added by Stats.2015, c. 293 (A.B.139), § 17, eff. Jan. 1, 2016.)*

Repeal

For repeal of Part 4, see Probate Code § 5600.

Law Revision Commission Comments

2015 Addition

Section 5612 adopts the rule that an instrument is deemed to be recorded when, being duly acknowledged or proved and certified, it is deposited in the recorder's office, with the proper officer, for record. See Civ. Code § 1170 (recorded). This definition applies to variants of the term defined, including "of record," "recordation," and the like. [36 Cal.L.Rev.Comm. Reports 103 (2006)].

§ 5614. "Revocable transfer on death deed" defined

(a) "Revocable transfer on death deed" means an instrument created pursuant to this part that does all of the following:

(1) Makes a donative transfer of real property to a named beneficiary.

(2) Operates on the transferor's death.

(3) Remains revocable until the transferor's death.

(b) A revocable transfer on death deed may also be known as a "revocable TOD deed." *(Added by Stats.2015, c. 293 (A.B.139), § 17, eff. Jan. 1, 2016.)*

Repeal

For repeal of Part 4, see Probate Code § 5600.

Law Revision Commission Comments

2015 Addition

Section 5614 adopts revocable TOD deed terminology, rather than "beneficiary deed" terminology used in some jurisdictions that have enacted comparable legislation.

A revocable TOD deed may be made for real property of the types described in Section 5610 ("real property" defined).

The beneficiary must be identified by name in a revocable TOD deed. See Section 5622 (beneficiary).

A revocable TOD deed creates no rights in the beneficiary until the death of the transferor, and is revocable until that time. See Sections 5630 (revocability) and 5650 (effect during transferor's life).

For a revocable TOD deed statutory form, see Section 5642. For construction of a revocable TOD deed, see Part 1 (commencing with Section 21101) of Division 11 (rules for interpretation of instruments). [44 Cal.L.Rev.Comm. Reports 573 (2015) [2015–16 AR Appx. 5]]

§ 5616. "Transferor" defined

"Transferor" means an owner of real property who makes a revocable transfer on death deed of the property. *(Added by Stats.2015, c. 293 (A.B.139), § 17, eff. Jan. 1, 2016.)*

Repeal

For repeal of Part 4, see Probate Code § 5600.

Law Revision Commission Comments

2015 Addition

Section 5616 is a specific application of Section 81 ("transferor" defined). [36 Cal.L.Rev.Comm. Reports 103 (2006)].

CHAPTER 2. EXECUTION AND REVOCATION

Repeal

For repeal of Part 4, see Probate Code § 5600.

ARTICLE 1. EXECUTION

Repeal

For repeal of Part 4, see Probate Code § 5600.

§ 5620. Who may make revocable transfer on death deed

An owner of real property who has the capacity to contract may make a revocable transfer on death deed of the property. *(Added by Stats.2015, c. 293 (A.B.139), § 17, eff. Jan. 1, 2016.)*

Repeal

For repeal of Part 4, see Probate Code § 5600.

Law Revision Commission Comments

2015 Addition

Section 5620 specifies the capacity that is required for execution of a revocable transfer on death deed. [44 Cal.L.Rev.Comm. Reports 573 (2015) [2015–16 AR Appx. 5]]

§ 5622. Identification of beneficiary

The transferor shall identify the beneficiary by name in a revocable transfer on death deed. *(Added by Stats.2015, c. 293 (A.B.139), § 17, eff. Jan. 1, 2016.)*

Repeal

For repeal of Part 4, see Probate Code § 5600.

Law Revision Commission Comments

2015 Addition

Subdivision (a) of Section 5622 makes explicit the requirement that a beneficiary be identified by name in the instrument. A class gift is not permissible.

A beneficiary must survive the transferor in order to take an interest under this section. Section 5652(b)(2). [44 Cal.L.Rev.Comm. Reports 573 (2015) [2015–16 AR Appx. 5]]

§ 5624. Signature, date and acknowledgment

A revocable transfer on death deed is not effective unless the transferor signs and dates the deed and acknowledges the deed before a notary public. *(Added by Stats.2015, c. 293 (A.B.139), § 17, eff. Jan. 1, 2016.)*

Repeal

For repeal of Part 4, see Probate Code § 5600.

Law Revision Commission Comments

2015 Addition

Section 5624 prescribes execution requirements. A revocable TOD deed is not invalid because it does not comply with the requirements for execution of a will. See Section 5000(a) (provision for nonprobate transfer on death in written instrument).

A properly executed revocable TOD deed is ineffective unless recorded within 60 days after it is executed. See Section 5626 (recordation, delivery, and acceptance). [44 Cal.L.Rev.Comm. Reports 573 (2015) [2015–16 AR Appx. 5]]

§ 5626. Recording; delivery to beneficiary not required; acceptance by beneficiary not required

(a) A revocable transfer on death deed is not effective unless the deed is recorded on or before 60 days after the date it was executed.

(b) The transferor is not required to deliver a revocable transfer on death deed to the beneficiary during the transferor's life.

(c) The beneficiary is not required to accept a revocable transfer on death deed from the transferor during the transferor's life. *(Added by Stats.2015, c. 293 (A.B.139), § 17, eff. Jan. 1, 2016.)*

Repeal

For repeal of Part 4, see Probate Code § 5600.

Law Revision Commission Comments

2015 Addition

Subdivision (a) of Section 5626 requires recordation of the revocable TOD deed, but does not require recordation by the transferor—an agent or other person authorized by the transferor may record the instrument. The deed is considered recorded for purposes of this section when it is deposited for record with the county recorder. See Section 5612 ("record" defined).

Subdivision (b) makes clear that delivery of a revocable TOD deed is not necessary, notwithstanding a Law Revision Commission Comment to Section 5000 to the effect that Section 5000 does not relieve against the delivery requirement of the law of deeds. The recordation requirement for a revocable TOD deed makes delivery unnecessary. Consideration is not required for a revocable TOD deed. See Civ. Code § 1040.

Subdivision (c) states the rule that, unlike an inter vivos deed, a revocable TOD deed does not require acceptance. Acceptance of a donative transfer is presumed. Disclaimer procedures are available to a beneficiary. See Sections 267, 279 (disclaimer).

A revocable TOD deed has no effect, and confers no rights on the beneficiary, until the transferor's death. See Section 5650 (effect during transferor's life). [44 Cal.L.Rev.Comm. Reports 573 (2015) [2015–16 AR Appx. 5]]

§ 5628. Effect of multiple recordings for same property

(a) If a revocable transfer on death deed is recorded for the same property for which another revocable transfer on death deed is recorded, the later executed deed is the operative instrument and its recordation revokes the earlier executed deed.

(b) Revocation of a revocable transfer on death deed does not revive an instrument earlier revoked by recordation of that deed. *(Added by Stats.2015, c. 293 (A.B.139), § 17, eff. Jan. 1, 2016.)*

Repeal

For repeal of Part 4, see Probate Code § 5600.

Law Revision Commission Comments

2015 Addition

Subdivision (a) of Section 5628 gives effect to the last executed of revocable TOD deeds recorded before the transferor's death. A revocable TOD deed is executed by signing, dating, and acknowledging before a notary public. See Section 5624 (execution). Execution is complete when the transferor acknowledges the deed before a notary public, not when the deed is signed and dated.

Under subdivision (b), recordation of a revocable TOD deed has the effect of revoking an earlier executed revocable TOD deed, regardless of the order of recordation of the deeds. Subsequent revocation of the later executed recorded deed does not revive an earlier executed deed. Instead, the property passes under failed transfer principles. See Section 21111 (failed transfer). [36 Cal.L.Rev. Comm. Reports 103 (2006)].

ARTICLE 2. REVOCATION

Repeal

For repeal of Part 4, see Probate Code § 5600.

§ 5630. Who may revoke revocable transfer on death deed

A transferor who has the capacity to contract may revoke a revocable transfer on death deed at any time. *(Added by Stats.2015, c. 293 (A.B.139), § 17, eff. Jan. 1, 2016.)*

Repeal

For repeal of Part 4, see Probate Code § 5600.

Law Revision Commission Comments

2015 Addition

Section 5630 states the rule that a transfer on death deed is revocable. The transferor's right of revocation may be subject to a contractual or court ordered limitation.

A TOD deed may be revocable in some circumstances even though the transferor lacks capacity. The transferor's agent under a durable power of attorney may not revoke a TOD deed unless expressly authorized. See Section 4264(f) (power of attorney). If the transferor's conservator seeks to revoke a TOD deed, the transferor's estate plan must be taken into account under general principles of substituted judgment, and notice must be given to the beneficiary. See Sections 2580–2586 (guardianship and conservatorship). [44 Cal.L.Rev.Comm. Reports 573 (2015) [2015–16 AR Appx. 5]].

§ 5632. Execution and recording of revocation

(a) An instrument revoking a revocable transfer on death deed shall be executed and recorded before the transferor's death in the same manner as execution and recordation of a revocable transfer on death deed.

(b) Joinder, consent, or agreement of, or notice to, the beneficiary is not required for revocation of a revocable transfer on death deed. *(Added by Stats.2015, c. 293 (A.B.139), § 17, eff. Jan. 1, 2016.)*

Repeal

For repeal of Part 4, see Probate Code § 5600.

Law Revision Commission Comments

2015 Addition

Under subdivision (a) of Section 5632 a revoking instrument must be signed, dated, acknowledged, and recorded by the transferor or a person acting at the transferor's direction. See Sections 5624 (execution), 5626 (recordation).

Subdivision (b) implements the principle that creation and recordation of a revocable TOD deed creates no rights in the beneficiary. See Section 5650 (effect during transferor's life). [36 Cal.L.Rev. Comm. Reports 103 (2006)].

ARTICLE 3. STATUTORY FORMS

Section
5642. Form of revocable transfer on death deed.
5644. Form of instrument revoking revocable transfer on death deed.

Repeal

For repeal of Part 4, see Probate Code § 5600.

§ 5642. Form of revocable transfer on death deed

A revocable transfer on death deed shall be substantially in the following form.

(a) The first page of the form shall be substantially the following:

SIMPLE REVOCABLE TRANSFER ON DEATH (TOD) DEED
(California Probate Code Section 5642)

Recording Requested By:
When Recorded Mail This Deed To
Name:
Address:
Assessor's Parcel Number: Space Above For Recorder's Use

This document is exempt from documentary transfer tax under Rev. & Tax. Code § 11930. This document is exempt from preliminary change of ownership report under Rev. & Tax. Code § 480.3.

IMPORTANT NOTICE: THIS DEED MUST BE RECORDED ON OR BEFORE 60 DAYS AFTER THE DATE IT IS SIGNED AND NOTARIZED

Use this deed to transfer the residential property described below directly to your named beneficiaries when you die. YOU SHOULD CAREFULLY READ ALL OF THE INFORMATION ON THE OTHER PAGES OF THIS FORM. You may wish to consult an attorney before using this deed. It may have results that you do not want. Provide only the information asked for in the form. DO NOT INSERT ANY OTHER INFORMATION OR INSTRUCTIONS. This form MUST be RECORDED on or before 60 days after the date it is signed and notarized or it will not be effective.

PROPERTY DESCRIPTION
Print the legal description of the residential property affected by this deed:
_____

BENEFICIARY(IES)
Print the FULL NAME(S) of the person(s) who will receive the property on your death (DO NOT use general terms like "my children") and state the RELATIONSHIP that each named person has to you (spouse, son, daughter, friend, etc.):
_____
_____
_____

TRANSFER ON DEATH
I transfer all of my interest in the described property to the named beneficiary(ies) on my death. I may revoke this deed. When recorded, this deed revokes any TOD deed that I made before signing this deed.
Sign and print your name below (your name should exactly match the name shown on your title documents):
_____ Date _____

NOTE: This deed only transfers MY ownership share of the property. The deed does NOT transfer the share of any co-owner of the property. Any co-owner who wants to name a TOD beneficiary must execute and RECORD a SEPARATE deed.

ACKNOWLEDGMENT OF NOTARY

A notary public or other officer completing this certificate verifies only the identity of the individual who signed the document to which this certificate is attached, and not the truthfulness, accuracy, or validity of that document.

State of California   )
County of _____   )

On _____ before me, (here insert name and title of the officer), personally appeared _____, who proved to me on the basis of satisfactory evidence to be the person(s) whose name(s) is/are subscribed to the within instrument and acknowledged to me that he/she/they executed the same in his/her/their authorized capacity(ies), and that by his/her/their signature(s) on the instrument the person(s), or the entity upon behalf of which the person(s) acted, executed the instrument.
I certify under PENALTY OF PERJURY under the laws of the State of California that the foregoing paragraph is true and correct.
WITNESS my hand and official seal.
Signature _____
(Seal)

(b) Subsequent pages of a form executed under this section shall be in substantially the following form:

COMMON QUESTIONS ABOUT THE USE OF THIS FORM

WHAT DOES THE TOD DEED DO? When you die, the identified property will transfer to your named beneficiary without probate. The TOD deed has no effect until you die. You can revoke it at any time.

CAN I USE THIS DEED TO TRANSFER BUSINESS PROPERTY? This deed can only be used to transfer (1) a parcel of property that contains one to four residential dwelling units, (2) a condominium unit, or (3) a parcel of agricultural land of 40 acres or less, which contains a single-family residence.

HOW DO I USE THE TOD DEED? Complete this form. Have it notarized. RECORD the form in the county where the property is located. The form MUST be recorded on or before 60 days after the date you sign it or the deed has no effect.

IS THE "LEGAL DESCRIPTION" OF THE PROPERTY NECESSARY? Yes.

HOW DO I FIND THE "LEGAL DESCRIPTION" OF THE PROPERTY? This information may be on the deed you received when you became an owner of the property. This information may also be available in the office of the county recorder for the county where the property is located. If you are not absolutely sure, consult an attorney.

HOW DO I "RECORD" THE FORM? Take the completed and notarized form to the county recorder for the county in which the property is located. Follow the instructions given by the county recorder to make the form part of the official property records.

WHAT IF I SHARE OWNERSHIP OF THE PROPERTY? This form only transfers YOUR share of the property. If a co-owner also wants to name a TOD beneficiary, that co-owner must complete and RECORD a separate form.

CAN I REVOKE THE TOD DEED IF I CHANGE MY MIND? Yes. You may revoke the TOD deed at any time. No one, including your beneficiary, can prevent you from revoking the deed.

HOW DO I REVOKE THE TOD DEED? There are three ways to revoke a recorded TOD deed: (1) Complete, have notarized, and RECORD a revocation form. (2) Create, have notarized, and RECORD a new TOD deed. (3) Sell or give away the property, or transfer it to a trust, before your death and RECORD the deed. A TOD deed can only affect property that you own when you die. A TOD deed cannot be revoked by will.

CAN I REVOKE A TOD DEED BY CREATING A NEW DOCUMENT THAT DISPOSES OF THE PROPERTY (FOR EXAMPLE, BY CREATING A NEW TOD DEED OR BY ASSIGNING THE PROPERTY TO A TRUST)? Yes, but only if the new document is RECORDED. To avoid any doubt, you may wish to RECORD a TOD deed revocation form before creating the new instrument. A TOD deed cannot be revoked by will, or by purporting to leave the subject property to anyone via will.

IF I SELL OR GIVE AWAY THE PROPERTY DESCRIBED IN A TOD DEED, WHAT HAPPENS WHEN I DIE? If the deed or other document used to transfer your property is RECORDED before your death, the TOD deed will have no effect. If the transfer document is not RECORDED before your death, the TOD deed will take effect.

I AM BEING PRESSURED TO COMPLETE THIS FORM. WHAT SHOULD I DO? Do NOT complete this form unless you freely choose to do so. If you are being pressured to dispose of your property in a way that you do not want, you may want to alert a family member, friend, the district attorney, or a senior service agency.

DO I NEED TO TELL MY BENEFICIARY ABOUT THE TOD DEED? No. But secrecy can cause later complications and might make it easier for others to commit fraud.

WHAT DOES MY BENEFICIARY NEED TO DO WHEN I DIE? Your beneficiary must RECORD evidence of your death (Prob. Code § 210), and file a change in ownership notice (Rev. & Tax. Code § 480). If you received Medi–Cal benefits, your beneficiary must notify the State Department of Health Care Services of your death and provide a copy of your death certificate (Prob. Code § 215).

WHAT IF I NAME MORE THAN ONE BENEFICIARY? Your beneficiaries will become co-owners in equal shares as tenants in common. If you want a different result, you should not use this form.

HOW DO I NAME BENEFICIARIES? You MUST name your beneficiaries individually, using each beneficiary's FULL name. You MAY NOT use general terms to describe beneficiaries, such as "my children." For each beneficiary that you name, you should briefly state that person's relationship to you (for example, my spouse, my son, my daughter, my friend, etc.).

WHAT IF A BENEFICIARY DIES BEFORE I DO? If all beneficiaries die before you, the TOD deed has no effect. If a beneficiary dies before you, but other beneficiaries survive you, the share of the deceased beneficiary will be divided equally between the surviving beneficiaries. If that is not the result you want, you should not use the TOD deed.

WHAT IS THE EFFECT OF A TOD DEED ON PROPERTY THAT I OWN AS JOINT TENANCY OR COMMUNITY PROPERTY WITH RIGHT OF SURVIVORSHIP? If you are the first joint tenant or spouse to die, the deed is VOID and has no effect. The property transfers to your joint tenant or surviving spouse and not according to this deed. If you are the last joint tenant or spouse to die, the deed takes effect and controls the ownership of your property when you die. If you do not want these results, do not use this form. The deed does NOT transfer the share of a co-owner of the property. Any co-owner who wants to name a TOD beneficiary must complete and RECORD a SEPARATE deed.

CAN I ADD OTHER CONDITIONS ON THE FORM? No. If you do, your beneficiary may need to go to court to clear title.

IS PROPERTY TRANSFERRED BY THE TOD DEED SUBJECT TO MY DEBTS? Yes.

DOES THE TOD DEED HELP ME TO AVOID GIFT AND ESTATE TAXES? No.

HOW DOES THE TOD DEED AFFECT PROPERTY TAXES? The TOD deed has no effect on your property taxes until your death. At that time, property tax law applies as it would to any other change of ownership.

DOES THE TOD DEED AFFECT MY ELIGIBILITY FOR MEDI–CAL? No.

AFTER MY DEATH, WILL MY HOME BE LIABLE FOR REIMBURSEMENT OF THE STATE FOR MEDI–CAL EXPENDITURES? Your home may be liable for reimbursement. If you have questions, you should consult an attorney.

(Added by Stats.2015, c. 293 (A.B.139), § 17, eff. Jan. 1, 2016.)

Repeal

For repeal of Part 4, see Probate Code § 5600.

Law Revision Commission Comments

2015 Addition

Section 5642 provides a form for creation of a revocable TOD deed. [44 Cal.L.Rev.Comm. Reports 573 (2015) [2015–16 AR Appx. 5]]

§ 5644. Form of instrument revoking revocable transfer on death deed

A transferor may revoke a revocable transfer on death deed by an instrument in substantially the following form:

Revocation of
Revocable Transfer on Death (TOD) Deed
(California Probate Code Section 5600)

Recording Requested By:

When Recorded Mail This
Deed To
Name:
Address:
Assessor's Parcel Number: Space Above For Recorder's
                                Use

This deed revocation is exempt from documentary transfer tax under Rev. & Tax. Code § 11930. This deed revocation is exempt from preliminary change of ownership report under Rev. & Tax. Code § 480.3.

IMPORTANT NOTICE: THIS FORM MUST BE RECORDED TO BE EFFECTIVE

This revocation form MUST be RECORDED before your death or it will not be effective. This revocation form only affects a transfer on death deed that YOU made. A transfer on death deed made by a co-owner of your property is not affected by this revocation form. A co-owner who wants to revoke a transfer on death deed that he/she made must complete and RECORD a SEPARATE revocation form.

PROPERTY DESCRIPTION

Print the legal description of the property affected by this revocation:

REVOCATION

I revoke any TOD deed to transfer the described property that I executed before executing this form.

SIGNATURE AND DATE

Sign and print your name below (your name should exactly match the name shown on your title documents):

_____ Date _____

ACKNOWLEDGMENT OF NOTARY

A notary public or other officer completing this certificate verifies only the identity of the individual who signed the document to which this certificate is attached, and not the truthfulness, accuracy, or validity of that document.

State of California)
County of _____)

On _____ before me, (here insert name and title of the officer), personally appeared _____, who proved to me on the basis of satisfactory evidence to be the person(s) whose name(s) is/are subscribed to the within instrument and acknowledged to me that he/she/they executed the same in his/her/their authorized capacity(ies), and that by his/her/their signature(s) on the instrument the person(s), or the entity upon behalf of which the person(s) acted, executed the instrument.

I certify under PENALTY OF PERJURY under the laws of the State of California that the foregoing paragraph is true and correct.

WITNESS my hand and official seal.

Signature _____

(Seal)

(Added by Stats.2015, c. 293 (A.B.139), § 17, eff. Jan. 1, 2016.)

Repeal

For repeal of Part 4, see Probate Code § 5600.

Law Revision Commission Comments

2015 Addition

Section 5644 provides a form for revocation of a revocable TOD deed. Use of the form is not mandatory, since other recorded instruments may revoke a TOD deed. See Sections 5628 (multiple deeds), 5660 (conflicting dispositive instruments). [44 Cal.L.Rev. Comm. Reports 573 (2015) [2015–16 AR Appx. 5]]

CHAPTER 3. EFFECT

Repeal

For repeal of Part 4, see Probate Code § 5600.

ARTICLE 1. GENERAL PROVISIONS

Repeal

For repeal of Part 4, see Probate Code § 5600.

§ 5650. Effect on ownership rights

During the transferor's life, execution and recordation of a revocable transfer on death deed:

(a) Does not affect the ownership rights of the transferor, and the transferor or the transferor's agent or other fiduciary may convey, assign, contract, encumber, or otherwise deal with the property, and the property is subject to process of the transferor's creditors, as if no revocable transfer on death deed were executed or recorded.

(b) Does not create any legal or equitable right in the beneficiary, and the property is not subject to process of the beneficiary's creditors.

(c) Does not transfer or convey any right, title, or interest in the property. *(Added by Stats.2015, c. 293 (A.B.139), § 17, eff. Jan. 1, 2016.)*

Repeal

For repeal of Part 4, see Probate Code § 5600.

Law Revision Commission Comments

2015 Addition

Section 5650 makes clear that a revocable TOD deed is effective only on the transferor's death and not before. A revocable TOD deed remains revocable until that time. See Section 5630 (revocability).

The transferor's execution and recordation of a revocable TOD deed has no effect on the ability of the transferor's creditors to subject the property to an involuntary lien or execution of a judgment.

The reference to the transferor's agent or other fiduciary in subdivision (a) includes a conservator. The authority of the fiduciary is subject to the qualification that the specific transaction entered into on behalf of the transferor must be within the scope of the fiduciary's authority. See, e.g., Section 4264(f) (power of attorney).

Subdivision (b) makes clear that the transferor's execution and recordation of a revocable TOD deed does not enable the creditors of a beneficiary to subject the property to an involuntary lien or execution of a judgment. The beneficiary is not entitled to notice of a trustee's sale, nor is the beneficiary's consent required to enable the transferor to refinance.

The beneficiary's joinder, consent, or agreement to any transaction by the transferor is unnecessary and irrelevant. If an obligation of the beneficiary incurred before the transferor's death attaches to the property on the transferor's death as a result of the doctrine of after-acquired title, that obligation is subordinate to any limitations on the transferor's interest in the property. See Sections 5652 (effect at death), 5670 (priority of secured creditor of transferor).

Subdivision (c) reinforces the concept that a revocable TOD deed does not effectuate a transfer before the transferor's death. Creation of a revocable TOD deed should not have the effect of a default on a loan secured by the property, since it is not a disposition of the property. [36 Cal.L.Rev.Comm. Reports 103 (2006)].

§ 5652. Rules for transfer of interest in property on transferor's death

(a) A revocable transfer on death deed transfers all of the transferor's interest in the property on the transferor's death according to the following rules:

(1) Subject to the beneficiary's right to disclaim the transfer, the interest in the property is transferred to the beneficiary in accordance with the deed.

(2) The interest of a beneficiary is contingent on the beneficiary surviving the transferor. Notwithstanding Section 21110, the interest of a beneficiary that fails to survive the transferor lapses.

(3) Except as provided in paragraph (4), if there is more than one beneficiary, they take the property as tenants in common, in equal shares.

(4) If there is more than one beneficiary, the share of a beneficiary that lapses or fails for any reason is transferred to the others in equal shares.

(b) Property is transferred by a revocable transfer on death deed subject to any limitation on the transferor's interest that is of record at the transferor's death, including, but not limited to, a lien, encumbrance, easement, lease, or other instrument affecting the transferor's interest, whether recorded before or after recordation of the revocable transfer on death deed. The holder of rights under that instrument may enforce those rights against the property notwithstanding its transfer by the revocable transfer on death deed.

(c) A revocable transfer on death deed transfers the property without covenant or warranty of title. *(Added by Stats.2015, c. 293 (A.B.139), § 17, eff. Jan. 1, 2016.)*

Repeal

For repeal of Part 4, see Probate Code § 5600.

Law Revision Commission Comments

2015 Addition

Under subdivision (a) of Section 5652, whatever interest the transferor owned at death in the property passes to the beneficiary. It should be noted, however, that this provision is not limited to the fee interest. If the transferor's ownership interest is a less than fee interest, the transferor's entire less than fee ownership interest passes to the beneficiary on the transferor's death.

Subdivision (b) conditions a transfer to a beneficiary on the beneficiary surviving the transferor.

Under subdivision (b), a beneficiary takes only what the transferor has at death. This is a specific application of the general rule that recordation of a revocable TOD deed does not affect the transferor's ownership rights or ability to deal with the property until death. See Section 5650 (effect during transferor's life). Likewise, if an obligation of the beneficiary attaches to the property as a result of the doctrine of after-acquired title, that obligation is subordinate to any limitations on the transferor's interest in the property, and a transfer by the beneficiary financed by a purchase money mortgage is subject to the priority of a recorded encumbrance on the transferor's interest notwithstanding Civil Code Section 2898 (priority of purchase money encumbrance).

Subdivision (c) emphasizes the point that a revocable TOD deed is basically a quitclaim, passing whatever interest the transferor had at death to the beneficiary. [44 Cal.L.Rev.Comm. Reports 573 (2015) [2015–16 AR Appx. 5]]

§ 5654. Medi–Cal eligibility

(a) For the purpose of determination of eligibility for health care under Chapter 7 (commencing with Section 14000) or Chapter 8 (commencing with Section 14200) of Part 3 of Division 9 of the Welfare and Institutions Code, execution and recordation of a revocable transfer on death deed is not a lifetime transfer of the property.

(b) Property transferred by a revocable transfer on death deed is subject to claims of the State Department of Health Care Services to the extent authorized by law. *(Added by Stats.2015, c. 293 (A.B.139), § 17, eff. Jan. 1, 2016.)*

Repeal

For repeal of Part 4, see Probate Code § 5600.

Law Revision Commission Comments

2015 Addition

Subdivision (a) of Section 5654 is a specific application of the general rule that execution and recordation of a revocable TOD deed divests the transferor of no interest in the property, and invests the beneficiary with no rights in the property, during the transferor's life. Section 5650 (effect during transferor's life).

Subdivision (b) is consistent with case law interpretation of the meaning and purpose of Welfare and Institutions Code Section 14009.5, providing for reimbursement to the state for Medi–Cal payments made during the decedent's life. See Bonta v. Burke, 98 Cal. App. 4th 788, 120 Cal. Rptr. 2d 72 (2002). [36 Cal.L.Rev.Comm. Reports 103 (2006)].

§ 5656. Application of property taxation and documentary transfer tax provisions

For the purpose of application of the property taxation and documentary transfer tax provisions of the Revenue and Taxation Code:

(a) Execution and recordation of, or revocation of, a revocable transfer on death deed of real property is not a change in ownership of the property and does not require declaration or payment of a documentary transfer tax or filing of a preliminary change of ownership report.

(b) Transfer of real property on the death of the transferor by a revocable transfer on death deed is a change in ownership of the property. *(Added by Stats.2015, c. 293 (A.B.139), § 17, eff. Jan. 1, 2016.)*

Repeal

For repeal of Part 4, see Probate Code § 5600.

Law Revision Commission Comments

2015 Addition

Section 5656 prescribes the effect of a revocable TOD deed or its revocation for purposes of property tax reassessment and documentary transfer taxation.

Under subdivision (a), mere recordation or revocation of a revocable TOD deed is not a transfer or change in ownership for taxation purposes. This is an application of existing law. See, e.g., Rev. & Tax Code §§ 480.3 (application of preliminary change of ownership requirement), 11930 (exemption from documentary transfer tax).

Under subdivision (b), a change in ownership pursuant to a revocable TOD deed does not occur until the transferor's death. The TOD beneficiary is responsible for filing the change in ownership statement required by Revenue and Taxation Code Section 480. See Section 5680 (beneficiary rights and duties). Although a transfer of property by a revocable TOD deed is a change in ownership for reassessment purposes, the transfer may qualify for exclusion under the Revenue and Taxation Code, depending on the nature of the parties to the transfer. See, e.g., Rev. & Tax. Code §§ 62–63.1. [36 Cal.L.Rev.Comm. Reports 103 (2006)].

ARTICLE 2. OTHER INSTRUMENTS AND FORMS OF TENURE

Repeal

For repeal of Part 4, see Probate Code § 5600.

§ 5660. Multiple instruments disposing of same property; operative instrument

If a revocable transfer on death deed recorded on or before 60 days after the date it was executed and another instrument both purport to dispose of the same property:

(a) If the other instrument is not recorded before the transferor's death, the revocable transfer on death deed is the operative instrument.

(b) If the other instrument is recorded before the transferor's death and makes a revocable disposition of the property, the later executed of the revocable transfer on death deed or the other instrument is the operative instrument.

(c) If the other instrument is recorded before the transferor's death and makes an irrevocable disposition of the property, the other instrument and not the revocable transfer on death deed is the operative instrument. *(Added by Stats.2015, c. 293 (A.B.139), § 17, eff. Jan. 1, 2016.)*

Repeal

For repeal of Part 4, see Probate Code § 5600.

Law Revision Commission Comments
2015 Addition

Section 5660 establishes the general rules governing a conflicting disposition of property that is subject to a recorded revocable TOD deed. A revocable TOD deed has no effect unless recorded. Section 5626 (recordation, delivery, and acceptance). A conflicting instrument may not affect a revocable TOD deed under this section unless recorded before the transferor's death.

This section does not apply if the transferor revokes a recorded revocable TOD deed before death. See Section 5630 (revocability).

Absent a total disposition of the property before death, the revocable TOD deed passes property subject to conflicting interests of record. See Section 5652 (effect at death). [36 Cal.L.Rev.Comm. Reports 103 (2006)].

§ 5664. Property held in joint tenancy or as community property with right of survivorship

If, at the time of the transferor's death, title to the property described in the revocable transfer on death deed is held in joint tenancy or as community property with right of survivorship, the revocable transfer on death deed is void. The transferor's interest in the property is governed by the right of survivorship and not by the revocable transfer on death deed. *(Added by Stats.2015, c. 293 (A.B.139), § 17, eff. Jan. 1, 2016.)*

Repeal

For repeal of Part 4, see Probate Code § 5600.

Law Revision Commission Comments
2015 Addition

Section 5664 addresses the effect of a revocable TOD deed that purports to transfer property held, at the time of the transferor's death, in joint tenancy or community property with a right of survivorship. [44 Cal.L.Rev.Comm. Reports 573 (2015) [2015–16 AR Appx. 5]]

§ 5666. Provisions applicable to revocable transfer on death deed of community property

(a) Chapter 2 (commencing with Section 5010) of Part 1 applies to a revocable transfer on death deed of community property.

(b) For the purpose of application of Chapter 2 (commencing with Section 5010) of Part 1 to a revocable transfer on death deed of community property, written consent to the deed, revocation of written consent to the deed, or modification of the deed, is ineffective unless recorded within the time required by that chapter for execution or service of the written consent, revocation, or modification. *(Added by Stats.2015, c. 293 (A.B.139), § 17, eff. Jan. 1, 2016.)*

Repeal

For repeal of Part 4, see Probate Code § 5600.

Law Revision Commission Comments
2015 Addition

Subdivision (a) of Section 5666 incorporates the general statutes governing the rights of spouses in a nonprobate transfer of community property. This is a specific application of the rule that general provisions of Part 1 of this division governing a nonprobate transfer apply to a revocable TOD deed. Section 5604(a)(2) (effect of other law).

Under the rules governing a nonprobate transfer of community property, a person has the power of disposition at death of the person's interest in community property without the joinder of the person's spouse.

Subdivision (b) makes clear that the general statute governing the rights of spouses in a nonprobate transfer of community property is qualified by the recording requirement in the case of a revocable TOD deed of community property. This is a specific application of the rule that general provisions of Part 1 of this division governing a nonprobate transfer are subject to a contrary rule in the revocable TOD deed law. See Section 5604(b); see also Section 5011(b) (rights of parties subject to "contrary state statute specifically applicable to instrument under which nonprobate transfer is made").

A third party that acts in reliance on apparent spousal rights under a revocable TOD deed is protected in that reliance. Section 5682 (bona fide purchaser protection). [44 Cal.L.Rev.Comm. Reports 573 (2015) [2015–16 AR Appx. 5]]

§ 5668. Provisions applicable to revocable transfer on death deed of community property with right of survivorship

A revocable transfer on death deed of community property with right of survivorship is subject to Section 5666, relating to a revocable transfer on death deed of community property. *(Added by Stats.2015, c. 293 (A.B.139), § 17, eff. Jan. 1, 2016.)*

Repeal

For repeal of Part 4, see Probate Code § 5600.

Law Revision Commission Comments
2015 Addition

Section 5668 addresses the effect of a revocable TOD deed on community property with right of survivorship. See Civ. Code § 682.1 (community property with right of survivorship). [44 Cal.L.Rev. Comm. Reports 573 (2015) [2015–16 AR Appx. 5]]

ARTICLE 3. CREDITORS

Section
5670. Creditor of transferor has priority over creditor of beneficiary.
5672. Liability of beneficiary for unsecured debts of transferor.
5674. Exceptions to beneficiary liability; aggregate personal liability of beneficiary.
5676. Proceedings for administration of transferor's estate commenced; beneficiary's liability to estate.

Repeal

For repeal of Part 4, see Probate Code § 5600.

§ 5670. Creditor of transferor has priority over creditor of beneficiary

Notwithstanding any other statute governing priorities among creditors, a creditor of the transferor whose right is evidenced at the time of the transferor's death by an encumbrance or lien of record on property transferred by a revocable transfer on death deed has priority against the property over a creditor of the beneficiary, regardless of whether the beneficiary's obligation was created before or after the transferor's death and regardless of whether the obligation is secured or unsecured, voluntary or involuntary, recorded or unrecorded. *(Added by Stats.2015, c. 293 (A.B.139), § 17, eff. Jan. 1, 2016.)*

Repeal

For repeal of Part 4, see Probate Code § 5600.

Law Revision Commission Comments
2015 Addition

Section 5670 makes clear that a creditor of the transferor has priority over a creditor of the beneficiary, at least to the extent the transferor's creditor has a lien or encumbrance of record at the time of the transferor's death. Thus the doctrine of after-acquired title (Civ. Code §§ 1106, 2930) does not create a priority in the beneficiary's creditors, even if the right of the transferor's creditor was created after the interest of the beneficiary's creditor. Likewise, the priority given by statute to a purchase money encumbrance by the beneficiary's transferee does not override the general priority of an encumbrance of record by a creditor of the transferor. See Civ. Code

§ 2898 (priority of purchase money encumbrance). [36 Cal.L.Rev. Comm. Reports 103 (2006)].

§ 5672. Liability of beneficiary for unsecured debts of transferor

Each beneficiary is personally liable to the extent provided in Section 5674 for the unsecured debts of the transferor. Any such debt may be enforced against the beneficiary in the same manner as it could have been enforced against the transferor if the transferor had not died. In any action based on the debt, the beneficiary may assert any defense, cross-complaint, or setoff that would have been available to the transferor if the transferor had not died. Nothing in this section permits enforcement of a claim that is barred under Part 4 (commencing with Section 9000) of Division 7. Section 366.2 of the Code of Civil Procedure applies in an action under this section. *(Added by Stats.2015, c. 293 (A.B.139), § 17, eff. Jan. 1, 2016.)*

Repeal

For repeal of Part 4, see Probate Code § 5600.

Law Revision Commission Comments
2015 Addition

Section 5672 is drawn from Section 13204, relating to the liability of a decedent's successor who takes real property of small value under the affidavit procedure. A beneficiary who wishes to avoid the liability imposed by this section may commence a probate proceeding and return the property to the estate under Section 5676. See Section 5674 (limitation on liability). See also Section 275 (disclaimer). [36 Cal.L.Rev.Comm. Reports 103 (2006)].

§ 5674. Exceptions to beneficiary liability; aggregate personal liability of beneficiary

(a) A beneficiary is not liable under Section 5672 if proceedings for the administration of the transferor's estate are commenced and the beneficiary satisfies the requirements of Section 5676.

(b) The aggregate of the personal liability of a beneficiary under Section 5672 shall not exceed the sum of the following:

(1) The fair market value at the time of the transferor's death of the property received by the beneficiary pursuant to the revocable transfer on death deed, less the amount of any liens and encumbrances on the property at that time.

(2) The net income the beneficiary received from the property.

(3) If the property has been disposed of, interest on the fair market value of the property from the date of disposition at the rate payable on a money judgment. For the purposes of this paragraph, "fair market value of the property" has the same meaning as defined in paragraph (2) of subdivision (a) of Section 5676. *(Added by Stats.2015, c. 293 (A.B.139), § 17, eff. Jan. 1, 2016.)*

Repeal

For repeal of Part 4, see Probate Code § 5600.

Law Revision Commission Comments
2015 Addition

Section 5674 is drawn from Section 13207, relating to limitation of liability of a decedent's successor who takes real property of small value under the affidavit procedure. [36 Cal.L.Rev.Comm. Reports 103 (2006)].

§ 5676. Proceedings for administration of transferor's estate commenced; beneficiary's liability to estate

(a) Subject to subdivisions (b), (c), and (d), if proceedings for the administration of the transferor's estate are commenced, each beneficiary is liable for:

(1) The restitution to the transferor's estate of the property the beneficiary received pursuant to the revocable transfer on death deed if the beneficiary still has the property, together with (A) the net income the beneficiary received from the property and (B) if the beneficiary encumbered the property after the transferor's death, the amount necessary to satisfy the balance of the encumbrance as of the date the property is restored to the estate.

(2) The restitution to the transferor's estate of the fair market value of the property if the beneficiary no longer has the property, together with (A) the net income the beneficiary received from the property prior to disposing of it and (B) interest from the date of disposition at the rate payable on a money judgment on the fair market value of the property. For the purposes of this paragraph, the "fair market value of the property" is the fair market value, determined as of the time of the disposition of the property, of the property the beneficiary received pursuant to the revocable transfer on death deed, less the amount of any liens and encumbrances on the property at the time of the transferor's death.

(b) Subject to subdivision (c), if proceedings for the administration of the transferor's estate are commenced and a beneficiary made a significant improvement to the property received by the beneficiary pursuant to the revocable transfer on death deed, the beneficiary is liable for whichever of the following the transferor's estate elects:

(1) The restitution of the property, as improved, to the estate of the transferor upon the condition that the estate reimburse the beneficiary for (A) the amount by which the improvement increases the fair market value of the property restored, determined as of the time of restitution, and (B) the amount paid by the beneficiary for principal and interest on any liens or encumbrances that were on the property at the time of the transferor's death.

(2) The restoration to the transferor's estate of the fair market value of the property, determined as of the time of the transferor's death, less the amount of any liens and encumbrances on the property at that time, together with interest on the net amount at the rate payable on a money judgment running from the time of the transferor's death.

(c) The property and amount required to be restored to the estate under this section shall be reduced by any property or amount paid by the beneficiary to satisfy a liability under Section 5672.

(d) An action to enforce the liability under this section may be brought only by the personal representative of the estate of the transferor. Whether or not the personal representative brings an action under this section, the personal representative may enforce the liability only to the extent of the beneficiary's liability under Section 5672. The reasonable cost of proceeding under this section shall be reimbursed as an extraordinary service under Sections 10801 and 10811.

Action under this section is optional. A personal representative is never required to act under this section.

(e) An action to enforce the liability under this section is forever barred three years after the transferor's death. The three-year period specified in this subdivision is not tolled for any reason. Nothing in this subdivision affects the requirements of Section 215, any law that may toll the limitations period for the commencement of a Medi–Cal estate recovery action, or the time for commencement of an action by the State Department of Health Care Services under Section 14009.5 of the Welfare and Institutions Code.

(f) If property is restored to the transferor's estate under this section, that property shall be treated as a specific gift and any proceeds remaining from the sale of the property after the payment of claims shall be returned to the beneficiary. *(Added by Stats.2015, c. 293 (A.B.139), § 17, eff. Jan. 1, 2016.)*

Repeal

For repeal of Part 4, see Probate Code § 5600.

Law Revision Commission Comments

2015 Addition

Section 5676 is drawn from Section 13206, relating to restoration of property to the estate by a decedent's successor who takes real property of small value under the affidavit procedure.

Subdivision (d) makes clear that liability for restitution of property to the estate under this section is limited to satisfaction of creditor claims, regardless of whether restitution under this section is made voluntarily or pursuant to a court proceeding. Any surplus belongs to the beneficiary.

Subdivision (f) makes clear that the beneficiary of revocable TOD-deeded property that is restored to the transferor's estate under this section is the beneficiary of a specific gift for purposes of abatement under Section 21402. [44 Cal.L.Rev.Comm. Reports 573 (2015) [2015–16 AR Appx. 5]]

CHAPTER 4. EFFECTUATION OF TRANSFER

Repeal

For repeal of Part 4, see Probate Code § 5600.

§ 5680. Establishment of transferor's death; change in ownership statement; notice to Director of Health Care Services; liability for estate and generation-skipping transfer taxes

(a) The beneficiary may establish the fact of the transferor's death under the procedure provided in Chapter 2 (commencing with Section 210) of Part 4 of Division 2. For the purpose of this subdivision, the beneficiary is a person empowered by statute to act on behalf of the transferor or the transferor's estate within the meaning of Section 103526 of the Health and Safety Code.

(b) For the purpose of filing the change in ownership statement required by Section 480 of the Revenue and Taxation Code, the beneficiary is a transferee of real property by reason of death.

(c) For the purpose of giving the notice to the Director of Health Care Services provided for in Section 215, the beneficiary is a beneficiary of the transferor.

(d) The beneficiary is liable to the transferor's estate for prorated estate and generation-skipping transfer taxes to the extent provided in Division 10 (commencing with Section 20100). *(Added by Stats.2015, c. 293 (A.B.139), § 17, eff. Jan. 1, 2016.)*

Repeal

For repeal of Part 4, see Probate Code § 5600.

Law Revision Commission Comments

2015 Addition

Subdivision (a) of Section 5680 establishes that a beneficiary may record an affidavit of death of the transferor to effectuate the transfer. See Section 212 (recordation is prima facie evidence of death to extent it "identifies real property located in county, title to which is affected by death"). Subdivision (a) authorizes the named beneficiary to obtain a certified copy of the transferor's death certificate under Health and Safety Code Section 103526 for the purpose of effectuating the transfer by revocable TOD deed.

Subdivision (b) cross-references the duty imposed on the beneficiary to file a change of ownership statement with the country recorder or assessor within 150 days after the transferor's death. See Rev. & Tax. Code § 480.

Subdivision (c) cross-references the duty imposed on the beneficiary to give the Director of Health Services notice of the death of a transferor who has received Medi–Cal benefits. See Section 215.

Subdivision (d) is a specific application of Division 10 (commencing with Section 20100), relating to proration of taxes. The beneficiary of a nonprobate transfer, such as a revocable TOD deed, is liable for a pro rata share of estate and generation-skipping transfer taxes paid by the transferor's estate. See Sections 20100 *et seq.* (proration of estate tax), 20200 *et seq.* (proration of tax on generation-skipping transfer).

A beneficiary may disclaim the property under Section 275 (disclaimer). [36 Cal.L.Rev.Comm. Reports 103 (2006)].

§ 5682. Rights and protections of beneficiary same as distributee from estate; conditions

If both of the following conditions are satisfied, a person dealing with a beneficiary of a revocable transfer on death deed of real property shall have the same rights and protections as the person would have if the beneficiary had been named as a distributee of the property in an order for distribution of the transferor's estate that had become final:

(a) The person acted in good faith and for a valuable consideration.

(b) An affidavit of death was recorded for the property under Chapter 2 (commencing with Section 210) of Part 4 of Division 2. *(Added by Stats.2015, c. 293 (A.B.139), § 17, eff. Jan. 1, 2016.)*

Repeal

For repeal of Part 4, see Probate Code § 5600.

Law Revision Commission Comments

2015 Addition

Section 5682 is drawn from Section 13203(a) (affidavit procedure for real property of small value). [36 Cal.L.Rev.Comm. Reports 103 (2006)].

CHAPTER 5. CONTEST

Repeal

For repeal of Part 4, see Probate Code § 5600.

§ 5690. Action for disqualification of beneficiary; person who may file; county for proceedings; lis pendens

(a)(1) An action for the disqualification of a beneficiary under Part 3.7 (commencing with Section 21360) of Division 11 may be brought to contest the validity of a transfer of property by a revocable transfer on death deed.

(2) An action to contest the validity of a transfer of property by a revocable transfer on death deed may be filed by the transferor's personal representative or an interested person under Part 19 (commencing with Section 850) of Division 2.

(b) The proper county for a contest proceeding is the proper county for proceedings concerning administration of the transferor's estate, whether or not proceedings concerning administration of the transferor's estate have been commenced at the time of the contest.

(c) On commencement of a contest proceeding, the contestant may record a lis pendens in the county in which the revocable transfer on death deed is recorded. *(Added by Stats.2015, c. 293 (A.B.139), § 17, eff. Jan. 1, 2016.)*

Repeal

For repeal of Part 4, see Probate Code § 5600.

Law Revision Commission Comments

2015 Addition

Section 5690 incorporates the procedure of Sections 850–859, relating to a conveyance or transfer of property claimed to belong to a decedent or other person. A person adversely affected by a revocable TOD deed has standing to contest the transfer. *Cf.* Section 48 ("interested person" defined).

Grounds for contest may include but are not limited to lack of capacity of the transferor (Section 5620), improper execution or recordation (Sections 5624–5626), invalidating cause for consent to a transfer of community property (Section 5015), and transfer to a disqualified person (Section 21380). See also Section 5696 (fraud, undue influence, duress, mistake, or other invalidating cause).

The proper county for proceedings for administration of a decedent's estate is the county of the decedent's domicile or, in the case of a nondomiciliary, the county of the decedent's death or, if the decedent died outside the state, where property of the decedent is located. Prob. Code §§ 7051, 7052.

Recordation of a lis pendens within 120 days after the transferor's death preserves remedies for the contestant. See Section 5694 (remedies). [44 Cal.L.Rev.Comm. Reports 573 (2015) [2015–16 AR Appx. 5]]

§ 5692. Time for commencing action; accrual of limitations period

(a) A contest proceeding pursuant to Section 5690 shall not be commenced before the transferor's death.

(b) For the purposes of the applicable limitations period, a contest proceeding accrues on the date of the transferor's death. *(Added by Stats.2015, c. 293 (A.B.139), § 17, eff. Jan. 1, 2016.)*

Repeal

For repeal of Part 4, see Probate Code § 5600.

Law Revision Commission Comments

2015 Addition

Subdivision (a) of Section 5692 limits the contest of a revocable TOD deed to a post-death challenge. A challenge before the transferor's death would be premature since a revocable TOD deed may be revoked at any time before the transfer occurs by reason of the transferor's death. However, the transferor's conservator may seek to revoke a revocable TOD deed pursuant to substituted judgment principles. See Section 5630 (revocability) & Comment and Section 5696(b); see also Sections 2580–2586 (substituted judgment).

Subdivision (b) provides that the limitations period for contesting a TOD deed commences on the transferor's death. [44 Cal.L.Rev. Comm. Reports 573 (2015) [2015–16 AR Appx. 5]]

§ 5694. Determination of invalid transfer; relief

If the court in a contest proceeding determines that a transfer of property by a revocable transfer on death deed is invalid, the court shall order the following relief:

(a) If the proceeding was commenced and a lis pendens was recorded within 120 days after the transferor's death, the court shall void the deed and order transfer of the property to the person entitled to it.

(b) If the proceeding was not commenced and a lis pendens was not recorded within 120 days after the transferor's death, the court shall grant appropriate relief but the court order shall not affect the rights in the property of a purchaser or encumbrancer for value and in good faith acquired before commencement of the proceeding and recordation of a lis pendens. *(Added by Stats.2015, c. 293 (A.B.139), § 17, eff. Jan. 1, 2016.)*

Repeal

For repeal of Part 4, see Probate Code § 5600.

Law Revision Commission Comments

2015 Addition

The 120–day period under Section 5694 represents a balance between the 40–day period applicable to disposition of an estate without administration under Sections 13100 (affidavit procedure for collection or transfer of personal property) and 13151 (court order determining succession to property), and the six month period applicable to the affidavit procedure for real property of small value

under Section 13200. [44 Cal.L.Rev.Comm. Reports 573 (2015) [2015–16 AR Appx. 5]]

§ 5696. Fraud, undue influence, duress, mistake, or other invalidating causes; petition by conservator or guardian of transferor

(a) Nothing in this chapter limits the application of principles of fraud, undue influence, duress, mistake, or other invalidating cause to a transfer of property by a revocable transfer on death deed.

(b) Notwithstanding subdivision (a) of Section 5692, the conservator or guardian of a transferor may, before the transferor's death, petition the court for invalidation of a revocable transfer on death deed executed by the transferor. *(Added by Stats.2015, c. 293 (A.B.139), § 17, eff. Jan. 1, 2016.)*

Repeal

For repeal of Part 4, see Probate Code § 5600.

Law Revision Commission Comments

2015 Addition

Subdivision (a) of Section 5696 is drawn from Section 5015 (nonprobate transfer of community property).

Subdivision (b) is new. [44 Cal.L.Rev.Comm. Reports 573 (2015) [2015–16 AR Appx. 5]]

Part 5

GIFTS IN VIEW OF IMPENDING DEATH

Section
5700. Gift defined.
5701. Application of general law of gifts.
5702. Gift in view of impending death defined.
5703. Presumption of gift in view of impending death.
5704. Revocation of gift in view of impending death.
5705. Rights of creditors of the giver.

§ 5700. Gift defined

As used in this part, "gift" means a transfer of personal property made voluntarily and without consideration. *(Added by Stats.1991, c. 1055 (S.B.271), § 18.)*

Law Revision Commission Comments

1991 Addition

Section 5700 continues the effect of prior law, when the provisions relating to gifts in view of impending death were located in the Civil Code. As defined in Section 5700, "gift" has the same meaning as defined in Section 1146 of the Civil Code. [20 Cal.L.Rev.Comm.Reports 2869 (1990)].

§ 5701. Application of general law of gifts

Except as provided in this part, a gift in view of impending death is subject to the general law relating to gifts of personal property. *(Added by Stats.1991, c. 1055 (S.B.271), § 18.)*

Law Revision Commission Comments

1991 Addition

Section 5701 codifies case law. See 4 B. Witkin, Summary of California Law *Personal Property* § 109, at 100–01 (9th ed. 1987). See also Civil Code §§ 1146–1148 (gifts of personal property).

The same essentials of intent, delivery, and acceptance apply to a gift in view of impending death as to gifts of personal property generally. 4 B. Witkin, *supra.* Thus, for example, a verbal gift is not valid unless the means of obtaining possession and control of the property are given, or, if the property is capable of delivery, unless there is actual, constructive, or symbolic delivery of the property to the donee. See Civil Code § 1147. [20 Cal.L.Rev.Comm.Reports 2869 (1990)].

Cross References

Gift defined for purposes of this Part, see Probate Code § 5700. Gift in view of impending death, see Probate Code § 5702.

§ 5702.   Gift in view of impending death defined

(a) A gift in view of impending death is one which is made in contemplation, fear, or peril of impending death, whether from illness or other cause, and with intent that it shall be revoked if the giver recovers from the illness or escapes from the peril.

(b) A reference in a statute to a gift in view of death means a gift in view of impending death. *(Added by Stats.1991, c. 1055 (S.B.271), § 18.)*

Law Revision Commission Comments

1991 Addition

Subdivision (a) of Section 5702 continues the substance of former Section 1149 of the Civil Code, with two exceptions:

(1) Section 5702 is phrased in terms of condition subsequent rather than condition precedent. If the giver intends the gift to become absolute only upon the giver's death, with title passing at the instant of death (condition precedent), the gift is testamentary. J. Cribbett & C. Johnson, Principles of the Law of Property 156 (3d ed. 1989). In such cases, the courts hold the attempted gift in view of death to be ineffective, and the property must be restored to the decedent's estate. See Yates v. Dundas, 80 Cal.App.2d 468, 182 P.2d 305 (1947). If the condition is subsequent, with the donee's title vesting immediately on delivery, subject to revocation if the giver survives the peril, the gift is not testamentary and can be sustained. J. Cribbett & C. Johnson, *supra;* see Yates v. Dundas, *supra.*

(2) Section 5702 changes the terminology to refer to a gift in view of "impending" death, and to define such a gift as one made in contemplation, fear, or peril of "impending" death. This codifies case law. See, e.g., Rosenberg v. Broy, 190 Cal.App.2d 591, 598, 12 Cal.Rptr. 103 (1961); 4 B. Witkin, Summary of California Law *Personal Property* § 108, at 100 (9th ed. 1987). This negates a possible construction that such a gift is any gift made in contemplation of death, whether imminent or remote, such as a gift to reduce estate taxes or to avoid probate. *Cf. In re* Estate of Pauson, 186 Cal. 358, 199 P. 331 (1921) (construing inheritance tax law).

Subdivision (b) is new.

A gift in view of impending death of community or quasi-community property is subject to the rights of the giver's spouse. See Civil Code § 5125; Prob.Code §§ 100–102.

To make an effective gift in view of impending death, the giver must have legal capacity. LaMar v. Bank of America Nat'l Trust & Sav. Ass'n, 218 Cal. 252, 22 P.2d 689 (1933); see Larsen v. Van Dieken, 34 Cal.App.2d 352, 93 P.2d 563 (1939).

A gift in view of impending death is not nullified because the giver dies by suicide. Berl v. Rosenberg, 169 Cal.App.2d 125, 130, 336 P.2d 975 (1959). [20 Cal.L.Rev.Comm.Reports 2869 (1990)].

Cross References

Gift defined for purposes of this Part, see Probate Code § 5700.

§ 5703.   Presumption of gift in view of impending death

A gift made during the last illness of the giver, or under circumstances which would naturally impress the giver with an expectation of speedy death, is presumed to be a gift in view of impending death. *(Added by Stats.1991, c. 1055 (S.B.271), § 18.)*

Law Revision Commission Comments

1991 Addition

Section 5703 continues the substance of former Section 1150 of the Civil Code. [20 Cal.L.Rev.Comm.Reports 2869 (1990)].

Cross References

Gift defined for purposes of this Part, see Probate Code § 5700. Gift in view of impending death, see Probate Code § 5702.

§ 5704.   Revocation of gift in view of impending death

(a) A gift in view of impending death is revoked by:

(1) The giver's recovery from the illness, or escape from the peril, under the presence of which it was made.

(2) The death of the donee before the death of the giver.

(b) A gift in view of impending death may be revoked by:

(1) The giver at any time.

(2) The giver's will if the will expresses an intention to revoke the gift.

(c) A gift in view of impending death is not affected by a previous will of the giver.

(d) Notwithstanding subdivisions (a) and (b), when the gift has been delivered to the donee, the rights of a purchaser or encumbrancer, acting before the revocation in good faith, for a valuable consideration, and without knowledge of the conditional nature of the gift, are not affected by the revocation. *(Added by Stats.1991, c. 1055 (S.B.271), § 18.)*

Law Revision Commission Comments

1991 Addition

Section 5704 continues the substance of former Sections 1151 and 1152 of the Civil Code, with three exceptions:

(1) The provision in former Section 1151 of the Civil Code that a gift in view of death is revoked by the occurrence of an event which would operate as a revocation of a will made at the same time is not continued.

(2) Paragraph (2) of subdivision (a) (revocation by death of donee) is new and codifies the case law rule of other U.S. jurisdictions. See 38 Am.Jur.2d *Gifts* § 90, at 889 (1968).

(3) The protection in subdivision (d) for an encumbrancer is new. The language "in good faith, for a valuable consideration, and without knowledge of the conditional nature of the gift" replaces the former reference to one who is "bona fide"; this change is nonsubstantive. [20 Cal.L.Rev.Comm.Reports 2869 (1990)].

Cross References

Gift defined for purposes of this Part, see Probate Code § 5700. Gift in view of impending death, see Probate Code § 5702.

§ 5705.   Rights of creditors of the giver

A gift in view of impending death is subject to Section 9653. *(Added by Stats.1991, c. 1055 (S.B.271), § 18.)*

Law Revision Commission Comments
1991 Addition

Section 5705 continues the substance of former Section 1153 of the Civil Code. [20 Cal.L.Rev.Comm.Reports 2869 (1990)].

Cross References

Gift defined for purposes of this Part, see Probate Code § 5700.
Gift in view of impending death, see Probate Code § 5702.

Division 6

WILLS AND INTESTATE SUCCESSION

Part 1

WILLS

Law Revision Commission Comments

1990 Enactment

This part supersedes Part 1 (commencing with Section 6100) of Division 6 the repealed Probate Code. The superseded part was enacted upon recommendation of the California Law Revision Commission. See Tentative Recommendation Relating to Wills and Intestate Succession, 16 Cal.L.Revision Comm'n Reports 2301 (1982). See also Report of Senate Committee on Judiciary on Assembly Bills 25 and 68, 17 Cal.L. Revision Comm'n Reports 867, 870–79 (1984). [20 Cal.L.Rev.Comm.Reports 1001 (1990)].

CHAPTER 1. GENERAL PROVISIONS

Application

Chapter 1 applicable where testator died on or after Jan. 1, 1985. For provisions applicable where testator died before Jan. 1, 1985, see Probate Code § 6103.

Cross References

Application of old and new law, see Probate Code § 3.

§ 6100. Persons who may make will

(a) An individual 18 or more years of age who is of sound mind may make a will.

(b) A conservator may make a will for the conservatee if the conservator has been so authorized by a court order pursuant to Section 2580. Nothing in this section shall impair the right of a conservatee who is mentally competent to make a will from revoking or amending a will made by the conservator or making a new and inconsistent will. *(Stats. 1990, c. 79 (A.B.759), § 14, operative July 1, 1991. Amended by Stats.1995, c. 730 (A.B.1466), § 7.)*

Law Revision Commission Comments

1990 Enactment

Section 6100 continues Section 6100 of the repealed Probate Code without change. This section is the same in substance as Section 2–501 of the Uniform Probate Code (1987). An emancipated minor is considered as being over the age of majority for the purpose of making or revoking a will. See Civil Code § 63. As to persons not mentally competent to make a will, see Section 6100.5. Section 6100 does not apply if the testator before January 1, 1985. See Section 6103. As to the application of any amendments made after that date, see Section 3.

Background on Section 6100 of Repealed Code

Section 6100 was added by 1983 Cal.Stat. ch. 842 § 55. The section continued the substance of a portion of the first sentence of former Probate Code Section 20 (repealed by 1983 Cal.Stat. ch. 842 § 18) and a portion of former Probate Code Section 21 (repealed by 1983 Cal.Stat. ch. 842 § 18). For background on the provisions of this part, see the Comment to this part under the part heading. [20 Cal.L.Rev.Comm.Reports 1001 (1990)].

Cross References

Civil death, capacity to make will, see Penal Code § 2601.
Joint or mutual wills, foreign wills, validity, see Probate Code §§ 6113, 12510, 12511.
Persons of unsound mind adjudged incapable powers establishment of conservatorship, see Civil Code § 40.

§ 6100.5. Persons not mentally competent to make a will; specified circumstances

(a) An individual is not mentally competent to make a will if at the time of making the will either of the following is true:

(1) The individual does not have sufficient mental capacity to be able to (A) understand the nature of the testamentary act, (B) understand and recollect the nature and situation of the individual's property, or (C) remember and understand the individual's relations to living descendants, spouse, and parents, and those whose interests are affected by the will.

(2) The individual suffers from a mental disorder with symptoms including delusions or hallucinations, which delusions or hallucinations result in the individual's devising property in a way which, except for the existence of the delusions or hallucinations, the individual would not have done.

(b) Nothing in this section supersedes existing law relating to the admissibility of evidence to prove the existence of mental incompetence or mental disorders.

(c) Notwithstanding subdivision (a), a conservator may make a will on behalf of a conservatee if the conservator has been so authorized by a court order pursuant to Section 2580. *(Stats.1990, c. 79 (A.B.759), § 14, operative July 1, 1991. Amended by Stats.1995, c. 730 (A.B.1466), § 8.)*

Law Revision Commission Comments

1990 Enactment

Section 6100.5 continues Section 6100.5 of the repealed Probate Code without substantive change.

Background on Section 6100.5 of Repealed Code

Section 6100.5 was a new provision added by 1985 Cal.Stat. ch. 940 § 1. [20 Cal.L.Rev.Comm.Reports 1001 (1990)].

§ 6101. Property which may be disposed of by will

A will may dispose of the following property:

(a) The testator's separate property.

(b) The one-half of the community property that belongs to the testator under Section 100.

(c) The one-half of the testator's quasi-community property that belongs to the testator under Section 101. *(Stats.1990, c. 79 (A.B.759), § 14, operative July 1, 1991.)*

Law Revision Commission Comments

1990 Enactment

Section 6101 continues Section 6101 of the repealed Probate Code without change. This section does not apply if the testator died before January 1, 1985. See Section 6103. As to the application of any amendments made after that date, see Section 3. For background on this section, see Recommendation and Study Relating to Rights of Surviving Spouse in Property Acquired by Decedent While Domiciled Elsewhere, 1 Cal.L. Revision Comm'n Reports E–1 (1957); Recommendation and Study Relating to Inter Vivos Marital Property Rights in Property Acquired While Domiciled Elsewhere, 3 Cal.L.Revision Comm'n Reports I–1 (1961); Recommendation Relating to Quasi–Community Property, 9 Cal.L. Revision Comm'n Reports 113 (1969).

Background on Section 6101 of Repealed Code

Section 6101 was added by 1983 Cal.Stat. ch. 842 § 55. Subdivision (a) continued a portion of the first sentence of former Probate Code Section 20 (repealed by 1983 Cal.Stat. ch. 842 § 18). Subdivision (b) continued a portion of former Probate Code Sections 21 (repealed by 1983 Cal.Stat. ch. 842 § 18) and 201 (repealed by 1983 Cal.Stat. ch. 842 § 19). Subdivision (c) continued a portion of former Probate Code Section 201.5 (repealed by 1983 Cal.Stat. ch. 842 § 19). For background on the provisions of this part, see the Comment to this part under the part heading. [20 Cal.L.Rev.Comm.Reports 1001 (1990)].

Cross References

Quasi-community property, defined, see Family Code § 125.
Separate property, damages for personal injuries, see Family Code § 781.

§ 6102. Persons to whom will may dispose of property

A will may make a disposition of property to any person, including but not limited to any of the following:

(a) An individual.

(b) A corporation.

(c) An unincorporated association, society, lodge, or any branch thereof.

(d) A county, city, city and county, or any municipal corporation.

(e) Any state, including this state.

(f) The United States or any instrumentality thereof.

(g) A foreign country or a governmental entity therein. *(Stats.1990, c. 79 (A.B.759), § 14, operative July 1, 1991.)*

Law Revision Commission Comments

1990 Enactment

Section 6102 continues Section 6102 of the repealed Probate Code without change. This section does not apply if the testator died before January 1, 1985. See Section 6103. As to the application of any amendments made after that date, see Section 3. For other provisions authorizing various entities to accept testamentary gifts, see, e.g., Cal. Const. art. 9, § 9 (University of California); Cal. Const. art. 20, § 2 (Stanford University and Huntington Library); Corp. Code § 10403 (corporation for prevention of cruelty to children or animals); Educ.Code §§ 19174 (county library), 33332 (State Department of Education), 70028 (California Maritime Academy); Harb. & Nav.Code §§ 6074 (harbor district), 6294 (port district), 6894 (river port district); Health & Safety Code §§ 8985, 9000 (public cemetery district), 32121 (hospital district); Pub.Res.Code §§ 5101 (monuments in memory of California pioneers), 5158, 5196 (park commissioners). See also Gov't Code §§ 11005, 11005.1 ("gifts" to state or state agency).

Background on Section 6102 of Repealed Code

Section 6102 was added by 1983 Cal.Stat. ch. 842 § 55. The section continued the substance of former Probate Code Section 27 (repealed by 1983 Cal.Stat. ch. 842 § 18), but omitted the obsolete reference in the former section to repealed provisions (former Sections 259–259.2). For background on the provisions of this part, see the Comment to this part under the part heading. [20 Cal.L.Rev.Comm.Reports 1001 (1990)].

§ 6103. Application of certain chapters

Except as otherwise specifically provided, Chapter 1 (commencing with Section 6100), Chapter 2 (commencing with Section 6110), Chapter 3 (commencing with Section 6120), Chapter 4 (commencing with Section 6130), Chapter 6 (commencing with Section 6200), and Chapter 7 (commencing with Section 6300) of this division, and Part 1 (commencing with Section 21101) of Division 11, do not apply where the testator died before January 1, 1985, and the law applicable prior to January 1, 1985, continues to apply where the testator died before January 1, 1985. *(Stats.1990, c. 79 (A.B.759), § 14, operative July 1, 1991. Amended by Stats. 2002, c. 138 (A.B.1784), § 6.)*

Law Revision Commission Comments

1990 Enactment

Section 6103 continues Section 6103 of the repealed Probate Code without substantive change. Section 6103 limits the application of Sections 6100–6303 in cases where the testator died before January 1, 1985, the operative date of those sections. As to the application of any amendments made after that date, see Section 3. For instances where the transitional rule is otherwise specifically provided, see Sections 6122, 6226, and 6247.

2002 Amendment

Section 6103 is amended to correct a cross-reference. Former Chapter 5 (rules of construction of wills) has been repealed and is superseded by Sections 21101–21140 (rules for interpretation of instruments). [31 Cal.L.Rev.Comm. Reports 220 (2001)].

Background on Section 6103 of Repealed Code

Section 6103 was a new provision added by 1984 Cal.Stat. ch. 892 § 21.7. See Recommendation Relating to Revision of Wills and Intestate Succession Law, 17 Cal.L. Revision Comm'n Reports 537 (1984). See also Communication of Law Revision Commission Concerning Assembly Bill 2290, 18 Cal.L. Revision Comm'n Reports 77, 85 (1986). [20 Cal.L.Rev.Comm.Reports 1001 (1990)].

§ 6104. Duress, menace, fraud, or undue influence; effect on execution or revocation

The execution or revocation of a will or a part of a will is ineffective to the extent the execution or revocation was procured by duress, menace, fraud, or undue influence. *(Stats.1990, c. 79 (A.B.759), § 14, operative July 1, 1991.)*

Law Revision Commission Comments

1990 Enactment

Section 6104 continues Section 6104 of the repealed Probate Code without change.

Background on Section 6104 of Repealed Code

Section 6104 was added by 1988 Cal.Stat. ch. 1199 § 74. The section restated former Probate Code Section 328.3 (added by 1983 Cal.Stat. ch. 842 § 26 and repealed by 1988 Cal.Stat. ch. 1199 § 40) without substantive change. For background on the provisions of this part, see the Comment to this part under the part heading. See also Comments to Conforming Revisions and Repeals, 19 Cal.L.Revision Comm'n Reports 1031, 1089 (1988). [20 Cal.L.Rev.Comm.Reports 1001 (1990)].

Cross References

Duress,
Generally, see Civil Code § 1569.
Fraud and mistake, rescission of contract, see Civil Code §§ 1689, 1690.
Fraud and undue influence, annulment of marriage, see Family Code § 2210.
Fraud and undue influence, extortion, see Penal Code § 518 et seq.
Fraud and undue influence, issues triable by and waiver of jury, see Probate Code § 8252.
Fraud and undue influence, reality or freedom of consent; causes for defeating, see Civil Code § 1567.
Undue influence, restoration of thing wrongfully acquired, see Civil Code §§ 1712, 1713.
Fraud,
Generally, see Civil Code § 1571 et seq.
Contracts exempting responsibility for fraud, contrary to policy of law, see Civil Code § 1668.
Damages, see Civil Code §§ 1709, 3288, 3294.
Deceit, see Civil Code § 1709 et seq.
Fraudulent instruments and transfers, see Civil Code § 3439 et seq.
Impeaching judgment for fraud, see Code of Civil Procedure § 1916.
Insurance contracts, concealment, see Insurance Code § 330 et seq.
Intent to defraud, see Penal Code § 8.
Interpretation of contract failing to express intent through fraud, see Civil Code § 1640.
Limitation of actions for relief on ground of fraud, see Code of Civil Procedure § 338.
Parol evidence to establish fraud, see Code of Civil Procedure § 1856.
Revision of contract for fraud, see Civil Code § 3399 et seq.
Specific performance barred by fraud, see Civil Code § 3391.
Statute of frauds, see Civil Code §§ 1623, 1624.

Menace, see Civil Code § 1570.
Undue influence,
Generally, see Civil Code § 1575.
Consent obtained by undue influence, see Civil Code § 1567.
Presumption of undue influence in transactions between trustee and beneficiary, see Probate Code § 16004.

§ 6105. Conditional validity

A will, the validity of which is made conditional by its own terms, shall be admitted to probate or rejected, or denied effect after admission to probate, in conformity with the condition. *(Stats.1990, c. 79 (A.B.759), § 14, operative July 1, 1991.)*

Law Revision Commission Comments

1990 Enactment

Section 6105 continues Section 6105 of the repealed Probate Code without change.

Background on Section 6105 of Repealed Code

Section 6105 was added by 1988 Cal.Stat. ch. 1199 § 74.5. The section restated former Probate Code Section 328.7 (added by 1983 Cal.Stat. ch. 842 § 27 and repealed by 1988 Cal.Stat. ch. 1199 § 40) without substantive change. For background on the provisions of this part, see the Comment to this part under the part heading. See also Comments to Conforming Revisions and Repeals, 19 Cal.L. Revision Comm'n Reports 1031, 1089 (1988). [20 Cal.L.Rev.Comm.Reports 1001 (1990)].

CHAPTER 2. EXECUTION OF WILLS

Section
6110. Necessity of writing; other requirements.
6111. Holographic wills; requirements.
6111.5. Extrinsic evidence; admissibility.
6112. Witnesses; interested witnesses.
6113. Validity; execution.

Application

Chapter 2 applicable where testator died on or after Jan. 1, 1985. For provisions applicable where testator died before Jan. 1, 1985, see Probate Code § 6103.

§ 6110. Necessity of writing; other requirements

(a) Except as provided in this part, a will shall be in writing and satisfy the requirements of this section.

(b) The will shall be signed by one of the following:

(1) By the testator.

(2) In the testator's name by some other person in the testator's presence and by the testator's direction.

(3) By a conservator pursuant to a court order to make a will under Section 2580.

(c)(1) Except as provided in paragraph (2), the will shall be witnessed by being signed, during the testator's lifetime, by at least two persons each of whom (A) being present at the same time, witnessed either the signing of the will or the testator's acknowledgment of the signature or of the will and (B) understand that the instrument they sign is the testator's will.

(2) If a will was not executed in compliance with paragraph (1), the will shall be treated as if it was executed in compliance with that paragraph if the proponent of the will

establishes by clear and convincing evidence that, at the time the testator signed the will, the testator intended the will to constitute the testator's will. *(Stats.1990, c. 79 (A.B.759), § 14, operative July 1, 1991. Amended by Stats.1996, c. 563 (S.B.392), § 20; Stats.2008, c. 53 (A.B.2248), § 1.)*

Law Revision Commission Comments

1990 Enactment

Section 6110 continues Section 6110 of the repealed Probate Code without change. This section does not apply if the testator died before January 1, 1985. See Section 6103. As to the application of any amendments made after that date, see Section 3.

The signing or acknowledgment of the will must take place in the presence of the witnesses, present at the same time, but does not require that the witnesses sign in the presence of each other. This is consistent with prior law. See, e.g., In re Estate of Armstrong, 8 Cal.2d 204, 209–10, 64 P.2d 1093 (1937).

The witness must understand that the instrument being witnessed is a will. The witness may obtain the necessary understanding by any means. For example, the witness may know that the instrument is a will by examining the instrument itself or from the circumstances surrounding the execution of the will. Nothing in Section 6110 requires that the testator disclose the contents of the will.

The introductory clause of Section 6110 recognizes that the validity of the execution of a will may be determined pursuant to some other provision of this part. See Sections 6111 (holographic will), 6221 (California statutory will), 6381–6385 (international will). The will may be valid if its execution complies with the law of another place. See Section 6113. See also Sections 6112 (devise to a witness to the will), 8220 (proof of will).

Background on Section 6110 of Repealed Code

Section 6110 was added by 1983 Cal.Stat. ch. 842 § 55. The section superseded former Probate Code Section 50 (repealed by 1983 Cal.Stat. ch. 842 § 18). Section 6110 relaxed the formalities required under former Section 50 by eliminating the requirements (1) that the testator's signature be "at the end" of the will, (2) that the testator "declare" to the witnesses that the instrument is his or her will, (3) that the witnesses' signatures be "at the end" of the will, (4) that the testator "request" the witnesses to sign the will, and (5) that the witnesses sign the will in the testator's presence. Section 6110 continued the requirements of former Section 50 that (1) the will be in writing, (2) that the will be signed by the testator or by someone else who signs the testator's name in the testator's presence and by the testator's direction, (3) that the will be signed or the testator acknowledge the signature in the presence of two witnesses who are present at the same time, and (4) that the witnesses sign the will.

The requirement of subdivision (c)(2) of Section 6110 that the witness understand that the instrument being witnesses is a will replaced the former requirement that the testator "declare" to the witnesses that the instrument is his or her will. The new requirement codified California decisional law which did not apply the former declaration requirement literally and held the requirement satisfied if it is apparent from the testator's conduct and the surrounding circumstances that the instrument is a will. See 7 B. Witkin, Summary of California Law Wills and Probate § 118, at 5633–34 (8th ed. 1974).

For background on the provisions of this part, see the Comment to this part under the part heading. [20 Cal.L.Rev.Comm.Reports 1001 (1990)].

Cross References

Interested persons as witnesses, see Probate Code § 6112.
Statutory will, validity notwithstanding this section, see Probate Code § 6226.

Subscribing witnesses, production and examination of, see Probate Code § 8253.
Writing defined, see Civil Code § 14; Code of Civil Procedure § 17.

§ 6111. Holographic wills; requirements

(a) A will that does not comply with Section 6110 is valid as a holographic will, whether or not witnessed, if the signature and the material provisions are in the handwriting of the testator.

(b) If a holographic will does not contain a statement as to the date of its execution and:

(1) If the omission results in doubt as to whether its provisions or the inconsistent provisions of another will are controlling, the holographic will is invalid to the extent of the inconsistency unless the time of its execution is established to be after the date of execution of the other will.

(2) If it is established that the testator lacked testamentary capacity at any time during which the will might have been executed, the will is invalid unless it is established that it was executed at a time when the testator had testamentary capacity.

(c) Any statement of testamentary intent contained in a holographic will may be set forth either in the testator's own handwriting or as part of a commercially printed form will. *(Stats.1990, c. 79 (A.B.759), § 14, operative July 1, 1991. Amended by Stats.1990, c. 710 (S.B.1775), § 13, operative July 1, 1991.)*

Law Revision Commission Comments

1990 Enactment

Section 6111 continues Section 6111 of the repealed Probate Code without change. This section does not apply if the testator died before January 1, 1985. See Section 6103. As to the application of any amendments made after that date, see Section 3.

Subdivision (a) of Section 6111 is the same in substance as Section 2–503 of the Uniform Probate Code (1987). The Uniform Probate Code does not contain a provision comparable to subdivision (b) of Section 6111. As to the construction of provisions drawn from uniform acts, see Section 2.

Paragraph (1) of subdivision (b) is a clarifying provision designed to deal with the situation where the holographic will and another will have inconsistent provisions as to the same property or otherwise have inconsistent provisions. To deal specifically with this situation, paragraph (1) requires either that the holographic will be dated or that the time of its execution be shown to be after the date of execution of the other will. If the date of execution of the holographic will cannot be established by a date in the will or by other evidence to be after the date of execution of the other will, the holographic will is invalid to the extent that the date of its execution is material in resolving the issue of whether it or the other inconsistent will is to be given effect. Where the conflict between the holographic will and the other will is to only a portion of the property governed by the holographic will, the invalidity of the holographic will as to the property governed by the other will does not affect the validity of the holographic will as to other property. Paragraph (1) also covers the situation where both wills are holographic and undated and have inconsistent provisions on a particular matter; in such a case, Section 6111 applies to both wills. If it cannot be established that one of the holographic wills was executed after the other, neither will is valid insofar as the two wills are inconsistent; but, in such case, the validity of the consistent provisions of the two wills is not affected by the failure to establish time of execution.

Paragraph (2) of subdivision (b) applies to the situation where the testator lacked testamentary capacity at any time during which the holographic will might have been executed. Thus, if the testator lacks testamentary capacity at the time of his or her death and the holographic will is found with the testator's personal effects, the will is invalid unless it is established that the will was executed at a time when the testator did have testamentary capacity. This could be established, for example, by evidence of a person who saw the testator make the holographic will and can testify that the testator had testamentary capacity at that time. Likewise, where a testator lacked testamentary capacity for a period prior to death and the undated holographic will is found in the testator's safe deposit box, it could be established that the will was executed at a time when the testator did have testamentary capacity if it were shown that the testator did not have access to the safe deposit box at any time after the testator lost the capacity to execute a will. Paragraph (2) does not invalidate a holographic will if it could not have been executed at a time when the testator lacked testamentary capacity. For example, if the testator becomes ill and requires hospitalization, loses his or her testamentary capacity and dies during the hospitalization period, and the testator's holographic will is found at the testator's home, the will must have been executed before the testator's hospitalization and therefore at a time when the testator had testamentary capacity.

This section was enacted upon recommendation of the California Law Revision Commission. See Recommendation Relating to Holographic and Nuncupative Wills, 16 Cal.L. Revision Comm'n Reports 301 (1982).

1990 Amendment

Section 6111 (enacted as a part of the new Probate Code by 1990 Cal.Stat. ch. 79 § 14) was amended by 1990 Cal.Stat. ch. 710 § 13 to continue language added to the repealed Probate Code by 1990 Cal.Stat. ch. 263 § 1. [20 Cal.L.Rev.Comm.Reports 1001 (1990)].

Background on Section 6111 of Repealed Code

Section 6111 was added by 1983 Cal.Stat. ch. 842 § 55. The section continued former Probate Code Section 53 (repealed by 1983 Cal.Stat. ch. 842 § 18). For background on the provisions of this part, see the Comment to this part under the part heading. [20 Cal.L.Rev.Comm.Reports 1001 (1990)].

§ 6111.5. Extrinsic evidence; admissibility

Extrinsic evidence is admissible to determine whether a document constitutes a will pursuant to Section 6110 or 6111, or to determine the meaning of a will or a portion of a will if the meaning is unclear. *(Added by Stats.1990, c. 710 (S.B. 1775), § 14, operative July 1, 1991.)*

Law Revision Commission Comments

1990 Addition

Section 6111.5 was added to the new Probate Code by 1990 Cal.Stat. ch. 710 § 14. The section continues Section 6111.5 of the repealed Probate Code (added by 1990 Cal.Stat. ch. 263 § 2) without change. [20 Cal.L.Rev.Comm.Reports 1001 (1990)].

Cross References

Executor indicated but not specifically named, see Probate Code § 8421.

§ 6112. Witnesses; interested witnesses

(a) Any person generally competent to be a witness may act as a witness to a will.

(b) A will or any provision thereof is not invalid because the will is signed by an interested witness.

(c) Unless there are at least two other subscribing witnesses to the will who are disinterested witnesses, the fact that the will makes a devise to a subscribing witness creates a presumption that the witness procured the devise by duress, menace, fraud, or undue influence. This presumption is a presumption affecting the burden of proof. This presumption does not apply where the witness is a person to whom the devise is made solely in a fiduciary capacity.

(d) If a devise made by the will to an interested witness fails because the presumption established by subdivision (c) applies to the devise and the witness fails to rebut the presumption, the interested witness shall take such proportion of the devise made to the witness in the will as does not exceed the share of the estate which would be distributed to the witness if the will were not established. Nothing in this subdivision affects the law that applies where it is established that the witness procured a devise by duress, menace, fraud, or undue influence. *(Stats.1990, c. 79 (A.B.759), § 14, operative July 1, 1991.)*

Law Revision Commission Comments

1990 Enactment

Section 6112 continues Section 6112 of the repealed Probate Code without substantive change. See also Section 76 ("subscribing witness" defined).

Subdivision (a) and the first sentence of subdivision (b) of Section 6112 are the same as Section 2–505 of the Uniform Probate Code (1987). As to the construction of provisions drawn from uniform acts, see Section 2. Section 6112 does not apply if the testator died before January 1, 1985. See Section 6103. As to the application of any amendments made after that date, see Section 3.

Section 6112 does not continue the pre–1983 rule that disqualified a subscribing witness from taking a share under the will larger than his or her intestate share unless there were two other disinterested subscribing witnesses. Under Section 6112, a witness may take under the will if the witness satisfies the burden of proving that the devise was not procured by duress, menace, fraud, or undue influence. The presumption of duress, menace, fraud, or undue influence established by Section 6112 only applies to the devise to the witness, and the presumption does not apply if there are two other witnesses to the will who are disinterested witnesses. See also Section 6104 (execution or revocation procured by duress, menace, fraud, or undue influence).

Where the will is witnessed by a person to whom a devise is made in a fiduciary capacity, under subdivision (c) the presumption of undue influence does not apply. Even though fraud or undue influence is not presumed in such a case, it may still be proven as a question of fact. See new subdivision (d) (last sentence).

If the witness fails to meet the burden of overcoming the presumption and the devise to that witness is not inconsistent with, and can be separated from, the remainder of the will, only the devise to the witness fails and not the entire will. In re Estate of Carson, 184 Cal. 437, 441, 194 P. 5 (1920); Estate of Molera, 23 Cal.App.3d 993, 1001, 100 Cal.Rptr. 696 (1972); Estate of Stauffer, 142 Cal.App.2d 35, 41, 297 P.2d 1029 (1956); In re Estate of Webster, 43 Cal.App.2d 6, 15–16, 110 P.2d 81 (1941).

Background on Section 6112 of Repealed Code

Section 6112 was added by 1983 Cal.Stat. ch. 842 § 55 and was amended by 1984 Cal.Stat. ch. 892 § 22, 1988 Cal.Stat. ch. 1199 § 75, and 1989 Cal.Stat. ch. 544 § 4. The section superseded former Probate Code Sections 51 and 52 (sections repealed by 1983 Cal.Stat. ch. 842 § 18). For background on the provisions of this part, see the Comment to this part under the part heading.

The 1984 amendment limited the scope of subdivision (b) and added subdivision (c) which continued the substance of a portion of former Probate Code Section 51. See Recommendation Relating to Revision of Wills and Intestate Succession Law, 17 Cal.L. Revision Comm'n Reports 537 (1984). See also Communication of Law Revision Commission Concerning Assembly Bill 2290, 18 Cal.L. Revision Comm'n 77, 86 (1986).

The 1988 amendment added subdivision (d) which restated former Probate Code Section 372.5 (added by 1983 Cal.Stat. ch. 842 § 30, amended by 1984 Cal.Stat. ch. 892 § 18, and repealed by 1988 Cal.Stat. ch. 1199 § 42) without substantive change. As to the 1988 amendment, see Comments to Conforming Revisions and Repeals, 19 Cal.L. Revision Comm'n Reports 1031, 1089 (1988).

The 1989 amendment revised subdivision (c) to make clear that, where the will is witnessed by a person to whom a devise is made in a fiduciary capacity, the presumption of undue influence does not apply. The references to a "subscribing" witness were deleted from subdivision (c) in recognition of the fact that a will need not be signed at the end. Former subdivision (d), relating to no contest clauses, was deleted and the matter dealt with comprehensively in Sections 21300 to 21307. See Recommendation Relating to No Contest Clauses, 20 Cal.L. Revision Comm'n Reports 7 (1990); see also Communication from the California Law Revision Commission Concerning Assembly Bill 158, 20 Cal.L. Revision Comm'n Reports 235 (1990). [20 Cal.L.Rev.Comm.Reports 1001 (1990)].

Cross References

Burden of proof, generally, see Evidence Code § 500 et seq.

§ 6113. Validity; execution

A written will is validly executed if its execution complies with any of the following:

(a) The will is executed in compliance with Section 6110 or 6111 or Chapter 6 (commencing with Section 6200) (California statutory will) or Chapter 11 (commencing with Section 6380) (Uniform International Wills Act).

(b) The execution of the will complies with the law at the time of execution of the place where the will is executed.

(c) The execution of the will complies with the law of the place where at the time of execution or at the time of death the testator is domiciled, has a place of abode, or is a national. *(Stats.1990, c. 79 (A.B.759), § 14, operative July 1, 1991.)*

Law Revision Commission Comments

1990 Enactment

Section 6113 continues Section 6113 of the repealed Probate Code without substantive change. This section applies whether or not the will was executed in California. This section does not apply if the testator died before January 1, 1985. See Section 6103. As to the application of any amendments made after that date, see Section 3.

Section 6113 is the same in substance as Section 2–506 of the Uniform Probate Code (1987). The references to the provisions relating to California statutory wills and international wills are added to the Uniform Probate Code provision. As to the construction of provisions drawn from uniform acts, see Section 2.

Background on Section 6113 of Repealed Code

Section 6113 was added by 1983 Cal.Stat. ch. 842 § 55. The section superseded former Probate Code Section 26 (repealed by 1983 Cal.Stat. ch. 842 § 18). Former Section 26 applied only where a will executed outside California was offered for probate in California; Section 6113 applied whether or not the will was executed in California. For background on the provisions of this part, see the Comment to this part under the part heading. [20 Cal.L.Rev.Comm.Reports 1001 (1990)].

Cross References

Foreign wills, probate of, see Probate Code §§ 12510, 12511.

CHAPTER 3.　REVOCATION AND REVIVAL

Section

Application

Chapter 3 applicable where testator died on or after Jan. 1, 1985. For provisions applicable where testator died before Jan. 1, 1985, see Probate Code § 6103.

§ 6120.　Acts constituting revocation

A will or any part thereof is revoked by any of the following:

(a) A subsequent will which revokes the prior will or part expressly or by inconsistency.

(b) Being burned, torn, canceled, obliterated, or destroyed, with the intent and for the purpose of revoking it, by either (1) the testator or (2) another person in the testator's presence and by the testator's direction. *(Stats.1990, c. 79 (A.B.759), § 14, operative July 1, 1991.)*

Law Revision Commission Comments

1990 Enactment

Section 6120 continues Section 6120 of the repealed Probate Code without change. This section is the same in substance as Section 2–507 of the Uniform Probate Code (1987). As to the construction of provisions drawn from uniform acts, see Section 2. This section does not apply if the testator died before January 1, 1985. See Section 6103. As to the application of any amendments made after that date, see Section 3.

Background on Section 6120 of Repealed Code

Section 6120 was added by 1983 Cal.Stat. ch. 842 § 55. The section superseded former Probate Code Sections 72 and 74 (sections repealed by 1983 Cal.Stat. ch. 842 § 18). The provision of former Section 74 requiring two witnesses to prove revocation of a will by someone other than the testator was not continued. Section 6120 otherwise was consistent with former Sections 72 and 74. For background on the provisions of this part, see the Comment to this part under the part heading. [20 Cal.L.Rev.Comm.Reports 1001 (1990)].

Cross References

Revocation of probate, see Probate Code §§ 8271, 8272.

Revocation procured by duress, menace, fraud or undue influence may be declared void, see Probate Code § 6104.

§ 6121. Duplicates

A will executed in duplicate or any part thereof is revoked if one of the duplicates is burned, torn, canceled, obliterated, or destroyed, with the intent and for the purpose of revoking it, by either (1) the testator or (2) another person in the testator's presence and by the testator's direction. *(Stats. 1990, c. 79 (A.B.759), § 14, operative July 1, 1991.)*

Law Revision Commission Comments
1990 Enactment

Section 6121 continues Section 6121 of the repealed Probate Code without change. This section does not apply if the testator died before January 1, 1985. See Section 6103. As to the application of any amendments made after that date, see Section 3.

Background on Section 6121 of Repealed Code

Section 6121 was added by 1983 Cal.Stat. ch. 842 § 55. The section continued the substance of former Probate Code Section 76 (repealed by 1983 Cal.Stat. ch. 842 § 18). For background on the provisions of this part, see the Comment to this part under the part heading. [20 Cal.L.Rev.Comm.Reports 1001 (1990)].

§ 6122. Dissolution or annulment of marriage; provisions revoked; other change in circumstances

(a) Unless the will expressly provides otherwise, if after executing a will the testator's marriage is dissolved or annulled, the dissolution or annulment revokes all of the following:

(1) Any disposition or appointment of property made by the will to the former spouse.

(2) Any provision of the will conferring a general or special power of appointment on the former spouse.

(3) Any provision of the will nominating the former spouse as executor, trustee, conservator, or guardian.

(b) If any disposition or other provision of a will is revoked solely by this section, it is revived by the testator's remarriage to the former spouse.

(c) In case of revocation by dissolution or annulment:

(1) Property prevented from passing to a former spouse because of the revocation passes as if the former spouse failed to survive the testator.

(2) Other provisions of the will conferring some power or office on the former spouse shall be interpreted as if the former spouse failed to survive the testator.

(d) For purposes of this section, dissolution or annulment means any dissolution or annulment which would exclude the spouse as a surviving spouse within the meaning of Section 78. A decree of legal separation which does not terminate the status of * * * spouses is not a dissolution for purposes of this section.

(e) Except as provided in Section 6122.1, no change of circumstances other than as described in this section revokes a will.

(f) Subdivisions (a) to (d), inclusive, do not apply to any case where the final judgment of dissolution or annulment of marriage occurs before January 1, 1985. That case is governed by the law in effect prior to January 1, 1985.

(Stats.1990, c. 79 (A.B.759), § 14, operative July 1, 1991. Amended by Stats.2001, c. 893 (A.B.25), § 50; Stats.2002, c. 664 (A.B.3034), § 179; Stats.2016, c. 50 (S.B.1005), § 86, eff. Jan. 1, 2017.)

Law Revision Commission Comments
1990 Enactment

Section 6122 continues Section 6122 of the repealed Probate Code without change. This section is the same in substance as Section 2–508 of the Uniform Probate Code (1987). As to the construction of provisions drawn from uniform acts, see Section 2. This section changed the former case law rule that dissolution or annulment of marriage had no effect on the will of either spouse. See In re Estate of Patterson, 64 Cal.App. 643, 646, 222 P. 374 (1923) cert. denied, 266 U.S. 594 (1925); 7 B. Witkin, Summary of California Law Wills and Probate § 150, at 5666 (8th ed. 1974). See also Section 36 ("dissolution of marriage" defined), Civil Code § 4352 (required notice in judgment of dissolution or nullity). For a comparable provision, see Section 6226 (California statutory will).

Subdivision (f) limits the application of subdivisions (a)–(d) to cases where the final judgment of dissolution or annulment of marriage occurs on or after the date this section of the repealed Probate Code first become operative.

Background on Section 6122 of Repealed Code

Section 6122 was added by 1983 Cal.Stat. ch. 842 § 55 and was amended by 1984 Cal.Stat. ch. 892 § 23. For background on the provisions of this part, see the Comment to this part under the part heading. The 1984 amendment added subdivision (f). See Communication of Law Revision Commission Concerning Assembly Bill 2290, 18 Cal.L.Revision Comm'n 77, 86 (1986). [20 Cal.L.Rev.Comm.Reports 1001 (1990)].

Cross References

Powers of appointment, generally, see Probate Code § 600 et seq.

§ 6122.1. Domestic partnership of testator; revocation by termination

(a) Unless the will expressly provides otherwise, if after executing a will the testator's domestic partnership is terminated, the termination revokes all of the following:

(1) Any disposition or appointment of property made by the will to the former domestic partner.

(2) Any provision of the will conferring a general or special power of appointment on the former domestic partner.

(3) Any provision of the will nominating the former domestic partner as executor, trustee, conservator, or guardian.

(b) If any disposition or other provision of a will is revoked solely by this section, it is revived by the testator establishing another domestic partnership with the former domestic partner.

(c) In case of revocation by termination of a domestic partnership:

(1) Property prevented from passing to a former domestic partner because of the revocation passes as if the former domestic partner failed to survive the testator.

(2) Other provisions of the will conferring some power or office on the former domestic partner shall be interpreted as if the former domestic partner failed to survive the testator.

(d) This section shall apply only to wills executed on or after January 1, 2002. *(Added by Stats.2001, c. 893 (A.B.25), § 51.)*

Application

For application of this section, see its terms.

§ 6123. Second will revoking first will; effect of revocation of second will

(a) If a second will which, had it remained effective at death, would have revoked the first will in whole or in part, is thereafter revoked by acts under Section 6120 or 6121, the first will is revoked in whole or in part unless it is evident from the circumstances of the revocation of the second will or from the testator's contemporary or subsequent declarations that the testator intended the first will to take effect as executed.

(b) If a second will which, had it remained effective at death, would have revoked the first will in whole or in part, is thereafter revoked by a third will, the first will is revoked in whole or in part, except to the extent it appears from the terms of the third will that the testator intended the first will to take effect. *(Stats.1990, c. 79 (A.B.759), § 14, operative July 1, 1991.)*

Law Revision Commission Comments

1990 Enactment

Section 6123 continues Section 6123 of the repealed Probate Code without change. This section is the same in substance as Section 2–509 of the Uniform Probate Code (1987). As to the construction of provisions drawn from uniform acts, see Section 2. This section does not apply if the testator died before January 1, 1985. See Section 6103. As to the application of any amendments made after that date, see Section 3.

Background on Section 6123 of Repealed Code

Section 6123 was added by 1983 Cal.Stat. ch. 842 § 55. The section superseded former Probate Code Section 75 (repealed by 1983 Cal.Stat. ch. 842 § 18). Section 6123 set forth a presumption against revival of a previously revoked will, the same as under former Section 75. However, unlike former Section 75, where revocation of the second will is by an act such as destruction, Section 6123 permitted the testator's intent that the first will be revived to be shown by extrinsic evidence, thus producing results generally more consistent with the testator's intent. For background on the provisions of this part, see the Comment to this part under the part heading. [20 Cal.L.Rev.Comm.Reports 1001 (1990)].

Cross References

Execution of wills, see Probate Code § 6110.
Revocation procured by duress, menace, fraud or undue influence may be declared void, see Probate Code § 6104.

§ 6124. Destruction of will with intent to revoke; presumption

If the testator's will was last in the testator's possession, the testator was competent until death, and neither the will nor a duplicate original of the will can be found after the testator's death, it is presumed that the testator destroyed the will with intent to revoke it. This presumption is a presumption affecting the burden of producing evidence. *(Stats.1990, c. 79 (A.B.759), § 14, operative July 1, 1991.)*

Law Revision Commission Comments

1990 Enactment

Section 6124 continues Section 6124 of the repealed Probate Code without change. This section codifies existing case law. See Estate of Obernolte, 91 Cal.App.3d 124, 153 Cal.Rptr. 798 (1979); 7 B. Witkin, Summary of California Law Wills and Probate § 381, at 5844 (8th ed. 1974). For a discussion of the showing required to overcome the case law presumption codified in Section 6124, see Estate of Moramarco, 86 Cal.App.2d 326, 194 P.2d 740 (1948); 7 B. Witkin, supra § 382, at 5845. The repeal of former Section 350 (repealed by 1983 Cal.Stat. ch. 842 § 28) (proof of lost or destroyed will) did not affect the case law presumption codified in Section 6124.

The presumption codified in Section 6124 does not apply if a duplicate original of the will is found after the testator's death. For example, if a duplicate original is in possession of the testator's attorney, it is less likely that the testator will preserve his or her duplicate original with the same care as if it were the only such instrument.

Background on Section 6124 of Repealed Code

Section 6124 was a new provision added by 1985 Cal.Stat. ch. 982 § 15.5. See Communication Concerning Assembly Bill 196, 18 Cal.L.Revision Comm'n Reports 367, 373 (1986). [20 Cal.L.Rev.Comm.Reports 1001 (1990)].

CHAPTER 4. REFERENCE TO MATTERS OUTSIDE THE WILL

Section
6130. Writing in existence at execution; incorporation by reference.
6131. References to acts and events.
6132. Writings that direct disposition of a testator's tangible personal property.

Application

Chapter 4 applicable where testator died on or after Jan. 1, 1985. For provisions applicable where testator died before Jan. 1, 1985, see Probate Code § 6103.

§ 6130. Writing in existence at execution; incorporation by reference

A writing in existence when a will is executed may be incorporated by reference if the language of the will manifests this intent and describes the writing sufficiently to permit its identification. *(Stats.1990, c. 79 (A.B.759), § 14, operative July 1, 1991.)*

Law Revision Commission Comments

1990 Enactment

Section 6130 continues Section 6130 of the repealed Probate Code without change. This section does not apply if the testator died before January 1, 1985. See Section 6103. As to the application of any amendments made after that date, see Section 3.

Section 6130 is the same as Section 2–510 of the Uniform Probate Code (1987). As to the construction of provisions drawn from uniform acts, see Section 2. Section 6130 codifies the doctrine of incorporation by reference which was recognized by prior California case law. See 7 B. Witkin, Summary of California Law Wills and Probate § 143, at 5660 (8th ed. 1974). The doctrine of incorporation by reference has been used, for example, to permit a validly executed will or codicil to incorporate by reference an earlier will which was defectively executed, and thereby to cure the defect of the former instrument. In re Estate of Plumel, 151 Cal. 77, 90 P. 192 (1907). See also Section 88 ("will" includes a codicil).

Section 6130 was a new provision added by 1983 Cal.Stat. ch. 842 § 55. For background on the provisions of this part, see the Comment to this part under the part heading. See also Communication of Law Revision Commission Concerning Assembly Bill 2290, 18 Cal.L.Revision Comm'n Reports 77, 86 (1986). [20 Cal.L.Rev.Comm.Reports 1001 (1990)].

Cross References

Will as including codicil, see Civil Code § 14.

§ 6131. References to acts and events

A will may dispose of property by reference to acts and events that have significance apart from their effect upon the dispositions made by the will, whether the acts and events occur before or after the execution of the will or before or after the testator's death. The execution or revocation of a will of another person is such an event. *(Stats.1990, c. 79 (A.B.759), § 14, operative July 1, 1991.)*

Law Revision Commission Comments

1990 Enactment

Section 6131 continues Section 6131 of the repealed Probate Code without change. This section is the same as Section 2–512 of the Uniform Probate Code (1987). As to the construction of provisions drawn from uniform acts, see Section 2. Section 6131 codifies the doctrine of acts and events of independent significance. See generally 7 B. Witkin, Summary of California Law Wills and Probate § 147, at 5662–63 (8th ed. 1974). The section does not apply if the testator died before January 1, 1985. See Section 6103. As to the application of any amendments made after that date, see Section 3.

Background on Section 6131 of Repealed Code

Section 6131 was a new provision added by 1983 Cal.Stat. ch. 842 § 55. For background on the provisions of this part, see the Comment to this part under the part heading. [20 Cal.L.Rev.Comm.Reports 1001 (1990)].

§ 6132. Writings that direct disposition of a testator's tangible personal property

(a) Notwithstanding any other provision, a will may refer to a writing that directs disposition of tangible personal property not otherwise specifically disposed of by the will, except for money that is common coin or currency and property used primarily in a trade or business. A writing directing disposition of a testator's tangible personal property is effective if all of the following conditions are satisfied:

(1) An unrevoked will refers to the writing.

(2) The writing is dated and is either in the handwriting of, or signed by, the testator.

(3) The writing describes the items and the recipients of the property with reasonable certainty.

(b) The failure of a writing to conform to the conditions described in paragraph (2) of subdivision (a) does not preclude the introduction of evidence of the existence of the testator's intent regarding the disposition of tangible personal property as authorized by this section.

(c) The writing may be written or signed before or after the execution of the will and need not have significance apart from its effect upon the dispositions of property made by the will. A writing that meets the requirements of this section shall be given effect as if it were actually contained in the will itself, except that if any person designated to receive property in the writing dies before the testator, the property shall pass as further directed in the writing and, in the absence of any further directions, the disposition shall lapse.

(d) The testator may make subsequent handwritten or signed changes to any writing. If there is an inconsistent disposition of tangible personal property as between writings, the most recent writing controls.

(e)(1) If the writing directing disposition of tangible personal property omits a statement as to the date of its execution, and if the omission results in doubt whether its provisions or the provisions of another writing inconsistent with it are controlling, then the writing omitting the statement is invalid to the extent of its inconsistency unless the time of its execution is established to be after the date of execution of the other writing.

(2) If the writing directing disposition of tangible personal property omits a statement as to the date of its execution, and it is established that the testator lacked testamentary capacity at any time during which the writing may have been executed, the writing is invalid unless it is established that it was executed at a time when the testator had testamentary capacity.

(f)(1) Concurrent with the filing of the inventory and appraisal required by Section 8800, the personal representative shall also file the writing that directs disposition of the testator's tangible personal property.

(2) Notwithstanding paragraph (1), if the writing has not been found or is not available at the time of the filing of the inventory and appraisal, the personal representative shall file the writing no later than 60 days prior to filing the petition for final distribution pursuant to Section 11640.

(g) The total value of tangible personal property identified and disposed of in the writing shall not exceed twenty-five thousand dollars ($25,000). If the value of an item of tangible personal property described in the writing exceeds five thousand dollars ($5,000), that item shall not be subject to this section and that item shall be disposed of pursuant to the remainder clause of the will. The value of an item of tangible personal property that is disposed of pursuant to the remainder clause of the will shall not be counted towards the twenty-five thousand dollar ($25,000) limit described in this subdivision.

(h) As used in this section, the following definitions shall apply:

(1) "Tangible personal property" means articles of personal or household use or ornament, including, but not limited to, furniture, furnishings, automobiles, boats, and jewelry, as well as precious metals in any tangible form, such as bullion or coins and articles held for investment purposes. The term "tangible personal property" does not mean real property, a mobilehome as defined in Section 798.3 of the Civil Code, intangible property, such as evidences of indebtedness, bank accounts and other monetary deposits, documents of title, or securities.

(2) "Common coin or currency" means the coins and currency of the United States that are legal tender for the payment of public and private debts, but does not include coins or currency kept or acquired for their historical, artistic,

collectable, or investment value apart from their normal use as legal tender for payment. *(Added by Stats.2006, c. 280 (A.B.2568), § 1.)*

CHAPTER 5. RULES OF CONSTRUCTION OF WILLS [REPEALED]

§§ 6140 to 6179. Repealed by Stats.1994, c. 806 (A.B.3686), § 21

CHAPTER 6. CALIFORNIA STATUTORY WILL

Cross References

California statutory will, form, see Probate Code § 6242.

ARTICLE 1. DEFINITIONS AND RULES OF CONSTRUCTION

Cross References

Application of old and new law, see Probate Code § 3.

§ 6200. Application of article

Unless the provision or context clearly requires otherwise, these definitions and rules of construction govern the construction of this chapter. *(Added by Stats.1991, c. 1055 (S.B.271), § 20.)*

Law Revision Commission Comments

1990 Enactment

Section 6200 continues Section 6200 of the repealed Probate Code without change. This section does not apply if the testator died before January 1, 1985. See Section 6103. As to the application of any amendments made after that date, see Section 3. See also Section 6247 (inclusion of clauses as existing on date of execution of will; statutory will executed on form prepared for use under prior law).

Background on Section 6200 of Repealed Code

Section 6200 was added by 1983 Cal.Stat. ch. 842 § 55. The section continued the substance of the introductory clause of former Probate Code Section 56 (repealed by 1983 Cal.Stat. ch. 842 § 18). For background on the provisions of this part, see the Comment to this part under the part heading. [20 Cal.L.Rev.Comm.Reports 1001 (1990)].

§ 6201. Testator

"Testator" means a person choosing to adopt a California statutory will. *(Added by Stats.1991, c. 1055 (S.B.271), § 20.)*

Law Revision Commission Comments

1990 Enactment

Section 6201 continues Section 6201 of the repealed Probate Code without change. This section does not apply if the testator died before January 1, 1985. See Section 6103. As to the application of any amendments made after that date, see Section 3. See also Section 6247 (inclusion of clauses as existing on date of execution of will; statutory will executed on form prepared for use under prior law).

Background on Section 6201 of Repealed Code

Section 6201 was added by 1983 Cal.Stat. ch. 842 § 55. The section continued subdivision (a) of former Probate Code Section 56 (repealed by 1983 Cal.Stat. ch. 842 § 18). For background on the provisions of this part, see the Comment to this part under the part heading. [20 Cal.L.Rev.Comm.Reports 1001 (1990)].

Cross References

Person defined for purposes of this Chapter, see Probate Code § 6210.

§ 6202. Repealed by Stats.2001, c. 417 (A.B.873), § 10

Law Revision Commission Comments

2001 Repeal

Section 6202 is repealed to eliminate the inconsistency in the operation of Section 6122 and Section 6227. Section 6122 revokes a disposition to a former spouse in a will executed before or during the testator's marriage to the former spouse. For the purposes of a statutory will, Section 6202 defines a "spouse" as a person who is married to the testator at the time the testator signs the statutory will. This means that Section 6227 only revokes a disposition to a former spouse in a statutory will that is executed after the testator's marriage to the former spouse. See Estate of Reeves, 233 Cal.App.3d 651, 284 Cal.Rptr. 650 (1991). [28 Cal.L.Rev. Comm. Reports 599 (1998)].

§ 6203. Executor

"Executor" means both the person so designated in a California statutory will and any other person acting at any time as the executor or administrator under a California statutory will. *(Added by Stats.1991, c. 1055 (S.B.271), § 20.)*

Law Revision Commission Comments

1990 Enactment

Section 6203 continues Section 6203 of the repealed Probate Code without change. This section does not apply if the testator died before January 1, 1985. See Section 6103. As to the application of any amendments made after that date, see Section 3. See also Section 6247 (inclusion of clauses as existing on date of execution of will; statutory will executed on form prepared for use under prior law).

Background on Section 6203 of Repealed Code

Section 6203 was added by 1983 Cal.Stat. ch. 842 § 55. The section continued subdivision (c) of former Probate Code Section 56 (repealed by 1983 Cal.Stat. ch. 842 § 18). For background on the provisions of this part, see the Comment to this part under the part heading. [20 Cal.L.Rev.Comm.Reports 1001 (1990)].

Cross References

Person defined for purposes of this Chapter, see Probate Code § 6210.

§ 6204. Trustee

"Trustee" means both the person so designated in a California statutory will and any other person acting at any time as the trustee under a California statutory will. *(Added by Stats.1991, c. 1055 (S.B.271), § 20.)*

Law Revision Commission Comments

1990 Enactment

Section 6204 continues Section 6204 of the repealed Probate Code without change. This section does not apply if the testator died before January 1, 1985. See Section 6103. As to the application of any amendments made after that date, see Section 3. See also Section 6247 (inclusion of clauses as existing on date of execution of will; statutory will executed on form prepared for use under prior law).

Background on Section 6204 of Repealed Code

Section 6204 was added by 1983 Cal.Stat. ch. 842 § 55. The section continued subdivision (d) of former Probate Code Section 56 (repealed by 1983 Cal.Stat. ch. 842 § 18). For background on the provisions of this part, see the Comment to this part under the part heading. [20 Cal.L.Rev.Comm.Reports 1001 (1990)].

Cross References

Person defined for purposes of this Chapter, see Probate Code § 6210.

§ 6205. Descendants

"Descendants" mean children, grandchildren, and their lineal descendants of all generations, with the relationship of parent and child at each generation being determined as provided in Section 21115. A reference to "descendants" in the plural includes a single descendant where the context so requires. *(Added by Stats.1991, c. 1055 (S.B.271), § 20. Amended by Stats.2002, c. 138 (A.B.1784), § 7.)*

Law Revision Commission Comments

1990 Enactment

Section 6205 continues Section 6205 of the repealed Probate Code without change. This section applies the rules of construction of wills for determining the parent-child relationship. This makes the construction of a California statutory will consistent with the construction of wills generally. This section applies to every California statutory will, including those executed before January 1, 1985. See Section 6247. As to the application of any amendments made after that date, see Section 3.

2002 Amendment

Section 6205 is amended to correct a cross-reference. [31 Cal.L.Rev.Comm. Reports 221 (2001)].

Background on Section 6205 of Repealed Code

Section 6205 was added by 1983 Cal.Stat. ch. 842 § 55 and was amended by 1984 Cal.Stat. ch. 892 § 33, 1985 Cal.Stat. ch. 359 § 5, and 1985 Cal.Stat. ch. 982 § 18. The section continued subdivision (e) of former Probate Code Section 56 (repealed by 1983 Cal.Stat. ch. 842 § 18). For background on the provisions of this part, see the Comment to this part under the part heading. The 1984 amendment revised Section 6205 to refer to the definitions of "parent" and "child" under Sections 26 and 54. The second sentence of Section 6205 (which was added by the 1984 amendment) continued subdivi-

sion (b) of former Probate Code Section 6206 (repealed by 1984 Cal.Stat. ch. 892 § 34). As to the 1984 amendment, see Recommendation Relating to Revision of Wills and Intestate Succession Law, 17 Cal.L.Revision Comm'n Reports 537 (1984). The 1985 amendment substituted the reference to Section 6152 (rules of construction for wills) for the former reference to the definitions of child and parent in Sections 26 and 54. Formerly Section 6205 applied the intestate succession rules for determining the parent-child relationship (see former Sections 6408, 6408.5) because Sections 26 and 54 incorporated those rules. As to the 1985 amendment, see Communication Concerning Assembly Bill 196, 18 Cal.L.Revision Comm'n Reports 367, 374 (1986). [20 Cal.L.Rev.Comm.Reports 1001 (1990)].

Cross References

Application of this section, see Probate Code § 6242.

§ 6206. Uniform gifts or transfers to minors acts; references include both acts; custodian defined

A reference in a California statutory will to the "Uniform Gifts to Minors Act of any state" or the "Uniform Transfers to Minors Act of any state" includes both the Uniform Gifts to Minors Act of any state and the Uniform Transfers to Minors Act of any state. A reference to a "custodian" means the person so designated in a California statutory will or any other person acting at any time as a custodian under a Uniform Gifts to Minors Act or Uniform Transfers to Minors Act. *(Added by Stats.1991, c. 1055 (S.B.271), § 20.)*

Law Revision Commission Comments

1990 Enactment

Section 6206 continues Section 6206 of the repealed Probate Code without change. This section applies to every California statutory will, including those executed before January 1, 1985. See Section 6247. As to the application of any amendments made after that date, see Section 3.

Background on Section 6206 of Repealed Code

Section 6206 was added by 1984 Cal.Stat. ch. 892 § 35. The section was added in recognition that the Uniform Gifts to Minors Act (1966) had been superseded by the Uniform Transfers to Minors Act (1986). See also Sections 6245, 6246. See Communication of Law Revision Commission Concerning Assembly Bill 2290, 18 Cal.L.Revision Comm'n Reports 77, 88 (1986). See also Recommendation Relating to Revision of Wills and Intestate Succession Law, 17 Cal.L.Revision Comm'n Reports 537 (1984). [20 Cal.L.Rev.Comm.Reports 1001 (1990)].

Cross References

Application of this section, see Probate Code § 6242.
Person defined for purposes of this Chapter, see Probate Code § 6210.

§ 6207. Masculine pronouns; plural and singular words

Masculine pronouns include the feminine, and plural and singular words include each other, where appropriate. *(Added by Stats.1991, c. 1055 (S.B.271), § 20.)*

Law Revision Commission Comments

1990 Enactment

Section 6207 continues Section 6207 of the repealed Probate Code without change. This section does not apply if the testator died before January 1, 1985. See Section 6103. As to the application of any amendments made after that date, see Section 3. See also Section 6247 (inclusion of clauses as existing on date of execution of will; statutory will executed on form prepared for use under prior law).

Background on Section 6207 of Repealed Code

Section 6207 was added by 1983 Cal.Stat. ch. 842 § 55. The section continued subdivision (g) of former Probate Code Section 56 (repealed by 1983 Cal.Stat. ch. 842 § 18). For background on the provisions of this part, see the Comment to this part under the part heading. [20 Cal.L.Rev.Comm.Reports 1001 (1990)].

§ 6208. Statutory will; "shall" and "may"

(a) If a California statutory will states that a person shall perform an act, the person is required to perform that act.

(b) If a California statutory will states that a person may do an act, the person's decision to do or not to do the act shall be made in the exercise of the person's fiduciary powers. *(Added by Stats.1991, c. 1055 (S.B.271), § 20.)*

Law Revision Commission Comments

1990 Enactment

Section 6208 continues Section 6208 of the repealed Probate Code without change. This section does not apply if the testator died before January 1, 1985. See Section 6103. As to the application of any amendments made after that date, see Section 3. See also Section 6247 (inclusion of clauses as existing on date of execution of will; statutory will executed on form prepared for use under prior law).

Background on Section 6208 of Repealed Code

Section 6208 was added by 1983 Cal.Stat. ch. 842 § 55. The section continued the substance of subdivision (h) of former Probate Code Section 56 (repealed by 1983 Cal.Stat. ch. 842 § 18). For background on the provisions of this part, see the Comment to this part under the part heading. [20 Cal.L.Rev.Comm.Reports 1001 (1990)].

Cross References

Person defined for purposes of this Chapter, see Probate Code § 6210.

§ 6209. Distribution to person's descendants; division; shares

Whenever a distribution under a California statutory will is to be made to a person's descendants, the property shall be divided into as many equal shares as there are then living descendants of the nearest degree of living descendants and deceased descendants of that same degree who leave descendants then living; and each living descendant of the nearest degree shall receive one share and the share of each deceased descendant of that same degree shall be divided among his or her descendants in the same manner. *(Added by Stats.1991, c. 1055 (S.B.271), § 20.)*

Law Revision Commission Comments

1990 Enactment

Section 6209 continues Section 6209 of the repealed Probate Code without change. The rule stated in Section 6209 is consistent with the general rule concerning taking by representation. See Section 240 (representation). Section 6209 does not apply if the testator died before January 1, 1985. See Section 6103. As to the application of any amendments made after that date, see Section 3. See also Section 6247 (inclusion of clauses as existing on date of execution of will; statutory will executed on form prepared for use under prior law).

Background on Section 6209 of Repealed Code

Section 6209 was added by 1983 Cal.Stat. ch. 842 § 55. The section continued the substance of subdivision (i) of former Probate Code Section 56 (repealed by 1983 Cal.Stat. ch. 842 § 18). For background on the provisions of this part, see the Comment to this part under the part heading. [20 Cal.L.Rev.Comm.Reports 1001 (1990)].

Cross References

Descendants defined for purposes of this Chapter, see Probate Code § 6205.
Person defined for purposes of this Chapter, see Probate Code § 6210.

§ 6210. Person

"Person" includes individuals and institutions. *(Added by Stats.1991, c. 1055 (S.B.271), § 20.)*

Law Revision Commission Comments

1990 Enactment

Section 6210 continues Section 6210 of the repealed Probate Code without change. This section does not apply if the testator died before January 1, 1985. See Section 6103. As to the application of any amendments made after that date, see Section 3. See also Section 6247 (inclusion of clauses as existing on date of execution of will; statutory will executed on form prepared for use under prior law).

Background on Section 6210 of Repealed Code

Section 6210 was added by 1983 Cal.Stat. ch. 842 § 55. The section continued subdivision (j) of former Probate Code Section 56 (repealed by 1983 Cal.Stat. ch. 842 § 18). For background on the provisions of this part, see the Comment to this part under the part heading. [20 Cal.L.Rev.Comm.Reports 1001 (1990)].

§ 6211. Survival; 120 hours

Reference to a person "if living" or who "survives me" means a person who survives the decedent by 120 hours. A person who fails to survive the decedent by 120 hours is deemed to have predeceased the decedent for the purpose of a California statutory will, and the beneficiaries are determined accordingly. If it cannot be established by clear and convincing evidence that a person who would otherwise be a beneficiary has survived the decedent by 120 hours, it is deemed that the person failed to survive for the required period. The requirement of this section that a person who survives the decedent must survive the decedent by 120 hours does not apply if the application of the 120-hour survival requirement would result in the escheat of property to the state. *(Added by Stats.1991, c. 1055 (S.B.271), § 20.)*

Law Revision Commission Comments

1990 Addition

Section 6211 was added to the new Probate Code by 1990 Cal.Stat. ch. 710 § 15 to provide a 120–hour survival rule for the beneficiary of a statutory will. Section 6211 is the same in substance as Section 6403 (requirement that heir survive decedent by 120 hours). Section 6211 does not apply if the testator died before the operative date of the section. See Section 6247. See also Section 230 (petition to determine for the purposes of Section 6211 whether one person survived another). For background on this section, see Recommendation Relating to Survival Requirement for Beneficiary of Statutory Will, 20 Cal.L.Revision Comm'n Reports 549 (1990). [20 Cal.L.Rev.Comm.Reports 1001 (1990)].

Application of this section, see Probate Code § 6242.
Person defined for purposes of this Chapter, see Probate Code § 6210.

ARTICLE 2.   GENERAL PROVISIONS

Section
6220.   Persons who may execute statutory wills.
6221.   Execution; procedure.
6221.5.   Repealed.
6222.   Execution of attestation clause.
6223.   Types; contents; prior law.
6224.   Property disposition clause; more than one or none selected; effect.
6225.   Titles of clauses; effect.
6226.   Revocation; codicils; additions or deletions; validity requirements.
6227.   Dissolution or annulment of testator's marriage or termination of testator's registered domestic partnership; provisions revoked; effect; application.

§ 6220.   Persons who may execute statutory wills

Any individual of sound mind and over the age of 18 may execute a California statutory will under the provisions of this chapter. *(Added by Stats.1991, c. 1055 (S.B.271), § 20.)*

Law Revision Commission Comments

1990 Enactment

Section 6220 continues Section 6220 of the repealed Probate Code without change. An emancipated minor is considered as being over the age of majority for the purpose of making or revoking a will. See Civil Code § 63. Section 6220 does not apply if the testator died before January 1, 1985. See Section 6103. As to the application of any amendments made after that date, see Section 3. See also Section 6247 (inclusion of clauses as existing on date of execution of will; statutory will executed on form prepared for use under prior law).

Background on Section 6220 of Repealed Code

Section 6220 was added by 1983 Cal.Stat. ch. 842 § 55. The section continued the substance of former Probate Code Section 56.1 (repealed by 1983 Cal.Stat. ch. 842 § 18). For background on the provisions of this part, see the Comment to this part under the part heading. [20 Cal.L.Rev.Comm.Reports 1001 (1990)].

§ 6221.   Execution; procedure

A California statutory will shall be executed only as follows:

(a) The testator shall complete the appropriate blanks and shall sign the will.

(b) Each witness shall observe the testator's signing and each witness shall sign his or her name in the presence of the testator. *(Added by Stats.1991, c. 1055 (S.B.271), § 20.)*

Law Revision Commission Comments

1990 Enactment

Section 6221 continues Section 6221 of the repealed Probate Code without change. This section does not apply if the testator died before January 1, 1985. See Section 6103. As to the application of any amendments made after that date, see Section 3. See also Section 6247 (inclusion of clauses as existing on date of execution of will; statutory will executed on form prepared for use under prior law).

Background on Section 6221 of Repealed Code

Section 6221 was added by 1983 Cal.Stat. ch. 842 § 55. The section continued the substance of a portion of former Probate Code Section 56.2 (repealed by 1983 Cal.Stat. ch. 842 § 18). For background on the provisions of this part, see the Comment to this part under the part heading. [20 Cal.L.Rev.Comm.Reports 1001 (1990)].

Cross References

Testator defined for purposes of this Chapter, see Probate Code § 6201.

§ 6221.5.   Repealed by Stats.1991, c. 1055 (S.B.271), § 19

§ 6222.   Execution of attestation clause

The execution of the attestation clause provided in the California statutory will by two or more witnesses satisfies Section 8220. *(Added by Stats.1991, c. 1055 (S.B.271), § 20.)*

Law Revision Commission Comments

1990 Enactment

Section 6222 continues Section 6222 of the repealed Probate Code without change. This section does not apply if the testator died before January 1, 1985. See Section 6103. As to the application of any amendments made after that date, see Section 3. See also Section 6247 (inclusion of clauses as existing on date of execution of will; statutory will executed on form prepared for use under prior law).

Background on Section 6222 of Repealed Code

Section 6222 was added by 1983 Cal.Stat. ch. 842 § 55. The section continued the substance of former Probate Code Section 56.3 (repealed by 1983 Cal.Stat. ch. 842 § 18). For background on the provisions of this part, see the Comment to this part under the part heading. [20 Cal.L.Rev.Comm.Reports 1001 (1990)].

§ 6223.   Types; contents; prior law

(a) There is only one California statutory will.

(b) The California statutory will includes all of the following:

(1) The contents of the California statutory will form set out in Section 6240, excluding the questions and answers at the beginning of the California statutory will.

(2) By reference, the full texts of each of the following:

(A) The definitions and rules of construction set forth in Article 1 (commencing with Section 6200).

(B) The property disposition clauses adopted by the testator. If no property disposition clause is adopted, Section 6224 shall apply.

(C) The mandatory clauses set forth in Section 6241.

(c) Notwithstanding this section, any California statutory will or California statutory will with trust executed on a form allowed under prior law shall be governed by the law that applied prior to January 1, 1992. *(Added by Stats.1991, c. 1055 (S.B.271), § 20.)*

Law Revision Commission Comments

1990 Enactment

Section 6223 continues Section 6223 of the repealed Probate Code without change. This section does not apply if the testator died before January 1, 1985. See Section 6103. As to the application of any amendments made after that date, see Section 3. See also

Section 6247 (inclusion of clauses as existing on date of execution of will; statutory will executed on form prepared for use under prior law).

Background on Section 6223 of Repealed Code

Section 6223 was added by 1983 Cal.Stat. ch. 842 § 55. The section continued former Probate Code Section 56.4 (repealed by 1983 Cal.Stat. ch. 842 § 18). For background on the provisions of this part, see the Comment to this part under the part heading. [20 Cal.L.Rev.Comm.Reports 1001 (1990)].

Cross References

Prior law, application where prior forms used, see Probate Code § 6242.
Testator defined for purposes of this Chapter, see Probate Code § 6201.

§ 6224. Property disposition clause; more than one or none selected; effect

If more than one property disposition clause appearing in paragraphs 2 or 3 of a California statutory will is selected, no gift is made. If more than one property disposition clause in paragraph 5 of a California statutory will form is selected, or if none is selected, the residuary estate of a testator who signs a California statutory will shall be distributed to the testator's heirs as if the testator did not make a will. *(Added by Stats.1991, c. 1055 (S.B.271), § 20.)*

Law Revision Commission Comments

1990 Enactment

Section 6224 continues Section 6224 of the repealed Probate Code without change. This section does not apply if the testator died before January 1, 1985. See Section 6103. As to the application of any amendments made after that date, see Section 3. See also Section 6247 (inclusion of clauses as existing on date of execution of will; statutory will executed on form prepared for use under prior law).

Background on Section 6224 of Repealed Code

Section 6224 was added by 1983 Cal.Stat. ch. 842 § 55. The section continued former Probate Code Section 56.5 (repealed by 1983 Cal.Stat. ch. 842 § 18). For background on the provisions of this part, see the Comment to this part under the part heading. [20 Cal.L.Rev.Comm.Reports 1001 (1990)].

Cross References

Testator defined for purposes of this Chapter, see Probate Code § 6201.

§ 6225. Titles of clauses; effect

Only the texts of property disposition clauses and the mandatory clauses shall be considered in determining their meaning. Their titles shall be disregarded. *(Added by Stats.1991, c. 1055 (S.B.271), § 20.)*

Law Revision Commission Comments

1990 Enactment

Section 6225 continues Section 6225 of the repealed Probate Code without change. This section does not apply if the testator died before January 1, 1985. See Section 6103. As to the application of any amendments made after that date, see Section 3. See also Section 6247 (inclusion of clauses as existing on date of execution of will; statutory will executed on form prepared for use under prior law).

Background on Section 6225 of Repealed Code

Section 6225 was added by 1983 Cal.Stat. ch. 842 § 55. The section continued former Probate Code Section 56.6 (repealed by 1983 Cal.Stat. ch. 842 § 18). For background on the provisions of this part, see the Comment to this part under the part heading. [20 Cal.L.Rev.Comm.Reports 1001 (1990)].

§ 6226. Revocation; codicils; additions or deletions; validity requirements

(a) A California statutory will may be revoked and may be amended by codicil in the same manner as other wills.

(b) Any additions to or deletions from the California statutory will on the face of the California statutory will form, other than in accordance with the instructions, shall be given effect only where clear and convincing evidence shows that they would effectuate the clear intent of the testator. In the absence of such a showing, the court either may determine that the addition or deletion is ineffective and shall be disregarded, or may determine that all or a portion of the California statutory will is invalid, whichever is more likely to be consistent with the intent of the testator.

(c) Notwithstanding Section 6110, a document executed on a California statutory will form is valid as a will if all of the following requirements are shown to be satisfied by clear and convincing evidence:

(1) The form is signed by the testator.

(2) The court is satisfied that the testator knew and approved of the contents of the will and intended it to have testamentary effect.

(3) The testamentary intent of the maker as reflected in the document is clear. *(Added by Stats.1991, c. 1055 (S.B. 271), § 20.)*

Law Revision Commission Comments

1990 Enactment

Section 6226 continues Section 6226 of the repealed Probate Code without substantive change.

Background on Section 6226 of Repealed Code

Section 6226 was added by 1983 Cal.Stat. ch. 842 § 55 and was amended by 1984 Cal.Stat. ch. 892 § 36. Section 6226 was a new provision drawn from and consistent with Section 6122. See the Comment to Section 6122. For background on the provisions of this part, see the Comment to this part under the part heading. The 1984 amendment revised subdivision (d) so that Section 6226 did not apply to a case where the final judgment of dissolution or annulment of marriage occurred before January 1, 1985. This made Section 6226 consistent with subdivision (f) of Section 6122. See Communication of Law Revision Commission Concerning Assembly Bill 2290, 18 Cal.L.Revision Comm'n Reports 77, 88 (1986). As to the application of any amendments made after that date, see Section 3. [20 Cal.L.Rev.Comm.Reports 1001 (1990)].

Cross References

Testator defined for purposes of this Chapter, see Probate Code § 6201.

§ 6227. Dissolution or annulment of testator's marriage or termination of testator's registered domestic partnership; provisions revoked; effect; application

(a) If after executing a California statutory will the testator's marriage is dissolved or annulled, or the testator's registered domestic partnership is terminated, the dissolution * * *, annulment, or termination revokes any disposition of property made by the will to the former spouse and any nomination of the former spouse as executor, trustee, guardian, or custodian made by the will. If any disposition or nomination is revoked solely by this section, it is revived by the testator's remarriage to, or entry into a subsequent registered domestic partnership with, the former spouse.

(b) In case of revocation by dissolution or annulment:

(1) Property prevented from passing to a former spouse because of the revocation passes as if the former spouse failed to survive the testator.

(2) Provisions nominating the former spouse as executor, trustee, guardian, or custodian shall be interpreted as if the former spouse failed to survive the testator.

(c) For purposes of this section, dissolution or annulment means any dissolution or annulment that would exclude the spouse as a surviving spouse within the meaning of Section 78. A decree of legal separation which does not terminate the status of * * * spouses is not a dissolution or annulment for purposes of this section.

(d) This section applies to any California statutory will, without regard to the time when the will was executed, but this section does not apply to any case where the final judgment of dissolution or annulment of marriage occurs before January 1, 1985; and, if the final judgment of dissolution or annulment of marriage occurs before January 1, 1985, the case is governed by the law that applied prior to January 1, 1985. *(Added by Stats.1991, c. 1055 (S.B.271), § 20. Amended by Stats.2016, c. 50 (S.B.1005), § 87, eff. Jan. 1, 2017.)*

Cross References

Application of this section, see Probate Code § 6242.
Executor defined for purposes of this Chapter, see Probate Code § 6203.
References to "custodian", see Probate Code § 6206.
Testator defined for purposes of this Chapter, see Probate Code § 6201.
Trustee defined for purposes of this Chapter, see Probate Code § 6204.

ARTICLE 3. FORM AND FULL TEXT OF CLAUSES

§ 6240. Statutory will form

The following is the California Statutory Will form:

QUESTIONS AND ANSWERS ABOUT THIS CALIFORNIA STATUTORY WILL

The following information, in question and answer form, is not a part of the California Statutory Will. It is designed to help you understand about Wills and to decide if this Will meets your needs. This Will is in a simple form. The complete text of each paragraph of this Will is printed at the end of the Will.

1. *What happens if I die without a Will?* If you die without a Will, what you own (your "assets") in your name alone will be divided among your spouse, domestic partner, children, or other relatives according to state law. The court will appoint a relative to collect and distribute your assets.

2. *What can a Will do for me?* In a Will you may designate who will receive your assets at your death. You may designate someone (called an "executor") to appear before the court, collect your assets, pay your debts and taxes, and distribute your assets as you specify. You may nominate someone (called a "guardian") to raise your children who are under age 18. You may designate someone (called a "custodian") to manage assets for your children until they reach any age from 18 to 25.

3. *Does a Will avoid probate?* No. With or without a Will, assets in your name alone usually go through the court probate process. The court's first job is to determine if your Will is valid.

4. *What is community property?* Can I give away my share in my Will? If you are married or in a domestic partnership and you or your spouse earned money during your marriage or domestic partnership from work and wages, that money (and the assets bought with it) is community property. Your Will can only give away your one-half of community property. Your Will cannot give away your spouse's one-half of community property.

5. *Does my Will give away all of my assets?* Do all assets go through probate? No. Money in a joint tenancy bank account automatically belongs to the other named owner without probate. If your spouse, domestic partner, or child is on the deed to your house as a joint tenant, the house automatically passes to him or her. Life insurance and retirement plan benefits may pass directly to the named beneficiary. A Will does not necessarily control how these types of "nonprobate" assets pass at your death.

6. *Are there different kinds of Wills?* Yes. There are handwritten Wills, typewritten Wills, attorney-prepared Wills, and statutory Wills. All are valid if done precisely as the law requires. You should see a lawyer if you do not want to use this Statutory Will or if you do not understand this form.

7. *Who may use this Will?* This Will is based on California law. It is designed only for California residents. You may use this form if you are single, married, a member of a domestic partnership, or divorced. You must be age 18 or older and of sound mind.

8. *Are there any reasons why I should NOT use this Statutory Will?* Yes. This is a simple Will. It is not designed to reduce death taxes or other taxes. Talk to a lawyer to do tax planning, especially if (i) your assets will be worth more than $600,000 or the current amount excluded from estate tax under federal law at your death, (ii) you own business-related assets, (iii) you want to create a trust fund for your children's education or other purposes, (iv) you own assets in some other state, (v) you want to disinherit your spouse, domestic partner, or descendants, or (vi) you have valuable interests in pension or profit-sharing plans. You should talk to a lawyer

who knows about estate planning if this Will does not meet your needs. This Will treats most adopted children like natural children. You should talk to a lawyer if you have stepchildren or foster children whom you have not adopted.

9. *May I add or cross out any words on this Will?* No. If you do, the Will may be invalid or the court may ignore the crossed out or added words. You may only fill in the blanks. You may amend this Will by a separate document (called a codicil). Talk to a lawyer if you want to do something with your assets which is not allowed in this form.

10. *May I change my Will?* Yes. A Will is not effective until you die. You may make and sign a new Will. You may change your Will at any time, but only by an amendment (called a codicil). You can give away or sell your assets before your death. Your Will only acts on what you own at death.

11. *Where should I keep my Will?* After you and the witnesses sign the Will, keep your Will in your safe deposit box or other safe place. You should tell trusted family members where your Will is kept.

12. *When should I change my Will?* You should make and sign a new Will if you marry, divorce, or terminate your domestic partnership after you sign this Will. Divorce, annulment, or termination of a domestic partnership automatically cancels all property stated to pass to a former * * * spouse or domestic partner under this Will, and revokes the designation of a former spouse or domestic partner as executor, custodian, or guardian. You should sign a new Will when you have more children, or if your spouse or a child dies, or a domestic partner dies or marries. You may want to change your Will if there is a large change in the value of your assets. You may also want to change your Will if you enter a domestic partnership or your domestic partnership has been terminated after you sign this Will.

13. *What can I do if I do not understand something in this Will?* If there is anything in this Will you do not understand, ask a lawyer to explain it to you.

14. *What is an executor?* An "executor" is the person you name to collect your assets, pay your debts and taxes, and distribute your assets as the court directs. It may be a person or it may be a qualified bank or trust company.

15. *Should I require a bond?* You may require that an executor post a "bond." A bond is a form of insurance to replace assets that may be mismanaged or stolen by the executor. The cost of the bond is paid from the estate's assets.

16. *What is a guardian? Do I need to designate one?* If you have children under age 18, you should designate a guardian of their "persons" to raise them.

17. *What is a custodian? Do I need to designate one?* A "custodian" is a person you may designate to manage assets for someone (including a child) who is under the age of 25 and who receives assets under your Will. The custodian manages the assets and pays as much as the custodian determines is proper for health, support, maintenance, and education. The custodian delivers what is left to the person when the person reaches the age you choose (from 18 to 25). No bond is required of a custodian.

18. *Should I ask people if they are willing to serve before I designate them as executor, guardian, or custodian?* Probably yes. Some people and banks and trust companies may not consent to serve or may not be qualified to act.

19. *What happens if I make a gift in this Will to someone and that person dies before I do?* A person must survive you by 120 hours to take a gift under this Will. If that person does not, then the gift fails and goes with the rest of your assets. If the person who does not survive you is a relative of yours or your spouse, then certain assets may go to the relative's descendants.

20. *What is a trust?* There are many kinds of trusts, including trusts created by Wills (called "testamentary trusts") and trusts created during your lifetime (called "revocable living trusts"). Both kinds of trusts are long-term arrangements in which a manager (called a "trustee") invests and manages assets for someone (called a "beneficiary") on the terms you specify. Trusts are too complicated to be used in this Statutory Will. You should see a lawyer if you want to create a trust.

21. *What is a domestic partner?* You have a domestic partner if you have met certain legal requirements and filed a form entitled "Declaration of Domestic Partnership" with the Secretary of State. Notwithstanding Section 299.6 of the Family Code, if you have not filed a Declaration of Domestic Partnership with the Secretary of State, you do not meet the required definition and should not use the section of the Statutory Will form that refers to domestic partners even if you have registered your domestic partnership with another governmental entity. If you are unsure if you have a domestic partner or if your domestic partnership meets the required definition, please contact the Secretary of State's office.

INSTRUCTIONS

1. *READ THE WILL.* Read the whole Will first. If you do not understand something, ask a lawyer to explain it to you.

2. *FILL IN THE BLANKS.* Fill in the blanks. Follow the instructions in the form carefully. Do not add any words to the Will (except for filling in blanks) or cross out any words.

3. *DATE AND SIGN THE WILL AND HAVE TWO WITNESSES SIGN IT.* Date and sign the Will and have two witnesses sign it. You and the witnesses should read and follow the Notice to Witnesses found at the end of this Will.

*You do not need to have this document notarized. Notarization will not fulfill the witness requirement.

CALIFORNIA STATUTORY WILL OF

```
┌─────────────────────────────────┐
│                                 │
│                                 │
│         Print Your Full Name    │
└─────────────────────────────────┘
```

1. <u>Will.</u> This is my Will. I revoke all prior Wills and codicils.

2. <u>Specific Gift of Personal Residence.</u> (Optional—use only if you want to give your personal residence to a different person or persons than you give the balance of your assets to under paragraph 5 below.) I give my interest in my principal personal residence at the time of my death (subject to mortgages and liens) as follows:

(Select one choice only and sign in the box after your choice.)

   a. <u>Choice One:</u> All to my spouse or domestic partner, registered with the California Secretary of State, if my spouse or domestic partner, registered with the California Secretary of State, survives me; otherwise to my descendants (my children and the descendants of my children)who survive me.

   b. <u>Choice Two:</u> Nothing to my spouse or domestic partner, registered with the California Secretary of State; all to my descendants (my children and the descendants of my children) who survive me.

   c. <u>Choice Three:</u> All to the following person if he or she survives me (Insert the name of the person.):

_____

   d. <u>Choice Four:</u> Equally among the following persons who survive me (Insert the names of two or more persons.):

_____
_____
_____

3. <u>Specific Gift of Automobiles, Household and Personal Effects.</u> (Optional—use only if you want to give automobiles and household and personal effects to a different person or persons than you give the balance of your assets to under paragraph 5 below.) I give all of my automobiles (subject to loans), furniture, furnishings, household items, clothing, jewelry, and other tangible articles of a personal nature at the time of my death as follows:

(Select one choice only and sign in the box after your choice.)

a. Choice One: All to my spouse or domestic partner, registered with the California Secretary of State, if my spouse, domestic partner, registered with the California Secretary of State, survives me; otherwise to my descendants (my children and the descendants of my children) who survive me.

b. Choice Two: Nothing to my spouse or domestic partner, registered with the California Secretary of State; all to my descendants (my children and the descendants of my children) who survive me.

c. Choice Three: All to the following person if he or she survives me (Insert the name of the person.):

_____

d. Choice Four: Equally among the following persons who survive me (Insert the names of two or more persons.):

_____

_____

_____

4. Specific Gifts of Cash. (Optional) I make the following cash gifts to the persons named below who survive me, or to the named charity, and I sign my name in the box after each gift. If I do not sign in the box, I do not make a gift. (Sign in the box after each gift you make.)

Name of Person or Charity to receive gift (name one only—please print)	Amount of Cash Gift
	Sign your name in this box to make this gift

Name of Person or Charity to receive gift (name one only—please print)	Amount of Cash Gift
	Sign your name in this box to make this gift

Name of Person or Charity to receive gift (name one only—please print)	Amount of Cash Gift
	Sign your name in this box to make this gift

Name of Person or Charity to receive gift (name one only—please print)	Amount of Cash Gift
	Sign your name in this box to make this gift

Name of Person or Charity to receive gift (name one only—please print)	Amount of Cash Gift
	Sign your name in this box to make this gift

5. <u>Balance of My Assets.</u> Except for the specific gifts made in paragraphs 2, 3 and 4 above, I give the balance of my assets as follows:

(Select <u>one</u> choice only and sign in the box after your choice. If I sign in more than one box or if I do not sign in any box, the court will distribute my assets as if I did not make a Will.)

a. <u>Choice One:</u> All to my spouse or domestic partner, registered with the California Secretary of State, if my spouse or domestic partner, registered with the California Secretary of State, survives me; otherwise to my descendants (my children and the descendants of my children) who survive me.

b. <u>Choice Two:</u> Nothing to my spouse or domestic partner, registered with the California Secretary of State; all to my descendants (my children and the descendants of my children) who survive me.

c. <u>Choice Three:</u> All to the following person if he or she survives me (Insert the name of the person.):

_____

561

d. <u>Choice Four:</u> Equally among the following persons who survive me (Insert the names of two or more persons.):

_____

_____

_____

_____

6. <u>Guardian of the Child's Person.</u> If, at my death, I have a child under age 18, whether the child is alive at the time this will is executed or born after the date this will is executed, and the child does not have a living parent, I nominate the individual named below as First Choice as guardian of the person of that child (to raise the child). If the First Choice does not serve, then I nominate the Second Choice, and then the Third Choice, to serve. Only an individual (not a bank or trust company) may serve.

Name of First Choice for Guardian of the Person

Name of Second Choice for Guardian of the Person

Name of Third Choice for Guardian of the Person

7. <u>Special Provision for Property of Persons Under Age 25.</u> (Optional—unless you use this paragraph, assets that go to a child or other person who is <u>under</u> age 18 may be given to the parent of the person, or to the Guardian named in paragraph 6 above as guardian of the person until age 18, and the court will require a bond, and assets that go to a child or other person who is age 18 or older will be given outright to the person. By using this paragraph you may provide that a custodian will hold the assets for the person until the person reaches any age from 18 to 25 which you choose.) If a beneficiary of this Will is under the age chosen below, **I** nominate the individual or bank or trust company named below as First Choice as custodian of the property. If the First Choice does not serve, then I nominate the Second Choice, and then the Third Choice, to serve.

Name of First Choice for Custodian of Assets

Name of Second Choice for Custodian of Assets

Name of Third Choice for Custodian of Assets

Insert any age from 18 to 25 as the age for the person to receive the property:

(If you do not choose an age, age 18 will apply.)

8. <u>Executor.</u> I nominate the individual or bank or trust company named below as First Choice as executor. If the First Choice does not serve, then I nominate the Second Choice, and then the Third Choice, to serve.

Name of First Choice for Executor

Name of Second Choice for Executor

Name of Third Choice for Executor

9. <u>Bond.</u> My signature in this box means a bond is <u>not</u> required for any person named as executor. A bond may be required if I do not sign in this box:

No bond shall be required.

(<u>Notice:</u> You must sign this Will in the presence of two (2) adult witnesses. The witnesses must sign their names in your presence. You must first read to them the following sentence.)

This is my Will: I ask the persons who sign below to be my witnesses.

Signed on _____ at _____ , California.
              (date)   (city)

                                     Signature of Maker of Will

(<u>Notice to Witnesses:</u> Two (2) adults must sign as witnesses. Each witness must read the following clause before signing. The witnesses should not receive assets under this Will.)

Each of us declares under penalty of perjury under the laws of the State of California that the following is true and correct:

    a. On the date written below the maker of this Will declared to us that this instrument was the maker's Will and requested us to act as witnesses to it;

    b. We understand this is the maker's Will;

    c. The maker signed this Will in our presence, all of us being present at the same time;

d. We now, at the maker's request, and in the maker's presence, sign below as witnesses;

e. We believe the maker is of sound mind and memory;

f. We believe that this Will was not procured by duress, menace, fraud or undue influence;

g. The maker is age 18 or older; and

h. Each of us is now age 18 or older, is a competent witness, and resides at the address set forth after his or her name.

Dated: _____ , _____

Signature of witness	Signature of witness

Print name here: Print name here:

_____   _____

Residence address: Residence address:

_____   _____

_____   _____

AT LEAST TWO WITNESSES <u>MUST</u> SIGN

(Added by Stats.1991, c. 1055 (S.B.271), § 20. Amended by Stats.2001, c. 893 (A.B.25), § 52; Stats.2003, c. 32 (A.B.167), § 5; Stats.2010, c. 88 (A.B.1986), § 1; Stats.2016, c. 50 (S.B.1005), § 88, eff. Jan. 1, 2017.)

Law Revision Commission Comments

1990 Enactment

Section 6240 continues Section 6240 of the repealed Probate Code without change. This section does not apply if the testator died before January 1, 1985. See Section 6103. As to the application of any amendments made after that date, see Section 3. See also Section 6247 (inclusion of clauses as existing on date of execution of will; statutory will executed on form prepared for use under prior law).

Background on Section 6240 of Repealed Code

Section 6240 was added by 1983 Cal.Stat. ch. 842 § 55. The section continued the substance of former Probate Code Section 56.7 (repealed by 1983 Cal.Stat. ch. 842 § 18). The language in parentheses in paragraph 3.3 concerning bond was new. For background on the provisions of this part, see the Comment to this part under the part heading. [20 Cal.L.Rev.Comm.Reports 1001 (1990)].

Cross References

Descendants defined for purposes of this Chapter, see Probate Code § 6205.

Executor defined for purposes of this Chapter, see Probate Code § 6203.

Person defined for purposes of this Chapter, see Probate Code § 6210.

References to a person who "survives me", see Probate Code § 6211.

References to "custodian", see Probate Code § 6206.

Trustee defined for purposes of this Chapter, see Probate Code § 6204.

§ 6241. Mandatory clauses

The mandatory clauses of the California statutory will form are as follows:

(a) *Intestate Disposition.* If the testator has not made an effective disposition of the residuary estate, the executor shall distribute it to the testator's heirs at law, their identities and respective shares to be determined according to the laws of the State of California in effect on the date of the testator's death relating to intestate succession of property not acquired from a predeceased spouse.

(b) *Powers of Executor.*

(1) In addition to any powers now or hereafter conferred upon executors by law, including all powers granted under the Independent Administration of Estates Act, the executor shall have the power to:

(A) Sell estate assets at public or private sale, for cash or on credit terms.

(B) Lease estate assets without restriction as to duration.

(C) Invest any surplus moneys of the estate in real or personal property, as the executor deems advisable.

(2) The executor may distribute estate assets otherwise distributable to a minor beneficiary to one of the following:

(A) The guardian of the minor's person or estate.

(B) Any adult person with whom the minor resides and who has the care, custody, or control of the minor.

(C) A custodian of the minor under the Uniform Transfers to Minors Act as designated in the California statutory will form.

The executor is free of liability and is discharged from any further accountability for distributing assets in compliance with the provisions of this paragraph.

(3) On any distribution of assets from the estate, the executor shall have the discretion to partition, allot, and distribute the assets in the following manner:

(A) In kind, including undivided interest in an asset or in any part of it.

(B) Partly in cash and partly in kind.

(C) Entirely in cash.

If a distribution is being made to more than one beneficiary, the executor shall have the discretion to distribute assets among them on a pro rata or non pro rata basis, with the assets valued as of the date of distribution.

(c) *Powers of Guardian.* A guardian of the person nominated in the California statutory will shall have the same authority with respect to the person of the ward as a parent having legal custody of a child would have. All powers granted to guardians in this paragraph may be exercised without court authorization. *(Added by Stats.1991, c. 1055 (S.B.271), § 20.)*

Law Revision Commission Comments

1990 Enactment

Section 6241 continues Section 6241 of the repealed Probate Code without change. This section does not apply if the testator died before January 1, 1985. See Section 6103. As to the application of any amendments made after that date, see Section 3. See also Section 6247 (inclusion of clauses as existing on date of execution of will; statutory will executed on form prepared for use under prior law).

Background on Section 6241 of Repealed Code

Section 6241 was added by 1983 Cal.Stat. ch. 842 § 55. The section continued the substance of former Probate Code Section 56.8 (repealed by 1983 Cal.Stat. ch. 842 § 18). The language in parentheses in paragraph 3.4 concerning bond was new. For background on the provisions of this part, see the Comment to this part under the part heading. [20 Cal.L.Rev.Comm.Reports 1001 (1990)].

Cross References

Executor defined for purposes of this Chapter, see Probate Code § 6203.
Person defined for purposes of this Chapter, see Probate Code § 6210.
References to "custodian", see Probate Code § 6206.

Testator defined for purposes of this Chapter, see Probate Code § 6201.

§ 6242. Property disposition and mandatory clauses; text; date of execution; application of various provisions; transitional provisions

(a) Except as specifically provided in this chapter, a California statutory will shall include only the texts of the property disposition clauses and the mandatory clauses as they exist on the day the California statutory will is executed.

(b) Sections 6205, 6206, and 6227 apply to every California statutory will, including those executed before January 1, 1985. Section 6211 applies only to California statutory wills executed after July 1, 1991.

(c) Notwithstanding Section 6222, and except as provided in subdivision (b), a California statutory will is governed by the law that applied prior to January 1, 1992, if the California statutory will is executed on a form that (1) was prepared for use under former Sections 56 to 56.14, inclusive, or former Sections 6200 to 6248, inclusive, of the Probate Code, and (2) satisfied the requirements of law that applied prior to January 1, 1992.

(d) A California statutory will does not fail to satisfy the requirements of subdivision (a) merely because the will is executed on a form that incorporates the mandatory clauses of Section 6241 that refer to former Section 1120.2. If the will incorporates the mandatory clauses with a reference to former Section 1120.2, the trustee has the powers listed in Article 2 (commencing with Section 16220) of Chapter 2 of Part 4 of Division 9. *(Added by Stats.1991, c. 1055 (S.B.271), § 20. Amended by Stats.2004, c. 183 (A.B.3082), § 279.)*

Law Revision Commission Comments

1990 Enactment

Section 6242 continues Section 6242 of the repealed Probate Code without change. This section does not apply if the testator died before January 1, 1985. See Section 6103. As to the application of any amendments made after that date, see Section 3. See also Section 6247 (inclusion of clauses as existing on date of execution of will; statutory will executed on form prepared for use under prior law). See also Sections 230–234 (proceeding to determine survival).

Background on Section 6242 of Repealed Code

Section 6242 was added by 1983 Cal.Stat. ch. 842 § 55. The section was the same as former Probate Code Section 56.9 (repealed by 1983 Cal.Stat. ch. 842 § 18). For background on the provisions of this part, see the Comment to this part under the part heading. [20 Cal.L.Rev.Comm.Reports 1001 (1990)].

Cross References

Trustee defined for purposes of this Chapter, see Probate Code § 6204.

§ 6243. Application of general law

Except as specifically provided in this chapter, the general law of California applies to a California statutory will. *(Added by Stats.1991, c. 1055 (S.B.271), § 20.)*

Law Revision Commission Comments

1990 Enactment

Section 6243 continues Section 6243 of the repealed Probate Code with the addition of language in subdivision (c) that provides for the distribution of the residuary estate according to the laws relating to intestate succession "of property not acquired from a predeceased spouse." This revision restores the substance of the language found in the provision when it was enacted as Probate Code Section 56.10 by 1982 Cal.Stat. ch. 1401, § 1 (later repealed by 1983 Cal.Stat. ch. 842).

Section 6243 applies to every California statutory will, including those executed before January 1, 1985. See Section 6247. As to the application of any amendments made after that date, see Section 3. See also Sections 230–234 (proceeding to determine survival).

Background on Section 6243 of Repealed Code

Section 6243 was added by 1983 Cal.Stat. ch. 842 § 55. The section continued the substance of former Probate Code Section 56.10 (repealed by 1983 Cal.Stat. ch. 842 § 18) except that the provision in the last paragraph of former Section 56.10 adopting the laws relating to the succession of separate property not acquired from a parent, grandparent, or predeceased spouse was replaced by a reference to the law relating to intestate succession. This change permitted community property and quasi-community property to be governed by the intestate succession rules applicable to that property and was based on the assumption that the special provisions relating to succession of property acquired from ancestors would not be continued. For background on the provisions of this part, see the Comment to this part under the part heading. [20 Cal.L.Rev.Comm.Reports 1001 (1990)].

§§ 6244 to 6248. Repealed by Stats.1991, c. 1055 (S.B.271), § 19

CHAPTER 7. UNIFORM TESTAMENTARY ADDITIONS TO TRUSTS ACT

Section
6300. Testamentary additions to trusts.
6301. Application to devises made prior to September 17, 1965.
6302. Repealed.
6303. Chapter citation.

Application

Chapter 7 applicable where testator died on or after Jan. 1, 1985. For provisions applicable where testator died before Jan. 1, 1985, see Probate Code § 6103 and Law Revision Commission Comments for sections in Chapter 7.

Cross References

Application of old and new law, see Probate Code § 3.
Designation of trustee in will as beneficiary of insurance, pension, death benefit, or employee benefit contract, see Probate Code § 6320 et seq.

§ 6300. Testamentary additions to trusts

A devise, the validity of which is determinable by the law of this state, may be made by a will to the trustee of a trust established or to be established by the testator or by the testator and some other person or by some other person (including a funded or unfunded life insurance trust, although the settlor has reserved any or all rights of ownership of the insurance contracts) if the trust is identified in the testator's will and its terms are set forth in a written instrument (other than a will) executed before or concurrently with the execution of the testator's will or in the valid last will of a person who has predeceased the testator (regardless of the existence, size, or character of the trust property). The devise is not invalid because the trust is amendable or revocable, or both, or because the trust was amended after the execution of the will or after the death of the testator. Unless the testator's will provides otherwise, the property so devised (1) is not deemed to be held under a testamentary trust of the testator but becomes a part of the trust to which it is given and (2) shall be administered and disposed of in accordance with the provisions of the instrument or will setting forth the terms of the trust, including any amendments thereto made before or after the death of the testator (regardless of whether made before or after the execution of the testator's will). Unless otherwise provided in the will, a revocation or termination of the trust before the death of the testator causes the devise to lapse. *(Stats.1990, c. 79 (A.B.759), § 14, operative July 1, 1991.)*

Law Revision Commission Comments

1990 Enactment

Section 6300 continues Section 6300 of the repealed Probate Code without substantive change. This section is the same in substance as Section 2–511 of the Uniform Probate Code (1987), except that Section 6300 permits the trust to be amended after the testator's death unless the testator's will provides that it may not be amended with respect to the testamentary assets. As to the construction of provisions drawn from uniform acts, see Section 2. See also Section 32 ("devise" means a disposition of real or personal property by will). Section 6300 does not apply if the testator died before January 1, 1985. See Section 6103. As to the application of any amendments made after that date, see Section 3. This chapter does not invalidate any devise made by a will executed prior to September 17, 1965. See Section 6301.

Background on Section 6300 of Repealed Code

Section 6300 was added by 1983 Cal.Stat. ch. 842 § 55 and was amended by 1984 Cal.Stat. ch. 892 § 39. The section continued the substance of former Probate Code Section 170 (repealed by 1983 Cal.Stat. ch. 842 § 18). For background on the provisions of this part, see the Comment to this part under the part heading. The 1984 amendment changed the former rule that with respect to the testamentary assets the trust may not be amended after the testator's death unless the testator's will so provides. Under the rule established by the 1984 amendment, the trust may be amended after the testator's death unless the testator's will provides that it may not be amended with respect to the testamentary assets. See Recommendation Relating to Revision of Wills and Intestate Succession Law, 17 Cal.L.Revision Comm'n Reports 537 (1984). [20 Cal.L.Rev.Comm.Reports 1001 (1990)].

§ 6301. Application to devises made prior to September 17, 1965

This chapter does not invalidate any devise made by a will executed prior to September 17, 1965. *(Stats.1990, c. 79 (A.B.759), § 14, operative July 1, 1991.)*

Law Revision Commission Comments

1990 Enactment

Section 6301 continues Section 6301 of the repealed Probate Code without change. This section does not apply if the testator died before January 1, 1985. See Section 6103. As to the application of any amendments made after that date, see Section 3.

Background on Section 6301 of Repealed Code

Section 6301 was added by 1983 Cal.Stat. ch. 842 § 55. The section continued the substance of former Probate Code Section 171 (repealed by 1983 Cal.Stat. ch. 842 § 18). September 17, 1965, was effective date of former Sections 170–173. See also Section 32 ("devise" means a disposition of real or personal property by will). For background on the provisions of this part, see the Comment to this part under the part heading. [20 Cal.L.Rev.Comm.Reports 1001 (1990)].

§ 6302. Repealed by Stats.1990, c. 79 (A.B.759), § 13, operative July 1, 1991

§ 6303. Chapter citation

This chapter may be cited as the Uniform Testamentary Additions to Trusts Act. *(Stats.1990, c. 79 (A.B.759), § 14, operative July 1, 1991.)*

Law Revision Commission Comments
1990 Enactment

Section 6303 continues Section 6303 of the repealed Probate Code without change. This section does not apply if the testator died before January 1, 1985. See Section 6103. As to the application of any amendments made after that date, see Section 3.

Background on Section 6303 of Repealed Code

Section 6303 was added by 1983 Cal.Stat. ch. 842 § 55. The section continued former Probate Code Section 173 (repealed by 1983 Cal.Stat. ch. 842 § 18). For background on the provisions of this part, see the Comment to this part under the part heading. [20 Cal.L.Rev.Comm.Reports 1001 (1990)].

CHAPTER 8. NONPROBATE TRANSFER TO TRUSTEE NAMED IN DECEDENT'S WILL

Section
6320. Definitions.
6321. Trustees; designation as beneficiary, payee, or owner.
6322. Creation of trust for valid disposition; necessity of effective designation.
6323. Necessity for administration.
6324. Effect of designator's debts.
6325. Court in which proceedings pending; jurisdiction; petition for order.
6326. Application of Division 9.
6327. Appealable orders.
6328. Payment or transfer; unclaimed benefits or rights or proceeds.
6329. Trusts not made pursuant to chapter; validity.
6330. Chapter as restatement and continuation of former law.

Cross References

Application of old and new law, see Probate Code § 3.
Uniform Testamentary Additions to Trusts Act, see Probate Code § 6300 et seq.

§ 6320. Definitions

As used in this chapter, unless the context otherwise requires:

(a) "Designation" means a designation made pursuant to Section 6321.

(b) "Instrument" includes all of the following:

(1) An insurance, annuity, or endowment contract (including any agreement issued or entered into by the insurer in connection therewith, supplemental thereto, or in settlement thereof).

(2) A pension, retirement benefit, death benefit, stock bonus, profit-sharing or employees' saving plan, employee benefit plan, or contract created or entered into by an employer for the benefit of some or all of his or her employees.

(3) A self-employed retirement plan, or an individual retirement annuity or account, established or held pursuant to the Internal Revenue Code.

(4) A multiple-party account, as defined in Section 5132.

(5) Any other written instrument of a type described in Section 5000. *(Stats.1990, c. 79 (A.B.759), § 14, operative July 1, 1991. Amended by Stats.1992, c. 178 (S.B.1496), § 31.4.)*

Law Revision Commission Comments
1992 Amendment [Revised Comment]

Former subdivision (a) of Section 6320 is redesignated as subdivision (b), and is amended to define "instrument" as used in Section 6321. Formerly, Section 6321 referred to a "contract or plan" which was defined in Section 6320. Former subdivision (b) is redesignated as subdivision (a) for purposes of alphabetization.

The basic definition of "instrument" is in Section 45. The definition of "instrument" in Section 6320 makes clear the scope and application of this chapter.

Paragraph (2) of subdivision (b) is amended to add "employee benefit plan." This includes both employee welfare benefit plans and employee pension benefit plans, and is consistent with the intent to make the definition of "instrument" broadly inclusive.

Paragraph (3) of subdivision (b) is amended to refer to individual "retirement" annuities or accounts, consistent with Section 408 of the Internal Revenue Code.

The former reference in paragraph (3) to the Internal Revenue Code as "now or hereafter amended" is revised to eliminate duplicative language. See Section 7 (reference to a law applies to all amendments and additions heretofore or hereafter made). [22 Cal.L.Rev.Comm.Reports 977 (1992)].

Background on Section 6320 of Repealed Code

Section 6320 was added by 1983 Cal.Stat. ch. 842 § 55. The section was drawn from former Probate Code Section 175 (repealed by 1983 Cal.Stat. ch. 842 § 18), but the language of paragraph (3) of Section 6320 was substituted for the former reference to the Self Employed Individuals' Tax Retirement Act of 1962. Subdivision (b) was new and was included for convenience in drafting. For background on the provisions of this part, see the Comment to this part under the part heading. [20 Cal.L.Rev.Comm.Reports 1001 (1990)].

§ 6321. Trustees; designation as beneficiary, payee, or owner

An instrument may designate as a primary or contingent beneficiary, payee, or owner a trustee named or to be named in the will of the person entitled to designate the beneficiary, payee, or owner. The designation shall be made in accordance with the provisions of the contract or plan or, in the absence of such provisions, in a manner approved by the insurer if an insurance, annuity, or endowment contract is involved, and by the trustee, custodian, or person or entity administering the contract or plan, if any. The designation may be made before or after the execution of the designator's will and is not required to comply with the formalities for execution of a will. *(Stats.1990, c. 79 (A.B.759), § 14, operative July 1, 1991. Amended by Stats.1992, c. 178 (S.B.1496), § 31.6.)*

Law Revision Commission Comments

1990 Enactment

Section 6321 continues Section 6321 of the repealed Probate Code without change.

1992 Amendment

Section 6321 is amended to use the term "instrument" in place of the former term "contract or plan." "Instrument" is defined in Section 6320. This amendment broadens the application of this chapter to all kinds of nonprobate transfers permitted under California law, including multiple-party accounts in financial institutions, public employees' death benefits (Gov't Code §§ 21332–21335), and beneficiary designations made under Section 5000.

Before benefits or rights are transferred to the trustee named in decedent's will, the will must be admitted to probate. See Section 6323. [21 Cal.L.Rev.Comm.Reports 201 (1991)].

Background on Section 6321 of Repealed Code

Section 6321 was added by 1983 Cal.Stat. ch. 842 § 55. The section continued a portion of former Probate Code Section 175 (repealed by 1983 Cal.Stat. ch. 842 § 18). For background on the provisions of this part, see the Comment to this part under the part heading. [20 Cal.L.Rev.Comm.Reports 1001 (1990)].

Cross References

Designation defined for purposes of this Chapter, see Probate Code § 6320.
Fiduciaries' wartime substitution law, see Probate Code § 350 et seq.
Instrument defined for purposes of this Chapter, see Probate Code § 6320.

§ 6322. Creation of trust for valid disposition; necessity of effective designation

The designation is ineffective unless the designator's will contains provisions creating the trust or makes a disposition valid under Section 6300. *(Stats.1990, c. 79 (A.B.759), § 14, operative July 1, 1991.)*

Law Revision Commission Comments

1990 Enactment

Section 6322 continues Section 6322 of the repealed Probate Code without change.

Background on Section 6322 of Repealed Code

Section 6322 was added by 1983 Cal.Stat. ch. 842 § 55. The section continued former Probate Code Section 176 (repealed by 1983 Cal.Stat. ch. 842 § 18). For background on the provisions of this part, see the Comment to this part under the part heading. [20 Cal.L.Rev.Comm.Reports 1001 (1990)].

Cross References

Designation defined for purposes of this Chapter, see Probate Code § 6320.

§ 6323. Necessity for administration

Subject to the provisions of Section 6325, the benefits or rights resulting from the designation are payable or transferable directly to the trustee, without becoming subject to administration, upon or at any time after admission of the designator's will to probate. A designation pursuant to this chapter does not have the effect of naming a trustee of a separate inter vivos trust but the rights and benefits or the proceeds thereof when paid to the trustee are, or become a part of, the testamentary trust or trusts established pursuant

to the designator's will or shall be added to an inter vivos trust or trusts if the disposition is governed by Section 6300. *(Stats.1990, c. 79 (A.B.759), § 14, operative July 1, 1991.)*

Law Revision Commission Comments

1990 Enactment

Section 6323 continues Section 6323 of the repealed Probate Code without substantive change.

Background on Section 6323 of Repealed Code

Section 6323 was added by 1983 Cal.Stat. ch. 842 § 55. The section continued former Probate Code Section 177 (repealed by 1983 Cal.Stat. ch. 842 § 18). For background on the provisions of this part, see the Comment to this part under the part heading. [20 Cal.L.Rev.Comm.Reports 1001 (1990)].

Cross References

Designation defined for purposes of this Chapter, see Probate Code § 6320.

§ 6324. Effect of designator's debts

Except as otherwise provided in the designator's will, the rights and benefits and their proceeds paid or transferred to the trustee are not subject to the debts of the designator to any greater extent than if they were paid or transferred to a named beneficiary, payee, or owner other than the estate of the designator. *(Stats.1990, c. 79 (A.B.759), § 14, operative July 1, 1991.)*

Law Revision Commission Comments

1990 Enactment

Section 6324 continues Section 6324 of the repealed Probate Code without change.

Background on Section 6324 of Repealed Code

Section 6324 was added by 1983 Cal.Stat. ch. 842 § 55. The section continued former Probate Code Section 178 (repealed by 1983 Cal.Stat. ch. 842 § 18). For background on the provisions of this part, see the Comment to this part under the part heading. [20 Cal.L.Rev.Comm.Reports 1001 (1990)].

§ 6325. Court in which proceedings pending; jurisdiction; petition for order

(a) The court in which the proceedings are pending for administration of the estate of the decedent has jurisdiction, before or after payment or transfer of benefits and rights or their proceeds to the trustee, to:

(1) Determine the validity of the trust.

(2) Determine the terms of the trust.

(3) Fill vacancies in the office of trustee.

(4) Require a bond of a trustee in its discretion and in such amount as the court may determine for the faithful performance of duties as trustee, subject to the provisions of Article 3 (commencing with Section 1570)of Chapter 16 of Division 1.1 of the Financial Code and Section 15602 of this code.

(5) Grant additional powers to the trustee, as provided in Section 16201.

(6) Instruct the trustee.

(7) Fix or allow payment of compensation of a trustee as provided in Sections 15680 to 15683, inclusive.

(8) Hear and determine adverse claims to the trust property by the personal representative, surviving spouse, or other third person.

(9) Determine the identity of the trustee and the trustee's acceptance or rejection of the office and, upon request, furnish evidence of trusteeship to a trustee.

(10) Order postponement of the payment or transfer of the benefits and rights or their proceeds.

(11) Authorize or direct removal of the trust or trust property to another jurisdiction pursuant to the procedure provided in Chapter 5 (commencing with Section 17400) of Part 5 of Division 9.

(12) Make any order incident to the foregoing or to the accomplishment of the purposes of this chapter.

(b) The personal representative of the designator's estate, any trustee named in the will or designation or successor to such trustee, or any person interested in the estate or trust may petition the court for an order under this section. Notice of hearing of the petition shall be given in the manner provided in Section 17203, except as the court may otherwise order. *(Stats.1990, c. 79 (A.B.759), § 14, operative July 1, 1991. Amended by Stats.2014, c. 71 (S.B.1304), § 138, eff. Jan. 1, 2015.)*

Law Revision Commission Comments

1990 Enactment

Section 6325 continues Section 6325 of the repealed Probate Code without substantive change. For general provisions, see Sections 1000–1004 (rules of practice), 1020–1023 (petitions and other papers), 1040–1050 (hearings and orders). For general provisions relating to notice of hearing, see Sections 1200–1221. See also Sections 1250–1252 (request for special notice), 1260–1265 (proof of giving notice).

Background on Section 6325 of Repealed Code

Section 6325 was added by 1983 Cal.Stat. ch. 842 § 55 and was amended by 1986 Cal.Stat. ch. 820 § 37. The section continued the substance of former Probate Code Section 179 (repealed by 1983 Cal.Stat. ch. 842 § 18). For background on the provisions of this part, see the Comment to this part under the part heading.

The 1986 amendment corrected cross-references and made other technical revisions. For changes in the law applicable to trust administration, see the Comments to the new sections referred to in Section 6325. Subdivision (a)(11) was amended to replace the reference to "assets" with "property"; this was a non-substantive change. See Section 62 ("property" defined). See also Recommendation Proposing the Trust Law, 18 Cal.L.Revision Comm'n Reports 501, 787–88 (1986). [20 Cal.L.Rev.Comm.Reports 1001 (1990)].

Cross References

Deposits with State Treasurer, see Financial Code § 1540 et seq. Designation defined for purposes of this Chapter, see Probate Code § 6320.

§ 6326. Application of Division 9

As to matters not specifically provided in Section 6325, the provisions of Division 9 (commencing with Section 15000) apply to the trust. *(Stats.1990, c. 79 (A.B.759), § 14, operative July 1, 1991.)*

Law Revision Commission Comments

1990 Enactment

Section 6326 continues Section 6326 of the repealed Probate Code without change.

Background on Section 6326 of Repealed Code

Section 6326 was added by 1983 Cal.Stat. ch. 842 § 55 and was amended by 1986 Cal.Stat. ch. 820 § 38. The section continued former Probate Code Section 180 (repealed by 1983 Cal.Stat. ch. 842 § 18). For background on the provisions of this part, see the Comment to this part under the part heading. The 1986 amendment revised the reference to refer to the statute governing trust administration. See Recommendation Proposing the Trust Law, 18 Cal.L.Revision Comm'n Reports 501, 788 (1986). [20 Cal.L.Rev.Comm.Reports 1001 (1990)].

§ 6327. Appealable orders

An appeal may be taken from any of the following:

(a) Any order described in Part 3 (commencing with Section 1300) of Division 3 made pursuant to this chapter.

(b) An order making or refusing to make a determination specified in paragraph (1), (2), or (8) of subdivision (a) of Section 6325.

(c) As provided in Section 1304 for an order made pursuant to Section 6326. *(Stats.1990, c. 79 (A.B.759), § 14, operative July 1, 1991. Amended by Stats.2003, c. 32 (A.B. 167), § 6.)*

Law Revision Commission Comments

1990 Enactment

Section 6327 continues Section 6327 of the repealed Probate Code without change.

2003 Amendment

Subdivision (a) of Section 6327 is amended to reflect relocation of the estate administration appeals statutes from former Section 7240 to Section 1300 et seq. See 1997 Cal. Stat. ch. 724, §§ 11, 18.

Subdivision (c) is amended to reflect relocation of the trust appeals statute from former Section 17207 to Section 1304. See 1997 Cal. Stat. ch. 724, §§ 11, 29. [33 Cal.L.Rev.Comm. Reports 158 (2003)].

Background on Section 6327 of Repealed Code

Section 6327 was added by 1983 Cal.Stat. ch. 842 § 55 and was amended by 1986 Cal.Stat. ch. 820 § 39, 1987 Cal.Stat. ch. 923 § 86, and 1988 Cal.Stat. ch. 1199 § 77. The section continued the substance of former Probate Code Section 181 (repealed by 1983 Cal.Stat. ch. 842 § 18). For background on the provisions of this part, see the Comment to this part under the part heading. The 1986 amendment to Section 6327 conformed the section to the revisions of Section 1240 and added subdivision (c). See the Comment to Section 1240. See also Recommendation Proposing the Trust Law, 18 Cal.L.Revision Comm'n Reports 501, 789 (1986). The 1987 amendment revised the cross-reference to former Section 1240. As to the 1987 amendment, see Communication from California Law Revision Commission Concerning Assembly Bill 708, 19 Cal.L.Revision Comm'n Reports 545, 559 (1988). See also Comments to Conforming Revisions and Repeals, 19 Cal.L.Revision Comm'n Reports 391, 449 (1988). The 1988 amendment corrected a section reference. As to the 1988 amendment, see Comments to Conforming Revisions and Repeals, 19 Cal.L.Revision Comm'n Reports 1031, 1090 (1988). [20 Cal.L.Rev.Comm.Reports 1001 (1990)].

§ 6328. Payment or transfer; unclaimed benefits or rights or proceeds

If no qualified trustee makes claim to the benefits or rights or proceeds within one year after the death of the designator, or if satisfactory evidence is furnished within such one-year period showing that no trustee can qualify to receive them, payment or transfer may be made, unless the designator has otherwise provided, by the obligor to the personal representative of the designator or to those thereafter entitled, and the obligor is discharged from liability. *(Stats.1990, c. 79 (A.B. 759), § 14, operative July 1, 1991.)*

Law Revision Commission Comments

1990 Enactment

Section 6328 continues Section 6328 of the repealed Probate Code without change.

Background on Section 6328 of Repealed Code

Section 6328 was added by 1983 Cal.Stat. ch. 842 § 55. The section continued the substance of former Probate Code Section 182 (repealed by 1983 Cal.Stat. ch. 842 § 18). For background on the provisions of this part, see the Comment to this part under the part heading. [20 Cal.L.Rev.Comm.Reports 1001 (1990)].

§ 6329. Trusts not made pursuant to chapter; validity

Enactment of this chapter does not invalidate trusts, otherwise valid, not made pursuant to the provisions of this chapter. *(Stats.1990, c. 79 (A.B.759), § 14, operative July 1, 1991.)*

Law Revision Commission Comments

1990 Enactment

Section 6329 continues Section 6329 of the repealed Probate Code without change.

Background on Section 6329 of Repealed Code

Section 6329 was added by 1983 Cal.Stat. ch. 842 § 55. The section continued a portion of former Probate Code Section 184 (repealed by 1983 Cal.Stat. ch. 842 § 18). For background on the provisions of this part, see the Comment to this part under the part heading. [20 Cal.L.Rev.Comm.Reports 1001 (1990)].

§ 6330. Chapter as restatement and continuation of former law

This chapter, insofar as it is substantially the same as former Chapter 10 (commencing with Section 175) of former Division 1, repealed by Section 18 of Chapter 842 of the Statutes of 1983, shall be construed as a restatement and continuation thereof and not as a new enactment. After December 31, 1984, a reference in a written instrument to the previously existing provisions relating to the subject matter of this chapter shall be deemed to be a reference to the corresponding provisions of this chapter. *(Stats.1990, c. 79 (A.B.759), § 14, operative July 1, 1991.)*

Law Revision Commission Comments

1990 Enactment

Section 6330 continues Section 6330 of the repealed Probate Code without change. The first sentence of Section 6330 is consistent with subdivision (a) of Section 2 of the Probate Code.

Background on Section 6330 of Repealed Code

Section 6330 was a new provision added by 1984 Cal.Stat. ch. 892 § 39.3. See Communication of Law Revision Commission Concerning Assembly Bill 2290, 18 Cal.L.Revision Comm'n Reports 77, 89 (1986). [20 Cal.L.Rev.Comm.Reports 1001 (1990)].

Cross References

Instrument defined for purposes of this Chapter, see Probate Code § 6320.

CHAPTER 9. DEVISE SUBJECT TO CALIFORNIA UNIFORM TRANSFERS TO MINORS ACT

Cross References

Application of old and new law, see Probate Code § 3.

§ 6340. Repealed by Stats.1984, c. 243, § 10

Law Revision Commission Comments

1984 Repeal

Section 6340 is superseded by Sections 3903 and 3905. [17 Cal.L.Rev.Comm.Reports 601 (1984)].

§ 6341. Devised property paid, delivered or transferred to custodians subject to Uniform Gifts to Minors Act or Uniform Transfers to Minors Act

If a testator's will provides that devised property shall be paid or delivered or transferred to a custodian subject to the California Uniform Gifts to Minors Act or the California Uniform Transfers to Minors Act:

(a) All of the provisions of the California Uniform Transfers to Minors Act, Part 9 (commencing with Section 3900) of Division 4, including, but not limited to, the definitions and the provisions concerning powers, rights, and immunities contained in that act, are applicable to the devise during the period prior to distribution of the property.

(b) Unless the will clearly requires otherwise, if the person named as the beneficiary for whose benefit the custodial property is to be held attains the age at which the custodianship was to terminate prior to the order of distribution, the devise shall be deemed to be a direct devise to the person named as the beneficiary for whose benefit the custodial property was to be held.

(c) The personal representative of the testator's estate, upon entry of an order for distribution, shall make distribution pursuant to the order for distribution by transferring the devised property in the form and manner provided by the California Uniform Transfers to Minors Act.

(d) If a vacancy in the custodianship exists prior to full distribution of the devised property by the personal representative, a successor custodian shall be appointed for any undistributed property in the manner provided by the California Uniform Transfers to Minors Act. *(Stats.1990, c. 79 (A.B.759), § 14, operative July 1, 1991.)*

Law Revision Commission Comments

1990 Enactment

Section 6341 continues Section 6341 of the repealed Probate Code without substantive change. Subdivision (a) makes the California Uniform Transfers to Minors Act applicable to a devise to a minor that the will makes subject to either the Uniform Transfers to Minors Act (1986) or to the superseded Uniform Gifts to Minors Act (1966). This avoids the requirement that a previously executed will be modified to substitute a reference to the Uniform Transfers to Minors Act in place of a reference to the superseded Uniform Gifts to Minors Act.

Background on Section 6341 of Repealed Code

Section 6341 was added by 1983 Cal.Stat. ch. 842 § 55 and was amended by 1984 Cal.Stat. ch. 243 § 11. The section as enacted continued the substance of former Probate Code Section 186.1 (repealed by 1983 Cal.Stat. ch. 842 § 18). See also Section 32 ("devise" means disposition of real or personal property by will). For background on the provisions of this part, see the Comment to this part under the part heading.

The 1984 amendment made a number of revisions and additions to Section 6341:

(1) The introductory clause was revised so that the section applied whether the testator's will referred to the California Uniform Transfers to Minors Act or to the superseded California Uniform Gifts to Minors Act.

(2) Subdivision (a) was revised to make the California Uniform Transfers Act applicable to a devise to a minor that the will makes subject to either the superseded act or the new Uniform Act.

(3) Subdivision (b) was added. This subdivision continued the substance of former Probate Code Section 6343 (repealed by 1984 Cal.Stat. ch. 243 § 13), but subdivision (b) did not apply unless the beneficiary had attained the age at which the custodianship was to terminate, which age could be older than 18 if the will so provided. See Sections 3920, 3920.5. Former Probate Code Section 6343 continued the substance of former Probate Code Section 186.3 (repealed by 1983 Cal.Stat. ch. 842 § 18).

(4) Subdivisions (c) and (d) were added. Subdivision (c) continued the substance of former Probate Code Section 6344 (repealed by 1984 Cal.Stat. ch. 243 § 14). Former Probate Code Section 6344 continued the substance of former Probate Code Section 186.4 (repealed by 1983 Cal.Stat. ch. 842 § 18). Subdivision (d) continued the substance of former Probate Code Section 6346 (repealed by 1984 Cal.Stat. ch. 243 § 15). Former Probate Code Section 6346 continued the substance of former Probate Code Section 186.6 (repealed by 1983 Cal.Stat. ch. 842 § 18).

Concerning the 1984 amendment, see Recommendation Relating to Uniform Transfers to Minors Act, 17 Cal.L.Revision Comm'n Reports 601 (1984). [20 Cal.L.Rev.Comm.Reports 1001 (1990)].

§§ 6342 to 6344. Repealed by Stats.1984, c. 243, §§ 12 to 14

§ 6345. Successor or substitute custodians; compensation

The will may provide for successor or substitute custodians and may specify the standard of compensation of the custodian. *(Stats.1990, c. 79 (A.B.759), § 14, operative July 1, 1991.)*

Law Revision Commission Comments

1990 Enactment

Section 6345 continues Section 6345 of the repealed Probate Code without substantive change.

Background on Section 6345 of Repealed Code

Section 6345 was added by 1983 Cal.Stat. ch. 842 § 55 and was amended by 1985 Cal.Stat. ch. 90 § 2. The section continued the substance of former Probate Code Section 186.5 (repealed by 1983 Cal.Stat. ch. 842 § 18). For background on the provisions of this part, see the Comment to this part under the part heading. The 1985 amendment made a technical, nonsubstantive revision. [20 Cal.L.Rev.Comm.Reports 1001 (1990)].

§ 6346. Repealed by Stats.1984, c. 243, § 15

§ 6347. Custodian; deemed devisee; notice; duty to participate in proceeding

(a) Except as otherwise provided in the will or ordered by a court, each custodian designated in the will and the person for whom the property is to be held shall be deemed a devisee for the purpose of receiving notices which may be required or permitted to be sent to a devisee in the estate of the testator.

(b) Unless required by the will or ordered by the court, a custodian does not have a duty to participate in the proceedings in the estate on behalf of the minor, and in no event does the custodian have a duty to so participate until the custodian has filed a written notice of acceptance of the office of custodian with the clerk of the court in which administration of the estate of the testator is pending. *(Stats.1990, c. 79 (A.B.759), § 14, operative July 1, 1991.)*

Law Revision Commission Comments

1990 Enactment

Section 6347 continues Section 6347 of the repealed Probate Code without change.

Background on Section 6347 of Repealed Code

Section 6347 was added by 1983 Cal.Stat. ch. 842 § 55. The section continued the substance of former Probate Code Section 186.7 (repealed by 1983 Cal.Stat. ch. 842 § 18). See also Section 34 ("devisee" means a person designated in a will to receive a devise of real or personal property). For background on the provisions of this part, see the Comment to this part under the part heading. [20 Cal.L.Rev.Comm.Reports 1001 (1990)].

§ 6348. Exclusive jurisdiction; court in which administration pending

Until distribution of the property pursuant to an order for distribution is completed, the court in which administration of the estate of the testator is pending has exclusive jurisdiction over all proceedings and matters concerning undistributed property, including, but not limited to, the appointment, declination, resignation, removal, bonding, and compensation of, and the delivery or transfer of the undistributed property to, a custodian. After distribution of any property is completed, the court has no further jurisdiction over the distributed property and the property shall be held subject to the California Uniform Transfers to Minors Act. *(Stats.1990, c. 79 (A.B.759), § 14, operative July 1, 1991.)*

1990 Enactment

Section 6348 continues Section 6348 of the repealed Probate Code without change.

Background on Section 6348 of Repealed Code

Section 6348 was added by 1983 Cal.Stat. ch. 842 § 55 and was amended by 1984 Cal.Stat. ch. 243 § 16. The section continued the substance of former Probate Code Section 186.8 (repealed by 1983 Cal.Stat. ch. 842 § 18). For background on the provisions of this part, see the Comment to this part under the part heading. The 1984 amendment substituted a reference to the California Uniform Transfers to Minors Act in place of the reference to the superseded California Uniform Gifts to Minors Act and deleted the phrase "in the same manner as if it had been a lifetime gift." The deleted phrase was unnecessary since the new Uniform Act covered gifts made by will. See Section 3905. Concerning the 1984 amendment, see Recommendation Relating to Uniform Transfers to Minors Act, 17 Cal.L.Revision Comm'n Reports 601 (1984).

§ 6349. Construction of chapter

(a) This chapter shall not be construed as providing an exclusive method for making devises to or for the benefit of minors.

(b) Nothing in this chapter limits any provision of the California Uniform Transfers to Minors Act, Part 9 (commencing with Section 3900) of Division 4. *(Stats.1990, c. 79 (A.B.759), § 14, operative July 1, 1991.)*

1990 Enactment

Section 6349 continues Section 6349 of the repealed Probate Code without change. Subdivision (b) makes clear that nothing in this chapter limits the California Uniform Transfers to Minors Act. See, e.g., Section 3906 (transfer to custodian by executor or administrator in the absence of a will or under a will that does not contain an authorization to do so).

Background on Section 6349 of Repealed Code

Section 6349 was added by 1983 Cal.Stat. ch. 842 § 55 and was amended by 1984 Cal.Stat. ch. 243 § 17. The section continued the substance of former Probate Code Section 186.9 (repealed by 1983 Cal.Stat. ch. 842 § 18). For background on the provisions of this part, see the Comment to this part under the part heading. The 1984 amendment added subdivision (b). Concerning the 1984 amendment, see Recommendation Relating to Uniform Transfers to Minors Act, 17 Cal.L.Revision Comm'n Reports 601 (1984). [20 Cal.L.Rev.Comm.Reports 1001 (1990)].

CHAPTER 11. UNIFORM INTERNATIONAL WILLS ACT

Cross References

Application of old and new law, see Probate Code § 3.

§ 6380. Definitions

In this chapter:

(a) "International will" means a will executed in conformity with Sections 6381 to 6384, inclusive.

(b) "Authorized person" and "person authorized to act in connection with international wills" means a person who by Section 6388, or by the laws of the United States including members of the diplomatic and consular service of the United States designated by Foreign Service Regulations, is empowered to supervise the execution of international wills. *(Stats. 1990, c. 79 (A.B.759), § 14, operative July 1, 1991.)*

1990 Enactment

Section 6380 continues Section 6380 of the repealed Probate Code without change. This section is the same in substance as Section 2–1001 of the Uniform Probate Code (1987) (Uniform International Wills Act). As to the construction of provisions drawn from uniform acts, see Section 2.

Background on Section 6380 of Repealed Code

Section 6380 was added by 1983 Cal.Stat. ch. 842 § 55. The section continued former Probate Code Section 60 (repealed by 1983 Cal.Stat. ch. 842 § 18). For background on the provisions of this part, see the Comment to this part under the part heading. [20 Cal.L.Rev.Comm.Reports 1001 (1990)].

§ 6381. Validity of wills; application of chapter to testamentary dispositions made by two or more persons

(a) A will is valid as regards form, irrespective particularly of the place where it is made, of the location of the assets and of the nationality, domicile, or residence of the testator, if it is made in the form of an international will complying with the requirements of this chapter.

(b) The invalidity of the will as an international will does not affect its formal validity as a will of another kind.

(c) This chapter does not apply to the form of testamentary dispositions made by two or more persons in one instrument. *(Stats.1990, c. 79 (A.B.759), § 14, operative July 1, 1991.)*

1990 Enactment

Section 6381 continues Section 6381 of the repealed Probate Code without change. This section is the same in substance as Section 2–1002 of the Uniform Probate Code (1987) (Uniform International Wills Act). As to the construction of provisions drawn from uniform acts, see Section 2.

Background on Section 6381 of Repealed Code

Section 6381 was added by 1983 Cal.Stat. ch. 842 § 55. The section continued former Probate Code Section 60.1 (repealed by 1983 Cal.Stat. ch. 842 § 18). For background on the provisions of this part, see the Comment to this part under the part heading. [20 Cal.L.Rev.Comm.Reports 1001 (1990)].

International will defined for purposes of this Chapter, see Probate Code § 6380.

§ 6382. Necessity of writing; witnesses; other requirements

(a) The will shall be made in writing. It need not be written by the testator himself or herself. It may be written in any language, by hand or by any other means.

(b) The testator shall declare in the presence of two witnesses and of a person authorized to act in connection with international wills that the document is the testator's will and that the testator knows the contents thereof. The testator need not inform the witnesses, or the authorized person, of the contents of the will.

(c) In the presence of the witnesses, and of the authorized person, the testator shall sign the will or, if the testator has previously signed it, shall acknowledge his or her signature.

(d) If the testator is unable to sign, the absence of the testator's signature does not affect the validity of the international will if the testator indicates the reason for his or her inability to sign and the authorized person makes note thereof on the will. In that case, it is permissible for any other person present, including the authorized person or one of the witnesses, at the direction of the testator, to sign the testator's name for the testator if the authorized person makes note of this also on the will, but it is not required that any person sign the testator's name for the testator.

(e) The witnesses and the authorized person shall there and then attest the will by signing in the presence of the testator. *(Stats.1990, c. 79 (A.B.759), § 14, operative July 1, 1991.)*

Law Revision Commission Comments

1990 Enactment

Section 6382 continues Section 6382 of the repealed Probate Code without substantive change. This section is the same in substance as Section 2–1003 of the Uniform Probate Code (1987) (Uniform International Wills Act). As to the construction of provisions drawn from uniform acts, see Section 2.

Background on Section 6382 of Repealed Code

Section 6382 was added by 1983 Cal.Stat. ch. 842 § 55. The section continued former Probate Code Section 60.2 (repealed by 1983 Cal.Stat. ch. 842 § 18). For background on the provisions of this part, see the Comment to this part under the part heading. [20 Cal.L.Rev.Comm.Reports 1001 (1990)].

Cross References

Authorized person defined for purposes of this Chapter, see Probate Code § 6380.
International will defined for purposes of this Chapter, see Probate Code § 6380.
Person authorized defined for purposes of this Chapter, see Probate Code § 6380.

§ 6383. Signatures; numbering; date; declaration concerning safekeeping; validity of will

(a) The signatures shall be placed at the end of the will. If the will consists of several sheets, each sheet shall be signed by the testator or, if the testator is unable to sign, by the person signing on his or her behalf or, if there is no such person, by the authorized person. In addition, each sheet shall be numbered.

(b) The date of the will shall be the date of its signature by the authorized person. That date shall be noted at the end of the will by the authorized person.

(c) The authorized person shall ask the testator whether the testator wishes to make a declaration concerning the safekeeping of the will. If so and at the express request of the testator, the place where the testator intends to have the will kept shall be mentioned in the certificate provided for in Section 6384.

(d) A will executed in compliance with Section 6382 is not invalid merely because it does not comply with this section. *(Stats.1990, c. 79 (A.B.759), § 14, operative July 1, 1991.)*

Law Revision Commission Comments

1990 Enactment

Section 6383 continues Section 6383 of the repealed Probate Code without substantive change. This section is the same in substance as Section 2–1004 of the Uniform Probate Code (1987) (Uniform International Wills Act). As to the construction of provisions drawn from uniform acts, see Section 2.

Background on Section 6383 of Repealed Code

Section 6383 was added by 1983 Cal.Stat. ch. 842 § 55. The section continued former Probate Code Section 60.3 (repealed by 1983 Cal.Stat. ch. 842 § 18). For background on the provisions of this part, see the Comment to this part under the part heading. [20 Cal.L.Rev.Comm.Reports 1001 (1990)].

Cross References

Authorized person defined for purposes of this Chapter, see Probate Code § 6380.

§ 6384. Certificate establishing fulfillment of requirements; form

The authorized person shall attach to the will a certificate to be signed by the authorized person establishing that the requirements of this chapter for valid execution of an international will have been fulfilled. The authorized person shall keep a copy of the certificate and deliver another to the testator. The certificate shall be substantially in the following form:

CERTIFICATE

(Convention of October 26, 1973)

1. I, _____,
    (name, address, and capacity)
    a person authorized to act in connection with international wills,
2. certify that on _____ at _____
    (date)   (place)
3. _____
    (testator)   (name, address, date and place of birth)
    in my presence and that of the witnesses
4. (a) _____
        (name, address, date and place of birth)
    (b) _____
        (name, address, date and place of birth)
    has declared that the attached document is his will and that he knows the contents thereof.
5. I furthermore certify that:

6. (a) in my presence and in that of the witnesses
    (1) the testator has signed the will or has acknowl-
        edged his signature previously affixed.
    (2) following a declaration of the testator stating that
        he was unable to sign his will for the following
        reason _____,
        I have mentioned this declaration on the will,*
        and the signature has been affixed by

        _____
                        (name and address)*
7. (b) the witnesses and I have signed the will;
8. (c) each page of the will has been signed by
        _____ and numbered;*
9. (d) I have satisfied myself as to the identity of the testator
        and of the witnesses as designated above;
10. (e) the witnesses met the conditions requisite to act as
        such according to the law under which I am acting;
11. (f) the testator has requested me to include the following
        statement concerning the safekeeping of his will:*

        _____
12.   PLACE OF EXECUTION
13.   DATE
14.   SIGNATURE and, if
                 necessary, SEAL

_____
*to be completed if appropriate

(Stats.1990, c. 79 (A.B.759), § 14, operative July 1, 1991.)

Law Revision Commission Comments
1990 Enactment

Section 6384 continues Section 6384 of the repealed Probate Code without substantive change. This section is the same in substance as Section 2–1005 of the Uniform Probate Code (1987) (Uniform International Wills Act). As to the construction of provisions drawn from uniform acts, see Section 2.

Background on Section 6384 of Repealed Code

Section 6384 was added by 1983 Cal.Stat. ch. 842 § 55. The section continued former Probate Code Section 60.4 (repealed by 1983 Cal.Stat. ch. 842 § 18). For background on the provisions of this part, see the Comment to this part under the part heading. [20 Cal.L.Rev.Comm.Reports 1001 (1990)].

Cross References

Authorized person defined for purposes of this Chapter, see Probate Code § 6380.
International will defined for purposes of this Chapter, see Probate Code § 6380.
Person authorized defined for purposes of this Chapter, see Probate Code § 6380.

§ 6385. Certificate of authorized person as conclusive of formal validity

In the absence of evidence to the contrary, the certificate of the authorized person is conclusive of the formal validity of the instrument as a will under this chapter. The absence or irregularity of a certificate does not affect the formal validity of a will under this chapter. *(Stats.1990, c. 79 (A.B.759), § 14, operative July 1, 1991.)*

Law Revision Commission Comments
1990 Enactment

Section 6385 continues Section 6385 of the repealed Probate Code without change. This section is the same in substance as Section 2–1006 of the Uniform Probate Code (1987) (Uniform International Wills Act). As to the construction of provisions drawn from uniform acts, see Section 2.

Background on Section 6385 of Repealed Code

Section 6385 was added by 1983 Cal.Stat. ch. 842 § 55. The section continued former Probate Code Section 60.5 (repealed by 1983 Cal.Stat. ch. 842 § 18). For background on the provisions of this part, see the Comment to this part under the part heading. [20 Cal.L.Rev.Comm.Reports 1001 (1990)].

Cross References

Authorized person defined for purposes of this Chapter, see Probate Code § 6380.

§ 6386. Revocation

The international will is subject to the ordinary rules of revocation of wills. *(Stats.1990, c. 79 (A.B.759), § 14, operative July 1, 1991.)*

Law Revision Commission Comments
1990 Enactment

Section 6386 continues Section 6386 of the repealed Probate Code without change. This section is the same in substance as Section 2–1007 of the Uniform Probate Code (1987) (Uniform International Wills Act). As to the construction of provisions drawn from uniform acts, see Section 2.

Background on Section 6386 of Repealed Code

Section 6386 was added by 1983 Cal.Stat. ch. 842 § 55. The section continued former Probate Code Section 60.6 (repealed by 1983 Cal.Stat. ch. 842 § 18). For background on the provisions of this part, see the Comment to this part under the part heading. [20 Cal.L.Rev.Comm.Reports 1001 (1990)].

Cross References

International will defined for purposes of this Chapter, see Probate Code § 6380.

§ 6387. Interpretation and application of chapter

Sections 6380 to 6386, inclusive, derive from Annex to Convention of October 26, 1973, Providing a Uniform Law on the Form of an International Will. In interpreting and applying this chapter, regard shall be had to its international origin and to the need for uniformity in its interpretation. *(Stats.1990, c. 79 (A.B.759), § 14, operative July 1, 1991.)*

Law Revision Commission Comments
1990 Enactment

Section 6387 continues Section 6387 of the repealed Probate Code without change. This section is the same in substance as Section 2–1008 of the Uniform Probate Code (1987) (Uniform International Wills Act). As to the construction of provisions drawn from uniform acts, see Section 2.

Background on Section 6387 of Repealed Code

Section 6387 was added by 1983 Cal.Stat. ch. 842 § 55. The section continued former Probate Code Section 60.7 (repealed by 1983 Cal.Stat. ch. 842 § 18). For background on the provisions of this part, see the Comment to this part under the part heading. [20 Cal.L.Rev.Comm.Reports 1001 (1990)].

International will defined for purposes of this Chapter, see Probate Code § 6380.

§ 6388. Law practitioners as authorized persons

Individuals who have been admitted to practice law before the courts of this state and who are in good standing as active law practitioners of this state are authorized persons in relation to international wills. *(Stats.1990, c. 79 (A.B.759), § 14, operative July 1, 1991.)*

Law Revision Commission Comments

1990 Enactment

Section 6388 continues Section 6388 of the repealed Probate Code without change. This section is the same in substance as Section 2–1009 of the Uniform Probate Code (1987) (Uniform International Wills Act). As to the construction of provisions drawn from uniform acts, see Section 2.

Background on Section 6388 of Repealed Code

Section 6388 was added by 1983 Cal.Stat. ch. 842 § 55. The section continued the first paragraph of former Probate Code Section 60.8 (repealed by 1983 Cal.Stat. ch. 842 § 18). For background on the provisions of this part, see the Comment to this part under the part heading. [20 Cal.L.Rev.Comm.Reports 1001 (1990)].

Cross References

Authorized person defined for purposes of this Chapter, see Probate Code § 6380.
International will defined for purposes of this Chapter, see Probate Code § 6380.

§ 6389. Registry system; authorized person; execution of international wills

The Secretary of State shall establish a registry system by which authorized persons may register in a central information center information regarding the execution of international wills, keeping that information in strictest confidence until the death of the maker and then making it available to any person desiring information about any will who presents a death certificate or other satisfactory evidence of the testator's death to the center. Information that may be received, preserved in confidence until death, and reported as indicated is limited to the name, social security or other individual identifying number established by law, if any, address, date and place of birth of the testator, and the intended place of deposit or safekeeping of the instrument pending the death of the maker. The Secretary of State, at the request of the authorized person, may cause the information it receives about execution of any international will to be transmitted to the registry system of another jurisdiction as identified by the testator, if that other system adheres to rules protecting the confidentiality of the information similar to those established in this state. *(Stats.1990, c. 79 (A.B.759), § 14, operative July 1, 1991.)*

Law Revision Commission Comments

1990 Enactment

Section 6389 continues Section 6389 of the repealed Probate Code without change. This section is the same in substance as Section 2–1010 of the Uniform Probate Code (1987) (Uniform International Wills Act). As to the construction of provisions drawn from uniform acts, see Section 2.

Background on Section 6389 of Repealed Code

Section 6389 was added by 1983 Cal.Stat. ch. 842 § 55. The section continued paragraph 2 of former Probate Code Section 60.8 (repealed by 1983 Cal.Stat. ch. 842 § 18). For background on the provisions of this part, see the Comment to this part under the part heading. [20 Cal.L.Rev.Comm.Reports 1001 (1990)].

Cross References

Authorized person defined for purposes of this Chapter, see Probate Code § 6380.
Inspection of public records, exemptions from disclosure, international wills, registration information, see Government Code § 6276.26.
International will defined for purposes of this Chapter, see Probate Code § 6380.
Other exemptions to inspection of public records, "wards and dependent children, release of description information about minor escapees" to "Youth service bureau", see Government Code § 6276.48.

§ 6390. Chapter as restatement and continuation of former law

After December 31, 1984, a reference in a written instrument, including a will, to the former law (repealed by Chapter 892 of the Statutes of 1984) shall be deemed to be a reference to the corresponding provision of this chapter. *(Stats.1990, c. 79 (A.B.759), § 14, operative July 1, 1991.)*

Law Revision Commission Comments

1990 Enactment

Section 6390 continues Section 6390 of the repealed Probate Code with the omission of the first sentence. The first sentence is unnecessary in light of subdivision (a) of Section 2.

Section 6390 makes clear that after the operative date of this chapter (January 1, 1985) a reference in a written instrument to the former law shall be deemed to be a reference to the corresponding provision of this chapter.

Background on Section 6390 of Repealed Code

Section 6390 was a new provision added by 1984 Cal.Stat. ch. 892 § 39.7. See Communication of Law Revision Commission Concerning Assembly Bill 2290, 18 Cal.L.Revision Comm'n Reports 77, 89 (1986). See also Recommendation Relating to Revision of Wills and Intestate Succession Law, 17 Cal.L.Revision Comm'n Reports 537 (1984). [20 Cal.L.Rev.Comm.Reports 1001 (1990)].

Part 2

INTESTATE SUCCESSION

Application

Application of Part 2 to estates of decedents who died on or after Jan. 1, 1985, see Probate Code § 6414.

Law Revision Commission Comments

1990 Enactment

This part supersedes Part 2 (commencing with Section 6400) of Division 6 the repealed Probate Code. The superseded part was enacted upon recommendation of the California Law Revision Commission. See Tentative Recommendation Relating to Wills and

Intestate Succession, 16 Cal.L.Revision Comm'n Reports 2301 (1982). See also Report of Senate Committee on Judiciary on Assembly Bills 25 and 68, 17 Cal.L.Revision Comm'n Reports 867, 871–83 (1984). [20 Cal.L.Rev.Comm.Reports 1001 (1990)].

Cross References
Biomedical and Behavioral Research, actions for physical or mental injuries or wrongful death, see Penal Code § 3524.
Claims and actions against public entities and employees, collateral source payments, see Government Code § 985.

CHAPTER 1. INTESTATE SUCCESSION GENERALLY

Cross References
Death of owner of family cemetery plot, disposition, sale, transfer, or donation of unoccupied portions of plot, see Health and Safety Code § 8650.
Death of owner of interment right, intestate succession, waiver of right, see Health and Safety Code § 9069.25.
Private cemeteries, death of owner of family plot without making disposition, see Health and Safety Code § 8650.

§ 6400. Property subject to intestacy provisions

Any part of the estate of a decedent not effectively disposed of by will passes to the decedent's heirs as prescribed in this part. *(Stats.1990, c. 79 (A.B.759), § 14, operative July 1, 1991.)*

Law Revision Commission Comments

1990 Enactment

Section 6400 continues Section 6400 of the repealed Probate Code without change. This section is the same in substance as Section 2–101 of the Uniform Probate Code (1987). As to the construction of provisions drawn from uniform acts, see Section 2. The section does not apply if the decedent died before January 1, 1985. As to the application of any amendments made after that date, see Section 3. If the decedent died before January 1, 1985, see Section 6414(b), (c). See also Section 6404 (escheat).

Background on Section 6400 of Repealed Code

Section 6400 was added by 1983 Cal.Stat. ch. 842 § 55. The section superseded former Probate Code Section 200 (repealed by 1983 Cal.Stat. ch. 842 § 19) and the first portion of former Probate

Code Section 220 (repealed by 1983 Cal.Stat. ch. 842 § 19). For background on the provisions of this part, see the Comment to this part under the part heading. [20 Cal.L.Rev.Comm.Reports 1001 (1990)].

Cross References
Acquisition of property by succession, see Civil Code § 1000.
Heir defined, see Probate Code § 44.
Property rights of the parties, see Family Code § 2550 et seq.
Tribal marriages and divorces, see Family Code § 295.
Unoccupied portions of a family plot, inalienable lots declared alienable, see Health and Safety Code § 8650.
Will, disposal of property, see Probate Code § 6101.
Wills,
Effects of duress, menace, fraud, or undue influence on execution or revocation, see Probate Code § 6104.
Execution of California statutory wills, see Probate Code § 6221 et seq.
Omitted spouse or child, see Probate Code § 6560 et seq.
Requirements for execution, see Probate Code § 6110 et seq.
Revocation and revival, see Probate Code § 6120 et seq.

§ 6401. Surviving spouse; intestate share; community or quasi-community property; separate property

(a) As to community property, the intestate share of the surviving spouse is the one-half of the community property that belongs to the decedent under Section 100.

(b) As to quasi-community property, the intestate share of the surviving spouse is the one-half of the quasi-community property that belongs to the decedent under Section 101.

(c) As to separate property, the intestate share of the surviving spouse is as follows:

(1) The entire intestate estate if the decedent did not leave any surviving issue, parent, brother, sister, or issue of a deceased brother or sister.

(2) One–half of the intestate estate in the following cases:

(A) Where the decedent leaves only one child or the issue of one deceased child.

(B) Where the decedent leaves no issue, but leaves a parent or parents or their issue or the issue of either of them.

(3) One–third of the intestate estate in the following cases:

(A) Where the decedent leaves more than one child.

(B) Where the decedent leaves one child and the issue of one or more deceased children.

(C) Where the decedent leaves issue of two or more deceased children. *(Stats.1990, c. 79 (A.B.759), § 14, operative July 1, 1991. Amended by Stats.2002, c. 447 (A.B.2216), § 1, operative July 1, 2003; Stats.2014, c. 913 (A.B.2747), § 32, eff. Jan. 1, 2015.)*

Law Revision Commission Comments

1990 Enactment

Section 6401 continues Section 6401 of the repealed Probate Code without substantive change. As to a surviving spouse's waiver of rights at death, see Sections 140–147.

Upon the death of a married person, one-half of the decedent's quasi-community property belongs to the surviving spouse (Section 101); in the case of intestate succession, the other one-half of the decedent's quasi-community property, which belongs to the decedent (Section 101), goes to the surviving spouse under subdivision (b) of Section 6401. The quasi-community property recaptured under

Section 102 does not belong to the decedent even though the property is restored to the decedent's estate; rather it is property that belongs to the surviving spouse. See Section 102 and the Comment thereto. Accordingly, the surviving spouse does not take the recaptured property by intestate succession. See also Section 66 (defining "quasi-community property").

Community property and quasi-community property that passes to the surviving spouse under subdivisions (a) and (b) is subject to Section 13502 (election to have community and quasi-community property administered) and Sections 13540–13542 (right of surviving spouse to deal with and dispose of community and quasi-community real property). As to the liability of the surviving spouse for debts of the deceased spouse, see Sections 13550–13554.

This section does not apply if the decedent died before January 1, 1985. See Section 6414(a). As to amendments made after that date, see Section 3. If the decedent died before January 1, 1985, see Section 6414(b), (c).

For background on this section, see Recommendation and Study Relating to Rights of Surviving Spouse in Property Acquired by Decedent While Domiciled Elsewhere, 1 Cal.L.Revision Comm'n Reports E–1 (1957); Recommendation and Study Relating to Inter Vivos Marital Property Rights in Property Acquired While Domiciled Elsewhere, 3 Cal.L.Revision Comm'n Reports I–1 (1961); Recommendation Relating to Quasi–Community Property, 9 Cal.L.Revision Comm'n Reports 113 (1969).

Background on Section 6401 of Repealed Code

Section 6401 was added by 1983 Cal.Stat. ch. 842 § 55 and was amended by 1984 Cal.Stat. ch. 892 § 40. Subdivision (a) of Section 6401 was the same in substance as a portion of former Probate Code Section 201 (repealed by 1983 Cal.Stat. ch. 842 § 19). Subdivision (b) was the same in substance as a portion of former Probate Code Section 201.5 (repealed by 1983 Cal.Stat. ch. 842 § 19). Subdivision (c) continued the rules under former law that determined the share the surviving spouse received of the decedent's separate estate. See former Prob.Code §§ 221, 223, 224 (repealed by 1983 Cal.Stat. ch. 842 § 19). The 1984 amendment made a nonsubstantive technical change. See Recommendation Relating to Revision of Wills and Intestate Succession Law, 17 Cal.L.Revision Comm'n Reports 537 (1984). For background on the provisions of this part, see the Comment to this part under the part heading. [20 Cal.L.Rev.Comm.Reports 1001 (1990)].

Cross References

Abatement of intestate share, application, see Probate Code § 21402.
Beneficiary of decedent's estate, successors to cause of action under this section, see Code of Civil Procedure § 377.10.
Child defined, see Probate Code § 26.
Community property,
  Debts, liability for, see Family Code §§ 910, 911.
  Definition, see Probate Code § 28; Civil Code § 687; Family Code § 760.
  Disposition of property held in revocable trust, see Probate Code § 13504.
  Disposition on divorce or separate maintenance, see Family Code § 2550.
  Division upon death of spouse, see Probate Code § 100.
  Election by surviving spouse or others to transfer property to trustee, see Probate Code § 13503.
  Election of surviving spouse to have property administered, see Probate Code § 13502.
  Interests of parties defined, see Family Code § 751.
  Management and control, see Family Code § 1100 et seq.
  Power of surviving spouse to deal with or dispose of property, see Probate Code § 13540 et seq.
  Presumptions regarding, see Family Code § 803.
  Simultaneous death, see Probate Code § 220 et seq.

Subject to support and education of children, see Family Code § 4008.
Debts of deceased spouse, liability of surviving spouse, see Probate Code § 13550 et seq.
Decedent's property, passage of title, see Probate Code §§ 7000, 7001.
Issue defined, see Probate Code § 50.
Offer to sell mobilehome park or entry into listing agreement for sale of park, see Civil Code § 798.80.
Parent defined, see Probate Code § 54.
Property defined, see Probate Code § 62.
Quasi-community property,
  Definition, see Probate Code § 66; Family Code § 125.
  Division upon death of spouse, see Probate Code § 101.
  Election of surviving spouse to have property administered, see Probate Code § 13502.
  Power of surviving spouse to deal with or dispose of property, see Probate Code § 13540 et seq.
  Requirements for restoration of transferred property to decedent's estate, see Probate Code § 102.
Registration and Titling of Manufactured Homes, Mobilehomes, and Commercial Coaches, death of owner, see Health and Safety Code § 18102.
Registration of vehicles and certificates of title, transfer upon death of owner, see Vehicle Code § 5910.
Surviving spouse, defined, see Probate Code § 78.
Transfer of a floating home marina, see Civil Code § 800.100.
Transfer of ownership of undocumented vessel upon death of owner, see Vehicle Code § 9916.

§ 6402. Intestate estate not passing to surviving spouse

Except as provided in Section 6402.5, the part of the intestate estate not passing to the surviving spouse, under Section 6401, or the entire intestate estate if there is no surviving spouse, passes as follows:

(a) To the issue of the decedent, the issue taking equally if they are all of the same degree of kinship to the decedent, but if of unequal degree those of more remote degree take in the manner provided in Section 240.

(b) If there is no surviving issue, to the decedent's parent or parents equally.

(c) If there is no surviving issue or parent, to the issue of the parents or either of them, the issue taking equally if they are all of the same degree of kinship to the decedent, but if of unequal degree those of more remote degree take in the manner provided in Section 240.

(d) If there is no surviving issue, parent or issue of a parent, but the decedent is survived by one or more grandparents or issue of grandparents, to the grandparent or grandparents equally, or to the issue of those grandparents if there is no surviving grandparent, the issue taking equally if they are all of the same degree of kinship to the decedent, but if of unequal degree those of more remote degree take in the manner provided in Section 240.

(e) If there is no surviving issue, parent or issue of a parent, grandparent or issue of a grandparent, but the decedent is survived by the issue of a predeceased spouse, to that issue, the issue taking equally if they are all of the same degree of kinship to the predeceased spouse, but if of unequal degree those of more remote degree take in the manner provided in Section 240.

(f) If there is no surviving issue, parent or issue of a parent, grandparent or issue of a grandparent, or issue of a predeceased spouse, but the decedent is survived by next of kin, to the next of kin in equal degree, but where there are two or more collateral kindred in equal degree who claim through different ancestors, those who claim through the nearest ancestor are preferred to those claiming through an ancestor more remote.

(g) If there is no surviving next of kin of the decedent and no surviving issue of a predeceased spouse of the decedent, but the decedent is survived by the parents of a predeceased spouse or the issue of those parents, to the parent or parents equally, or to the issue of those parents if both are deceased, the issue taking equally if they are all of the same degree of kinship to the predeceased spouse, but if of unequal degree those of more remote degree take in the manner provided in Section 240. *(Stats.1990, c. 79 (A.B.759), § 14, operative July 1, 1991. Amended by Stats.2002, c. 447 (A.B.2216), § 2, operative July 1, 2003; Stats.2014, c. 913 (A.B.2747), § 32.5, eff. Jan. 1, 2015.)*

Law Revision Commission Comments
1990 Enactment

Section 6402 continues Section 6402 of the repealed Probate Code without substantive change. Except to the extent indicated below, subdivisions (a)–(d) are the same in substance as Section 2–103 of the Uniform Probate Code (1987). As to the construction of provisions drawn from uniform acts, see Section 2.

Under subdivision (d), grandchildren or more remote lineal descendants of the deceased take ahead of great-grandparents. Subdivision (d) does not adopt the scheme of paragraph (4) of Section 2–103 of the Uniform Probate Code (1987). (Under that provision of the Uniform Probate Code, half of the estate goes to paternal grandparents or to the issue of the paternal grandparents if both are deceased, and the other half goes to maternal grandparents or to the issue of the maternal grandparents if both are deceased.)

If there are no takers under Sections 6401–6402.5, the decedent's estate escheats to the state. See Section 6404.

This section does not apply if the decedent died before January 1, 1985. See Section 6414(a). As to the application of any amendments made after that date, see Section 3. If the decedent died before January 1, 1985, see Section 6414(b), (c).

Background on Section 6402 of Repealed Code

Section 6402 was added by 1983 Cal.Stat. ch. 842 § 55 and was amended by 1984 Cal.Stat. ch. 892 § 41 and 1985 Cal.Stat. ch. 982 § 19. Subdivision (a) was consistent with former Probate Code Section 222 (repealed by 1983 Cal.Stat. ch. 842 § 19) except that the rule of representation was changed. See Section 240 and the Comment thereto. Subdivisions (b) and (c) were consistent with former Probate Code Section 225 (repealed by 1983 Cal.Stat. ch. 842 § 19) except for the new rule of representation.

Subdivisions (d), (e), (f), and (g) superseded former Probate Code Section 226 (repealed by 1983 Cal.Stat. ch. 842 § 19) and a portion of former Probate Code Section 229 (repealed by 1983 Cal.Stat. ch. 842 § 19). Subdivision (d) was consistent with former Probate Code Section 226 (repealed by 1983 Cal.Stat. ch. 842 § 19) pursuant to which the estate went to the next of kin, except that under subdivision (d) grandchildren or more remote lineal descendants of the grandparents of the deceased took ahead of great-grandparents. By way of contrast, under former Section 226 great-grandparents (related in the third degree) took ahead of grandchildren of the deceased's grandparents (fourth degree). Subdivision (e) was drawn from former Probate Code Section 229 (repealed by 1983 Cal.Stat. ch. 842 § 19) and gave the decedent's stepchildren and issue of deceased stepchildren a right to inherit if there is no one to inherit under

subdivisions (a) through (d). Subdivision (f) was drawn from former Probate Code Section 226 (repealed by 1983 Cal.Stat. ch. 842 § 19). Subdivision (g) was drawn from former Section 229 and gave parents and issue of deceased parents of a predeceased spouse of the decedent a right to inherit if there is no one to inherit under subdivisions (a) through (f). See also Section 6402.5 (succession to the portion of the decedent's estate attributable to the decedent's predeceased spouse). The 1984 amendment made a nonsubstantive technical change. See Communication of Law Revision Commission Concerning Assembly Bill 2290, 18 Cal.L.Revision Comm'n Reports 77, 89 (1986). See also Recommendation Relating to Revision of Wills and Intestate Succession Law, 17 Cal.L.Revision Comm'n Reports 537 (1984). The 1985 amendment substituted the references to Section 240 for the former references to taking "by representation." This change was nonsubstantive. See Communication Concerning Assembly Bill 196, 18 Cal.L.Revision Comm'n Reports 367, 375 (1986). See also Recommendation Relating to Distribution Under a Will or Trust, 18 Cal.L.Revision Comm'n Reports 269, 284–85 (1986). For background on the provisions of this part, see the Comment to this part under the part heading. [20 Cal.L.Rev.Comm.Reports 1001 (1990)].

Cross References

Abatement of intestate share, application, see Probate Code § 21402.

Beneficiary of decedent's estate, successors to cause of action under this section, see Code of Civil Procedure § 377.10.

Escheat of decedent's property, see Probate Code § 6800 et seq.

Halfbloods, adopted persons, persons born out of wedlock, stepchildren, foster children and their issue as kindred or issue, see Probate Code § 21115.

Issue defined, see Probate Code § 50.

Offer to sell mobilehome park or entry into listing agreement for sale of park, see Civil Code § 798.80.

Parent defined, see Probate Code § 54.

Parental inheritance through a child, conditions preventing inheritance, parent treated as predeceasing child, see Probate Code § 6452.

Registration and Titling of Manufactured Homes, Mobilehomes, and Commercial Coaches, death of owner, see Health and Safety Code § 18102.

Registration of vehicles and certificates of title, transfer upon death of owner, see Vehicle Code § 5910.

Surviving spouse defined, see Probate Code § 78.

Taking by representation, manner, see Probate Code § 240.

Transfer of a floating home marina, see Civil Code § 800.100.

Transfer of ownership of undocumented vessel upon death of owner, see Vehicle Code § 9916.

§ 6402.5. Predeceased spouse; portion of decedent's estate attributable to decedent's predeceased spouse

(a) For purposes of distributing real property under this section if the decedent had a predeceased spouse who died not more than 15 years before the decedent and there is no surviving spouse or issue of the decedent, the portion of the decedent's estate attributable to the decedent's predeceased spouse passes as follows:

(1) If the decedent is survived by issue of the predeceased spouse, to the surviving issue of the predeceased spouse; if they are all of the same degree of kinship to the predeceased spouse they take equally, but if of unequal degree those of more remote degree take in the manner provided in Section 240.

(2) If there is no surviving issue of the predeceased spouse but the decedent is survived by a parent or parents of the

predeceased spouse, to the predeceased spouse's surviving parent or parents equally.

(3) If there is no surviving issue or parent of the predeceased spouse but the decedent is survived by issue of a parent of the predeceased spouse, to the surviving issue of the parents of the predeceased spouse or either of them, the issue taking equally if they are all of the same degree of kinship to the predeceased spouse, but if of unequal degree those of more remote degree take in the manner provided in Section 240.

(4) If the decedent is not survived by issue, parent, or issue of a parent of the predeceased spouse, to the next of kin of the decedent in the manner provided in Section 6402.

(5) If the portion of the decedent's estate attributable to the decedent's predeceased spouse would otherwise escheat to the state because there is no kin of the decedent to take under Section 6402, the portion of the decedent's estate attributable to the predeceased spouse passes to the next of kin of the predeceased spouse who shall take in the same manner as the next of kin of the decedent take under Section 6402.

(b) For purposes of distributing personal property under this section if the decedent had a predeceased spouse who died not more than five years before the decedent, and there is no surviving spouse or issue of the decedent, the portion of the decedent's estate attributable to the decedent's predeceased spouse passes as follows:

(1) If the decedent is survived by issue of the predeceased spouse, to the surviving issue of the predeceased spouse; if they are all of the same degree of kinship to the predeceased spouse they take equally, but if of unequal degree those of more remote degree take in the manner provided in Section 240.

(2) If there is no surviving issue of the predeceased spouse but the decedent is survived by a parent or parents of the predeceased spouse, to the predeceased spouse's surviving parent or parents equally.

(3) If there is no surviving issue or parent of the predeceased spouse but the decedent is survived by issue of a parent of the predeceased spouse, to the surviving issue of the parents of the predeceased spouse or either of them, the issue taking equally if they are all of the same degree of kinship to the predeceased spouse, but if of unequal degree those of more remote degree take in the manner provided in Section 240.

(4) If the decedent is not survived by issue, parent, or issue of a parent of the predeceased spouse, to the next of kin of the decedent in the manner provided in Section 6402.

(5) If the portion of the decedent's estate attributable to the decedent's predeceased spouse would otherwise escheat to the state because there is no kin of the decedent to take under Section 6402, the portion of the decedent's estate attributable to the predeceased spouse passes to the next of kin of the predeceased spouse who shall take in the same manner as the next of kin of the decedent take under Section 6402.

(c) For purposes of disposing of personal property under subdivision (b), the claimant heir bears the burden of proof to show the exact personal property to be disposed of to the heir.

(d) For purposes of providing notice under any provision of this code with respect to an estate that may include personal property subject to distribution under subdivision (b), if the aggregate fair market value of tangible and intangible personal property with a written record of title or ownership in the estate is believed in good faith by the petitioning party to be less than ten thousand dollars ($10,000), the petitioning party need not give notice to the issue or next of kin of the predeceased spouse. If the personal property is subsequently determined to have an aggregate fair market value in excess of ten thousand dollars ($10,000), notice shall be given to the issue or next of kin of the predeceased spouse as provided by law.

(e) For the purposes of disposing of property pursuant to subdivision (b), "personal property" means that personal property in which there is a written record of title or ownership and the value of which in the aggregate is ten thousand dollars ($10,000) or more.

(f) For the purposes of this section, the "portion of the decedent's estate attributable to the decedent's predeceased spouse" means all of the following property in the decedent's estate:

(1) One-half of the community property in existence at the time of the death of the predeceased spouse.

(2) One-half of any community property, in existence at the time of death of the predeceased spouse, which was given to the decedent by the predeceased spouse by way of gift, descent, or devise.

(3) That portion of any community property in which the predeceased spouse had any incident of ownership and which vested in the decedent upon the death of the predeceased spouse by right of survivorship.

(4) Any separate property of the predeceased spouse which came to the decedent by gift, descent, or devise of the predeceased spouse or which vested in the decedent upon the death of the predeceased spouse by right of survivorship.

(g) For the purposes of this section, quasi-community property shall be treated the same as community property.

(h) For the purposes of this section:

(1) Relatives of the predeceased spouse conceived before the decedent's death but born thereafter inherit as if they had been born in the lifetime of the decedent.

(2) A person who is related to the predeceased spouse through two lines of relationship is entitled to only a single share based on the relationship which would entitle the person to the larger share. (Stats.1990, c. 79 (A.B.759), § 14, operative July 1, 1991.)

Law Revision Commission Comments

1990 Enactment

Section 6402.5 continues Section 6402.5 of the repealed Probate Code without change. This section does not apply if the decedent died before January 1, 1985. See Section 6414(a). As to the application of any amendments made after that date, see Section 3. If the decedent died before January 1, 1985, see Section 6414(b), (c).

Background on Section 6402.5 of Repealed Code

Section 6402.5 was added by 1983 Cal.Stat. ch. 842 § 55 and was amended by 1985 Cal.Stat. ch. 982 § 20 and 1986 Cal.Stat. ch. 873 § 1. As enacted in 1983, the section continued the substance of subdivisions (a), (b), and (e) of former Probate Code Section 229 (repealed by 1983 Cal.Stat. ch. 842 § 19) with the following changes:

(1) The application of Section 6402.5 was limited to real property and the section applied only where the predeceased spouse died not more than 15 years before the decedent. Former Section 229 was not so limited. The rules for determining what constitutes "the portion of the decedent's estate attributable to the decedent's predeceased spouse" were the same as under subdivision (b) of former Section 229.

(2) The provisions of Section 6402.5 relating to taking by representation were consistent with the general provisions relating to taking by representation. See Section 240.

(3) Paragraph (4) of subdivision (b) of former Section 229 was not continued. The omitted provision was made obsolete by 1980 Cal.Stat. ch. 119, which provided that property set aside as a probate homestead for a surviving spouse shall in no case be set aside beyond the lifetime of the surviving spouse; after the 1980 enactment, the probate homestead is not a part of the estate of that spouse when that spouse dies.

(4) Subdivision (c), now subdivision (g), was included in Section 6402.5 to make clear that quasi-community real property (see Section 66) is to be treated the same as community real property for the purposes of this section. Former Section 229 contained no provision that dealt specifically with quasi-community property.

(5) The special rule provided in subdivision (c) of former Section 229 was not continued. Insofar as the property described in that subdivision is a "portion of the decedent's estate attributable to the decedent's predeceased spouse" and the spouse died not more than 15 years before the decedent, the property is governed by the general provisions of Section 6402.5.

(6) Subdivision (d) of former Section 229 was superseded by subdivisions (e) and (g) of Section 6402.

The 1985 amendment substituted the references to Section 240 for the former reference to taking "by representation." This change was nonsubstantive. See Recommendation Relating to Distribution Under a Will or Trust, 18 Cal.L.Revision Comm'n Reports 269, 285–87 (1986). The 1986 amendment made the section applicable to personal property. For background on the provisions of this part, see the Comment to this part under the part heading. [20 Cal.L.Rev.Comm.Reports 1001 (1990)].

Cross References

Burden of proof, generally, see Evidence Code § 500 et seq.
Degree of kinship, manner of taking, see Probate Code § 240.
Escheat of decedent's property, see Probate Code § 6800 et seq.
Halfbloods, adopted persons, persons born out of wedlock, stepchildren, foster children and their issue as kindred or issue, see Probate Code § 21115.
Inventory of estate, community and separate property, see Probate Code § 8850.
Issue defined, see Probate Code § 50.
Notice, general provisions, see Probate Code § 1200 et seq.
Parent defined, see Probate Code § 54.
Predeceased spouse defined, see Probate Code § 59.
Quasi-community property defined, see Probate Code § 66.
Real property defined, see Probate Code § 68.
Separate and community property, see Family Code § 751 et seq.
Separate property of married person, see Family Code § 770.
Surviving spouse defined, see Probate Code § 78.

Taking by representation, manner, see Probate Code § 240.

§ 6403. Failure to survive decedent by 120 hours; deemed predeceased; application of section

(a) A person who fails to survive the decedent by 120 hours is deemed to have predeceased the decedent for the purpose of intestate succession, and the heirs are determined accordingly. If it cannot be established by clear and convincing evidence that a person who would otherwise be an heir has survived the decedent by 120 hours, it is deemed that the person failed to survive for the required period. The requirement of this section that a person who survives the decedent must survive the decedent by 120 hours does not apply if the application of the 120-hour survival requirement would result in the escheat of property to the state.

(b) This section does not apply to the case where any of the persons upon whose time of death the disposition of property depends died before January 1, 1990, and such case continues to be governed by the law applicable before January 1, 1990. *(Stats.1990, c. 79 (A.B.759), § 14, operative July 1, 1991.)*

Law Revision Commission Comments

1990 Enactment

Section 6403 continues Section 6403 of the repealed Probate Code without substantive change. The section is the same in substance as Section 2–104 of the Uniform Probate Code (1987) insofar as that section relates to taking by intestate succession. As to the construction of provisions drawn from uniform acts, see Section 2.

Where Section 6403 applies, the 120–hour survival requirement is used to determine whether one person survived another for the purposes of Sections 103 (simultaneous death of husband and wife) and 234 (proceedings to determine survival).

For a provision governing disposition of community property and quasi-community property where a married person does not survive his or her spouse, see Section 103. See also Sections 230–234 (proceeding to determine whether one person survived another).

Section 6403 does not apply if the decedent died before January 1, 1985. See Section 6414(a). As to the application of any amendments made after that date, see Section 3. If the decedent died before January 1, 1985, see Section 6414(b), (c).

Background on Section 6403 of Repealed Code

Section 6403 was a new provision added by 1983 Cal.Stat. ch. 842 § 55 and amended by 1989 Cal.Stat. ch. 544 § 5 to provide a 120–hour survival rule. See Recommendation Relating to 120–Hour Survival Requirement, 20 Cal.L.Revision Commission Reports 21 (1990); see also Communication from the California Law Revision Commission Concerning Assembly Bill 158, 20 Cal.L.Revision Commission Reports 235, 236 (1990). For background on the provisions of this part, see the Comment to this part under the part heading. [20 Cal.L.Rev.Comm.Reports 1001 (1990)].

Cross References

Escheat of decedents' property, see Probate Code § 6800 et seq.
Heir defined, see Probate Code § 44.
Person defined, see Probate Code § 56.
Simultaneous death, administration and distribution of community or quasi-community property, see Probate Code § 103.
Survival, proceedings to determine, see Probate Code § 230 et seq.

§ 6404. Application of escheat provisions

Part 4 (commencing with Section 6800) (escheat) applies if there is no taker of the intestate estate under the provisions of this part. *(Stats.1990, c. 79 (A.B.759), § 14, operative July 1, 1991.)*

1990 Enactment

Section 6404 continues Section 6404 of the repealed Probate Code without change. This section is comparable to Section 2–105 of the Uniform Probate Code (1987). As to the construction of provisions drawn from uniform acts, see Section 2. For provisions relating to escheat, see Sections 6800–6806. See also Code Civ.Proc. §§ 1300–1615 (unclaimed property). Section 6404 does not apply if the decedent died before January 1, 1985. See Section 6414(a). As to the application of any amendments made after that date, see Section 3. If the decedent died before January 1, 1985, see Section 6414(b), (c).

Background on Section 6404 of Repealed Code

Section 6404 was a new provision added by 1983 Cal.Stat. ch. 842 § 55. For background on the provisions of this part, see the Comment to this part under the part heading. [20 Cal.L.Rev.Comm.Report 1001 (1990)].

Cross References

Escheat of decedent's property, see Probate Code § 6800 et seq.

§ 6406. Relatives of halfblood

Except as provided in Section 6451, relatives of the halfblood inherit the same share they would inherit if they were of the whole blood. *(Stats.1990, c. 79 (A.B.759), § 14, operative July 1, 1991. Amended by Stats.1993, c. 529 (A.B.1137), § 3.)*

Law Revision Commission Comments

1990 Enactment

Section 6406 continues Section 6406 of the repealed Probate Code without change. This section is the same as Section 2–107 of the Uniform Probate Code (1987). As to the construction of provisions drawn from uniform acts, see Section 2. See also Section 6152 (construction of wills). Section 6406 does not apply if the decedent died before January 1, 1985. See Section 6414(a). As to the application of any amendments made after that date, see Section 3. If the decedent died before January 1, 1985, see Section 6414(b), (c).

1993 Amendment

Section 6406 is amended to recognize the exception in Section 6451. This amendment is clarifying. [23 Cal.L.Rev.Comm. Reports 901 (1993) (Annual Report, App. 9)].

Background on Section 6406 of Repealed Code

Section 6406 was added by 1983 Cal.Stat. ch. 842 § 55. The section superseded former Probate Code Section 254 (repealed by 1983 Cal.Stat. ch. 842 § 19). Under former Section 254, halfblood relatives of the decedent who were not of the blood of an ancestor of the decedent were excluded from inheriting property of the decedent which had come to the decedent from such ancestor. Section 6406 eliminated this rule and puts halfbloods on the same footing as wholeblood relatives of the decedent. For background on the provisions of this part, see the Comment to this part under the part heading. [20 Cal.L.Rev.Comm.Reports 1001 (1990)].

Cross References

Halfbloods, adopted persons, persons born out of wedlock, stepchildren, foster children and their issue as kindred or issue, see Probate Code § 21115.

§ 6407. Unborn relatives of decedent

Relatives of the decedent conceived before the decedent's death but born thereafter inherit as if they had been born in the lifetime of the decedent. *(Stats.1990, c. 79 (A.B.759), § 14, operative July 1, 1991.)*

Law Revision Commission Comments

1990 Enactment

Section 6407 continues Section 6407 of the repealed Probate Code without change. This section is the same in substance as Section 2–108 of the Uniform Probate Code (1987). As to the construction of provisions drawn from uniform acts, see Section 2. Section 6407 is consistent with Civil Code Section 29. See also Section 6150(c) (person conceived before but born after a testator's death or after time the devise is to take effect in enjoyment takes if answering the class description). Section 6407 does not apply if the decedent died before January 1, 1985. See Section 6414(a). As to the application of any amendments made after that date, see Section 3. If the decedent died before January 1, 1985, see Section 6414(b), (c).

Background on Section 6407 of Repealed Code

Section 6407 was added by 1983 Cal.Stat. ch. 842 § 55. The section superseded the second sentence of former Probate Code Section 250 (repealed by 1983 Cal.Stat. ch. 842 § 19). For background on the provisions of this part, see the Comment to this part under the part heading. [20 Cal.L.Rev.Comm.Reports 1001 (1990)].

Cross References

Defeat of future interests, birth of posthumous child, see Civil Code § 739.
Future interests of posthumous children, see Civil Code § 698.
Omitted children, see Probate Code § 6570 et seq.
Unborn child deemed an existing person, see Civil Code § 43.1.

§ 6408. Repealed by Stats.1993, c. 529 (A.B.1137), § 4

Law Revision Commission Comments

Repeal

Former Section 6408 is superseded by Sections 6450–6455. [23 Cal.L.Rev.Comm. Reports 901 (1993) (Annual Report, App. 9)].

§ 6408.5. Repealed by Stats.1990, c. 79 (A.B.759), § 13, operative July 1, 1991

Law Revision Commission Comments

1990 Repeal

Former Section 6408.5 is continued in Section 6408 without substantive change. Subdivision (a) of former Section 6408.5 is continued in subdivision (b) of Section 6408 without substantive change. Subdivision (b) of former Section 6408.5 is continued in subdivision (c) of Section 6408 without change. Subdivision (c) of former Section 6408.5 is continued in subdivision (d) of Section 6408 without change. [20 Cal.L.Rev.Comm.Reports 1001 (1990)].

§ 6409. Property given to heirs during decedent's lifetime; advancement against share

(a) If a person dies intestate as to all or part of his or her estate, property the decedent gave during lifetime to an heir is treated as an advancement against that heir's share of the intestate estate only if one of the following conditions is satisfied:

(1) The decedent declares in a contemporaneous writing that the gift is an advancement against the heir's share of the estate or that its value is to be deducted from the value of the heir's share of the estate.

(2) The heir acknowledges in writing that the gift is to be so deducted or is an advancement or that its value is to be deducted from the value of the heir's share of the estate.

(b) Subject to subdivision (c), the property advanced is to be valued as of the time the heir came into possession or enjoyment of the property or as of the time of death of the decedent, whichever occurs first.

(c) If the value of the property advanced is expressed in the contemporaneous writing of the decedent, or in an acknowledgment of the heir made contemporaneously with the advancement, that value is conclusive in the division and distribution of the intestate estate.

(d) If the recipient of the property advanced fails to survive the decedent, the property is not taken into account in computing the intestate share to be received by the recipient's issue unless the declaration or acknowledgment provides otherwise. *(Stats.1990, c. 79 (A.B.759), § 14, operative July 1, 1991. Amended by Stats.2002, c. 138 (A.B.1784), § 8.)*

Law Revision Commission Comments

1990 Enactment

Section 6409 continues Section 6409 of the repealed Probate Code without change. Subdivisions (a), (b), and (d) are the same in substance as Section 2–110 of the Uniform Probate Code (1987). As to the construction of provisions drawn from uniform acts, see Section 2. For a comparable rule concerning ademption by satisfaction, see Section 6174. See also Section 11640 (hearing and order resolving questions arising under Section 6409). Section 6409 does not apply if the decedent died before January 1, 1985. See Section 6414(a). As to the application of any amendments made after that date, see Section 3. If the decedent died before January 1, 1985, see Section 6414(b), (c). As to the effect of a disclaimer, see Section 282.

2002 Amendment

Section 6409 is amended for conformity with Section 21135. It is consistent with Uniform Probate Code Section 2–109 (1990). [31 Cal.L.Rev.Comm. Reports 221 (2001)].

Background on Section 6409 of Repealed Code

Section 6409 was added by 1983 Cal.Stat. ch. 842 § 55 and was amended by 1984 Cal.Stat. ch. 892 § 43. Subdivisions (a), (b), and (d) superseded the last portion of former Probate Code Section 1050 (repealed by 1983 Cal.Stat. ch. 842 § 44). Subdivisions (b) and (c) superseded a portion of former Probate Code Section 1052 (repealed by 1983 Cal.Stat. ch. 842 § 46).

Section 6409 was consistent with former law with two exceptions:

(1) Under former Probate Code Section 1053 (repealed by 1983 Cal.Stat. ch. 842 § 47), if the donee of an advancement predeceased the donor, the advancement was deducted from the shares the heirs of the donee would receive from the donor's estate, while under Section 6409 the advancement was not charged against the donee's issue unless the declaration or acknowledgment provides otherwise.

(2) The provisions relating to the valuation of the property, which superseded former Probate Code Section 1052 (repealed by 1983 Cal.Stat. ch. 842 § 46), were consistent with the provisions of Section 6174 relating to ademption by satisfaction. See the Comment to Section 6174.

The 1984 amendment revised the section to cover advancements where there is a partial intestacy. See Communication of Law Revision Commission Concerning Assembly Bill 2290, 18 Cal.L.Revision Comm'n Reports 77, 90 (1986).

For background on the provisions of this part, see the Comment to this part under the part heading. [20 Cal.L.Rev.Comm.Reports 1001 (1990)].

Cross References

Ademption by satisfaction, see Probate Code § 21135.
Child or issue omitted from will, see Probate Code § 6570 et seq.
Disclaimers, treatment of beneficiary of disclaimed interest, see Probate Code § 282.
Final distribution of estate, hearing on questions arising under this section, see Probate Code § 11640.
Hearings and orders on questions arising under this section, see Probate Code § 11640.
Heirs defined, see Probate Code § 44.
Issue defined, see Probate Code § 50.
Satisfaction of testamentary gift during lifetime of testator, see Probate Code § 21135.
Transferee dying in lifetime of testator, see Probate Code § 21110.

§ 6410. Debt owed to decedent; predeceased debtor

(a) A debt owed to the decedent is not charged against the intestate share of any person except the debtor.

(b) If the debtor fails to survive the decedent, the debt is not taken into account in computing the intestate share of the debtor's issue. *(Stats.1990, c. 79 (A.B.759), § 14, operative July 1, 1991.)*

Law Revision Commission Comments

1990 Enactment

Section 6410 continues Section 6410 of the repealed Probate Code without change. This section is the same in substance as Section 2–111 of the Uniform Probate Code (1987) and is consistent with prior California case law. See Estate of Berk, 196 Cal.App.2d 278, 16 Cal.Rptr. 492 (1961). As to the construction of provisions drawn from uniform acts, see Section 2. As to the effect of a disclaimer, see Section 282. This section does not apply if the decedent died before January 1, 1985. See Section 6414(a). As to the application of any amendments made after that date, see Section 3. If the decedent died before January 1, 1985, see Section 6414(b), (c).

Background on Section 6410 of Repealed Code

Section 6410 was a new provision added by 1983 Cal.Stat. ch. 842 § 55. For background on the provisions of this part, see the Comment to this part under the part heading. [20 Cal.L.Rev.Comm.Reports 1001 (1990)].

Cross References

Issue defined, see Probate Code § 50.
Person defined, see Probate Code § 56.

§ 6411. Aliens

No person is disqualified to take as an heir because that person or a person through whom he or she claims is or has been an alien. *(Stats.1990, c. 79 (A.B.759), § 14, operative July 1, 1991.)*

Law Revision Commission Comments

1990 Enactment

Section 6411 continues Section 6411 of the repealed Probate Code without change. This section is the same in substance as Section 2–112 of the Uniform Probate Code (1987) and is consistent with other provisions of California law. See Cal. Const. art. 1, § 20; Civil Code § 671. As to the construction of provisions drawn from uniform acts, see Section 2. This section does not apply if the decedent died before January 1, 1985. See Section 6414(a). As to the application of any amendments made after that date, see Section 3. If the decedent died before January 1, 1985, see Section 6414(b), (c).

Background on Section 6411 of Repealed Code

Section 6411 was a new provision added by 1983 Cal.Stat. ch. 842 § 55. For background on the provisions of this part, see the Comment to this part under the part heading. [20 Cal.L.Rev.Comm.Reports 1001 (1990)].

Cross References

Heirs defined, see Probate Code § 44.
Ownership of property, authorization, see Civil Code § 671.
Person defined, see Probate Code § 56.

§ 6412. Dower and curtesy; nonrecognition

Except to the extent provided in Section 120, the estates of dower and curtesy are not recognized. *(Stats.1990, c. 79 (A.B.759), § 14, operative July 1, 1991.)*

Law Revision Commission Comments

1990 Enactment

Section 6412 continues Section 6412 of the repealed Probate Code without change. This section is the same in substance as Section 2–113 of the Uniform Probate Code (1987). As to the construction of provisions drawn from uniform acts, see Section 2. The introductory clause is not found in the Uniform Probate Code and is included to recognize that Section 120 gives the surviving spouse rights in California real property of a nondomiciliary decedent that may be akin to dower or curtesy in the decedent's state of domicile. This section applies whether the decedent died before, on, or after January 1, 1985. See Section 6414(b). As to the application of any amendments made after that date, see Section 3.

Background on Section 6412 of Repealed Code

Section 6412 was added by 1983 Cal.Stat. ch. 842 § 55 and was amended by 1984 Cal.Stat. ch. 892 § 44. The section continued the substance of former Section 5129 of the Civil Code (repealed by 1983 Cal.Stat. ch. 842 § 9). The 1984 amendment revised Section 6412 to recognize that Section 120 gives the surviving spouse rights in California real property of a nondomiciliary decedent that may be akin to dower or curtesy in the decedent's state of domicile. This amendment was clarifying, and not substantive. See Recommendation Relating to Revision of Wills and Intestate Succession Law, 17 Cal.L.Revision Comm'n Reports 537, 582 (1984). For background on the provisions of this part, see the Comment to this part under the part heading. [20 Cal.L.Rev.Comm.Reports 1001 (1990)].

Cross References

Spouses, effect of will of nondomiciliary decedent disposing of real property within state on surviving spouse's rights, see Probate Code § 120.

§ 6413. Relation through two lines of relationships; single share

A person who is related to the decedent through two lines of relationship is entitled to only a single share based on the relationship which would entitle the person to the larger share. *(Stats.1990, c. 79 (A.B.759), § 14, operative July 1, 1991.)*

Law Revision Commission Comments

1990 Enactment

Section 6413 continues Section 6413 of the repealed Probate Code without change. This section is the same in substance as Section 2–114 of the Uniform Probate Code (1987). As to the construction of provisions drawn from uniform acts, see Section 2. The section has potential application, for example, in a case where the natural parents of a child are killed in an accident and the child is adopted by a brother or sister of the natural mother of child, leaving the child as natural and adopted grandchild of the parents of the natural mother. See also Uniform Probate Code § 2–114 comment (1987). Section 6413 does not apply if the decedent died before January 1, 1985. See Section 6414(a). As to the application of any amendments made after that date, see Section 3. If the decedent died before January 1, 1985, see Section 6414(b), (c).

Background on Section 6413 of Repealed Code

Section 6413 was a new provision added by 1983 Cal.Stat. ch. 842 § 55. For background on the provisions of this part, see the Comment to this part under the part heading. [20 Cal.L.Rev.Comm.Reports 1001 (1990)].

Cross References

Distribution of intestate estate, division of property, see Probate Code § 240 et seq.
Person defined, see Probate Code § 56.

§ 6414. Application of part

(a) Except as provided in subdivision (b), this part does not apply where the decedent died before January 1, 1985, and the law applicable prior to January 1, 1985, continues to apply where the decedent died before January 1, 1985.

(b) Section 6412 applies whether the decedent died before, on, or after January 1, 1985.

(c) Where any of the following provisions is applied in a case where the decedent died before January 1, 1985, any reference in that provision to this part shall be deemed to be a reference to former Division 2 (commencing with Section 200) which was repealed by Section 19 of Chapter 842 of the Statutes of 1983:

(1) Section 377 of the Code of Civil Procedure.

(2) Section 3524 of the Penal Code. *(Stats.1990, c. 79 (A.B.759), § 14, operative July 1, 1991.)*

Law Revision Commission Comments

1990 Enactment

Section 6414 continues Section 6414 of the repealed Probate Code without substantive change. This section limits the application of Sections 6400–6411 and 6413 to cases where the decedent died on or after January 1, 1985, the operative date of those sections. As to the application of any amendments made after that date, see Section 3. Subdivision (c) makes clear that cross-references to a provision of this part contained in Code of Civil Procedure Section 377 (wrongful death) and Penal Code Section 3524 (injury or death of prisoner during biomedical or behavioral research) are deemed to be references to the corresponding provision of former law in cases where the decedent died before January 1, 1985, the operative date of this part.

Background on Section 6414 of Repealed Code

Section 6414 was a new provision added by 1984 Cal.Stat. ch. 892 § 44.5. See Communication of Law Revision Commission Concerning Assembly Bill 2290, 18 Cal.L.Revision Comm'n Reports 77, 90 (1986). See also Recommendation Relating to Revision of Wills and Intestate Succession Law, 17 Cal.L.Revision Comm'n Reports 537 (1984). The section was amended by 1989 Cal.Stat. ch. 21 § 12 to delete the reference to Section 300 of the Probate Code, which had been repealed. See Communication from the California Law Revision Commission Concerning Assembly Bill 156, 20 Cal.L.Revision Comm'n Reports 227, 229–30 (1990). For background on the provisions of this part, see the Comment to this part under the part heading. [20 Cal.L.Rev.Comm.Reports 1001 (1990)].

CHAPTER 2. PARENT AND CHILD RELATIONSHIP

§ 6450. Relationship existence

Subject to the provisions of this chapter, a relationship of parent and child exists for the purpose of determining intestate succession by, through, or from a person in the following circumstances:

(a) The relationship of parent and child exists between a person and the person's natural parents, regardless of the marital status of the natural parents.

(b) The relationship of parent and child exists between an adopted person and the person's adopting parent or parents. *(Added by Stats.1993, c. 529 (A.B.1137), § 5.)*

Law Revision Commission Comments
1993 Addition

Section 6450 continues former Section 6408(a) without substantive change. The language "[s]ubject to the provisions of this chapter" is placed in the introductory clause because Sections 6451, 6452, and 6454 modify the relationship of parent and child between an adopted person and the person's adopting parent or parents, as well as the relationship of parent and child between a person and the person's natural parents. See also Section 6453 (establishing natural parent-child relationship). In former Section 6408, application of the "except" clause was limited to the relationship of parent and child between a person and the person's natural parents.

The definitions of "child" (Section 26), "issue" (Section 50), and "parent" (Section 54) adopt the rules set out in this chapter. See also Section 6152 (construction of wills). [23 Cal.L.Rev.Comm. Reports 901 (1993) (Annual Report, App. 9)].

§ 6451. Adoption

(a) An adoption severs the relationship of parent and child between an adopted person and a natural parent of the adopted person unless both of the following requirements are satisfied:

(1) The natural parent and the adopted person lived together at any time as parent and child, or the natural parent was married to or cohabiting with the other natural parent at the time the person was conceived and died before the person's birth.

(2) The adoption was by the spouse of either of the natural parents or after the death of either of the natural parents.

(b) Neither a natural parent nor a relative of a natural parent, except for a wholeblood brother or sister of the adopted person or the issue of that brother or sister, inherits from or through the adopted person on the basis of a parent and child relationship between the adopted person and the natural parent that satisfies the requirements of paragraphs

(1) and (2) of subdivision (a), unless the adoption is by the spouse or surviving spouse of that parent.

(c) For the purpose of this section, a prior adoptive parent and child relationship is treated as a natural parent and child relationship. *(Added by Stats.1993, c. 529 (A.B.1137), § 5.)*

Law Revision Commission Comments
1993 Addition [Revised Comment]

Section 6451 continues the substance of subdivisions (b) and (c) of former Section 6408.

In case of an adoption coming within subdivision (a), the adopted child may inherit from or through the adoptive parent, and also from or through the natural parent who gave up the child for adoption or through the natural parent who died preceding the adoption. The following examples indicate in various situations whether an adopted child or the issue of an adopted child may inherit from or through the child's natural parent.

Example 1. Child never lived with either mother or father. Both parents relinquish child for adoption. The adopted child's relationship with both natural parents' families is severed. The requirements of subdivision (a)(1) are not satisfied.

Example 2. Child's mother and father were married or lived together as a family. Child lives with mother and father. Father dies. Mother relinquishes child for adoption. For the purpose of inheritance, the adopted child remains a member of both the deceased father's family and of the relinquishing mother's family. The requirement of subdivision (a) is satisfied because the adoption was "after the death of either of the natural parents."

Example 3. Child's mother and father were married or lived together as a family until father died. Child lives with mother but not father because father died prior to child's birth. Mother relinquishes child for adoption. For the purpose of inheritance, the adopted child remains a member of both the deceased father's family and of the relinquishing mother's family. Child remains a member of the deceased father's family because the father died before the birth of the child (satisfying the subdivision (a)(1) requirement) and the adoption was after the death of the father (satisfying the subdivision (a)(2) requirement).

Under subdivision (a), a non-stepparent adoption severs the relationship between the adopted person and his or her natural "parent." Thus, for example, if a person is adopted by only one adopting parent, that severs the parent-child relationship between the adopted person and his or her natural parent of the same gender as the adopting parent. The parent-child relationship continues to exist between the adopted person and his or her other natural parent.

In case of an adoption described in subdivision (b), the natural relatives cannot inherit from the adopted child, even though under Section 6450(a) the child could inherit from the natural relatives.

In subdivision (b), the reference to inheritance on the basis of a parent-child relationship "that satisfies the requirements of paragraphs (1) and (2) of subdivision (a)" is added to make clear that, for a wholeblood brother or sister to inherit from or through the adoptee, the requirements of these two paragraphs must be satisfied. Under these two paragraphs, the relationship of parent and child does not exist between an adopted person and the person's natural parent unless the living-together or other requirements of paragraph (1) of subdivision (a) are satisfied, and the adoption was after the death of either natural parent. This changes the rule of *In re* Estate of Reedy, 22 Cal.Rptr.2d 478 (1993), *petition for hearing in California Supreme Court filed.* If the adoption was by the spouse of either natural parent, by its terms subdivision (b) does not apply.

Subdivision (b) omits the reference to the adoptee's "issue" that was in the parenthetical "except" clause in subdivision (c) of former Section 6408. The former reference to "issue" was unnecessary. Issue of the adoptee do not inherit from or through the adoptee on the basis of a parent-child relationship between the adoptee and the adoptee's parents. Rather they inherit from or through the adoptee on the basis of the parent-child relationship between themselves and the adoptee.

Subdivision (c) is new, and makes clear that, for the purpose of this section, a prior adoptive parent and child relationship is treated as a natural parent and child relationship. Thus, for example, if a person is adopted by one set of parents, and later is adopted by a second set of parents, the second adoption severs the parent-child relationship between the adoptee and the first set of adoptive parents unless paragraphs (1) and (2) of subdivision (a) are satisfied, substituting "adoptive" for "natural" in those paragraphs. This is a clarification, and may be a change in prior law.

"Wholeblood" relatives were defined in *In re* Estate of Belshaw, 190 Cal. 278, 285, 212 P. 13 (1923), to mean persons having both natural parents in common. One effect of subdivision (c) is to broaden "wholeblood" in subdivision (b) to include adoptive siblings in an appropriate case. For example, assume a person, *P,* is born to two parents, a brother, *B,* is born to the same two parents, and a half-sister, *S,* is born to the mother and later adopted by the father. *B* is a wholeblood sibling of *P* because they have both natural parents in common. For the purpose of inheritance, *S* is treated as a wholeblood sibling of *P,* because under subdivision (c) the effect of the adoption is to treat *S* as the natural child of the adopting father. If *P* is later adopted by two adopting parents, under subdivision (b) the adoption cuts off inheritance by most of *P's* natural relatives, except that both *B* and *S* may inherit from or through *P* if the requirements of paragraphs (1) and (2) of subdivision (a) are satisfied. [23 Cal.L.Rev.Comm. Reports 1009 (1993)].

§ 6452. Conditions preventing a parent from inheriting from or through a child

(a) A parent does not inherit from or through a child on the basis of the parent and child relationship if any of the following apply:

(1) The parent's parental rights were terminated and the parent-child relationship was not judicially reestablished.

(2) The parent did not acknowledge the child.

(3) The parent left the child during the child's minority without an effort to provide for the child's support or without communication from the parent, for at least seven consecutive years that continued until the end of the child's minority, with the intent on the part of the parent to abandon the child. The failure to provide support or to communicate for the prescribed period is presumptive evidence of an intent to abandon.

(b) A parent who does not inherit from or through the child as provided in subdivision (a) shall be deemed to have predeceased the child, and the intestate estate shall pass as otherwise required under Section 6402. *(Added by Stats. 2013, c. 39 (A.B.490), § 2.)*

§ 6453. Natural parents

For the purpose of determining whether a person is a "natural parent" as that term is used in this chapter:

(a) A natural parent and child relationship is established where that relationship is presumed and not rebutted pursuant to the Uniform Parentage Act (Part 3 (commencing with Section 7600) of Division 12 of the Family Code).

(b) A natural parent and child relationship may be established pursuant to any other provisions of the Uniform Parentage Act, except that the relationship may not be established by an action under subdivision (c) of Section 7630

of the Family Code unless any of the following conditions exist:

(1) A court order was entered during the father's lifetime declaring paternity.

(2) Paternity is established by clear and convincing evidence that the father has openly held out the child as his own.

(3) It was impossible for the father to hold out the child as his own and paternity is established by clear and convincing evidence.

(c) A natural parent and child relationship may be established pursuant to Section 249.5. *(Added by Stats.1993, c. 529 (A.B.1137), § 5. Amended by Stats.2004, c. 775 (A.B.1910), § 9.)*

Law Revision Commission Comments
1993 Addition [Revised Comment]

Subdivision (a) and paragraphs (1) and (2) of subdivision (b) of Section 6453 continue the substance of former Section 6408(f), except that former Section 6408(f)(2) required the father to have "openly and notoriously held out the child as his own." Paragraph (2) of subdivision (b) of Section 6453 omits "and notoriously," and merely requires the father to have "openly held out" the child as his own. [23 Cal.L.Rev.Comm. Reports 1009 (1993)].

§ 6454. Foster parent or stepparent

For the purpose of determining intestate succession by a person or the person's issue from or through a foster parent or stepparent, the relationship of parent and child exists between that person and the person's foster parent or stepparent if both of the following requirements are satisfied:

(a) The relationship began during the person's minority and continued throughout the joint lifetimes of the person and the person's foster parent or stepparent.

(b) It is established by clear and convincing evidence that the foster parent or stepparent would have adopted the person but for a legal barrier. *(Added by Stats.1993, c. 529 (A.B.1137), § 5.)*

Law Revision Commission Comments
1993 Addition

Section 6454 continues the substance of former Section 6408(e). Section 6454 applies, for example, where a foster child or stepchild is not adopted because a parent of the child refuses to consent to the adoption. See also Estate of Lind, 209 Cal.App.3d 1424, 257 Cal.Rptr. 853 (2d Dist.1989), review denied; Estate of Claffey, 209 Cal.App.3d 254, 257 Cal.Rptr. 197 (1989).

In the introductory clause of Section 6454, "issue" is substituted for "descendants" in former Section 6408(e). This change is nonsubstantive, and is for consistency with other provisions in this part. See, e.g., Sections 6401, 6402, 6402.5, 6451, 6452, 6455.

Even though the requirements of Section 6454 are satisfied, the natural parent may continue to inherit from the child under Section 6450(a). The foster parent or stepparent may not inherit from the child: Subdivision (b) of Section 6450 does not apply because the adoption was not completed, and Section 6454 does not apply because the section applies only to inheritance by the foster child or stepchild or the child's issue "from" or "through" a foster parent or stepparent, not to inheritance "by" a foster parent or stepparent. The child, however, may inherit both from the natural parent under Section 6450(a), and from the foster parent or stepparent under Section 6454. [23 Cal.L.Rev.Comm. Reports 901 (1993) (Annual Report, App. 9)].

§ 6455. Equitable adoption; application

Nothing in this chapter affects or limits application of the judicial doctrine of equitable adoption for the benefit of the child or the child's issue. *(Added by Stats.1993, c. 529 (A.B.1137), § 5.)*

Law Revision Commission Comments

1993 Addition

Section 6455 continues the substance of subdivision (g) of former Section 6408. "Issue" is substituted in Section 6455 for "descendants" in former Section 6408(g). This change is nonsubstantive, and is for consistency with other provisions in this part. See, e.g., Sections 6401, 6402, 6402.5, 6451, 6452, 6454.

Concerning equitable adoption, see Estate of Wilson, 111 Cal. App.3d 242, 168 Cal.Rptr. 533 (1980). [23 Cal.L.Rev.Comm. Reports 901 (1993) (Annual Report, App. 9)].

Part 3

FAMILY PROTECTION

Law Revision Commission Comments

1990 Enactment

This part supersedes Part 3 (commencing with Section 6500) of Division 6 [of] the repealed Probate Code. The superseded part was enacted upon recommendation of the California Law Revision Commission. See Tentative Recommendation Relating to Wills and Intestate Succession, 16 Cal.L.Revision Comm'n Reports 2301 (1982). See also Report of Senate Committee on Judiciary on Assembly Bills 25 and 68, 17 Cal.L.Revision Comm'n Reports 867, 871–83 (1984). [20 Cal.L.Rev.Comm.Reports 1001 (1990)].

CHAPTER 1. TEMPORARY POSSESSION OF FAMILY DWELLING AND EXEMPT PROPERTY

§ 6500. Possession of family dwelling; exempt property; duration

Until the inventory is filed and for a period of 60 days thereafter, or for such other period as may be ordered by the court for good cause on petition therefor, the decedent's surviving spouse and minor children are entitled to remain in possession of the family dwelling, the wearing apparel of the family, the household furniture, and the other property of the decedent exempt from enforcement of a money judgment. *(Stats.1990, c. 79 (A.B.759), § 14, operative July 1, 1991.)*

Law Revision Commission Comments

1990 Enactment

Section 6500 continues Section 6500 of the repealed Probate Code without change. See also Code Civ.Proc. §§ 695.010–695.070, 703.010–704.995, 706.050–706.051 (property exempt from enforcement of money judgment). Other exemptions are listed in the Comment to Code of Civil Procedure Section 703.010. As to a surviving spouse's waiver of rights at death, see Sections 140–147. For background on this section, see Recommendation Relating to Probate Homestead, 15 Cal.L.Revision Comm'n Reports 401, 420 (1980).

Background on Section 6500 of Repealed Code

Section 6500 was added by 1983 Cal.Stat. ch. 842 § 55. The section continued the substance of subdivision (a) of former Probate Code Section 660 (repealed by 1983 Cal.Stat. ch. 842 § 39). For background on the provisions of this part, see the Comment to this part under the part heading. [20 Cal.L.Rev.Comm.Reports 1001 (1990)].

Cross References

Conservatorships and other protective proceedings, educational requirements for court-appointed, nonprofessional conservators and guardians, see Probate Code § 1457.

Enforcement of money judgments, exemptions, see Code of Civil Procedure § 703.010 et seq.

§ 6501. Petition for order

A petition for an order under Section 6500 may be filed by any interested person. Notice of the hearing on the petition shall be given as provided in Section 1220. *(Stats.1990, c. 79 (A.B.759), § 14, operative July 1, 1991.)*

Law Revision Commission Comments

1990 Enactment

Section 6501 continues Section 6501 of the repealed Probate Code without change. For general provisions, see Sections 1000–1004 (rules of practice), 1020–1023 (petitions and other papers), 1040–1050 (hearings and orders). For general provisions relating to notice of hearing, see Sections 1200–1221. See also Sections 1250–1252 (request for special notice), 1260–1265 (proof of giving notice). The requirement that notice be given as provided in Section 1220 does not apply to a particular notice where the notice was delivered, mailed, posted, or first published before July 1, 1991. In such a case, the applicable law in effect before July 1, 1991, continues to apply to the giving of the notice. Section 1200(c). As to the application of any amendments made after that date, see Section 3. See also Section 48 ("interested person" defined).

Background on Section 6501 of Repealed Code

Section 6501 was a new provision added by 1983 Cal.Stat. ch. 842 § 55 and was amended by 1987 Cal.Stat. ch. 923 § 87. The section was drawn from former Probate Code Section 662 (probate homestead) (repealed by 1983 Cal.Stat. ch. 842 § 39). The 1987 amendment (1) revised the cross-reference to the procedure for mailing notice of the hearing and (2) deleted the provision requiring the clerk to set the petition for hearing, this provision being unnecessary in view of Section 1285 which is a general provision that imposes this duty on the clerk. As to the 1987 amendment, see Communication from California Law Revision Commission Concerning Assembly Bill 708, 19 Cal.L.Revision Comm'n Reports 545, 560 (1988); Comments to Conforming Revisions and Repeals, 19 Cal.L.Revision Comm'n Reports 391, 449 (1988). For background on the provisions of this part, see the Comment to this part under the part heading. [20 Cal.L.Rev.Comm.Reports 1001 (1990)].

CHAPTER 2. SETTING ASIDE EXEMPT PROPERTY OTHER THAN FAMILY DWELLING

Section
6510.   Exempt property; setting apart by court.
6511.   Petition; notice.

§ 6510. Exempt property; setting apart by court

Upon the filing of the inventory or at any subsequent time during the administration of the estate, the court in its discretion may on petition therefor set apart all or any part of the property of the decedent exempt from enforcement of a money judgment, other than the family dwelling, to any one or more of the following:

(a) The surviving spouse.

(b) The minor children of the decedent. *(Stats.1990, c. 79 (A.B.759), § 14, operative July 1, 1991.)*

Law Revision Commission Comments

1990 Enactment

Section 6510 continues Section 6510 of the repealed Probate Code without change. This section permits, for example, the minor children to receive the furniture and household furnishings for a probate homestead set apart for the use of the minor children. See the Comment to Section 6521. See also the Comment to Section 6500 for a listing of provisions relating to property exempt from enforcement of a money judgment. As to a surviving spouse's waiver of rights at death, see Sections 140–147.

Background on Section 6510 of Repealed Code

Section 6510 was added by 1983 Cal.Stat. ch. 842 § 55. The section continued the substance of a portion of subdivision (b) of former Probate Code Section 660 (repealed by 1983 Cal.Stat. ch. 842 § 39), except that Section 6510 permitted the court to award the exempt property to the decedent's minor children even where there is a surviving spouse, while the former section permitted an award to the minor children only in case of the death of the surviving spouse. This change in the former law adopted the rule as to a probate homestead under former Probate Code Section 661 (repealed by 1983 Cal.Stat. ch. 842 § 39), the substance of which is continued in Section 6521, and applied it to property exempt from a money judgment other than the family dwelling. For background on the provisions of this part, see the Comment to this part under the part heading. [20 Cal.L.Rev.Comm.Reports 1001 (1990)].

Cross References

Enforcement of money judgments, exemptions, see Code of Civil
    Procedure § 703.010 et seq.
Family allowance, generally, see Probate Code § 6540 et seq.

§ 6511. Petition; notice

A petition for an order under Section 6510 may be filed by any interested person. Notice of the hearing on the petition shall be given as provided in Section 1220. *(Stats.1990, c. 79 (A.B.759), § 14, operative July 1, 1991.)*

Law Revision Commission Comments

1990 Enactment

Section 6511 continues Section 6511 of the repealed Probate Code without change. For general provisions, see Sections 1000–1004 (rules of practice), 1020–1023 (petitions and other papers), 1040–1050 (hearings and orders). For general provisions relating to notice of hearing, see Sections 1200–1221. See also Sections 1250–1252 (request for special notice), 1260–1265 (proof of giving notice). The requirement that notice be given as provided in Section 1220 does not apply to a particular notice where the notice was delivered, mailed, posted, or first published before July 1, 1991. In such a case, the applicable law in effect before July 1, 1991, continues to apply to the giving of the notice. Section 1200(c). As to the application of any amendments made after that date, see Section 3. See also Section 48 ("interested person" defined). As to the right to appeal from an order under this section, see Section 7240 and the Comment thereto.

Background on Section 6511 of Repealed Code

Section 6511 was a new provision added by 1983 Cal.Stat. ch. 842 § 55 and was amended by 1987 Cal.Stat. ch. 923 § 88. The section was drawn from former Probate Code Section 662 (probate homestead) (repealed by 1983 Cal.Stat. ch. 842 § 39). The 1987 amendment (1) revised the cross-reference to the procedure for mailing notice of the hearing and (2) deleted the provision requiring the clerk to set the petition for hearing, this provision being unnecessary in view of Section 1285 (now Section 1041), a general provision that imposes this duty on the clerk. As to the 1987 amendment, see Communication from California Law Revision Commission Concerning Assembly Bill 708, 19 Cal.L.Revision Comm'n Reports 545, 560 (1988); Comments to Conforming Revisions and Repeals, 19 Cal.L.Revision Comm'n Reports 391, 449 (1988). [20 Cal.L.Rev.Comm.Reports 1001 (1990)].

CHAPTER 3. SETTING ASIDE PROBATE HOMESTEAD

Section
6520.   Authority; setting aside probate homestead.
6521.   Persons for whose use homestead shall be set apart.
6522.   Property out of which selected; preference.
6523.   Facts considered; conditions.
6524.   Period; rights of parties.
6525.   Petition; notice.
6526.   Liability for claims against estate; homestead exemption.
6527.   Modification, terms and conditions; termination; petition for order; notice of hearing.
6528.   Relationship to existing law.

Law Revision Commission Comments

1990 Enactment

This chapter supersedes Chapter 3 (commencing with Section 6520) of Part 3 of Division 6 of the repealed Probate Code. The superseded chapter was enacted upon recommendation of the California Law Revision Commission. See Recommendation Relating to Probate Homestead, 15 Cal.L.Revision Comm'n Reports 401 (1980). See also Recommendation and Study Relating to Rights of Surviving Spouse in Property Acquired by Decedent While Domiciled Elsewhere, 1 Cal.L.Revision Comm'n Reports E–1 (1957); Recommendation and Study Relating to Inter Vivos Marital Property Rights in Property Acquired While Domiciled Elsewhere, 3 Cal.L.Revision Comm'n Reports I–1 (1961). [20 Cal.L.Rev.Comm.Reports 1001 (1990)].

§ 6520. Authority; setting aside probate homestead

Upon the filing of the inventory or at any subsequent time during the administration of the estate, the court in its discretion may on petition therefor select and set apart one probate homestead in the manner provided in this chapter. *(Stats.1990, c. 79 (A.B.759), § 14, operative July 1, 1991.)*

1990 Enactment

Section 6520 continues Section 6520 of the repealed Probate Code without change. Under this section, establishment of a probate homestead is discretionary with the court. The factors to be used by the court in exercising discretion are set forth in Section 6523.

Background on Section 6520 of Repealed Code

Section 6520 was added by 1983 Cal.Stat. ch. 842 § 55. The section continued the substance of a portion of subdivision (b) of former Probate Code Section 660 (repealed by 1983 Cal.Stat. ch. 842 § 39). For background on the provisions of this chapter, see the Comment to this chapter under the chapter heading. [20 Cal.L.Rev.Comm.Reports 1001 (1990)].

Cross References

Exemptions generally, see Code of Civil Procedure § 703.010 et seq.
Protection of homesteads, see Cal. Const. Art. 20, § 1.5.
Recordation of order setting apart homestead, see Probate Code § 7263.

§ 6521. Persons for whose use homestead shall be set apart

The probate homestead shall be set apart for the use of one or more of the following persons:

(a) The surviving spouse.

(b) The minor children of the decedent. *(Stats.1990, c. 79 (A.B.759), § 14, operative July 1, 1991.)*

Law Revision Commission Comments

1990 Enactment

Section 6521 continues Section 6521 of the repealed Probate Code without change. This section permits the probate homestead to be set apart for minor children of the decedent even if there is a surviving spouse. This may be desirable, for example, if the minor children live apart from the surviving spouse or where the minor children are not children of the surviving spouse. As to a surviving spouse's waiver of rights at death, see Section 140–147.

Background on Section 6521 of Repealed Code

Section 6521 was added by 1983 Cal.Stat. ch. 842 § 55. The section continued subdivision (a) of former Probate Code Section 661 (repealed by 1983 Cal.Stat. ch. 842 § 39). For background on the provisions of this chapter, see the Comment to this chapter under the chapter heading. [20 Cal.L.Rev.Comm.Reports 1001 (1990)].

Cross References

Declared homesteads, see Code of Civil Procedure § 704.910 et seq.
Recordation of order setting apart homestead, see Probate Code § 7263.
Small estate set-aside, see Probate Code § 6600 et seq.

§ 6522. Property out of which selected; preference

(a) The probate homestead shall be selected out of the following property, giving first preference to the community and quasi-community property of, or property owned in common by, the decedent and the person entitled to have the homestead set apart:

(1) If the homestead is set apart for the use of the surviving spouse or for the use of the surviving spouse and minor children, out of community property or quasi-community property.

(2) If the homestead is set apart for the use of the surviving spouse or for the use of the minor children or for the use of the surviving spouse and minor children, out of property owned in common by the decedent and the persons entitled to have the homestead set apart, or out of the separate property of the decedent or, if the decedent was not married at the time of death, out of property owned by the decedent.

(b) The probate homestead shall not be selected out of property the right to possession of which is vested in a third person unless the third person consents thereto. As used in this subdivision, "third person" means a person whose right to possession of the property (1) existed at the time of the death of the decedent or came into existence upon the death of the decedent and (2) was not created by testate or intestate succession from the decedent. *(Stats.1990, c. 79 (A.B.759), § 14, operative July 1, 1991. Amended by Stats.1990, c. 710 (S.B.1775), § 17, operative July 1, 1991.)*

Law Revision Commission Comments

1990 Enactment

Section 6522 continues Section 6522 of the repealed Probate Code without change. This section does not require that the probate homestead be selected out of real property. The probate homestead may be selected out of personal property such as a mobilehome. Under Section 6522, the court may select a homestead out of separate property of the decedent despite the availability of community or quasi-community property or property held in common by the decedent and the person in whose use the homestead is set apart. However, the court must give preference to property other than the separate property of the decedent for selection as a probate homestead.

Subdivision (b) limits the property from which the homestead may be selected. A probate homestead may not be created on property of which a third person has the right to possession, whether by partial ownership, lease, or otherwise, without the person's consent. The probate homestead can affect the possessory rights only of testate and intestate successors of the decedent. See also Sections 28 ("community property" defined), 66 ("quasi-community property" defined). As to a surviving spouse's waiver of rights at death, see Sections 140–147.

1990 Amendment

Section 6522 (enacted as a part of the new Probate Code by 1990 Cal.Stat. ch. 79 § 14) was amended by 1990 Cal.Stat. ch. 710 § 17 to remove any implication that the decedent's separate property may not be used for a probate homestead for both the surviving spouse and the minor children. [20 Cal.L.Rev.Comm.Reports 1001 (1990)].

Background on Section 6522 of Repealed Code

Section 6522 was added by 1983 Cal.Stat. ch. 842 § 55. The section continued subdivisions (b) and (c) of former Probate Code Section 661 (repealed by 1983 Cal.Stat. ch. 842 § 39). For background on the provisions of this chapter, see the Comment to this chapter under the chapter heading. [20 Cal.L.Rev.Comm.Reports 1001 (1990)].

§ 6523. Facts considered; conditions

(a) In selecting and setting apart the probate homestead, the court shall consider the needs of the surviving spouse and minor children, the liens and encumbrances on the property, the claims of creditors, the needs of the heirs or devisees of the decedent, and the intent of the decedent with respect to the property in the estate and the estate plan of the decedent as expressed in inter vivos and testamentary transfers or by other means.

(b) The court, in light of subdivision (a) and other relevant considerations as determined by the court in its discretion, shall:

(1) Select as a probate homestead the most appropriate property available that is suitable for that use, including in addition to the dwelling itself such adjoining property as appears reasonable.

(2) Set the probate homestead so selected apart for such a term and upon such conditions (including, but not limited to, assignment by the homestead recipient of other property to the heirs or devisees of the property set apart as a homestead) as appear proper. *(Stats.1990, c. 79 (A.B.759), § 14, operative July 1, 1991.)*

Law Revision Commission Comments
1990 Enactment

Section 6523 continues Section 6523 of the repealed Probate Code without change. Under this section, the court has broad discretion in selecting the probate homestead and may take into account a wide variety of factors in exercising its discretion. This section expressly authorizes the court to condition the homestead on any terms that appear proper to the court. The court may select the homestead out of the separate property of the decedent but must give a preference to community or quasi-community property of or other property held in common by the decedent and the person for whose use the homestead is set apart. See Section 6522 and the Comment thereto. The court must select the most appropriate property as the homestead and is not limited to the existing dwelling. The court is not limited to existing lots or parcels, but must set apart only so much of the property as is reasonable under the circumstances of the case. As to a surviving spouse's waiver of rights at death, see Sections 140–147.

Background on Section 6523 of Repealed Code

Section 6523 was added by 1983 Cal.Stat. ch. 842 § 55. The section continued former Probate Code Section 664 (repealed by 1983 Cal.Stat. ch. 842 § 39). For background on the provisions of this chapter, see the Comment to this chapter under the chapter heading. [20 Cal.L.Rev.Comm.Reports 1001 (1990)].

§ 6524. Period; rights of parties

The property set apart as a probate homestead shall be set apart only for a limited period, to be designated in the order, and in no case beyond the lifetime of the surviving spouse, or, as to a child, beyond its minority. Subject to the probate homestead right, the property of the decedent remains subject to administration including testate and intestate succession. The rights of the parties during the period for which the probate homestead is set apart are governed, to the extent applicable, by the Legal Estates Principal and Income Law, Chapter 2.6 (commencing with Section 731) of Title 2 of Part 1 of Division 2 of the Civil Code. *(Stats.1990, c. 79 (A.B.759), § 14, operative July 1, 1991.)*

Law Revision Commission Comments
1990 Enactment

Section 6524 continues Section 6524 of the repealed Probate Code without change. This section requires that the probate homestead be set apart only for a limited period, regardless whether the homestead is selected out of the separate property of the decedent or otherwise. Under this section, the property set aside as a probate homestead remains subject to administration. The testate or intestate successors of the decedent or other successors to the property set aside as a probate homestead take the property subject to the

probate homestead right. Any portion of the probate homestead that is the property of the person for whom the homestead was set apart remains vested in the person at the termination of the probate homestead right. The rights of the homestead recipients and remaindermen are governed by the Legal Estates Principal and Income Law, but the court setting apart the homestead may vary the requirements of that law where appropriate to do so. See Civil Code § 731.04. As to the rights of creditors during and after administration, see Section 6526.

Background on Section 6524 of Repealed Code

Section 6524 was added by 1983 Cal.Stat. ch. 842 § 55. The section continued subdivision (d) of former Probate Code Section 661 (repealed by 1983 Cal.Stat. ch. 842 § 39). For background on the provisions of this chapter, see the Comment to this chapter under the chapter heading. [20 Cal.L.Rev.Comm.Reports 1001 (1990)].

Cross References

Apportionment of receipts and expenditures, tenants and remaindermen, see Civil Code § 731.04.

§ 6525. Petition; notice

(a) A petition to select and set apart a probate homestead may be filed by any interested person.

(b) Notice of the hearing on the petition shall be given as provided in Section 1220 to all of the following persons:

(1) Each person listed in Section 1220.

(2) Each known heir whose interest in the estate would be affected by the petition.

(3) Each known devisee whose interest in the estate would be affected by the petition. *(Stats.1990, c. 79 (A.B.759), § 14, operative July 1, 1991.)*

Law Revision Commission Comments
1990 Enactment

Section 6525 restates Section 6525 of the repealed Probate Code with the addition of the requirement that notice of the hearing be given to each known heir or devisee whose interest in the estate would be affected by the petition. See Section 1206 (notice to known heirs or known devisees). For general provisions, see Sections 1000–1004 (rules of practice), 1020–1023 (petitions and other papers), 1040–1050 (hearings and orders). For general provisions relating to notice of hearing, see Sections 1200–1221. See also Sections 1250–1252 (request for special notice), 1260–1265 (proof of giving notice). The requirement that notice be given as provided in Section 1220 does not apply to a particular notice where the notice was delivered, mailed, posted, or first published before July 1, 1991. In such a case, the applicable law in effect before July 1, 1991, continues to apply to the giving of the notice. Section 1200(c). As to the application of any amendments made after that date, see Section 3. See also Section 48 ("interested person" defined). As to the right to appeal from an order under this chapter, see Section 7240 and the Comment thereto.

Background on Section 6525 of Repealed Code

Section 6525 was added by 1983 Cal.Stat. ch. 842 § 55 and was amended by 1987 Cal.Stat. ch. 923 § 89. The section continued the substance of former Probate Code Section 662 (repealed by 1983 Cal.Stat. ch. 842 § 39). The 1987 amendment (1) revised the cross-reference to the procedure for mailing notice of the hearing and (2) deleted the provision requiring the clerk to set the petition for hearing, this provision being unnecessary in view of Section 1285 which is a general provision that imposes this duty on the clerk. As to the 1987 amendment, see Communication from California Law Revision Commission Concerning Assembly Bill 708, 19 Cal.L.Revision Comm'n Reports 545, 560 (1988); Comments to Conforming Revisions and Repeals, 19 Cal.L.Revision Comm'n Reports 391, 449 (1988). For background on the provisions of this chapter, see the Comment to this chapter under the chapter heading. [20 Cal.L.Rev.Comm.Reports 1001 (1990)].

§ 6526. Liability for claims against estate; homestead exemption

(a) Property of the decedent set apart as a probate homestead is liable for claims against the estate of the decedent, subject to the probate homestead right. The probate homestead right in property of the decedent is liable for claims that are secured by liens and encumbrances on the property at the time of the decedent's death but is exempt to the extent of the homestead exemption as to any claim that would have been subject to a homestead exemption at the time of the decedent's death under Article 4 (commencing with Section 704.710) of Chapter 4 of Division 2 of Title 9 of Part 2 of the Code of Civil Procedure.

(b) The probate homestead right in the property of the decedent is not liable for claims against the person for whose use the probate homestead is set apart.

(c) Property of the decedent set apart as a probate homestead is liable for claims against the testate or intestate successors of the decedent or other successors to the property after administration, subject to the probate homestead right. *(Stats.1990, c. 79 (A.B.759), § 14, operative July 1, 1991.)*

Law Revision Commission Comments

1990 Enactment

Section 6526 continues Section 6526 of the repealed Probate Code without change. Subdivision (a) sets the rules governing liability of probate homestead property for debts of the decedent. The first sentence makes clear that such property may be used to satisfy debts of the decedent, but any sale is subject to the probate homestead right of occupancy by the person for whose use the homestead is set apart. This codifies the rule of In re Estate of Tittel, 139 Cal. 149, 72 P. 909 (1903). The second sentence recognizes the common law rule that the probate homestead does not affect prior liens and encumbrances. See, e.g., In re Estate of McCauley, 50 Cal. 544 (1875); In re Estate of Huelsman, 127 Cal. 275, 59 P. 776 (1899). However, the court may select as a probate homestead property not subject to liens and encumbrances or property whose liens and encumbrances will be discharged in probate. See Section 6523 (discretion of court). Preexisting liens and encumbrances on the property may be satisfied out of the probate homestead right. If the property would have been exempt from enforcement of a claim secured by a lien or encumbrance at the time of the decedent's death, however, the homestead recipient may claim a homestead exemption for the probate homestead right.

Subdivision (b) states the rule governing liability of the probate homestead right for debts of the person for whose use the homestead is set apart. Subdivision (b) creates an absolute exemption for the probate homestead right, both as to prior and subsequently incurred debts, regardless of liens created on the probate homestead right. Subdivision (b) does not preclude a creditor of the person for whose use the probate homestead is set apart from reaching any interest in the property the person may have apart from the probate homestead right; this may occur where the homestead was selected out of community property of or property held in common by the decedent and the person for whose use the homestead is set apart. In such a situation, the exemption from execution for a dwelling may be available to the person for whose use the homestead is set apart to protect his or her property interest.

Subdivision (c) states the rule governing liability of probate homestead property for debts of the heirs or devisees or other persons who may have acquired the property through administration. The probate homestead property is subject to administration and devolves as any other property, subject to the right of use of the homestead by the persons for whose use it is set apart. See Section 6524. Under subdivision (c) of Section 6526, the remainder interest but not the probate homestead right is subject to claims of creditors.

Background on Section 6526 of Repealed Code

Section 6526 was added by 1983 Cal.Stat. ch. 842 § 55. The section continued former Probate Code Section 663 (repealed by 1983 Cal.Stat. ch. 842 § 39). For background on the provisions of this chapter, see the Comment to this chapter under the chapter heading. [20 Cal.L.Rev.Comm.Reports 1001 (1990)].

Cross References

Protection of homesteads, see Cal. Const. Art. 20, § 1.5.

§ 6527. Modification, terms and conditions; termination; petition for order; notice of hearing

(a) The court may by order modify the term or conditions of the probate homestead right or terminate the probate homestead right at any time prior to entry of an order for final distribution of the decedent's estate if in the court's discretion to do so appears appropriate under the circumstances of the case.

(b) A petition for an order under this section may be filed by any of the following:

(1) The person for whose use the probate homestead is set apart.

(2) The testate or intestate successors of the decedent or other successors to the property set apart as a probate homestead.

(3) Persons having claims secured by liens or encumbrances on the property set apart as a probate homestead.

(c) Notice of the hearing on the petition shall be given to all the persons listed in subdivision (b) as provided in Section 1220. *(Stats.1990, c. 79 (A.B.759), § 14, operative July 1, 1991.)*

Law Revision Commission Comments

1990 Enactment

Section 6527 continues Section 6527 of the repealed Probate Code without change. This section gives the court authority to modify the probate homestead right until the entry of an order for final distribution in recognition of the possibility of changed circumstances. For general provisions, see Sections 1000–1004 (rules of practice), 1020–1023 (petitions and other papers), 1040–1050 (hearings and orders). For general provisions relating to notice of hearing, see Sections 1200–1221. See also Sections 1250–1252 (request for special notice), 1260–1265 (proof of giving notice). See also Section 48 ("interested person" defined).

Background on Section 6527 of Repealed Code

Section 6527 was added by 1983 Cal.Stat. ch. 842 § 55 and was amended by 1987 Cal.Stat. ch. 923 § 90 and 1988 Cal.Stat. ch. 1199 § 77.5. The section continued the substance of former Probate Code Section 665 (repealed by 1983 Cal.Stat. ch. 842 § 39) with the addition of subdivision (c). The 1987 amendment (1) revised the cross-reference to the procedure for mailing notice of the hearing and (2) deleted the provision formerly in subdivision (c) excusing giving notice to oneself, this provision now being generalized in Section 1201. As to the 1987 amendment, see Communication from

California Law Revision Commission Concerning Assembly Bill 708, 19 Cal.L.Revision Comm'n Reports 545, 561 (1988); Comments to Conforming Revisions and Repeals, 19 Cal.L.Revision Comm'n Reports 391, 450 (1988). The 1988 amendment conformed terminology to revisions made to the Probate Code in 1988. As to the 1988 amendment, see Comments to Conforming Revisions and Repeals, 19 Cal.L.Revision Comm'n Reports 1031, 1090 (1988). For background on the provisions of this chapter, see the Comment to this chapter under the chapter heading. [20 Cal.L.Rev.Comm.Reports 1001 (1990)].

§ 6528. Relationship to existing law

Nothing in this chapter terminates or otherwise affects a declaration of homestead by, or for the benefit of, a surviving spouse or minor child of the decedent with respect to the community, quasi-community, or common interest of the surviving spouse or minor child in property in the decedent's estate. This section is declaratory of, and does not constitute a change in, existing law. *(Stats.1990, c. 79 (A.B.759), § 14, operative July 1, 1991.)*

Law Revision Commission Comments

1990 Enactment

Section 6528 continues Section 6528 of the repealed Probate Code without change. This section makes clear the relationship between the probate homestead law and the declared homestead law. See Code Civ.Proc. §§ 704.910–704.990 (declared homestead). Although there is no longer a right of survivorship created by a declaration of homestead (1980 Cal.Stat. ch. 119, § 22), in the sense that the survivor no longer takes the decedent's interest in the property over a contrary testamentary disposition, a homestead declaration made by or for the benefit of a survivor nonetheless remains effective as to the survivor's interest in the property, notwithstanding dictum to the contrary in Estate of Grigsby, 134 Cal.App.3d 611, 184 Cal.Rptr. 886 (1982).

Background on Section 6528 of Repealed Code

Section 6528 was a new provision added by 1983 Cal.Stat. ch. 842 § 55. For background on the provisions of this chapter, see the Comment to this chapter under the chapter heading. [20 Cal.L.Rev.Comm.Reports 1001 (1990)].

CHAPTER 4. FAMILY ALLOWANCE

Cross References

Application of old and new law, see Probate Code § 3.

§ 6540. Persons entitled to allowance

(a) The following are entitled to such reasonable family allowance out of the estate as is necessary for their maintenance according to their circumstances during administration of the estate:

(1) The surviving spouse of the decedent.

(2) Minor children of the decedent.

(3) Adult children of the decedent who are physically or mentally incapacitated from earning a living and were actually dependent in whole or in part upon the decedent for support.

(b) The following may be given such reasonable family allowance out of the estate as the court in its discretion determines is necessary for their maintenance according to their circumstances during administration of the estate:

(1) Other adult children of the decedent who were actually dependent in whole or in part upon the decedent for support.

(2) A parent of the decedent who was actually dependent in whole or in part upon the decedent for support.

(c) If a person otherwise eligible for family allowance has a reasonable maintenance from other sources and there are one or more other persons entitled to a family allowance, the family allowance shall be granted only to those who do not have a reasonable maintenance from other sources. *(Stats. 1990, c. 79 (A.B.759), § 14, operative July 1, 1991.)*

Law Revision Commission Comments

1990 Enactment

Section 6540 continues Section 6540 of the repealed Probate Code without change. The right of a surviving spouse to a family allowance may be waived in whole or in part, whether the waiver is executed before or during marriage. See Sections 140–147. As to the priority of the family allowance, see Section 11420. See also Sections 21400–21406 (abatement of shares of beneficiaries).

Background on Section 6540 of Repealed Code

Section 6540 was added by 1983 Cal.Stat. ch. 842 § 55. Subdivision (a) continued the substance of subdivision (a) of former Probate Code Section 680 (repealed by 1983 Cal.Stat. ch. 842 § 39). Subdivision (b) continued the substance of subdivision (b) of former Probate Code Section 680, with the addition of discretionary authority for the court to award family allowance to a parent of the decedent who was actually dependent in whole or in part on the decedent for support. Subdivision (c) continued the substance of former Probate Code Section 682 (repealed by 1983 Cal.Stat. ch. 842 § 39). For background on the provisions of this part, see the Comment to this part under the part heading. [20 Cal.L.Rev.Comm.Reports 1001 (1990)].

Cross References

Order of payment of expenses, charges and debts, see Probate Code § 11420.
Sale of property to pay family allowance, see Probate Code §§ 10252, 10259.

§ 6541. Grant or modification; petition; hearing; notice

(a) The court may grant or modify a family allowance on petition of any interested person.

(b) With respect to an order for the family allowance provided for in subdivision (a) of Section 6540:

(1) Before the inventory is filed, the order may be made or modified either (A) ex parte or (B) after notice of the hearing on the petition has been given as provided in Section 1220.

(2) After the inventory is filed, the order may be made or modified only after notice of the hearing on the petition has been given as provided in Section 1220.

(c) An order for the family allowance provided in subdivision (b) of Section 6540 may be made only after notice of the hearing on the petition has been given as provided in Section 1220 to all of the following persons:

(1) Each person listed in Section 1220.

(2) Each known heir whose interest in the estate would be affected by the petition.

(3) Each known devisee whose interest in the estate would be affected by the petition. *(Stats.1990, c. 79 (A.B.759), § 14, operative July 1, 1991.)*

Law Revision Commission Comments

1990 Enactment

Section 6541 continues Section 6541 of the repealed Probate Code without substantive change. See also Section 1206 (notice to known heirs or known devisees). For general provisions, see Sections 1000–1004 (rules of practice), 1020–1023 (petitions and other papers), 1040–1050 (hearings and orders). For general provisions relating to notice of hearing, see Sections 1200–1221. See also Sections 1250–1252 (request for special notice), 1260–1265 (proof of giving notice). The notice provisions referred to in Section 6541 do not apply to a particular notice where the notice was delivered, mailed, posted, or first published before July 1, 1991. In such a case, the applicable law in effect before July 1, 1991, continues to apply to the giving of the notice. Section 1200(c). As to the application of any amendments made after that date, see Section 3. See also Section 48 ("interested person" defined).

Background on Section 6541 of Repealed Code

Section 6541 was added by 1983 Cal.Stat. ch. 842 § 55 and was amended by 1987 Cal.Stat. ch. 923 § 91. The section continued the substance of a portion of former Probate Code Section 681 (repealed by 1983 Cal.Stat. ch. 842 § 39). The 1987 amendments revised the provisions relating to notice. As to the 1987 amendment, see Communication from California Law Revision Commission Concerning Assembly Bill 708, 19 Cal.L.Revision Comm'n Reports 545, 561 (1988); Comments to Conforming Revisions and Repeals, 19 Cal.L.Revision Comm'n Reports 391, 450 (1988). For background on the provisions of this part, see the Comment to this part under the part heading. [20 Cal.L.Rev.Comm.Reports 1001 (1990)].

Cross References

Time for and place of filing inventory, see Probate Code § 8800.

§ 6542. Commencement; retroactive allowances

A family allowance commences on the date of the court's order or such other time as may be provided in the court's order, whether before or after the date of the order, as the court in its discretion determines, but the allowance may not be made retroactive to a date earlier than the date of the decedent's death. *(Stats.1990, c. 79 (A.B.759), § 14, operative July 1, 1991.)*

Law Revision Commission Comments

1990 Enactment

Section 6542 continues Section 6542 of the repealed Probate Code without change.

Background on Section 6542 of Repealed Code

Section 6542 was added by 1983 Cal.Stat. ch. 842 § 55. The section codified the previously existing practice. The prohibition against an order which is retroactive to a date earlier to a date earlier than the date of decedent's death continued the substance of a portion of subdivision (c) of former Probate Code Section 680 (repealed by 1983 Cal.Stat. ch. 842 § 39). For background on the provisions of this part, see the Comment to this part under the part heading. [20 Cal.L.Rev.Comm.Reports 1001 (1990)].

§ 6543. Termination; limitation; continuation

(a) A family allowance shall terminate no later than the entry of the order for final distribution of the estate or, if the estate is insolvent, no later than one year after the granting of letters.

(b) Subject to subdivision (a), a family allowance shall continue until modified or terminated by the court or until such time as the court may provide in its order. *(Stats.1990, c. 79 (A.B.759), § 14, operative July 1, 1991.)*

Law Revision Commission Comments

1990 Enactment

Section 6543 restates Section 6543 of the repealed Probate Code without substantive change. The phrase "entry of the order for final distribution of the estate" has been substituted for "final settlement of the estate." See also Section 12203 (continuation of administration of the estate in order to pay family allowance).

Background on Section 6543 of Repealed Code

Section 6543 was added by 1983 Cal.Stat. ch. 842 § 55. Subdivision (a) continued portions of former Probate Code Section 680 (repealed by 1983 Cal.Stat. ch. 842 § 39). Subdivision (b) continued a portion of the first sentence of subdivision (a) of former Probate Code Section 681 (repealed by 1983 Cal.Stat. ch. 842 § 39). The authority in subdivision (b) for the court to make an order terminating a family allowance or to include a termination date in its original order was new, but was implied under the former sections. For background on the provisions of this part, see the Comment to this part under the part heading. [20 Cal.L.Rev.Comm.Reports 1001 (1990)].

§ 6544. Costs

The costs of proceedings under this chapter shall be paid by the estate as expenses of administration. *(Stats.1990, c. 79 (A.B.759), § 14, operative July 1, 1991.)*

Law Revision Commission Comments

1990 Enactment

Section 6544 continues Section 6544 of the repealed Probate Code without change.

Background on Section 6544 of Repealed Code

Section 6544 was added by 1983 Cal.Stat. ch. 842 § 55. The section continued the substance of former Probate Code Section 683 (repealed by 1983 Cal.Stat. ch. 842 § 39). For background on the provisions of this part, see the Comment to this part under the part heading. [20 Cal.L.Rev.Comm.Reports 1001 (1990)].

Cross References

Costs, discretion to order payment by parties or from estate, see Probate Code § 1002.

§ 6545. Perfection of appeal; stay of proceedings

Notwithstanding Chapter 2 (commencing with Section 916) of Title 13 of Part 2 of the Code of Civil Procedure, the perfecting of an appeal from an order made under this chapter does not stay proceedings under this chapter or the enforcement of the order appealed from if the person in whose favor the order is made gives an undertaking in double the amount of the payment or payments to be made to that person. The undertaking shall be conditioned that if the order appealed from is modified or reversed so that the payment or any part thereof to the person proves to have been unwarranted, the payment or part thereof shall, unless deducted from any preliminary or final distribution ordered in favor of the person, be repaid and refunded into the estate within 30 days after the court so orders following the modification or reversal, together with interest and costs. *(Stats.1990, c. 79 (A.B.759), § 14, operative July 1, 1991.)*

Law Revision Commission Comments

1990 Enactment

Section 6545 continues Section 6545 of the repealed Probate Code without change. Concerning enforcement of liability on the undertaking, see Code Civ.Proc. §§ 996.410–996.495.

Background on Section 6545 of Repealed Code

Section 6545 was added by 1983 Cal.Stat. ch. 842 § 55. The section continued the substance of a portion of former Probate Code Section 684 (repealed by 1983 Cal.Stat. ch. 842 § 39). For background on the requirement of an undertaking, see Recommendation Relating to Statutory Bonds and Undertakings, 16 Cal.L.Revision Comm'n Reports 501, 610 (1982). For background on the provisions of this part, see the Comment to this part under the part heading. [20 Cal.L.Rev.Comm.Reports 1001 (1990)].

CHAPTER 5. SPOUSE OR CHILD OMITTED FROM WILL [REPEALED]

Section
6560 to 6580. Repealed.

Repeal

Chapter 5, "Spouse or Child Omitted from Will", enacted by Stats.1990, c. 79 (A.B.759), § 14, consisting of §§ 6560 to 6580, was repealed by Stats.1997, c. 724 (A.B.1172), § 17.

Application

Provisions of this chapter have continuing application for estates of decedents who died before Jan. 1, 1998, see Probate Code § 21630.

Chapter not applicable where testator died before Jan. 1, 1985, see Probate Code § 6580.

§§ 6560 to 6580. Repealed by Stats.1997, c. 724 (A.B.1172), § 17

CHAPTER 6. SMALL ESTATE SET–ASIDE

Section
6600. Decedent's estate defined.
6601. Minor child.
6602. Petition requesting order to set aside estate; maximum value.
6603. Venue.
6604. Contents of petition.
6605. Procedure for filing petition; time for filing.
6606. Who may file.
6607. Notice of hearing; concurrent with hearing of petition for probate or administration.
6608. Inventory and appraisal; filing.
6609. Determination of whether to make order; assignment of estate; unpaid liabilities; title to property.
6610. Effect of order.
6611. Unsecured debts; liability; actions and proceedings.

Section
6612. Determinations not to make order under § 6609; action on petition for probate or administration.
6613. Attorney's fees.
6614. Application of law.
6615. References to former sections deemed references to comparable provisions of this chapter.

Application

Provisions applicable to decedents who died on or after July 1, 1987, see Probate Code § 6614.

Law Revision Commission Comments

1990 Enactment

This chapter supersedes Chapter 6 (commencing with Section 6600) of Part 3 of Division 6 of the repealed Probate Code. The superseded chapter was enacted upon recommendation of the California Law Revision Commission. See Recommendation Relating to Small Estate Set–Aside, 18 Cal.L.Revision Comm'n Reports 1101 (1986). See also Communication from California Law Revision Commission Concerning Assembly Bill 2625, 18 Cal.L.Revision Comm'n Reports 1743, 1750–53 (1986). The Commission, in cooperation with California Continuing Education of the Bar, published the recommended legislation as enacted with official comments. See Selected 1986 Trust and Probate Legislation, 18 Cal.L.Revision Comm'n Reports 1201, 1597–1621 (1986). [20 Cal.L.Rev.Comm.Reports 1001 (1990)].

Cross References

Application of old and new law, see Probate Code § 3.

§ 6600. Decedent's estate defined

(a) Subject to subdivision (b), for the purposes of this chapter, "decedent's estate" means all the decedent's personal property, wherever located, and all the decedent's real property located in this state.

(b) For the purposes of this chapter:

(1) Any property or interest or lien thereon which, at the time of the decedent's death, was held by the decedent as a joint tenant, or in which the decedent had a life or other interest terminable upon the decedent's death, shall be excluded in determining the estate of the decedent or its value.

(2) A multiple-party account to which the decedent was a party at the time of the decedent's death shall be excluded in determining the estate of the decedent or its value, whether or not all or a portion of the sums on deposit are community property, to the extent that the sums on deposit belong after the death of the decedent to a surviving party, P.O.D. payee, or beneficiary. As used in this paragraph, the terms "multiple-party account," "party," "P.O.D. payee," and "beneficiary" have the meanings given those terms in Article 2 (commencing with Section 5120) of Chapter 1 of Part 2 of Division 5. *(Stats.1990, c. 79 (A.B.759), § 14, operative July 1, 1991.)*

Law Revision Commission Comments

1990 Enactment

Section 6600 continues Section 6600 of the repealed Probate Code without substantive change. As to a surviving spouse's waiver of rights at death, see Sections 140–47.

As defined in subdivision (a), "decedent's estate" is not limited to probate assets. The term includes all personal property, wherever located, and all real property located in this state, excluding the property described in subdivision (b). Subdivision (a) requires, for example, that the decedent's one-half share of the community and quasi-community property be included in determining the decedent's estate or its value, whether or not the decedent's interest is set apart to the surviving spouse under Sections 13650–13660, unless the interest is excluded in determining the estate of the decedent under subdivision (b) as would be the case, for example, if the property is held in joint tenancy. This is consistent with prior law. Estate of Pezzola, 112 Cal.App.3d 752, 169 Cal.Rptr. 464 (1980).

Subdivision (b) excludes any interest that terminates at death in determining the estate of the decedent or its value. If the interest is one that passes to another on the death of the decedent by virtue of a joint tenancy, a pay-on-death provision, or a contractual provision that provides that the interest is to be transferred or paid to another upon the death of the decedent, subdivision (b)(1) requires that the value of the interest be excluded in determining the estate of the decedent or its value. For example, if there is a policy of insurance on the decedent's life and the proceeds are payable to a named beneficiary (not to the decedent's estate), the insurance proceeds are excluded in determining the estate of the decedent or its value. Similarly, for example, if the decedent has a retirement plan that provides benefits to a surviving spouse, those benefits are excluded in determining the estate of the decedent or its value. Subdivision (b) also excludes, for example, life interests in trusts and life estates. See O. McCarroll, 1 California Decedent Estate Administration Supplement § 3.24, at 84–85 (Cal.Cont.Ed.Bar 1985).

This section does not apply if the decedent died before July 1, 1987. See Section 6614. As to the application of any amendments made after that date, see Section 3. A reference to a provision of the former statute is deemed to be a reference to the comparable provisions of this chapter. See Section 6615.

Background on Section 6600 of Repealed Code

Section 6600 was added by 1986 Cal.Stat. ch. 783 § 23 and amended by 1989 Cal.Stat. ch. 397 § 38. Subdivision (a) was a new provision that defined "decedent's estate." This definition replaced the phrase "the whole estate" used in former Probate Code Section 640 (repealed by 1986 Cal.Stat. ch. 783 § 9). Subdivision (a) made clear that real property located outside California is not included in determining the estate of the decedent or its value. The rule under former law was unclear. See Broll, Summary Administration, in 1 California Decedent Estate Administration § 3.24, at 129 (Cal. Cont.Ed.Bar 1971). Apparently real property outside California was not included under former law, since former Section 644 required "an inventory and appraisement to be prepared in the manner prescribed by law and filed within such time as the court may allow," and an inventory and appraisement does not include real property located outside California.

Subdivision (b) continued former Probate Code Section 647 (repealed by 1986 Cal.Stat. ch. 783 § 9) without substantive change. As to paragraph (2) of subdivision (b), see Recommendation Relating to Nonprobate Transfers, 16 Cal.L.Revision Comm'n Reports 129, 159 (1982).

The 1989 amendment conformed a reference to the definitional provisions to the renumbering of those provisions made by 1989 Cal.Stat. ch. 397. For background on the provisions of this chapter, see the Comment to this chapter under the chapter heading. [20 Cal.L.Rev.Comm.Reports 1001 (1990)].

§ 6601. Minor child

As used in this chapter, "minor child" means a child of the decedent who was under the age of 18 at the time of the decedent's death and who survived the decedent. (Stats. 1990, c. 79 (A.B.759), § 14, operative July 1, 1991.)

Law Revision Commission Comments

1990 Enactment

Section 6601 continues Section 6601 of the repealed Probate Code without change. This determination whether a child is a minor is made at the time of the death of the decedent. This section does not apply if the decedent died before July 1, 1987. See Section 6614. As to the application of any amendments made after that date, see Section 3. A reference to a provision of the former statute is deemed to be a reference to the comparable provisions of this chapter. See Section 6615.

Background on Section 6601 of Repealed Code

Section 6601 was a new provision added by 1986 Cal.Stat. ch. 783 § 23. The section changed the rule under former Probate Code Section 645 (repealed by 1986 Cal.Stat. ch. 783 § 9) that, if the other statutory requirements were satisfied, the court could order that the estate be set aside "to such child or children of the decedent as may then be minors." The apparent result of this provision was that a child who was a minor at the time of the decedent's death was deprived of the right to a small estate set aside if the order was not made while the child was still a minor. The definition under Section 6601 avoided this result. For background on the provisions of this chapter, see the Comment to this chapter under the chapter heading. [20 Cal.L.Rev.Comm.Reports 1001 (1990)].

§ 6602. Petition requesting order to set aside estate; maximum value

A petition may be filed under this chapter requesting an order setting aside the decedent's estate to the decedent's surviving spouse and minor children, or one or more of them, as provided in this chapter, if the net value of the decedent's estate, over and above all liens and encumbrances at the date of death and over and above the value of any probate homestead interest set apart out of the decedent's estate under Section 6520, does not exceed twenty thousand dollars ($20,000). (Stats.1990, c. 79 (A.B.759), § 14, operative July 1, 1991.)

Law Revision Commission Comments

1990 Enactment

Section 6602 continues Section 6602 of the repealed Probate Code without change. The purpose of this chapter is to insure the support of the dependent surviving spouse and minor children (or any one or more of them) when the breadwinner is taken by death leaving but a small estate. This right to have a small estate set aside effectively forecloses the rights of a third person to inherit or otherwise receive a part of that estate under the decedent's will. Estate of Pezzola, 112 Cal.App.3d 752, 169 Cal.Rptr. 464 (1980). Section 6602 limits the use of this chapter to a case where the decedent's estate, less liens and encumbrances and the value of any probate homestead interest, does not exceed $20,000. See also Section 6600 (defining "decedent's estate") and the Comment thereto. As to a surviving spouse's waiver of rights at death, see Sections 140–147.

This section does not apply if the decedent died before July 1, 1987. See Section 6614. As to the application of any amendments made after that date, see Section 3. A reference to a provision of the former statute is deemed to be a reference to the comparable provisions of this chapter. See Section 6615.

Background on Section 6602 of Repealed Code

Section 6602 was added by 1986 Cal.Stat. ch. 783 § 23. The section superseded former Probate Code Section 640 (repealed by 1986 Cal.Stat. ch. 783 § 9). For background on the provisions of this chapter, see the Comment to this chapter under the chapter heading. [20 Cal.L.Rev.Comm.Reports 1001 (1990)].

Cross References

Decedent's estate defined for purposes of this Chapter, see Probate Code § 6600.

Fee for filing petition commencing or opposition papers concerning setting aside decedent's estate of small value, see Government Code § 70656.

Minor child defined for purposes of this Chapter, see Probate Code § 6601.

§ 6603. Venue

The petition shall be filed in the superior court of a county in which the estate of the decedent may be administered. *(Stats.1990, c. 79 (A.B.759), § 14, operative July 1, 1991.)*

Law Revision Commission Comments

1990 Enactment

Section 6603 continues Section 6603 of the repealed Probate Code without change. This section specifies the county in which the petition is to be filed. The section is consistent with a provision of Section 13650 (determination or confirmation of property passing or belonging to surviving spouse). This section does not apply if the decedent died before July 1, 1987. See Section 6614. As to the application of any amendments made after that date, see Section 3. A reference to a provision of the former statute is deemed to be a reference to the comparable provisions of this chapter. See Section 6615.

Background on Section 6603 of Repealed Code

Section 6603 was a new provision added by 1986 Cal.Stat. ch. 783 § 23. For background on the provisions of this chapter, see the Comment to this chapter under the chapter heading. [20 Cal.L.Rev.Comm.Reports 1001 (1990)].

§ 6604. Contents of petition

(a) The petition shall allege that this chapter applies and request that an order be made setting aside the estate of the decedent as provided in this chapter.

(b) The petition shall include the following:

(1) If proceedings for administration of the estate are not pending, the facts necessary to determine the county in which the estate of the decedent may be administered.

(2) The name, age, address, and relation to the decedent of each heir and devisee of the decedent, so far as known to the petitioner.

(3) A specific description and estimate of the value of the decedent's estate and a list of all liens and encumbrances at the date of death.

(4) A specific description and estimate of the value of any of the decedent's real property located outside this state that passed to the surviving spouse and minor children of the decedent, or any one or more of them, under the will of the decedent or by intestate succession.

(5) A specific description and estimate of the value of any of the decedent's property described in subdivision (b) of Section 6600 that passed to the surviving spouse and minor children of the decedent, or any one or more of them, upon the death of the decedent.

(6) A designation of any property as to which a probate homestead is set apart out of the decedent's estate under Section 6520.

(7) A statement of any unpaid liabilities for expenses of the last illness, funeral charges, and expenses of administration.

(8) The requested disposition of the estate of the decedent under this chapter and the considerations that justify the requested disposition. *(Stats.1990, c. 79 (A.B.759), § 14, operative July 1, 1991.)*

Law Revision Commission Comments

1990 Enactment

Section 6604 continues Section 6604 of the repealed Probate Code without substantive change. Paragraph (1) of subdivision (b) implements Section 6603 (venue). Paragraph (2) of subdivision (b) is designed to implement the provision for giving notice of the hearing on the petition under this chapter. See Section 6607. Paragraph (7) of subdivision (b) is consistent with subdivision (d) of Section 6609 (court shall ensure that expenses of last illness, funeral charges, and expenses of administration are paid).

Paragraph (8) of subdivision (b) requires that the petition contain the information necessary so that the court may make an appropriate order under Section 6609. If the court makes an order under Section 6609, the court may set aside the small estate to the surviving spouse and minor children of the decedent, or to any one or more of them. See the Comment to 6609. The petition, for example, may request that the small estate be set aside to one of the minor children and that the other minor children and the spouse be excluded, or it may request that the small estate be set aside in unequal shares to the minor children. In determining whether to make such an order, the court must take into account the various considerations listed in subdivision (b) of Section 6609.

For general provisions, see Sections 1020–1023 (petitions and other papers). This section does not apply if the decedent died before July 1, 1987. See Section 6614. As to the application of any amendments made after that date, see Section 3. A reference to a provision of the former statute is deemed to be a reference to the comparable provisions of this chapter. See Section 6615.

Background on Section 6604 of Repealed Code

Section 6604 was added by 1986 Cal.Stat. ch. 783 § 23. Subdivision (a) continued the first portion of the first sentence of former Probate Code Section 641 (repealed by 1986 Cal.Stat. ch. 783 § 9) without substantive change. Subdivision (b) superseded the last sentence of former Section 641 which specified the contents of the petition. Paragraphs (1) and (2) of subdivision (b) were new. Paragraphs (3), (4), and (5) of subdivision (b) superseded the provision of former Probate Code Section 641 that required that the petition include "a specific description and an estimate of the value of all of the decedent's property" and "a list of all liens and encumbrances at the date of death." Paragraph (6) of subdivision (b) continued a requirement of former Probate Code Section 641 without substantive change. Paragraphs (7) and (8) of subdivision (b) were new. For background on the provisions of this chapter, see the Comment to this chapter under the chapter heading. [20 Cal.L.Rev.Comm.Reports 1001 (1990)].

Cross References

Decedent's estate defined for purposes of this Chapter, see Probate Code § 6600.

Minor child defined for purposes of this Chapter, see Probate Code § 6601.

Probate of will, petition, see Probate Code § 8006.

Verification of pleadings, see Code of Civil Procedure § 446.

§ 6605. Procedure for filing petition; time for filing

(a) If proceedings for the administration of the estate of the decedent are pending, a petition under this chapter shall be filed in those proceedings without the payment of an additional fee.

(b) If proceedings for the administration of the estate of the decedent have not yet been commenced, a petition under this chapter may be filed concurrently with a petition for the probate of the decedent's will or for administration of the estate of the decedent, or, if no petition for probate or for administration is being filed, a petition under this chapter may be filed independently.

(c) A petition may be filed under this chapter at any time prior to the entry of the order for final distribution of the estate. *(Stats.1990, c. 79 (A.B.759), § 14, operative July 1, 1991.)*

Law Revision Commission Comments

1990 Enactment

Section 6605 continues Section 6605 of the repealed Probate Code without substantive change. This section does not apply if the decedent died before July 1, 1987. See Section 6614. As to the application of any amendments made after that date, see Section 3. A reference to a provision of the former statute is deemed to be a reference to the comparable provisions of this chapter. See Section 6615.

Background on Section 6605 of Repealed Code

Section 6605 was added by 1986 Cal.Stat. ch. 783 § 23. Subdivisions (a) and (b) continued the substance of portions of former Probate Code Section 641 (repealed by 1986 Cal.Stat. ch. 783 § 9) with language added to subdivision (a) to provide that a petition under this chapter may be filed in a pending probate proceeding "without the payment of an additional fee." The added language was drawn from Section 13652 (determination or confirmation of property passing or belonging to surviving spouse). Subdivision (c), which permitted a petition to be filed at any time prior to the final distribution of the estate, replaced the provision of former Section 641 which permitted a petition to be "filed at any time before the hearing on the petition for probate of the will or for letters of administration or after the filing of the inventory." For background on the provisions of this chapter, see the Comment to this chapter under the chapter heading. [20 Cal.L.Rev.Comm.Reports 1001 (1990)].

§ 6606. Who may file

(a) A petition may be filed under this chapter by any of the following:

(1) The person named in the will of the decedent as executor.

(2) The surviving spouse of the decedent.

(3) The guardian of a minor child of the decedent.

(4) A child of the decedent who was a minor at the time the decedent died.

(5) The personal representative if a personal representative has been appointed for the decedent's estate.

(b) The guardian of a minor child of the decedent may file the petition without authorization or approval of the court in which the guardianship proceeding is pending. *(Stats.1990, c. 79 (A.B.759), § 14, operative July 1, 1991.)*

Law Revision Commission Comments

1990 Enactment

Section 6606 continues Section 6606 of the repealed Probate Code without substantive change. Paragraph (4) of subdivision (a) recognizes that the court is authorized to set aside a small estate to a child who is a minor at the time of the decedent's death (as distinguished from a requirement that the child be a minor at the time the petition is filed or the time the court order under this chapter is made or some other time). See Section 6609(c). See also Section 6601 (defining "minor child"). Subdivision (b) is consistent with Section 13650(c) (determination or confirmation of property passing or belonging to surviving spouse). See also Section 13051(a) (collection or transfer of small estate without administration). As to a surviving spouse's waiver of rights at death, see Sections 140–147.

This section does not apply if the decedent died before July 1, 1987. See Section 6614. As to the application of any amendments made after that date, see Section 3. A reference to a provision of the former statute is deemed to be a reference to the comparable provisions of this chapter. See Section 6615.

Background on Section 6606 of Repealed Code

Section 6606 was added by 1986 Cal.Stat. ch. 783 § 23. The section continued the provisions of former Probate Code Section 641 (repealed by 1986 Cal.Stat. ch. 783 § 9) that described the persons authorized to file a petition and added paragraph (4) of subdivision (a) and all of subdivision (b), which were new provisions. For background on the provisions of this chapter, see the Comment to this chapter under the chapter heading. [20 Cal.L.Rev.Comm.Reports 1001 (1990)].

Cross References

Decedent's estate defined for purposes of this Chapter, see Probate Code § 6600.
Minor child defined for purposes of this Chapter, see Probate Code § 6601.

§ 6607. Notice of hearing; concurrent with hearing of petition for probate or administration

(a) Where proceedings for the administration of the estate of the decedent are not pending when the petition is filed under this chapter and the petition under this chapter is not joined with a petition for the probate of the decedent's will or for administration of the estate of the decedent, the petitioner shall give notice of the hearing on the petition as provided in Section 1220 to (1) each person named as executor in the decedent's will and to (2) each heir or devisee of the decedent, if known to the petitioner. A copy of the petition shall be sent with the notice of hearing to the surviving spouse, each child, and each devisee who is not petitioning.

(b) If the petition under this chapter is filed with a petition for the probate of the decedent's will or with a petition for administration of the estate of the deceased spouse, notice of the hearing on the petition shall be given to the persons and in the manner prescribed by Section 8003 and shall be included in the notice required by that section.

(c) If proceedings for the administration of the estate of the decedent are pending when the petition is filed under this chapter and the hearing of the petition for probate of the will or administration of the estate of the decedent is set for a day more than 15 days after the filing of the petition filed under this chapter, the petition under this chapter shall be set for hearing at the same time as the petition for probate of the will or for administration of the estate, and notice of hearing on the petition filed under this chapter shall be given by the petitioner as provided in Section 1220. If the hearing of the petition for probate of the will or for administration of the estate is not set for hearing for a day more than 15 days after the filing of the petition under this chapter, (1) the petition filed under this chapter shall be set for hearing at least 15 days after the date on which it is filed, (2) notice of the hearing on the petition filed under this chapter shall be given by the petitioner as provided in Section 1220, and (3) if the petition for probate of the will or for administration of the estate has not already been heard, that petition shall be continued until that date and heard at the same time unless the court otherwise orders. *(Stats.1990, c. 79 (A.B.759), § 14, operative July 1, 1991.)*

Law Revision Commission Comments
1990 Enactment

Section 6607 continues Section 6607 of the repealed Probate Code without substantive change. See also Section 1206 (notice to known heirs or known devisees). Subdivision (b) is comparable to subdivision (a) of Section 13655 (determination or confirmation of property passing or belonging to surviving spouse). For general provisions relating to notice of hearing, see Sections 1200–1221. See also Sections 1250–1252 (request for special notice), 1260–1265 (proof of giving notice). This section does not apply if the decedent died before July 1, 1987. See Section 6614. As to the application of any amendments made after that date, see Section 3. A reference to a provision of the former statute is deemed to be a reference to the comparable provisions of this chapter. See Section 6615.

The notice provisions referred to in Section 6607 do not apply to a particular notice where the notice was delivered, mailed, posted, or first published before July 1, 1991. In such a case, the applicable law in effect before July 1, 1991, continues to apply to the giving of the notice. See Section 1200(c).

Background on Section 6607 of Repealed Code

Section 6607 was added by 1986 Cal.Stat. ch. 783 § 23 and was amended by 1987 Cal.Stat. ch. 923 § 92 and 1988 Cal.Stat. ch. 1199 § 78. Subdivision (a) continued the substance of subdivision (a) of former Probate Code Section 643 (repealed by 1986 Cal.Stat. ch. 783 § 9) but specified the persons to whom the notice of hearing is to be mailed in place of the reference to former Section 1200.5 contained in former Section 643 and added the requirement that a copy of the petition be mailed with the notice of hearing given to the surviving spouse, each child, and each devisee, who is not petitioning. Subdivision (b) superseded former Probate Code Section 642 (repealed by 1986 Cal.Stat. ch. 783 § 9). Subdivision (c) continued subdivision (b) of former Probate Code Section 643 (repealed by 1986 Cal.Stat. ch. 783 § 9) without substantive change but with the addition of the phrase "unless the court otherwise orders" at the end of the subdivision. The 1987 amendment revised the provisions relating to notice. As to the 1987 amendment, see Communication from California Law Revision Commission Concerning Assembly Bill 708, 19 Cal.L.Revision Comm'n Reports 545, 561–62 (1988); Comments to Conforming Revisions and Repeals, 19 Cal.L.Revision Comm'n Reports 391, 450 (1988). The 1988 amendment corrected section references and conformed terminology to revisions made in the Probate Code in 1988. As to the 1988 amendment, see Comments to Conforming Revisions and Repeals, 19 Cal.L.Revision Comm'n Reports 1031, 1090 (1988). For background on the provisions of this chapter, see the Comment to this chapter under the chapter heading. [20 Cal.L.Rev.Comm.Reports 1001 (1990)].

§ 6608. Inventory and appraisal; filing

If a petition is filed under this chapter, the personal representative, or the petitioner if no personal representative has been appointed, shall file with the clerk of the court, prior to the hearing of the petition, an inventory and appraisal made as provided in Part 3 (commencing with Section 8800) of Division 7. The personal representative or the petitioner, as the case may be, may appraise the assets which a personal representative could appraise under Section 8901. *(Stats. 1990, c. 79 (A.B.759), § 14, operative July 1, 1991.)*

Law Revision Commission Comments
1990 Enactment

Section 6608 continues Section 6608 of the repealed Probate Code without substantive change. This section does not apply if the decedent died before July 1, 1987. See Section 6614. As to the application of any amendments made after that date, see Section 3. A reference to a provision of the former statute is deemed to be a reference to the comparable provisions of this chapter. See Section 6615.

Background on Section 6608 of Repealed Code

Section 6608 was added by 1986 Cal.Stat. ch. 783 § 23 and was amended by 1988 Cal.Stat. ch. 1199 § 78.5. The section continued the requirement of former Probate Code Section 644 (repealed by 1986 Cal.Stat. ch. 783 § 9) that an inventory and appraisement be filed. The former provision was revised to conform to the then existing provisions relating to inventory and appraisement. See former Probate Code Sections 600–611 (repealed by 1988 Cal.Stat. ch. 1199 § 51). The requirement that the inventory and appraisement be filed before the hearing of the petition was substituted for the requirement of former Section 644 that the inventory and appraisement be filed within such time as the court may allow. The 1988 amendment corrected section references and conformed terminology to revisions made in the Probate Code in 1988. As to the 1988 amendment, see Comments to Conforming Revisions and Repeals, 19 Cal.L.Revision Comm'n Reports 1031, 1090 (1988). For background on the provisions of this chapter, see the Comment to this chapter under the chapter heading. [20 Cal.L.Rev.Comm.Reports 1001 (1990)].

§ 6609. Determination of whether to make order; assignment of estate; unpaid liabilities; title to property

(a) If the court determines that the net value of the decedent's estate, over and above all liens and encumbrances at the date of death of the decedent and over and above the value of any probate homestead interest set apart out of the decedent's estate under Section 6520, does not exceed twenty thousand dollars ($20,000) as of the date of the decedent's death, the court shall make an order under this section unless the court determines that making an order under this section would be inequitable under the circumstances of the particular case.

(b) In determining whether to make an order under this section, the court shall consider the needs of the surviving spouse and minor children, the liens and encumbrances on the property of the decedent's estate, the claims of creditors, the needs of the heirs or devisees of the decedent, the intent of the decedent with respect to the property in the estate and the estate plan of the decedent as expressed in inter vivos and testamentary transfers or by other means, and any other relevant considerations. If the surviving spouse has remarried at the time the petition is heard, it shall be presumed that the needs of the surviving spouse do not justify the setting aside of the small estate, or any portion thereof, to the surviving spouse. This presumption is a presumption affecting the burden of proof.

(c) Subject to subdivision (d), if the court makes an order under this section, the court shall assign the whole of the decedent's estate, subject to all liens and encumbrances on property in the estate at the date of the decedent's death, to the surviving spouse and the minor children of the decedent, or any one or more of them.

(d) If there are any liabilities for expenses of the last illness, funeral charges, or expenses of administration that are unpaid at the time the court makes an order under this section, the court shall make such orders as are necessary so that those unpaid liabilities are paid.

(e) Title to property in the decedent's estate vests absolutely in the surviving spouse, minor children, or any or all of them, as provided in the order, subject to all liens and encumbrances on property in the estate at the date of the decedent's death, and there shall be no further proceedings in the administration of the decedent's estate unless additional property in the decedent's estate is discovered. *(Stats.1990, c. 79 (A.B.759), § 14, operative July 1, 1991.)*

Law Revision Commission Comments
1990 Enactment

Section 6609 continues Section 6609 of the repealed Probate Code without substantive change. The court may decline to set aside a small estate if the court determines that it would be inequitable to do so. An appeal may be taken from an order made under this section. See Section 7240.

The court may assign the estate to the minor child or minor children of the decedent even if there is a surviving spouse. This may be desirable, for example, if the minor children live apart from the surviving spouse or where the minor children are not children of the surviving spouse. In this respect, Section 6609 is consistent with Section 6510 (setting aside exempt property other than family dwelling) and Section 6521 (setting apart probate homestead).

The court may assign the estate to a surviving spouse even if the surviving spouse has remarried. Permitting the small estate to be set aside to a surviving spouse, whether or not remarried, makes Section 6609 consistent with Section 6510 (setting aside exempt property other than family dwelling) and Section 6521 (setting apart probate homestead). The last two sentences of subdivision (b) place on the remarried surviving spouse the burden of proof to establish the need for the small estate set aside.

Subdivision (b) specifies matters to be considered in determining whether to make an order under the section. Under some circumstances, the court may order that the small estate be set aside to one of the minor children and that the other minor children and the spouse be excluded, or that the small estate be set aside in unequal shares to the minor children, or that the small estate be set aside to the surviving spouse and that the minor children be excluded. In determining the assignment to make, the court must take into account the various considerations listed in subdivision (b). See also Section 6604(b)(8) (petition must include the requested disposition of the decedent's estate and the considerations justifying the requested disposition).

Under subdivision (d), the court may set aside a small estate whether or not expenses of last illness, funeral charges, and expenses of administration have been paid, but the court must make an appropriate order to ensure that they will be paid.

For general provisions, see Sections 1000–1004 (rules of practice), 1040–1050 (hearings and orders). This section does not apply if the decedent died before July 1, 1987. See Section 6614. As to the application of any amendments made after that date, see Section 3. A reference to a provision of the former statute is deemed to be a reference to the comparable provisions of this chapter. See Section 6615.

Background on Section 6609 of Repealed Code

Section 6609 was added by 1986 Cal.Stat. ch. 783 § 23. The section superseded former Probate Code Section 645 (repealed by 1986 Cal.Stat. ch. 783 § 9).

Section 6609 made these significant substantive changes in the former law:

(1) Under Section 6609, the court may decline to set aside a small estate if the court determines that it would be inequitable to do so. Under former Section 645, the court had no discretion; the court was required to set aside the small estate if the court made the findings prescribed by that section.

(2) Under Section 6609, the court may assign the estate to the minor child or minor children of the decedent even if there is a surviving spouse. Former law did not permit the small estate to be assigned to the minor child or children if there was an unmarried surviving spouse.

(3) Under Section 6609, the court may assign the estate to a surviving spouse even if the surviving spouse has remarried. Under former Section 645, the small estate could be set aside only to a "surviving spouse who has not theretofore remarried."

Subdivision (b) of Section 6609, which specifies matters to be considered in determining whether to make an order under the section, was a new provision drawn from subdivision (a) of Section 6523 which specifies matters to be considered in selecting and setting apart a probate homestead.

The word "mortgages," which was found in former Section 645, was omitted as unnecessary, mortgages being included within the phrase "liens and encumbrances."

Subdivision (d) of Section 6609 superseded the portion of the first sentence of former Section 645 that required expenses of last illness, funeral charges, and expenses of administration to be paid before the court could set aside a small estate. Under subdivision (d), the court may set aside a small estate whether or not such expenses have been paid, but the court must make an appropriate order to ensure that they will be paid.

Subdivision (e) of Section 6609 continued the last sentence of former Section 645, revised to reflect the new authority of the court to assign the small estate to one or more of the minor children of the decedent where there is a surviving spouse.

For background on the provisions of this chapter, see the Comment to this chapter under the chapter heading. [20 Cal.L.Rev.Comm.Reports 1001 (1990)].

Cross References

Administration of estates of decedents, see Probate Code §§ 7000, 7001.
Burden of proof, generally, see Evidence Code § 500 et seq.
Decedent's estate defined for purposes of this Chapter, see Probate Code § 6600.
Family allowance, see Probate Code § 6540 et seq.
Minor child defined for purposes of this Chapter, see Probate Code § 6601.

§ 6610. Effect of order

Upon becoming final, an order under Section 6609 shall be conclusive on all persons, whether or not they are then in being. *(Stats.1990, c. 79 (A.B.759), § 14, operative July 1, 1991.)*

Law Revision Commission Comments
1990 Enactment

Section 6610 continues Section 6610 of the repealed Probate Code without change. This section gives the order the same effect as an order under Section 13657 (effect of order determining or confirming property passing or belonging to surviving spouse). For general provisions, see Sections 1040–1050 (hearings and orders). This section does not apply if the decedent died before July 1, 1987. See Section 6614. As to the application of any amendments made after that date, see Section 3. A reference to a provision of the former statute is deemed to be a reference to the comparable provisions of this chapter. See Section 6615.

Background on Section 6610 of Repealed Code

Section 6610 was added by 1986 Cal.Stat. ch. 783 § 23. The section superseded former Probate Code Section 645.1 (repealed by 1986 Cal.Stat. ch. 783 § 9). The language in former Section 645.1 referring to fraud or the erroneously assumed deceased appearing has been omitted from Section 6610 as unnecessary. The omission of this language make no substantive change in the effect of the section. See McMillan v. Boese, 45 Cal.App.2d 764, 115 P.2d 37 (1941). For background on the provisions of this chapter, see the Comment to this chapter under the chapter heading. [20 Cal.L.Rev.Comm.Reports 1001 (1990)].

§ 6611. Unsecured debts; liability; actions and proceedings

(a) Subject to the limitations and conditions specified in this section, the person or persons in whom title vested pursuant to Section 6609 are personally liable for the unsecured debts of the decedent.

(b) The personal liability of a person under this section does not exceed the fair market value at the date of the decedent's death of the property title to which vested in that person pursuant to Section 6609, less the total of all of the following:

(1) The amount of any liens and encumbrances on that property.

(2) The value of any probate homestead interest set apart under Section 6520 out of that property.

(3) The value of any other property set aside under Section 6510 out of that property.

(c) In any action or proceeding based upon an unsecured debt of the decedent, the surviving spouse of the decedent, the child or children of the decedent, or the guardian of the minor child or children of the decedent, may assert any defense, cross-complaint, or setoff which would have been available to the decedent if the decedent had not died.

(d) If proceedings are commenced in this state for the administration of the estate of the decedent and the time for filing claims has commenced, any action upon the personal liability of a person under this section is barred to the same extent as provided for claims under Part 4 (commencing with Section 9000) of Division 7, except as to the following:

(1) Creditors who commence judicial proceedings for the enforcement of the debt and serve the person liable under this section with the complaint therein prior to the expiration of the time for filing claims.

(2) Creditors who have or who secure an acknowledgment in writing of the person liable under this section that that person is liable for the debts.

(3) Creditors who file a timely claim in the proceedings for the administration of the estate of the decedent.

(e) Section 366.2 of the Code of Civil Procedure applies in an action under this section. *(Stats.1990, c. 79 (A.B.759), § 14, operative July 1, 1991. Amended by Stats.1990, c. 140*

(S.B.1855), § 4.1, operative July 1, 1991; Stats.1992, c. 178 (S.B.1496), § 32.)

Law Revision Commission Comments
1990 Enactment

Section 6611 continues Section 6611 of the repealed Probate Code without substantive change. The personal liability of a person who takes only a share or portion of the decedent's estate is limited to the net value of the share or portion (fair market value less liens and encumbrances and any probate homestead or exempt property set apart out of the share), rather than the net value of the entire estate.

Subdivision (e) is drawn from Section 13552 (liability for debts of deceased spouse). The subdivision is a limitation on the one-year limitation period of subdivision (c) where estate proceedings are commenced, and provides the same period as for creditors' claims in estate proceedings generally.

This section does not apply if the decedent died before July 1, 1987. See Section 6614. As to the application of any amendments made after that date, see Section 3. A reference to a provision of the former statute is deemed to be a reference to the comparable provisions of this chapter. See Section 6615.

1990 Amendment

Section 6611 (enacted as a part of the new Probate Code by 1990 Cal.Stat. ch. 79 § 14) was amended by 1990 Cal.Stat. ch. 140 § 4.1 to delete former subdivision (c), which conflicted with Code of Civil Procedure Section 353 (statute of limitations), and to make clear that the general one-year statute of limitations applicable to all causes of action against a decedent is applicable to liability for the decedent's debts under Section 6611. For background on the 1990 amendment, see Recommendation Relating to Notice to Creditors in Estate Administration, 20 Cal.L.Revision Comm'n Reports 507 (1990). [20 Cal.L.Rev.Comm.Reports 1001 (1990)].

1992 Amendment

Section 6611 is amended to revise a section reference. This revision is a technical, nonsubstantive change. [22 Cal.L.Rev.Comm.Reports 895 (1992)].

Background on Section 6611 of Repealed Code

Section 6611 was added by 1986 Cal.Stat. ch. 783 § 23 and was amended by 1987 Cal.Stat. ch. 923 § 92.5. The section continued former Probate Code Section 645.3 (repealed by 1986 Cal.Stat. ch. 783 § 9) without substantive change, except as follows:

(1) Subdivision (b) of Section 6611 made clear that the personal liability of a person who takes only a share or portion of the decedent's estate is limited to the net value of the share or portion (fair market value less liens and encumbrances and any probate homestead or exempt property set apart out of the share), rather than the net value of the entire estate.

(2) Subdivision (e) of Section 6611 was new.

The 1987 amendment revised the provisions relating to notice. As to the 1987 amendment, see Communication from California Law Revision Commission Concerning Assembly Bill 708, 19 Cal.L.Revision Comm'n Reports 545, 560 (1988); Comments to Conforming Revisions and Repeals, 19 Cal.L.Revision Comm'n Reports 391, 450 (1988). For background on the provisions of this chapter, see the Comment to this chapter under the chapter heading. [20 Cal.L.Rev.Comm.Reports 1001 (1990)].

Cross References

Minor child defined for purposes of this Chapter, see Probate Code § 6601.

§ 6612. Determinations not to make order under § 6609; action on petition for probate or administration

If a petition filed under this chapter is filed with a petition for the probate of the decedent's will or for administration of the estate of the decedent and the court determines not to make an order under Section 6609, the court shall act on the petition for probate of the decedent's will or for administration of the estate of the decedent in the same manner as if no petition had been filed under this chapter, and the estate shall then be administered in the same manner as if no petition had been filed under this chapter. *(Stats.1990, c. 79 (A.B.759), § 14, operative July 1, 1991.)*

Law Revision Commission Comments

1990 Enactment

Section 6612 continues Section 6612 of the repealed Probate Code without change. Under Section 6609, the court is required to deny a petition filed under this chapter if the decedent's estate is not a small estate (see Sections 6600, 6609), or if there is neither a surviving spouse nor a minor child. The court also may decline to order a small estate set-aside when it would be inequitable to do so. See Section 6609.

For general provisions, see Sections 1000–1004 (rules of practice), 1020–1023 (petitions and other papers), 1040–1050 (hearings and orders). This section does not apply if the decedent died before July 1, 1987. See Section 6614. As to the application of any amendments made after that date, see Section 3. A reference to a provision of the former statute is deemed to be a reference to the comparable provisions of this chapter. See Section 6615.

Background on Section 6612 of Repealed Code

Section 6612 was added by 1986 Cal.Stat. ch. 783 § 23. The section was drawn from former Probate Code Section 646 (repealed by 1986 Cal.Stat. ch. 783 § 9) but the language of the former section was revised to recognize that the court has discretion to deny a petition filed under this chapter. See Section 6609. For background on the provisions of this chapter, see the Comment to this chapter under the chapter heading. [20 Cal.L.Rev.Comm.Reports 1001 (1990)].

Cross References

Administration of estates of decedents, see Probate Code § 7000 et seq.

§ 6613. Attorney's fees

The attorney's fees for services performed in connection with the filing of a petition and the obtaining of a court order under this chapter shall be determined by private agreement between the attorney and the client and are not subject to approval by the court. If there is no agreement between the attorney and the client concerning the attorney's fees for services performed in connection with the filing of a petition and obtaining of a court order under this chapter and there is a dispute concerning the reasonableness of the attorney's fees for those services, a petition may be filed with the court in the same proceeding requesting that the court determine the reasonableness of the attorney's fees for those services. If there is an agreement between the attorney and the client concerning the attorney's fees for services performed in connection with the filing of a petition and obtaining a court order under this chapter and there is a dispute concerning the meaning of the agreement, a petition may be filed with the court in the same proceeding requesting that the court determine the dispute. *(Stats.1990, c. 79 (A.B.759), § 14, operative July 1, 1991.)*

Law Revision Commission Comments

1990 Enactment

Section 6613 continues Section 6613 of the repealed Probate Code without substantive change. This section is the same as Section 13660 (petition for determination or confirmation of property passing or belonging to surviving spouse). Section 6613 continues former law and practice but gives the probate court authority to determine disputes concerning the attorney's fee for services performed in connection with the filing of a petition and the obtaining of a court order under this chapter. The court has no jurisdiction to determine disputes concerning attorney's fees for other services, such as termination of joint tenancies, collection of insurance, and the like.

For general provisions, see Sections 1000–1004 (rules of practice), 1020–1023 (petitions and other papers), 1040–1050 (hearings and orders). For general provisions relating to notice of hearing, see Sections 1200–1221. See also Sections 1250–1252 (request for special notice), 1260–1265 (proof of giving notice). This section does not apply if the decedent died before July 1, 1987. See Section 6614. As to the application of any amendments made after that date, see Section 3. A reference to a provision of the former statute is deemed to be a reference to the comparable provisions of this chapter. See Section 6615.

Background on Section 6613 of Repealed Code

Section 6613 was a new provision added by 1986 Cal.Stat. ch. 783 § 23. For background on the provisions of this chapter, see the Comment to this chapter under the chapter heading. [20 Cal.L.Rev.Comm.Reports 1001 (1990)].

§ 6614. Application of law

Sections 6600 to 6613, inclusive, do not apply if the decedent died before July 1, 1987. If the decedent died before July 1, 1987, the case continues to be governed by the law applicable to the case prior to July 1, 1987. *(Stats.1990, c. 79 (A.B.759), § 14, operative July 1, 1991.)*

Law Revision Commission Comments

1990 Enactment

Section 6614 continues Section 6614 of the repealed Probate Code without substantive change. This section makes clear that Sections 6600–6613 do not apply if the decedent died before July 1, 1987, the operative date of those sections. If the decedent died before that date, the right to a small estate set-aside is determined under the law that was applicable prior to July 1, 1987. The application of Sections 6600 to 6613 does not apply if the decedent died before July 1, 1987 because in a case where the decedent died before that date there was a right to have a small estate set-aside. Under Sections 6600 to 6613, the court may decline to order a small estate set-aside when it would be inequitable to do so. See Section 6609.

Background on Section 6614 of Repealed Code

Section 6614 was added by 1986 Cal.Stat. ch. 783 § 23. The section superseded former Probate Code Section 647.5 (repealed by 1986 Cal.Stat. ch. 783 § 9). For background on the provisions of this chapter, see the Comment to this chapter under the chapter heading. [20 Cal.L.Rev.Comm.Reports 1001 (1990)].

§ 6615. References to former sections deemed references to comparable provisions of this chapter

A reference in any statute of this state or in a written instrument, including a will or trust, to a provision of former Sections 640 to 647.5, inclusive, repealed by Chapter 783 of the Statutes of 1986, shall be deemed to be a reference to the comparable provisions of this chapter. *(Stats.1990, c. 79 (A.B.759), § 14, operative July 1, 1991.)*

Law Revision Commission Comments

1990 Enactment

Section 6615 continues Section 6615 of the repealed Probate Code without substantive change. This section makes clear that, after the operative date of this chapter of the repealed Probate Code (July 1, 1987), a reference in a statute or written instrument to a provision of former law will be deemed to be a reference to the comparable provision of this chapter.

Background on Section 6615 of Repealed Code

Section 6615 was a new provision added by 1986 Cal.Stat. ch. 783 § 23. The section was drawn from former Probate Code Section 1490 and from former Probate Code Section 649.6 (repealed by 1986 Cal.Stat. ch. 783 § 9). For background on the provisions of this chapter, see the Comment to this chapter under the chapter heading. [20 Cal.L.Rev.Comm.Reports 1001 (1990)].

Part 4

ESCHEAT OF DECEDENT'S PROPERTY

Section

6800. Failure to leave person to take by testate or intestate succession; escheat.
6801. Real property.
6802. Personal property.
6803. Personal property subject to control of superior court of state; property going to another jurisdiction.
6804. Intangible property.
6805. Intangible property subject to control of superior court of state; property going to another jurisdiction.
6806. Property distributable from trusts; benefit plans; reversion to trust or fund from which distributable.

Law Revision Commission Comments

1990 Enactment

This part supersedes Part 4 (commencing with Section 6800) of Division 6 of the repealed Probate Code. The superseded part was enacted upon recommendation of the California Law Revision Commission. See Tentative Recommendation Relating to Wills and Intestate Succession, 16 Cal.L.Revision Comm'n Reports 2301 (1982). See also Recommendation Relating to Escheat, 8 Cal.L.Revision Comm'n Reports 1001 (1967). [20 Cal.L.Rev.Comm.Reports 1001 (1990)].

§ 6800. Failure to leave person to take by testate or intestate succession; escheat

(a) If a decedent, whether or not the decedent was domiciled in this state, leaves no one to take the decedent's estate or any portion thereof by testate succession, and no one other than a government or governmental subdivision or agency to take the estate or a portion thereof by intestate succession, under the laws of this state or of any other jurisdiction, the same escheats at the time of the decedent's death in accordance with this part.

(b) Property that escheats to the state under this part, whether held by the state or its officers, is subject to the same charges and trusts to which it would have been subject if it had passed by succession and is also subject to the provisions of Title 10 (commencing with Section 1300) of Part 3 of the Code of Civil Procedure relating to escheated estates. *(Stats. 1990, c. 79 (A.B.759), § 14, operative July 1, 1991.)*

Law Revision Commission Comments

1990 Enactment

Section 6800 continues Section 6800 of the repealed Probate Code without substantive change.

Background on Section 6800 of Repealed Code

Section 6800 was added by 1983 Cal.Stat. ch. 842 § 55. The section continued the substance of subdivisions (a) and (b) of former Probate Code Section 231 (repealed by 1983 Cal.Stat. ch. 842 § 19). For background on the provisions of this part, see the Comment to this part under the part heading. [20 Cal.L.Rev.Comm.Reports 1001 (1990)].

Cross References

Construction of instruments, transfers of present or future interests to heirs, see Probate Code § 21114.
Estates of deceased persons, payment to state, see Code of Civil Procedure § 1443.

§ 6801. Real property

Real property in this state escheats to this state in accordance with Section 6800. *(Stats.1990, c. 79 (A.B.759), § 14, operative July 1, 1991.)*

Law Revision Commission Comments

1990 Enactment

Section 6801 continues Section 6801 of the repealed Probate Code without change.

Background on Section 6801 of Repealed Code

Section 6801 was added by 1983 Cal.Stat. ch. 842 § 55. The section continued former Probate Code Section 232 (repealed by 1983 Cal.Stat. ch. 842 § 19). For background on the provisions of this part, see the Comment to this part under the part heading. [20 Cal.L.Rev.Comm.Reports 1001 (1990)].

§ 6802. Personal property

All tangible personal property owned by the decedent, wherever located at the decedent's death, that was customarily kept in this state prior to the decedent's death, escheats to this state in accordance with Section 6800. *(Stats.1990, c. 79 (A.B.759), § 14, operative July 1, 1991.)*

Law Revision Commission Comments

1990 Enactment

Section 6802 continues Section 6802 of the repealed Probate Code without change.

Background on Section 6802 of Repealed Code

Section 6802 was added by 1983 Cal.Stat. ch. 842 § 55. The section continued former Probate Code Section 233 (repealed by 1983 Cal.Stat. ch. 842 § 19). For background on the provisions of this part, see the Comment to this part under the part heading. [20 Cal.L.Rev.Comm.Reports 1001 (1990)].

§ 6803. Personal property subject to control of superior court of state; property going to another jurisdiction

(a) Subject to subdivision (b), all tangible personal property owned by the decedent that is subject to the control of a superior court of this state for purposes of administration under this code escheats to this state in accordance with Section 6800.

(b) The property described in subdivision (a) does not escheat to this state but goes to another jurisdiction if the other jurisdiction claims the property and establishes all of the following:

(1) The other jurisdiction is entitled to the property under its law.

(2) The decedent customarily kept the property in that jurisdiction prior to the decedent's death.

(3) This state has the right to escheat and take tangible personal property being administered as part of a decedent's estate in that jurisdiction if the decedent customarily kept the property in this state prior to the decedent's death. *(Stats. 1990, c. 79 (A.B.759), § 14, operative July 1, 1991.)*

Law Revision Commission Comments

1990 Enactment

Section 6803 continues Section 6803 of the repealed Probate Code without substantive change. The words "and disposition" have been omitted as unnecessary, "administration" covering "disposition" as well as all other aspects of administration of a decedent's estate.

Background on Section 6803 of Repealed Code

Section 6803 was added by 1983 Cal.Stat. ch. 842 § 55 and was amended by 1988 Cal.Stat. ch. 1199 § 79. The section continued former Probate Code Section 234 (repealed by 1983 Cal.Stat. ch. 842 § 19). The 1988 amendment corrected a section reference. As to the 1988 amendment, see Comments to Conforming Revisions and Repeals, 19 Cal.L.Revision Comm'n Reports 1031, 1091 (1988). For background on the provisions of this part, see the Comment to this part under the part heading. [20 Cal.L.Rev.Comm.Reports 1001 (1990)].

§ 6804. Intangible property

All intangible property owned by the decedent escheats to this state in accordance with Section 6800 if the decedent was domiciled in this state at the time of the decedent's death. *(Stats.1990, c. 79 (A.B.759), § 14, operative July 1, 1991.)*

Law Revision Commission Comments

1990 Enactment

Section 6804 continues Section 6804 of the repealed Probate Code without change.

Background on Section 6804 of Repealed Code

Section 6804 was added by 1983 Cal.Stat. ch. 842 § 55. The section continued former Probate Code Section 235 (repealed by 1983 Cal.Stat. ch. 842 § 19). For background on the provisions of this part, see the Comment to this part under the part heading. [20 Cal.L.Rev.Comm.Reports 1001 (1990)].

Cross References

Determination of residence and domicile, see Elections Code §§ 349, 2020 et seq.; Revenue and Taxation Code § 17014 et seq.; Welfare and Institutions Code § 17101.
Escheat of intangible personal property, see Code of Civil Procedure § 1510 et seq.

§ 6805. Intangible property subject to control of superior court of state; property going to another jurisdiction

(a) Subject to subdivision (b), all intangible property owned by the decedent that is subject to the control of a superior court of this state for purposes of administration under this code escheats to this state in accordance with Section 6800 whether or not the decedent was domiciled in this state at the time of the decedent's death.

(b) The property described in subdivision (a) does not escheat to this state but goes to another jurisdiction if the other jurisdiction claims the property and establishes all of the following:

(1) The other jurisdiction is entitled to the property under its laws.

(2) The decedent was domiciled in that jurisdiction at the time of the decedent's death.

(3) This state has the right to escheat and take intangible property being administered as part of a decedent's estate in that jurisdiction if the decedent was domiciled in this state at the time of the decedent's death. *(Stats.1990, c. 79 (A.B. 759), § 14, operative July 1, 1991.)*

Law Revision Commission Comments

1990 Enactment

Section 6805 continues Section 6805 of the repealed Probate Code without substantive change. The words "and disposition" have been omitted as unnecessary, "administration" covering "disposition" as well as all other aspects of administration of a decedent's estate.

Background on Section 6805 of Repealed Code

Section 6805 was added by 1983 Cal.Stat. ch. 842 § 55 and was amended by 1988 Cal.Stat. ch. 1199 § 79.5. The section continued former Probate Code Section 236 (repealed by 1983 Cal.Stat. ch. 842 § 19). The 1988 amendment corrected a section reference. As to the 1988 amendment, see Comments to Conforming Revisions and Repeals, 19 Cal.L.Revision Comm'n Reports 1031, 1091 (1988). For background on the provisions of this part, see the Comment to this part under the part heading. [20 Cal.L.Rev.Comm.Reports 1001 (1990)].

Cross References

Determination of residence and domicile, see Revenue and Taxation Code § 17014 et seq.; Welfare and Institutions Code § 17101.
Residence and domicile, see Elections Code §§ 349, 2020 et seq.

§ 6806. Property distributable from trusts; benefit plans; reversion to trust or fund from which distributable

Notwithstanding any other provision of law, a benefit consisting of money or other property distributable from a trust established under a plan providing health and welfare, pension, vacation, severance, retirement benefit, death benefit, unemployment insurance or similar benefits does not pass to or escheat to the state under this part but goes to the trust or fund from which it is distributable, subject to the provisions of Section 1521 of the Code of Civil Procedure. However, if such plan has terminated and the trust or fund has been distributed to the beneficiaries thereof prior to distribution of such benefit from the estate, such benefit passes to the state and escheats to the state under this part. *(Stats.1990, c. 79 (A.B.759), § 14, operative July 1, 1991.)*

Law Revision Commission Comments

1990 Enactment

Section 6806 continues Section 6806 of the repealed Probate Code without substantive change.

Background on Section 6806 of Repealed Code

Section 6806 was added by 1983 Cal.Stat. ch. 842 § 55. The section continued subdivision (c) of former Probate Code Section 231 (repealed by 1983 Cal.Stat. ch. 842 § 19). For background on the provisions of this part, see the Comment to this part under the part heading.   [20 Cal.L.Rev.Comm.Reports 1001 (1990)].

Division 7

ADMINISTRATION OF ESTATES OF DECEDENTS

Cross References

Real property, transfer fee defined, see Civil Code § 1098.

Part 1

GENERAL PROVISIONS

CHAPTER 1. PASSAGE OF DECEDENT'S PROPERTY

Law Revision Commission Comments

1990 Enactment

This chapter supersedes Chapter 1 of Part 1 (commencing with Section 7000) of Division 7 of the repealed Probate Code. The superseded chapter was enacted upon recommendation of the California Law Revision Commission. See Recommendation Relating to Rules of Procedure in Probate, 19 Cal.L.Revision Comm'n Reports 917 (1988). [20 Cal.L.Rev.Comm.Reports 1001 (1990)].

Cross References

Application of old and new law, see Probate Code § 3.

§ 7000. Passage to devisee or intestate heirs

Subject to Section 7001, title to a decedent's property passes on the decedent's death to the person to whom it is devised in the decedent's last will or, in the absence of such a devise, to the decedent's heirs as prescribed in the laws governing intestate succession. *(Stats.1990, c. 79 (A.B.759), § 14, operative July 1, 1991.)*

Law Revision Commission Comments

1990 Enactment

Section 7000 continues Section 7000 of the repealed Probate Code without change. The decedent's heirs are determined as provided in Part 2 (commencing with Section 6400) of Division 6 (intestate succession). The rule stated in Section 7000 is subject to limitations. See Section 7001 and the Comment thereto.

Background on Section 7000 of Repealed Code

Section 7000 was added by 1988 Cal.Stat. ch. 1199 § 80.5. The section restated the first part of former Probate Code Section 300 (repealed by 1988 Cal.Stat. ch. 1199 § 40) without substantive change. For background on the provisions of this chapter, see the Comment to this chapter under the chapter heading. [20 Cal.L.Rev.Comm.Reports 1001 (1990)].

Cross References

Acquisition of estate and collection of debts by executor or administrator, see Probate Code § 9650.
Collection or transfer of estates without administration, see Probate Code § 13100 et seq.
Conveyances of real property vest in purchaser title of decedent, see Probate Code § 10314.
Family allowance generally, see Probate Code § 6540 et seq.
Leasing of real property of estate, see Probate Code § 9942 et seq.
Payment of debts, expenses and charges, generally, see Probate Code § 11401 et seq.
Powers and duties of joint personal representatives, see Probate Code § 9630 et seq.
Provision by will for payment of debts, expense, or family allowance, see Probate Code § 21401.
Sale of property,
  Personal, see Probate Code § 10252 et seq.
  Real, see Probate Code § 10300 et seq.
Setting aside probate homestead, see Probate Code § 6521 et seq.
Succession of property generally, see Probate Code § 6100 et seq.
Testamentary disposition, when vesting, see Probate Code § 21116.

§ 7001. Administration of decedent's property; rights of beneficiaries and creditors

The decedent's property is subject to administration under this code, except as otherwise provided by law, and is subject to the rights of beneficiaries, creditors, and other persons as provided by law. *(Stats.1990, c. 79 (A.B.759), § 14, operative July 1, 1991.)*

Law Revision Commission Comments

1990 Enactment

Section 7001 continues Section 7001 of the repealed Probate Code without change. Administration of the decedent's estate includes possession by the personal representative, control by the court, sale and other disposition of the property, charges of administration, and payment of debts and family allowance. The requirement of administration is subject to exceptions. See, e.g., Sections 5000 (contract rights), 5100–5407 (multiple party accounts), 13000–13660 (disposition without administration), 15000–18201 (trusts), and the law governing joint tenancy. For provisions relating to the rights of beneficiaries, creditors, and others, see, e.g., Sections 100–105 (effect of death of married person on community and quasi-community property), 260–295 (disclaimers), 6146–6147 (lapsed gifts), 6510–6511 (exempt property), 6520–6528 (probate homestead), 6540–6545 (family allowance), 6560–6573 (omitted spouse and children), 6600–6615 (small estate set-aside), 21400–21406 (abatement).

Background on Section 7001 of Repealed Code

Section 7001 was added by 1988 Cal.Stat. ch. 1199 § 80.5. The section restated the last part of former Probate Code Section 300 (repealed by 1988 Cal.Stat. ch. 1199 § 40) without substantive change. For background on the provisions of this chapter, see the Comment to this chapter under the chapter heading. [20 Cal.L.Rev.Comm.Reports 1001 (1990)].

CHAPTER 2.　JURISDICTION AND COURTS

Law Revision Commission Comments

1990 Enactment

This chapter supersedes Chapter 2 of Part 1 (commencing with Section 7050) of Division 7 of the repealed Probate Code. The superseded chapter was enacted upon recommendation of the California Law Revision Commission. See Recommendation Relating to Rules of Procedure in Probate, 19 Cal.L.Revision Comm'n Reports 917 (1988). See also Communication from the California Law Revision Commission Concerning Assembly Bill 2841, 19 Cal.L.Revision Comm'n Reports 1201, 1229–30 (1988). [20 Cal.L.Rev.Comm.Reports 1001 (1990)].

ARTICLE 1.　JURISDICTION AND VENUE

Section
7050.　Jurisdiction over estate administration.
7051.　Venue; county of domicile.
7052.　Venue; nondomiciliary decedents; location of property.

§ 7050.　Jurisdiction over estate administration

The superior court has jurisdiction of proceedings under this code concerning the administration of the decedent's estate. *(Stats.1990, c. 79 (A.B.759), § 14, operative July 1, 1991. Amended by Stats.1994, c. 806 (A.B.3686), § 22.)*

Law Revision Commission Comments

1990 Enactment

Section 7050 continues Section 7050 of the repealed Probate Code without change. Subdivision (a) is comparable to Section 2200 (jurisdiction of guardianship and conservatorship proceedings). Proceedings concerning administration of a decedent's estate include the probate of wills (Sections 8200–8272), appointment of personal representatives (Sections 8400–8577), and estate management (Sections 9600–10382). Where appropriate, the reference to the superior court in subdivision (a) means the department or judge of the court that deals with probate matters.

Subdivision (b) makes clear that the probate court, when considering cases brought before it under this division, has all the powers of the superior court exercising its general jurisdiction. Hence, while preserving the division of business among different departments of the superior court, this section rejects the limitation on the powers of the probate court that has been cited in appellate decisions. See, e.g., Copley v. Copley, 80 Cal.App.3d 97, 106–08, 145 Cal.Rptr. 437 (1978). See also Section 17001 (full-power court under Trust Law). For general provisions, see Sections 1000–1004 (rules of practice),

1020–1023 (petitions and other papers), 1040–1050 (hearings and orders).

Background on Section 7050 of Repealed Code

Section 7050 was added by 1988 Cal.Stat. ch. 1199 § 80.5. Subdivision (a) restated a provision of former Probate Code Section 300 and the introductory part of former Probate Code Section 301 (provisions repealed by 1988 Cal.Stat. ch. 1199 § 40) without substantive change. Subdivision (b) expanded a provision of former Probate Code Section 321 ("judge may make and issue all necessary orders and writs to enforce production of wills and attendance of witnesses") (repealed by 1988 Cal.Stat. ch. 1199 § 40) and abandoned the former rule that the superior court sitting in probate was a court of limited jurisdiction. See 7B. Witkin, Summary of California Law Wills and Probate §§ 233–34, at 5741–43 (8th ed. 1974). Subdivision (b) was revised by 1989 Cal.Stat. ch. 21 § 13 to make clear that the subdivision applies in estate administration proceedings throughout the code, whether pursuant to this division or any other division of the code. See Communication from the California Law Revision Commission Concerning Assembly Bill 156, 20 Cal.L.Revision Comm'n Reports 227, 230 (1990). For background on the provisions of this chapter, see the Comment to this chapter under the chapter heading. [20 Cal.L.Rev.Comm.Reports 1001 (1990)].

Cross References

Administration of estates of persons missing over five years, see Probate Code § 12401 et seq.
Appointment of personal representatives, see Probate Code § 8402.
Disqualification of judge for interest and transfer of proceedings, see Probate Code § 7060.
Escheat proceedings, jurisdiction and venue, see Code of Civil Procedure § 1410.
Jurisdiction of superior court, see Cal. Const. Art. 6, § 5.

§ 7051.　Venue; county of domicile

If the decedent was domiciled in this state at the time of death, the proper county for proceedings concerning administration of the decedent's estate is the county in which the decedent was domiciled, regardless of where the decedent died. *(Stats.1990, c. 79 (A.B.759), § 14, operative July 1, 1991.)*

Law Revision Commission Comments

1990 Enactment

Section 7051 continues Section 7051 of the repealed Probate Code without change.

Background on Section 7051 of Repealed Code

Section 7051 was added by 1988 Cal.Stat. ch. 1199 § 80.5. The section restated without substantive change the venue provisions of former Probate Code Section 301 (repealed by 1988 Cal.Stat. ch. 1199 § 40) applicable to domiciliaries. The substitution of "domicile" for "residence" codified case law. See, e.g., Estate of Phillips, 269 Cal.App.2d 656, 659, 75 Cal.Rptr. 301 (1969); In re Brace's Estate, 180 Cal.App.2d 797, 802, 4 Cal.Rptr. 683 (1960); In re Glassford's Estate, 114 Cal.App.2d 181, 186, 249 P.2d 908 (1952). For background on the provisions of this chapter, see the Comment to this chapter under the chapter heading. [20 Cal.L.Rev.Comm.Reports 1001 (1990)].

§ 7052.　Venue; nondomiciliary decedents; location of property

If the decedent was not domiciled in this state at the time of death, the proper county for proceedings under this code concerning the administration of the decedent's estate is one of the following:

(a) If property of the nondomiciliary decedent is located in the county in which the nondomiciliary decedent died, the county in which the nondomiciliary decedent died.

(b) If no property of the nondomiciliary decedent is located in the county in which the nondomiciliary decedent died or if the nondomiciliary decedent did not die in this state, any county in which property of the nondomiciliary decedent is located, regardless of where the nondomiciliary decedent died. If property of the nondomiciliary decedent is located in more than one county, the proper county is the county in which a petition for ancillary administration is first filed, and the court in that county has jurisdiction of the administration of the estate. *(Stats.1990, c. 79 (A.B.759), § 14, operative July 1, 1991.)*

Law Revision Commission Comments

1990 Enactment

Section 7052 continues Section 7052 of the repealed Probate Code without substantive change. See also Section 12511 (ancillary administration).

Background on Section 7052 of Repealed Code

Section 7052 was added by 1988 Cal.Stat. ch. 1199 § 80.5. The section restated the nondomiciliary venue provisions of former Probate Code Section 301 (repealed by 1988 Cal.Stat. ch. 1199 § 40) without substantive change. The substitution of "domicile" for "residence" codified case law. See the Background portion of the Comment to Section 7051. For background on the provisions of this chapter, see the Comment to this chapter under the chapter heading. [20 Cal.L.Rev.Comm.Reports 1001 (1990)].

ARTICLE 2. DISQUALIFICATION OF JUDGE

Section
7060. Grounds for disqualification; interest or participation of judge; application of law.

§ 7060. Grounds for disqualification; interest or participation of judge; application of law

(a) In addition to any other ground provided by law for disqualification of a judge, a judge is disqualified from acting in proceedings under this code concerning the administration of the decedent's estate, except to order the transfer of a proceeding as provided in Article 3 (commencing with Section 7070), if any of the following circumstances exist:

(1) The judge is interested as a beneficiary or creditor.

(2) The judge is named as executor or trustee in the will.

(3) The judge is otherwise interested.

(b) A judge who participates in any manner in the drafting or execution of a will, including acting as a witness to the will, is disqualified from acting in any proceeding prior to and including the admission of the will to probate or in any proceeding involving its validity or interpretation.

(c) The amendments made to former Section 303 by Section 27 of Chapter 923 of the Statutes of 1987 do not apply in any proceeding commenced prior to July 1, 1988. *(Stats.1990, c. 79 (A.B.759), § 14, operative July 1, 1991.)*

Law Revision Commission Comments

1990 Enactment

Section 7060 continues Section 7060 of the repealed Probate Code without change. For general provisions on disqualification, see Code Civ.Proc. §§ 170–170.8.

Background on Section 7060 of Repealed Code

Section 7060 was added by 1988 Cal.Stat. ch. 1199 § 80.5. Subdivisions (a) and (b) restated subdivision (a) of former Probate Code Section 303 (repealed by 1988 Cal.Stat. ch. 1199 § 40) without substantive change. Subdivision (c) restated subdivision (c) of former Section 303 (repealed by 1988 Cal.Stat. ch. 1199 § 40) without substantive change. See Communication from the California Law Revision Commission Concerning Assembly Bill 2841, 19 Cal.L.Revision Comm'n Reports, 1201, 1230 (1988). Subdivision (a) was revised by 1989 Cal.Stat. ch. 21 § 14 to make clear that the subdivision applies in estate administration proceedings throughout the code, whether pursuant to this division or any other division of the code. See Communication from the California Law Revision Commission Concerning Assembly Bill 156, 20 Cal.L.Revision Comm'n Reports 227, 230 (1990). For background on the provisions of this chapter, see the Comment to this chapter under the chapter heading. [20 Cal.L.Rev.Comm.Reports 1001 (1990)].

Cross References

Appeal from order of change of venue, see Code of Civil Procedure § 963.
Change of place of trial, see Code of Civil Procedure §§ 397, 398.
Costs on transfer of actions, see Code of Civil Procedure § 399.
Disqualification of judges, see Code of Civil Procedure § 170 et seq.
Initiative and referendum of cities and counties, see Cal. Const. Art. 2, § 11.
Relationship between judge and receiver, see Code of Civil Procedure § 566.
Superior Courts, generally, see Cal. Const. Art. 6, § 5 et seq.

ARTICLE 3. TRANSFER OF PROCEEDINGS

Section
7070. Lack of qualified judge; transfer; assignment by Judicial Council.
7071. County to which transferred; location of property; adjoining county.
7072. Retransfer to original county.

§ 7070. Lack of qualified judge; transfer; assignment by Judicial Council

The court or judge shall order a proceeding under this code concerning the administration of the decedent's estate transferred to another county if there is no judge of the court in which the proceeding is pending who is qualified to act. This section does not apply if a judge qualified to act is assigned by the chairman of the Judicial Council to sit in the county and hear the proceeding. *(Stats.1990, c. 79 (A.B.759), § 14, operative July 1, 1991.)*

Law Revision Commission Comments

1990 Enactment

Section 7070 continues Section 7070 of the repealed Probate Code with a revision to make clear that the section applies in estate administration proceedings throughout the code, whether pursuant to this division or any other division of the code.. Transfer of a proceeding under this article is in the same manner and with the same effect as transfer of actions and proceedings under the Code of Civil Procedure. See Section 1000 (general rules of practice govern);

Code Civ.Proc. § 399 (transmittal of papers; jurisdiction of receiving court).

Background on Section 7070 of Repealed Code

Section 7070 was added by 1988 Cal.Stat. ch. 1199 § 80.5. The section restated part of subdivision (b) of former Probate Code Section 303 (repealed by 1988 Cal.Stat. ch. 1199 § 40) without substantive change. For background on the provisions of this chapter, see the Comment to this chapter under the chapter heading. [20 Cal.L.Rev.Comm.Reports 1001 (1990)].

§ 7071. County to which transferred; location of property; adjoining county

Transfer of a proceeding under this article shall be to another county in which property of the decedent is located or, if there is no other county in which property of the decedent is located, to an adjoining county. *(Stats.1990, c. 79 (A.B.759), § 14, operative July 1, 1991.)*

Law Revision Commission Comments

1990 Enactment

Section 7071 continues Section 7071 of the repealed Probate Code without change.

Background on Section 7071 of Repealed Code

Section 7071 was a new provision added by 1988 Cal.Stat. ch. 1199 § 80.5. The provision for transfer to an adjoining county continued a provision of subdivision (b) of former Probate Code Section 303 (repealed by 1988 Cal.Stat. ch. 1199 § 40). For background on the provisions of this chapter, see the Comment to this chapter under the chapter heading. [20 Cal.L.Rev.Comm.Reports 1001 (1990)].

§ 7072. Retransfer to original county

Upon petition of the personal representative or other interested person before entry of the order for final distribution of the estate, a proceeding transferred under this article may be retransferred to the court in which the proceeding was originally commenced if the court determines that both of the following conditions are satisfied:

(a) Another person has become judge of the court where the proceeding was originally commenced who is not disqualified to act in the administration of the estate.

(b) The convenience of the parties interested would be promoted by the retransfer. *(Stats.1990, c. 79 (A.B.759), § 14, operative July 1, 1991.)*

Law Revision Commission Comments

1990 Enactment

Section 7072 continues Section 7072 of the repealed Probate Code with the substitution of "before entry of the order for final distribution of the estate" for "before the administration of the estate is closed.". For general provisions, see Sections 1000–1004 (rules of practice), 1020–1023 (petitions and other papers), 1040–1050 (hearings and orders). For general provisions relating to notice of hearing, see Sections 1200–1221. See also Sections 1250–1252 (request for special notice), 1260–1265 (proof of giving notice).

Background on Section 7072 of Repealed Code

Section 7072 was added by 1988 Cal.Stat. ch. 1199 § 80.5. The section restated part of former Probate Code Section 305 (repealed by 1988 Cal.Stat. ch. 1199 § 40) but made retransfer permissive rather than mandatory. For background on the provisions of this chapter, see the Comment to this chapter under the chapter heading. [20 Cal.L.Rev.Comm.Reports 1001 (1990)].

Cross References

Change of place of trial, grounds, see Code of Civil Procedure § 397.
Jurisdiction of transferee court, see Code of Civil Procedure § 399.
Transfer, court having proper jurisdiction, see Code of Civil Procedure § 398.

CHAPTER 3. RULES OF PROCEDURE

Law Revision Commission Comments

1990 Enactment

This chapter supersedes Chapter 3 of Part 1 (commencing with Section 7200) of Division 7 of the repealed Probate Code. The superseded chapter was enacted upon recommendation of the California Law Revision Commission. See Recommendation Relating to Rules of Procedure in Probate, 19 Cal.L.Revision Comm'n Reports 917 (1988). See also Communication from the California Law Revision Commission Concerning Assembly Bill 2841, 19 Cal.L.Revision Comm'n Reports 1201, 1230–31 (1988); Recommendation Relating to Notice in Probate Proceedings, 19 Cal.L.Revision Comm'n Reports 357, 383–90 (1988). [20 Cal.L.Rev.Comm.Reports 1001 (1990)].

ARTICLE 1. TRIAL BY JURY [REPEALED]

§ 7200. Repealed by Stats.1999, c. 175 (A.B.239), § 4

ARTICLE 2. NEW TRIALS

Section
7220. Cases where motion for new trial allowed.

§ 7220. Cases where motion for new trial allowed

In proceedings under this code concerning the administration of the decedent's estate, a motion for a new trial may be made only in the following cases:

(a) Contest of a will or revocation of probate of a will.

(b) Cases in which a right to jury trial is expressly granted, whether or not the case was tried by a jury. *(Stats.1990, c. 79 (A.B.759), § 14, operative July 1, 1991.)*

Law Revision Commission Comments

1990 Enactment

Section 7220 continues Section 7220 of the repealed Probate Code without substantive change. There is no right to a jury trial unless expressly provided by statute. See Section 7200 (trial by jury).

Background on Section 7220 of Repealed Code

Section 7220 was added by 1988 Cal.Stat. ch. 1199 § 80.5. The section restated former Probate Code Section 1281 (repealed by 1988 Cal.Stat. ch. 1199 § 64.5) without substantive change. Former Section 1281 continued former Probate Code Section 1231 (repealed by 1987 Cal.Stat. ch. 923 § 59) without change. For background on the provisions of this chapter, see the Comment to this chapter under the chapter heading. [20 Cal.L.Rev.Comm.Reports 1001 (1990)].

Contests of wills,
After probate, see Probate Code § 8270 et seq.
Before probate, see Probate Code §§ 8004 et seq., 8250 et seq.
New trial, generally, see Code of Civil Procedure § 655 et seq.

ARTICLE 3.   APPEALS [REPEALED]

§§ 7240 to 7242.   Repealed by Stats.1997, c. 724 (A.B.1172), § 18

ARTICLE 3.5.   JUDGMENTS AND ORDERS

Section
7250.   Release of heirs' or devisees' claims against personal representative and sureties; order; application to orders, etc., made before July 1, 1988.

§ 7250.   Release of heirs' or devisees' claims against personal representative and sureties; order; application to orders, etc., made before July 1, 1988

(a) When a judgment or order made pursuant to the provisions of this code concerning the administration of the decedent's estate becomes final, it releases the personal representative and the sureties from all claims of the heirs or devisees and of any persons affected thereby based upon any act or omission directly authorized, approved, or confirmed in the judgment or order.   For the purposes of this section, "order" includes an order settling an account of the personal representative, whether an interim or final account.

(b) Nothing in this section affects any order, judgment, or decree made, or any action taken, before July 1, 1988.   The validity of any action taken before July 1, 1988, is determined by the applicable law in effect before July 1, 1988, and not by this section.

(c) This section shall not apply where the judgment or order is obtained by fraud or conspiracy or by misrepresentation contained in the petition or account or in the judgment as to any material fact.   For purposes of this subdivision, misrepresentation includes, but shall not be limited to, the omission of a material fact.   *(Stats.1990, c. 79 (A.B.759), § 14, operative July 1, 1991.   Amended by Stats.1993, c. 794 (A.B.516), § 2.)*

Law Revision Commission Comments

1990 Enactment

Subdivision (a) of Section 7250 continues Section 9612 of the repealed Probate Code without substantive change.   Subdivision (b) is new but continues the substance of subdivision (b) and paragraph (3) of subdivision (c) of Section 9645 of the repealed Probate Code insofar as those provisions applied to Section 9612 of the repealed Probate Code.

Section 7250 is comparable to subdivision (a) of Section 2103 (Guardianship–Conservatorship Law).   The section is subject to case law exceptions relating to extrinsic fraud.   See, e.g., Bank of America v. Superior Court, 181 Cal.App.3d 705, 226 Cal.Rptr. 685 (1986); Lazzarone v. Bank of America, 181 Cal.App.3d 581, 226 Cal.Rptr. 855 (1986); 8 B. Witkin, California Procedure Attack on Judgment in Trial Court § 198, at 596–97, §§ 204–07, at 602–07 (3d ed. 1985).   See also Section 8007 (effect of order admitting will to probate or appointing a personal representative), 8272 (effect of revocation of probate of will on acts of personal representative before the

revocation), 8406 (effect of reversal of order appointing personal representative on acts of personal representative before reversal), 8525 (acts before a vacancy occurs), 9805 (liability on note and security instrument), 9806 (effectiveness of encumbrance), 9838 (effectiveness of order authorizing a compromise or settlement that requires the transfer of real property of estate), 9868 (order for execution of conveyance or transfer of property claimed to belong to decedent or other person), 9923 (order for exchange of property), 9948 (order for lease), 9966 (order authorizing granting of option to purchase property), 9983 (order that property be transferred pursuant to option to purchase given in will), 10264 (order for sale of personal property), 10316 (order for sale of real property), 11705 (order determining persons entitled to distribution of decedent's estate and their shares), 12250 (order discharging personal representative).

Background on Section 7250 of the new Probate Code

Section 7250 continues the substance of Section 9612 of the repealed Probate Code.   Section 9612 was a new provision added by 1987 Cal.Stat. ch. 923 § 93.   The section generalized provisions such as the last sentence of former Probate Code Section 718.5 (repealed by 1987 Cal.Stat. ch. 923 § 37).   For background, see Recommendation Relating to Supervised Administration of Decedent's Estate, 19 Cal.L. Revision Comm'n Reports 5 (1988).   The section was amended by 1989 Cal.Stat. ch. 21 § 23 to make clear that the section applies in estate administration proceedings throughout the code, whether pursuant to this division or any other division of the code. [20 Cal.L.Rev.Comm.Reports 1001 (1990)].

ARTICLE 4.   ORDERS AND TRANSACTIONS AFFECTING PROPERTY

Section
7260.   "Transaction" defined.
7261.   Court-ordered real property transaction; statement in instrument.
7262.   Effect of court-ordered transaction.
7263.   Recording order affecting title to real property.

§ 7260.   "Transaction" defined

As used in this article, "transaction" means a transaction affecting title to property in the estate, including, but not limited to, the following:

(a) In the case of real property, a conveyance (including a sale, option, or order confirming a sale or option), a lease, the creation of a mortgage, deed of trust, or other lien or encumbrance, the setting apart of a probate homestead, or the distribution of property.

(b) In the case of personal property, a transfer of the property or the creation of a security interest or other lien on the property.   *(Stats.1990, c. 79 (A.B.759), § 14, operative July 1, 1991.)*

Law Revision Commission Comments

1990 Enactment

Section 7260 continues Section 7260 of the repealed Probate Code without change.   This section is comparable to Section 2111(a) (Guardianship–Conservatorship Law).

Background on Section 7260 of Repealed Code

Section 7260 was a new provision added by 1988 Cal.Stat. ch. 1199 § 80.5.   For background on the provisions of this chapter, see the Comment to this chapter under the chapter heading.   [20 Cal.L.Rev.Comm.Reports 1001 (1990)].

§ 7261. Court-ordered real property transaction; statement in instrument

If a transaction affecting real property in the estate is executed by the personal representative in accordance with the terms of a court order, the instrument shall include a statement that the transaction is made by authority of the order authorizing or directing the transaction and shall give the date of the order. *(Stats.1990, c. 79 (A.B.759), § 14, operative July 1, 1991.)*

Law Revision Commission Comments

1990 Enactment

Section 7261 continues Section 7261 of the repealed Probate Code without change. This section is comparable to Section 2111(c) (Guardianship–Conservatorship Law) and is consistent with several provisions in other parts of the code. See Sections 9805 (execution of encumbrance), 9838 (compromise or settlement), 9948 (execution of lease), 10314 (conveyance or assignment after confirmation). See also Section 7250 (effect of court authorization or approval).

Background on Section 7261 of Repealed Code

Section 7261 was a new provision added by 1988 Cal.Stat. ch. 1199 § 80.5. For background on the provisions of this chapter, see the Comment to this chapter under the chapter heading. [20 Cal.L.Rev.Comm.Reports 1001 (1990)].

§ 7262. Effect of court-ordered transaction

A transaction executed by the personal representative in accordance with an order authorizing or directing the transaction has the same effect as if the decedent were living at the time of the transaction and had carried it out in person while having legal capacity to do so. *(Stats.1990, c. 79 (A.B.759), § 14, operative July 1, 1991.)*

Law Revision Commission Comments

1990 Enactment

Section 7262 continues Section 7262 of the repealed Probate Code without change. This section is comparable to Section 2111(d) (Guardianship–Conservatorship Law) and is consistent with several provisions in other parts of the code. See also Sections 7250 (effect of court authorization or approval), 9805 (liability on note or security instrument), 9806 (effectiveness of encumbrance), 9838 (compromise or settlement), 9868 (effectiveness of order in proceedings involving property claimed by another), 9948 (effectiveness of lease), 10314 (conveyance or assignment after confirmation). See also Section 8007 (effect of order admitting will to probate or appointing a personal representative), 8272 (effect of revocation of probate of will on acts of personal representative before the revocation), 8406 (effect of reversal of order appointing personal representative on acts of personal representative before reversal), 9868 (effect of order for execution of conveyance or transfer of property claimed to belong to decedent or other person), 9923 (effect of order for exchange of property), 9948 (effect of order for lease), 9966 (effect of order authorizing granting of option to purchase property), 9983 (effect of order that property be transferred pursuant to option to purchase given in will), 10264 (effect of order for sale of personal property), 10314 (effect of conveyance or assignment made in connection with order for sale of real property), 10316 (effect of order for sale of real property), 11605 (effect of order for distribution), 11705 (order determining persons entitled to distribution of decedent's estate and their shares), 12408 (order for final distribution of estate of missing person), 13657 (order determining that property is property passing to surviving spouse or confirming the ownership of the surviving spouse of property belonging to the surviving spouse).

Whether or not after-acquired title is passed by an instrument executed by the personal representative depends on the terms of the instrument. See generally 4 B. Witkin, Summary of California Law Real Property § 136, at 351–52, § 212, at 417–18 (9th ed. 1987). But see Section 9838 (compromise or settlement).

Background on Section 7262 of Repealed Code

Section 7262 was a new provision added by 1988 Cal.Stat. ch. 1199 § 80.5. For background on the provisions of this chapter, see the Comment to this chapter under the chapter heading. [20 Cal.L.Rev.Comm.Reports 1001 (1990)].

§ 7263. Recording order affecting title to real property

If an order is made setting apart a probate homestead, confirming a sale or making a distribution of real property, or determining any other matter affecting title to real property in the estate, the personal representative shall record a certified copy of the order in the office of the county recorder in each county in which any portion of the real property is located. *(Stats.1990, c. 79 (A.B.759), § 14, operative July 1, 1991.)*

Law Revision Commission Comments

1990 Enactment

Section 7263 continues Section 7263 of the repealed Probate Code without substantive change. Recordation of an order for distribution of real property has the effect of a receipt by the distributee. See Section 11751. See also Sections 9838 (compromise or settlement), 11902 (recording order for distribution of property to state).

Background on Section 7263 of Repealed Code

Section 7263 was added by 1988 Cal.Stat. ch. 1199 § 80.5. The section restated all but the last clause of former Probate Code Section 1292 (repealed by 1988 Cal.Stat. ch. 1199 § 64.5) (recordation of order affecting real property) without substantive change. Former Section 1292 continued former Probate Code Section 1222 (repealed by 1987 Cal.Stat. ch. 923 § 59) without substantive change. For background on the provisions of this chapter, see the Comment to this chapter under the chapter heading. [20 Cal.L.Rev.Comm.Reports 1001 (1990)].

Cross References

Recordation of orders,
    Leasing of property, see Probate Code § 9945 et seq.
    Mortgages, authorization, see Probate Code § 9804.
    Sale, confirmation, see Probate Code § 10314.

ARTICLE 5. UNITED STATES AS INTERESTED PERSON

Section
7280. Rights of United States where federal allowance is made to estate.

§ 7280. Rights of United States where federal allowance is made to estate

Where compensation, pension, insurance, or other allowance is made or awarded by a department or bureau of the United States government to a decedent's estate, the department or bureau has the same right as an interested person to do any of the following:

(a) Request special notice.

(b) Commence and prosecute an action on the bond of a personal representative.

(c) Contest an account of a personal representative. *(Stats.1990, c. 79 (A.B.759), § 14, operative July 1, 1991.)*

Law Revision Commission Comments

1990 Enactment

Section 7280 restates Section 7280 of the repealed Probate Code without substantive change. See Section 58 ("personal representative" defined).

Background on Section 7280 of Repealed Code

Section 7280 was added by 1988 Cal.Stat. ch. 1199 § 80.5. The section restated former Probate Code Section 1288 (repealed by 1988 Cal.Stat. ch. 1199 § 64.5) without substantive change. Former Section 1288 restated former Probate Code Section 1203 (repealed by 1987 Cal.Stat. ch. 923 § 59) without substantive change. For background on the provisions of this chapter, see the Comment to this chapter under the chapter heading. [20 Cal.L.Rev.Comm.Reports 1001 (1990)].

CHAPTER 4. PUBLIC ADMINISTRATORS

Law Revision Commission Comments

1990 Enactment

This chapter supersedes Chapter 4 of Part 1 (commencing with Section 7600) of Division 7 of the repealed Probate Code. The superseded chapter was enacted upon recommendation of the California Law Revision Commission. See Recommendation Relating to Public Guardians and Administrators, 19 Cal.L.Revision Comm'n Reports 707 (1988). [20 Cal.L.Rev.Comm.Reports 1001 (1990)].

ARTICLE 1. TAKING TEMPORARY POSSESSION OR CONTROL OF PROPERTY

§ 7600. Property of decedent subject to loss, etc.; duty of public employee to inform public administrator

If a public officer or employee knows of property of a decedent that is subject to loss, injury, waste, or misappropriation and that ought to be in the possession or control of the public administrator, the officer or employee shall inform the public administrator. *(Stats.1990, c. 79 (A.B.759), § 14, operative July 1, 1991.)*

Law Revision Commission Comments

1990 Enactment

Section 7600 continues Section 7600 of the repealed Probate Code without change.

Background on Section 7600 of Repealed Code

Section 7600 was added by 1988 Cal.Stat. ch. 1199 § 80.5. The section restated former Probate Code Section 1146 (repealed by 1988 Cal.Stat. ch. 1199 § 57.5) without substantive change. For background on the provisions of this chapter, see the Comment to this chapter under the chapter heading. [20 Cal.L.Rev.Comm.Reports 1001 (1990)].

Cross References

Civil executive officers defined, see Government Code § 1001.
Property taxation, cancellations, escheated property not distributed, validity of taxes, probate, see Revenue and Taxation Code § 4986.6.

§ 7600.5. Death of person without known next of kin in health care facility; notice to public administrator; liability for failure to give notice

If a person dies in a hospital, convalescent hospital, or board and care facility without known next of kin, the person in charge of the hospital or facility shall give immediate notice of that fact to the public administrator of the county in which the hospital or facility is located. If the notice required by this section is not given, the hospital or facility is liable for (1) any cost of interment incurred by the estate or the county as a result of the failure and (2) any loss to the estate or beneficiaries caused by loss, injury, waste, or misappropriation of property of the decedent as a result of the failure. *(Stats.1990, c. 79 (A.B.759), § 14, operative July 1, 1991.)*

Law Revision Commission Comments

1990 Enactment

Section 7600.5 continues Section 7600.5 of the repealed Probate Code without change.

Background on Section 7600.5 of Repealed Code

Section 7600.5 was added by 1988 Cal.Stat. ch. 1199 § 80.5. The section superseded former Probate Code Section 1145 (repealed by 1988 Cal.Stat. ch. 1199 § 57.5). For background on the provisions of this chapter, see the Comment to this chapter under the chapter heading. [20 Cal.L.Rev.Comm.Reports 1001 (1990)].

§ 7600.6. Decedent's remains; inability to contact next-of-kin; notification by funeral director

A funeral director in control of the decedent's remains pursuant to subdivision (b) of Section 7100 of the Health and Safety Code shall notify the public administrator if none of the persons described in paragraphs (1) to (4), inclusive, of subdivision (a) of Section 7100 of the Health and Safety Code exist, can be found after reasonable inquiry, or can be contacted by reasonable means. *(Added by Stats.1997, c. 93 (S.B.696), § 1. Amended by Stats.1998, c. 253 (S.B.1360), § 3.)*

§ 7601. Property over which county public administrator shall take prompt possession or control

(a) If no personal representative has been appointed, the public administrator of a county shall take prompt possession or control of property of a decedent in the county that is deemed by the public administrator to be subject to loss, injury, waste, or misappropriation, or that the court orders into the possession or control of the public administrator after notice to the public administrator as provided in Section 1220.

(b) If property described in subdivision (a) is beyond the ability of the public administrator to take possession or control, the public administrator is not liable for failing to take possession or control of the property. *(Stats.1990, c. 79 (A.B.759), § 14, operative July 1, 1991. Amended by Stats. 2004, c. 888 (A.B.2687), § 2.)*

Law Revision Commission Comments

1990 Enactment

Section 7601 continues Section 7601 of the repealed Probate Code without change. The public administrator may also be appointed special administrator for the property. See Sections 8540–8541 (special administrators).

Background on Section 7601 of Repealed Code

Section 7601 was added by 1988 Cal.Stat. ch. 1199 § 80.5. The section restated the first sentence of subdivision (a) of former Probate Code Section 1140 (repealed by 1988 Cal.Stat. ch. 1199 § 57.5), with the addition of (1) misappropriation as a ground for taking possession or control, (2) express provisions relating to notice and hearing, and (3) an express immunity in the case of property that is beyond the control of the public administrator. For background on the provisions of this chapter, see the Comment to this chapter under the chapter heading. [20 Cal.L.Rev.Comm.Reports 1001 (1990)].

Cross References

Appointment to take charge of estate, see Probate Code § 8540.
Costs and fees of public administrator in case of appointment of another as executor or administrator, see Probate Code § 7604.
Direction to public administrator to commence administration if proceedings have not been begun six months from death, see Code of Civil Procedure § 1420.
Escheated property discovered prior to tax sale, duty to probate, see Revenue and Taxation Code § 4986.6.
Powers and duties of joint personal representatives, see Probate Code § 9630.
Property taxation, cancellations, escheated property not distributed, validity of taxes, probate, see Revenue and Taxation Code § 4986.6.
Public administrator as ex officio public guardian, see Government Code § 27432.
Special administrators, generally, see Probate Code § 8540 et seq.

§ 7602. Searches required of public administrator; outcomes and required responses

(a) A public administrator who is authorized to take possession or control of property of a decedent under this article shall make a prompt search for other property, a will, and instructions for disposition of the decedent's remains.

(b) If a will is found, the public administrator or custodian of the will shall deliver the will as provided in Section 8200.

(c) If instructions for disposition of the decedent's remains are found, the public administrator shall promptly deliver the instructions to the person upon whom the right to control disposition of the decedent's remains devolves as provided in Section 7100 of the Health and Safety Code.

(d) If other property is located, the public administrator shall take possession or control of any property that, in the sole discretion of the public administrator, is deemed to be subject to loss, injury, waste, or misappropriation and that is located anywhere in this state or that is subject to the laws of this state. The public administrator does not have any liability for loss, injury, waste, or misappropriation of property of which he or she is unable to take possession or control. *(Stats.1990, c. 79 (A.B.759), § 14, operative July 1, 1991. Amended by Stats.2004, c. 888 (A.B.2687), § 3.)*

Law Revision Commission Comments

1990 Enactment

Section 7602 continues Section 7602 of the repealed Probate Code without change.

Background on Section 7602 of Repealed Code

Section 7602 was added by 1988 Cal.Stat. ch. 1199 § 80.5. The section restated the first portion of subdivision (a) and subdivision (b) of former Probate Code Section 1141 (repealed by 1988 Cal.Stat. ch. 1199 § 57.5) but eliminated the requirement that there be reasonable grounds to believe that the public administrator may be appointed personal representative. For background on the provisions of this chapter, see the Comment to this chapter under the chapter heading. [20 Cal.L.Rev.Comm.Reports 1001 (1990)].

Cross References

Property taxation, cancellations, escheated property not distributed, validity of taxes, probate, see Revenue and Taxation Code § 4986.6.

§ 7603. Certification of public administrator's authority; recording; effect on financial institutions or others; safe deposit box; surrender of property

(a) A public administrator who is authorized to take possession or control of property of a decedent pursuant to this article may issue a written certification of that fact. The written certification is effective for 30 days after the date of issuance.

(b) The public administrator may record a copy of the written certification in any county in which is located real property of which the public administrator is authorized to take possession or control under this article.

(c) A financial institution, government or private agency, retirement fund administrator, insurance company, licensed securities dealer, or other person shall, without the necessity of inquiring into the truth of the written certification, without requiring a death certificate, without charge, and without court order or letters being issued:

(1) Provide the public administrator complete information concerning property held in the sole name of the decedent, including the names and addresses of any beneficiaries.

(2) Grant the public administrator access to a safe-deposit box rented in the sole name of the decedent for the purpose of inspection and removal of any will or instructions for disposition of the decedent's remains. Costs and expenses incurred in drilling or forcing a safe-deposit box shall be borne by the estate of the decedent.

(3) Surrender to the public administrator any property of the decedent that, in the sole discretion of the public administrator, is deemed to be subject to loss, injury, waste, or misappropriation.

(d) Receipt of the written certification provided by this section:

(1) Constitutes sufficient acquittance for providing information or granting access to the safe-deposit box, for removal of the decedent's will and instructions for disposition of the decedent's remains, and for surrendering property of the decedent.

(2) Fully discharges the financial institution, government or private agency, retirement fund administrator, insurance company, licensed securities dealer, or other person from any liability for any act or omission of the public administrator with respect to the property or the safe-deposit box. *(Stats. 1990, c. 79 (A.B.759), § 14, operative July 1, 1991. Amended by Stats.2004, c. 888 (A.B.2687), § 4.)*

Law Revision Commission Comments
1990 Enactment

Section 7603 restates Section 7603 of the repealed Probate Code without substantive change. The reference to the county recorder has been omitted from subdivision (d)(2) as unnecessary since the county recorder's only involvement is to record the written certification of the public administrator in the county real property records. Other nonsubstantive changes have been made. This section is comparable to Section 2901 (providing information and access to public guardian).

Background on Section 7603 of Repealed Code

Section 7603 was added by 1988 Cal.Stat. ch. 1199 § 80.5. The section restated the last portion of subdivision (a) and subdivision (c) of former Probate Code Section 1141 (repealed by 1988 Cal.Stat. ch. 1199 § 57.5) with the elimination of the requirement that there be reasonable grounds to believe the public administrator may be appointed personal representative and with the addition of subdivisions (b) and (c)(3) and the imposition of a five-day effective period for the written certification. For background on the provisions of this chapter, see the Comment to this chapter under the chapter heading. [20 Cal.L.Rev.Comm.Reports 1001 (1990)].

Cross References

Property taxation, cancellations, escheated property not distributed, validity of taxes, probate, see Revenue and Taxation Code § 4986.6.

§ 7604. Possession or control of decedent's property by public administrator; another person appointed personal representative or subsequently takes control or possession; costs and compensation

If the public administrator takes possession or control of property of a decedent under this article, but another person is subsequently appointed personal representative or subsequently takes control or possession, the public administrator is entitled to reasonable costs incurred for the preservation of the estate, together with reasonable compensation for ser-

vices. The costs and compensation are a proper expense of administration. *(Stats.1990, c. 79 (A.B.759), § 14, operative July 1, 1991. Amended by Stats.1994, c. 806 (A.B.3686), § 24.)*

Law Revision Commission Comments
1990 Enactment

Section 7604 continues Section 7604 of the repealed Probate Code without substantive change. The public administrator's compensation and expenses under this section are an expense of administration and thus subject to court order for payment. See Section 11422 (payment of debts on court order). For a comparable provision relating to the public guardian, see Section 2902.

Background on Section 7604 of Repealed Code

Section 7604 was added by 1988 Cal.Stat. ch. 1199 § 80.5. The section restated former Probate Code Section 1144.5 (repealed by 1988 Cal.Stat. ch. 1199 § 57.5). For background on the provisions of this chapter, see the Comment to this chapter under the chapter heading. [20 Cal.L.Rev.Comm.Reports 1001 (1990)].

Cross References

Compensation and allowances, see Probate Code § 7622.
Fees of public administrator,
 Charge and collection, see Government Code § 27441.
 Salary, see Government Code § 27442.

§ 7605. Continuing education requirements; compliance by public administrator

On or before January 1, 2010, the public administrator shall comply with the continuing education requirements that are established by the California State Association of Public Administrators, Public Guardians, and Public Conservators. *(Added by Stats.2008, c. 237 (A.B.2343), § 3.)*

ARTICLE 2. APPOINTMENT AS PERSONAL REPRESENTATIVE

§ 7620. Petition for appointment; court-ordered appointment

The public administrator of the county in which the estate of a decedent may be administered shall promptly:

(a) Petition for appointment as personal representative of the estate if no person having higher priority has petitioned for appointment and the total value of the property in the decedent's estate exceeds one hundred fifty thousand dollars ($150,000).

(b) Petition for appointment as personal representative of any other estate the public administrator determines is proper.

(c) Accept appointment as personal representative of an estate when so ordered by the court, whether or not on petition of the public administrator, after notice to the public administrator as provided in Section 7621.

(d) Proceed with summary disposition of the estate as authorized by Article 4 (commencing with Section 7660), if the total value of the property in the decedent's estate does not exceed the amount prescribed in Section 13100 and a person having higher priority has not assumed responsibility for administration of the estate. *(Stats.1990, c. 79 (A.B.759), § 14, operative July 1, 1991. Amended by Stats.2004, c. 888 (A.B.2687), § 5; Stats.2011, c. 117 (A.B.1305), § 1.)*

Law Revision Commission Comments
1990 Enactment

Section 7620 continues Section 7620 of the repealed Probate Code without change. For priority for appointment as personal representative, see Section 8461. See also Sections 7050–7051 (jurisdiction and venue of probate proceedings). For general provisions, see Sections 1000–1004 (rules of practice), 1020–1023 (petitions and other papers), 1040–1050 (hearings and orders). As to the surviving spouse's waiver of rights at death, see Sections 140–147.

Background on Section 7620 of Repealed Code

Section 7620 was added by 1988 Cal.Stat. ch. 1199 § 80.5. Subdivisions (a) and (b) of Section 7620 restated the second sentence of subdivision (a) of former Probate Code Section 1140 (repealed by 1988 Cal.Stat. ch. 1199 § 57.5) without substantive change. Subdivision (c) was new. For background on the provisions of this chapter, see the Comment to this chapter under the chapter heading. [20 Cal.L.Rev.Comm.Reports 1001 (1990)].

Cross References

Property taxation, cancellations, escheated property not distributed, validity of taxes, probate, see Revenue and Taxation Code § 4986.6.

§ 7621. Procedures for appointment; motion by court; oath and bond; bond fees

(a) Except as otherwise provided in this section, appointment of the public administrator as personal representative shall be made, and letters issued, in the same manner and pursuant to the same procedure as for appointment of and issuance of letters to personal representatives generally.

(b) Appointment of the public administrator may be made on the court's own motion, after notice to the public administrator as provided in Section 1220.

(c) Letters may be issued to "the public administrator" of the county without naming the public administrator.

(d) The public administrator's oath and official bond are in lieu of the personal representative's oath and bond. Every estate administered under this chapter shall be charged an annual bond fee in the amount of twenty-five dollars ($25) plus one-fourth of one percent of the amount of an estate greater than ten thousand dollars ($10,000). The amount charged is an expense of administration and that amount shall be deposited in the county treasury. If a successor personal representative is appointed, the amount of the bond fee shall be prorated over the period of months during which the public administrator acted as personal representative. Upon final distribution by the public administrator, any amount of bond charges in excess of one year shall be a

prorated charge to the estate. *(Stats.1990, c. 79 (A.B.759), § 14, operative July 1, 1991. Amended by Stats.1995, c. 160 (A.B.128), § 1.)*

Law Revision Commission Comments
1990 Enactment

Section 7621 continues Section 7621 of the repealed Probate Code without substantive change. Letters issued to "the public administrator" under subdivision (c) are sufficient to enable a successor public administrator to act without issuance of new letters. See Gov't Code § 27444 (expiration of term of office). Subdivision (d) is comparable to Section 2942(c) (public guardian). The amount allowed under subdivision (d) is half the amount allowed for the bond of a personal representative generally under former Section 541.5 (repealed by 1988 Cal.Stat. ch. 1199, § 48). Removal of the public administrator is subject to the same procedures as removal of administrators generally, including removal at the request of a person having a higher priority for appointment. See Section 8503.

Background on Section 7621 of Repealed Code

Section 7621 was added by 1988 Cal.Stat. ch. 1199 § 80.5. The section restated subdivision (b) of former Probate Code Section 1140 (repealed by 1988 Cal.Stat. ch. 1199 § 57.5), with the addition in Section 7621 of subdivisions (b) and (c) and the provision of subdivision (d) allowing the county to recoup a bond fee. For background on the provisions of this chapter, see the Comment to this chapter under the chapter heading. [20 Cal.L.Rev.Comm.Reports 1001 (1990)].

§ 7622. Manner of administration by public administrator; compensation and allowances

Except as otherwise provided in this chapter:

(a) The public administrator shall administer the estate in the same manner as a personal representative generally, and the provisions of this code concerning the administration of the decedent's estate apply to administration by the public administrator.

(b) The public administrator is entitled to receive the same compensation as is granted by this division to a personal representative generally. The attorney for the public administrator is entitled to receive the same compensation as is granted by this division to an attorney for a personal representative generally. However, the compensation of the public administrator and the public administrator's attorney may not be less than the compensation in effect at the time of appointment of the public administrator or the minimum amount provided in subdivision (b) of Section 7666, whichever is greater. *(Stats.1990, c. 79 (A.B.759), § 14, operative July 1, 1991. Amended by Stats.1991, c. 82 (S.B.896), § 22, eff. June 30, 1991, operative July 1, 1991; Stats.2004, c. 888 (A.B.2687), § 6.)*

Law Revision Commission Comments
1991 Amendment [Revised Comment]

Section 7622 is amended to add the second sentence to subdivision (b). This restores the substance of a portion of the first sentence of subdivision (b) of former Section 7622 of the repealed Probate Code.

The reference in subdivision (b) to the "same compensation" as is granted by this division to personal representatives generally, and attorneys for personal representatives generally, includes allowances of compensation. See Part 7 (commencing with Section 10800) (compensation of personal representative and estate attorney), particularly Chapter 2 (commencing with Section 10830) (allowance of compensation by court). [21 Cal.L.Rev.Comm.Reports 67 (1991)].

Background on Section 7622 of Repealed Code

Section 7622 was added by 1988 Cal.Stat. ch. 1199 § 80.5. The section restated former Probate Code Section 1142 (repealed by 1988 Cal.Stat. ch. 1199 § 57.5) without substantive change. The section was amended by 1989 Cal.Stat. ch. 21 § 16 to make clear that the section applies in estate administration proceedings throughout the code, whether pursuant to this division or any other division of the code, and to incorporate provisions added by Chapter 280 of the Statutes of 1988. See Communication from the California Law Revision Commission Concerning Assembly Bill 156, 20 Cal.L.Revision Comm'n Reports 227, 230 (1990). For background on the provisions of this chapter, see the Comment to this chapter under the chapter heading. [20 Cal.L.Rev.Comm.Reports 1001 (1990)].

Cross References

Attorneys fees, see Probate Code § 10810 et seq.
Compensation of special administrators and attorneys, see Probate Code § 8547.
Compensations for personal representatives, see Probate Code § 10800 et seq.
Distribution, see Probate Code § 11600 et seq.
Powers and duties of joint personal representatives, generally, see Probate Code § 9630 et seq.
Special administrators, generally, see Probate Code § 8540 et seq.

§ 7623. Additional compensation; person having priority for appointment failing to petition; appointment after resignation or removal of personal representative

(a) As used in this section, "additional compensation" means the difference between the reasonable compensation of the public administrator in administering the estate and the compensation awarded the public administrator under Chapter 1 (commencing with Section 10800) of Part 7.

(b) The public administrator may be awarded additional compensation if any of the following conditions are satisfied:

(1) A person having priority for appointment as personal representative has been given notice under Section 8110 of the public administrator's petition for appointment, and the person has not petitioned for appointment in preference to the public administrator.

(2) The public administrator has been appointed after the resignation or removal of a personal representative. *(Stats. 1990, c. 79 (A.B.759), § 14, operative July 1, 1991.)*

Law Revision Commission Comments
1990 Enactment

Section 7623 continues Section 7623 of the repealed Probate Code without substantive change.

Background on Section 7623 of Repealed Code

Section 7623 was added by 1988 Cal.Stat. ch. 1199 § 80.5. The section restated former Probate Code Section 1142.3 (repealed by 1988 Cal.Stat. ch. 1199 § 57.5) without substantive change. For background on the provisions of this chapter, see the Comment to this chapter under the chapter heading. [20 Cal.L.Rev.Comm.Reports 1001 (1990)].

Cross References

Costs and fees of public administrator in case of appointment of another as executor or administrator, allowance, see Probate Code § 7604.

Order of priority, persons entitled to appointment, see Probate Code § 8461.
Special administrators,
Generally, see Probate Code § 8540 et seq.
Compensation, see Probate Code § 8547.

§ 7624. Money remaining after final distribution of an estate; payment to county treasurer; failure to make payment

(a) If after final distribution of an estate any money remains in the possession of the public administrator that should be paid over to the county treasurer pursuant to Chapter 5 (commencing with Section 11850) of Part 10, the court shall order payment to be made within 60 days.

(b) Upon failure of the public administrator to comply with an order made pursuant to subdivision (a), the district attorney of the county shall promptly institute proceedings against the public administrator and the sureties on the official bond for the amount ordered to be paid, plus costs. *(Stats.1990, c. 79 (A.B.759), § 14, operative July 1, 1991.)*

Law Revision Commission Comments
1990 Enactment

Section 7624 continues Section 7624 of the repealed Probate Code without change.

Background on Section 7624 of Repealed Code

Section 7624 was added by 1988 Cal.Stat. ch. 1199 § 80.5. The section restated former Probate Code Section 1154 (repealed by 1988 Cal.Stat. ch. 1199 § 57.5), referring to the general provisions for deposit of funds in the county treasury instead of to "unclaimed" property and allowing 60 instead of 10 days for payment to be made. For background on the provisions of this chapter, see the Comment to this chapter under the chapter heading. [20 Cal.L.Rev.Comm.Reports 1001 (1990)].

Cross References

Official bonds,
Generally, see Government Code § 1450 et seq.
Prescription of amount, see Government Code § 24150.

ARTICLE 3. DEPOSIT OF MONEY OF ESTATE

Section
7640. Deposit with financial institution or county treasurer; discharge of responsibility.
7641. Withdrawals.
7642. Interest or dividends.
7643. County treasurer's duties; safekeeping; payment; delivery to state if no beneficiaries or claimants.
7644. Abandoned deposit in financial institution; presumption; payment to state.

Cross References

Application of old and new law, see Probate Code § 3.

§ 7640. Deposit with financial institution or county treasurer; discharge of responsibility

(a) The public administrator shall, upon receipt, deposit all money of the estate in an insured account in a financial institution or with the county treasurer of the county in which the proceedings are pending.

(b) Upon deposit under this section the public administrator is discharged from further responsibility for the money deposited until the public administrator withdraws the money. *(Stats.1990, c. 79 (A.B.759), § 14, operative July 1, 1991.)*

Law Revision Commission Comments

1990 Enactment

Section 7640 continues Section 7640 of the repealed Probate Code without change.

Background on Section 7640 of Repealed Code

Section 7640 was added by 1988 Cal.Stat. ch. 1199 § 80.5. The section restated the first sentence of former Probate Code Section 1147 (repealed by 1988 Cal.Stat. ch. 1199 § 57.5) without substantive change. For background on the provisions of this chapter, see the Comment to this chapter under the chapter heading. [20 Cal.L.Rev.Comm.Reports 1001 (1990)].

Cross References

Financial institution, defined, see Probate Code § 40.

§ 7641. Withdrawals

Money deposited in a financial institution or with the county treasurer under this article may be withdrawn upon the order of the public administrator when required for the purposes of administration. *(Stats.1990, c. 79 (A.B.759), § 14, operative July 1, 1991.)*

Law Revision Commission Comments

1990 Enactment

Section 7641 continues Section 7641 of the repealed Probate Code without change.

Background on Section 7641 of Repealed Code

Section 7641 was added by 1988 Cal.Stat. ch. 1199 § 80.5. The section restated the second sentence of former Probate Code Section 1147 (repealed by 1988 Cal.Stat. ch. 1199 § 57.5) without substantive change. For background on the provisions of this chapter, see the Comment to this chapter under the chapter heading. [20 Cal.L.Rev.Comm.Reports 1001 (1990)].

§ 7642. Interest or dividends

(a) The public administrator shall credit each estate with the highest rate of interest or dividends that the estate would have received if the funds available for deposit had been individually and separately deposited.

(b) Interest or dividends credited to the account of the public administrator in excess of the amount credited to the estates pursuant to subdivision (a) shall be deposited in the county general fund. *(Stats.1990, c. 79 (A.B.759), § 14, operative July 1, 1991.)*

Law Revision Commission Comments

1990 Enactment

Section 7642 continues Section 7642 of the repealed Probate Code without change.

Background on Section 7642 of Repealed Code

Section 7642 was added by 1988 Cal.Stat. ch. 1199 § 80.5. The section restated the second paragraph of former Probate Code Section 1147 (repealed by 1988 Cal.Stat. ch. 1199 § 57.5) without substantive change. For background on the provisions of this chapter, see the Comment to this chapter under the chapter heading. [20 Cal.L.Rev.Comm.Reports 1001 (1990)].

§ 7643. County treasurer's duties; safekeeping; payment; delivery to state if no beneficiaries or claimants

(a) The county treasurer shall receive and safely keep all money deposited with the county treasurer under this chapter and pay the money out on the order of the public administrator when required for the purposes of administration. The county treasurer and sureties on the official bond of the county treasurer are responsible for the safekeeping and payment of the money.

(b) The county treasurer shall deliver to the State Treasurer or the Controller all money in the possession of the county treasurer belonging to the estate, if there are no beneficiaries or other persons entitled to the money, or the beneficiaries or other persons entitled to the money do not appear and claim it. Delivery shall be made under the provisions of Article 1 (commencing with Section 1440) of Chapter 6 of Title 10 of Part 3 of the Code of Civil Procedure. *(Stats.1990, c. 79 (A.B.759), § 14, operative July 1, 1991.)*

Law Revision Commission Comments

1990 Enactment

Section 7643 continues Section 7643 of the repealed Probate Code without change.

Background on Section 7643 of Repealed Code

Section 7643 was added by 1988 Cal.Stat. ch. 1199 § 80.5. The section restated former Probate Code Section 1148 (repealed by 1988 Cal.Stat. ch. 1199 § 57.5) without substantive change. For background on the provisions of this chapter, see the Comment to this chapter under the chapter heading. [20 Cal.L.Rev.Comm.Reports 1001 (1990)].

Cross References

Abandoned money, presumption of payment or delivery, see Code of Civil Procedure § 1449.

Attorney General application for order directing deposit of property which may become payable to state pursuant to this section, see Code of Civil Procedure § 1421.

Bank, defined, see Financial Code §§ 102, 109.

Banked money, see Probate Code § 9700.

County treasurer, duties generally, see Government Code § 27000 et seq.

Deposit in county treasury where creditor not found, see Probate Code § 11428.

Deposits by public administrator, see Financial Code § 1380.

Deposits in county treasury, delivery of copy of order of distribution by personal representative, see Probate Code § 11853.

Escheat,

  Generally, see Probate Code § 6800 et seq.

  Money under $50 on deposit with county treasurer received from public administrator, see Code of Civil Procedure § 1444.5.

Escheat proceedings in decedents' estates, see Code of Civil Procedure § 1420 et seq.

Estates of deceased persons, payment to state, see Code of Civil Procedure § 1443.

Official bonds, generally, see Government Code § 1450 et seq.

Payment to state under this section, see Code of Civil Procedure § 1443.

Prescribing amount of official bond of treasurer, see Government Code § 24150.

Unclaimed property, see Code of Civil Procedure §§ 1300, 1500 et seq.; Financial Code §§ 874, 3121, 3150, 3162; Government Code § 13470; Penal Code § 5061 et seq.; Probate Code §§ 6800 et seq., 11854; Welfare and Institutions Code §§ 1015 et seq., 4126 et seq.

Unknown whereabouts of distributee, minors, deposits with county treasurer, see Probate Code § 11850.

§ 7644. Abandoned deposit in financial institution; presumption; payment to state

(a) If a deposit in a financial institution is made under this article, money remaining unclaimed at the expiration of five years after the date of the deposit, together with the increase and proceeds of the deposit, shall be presumed abandoned in any of the following circumstances:

(1) The deposit belongs to the estate of a known decedent for which a personal representative has never been appointed.

(2) The deposit belongs to the estate of a known decedent for which a personal representative has been appointed but no order of distribution has been made due to the absence of interested persons or the failure of interested persons diligently to protect their interests by taking reasonable steps for the purpose of securing a distribution of the estate.

(b) The Controller may, at any time after the expiration of the five-year period, file a petition with the court setting forth the fact that the money has remained on deposit in a financial institution under the circumstances described in subdivision (a) for the five-year period, and requesting an order declaring that the money is presumptively abandoned and directing the holder of the money to pay the money to the State Treasurer.

(c) Upon presentation of a certified copy of a court order made under subdivision (b), the financial institution shall forthwith transmit the money to the State Treasurer for deposit in the State Treasury. The deposit shall be made as provided in Section 1310 of the Code of Civil Procedure. All money deposited in the State Treasury under the provisions of this section shall be deemed to be deposited in the State Treasury under the provisions of Article 1 (commencing with Section 1440) of Chapter 6 of Title 10 of Part 3 of the Code of Civil Procedure. The deposit shall be transmitted, received, accounted for, and disposed of as provided by Title 10 (commencing with Section 1300) of Part 3 of the Code of Civil Procedure. *(Stats.1990, c. 79 (A.B.759), § 14, operative July 1, 1991.)*

Law Revision Commission Comments
1990 Enactment

Section 7644 continues Section 7644 of the repealed Probate Code without change. For general provisions, see Sections 1000–1004 (rules of practice), 1020–1023 (petitions and other papers), 1040–1050 (hearings and orders). For general provisions relating to notice of hearing, see Sections 1200–1221. See also Sections 1250–1252 (request for special notice), 1260–1265 (proof of giving notice).

Background on Section 7644 of Repealed Code

Section 7644 was added by 1988 Cal.Stat. ch. 1199 § 80.5. The section restated former Probate Code Section 1147.5 (repealed by 1988 Cal.Stat. ch. 1199 § 57.5) without substantive change. For background on the provisions of this chapter, see the Comment to this chapter under the chapter heading. [20 Cal.L.Rev.Comm.Reports 1001 (1990)].

Cross References

Presumptively abandoned property paid or delivered to Treasurer or Controller under this section, see Code of Civil Procedure § 1449.

Savings association defined, see Financial Code § 5102.

ARTICLE 4. SUMMARY DISPOSITION OF SMALL ESTATES

Cross References

Application of old and new law, see Probate Code § 3.
Petition for appointment, and court-ordered appointment, of personal representative, see Probate Code § 7620.

§ 7660. Estates subject to summary disposition; certification of authority for summary administration; existence of will; contents of petition; summary disposition of estate

(a) If a public administrator takes possession or control of an estate pursuant to this chapter, the public administrator may, acting as personal representative of the estate, summarily dispose of the estate in the manner provided in this article in either of the following circumstances:

(1) The total value of the property in the decedent's estate does not exceed the amount prescribed in Section 13100. The authority provided by this paragraph may be exercised only upon order of the court. The order may be made upon ex parte application. The fee to be allowed to the clerk for the filing of the application is two hundred five dollars ($205). The authority for this summary administration of the estate shall be evidenced by a court order for summary disposition.

(2) The total value of the property in the decedent's estate does not exceed fifty thousand dollars ($50,000). The authority provided by this paragraph may be exercised without court authorization.

(A) A public administrator who is authorized to summarily dispose of property of a decedent pursuant to this paragraph may issue a written certification of Authority for Summary Administration. The written certification is effective for 30 days after the date of issuance.

(B) A financial institution, government or private agency, retirement fund administrator, insurance company, licensed securities dealer, or other person shall, without the necessity of inquiring into the truth of the written certification of Authority for Summary Administration and without court order or letters being issued, do all of the following:

(i) Provide the public administrator complete information concerning any property held in the name of the decedent, including the names and addresses of any beneficiaries or joint owners.

(ii) Grant the public administrator access to a safe-deposit box or storage facility rented in the name of the decedent for the purpose of inspection and removal of property of the decedent. Costs and expenses incurred in accessing a safe-deposit box or storage facility shall be borne by the estate of the decedent.

(iii) Surrender to the public administrator any property of the decedent that is held or controlled by the financial institution, agency, retirement fund administrator, insurance company, licensed securities dealer, or other person.

(C) Receipt by a financial institution, government or private agency, retirement fund administrator, insurance company, licensed securities dealer, or other person of the written certification provided by this article shall do both of the following:

(i) Constitute sufficient acquittance for providing information or granting access to a safe-deposit box or a storage facility and for surrendering any property of the decedent.

(ii) Fully discharge the financial institution, government or private agency, retirement fund administrator, insurance company, licensed securities dealer, or other person from liability for any act or omission of the public administrator with respect to the property, a safe-deposit box, or a storage facility.

(b) Summary disposition may be made notwithstanding the existence of the decedent's will, if the will does not name an executor or if the named executor refuses to act.

(c) Nothing in this article precludes the public administrator from filing a petition with the court under any other provision of this code concerning the administration of the decedent's estate.

(d) Petitions filed pursuant to this article shall contain the information required by Section 8002.

(e) If a public administrator takes possession or control of an estate pursuant to this chapter, this article conveys the authority of a personal representative as described in Section 9650 to the public administrator to summarily dispose of the estates pursuant to the procedures described in paragraphs (1) and (2) of subdivision (a).

(f) The fee charged under paragraph (1) of subdivision (a) shall be distributed as provided in Section 68085.4 of the Government Code. When an application is filed under that paragraph, no other fees shall be charged in addition to the uniform filing fee provided for in Section 68085.4 of the Government Code. *(Stats.1990, c. 79 (A.B.759), § 14, operative July 1, 1991. Amended by Stats.1997, c. 63 (A.B.1165), § 1; Stats.1997, c. 93 (S.B.696), § 2.5; Stats.2004, c. 888 (A.B.2687), § 7; Stats.2005, c. 75 (A.B.145), § 149, eff. July 19, 2005, operative Jan. 1, 2006; Stats.2008, c. 311 (S.B.1407), § 29; Stats.2009–2010, 4th Ex.Sess., c. 22 (S.B.13), § 32, eff. July 28, 2009; Stats.2011, c. 117 (A.B.1305), § 2; Stats.2012, c. 162 (S.B.1171), § 139.)*

Law Revision Commission Comments
1990 Enactment

Section 7660 continues Section 7660 of the repealed Probate Code without substantive change. Petitions under other provisions of this code include petitions for interpretation of a will or determination of persons entitled to distribution. See, e.g., Sections 9611 (petition for instructions), 11700–11705 (determination of persons entitled to distribution). For general provisions, see Sections 1000–1004 (rules of practice), 1020–1023 (petitions and other papers), 1040–1050 (hearings and orders).

Background on Section 7660 of Repealed Code

Section 7660 was added by 1988 Cal.Stat. ch. 1199 § 80.5. Subdivisions (a) and (b) superseded portions of subdivisions (a) and (b) of former Probate Code Section 1143 (repealed by 1988 Cal.Stat. ch. 1199 § 57.5). Subdivision (c) restated subdivision (d) of former Probate Code Section 1143 (repealed by 1988 Cal.Stat. ch. 1199 § 57.5). For background on the provisions of this chapter, see the Comment to this chapter under the chapter heading. [20 Cal.L.Rev.Comm.Reports 1001 (1990)].

Cross References

Certain fees to be deposited into bank account, distribution and transmittal, see Government Code § 68085.4.

Collection or transfer of estates without administration, see Probate Code § 13002 et seq.

County counsel or private counsel as attorney for public administrator under this section, see Government Code § 27643.

Deposit of fees or fines collected pursuant to this section in the Trial Court Trust Fund, effect of prior agreements or practices, long-term revenue allocation schedule proposal, see Government Code § 68085.5.

Organization and government of courts, collection of fees and fines pursuant to this section, deposits, see Government Code § 68085.1.

Personal representative and general personal representative, see Probate Code § 58.

Property taxation, cancellations, escheated property not distributed, validity of taxes, probate, see Revenue and Taxation Code § 4986.6.

Public employees' retirement, death benefits,
 Lump-sum benefit or uncashed lump-sum death benefit warrant payable to beneficiary, payment to public administrator for estates with total value not exceeding the amount prescribed in this section, see Government Code § 21507.
 Order of payment, absence of beneficiary designation, payment to public administrator for estates with total value not exceeding the amount prescribed in this section, see Government Code § 21493.
 Order of payment, valid beneficiary designation, payment to public administrator for estates with total value not exceeding the amount prescribed in this section, see Government Code § 21494.
 Retirement allowance accrued and unpaid at time of death and balance of prepaid complementary health premiums, payment to public administrator for estates with total value not exceeding the amount prescribed in this section, see Government Code § 21506.

Unclaimed property, filing of claim, "owner" defined, see Code of Civil Procedure § 1540.

§ 7661. Authority of public administrator

A public administrator acting under authority of this article may:

(a) Withdraw money or take possession of any other property of the decedent that is in the possession or control of a financial institution, government or private agency, retirement fund administrator, insurance company, licensed securities dealer, or other person.

(b) Collect any debts owed to the decedent, including, but not limited to, any rents, issues, or profits from the real and personal property in the estate until the estate is distributed.

(c) Sell any personal property of the decedent, including, but not limited to, stocks, bonds, mutual funds and other types of securities. Sales may be made with or without notice, as the public administrator elects. Title to the property sold passes without the need for confirmation by the court.

(d) Sell any real property of the decedent. The sale shall be accomplished through one of the following procedures:

(1) The sale may be conducted subject to Article 6 (commencing with Section 10300) of Chapter 18 of Part 5.

(2) With approval specified in the original court order for summary disposition of the estate, the sale of real property may be accomplished using a Notice of Proposed Action according to the following requirements:

(A) The publication of the sale shall be accomplished according to Sections 10300 to 10307, inclusive.

(B) The appraisal of the property and determination of the minimum sale price of 90 percent of the appraised value shall be accomplished according to Section 10309.

(C) If an offer meets the approval of the public administrator and the offered price is at least 90 percent of the appraised value, a notice of proposed action shall be made according to Sections 10581 to 10588, inclusive. If objection is not made to the notice of proposed action, the sale may be completed without a court confirmation of the sale. The sale may be consummated by recording a public administrator's deed and a copy of the court order for summary disposition that authorized the use of the notice of proposed action.

(D) If an objection to the notice of proposed action is made pursuant to Section 10587, the sale shall be confirmed in court according to Sections 10308 to 10316, inclusive. The sale may be consummated by recording an administrator's deed and a copy of the court order confirming the sale.

(E) If objection to the notice of proposed action is not made under Section 10587, the public administrator may still elect to have the sale confirmed in court according to Sections 10308 to 10316, inclusive, if the public administrator deems that is in the best interest of the estate. Title to the property sold passes with the public administrator's deed. *(Stats.1990, c. 79 (A.B.759), § 14, operative July 1, 1991. Amended by Stats.2004, c. 888 (A.B.2687), § 8.)*

Law Revision Commission Comments
1990 Enactment
Section 7661 continues Section 7661 of the repealed Probate Code without change.

Background on Section 7661 of Repealed Code
Section 7661 was added by 1988 Cal.Stat. ch. 1199 § 80.5. The section restated portions of former Probate Code Sections 1143 and 1144 (provisions repealed by 1988 Cal.Stat. ch. 1199 § 57.5), expanding the ability to withdraw funds to include other financial institutions besides banks. For background on the provisions of this chapter, see the Comment to this chapter under the chapter heading. [20 Cal.L.Rev.Comm.Reports 1001 (1990)].

Cross References
Disposition of unclaimed property of estates of deceased persons, see Code of Civil Procedure § 1440 et seq.
Sale of personal property, see Probate Code § 10252 et seq.
Unclaimed personal property, sale by personal representative, see Probate Code § 11851.
Unclaimed property, filing of claim, "owner" defined, see Code of Civil Procedure § 1540.

§ 7662. Payments from estate; priority; administration costs; expenses of last illness and disposition of remains; creditor claims
The public administrator acting under authority of this article shall pay out the money of the estate in the order prescribed in Section 11420, for expenses of administration, charges against the estate, and claims presented to the public administrator before distribution of the decedent's property pursuant to Section 7663. A creditor whose claim is paid under this section is not liable for contribution to a creditor whose claim is presented after the payment. *(Stats.1990, c. 79 (A.B.759), § 14, operative July 1, 1991. Amended by Stats.1990, c. 710 (S.B.1775), § 18, operative July 1, 1991; Stats.1991, c. 82 (S.B.896), § 23, eff. June 30, 1991, operative July 1, 1991.)*

Law Revision Commission Comments
1990 Enactment and Amendment
Section 7662 (enacted as a part of the new Probate Code by 1990 Cal.Stat. ch. 79 § 14) was amended by 1990 Cal.Stat. ch. 710 § 18. The section as amended continues Section 7662 of the repealed Probate Code revised to incorporate the order of payment prescribed by Section 11420.

Tax and other claims of public entities are entitled to priority under Section 11420. Because no notice to creditors is given pursuant to this article, the time for making claims is extended to the time of distribution of the decedent's property, and recipients of the property remain liable for creditor claims. See Section 7664 (liability for decedent's unsecured debts). Distribution may not be made until at least four months after commencement of administration. See Section 7663 (distribution of property).

1991 Amendment
Section 7662 is amended to correct a typographical error [20 Cal.L.Rev.Comm.Reports 2909 (1990)].

Background on Section 7662 of Repealed Code
Section 7662 was added by 1988 Cal.Stat. ch. 1199 § 80.5. The section restated the second sentence of subdivision (a) of former Probate Code Section 1143 and a portion of subdivision (b) of former Probate Code Section 1143 (provisions repealed by 1988 Cal.Stat. ch. 1199 § 57.5), with the addition of specific references to fees and costs of administration. For background on the provisions of this chapter, see the Comment to this chapter under the chapter heading. [20 Cal.L.Rev.Comm.Reports 1001 (1990)].

Cross References
Liability of estate for interment, see Health and Safety Code §§ 7100, 7101.
Money or property distributed to state, permanent escheat, see Code of Civil Procedure § 1441.

§ 7663. Distributions to beneficiaries; deposit with county treasurer if no beneficiaries
(a) After payment of debts pursuant to Section 7662, but in no case before four months after court authorization of the

public administrator to act under this article or after the public administrator takes possession or control of the estate, the public administrator shall distribute to the decedent's beneficiaries any money or other property of the decedent remaining in the possession of the public administrator.

(b) If there are no beneficiaries, the public administrator shall deposit the balance with the county treasurer for use in the general fund of the county, subject to Article 3 (commencing with Section 50050) of Chapter 1 of Part 1 of Division 1 of Title 5 of the Government Code. If the amount deposited exceeds five thousand dollars ($5,000), the public administrator shall at the time of the deposit give the Controller written notice of the information specified in Section 1311 of the Code of Civil Procedure. *(Stats.1990, c. 79 (A.B.759), § 14, operative July 1, 1991. Amended by Stats.1990, c. 324 (S.B.1774), § 2, eff. July 17, 1990, operative July 1, 1991; Stats.1996, c. 401 (S.B.1582), § 2.)*

Law Revision Commission Comments

1990 Enactment

Section 7663 continues Section 7663 of the repealed Probate Code without substantive change. The California Veterans' Home is considered a beneficiary for the purpose of application of this section. See Mil. & Vet.Code § 1035.05.

1990 Amendment

Section 7663 (enacted as a part of the new Probate Code by 1990 Cal.Stat. ch. 79 § 14) was amended by 1990 Cal.Stat. ch. 324 § 2 to make clear that the procedure for disposition of unclaimed funds in the county treasury provided by Government Code Sections 50050–50056 applies to funds deposited by the public administrator under subdivision (b). Although the county treasurer has the duty to administer the funds deposited, a public record of the deposit is maintained by the State Controller under this section as well as by the public administrator pursuant to Section 7665.

It should be noted that, while claims for funds deposited under subdivision (b) are processed under the general Government Code provisions, claims for funds deposited with the county treasurer under Section 11850 are processed by the court under Section 11854. Deposit with the county treasurer under subdivision (b) is an exception to the deposit procedure generally applicable in estate administration. See Sections 11900 (distribution to state) and 7622 (general administration rules apply except as otherwise provided in this chapter). For background on the 1990 amendment, see Recommendation Relating to Disposition of Small Estate by Public Administrator, 20 Cal.L.Revision Comm'n Reports 529 (1990). [20 Cal.L.Rev.Comm.Reports 1001 (1990)].

Background on Section 7663 of Repealed Code

Section 7663 was added by 1988 Cal.Stat. ch. 1199 § 80.5. The section restated a portion of subdivision (b) of former Probate Code Section 1143 and superseded the second sentence of the second paragraph of, and the third paragraph of, former Probate Code Section 1144 (provisions repealed by 1988 Cal.Stat. ch. 1199 § 57.5). Section 7663 made clear that distribution may not be made until at least four months after commencement of administration, and required that all unclaimed summary disposition funds go to the county (as opposed to only those from the smallest estates as was the case under the prior law). For background on the provisions of this chapter, see the Comment to this chapter under the chapter heading. [20 Cal.L.Rev.Comm.Reports 1001 (1990)].

Cross References

Distribution to state, see Probate Code § 11900.

Escheat,
  Generally, see Code of Civil Procedure § 1410 et seq.; Probate Code § 6800 et seq.
  Money under $50 on deposit with county treasurer received from public administrator, see Code of Civil Procedure § 1444.5.

§ 7664. Liability for unsecured debts; enforcement; defenses

A person to whom property is distributed under this article is personally liable for the unsecured debts of the decedent. Such a debt may be enforced against the person in the same manner as it could have been enforced against the decedent if the decedent had not died. In an action based on the debt, the person may assert any defenses available to the decedent if the decedent had not died. The aggregate personal liability of a person under this section shall not exceed the fair market value of the property distributed to the person, valued as of the date of the distribution, less the amount of any liens and encumbrances on the property on that date. Section 366.2 of the Code of Civil Procedure applies in an action under this section. *(Stats.1990, c. 79 (A.B.759), § 14, operative July 1, 1991. Amended by Stats.1990, c. 140 (S.B.1855), § 5.1, operative July 1, 1991; Stats.1992, c. 178 (S.B.1496), § 33.)*

Law Revision Commission Comments

1990 Enactment

Section 7664 continues Section 7664 of the repealed Probate Code without substantive change. This section was drawn from Sections 13109 and 13112 (affidavit procedure for collection or transfer of personal property).

1990 Amendment

Section 7664 (enacted as a part of the new Probate Code by 1990 Cal.Stat. ch. 79 § 14) was amended by 1990 Cal.Stat. ch. 140 § 5.1 to make clear that the general one-year statute of limitations applicable to all causes of action against a decedent is applicable to liability for the decedent's debts under Section 7664. For background on the 1990 amendment, see Recommendation Relating to Notice to Creditors in Estate Administration, 20 Cal.L.Revision Comm'n Reports 507 (1990). [20 Cal.L.Rev.Comm.Reports 1001 (1990)].

1992 Amendment

Section 7664 is amended to revise a section reference. This revision is a technical, nonsubstantive change. [22 Cal.L.Rev.Comm.Reports 895 (1992)].

Background on Section 7664 of Repealed Code

Section 7664 was a new provision added by 1988 Cal.Stat. ch. 1199 § 80.5. For background on the provisions of this chapter, see the Comment to this chapter under the chapter heading. [20 Cal.L.Rev.Comm.Reports 1001 (1990)].

Cross References

Death of party before expiration of statute of limitations, limitation upon action by or against representatives or estates, see Code of Civil Procedure §§ 366.1, 366.2, 377 et seq.

§ 7665. Statement showing property and disposition; filing; receipts for distributions; retention of receipts and records of expenditures

(a) The public administrator shall file with the clerk a statement showing the property of the decedent that came into possession of the public administrator and the disposition made of the property, together with receipts for all distributions. This subdivision does not apply to proceedings under paragraph (2) of subdivision (a) of Section 7660.

(b) The public administrator shall maintain a file of all receipts and records of expenditures for a period of three years after disposition of the property pursuant to Section 7663. *(Stats.1990, c. 79 (A.B.759), § 14, operative July 1, 1991.)*

Law Revision Commission Comments

1990 Enactment

Section 7665 continues Section 7665 of the repealed Probate Code without change.

Background on Section 7665 of Repealed Code

Section 7665 was added by 1988 Cal.Stat. ch. 1199 § 80.5. Subdivision (a) of Section 7665 restated the substance of the first sentence of the second paragraph of former Probate Code Section 1144 (repealed by 1988 Cal.Stat. ch. 1199 § 57.5). Receipts and records for expenditures are preserved in the public administrator's files for three years pursuant to subdivision (b). For background on the provisions of this chapter, see the Comment to this chapter under the chapter heading. [20 Cal.L.Rev.Comm.Reports 1001 (1990)].

§ 7666. Compensation; administrator; attorney

(a) Except as provided in Section 7623 and in subdivision (b), the compensation payable to the public administrator and the attorney, if any, for the public administrator for the filing of an application pursuant to this chapter and for performance of any duty or service connected therewith is that set out in Part 7 (commencing with Section 10800).

(b) The public administrator is entitled to a minimum compensation of one thousand dollars ($1,000). *(Stats.1990, c. 79 (A.B.759), § 14, operative July 1, 1991. Amended by Stats.1990, c. 710 (S.B.1775), § 19, operative July 1, 1991; Stats.1991, c. 1019 (S.B.1022), § 8; Stats.1998, c. 103 (S.B. 1487), § 3; Stats.2004, c. 888 (A.B.2687), § 9.)*

Law Revision Commission Comments

1990 Enactment and Amendment

Section 7666 (enacted as a part of the new Probate Code by 1990 Cal.Stat. ch. 79 § 14) was amended by 1990 Cal.Stat. ch. 710 § 19. The section as amended continues Section 7666 of the repealed Probate Code without substantive change.

Background on Section 7666 of Repealed Code

Section 7666 was added by 1988 Cal.Stat. ch. 1199 § 80.5. The section superseded subdivision (c) of former Probate Code Section 1143 and the second sentence of former Probate Code Section 1144 (provisions repealed by 1988 Cal.Stat. ch. 1199 § 57.5). The 1990 amendment added language found in the repealed code section relating to the compensation of the attorney of the public administrator. As originally enacted in the new Probate Code, Section 7666 had been revised to reflect the fact that Assembly Bill 831 of the 1989–1990 regular session would have substituted an agreed fee system for the statutory fee system for probate attorney fees. However, Assembly Bill 831 was not enacted, and Section 7666 was amended by 1990 Cal.Stat. ch. 710 § 19 to reflect this fact. See the Comment to Section 900. For background on the provisions of this chapter, see the Comment to this chapter under the chapter heading. [20 Cal.L.Rev.Comm. Reports 1001 (1990)].

Cross References

Applicability of code provisions to courts, exceptions, see Code of Civil Procedure § 34.
Attorney for a public administrator, see Government Code § 27643.
Contents of petition for probate of will, see Probate Code § 8002.
Contests before and after probate, see Probate Code §§ 8004, 8270.
Death, establishment of fact, see Probate Code § 200 et seq.
Manner of administration by public administrator, compensation and allowances, see Probate Code § 7622.

Part 2

OPENING ESTATE ADMINISTRATION

Law Revision Commission Comments

1990 Enactment

This part supersedes Part 2 (commencing with Section 8000) of Division 7 of the repealed Probate Code. The superseded part was enacted upon recommendation of the California Law Revision Commission. See Recommendation Relating to Opening Estate Administration, 19 Cal.L.Revision Comm'n Reports 787 (1988). See also Communication from the California Law Revision Commission Concerning Assembly Bill 2841, 19 Cal.L.Revision Comm'n Reports 1201, 1231–35 (1988); Communication from the California Law Revision Commission Concerning Assembly Bill 158, 20 Cal.L.Revision Comm'n Reports 235, 236 (1990). [20 Cal.L.Rev.Comm.Reports 1001 (1990)].

Cross References

Application of old and new law, see Probate Code § 3.
Nondomiciliary decedent's will, ancillary administration pursuant to this part, see Probate Code § 12520.

CHAPTER 1. COMMENCEMENT OF PROCEEDINGS

Section
8000. Time of commencement; who may commence; petition; status of will.
8001. Executor named in will; time to petition before right to be personal representative is waived.
8002. Contents of petition; attachment of will.
8003. Hearing; time; notice.
8004. Contesting appointment of personal representative; grounds; replacement; contesting will.
8005. Hearing; examination and compelling attendance of witnesses; matters to be established.
8006. Establishment of jurisdictional facts; order determining time and place of death and jurisdiction, admitting will to probate, and appointing personal representative; effect of defect of form or error in petition.
8007. Collateral attack on order admitting will to probate or appointing personal representative; fraud in procurement of order; erroneous determination of death.

§ 8000. Time of commencement; who may commence; petition; status of will

(a) At any time after a decedent's death, any interested person may commence proceedings for administration of the estate of the decedent by a petition to the court for an order determining the date and place of the decedent's death and for either or both of the following:

(1) Appointment of a personal representative.

(2) Probate of the decedent's will.

(b) A petition for probate of the decedent's will may be made regardless of whether the will is in the petitioner's possession or is lost, destroyed, or beyond the jurisdiction of the state. *(Stats.1990, c. 79 (A.B.759), § 14, operative July 1, 1991.)*

Law Revision Commission Comments

1990 Enactment

Section 8000 continues Section 8000 of the repealed Probate Code without change. The court having jurisdiction is the superior court of the proper county. See Sections 7050 (jurisdiction in superior court), 7051–7052 (venue), 7070–7072 (transfer of proceedings).

Background on Section 8000 of Repealed Code

Section 8000 was added by 1988 Cal.Stat. ch. 1199 § 81.5. The section restated former law without substantive change. See, e.g., former Probate Code Section 323 (petition for probate of will) (repealed by 1988 Cal.Stat. ch. 1199 § 40). For background on the provisions of this part, see the Comment to this part under the part heading. [20 Cal.L.Rev.Comm.Reports 1001 (1990)].

§ 8001. Executor named in will; time to petition before right to be personal representative is waived

Unless good cause for delay is shown, if a person named in a will as executor fails to petition the court for administration of the estate within 30 days after the person has knowledge of the death of the decedent and that the person is named as executor, the person may be held to have waived the right to appointment as personal representative. *(Stats.1990, c. 79 (A.B.759), § 14, operative July 1, 1991.)*

Law Revision Commission Comments

1990 Enactment

Section 8001 continues Section 8001 of the repealed Probate Code without change. It is within the discretion of the court whether to hold the person named as executor to have waived the right to appointment. If the court so holds, the court may appoint another competent person as personal representative. See Section 8440 (administrators with the will annexed).

Background on Section 8001 of Repealed Code

Section 8001 was added by 1988 Cal.Stat. ch. 1199 § 81.5. The section restated former Probate Code Section 324 (repealed by 1988 Cal.Stat. ch. 1199 § 40) without substantive change. For background on the provisions of this part, see the Comment to this part under the part heading. [20 Cal.L.Rev.Comm.Reports 1001 (1990)].

Cross References

Administrators with will annexed; priority of appointment, see Probate Code § 8441.
Death, establishment of fact, see Probate Code § 200 et seq.
Executor; administrator with will annexed, see Probate Code § 8440.

§ 8002. Contents of petition; attachment of will

(a) The petition shall contain all of the following information:

(1) The date and place of the decedent's death.

(2) The street number, street, and city, or other address, and the county, of the decedent's residence at the time of death.

(3) The name, age, address, and relation to the decedent of each heir and devisee of the decedent, so far as known to or reasonably ascertainable by the petitioner.

(4) The character and estimated value of the property in the estate.

(5) The name of the person for whom appointment as personal representative is petitioned.

(b) If the decedent left a will:

(1) The petitioner shall attach to the petition a photographic copy of the will. In the case of a holographic will or other will of which material provisions are handwritten, the petitioner shall also attach a typed copy of the will.

(2) If the will is in a foreign language, the petitioner shall attach an English language translation. On admission of the will to probate, the court shall certify to a correct translation into English, and the certified translation shall be filed with the will.

(3) The petition shall state whether the person named as executor in the will consents to act or waives the right to appointment. *(Stats.1990, c. 79 (A.B.759), § 14, operative July 1, 1991.)*

Law Revision Commission Comments

1990 Enactment

Section 8002 continues Section 8002 of the repealed Probate Code without substantive change. For general provisions relating to petitions, see Sections 1020–1023.

Background on Section 8002 of Repealed Code

Section 8002 was added by 1988 Cal.Stat. ch. 1199 § 81.5. The section superseded portions of former Probate Code Sections 326 (petition for probate of will) (repealed by 1988 Cal.Stat. ch. 1199 § 40), 332 (admission of will to probate) (repealed by 1988 Cal.Stat. ch. 1199 § 40), and 440 (petition for letters of administration) (repealed by 1988 Cal.Stat. ch. 1199 § 45). It substituted the "address" for the "residences" of heirs and devisees, added an express requirement that a copy of the will be attached, required that a typed copy of a holographic or handwritten will be attached to the petition, and provided for notice to heirs and devisees reasonably ascertainable by the petitioner. For background on the provisions of this part, see the Comment to this part under the part heading. [20 Cal.L.Rev.Comm.Reports 1001 (1990)].

Cross References

Lost or destroyed wills, written statement with petition, see Probate Code § 8223.

§ 8003. Hearing; time; notice

(a) The hearing on the petition shall be set for a day not less than 15 nor more than 30 days after the petition is filed. At the request of the petitioner made at the time the petition is filed, the hearing on the petition shall be set for a day not less than 30 nor more than 45 days after the petition is filed. The court may not shorten the time for giving the notice of hearing under this section.

(b) The petitioner shall serve and publish notice of the hearing in the manner prescribed in Chapter 2 (commencing with Section 8100). *(Stats.1990, c. 79 (A.B.759), § 14, operative July 1, 1991.)*

Law Revision Commission Comments

1990 Enactment

Section 8003 continues Section 8003 of the repealed Probate Code with the addition of the last sentence of subdivision (a). The added sentence continues without substantive change a portion of subdivision (b) of Section 1203 of the repealed Probate Code.

Background on Section 8003 of Repealed Code

Section 8003 was added by 1988 Cal.Stat. ch. 1199 § 81.5. The section restated former Probate Code Section 327 (probate of will) (repealed by 1988 Cal.Stat. ch. 1199 § 40) and a portion of former Probate Code Section 441 (application for letters) (repealed by 1988 Cal.Stat. ch. 1199 § 45), except that the petitioner rather than the clerk has the duty of giving notice. For background on the provisions of this part, see the Comment to this part under the part heading. [20 Cal.L.Rev.Comm.Reports 1001 (1990)].

Cross References

Computation of time generally, see Code of Civil Procedure § 12 et seq.
Evidence of publication, see Code of Civil Procedure §§ 2010, 2011.
Notices, see Probate Code § 1200 et seq.
Publications, generally, see Government Code § 6000 et seq.

§ 8004. Contesting appointment of personal representative; grounds; replacement; contesting will

(a) If appointment of the personal representative is contested, the grounds of opposition may include a challenge to the competency of the personal representative or the right to appointment. If the contest asserts the right of another person to appointment as personal representative, the contestant shall also file a petition and serve notice in the manner provided in Article 2 (commencing with Section 8110) of Chapter 2, and the court shall hear the two petitions together.

(b) If a will is contested, the applicable procedure is that provided in Article 3 (commencing with Section 8250) of Chapter 3. *(Stats.1990, c. 79 (A.B.759), § 14, operative July 1, 1991.)*

Law Revision Commission Comments

1990 Enactment

Section 8004 continues Section 8004 of the repealed Probate Code without change. See also Sections 1043 (response or objection), 1045 (continuance or postponement).

Background on Section 8004 of Repealed Code

Section 8004 was added by 1988 Cal.Stat. ch. 1199 § 81.5. Subdivision (a) restated portions of former Probate Code Sections 370 (repealed by 1988 Cal.Stat. ch. 1199 § 42), 407 (repealed by 1988 Cal.Stat. ch. 1199 § 43), and 442 (repealed by 1988 Cal.Stat. ch. 1199 § 45) without substantive change. Subdivision (b) was a new provision. For background on the provisions of this part, see the Comment to this part under the part heading. [20 Cal.L.Rev.Comm.Reports 1001 (1990)].

Cross References

Contests after probate, see Probate Code § 8270.

Personal representatives, competency and priority in appointment of, see Probate Code § 8402 et seq.

§ 8005. Hearing; examination and compelling attendance of witnesses; matters to be established

(a) At the hearing on the petition, the court may examine and compel any person to attend as a witness concerning any of the following matters:

(1) The time, place, and manner of the decedent's death.

(2) The place of the decedent's domicile and residence at the time of death.

(3) The character and value of the decedent's property.

(4) Whether or not the decedent left a will.

(b) The following matters shall be established:

(1) The jurisdictional facts, including:

(A) The date and place of the decedent's death.

(B) That the decedent was domiciled in this state or left property in this state at the time of death.

(C) The publication of notice under Article 3 (commencing with Section 8120) of Chapter 2.

(2) The existence or nonexistence of the decedent's will.

(3) That notice of the hearing was served as provided in Article 2 (commencing with Section 8110) of Chapter 2. *(Stats.1990, c. 79 (A.B.759), § 14, operative July 1, 1991.)*

Law Revision Commission Comments

1990 Enactment

Section 8005 continues Section 8005 of the repealed Probate Code without change. For general provisions, see Sections 1040–1048 (hearings and orders), 1260–1265 (proof of giving notice).

Background on Section 8005 of Repealed Code

Section 8005 was added by 1988 Cal.Stat. ch. 1199 § 81.5. The section restated former Probate Code Section 443 (repealed by 1988 Cal.Stat. ch. 1199 § 45) and a portion of the first sentence of former Probate Code Section 407 (repealed by 1988 Cal.Stat. ch. 1199 § 43), with the addition of the references to notice. For background on the provisions of this part, see the Comment to this part under the part heading. [20 Cal.L.Rev.Comm.Reports 1001 (1990)].

Cross References

Affidavit, use of in examination of witness, see Code of Civil Procedure § 2009.
Character and estimated value of the property of estate, see Probate Code § 8002.
Establishing fact of death or heirship, see Probate Code § 200 et seq.
Recital of jurisdictional facts generally, see Probate Code § 1047.
Witnesses,
  Compelling attendance of, see Code of Civil Procedure §§ 128, 177, 1985 et seq.
  Examination of, see Evidence Code § 777 et seq.

§ 8006. Establishment of jurisdictional facts; order determining time and place of death and jurisdiction, admitting will to probate, and appointing personal representative; effect of defect of form or error in petition

(a) If the court finds that the matters referred to in paragraph (1) of subdivision (b) of Section 8005 are established, the court shall make an order determining the time and place of the decedent's death and the jurisdiction of the court. Where appropriate and on satisfactory proof, the order shall admit the decedent's will to probate and appoint a personal representative. The date the will is admitted to probate shall be included in the order.

(b) If through defect of form or error the matters referred to in paragraph (1) of subdivision (b) of Section 8005 are incorrectly stated in the petition but actually are established, the court has and retains jurisdiction to correct the defect or error at any time. No such defect or error makes void an order admitting the will to probate or appointing a personal representative or an order made in any subsequent proceeding. *(Stats.1990, c. 79 (A.B.759), § 14, operative July 1, 1991.)*

Law Revision Commission Comments

1990 Enactment

Section 8006 continues Section 8006 of the repealed Probate Code without change. For the minute order admitting a will to probate, see Section 8225.

Background on Section 8006 of Repealed Code

Section 8006 was added by 1988 Cal.Stat. ch. 1199 § 81.5. Subdivision (a) was a new provision. Subdivision (b) restated the last paragraph of former Probate Code Sections 326 (repealed by 1988 Cal.Stat. ch. 1199 § 40) and 440 (repealed by 1988 Cal.Stat. ch. 1199 § 45) without substantive change. For background on the provisions of this part, see the Comment to this part under the part heading. [20 Cal.L.Rev.Comm.Reports 1001 (1990)].

§ 8007. Collateral attack on order admitting will to probate or appointing personal representative; fraud in procurement of order; erroneous determination of death

(a) Except as provided in subdivision (b), an order admitting a will to probate or appointing a personal representative, when it becomes final, is a conclusive determination of the jurisdiction of the court and cannot be collaterally attacked.

(b) Subdivision (a) does not apply in either of the following cases:

(1) The presence of extrinsic fraud in the procurement of the court order.

(2) The court order is based on the erroneous determination of the decedent's death. *(Stats.1990, c. 79 (A.B.759), § 14, operative July 1, 1991.)*

Law Revision Commission Comments

1990 Enactment

Section 8007 continues Section 8007 of the repealed Probate Code without change, except that subdivision (b)(1) is revised to make clear that the fraud referred to is extrinsic fraud. This is consistent with case law. See Estate of Robinson, 19 Cal.2d 534, 121 P.2d 734 (1942); Estate of Crisler, 83 Cal.App.2d 431, 188 P.2d 772 (1948).

Background on Section 8007 of Repealed Code

Section 8007 was added by 1988 Cal.Stat. ch. 1199 § 81.5. The section restated former Probate Code Section 302 (repealed by 1988 Cal.Stat. ch. 1199 § 40) without substantive change and extended it to cover probate of a will as well as appointment of a personal representative. This had the effect of codifying the rule in Estate of Sanders, 40 Cal.3d 607, 710 P.2d 232, 221 Cal.Rptr. 432 (1985). For background on the provisions of this part, see the Comment to this part under the part heading. [20 Cal.L.Rev.Comm.Reports 1001 (1990)].

Cross References

Conclusive judgment or order of court, see Code of Civil Procedure § 1908.5.
Conclusiveness of final order, see Code of Civil Procedure § 1908.
Judicial orders, disputable presumption, see Code of Civil Procedure § 1909.
Probate, conclusiveness of, see Probate Code § 8226.

CHAPTER 2. NOTICE OF HEARING

ARTICLE 1. CONTENTS

Cross References

Application of old and new law, see Probate Code § 3.

§ 8100. Notice of hearing; contents

The notice of hearing of a petition for administration of a decedent's estate, whether served under Article 2 (commencing with Section 8110) or published under Article 3 (commencing with Section 8120), shall state substantially as follows:

NOTICE OF PETITION TO ADMINISTER ESTATE OF _____, ESTATE NO. _____

To all heirs, beneficiaries, creditors, and contingent creditors of _____ and persons who may be otherwise interested in the will or estate, or both:

A petition has been filed by _____ in the Superior Court of California, County of _____, requesting that _____ be appointed as personal representative to administer the estate of _____ [and for probate of the decedent's will, which is available for examination in the court file].

[The petition requests authority to administer the estate under the Independent Administration of Estates Act. This will avoid the need to obtain court approval for many actions taken in connection with the estate. However, before taking certain actions, the personal representative will be required to give notice to interested persons unless they have waived notice or have consented to the proposed action. The petition will be granted unless good cause is shown why it should not be.]

The petition is set for hearing in Dept. No. _____ at _____

(Address)

on _____ at _____.

(Date of hearing)   (Time of hearing)

IF YOU OBJECT to the granting of the petition, you should appear at the hearing and state your objections or file written objections with the court before the hearing. Your appearance may be in person or by your attorney.

IF YOU ARE A CREDITOR or a contingent creditor of the deceased, you must file your claim with the court and mail a copy to the personal representative appointed by the court within the later of either (1) four months from the date of first issuance of letters to a general personal representative, as defined in subdivision (b) of Section 58 of the California Probate Code, or (2) 60 days from the date of mailing or personal delivery of the notice to you under Section 9052 of the California Probate Code.

YOU MAY EXAMINE the file kept by the court. If you are interested in the estate, you may request special notice of the filing of an inventory and appraisal of estate assets or of any petition or account as provided in Section 1250 of the California Probate Code.

_____

(Name and address of petitioner or petitioner's attorney)

(Stats.1990, c. 79 (A.B.759), § 14, operative July 1, 1991. Amended by Stats.2012, c. 207 (A.B.2683), § 2.)

Law Revision Commission Comments

1990 Enactment

Section 8100 continues Section 8100 of the repealed Probate Code without change.

Background on Section 8100 of Repealed Code

Section 8100 was added by 1988 Cal.Stat. ch. 1199 § 81.5. The section restated the second sentence of former Probate Code Section 328 and subdivision (b) of former Probate Code Section 333 and continued the substance of subdivision (e) of former Section 333 (provisions repealed by 1988 Cal.Stat. ch. 1199 § 40), except that reference to notice of the decedent's death was eliminated from the caption, the type size was not specified (but see Section 8123 concerning type size), and a reference to the decedent's will was added. Section 8100 also restated the last sentence of former Probate Code Section 441 (repealed by 1988 Cal.Stat. ch. 1199 § 45) without substantive change and incorporated the substance of subdivision (c) of Probate Code Section 10451. Section 8100 consolidated the published notice with the general notice served on heirs or beneficiaries, so that there is a single form of notice. For background on the provisions of this part, see the Comment to this part under the part heading. [20 Cal.L.Rev.Comm.Reports 1001 (1990)].

Cross References

Creditor and contingent creditor information, omission in subsequent publication of notice, see Probate Code § 8125.

ARTICLE 2. SERVICE OF NOTICE OF HEARING

Cross References

Application of old and new law, see Probate Code § 3.

§ 8110. Time for service; manner; persons to be served

At least 15 days before the hearing of a petition for administration of a decedent's estate, the petitioner shall serve notice of the hearing by mail or personal delivery on all of the following persons:

(a) Each heir of the decedent, so far as known to or reasonably ascertainable by the petitioner.

(b) Each devisee, executor, and alternative executor named in any will being offered for probate, regardless of whether the devise or appointment is purportedly revoked in a subsequent instrument. *(Stats.1990, c. 79 (A.B.759), § 14, operative July 1, 1991. Amended by Stats.1996, c. 563 (S.B.392), § 22.)*

Law Revision Commission Comments

1990 Enactment

Section 8110 continues Section 8110 of the repealed Probate Code without change. For general provisions relating to notice, see Sections 1200–1221. See also Sections 1260–1265 (proof of giving of notice). Cf. Section 9050 (notice to creditors).

Background on Section 8110 of Repealed Code

Section 8110 was added by 1988 Cal.Stat. ch. 1199 § 81.5. The section restated the first part of the first sentence of former Probate Code Section 328 (repealed by 1988 Cal.Stat. ch. 1199 § 40) and a portion of the second sentence of former Probate Code Section 441 (repealed by 1988 Cal.Stat. ch. 1199 § 45), but limits service on heirs to known heirs. For background on the provisions of this part, see the Comment to this part under the part heading. [20 Cal.L.Rev.Comm.Reports 1001 (1990)].

Cross References

Notices, see Probate Code § 1200 et seq.
Publication of notice upon petition for letters of administration, see Probate Code § 8003.
Revocation of letters of administration, see Probate Code § 8501.

§ 8111. Charitable devise or trust without designated devisee or resident trustee; service on Attorney General

If the decedent's will involves or may involve a testamentary trust of property for charitable purposes other than a charitable trust with a designated trustee resident in this state, or involves or may involve a devise for charitable purposes without an identified devisee, notice of hearing accompanied by a copy of the petition and of the will shall be served on the Attorney General as provided in Section 1209. *(Stats.1990, c. 79 (A.B.759), § 14, operative July 1, 1991.)*

Law Revision Commission Comments

1990 Enactment

Section 8111 continues Section 8111 of the repealed Probate Code without substantive change.

Background on Section 8111 of Repealed Code

Section 8111 was added by 1988 Cal.Stat. ch. 1199 § 81.5. The section restated the second paragraph of former Probate Code Section 328 (repealed by 1988 Cal.Stat. ch. 1199 § 40) without substantive change. For background on the provisions of this part, see the Comment to this part under the part heading. [20 Cal.L.Rev.Comm.Reports 1001 (1990)].

§ 8112. Creditors; public entities with claims; notice by general personal representative

A general personal representative shall give notice of administration of the estate of the decedent to creditors under Chapter 2 (commencing with Section 9050), and to public entities under Chapter 5 (commencing with Section 9200), of Part 4. *(Stats.1990, c. 79 (A.B.759), § 14, operative July 1, 1991.)*

Law Revision Commission Comments

1990 Enactment

Section 8112 continues Section 8112 of the repealed Probate Code without change.

Background on Section 8112 of Repealed Code

Section 8112 was a new provision added by 1988 Cal.Stat. ch. 1199 § 81.5. For background on the provisions of this part, see the Comment to this part under the part heading. [20 Cal.L.Rev.Comm.Reports 1001 (1990)].

§ 8113. Foreign citizen's death without will, etc.; notice to diplomat or consul

If a citizen of a foreign country dies without leaving a will or leaves a will without naming an executor, or if it appears that property will pass to a citizen of a foreign country, notice shall be given to a recognized diplomatic or consular official of the foreign country maintaining an office in the United States. *(Stats.1990, c. 79 (A.B.759), § 14, operative July 1, 1991.)*

Law Revision Commission Comments

1990 Enactment

Section 8113 continues Section 8113 of the repealed Probate Code without change. This section applies only if there is a recognized diplomatic or consular official of the particular foreign country maintaining an office in the United States. Whether a country has recognized diplomatic or consular representation in the United States may be ascertained from the United States Department of State.

Background on Section 8113 of Repealed Code

Section 8113 was a new provision added by 1988 Cal.Stat. ch. 1199 § 81.5. The section was drawn from Section 7.06 of the Los Angeles County Probate Policy Memorandum in California Local Probate Rules (10th ed. Cal.Cont.Ed.Bar 1989). For background on the provisions of this part, see the Comment to this part under the part heading. [20 Cal.L.Rev.Comm.Reports 1001 (1990)].

ARTICLE 3.   PUBLICATION

Cross References

Application of old and new law, see Probate Code § 3.

§ 8120. Published notice in addition to served notice

In addition to service of the notice of hearing as provided in Article 2 (commencing with Section 8110), notice of hearing of a petition for administration of a decedent's estate shall also be published before the hearing in the manner provided in this article. *(Stats.1990, c. 79 (A.B.759), § 14, operative July 1, 1991.)*

Law Revision Commission Comments

1990 Enactment

Section 8120 continues Section 8120 of the repealed Probate Code without change.

Background on Section 8120 of Repealed Code

Section 8120 was a new provision added by 1988 Cal.Stat. ch. 1199 § 81.5. For background on the provisions of this part, see the Comment to this part under the part heading. [20 Cal.L.Rev.Comm.Reports 1001 (1990)].

§ 8121.   Time of publication; number; newspaper

(a) The first publication date of the notice shall be at least 15 days before the hearing. Three publications in a newspaper published once a week or more often, with at least five days intervening between the first and last publication dates, not counting the publication dates, are sufficient.

(b) Notice shall be published in a newspaper of general circulation in the city where the decedent resided at the time of death, or where the decedent's property is located if the court has jurisdiction under Section 7052. If there is no such newspaper, or if the decedent did not reside in a city, or if the property is not located in a city, then notice shall be published in a newspaper of general circulation in the county which is circulated within the area of the county in which the decedent resided or the property is located. If there is no such newspaper, notice shall be published in a newspaper of general circulation published in this state nearest to the county seat of the county in which the decedent resided or the property is located, and which is circulated within the area of the county in which the decedent resided or the property is located.

(c) For purposes of this section, "city" means a charter city as defined in Section 34101 of the Government Code or a general law city as defined in Section 34102 of the Government Code. *(Stats.1990, c. 79 (A.B.759), § 14, operative July 1, 1991.)*

Law Revision Commission Comments

1990 Enactment

Section 8121 continues Section 8121 of the repealed Probate Code without substantive change.

Background on Section 8121 of Repealed Code

Section 8121 was added by 1988 Cal.Stat. ch. 1199 § 81.5. The section restated subdivision (a) of former Probate Code Section 333 (repealed by 1988 Cal.Stat. ch. 1199 § 40) but omitted the posting provision, which was no longer necessary. The reference to the first publication date clarified the former provision that publication of notice "pursuant to this section shall be for at least 15 days." The former reference to the "community" where the decedent resided was replaced by a reference to the "area of the county," since some decedents do not reside in communities. For background on the provisions of this part, see the Comment to this part under the part heading. [20 Cal.L.Rev.Comm.Reports 1001 (1990)].

§ 8122. Substantial compliance with requirements

The Legislature finds and declares that, to be most effective, notice of hearing should be published in compliance with Section 8121. However, the Legislature recognizes the possibility that in unusual cases due to confusion over jurisdictional boundaries or oversight such notice may inadvertently be published in a newspaper that does not satisfy Section 8121. Therefore, to prevent a minor error in publication from invalidating what would otherwise be a proper proceeding, the Legislature further finds and declares that notice published in a good faith attempt to comply with Section 8121 is sufficient to provide notice of hearing and to establish jurisdiction if the court expressly finds that the notice was published in a newspaper of general circulation published within the county and widely circulated within a true cross-section of the area of the county in which the decedent resided or the property was located in substantial compliance with Section 8121. *(Stats.1990, c. 79 (A.B.759), § 14, operative July 1, 1991.)*

Law Revision Commission Comments

1990 Enactment

Section 8122 continues Section 8122 of the repealed Probate Code without change.

Background on Section 8122 of Repealed Code

Section 8122 was added by 1988 Cal.Stat. ch. 1199 § 81.5. The section restated former Probate Code Section 334 (repealed by 1988 Cal.Stat. ch. 1199 § 40) without substantive change. For background on the provisions of this part, see the Comment to this part under the part heading. [20 Cal.L.Rev.Comm.Reports 1001 (1990)].

§ 8123. Type size

The caption of a notice under this article shall be in 8-point type or larger and the text shall be in 7-point type or larger. *(Stats.1990, c. 79 (A.B.759), § 14, operative July 1, 1991.)*

Law Revision Commission Comments

1990 Enactment

Section 8123 continues Section 8123 of the repealed Probate Code without change. See also Code Civ.Proc. § 1019 (type size variations).

Background on Section 8123 of Repealed Code

Section 8123 was added by 1988 Cal.Stat. ch. 1199 § 81.5. The section restated the introductory portion of subdivision (b) of former Probate Code Section 333 (repealed by 1988 Cal.Stat. ch. 1199 § 40) without substantive change. For background on the provisions of this part, see the Comment to this part under the part heading. [20 Cal.L.Rev.Comm.Reports 1001 (1990)].

§ 8124. Affidavit; prerequisite for hearing petition

A petition for administration of a decedent's estate shall not be heard by the court unless an affidavit showing due publication of the notice of hearing has been filed with the court. The affidavit shall contain a copy of the notice and state the date of its publication. *(Stats.1990, c. 79 (A.B.759), § 14, operative July 1, 1991.)*

Law Revision Commission Comments

1990 Enactment

Section 8124 continues Section 8124 of the repealed Probate Code without change. See also Sections 1260–1265 (proof of giving of notice).

Background on Section 8124 of Repealed Code

Section 8124 was added by 1988 Cal.Stat. ch. 1199 § 81.5. The section restated subdivision (c) of former Probate Code Section 333 (repealed by 1988 Cal.Stat. ch. 1199 § 40) without substantive change. For background on the provisions of this part, see the Comment to this part under the part heading. [20 Cal.L.Rev.Comm.Reports 1001 (1990)].

§ 8125. Creditor and contingent creditor information; omission in subsequent publication

Notwithstanding Section 8100, after the notice of hearing is published and an affidavit filed, any subsequent publication of the notice ordered by the court may omit the information for creditors and contingent creditors. *(Stats.1990, c. 79 (A.B.759), § 14, operative July 1, 1991.)*

Law Revision Commission Comments

1990 Enactment

Section 8125 continues Section 8125 of the repealed Probate Code without change.

Background on Section 8125 of Repealed Code

Section 8125 was added by 1988 Cal.Stat. ch. 1199 § 81.5. The section restated subdivision (d) of former Probate Code Section 333 (repealed by 1988 Cal.Stat. ch. 1199 § 40) without substantive change. For background on the provisions of this part, see the Comment to this part under the part heading. [20 Cal.L.Rev.Comm.Reports 1001 (1990)].

CHAPTER 3. PROBATE OF WILL

ARTICLE 1. PRODUCTION OF WILL

Cross References

Application of old and new law, see Probate Code § 3.

§ 8200. Custodian of will; duties upon testator's death; liability; copies of delivered will to be released by clerk; fees

(a) Unless a petition for probate of the will is earlier filed, the custodian of a will shall, within 30 days after having knowledge of the death of the testator, do both of the following:

(1) Deliver the will to the clerk of the superior court of the county in which the estate of the decedent may be administered.

(2) Mail a copy of the will to the person named in the will as executor, if the person's whereabouts is known to the custodian, or if not, to a person named in the will as a beneficiary, if the person's whereabouts is known to the custodian.

(b) A custodian of a will who fails to comply with the requirements of this section shall be liable for all damages sustained by any person injured by the failure.

(c) The clerk shall release a copy of a will delivered under this section for attachment to a petition for probate of the will or otherwise on receipt of payment of the required fee and either a court order for production of the will or a certified copy of a death certificate of the decedent.

(d) The fee for delivering a will to the clerk of the superior court pursuant to paragraph (1) of subdivision (a) shall be as provided in Section 70626 of the Government Code. If an estate is commenced for the decedent named in the will, the fee for any will delivered pursuant to paragraph (1) of subdivision (a) shall be reimbursable from the estate as an expense of administration. *(Stats.1990, c. 79 (A.B.759), § 14, operative July 1, 1991. Amended by Stats.1994, c. 806 (A.B.3686), § 25; Stats.2012, c. 41 (S.B.1021), § 86, eff. June 27, 2012; Stats.2013, c. 61 (S.B.826), § 2.)*

Law Revision Commission Comments
1990 Enactment
Section 8200 continues Section 8200 of the repealed Probate Code without change.

Background on Section 8200 of Repealed Code
Section 8200 was added by 1988 Cal.Stat. ch. 1199 § 81.5. The section superseded former Probate Code Section 320 (repealed by 1988 Cal.Stat. ch. 1199 § 40). Section 8200 required delivery of the original will in all cases, precluded charging a filing fee, and added a procedure for production of the delivered will. For background on the provisions of this part, see the Comment to this part under the part heading. [20 Cal.L.Rev.Comm.Reports 1001 (1990)].

Cross References
Contents of petition for probate of will, see Probate Code § 8002.
Creation, maintenance and preservation of trial court records, provisions not applicable to original wills and codicils, see Government Code § 68150.
Delivery of records and public papers to county clerk on death of notary public, see Government Code § 8209.
Destruction of court records, notice, retention periods, see Government Code § 68152.
Fee for delivering will to clerk of superior court as required by this section, see Government Code § 70626.
Reproduction of will held for at least 10 years by clerk of the superior court, see Government Code § 26810.

§ 8201. Order to produce
If, on petition to the superior court of the county in which the estate of the decedent is being or may be administered alleging that a person has possession of a decedent's will, the court is satisfied that the allegation is true, the court shall order the person to produce the will. *(Stats.1990, c. 79 (A.B.759), § 14, operative July 1, 1991.)*

Law Revision Commission Comments
1990 Enactment
Section 8201 continues Section 8201 of the repealed Probate Code without change. The court or judge has general authority to enforce the production of wills and the attendance of witnesses. See Section 7050 (authority of court or judge).

Background on Section 8201 of Repealed Code
Section 8201 was added by 1988 Cal.Stat. ch. 1199 § 81.5. The section restated a portion of former Probate Code Section 321 (repealed by 1988 Cal.Stat. ch. 1199 § 40). For background on the provisions of this part, see the Comment to this part under the part heading. [20 Cal.L.Rev.Comm.Reports 1001 (1990)].

Cross References
Orders,
Generally, see Probate Code § 1047 et seq.
Motions and orders, see Code of Civil Procedure § 1003 et seq.

§ 8202. Will detained in court of other state or country; certified copy; proof
If the will of a person who was domiciled in this state at the time of death is detained in a court of any other state or country and cannot be produced for probate in this state, a certified photographic copy of the will may be admitted to probate in this state with the same force and effect as the original will. The same proof shall be required as if the original will were produced. *(Stats.1990, c. 79 (A.B.759), § 14, operative July 1, 1991.)*

Law Revision Commission Comments
1990 Enactment
Section 8202 continues Section 8202 of the repealed Probate Code without change. Proof of a certified copy may be made in the same manner as proof of an original will. Thus the court may authorize a copy to be presented to the witnesses and the witnesses may be asked the same questions with respect to the copy as if the original will were present. See Article 2 (commencing with Section 8220) (proof of will). Proof may also be made by an affidavit in the will that incorporates an attestation clause. Section 8220(b) (evidence of subscribing witness).

Background on Section 8202 of Repealed Code
Section 8202 was added by 1988 Cal.Stat. ch. 1199 § 81.5. The section restated former Probate Code Section 330 (repealed by 1988 Cal.Stat. ch. 1199 § 40) with clarifications that domicile, rather than residence, is the determining factor and that a certified, rather than authenticated, copy of the will is necessary. For background on the provisions of this part, see the Comment to this part under the part heading. [20 Cal.L.Rev.Comm.Reports 1001 (1990)].

Cross References
Photographic copies,
Business records, see Evidence Code § 1550.
Public writings, see Evidence Code § 1551.

§ 8203. Transfers of wills between counties; petition; order; filing of copies
If a will has been delivered to the clerk of the superior court in a county in which no proceeding is pending to administer the testator's estate, that court may order the will transferred to the clerk of the superior court in a county in

which such a proceeding is pending. A petition for the transfer may be presented and heard without notice, but shall not be granted without proof that a copy of the petition has been mailed to the petitioner and any persons who have requested special notice in the proceeding in the court to which the will is to be transferred. The petition and order shall include the case number of the proceeding in the court to which transfer is prayed. Certified copies of the petition, any supporting documents, and the order shall be transmitted by the clerk along with the original will, and these copies shall be filed in the proceeding by the clerk of the recipient court. *(Added by Stats.1992, c. 871 (A.B.2975), § 10.)*

Cross References

Destruction of court records, notice, retention periods, see Government Code § 68152.

ARTICLE 2. PROOF OF WILL

Section
8220. Subscribing witness; affidavit; deposition.
8221. Subscribing witness unavailable; handwriting; witnesses' signatures; affidavit of person with personal knowledge.
8222. Holographic will.
8223. Lost or destroyed will.
8224. Preserving testimony; reporter's transcript; admissibility in subsequent proceeding.
8225. Admission of will to probate; recording in minutes; filing will.
8226. Conclusiveness of admission of will to probate; contest or petition for revocation; admission of subsequent will; prior distributions; petition for probate; time limits.

Cross References

Application of old and new law, see Probate Code § 3.

§ 8220. Subscribing witness; affidavit; deposition

Unless there is a contest of a will:

(a) The will may be proved on the evidence of one of the subscribing witnesses only, if the evidence shows that the will was executed in all particulars as prescribed by law.

(b) Evidence of execution of a will may be received by an affidavit of a subscribing witness to which there is attached a photographic copy of the will, or by an affidavit in the original will that includes or incorporates the attestation clause.

(c) If no subscribing witness resides in the county, but the deposition of a witness can be taken elsewhere, the court may direct the deposition to be taken. On the examination, the court may authorize a photographic copy of the will to be made and presented to the witness, and the witness may be asked the same questions with respect to the photographic copy as if the original will were present. *(Stats.1990, c. 79 (A.B.759), § 14, operative July 1, 1991.)*

Law Revision Commission Comments

1990 Enactment

Section 8220 continues Section 8220 of the repealed Probate Code without change. See also Section 6221.5 (California Statutory Will).

Background on Section 8220 of Repealed Code

Section 8220 was added by 1988 Cal.Stat. ch. 1199 § 81.5. The section restated the first two sentences of former Probate Code Section 329 (repealed by 1988 Cal.Stat. ch. 1199 § 40) and the last sentence of former Probate Code Section 1283 (enacted by 1987 Cal.Stat. ch. 923 § 60.5 and repealed by 1988 Cal.Stat. ch. 1199 § 64.5) without substantive change. Former Section 1283 continued former Probate Code Section 1233 (repealed by 1987 Cal.Stat. ch. 923 § 59) without change. For background on the provisions of this part, see the Comment to this part under the part heading. [20 Cal.L.Rev.Comm.Reports 1001 (1990)].

Cross References

Contests before probate, see Probate Code § 8004.
Depositions, see Code of Civil Procedure §§ 2004, 2025 et seq.
Execution, proof of, see Evidence Code §§ 1413, 1415.
Execution of wills, see Probate Code § 6110.
Foreign wills, see Probate Code § 12510 et seq.
Minute entry of admission to probate, see Probate Code § 8225.
Photographic copies, business records, see Evidence Code § 1550.
Private writings, see Code of Civil Procedure § 1929 et seq.
Witnesses,
    Generally, see Code of Civil Procedure § 1878.
    Experts, see Evidence Code §§ 721, 730 et seq., 802.
    Subscribing witness defined, see Code of Civil Procedure § 1935.

§ 8221. Subscribing witness unavailable; handwriting; witnesses' signatures; affidavit of person with personal knowledge

If no subscribing witness is available as a witness within the meaning of Section 240 of the Evidence Code, the court may, if the will on its face conforms to all requirements of law, permit proof of the will by proof of the handwriting of the testator and one of the following:

(a) Proof of the handwriting of any one subscribing witness.

(b) Receipt in evidence of one of the following documents reciting facts showing due execution of the will:

(1) A writing in the will bearing the signatures of all subscribing witnesses.

(2) An affidavit of a person with personal knowledge of the circumstances of the execution. *(Stats.1990, c. 79 (A.B. 759), § 14, operative July 1, 1991.)*

Law Revision Commission Comments

1990 Enactment

Section 8221 continues Section 8221 of the repealed Probate Code without change. If the subscribing witnesses are competent at the time of attesting the execution, their subsequent incompetency, from whatever cause, will not prevent the probate of the will if it is otherwise satisfactorily proved. Cf. Evid.Code § 240 ("unavailable as a witness").

Background on Section 8221 of Repealed Code

Section 8221 was added by 1988 Cal.Stat. ch. 1199 § 81.5. The section restated the fourth sentence of former Probate Code Section 329 (repealed by 1988 Cal.Stat. ch. 1199 § 40), except that the writing need not appear "at the end" of the will. The signatures of subscribing witnesses no longer must appear at the end. See Section 6110 (execution) and Comment thereto. For background on the provisions of this part, see the Comment to this part under the part heading. [20 Cal.L.Rev.Comm.Reports 1001 (1990)].

§ 8221

Cross References

Handwriting, proof, see Evidence Code § 1416.

§ 8222. Holographic will

A holographic will may be proved in the same manner as other writings. *(Stats.1990, c. 79 (A.B.759), § 14, operative July 1, 1991.)*

Law Revision Commission Comments

1990 Enactment

Section 8222 continues Section 8222 of the repealed Probate Code without change. See Evid.Code §§ 1400–1454 (authentication and proof of writings). See also Section 6111 (requirements for valid holographic will).

Background on Section 8222 of Repealed Code

Section 8222 was added by 1988 Cal.Stat. ch. 1199 § 81.5. The section restated former Probate Code Section 331 (repealed by 1988 Cal.Stat. ch. 1199 § 40) without substantive change. For background on the provisions of this part, see the Comment to this part under the part heading. [20 Cal.L.Rev.Comm.Reports 1001 (1990)].

Cross References

Form of holographic will, see Probate Code § 6111.
Private writings, generally, see Code of Civil Procedure § 1929 et seq.

§ 8223. Lost or destroyed will

The petition for probate of a lost or destroyed will shall include a written statement of the testamentary words or their substance. If the will is proved, the provisions of the will shall be set forth in the order admitting the will to probate. *(Stats.1990, c. 79 (A.B.759), § 14, operative July 1, 1991.)*

Law Revision Commission Comments

1990 Enactment

Section 8223 continues Section 8223 of the repealed Probate Code without change. See also Section 6124 (presumption that will that cannot be found after the testator's death was destroyed with intent to revoke it).

Background on Section 8223 of Repealed Code

Section 8223 was added by 1988 Cal.Stat. ch. 1199 § 81.5. The section restated the first two sentences of former Probate Code Section 351 (repealed by 1988 Cal.Stat. ch. 1199 § 40), except that the requirement that the order admitting the will to probate be "entered at length in the minutes" was omitted. For background on the provisions of this part, see the Comment to this part under the part heading. [20 Cal.L.Rev.Comm.Reports 1001 (1990)].

Cross References

Conclusiveness of order, see Code of Civil Procedure § 1908.
Contents of petition for probate, effect of defects, see Probate Code § 8002.
Contests of wills before and after probate, see Probate Code § 8004.
Recording of will on admission to probate, see Probate Code § 8225.

§ 8224. Preserving testimony; reporter's transcript; admissibility in subsequent proceeding

The testimony of each witness in a proceeding concerning the execution or provisions of a will, the testamentary capacity of the decedent, and other issues of fact, may be reduced to writing, signed by the witness, and filed, whether or not the will is contested. The testimony so preserved, or an official reporter's transcript of the testimony, is admissible in evidence in any subsequent proceeding concerning the will if the witness has become unavailable as a witness within the meaning of Section 240 of the Evidence Code. *(Stats.1990, c. 79 (A.B.759), § 14, operative July 1, 1991.)*

Law Revision Commission Comments

1990 Enactment

Section 8224 continues Section 8224 of the repealed Probate Code without change. See also Section 8220 (evidence of subscribing witness).

Background on Section 8224 of Repealed Code

Section 8224 was added by 1988 Cal.Stat. ch. 1199 § 81.5. The section restated and broadened former Probate Code Section 374 (will contests) (repealed by 1988 Cal.Stat. ch. 1199 § 42) and the last sentence of former Probate Code Section 351 (proof of lost or destroyed will) (repealed by 1988 Cal.Stat. ch. 1199 § 40). The former provisions were treated as permissive rather than mandatory in practice and by case law. For background on the provisions of this part, see the Comment to this part under the part heading. [20 Cal.L.Rev.Comm.Reports 1001 (1990)].

Cross References

Comments of court on evidence and credibility of witnesses, see Cal. Const. Art. 6, § 10.
Mode of taking testimony of witnesses, see Code of Civil Procedure § 2002 et seq.
Proceedings to perpetuate testimony, see Code of Civil Procedure § 2035 et seq.
Subscribing witness,
    Definition, see Code of Civil Procedure § 1935.
    Deposition, see Code of Civil Procedure § 2021.

§ 8225. Admission of will to probate; recording in minutes; filing will

When the court admits a will to probate, that fact shall be recorded in the minutes by the clerk and the will shall be filed. *(Stats.1990, c. 79 (A.B.759), § 14, operative July 1, 1991.)*

Law Revision Commission Comments

1990 Enactment

Section 8225 continues Section 8225 of the repealed Probate Code without change. See also Section 8002(b) (contents of petition).

Background on Section 8225 of Repealed Code

Section 8225 was added by 1988 Cal.Stat. ch. 1199 § 81.5. The section superseded the first sentence of former Probate Code Section 332 (repealed by 1988 Cal.Stat. ch. 1199 § 40). For background on the provisions of this part, see the Comment to this part under the part heading. [20 Cal.L.Rev.Comm.Reports 1001 (1990)].

§ 8226. Conclusiveness of admission of will to probate; contest or petition for revocation; admission of subsequent will; prior distributions; petition for probate; time limits

(a) If no person contests the validity of a will or petitions for revocation of probate of the will within the time provided in this chapter, admission of the will to probate is conclusive, subject to Section 8007.

(b) Subject to subdivision (c), a will may be admitted to probate notwithstanding prior admission to probate of another will or prior distribution of property in the proceeding.

The will may not affect property previously distributed, but the court may determine how any provision of the will affects property not yet distributed and how any provision of the will affects provisions of another will.

(c) If the proponent of a will has received notice of a petition for probate or a petition for letters of administration for a general personal representative, the proponent of the will may petition for probate of the will only within the later of either of the following time periods:

(1) One hundred twenty days after issuance of the order admitting the first will to probate or determining the decedent to be intestate.

(2) Sixty days after the proponent of the will first obtains knowledge of the will. *(Stats.1990, c. 79 (A.B.759), § 14, operative July 1, 1991. Amended by Stats.1997, c. 724 (A.B.1172), § 19.)*

Law Revision Commission Comments

1990 Enactment

Section 8226 continues Section 8226 of the repealed Probate Code without change. The conclusive effect under subdivision (a) of admission of a will to probate does not apply in case of extrinsic fraud or other jurisdictional defects. See Section 8007. See also, e.g., Estate of Sanders, 40 Cal.3d 607, 710 P.2d 232, 221 Cal.Rptr. 432 (1985) (extrinsic fraud). The time within which a contest must be made is before or at the hearing (Section 1043), and the time within which revocation of probate may be sought is 120 days after the will is admitted or, in the case of a minor or incompetent person, before the close of estate administration (Section 8270).

Subdivision (b) is consistent with Estate of Moore, 180 Cal. 570, 182 P. 285 (1919) (admission of will does not preclude probate of another will). If more than one will is admitted to probate, the court should resolve any conflicts in provisions, including what provisions control nomination of an executor. Admission of a will to probate may not affect property previously distributed, but the court may order adjustments of gifts in light of a will later admitted to probate. The court may not, however, rescind a distribution once made as a result of a later discovery of a will.

One effect of subdivision (b) is to preclude probate of a will after close of administration as a general rule. In the case of after-discovered property, however, a later will would be admissible under subdivision (b) to govern distribution of the after-discovered property, notwithstanding Section 11642 (after-acquired or after-discovered property).

Background on Section 8226 of Repealed Code

Section 8226 was added by 1988 Cal.Stat. ch. 1199 § 81.5. Subdivision (a) restated the first portion of former Probate Code Section 384 (repealed by 1988 Cal.Stat. ch. 1199 § 42) without substantive change. Subdivision (b) superseded former Probate Code Section 385 (repealed by 1988 Cal.Stat. ch. 1199 § 42). For background on the provisions of this part, see the Comment to this part under the part heading. [20 Cal.L.Rev.Comm.Reports 1001 (1990)].

Cross References

Conclusiveness of judgment, see Code of Civil Procedure § 1908.
Subsequent probate, see Probate Code § 8504.
Subsequent will, effect, see Probate Code §§ 6120, 6123.

Time specified for contest of will, see Probate Code § 8270.

ARTICLE 3. CONTEST OF WILL

Section
8250. Summons; persons to be served; time for responsive pleading; executor's duty to defend.
8251. Joint or separate answer; demurrer; failure to respond timely to summons.
8252. Burden of proof; later will revoking former; contested issues of fact affecting validity.
8253. Subscribing witnesses; production and examination; unavailability; other witnesses.
8254. Court orders; judgment; appointment of personal representative.

Cross References

Application of old and new law, see Probate Code § 3.

§ 8250. Summons; persons to be served; time for responsive pleading; executor's duty to defend

(a) When a will is contested under Section 8004, the contestant shall file with the court an objection to probate of the will. Thereafter, a summons shall be issued and served, with a copy of the objection, on the persons required by Section 8110 to be served with notice of hearing of a petition for administration of the decedent's estate. The summons shall be issued and served as provided in Chapter 3 (commencing with Section 412.10) and Chapter 4 (commencing with Section 413.10) of Title 5 of Part 2 of the Code of Civil Procedure. The summons shall contain a direction that the persons summoned file with the court a written pleading in response to the contest within 30 days after service of the summons.

(b) A person named as executor in the will is under no duty to defend a contest until the person is appointed personal representative. *(Stats.1990, c. 79 (A.B.759), § 14, operative July 1, 1991. Amended by Stats.1998, c. 581 (A.B.2801), § 24; Stats.2011, c. 308 (S.B.647), § 11.)*

Law Revision Commission Comments

1990 Enactment

Section 8250 continues Section 8250 of the repealed Probate Code without substantive change. Subdivision (a) is revised to make clear that a will contest is initiated by filing an objection to probate of the will. Service of the summons must be made in the manner provided by law for service of summons in a civil action. Section 1000 (general rules of practice). Section 8250 does not limit the persons to be notified, and thus requires notice to all affected persons wherever residing, including minors and incompetents. Failure of a person to respond precludes the person from further participating in the contest but does not otherwise affect the person's interest. Section 8251 (responsive pleading).

Background on Section 8250 of Repealed Code

Section 8250 was added by 1988 Cal.Stat. ch. 1199 § 81.5. The section restated the last portion of the first sentence of former Probate Code Section 370 (repealed by 1988 Cal.Stat. ch. 1199 § 42), but replaced the citation with a summons. For background on the provisions of this part, see the Comment to this part under the part heading. [20 Cal.L.Rev.Comm.Reports 1001 (1990)].

Fees for filing papers in probate proceedings, see Government Code § 70650.

§ 8251. Joint or separate answer; demurrer; failure to respond timely to summons

(a) The petitioner and any other interested person may jointly or separately answer the objection or demur to the objection within the time prescribed in the summons.

(b) Demurrer may be made on any of the grounds of demurrer available in a civil action. If the demurrer is sustained, the court may allow the contestant a reasonable time, not exceeding 15 days, within which to amend the objection. If the demurrer is overruled, the petitioner and other interested persons may, within 15 days thereafter, answer the objection.

(c) If a person fails timely to respond to the summons:

(1) The case is at issue notwithstanding the failure and the case may proceed on the petition and other documents filed by the time of the hearing, and no further pleadings by other persons are necessary.

(2) The person may not participate further in the contest, but the person's interest in the estate is not otherwise affected. Nothing in this paragraph precludes further participation by the petitioner.

(3) The person is bound by the decision in the proceeding. *(Stats.1990, c. 79 (A.B.759), § 14, operative July 1, 1991.)*

Law Revision Commission Comments

1990 Enactment

Section 8251 continues Section 8251 of the repealed Probate Code without substantive change. Subdivision (c)(2) is revised to make clear that failure to respond by the petitioner for probate of a will does not preclude the petitioner from further participation. Relief from a failure timely to respond or from a judgment in the will contest may be available under Code of Civil Procedure Section 473. See Section 1000 (general rules of practice).

Background on Section 8251 of Repealed Code

Section 8251 was added by 1988 Cal.Stat. ch. 1199 § 81.5. Subdivisions (a) and (b) restated the second, third, and fourth sentences of former Probate Code Section 370 (repealed by 1988 Cal.Stat. ch. 1199 § 42), but did not make receipt of written notice a condition for time to answer after a demurrer is overruled. Subdivision (c) was a new provision. For background on the provisions of this part, see the Comment to this part under the part heading. [20 Cal.L.Rev.Comm.Reports 1001 (1990)].

§ 8252. Burden of proof; later will revoking former; contested issues of fact affecting validity

(a) At the trial, the proponents of the will have the burden of proof of due execution. The contestants of the will have the burden of proof of lack of testamentary intent or capacity, undue influence, fraud, duress, mistake, or revocation. If the will is opposed by the petition for probate of a later will revoking the former, it shall be determined first whether the later will is entitled to probate.

(b) The court shall try and determine any contested issue of fact that affects the validity of the will. *(Stats.1990, c. 79 (A.B.759), § 14, operative July 1, 1991.)*

Law Revision Commission Comments

1990 Enactment

Section 8252 continues Section 8252 of the repealed Probate Code without change. Subdivision (a) is drawn from Uniform Probate Code Section 3–407 (1987). As to the construction of provisions drawn from uniform acts, see Section 2. Nothing in subdivision (a) precludes consolidation for trial of two wills offered for probate. Subdivision (b) eliminates jury trial in will contests. See also Section 7200 (right to trial by jury).

Background on Section 8252 of Repealed Code

Section 8252 was added by 1988 Cal.Stat. ch. 1199 § 81.5. The section superseded former Probate Code Section 371 (repealed by 1988 Cal.Stat. ch. 1199 § 42). Section 8252 eliminated the jury trial in will contests. A jury trial is not constitutionally required. Under former law, there was a high percentage of reversals on appeal of jury verdicts, with the net result that the whole jury and appeal process served mainly to postpone enjoyment of the estate, enabling contestants as a practical matter to force compromise settlements to which they would not otherwise be entitled. See Recommendation Relating to Opening Estate Administration, 19 Cal.L.Revision Comm'n Reports 787, 793–94 (1988). For background on the provisions of this part, see the Comment to this part under the part heading. [20 Cal.L.Rev.Comm.Reports 1001 (1990)].

Cross References

Contests after probate, see Probate Code §§ 8271, 8272.
Issues of law, see Code of Civil Procedure § 591.
Questions of fact, see Evidence Code § 312.

§ 8253. Subscribing witnesses; production and examination; unavailability; other witnesses

At the trial, each subscribing witness shall be produced and examined. If no subscribing witness is available as a witness within the meaning of Section 240 of the Evidence Code, the court may admit the evidence of other witnesses to prove the due execution of the will. *(Stats.1990, c. 79 (A.B.759), § 14, operative July 1, 1991.)*

Law Revision Commission Comments

1990 Enactment

Section 8253 continues Section 8253 of the repealed Probate Code without change. The court may admit proof of the handwriting of the testator and of any of the subscribing witnesses as evidence of the due execution of the will where no witness is available. See Section 8221 (proof where no subscribing witness available).

Background on Section 8253 of Repealed Code

Section 8253 was added by 1988 Cal.Stat. ch. 1199 § 81.5. The section restated former Probate Code Section 372 (repealed by 1988 Cal.Stat. ch. 1199 § 42) but did not continue the former limitation on production of witnesses outside the county. See Section 1000 (general rules of practice); Code Civ.Proc. § 1989 (compelling attendance of witnesses). For background on the provisions of this part, see the Comment to this part under the part heading. [20 Cal.L.Rev.Comm.Report 1001 (1990)].

Cross References

Affidavit of subscribing witness in proceedings, see Probate Code § 8220.
Conclusiveness of probate where no one contests validity of will, see Probate Code § 8226.
Definitions,
  Affidavit, see Code of Civil Procedure § 2003.
  Deposition, see Code of Civil Procedure § 2004.

Depositions,
Generally, see Code of Civil Procedure § 2025 et seq.
Subscribing witnesses, see Probate Code § 8220.
Evidence of subscribing witnesses, see Probate Code § 8220.
Holographic will, proof of, see Probate Code § 8222.
Mode of taking testimony of witnesses, see Code of Civil Procedure § 2002 et seq.
Nondomiciliary decedent's will, probate, see Probate Code § 12510 et seq.
Service of summons in contests after probate, see Probate Code § 8271.
Use of certified copy of will when original is detained beyond jurisdiction of state, see Probate Code § 8202.
Witnesses,
Generally, see Probate Code § 6112.
Devises to, see Probate Code § 6112.
Holographic will, see Probate Code § 6111.
Number of, see Probate Code § 6110.

§ 8254. Court orders; judgment; appointment of personal representative

The court may make appropriate orders, including orders sustaining or denying objections, and shall render judgment either admitting the will to probate or rejecting it, in whole or in part, and appointing a personal representative. *(Stats. 1990, c. 79 (A.B.759), § 14, operative July 1, 1991.)*

Law Revision Commission Comments

1990 Enactment

Section 8254 continues Section 8254 of the repealed Probate Code without change.

Background on Section 8254 of Repealed Code

Section 8254 was added by 1988 Cal.Stat. ch. 1199 § 81.5. The section superseded former Probate Code Section 373 (repealed by 1988 Cal.Stat. ch. 1199 § 42). For background on the provisions of this part, see the Comment to this part under the part heading. [20 Cal.L.Rev.Comm.Reports 1001 (1990)].

Cross References

Conclusiveness of judgment, see Code of Civil Procedure § 1908.
Conduct of trial, generally, see Code of Civil Procedure § 607 et seq.
Decree of final distribution, conclusiveness, see Probate Code §§ 11603, 11605, 11641.
Enforcement of judgment in civil actions, see Code of Civil Procedure § 681.010 et seq.
Entry and enforcement of orders, see Probate Code §§ 1048, 1049.
General and special verdicts, see Code of Civil Procedure § 624 et seq.
Manner of giving and entering judgment, generally, see Code of Civil Procedure § 664 et seq.
Submitting a controversy without action, see Code of Civil Procedure § 1138 et seq.
Vacating verdict, grounds for, see Code of Civil Procedure § 657.

ARTICLE 4. REVOCATION OF PROBATE

Section
8270. Time to petition for revocation; eligible persons; contents of petition; minors or incompetent persons.
8271. Summons; persons to be served; time for responsive pleading; failure timely to respond; manner of service and proceedings.
8272. Sufficiency of proof; order revoking probate; effect of revocation; liability of personal representative; good faith transactions.

Cross References

Application of old and new law, see Probate Code § 3.

§ 8270. Time to petition for revocation; eligible persons; contents of petition; minors or incompetent persons

(a) Within 120 days after a will is admitted to probate, any interested person, other than a party to a will contest and other than a person who had actual notice of a will contest in time to have joined in the contest, may petition the court to revoke the probate of the will. The petition shall include objections setting forth written grounds of opposition.

(b) Notwithstanding subdivision (a), a person who was a minor or who was incompetent and had no guardian or conservator at the time a will was admitted to probate may petition the court to revoke the probate of the will at any time before entry of an order for final distribution. *(Stats.1990, c. 79 (A.B.759), § 14, operative July 1, 1991.)*

Law Revision Commission Comments

1990 Enactment

Section 8270 continues Section 8270 of the repealed Probate Code without change. A will is admitted to probate when it is recorded in the minutes by the clerk. Section 8225 (admission of will to probate).

Background on Section 8270 of Repealed Code

Section 8270 was added by 1988 Cal.Stat. ch. 1199 § 81.5. Subdivision (a) restated former Probate Code Section 380 (repealed by 1988 Cal.Stat. ch. 1199 § 42) but omitted reference to some of the specific grounds of opposition. Subdivision (b) superseded the last portion of former Probate Code Section 384 (repealed by 1988 Cal.Stat. ch. 1199 § 42). Subdivision (b) limited the previously indefinite right of minors and incompetents to petition for revocation. For background on the provisions of this part, see the Comment to this part under the part heading. [20 Cal.L.Rev.Comm.Reports 1001 (1990)].

Cross References

Conclusiveness of probate, see Probate Code § 8226.
Contests before probate, see Probate Code § 8250 et seq.
Fees for filing papers in probate proceedings, see Government Code § 70650.
Final order in a probate proceeding, see Code of Civil Procedure § 1908.
Jurisdiction and venue of probate proceedings, see Probate Code § 7050 et seq.
Revocation of probate, effect of, see Probate Code § 8272.

§ 8271. Summons; persons to be served; time for responsive pleading; failure timely to respond; manner of service and proceedings

(a) On the filing of the petition, a summons shall be directed to the personal representative and to the heirs and devisees of the decedent, so far as known to the petitioner. The summons shall contain a direction that the persons summoned file with the court a written pleading in response to the petition within 30 days after service of the summons. Failure of a person timely to respond to the summons precludes the person from further participation in the revocation proceeding, but does not otherwise affect the person's interest in the estate.

(b) The summons shall be issued and served with a copy of the petition and proceedings had as in the case of a contest of the will.

(c) If a person fails timely to respond to the summons:

(1) The case is at issue notwithstanding the failure and the case may proceed on the petition and other documents filed by the time of the hearing, and no further pleadings by other persons are necessary.

(2) The person may not participate further in the contest, but the person's interest in the estate is not otherwise affected.

(3) The person is bound by the decision in the proceeding. *(Stats.1990, c. 79 (A.B.759), § 14, operative July 1, 1991. Amended by Stats.1998, c. 581 (A.B.2801), § 25.)*

Law Revision Commission Comments

1990 Enactment

Section 8271 continues Section 8271 of the repealed Probate Code without change. The summons must be directed to the devisees mentioned in the will as to which revocation of probate is sought, as well as to heirs and any personal representative appointed by the court. The summons may be directed to minors or incompetent persons, or to the personal representative of a deceased person. For the burden of proof on proponents and contestants of the will, see Section 8252 (trial). Relief from a failure timely to respond or from a judgment in the will contest may be available under Code of Civil Procedure Section 473. See Section 1000 (general rules of practice).

Background on Section 8271 of Repealed Code

Section 8271 was added by 1988 Cal.Stat. ch. 1199 § 81.5. Subdivision (a) superseded former Probate Code Section 381 (repealed by 1988 Cal.Stat. ch. 1199 § 42), substituting a summons for the citation. The former requirement that the summons be issued within the time allowed for filing the petition was not continued. Subdivision (b) restated the first sentence of former Section 382 (repealed by 1988 Cal.Stat. ch. 1199 § 42), except that the provision for a jury trial was not continued. See Section 7200 (trial by jury). Subdivision (c) was a new provision. For background on the provisions of this part, see the Comment to this part under the part heading. [20 Cal.L.Rev.Comm.Reports 1001 (1990)].

Cross References

Guardians of minors and incompetents, see Probate Code § 1500 et seq.
Service of summons, see Probate Code § 8250.

§ 8272. Sufficiency of proof; order revoking probate; effect of revocation; liability of personal representative; good faith transactions

(a) If it appears on satisfactory proof that the will should be denied probate, the court shall revoke the probate of the will.

(b) Revocation of probate of a will terminates the powers of the personal representative. The personal representative is not liable for any otherwise proper act done in good faith before the revocation, nor is any transaction void by reason of the revocation if entered into with a third person dealing in good faith and for value. *(Stats.1990, c. 79 (A.B.759), § 14, operative July 1, 1991.)*

Law Revision Commission Comments

1990 Enactment

Section 8272 continues Section 8272 of the repealed Probate Code without change. Subdivision (b) is consistent with Section 8406 (reversal of order appointing personal representative).

Background on Section 8272 of Repealed Code

Section 8272 was added by 1988 Cal.Stat. ch. 1199 § 81.5. The section restated the second, third, and fourth sentences of former Probate Code Section 382 (repealed by 1988 Cal.Stat. ch. 1199 § 42), except that the references to jury trial and invalidity of the will were not continued. See Section 7200 (trial by jury). Section 8272 also added protection for bona fide purchasers and encumbrancers for value. For background on the provisions of this part, see the Comment to this part under the part heading. [20 Cal.L.Rev.Comm.Reports 1001 (1990)].

Cross References

Contests before probate, see Probate Code § 8250 et seq.
Rules of practice, see Probate Code § 1000 et seq.
Service of summons, generally, see Code of Civil Procedure § 413.10 et seq.

CHAPTER 4.   APPOINTMENT OF PERSONAL REPRESENTATIVE

Cross References

Application of old and new law, see Probate Code § 3.
Counsel for public administrator appointed pursuant to this chapter, see Government Code § 27643.

ARTICLE 1.   GENERAL PROVISIONS

§ 8400. Power to administer estate; appointment effective upon issuance of letters; named executor; funeral expenses; preservation of estate

(a) A person has no power to administer the estate until the person is appointed personal representative and the appointment becomes effective. Appointment of a personal representative becomes effective when the person appointed is issued letters.

(b) Subdivision (a) applies whether or not the person is named executor in the decedent's will, except that a person named executor in the decedent's will may, before the appointment is made or becomes effective, pay funeral expenses and take necessary measures for the maintenance and preservation of the estate.

(c) The order appointing a personal representative shall state in capital letters on the first page of the order, in at least 12–point type, the following: "WARNING: THIS APPOINTMENT IS NOT EFFECTIVE UNTIL LETTERS HAVE ISSUED." *(Stats.1990, c. 79 (A.B.759), § 14, operative July 1, 1991. Amended by Stats.1996, c. 862 (A.B.2751), § 16.)*

Law Revision Commission Comments
1990 Enactment

Section 8400 continues Section 8400 of the repealed Probate Code without change. Letters may not be issued until the person appointed takes the oath of office and gives any required bond. See Section 8403 (oath) and Article 5 (commencing with Section 8480) (bond). It should be noted that a petitioner for appointment as personal representative may deliver or deposit property of the decedent in the petitioner's possession in a controlled account. See Section 8401. A person named executor in the will is under no duty to defend a contest of the will until appointment as executor. See Section 8250 (summons). See also Sections 300–301 (trust company as personal representative), 9605 (appointment does not discharge any claim the decedent has against personal representative).

Background on Section 8400 of Repealed Code

Section 8400 was added by 1988 Cal.Stat. ch. 1199 § 81.5. The section restated former Probate Code Section 400 (repealed by 1988 Cal.Stat. ch. 1199 § 43) without substantive change. For background on the provisions of this part, see the Comment to this part under the part heading. [20 Cal.L.Rev.Comm.Reports 1001 (1990)].

Cross References

Custody and duty of interment of decedent, see Health and Safety Code § 7100 et seq.
Personal representatives, powers and duties generally, see Probate Code § 9600 et seq.
Special administrators, nature and extent of functions, see Probate Code § 8540 et seq.
Time for payment of funeral expenses, see Probate Code § 11421.

§ 8401. Petitioner for appointment; deposit of property in institution; written receipt; withdrawal; liability of institution

(a) Notwithstanding Section 8400, a petitioner for appointment as personal representative may deliver property in the petitioner's possession to a trust company or financial institution for deposit, or allow a trust company or financial institution to retain on deposit property already in its possession, as provided in Chapter 3 (commencing with Section 9700) of Part 5.

(b) The petitioner shall obtain and file with the court a written receipt including the agreement of the trust company or financial institution that the property on deposit, including any earnings thereon, shall not be allowed to be withdrawn except on order of the court.

(c) In receiving and retaining property under this section, the trust company or financial institution is protected to the same extent as though it had received the property from a person who had been appointed personal representative. *(Stats.1990, c. 79 (A.B.759), § 14, operative July 1, 1991.)*

Law Revision Commission Comments
1990 Enactment

Section 8401 continues Section 8401 of the repealed Probate Code without change. See also Section 8483 (reduction of bond by deposit of assets).

Background on Section 8401 of Repealed Code

Section 8401 was added by 1988 Cal.Stat. ch. 1199 § 81.5. The section restated subdivision (b) of former Probate Code Section 541.1 (repealed by 1988 Cal.Stat. ch. 1199 § 48) and extended the coverage of the section to include "personal property" in addition to "money" and "securities." Section 8401 was amended by 1989 Cal.Stat. ch. 544 § 6 to refer to the procedures in Sections 9700–9705 for depositing money in an insured account in a financial institution and depositing personal property with a trust company. This continued a provision of former Section 541.1(b). For background on the provisions of this part, see the Comment to this part under the part heading. [20 Cal.L.Rev.Comm.Reports 1001 (1990)].

Cross References

Deposits on court order, reduction of bond, see Financial Code § 1586.

§ 8402. Persons ineligible for appointment; minors; incapable persons; grounds for removal existing; non-U.S. residents; surviving business partner

(a) Notwithstanding any other provision of this chapter, a person is not competent to act as personal representative in any of the following circumstances:

(1) The person is under the age of majority.

(2) The person is subject to a conservatorship of the estate or is otherwise incapable of executing, or is otherwise unfit to execute, the duties of the office.

(3) There are grounds for removal of the person from office under Section 8502.

(4) The person is not a resident of the United States.

(5) The person is a surviving business partner of the decedent and an interested person objects to the appointment.

(b) Paragraphs (4) and (5) of subdivision (a) do not apply to a person named as executor or successor executor in the decedent's will. *(Stats.1990, c. 79 (A.B.759), § 14, operative July 1, 1991. Amended by Stats.2016, c. 703 (A.B.2881), § 19, eff. Jan. 1, 2017.)*

Law Revision Commission Comments
1990 Enactment

Section 8402 continues Section 8402 of the repealed Probate Code without change. Paragraph (3) of subdivision (a) enables the court to deny appointment of a personal representative if the personal representative would be subject to removal, for example, for a conflict of interest that is sufficient to require removal. This would reverse the result in cases such as Estate of Backer, 164 Cal.App.3d 1159, 211 Cal.Rptr. 163 (1985). For contest of appointment, see Section 8004.

Background on Section 8402 of Repealed Code

Section 8402 was added by 1988 Cal.Stat. ch. 1199 § 81.5. Paragraph (a)(1) restated a provision of former Probate Code Section 401 (repealed by 1988 Cal.Stat. ch. 1199 § 43) without substantive change. Paragraph (a)(2) superseded the remainder of former Section 401. Paragraph (a)(3) was a new provision. Paragraph (a)(4) and subdivision (b) restated former Probate Code Section 420 (repealed by 1988 Cal.Stat. ch. 1199 § 45) without substantive change. Paragraph (a)(5) and subdivision (b) restated former Probate Code Section 421 (repealed by 1988 Cal.Stat. ch. 1199 § 45) without substantive change. For background on the provisions of this part, see the Comment to this part under the part heading. [20 Cal.L.Rev.Comm.Reports 1001 (1990)].

Cross References

Administrators, appointment of nominated persons, priority, considerations, nominees required to obtain a bond, resignation upon cessation of California residency, submission to jurisdiction of court, see Probate Code § 8465.
Challenge of competency of applicant for letters of administration, see Probate Code § 8004.
Corporations or trust companies as personal representatives, see Probate Code § 300.
Homicide, loss of rights to decedent's property, see Probate Code § 250 et seq.
Inventory and appraisal of partnership interest of decedent,
 Generally, see Probate Code § 8850.
 Administrators with will annexed, see Probate Code § 8440 et seq.
 Special administrators, see Probate Code § 8540 et seq.
Minor named as executor, see Probate Code § 8424.
Minors, definition, see Family Code § 6500.
Nonresident personal representative, see Probate Code § 8570 et seq.
Personal representatives and administrators,
 Bond, see Probate Code § 8480 et seq.
 Priority for appointment as administrator, see Probate Code § 8461 et seq.
 Probate of foreign wills, see Probate Code § 12510 et seq.
 Renouncement of right to appointment by failure to petition, see Probate Code § 8001.
 Suspension and removal, grounds for, see Probate Code § 8500 et seq.
 Vacancy, effect, see Probate Code § 8521 et seq.
Sale of partnership interest of decedent, see Probate Code § 10204.
Trust companies authorized to act as personal representatives, see Probate Code § 300.

§ 8403. Oath

(a) Before letters are issued, the personal representative shall take and subscribe an oath to perform, according to law, the duties of the office. The oath may be taken and dated on or after the time the petition for appointment as personal representative is signed, and may be filed with the clerk at any time after the petition is granted.

(b) The oath constitutes an acceptance of the office and shall be attached to or endorsed on the letters. *(Stats.1990, c. 79 (A.B.759), § 14, operative July 1, 1991.)*

Law Revision Commission Comments
1990 Enactment

Section 8403 continues Section 8403 of the repealed Probate Code without change. The requirement of an oath may be satisfied by a written affirmation. See Code Civ.Proc. § 2015.6. See also Adams v. Sharp, 61 Cal.2d 775, 394 P.2d 943, 40 Cal.Rptr. 255 (1964) (oath taken out of state).

Background on Section 8403 of Repealed Code

Section 8403 was added by 1988 Cal.Stat. ch. 1199 § 81.5. The section restated former Probate Code Section 540 (repealed by 1988 Cal.Stat. ch. 1199 § 48) but permitted the oath to be signed at the time the petition is signed. For background on the provisions of this part, see the Comment to this part under the part heading. [20 Cal.L.Rev.Comm.Reports 1001 (1990)].

Cross References

Form of letters, see Probate Code § 8405.
Public administrator, official oath in lieu of personal representative's oath, see Probate Code § 7621.
Special administrator, oath, see Probate Code § 8542.
Trust companies, oath, see Probate Code § 301.

§ 8404. Statement of duties and liabilities of personal representative; acknowledgment of receipt; form of statement; supersedure by law

(a) Before letters are issued, the personal representative (other than a trust company or a public administrator) shall file an acknowledgment of receipt of a statement of duties and liabilities of the office of personal representative. The statement shall be in the form prescribed by the Judicial Council.

(b) The court may by local rule require the acknowledgment of receipt to include the personal representative's birth date and driver's license number, if any, provided that the court ensures their confidentiality.

(c) The statement of duties and liabilities prescribed by the Judicial Council does not supersede the law on which the statement is based. *(Stats.1990, c. 79 (A.B.759), § 14, operative July 1, 1991. Amended by Stats.1994, c. 806 (A.B.3686), § 26.)*

Law Revision Commission Comments
1990 Enactment

Section 8404 continues Section 8404 of the repealed Probate Code with the following revisions:

(1) Subdivision (a) has been revised to except the public administrator from the requirement of filing an acknowledgment of receipt of the statement of duties and liabilities.

(2) The second sentence of subdivision (a) has been revised to eliminate the reference to the form provided in former subdivision (c).

(3) The form stating the personal representative's duties and liabilities in former subdivision (c) has been omitted because the form was superseded by the Judicial Council Form DE 147 (July 1, 1989).

Although the statement of duties and liabilities must be in the form prescribed by the Judicial Council, the attorney for the personal representative may supplement, explain, or otherwise address the subject matter separately, where appropriate.

Background on Section 8404 of Repealed Code

Section 8404 was added by 1988 Cal.Stat. ch. 1199 § 81.5. The section was a new provision drawn from general instructions given to personal representatives by a number of courts. Section 8404 was amended by 1989 Cal.Stat. ch. 21 § 17 to amend item 4 in subdivision (c) to conform with Section 8800. See Communication from the California Law Revision Commission Concerning Assembly Bill 156, 20 Cal.L.Revision Comm'n Reports 227, 230 (1990). For background on the provisions of this part, see the Comment to this part under the part heading. [20 Cal.L.Rev.Comm.Reports 1001 (1990)].

§ 8405. Letters; contents

Letters shall be signed by the clerk under the seal of the court and shall include:

(a) The county from which the letters are issued.

(b) The name of the person appointed as personal representative and whether the personal representative is an executor, administrator, administrator with the will annexed, or special administrator.

(c) A notation whether the personal representative is authorized to act under the Independent Administration of Estates Act (Part 6 (commencing with Section 10400) of Division 7), and if so authorized whether the independent administration authority includes or excludes the power to do any of the following:

(1) Sell real property.

(2) Exchange real property.

(3) Grant an option to purchase real property.

(4) Borrow money with the loan secured by an encumbrance upon real property. *(Stats.1990, c. 79 (A.B.759), § 14, operative July 1, 1991.)*

Law Revision Commission Comments
1990 Enactment

Section 8405 continues Section 8405 of the repealed Probate Code with the addition of the requirement in subdivision (c) that the letters include a notation whether the independent administration authority includes or excludes the power to borrow money with the loan secured by an encumbrance upon real property. This is consistent with subdivision (c) of Section 10452 of the repealed Probate Code, which is superseded by subdivision (c) of Section 8405, and with subdivision (b) of Section 10501. The Judicial Council may prescribe the form of letters. See Section 1001 (Judicial Council and local court rules). See also Section 10454 (new letters to be issued when court orders limits or revokes independent administration authority).

Background on Section 8405 of Repealed Code

Section 8405 was added by 1988 Cal.Stat. ch. 1199 § 81.5. The section superseded former Probate Code Sections 500, 501, and 502 (provisions repealed by 1988 Cal.Stat. ch. 1199 § 47). The section was amended by 1989 Cal.Stat. ch. 21 § 18 to conform with Sections 10403 (limited authority) and 10452 (endorsement on letters) of the repealed Probate Code. See Communication from the California Law Revision Commission Concerning Assembly Bill 156, 20 Cal.L.Revision Comm'n Reports 227, 230 (1990). For background on the provisions of this part, see the Comment to this part under the part heading. [20 Cal.L.Rev.Comm.Reports 1001 (1990)].

Cross References

Documents to which seal must be affixed, see Code of Civil Procedure § 153.

§ 8406. Repealed by Stats.1997, c. 724 (A.B.1172), § 20

ARTICLE 2. EXECUTORS

Section
8420. Right to appointment as personal representative.
8421. Person apparently intended as executor by will; right to appointment as personal representative.
8422. Power in will to designate executor or coexecutor; bond; designation; executor authority to name coexecutor or successor.

Section
8423. Trust company named as executor; sale to, merger with, etc., another trust company.
8424. Minor named as executor.
8425. Court appointment of fewer than all persons named in will as executors; authority of appointees.

Cross References

Application of old and new law, see Probate Code § 3.

§ 8420. Right to appointment as personal representative

The person named as executor in the decedent's will has the right to appointment as personal representative. *(Stats. 1990, c. 79 (A.B.759), § 14, operative July 1, 1991.)*

Law Revision Commission Comments
1990 Enactment

Section 8420 continues Section 8420 of the repealed Probate Code without change. This section is an express statement of the concept that the named executor has first priority for appointment as personal representative. The section does not apply if the person named is not qualified for appointment under Section 8402 (qualifications) or has waived the right to appointment. See also Section 9605 (appointment does not discharge any claim the decedent has against personal representative).

Background on Section 8420 of Repealed Code

Section 8420 was a new provision added by 1988 Cal.Stat. ch. 1199 § 81.5. Cf. former Probate Code Section 407 (repealed by 1988 Cal.Stat. ch. 1199 § 43). For background on the provisions of this part, see the Comment to this part under the part heading. [20 Cal.L.Rev.Comm.Reports 1001 (1990)].

§ 8421. Person apparently intended as executor by will; right to appointment as personal representative

If a person is not named as executor in a will but it appears by the terms of the will that the testator intended to commit the execution of the will and the administration of the estate to the person, the person is entitled to appointment as personal representative in the same manner as if named as executor. *(Stats.1990, c. 79 (A.B.759), § 14, operative July 1, 1991.)*

Law Revision Commission Comments
1990 Enactment

Section 8421 continues Section 8421 of the repealed Probate Code without change.

Background on Section 8421 of Repealed Code

Section 8421 was added by 1988 Cal.Stat. ch. 1199 § 81.5. The section restated former Probate Code Section 402 (repealed by 1988 Cal.Stat. ch. 1199 § 43) without substantive change. For background on the provisions of this part, see the Comment to this part under the part heading. [20 Cal.L.Rev.Comm.Reports 1001 (1990)].

Cross References

Interpretation of wills, see Probate Code § 21102 et seq.
Priority of appointment of administrator, see Probate Code § 8461.

§ 8422. Power in will to designate executor or coexecutor; bond; designation; executor authority to name coexecutor or successor

(a) The testator may by will confer on a person the power to designate an executor or coexecutor, or successor executor or coexecutor. The will may provide that the persons so designated may serve without bond.

(b) A designation shall be in writing and filed with the court. Unless the will provides otherwise, if there are two or more holders of the power to designate, the designation shall be unanimous, unless one of the holders of the power is unable or unwilling to act, in which case the remaining holder or holders may exercise the power.

(c) Except as provided in this section, an executor does not have authority to name a coexecutor, or a successor executor or coexecutor. *(Stats.1990, c. 79 (A.B.759), § 14, operative July 1, 1991.)*

Law Revision Commission Comments

1990 Enactment

Section 8422 continues Section 8422 of the repealed Probate Code without change. An executor designated under this section must be appointed by the court. See Section 8400 (appointment necessary).

Background on Section 8422 of Repealed Code

Section 8422 was added by 1988 Cal.Stat. ch. 1199 § 81.5. The section restated former Probate Code Section 403 (repealed by 1988 Cal.Stat. ch. 1199 § 43) without substantive change. For background on the provisions of this part, see the Comment to this part under the part heading. [20 Cal.L.Rev.Comm.Reports 1001 (1990)].

§ 8423. Trust company named as executor; sale to, merger with, etc., another trust company

If the executor named in the will is a trust company that has sold its business and assets to, has consolidated or merged with, or is in any manner provided by law succeeded by, another trust company, the court may, and to the extent required by the Banking Law (Division 1 (commencing with Section 99) of the Financial Code) shall, appoint the successor trust company as executor. *(Stats.1990, c. 79 (A.B.759), § 14, operative July 1, 1991.)*

Law Revision Commission Comments

1990 Enactment

Section 8423 continues Section 8423 of the repealed Probate Code without change. A trust company is an entity that has qualified to engage in and conduct a trust business in this state. A trust company may act as an executor. See Sections 83, 300; Fin.Code § 1580.

Background on Section 8423 of Repealed Code

Section 8423 was added by 1988 Cal.Stat. ch. 1199 § 81.5. The section restated former Probate Code Section 404 (repealed by 1988 Cal.Stat. ch. 1199 § 43) without substantive change. For background on the provisions of this part, see the Comment to this part under the part heading. [20 Cal.L.Rev.Comm.Reports 1001 (1990)].

Cross References

Trust companies authorized to act as personal representatives, see Probate Code § 300; Financial Code § 1580.

§ 8424. Minor named as executor

(a) If a person named as executor is under the age of majority and there is another person named as executor, the other person may be appointed and may administer the estate until the majority of the minor, who may then be appointed as coexecutor.

(b) If a person named as executor is under the age of majority and there is no other person named as executor,

another person may be appointed as personal representative, but the court may revoke the appointment on the majority of the minor, who may then be appointed as executor. *(Stats. 1990, c. 79 (A.B.759), § 14, operative July 1, 1991.)*

Law Revision Commission Comments

1990 Enactment

Section 8424 continues Section 8424 of the repealed Probate Code without change. The court may exercise its discretion under this section.

Background on Section 8424 of Repealed Code

Section 8424 was added by 1988 Cal.Stat. ch. 1199 § 81.5. The section restated without substantive change the portion of former Probate Code Section 405 (repealed by 1988 Cal.Stat. ch. 1199 § 43) that related to a minor named as executor. For background on the provisions of this part, see the Comment to this part under the part heading. [20 Cal.L.Rev.Comm.Reports 1001 (1990)].

Cross References

Joint personal representatives,
   Vacancy of fewer than all personal representatives, see Probate Code §§ 8521, 9630.
   Vacancy where no personal representatives remain, see Probate Code § 8522.
Letters, contents, see Probate Code § 8405.
Minor, definition, see Family Code § 6500.
Multiple executors, authority of those remaining where one or more absent or disqualified, see Probate Code § 9630.

§ 8425. Court appointment of fewer than all persons named in will as executors; authority of appointees

If the court does not appoint all the persons named in the will as executors, those appointed have the same authority to act in every respect as all would have if appointed. *(Stats. 1990, c. 79 (A.B.759), § 14, operative July 1, 1991.)*

Law Revision Commission Comments

1990 Enactment

Section 8425 continues Section 8425 of the repealed Probate Code without change.

Background on Section 8425 of Repealed Code

Section 8425 was added by 1988 Cal.Stat. ch. 1199 § 81.5. The section restated former Probate Code Section 408 (repealed by 1988 Cal.Stat. ch. 1199 § 43) without substantive change. For background on the provisions of this part, see the Comment to this part under the part heading. [20 Cal.L.Rev.Comm.Reports 1001 (1990)].

Cross References

Multiple executors, authority of those remaining where one or more absent or disqualified, see Probate Code § 9630.

ARTICLE 3. ADMINISTRATORS WITH THE WILL ANNEXED

Application of old and new law, see Probate Code § 3.

§ 8440. Appointment as personal representative; no executor named; named executors waive right or are unwilling or unable

An administrator with the will annexed shall be appointed as personal representative if no executor is named in the will or if the sole executor or all the executors named in the will have waived the right to appointment or are for any reason unwilling or unable to act. *(Stats.1990, c. 79 (A.B.759), § 14, operative July 1, 1991.)*

Law Revision Commission Comments

1990 Enactment

Section 8440 continues Section 8440 of the repealed Probate Code without change. A person named as an executor may be unwilling or unable to act because the person is dead or incompetent, renounces or fails to petition for appointment, fails to appear and qualify, or dies or is removed from office after appointment and before the completion of administration.

No executor of a deceased executor is, as such, authorized to administer the estate of the first testator. Section 8522 (vacancy where no personal representatives remain). However, the deceased executor may have the power to designate a successor executor. See Section 8422 (power to designate executor). And the executor of the deceased executor may qualify independently for appointment as an administrator with the will annexed under this section. See also Sections 300–301 (trust company as personal representative), 9605 (appointment does not discharge any claim the decedent has against personal representative).

Background on Section 8440 of Repealed Code

Section 8440 was added by 1988 Cal.Stat. ch. 1199 § 81.5. The section superseded former Probate Code Section 406 (repealed by 1988 Cal.Stat. ch. 1199 § 43). For background on the provisions of this part, see the Comment to this part under the part heading. [20 Cal.L.Rev.Comm.Reports 1001 (1990)].

Cross References
Joint personal representatives,
    Death of one or more, see Probate Code §§ 8521, 9630.
    Vacancy in office, see Probate Code § 8522.
Jurisdictional limitation on foreign executor's authority, see Code of Civil Procedure § 1913.
Renouncement of right to appointment by failure to petition, see Probate Code § 8001.

§ 8441. Priority for appointment

(a) Except as provided in subdivision (b), persons and their nominees are entitled to appointment as administrator with the will annexed in the same order of priority as for appointment of an administrator.

(b) A person who takes under the will has priority over a person who does not, but the court in its discretion may give priority to a person who does not take under the will if the person is entitled to a statutory interest that is a substantially greater portion of the estate than the devise to the person who takes under the will and the priority appears appropriate under the circumstances. A person who takes more than 50 percent of the value of the estate under the will or the person's nominee, or the nominee of several persons who together take more than 50 percent of the value of the estate under the will, has priority over other persons who take under

the will. *(Stats.1990, c. 79 (A.B.759), § 14, operative July 1, 1991.)*

Law Revision Commission Comments

1990 Enactment

Section 8441 continues Section 8441 of the repealed Probate Code without change. For priority for appointment of an administrator, see Section 8461. Subdivision (b) gives priority to devisees, who need not be entitled to succeed to all or part of the estate under the law of succession in order to have priority. However, subdivision (b) also gives the court discretion to disregard the priority of a devisee in an appropriate case where another person would take a substantial statutory intestate or omitted heir share. See also Sections 140–147 (surviving spouse's waiver of rights at death), 9605 (appointment does not discharge claim decedent has against personal representative).

Background on Section 8441 of Repealed Code

Section 8441 was added by 1988 Cal.Stat. ch. 1199 § 81.5. The section superseded the second and third sentences of former Probate Code Section 409 (repealed by 1988 Cal.Stat. ch. 1199 § 43). The express references to nominees were new. For background on the provisions of this part, see the Comment to this part under the part heading. [20 Cal.L.Rev.Comm.Reports 1001 (1990)].

Cross References
Letters of administration with will annexed, form for, see Probate Code § 8405.
Joint personal representatives,
    Competency and priority of appointment, see Probate Code § 8402 et seq.
    Powers and duties, see Probate Code § 9630 et seq.
    Sales under direction of will, see Probate Code § 10000.

§ 8442. Authority over estate

(a) Subject to subdivision (b), an administrator with the will annexed has the same authority over the decedent's estate as an executor named in the will would have.

(b) If the will confers a discretionary power or authority on an executor that is not conferred by law and the will does not extend the power or authority to other personal representatives, the power or authority shall not be deemed to be conferred on an administrator with the will annexed, but the court in its discretion may authorize the exercise of the power or authority. *(Stats.1990, c. 79 (A.B.759), § 14, operative July 1, 1991.)*

Law Revision Commission Comments

1990 Enactment

Section 8442 continues Section 8442 of the repealed Probate Code without change. The acts of the administrator with the will annexed are as effectual for all purposes as the acts of an executor would be.

Background on Section 8442 of Repealed Code

Section 8442 was added by 1988 Cal.Stat. ch. 1199 § 81.5. The section restated the first sentence of former Probate Code Section 409 (repealed by 1988 Cal.Stat. ch. 1199 § 43), with the addition of court discretion to permit exercise of a discretionary power or authority. For background on the provisions of this part, see the Comment to this part under the part heading. [20 Cal.L.Rev.Comm.Reports 1001 (1990)].

Cross References

Successor personal representative, powers limited by this section, see Probate Code § 8524.

ARTICLE 4. ADMINISTRATORS

§ 8460. Intestate decedent; appointment of administrator; number

(a) If the decedent dies intestate, the court shall appoint an administrator as personal representative.

(b) The court may appoint one or more persons as administrator. *(Stats.1990, c. 79 (A.B.759), § 14, operative July 1, 1991.)*

Law Revision Commission Comments

1990 Enactment

Section 8460 continues Section 8460 of the repealed Probate Code without change. See also Section 9605 (appointment does not discharge any claim decedent has against personal representative).

Background on Section 8460 of Repealed Code

Section 8460 was added by 1988 Cal.Stat. ch. 1199 § 81.5. The section restated the introductory portion of subdivision (a) of former Probate Code Section 422 (repealed by 1988 Cal.Stat. ch. 1199 § 45) without substantive change. For background on the provisions of this part, see the Comment to this part under the part heading. [20 Cal.L.Rev.Comm.Reports 1001 (1990)].

§ 8461. Persons entitled to appointment; priority

Subject to the provisions of this article, a person in the following relation to the decedent is entitled to appointment as administrator in the following order of priority:

(a) Surviving spouse or domestic partner as defined in Section 37.

(b) Children.

(c) Grandchildren.

(d) Other issue.

(e) Parents.

(f) Brothers and sisters.

(g) Issue of brothers and sisters.

(h) Grandparents.

(i) Issue of grandparents.

(j) Children of a predeceased spouse or domestic partner.

(k) Other issue of a predeceased spouse or domestic partner.

(*l*) Other next of kin.

(m) Parents of a predeceased spouse or domestic partner.

(n) Issue of parents of a predeceased spouse or domestic partner.

(*o*) Conservator or guardian of the estate acting in that capacity at the time of death who has filed a first account and is not acting as conservator or guardian for any other person.

(p) Public administrator.

(q) Creditors.

(r) Any other person. *(Stats.1990, c. 79 (A.B.759), § 14, operative July 1, 1991. Amended by Stats.1990, c. 710 (S.B.1775), § 20, operative July 1, 1991; Stats.2001, c. 893 (A.B.25), § 53.)*

Law Revision Commission Comments

1990 Enactment

Section 8461 continues Section 8461 of the repealed Probate Code without change. The general order of priority prescribed in Section 8461 is subject to limitation in the succeeding sections of this article. See, e.g., Sections 8462 (priority of relatives), 8463 (surviving spouse). A person appointed must be legally competent. See Section 8402 (qualifications). See also Sections 140–147 (surviving spouse's waiver of rights at death), 300–301 (trust company as personal representative), 12252 (appointment where subsequent administration necessary after personal representative has been discharged), 12513 (priority of sister state personal representative).

1990 Amendment

Section 8461 (enacted as a part of the new Probate Code by 1990 Cal.Stat. ch. 79 § 14) was amended by 1990 Cal.Stat. ch. 710 § 20. The amendment revised subdivision (*o*) to limit the priority for a conservator or guardian of the estate to the case where a first account has been filed (Section 2620) and the conservator or guardian is not acting in that capacity for any other person. See also Section 8469 (court discretion to give priority to conservator or guardian where requirements of Section 8461 not met). For background on the 1990 amendment, see Recommendation Relating to Priority of Conservator or Guardian for Appointment as Administrator, 20 Cal.L.Revision Comm'n Reports 607 (1990). [20 Cal.L.Rev.Comm.Reports 1001 (1990)].

Background on Section 8461 of Repealed Code

Section 8461 was added by 1988 Cal.Stat. ch. 1199 § 81.5. The section restated a portion of subdivision (a) of former Probate Code Section 422 (repealed by 1988 Cal.Stat. ch. 1199 § 45), with the addition of subdivisions (d), (g), (h), and (i) to reflect changes in the law governing intestate succession. See Section 6402 (intestate share of heirs other than surviving spouse). Section 8461 was amended by 1989 Cal.Stat. ch. 544 § 8 to conform the priorities for appointment as administrator more closely to the priorities to take from the decedent by intestate succession. See Section 6402. For background on the provisions of this part, see the Comment to this part under the part heading. [20 Cal.L.Rev.Comm.Reports 1001 (1990)].

Cross References

Executor, administrator with will annexed, see Probate Code § 8440.

Failure of persons having priority to claim appointment, see Probate Code § 8468.

Preference in appointment of special administrator, see Probate Code § 8541.

Priority of appointment of administrators with will annexed, see Probate Code § 8441.

Public administrators generally, see Probate Code § 7601 et seq.

Succession of persons to decedent's separate property, generally, see Probate Code § 6400 et seq.

Vacancy in office, order of appointment of successors, see Probate Code § 8522.

§ 8462. Surviving spouse or domestic partner, relative, or relative of predeceased spouse or domestic partner; conditions of priority

The surviving spouse or domestic partner of the decedent, a relative of the decedent, or a relative of a predeceased spouse or domestic partner of the decedent, has priority under Section 8461 only if one of the following conditions is satisfied:

(a) The surviving spouse, domestic partner, or relative is entitled to succeed to all or part of the estate.

(b) The surviving spouse, domestic partner, or relative either takes under the will of, or is entitled to succeed to all or part of the estate of, another deceased person who is entitled to succeed to all or part of the estate of the decedent. *(Stats.1990, c. 79 (A.B.759), § 14, operative July 1, 1991. Amended by Stats.2001, c. 893 (A.B.25), § 54.)*

Law Revision Commission Comments
1990 Enactment

Section 8462 continues Section 8462 of the repealed Probate Code without change. See also Sections 140–147 (surviving spouse's waiver of rights at death).

Background on Section 8462 of Repealed Code

Section 8462 was added by 1988 Cal.Stat. ch. 1199 § 81.5. The section restated subdivision (b) of former Probate Code Section 422 (repealed by 1988 Cal.Stat. ch. 1199 § 45) with the addition of language recognizing the priority of relatives of a predeceased spouse and the expansion of subdivision (b) to include any relative of the decedent who satisfies the prescribed conditions. For background on the provisions of this part, see the Comment to this part under the part heading. [20 Cal.L.Rev.Comm.Reports 1001 (1990)].

§ 8463. Surviving spouse; living apart and party to action for separate maintenance, annulment, or dissolution; priority

If the surviving spouse is a party to an action for separate maintenance, annulment, or dissolution of the marriage of the decedent and the surviving spouse, and was living apart from the decedent on the date of the decedent's death, the surviving spouse has priority next after brothers and sisters and not the priority prescribed in Section 8461. *(Stats.1990, c. 79 (A.B.759), § 14, operative July 1, 1991.)*

Law Revision Commission Comments
1990 Enactment

Section 8463 continues Section 8463 of the repealed Probate Code without change. There is an inherent conflict of interest between the surviving spouse and other heirs of the decedent in the situation described in this section. As to the surviving spouse's waiver of rights at death, see Sections 140–147.

Background on Section 8463 of Repealed Code

Section 8463 was added by 1988 Cal.Stat. ch. 1199 § 81.5. The section superseded subdivision (a)(6) and the second paragraph of subdivision (a)(1) of former Probate Code Section 422 (repealed by 1988 Cal.Stat. ch. 1199 § 45). For background on the provisions of this part, see the Comment to this part under the part heading. [20 Cal.L.Rev.Comm.Reports 1001 (1990)].

§ 8464. Minor; appointment of guardian or conservator

If a person otherwise entitled to appointment as administrator is a person under the age of majority or a person for whom a guardian or conservator of the estate has been appointed, the court in its discretion may appoint the guardian or conservator or another person entitled to appointment. *(Stats.1990, c. 79 (A.B.759), § 14, operative July 1, 1991.)*

Law Revision Commission Comments
1990 Enactment

Section 8464 continues Section 8464 of the repealed Probate Code without change.

Background on Section 8464 of Repealed Code

Section 8464 was added by 1988 Cal.Stat. ch. 1199 § 81.5. The section restated former Probate Code Section 426 (repealed by 1988 Cal.Stat. ch. 1199 § 45) without substantive change. For background on the provisions of this part, see the Comment to this part under the part heading. [20 Cal.L.Rev.Comm.Reports 1001 (1990)].

Cross References

Powers and duties of guardians to appear for minors and incompetents, see Code of Civil Procedure § 372.

§ 8465. Appointment of nominated persons; priority; considerations; nominees required to obtain a bond; resignation upon cessation of California residency; submission to jurisdiction of court

(a) The court may appoint as administrator a person nominated by any of the following persons:

(1) A person otherwise entitled to appointment.

(2) A person who would otherwise be entitled for appointment but who is ineligible for appointment under paragraph (4) of subdivision (a) of Section 8402 because he or she is not a resident of the United States.

(3) The guardian or conservator of the estate of a person otherwise entitled to appointment. The nomination shall be made in writing and filed with the court.

(b) If a person making a nomination for appointment of an administrator is the surviving spouse or domestic partner, child, grandchild, other issue, parent, brother or sister, or grandparent of the decedent, the nominee has priority next after those in the class of the person making the nomination.

(c) If a person making a nomination for appointment of an administrator is other than a person described in subdivision (b), the court in its discretion may appoint either the nominee or a person of a class lower in priority to that of the person making the nomination, but other persons of the class of the person making the nomination have priority over the nominee.

(d) If a person making a nomination for appointment of an administrator is a person described in paragraph (2) of subdivision (a), the court shall not appoint a nominee who is not a California resident to act as administrator. For California residents nominated under paragraph (2) of subdivision (a), the court shall consider whether the nominee is capable of faithfully executing the duties of the office. The court may in its discretion deny the appointment and appoint another person. In determining whether to appoint the nominee, the factors the court may consider include, but are not limited to, the following:

(1) Whether the nominee has a conflict of interest with the heirs or any other interested party.

(2) Whether the nominee had a business or personal relationship with the decedent or decedent's family before the decedent's death.

(3) Whether the nominee is engaged in or acting on behalf of an individual, a business, or other entity that solicits heirs to obtain the person's nomination for appointment as administrator.

(4) Whether the nominee has been appointed as a personal representative in any other estate.

(e) If the court decides to appoint a nominee under the circumstances described in subdivision (d), the court shall require the nominee to obtain bond, unless the court orders otherwise for good cause. Any order for good cause must be supported by specific findings of fact, and shall consider the need for the protection of creditors, heirs, and any other interested parties. Before waiving a bond, the court shall consider all other alternatives, including, but not limited to, the deposit of property in the estate pursuant to Chapter 3 (commencing with Section 9700) of Part 5 on the condition that the property, including any earnings thereon, will not be withdrawn except on authorization of the court. The waiver of all of the heirs of the requirement of a bond shall not constitute good cause.

(f) If the appointed nominee ceases to be a California resident following his or her appointment, he or she shall be deemed to have resigned as administrator for the purposes of Article 7 (commencing with Section 8520). The court shall not lose jurisdiction of the proceeding by any resignation under this subdivision.

(g) By accepting appointment as personal representative, the nominee shall submit personally to the jurisdiction of the court. *(Stats.1990, c. 79 (A.B.759), § 14, operative July 1, 1991. Amended by Stats.2001, c. 893 (A.B.25), § 55; Stats. 2012, c. 635 (A.B.1670), § 1; Stats.2015, c. 54 (A.B.548), § 1, eff. Jan. 1, 2016.)*

Law Revision Commission Comments
1990 Enactment

Section 8465 continues Section 8465 of the repealed Probate Code without change. The nominee is not entitled to appointment unless legally competent. See Section 8402 (qualifications).

Background on Section 8465 of Repealed Code

Section 8465 was added by 1988 Cal.Stat. ch. 1199 § 81.5. The section restated without substantive change provisions found in former Probate Code Section 423 (repealed by 1988 Cal.Stat. ch. 1199 § 45). "Grandparent" and "issue" were added to subdivision

(b) consistent with Section 8461 (priority for appointment). For background on the provisions of this part, see the Comment to this part under the part heading. [20 Cal.L.Rev.Comm.Reports 1001 (1990)].

Cross References
Competency of person to serve as administrator, see Probate Code § 8402.

§ 8466. Creditor; court denial of appointment

If a person whose only priority is that of a creditor claims appointment as administrator, the court in its discretion may deny the appointment and appoint another person. *(Stats. 1990, c. 79 (A.B.759), § 14, operative July 1, 1991.)*

Law Revision Commission Comments
1990 Enactment

Section 8466 continues Section 8466 of the repealed Probate Code without change. Any person appointed under this section must be legally competent. See Section 8402 (qualifications). See also Section 9605 (appointment of person as personal representative does not discharge any claim the decedent has against the person).

Background on Section 8466 of Repealed Code

Section 8466 was added by 1988 Cal.Stat. ch. 1199 § 81.5. The section restated the last portion of former Probate Code Section 425 (repealed by 1988 Cal.Stat. ch. 1199 § 45) but omitted the requirement that there be a request of another creditor before the court may appoint another person. For background on the provisions of this part, see the Comment to this part under the part heading. [20 Cal.L.Rev.Comm.Reports 1001 (1990)].

§ 8467. Persons with equal priority

If several persons have equal priority for appointment as administrator, the court may appoint one or more of them, or if such persons are unable to agree, the court may appoint the public administrator or a disinterested person in the same or the next lower class of priority as the persons who are unable to agree. *(Stats.1990, c. 79 (A.B.759), § 14, operative July 1, 1991.)*

Law Revision Commission Comments
1990 Enactment

Section 8467 continues Section 8467 of the repealed Probate Code without change.

Background on Section 8467 of Repealed Code

Section 8467 was added by 1988 Cal.Stat. ch. 1199 § 81.5. The section restated the first portion of former Probate Code Section 425 (repealed by 1988 Cal.Stat. ch. 1199 § 45), with the addition of authority to appoint the public administrator or a disinterested person where there is a conflict between persons of equal priority. For background on the provisions of this part, see the Comment to this part under the part heading. [20 Cal.L.Rev.Comm.Reports 1001 (1990)].

Cross References
Joint personal representatives,
  Death, removal, or resignation, completion of administration, see Probate Code §§ 8521, 9630.
Vacancy in office, see Probate Code § 8522.

§ 8468. Failure to claim appointment

If persons having priority fail to claim appointment as administrator, the court may appoint any person who claims appointment. *(Stats.1990, c. 79 (A.B.759), § 14, operative July 1, 1991.)*

1990 Enactment

Section 8468 continues Section 8468 of the repealed Probate Code without change. A person appointed under this section must be legally competent. See Section 8402 (qualifications).

Background on Section 8468 of Repealed Code

Section 8468 was added by 1988 Cal.Stat. ch. 1199 § 81.5. The section restated former Probate Code Section 427 (repealed by 1988 Cal.Stat. ch. 1199 § 45) without substantive change. For background on the provisions of this part, see the Comment to this part under the part heading. [20 Cal.L.Rev.Comm.Reports 1001 (1990)].

Cross References

Qualifications for appointment as administrator, see Probate Code § 8402.

§ 8469. Conservator or guardian serving at time of death; priority; petition; notice

(a) For good cause, the court may allow the priority given by Section 8461 to a conservator or guardian of the estate of the decedent serving in that capacity at the time of death that has not filed a first account, or that is acting as guardian or conservator for another person, or both.

(b) If the petition for appointment as administrator requests the court to allow the priority permitted by subdivision (a), the petitioner shall, in addition to the notice otherwise required by statute, serve notice of the hearing by mail or personal delivery on the public administrator. *(Added by Stats.1990, c. 710 (S.B.1775), § 21, operative July 1, 1991.)*

Law Revision Commission Comments

1990 Addition

Section 8469 was added to the new Probate Code by 1990 Cal.Stat. ch. 710 § 21. The section permits the court to allow the priority given by Section 8461 to a conservator or guardian of the estate of the decedent serving in that capacity at the time of death, notwithstanding that the conservator or guardian fails to satisfy the other requirements of Section 8461. For background on this section, see Recommendation Relating to Priority of Conservator or Guardian for Appointment as Administrator, 20 Cal.L.Revision Comm'n Reports 607 (1990). [20 Cal.L.Rev.Comm.Reports 1001 (1990)].

ARTICLE 5. BOND

Cross References

Application of old and new law, see Probate Code § 3.

§ 8480. Personal representatives; approved bond required before issuance of letters; two or more appointees; beneficiaries and condition; failure to give bond or supplemental bond, etc.

(a) Except as otherwise provided by statute, every person appointed as personal representative shall, before letters are issued, give a bond approved by the court. If two or more persons are appointed, the court may require either a separate bond from each or a joint and several bond. If a joint bond is furnished, the liability on the bond is joint and several.

(b) The bond shall be for the benefit of interested persons and shall be conditioned on the personal representative's faithful execution of the duties of the office according to law.

(c) If the person appointed as personal representative fails to give the required bond, letters shall not be issued. If the person appointed as personal representative fails to give a new, additional, or supplemental bond, or to substitute a sufficient surety, under court order, the person may be removed from office. *(Stats.1990, c. 79 (A.B.759), § 14, operative July 1, 1991. Amended by Stats.1998, c. 77 (S.B. 1841), § 3.)*

Law Revision Commission Comments

1990 Enactment

Section 8480 continues Section 8480 of the repealed Probate Code without change. Subdivision (c) is a specific application of Code of Civil Procedure Section 996.010. For statutory exceptions to the bond requirement, see Sections 301 (trust company), 8481 (waiver of bond). See also Code Civ.Proc. §§ 995.310 (sureties on bond), 995.320 (contents of bond), 995.840 (court approval of bond).

Background on Section 8480 of Repealed Code

Section 8480 was added by 1988 Cal.Stat. ch. 1199 § 81.5. Subdivisions (a) and (b) restated without substantive change former Probate Code Section 410 (repealed by 1988 Cal.Stat. ch. 1199 § 43), the first sentence of subdivision (a) of former Probate Code Section 541 (repealed by 1988 Cal.Stat. ch. 1199 § 48), and former Probate Code Section 544 (repealed by 1988 Cal.Stat. ch. 1199 § 48). Subdivision (c) continued the effect of a portion of former Probate Code Section 549 (repealed by 1988 Cal.Stat. ch. 1199 § 48). For background on the provisions of this part, see the Comment to this part under the part heading. [20 Cal.L.Rev.Comm.Reports 1001 (1990)].

Cross References

Action for misconduct or neglect on sale, see Probate Code § 10380.
Deposited property, see Probate Code § 8401.
Former personal representative, action on bond against by successor, see Probate Code § 9822.
Liability for failure to pay debt, see Probate Code § 11424.
Official bonds, see Government Code § 1450 et seq.
Powers and duties of personal representatives covered by bond, see Probate Code § 9630 et seq.
Trust companies, exemption from special bond, see Probate Code § 301.

§ 8481. Waiver of bond requirement

(a) A bond is not required in either of the following cases:

(1) The will waives the requirement of a bond.

(2) All beneficiaries waive in writing the requirement of a bond and the written waivers are attached to the petition for appointment of a personal representative. This paragraph does not apply if the will requires a bond.

(b) Notwithstanding the waiver of a bond by a will or by all the beneficiaries, on petition of any interested person or on its own motion, the court may for good cause require that a bond be given, either before or after issuance of letters. *(Stats.1990, c. 79 (A.B.759), § 14, operative July 1, 1991.)*

Law Revision Commission Comments
1990 Enactment

Section 8481 continues Section 8481 of the repealed Probate Code without change. Unless the will requires a bond, the court must dispense with the bond if the bond is properly waived unless good cause is shown under subdivision (b) to require a bond. For provisions on reduction or increase of the amount of the bond, see Code Civ.Proc. §§ 996.010–996.030 (insufficient and excessive bonds).

Background on Section 8481 of Repealed Code

Section 8481 was added by 1988 Cal.Stat. ch. 1199 § 81.5. Subdivision (a)(1) restated without substantive change portions of subdivision (c) of former Probate Code Section 462 (repealed by 1988 Cal.Stat. ch. 1199 § 46) and subdivision (a) of former Probate Code Section 541 (repealed by 1988 Cal.Stat. ch. 1199 § 48). Subdivision (a)(2) restated subdivision (b) of former Section 541 (repealed by 1988 Cal.Stat. ch. 1199 § 48) without substantive change. Subdivision (b) restated the substance of the first sentence of former Probate Code Section 543 (repealed by 1988 Cal.Stat. ch. 1199 § 48) but did not continue the substance of the second sentence of the former section. For background on the provisions of this part, see the Comment to this part under the part heading. [20 Cal.L.Rev.Comm.Reports 1001 (1990)].

Cross References

Additional bond of special administrator, see Probate Code § 8545.

§ 8482. Amount; additional bond for sale of real property

(a) The court in its discretion may fix the amount of the bond, but the amount of the bond shall be not more than the sum of:

(1) The estimated value of the personal property.

(2) The probable annual gross income of the estate.

(3) If independent administration is granted as to real property, the estimated value of the decedent's interest in the real property.

(b) Notwithstanding subdivision (a), if the bond is given by an admitted surety insurer, the court may establish a fixed minimum amount for the bond, based on the minimum premium required by the admitted surety insurer.

(c) If the bond is given by personal sureties, the amount of the bond shall be twice the amount fixed by the court under subdivision (a).

(d) Before confirming a sale of real property the court shall require such additional bond as may be proper, not exceeding the maximum requirements of this section, treating the expected proceeds of the sale as personal property. *(Stats.1990, c. 79 (A.B.759), § 14, operative July 1, 1991.)*

Law Revision Commission Comments
1990 Enactment

Section 8482 continues Section 8482 of the repealed Probate Code without change. See also Section 301 (trust company as personal representative).

Background on Section 8482 of Repealed Code

Section 8482 was added by 1988 Cal.Stat. ch. 1199 § 81.5. Subdivisions (a) and (b) superseded the last sentence of subdivision (a) of former Probate Code Section 541 (repealed by 1988 Cal.Stat. ch. 1199 § 48), making explicit the authority of the court to impose a fixed minimum bond. Subdivision (c) superseded former Probate Code Section 542 (repealed by 1988 Cal.Stat. ch. 1199 § 48). The section was amended by 1989 Cal.Stat. ch. 21 § 19 to make clear that the fixed minimum bond may exceed the maximum established by subdivision (a). See Communication from the California Law Revision Commission Concerning Assembly Bill 156, 20 Cal.L.Revision Comm'n Reports 227, 230 (1990). For background on the provisions of this part, see the Comment to this part under the part heading. [20 Cal.L.Rev.Comm.Reports 1001 (1990)].

§ 8483. Property of estate deposited with institution; court order restricting withdrawal; amount of bond

(a) This section applies where property in the estate has been deposited pursuant to Chapter 3 (commencing with Section 9700) of Part 5 on condition that the property, including any earnings thereon, will not be withdrawn except on authorization of the court.

(b) In a proceeding to determine the amount of the bond of the personal representative (whether at the time of appointment or subsequently), on production of a receipt showing the deposit of property of the estate in the manner described in subdivision (a), the court may order that the property shall not be withdrawn except on authorization of the court and may, in its discretion, do either of the following:

(1) Exclude the property in determining the amount of the required bond or reduce the amount of the bond to an amount the court determines is reasonable.

(2) If a bond has already been given or the amount fixed, reduce the amount to an amount the court determines is reasonable. *(Stats.1990, c. 79 (A.B.759), § 14, operative July 1, 1991.)*

Law Revision Commission Comments
1990 Enactment

Section 8483 continues Section 8483 of the repealed Probate Code without substantive change. For a comparable provision, see Section 2328 (Guardianship–Conservatorship Law). For the authority of a petitioner for appointment as personal representative to make a deposit described in this section, see Section 8401 (deposit in controlled account).

Background on Section 8483 of Repealed Code

Section 8483 was added by 1988 Cal.Stat. ch. 1199 § 81.5. The section restated subdivision (a) of former Probate Code Section 541.1 (repealed by 1988 Cal.Stat. ch. 1199 § 48) and extended the coverage of the provision to include "personal property" in addition to "money" and "securities." Section 8483 was amended by 1989 Cal.Stat. ch. 544 § 9 to refer to the procedures in Sections 9700–9705 for depositing money in an insured account in a financial institution and depositing personal property with a trust company. This continued a provision of former Section 541.1(a). For background on the provisions of this part, see the Comment to this part under the part heading. [20 Cal.L.Rev.Comm.Reports 1001 (1990)].

§ 8484. Petition to reduce amount; affidavit; notice of hearing

If a personal representative petitions to have the amount of the bond reduced, the petition shall include an affidavit setting forth the condition of the estate and notice of hearing shall be given as provided in Section 1220. *(Stats.1990, c. 79 (A.B.759), § 14, operative July 1, 1991.)*

Law Revision Commission Comments

1990 Enactment

Section 8484 continues Section 8484 of the repealed Probate Code without change. For general provisions, see Sections 1020–1023 (petitions), 1200–1221 (notice of hearing), 1250–1252 (request for special notice), 1260–1265 (proof of giving of notice).

Background on Section 8484 of Repealed Code

Section 8484 was added by 1988 Cal.Stat. ch. 1199 § 81.5. The section restated former Probate Code Section 553.3 (repealed by 1988 Cal.Stat. ch. 1199 § 48) without substantive change. For background on the provisions of this part, see the Comment to this part under the part heading. [20 Cal.L.Rev.Comm.Reports 1001 (1990)].

§ 8485. Substitution or release of surety; account

A personal representative who petitions for substitution or release of a surety shall file with the petition an account in the form provided in Section 10900. The court shall not order a substitution or release unless the account is approved. *(Stats.1990, c. 79 (A.B.759), § 14, operative July 1, 1991.)*

Law Revision Commission Comments

1990 Enactment

Section 8485 continues Section 8485 of the repealed Probate Code without change. A copy of the petition and a notice of hearing must be served on the surety. Code Civ.Proc. § 996.110(c). For general provisions, see Sections 1020–1023 (petitions), 1200–1221 (notice of hearing), 1250–1252 (request for special notice), 1260–1265 (proof of giving of notice).

Background on Section 8485 of Repealed Code

Section 8485 was added by 1988 Cal.Stat. ch. 1199 § 81.5. The section restated former Probate Code Section 553.5 (repealed by 1988 Cal.Stat. ch. 1199 § 48) without substantive change. For background on the provisions of this part, see the Comment to this part under the part heading. [20 Cal.L.Rev.Comm.Reports 1001 (1990)].

§ 8486. Cost of bond

The personal representative shall be allowed the reasonable cost of the bond for every year it remains in force. *(Stats.1990, c. 79 (A.B.759), § 14, operative July 1, 1991.)*

Law Revision Commission Comments

1990 Enactment

Section 8486 continues Section 8486 of the repealed Probate Code without change.

Background on Section 8486 of Repealed Code

Section 8486 was added by 1988 Cal.Stat. ch. 1199 § 81.5. The section superseded former Probate Code Section 541.5 (repealed by 1988 Cal.Stat. ch. 1199 § 48). Unlike the former provision, Section 8486 did not prescribe a fixed or maximum amount, but left the reasonableness of the amount to be determined by market forces. For background on the provisions of this part, see the Comment to this part under the part heading. [20 Cal.L.Rev.Comm.Reports 1001 (1990)].

Cross References

Testamentary trustee's bond, allowance for cost, see Probate Code § 15602.

§ 8487. Bond and Undertaking Law; application

The provisions of the Bond and Undertaking Law (Chapter 2 (commencing with Section 995.010) of Title 14 of Part 2 of the Code of Civil Procedure) apply to a bond given under this division, except to the extent this division is inconsistent. *(Stats.1990, c. 79 (A.B.759), § 14, operative July 1, 1991.)*

Law Revision Commission Comments

1990 Enactment

Section 8487 continues Section 8487 of the repealed Probate Code without substantive change. The Bond and Undertaking Law permits the beneficiary to enforce liability on the bond either by motion in the probate court or by separate civil action. Code Civ.Proc. §§ 996.430, 996.440. Ordinarily, liability on the bond may not be enforced until the personal representative has made a final accounting, the probate court has made an order surcharging the personal representative, and the order has become final. Alexandrou v. Alexander, 37 Cal.App.3d 306, 311, 112 Cal.Rptr. 307 (1974). However, this is not necessary where the personal representative dies or is removed before final accounting, or where the amount of liability is ascertainable without accounting. Id. See also Section 8488 (limitation period for action against sureties on personal representative's bond is four years after discharge).

Background on Section 8487 of Repealed Code

Section 8487 was a new provision added by 1988 Cal.Stat. ch. 1199 § 81.5. The section was a specific application of previously existing law. See Code Civ.Proc. § 995.020 (application of Bond and Undertaking Law). For background on the provisions of this part, see the Comment to this part under the part heading. [20 Cal.L.Rev.Comm.Reports 1001 (1990)].

§ 8488. Condition of bond breached; action against sureties; limitation of actions

(a) In case of a breach of a condition of the bond, an action may be brought against the sureties on the bond for the use and benefit of the decedent's estate or of any person interested in the estate.

(b) No action may be maintained against the sureties on the bond of the personal representative unless commenced within four years from the discharge or removal of the personal representative or within four years from the date the order surcharging the personal representative becomes final, whichever is later.

(c) In any case, and notwithstanding subdivision (c) of Section 7250, no action may be maintained against the sureties on the bond unless commenced within six years from the date the judgment under Section 7250 or the later of the orders under subdivision (b) of this section becomes final. *(Stats.1990, c. 79 (A.B.759), § 14, operative July 1, 1991. Amended by Stats.1993, c. 794 (A.B.516), § 3; Stats.1994, c. 806 (A.B.3686), § 27.)*

Law Revision Commission Comments

1990 Enactment

Section 8488 continues Section 8488 of the repealed Probate Code without change. This section is comparable to Section 2333 (Guardianship–Conservatorship Law).

Background on Section 8488 of Repealed Code

Section 8488 was a new provision added by 1988 Cal.Stat. ch. 1199 § 81.5. For background on the provisions of this part, see the Comment to this part under the part heading. [20 Cal.L.Rev.Comm.Reports 1001 (1990)].

ARTICLE 6.   REMOVAL FROM OFFICE

Section
8500. Petition for removal of personal representative; court-initiated removal; hearing; status pending hearing; procedure; compelled attendance.
8501. Revocation of letters; cessation of authority.
8502. Grounds for removal.
8503. Removal of administrator; petition of person higher in priority; court refusal to grant.
8504. Administrator appointed on ground of intestacy; later admission of will; executor or administrator with the will annexed; admission of later will.
8505. Contempt for disobeying court order.

Cross References

Application of old and new law, see Probate Code § 3.

§ 8500.   Petition for removal of personal representative; court-initiated removal; hearing; status pending hearing; procedure; compelled attendance

(a) Any interested person may petition for removal of the personal representative from office. A petition for removal may be combined with a petition for appointment of a successor personal representative under Article 7 (commencing with Section 8520). The petition shall state facts showing cause for removal.

(b) On a petition for removal, or if the court otherwise has reason to believe from the court's own knowledge or from other credible information, whether on the settlement of an account or otherwise, that there are grounds for removal, the court shall issue a citation to the personal representative to appear and show cause why the personal representative should not be removed. The court may suspend the powers of the personal representative and may make such orders as are necessary to deal with the property pending the hearing.

(c) Any interested person may appear at the hearing and file a written declaration showing that the personal representative should be removed or retained. The personal representative may demur to or answer the declaration. The court may compel the attendance of the personal representative and may compel the personal representative to answer questions, on oath, concerning the administration of the estate. Failure to attend or answer is cause for removal of the personal representative from office.

(d) The issues shall be heard and determined by the court. If the court is satisfied from the evidence that the citation has been duly served and cause for removal exists, the court shall remove the personal representative from office. *(Stats.1990, c. 79 (A.B.759), § 14, operative July 1, 1991.)*

Law Revision Commission Comments

1990 Enactment

Section 8500 continues Section 8500 of the repealed Probate Code without change. The court may enforce its orders by any proper means, including contempt. See Section 7050 (jurisdiction and authority of court or judge). For general provisions, see Sections 1020–1023 (petitions), 1040–1050 (hearings and orders), 1200–1221 (notice of hearing), 1240–1242 (citations), 1250–1252 (request for special notice), 1260–1265 (proof of giving of notice). See also Section 10952 (unless the court extends the time, the personal representative must file account not later than 60 days after removal).

Background on Section 8500 of Repealed Code

Section 8500 was added by 1988 Cal.Stat. ch. 1199 § 81.5. The section superseded portions of former Probate Code Section 451 (repealed by 1988 Cal.Stat. ch. 1199 § 45). Subdivision (b) restated portions of the first sentence of former Probate Code Section 521 (repealed by 1988 Cal.Stat. ch. 1199 § 47) without substantive change. Subdivision (c) restated former Probate Code Sections 522 and 523 (provisions repealed by 1988 Cal.Stat. ch. 1199 § 47) without substantive change. For background on the provisions of this part, see the Comment to this part under the part heading. [20 Cal.L.Rev.Comm.Reports 1001 (1990)].

Cross References

Admissibility of affidavits or verified petitions in uncontested probate proceedings, see Code of Civil Procedure § 2009.
Appeal from orders revoking letters, right to, see Probate Code § 7240.
Conclusiveness of judgment or final order, see Code of Civil Procedure § 1908.
Contempt in general, see Code of Civil Procedure § 1209 et seq.
Removal of personal representative, grounds for,
    Account, neglect or refusal to, see Probate Code § 11052
    Inventory, failure to file, see Probate Code § 8804
    New sureties, failure to give sufficient security, see Code of Civil Procedure § 996.140.
    Sufficient or additional security, failure to give, see Probate Code § 8480.
Rules of practice, see Probate Code § 1000.
Searches and seizures, see Cal. Const. Art. 1, § 13.
Suspension of powers by judge in chambers, power to, see Code of Civil Procedure § 166.
Suspension of powers of personal representative, see Probate Code § 9614.

§ 8501.   Revocation of letters; cessation of authority

On removal of a personal representative from office, the court shall revoke any letters issued to the personal representative, and the authority of the personal representative ceases. *(Stats.1990, c. 79 (A.B.759), § 14, operative July 1, 1991.)*

Law Revision Commission Comments

1990 Enactment

Section 8501 continues Section 8501 of the repealed Probate Code without change. See also Sections 10952 (unless the court extends the time, the personal representative must file account not later than 60 days after removal), 10953 (filing account for incapacitated personal representative).

Background on Section 8501 of Repealed Code

Section 8501 was a new provision added by 1988 Cal.Stat. ch. 1199 § 81.5. The section generalized a provision found in former Probate Code Section 549 (repealed by 1988 Cal.Stat. ch. 1199 § 48). For background on the provisions of this part, see the Comment to this part under the part heading. [20 Cal.L.Rev.Comm.Reports 1001 (1990)].

§ 8502. Grounds for removal

A personal representative may be removed from office for any of the following causes:

(a) The personal representative has wasted, embezzled, mismanaged, or committed a fraud on the estate, or is about to do so.

(b) The personal representative is incapable of properly executing the duties of the office or is otherwise not qualified for appointment as personal representative.

(c) The personal representative has wrongfully neglected the estate, or has long neglected to perform any act as personal representative.

(d) Removal is otherwise necessary for protection of the estate or interested persons.

(e) Any other cause provided by statute. *(Stats.1990, c. 79 (A.B.759), § 14, operative July 1, 1991.)*

Law Revision Commission Comments
1990 Enactment

Section 8502 continues Section 8502 of the repealed Probate Code without change. A conflict of interest may be ground for removal under subdivision (d); it should be noted, however, that not every conflict necessarily requires removal for protection of the estate, depending on the circumstances of the particular case. Other causes for removal are provided in this article and elsewhere by statute. See, e.g., Section 8500 (failure to attend and answer). For removal provisions elsewhere in statute, see, e.g., Sections 8480 (failure to give required bond), 8577 (failure of nonresident personal representative to file statement of address or statement of change of address), 8804 (failure to file inventory and appraisal within time allowed), 8941 (failure to comply with court order that information necessary to complete appraisal be delivered to probate referee), 10592 (failure to comply with Independent Administration of Estates Act), 11051 (purposeful evasion of personal service of citation), 11052 (failure, after having been cited, to appear and file a required account), 12204 (failure to comply with order concerning closing estate administration). See also Section 10953 (filing account for incapacitated personal representative).

Background on Section 8502 of Repealed Code

Section 8502 was added by 1988 Cal.Stat. ch. 1199 § 81.5. The section restated former Probate Code Section 524 and portions of the first sentence of former Probate Code Section 521 (provisions repealed by 1988 Cal.Stat. ch. 1199 § 47), except that permanent removal from the state is not continued as a ground for dismissal. See Article 9 (commencing with Section 8570) (nonresident personal representative). For background on the provisions of this part, see the Comment to this part under the part heading. [20 Cal.L.Rev.Comm.Reports 1001 (1990)].

Cross References

Accounts, when required, see Probate Code § 10950 et seq.

§ 8503. Removal of administrator; petition of person higher in priority; court refusal to grant

(a) Subject to subdivision (b), an administrator may be removed from office on the petition of the surviving spouse or a relative of the decedent entitled to succeed to all or part of the estate, or the nominee of the surviving spouse or relative, if such person is higher in priority than the administrator.

(b) The court in its discretion may refuse to grant the petition:

(1) Where the petition is by a person or the nominee of a person who had actual notice of the proceeding in which the administrator was appointed and an opportunity to contest the appointment.

(2) Where to do so would be contrary to the sound administration of the estate. *(Stats.1990, c. 79 (A.B.759), § 14, operative July 1, 1991.)*

Law Revision Commission Comments
1990 Enactment

Section 8503 continues Section 8503 of the repealed Probate Code without change. A petition under this section should be accompanied by a petition for appointment of a successor who has higher priority than the existing personal representative. Subdivision (b)(2) is intended to cover the situation, for example, where administration is nearly complete or has otherwise progressed to a point where replacement of the administrator would be inappropriate.

Background on Section 8503 of Repealed Code

Section 8503 was added by 1988 Cal.Stat. ch. 1199 § 81.5. Subdivision (a) superseded former Probate Code Sections 450 and 452 (provisions repealed by 1988 Cal.Stat. ch. 1199 § 45). Subdivision (b)(1) restated former Probate Code Section 453 (repealed by 1988 Cal.Stat. ch. 1199 § 45) without substantive change. Subdivision (b)(2) was a new provision. For background on the provisions of this part, see the Comment to this part under the part heading. [20 Cal.L.Rev.Comm.Reports 1001 (1990)].

Cross References

Appointment of personal representatives,
  Competency, see Probate Code § 8402.
  Petition, see Probate Code § 8000 et seq.
Granting administration to nominee, see Probate Code § 8465.
Order of priority of persons, see Probate Code § 8461 et seq.
Suspension and removal, generally, see Probate Code § 8500 et seq.
Vacancy, effect, see Probate Code § 8520 et seq.

§ 8504. Administrator appointed on ground of intestacy; later admission of will; executor or administrator with the will annexed; admission of later will

(a) After appointment of an administrator on the ground of intestacy, the personal representative shall be removed from office on the later admission to probate of a will.

(b) After appointment of an executor or administrator with the will annexed, the personal representative shall be removed from office on admission to probate of a later will. *(Stats.1990, c. 79 (A.B.759), § 14, operative July 1, 1991.)*

Law Revision Commission Comments
1990 Enactment

Section 8504 continues Section 8504 of the repealed Probate Code without change. See also Section 8226 (effect of admission of will to probate).

Background on Section 8504 of Repealed Code

Section 8504 was added by 1988 Cal.Stat. ch. 1199 § 81.5. The section restated the first portion of the first sentence of former Probate Code Section 510 (repealed by 1988 Cal.Stat. ch. 1199 § 47) without substantive change. For background on the provisions of this part, see the Comment to this part under the part heading. [20 Cal.L.Rev.Comm.Reports 1001 (1990)].

Cross References

Revocation of probate, effect on powers of personal representatives, see Probate Code § 8272.
Validity of acts prior to vacancy, see Probate Code § 8525.

§ 8505. Contempt for disobeying court order

(a) A personal representative may be removed from office if the personal representative is found in contempt for disobeying an order of the court.

(b) Notwithstanding any other provision of this article, a personal representative may be removed from office under this section by a court order reciting the facts and without further showing or notice. *(Stats.1990, c. 79 (A.B.759), § 14, operative July 1, 1991.)*

Law Revision Commission Comments
1990 Enactment

Section 8505 continues Section 8505 of the repealed Probate Code without change. See also Sections 8501 (revocation of letters), 8524 (successor personal representative).

Background on Section 8505 of Repealed Code

Section 8505 was added by 1988 Cal.Stat. ch. 1199 § 81.5. The section restated former Probate Code Section 526 (repealed by 1988 Cal.Stat. ch. 1199 § 47), omitting the requirement of 30 days custody. For background on the provisions of this part, see the Comment to this part under the part heading. [20 Cal.L.Rev.Comm.Reports 1001 (1990)].

Cross References

Contempt in general, see Code of Civil Procedure § 1209 et seq.

ARTICLE 7. CHANGES IN ADMINISTRATION

Section
8520. Vacancy in office of personal representative.
8521. Vacancy in office of fewer than all personal representatives; amended letters.
8522. Successor personal representative; appointment; petition; notice; personal representative of deceased personal representative.
8523. Property of estate between time of vacancy and appointment of successor; court orders.
8524. Powers and duties of successor personal representative; preservation of claims, etc., given former representative.
8525. Validity of acts prior to vacancy; liability regarding vacant office; settlement of accounts, etc.

Cross References

Administrators, appointment of nominated persons, priority, considerations, nominees required to obtain a bond, resignation upon cessation of California residency, submission to jurisdiction of court, see Probate Code § 8465.
Application of old and new law, see Probate Code § 3.

§ 8520. Vacancy in office of personal representative

A vacancy occurs in the office of a personal representative who resigns, dies, or is removed from office under Article 6 (commencing with Section 8500), or whose authority is otherwise terminated. *(Stats.1990, c. 79 (A.B.759), § 14, operative July 1, 1991.)*

Law Revision Commission Comments
1990 Enactment

Section 8520 continues Section 8520 of the repealed Probate Code without change. A personal representative who resigns is not excused from liability until accounts are settled and property is delivered to the successor. See Section 8525(b) (effect of vacancy). See also Sections 10952 (unless the court extends the time, the personal representative must file account not later than 60 days after resignation), 10953 (filing account for dead or incapacitated personal representative).

Background on Section 8520 of Repealed Code

Section 8520 was a new provision added by 1988 Cal.Stat. ch. 1199 § 81.5. Section 8520 generalized provisions found in various parts of former law. For background on the provisions of this part, see the Comment to this part under the part heading. [20 Cal.L.Rev.Comm.Reports 1001 (1990)].

§ 8521. Vacancy in office of fewer than all personal representatives; amended letters

(a) Unless the will provides otherwise or the court in its discretion orders otherwise, if a vacancy occurs in the office of fewer than all personal representatives, the remaining personal representatives shall complete the administration of the estate.

(b) The court, on the filing of a petition alleging that a vacancy has occurred in the office of fewer than all personal representatives, may order the clerk to issue appropriate amended letters to the remaining personal representatives. *(Stats.1990, c. 79 (A.B.759), § 14, operative July 1, 1991.)*

Law Revision Commission Comments
1990 Enactment

Section 8521 continues Section 8521 of the repealed Probate Code without change. See also Section 9630 (effect of death, removal, or resignation of one of several joint personal representatives).

Background on Section 8521 of Repealed Code

Section 8521 was added by 1988 Cal.Stat. ch. 1199 § 81.5. The section restated former Probate Code Section 511 (repealed by 1988 Cal.Stat. ch. 1199 § 47) without substantive change. For background on the provisions of this part, see the Comment to this part under the part heading. [20 Cal.L.Rev.Comm.Reports 1001 (1990)].

Cross References

Authority of majority in case of absences or disqualifications, see Probate Code § 9630.
Competency requirements, see Probate Code § 8402.

§ 8522. Successor personal representative; appointment; petition; notice; personal representative of deceased personal representative

(a) If a vacancy occurs in the office of a personal representative and there are no other personal representatives, the court shall appoint a successor personal representative.

(b) Appointment of a successor personal representative shall be made on petition and service of notice on interested persons in the manner provided in Article 2 (commencing with Section 8110) of Chapter 2, and shall be subject to the same priority as for an original appointment of a personal representative. The personal representative of a deceased personal representative is not, as such, entitled to appointment as successor personal representative. *(Stats.1990, c. 79 (A.B.759), § 14, operative July 1, 1991.)*

Law Revision Commission Comments

1990 Enactment

Section 8522 continues Section 8522 of the repealed Probate Code without change.

Background on Section 8522 of Repealed Code

Section 8522 was added by 1988 Cal.Stat. ch. 1199 § 81.5. The section restated former Probate Code Section 512 (repealed by 1988 Cal.Stat. ch. 1199 § 47) and a portion of former Probate Code Section 451 (repealed by 1988 Cal.Stat. ch. 1199 § 45) without substantive change, and generalized the first sentence of former Probate Code Section 406 (repealed by 1988 Cal.Stat. ch. 1199 § 43). For background on the provisions of this part, see the Comment to this part under the part heading. [20 Cal.L.Rev.Comm.Reports 1001 (1990)].

Cross References

Authority of executor to appoint executor, see Probate Code § 8422.

§ 8523. Property of estate between time of vacancy and appointment of successor; court orders

The court may make orders that are necessary to deal with the estate of the decedent between the time a vacancy occurs in the office of personal representative and appointment of a successor. Those orders may include appointment of a special administrator. *(Stats.1990, c. 79 (A.B.759), § 14, operative July 1, 1991.)*

Law Revision Commission Comments

1990 Enactment

Section 8523 continues Section 8523 of the repealed Probate Code without substantive change. See also Sections 10952 (unless the court extends the time, the personal representative must file account not later than 60 days after termination of authority), 10953 (filing account for dead or incapacitated personal representative).

Background on Section 8523 of Repealed Code

Section 8523 was added by 1988 Cal.Stat. ch. 1199 § 81.5. The section superseded the second sentence of former Probate Code Section 520 (repealed by 1988 Cal.Stat. ch. 1199 § 47). For background on the provisions of this part, see the Comment to this part under the part heading. [20 Cal.L.Rev.Comm.Reports 1001 (1990)].

§ 8524. Powers and duties of successor personal representative; preservation of claims, etc., given former representative

(a) A successor personal representative is entitled to demand, sue for, recover and collect all the estate of the decedent remaining unadministered, and may prosecute to final judgment any suit commenced by the former personal representative before the vacancy.

(b) No notice, process, or claim given to or served on the former personal representative need be given to or served on the successor in order to preserve any position or right the person giving the notice or filing the claim may thereby have obtained or preserved with reference to the former personal representative.

(c) Except as provided in subdivision (b) of Section 8442 (authority of administrator with will annexed) or as otherwise ordered by the court, the successor personal representative has the powers and duties in respect to the continued administration that the former personal representative would have had. *(Stats.1990, c. 79 (A.B.759), § 14, operative July 1, 1991.)*

Law Revision Commission Comments

1990 Enactment

Section 8524 continues Section 8524 of the repealed Probate Code without substantive change. Subdivisions (b) and (c) are drawn from Section 3–613 of the Uniform Probate Code (1987). As to the construction of provisions drawn from uniform acts, see Section 2.

Background on Section 8524 of Repealed Code

Section 8524 was added by 1988 Cal.Stat. ch. 1199 § 81.5. Subdivision (a) restated and broadened the application of a portion of former Probate Code Section 466 (repealed by 1988 Cal.Stat. ch. 1199 § 46) and the second sentence of former Probate Code Section 510 (repealed by 1988 Cal.Stat. ch. 1199 § 47). Subdivisions (b) and (c) were new provisions. For background on the provisions of this part, see the Comment to this part under the part heading. [20 Cal.L.Rev.Comm.Reports 1001 (1990)].

Cross References

Duties of personal representatives, see Probate Code § 9600 et seq. Parties, substitution of, see Code of Civil Procedure §§ 368.5, 386.

§ 8525. Validity of acts prior to vacancy; liability regarding vacant office; settlement of accounts, etc.

(a) The acts of the personal representative before a vacancy occurs are valid to the same extent as if no vacancy had later occurred.

(b) The liability of a personal representative whose office is vacant, or of the surety on the bond, is not discharged, released, or affected by the vacancy or by appointment of a successor, but continues until settlement of the accounts of the personal representative and delivery of all the estate of the decedent to the successor personal representative or other person appointed by the court to receive it. The personal representative shall render an account of the administration within the time that the court directs. *(Stats. 1990, c. 79 (A.B.759), § 14, operative July 1, 1991.)*

Law Revision Commission Comments

1990 Enactment

Section 8525 continues Section 8525 of the repealed Probate Code without substantive change. See also Sections 10952 (unless the court extends the time, the personal representative must file account not later than 60 days after termination of authority), 10953 (filing account for dead or incapacitated personal representative).

Background on Section 8525 of Repealed Code

Section 8525 was added by 1988 Cal.Stat. ch. 1199 § 81.5. Subdivision (a) restated former Probate Code Section 525 (repealed by 1988 Cal.Stat. ch. 1199 § 47) without substantive change. The first sentence of subdivision (b) restated the third sentence of former Probate Code Section 520 (repealed by 1988 Cal.Stat. ch. 1199 § 47) without substantive change. The second sentence of subdivision (b) restated the last portion of the first sentence of former Probate Code Section 510 (repealed by 1988 Cal.Stat. ch. 1199 § 47) without substantive change. For background on the provisions of this part, see the Comment to this part under the part heading. [20 Cal.L.Rev.Comm.Reports 1001 (1990)].

Accounting after authority ceases, see Probate Code § 10952.

Bonds, conditions and liabilities on, see Code of Civil Procedure § 996.460 et seq.; Probate Code § 8480 et seq.

Liability of personal representative for acts done in good faith before revocation of probate, see Probate Code § 8272.

Order settling final account or for final distribution, notice, see Probate Code §§ 11000, 11641.

Reversal of order appointing personal representative, effect on transactions, see Probate Code § 8406.

ARTICLE 8.   SPECIAL ADMINISTRATORS

Section

8540. Circumstances requiring immediate appointment; powers; term of office.

8541. Notice; preference; appointment to perform particular act; errors in appointment.

8542. Letters; conditions; bond; oath; notation for performance of particular act.

8543. Bond requirement; waiver.

8544. Powers; with and without further court order; liability to decedent's creditors; duties of special administrator appointed to perform particular act.

8545. General personal representative powers granted to special administrator; additional bond; letters.

8546. Cessation of powers; issuance of letters to general personal representative; delivery of property; pending transactions; list of creditor claims; verified account.

8547. Compensation; special administrator; attorney; extraordinary services; amount.

Cross References

Application of old and new law, see Probate Code § 3.

§ 8540.   Circumstances requiring immediate appointment; powers; term of office

(a) If the circumstances of the estate require the immediate appointment of a personal representative, the court may appoint a special administrator to exercise any powers that may be appropriate under the circumstances for the preservation of the estate.

(b) The appointment may be for a specified term, to perform particular acts, or on any other terms specified in the court order. *(Stats.1990, c. 79 (A.B.759), § 14, operative July 1, 1991.)*

Law Revision Commission Comments

1990 Enactment

Section 8540 continues Section 8540 of the repealed Probate Code without substantive change. Under subdivision (a), grounds for appointment of a special administrator would include situations where (1) no application is made for appointment of a personal representative, (2) there is delay in appointment of a personal representative, (3) a sufficient bond is not given as required by statute or letters are otherwise granted irregularly, (4) the personal representative dies, resigns, or is suspended or removed from office, (5) an appeal is taken from an order revoking probate of a will, (6) there is a will contest pending, (7) appointment is necessary to maintain a lawsuit on the decedent's cause of action, or where (8) for any other cause the personal representative is unable to act. Appointment may be made on the court's own motion or on petition of an interested person.

Subdivision (b) is drawn from Section 3–617 of the Uniform Probate Code (1987). As to the construction of provisions drawn from uniform acts, see Section 2. See also Section 8544 (special powers, duties, and obligations).

A judge may appoint a special administrator in chambers. See Code Civ.Proc. § 166 (actions in chambers). The public administrator may serve as special administrator. See Section 8541.

Background on Section 8540 of Repealed Code

Section 8540 was added by 1988 Cal.Stat. ch. 1199 § 81.5. Subdivision (a) superseded the first clause of former Probate Code Section 460 (repealed by 1988 Cal.Stat. ch. 1199 § 46) and generalized provisions of former Probate Code Sections 465 (repealed by 1988 Cal.Stat. ch. 1199 § 46) and 520 (repealed by 1988 Cal.Stat. ch. 1199 § 47). Subdivision (b) was a new provision. For background on the provisions of this part, see the Comment to this part under the part heading. [20 Cal.L.Rev.Comm.Reports 1001 (1990)].

Cross References

Judicial powers in chambers in matters of probate, see Code of Civil Procedure § 166.

§ 8541.   Notice; preference; appointment to perform particular act; errors in appointment

(a) Appointment of a special administrator may be made at any time without notice or on such notice to interested persons as the court deems reasonable.

(b) In making the appointment, the court shall ordinarily give preference to the person entitled to appointment as personal representative. The court may appoint the public administrator.

(c) In the case of an appointment to perform a particular act, request for approval of the act may be included in the petition for appointment, and approval may be made on the same notice and at the same time as the appointment.

(d) The court may act, if necessary, to remedy any errors made in the appointment. *(Stats.1990, c. 79 (A.B.759), § 14, operative July 1, 1991.)*

Law Revision Commission Comments

1990 Enactment

Section 8541 continues Section 8541 of the repealed Probate Code without change. The appointment of, or refusal to appoint, a person as special administrator is not appealable. See Section 7240 (appealable orders and refusals to make orders). The public administrator may no longer be directed by the court to "take charge" of the estate (as under former law) but may be appointed as special administrator. Appointment of a special administrator may be made by the judge in chambers. See Code Civ.Proc. § 166 (actions in chambers).

Background on Section 8541 of Repealed Code

Section 8541 was added by 1988 Cal.Stat. ch. 1199 § 81.5. The section restated former Probate Code Section 461 and the last clause of former Probate Code Section 460 (provisions repealed by 1988 Cal.Stat. ch. 1199 § 46), with the addition of subdivisions (c) and (d). For background on the provisions of this part, see the Comment to this part under the part heading. [20 Cal.L.Rev.Comm.Reports 1001 (1990)].

Cross References

Appealable orders, see Probate Code § 7240.

Competency for appointment, see Probate Code § 8402.

Judicial powers in chambers in matters of probate, see Code of Civil Procedure § 166.
Jurisdiction and venue, see Probate Code § 7050 et seq.
Public administrators, duties and powers, see Probate Code § 7600 et seq.
Suspension or removal, see Probate Code § 8500 et seq.

§ 8542. Letters; conditions; bond; oath; notation for performance of particular act

(a) The clerk shall issue letters to the special administrator after both of the following conditions are satisfied:

(1) The special administrator gives any bond that may be required by the court under Section 8480.

(2) The special administrator takes the usual oath attached to or endorsed on the letters.

(b) Subdivision (a) does not apply to the public administrator.

(c) The letters of a special administrator appointed to perform a particular act shall include a notation of the particular act the special administrator was appointed to perform. *(Stats.1990, c. 79 (A.B.759), § 14, operative July 1, 1991.)*

Law Revision Commission Comments
1990 Enactment

Section 8542 continues Section 8542 of the repealed Probate Code without substantive change.

Subdivision (a)(2) is revised to permit the oath to be "attached to" the letters. This revision conforms the provision to Section 8403(b) (general requirement of oath).

The bond must be conditioned that the special administrator will faithfully execute the duties of the office according to law. See Section 8480 (bond required). The judge may approve the bond in chambers. See Code Civ.Proc. § 166 (actions in chambers).

Background on Section 8542 of Repealed Code

Section 8542 was added by 1988 Cal.Stat. ch. 1199 § 81.5. Subdivisions (a) and (b) restated subdivisions (a) and (b) of former Probate Code Section 462 (repealed by 1988 Cal.Stat. ch. 1199 § 46) without substantive change. Subdivision (c) was a new provision. For background on the provisions of this part, see the Comment to this part under the part heading. [20 Cal.L.Rev.Comm.Reports 1001 (1990)].

Cross References
Additional bond, see Probate Code § 8545.
Bonds in general, see Probate Code § 8480 et seq.
Contents of letters, see Probate Code § 8405.
Trust companies not required to give bond, see Probate Code § 301.

§ 8543. Bond requirement; waiver

Subject to subdivision (b) of Section 8481, the court shall direct that no bond be given in either of the following cases:

(a) The will waives the requirement of a bond and the person named as executor in the will is appointed special administrator.

(b) All beneficiaries waive in writing the requirement of a bond and the written waivers are attached to the petition for appointment of the special administrator. This paragraph does not apply if the will requires a bond. *(Stats.1990, c. 79 (A.B.759), § 14, operative July 1, 1991.)*

Law Revision Commission Comments
1990 Enactment

Section 8543 continues the substance of Section 8543 of the repealed Probate Code with the addition of the provision relating to waiver of bond by all the beneficiaries. This addition conforms Section 8543 to Section 8481 (waiver of bond of personal representative). Notwithstanding waiver of bond in the will or by all the beneficiaries, the court, on petition of an interested person or on its own motion, may for good cause require that a bond be given, either before or after issuance of letters. See Section 8481(b).

Background on Section 8543 of Repealed Code

Section 8543 was added by 1988 Cal.Stat. ch. 1199 § 81.5. The section restated a portion of subdivision (c) of former Probate Code Section 462 (repealed by 1988 Cal.Stat. ch. 1199 § 46) without substantive change. For background on the provisions of this part, see the Comment to this part under the part heading. [20 Cal.L.Rev.Comm.Reports 1001 (1990)].

§ 8544. Powers; with and without further court order; liability to decedent's creditors; duties of special administrator appointed to perform particular act

(a) Except to the extent the order appointing a special administrator prescribes terms, the special administrator has the power to do all of the following without further order of the court:

(1) Take possession of all of the real and personal property of the estate of the decedent and preserve it from damage, waste, and injury.

(2) Collect all claims, rents, and other income belonging to the estate.

(3) Commence and maintain or defend suits and other legal proceedings.

(4) Sell perishable property.

(b) Except to the extent the order prescribes terms, the special administrator has the power to do all of the following on order of the court:

(1) Borrow money, or lease, mortgage, or execute a deed of trust on real property, in the same manner as an administrator.

(2) Pay the interest due or all or any part of an obligation secured by a mortgage, lien, or deed of trust on property in the estate, where there is danger that the holder of the security may enforce or foreclose on the obligation and the property exceeds in value the amount of the obligation. This power may be ordered only on petition of the special administrator or any interested person, with any notice that the court deems proper, and shall remain in effect until appointment of a successor personal representative. The order may also direct that interest not yet accrued be paid as it becomes due, and the order shall remain in effect and cover the future interest unless and until for good cause set aside or modified by the court in the same manner as for the original order.

(3) Exercise other powers that are conferred by order of the court.

(c) Except where the powers, duties, and obligations of a general personal representative are granted under Section 8545, the special administrator is not a proper party to an action on a claim against the decedent.

(d) A special administrator appointed to perform a particular act has no duty to take any other action to protect the estate. *(Stats.1990, c. 79 (A.B.759), § 14, operative July 1, 1991.)*

Law Revision Commission Comments
1990 Enactment

Section 8544 continues Section 8544 of the repealed Probate Code without substantive change. Subdivision (c) is revised to eliminate any implication that a general personal representative is personally liable on a creditor's claim. Among the other powers that the court may grant the special administrator is the power to disclaim. See Section 277(b) (disclaimer on behalf of decedent to be made by personal representative of decedent). See also Section 58 ("personal representative" includes a special administrator).

Background on Section 8544 of Repealed Code

Section 8544 was added by 1988 Cal.Stat. ch. 1199 § 81.5. Subdivisions (a), (b), and (c) restated former Probate Code Section 463 (repealed by 1988 Cal.Stat. ch. 1199 § 46) without substantive change and superseded a portion of former Probate Code Section 460 (repealed by 1988 Cal.Stat. ch. 1199 § 46). Subdivision (b)(2) restated former Probate Code Section 464 (repealed by 1988 Cal.Stat. ch. 1199 § 46), with the addition of a provision that the order remains in effect until appointment of a successor. Subdivision (d) was a new provision. For background on the provisions of this part, see the Comment to this part under the part heading. [20 Cal.L.Rev.Comm.Reports 1001 (1990)].

Cross References

Acquisition of estate and collection of debts, see Probate Code § 9650.
Authorized actions, see Probate Code § 9820 et seq.
Borrowing, refinancing and encumbering property, see Probate Code § 9800 et seq.
Payment of debts, see Probate Code § 11420 et seq.
Powers and duties of personal representatives, generally, see Probate Code § 9600 et seq.
Presentation and payment of claims, see Probate Code § 9000 et seq.
Proxies, who may authorize, see Corporations Code § 705.
Rules as to payment of claims, see Probate Code § 9300 et seq.
Sales by personal representatives,
  Generally, see Probate Code § 10000 et seq.
  Personal property, see Probate Code § 10250 et seq.
  Real property, see Probate Code § 10300 et seq.
Voting corporate shares in name of deceased, see Corporations Code § 702.

§ 8545. General personal representative powers granted to special administrator; additional bond; letters

(a) Notwithstanding Section 8544, the court may grant a special administrator the same powers, duties, and obligations as a general personal representative where to do so appears proper. Notwithstanding Section 8541, if letters have not previously been issued to a general personal representative, the grant shall be on the same notice required under Section 8003 for appointment of a personal representative, unless the appointment is made at a hearing on a petition for appointment of a general personal representative and the notice of that petition required under Section 8003 has been given.

(b) Subject to Section 8543, the court may require as a condition of the grant that the special administrator give any additional bond that the court deems proper. From the time of approving and filing any required additional bond, the special administrator shall have the powers, duties, and obligations of a general personal representative.

(c) If a grant is made under this section, the letters shall recite that the special administrator has the powers, duties, and obligations of a general personal representative. *(Stats. 1990, c. 79 (A.B.759), § 14, operative July 1, 1991. Amended by Stats.1994, c. 806 (A.B.3686), § 28.)*

Law Revision Commission Comments
1990 Enactment

Section 8545 continues Section 8545 of the repealed Probate Code with the addition of the introductory clause of subdivision (b) which makes clear that the provisions relating to waiver of the bond requirement apply to subdivision (b). Instances where it might be proper to grant general powers, duties, and obligations include situations where:

(1) The special administrator is appointed pending determination of a will contest or pending an appeal from an order appointing or removing the personal representative.

(2) After appointment of the special administrator a will contest is instituted.

(3) An appeal is taken from an order revoking probate of a will.

A special administrator with general powers has the power to make distributions to the same extent as any other general administrator, unless limited by the court. See, e.g., Estate of Buchman, 132 Cal.App.2d 81, 281 P.2d 608 (1955) cert. denied 350 U.S. 873 (1955).

Background on Section 8545 of Repealed Code

Section 8545 was added by 1988 Cal.Stat. ch. 1199 § 81.5. The section superseded former Probate Code Section 465 (repealed by 1988 Cal.Stat. ch. 1199 § 46). For background on the provisions of this part, see the Comment to this part under the part heading. [20 Cal.L.Rev.Comm.Reports 1001 (1990)].

Cross References

Fees for filing papers in probate proceedings, see Government Code § 70650.
Powers and duties of personal representatives, see Probate Code § 9600 et seq.
Suspension of powers of personal representative pending petition, see Probate Code § 9614.
Vacancy, see Probate Code § 8520 et seq.

§ 8546. Cessation of powers; issuance of letters to general personal representative; delivery of property; pending transactions; list of creditor claims; verified account

(a) The powers of a special administrator cease on issuance of letters to a general personal representative or as otherwise directed by the court.

(b) The special administrator shall promptly deliver to the general personal representative:

(1) All property of the estate in the possession of the special administrator. The court may authorize the special administrator to complete a sale or other transaction affecting property in the possession of the special administrator.

(2) A list of all creditor claims of which the special administrator has knowledge. The list shall show the name and address of each creditor, the amount of the claim, and what action has been taken with respect to the claim. A copy of the list shall be filed in the court.

(c) The special administrator shall account in the same manner as a general personal representative is required to account. If the same person acts as both special administrator and general personal representative, the account of the special administrator may be combined with the first account of the general personal representative. *(Stats.1990, c. 79 (A.B.759), § 14, operative July 1, 1991.)*

Law Revision Commission Comments

1990 Enactment

Section 8546 continues Section 8546 of the repealed Probate Code without substantive change. The requirement that the account be verified has been omitted as unnecessary in view of Section 1021(b)(2). The personal representative may prosecute to final judgment any suit commenced by the special administrator. See Section 8524 (successor personal representative).

Background on Section 8546 of Repealed Code

Section 8546 was added by 1988 Cal.Stat. ch. 1199 § 81.5. Subdivisions (a) and (b) restated former Probate Code Section 466 (repealed by 1988 Cal.Stat. ch. 1199 § 46), with the addition of language expressly permitting court authorization of the special administrator to complete ongoing transactions. Subdivision (c) restated the first sentence of former Probate Code Section 467 (repealed by 1988 Cal.Stat. ch. 1199 § 46), with the addition of language permitting a consolidated account where the special administrator and general personal representative are the same person. For background on the provisions of this part, see the Comment to this part under the part heading. [20 Cal.L.Rev.Comm.Reports 1001 (1990)].

Cross References

Accounts, see Probate Code § 10900 et seq.

§ 8547. Compensation; special administrator; attorney; extraordinary services; amount

(a) Subject to the limitations of this section, the court shall fix the compensation of the special administrator and the compensation of the attorney of the special administrator.

(b) The compensation of the special administrator shall not be allowed until the close of administration, unless the general personal representative joins in the petition for allowance of the special administrator's compensation or the court in its discretion so allows. Compensation for extraordinary services of a special administrator may be allowed on settlement of the final account of the special administrator. The total compensation paid to the special administrator and general personal representative shall not, together, exceed the sums provided in Part 7 (commencing with Section 10800) for compensation for the ordinary and extraordinary services of a personal representative. If the same person does not act as both special administrator and general personal representative, the compensation shall be divided in such proportions as the court determines to be just or as may be agreed to by the special administrator and general personal representative.

(c) The total compensation paid to the attorneys both of the special administrator and the general personal representative shall not, together, exceed the sums provided in Part 7 (commencing with Section 10800) as compensation for the ordinary and extraordinary services of attorneys for personal representatives. When the same attorney does not act for both the special administrator and general personal representative, the compensation shall be divided between the attorneys in such proportions as the court determines to be just or as agreed to by the attorneys.

(d) Compensation of an attorney for extraordinary services to a special administrator may be awarded in the same manner and subject to the same standards as for extraordinary services to a general personal representative, except that the award of compensation to the attorney may be made on settlement of the final account of the special administrator. *(Stats.1990, c. 79 (A.B.759), § 14, operative July 1, 1991. Amended by Stats.1990, c. 710 (S.B.1775), § 22, operative July 1, 1991.)*

Law Revision Commission Comments

1990 Enactment and Amendment [Revised Comment]

Section 8547 (enacted as a part of the new Probate Code by 1990 Cal.Stat. ch. 79, § 14) was amended by 1990 Cal.Stat. ch. 710, § 22. The section as amended continues Section 8547 of the repealed Probate Code without substantive change.

Under subdivision (d), compensation of an attorney for extraordinary services to a special administrator is made on the same basis as compensation for extraordinary services to a general personal representative. This includes services by a paralegal performing the extraordinary services under the direction and supervision of an attorney. See Section 10811 (additional compensation for extraordinary services). [21 Cal.L.Rev.Comm.Reports 67 (1991)].

Background on Section 8547 of Repealed Code

Section 8547 was added by 1988 Cal.Stat. ch. 1199 § 81.5. Subdivisions (a)–(c) of Section 8547 of the repealed Probate Code restated former Probate Code Sections 467–468 (repealed by 1988 Cal.Stat. ch. 1199 § 46), with the addition of provisions limiting payment of the special administrator until close of administration (except for extra allowances) and recognizing agreements of the special administrator, personal representative, and attorneys as to division of fees and commissions. Subdivision (d) of Section 8547 of the repealed Probate Code superseded former Probate Code Section 469 (repealed by 1988 Cal.Stat. ch. 1199 § 46), and was amended by 1989 Cal.Stat. ch. 21 § 20 to incorporate material omitted in the recodification of former Section 469. See Communication from the California Law Revision Commission Concerning Assembly Bill 156, 20 Cal.L.Revision Comm'n Reports 227, 230 (1990). The 1990 amendment added a reference in subdivision (a) to fixing the compensation of the attorney for the special administrator and restored subdivisions (c) and (d) so that the amended section conformed to Section 8547 of the repealed code. As originally enacted in the new Probate Code, Section 8547 had been revised to reflect the fact that Assembly Bill 831 of the 1989–1990 regular session would have substituted an agreed fee system for the statutory fee system for probate attorney fees. However, Assembly Bill 831 was not enacted, and Section 8547 was amended by 1990 Cal.Stat. ch. 710 § 22 to reflect this fact. See the Comment to Section 900. For background on the provisions of this part, see the Comment to this part under the part heading. [20 Cal.L.Rev.Comm.Reports 1001 (1990)].

Cross References

Compensation of personal representative and estate attorney, see Probate Code §§ 10800 et seq., 10810 et seq.

ARTICLE 9. NONRESIDENT PERSONAL REPRESENTATIVE

Cross References

Application of old and new law, see Probate Code § 3.

§ 8570. Definition

As used in this article, "nonresident personal representative" means a nonresident of this state appointed as personal representative, or a resident of this state appointed as personal representative who later removes from and resides without this state. *(Stats.1990, c. 79 (A.B.759), § 14, operative July 1, 1991. Amended by Stats.1991, c. 1055 (S.B.271), § 22.)*

Law Revision Commission Comments

1991 Amendment

Section 8570 is amended to change "the state" to "this state" in three places. This change is nonsubstantive. [20 Cal.L.Rev.Comm.Reports 2907 (1990)].

Background on Section 8570 of Repealed Code

Section 8570 was a new provision added by 1988 Cal.Stat. ch. 1199 § 81.5. For background on the provisions of this part, see the Comment to this part under the part heading. [20 Cal.L.Rev.Comm.Reports 1001 (1990)].

§ 8571. Bond

Notwithstanding any other provision of this chapter and notwithstanding a waiver of a bond, the court in its discretion may require a nonresident personal representative to give a bond in an amount determined by the court. *(Stats.1990, c. 79 (A.B.759), § 14, operative July 1, 1991.)*

Law Revision Commission Comments

1990 Enactment

Section 8571 continues Section 8571 of the repealed Probate Code without change. This section is a specific application of subdivision (b) of Section 8481 (waiver of bond).

Background on Section 8571 of Repealed Code

Section 8571 was a new provision added by 1988 Cal.Stat. ch. 1199 § 81.5. For background on the provisions of this part, see the Comment to this part under the part heading. [20 Cal.L.Rev.Comm.Reports 1001 (1990)].

§ 8572. Appointment of Secretary of State as attorney

(a) Acceptance of appointment by a nonresident personal representative is equivalent to and constitutes an irrevocable and binding appointment by the nonresident personal representative of the Secretary of State to be the attorney of the personal representative for the purpose of this article. The appointment of the nonresident personal representative also applies to any personal representative of a deceased nonresident personal representative.

(b) All lawful processes, and notices of motion under Section 377.41 of the Code of Civil Procedure, in an action or proceeding against the nonresident personal representative with respect to the estate or founded on or arising out of the acts or omissions of the nonresident personal representative in that capacity may be served on the Secretary of State as the attorney for service of the nonresident personal representative. *(Stats.1990, c. 79 (A.B.759), § 14, operative July 1, 1991. Amended by Stats.1993, c. 589 (A.B.2211), § 129.)*

Law Revision Commission Comments

1993 Amendment

Subdivision (b) of Section 8572 is amended to substitute a reference to the provision that replaced the relevant part of former Code of Civil Procedure Section 385. This is a technical, nonsubstantive change. [23 Cal.L.Rev.Comm. Reports 901 (1993) (Annual Report, App. 6)].

Background on Section 8572 of Repealed Code

Section 8572 was added by 1988 Cal.Stat. ch. 1199 § 81.5. The section restated former Probate Code Section 405.1 (repealed by 1988 Cal.Stat. ch. 1199 § 43) without substantive change. For background on the provisions of this part, see the Comment to this part under the part heading. [20 Cal.L.Rev.Comm.Reports 1001 (1990)].

Cross References

Death of party, transfer of interest in and continuation of action, see Code of Civil Procedure § 377.20 et seq.

§ 8573. Address; statement

A nonresident personal representative shall sign and file with the court a statement of the permanent address of the nonresident personal representative. If the permanent address is changed, the nonresident personal representative shall promptly file in the same manner a statement of change of address. *(Stats.1990, c. 79 (A.B.759), § 14, operative July 1, 1991.)*

Law Revision Commission Comments

1990 Enactment

Section 8573 continues Section 8573 of the repealed Probate Code without change. Failure to comply with this section is cause for removal from office. See Section 8577.

Background on Section 8573 of Repealed Code

Section 8573 was added by 1988 Cal.Stat. ch. 1199 § 81.5. The section restated former Probate Code Section 405.2 (repealed by 1988 Cal.Stat. ch. 1199 § 43), with the omission of the acknowledgment requirement. For background on the provisions of this part, see the Comment to this part under the part heading. [20 Cal.L.Rev.Comm.Reports 1001 (1990)].

§ 8574. Service of process or notice in civil action

(a) Service of process or notice of a motion under Section 377.41 of the Code of Civil Procedure in any action or proceeding against the nonresident personal representative shall be made by delivering to and leaving with the Secretary of State two copies of the summons and complaint or notice of motion and either of the following:

(1) A copy of the statement by the nonresident personal representative under Section 8573.

(2) If the nonresident personal representative has not filed a statement under Section 8573, a copy of the letters issued to the nonresident personal representative together with a written statement signed by the party or attorney of the party

seeking service that sets forth an address for use by the Secretary of State.

(b) The Secretary of State shall promptly mail by registered mail one copy of the summons and complaint or notice of motion to the nonresident personal representative at the address shown on the statement delivered to the Secretary of State.

(c) Personal service of process, or notice of motion, on the nonresident personal representative wherever found shall be the equivalent of service as provided in this section. *(Stats. 1990, c. 79 (A.B.759), § 14, operative July 1, 1991. Amended by Stats.1993, c. 589 (A.B.2211), § 130.)*

Law Revision Commission Comments

1993 Amendment

Subdivision (a) of Section 8574 is amended to substitute a reference to the provision that replaced the relevant part of former Code of Civil Procedure Section 385. This is a technical, nonsubstantive change. [23 Cal.L.Rev.Comm. Reports 901 (1993) (Annual Report, App. 6)].

Background on Section 8574 of Repealed Code

Section 8574 was added by 1988 Cal.Stat. ch. 1199 § 81.5. The section restated former Probate Code Section 405.3 (repealed by 1988 Cal.Stat. ch. 1199 § 43) without substantive change. For background on the provisions of this part, see the Comment to this part under the part heading. [20 Cal.L.Rev.Comm.Reports 1001 (1990)].

§ 8575. Proof of service

Proof of compliance with Section 8574 shall be made in the following manner:

(a) In the event of service by mail, by certificate of the Secretary of State, under official seal, showing the mailing. The certificate shall be filed with the court from which process issued.

(b) In the event of personal service outside this state, by the return of any duly constituted public officer qualified to serve like process, or notice of motion, of and in the jurisdiction where the nonresident personal representative is found, showing the service to have been made. The return shall be attached to the original summons, or notice of motion, and filed with the court from which process issued. *(Stats.1990, c. 79 (A.B.759), § 14, operative July 1, 1991. Amended by Stats.1991, c. 1055 (S.B.271), § 23.)*

Law Revision Commission Comments

1990 Enactment

Section 8575 continues Section 8575 of the repealed Probate Code without change.

1991 Amendment

Subdivision (b) of Section 8575 is amended to change "the state" to "this state." This change is nonsubstantive. [20 Cal.L.Rev.Comm.Reports 2907 (1990)].

Background on Section 8575 of Repealed Code

Section 8575 was added by 1988 Cal.Stat. ch. 1199 § 81.5. The section restated former Probate Code Section 405.4 (repealed by 1988 Cal.Stat. ch. 1199 § 43) without substantive change. For background on the provisions of this part, see the Comment to this

part under the part heading. [20 Cal.L.Rev.Comm.Reports 1001 (1990)].

§ 8576. Force and validity of service; time limits; answer; notice of motion

(a) Except as provided in this section, service made under Section 8574 has the same legal force and validity as if made personally in this state.

(b) A nonresident personal representative served under Section 8574 may appear and answer the complaint within 30 days from the date of service.

(c) Notice of motion shall be served on a nonresident personal representative under Section 8574 not less than 30 days before the date of the hearing on the motion. *(Stats. 1990, c. 79 (A.B.759), § 14, operative July 1, 1991.)*

Law Revision Commission Comments

1990 Enactment

Section 8576 continues Section 8576 of the repealed Probate Code without change.

Background on Section 8576 of Repealed Code

Section 8576 was added by 1988 Cal.Stat. ch. 1199 § 81.5. The section restated former Probate Code Section 405.5 (repealed by 1988 Cal.Stat. ch. 1199 § 43) without substantive change. For background on the provisions of this part, see the Comment to this part under the part heading. [20 Cal.L.Rev.Comm.Reports 1001 (1990)].

§ 8577. Address statement; failure to comply; removal from office; liability

(a) Failure of a nonresident personal representative to comply with Section 8573 is cause for removal from office.

(b) Nothing in this section limits the liability of, or the availability of any other remedy against, a nonresident personal representative who is removed from office under this section. *(Stats.1990, c. 79 (A.B.759), § 14, operative July 1, 1991.)*

Law Revision Commission Comments

1990 Enactment

Section 8577 continues Section 8577 of the repealed Probate Code without change.

Background on Section 8577 of Repealed Code

Section 8577 was added by 1988 Cal.Stat. ch. 1199 § 81.5. Subdivision (a) restated former Probate Code Section 405.6 (repealed by 1988 Cal.Stat. ch. 1199 § 43) without substantive change. Subdivision (b) was a new provision. For background on the provisions of this part, see the Comment to this part under the part heading. [20 Cal.L.Rev.Comm.Reports 1001 (1990)].

Part 3

INVENTORY AND APPRAISAL

Law Revision Commission Comments
1990 Enactment

This part supersedes Part 3 (commencing with Section 8800) of Division 7 of the repealed Probate Code. The superseded part was enacted upon recommendation of the California Law Revision Commission. See Recommendation Relating to Inventory and Appraisal, 19 Cal.L.Revision Comm'n Reports 741 (1988). See also Communication from the California Law Revision Commission Concerning Assembly Bill 2841, 19 Cal.L.Revision Comm'n Reports 1201, 1235–38 (1988).

The inventory and appraisal procedure provided in this part applies to valuation in administration of decedents' estates, but may be incorporated in other proceedings. For example, in a small estate set-aside proceeding under Chapter 6 (commencing with Section 6600) of Part 3 of Division 6, an inventory and appraisal of the decedent's estate is required as provided in Section 6608. No inventory and appraisal of the decedent's estate is required where it is disposed of without administration under Division 8 (commencing with Section 13000) except to the extent an inventory and appraisal is required pursuant to Section 13103 (affidavit procedure for collection or transfer of personal property), subdivision (b) of Section 13152 (court order determining succession to real property), subdivision (c) of Section 13200 (affidavit procedure for real property of small value), or Section 13658 (property passing or belonging to surviving spouse).

CHAPTER 1. GENERAL PROVISIONS

Section
8800. Filing; time; change in ownership statement.
8801. Supplemental inventory and appraisal; filing; time.
8802. List of items; fair market value.
8803. Mailing copy; persons requesting special notice.
8804. Failure to file; compelled filing; removal from office; liability; attorney fees.

Cross References
Application of old and new law, see Probate Code § 3.

§ 8800. Filing; time; change in ownership statement

(a) The personal representative shall file with the court clerk an inventory of property to be administered in the decedent's estate together with an appraisal of property in the inventory. An inventory and appraisal shall be combined in a single document.

(b) The inventory and appraisal shall be filed within four months after letters are first issued to a general personal representative. The court may allow such further time for filing an inventory and appraisal as is reasonable under the circumstances of the particular case.

(c) The personal representative may file partial inventories and appraisals where appropriate under the circumstances of the particular case, but all inventories and appraisals shall be filed before expiration of the time allowed under subdivision (b).

(d) Concurrent with the filing of the inventory and appraisal pursuant to this section, the personal representative shall also file a certification that the requirements of Section 480 of the Revenue and Taxation Code either:

(1) Are not applicable because the decedent owned no real property in California at the time of death.

(2) Have been satisfied by the filing of a change in ownership statement with the county recorder or assessor of each county in California in which the decedent owned property at the time of death. *(Stats.1990, c. 79 (A.B.759), § 14, operative July 1, 1991. Amended by Stats.1992, c. 1180 (S.B.1639), § 1.)*

Law Revision Commission Comments
1990 Enactment

Section 8800 continues Section 8800 of the repealed Probate Code without change. The four-month period may be extended by the court either on prior authorization or by subsequent excuse. A further time might be reasonable, for example, in an estate for which a federal estate tax return is necessary and additional time is required in order to ensure that the property is valued consistently. See also Code Civ.Proc. § 166 (actions in chambers).

Background on Section 8800 of Repealed Code

Section 8800 was added by 1988 Cal.Stat. ch. 1199 § 82.5. The section superseded the first portion of the first sentence of former Probate Code Section 600 (repealed by 1988 Cal.Stat. ch. 1199 § 51). It extended the time for filing the inventory and appraisal from three to four months. For background on the provisions of this part, see the Comment to this part under the part heading. [20 Cal.L.Rev.Comm.Reports 1001 (1990)].

Cross References
Authority of judge at chambers to receive inventory and account, see Code of Civil Procedure § 166.
Powers and duties of personal representatives generally, see Probate Code § 9650.
Presentation of claims against decedent, see Probate Code § 9150.
Reappraisal, see Probate Code § 10309.
Reimbursement of graduated filing fee by successful subsequent petitioner, probate rules, see California Rules of Court, Rule 7.151.

§ 8801. Supplemental inventory and appraisal; filing; time

If the personal representative acquires knowledge of property to be administered in the decedent's estate that is not included in a prior inventory and appraisal, the personal representative shall file a supplemental inventory and appraisal of the property in the manner prescribed for an original inventory and appraisal. The supplemental inventory and appraisal shall be filed within four months after the personal representative acquires knowledge of the property. The court may allow such further time for filing a supplemental inventory and appraisal as is reasonable under the circumstances of the particular case. *(Stats.1990, c. 79 (A.B.759), § 14, operative July 1, 1991.)*

Law Revision Commission Comments
1990 Enactment

Section 8801 continues Section 8801 of the repealed Probate Code without change. For enforcement of this requirement, see Section 8804 (failure to timely file inventory and appraisal).

Background on Section 8801 of Repealed Code

Section 8801 was added by 1988 Cal.Stat. ch. 1199 § 82.5. The section superseded former Probate Code Section 611 (repealed by 1988 Cal.Stat. ch. 1199 § 51), extending the two-month time for filing to four months, parallel to Section 8800 (inventory and appraisal required). For background on the provisions of this part, see the Comment to this part under the part heading. [20 Cal.L.Rev.Comm.Reports 1001 (1990)].

§8802. List of items; fair market value

The inventory and appraisal shall separately list each item and shall state the fair market value of the item at the time of the decedent's death in monetary terms opposite the item. *(Stats.1990, c. 79 (A.B.759), § 14, operative July 1, 1991.)*

Law Revision Commission Comments

1990 Enactment

Section 8802 continues Section 8802 of the repealed Probate Code without change.

Background on Section 8802 of Repealed Code

Section 8802 was added by 1988 Cal.Stat. ch. 1199 § 82.5. The section restated the fifth sentence of former Probate Code Section 600 (repealed by 1988 Cal.Stat. ch. 1199 § 51). For background on the provisions of this part, see the Comment to this part under the part heading. [20 Cal.L.Rev.Comm.Reports 1001 (1990)].

§8803. Mailing copy; persons requesting special notice

On the filing of an inventory and appraisal or a supplemental inventory and appraisal, the personal representative shall, pursuant to Section 1252, mail a copy to each person who has requested special notice. *(Stats.1990, c. 79 (A.B.759), § 14, operative July 1, 1991.)*

Law Revision Commission Comments

1990 Enactment

Section 8803 continues Section 8803 of the repealed Probate Code without change.

Background on Section 8803 of Repealed Code

Section 8803 was a new provision added by 1988 Cal.Stat. ch. 1199 § 82.5. For background on the provisions of this part, see the Comment to this part under the part heading. [20 Cal.L.Rev.Comm.Reports 1001 (1990)].

§8804. Failure to file; compelled filing; removal from office; liability; attorney fees

If the personal representative refuses or negligently fails to file an inventory and appraisal within the time allowed under this chapter, upon petition of an interested person:

(a) The court may compel the personal representative to file an inventory and appraisal pursuant to the procedure prescribed in Chapter 4 (commencing with Section 11050) of Part 8.

(b) The court may remove the personal representative from office.

(c) The court may impose on the personal representative personal liability for injury to the estate or to an interested person that directly results from the refusal or failure. The liability may include attorney's fees, in the court's discretion. Damages awarded pursuant to this subdivision are a liability on the bond of the personal representative, if any. *(Stats. 1990, c. 79 (A.B.759), § 14, operative July 1, 1991.)*

Law Revision Commission Comments

1990 Enactment

Section 8804 continues Section 8804 of the repealed Probate Code without change. The time allowed under this chapter for filing an inventory and appraisal includes any court extension of the statutory times under Sections 8800 (inventory and appraisal required) and 8801 (supplemental inventory and appraisal). Section 8804 is limited to negligent or willful noncompliance by the personal representative and does not apply where the personal representative is unable to file the inventory and appraisal due to the probate referee's delay, or where the personal representative made a good faith effort to file but was unable to do so due to circumstances beyond the personal representative's control. For delay caused by the probate referee, see Article 3 (commencing with Section 8940) of Chapter 3.

Subdivision (a) incorporates the procedure for compelling an account. Subdivision (b) provides for removal as an independent sanction. For the removal procedure, see Article 6 (commencing with Section 8500) of Chapter 4 of Part 2 of Division 7. This supplements the removal sanction that is part of the procedure under subdivision (a) to compel a filing.

Under subdivision (c), liability for injury arising from the refusal or failure of the personal representative to timely file the inventory and appraisal may include attorney's fees incurred in proceedings to compel the filing. Liability of the personal representative and of the sureties on the bond is joint and several. See Code Civ.Proc. § 996.460. See generally Code Civ.Proc. § 996.410 et seq.

Background on Section 8804 of Repealed Code

Section 8804 was added by 1988 Cal.Stat. ch. 1199 § 82.5. The section restated former Probate Code Section 610 and a portion of former Probate Code Section 611 (provisions repealed by 1988 Cal.Stat. ch. 1199 § 51) without substantive change. Subdivision (a) was a new provision. For background on the provisions of this part, see the Comment to this part under the part heading. [20 Cal.L.Rev.Comm.Reports 1001 (1990)].

Cross References

Grounds for removal, see Probate Code § 8502.

CHAPTER 2. INVENTORY

ARTICLE 1. GENERAL PROVISIONS

Cross References

Application of old and new law, see Probate Code § 3.

§8850. Included property; particular specification; money owed; partnership interest; cash; community, quasi-community, and separate property

(a) The inventory, including partial and supplemental inventories, shall include all property to be administered in the decedent's estate.

(b) The inventory shall particularly specify the following property:

(1) Money owed to the decedent, including debts, bonds, and notes, with the name of each debtor, the date, the sum originally payable, and the endorsements, if any, with their dates. The inventory shall also specify security for the payment of money to the decedent, including mortgages and

deeds of trust. If security for the payment of money is real property, the inventory shall include the recording reference or, if not recorded, a legal description of the real property.

(2) A statement of the interest of the decedent in a partnership, appraised as a single item.

(3) All money and other cash items, as defined in Section 8901, of the decedent.

(c) The inventory shall show, to the extent ascertainable by the personal representative, the portions of the property that are community, quasi-community, and separate property of the decedent. *(Stats.1990, c. 79 (A.B.759), § 14, operative July 1, 1991.)*

Law Revision Commission Comments
1990 Enactment

Section 8850 continues Section 8850 of the repealed Probate Code without change. Subdivision (b)(1) includes a requirement of precise identification of real property security in order to achieve an accurate inventory for appraisal of the underlying obligation.

Background on Section 8850 of Repealed Code

Section 8850 was added by 1988 Cal.Stat. ch. 1199 § 82.5. Subdivisions (a) and (b) restated the third and fourth sentences of former Probate Code Section 600 (repealed by 1988 Cal.Stat. ch. 1199 § 51) without substantive change. Subdivision (c) restated former Probate Code Section 601 (repealed by 1988 Cal.Stat. ch. 1199 § 51), with the addition of the reference to quasi-community property. For background on the provisions of this part, see the Comment to this part under the part heading. [20 Cal.L.Rev.Comm.Reports 1001 (1990)].

Cross References

Community property,
  Generally, see Probate Code § 6401 et seq.
  Interests of parties defined, see Family Code § 751.
  Liability for debt of either spouse, see Family Code § 910.
  Personal property, see Family Code § 1100.
  Presumptions as to property acquired by married person, see Family Code § 803.
  Real property, see Family Code § 1102.

§ 8851. Discharge or devise in will of debt or demand; creditors; distribution

The discharge or devise in a will of any debt or demand of the testator against the executor or any other person is not valid against creditors of the testator, but is a specific devise of the debt or demand. The debt or demand shall be included in the inventory. If necessary, the debt or demand shall be applied in the payment of the debts of the testator. If not necessary for that purpose, the debt or demand shall be distributed in the same manner and proportion as other specific devises. *(Stats.1990, c. 79 (A.B.759), § 14, operative July 1, 1991.)*

Law Revision Commission Comments
1990 Enactment

Section 8851 continues Section 8851 of the repealed Probate Code without change.

Background on Section 8851 of Repealed Code

Section 8851 was added by 1988 Cal.Stat. ch. 1199 § 82.5. The section restated former Probate Code Section 603 (repealed by 1988 Cal.Stat. ch. 1199 § 51) without substantive change. For background

on the provisions of this part, see the Comment to this part under the part heading. [20 Cal.L.Rev.Comm.Reports 1001 (1990)].

Cross References

Legacies, order of abatement, see Probate Code § 21400.
Powers and duties of personal representatives, generally, see Probate Code § 9650 et seq.
Priority in payment of debts, see Probate Code § 11420.
Provision in will for payment of debts, see Probate Code § 21401.
Specific gift, see Probate Code § 21117.

§ 8852. Oath; disagreement among personal representatives as to inventory; court determination

(a) The personal representative shall take and subscribe an oath that the inventory contains a true statement of the property to be administered in the decedent's estate of which the personal representative has knowledge, and particularly of money of the decedent and debts or demands of the decedent against the personal representative. The oath shall be endorsed upon or attached to the inventory.

(b) If there is more than one personal representative, each shall take and subscribe the oath. If the personal representatives are unable to agree as to property to be included in the inventory, any personal representative may petition for a court order determining whether the property is to be administered in the decedent's estate. The determination shall be made pursuant to the procedure provided in Part 19 (commencing with Section 850) of Division 2 or, if there is an issue of property belonging or passing to the surviving spouse, pursuant to Chapter 5 (commencing with Section 13650) of Part 2 of Division 8. *(Stats.1990, c. 79 (A.B.759), § 14, operative July 1, 1991. Amended by Stats.2003, c. 32 (A.B. 167), § 7.)*

Law Revision Commission Comments
1990 Enactment

Section 8852 continues Section 8852 of the repealed Probate Code without change. The requirement of an oath may be satisfied by a written affirmation. See Code Civ.Proc. § 2015.6. Subdivision (b) is an exception to the rule of Section 9630 (where there is more than one personal representative, a majority may act).

2003 Amendment

Section 8852 is amended to reflect relocation (from former Section 9860 *et seq.* to Section 850 *et seq.*) of the statutes relating to conveyance or transfer of property claimed to belong to the decedent or another person. See 2001 Cal. Stat. ch. 49, §§ 1, 4. [33 Cal.L.Rev.Comm. Reports 159 (2003)].

Background on Section 8852 of Repealed Code

Section 8852 was added by 1988 Cal.Stat. ch. 1199 § 82.5. Subdivision (a) restated former Probate Code Section 604 (repealed by 1988 Cal.Stat. ch. 1199 § 51) without substantive change. Subdivision (b) was a new provision. For background on the provisions of this part, see the Comment to this part under the part heading. [20 Cal.L.Rev.Comm.Reports 1001 (1990)].

Cross References

Appraiser of estate, oath of, see Probate Code § 8905.

Letters of administration, taking of oath, see Probate Code § 8403.

ARTICLE 2. DISCOVERY OF PROPERTY OF DECEDENT

Section
8870. Citation; interrogatories or examination in court; issuing court; contempt; notice requirements.
8871. Interrogatories; perjury; filing.
8872. Examination; witnesses; truth of allegations; order to disclose; expenses including attorney's fee.
8873. Citation; person controlling property in estate; account; contempt.
8874. Repealed.

Cross References

Application of old and new law, see Probate Code § 3.

§ 8870. Citation; interrogatories or examination in court; issuing court; contempt; notice requirements

(a) On petition by the personal representative or an interested person, the court may order that a citation be issued to a person to answer interrogatories, or to appear before the court and be examined under oath, or both, concerning any of the following allegations:

(1) The person has wrongfully taken, concealed, or disposed of property in the estate of the decedent.

(2) The person has knowledge or possession of any of the following:

(A) A deed, conveyance, bond, contract, or other writing that contains evidence of or tends to disclose the right, title, interest, or claim of the decedent to property.

(B) A claim of the decedent.

(C) A lost will of the decedent.

(b) If the person does not reside in the county in which the estate is being administered, the superior court either of the county in which the person resides or of the county in which the estate is being administered may issue a citation under this section.

(c) Disobedience of a citation issued pursuant to this section may be punished as a contempt of the court issuing the citation.

(d) Notice to the personal representative of a proceeding under subdivision (a) shall be given for the period and in the manner provided in Section 1220. Other persons requesting notice of the hearing pursuant to Section 1250 shall be notified by the person filing the petition as set forth in Section 1252. *(Stats.1990, c. 79 (A.B.759), § 14, operative July 1, 1991. Amended by Stats.1996, c. 563 (S.B.392), § 23.)*

Law Revision Commission Comments

1990 Enactment

Section 8870 continues Section 8870 of the repealed Probate Code without substantive change. See also Code Civ.Proc. § 166 (actions in chambers). For general provisions, see Sections 1020–1023 (petitions and other papers), 1240–1242 (citations).

Background on Section 8870 of Repealed Code

Section 8870 was added by 1988 Cal.Stat. ch. 1199 § 82.5. Subdivisions (a) and (b) restated the first two sentences of former Probate Code Section 613 (repealed by 1988 Cal.Stat. ch. 1199 § 51).

Subdivision (c) superseded the first sentence of former Probate Code Section 614 (repealed by 1988 Cal.Stat. ch. 1199 § 51). For background on the provisions of this part, see the Comment to this part under the part heading. [20 Cal.L.Rev.Comm.Reports 1001 (1990)].

Cross References

Compelling attendance of witnesses, see Code of Civil Procedure §§ 177, 2064, 2065.
Contempts, acts or omissions constituting, see Code of Civil Procedure § 1209 et seq.

§ 8871. Interrogatories; perjury; filing

Interrogatories may be put to a person cited to answer interrogatories pursuant to Section 8870. The interrogatories and answers shall be in writing. The answers shall be signed under penalty of perjury by the person cited. The interrogatories and answers shall be filed with the court. *(Stats.1990, c. 79 (A.B.759), § 14, operative July 1, 1991.)*

Law Revision Commission Comments

1990 Enactment

Section 8871 continues Section 8871 of the repealed Probate Code without change.

Background on Section 8871 of Repealed Code

Section 8871 was added by 1988 Cal.Stat. ch. 1199 § 82.5. The section restated the third sentence and a portion of the first sentence of former Probate Code Section 614 (repealed by 1988 Cal.Stat. ch. 1199 § 51) without substantive change. For background on the provisions of this part, see the Comment to this part under the part heading. [20 Cal.L.Rev.Comm.Reports 1001 (1990)].

§ 8872. Examination; witnesses; truth of allegations; order to disclose; expenses including attorney's fee

(a) At an examination witnesses may be produced and examined on either side.

(b) If upon the examination it appears that the allegations of the petition are true, the court may order the person to disclose the person's knowledge of the facts to the personal representative.

(c) If upon the examination it appears that the allegations of the petition are not true, the person's necessary expenses, including a reasonable attorney's fee, shall be charged against the petitioner or allowed out of the estate, in the discretion of the court. *(Stats.1990, c. 79 (A.B.759), § 14, operative July 1, 1991.)*

Law Revision Commission Comments

1990 Enactment

Section 8872 continues Section 8872 of the repealed Probate Code without change. The court order of disclosure is enforceable in the same manner as other court orders. See, e.g., Code Civ.Proc. § 1209 (contempt). See also Section 1000 (general rules of practice).

Background on Section 8872 of Repealed Code

Section 8872 was added by 1988 Cal.Stat. ch. 1199 § 82.5. Subdivisions (a) and (b) restated the second and fourth sentences of former Probate Code Section 614 (repealed by 1988 Cal.Stat. ch. 1199 § 51). Subdivision (c) superseded the third sentence of former Probate Code Section 613 (repealed by 1988 Cal.Stat. ch. 1199 § 51). For background on the provisions of this part, see the Comment to this part under the part heading. [20 Cal.L.Rev.Comm.Reports 1001 (1990)].

§ 8873. Citation; person controlling property in estate; account; contempt

(a) On petition by the personal representative, the court may issue a citation to a person who has possession or control of property in the decedent's estate to appear before the court and make an account under oath of the property and the person's actions with respect to the property.

(b) Disobedience of a citation issued pursuant to this section may be punished as a contempt of the court issuing the citation. *(Stats.1990, c. 79 (A.B.759), § 14, operative July 1, 1991.)*

Law Revision Commission Comments

1990 Enactment

Section 8873 continues Section 8873 of the repealed Probate Code without change. The duty to account under this section includes both property entrusted to a person and property that comes into the person's possession, including money, accounts, and other property and papers. For general provisions governing issuance and enforcement of citations, see Sections 1240–1242. See also Code Civ.Proc. § 166 (actions in chambers).

Background on Section 8873 of Repealed Code

Section 8873 was added by 1988 Cal.Stat. ch. 1199 § 82.5. The section restated former Probate Code Section 615 (repealed by 1988 Cal.Stat. ch. 1199 § 51) without substantive change. For background on the provisions of this part, see the Comment to this part under the part heading. [20 Cal.L.Rev.Comm.Reports 1001 (1990)].

§ 8874. Repealed by Stats.1994, c. 806 (A.B.3686), § 29

CHAPTER 3. APPRAISAL

ARTICLE 1. PROCEDURE

Cross References

Application of old and new law, see Probate Code § 3.

§ 8900. Personal representative, probate referee, or independent expert

The appraisal of property in the inventory shall be made by the personal representative, probate referee, or independent expert as provided in this chapter. *(Stats.1990, c. 79 (A.B. 759), § 14, operative July 1, 1991.)*

Law Revision Commission Comments

1990 Enactment

Section 8900 continues Section 8900 of the repealed Probate Code without change. Designation of a probate referee is made pursuant to Article 2 (commencing with Section 8920). The appraisal is made of the fair market value of the property at the time of the decedent's death. See Section 8802 (form of inventory and appraisal). See also Section 8904 (appraisal by independent expert).

Background on Section 8900 of Repealed Code

Section 8900 was added by 1988 Cal.Stat. ch. 1199 § 82.5. The section restated the introductory clause of subdivision (a) of former Probate Code Section 605 (repealed by 1988 Cal.Stat. ch. 1199 § 51) with the addition of the reference to an independent expert. For background on the provisions of this part, see the Comment to this part under the part heading. [20 Cal.L.Rev.Comm.Reports 1001 (1990)].

§ 8901. Property appraised by personal representative; cash items; checks; accounts; insurance; pensions; annuities

The personal representative shall appraise the following property, excluding items whose fair market value is, in the opinion of the personal representative, an amount different from the face value of the property:

(a) Money and other cash items. As used in this subdivision, a "cash item" is a check, draft, money order, or similar instrument issued on or before the date of the decedent's death that can be immediately converted to cash.

(b) The following checks issued after the date of the decedent's death:

(1) Checks for wages earned before death.

(2) Refund checks, including tax and utility refunds, and Medicare, medical insurance, and other health care reimbursements and payments.

(c) Accounts (as defined in Section 21) in financial institutions.

(d) Cash deposits and money market mutual funds, as defined in subdivision (b) of Section 9730, whether in a financial institution or otherwise, including a brokerage cash account. All other mutual funds, stocks, bonds, and other securities shall be appraised pursuant to Sections 8902 to 8909, inclusive.

(e) Proceeds of life and accident insurance policies and retirement plans and annuities payable on death in lump sum amounts. *(Stats.1990, c. 79 (A.B.759), § 14, operative July 1, 1991. Amended by Stats.1994, c. 806 (A.B.3686), § 30.)*

Section 8901 continues Section 8901 of the repealed Probate Code without change. The personal representative may appraise an item listed in subdivision (b) or (d), as well as items listed in subdivisions (a), (c), and (e), only if its fair market value can be determined solely from its face without calculation or reference to other sources. See introductory clause of Section 8901.

Background on Section 8901 of Repealed Code

Section 8901 was added by 1988 Cal.Stat. ch. 1199 § 82.5. Subdivisions (a), (c), and (e) restated paragraph (1) of subdivision (a) of former Section 605 (repealed by 1988 Cal.Stat. ch. 1199 § 51) with the addition of annuities in subdivision (e). The definition of "cash item" in subdivision (a) was consistent with existing practice. California Probate Referees' Ass'n, Probate Referees' Procedures Guide 9 (1985). Subdivisions (b) and (d) were new provisions. For background on the provisions of this part, see the Comment to this part under the part heading. [20 Cal.L.Rev.Comm.Reports 1001 (1990)].

§ 8902. Probate referee; inventory from personal representative; appraisal

Except as otherwise provided by statute:

(a) The personal representative shall deliver the inventory to the probate referee designated by the court, together with necessary supporting data to enable the probate referee to make an appraisal of the property in the inventory to be appraised by the probate referee.

(b) The probate referee shall appraise all property other than that appraised by the personal representative. *(Stats. 1990, c. 79 (A.B.759), § 14, operative July 1, 1991.)*

Section 8902 continues Section 8902 of the repealed Probate Code without change. A statutory exception to the duty to deliver an inventory to the probate referee occurs in the case of a waiver of appraisal by the probate referee. See Section 8903. The personal representative must furnish the referee such information as the referee requires concerning the assets appraised by the personal representative or to be appraised by the probate referee. See Sections 450–453 (powers of probate referee). Designation of a probate referee is made pursuant to Article 2 (commencing with Section 8920).

The probate referee may serve an appraisal function in areas outside of decedent estate administration. For example, in a small estate set-aside proceeding under Chapter 6 (commencing with Section 6600) of Part 3 of Division 6, an inventory and appraisal of the decedent's estate is required as provided in Section 6608. No inventory and appraisal of the decedent's estate is required where it is disposed of without administration under Division 8 (commencing with Section 13000) except to the extent an inventory and appraisal is required pursuant to Section 13103 (affidavit procedure for collection or transfer of personal property), subdivision (b) of Section 13152 (court order determining succession to real property), subdivision (c) of Section 13200 (affidavit procedure for real property of small value), or Section 13658 (property passing or belonging to surviving spouse).

There are statutory exceptions to appraisal by the probate referee. See, e.g., Section 2610 (inventory and appraisal of conservatorship under Lanterman–Petris–Short Act). For waiver of the probate referee, see Section 8903. For appraisal by an independent expert, see Section 8904.

Background on Section 8902 of Repealed Code

Section 8902 was added by 1988 Cal.Stat. ch. 1199 § 82.5. Subdivision (a) codified the previously existing practice. Subdivision (b) restated a portion of paragraph (2) of subdivision (a) of former Probate Code Section 605 (repealed by 1988 Cal.Stat. ch. 1199 § 51). For background on the provisions of this part, see the Comment to this part under the part heading. [20 Cal.L.Rev.Comm.Reports 1001 (1990)].

§ 8903. Waiver of probate referee's appraisal; petition; hearing; notice; opposition by probate referee; costs and attorney fees

(a) The court may, for good cause, waive appraisal by a probate referee in the manner provided in this section.

(b) The personal representative may apply for a waiver together with the petition for appointment of the personal representative or together with another petition, or may apply for a waiver in a separate petition filed in the administration proceedings, but the application may not be made later than the time the personal representative delivers the inventory to the probate referee, if a probate referee has been designated. A copy of the proposed inventory and appraisal and a statement that sets forth the good cause that justifies the waiver shall be attached to the petition.

(c) The hearing on the waiver shall be not sooner than 15 days after the petition is filed. Notice of the hearing on the petition, together with a copy of the petition and a copy of the proposed inventory and appraisal, shall be given as provided in Section 1220 to all of the following persons:

(1) Each person listed in Section 1220.

(2) Each known heir whose interest in the estate would be affected by the waiver.

(3) Each known devisee whose interest in the estate would be affected by the waiver.

(4) The Attorney General, at the office of the Attorney General in Sacramento, if any portion of the estate is to escheat to the state and its interest in the estate would be affected by the waiver.

(5) The probate referee, if a probate referee has been designated.

(d) A probate referee to whom notice is given under this section may oppose the waiver. If the opposition fails and the court determines the opposition was made without substantial justification, the court shall award litigation expenses, including reasonable attorney's fees, against the probate referee. If the opposition succeeds, the court may designate a different probate referee to appraise property in the estate.

(e) If the petition is granted, the inventory and appraisal attached to the petition shall be filed pursuant to Section 8800. *(Stats.1990, c. 79 (A.B.759), § 14, operative July 1, 1991.)*

Section 8903 restates Section 8903 of the repealed Probate Code without substantive change. If a probate referee opposes a waiver petition without substantial justification, the court must award litigation expenses against the referee. Moreover, a probate referee who opposes the petition ordinarily should not appraise the property in the estate. Neither the probate referee who opposed the petition, nor any other probate referee in the same office or with whom the referee has a financial arrangement, should appraise, share in the commission, or in any other manner benefit from the appraisal of property in the estate as a result of the opposition. However, the court in an unusual case may allow an appraisal by the opposing referee. For example, in a small county with only one referee where it is a problem to obtain a referee from another county, the court might designate the opposing referee if in the court's judgment the situation is such that it is satisfactory to allow the opposing referee to appraise the property.

A waiver petition may be made under Section 8903 at any time before an inventory is delivered to the probate referee, including a combined waiver and petition to open administration or a combined waiver and petition for final distribution.

For general provisions, see Sections 1000–1004 (rules of practice), 1020–1023 (petitions and other papers), 1040–1050 (hearings and orders), 1200–1230 (notice of hearing), 1250–1252 (request for special notice), 1260–1265 (proof of giving of notice).

Background on Section 8903 of Repealed Code

Section 8903 was added by 1988 Cal.Stat. ch. 1199 § 82.5. The section restated paragraphs (2) and (3) of subdivision (a) of former Probate Code Section 605 (repealed by 1988 Cal.Stat. ch. 1199 § 51), with the following revisions:

(1) A provision was added to make clear that the application for waiver is made by petition and to specify the time within which the petition must be made.

(2) A provision was added that the inventory and appraisal attached to the petition is to be filed pursuant to Section 8800 (inventory and appraisal required).

(3) The court was required to award litigation expenses against a probate referee who opposes a waiver petition without substantial justification.

(4) The court was given authority to appoint another referee to appraise the property in the estate if the opposition succeeds.

For background on the provisions of this part, see the Comment to this part under the part heading. [20 Cal.L.Rev.Comm.Reports 1001 (1990)].

§ 8904. Independent expert; special item of tangible personal property; election by personal representative; court determination; costs and attorney fees

(a) A unique, artistic, unusual, or special item of tangible personal property that would otherwise be appraised by the probate referee may, at the election of the personal representative, be appraised by an independent expert qualified to appraise the item.

(b) The personal representative shall make the election provided in subdivision (a) by a notation on the inventory delivered to the probate referee indicating the property to be appraised by an independent expert. The probate referee may, within five days after delivery of the inventory, petition for a court determination whether the property to be appraised by an independent expert is a unique, artistic, unusual, or special item of tangible personal property. If the petition fails and the court determines that the petition was made without substantial justification, the court shall award litigation expenses, including reasonable attorney's fees, against the probate referee. *(Stats.1990, c. 79 (A.B.759), § 14, operative July 1, 1991.)*

Law Revision Commission Comments
1990 Enactment

Section 8904 continues Section 8904 of the repealed Probate Code without change. If the Judicial Council adopts a form for the inventory and appraisal filed with the court, the independent expert appraisal must be filed in that form or otherwise comply with Judicial Council rules for completing the form. See Section 1001 (Judicial Council and local court rules). See also Section 8802 (form of inventory and appraisal).

Background on Section 8904 of Repealed Code

Section 8904 was a new provision added by 1988 Cal.Stat. ch. 1199 § 82.5. For background on the provisions of this part, see the Comment to this part under the part heading. [20 Cal.L.Rev.Comm.Reports 1001 (1990)].

§ 8905. Signature; oath

A person who appraises property, whether a personal representative, probate referee, or independent expert, shall sign the appraisal as to property appraised by that person, and shall take and subscribe an oath that the person has truly, honestly, and impartially appraised the property to the best of the person's ability. *(Stats.1990, c. 79 (A.B.759), § 14, operative July 1, 1991.)*

Law Revision Commission Comments
1990 Enactment

Section 8905 continues Section 8905 of the repealed Probate Code without change. The requirement of subscription of an oath may be satisfied by a written affirmation or a declaration under penalty of perjury. See Code Civ.Proc. §§ 2015.5–2015.6.

Background on Section 8905 of Repealed Code

Section 8905 was added by 1988 Cal.Stat. ch. 1199 § 82.5. The section restated former Probate Code Section 608 (repealed by 1988 Cal.Stat. ch. 1199 § 51), with the inclusion of an independent appraisal expert. See Section 8904. For background on the provisions of this part, see the Comment to this part under the part heading. [20 Cal.L.Rev.Comm.Reports 1001 (1990)].

Cross References

Personal representative, oath of, see Probate Code § 8852.

§ 8906. Objection to appraisal; hearing; notice; burden of proof; costs and attorney fees

(a) At any time before the hearing on the petition for final distribution of the estate, the personal representative or an interested person may file with the court a written objection to the appraisal.

(b) The clerk shall fix a time, not less than 15 days after the filing, for a hearing on the objection.

(c) The person objecting shall give notice of the hearing, together with a copy of the objection, as provided in Section 1220. If the appraisal was made by a probate referee, the person objecting shall also mail notice of the hearing and a copy of the objection to the probate referee at least 15 days before the date set for the hearing.

(d) The person objecting to the appraisal has the burden of proof.

(e) Upon completion of the hearing, the court may make any orders that appear appropriate. If the court determines the objection was filed without reasonable cause or good faith, the court may order that the fees of the personal representative and attorney and any costs incurred for defending the appraisal be made a charge against the person filing the objection. *(Stats.1990, c. 79 (A.B.759), § 14, operative July 1, 1991.)*

Law Revision Commission Comments

1990 Enactment

Section 8906 continues Section 8906 of the repealed Probate Code without substantive change. See also Section 8908 (appraisal report, backup data, and justification of appraisal). For objection to the inventory, other procedures are available. See, e.g., Chapter 11 (commencing with Section 9860) of Part 5 (conveyance or transfer of property claimed to belong to decedent or other person).

For general provisions, see Sections 1000–1004 (rules of practice), 1020–1023 (petitions and other papers), 1040–1050 (hearings and orders), 1200–1230 (notice of hearing), 1250–1252 (request for special notice), 1260–1265 (proof of giving of notice).

Background on Section 8906 of Repealed Code

Section 8906 was added by 1988 Cal.Stat. ch. 1199 § 82.5. The section restated former Probate Code Section 608.5 (repealed by 1988 Cal.Stat. ch. 1199 § 51), but added provision for an award of fees and costs in the event of a frivolous objection. It was drawn from former Probate Code Section 927 (repealed by 1988 Cal.Stat. ch. 1199 § 54.5) and from former Revenue and Taxation Code Sections 14510–14513 (provisions repealed by 1982 Cal.Stat. ch. 1535 § 14). For background on the provisions of this part, see the Comment to this part under the part heading. [20 Cal.L.Rev.Comm.Reports 1001 (1990)].

§ 8907. Extraordinary services compensation

Neither the personal representative nor the attorney for the personal representative is entitled to receive compensation for extraordinary services by reason of appraising any property in the estate. *(Stats.1990, c. 79 (A.B.759), § 14, operative July 1, 1991. Amended by Stats.1991, c.82 (S.B.896), §24, eff. June 30, 1991, operative July 1, 1991.)*

Law Revision Commission Comments

1990 Enactment

Section 8907 continues Section 8907 of the repealed Probate Code with the omission of the reference to the personal representative's attorney. It should be noted that the limitation in this section applies only to appraisal of property; it does not affect estate tax work performed by the attorney.

1991 Amendment

Section 8907 is amended to add a reference to compensation of the attorney for the personal representative. This restores the substance of a portion of former Section 8907 of the repealed Probate Code.

Background on Section 8907 of Repealed Code

Section 8907 was added by 1988 Cal.Stat. ch. 1199 § 82.5. The section restated subdivision (c) of former Probate Code Section 605 (repealed by 1988 Cal.Stat. ch. 1199 § 51) and expanded it to preclude extra compensation not only for appraising cash items but also for appraising other property in the estate. For background on the provisions of this part, see the Comment to this part under the part heading. [20 Cal.L.Rev.Comm.Reports 1001 (1990)].

§ 8908. Probate referee; appraisal report or backup data; justification of appraisal; fee

A probate referee who appraises property in the estate shall, upon demand by the personal representative or by a beneficiary:

(a) Provide any appraisal report or backup data in the possession of the probate referee used by the referee to appraise an item of property. The probate referee shall not disclose any information that is required by law to be confidential. The probate referee shall provide the appraisal report or backup data without charge. The cost of providing the appraisal report or backup data shall not be allowed as an expense of appraisal but is included in the commission for services of the probate referee.

(b) Justify the appraisal of an item of property if the appraisal is contested, whether by objection pursuant to Section 8906, by tax audit, or otherwise. The probate referee may be entitled to an additional fee for services provided to justify the appraisal, to be agreed upon by the personal representative or beneficiary and referee. If the personal representative or beneficiary and the probate referee are unable to agree, the court shall determine what fee, if any, is appropriate. *(Stats.1990, c. 79 (A.B.759), § 14, operative July 1, 1991.)*

Law Revision Commission Comments

1990 Enactment

Section 8908 continues Section 8908 of the repealed Probate Code without change. Backup data required pursuant to subdivision (a) might include, for example, a listing of comparable sales used in the appraisal. Confidential information that may not be disclosed includes tax assessor information obtained by the probate referee pursuant to Section 408 of the Revenue and Taxation Code. The determination of an appropriate fee under subdivision (b) will depend in part upon the quality of the appraisal and whether the contest of the appraisal is reasonable.

Background on Section 8908 of Repealed Code

Section 8908 was a new provision added by 1988 Cal.Stat. ch. 1199 § 82.5. For background on the provisions of this part, see the Comment to this part under the part heading. [20 Cal.L.Rev.Comm.Reports 1001 (1990)].

§ 8909. Retention of appraisal reports and backup data; offer to personal representative

A probate referee who appraises property in an estate shall retain possession of all appraisal reports and backup data used by the referee to appraise the property for a period of three years after the appraisal is filed. The probate referee shall, during the three-year period, offer the personal representative the reports and data used by the referee to appraise the property and deliver the reports and data to the personal representative on request. Any reports and data not requested by the personal representative may be destroyed at the end of the three-year period without further notice. *(Stats. 1990, c. 79 (A.B.759), § 14, operative July 1, 1991.)*

Law Revision Commission Comments

1990 Enactment

Section 8909 continues Section 8909 of the repealed Probate Code without change.

Background on Section 8909 of Repealed Code

Section 8909 was a new provision added by 1988 Cal.Stat. ch. 1199 § 82.5. For background on the provisions of this part, see the Comment to this part under the part heading. [20 Cal.L.Rev.Comm.Reports 1001 (1990)].

ARTICLE 2. DESIGNATION AND REMOVAL OF PROBATE REFEREE

Section

8920. Designation by court; persons appointed by county; referee from another county.
8921. Designation requested by personal representative; good cause; same or similar property or related appraisal.
8922. Court authority and discretion; non-designation of Controller appointee.
8923. Ineligible persons.
8924. Removal; for cause; hearing; notice; first-designated referee without cause; affidavit; designation of another referee.

Cross References

Application of old and new law, see Probate Code § 3.

§ 8920. Designation by court; persons appointed by county; referee from another county

The probate referee, when designated by the court, shall be among the persons appointed by the Controller to act as a probate referee for the county. If there is no person available who is able to act or if, pursuant to authority of Section 8922 or otherwise, the court does not designate a person appointed for the county, the court may designate a probate referee from another county. *(Stats.1990, c. 79 (A.B.759), § 14, operative July 1, 1991.)*

Law Revision Commission Comments

1990 Enactment

Section 8920 continues Section 8920 of the repealed Probate Code without change. Where there is no person able to act, whether because all are disqualified or removed or because there are an insufficient number appointed or because the court elects not to designate a particular probate referee or otherwise, the court may designate a probate referee from another county. For designation of a probate referee for sale of real property, see Section 10309 (minimum price for private sale of real property). The designation of a probate referee may be made by the judge in chambers. See Code Civ.Proc. § 166 (actions in chambers).

Background on Section 8920 of Repealed Code

Section 8920 was added by 1988 Cal.Stat. ch. 1199 § 82.5. The section restated a portion of paragraph (2) of subdivision (a) of former Probate Code Section 605 (repealed by 1988 Cal.Stat. ch. 1199 § 51) and made clear that the probate referee is designated from the panel appointed for the county by the State Controller. See Section 400 (appointment by Controller). The provision that the court may appoint a probate referee from another county under specified circumstances codified the previously existing practice. For background on the provisions of this part, see the Comment to this part under the part heading. [20 Cal.L.Rev.Comm.Reports 1001 (1990)].

§ 8921. Designation requested by personal representative; good cause; same or similar property or related appraisal

The court may designate a person requested by the personal representative as probate referee, on a showing by the personal representative of good cause for the designation. The following circumstances are included within the meaning of good cause, as used in this section:

(a) The probate referee has recently appraised the same property that will be appraised in the administration proceeding.

(b) The probate referee will be making related appraisals in another proceeding.

(c) The probate referee has recently appraised similar property in another proceeding. *(Stats.1990, c. 79 (A.B.759), § 14, operative July 1, 1991.)*

Law Revision Commission Comments

1990 Enactment

Section 8921 continues Section 8921 of the repealed Probate Code without change.

Background on Section 8921 of Repealed Code

Section 8921 was a new provision added by 1988 Cal.Stat. ch. 1199 § 82.5. For background on the provisions of this part, see the Comment to this part under the part heading. [20 Cal.L.Rev.Comm.Reports 1001 (1990)].

§ 8922. Court authority and discretion; non-designation of Controller appointee

The court has authority and discretion not to designate a particular person as probate referee even though appointed by the Controller to act as a probate referee for the county. *(Stats.1990, c. 79 (A.B.759), § 14, operative July 1, 1991.)*

Law Revision Commission Comments

1990 Enactment

Section 8922 continues Section 8922 of the repealed Probate Code without change. The court may, but is not required to, designate probate referees in rotation from the panel for the county, or may use any other system of designation. The court may refuse to designate a particular person as probate referee if experience with that person is unsatisfactory, if experience with that person's office or staff (including office or staff shared with other probate referees) is generally unsatisfactory, or for other proper reasons in the court's discretion. Among the proper reasons for refusal to designate a particular person as probate referee is that the person is habitually unduly slow in making appraisals, due to overwork or otherwise. This example is given by way of illustration and is not intended as a comprehensive listing of reasons. Where there is no satisfactory probate referee for the county, or a sufficient number of satisfactory probate referees for the county is lacking, the court may designate a probate referee from the panel appointed for another county. See Section 8920 (designation by court).

Background on Section 8922 of Repealed Code

Section 8922 was a new provision added by 1988 Cal.Stat. ch. 1199 § 82.5. For background on the provisions of this part, see the Comment to this part under the part heading. [20 Cal.L.Rev.Comm.Reports 1001 (1990)].

§ 8923. Ineligible persons

The court may not designate as probate referee any of the following persons:

(a) The court clerk.

(b) A partner or employee of the judge or commissioner who orders the designation.

(c) The spouse of the judge or commissioner who orders the designation.

(d) A person, or the spouse of a person, who is related within the third degree either (1) to the judge or commissioner who orders the designation or (2) to the spouse of the judge or commissioner who orders the designation. *(Stats. 1990, c. 79 (A.B.759), § 14, operative July 1, 1991.)*

Law Revision Commission Comments
1990 Enactment

Section 8923 continues Section 8923 of the repealed Probate Code without change. The prohibition in subdivision (a) includes deputy clerks as well. See Gov't Code § 24100.

Background on Section 8923 of Repealed Code

Section 8923 was added by 1988 Cal.Stat. ch. 1199 § 82.5. The section restated former Probate Code Section 606 (repealed by 1988 Cal.Stat. ch. 1199 § 51) with the addition of references to a commissioner. For background on the provisions of this part, see the Comment to this part under the part heading. [20 Cal.L.Rev.Comm.Reports 1001 (1990)].

§ 8924. Removal; for cause; hearing; notice; first-designated referee without cause; affidavit; designation of another referee

(a) The court shall remove the designated probate referee in any of the following circumstances:

(1) The personal representative shows cause, including incompetence or undue delay in making the appraisal, that in the opinion of the court warrants removal of the probate referee. The showing shall be made at a hearing on petition of the personal representative. The personal representative shall mail notice of the hearing on the petition to the probate referee at least 15 days before the date set for the hearing.

(2) The personal representative has the right to remove the first probate referee who is designated by the court. No cause need be shown for removal under this paragraph. The personal representative may exercise the right at any time before the personal representative delivers the inventory to the probate referee. The personal representative shall exercise the right by filing an affidavit or declaration under penalty of perjury with the court and mailing a copy to the probate referee. Thereupon, the court shall remove the probate referee without any further act or proof.

(3) Any other cause provided by statute.

(b) Upon removal of the probate referee, the court shall designate another probate referee in the manner prescribed in Section 8920. *(Stats.1990, c. 79 (A.B.759), § 14, operative July 1, 1991.)*

Law Revision Commission Comments
1990 Enactment

Section 8924 continues Section 8924 of the repealed Probate Code without substantive change. Other causes provided by statute for

removal of a probate referee include failure to make a timely appraisal or report. See Section 8941 (hearing and order). If experience with all the probate referees in a particular office is unsatisfactory, a referee from that office can be removed pursuant to Section 8924 or designation of a referee from that office can be avoided pursuant to Section 8922 (discretion not to designate a person as probate referee).

For general provisions, see Sections 1000–1004 (rules of practice), 1020–1023 (petitions and other papers), 1040–1050 (hearings and orders), 1200–1230 (notice of hearing), 1250–1252 (request for special notice), 1260–1265 (proof of giving of notice).

Background on Section 8924 of Repealed Code

Section 8924 was a new provision added by 1988 Cal.Stat. ch. 1199 § 82.5. For background on the provisions of this part, see the Comment to this part under the part heading. [20 Cal.L.Rev.Comm.Reports 1001 (1990)].

ARTICLE 3. TIME FOR PROBATE REFEREE APPRAISAL

Section
8940. Appraisal or status report; time; disposition.
8941. Report of status of appraisal; hearing; compelling attendance; late report; court orders; removal of referee; reduction of commission; information from personal representative.

Cross References
Application of old and new law, see Probate Code § 3.

§ 8940. Appraisal or status report; time; disposition

(a) The probate referee shall promptly and with reasonable diligence appraise the property scheduled for appraisal by the probate referee in the inventory that the personal representative delivers to the referee.

(b) The probate referee shall, not later than 60 days after delivery of the inventory, do one of the following:

(1) Return the completed appraisal to the personal representative.

(2) Make a report of the status of the appraisal. The report shall show the reason why the property has not been appraised and an estimate of the time needed to complete the appraisal. The report shall be delivered to the personal representative and filed with the court. *(Stats.1990, c. 79 (A.B.759), § 14, operative July 1, 1991.)*

Law Revision Commission Comments
1990 Enactment

Section 8940 continues Section 8940 of the repealed Probate Code without change. The personal representative must deliver an inventory together with supporting data to the probate referee. Section 8902 (appraisal by probate referee). Subdivision (a) of Section 8940 requires the probate referee to act promptly and diligently in making the appraisal, which in the ordinary case should occur well before the 60–day period provided in subdivision (b) has run. The 60–day period provided in subdivision (b) should be viewed as an unusually long period and not as the norm for accomplishing the appraisal.

Background on Section 8940 of Repealed Code

Section 8940 was a new provision added by 1988 Cal.Stat. ch. 1199 § 82.5. The section was drawn from a portion of former Probate Code Section 1025.5 (time for closing estate) (repealed by 1988

Cal.Stat. ch. 1199 § 55.5). For background on the provisions of this part, see the Comment to this part under the part heading. [20 Cal.L.Rev.Comm.Reports 1001 (1990)].

§ 8941. Report of status of appraisal; hearing; compelling attendance; late report; court orders; removal of referee; reduction of commission; information from personal representative

(a) The court shall, on petition of the personal representative or probate referee, or may, on the court's own motion, hear the report of the status of the appraisal. The court may issue a citation to compel the personal representative or the probate referee to attend the hearing.

(b) If the probate referee does not make the report of the status of the appraisal within the time required by this article or prescribed by the court, the court shall, on petition of the personal representative or may, on its own motion, cite the probate referee to appear before the court and show the reason why the property has not been appraised.

(c) Upon the hearing, the court may order any of the following:

(1) That the appraisal be completed within a time that appears reasonable.

(2) That the probate referee be removed. Upon removal of the probate referee the court shall designate another probate referee in the manner prescribed in Section 8920.

(3) That the commission of the probate referee be reduced by an amount the court deems appropriate, regardless of whether the commission otherwise allowable under the provisions of Sections 8960 to 8964 would be reasonable compensation for the services rendered.

(4) That the personal representative deliver to the probate referee all information necessary to allow the probate referee to complete the appraisal. Failure to comply with such an order is grounds for removal of the personal representative.

(5) Such other orders as may be appropriate. *(Stats.1990, c. 79 (A.B.759), § 14, operative July 1, 1991.)*

Law Revision Commission Comments
1990 Enactment

Section 8941 continues Section 8941 of the repealed Probate Code without change. Reduction of the probate referee's commission under subdivision (c)(3) may be appropriate if the time taken was within the control of the referee and was not in the best interest of the estate or interested persons. In making such a determination, the court should take into account any previous action taken under this article as a result of the delay. Removal of the personal representative under subdivision (c)(4) may be appropriate where the personal representative's failure to supply necessary information is hindering completion of the appraisal.

For general provisions, see Sections 1000–1004 (rules of practice), 1020–1023 (petitions and other papers), 1040–1050 (hearings and orders), 1200–1230 (notice of hearing), 1240–1242 (citations), 1250–1252 (request for special notice), 1260–1265 (proof of giving of notice).

Background on Section 8941 of Repealed Code

Section 8941 was a new provision added by 1988 Cal.Stat. ch. 1199 § 82.5. The section was drawn from a portion of former Probate Code Section 1025.5 (time for closing estate) (repealed by 1988 Cal.Stat. ch. 1199 § 55.5). For background on the provisions of this

part, see the Comment to this part under the part heading. [20 Cal.L.Rev.Comm.Reports 1001 (1990)].

ARTICLE 4. COMMISSION AND EXPENSES OF PROBATE REFEREE

Cross References
Application of old and new law, see Probate Code § 3.

§ 8960. Payment from estate; withholding appraisal until paid; priority; payment in course of administration

(a) The commission and expenses provided by this article as compensation for the services of the probate referee shall be paid from the estate.

(b) The probate referee may not withhold the appraisal until the commission and expenses are paid, but shall deliver the appraisal to the personal representative promptly upon completion.

(c) The commission and expenses of the probate referee are an expense of administration, entitled to the priority for payment provided by Section 11420, and shall be paid in the course of administration. *(Stats.1990, c. 79 (A.B.759), § 14, operative July 1, 1991.)*

Law Revision Commission Comments
1990 Enactment

Section 8960 continues Section 8960 of the repealed Probate Code without change. Section 11420 provides the highest priority for payment of expenses of administration, which take precedence over all other debts.

Background on Section 8960 of Repealed Code

Section 8960 was added by 1988 Cal.Stat. ch. 1199 § 82.5. Subdivision (a) restated a portion of the first sentence of the first paragraph of former Probate Code Section 609 (repealed by 1988 Cal.Stat. ch. 1199 § 51) without substantive change. Subdivisions (b) and (c) were new provisions. For background on the provisions of this part, see the Comment to this part under the part heading. [20 Cal.L.Rev.Comm.Reports 1001 (1990)].

§ 8961. Computation of commission; eligible expenses; verified account

As compensation for services the probate referee shall receive all of the following:

(a) A commission of one-tenth of one percent of the total value of the property for each estate appraised, subject to Section 8963. The commission shall be computed excluding property appraised by the personal representative pursuant to Section 8901 or by an independent expert pursuant to Section 8904.

(b) Actual and necessary expenses for each estate appraised. The referee shall file with, or list on, the inventory and appraisal a verified account of the referee's expenses. *(Stats.1990, c. 79 (A.B.759), § 14, operative July 1, 1991.)*

Law Revision Commission Comments

1990 Enactment

Section 8961 continues Section 8961 of the repealed Probate Code without change. The commission provided by this section is subject to a maximum and minimum limitation pursuant to Section 8963.

Background on Section 8961 of Repealed Code

Section 8961 was added by 1988 Cal.Stat. ch. 1199 § 82.5. The section restated a portion of the first sentence and the second sentence of the first paragraph, and the second paragraph, of former Probate Code Section 609 (repealed by 1988 Cal.Stat. ch. 1199 § 51) without substantive change. For background on the provisions of this part, see the Comment to this part under the part heading. [20 Cal.L.Rev.Comm.Reports 1001 (1990)].

§ 8962. [Blank]

§ 8963. Minimum and maximum commission; allowance exceeding usual maximum; hearing; notice

(a) Notwithstanding Section 8961 and subject to subdivision (b), the commission of the probate referee shall in no event be less than seventy-five dollars ($75) nor more than ten thousand dollars ($10,000) for any estate appraised.

(b) Upon application of the probate referee, the court may allow a commission in excess of ten thousand dollars ($10,-000) if the court determines that the reasonable value of the referee's services exceeds that amount. Notice of the hearing under this subdivision shall be given as provided in Section 1220 to all of the following persons:

(1) Each person listed in Section 1220.

(2) Each known heir whose interest in the estate would be affected by the petition.

(3) Each known devisee whose interest in the estate would be affected by the petition.

(4) The Attorney General, at the office of the Attorney General in Sacramento, if any portion of the estate is to escheat to the state and its interest in the estate would be affected by the petition.

(5) Each person who has requested special notice of petitions filed in the proceeding. *(Stats.1990, c. 79 (A.B.759), § 14, operative July 1, 1991.)*

Law Revision Commission Comments

1990 Enactment

Section 8963 restates Section 8963 of the repealed Probate Code without substantive change. For general provisions, see Sections 1000–1004 (rules of practice), 1020–1023 (petitions and other papers), 1040–1050 (hearings and orders), 1200–1230 (notice of hearing), 1250–1252 (request for special notice), 1260–1265 (proof of giving of notice).

Background on Section 8963 of Repealed Code

Section 8963 was added by 1988 Cal.Stat. ch. 1199 § 82.5. The section restated a portion of the first sentence of the first paragraph and the third paragraph of former Probate Code Section 609 (repealed by 1988 Cal.Stat. ch. 1199 § 51) with the addition of the provision for notice in the case of an increase in commission. For background on the provisions of this part, see the Comment to this part under the part heading.

§ 8964. More than one referee; share of commission; total

If more than one probate referee appraises or participates in the appraisal of property in the estate, each is entitled to the share of the commission agreed upon by the referees or, absent an agreement, that the court allows. In no case shall the total commission for all referees exceed the maximum commission that would be allowable for a single referee. *(Stats.1990, c. 79 (A.B.759), § 14, operative July 1, 1991.)*

Law Revision Commission Comments

1990 Enactment

Section 8964 continues Section 8964 of the repealed Probate Code without change. Each referee is entitled to actual and necessary expenses allowed by the court, regardless of the amount of the commission. The amount of the commission split by the referees may exceed the statutory maximum in a case where the court determines that the reasonable value of the services in the case exceeds the statutory amount. See Section 8963(b).

Background on Section 8964 of Repealed Code

Section 8964 was added by 1988 Cal.Stat. ch. 1199 § 82.5. The section restated former Probate Code Section 609.5 (repealed by 1988 Cal.Stat. ch. 1199 § 51) without substantive change. Reference to division of expenses was omitted, since each referee is entitled to actual and necessary expenses allowed by the court, regardless of the amount of the commission. For background on the provisions of this part, see the Comment to this part under the part heading. [20 Cal.L.Rev.Comm.Reports 1001 (1990)].

ARTICLE 5. TRANSITIONAL PROVISION

Cross References

Application of old and new law, see Probate Code § 3.

§ 8980. Inventory delivered for appraisal before July 1, 1989; applicable law

If an inventory is delivered to a probate referee for appraisal before July 1, 1989, all matters relating to the appraisal by the referee, including the property to be included in the appraisal, waiver of the appraisal, and compensation of the referee, are governed by the applicable law in effect before July 1, 1989, and are not governed by this chapter. *(Stats.1990, c. 79 (A.B.759), § 14, operative July 1, 1991.)*

Law Revision Commission Comments

1990 Enactment

Section 8980 continues Section 8980 of the repealed Probate Code without change. This section is an exception to the general rule that all provisions of this part applied immediately on its operative date (July 1, 1989) to pending proceedings. See Section 3.

Background on Section 8980 of Repealed Code

Section 8980 was a new provision added by 1988 Cal.Stat. ch. 1199 § 82.5. For background on the provisions of this part, see the Comment to this part under the part heading.

Part 4

CREDITOR CLAIMS

Application

Applicable in proceedings commenced on or after July 1, 1988, see Probate Code § 9004.

Law Revision Commission Comments

1990 Enactment

This part supersedes Part 4 (commencing with Section 9000) of Division 7 of the repealed Probate Code. The superseded part was enacted upon recommendation of the California Law Revision Commission. See Recommendation Relating to Creditor Claims Against Decedent's Estate, 19 Cal.L.Revision Comm'n Reports 299 (1988); Communication from California Law Revision Commission Concerning Assembly Bill 708, 19 Cal.L.Revision Comm'n Reports 545, 562–66 (1988). [20 Cal.L.Rev.Comm.Reports 1001 (1990)].

Cross References

Contingent, disputed, or "not due" debts, see Probate Code § 11460 et seq.
Determination of contest in irrevocable instrument, see Probate Code § 21320.

CHAPTER 1.   GENERAL PROVISIONS

Section
9000.   "Claim" defined.
9001.   Notice to creditors of requirements of part; notice or requests to public entities.
9002.   Filing of claims; claims barred.
9003.   Claims included among debts to be paid.
9004.   Application of law.

Application

Applicable in proceedings commenced on or after July 1, 1988, see Probate Code § 9004.

Cross References

Application of old and new law, see Probate Code § 3.
Death of person against whom action may be brought, limitation period for claims, see Code of Civil Procedure § 366.2.

§ 9000.   "Claim" defined

As used in this division:

(a) "Claim" means a demand for payment for any of the following, whether due, not due, accrued or not accrued, or contingent, and whether liquidated or unliquidated:

(1) Liability of the decedent, whether arising in contract, tort, or otherwise.

(2) Liability for taxes incurred before the decedent's death, whether assessed before or after the decedent's death, other than property taxes and assessments secured by real property liens.

(3) Liability of the estate for funeral expenses of the decedent.

(b) "Claim" does not include a dispute regarding title of a decedent to specific property alleged to be included in the decedent's estate.

(c) "Creditor" means a person who may have a claim against estate property. *(Stats.1990, c. 79 (A.B.759), § 14, operative July 1, 1991.   Amended by Stats.1996, c. 862 (A.B.2751), § 17;   Stats.2007, c. 159 (A.B.341), § 1.)*

Law Revision Commission Comments

1990 Enactment

Section 9000 continues Section 9000 of the repealed Probate Code without change. A claim not filed as provided in this part is barred. See Section 9002 (claim requirement).

Subdivision (a)(1) uses language drawn from a portion of Section 1–201(4) of the Uniform Probate Code (1987). As to the construction of provisions drawn from uniform acts, see Section 2.

A claim for a tax liability is required only as to liabilities incurred by the decedent up until the time of death, regardless whether the actual assessment for the tax liability was made before or after the time of death. See subdivision (a)(2) of Section 9000 and Chapter 5 (commencing with Section 9200) (claims by public entities). Liabilities for estate and gift taxes are not subject to claim requirements, these liabilities being liabilities arising after death. Secured property taxes and assessments, whether incurred before or after death, are not subject to claim requirements. See subdivision (a)(2).

While the term "claim" does not include administration expenses such as compensation of the personal representative and the estate attorney, it does include funeral expenses under subdivision (a)(3).

A claim need not be filed in the case of foreclosure of a lien on property in the decedent's estate. See Section 9391 (enforcement of security interest). With regard to title to property, see Sections 9860–9868 (conveyance or transfer of property claimed to belong to decedent or other person).

This part does not apply to any proceeding for the administration of a decedent's estate commenced before July 1, 1988. See Section 9004. As to the application of any amendments made after that date, see Section 3.

Background on Section 9000 of Repealed Code

Section 9000 was a new provision added by 1987 Cal.Stat. ch. 923 § 93. The section was drawn from former Probate Code Section 707 (repealed by 1988 Cal.Stat. ch. 1199 § 53) and Section 1–201(4) of the Uniform Probate Code (1987). As to the construction of provisions drawn from uniform acts, see Section 2. For background on the provisions of this part, see the Comment to this part under the part heading.

Subdivision (a)(1) of Section 9000 defined "claim" broadly to include all claims against the decedent whether in "contract, tort, or otherwise." The phrase "tort, or otherwise" included but was broader than the scope of the following language of former Section 707: "all claims for damages for injuries to, or death of, a person or injury to property and all claims against the executor or administrator of any testator or intestate who in his or her lifetime has wasted, destroyed, taken or carried away or converted to his or her own use, the property of another person or committed any trespass on the real property of another person."

Subdivision (a)(2) restated subdivision (c) of former Probate Code Section 707.5 (repealed by 1987 Cal.Stat. ch. 923 § 37), with clarifying changes relating to tax liability of the decedent.

Subdivision (a)(3) restated a provision of subdivision (a) of former Section 707 (repealed by 1988 Cal.Stat. ch. 1199 § 53) without substantive change. [20 Cal.L.Rev.Comm.Reports 1001 (1990)].

§ 9001. Notice to creditors of requirements of part; notice or requests to public entities

(a) The publication of notice under Section 8120 and the giving of notice of administration of the estate of the decedent under Chapter 2 (commencing with Section 9050) constitute notice to creditors of the requirements of this part.

(b) Nothing in subdivision (a) affects a notice or request to a public entity required by Chapter 5 (commencing with Section 9200). *(Stats.1990, c. 79 (A.B.759), § 14, operative July 1, 1991.)*

Law Revision Commission Comments

1990 Enactment

Section 9001 continues Section 9001 of the repealed Probate Code without change. This part does not apply to any proceeding for the administration of a decedent's estate commenced before July 1, 1988. See Section 9004. As to the application of any amendments made after that date, see Section 3.

Background on Section 9001 of Repealed Code

Section 9001 was added by 1987 Cal.Stat. ch. 923 § 93. Subdivision (a) restated the first portion of former Probate Code Section 700 (repealed by 1987 Cal.Stat. ch. 923 § 37), with the addition of the reference to notice to creditors under Chapter 2 (commencing with Section 9050). Subdivision (b) was new. For background on the provisions of this part, see the Comment to this part under the part heading. The section was amended by 1988 Cal.Stat. ch. 1199 § 83. The 1988 amendment corrected a section reference. See Comments to Conforming Revisions and Repeals, 19 Cal.L.Revision Comm'n Reports 1031, 1091 (1988). [20 Cal.L.Rev.Comm.Reports 1001 (1990)].

Cross References

Constructive notice, generally, see Civil Code § 19.
Filing or presentment of claim as prerequisite to action thereon, see Probate Code § 9391.
Publications, generally, see Government Code § 6000 et seq.

§ 9002. Filing of claims; claims barred

Except as otherwise provided by statute:

(a) All claims shall be filed in the manner and within the time provided in this part.

(b) A claim that is not filed as provided in this part is barred. *(Stats.1990, c. 79 (A.B.759), § 14, operative July 1, 1991.)*

Law Revision Commission Comments

1990 Enactment

Section 9002 continues Section 9002 of the repealed Probate Code without change. This section applies to all claims, whether due, not due, or contingent, and whether liquidated or unliquidated, and whether in contract, tort, or otherwise, including claims for funeral expenses. See Section 9000 ("claim" defined) and the Comment thereto. The requirement that a claim be filed as provided in this part is subject to exception under other provisions. See Section 9154 (waiver of formal defects). See also Sections 9390 (claim covered by insurance), 9391 (enforcement of security interest). This part does not apply to any proceeding for the administration of a decedent's estate commenced before July 1, 1988. See Section 9004. As to the application of any amendments made after that date, see Section 3.

Background on Section 9002 of Repealed Code

Section 9002 was added by 1987 Cal.Stat. ch. 923 § 93. Subdivision (a) restated a portion of the first sentence of subdivision (a) of former Probate Code Section 707 (repealed by 1987 Cal.Stat. ch. 923 § 37) without substantive change. Subdivision (b) restated a portion of the second sentence of subdivision (a) of former Section 707 without substantive change. Subdivision (c) restated subdivision (a) of former Probate Code Section 716 (repealed by 1988 Cal.Stat. ch. 1199 § 53) without substantive change. For background on the provisions of this part, see the Comment to this part under the part heading. The section was amended by 1988 Cal.Stat. ch. 1199 § 83.5 to delete subdivision (c) which was superseded by Chapter 8 (commencing with Section 9350) (claims in litigation). See Comments to Conforming Revisions and Repeals, 19 Cal.L.Revision Comm'n Reports 1031, 1091 (1988). [20 Cal.L.Rev.Comm.Reports 1001 (1990)].

Cross References

Claims in litigation, transitional provisions, see Probate Code § 9399.

§ 9003. Claims included among debts to be paid

A claim that is established under this part shall be included among the debts to be paid in the course of administration. *(Stats.1990, c. 79 (A.B.759), § 14, operative July 1, 1991.)*

Law Revision Commission Comments

1990 Enactment

Section 9003 continues Section 9003 of the repealed Probate Code without change. For payment of debts, see Part 9 (commencing with Section 11400). See also Section 11421 (immediate payment of priority debts). This part does not apply to any proceeding for the administration of a decedent's estate commenced before July 1, 1988. See Section 9004. As to the application of any amendments made after that date, see Section 3.

Background on Section 9003 of Repealed Code

Section 9003 was added by 1987 Cal.Stat. ch. 923 § 93. The section restated the first portion of the first sentence of former Probate Code Section 713 (repealed by 1987 Cal.Stat. ch. 923 § 37) without substantive change. For background on the provisions of this part, see the Comment to this part under the part heading. [20 Cal.L.Rev.Comm.Reports 1001 (1990)].

Cross References

Presentment of claims, see Probate Code § 9250.

§ 9004. Application of law

(a) This part does not apply in any proceeding for administration of a decedent's estate commenced before July 1, 1988.

(b) The applicable law in effect before July 1, 1988, governing the subject matter of this part continues to apply in any proceeding for administration of a decedent's estate commenced before July 1, 1988, notwithstanding its repeal by Chapter 923 of the Statutes of 1987. *(Stats.1990, c. 79 (A.B.759), § 14, operative July 1, 1991.)*

Law Revision Commission Comments

1990 Enactment

Section 9004 continues Section 9004 of the repealed Probate Code without substantive change.

Background on Section 9004 of Repealed Code

Section 9004 was a new provision added by 1987 Cal.Stat. ch. 923 § 93. For background on the provisions of this part, see the Comment to this part under the part heading. [20 Cal.L.Rev.Comm.Reports 1001 (1990)].

CHAPTER 2. NOTICE TO CREDITORS

Section

9050. Known or reasonably ascertained creditors of decedent; notice of administration.
9051. Time of notice.
9052. Form of notice.
9053. Liability of personal representative; giving or failing to give notice; search for creditors.
9054. Conditions under which notice not required.

Application

Applicable in proceedings commenced on or after July 1, 1988, see Probate Code § 9004.

Cross References

Application of old and new law, see Probate Code § 3.

§ 9050. Known or reasonably ascertained creditors of decedent; notice of administration

(a) Subject to Section 9054, the personal representative shall give notice of administration of the estate to the known or reasonably ascertainable creditors of the decedent. The notice shall be given as provided in Section 1215. For the purpose of this subdivision, a personal representative has knowledge of a creditor of the decedent if the personal representative is aware that the creditor has demanded payment from the decedent or the estate.

(b) The giving of notice under this chapter is in addition to the publication of the notice under Section 8120. *(Stats.1990, c. 79 (A.B.759), § 14, operative July 1, 1991. Amended by Stats.1990, c. 140 (S.B.1855), § 6.1, operative July 1, 1991; Stats.1991, c. 82 (S.B.896), § 25, eff. June 30, 1991, operative July 1, 1991; Stats.1996, c. 862 (A.B.2751), § 18.)*

Law Revision Commission Comments

1990 Enactment

Section 9050 continues Section 9050 of the repealed Probate Code without substantive change. This section is designed to satisfy due process requirements by ensuring reasonable notice to creditors within the practicalities of administration of the estate of a decedent. Notice may be given either by mail or personal delivery. See Sections 1215–1216. See also Sections 52 ("letters" defined), 58 (meaning of "general personal representative").

The personal representative is not required to make a search for possible creditors under this section. See Section 9053(d). The personal representative is required only to notify creditors who are actually known to the personal representative either because information comes to the attention of the personal representative in the course of administration or because the creditor has demanded payment during administration. Information received by the personal representative may be written or oral; but actual, as opposed to constructive, knowledge is required before a duty to give notice is imposed on the personal representative. The personal representative is protected by statute from a failure to give notice unless the failure is in bad faith. See Section 9053(b). However, the personal representative may not willfully ignore information that would likely impart knowledge of a creditor. For example, the personal represen-

tative may not refuse to inspect a file of the decedent marked "unpaid bills" of which the personal representative is aware. Inferences and presumptions may be available to demonstrate the personal representative's knowledge.

The personal representative is not required to notify persons who are potentially creditors because of possible liability of the decedent, but only creditors who have made their claims known. In a case where there is doubt whether notice to a particular person is required under this standard, the personal representative should give notice. The personal representative is protected from liability in this event. See Section 9053(a).

The purpose of the notice is to alert creditors to the need to file a formal claim. For this reason, the personal representative need not give notice to a creditor who has already filed a formal claim or to a creditor whose demand for payment the personal representative elects to allow as a claim notwithstanding the creditor's failure to comply with formal claim requirements. See Section 9054 (when notice not required).

This part does not apply to any proceeding for the administration of a decedent's estate commenced before July 1, 1988. See Section 9004. As to the application of any amendments made after that date, see Section 3.

1990 Amendment [Revised Comment]

Section 9050 is amended to require the personal representative to give notice to a creditor if the personal representative has knowledge of the creditor at any time during estate administration. If the personal representative first has knowledge of the creditor more than four months after letters were issued, the personal representative must give notice within 30 days after the personal representative first has knowledge of the creditor. Section 9051(c) (time of notice). Such a notice does not extend the creditor's time to file a claim. Section 9100 (claim period). However, the creditor may petition to file a late claim. Section 9103 (late claims). [20 Cal.L.Rev.Comm.Reports 2287 (1990)].

1991 Amendment

Section 9050 is amended to add the introductory clause to subdivision (a). This restores language in Section 9050 as enacted by 1990 Cal.Stat. ch. 79 which was superseded by a later enactment, 1990 Cal.Stat. ch. 140 [20 Cal.Rev.Comm.Reports 2909 (1990)].

Background on Section 9050 of Repealed Code

Section 9050 was a new provision added by 1987 Cal.Stat. ch. 923 § 93. For background on the provisions of this part, see the Comment to this part under the part heading. The section was amended by 1988 Cal.Stat. ch. 1199 § 84 to correct a section reference. See Comments to Conforming Revisions and Repeals, 19 Cal.L.Revision Comm'n Reports 1031, 1091 (1988). [20 Cal.L.Rev.Comm.Reports 1001 (1990)].

Cross References

Liability of marital property, personal liability for debts incurred by spouse, statute of limitations, see Family Code § 914.

§ 9051. Time of notice

The notice shall be given within the later of:

(a) Four months after the date letters are first issued.

(b) Thirty days after the personal representative first has knowledge of the creditor. *(Stats.1990, c. 79 (A.B.759), § 14, operative July 1, 1991. Amended by Stats.1990, c. 140 (S.B.1855), § 7.1, operative July 1, 1991; Stats.1996, c. 862 (A.B.2751), § 19.)*

Law Revision Commission Comments

1990 Enactment

Section 9051 continues Section 9051 of the repealed Probate Code without substantive change. Failure of the personal representative to give notice within the time required by Section 9051 does not preclude a creditor from filing a claim within the time provided in Section 9100 (claim period). This part does not apply to any proceeding for the administration of a decedent's estate commenced before July 1, 1988. See Section 9004. As to the application of any amendments made after that date, see Section 3. See also Sections 52 ("letters" defined), 58 (meaning of "general personal representative").

1990 Amendment [Revised Comment]

Section 9051 is amended to require the personal representative to give notice to a creditor within 30 days after the personal representative first has knowledge of the creditor, in cases where the personal representative first has knowledge of the creditor more than four months after letters were issued. This implements the requirement of Section 9050 (notice required) that the personal representative must give notice to the creditor even if the personal representative first has knowledge of the creditor after expiration of the claim filing period. Such a notice does not extend the creditor's time to file a claim. Section 9100 (claim period). However, the creditor may petition to file a late claim. Section 9103 (late claims). [20 Cal.L.Rev.Comm.Reports 2287 (1990)].

1990 Amendment

Section 9051 (enacted as a part of the new Probate Code by 1990 Cal.Stat. ch. 79 § 14) was amended by 1990 Cal.Stat. ch. 140 § 7.1 to require the personal representative to give notice to a creditor within 30 days after the personal representative first has knowledge of the creditor, in cases where the personal representative first has knowledge of the creditor more than four months after letters were issued. This implements the requirement of Section 9050 (notice required) that the personal representative must give notice to the creditor even if the personal representative first has knowledge of the creditor after expiration of the claim filing period. Such a notice does not extend the creditor's time to file a claim. See Section 9100 (claim period). However, the creditor may petition to file a late claim. See Section 9103 (late claims). For background on the 1990 amendment, see Recommendation Relating to Notice to Creditors in Estate Administration, 20 Cal.L. Revision Comm'n Reports 507 (1990). [20 Cal.L.Rev.Comm.Reports 1001 (1990)].

Background on Section 9051 of Repealed Code

Section 9051 was a new provision added by 1987 Cal.Stat. ch. 923 § 93. For background on the provisions of this part, see the Comment to this part under the part heading. [20 Cal.L.Rev.Comm.Reports 1001 (1990)].

§ 9052. Form of notice

The notice shall be in substantially the following form:

NOTICE OF ADMINISTRATION OF
ESTATE OF _____, DECEDENT
Notice to creditors:

Administration of the estate of _____ (deceased) has been commenced by _____ (personal representative) in Estate No. _____ in the Superior Court of California, County of _____. You must file your claim with the court and mail or deliver a copy to the personal representative within the last to occur of four months after _____ (the date letters were first issued to a general personal representative, as defined in subdivision (b) of Section 58 of the California Probate Code), or 60 days after the date this notice was mailed to you or, in the case of personal delivery, 60 days after the date this notice was delivered to you,,[1] or you must petition to file a late claim as provided in Section 9103 of the California Probate Code. Failure to file a claim with the court and serve a copy of the claim on the personal representative will, in most instances, invalidate your claim. A claim form may be obtained from the court clerk. For your protection, you are encouraged to file your claim by certified mail, with return receipt requested.

_____   _____
(Date of mailing this notice)   (Name and address of personal
                                  representative or attorney)

(Stats.1990, c. 79 (A.B.759), § 14, operative July 1, 1991. Amended by Stats.1990, c. 140 (S.B.1855), § 8.1, operative July 1, 1991; Stats.1996, c. 862 (A.B.2751), § 20; Stats.2012, c. 207 (A.B.2683), § 3.) [1]

[1] So in enrolled bill.

Law Revision Commission Comments

1990 Enactment

Section 9052 continues Section 9052 of the repealed Probate Code without substantive change. This section prescribes the form of notice given to creditors. The Judicial Council may adopt a different form. See Section 1001. This part does not apply to any proceeding for the administration of a decedent's estate commenced before July 1, 1988. See Section 9004. As to the application of any amendments made after that date, see Section 3.

1990 Amendment [Revised Comment]

Section 9052 is amended to revise the form of notice of administration to inform the creditor of the opportunity to petition to file a late claim. This implements the requirement of Section 9050 (notice required) that the personal representative must give notice to the creditor even if the personal representative first has knowledge of the creditor after expiration of the claim filing period. Such a notice does not extend the creditor's time to file a claim. Section 9100 (claim period). However, the creditor may petition to file a late claim. Section 9103 (late claims). [20 Cal.L.Rev.Comm.Reports 2287 (1990)].

1990 Amendment

Section 9052 (enacted as a part of the new Probate Code by 1990 Cal.Stat. ch. 79 § 14) was amended by 1990 Cal.Stat. ch. 140 § 8.1 to revise the form of notice of administration so that it would inform the creditor of the opportunity to petition to file a late claim. This implements the requirement of Section 9050 that the personal representative give notice to the creditor even if the personal representative first has knowledge of the creditor after expiration of the claim filing period. Such a notice does not extend the creditor's time to file a claim. See Section 9100 (claim period). However, the creditor may petition to file a late claim. See Section 9103 (late claims). For background on the 1990 amendment, see Recommendation Relating to Notice to Creditors in Estate Administration, 20 Cal.L. Revision Comm'n Reports 507 (1990). [20 Cal.L.Rev.Comm.Reports 1001 (1990)].

Background on Section 9052 of Repealed Code

Section 9052 was a new provision added by 1987 Cal.Stat. ch. 923 § 93. For background on the provisions of this part, see the Comment to this part under the part heading. The section was amended by 1988 Cal.Stat. ch. 113 § 15. The 1988 amendment revised the section for clarity. [20 Cal.L.Rev.Comm.Reports 1001 (1990)].

Cross References

Administration of decedent's estate, hearing petition, notice, see Probate Code § 8100.

§ 9053. Liability of personal representative; giving or failing to give notice; search for creditors

(a) If the personal representative believes that notice to a particular creditor is or may be required by this chapter and gives notice based on that belief, the personal representative is not liable to any person for giving the notice, whether or not required by this chapter.

(b) If the personal representative fails to give notice required by this chapter, the personal representative is not liable to any person for the failure, unless a creditor establishes all of the following:

(1) The failure was in bad faith.

(2) The creditor had no actual knowledge of the administration of the estate before expiration of the time for filing a claim, and payment would have been made on the creditor's claim in the course of administration if the claim had been properly filed.

(3) Within 16 months after letters were first issued to a general personal representative, the creditor did both of the following:

(A) Filed a petition requesting that the court in which the estate was administered make an order determining the liability of the personal representative under this subdivision.

(B) At least 30 days before the hearing on the petition, caused notice of the hearing and a copy of the petition to be served on the personal representative in the manner provided in Chapter 4 (commencing with Section 413.10) of Title 5 of Part 2 of the Code of Civil Procedure.

(c) Nothing in this section affects the liability of the estate, if any, for the claim of a creditor, and the personal representative is not liable for the claim to the extent it is paid out of the estate or could be paid out of the estate pursuant to Section 9103.

(d) A personal representative has a duty to make reasonably diligent efforts to identify reasonably ascertainable creditors of the decedent. *(Stats.1990, c. 79 (A.B.759), § 14, operative July 1, 1991. Amended by Stats.1991, c. 1055 (S.B.271), § 24; Stats.1996, c. 862 (A.B.2751), § 21; Stats. 1999, c. 263 (A.B.1051), § 4.)*

Law Revision Commission Comments

1990 Enactment

Section 9053 continues Section 9053 of the repealed Probate Code without change. Subdivision (a) is intended to encourage full and adequate notice in cases where it is a close question whether a personal representative has actual knowledge of a creditor within the meaning of Section 9050. If, for example, the personal representative believes that notice may be required and if the notice given generates claims or litigation that would not otherwise have arisen, Section 9053 immunizes the personal representative from liability even though notice turns out not to have been legally required.

Subdivision (b) protects the personal representative from liability for a failure to give notice to a creditor, unless the creditor establishes that the failure was in bad faith and satisfies the other requirements of the subdivision. As provided in subdivision (c), the remedy, if any, of a creditor who suffers loss as a result of a good-faith or inadvertent failure to give notice is against the estate and not against the personal representative.

Subdivision (d) implements the principle that the personal representative need not make a special search for creditors, but must only notify those who come to the attention of the personal representative during the course of administration. See Section 9050 (notice required). However, subdivision (d) does not authorize the personal representative willfully to ignore information that would likely impart knowledge of a creditor. Evidentiary inferences and presumptions may be available to prove knowledge of the personal representative in a disputed case.

This part does not apply to any proceeding for the administration of a decedent's estate commenced before July 1, 1988. See Section 9004. As to the application of any amendments made after that date, see Section 3.

1991 Amendment

Section 9053 is amended to extend liability to a bad faith personal representative in a case where the estate is open but the debt cannot be satisfied out of the estate due to preliminary distributions that cannot be recovered under Section 9103 (late claims). [20 Cal.L.Rev.Comm.Reports 2719 (1990)].

Background on Section 9053 of Repealed Code

Section 9053 was a new provision added by 1987 Cal.Stat. ch. 923 § 93. For background on the provisions of this part, see the Comment to this part under the part heading. The section was amended by 1989 Cal.Stat. ch. 544 § 9.5. The amendment made clear that the burden of proof of bad faith of the personal representative is on the person seeking to impose liability and to state the conditions necessary to impose liability. The amendment also deleted references to the attorney for the personal representative since the chapter imposes no duty on the attorney to give notice. [20 Cal.L.Rev.Comm.Reports 1001 (1990)].

§ 9054. Conditions under which notice not required

Notwithstanding Section 9050, the personal representative need not give notice to a creditor even though the personal representative has knowledge of the creditor if any of the following conditions is satisfied:

(a) The creditor has filed a claim as provided in this part.

(b) The creditor has demanded payment and the personal representative elects to treat the demand as a claim under Section 9154. *(Stats.1990, c. 79 (A.B.759), § 14, operative July 1, 1991.)*

Law Revision Commission Comments

1990 Enactment

Section 9054 continues Section 9054 of the repealed Probate Code without change. This section eliminates the need for notice to a creditor who has filed a satisfactory claim in the administration proceeding. The personal representative may waive formal defects in a demand for payment made during the four-month claim period and accept the demand as a statutory claim, thereby avoiding the need for additional notice to the creditor. See Section 9154 (waiver of formal defects). This part does not apply to any proceeding for the administration of a decedent's estate commenced before July 1, 1988. See Section 9004. As to the application of any amendments made after that date, see Section 3.

Background on Section 9054 of Repealed Code

Section 9054 was a new provision added by 1987 Cal.Stat. ch. 923 § 93. For background on the provisions of this part, see the Comment to this part under the part heading. [20 Cal.L.Rev.Comm.Reports 1001 (1990)].

CHAPTER 3. TIME FOR FILING CLAIMS

Application

Applicable in proceedings commenced on or after July 1, 1988, see § 9004.

Cross References

Application of old and new law, see Probate Code § 3.

§ 9100. Expiration date for filing

(a) A creditor shall file a claim before expiration of the later of the following times:

(1) Four months after the date letters are first issued to a general personal representative.

(2) Sixty days after the date notice of administration is mailed or personally delivered to the creditor. Nothing in this paragraph extends the time provided in Section 366.2 of the Code of Civil Procedure.

(b) A reference in another statute to the time for filing a claim means the time provided in paragraph (1) of subdivision (a).

(c) Nothing in this section shall be interpreted to extend or toll any other statute of limitations or to revive a claim that is barred by any statute of limitations. The reference in this subdivision to a "statute of limitations" includes Section 366.2 of the Code of Civil Procedure. *(Stats.1990, c. 79 (A.B.759), § 14, operative July 1, 1991. Amended by Stats.1990, c. 140 (S.B.1855), § 9.1, operative July 1, 1991; Stats.1996, c. 862 (A.B.2751), § 22; Stats.1999, c. 263 (A.B.1051), § 5; Stats. 2007, c. 159 (A.B.341), § 2.)*

Law Revision Commission Comments
1990 Enactment

Section 9100 continues Section 9100 of the repealed Probate Code with a revision in subdivision (b) that makes clear that a reference in another statute to the time for filing claims means a time that expires four months after the date letters are first issued to a general personal representative. If letters are issued by more than one court or if subsequent letters are issued by the same court, the four-month period of paragraph (1) of subdivision (a) commences on the first issuance of letters to a general personal representative. In the case of a special administrator granted the powers of a general personal representative, the claim period commences to run on first issuance of letters reciting the general powers of the special administrator. See Sections 52 ("letters" defined), 58 (meaning of "general personal representative"). This part does not apply to any proceeding for the administration of a decedent's estate commenced before July 1, 1988. See Section 9004. As to the application of any amendments made after that date, see Section 3.

1990 Amendment [Revised Comment]

Section 9100 is amended to make clear that notice to a creditor given after expiration of the claim filing period under Sections 9050 (notice required) and 9051 (time of notice) does not extend the

creditor's time to file a claim. However, the creditor may petition to file a late claim. Section 9103 (late claims). [20 Cal.L.Rev.Comm.Reports 2287 (1990)].

1990 Amendment

Section 9100 (enacted as a part of the new Probate Code by 1990 Cal.Stat. ch. 79 § 14) was amended by 1990 Cal.Stat. ch. 140 § 9.1 to make clear that notice to a creditor given after expiration of the claim filing period under Sections 9050 (notice required) and 9051 (time of notice) does not extend the creditor's time to file a claim. However, the creditor may petition to file a late claim. See Section 9103 (late claims). For background on the 1990 amendment, see Recommendation Relating to Notice to Creditors in Estate Administration, 20 Cal.L.Revision Comm'n Reports 507 (1990). [20 Cal.L.Rev.Comm.Reports 1001 (1990)].

Background on Section 9100 of Repealed Code

Section 9100 was added by 1987 Cal.Stat. ch. 923 § 93. The section superseded the last portion of subdivision (a) and all of subdivision (c) of former Probate Code Section 700 (repealed by 1987 Cal.Stat. ch. 923 § 37). For background on the provisions of this part, see the Comment to this part under the part heading. [20 Cal.L.Rev.Comm.Reports 1001 (1990)].

§ 9101. Vacancy in office of personal representative

A vacancy in the office of the personal representative that occurs before expiration of the time for filing a claim does not extend the time. *(Stats.1990, c. 79 (A.B.759), § 14, operative July 1, 1991.)*

Law Revision Commission Comments
1990 Enactment

Section 9101 continues Section 9101 of the repealed Probate Code without change. A vacancy includes the resignation, death, or removal of the personal representative from office. See Section 8520. This part does not apply to any proceeding for the administration of a decedent's estate commenced before July 1, 1988. See Section 9004. As to the application of any amendments made after that date, see Section 3.

Background on Section 9101 of Repealed Code

Section 9101 was added by 1987 Cal.Stat. ch. 923 § 93. The section restated subdivision (b) of former Probate Code Section 700 (repealed by 1987 Cal.Stat. ch. 923 § 37) without substantive change. For background on the provisions of this part, see the Comment to this part under the part heading. [20 Cal.L.Rev.Comm.Reports 1001 (1990)].

§ 9102. Claims acted on by personal representative or by court after expiration of time

A claim that is filed before expiration of the time for filing the claim is timely even if acted on by the personal representative or by the court after expiration of the time for filing claims. *(Stats.1990, c. 79 (A.B.759), § 14, operative July 1, 1991. Amended by Stats.2007, c. 159 (A.B.341), § 3.)*

Law Revision Commission Comments
1990 Enactment

Section 9102 continues Section 9102 of the repealed Probate Code without change. This part does not apply to any proceeding for the administration of a decedent's estate commenced before July 1, 1988. See Section 9004. As to the application of any amendments made after that date, see Section 3.

Background on Section 9102 of Repealed Code

Section 9102 was added by 1987 Cal.Stat. ch. 93. The section restated the last sentence of former Probate Code Section 712 (repealed by 1987 Cal.Stat. ch. 923 § 37) without substantive change. For background on the provisions of this part, see the Comment to this part under the part heading. [20 Cal.L.Rev.Comm.Reports 1001 (1990)].

§ 9103. Claims allowed to be filed after expiration of time; property distributed prior to claim; notice of hearing

(a) Upon petition by a creditor or the personal representative, the court may allow a claim to be filed after expiration of the time for filing a claim provided in Section 9100 if either of the following conditions is satisfied:

(1) The personal representative failed to send proper and timely notice of administration of the estate to the creditor, and that petition is filed within 60 days after the creditor has actual knowledge of the administration of the estate.

(2) The creditor had no knowledge of the facts reasonably giving rise to the existence of the claim more than 30 days prior to the time for filing a claim as provided in Section 9100, and the petition is filed within 60 days after the creditor has actual knowledge of both of the following:

(A) The existence of the facts reasonably giving rise to the existence of the claim.

(B) The administration of the estate.

(b) Notwithstanding subdivision (a), the court shall not allow a claim to be filed under this section after the court makes an order for final distribution of the estate.

(c) The court may condition the claim on terms that are just and equitable, and may require the appointment or reappointment of a personal representative if necessary. The court may deny the creditor's petition if a payment to general creditors has been made and it appears that the filing or establishment of the claim would cause or tend to cause unequal treatment among creditors.

(d) Regardless of whether the claim is later established in whole or in part, payments otherwise properly made before a claim is filed under this section are not subject to the claim. Except to the extent provided in Section 9392 and subject to Section 9053, the personal representative or payee is not liable on account of the prior payment. Nothing in this subdivision limits the liability of a person who receives a preliminary distribution of property to restore to the estate an amount sufficient for payment of the distributee's proper share of the claim, not exceeding the amount distributed.

(e) Notice of hearing on the petition shall be given as provided in Section 1220.

(f) Nothing in this section authorizes allowance or approval of a claim barred by, or extends the time provided in, Section 366.2 of the Code of Civil Procedure. *(Stats.1990, c. 79 (A.B.759), § 14, operative July 1, 1991. Amended by Stats.1990, c. 140 (S.B.1855), § 10.1, operative July 1, 1991; Stats.1991, c. 1055 (S.B.271), § 25; Stats.1992, c. 178 (S.B. 1496), § 34; Stats.1996, c. 862 (A.B.2751), § 23; Stats.2007, c. 159 (A.B.341), § 4.)*

Law Revision Commission Comments

1990 Enactment

Section 9103 continues Section 9103 of the repealed Probate Code with clarifying revisions in paragraphs (1) and (2) of subdivision (a) and in subdivisions (d) and (e). For general provisions, see Sections 1000–1004 (rules of practice), 1020–1023 (petitions and other papers), 1040–1050 (hearings and orders), 1200–1230 (notice of hearing), 1250–1252 (request for special notice), 1260–1265 (proof of giving of notice). See also Sections 52 ("letters" defined), 58 (meaning of "general personal representative").

This section does not excuse the duty of the personal representative to give timely notice to a known creditor pursuant to Chapter 2 (commencing with Section 9050). A creditor has knowledge of the administration of an estate within the meaning of subdivision (a)(1) of Section 9103 if the creditor has actual knowledge of the administration through receipt of notice given under Section 9050 or otherwise, such as information from a newspaper clipping service that comes to the attention of the creditor. Constructive knowledge through publication of a notice of death or other information that does not come to the attention of the creditor is not knowledge for the purpose of subdivision (a)(1). The standard applicable to the creditor's attorney is different. The creditor is not held responsible for any actual knowledge the attorney may have of the decedent's death unless the attorney is representing the creditor in the matter involving the decedent.

This section does not apply to certain public entity claims which involve a written notice or request to the public entity and a response time governed by other law. See Sections 9201 (claims governed by special statutes), 9202 (claim by Director of Health Services).

This part does not apply to any proceeding for the administration of a decedent's estate commenced before July 1, 1988. See Section 9004. As to the application of any amendments made after that date, see Section 3.

1990 Amendment

Section 9103 (enacted as a part of the new Probate Code by 1990 Cal.Stat. ch. 79 § 14) was amended by 1990 Cal.Stat. ch. 140 § 10.1 to delete former subdivision (b), which limited the types of claims eligible for late claim treatment. It should be noted that a creditor who is omitted because the creditor had no knowledge of the administration is not limited to the remedy provided in this section. If assets have been distributed, a remedy may be available against distributees under Section 9392 (liability of distributee). If the creditor can establish that the lack of knowledge is a result of the personal representative's bad faith failure to notify known creditors under Chapter 2 (commencing with Section 9050) (notice to creditors), recovery may be available against the personal representative personally or on the bond, if any. See Section 11429 (unpaid creditor). See also Section 9053 (immunity of personal representative).

The 1990 amendment renumbered former subdivision (c) to be subdivision (b) and revised new subdivision (b)(2) to make clear that a late claim should not be permitted if the statute of limitations has run on the claim. This is the consequence of the rule stated in Section 9253 that a claim barred by the statute of limitations may not be allowed by the personal representative or approved by the court or judge. Under Code of Civil Procedure Section 353, the statute of limitations runs one year after the decedent's death.

For background on the 1990 amendment, see Recommendation Relating to Notice to Creditors in Estate Administration, 20 Cal.L.Revision Comm'n Reports 507 (1990). [20 Cal.L.Rev.Comm.Reports 1001 (1990)].

1991 Amendment

Subdivisions (c) and (d) of Section 9103 are amended so that they do not immunize a distribution made under an order for preliminary distribution from subsequent liability for a late claim. Only a distribution made under an order for final distribution is entitled to the immunity provided in subdivision (b). *Cf.* Section 11622(c) (bond for preliminary distribution). [20 Cal.L.Rev.Comm.Reports 2785 (1990)].

1992 Amendment

Section 9103 is amended to revise a section reference. This revision is a technical, nonsubstantive change. [22 Cal.L.Rev.Comm.Reports 895 (1992)].

Background on Section 9103 of Repealed Code

Section 9103 was added by 1987 Cal.Stat. ch. 923 § 93. The section superseded the second, third, and fourth sentences of subdivision (a) of former Probate Code Section 707 (repealed by 1987 Cal.Stat. ch. 923 § 37). For background on the provisions of this part, see the Comment to this part under the part heading.

Section 9103 was amended by 1988 Cal.Stat. ch. 113 § 15.1 to eliminate the requirement that the creditor establish the existence of the required conditions by "clear and convincing evidence." See Communication from the California Law Revision Commission Concerning Assembly Bill 2779, 19 Cal.L.Revision Comm'n Reports 1191, 1194 (1988). See also Comments to Conforming Revisions and Repeals, 19 Cal.L.Revision Comm'n Reports 1031, 1091–92 (1988).

Section 9103 was again amended by 1988 Cal.Stat. ch. 1199 § 84.5 to combine the section with the fourth sentence of the first paragraph and the second and third paragraphs of former Probate Code Section 709 (repealed by 1988 Cal.Stat. ch. 1199 § 53), which related to late claims in pending actions, and with former Probate Code Section 720 (repealed by 1988 Cal.Stat. ch. 1199 § 53), which related to late claims involving causes of action not pending. This combination of provisions resulted in changes for purposes of clarification, generalization, and uniformity. The amendment also added paragraph (2) of subdivision (a) to Section 9103. This paragraph was a new provision. See Communication from the California Law Revision Commission Concerning Assembly Bill 2841, 19 Cal.L.Revision Comm'n Reports 1201, 1238–39 (1988). [20 Cal.L.Rev.Comm.Reports 1001 (1990)].

§ 9104. Amendment or revision of claims

(a) Subject to subdivision (b), if a claim is filed within the time provided in this chapter, the creditor may later amend or revise the claim. The amendment or revision shall be filed in the same manner as the claim.

(b) An amendment or revision may not be made to increase the amount of the claim after the time for filing a claim has expired. An amendment or revision to specify the amount of a claim that, at the time of filing, was not due, was contingent, or was not yet ascertainable, is not an increase in the amount of the claim within the meaning of this subdivision.

(c) An amendment or revision may not be made for any purpose after the earlier of the following times:

(1) The time the court makes an order for final distribution of the estate.

(2) One year after letters are first issued to a general personal representative. This paragraph does not extend the time provided by Section 366.2 of the Code of Civil Procedure or authorize allowance or approval of a claim barred by that section. *(Stats.1990, c. 79 (A.B.759), § 14, operative July 1, 1991. Amended by Stats.2007, c. 159 (A.B.341), § 5.)*

Law Revision Commission Comments
1990 Enactment

Section 9104 continues Section 9104 of the repealed Probate Code without substantive change. A claim is timely if filed within the time prescribed by Section 9100 or allowed by the court under Section 9103. A sentence is added to subdivision (b) to codify a statement in the Comment to Section 9104 of the repealed Probate Code. This addition is not a substantive change.

If letters are issued by more than one court or if subsequent letters are issued by the same court, the one year amendment or revision period commences on the first issuance of letters to a general personal representative. In the case of a special administrator granted the powers of a general personal representative, the period commences to run on first issuance of letters reciting the general powers of the special administrator. See Sections 52 ("letters" defined), 58 (meaning of "general personal representative").

This part does not apply to any proceeding for the administration of a decedent's estate commenced before July 1, 1988. See Section 9004. As to the application of any amendments made after that date, see Section 3.

Background on Section 9104 of Repealed Code

Section 9104 was a new provision added by 1987 Cal.Stat. ch. 923 § 93. For background on the provisions of this part, see the Comment to this part under the part heading. [20 Cal.L.Rev.Comm.Reports 1001 (1990)].

CHAPTER 4. FILING OF CLAIMS

Section
9150. Persons entitled to file; place of filing; service; invalidation of claim.
9151. Affidavits; vouchers or proof.
9152. Written instruments attached to claims; copies; mortgages, deeds of trust; liens.
9153. Forms.
9154. Demand for payment as a claim; waiver of formal defects.

Application

Applicable in proceedings commenced on or after July 1, 1988, see Probate Code § 9004.

Cross References

Application of old and new law, see Probate Code § 3.

§ 9150. Persons entitled to file; place of filing; service; invalidation of claim

(a) A claim may be filed by the creditor or a person acting on behalf of the creditor.

(b) A claim shall be filed with the court and a copy shall be served on the personal representative, or on a person who is later appointed and qualified as personal representative.

(c) Service of the claim on the personal representative shall be made within the later of 30 days of the filing of the claim or four months after letters issue to a personal representative with general powers. Service shall not be required after the claim has been allowed or rejected.

(d) If the creditor does not file the claim with the court and serve the claim on the personal representative as provided in this section, the claim shall be invalid. *(Stats. 1990, c. 79 (A.B.759), § 14, operative July 1, 1991. Amended by Stats.1996, c. 862 (A.B.2751), § 24.)*

Law Revision Commission Comments
1990 Enactment

Section 9150 continues Section 9150 of the repealed Probate Code without change. A person acting on behalf of the creditor may include the personal representative of the estate of the creditor or the guardian or conservator of the estate of the creditor.

Under Section 9150, if the claimant mails a copy of the claim to the personal representative but fails to file it with the court, the claim is not properly filed. Thus the holding in Estate of Schweitzer, 182 Cal.App.3d 330, 227 Cal.Rptr. 11 (1986) (sending settlement agreement to executor's attorney was sufficient), is no longer good law. However, the requirement that the claim be filed with the court does not preclude application of estoppel or other equitable doctrines in an appropriate case. See Section 9154(b). See also Section 9154(a) (waiver of formal defects). When a claim is filed with the court, the court clerk must accept it as filed and may not reject it for formal defects. For general provisions relating to mailing, see Sections 1215–1217.

This part does not apply to any proceeding for the administration of a decedent's estate commenced before July 1, 1988. See Section 9004. As to the application of any amendments made after that date, see Section 3.

Background on Section 9150 of Repealed Code

Section 9150 was added by 1987 Cal.Stat. ch. 923 § 93. Subdivision (a) of Section 9150 generalized a provision of the first sentence of former Probate Code Section 704.2 (repealed by 1987 Cal.Stat. ch. 923 § 37).

Subdivision (b) of Section 9150 superseded subdivision (a) of former Probate Code Section 700 (repealed by 1987 Cal.Stat. ch. 923 § 37). Under former Section 700, the creditor was required either to file the claim with the court or to present it to the personal representative. Section 9150 required the claim to be filed with the court and a copy to be mailed to the personal representative. See also new Section 9153 (form of claim).

For background on the provisions of this part, see the Comment to this part under the part heading. [20 Cal.L.Rev.Comm.Reports 1001 (1990)].

§ 9151. Affidavits; vouchers or proof

(a) A claim shall be supported by the affidavit of the creditor or the person acting on behalf of the creditor stating:

(1) The claim is a just claim.

(2) If the claim is due, the facts supporting the claim, the amount of the claim, and that all payments on and offsets to the claim have been credited.

(3) If the claim is not due or contingent, or the amount is not yet ascertainable, the facts supporting the claim.

(4) If the affidavit is made by a person other than the creditor, the reason it is not made by the creditor.

(b) The personal representative may require satisfactory vouchers or proof to be produced to support the claim. An original voucher may be withdrawn after a copy is provided. If a copy is provided, the copy shall be attached to the claim. *(Stats.1990, c. 79 (A.B.759), § 14, operative July 1, 1991.)*

Law Revision Commission Comments
1990 Enactment

Section 9151 continues Section 9151 of the repealed Probate Code without substantive change. The claim may be supported by a declaration under penalty of perjury in lieu of an affidavit. See Code Civ.Proc. § 2015.5. The affidavit may be made on information and belief. Cf. Code Civ.Proc. § 446. A person acting on behalf of the creditor may include the personal representative of the estate of the creditor or the guardian or conservator of the estate of the creditor. As to a claim barred by the statute of limitations, see Section 9253. This part does not apply to any proceeding for the administration of a decedent's estate commenced before July 1, 1988. See Section 9004. As to the application of any amendments made after that date, see Section 3.

Background on Section 9151 of Repealed Code

Section 9151 was added by 1987 Cal.Stat. ch. 923 § 93. The section restated former Probate Code Section 705 (repealed by 1987 Cal.Stat. ch. 923 § 37) without substantive change. For background on the provisions of this part, see the Comment to this part under the part heading. [20 Cal.L.Rev.Comm.Reports 1001 (1990)].

Cross References

Affidavits,
   Generally, see Code of Civil Procedure § 2009 et seq.
   Definition, see Code of Civil Procedure § 2003.
Future, contingent, or disputed claims, deposit in financial institution, see Probate Code § 11463.
Payment of debts without verified claim filed and established, see Probate Code § 11005.

§ 9152. Written instruments attached to claims; copies; mortgages, deeds of trust; liens

(a) If a claim is based on a written instrument, either the original or a copy of the original with all endorsements shall be attached to the claim. If a copy is attached, the original instrument shall be exhibited to the personal representative or court or judge on demand unless it is lost or destroyed, in which case the fact that it is lost or destroyed shall be stated in the claim.

(b) If the claim or a part of the claim is secured by a mortgage, deed of trust, or other lien that is recorded in the office of the recorder of the county in which the property subject to the lien is located, it is sufficient to describe the mortgage, deed of trust, or lien and the recording reference for the instrument that created the mortgage, deed of trust, or other lien. *(Stats.1990, c. 79 (A.B.759), § 14, operative July 1, 1991.)*

Law Revision Commission Comments
1990 Enactment

Section 9152 continues Section 9152 of the repealed Probate Code without substantive change. A creditor need not file a claim in order to enforce a secured obligation against the security if recourse against other property in the estate is waived. See Section 9391 (enforcement of security interest). This part does not apply to any proceeding for the administration of a decedent's estate commenced before July 1, 1988. See Section 9004. As to the application of any amendments made after that date, see Section 3.

Background on Section 9152 of Repealed Code

Section 9152 was added by 1987 Cal.Stat. ch. 923 § 93. The section restated former Probate Code Section 706 (repealed by 1987 Cal.Stat. ch. 923 § 37) without substantive change. For background on the provisions of this part, see the Comment to this part under the part heading. [20 Cal.L.Rev.Comm.Reports 1001 (1990)].

Cross References

Grants and mortgages, recording in separate books, see Civil Code § 1171.
Mode of recording instruments, generally, see Civil Code § 1169 et seq.

Mortgage or lien, filing or presenting as prerequisite to action on, see Probate Code § 9391.

Rules as to payment of claims, see Probate Code § 9300 et seq.

§ 9153. Forms

A claim form adopted by the Judicial Council shall inform the creditor that the claim must be filed with the court and a copy mailed or delivered to the personal representative. The claim form shall include a proof of mailing or delivery of a copy of the claim to the personal representative, which may be completed by the creditor. *(Stats.1990, c. 79 (A.B.759), § 14, operative July 1, 1991.)*

Law Revision Commission Comments

1990 Enactment

Section 9153 continues Section 9153 of the repealed Probate Code with the omission of subdivision (a) of Section 9153 of the repealed Probate Code. That subdivision, which gave the Judicial Council authority to prescribe forms, was unnecessary in view of Section 1001(b), a general provision that gives the Judicial Council authority to prescribe forms. This part does not apply to any proceeding for the administration of a decedent's estate commenced before July 1, 1988. See Section 9004. As to the application of any amendments made after that date, see Section 3.

Background on Section 9153 of Repealed Code

Section 9153 was a new provision added by 1987 Cal.Stat. ch. 923 § 93. For background on the provisions of this part, see the Comment to this part under the part heading. [20 Cal.L.Rev.Comm.Reports 1001 (1990)].

§ 9154. Demand for payment as a claim; waiver of formal defects

(a) Notwithstanding any other provision of this part, if a creditor makes a written demand for payment within four months after the date letters are first issued to a general personal representative, the personal representative may waive formal defects and elect to treat the demand as a claim that is filed and established under this part by paying the amount demanded before the expiration of 30 days after the four-month period if all of the following conditions are satisfied:

(1) The debt was justly due.

(2) The debt was paid in good faith.

(3) The amount paid was the true amount of the indebtedness over and above all payments and offsets.

(4) The estate is solvent.

(b) Nothing in this section limits application of (1) the doctrines of waiver, estoppel, laches, or detrimental reliance or (2) any other equitable principle. *(Stats.1990, c. 79 (A.B.759), § 14, operative July 1, 1991.)*

Law Revision Commission Comments

1990 Enactment

Section 9154 continues Section 9154 of the repealed Probate Code without substantive change. Subdivision (a) authorizes the personal representative to waive technical claim requirements, such as the form and manner of filing a claim, in appropriate cases. This may be useful, for example, for regular bills received by the personal representative in the ordinary course of business concerning which there is no dispute. This authority enables the personal representative to avoid the need for additional notice to the creditor. See

Section 9054 (when notice not required). For approval of the personal representative's account where payment is made without prior court order, see Sections 11005 (settlement of account), 11422 (payment of debts on court order). See also Sections 52 ("letters" defined), 58 (meaning of "general personal representative"). As to a claim barred by the statute of limitations, see Section 9253.

Subdivision (b) recognizes expressly equitable principles that might permit payment of an informal claim notwithstanding a failure to satisfy all requirements of subdivision (a). Under the facts in Estate of Sturm, 201 Cal.App.3d 14, 246 Cal.Rptr. 852 (1988), for example, recognition and partial payment of the debt by the personal representative within the four-month and thirty-day limitation of subdivision (a) could serve as an equitable basis for allowing completion of payments beyond that period.

This part does not apply to any proceeding for the administration of a decedent's estate commenced before July 1, 1988. See Section 9004. As to the application of any amendments made after that date, see Section 3.

Background on Section 9154 of Repealed Code

Section 9154 was added by 1987 Cal.Stat. ch. 923 § 93. Section 9154 was drawn from former Probate Code Section 929 (repealed by 1988 Cal.Stat. ch. 1199 § 54.5) (accounts). For background on the provisions of this part, see the Comment to this part under the part heading. Section 9154 was amended by 1989 Cal.Stat. ch. 21 § 21 to add subdivision (b). See Communication from the California Law Revision Commission Concerning Assembly Bill 156, 20 Cal.L.Revision Comm'n Reports 227, 230–31 (1990). [20 Cal.L.Rev.Comm.Reports 1001 (1990)].

Cross References

Allowance of debt payment without filing of claim, see Probate Code § 11005.

CHAPTER 5. CLAIMS BY PUBLIC ENTITIES

Application

Applicable in proceedings commenced on or after July 1, 1988, see § 9004.

Cross References

Application of old and new law, see Probate Code § 3.

§ 9200. Time for filing; "public entity" defined

(a) Except as provided in this chapter, a claim by a public entity shall be filed within the time otherwise provided in this part. A claim not so filed is barred, including any lien imposed for the claim.

(b) As used in this chapter, "public entity" has the meaning provided in Section 811.2 of the Government Code, and includes an officer authorized to act on behalf of the public entity. *(Stats.1990, c. 79 (A.B.759), § 14, operative July 1, 1991.)*

Law Revision Commission Comments
1990 Enactment

Section 9200 continues Section 9200 of the repealed Probate Code without change. "Public entity" is defined in Government Code Section 811.2 to include the State, the Regents of the University of California, a county, city, district, public authority, public agency, and any other political subdivision or public corporation in the State. This section does not govern obligations owed to the United States which are governed by federal law. This part does not apply to any proceeding for the administration of a decedent's estate commenced before July 1, 1988. See Section 9004. As to the application of any amendments made after that date, see Section 3.

Background on Section 9200 of Repealed Code

Section 9200 was added by 1987 Cal.Stat. ch. 923 § 93. The section restated subdivision (a) of former Probate Code Section 707.5 (repealed by 1987 Cal.Stat. ch. 923 § 37), with the addition of the reference to an authorized officer. See, e.g., Section 9202 (claim by Director of Health Services). For background on the provisions of this part, see the Comment to this part under the part heading. [20 Cal.L.Rev.Comm.Reports 1001 (1990)].

§ 9201. Claims arising under laws, acts, or codes; forms; written notice or request

(a) Notwithstanding any other statute, if a claim of a public entity arises under a law, act, or code listed in subdivision (b):

(1) The public entity may provide a form to be used for the written notice or request to the public entity required by this chapter. Where appropriate, the form may require the decedent's social security number, if known.

(2) The claim is barred only after written notice or request to the public entity and expiration of the period provided in the applicable section. If no written notice or request is made, the claim is enforceable by the remedies, and is barred at the time, otherwise provided in the law, act, or code.

(b)

Law, Act, or Code	Applicable Section
Sales and Use Tax Law (commencing with Section 6001 of the Revenue and Taxation Code)	Section 6487.1 of the Revenue and Taxation Code
Bradley–Burns Uniform Local Sales and Use Tax Law (commencing with Section 7200 of the Revenue and Taxation Code)	Section 6487.1 of the Revenue and Taxation Code
Transactions and Use Tax Law (commencing with Section 7251 of the Revenue and Taxation Code)	Section 6487.1 of the Revenue and Taxation Code
Motor Vehicle Fuel License Tax Law (commencing with Section 7301 of the Revenue and Taxation Code)	Section 7675.1 of the Revenue and Taxation Code
Use Fuel Tax Law (commencing with Section 8601 of the Revenue and Taxation Code)	Section 8782.1 of the Revenue and Taxation Code
Administration of Franchise and Income Tax Law (commencing with Section 18401 of the Revenue and Taxation Code)	Section 19517 of the Revenue and Taxation Code
Cigarette Tax Law (commencing with Section 30001 of the Revenue and Taxation Code)	Section 30207.1 of the Revenue and Taxation Code
Alcoholic Beverage Tax Law (commencing with Section 32001 of the Revenue and Taxation Code)	Section 32272.1 of the Revenue and Taxation Code
Unemployment Insurance Code	Section 1090 of the Unemployment Insurance Code
State Hospitals (commencing with Section 7200 of the Welfare and Institutions Code)	Section 7277.1 of the Welfare and Institutions Code
Medi–Cal Act (commencing with Section 14000 of the Welfare and Institutions Code)	Section 9202 of the Probate Code
Waxman–Duffy Prepaid Health Plan Act (commencing with Section 14200 of the Welfare and Institutions Code)	Section 9202 of the Probate Code

(Stats.1990, c. 79 (A.B.759), § 14, operative July 1, 1991. Amended by Stats.1990, c. 140 (S.B.1855), § 11.1, operative July 1, 1991; Stats.1999, c. 987 (S.B.1229), § 2, eff. Oct. 10, 1999; Stats.2014, c. 144 (A.B.1847), § 49, eff. Jan. 1, 2015.)

Law Revision Commission Comments
1990 Enactment

Section 9201 continues Section 9201 of the repealed Probate Code without substantive change. This section makes explicit the authority of the public entity to use an appropriate form for efficient administration of the relevant law under which collection is sought, notwithstanding Section 9052 (form of notice). Section 9201 also makes explicit the authority of the public entity to use available statutory remedies to enforce the liability where it has not been given notice of estate administration. This part does not apply to any proceeding for the administration of a decedent's estate commenced before July 1, 1988. See Section 9004. As to the application of any amendments made after that date, see Section 3.

1990 Amendment

Section 9201 (enacted as a part of the new Probate Code by 1990 Cal.Stat. ch. 79 § 14) was amended by 1990 Cal.Stat. ch. 140 § 11.1 to make clear that the section applies notwithstanding statutes located in places other than this part. Specifically, Section 9201 applies notwithstanding Code of Civil Procedure Section 353 (general statute of limitations running one year from the decedent's death). For background on the 1990 amendment, see Recommendation Relating to Notice to Creditors in Estate Administration, 20 Cal.L. Revision Comm'n Reports 507 (1990). [20 Cal.L.Rev.Comm.Reports 1001 (1990)].

Background on Section 9201 of Repealed Code

Section 9201 was added by 1987 Cal.Stat. ch. 923 § 93. The section restated subdivision (b) of former Probate Code Section 707.5 and a portion of the first sentence of subdivision (a) of former Probate Code Section 700.1 (provisions repealed by 1987 Cal.Stat. ch. 923 § 37). For background on the provisions of this part, see the Comment to this part under the part heading. [20 Cal.L.Rev.Comm.Reports 1001 (1990)].

§ 9202. Death of person or surviving spouse of person receiving public health care; notice to Director of Health Care Services; death of person with heir in correctional facility; notice to director of Victim Compensation Board; notice of estate administration to Franchise Tax Board

(a) Not later than 90 days after the date letters are first issued to a general personal representative, the general personal representative or estate attorney shall give the Director of Health Care Services notice of the decedent's death in the manner provided in Section 215 if the general personal representative knows or has reason to believe that the decedent received health care under Chapter 7 (commencing with Section 14000) or Chapter 8 (commencing with Section 14200) of Part 3 of Division 9 of the Welfare and Institutions Code, or was the surviving spouse of a person who received that health care. The director has four months after notice is given in which to file a claim.

(b) Not later than 90 days after the date letters are first issued to a general personal representative, the general personal representative or estate attorney shall give the Director of the California Victim Compensation * * * Board notice of the decedent's death in the manner provided in Section 216 if the general personal representative or estate attorney knows that an heir or beneficiary is or has previously been confined in a prison or facility under the jurisdiction of the Department of Corrections and Rehabilitation or confined in any county or city jail, road camp, industrial farm, or other local correctional facility. The director of the board shall have four months after that notice is received in which to pursue collection of any outstanding restitution fines or orders.

(c)(1) Not later than 90 days after the date letters are first issued to a general personal representative, the general personal representative or estate attorney shall give the Franchise Tax Board notice of the administration of the estate. The notice shall be given as provided in Section 1215.

(2) The provisions of this subdivision shall apply to estates for which letters are first issued on or after July 1, 2008.

(d) Nothing in this section shall be interpreted as requiring the estate attorney, the beneficiary, the personal representative, or the person in possession of property of the decedent to conduct an additional investigation to determine whether a decedent has an heir or beneficiary who has been confined in a prison or facility under the jurisdiction of the Department of Corrections and Rehabilitation, or its Division of Juvenile Facilities, or confined in any county or city jail, road camp, industrial farm, or other local correctional facility. *(Stats. 1990, c. 79 (A.B.759), § 14, operative July 1, 1991. Amended by Stats.1993, c. 69 (S.B.35), § 5, eff. June 30, 1993; Stats. 2005, c. 238 (S.B.972), § 4; Stats.2007, c. 105 (A.B.361), § 1; Stats.2014, c. 508 (A.B.2685), § 4, eff. Jan. 1, 2015; Stats.2016, c. 31 (S.B.836), § 261, eff. June 27, 2016.)*

Law Revision Commission Comments
1990 Enactment

Section 9202 continues Section 9202 of the repealed Probate Code without change. This part does not apply to any proceeding for the administration of a decedent's estate commenced before July 1, 1988. See Section 9004. As to the application of any amendments made after that date, see Section 3. See also Sections 52 ("letters" defined), 58 (meaning of "general personal representative"). Section 215 requires that a report of death be made to the Director of Health Services by the estate attorney (or if no estate attorney, by the beneficiary, the personal representative, or the person in possession of property of the decedent) where the decedent received or may have received health care under the provisions of Chapter 7 (commencing with Section 14000) or Chapter 8 (commencing with Section 14200) of Part 3 of Division 9 of the Welfare and Institutions Code.

Background on Section 9202 of Repealed Code

Section 9202 was added by 1987 Cal.Stat. ch. 923 § 93. The section restated the first sentence of subdivision (a), all of subdivision (b), and the first sentence of subdivision (c) of former Probate Code Section 700.1 (repealed by 1987 Cal.Stat. ch. 923 § 37), except that notice by beneficiaries and persons in possession of the decedent's property was omitted from Section 9202. For notice by these persons, see Section 215 (report to Director of Health Services). Under Section 9202, the time within which the notice must be made to the Director of Health Services was made to run from the date of issuance of letters rather than from the date of death as was provided in former Section 700.1. For background on the provisions of this part, see the Comment to this part under the part heading. [20 Cal.L.Rev.Comm.Reports 1001 (1990)].

§ 9203. Failure to give written notice or request; claims against distributees

(a) Failure of a person to give the written notice or request required by this chapter does not affect the validity of any proceeding under this code concerning the administration of the decedent's estate.

(b) If property in the estate is distributed before expiration of the time allowed a public entity to file a claim, the public entity has a claim against the distributees to the full extent of the public entity's claim, or each distributee's share of the distributed property, whichever is less. The public entity's claim against distributees includes interest at a rate equal to that specified in Section 19521 of the Revenue and Taxation Code, from the date of distribution or the date of filing the claim by the public entity, whichever is later, plus other accruing costs as in the case of enforcement of a money judgment. *(Stats.1990, c. 79 (A.B.759), § 14, operative July 1, 1991. Amended by Stats.1993, c. 69 (S.B.35), § 6, eff. June 30, 1993; Stats.1999, c. 987 (S.B.1229), § 3, eff. Oct. 10, 1999.)*

Law Revision Commission Comments
1990 Enactment

Section 9203 continues Section 9203 of the repealed Probate Code without substantive change. This part does not apply to any proceeding for the administration of a decedent's estate commenced before July 1, 1988. See Section 9004. As to the application of any amendments made after that date, see Section 3.

Background on Section 9203 of Repealed Code

Section 9203 was added by 1987 Cal.Stat. ch. 923 § 93. The section restated the second and third sentences of subdivision (c) and all of subdivision (d) of former Probate Code Section 700.1 (repealed by 1987 Cal.Stat. ch. 923 § 37), and generalized them to apply to all public entities. For background on the provisions of this part, see the Comment to this part under the part heading. [20 Cal.L.Rev.Comm.Reports 1001 (1990)].

§ 9204. Priority of claims

Nothing in this chapter shall be construed to affect the order of priority of claims provided for under other provisions of law. *(Stats.1990, c. 79 (A.B.759), § 14, operative July 1, 1991.)*

Law Revision Commission Comments
1990 Enactment

Section 9204 continues Section 9204 of the repealed Probate Code without change. This part does not apply to any proceeding for the administration of a decedent's estate commenced before July 1, 1988.

See Section 9004. As to the application of any amendments made after that date, see Section 3.

Background on Section 9204 of Repealed Code

Section 9204 was added by 1987 Cal.Stat. ch. 923 § 93. The section restated subdivision (d) of former Probate Code Section 707.5 (repealed by 1987 Cal.Stat. ch. 923 § 37) without substantive change. For background on the provisions of this part, see the Comment to this part under the part heading. [20 Cal.L.Rev.Comm.Reports 1001 (1990)].

§ 9205. Liability for restitution of amounts illegally acquired

This chapter does not apply to liability for the restitution of amounts illegally acquired through the means of a fraudulent, false, or incorrect representation, or a forged or unauthorized endorsement. *(Stats.1990, c. 79 (A.B.759), § 14, operative July 1, 1991.)*

Law Revision Commission Comments

1990 Enactment

Section 9205 continues Section 9205 of the repealed Probate Code without change. This part does not apply to any proceeding for the administration of a decedent's estate commenced before July 1, 1988. See Section 9004. As to the application of any amendments made after that date, see Section 3.

Background on Section 9205 of Repealed Code

Section 9205 was added by 1987 Cal.Stat. ch. 923 § 93. The section restated subdivision (e) of former Probate Code Section 707.5 (repealed by 1987 Cal.Stat. ch. 923 § 37), omitting the reference to a "claim," which is included in "representation." For background on the provisions of this part, see the Comment to this part under the part heading. [20 Cal.L.Rev.Comm.Reports 1001 (1990)].

CHAPTER 6. ALLOWANCE AND REJECTION OF CLAIMS

Section

Application

Applicable in proceedings commenced on or after July 1, 1988, see § 9004.

Cross References

Application of old and new law, see Probate Code § 3.

§ 9250. Allowance or rejection in whole or part; filing; notice; contents; form

(a) When a claim is filed, the personal representative shall allow or reject the claim in whole or in part.

(b) The allowance or rejection shall be in writing. The personal representative shall file the allowance or rejection with the court clerk and give notice to the creditor as provided in Part 2 (commencing with Section 1200) of Division 3, together with a copy of the allowance or rejection.

(c) The allowance or rejection shall contain the following information:

(1) The name of the creditor.

(2) The total amount of the claim.

(3) The date of issuance of letters.

(4) The date of the decedent's death.

(5) The estimated value of the decedent's estate.

(6) The amount allowed or rejected by the personal representative.

(7) Whether the personal representative is authorized to act under the Independent Administration of Estates Act (Part 6 (commencing with Section 10400)).

(8) A statement that the creditor has 90 days in which to act on a rejected claim.

(d) The Judicial Council may prescribe an allowance or rejection form, which may be part of the claim form. Use of a form prescribed by the Judicial Council is deemed to satisfy the requirements of this section.

(e) This section does not apply to a demand the personal representative elects to treat as a claim under Section 9154. *(Stats.1990, c. 79 (A.B.759), § 14, operative July 1, 1991. Amended by Stats.1999, c. 263 (A.B.1051), § 6; Stats.2007, c. 159 (A.B.341), § 6.)*

Law Revision Commission Comments

1990 Enactment

Section 9250 continues Section 9250 of the repealed Probate Code without substantive change. See also Section 9807 (payment of established claim where resort to security insufficient to pay claim).

Under the Independent Administration of Estates Act, the personal representative may allow, pay, reject, contest, or compromise any claim without court supervision. Section 10552 (acting on claims against estate). However, court supervision is necessary where the personal representative or the attorney for the personal representative is the creditor. See Section 9252.

This part does not apply to any proceeding for the administration of a decedent's estate commenced before July 1, 1988. See Section 9004. As to the application of any amendments made after that date, see Section 3.

Background on Section 9250 of Repealed Code

Section 9250 was added by 1987 Cal.Stat. ch. 923 § 93. The section superseded the third sentence of former Probate Code Section 710, the first sentence of former Probate Code Section 711, and the first sentence of former Probate Code Section 714 (provisions repealed by 1987 Cal.Stat. ch. 923 § 37). For background on the provisions of this part, see the Comment to this part under the part heading. Subdivision (e) was added to the section by 1989 Cal.Stat. ch. 21 § 22 to make clear that an informally paid claim under Section 9154 (waiver of formal defects) is not subject to the requirements of the section. See Communication from the California Law Revision Commission Concerning Assembly Bill 156, 20 Cal.L.Revision Comm'n Reports 227, 231 (1990). [20 Cal.L.Rev.Comm.Reports 1001 (1990)].

§ 9251. Personal representative not authorized to act under Independent Administration of Estates Act

If the personal representative is not authorized to act under the Independent Administration of Estates Act (Part 6 (commencing with Section 10400)):

(a) Immediately on the filing of the allowance of a claim, the clerk shall present the claim and allowance to the court or judge for approval or rejection.

(b) On presentation of a claim and allowance, the court or judge may, in its discretion, examine the creditor and others on oath and receive any evidence relevant to the validity of the claim. The court or judge shall endorse on the claim whether the claim is approved or rejected and the date. *(Stats.1990, c. 79 (A.B.759), § 14, operative July 1, 1991.)*

Law Revision Commission Comments

1990 Enactment

Section 9251 continues Section 9251 of the repealed Probate Code without substantive change. This part does not apply to any proceeding for the administration of a decedent's estate commenced before July 1, 1988. See Section 9004. As to the application of any amendments made after that date, see Section 3.

Background on Section 9251 of Repealed Code

Section 9251 was added by 1987 Cal.Stat. ch. 923 § 93. The section superseded the second sentence of former Probate Code Section 708, the last two sentences of former Probate Code Section 710, the second sentence of former Probate Code Section 711, and the second sentence of former Probate Code Section 713 (provisions repealed by 1987 Cal.Stat. ch. 923 § 37). For background on the provisions of this part, see the Comment to this part under the part heading. [20 Cal.L.Rev.Comm.Reports 1001 (1990)].

Cross References

Power of judge to approve claims filed with clerk, see Code of Civil Procedure § 166.

§ 9252. Personal representative or attorney of personal representative as creditor of decedent

(a) If the personal representative or the attorney for the personal representative is a creditor of the decedent, the clerk shall present the claim to the court or judge for approval or rejection. The court or judge may in its discretion require the creditor to file a petition and give notice of hearing.

(b) If the court or judge approves the claim, the claim is established and shall be included with other established claims to be paid in the course of administration.

(c) If the court or judge rejects the claim, the personal representative or attorney may bring an action against the estate. Summons shall be served on the judge, who shall appoint an attorney at the expense of the estate to defend the action. *(Stats.1990, c. 79 (A.B.759), § 14, operative July 1, 1991.)*

Law Revision Commission Comments

1990 Enactment

Section 9252 continues Section 9252 of the repealed Probate Code without change. For general provisions, see Sections 1000–1004 (rules of practice), 1020–1023 (petitions and other papers), 1040–1050 (hearings and orders), 1200–1230 (notice of hearing), 1250–

1252 (request for special notice), 1260–1265 (proof of giving of notice).

An approved claim is paid as other claims in the course of administration. If the personal representative or attorney fails to recover in an action on the claim, the personal representative or attorney must pay costs, and may be required to pay reasonable litigation expenses, including attorney's fees. See Section 9354 (action on rejected claim). This part does not apply to any proceeding for the administration of a decedent's estate commenced before July 1, 1988. See Section 9004. As to the application of any amendments made after that date, see Section 3.

Background on Section 9252 of Repealed Code

Section 9252 was added by 1987 Cal.Stat. ch. 923 § 93. The section restated former Probate Code Section 703 (repealed by 1987 Cal.Stat. ch. 923 § 37), expanding it to cover the personal representative's attorney and adding the second sentence of subdivision (a) of Section 9252 giving the court authority to require a noticed hearing. For background on the provisions of this part, see the Comment to this part under the part heading. [20 Cal.L.Rev.Comm.Reports 1001 (1990)].

Cross References

Compensation, see Probate Code § 10800 et seq.
Costs, allowance in discretion of court, see Code of Civil Procedure § 1268.710
Debts owed by representative to estate, see Probate Code §§ 8800, 8851, 9605.
Payment of debts, expenses, and charges, generally, see Probate Code § 11420.

§ 9253. Claims barred by limitations

A claim barred by the statute of limitations may not be allowed by the personal representative or approved by the court or judge. *(Stats.1990, c. 79 (A.B.759), § 14, operative July 1, 1991.)*

Law Revision Commission Comments

1990 Enactment

Section 9253 continues Section 9253 of the repealed Probate Code without change. See also Sections 9350–9354 (tolling of statute of limitations; action on rejected claim). This part does not apply to any proceeding for the administration of a decedent's estate commenced before July 1, 1988. See Section 9004. As to the application of any amendments made after that date, see Section 3.

Background on Section 9253 of Repealed Code

Section 9253 was added by 1987 Cal.Stat. ch. 923 § 93. Subdivisions (a) and (d) were new. Subdivisions (b) and (c) restated the first and third sentences of former Probate Code Section 708 (repealed by 1987 Cal.Stat. ch. 923 § 37) without substantive change. For background on the provisions of this part, see the Comment to this part under the part heading.

Section 9253 was amended by 1988 Cal.Stat. ch. 1199 § 85 to delete all of Section 9253 except former subdivision (b) which was continued as Section 9253 of the repealed Probate Code without change. Former subdivisions (a) and (c) were restated in Section 9352 of the repealed Probate Code (tolling of statute of limitations) without substantive change. Former subdivision (d) was combined with subdivision (a) of Section 9257 of the repealed Probate Code and restated in Section 9353 of the repealed Probate Code (bar of rejected claims) without substantive change. See Comments to Conforming Revisions and Repeals, 19 Cal.L.Revision Comm'n Reports 1031, 1092 (1988). [20 Cal.L.Rev.Comm.Reports 1001 (1990)].

Claims in litigation, transitional provisions, see Probate Code § 9399.
Expiration date for filing claim, see Probate Code § 9100.
Time of commencing civil actions,
  Generally, see Code of Civil Procedure §§ 312 et seq., 350 et seq.
  Periods of limitation for actions other than for recovery of real
    property, see Code of Civil Procedure § 335 et seq.
Unfiled claim as barred, see Probate Code § 9002.

§ 9254. Contest of validity of allowed or approved claim; burden of proof

(a) The validity of an allowed or approved claim may be contested by any interested person at any time before settlement of the report or account of the personal representative in which it is first reported as an allowed or approved claim. The burden of proof is on the contestant, except where the personal representative has acted under the Independent Administration of Estates Act (Part 6 (commencing Section 10400)), in which case the burden of proof is on the personal representative.

(b) Subdivision (a) does not apply to a claim established by a judgment. (Stats.1990, c. 79 (A.B.759), § 14, operative July 1, 1991.)

Law Revision Commission Comments

1990 Enactment

Section 9254 continues Section 9254 of the repealed Probate Code without substantive change. See also Section 48 ("interested person" defined). For claims established by judgments, see Chapter 7 (commencing with Section 9300). See also Section 9807 (payment of established claim where resort to security insufficient to pay claim). This part does not apply to any proceeding for the administration of a decedent's estate commenced before July 1, 1988. See Section 9004. As to the application of any amendments made after that date, see Section 3.

Background on Section 9254 of Repealed Code

Section 9254 was added by 1987 Cal.Stat. ch. 923 § 93. The section restated a portion of the first sentence of former Probate Code Section 713 (repealed by 1987 Cal.Stat. ch. 923 § 37), with the addition of the provision relating to burdens of proof. For background on the provisions of this part, see the Comment to this part under the part heading. [20 Cal.L.Rev.Comm.Reports 1001 (1990)].

Cross References

Claims not established by judgment may be contested for cause shown, see Probate Code § 11001.
Expenses, charges and debts, order of payment, see Probate Code § 11420.
Judgment on claims, conclusiveness of, see Code of Civil Procedure § 1908; Probate Code § 9300.
Power of judge to approve claims in chambers, see Code of Civil Procedure § 166.

§ 9255. Partial allowance or approval of claim; refusal to accept; actions on claims; costs

(a) The personal representative may allow a claim, or the court or judge may approve a claim, in part. The allowance or approval shall state the amount for which the claim is allowed or approved.

(b) A creditor who refuses to accept the amount allowed or approved in satisfaction of the claim may bring an action on the claim in the manner provided in Chapter 8 (commencing with Section 9350). The creditor may not recover costs in the action unless the creditor recovers an amount greater than that allowed or approved. (Stats.1990, c. 79 (A.B.759), § 14, operative July 1, 1991.)

Law Revision Commission Comments

1990 Enactment

Section 9255 continues Section 9255 of the repealed Probate Code without change. As to a claim barred by the statute of limitations, see Section 9253. This part does not apply to any proceeding for the administration of a decedent's estate commenced before July 1, 1988. See Section 9004. As to the application of any amendments made after that date, see Section 3.

Background on Section 9255 of Repealed Code

Section 9255 was added by 1987 Cal.Stat. ch. 923 § 93. The section restated former Probate Code Section 717 (repealed by 1987 Cal.Stat. ch. 923 § 37) without substantive change. For background on the provisions of this part, see the Comment to this part under the part heading. Section 9255 was amended by 1988 Cal.Stat. ch. 1199 § 85.3 to correct a section reference. See communication from the California Law Revision Commission Concerning Assembly Bill 2841, 19 Cal.L.Revision Comm'n Reports 1201, 1239 (1988). [20 Cal.L.Rev.Comm.Reports 1001 (1990)].

Cross References

Compromise or settlement of claims, see Probate Code § 9830.
Costs, discretion of court to order payment by parties or from estate, see Probate Code § 1002.

§ 9256. Refusal or neglect to act on claim as notice of rejection

If within 30 days after a claim is filed the personal representative or the court or judge has refused or neglected to act on the claim, the refusal or neglect may, at the option of the creditor, be deemed equivalent to giving a notice of rejection on the 30th day. (Stats.1990, c. 79 (A.B.759), § 14, operative July 1, 1991.)

Law Revision Commission Comments

1990 Enactment

Section 9256 continues Section 9256 of the repealed Probate Code without change. This part does not apply to any proceeding for the administration of a decedent's estate commenced before July 1, 1988. See Section 9004.

Background on Section 9256 of Repealed Code

Section 9256 was added by 1987 Cal.Stat. ch. 923 § 93. The section superseded the first sentence of former Probate Code Section 712 (repealed by 1987 Cal.Stat. ch. 923 § 37). Section 9256 substituted a 30–day period for the 10–day period formerly provided in former Section 712. For background on the provisions of this part, see the Comment to this part under the part heading. [20 Cal.L.Rev.Comm.Reports 1001 (1990)].

Cross References

Claims in litigation, actions to be commenced within three months after notice of rejection or after claim becomes due, see Probate Code § 9353.

§ 9257. Repealed by Stats.1988, c. 1199, § 85.5, operative July 1, 1989

1988 Repeal

Subdivision (a) of former Section 9257 is combined with former subdivision (d) of Section 9253 and restated in Section 9353 (bar of rejected claims) without substantive change. Subdivisions (b)–(d) are restated in Section 9354(a)–(c) (action on claim) without substantive change [19 Cal.L.Rev.Comm. Reports 1092 (1988)].

CHAPTER 7. CLAIMS ESTABLISHED BY JUDGMENT

Application

Applicable in proceedings commenced on or after July 1, 1988, see § 9004.

Law Revision Commission Comments
1990 Enactment

This chapter supersedes Chapter 7 (commencing with Section 9300) of Part 4 of Division 7 of the repealed Probate Code. Provisions included in this chapter of the repealed Probate Code were enacted upon recommendation of the California Law Revision Commission. See Recommendation Relating to Enforcement of Obligations After Death, 15 Cal.L.Revision Comm'n Reports 1327 (1980). See also Recommendation Relating to Creditor Claims Against Decedent's Estate, 19 Cal.L.Revision Comm'n Reports 299 (1988). [20 Cal.L.Rev.Comm.Reports 1001 (1990)].

Cross References

Application of old and new law, see Probate Code § 3.

§ 9300. Payment in course of administration; enforcement against estate property; filing

(a) Except as provided in Section 9303, after the death of the decedent all money judgments against the decedent or against the personal representative on a claim against the decedent or estate are payable in the course of administration and are not enforceable against property in the estate of the decedent under the Enforcement of Judgments Law (Title 9 (commencing with Section 680.010) of Part 2 of the Code of Civil Procedure).

(b) Subject to Section 9301, a judgment referred to in subdivision (a) shall be filed in the same manner as other claims. *(Stats.1990, c. 79 (A.B.759), § 14, operative July 1, 1991.)*

Law Revision Commission Comments
1990 Enactment

Section 9300 continues Section 9300 of the repealed Probate Code without change. See also Code Civ.Proc. § 686.020. For an exception to the rule of Section 9300, see Section 9303 (property under levy of execution). Section 9300 applies to federal as well as state judgments. This part does not apply to any proceeding for the administration of a decedent's estate commenced before July 1, 1988.

See Section 9004. As to the application of any amendments made after that date, see Section 3.

Background on Section 9300 of Repealed Code

Section 9300 was added by 1987 Cal.Stat. ch. 923 § 93. The section restated subdivisions (a) and (b) of former Probate Code Section 730 (repealed by 1987 Cal.Stat. ch. 923 § 37) and extended those provisions to all money judgments. For background on the provisions of this chapter, see the Comment to this chapter under the chapter heading. [20 Cal.L.Rev.Comm.Reports 1001 (1990)].

Cross References

Claim of plaintiff in action pending against decedent at time of death, see Probate Code § 9370.
Death of party after verdict, entry of judgment authorized, see Code of Civil Procedure § 669.
Enforcement of judgment after death of party, see Code of Civil Procedure §§ 686.010, 686.020.
Manner of giving and entering judgment, see Code of Civil Procedure § 664 et seq.
Payment of allowed claims in due course of administration, see Probate Code § 9003.

§ 9301. Validity of claim conclusively established; contents; abstracts

When a money judgment against a personal representative in a representative capacity becomes final, it conclusively establishes the validity of the claim for the amount of the judgment. The judgment shall provide that it is payable out of property in the decedent's estate in the course of administration. An abstract of the judgment shall be filed in the administration proceedings. *(Stats.1990, c. 79 (A.B.759), § 14, operative July 1, 1991.)*

Law Revision Commission Comments
1990 Enactment

Section 9301 continues Section 9301 of the repealed Probate Code without change. This part does not apply to any proceeding for the administration of a decedent's estate commenced before July 1, 1988. See Section 9004. As to the application of any amendments made after that date, see Section 3.

Background on Section 9301 of Repealed Code

Section 9301 was added by 1987 Cal.Stat. ch. 923 § 93. The section restated former Probate Code Section 731 (repealed by 1987 Cal.Stat. ch. 923 § 37) without substantive change. For background on the provisions of this chapter, see the Comment to this chapter under the chapter heading. [20 Cal.L.Rev.Comm.Reports 1001 (1990)].

Cross References

Judgment defined, see Code of Civil Procedure § 577.
Judgments, conclusiveness of, see Code of Civil Procedure §§ 577, 1908.

§ 9302. Judgments for possession or sale of property; demands for money not satisfied

(a) Notwithstanding the death of the decedent, a judgment for possession of property or a judgment for sale of property may be enforced under the Enforcement of Judgments Law (Title 9 (commencing with Section 680.010) of Part 2 of the Code of Civil Procedure). Nothing in this subdivision authorizes enforcement under the Enforcement of Judgments Law against any property in the estate of the decedent other than the property described in the judgment for possession or sale.

(b) After the death of the decedent, a demand for money that is not satisfied from the property described in a judgment for sale of property shall be filed as a claim in the same manner as other claims and is payable in the course of administration. *(Stats.1990, c. 79 (A.B.759), § 14, operative July 1, 1991.)*

Law Revision Commission Comments
1990 Enactment

Section 9302 continues Section 9302 of the repealed Probate Code without change. The first sentence permits the use of the Enforcement of Judgments Law to enforce an order for sale in a judgment foreclosing a lien and to enforce other judgments for possession or sale of property. The remainder of the section deals with claims for money in connection with a judgment for possession or sale of property. A judgment for possession of property may include damages and costs which ordinarily would be recovered by levy on other property of the judgment debtor. There may also be accrued costs, interest, and the levying officer's costs in enforcing a judgment for possession, and these also would ordinarily be recovered by the judgment creditor by levy on other property of the judgment debtor. Section 9302 makes clear that, after the death of the judgment debtor, these claims for money cannot be enforced by levy against other property of the decedent; instead, amounts due under a judgment for possession are enforced in the same manner as a money judgment and thus are governed by the general rule applicable to money judgments under Section 9300.

This part does not apply to any proceeding for the administration of a decedent's estate commenced before July 1, 1988. See Section 9004. As to the application of any amendments made after that date, see Section 3.

Background on Section 9302 of Repealed Code

Section 9302 was added by 1987 Cal.Stat. ch. 923 § 93. The section restated subdivision (d) of former Probate Code Section 730 (repealed by 1987 Cal.Stat. ch. 923 § 37) without substantive change. The former reference to unsatisfied demands for money under a judgment for possession was omitted. Amounts due under a judgment for possession are enforced in the same manner as a money judgment and thus are governed by the general rule applicable to money judgments under Section 9300. See Code Civ.Proc. §§ 680.270, 712.040, 714.020. For background on the provisions of this chapter, see the Comment to this chapter under the chapter heading. [20 Cal.L.Rev.Comm.Reports 1001 (1990)].

§ 9303. Execution liens

If property of the decedent is subject to an execution lien at the time of the decedent's death, enforcement against the property may proceed under the Enforcement of Judgments Law (Title 9 (commencing with Section 680.010) of Part 2 of the Code of Civil Procedure) to satisfy the judgment. The levying officer shall account to the personal representative for any surplus. If the judgment is not satisfied, the balance of the judgment remaining unsatisfied is payable in the course of administration. *(Stats.1990, c. 79 (A.B.759), § 14, operative July 1, 1991.)*

Law Revision Commission Comments
1990 Enactment

Section 9303 continues Section 9303 of the repealed Probate Code without change. This part does not apply to any proceeding for the administration of a decedent's estate commenced before July 1, 1988.

See Section 9004. As to the application of any amendments made after that date, see Section 3.

Background on Section 9303 of Repealed Code

Section 9303 was added by 1987 Cal.Stat. ch. 923 § 93. The section restated subdivision (c) of former Probate Code Section 730 (repealed by 1987 Cal.Stat. ch. 923 § 37) without substantive change. For background on the provisions of this chapter, see the Comment to this chapter under the chapter heading. [20 Cal.L.Rev.Comm.Reports 1001 (1990)].

§ 9304. Attachment liens; conversion into judgment liens; exemptions

(a) An attachment lien may be converted into a judgment lien on property in the estate subject to the attachment lien, with the same priority as the attachment lien, in either of the following cases:

(1) Where the judgment debtor dies after entry of judgment in an action in which the property was attached.

(2) Where a judgment is entered after the death of the defendant in an action in which the property was attached.

(b) To convert the attachment lien into a judgment lien, the levying officer shall, after entry of judgment in the action in which the property was attached and before the expiration of the attachment lien, do one of the following:

(1) Serve an abstract of the judgment, and a notice that the attachment lien has become a judgment lien, on the person holding property subject to the attachment lien.

(2) Record or file, in any office where the writ of attachment and notice of attachment are recorded or filed, an abstract of the judgment and a notice that the attachment lien has become a judgment lien. If the attached property is real property, the plaintiff or the plaintiff's attorney may record the required abstract and notice with the same effect as if recorded by the levying officer.

(c) After the death of the decedent, any members of the decedent's family who were supported in whole or in part by the decedent may claim an exemption provided in Section 487.020 of the Code of Civil Procedure for property levied on under the writ of attachment if the right to the exemption exists at the time the exemption is claimed. The personal representative may claim the exemption on behalf of members of the decedent's family. The claim of exemption may be made at any time before the time the abstract and notice are served, recorded, or filed under subdivision (b) with respect to the property claimed to be exempt. The claim of exemption shall be made in the same manner as an exemption is claimed under Section 482.100 of the Code of Civil Procedure. *(Stats.1990, c. 79 (A.B.759), § 14, operative July 1, 1991.)*

Law Revision Commission Comments
1990 Enactment

Section 9304 continues Section 9304 of the repealed Probate Code without substantive change. The reference in subdivision (c) to Section 462.100 has been corrected to refer to Section 482.100.

Section 9304 makes the judgment a lien on the attached property for the purpose of determining the order of priority for payment of claims against the estate under Section 11420 and for the purpose of permitting foreclosure of the lien under Section 9391.

Under Section 9304, the judgment does not become a lien on property subject to the attachment lien which is not included in the decedent's estate because it was transferred by the decedent; the attachment lien continues on the property transferred and can be enforced after judgment notwithstanding the death of the decedent. Everett v. Hayes, 94 Cal.App. 31, 270 P. 458 (1928).

Subdivision (b) of Section 9304 is comparable to subdivision (c) of Code of Civil Procedure Section 488.510 (extension of attachment lien).

Subdivision (c) of Section 9304 makes clear that after the death of the decedent, an exemption claim may be made by or on behalf of any one or more members of the decedent's family who were supported in whole or in part by the decedent. Subdivision (c) is consistent with Code of Civil Procedure Section 482.100 which permits the defendant to claim an exemption if the right to the exemption is the result of a change in circumstances occurring after (1) the denial of a claim of exemption for the property earlier in the action or (2) the expiration of the time for claiming the exemption earlier in the action. However, a showing of a change in circumstances is not required under subdivision (c), the death of the decedent whose property was attached being considered a sufficient change in circumstances to permit the claim of exemption by or on behalf of the surviving member or members of the decedent's family.

The only limit on the time within which the exemption must be claimed is that the claim must be made prior to the time the abstract and notice are served, recorded, or filed under subdivision (b). The right to the exemption is determined as of the time the claim is made by or on behalf of the surviving member or members of the decedent's family.

The primary purpose of subdivision (c) is to preserve the effect, after the death of the decedent, of the exemption provided by subdivision (b) of Code of Civil Procedure Section 487.020 (property "necessary for the support of [the defendant's family] supported in whole or in part by the defendant"). However, subdivision (c) also permits the claim of any of the other exemptions provided by Section 487.020.

This part does not apply to any proceeding for the administration of a decedent's estate commenced before July 1, 1988. See Section 9004. As to the application of any amendments made after that date, see Section 3.

Background on Section 9304 of Repealed Code

Section 9304 was added by 1987 Cal.Stat. ch. 923 § 93. The section restated former Probate Code Section 732 (repealed by 1987 Cal.Stat. ch. 923 § 37) without substantive change. For background on the provisions of this chapter, see the Comment to this chapter under the chapter heading. [20 Cal.L.Rev.Comm.Reports 1001 (1990)].

Cross References

Claims when filed or presented to be supported by affidavits, see Probate Code § 9151.
Execution upon judgment after death of party, see Code of Civil Procedure § 686.010.
Judgment defined, see Code of Civil Procedure § 577.
Presentment of claims generally, see Probate Code § 9100 et seq.
Redemption of property generally, see Code of Civil Procedure § 701.680.

CHAPTER 8. CLAIMS IN LITIGATION

Application

Part not applicable in proceeding commenced before July 1, 1988, see Probate Code § 9004. Chapter not applicable to action commenced before July 1, 1989, see Probate Code § 9399.

Law Revision Commission Comments

1990 Enactment

This chapter supersedes Chapter 8 (commencing with Section 9350) of Part 4 of Division 7 of the repealed Probate Code. The superseded chapter was enacted upon recommendation of the California Law Revision Commission. See Recommendation Relating to Litigation Involving Decedents, 19 Cal.L.Revision Comm'n Reports 899 (1988). See also Communication from the California Law Revision Commission Concerning Assembly Bill 2841, 19 Cal.L.Revision Comm'n Reports 1201, 1239–41 (1988). [20 Cal.L.Rev.Comm.Reports 1001 (1990)].

ARTICLE 1. CLAIM WHERE NO PENDING ACTION OR PROCEEDING

Application

Part not applicable in proceeding commenced before July 1, 1988, see Probate Code § 9004. Chapter not applicable to action commenced before July 1, 1989, see Probate Code § 9399.

Cross References

Application of old and new law, see Probate Code § 3.
Death of person against whom action may be brought, limitation period for claims, see Code of Civil Procedure § 366.2.

§ 9350. Application of article

This article applies to any claim other than a claim on an action or proceeding pending against the decedent at the time of death. *(Stats.1990, c. 79 (A.B.759), § 14, operative July 1, 1991.)*

Law Revision Commission Comments

1990 Enactment

Section 9350 continues Section 9350 of the repealed Probate Code without change. Provisions governing claims on pending actions or proceedings are located in Section 9370 (claims on pending action or proceeding), not in this article. This chapter does not apply to any proceeding for the administration of a decedent's estate commenced before July 1, 1989. See Section 9399. As to the application of any amendments made after that date, see Section 3.

Background on Section 9350 of Repealed Code

Section 9350 was a new provision added by 1988 Cal.Stat. ch. 1199 § 86. For background on the provisions of this chapter, see the Comment to this chapter under the chapter heading. [20 Cal.L.Rev.Comm.Reports 1001 (1990)].

§ 9351. Claim filing and rejection; prerequisite to commencing action

An action may not be commenced against a decedent's personal representative on a cause of action against the decedent unless a claim is first filed as provided in this part and the claim is rejected in whole or in part. *(Stats.1990, c. 79 (A.B.759), § 14, operative July 1, 1991.)*

Law Revision Commission Comments

1990 Enactment

Section 9351 continues Section 9351 of the repealed Probate Code without change. For the time within which a claim must be filed, see Section 9100 (claim period). For late claims, see Section 9103. An action may be brought to enforce a liability of the decedent without first filing a claim in the case of a secured obligation. Section 9391 (enforcement of security interest). This chapter does not apply to any proceeding for the administration of a decedent's estate commenced before July 1, 1989. See Section 9399. As to the application of any amendments made after that date, see Section 3.

Section 9351 relates only to an action against the personal representative. It does not affect actions against other persons who may be liable for the decedent's debts. See, e.g., Sections 13109 (affidavit procedure), 13550–13554 (debts of deceased spouse). See also Sections 550–554 (liability of decedent covered by insurance).

Background on Section 9351 of Repealed Code

Section 9351 was added by 1988 Cal.Stat. ch. 1199 § 86. The section restated subdivision (c) of former Probate Code Section 9002 (claim requirement) (as that section existed prior to its amendment by 1988 Cal.Stat. ch. 1199 § 83.5) with the addition of the implied requirement that the claim was rejected in whole or in part. For background on the provisions of this chapter, see the Comment to this chapter under the chapter heading. [20 Cal.L.Rev.Comm.Reports 1001 (1990)].

§ 9352. Tolling statute of limitations

(a) The filing of a claim or a petition under Section 9103 to file a claim tolls the statute of limitations otherwise applicable to the claim until allowance, approval, or rejection.

(b) The allowance or approval of a claim in whole or in part further tolls the statute of limitations during the administration of the estate as to the part allowed or approved. *(Stats.1990, c. 79 (A.B.759), § 14, operative July 1, 1991. Amended by Stats.1991, c. 1055 (S.B.271), § 26.)*

Law Revision Commission Comments

1990 Enactment

Section 9352 continues Section 9352 of the repealed Probate Code without change. See also Section 9253 (claim barred by statute of limitations may not be allowed or approved). This chapter does not apply to any proceeding for the administration of a decedent's estate commenced before July 1, 1989. See Section 9399. As to the application of any amendments made after that date, see Section 3.

1991 Amendment

Subdivision (a) of Section 9352 is amended to provide that filing a petition for a late claim tolls the statute of limitations applicable to the claim. [20 Cal.L.Rev.Comm.Reports 2719 (1990)].

Background on Section 9352 of Repealed Code

Section 9352 was added by 1988 Cal.Stat. ch. 1199 § 86. The section restated subdivisions (a) and (c) of former Probate Code Section 9253 (as that section existed prior to its amendment by 1988 Cal.Stat. ch. 1199 § 85) without substantive change. For background

on the provisions of this chapter, see the Comment to this chapter under the chapter heading. [20 Cal.L.Rev.Comm.Reports 1001 (1990)].

§ 9353. Rejected claim; barring regardless of statute of limitations; time limits

(a) Regardless of whether the statute of limitations otherwise applicable to a claim will expire before or after the following times, a claim rejected in whole or in part is barred as to the part rejected unless, within the following times, the creditor commences an action on the claim or the matter is referred to a referee or to arbitration:

(1) If the claim is due at the time the notice of rejection is given, 90 days after the notice is given.

(2) If the claim is not due at the time the notice of rejection is given, 90 days after the claim becomes due.

(b) The time during which there is a vacancy in the office of the personal representative shall be excluded from the period determined under subdivision (a). *(Stats.1990, c. 79 (A.B.759), § 14, operative July 1, 1991. Amended by Stats. 2007, c. 159 (A.B.341), § 7.)*

Law Revision Commission Comments

1990 Enactment

Section 9353 continues Section 9353 of the repealed Probate Code without change. See also Section 9253 (claim barred by statute of limitations may not be allowed or approved). This chapter does not apply to any proceeding for the administration of a decedent's estate commenced before July 1, 1989. See Section 9399. As to the application of any amendments made after that date, see Section 3.

Background on Section 9353 of Repealed Code

Section 9353 was added by 1988 Cal.Stat. ch. 1199 § 86. The section restated subdivision (d) of former Probate Code Section 9253 (as that section existed prior to its amendment by 1988 Cal.Stat. ch. 1199 § 85) and subdivision (a) of former Probate Code Section 9257 (repealed by 1988 Cal.Stat. ch. 1199 § 85.5) without substantive change. The provision relating to partial rejection was new. For background on the provisions of this chapter, see the Comment to this chapter under the chapter heading. [20 Cal.L.Rev.Comm.Reports 1001 (1990)].

Cross References

Action to recover property sold by personal representatives, limitation period, see Probate Code § 10382.
Claims barred by limitations, see Probate Code § 9253.
Death of party before expiration of limitation period, see Code of Civil Procedure §§ 366.1, 366.2, 377 et seq.
Effect of absence from state on limitation period, see Code of Civil Procedure § 351.
Notice of rejection, refusal or neglect to act on claim deemed equivalent to, see Probate Code § 9256.
Pleading and proof of statute of limitations, see Code of Civil Procedure § 458.
Recovery of property sold by guardian, limitation of actions, see Probate Code § 2548.
Time of commencing actions,
Actions other than for recovery of real property, see Code of Civil Procedure § 335 et seq.
General limitations, special cases, see Code of Civil Procedure § 312 et seq.

§ 9354. Venue; notice of pendency of action; service of process or notice; property not subject to claim; liability; costs; attorney fees

(a) In addition to any other county in which an action may be commenced, an action on the claim may be commenced in the county in which the proceeding for administration of the decedent's estate is pending.

(b) The plaintiff shall file a notice of the pendency of the action with the court clerk in the estate proceeding, together with proof of giving a copy of the notice to the personal representative as provided in Section 1215. Personal service of a copy of the summons and complaint on the personal representative is equivalent to the filing and giving of the notice. Any property distributed under court order, or any payment properly made, before the notice is filed and given is not subject to the claim. The personal representative, distributee, or payee is not liable on account of the prior distribution or payment.

(c) The prevailing party in the action shall be awarded court costs and, if the court determines that the prosecution or defense of the action against the prevailing party was unreasonable, the prevailing party shall be awarded reasonable litigation expenses, including attorney's fees. *(Stats. 1990, c. 79 (A.B.759), § 14, operative July 1, 1991.)*

Law Revision Commission Comments

1990 Enactment

Section 9354 continues Section 9354 of the repealed Probate Code without change. See also Section 7050 (jurisdiction in superior court). This chapter does not apply to any proceeding for the administration of a decedent's estate commenced before July 1, 1989. See Section 9399. As to the application of any amendments made after that date, see Section 3.

Background on Section 9354 of Repealed Code

Section 9354 was added by 1988 Cal.Stat. ch. 1199 § 86. The section restated subdivisions (b)–(d) of former Probate Code Section 9257 (repealed by 1988 Cal.Stat. ch. 1199 § 85.5) without substantive change. For background on the provisions of this chapter, see the Comment to this chapter under the chapter heading. [20 Cal.L.Rev.Comm.Reports 1001 (1990)].

Cross References

Actions by and against personal representatives, see Probate Code § 9820 et seq.
Manner of commencing civil actions, generally, see Code of Civil Procedure § 411.10 et seq.
Pending action, definition, see Code of Civil Procedure § 1049.

ARTICLE 2. CLAIM WHERE ACTION OR PROCEEDING PENDING

Section
9370. Continuation of action pending at time of death; filing and rejection of claim; order for substitution; proof of compliance.

Application

Part not applicable in proceeding commenced before July 1, 1988, see Probate Code § 9004. Chapter not applicable to action commenced before July 1, 1989, see Probate Code § 9399.

Cross References

Application of old and new law, see Probate Code § 3.

§ 9370. Continuation of action pending at time of death; filing and rejection of claim; order for substitution; proof of compliance

(a) An action or proceeding pending against the decedent at the time of death may not be continued against the decedent's personal representative unless all of the following conditions are satisfied:

(1) A claim is first filed as provided in this part.

(2) The claim is rejected in whole or in part.

(3) Within three months after the notice of rejection is given, the plaintiff applies to the court in which the action or proceeding is pending for an order to substitute the personal representative in the action or proceeding. This paragraph applies only if the notice of rejection contains a statement that the plaintiff has three months within which to apply for an order for substitution.

(b) No recovery shall be allowed in the action against property in the decedent's estate unless proof is made of compliance with this section. *(Stats.1990, c. 79 (A.B.759), § 14, operative July 1, 1991.)*

Law Revision Commission Comments

1990 Enactment

Section 9370 continues Section 9370 of the repealed Probate Code without change. The personal representative must notify creditors, including plaintiffs in actions against the decedent, if the personal representative has actual knowledge of the creditor. See Section 9050 (notice required). In addition, the substitution requirement applies only if the personal representative notifies plaintiffs whose claims are rejected of the requirement. For late claims, see Section 9103. This chapter does not apply to any proceeding for the administration of a decedent's estate commenced before July 1, 1989. See Section 9399. As to the application of any amendments made after that date, see Section 3.

Background on Section 9370 of Repealed Code

Section 9370 was added by 1988 Cal.Stat. ch. 1199 § 86. Subdivision (a) restated the first sentence of former Probate Code Section 709 (enacted by 1987 Cal.Stat. ch. 923 § 38 and repealed by 1988 Cal.Stat. ch. 1199 § 53) with the addition of the implied requirement that the claim be rejected in whole or in part and that the plaintiff act to substitute the personal representative as a party within three months after rejection of the claim. Subdivision (b) restated the second sentence of former Probate Code Section 709 (enacted by 1987 Cal.Stat. ch. 923 § 38 and repealed by 1988 Cal.Stat. ch. 1199 § 53) without substantive change. For background on the provisions of this chapter, see the Comment to this chapter under the chapter heading. [20 Cal.L.Rev.Comm.Reports 1001 (1990)].

Cross References

Continuance of proceedings by representative notwithstanding death or disability of party, see Code of Civil Procedure §§ 375, 377.20 et seq.

ARTICLE 3. LITIGATION WHERE NO CLAIM REQUIRED

Section
9390. Insurance protecting decedent from liability; claim; insurer reimbursement; waiver.

Section
9391. Enforcement of liens.
9392. Personal liability for creditor claims.

Application

Part not applicable in proceeding commenced before July 1, 1988, see Probate Code § 9004. Chapter not applicable to action commenced before July 1, 1989, see Probate Code § 9399.

Cross References

Application of old and new law, see Probate Code § 3.

§ 9390. Insurance protecting decedent from liability; claim; insurer reimbursement; waiver

(a) An action to establish the decedent's liability for which the decedent was protected by insurance may be commenced or continued under Section 550, and a judgment in the action may be enforced against the insurer, without first filing a claim as provided in this part.

(b) Unless a claim is first made as provided in this part, an action to establish the decedent's liability for damages outside the limits or coverage of the insurance may not be commenced or continued under Section 550.

(c) If the insurer seeks reimbursement under the insurance contract for any liability of the decedent, including, but not limited to, deductible amounts in the insurance coverage and costs and attorney's fees for which the decedent is liable under the contract, an insurer defending an action under Section 550 shall file a claim as provided in this part. Failure to file a claim is a waiver of reimbursement under the insurance contract for any liability of the decedent. *(Stats. 1990, c. 79 (A.B.759), § 14, operative July 1, 1991. Amended by Stats.1990, c. 710 (S.B.1775), § 23, operative July 1, 1991.)*

Law Revision Commission Comments

1990 Enactment

Section 9390 continues Section 9390 of the repealed Probate Code without change. Nothing in this section affects any applicable statutes of limitation relating to the action. Cf. Code Civ.Proc. § 353 (death of party before expiration of limitation period); Prob.Code § 551 (statute of limitations). This chapter does not apply to any proceeding for the administration of a decedent's estate commenced before July 1, 1989. See Section 9399. As to the application of any amendments made after that date, see Section 3.

1990 Amendment

Section 9390 (enacted as a part of the new Probate Code by 1990 Cal.Stat. ch. 79 § 14) was amended by 1990 Cal.Stat. ch. 710 § 23. The 1990 amendment amended subdivision (c) to make clear that the subdivision is not an independent authorization for reimbursement of the insurer's costs and attorney's fees, but only a procedure for recovering those costs and attorney's fees if the decedent is liable under the contract. This amendment is a clarification of, and not a change in, existing law. [20 Cal.L.Rev.Comm.Reports 1001 (1990)].

Background on Section 9390 of Repealed Code

Section 9390 was added by 1988 Cal.Stat. ch. 1199 § 86. The section replaced part of the first sentence of former Probate Code Section 707, the third sentence of former Probate Code Section 709, part of former Probate Code Section 709.1, and subdivision (a) of former Probate Code Section 721 (provisions enacted by 1987 Cal.Stat. ch. 923 § 38 and repealed by 1988 Cal.Stat. ch. 1199 § 53).

For background on the provisions of this chapter, see the Comment to this chapter under the chapter heading.

Section 9390, in conjunction with Section 550, made the following significant changes in the former scheme:

(1) The new provisions applied uniformly to actions pending at the death of the decedent and actions commenced after the decedent's death.

(2) Court approval was not required under the new provisions before the plaintiff could commence an action against the estate for the insured amount.

(3) Under the new provisions, the estate of the decedent need not have otherwise qualified for treatment under Sections 13100–13115 (affidavit procedure for collection or transfer of personal property).

(4) The new provisions applied in any case where there is a claim for damages for which the decedent was insured, whether for injury to or death of a person caused by the wrongful act or neglect of the decedent, or otherwise.

(5) The new provisions excused a claim in probate only where the plaintiff is proceeding under Section 550, whether or not the insurer has otherwise accepted the defense of the cause or an appearance has been made on behalf of the decedent. [20 Cal.L.Rev.Comm.Reports 1001 (1990)].

§ 9391. Enforcement of liens

Except as provided in Section 10361, the holder of a mortgage or other lien on property in the decedent's estate, including, but not limited to, a judgment lien, may commence an action to enforce the lien against the property that is subject to the lien, without first filing a claim as provided in this part, if in the complaint the holder of the lien expressly waives all recourse against other property in the estate. Section 366.2 of the Code of Civil Procedure does not apply to an action under this section. The personal representative shall have the authority to seek to enjoin any action of the lienholder to enforce a lien against property that is subject to the lien. *(Stats.1990, c. 79 (A.B.759), § 14, operative July 1, 1991. Amended by Stats.1990, c. 140 (S.B.1855), § 12.1, operative July 1, 1991; Stats.1992, c. 178 (S.B.1496), § 35; Stats.1996, c. 563 (S.B.392), § 24; Stats.1996, c. 862 (A.B. 2751), § 25.)*

Law Revision Commission Comments

1990 Enactment

Section 9391 continues Section 9391 of the repealed Probate Code without change. This chapter does not apply to any proceeding for the administration of a decedent's estate commenced before July 1, 1989. See Section 9399. As to the application of any amendments made after that date, see Section 3.

1990 Amendment

Section 9391 (enacted as a part of the new Probate Code by 1990 Cal.Stat. ch. 79 § 14) was amended by 1990 Cal.Stat. ch. 140 § 12.1 to except an action to enforce a lien from the one-year statute of limitations in Code of Civil Procedure Section 353. The statute of limitations otherwise applicable to an action to enforce the lien continues to apply notwithstanding Section 353. For background on the 1990 amendment, see Recommendation Relating to Notice to Creditors in Estate Administration, 20 Cal.L.Revision Comm'n Reports 507 (1990). [20 Cal.L.Rev.Comm.Reports 1001 (1990)].

1992 Amendment

Section 9391 is amended to revise a section reference. This revision is a technical, nonsubstantive change. [22 Cal.L.Rev.Comm.Reports 895 (1992)].

Background on Section 9391 of Repealed Code

Section 9391 was added by 1988 Cal.Stat. ch. 1199 § 86. The section restated former Probate Code Section 716 (enacted by 1987 Cal.Stat. ch. 923 § 38 and repealed by 1988 Cal.Stat. ch. 1199 § 53), omitting the provision relating to attorney's fees. For background on the provisions of this chapter, see the Comment to this chapter under the chapter heading. [20 Cal.L.Rev.Comm.Reports 1001 (1990)].

Cross References

Actions for the foreclosure of mortgages, see Code of Civil Procedure § 725a et seq.

Attorney's fees on foreclosure of mortgage, see Code of Civil Procedure §§ 726, 730.

Claim founded on written instrument, presentation of copy, secured claims, see Probate Code § 9152.

Mortgages in general, see Civil Code § 2920 et seq.

Place of trial in foreclosure actions on real property, see Code of Civil Procedure § 392.

Sale of encumbered property, see Probate Code § 10361 et seq.

§ 9392. Personal liability for creditor claims

(a) Subject to subdivision (b), a person to whom property is distributed is personally liable for the claim of a creditor, without a claim first having been filed, if all of the following conditions are satisfied:

(1) The identity of the creditor was known to, or reasonably ascertainable by, a general personal representative within four months after the date letters were first issued to the personal representative, and the claim of the creditor was not merely conjectural.

(2) Notice of administration of the estate was not given to the creditor under Chapter 2 (commencing with Section 9050) and neither the creditor nor the attorney representing the creditor in the matter has actual knowledge of the administration of the estate before the time the court made an order for final distribution of the property.

(3) The statute of limitations applicable to the claim under Section 366.2 of the Code of Civil Procedure has not expired at the time of commencement of an action under this section.

(b) Personal liability under this section is applicable only to the extent the claim of the creditor cannot be satisfied out of the estate of the decedent and is limited to a pro rata portion of the claim of the creditor, based on the proportion that the value of the property distributed to the person out of the estate bears to the total value of all property distributed to all persons out of the estate. Personal liability under this section for all claims of all creditors shall not exceed the value of the property distributed to the person out of the estate. As used in this section, the value of property is the fair market value of the property on the date of the order for distribution, less the amount of any liens and encumbrances on the property at that time.

(c) Nothing in this section affects the rights of a purchaser or encumbrancer of property in good faith and for value from a person who is personally liable under this section. *(Added by Stats.1990, c. 140 (S.B.1855), § 13.1, operative July 1, 1991. Amended by Stats.1992, c. 178 (S.B.1496), § 36.)*

Law Revision Commission Comments
1990 Addition [Revised Comment]

Section 9392 is new. It implements the rule of Tulsa Professional Collection Services, Inc. v. Pope, 108 S.Ct. 1340 (1988), that the claim of a known or reasonably ascertainable creditor whose claim is not merely conjectural but who is not given actual notice of administration may not be cut off by a short claim filing requirement. Section 9392 is intended as a limited remedy to cure due process failures only, and is not intended as a general provision applicable to all creditors.

A creditor who has knowledge of estate administration must file a claim or, if the claim filing period has expired, must petition for leave to file a late claim. See Sections 9100 (time for filing claims) and 9103 (late claims). This rule applies whether the creditor's knowledge is acquired through notification under Section 9050 (notice required), by virtue of publication under Section 8120 (publication required), or otherwise.

Under Section 9392, a creditor who has no knowledge of estate administration before an order is made for distribution of property has a remedy against distributees to the extent payment cannot be obtained from the estate. There is a one year statute of limitations, commencing with the date of the decedent's death, for an action under this section by the creditor. Code Civ.Proc. § 353. Subdivision (c) is a specific application of the general purpose of this section to subject a distributee to personal liability but not to require rescission of a distribution already made.

An omitted creditor may also have a cause of action against a personal representative who in bad faith fails to give notice to a known creditor. See Sections 9053 (immunity of personal representative) and Section 11429 (unpaid creditor). [20 Cal.L.Rev.Comm.Reports 2287 (1990)].

1992 Amendment

Section 9392 is amended to revise a section reference. This revision is a technical, nonsubstantive change. [22 Cal.L.Rev.Comm.Reports 895 (1992)].

ARTICLE 4. TRANSITIONAL PROVISION

Section
9399. Application of chapter; former law.

Application

Part not applicable in proceeding commenced before July 1, 1988, see Probate Code § 9004.

Cross References

Application of old and new law, see Probate Code § 3.

§ 9399. Application of chapter; former law

(a) This chapter does not apply to an action commenced before July 1, 1989.

(b) The applicable law in effect before July 1, 1989,[1] continues to apply to an action commenced before July 1, 1989, notwithstanding its repeal by Chapter 1199 of the Statutes of 1988. *(Stats.1990, c. 79 (A.B.759), § 14, operative July 1, 1991.)*

[1] See Probate Code § 707 et seq. (repealed).

Law Revision Commission Comments
1990 Enactment

Section 9399 continues Section 9399 of the repealed Probate Code without substantive change. This section is an exception to the general rule of Section 3 that a "new law" applies on its operative date to pending probate proceedings. Where litigation was commenced before July 1, 1989, either against the decedent or against the personal representative, any claim requirements applicable to the litigation are governed by the relevant law in effect before July 1, 1989, and not by this chapter.

Background on Section 9399 of Repealed Code

Section 9399 was a new provision added by 1988 Cal.Stat. ch. 1199 § 86. For background on the provisions of this chapter, see the Comment to this chapter under the chapter heading. [20 Cal.L.Rev.Comm.Reports 1001 (1990)].

Part 5

ESTATE MANAGEMENT

Law Revision Commission Comments

1990 Enactment

This part supersedes Part 5 (commencing with Section 9600) of Division 7 of the repealed Probate Code. The superseded part was enacted upon recommendation of the California Law Revision Commission. See Recommendation Relating to Supervised Administration of Decedent's Estate, 19 Cal.L.Revision Comm'n Reports 5 (1988); Communication from California Law Revision Commission Concerning Assembly Bill 708, 19 Cal.L.Revision Comm'n Reports 545 (1988). [20 Cal.L.Rev.Comm.Reports 1001 (1990)].

Cross References

Independent Administration of Estates Act, generally, see Probate Code § 10400 et seq.

CHAPTER 1. GENERAL PROVISIONS

ARTICLE 1. DUTIES AND LIABILITIES OF PERSONAL REPRESENTATIVE

Cross References

Application of old and new law, see Probate Code § 3.

§ 9600. Management and control of estate; ordinary care and diligence

(a) The personal representative has the management and control of the estate and, in managing and controlling the estate, shall use ordinary care and diligence. What constitutes ordinary care and diligence is determined by all the circumstances of the particular estate.

(b) The personal representative:

(1) Shall exercise a power to the extent that ordinary care and diligence require that the power be exercised.

(2) Shall not exercise a power to the extent that ordinary care and diligence require that the power not be exercised. *(Stats.1990, c. 79 (A.B.759), § 14, operative July 1, 1991.)*

Law Revision Commission Comments

1990 Enactment

Section 9600 continues Section 9600 of the repealed Probate Code without change. This section is comparable to Section 2401 (Guardianship–Conservatorship Law) and is consistent with prior law. See, e.g., Estate of Beach, 15 Cal.3d 623, 631, 542 P.2d 994, 125 Cal.Rptr. 570 (1975) (executor required to exercise "that degree of prudence and diligence which a man of ordinary judgment would be expected to bestow upon his own affairs of a like nature"); Lobro v. Watson, 42 Cal.App.3d 180, 189, 116 Cal.Rptr. 533 (1974) (personal representative "required to exercise the degree of care and prudence that an ordinary person would employ in handling his or her own affairs").

In determining what constitutes ordinary care and diligence, a professional personal representative is held to a higher standard of care based on its presumed expertise than is a lay personal representative. See Estate of Beach, 15 Cal.3d at 635. Section 9600 applies to all powers and duties of the personal representative, whether or not prior court authorization is required. See also Section 7250 (effect of court authorization or approval).

Subdivision (b) of Section 9600 makes clear that ordinary care and diligence may require that the personal representative exercise a power. For example, the personal representative has the duty to take all steps reasonably necessary for the protection and preservation of the estate property, and this duty requires that the personal representative obtain and maintain insurance on the estate property to the extent reasonably necessary. See Section 9656. At the same time, subdivision (b) also makes clear that the extent to which a power should be exercised is limited to what is required by the exercise of ordinary care and diligence under all the circumstances. Thus, for example, the personal representative is not authorized to obtain or maintain more insurance on the estate property than is reasonably necessary. In determining when a power is required to be exercised and when it may not be exercised, the personal representative has some discretion. For example, the personal representative has discretion to determine the amount of insurance, and so long as the amount of insurance is not unreasonably high or low under the circumstances, the personal representative has complied with the duty to use ordinary care and diligence.

The liability of a personal representative whose office is vacant, and of surety on bond, continues until settlement of accounts and delivery of all of the estate to successor personal representative or other person appointed by the court to receive it. See Section 8525.

As to orders made, or actions taken, before July 1, 1988, and matters pending on July 1, 1988, see Section 9645. As to the application of any amendments made after that date, see Section 3.

Background on Section 9600 of Repealed Code

Section 9600 was a new provision added by 1987 Cal.Stat. ch. 923 § 93. For background on the provisions of this part, see the Comment to this part under the part heading. [20 Cal.L.Rev.Comm.Reports 1001 (1990)].

§ 9601. Breach of fiduciary duty; liability

(a) If a personal representative breaches a fiduciary duty, the personal representative is chargeable with any of the following that is appropriate under the circumstances:

(1) Any loss or depreciation in value of the decedent's estate resulting from the breach of duty, with interest.

(2) Any profit made by the personal representative through the breach of duty, with interest.

(3) Any profit that would have accrued to the decedent's estate if the loss of profit is the result of the breach of duty.

(b) If the personal representative has acted reasonably and in good faith under the circumstances as known to the personal representative, the court, in its discretion, may excuse the personal representative in whole or in part from liability under subdivision (a) if it would be equitable to do so. *(Stats.1990, c. 79 (A.B.759), § 14, operative July 1, 1991.)*

Law Revision Commission Comments

1990 Enactment

Section 9601 continues Section 9601 of the repealed Probate Code without change. See also Section 9603 (other remedies not affected). Section 9601 is comparable to Sections 2401.3 (guardians and conservators) and 16440 (trustees) and is in general accord with prior law. See In re Estate of Elizalde, 182 Cal. 427, 435, 188 P. 560 (1920) (liability for misappropriated funds plus interest where no showing that larger profit was received); Estate of Gerber, 73 Cal.App.3d 96, 113, 140 Cal.Rptr. 577 (1977) (liability for interest due to delay in payment of estate taxes); Estate of Guiol, 28 Cal.App.3d 818, 824–25, 105 Cal.Rptr. 35 (1972) (breach of duty for turning estate assets over to attorney and failing to protect assets); Estate of McSweeney, 123 Cal.App.2d 787, 791–92, 268 P.2d 107 (1954) (liability for using estate funds for individual needs) (dictum); Estate of Pardue, 57 Cal.App.2d 918, 920–21, 135 P.2d 394 (1943) (liability for rental value of property). See also Sections 9631 (liability of joint personal representative for breach of duty by another personal representative), 10380 (liability for neglect or misconduct in sale of estate property), 10381 (liquidated damages for fraudulent sale), 10382 (limitation of actions for recovery of property).

Under subdivision (a), the court has discretion to choose the measure of liability in paragraph (1), (2) or (3) that is appropriate under the circumstances. The reference to "profit made by the personal representative" in paragraph (2) of subdivision (a) refers to personal profit rather than profit to the estate.

The liability of a personal representative whose office is vacant, and of surety on bond, continues until settlement of accounts and delivery of all of the estate to successor personal representative or other person appointed by the court to receive it. See Section 8525.

As to orders made, or actions taken, before July 1, 1988, and matters pending on July 1, 1988, see Section 9645. As to the application of any amendments made after that date, see Section 3.

Background on Section 9601 of Repealed Code

Section 9601 was a new provision added by 1987 Cal.Stat. ch. 923 § 93. For background on the provisions of this part, see the Comment to this part under the part heading. [20 Cal.L.Rev.Comm.Reports 1001 (1990)].

§ 9602. Interest; amount of liability; excuse from liability

(a) If the personal representative is liable for interest pursuant to Section 9601, the personal representative is liable for the greater of the following amounts:

(1) The amount of interest that accrues at the legal rate on judgments.

(2) The amount of interest actually received.

(b) If the personal representative has acted reasonably and in good faith under the circumstances as known to the personal representative, the court, in its discretion, may excuse the personal representative in whole or in part from liability under subdivision (a) if it would be equitable to do so. *(Stats.1990, c. 79 (A.B.759), § 14, operative July 1, 1991. Amended by Stats.1998, c. 77 (S.B.1841), § 4.)*

Law Revision Commission Comments

1990 Enactment

Section 9602 continues Section 9602 of the repealed Probate Code without change. See also Section 9603 (other remedies not affected). Section 9602 is comparable to Section 16441 (measure of liability for interest for breach of trust). See the Comment to Section 16441. See also Code Civ.Proc. § 685.010 (rate of interest on judgments). Section 9602 is consistent with the prior case law rule that executors are liable for interest at the legal rate. See In re Estate of Piercy, 168 Cal. 755, 757–58, 145 P. 91 (1914); In re Estate of Hilliard, 83 Cal. 423, 427–28, 23 P. 393 (1890); In re Estate of Holbert, 39 Cal. 597, 601 (1870) (liability for interest or profit, whichever is greater); Estate of McSweeney, 123 Cal.App.2d 787, 791–93, 268 P.2d 107 (1954); see also In re Estate of Guglielmi, 138 Cal.App. 80, 90, 31 P.2d 1078 (1934). Unlike the prior case law rule, however, Section 9602 does not allow for annual compounding even where the personal representative is negligent. As to orders made, or actions taken, before July 1, 1988, and matters pending on July 1, 1988, see Section 9645. As to the application of any amendments made after that date, see Section 3.

Background on Section 9602 of Repealed Code

Section 9602 was a new provision added by 1987 Cal.Stat. ch. 923 § 93. For background on the provisions of this part, see the Comment to this part under the part heading. [20 Cal.L.Rev.Comm.Reports 1001 (1990)].

§ 9603. Other remedies under statutory or common law

The provisions of Sections 9601 and 9602 for liability of a personal representative for breach of a fiduciary duty do not prevent resort to any other remedy available against the personal representative under the statutory or common law. *(Stats.1990, c. 79 (A.B.759), § 14, operative July 1, 1991.)*

Law Revision Commission Comments

1990 Enactment

Section 9603 continues Section 9603 of the repealed Probate Code without change. This section is comparable to Sections 2401.7 (guardians and conservators) and 16442 (trustees). The section makes clear that Section 9601 does not prevent resort to any other remedy available against the personal representative under the statutory or common law. The section merely retains remedies that existed before the enactment of Sections 9601 and 9602; it does not create any new remedies against a personal representative. As to orders made, or actions taken, before July 1, 1988, and matters pending on July 1, 1988, see Section 9645. As to the application of any amendments made after that date, see Section 3.

Background on Section 9603 of Repealed Code

Section 9603 was a new provision added by 1987 Cal.Stat. ch. 923 § 93. For background on the provisions of this part, see the Comment to this part under the part heading. [20 Cal.L.Rev.Comm.Reports 1001 (1990)].

§ 9604. Agreements to answer in damages or pay debt of decedent out of personal representative's estate

No personal representative is chargeable upon a special promise to answer in damages for a liability of the decedent or to pay a debt of the decedent out of the personal representative's own estate unless the agreement for that purpose, or some memorandum or note thereof, is in writing and is signed by one of the following:

(a) The personal representative.

(b) Some other person specifically authorized by the personal representative in writing to sign the agreement or the memorandum or note. *(Stats.1990, c. 79 (A.B.759), § 14, operative July 1, 1991.)*

Law Revision Commission Comments

1990 Enactment

Section 9604 continues Section 9604 of the repealed Probate Code without change. As to orders made, or actions taken, before July 1, 1988, and matters pending on July 1, 1988, see Section 9645. As to the application of any amendments made after that date, see Section 3.

Background on Section 9604 of Repealed Code

Section 9604 was added by 1987 Cal.Stat. ch. 923 § 93. The section restated former Probate Code Section 737 (repealed by 1987 Cal.Stat. ch. 923 § 37) without substantive change. For background on the provisions of this part, see the Comment to this part under the part heading. [20 Cal.L.Rev.Comm.Reports 1001 (1990)].

Cross References

Creditors, liability for payment to, see Probate Code § 11424.
Decree of distribution, see Probate Code § 11603.

Obligations which need not be in writing generally, see Civil Code § 2794.

§ 9605. Personal representative; claims of decedent against person appointed

Appointment of a person as personal representative does not discharge any claim the decedent has against the person. *(Stats.1990, c. 79 (A.B.759), § 14, operative July 1, 1991.)*

Law Revision Commission Comments

1990 Enactment

Section 9605 continues Section 9605 of the repealed Probate Code without change. See also Section 8851 (discharge or devise of claims).

Background on Section 9605 of Repealed Code

Section 9605 was added by 1988 Cal.Stat. ch. 1199 § 86.5. The section restated parts of former Probate Code Section 602 (repealed by 1988 Cal.Stat. ch. 1199 § 51) and extended the provisions from executors to all personal representatives. For background on this section, see Communication from the California Law Revision Commission Concerning Assembly Bill 2841, 19 Cal.L.Revision Comm'n Reports 1201, 1241 (1988). For background on the provisions of this part, see also the Comment to this part under part heading. [20 Cal.L.Rev.Comm.Reports 1001 (1990)].

§ 9606. Failure to reveal representative capacity or identify estate in instrument

Unless otherwise provided in the instrument or in this division, a personal representative is not personally liable on an instrument, including but not limited to a note, mortgage, deed of trust, or other contract, properly entered into in the personal representative's fiduciary capacity in the course of administration of the estate unless the personal representative fails to reveal the personal representative's representative capacity or identify the estate in the instrument. *(Stats.1990, c. 79 (A.B.759), § 14, operative July 1, 1991.)*

Law Revision Commission Comments

1990 Enactment

Section 9606 is new. It generalizes provisions formerly found in Section 9805(b) and is comparable to Sections 18000 (trust law) and 2110 (guardianship-conservatorship law). [20 Cal.L.Rev.Comm.Reports 1001 (1990)].

ARTICLE 2. COURT SUPERVISION

Cross References

Application of old and new law, see Probate Code § 3.

§ 9610. Powers and duties exercisable without court authorization

Unless this part specifically provides a proceeding to obtain court authorization or requires court authorization, the powers and duties set forth in this part may be exercised by the personal representative without court authorization, instruction, approval, or confirmation. Nothing in this section precludes the personal representative from seeking court authorization, instructions, approval, or confirmation. *(Stats. 1990, c. 79 (A.B.759), § 14, operative July 1, 1991.)*

Law Revision Commission Comments
1990 Enactment

Section 9610 continues Section 9610 of the repealed Probate Code without change. This section is comparable to subdivision (a) of Section 2450 (Guardianship–Conservatorship Law). The section is consistent with prior law under which a personal representative could perform many acts without prior court approval. See In re Estate of Fulmer, 203 Cal. 693, 697–98, 265 P. 920 (1928); Estate of Palm, 68 Cal.App.2d 204, 212, 156 P.2d 62 (1945).

In a case where Section 9610 authorizes the personal representative to act without court authorization and the personal representative decides to take the action without obtaining court authorization, the personal representative must use ordinary care and diligence in taking the action. See Section 9600. As to the effect of court authorization or approval, see Section 7250. As to when the personal representative is required to exercise a power and when the personal representative may not exercise a power, see Section 9600(b).

As to orders made, or actions taken, before July 1, 1988, and matters pending on July 1, 1988, see Section 9645. As to the application of any amendments made after that date, see Section 3.

Background on Section 9610 of Repealed Code

Section 9610 was a new provision added by 1987 Cal.Stat. ch. 923 § 93. For background on the provisions of this part, see the Comment to this part under the part heading. [20 Cal.L.Rev.Comm.Reports 1001 (1990)].

Cross References

Powers and duties of personal representative, see Probate Code § 9650.

§ 9611. Authorization and instruction of personal representative; confirmation of acts; petitions; notice

(a) In all cases where no other procedure is provided by statute, upon petition of the personal representative, the court may authorize and instruct the personal representative, or approve and confirm the acts of the personal representative, in the administration, management, investment, disposition, care, protection, operation, or preservation of the estate, or the incurring or payment of costs, fees, or expenses in connection therewith. Section 9613 does not preclude a petition for instructions under this section.

(b) Notice of the hearing on the petition shall be given as provided in Section 1220. *(Stats.1990, c. 79 (A.B.759), § 14, operative July 1, 1991.)*

Law Revision Commission Comments
1990 Enactment

Section 9611 continues Section 9611 of the repealed Probate Code without change. For general provisions, see Sections 1000–1004 (rules of practice), 1020–1023 (petitions and other papers), 1040–1050 (hearings and orders), 1200–1230 (notice of hearing), 1250–1252 (request for special notice), 1260–1265 (proof of giving of notice).

Section 9611 permits a petition for instructions only where no other procedure is provided by statute. For example, a petition for

instructions is used to obtain court authorization to incorporate the decedent's unincorporated business, there being no specific provision governing that matter. Compare Section 10512 (independent administration authority).

If another procedure is provided by statute but the personal representative is uncertain whether the statute providing the other procedure is applicable to the particular case, the personal representative may petition in the alternative, giving notice that is sufficient to satisfy the requirements of both Section 9611 and the other possibly applicable statute.

Only the personal representative may petition for instructions under Section 9611. But see Section 9613 (right of interested person to petition for order directing personal representative to act to avoid great or irreparable injury).

Subdivision (a) makes clear that the court may not only instruct the personal representative in advance, but may also confirm actions already taken. As to the effect of court authorization or approval, see Section 7250. As to orders made, or actions taken, before July 1, 1988, and matters pending on July 1, 1988, see Section 9645. As to the application of any amendments made after that date, see Section 3. See also Section 9603 (other remedies not affected).

Background on Section 9611 of Repealed Code

Section 9611 was added by 1987 Cal.Stat. ch. 923 § 93. Section 9611 continued former Probate Code Section 588 (repealed by 1987 Cal.Stat. ch. 923 § 35) insofar as that section authorized only the personal representative to petition for instructions. In this respect, the authorization was more limited than the authorization of the Guardianship–Conservatorship Law, which authorizes a creditor or other interested person to file a petition for instructions (Section 2403). The words "from time to time," which appeared in former Section 588, were omitted as unnecessary, since there is no limit on the number of times instructions or confirmations can be requested. Subdivision (b) required that notice be given at least 15 days before the hearing pursuant to Section 1220 instead of at least 10 days before the hearing as required by former Probate Code Section 1200.5 (repealed by 1987 Cal.Stat. ch. 923 § 59). For background on the provisions of this part, see the Comment to this part under the part heading. [20 Cal.L.Rev.Comm.Reports 1001 (1990)].

§ 9612. Repealed by Stats.1990, c. 79 (A.B.759), § 13, operative July 1, 1991

Law Revision Commission Comments
1990 Repeal

Section 9612 of the repealed Probate Code is continued without substantive change in Section 7250(a) (effect of court authorization or approval). [20 Cal.L.Rev.Comm.Reports 1001 (1990)].

§ 9613. Orders directing personal representative; notice

(a) On petition of any interested person, and upon a showing that if the petition is not granted the estate will suffer great or irreparable injury, the court may direct the personal representative to act or not to act concerning the estate. The order may include terms and conditions the court determines are appropriate under the circumstances.

(b) Notice of the hearing on the petition shall be given as provided in Section 1220. *(Stats.1990, c. 79 (A.B.759), § 14, operative July 1, 1991.)*

Law Revision Commission Comments
1990 Enactment

Section 9613 continues Section 9613 of the repealed Probate Code without substantive change. For general provisions, see Sections 1000–1004 (rules of practice), 1020–1023 (petitions and other papers), 1040–1050 (hearings and orders), 1200–1230 (notice of hearing), 1250–1252 (request for special notice), 1260–1265 (proof of giving of notice).

Section 9613 permits the court to direct the personal representative to act or not to act concerning the estate. The showing of irreparable injury under Section 9613 is analogous to the irreparable injury that must be shown for injunctive relief. Cf. Code Civ.Proc. § 526(2); 6 B. Witkin, California Procedure Provisional Remedies § 254, at 221 (3d ed. 1985 & Supp.1988). The existence of a remedy under Section 9613 does not limit the right of a personal representative to petition for instructions. See Section 9611. As to orders and transactions affecting property, see Sections 7260–7263. As to orders made, or actions taken, before July 1, 1988, and matters pending on July 1, 1988, see Section 9645. As to the application of any amendments made after that date, see Section 3.

Background on Section 9613 of Repealed Code

Section 9613 was a new provision added by 1987 Cal.Stat. ch. 923 § 93. For background on the provisions of this part, see the Comment to this part under the part heading. [20 Cal.L.Rev.Comm.Reports 1001 (1990)].

§ 9614. Suspension of powers of personal representative; hearing

(a) On petition of an interested person, the court may suspend the powers of the personal representative in whole or in part, for a time, as to specific property or circumstances or as to specific duties of the office, or may make any other order to secure proper performance of the duties of the personal representative, if it appears to the court that the personal representative otherwise may take some action that would jeopardize unreasonably the interest of the petitioner. Persons with whom the personal representative may transact business may be made parties.

(b) The matter shall be set for hearing within 10 days unless the parties agree otherwise. Notice as the court directs shall be given to the personal representative and attorney of record, if any, and to any other parties named in the petition.

(c) The court may, in its discretion, if it determines that the petition was brought unreasonably and for the purpose of hindering the personal representative in the performance of the duties of the office, assess attorney's fees against the petitioner and make the assessment a charge against the interest of the petitioner. *(Stats.1990, c. 79 (A.B.759), § 14, operative July 1, 1991.)*

Law Revision Commission Comments

1990 Enactment

Section 9614 continues Section 9614 of the repealed Probate Code without change. For general provisions, see Sections 1000–1004 (rules of practice), 1020–1023 (petitions and other papers), 1040–1050 (hearings and orders), 1200–1230 (notice of hearing), 1250–1252 (request for special notice), 1260–1265 (proof of giving of notice).

Section 9614 is drawn from Section 3–607 of the Uniform Probate Code (1987). As to the construction of provisions drawn from uniform acts, see Section 2. The section includes but is not limited to the situation (1) where the personal representative is appointed before or pending probate of a will or is appointed under a previous will or (2) where there is litigation over the bond of the personal representative and it is alleged that the estate is being wasted. For background on this section, see Comments to Conforming Revisions and Repeals, 19 Cal.L.Revision Comm'n Reports 1031, 1092–93 (1988).

Background on Section 9614 of Repealed Code

Section 9614 was added by 1988 Cal.Stat. ch. 1199 § 87. The section superseded former Probate Code Sections 352 (repealed by 1988 Cal.Stat. ch. 1199 § 40) and 550 (repealed by 1988 Cal.Stat. ch. 1199 § 48). The provision for assessment of attorney's fees was new. For background on the provisions of this part, see also the Comment to this part under the part heading. [20 Cal.L.Rev.Comm.Reports 1001 (1990)].

Cross References

Appointment of special administrator during delay, see Probate Code § 8540.

Removal of personal representative, see Probate Code § 8500 et seq.

ARTICLE 3. SUMMARY DETERMINATION OF DISPUTES

Section
9620. Written agreements to refer disputes to judge.
9621. Written agreements to submit disputes to arbitration.

Cross References

Application of old and new law, see Probate Code § 3.

§ 9620. Written agreements to refer disputes to judge

If there is a dispute relating to the estate between the personal representative and a third person, the personal representative may do either of the following:

(a) Enter into an agreement in writing with the third person to refer the dispute to a temporary judge designated in the agreement. The agreement shall be filed with the clerk, who shall thereupon, with the approval of the court, enter an order referring the matter to the designated person. The temporary judge shall proceed promptly to hear and determine the matter in controversy by summary procedure, without pleadings or discovery. The decision of the designated person is subject to Section 632 of the Code of Civil Procedure. Judgment shall be entered on the decision and shall be as valid and effective as if rendered by a judge of the court in an action against the personal representative or the third person commenced by ordinary process.

(b) Enter into an agreement in writing with the third person that a judge, pursuant to the agreement and with the written consent of the judge, both filed with the clerk within the time specified in Section 9353 for bringing an independent suit on the matter in dispute, may hear and determine the dispute pursuant to the procedure provided in subdivision (a). *(Stats.1990, c. 79 (A.B.759), § 14, operative July 1, 1991.)*

Law Revision Commission Comments

1990 Enactment

Section 9620 continues Section 9620 of the repealed Probate Code without substantive change.

Section 9620 is designed to reduce the cost of administration of estates and to ease the court's workload by encouraging disposition of disputes by summary proceedings rather than by litigation. See Review of Selected 1968 Code Legislation 226–28 (Cal.Cont.Ed.Bar 1968). Nothing in Section 9620 limits the alternative of reference and trial by a referee under Code of Civil Procedure Sections 638–645.1, and those provisions remain applicable to probate matters. Summary proceedings under Section 9620 do not include a right to jury trial. See Estate of Beach, 15 Cal.3d 623, 642, 542 P.2d 994, 125 Cal.Rptr. 570 (1975). See also Section 7200 (right to jury trial).

Under Section 9620, any member of the State Bar (including a court commissioner or referee) may be appointed as a temporary judge. See also Cal. Const. art. VI, § 21 ("On stipulation of the parties litigant the court may order a cause to be tried by a temporary judge who is a member of the State Bar, sworn and empowered to act until final determination of the cause."); Code Civ.Proc. § 259(5) (power of court commissioner to act as temporary judge). Section 9620 does not require that the temporary judge try the matter in a regular courtroom; the temporary judge may try the matter at his or her office or at any other place.

As to orders made, or actions taken, before July 1, 1988, and matters pending on July 1, 1988, see Section 9645. As to the application of any amendments made after that date, see Section 3.

Background on Section 9620 of Repealed Code

Section 9620 was added by 1987 Cal.Stat. ch. 923 § 93 and was amended by 1988 Cal.Stat. ch. 1199 § 87.5 and 1989 Cal.Stat. ch. 21 § 24. The section restated and generalized paragraph (2) of former Probate Code Section 718 (repealed by 1987 Cal.Stat. ch. 923 § 37). Former Section 718 was limited to claims filed or presented, but Section 9620 applied to any dispute relating to the estate, including but not limited to one concerning a claim by or against the decedent or the estate. Paragraph (2) of former Section 718 required a written decision; this requirement was replaced by a provision that adopted the statement of decision provision of Code of Civil Procedure Section 632.

The reference in paragraph (2) of former Section 718 to "a commissioner or referee who is regularly attached to the court and designated in the agreement or to a judge pro tempore designated in the agreement" was replaced by a reference to "a temporary judge designated in the agreement." This substitution made no substantive change in the law but made the provision conform to the language used in Section 21 of Article 6 of the California Constitution ("On stipulation of the parties litigant the court may order a cause to be tried by a temporary judge who is a member of the State Bar, sworn and empowered to act until final determination of the cause.").

The 1988 and 1989 amendments corrected a section reference.

For background on the provisions of this part, see the Comment to this part under the part heading. [20 Cal.L.Rev.Comm.Reports 1001 (1990)].

Cross References

Appointment of referee to examine accounts of representatives, see Probate Code § 11002.
Evidence on trial of question of fact before referee, see Evidence Code § 300.
Judgment roll as including finding of referee, see Code of Civil Procedure § 670.
Referees' fees, see Code of Civil Procedure § 1023.
References and trials by referees, generally, see Code of Civil Procedure § 638 et seq.
Review of decision, see Code of Civil Procedure § 645.

§ 9621. Written agreements to submit disputes to arbitration

If there is a dispute relating to the estate between the personal representative and a third person, the personal representative may enter into an agreement in writing with the third person to submit the dispute to arbitration under Title 9 (commencing with Section 1280) of Part 3 of the Code of Civil Procedure. The agreement is not effective unless it is first approved by the court and a copy of the approved agreement is filed with the court. Notice of the hearing on the petition for approval of the agreement shall be given as provided in Section 1220. The order approving the agree-

ment may be made ex parte. *(Stats.1990, c. 79 (A.B.759), § 14, operative July 1, 1991.)*

Law Revision Commission Comments
1990 Enactment

Section 9621 continues Section 9621 of the repealed Probate Code without substantive change. The provision giving the court authority to order notice be given for a shorter period or that notice be dispensed with has been omitted as unnecessary in view of the general provisions giving the court this authority. See Sections 1203, 1220(c). For general provisions relating to notice, see Sections 1200–1230 (notice of hearing), 1250–1252 (request for special notice), 1260–1265 (proof of giving of notice). As to orders made, or actions taken, before July 1, 1988, and matters pending on July 1, 1988, see Section 9645. As to the application of any amendments made after that date, see Section 3.

Section 9621 is comparable to Section 2406 (Guardianship–Conservatorship Law). Arbitration pursuant to Section 9621 is conducted under Code of Civil Procedure Sections 1280–1294.2. This is "conventional" or "ordinary" arbitration. See 6 B. Witkin, California Procedure Proceedings Without Trial § 320, at 612–13 (3d ed. 1985 & Supp.1988). In conventional or ordinary arbitration, there is no right to trial de novo, and, although the court may correct or vacate an award, the grounds for so doing are limited. See Code Civ.Proc. §§ 1285–1294.2. There is no right to a jury trial when an arbitration award as contemplated by Section 9621 is confirmed. See Code Civ.Proc. § 1286; Madden v. Kaiser Foundation Hospitals, 17 Cal.3d 699, 712–14, 552 P.2d 1178, 131 Cal.Rptr. 882 (1976).

Background on Section 9621 of Repealed Code

Section 9621 was a new provision added by 1987 Cal.Stat. ch. 923 § 93. For background on the provisions of this part, see the Comment to this part under the part heading. [20 Cal.L.Rev.Comm.Reports 1001 (1990)].

ARTICLE 4. JOINT PERSONAL REPRESENTATIVES

Section
9630. Powers and duties.
9631. Breach of fiduciary duty; liability.

Cross References
Application of old and new law, see Probate Code § 3.

§ 9630. Powers and duties

(a) Subject to subdivisions (b), (c), and (d):

(1) Where there are two personal representatives, both must concur to exercise a power.

(2) Where there are more than two personal representatives, a majority must concur to exercise a power.

(b) If one of the joint personal representatives dies or is removed or resigns, the powers and duties continue in the remaining joint personal representatives as if they were the only personal representatives until further appointment is made by the court.

(c) Where joint personal representatives have been appointed and one or more are (1) absent from the state and unable to act, or (2) otherwise unable to act, or (3) legally disqualified from serving, the court may, by order made with or without notice, authorize the remaining joint personal representatives to act as to all matters embraced within its order.

(d) Where there are two or more personal representatives, any of them may:

(1) Oppose a petition made by one or more of the other personal representatives or by any other person.

(2) Petition the court for an order requiring the personal representatives to take a specific action for the benefit of the estate or directing the personal representatives not to take a specific action. If a procedure is provided by statute for a petition to authorize the specific action by the personal representatives, the petitioner shall file the petition under the provision relating to that procedure. Otherwise, the petitioner shall file the petition under Section 9611. *(Stats.1990, c. 79 (A.B.759), § 14, operative July 1, 1991.)*

Law Revision Commission Comments
1990 Enactment

Section 9630 continues Section 9630 of the repealed Probate Code without change. See also Section 8521 (effect of vacancy in office of fewer than all personal representatives).

Under Section 9630, absence from the state does not suspend the power of a personal representative to act. See Sections 8570–8577. And, absent a court order authorizing the remaining personal representatives to act, if one of several joint personal representatives is absent from California, the same number of joint personal representatives must concur in the action as would be required if the absent personal representative were still in California.

Paragraph (1) of subdivision (a) codifies case law. See Bullis v. Security Pac. Nat'l Bank, 21 Cal.3d 801, 810, 582 P.2d 109, 148 Cal.Rptr. 22 (1978). The language used in subdivisions (b) and (c) is comparable to language used in Section 2105 (Guardianship–Conservatorship Law). Paragraph (2) of subdivision (d) is drawn from the law in other states. See Annot., 85 A.L.R.3d 1124 (1978 and Supp.1988). For general provisions relating to petitions, see Sections 1020–1023.

As to orders made, or actions taken, before July 1, 1988, and matters pending on July 1, 1988, see Section 9645. As to the application of any amendments made after that date, see Section 3.

Background on Section 9630 of Repealed Code

Section 9630 was added by 1987 Cal.Stat. ch. 923 § 93. The section replaced former Probate Code Section 570 (repealed by 1987 Cal.Stat. ch. 923 § 35). Paragraph (1) of subdivision (a) codified case law. See Bullis v. Security Pac. Nat'l Bank, 21 Cal.3d 801, 810, 582 P.2d 109, 148 Cal.Rptr. 22 (1978). Paragraph (2) of subdivision (a) restated the second sentence of former Section 570 without substantive change. Subdivisions (b) and (c) replaced the first sentence of former Section 570 with language drawn in part from Section 2105 (Guardianship–Conservatorship Law). Subdivision (d) was new. Paragraph (1) of subdivision (d) was drawn from a portion of the last sentence of former Probate Code Section 1000 and of the second sentence of former Probate Code Section 1020 (provisions repealed by 1988 Cal.Stat. ch. 1199 § 55.5). For background on the provisions of this part, see the Comment to this part under the part heading. [20 Cal.L.Rev.Comm.Reports 1001 (1990)].

Cross References

Death or other disability of co-representative, see Probate Code § 8521.
Liability of co-trustees, see Probate Code § 16402.

§ 9631. Breach of fiduciary duty; liability

(a) Except as provided in subdivision (b), where there is more than one personal representative, one personal representative is not liable for a breach of fiduciary duty committed by another of the personal representatives.

(b) Where there is more than one personal representative, one personal representative is liable for a breach of fiduciary duty committed by another of the personal representatives under any of the following circumstances:

(1) Where the personal representative participates in a breach of fiduciary duty committed by the other personal representative.

(2) Where the personal representative improperly delegates the administration of the estate to the other personal representative.

(3) Where the personal representative approves, knowingly acquiesces in, or conceals a breach of fiduciary duty committed by the other personal representative.

(4) Where the personal representative's negligence enables the other personal representative to commit a breach of fiduciary duty.

(5) Where the personal representative knows or has information from which the personal representative reasonably should have known of the breach of fiduciary duty by the other personal representative and fails to take reasonable steps to compel the other personal representative to redress the breach.

(c) The liability of a personal representative for a breach of fiduciary duty committed by another of the personal representatives that occurred before July 1, 1988, is governed by prior law and not by this section. *(Stats.1990, c. 79 (A.B.759), § 14, operative July 1, 1991.)*

Law Revision Commission Comments
1990 Enactment

Section 9631 continues Section 9631 of the repealed Probate Code without change. This section is comparable to the law applicable to guardians and conservators (Section 2105.5) and trustees (Section 16402). Subdivision (b), which imposes liability on one personal representative for a breach of fiduciary duty by another representative under certain circumstances, is generally consistent with prior case law. See In re Estate of Osborn, 87 Cal. 1, 25 P. 157 (1890). As to orders made, or actions taken, before July 1, 1988, and matters pending on July 1, 1988, see Section 9645. As to the application of any amendments made after that date, see Section 3.

Background on Section 9631 of Repealed Code

Section 9631 was added by 1987 Cal.Stat. ch. 923 § 93. The section replaced a provision formerly found in the last portion of the first sentence of former Probate Code Section 920 (before its amendment by 1987 Cal.Stat. ch. 923 § 44; repealed by 1988 Cal.Stat. ch. 1199 § 54.5) (personal representative not liable for act or negligence of coexecutor or coadministrator except for collusion or gross negligence). For background on the provisions of this part, see the Comment to this part under the part heading. [20 Cal.L.Rev.Comm.Reports 1001 (1990)].

ARTICLE 5. INDEPENDENT ADMINISTRATION

Section
9640. Part not to limit or restrict authority of personal representative.

§ 9640. Part not to limit or restrict authority of personal representative

Nothing in this part limits or restricts any authority granted to a personal representative under the Independent Administration of Estates Act (Part 6 (commencing with Section 10400)) to administer the estate under that part. *(Stats.1990, c. 79 (A.B.759), § 14, operative July 1, 1991.)*

Law Revision Commission Comments

1990 Enactment

Section 9640 continues Section 9640 of the repealed Probate Code without substantive change. As to orders made, or actions taken, before July 1, 1988, and matters pending on July 1, 1988, see Section 9645. As to the application of any amendments made after that date, see Section 3.

Background on Section 9640 of Repealed Code

Section 9640 was a new provision added by 1987 Cal.Stat. ch. 923 § 93. For background on the provisions of this part, see the Comment to this part under the part heading. [20 Cal.L.Rev.Comm.Reports 1001 (1990)].

ARTICLE 6. TRANSITIONAL PROVISION

§ 9645. Application of law; continuation of actions, orders, judgments

(a) Subject to subdivisions (b) and (c), any petition or other matter filed or commenced before July 1, 1988, shall be continued under this part, so far as applicable, except where the court determines that application of a particular provision of this part would substantially interfere with the rights of the parties or other interested persons, in which case the particular provision of this part does not apply and the applicable law in effect before July 1, 1988, applies.

(b) Nothing in this part affects any order, judgment, or decree made, or any action taken, before July 1, 1988.

(c) Notwithstanding the enactment of this part:

(1) An order, judgment, or decree made before July 1, 1988, shall continue in full force and effect in accordance with its terms or until modified or terminated by the court.

(2) The validity of an order, judgment, or decree made before July 1, 1988, is determined by the applicable law in effect before July 1, 1988, and not by this part.

(3) The validity of any action taken before July 1, 1988, is determined by the applicable law in effect before July 1, 1988, and not by this part. *(Stats.1990, c. 79 (A.B.759), § 14, operative July 1, 1991.)*

Law Revision Commission Comments

1990 Enactment

Section 9645 continues Section 9645 of the repealed Probate Code without substantive change. This section limits the application of this part to petitions and other matters that were pending on July 1, 1988 (operative date of this part of repealed Probate Code); this part applies to these pending petitions and other pending matters unless the court with respect to a particular matter determines that application of a particular provision of this part would substantially interfere with the effective conduct of the matter or with the rights of the parties or other interested persons. If the court makes such a determination, the matter is governed by prior law which is preserved for this purpose.

Background on Section 9645 of Repealed Code

Section 9645 was a new provision added by 1987 Cal.Stat. ch. 923 § 93. For background on the provisions of this part, see the Comment to this part under the part heading. [20 Cal.L.Rev.Comm.Reports 1001 (1990)].

CHAPTER 2. ESTATE MANAGEMENT GENERALLY

§ 9650. Powers and duties of personal representatives

(a) Except as provided by statute and subject to subdivision (c):

(1) The personal representative has the right to, and shall take possession or control of, all the property of the decedent to be administered in the decedent's estate and shall collect all debts due to the decedent or the estate. The personal representative is not accountable for any debts that remain uncollected without his or her fault.

(2) The personal representative is entitled to receive the rents, issues, and profits from the real and personal property in the estate until the estate is distributed.

(b) The personal representative shall pay taxes on, and take all steps reasonably necessary for the management, protection, and preservation of, the estate in his or her possession.

(c) Real property or tangible personal property may be left with or surrendered to the person presumptively entitled to it unless or until, in the judgment of the personal representative, possession of the property by the personal representative will be necessary for purposes of administration. The person holding the property shall surrender it to the personal representative on request by the personal representative. *(Stats.1990, c. 79 (A.B.759), § 14, operative July 1, 1991.)*

Law Revision Commission Comments

1990 Enactment

Section 9650 continues Section 9650 of the repealed Probate Code without substantive change. The introductory clause of subdivision (a) recognizes that the subdivision is subject to other provisions of law governing possession of the estate. See, e.g., Sections 6500 (temporary possession of family dwelling and exempt property), 9780 (abandonment of tangible personal property). The first sentence of paragraph (1) of subdivision (a) uses language drawn in part from Section 3–709 of the Uniform Probate Code (1987). For a comparable provision in the Guardianship–Conservatorship Law, see Section 2451 (collection of debts and benefits). Where necessary, the personal representative may bring an action to recover possession of estate property or to determine title thereto. See Sections 9820 (action or proceeding for benefit of estate), 9654 (action by heirs or devisees for possession or to quiet title to real property of estate). See also Sections 7050 (estate subject to control of superior court), 9605 (appointment of person as personal representative does not discharge any claim the decedent has against the person).

Subdivision (b) is drawn from Section 3–709 of the Uniform Probate Code (1987). Under subdivision (b), the personal representative not only has a duty to maintain estate property in a reasonably good condition but also has, for example, a duty to obtain and maintain reasonably necessary insurance on estate property. Cf. Section 9656 (authority to insure). See also Section 9610 (extent of court supervision).

Subdivision (c) is drawn from Section 3–709 of the Uniform Probate Code (1987). This subdivision is designed to avoid disruption of possession of the decedent's assets by the heirs or devisees whenever possible. But, if the personal representative decides that possession of an asset is necessary or desirable for purposes of administration, the heir or devisee must surrender the asset to the personal representative. It may be possible for the heir or devisee to question the judgment of the personal representative in a later proceeding to surcharge for breach of fiduciary duty, but this possibility should not interfere with the personal representative's administrative authority as it relates to possession of the estate. On the other hand, the personal representative may be liable for failing to take possession of estate property if the property is thereby lost to those entitled to it. In re Estate of Boggs, 33 Cal.App.2d 30, 33, 90 P.2d 814 (1939). However, where the property is in the possession of the person who will ultimately receive it (as authorized under subdivision (c) of Section 9650), the personal representative is not liable to the person having the property if it is not properly cared for by that person.

As to the construction of provisions drawn from uniform acts, see Section 2. As to orders made, or actions taken, before July 1, 1988, and matters pending on July 1, 1988, see Section 9645. As to the application of any amendments made after that date, see Section 3.

Background on Section 9650 of Repealed Code

Section 9650 was added by 1987 Cal.Stat. ch. 923 § 93. The first sentence of paragraph (1) of subdivision (a) restated subdivision (a) of former Probate Code Section 571 without substantive change and superseded a portion of the first sentence of former Probate Code Section 581 (provisions repealed by 1987 Cal.Stat. ch. 923 § 35). The second sentence of paragraph (1) of subdivision (a) restated a provision formerly found in the first sentence of Probate Code Section 920 (before its amendment by 1987 Cal.Stat. ch. 923 § 44; repealed by 1988 Cal.Stat. ch. 1199 § 54.5) without substantive change. Paragraph (2) of subdivision (a) restated the last portion of the first sentence of former Probate Code Section 581 without substantive change.

Subdivision (b) replaced the second sentence of former Section 581 (repealed by 1987 Cal.Stat. ch. 923 § 35) which imposed on the personal representative the duty of keeping in good tenantable repair all houses, buildings, and fixtures on estate property under the control of the personal representative.

Subdivision (c) replaced the third sentence of former Section 581 and all of former Probate Code Section 582 (provisions repealed by 1987 Cal.Stat. ch. 923 § 35). Under subdivision (c), the expiration of the time to file or present claims no longer has significance in this context. Under former Section 582, after the time to file or present claims expired, the personal representative had to deliver possession of real property to the heirs or devisees unless needed to pay debts. Under former Section 581, the personal representative could not recover property from an heir or devisee unless the personal representative could prove it was needed in estate administration. By contrast, the sole question under subdivision (c) of Section 9650 is whether, in the judgment of the personal representative, the property is "necessary for purposes of administration."

For background on the provisions of this part, see the Comment to this part under the part heading. [20 Cal.L.Rev.Comm.Reports 1001 (1990)].

Cross References

Borrowing money and mortgaging property, generally, see Probate Code § 9800.

Death of mate or seaman on voyage, right of personal representative to wages, see Harbors and Navigation Code § 874.

Distribution of property in general, see Probate Code § 11600 et seq.

Estates subject to summary disposition, certification of authority for summary administration, existence of will, contents of petition, summary disposition of estate, see Probate Code § 7660.

Income tax credits, see Revenue and Taxation Code § 17733.

Personal representative or special administrator to take possession and preserve estate, see Probate Code § 8540.

Possession,

    Special administrator, see Probate Code § 8540 et seq.

Power of representative to engage agents or brokers to sell property, see Probate Code § 10150.

Presumption as to time of vesting of testamentary disposition, see Probate Code § 21116.

Time for filing inventory and appraisement of estate, see Probate Code § 8800.

§ 9651. Liability of personal representative; possession of property; compensation for services

(a) A personal representative who in good faith takes into possession real or personal property, and reasonably believes that the property is part of the estate of the decedent, is not:

(1) Criminally liable for so doing.

(2) Civilly liable to any person for so doing.

(b) The personal representative shall make reasonable efforts to determine the true nature of, and title to, the property so taken into possession.

(c) During his or her possession, the personal representative is entitled to receive all rents, issues, and profits of the property. If the property is later determined not to be part of the estate of the decedent, the personal representative shall deliver the property, or cause it to be delivered, to the person legally entitled to it, together with all rents, issues, and profits of the property received by the personal representative, less any expenses incurred in protecting and maintaining the property and in collecting rents, issues, and profits. The personal representative may request court approval before delivering the property pursuant to this subdivision.

(d) The court may allow the personal representative reasonable compensation for services rendered in connection with the duties specified in this section as to property later determined not to be part of the estate of the decedent, if the court makes one of the following findings:

(1) The services were of benefit to the estate. If the court makes this finding, the compensation and the expenses and costs of litigation, including attorney's fees of the attorney hired by the personal representative to handle the matter, are a proper expense of administration.

(2) The services were essential to preserve, protect, and maintain the property. If the court makes this finding, the court shall award compensation and the expenses and costs of litigation, including attorney's fees of the attorney hired by the personal representative to handle the matter, as an expense deductible from the rents, issues, and profits received by the personal representative, or, if these are insufficient, as a lien against the property. *(Stats.1990, c. 79 (A.B.759), § 14, operative July 1, 1991.)*

Law Revision Commission Comments

1990 Enactment

Section 9651 continues Section 9651 of the repealed Probate Code except that the section omits the language that provided for the court awarding the attorney for the personal representative reasonable compensation for services rendered in connection with the duties specified in the section. As to orders made, or actions taken, before July 1, 1988, and matters pending on July 1, 1988, see Section 9645.

Background on Section 9651 of Repealed Code

Section 9651 was added by 1987 Cal.Stat. ch. 923 § 93. The section restated subdivision (c) of former Probate Code Section 571 (repealed by 1987 Cal.Stat. ch. 923 § 35) without substantive change. For background on the provisions of this part, see the Comment to this part under the part heading.

Chapter 2.5 (consisting of Sections 9680 to 9686, inclusive, was recommended for enactment by the California Law Revision Commission. See Recommendations Relating to Probate Law: Hiring and Paying Attorneys, Advisors, and Others: Compensation of Personal Representative, 20 Cal.L.Revision Comm'n Reports 31 (1990). The Recommendation Proposing New Probate Code, 20 Cal.L.Revision Comm'n Reports 1001 (1990), included Comments to those sections. However, since the sections recommended by the Commission were not enacted by the Legislature, the Comments to the provisions of Chapter 2.5 (commencing with Section 9680) are no longer relevant to the new Probate Code which does not contain the sections. [20 Cal.L.Rev.Comm.Reports 1001 (1990)].

§ 9652. Investment of cash

(a) Except as provided in subdivisions (b) and (c), the personal representative shall keep all cash in his or her possession invested in interest-bearing accounts or other investments authorized by law.

(b) The requirement of subdivision (a) does not apply to the amount of cash that is reasonably necessary for orderly administration of the estate.

(c) The requirement of subdivision (a) does not apply to the extent that the testator's will otherwise provides. *(Stats. 1990, c. 79 (A.B.759), § 14, operative July 1, 1991.)*

Law Revision Commission Comments

1990 Enactment

Section 9652 continues Section 9652 of the repealed Probate Code without change. For the provisions concerning investments authorized by law, see Sections 9700, 9730, 9731. See also Section 9705 (interest on deposits by trust company). As to orders made, or actions taken, before July 1, 1988, and matters pending on July 1, 1988, see Section 9645. As to the application of any amendments made after that date, see Section 3.

Background on Section 9652 of Repealed Code

Section 9652 was added by 1987 Cal.Stat. ch. 923 § 93. The section restated a provision formerly found in Section 920.3 (before its amendment by 1987 Cal.Stat. ch. 923 § 45; repealed by 1988 Cal.Stat. ch. 1199 § 54.5) without substantive change. For background on the provisions of this part, see the Comment to this part under the part heading. [20 Cal.L.Rev.Comm.Reports 1001 (1990)].

§ 9653. Actions to recover property fraudulently conveyed, gifts in view of impending death, or transfers to designated beneficiaries on death; costs; priorities

(a) On application of a creditor of the decedent or the estate, the personal representative shall commence and prosecute an action for the recovery of real or personal property of the decedent for the benefit of creditors if the personal representative has insufficient assets to pay creditors and the decedent during lifetime did any of the following with respect to the property:

(1) Made a conveyance of the property, or any right or interest in the property, that is voidable as to creditors under the Uniform Voidable Transactions Act (Chapter 1 (commencing with Section 3439) of Title 2 of Part 2 of Division 4 of the Civil Code).

(2) Made a gift of the property in view of impending death.

(3) Made a direction to transfer a vehicle, undocumented vessel, manufactured home, mobilehome, commercial coach, truck camper, or floating home to a designated beneficiary on the decedent's death pursuant to Section 18102.2 of the Health and Safety Code, or Section 5910.5 or 9916.5 of the Vehicle Code, and the property has been transferred as directed.

(b) A creditor making application under this section shall pay such part of the costs and expenses of the suit and attorney's fees, or give an undertaking to the personal representative for that purpose, as the personal representative and the creditor agree, or, absent an agreement, as the court or judge orders.

(c) The property recovered under this section shall be sold for the payment of debts in the same manner as if the decedent had died seized or possessed of the property. The proceeds of the sale shall be applied first to payment of the costs and expenses of suit, including attorney's fees, and then to payment of the debts of the decedent in the same manner as other property in possession of the personal representative. After all the debts of the decedent have been paid, the remainder of the proceeds shall be paid to the person from whom the property was recovered. The property may be sold in its entirety or in such portion as necessary to pay the debts. *(Stats.1990, c. 79 (A.B.759), § 14, operative July 1, 1991. Amended by Stats.1991, c. 1055 (S.B.271), § 27, operative Jan. 1, 1993; Stats.2015, c. 44 (S.B.161), § 27, eff. Jan. 1, 2016.)*

Law Revision Commission Comments

1990 Enactment

Section 9653 continues Section 9653 of the repealed Probate Code without substantive change. Under subdivision (a), the personal representative must prosecute the action, but may settle the action as in other actions generally. In addition, the personal representative may, with court approval, assign to the creditor the right to bring the action. See Webb v. Pillsbury, 23 Cal.2d 324, 328–29, 144 P.2d 1 (1943). The requirement of subdivision (a) that the transfer must have been "during lifetime" does not preclude recovery of property given by a transfer which takes effect at death, such as a joint tenancy or life insurance. See, e.g., Rupp v. Kahn, 246 Cal.App.2d 188, 55 Cal.Rptr. 108 (1966) (joint tenancy); Headen v. Miller, 141 Cal. App.3d 169, 190 Cal.Rptr. 198 (1983) (life insurance).

The authority in paragraph (2) of subdivision (a) for a creditor to recover a gift made in view of death (Civil Code § 1149) is qualified by the requirement in the introductory clause of subdivision (a) that there be insufficient estate assets to pay creditors. See also Adams v. Prather, 176 Cal. 33, 40–42, 167 P. 534 (1917) (gift rendering estate insolvent); Civil Code §§ 1149–1153 (gifts in view of death).

In cases where Section 9653 applies, the personal representative must take action to recover the property even in the absence of a request by a creditor. Goldstein v. Prien, 143 Cal.App.2d 123, 127, 299 P.2d 344 (1956). See also Section 9820 (actions or proceedings for benefit of estate).

As to orders made, or actions taken, before July 1, 1988, and matters pending on July 1, 1988, see Section 9645. As to the application of any amendments made after that date, see Section 3.

1991 Amendment [Revised Comment]

Paragraph (2) of subdivision (a) of Section 9653 is amended to refer to a gift in view of "impending" death, consistent with Sections 5701–5705.

Paragraph (3) is added to subdivision (a) to provide for recovery of property transferred by TOD beneficiary designation. [21 Cal.L.Rev.Comm.Reports 71 (1991)].

Background on Section 9653 of Repealed Code

Section 9653 was added by 1987 Cal.Stat. ch. 923 § 93. Subdivision (a) restated former Probate Code Section 579 (repealed by 1987 Cal.Stat. ch. 923 § 35) without substantive change, except that the former provision that the personal representative must prosecute the action to recover the property "to final judgment" was not continued. Under subdivision (a), the personal representative must prosecute the action, but may settle the action as in other actions generally.

The reference in paragraph (1) of subdivision (a) to conveyances fraudulent as to creditors under the Uniform Fraudulent Transfer Act (Civil Code §§ 3439–3439.12) replaced the former reference to conveyances made with intent to defraud creditors, to avoid any obligation due another, or that is void as against creditors. This change was nonsubstantive. See Webb v. Pillsbury, 23 Cal.2d 324, 144 P.2d 1 (1943); Estate of Heigho, 186 Cal.App.2d 360, 365–66, 9 Cal.Rptr. 196 (1960); Goldstein v. Prien, 143 Cal.App.2d 123, 127, 299 P.2d 344 (1956).

The authority in paragraph (2) of subdivision (a) for a creditor to recover a gift made in view of death (Civil Code § 1149) is qualified by the requirement in the introductory clause of subdivision (a) that there be insufficient estate assets to pay creditors. This continued a provision in former Section 579 (repealed by 1987 Cal.Stat. ch. 923 § 35).

Subdivisions (b) and (c) restated former Probate Code Section 580 (repealed by 1987 Cal.Stat. ch. 923 § 35) with the following additions:

(1) Authority was added in subdivision (b) for the court to require the creditor to pay all or part of the personal representative's attorney's fees.

(2) The provision in subdivision (c) for application of the proceeds of sale first to costs and expenses of suit was new. The last sentence of subdivision (c) was new.

For background on the provisions of this part, see the Comment to this part under the part heading. [20 Cal.L.Rev.Comm.Reports 1001 (1990)].

Cross References

Action to set aside fraudulent conveyances, undertaking, see Civil Code § 3445 et seq.
Attorney General, proceedings to set aside fraudulent conveyances, see Government Code § 12517.
Costs,
    Allowance, see Code of Civil Procedure § 1026.
    Attorney's fees, see Code of Civil Procedure § 1021 et seq.
    Discretion of court to order payment, see Probate Code § 1002.
    Personal representatives, trustee of an express trust, guardian or conservator, actions by or against, see Code of Civil Procedure § 1026.
    Right to, see Code of Civil Procedure § 1021 et seq.
    Security for where plaintiff is a nonresident or foreign corporation, see Code of Civil Procedure § 1030.
Fraudulent instruments and transfers, see Civil Code § 3439 et seq.
Gifts in view of impending death, see Probate Code § 5705.
Preference of creditors, payment or security, see Civil Code § 3432.
Revocation of gift in view of death, see Probate Code § 5704.
Sales of estate property, generally, see Probate Code § 21400 et seq.

§ 9654. Actions for possession of property or to quiet title

The heirs or devisees may themselves, or jointly with the personal representative, maintain an action for possession of property or to quiet title to property against any person except the personal representative. *(Stats.1990, c. 79 (A.B. 759), § 14, operative July 1, 1991.)*

Law Revision Commission Comments
1990 Enactment

Section 9654 continues Section 9654 of the repealed Probate Code without change. See also Sections 9650 (right of personal representative to possession or control of estate), 9820 (authority of personal representative to maintain action for benefit of estate).

As to orders made, or actions taken, before July 1, 1988, and matters pending on July 1, 1988, see Section 9645. As to the application of any amendments made after that date, see Section 3.

Background on Section 9654 of Repealed Code

Section 9654 was added by 1987 Cal.Stat. ch. 923 § 93. The section restated the fourth sentence of former Probate Code Section 581 (repealed by 1987 Cal.Stat. ch. 923 § 35) and broadened it to apply to personal property as well as to real property. For background on the provisions of this part, see the Comment to this part under the part heading. [20 Cal.L.Rev.Comm.Reports 1001 (1990)].

§ 9655. Corporate stock

With respect to a share of stock of a domestic or foreign corporation held in the estate, a membership in a nonprofit corporation held in the estate, or other property held in the estate, a personal representative may do any one or more of the following:

(a) Vote in person, and give proxies to exercise, any voting rights with respect to the share, membership, or other property.

(b) Waive notice of a meeting or give consent to the holding of a meeting.

(c) Authorize, ratify, approve, or confirm any action which could be taken by shareholders, members, or property owners. *(Stats.1990, c. 79 (A.B.759), § 14, operative July 1, 1991.)*

Law Revision Commission Comments
1990 Enactment

Section 9655 continues Section 9655 of the repealed Probate Code without substantive change. The personal representative may act under Section 9655 without prior court authorization. See Section 9610. This section is comparable to Section 2458 (Guardianship–Conservatorship Law).

The word "meeting" in subdivision (b) includes a meeting of shareholders, members, or property owners, but is not so limited. Subdivision (c) permits authorization of action taken at a defectively noticed meeting by approval of the minutes of the meeting if the approval satisfies the requirements of the Corporations Code or other applicable law. See also Corp.Code §§ 702(a) (personal representative may vote share), 705(a) (person entitled to vote shares may give proxy). As to orders made, or actions taken, before July 1, 1988, and matters pending on July 1, 1988, see Section 9645. As to the application of any amendments made after that date, see Section 3.

Background on Section 9655 of Repealed Code

Section 9655 was added by 1987 Cal.Stat. ch. 923 § 93. The section was consistent with former Probate Code Section 589 (repealed by 1987 Cal.Stat. ch. 923 § 35). Former Section 589 permitted the personal representative to authorize "by a writing" any action which could be taken by shareholders. The requirement of a writing was not continued, but this change was not significant. Whether a writing is required in such cases is governed by the Corporations Code, which generally does require a writing for ratification by shareholders or members. For example, the transactions of an improperly called or noticed meeting may be ratified only by a signed instrument. Corp.Code § 601(e). Also, a writing is required for shareholder consent to action taken without a meeting. Corp.Code § 603. For background on the provisions of this part, see the Comment to this part under the part heading. [20 Cal.L.Rev.Comm.Reports 1001 (1990)].

Cross References

Persons entitled to vote, see Corporations Code § 701.
Proxies by fiduciaries, see Corporations Code § 703.
Voting corporate shares in name of two or more persons, see Corporations Code § 704.

§ 9656. Insurance

The personal representative may insure the property of the estate against damage or loss and may insure himself or herself against liability to third persons. *(Stats.1990, c. 79 (A.B.759), § 14, operative July 1, 1991.)*

Law Revision Commission Comments
1990 Enactment

Section 9656 continues Section 9656 of the repealed Probate Code without change. The personal representative may act under Section 9656 without prior court authorization. See Section 9610. The personal representative is required to exercise the power granted by this section to the extent that ordinary care and diligence require that the power be exercised, and may not exercise the power to the extent that ordinary care and diligence require that the power not be exercised. See Section 9600(b). For example, if the estate includes real property, the personal representative ordinarily will have the responsibility to maintain a reasonable amount of insurance on improvements on property and may insure himself or herself against personal liability arising out of the duty to maintain the property. Where the personal representative properly exercises the power

under this section, the cost of insurance for estate property or to protect the personal representative against liability is a proper expense of estate administration. As to orders made, or actions taken, before July 1, 1988, and matters pending on July 1, 1988, see Section 9645. As to the application of any amendments made after that date, see Section 3.

Background on Section 9656 of Repealed Code

Section 9656 was added by 1987 Cal.Stat. ch. 923 § 93. The section was drawn from subdivision (i) of former Probate Code Section 591.6 (repealed by 1987 Cal.Stat. ch. 923 § 35). The section continued a power implied under former law. For background on the provisions of this part, see the Comment to this part under the part heading. [20 Cal.L.Rev.Comm.Reports 1001 (1990)].

§ 9657. Profit or loss from increase or decrease of estate

The personal representative shall not make profit by the increase, nor suffer loss by the decrease or destruction without his or her fault, of any part of the estate. *(Stats.1990, c. 79 (A.B.759), § 14, operative July 1, 1991.)*

Law Revision Commission Comments
1990 Enactment

Section 9657 continues Section 9657 of the repealed Probate Code without change. See also Section 10005 (property sold for more or less than appraised value). As to orders made, or actions taken, before July 1, 1988, and matters pending on July 1, 1988, see Section 9645. As to the application of any amendments made after that date, see Section 3.

Background on Section 9657 of Repealed Code

Section 9657 was added by 1987 Cal.Stat. ch. 923 § 93. The section restated the former second sentence of former Probate Code Section 920 (prior to its amendment by 1987 Cal.Stat. ch. 923 § 44) without substantive change. For background on the provisions of this part, see the Comment to this part under the part heading. [20 Cal.L.Rev.Comm.Reports 1001 (1990)].

Cross References

Standard of care required of personal representative, see Probate Code § 9600.

CHAPTER 2.5. HIRING AND PAYING ATTORNEYS, ADVISERS, AND OTHERS [HEADING REPEALED]

CHAPTER 3. DEPOSIT OF MONEY AND PERSONAL PROPERTY WITH FINANCIAL INSTITUTIONS

Section
9700. Deposit and withdrawal of money.
9701. Deposit and withdrawal of personal property.
9702. Securities.
9703. Order of deposit of property subject to withdrawal only upon court authorization; notice.
9704. Delivery of property pursuant to decree; receipts.
9705. Interest on deposits.

Cross References

Administrators, appointment of nominated persons, priority, considerations, nominees required to obtain a bond, resignation upon cessation of California residency, submission to jurisdiction of court, see Probate Code § 8465.

§ 9700. Deposit and withdrawal of money

The personal representative may deposit money of the estate in an insured account in a financial institution in this state. Unless otherwise provided by court order, the money may be withdrawn without order of the court. *(Stats.1990, c. 79 (A.B.759), § 14, operative July 1, 1991.)*

Law Revision Commission Comments

1990 Enactment

Section 9700 continues Section 9700 of the repealed Probate Code without substantive change. The first sentence provides authority for the deposit or investment of estate money without court authorization. See Section 9610 (prior court authorization not required). The extent of the personal representative's responsibility for deposited funds is determined under Section 9600 (duty to use ordinary care and diligence). This is consistent with Section 2453 (Guardianship–Conservatorship Law). See also the Comment to Section 2453. See also Section 46 (defining "insured account in a financial institution").

If the deposit is withdrawable only upon court order, provisions for reducing the amount of the bond are found in Section 8483 and Financial Code Section 1586. See also Section 9703 (deposits withdrawable only upon court order). For provisions relating to deposits pursuant to court order, see Fin.Code § 764 (deposit with bank or trust company); Prob.Code §§ 8401, 8483 (exclusion of deposited property in computing amount of bond). See also Fin.Code §§ 6850–6851 (account of fiduciary under savings association law).

As to orders made, or actions taken, before July 1, 1988, and matters pending on July 1, 1988, see Section 9645. As to the application of any amendments made after that date, see Section 3.

Background on Section 9700 of Repealed Code

Section 9700 was added by 1987 Cal.Stat. ch. 923 § 93. The section replaced former Probate Code Section 585 (repealed by 1987 Cal.Stat. ch. 923 § 35) and expanded the deposits and investments permitted under former Section 585 to include investments in insured credit unions. This made the coverage of Section 9700 consistent with the coverage under Section 2453 (Guardianship–Conservatorship Law). The references in former Section 585 to statutory provisions that provided for the deposit or investment of money pursuant to a court order were omitted as unnecessary. The provision of former Section 585 discharging the personal representative from responsibility for deposited money until withdrawn was not continued. The extent of the personal representative's responsibility for deposited funds is determined under Section 9600 (duty to use ordinary care and diligence). [20 Cal.L.Rev.Comm.Reports 1001 (1990)].

Cross References

Financial institution, defined, see Probate Code § 40.

§ 9701. Deposit and withdrawal of personal property

The personal representative may deposit personal property of the estate with a trust company for safekeeping. Unless otherwise provided by court order, the personal property may be withdrawn without order of the court. *(Stats.1990, c. 79 (A.B.759), § 14, operative July 1, 1991.)*

Law Revision Commission Comments

1990 Enactment

Section 9701 continues Section 9701 of the repealed Probate Code without change. The first sentence provides authority for the deposit without court authorization of personal property of the estate with a trust company (defined in Section 83). See Section 9610 (prior court authorization not required). If personal property is deposited with a

trust company and the deposit is withdrawable only upon court order, provisions for reducing the amount of the bond are found in Section 8483 and Financial Code Section 1586. For other provisions relating to property deposited with a financial institution under court order, see Prob.Code §§ 8401, 9700–9705; Fin.Code § 1586. As to orders made, or actions taken, before July 1, 1988, and matters pending on July 1, 1988, see Section 9645. As to the application of any amendments made after that date, see Section 3.

Background on Section 9701 of Repealed Code

Section 9701 was added by 1987 Cal.Stat. ch. 923 § 93. The section replaced former Probate Code Section 586 (repealed by 1987 Cal.Stat. ch. 923 § 35) which permitted personal assets to be deposited with a trust company, and the bond of the personal representative reduced, "as provided by Division 1 of the Financial Code." The omission in Section 9701 of the quoted language did not change the law: If personal property is deposited with a trust company and the deposit is withdrawable only upon court order, provisions for reducing the amount of the bond are found in Section 8483 and Financial Code Section 1586. See also Section 9703 (deposits withdrawable only upon court order). For background on the provisions of this part, see the Comment to this part under the part heading. [20 Cal.L.Rev.Comm.Reports 1001 (1990)].

Cross References

Deposits with financial institutions under court order, see Financial Code § 1586; Probate Code §§ 8401, 9703.
Trust company, defined, see Probate Code § 83.

§ 9702. Securities

(a) A trust company serving as personal representative may deposit securities that constitute all or part of the estate in a securities depository, as provided in Section 1612 of the Financial Code.

(b) If securities have been deposited with a trust company by a personal representative pursuant to Section 9701, the trust company may deposit the securities in a securities depository, as provided in Section 1612 of the Financial Code.

(c) The securities depository may hold securities deposited with it in the manner authorized by Section 1612 of the Financial Code. *(Stats.1990, c. 79 (A.B.759), § 14, operative July 1, 1991. Amended by Stats.2014, c. 71 (S.B.1304), § 139, eff. Jan. 1, 2015.)*

Law Revision Commission Comments

1990 Enactment

Section 9702 continues Section 9702 of the repealed Probate Code without change. The personal representative may deposit securities under subdivision (a) without prior court authorization. See Section 9610. See also Section 83 (defining "trust company"). As to orders made, or actions taken, before July 1, 1988, and matters pending on July 1, 1988, see Section 9645. As to the application of any amendments made after that date, see Section 3.

Background on Section 9702 of Repealed Code

Section 9702 was added by 1987 Cal.Stat. ch. 923 § 93. Subdivisions (a) and (c) restated former Probate Code Section 590 (repealed by 1987 Cal.Stat. ch. 923 § 35) without substantive change. Subdivision (b) also restated former Probate Code Section 586.1 (repealed by 1987 Cal.Stat. ch. 923 § 35) without substantive change. For background on the provisions of this part, see the Comment to this part under the part heading. [20 Cal.L.Rev.Comm.Reports 1001 (1990)].

Securities, defined, see Probate Code §§ 70, 10200.

§ 9703. Order of deposit of property subject to withdrawal only upon court authorization; notice

(a) Upon application of the personal representative, the court may, with or without notice, order that money or other personal property be deposited pursuant to Section 9700 or 9701 and be subject to withdrawal only upon authorization of the court.

(b) The personal representative shall deliver a copy of the court order to the financial institution or trust company at the time the deposit is made.

(c) No financial institution or trust company accepting a deposit pursuant to Section 9700 or 9701 shall be on notice of the existence of an order that the money or other property is subject to withdrawal only upon authorization of the court unless it has actual notice of the order. *(Stats.1990, c. 79 (A.B.759), § 14, operative July 1, 1991.)*

Law Revision Commission Comments
1990 Enactment

Section 9703 continues Section 9703 of the repealed Probate Code without change. Where the deposit is withdrawable only upon court order, provisions for reducing the amount of the bond governed by Probate Code Section 8483 and Financial Code Section 1586. Only the personal representative may make an application under Section 9703. An interested person (such as an heir, devisee, or creditor) may neither make the application under Section 9703 nor petition for instructions under Section 9611. But see Section 9613 (right of interested person to petition for order directing personal representative in order to avoid great or irreparable injury). Section 9703 is comparable to a provision of the Guardianship–Conservatorship Law (Section 2456). As to orders made, or actions taken, before July 1, 1988, and matters pending on July 1, 1988, see Section 9645. As to the application of any amendments made after that date, see Section 3.

Background on Section 9703 of Repealed Code

Section 9703 was a new provision added by 1987 Cal.Stat. ch. 923 § 93. The section was based on authority implied under former Probate Code Sections 541.1 (repealed by 1988 Cal.Stat. ch. 1199 § 48), 585 (repealed by 1987 Cal.Stat. ch. 923 § 35), and 586 (repealed by 1987 Cal.Stat. ch. 923 § 35), except that Section 9703 included investments in shares of insured credit unions which were not included under former Sections 541.1 and 585. For background on the provisions of this part, see the Comment to this part under the part heading. [20 Cal.L.Rev.Comm.Reports 1001 (1990)].

Cross References

Reduction of bond, deposits withdrawable only upon court order, see Probate Code § 8483; Financial Code § 1586.

§ 9704. Delivery of property pursuant to decree; receipts

When an order for distribution of money or personal property deposited pursuant to this chapter is made, the financial institution, trust company, or securities depository may deliver the property directly to the distributees and shall file receipts therefor with the clerk. *(Stats.1990, c. 79 (A.B.759), § 14, operative July 1, 1991.)*

Law Revision Commission Comments
1990 Enactment

Section 9704 continues Section 9704 of the repealed Probate Code without change. As to orders made, or actions taken, before July 1, 1988, and matters pending on July 1, 1988, see Section 9645. As to the application of any amendments made after that date, see Section 3.

Background on Section 9704 of Repealed Code

Section 9704 was added by 1987 Cal.Stat. ch. 923 § 93 and was amended by 1988 Cal.Stat. ch. 1199 § 88. The section continued former Probate Code Section 586.5 (repealed by 1987 Cal.Stat. ch. 923 § 35) and expanded it to apply to all types of financial institutions where money or property may be deposited pursuant to this chapter. Former Section 586.5 applied only to a bank or trust company. For background on the provisions of this part, see the Comment to this part under the part heading.

The 1988 amendment conformed the terminology of the section to terminology used in other provisions enacted in 1988. [20 Cal.L.Rev.Comm.Reports 1001 (1990)].

§ 9705. Interest on deposits

(a) Subject to subdivision (b), where a trust company is a personal representative and in the exercise of reasonable judgment deposits money of the estate in an account in any department of the corporation or association of which it is a part, it is chargeable with interest thereon at the rate of interest prevailing among banks of the locality on such deposits.

(b) Where it is to the advantage of the estate, the amount of cash that is reasonably necessary for orderly administration of the estate may be deposited in a checking account that does not earn interest which is maintained in a department of the corporation or association of which the trust company is a part. *(Stats.1990, c. 79 (A.B.759), § 14, operative July 1, 1991.)*

Law Revision Commission Comments
1990 Enactment

Section 9705 continues Section 9705 of the repealed Probate Code without change. The type of account into which moneys of the estate are to be deposited depends on the type of account which best serves the needs of the estate. The time within which the estate may be distributed, the time of the receipt of the funds, and the immediate need for funds in order to meet the requirements of administration are all factors to be considered in determining the type of account in which the funds should be deposited. For example, where there is a substantial sum in excess of the immediate requirements and the sum is to be held over a period of time, the personal representative should deposit the funds in an account (which would include purchase of a certificate of deposit where appropriate under the circumstances) which not only would safeguard the funds but also allow a rate of interest on the funds that is advantageous to the estate. See In re Estate of Smith, 112 Cal.App. 680, 685–86, 297 P. 927 (1931); see also Estate of Buchman, 138 Cal.App.2d 228, 238–39, 291 P.2d 547 (1955); Fin.Code § 6515 (saving association as personal representative); Prob.Code §§ 2453.5 (trust company as guardian or conservator), 9600 (duty of personal representative to manage estate using ordinary care and diligence), 16225 (trustee's power to deposit trust funds).

Consistent with subdivision (b) of Section 9652, subdivision (b) of Section 9705 makes clear that a noninterest bearing checking account may be maintained where it is to the advantage of the estate to do so. It may, for example, be to the advantage of the estate to maintain a noninterest bearing checking account where the net cost of a checking account that would bear interest (service charges, less interest) would be more than the cost of a checking account that would not bear interest.

As to orders made, or actions taken, before July 1, 1988, and matters pending on July 1, 1988, see Section 9645. As to the application of any amendments made after that date, see Section 3.

Background on Section 9705 of Repealed Code

Section 9705 was added by 1987 Cal.Stat. ch. 923 § 93. Subdivision (a) restated former Probate Code Section 920.5 (repealed by 1987 Cal.Stat. ch. 923 § 46) without substantive change. The reference in Section 9705 to an "association" was new. See Fin.Code § 1502 (national banking association authorized to transact trust business). Subdivision (b) was new. For background on the provisions of this part, see the Comment to this part under the part heading. [20 Cal.L.Rev.Comm.Reports 1001 (1990)].

Cross References

Capacity of trust company to act as guardian or conservator, see Probate Code § 2453.5.
Capacity of trust company to act as personal representative, see Probate Code §§ 83, 300; Financial Code §§ 1580, 1586, 1587.
Management of estate using ordinary care and diligence, duty of personal representative, see Probate Code § 9600.
Personal representatives, generally, see Probate Code § 8400 et seq.
Security required of trust company, see Probate Code §§ 83, 301; Financial Code § 1540 et seq.
Special administrators, generally, see Probate Code § 8540 et seq.
Trust company defined, see Financial Code § 107.
Trust funds, power of trustee to deposit, see Probate Code § 16225.

CHAPTER 4. INVESTMENTS AND PURCHASE OF PROPERTY

Section
9730.   Permissible investments of estate money.
9731.   Orders; investments in United States or state securities; petition.
9732.   Manner of investment provided by will; orders; petition; notice.
9733.   Annuities.
9734.   Option rights.
9735.   Purchase of securities or commodities required to perform incomplete contract of sale.
9736.   Securities held in name of nominee.
9737.   Subscription rights.

§ 9730. Permissible investments of estate money

Pending distribution of the estate, the personal representative may invest money of the estate in possession of the personal representative in any one or more of the following:

(a) Direct obligations of the United States, or of the State of California, maturing not later than one year from the date of making the investment.

(b) An interest in a money market mutual fund registered under the Investment Company Act of 1940 (15 U.S.C. Sec. 80a–1, et seq.) or an investment vehicle authorized for the collective investment of trust funds pursuant to Section 9.18 of Part 9 of Title 12 of the Code of Federal Regulations, the portfolios of which are limited to United States government obligations maturing not later than five years from the date of investment and to repurchase agreements fully collateralized by United States government obligations.

(c) Units of a common trust fund described in Section 1585 of the Financial Code. The common trust fund shall have as its objective investment primarily in short term fixed income obligations and shall be permitted to value investments at cost pursuant to regulations of the appropriate regulatory authority. *(Stats.1990, c. 79 (A.B.759), § 14, operative July 1, 1991. Amended by Stats.2014, c. 71 (S.B. 1304), § 140, eff. Jan. 1, 2015.)*

Law Revision Commission Comments

1990 Enactment

Section 9730 continues Section 9730 of the repealed Probate Code without substantive change. The investments described in Section 9730 may be made without prior court authorization. See Section 9610. The personal representative is required to exercise the power granted by this section to the extent that ordinary care and diligence require that the power be exercised and may not exercise the power to the extent that ordinary care and diligence require that the power not be exercised. See Section 9600(b). As to the effect of court authorization or approval, see Section 7250. Subdivision (b) uses language comparable to that used in Section 16224 (powers of trustees). As to orders made, or actions taken, before July 1, 1988, and matters pending on July 1, 1988, see Section 9645. As to the application of any amendments made after that date, see Section 3.

Background on Section 9730 of Repealed Code

Section 9730 was added by 1987 Cal.Stat. ch. 923 § 93. Subdivision (a) continued without substantive change the portion of former Probate Code Section 584.1 (repealed by 1987 Cal.Stat. ch. 923 § 35) relating to investments in direct obligations of the United States and added authority to invest in direct obligations of the State of California maturing not later than one year from the date of making the investment. Subdivision (b) replaced a portion of former Section 584.1 (repealed by 1987 Cal.Stat. ch. 923 § 35) with language drawn from Section 16224 (powers of trustees). The words "and reinvest" which were found in former Section 584.1 were omitted as unnecessary; under Section 9730 "invest" included reinvestment. Subdivision (c) restated former Probate Code Section 585.1 (repealed by 1987 Cal.Stat. ch. 923 § 35) without substantive change. For background on the provisions of this part, see the Comment to this part under the part heading. [20 Cal.L.Rev.Comm.Reports 1001 (1990)].

Cross References

Management and control of estate, ordinary care and diligent, see Probate Code § 9600.
Powers and duties exercisable without court authorization, see Probate Code § 9610.

§ 9731. Orders; investments in United States or state securities; petition

(a) Pending distribution of the estate, upon a showing that it is to the advantage of the estate, the court may order that money of the estate in possession of the personal representative be invested in securities of the United States or of this state.

(b) To obtain an order under this section, the personal representative or any interested person shall file a petition stating the types of securities that are proposed to be purchased and the advantage to the estate of the purchase.

(c) Notice of the hearing on the petition shall be given as provided in Section 1220. *(Stats.1990, c. 79 (A.B.759), § 14, operative July 1, 1991.)*

Law Revision Commission Comments

1990 Enactment

Section 9731 continues Section 9731 of the repealed Probate Code without substantive change. For general provisions, see Sections 1000–1004 (rules of practice), 1020–1023 (petitions and other papers), 1040–1050 (hearings and orders), 1200–1230 (notice of hearing), 1250–1252 (request for special notice), 1260–1265 (proof of giving of notice). As to orders made, or actions taken, before July 1, 1988, and matters pending on July 1, 1988, see Section 9645. As to the application of any amendments made after that date, see Section 3.

Background on Section 9731 of Repealed Code

Section 9731 was added by 1987 Cal.Stat. ch. 923 § 93. The section restated a portion of former Probate Code Section 584 (repealed by 1987 Cal.Stat. ch. 923 § 35) without substantive change except that (1) the order now may be obtained only pending the settlement of the estate whereas former Section 584 permitted the order also to be obtained at the time of settlement of the estate, (2) the portion of subdivision (b) stating the contents of the petition was new, and (3) subdivision (c) required that notice be given at least 15 days before the hearing pursuant to Section 1220 instead of at least 10 days before the hearing as required by former Probate Code Section 1200.5 (repealed by 1987 Cal.Stat. ch. 923 § 59).

The language of former Section 584 (repealed by 1987 Cal.Stat. ch. 923 § 35) that permitted the order to be obtained at the time of settlement of the estate was omitted from Section 9731. The omitted language appeared to be included in former Section 584 only to apply to the provision of former Section 584 that permitted the purchase of an annuity expressly granted to a legatee by the decedent's will. The omitted language was continued in Section 9733 which continued the substance of that provision of former Section 584.

For background on the provisions of this part, see the Comment to this part under the part heading. [20 Cal.L.Rev.Comm.Reports 1001 (1990)].

Cross References

Deposits in banks and trust companies, see Probate Code §§ 9700, 9701.

Hearings and orders, generally, see Probate Code § 1040 et seq.

Notice of hearing, see Probate Code § 1200 et seq.

Petitions and other papers, generally, see Probate Code § 1020 et seq.

Proof of giving notice, see Probate Code § 1260 et seq.

§ 9732. Manner of investment provided by will; orders; petition; notice

(a) The court may order that money of the estate in possession of the personal representative be invested in any manner provided by the will if all of the following conditions are satisfied:

(1) The time for filing claims has expired.

(2) All debts (as defined in Section 11401) have been paid or are sufficiently secured by mortgage or otherwise, or there is sufficient cash in the estate aside from the money to be invested to pay all the debts, or the court is otherwise satisfied that all the debts will be paid.

(3) The estate is not in a condition to be finally distributed.

(b) To obtain an order under this section, the personal representative or any interested person shall file a petition showing the general condition of the estate and the types of investments that are proposed to be made.

(c) Notice of the hearing on the petition shall be given as provided in Section 1220. In addition, the petitioner shall cause notice of the hearing and a copy of the petition to be mailed to all known devisees of property which is proposed to be invested. Where the property proposed to be invested is devised to a trust or trustee, notice of the hearing and a copy of the petition shall be mailed to the trustee or, if the trustee has not yet accepted the trust, to the person named in the will as trustee. Mailing pursuant to this subdivision shall be to the person's last known address as provided in Section 1220.

(d) If no objection has been filed by an interested person, the court may make an order authorizing or directing the personal representative to invest such portion of the money of the estate as the court deems advisable in the types of investments proposed in the petition and authorized by the will. If there is no objection by an interested person and no substantial reason why some or all of the investment powers given by the will should not be exercised, the court shall make the order. The order may be for a limited period or until the administration of the estate is completed. Upon petition of the personal representative or any interested person, the order may be renewed, modified, or terminated at any time. *(Stats.1990, c. 79 (A.B.759), § 14, operative July 1, 1991.)*

Law Revision Commission Comments

1990 Enactment

Section 9732 continues Section 9732 of the repealed Probate Code without substantive change. The phrase "debts (as defined in Section 11401)" has been substituted for the phrase "uncontested claims" to conform to the terminology used in the provisions relating to creditors' claims. The references to the trustee being "appointment" and to the "nomination" of the trustee have been replaced by references to the trustee having "accepted the trust" and to the person "named in the will" as trustee. These revisions reflect the fact that trusts are no longer generally under court supervision. See Sections 17300–17354. See also Sections 17000–17210 (judicial proceedings concerning trusts). For general provisions, see Sections 1000–1004 (rules of practice), 1020–1023 (petitions and other papers), 1040–1050 (hearings and orders), 1200–1230 (notice of hearing), 1250–1252 (request for special notice), 1260–1265 (proof of giving of notice).

If the money cannot be invested as provided in the will because the requirements of Section 9732 are not satisfied, the money can be invested under other provisions. See Sections 9700 (deposit in insured account), 9703 (accounts and deposits withdrawable only upon court order), 9730 (investments permitted without court authorization), 9731 (investments in federal or state securities with court authorization).

As to orders made, or actions taken, before July 1, 1988, and matters pending on July 1, 1988, see Section 9645. As to the application of any amendments made after that date, see Section 3.

Background on Section 9732 of Repealed Code

Section 9732 was added by 1987 Cal.Stat. ch. 923 § 93. The section replaced former Probate Code Sections 584.5 and 584.6 (repealed by 1987 Cal.Stat. ch. 923 § 35).

Subdivision (a) restated the first sentence of former Probate Code Section 584.5 with the substitution of "may order" for "may authorize" and the inclusion of additional language in paragraph (2) to make clear that an order may be made if the court is satisfied that all uncontested claims will be paid. The word "reinvested" which was found in the former provision was omitted as unnecessary. The limitation in the former provision that only "surplus" money could be invested was omitted as unnecessary.

Subdivision (b) restated a portion of the second sentence of former Probate Code Section 584.5 without substantive change except that the personal representative or "any interested person" is now authorized to file a petition. Former Section 584.5 permitted the personal representative to file an initial petition, while former Section 584.6 permitted any person interested to file a petition for renewal, modification, or termination of the order.

Subdivision (c) restated the fourth and fifth sentences of former Probate Code Section 584.5 (repealed by 1987 Cal.Stat. ch. 923 § 35) with the following changes:

(1) Language was added to require notice to the person nominated as trustee if a trustee has not yet been appointed for a trust that is a devisee.

(2) The former requirement that notice be mailed to all persons in being who will or may participate in the corpus or income of the trust was not continued.

(3) Notice must be given at least 15 days before the hearing pursuant to Section 1220 instead of at least 10 days before the hearing as required by former Probate Code Section 1200.5 (repealed by 1987 Cal.Stat. ch. 923 § 59).

The third sentence of former Probate Code Section 584.5, which required the clerk to set the petition for hearing by the court, was continued in former Probate Code Section 1285 (repealed by 1988 Cal.Stat. ch. 1199 § 64.5), now Section 1041. The language of the fourth and fifth sentences of former Section 584.5 requiring notice to persons "whether or not they have requested special notice or given notice of appearance" was omitted as unnecessary.

Subdivision (d) restated a portion of the first sentence of former Probate Code Section 584.5 (repealed by 1987 Cal.Stat. ch. 923 § 35) (court "may" authorize) and the first and second sentences of former Probate Code Section 584.6 (repealed by 1987 Cal.Stat. ch. 923 § 35) without substantive change. The language of former Section 584.6 that "the court shall hear the petition if no objection thereto has been filed" was revised to say that the court may make an order if no objection has been filed. This revision made the language consistent with the original intent of the section. See Review of Selected 1968 Code Legislation 224 (Cal.Cont.Ed.Bar 1968).

For background on the provisions of this part, see the Comment to this part under the part heading. [20 Cal.L.Rev.Comm.Reports 1001 (1990)].

§ 9733. Annuities

(a) Pending distribution of the estate or at the time the court makes an order for final distribution of the estate, on petition of the personal representative or any interested person, the court may, upon good cause shown, order that the personal representative purchase an annuity from an insurer admitted to do business in this state to satisfy a devise of an annuity or other direction in the will for periodic payments to a devisee.

(b) Notice of the hearing on the petition shall be given as provided in Section 1220. *(Stats.1990, c. 79 (A.B.759), § 14, operative July 1, 1991.)*

Law Revision Commission Comments

1990 Enactment

Section 9733 continues Section 9733 of the repealed Probate Code without substantive change. The reference to the "time of settlement of the estate" has been replaced by a more precise reference to the "time the court makes an order for final distribution of the estate." For general provisions, see Sections 1000–1004 (rules of practice), 1020–1023 (petitions and other papers), 1040–1050 (hearings and orders), 1200–1230 (notice of hearing), 1250–1252 (request for special notice), 1260–1265 (proof of giving of notice). As to orders made, or actions taken, before July 1, 1988, and matters

pending on July 1, 1988, see Section 9645. As to the application of any amendments made after that date, see Section 3. As to independent administration authority, see Section 10557.

Background on Section 9733 of Repealed Code

Section 9733 was added by 1987 Cal.Stat. ch. 923 § 93. Section 9733 superseded a portion of former Probate Code Section 584 (repealed by 1987 Cal.Stat. ch. 923 § 35). Subdivision (a) made clear that an annuity may be purchased to satisfy not only a devise of an annuity as under former Section 584 but also to satisfy any other direction in the will for periodic payments to a devisee. Subdivision (b) required that notice be given at least 15 days before the hearing pursuant to Section 1220 instead of at least 10 days before the hearing as required by former Probate Code Section 1200.5 (repealed by 1987 Cal.Stat. ch. 923 § 59). For background on the provisions of this part, see the Comment to this part under the part heading. [20 Cal.L.Rev.Comm.Reports 1001 (1990)].

Cross References

Management and control of estate, ordinary care and diligence, see Probate Code § 9600.

§ 9734. Option rights

(a) If an asset of the estate consists of an option right, the personal representative may exercise the option after authorization by order of court upon a showing that the exercise would be to the advantage of the estate and would be in the best interest of the interested persons. The personal representative may use any funds or property in the estate to acquire the property covered by the option.

(b) A petition under this section may be filed by the personal representative or any interested person.

(c) Notice of the hearing on the petition shall be given as provided in Section 1220. *(Stats.1990, c. 79 (A.B.759), § 14, operative July 1, 1991.)*

Law Revision Commission Comments

1990 Enactment

Section 9734 continues Section 9734 of the repealed Probate Code without change. The personal representative is required to exercise the power granted by this section (by filing a petition with the court) to the extent that ordinary care and diligence require that the power be exercised and may not exercise the power to the extent that ordinary care and diligence require that the power not be exercised. See Section 9600(b). For general provisions, see Sections 1000–1004 (rules of practice), 1020–1023 (petitions and other papers), 1040–1050 (hearings and orders), 1200–1230 (notice of hearing), 1250–1252 (request for special notice), 1260–1265 (proof of giving of notice). See also Sections 7250 (effect of court authorization or approval), 10202 (sale of subscription rights). As to orders made, or actions taken, before July 1, 1988, and matters pending on July 1, 1988, see Section 9645. As to the application of any amendments made after that date, see Section 3. As to independent administration authority, see Section 10558.

Background on Section 9734 of Repealed Code

Section 9734 was added by 1987 Cal.Stat. ch. 923 § 93. The section restated former Probate Code Section 584.2 (repealed by 1987 Cal.Stat. ch. 923 § 35) without the limitation of former Section 584.2 that the option right be one that "is nontransferable save only by testate or intestate succession from the decedent." In addition, subdivision (c) required that notice be given at least 15 days before the hearing pursuant to Section 1220 instead of at least 10 days before the hearing as required by former Probate Code Section 1200.5 (repealed by 1987 Cal.Stat. ch. 923 § 59). The provision of the last sentence of former Section 584.2 giving the court authority to shorten the time of notice or to dispense with notice was omitted as unnecessary because the court is given this authority by general provisions. See Sections 1203 (shortening period of notice), 1220(c) (dispensing with notice).

The requirement of former Section 584.2 that the exercise of the option right would "add value to the estate" was omitted as unnecessary, this requirement being included in the requirement of Section 9734 that exercise of the option right be "to the advantage of the estate" and "in the best interest of the interested persons."

Under subdivision (b) of Section 9734, the personal representative "or any interested person" was authorized to file a petition. Under former Section 584.2, it was unclear whether an interested person was authorized to file a petition.

The provision of former Section 584.2 that the petition shall be filed with the clerk was omitted as unnecessary. The provision of former Section 584.2 that the clerk shall set the petition for hearing by the court was continued in Section 1285 (repealed by 1988 Cal.Stat. ch. 1199 § 64.5), now Section 1041.

For background on the provisions of this part, see the Comment to this part under the part heading. [20 Cal.L.Rev.Comm.Reports 1001 (1990)].

Cross References

Management and control of estate, ordinary care and diligence, see Probate Code § 9600.
Petitions and other papers, generally, see Probate Code § 1020 et seq.
Proof of giving notice of hearing etc., see Probate Code § 1260 et seq.

§ 9735. Purchase of securities or commodities required to perform incomplete contract of sale

(a) After authorization by order of court, the personal representative may purchase securities or commodities required to perform an incomplete contract of sale where the decedent died having sold but not delivered securities or commodities not owned by the decedent. The court's order shall fix the terms and conditions of purchase.

(b) A petition under this section may be filed by the personal representative or by any party to the contract. Notice of the hearing on the petition shall be given as provided in Section 1220.

(c) No notice of hearing need be given where the maximum purchase price is fixed or where the securities or commodities are to be purchased on an established stock, bond, or commodity exchange. *(Stats.1990, c. 79 (A.B.759), § 14, operative July 1, 1991.)*

Law Revision Commission Comments
1990 Enactment

Section 9735 continues Section 9735 of the repealed Probate Code without substantive change. The personal representative is required to exercise the power granted by this section (by filing a petition with the court) to the extent that ordinary care and diligence require that the power be exercised and may not exercise the power to the extent that ordinary care and diligence require that the power not be exercised. See Section 9600(b). See also Section 7250 (effect of court authorization or approval). Only the personal representative or a party to the contract may petition under Section 9735. But see Section 9613 (interested person may petition for order directing personal representative to act or not to act upon showing that if petition is not granted estate will suffer great or irreparable injury). For general provisions, see Sections 1000–1004 (rules of practice), 1020–1023 (petitions and other papers), 1040–1050 (hearings and

orders), 1200–1230 (notice of hearing), 1250–1252 (request for special notice), 1260–1265 (proof of giving of notice). As to orders made, or actions taken, before July 1, 1988, and matters pending on July 1, 1988, see Section 9645. As to the application of any amendments made after that date, see Section 3. As to independent administration authority, see Section 10559.

Background on Section 9735 of Repealed Code

Section 9735 was added by 1987 Cal.Stat. ch. 923 § 93. The section restated former Probate Code Section 771.3 (repealed by 1987 Cal.Stat. ch. 923 § 39) without substantive change, except that subdivision (b) required that notice be given at least 15 days before the hearing pursuant to Section 1220 instead of at least 10 days before the hearing as required by former Probate Code Section 1200.5 (repealed by 1987 Cal.Stat. ch. 923 § 59). The provision of the third sentence of former Section 771.3 giving the court authority to shorten the time of notice or to dispense with notice was omitted as unnecessary because the court is given this authority by general provisions. See Sections 1203 (shortening period of notice), 1220(c) (dispensing with notice). For background on the provisions of this part, see the Comment to this part under the part heading. [20 Cal.L.Rev.Comm.Reports 1001 (1990)].

Cross References

Interested parties, petition, see Probate Code § 9613.
Management and control of estate, ordinary care and diligence, see Probate Code § 9600.
Notice of hearing, generally, see Probate Code § 1200 et seq.
Petitions and other papers, generally, see Probate Code § 1020 et seq.
Proof of giving notice, see Probate Code § 1260 et seq.

§ 9736. Securities held in name of nominee

The personal representative may hold a security in the name of a nominee or in any other form without disclosure of the estate so that title to the security may pass by delivery. *(Stats.1990, c. 79 (A.B.759), § 14, operative July 1, 1991.)*

Law Revision Commission Comments
1990 Enactment

Section 9736 continues Section 9736 of the repealed Probate Code without change. This section is comparable to Section 16238 (Trust Law). See also Corp.Code § 702(a) (personal representative may vote shares without transfer into personal representative's name); Fin.Code § 1563 (trust company may register securities in name of nominee). As to orders made, or actions taken, before July 1, 1988, and matters pending on July 1, 1988, see Section 9645. As to the application of any amendments made after that date, see Section 3. As to independent administration authority, see Section 10560.

Background on Section 9736 of Repealed Code

Section 9736 was a new provision added by 1987 Cal.Stat. ch. 923 § 93. For background on the provisions of this part, see the Comment to this part under the part heading. [20 Cal.L.Rev.Comm.Reports 1001 (1990)].

§ 9737. Subscription rights

(a) If an estate by reason of owning securities also owns or receives subscription rights for the purchase of additional securities, the personal representative may exercise the subscription rights after authorization by order of court upon a showing that it is to the advantage of the estate.

(b) To obtain an order under this section, the personal representative or any interested person shall file a petition stating the nature of the subscription rights and the advantage to the estate of exercising them.

(c) Notice of the hearing on the petition shall be given as provided in Section 1220. *(Stats.1990, c. 79 (A.B.759), § 14, operative July 1, 1991.)*

Law Revision Commission Comments

1990 Enactment

Section 9737 continues Section 9737 of the repealed Probate Code without change. See also Sections 9734 (exercise of option right), 10202 (sale of subscription rights). For general provisions, see Sections 1000–1004 (rules of practice), 1020–1023 (petitions and other papers), 1040–1050 (hearings and orders), 1200–1230 (notice of hearing), 1250–1252 (request for special notice), 1260–1265 (proof of giving of notice). As to orders made, or actions taken, before July 1, 1988, and matters pending on July 1, 1988, see Section 9645. As to the application of any amendments made after that date, see Section 3. As to independent administration authority, see Section 10561.

Background on Section 9737 of Repealed Code

Section 9737 was a new provision added by 1987 Cal.Stat. ch. 923 § 93. For background on the provisions of this part, see the Comment to this part under the part heading. [20 Cal.L.Rev.Comm.Reports 1001 (1990)].

Cross References

Management and control of estate, ordinary care and diligence, see Probate Code § 9600.
Option rights, exercise, see Probate Code § 9734.
Proof of giving notice, see Probate Code § 1260 et seq.
Sale of subscription rights, see Probate Code § 10202.

CHAPTER 5. OPERATION OF DECEDENT'S BUSINESS

Section
9760. Continuation of operation; time; orders; petition; notice.
9761. Partnerships; orders for accounting.
9762. Partnerships; participation of personal representative; orders.
9763. Partnerships; actions against surviving partners; exercise of limited partner rights.
9764. Deceased attorney; petition for appointment; notice and hearing; contents; compensation.

§ 9760. Continuation of operation; time; orders; petition; notice

(a) As used in this section, "decedent's business" means an unincorporated business or venture in which the decedent was engaged or which was wholly or partly owned by the decedent at the time of the decedent's death, but does not include a business operated by a partnership in which the decedent was a partner.

(b) If it is to the advantage of the estate and in the best interest of the interested persons, the personal representative, with or without court authorization, may continue the operation of the decedent's business; but the personal representative may not continue the operation of the decedent's business for a period of more than six months from the date letters are first issued to a personal representative unless a court order has been obtained under this section authorizing the personal representative to continue the operation of the business.

(c) The personal representative or any interested person may file a petition requesting an order (1) authorizing the personal representative to continue the operation of the decedent's business or (2) directing the personal representative to discontinue the operation of the decedent's business. The petition shall show the advantage to the estate and the benefit to the interested persons of the order requested. Notice of the hearing on the petition shall be given as provided in Section 1220.

(d) If a petition is filed under this section, the court may make an order that either:

(1) Authorizes the personal representative to continue the operation of the decedent's business to such an extent and subject to such restrictions as the court determines to be to the advantage of the estate and in the best interest of the interested persons.

(2) Directs the personal representative to discontinue the operation of the decedent's business within the time specified in, and in accordance with the provisions of, the order. *(Stats.1990, c. 79 (A.B.759), § 14, operative July 1, 1991.)*

Law Revision Commission Comments

1990 Enactment

Section 9760 continues Section 9760 of the repealed Probate Code without substantive change. This section does not apply to a business operated by a partnership in which the decedent was a partner. See Sections 9761–9763 (operation of decedent's partnership).

Section 9760 requires court authorization to continue operation of the decedent's nonpartnership business for a period of more than six months from the date letters are first issued to any personal representative, whether the personal representative is a special personal representative or a general personal representative. The six-month period commences to run from the time the first special or general personal representative is issued letters. The six-month limitation recognizes that operation of the business may result in the loss of estate assets if the business proves to be unprofitable.

Although Section 9760 makes clear that the personal representative may continue to operate the decedent's nonpartnership business without prior court authorization for the six-month period, it is generally advisable for the personal representative to obtain an order under Section 9760 authorizing continued operation of the business. See Gould, *First Steps in Handling A Decedent's Estate,* in 1 California Decedent Estate Practice § 2.38, at 2–48 (Cal.Cont.Ed.Bar rev. 1989). If the personal representative operates the decedent's business without prior authorization of the court, the court may nonetheless ratify the acts and expenditures of the personal representative after the fact. See In re Estate of Maddalena, 42 Cal.App.2d 12, 19, 108 P.2d 17 (1940). Under Section 9760, the personal representative may obtain ratification only upon the showing that it was to the advantage of the estate and in the best interest of interested persons to continue the operation of the decedent's business. See subdivision (b).

The personal representative is required to exercise the power granted by this section to the extent that ordinary care and diligence require that the power be exercised and may not exercise the power to the extent that ordinary care and diligence require that the power not be exercised. See Section 9600(b). See also Section 7250 (effect of court authorization or approval).

For general provisions, see Sections 1000–1004 (rules of practice), 1020–1023 (petitions and other papers), 1040–1050 (hearings and orders), 1200–1230 (notice of hearing), 1250–1252 (request for special notice), 1260–1265 (proof of giving of notice). As to orders made, or actions taken, before July 1, 1988, and matters pending on July 1, 1988, see Section 9645. As to the application of any amendments made after that date, see Section 3. As to independent administration authority, see Section 10534.

Background on Section 9760 of Repealed Code

Section 9760 was added by 1987 Cal.Stat. ch. 923 § 93.

Subdivision (a) was a new provision. The first portion of subdivision (a) used language taken from paragraph (6) of subdivision (b) of former Probate Code Section 591.3 (repealed by 1987 Cal.Stat. ch. 923 § 35). Subdivision (a) also made clear that Section 9760 did not apply to a business operated by a partnership in which the decedent was a partner. See Prob.Code §§ 9761–9762 (operation of decedent's partnership).

Subdivision (b) provided that the personal representative could not continue the operation of the business for a period of more than six months from the date letters were first issued unless a court order had been obtained permitting continued operation of the business. This was a new limitation. Under prior law, if the personal representative continued the operation of the decedent's business without a court order, but acted in good faith and as a cautious and prudent person would act under similar circumstances, the personal representative was not personally liable for expenses of operating the business. In re Estate of Maddalena, 42 Cal.App.2d 12, 18, 108 P.2d 17 (1940).

Subdivisions (c) and (d) replaced a portion of the first sentence of former Probate Code Section 572 (repealed by 1987 Cal.Stat. ch. 923 § 35). Under subdivision (c) of Section 9760, the personal representative or "any interested person" was authorized to file a petition. It was unclear under former Section 572 whether an interested person was authorized to file a petition.

The requirement that notice of the hearing on the petition shall be given as provided in Probate Code Section 1220 was substituted for the requirement of former Section 572 that the order be made after notice to all persons interested in the estate, given in such manner as may be directed by the court or a judge thereof.

For background on the provisions of this part, see the Comment to this part under the part heading. [20 Cal.L.Rev.Comm.Reports 1001 (1990)].

§ 9761. Partnerships; orders for accounting

If a partnership existed between the decedent and another person at the time of the decedent's death, on application of the personal representative, the court may order any surviving partner to render an account pursuant to Section 15510, 15634, or 16807 of the Corporations Code. An order under this section may be enforced by the court's power to punish for contempt. *(Stats.1990, c. 79 (A.B.759), § 14, operative July 1, 1991. Amended by Stats.2003, c. 32 (A.B.167), § 8.)*

Law Revision Commission Comments
1990 Enactment

Section 9761 continues Section 9761 of the repealed Probate Code without change. The standard for ordering an account is provided in the statutes governing partnerships. As to a general partnership, see Corp.Code §§ 15022 (right to formal account where "just and reasonable"), 15043 (right to account of deceased partner's interest accrues to personal representative); see also Corp.Code §§ 15019 (right to inspect partnership books), 15020 (right to information on demand). As to a limited partnership, see Corp.Code §§ 15510(1)(a)–(b) (right to information), 15521 (personal representative's exercise of rights), 15634 (right to information), 15675 (personal representative's exercise of rights). The court has jurisdiction and discretion to order any surviving partner to render an account to the extent provided in the sections of the Corporation Code referred to in Section 9761. See also Sections 1000–1004 (rules of practice).

The order to account under this section is enforceable by the power to punish for contempt under Code of Civil Procedure Section 717.010. Only the personal representative may apply for an account under Section 9761. An interested person may neither make application under this section nor petition for instructions under Section 9611. But see Section 9613 (right of interested person to petition for order directing personal representative in order to avoid great or irreparable injury).

As to orders made, or actions taken, before July 1, 1988, and matters pending on July 1, 1988, see Section 9645. As to the application of any amendments made after that date, see Section 3.

2003 Amendment

Section 9761 is amended to reflect the repeal of former Corporations Code Section 15043 and its replacement by provisions of the Uniform Partnership Act of 1994 relating to winding up partnership business. See 1996 Cal. Stat. ch. 1003, §§ 1.2, 2. [33 Cal.L.Rev. Comm. Reports 159 (2003)].

Background on Section 9761 of Repealed Code

Section 9761 was added by 1987 Cal.Stat. ch. 923 § 93. The section replaced the authority provided in former Probate Code Section 571 (repealed by 1987 Cal.Stat. ch. 923 § 35) to order an accounting where necessary and to enforce the order "by attachment." The standard for ordering an accounting is provided in the statutes governing partnerships. For background on the provisions of this part, see the Comment to this part under the part heading. [20 Cal.L.Rev.Comm.Reports 1001 (1990)].

Cross References

Contempt, enforcement of order, see Code of Civil Procedure § 717.010.
Limited partnerships, information and accounts, see Corporations Code §§ 15510, 15634.
Partnership books and papers, right to demand information, see Corporations Code § 15020.
Partnerships, right to accounting, see Corporations Code §§ 15019, 15022.
Special civil proceedings, of contempts, see Code of Civil Procedure § 1209 et seq.

§ 9762. Partnerships; participation of personal representative; orders

(a) After authorization by order of court upon a showing that it would be to the advantage of the estate and in the best interest of the interested persons, the personal representative may continue as a general or a limited partner in any partnership in which the decedent was a general partner at the time of death. In its order, the court may specify any terms and conditions of the personal representative's participation as a partner that the court determines are to the advantage of the estate and in the best interest of the interested persons, but any terms and conditions that are inconsistent with the terms of any written partnership agreement are subject to the written consent of all of the surviving partners.

(b) If there is a written partnership agreement permitting the decedent's personal representative to participate as a partner, the personal representative has all the rights, powers, duties, and obligations provided in the written partnership agreement, except as otherwise ordered by the court pursuant to subdivision (a).

(c) If there is not a written partnership agreement, the personal representative has the rights, powers, duties, and obligations that the court specifies in its order pursuant to subdivision (a).

(d) To obtain an order under this section, the personal representative or any interested person shall file a petition showing that the order requested would be to the advantage of the estate and in the best interest of the interested persons. Notice of the hearing on the petition shall be given as provided in Section 1220. In addition, unless the court otherwise orders, the petitioner, not less than 15 days before the hearing, shall cause notice of hearing and a copy of the petition to be mailed to each of the surviving general partners at his or her last known address. *(Stats.1990, c. 79 (A.B.759), § 14, operative July 1, 1991.)*

Law Revision Commission Comments
1990 Enactment

Section 9762 continues Section 9762 of the repealed Probate Code without change. This section is limited to a partnership in which the decedent was a general partner at the time of the decedent's death. As to a partnership in which the decedent was a limited partner, see Section 9763. If the court determines that notice as provided in Section 1220 is not sufficient, the court can require such further and additional notice to be given as the court considers proper. See Section 1202.

The personal representative is required to exercise the power granted by this section (by filing a petition with the court) to the extent that ordinary care and diligence require that the power be exercised and may not exercise the power to the extent that ordinary care and diligence require that the power not be exercised. See Section 9600(b). See also Section 7250 (effect of court authorization or approval).

Nothing in Section 9762 authorizes the personal representative to perform acts as a partner for which a professional license is required, or authorizes otherwise prohibited fee-sharing by a licensed professional with unlicensed persons. See, e.g., Rules of Professional Conduct of the State Bar of California, Rule 1–320 (payment of fees to deceased lawyer's estate or other specified person). Section 9762 is subject to regulatory provisions governing use of a license after death of a licensee. See, e.g., Bus. & Prof.Code § 7076 (temporary continuance of licensed contractor's business by family member of deceased licensee).

For general provisions, see Sections 1000–1004 (rules of practice), 1020–1023 (petitions and other papers), 1040–1050 (hearings and orders), 1200–1230 (notice of hearing), 1250–1252 (request for special notice), 1260–1265 (proof of giving of notice). As to orders made, or actions taken, before July 1, 1988, and matters pending on July 1, 1988, see Section 9645. As to the application of any amendments made after that date, see Section 3. As to independent administration authority, see Section 10534.

Background on Section 9762 of Repealed Code

Section 9762 was added by 1987 Cal.Stat. ch. 923 § 93. The section restated a portion of the first sentence and all of the second sentence of former Probate Code Section 572 (repealed by 1987 Cal.Stat. ch. 923 § 35) without substantive change except as indicated below.

The coverage of Section 9762 was limited to a partnership in which the decedent was a general partner at the time of the decedent's death. Insofar as former Section 572 may have applied to a partnership in which the decedent was a limited partner, the section was superseded by Section 9763.

The authority of the surviving partners under the second sentence of subdivision (a) of Section 9762 to consent to participation by the personal representative notwithstanding the terms of the partnership agreement was new. Former law did not appear to allow the personal representative to continue participation in the partnership

where to do so would be inconsistent with the terms of the partnership agreement. See former Prob.Code § 572. But cf. Corp.Code § 15023 (continuation of terminated partnership).

The requirement in subdivision (d) of Section 9762 that notice of the hearing on the petition be given as provided in Probate Code Section 1220 and by mail to each of the surviving partners replaced the requirement of former Section 572 that the order be made after notice to all persons interested in the estate, given in such manner as may be directed by the court or a judge thereof.

For background on the provisions of this part, see the Comment to this part under the part heading. [20 Cal.L.Rev.Comm.Reports 1001 (1990)].

§ 9763. Partnerships; actions against surviving partners; exercise of limited partner rights

(a) If the decedent was a general partner, the personal representative may commence and maintain any action against the surviving partner that the decedent could have commenced and maintained.

(b) The personal representative may exercise the decedent's rights as a limited partner as provided in Section 15675 of the Corporations Code. *(Stats.1990, c. 79 (A.B.759), § 14, operative July 1, 1991.)*

Law Revision Commission Comments
1990 Enactment

Section 9763 continues Section 9763 of the repealed Probate Code without change. Under Section 15675 of the Corporations Code, referred to in subdivision (b) of Section 9763, court approval is not required, but the personal representative may exercise the decedent's rights only for the purpose of settling the estate. As to orders made, or actions taken, before July 1, 1988, and matters pending on July 1, 1988, see Section 9645. As to the application of any amendments made after that date, see Section 3.

Background on Section 9763 of Repealed Code

Section 9763 was added by 1987 Cal.Stat. ch. 923 § 93. Subdivision (a) restated the last part of the last sentence of subdivision (b) of former Probate Code Section 571 (repealed by 1987 Cal.Stat. ch. 923 § 35) without substantive change. Subdivision (b) replaced the provisions of former Probate Code Section 572 (repealed by 1987 Cal.Stat. ch. 923 § 35) that may have required court approval for the personal representative to exercise the decedent's rights as a limited partner. For background on the provisions of this part, see the Comment to this part under the part heading. [20 Cal.L.Rev.Comm.Reports 1001 (1990)].

§ 9764. Deceased attorney; petition for appointment; notice and hearing; contents; compensation

(a) The personal representative of the estate of a deceased attorney who was engaged in a practice of law at the time of his or her death or other person interested in the estate may bring a petition for appointment of an active member of the State Bar of California to take control of the files and assets of the practice of the deceased member.

(b) The petition may be filed and heard on such notice that the court determines is in the best interests of the estate of the deceased member. If the petition alleges that the immediate appointment of a practice administrator is required to safeguard the interests of the estate, the court may dispense with notice only if the personal representative is the petitioner or has joined in the petition or has otherwise waived notice of hearing on the petition.

(c) The petition shall indicate the powers sought for the practice administrator from the list of powers set forth in Section 6185 of the Business and Professions Code. These powers shall be specifically listed in the order appointing the practice administrator.

(d) The petition shall allege the value of the assets that are to come under the control of the practice administrator, including, but not limited by the amount of funds in all accounts used by the deceased member. The court shall require the filing of a surety bond in the amount of the value of the personal property to be filed with the court by the practice administrator. No action may be taken by the practice administrator unless a bond has been fully filed with the court.

(e) The practice administrator shall not be the attorney representing the personal representative.

(f) The court shall appoint the attorney nominated by the deceased member in a writing, including, but not limited to, the deceased member's will, unless the court concludes that the appointment of the nominated person would be contrary to the best interests of the estate or would create a conflict of interest with any of the clients of the deceased member.

(g) The practice administrator shall be compensated only upon order of the court making the appointment for his or her reasonable and necessary services. The law practice shall be the source of the compensation for the practice administrator unless the assets are insufficient in which case, the compensation of the practice administrator shall be charged against the assets of the estate as a cost of administration. The practice administrator shall also be entitled to reimbursement of his or her costs.

(h) Upon conclusion of the services of the practice administrator, the practice administrator shall render an accounting and petition for its approval by the superior court making the appointment. Upon settlement of the accounting, the practice administrator shall be discharged and the surety on his or her bond exonerated.

(i) For the purposes of this section, the person appointed to take control of the practice of the deceased member shall be referred to as the "practice administrator" and the decedent shall be referred to as the "deceased member." *(Added by Stats.1998, c. 682 (A.B.2069), § 5.)*

CHAPTER 6. ABANDONMENT OF TANGIBLE PERSONAL PROPERTY

§ 9780. Power to dispose or abandon property

Unless the property is specifically devised, subject to the requirements of this chapter, the personal representative may dispose of or abandon tangible personal property where the cost of collecting, maintaining, and safeguarding the property would exceed its fair market value. *(Stats.1990, c. 79 (A.B.759), § 14, operative July 1, 1991.)*

Law Revision Commission Comments
1990 Enactment

Section 9780 continues Section 9780 of the repealed Probate Code without change. This section is consistent with prior case law. See In re Estate of Barreiro, 125 Cal.App. 153, 178–79, 13 P.2d 1017 (1932). The section also is consistent with the Guardianship–Conservatorship Law (Section 2465) and with the Uniform Probate Code (§ 3–715(6), (11) (1987)). As to the construction of provisions drawn from uniform acts, see Section 2.

This chapter (commencing with Section 9780) applies only to tangible personal property. As to intangible personal property, Section 9820 gives the personal representative the power to commence and maintain actions and proceedings for the benefit of the estate. See also the Comment to Section 9820 and Section 6154 (defining "specific devise").

The personal representative is required to exercise the power granted by this chapter to the extent that ordinary care and diligence require that the power be exercised and may not exercise the power to the extent that ordinary care and diligence require that the power not be exercised. See Section 9600(b). See also Section 7250 (effect of court authorization or approval).

As to orders made, or actions taken, before July 1, 1988, and matters pending on July 1, 1988, see Section 9645. As to the application of any amendments made after that date, see Section 3.

Background on Section 9780 of the Repealed Code

Section 9780 was a new provision added by 1987 Cal.Stat. ch. 923 § 93. For background on the provisions of this part, see the Comment to this part under the part heading. [20 Cal.L.Rev.Comm.Reports 1001 (1990)].

§ 9781. Court authorization or approval

Unless otherwise provided in the will, subject to the requirements of this chapter, the personal representative may exercise the power provided in Section 9780 without court authorization or approval. *(Stats.1990, c. 79 (A.B.759), § 14, operative July 1, 1991.)*

Law Revision Commission Comments
1990 Enactment

Section 9781 continues Section 9781 of the repealed Probate Code without change. See the Comment to Section 9780.

Background on Section 9781 of Repealed Code

Section 9781 was a new provision added by 1987 Cal.Stat. ch. 923 § 93. For background on the provisions of this part, see the Comment to this part under the part heading. [20 Cal.L.Rev.Comm.Reports 1001 (1990)].

§ 9782. Notice of proposed disposition or abandonment; persons notified; contents; delivery

(a) Except as provided in Section 9785, before disposing of or abandoning property under Section 9780, the personal representative shall give notice of the proposed disposition or abandonment as provided in subdivision (c) to all of the following:

(1) Each known devisee whose interest in the estate would be affected by the proposed action.

(2) Each known heir whose interest in the estate would be affected by the proposed action.

(3) Each person who has filed a request for special notice pursuant to Section 1250.

(4) The Attorney General, at the office of the Attorney General in Sacramento, if any portion of the estate is to escheat to the state and its interest in the estate would be affected by the proposed action.

(b) The notice of the proposed disposition or abandonment shall describe the property to be disposed of or abandoned, indicate the manner in which the property is to be disposed of or abandoned, and specify the date on or after which the property will be disposed of or abandoned.

(c) The notice shall be delivered personally to each person required to be given notice or shall be sent by mail to the person at the person's last known address. If the notice is delivered personally, it shall be delivered to the person not less than five days before the date specified in the notice as the date on or after which the property will be disposed of or abandoned. If the notice is sent by mail, it shall be deposited in the mail not less than 10 days before the date specified in the notice as the date on or after which the property will be disposed of or abandoned. *(Stats.1990, c. 79 (A.B.759), § 14, operative July 1, 1991.)*

Law Revision Commission Comments

1990 Enactment

Section 9782 continues Section 9782 of the repealed Probate Code without substantive change. See the Comment to Section 9780. For general provisions relating to notice, see Sections 1200–1215, 1250–1252.

Background on Section 9782 of Repealed Code

Section 9782 was a new provision added by 1987 Cal.Stat. ch. 923 § 93. [20 Cal.L.Rev.Comm.Reports 1001 (1990)].

Cross References

Notice provisions, generally, see Probate Code §§ 1200 et seq., 1250 et seq.

§ 9783. Objections to disposition or abandonment

A person described in Section 9782 may deliver or mail a written objection to the disposition or abandonment to the personal representative on or before the date specified in the notice as the date on or after which the property will be disposed of or abandoned. Subject to Section 9788, after receipt of the written objection, the personal representative shall not dispose of or abandon the property without authorization by order of the court obtained under Section 9611. *(Stats.1990, c. 79 (A.B.759), § 14, operative July 1, 1991.)*

Law Revision Commission Comments

1990 Enactment

Section 9783 continues Section 9783 of the repealed Probate Code without change. See the Comment to Section 9780. See also Section 1215 (mailing in general).

Background on Section 9783 of Repealed Code

Section 9783 was a new provision added by 1987 Cal.Stat. ch. 923 § 93. [20 Cal.L.Rev.Comm.Reports 1001 (1990)].

§ 9784. Restraining orders; notice; conditions

(a) A person described in Section 9782 who objects to the disposition or abandonment of property by the personal representative under Section 9780 may apply to the court in which proceedings for administration of the estate are pending for an order restraining the personal representative from disposing of or abandoning the property without prior court authorization.

(b) The court shall grant the requested order without requiring notice to the personal representative and without cause being shown for the order if the court is satisfied that the estate will not suffer any loss or unreasonable expense if the order is granted. As a condition of granting the order, the court may require the person applying for the order (1) to pay the costs of storing and protecting the property or (2) to provide security by bond or cash deposit that the costs will be paid.

(c) The personal representative is deemed to have notice of the restraining order if it is served upon the personal representative in the manner provided in Section 415.10 or 415.30 of the Code of Civil Procedure, or in the manner authorized by the court, before the date specified in the notice as the date on or after which the property will be disposed of or abandoned. *(Stats.1990, c. 79 (A.B.759), § 14, operative July 1, 1991.)*

Law Revision Commission Comments

1990 Enactment

Section 9784 continues Section 9784 of the repealed Probate Code without substantive change. See the Comment to Section 9780.

Background on Section 9784 of Repealed Code

Section 9784 was a new provision added by 1987 Cal.Stat. ch. 923 § 93. [20 Cal.L.Rev.Comm.Reports 1001 (1990)].

Cross References

Hearings and orders, generally, see Probate Code § 1040 et seq.
Notice of hearing, see Probate Code § 1200 et seq.
Petitions and other papers, see Probate Code § 1020 et seq.
Proof of giving notice, generally, see Probate Code § 1260 et seq.
Rules of practice, generally, see Probate Code § 1000 et seq.

§ 9785. Notice of proposed disposition or abandonment; persons not required to be notified

Notice of the proposed disposition or abandonment need not be given to any of the following:

(a) A person who consents in writing to the proposed disposition or abandonment.

(b) A person who, in writing, waives the right to notice of the proposed disposition or abandonment. *(Stats.1990, c. 79 (A.B.759), § 14, operative July 1, 1991.)*

Law Revision Commission Comments

1990 Enactment

Section 9785 continues Section 9785 of the repealed Probate Code without substantive change. See the Comment to Section 9780.

Section 9785 was a new provision added by 1987 Cal.Stat. ch. 923 § 93. [20 Cal.L.Rev.Comm.Reports 1001 (1990)].

Cross References

Notice of hearing, generally, see Probate Code § 1200 et seq.
Proof of giving notice, see Probate Code § 1260 et seq.

§ 9786. Notice of hearing for court authorization; persons notified

A person who objects to the disposition or abandonment as provided in Section 9783, or who serves a restraining order issued under Section 9784 in the manner provided in that section, shall be given notice of any court hearing on a petition for court authorization of the disposition or abandonment of the property. *(Stats.1990, c. 79 (A.B.759), § 14, operative July 1, 1991.)*

Law Revision Commission Comments

1990 Enactment

Section 9786 continues Section 9786 of the repealed Probate Code without change. See the Comment to Section 9780.

Background on Section 9786 of Repealed Code

Section 9786 was a new provision added by 1987 Cal.Stat. ch. 923 § 93. [20 Cal.L.Rev.Comm.Reports 1001 (1990)].

Cross References

Notice of hearing, generally, see Probate Code § 1200 et seq.
Proof of giving notice, see Probate Code § 1260 et seq.

§ 9787. Waiver of right to court review

(a) Except as provided in subdivision (b), a person described in Section 9782 who receives notice of the proposed disposition or abandonment as provided in Section 9782, waives the right to have the court later review the disposition or abandonment of the property unless the person does one of the following:

(1) Delivers or mails a written objection as provided in Section 9783.

(2) Serves a restraining order obtained under Section 9784 before whichever of the following is the later time:

(A) The date specified in the notice of proposed disposition or abandonment as the date on or after which the property will be disposed of or abandoned.

(B) The date the property has actually been disposed of or abandoned.

(b) Subject to Section 9785, the court may review the disposition or abandonment of the property upon the motion of a person described in subdivision (a) of Section 9782 who establishes that he or she did not actually receive notice of the proposed disposition or abandonment before the time to object expired. *(Stats.1990, c. 79 (A.B.759), § 14, operative July 1, 1991.)*

Law Revision Commission Comments

1990 Enactment

Section 9787 continues Section 9787 of the repealed Probate Code without change. See the Comment to Section 9780.

Background on Section 9787 of Repealed Code

Section 9787 was a new provision added by 1987 Cal.Stat. ch. 923 § 93. [20 Cal.L.Rev.Comm.Reports 1001 (1990)].

Cross References

Appeals, rules of procedure, see Probate Code § 7240 et seq.
Review of proceedings leading to partition, allotment, or other division of estate, see Probate Code § 11956.

§ 9788. Failure to take possession of property upon request; liability for safekeeping

(a) Notwithstanding Sections 9783 and 9784, the personal representative may abandon or dispose of the property without court authorization if the person who made the objection or obtained the restraining order fails to take possession of the property at his or her expense within 10 days after the personal representative requests that the person do so.

(b) A person who takes possession of estate property pursuant to this section is liable for the safekeeping of the property until a court order is made relieving the person of this obligation. *(Stats.1990, c. 79 (A.B.759), § 14, operative July 1, 1991.)*

Law Revision Commission Comments

1990 Enactment

Section 9788 continues Section 9788 of the repealed Probate Code without change. See the Comment to Section 9780.

Background on Section 9788 of Repealed Code

Section 9788 was a new provision added by 1987 Cal.Stat. ch. 923 § 93. [20 Cal.L.Rev.Comm.Reports 1001 (1990)].

CHAPTER 7. BORROWING, REFINANCING, AND ENCUMBERING PROPERTY

§ 9800. Power to borrow money and give security interests; purposes; consent of surviving spouse

(a) Subject to subdivision (c), after authorization by order of court obtained under this chapter upon a showing that it would be to the advantage of the estate, the personal representative may borrow money on a note, either unsecured or to be secured by a security interest or other lien on the personal property of the estate, or any part thereof, or to be secured by a mortgage or deed of trust on the real property of the estate, or any part thereof, and may give a security interest or other lien on the personal property of the estate, or any part thereof, or a mortgage or deed of trust on the real property of the estate, or any part thereof, in order to do any one or more of the following:

(1) Pay the debts of the decedent or the estate, devises, expenses of administration, and charges against the estate.

(2) Pay, reduce, extend, or renew a security interest or lien or mortgage or deed of trust already existing on property of the estate.

(3) Improve, use, operate, or preserve property in the estate.

(b) The personal representative shall apply the money to the purpose specified in the order.

(c) Where the surviving spouse has elected to have his or her share of the community real property administered in the decedent's estate, the personal representative is authorized to borrow money to be secured by a mortgage or deed of trust on the community real property of the estate, or any part thereof, only with the written consent of the surviving spouse. *(Stats.1990, c. 79 (A.B.759), § 14, operative July 1, 1991.)*

Law Revision Commission Comments

1990 Enactment

Section 9800 continues Section 9800 of the repealed Probate Code without substantive change, except that the requirement under subdivision (c) that the written consent of the surviving spouse be obtained has been limited to the case where the loan is to be secured by the "community" real property of the estate, or any part thereof. This limitation makes clear that the consent of the surviving spouse is required only where the surviving spouse has elected to have his or her share of the community real property administered in the estate and the loan is to be secured by community real property. The consent of the surviving spouse is not required where the surviving spouse has not elected to have his or her share of the community real property administered in the estate or where the loan is to be secured by estate property that is the separate property of the decedent. Taxes owed by the decedent or the estate are included under paragraph (1) of subdivision (a) as "charges against the estate." See Section 11401(c). For a provision comparable to paragraph (3) of subdivision (a), see Section 2552 (Guardianship–Conservatorship Law). Subdivision (b) is comparable to the second sentence of subdivision (a) of Section 2551 (Guardianship–Conservatorship Law).

The personal representative is required to exercise the power granted by this section (by filing a petition with the court) to the extent that ordinary care and diligence require that the power be exercised and may not exercise the power to the extent that ordinary care and diligence require that the power not be exercised. See Section 9600(b). See also Section 7250 (effect of court authorization or approval).

As to orders made, or actions taken, before July 1, 1988, and matters pending on July 1, 1988, see Section 9645. As to the application of any amendments made after that date, see Section 3. As to independent administration authority, see Section 10514.

Background on Section 9800 of Repealed Code

Section 9800 was added by 1987 Cal.Stat. ch. 923 § 93. Subdivision (a) restated a portion of the first sentence, and all of the third sentence, of former Probate Code Section 830 (repealed by 1987 Cal.Stat. ch. 923 § 41) without substantive change. Clarifying language was added to paragraph (1) of subdivision (a) to make clear that debts of the estate are included. Paragraph (3) of subdivision (a) was new. Subdivision (b) was drawn from the second sentence of

subdivision (a) of Section 2551 (Guardianship–Conservatorship Law). Subdivision (c) was a new provision.

"Security interest" was substituted in Section 9800 for "chattel mortgage" and "pledge" which appeared in former Section 830 (repealed by 1987 Cal.Stat. ch. 923 § 41). Under the California Commercial Code, the security interest replaces the chattel mortgage and pledge. See Uniform Law Commissioners' Comment to Uniform Commercial Code Section 9–101 (1971); see also California State Bar Committee on the Commercial Code, A Special Report, The Uniform Commercial Code, 37 Cal.St.B.J. 117, 198–99 (1962).

The word "note" was used in Section 9800 in place of the phrase "note or notes" used in former Section 830 (repealed by 1987 Cal.Stat. ch. 923 § 41). This was not a substantive change. See Section 10 (singular number includes the plural).

For background on the provisions of this part, see the Comment to this part under the part heading. [20 Cal.L.Rev.Comm.Reports 1001 (1990)].

Cross References

Borrowing money and giving security, conservatorship or guardianship, see Probate Code § 2551.

Judicial authorization or approval, effect of, see Probate Code § 7250.

Management and control of estate, ordinary care and diligence, see Probate Code § 9600.

Orders, see Probate Code § 1046 et seq.

Pay interest on or obligation secured by liens, see Probate Code § 8544.

Payment of debts, charge against estate, see Probate Code § 11401.

§ 9801.   Property interests less than entire ownership; joint borrowing; joint and several notes and security interests

If property of the estate consists of an undivided interest in real or personal property, or any other interest therein less than the entire ownership, upon a showing that it would be to the advantage of the estate to borrow money to improve, use, operate, or preserve the property jointly with the owners of the other interests therein, or to pay, reduce, extend, or renew a security interest, lien, mortgage, or deed of trust already existing on all of the property, the personal representative, after authorization by order of the court obtained under this chapter, may join with the owners of the other interests in borrowing money and the execution of a joint and several note and such security interest, lien, mortgage, or deed of trust as may be required to secure the payment of the note. The note may be for such sum as is required for the purpose. *(Stats.1990, c. 79 (A.B.759), § 14, operative July 1, 1991.)*

Law Revision Commission Comments

1990 Enactment

Section 9801 continues Section 9801 of the repealed Probate Code without change. This section is comparable to subdivision (b) of Section 2552 (Guardianship–Conservatorship Law). The personal representative is required to exercise the power granted by this section (by filing a petition with the court) to the extent that ordinary care and diligence require that the power be exercised and may not exercise the power to the extent that ordinary care and diligence require that the power not be exercised. See Section 9600(b). See also Section 7250 (effect of court authorization or approval). As to orders made, or actions taken, before July 1, 1988, and matters pending on July 1, 1988, see Section 9645. As to the application of any amendments made after that date, see Section 3. As to independent administration authority, see Section 10514.

Background on Section 9801 of Repealed Code

Section 9801 was added by 1987 Cal.Stat. ch. 923 § 93. Section 9801 continued the second sentence of former Probate Code Section 830 (repealed by 1987 Cal.Stat. ch. 923 § 41) without substantive change. The word "note" was substituted in Section 9801 for the phrase "note or notes" used in former Section 830 and the word "owners" was substituted in Section 9801 for the phrase "owner or owners" used in former Section 830. These were not substantive changes. See Section 10 (singular number includes the plural, and the plural, the singular). For background on the provisions of this part, see the Comment to this part under the part heading. [20 Cal.L.Rev.Comm.Reports 1001 (1990)].

§ 9802. Petitions for orders

(a) The personal representative or any interested person may file a petition for an order under this chapter.

(b) The petition shall state the purpose for which the order is sought and the necessity for or the advantage to accrue from the order. If applicable, the petition shall also show the amount of money proposed to be borrowed, the rate of interest to be paid, the length of time the note is to run, and a general description of the property proposed to be mortgaged or subjected to the deed of trust, security interest, or other lien. *(Stats.1990, c. 79 (A.B.759), § 14, operative July 1, 1991.)*

Law Revision Commission Comments

1990 Enactment

Section 9802 continues Section 9802 of the repealed Probate Code without change. For general provisions relating to petitions, see Sections 1020–1023. As to orders made, or actions taken, before July 1, 1988, and matters pending on July 1, 1988, see Section 9645. As to the application of any amendments made after that date, see Section 3.

Background on Section 9802 of Repealed Code

Section 9802 was added by 1987 Cal.Stat. ch. 923 § 93. The section restated the first sentence of former Probate Code Section 831 (repealed by 1987 Cal.Stat. ch. 923 § 41) without substantive change. For background on the provisions of this part, see the Comment to this part under the part heading. [20 Cal.L.Rev.Comm.Reports 1001 (1990)].

Cross References

Petitions, generally, see Probate Code § 1020 et seq.

§ 9803. Notice of hearing on petition

Notice of the hearing on the petition shall be given as provided in Section 1220. *(Stats.1990, c. 79 (A.B.759), § 14, operative July 1, 1991.)*

Law Revision Commission Comments

1990 Enactment

Section 9803 continues Section 9803 of the repealed Probate Code without change. For general provisions relating to notice, see Sections 1200–1230 (notice of hearing), 1250–1252 (request for special notice), 1260–1265 (proof of giving of notice). As to orders made, or actions taken, before July 1, 1988, and matters pending on July 1, 1988, see Section 9645. As to the application of any amendments made after that date, see Section 3.

Background on Section 9803 of Repealed Code

Section 9803 was added by 1987 Cal.Stat. ch. 923 § 93. The section restated the last portion of the second sentence of former

Probate Code Section 831 (repealed by 1987 Cal.Stat. ch. 923 § 41) without substantive change, except that the section required that notice be given at least 15 days before the hearing pursuant to Section 1220 instead of at least 10 days before the hearing as required by former Probate Code Section 1200.5 (repealed by 1987 Cal.Stat. ch. 923 § 59). For background on the provisions of this part, see the Comment to this part under the part heading. [20 Cal.L.Rev.Comm.Reports 1001 (1990)].

Cross References

Proof of giving notice, see Probate Code § 1260 et seq.
Request for special notice, see Probate Code § 1250 et seq.

§ 9804. Orders authorizing borrowing or giving security interests; consent of spouse

(a) Subject to subdivision (c), if the court is satisfied that it will be to the advantage of the estate, the court shall make an order that authorizes or requires that the personal representative do any one or more of the following:

(1) Borrow money and execute a note.

(2) Execute a mortgage or deed of trust or give other security by security interest or other lien.

(3) Pay, reduce, extend, or renew a security interest or lien or mortgage or deed of trust already existing upon property of the estate.

(b) The court in its order may do any one or more of the following:

(1) Order that the amount specified in the petition, or a lesser amount, be borrowed.

(2) Prescribe the maximum rate of interest and the period of the loan.

(3) Require that the interest and the whole or any part of the principal be paid from time to time out of the whole estate or any part thereof.

(4) Require that the personal property used as security, or any buildings on real property to be mortgaged or subjected to the deed of trust, be insured for the further security of the lender and that the premiums be paid out of the estate.

(5) Specify the purpose for which the money to be borrowed is to be applied.

(6) Specify the terms and conditions of any extension or renewal agreement.

(7) Prescribe such other terms and conditions concerning the transaction as the court determines to be to the advantage of the estate.

(c) Where the surviving spouse has elected to have his or her share of the community real property administered in the decedent's estate, an order authorizing or requiring the personal representative to borrow money to be secured by a mortgage or deed of trust upon the community real property of the estate, or any part thereof, may be made only if the written consent of the surviving spouse has been filed with the court. *(Stats.1990, c. 79 (A.B.759), § 14, operative July 1, 1991.)*

Law Revision Commission Comments

1990 Enactment

Section 9804 continues Section 9804 of the repealed Probate Code without substantive change, except that the requirement under subdivision (c) that the written consent of the surviving spouse be filed with court has been limited to the case where the loan is to be secured by the "community" real property of the estate, or any part thereof. See the discussion in the Comment to Section 9800 concerning a similar change in that section. Paragraph (7) of subdivision (b) makes clear that the court has flexibility to fashion an appropriate order. Subdivision (c) is comparable to subdivision (c) of Section 9800. As to the recording of the order, see Section 7263. See also Sections 7250 (effect of court authorization or approval), 7260–7263 (orders and transactions affecting real property). For general provisions relating to hearings and orders, see Sections 1040–1050. As to orders made, or actions taken, before July 1, 1988, and matters pending on July 1, 1988, see Section 9645. As to the application of any amendments made after that date, see Section 3. As to independent administration authority, see Section 10514.

Background on Section 9804 of Repealed Code

Section 9804 was added by 1987 Cal.Stat. ch. 923 § 93. The section restated the last portion of the first sentence of former Probate Code Section 830 and the first and second sentences of former Probate Code Section 832 (provisions repealed by 1987 Cal.Stat. ch. 923 § 41) without substantive change. The provision of former Section 832 that the court may direct in what coin or currency the loan shall be paid was omitted as obsolete. This omission was consistent with the 1982 amendment to Section 667 of the Code of Civil Procedure (1982 Cal.Stat. ch. 497 § 37). Paragraphs (5) and (6) of subdivision (b) were new and stated matters that were implied under former Section 830. Paragraph (7) was new. For background on the provisions of this part, see the Comment to this part under the part heading. [20 Cal.L.Rev.Comm.Reports 1001 (1990)].

Cross References
Entry and filing of orders, see Probate Code § 1048.
Hearings and orders, generally, see Probate Code § 1040 et seq.
Judicial authorization or approval, effect of, see Probate Code § 7250.
Necessary recitals in orders, see Probate Code § 1047.
Notices, see Probate Code § 1200 et seq.
Real estate, orders and transactions affecting, see Probate Code § 7260 et seq.
Recordation, see Probate Code § 7263.

§ 9805. Execution and delivery of mortgage, deed of trust, or security instrument

(a) The personal representative shall execute and deliver the mortgage or deed of trust, or execute and deliver the instrument creating the security interest, setting forth therein that it is made by authority of the order, giving the date of the order.

(b) The note and the mortgage or deed of trust or other instrument creating the security interest, if any, shall be signed by the personal representative and shall be acknowledged by the personal representative if the instrument creates a lien on real property. *(Stats.1990, c. 79 (A.B.759), § 14, operative July 1, 1991.)*

Law Revision Commission Comments
1990 Enactment
Section 9805 continues Section 9805 of the repealed Probate Code without change, except that subdivision (b) was revised to delete the provision relating to the personal liability of the personal representative. This matter is governed by Section 9606 (liability of personal representative who signs instrument). See also Sections 7250 (effect of court authorization or approval), 7260–7263 (orders and transactions affecting real property). As to orders made, or actions taken, before July 1, 1988, and matters pending on July 1, 1988, see Section

9645. As to the application of any amendments made after that date, see Section 3. As to independent administration authority, see Section 10514.

Background on Section 9805 of Repealed Code

Section 9805 was added by 1987 Cal.Stat. ch. 923 § 93. The section restated former Probate Code Section 833 (repealed by 1987 Cal.Stat. ch. 923 § 41) without substantive change, except that Section 9805 applied to an instrument creating a security interest in personal property as well as to a mortgage or deed of trust on real property. Former Section 833 did not refer to an instrument creating a security interest in personal property. For background on the provisions of this part, see the Comment to this part under the part heading. [20 Cal.L.Rev.Comm.Reports 1001 (1990)].

Cross References
Authorization or approval of court, see Probate Code § 7250.
Orders and transactions affecting real estate, see Probate Code § 7260 et seq.

§ 9806. Effect of mortgage, deed of trust, or security interest; jurisdiction; omissions and errors in proceedings

(a) Every mortgage, deed of trust, or security interest made pursuant to a court order obtained under this chapter is effectual to mortgage, or to subject to the deed of trust or security interest, all of the following:

(1) All right, title, and interest which the decedent had to the property described therein at the time of the decedent's death.

(2) Any right, title, or interest in the property acquired by the estate of the decedent, by operation of law or otherwise, since the time of the decedent's death.

(3) Any right, title, or interest in the community real property belonging to the decedent's surviving spouse whose written consent has been filed with the court and which is referred to in the court order obtained under this chapter.

(b) Jurisdiction of the court to administer the estate of the decedent vests the court with jurisdiction to make the order for the note and for the security interest, lien, mortgage, or deed of trust. This jurisdiction shall conclusively inure to the benefit of the owner of the security interest or lien, mortgagee named in the mortgage, or the trustee and beneficiary named in the deed of trust, and their heirs and assigns.

(c) No omission, error, or irregularity in the proceedings under this chapter shall impair or invalidate the proceedings or the note, security interest, lien, mortgage, or deed of trust given pursuant to an order under this chapter. Subject to Section 9807, the owner of the security interest or lien, the mortgagee named in the mortgage, or the trustee and beneficiary named in the deed of trust, and their heirs and assigns, have and possess the same rights and remedies on the note and the security interest or lien or mortgage or deed of trust as if it had been made by the decedent prior to his or her death. *(Stats.1990, c. 79 (A.B.759), § 14, operative July 1, 1991.)*

Law Revision Commission Comments
1990 Enactment
Section 9806 continues Section 9806 of the repealed Probate Code with the addition of paragraph (3) of subdivision (a). This addition covers the situation where the community real property interest of

the surviving spouse has been included in an encumbrance made pursuant to Sections 9800(c) and 9804(c). As to orders made, or actions taken, before July 1, 1988, and matters pending on July 1, 1988, see Section 9645. As to the application of any amendments made after that date, see Section 3. As to independent administration authority, see Section 10514.

Background on Section 9806 of Repealed Code

Section 9806 was added by 1987 Cal.Stat. ch. 923 § 93. The section restated without substantive change the first and second sentences and the first portion of the third sentence of former Probate Code Section 834 (repealed by 1987 Cal.Stat. ch. 923 § 41). The words "or prior thereto" which appeared in the first sentence of former Section 834 were omitted. Those words should have been deleted from Section 834 in 1931 when former Code of Civil Procedure Section 1578 (which applied not only to decedents' estates but also to estates of guardians of minors and incompetent persons) was repealed and Section 834 (which applied only to decedents' estates) was enacted. See 1931 Cal.Stat. ch. 281 §§ 834, 1533, 1538. For background on the provisions of this part, see the Comment to this part under the part heading. [20 Cal.L.Rev.Comm.Reports 1001 (1990)].

Cross References

Necessary recitals in orders, see Probate Code § 1047.

§ 9807. Judgments or claims for deficiency; unsatisfied indebtedness as claim

(a) Except as provided in subdivision (b), no judgment or claim for any deficiency shall be had or allowed against the personal representative or the estate if (1) there is a foreclosure or sale under a security interest, lien, mortgage, or deed of trust and (2) the proceeds of sale of the encumbered property are insufficient to pay the note, the security interest, lien, mortgage, or deed of trust, and the costs or expenses of sale.

(b) If the note, security interest, mortgage, or deed of trust was given to pay, reduce, extend, or renew a lien, security interest, mortgage, or deed of trust existing on property of the estate at the time of death of the decedent and the indebtedness secured thereby was a claim established under Part 4 (commencing with Section 9000), the part of the indebtedness remaining unsatisfied shall be classed with other established claims. *(Stats.1990, c. 79 (A.B.759), § 14, operative July 1, 1991.)*

Law Revision Commission Comments

1990 Enactment

Section 9807 continues Section 9807 of the repealed Probate Code without substantive change, except that the words "and paid" are omitted from subdivision (b). Established claims referred to in subdivision (b) are paid or provided for with other established claims. See also Section 9003 (payment of established claims). As to orders made, or actions taken, before July 1, 1988, and matters pending on July 1, 1988, see Section 9645. As to the application of any amendments made after that date, see Section 3.

Background on Section 9807 of Repealed Code

Section 9807 was added by 1987 Cal.Stat. ch. 923 § 93. The section restated the last portion of the third sentence of former Probate Code Section 834 (repealed by 1987 Cal.Stat. ch. 923 § 41) without substantive change. For background on the provisions of this part, see the Comment to this part under the part heading. [20 Cal.L.Rev.Comm.Reports 1001 (1990)].

Cross References

Allowance and rejection of claims, see Probate Code § 9250 et seq.
Claims by public entities, priority, see Probate Code § 9204.
Claims established by judgment, see Probate Code § 9300 et seq.
Deficiency judgments, foreclosure of mortgages, see Code of Civil Procedure §§ 580a et seq., 725a, 726.
Established claims, payment, see Probate Code § 9003.
Filing of claims, see Probate Code § 9150 et seq.
Order of priority, payment of mortgages, see Probate Code § 11420.

CHAPTER 8. ACTIONS AND PROCEEDINGS BY OR AGAINST PERSONAL REPRESENTATIVE

§ 9820. Powers of personal representatives

The personal representative may:

(a) Commence and maintain actions and proceedings for the benefit of the estate.

(b) Defend actions and proceedings against the decedent, the personal representative, or the estate. *(Stats.1990, c. 79 (A.B.759), § 14, operative July 1, 1991.)*

Law Revision Commission Comments

1990 Enactment

Section 9820 continues Section 9820 of the repealed Probate Code without change. This section is comparable to Section 2462 (Guardianship–Conservatorship Law). The authority in subdivision (b) for defense of actions and proceedings against the personal representative refers to actions and proceedings against the personal representative in his or her representative capacity, not those against him or her individually.

The personal representative may act under Section 9820 without prior court authorization. See Section 9610. See also Halleck v. Mixer, 16 Cal. 574, 580 (1860). The personal representative must exercise ordinary care and diligence in determining whether to exercise a power granted by Section 9820 and in exercising the power. See Section 9600. For example, the personal representative may decline to bring an action to collect property in a case where the cost of collection is likely to exceed the amount likely to be collected. See Section 9600(b). The personal representative may seek instructions from the court if in doubt as to the appropriate action to take. See Section 9611. See also Section 9613 (right of interested person to petition for order directing personal representative in order to avoid great or irreparable injury). As to the effect of court authorization or approval, see Section 7250.

Section 9820 gives authority to the personal representative to defend actions and proceedings, but procedural requirements are governed by the Code of Civil Procedure. If the defendant in a pending action dies and the cause of action survives or continues, the court in which the civil action is pending may, on motion, allow the action to be continued against the personal representative. Code Civ.Proc. § 385.

The personal representative and third party may agree to use a summary procedure for determination of a dispute. See Sections 9620 (submission to temporary judge), 9621 (submission to arbitration).

See also Sections 550–555 (liability of decedent covered by insurance), 8874 (action for double damages), 9650 (possession and management of decedent's estate), 9653 (duty to recover property transferred in fraud of creditors), 9654 (action by heirs or devisees for possession of or to quiet title to real property), 9763 (action against decedent's surviving partner), 9780 (abandonment of tangible personal property where cost of collection would exceed its value), 9823 (partition action); Code Civ.Proc. §§ 376 (action against personal representative of person causing injury to minor child), 377 (wrongful death action against personal representative of person causing death). As to orders made, or actions taken, before July 1, 1988, and matters pending on July 1, 1988, see Section 9645. As to the application of any amendments made after that date, see Section 3.

Background on Section 9820 of Repealed Code

Section 9820 was a new provision added by 1987 Cal.Stat. ch. 923 § 93. The section was consistent with prior law (see former Prob.Code §§ 573, 575, 576; repealed by 1987 Cal.Stat. ch. 923 § 35). For background on the provisions of this part, see the Comment to this part under the part heading. [20 Cal.L.Rev.Comm.Reports 1001 (1990)].

Cross References

Abandonment of personal property, see Probate Code § 9780.
Children and minors, personal injury actions against representatives of person causing injury, see Code of Civil Procedure § 376.
Comparable provision, guardianship and conservatorship, see Probate Code § 2462.
Continuation of actions, nonabatement on death, disability, etc., see Code of Civil Procedure §§ 375, 377.20 et seq.
Double damages, see Probate Code § 9869.
Fraudulent conveyances, duty to recover property, see Probate Code § 9653.
Insurance, covered decedents, see Probate Code § 550 et seq.
Management and control of estate, ordinary care and diligence, see Probate Code § 9600.
Partition actions, see Probate Code § 9823.
Partnerships, actions against survivors, see Probate Code § 9763.
Petition of personal representative for instruction, see Probate Code § 9611.
Petitions for orders directing personal representative to avoid injury to estate, see Probate Code § 9613.
Possession and management of decedent's estate, actions involving, see Probate Code § 9650.
Possession of real estate, action to recover by heirs or devisees, see Probate Code § 9654.
Powers and duties exercisable without court authorization, see Probate Code § 9610.
Quiet title actions, heirs or devisees, see Probate Code § 9654.
Summary determination of disputes, see Probate Code §§ 9620, 9621.
Wrongful death action, see Code of Civil Procedure § 377.60 et seq.

§ 9822. Actions on bond of former personal representative

The personal representative may bring an action on the bond of any former personal representative of the same estate, for the use and benefit of all interested persons. *(Stats.1990, c. 79 (A.B.759), § 14, operative July 1, 1991.)*

Law Revision Commission Comments

1990 Enactment

Section 9822 continues Section 9822 of the repealed Probate Code without change. The personal representative may act under this section without prior court authorization. See Section 9610.

The personal representative is required to exercise the power granted by this section to the extent that ordinary care and diligence require that the power be exercised and may not exercise the power to the extent that ordinary care and diligence require that the power not be exercised. See Section 9600(b). As to the effect of court authorization or approval, see Section 7250.

The authority given by Section 9822 is not exclusive: Liability on the bond of a former personal representative may be enforced on motion as well as by an action. See Code Civ.Proc. §§ 995.020, 996.440(a); Estate of Johnson, 162 Cal.App.3d 917, 919, 208 Cal.Rptr. 821 (1984) (liability on bond determined on settlement of account).

As to orders made, or actions taken, before July 1, 1988, and matters pending on July 1, 1988, see Section 9645. As to the application of any amendments made after that date, see Section 3.

Background on Section 9822 of Repealed Code

Section 9822 was added by 1987 Cal.Stat. ch. 923 § 93. The section restated former Probate Code Section 576 (repealed by 1987 Cal.Stat. ch. 923 § 35) without substantive change. The former reference to the personal representative acting "as such" was omitted as unnecessary. For background on the provisions of this part, see the Comment to this part under the part heading. [20 Cal.L.Rev.Comm.Reports 1001 (1990)].

Cross References

Accounting for deceased or incapacitated personal representative by his representative or guardian, see Probate Code § 10953.
Bonds of personal representatives, see Probate Code § 8480 et seq.
Commencement and maintenance of actions by special administrators, see Probate Code § 8544.
Limitation of actions against sureties on bond of guardian, see Probate Code § 2333.
Nature of liability on bond, see Code of Civil Procedure § 996.460 et seq.
Trust company, bond or security of, see Probate Code § 301.

§ 9823. Partition actions

(a) If the decedent leaves an undivided interest in any property, an action for partition of the property may be brought against the personal representative.

(b) The personal representative may bring an action against the other cotenants for partition of any property in which the decedent left an undivided interest. *(Stats.1990, c. 79 (A.B.759), § 14, operative July 1, 1991.)*

Law Revision Commission Comments

1990 Enactment

Section 9823 continues Section 9823 of the repealed Probate Code without change. This section is a specific example of the general authority given the personal representative by Section 9820. The personal representative is required to exercise the power granted by Section 9823 to the extent that ordinary care and diligence require that the power be exercised and may not exercise the power to the extent that ordinary care and diligence require that the power not be exercised. See Section 9600(b). As to the effect of court authorization or approval, see Section 7250.

When a partition action is brought against the personal representative, the rules of venue for partition actions generally apply. See Code Civ.Proc. § 872.110.

Under subdivision (b), court authorization is not required for the personal representative to commence a partition action. See Section 9610. This continues prior law. See Review of Selected 1969 Code Legislation 187 (Cal.Cont.Ed.Bar 1969).

The personal representative and third party may agree to use a summary procedure for determination of a dispute. See Sections 9620 (submission to temporary judge), 9621 (submission to arbitration).

As to orders made, or actions taken, before July 1, 1988, and matters pending on July 1, 1988, see Section 9645. As to the application of any amendments made after that date, see Section 3.

Background on Section 9823 of Repealed Code

Section 9823 was added by 1987 Cal.Stat. ch. 923 § 93. The section continued former Probate Code Section 575 (repealed by 1987 Cal.Stat. ch. 923 § 35) without substantive change. For background on the provisions of this part, see the Comment to this part under the part heading. [20 Cal.L.Rev.Comm.Reports 1001 (1990)].

Cross References

Actions for partition, see Code of Civil Procedure § 872.010 et seq.
Authorization or approval of court, effect, see Probate Code § 7250.
Mode and proof of giving notice in certain instances, see Probate Code § 1200.
Ordinary care and diligence, management of estate, see Probate Code § 9600.
Partition before distribution, see Probate Code § 11950 et seq.
Summary determination of disputes, see Probate Code §§ 9620, 9621.

CHAPTER 9. COMPROMISE OF CLAIMS AND ACTIONS; EXTENSION, RENEWAL, OR MODIFICATION OF OBLIGATIONS

Section
9830. Powers of personal representative; limitation of authority.
9831. Claims by or against decedent, personal representative, or estate; court authorization.
9832. Real property interests; leases; court authorization.
9833. Transfer or encumbrance of estate property; creation of unsecured liability in excess of $25,000; court authorization.
9834. Claims by estate against personal representative or attorney; modification of obligations; court authorization.
9835. Wrongful death or injury actions; court authorization.
9836. Authorization from court administering estate required.
9837. Petitions for court orders; persons allowed to file; contents; notice of hearing.
9838. Conveyances in compliance with court orders; contents; recording orders; effect.
9839. Payment of less than full claim; crediting accounts.

§ 9830. Powers of personal representative; limitation of authority

(a) Unless this chapter or some other applicable statute requires court authorization or approval, if it is to the advantage of the estate, the personal representative may do any of the following without court authorization, instruction, approval, or confirmation:

(1) Compromise or settle a claim, action, or proceeding by or for the benefit of, or against, the decedent, the personal representative, or the estate, including the giving of a covenant not to sue.

(2) Extend, renew, or in any manner modify the terms of an obligation owing to or in favor of the decedent or the estate.

(3) Release, in whole or in part, any claim belonging to the estate to the extent that the claim is uncollectible.

(b) Nothing in this section precludes the personal representative from seeking court authorization pursuant to the provisions of this chapter.

(c) Upon petition of an interested person or upon the court's own motion, the court may limit the authority of the personal representative under subdivision (a). Notice of the hearing on the petition shall be given as provided in Section 1220. *(Stats.1990, c. 79 (A.B.759), § 14, operative July 1, 1991.)*

Law Revision Commission Comments
1990 Enactment

Section 9830 continues Section 9830 of the repealed Probate Code without change. This section is comparable to Section 2500 (Guardianship–Conservatorship Law). Under Section 9830, unless otherwise provided by statute, the personal representative may, but is not required to, obtain court authorization.

Section 9830 requires that the action taken be to the advantage of the estate. In addition, the personal representative must exercise ordinary care and diligence in determining whether to exercise a power granted by Section 9830 and in exercising the power. See Section 9600(b). The personal representative may seek prior authorization from the court under Sections 9836–9837 if in doubt as to the appropriate action to take. As to the effect of court authorization, see Section 7250. For other provisions that may apply to a compromise or settlement, see, e.g., Labor Code § 5001 (compromise of worker's compensation claim).

Although there is no general requirement under this chapter that authorization of the court be obtained, certain matters (specified in Sections 9831–9835) do require authorization by the court. Thus, court authorization is required if any provision of this chapter is applicable, even though court authorization might not be required under another provision of this chapter.

For example, if the compromise, modification, or release affects title to real property, court authorization is required. This scheme is comparable to that under the Guardianship–Conservatorship Law. See Sections 2500–2507. In addition, under subdivision (c) of Section 9830, the court may limit the authority of the personal representative under this section. For example, the court may require prior court authorization for any compromise or settlement of a particular matter or of a particular kind of matter. Or the court may order that no compromise or settlement be made unless it has first been authorized by the court. Under subdivision (c), a creditor or other interested person may request that the court make an order that, for example, limits the authority of the personal representative to take action under this section without prior authorization by order of the court.

For general provisions, see Sections 1000–1004 (rules of practice), 1020–1023 (petitions and other papers), 1040–1050 (hearings and orders), 1200–1230 (notice of hearing), 1250–1252 (request for special notice), 1260–1265 (proof of giving of notice). As to orders made, or actions taken, before July 1, 1988, and matters pending on July 1, 1988, see Section 9645. As to the application of any amendments made after that date, see Section 3. As to independent administration authority, see Sections 10552(b), 10554.

Background on Section 9830 of Repealed Code

Section 9830 was added by 1987 Cal.Stat. ch. 923 § 93. The section replaced the first, second, and third sentences of former Probate Code Section 578 (repealed by 1987 Cal.Stat. ch. 923 § 35) and the first sentence of former Probate Code Section 718.5 (repealed by 1987 Cal.Stat. ch. 923 § 37). For background on the provisions of this part, see the Comment to this part under the part heading.

The provisions of former Sections 578 and 718.5 authorized the personal representative to do the acts described in subdivision (a) "with the approval of the court." Under Section 9830, unless otherwise provided by statute, the personal representative may, but is not required to, obtain court authorization. By permitting but not requiring prior court authorization, Section 9830 continued prior law.

See Moulton v. Holmes, 57 Cal. 337, 343–44 (1881); Estate of Coffey, 161 Cal.App.2d 259, 264–65, 326 P.2d 511 (1958); Taylor v. Sanson, 24 Cal.App. 515, 517–18, 141 P. 1060 (1914); see also Estate of Lucas, 23 Cal.2d 454, 463–65, 144 P.2d 340 (1943).

Chapter 9 (commencing with Section 9830) limited the authority the personal representative had under prior law to compromise claims and actions without court approval. Although there was no general requirement under Chapter 9 that authorization of the court be obtained, certain matters (specified in Sections 9831–9835) did require authorization by the court. In addition, (c) of Section 9830 provided that the court may limit the authority of the personal representative under Section 9830. [20 Cal.L.Rev.Comm.Reports 1001 (1990)].

Cross References

Accord and satisfaction, see Civil Code § 1521 et seq.
Authorization from court,
  Generally, see Probate Code §§ 9836, 9837.
  Effect, see Probate Code § 7250.
Collection of debts by personal representative, see Probate Code § 9650.
Comparable provision, guardianship and conservatorship, see Probate Code § 2500.
Compromise offer not an admission, not admissible, see Evidence Code § 1152 et seq.
Extinction of obligation by due offer of payment, see Civil Code § 1500.
Independent administration, compromise and settlement,
  Court supervision, see Probate Code § 10501.
  Powers, see Probate Code § 10552.
Management and control of estate, ordinary care and diligence, see Probate Code § 9600.
Minor's disputed claim, compromise or covenant not to sue on, see Probate Code § 3500.
Offer of defendant to compromise, see Code of Civil Procedure § 998.
Receivers, compromise of debts or suits, see Code of Civil Procedure § 568.
Release, see Civil Code § 1541 et seq.
Unsealed agreement for compromise or settlement of debt, validity, see Code of Civil Procedure § 1934.

§ 9831. Claims by or against decedent, personal representative, or estate; court authorization

Unless the time for filing creditor claims has expired, authorization by order of court is required for a compromise or settlement of a claim, action, or proceeding by or for the benefit of, or against, the decedent, the personal representative, or the estate. *(Stats.1990, c. 79 (A.B.759), § 14, operative July 1, 1991.)*

Law Revision Commission Comments

1990 Enactment

Section 9831 continues Section 9831 of the repealed Probate Code without substantive change. This section requires authorization by order of court obtained under Sections 9836–9837 if the compromise or settlement is to be made before the time for filing creditors' claims has expired. As to when the time for filing creditors' claims has expired, see Section 9100.

Even though the time for filing creditor claims has expired, court authorization of compromise or settlement may be required under another provision of this chapter. See Section 9830 and the Comment thereto. For example, if the transaction requires transfer of property in excess of $25,000, Section 9833 requires court consent whether or not the time for filing creditors' claims has expired. Or, if the compromise or settlement involves a claim by the estate against

the personal representative, Section 9833 requires court authorization regardless of the creditors' claim filing period.

Section 9831 requires court authorization only for a compromise or settlement of a claim, action, or proceeding by or for the benefit of, or against, the decedent, the personal representative, or the estate. The section does not require court authorization in order to extend, renew, or in any manner modify the terms of an obligation owing to or running in favor of the decedent or the estate. See generally Section 9830(a)(2).

As to orders made, or actions taken, before July 1, 1988, and matters pending on July 1, 1988, see Section 9645. As to the application of any amendments made after that date, see Section 3.

Background on Section 9831 of Repealed Code

Section 9831 was added by 1987 Cal.Stat. ch. 923 § 93. The section replaced the first sentence of former Probate Code Section 718.5 (repealed by 1987 Cal.Stat. ch. 923 § 37). For background on the provisions of this part, see the Comment to this part under the part heading. [20 Cal.L.Rev.Comm.Reports 1001 (1990)].

§ 9832. Real property interests; leases; court authorization

(a) Except as provided in subdivision (b), authorization by order of court is required for a compromise, settlement, extension, renewal, or modification which affects any of the following:

(1) Title to real property.

(2) An interest in real property or a lien or encumbrance on real property.

(3) An option to purchase real property or an interest in real property.

(b) If it is to the advantage of the estate, the personal representative without prior court authorization may extend, renew, or modify a lease of real property in either of the following cases:

(1) Where under the lease as extended, renewed, or modified the rental does not exceed five thousand dollars ($5,000) a month and the term does not exceed one year.

(2) Where the lease is from month to month, regardless of the amount of the rental.

(c) For the purposes of subdivision (b), if the lease as extended, renewed, or modified gives the lessee the right to extend the term of the lease, the length of the term shall be considered as though the right to extend had been exercised. *(Stats.1990, c. 79 (A.B.759), § 14, operative July 1, 1991. Amended by Stats.1990, c. 710 (S.B.1775), § 24, operative July 1, 1991.)*

Law Revision Commission Comments

1990 Enactment

Section 9832 continues Section 9832 of the repealed Probate Code without substantive change. This section is comparable to Section 2501 (Guardianship–Conservatorship Law).

Except as provided in subdivision (b), a transaction described in Section 9832 requires authorization by order of court obtained under Sections 9836–9837. Subdivision (b), which provides an exception to the requirement of court authorization, is consistent with Section 9941 (leases permitted without court authorization).

In determining whether to extend, renew, or modify a lease under subdivision (b) without prior court authorization, and in extending, renewing, or modifying the lease under that subdivision, the personal representative is required to exercise ordinary care and diligence.

See Section 9600(b). As to the effect of court authorization or approval, see Section 7250.

1990 Amendment

Section 9832 (enacted as a part of the new Probate Code by 1990 Cal.Stat. ch. 79 § 14) was amended by 1990 Cal.Stat. ch. 710 § 24 to increase the limit on extending, renewing, or modifying a lease without court authorization from $1,500 to $5,000. See also 9941 (execution of lease by personal representative). For a comparable provision relating to guardians and conservators, see Section 2501. For background on the 1990 amendment, see Recommendation Relating to Execution or Modification of Lease Without Court Order, 20 Cal.L. Revision Comm'n Reports 557 (1990). [20 Cal.L.Rev.Comm.Reports 1001 (1990)].

Background on Section 9832 of Repealed Code

Section 9832 was a new provision added by 1987 Cal.Stat. ch. 923 § 93. For background on the provisions of this part, see the Comment to this part under the part heading. [20 Cal.L.Rev.Comm.Reports 1001 (1990)].

§ 9833. Transfer or encumbrance of estate property; creation of unsecured liability in excess of $25,000; court authorization

Authorization by order of court is required for a compromise or settlement of a matter when the transaction requires the transfer or encumbrance of property of the estate, or the creation of an unsecured liability of the estate, or both, in an amount or value in excess of twenty-five thousand dollars ($25,000). *(Stats.1990, c. 79 (A.B.759), § 14, operative July 1, 1991.)*

Law Revision Commission Comments

1990 Enactment

Section 9833 continues Section 9833 of the repealed Probate Code without change. This section is comparable to Section 2502 (Guardianship–Conservatorship Law). The section requires authorization by order of court obtained under Sections 9836–9837 where the amount to be paid or charged against the estate exceeds $25,000. Section 9833 does not apply to a claim by the estate.

Although Section 9833 does not require court authorization for a compromise or settlement where the amount to be paid or charged against the estate is not more than $25,000, another provision may require court authorization in the particular case as, for example, under Section 9832 (matter affecting real property).

As to orders made, or actions taken, before July 1, 1988, and matters pending on July 1, 1988, see Section 9645. As to the application of any amendments made after that date, see Section 3.

Background on Section 9833 of Repealed Code

Section 9833 was a new provision added by 1987 Cal.Stat. ch. 923 § 93. For background on the provisions of this part, see the Comment to this part under the part heading. [20 Cal.L.Rev.Comm.Reports 1001 (1990)].

Cross References

Authorization of court administering estate, see Probate Code § 9836.

Petitions for court orders, see Probate Code § 9837.

§ 9834. Claims by estate against personal representative or attorney; modification of obligations; court authorization

Authorization by order of court is required for any of the following:

(a) A compromise or settlement of a claim by the estate against the personal representative or the personal representative's attorney, whether or not the claim arises out of the administration of the estate.

(b) An extension, renewal, or modification of the terms of a debt or similar obligation of the personal representative, or the personal representative's attorney, owing to, or in favor of, the estate. *(Stats.1990, c. 79 (A.B.759), § 14, operative July 1, 1991.)*

Law Revision Commission Comments

1990 Enactment

Section 9834 continues Section 9834 of the repealed Probate Code without change. This section is comparable to Section 2503 (Guardianship–Conservatorship Law) except that Section 9834 also covers transactions involving the personal representative's attorney. Section 9834 requires authorization by order of court obtained under Sections 9836–9837 for a compromise, settlement, extension, renewal, or modification described in the section. Section 9834 requires court authorization because the section involves matters that may involve a conflict of interest for the personal representative.

The term "the personal representative's attorney" is used in a broad sense and includes the associates, partners, and attorneys of counsel with the law firm of the attorney selected by the personal representative and also associates, partners, and attorneys of counsel with other law firms associated in the estate proceeding with the firm of the attorney selected by the personal representative.

As to orders made, or actions taken, before July 1, 1988, and matters pending on July 1, 1988, see Section 9645. As to the application of any amendments made after that date, see Section 3.

Background on Section 9834 of Repealed Code

Section 9834 was a new provision added by 1987 Cal.Stat. ch. 923 § 93. For background on the provisions of this part, see the Comment to this part under the part heading. [20 Cal.L.Rev.Comm.Reports 1001 (1990)].

Cross References

Authorization of court administering estate, see Probate Code § 9836.

Comparable provision, guardianship and conservatorship, see Probate Code § 2503.

Petitions for court orders, see Probate Code § 9837.

§ 9835. Wrongful death or injury actions; court authorization

Authorization by order of court is required for the compromise or settlement of a claim or right of action given to the personal representative by any law for the wrongful death or injury of the decedent, including any action brought by the personal representative in attempting enforcement of the claim or right of action. Authorization to compromise or settle the claim or right of action includes authorization to give a covenant not to sue. *(Stats.1990, c. 79 (A.B.759), § 14, operative July 1, 1991.)*

Law Revision Commission Comments

1990 Enactment

Section 9835 continues Section 9835 of the repealed Probate Code without change. This section requires authorization by order of court obtained under Sections 9836–9837 for a compromise or settlement described in the section. For provisions giving the personal representative a right of action for wrongful death of the decedent, see Code Civ.Proc. § 377 (wrongful death of adult or certain minors); Labor Code § 2803 (wrongful death of employee). As to orders made, or actions taken, before July 1, 1988, and matters pending on July 1, 1988, see Section 9645. As to the application of any amendments made after that date, see Section 3.

Background on Section 9835 of Repealed Code

Section 9835 was added by 1987 Cal.Stat. ch. 923 § 93. The section continued the substance of the first paragraph of former Probate Code Section 578a (repealed by 1987 Cal.Stat. ch. 923 § 35). For background on the provisions of this part, see the Comment to this part under the part heading. [20 Cal.L.Rev.Comm.Reports 1001 (1990)].

Cross References

Accord and satisfaction, see Civil Code § 1521 et seq.
Compromise offer not an admission, not admissible, see Evidence Code § 1152 et seq.
Damages for wrongs, see Civil Code § 3333 et seq.
Death of employee does not abate right of action, see Labor Code § 3851.
Death of party before expiration of time limited for commencement of action, see Code of Civil Procedure §§ 366.1, 366.2, 377 et seq.
Limitation of actions for wrongful death, see Code of Civil Procedure § 340.
Offer of defendant to compromise, see Code of Civil Procedure § 998.
Release, see Civil Code § 1541 et seq.
Survival of actions, see Code of Civil Procedure § 377.20 et seq.
Wrongful death, action by personal representative, see Code of Civil Procedure § 377.60 et seq.
Wrongful death of employee, action by personal representative, see Labor Code § 2803.

§ 9836. Authorization from court administering estate required

The court authorization required by this chapter shall be obtained from the court in which the estate is being administered. *(Stats.1990, c. 79 (A.B.759), § 14, operative July 1, 1991.)*

Law Revision Commission Comments

1990 Enactment

Section 9836 continues Section 9836 of the repealed Probate Code without change. This section applies whether or not the claim or matter is the subject of a pending action or proceeding. As to orders made, or actions taken, before July 1, 1988, and matters pending on July 1, 1988, see Section 9645. As to the application of any amendments made after that date, see Section 3.

Background on Section 9836 of Repealed Code

Section 9836 was a new provision added by 1987 Cal.Stat. ch. 923 § 93. For background on the provisions of this part, see the Comment to this part under the part heading. [20 Cal.L.Rev.Comm.Reports 1001 (1990)].

§ 9837. Petitions for court orders; persons allowed to file; contents; notice of hearing

(a) A petition for an order authorizing a compromise, settlement, extension, renewal, or modification under this chapter may be filed by any of the following:

(1) The personal representative.

(2) Any interested person who has obtained the written approval of the personal representative to file the petition.

(b) The petition shall show the terms of the compromise, settlement, extension, renewal, or modification and its advantage to the estate.

(c) Notice of the hearing on the petition shall be given as provided in Section 1220. *(Stats.1990, c. 79 (A.B.759), § 14, operative July 1, 1991.)*

Law Revision Commission Comments

1990 Enactment

Section 9837 continues Section 9837 of the repealed Probate Code without change. Subdivision (a)(2) permits any interested person who has obtained the written approval of the personal representative to file the petition for an order described in the introductory portion of subdivision (a). In some cases, the personal representative may desire to have an outside party bear the legal expense of obtaining the court approval, or the estate beneficiaries may be interested in seeking court approval of a modification. For general provisions, see Sections 1020–1023 (petitions), 1200–1230 (notice of hearing), 1250–1252 (request for special notice), 1260–1265 (proof of giving of notice). As to orders made, or actions taken, before July 1, 1988, and matters pending on July 1, 1988, see Section 9645. As to the application of any amendments made after that date, see Section 3.

Background on Section 9837 of Repealed Code

Section 9837 was added by 1987 Cal.Stat. ch. 923 § 93. The section restated the fourth and fifth sentences of former Probate Code Section 578 (repealed by 1987 Cal.Stat. ch. 923 § 35), the third and fourth sentences of former Probate Code Section 578a (repealed by 1987 Cal.Stat. ch. 923 § 35), and the second and third sentences of former Probate Code Section 718.5 (repealed by 1987 Cal.Stat. ch. 923 § 37), with the following changes:

(1) The authority for the filing of a petition by an interested person with the written approval of the personal representative was new.

(2) Subdivision (c) required that notice be given at least 15 days before the hearing pursuant to Probate Code Section 1220 instead of at least 10 days before the hearing as required by former Probate Code Section 1200.5 (repealed by 1987 Cal.Stat. ch. 923 § 59).

For background on the provisions of this part, see the Comment to this part under the part heading. [20 Cal.L.Rev.Comm.Reports 1001 (1990)].

§ 9838. Conveyances in compliance with court orders; contents; recording orders; effect

(a) If an order made under Section 9837 authorizes a compromise or settlement that requires the transfer of real property of the estate, the personal representative shall execute a conveyance of the real property to the person entitled thereto under the compromise or settlement. The conveyance shall refer to the order authorizing the compromise or settlement and directing that the conveyance be executed. A certified copy of the order shall be recorded in the office of the county recorder in each county in which any portion of the real property is located.

(b) A conveyance made in compliance with the court order authorizing the compromise or settlement and directing the conveyance to be executed vests in the person to whom the property is transferred both of the following:

(1) All the right, title, and interest which the decedent had in the property at the time of the decedent's death.

(2) Any other or additional right, title, or interest in the property acquired by the estate of the decedent, by operation

of law or otherwise, prior to the transfer. *(Stats.1990, c. 79 (A.B.759), § 14, operative July 1, 1991.)*

Law Revision Commission Comments

1990 Enactment

Section 9838 continues Section 9838 of the repealed Probate Code without substantive change. See also Sections 7250 (effect of court authorization or approval), 7260–7263 (orders and transactions affecting real property). As to orders made, or actions taken, before July 1, 1988, and matters pending on July 1, 1988, see Section 9645. As to the application of any amendments made after that date, see Section 3.

Background on Section 9838 of Repealed Code

Section 9838 was added by 1987 Cal.Stat. ch. 923 § 93. The section restated the fourth sentence of former Probate Code Section 718.5 (repealed by 1987 Cal.Stat. ch. 923 § 37) without substantive change. For background on the provisions of this part, see the Comment to this part under the part heading. [20 Cal.L.Rev.Comm.Reports 1001 (1990)].

§ 9839. Payment of less than full claim; crediting accounts

If the personal representative pays a claim for less than its full amount, the personal representative's accounts may be credited only for the amount actually paid. *(Stats.1990, c. 79 (A.B.759), § 14, operative July 1, 1991.)*

Law Revision Commission Comments

1990 Enactment

Section 9839 continues Section 9839 of the repealed Probate Code without change. As to orders made, or actions taken, before July 1, 1988, and matters pending on July 1, 1988, see Section 9645. As to the application of any amendments made after that date, see Section 3.

Background on Section 9839 of Repealed Code

Section 9839 was added by 1987 Cal.Stat. ch. 923 § 93. The section restated the second half of the first paragraph of former Probate Code Section 583 (repealed by 1987 Cal.Stat. ch. 923 § 35) without substantive change. For background on the provisions of this part, see the Comment to this part under the part heading. [20 Cal.L.Rev.Comm.Reports 1001 (1990)].

CHAPTER 10. ACCEPTANCE OF DEED IN LIEU OF FORECLOSURE OR TRUSTEE'S SALE; GRANT OF PARTIAL SATISFACTION OR PARTIAL RECONVEYANCE

Section
9850. Power of personal representative to accept deed; court authorization; petition; notice of hearing.
9851. Partial satisfaction of mortgages; partial reconveyance under trust deed; court authorization; petition; notice of hearing.

Cross References
Application of old and new law, see Probate Code § 3.

§ 9850. Power of personal representative to accept deed; court authorization; petition; notice of hearing

(a) If it is to the advantage of the estate to accept a deed to property which is subject to a mortgage or deed of trust in lieu of foreclosure of the mortgage or sale under the deed of trust, the personal representative may, after authorization by

order of the court and upon such terms and conditions as may be imposed by the court, accept a deed conveying the property to the heirs or devisees of the decedent, subject to administration.

(b) To obtain an order under this section, the personal representative or any interested person shall file a petition showing the advantage to the estate of accepting the deed. Notice of the hearing on the petition shall be given as provided in Section 1220.

(c) The court shall make an order under this section only if the advantage to the estate of accepting the deed is shown by clear and convincing evidence. *(Stats.1990, c. 79 (A.B.759), § 14, operative July 1, 1991.)*

Law Revision Commission Comments

1990 Enactment

Section 9850 continues Section 9850 of the repealed Probate Code without change. Among the factors to be taken into consideration by the court in determining whether it is to the advantage of the estate to take a deed in lieu of foreclosure are (1) whether there are subordinate liens that will continue on the property if the deed is taken that would be eliminated if the mortgage is foreclosed or the property is sold under the deed of trust and (2) whether there is a right to a deficiency judgment that would continue if the mortgage were foreclosed and the property were to fail to yield enough to pay the amount of the encumbrance. These factors would not necessarily preclude the granting of the order, such as where the subordinate lien that would continue is for only a small amount or where the deficiency judgment would be uncollectible.

The personal representative is required to exercise the power granted by this section (by filing a petition with the court) to the extent that ordinary care and diligence require that the power be exercised. See Section 9600(b). As to the effect of court authorization or approval, see Section 7250. For general provisions, see Sections 1000–1004 (rules of practice), 1020–1023 (petitions and other papers), 1040–1050 (hearings and orders), 1200–1230 (notice of hearing), 1250–1252 (request for special notice), 1260–1265 (proof of giving of notice). As to orders made, or actions taken, before July 1, 1988, and matters pending on July 1, 1988, see Section 9645. As to the application of any amendments made after that date, see Section 3. As to independent administration authority, see Section 10563.

Background on Section 9850 of Repealed Code

Section 9850 was added by 1987 Cal.Stat. ch. 923 § 93. The section restated the substance of former Probate Code Section 718.6 (repealed by 1987 Cal.Stat. ch. 923 § 37), except that (1) Section 9850 required that the advantage to the estate be shown by clear and convincing evidence and (2) subdivision (b) of Section 9850 required that notice be given at least 15 days before the hearing pursuant to Section 1220 instead of at least 10 days before the hearing as required by former Probate Code Section 1200.5 (repealed by 1987 Cal.Stat. ch. 923 § 59). For background on the provisions of this part, see the Comment to this part under the part heading. [20 Cal.L.Rev.Comm.Reports 1001 (1990)].

Cross References
Order, recordation of, see Probate Code § 7263.

§ 9851. Partial satisfaction of mortgages; partial reconveyance under trust deed; court authorization; petition; notice of hearing

(a) Except as provided in subdivision (c), if it is to the advantage of the estate for the personal representative to give a partial satisfaction of a mortgage or to cause a partial reconveyance to be executed by a trustee under a trust deed held by the estate, the personal representative may, after authorization by order of the court and upon such terms and conditions as may be imposed by the court, give the partial satisfaction or cause the partial reconveyance to be executed by the trustee.

(b) To obtain an order under this section, the personal representative or any interested person shall file a petition showing the advantage to the estate of giving the partial satisfaction or causing the partial reconveyance. Notice of the hearing on the petition shall be given as provided in Section 1220.

(c) No authorization by the court is necessary for the personal representative to give a partial satisfaction of a mortgage or to cause a partial reconveyance to be executed by a trustee under a deed of trust held by the estate if the partial satisfaction or partial reconveyance is executed pursuant to the terms of the mortgage or deed of trust held by the estate. *(Stats.1990, c. 79 (A.B.759), § 14, operative July 1, 1991.)*

Law Revision Commission Comments
1990 Enactment

Section 9851 continues Section 9851 of the repealed Probate Code without substantive change. The personal representative is required to exercise the power granted by subdivision (a) (by filing a petition with the court) to the extent that ordinary care and diligence require that the power be exercised. See Section 9600(b). As to the effect of court authorization or approval, see Section 7250. For general provisions, see Sections 1000–1004 (rules of practice), 1020–1023 (petitions and other papers), 1040–1050 (hearings and orders), 1200–1230 (notice of hearing), 1250–1252 (request for special notice), 1260–1265 (proof of giving of notice). As to orders made, or actions taken, before July 1, 1988, and matters pending on July 1, 1988, see Section 9645. As to the application of any amendments made after that date, see Section 3. As to independent administration authority, see Section 10564.

Background on Section 9851 of Repealed Code

Section 9851 was added by 1987 Cal.Stat. ch. 923 § 93. The section restated former Probate Code Section 718.7 (repealed by 1987 Cal.Stat. ch. 923 § 37) without substantive change, except that subdivision (b) of Section 9851 required that notice be given at least 15 days before the hearing pursuant to Section 1220 instead of at least 10 days before the hearing as required by former Probate Code Section 1200.5 (repealed by 1987 Cal.Stat. ch. 923 § 59). For background on the provisions of this part, see the Comment to this part under the part heading. [20 Cal.L.Rev.Comm.Reports 1001 (1990)].

Cross References

Mortgages in general, see Civil Code § 2920 et seq.
Satisfaction of mortgages by foreign executors, administrators and guardians, see Civil Code § 2939.5.

CHAPTER 11.　CONVEYANCE OR TRANSFER OF PROPERTY CLAIMED TO BELONG TO DECEDENT OR OTHER PERSON [REPEALED]

§§ 9860 to 9862.　Repealed by Stats.2001, c. 49 (S.B.669), § 4

§ 9863.　Repealed by Stats.1988, c. 1199, § 88.5, operative July 1, 1989

Law Revision Commission Comments
1988 Repeal

Former Section 9863 is generalized in Section 1004. [19 Cal. L.Rev.Comm. Reports 1093 (1988)].

§§ 9864 to 9869.　Repealed by Stats.2001, c. 49 (S.B.669), § 4

CHAPTER 12.　PURCHASE OF CLAIMS OR ESTATE PROPERTY BY PERSONAL REPRESENTATIVE OR PERSONAL REPRESENTATIVE'S ATTORNEY

Section
9880.　Purchases or interests prohibited.
9881.　Orders authorizing purchase; requirements.
9882.　Orders authorizing purchase; will authorization.
9883.　Petitions; confirmation of sale; notice of hearing; orders; conveyance.
9884.　Purchases pursuant to contract.
9885.　Options to purchase.

Cross References
Application of old and new law, see Probate Code § 3.

§ 9880.　Purchases or interests prohibited

Except as provided in this chapter, neither the personal representative nor the personal representative's attorney may do any of the following:

(a) Purchase any property of the estate or any claim against the estate, directly or indirectly.

(b) Be interested in any such purchase. *(Stats.1990, c. 79 (A.B.759), § 14, operative July 1, 1991.)*

Law Revision Commission Comments
1990 Enactment

Section 9880 continues Section 9880 of the repealed Probate Code without substantive change. The term "personal representative's attorney" is to be given a broad meaning for the purposes of this chapter and includes the associates, partners, and attorneys of counsel with the law firm of the attorney retained by the personal representative and also associates, partners, and attorneys of counsel with other law firms associated in the estate proceeding with the firm of the attorney retained by the personal representative. See also Section 9605 (appointment of person as personal representative does not discharge any claim the decedent has against the person). As to orders made, or actions taken, before July 1, 1988, and matters pending on July 1, 1988, see Section 9645. As to the application of any amendments made after that date, see Section 3.

Background on Section 9880 of Repealed Code

Section 9880 was added by 1987 Cal.Stat. ch. 923 § 93. The section restated the first portion of the first paragraph of former Probate Code Section 583 (repealed by 1987 Cal.Stat. ch. 923 § 35) without substantive change except that the prohibition was extended to the personal representative's attorney. For background on the provisions of this part, see the Comment to this part under the part heading. [20 Cal.L.Rev.Comm.Reports 1001 (1990)].

§ 9881.　Orders authorizing purchase; requirements

Upon a petition filed under Section 9883, the court may make an order under this section authorizing the personal representative or the personal representative's attorney to purchase property of the estate if all of the following requirements are satisfied:

(a) Written consent to the purchase is signed by (1) each known heir whose interest in the estate would be affected by the proposed purchase and (2) each known devisee whose interest in the estate would be affected by the proposed purchase.

(b) The written consents are filed with the court.

(c) The purchase is shown to be to the advantage of the estate. *(Stats.1990, c. 79 (A.B.759), § 14, operative July 1, 1991.)*

Law Revision Commission Comments
1990 Enactment

Section 9881 continues Section 9881 of the repealed Probate Code without substantive change. See also Sections 7260–7263 (orders and transactions affecting property). As to orders made, or actions taken, before July 1, 1988, and matters pending on July 1, 1988, see Section 9645. As to the application of any amendments made after that date, see Section 3.

Background on Section 9881 of Repealed Code

Section 9881 was a new provision added by 1987 Cal.Stat. ch. 923 § 93. For background on the provisions of this part, see the Comment to this part under the part heading. [20 Cal.L.Rev.Comm.Reports 1001 (1990)].

§ 9882. Orders authorizing purchase; will authorization

Upon a petition filed under Section 9883, the court may make an order under this section authorizing the personal representative or the personal representative's attorney to purchase property of the estate if the will of the decedent authorizes the personal representative or the personal representative's attorney to purchase the property. *(Stats.1990, c. 79 (A.B.759), § 14, operative July 1, 1991.)*

Law Revision Commission Comments
1990 Enactment

Section 9882 continues Section 9882 of the repealed Probate Code without change. See also Sections 7260–7263 (orders and transactions affecting property). As to orders made, or actions taken, before July 1, 1988, and matters pending on July 1, 1988, see Section 9645. As to the application of any amendments made after that date, see Section 3.

Background on Section 9882 of Repealed Code

Section 9882 was added by 1987 Cal.Stat. ch. 923 § 93. The section superseded the first portion of the third paragraph of former Probate Code Section 583 (repealed by 1987 Cal.Stat. ch. 923 § 35) which provided that the prohibition against purchase by the personal representative did not prohibit the purchase of property of the estate by the personal representative pursuant to the will of the decedent. Section 9880 extended this prohibition against purchase to include the personal representative's attorney, and Section 9882 expanded the provision of former Section 583 to permit the court to make an order authorizing purchase by the personal representative's attorney pursuant to the will of the decedent. For background on the provisions of this part, see the Comment to this part under the part heading. [20 Cal.L.Rev.Comm.Reports 1001 (1990)].

§ 9883. Petitions; confirmation of sale; notice of hearing; orders; conveyance

(a) The personal representative may file a petition requesting that the court make an order under Section 9881 or 9882. The petition shall set forth the facts upon which the request for the order is based.

(b) If court confirmation of the sale is required, the court may make its order under Section 9881 or 9882 at the time of the confirmation.

(c) Notice of the hearing on the petition shall be given as provided in Section 1220 to all of the following persons:

(1) Each person listed in Section 1220.

(2) Each known heir whose interest in the estate would be affected by the proposed purchase.

(3) Each known devisee whose interest in the estate would be affected by the proposed purchase.

(d) If the court is satisfied that the purchase should be authorized, the court shall make an order authorizing the purchase upon the terms and conditions specified in the order, and the personal representative may execute a conveyance or transfer according to the terms of the order. Unless otherwise provided in the will or in the order of the court, the sale of the property shall be made in the same manner as the sale of other estate property of the same nature. *(Stats.1990, c. 79 (A.B.759), § 14, operative July 1, 1991.)*

Law Revision Commission Comments
1990 Enactment

Section 9883 continues Section 9883 of the repealed Probate Code without substantive change. Only the personal representative may petition under Section 9883. An interested person may neither petition under Section 9883 nor petition for instructions under Section 9611. But see Section 9613 (right of interested person to petition for order directing personal representative in order to avoid great or irreparable injury). Persons who requested special notice also must be given notice. See Sections 1250–1252. As to giving notice to known heirs and known devisees, see Section 1206. See also Sections 7260–7263 (orders and transactions affecting property). For general provisions, see Sections 1000–1004 (rules of practice), 1020–1023 (petitions and other papers), 1040–1050 (hearings and orders), 1200–1230 (notice of hearing), 1250–1252 (request for special notice), 1260–1265 (proof of giving of notice). As to orders made, or actions taken, before July 1, 1988, and matters pending on July 1, 1988, see Section 9645. As to the application of any amendments made after that date, see Section 3.

Background on Section 9883 of Repealed Code

Section 9883 was added by 1987 Cal.Stat. ch. 923 § 93. Subdivision (a) continued the substance of the first sentence of former Probate Code Section 851 (repealed by 1987 Cal.Stat. ch. 923 § 41) which was made applicable to purchases by the personal representative of estate property by the last sentence of former Probate Code Section 583 (repealed by 1987 Cal.Stat. ch. 923 § 35). Section 9883 expanded the former provision to apply to a purchase by the personal representative's attorney. See Section 9881. Subdivision (b) was new. Subdivisions (c) and (d) superseded the portion of the last sentence of former Section 583 relating to notice. The first sentence of subdivision (e) continued the substance of the last portion of the first sentence of former Probate Code Section 852 and the first portion of the second sentence of former Probate Code Section 853 (provisions repealed by 1987 Cal.Stat. ch. 923 § 41). These provisions were applied to purchases by the personal representative of estate property by the last sentence of former Section 583. The second sentence of subdivision (e) was new. For background on the provisions of this part, see the Comment to this part under the part heading. [20 Cal.L.Rev.Comm.Reports 1001 (1990)].

§ 9884. Purchases pursuant to contract

This chapter does not prohibit the purchase of property of the estate by the personal representative or the personal representative's attorney pursuant to a contract in writing made during the lifetime of the decedent if the contract is one that can be specifically enforced and the requirements of Part 19 (commencing with Section 850) of Division 2 are satisfied. *(Stats.1990, c. 79 (A.B.759), § 14, operative July 1, 1991. Amended by Stats.2003, c. 32 (A.B.167), § 9.)*

Law Revision Commission Comments

1990 Enactment

Section 9884 continues Section 9884 of the repealed Probate Code without change. An order authorizing the personal representative or the attorney for the personal representative to purchase property pursuant to a contract of the decedent to sell the property is obtained under Chapter 11 (commencing with Section 9860), not under this chapter. See also Section 9860(a)(1), (2). As to orders made, or actions taken, before July 1, 1988, and matters pending on July 1, 1988, see Section 9645. As to the application of any amendments made after that date, see Section 3.

2003 Amendment

Section 9884 is amended to reflect relocation (from former Section 9860 *et seq.* to Section 850 *et seq.*) of the statutes relating to conveyance or transfer of property claimed to belong to the decedent or another person. See 2001 Cal. Stat. ch. 49, §§ 1, 4. [33 Cal.L.Rev.Comm. Reports 160 (2003)].

Background on Section 9884 of Repealed Code

Section 9884 was added by 1987 Cal.Stat. ch. 923 § 93. The section restated a portion of the third paragraph of former Probate Code Section 583 (repealed by 1987 Cal.Stat. ch. 923 § 35) without substantive change. Language was included in Section 9884 to recognize the expansion of Sections 9880 and 9881 to cover purchases by the personal representative's attorney. For background on the provisions of this part, see the Comment to this part under the part heading. [20 Cal.L.Rev.Comm.Reports 1001 (1990)].

§ 9885. Options to purchase

This chapter does not prevent the exercise by the personal representative or the personal representative's attorney of an option to purchase property of the estate given in the will of the decedent if the requirements of Chapter 17 (commencing with Section 9980) are satisfied. *(Stats.1990, c. 79 (A.B.759), § 14, operative July 1, 1991.)*

Law Revision Commission Comments

1990 Enactment

Section 9885 continues Section 9885 of the repealed Probate Code without change. An order authorizing the personal representative or the attorney for the personal representative to exercise an option to purchase property of the estate is obtained under Chapter 17 (commencing with Section 9980), not under this chapter. Under Section 9981, the decedent's will must have been admitted to probate. As to orders made, or actions taken, before July 1, 1988, and matters pending on July 1, 1988, see Section 9645. As to the application of any amendments made after that date, see Section 3.

Background on Section 9885 of Repealed Code

Section 9885 was added by 1987 Cal.Stat. ch. 923 § 93. The section restated the second paragraph of former Probate Code Section 583 (repealed by 1987 Cal.Stat. ch. 923 § 35) without substantive change. Language was included in Section 9885 to recognize the expansion of Sections 9880 and 9881 to cover purchases by the personal representative's attorney. For background on the provisions of this part, see the Comment to this part under the part heading. [20 Cal.L.Rev.Comm.Reports 1001 (1990)].

CHAPTER 13. DEDICATION OR CONVEYANCE TO GOVERNMENTAL ENTITY; EASEMENTS AND ACCESS RIGHTS

Cross References

Application of old and new law, see Probate Code § 3.

§ 9900. Powers of personal representative

If it is to the advantage of the estate and in the best interest of the interested persons, the personal representative, after authorization by order of the court obtained under this chapter and upon such terms and conditions as the court may prescribe, may do any of the following either with or without consideration:

(a) Dedicate or convey real property of the estate for any purpose to any of the following:

(1) This state or any public entity in this state.

(2) The United States or any agency or instrumentality of the United States.

(b) Dedicate or convey an easement over real property of the estate to any person for any purpose.

(c) Convey, release, or relinquish to this state or any public entity in this state any access rights to any street, highway, or freeway from any real property of the estate.

(d) Consent as a lienholder to a dedication, conveyance, release, or relinquishment under subdivision (a), (b), or (c) by the owner of property subject to the lien. *(Stats.1990, c. 79 (A.B.759), § 14, operative July 1, 1991.)*

Law Revision Commission Comments

1990 Enactment

Section 9900 continues Section 9900 of the repealed Probate Code without change. The authority in subdivision (a) for the dedication or conveyance of real property of the estate includes the entire interest or any lesser interest in the property. Section 9900 is similar to subdivision (a) of Section 2556 (Guardianship–Conservatorship Law).

The personal representative is required to exercise the power granted by this section (by filing a petition with the court) to the extent that ordinary care and diligence require that the power be exercised. See Section 9600(b). As to the effect of court authorization or approval, see Section 7250. See also Sections 7260–7263 (orders and transactions affecting property).

As to orders made, or actions taken, before July 1, 1988, and matters pending on July 1, 1988, see Section 9645. As to the application of any amendments made after that date, see Section 3.

Background on Section 9900 of Repealed Code

Section 9900 was added by 1987 Cal.Stat. ch. 923 § 93. The section restated a portion of former Probate Code Section 587 (repealed by 1987 Cal.Stat. ch. 923 § 35) with the following changes:

(1) Language was added to Section 9900 to recognize that the court may prescribe terms and conditions in its order.

(2) Subdivision (d) of Section 9900 was new.

(3) In the introductory clause of Section 9900, "advantage of the estate and in the best interest of the interested persons" was substituted for "advantage, benefit, and best interest of the estate,

and those interested therein" which was used in former Section 587. This change was nonsubstantive.

For background on the provisions of this part, see the Comment to this part under the part heading. [20 Cal.L.Rev.Comm.Reports 1001 (1990)].

§ 9901. Petitions for orders; notice of hearing

(a) The personal representative or any interested person may file a petition for an order under this chapter.

(b) Notice of the hearing on the petition shall be given as provided in Section 1220. *(Stats.1990, c. 79 (A.B.759), § 14, operative July 1, 1991.)*

Law Revision Commission Comments
1990 Enactment

Section 9901 continues Section 9901 of the repealed Probate Code without change. See also Sections 7260–7263 (orders and transactions affecting property). For general provisions, see Sections 1000–1004 (rules of practice), 1020–1023 (petitions and other papers), 1040–1050 (hearings and orders), 1200–1230 (notice of hearing), 1250–1252 (request for special notice), 1260–1265 (proof of giving of notice). As to orders made, or actions taken, before July 1, 1988, and matters pending on July 1, 1988, see Section 9645. As to the application of any amendments made after that date, see Section 3.

Background on Section 9901 of Repealed Code

Section 9901 was added by 1987 Cal.Stat. ch. 923 § 93. The section restated a portion of former Probate Code Section 587 (repealed by 1987 Cal.Stat. ch. 923 § 35) without substantive change except that subdivision (b) of Section 9901 required that notice be given at least 15 days before the hearing pursuant to Section 1220 instead of at least 10 days before the hearing as required by former Probate Code Section 1200.5 (repealed by 1987 Cal.Stat. ch. 923 § 59). For background on the provisions of this part, see the Comment to this part under the part heading. [20 Cal.L.Rev.Comm.Reports 1001 (1990)].

CHAPTER 14. EXCHANGE OF PROPERTY

Section
9920. Powers of personal representative.
9921. Petitions.
9922. Notice of hearing.
9923. Omissions or errors in proceedings.

Cross References

Application of old and new law, see Probate Code § 3.

§ 9920. Powers of personal representative

If it is to the advantage of the estate to exchange property of the estate for other property, the personal representative may, after authorization by order of court obtained under this chapter and upon such terms and conditions as may be prescribed by the court, exchange the property for the other property. The terms and conditions prescribed by the court may include the payment or receipt of part cash by the personal representative. *(Stats.1990, c. 79 (A.B.759), § 14, operative July 1, 1991.)*

Law Revision Commission Comments
1990 Enactment

Section 9920 continues Section 9920 of the repealed Probate Code without substantive change. Section 9920 is similar to subdivision (a) of Section 2557 (Guardianship–Conservatorship Law). The personal

representative is required to exercise the power granted by Section 9920 (by filing a petition with the court) to the extent that ordinary care and diligence require that the power be exercised. See Section 9600(b). As to the effect of court authorization, see Section 7250. See also Sections 7260–7263 (orders and transactions affecting property). As to orders made, or actions taken, before July 1, 1988, and matters pending on July 1, 1988, see Section 9645. As to the application of any amendments made after that date, see Section 3.

Background on Section 9920 of Repealed Code

Section 9920 was added by 1987 Cal.Stat. ch. 923 § 93. The section restated a portion of the first sentence of former Probate Code Section 860 (repealed by 1987 Cal.Stat. ch. 923 § 41) without substantive change. The language "advantage of the estate" was substituted for the former language "advantage or best interests of the estate." This change was nonsubstantive. For background on the provisions of this part, see the Comment to this part under the part heading. [20 Cal.L.Rev.Comm.Reports 1001 (1990)].

§ 9921. Petitions

To obtain an order under this chapter, the personal representative or any interested person shall file a petition containing all of the following:

(a) A description of the property.

(b) The terms and conditions of the proposed exchange.

(c) A showing that the proposed exchange is to the advantage of the estate. *(Stats.1990, c. 79 (A.B.759), § 14, operative July 1, 1991.)*

Law Revision Commission Comments
1990 Enactment

Section 9921 continues Section 9921 of the repealed Probate Code without substantive change. For general provisions relating to petitions, see Sections 1020–1023. As to orders made, or actions taken, before July 1, 1988, and matters pending on July 1, 1988, see Section 9645. As to the application of any amendments made after that date, see Section 3. As to independent administration authority, see Section 10537.

Background on Section 9921 of Repealed Code

Section 9921 was added by 1987 Cal.Stat. ch. 923 § 93. The section restated a portion of the first sentence of former Probate Code Section 860 (repealed by 1987 Cal.Stat. ch. 923 § 41) without substantive change. The requirement that the petition contain a description of the property and the terms and conditions of the proposed exchange was new. The phrase "advantage of the estate" was substituted for the former phrase "advantage or best interests of the estate." This change was nonsubstantive. For background on the provisions of this part, see the Comment to this part under the part heading. [20 Cal.L.Rev.Comm.Reports 1001 (1990)].

§ 9922. Notice of hearing

(a) Except as provided in subdivision (b), notice of the hearing on the petition shall be given as provided in Section 1220.

(b) If the petition is for authorization to exchange securities as defined in Section 10200 for different securities, the court, upon a showing of good cause, may order that the notice be given for a shorter period or that the notice be dispensed with. The order provided by this subdivision may be made ex parte. *(Stats.1990, c. 79 (A.B.759), § 14, operative July 1, 1991.)*

Law Revision Commission Comments
1990 Enactment

Section 9922 continues Section 9922 of the repealed Probate Code without change. Subdivision (b) of Section 9922 is comparable to subdivision (c) of Section 2557 (Guardianship–Conservatorship Law). For general provisions relating to notice, see Sections 1200–1230 (notice of hearing), 1250–1252 (request for special notice), 1260–1265 (proof of giving of notice). As to orders made, or actions taken, before July 1, 1988, and matters pending on July 1, 1988, see Section 9645. As to the application of any amendments made after that date, see Section 3.

Background on Section 9922 of Repealed Code

Section 9922 was added by 1987 Cal.Stat. ch. 923 § 93. The section restated the second and third sentences of former Probate Code Section 860 (repealed by 1987 Cal.Stat. ch. 923 § 41) without substantive change, except that subdivision (a) of Section 9922 required that notice be given at least 15 days before the hearing pursuant to Section 1220 instead of at least 10 days before the hearing as required by former Probate Code Section 1200.5 (repealed by 1987 Cal.Stat. ch. 923 § 59). The last sentence of subdivision (b) was new. For background on the provisions of this part, see the Comment to this part under the part heading. [20 Cal.L.Rev.Comm.Reports 1001 (1990)].

§ 9923. Omissions or errors in proceedings

No omission, error, or irregularity in the proceedings under this chapter shall impair or invalidate the proceedings or the exchange made pursuant to an order made under this chapter. *(Stats.1990, c. 79 (A.B.759), § 14, operative July 1, 1991.)*

Law Revision Commission Comments
1990 Enactment

Section 9923 continues Section 9923 of the repealed Probate Code without change. This section is comparable to Sections 9948(d) (leases), 9966 (option to purchase real property), 9983 (option to purchase given in will), 10264 (sale of personal property), and 10316 (sale of real property). See also Sections 7260–7263 (orders and transactions affecting property).

If the court lacks jurisdiction, Section 9923 does not cure the defect. See Texas Co. v. Bank of America Nat'l Trust & Sav. Ass'n, 5 Cal.2d 35, 41–44, 53 P.2d 127 (1935). Section 9923 does not limit the court's authority to set aside an order made through mistake, inadvertence, surprise, or excusable neglect. See Code Civ.Proc. § 473; Estate of Lee, 159 Cal.App.2d 109, 111–12, 323 P.2d 448 (1958); Estate of Herz, 147 Cal.App.2d 100, 106–07, 305 P.2d 278 (1956); Estate of McCrae, 133 Cal.App.2d 634, 637–39, 284 P.2d 914 (1955); Estate of Moreland, 49 Cal.App.2d 484, 487–88, 121 P.2d 867 (1942). As to orders made, or actions taken, before July 1, 1988, and matters pending on July 1, 1988, see Section 9645. As to the application of any amendments made after that date, see Section 3.

Background on Section 9923 of Repealed Code

Section 9923 was a new provision added by 1987 Cal.Stat. ch. 923 § 93. For background on the provisions of this part, see the Comment to this part under the part heading. [20 Cal.L.Rev.Comm.Reports 1001 (1990)].

CHAPTER 15. LEASES

Cross References
Application of old and new law, see Probate Code § 3.

§ 9940. "Lease" defined; term of lease

For the purpose of this chapter:

(a) "Lease" includes, without limitation, a lease that includes an option to purchase real propery [1] of the estate.

(b) If a lease gives the lessee the right to extend the term of the lease, the length of the term shall be considered as though the right to extend had been exercised. *(Stats.1990, c. 79 (A.B.759), § 14, operative July 1, 1991.)*

[1] So in enrolled bill.

Law Revision Commission Comments
1990 Enactment

Section 9940 continues Section 9940 of the repealed Probate Code without change. Subdivision (b) is consistent with Section 10203(b)(1) (sale of leasehold interest). As to orders made, or actions taken, before July 1, 1988, and matters pending on July 1, 1988, see Section 9645. As to the application of any amendments made after that date, see Section 3.

Background on Section 9940 of Repealed Code

Section 9940 was added by 1987 Cal.Stat. ch. 923 § 93. Subdivision (a) restated the first portion of former Probate Code Section 845 (repealed by 1987 Cal.Stat. ch. 923 § 41) without substantive change. Subdivision (b) was new. For background on the provisions of this part, see the Comment to this part under the part heading. [20 Cal.L.Rev.Comm.Report 1001 (1990)].

§ 9941. Leases without court authorization

If it is to the advantage of the estate, the personal representative may lease, as lessor, real property of the estate without authorization of the court in either of the following cases:

(a) Where the rental does not exceed five thousand dollars ($5,000) a month and the term does not exceed one year.

(b) Where the lease is from month to month, regardless of the amount of the rental. *(Stats.1990, c. 79 (A.B.759), § 14, operative July 1, 1991. Amended by Stats.1990, c. 710 (S.B.1775), § 25, operative July 1, 1991.)*

Law Revision Commission Comments
1990 Enactment

Section 9941 continues Section 9941 of the repealed Probate Code without change. The personal representative may act under Section 9941 without prior court authorization, but the personal representative must exercise ordinary care and diligence in determining whether or not to lease the real property and in the leasing of the property. See Section 9600(b). The personal representative may seek approval from the court under Sections 9943–9947 if in doubt as to the appropriate action to take. As to the effect of court authorization, see Section 7250. For a similar provision, see Section 2555 (Guardianship–Conservatorship Law). If the lease gives the lessee an option to extend the lease beyond a one-year term, court approval of the lease is required. See Sections 9940(b), 9941–9942. As to orders made, or actions taken, before July 1, 1988, and matters pending on July 1, 1988, see Section 9645. As to the application of any amendments made after that date, see Section 3. As to independent administration authority, see Section 10536.

1990 Amendment

Section 9941 (enacted as a part of the new Probate Code by 1990 Cal.Stat. ch. 79 § 14) was amended by 1990 Cal.Stat. ch. 710 § 25 to increase the limit on executing a lease without court authorization from $1,500 to $5,000. See also Section 9832 (extension, renewal, or modification of lease by personal representative). For a comparable provision relating to guardians and conservators, see Section 2555. For background on the 1990 amendment, see Recommendation Relating to Execution or Modification of Lease Without Court Order, 20 Cal.L.Revision Comm'n Reports 557 (1990). [20 Cal.L.Rev.Comm.Reports 1001 (1990)].

Background on Section 9941 of Repealed Code

Section 9941 was added by 1987 Cal.Stat. ch. 923 § 93. The section superseded former Probate Code Section 844 (repealed by 1987 Cal.Stat. ch. 923 § 41). Subdivision (a) of Section 9941 increased the maximum rental under former Probate Code Section 844 from $250 a month to $1,500 a month. Court supervision for leases for less than $1,500 a month added little protection to the estate, since overbids on these leases were rare and the one-year maximum limit on the lease term ensures that the lease will terminate before or soon after distribution of the average estate. See Review of 1963 Code Legislation, 38 Cal.St.B.J. 601, 777 (1963). For background on the provisions of this part, see the Comment to this part under the part heading. [20 Cal.L.Rev.Comm.Reports 1001 (1990)].

§ 9942. Leases with court authorization; options to purchase property; petitions

(a) The personal representative may lease, as lessor, real property of the estate after authorization by order of court obtained under this chapter upon a showing that the proposed lease is to the advantage of the estate.

(b) If the proposed lease includes an option to purchase real property of the estate, a petition for an order authorizing the lease shall be filed under this chapter but the applicable provisions for court approval both in this chapter and in Chapter 16 (commencing with Section 9960) apply to the execution of the lease. *(Stats.1990, c. 79 (A.B.759), § 14, operative July 1, 1991.)*

Law Revision Commission Comments
1990 Enactment

Section 9942 continues Section 9942 of the repealed Probate Code without change. The personal representative is required to exercise the power granted by this section (by filing a petition with the court) to the extent that ordinary care and diligence require that the power be exercised. See Section 9600(b). As to the effect of court authorization or approval, see Section 7250. As to orders made, or actions taken, before July 1, 1988, and matters pending on July 1, 1988, see Section 9645. As to the application of any amendments made after that date, see Section 3. As to independent administration authority, see Section 10536.

Background on Section 9942 of Repealed Code

Section 9942 was added by 1987 Cal.Stat. ch. 923 § 93. Subdivision (a) restated former Probate Code Section 840 (repealed by 1987 Cal.Stat. ch. 923 § 41) without substantive change. Subdivision (b) restated former Probate Code Section 845 (repealed by 1987

Cal.Stat. ch. 923 § 41) without substantive change. For background on the provisions of this part, see the Comment to this part under the part heading. [20 Cal.L.Rev.Comm.Reports 1001 (1990)].

§ 9943. Petitions for orders

(a) To obtain an order under this chapter, the personal representative or any interested person shall file a petition containing all of the following:

(1) A general description of the real property proposed to be leased.

(2) The term, rental, and general conditions of the proposed lease.

(3) A showing that the proposed lease is to the advantage of the estate.

(b) If the lease is proposed to be for a term longer than 10 years, the petition shall also state facts showing the need for the longer lease and its advantage to the estate and its benefit to the interested persons. *(Stats.1990, c. 79 (A.B.759), § 14, operative July 1, 1991.)*

Law Revision Commission Comments
1990 Enactment

Section 9943 continues Section 9943 of the repealed Probate Code without substantive change. For a comparable provision, see Section 2553(b) (Guardianship–Conservatorship Law). For general provisions relating to petitions, see Sections 1020–1023. As to orders made, or actions taken, before July 1, 1988, and matters pending on July 1, 1988, see Section 9645. As to the application of any amendments made after that date, see Section 3.

Background on Section 9943 of Repealed Code

Section 9943 was added by 1987 Cal.Stat. ch. 923 § 93. Subdivision (a) restated the first sentence of former Probate Code Section 841 (repealed by 1987 Cal.Stat. ch. 923 § 41) without substantive change. Subdivision (b) restated a portion of the first sentence of former Probate Code Section 842.1 (repealed by 1987 Cal.Stat. ch. 923 § 41) without substantive change. For background on the provisions of this part, see the Comment to this part under the part heading. [20 Cal.L.Rev.Comm.Reports 1001 (1990)].

Cross References

Contents of orders authorizing leases by guardians, see Probate Code § 2554.

Orders, generally, see Probate Code § 1046 et seq.

§ 9944. Notice of hearing

(a) Notice of the hearing on the petition shall be given as provided in Section 1220 and posted as provided in Section 1230.

(b) Notice of the hearing on the petition also shall be given as provided in Section 10300, but this notice is not required if the will authorizes or directs the personal representative to lease or sell property.

(c) If the lease is proposed to be for a term longer than 10 years, in addition to the notice required by subdivision (a), notice of the hearing shall be given as provided in Section 1220 to all of the following persons:

(1) Each known heir whose interest in the estate would be affected by the proposed lease.

(2) Each known devisee whose interest in the estate would be affected by the proposed lease. *(Stats.1990, c. 79 (A.B. 759), § 14, operative July 1, 1991.)*

Law Revision Commission Comments

1990 Enactment

Section 9944 continues Section 9944 of the repealed Probate Code without substantive change. For general provisions relating to notice, see Sections 1200–1230 (notice of hearing), 1250–1252 (request for special notice), 1260–1265 (proof of giving of notice). As to orders made, or actions taken, before July 1, 1988, and matters pending on July 1, 1988, see Section 9645. As to the application of any amendments made after that date, see Section 3.

Background on Section 9944 of Repealed Code

Section 9944 was added by 1987 Cal.Stat. ch. 923 § 93. Subdivisions (a) and (b) restated a portion of the second sentence and all of the third sentence of former Probate Code Section 841 (repealed by 1987 Cal.Stat. ch. 923 § 41) without substantive change, except that (1) subdivision (a) of Section 9944 required that notice be given at least 15 days before the hearing pursuant to Section 1220 instead of at least 10 days before the hearing as required by former Probate Code Section 1200.5 (repealed by 1987 Cal.Stat. ch. 923 § 59) and (2) the provision in subdivision (b) dispensing with notice was expanded to include the case where the will authorizes or directs sale of the property as well as authorizing or directing its leasing.

Subdivision (c) restated the second sentence of former Probate Code Section 842.1 (repealed by 1987 Cal.Stat. ch. 923 § 41) without substantive change except that subdivision (c) of Section 9944 required that notice be given at least 15 days before the hearing instead of at least 20 days before the hearing as required under former Section 842.1. The authority under former Section 842.1 for the court to require additional notice was omitted as unnecessary in view of the general provision which gives the court this authority. See Section 1202.

For background on the provisions of this part, see the Comment to this part under the part heading. [20 Cal.L.Rev.Comm.Reports 1001 (1990)].

Cross References

Interested person, defined, see Probate Code § 48.

§ 9945. Hearings; offer to lease; orders to make lease

(a) At the hearing, the court shall entertain and consider any other offer made in good faith at the hearing to lease the same property on more favorable terms.

(b) If the court is satisfied that it will be to the advantage of the estate, and, if the lease is for more than 10 years, that it is to the benefit of interested persons, the court shall make an order authorizing the personal representative to make the lease to the person on the terms and conditions stated in the order. The court shall not make an order authorizing the personal representative to make the lease to any person other than the lessee named in the petition unless the offer made at the hearing is acceptable to the personal representative. *(Stats.1990, c. 79 (A.B.759), § 14, operative July 1, 1991.)*

Law Revision Commission Comments

1990 Enactment

Section 9945 continues Section 9945 of the repealed Probate Code without change. For general provisions relating to hearings and orders, see Section 1040–1050. As to the effect of court authorization or approval, see Section 7250. See also Sections 7260–7263 (orders and transactions affecting property). For a comparable provision, see Section 2553 (Guardianship–Conservatorship Law). As to orders made, or actions taken, before July 1, 1988, and matters pending on July 1, 1988, see Section 9645. As to the application of any amendments made after that date, see Section 3.

Background on Section 9945 of Repealed Code

Section 9945 was added by 1987 Cal.Stat. ch. 923 § 93. The section restated the first sentence of former Probate Code Section 842 (repealed by 1987 Cal.Stat. ch. 923 § 41), and a portion of the first sentence of former Probate Code Section 842.1 (repealed by 1987 Cal.Stat. ch. 923 § 41), without substantive change. For background on the provisions of this part, see the Comment to this part under the part heading. [20 Cal.L.Rev.Comm.Reports 1001 (1990)].

§ 9946. Orders authorizing lease; contents

(a) Subject to Section 9947, an order authorizing the execution of a lease shall set forth the minimum rental or royalty or both and the period of the lease.

(b) The order may authorize other terms and conditions of the lease, including, with respect to a lease for the purpose of exploration for or production or removal of minerals, oil, gas, or other hydrocarbon substances, or geothermal energy, any one or more of the following provisions:

(1) A provision for the payment of rental and royalty to a depositary.

(2) A provision for the appointment of a common agent to represent the interests of all the lessors.

(3) A provision for the payment of a compensatory royalty in lieu of rental and in lieu of drilling and producing operations on the land covered by the lease.

(4) A provision empowering the lessee to enter into any agreement authorized by Section 3301 of the Public Resources Code with respect to the land covered by the lease.

(5) A provision for a community oil lease or a pooling or unitization by the lessee.

(c) If the lease covers additional property owned by other persons or an undivided or other interest of the decedent less than the entire ownership in the property, the order may authorize the lease to provide for division of rental and royalty in the proportion that the land or interest of each owner bears to the total area of the land or total interests covered by the lease. *(Stats.1990, c. 79 (A.B.759), § 14, operative July 1, 1991.)*

Law Revision Commission Comments

1990 Enactment

Section 9946 continues Section 9946 of the repealed Probate Code without change. As to the maximum term of the lease, see Section 9947. For comparable provisions, see Section 2554(a)–(c) (Guardianship–Conservatorship Law). As to orders made, or actions taken, before July 1, 1988, and matters pending on July 1, 1988, see Section 9645. As to the application of any amendments made after that date, see Section 3. As to independent administration authority, see Section 10536.

Background on Section 9946 of Repealed Code

Section 9946 was added by 1987 Cal.Stat. ch. 923 § 93. The section restated a portion of the second and all of the third and fourth sentences of former Probate Code Section 842 (repealed by 1987 Cal.Stat. ch. 923 § 41) without substantive change. The reference in subdivision (b) to geothermal energy and to a community oil lease was new. For background on the provisions of this part, see the Comment to this part under the part heading. [20 Cal.L.Rev.Comm.Reports 1001 (1990)].

Creation of interest in real property by operation of law, see Code of Civil Procedure §§ 1971, 1972.

Leases by guardian, see Probate Code § 2554.

Mine and mineral, definition of, see Public Resources Code § 2200.

Oil, gas, and mineral leases, generally, see Public Resources Code § 6801 et seq.

Orders, entry and filing, see Probate Code § 1048.

Recitals of jurisdictional facts in orders, see Probate Code § 1047.

Recordation of leases, see Civil Code § 1214.

Recordations of orders, see Probate Code § 7263.

§ 9947. Period of lease

(a) Except as provided in this section, the term of the lease shall be for such period as the court may authorize.

(b) Except as provided in subdivision (c), the court shall not authorize a lease for longer than 10 years if any heir or devisee who has an interest in the property to be leased objects at the hearing.

(c) If the lease is for the purpose of exploration for or production or removal of minerals, oil, gas, or other hydrocarbon substances, or geothermal energy, the court may authorize that the lease be for a fixed period and any of the following:

(1) So long thereafter as minerals, oil, gas, or other hydrocarbon substances or geothermal energy are produced in paying quantities from the property leased or mining or drilling operations are conducted thereon.

(2) If the lease provides for the payment of a compensatory royalty, so long thereafter as such compensatory royalty is paid.

(3) If the land covered by the lease is included in an agreement authorized by Section 3301 of the Public Resources Code, so long thereafter as oil, gas, or other hydrocarbon substances are produced in paying quantities from any of the lands included in any such agreement or drilling operations are conducted thereon. *(Stats.1990, c. 79 (A.B.759), § 14, operative July 1, 1991.)*

Law Revision Commission Comments

1990 Enactment

Section 9947 continues Section 9947 of the repealed Probate Code without substantive change. Subdivision (c) of Section 9947 is comparable to subdivision (d) of Section 2554 (Guardianship–Conservatorship Law). As to orders made, or actions taken, before July 1, 1988, and matters pending on July 1, 1988, see Section 9645. As to the application of any amendments made after that date, see Section 3. As to independent administration authority, see Section 10536.

Background on Section 9947 of Repealed Code

Section 9947 was added by 1987 Cal.Stat. ch. 923 § 93. Subdivisions (a) and (b) restated without substantive change the portion of the second sentence of former Probate Code Section 842 that concerned the period of the lease and the third sentence of former Probate Code Section 842.1 (provisions repealed by 1987 Cal.Stat. ch. 923 § 41). Subdivision (c) restated the fifth sentence of former Section 842 (repealed by 1987 Cal.Stat. ch. 923 § 41) without substantive change. The reference to geothermal energy was new.

For background on the provisions of this part, see the Comment to this part under the part heading. [20 Cal.L.Rev.Comm.Reports 1001 (1990)].

Duration of leases, limits, see Civil Code §§ 717, 718.

§ 9948. Execution of lease; effect; jurisdiction; omissions or errors in proceedings

(a) The personal representative shall execute, acknowledge, and deliver the lease as directed, setting forth therein that it is made by authority of the order, giving the date of the order.

(b) A lease made pursuant to an order obtained under this chapter is effectual to lease the premises described in the order at the rent, for the term, and upon the terms and conditions prescribed in the order.

(c) Jurisdiction of the court in proceedings under this code concerning the administration of the estate of the decedent vests the court with jurisdiction to make the order for the lease. This jurisdiction shall conclusively inure to the benefit of the lessee and the lessee's heirs and assigns.

(d) No omission, error, or irregularity in the proceedings under this chapter shall impair or invalidate the proceedings or the lease made pursuant to an order made under this chapter. *(Stats.1990, c. 79 (A.B.759), § 14, operative July 1, 1991.)*

Law Revision Commission Comments

1990 Enactment

Section 9948 continues Section 9948 of the repealed Probate Code without substantive change. A certified copy of the order must be recorded. See Section 7263. See generally Sections 7260–7263 (orders and transactions affecting property).

If the court lacks jurisdiction, subdivision (d) does not cure the defect. See Texas Co. v. Bank of America Nat'l Trust & Sav. Ass'n, 5 Cal.2d 35, 41–44, 53 P.2d 127 (1935). Subdivision (d) does not limit the court's authority to set aside an order made through mistake, inadvertence, surprise, or excusable neglect. See Code Civ.Proc. § 473; Estate of Lee, 159 Cal.App.2d 109, 111–12, 323 P.2d 448 (1958); Estate of Herz, 147 Cal.App.2d 100, 106–07, 305 P.2d 278 (1956); Estate of McCrae, 133 Cal.App.2d 634, 637–39, 284 P.2d 914 (1955); Estate of Moreland, 49 Cal.App.2d 484, 487–88, 121 P.2d 867 (1942). For provisions comparable to subdivision (d), see Sections 9923 (exchanges), 9966 (option to purchase real property), 9983 (option to purchase given in will), 10264 (sale of personal property), 10316 (sale of real property). For a comparable provision of the Guardianship–Conservatorship Law, see Section 2553(d).

Section 9948 does not deal with the rights of the lessee and a subsequent lessee or purchaser of the property except to the extent that the section protects the lessee from a claim by a third party that there was an omission, error, or irregularity in the proceedings under this chapter. Section 9948 is limited to defining the relationship between the personal representative and the beneficiaries and creditors of the estate, the relationship between the personal representative and the lessee, and the relationship between the personal representative and the court from which the authority of the personal representative is derived.

As to orders made, or actions taken, before July 1, 1988, and matters pending on July 1, 1988, see Section 9645. As to the application of any amendments made after that date, see Section 3.

Background on Section 9948 of Repealed Code

Section 9948 was added by 1987 Cal.Stat. ch. 923 § 93. Subdivisions (a), (b), and (c) restated the first, second, and third sentences of former Probate Code Section 843 (repealed by 1987 Cal.Stat. ch. 923 § 41) without substantive change. Subdivision (d) restated the last sentence of former Section 843 without substantive change. For background on the provisions of this part, see the Comment to this part under the part heading. [20 Cal.L.Rev.Comm.Reports 1001 (1990)].

CHAPTER 16. GRANTING OPTION TO PURCHASE REAL PROPERTY

Cross References

Application of old and new law, see Probate Code § 3.

§ 9960. Power of personal representative

After authorization by order of court obtained under this chapter, the personal representative may grant an option to purchase real property of the estate for a period within or beyond the period of administration. *(Stats.1990, c. 79 (A.B.759), § 14, operative July 1, 1991.)*

Law Revision Commission Comments

1990 Enactment

Section 9960 continues Section 9960 of the repealed Probate Code without change. The personal representative is required to exercise the power granted by this section (by filing a petition with the court) to the extent that ordinary care and diligence require that the power be exercised. See Section 9600(b). As to the effect of court authorization or approval, see Section 7250. A certified copy of the order must be recorded. Section 7263. See generally Sections 7260–7263 (orders and transactions affecting property). As to orders made, or actions taken, before July 1, 1988, and matters pending on July 1, 1988, see Section 9645. As to the application of any amendments made after that date, see Section 3. As to independent administration authority, see Section 10515.

Background on Section 9960 of Repealed Code

Section 9960 was added by 1987 Cal.Stat. ch. 923 § 93. The section restated the first sentence of former Probate Code Section 584.3 (repealed by 1987 Cal.Stat. ch. 923 § 35) without substantive change. For background on the provisions of this part, see the Comment to this part under the part heading. [20 Cal.L.Rev.Comm.Reports 1001 (1990)].

§ 9961. Petitions

To obtain an order under this chapter, the personal representative shall file a petition containing all of the following:

(a) A description of the real property.

(b) The terms and conditions of the proposed option.

(c) A showing that granting the option is to the advantage of the estate. *(Stats.1990, c. 79 (A.B.759), § 14, operative July 1, 1991.)*

Law Revision Commission Comments

1990 Enactment

Section 9961 continues Section 9961 of the repealed Probate Code without substantive change. Only the personal representative may file a petition under this section. An interested person may neither petition under this section nor petition for instructions under Section 9611. But see Section 9613 (right of interested person to petition for order directing personal representative in order to avoid great or irreparable injury). For general provisions relating to petitions, see Sections 1020–1023. As to orders made, or actions taken, before July 1, 1988, and matters pending on July 1, 1988, see Section 9645. As to the application of any amendments made after that date, see Section 3.

Background on Section 9961 of Repealed Code

Section 9961 was added by 1987 Cal.Stat. ch. 923 § 93. The section restated subdivision (a) of former Probate Code Section 584.3 (repealed by 1987 Cal.Stat. ch. 923 § 35) without substantive change. For background on the provisions of this part, see the Comment to this part under the part heading. [20 Cal.L.Rev.Comm.Reports 1001 (1990)].

§ 9962. Purchase price; appraisals

The purchase price of the real property subject to the option shall be at least 90 percent of the appraised value of the real property. The appraisal shall be made in the manner provided in subdivision (c) of Section 10309 within one year prior to the hearing of the petition. *(Stats.1990, c. 79 (A.B.759), § 14, operative July 1, 1991.)*

Law Revision Commission Comments

1990 Enactment

Section 9962 continues Section 9962 of the repealed Probate Code, with a revision incorporating the appraisal procedure of Section 10309(c). Under that provision, if a new appraisal is needed, the new appraisal need not be made by a probate referee if the original appraisal of the property was made by a person other than a probate referee. If the original appraisal of the property was made by a probate referee, the new appraisal may be made by the probate referee who made the original appraisal without further order of the court or further request for the appointment of a new probate referee. If appraisal by a probate referee is required, a new probate referee must be appointed, using the same procedure as for the appointment of an original referee, to make the new appraisal if the original probate referee is dead, has been removed, or is otherwise unable to act, or if there is other reason to appoint another probate referee. The requirement that the appraisal be made within one year prior to the hearing of the petition is consistent with the requirement of Section 10309(a)(1) (minimum price for private sale of real property). The requirement that the purchase price be at least 90 percent of appraised value is consistent with the general provision prescribing the minimum price for private sales of real property. See Section 10309. As to orders made, or actions taken, before July 1, 1988, and matters pending on July 1, 1988, see Section 9645. As to the application of any amendments made after that date, see Section 3.

Background on Section 9962 of Repealed Code

Section 9962 was added by 1987 Cal.Stat. ch. 923 § 93. The section restated subdivision (b) of former Probate Code Section 584.3 (repealed by 1987 Cal.Stat. ch. 923 § 35) without substantive change except that a requirement that the appraisal be made within one year prior to the hearing of the petition was substituted for the former requirement that the appraisal be made within 90 days prior to the filing of the petition. This substitution made Section 9962 consistent with the requirement of Section 10309(a)(1) (minimum price for private sale of real property). For background on the provisions of this part, see the Comment to this part under the part heading. [20 Cal.L.Rev.Comm.Reports 1001 (1990)].

§ 9963. Notice of hearing

Notice of the hearing on the petition shall be posted as provided in Section 1230 and given as provided in Section 1220 to all of the following persons:

(a) Each person listed in Section 1220.

(b) Each known heir whose interest in the estate would be affected by the granting of the option.

(c) Each known devisee whose interest in the estate would be affected by the granting of the option. *(Stats.1990, c. 79 (A.B.759), § 14, operative July 1, 1991.)*

Law Revision Commission Comments

1990 Enactment

Section 9963 continues Section 9963 of the repealed Probate Code without substantive change. For general provisions relating to notice, see Sections 1200–1230 (notice of hearing), 1250–1252 (request for special notice), 1260–1265 (proof of giving of notice). As to orders made, or actions taken, before July 1, 1988, and matters pending on July 1, 1988, see Section 9645. As to the application of any amendments made after that date, see Section 3.

Background on Section 9963 of Repealed Code

Section 9963 was added by 1987 Cal.Stat. ch. 923 § 93. The section restated subdivision (c) of former Probate Code Section 584.3 (repealed by 1987 Cal.Stat. ch. 923 § 35) without substantive change, except that:

(1) Section 9963 required notice by mail (Section 1220) in addition to the notice by posting (Section 1230) which was required by former Section 584.3.

(2) Section 9963 required notice to be mailed at least 15 days before the hearing as provided in Section 1220 instead of at least 10 days before the hearing as required under subdivision (c) of former Section 584.3.

(3) Section 9963 limited the giving of notice to known heirs and known devisees to those "whose interest in the estate would be affected by the granting of the option."

For background on the provisions of this part, see the Comment to this part under the part heading. [20 Cal.L.Rev.Comm.Reports 1001 (1990)].

§ 9964. Orders authorizing grant of option; higher bids

(a) The court shall make an order authorizing the personal representative to grant the option upon the terms and conditions stated in the order if the court is satisfied as to all of the following:

(1) Good reason exists to grant the option and granting the option will be to the advantage of the estate.

(2) It does not appear that a higher offer with respect to the purchase price of the real property subject to the option may be obtained. An offer is a higher offer with respect to purchase price only if the offer satisfies the requirements of Section 10311 governing increased bids in real property sales.

(3) It does not appear that a better offer with respect to the terms of the option may be obtained. An offer is a better offer with respect to the terms of the option only if the offer is materially more advantageous to the estate.

(b) A higher offer made either for cash or on credit, whether on the same or different credit terms, or a better

offer, shall be considered only if the personal representative informs the court in person or by counsel, before the court makes its order authorizing the granting of the option, that the offer is acceptable. *(Stats.1990, c. 79 (A.B.759), § 14, operative July 1, 1991.)*

Law Revision Commission Comments

1990 Enactment

Section 9964 continues Section 9964 of the repealed Probate Code without change. For general provisions relating to hearings and orders, see Section 1040–1050. As to orders made, or actions taken, before July 1, 1988, and matters pending on July 1, 1988, see Section 9645. As to the application of any amendments made after that date, see Section 3.

Background on Section 9964 of Repealed Code

Section 9964 was added by 1987 Cal.Stat. ch. 923 § 93. The section restated the second, third, and fourth sentences of subdivision (d) of former Probate Code Section 584.3 (repealed by 1987 Cal.Stat. ch. 923 § 35) without substantive change. For background on the provisions of this part, see the Comment to this part under the part heading. [20 Cal.L.Rev.Comm.Reports 1001 (1990)].

§ 9965. Options subject to provisions of Civil Code

An option granted pursuant to an order made under this chapter, whether within or beyond the administration of the estate, is subject to Chapter 4 (commencing with Section 884.010) of Title 5 of Part 2 of Division 2 of the Civil Code. *(Stats.1990, c. 79 (A.B.759), § 14, operative July 1, 1991.)*

Law Revision Commission Comments

1990 Enactment

Section 9965 continues Section 9965 of the repealed Probate Code without change. If an option granted pursuant to this chapter is recorded, the option expires of record unless a notice of exercise or an extension of the option is recorded within six months after the option expires according to its terms or, if the option has no expiration date, within six months after the option is recorded. Civil Code § 884.010. As to orders made, or actions taken, before July 1, 1988, and matters pending on July 1, 1988, see Section 9645. As to the application of any amendments made after that date, see Section 3.

Background on Section 9965 of Repealed Code

Section 9965 was added by 1987 Cal.Stat. ch. 923 § 93. The section restated the second sentence of subdivision (e) of former Probate Code Section 584.3 (repealed by 1987 Cal.Stat. ch. 923 § 35) without substantive change. For background on the provisions of this part, see the Comment to this part under the part heading. [20 Cal.L.Rev.Comm.Reports 1001 (1990)].

§ 9966. Omissions or errors in proceedings

No omission, error, or irregularity in the proceedings under this chapter shall impair or invalidate the proceedings or the granting of an option pursuant to an order made under this chapter. *(Stats.1990, c. 79 (A.B.759), § 14, operative July 1, 1991.)*

Law Revision Commission Comments

1990 Enactment

Section 9966 continues Section 9966 of the repealed Probate Code without change. This section is comparable to Sections 9923 (exchanges), 9948(d) (leases), 9983 (option to purchase given in will), 10264 (sale of personal property), and 10316 (sale of real property).

If the court lacks jurisdiction, Section 9966 does not cure the defect. See Texas Co. v. Bank of America Nat'l Trust & Sav. Ass'n, 5 Cal.2d 35, 41–44, 53 P.2d 127 (1935). Section 9966 does not limit the court's authority to set aside an order made through mistake, inadvertence, surprise, or excusable neglect. See Code Civ.Proc. § 473; Estate of Lee, 159 Cal.App.2d 109, 111–12, 323 P.2d 448 (1958); Estate of Herz, 147 Cal.App.2d 100, 106–07, 305 P.2d 278 (1956); Estate of McCrae, 133 Cal.App.2d 634, 637–39, 284 P.2d 914 (1955); Estate of Moreland, 49 Cal.App.2d 484, 487–88, 121 P.2d 867 (1942).

As to orders made, or actions taken, before July 1, 1988, and matters pending on July 1, 1988, see Section 9645. As to the application of any amendments made after that date, see Section 3.

Background on Section 9966 of Repealed Code

Section 9966 is a new provision added by 1987 Cal.Stat. ch. 923 § 93. For background on the provisions of this part, see the Comment to this part under the part heading. [20 Cal.L.Rev.Comm.Reports 1001 (1990)].

CHAPTER 17. OPTION TO PURCHASE GIVEN IN WILL

Section

Cross References

Application of old and new law, see Probate Code § 3.

§ 9980. Exercise of option; time limitation; distribution subject to option

(a) Where an option to purchase real or personal property is given in a will, the person given the option has the right to exercise the option at any time within the time limits provided by the will. For the purposes of this section, if a time limitation in the will is measured from the death of the testator, that time shall be extended by the period between the testator's death and the issuance of letters testamentary or of administration with the will annexed or by six months, whichever is the shorter period.

(b) If the will does not provide a time limit for exercise of the option, the time limit is one year from the death of the decedent.

(c) Subject to subdivision (b), if the option given in the will is exercisable under the terms of the will after the time that the estate would otherwise be closed, the property subject to the option shall be distributed subject to the option. *(Stats. 1990, c. 79 (A.B.759), § 14, operative July 1, 1991.)*

Law Revision Commission Comments

1990 Enactment

Section 9980 continues Section 9980 of the repealed Probate Code without change. As to orders made, or actions taken, before July 1, 1988, and matters pending on July 1, 1988, see Section 9645. As to the application of any amendments made after that date, see Section 3.

Background on Section 9980 of Repealed Code

Section 9980 was added by 1987 Cal.Stat. ch. 923 § 93. Subdivision (a) restated subdivision (a) of former Probate Code Section 854 (repealed by 1987 Cal.Stat. ch. 923 § 41) without substantive change. Subdivision (b) restated subdivision (d) of former Section 854 without change. Subdivision (c) restated subdivision (c) of former Section 854 without substantive change. For background on the provisions of this part, see the Comment to this part under the part heading. [20 Cal.L.Rev.Comm.Reports 1001 (1990)].

§ 9981. Orders to transfer or convey property; petitions; notice of hearing

(a) Where an option to purchase real or personal property is given in a will admitted to probate, the court may make an order under this chapter directing the personal representative to transfer or convey the property to the person given the option upon compliance with the terms and conditions stated in the will.

(b) The personal representative or the person given the option to purchase the property may file a petition for an order pursuant to this chapter.

(c) Notice of the hearing on the petition shall be given as provided in Section 1220. *(Stats.1990, c. 79 (A.B.759), § 14, operative July 1, 1991.)*

Law Revision Commission Comments

1990 Enactment

Section 9981 continues Section 9981 of the repealed Probate Code without change. For general provisions, see Sections 1000–1004 (rules of practice), 1020–1023 (petitions and other papers), 1040–1050 (hearings and orders), 1200–1230 (notice of hearing), 1250–1252 (request for special notice), 1260–1265 (proof of giving of notice). As to orders made, or actions taken, before July 1, 1988, and matters pending on July 1, 1988, see Section 9645. As to the application of any amendments made after that date, see Section 3. As to independent administration authority, see Section 10516.

Background on Section 9981 of Repealed Code

Section 9981 was added by 1987 Cal.Stat. ch. 923 § 93. Subdivisions (a) and (b) restated the first sentence of subdivision (b) of former Probate Code Section 854 (repealed by 1987 Cal.Stat. ch. 923 § 41) without substantive change. The requirement of former Section 854 that the petition be filed "within any time limits provided in the will" was omitted as unnecessary in view of the requirement of subdivision (a) of Section 9981 that the person given the option must comply with the terms and conditions stated in the will. Subdivision (c) continued the third sentence of subdivision (b) of former Section 854 (repealed by 1987 Cal.Stat. ch. 923 § 41) without substantive change, except that Section 9981 required that notice be given at least 15 days before the hearing pursuant to Section 1220 instead of at least 10 days before the hearing as required by former Probate Code Section 1200.5 (repealed by 1987 Cal.Stat. ch. 923 § 59). For background on the provisions of this part, see the Comment to this part under the part heading. [20 Cal.L.Rev.Comm.Reports 1001 (1990)].

§ 9982. Orders; requirements

The court shall not make an order under this chapter unless one of the following requirements is satisfied:

(a) The court determines that the rights of creditors will not be impaired by the making of the order.

(b) The court requires a bond in an amount and with such surety as the court shall direct or approve. *(Stats.1990, c. 79 (A.B.759), § 14, operative July 1, 1991.)*

Law Revision Commission Comments

1990 Enactment

Section 9982 continues Section 9982 of the repealed Probate Code without change. As to orders made, or actions taken, before July 1, 1988, and matters pending on July 1, 1988, see Section 9645. As to the application of any amendments made after that date, see Section 3.

Background on Section 9982 of Repealed Code

Section 9982 was added by 1987 Cal.Stat. ch. 923 § 93. The section restated the fourth sentence of subdivision (b) of former Probate Code Section 854 (repealed by 1987 Cal.Stat. ch. 923 § 41) without substantive change. For background on the provisions of this part, see the Comment to this part under the part heading. [20 Cal.L.Rev.Comm.Reports 1001 (1990)].

§ 9983. Omissions or errors in proceedings

No omission, error, or irregularity in the proceedings under this chapter shall impair or invalidate the proceedings or the transfer or conveyance made pursuant to an order made under this chapter. *(Stats.1990, c. 79 (A.B.759), § 14, operative July 1, 1991.)*

Law Revision Commission Comments

1990 Enactment

Section 9983 continues Section 9983 of the repealed Probate Code without change. This section is comparable to Sections 9923 (exchanges), 9948(d) (leases), 9966 (option to purchase real property), 10264 (sale of personal property), and 10316 (sale of real property).

If the court lacks jurisdiction, Section 9983 does not cure the defect. See Texas Co. v. Bank of America Nat'l Trust & Sav. Ass'n, 5 Cal.2d 35, 41–44, 53 P.2d 127 (1935). Section 9983 does not limit the court's authority to set aside an order made through mistake, inadvertence, surprise, or excusable neglect. See Code Civ.Proc. § 473; Estate of Lee, 159 Cal.App.2d 109, 111–12, 323 P.2d 448 (1958); Estate of Herz, 147 Cal.App.2d 100, 106–07, 305 P.2d 278 (1956); Estate of McCrae, 133 Cal.App.2d 634, 637–39, 284 P.2d 914 (1955); Estate of Moreland, 49 Cal.App.2d 484, 487–88, 121 P.2d 867 (1942). As to orders made, or actions taken, before July 1, 1988, and matters pending on July 1, 1988, see Section 9645. As to the application of any amendments made after that date, see Section 3.

Background on Section 9983 of Repealed Code

Section 9983 was a new provision added by 1987 Cal.Stat. ch. 923 § 93. For background on the provisions of this part, see the Comment to this part under the part heading. [20 Cal.L.Rev.Comm.Reports 1001 (1990)].

CHAPTER 18. SALES

ARTICLE 1. GENERAL PROVISIONS

Cross References

Application of old and new law, see Probate Code § 3.

§ 10000. Powers of personal representative

Subject to the limitations, conditions, and requirements of this chapter, the personal representative may sell real or personal property of the estate in any of the following cases:

(a) Where the sale is necessary to pay debts, devises, family allowance, expenses of administration, or taxes.

(b) Where the sale is to the advantage of the estate and in the best interest of the interested persons.

(c) Where the property is directed by the will to be sold.

(d) Where authority is given in the will to sell the property. *(Stats.1990, c. 79 (A.B.759), § 14, operative July 1, 1991.)*

Law Revision Commission Comments

1990 Enactment

Section 10000 continues Section 10000 of the repealed Probate Code without change. The personal representative is required to exercise the power granted by this section to the extent that ordinary care and diligence require that the power be exercised and may not exercise the power to the extent that ordinary care and diligence require that the power not be exercised. See Section 9600(b). As to the effect of court authorization or approval, see Section 7250. See also Sections 7260–7263 (orders and transactions affecting property). As to orders made, or actions taken, before July 1, 1988, and matters pending on July 1, 1988, see Section 9645. As to the application of any amendments made after that date, see Section 3.

Background on Section 10000 of Repealed Code

Section 10000 was added by 1987 Cal.Stat. ch. 923 § 93. Subdivisions (a) and (b) restated a portion of the second sentence of former Probate Code Section 754 (repealed by 1987 Cal.Stat. ch. 923 § 39) without substantive change. The reference to "taxes" was added to subdivision (a) of Section 10000, consistent with the likely construction of former Section 754. The phrase "to the advantage of the estate and in the best interest of the interested persons" was substituted in subdivision (b) of Section 10000 for the phrase "for the advantage, benefit, and best interests of the estate and those interested therein" which was used in former Section 754. This substitution made no substantive change in the provision. Subdivisions (c) and (d) restated portions of the first sentence of former Probate Code Section 757 (repealed by 1987 Cal.Stat. ch. 923 § 39) without substantive change. For background on the provisions of this part, see the Comment to this part under the part heading. [20 Cal.L.Rev.Comm.Reports 1001 (1990)].

Cross References

Borrowing, refinancing, and encumbering property, see Probate Code § 9800 et seq.

Direction for conversion of real estate, effect of, see Probate Code § 21107.

Family allowance, see Probate Code § 6540 et seq.
Personal property, sales, see Probate Code § 10250 et seq.
Real property, sale,
   Generally, see Probate Code § 10300 et seq.
   Sales to be reported to and confirmed by court, see Probate Code
    § 10308.

§ 10001. Orders requiring sale of property; petitions; notice of hearing

(a) If the personal representative neglects or refuses to sell the property, any interested person may petition the court for an order requiring the personal representative to sell real or personal property of the estate in any of the following cases:

(1) Where the sale is necessary to pay debts, devises, family allowance, expenses of administration, or taxes.

(2) Where the sale is to the advantage of the estate and in the best interest of the interested persons.

(3) Where the property is directed by the will to be sold.

(b) Notice of the hearing on the petition shall be given as provided in Section 1220.

(c) Notice of the hearing on the petition also shall be given to the personal representative by citation served at least five days before the hearing. *(Stats.1990, c. 79 (A.B.759), § 14, operative July 1, 1991.)*

Law Revision Commission Comments

1990 Enactment

Section 10001 continues Section 10001 of the repealed Probate Code without change. See also Sections 7260–7263 (orders and transactions affecting property). For general provisions, see Sections 1000–1004 (rules of practice), 1020–1023 (petitions and other papers), 1040–1050 (hearings and orders), 1200–1230 (notice of hearing), 1240–1242 (citations), 1250–1252 (request for special notice), 1260–1265 (proof of giving of notice). As to orders made, or actions taken, before July 1, 1988, and matters pending on July 1, 1988, see Section 9645. As to the application of any amendments made after that date, see Section 3.

Background on Section 10001 of Repealed Code

Section 10001 was added by 1987 Cal.Stat. ch. 923 § 93. The section restated former Probate Code Section 758 (repealed by 1987 Cal.Stat. ch. 923 § 39) without substantive change, except for the addition of subdivision (b) which was new. The reference to "taxes" was added to subdivision (a)(1), consistent with the addition of "taxes" to subdivision (a) of Section 10000. The phrase "to the advantage of the estate and in the best interest of the interested persons" was substituted in subdivision (a)(2) of Section 10001 for the phrase "for the advantage, benefit and best interests of the estate and those interested therein" which was used in former Section 758. This substitution made no substantive change and made subdivision (a)(2) of Section 10001 consistent with subdivision (b) of Section 10000. For background on the provisions of this part, see the Comment to this part under the part heading. [20 Cal.L.Rev.Comm.Reports 1001 (1990)].

Cross References

Notice generally, see Probate Code § 1200.

§ 10002. Will directions as to mode of sale; orders relieving duty of compliance; petition; notice

(a) Subject to subdivision (b), if directions are given in the will as to the mode of selling or the particular property to be sold, the personal representative shall comply with those directions.

(b) If the court determines that it would be to the advantage of the estate and in the best interest of the interested persons, the court may make an order relieving the personal representative of the duty to comply with the directions in the will. The order shall specify the mode and the terms and conditions of selling or the particular property to be sold, or both. The personal representative or any interested person may file a petition for an order under this subdivision. Notice of the hearing on the petition shall be given as provided in Section 1220. *(Stats.1990, c. 79 (A.B. 759), § 14, operative July 1, 1991.)*

Law Revision Commission Comments

1990 Enactment

Section 10002 continues Section 10002 of the repealed Probate Code without change. Subdivision (b) permits the court to dispense in whole or in part with the directions given in the will where good cause is shown why the personal representative should not be required to comply with the directions. The court may make an order under subdivision (b), for example, where the property directed to be sold to pay the decedent's debts has greatly increased in value since the will was executed and there is sufficient cash in the estate to pay the debts and paying the debts with the cash would not adversely affect any of the interested persons. Or the court may determine that the mode of selling directed in the will is not appropriate under the circumstances existing at the time the property is to be sold. For general provisions, see Sections 1000–1004 (rules of practice), 1020–1023 (petitions and other papers), 1040–1050 (hearings and orders), 1200–1230 (notice of hearing), 1250–1252 (request for special notice), 1260–1265 (proof of giving of notice). See also Sections 7260–7263 (orders and transactions affecting property). As to orders made, or actions taken, before July 1, 1988, and matters pending on July 1, 1988, see Section 9645. As to the application of any amendments made after that date, see Section 3.

Background on Section 10002 of Repealed Code

Section 10002 was added by 1987 Cal.Stat. ch. 923 § 93. Subdivision (a) restated the last sentence of former Probate Code Section 757 (repealed by 1987 Cal.Stat. ch. 923 § 39) without substantive change. Subdivision (b) was new. For background on the provisions of this part, see the Comment to this part under the part heading. [20 Cal.L.Rev.Comm.Reports 1001 (1990)].

Cross References

Sales of real property of an estate, requirements for sales to be reported to and confirmed by court, see Probate Code § 10308.

§ 10003. Mode of sale

Subject to Part 4 (commencing with Section 21400) of Division 11 and to Sections 10001 and 10002, if estate property is required or permitted to be sold, the personal representative may:

(a) Use discretion as to which property to sell first.

(b) Sell the entire interest of the estate in the property or any lesser interest therein.

(c) Sell the property either at public auction or private sale. *(Stats.1990, c. 79 (A.B.759), § 14, operative July 1, 1991.)*

Law Revision Commission Comments

1990 Enactment

Section 10003 continues Section 10003 of the repealed Probate Code without change. Under subdivision (a) there is no priority between personal and real property in selling property, whatever the reason that causes the property to be sold. For the rules of abatement, see Sections 21400–21406. As to orders made, or actions taken, before July 1, 1988, and matters pending on July 1, 1988, see Section 9645. As to the application of any amendments made after that date, see Section 3.

Background on Section 10003 of Repealed Code

Section 10003 was added by 1987 Cal.Stat. ch. 923 § 93 and was amended by 1988 Cal.Stat. ch. 1199 § 89. Subdivision (a) restated the first sentence and a portion of the second sentence of former Probate Code Section 754 (repealed by 1987 Cal.Stat. ch. 923 § 39) without substantive change except that the former provision provided that there was no priority between personal and real property in selling property "to pay debts, legacies, family allowance or expenses." Under subdivision (a) of Section 10003 there was no priority between personal and real property in selling property, whatever the reason that causes the property to be sold. Subdivision (b) restated the third sentence of former Section 754 (repealed by 1987 Cal.Stat. ch. 923 § 39) without substantive change. Subdivision (c) restated a portion of the second sentence of former Section 754 and a portion of the first sentence of former Probate Code Section 757 (provisions repealed by 1987 Cal.Stat. ch. 923 § 39) without substantive change. The 1988 amendment corrected a section reference. For background on the provisions of this part, see the Comment to this part under the part heading. [20 Cal.L.Rev.Comm.Reports 1001 (1990)].

Cross References

Sales of real property of an estate, requirements for sales to be reported to and confirmed by court, see Probate Code § 10308.

§ 10004. Assets as a unit; appraisal; sale

(a) Where the personal representative determines in his or her discretion that, by use or relationship, any assets of the estate, whether real or personal, constitute a unit for purposes of sale, the personal representative may cause the property to be appraised as a unit.

(b) Whether or not the property is appraised as a unit, the personal representative may sell all the assets described in subdivision (a) as a unit and under one bid if the court finds the sale of the assets as a unit to be to the advantage of the estate.

(c) No private sale of the assets as a unit may be made for less than 90 percent of the sum of the appraised values of the personal property and the sum of the appraised values of the real property, appraised separately, or for less than 90 percent of the appraised value if appraised as a unit.

(d) If the assets to be sold as a unit include any real property, the sale shall be made in the manner provided for the sale of real property, and the bid and sale are subject to the limitations and restrictions established for the sale of real property. If the assets to be sold as a unit are entirely personal property, the property shall be sold in the manner provided for the sale of personal property. *(Stats.1990, c. 79 (A.B.759), § 14, operative July 1, 1991.)*

Law Revision Commission Comments

1990 Enactment

Section 10004 continues Section 10004 of the repealed Probate Code without substantive change. The personal representative is required to exercise the power granted by this section (by filing a petition with the court) to the extent that ordinary care and diligence require that the power be exercised. See Section 9600(b). As to the effect of court authorization or approval, see Section 7250. As to orders made, or actions taken, before July 1, 1988, and matters pending on July 1, 1988, see Section 9645. As to the application of any amendments made after that date, see Section 3.

Background on Section 10004 of Repealed Code

Section 10004 was added by 1987 Cal.Stat. ch. 923 § 93. The section restated former Probate Code Section 754.5 (repealed by 1987 Cal.Stat. ch. 923 § 39) without substantive change. For background on the provisions of this part, see the Comment to this part under the part heading. [20 Cal.L.Rev.Comm.Reports 1001 (1990)].

Cross References

Appraisement generally, see Probate Code § 8800 et seq.
Real property, sale generally, see Probate Code § 10300 et seq.

§ 10005. Proceeds of sale

(a) If any property in the estate is sold for more than the appraised value, the personal representative shall account for the proceeds of sale, including the excess over the appraised value.

(b) If any property in the estate is sold for less than the appraised value and the sale has been made in accordance with law, the personal representative is not responsible for the loss. *(Stats.1990, c. 79 (A.B.759), § 14, operative July 1, 1991.)*

Law Revision Commission Comments

1990 Enactment

Section 10005 continues Section 10005 of the repealed Probate Code without change. See also Sections 9657 (personal representative may not profit from increase, nor suffer loss from decrease or destruction without fault), 10900 (contents of account), 10950–10954 (duty to account). As to orders made, or actions taken, before July 1, 1988, and matters pending on July 1, 1988, see Section 9645. As to the application of any amendments made after that date, see Section 3.

Background on Section 10005 of Repealed Code

Section 10005 was added by 1987 Cal.Stat. ch. 923 § 93 and was amended by 1988 Cal.Stat. ch. 1199 § 89.5. The section restated a provision formerly found in the last sentence of former Probate Code Section 920 (prior to its amendment by 1987 Cal.Stat. ch. 923 § 44) without substantive change. The language in subdivision (a) requiring the personal representative to account for the "proceeds of sale" was new, but was consistent with case law. See In re Estate of Radovich, 74 Cal. 536, 538–40, 16 P. 321 (1888).

The language in subdivision (b) that the personal representative is not responsible for a loss where a sale is made "in accordance with law" replaced the former reference to a sale which is "justly" made. The new language was consistent with case law. See In re Estate of Guglielmi, 138 Cal.App. 80, 86–88, 31 P.2d 1078 (1934).

The 1988 amendment conformed the terminology used in Section 10005 to the terminology used in other provisions enacted in 1988.

For background on the provisions of this part, see the Comment to this part under the part heading. [20 Cal.L.Rev.Comm.Reports 1001 (1990)].

§ 10006. Cotenancy

If property in the estate is to be sold as an undivided interest in a cotenancy, the other cotenants may file in the estate proceeding written consent to have their interests sold pursuant to this chapter. Thereafter, the court's orders made pursuant to this chapter are as binding on the consenting cotenants as on the personal representative. *(Stats.1990, c. 79 (A.B.759), § 14, operative July 1, 1991.)*

Law Revision Commission Comments

1990 Enactment

Section 10006 is new and is to facilitate estate sales of the decedent's interest in a joint tenancy or tenancy in common. Section 10006 is consistent with existing practice. See 1 California Decedent Estate Practice § 6.19 (Cal.Cont.Ed.Bar rev. ed. Feb. 1989) (probate court may by stipulation consider any matter in connection with and in aid of proceeding). [20 Cal.L.Rev.Comm.Reports 1001 (1990)].

ARTICLE 2. CONTRACT WITH AGENT, BROKER, OR AUCTIONEER

Section
10150. Contracts with agents or brokers; terms; liability of estate or personal representative.
10151. Contracts with auctioneers; terms; liability of estate or personal representative.

Cross References

Application of old and new law, see Probate Code § 3.

§ 10150. Contracts with agents or brokers; terms; liability of estate or personal representative

(a) The personal representative may enter into a written contract with either or both of the following:

(1) A licensed real estate broker to secure a purchaser for any real property of the estate. The broker may associate other licensed real estate brokers for this purpose, including use of a multiple listing service as defined in Section 1087 of the Civil Code.

(2) One or more agents or brokers to secure a purchaser for any personal property of the estate. If the particular property to be sold or the particular manner of sale requires that the agent or broker be licensed, the contract may be made only with an agent or broker that is so licensed.

(b) The contract may provide for payment of a fee, commission, or other compensation out of the proceeds of sale, but the contract is binding and valid as against the estate only for such amount as the court allows pursuant to Article 3 (commencing with Section 10160). No liability of any kind is incurred by the estate under the contract or a sale unless the sale is confirmed by the court, except for the obligations of the estate to the purchaser of personal property as to which title passes pursuant to Section 10259 without court confirmation or approval. The personal representative is not personally liable on the contract by reason of execution of the contract.

(c) The contract may grant an exclusive right to sell property for a period not in excess of 90 days if, prior to execution of the contract granting an exclusive right to sell, the personal representative obtains permission of the court to enter into the contract upon a showing of necessity and advantage to the estate. The court may grant the permission when the personal representative is appointed or at any subsequent time upon ex parte application. The personal representative may execute one or more extensions of the contract granting an exclusive right to sell property, each extension being for a period not to exceed 90 days, if for each extension the personal representative obtains permission of the court upon ex parte application to extend the contract upon a showing of necessity and advantage to the estate of the extension. *(Stats.1990, c. 79 (A.B.759), § 14, operative July 1, 1991.)*

Law Revision Commission Comments

1990 Enactment

Section 10150 restates Section 10150 of the repealed Probate Code without substantive change. For various licensing provisions, see Bus. & Prof.Code §§ 5731 (auctioneer), 10000–10581 (real estate brokers); Fin.Code § 22200 (personal property brokers); Health & Safety Code §§ 18006, 18045 (sale of mobilehomes and manufactured housing). See also Section 10160 (no liability unless actual sale made, confirmed, and consummated).

Under subdivision (c), the contract granting the exclusive right to sell may be extended for any number of additional periods (each period not to exceed 90 days) if the personal representative obtains permission of the court for each extension. As to orders made, or actions taken, before July 1, 1988, and matters pending on July 1, 1988, see Section 9645. As to the application of any amendments made after that date, see Section 3. As to independent administration authority, see Section 10538.

Background on Section 10150 of Repealed Code

Section 10150 was added by 1987 Cal.Stat. ch. 923 § 93. Subdivision (a) restated a portion of the first sentence of former Probate Code Section 760 (repealed by 1987 Cal.Stat. ch. 923 § 39) except that:

(1) The reference in former Section 760 to a "bona fide agent or broker" was not continued. Instead (1) a reference to a "licensed real estate broker" was made in paragraph (1) of subdivision (a) and (2) the second sentence of paragraph (2) of subdivision (a) was added.

(2) The reference in former Section 760 to a "multiple group of agents or brokers" was replaced by the second sentence of paragraph (1) of subdivision (a).

The first sentence of subdivision (b) restated the last portion of the first sentence and the fourth sentence of former Section 760 (repealed by 1987 Cal.Stat. ch. 923 § 39) without substantive change. The second sentence of subdivision (b) restated the last portion of the last sentence of former Section 760 with the addition of the phrase "except for the obligations of the estate to the purchaser of personal property as to which title passes pursuant to Section 10259 without court confirmation or approval." This additional phrase was drawn from former Probate Code Section 760.5 (repealed by 1987 Cal.Stat. ch. 923 § 39), which was continued as Section 10151. The last sentence of subdivision (b) restated the first portion of the last sentence of former Section 760 without substantive change.

The first two sentences of subdivision (c) restated the second paragraph of former Section 760 (repealed by 1987 Cal.Stat. ch. 923 § 39) without substantive change. The last sentence of subdivision (c) was new.

For background on the provisions of this part, see the Comment to this part under the part heading. [20 Cal.L.Rev.Comm.Reports 1001 (1990)].

Cross References

Agency listings, application of statutes to contracts under this section, see Civil Code § 1089.5.

Sales of real property of an estate, requirements for sales to be reported to and confirmed by court, see Probate Code § 10308. Security sales through stock or bond exchange, see Probate Code § 10200.

§ 10151. Contracts with auctioneers; terms; liability of estate or personal representative

(a) The personal representative may enter into a written contract with any of the following:

(1) Where the public auction sale will be held in this state, an auctioneer who is qualified to conduct business under Title 2.95 (commencing with Section 1812.600) of Part 4 of Division 3 of the Civil Code.

(2) Where the public auction sale will be held outside this state pursuant to an order made under Section 10254, an auctioneer who is legally permitted in the jurisdiction where the sale will be held to conduct a public auction sale and to secure purchasers by that method for the personal property authorized to be sold by public auction sale in that jurisdiction under the court order.

(b) The contract shall be one that is legally enforceable under the law of the jurisdiction where made.

(c) The contract may provide for payment to the auctioneer of a fee, commission, or other compensation out of the proceeds of sale and for reimbursement of expenses, but the contract is binding and valid as against the estate only for such amounts as the court allows pursuant to Section 10167. No liability of any kind is incurred by the estate under the contract or a sale unless the sale is approved by the court, except for the obligations of the estate to the purchaser of personal property as to which title passes pursuant to Section 10259 without court confirmation or approval. The personal representative is not personally liable on the contract by reason of execution of the contract.

(d) The contract may provide that personal property of two or more estates being administered by the same personal representative may be sold at the same public auction sale. Items of personal property may be sold separately or in a lot with other items from the same estate. A sale pursuant to the contract shall be with reserve. The auctioneer shall comply with the instructions of the personal representative with respect to withdrawal of items, risk of loss, place of delivery, warranties, and other matters. *(Stats.1990, c. 79 (A.B.759), § 14, operative July 1, 1991. Amended by Stats. 2003, c. 32 (A.B.167), § 10.)*

Law Revision Commission Comments
1990 Enactment

Section 10151 restates Section 10151 of the repealed Probate Code without substantive change. See also Sections 10254 (sales at public auction), 10259 (unless court subsequently approves the sale, personal representative responsible for the value of property title to which passes without court confirmation or approval). As to orders made, or actions taken, before July 1, 1988, and matters pending on July 1, 1988, see Section 9645. As to the application of any amendments made after that date, see Section 3.

2003 Amendment

Section 10151 is amended to reflect repeal of the Auctioneer and Auction Licensing Act (Bus. & Prof. Code § 5700 *et seq.*) and its replacement by the Auctioneer and Auction Companies law (Civ.

Code § 1812.600 *et seq.*). See 1993 Cal. Stat. ch. 1170, §§ 1, 2. [33 Cal.L.Rev.Comm. Reports 161 (2003)].

Background on Section 10151 of Repealed Code

Section 10151 was added by 1987 Cal.Stat. ch. 923 § 93.

Subdivision (a) restated the first sentence of former Probate Code Section 760.5 (repealed by 1987 Cal.Stat. ch. 923 § 39) with the following changes:

(1) The reference in former Section 760.5 to a "bona fide" auctioneer "authorized to act as such in the locality" was replaced by the reference to an auctioneer licensed under the Auctioneer and Auction Licensing Act (Bus. & Prof.Code §§ 5700–5791.5). Where the sale is to be made in another jurisdiction, Section 10151 referred to a person permitted to sell the property by public auction sale in that jurisdiction.

(2) The provision of former Section 760.5 authorizing auction sale of "tangible" personal property was revised to authorize auction sale of all personal property an auctioneer may auction under the Auctioneer and Auction Licensing Act (see, e.g., Bus. & Prof.Code §§ 5701(j), 5774, 5775–5776).

Subdivision (b) was new. Subdivisions (c) and (d) restated the remainder of former Section 760.5 without substantive change. For background on the provisions of this part, see the Comment to this part heading. [20 Cal.L.Rev.Comm.Reports 1001 (1990)].

ARTICLE 3. COMPENSATION OF AGENT, BROKER, OR AUCTIONEER

Section

10160.	Liability of estate.
10160.5.	Broker who is or has interest in purchaser.
10161.	Amount of compensation; right to compensation.
10162.	Agents or brokers procuring purchaser to whom sale confirmed; compensation on partial amount of sale.
10162.3.	Agents or brokers procuring purchaser to whom sale confirmed; compensation on full amount of sale.
10162.5.	Agents or brokers with exclusive right to sell property; compensation on full amount or amount of original bid.
10162.6.	Agents or brokers with exclusive right to sell property; sale confirmed to purchaser named in contract.
10162.7.	Agents or brokers with exclusive right to sell property; sale to purchaser procured by another agent or broker.
10163.	Original bid by purchaser not procured by agent or broker; sale to purchaser procured by agent or broker.
10164.	Purchaser in sale on increased bid not procured by agent or broker; compensation of original bid agent or broker.
10165.	Purchaser in sale on increased bid procured by agent or broker; allocation of compensation.
10166.	Bids with condition that agent or broker be paid certain amount.
10167.	Auctioneers.
10168.	Effect of article on agreements between cooperating agents or brokers.

Cross References

Application of old and new law, see Probate Code § 3.

Sales of real property of an estate, requirements for sales to be reported to and confirmed by court, see Probate Code § 10308.

§ 10160.   Liability of estate

The estate is not liable to an agent, broker, or auctioneer under a contract for the sale of property or for any fee, commission, or other compensation or expenses in connection with a sale of property unless the following requirements are satisfied:

(a) An actual sale is made.

(b) If court confirmation or approval is required, the sale is confirmed or approved by the court as required.

(c) The sale is consummated. *(Stats.1990, c. 79 (A.B.759), § 14, operative July 1, 1991.)*

Law Revision Commission Comments
1990 Enactment

Section 10160 continues Section 10160 of the repealed Probate Code without change. Subdivision (c) makes clear that the sale must be consummated before the estate is liable to the agent, broker, or auctioneer. In the case of real property, the requirement that an actual sale be made and be consummated requires that the estate receive the purchase price and that a deed be given to the purchaser and a mortgage or deed of trust be taken for payments due in the future. See Estate of Rule, 25 Cal.2d 1, 16, 152 P.2d 1003 (1944); Wilson v. Fleming, 106 Cal.App. 542, 549, 289 P. 658 (1930). As to when court confirmation or approval is not required, see Section 10259 (personal property). As to orders made, or actions taken, before July 1, 1988, and matters pending on July 1, 1988, see Section 9645. As to the application of any amendments made after that date, see Section 3.

Background on Section 10160 of Repealed Code

Section 10160 was added by 1987 Cal.Stat. ch. 923 § 93. The section restated the last portion of the last sentence of former Probate Code Section 760 and a portion of the third sentence of former Probate Code Section 760.5 (provisions repealed by 1987 Cal.Stat. ch. 923 § 39) with the addition of subdivision (c). For background on the provisions of this part, see the Comment to this part under the part heading. [20 Cal.L.Rev.Comm.Reports 1001 (1990)].

§ 10160.5.   Broker who is or has interest in purchaser

The estate is not liable to an agent or broker under a contract for the sale of property or for any fee, commission, or other compensation or expenses in connection with sale of the property in either of the following cases:

(a) Where the agent or broker, directly or indirectly, is the purchaser of the property.

(b) Where the agent or broker representing the purchaser to whom the sale is confirmed has any interest in the purchaser. *(Stats.1990, c. 79 (A.B.759), § 14, operative July 1, 1991.)*

Law Revision Commission Comments
1990 Enactment

Section 10160.5 restates Section 10160.5 of the repealed Probate Code, with revisions making the section applicable to both real and personal property and to both agents and brokers. This section extends to the situation where there is not complete identity between broker and purchaser but the broker does have an interest in the purchasing entity, whether that interest is substantial or insubstantial.

Thus, for example, the broker would not be entitled to a commission if the purchaser is a corporation in which the broker owns stock.

Background on Section 10160.5 of Repealed Code

Section 10160.5 was a new provision added by 1989 Cal.Stat. ch. 544 § 10. The section changed the rule in Estate of Levinthal, 105 Cal.App.3d 691, 164 Cal.Rptr. 628 (1980), that a broker in an estate sale is entitled to a commission even though the purchaser is an entity in which the broker has an interest. The section was consistent with the rule in Estate of Toy, 72 Cal.App.3d 392, 140 Cal.Rptr. 183 (1977) (broker may not receive commission where there is complete identity between broker and purchaser), and broadened that rule to apply in the *Levinthal* situation. For background on the provisions of this chapter, see the Comment to this chapter under the chapter heading. [20 Cal.L.Rev.Comm.Reports 1001 (1990)].

§ 10161.   Amount of compensation; right to compensation

(a) Subject to the provisions of this article, whether or not the agent or broker has a contract with the personal representative, the fee, commission, or other compensation of an agent or broker in connection with a sale of property shall be the amount the court, in its discretion, determines to be a reasonable compensation for the services of the agent or broker to the estate.

(b) Unless the agent or broker holds a contract granting an exclusive right to sell the property, an agent or broker is not entitled to any fee, commission, or other compensation for services to the estate in connection with a sale except in the following cases:

(1) Where the agent or broker produces the original bid which is returned to the court for confirmation.

(2) Where the property is sold on an increased bid, made at the time of the hearing on the petition for confirmation, to a purchaser procured by the agent or broker.

(c) If the agent or broker has a contract with the personal representative, the amount of the compensation of the agent or broker in connection with the sale of property shall not exceed the amount provided for in the contract. *(Stats.1990, c. 79 (A.B.759), § 14, operative July 1, 1991.)*

Law Revision Commission Comments
1990 Enactment

Section 10161 continues Section 10161 of the repealed Probate Code without change. For provisions concerning court determination of the compensation of the agent or broker, see Sections 10261(d) (personal property), 10313(b) (real property). As to orders made, or actions taken, before July 1, 1988, and matters pending on July 1, 1988, see Section 9645. As to the application of any amendments made after that date, see Section 3.

Subdivision (a).   Rate or Amount of Compensation

Subdivision (a) of Section 10161 provides for judicial control over the reasonableness of the compensation of brokers and agents. A local court rule may, for example, fix reasonable compensation as a commission of 6 percent of the original bid or sales price (whichever is appropriate under the provisions of this article), and the court may determine what constitutes reasonable compensation by applying the court rule. Where an agent or broker holding a nonexclusive contract either produces the original bid returned to the court for confirmation or produces the successful overbidder, the compensation to which the agent or broker is entitled is the amount determined by the court to be a reasonable compensation for the services of the agent or broker to the estate and is subject to the provisions of this article.

The court has considerable flexibility in determining the compensation of the agent or broker or the agents or brokers in connection with a sale of property. Subject to the provisions of this article, compensation may be fixed, for example, as a percentage of the amount of the bid returned to the court for confirmation (see, e.g., Section 10164(b)) or as a percentage of the amount for which the sale is confirmed (see, e.g., Section 10165). The court may use one percentage (e.g., 6 percent) for improved property and another (e.g., 10 percent) for unimproved property. Or the court may use a schedule with the percentage decreasing as the value of the property increases (e.g., 6 percent for the first $100,000; 5 percent for amounts in excess of $100,000). The method of computing the compensation may be prescribed by court rule, but the court rule must not conflict with the provisions of this article. Nothing in this article precludes the court from fixing the compensation using a different method than a percentage of the amount bid or the amount for which the sale is confirmed. The personal representative and the agent or broker may provide in their contract for the amount or manner of computing the compensation for the sale and, although the court may fix the compensation at less than the amount provided for in the contract, the compensation allowed by the court in such a case may not exceed the contract amount. See Section 10161(c). See also Sections 10261(d), 10313(b) (court to fix compensation of agents and brokers).

The compensation of an agent or broker may be for the sale of real or personal property. See Section 10150. For a limitation on the amount of compensation that may be allowed to the agent or broker who produces the successful overbidder, see Section 10162. See also Section 10166 (invalidity of provision in bid that certain amount of bid be paid to agent or broker).

Subdivision (b). Requirements for Compensation

Subdivision (b) makes clear that an agent or broker holding a nonexclusive contract is not entitled to compensation unless the agent or broker produces the original bid returned to the court for confirmation or produces the overbidder to whom the sale is confirmed at the confirmation hearing. For example, the agent or broker holding a nonexclusive contract is not entitled to compensation in the following cases:

(1) Where the bid returned to the court for confirmation was submitted by a bidder not produced by an agent or broker and the sale is confirmed to that bidder.

(2) Where the bid returned to the court for confirmation was submitted by a bidder produced by another agent or broker and the sale is confirmed to that bidder. See Section 10162.3.

(3) Where the bid returned to the court for confirmation was submitted by a bidder not produced by the agent or broker who holds a nonexclusive contract and the court at the confirmation hearing confirms the sale of the property to an overbidder not produced by the agent or broker holding the nonexclusive contract. See Sections 10163, 10164, 10165(a)(1), (b), (c)(2).

Subdivision (c). Compensation Subject to Contractual Limits

Subdivision (c) makes clear that the amount of the compensation of the agent or broker may not exceed the amount provided for in the contract. For example, if the contract provides for a 5 percent commission and the applicable court rule would allow a 6 percent commission, the commission awarded by the court may not exceed the 5 percent rate provided for in the contract. See also Section 10166 (invalidity of provision in bid that certain amount of bid be paid to agent or broker). In all of the examples set out below, it should be remembered that the compensation due an agent or broker holding a contract with the personal representative would be subject to the terms of the contract. Thus, the amount of compensation could be less than the amount indicated in the example.

Examples of Application of Article

The following examples illustrate the effect of Sections 10161–10166. In these examples, Broker A refers to the broker holding an exclusive or nonexclusive contract with the personal representative

(as indicated in the particular example). Broker B refers to a broker who does not hold a contract with the personal representative and who produces the bid returned to the court for confirmation. Broker C refers to a broker who does not have a contract with the personal representative and who produces a successful overbidder. (This broker is referred to as Broker C whether or not a Broker A or Broker B is involved in the transaction).

Example 1. Broker with contract produces original bid; no overbid. The personal representative enters into a written contract (either exclusive or nonexclusive) with Broker A for the sale of real property of the estate. The contract provides for a commission to Broker A of 6 percent of the sale price. Broker A finds a bidder whose bid is confirmed by the court. Broker A is entitled to a commission on the amount for which the sale is confirmed. See Section 10161(b), 10162.3. The court is not bound by the 6 percent commission provided in the contract. The court may fix a commission in the amount the court determines to be reasonable compensation for the services of Broker A to the estate, but not an amount in excess of the amount provided in the contract. See Section 10161(a), (c).

Example 2. Broker with contract produces original bid; successful overbidder not produced by broker. The personal representative enters into a written contract (either exclusive or nonexclusive) with Broker A for the sale of real property of the estate. The contract provides for a commission to Broker A of 6 percent of the sale price. Broker A finds a bidder whose bid is returned to the court for confirmation. At the confirmation hearing, the highest bid is made by a different bidder not produced by a broker. The court confirms the sale to the overbidder. Broker A is entitled to a commission on the amount of the original bid, but not the overbid. See Sections 10162.5(b), 10164(b).

For example, Broker A returns a $100,000 bid for confirmation. At the hearing, a different bidder not produced by a broker bids $110,000 and the sale is confirmed to the overbidder. Broker A receives a $6,000 commission on the original bid (6 percent of $100,000 = $6,000). There is no commission paid on the $10,000 amount by which the overbid exceeds the original bid.

Example 3. Exclusive listing contract; original bidder produced by Broker B; successful overbidder not produced by broker. The personal representative enters into an exclusive listing contract with Broker A. The original bid returned to court for confirmation is produced by Broker B. At the confirmation hearing, the highest bid is made by a different bidder not produced by a broker. The court confirms the sale to the overbidder. The commission is determined as in Example 2 (reasonable commission on amount of original bid). The commission is divided between Broker A and Broker B as provided in any agreement between them or, if there is no agreement, is divided equally. See Section 10164(c).

For example, suppose that the original bid returned to the court by Broker B is $100,000 and a bidder not produced by a broker makes an overbid of $110,000 on which the sale is confirmed. The court determines that a reasonable commission is 6 percent, which yields $6,000 (6 percent of $100,000 = $6,000). If there is no agreement between the brokers, Broker A and Broker B each receive $3,000, which is half of the commission on the original bid returned to the court for confirmation (6 percent of $100,000 = $6,000; half of $6,000 = $3,000).

Example 4. No exclusive listing contract; original bidder not produced by broker; successful overbidder produced by Broker C. The personal representative has not entered into an exclusive listing contract with an agent or broker. The original bid is made by a bidder not produced by a broker. A successful overbidder is produced by Broker C. The reasonable commission allowed by the court is paid entirely to Broker C. See Section 10163. Subject to Section 10162, the commission is allowed on the full amount for which the sale is confirmed. See Section 10163(b). For example, where the commission is fixed by the court in a percentage amount, the percentage is applied to the full amount for which the sale is confirmed. See Section 10163. As noted, the commission of Broker C is subject to the limitation that it may not exceed half of the difference between the amount of the original bid and the amount of the successful overbid. See Section 10162. (The result would be the same in this example where the successful overbidder was produced by Broker A, holding a nonexclusive contract.)

For example, suppose that the original bid returned to court was for $100,000 made by a bidder not produced by a broker. Broker C brings in an increased bid of $110,000 on which the sale is confirmed. Under Section 10163, Broker C is entitled to a commission on the amount for which the sale is confirmed. The court determines that a reasonable commission is 6 percent, which yields $6,600 (6 percent of $110,000 = $6,600). However, Broker C is entitled only to a commission of $5,000, instead of $6,600, by operation of Section 10162 which limits the commission of a broker producing the successful overbidder to half of the difference between the original bid and the overbid ($110,000 − $100,000 = $10,000; half of $10,000 = $5,000).

Example 5. Exclusive listing contract; original bidder not produced by broker; successful overbidder produced by Broker A. The personal representative enters into an exclusive listing contract with Broker A. The contract provides for a commission to Broker A of 6 percent of the sale price. The bid returned to court for confirmation is made by a bidder not produced by a broker. At the confirmation hearing, the highest bid is made by a different bidder produced by Broker A. The court confirms the sale to the overbidder. Broker A is entitled to a commission on the amount for which the sale is confirmed. See Section 10163(a). The limitation on the commission of an overbidder provided by Section 10162 does not apply in this case because the overbid is produced by a broker with an exclusive listing contract. See Section 10162(b).

For example, suppose that the original bid returned to court was for $100,000 made by a bidder not produced by a broker. Broker A (with exclusive contract) brings in an increased bid of $110,000 on which the sale is confirmed. Broker A is entitled to a commission on the amount for which the sale is confirmed. The court determines that a reasonable commission is 6 percent, which yields $6,600 (6 percent of $110,000 = $6,600). Broker A receives the entire $6,600 commission.

Example 6. No exclusive listing contract; original bidder produced by Broker A; successful overbidder produced by Broker C. The personal representative enters into a nonexclusive contract with Broker A for the sale of real property of the estate. The contract provides for a commission to Broker A of 6 percent of the sale price. Broker A finds a bidder whose bid is returned to the court for confirmation. At the confirmation hearing, the highest bid is made by a different bidder produced by Broker C who does not hold a contract with the personal representative. The court confirms the sale to the overbidder. Broker A is entitled to half of the commission on the original bid. Broker C is entitled to the other half of the commission on the original bid plus all of the commission on the overbid. See Section 10165(a)(1), (b), (c)(2).

For example, suppose that Broker A returns a $100,000 bid for confirmation and Broker C brings in an increased bid of $110,000 on which the sale is confirmed. The court approves a 6 percent commission, which yields $6,600 (6 percent of $110,000 = $6,600). Broker A receives $3,000 which is half of the commission on the original bid (6 percent of $100,000 = $6,000; half of $6,000 = $3,000). Broker C receives $3,600, which consists of the other half of the commission on the original bid ($3,000) and all of the commission on the amount of the difference between the original bid and the confirmed overbid ($110,000 − $100,000 = $10,000; 6 percent of $10,000 = $600).

If the original bidder in this example were produced by Broker B, who does not have a contract with the personal representative, Broker B would be entitled to the same commission as the broker with a nonexclusive contract in this example, except that the amount

of the commission would be subject only to control of the court, and not to contractual limitations. See Example 10.

Example 7. No exclusive listing contract; original bidder produced by Broker B; successful overbidder not produced by broker. The personal representative enters into a nonexclusive contract with Broker A for the sale of real property of the estate. Broker B finds a bidder whose bid is returned to the court for confirmation. At the confirmation hearing, the highest bid is made by a different bidder not produced by a broker. The court confirms the sale to the overbidder. Broker B is entitled to a commission on the amount of the original bid. See Section 10164(a)–(b). Broker A is not entitled to a commission. See Section 10161(b).

For example, suppose Broker B returns a $100,000 bid for confirmation and a bidder not produced by a broker makes an overbid of $110,000 on which the sale is confirmed. The court approves a 6 percent commission, which yields $6,000 (6 percent of $100,000 = $6,000). Broker B receives the entire $6,000 commission on the original bid. Broker A receives nothing.

Example 8. Exclusive listing contract; original bidder produced by Broker B; successful overbidder produced by Broker C. The personal representative enters into an exclusive contract with Broker A for the sale of real property of the estate. The contract provides for a commission to Broker A of 6 percent of the sale price. Broker B produces a bidder whose bid is returned to the court for confirmation. At the confirmation hearing, the highest bid is made by a different bidder produced by Broker C. The court confirms the sale to the overbidder. Under Section 10165, Broker A and Broker B are entitled to share half of the commission on the original bid; Broker C is entitled to the other half of the commission on the original bid plus all of the commission on the overbid. The division of the commission between Broker A and Broker B is determined by their agreement. See Section 10165(a)(1), (b), (c)(3).

For example, suppose Broker B returns a $100,000 bid for confirmation and Broker C brings in an increased bid of $110,000 on which the sale is confirmed. The court approves a 6 percent commission, which yields $6,600 (6 percent of $110,000 = $6,600). Broker A (with exclusive contract) and Broker B (broker producing bidder whose bid was returned to the court for confirmation) are entitled to share half of the commission on the original bid (6 percent of $100,000 = $6,000; half of $6,000 = $3,000). Thus, Broker A and Broker B each receive $1,500 (half of $3,000), unless otherwise provided in their agreement. Broker C receives $3,600, which consists of the other half of the commission on the original bid ($3,000) plus all of the commission on the difference between the original bid and the amount for which the sale is confirmed ($110,000 − $100,000 = $10,000; 6 percent of $10,000 = $600).

Example 9. Exclusive listing contract; original bid produced by Broker B; successful overbidder produced by Broker A. The personal representative enters into an exclusive contract with Broker A for the sale of real property of the estate. The contract provides for a commission to Broker A of 6 percent of the sale price. Broker B finds a bidder whose bid is returned to the court for confirmation. At the confirmation hearing, the highest bid is made by a different bidder produced by Broker A. The court confirms the sale to the overbidder. Broker B is entitled to half of the commission on the original bid. Broker A is entitled to the other half of the commission on the original bid plus all of the commission on the overbid. See Section 10165(a)(1), (b), (c)(5).

For example, suppose that Broker B returns a $100,000 bid for confirmation, and Broker A brings in an increased bid of $110,000 on which the sale is confirmed. The court approves a 6 percent commission, which yields $6,600 (6 percent of $110,000 = $6,600). Broker A (with exclusive contract) receives $3,600, which consists of half of the commission on the original bid (half of 6 percent of $100,000 = $3,000) and all of the commission on the difference between the original bid and confirmed overbid ($110,000 − $100,000 = $10,000; 6 percent of $10,000 = $600). Broker B (who produced original bid) receives the other half of the commission on the original bid (half of 6 percent of $100,000 = $3,000).

Example 10. No exclusive listing contract; original bidder produced by Broker B; no overbid. The personal representative has not entered into an exclusive contract with a broker. Broker B produces a bidder whose bid is confirmed by the court. The reasonable compensation allowed by the court on the amount for which the sale is confirmed is paid to Broker B. See Section 10162.3.

Example 11. Exclusive listing contract; original bidder not produced by broker; no overbid. The personal representative enters into an exclusive contract with Broker A for the sale of real property of the estate. The bid returned to court for confirmation is made by a bidder not produced by a broker. The sale is confirmed to the original bidder on that bid. The reasonable compensation allowed by the court on the amount for which the sale is confirmed is paid to Broker A. See Section 10162.5(a)(1).

Example 12. Exclusive listing contract; original bidder not produced by broker; successful overbidder not produced by broker. The personal representative enters into an exclusive contract with Broker A for the sale of real property of the estate. The bid returned to court for confirmation is made by a bidder not produced by a broker. At the confirmation hearing, the highest bid is made by a different bidder not produced by a broker. The court confirms the sale to the overbidder. The commission is allowed on the amount of the original bid. See Section 10162.5(b). For example, where the commission is fixed by the court in a percentage amount, the percentage is applied to the amount of the original bid, not the amount of the successful overbid.

For example, suppose that the original bid returned to court was for $100,000 made by a bidder not produced by a broker and that a different bidder not produced by a broker makes an overbid of $110,000 on which the sale is confirmed. The court determines that a reasonable commission is 6 percent. Broker A (holder of exclusive contract) receives a $6,000 commission on the original bid (6 percent of $100,000 = $6,000). There is no commission paid on the $10,000 amount by which the overbid exceeds the original bid.

Example 13. Exclusive listing contract; original bidder not produced by broker; successful overbidder produced by Broker C. The personal representative enters into an exclusive contract with Broker A for the sale of real property of the estate. The bid returned to court for confirmation is made by a bidder not produced by a broker. At the confirmation hearing, the highest bid is made by a different bidder produced by Broker C. The court confirms the sale to the overbidder. Broker A is entitled to half of the commission on the original bid. Subject to Section 10162, Broker C is entitled to the other half of the commission on the original bid plus all of the commission on the overbid. See Section 10165(a)(2), (b), (c)(4).

For example, suppose that the original bid returned to court was for $100,000 made by a bidder not produced by a broker and that Broker C brings in an increased bid of $110,000 on which the sale is confirmed. The court determines that a reasonable commission is 6 percent, which yields $6,600 (6 percent of $110,000 = $6,600). Broker A (holder of exclusive contract) receives $3,000, which is half of the commission on the original bid (half of 6 percent of $100,000 = $3,000). Broker C receives $3,600, which consists of the other half of the commission on the original bid (half of 6 percent of $100,000 = $3,000) and all of the commission on the difference between the original bid and the confirmed overbid ($110,000 − $100,000 = $10,000; 6 percent of $10,000 = $600). Since the $3,600 commission does not exceed half of the amount by which the overbid exceeds the original bid (half of $10,000 = $5,000), Section 10162 is not violated and Broker C is entitled to the full $3,600 commission.

Example 14. Exclusive listing contract; original bidder produced by Broker B; no overbid. The personal representative enters into an exclusive contract with Broker A for the sale of real property of the estate. The bid returned to court for confirmation is made by a bidder produced by Broker B. The sale is confirmed to that bidder on that bid. The reasonable compensation allowed by the court on the amount for which the sale is confirmed is divided between Broker A and Broker B as provided in any agreement between them, or, if there is no agreement, is divided equally. See Section 10162.7.

For example, suppose that Broker B produces the original bid of $100,000 and the sale is confirmed at that amount. The court determines that a reasonable commission is 6 percent, which yields $6,000 (6 percent of $100,000 = $6,000). The $6,000 is divided between Broker A and Broker B as provided in their agreement or, absent an agreement, is divided equally so that Broker A receives $3,000 and Broker B receives $3,000.

Example 15. No exclusive listing contract; original bidder produced by Broker B; one or more other overbidders; successful overbid by original bidder produced by Broker B. The bid returned to the court for confirmation is made by a bidder produced by Broker B. At the confirmation hearing, an increased bid is made by a different bidder produced by Broker D. Another increased bid is made by a third bidder not produced by a broker. A further increased bid is made by the original bidder, produced by Broker B. The court confirms the sale to the overbidder produced by Broker B. Under Section 10162.3, Broker B is entitled to a commission on the full amount for which the sale is confirmed.

For example, suppose that the original bid returned to court is $100,000, Broker D brings in an overbid of $120,000, the unrepresented bidder bids $130,000, and the original bidder produced by Broker B makes an overbid of $140,000 on which the sale is confirmed. The court determines that a reasonable commission is 6 percent, which yields $8,400 (6 percent of $140,000 = $8,400). Broker B is entitled to the full commission of $8,400. Broker D receives nothing, as provided in Section 10161(b).

Example 16. Exclusive listing contract; original bidder produced by Broker B; one or more other overbidders; successful overbid by original bidder produced by Broker B. The personal representative enters into an exclusive contract with Broker A for the sale of real property of the estate. The bid returned to the court for confirmation is made by a bidder produced by Broker B. At the confirmation hearing, an increased bid is made by a different bidder produced by Broker D. Another increased bid is made by a third bidder not produced by a broker. A further increased bid is made by the original bidder, produced by Broker B. The court confirms the sale to the overbidder produced by Broker B. Under Section 10162.7, in the absence of an agreement between Broker A and Broker B, the reasonable compensation allowed by the court on the original bid is divided equally between Broker A and Broker B, and all of the commission on the overbid is paid to Broker B.

For example, suppose that the original bid returned to court is $100,000, Broker D brings in an overbid of $120,000, the unrepresented bidder bids $130,000, and the original bidder produced by Broker B makes an overbid of $140,000 on which the sale is confirmed. The court determines that a reasonable commission is 6 percent, which yields $8,400 (6 percent of $140,000 = $8,400). Broker B receives $5,400, which consists of half of the commission on the original bid (half of 6 percent of $100,000 = $3,000) and all of the commission on the difference between the original bid and confirmed overbid ($140,000 − $100,000 = $40,000; 6 percent of $40,000 = $2,400). Broker A receives the other half of the commission on the original bid (half of 6 percent of $100,000 = $3,000). Broker D receives nothing.

Example 17. Exclusive listing contract; agreement between Broker A and Broker B; original bidder produced by Broker B; one or more other overbidders; successful overbid by original bidder produced by Broker B. The personal representative enters into an exclusive contract with Broker A for the sale of real property of the estate. The bid returned to the court for confirmation is made by a bidder produced by Broker B. Broker A and Broker B have an agreement to split the commission on the full amount for which the sale is confirmed. At the confirmation hearing, an increased bid is made by a different bidder produced by Broker D. Another increased bid is made by a third bidder not produced by a broker. A further increased bid is made by the original bidder produced by Broker B. The court confirms the sale to the overbidder produced by Broker B. Under Section 10162.7, the reasonable compensation allowed by the court on the full amount for which the sale is confirmed is divided between Broker A and Broker B pursuant to their agreement.

For example, suppose that the original bid returned to court is $100,000, Broker D brings in an overbid of $120,000, the unrepresented bidder bids $130,000, and the original bidder produced by Broker B makes an overbid of $140,000 on which the sale is confirmed. The court determines that a reasonable commission is 6 percent, which yields $8,400 (6 percent of $140,000 = $8,400). Broker A and Broker B each receive $4,200 pursuant to their agreement. Broker D receives nothing.

Example 18. Exclusive listing contract; original bidder not produced by broker; successful overbidder produced by Broker C. The personal representative enters into an exclusive contract with Broker A for the sale of real property of the estate. The contract provides for a commission to Broker A of 6 percent of the sale price. The bid returned to the court for confirmation is made by a bidder not produced by a broker. At the confirmation hearing, the highest bid is made by a different bidder produced by Broker C. The court confirms the sale to the overbidder. Under Section 10165(b), Broker C is entitled to half of the commission on the original bid plus all of the commission on the overbid, subject to the limitation on overbids in Section 10162. Under Section 10165(c)(4), Broker A is entitled to the other half of the commission on the original bid.

For example, suppose that the original bid returned to court is $100,000 and Broker C brings in an overbid of $110,000 on which the sale is confirmed. The court approves a 6 percent commission, which yields $6,600 (6 percent of $110,000 = $6,600). Broker C receives $3,600, which consists of half of the commission on the original bid (half of 6 percent of $100,000 = $3,000) and all of the commission on the difference between the original bid and confirmed overbid ($110,000 − $100,000 = $10,000; 6 percent of $10,000 = $600). Broker A (the broker holding the exclusive contract) receives the other half of the commission on the original bid (half of 6 percent of $100,000 = $3,000).

Example 19. Exclusive listing contract; original bidder produced by Broker B; successful overbidder produced by Broker A. The personal representative enters into an exclusive contract with Broker A for the sale of real property of the estate. The contract provides for a commission to Broker A of 6 percent of the sale price. The bid returned to the court for confirmation is made by a bidder produced by Broker B. At the confirmation hearing, the highest bid is made by a different bidder produced by Broker A. The court confirms the sale to the overbidder. Broker A is entitled to half of the commission on the original bid plus all of the commission on the overbid. See Section 10165(b). Broker B is entitled to the other half of the commission on the original bid. See Section 10165(c)(5).

For example, suppose that the original bid returned to court is $100,000 made by a bidder produced by Broker B. Broker A brings in an overbid of $110,000 on which the sale is confirmed. The court approves a 6 percent commission, which yields $6,600 (6 percent of $110,000 = $6,600). Broker A receives $3,600, which consists of half of the commission on the original bid (half of 6 percent of $100,000 = $3,000) and all of the commission on the difference between the original bid and confirmed overbid ($110,000 − $100,000 = $10,000; 6 percent of $10,000 = $600). Broker B receives the other half of the commission on the original bid (half of 6 percent of $100,000 = $3,000).

Background on Section 10161 of Repealed Code

Section 10161 was added by 1987 Cal.Stat. ch. 923 § 93. Subdivision (a) restated a portion of the fourth sentence of former Probate Code Section 760 (contract binding "for an amount to be allowed by the court"), a portion of former Probate Code Section 761.5

(overbidder's agent entitled to "reasonable compensation" fixed by the court), and a portion of the second and third sentences of former Probate Code Section 785 (overbidder's agent entitled to "reasonable compensation" fixed by the court) (provisions repealed by 1987 Cal.Stat. ch. 923 § 39), without substantive change. Subdivision (a) used language drawn primarily from the last portion of former Section 761.5. Subdivisions (b) and (c) were new provisions. For background on the provisions of this part, see the Comment to this part under the part heading. [20 Cal.L.Rev.Comm.Reports 1001 (1990)].

Cross References

Compensation of agent in real property sales, see Probate Code § 10313.

§ 10162. Agents or brokers procuring purchaser to whom sale confirmed; compensation on partial amount of sale

(a) Subject to subdivision (b), where the bid returned to the court for confirmation is made by a person who is not represented by an agent or broker and the successful bidder is represented by an agent or broker, the compensation of the agent or broker who procured the purchaser to whom the sale is confirmed shall not exceed one-half of the difference between the amount of the bid in the original return and the amount of the successful bid.

(b) This section does not limit the compensation of the agent or broker who holds a contract under Section 10150 granting him or her the exclusive right to sell the property. *(Stats.1990, c. 79 (A.B.759), § 14, operative July 1, 1991.)*

Law Revision Commission Comments
1990 Enactment

Section 10162 continues Section 10162 of the repealed Probate Code without change. For examples of the operation of this section, see Examples 4, 5, 13, and 18 in the Comment to Section 10161. As to orders made, or actions taken, before July 1, 1988, and matters pending on July 1, 1988, see Section 9645. As to the application of any amendments made after that date, see Section 3.

Background on Section 10162 of Repealed Code

Section 10162 was added by 1987 Cal.Stat. ch. 923 § 93. The section restated the fourth sentence of former Probate Code Section 785 (repealed by 1987 Cal.Stat. ch. 923 § 39) with the following changes:

(1) Section 10162 was limited to the case where the original bid returned to the court for confirmation is made by a person not produced by an agent or broker.

(2) Section 10162 covered sales of real and personal property. Former Section 785 applied only to real property sales.

(3) Section 10162 did not limit the compensation of the agent or broker who holds a contract under Section 10150 granting him or her the exclusive right to sell the property. Former Section 785 did not limit the compensation of the agent or broker who held the contract with the personal representative, whether or not the contract granted the exclusive right to sell the property.

For background on the provisions of this part, see the Comment to this part under the part heading. [20 Cal.L.Rev.Comm.Reports 1001 (1990)].

§ 10162.3. Agents or brokers procuring purchaser to whom sale confirmed; compensation on full amount of sale

(a) This section applies if all of the following circumstances exist:

(1) There is no agent or broker holding a contract under Section 10150 granting the exclusive right to sell the property.

(2) The bid returned to court for confirmation is made by a purchaser represented by an agent or broker.

(3) The court confirms the sale to that purchaser either on the bid returned to court for confirmation or on an increased bid made at the time of the hearing on the petition for confirmation.

(b) If all the circumstances described in subdivision (a) exist, the court shall allow the agent or broker who procured the purchaser to whom the sale is confirmed the compensation determined under Section 10161 on the full amount for which the sale is confirmed. *(Stats.1990, c. 79 (A.B.759), § 14, operative July 1, 1991.)*

Law Revision Commission Comments

1990 Enactment

Section 10162.3 continues Section 10162.3 of the repealed Probate Code without change. This section provides the rule that applies where there is no exclusive contract and the sale is made on a bid returned to the court by a purchaser produced by an agent or broker. The reference to Section 10161 in Section 10162.3 recognizes that the court has discretion to determine the total amount of compensation to be paid. Under subdivision (b), where the original bidder becomes the successful overbidder at the end of the auction in court, the agent or broker is entitled to compensation on the full amount for which the sale is confirmed. For examples of the operation of this section, see Examples 1, 10, and 15 in the Comment to Section 10161.

As to orders made, or actions taken, before July 1, 1988, and matters pending on July 1, 1988, see Section 9645. As to the application of any amendments made after that date, see Section 3.

Background on Section 10162.3 of Repealed Code

Section 10162.3 was added by 1987 Cal.Stat. ch. 923 § 93 and amended by 1989 Cal.Stat. ch. 544 § 11. The 1989 amendment to Section 10162.3 revised subdivision (a)(3) to provide for the compensation in a situation where the sale is confirmed to a successful overbidder produced by an agent or broker and who also made the original bid returned to the court for confirmation. The 1989 amendment also replaced the word "person" in Section 10162.3(a)(2) with "purchaser" for consistency with subdivision (a)(3).

For background on the provisions of this part, see the Comment to this part under the part hearing. [20 Cal.L.Rev.Comm.Reports 1001 (1990)].

§ 10162.5. Agents or brokers with exclusive right to sell property; compensation on full amount or amount of original bid

Subject to Section 10162.6, where an agent or broker holds a contract under Section 10150 granting the exclusive right to sell the property, the court shall allow to the agent or broker holding the contract the compensation determined under Section 10161 on:

(a) The full amount for which the sale is confirmed in either of the following circumstances:

(1) The bid returned to the court for confirmation is made by a purchaser who is not represented by an agent or broker and the court confirms the sale to that purchaser on that bid.

(2) The bid returned to the court for confirmation is made by a purchaser who is represented by the agent or broker holding the contract and the court confirms the sale to that

purchaser on an increased bid made at the time of the hearing on the petition for confirmation.

(b) The amount of the original bid if both of the following circumstances exist:

(1) The bid returned to court for confirmation is made by a purchaser who is not represented by an agent or broker or who is represented by the agent or broker holding a contract under Section 10150 granting the exclusive right to sell the property.

(2) The court confirms the sale on an increased bid, made at the time of the hearing on the petition for confirmation, to a purchaser who was not procured by a bona fide agent or broker. *(Stats.1990, c. 79 (A.B.759), § 14, operative July 1, 1991.)*

Law Revision Commission Comments

1990 Enactment

Section 10162.5 continues Section 10162.5 of the repealed Probate Code without change, except that the introductory clause is added to subdivision (a) to recognize the special rules in Section 10162.6 (exclusive contract providing that no compensation payable if sale confirmed to particular person named in contract). This section provides the rules that apply where there is an exclusive contract and no other agent or broker produces the purchaser to whom the sale is confirmed. The reference to Section 10161 in Section 10162.5 recognizes that the court has discretion to determine the amount of compensation to be paid. For examples of the operation of this section, see Examples 2, 11, and 12 in the Comment to Section 10161.

Under subdivision (a)(2), where the original bidder becomes the successful overbidder at the end of the auction in court, the agent or broker holding the exclusive listing contract is entitled to compensation on the full amount for which the sale is confirmed. For an illustration of the application of the rule in subdivision (b), see Example 2 in the Comment to Section 10161.

As to orders made, or actions taken, before July 1, 1988, and matters pending on July 1, 1988, see Section 9645. As to the application of any amendments made after that date, see Section 3.

Background on Section 10162.5 of Repealed Code

Section 10162.5 was added by 1987 Cal.Stat. ch. 923 § 93 and amended by 1989 Cal.Stat. ch. 544 § 12. The 1989 amendment revised subdivision (a) to provide for the compensation in a situation where the sale is confirmed to a successful overbidder produced by the agent or broker holding the contract and who also made the original bid returned to the court for confirmation. The 1989 amendment also revised subdivision (b)(1) to apply the rule in subdivision (b) to situations where the bid returned to court is produced by an agent with an exclusive listing. The 1989 amendment replaced the word "person" in subdivisions (a)(1) and (b)(1) with "purchaser" for consistency with the remainder of the section. For background on the provisions of this part, see the Comment to this part under the part heading. [20 Cal.L.Rev.Comm.Reports 1001 (1990)].

§ 10162.6. Agents or brokers with exclusive right to sell property; sale confirmed to purchaser named in contract

(a) This section applies if both of the following circumstances exist:

(1) An agent or broker holds a contract under Section 10150 granting the exclusive right to sell the property.

(2) The contract provides that no compensation is payable to the agent or broker holding the contract if sale is confirmed to a particular purchaser named in the contract.

(b) If the court confirms the sale to the purchaser named in the contract, whether on an original bid returned to the court or on an increased bid made at the time of the hearing on the petition for confirmation, the compensation of any agents or brokers involved in the sale is determined as provided in this article, except that no compensation is payable to the agent or broker holding the contract.

(c) If the court confirms the sale to a purchaser other than the person named in the contract, whether on an original bid returned to the court or on an increased bid made at the time of the hearing on the petition for confirmation, the compensation of the agent or broker holding the contract, and of any other agents or brokers involved in the sale, is determined under this article as if the limitation in the contract did not exist. *(Stats.1990, c. 79 (A.B.759), § 14, operative July 1, 1991.)*

Law Revision Commission Comments
1990 Enactment

Section 10162.6 is new, and deals with the situation where the personal representative makes an exclusive listing contract with a broker (Broker A) to sell estate property, but the contract provides that no commission is payable to Broker A if sale is confirmed to a particular purchaser (or purchasers) named in the contract. See subdivision (a). Special rules apply in this situation, as provided in subdivisions (b) and (c).

Subdivision (b) applies to the situation where the sale is made to the purchaser named in the contract. In this case, Broker A is not entitled to any commission, even if Broker A produced the original bid returned to the court. Under subdivision (b), if sale is confirmed to the named person, the commission that would have been paid to Broker A, except for the limitation in the contract, is not paid. In this case, the estate receives the benefit of the commission, just as if the estate were acting as the agent with the exclusive listing contract. The compensation due any other brokers involved in the sale is determined under the normal rules that apply where there is a broker with an exclusive listing contract.

Subdivision (c) makes clear that the limitation in the exclusive listing contract does not affect the compensation of the broker holding the contract or any other brokers in a case where the sale is not made to the person named in the exclusive listing contract. In such case, the rules governing compensation where there is an exclusive listing contract apply and the limitation concerning the person named in the contract is ignored.

The following examples illustrate the application of this section. In these examples, Broker A refers to the broker holding the exclusive listing contract with the limitation that no compensation is due Broker A if sale is made to Bidder X. Broker B refers to a broker who does not hold a contract with the personal representative and who produces the bid returned to the court for confirmation. Broker C refers to a broker who does not have a contract with the personal representative and who produces a successful overbid.

Example 1. Exclusive listing contract excluding compensation if sale to Bidder X; Bidder X is original bidder, not produced by broker; no overbid. The original bid returned to court for confirmation is made by Bidder X who is not represented by a broker. The sale is confirmed to the original bidder on that bid. Under subdivision (b) and Section 10162.5(a), no commission is payable. This example is comparable to Example 11 in the Comment to Section 10161, except that Broker A receives no compensation.

Example 2. Exclusive listing contract excluding compensation if sale to Bidder X; Bidder X produced by Broker B; no overbid. The

original bid returned to court for confirmation is made by Bidder X produced by Broker B. The sale is confirmed to that bidder on that bid. The reasonable compensation allowed by the court on the amount for which the sale is confirmed is divided equally. Under subdivision (b) and Section 10162.7, one-half of the commission is paid to Broker B and the other half, which would have been paid to Broker A except for the limitation in the contract, is not paid. This example is comparable to Example 14 in the Comment to Section 10161, except that Broker A receives no compensation.

Example 3. Exclusive listing contract excluding compensation if sale to Bidder X; original bidder not produced by broker; successful overbid by Bidder X, not produced by broker. The original bid returned to court for confirmation is made by a bidder who is not represented by a broker. At the confirmation hearing, the highest bid is made by Bidder X who is not produced by a broker. The court confirms the sale to Bidder X. Under subdivision (b) and Section 10162.5(b), no commission is payable. This example is comparable to Example 12 in the Comment to Section 10161, except that Broker A receives no compensation.

The result would be the same where the original bidder in this example is produced by Broker A.

Example 4. Exclusive listing contract excluding compensation if sale to Bidder X; original bidder not produced by broker; successful overbid by Bidder X produced by Broker C. The original bid returned to court for confirmation is made by a bidder who is not represented by a broker. At the confirmation hearing, the highest bid is made by Bidder X who is produced by Broker C. The court confirms the sale to Bidder X. Under subdivision (b), and subject to Section 10162, Broker C is entitled to half of the commission on the original bid plus all of the commission on the overbid; the other half of the commission on the original bid is not paid. See Section 10165(a)(2), (b), (c)(4). This example is comparable to Example 13 in the Comment to Section 10161, except that Broker A receives no compensation.

The result would be the same where the original bidder in this example is produced by Broker A.

Example 5. Exclusive listing contract excluding compensation if sale to Bidder X; original bidder produced by Broker B; successful overbid by Bidder X not produced by broker. The original bid returned to court for confirmation is made by a bidder produced by Broker B. At the confirmation hearing, the highest bid is made by Bidder X who is not produced by a broker. The court confirms the sale to Bidder X. Under subdivision (b) and Section 10164(c), Broker B is entitled to half of the commission on the original bid. The other half of the commission on the original bid is not paid. This example is comparable to Example 3 in the Comment to Section 10161, except that Broker A receives no compensation.

Example 6. Exclusive listing contract excluding compensation if sale to Bidder X; original bidder produced by Broker B; successful overbid by Bidder X produced by Broker C. The original bid returned to court for confirmation is made by a bidder produced by Broker B. At the confirmation hearing, the highest bid is made by Bidder X who is produced by Broker C. The court confirms the sale to Bidder X. Under subdivision (b), Broker B is entitled to one-fourth of the commission on the original bid and Broker C is entitled to half of the commission on the original bid plus all of the commission on the overbid. The other fourth of the commission on the original bid is not paid. See Section 10165(a)(1), (b), (c)(3). This example is comparable to Example 8 in the Comment to Section 10161, except that Broker A receives no compensation.

Example 7. Exclusive listing contract excluding compensation if sale to Bidder X; original bid by Bidder X, not produced by broker; successful overbidder not produced by broker. The original bid returned to court for confirmation is made by Bidder X who is not represented by a broker. At the confirmation hearing, the highest bid is made by a different bidder not produced by a broker. The court confirms the sale to the overbidder. Under subdivision (c) and Section 10162.5(b), Broker A receives a commission on the amount of the original bid and the limitation in the contract has no effect. This result in this example is the same as Example 12 in the Comment to Section 10161.

Example 8. Exclusive listing contract excluding compensation if sale to Bidder X; original bid by Bidder X produced by Broker B; successful overbidder not produced by broker. The original bid returned to court for confirmation is made by Bidder X produced by Broker B. At the confirmation hearing, the highest bid is made by a different bidder not produced by a broker. The court confirms the sale to the overbidder. Under subdivision (c), the commission on the original bid is divided equally between Broker A and Broker B. The limitation in the contract has no effect. This result in this example is the same as Example 3 in the Comment to Section 10161. [20 Cal.L.Rev.Comm.Reports 1001 (1990)].

§ 10162.7. Agents or brokers with exclusive right to sell property; sale to purchaser procured by another agent or broker

(a) Subject to Section 10162.6, this section applies if all of the following circumstances exist:

(1) There is an agent or broker holding a contract under Section 10150 granting the exclusive right to sell the property.

(2) The bid returned to court for confirmation is made by a purchaser procured by another agent or broker.

(3) The court confirms the sale to that purchaser either on the bid returned to court for confirmation or on an increased bid made at the time of the hearing on the petition for confirmation.

(b) If all the circumstances described in subdivision (a) exist, the court shall allow the compensation determined under Section 10161 on the full amount for which the sale is confirmed. The compensation allowed by the court shall be divided between the agent or broker holding the contract and the other agent or broker as is provided in any agreement between the agent or broker holding the contract and the other agent or broker. If there is no agreement, the compensation on the amount of the original bid returned to the court shall be divided equally between the agent or broker holding the contract and the other agent or broker and, if the sale is confirmed on an increased bid, the other agent or broker shall be paid all of the compensation on the difference between the original bid and the amount for which the sale is confirmed. *(Stats.1990, c. 79 (A.B.759), § 14, operative July 1, 1991.)*

Law Revision Commission Comments

1990 Enactment

Section 10162.7 continues Section 10162.7 of the repealed Probate Code without change, except that the introductory clause is added to subdivision (a) to recognize the special rules in Section 10162.6 (exclusive contract providing that no compensation payable if sale confirmed to particular person named in contract). This section provides the rule that applies where there is an exclusive contract and the sale is made to a purchaser produced by another agent or broker on the bid returned to court or on an overbid by the same purchaser. The reference to Section 10161 in Section 10162.7 recognizes that the court has discretion to determine the total amount of compensation to be paid. Under subdivision (b), in the absence of an agreement between the two brokers, they split the commission on the amount of the original bid and the broker representing the successful overbidder receives all of the commission on the overbid. For examples of the operation of this section, see Examples 14, 16, and 17 in the Comment to Section 10161.

As to orders made, or actions taken, before July 1, 1988, and matters pending on July 1, 1988, see Section 9645. As to the application of any amendments made after that date, see Section 3.

Background on Section 10162.7 of Repealed Code

Section 10162.7 was added by 1987 Cal.Stat. ch. 923 § 93 and amended by 1989 Cal.Stat. ch. 544 § 13. The 1989 amendment revised subdivisions (a)(3) and (b) of Section 10162.7 to provide for the compensation in a situation where there is an agent or broker holding an exclusive listing contract and the sale is confirmed to a successful overbidder (produced by another agent or broker) who also made the original bid returned to the court for confirmation. For background on the provisions of this part, see the Comment to this part under the part heading. [20 Cal.L.Rev.Comm.Reports 1001 (1990)].

§ 10163. Original bid by purchaser not procured by agent or broker; sale to purchaser procured by agent or broker

Subject to Sections 10162 and 10162.6, where the original bid returned to the court for confirmation was made by a purchaser who was not procured by an agent or broker, the court shall allow the compensation determined under Section 10161 on the full amount for which the sale is confirmed to the agent or broker who procured the purchaser to whom the sale is confirmed if either of the following conditions is satisfied:

(a) The court confirms a sale on an increased bid, made at the time of the hearing on the petition for confirmation, to a purchaser procured by an agent or broker holding a contract under Section 10150 granting the exclusive right to sell the property.

(b) There is no agent or broker holding a contract under Section 10150 granting the exclusive right to sell the property and the court confirms a sale on an increased bid, made at the time of the hearing on the petition for confirmation, to a purchaser procured by a bona fide agent or broker. *(Stats. 1990, c. 79 (A.B.759), § 14, operative July 1, 1991.)*

Law Revision Commission Comments

1990 Enactment

Section 10163 continues Section 10163 of the repealed Probate Code without change, except that the introductory clause of subdivision (a) is revised to recognize the special rules in Section 10162.6 (exclusive contract providing that no compensation payable if sale confirmed to particular person named in contract). The reference to Section 10161 in Section 10163 makes clear that the court has discretion to determine the total amount of compensation to be paid. Section 10163 applies where there is no agent or broker holding an exclusive right to sell the property or where the agent or broker representing the overbidder holds an exclusive right to sell the property. For examples of the operation of this section, see Examples 4 and 5 in the Comment to Section 10161. For a limitation on the amount of compensation that may be allowed to the agent or broker who produces the successful overbidder, see Section 10162.

As to orders made, or actions taken, before July 1, 1988, and matters pending on July 1, 1988, see Section 9645. As to the application of any amendments made after that date, see Section 3.

Background on Section 10163 of Repealed Code

Section 10163 was added by 1987 Cal.Stat. ch. 923 § 93 and amended by 1989 Cal.Stat. ch. 544 § 14. Section 10163 restated the substance of former Probate Code Section 761.5 (repealed by 1987 Cal.Stat. ch. 923 § 39). Section 10163 referred to Section 10161 which restated the last portion of former Section 761.5 without substantive change. The 1989 amendment extended the rule of Section 10163 to cases where the successful overbidder is produced by an agent or broker holding an exclusive listing contract. For background on the provisions of this part, see the Comment to this part under the part heading. [20 Cal.L.Rev.Comm.Reports 1001 (1990)].

§ 10164. Purchaser in sale on increased bid not procured by agent or broker; compensation of original bid agent or broker

(a) This section applies only where the court confirms a sale on an increased bid, made at the time of the hearing on the petition for confirmation, to a purchaser who was not procured by a bona fide agent or broker.

(b) Except as provided in subdivision (c), the court shall allow the compensation determined under Section 10161 on the amount of the original bid to the agent or broker whose original bid was returned to the court.

(c) If an agent or broker holds a contract under Section 10150 granting the exclusive right to sell the property and the original bid returned to the court is made by a purchaser who was procured by another agent or broker, the compensation determined under Section 10161 on the amount of the original bid shall be divided between the agent or broker holding the contract and the other agent or broker as is provided in any agreement between the agent or broker holding the contract and the other agent or broker. If there is no agreement, the compensation shall be divided equally between the agent or broker holding the contract and the other agent or broker. *(Stats.1990, c. 79 (A.B.759), § 14, operative July 1, 1991.)*

Law Revision Commission Comments

1990 Enactment

Section 10164 continues Section 10164 of the repealed Probate Code without change. The references to Section 10161 in Section 10164 make clear that the court has discretion to determine the total amount of compensation to be paid and allocated. For examples of the operation of Section 10164, see Examples 2, 3, and 7 in the Comment to Section 10161.

As to orders made, or actions taken, before July 1, 1988, and matters pending on July 1, 1988, see Section 9645. As to the application of any amendments made after that date, see Section 3.

Background on Section 10164 of Repealed Code

Section 10164 was added by 1987 Cal.Stat. ch. 923 § 93. Subdivision (b) restated the last sentence of former Probate Code Section 761 (repealed by 1987 Cal.Stat. ch. 923 § 39) without substantive change. Subdivision (c) was a new provision that covered the situation where an agent or broker holds an exclusive right to sell contract and the original bid returned to the court is made by a purchaser who was produced by another agent or broker. Former Section 761 failed to cover this situation. If there is an agreement concerning the sharing of commissions, subdivision (c) of Section 10164 required that the court divide the commission as provided in the agreement, rather than requiring the court to "give consideration" to the agreement as under the second sentence of former Probate Code Section 760 (repealed by 1987 Cal.Stat. ch. 923 § 39). For background on the provisions of this part, see the Comment to this part under the part heading. [20 Cal.L.Rev.Comm.Reports 1001 (1990)].

§ 10165. Purchaser in sale on increased bid procured by agent or broker; allocation of compensation

(a) Subject to Section 10162.6, where the court confirms a sale on an increased bid, made at the time of the hearing on the petition for confirmation, to a purchaser procured by a bona fide agent or broker, the court shall allow the compensation determined under Section 10161 on the full amount for which the sale is confirmed, as provided in this section, if either of the following conditions is satisfied:

(1) The original bid returned to the court for confirmation was made by a purchaser who was procured by another agent or broker.

(2) The original bid returned to the court for confirmation was made by a purchaser who was not represented by an agent or broker, and another agent or broker holds a contract under Section 10150 granting the exclusive right to sell the property.

(b) The agent or broker who procured the purchaser to whom the sale is confirmed shall be paid one-half of the compensation on the amount of the original bid and all of the compensation on the difference between the original bid and the amount for which the sale is confirmed.

(c) The other one-half of the compensation on the amount of the original bid shall be paid as follows:

(1) If the original bid returned to the court is made by a purchaser who was procured by the agent or broker holding a contract under Section 10150 granting the exclusive right to sell the property, the entire one-half of the compensation on the original bid shall be paid to that agent or broker.

(2) If the original bid returned to the court is made by a purchaser who was procured by a bona fide agent or broker and there is no agent or broker holding a contract under Section 10150 granting the exclusive right to sell the property, the entire one-half of the compensation on the original bid shall be paid to that agent or broker.

(3) If there is an agent or broker who holds a contract under Section 10150 granting the exclusive right to sell the property and the original bid returned to the court is made by a purchaser who was procured by another agent or broker, the one-half of the compensation on the amount of the original bid shall be divided between the agent or broker holding the contract granting the exclusive right to sell the property and the other agent or broker whose original bid was returned to the court for confirmation as is provided in any agreement between the agent or broker holding the contract and the other agent or broker. If there is no agreement, the one-half of the compensation on the amount of the original bid shall be divided equally between the agent or broker holding the contract and the other agent or broker whose original bid was returned to the court for confirmation.

(4) If there is an agent or broker who holds a contract under Section 10150 granting the exclusive right to sell the property and the original bid returned to the court is made by a purchaser who is not represented by an agent or broker and the court confirms the sale on an increased bid, made at the time of the hearing on the petition for confirmation, to a purchaser procured by another agent or broker, the entire one-half of the compensation on the original bid shall be paid to the agent or broker holding the contract.

(5) If the agent or broker compensated under subdivision (b) holds a contract under Section 10150 granting the exclusive right to sell the property, the entire one-half of the compensation on the original bid shall be paid to the other agent or broker who procured the original bid returned to the court. *(Stats.1990, c. 79 (A.B.759), § 14, operative July 1, 1991.)*

Law Revision Commission Comments
1990 Enactment

Section 10165 continues Section 10165 of the repealed Probate Code without substantive change. The introductory clause is added to subdivision (a) to recognize the special rules in Section 10162.6 (exclusive contract providing that no compensation payable if sale confirmed to particular person named in contract). Subdivision (a) describes the circumstances that must exist before Section 10165 applies. The section applies only where the court confirms a sale on an increased bid made at the time of the hearing on the petition for confirmation. The successful overbidder must be one produced by a bona fide agent or broker. In addition, before the section applies one of the following requirements also must be satisfied:

(1) The original bid returned to court for confirmation was made by a purchaser who was produced by another agent or broker (i.e., an agent or broker other than the one who produced the successful overbidder).

(2) An agent or broker (other than the one who produced the successful overbidder) holds an exclusive sales contract. All that is required to satisfy this requirement is that an exclusive right to sell the property has been granted to the agent or broker; there is no requirement that the agent or broker holding the exclusive sales contract have produced the purchaser whose original bid was returned to the court for confirmation.

The reference in subdivision (a) to Section 10161 makes clear that the court has discretion to determine the total amount of compensation to be allocated under Section 10165. See the Comment to Section 10161. If there is an agreement concerning the sharing of commissions, subdivision (c) requires that the court divide the commission as provided in the agreement. Paragraph (3) of subdivision (c) makes clear that the agent or broker holding an exclusive right to sell contract is allowed a commission whether or not he or she returns a bid to the court. If the agent or broker who holds the contract under Section 10150 has not been granted an exclusive right to sell the property, the agent or broker is allowed a commission only if he or she returns the original bid to the court or produces the successful overbidder to whom the sale of the property is confirmed at the confirmation hearing. See Section 10161(b). For examples of the operation of this section, see Examples 6, 8, 9, 13, 18, and 19 in the Comment to Section 10161.

As to orders made, or actions taken, before July 1, 1988, and matters pending on July 1, 1988, see Section 9645. As to the application of any amendments made after that date, see Section 3.

Background on Section 10165 of Repealed Code

Section 10165 was added by 1987 Cal.Stat. ch. 923 § 93 and amended by 1989 Cal.Stat. ch. 544 § 15. Subdivision (a) was a new provision that described the circumstances that must exist before Section 10165 applied. Subdivision (b) restated a portion of the first sentence of former Probate Code Section 761 (repealed by 1987 Cal.Stat. ch. 923 § 39) without substantive change. Paragraphs (1) and (2) of subdivision (c) restated a portion of the first sentence of former Section 761 without substantive change. Paragraph (3) of subdivision (c) was a new provision that covered the situation where an agent or broker holds an exclusive right to sell contract and the original bid returned to the court is made by a purchaser who was produced by another agent or broker. Former Section 761 failed to cover this situation. Paragraph (3) made clear that the agent or broker holding an exclusive right to sell contract is allowed a

commission whether or not he or she returns a bid to the court. In this respect, paragraph (3) was consistent with what appears to have been prior law. See 1 H. Miller & M. Starr, Current Law of California Real Estate § 2:50, at 301 (rev. ed. 1975). If there is an agreement concerning the sharing of commissions, subdivision (c) required that the court divide the commission as provided in the agreement, rather than requiring the court to "give consideration" to the agreement as was the case under the second sentence of former Probate Code Section 760 (repealed by 1987 Cal.Stat. ch. 923 § 39).

The 1989 amendment revised Section 10165 by adding paragraphs (4) and (5) to subdivision (c) to cover situations not previously covered in Section 10165. Subdivision (a)(2) was amended to clarify the application of the section.

For background on the provisions of this part, see the Comment to this part under the part heading. [20 Cal.L.Rev.Comm.Reports 1001 (1990)].

Cross References

Compensation of agent in real property sales, see Probate Code § 10313.

§ 10166. Bids with condition that agent or broker be paid certain amount

Notwithstanding that a bid contains a condition that a certain amount of the bid shall be paid to an agent or broker by the personal representative, only such compensation as is proper under this article shall be allowed. Acceptance of the bid by the court binds the bidder even though the compensation allowed by the court is less than that specified by the condition. *(Stats.1990, c. 79 (A.B.759), § 14, operative July 1, 1991.)*

Law Revision Commission Comments
1990 Enactment

Section 10166 continues Section 10166 of the repealed Probate Code without change. As to orders made, or actions taken, before July 1, 1988, and matters pending on July 1, 1988, see Section 9645. As to the application of any amendments made after that date, see Section 3.

Background on Section 10166 of Repealed Code

Section 10166 was added by 1987 Cal.Stat. ch. 923 § 93. The section restated the last portion of the sixth sentence of former Probate Code Section 785 (real property) (repealed by 1987 Cal.Stat. ch. 923 § 39) without substantive change, and generalized it to apply also to sales of personal property. For background on the provisions of this part, see the Comment to this part under the part heading. [20 Cal.L.Rev.Comm.Reports 1001 (1990)].

§ 10167. Auctioneers

(a) Subject to subdivision (b), whether or not the auctioneer has a contract with the personal representative, the fees, compensation, and expenses of an auctioneer in connection with a sale of property shall be the amount the court, in its discretion, determines to be a reasonable compensation for the services of the auctioneer to the estate.

(b) If the auctioneer has a contract with the personal representative, the amount of the compensation of the auctioneer in connection with the sale of property shall not exceed the amount provided for in the contract. *(Stats.1990, c. 79 (A.B.759), § 14, operative July 1, 1991.)*

Law Revision Commission Comments

1990 Enactment

Section 10167 continues Section 10167 of the repealed Probate Code without change. The language used in this section is comparable to the language used in Section 10161 (compensation of agent or broker). The compensation to an auctioneer may be for the sale of personal property only. See Section 10151. As to orders made, or actions taken, before July 1, 1988, and matters pending on July 1, 1988, see Section 9645. As to the application of any amendments made after that date, see Section 3.

Background on Section 10167 of Repealed Code

Section 10167 was a new provision added by 1987 Cal.Stat. ch. 923 § 93. The section was consistent with the second sentence of former Probate Code Section 760.5 (auctioneer's fee "to be determined by the court") (repealed by 1987 Cal.Stat. ch. 923 § 39). For background on the provisions of this part, see the Comment to this part under the part heading. [20 Cal.L.Rev.Comm.Reports 1001 (1990)].

§ 10168. Effect of article on agreements between cooperating agents or brokers

This article does not supersede any agreement cooperating agents or brokers may have among themselves to divide the compensation payable under this article. *(Added by Stats. 1990, c. 710 (S.B.1775), § 26, operative July 1, 1991.)*

Law Revision Commission Comments

1990 Enactment

Section 10168 was added to the new Probate Code by 1990 Cal.Stat. ch. 710 § 26. The section provides a general rule consistent with the special rules concerning division of compensation between cooperating agents and brokers in Sections 10162.7(b), 10164(c), and 10165(c)(3). [20 Cal.L.Rev.Comm.Reports 1001 (1990)].

ARTICLE 4. SPECIAL PROVISIONS APPLICABLE TO PARTICULAR TYPES OF PROPERTY

Cross References

Application of old and new law, see Probate Code § 3.

§ 10200. Securities; definition; sale or surrender for redemption or conversion; notice of hearing and of sale or redemption

(a) As used in this section, "securities" means "security" as defined in Section 70, land trust certificates, certificates of beneficial interest in trusts, investment trust certificates, mortgage participation certificates, or certificates of deposit for any of the foregoing, but does not include notes secured by a mortgage or deed of trust unless the note or notes have been authorized or permitted to be issued by the Commissioner of Corporations or have been made by a public utility subject to the Public Utilities Act (Part 1 (commencing with Section 201) of Division 1 of the Public Utilities Code).

(b) After authorization by order of court, securities may be sold or may be surrendered for redemption or conversion. Title to the securities sold or surrendered as authorized by an order obtained under this section passes without the need for subsequent court confirmation.

(c) To obtain an order under this section, the personal representative or any interested person shall file a petition stating the terms and conditions and the advantage to the estate of the proposed sale or redemption or conversion. If the court authorizes the sale, redemption, or conversion, the court's order shall fix the terms and conditions of sale, redemption, or conversion.

(d) Notice of the hearing on the petition shall be given as provided in Section 1220 and posted as provided in Section 1230, but the court may order that the notice be given for a shorter period or dispensed with.

(e) No notice of sale or of the redemption or conversion need be given if any of the following conditions are satisfied:

(1) The minimum selling price is fixed by the court.

(2) The securities are to be sold on an established stock or bond exchange.

(3) The securities to be sold are securities designated as a national market system security on an interdealer quotation system, or subsystem thereof, by the National Association of Securities Dealers, Inc., sold through a broker-dealer registered under the Securities Exchange Act of 1934 during the regular course of business of the broker-dealer.

(4) The securities are to be surrendered for redemption or conversion. *(Stats.1990, c. 79 (A.B.759), § 14, operative July 1, 1991.)*

Law Revision Commission Comments

1990 Enactment

Section 10200 continues Section 10200 of the repealed Probate Code without change. The personal representative is required to exercise the power granted by this section to the extent that ordinary care and diligence require that the power be exercised and may not exercise the power to the extent that ordinary care and diligence require that the power not be exercised. See Section 9600(b). As to the effect of court authorization or approval, see Section 7250. See also Section 10201 (sale or withdrawal of savings accounts and mutual capital certificates without court order). For general provisions, see Sections 1000–1004 (rules of practice), 1020–1023 (petitions and other papers), 1040–1050 (hearings and orders), 1200–1230 (notice of hearing), 1250–1252 (request for special notice), 1260–1265 (proof of giving of notice). As to orders made, or actions taken, before July 1, 1988, and matters pending on July 1, 1988, see Section 9645. As to the application of any amendments made after that date, see Section 3.

Background on Section 10200 of Repealed Code

Section 10200 was added by 1987 Cal.Stat. ch. 923 § 93. The section restated subdivisions (a) and (b) of former Probate Code Section 771 (repealed by 1987 Cal.Stat. ch. 923 § 39) without substantive change, except that (1) the first sentence of subdivision

(c) and paragraph (3) of subdivision (e) were new, and (2) Section 10200 required that notice under subdivision (d) be given at least 15 days before the hearing pursuant to Sections 1220 and 1230 instead of at least 10 days before the hearing as required under former Probate Code Sections 1200 and 1200.5 (provisions repealed by 1987 Cal.Stat. ch. 923 § 59). For background on the provisions of this part, see the Comment to this part under the part heading. [20 Cal.L.Rev.Comm.Reports 1001 (1990)].

Cross References

Commissioner of corporations, powers and duties, generally, see Corporations Code § 25300.

Participation certificates, issued by trust company, see Financial Code § 1565.

Savings association stocks and shares, generally, see Financial Code § 5620 et seq.

§ 10201. Savings accounts, mutual capital certificates of savings association or federal association; sale on surrender for withdrawal

(a) For purposes of this section:

(1) "Federal association" is defined in Section 5102 of the Financial Code.

(2) "Mutual capital certificate" is defined in Section 5111 of the Financial Code.

(3) "Savings account" is defined in Section 5116 of the Financial Code.

(4) "Savings association" is defined in Section 5102 of the Financial Code.

(5) "Withdrawal value" is defined in Section 5124 of the Financial Code.

(b) Notwithstanding Section 10200, savings accounts and mutual capital certificates of a savings association or federal association may be sold or surrendered for withdrawal by the personal representative, and title thereto passed, without notice of sale, prior order of court, or subsequent confirmation by the court, if an amount of money is obtained upon the sale or withdrawal not less than the withdrawal value of the savings account or the value of the mutual capital certificate.

(c) Notwithstanding Section 10200, credit union share accounts and certificates for funds may be sold or withdrawn by the personal representative, and title thereto passed, without notice of sale, prior order of court, or subsequent confirmation by the court, if an amount of money is obtained upon the sale or withdrawal not less than the withdrawal value of the share account or the value of the certificate for funds. *(Stats.1990, c. 79 (A.B.759), § 14, operative July 1, 1991.)*

Law Revision Commission Comments

1990 Enactment

Section 10201 continues Section 10201 of the repealed Probate Code without substantive change. As to orders made, or actions taken, before July 1, 1988, and matters pending on July 1, 1988, see Section 9645. As to the application of any amendments made after that date, see Section 3.

Background on Section 10201 of Repealed Code

Section 10201 was added by 1987 Cal.Stat. ch. 923 § 93. Subdivisions (a) and (b) restated subdivision (c) of former Probate Code Section 771 (repealed by 1987 Cal.Stat. ch. 923 § 39) without substantive change. Subdivision (c) was new. For background on

the provisions of this part, see the Comment to this part under the part heading. [20 Cal.L.Rev.Comm.Reports 1001 (1990)].

Cross References

Certificate of deposit, generally, see Financial Code § 1206.

§ 10202. Subscription rights to securities; sale

Notwithstanding Section 10200, if an estate by reason of owning securities, also owns or receives subscription rights for the purchase of additional securities, the personal representative may sell all or part of the subscription rights without notice of sale, prior order of court, or subsequent confirmation by the court. *(Stats.1990, c. 79 (A.B.759), § 14, operative July 1, 1991.)*

Law Revision Commission Comments

1990 Enactment

Section 10202 continues Section 10202 of the repealed Probate Code without change. The personal representative is required to exercise the power granted by this section to the extent that ordinary care and diligence require that the power be exercised and may not exercise the power to the extent that ordinary care and diligence require that the power not be exercised. See Section 9600(b). See also Sections 9734 (exercise of option rights), 9737 (exercise of subscription rights). As to orders made, or actions taken, before July 1, 1988, and matters pending on July 1, 1988, see Section 9645. As to the application of any amendments made after that date, see Section 3.

Background on Section 10202 of Repealed Code

Section 10202 was added by 1987 Cal.Stat. ch. 923 § 93. The section restated former Probate Code Section 771.5 (repealed by 1987 Cal.Stat. ch. 923 § 39) without substantive change except that language was added in Section 10202 to make clear that notice of sale and confirmation of sale is not required. This new language made Section 10202 consistent with subdivision (e) of Section 10200 and with Section 10201. The words "stocks" and "bonds" which appeared in former Section 771.5 were omitted in view of the broad definition of "securities" provided in Section 70. For background on the provisions of this part, see the Comment to this part under the part heading. [20 Cal.L.Rev.Comm.Reports 1001 (1990)].

§ 10203. Sale to be made as in case of personal property; sale of leasehold interest

(a) Except as provided in subdivision (b), where property to be sold consists of a leasehold interest, the sale shall be made as in the case of the sale of personal property of the estate.

(b) The sale of a leasehold interest shall be made as in the case of the sale of real property of the estate if the interest to be sold consists of any of the following:

(1) A leasehold interest in real property with an unexpired term of 10 years or longer. For this purpose, the leasehold interest shall be considered to have an unexpired term of 10 years or longer if the lessee has the right to extend the term and the term, if extended, would exceed 10 years.

(2) A leasehold interest in real property together with an option to purchase the leased property or some part thereof.

(3) A lease for the purpose of production of minerals, oil, gas, or other hydrocarbon substances, or geothermal energy. *(Stats.1990, c. 79 (A.B.759), § 14, operative July 1, 1991.)*

Law Revision Commission Comments

1990 Enactment

Section 10203 continues Section 10203 of the repealed Probate Code without change. The second sentence of paragraph (1) of subdivision (b) is consistent with subdivision (b) of Section 9940 (leasing property of estate). As to orders made, or actions taken, before July 1, 1988, and matters pending on July 1, 1988, see Section 9645. As to the application of any amendments made after that date, see Section 3.

Background on Section 10203 of Repealed Code

Section 10203 was added by 1987 Cal.Stat. ch. 923 § 93. The section continued former Probate Code Section 754.6 (repealed by 1987 Cal.Stat. ch. 923 § 39) without substantive change, except that the second sentence of paragraph (1) of subdivision (b) of Section 10203 was new, and paragraph (3) of subdivision (b) of Section 10203 broadened the former provision to include, in addition to an oil or gas lease, a lease for the production of minerals, other hydrocarbon substances, or geothermal resources. This made Section 10203 consistent with Sections 9940(b) and 9946 (leases). For background on the provisions of this part, see the Comment to this part under the part heading. [20 Cal.L.Rev.Comm.Reports 1001 (1990)].

Cross References

Personal property, sale, see Probate Code § 10250 et seq.
Real property, sale, see Probate Code § 10300 et seq.

§ 10204. Partnership interests; sale

Property of the estate that consists of a partnership interest or an interest belonging to an estate by virtue of a partnership formerly existing may be sold in the same manner as other personal property. *(Stats.1990, c. 79 (A.B.759), § 14, operative July 1, 1991.)*

Law Revision Commission Comments

1990 Enactment

Section 10204 continues Section 10204 of the repealed Probate Code without change. A partner's interest in the partnership is that partner's share of the profits and surplus and is itself personal property. Corp.Code § 15026; Kenworthy v. Hadden, 87 Cal. App.3d 696, 701, 151 Cal.Rptr. 169 (1978); see generally Annot., 80 A.L.R.2d 1107 (1961 & Supp.1989) (effect of Section 26 of the Uniform Partnership Act (1914) as converting realty into personalty). See also Section 10261 (confirmation of sale of partnership interest). As to orders made, or actions taken, before July 1, 1988, and matters pending on July 1, 1988, see Section 9645. As to the application of any amendments made after that date, see Section 3.

Background on Section 10204 of Repealed Code

Section 10204 was added by 1987 Cal.Stat. ch. 923 § 93. The section continued a portion of the first sentence of former Probate Code Section 774 (repealed by 1987 Cal.Stat. ch. 923 § 39) without substantive change. For background on the provisions of this part, see the Comment to this part under the part heading. [20 Cal.L.Rev.Comm.Reports 1001 (1990)].

Cross References

Appraisement of partnership interest, see Probate Code §§ 8800, 8850.
Partnership and partnership interest defined, see Civil Code § 684; Revenue and Taxation Code § 17008.
Sale of personal property, notice of, see Probate Code § 10250 et seq.
Uniform partnership act, effect on partnership provisions of this section, see Corporations Code § 15045.

Vesting of decedent's right in specific partnership property in surviving partners, see Corporations Code § 15025.

§ 10205. Chose in action; sale

A chose in action belonging to the estate may be sold in the same manner as other personal property. *(Stats.1990, c. 79 (A.B.759), § 14, operative July 1, 1991.)*

Law Revision Commission Comments

1990 Enactment

Section 10205 continues Section 10205 of the repealed Probate Code without change. As to orders made, or actions taken, before July 1, 1988, and matters pending on July 1, 1988, see Section 9645. As to the application of any amendments made after that date, see Section 3.

Background on Section 10205 of Repealed Code

Section 10205 was added by 1987 Cal.Stat. ch. 923 § 93. The section continued a portion of the first sentence of former Probate Code Section 774 (repealed by 1987 Cal.Stat. ch. 923 § 39) without substantive change. For background on the provisions of this part, see the Comment to this part under the part heading. [20 Cal.L.Rev.Comm.Reports 1001 (1990)].

§ 10206. Contracts for purchase of real property; sale; bond required

(a) Except as otherwise provided in this section, if the decedent at the time of death was possessed of a contract for the purchase of real property and the decedent's interest in the property and under the contract is to be sold, the sale shall be made as in the case of the sale of real property of the estate.

(b) If the decedent's interest in the property and under the contract is sold, the sale shall be made subject to all payments which are due at the time of sale or which may thereafter become due on the contract. Except as provided in subdivision (d), if there are any payments due or to become due, the court shall not confirm the sale until the purchaser executes a bond to the personal representative that satisfies the requirements of subdivision (c).

(c) The bond shall be for the benefit and indemnity of the personal representative and the persons entitled to the interest of the decedent in the real property contracted for. The amount of the bond shall be equal to the amount of payments then due and thereafter to become due on the contract, with such sureties as the court may approve. The bond shall be conditioned that the purchaser will (1) make all payments for the property which are then due or which become due after the date of the sale and (2) fully indemnify the personal representative and the person entitled to the interest of the decedent against all demands, costs, charges, and expenses, by reason of any covenant or agreement contained in the contract.

(d) The bond need not be given in either of the following cases:

(1) Where no claim has been made against the estate on the contract and the time for filing claims has expired.

(2) Where the person entitled to payment under the contract waives all recourse to the assets of the estate for payment and releases the estate and the personal representa-

tive from liability for payment. *(Stats.1990, c. 79 (A.B.759), § 14, operative July 1, 1991.)*

Law Revision Commission Comments

1990 Enactment

Section 10206 continues Section 10206 of the repealed Probate Code without substantive change. The reference to the "judge" approving the sureties on the bond has been omitted as unnecessary in view of Code of Civil Procedure Section 166(a)(5) (powers of judge at chambers).

The bond covers whatever is required under the contract to be paid. This includes, for example, both principal and interest payments required to be made under the contract. See also Section 10314 (assignment of contract right to purchaser after furnishing of bond and confirmation of sale).

Treating the sale of the decedent's contract right to purchase real property in the same manner as sale of real property generally is consistent with the general treatment of such interests as real property at the decedent's death. See Fleishman v. Woods, 135 Cal. 256, 259, 67 P. 276 (1901) (equitable estate of vendee "is alienable, descendible, and devisable in like manner as real estate held by a legal title"); Retsloff v. Smith, 79 Cal.App. 443, 448, 249 P. 886 (1926) ("[i]f the purchaser dies while the contract is in force and effect, his interest passes to his heirs as real property").

As to orders made, or actions taken, before July 1, 1988, and matters pending on July 1, 1988, see Section 9645. As to the application of any amendments made after that date, see Section 3.

Background on Section 10206 of Repealed Code

Section 10206 was added by 1987 Cal.Stat. ch. 923 § 93. Subdivision (a) restated former Probate Code Section 800 (repealed by 1987 Cal.Stat. ch. 923 § 39) without substantive change. The remainder of Section 10206 restated former Probate Code Section 801 (repealed by 1987 Cal.Stat. ch. 923 § 39) without substantive change. For background on the provisions of this part, see the Comment to this part under the part heading. [20 Cal.L.Rev.Comm.Reports 1001 (1990)].

Cross References

Confirmation of sales, generally, see Probate Code §§ 10260 et seq., 10308 et seq.
Provisions applicable to sales in general, see Probate Code § 21400 et seq.
Sale of,
    Decedent's property to complete contract, see Probate Code § 9860 et seq.
    Real property, see Probate Code § 10300 et seq.

§ 10207. Rural property suitable for shift-in-land-use loan to develop grazing or pasture facilities; court order for sale

(a) Real property suitable for a shift-in-land-use loan to develop grazing or pasture facilities may be sold under this section by the personal representative to a grazing or pasture association in conformity with the federal Consolidated Farm and Rural Development Act (7 U.S.C. Sec. 1921, et seq.) after authorization by order of the court.

(b) The personal representative or any interested person may file a petition for an order under this section. Notice of the hearing on the petition shall be given as provided in Section 1220.

(c) An order for sale of property under this section may be made only if the court determines both of the following:

(1) Either the sale is made pursuant to the will of the decedent or all of the following have consented to the sale:

(A) Each known heir whose interest in the estate would be affected by the sale.

(B) Each known devisee who has an interest in the property under the decedent's will.

(2) The sale will not jeopardize the rights of creditors of the estate.

(d) If the court makes an order authorizing sale of the property, the personal representative may make the sale in accord with the terms and conditions set out in the order, subject to the following requirements:

(1) Except as provided in Sections 10002, 10301, 10303, and 10503, notice of the time and place of the sale shall be published pursuant to Section 10300.

(2) The price of the sale made shall be not less than the value of the property as established by an independent and competent appraiser mutually acceptable to the federal government, the grazing or pasture association, and the personal representative.

(3) Except as provided in Sections 10002 and 10503, the sale shall be reported to and confirmed by the court as provided in Article 6 (commencing with Section 10300) before title to the property passes, but the sale may be made irrespective of whether a higher bid is made to the court at the hearing on the petition to confirm the sale. *(Stats.1990, c. 79 (A.B.759), § 14, operative July 1, 1991.)*

Law Revision Commission Comments

1990 Enactment

Section 10207 continues Section 10207 of the repealed Probate Code without change. For general provisions, see Sections 1000–1004 (rules of practice), 1020–1023 (petitions and other papers), 1040–1050 (hearings and orders), 1200–1230 (notice of hearing), 1250–1252 (request for special notice), 1260–1265 (proof of giving of notice).

Subdivision (a) of former Probate Code Section 794 (repealed by 1987 Cal.Stat. ch. 923 § 39) (finding and declaration of legislative purpose) from which Section 10207 was drawn is not continued as a codified provision, but may be found in 1978 Cal.Stat. ch. 40.

As to orders made, or actions taken, before July 1, 1988, and matters pending on July 1, 1988, see Section 9645. As to the application of any amendments made after that date, see Section 3.

Background on Section 10207 of Repealed Code

Section 10207 was added by 1987 Cal.Stat. ch. 923 § 93. The section restated subdivision (b) of former Probate Code Section 794 (repealed by 1987 Cal.Stat. ch. 923 § 39) with the addition of subdivision (b) and language that makes clear that the sale may be made only with the consent of the "known" heirs and the "known" devisees. For background on the provisions of this part, see the Comment to this part under the part heading. [20 Cal.L.Rev.Comm.Reports 1001 (1990)].

Cross References

Sales of real property of an estate, requirements for sales to be reported to and confirmed by court, see Probate Code § 10308.

ARTICLE 5. SALE OF PERSONAL PROPERTY

Section
10250. Notice of sale.

Cross References

Application of old and new law, see Probate Code § 3.

§ 10250. Notice of sale

Subject to Sections 10251 and 10252 and except as otherwise provided by statute, personal property of the estate may be sold only after notice of sale is given by one or both of the following methods, as the personal representative may determine:

(a) Posting at the county courthouse of the county in which the proceedings are pending at least 15 days before:

(1) In the case of a private sale, the day specified in the notice of sale as the day on or after which the sale is to be made.

(2) In the case of a public auction sale, the day of the auction.

(b) Publication pursuant to Section 6063a of the Government Code in a newspaper in the county in which the proceedings are pending, such publication to be completed before:

(1) In the case of a private sale, the day specified in the notice of sale as the day on or after which the sale is to be made.

(2) In the case of a public auction sale, the day of the auction. *(Stats.1990, c. 79 (A.B.759), § 14, operative July 1, 1991.)*

Law Revision Commission Comments

1990 Enactment

Section 10250 continues Section 10250 of the repealed Probate Code without change. As to when property of the estate may or must be sold, see Sections 10000, 10001. See also Section 10251 (shortening time of notice of sale). For provisions permitting sale of personal property without notice of sale, see Sections 10200 (securities), 10201 (savings accounts and mutual capital certificates), 10202 (subscription rights), 10252 (perishable property; property directed or authorized by will to be sold; property sold to pay family allowance). See also Section 9640 (independent administration authority not limited). As to orders made, or actions taken, before July 1, 1988, and matters pending on July 1, 1988, see Section 9645.

As to the application of any amendments made after that date, see Section 3.

Background on Section 10250 of Repealed Code

Section 10250 was added by 1987 Cal.Stat. ch. 923 § 93. The section restated the first sentence of former Probate Code Section 772 (repealed by 1987 Cal.Stat. ch. 923 § 39) without substantive change, except that subdivision (a) extended the former 10–day period for posting of notice of sale to 15 days. For background on the provisions of this part, see the Comment to this part under the part heading. [20 Cal.L.Rev.Comm.Reports 1001 (1990)].

Cross References

Publications, generally, see Government Code § 6000 et seq.

§ 10251. Shortened time of notice of sale; method of notice

(a) If it is shown that it will be to the advantage of the estate, the court or judge may by order shorten the time of notice of sale to not less than five days.

(b) If the court or judge makes an order under subdivision (a), notice of sale shall be given by one or both of the following methods, as the personal representative may determine:

(1) By posting as provided in Section 10250 except that the posting shall be for at least five days instead of 15 days as required by Section 10250.

(2) By publication as provided in Section 10250 except that the publication shall be pursuant to Section 6061 of the Government Code. *(Stats.1990, c. 79 (A.B.759), § 14, operative July 1, 1991.)*

Law Revision Commission Comments

1990 Enactment

Section 10251 continues Section 10251 of the repealed Probate Code without change. As to orders made, or actions taken, before July 1, 1988, and matters pending on July 1, 1988, see Section 9645. As to the application of any amendments made after that date, see Section 3.

Background on Section 10251 of Repealed Code

Section 10251 was added by 1987 Cal.Stat. ch. 923 § 93. The section restated the second sentence of former Probate Code Section 772 (repealed by 1987 Cal.Stat. ch. 923 § 39) without substantive change. The reference in Section 10251 to a court "or judge" was drawn from former Probate Code Section 782 (real property) (repealed by 1987 Cal.Stat. ch. 923 § 39). For background on the provisions of this part, see the Comment to this part under the part heading. [20 Cal.L.Rev.Comm.Reports 1001 (1990)].

§ 10252. Sales with or without notice as determined by personal representative

Personal property may be sold with or without notice, as the personal representative may determine, in any of the following cases:

(a) Where the property is directed by the will to be sold.

(b) Where authority is given in the will to sell the property.

(c) Where the property is perishable, will depreciate in value if not disposed of promptly, or will incur loss or expense by being kept.

(d) Where sale of the property is necessary to provide for the payment of a family allowance pending receipt of other sufficient funds. *(Stats.1990, c. 79 (A.B.759), § 14, operative July 1, 1991.)*

Law Revision Commission Comments
1990 Enactment

Section 10252 continues Section 10252 of the repealed Probate Code without change. Under Section 10252, it is not necessary that the will specifically grant the personal representative authority to sell without notice. If the will directs or authorizes the sale, whether or not notice should be given is within the discretion of the personal representative. See Bagley v. City and County of San Francisco, 19 Cal.App. 255, 271, 125 P. 931 (1912). However, unless there is some other statutory provision dispensing with the need for confirmation of the sale in the particular case, a sale of personal property made pursuant to a direction or authorization in the will must be confirmed by the court before title to the property passes to the purchaser. See Section 10260. For other provisions permitting sale of personal property without notice of sale, see Sections 10200 (securities), 10201 (savings accounts and mutual capital certificates), 10202 (subscription rights). As to orders made, or actions taken, before July 1, 1988, and matters pending on July 1, 1988, see Section 9645. As to the application of any amendments made after that date, see Section 3.

Background on Section 10252 of Repealed Code

Section 10252 was added by 1987 Cal.Stat. ch. 923 § 93. Subdivisions (a) and (b) restated a portion of the first sentence of former Probate Code Section 757 (repealed by 1987 Cal.Stat. ch. 923 § 39) without substantive change. Subdivisions (c) and (d) restated the first portion of former Probate Code Section 770 (repealed by 1987 Cal.Stat. ch. 923 § 39) without substantive change. For background on the provisions of this part, see the Comment to this part under the part heading. [20 Cal.L.Rev.Comm.Reports 1001 (1990)].

Cross References

Family allowance, generally, see Probate Code § 6540 et seq.
Special administrator, sale of perishable property by, see Probate Code § 8544.

§ 10253. Contents of notice of sale

(a) The notice of sale given pursuant to Section 10250 shall state all of the following:

(1) Whether the sale is to be a private sale or a public auction sale.

(2) In the case of a private sale, the place at which bids or offers will be received and a day on or after which the sale will be made or, in the case of a public auction sale, the time and place of sale.

(3) A brief description of the personal property to be sold.

(b) The notice of sale may state other matters in addition to those required by subdivision (a), including terms and conditions of sale. *(Stats.1990, c. 79 (A.B.759), § 14, operative July 1, 1991.)*

Law Revision Commission Comments
1990 Enactment

Section 10253 continues Section 10253 of the repealed Probate Code without change. As to orders made, or actions taken, before July 1, 1988, and matters pending on July 1, 1988, see Section 9645. As to the application of any amendments made after that date, see Section 3.

Background on Section 10253 of Repealed Code

Section 10253 was added by 1987 Cal.Stat. ch. 923 § 93. Subdivision (a) restated the third sentence and a portion of the fourth

sentence of former Probate Code Section 772 (repealed by 1987 Cal.Stat. ch. 923 § 39) without substantive change. Subdivision (b) was new and codified the prior practice. For background on the provisions of this part, see the Comment to this part under the part heading. [20 Cal.L.Rev.Comm.Reports 1001 (1990)].

§ 10254. Auction sales

(a) Unless the court orders otherwise pursuant to subdivision (b):

(1) A sale of personal property at a public auction sale shall be made within this state at the courthouse door, at the auction house, at some other public place, or at the residence of the decedent.

(2) No public auction sale shall be made of any tangible personal property that is not present at the time of sale.

(b) Upon petition of the personal representative or any interested person, the court may order either or both of the following:

(1) That a sale of personal property at public auction be made at any place within or without the United States.

(2) That tangible personal property need not be present at the time of sale.

(c) The personal representative may postpone a public auction sale of personal property from time to time if all of the following conditions are satisfied:

(1) The personal representative believes that the postponement is to the advantage of the estate.

(2) Notice of the postponement is given by public declaration at the time and place appointed for the sale.

(3) The postponement, together with previous postponements of sale of the property, does not exceed three months. *(Stats.1990, c. 79 (A.B.759), § 14, operative July 1, 1991.)*

Law Revision Commission Comments
1990 Enactment

Section 10254 continues Section 10254 of the repealed Probate Code without substantive change. Under paragraph (1) of subdivision (b), the court may order, for example, that rare art works be sold in some other country when to do so will afford a better market. See also Section 10151 (manner of sale pursuant to contract with auctioneer). For the provision concerning passage of title to personal property sold at public auction without court confirmation or approval, see Section 10259. The overbid provision does not apply where property is sold at public auction. See Sections 10259(b), 10262(c). For general provisions relating to petitions, see Sections 1020–1023. As to orders made, or actions taken, before July 1, 1988, and matters pending on July 1, 1988, see Section 9645. As to the application of any amendments made after that date, see Section 3.

Background on Section 10254 of Repealed Code

Section 10254 was added by 1987 Cal.Stat. ch. 923 § 93. The section restated the fifth, sixth, and seventh sentences of former Probate Code Section 772 (repealed by 1987 Cal.Stat. ch. 923 § 39) without substantive change, except that the former requirement that personal property be present at the time of sale was limited by Section 10254 to "tangible" personal property, and the authority for the court to order that the auction be held somewhere other than as required in paragraph (1) of subdivision (a) was new. For background on the provisions of this part, see the Comment to this part under the part heading. [20 Cal.L.Rev.Comm.Reports 1001 (1990)].

§ 10255. Private sales

(a) A private sale of personal property may not be made before the day stated in the notice of sale as the day on or after which the sale will be made, nor later than one year after that day.

(b) In the case of a private sale of personal property, the bids or offers shall be in writing and shall be left at the place designated in the notice of sale, or be delivered to the personal representative personally or to the person specified in the notice of sale, at any time after the first publication or posting of notice of sale and before the making of the sale. *(Stats.1990, c. 79 (A.B.759), § 14, operative July 1, 1991.)*

Law Revision Commission Comments

1990 Enactment

Section 10255 continues Section 10255 of the repealed Probate Code without change. Subdivision (b) permits the notice of sale to require, for example, that bids be delivered to the attorney for the personal representative. As to orders made, or actions taken, before July 1, 1988, and matters pending on July 1, 1988, see Section 9645. As to the application of any amendments made after that date, see Section 3.

Background on Section 10255 of Repealed Code

Section 10255 was added by 1987 Cal.Stat. ch. 923 § 93. Subdivision (a) restated a portion of the fourth sentence of former Probate Code Section 772 (repealed by 1987 Cal.Stat. ch. 923 § 39). Subdivision (b) was new and codified existing practice. For background on the provisions of this part, see the Comment to this part under the part heading. [20 Cal.L.Rev.Comm.Reports 1001 (1990)].

§ 10256. Bids

Whether a sale of personal property is private or at public auction, bids shall substantially comply with any terms specified in the notice of sale. *(Stats.1990, c. 79 (A.B.759), § 14, operative July 1, 1991.)*

Law Revision Commission Comments

1990 Enactment

Section 10256 continues Section 10256 of the repealed Probate Code without change. This section is consistent with prior case law. See In re Estate of Dargie, 33 Cal.App.2d 148, 155–57, 91 P.2d 126 (1939) (personal property); cf. Estate of Hunter, 194 Cal.App.2d 859, 865–68, 15 Cal.Rptr. 556 (1961) (real property). For the section prescribing required and optional contents of the notice of sale, see Section 10253. As to orders made, or actions taken, before July 1, 1988, and matters pending on July 1, 1988, see Section 9645. As to the application of any amendments made after that date, see Section 3.

Background on Section 10256 of Repealed Code

Section 10256 was a new provision added by 1987 Cal.Stat. ch. 923 § 93. For background on the provisions of this part, see the Comment to this part under the part heading. [20 Cal.L.Rev.Comm.Reports 1001 (1990)].

§ 10257. Cash or credit sales; conditions of credit sale

(a) Personal property may be sold for cash or on credit.

(b) Except as may otherwise be ordered by the court pursuant to Section 10258, if a sale is made on credit, not less than 25 percent of the purchase price shall be paid in cash at the time of sale, and the personal representative shall do one of the following:

(1) Take the note of the purchaser for the balance of the purchase money, with a security interest in the personal propery [1] sold, to secure the payment of the balance.

(2) Enter into a conditional sale contract under which title is retained until the balance is paid.

(c) The terms of the note and security interest or conditional sale contract shall be approved by the court at the time of confirmation of sale.

(d) Where property sold by the personal representative for part cash and part deferred payments consists of an undivided interest in personal property or any other interest therein less than the entire ownership and the owner or owners of the remaining interests therein join in the sale, the note and security interest may be made to the personal representative and such others having an interest in the property. The interest of the personal representative in the note and security interest shall be in the same interest and in the same proportions as the estate's interest in the property prior to the sale. *(Stats.1990, c. 79 (A.B.759), § 14, operative July 1, 1991.)*

[1] So in enrolled bill.

Law Revision Commission Comments

1990 Enactment

Section 10257 continues Section 10257 of the repealed Probate Code without change. Concerning the requirement that 25 percent of the purchase price be paid in cash at the time of sale, see Consolidated Copperstate Lines v. Frasher, 141 Cal.App.2d 916, 924–26, 297 P.2d 692 (1956). See also Section 10258 (court order relaxing requirements for credit sale). As to orders made, or actions taken, before July 1, 1988, and matters pending on July 1, 1988, see Section 9645. As to the application of any amendments made after that date, see Section 3.

Background on Section 10257 of Repealed Code

Section 10257 was added by 1987 Cal.Stat. ch. 923 § 93. Subdivisions (a), (b), and (c) restated the first, second, third, and fourth sentences of former Probate Code Section 773 (repealed by 1987 Cal.Stat. ch. 923 § 39) without substantive change. "Security interest" was substituted in Section 10257 for "pledge" and "chattel mortgage" which appeared in former Section 773. Under the California Commercial Code, the security interest replaces the pledge and chattel mortgage. See California State Bar Committee on the Commercial Code, A Special Report, The Uniform Commercial Code, 37 Cal.St.B.J. 117, 198–99 (1962). Subdivision (d) restated the second and third sentences of former Probate Code Section 787 (repealed by 1987 Cal.Stat. ch. 923 § 39) without substantive change as it applied to personal property. For background on the provisions of this part, see the Comment to this part under the part heading. [20 Cal.L.Rev.Comm.Reports 1001 (1990)].

Cross References

Sale of real property on credit, see Probate Code § 10315.
Sales, passage of title upon confirmation of court, see Probate Code §§ 10260, 10308.

§ 10258. Credit sales; exceptions to statutory requirements by court order; notice

(a) On petition of the personal representative, the court may by order authorize a sale of personal property on credit on terms providing for less than 25 percent of the purchase price to be paid in cash at the time of sale, or may waive or modify the requirement that a security interest or other lien shall be retained or taken to secure payment of the balance of the purchase price, where it is shown that the terms are to the advantage of the estate and the property to be sold is of such a nature that it is impracticable to sell the property for a larger cash payment at the time of sale or to retain a security interest or other lien in the property. The order of the court shall fix the terms and conditions of the sale.

(b) Notice of the hearing on the petition shall be posted as provided in Section 1230 and given as provided in Section 1220 to all of the following persons:

(1) Each person listed in Section 1220.

(2) Each known heir whose interest in the estate would be affected by the sale.

(3) Each known devisee whose interest in the estate would be affected by the sale. *(Stats.1990, c. 79 (A.B.759), § 14, operative July 1, 1991.)*

Law Revision Commission Comments

1990 Enactment

Section 10258 continues Section 10258 of the repealed Probate Code without substantive change. This section permits the court to vary the requirements of Section 10257 where it is impractical to meet those requirements, such as in the sale of an insurance business, a liquor license, the goodwill of a business, or the stock in trade of a merchant. Only the personal representative may petition under Section 10258. An interested person may neither petition under Section 10258 nor petition for instructions under Section 9611. But see Section 9613 (right of interested person to petition for order directing personal representative in order to avoid great or irreparable injury). For general provisions, see Sections 1000–1004 (rules of practice), 1020–1023 (petitions and other papers), 1040–1050 (hearings and orders), 1200–1230 (notice of hearing), 1250–1252 (request for special notice), 1260–1265 (proof of giving of notice). As to orders made, or actions taken, before July 1, 1988, and matters pending on July 1, 1988, see Section 9645. As to the application of any amendments made after that date, see Section 3.

Background on Section 10258 of Repealed Code

Section 10258 was added by 1987 Cal.Stat. ch. 923 § 93. The section restated the fifth, sixth, seventh, and eighth sentences of former Probate Code Section 773 (repealed by 1987 Cal.Stat. ch. 923 § 39) without substantive change, except that subdivisions (b) and (c) of Section 10258 required that notice be given at least 15 days before the hearing pursuant to Probate Code Sections 1220 and 1230 instead of at least 10 days before the hearing as required under former Probate Code Sections 1200 and 1200.5 (provisions repealed by 1987 Cal.Stat. ch. 923 § 59). For background on the provisions of this part, see the Comment to this part under the part heading. [20 Cal.L.Rev.Comm.Reports 1001 (1990)].

§ 10259. Title to certain property passing upon sale without need for court confirmation or approval

(a) Title to the following personal property passes upon sale without the need for court confirmation or approval:

(1) Personal property which is perishable, which will depreciate in value if not disposed of promptly, or which will incur loss or expense by being kept.

(2) Personal property the sale of which is necessary to provide for the payment of a family allowance pending receipt of other sufficient funds.

(b) Title to personal property sold at public auction passes without the need for court confirmation or approval upon receipt of the purchase price and:

(1) In the case of tangible personal property, the delivery of the property to the purchaser.

(2) In the case of intangible personal property, the delivery to the purchaser of the instrument that transfers the title to the property to the purchaser.

(c) The personal representative is responsible for the actual value of the property described in subdivision (a) or (b) unless the sale is reported to and approved by the court. *(Stats.1990, c. 79 (A.B.759), § 14, operative July 1, 1991.)*

Law Revision Commission Comments

1990 Enactment

Section 10259 continues Section 10259 of the repealed Probate Code without change. For other provisions dispensing with the requirement of court confirmation, see Sections 10200 (securities), 10201 (mutual capital certificates, savings accounts), 10202 (subscription rights). For special confirmation provisions, see Sections 10206 (decedent's interest under contract to purchase real property), 10207 (property sold to grazing or pasture association). As to orders made, or actions taken, before July 1, 1988, and matters pending on July 1, 1988, see Section 9645. As to the application of any amendments made after that date, see Section 3.

Background on Section 10259 of Repealed Code

Section 10259 was added by 1987 Cal.Stat. ch. 923 § 93. The section restated a portion of former Probate Code Section 770 and the last sentence of former Probate Code Section 772 (provisions repealed by 1987 Cal.Stat. ch. 923 § 39) without substantive change. Paragraph (2) of subdivision (b) was new and reflected the expansion of the authority to sell at public auction to include intangible personal property. See Section 10254. For background on the provisions of this part, see the Comment to this part under the part heading. [20 Cal.L.Rev.Comm.Reports 1001 (1990)].

Cross References

Confirmation of sale by court, provisions of this section excepted from, see Probate Code § 10260 et seq.

Non-applicability of this section to bids in excess of original bids, see Probate Code § 10262.

Sales of property, title passes upon confirmation by court, see Probate Code §§ 10260, 10308.

§ 10260. Sales to be reported to and confirmed by court before title passes; exceptions

(a) Except as provided in Sections 10200, 10201, 10202, 10259, and 10503, all sales of personal property shall be reported to and be confirmed by the court before title to the property passes to the purchaser, notwithstanding that the property is directed by the will to be sold or authority is given in the will to sell the property.

(b) If the personal representative fails to file the report and a petition for confirmation of the sale within 30 days after the sale, the purchaser at the sale may file the report and petition for confirmation of the sale.

(c) Notice of the hearing on the petition for confirmation filed under subdivision (a) or (b) shall be given as provided in Section 1220 and posted as provided in Section 1230. *(Stats.1990, c. 79 (A.B.759), § 14, operative July 1, 1991.)*

Law Revision Commission Comments

1990 Enactment

Section 10260 continues Section 10260 of the repealed Probate Code without change. For provisions dispensing with the requirement of court confirmation, see Sections 10200 (securities), 10201 (mutual capital certificates; savings accounts), 10202 (subscription rights), 10259 (personal property which is perishable, which will depreciate in value if not disposed of promptly, or which will incur loss or expense by being kept; personal property the sale of which is necessary to provide for the payment of a family allowance pending receipt of other sufficient funds; personal property sold at public auction). See also Sections 10150 (liability on contract with agent or broker), 10151 (liability on contract with auctioneer), 10160–10167 (compensation of agent, broker, or auctioneer). For general provisions, see Sections 1000–1004 (rules of practice), 1020–1023 (petitions and other papers), 1040–1050 (hearings and orders), 1200–1230 (notice of hearing), 1250–1252 (request for special notice), 1260–1265 (proof of giving of notice).

When property is directed by the will to be sold, or authority is given in the will to sell property, the personal representative may sell the property with or without notice of sale (Section 10252), but the personal representative must make a return of sale and obtain confirmation of the sale as in other cases and no title passes until the sale is confirmed by the court. See the last portion of subdivision (a) of Section 10260. See also Section 10261(a) (when sale is directed or authorized by will, necessity and advantage of sale need not be shown at hearing on petition for confirmation of the sale). The provision for overbids at the confirmation hearing also applies to a sale authorized or directed by the will. See Section 10262. However, if the will provides for the mode of sale, the directions in the will must be followed unless the court otherwise orders. See Section 10002.

As to orders made, or actions taken, before July 1, 1988, and matters pending on July 1, 1988, see Section 9645. As to the application of any amendments made after that date, see Section 3.

Background on Section 10260 of Repealed Code

Section 10260 was added by 1987 Cal.Stat. ch. 923 § 93. The section restated former Probate Code Section 755 (repealed by 1987 Cal.Stat. ch. 923 § 39) as it applied to personal property without substantive change, with the following exceptions:

(1) Subdivision (b) substituted the requirement that the report and petition be "filed" within 30 days after each sale for the requirement of former Section 755 that the report and petition be "made" within 30 days after each sale.

(2) Subdivision (b) gave the purchaser the right to file the report and petition if the personal representative fails to file the report and petition within 30 days after the sale. The former provision required that the report and petition be filed within 30 days but did not state the remedy, if any, the purchaser had if the report and petition were not filed within the 30-day period.

(3) Subdivision (c) required that notice be given at least 15 days before the hearing pursuant to Section 1220 instead of at least 10 days before the hearing as required by former Probate Code Section 1200.5 (repealed by 1987 Cal.Stat. ch. 923 § 59).

For background on the provisions of this part, see the Comment to this part under the part heading. [20 Cal.L.Rev.Comm.Reports 1001 (1990)].

Cross References

Real property sales, confirmation, see Probate Code § 10308 et seq. Sale of perishable and easily depreciated property, see Probate Code § 10252.

Securities, transfer of title without confirmation, see Probate Code § 10200.

§ 10261. Hearing to confirm sale; necessity of sale; objections; compensation of agent or broker

(a) Except as provided in this subdivision, at the hearing on the petition for confirmation of the sale, the court shall examine into the necessity for the sale or the advantage to the estate and the benefit to the interested persons in making the sale. If the decedent's will authorizes or directs the property to be sold, there need be no showing of the necessity of the sale or the advantage to the estate and the benefit to the interested persons in making the sale.

(b) Any interested person may file written objections to the confirmation of the sale at or before the hearing and may testify and produce witnesses in support of the objections.

(c) Before confirming the sale of a partnership interest, whether made to the surviving partner or to any other person, the court shall do both of the following:

(1) Inquire into the condition of the partnership affairs.

(2) Examine any surviving partner if that surviving partner is a resident within the state at the time of the hearing and able to be present in court. The court may issue a citation to compel the surviving partner to attend the hearing.

(d) Upon its own motion or upon the request of the personal representative, the agent or broker, or any other interested person, made at the time of the confirmation hearing or at another time, the court shall fix the compensation of the agent or broker as provided in Article 3 (commencing with Section 10160). *(Stats.1990, c. 79 (A.B. 759), § 14, operative July 1, 1991.)*

Law Revision Commission Comments

1990 Enactment

Section 10261 continues Section 10261 of the repealed Probate Code without change. Subdivision (d) is comparable to subdivision (b) of Section 10313 (real property sales). As to when property of the estate may be sold, see Section 10000. For general provisions relating to hearings and orders, see Section 1040–1050.

Unlike the statutes governing the sale of real property (see Sections 10309, 10313), those for sale of personal property do not require that the purchase price of the property be within a specified percentage range of the amount for which the property is appraised by the probate referee.

As to orders made, or actions taken, before July 1, 1988, and matters pending on July 1, 1988, see Section 9645. As to the application of any amendments made after that date, see Section 3.

Background on Section 10261 of Repealed Code

Section 10261 was added by 1987 Cal.Stat. ch. 923 § 93. The first sentence of subdivision (a) was a new provision drawn from a portion of the first sentence of former Probate Code Section 785 (real property) (repealed by 1987 Cal.Stat. ch. 923 § 39). The second sentence of subdivision (a) restated a portion of the second sentence of former Probate Code Section 757 (repealed by 1987 Cal.Stat. ch. 923 § 39) without substantive change.

Subdivision (b) restated the first sentence of former Probate Code Section 756 (repealed by 1987 Cal.Stat. ch. 923 § 39) insofar as it applied to personal property with the addition of the phrase "at or before the hearing."

Subdivision (c) restated the second sentence of former Probate Code Section 774 (repealed by 1987 Cal.Stat. ch. 923 § 39) but provided for examination of the surviving partner if the surviving partner is able to be present at the hearing and is "a resident within the state at the time of the hearing" and included a new provision that made clear that the court may issue a citation to compel the surviving partner to attend the hearing. The court has jurisdiction and discretion to order any surviving partner to appear for examination. Under former Section 774, the provision for examination of the surviving partner applied only where the surviving partner is able to be present at the hearing and is "in the county."

Subdivision (d) was new and was drawn from portions of the second and third sentences of former Section 785 (real property sales) (repealed by 1987 Cal.Stat. ch. 923 § 39).

For background on the provisions of this part, see the Comment to this part under the part heading. [20 Cal.L.Rev.Comm.Reports 1001 (1990)].

Cross References

Hearing for private sale of real property, see Probate Code § 10310. Notice requirements for,
    Personal property, see Probate Code § 10252 et seq.
    Real property, see Probate Code § 10300 et seq.
Sale of partnership interests, see Probate Code § 10204.

§ 10262. Written bids made at hearing to confirm sale; disposition of property by court

(a) Except as provided in subdivision (b), if a written offer to purchase the property is made to the court at the hearing on the petition for confirmation of the sale and the new bid is at least 10 percent more than the amount stated in the report made to the court, the court in its discretion may accept the new bid and confirm the sale to the offeror, or may order a new sale, if all of the following conditions are satisfied:

(1) The original bid as stated in the report to the court is more than one hundred dollars ($100) or, if the original bid is less than one hundred dollars ($100), the new bid is at least one hundred dollars ($100) more than the original bid.

(2) The new bid is made by a responsible person.

(3) The new bid complies with all provisions of law.

(b) If there is more than one offer that satisfies the requirements of subdivision (a), the court shall do one of the following:

(1) Accept the highest such offer and confirm the sale to the offeror.

(2) Order a new sale.

(c) This section does not apply to a sale of property described in Section 10259. *(Stats.1990, c. 79 (A.B.759), § 14, operative July 1, 1991.)*

Law Revision Commission Comments

1990 Enactment

Section 10262 continues Section 10262 of the repealed Probate Code without change. See also Section 10207 (sale to grazing or pasture association permitted irrespective of whether higher bid made at confirmation hearing). Unlike the statutes governing the sale of real property (see Sections 10309, 10313), those for sale of personal property do not require that the purchase price of the property be within a specified percentage range of the amount for which the property is appraised by the probate referee. As to orders made, or actions taken, before July 1, 1988, and matters pending on July 1, 1988, see Section 9645. As to the application of any amendments made after that date, see Section 3.

Background on Section 10262 of Repealed Code

Section 10262 was added by 1987 Cal.Stat. ch. 923 § 93. The section restated former Probate Code Section 756.5 (repealed by 1987 Cal.Stat. ch. 923 § 39) without substantive change, except that Section 10262 permitted an overbid where the original bid is less than $100 and the overbid is not less than $100 more than the original bid. Former Section 756.5 did not permit an overbid where the original bid was less than $100. Subdivision (b) was a new provision drawn from the second sentence of former Probate Code Section 785 (repealed by 1987 Cal.Stat. ch. 923 § 39). For background on the provisions of this part, see the Comment to this part under the part heading. [20 Cal.L.Rev.Comm.Reports 1001 (1990)].

Cross References

Sale of partnership interests, see Probate Code § 10204.
Securities, sale of without confirmation, see Probate Code § 10200.

§ 10263. Notice of sale; proof

If notice of the sale was required, before an order is made confirming the sale, it shall be proved to the satisfaction of the court that notice of the sale was given as required by this article, and the order of confirmation shall show that such proof was made. *(Stats.1990, c. 79 (A.B.759), § 14, operative July 1, 1991.)*

Law Revision Commission Comments

1990 Enactment

Section 10263 continues Section 10263 of the repealed Probate Code without change. As to proof of giving of notice, see Sections 1260–1265. As to orders made, or actions taken, before July 1, 1988, and matters pending on July 1, 1988, see Section 9645. As to the application of any amendments made after that date, see Section 3.

Background on Section 10263 of Repealed Code

Section 10263 was added by 1987 Cal.Stat. ch. 923 § 93. The section restated the last sentence of former Probate Code Section 756 (repealed by 1987 Cal.Stat. ch. 923 § 39) without substantive change as it applied to personal property. For background on the provisions of this part, see the Comment to this part under the part heading. [20 Cal.L.Rev.Comm.Reports 1001 (1990)].

§ 10264. Sales pursuant to court order; effect of irregularity in proceedings

No omission, error, or irregularity in the proceedings under this article shall impair or invalidate the proceedings or the sale pursuant to an order made under this article. *(Stats. 1990, c. 79 (A.B.759), § 14, operative July 1, 1991.)*

Law Revision Commission Comments

1990 Enactment

Section 10264 continues Section 10264 of the repealed Probate Code without change. This section is comparable to Sections 9923 (exchanges), 9948(d) (leases), 9966 (option to purchase real property), 9983 (option to purchase given in will), and 10316 (sale of real property).

If the court lacks jurisdiction, Section 10264 does not cure the defect. See Texas Co. v. Bank of America Nat'l Trust & Sav. Ass'n, 5 Cal.2d 35, 41–44, 53 P.2d 127 (1935). Section 10264 does not limit the court's authority to set aside an order made through mistake, inadvertence, surprise, or excusable neglect. See Code Civ.Proc. § 473; Estate of Lee, 159 Cal.App.2d 109, 111–12, 323 P.2d 448 (1958); Estate of Herz, 147 Cal.App.2d 100, 106–07, 305 P.2d 278 (1956); Estate of McCrae, 133 Cal.App.2d 634, 637–39, 284 P.2d 914 (1955); Estate of Moreland, 49 Cal.App.2d 484, 487–88, 121 P.2d 867 (1942).

As to orders made, or actions taken, before July 1, 1988, and matters pending on July 1, 1988, see Section 9645. As to the application of any amendments made after that date, see Section 3.

Background on Section 10264 of Repealed Code

Section 10264 was a new provision added by 1987 Cal.Stat. ch. 923 § 93. For background on the provisions of this part, see the Comment to this part under the part heading. [20 Cal.L.Rev.Comm.Reports 1001 (1990)].

ARTICLE 6.   SALE OF REAL PROPERTY

Section

Cross References

Options to purchase real property, see Probate Code § 9960 et seq.
Powers and duties of conservator, manner of sale of property to conform with provisions this article, see Probate Code § 2543.
Real and personal property, appraisal and sale of assets as a unit, see Probate Code § 10004.
Real property, defined, see Probate Code § 68.
Rural property suitable for shift-in-land-use loan to develop grazing or pasture facilities, sale, see Probate Code § 10207.

§ 10300.   Notice of sale

(a) Except as provided in Sections 10301 to 10303, inclusive, and in Section 10503, real property of the estate may be sold only after notice of sale has been published pursuant to Section 6063a of the Government Code (1) in a newspaper published in the county in which the real property or some portion thereof is located or (2) if there is no such newspaper, in such newspaper as the court or judge may direct.

(b) The publication of notice of sale shall be completed before:

(1) In the case of a private sale, the day specified in the notice as the day on or after which the sale is to be made.

(2) In the case of a public auction sale, the day of the auction. *(Stats.1990, c. 79 (A.B.759), § 14, operative July 1, 1991.)*

Law Revision Commission Comments
1990 Enactment

Section 10300 continues Section 10300 of the repealed Probate Code without substantive change. For provisions permitting sale of real property without notice of sale, see Sections 10301 (property appraised at not more than $5,000), 10303 (property authorized or directed by will to be sold). See also Section 9640 (independent administration authority not limited). As to when property of the estate may or must be sold, see Sections 10000, 10001, 10303. As to orders made, or actions taken, before July 1, 1988, and matters pending on July 1, 1988, see Section 9645. As to the application of any amendments made after that date, see Section 3.

Background on Section 10300 of Repealed Code

Section 10300 was added by 1987 Cal.Stat. ch. 923 § 93. The section restated the first sentence of former Probate Code Section 780 (repealed by 1987 Cal.Stat. ch. 923 § 39) without substantive change, except that the requirement that the notice state the "time and place" of sale was continued in Section 10304. For background on the provisions of this part, see the Comment to this part under the part heading. [20 Cal.L.Rev.Comm.Reports 1001 (1990)].

Cross References

Authority of public administrator, see Probate Code § 7661.
Independent administration of estates,
    Personal representatives, limitations of authority, see Probate Code § 9640.
    Property sold under independent administration, see Probate Code § 10503.
Powers and duties of conservator, manner of sale of property to conform with provisions this article, see Probate Code § 2543.
Publications, generally, see Government Code § 6000 et seq.

§ 10301.   Real property valued at not exceeding $5000; notice

(a) If it appears from the inventory and appraisal that the value of the real property to be sold does not exceed five thousand dollars ($5,000), the personal representative may in his or her discretion dispense with publication of notice of sale and, in lieu of publication, post the notice of sale at the courthouse of the county in which the real property or some portion thereof is located.

(b) Except as provided in Section 10302, posting pursuant to this section shall be for at least 15 days before:

(1) In the case of a private sale, the day specified in the notice of sale as the day on or after which the sale is to be made.

(2) In the case of a public auction sale, the day of the auction. *(Stats.1990, c. 79 (A.B.759), § 14, operative July 1, 1991.)*

Law Revision Commission Comments
1990 Enactment

Section 10301 continues Section 10301 of the repealed Probate Code without substantive change. As to orders made, or actions taken, before July 1, 1988, and matters pending on July 1, 1988, see Section 9645. As to the application of any amendments made after that date, see Section 3.

Background on Section 10301 of Repealed Code

Section 10301 was added by 1987 Cal.Stat. ch. 923 § 93 and was amended by 1988 Cal.Stat. ch. 1199 § 90. The section restated the second sentence of former Probate Code Section 780 (repealed by 1987 Cal.Stat. ch. 923 § 39), except that:

(1) Section 10301 increased the amount from $1,000 to $5,000. The last previous increase in the amount was to $1,000 in 1959. The increase to $5,000 recognized to a limited extent the effect of inflation during the previous 30 years.

(2) The former 10–day period for posting of notice of sale was extended to 15 days under subdivision (b).

The 1988 amendment conformed the terminology used in Section 10301 to the terminology used in other provisions enacted in 1988. For background on the provisions of this part, see the Comment to this part under the part heading. [20 Cal.L.Rev.Comm.Reports 1001 (1990)].

Cross References

Auctioneer and auction companies, generally, see Civil Code § 1812.600 et seq.
Authority of public administrator, see Probate Code § 7661.
Personal representative, defined, see Probate Code § 58.

§ 10302. Shortened time of notice of sale; method of notice

(a) If it is shown that it will be to the advantage of the estate, the court or judge may by order shorten the time of notice of sale to not less than five days.

(b) Except as provided in subdivision (c), if the court or judge makes an order under subdivision (a), notice of sale shall be published as provided in Section 10300 except that the publication shall be pursuant to Section 6061 of the Government Code.

(c) In a case described in Section 10301, if the court makes an order under subdivision (a), notice of sale shall be posted as provided in Section 10301 except that the notice of sale shall be posted at least five days before the sale instead of 15 days as required by Section 10301. *(Stats.1990, c. 79 (A.B.759), § 14, operative July 1, 1991.)*

Law Revision Commission Comments

1990 Enactment

Section 10302 continues Section 10302 of the repealed Probate Code without change. As to orders made, or actions taken, before July 1, 1988, and matters pending on July 1, 1988, see Section 9645. As to the application of any amendments made after that date, see Section 3.

Background on Section 10302 of Repealed Code

Section 10302 was added by 1987 Cal.Stat. ch. 923 § 93. The section restated the last portion of the first sentence of former Probate Code Section 782 (repealed by 1987 Cal.Stat. ch. 923 § 39) without substantive change, except that Section 10302 required posting to be for at least five days instead of "one week" as required by former Section 782. The five-day posting period required by Section 10302 was consistent with the posting period required by Section 10251 (shortening time of notice of sale of personal property) which continued the five-day posting period required by former Probate Code Section 772 (repealed by 1987 Cal.Stat. ch. 923 § 39). For background on the provisions of this part, see the Comment to this part under the part heading. [20 Cal.L.Rev.Comm.Reports 1001 (1990)].

Cross References

Authority of public administrator, see Probate Code § 7661.
Discretion of personal representative to sell at public or private sale,
  Under direction of will, see Probate Code § 10000.

Report and confirmation of sale, see Probate Code § 10260.

§ 10303. Sales without notice

Real property may be sold with or without notice, as the personal representative may determine, in either of the following cases:

(a) Where the property is directed by the will to be sold.

(b) Where authority is given in the will to sell the property. *(Stats.1990, c. 79 (A.B.759), § 14, operative July 1, 1991.)*

Law Revision Commission Comments

1990 Enactment

Section 10303 continues Section 10303 of the repealed Probate Code without change. Under Section 10303, it is not necessary that the will specifically grant the personal representative authority to sell without notice. If the will directs or authorizes the sale, whether or not notice should be given is within the discretion of the personal representative. See Bagley v. City and County of San Francisco, 19 Cal.App. 255, 271, 125 P. 931 (1912). However, a sale of real property made pursuant to a direction or authorization in the will must be confirmed by the court before title to the property passes to the purchaser. See Section 10308. As to orders made, or actions taken, before July 1, 1988, and matters pending on July 1, 1988, see Section 9645. As to the application of any amendments made after that date, see Section 3.

Background on Section 10303 of Repealed Code

Section 10303 was added by 1987 Cal.Stat. ch. 923 § 93. The section restated a portion of the first sentence of former Probate Code Section 757 (repealed by 1987 Cal.Stat. ch. 923 § 39) without substantive change as it applied to real property. For background on the provisions of this part, see the Comment to this part under the part heading. [20 Cal.L.Rev.Comm.Reports 1001 (1990)].

Cross References

Authority of public administrator, see Probate Code § 7661.
Personal representative, defined, see Probate Code § 58.

§ 10304. Contents of notice of sale

(a) The notice of sale given pursuant to this article shall state all of the following:

(1) Whether the sale is to be a private sale or a public auction sale.

(2) In the case of a private sale, the place at which bids or offers will be received and a day on or after which the sale will be made or, in the case of a public auction sale, the time and place of sale.

(3) The street address or other common designation or, if none, a legal description of the real property to be sold.

(b) The notice of sale may state other matters in addition to those required by subdivision (a), including terms and conditions of sale. *(Stats.1990, c. 79 (A.B.759), § 14, operative July 1, 1991.)*

Law Revision Commission Comments

1990 Enactment

Section 10304 continues Section 10304 of the repealed Probate Code without change. As to orders made, or actions taken, before July 1, 1988, and matters pending on July 1, 1988, see Section 9645. As to the application of any amendments made after that date, see Section 3.

Background on Section 10304 of Repealed Code

Section 10304 was added by 1987 Cal.Stat. ch. 923 § 93. Paragraphs (1) and (2) of subdivision (a) restated a portion of the first sentence of former Probate Code Section 780 and a portion of the first sentence of former Probate Code Section 782 (provisions repealed by 1987 Cal.Stat. ch. 923 § 39) without substantive change. Paragraph (3) of subdivision (a) superseded the third and fourth sentences of former Section 780 (repealed by 1987 Cal.Stat. ch. 923 § 39). Subdivision (b) was new and codified existing practice. For background on the provisions of this part, see the Comment to this part under the part heading. [20 Cal.L.Rev.Comm.Reports 1001 (1990)].

Cross References

Auctioneer and auction companies, generally, see Civil Code § 1812.600 et seq.
Authority of public administrator, see Probate Code § 7661.

§ 10305. Auction sales; postponement of auction

(a) A sale of real property at public auction shall be made in the county in which the property is located. If the property is located in two or more counties, it may be sold in any one of them.

(b) A sale of real property at public auction shall be made between 9 a.m. and 9 p.m., and the sale shall be made on the day specified in the notice of sale unless the sale is postponed.

(c) The personal representative may postpone a public auction sale of real property from time to time if all of the following conditions are satisfied:

(1) The personal representative believes that the postponement is to the advantage of the estate.

(2) Notice of the postponement is given by public declaration at the time and place appointed for the sale.

(3) The postponement, together with previous postponements of sale of the property, does not exceed three months in all. *(Stats.1990, c. 79 (A.B.759), § 14, operative July 1, 1991.)*

Law Revision Commission Comments
1990 Enactment

Section 10305 continues Section 10305 of the repealed Probate Code with the substitution of the requirement that the postponement "is to the advantage of the estate" for the requirement that the postponement "will serve the interests of all persons concerned." Under subdivision (c), the notice of the postponement is given by public declaration at the time and place specified in the notice of sale unless the auction at that time and place was previously postponed and set for a new date. If the sale is to be again postponed, the notice of the postponement is given by public declaration at the time and place of the new auction as announced in the declaration that postponed the first auction. As to orders made, or actions taken, before July 1, 1988, and matters pending on July 1, 1988, see Section 9645. As to the application of any amendments made after that date, see Section 3.

Background on Section 10305 of Repealed Code

Section 10305 was added by 1987 Cal.Stat. ch. 923 § 93. Subdivisions (a) and (b) restated former Probate Code Section 781 (repealed by 1987 Cal.Stat. ch. 923 § 39) with the following change: Section 10305 required that an auction sale of real property be held between 9:00 a.m. and 9:00 p.m., instead of between 9 a.m. and sunset as formerly required. Subdivision (c) restated former Probate Code

Section 783 (repealed by 1987 Cal.Stat. ch. 923 § 39) without substantive change. See also Estate of Hunter, 194 Cal.App.2d 859, 863–64, 15 Cal.Rptr. 556 (1961) (former Section 783 applied to public auction sales but not to private sales). For background on the provisions of this part, see the Comment to this part under the part heading. [20 Cal.L.Rev.Comm.Reports 1001 (1990)].

Cross References

Auctioneer and auction companies, generally, see Civil Code § 1812.600 et seq.
Auctioneers, powers, see Civil Code §§ 2362, 2363.
Authority of public administrator, see Probate Code § 7661.
Discretion of personal representative to sell at public or private sale, Under direction of will, see Probate Code § 10000.
Execution sales, see Code of Civil Procedure §§ 701.570, 701.640.
Personal representative, defined, see Probate Code § 58.
Real and personal property, requirements for appraisal and sale of assets as a unit, see Probate Code § 10004.

§ 10306. Private sales; bids

(a) A private sale of real property may not be made before the day stated in the notice of sale as the day on or after which the sale will be made, nor later than one year after that day.

(b) In the case of a private sale of real property, the bids or offers shall be in writing and shall be left at the place designated in the notice of sale, or be delivered to the personal representative personally or to the person specified in the notice of sale, at any time after the first publication or posting of notice of sale and before the making of the sale. *(Stats.1990, c. 79 (A.B.759), § 14, operative July 1, 1991.)*

Law Revision Commission Comments
1990 Enactment

Section 10306 continues Section 10306 of the repealed Probate Code without change. Under subdivision (b), the notice of sale may, for example, require that bids be delivered to the attorney for the personal representative. As to orders made, or actions taken, before July 1, 1988, and matters pending on July 1, 1988, see Section 9645. As to the application of any amendments made after that date, see Section 3.

Background on Section 10306 of Repealed Code

Section 10306 was added by 1987 Cal.Stat. ch. 923 § 93. Subdivision (a) restated a portion of the first sentence of former Probate Code Section 782 (repealed by 1987 Cal.Stat. ch. 923 § 39) without substantive change.

Subdivision (b) restated the last sentence of former Section 782 (repealed by 1987 Cal.Stat. ch. 923 § 39) with the following changes:

(1) The former authority for filing bids with the clerk of the court was not continued.

(2) Subdivision (b) made clear that the notice of sale may indicate the person to whom bids are to be delivered.

For background on the provisions of this part, see the Comment to this part under the part heading. [20 Cal.L.Rev.Comm.Reports 1001 (1990)].

Cross References

Authority of public administrator, see Probate Code § 7661.
Personal representative, defined, see Probate Code § 58.

Real and personal property, requirements for appraisal and sale of assets as a unit, see Probate Code § 10004.

§ 10307. Bids to comply with terms in notice of sale

Whether a sale of real property is private or at public auction, bids shall substantially comply with any terms specified in the notice of sale. *(Stats.1990, c. 79 (A.B.759), § 14, operative July 1, 1991.)*

Law Revision Commission Comments
1990 Enactment

Section 10307 continues Section 10307 of the repealed Probate Code without change. This section is consistent with prior case law. See Estate of Hunter, 194 Cal.App.2d 859, 865–68, 15 Cal.Rptr. 556 (1961) (real property); cf. In re Estate of Dargie, 33 Cal.App.2d 148, 155–57, 91 P.2d 126 (1939) (personal property). See also Section 10304 (required and optional contents of notice of sale). As to orders made, or actions taken, before July 1, 1988, and matters pending on July 1, 1988, see Section 9645. As to the application of any amendments made after that date, see Section 3.

Background on Section 10307 of Repealed Code

Section 10307 was a new provision added by 1987 Cal.Stat. ch. 923 § 93. For background on the provisions of this part, see the Comment to this part under the part heading. [20 Cal.L.Rev.Comm.Reports 1001 (1990)].

Cross References

Auctioneer and auction companies, generally, see Civil Code § 1812.600 et seq.
Authority of public administrator, see Probate Code § 7661.
Real and personal property, requirements for appraisal and sale of assets as a unit, see Probate Code § 10004.

§ 10308. Sales to be reported to and confirmed by court before title passes; exceptions

(a) Except as provided in Section 10503, all sales of real property shall be reported to and be confirmed by the court before title to the property passes to the purchaser, whether the sale is a private sale or a public auction sale and notwithstanding that the property is directed by the will to be sold or authority is given in the will to sell the property.

(b) If the personal representative fails to file the report and a petition for confirmation of the sale within 30 days after the sale, the purchaser at the sale may file the report and petition for confirmation of the sale.

(c) Notice of the hearing on the petition for confirmation filed under subdivision (a) or (b) shall be given as provided in Section 1220 to the persons designated by that section and to the purchasers named in the petition, and posted as provided in Section 1230. *(Stats.1990, c. 79 (A.B.759), § 14, operative July 1, 1991. Amended by Stats.1992, c. 871 (A.B.2975), § 11.)*

Law Revision Commission Comments
1990 Enactment

Section 10308 continues Section 10308 of the repealed Probate Code without change. The introductory clause of subdivision (a) recognizes that a sale of real property under independent administration authority does not require court confirmation. See Sections 9640, 10503. Subdivision (a) requires confirmation whether the sale is public or private and whether or not made pursuant to a will. For special confirmation provisions, see Sections 10206 (decedent's

interest under contract to purchase real property), 10207 (property sold to grazing or pasture association). See also Sections 10150 (liability on contract with agent or broker), 10160–10166 (compensation of agent or broker). For general provisions, see Sections 1000–1004 (rules of practice), 1020–1023 (petitions and other papers), 1040–1050 (hearings and orders), 1200–1230 (notice of hearing), 1250–1252 (request for special notice), 1260–1265 (proof of giving of notice). As to orders made, or actions taken, before July 1, 1988, and matters pending on July 1, 1988, see Section 9645. As to the application of any amendments made after that date, see Section 3.

Background on Section 10308 of Repealed Code

Section 10308 was added by 1987 Cal.Stat. ch. 923 § 93. The section restated former Probate Code Section 755 (repealed by 1987 Cal.Stat. ch. 923 § 39) as it applied to real property without substantive change, with the following exceptions:

(1) Subdivision (b) gave the purchaser the right to file the report of sale and the petition for confirmation of the sale if the personal representative fails to file the report and petition within 30 days after the sale. The former provision required that the report and petition be filed within 30 days but did not state the remedy, if any, the purchaser had if the report and petition were not filed within the 30–day period.

(2) Subdivision (c) required that notice be given at least 15 days before the hearing pursuant to Section 1220 instead of at least 10 days before the hearing as required by former Probate Code Section 1200.5 (repealed by 1987 Cal.Stat. ch. 923 § 59).

The language in subdivision (a) that confirmation is required whether the sale is public or private and whether made pursuant to a will was new, but continued the effect of former Section 755. See 1 H. Miller & M. Starr, Current Law of California Real Estate § 2:49, at 296 (rev. ed. 1975); former Prob.Code § 757 (repealed by 1987 Cal.Stat. ch. 923 § 39).

For background on the provisions of this part, see the Comment to this part under the part heading. [20 Cal.L.Rev.Comm.Reports 1001 (1990)].

Cross References

Auctioneer and auction companies, generally, see Civil Code § 1812.600 et seq.
Authority of public administrator, see Probate Code § 7661.
Contracts for purchase of real property, bond requirements prior to court confirmation of sale of decedent's interest, see Probate Code § 10206.
Hearings and orders, requirements, see Probate Code § 1040 et seq.
Independent administration authority,
    Application of limitations or restrictions on administration of estates by personal representatives, see Probate Code § 9640.
    Exception to report and confirmation requirements for sale of estate property, see Probate Code § 10503.
Notice of hearing,
    Mailing requirements, see Probate Code § 1220.
    Posting requirements, see Probate Code § 1230.
Notices, generally, see Probate Code § 1200 et seq.
Petitions and other papers, requirements, see Probate Code § 1020 et seq.
Real and personal property, requirements for appraisal and sale of assets as a unit, see Probate Code § 10004.
Rural property suitable for shift-in-land-use loan to develop grazing or pasture facilities, conditions required for court confirmation of sale, see Probate Code § 10207.
Will, defined, see Probate Code § 88.
Wills, compliance with directions as to mode of sale or property to be sold, see Probate Code § 10002.

§ 10309. Court confirmation of sale; conditions; appraisals

(a) Except as provided in Section 10207, no sale of real property at private sale shall be confirmed by the court unless all of the following conditions are satisfied:

(1) The real property has been appraised within one year prior to the date of the confirmation hearing.

(2) The valuation date used in the appraisal described in paragraph (1) is within one year prior to the date of the confirmation hearing.

(3) The sum offered for the property is at least 90 percent of the appraised value of the property as determined by the appraisal described in paragraph (1).

(b) An appraisal of the property may be had at any time before the sale or the confirmation of sale in any of the following cases:

(1) Where the property has not been previously appraised.

(2) Where the property has not been appraised within one year before the date of the confirmation hearing.

(3) Where the valuation date used in the latest appraisal is more than one year before the date of the confirmation hearing.

(4) Where the court is satisfied that the latest appraisal is too high or too low.

(c) A new appraisal made pursuant to subdivision (b) need not be made by a probate referee if the original appraisal of the property was made by a person other than a probate referee. If the original appraisal of the property was made by a probate referee, the new appraisal may be made by the probate referee who made the original appraisal without further order of the court or further request for the appointment of a new probate referee. If appraisal by a probate referee is required, a new probate referee shall be appointed, using the same procedure as for the appointment of an original referee, to make the new appraisal if the original probate referee is dead, has been removed, or is otherwise unable to act, or if there is other reason to appoint another probate referee. *(Stats.1990, c. 79 (A.B.759), § 14, operative July 1, 1991.)*

Law Revision Commission Comments

1990 Enactment

Section 10309 continues Section 10309 of the repealed Probate Code without change. All sales of real property must be confirmed by the court, whether the sale is private or at public auction (Section 10308), and all sales must be for a sum not disproportionate to the value of the property (Section 10313(a)(4)). However, the requirement of Section 10309 that the offer be at least 90 percent of the appraised value applies only to private sales; the 90 percent requirement does not apply to sales made at public auction. See also Section 10004 (sale of real and personal property as a unit). For provisions on appointment of probate referees, see Sections 8920–8924. As to orders made, or actions taken, before July 1, 1988, and matters pending on July 1, 1988, see Section 9645. As to the application of any amendments made after that date, see Section 3.

Background on Section 10309 of Repealed Code

Section 10309 was added by 1987 Cal.Stat. ch. 923 § 93. The section restated former Probate Code Section 784 (repealed by 1987 Cal.Stat. ch. 923 § 39) without substantive change, except that (1) Section 10309 required that the appraisal and valuation date used for the appraisal be within one year of the confirmation hearing rather than the date of sale, and (2) subdivision (c) permitted the appointment of a new probate referee if "there is other reason to appoint another probate referee" in place of the provision of former Section 784 that permitted appointment of new probate referee "for

just cause." The introductory "except" clause of subdivision (a) continued one effect of the "notwithstanding" clause of subdivision (b) of former Probate Code Section 794 (repealed by 1987 Cal.Stat. ch. 923 § 39).

Paragraph (2) of subdivision (a) referred to the "valuation date" of the appraisal. This was consistent with the intent of former Section 784, pursuant to which an appraisement was deemed to relate back to the valuation date. See 1 A. Marshall, California Probate Procedure § 1403, at 14–200 (4th ed. rev. 1984). For background on the provisions of this part, see the Comment to this part under the part heading. [20 Cal.L.Rev.Comm.Reports 1001 (1990)].

Cross References

Authority of public administrator, see Probate Code § 7661.
Inventory and appraisement, generally, see Probate Code § 8800 et seq.
Objections to confirmation, proceedings, see Probate Code §§ 10261 et seq., 10310 et seq.
Powers and duties of conservator, sale of personal residence, required compliance with provisions of this section, see Probate Code § 2591.5.
Probate referees, designation and removal, see Probate Code § 8920 et seq.
Real and personal property, requirements for appraisal and sale of assets as a unit, see Probate Code § 10004.
Report and confirmation of sale, see Probate Code § 10260.
Rural property suitable for shift-in-land-use loan to develop grazing or pasture facilities, conditions required for court confirmation of sale, see Probate Code § 10207.

§ 10310. Hearing to confirm sale; necessity of sale; objections

(a) Except as provided in this subdivision, at the hearing on the petition for confirmation of the sale of the real property, the court shall examine into the necessity for the sale or the advantage to the estate and the benefit to the interested persons in making the sale. If the decedent's will authorizes or directs the property to be sold, there need be no showing of the necessity of the sale or the advantage to the estate and benefit to the interested persons in making the sale.

(b) The court shall examine into the efforts of the personal representative to obtain the highest and best price for the property reasonably attainable.

(c) Any interested person may file written objections to the confirmation of the sale at or before the hearing and may testify and produce witnesses in support of the objections. *(Stats.1990, c. 79 (A.B.759), § 14, operative July 1, 1991.)*

Law Revision Commission Comments

1990 Enactment

Section 10310 continues Section 10310 of the repealed Probate Code without change. For general provisions relating to hearings and orders, see Section 1040–1050. As to orders made, or actions taken, before July 1, 1988, and matters pending on July 1, 1988, see Section 9645. As to the application of any amendments made after that date, see Section 3.

Background on Section 10310 of Repealed Code

Section 10310 was added by 1987 Cal.Stat. ch. 923 § 93. The first sentence of subdivision (a) restated a portion of the first sentence of former Probate Code Section 785 (repealed by 1987 Cal.Stat. ch. 923 § 39) without substantive change. The second sentence of subdivision (a) restated a portion of the second sentence of former Probate

Code Section 757 (repealed by 1987 Cal.Stat. ch. 923 § 39) without substantive change.

The phrase "advantage of the estate and the benefit to the interested persons" was substituted in subdivision (a) of Section 10310 for the phrase "advantage, benefit and interest of the estate" used in former Section 785. This substitution made no substantive change in the provision and made the provision consistent with subdivision (b) of Section 10000.

Subdivision (b) restated a portion of the first sentence of former Section 785 with the substitution of the phrase "to obtain the highest and best price for the property reasonably attainable" for the former language "to expose the property to the market, and must examine the return and witnesses in relation to the sale."

Subdivision (c) restated the first sentence of former Probate Code Section 756 (repealed by 1987 Cal.Stat. ch. 923 § 39) insofar as it applied to real property with the addition of the phrase "at or before the hearing."

For background on the provisions of this part, see the Comment to this part under the part heading. [20 Cal.L.Rev.Comm.Reports 1001 (1990)].

Cross References

Authority of public administrator, see Probate Code § 7661.
Hearings and orders, generally, see Probate Code § 1040 et seq.
Notice of private sale, contents and publication, see Probate Code § 10302 et seq.
Objections to confirmation, hearing, see Probate Code § 10261 et seq.
Personal representative, defined, see Probate Code § 58.
Real and personal property, requirements for appraisal and sale of assets as a unit, see Probate Code § 10004.
Report and confirmation of sales, see Probate Code §§ 10260, 10308.
Will, defined, see Probate Code § 88.

§ 10311. Written bids made at hearing to confirm sale; disposition of property by court

(a) Subject to subdivisions (b), (c), (d), and (e), and except as provided in Section 10207, if a written offer to purchase the real property is made to the court at the hearing on the petition for confirmation of the sale, the court shall accept the offer and confirm the sale to the offeror if all of the following conditions are satisfied:

(1) The offer is for an amount at least 10 percent more on the first ten thousand dollars ($10,000) of the original bid and 5 percent more on the amount of the original bid in excess of ten thousand dollars ($10,000).

(2) The offer is made by a responsible person.

(3) The offer complies with all provisions of law.

(b) Subject to subdivisions (c), (d), and (e), if there is more than one offer that satisfies the requirements of subdivision (a), the court shall accept the highest such offer and confirm the sale to the person making that offer.

(c) The court may, in its discretion, decline to accept the offer that satisfies the requirements of subdivisions (a) and (b); and, in such case, the court shall order a new sale.

(d) If the sale returned for confirmation is on credit and the higher offer is for cash or on credit, whether on the same or different credit terms, or the sale returned for confirmation is for cash and the higher offer is on credit, the court may not consider the higher offer unless the personal representative informs the court in person or by counsel prior to confirmation of sale that the higher offer is acceptable.

(e) For the purpose of this section, the amount of the original bid and any higher offer shall be determined by the court without regard to any of the following:

(1) Any commission on the amount of the bid to which an agent or broker may be entitled under a contract with the personal representative.

(2) Any condition of the bid that a certain amount of the bid be paid to an agent or broker by the personal representative. *(Stats.1990, c. 79 (A.B.759), § 14, operative July 1, 1991.)*

Law Revision Commission Comments

1990 Enactment

Section 10311 continues Section 10311 of the repealed Probate Code without change. If the court orders a new sale under subdivision (c), notice of the new sale shall be given and the new sale shall be conducted as if no previous sale had taken place. See Section 10313(d). See also Sections 10162 (limitation on compensation of agent or broker producing successful overbidder), 10166 (effect of condition in bid that certain amount of bid be paid to agent or broker). As to compensation of agents and brokers generally, see Sections 10160–10167.

As under prior law, the overbid procedure applies both to private sales and to public auction sales. See 1 H. Miller & M. Starr, Current Law of California Real Estate § 2:63, at 735–36 (2d ed. 1989).

As to orders made, or actions taken, before July 1, 1988, and matters pending on July 1, 1988, see Section 9645. As to the application of any amendments made after that date, see Section 3.

Background on Section 10311 of Repealed Code

Section 10311 was added by 1987 Cal.Stat. ch. 923 § 93. Subdivision (a) restated a portion of the second sentence of former Probate Code Section 785 (repealed by 1987 Cal.Stat. ch. 923 § 39) without substantive change. The reference to Section 10207 in the introductory clause of subdivision (a) continued one effect of the "notwithstanding" clause of subdivision (b) of former Probate Code Section 794 (repealed by 1987 Cal.Stat. ch. 923 § 39). Subdivision (b) restated a portion of the third sentence of former Section 785 without substantive change. Subdivision (c) restated portions of the second and third sentences of former Section 785 without substantive change. Subdivision (d) restated former Probate Code Section 785.1 (repealed by 1987 Cal.Stat. ch. 923 § 39) and the last sentence of former Section 785 without substantive change. Subdivision (e) restated the fifth sentence and a portion of the sixth sentence of former Section 785 without substantive change. For background on the provisions of this part, see the Comment to this part under the part heading. [20 Cal.L.Rev.Comm.Reports 1001 (1990)].

Cross References

Agents and brokers,
    Compensation, see Probate Code § 10160 et seq.
    Contracts, see Probate Code § 10150 et seq.
Authority of public administrator, see Probate Code § 7661.
Hearings and orders, generally, see Probate Code § 1040 et seq.
Independent administration authority, application of limitations or restrictions on administration of estates by personal representatives, see Probate Code § 9640.
Personal representative, defined, see Probate Code § 58.
Real and personal property, requirements for appraisal and sale of assets as a unit, see Probate Code § 10004.
Rural property suitable for shift-in-land-use loan to develop grazing or pasture facilities, conditions required for court confirmation of sale, see Probate Code § 10207.

§ 10312. Proof required that notice of sale was made

If notice of the sale was required, before an order is made confirming the sale it shall be proved to the satisfaction of the court that notice of the sale was given as required by this article, and the order of confirmation shall show that the proof was made. *(Stats.1990, c. 79 (A.B.759), § 14, operative July 1, 1991.)*

Law Revision Commission Comments

1990 Enactment

Section 10312 continues Section 10312 of the repealed Probate Code without change. As to when notice of sale is required, see Sections 10300–10303. As to proof of giving of notice, see Sections 1260–1265. As to orders made, or actions taken, before July 1, 1988, and matters pending on July 1, 1988, see Section 9645. As to the application of any amendments made after that date, see Section 3. For a comparable provision, see Section 10263 (personal property).

Background on Section 10312 of Repealed Code

Section 10312 was added by 1987 Cal.Stat. ch. 923 § 93. The section restated the last sentence of former Probate Code Section 756 (repealed by 1987 Cal.Stat. ch. 923 § 39) without substantive change as it applied to real property. For background on the provisions of this part, see the Comment to this part under the part heading. [20 Cal.L.Rev.Comm.Reports 1001 (1990)].

Cross References

Authority of public administrator, see Probate Code § 7661.
Independent administration authority, exception to report and confirmation requirements for sale of estate property, see Probate Code § 10503.
Notices, generally, see Probate Code § 1200 et seq.

§ 10313. Court order confirming sale; conditions; compensation of agent or broker; order for new sale

(a) The court shall make an order confirming the sale to the person making the highest offer that satisfies the requirements of this article, and directing conveyances or assignments or both to be executed, if it appears to the court that all of the following requirements are satisfied:

(1) Either the sale was authorized or directed to be made by the decedent's will or good reason existed for the sale.

(2) If notice of the sale was required, the proof required by Section 10312 has been made.

(3) The sale was legally made and fairly conducted.

(4) The amount for which the sale is to be confirmed is not disproportionate to the value of the property.

(5) In the case of a private sale, the sale complied with the requirements of Section 10309.

(6) If the sale is confirmed to the original bidder, it does not appear that a sum exceeding the original bid by at least 10 percent more on the first ten thousand dollars ($10,000) of the original bid and 5 percent more on the amount of the original bid in excess of ten thousand dollars ($10,000), exclusive of the expenses of a new sale, may be obtained.

(b) Upon its own motion or upon the request of the personal representative, the agent or broker, or any other interested person, made at the time of the confirmation hearing or at another time, the court shall fix the compensation of the agent or broker as provided in Article 3 (commencing with Section 10160).

(c) If it appears to the court that the requirements of subdivision (a) are not satisfied, the court shall vacate the sale and order a new sale.

(d) If the court orders a new sale under subdivision (c) of this section or under subdivision (c) of Section 10311, notice of the new sale shall be given and the new sale shall in all respects be conducted as if no previous sale had taken place. *(Stats.1990, c. 79 (A.B.759), § 14, operative July 1, 1991.)*

Law Revision Commission Comments

1990 Enactment

Section 10313 continues Section 10313 of the repealed Probate Code without change. Paragraph (1) of subdivision (a) recognizes that it is not necessary to show that good reason existed for the sale if the sale was authorized or directed by the decedent's will. Paragraph (5) of subdivision (a) recognizes that the 90 percent requirement of Section 10309 applies only to private sales, and not to public auction sales. See also Sections 10150 (contract with agent or broker), 10160–10166 (compensation of agent or broker). As to orders made, or actions taken, before July 1, 1988, and matters pending on July 1, 1988, see Section 9645. As to the application of any amendments made after that date, see Section 3.

Background on Section 10313 of Repealed Code

Section 10313 was added by 1987 Cal.Stat. ch. 923 § 93. Subdivision (a) restated portions of the first, second, and third sentences of former Probate Code Section 785 (repealed by 1987 Cal.Stat. ch. 923 § 39) without substantive change. Paragraph (1) of subdivision (a) recognized that it is not necessary to show that good reason existed for the sale if the sale was authorized or directed by the decedent's will. This continued the last portion of the second sentence of former Probate Code Section 757 (repealed by 1987 Cal.Stat. ch. 923 § 39) as it applied to real property. Paragraph (5) of subdivision (a) recognized that the 90 percent requirement of Section 10309 applies only to private sales and not to public auction sales. This continued a portion of the first sentence of former Probate Code Section 784 (repealed by 1987 Cal.Stat. ch. 923 § 39). See 1 A. Marshall, California Probate Procedure § 1407, at 14–204 (4th ed. rev. 1984); 1 H. Miller & M. Starr, Current Law of California Real Estate § 2:49, at 296 n. 19 (rev. ed. 1975).

Subdivision (b) restated portions of the second and third sentences of former Section 785 (without substantive change. Subdivisions (c) and (d) continued the last portion of the first sentence of former Section 785 without substantive change.

For background on the provisions of this part, see the Comment to this part under the part heading. [20 Cal.L.Rev.Comm.Reports 1001 (1990)].

Cross References

Agents and brokers,
    Compensation, see Probate Code § 10160 et seq.
    Contracts, see Probate Code § 10150 et seq.
Appraisal and sale of assets as a unit, see Probate Code § 10004.
Authority of public administrator, see Probate Code § 7661.
Independent administration authority,
    Application of limitations or restrictions on administration of estates by personal representatives, see Probate Code § 9640.
    Exception to report and confirmation requirements for sale of estate property, see Probate Code § 10503.
Notices, generally, see Probate Code § 1200 et seq.
Personal representative, defined, see Probate Code § 58.
Petitions and other papers, requirements, see Probate Code § 1020 et seq.
Will, defined, see Probate Code § 88.

Wills, compliance with directions as to mode of sale or property to be sold, see Probate Code § 10002.

§ 10314. Execution of conveyance or assignment of contract to purchase real property; copy of order to be recorded; rights vested by conveyance or assignment

(a) Except as provided in subdivision (b), upon confirmation of the sale, the personal representative shall execute a conveyance to the purchaser which shall refer to the order confirming the sale and directing the conveyance to be executed. A certified copy of the order shall be recorded in the office of the recorder of the county in which the real property or some portion thereof is located.

(b) Upon confirmation of a sale of the decedent's interest under a contract for the purchase of real property by the decedent and after the purchaser has given a bond if one is required under Section 10206, the personal representative shall execute an assignment of the contract to the purchaser.

(c) A conveyance made in compliance with the court order confirming the sale and directing the conveyance to be executed vests in the purchaser both of the following:

(1) All the right, title, and interest which the decedent had in the property at the time of the decedent's death.

(2) Any other or additional right, title, or interest in the property acquired by the estate of the decedent, by operation of law or otherwise, prior to the sale.

(d) An assignment made in compliance with the court order confirming the sale of the decedent's interest under a contract for the purchase of real property by the decedent vests in the purchaser all the right, title, and interest of the estate, or of the persons entitled to the interest of the decedent, at the time of sale in the property assigned. The purchaser of the decedent's interest under the contract for the purchase of the real property by the decedent has the same rights and remedies against the vendor of the property as the decedent would have had if living. *(Stats.1990, c. 79 (A.B.759), § 14, operative July 1, 1991.)*

Law Revision Commission Comments
1990 Enactment

Section 10314 continues Section 10314 of the repealed Probate Code without substantive change. As to the effect of court authorization or approval, see Section 7250. See also Sections 7260–7263 (orders and transactions affecting property). As to orders made, or actions taken, before July 1, 1988, and matters pending on July 1, 1988, see Section 9645. As to the application of any amendments made after that date, see Section 3.

Background on Section 10314 of Repealed Code

Section 10314 was added by 1987 Cal.Stat. ch. 923 § 93. Subdivision (a) restated the first sentence of former Probate Code Section 786 (repealed by 1987 Cal.Stat. ch. 923 § 39) without substantive change. Subdivision (b) restated the first portion of former Probate Code Section 802 (repealed by 1987 Cal.Stat. ch. 923 § 39). Subdivision (c) restated the second sentence of former Section 786 without substantive change. Subdivision (d) restated the last portion of former Section 802 without substantive change. For background on the provisions of this part, see the Comment to this part under the part heading. [20 Cal.L.Rev.Comm.Reports 1001 (1990)].

Cross References

Authority of public administrator, see Probate Code § 7661.

Contracts for purchase of real property, bond requirements for court confirmation of sale of decedents' interest, see Probate Code § 10206.
Court-ordered real property transactions, inclusion in instrument of statement on authority of the order, see Probate Code § 7261.
Court-ordered transactions, effect of execution by personal representative, see Probate Code § 7262.
Liability of personal representatives and sureties, effect of final order, see Probate Code § 7250.
Personal representative, defined, see Probate Code § 58.
Recordation of orders affecting real estate, see Probate Code § 7263.

§ 10315. Credit sales; purchaser's note; mortgage or deed of trust on property

(a) If a sale is made on credit, the personal representative shall take the note of the purchaser for the unpaid portion of the purchase money, with a mortgage or deed of trust on the property to secure payment of the note. The mortgage or deed of trust shall be subject only to encumbrances existing at the date of sale and such other encumbrances as the court may approve.

(b) Where property sold by the personal representative for part cash and part deferred payments consists of an undivided interest in real property or any other interest therein less than the entire ownership and the owner or owners of the remaining interests therein join in the sale, the note and deed of trust or mortgage may be made to the personal representative and such others having an interest in the property. The interest of the personal representative in the note and deed of trust or mortgage shall be in the same interest and in the same proportions as the estate's interest in the property prior to the sale. *(Stats.1990, c. 79 (A.B.759), § 14, operative July 1, 1991.)*

Law Revision Commission Comments
1990 Enactment

Section 10315 continues Section 10315 of the repealed Probate Code without change. As to orders made, or actions taken, before July 1, 1988, and matters pending on July 1, 1988, see Section 9645. As to the application of any amendments made after that date, see Section 3.

Background on Section 10315 of Repealed Code

Section 10315 was added by 1987 Cal.Stat. ch. 923 § 93. The section restated former Probate Code Section 787 (repealed by 1987 Cal.Stat. ch. 923 § 39) without substantive change as it applied to real property. For background on the provisions of this part, see the Comment to this part under the part heading. [20 Cal.L.Rev.Comm.Reports 1001 (1990)].

Cross References

Authority of public administrator, see Probate Code § 7661.
Mortgages on real property, see Civil Code § 2955 et seq.
Personal representative, defined, see Probate Code § 58.
Sales of personal property, credit terms on, see Probate Code § 10257.

§ 10316. Sales pursuant to court order; effect of irregularity in proceedings

No omission, error, or irregularity in the proceedings under this article shall impair or invalidate the proceedings or the sale pursuant to an order made under this article. *(Stats. 1990, c. 79 (A.B.759), § 14, operative July 1, 1991.)*

Law Revision Commission Comments

1990 Enactment

Section 10316 continues Section 10316 of the repealed Probate Code without change. This section is comparable to Sections 9923 (exchanges), 9948(d) (leases), 9966 (option to purchase real property), 9983 (option to purchase given in will), and 10264 (sale of personal property).

If the court lacks jurisdiction, Section 10316 does not cure the defect. See Texas Co. v. Bank of America Nat'l Trust & Sav. Ass'n, 5 Cal.2d 35, 41–44, 53 P.2d 127 (1935). Section 10316 does not limit the court's authority to set aside an order made through mistake, inadvertence, surprise, or excusable neglect. See Code Civ.Proc. § 473; Estate of Lee, 159 Cal.App.2d 109, 111–12, 323 P.2d 448 (1958); Estate of Herz, 147 Cal.App.2d 100, 106–07, 305 P.2d 278 (1956); Estate of McCrae, 133 Cal.App.2d 634, 637–39, 284 P.2d 914 (1955); Estate of Moreland, 49 Cal.App.2d 484, 487–88, 121 P.2d 867 (1942).

As to orders made, or actions taken, before July 1, 1988, and matters pending on July 1, 1988, see Section 9645. As to the application of any amendments made after that date, see Section 3.

Background on Section 10316 of Repealed Code

Section 10316 was a new provision added by 1987 Cal.Stat. ch. 923 § 93. For background on the provisions of this part, see the Comment to this part under the part heading. [20 Cal.L.Rev.Comm.Reports 1001 (1990)].

Cross References

Authority of public administrator, see Probate Code § 7661.

ARTICLE 7. VACATING SALE FOR PURCHASER'S DEFAULT; LIABILITY OF DEFAULTING PURCHASER FOR DAMAGES

Section
10350. Notice of hearing to vacate sale; notice and resale of property; liability of defaulting purchaser.
10351. Confirmation of sale to new high bidder; notice to defaulting purchaser.

Cross References

Powers and duties of conservator, manner of sale of property to conform with provisions this article, see Probate Code § 2543.

§ 10350. Notice of hearing to vacate sale; notice and resale of property; liability of defaulting purchaser

(a) If after court confirmation of sale of real or personal property the purchaser fails to comply with the terms of sale, the court may, on petition of the personal representative, vacate the order of confirmation, order a resale of the property, and award damages to the estate against the purchaser.

(b) Notice of the hearing on the petition shall be given as provided in Section 1220 to the persons designated by that section and the notice and a copy of the petition shall be given to the buyers and brokers named in the order confirming sale, except that notice need not be given to a defaulting purchaser whose written consent to the petition is filed with the court before the hearing.

(c) Notice of the resale of the property shall be given as provided in this chapter for a sale of the property in the first instance.

(d) Proceedings after notice of the resale shall be as provided in this chapter for a sale of the property in the first instance.

(e) If the property is resold, the defaulting purchaser is liable to the estate for damages equal to the sum of the following:

(1) The difference between the contract price of the first sale and the amount paid by the purchaser at the resale.

(2) Expenses made necessary by the purchaser's breach.

(3) Other consequential damages. *(Stats.1990, c. 79 (A.B. 759), § 14, operative July 1, 1991. Amended by Stats.1992, c. 871 (A.B.2975), § 12.)*

Law Revision Commission Comments

1990 Enactment

Section 10350 continues Section 10350 of the repealed Probate Code without change. For general provisions, see Sections 1000–1004 (rules of practice), 1020–1023 (petitions and other papers), 1040–1050 (hearings and orders), 1200–1230 (notice of hearing), 1250–1252 (request for special notice), 1260–1265 (proof of giving of notice).

Under paragraph (1) of subdivision (e), the estate's loss of bargain is measured by the contract price for the first sale less the price obtained on the second sale. This differs from damages for defaults generally in that, under the general rule, the resale price is merely some evidence of value. See 1 B. Witkin, Summary of California Law Contracts § 847, at 763–64 (9th ed. 1987).

Under paragraph (2) of subdivision (e), the recoverable expenses of sale are those made necessary by the purchaser's breach, the same as under general law. Estate of Williamson, 150 Cal.App.2d 334, 339, 310 P.2d 77 (1957). Such expenses may include expenses of resale to the extent they exceed the expenses assumed by the estate under the breached contract. Jensen v. Dalton, 9 Cal.App.3d 654, 657–58, 88 Cal.Rptr. 426 (1970).

Under paragraph (3) of subdivision (e), consequential damages are recoverable as under general law. See also 1 B. Witkin, supra, §§ 848–49, at 764–66. In the case of real property, such consequential damages may include sewer assessments, taxes, and fees for utilities (Jensen v. Dalton, 9 Cal.App.3d at 658), and insurance, security, storage, and pool and gardening expenses.

As to orders made, or actions taken, before July 1, 1988, and matters pending on July 1, 1988, see Section 9645. As to the application of any amendments made after that date, see Section 3.

Background on Section 10350 of Repealed Code

Section 10350 was added by 1987 Cal.Stat. ch. 923 § 93. Subdivisions (a) and (b) restated the first sentence of former Probate Code Section 775 and the first sentence of former Probate Code Section 788 (provisions repealed by 1987 Cal.Stat. ch. 923 § 39) without substantive change except that the provision in subdivision (b) that notice need not be given to a defaulting purchaser who has filed a written consent was new and was drawn from former Probate Code Sections 776 and 789 (provisions repealed by 1987 Cal.Stat. ch. 923 § 39).

Subdivision (c) restated the substance of a portion of the second sentence of former Section 788 (resale of real property) and superseded the third sentence and a portion of the second sentence of former Section 775 (resale of personal property) (provisions repealed by 1987 Cal.Stat. ch. 923 § 39).

Subdivision (d) restated a portion of the second sentence of former Section 775 and a portion of the second sentence of former Section 788 without substantive change (provisions repealed by 1987 Cal.Stat. ch. 923 § 39).

Subdivision (e) superseded the last sentence of former Section 775 and the last sentence of former Section 788 (provisions repealed by 1987 Cal.Stat. ch. 923 § 39). Paragraph (1) of subdivision (e) continued prior law. Under former Sections 775 and 788, if the amount realized on resale did not cover the bid and expenses of the first (incomplete) sale, the defaulting purchaser was liable for the "deficiency." See also Estate of Williamson, 150 Cal.App.2d 334, 339, 310 P.2d 77 (1957). Under paragraph (1) of subdivision (e), as under former Sections 775 and 788, the estate's loss of bargain is measured by the contract price for the first sale less the price obtained on the second sale. Paragraph (2) of subdivision (e) changed prior law. Under former Sections 775 and 788, if there was a resale of the property, recoverable expenses were those of the first (incomplete) sale, not those of the resale. Estate of Williamson, 150 Cal.App.2d 334, 339, 310 P.2d 77 (1957). Under paragraph (2), the recoverable expenses of sale were those made necessary by the purchaser's breach, the same as under general law. Id. at 339. Paragraph (3) of subdivision (e) was new.

For background on the provisions of this part, see the Comment to this part under the part heading. [20 Cal.L.Rev.Comm.Reports 1001 (1990)].

Cross References

Confirmation of sale by court,
Personal property, application, see Probate Code § 10260 et seq.
Real property, see Probate Code § 10308 et seq.
Hearings, generally, see Probate Code § 1040 et seq.
Notice,
Generally, see Probate Code § 1200 et seq.
Personal property sales, see Probate Code § 10300 et seq.
Real property sales, see Probate Code § 10300 et seq.
Notice of hearing,
Mailing requirements, see Probate Code § 1220.
Posting requirements, see Probate Code § 1230.
Petitions and other papers, requirements, see Probate Code § 1020 et seq.
Powers and duties of conservator, manner of sale of property to conform with provisions this article, see Probate Code § 2543.
Real property,
Defined, see Probate Code § 68.
Proceedings for sale, see Probate Code § 10305 et seq.

§ 10351. Confirmation of sale to new high bidder; notice to defaulting purchaser

(a) The court may vacate the order of confirmation of a sale of real or personal property and make an order confirming the sale to the new high bidder if both of the following requirements are satisfied:

(1) A petition is filed within 60 days after confirmation of the sale showing that (A) the purchaser at the sale has failed to complete the purchase and (B) a bid has been made for the property in the same or a higher amount, on the same or better terms, and in the manner prescribed in the original notice of sale.

(2) The sale has not been vacated pursuant to Section 10350.

(b) Notice of the hearing on the petition shall be given as provided in Section 1220 to the persons designated by that section and the notice and a copy of the petition shall be given to the buyers and brokers named in the order confirming sale, except that notice need not be given to a defaulting purchaser whose written consent to the vacation of the order confirming the sale is filed with the court prior to the hearing.

(c) If the report and petition for confirmation of the second sale are not filed within 60 days of the confirmation of the first sale, the property may be resold only in the manner provided in Section 10350. *(Stats.1990, c. 79 (A.B.759), § 14, operative July 1, 1991. Amended by Stats.1992, c. 871 (A.B.2975), § 13.)*

Law Revision Commission Comments

1990 Enactment

Section 10351 continues Section 10351 of the repealed Probate Code without change. The 60–day period allowed for filing the petition does not require that the personal representative delay until the 60 days have expired before petitioning the court for an order directing the resale of the property. See Section 10350. For general provisions, see Sections 1000–1004 (rules of practice), 1020–1023 (petitions and other papers), 1040–1050 (hearings and orders), 1200–1230 (notice of hearing), 1250–1252 (request for special notice), 1260–1265 (proof of giving of notice). As to orders made, or actions taken, before July 1, 1988, and matters pending on July 1, 1988, see Section 9645. As to the application of any amendments made after that date, see Section 3.

Background on Section 10351 of Repealed Code

Section 10351 was added by 1987 Cal.Stat. ch. 923 § 93. The section restated former Probate Code Sections 776 and 789 (provisions repealed by 1987 Cal.Stat. ch. 923 § 39) without substantive change, except that Section 10351 increased the 45–day period provided in the former sections to 60 days. For background on the provisions of this part, see the Comment to this part under the part heading. [20 Cal.L.Rev.Comm.Reports 1001 (1990)].

Cross References

Confirmation of sale by court,
Personal property sales, see Probate Code § 10260 et seq.
Real property sales, see Probate Code § 10308 et seq.
Hearings, generally, see Probate Code § 1040 et seq.
Notice,
Generally, see Probate Code § 1200 et seq.
Personal property sales, see Probate Code § 10250 et seq.
Real property sales, see Probate Code § 10300 et seq.
Notice of hearing,
Mailing requirements, see Probate Code § 1220.
Posting requirements, see Probate Code § 1230.
Petitions and other papers, requirements, see Probate Code § 1020 et seq.
Real property, defined, see Probate Code § 68.

ARTICLE 8. APPLICATION OF SALE PROCEEDS OF ENCUMBERED PROPERTY; SALE TO LIENHOLDER

Powers and duties of conservator, manner of sale of property to conform with provisions this article, see Probate Code § 2543.

§ 10360. Definitions

As used in this article:

(a) "Amount secured by the lien" includes interest and any costs and charges secured by the lien.

(b) "Encumbered property" means real or personal property that is subject to a lien for a secured debt which is a valid claim against the estate and which has been allowed or approved.

(c) "Lien" means a mortgage, deed of trust, or other lien. *(Stats.1990, c. 79 (A.B.759), § 14, operative July 1, 1991.)*

Law Revision Commission Comments

1990 Enactment

Section 10360 continues Section 10360 of the repealed Probate Code without change. As to orders made, or actions taken, before July 1, 1988, and matters pending on July 1, 1988, see Section 9645. As to the application of any amendments made after that date, see Section 3.

Background on Section 10360 of Repealed Code

Section 10360 was a new provision added by 1987 Cal.Stat. ch. 923 § 93. For background on the provisions of this part, see the Comment to this part under the part heading. [20 Cal.L.Rev.Comm.Reports 1001 (1990)].

Cross References

Powers and duties of conservator, manner of sale of property to conform with provisions this article, see Probate Code § 2543.

§ 10361. Application of proceeds from sale of encumbered property; priorities; continuation of lien

(a) If encumbered property is sold, the purchase money shall be applied in the following order:

(1) Expenses of administration which are reasonably related to the administration of the property sold as provided in paragraph (1) of subdivision (a) of Section 11420.

(2) The payment of the expenses of the sale.

(3) The payment and satisfaction of the amount secured by the lien on the property sold if payment and satisfaction of the lien is required under the terms of the sale.

(4) Application in the course of administration.

(b) The application of the purchase money, after the payment of those expenses set forth in paragraphs (1) and (2) of subdivision (a), to the payment and satisfaction of the amount secured by the lien on the property sold shall be made without delay; and, subject to Section 10362, the property sold remains subject to the lien until the purchase money has been actually so applied. *(Stats.1990, c. 79 (A.B.759), § 14, operative July 1, 1991. Amended by Stats. 1996, c. 862 (A.B.2751), § 26.)*

Law Revision Commission Comments

1990 Enactment

Section 10361 continues Section 10361 of the repealed Probate Code without substantive change. This section requires that the lien be paid and satisfied only if required under the terms of the sale.

This permits the property to be sold subject to the lien, a term of sale that might be beneficial to the estate if the terms of the existing financing are better than can be obtained at the time of the sale. If the expenses of sale are unreasonable in amount, the personal representative is liable for the excess amount. See Sections 9600–9603. As to orders made, or actions taken, before July 1, 1988, and matters pending on July 1, 1988, see Section 9645. As to the application of any amendments made after that date, see Section 3.

Background on Section 10361 of Repealed Code

Section 10361 was added by 1987 Cal.Stat. ch. 923 § 93. The section restated former Probate Code Section 762 (repealed by 1987 Cal.Stat. ch. 923 § 39) with the following changes:

(1) Section 10361 required that the amount secured by the lien on the property sold be paid and satisfied (if required under the terms of the sale) before payment of the expenses of the sale. Former Section 762 required that the necessary expenses of the sale be paid before the lien on the property sold was paid and satisfied, and did not specifically permit sale of the property subject to the lien.

(2) Section 10361 provided that the purchase money be used to pay the expenses of sale. Former Section 762 required that the "necessary" expenses of the sale be paid.

For background on the provisions of this part, see the Comment to this part under the part heading. [20 Cal.L.Rev.Comm.Reports 1001 (1990)].

Cross References

Deed of trust, mortgage as including, see Insurance Code § 29.
Definitions,
    Lien, see Civil Code § 2872; Code of Civil Procedure § 1180; Insurance Code § 29.
    Mortgage, see Civil Code § 2920; Insurance Code § 29.
Determination of validity of lien, purchase by lien holder, see Probate Code § 10363.
Liability of personal representative, see Probate Code § 9601 et seq.

§ 10361.5. Administration expenses; petition to determine amount prior to lien satisfaction; hearing; notice

The personal representative or any interested party may, at any time before payment is made to satisfy all liens on the encumbered property sold, petition for an order determining the amount of expenses of administration that are reasonably related to the administration of that encumbered property as provided in paragraph (1) of subdivision (a) of Section 11420. The petition may be heard as part of a petition for confirmation of sale of personal or real property as provided in Section 10260 or 10308, respectively or may be heard separately. If the petition is presented as part of a petition for confirmation of sale of real or personal property, the notice of hearing otherwise required by this code for a petition for confirmation of sale shall be given in addition to the notice requirements under Section 10361.6. *(Added by Stats.1996, c. 862 (A.B.2751), § 27.)*

§ 10361.6. Notice of hearing and copy of petition; service; specified persons; alteration of time for notice

(a) At least 30 days prior to the day of the hearing, the petitioner shall cause notice of the hearing and a copy of the petition to be served in the manner provided in Chapter 4 (commencing with Section 413.10) of Title 5 of Part 3 of the Code of Civil Procedure on all of the following persons:

(1) The personal representative, if the personal representative is not the petitioner.

(2) The holder of any mortgage or other lien secured by the property that is sold.

(3) All agents or brokers entitled to compensation from the proceeds of the property that is sold.

(b) Except for those persons given notice pursuant to subdivision (a), notice of the hearing, together with a copy of the petition, shall be given as provided in Section 1220 to all of the following persons:

(1) Each person listed in Section 1220.

(2) Each known heir whose interest in the estate would be affected by the petition.

(3) Each known devisee whose interest in the estate would be affected by the petition.

(4) The Attorney General, at the office of the Attorney General in Sacramento, if any portion of the estate is to escheat to the state and its interest in the estate would be affected by the petition.

(c) The court may not shorten the time for giving the notice of hearing under this section. *(Added by Stats.1996, c. 862 (A.B.2751), § 28.)*

§ 10362. Payment of purchase money to clerk of court; satisfaction of lien and expenses; surplus

(a) If encumbered property is sold, the purchase money, or so much of the purchase money as is sufficient to pay the amount secured by the lien on the property sold and the expenses of the sale, may be paid to the clerk of the court. Upon the payment being so made, the lien on the property sold ceases.

(b) The clerk of court without delay shall use the money paid to the clerk under this section to pay the expenses of the sale and to pay and satisfy the amount secured by the lien on the property sold. The clerk shall at once return the surplus, if any, to the personal representative unless the court, for good cause shown and after notice to the personal representative, otherwise orders. *(Stats.1990, c. 79 (A.B.759), § 14, operative July 1, 1991.)*

Law Revision Commission Comments
1990 Enactment

Section 10362 continues Section 10362 of the repealed Probate Code without change. As to orders made, or actions taken, before July 1, 1988, and matters pending on July 1, 1988, see Section 9645. As to the application of any amendments made after that date, see Section 3.

Background on Section 10362 of Repealed Code

Section 10362 was added by 1987 Cal.Stat. ch. 923 § 93. The section restated former Probate Code Section 763 (repealed by 1987 Cal.Stat. ch. 923 § 39) without substantive change. For background on the provisions of this part, see the Comment to this part under the part heading. [20 Cal.L.Rev.Comm.Reports 1001 (1990)].

Cross References

Deed of trust, mortgage as including, see Insurance Code § 29.
Definitions,
  Lien, see Civil Code § 2872; Code of Civil Procedure § 1180; Insurance Code § 29.
  Mortgage, see Civil Code § 2920; Insurance Code § 29.

§ 10363. Purchase by lienholder

(a) At a sale of real or personal property subject to a lien, the lienholder may become the purchaser of the property, even though no claim for the amount secured by the lien on the property sold has been, or could have been, filed, allowed, or approved.

(b) Unless the property is sold subject to the lien:

(1) If the lienholder becomes the purchaser of the property and the amount secured by the lien on the property is a valid claim against the estate and has been allowed or approved, the receipt of the lienholder for the amount due the lienholder from the proceeds of the sale is a payment pro tanto.

(2) If the lienholder becomes the purchaser of the property and no claim for the amount secured by the lien on the property has been filed, allowed, or approved, the court may at the hearing on the petition for confirmation of the sale examine into the validity and enforceability of the lien and the amount secured by the lien, and the court may authorize the personal representative to accept the receipt of the lienholder for the amount secured by the lien as payment pro tanto.

(3) If the lienholder becomes the purchaser of the property and the amount for which the property is purchased is insufficient to pay the expenses of the sale and to discharge the lienholder's lien, whether or not a claim has been filed, allowed, or approved, the lienholder shall pay to the clerk of the court an amount sufficient to cover the expenses of the sale.

(c) Nothing permitted under this section shall be deemed to be an allowance or approval of a claim based upon the lien or the amount secured by the lien. *(Stats.1990, c. 79 (A.B.759), § 14, operative July 1, 1991.)*

Law Revision Commission Comments
1990 Enactment

Section 10363 continues Section 10363 of the repealed Probate Code without change. As to orders made, or actions taken, before July 1, 1988, and matters pending on July 1, 1988, see Section 9645. As to the application of any amendments made after that date, see Section 3.

Background on Section 10363 of Repealed Code

Section 10363 was added by 1987 Cal.Stat. ch. 923 § 93. The section restated former Probate Code Section 764 (repealed by 1987 Cal.Stat. ch. 923 § 39) without substantive change except for revisions necessary to reflect the new authorization under Section 10361 to sell property subject to the lien on the property. For background on the provisions of this part, see the Comment to this part under the part heading. [20 Cal.L.Rev.Comm.Reports 1001 (1990)].

Cross References

Application of purchase money from sale of encumbered property, see Probate Code § 10361.
Deed of trust, mortgage as including, see Insurance Code § 29.
Definitions,
  Lien, see Civil Code § 2872; Code of Civil Procedure § 1180; Insurance Code § 29.
  Mortgage, see Civil Code § 2920; Insurance Code § 29.

Hearing of petition for confirmation of sale, see Probate Code §§ 10260 et seq., 10308 et seq.

ARTICLE 9.   DAMAGES AND RECOVERY OF PROPERTY

Section
10380.   Liability of personal representative.
10381.   Fraudulent sale of real property.
10382.   Limitation of actions.

Cross References

Powers and duties of conservator, manner of sale of property to conform with provisions this article, see Probate Code § 2543.

§ 10380.   Liability of personal representative

The personal representative is liable to an interested person for damages suffered by the interested person by reason of the neglect or misconduct of the personal representative in the proceedings in relation to a sale. *(Stats.1990, c. 79 (A.B.759), § 14, operative July 1, 1991.)*

Law Revision Commission Comments

1990 Enactment

Section 10380 continues Section 10380 of the repealed Probate Code without change. When the personal representative is liable, the liability may be enforced against the bond of the personal representative or by other means of enforcement of a judgment. See Sections 8480, 8487; Code Civ.Proc. § 996.410. See also Guggenhime & Wald, Bonds and Protection of Assets, in 1 California Decedent Estate Practice § 8.28 (Cal.Cont.Ed.Bar rev. 1989). But see the Comment to Section 10381 (liquidated damages for fraudulent sale of real property). As to orders made, or actions taken, before July 1, 1988, and matters pending on July 1, 1988, see Section 9645. As to the application of any amendments made after that date, see Section 3.

Background on Section 10380 of Repealed Code

Section 10380 was added by 1987 Cal.Stat. ch. 923 § 93. The section restated former Probate Code Section 759 (repealed by 1987 Cal.Stat. ch. 923 § 39) without substantive change. The language that "[t]he personal representative is liable to an interested person" replaced the former language that "the party aggrieved may recover the damage by enforcing the liability upon the bond of the executor or administrator, or otherwise." This change was nonsubstantive. For background on the provisions of this part, see the Comment to this part under the part heading. [20 Cal.L.Rev.Comm.Reports 1001 (1990)].

Cross References

Amount and requisites of bond, see Probate Code § 8482 et seq.
Bond and Undertaking Law,
   Application, see Probate Code § 8487.
   Law, generally, see Code of Civil Procedure § 995.010 et seq.
Interested person, defined, see Probate Code § 48.
Liability of principals and sureties, enforcement of liability by beneficiary, see Code of Civil Procedure § 996.410.
Personal representative, defined, see Probate Code § 58.
Powers and duties of conservator, manner of sale of property to conform with provisions this article, see Probate Code § 2543.

§ 10381.   Fraudulent sale of real property

In addition to any other damages for which the personal representative is liable, if the personal representative fraudulently sells real property of the estate contrary to or otherwise than under the provisions of this chapter, the person having an estate of inheritance in the real property may recover from the personal representative, as liquidated damages, an amount equal to double the fair market value of the real property sold on the date of sale. *(Stats.1990, c. 79 (A.B. 759), § 14, operative July 1, 1991.)*

Law Revision Commission Comments

1990 Enactment

Section 10381 continues Section 10381 of the repealed Probate Code without change. See also Sections 9601–9603 (measure of liability for breach of fiduciary duty), 10380 (damages for neglect or misconduct of personal representative); Civil Code §§ 761–783.1 (estates in real property). Although the person may recover liquidated damages from the personal representative under Section 10381, the surety on the personal representative's bond is liable only for the damages under Section 10380 up to the limits on the bond. See Weihe v. Statham, 67 Cal. 245, 7 P. 673 (1885). See also Section 10380. As to orders made, or actions taken, before July 1, 1988, and matters pending on July 1, 1988, see Section 9645. As to the application of any amendments made after that date, see Section 3.

Background on Section 10381 of Repealed Code

Section 10381 was added by 1987 Cal.Stat. ch. 923 § 93. The section restated former Probate Code Section 792 (repealed by 1987 Cal.Stat. ch. 923 § 39) without substantive change except (1) the damages were made double the value of the "real property" sold rather than double the value of the "land" sold and language was added to make clear that the damages are to be computed using the value of the property on the date it was sold and (2) Section 10381 made clear that the liquidated damages provided for in the section are in addition to any other recoverable damages. For background on the provisions of this part, see the Comment to this part under the part heading. [20 Cal.L.Rev.Comm.Reports 1001 (1990)].

Cross References

Double liability by persons other than representatives for wrongful disposition of property, see Probate Code § 8874.
Estates in real property, generally, see Civil Code § 761 et seq.
Liability of personal representative for breach of fiduciary duty, see Probate Code § 9601 et seq.
Purchase of property or claims by representatives, see Probate Code § 9880 et seq.

§ 10382.   Limitation of actions

(a) No action for the recovery of property sold by a personal representative on the claim that the sale is void may be maintained by an heir or other person claiming under the decedent unless the action is commenced within whichever of the following is the later time:

(1) Three years after the settlement of the final account of the personal representative.

(2) Three years after the discovery of any fraud upon which the action is based.

(b) The limitation established by subdivision (a) is not tolled for any reason. *(Stats.1990, c. 79 (A.B.759), § 14, operative July 1, 1991.)*

Law Revision Commission Comments

1990 Enactment

Section 10382 continues Section 10382 of the repealed Probate Code without change. As to orders made, or actions taken, before July 1, 1988, and matters pending on July 1, 1988, see Section 9645.

As to the application of any amendments made after that date, see Section 3.

Background on Section 10382 of Repealed Code

Section 10382 was added by 1987 Cal.Stat. ch. 923 § 93. Subdivision (a) continued the first sentence of former Probate Code Section 793 (repealed by 1987 Cal.Stat. ch. 923 § 39) without substantive change. Subdivision (b) replaced the second sentence of former Section 793 which provided for tolling of the limitation for minors and others under legal disability. For background on the provisions of this part, see the Comment to this part under the part heading. [20 Cal.L.Rev.Comm.Reports 1001 (1990)].

Cross References

Limitation of actions for recovery of real property, see Code of Civil Procedure § 315 et seq.

Part 6

INDEPENDENT ADMINISTRATION OF ESTATES

Application

Application of Part 6, see Probate Code § 10406.

Law Revision Commission Comments

1990 Enactment

THIS part supersedes Part 6 (commencing with Section 10400) of Division 7 of the repealed Probate Code. The superseded part was enacted upon recommendation of the California Law Revision Commission. See Recommendation Relating to Independent Administration of Estates Act, 19 Cal.L.Revision Comm'n Reports 205 (1988); Communication from California Law Revision Commission Concerning Assembly Bill 708, 19 Cal.L.Revision Comm'n Reports 545, 583–611 (1988). See also Recommendation Relating to Independent Administration of Decedent's Estate, 17 Cal.L.Revision Comm'n Reports 405 (1984); Communication Concerning Assembly Bill 196, 18 Cal.L.Revision Comm'n Reports 367, 370–73 (1986). [20 Cal.L.Rev.Comm.Reports 1001 (1990)].

Cross References

Estate management provisions not limiting authority given personal representatives under this part, see Probate Code § 9640. Powers and duties of conservator, manner of sale of property excluded from application of this Part, see Probate Code § 2543.

CHAPTER 1. GENERAL PROVISIONS

§ 10400. Short title

This part shall be known and may be cited as the Independent Administration of Estates Act. *(Stats.1990, c. 79 (A.B.759), § 14, operative July 1, 1991.)*

Application

Application of Part 6, see Probate Code § 10406.

Law Revision Commission Comments

1990 Enactment

Section 10400 continues Section 10400 of the repealed Probate Code without change.

Background on Section 10400 of Repealed Code

Section 10400 was added by 1987 Cal.Stat. ch. 923 § 93. The section restated former Probate Code Section 591 (repealed by 1987 Cal.Stat. ch. 923 § 35) without substantive change. For background on the provisions of this part, see the Comment to this part under the part heading. [20 Cal.L.Rev.Comm.Reports 1001 (1990)].

Cross References

Powers and duties of conservator, manner of sale of property excluded from application of this Part, see Probate Code § 2543.

§ 10401. Court supervision

As used in this part, "court supervision" means the judicial order, authorization, approval, confirmation, or instructions that would be required if authority to administer the estate had not been granted under this part. *(Stats.1990, c. 79 (A.B.759), § 14, operative July 1, 1991.)*

Application

Application of Part 6, see Probate Code § 10406.

Law Revision Commission Comments

1990 Enactment

Section 10401 continues Section 10401 of the repealed Probate Code without change. See also Section 10503 (requirements applicable to court confirmation of sales of real property do not apply to sales under independent administration). As to the order, authorization, approval, confirmation, or instructions required for estate management transactions when the personal representative has not been granted independent administration authority, see generally Part 5 (commencing with Section 9600) of Division 7.

Background on Section 10401 of Repealed Code

Section 10401 was added by 1987 Cal.Stat. ch. 923 § 93. The section restated a portion of the second sentence of subdivision (a) of former Probate Code Section 591.2 (repealed by 1987 Cal.Stat. ch. 923 § 35) without substantive change. For background on the provisions of this part, see the Comment to this part under the part heading. [20 Cal.L.Rev.Comm.Reports 1001 (1990)].

Cross References

Estate management, generally, see Probate Code § 9600 et seq.

Exception to report and confirmation requirements for sale of estate property, see Probate Code § 10503.

§ 10402. Full authority

As used in this part, "full authority" means authority to administer the estate under this part that includes all the powers granted under this part. *(Stats.1990, c. 79 (A.B.759), § 14, operative July 1, 1991.)*

Application

Application of Part 6, see Probate Code § 10406.

Law Revision Commission Comments

1990 Enactment

Section 10402 continues Section 10402 of the repealed Probate Code without change. As to the exercise of powers under this part, see generally Section 10502 and the Comment thereto.

Background on Section 10402 of Repealed Code

Section 10402 was a new provision added by 1987 Cal.Stat. ch. 923 § 93. Sections 10402 and 10403 were new definitions that recognized the use in former practice of the terms "full authority" and "limited authority" to describe the powers of a personal representative who has obtained independent administration authority. For background on the provisions of this part, see the Comment to this part under the part heading. [20 Cal.L.Rev.Comm.Reports 1001 (1990)].

Cross References

Authority for independent administration of estates,
    Objections, see Probate Code § 10452.
    Petitions, see Probate Code § 10450.
Court supervision, see Probate Code § 10501.
Personal representatives authorized for independent administration
    of estates, powers, see Probate Code § 10502.

§ 10403. Limited authority

As used in this part, "limited authority" means authority to administer the estate under this part that includes all the powers granted under this part except the power to do any of the following:

(a) Sell real property.

(b) Exchange real property.

(c) Grant an option to purchase real property.

(d) Borrow money with the loan secured by an encumbrance upon real property. *(Stats.1990, c. 79 (A.B.759), § 14, operative July 1, 1991.)*

Application

Application of Part 6, see Probate Code § 10406.

Law Revision Commission Comments

1990 Enactment

Section 10403 continues Section 10403 of the repealed Probate Code without change. As to the exercise of powers under this part, see generally Section 10502 and the Comment thereto. In connection with subdivision (d), see Sections 10450(b)(2), 10452, 10501(b). See also the Comment to Section 10501. If the personal representative was granted independent administration authority prior to July 1, 1988, the personal representative may use that existing authority on and after July 1, 1988, to borrow money on a loan secured by an encumbrance upon real property, whether or not that existing authority includes authority to sell real property. See Section

10406(b). As to the reason why the personal representative may request only limited authority, see the Comment to Section 10450.

Background on Section 10403 of Repealed Code

Section 10403 was a new provision added by 1987 Cal.Stat. ch. 923 § 93. Sections 10402 and 10403 were new definitions that recognized the use in former practice of the terms "full authority" and "limited authority" to describe the powers of a personal representative who has obtained independent administration authority.

Section 10403 was consistent with subdivision (b)(2) of former Probate Code Section 591.1 (repealed by 1987 Cal.Stat. ch. 923 § 35), except for the addition of subdivision (d) of Section 10403 which was a new limitation on the powers of a personal representative who has only limited authority. Subdivision (d) was consistent with the portion of subdivision (b) of Probate Code Section 10501 which required court supervision if the personal representative has limited authority and proposes to borrow money with the loan secured by an encumbrance upon real property of the estate.

For background on the provisions of this part, see the Comment to this part under the part heading. [20 Cal.L.Rev.Comm.Reports 1001 (1990)].

Cross References

Authority for independent administration of estates,
    Objections, see Probate Code § 10452.
    Petitions, see Probate Code § 10450.
Court supervision, see Probate Code § 10501.
Personal representatives authorized for independent administration
    of estates, powers, see Probate Code § 10502.
Real property, defined, see Probate Code § 68.

§ 10404. Provision in will prohibiting independent administration

The personal representative may not be granted authority to administer the estate under this part if the decedent's will provides that the estate shall not be administered under this part. *(Stats.1990, c. 79 (A.B.759), § 14, operative July 1, 1991.)*

Application

Application of Part 6, see Probate Code § 10406.

Law Revision Commission Comments

1990 Enactment

Section 10404 continues Section 10404 of the repealed Probate Code without change. For purposes of Section 10404, a provision in the decedent's will that the estate shall not be administered under former Article 2 of Chapter 8 of Division 3 of the repealed Probate Code (former Probate Code Sections 591–591.9, repealed by 1987 Cal.Stat. ch. 923 § 35), or under the Independent Administration of Estates Act, is a provision that the estate shall not be administered under this part. See also Section 10502(b) (decedent's will may restrict powers exercisable under independent administration authority). As to the application of this part where independent administration authority was granted under the repealed Probate Code, see Section 10406.

Background on Section 10404 of Repealed Code

Section 10404 was added by 1987 Cal.Stat. ch. 923 § 93. Section 10404 restated the second sentence of subdivision (a) of former Probate Code Section 591.1 (repealed by 1987 Cal.Stat. ch. 923 § 35) without substantive change. For background on the provisions of this part, see the Comment to this part under the part heading. [20 Cal.L.Rev.Comm.Reports 1001 (1990)].

Personal representative,
   Defined, see Probate Code § 58.
   Restrictions on powers, see Probate Code § 10502.
Will, defined, see Probate Code § 88.

§ 10404.5. Repealed by Stats.1990, c. 710 (S.B.1775), § 27, operative July 1, 1991

Law Revision Commission Comments

1990 Repeal

Section 10404.5 (enacted as a part of the new Probate Code by 1990 Cal.Stat. ch. 79 § 14) was repealed by 1990 Cal.Stat. ch. 710 § 27. Section 10404.5 was included in the new Probate Code because Assembly Bill 831 of the 1989–1990 regular session would have extended the independent administration provisions to cover probate attorney fees. However, Assembly Bill 831 was not enacted, and as a result Section 10404.5 became unnecessary. See the Comment to Section 900. [20 Cal.L.Rev.Comm.Reports 1001 (1990)].

§ 10405. Administration by special administrator

A special administrator may be granted authority to administer the estate under this part if the special administrator is appointed with, or has been granted, the powers of a general personal representative. *(Stats.1990, c. 79 (A.B.759), § 14, operative July 1, 1991.)*

Application

Application of Part 6, see Probate Code § 10406.

Law Revision Commission Comments

1990 Enactment

Section 10405 continues Section 10405 of the repealed Probate Code without change. This section permits independent administration authority to be granted to a special administrator if the special administrator is appointed with, or has been granted, the powers of a general administrator. See Section 8545. This authority is useful, for example, in an estate with a lengthy will contest where virtually all of the administration is handled by the special administrator, and the only act which occurs after the final resolution of the will contest is the distribution of the estate assets. In such a case, the special administrator may obtain independent administration authority unless good cause is shown why the authority should not be granted.

An applicant for letters of special administration with powers of a general administrator can obtain independent administration authority only as provided in Sections 10450–10453. The applicant must petition for the authority as provided in Section 10450; notice of the hearing must be given in compliance with the requirements of Section 10451; and the provisions of Sections 10452 and 10453 are applicable.

If there is an urgent need for appointment of a special administrator, the petition for independent administration authority can be filed under Chapter 2 (commencing with Section 10450) after the special administrator has been appointed. Using this procedure will permit the special administrator to be appointed without delay and yet permit compliance with the notice of hearing requirements of Section 10451 for the hearing on the petition for independent administration authority.

If the special administrator is not granted the powers of a general administrator at the time of appointment but is later granted the powers of a general administrator, the special administrator may be granted authority to administer the estate under this part at the same time the special administrator is granted the powers of a general administrator or at any time after the personal representative has been granted the powers of a general administrator.

As to the application of this part where independent administration authority was granted under the repealed Probate Code, see Section 10406.

Background on Section 10405 of Repealed Code

Section 10405 was added by 1987 Cal.Stat. ch. 923 § 93 and was amended by 1988 Cal.Stat. ch. 1199 § 90.5. Section 10405 replaced the third sentence of subdivision (a) of former Probate Code Section 591.1 (repealed by 1987 Cal.Stat. ch. 923 § 35). That sentence provided that the independent administration provisions did not apply to special administrators. The 1988 amendment conformed Section 10405 to the terminology used in other provisions enacted or revised in 1988. For background on the provisions of this part, see the Comment to this part under the part heading. [20 Cal.L.Rev.Comm.Reports 1001 (1990)].

Cross References

Authority for independent administration of estates,
   Objections, see Probate Code § 10452.
   Petitions, see Probate Code § 10450.
   Powers authorized, see Probate Code § 10502.
General personal representative, defined, see Probate Code § 58.
Powers of general personal representative granted to special administrator, see Probate Code § 8545.

§ 10406. Application of part; authority to administer granted; independent administration granted under prior law; authority

(a) Subject to subdivision (b), this part applies in any case where authority to administer the estate is granted under this part or where independent administration authority was granted under prior law.

(b) If the personal representative was granted independent administration authority prior to July 1, 1988, the personal representative may use that existing authority on and after July 1, 1988, to borrow money on a loan secured by an encumbrance upon real property, whether or not that existing authority includes the authority to sell real property. *(Stats. 1990, c. 79 (A.B.759), § 14, operative July 1, 1991. Amended by Stats.1990, c. 710 (S.B.1775), § 28, operative July 1, 1991.)*

Law Revision Commission Comments

1990 Enactment and Amendment

Section 10406 (enacted as a part of the new Probate Code by 1990 Cal.Stat. ch. 79 § 14) was amended by 1990 Cal.Stat. ch. 710 § 28.

The 1990 amendment deleted subdivision (c). This subdivision was included in the new Probate Code section because Assembly Bill 831 of the 1989–1990 regular session would have extended the independent administration provisions to cover probate attorney fees. However, Assembly Bill 831 was not enacted, and as a result subdivision (c) became unnecessary. See the Comment to Section 900.

Section 10406 as amended in 1990 continues Section 10406 of the repealed Probate Code with the changes described below.

Subdivision (a) supersedes subdivisions (a) and (b) of Section 10406 of the repealed Probate Code. Under the superseded provisions, a personal representative who was granted authority prior to January 1, 1985, to administer the estate under the Independent Administration of Estates Act was governed by the provisions of the Independent Administration of Estates Act that were applicable at the time the petition requesting independent administration authority was granted. But the superseded provisions included an exception that allowed a personal representative who was granted independent administration authority prior to January 1, 1985, to exercise the authority granted by this part of the repealed Probate Code where a petition was filed after that date requesting authority to administer the estate under the independent administration statute in effect at the time the petition was filed and the petition was granted. Subdivision (a) Section 10406 abandons this now obsolete scheme and simplifies the law by providing that—subject to subdivision (b)—this part applies to all proceedings where independent administration authority has been granted, whether under the new Probate Code, under the provisions of the repealed Probate Code, or under the provisions of the Probate Code in effect prior to January 1, 1985. As to the application of any amendments made after that date, see Section 3.

Subdivision (b) continues subdivision (c) of Section 10405 of the repealed Probate Code without change. Subdivision (b) preserves the authority of a personal representative prior to July 1, 1988, to borrow money secured by real property where the personal representative was granted authority that did not include the authority to sell, exchange, or grant an option to purchase real property. Under the law in effect prior to July 1, 1988, such a personal representative had authority to borrow money with the loan secured by an encumbrance upon real property of the estate. This part of the repealed Probate Code (which became operative on July 1, 1988) added an additional limitation on the authority of a personal representative whose authority does not include authority to sell, exchange, or grant an option to purchase real property: Such a personal representative does not have authority to borrow money with the loan secured by an encumbrance upon real property of the estate. See Section 10403 (defining "limited authority") and the Comment to that section; see also Section 10501(b) and the Comment to that section. Subdivision (b) of Section 10406 makes clear that this additional limitation does not apply to a personal representative who was granted independent administration authority prior to July 1, 1988. Such a personal representative may borrow money on or after July 1, 1988, on a loan secured by real property of the estate, notwithstanding that the personal representative does not have authority to sell real property of the estate.

Background on Section 10406 of Repealed Code

Section 10406 was a new provision added by 1987 Cal.Stat. ch. 923 § 93. For background on the provisions of this part, see the Comment to this part under the part heading. [20 Cal.L.Rev.Comm.Reports 1001 (1990)].

CHAPTER 2. GRANTING OR REVOKING INDEPENDENT ADMINISTRATION AUTHORITY

Section

§ 10450. Petition for authority for independent administration of estate

(a) To obtain authority to administer the estate under this part, the personal representative shall petition the court for that authority either in the petition for appointment of the personal representative or in a separate petition filed in the estate proceedings.

(b) The petition may request either of the following:

(1) Full authority to administer the estate under this part.

(2) Limited authority to administer the estate under this part. *(Stats.1990, c. 79 (A.B.759), § 14, operative July 1, 1991.)*

Application

Application of Part 6, see Probate Code § 10406.

Law Revision Commission Comments
1990 Enactment

Section 10450 continues Section 10450 of the repealed Probate Code without change. Subdivision (b) permits the petitioner either (1) to request full authority (this authority permits the personal representative to administer the estate using all of the powers granted by this part) or (2) to request limited authority. Limited authority permits the personal representative to exercise all of the powers granted by this part except the power to sell, exchange, or grant an option to purchase real property or to borrow money with the loan secured by an encumbrance upon real property. See Sections 10402 (defining "full authority"), 10403 (defining "limited authority"). See also Sections 8405 (notation on letters), 10501(b) (matters requiring court supervision). For example, the personal representative granted limited authority cannot use the independent administration procedure to sell or exchange real property, but the personal representative is authorized to use independent administration authority to sell listed and certain over the counter securities without giving notice of proposed action (see paragraphs (1) and (2) of subdivision (b) of Section 10537) and to invest in certain securities using the notice of proposed action procedure (see subdivision (c) of Section 10533).

If a bond is required and the bond is given by a corporate surety, the amount of the bond of the personal representative who is granted full authority is fixed by the court at not more than the estimated value of the personal property, the estimated value of the decedent's interest in the real property authorized to be sold under this part, and the probable annual gross income of the estate; if the bond is given by personal sureties, the amount is fixed at not less than twice that amount. See Section 10453(a). The estimated value of the decedent's interest in the real property authorized to be sold under this part is excluded in determining the amount of the required bond if the personal representative has only limited authority. See Section 10453(b). Thus, in some cases, a significant saving in the bond premium can be realized by seeking only limited authority. Because of this consideration, limited authority ordinarily is sought only where a bond is required and the personal representative seeks to avoid the increased bond premium that is required when full authority is granted. Accordingly, a personal representative who is not required to provide a bond almost always will request full authority; and a personal representative who is required to provide a bond for an estate that includes real property ordinarily will request limited authority unless the personal representative wishes to use independent administration authority for a sale of some or all of the real property or to borrow money secured by the real property.

The personal representative, despite the grant of independent administration authority, may seek court supervision of a particular transaction. See Section 10500(b). Hence, for example, even though the personal representative has been granted full authority (independent administration authority that encompasses real property transactions), the personal representative may decide to sell real property under the supervised administration procedures (using the statutory procedure that governs a real property sale when independent administration authority has not been granted). See the Comment to Section 10500. Likewise, the personal representative may decide to seek court approval or instructions concerning a transaction rather than to use independent administration authority in a case where there is a lack of agreement as to the desirability of the transaction among the persons interested in the estate or where some of the heirs or devisees who would receive notice of proposed action lack the capacity to object to the proposed action (see subdivision (c) of Section 10590) or for some other reason.

Authority to administer the estate under this part may not be granted where the decedent's will provides that the estate shall not be administered under this part. See Section 10404. Likewise, the authority of the personal representative to exercise particular powers under the Independent Administration of Estates Act may be restricted by the decedent's will. See Section 10502. A special administrator may be granted independent administration authority only if the special administrator is appointed with or has been granted the powers of a general administrator. See Section 10405 and the Comment thereto.

As to the application of this part where independent administration authority was granted under the repealed Probate Code, see Section 10406.

Background on Section 10450 of Repealed Code

Section 10450 was added by 1987 Cal.Stat. ch. 923 § 93. Subdivision (a) restated the first sentence of subdivision (a) of former Probate Code Section 591.1 (repealed by 1987 Cal.Stat. ch. 923 § 35) without substantive change. Subdivision (b) restated subdivision (b) of former Section 591.1 without substantive change, except that subdivision (b) of Section 10450 uses the defined terms "full authority" and "limited authority." See Sections 10402 (defining "full authority"), 10403 (defining "limited authority"). See also Sections 1020–1023 (petitions and other papers), 8405 (endorsement on letters), 10501(b) (matters requiring court supervision). For background on the provisions of this part, see the Comment to this part under the part heading. [20 Cal.L.Rev.Comm.Reports 1001 (1990)].

Cross References

Court supervision, request by personal representative, see Probate Code § 10500.
Court supervision of certain actions, see Probate Code § 10501.
Full authority, defined, see Probate Code § 10402.
Limited authority, defined, see Probate Code § 10403.
Notation on letters, authorization under Independent Administration of Estates Act, see Probate Code § 8405.
Personal representative, defined, see Probate Code § 58.
Wills, provision prohibiting independent administration, see Probate Code § 10404.

§ 10451. Notice of hearing on petition; persons required to receive notice; contents

(a) If the authority to administer the estate under this part is requested in the petition for appointment of the personal representative, notice of the hearing on the petition shall be given for the period and in the manner applicable to the petition for appointment.

(b) Where proceedings for the administration of the estate are pending at the time a petition is filed under Section 10450, notice of the hearing on the petition shall be given as provided in Section 1220 to all of the following persons:

(1) Each person listed in Section 1220.

(2) Each known heir whose interest in the estate would be affected by the petition.

(3) Each known devisee whose interest in the estate would be affected by the petition.

(4) Each person named as executor in the will of the decedent.

(c) The notice of hearing of the petition for authority to administer the estate under this part, whether included in the petition for appointment or in a separate petition, shall include the substance of the following statement: "The petition requests authority to administer the estate under the Independent Administration of Estates Act. This will avoid the need to obtain court approval for many actions taken in connection with the estate. However, before taking certain actions, the personal representative will be required to give notice to interested persons unless they have waived notice or have consented to the proposed action. Independent administration authority will be granted unless good cause is shown why it should not be." *(Stats.1990, c. 79 (A.B.759), § 14, operative July 1, 1991.)*

Application

Application of Part 6, see Probate Code § 10406.

Law Revision Commission Comments

1990 Enactment

Section 10451 continues Section 10451 of the repealed Probate Code without substantive change. For general provisions, see Sections 1020–1023 (petitions and other papers), 1200–1230 (notice of hearing), 1250–1252 (request for special notice), 1260–1265 (proof of giving of notice). As to the application of this part where independent administration authority was granted under the repealed Probate Code, see Section 10406.

Background on Section 10451 of Repealed Code

Section 10451 was added by 1987 Cal.Stat. ch. 923 § 93. Subdivision (a) restated subdivision (c) of former Probate Code Section 591.1 (repealed by 1987 Cal.Stat. ch. 923 § 35) without substantive change.

Subdivision (b) restated subdivision (d) of former Section 591.1 (repealed by 1987 Cal.Stat. ch. 923 § 35) with the following additions and changes:

(1) The requirement that notice be given to each known heir whose interest in the estate is affected by the petition replaced the former requirement of notice to "all known heirs of the decedent."

(2) The requirement that notice be given to each known devisee whose interest in the estate is affected by the petition replaced the former requirement of notice to "all legatees and devisees." See Section 34 (defining "devisee"). See also Section 1206 (notice to known devisees).

(3) The requirement that notice be given to each person named as personal representative in the will of the decedent was new.

The reference in former Section 591.1 to former Probate Code Section 1200 (notice by posting) (repealed by 1987 Cal.Stat. ch. 923 § 59) was corrected in subdivision (b) of Section 10451 to refer to Section 1220 (notice by mail) of the repealed Probate Code. Section 1220 of the repealed Probate Code required 15 days' notice instead of the ten days' notice required under former Probate Code Sections 1200 and 1200.5 (provisions repealed by 1987 Cal.Stat. ch. 923 § 59).

Subdivision (c) restated subdivision (e) of former Section 591.1 (repealed by 1987 Cal.Stat. ch. 923 § 35) with the addition in Section 10451 of the last three sentences of the statement which were new.

For background on the provisions of this part, see the Comment to this part under the part heading. [20 Cal.L.Rev.Comm.Reports 1001 (1990)].

Cross References

Devisee, defined, see Probate Code § 34.
Heir, defined, see Probate Code § 44.
Notice of hearing, mailing requirements, see Probate Code § 1220.
Notices, generally, see Probate Code § 1200 et seq.
Personal representative, defined, see Probate Code § 58.

Petitions and other papers, generally, see Probate Code § 1020 et seq.

§ 10452. Objections; grant of authority; limited authority

Unless an interested person objects as provided in Section 1043 to the granting of authority to administer the estate under this part and the court determines that the objecting party has shown good cause why the authority to administer the estate under this part should not be granted, the court shall grant the requested authority. If the objecting party has shown good cause why only limited authority should be granted, the court shall grant only limited authority. *(Stats. 1990, c. 79 (A.B.759), § 14, operative July 1, 1991.)*

Application

Application of Part 6, see Probate Code § 10406.

Law Revision Commission Comments

1990 Enactment

Section 10452 restates Section 10452 of the repealed Probate Code without substantive change. The making of an objection to the granting of independent administration authority is governed by Section 1043. The second sentence of Section 10452 makes clear that the court, for good cause shown, may grant only limited authority rather than full authority. See Sections 10402 (defining "full authority"), 10403 (defining "limited authority"). See also Section 10450(b)(2) (petition for limited authority). As to the application of this part where independent administration authority was granted under the repealed Probate Code, see Section 10406.

Background on Section 10452 of Repealed Code

Section 10452 was added by 1987 Cal.Stat. ch. 923 § 93. Subdivision (a) superseded subdivision (f) of former Probate Code Section 591.1 (repealed by 1987 Cal.Stat. ch. 923 § 35). Subdivisions (b) and (c) of Section 10452 of the repealed Probate Code restated subdivision (g) of former Section 591.1 without substantive change, except that the endorsement on the letters required by subdivision (c) of Section 10452 where limited authority is granted was made consistent with subdivision (b) of Section 10501. Subdivision (c) was deleted by 1989 Cal.Stat. ch. 21 § 25 because it duplicated Section 8405(c). See *Communication from the California Law Revision Commission Concerning Assembly Bill 156,* 20 Cal.L.Revision Comm'n Reports 227, 231 (1990). For background on the provisions of this part, see the Comment to this part under the part heading. [20 Cal.L.Rev.Comm.Reports 1001 (1990)].

Cross References

Full authority, defined, see Probate Code § 10402.
Interested person, defined, see Probate Code § 48.
Limited authority, defined, see Probate Code § 10403.

§ 10453. Bond of personal representative; amount

(a) If the personal representative is otherwise required to file a bond and has full authority, the court, in its discretion, shall fix the amount of the bond at not more than the estimated value of the personal property, the estimated value of the decedent's interest in the real property authorized to be sold under this part, and the probable annual gross income of the estate, or, if the bond is to be given by personal sureties, at not less than twice that amount.

(b) If the personal representative is otherwise required to file a bond and has limited authority, the court, in its discretion, shall fix the amount of the bond at not more than the estimated value of the personal property and the probable

annual gross income of the estate, or, if the bond is to be given by personal sureties, at not less than twice that amount. *(Stats.1990, c. 79 (A.B.759), § 14, operative July 1, 1991.)*

Application

Application of Part 6, see Probate Code § 10406.

Law Revision Commission Comments

1990 Enactment

Section 10453 continues Section 10453 of the repealed Probate Code with clarifying revisions that conform the section to Section 8482 (bond of personal representative). This section applies only where the personal representative is otherwise required to file a bond. See Sections 301 (no bond required of trust company serving as personal representative), 8481 (waiver of bond in will or by all the heirs or beneficiaries under will). Subdivision (b) makes clear that the amount of the bond does not include the estimated value of the decedent's interest in real property where only limited authority is granted. As to the application of this part where independent administration authority was granted under the repealed Probate Code, see Section 10406.

Background on Section 10453 of Repealed Code

Section 10453 was added by 1987 Cal.Stat. ch. 923 § 93. Subdivision (a) restated subdivision (b) of former Probate Code Section 591.9 (repealed by 1987 Cal.Stat. ch. 923 § 35) but made clear that the court is required to fix the amount of the bond at not more than the amount specified in the section rather than at "not less than" that amount as provided in former Probate Code Section 591.9. Subdivision (b) was a new provision that was consistent with the provision of former Probate Code Section 541 (repealed by 1988 Cal.Stat. ch. 1199 § 48) that excluded the value of real property in determining amount of the bond. For background on the provisions of this part, see the Comment to this part under the part heading. [20 Cal.L.Rev.Comm.Reports 1001 (1990)].

Cross References

Bond, defined, see Code of Civil Procedure § 995.140.
Bond and Undertaking Law,
    Generally, see Code of Civil Procedure § 995.010 et seq.
    Application, see Probate Code § 8487.
Bonds of personal representatives, amounts and requirements, see Probate Code § 8482 et seq.
Liability of principals and sureties, enforcement of liability by beneficiary, see Code of Civil Procedure § 996.410.
Limited authority, defined, see Probate Code § 10403.
Real property, defined, see Probate Code § 68.
Trust companies serving as personal representatives, bond requirements, see Probate Code § 301.
Wills, waiver of bond requirements, see Probate Code § 8481.

§ 10454. Petition requesting modification or revocation of authority of personal representative; notice; court order

(a) Any interested person may file a petition requesting that the court make either of the following orders:

(1) An order revoking the authority of the personal representative to continue administration of the estate under this part.

(2) An order revoking the full authority of the personal representative to administer the estate under this part and granting the personal representative limited authority to administer the estate under this part.

(b) The petition shall set forth the basis for the requested order.

(c) Notice of the hearing on the petition shall be given as provided in Section 1220. In addition, the personal representative shall be served with a copy of the petition and a notice of the time and place of the hearing at least 15 days prior to the hearing. Service on the personal representative shall be made in the manner provided in Section 415.10 or 415.30 of the Code of Civil Procedure or in such manner as may be authorized by the court.

(d) If the court determines that good cause has been shown, the court shall make an order revoking the authority of the personal representative to continue administration of the estate under this part. Upon the making of the order, new letters shall be issued without the notation described in subdivision (c) of Section 8405.

(e) If the personal representative was granted full authority and the court determines that good cause has been shown, the court shall make an order revoking the full authority and granting the personal representative limited authority. Upon the making of the order, new letters shall be issued with the notation described in subdivision (c) of Section 8405 that is required where the authority granted is limited authority. (Stats.1990, c. 79 (A.B.759), § 14, operative July 1, 1991.)

Application

Application of Part 6, see Probate Code § 10406.

Law Revision Commission Comments

1990 Enactment

Section 10454 continues Section 10454 of the repealed Probate Code without change. For general provisions, see Sections 1000–1004 (rules of practice), 1020–1023 (petitions and other papers), 1040–1050 (hearings and orders), 1200–1230 (notice of hearing), 1250–1252 (request for special notice), 1260–1265 (proof of giving of notice). As to the application of this part where independent administration authority was granted under the repealed Probate Code, see Section 10406.

Background on Section 10454 of Repealed Code

Section 10454 was added by 1987 Cal.Stat. ch. 923 § 93. The section restated former Probate Code Section 591.7 (repealed by 1987 Cal.Stat. ch. 923 § 35) with the following changes:

(1) Section 10454 made clear that an order may be made which revokes full authority and instead grants limited authority.

(2) The requirement that notice of the hearing be given as provided in Section 1220 was new. Former Section 591.7 required notice of hearing only to the personal representative. Giving notice of hearing as provided in Section 1220 gives notice to other persons who may be interested in the petition.

Section 10454 was amended by 1989 Cal.Stat. ch. 544 § 16 to reflect the deletion of subdivision (c) from former Section 10452 (amended by 1989 Cal.Stat. ch. 21 § 25), the substance of this provision being found in Section 8405(c). See *Communication from the California Law Revision Commission Concerning Assembly Bill 158,* 20 Cal.L.Revision Comm'n Reports 235, 242 (1990).

For background on the provisions of this part, see the Comment to this part under the part heading. [20 Cal.L.Rev.Comm.Reports 1001 (1990)].

Cross References

Full authority, defined, see Probate Code § 10402.

Hearings and orders, general requirements, see Probate Code § 1040 et seq.

Letters of administration, notation of authority to act under Independent Administration of Estates Act, see Probate Code § 8405.

Limited authority, defined, see Probate Code § 10403.

Notice of hearing, mailing requirements, see Probate Code § 1220.

Notices, proof requirements, see Probate Code § 1260 et seq.

Personal representative, defined, see Probate Code § 58.

Petitions and other papers, general requirements, see Probate Code § 1020 et seq.

Rules of practice, see Probate Code § 1000 et seq.

Service of summons, see Code of Civil Procedure §§ 415.10, 415.30.

Special notice, requests, see Probate Code § 1250 et seq.

CHAPTER 3. ADMINISTRATION UNDER INDEPENDENT ADMINISTRATION AUTHORITY

ARTICLE 1. GENERAL PROVISIONS

§ 10500. Authority to administer estate without court supervision; request for supervision

(a) Subject to the limitations and conditions of this part, a personal representative who has been granted authority to administer the estate under this part may administer the estate as provided in this part without court supervision, but in all other respects the personal representative shall administer the estate in the same manner as a personal representative who has not been granted authority to administer the estate under this part.

(b) Notwithstanding subdivision (a), the personal representative may obtain court supervision as provided in this code of any action to be taken by the personal representative during administration of the estate. (Stats.1990, c. 79 (A.B.759), § 14, operative July 1, 1991.)

Application

Application of Part 6, see Probate Code § 10406.

Law Revision Commission Comments

1990 Enactment

Section 10500 continues Section 10500 of the repealed Probate Code without change.

As the introductory clause of subdivision (a) recognizes, a personal representative who has been granted only limited authority under this part may not exercise authority with respect to matters not included within the scope of the authority granted. See Section 10501(b) (limited authority excludes power to sell, exchange, or grant option to purchase real property, or to borrow money with the loan secured by an encumbrance upon real property, using independent administration procedure). See also Sections 10403, 10450(b)(2), 10452 (limited authority); Section 10502 (decedent's will may restrict powers exercisable under independent administration authority).

Notwithstanding that full authority has been granted, some actions can be taken only under court supervision. See Section 10501 (court supervision required for allowance of compensation of the personal representative and attorney for personal representative, settlement of accounts, preliminary and final distributions and discharge, and certain transactions involving a possible conflict of interest on the part of the personal representative or the personal representative's attorney). See also Section 10401 (defining "court supervision").

The introductory clause of subdivision (a) also recognizes that independent administration authority must be exercised in compliance with the provisions of this part. Some actions can be taken only if the notice of proposed action procedure is followed. See Article 2 (commencing with Section 10510), Article 3 (commencing with Section 10530) (actions requiring notice of proposed action); see also Chapter 4 (commencing with Section 10580) (notice of proposed action procedure). For a general provision concerning the exercise of powers under this part, see Section 10502. See also the Comment to Section 10502.

Subdivision (b) makes clear that the personal representative may obtain court supervision of an action even though the personal representative is authorized to take the action using the independent administration procedure. For example, even though the personal representative has been granted full authority (full authority includes the power to sell real property using the independent administration procedure), the personal representative may nevertheless determine to sell the real property using the court supervised procedure for a real property sale. If the personal representative determines to use the court supervised procedure, all the requirements of the court supervised procedure apply to the same extent that they would apply if the personal representative had not been granted independent administration authority. See Section 10401 (defining "court supervision"). For example, except as provided in Sections 10301–10303, the requirement that notice of sale be published must be satisfied. See Section 10300. See also Section 10303 (notice of sale need not be published where decedent's will directs or authorizes the sale).

Where the personal representative decides to obtain court supervision of an action even though the personal representative is authorized to take the action using the independent administration procedure and no other procedure is provided by statute for court supervision of the particular proposed action, the personal representative may petition for instructions under Section 9611. For example, there being no specific procedure for obtaining authority under supervised administration for incorporation of the decedent's unincorporated business (see Section 10512), the personal representative may elect to petition for instructions under Section 9611 rather than using the notice of proposed action procedure under Chapter 4 (commencing with Section 10580). See also Section 10580(b) (personal representative may use notice of proposed action procedure for an action that could be taken without giving notice of proposed action).

As to the application of this part where independent administration authority was granted under the repealed Probate Code, see Section 10406.

Background on Section 10500 of Repealed Code

Section 10500 was added by 1987 Cal.Stat. ch. 923 § 93. Subdivision (a) restated the first sentence and the first portion of the second sentence of subdivision (a) of former Probate Code Section 591.2 (repealed by 1987 Cal.Stat. ch. 923 § 35) without substantive change. See also Section 10401 (defining "court supervision"). Subdivision (b) restated the first sentence of subdivision (b) of former Section 591.2 (repealed by 1987 Cal.Stat. ch. 923 § 35) without substantive change. For background on the provisions of this part, see the Comment to this part under the part heading. [20 Cal.L.Rev.Comm.Reports 1001 (1990)].

§ 10501. Court supervision required for certain actions; exceptions

(a) Notwithstanding any other provision of this part, whether the personal representative has been granted full authority or limited authority, a personal representative who has obtained authority to administer the estate under this part is required to obtain court supervision, in the manner provided in this code, for any of the following actions:

(1) Allowance of the personal representative's compensation.

(2) Allowance of compensation of the attorney for the personal representative.

(3) Settlement of accounts.

(4) Subject to Section 10520, preliminary and final distributions and discharge.

(5) Sale of property of the estate to the personal representative or to the attorney for the personal representative.

(6) Exchange of property of the estate for property of the personal representative or for property of the attorney for the personal representative.

(7) Grant of an option to purchase property of the estate to the personal representative or to the attorney for the personal representative.

(8) Allowance, payment, or compromise of a claim of the personal representative, or the attorney for the personal representative, against the estate.

(9) Compromise or settlement of a claim, action, or proceeding by the estate against the personal representative or against the attorney for the personal representative.

(10) Extension, renewal, or modification of the terms of a debt or other obligation of the personal representative, or the attorney for the personal representative, owing to or in favor of the decedent or the estate.

(b) Notwithstanding any other provision of this part, a personal representative who has obtained only limited authority to administer the estate under this part is required to obtain court supervision, in the manner provided in this code, for any of the following actions:

(1) Sale of real property.

(2) Exchange of real property.

(3) Grant of an option to purchase real property.

(4) Borrowing money with the loan secured by an encumbrance upon real property.

(c) Paragraphs (5) to (10), inclusive, of subdivision (a) do not apply to a transaction between the personal representative as such and the personal representative as an individual where all of the following requirements are satisfied:

(1) Either (A) the personal representative is the sole beneficiary of the estate or (B) all the known heirs or devisees have consented to the transaction.

(2) The period for filing creditor claims has expired.

(3) No request for special notice is on file or all persons who filed a request for special notice have consented to the transaction.

(4) The claim of each creditor who filed a claim has been paid, settled, or withdrawn, or the creditor has consented to the transaction. *(Stats.1990, c. 79 (A.B.759), § 14, operative July 1, 1991. Amended by Stats.1990, c. 710 (S.B.1775), § 29, operative July 1, 1991; Stats.1992, c. 178 (S.B.1496), § 37.)*

Application

Application of Part 6, see Probate Code § 10406.

Law Revision Commission Comments

1990 Enactment and Amendment

Section 10501 (enacted as a part of the new Probate Code by 1990 Cal.Stat. ch. 79 § 14) was amended by 1990 Cal.Stat. ch. 710 § 29.

As originally enacted, Section 10501 had revised the language taken from Section 10501 of the repealed Probate Code to reflect the fact that Assembly Bill 831 of the 1989–1990 regular session would have extended the independent administration provisions to cover probate attorney fees. However, Assembly Bill 831 was not enacted, and as a result the revisions the new Probate Code made in Section 10501 became unnecessary and were deleted by the 1990 amendment. See the Comment to Section 900.

Section 10501 as amended continues Section 10501 of the repealed Probate Code without substantive change.

The types of actions described in paragraphs (5)–(10) of subdivision (a) are ones where there often will be a conflict of interest.

Paragraphs (5)–(7) of subdivision (a) make clear that the personal representative cannot use the independent administration procedure to do any of the following:

(1) Sell estate property to the personal representative or the personal representative's attorney.

(2) Exchange estate property for property of the personal representative or the personal representative's attorney.

(3) Grant an option to purchase estate property to the personal representative or the personal representative's attorney.

The prohibitions of paragraphs (5)–(7) are subject to the qualification that the independent administration procedure may be used for the transaction when it is between the personal representative as such and the personal representative as an individual and the requirements of subdivision (c) of Section 10501 are satisfied. Special supervised administration provisions govern the transactions described in paragraphs (5)–(7). See, e.g., Sections 9880–9885. A purchase by or exchange with the personal representative or the personal representative's attorney may be accomplished only to the extent allowed under these special provisions and is subject to their limitations and requirements. Under these provisions, the purchase is permitted only if all known heirs or devisees give written consent to the purchase (Section 9881) and the court approves the purchase (Section 9883). The personal representative or personal representative's attorney may purchase property of the estate pursuant to a contract made during the lifetime of the decedent only if the statutory supervised administration requirements are satisfied. See Sections 9860–9868, 9884. The personal representative or personal representative's attorney may exercise an option to purchase property of the estate given in the will of the decedent only if the statutory supervised administration requirements are satisfied. See Sections 9885, 9980–9983.

Paragraph (8) of subdivision (a) makes clear that the personal representative may not use the independent administration procedure for a claim against the estate by the personal representative or the personal representative's attorney. The personal representative must submit the claim for allowance or rejection by the judge pursuant to Section 9252. Paragraph (8) is subject to the qualification that the independent administration procedure may be used for a claim of the personal representative against the estate if the requirements of subdivision (c) are satisfied.

Paragraphs (9) and (10) of subdivision (a) preclude the use of independent administration to compromise or settle a claim, action, or proceeding of the estate against the personal representative or the personal representative's attorney or to modify the terms of a debt or similar obligation of the personal representative or the personal representative's attorney to the estate. A special provision governs these transactions. See Sections 9830, 9834. Independent administration procedure may be used for the actions described in paragraphs (9) and (10) between the personal representative as such and the personal representative as an individual if the requirements of subdivision (c) are satisfied.

Paragraph (4) of subdivision (b) requires court supervision if the personal representative has limited authority and proposes to borrow money with the loan secured by an encumbrance upon real property of the estate. This limitation on borrowing money does not affect the powers of a personal representative who was granted independent administration authority prior to July 1, 1988. See Section 10406(b). In connection with subdivision (b), see Sections 10403, 10450(b)(2), 10452 (limited authority). See also Section 10502 (decedent's will may restrict powers exercisable under independent administration authority).

Subdivision (c) permits the use of the independent administration procedure for a transaction between the personal representative as such and the personal representative as an individual under the circumstances described in the subdivision. Subdivision (c) does not permit use of the independent administration procedure where the transaction involves the personal representative's attorney; such a transaction is subject to the applicable court supervision provisions referred to above.

The term "the attorney for the personal representative" is used in a broad sense and includes the associates, partners, and attorneys of counsel with the law firm of the attorney selected by the personal representative and also associates, partners, and attorneys of counsel with other law firms associated in the estate proceeding with the firm of the attorney selected by the personal representative.

As to the application of this part where independent administration authority was granted under the repealed Probate Code, see Section 10406.

1992 Amendment

Paragraph (4) of subdivision (a) of Section 10501 is amended to make it subject to Section 10520 (preliminary distribution using notice of proposed action procedure). [21 Cal.L.Rev.Comm.Reports 209 (1991)].

Background on Section 10501 of Repealed Code

Section 10501 was added by 1987 Cal.Stat. ch. 923 § 93.

Paragraphs (1)–(4) of subdivision (a) restated without substantive change clauses (1)–(3) of the second sentence of subdivision (a) of former Probate Code Section 591.2 (repealed by 1987 Cal.Stat. ch. 923 § 35). Paragraphs (5)–(10) of subdivision (a) were new. Prior law did not expressly provide that the independent administration procedure could not be used for the types of actions listed in those paragraphs.

Paragraphs (1)–(3) of subdivision (b) restated without substantive change clause (4) of the second sentence of subdivision (a) of former Section 591.2 (repealed by 1987 Cal.Stat. ch. 923 § 35). Paragraph (4) of subdivision (b) was new and required court supervision if the personal representative had limited authority and proposed to borrow money with the loan secured by an encumbrance upon real property of the estate. Under former law, the personal representative with limited authority could use independent administration authority to borrow money with the loan secured by an encumbrance upon real property.

Subdivision (c) was new.

For background on the provisions of this part, see the Comment to this part under the part heading. [20 Cal.L.Rev.Comm.Reports 1001 (1990)].

Cross References

Fee for filing petition or opposition paper concerning appealable order filed after issuance of letters in probate court, see Government Code § 70658.

Filing fees, exemption for subsequent papers for proceedings required by this section, see Government Code § 26827.4.

§ 10502. Powers of personal representative authorized for independent administration of estate

(a) Subject to the conditions and limitations of this part and to Section 9600, a personal representative who has been granted authority to administer the estate under this part has the powers described in Article 2 (commencing with Section 10510), Article 3 (commencing with Section 10530), and Article 4 (commencing with Section 10550).

(b) The will may restrict the powers that the personal representative may exercise under this part. *(Stats.1990, c. 79 (A.B.759), § 14, operative July 1, 1991.)*

Application

Application of Part 6, see Probate Code § 10406.

Law Revision Commission Comments
1990 Enactment

Section 10502 continues Section 10502 of the repealed Probate Code without change.

The reference to Section 9600 (duty to manage estate using ordinary care and diligence) in subdivision (a) of Section 10502 recognizes that the personal representative acts in a fiduciary capacity in exercising the powers under this part. The personal representative is required to exercise the power granted under this part to the extent that ordinary care and diligence requires that the power be exercised and may not exercise the power to the extent that ordinary care and diligence requires that the power not be exercised. See Section 9600(b). As to the effect of court authorization or approval, see Section 7250. See also Section 10590 (court review of action taken pursuant to independent administration authority).

As the introductory clause of subdivision (a) of Section 10502 recognizes, the powers of the personal representative are subject to the conditions and limitations of this part. Thus, a personal representative who has been granted only limited authority under this part may not exercise independent administration authority with respect to matters not included within the scope of the authority granted. See Section 10501(b) (limited authority excludes power to sell, exchange, or grant option to purchase real property, or to borrow money secured by encumbrance on real property, using independent administration procedure). See also Sections 10403, 10450(b)(2), 10452 (limited authority); Section 10501 (matters requiring court supervision notwithstanding grant of independent administration authority).

Subdivision (b) of Section 10502 states another limitation on the exercise of powers by the personal representative: The decedent's will may limit the powers of the personal representative under this part. See also Section 10404 (part not applicable if decedent's will so provides).

A further limitation on the exercise of independent administration powers is that in some cases powers described in this chapter may be exercised only if notice of proposed action is given or the person entitled to notice of proposed action has waived the notice or has consented to the proposed action. If a person entitled to notice of proposed action makes a timely objection to the proposed action, it may be taken only under court supervision. See Chapter 4 (commencing with Section 10580) (notice of proposed action procedure). As to when notice of proposed action is required, see Article 2 (commencing with Section 10510) and Article 3 (commencing with Section 10530).

As to the application of this part where independent administration authority was granted under the repealed Probate Code, see Section 10406.

Background on Section 10502 of Repealed Code

Section 10502 was added by 1987 Cal.Stat. ch. 923 § 93. The section restated the introductory clause of former Probate Code Section 591.6 (repealed by 1987 Cal.Stat. ch. 923 § 35) without substantive change except that the portion of former Section 591.6 giving the executor or administrator powers "in addition to any other powers granted by this code" was superseded by Section 10551.

The reference to Section 9600 (duty to manage estate using ordinary care and diligence) was new and was added to Section 10502 to recognize that the personal representative acts in a fiduciary capacity in exercising the powers under this part. This reference continued and generalized the substantive effect of the phrase "the applicable fiduciary duties" which appeared in former Probate Code Section 591.9 (repealed by 1987 Cal.Stat. ch. 923 § 35).

For background on the provisions of this part, see the Comment to this part under the part heading. [20 Cal.L.Rev.Comm.Reports 1001 (1990)].

§ 10503. Sale of property of estate; court confirmation of sales not required; limitations

Subject to the limitations and requirements of this part, when the personal representative exercises the authority to sell property of the estate under this part, the personal representative may sell the property either at public auction or private sale, and with or without notice, for such price, for cash or on credit, and upon such terms and conditions as the personal representative may determine, and the requirements applicable to court confirmation of sales of real property (including, but not limited to, publication of notice of sale, court approval of agents' and brokers' commissions, sale at not less than 90 percent of appraised value, and court examination into the necessity for the sale, advantage to the estate and benefit to interested persons, and efforts of the personal representative to obtain the highest and best price for the property reasonably attainable), and the requirements applicable to court confirmation of sales of personal property, do not apply to the sale. *(Stats.1990, c. 79 (A.B.759), § 14, operative July 1, 1991.)*

Application

Application of Part 6, see Probate Code § 10406.

Law Revision Commission Comments
1990 Enactment

Section 10503 continues Section 10503 of the repealed Probate Code without change. This section concerns the manner of sale of property when the personal representative exercises the power to sell property. The power to sell property is found in other provisions of this chapter. See Sections 10511 (real property) and 10537 (personal property). See also Sections 10515 (granting option to purchase real property), 10516 (transferring to person given option to purchase in will), 10517 (completing contract of decedent to convey or transfer property), 10538 (granting exclusive right to sell property). The personal representative acts in a fiduciary capacity in exercising the powers granted by this part. See Sections 9600, 10502, and the Comment to Section 10502.

Section 10503 makes clear that sales under independent administration authority are not subject to the statutory requirements that apply to sales made under court supervision. Thus, for example, the commission of the realtor who lists or obtains the purchaser of real property sold under independent administration authority is not subject to the approval of the court and the provisions concerning contracts and commissions of agents or brokers (Sections 10150–10166) are not applicable. Nor does the 90–percent–of–appraised–value requirement apply when a sale is made under independent administration authority. Nor does the court examine into the efforts of the personal representative to obtain the highest and best price for the property reasonably attainable as is the case where there is a court hearing on the confirmation of a real property sale. Publication of notice of sale is not required where the sale is made under independent administration authority. Likewise, notice of sale, court confirmation, and approval of the commission of the agent, broker, or auctioneer is not required where a sale of personal property is made under independent administration authority.

The personal representative who has been granted only limited authority may not exercise independent administration authority with respect to the sale, exchange, or granting of an option to purchase real property. See Section 10501(b) (limited authority excludes power to sell, exchange, or grant option to purchase real property using independent administration procedure). See also Sections 10403, 10450(b)(2), 10452 (limited authority). The decedent's will may restrict the exercise of the power to sell property. See Section 10502. See also the Comment to Section 10502. In addition, except in certain narrowly limited circumstances, independent administration authority may not be used to sell estate property to the personal representative or the personal representative's attorney. See Section 10501.

Unless notice has been waived or consent to the proposed action has been obtained, notice of proposed action under Chapter 4 (commencing with Section 10580) is required to sell or exchange real property (Section 10511) or to sell or exchange personal property except for certain kinds of property (Section 10537). Absent waiver of notice or consent to the proposed action, notice of proposed action also is required for selling the decedent's unincorporated business (Section 10512), granting an option to purchase real property (Section 10515), transferring to a person given an option to purchase in the decedent's will (Section 10516), completing a contract by decedent to convey property (Section 10517), or granting an extension of an exclusive right to sell property that will cause the entire period covered by the right to exceed 270 days (Section 10538).

The personal representative has the power to execute any conveyance needed to effectuate the sale. See Section 10555.

As to the application of this part where independent administration authority was granted under the repealed Probate Code, see Section 10406.

Background on Section 10503 of Repealed Code

Section 10503 was added by 1987 Cal.Stat. ch. 923 § 93. The section restated subdivision (a) of former Probate Code Section 591.9 (repealed by 1987 Cal.Stat. ch. 923 § 35) without substantive change. The phrase "for cash or on credit" was continued in Section 10503 from subdivision (a) of former Probate Code Section 591.6 (repealed by 1987 Cal.Stat. ch. 923 § 35). The phrase "the applicable fiduciary duties" which appeared in subdivision (a) of former Section 591.9 was replaced by Section 10502 (personal representative acts in a fiduciary capacity in exercising the powers granted by this part). See also Section 9600 and the Comment to Section 10502. For background on the provisions of this part, see the Comment to this

part under the part heading. [20 Cal.L.Rev.Comm.Reports 1001 (1990)].

Cross References

Rural property suitable for shift-in-land-use loan to develop grazing or pasture facilities, sale, see Probate Code § 10207.

ARTICLE 2. POWERS EXERCISABLE ONLY AFTER GIVING NOTICE OF PROPOSED ACTION

Section
10510. Exercise of powers.
10511. Sale or exchange of real property.
10512. Sale or incorporation of business.
10513. Abandonment of tangible personal property.
10514. Power to borrow or encumber property.
10515. Grant of option to purchase real property of estate.
10516. Transfer of property to person exercising option to purchase provided by will.
10517. Conveyance or transfer of real or personal property.
10518. Determination of claims to property.
10519. Disclaimers.
10520. Preliminary distributions after time for filing claims expired.

Cross References

Application of old and new law, see Probate Code § 3.

§ 10510. Exercise of powers

The personal representative may exercise the powers described in this article only if the requirements of Chapter 4 (commencing with Section 10580) (notice of proposed action procedure) are satisfied. *(Stats.1990, c. 79 (A.B.759), § 14, operative July 1, 1991.)*

Application

Application of Part 6, see Probate Code § 10406.

Law Revision Commission Comments

1990 Enactment

Section 10510 continues Section 10510 of the repealed Probate Code without change. This section conditions the exercise of the powers described in this article: Those powers may be exercised only if the requirements of Chapter 4 (commencing with Section 10580) (notice of proposed action procedure) are satisfied.

The personal representative is required to exercise a power granted under this article to the extent that ordinary care and diligence requires that the power be exercised and may not exercise the power to the extent that ordinary care and diligence requires that the power not be exercised. See Section 9600(b). See also Section 10502 (introductory clause) and the Comment thereto. As to the effect of court authorization or approval, see Section 7250. See also Section 10590 (court review of action taken pursuant to independent administration authority).

The personal representative may not take certain actions under independent administration authority where there is a conflict of interest between the interest of the personal representative and the interest of the estate. See Section 10501 (except in certain narrowly limited circumstances, personal representative cannot use independent administration procedure to sell property of the estate to the personal representative or the personal representative's attorney, to exchange estate property for property of the personal representative or the personal representative's attorney, or to grant to the personal representative or to the personal representative's attorney an option to purchase property of the estate). See also the Comment to Section 10501.

A personal representative who has been granted only limited authority may not exercise independent administration authority with respect to matters not included within the scope of the authority granted. See Section 10502 and the Comment thereto. See also Section 10501(b) (limited authority excludes power to sell, exchange, or grant option to purchase real property, or to borrow money secured by encumbrance on real property, using independent administration procedure); Sections 10403, 10450(b)(2), 10452 (limited authority); Section 10501 (matters requiring court supervision notwithstanding grant of independent administration authority). The decedent's will may limit the powers of the personal representative under this part. See Section 10502.

As to the application of this part where independent administration authority was granted under the repealed Probate Code, see Section 10406.

Background on Section 10510 of Repealed Code

Section 10510 was added by 1987 Cal.Stat. ch. 923 § 93. The section continued the substance of the phrase "which powers can be exercised in the manner provided in this article" which was found in the introductory portion of former Probate Code Section 591.6 (repealed by 1987 Cal.Stat. ch. 923 § 35). For background on the provisions of this part, see the Comment to this part under the part heading. [20 Cal.L.Rev.Comm.Reports 1001 (1990)].

§ 10511. Sale or exchange of real property

The personal representative who has full authority has the power to sell or exchange real property of the estate. *(Stats.1990, c. 79 (A.B.759), § 14, operative July 1, 1991.)*

Application

Application of Part 6, see Probate Code § 10406.

Law Revision Commission Comments

1990 Enactment

Section 10511 continues Section 10511 of the repealed Probate Code without change. Concerning the exercise of powers described in this article, see Sections 10502 and 10510 and the Comments to those sections. The power described in Section 10511 may be exercised only if the requirements of Chapter 4 (commencing with Section 10580) (notice of proposed action procedure) are satisfied. See Section 10510. For a general provision concerning the manner of sale of real property under independent administration, see Section 10503. The personal representative has power to make any conveyance needed to effectuate the power granted by Section 10511. See Section 10555.

A personal representative who has been granted only limited authority may not sell or exchange real property using the independent administration procedure. See Section 10501(b) (limited authority excludes power to sell or exchange real property using independent administration procedure). See also Sections 10403, 10450(b)(2), 10452 (limited authority).

Except in certain narrowly limited circumstances, the personal representative may not use independent administration authority to sell property of the estate to the personal representative or the personal representative's attorney or to exchange estate property for property of the personal representative or the personal representative's attorney. See Section 10501 and the Comment thereto.

As to the application of this part where independent administration authority was granted under the repealed Probate Code, see Section 10406.

Background on Section 10511 of Repealed Code

Section 10511 was added by 1987 Cal.Stat. ch. 923 § 93. Section 10511, together with Section 10510, restated without substantive change a portion of subdivision (a) of former Probate Code Section 591.6 (powers of personal representative) and subdivision (b)(1) of former Probate Code Section 591.3 (notice of proposed action required) (provisions repealed by 1987 Cal.Stat. ch. 923 § 35). For background on the provisions of this part, see the Comment to this part under the part heading. [20 Cal.L.Rev.Comm.Reports 1001 (1990)].

§ 10512. Sale or incorporation of business

The personal representative has the power to sell or incorporate any of the following:

(a) An unincorporated business or venture in which the decedent was engaged at the time of the decedent's death.

(b) An unincorporated business or venture which was wholly or partly owned by the decedent at the time of the decedent's death. *(Stats.1990, c. 79 (A.B.759), § 14, operative July 1, 1991.)*

Application

Application of Part 6, see Probate Code § 10406.

Law Revision Commission Comments

1990 Enactment

Section 10512 continues Section 10512 of the repealed Probate Code without change. Concerning the exercise of powers described in this article, see Sections 10502 and 10510 and the Comments thereto. The power described in Section 10512 may be exercised only if the requirements of Chapter 4 (commencing with Section 10580) (notice of proposed action procedure) are satisfied. See Section 10510. Real or personal property or both may be sold in connection with the sale of the decedent's business. For a general provision concerning the manner of sale of real property under independent administration, see Section 10503. The personal representative has power to execute any conveyance needed to effectuate the power granted by Section 10512. See Section 10555. As to the power to continue the operation of the decedent's business, see Section 10534.

If the business includes ownership of real property, the personal representative who has been granted only limited authority may not sell or exchange the real property using the independent administration procedure. See Section 10501(b) (limited authority excludes power to sell or exchange real property using independent administration procedure). See also Sections 10403, 10450(b)(2), 10452 (limited authority).

Except in certain narrowly limited circumstances, the personal representative may not use independent administration authority to sell property of the estate to the personal representative or the personal representative's attorney. See Section 10501 and the Comment thereto.

As to the application of this part where independent administration authority was granted under the repealed Probate Code, see Section 10406.

Background on Section 10512 of Repealed Code

Section 10512 was added by 1987 Cal.Stat. ch. 923 § 93. Section 10512, together with Section 10510, restated the last portion of subdivision (b)(6) of former Probate Code Section 591.3 (repealed by 1987 Cal.Stat. ch. 923 § 35) without substantive change. For background on the provisions of this part, see the Comment to this part under the part heading. [20 Cal.L.Rev.Comm.Reports 1001 (1990)].

§ 10513. Abandonment of tangible personal property

The personal representative has the power to abandon tangible personal property where the cost of collecting, maintaining, and safeguarding the property would exceed its fair market value. *(Stats.1990, c. 79 (A.B.759), § 14, operative July 1, 1991.)*

Application

Application of Part 6, see Probate Code § 10406.

Law Revision Commission Comments
1990 Enactment

Section 10513 continues Section 10513 of the repealed Probate Code without change. The language used in Section 10513 is comparable to that used in the provision governing supervised administration. See Sections 9780–9788. Section 10513 applies only to tangible personal property. As to the power with respect to real property and intangible personal property, see Sections 10552 (compromising or settling claim, action, or proceeding), 10553 (commencing and defending actions and proceedings).

Concerning the exercise of powers described in this article, see Sections 10502 and 10510 and the Comments thereto. The power described in Section 10513 may be exercised only if the requirements of Chapter 4 (commencing with Section 10580) (notice of proposed action procedure) are satisfied. See Section 10510. As to the application of this part where independent administration authority was granted under the repealed Probate Code, see Section 10406.

Background on Section 10513 of Repealed Code

Section 10513 was added by 1987 Cal.Stat. ch. 923 § 93. The section superseded subdivision (d) of former Probate Code Section 591.6 (repealed by 1987 Cal.Stat. ch. 923 § 35) which did not require notice of proposed action to abandon property and was not limited to tangible personal property. The language "or any interest therein," which appeared in subdivision (d) of former Section 591.6 was omitted from Section 10513. This language was unnecessary in view of the definition of property which includes "any interest therein." See Section 62 (defining "property"). For background on the provisions of this part, see the Comment to this part under the part heading. [20 Cal.L.Rev.Comm.Reports 1001 (1990)].

§ 10514. Power to borrow or encumber property

(a) Subject to subdivision (b), the personal representative has the following powers:

(1) The power to borrow.

(2) The power to place, replace, renew, or extend any encumbrance upon any property of the estate.

(b) Only a personal representative who has full authority has the power to borrow money with the loan secured by an encumbrance upon real property. *(Stats.1990, c. 79 (A.B. 759), § 14, operative July 1, 1991.)*

Application

Application of Part 6, see Probate Code § 10406.

Law Revision Commission Comments
1990 Enactment

Section 10514 continues Section 10514 of the repealed Probate Code without change. Concerning the exercise of powers described in this article, see Sections 10502 and 10510 and the Comments thereto. The power described in Section 10514 may be exercised only if the requirements of Chapter 4 (commencing with Section 10580) (notice of proposed action procedure) are satisfied. See Section 10510. For provisions relating to supervised administration, see Sections 9800–9807.

A personal representative who has been granted only limited authority may not borrow money with the loan secured by an encumbrance upon real property of the estate using the independent administration procedure. See Section 10501(b)(4). See also Sections 10403, 10450(b)(2), 10452 (limited authority). If the personal representative was granted independent administration authority prior to July 1, 1988, the personal representative may use that existing authority on and after July 1, 1988, to borrow money on a loan secured by an encumbrance upon real property, whether or not that existing authority includes authority to sell real property. See Section 10406(b).

Background on Section 10514 of Repealed Code

Section 10514 was added by 1987 Cal.Stat. ch. 923 § 93. Section 10514, together with Section 10510, restated subdivision (c) of former Probate Code Section 591.6 (powers of personal representative) and subdivision (b)(10) of former Probate Code Section 591.3 (provisions repealed by 1987 Cal.Stat. ch. 923 § 35) with the addition of subdivision (b) which made Section 10514 consistent with Section 10501(b)(4). See the Comment to Section 10501. For background on the provisions of this part, see the Comment to this part under the part heading. [20 Cal.L.Rev.Comm.Reports 1001 (1990)].

§ 10515. Grant of option to purchase real property of estate

The personal representative who has full authority has the power to grant an option to purchase real property of the estate for a period within or beyond the period of administration. *(Stats.1990, c. 79 (A.B.759), § 14, operative July 1, 1991.)*

Application

Application of Part 6, see Probate Code § 10406.

Law Revision Commission Comments
1990 Enactment

Section 10515 continues Section 10515 of the repealed Probate Code without change. Concerning the exercise of powers described in this article, see Sections 10502 and 10510 and the Comments thereto. The power described in Section 10515 may be exercised only if the requirements of Chapter 4 (commencing with Section 10580) (notice of proposed action procedure) are satisfied. See Section 10510. See also Section 10503 (manner of sale of property under independent administration authority).

A personal representative who has been granted only limited authority may not grant an option to purchase real property of the estate using the independent administration procedure. See Section 10501(b) (limited authority excludes power to grant an option to purchase real property). See also Sections 10403, 10450(b)(2), 10452 (limited authority). For the comparable provision under supervised administration, see Section 9960.

Except in certain narrowly limited circumstances, independent administration authority may not be used to grant an option to the personal representative or the personal representative's attorney to purchase property of the estate. See Section 10501 and the Comment thereto.

As to the application of this part where independent administration authority was granted under the repealed Probate Code, see Section 10406.

Background on Section 10515 of Repealed Code

Section 10515 was added by 1987 Cal.Stat. ch. 923 § 93. Section 10515, together with Section 10510, restated without substantive change the last portion of subdivision (a) of former Probate Code Section 591.6 (powers of personal representative) and subdivision (b)(2) of former Probate Code Section 591.3 (notice of proposed action required) (provisions repealed by 1987 Cal.Stat. ch. 923 § 35). For background on the provisions of this part, see the Comment to this part under the part heading. [20 Cal.L.Rev.Comm.Reports 1001 (1990)].

§ 10516. Transfer of property to person exercising option to purchase provided by will

If the will gives a person the option to purchase real or personal property and the person has complied with the terms and conditions stated in the will, the personal representative has the power to convey or transfer the property to the person. *(Stats.1990, c. 79 (A.B.759), § 14, operative July 1, 1991.)*

Application

Application of Part 6, see Probate Code § 10406.

Law Revision Commission Comments

1990 Enactment

Section 10516 continues Section 10516 of the repealed Probate Code without change. For the comparable provision under supervised administration, see Section 9980.

Concerning the exercise of powers described in this article, see Sections 10502 and 10510 and the Comments thereto. The power described in Section 10516 may be exercised only if the requirements of Chapter 4 (commencing with Section 10580) (notice of proposed action procedure) are satisfied. See Section 10510. The personal representative has the power to execute any conveyance needed to effectuate the power granted by Section 10516. See Section 10555.

The personal representative has the specific power described in Section 10516 even though the personal representative has only limited authority. The limitations of Section 10501 that independent administration authority may not be used for certain transactions involving the transfer of estate property to the personal representative or the personal representative's attorney do not apply to the exercise of the power granted by Section 10516.

As to the application of this part where independent administration authority was granted under the repealed Probate Code, see Section 10406.

Background on Section 10516 of Repealed Code

Section 10516 was added by 1987 Cal.Stat. ch. 923 § 93. Section 10516 was a new provision, but the power to transfer to a person given an option in the will probably was embraced within the power to "convey" in subdivision (a) of former Probate Code Section 591.6 (repealed by 1987 Cal.Stat. ch. 923 § 35). For background on the provisions of this part, see the Comment to this part under the part heading. [20 Cal.L.Rev.Comm.Reports 1001 (1990)].

§ 10517. Conveyance or transfer of real or personal property

The personal representative has the power to convey or transfer real or personal property to complete a contract entered into by the decedent to convey or transfer the property. *(Stats.1990, c. 79 (A.B.759), § 14, operative July 1, 1991.)*

Application

Application of Part 6, see Probate Code § 10406.

Law Revision Commission Comments

1990 Enactment

Section 10517 continues Section 10517 of the repealed Probate Code without change. For the comparable provision under supervised administration, see Section 9860.

Concerning the exercise of powers described in this article, see Sections 10502 and 10510 and the Comments thereto. The power described in Section 10517 may be exercised only if the requirements of Chapter 4 (commencing with Section 10580) (notice of proposed action procedure) are satisfied. See Section 10510. The personal representative has the power to execute any conveyance needed to effectuate the power granted by Section 10517. See Section 10555.

The personal representative has the specific power described in Section 10517 even though the personal representative has only limited authority. The limitations of Section 10501 that independent administration authority may not be used for certain transactions involving the transfer of estate property to the personal representative or the personal representative's attorney do not apply to the exercise of the power granted by Section 10517.

As to the application of this part where independent administration authority was granted under the repealed Probate Code, see Section 10406.

Background on Section 10517 of Repealed Code

Section 10517 was added by 1987 Cal.Stat. ch. 923 § 93. The section restated subdivision (b)(9) of former Probate Code Section 591.3 (repealed by 1987 Cal.Stat. ch. 923 § 35) without substantive change. For background on the provisions of this part, see the Comment to this part under the part heading. [20 Cal.L.Rev.Comm.Reports 1001 (1990)].

§ 10518. Determination of claims to property

The personal representative has the power to allow, compromise, or settle any of the following:

(a) A third-party claim to real or personal property if the decedent died in possession of, or holding title to, the property.

(b) The decedent's claim to real or personal property title to or possession of which is held by another. *(Stats.1990, c. 79 (A.B.759), § 14, operative July 1, 1991.)*

Application

Application of Part 6, see Probate Code § 10406.

Law Revision Commission Comments

1990 Enactment

Section 10518 continues Section 10518 of the repealed Probate Code with the substitution of the more precise and accurate words "allow, compromise, or settle" for "determine." For the comparable provision under supervised administration, see Section 9860.

Concerning the exercise of powers described in this article, see Sections 10502 and 10510 and the Comments thereto. The power described in Section 10518 may be exercised only if the requirements of Chapter 4 (commencing with Section 10580) (notice of proposed action procedure) are satisfied. See Section 10510. Except in certain narrowly limited circumstances, independent administration authority may not be used to compromise or settle a claim of the personal representative or the personal representative's attorney against the estate. See Section 10501 and the Comment thereto.

As to the application of this part where independent administration authority was granted under the repealed Probate Code, see Section 10406.

Background on Section 10518 of Repealed Code

Section 10518 was added by 1987 Cal.Stat. ch. 923 § 93. The section restated subdivision (b)(11) of former Probate Code Section 591.3 (repealed by 1987 Cal.Stat. ch. 923 § 35) without substantive change. For background on the provisions of this part, see the Comment to this part under the part heading. [20 Cal.L.Rev.Comm.Reports 1001 (1990)].

§ 10519. Disclaimers

The personal representative has the power to make a disclaimer. *(Stats.1990, c. 79 (A.B.759), § 14, operative July 1, 1991.)*

Application

Application of Part 6, see Probate Code § 10406.

Law Revision Commission Comments

1990 Enactment

Section 10519 continues Section 10519 of the repealed Probate Code without change. For the provisions relating to disclaimers, see Part 8 (commencing with Section 260) of Division 2. Concerning the exercise of powers described in this article, see Sections 10502 and 10510 and the Comments thereto. The power described in Section 10519 may be exercised only if the requirements of Chapter 4 (commencing with Section 10580) (notice of proposed action procedure) are satisfied. See Section 10510. As to the application of this part where independent administration authority was granted under the repealed Probate Code, see Section 10406.

Background on Section 10519 of Repealed Code

Section 10519 was added by 1987 Cal.Stat. ch. 923 § 93. The section restated subdivision (n) of former Probate Code Section 591.6 (powers of personal representative) (repealed by 1987 Cal.Stat. ch. 923 § 35) except that notice of proposed action was not required to exercise this power under former law. For background on the provisions of this part, see the Comment to this part under the part heading. [20 Cal.L.Rev.Comm.Reports 1001 (1990)].

§ 10520. Preliminary distributions after time for filing claims expired

If the time for filing claims has expired and it appears that the distribution may be made without loss to creditors or injury to the estate or any interested person, the personal representative has the power to make preliminary distributions of the following:

(a) Income received during administration to the persons entitled under Chapter 8 (commencing with Section 12000) of Part 10.

(b) Household furniture and furnishings, motor vehicles, clothing, jewelry, and other tangible articles of a personal nature to the persons entitled to the property under the decedent's will, not to exceed an aggregate fair market value to all persons of fifty thousand dollars ($50,000) computed cumulatively through the date of distribution. Fair market value shall be determined on the basis of the inventory and appraisal.

(c) Cash to general pecuniary devisees entitled to it under the decedent's will, not to exceed ten thousand dollars ($10,000) to any one person. *(Added by Stats.1992, c. 178 (S.B.1496), § 38.)*

Application

Application of Part 6, see Probate Code § 10406.

Law Revision Commission Comments

1992 Addition

Section 10520 is new. The section permits the personal representative to take the specified action after giving notice of proposed action, but without court approval. Sections 10500, 10510. A person given notice of proposed action who fails to object waives the right to have the court later review the proposed action. Section 10590.

Section 10520 is an optional procedure; the personal representative may seek court approval if the personal representative so desires. See Section 10500(b). If the personal representative seeks court approval of a preliminary distribution, the personal representative may give notice as provided in Section 11623(a)(1) or may give notice as provided in Section 11601, the general provision applicable to court-supervised distribution. See Section 11623(b). [21 Cal.L.Rev.Comm.Reports 209 (1991)].

ARTICLE 3. POWERS THE EXERCISE OF WHICH REQUIRES GIVING OF NOTICE OF PROPOSED ACTION UNDER SOME CIRCUMSTANCES

Section

10530. Notice required for exercise of power.
10531. Management and control of property.
10532. Contracts, power to enter contracts with or without notice.
10533. Deposits and investments of money of estate.
10534. Continuation of partnership or other business.
10535. Payment of family allowance.
10536. Lease of estate property; exploration, production or removal of minerals, oil or gas.
10537. Sale or exchange of personal property.
10538. Grant of exclusive right to sell property.

Cross References

Application of old and new law, see Probate Code § 3.

§ 10530. Notice required for exercise of power

Except to the extent that this article otherwise provides, the personal representative may exercise the powers described in this article without giving notice of proposed action under Chapter 4 (commencing with Section 10580). *(Stats.1990, c. 79 (A.B.759), § 14, operative July 1, 1991.)*

Application

Application of Part 6, see Probate Code § 10406.

Law Revision Commission Comments

1990 Enactment

Section 10530 continues Section 10530 of the repealed Probate Code without change.

The powers set out in this article are powers that under some circumstances may be exercised without giving notice of proposed action and in other circumstances may be exercised only if notice of proposed action procedure requirements are satisfied. Section 10530 permits the exercise of powers described in this article without giving notice of proposed action under Chapter 4 (commencing with Section 10580) except to the extent otherwise provided in this article.

The personal representative is required to exercise a power granted under this article to the extent that ordinary care and diligence requires that the power be exercised and may not exercise the power to the extent that ordinary care and diligence requires that the power not be exercised. See Section 9600(b). See also Section 10502 (introductory clause) and the Comment thereto. As to the effect of court authorization or approval, see Section 7250. See also Section 10590 (court review of action taken pursuant to independent administration authority).

Subdivision (b) of Section 10580 permits a personal representative to use the procedure provided in Chapter 4 (notice of proposed action procedure) with respect to an action that the personal representative proposes to take under a power granted by this article even though the action is not one for which notice of proposed action is required under this article. For example, the personal representative may want to proceed under Chapter 4 where the proposed action is the making of a contract that will be fully performed within two years. Entering into such a contract ordinarily does not require notice of proposed action. See Section 10532. Or, for example, the personal representative may want to proceed under Chapter 4 where the proposed action is the entering into a lease of real property for a term not in excess of one year. This action does not require notice of proposed action. See Section 10536(b). If the procedure provided by Chapter 4 is used with respect to the proposed action, the person who fails to object to the proposed action waives the right to have the court later review the action taken. See Section 10590 and the Comment thereto. See also Section 10589(b) and the Comment thereto.

The personal representative may not take certain actions under independent administration authority where there is a potential for conflict of interest between the interest of the personal representative and the interest of the estate. See Section 10501 and the Comment thereto.

The decedent's will may limit the powers of the personal representative under this part. See Section 10502.

As to the application of this part where independent administration authority was granted under the repealed Probate Code, see Section 10406.

Background on Section 10530 of Repealed Code

Section 10530 was added by 1987 Cal.Stat. ch. 923 § 93. For background on the provisions of this part, see the Comment to this part under the part heading. [20 Cal.L.Rev.Comm.Reports 1001 (1990)].

§ 10531.   Management and control of property

(a) The personal representative has the power to manage and control property of the estate, including making allocations and determinations under the Uniform Principal and Income Act, Chapter 3 (commencing with Section 16320) of Part 4 of Division 9. Except as provided in subdivision (b), the personal representative may exercise this power without giving notice of proposed action under Chapter 4 (commencing with Section 10580).

(b) The personal representative shall comply with the requirements of Chapter 4 (commencing with Section 10580) in any case where a provision of Chapter 3 (commencing with Section 10500) governing the exercise of a specific power so requires. *(Stats.1990, c. 79 (A.B.759), § 14, operative July 1, 1991. Amended by Stats.1999, c. 145 (A.B.846), § 3.)*

Application

Application of Part 6, see Probate Code § 10406.

Law Revision Commission Comments
1990 Enactment

Section 10531 continues Section 10531 of the repealed Probate Code without change. Concerning the exercise of powers described

in this article, see Sections 10502 and 10530 and the Comments thereto. See also Section 10501 (matters requiring court supervision notwithstanding grant of independent administration authority). As to the application of this part where independent administration authority was granted under the repealed Probate Code, see Section 10406.

1999 Amendment

Subdivision (a) of Section 10531 is amended to make clear that decisions made by a personal representative under the Uniform Principal and Income Act are in the general category of management and control of estate property. Unlike the former Revised Uniform Principal and Income Act (former Sections 16300–16315), the new Uniform Principal and Income Act applies to both trusts and decedents' estates. See, e.g., Sections 16323 ("fiduciary" defined), 16335 (general fiduciary duties). [29 Cal.L.Rev.Comm. Reports 245 (1999)].

Background on Section 10531 of Repealed Code

Section 10531 was added by 1987 Cal.Stat. ch. 923 § 93. The first sentence of Section 10531 restated without substantive change the part of the first portion of subdivision (a) of former Probate Code Section 591.6 (repealed by 1987 Cal.Stat. ch. 923 § 35) that gave the personal representative the power to manage and control property of the estate. The second sentence of subdivision (a) and subdivision (b) of Section 10531 were new provisions that made clear that the requirements of Chapter 4 (commencing with Section 10580) (notice of proposed action procedure) must be satisfied where a provision governing the exercise of a specific power so requires.

The provision of subdivision (a) of former Section 591.6 relating to "exchanges" was superseded by Sections 10511 (real property) and 10537 (personal property).

The portion of subdivision (a) of former Section 591.6 that gave the personal representative the power to "convey" property was superseded by various provisions of this chapter which gave the personal representative the power to take particular actions that may involve a conveyance and by Section 10555 which made clear that the personal representative is authorized to execute a conveyance in any case where a power is exercised and the conveyance is necessary to effectuate the exercise of the power.

The portion of subdivision (a) of former Section 591.6 that gave the personal representative the power to "divide" or "partition" property of the estate was not continued. Insofar as the power to "partition" related to partition proceedings, the inclusion of the word in Section 10531 was unnecessary in view of Section 10553 which authorizes the personal representative to institute, maintain, and defend actions and proceedings. Insofar as the power to "divide" or "partition" may have related to division or partition before distribution, the inclusion of this power as an independent administration power was unnecessary to authorize partition or division without court supervision if there is an agreement of the heirs or devisees. See Sections 1100–1106 (repealed and reenacted as Sections 11950–11956). If there is no agreement, the matter is to be decided under the provisions of Sections 11950–11956 rather than by using the independent administration procedure.

For background on the provisions of this part, see the Comment to this part under the part heading. [20 Cal.L.Rev.Comm.Reports 1001 (1990)].

§ 10532.   Contracts, power to enter contracts with or without notice

(a) The personal representative has the power to enter into a contract in order to carry out the exercise of a specific power granted by this part, including, but not limited to, the powers granted by Sections 10531 and 10551. Except as provided in subdivision (b), the personal representative may exercise this power without giving notice of proposed action under Chapter 4 (commencing with Section 10580).

(b) The personal representative shall comply with the requirements of Chapter 4 (commencing with Section 10580) where the contract is one that by its provisions is not to be fully performed within two years, except that the personal representative is not required to comply with those requirements if the personal representative has the unrestricted right under the contract to terminate the contract within two years.

(c) Nothing in this section excuses compliance with the requirements of Chapter 4 (commencing with Section 10580) when the contract is made to carry out the exercise of a specific power and the provision that grants that power requires compliance with Chapter 4 (commencing with Section 10580) for the exercise of the power. *(Stats.1990, c. 79 (A.B.759), § 14, operative July 1, 1991.)*

Application

Application of Part 6, see Probate Code § 10406.

Law Revision Commission Comments
1990 Enactment

Section 10532 continues Section 10532 of the repealed Probate Code without change. Concerning the exercise of powers described in this article, see Sections 10502 and 10530 and the Comments thereto. See also Section 10501 (matters requiring court supervision notwithstanding grant of independent administration authority).

Where a contract is made to effectuate an independent administration power, the requirements of Chapter 4 (commencing with Section 10580) (notice of proposed action procedure) must be satisfied if the contract fits the description of subdivision (b) of Section 10532. For example, the power to lease personal property of the estate under independent administration authority is governed by the limitation of subdivision (b) of Section 10532. See Section 10536(c). But the power to lease real property of the estate under independent administration authority is subject to a more stringent requirement concerning giving of notice of proposed action (see subdivision (b) of Section 10536), and subdivision (c) of Section 10532 makes clear that this more stringent requirement must be satisfied.

The power to make contracts under independent administration authority in connection with the management and control of the estate is included in the power granted by Section 10531. Other specific powers granted in this chapter—including the powers granted by Section 10551 (powers that any personal representative may exercise without court supervision)—by implication include the power to make a contract where necessary to effectuate the specific power granted.

Subdivision (c) makes clear that if a power given by another section is exercised and a contract is executed to carry out that power, the provisions of Chapter 4 (commencing with Section 10580) apply if the section that governs the exercise of the power requires compliance with Chapter 4.

As to the application of this part where independent administration authority was granted under the repealed Probate Code, see Section 10406.

Background on Section 10532 of Repealed Code

Section 10532 was added by 1987 Cal.Stat. ch. 923 § 93.

Subdivisions (a) and (b) restated subdivision (b)(5) of former Probate Code Section 591.3 (repealed by 1987 Cal.Stat. ch. 923 § 35) with two revisions:

(1) A new provision—that the contract is one that cannot be terminated by the personal representative within two years—was added in subdivision (b) of Section 10532. This provision made clear

that notice of proposed action is not required by Section 10532 if a contract is one that by its terms can be terminated by the personal representative within two years. A contract that can be terminated within two years is to be treated the same as a contract that is to be fully performed within two years.

(2) The word "fully" was added to subdivision (b) of Section 10532 to make clear that the requirement that the contract be one that will be performed within two years is satisfied only if the contract is one that will be "fully" performed within two years.

Subdivision (c) was new. For background on the provisions of this part, see the Comment to this part under the part heading. [20 Cal.L.Rev.Comm.Reports 1001 (1990)].

§ 10533. Deposits and investments of money of estate

(a) The personal representative has the power to do all of the following:

(1) Deposit money belonging to the estate in an insured account in a financial institution in this state.

(2) Invest money of the estate in any one or more of the following:

(A) Direct obligations of the United States, or of the State of California, maturing not later than one year from the date of making the investment.

(B) An interest in a money market mutual fund registered under the Investment Company Act of 1940 (15 U.S.C. Sec. 80a-1, et seq.) or an investment vehicle authorized for the collective investment of trust funds pursuant to Section 9.18 of Part 9 of Title 12 of the Code of Federal Regulations, the portfolios of which are limited to United States government obligations maturing not later than five years from the date of investment and to repurchase agreements fully collateralized by United States government obligations.

(C) Units of a common trust fund described in Section 1564 of the Financial Code. The common trust fund shall have as its objective investment primarily in short term fixed income obligations and shall be permitted to value investments at cost pursuant to regulations of the appropriate regulatory authority.

(D) Eligible securities for the investment of surplus state moneys as provided for in Section 16430 of the Government Code.

(3) Invest money of the estate in any manner provided by the will.

(b) Except as provided in subdivision (c), the personal representative may exercise the powers described in subdivision (a) without giving notice of proposed action under Chapter 4 (commencing with Section 10580).

(c) The personal representative shall comply with the requirements of Chapter 4 (commencing with Section 10580) where the personal representative exercises the power to make any investment pursuant to the power granted by subparagraph (D) of paragraph (2) of subdivision (a) or paragraph (3) of subdivision (a), except that the personal representative may invest in direct obligations of the United States, or of the State of California, maturing not later than one year from the date of making the investment without complying with the requirements of Chapter 4 (commencing with Section 10580). *(Stats.1990, c. 79 (A.B.759), § 14, operative July 1, 1991.)*

Application

Application of Part 6, see Probate Code § 10406.

Law Revision Commission Comments

1990 Enactment

Section 10533 continues Section 10533 of the repealed Probate Code without change. This section uses language from the supervised administration provisions. See Sections 9700 (investment in insured account in a financial institution in this state), 9730 (investment in direct obligations of United States or the State of California, money market mutual fund, investment vehicle authorized for the collective investment of trust funds, units of common trust fund).

Concerning the exercise of powers described in this article, see Sections 10502 and 10530 and the Comments thereto. See also Section 10501 (matters requiring court supervision notwithstanding grant of independent administration authority). For authorization to exercise security subscription or conversion rights under independent administration authority, see Section 10561. See also 10560 (holding securities in name of nominee or in other form). As to the application of this part where independent administration authority was granted under the repealed Probate Code, see Section 10406.

Background on Section 10533 of Repealed Code

Section 10533 was added by 1987 Cal.Stat. ch. 923 § 93. The section superseded subdivision (b) of former Probate Code Section 591.6 (powers of personal representative) and subdivision (b)(8) of former Probate Code Section 591.3 (notice of proposed action required—with certain specified exceptions—for investing funds of the estate) (provisions repealed by 1987 Cal.Stat. ch. 923 § 35). For background on the provisions of this part, see the Comment to this part under the part heading. [20 Cal.L.Rev.Comm.Reports 1001 (1990)].

§ 10534. Continuation of partnership or other business

(a) Subject to the partnership agreement and the provisions of the Uniform Partnership Act of 1994 (Chapter 5 (commencing with Section 16100) of Title 2 of the Corporations Code), the personal representative has the power to continue as a general partner in any partnership in which the decedent was a general partner at the time of death.

(b) The personal representative has the power to continue operation of any of the following:

(1) An unincorporated business or venture in which the decedent was engaged at the time of the decedent's death.

(2) An unincorporated business or venture which was wholly or partly owned by the decedent at the time of the decedent's death.

(c) Except as provided in subdivision (d), the personal representative may exercise the powers described in subdivisions (a) and (b) without giving notice of proposed action under Chapter 4 (commencing with Section 10580).

(d) The personal representative shall comply with the requirements of Chapter 4 (commencing with Section 10580) if the personal representative continues as a general partner under subdivision (a), or continues the operation of any unincorporated business or venture under subdivision (b), for a period of more than six months from the date letters are first issued to a personal representative. *(Stats.1990, c. 79 (A.B.759), § 14, operative July 1, 1991. Amended by Stats. 2003, c. 32 (A.B.167), § 11.)*

Application

Application of Part 6, see Probate Code § 10406.

Law Revision Commission Comments

1990 Enactment

Section 10534 continues Section 10534 of the repealed Probate Code without change. Concerning the exercise of powers described in this article, see Sections 10502 and 10530 and the Comments thereto. See also Section 10501 (matters requiring court supervision notwithstanding grant of independent administration authority). For the provisions governing supervised administration, see Sections 9760–9763.

The partnership agreement may contain a provision governing the continuance of the personal representative as a partner in the case of the death of a partner, but the power to continue as a general partner is subject to the provisions of the Uniform Partnership Act. See Corp.Code §§ 15001–15045.

Subdivision (d) requires notice of proposed action if the personal representative continues the operation of the business for more than six months from the date letters are first issued to any personal representative, whether the personal representative is a special personal representative or a general personal representative. The six-month period commences to run from the time the first special or general personal representative is issued letters.

Although notice of proposed action is not required in order to continue the operation of the decedent's business for the first six months, the personal representative has the option of giving notice of proposed action if the personal representative plans to continue the business during this period. See Section 10580(b). If notice of proposed action is given, a person who fails to object to the proposed action waives the right to have the court later review the action taken. See Section 10590 and the Comment thereto. See also the Comment to Section 10530.

As to the application of this part where independent administration authority was granted under the repealed Probate Code, see Section 10406.

2003 Amendment

Section 10534 is amended to reflect repeal of the Uniform Partnership Act and its replacement by the Uniform Partnership Act of 1994. See 1996 Cal. Stat. ch. 1003, §§ 1.2, 2. [33 Cal.L.Rev.Comm. Reports 162 (2003)].

Background on Section 10534 of Repealed Code

Section 10534 was added by 1987 Cal.Stat. ch. 923 § 93. The section superseded subdivision (*l*) of former Probate Code Section 591.6 (powers of personal representative) and the first portion of subdivision (b)(6) of former Probate Code Section 591.3 (notice of proposed action) (provisions repealed by 1987 Cal.Stat. ch. 923 § 35). The former provisions did not distinguish between nonpartnership businesses and partnerships in which the decedent was a general partner. However, Sections 9760–9763 relating to supervised administration made that distinction, and Section 10534 was drafted to conform to the supervised administration provisions.

The phrase "to such extent as he or she shall deem to be for the best interest of the estate and those interested therein" which was found in former Section 591.6 was omitted as unnecessary. The introductory clause of Section 10502 recognized that the personal representative is required to exercise a power granted under this chapter to the extent that ordinary care and diligence requires that the power be exercised and may not exercise the power to the extent that ordinary care and diligence requires that the power not be exercised. See Section 9600(b). See also the Comment to Section 10502. For background on the provisions of this part, see the Comment to this part under the part heading. [20 Cal.L.Rev.Comm.Reports 1001 (1990)].

§ 10535. Payment of family allowance

(a) The personal representative has the power to pay a reasonable family allowance. Except as provided in subdivision (b), the personal representative may exercise this power without giving notice of proposed action under Chapter 4 (commencing with Section 10580).

(b) The personal representative shall comply with the requirements of Chapter 4 (commencing with Section 10580) for all of the following:

(1) Making the first payment of a family allowance.

(2) Making the first payment of a family allowance for a period commencing more than 12 months after the death of the decedent.

(3) Making any increase in the amount of the payment of a family allowance. *(Stats.1990, c. 79 (A.B.759), § 14, operative July 1, 1991.)*

Application

Application of Part 6, see Probate Code § 10406.

Law Revision Commission Comments

1990 Enactment

Section 10535 continues Section 10535 of the repealed Probate Code without change. Concerning the exercise of powers described in this article, see Sections 10502 and 10530 and the Comments thereto. See also Section 10501 (matters requiring court supervision notwithstanding grant of independent administration authority). For provisions relating to payment of the family allowance, see Sections 6540–6545.

Although notice of proposed action is required for the first payment of a family allowance, the personal representative can continue to make the payment (without any increase) without giving notice of proposed action, except that another notice of proposed action is required if the family allowance is to be continued for a period commencing more than 12 months after the death of the decedent. Notice of proposed action also must be given if (1) there is to be an increase in the amount of the payment of a family allowance or (2) a family allowance is proposed to be paid to a person who previously has not been receiving a family allowance, even where notice of proposed action previously has been given with reference to the payment of a family allowance to another person.

As to the application of this part where independent administration authority was granted under the repealed Probate Code, see Section 10406.

Background on Section 10535 of Repealed Code

Section 10535 was added by 1987 Cal.Stat. ch. 923 § 93. The first sentence of subdivision (a) of Section 10535 restated subdivision (m) of former Probate Code Section 591.6 (powers of personal representative) (repealed by 1987 Cal.Stat. ch. 923 § 35) without substantive change. The second sentence of subdivision (a) and subdivision (b) of Section 10535 restated subdivision (b)(7) of former Probate Code Section 591.3 (notice of proposed action required under some circumstances) (repealed by 1987 Cal.Stat. ch. 923 § 35) without substantive change. For background on the provisions of this part, see the Comment to this part under the part heading. [20 Cal.L.Rev.Comm.Reports 1001 (1990)].

§ 10536. Lease of estate property; exploration, production or removal of minerals, oil or gas

(a) The personal representative has the power to enter as lessor into a lease of property of the estate for any purpose (including, but not limited to, exploration for and production or removal of minerals, oil, gas, or other hydrocarbon substances or geothermal energy, including a community oil lease or a pooling or unitization agreement) for such period, within or beyond the period of administration, and for such rental or royalty or both, and upon such other terms and conditions as the personal representative may determine. Except as provided in subdivisions (b) and (c), the personal representative may exercise this power without giving notice of proposed action under Chapter 4 (commencing with Section 10580).

(b) The personal representative shall comply with the requirements of Chapter 4 (commencing with Section 10580) where the personal representative enters into a lease of real property for a term in excess of one year. If the lease gives the lessee the right to extend the term of the lease, the lease shall be considered as if the right to extend has been exercised.

(c) The personal representative shall comply with the requirements of Chapter 4 (commencing with Section 10580) where the personal representative enters into a lease of personal property and the lease is one described in subdivision (b) of Section 10532. *(Stats.1990, c. 79 (A.B.759), § 14, operative July 1, 1991.)*

Application

Application of Part 6, see Probate Code § 10406.

Law Revision Commission Comments

1990 Enactment

Section 10536 continues Section 10536 of the repealed Probate Code without change.

The first sentence of subdivision (a) makes clear that the personal representative is authorized to determine the period, rental or royalty, and other terms and conditions of the lease. For the comparable provision under supervised administration, see Sections 9940–9948. For the comparable provisions of the Trust Law, see Sections 16231, 16232.

Concerning the exercise of powers described in this article, see Sections 10502 and 10530 and the Comments thereto. See also Section 10501 (matters requiring court supervision notwithstanding grant of independent administration authority). As to the application of this part where independent administration authority was granted under the repealed Probate Code, see Section 10406.

If the lease gives the lessee the option to extend the lease beyond the one-year term, notice of proposed action is required. The option to extend is taken into account in determining the term of the lease for the purpose of subdivision (b). This is consistent with the rule governing personal property leases under supervised administration. See Section 9940.

Background on Section 10536 of Repealed Code

Section 10536 was added by 1987 Cal.Stat. ch. 923 § 93. Subdivision (a) superseded the portion of subdivision (a) of former Probate Code Section 591.6 (repealed by 1987 Cal.Stat. ch. 923 § 35) relating to leases. The second sentence of subdivision (a) and subdivision (b) restated subdivision (b)(4) of former Probate Code Section 591.3 (repealed by 1987 Cal.Stat. ch. 923 § 35) with the addition of a provision dealing specifically with a lease that gives the lessee the option to extend the term of the lease.

Subdivision (c) was a new provision that was consistent with prior law. Under prior law, a lease of personal property was governed by subdivision (b)(5) of former Section 591.3 (contracts other than leases of real property) (repealed by 1987 Cal.Stat. ch. 923 § 35), which was replaced by subdivisions (a) and (b) of Section 10532.

For background on the provisions of this part, see the Comment to this part under the part heading. [20 Cal.L.Rev.Comm.Reports 1001 (1990)].

§ 10537. Sale or exchange of personal property

(a) The personal representative has the power to sell personal property of the estate or to exchange personal property of the estate for other property upon such terms and conditions as the personal representative may determine. Except as provided in subdivision (b), the personal representative shall comply with the requirements of Chapter 4 (commencing with Section 10580) in exercising this power.

(b) The personal representative may exercise the power granted by subdivision (a) without giving notice of proposed action under Chapter 4 (commencing with Section 10580) in case of the sale or exchange of any of the following:

(1) A security sold on an established stock or bond exchange.

(2) A security designated as a national market system security on an interdealer quotation system, or subsystem thereof, by the National Association of Securities Dealers, Inc., sold through a broker-dealer registered under the Securities Exchange Act of 1934 [1] during the regular course of business of the broker-dealer.

(3) Personal property referred to in Section 10202 or 10259 when sold for cash.

(4) A security described in Section 10200 surrendered for redemption or conversion. *(Stats.1990, c. 79 (A.B.759), § 14, operative July 1, 1991.)*

[1] 15 U.S.C.A. § 78a et seq.

Application

Application of Part 6, see Probate Code § 10406.

Law Revision Commission Comments

1990 Enactment

Section 10537 continues Section 10537 of the repealed Probate Code without change. For the comparable provisions under supervised administration, see Sections 9920 (exchanges), 10250–10264 (sales).

Concerning the exercise of powers described in this article, see Sections 10502 and 10530 and the Comments thereto. See also Section 10501 (matters requiring court supervision notwithstanding grant of independent administration authority). For a general provision concerning the power to sell property under independent administration, see Section 10503. Except in certain narrowly limited circumstances, independent administration authority may not be used for the sale of property to the personal representative or the personal representative's attorney or for the exchange of property of the estate for property of the personal representative or the personal representative's attorney. See Section 10501.

Notice of proposed action must be given for the sale or exchange of personal property. Exceptions to this requirement are set forth in subdivision (b) of Section 10537. See also Sections 10510, 10512 (notice of proposed action required for sale of decedent's unincorporated business).

Paragraph (2) of subdivision (b) authorizes the sale of certain over-the-counter stocks. No notice of sale is required, nor is court confirmation required, for the sale of these over-the-counter stocks under supervised administration. See Section 10200. Quotations for these over-the-counter stocks are published daily in newspapers.

For the provision relating to supervised administration that is comparable to paragraph (1) of subdivision (b), see Section 10200.

The reference to Section 10259 in paragraph (3) of subdivision (b) makes clear that notice of proposed action is not required for the sale of personal property at public auction for cash.

The reference to Section 10202 in paragraph (3) of subdivision (b) makes clear that notice of proposed action is not required to sell security subscription or conversion rights when sold for cash. If rights are not sold for cash, Section 10537 requires that notice of proposed action be given for the sale. Under supervised administration, the sale of subscription rights for the purchase of securities is permitted without court supervision. See Section 10202. As to the sale or surrender for redemption or conversion of securities under supervised administration, see Section 10200. As to the exercise of a security subscription or conversion right under independent administration authority, see Sections 10550 and 10561 (notice of proposed action not required).

Paragraph (4) of subdivision (b) makes clear that a security described in Section 10200 may be surrendered for redemption or conversion without giving notice of proposed action. Section 10200 governs the surrender of securities for redemption or conversion.

As to the application of this part where independent administration authority was granted under the repealed Probate Code, see Section 10406.

Background on Section 10537 of Repealed Code

Section 10537 was added by 1987 Cal.Stat. ch. 923 § 93. The section superseded portions of subdivisions (a) and (g) of former Probate Code Section 591.6 which related to sales or exchanges of personal property (powers of personal representative) and all of subdivision (b)(3) of former Probate Code Section 591.3 (notice of proposed action) (provisions repealed by 1987 Cal.Stat. ch. 923 § 35).

Subdivision (a) continued the general requirement of subdivision (b)(3) of former Section 591.3 (repealed by 1987 Cal.Stat. ch. 923 § 35) that notice of proposed action be given for the sale or exchange of personal property.

Paragraph (1) of subdivision (b) restated without substantive change an exception found in subdivision (b)(3) of former Section 591.3 (repealed by 1987 Cal.Stat. ch. 923 § 35). Paragraph (2) of subdivision (b) was new.

Paragraph (3) of subdivision (b) superseded the exception found in subdivision (b)(3) of former Section 591.3 (repealed by 1987 Cal.Stat. ch. 923 § 35) for assets referred to in former Probate Code Sections 770 and 771.5 (provisions repealed by 1987 Cal.Stat. ch. 923 § 39) when sold for cash. Paragraph (3) of subdivision (b) of Section 10537 expanded the exception provided under former Sections 770 and 771.5 to the extent indicated below:

(1) New Section 10259 (supervised administration) of the repealed Probate Code continued the substance of former Section 770 (perishable and other property) (repealed by 1987 Cal.Stat. ch. 923 § 39) which was referred to in former Section 591.3(b)(3), and the substance of the last sentence of former Probate Code Section 772 (personal property sold at public auction) (repealed by 1987 Cal.Stat. ch. 923 § 39) which was not referred to in subdivision (b)(3) of former Section 591.3 (repealed by 1987 Cal.Stat. ch. 923 § 35).

(2) Former Section 771.5 (repealed by 1987 Cal.Stat. ch. 923 § 39) was restated without substantive change in new Section 10202 of the repealed Probate Code.

Paragraph (4) of subdivision (b) was new.

For background on the provisions of this part, see the Comment to this part under the part heading. [20 Cal.L.Rev.Comm.Reports 1001 (1990)].

§ 10538. Grant of exclusive right to sell property

(a) The personal representative has the following powers:

(1) The power to grant an exclusive right to sell property for a period not to exceed 90 days.

(2) The power to grant to the same broker one or more extensions of an exclusive right to sell property, each extension being for a period not to exceed 90 days.

(b) Except as provided in subdivision (c), the personal representative may exercise the powers described in subdivision (a) without giving notice of proposed action under Chapter 4 (commencing with Section 10580).

(c) The personal representative shall comply with the requirements of Chapter 4 (commencing with Section 10580) where the personal representative grants to the same broker an extension of an exclusive right to sell property and the period of the extension, together with the periods of the original exclusive right to sell the property and any previous extensions of that right, is more than 270 days. *(Stats.1990, c. 79 (A.B.759), § 14, operative July 1, 1991.)*

Application

Application of Part 6, see Probate Code § 10406.

Law Revision Commission Comments

1990 Enactment

Section 10538 continues Section 10538 of the repealed Probate Code without change.

Under paragraph (1) of subdivision (a), the personal representative may grant an exclusive right to sell to one broker; and, when that exclusive right expires, grant another broker the exclusive right to sell the same property. The granting of the exclusive right to sell to the new broker is not an extension of the exclusive right to sell within the meaning of paragraph (2) or subdivision (c).

Paragraph (2) of subdivision (a) makes clear that the exclusive right to sell agreement can be extended, each extension being for a period not to exceed 90 days. This addition conforms the independent administration authority under Section 10538 to the supervised administration provision found in Section 10150(c).

Concerning the exercise of powers described in this article, see Sections 10502 and 10530 and the Comments thereto. See also Section 10501 (matters requiring court supervision notwithstanding grant of independent administration authority). For a general provision governing the manner of sale of property, see Section 10503. Notice of proposed action is required for (1) selling or exchanging real property and (2) selling or exchanging personal property (with certain exceptions). See Sections 10510, 10511, 10537.

Although notice of proposed action is not required in order to grant an exclusive right to sell property for a period not to exceed 90 days, or to extend the broker's exclusive right to sell so long as the total period does not exceed 270 days, the personal representative may give notice of proposed action if the personal representative so desires. See Section 10580(b).

The personal representative does not have the power to sell real property using independent administration procedures if the personal representative has limited authority. See Sections 10501(b). See also Sections 10403, 10450(b)(2), 10452 (limited authority).

As to the application of this part where independent administration authority was granted under the repealed Probate Code, see Section 10406.

Background on Section 10538 of Repealed Code

Section 10538 was added by 1987 Cal.Stat. ch. 923 § 93. Paragraph (1) of subdivision (a) restated subdivision (o) of former Probate Code Section 591.6 (repealed by 1987 Cal.Stat. ch. 923 § 35)

without substantive change. Paragraph (2) of subdivision (a) was new. Subdivisions (b) and (c) were new.

The phrase "where necessary and advantageous to the estate" which was found in subdivision (o) of former Section 591.6 was omitted as unnecessary. The introductory clause of Section 10502 recognizes that the personal representative is required to exercise the power granted under this article to the extent that ordinary care and diligence requires that the power be exercised and may not exercise the power to the extent that ordinary care and diligence requires that the power not be exercised. See Section 9600(b). See also the Comment to Section 10502.

For background on the provisions of this part, see the Comment to this part under the part heading. [20 Cal.L.Rev.Comm.Reports 1001 (1990)].

ARTICLE 4. POWERS EXERCISABLE WITHOUT GIVING NOTICE OF PROPOSED ACTION

Cross References

Application of old and new law, see Probate Code § 3.

§ 10550. Exercise of powers

The personal representative may exercise the powers described in this article without giving notice of proposed action under Chapter 4 (commencing with Section 10580). *(Stats.1990, c. 79 (A.B.759), § 14, operative July 1, 1991.)*

Application

Application of Part 6, see Probate Code § 10406.

Law Revision Commission Comments

1990 Enactment

Section 10550 continues Section 10550 of the repealed Probate Code without change. This section permits the exercise of the powers described in this article without giving notice of proposed action under Chapter 4 (commencing with Section 10580). However, subdivision (b) of Section 10580 permits a personal representative to use the notice of proposed action procedure provided in Chapter 4 with respect to an action that the personal representative proposes to take even though the action is not one for which notice of proposed action is required. For example, the personal representative may want to proceed under Chapter 4 where the proposed action is the compromise of a claim by or against the estate (see Section 10552).

This action is one that ordinarily does not require notice of proposed action. If the procedure provided by Chapter 4 is used with respect to the proposed action, the person who fails to object to the proposed action waives the right to have the court later review the action taken. See Section 10590 and the Comment thereto. See also Section 10589(b) and the Comment thereto. Use of the notice of proposed action procedure avoids the need to petition the court for instructions on the proposed compromise (unless there is an objection to the proposed action) in order to preclude a later challenge to the accounts of the personal representative.

The personal representative is required to exercise a power granted under this article to the extent that ordinary care and diligence requires that the power be exercised and may not exercise the power to the extent that ordinary care and diligence requires that the power not be exercised. See Section 9600(b). See also the Comment to Section 10502. As to the effect of court authorization or approval, see Section 7250. See also Section 10590 (court review of action taken pursuant to independent administration authority).

The decedent's will may limit the powers of the personal representative under this part. See Section 10502. As to the application of this part where independent administration authority was granted under the repealed Probate Code, see Section 10406.

Background on Section 10550 of Repealed Code

Section 10550 was added by 1987 Cal.Stat. ch. 923 § 93. For background on the provisions of this part, see the Comment to this part under the part heading. [20 Cal.L.Rev.Comm.Reports 1001 (1990)].

§ 10551. Additional powers

In addition to the powers granted to the personal representative by other sections of this chapter, the personal representative has all the powers that the personal representative could exercise without court supervision under this code if the personal representative had not been granted authority to administer the estate under this part. (Stats.1990, c. 79 (A.B.759), § 14, operative July 1, 1991.)

Application

Application of Part 6, see Probate Code § 10406.

Law Revision Commission Comments

1990 Enactment

Section 10551 continues Section 10551 of the repealed Probate Code without change. Concerning the exercise of powers described in this chapter, see Sections 10502 and 10550 and the Comments thereto. Notice of proposed action is not required to exercise the power granted by Section 10551. See Section 10550.

The inclusion of Section 10551 makes it unnecessary to list in this article those powers that a personal representative not having independent administration authority can exercise without court supervision. This is the reason why some powers listed in former Probate Code Section 591.6 (repealed by 1987 Cal.Stat. ch. 923 § 35) of the repealed Probate Code are not listed in this article. Accordingly, the following powers listed in former Section 591.6 are not listed in this article: Power to vote a security, in person or by general or limited proxy (authorized without court supervision by Section 9655); power to insure estate and personal representative (authorized without court supervision by Section 9656). Section 10551 gives the personal representative who has been granted independent administration authority these powers as well as any other powers that can be exercised without court supervision by a personal representative who has not been granted independent administration authority.

As to the application of this part where independent administration authority was granted under the repealed Probate Code, see Section 10406.

Background on Section 10551 of Repealed Code

Section 10551 was added by 1987 Cal.Stat. ch. 923 § 93. The section superseded the phrase "in addition to any other powers granted by this code" which appeared in the introductory portion of former Probate Code Section 591.6 (repealed by 1987 Cal.Stat. ch. 923 § 35). For background on the provisions of this part, see the Comment to this part under the part heading. [20 Cal.L.Rev.Comm.Reports 1001 (1990)].

§ 10552. Claims of or against estate; payment, contest, compromise, release, or filing after expiration date

The personal representative has the power to do all of the following:

(a) Allow, pay, reject, or contest any claim by or against the estate.

(b) Compromise or settle a claim, action, or proceeding by or for the benefit of, or against, the decedent, the personal representative, or the estate.

(c) Release, in whole or in part, any claim belonging to the estate to the extent that the claim is uncollectible.

(d) Allow a claim to be filed after the expiration of the time for filing the claim. (Stats.1990, c. 79 (A.B.759), § 14, operative July 1, 1991. Amended by Stats.1996, c. 862 (A.B.2751), § 29.)

Application

Application of Part 6, see Probate Code § 10406.

Law Revision Commission Comments

1990 Enactment

Section 10552 continues Section 10552 of the repealed Probate Code without change. Concerning the exercise of powers described in this chapter, see Sections 10502 and 10550 and the Comments thereto. Subdivision (b) is comparable to Section 9830 (supervised administration). As to the payment of taxes, assessments, and other expenses incurred in the collection, care, and administration of the estate, see Section 10556. For provisions relating to claims, see Part 4 (commencing with Section 9000). See also Part 9 (commencing with Section 11400) (payment of debts).

Notice of proposed action is not required to exercise the power granted by Section 10552. See Section 10550 and the Comment thereto. Notice of proposed action is required (1) for determining third-party claims to real or personal property if the decedent died in possession of, or holding title to, the property and (2) for determining decedent's claim to real or personal property title to or possession of which is held by another. See Section 10518.

Except in certain narrowly limited circumstances, Section 10501 prohibits use of independent administration authority to:

(1) Compromise or settle a claim, action, or proceeding by the estate against the personal representative or the personal representative's attorney.

(2) Pay or compromise a claim of the personal representative against the estate or a claim of the personal representative's attorney against the estate, whether or not an action or proceeding is commenced on the claim.

Notwithstanding the granting of independent administration authority, the personal representative is required to obtain court supervision for allowance of compensation of the personal representative. See Section 10501.

As to the application of this part where independent administration authority was granted under the repealed Probate Code, see Section 10406.

Background on Section 10552 of Repealed Code

Section 10552 was added by 1987 Cal.Stat. ch. 923 § 93. Subdivision (a) restated the first clause of subdivision (j) of former Probate Code Section 591.6 (repealed by 1987 Cal.Stat. ch. 923 § 35) without substantive change. The words "by compromise," which appeared at the end of the first clause of subdivision (j) of former Section 591.6, were omitted at the end of subdivision (a) of Section 10552 because those words were unnecessary and their omission did not make a substantive change in the meaning of the provision. Subdivision (b) superseded a portion of the last clause of subdivision (j) of former Section 591.6. Subdivision (c) continued without change language found in the second clause of subdivision (j) of former Section 591.6. For background on the provisions of this part, see the Comment to this part under the part heading. [20 Cal.L.Rev.Comm.Reports 1001 (1990)].

§ 10553. Commencement or defense of actions and proceedings against decedent or estate

The personal representative has the power to do all of the following:

(a) Commence and maintain actions and proceedings for the benefit of the estate.

(b) Defend actions and proceedings against the decedent, the personal representative, or the estate. *(Stats.1990, c. 79 (A.B.759), § 14, operative July 1, 1991.)*

Application

Application of Part 6, see Probate Code § 10406.

Law Revision Commission Comments

1990 Enactment

Section 10553 continues Section 10553 of the repealed Probate Code without change. The language used in this section conforms to the language used in the provision relating to supervised administration. See Section 9820. The authority with respect to actions and proceedings is not limited and includes, for example, commencing, maintaining, or defending partition actions. See Section 9823 (supervised administration).

Concerning the exercise of powers described in this chapter, see Sections 10502 and 10550 and the Comments thereto. Notice of proposed action is not required to exercise the power granted by Section 10553. See Section 10550. Notice of proposed action is required for determining third-party claims to real or personal property if the decedent died in possession of, or holding title to, the property and for determining decedent's claim to real or personal property title to or possession of which is held by another. See Section 10518.

Except in certain narrowly limited circumstances, Section 10501 prohibits use of independent administration authority to:

(1) Compromise or settle a claim, action, or proceeding by the estate against the personal representative or the personal representative's attorney.

(2) Pay or compromise a claim of the personal representative or the personal representative's attorney against the estate, whether or not an action or proceeding is commenced on the claim.

As to the application of this part where independent administration authority was granted under the repealed Probate Code, see Section 10406.

Background on Section 10553 of Repealed Code

Section 10553 was added by 1987 Cal.Stat. ch. 923 § 93. The section restated without substantive change the portion of subdivision (j) of former Probate Code Section 591.6 (repealed by 1987 Cal.Stat. ch. 923 § 35) which authorized the personal representative to "institute" and "defend" actions and proceedings. For background on the provisions of this part, see the Comment to this part under the part heading. [20 Cal.L.Rev.Comm.Reports 1001 (1990)].

§ 10554. Modification of obligation to or in favor of decedent

The personal representative has the power to extend, renew, or in any manner modify the terms of an obligation owing to or in favor of the decedent or the estate. *(Stats. 1990, c. 79 (A.B.759), § 14, operative July 1, 1991.)*

Application

Application of Part 6, see Probate Code § 10406.

Law Revision Commission Comments

1990 Enactment

Section 10554 continues Section 10554 of the repealed Probate Code without change. For the comparable provision under supervised administration, see Section 9830(a)(2).

Concerning the exercise of powers described in this chapter, see Sections 10502 and 10550 and the Comments thereto. Notice of proposed action is not required to exercise the power granted by Section 10554. See Section 10550.

The power granted by Section 10554 is not limited to modifying the terms of an indebtedness owing to the decedent or the estate. It extends to the modification of the terms of an obligation as well. For example, if the lessee has an obligation (not involving the payment of money) to the estate under the terms of a lease (such as a requirement as to the hours of business of the lessee), Section 10554 authorizes the personal representative to modify that term of the lease, it being one of the terms of the obligation in favor of the estate.

Except in certain narrowly limited circumstances, independent administration authority may not be used to extend, renew, or modify the terms of a debt or other obligation of the personal representative or the personal representative's attorney owing to or in favor of the estate. Notwithstanding the granting of independent administration authority, the personal representative is required to obtain court supervision for allowance of compensation of the personal representative. See Section 10501.

As to the application of this part where independent administration authority was granted under the repealed Probate Code, see Section 10406.

Background on Section 10554 of Repealed Code

Section 10554 was a new provision added by 1987 Cal.Stat. ch. 923 § 93. For background on the provisions of this part, see the Comment to this part under the part heading. [20 Cal.L.Rev.Comm.Reports 1001 (1990)].

§ 10555. Transfer or conveyance of property

The personal representative has the power to convey or transfer property in order to carry out the exercise of a specific power granted by this part. *(Stats.1990, c. 79 (A.B.759), § 14, operative July 1, 1991.)*

Application

Application of Part 6, see Probate Code § 10406.

Law Revision Commission Comments

1990 Enactment

Section 10555 continues Section 10555 of the repealed Probate Code without change.

Concerning the exercise of powers described in this chapter, see Sections 10502 and 10550 and the Comments thereto. Under this part, there must be a specific power to act in the specific circumstances (such as the power to make a sale or exchange) in order to authorize the personal representative to execute a conveyance. Where the personal representative acts under one of these specific powers (and complies with the notice of proposed action procedure if notice of proposed action is required), Section 10555 gives the personal representative power to execute any conveyance that is necessary to effectuate the exercise of the specific power without giving notice of proposed action with respect to the execution of the conveyance.

Although notice of proposed action is not required to exercise the power granted by Section 10555 (see Section 10550), the personal representative may use the notice of proposed action procedure if the personal representative so desires. See Section 10580(b) and the Comment to Section 10550.

As to the application of this part where independent administration authority was granted under the repealed Probate Code, see Section 10406.

Background on Section 10555 of Repealed Code

Section 10555 was added by 1987 Cal.Stat. ch. 923 § 93. The section superseded the portion of subdivision (a) of former Probate Code Section 591.6 (repealed by 1987 Cal.Stat. ch. 923 § 35) that gave the personal representative the power to "convey" property. See the discussion in the Comment to Section 10551 concerning that portion of former Section 591.6. For background on the provisions of this part, see the Comment to this part under the part heading. [20 Cal.L.Rev.Comm.Reports 1001 (1990)].

§ 10556.   Payment of taxes, assessments or expenses

The personal representative has the power to pay all of the following:

(a) Taxes and assessments.

(b) Expenses incurred in the collection, care, and administration of the estate. *(Stats.1990, c. 79 (A.B.759), § 14, operative July 1, 1991.)*

Application

Application of Part 6, see Probate Code § 10406.

Law Revision Commission Comments

1990 Enactment

Section 10556 continues Section 10556 of the repealed Probate Code without change. As to the payment of claims against the estate, see Section 10552. For provisions relating to payment of debts, expenses, and charges, see Part 9 (commencing with Section 11400). See also Section 10552 (compromise or settling claim against decedent, personal representative, or estate).

Concerning the exercise of powers described in this chapter, see Sections 10502 and 10550 and the Comments thereto. Notice of proposed action is not required to exercise the power granted by Section 10556. See Section 10550. But see Section 10501 (notwithstanding grant of independent administration authority, personal representative is required to obtain court supervision for allowance of compensation of the personal representative). Although notice of proposed action is not required to exercise the power described in Section 10556, the personal representative may use the notice of proposed action procedure if the personal representative so desires. See Section 10580(b) and the Comment to Section 10550.

As to the application of this part where independent administration authority was granted under the repealed Probate Code, see Section 10406.

Background on Section 10556 of Repealed Code

Section 10556 was added by 1987 Cal.Stat. ch. 923 § 93. The section restated subdivision (k) of former Probate Code Section 591.6 (repealed by 1987 Cal.Stat. ch. 923 § 35) without substantive change. For background on the provisions of this part, see the Comment to this part under the part heading. [20 Cal.L.Rev.Comm.Reports 1001 (1990)].

§ 10557.   Purchase of annuity

The personal representative has the power to purchase an annuity from an insurer admitted to do business in this state to satisfy a devise of an annuity or other direction in the will for periodic payments to a devisee. *(Stats.1990, c. 79 (A.B.759), § 14, operative July 1, 1991.)*

Application

Application of Part 6, see Probate Code § 10406.

Law Revision Commission Comments

1990 Enactment

Section 10557 continues Section 10557 of the repealed Probate Code without change. For the comparable provision under supervised administration, see Section 9733. Concerning the exercise of powers described in this chapter, see Sections 10502 and 10550 and the Comments thereto. Notice of proposed action is not required to exercise the power granted by Section 10557. See Section 10550. But the personal representative may use the notice of proposed action procedure if the personal representative so desires. See Section 10580(b) and the Comment to Section 10550. As to the application of this part where independent administration authority was granted under the repealed Probate Code, see Section 10406.

Background on Section 10557 of Repealed Code

Section 10557 was a new provision added by 1987 Cal.Stat. ch. 923 § 93. For background on the provisions of this part, see the Comment to this part under the part heading. [20 Cal.L.Rev.Comm.Reports 1001 (1990)].

§ 10558.   Exercise of option

The personal representative has the power to exercise an option right that is property of the estate. *(Stats.1990, c. 79 (A.B.759), § 14, operative July 1, 1991.)*

Application

Application of Part 6, see Probate Code § 10406.

Law Revision Commission Comments

1990 Enactment

Section 10558 continues Section 10558 of the repealed Probate Code without substantive change. For the comparable provision under supervised administration, see Section 9734. See also Section 10561 (exercising security subscription or conversion right under independent administration authority). Concerning the exercise of powers described in this chapter, see Sections 10502 and 10550 and the Comments thereto. Notice of proposed action is not required to exercise the power granted by Section 10558. See Section 10550. But the personal representative may use the notice of proposed action procedure if the personal representative so desires. See Section 10580(b) and the Comment to Section 10550. As to the application of this part where independent administration authority was granted under the repealed Probate Code, see Section 10406.

Section 10558 was a new provision added by 1987 Cal.Stat. ch. 923 § 93. For background on the provisions of this part, see the Comment to this part under the part heading. [20 Cal.L.Rev.Comm.Reports 1001 (1990)].

§ 10559. Purchase of securities or commodities to perform contract of sale

The personal representative has the power to purchase securities or commodities required to perform an incomplete contract of sale where the decedent died having sold but not delivered securities or commodities not owned by the decedent. *(Stats.1990, c. 79 (A.B.759), § 14, operative July 1, 1991.)*

Application

Application of Part 6, see Probate Code § 10406.

Law Revision Commission Comments

1990 Enactment

Section 10559 continues Section 10559 of the repealed Probate Code without change. For the comparable provision under supervised administration, see Section 9735. Concerning the exercise of powers described in this chapter, see Sections 10502 and 10550 and the Comments thereto. Notice of proposed action is not required to exercise the power granted by Section 10559. See Section 10550. But the personal representative may use the notice of proposed action procedure if the personal representative so desires. See Section 10580(b) and the Comment to Section 10550. As to the application of this part where independent administration authority was granted under the repealed Probate Code, see Section 10406.

Background on Section 10559 of Repealed Code

Section 10559 was a new provision added by 1987 Cal.Stat. ch. 923 § 93. For background on the provisions of this part, see the Comment to this part under the part heading. [20 Cal.L.Rev.Comm.Reports 1001 (1990)].

§ 10560. Holding security in name of nominee

The personal representative has the power to hold a security in the name of a nominee or in any other form without disclosure of the estate, so that title to the security may pass by delivery. *(Stats.1990, c. 79 (A.B.759), § 14, operative July 1, 1991.)*

Application

Application of Part 6, see Probate Code § 10406.

Law Revision Commission Comments

1990 Enactment

Section 10560 continues Section 10560 of the repealed Probate Code without change. For the comparable provision under supervised administration, see Section 9736. Concerning the exercise of powers described in this chapter, see Sections 10502 and 10550 and the Comments thereto. Notice of proposed action is not required to exercise the power granted by Section 10560. See Section 10550. But the personal representative may use the notice of proposed action procedure if the personal representative so desires. See Section 10580(b) and the Comment to Section 10550. As to the application of this part where independent administration authority was granted under the repealed Probate Code, see Section 10406.

Background on Section 10560 of Repealed Code

Section 10560 was added by 1987 Cal.Stat. ch. 923 § 93. The section restated subdivision (h) of former Probate Code Section 591.6 (repealed by 1987 Cal.Stat. ch. 923 § 35), except that Section 10560 did not continue the provision of former Section 591.6 that made the personal representative "liable for any act of the nominee in connection with the security so held." The liability of the personal representative is now determined under Section 9600 which requires the personal representative to use ordinary care and diligence in managing and controlling the estate and not to exercise a power to the extent that ordinary care and diligence requires that the power not be exercised. See Section 9600 and the Comment thereto. See also Section 10502 and the Comment thereto. For background on the provisions of this part, see the Comment to this part under the part heading. [20 Cal.L.Rev.Comm.Reports 1001 (1990)].

§ 10561. Exercise of security subscription or conversion rights

The personal representative has the power to exercise security subscription or conversion rights. *(Stats.1990, c. 79 (A.B.759), § 14, operative July 1, 1991.)*

Application

Application of Part 6, see Probate Code § 10406.

Law Revision Commission Comments

1990 Enactment

Section 10561 continues Section 10561 of the repealed Probate Code without change. For the comparable provision under supervised administration, see Section 9737 (exercise of security subscription rights). As to the sale under independent administration authority of security subscription or conversion rights, see Section 10537 (notice of proposed action not required if sold for cash). Concerning the exercise of powers described in this chapter, see Sections 10502 and 10550 and the Comments thereto. Notice of proposed action is not required to exercise the power granted by Section 10561. See Section 10550. But the personal representative may use the notice of proposed action procedure if the personal representative so desires. See Section 10580(b) and the Comment to Section 10550. As to the application of this part where independent administration authority was granted under the repealed Probate Code, see Section 10406.

Background on Section 10561 of Repealed Code

Section 10561 was added by 1987 Cal.Stat. ch. 923 § 93. The section restated the substance of the portion of subdivision (g) of former Probate Code Section 591.6 (repealed by 1987 Cal.Stat. ch. 923 § 35) that related to the exercise of subscription or conversion rights with the expansion of the scope of the provision to cover "securities" instead of "stock." See Section 70 (defining "security"). For background on the provisions of this part, see the Comment to this part under the part heading. [20 Cal.L.Rev.Comm.Reports 1001 (1990)].

§ 10562. Repair and improvement of property

The personal representative has the power to make repairs and improvements to real and personal property of the estate. *(Stats.1990, c. 79 (A.B.759), § 14, operative July 1, 1991.)*

Application

Application of Part 6, see Probate Code § 10406.

Law Revision Commission Comments

1990 Enactment

Section 10562 continues Section 10562 of the repealed Probate Code without change. Concerning the exercise of powers described in this chapter, see Sections 10502 and 10550 and the Comments thereto. Notice of proposed action is not required to exercise the power granted by Section 10562. See Section 10550. But the personal representative may use the notice of proposed action procedure if the personal representative so desires. See Section 10580(b) and the Comment to Section 10550. As to the application of this part where independent administration authority was granted under the repealed Probate Code, see Section 10406.

Background on Section 10562 of Repealed Code

Section 10562 was added by 1987 Cal.Stat. ch. 923 § 93. The section restated subdivision (e) of former Probate Code Section 591.6 (repealed by 1987 Cal.Stat. ch. 923 § 35) without substantive change. The phrase "repairs and improvements to real and personal property of the estate" was substituted in Section 10562 for the language "make ordinary or extraordinary repairs or alterations in buildings or other property" which was used in former Section 591.6. The language "ordinary or extraordinary" was omitted because the distinction was irrelevant: Whether a repair or improvement should or should not be made does not depend on whether it is ordinary or extraordinary. The personal representative is required to exercise a power to the extent that ordinary care and diligence requires that the power be exercised and may not exercise the power to the extent that ordinary care and diligence requires that the power not be exercised. See Section 9600(b). See also the Comment to Section 10502. For background on the provisions of this part, see the Comment to this part under the part heading. [20 Cal.L.Rev.Comm.Reports 1001 (1990)].

§ 10563. Acceptance of deed or deed in trust in lieu of foreclosure

The personal representative has the power to accept a deed to property which is subject to a mortgage or deed of trust in lieu of foreclosure of the mortgage or sale under the deed of trust. *(Stats.1990, c. 79 (A.B.759), § 14, operative July 1, 1991.)*

Application

Application of Part 6, see Probate Code § 10406.

Law Revision Commission Comments

1990 Enactment

Section 10563 continues Section 10563 of the repealed Probate Code without change. For the comparable provision under supervised administration, see Section 9850. Concerning the exercise of powers described in this chapter, see Sections 10502 and 10550 and the Comments thereto. Notice of proposed action is not required to exercise the power granted by Section 10563. See Section 10550. But the personal representative may use the notice of proposed action procedure if the personal representative so desires. See Section 10580(b) and the Comment to Section 10550. As to the application of this part where independent administration authority was granted under the repealed Probate Code, see Section 10406.

Background on Section 10563 of Repealed Code

Section 10563 was a new provision added by 1987 Cal.Stat. ch. 923 § 93. For background on the provisions of this part, see the Comment to this part under the part heading. [20 Cal.L.Rev.Comm.Reports 1001 (1990)].

§ 10564. Satisfaction of mortgage or reconveyance under deed of trust

The personal representative has the power to give a partial satisfaction of a mortgage or to cause a partial reconveyance to be executed by a trustee under a deed of trust held by the estate. *(Stats.1990, c. 79 (A.B.759), § 14, operative July 1, 1991.)*

Application

Application of Part 6, see Probate Code § 10406.

Law Revision Commission Comments

1990 Enactment

Section 10564 continues Section 10564 of the repealed Probate Code without change. For the comparable provision under supervised administration, see Section 9851. Concerning the exercise of powers described in this chapter, see Sections 10502 and 10550 and the Comments thereto. Notice of proposed action is not required to exercise the power granted by Section 10564. See Section 10550. But the personal representative may use the notice of proposed action procedure if the personal representative so desires. See Section 10580(b) and the Comment to Section 10550. As to the application of this part where independent administration authority was granted under the repealed Probate Code, see Section 10406.

Background on Section 10564 of Repealed Code

Section 10564 was a new provision added by 1987 Cal.Stat. ch. 923 § 93. For background on the provisions of this part, see the Comment to this part under the part heading. [20 Cal.L.Rev.Comm.Reports 1001 (1990)].

§ 10565. Repealed by Stats.1990, c. 710 (S.B.1775), § 30, operative July 1, 1991

Law Revision Commission Comments

1990 Enactment and Repeal

Section 10565 (enacted as a part of the new Probate Code by 1990 Cal.Stat. ch. 79 § 14) was repealed by 1990 Cal.Stat. ch. 710 § 30. This section was included in the new Probate Code because Assembly Bill 831 of the 1989–1990 regular session would have extended the independent administration provisions to cover probate attorney fees. However, Assembly Bill 831 was not enacted, and as a result Section 10565 became unnecessary. See the Comment to Section 900. [20 Cal.L.Rev.Comm.Reports 1001 (1990)].

CHAPTER 4. NOTICE OF PROPOSED ACTION PROCEDURE

Cross References

Application of old and new law, see Probate Code § 3.

§ 10580. Actions requiring notice; giving of notice where not required

(a) A personal representative who has been granted authority to administer the estate under this part shall give notice of proposed action as provided in this chapter prior to the taking of the proposed action without court supervision if the provision of Chapter 3 (commencing with Section 10500) giving the personal representative the power to take the action so requires. Nothing in this subdivision authorizes a personal representative to take an action under this part if the personal representative does not have the power to take the action under this part.

(b) A personal representative who has been granted authority to administer the estate under this part may give notice of proposed action as provided in this chapter even if the provision of Chapter 3 (commencing with Section 10500) giving the personal representative the power to take the action permits the personal representative to take the action without giving notice of proposed action. Nothing in this subdivision requires the personal representative to give notice of proposed action where not required under subdivision (a) or authorizes a personal representative to take any action that the personal representative is not otherwise authorized to take. *(Stats.1990, c. 79 (A.B.759), § 14, operative July 1, 1991.)*

Application

Application of Part 6, see Probate Code § 10406.

Law Revision Commission Comments

1990 Enactment

Section 10580 continues Section 10580 of the repealed Probate Code without substantive change.

Subdivision (b) permits a personal representative to use the notice of proposed action procedure provided in this article with respect to an action that the personal representative proposes to take even though the action is not one for which notice of proposed action is required. For example, the personal representative may want to proceed under subdivision (b) of Section 10580 where the proposed action is the compromise of a claim against the estate (see Section 10552). This action is one that ordinarily does not require notice of proposed action. See the Comment to Section 10550. If the procedure provided by this article is used with respect to the proposed action, the person who fails to object to the proposed action waives the right to have the court later review the action taken. See Section 10590 and the Comment thereto. See also Section 10589(b) and the Comment thereto. Use of the notice of proposed

action procedure avoids the need to petition the court for instructions on the proposed compromise in order to preclude a later challenge to the accounts of the personal representative.

The personal representative need not take an action under independent administration authority even though authorized to do so; if the personal representative so desires, the action may be taken using the applicable court supervised administration procedure. See Section 10500(b) and the Comment to Section 10500.

The second sentence of subdivision (a) makes clear that if the personal representative has only limited authority, the mere fact that the power is listed in Chapter 3 (commencing with Section 10500) gives the personal representative no right or authority to exercise the power using the procedure provided in this chapter. See Section 10403 (limited authority does not include authority to sell, exchange, or grant an option to purchase real property or to borrow money with the loan secured by an encumbrance upon real property). Where the personal representative has only limited authority and does not have the power to take the proposed action under this part because the power to do so is not within the authority granted to the personal representative, the personal representative may exercise the power only pursuant to the provisions relating to court supervision, and the provisions of this part have no application to the transaction. See Sections 10501 and 10502 and the Comments thereto.

As to the application of this part where independent administration authority was granted under the repealed Probate Code, see Section 10406.

Background on Section 10580 of Repealed Code

Section 10580 was added by 1987 Cal.Stat. ch. 923 § 93. The first sentence of subdivision (a) restated paragraph (1) of subdivision (a) of former Probate Code Section 591.3 (repealed by 1987 Cal.Stat. ch. 923 § 35) without substantive change except that a reference to Chapter 3 (commencing with Section 10500) was substituted for the reference to subdivision (b) of former Section 591.3; Chapter 3 superseded subdivision (b) of former Section 591.3. The second sentence of subdivision (a) was a new provision that made no substantive change in prior law. Subdivision (b) was new. For background on the provisions of this part, see the Comment to this part under the part heading. [20 Cal.L.Rev.Comm.Reports 1001 (1990)].

§ 10581. Parties to whom notice must be given

Except as provided in Sections 10582 and 10583, notice of proposed action shall be given to all of the following:

(a) Each known devisee whose interest in the estate would be affected by the proposed action.

(b) Each known heir whose interest in the estate would be affected by the proposed action.

(c) Each person who has filed a request under Chapter 6 (commencing with Section 1250) of Part 2, of Division 3 for special notice of petitions filed in the administration proceeding.

(d) The Attorney General, at the office of the Attorney General in Sacramento, if any portion of the estate is to escheat to the state and its interest in the estate would be affected by the proposed action. *(Stats.1990, c. 79 (A.B.759), § 14, operative July 1, 1991.)*

Application

Application of Part 6, see Probate Code § 10406.

Law Revision Commission Comments

1990 Enactment

Section 10581 continues Section 10581 of the repealed Probate Code without substantive change. As to giving notice to known heirs and known devisees, see Section 1206. As to the application of this part where independent administration authority was granted under the repealed Probate Code, see Section 10406.

Background on Section 10581 of Repealed Code

Section 10581 was added by 1987 Cal.Stat. ch. 923 § 93. The section restated the introductory clause and paragraph (2) of subdivision (a) of former Probate Code Section 591.3 (repealed by 1987 Cal.Stat. ch. 923 § 35) with the following revisions:

(1) In subdivision (a) of Section 10581, "Each known devisee" was substituted for "the devisees and legatees." See Section 34 (defining "devisee").

(2) In subdivision (b) of Section 10581, "each known heir" was substituted for "the heirs" and language was added to make clear that notice of proposed action need be given only to heirs whose interest in the estate is affected by the proposed action.

(3) Language was added in subdivision (d) of Section 10581 to make clear that notice of proposed action need be given to the State of California only if its interest in the estate is affected by the proposed action.

For background on the provisions of this part, see the Comment to this part under the part heading. [20 Cal.L.Rev.Comm.Reports 1001 (1990)].

Cross References

Authority of public administrator, see Probate Code § 7661.

§ 10582. Party consenting to action; waiver of notice

Notice of proposed action need not be given to any person who consents in writing to the proposed action. The consent may be executed at any time before or after the proposed action is taken. *(Stats.1990, c. 79 (A.B.759), § 14, operative July 1, 1991.)*

Application

Application of Part 6, see Probate Code § 10406.

Law Revision Commission Comments

1990 Enactment

Section 10582 continues Section 10582 of the repealed Probate Code without change. This section provides a method that can be used to avoid the delay that otherwise would result from the requirement (see Sections 10586, 10587) that a person given notice of proposed action be allowed at least 15 days within which to object to the proposed action. Concerning the effect of a consent, see Section 10590. Concerning revocation of a consent, see Section 10584. As to the application of this part where independent administration authority was granted under the repealed Probate Code, see Section 10406.

Background on Section 10582 of Repealed Code

Section 10582 was added by 1987 Cal.Stat. ch. 923 § 93. The section restated subdivision (c) of former Probate Code Section 591.3 (repealed by 1987 Cal.Stat. ch. 923 § 35) without substantive change. For background on the provisions of this part, see the Comment to this part under the part heading. [20 Cal.L.Rev.Comm.Reports 1001 (1990)].

Cross References

Authority of public administrator, see Probate Code § 7661.

§ 10583. Waiver of notice; particular proposed actions; general waiver

(a) Notice of proposed action need not be given to any person who, in writing, waives the right to notice of proposed action with respect to the particular proposed action. The waiver may be executed at any time before or after the proposed action is taken. The waiver shall describe the particular proposed action and may waive particular aspects of the notice, such as the delivery, mailing, or time requirements of Section 10586, or the giving of the notice in its entirety for the particular proposed action.

(b) Notice of proposed action need not be given to any person who has executed the Statutory Waiver of Notice of Proposed Action Form prescribed by the Judicial Council and in that form has made either of the following:

(1) A general waiver of the right to notice of proposed action.

(2) A waiver of the right to notice of proposed action for all transactions of a type which includes the particular proposed action. *(Stats.1990, c. 79 (A.B.759), § 14, operative July 1, 1991.)*

Application

Application of Part 6, see Probate Code § 10406.

Law Revision Commission Comments

1990 Enactment

Section 10583 continues Section 10583 of the repealed Probate Code with a revision in the introductory clause of subdivision (b) to require use of the Judicial Council Statutory Waiver of Notice of Proposed Action Form.

Subdivision (a) permits waiver of notice of proposed action only with respect to a particular proposed action. A person entitled to notice of proposed action may execute a written waiver under subdivision (a) that would, for example, permit notice of a particular proposed real property transaction to be given to the person by telephone so that the proposed action can be expeditiously completed if the person does not object. In such a case, if the person is agreeable to the sale of the real property, the waiver could be drafted in terms that would permit the personal representative to call the person on the telephone to notify the person of an offer to buy the property and to permit the sale of the property at the price and on the terms offered if the person called is agreeable or at a price and on the terms of a counter-offer that is agreeable to the person called.

Subdivision (b) applies when a Statutory Waiver of Notice of Proposed Action Form is used. Under subdivision (b), a person may, for example, execute the Judicial Council statutory waiver form to waive the right of notice of proposed action with respect to investing funds of the estate and borrowing money without waiving the right to notice of proposed action with respect to sales of real property. Or the person may waive the right to receive notice of proposed action with respect to any and all actions the personal representative might decide to take.

Concerning the effect of a waiver, see Section 10590. Concerning revocation of a waiver, see Section 10584. As to the application of this part where independent administration authority was granted under the repealed Probate Code, see Section 10406.

Background on Section 10583 of Repealed Code

Section 10583 was added by 1987 Cal.Stat. ch. 923 § 93. Subdivision (a) restated subdivision (d) of former Probate Code Section 591.3 (repealed by 1987 Cal.Stat. ch. 923 § 35) without substantive change. Subdivision (b) was new. For background on the provisions of this part, see the Comment to this part under the part heading. [20 Cal.L.Rev.Comm.Reports 1001 (1990)].

Cross References

Authority of public administrator, see Probate Code § 7661.

§ 10584. Revocation of waiver

(a) A waiver or consent may be revoked only in writing and is effective only when the writing is received by the personal representative.

(b) A copy of the revocation may be filed with the court, but the effectiveness of the revocation is not dependent upon a copy being filed with the court. *(Stats.1990, c. 79 (A.B.759), § 14, operative July 1, 1991.)*

Application

Application of Part 6, see Probate Code § 10406.

Law Revision Commission Comments

1990 Enactment

Section 10584 continues Section 10584 of the repealed Probate Code without change. This section prescribes the requirements for revocation of a consent or waiver. Subdivision (b) permits, but does not require, a copy of the revocation to be filed with the court. Such a filing may be of some value in proving that the consent or waiver was revoked. As to the application of this part where independent administration authority was granted under the repealed Probate Code, see Section 10406.

Background on Section 10584 of Repealed Code

Section 10584 was a new provision added by 1987 Cal.Stat. ch. 923 § 93. For background on the provisions of this part, see the Comment to this part under the part heading. [20 Cal.L.Rev.Comm.Reports 1001 (1990)].

Cross References

Authority of public administrator, see Probate Code § 7661.

§ 10585. Contents of notice; necessary information; form to be used

(a) The notice of proposed action shall state all of the following:

(1) The name and mailing address of the personal representative.

(2) The person and telephone number to call to get additional information.

(3) The action proposed to be taken, with a reasonably specific description of the action. Where the proposed action involves the sale or exchange of real property, or the granting of an option to purchase real property, the notice of proposed action shall state the material terms of the transaction, including, if applicable, the sale price and the amount of, or method of calculating, any commission or compensation paid or to be paid to an agent or broker in connection with the transaction.

(4) The date on or after which the proposed action is to be taken.

(b) The notice of proposed action may be given using the most current Notice of Proposed Action form prescribed by the Judicial Council.

(c) If the most current form prescribed by the Judicial Council is not used to give notice of proposed action, the notice of proposed action shall satisfy all of the following requirements:

(1) The notice of proposed action shall be in substantially the same form as the form prescribed by the Judicial Council.

(2) The notice of proposed action shall contain the statements described in subdivision (a).

(3) The notice of proposed action shall contain a form for objecting to the proposed action in substantially the form set out in the Judicial Council form. *(Stats.1990, c. 79 (A.B.759), § 14, operative July 1, 1991.)*

Application

Application of Part 6, see Probate Code § 10406.

Law Revision Commission Comments

1990 Enactment

Section 10585 continues Section 10585 of the repealed Probate Code without change. As to the application of this part where independent administration authority was granted under the repealed Probate Code, see Section 10406.

Background on Section 10585 of Repealed Code

Section 10585 was added by 1987 Cal.Stat. ch. 923 § 93. The section replaced the second, third, and fifth sentences of subdivision (a) of former Probate Code Section 591.4 and all of former Probate Code Section 591.8 (provisions repealed by 1987 Cal.Stat. ch. 923 § 35). Section 10585 made no change in former practice, but substituted subdivision (c) of Section 10585 for the statutory form set out in former Section 591.8 (repealed by 1987 Cal.Stat. ch. 923 § 35) which had been superseded by a Judicial Council form. For background on the provisions of this part, see the Comment to this part under the part heading. [20 Cal.L.Rev.Comm.Reports 1001 (1990)].

Cross References

Authority of public administrator, see Probate Code § 7661.

§ 10585.5. Repealed by Stats.1990, c. 710 (S.B.1775), § 31, operative July 1, 1991

Law Revision Commission Comments

1990 Enactment and Repeal

Section 10585.5 (enacted as a part of the new Probate Code by 1990 Cal.Stat. ch. 79 § 14) was repealed by 1990 Cal.Stat. ch. 710 § 31. This section was included in the new Probate Code because Assembly Bill 831 of the 1989–1990 regular session would have extended the independent administration provisions to cover probate attorney fees. However, Assembly Bill 831 was not enacted, and as a result Section 10585.5 became unnecessary. See the Comment to Section 900. [20 Cal.L.Rev.Comm. Reports 1001 (1990)].

§ 10586. Mail or delivery of notice

The notice of proposed action shall be mailed or personally delivered to each person required to be given notice of proposed action not less than 15 days before the date specified in the notice of proposed action on or after which the proposed action is to be taken. If mailed, the notice of proposed action shall be addressed to the person at the person's last known address. Sections 1215 and 1216 apply to the mailing or delivery of the notice of proposed action. *(Stats.1990, c. 79 (A.B.759), § 14, operative July 1, 1991.)*

Application

Application of Part 6, see Probate Code § 10406.

Law Revision Commission Comments

1990 Enactment

Section 10586 continues Section 10586 of the repealed Probate Code without change. As to the manner of mailing, see Section 1215. As to the application of this part where independent administration authority was granted under the repealed Probate Code, see Section 10406.

Background on Section 10586 of Repealed Code

Section 10586 was added by 1987 Cal.Stat. ch. 923 § 93. The section superseded the first and fourth sentences of subdivision (a) of former Probate Code Section 591.4 (repealed by 1987 Cal.Stat. ch. 923 § 35). Unlike former Section 591.4, the time is not extended under Section 10586 if the notice of proposed action is given by mail. The mailing is complete when the notice of proposed action is deposited in the mail. See Section 1215. For background on the provisions of this part, see the Comment to this part under the part heading. [20 Cal.L.Rev.Comm.Reports 1001 (1990)].

Cross References

Authority of public administrator, see Probate Code § 7661.

§ 10587. Objection to proceedings; method of objecting; notice to personal representative

(a) Any person entitled to notice of proposed action under Section 10581 may object to the proposed action as provided in this section.

(b) The objection to the proposed action is made by delivering or mailing a written objection to the proposed action to the personal representative at the address stated in the notice of proposed action. The person objecting to the proposed action either may use the Judicial Council form or may make the objection in any other writing that identifies the proposed action with reasonable certainty and indicates that the person objects to the taking of the proposed action.

(c) The personal representative is deemed to have notice of the objection to the proposed action if it is delivered or received at the address stated in the notice of proposed action before whichever of the following times is the later:

(1) The date specified in the notice of proposed action on or after which the proposed action is to be taken.

(2) The date the proposed action is actually taken. *(Stats. 1990, c. 79 (A.B.759), § 14, operative July 1, 1991.)*

Application

Application of Part 6, see Probate Code § 10406.

Law Revision Commission Comments

1990 Enactment

Section 10587 continues Section 10587 of the repealed Probate Code without change. This section applies whether the notice of proposed action is given pursuant to subdivision (a) of Section 10580 (giving of notice mandatory) or under subdivision (b) of that section (giving of notice permissive). See also Section 10590 (effect of failure to object).

Subdivision (a) permits a person not given notice of proposed action to object to the proposed action. For example, the personal representative may for some reason fail to give notice of proposed action to a person entitled to the notice. The person may be informed of the proposed action by a relative who did receive a notice of proposed action. If the person entitled to the notice objects to the proposed action, the proposed action can be taken only under court supervision. See Section 10589. However, the person is not required to object to the proposed action in order to protect the right to have the court later review the action. Since the person was not given notice of proposed action, the person's right to have the court later review the proposed action is not affected. See Section 10590.

As an alternative to or in addition to objecting to the proposed action, a person who wants to prevent the proposed action from being taken other than under court supervision may apply for a restraining order under Section 10588.

As to the application of this part where independent administration authority was granted under the repealed Probate Code, see Section 10406.

Background on Section 10587 of Repealed Code

Section 10587 was added by 1987 Cal.Stat. ch. 923 § 93. The section restated subdivision (a)(2) of former Probate Code Section 591.5 (repealed by 1987 Cal.Stat. ch. 923 § 35) without substantive change. The second sentence of subdivision (b) was drawn from the last sentence of subdivision (b) of former Probate Code Section 591.8 (repealed by 1987 Cal.Stat. ch. 923 § 35). For background on the provisions of this part, see the Comment to this part under the part heading. [20 Cal.L.Rev.Comm.Reports 1001 (1990)].

Cross References

Authority of public administrator, see Probate Code § 7661.

§ 10588. Restraining order prohibiting action without court supervision; notice of order to personal representative

(a) Any person who is entitled to notice of proposed action for a proposed action described in subdivision (a) of Section 10580, or any person who is given notice of a proposed action described in subdivision (b) of Section 10580, may apply to the court having jurisdiction over the proceeding for an order restraining the personal representative from taking the proposed action without court supervision. The court shall grant the requested order without requiring notice to the personal representative and without cause being shown for the order.

(b) The personal representative is deemed to have notice of the restraining order if it is served upon the personal representative in the same manner as is provided for in Section 415.10 or 415.30 of the Code of Civil Procedure, or in the manner authorized by the court, before whichever of the following times is the later:

(1) The date specified in a notice of proposed action on or after which the proposed action is to be taken.

(2) The date the proposed action is actually taken. *(Stats. 1990, c. 79 (A.B.759), § 14, operative July 1, 1991.)*

Application

Application of Part 6, see Probate Code § 10406.

1990 Enactment

Section 10588 continues Section 10588 of the repealed Probate Code without change. This section applies whether the notice of proposed action is given pursuant to subdivision (a) of Section 10580 (giving of notice mandatory) or under subdivision (b) of that section (giving of notice permissive). See also Section 10590 (effect of failure to object).

Where notice of proposed action is mandatory (see subdivision (a) of Section 10580), a person who is entitled to notice of proposed action but has not been given notice of proposed action may nevertheless obtain a restraining order under Section 10588. See the discussion in the Comment to Section 10587. Where notice of proposed action is not required (see subdivision (b) of Section 10580), a person can obtain a restraining order under Section 10588 only if the person has been given notice of the proposed action. If other persons have been given a notice of proposed action under subdivision (b) of Section 10580 but the person who objects to the proposed action has not been given the notice, the person entitled to notice under Section 10581 can object to the proposed action as provided in Section 10587 but may not obtain a restraining order under Section 10588.

As to the application of this part where independent administration authority was granted under the repealed Probate Code, see Section 10406.

Background on Section 10588 of Repealed Code

Section 10588 was added by 1987 Cal.Stat. ch. 923 § 93. The section restated subdivision (a)(1) of former Probate Code Section 591.5 (repealed by 1987 Cal.Stat. ch. 923 § 35) without substantive change except that Section 10588 made clear the time within which the order must be served on the personal representative and also recognized the new provision found in subdivision (b) of Section 10580. For background on the provisions of this part, see the Comment to this part under the part heading. [20 Cal.L.Rev.Comm.Reports 1001 (1990)].

Cross References

Authority of public administrator, see Probate Code § 7661.

§ 10589. Personal representative under notice of objection or restraining order; court supervision or order required for action; notice of hearing

(a) If the proposed action is one that would require court supervision if the personal representative had not been granted authority to administer the estate under this part and the personal representative has notice of a written objection made under Section 10587 to the proposed action or a restraining order issued under Section 10588, the personal representative shall, if the personal representative desires to take the proposed action, take the proposed action under the provisions of this code dealing with court supervision of that kind of action.

(b) If the proposed action is one that would not require court supervision even if the personal representative had not been granted authority to administer the estate under this part but the personal representative has given notice of the proposed action and has notice of a written objection made under Section 10587 to the proposed action or a restraining order issued under Section 10588, the personal representative shall, if he or she desires to take the proposed action, request instructions from the court concerning the proposed action. The personal representative may take the proposed action only under such order as may be entered by the court.

(c) A person who objects to a proposed action as provided in Section 10587 or serves a restraining order issued under Section 10588 in the manner provided in that section shall be given notice of any hearing on a petition for court authorization or confirmation of the proposed action. (Stats.1990, c. 79 (A.B.759), § 14, operative July 1, 1991. Amended by Stats.1991, c. 82 (S.B.896), § 26, eff. June 30, 1991, operative July 1, 1991.)

Application

Application of Part 6, see Probate Code § 10406.

1990 Enactment

Section 10589 continues Section 10589 of the repealed Probate Code without substantive change.

Where notice of proposed action is required, subdivision (a) requires that the proposed action be taken only under court supervision if the personal representative has notice of a written objection or a restraining order with respect to the proposed action. And, when the proposed action is taken under court supervision, all the requirements of the court supervised procedure apply to the same extent that they would apply if the personal representative had not been granted independent administration authority. See Section 10401 (defining "court supervision"). For example, except as provided in Sections 10301–10303, if the proposed action is the sale of real property, notice of sale must be published. See Section 10300.

Subdivision (a) applies not only to a case where notice of proposed action is required but also to a case where notice of proposed action is not required to be given for a proposed action that would require court supervision if independent administration authority had not been granted. See Section 10580(b) (personal representative may give notice of proposed action with respect to a proposed action that could be taken without giving notice of proposed action). If the personal representative elects to give notice of proposed action in such a case, even though not required, subdivision (a) permits the personal representative to take the proposed action only under court supervision if the personal representative has notice of a written objection to the proposed action or of a restraining order issued with respect to the proposed action.

Subdivision (b) applies where the personal representative decides to give notice of proposed action in a case where the personal representative would be authorized to take the proposed action without court supervision even if the personal representative had not been granted independent administration authority. In such a case, if the personal representative has notice of a written objection to the proposed action or of a restraining order issued with respect to the proposed action, subdivision (b) requires that the proposed action be taken only after authorization by court order obtained in a proceeding on a petition for instructions.

The benefit of the procedure provided by subdivision (b) of Section 10580 and subdivisions (a) and (b) of Section 10589 is that the procedure permits a court review of the proposed action before it is taken if the personal representative has notice of an objection rather than having the objection first made after the action has been taken. For further discussion, see the Comment to Section 10580.

What are the consequences if the personal representative goes ahead with the proposed transaction without court supervision after the personal representative has notice of a written objection to the transaction? As far as the third party to the transaction is concerned, the third party is protected if the third party is a bona fide purchaser or a third person dealing in good faith with the personal representative who changes his or her position in reliance upon the action, conveyance, or transfer, without actual notice of the failure of the personal representative to comply with the court supervision requirements. See Section 10591. As far as the personal representative is concerned, there are two sanctions that would apply where the personal representative goes ahead with a transaction knowing that there is a written objection to the transaction. First, the personal representative can be surcharged if the personal representative violates the standard of ordinary care and diligence established by Section 9600. In view of the objection, the burden is on the personal representative to establish that the action taken satisfied the requirements of Section 9600. Second, taking an action without obtaining court supervision where there has been an objection to the proposed action is grounds for removal of the personal representative. See Section 10592 and the Comment thereto. If the objection was made by serving a restraining order with respect to the proposed action, the personal representative also would be subject to sanctions for violation of the court order.

Subdivision (c) of Section 10589 requires that notice of hearing be given to a person who has made a written objection under Section 10587 or has served a restraining order under Section 10588. Subdivision (c) requires that notice of hearing be given of the hearing on a petition for instructions, or a petition under Section 9684, for an order authorizing a proposed action described in subdivision (b) as well as of a hearing on a petition for court authorization or confirmation of a proposed action described in subdivision (a).

As to the application of this part where independent administration authority was granted under the repealed Probate Code, see Section 10406.

1991 Amendment

Section 10589 is amended to delete language that was included to conform to the agreed fee system for probate attorney fees. The new Probate Code retains the statutory fee system. The deleted language is inconsistent with the statutory fee system.

Background on Section 10589 of Repealed Code

Section 10589 was added by 1987 Cal.Stat. ch. 923 § 93. Subdivision (a) restated the first sentence of subdivision (b) of former Probate Code Section 591.5 (repealed by 1987 Cal.Stat. ch. 923 § 35) without substantive change. Subdivision (b) was new. Subdivision (c) restated subdivision (e) of former Section 591.5 (repealed by 1987 Cal.Stat. ch. 923 § 35) without substantive change. For background on the provisions of this part, see the Comment to this part under the part heading. [20 Cal.L.Rev.Comm.Reports 1001 (1990)].

§ 10590. Review of action taken; parties with right to review or object; waiver of right; review by court on own motion

(a) Except as provided in subdivision (c), only a person described in Section 10581 has a right to have the court review the proposed action after it has been taken or otherwise to object to the proposed action after it has been taken. Except as provided in subdivisions (b) and (c), a person described in Section 10581 waives the right to have the court review the proposed action after it has been taken, or otherwise to object to the proposed action after it has been taken, if either of the following circumstances exists:

(1) The person has been given notice of a proposed action, as provided in Sections 10580 to 10586, inclusive, and fails to object as provided in subdivision (d).

(2) The person has waived notice of or consented to the proposed action as provided in Sections 10582 to 10584, inclusive.

(b) Unless the person has waived notice of or consented to the proposed action as provided in Sections 10582 to 10584, inclusive, the court may review the action taken upon motion of a person described in Section 10581 who establishes that

he or she did not actually receive the notice of proposed action before the time to object under subdivision (d) expires.

(c) The court may review the action of the personal representative upon motion of an heir or devisee who establishes all of the following:

(1) At the time the notice was given, the heir or devisee lacked capacity to object to the proposed action or was a minor.

(2) No notice of proposed action was actually received by the guardian, conservator, or other legal representative of the heir or devisee.

(3) The guardian, conservator, or other legal representative did not waive notice of proposed action.

(4) The guardian, conservator, or other legal representative did not consent to the proposed action.

(d) For the purposes of this section, an objection to a proposed action is made only by one or both of the following methods:

(1) Delivering or mailing a written objection as provided in Section 10587 within the time specified in subdivision (c) of that section.

(2) Serving a restraining order obtained under Section 10588 in the manner prescribed and within the time specified in subdivision (b) of that section. *(Stats.1990, c. 79 (A.B. 759), § 14, operative July 1, 1991.)*

Application

Application of Part 6, see Probate Code § 10406.

Law Revision Commission Comments

1990 Enactment

Section 10590 continues Section 10590 of the repealed Probate Code without substantive change. The introductory portion of subdivision (c) has been rephrased to make clear that the person seeking review of the action of the personal representative must make a motion and establish the matters listed in the subdivision.

Section 10590 applies only where notice of proposed action was given as provided in Sections 10580–10586 or where the notice was waived or consent was given to the proposed action. See Sections 10585 (contents of notice), 10586 (delivery or mailing required). See also Sections 10582–10584 (waiver or consent). Subject to subdivision (c), only a person described in Section 10581 may obtain review of the action and then only if the person was not given a proper notice of proposed action and had not waived the notice or consented to the proposed action.

To satisfy the requirements of Section 10590, the notice must include a description of the proposed action in reasonably specific terms, with additional information if the proposed action involves a sale or exchange of real property or an option to purchase real property. See Section 10585.

Under Section 10590, a creditor who does not request special notice is not entitled to notice of proposed action (see Section 10581) and is not entitled to obtain review of the action taken. A creditor who requests special notice pursuant to Section 1250 is entitled to notice of proposed action. See Section 10581(c).

Subdivision (c) deals with the case where the heir or devisee entitled to notice of proposed action lacked capacity to object to the proposed action or was a minor. Upon motion of the heir or devisee (or the legal representative of the heir or devisee if the heir or devisee lacks the capacity to make the motion), the court will review the proposed action if the matters established in paragraphs (1)–(4)

of subdivision (c) are established. As to the right of a person having capacity who failed to object to the action to obtain court review, see subdivision (b).

Paragraph (2) of subdivision (a) and the introductory clause of subdivision (b) make clear that the court is not authorized to review the proposed action on motion of a person who consented to the proposed action (Section 10582) or waived the notice of proposed action (Section 10583). See the Comments to Sections 10582 and 10583. See also Section 10584 (revocation of consent or waiver).

A guardian ad litem can be appointed to object, waive, or consent to proposed actions under the Independent Administration of Estates Act where the person entitled to notice of proposed action lacks the capacity to act with respect to the proposed action. See Section 1003.

As to the application of this part where independent administration authority was granted under the repealed Probate Code, see Section 10406.

Background on Section 10590 of Repealed Code

Section 10590 was added by 1987 Cal.Stat. ch. 923 § 93. Subdivisions (a) and (b) restated the substance of the second sentence and a portion of the third sentence of subdivision (d) of former Probate Code Section 591.5 (repealed by 1987 Cal.Stat. ch. 923 § 35), but Section 10590 limited the right to obtain court review on the court's own motion. Subdivision (c) superseded the portion of the third sentence of subdivision (d) of former Section 591.5 which permitted the court to review the proposed action on its own motion. Subdivision (d) continued the substantive effect of the first sentence of subdivision (d) of former Section 591.5. For background on the provisions of this part, see the Comment to this part under the part heading. [20 Cal.L.Rev.Comm.Reports 1001 (1990)].

Cross References

Account contest for action taken not approved subject to this section, see Probate Code § 11001.

§ 10591. Failure of personal representative to comply with requirements; validity of actions or title to property conveyed or transferred; duty to investigate compliance

(a) The failure of the personal representative to comply with subdivision (a) of Section 10580 and with Sections 10581, 10585, 10586, and 10589, and the taking of the action by the personal representative without such compliance, does not affect the validity of the action so taken or the title to any property conveyed or transferred to bona fide purchasers or the rights of third persons who, dealing in good faith with the personal representative, changed their position in reliance upon the action, conveyance, or transfer without actual notice of the failure of the personal representative to comply with those provisions.

(b) No person dealing with the personal representative has any duty to inquire or investigate whether or not the personal representative has complied with the provisions listed in subdivision (a). *(Stats.1990, c. 79 (A.B.759), § 14, operative July 1, 1991.)*

Application

Application of Part 6, see Probate Code § 10406.

Law Revision Commission Comments

1990 Enactment

Section 10591 continues Section 10591 of the repealed Probate Code without change. As to the application of this part where

independent administration authority was granted under the repealed Probate Code, see Section 10406.

Background on Section 10591 of Repealed Code

Section 10591 was added by 1987 Cal.Stat. ch. 923 § 93. The section restated subdivision (b) of former Probate Code Section 591.4 and subdivision (c) of former Probate Code Section 591.5 (provisions repealed by 1987 Cal.Stat. ch. 923 § 35) without substantive change. For background on the provisions of this part, see the Comment to this part under the part heading. [20 Cal.L.Rev.Comm.Reports 1001 (1990)].

§ 10592. Removal of personal representative from office

(a) In a case where notice of proposed action is required by this chapter, the court in its discretion may remove the personal representative from office unless the personal representative does one of the following:

(1) Gives notice of proposed action as provided in this chapter.

(2) Obtains a waiver of notice of proposed action as provided in this chapter.

(3) Obtains a consent to the proposed action as provided in this chapter.

(b) The court in its discretion may remove the personal representative from office if the personal representative takes a proposed action in violation of Section 10589. *(Stats.1990, c. 79 (A.B.759), § 14, operative July 1, 1991.)*

Application

Application of Part 6, see Probate Code § 10406.

Law Revision Commission Comments

1990 Enactment

Section 10592 continues Section 10592 of the repealed Probate Code without substantive change. The court has discretion whether to remove the personal representative. In determining whether to remove the personal representative, the court should consider all the circumstances of the particular case. Among the significant considerations are whether the personal representative violated the statute with the intent to deprive the person entitled to notice of his or her rights or whether the failure was inadvertent or merely negligent. As to the application of this part where independent administration authority was granted under the repealed Probate Code, see Section 10406.

Background on Section 10592 of Repealed Code

Section 10592 was added by 1987 Cal.Stat. ch. 923 § 93. The section was drawn from the last sentence of subdivision (b) of former Probate Code Section 591.5 (repealed by 1987 Cal.Stat. ch. 923 § 35). Section 10592 expanded the provision of former law to permit removal from office for failure to give notice of proposed action as required by this chapter. For background on the provisions of this part, see the Comment to this part under the part heading. [20 Cal.L.Rev.Comm.Reports 1001 (1990)].

§ 10600. Repealed by Stats.1990, c. 79 (A.B.759), § 13, operative July 1, 1991

Law Revision Commission Comments

1990 Repeal

Section 10600 of the repealed Probate Code is omitted from the new Probate Code because it is unnecessary. See Section 1001 (Judicial Council forms). [20 Cal.L.Rev.Comm.Reports 1001 (1990)].

Part 7

COMPENSATION OF PERSONAL REPRESENTATIVE AND ATTORNEY FOR THE PERSONAL REPRESENTATIVE

Law Revision Commission Comments

1990 Enactment

This part supersedes Sections 900, 901, 902, 903, 904, 910, and 911 of the repealed Probate Code. For background, see Recommendations Relating to Probate Law: Hiring and Paying Attorneys, Advisors, and Others; Compensation of Personal Representative, 20 Cal.L.Revision Comm'n Reports 31 (1990); Revised and Supplemental Comments to the New Probate Code, 20 Cal.L.Revision Comm'n Reports 2001 (1990). See also the Comment to Section 900. [20 Cal.L.Rev.Comm.Reports 1001 (1990)].

Cross References

Public guardian or public administrator appointed as trust that provides outright distribution of entire trust estate, see Probate Code § 15688.

CHAPTER 1. AMOUNT OF COMPENSATION

ARTICLE 1. COMPENSATION OF PERSONAL REPRESENTATIVE

§ 10800. Based on value of estate

(a) Subject to the provisions of this part, for ordinary services the personal representative shall receive compensation based on the value of the estate accounted for by the personal representative, as follows:

(1) Four percent on the first one hundred thousand dollars ($100,000).

(2) Three percent on the next one hundred thousand dollars ($100,000).

(3) Two percent on the next eight hundred thousand dollars ($800,000).

(4) One percent on the next nine million dollars ($9,000,000).

(5) One-half of one percent on the next fifteen million dollars ($15,000,000).

(6) For all amounts above twenty-five million dollars ($25,000,000), a reasonable amount to be determined by the court.

(b) For the purposes of this section, the value of the estate accounted for by the personal representative is the total amount of the appraisal value of property in the inventory, plus gains over the appraisal value on sales, plus receipts, less losses from the appraisal value on sales, without reference to encumbrances or other obligations on estate property. *(Stats.1990, c. 79 (A.B.759), § 14, operative July 1, 1991. Amended by Stats.1991, c. 82 (S.B.896), § 27, eff. June 30, 1991, operative July 1, 1991; Stats.2001, c. 699 (A.B.232), § 2.)*

Law Revision Commission Comments

1990 Enactment

Subdivision (a) of Section 10800 restates a portion of the first sentence of Section 901 of the repealed Probate Code without substantive change. Subdivision (b) restates the first sentence of the second paragraph of Section 901 of the repealed Probate Code without substantive change.

Compensation is computed using the total amount of the appraisal of property in the inventory (see Sections 8800–8802, 8850, 8900), plus gains over the appraisal value on sales, plus receipts, less losses from the appraisal value on sales, without reference to encumbrances or other obligations on estate property. Property is appraised at its fair market value at the time of the decedent's death. See Section 8802. The amount of any liens or encumbrances on the property is not subtracted from the fair market value used for the purpose of computing the compensation under this section.

A court order allowing the compensation to the personal representative is required before the compensation may be paid, and the compensation allowed is paid out of the estate. See Sections 10830, 10831. As to allowing a portion of the compensation of the personal representative (on account of services rendered up to the time of allowance), see Section 10830. See also Section 12205 (reduction of compensation for delay in closing estate administration).

As to the right of an attorney to receive dual compensation for services as personal representative and as estate attorney, see Section 10804.

Under the introductory clause of Section 10800, the section is subject to Section 10802. Section 10802 provides that, if the decedent's will makes provision for the compensation of the personal representative and the court does not relieve the personal representative from those provisions, the compensation provided by the will shall be the full and only compensation for the services of the personal representative. See also the discussion in the Comment to Section 10802.

As to the law applicable to a proceeding commenced before July 1, 1991, see Section 10850. As to the application of any amendments made after that date, see Section 3.

Section 10800 does not continue the last sentence of former Probate Code Section 901. Before 1965, the usual practice was to use gross value of real property to calculate the statutory fee unless the property was sold during probate, in which case only the decedent's equity in the property was used. Under the 1965 revision to former Probate Code Section 901 (amended 1965 Cal.Stat. ch. 115), gross value was used, whether or not a sale had taken place. See Review of Selected 1965 Code Legislation 222 (Cal.Cont.Ed.Bar 1965). Subdivision (b) of Section 10800 continues the substance of the 1965 revision. The last sentence of former Section 901 was included in 1965 to make clear that the former practice was being changed; it is no longer necessary to continue this sentence.

For background on the provisions of this part, see the Comment to this part, see the Comment to this part under the part heading. [20 Cal.L.Rev.Comm.Reports 1001 (1990)].

1991 Amendment

Section 10800 is amended to add the word "value" which was inadvertently omitted from subdivision (b).

§ 10801. Additional compensation; employment of tax experts

(a) Subject to the provisions of this part, in addition to the compensation provided by Section 10800, the court may allow additional compensation for extraordinary services by the personal representative in an amount the court determines is just and reasonable.

(b) The personal representative may also employ or retain tax counsel, tax auditors, accountants, or other tax experts for the performance of any action which such persons, respectively, may lawfully perform in the computation, reporting, or making of tax returns, or in negotiations or litigation which may be necessary for the final determination and payment of taxes, and pay from the funds of the estate for such services. *(Stats.1990, c. 79 (A.B.759), § 14, operative July 1, 1991. Amended by Stats.1991, c. 82 (S.B.896), § 28, eff. June 30, 1991, operative July 1, 1991.)*

Law Revision Commission Comments

1990 Enactment

Section 10801 restates the first sentence of Section 902 of the repealed Probate Code without substantive change. See also Section 12205 (reduction of compensation for delay in closing estate administration). As to the law applicable to a proceeding commenced before July 1, 1991, see Section 10850. As to the application of any amendments made after that date, see Section 3.

Even though services are extraordinary, the court has discretion whether or not to award compensation for them. Estate of Walker, 221 Cal.App.2d 792, 795–96, 34 Cal.Rptr. 832 (1963) (extraordinary services by executor and estate attorney).

The listing in Section 902 of the repealed Probate Code of examples of what constituted extraordinary services is not continued in Section 10801. The former list was incomplete. See Estate of Buchman, 138 Cal.App.2d 228, 236, 291 P.2d 547 (1955) (special administrator and estate attorney). Omission of the list is not intended to change the law.

For background on the provisions of this part, see the Comment to this part under the part heading.

Under Sections 10800 and 10801, the following services by the personal representative may be considered as extraordinary:

(1) Sales or mortgages of real or personal property. Estate of McSweeney, 123 Cal.App.2d 787, 798, 268 P.2d 107 (1954) (extraordinary fees of executor and estate attorney).

(2) Carrying on decedent's business. Estate of King, 19 Cal.2d 354, 358–60. 121 P.2d 716 (1942) (extraordinary fees of executrix); Estate of Scherer, 58 Cal.App.2d 133, 136 P.2d 103 (1943) (extraordinary fees of executor); In re Estate of Allen, 42 Cal.App.2d 346, 353, 108 P.2d 973 (1941) (extraordinary fees of administratrix and estate attorney).

(3) Court proceedings to determine testator's intention concerning undisclosed beneficiaries. Estate of Feldman, 78 Cal.App.2d 778, 793–94, 178 P.2d 498 (1947) (extraordinary fees of executor and estate attorney).

(4) Defense of personal representative's account (answering interrogatories; attending depositions; conferring with attorneys to prepare for depositions, interrogatories, and trial; attending trial).

Estate of Beach, 15 Cal.3d 623, 644–45, 542 P.2d 994, 125 Cal.Rptr. 570 (1975), cert. denied, 434 U.S. 1046 (1978) (extraordinary fees of executor and estate attorney).

(5) Securing a loan to pay debts of the estate. In re O'Connor's Estate, 200 Cal. 646, 651, 254 P. 269 (1927) (extraordinary fees of executor and estate attorney).

The foregoing is not an exhaustive list. Other extraordinary services are or may in the future be added to this list by case law or court rule. See generally Feinfield, Fees and Commissions, in 2 California Decedent Estate Practice § 20.28 (Cal.Cont.Ed.Bar, Feb. 1989); Los Angeles County Probate Policy Memorandum § 15.08, reprinted in California Local Probate Rules (10th ed. Cal. Cont.Ed.Bar 1989).

Under the introductory clause of Section 10801, the section is subject to the provisions of this part. Thus, for example, Section 10801 is subject to Section 10802. Section 10802 provides that, if the decedent's will makes provision for the compensation of the personal representative and the court does not relieve the personal representative from those provisions, the compensation provided by the will shall be the full and only compensation for the services of the personal representative. See also the discussion in the Comment to Section 10802. Likewise, Section 10801 is subject to Section 10804. Section 10804 provides that, unless expressly authorized by the decedent's will, a personal representative who is an attorney may not receive compensation for services as estate attorney. [20 Cal.L.Rev.Comm.Reports 1001 (1990)].

1991 Amendment

Section 10801 is amended to add subdivision (b). Subdivision (b) continues the substance of the last paragraph of former Section 902 of the repealed Probate Code.

Cross References

Compensations and allowances,
  Public administrator's, see Probate Code § 7622.
  Special administrator's, see Probate Code § 8547.
Duties and powers of joint personal representatives, generally, see Probate Code § 9630.

§ 10802. Compensation provided by will; petition for relief from provision; notice

(a) Except as otherwise provided in this section, if the decedent's will makes provision for the compensation of the personal representative, the compensation provided by the will shall be the full and only compensation for the services of the personal representative.

(b) The personal representative may petition the court to be relieved from a provision of the will that provides for the compensation of the personal representative.

(c) Notice of the hearing on the petition shall be given as provided in Section 1220 to all of the following persons:

(1) Each person listed in Section 1220.

(2) Each known heir whose interest in the estate would be affected by the petition.

(3) Each known devisee whose interest in the estate would be affected by the petition.

(4) The Attorney General, at the office of the Attorney General in Sacramento, if any portion of the estate is to escheat to the state and its interest in the estate would be affected by the petition.

(d) If the court determines that it is to the advantage of the estate and in the best interest of the persons interested in the estate, the court may make an order authorizing compensation for the personal representative in an amount greater than provided in the will. *(Stats.1990, c. 79 (A.B.759), § 14, operative July 1, 1991.)*

Law Revision Commission Comments
1990 Enactment

Section 10802 is a new provision. Subdivision (a) restates a portion of Section 900 of the repealed Probate Code without substantive change. The remainder of the section supersedes the portions of Sections 900 and 901 of the repealed Probate Code that permitted the personal representative to renounce the compensation provided by the will. The former ability to renounce the compensation provided by the will has been replaced by a new requirement that court approval must be obtained for the personal representative to receive greater compensation than provided under the will.

Subdivision (a) gives the testator the ability to provide for alternative methods of compensation in the will. For example, the will can eliminate the distinction between ordinary and extraordinary services and substitute an hourly rate or rates for the various services to be provided by the personal representative. The statutory compensation provisions are thus default provisions that apply where the will does not make provision for the compensation of the personal representative. Subdivision (a) also permits the personal representative to receive a greater amount of compensation than the statutory compensation if the decedent's will makes provision for the greater amount of compensation. Cf. Estate of Van Every, 67 Cal.App.2d 164, 153 P.2d 614 (1944) ($4,000 bequest to attorney in lieu of $1,696.33 statutory fee).

As to the law applicable to a proceeding commenced before July 1, 1991, see Section 10850. As to the application of any amendments made after that date, see Section 3.

For general provisions, see Sections 1000–1004 (rules of practice), 1020–1023 (petitions and other papers), 1040–1050 (hearings and orders). For general provisions relating to notice of hearing, see Sections 1200–1220. See also Sections 1206 (notice to known heirs or devisees), 1215–1217 (mailing in general), 1250–1252 (request for special notice), 1260–1265 (proof of giving notice). The court for good cause may dispense with the notice otherwise required to be given pursuant to this section. See Section 1220(c).

For background on the provisions of this part, see the Comment to this part under the part heading. [20 Cal.L.Rev.Comm.Reports 1001 (1990)].

Cross References

Allowance of costs against personal representative, see Code of Civil Procedure § 1026.
Compensation and allowances of public administrator, see Probate Code § 7622.
Compensation and allowances of special administrator, see Probate Code § 8547.
Payment of expenses of administration, see Probate Code §§ 11420, 11422.

§ 10803. Agreement between personal representative and heir or devisee

An agreement between the personal representative and an heir or devisee for higher compensation than that provided by this part is void. *(Stats.1990, c. 79 (A.B.759), § 14, operative July 1, 1991.)*

Law Revision Commission Comments
1990 Enactment

Section 10803 restates Section 903 of the repealed Probate Code without substantive change. This section applies to compensation for both ordinary and extraordinary services. Nothing prevents the personal representative from waiving all compensation or agreeing to take less than the statutory compensation. See In re Estate of Marshall, 118 Cal. 379, 381, 50 P. 540 (1897) (statutory compensation allowed when evidence of alleged agreement for lower compensation was insufficient). See also Feinfield, Fees and Commissions, in 2 California Decedent Estate Practice § 20.5 (Cal.Cont.Ed.Bar, Feb. 1989). As to the law applicable to a proceeding commenced before July 1, 1991, see Section 10850. As to the application of any amendments made after that date, see Section 3. For background on the provisions of this part, see the Comment to this part under the part heading. [20 Cal.L.Rev.Comm.Reports 1001 (1990)].

§ 10804. Personal representative who is an attorney

Notwithstanding any provision in the decedent's will, a personal representative who is an attorney shall be entitled to receive the personal representative's compensation as provided in this part, but shall not receive compensation for services as the attorney for the personal representative unless the court specifically approves the right to the compensation in advance and finds that the arrangement is to the advantage, benefit, and best interests of the decedent's estate. *(Stats. 1990, c. 79 (A.B.759), § 14, operative July 1, 1991. Amended by Stats.1993, c. 293 (A.B.21), § 5; Stats.1996, c. 563 (S.B. 392), § 26; Stats.2001, c. 699 (A.B.232), § 3.)*

Law Revision Commission Comments
1990 Enactment

Section 10804 is a new provision that codifies the general case law rule that the personal representative cannot serve as the estate attorney and receive dual compensation. See In re Estate of Parker, 200 Cal. 132, 251 P. 907 (1926); Estate of Downing, 134 Cal.App.3d 256, 184 Cal.Rptr. 511 (1982); Estate of Haviside, 102 Cal.App.3d 365, 368–69, 162 Cal.Rptr. 393 (1980). The provision that dual compensation may be paid if expressly authorized by the decedent's will also codifies case law. See Estate of Thompson, 50 Cal.2d 613, 328 P.2d 1 (1958); Estate of Crouch, 240 Cal.App.2d 801, 49 Cal.Rptr. 926 (1966). See generally Feinfield, Fees and Commissions, in 2 California Decedent Estate Practice §§ 20.10–20.12 (Cal.Cont.Ed.Bar, Feb. 1989).

The term "estate attorney" is to be given a broad meaning for the purposes of this section and includes the associates, partners, and attorneys of counsel with the law firm of the attorney retained by the personal representative as estate attorney, and also associates, partners, and attorneys of counsel with other law firms associated in the estate proceeding with the firm of the attorney retained by the personal representative as estate attorney, if the personal representative will share in the compensation that would be paid to the law firm. See also In re Estate of Parker, 200 Cal. 132, 251 P. 907 (1926). As to the law applicable to a proceeding commenced before July 1, 1991, see Section 10850. As to the application of any amendments made after that date, see Section 3.

For background on the provisions of this part, see the Comment to this part under the part heading. [20 Cal.L.Rev.Comm.Reports 1001 (1990)].

§ 10805. Two or more personal representatives

If there are two or more personal representatives, the personal representative's compensation shall be apportioned among the personal representatives by the court according to the services actually rendered by each personal representative or as agreed to by the personal representatives. *(Stats.1990, c. 79 (A.B.759), § 14, operative July 1, 1991.)*

Law Revision Commission Comments

1990 Enactment

Section 10805 restates the second sentence of Section 901 of the repealed Probate Code without substantive change, with the addition of the reference to an agreement between the personal representatives concerning apportionment of their compensation. The added language was drawn from Section 8547 (division of compensation between special administrator and general personal representative). For background on the provisions of this part, see the Comment to this part under the part heading. As to the law applicable to a proceeding commenced before July 1, 1991, see Section 10850. As to the application of any amendments made after that date, see Section 3. [20 Cal.L.Rev.Comm.Reports 1001 (1990)].

ARTICLE 2. COMPENSATION OF ATTORNEY FOR THE PERSONAL REPRESENTATIVE

Section

Law Revision Commission Comments

1991 Addition

Sections 10810–10814 continue the effect of the first sentence of former Section 10810 which provided that attorneys for personal representatives shall be allowed as compensation for ordinary services the same amounts as are allowed as compensation to personal representatives, and such further amount as the court deems just and reasonable for extraordinary services. [20 Cal.L.Rev. Comm. Reports 2913 (1990)].

§ 10810. Compensation for conducting ordinary proceedings

(a) Subject to the provisions of this part, for ordinary services the attorney for the personal representative shall receive compensation based on the value of the estate accounted for by the personal representative, as follows:

(1) Four percent on the first one hundred thousand dollars ($100,000).

(2) Three percent on the next one hundred thousand dollars ($100,000).

(3) Two percent on the next eight hundred thousand dollars ($800,000).

(4) One percent on the next nine million dollars ($9,000,-000).

(5) One-half of 1 percent on the next fifteen million dollars ($15,000,000).

(6) For all amounts above twenty-five million dollars ($25,000,000), a reasonable amount to be determined by the court.

(b) For the purposes of this section, the value of the estate accounted for by the personal representative is the total amount of the appraisal of property in the inventory, plus gains over the appraisal value on sales, plus receipts, less losses from the appraisal value on sales, without reference to encumbrances or other obligations on estate property. *(Added by Stats.1991, c. 82 (S.B.896), § 30, eff. June 30, 1991,*

operative July 1, 1991. Amended by Stats.2001, c. 699 (A.B.232), § 4.)

Law Revision Commission Comments

1991 Addition

Section 10810 is new. It continues the effect of the first portion of the first sentence of former Section 910 of the repealed Probate Code, which provided that attorneys for personal representatives shall be allowed as compensation for ordinary services the same amounts as are allowed as compensation to personal representatives. [20 Cal.L.Rev.Comm.Reports 2913 (1990)].

Cross References

Accounting by attorney for deceased or incapacitated personal representative as extraordinary service, see Probate Code § 10953.
Attorneys, generally, see Business and Professions Code § 6000 et seq.
Authority of attorney,
  Generally, see Code of Civil Procedure § 283.
  Right to appeal on death of client, see Code of Civil Procedure § 903.
  Satisfaction of judgment, see Code of Civil Procedure §§ 283, 724.010 et seq.
  Verification of pleadings, see Code of Civil Procedure § 446.
Change of attorney, see Code of Civil Procedure § 284.
Claims of personal representative, attorneys' fees, see Probate Code § 9252.
Compensation of guardian, conservator, and attorney, see Probate Code § 2640 et seq.
Compensation of special administrator and attorney for special administrator, see Probate Code § 8547.
Continuation of administration, see Probate Code § 12201.
Death or removal of attorney, see Code of Civil Procedure § 286.
Dismissal of action, consent of attorney, see Code of Civil Procedure § 581.
Duties of attorney, see Business and Professions Code § 6068.
Lawyer-client privilege, see Evidence Code § 950 et seq.
Order as appealable, see Probate Code § 7240.
Partition, attorney's fees on, see Probate Code § 11955.
Reduction of compensation, excessive time for administration of estate, see Probate Code § 12205.
Restrictions respecting attorney as receiver, see Code of Civil Procedure § 566.
Service on attorney, see Code of Civil Procedure § 1010 et seq.

§ 10811. Extraordinary services; additional compensation; contingent fee

(a) Subject to the provisions of this part, in addition to the compensation provided by Section 10810, the court may allow additional compensation for extraordinary services by the attorney for the personal representative in an amount the court determines is just and reasonable.

(b) Extraordinary services by the attorney for which the court may allow compensation include services by a paralegal performing the extraordinary services under the direction and supervision of an attorney. The petition for compensation shall set forth the hours spent and services performed by the paralegal.

(c) An attorney for the personal representative may agree to perform extraordinary service on a contingent fee basis subject to the following conditions:

(1) The agreement is written and complies with all the requirements of Section 6147 of the Business and Professions Code.

(2) The agreement is approved by the court following a hearing noticed as provided in Section 10812.

(3) The court determines that the compensation provided in the agreement is just and reasonable and the agreement is to the advantage of the estate and in the best interests of the persons who are interested in the estate. *(Added by Stats. 1991, c. 82 (S.B.896), § 30, eff. June 30, 1991, operative July 1, 1991. Amended by Stats.1993, c. 527 (A.B.908), § 4.)*

Law Revision Commission Comments

1991 Addition [Revised Comment]

Section 10811 is new. It continues the substance of the last portion of the first sentence, and all of the second and third sentences, of former Section 910 of the repealed Probate Code. [21 Cal.L.Rev.Comm.Reports 67 (1991)].

§ 10812. Compensation provided by will; petition for relief

(a) Except as otherwise provided in this section, if the decedent's will makes provision for the compensation of the attorney for the personal representative, the compensation provided by the will shall be the full and only compensation for the services of the attorney for the personal representative.

(b) The personal representative or the attorney for the personal representative may petition the court to be relieved from a provision of the will that provides for the compensation of the attorney for the personal representative.

(c) Notice of the hearing on the petition shall be given as provided in Section 1220 to all of the following persons:

(1) Each person listed in Section 1220.

(2) Each known heir whose interest in the estate would be affected by the petition.

(3) Each known devisee whose interest in the estate would be affected by the petition.

(4) The Attorney General, at the office of the Attorney General in Sacramento, if any portion of the estate is to escheat to the state and its interest in the estate would be affected by the petition.

(5) If the court determines that it is to the advantage of the estate and in the best interest of the persons interested in the estate, the court may make an order authorizing compensation of the attorney for the personal representative in an amount greater than provided in the will. *(Added by Stats.1991, c. 82 (S.B.896), § 30, eff. June 30, 1991, operative July 1, 1991.)*

Law Revision Commission Comments

1991 Addition

Section 10812 supersedes the portions of former Section 900 and 901 of the repealed Probate Code that permitted the estate attorney to renounce the compensation provided by the will and to receive the statutory compensation. Those portions applied to personal representatives, and were made applicable to estate attorneys by the first sentence of former Section 910 of the repealed Probate Code. Instead, Section 10812, like Section 10802 (personal representative), imposes a requirement that court approval by obtained before the estate attorney may be relieved from the provisions of the will

governing compensation. [20 Cal.L.Rev.Comm.Reports 2913 (1990)].

§ 10813. Agreements for higher compensation

An agreement between the personal representative and the attorney for higher compensation for the attorney than that provided by this part is void. *(Added by Stats.1991, c. 82 (S.B.896), § 30, eff. June 30, 1991, operative July 1, 1991.)*

Law Revision Commission Comments

1991 Addition

Section 10813 continues the effect of former Section 903 of the repealed Probate Code which applied to personal representatives, and was made applicable to estate attorneys by the first sentence of former Section 910 of the repealed Probate Code. Section 10812 is comparable to Section 10803 (personal representatives). [20 Cal.L.Rev.Comm.Reports 2019 (1990)].

§ 10814. Apportionment of compensation

If there are two or more attorneys for the personal representative, the attorney's compensation shall be apportioned among the attorneys by the court according to the services actually rendered by each attorney or as agreed to by the attorneys. *(Added by Stats.1991, c. 82 (S.B.896), § 30, eff. June 30, 1991, operative July 1, 1991.)*

Law Revision Commission Comments

1991 Addition

Section 10814 continues the effect of the second sentence of former Section 901 of the repealed Probate Code which applied to personal representatives, and was made applicable to estate attorneys by the first sentence of former Section 910 of the repealed Probate Code. Section 10812 is comparable to Section 10805 (personal representatives). [20 Cal.L.Rev.Comm.Reports 2913 (1990)].

CHAPTER 2. ALLOWANCE OF COMPENSATION BY COURT

§ 10830. Allowance on compensation; personal representative or attorney; petition; notice; hearing

(a) At any time after four months from the issuance of letters:

(1) The personal representative may file a petition requesting an allowance on the compensation of the personal representative.

(2) The personal representative or the attorney for the personal representative may file a petition requesting an allowance on the compensation of the attorney for the personal representative.

(b) Notice of the hearing on the petition shall be given as provided in Section 1220 to all of the following:

(1) Each person listed in Section 1220.

(2) Each known heir whose interest in the estate would be affected by the payment of the compensation.

(3) Each known devisee whose interest in the estate would be affected by the payment of the compensation.

(4) The Attorney General, at the office of the Attorney General in Sacramento, if any portion of the estate is to escheat to the state and its interest in the estate would be affected by the petition.

(c) On the hearing, the court may make an order allowing the portion of the compensation of the personal representative or the attorney for the personal representative, as the case may be, on account of services rendered up to that time, that the court determines is proper. The order shall authorize the personal representative to charge against the estate the amount allowed. *(Stats.1990, c. 79 (A.B.759), § 14, operative July 1, 1991. Amended by Stats.1990, c. 710 (S.B.1775), § 35, operative July 1, 1991.)*

Law Revision Commission Comments

1990 Enactment and Amendment

Section 10830 (enacted as a part of the new Probate Code by 1990 Cal.Stat. ch. 79 § 14) was amended by 1990 Cal.Stat. ch. 710 § 35. The section as amended is drawn from Sections 904 and 911 of the repealed Probate Code. As originally enacted in the new Probate Code, Section 10830 had been revised to reflect the fact that Assembly Bill 831 of the 1989–1990 regular session would have substituted an agreed fee system for the statutory fee system for probate attorney fees. However, Assembly Bill 831 was not enacted, and Section 10830 was amended by 1990 Cal.Stat. ch. 710 § 35 to reflect this fact. See the Comment to Section 900.

As to the priority for payment, see Section 11420. As to the law applicable to a proceeding commenced before July 1, 1991, see Section 10850. As to the application of any amendments made after that date, see Section 3.

For general provisions, see Sections 1000–1004 (rules of practice), 1020–1023 (petitions and other papers), 1040–1050 (hearings and orders). For general provisions relating to notice of hearing, see Sections 1200–1220. See also Sections 1206 (notice to known heirs or devisees), 1215–1217 (mailing in general), 1250–1252 (request for special notice), 1260–1265 (proof of giving notice). The court for good cause may dispense with the notice otherwise required to be given to a person under Section 10830. See Section 1220(c). For a limitation on the court's authority to award a partial allowance of fees for extraordinary services, see Section 10832. See also Sections 8547 (compensation of special administrator), 10954(c) (final report to show compensation), 12205 (reduction of compensation for delay in closing estate administration). See also Section 52 (defining "letters").

For background on the provisions of this part, see the Comment to this part under the part heading. [20 Cal.L.Rev.Comm.Reports 1001 (1990)].

Cross References

Compensation and allowances,
  Public administrator's, see Probate Code § 7622.
  Special administrator's, see Probate Code § 8547.
Expenses of administration, charge against estate, see Probate Code § 11401.
Notices, generally, see Probate Code § 1200 et seq.

§ 10831. Order fixing and allowing compensation; personal representative or attorney; petition; notice; hearing

(a) At the time of the filing of the final account and petition for an order for final distribution:

(1) The personal representative may petition the court for an order fixing and allowing the personal representative's compensation for all services rendered in the estate proceeding.

(2) The personal representative or the attorney for the personal representative may petition the court for an order fixing and allowing the compensation, of the attorney for all services rendered in the estate proceeding.

(b) The request for compensation may be included in the final account or the petition for final distribution or may be made in a separate petition.

(c) Notice of the hearing on the petition shall be given as provided in Section 1220 to all of the following:

(1) Each person listed in Section 1220.

(2) Each known heir whose interest in the estate would be affected by the payment of the compensation.

(3) Each known devisee whose interest in the estate would be affected by the payment of the compensation.

(4) The Attorney General, at the office of the Attorney General in Sacramento, if any portion of the estate is to escheat to the state and its interest in the estate would be affected by the petition.

(d) On the hearing, the court shall make an order fixing and allowing the compensation for all services rendered in the estate proceeding. In the case of an allowance to the personal representative, the order shall authorize the personal representative to charge against the estate the amount allowed, less any amount previously charged against the estate pursuant to Section 10830. In the case of the attorney's compensation the order shall require the personal representative to pay the attorney out of the estate the amount allowed, less any amount paid to the attorney out of the estate pursuant to Section 10830. *(Stats.1990, c. 79 (A.B.759), § 14, operative July 1, 1991. Amended by Stats. 1990, c. 710 (S.B.1775), § 36, operative July 1, 1991.)*

Law Revision Commission Comments

1990 Enactment and Amendment

Section 10831 (enacted as a part of the new Probate Code by 1990 Cal.Stat. ch. 79 § 14) was amended by 1990 Cal.Stat. ch. 710 § 36. As originally enacted in the new Probate Code, Section 10831 had been drafted to reflect the fact that Assembly Bill 831 of the 1989–1990 regular session would have substituted an agreed fee system for the statutory fee system for probate attorney fees. However, Assembly Bill 831 was not enacted, and Section 10831 was amended by 1990 Cal.Stat. ch. 710 § 36 to reflect this fact. See the Comment to Section 900.

Amended Section 10831 is a new provision drawn from Probate Code Section 10830 and is in accord with existing practice. See Feinfield, Fees and Commissions, in 2 California Decedent Estate Practice § 20.34 (Cal.Cont.Ed.Bar, Feb. 1989). Final compensation is not to be paid until there is a final account and a final distribution. As to the priority for payment, see Section 11420. As to the law applicable to a proceeding commenced before July 1, 1991, see Section 10850. As to the application of any amendments made after that date, see Section 3.

For general provisions, see Sections 1000–1004 (rules of practice), 1020–1023 (petitions and other papers), 1040–1050 (hearings and orders). For general provisions relating to notice of hearing, see Sections 1200–1220. See also Sections 1206 (notice to known heirs or devisees), 1215–1217 (mailing in general), 1250–1252 (request for special notice), 1260–1265 (proof of giving notice). See also Sections 8547 (compensation of special administrator), 10954(c) (final report to show compensation), 12205 (reduction of compensation for delay in closing estate administration).

For background on the provisions of this part, see the Comment to this part under the part heading. [20 Cal.L.Rev.Comm.Reports 1001 (1990)].

§ 10832. Compensation for extraordinary services before final distribution

Notwithstanding Sections 10830 and 10831, the court may allow compensation to the personal representative or to the attorney for the personal representative for extraordinary services before final distribution when any of the following requirements is satisfied:

(a) It appears likely that administration of the estate will continue, whether due to litigation or otherwise, for an unusually long time.

(b) Present payment will benefit the estate or the beneficiaries of the estate.

(c) Other good cause is shown. *(Stats.1990, c. 79 (A.B. 759), § 14, operative July 1, 1991. Amended by Stats.1994, c. 806 (A.B.3686), § 33.)*

Law Revision Commission Comments

1990 Enactment

Section 10832 is a new provision drawn from local court rules. In some cases, present payment will benefit the estate. For example, compensation may be allowed near the end of a tax year to absorb estate income so that the income will not be taxable. Partial payment also may be allowed at any time during the year if good cause is shown. As to the law applicable to a proceeding commenced before July 1, 1991, see Section 10850. As to the application of any amendments made after that date, see Section 3. For background on the provisions of this part, see the Comment to this part under the part heading. [20 Cal.L.Rev.Comm.Reports 1001 (1990)].

CHAPTER 3. APPLICATION OF PART

§ 10850. Proceedings commenced before July 1, 1991

(a) This part does not apply in any proceeding for administration of a decedent's estate commenced before July 1, 1991.

(b) Notwithstanding its repeal, the applicable law in effect before July 1, 1991, governing the subject matter of this part continues to apply in any proceeding for administration of a decedent's estate commenced before July 1, 1991. *(Stats. 1990, c. 79 (A.B.759), § 14, operative July 1, 1991. Amended by Stats.1990, c. 710 (S.B.1775), § 37, operative July 1, 1991.)*

Law Revision Commission Comments

1990 Enactment and Amendment

Section 10850 (enacted as a part of the new Probate Code by 1990 Cal.Stat. ch. 79 § 14) was amended by 1990 Cal.Stat. ch. 710 § 37. The amended section limits the application of this part to proceedings commenced on or after July 1, 1991. Thus, for example, the allowance of compensation of the personal representative or the attorney for the personal representative in a proceeding commenced

before July 1, 1991, is governed by the applicable law in effect before July 1, 1991. See former Prob.Code §§ 900, 901, 902, 903, 904, 910, and 911 (repealed by 1990 Cal.Stat. ch. 79 § 13) (compensation of personal representative and attorney for personal representative). For background, see Recommendations Relating to Probate Law: Hiring and Paying Attorneys, Advisors, and Others; Compensation of Personal Representative, 20 Cal.L.Revision Comm'n Reports 31 (1990); Revised and Supplemental Comments to the New Probate Code, 20 Cal.L.Revision Comm'n Reports 2001 (1990). [20 Cal.L.Rev.Comm.Reports 1001 (1990)].

Part 8

ACCOUNTS

Law Revision Commission Comments

1990 Enactment

This part supersedes Part 8 (commencing with Section 10900) of Division 7 of the repealed Probate Code. The superseded part was enacted upon recommendation of the California Law Revision Commission. See Recommendation Relating to Accounts, 19 Cal.L.Revision Comm'n Reports 877 (1988). See also Communication from the California Law Revision Commission Concerning Assembly Bill 2841, 19 Cal.L.Revision Comm'n Reports 1201, 1241–42 (1988); Communication from the California Law Revision Commission Concerning Assembly Bill 158, 20 Cal.L.Revision Comm'n Reports 235.242 (1990). [20 Cal.L.Rev.Comm.Reports 1001 (1990)].

CHAPTER 1. GENERAL PROVISIONS

Cross References

Application of old and new law, see Probate Code § 3.

§ 10900. Financial statement; report of administration; included items

(a) An account shall include both a financial statement and a report of administration as provided in Chapter 4 (commencing with Section 1060) of Part 1 of Division 3, and this section.

(b) The statement of liabilities in the report of administration shall include the following information:

(1) Whether notice to creditors was given under Section 9050.

(2) Creditor claims filed, including the date of filing the claim, the name of the claimant, the amount of the claim, and the action taken on the claim.

(3) Creditor claims not paid, satisfied, or adequately provided for. As to each such claim, the statement shall indicate whether the claim is due and the date due, the date any notice of rejection was given, and whether the creditor has brought an action on the claim. The statement shall identify any real or personal property that is security for the claim, whether by mortgage, deed of trust, lien, or other encumbrance.

(c) The amendments to this section made by Assembly Bill 2751 of the 1995–96 Regular Session shall become operative on July 1, 1997. *(Stats.1990, c. 79 (A.B.759), § 14, operative July 1, 1991. Amended by Stats.1990, c. 710 (S.B.1775), § 38, operative July 1, 1991; Stats.1996, c. 862 (A.B.2751), § 30, operative July 1, 1997.)*

Law Revision Commission Comments
1990 Enactment and Amendment

Section 10900 (enacted as a part of the new Probate Code by 1990 Cal.Stat. ch. 79 § 14) was amended by 1990 Cal.Stat. ch. 710 § 38. As originally enacted in the new Probate Code, Section 10900 had been revised to reflect the fact that Assembly Bill 831 of the 1989–1990 regular session would have substituted an agreed fee system for the statutory fee system for probate attorney fees. However, Assembly Bill 831 was not enacted, and Section 10900 was amended by 1990 Cal.Stat. ch. 710 § 38 to reflect this fact. See the Comment to Section 900.

Section 10900 as amended continues Section 10900 of the repealed Probate Code without change. See also Sections 9657 (personal representative not to profit from increase, nor to suffer loss from decrease or destruction of estate without fault), 9839 (paying claim for less than its full amount), 10005 (sale for more or less than appraised value).

Subdivision (b) is based on concepts developed in Note, California Probate Accounting Procedures, 39 S.Cal.L.Rev. 316 (1966). In the financial statement, each schedule should contain a breakdown of the summary item into its component parts. For instance, the summary item of receipts might be broken down into the totals of interest income, dividend income, royalties received, and miscellaneous receipts. The exact breakdown will vary, depending on the nature of the estate. It would be unnecessary to show in the summary item more than the total amount of each component part making up the total. For illustrative material, see National Fiduciary Accounting Standards Project: Uniform Fiduciary Accounting Principles and Model Accounting Formats, in 9 Probate Notes 224–47 (American College of Probate Counsel 1984).

Since the purpose of the report of administration (subdivisions (c) and (d)) is to provide a complete summary of the estate's administration, additional statements may be necessary in order to clarify certain events or circumstances and to permit interested persons to understand the report. In certain instances, the report of administration may include such information as a statement that cash was invested in interest-bearing accounts or other proper investments (Section 9652). If a final account is waived, the final report of administration must include the amount of the compensation paid or payable to the personal representative and the attorney for the personal representative and must set forth the basis for determining the amount of the compensation. See Section 10954(c). See also Section 10831 (request for compensation may be included in the final account).

Likewise, the financial statement must include the information required by this section. This section does not, however, preclude a financial statement from including any other relevant information, such as a separate statement of account as to specific gifts, allocation of principal and income, taxable income and distributable net income, and current values of property in the estate.

Background on Section 10900 of Repealed Code

Section 10900 was added by 1988 Cal.Stat. ch. 1199 § 91. The section superseded former Probate Code Section 920.3 and the first sentence of former Probate Code Section 921 (provisions repealed by 1988 Cal.Stat. ch. 1199 § 54.5). For background on the provisions of this part, see the Comment to this part under the part heading. [20 Cal.L.Rev.Comm.Reports 1001 (1990)].

Cross References

Account by personal representatives seeking reduction of bond and discharge of surety, see Probate Code §§ 8484, 8485.
Attachment in general, see Code of Civil Procedure § 481.010 et seq.
Claims against the estate, generally, see Probate Code § 9100 et seq.
Contempt, see Code of Civil Procedure § 1209 et seq.; Probate Code § 8505.
Deposit or withdrawal of estate funds in bank, see Probate Code § 9700.
Final distribution, generally, see Probate Code § 11600 et seq.
Investment of funds of estate, see Probate Code § 9731 et seq.
Payment of debts, order for, see Probate Code § 11420.
Persons interested in the estate,
  Allowed claims, contest of validity, see Probate Code § 9254.
  Borrowing money and mortgaging of property, see Probate Code § 9802.
  Contests before probate, see Probate Code §§ 8004, 8250.
  Lease of property, see Probate Code § 9943.
  Petition for probate, see Probate Code § 8000.
  Proration of federal estate taxes among, see Probate Code § 20110.
  Removal of personal representative, see Probate Code § 8500.
  Sale of property, petition for order requiring, see Probate Code § 10001.
Property acquired or discovered after final distribution order made, see Probate Code § 11642.
Removal of personal representative for failure to file an account, see Probate Code §§ 11051, 11052.

§ 10901. Documents supporting accounts; inspection and audit; court or interested person

On court order, or on request by an interested person filed with the clerk and a copy served on the personal representative, the personal representative shall produce for inspection and audit by the court or interested person the documents specified in the order or request that support an account. *(Stats.1990, c. 79 (A.B.759), § 14, operative July 1, 1991.)*

Law Revision Commission Comments
1990 Enactment

Section 10901 continues Section 10901 of the repealed Probate Code without change.

Background on Section 10901 of Repealed Code

Section 10901 was added by 1988 Cal.Stat. ch. 1199 § 91. The section superseded former Probate Code Section 925 (repealed by 1988 Cal.Stat. ch. 1199 § 54.5), extending the voucher procedure to supporting documents generally. For background on the provisions of this part, see the Comment to this part under the part heading. [20 Cal.L.Rev.Comm.Reports 1001 (1990)].

§ 10902. Receipt of assets from conservator or guardian of deceased person; incorporation of accounting by reference; reliance

When a personal representative receives assets from the conservator of a deceased conservatee or the guardian of a deceased ward, the personal representative may incorporate by reference any accounting provided by the conservator or guardian for the decedent for the period subsequent to the date of death, and the personal representative is entitled to rely on the accounting by such other fiduciary, and shall not have a duty to independently investigate or verify the transactions reported in such an account. *(Added by Stats. 1996, c. 862 (A.B.2751), § 32, operative July 1, 1997.)*

Law Revision Commission Comments

1990 Enactment

Section 10902 continues Section 10902 of the repealed Probate Code without substantive change.

Background on Section 10902 of Repealed Code

Section 10902 was added by 1989 Cal.Stat. ch. 21 § 26. See Communication from the California Law Revision Commission Concerning Assembly Bill 156, 20 Cal.L.Revision Comm'n Reports 227, 231 (1990). [20 Cal.L.Rev.Comm.Reports 1001 (1990)].

CHAPTER 2. WHEN ACCOUNT REQUIRED

Section
10950. Court's motion or interested person's petition; when account required.
10951. Final account; petition for final distribution order.
10952. Termination of personal representative's authority.
10953. Deceased, incapacitated, or absconding personal representative; legal representative; compensation; extraordinary services.
10954. Account not required; waiver; acknowledgment of or provision for satisfaction of interest; execution; final report of administration; creditor petition for account.

Cross References

Application of old and new law, see Probate Code § 3.

§ 10950. Court's motion or interested person's petition; when account required

(a) On its own motion or on petition of an interested person, the court may order an account at any time.

(b) The court shall order an account on petition of an interested person made more than one year after the last account was filed or, if no previous account has been filed, made more than one year after issuance of letters to the personal representative.

(c) The court order shall specify the time within which the personal representative must file an account. *(Stats.1990, c. 79 (A.B.759), § 14, operative July 1, 1991.)*

Law Revision Commission Comments

1990 Enactment

Section 10950 continues Section 10950 of the repealed Probate Code without change. This section is subject to Section 10954 (when account is not required). For general provisions, see Sections 1000–1004 (rules of practice), 1020–1023 (petitions and other papers), 1040–1050 (hearings and orders). For general provisions relating to notice of hearing, see Sections 1200–1220. See also Sections 1215–1217 (mailing in general), 1250–1252 (request for special notice), 1260–1265 (proof of giving notice).

Background on Section 10950 of Repealed Code

Section 10950 was added by 1988 Cal.Stat. ch. 1199 § 91. The section superseded portions of the first sentences of former Probate Code Sections 921 and 922 (provisions repealed by 1988 Cal.Stat. ch.

1199 § 54.5). For background on the provisions of this part, see the Comment to this part under the part heading. [20 Cal.L.Rev.Comm.Reports 1001 (1990)].

Cross References

Report of status of administration, account, see Probate Code § 12201.

§ 10951. Final account; petition for final distribution order

The personal representative shall file a final account and petition for an order for final distribution of the estate when the estate is in a condition to be closed. *(Stats.1990, c. 79 (A.B.759), § 14, operative July 1, 1991.)*

Law Revision Commission Comments

1990 Enactment

Section 10951 continues Section 10951 of the repealed Probate Code without change. This section is consistent with Section 11640 (petition and order for final distribution). The section is subject to Section 10954 (when account is not required). It should be noted that a supplemental account may be required under Section 11642 (after-acquired or after-discovered property). The liability of a personal representative whose office is vacant, and of surety on bond, continues until settlement of accounts and delivery of all of the estate to successor personal representative or other person appointed by the court to receive it. See Section 8525. See also Section 10831 (request for compensation may be included in the final account).

Background on Section 10951 of Repealed Code

Section 10951 was added by 1988 Cal.Stat. ch. 1199 § 91. The section superseded the second sentence of former Probate Code Section 922 (repealed by 1988 Cal.Stat. ch. 1199 § 54.5). For background on the provisions of this part, see the Comment to this part under the part heading. [20 Cal.L.Rev.Comm.Reports 1001 (1990)].

§ 10952. Termination of personal representative's authority

A personal representative who resigns or is removed from office or whose authority is otherwise terminated shall, unless the court extends the time, file an account not later than 60 days after termination of authority. If the personal representative fails to so file the account, the court may compel the account pursuant to Chapter 4 (commencing with Section 11050). *(Stats.1990, c. 79 (A.B.759), § 14, operative July 1, 1991.)*

Law Revision Commission Comments

1990 Enactment

Section 10952 continues Section 10952 of the repealed Probate Code without change. This section is subject to Section 10954 (when account is not required). For an account where the personal representative dies, absconds, or becomes incapacitated, see Section 10953.

Background on Section 10952 of Repealed Code

Section 10952 was added by 1988 Cal.Stat. ch. 1199 § 91. The section superseded former Probate Code Section 923 (repealed by 1988 Cal.Stat. ch. 1199 § 54.5). For background on the provisions of this part, see the Comment to this part under the part heading. [20 Cal.L.Rev.Comm.Reports 1001 (1990)].

Cross References

Account by personal representative,
  Removal from office, see Probate Code § 8504.
  Vacancy of office, see Probate Code § 8525.
Revocation of letters of administration, see Probate Code § 8501.

§ 10953. Deceased, incapacitated, or absconding personal representative; legal representative; compensation; extraordinary services

(a) As used in this section:

(1) "Incapacitated" means lack of capacity to serve as personal representative.

(2) "Legal representative" means the personal representative of a deceased personal representative or the conservator of the estate of an incapacitated personal representative.

(b) If a personal representative dies or becomes incapacitated and a legal representative is appointed for the deceased or incapacitated personal representative, the legal representative shall not later than 60 days after appointment, unless the court extends the time, file an account of the administration of the deceased or incapacitated personal representative.

(c) If a personal representative dies or becomes incapacitated and no legal representative is appointed for the deceased or incapacitated personal representative, or if the personal representative absconds, the court may compel the attorney for the deceased, incapacitated, or absconding personal representative or attorney of record in the estate proceeding to file an account of the administration of the deceased, incapacitated, or absconding personal representative.

(d) The legal representative or attorney shall exercise reasonable diligence in preparing an account under this section. Verification of the account may be made on information and belief. The court shall settle the account as in other cases. The court shall allow reasonable compensation to the legal representative or the attorney for preparing the account. The amount allowed is a charge against the estate that was being administered by the deceased, incapacitated, or absconding personal representative. Legal services for which compensation shall be allowed to the attorney under this subdivision include those services rendered by any paralegal performing the services under the direction and supervision of an attorney. The petition or application for compensation shall set forth the hours spent and services performed by the paralegal. *(Stats.1990, c. 79 (A.B.759), § 14, operative July 1, 1991.)*

Law Revision Commission Comments
1990 Enactment

Section 10953 continues Section 10953 of the repealed Probate Code without substantive change. The court referred to in this section is the court in which the estate of the original decedent is being administered.

Background on Section 10953 of Repealed Code

Section 10953 was added by 1988 Cal.Stat. ch. 1199 § 91. The section restated former Probate Code Section 932 (repealed by 1988 Cal.Stat. ch. 1199 § 54.5) with changes for internal consistency. For background on the provisions of this part, see the Comment to this part under the part heading. [20 Cal.L.Rev.Comm.Reports 1001 (1990)].

Cross References

Appointment as personal representative with will annexed on vacancy of office, see Probate Code §§ 8440, 8522.
Compensation for attorney rendering account for dead, incapacitated or absconding guardian or conservator, see Probate Code § 2632.
Compensation of guardian, conservator, and attorney, see Probate Code § 2640 et seq.
Conservatorships, see Probate Code § 1800 et seq.
Incompetency, see Probate Code § 8402.
Special administrators, appointment, see Probate Code § 8540.

§ 10954. Account not required; waiver; acknowledgment of or provision for satisfaction of interest; execution; final report of administration; creditor petition for account

(a) Notwithstanding any other provision of this part, the personal representative is not required to file an account if any of the following conditions is satisfied as to each person entitled to distribution from the estate:

(1) The person has executed and filed a written waiver of account or a written acknowledgment that the person's interest has been satisfied.

(2) Adequate provision has been made for satisfaction in full of the person's interest. This paragraph does not apply to a residuary devisee or a devisee whose interest in the estate is subject to abatement, payment of expenses, or accrual of interest or income.

(b) A waiver or acknowledgment under subdivision (a) shall be executed as follows:

(1) If the person entitled to distribution is an adult and competent, by that person.

(2) If the person entitled to distribution is a minor, by a person authorized to receive money or property belonging to the minor. If the waiver or acknowledgment is executed by a guardian of the estate of the minor, the waiver or acknowledgment may be executed without the need to obtain approval of the court in which the guardianship proceeding is pending.

(3) If the person entitled to distribution is a conservatee, by the conservator of the estate of the conservatee. The waiver or acknowledgment may be executed without the need to obtain approval of the court in which the conservatorship proceeding is pending.

(4) If the person entitled to distribution is a trust, by the trustee, but only if the named trustee's written acceptance of the trust is filed with the court. In the case of a trust that is subject to the continuing jurisdiction of the court pursuant to Chapter 4 (commencing with Section 17300) of Part 5 of Division 9, the waiver or acknowledgment may be executed without the need to obtain approval of the court.

(5) If the person entitled to distribution is an estate, by the personal representative of the estate. The waiver or acknowledgment may be executed without the need to obtain approval of the court in which the estate is being administered.

(6) If the person entitled to distribution is incapacitated, unborn, unascertained, or is a person whose identity or address is unknown, or is a designated class of persons who are not ascertained or are not in being, and there is a

guardian ad litem appointed to represent the person entitled to distribution, by the guardian ad litem.

(7) If the person entitled to distribution has designated an attorney in fact who has the power under the power of attorney to execute the waiver or acknowledgment, by either of the following:

(A) The person entitled to distribution if an adult and competent.

(B) The attorney in fact.

(c) Notwithstanding subdivision (a):

(1) The personal representative shall file a final report of administration at the time the final account would otherwise have been required. The final report shall include the amount of compensation paid or payable to the personal representative and to the attorney for the personal representative and shall set forth the basis for determining the amounts.

(2) A creditor whose interest has not been satisfied may petition under Section 10950 for an account. *(Stats.1990, c. 79 (A.B.759), § 14, operative July 1, 1991. Amended by Stats.1990, c. 710 (S.B.1775), § 39, operative July 1, 1991.)*

Law Revision Commission Comments
1990 Enactment and Amendment

Section 10954 (enacted as a part of the new Probate Code by 1990 Cal.Stat. ch. 79 § 14) was amended by 1990 Cal.Stat. ch. 710 § 39. As originally enacted in the new Probate Code, Section 10954 had been revised to reflect the fact that Assembly Bill 831 of the 1989–1990 regular session would have substituted an agreed fee system for the statutory fee system for probate attorney fees. However, Assembly Bill 831 was not enacted, and Section 10954 was amended by 1990 Cal.Stat. ch. 710 § 39 to reflect this fact. See the Comment to Section 900.

Section 10954 as amended continues Section 10954 of the repealed Probate Code with the following revisions:

(1) Paragraph (7) of subdivision (b) is added to recognize the authority of an attorney in fact to execute a waiver or acknowledgment under Section 10954.

(2) The phrase "fees and commissions" is changed to "compensation", consistent with the terminology used in Part 7 (commencing with Section 10800) (compensation of personal representative and estate attorney).

Section 10954 supersedes local court rules. The section applies notwithstanding any other provision of this part, including but not limited to Section 10950 (court-ordered account).

Under paragraph (2) of subdivision (b), a waiver may be made on behalf of a minor by the minor's parent or guardian of the estate. The minor's parent or guardian of the estate is the person authorized to receive money or property belonging to the minor. See Sections 3400–3402. If waiver is by the guardian of the estate of the minor, approval of the guardianship court is not required. Similarly, paragraph (3) of subdivision (b) permits a conservator of the estate to waive the account without approval of the conservatorship court. Paragraph (4) of subdivision (b) permits a trustee who has consented to act to waive the account on behalf of the trust.

A guardian, conservator, trustee, or personal representative who waives accounting under this section acts in a fiduciary capacity and is held to the same standard that applies to other actions taken in the fiduciary capacity.

Background on Section 10954 of Repealed Code

Section 10954 was added by 1988 Cal.Stat. ch. 1199 § 91. The section restated former Probate Code Section 933 (repealed by 1988

Cal.Stat. ch. 1199 § 54.5), but excluded from those whose waiver is required beneficiaries whose interest will be satisfied in full. The section also made clear that an unpaid creditor may seek to require an account notwithstanding a waiver by beneficiaries. In subdivision (b)(4) of Section 10954, a reference to the trustee's written acceptance of the trust replaced the former reference to a trustee's consent to act, and a provision excusing court approval was added for court-supervised trusts. See Section 15600 (acceptance of trust by trustee). Court approval was also excused in subdivision (b)(5) for waiver by the personal representative. Subdivision (b)(6) was substituted for the former provision precluding waiver if a person entitled to distribution is unascertained.

For background on the provisions of this part, see the Comment to this part under the part heading. [20 Cal.L.Rev.Comm.Reports 1001 (1990)].

Cross References

Final accounts or reports in estates with nonresident beneficiaries, probate rules, see California Rules of Court, Rule 7.551.

CHAPTER 3. SETTLEMENT OF ACCOUNT

Cross References

Application of old and new law, see Probate Code § 3.

§ 11000. Notice of hearing; persons given; contents

(a) The personal representative shall give notice of the hearing as provided in Section 1220 to all of the following persons:

(1) Each person listed in Section 1220.

(2) Each known heir whose interest in the estate would be affected by the account.

(3) Each known devisee whose interest in the estate would be affected by the account.

(4) The Attorney General, at the office of the Attorney General in Sacramento, if any portion of the estate is to escheat to the state and its interest would be affected by the account.

(5) If the estate is insolvent, each creditor who has filed a claim that is allowed or approved but is unpaid in whole or in part.

(b) If the petition for approval of the account requests allowance of all or a portion of the compensation of the personal representative or the attorney for the personal representative, the notice of hearing shall so state.

(c) If the account is a final account and is filed together with a petition for an order for final distribution of the estate, the notice of hearing shall so state. *(Stats.1990, c. 79 (A.B.759), § 14, operative July 1, 1991. Amended by Stats. 1990, c. 710 (S.B.1775), § 40, operative July 1, 1991.)*

Law Revision Commission Comments
1990 Enactment and Amendment

Section 11000 (enacted as a part of the new Probate Code by 1990 Cal.Stat. ch. 79 § 14) was amended by 1990 Cal.Stat. ch. 710 § 40. As originally enacted in the new Probate Code, Section 11000 revised Section 11000 of the repealed Probate Code to reflect the fact that Assembly Bill 831 of the 1989–1990 regular session would have substituted an agreed fee system for the statutory fee system for probate attorney fees. However, Assembly Bill 831 was not enacted, and Section 11000 of the new Probate Code was amended by 1990 Cal.Stat. ch. 710 § 40 to reflect this fact. See the Comment to Section 900.

Section 11000 as amended continues Section 11000 of the repealed Probate Code without change. For general provisions relating to notice of hearing, see Sections 1200–1220. See also Sections 1206 (notice to known heirs or devisees), 1215–1217 (mailing in general), 1250–1252 (request for special notice), 1260–1265 (proof of giving notice).

Background on Section 11000 of Repealed Code

Section 11000 was added by 1988 Cal.Stat. ch. 1199 § 91. Subdivisions (a) and (b) restated subdivisions (b) and (c) of former Probate Code Section 926 (repealed by 1988 Cal.Stat. ch. 1199 § 54.5) without substantive change. Subdivisions (b)(4) and (c) were new. Subdivision (d) restated the first portion of the second sentence of subdivision (a) of former Probate Code Section 926 (repealed by 1988 Cal.Stat. ch. 1199 § 54.5) without substantive change. For background on the provisions of this part, see the Comment to this part under the part heading. [20 Cal.L.Rev.Comm.Reports 1001 (1990)].

Cross References

Continuance of administration, see Probate Code § 11640.
Escheat, see Probate Code § 6800 et seq.; Code of Civil Procedure § 1300 et seq.
Final distribution, generally, see Probate Code § 11600 et seq.
Notice, see Probate Code § 1200 et seq.
Partition before distribution, notice of hearing, see Probate Code § 11952.

§ 11001. Contesting for cause

All matters relating to an account may be contested for cause shown, including, but not limited to:

(a) The validity of an allowed or approved claim not reported in a previous account and not established by judgment.

(b) The value of property for purposes of distribution.

(c) Actions taken by the personal representative not previously authorized or approved by the court, subject to Section 10590 (Independent Administration of Estates Act). *(Stats.1990, c. 79 (A.B.759), § 14, operative July 1, 1991.)*

Law Revision Commission Comments
1990 Enactment

Section 11001 continues Section 11001 of the repealed Probate Code without change. See also Section 1043 (response or objection).

Subdivision (b) permits a contest of the value of property for purposes of distribution only, and not of the inventory and appraisal; a separate procedure is provided for a direct contest of appraisal values. See Section 8906 (objection to appraisal). Subdivision (c) makes clear the right of an interested person to obtain court review of actions by the personal representative through a contest of an account.

Background on Section 11001 of Repealed Code

Section 11001 was added by 1988 Cal.Stat. ch. 1199 § 91. The section restated the first and fourth sentences of former Probate Code Section 927 (repealed by 1988 Cal.Stat. ch. 1199 § 54.5). Subdivision (c) was a new provision. For background on the provisions of this part, see the Comment to this part under the part heading. [20 Cal.L.Rev.Comm.Reports 1001 (1990)].

Cross References

Allowed claims, contesting validity of, see Probate Code § 9254.
Notice, creditors, see Probate Code § 9001 et seq.
Persons interested in the estate,
  Accounting by interested person or personal representative, see Probate Code § 10950.
  Allowed claims, contest of validity, see Probate Code § 9254.
  Borrowing money and mortgaging of property, see Probate Code § 9802.
  Contests before probate, see Probate Code § 8004.
  Contests of petition, hearing, see Probate Code § 1043.
  Final distribution, petition for, see Probate Code §§ 11600 et seq., 11640.
  Lease of property, see Probate Code § 9943.
  Petition for probate, see Probate Code § 8000.
  Preliminary distribution, petition for, see Probate Code § 11600 et seq.
  Proration of federal estate taxes among, see Probate Code § 20110.
  Removal of executor or administrator, see Probate Code § 8500.
  Sale of property, petition for order requiring, see Probate Code § 10001.
Real party in interest, necessity of prosecution in name of, see Code of Civil Procedure § 367.
Referees' fees, see Code of Civil Procedure § 1023.
References and trials by referees, see Code of Civil Procedure § 638 et seq.

§ 11002. Hearings; appearance by personal representative; referee examination of account; compensation of referee

(a) The court may conduct any hearing that may be necessary to settle the account, and may cite the personal representative to appear before the court for examination.

(b) The court may appoint one or more referees to examine the account and make a report on the account, subject to confirmation by the court. The court may allow a reasonable compensation to the referee to be paid out of the estate.

(c) The court may make any orders that the court deems necessary to effectuate the provisions of this section. *(Stats. 1990, c. 79 (A.B.759), § 14, operative July 1, 1991.)*

Law Revision Commission Comments
1990 Enactment

Section 11002 continues Section 11002 of the repealed Probate Code without change. There is no jury trial of a contest of an allowed claim. See Section 7200 (trial by jury). For general provisions, see Sections 1000–1004 (rules of practice), 1040–1050 (hearings and orders), 1240–1242 (citations), 1260–1265 (proof of giving notice of hearing). The provision for payment of referee compensation out of the estate is subject to Section 11003 (litigation expenses).

Background on Section 11002 of Repealed Code

Section 11002 was added by 1988 Cal.Stat. ch. 1199 § 91. The section restated the third and fifth sentences of former Probate Code Section 927 (repealed by 1988 Cal.Stat. ch. 1199 § 54.5), replacing the provision for examination under oath with a provision for a citation. The provision of former Probate Code Section 928 (repealed by 1988 Cal.Stat. ch. 1199 § 54.5) for jury trial of a contest of an allowed claim was not continued. For background on the provisions of this part, see the Comment to this part under the part heading. [20 Cal.L.Rev.Comm.Reports 1001 (1990)].

§ 11003. Costs; attorney fees; liability of contestant or personal representative found in bad faith

(a) If the court determines that the contest was without reasonable cause and in bad faith, the court may award against the contestant the compensation and costs of the personal representative and other expenses and costs of litigation, including attorney's fees, incurred to defend the account. The amount awarded is a charge against any interest of the contestant in the estate and the contestant is personally liable for any amount that remains unsatisfied.

(b) If the court determines that the opposition to the contest was without reasonable cause and in bad faith, the court may award the contestant the costs of the contestant and other expenses and costs of litigation, including attorney's fees, incurred to contest the account. The amount awarded is a charge against the compensation or other interest of the personal representative in the estate and the personal representative is liable personally and on the bond, if any, for any amount that remains unsatisfied. *(Stats.1990, c. 79 (A.B.759), § 14, operative July 1, 1991.)*

Law Revision Commission Comments

1990 Enactment

Section 11003 continues Section 11003 of the repealed Probate Code without change. Litigation costs under Section 11003 include the costs of a referee appointed under Section 11002.

Background on Section 11003 of Repealed Code

Section 11003 was added by 1988 Cal.Stat. ch. 1199 § 91. Subdivision (a) superseded the second sentence of former Probate Code Section 927 (repealed by 1988 Cal.Stat. ch. 1199 § 54.5). Subdivision (b) was a new provision. For background on the provisions of this part, see the Comment to this part under the part heading. [20 Cal.L.Rev.Comm.Reports 1001 (1990)].

§ 11004. Expenses of personal representative

The personal representative shall be allowed all necessary expenses in the administration of the estate, including, but not limited to, necessary expenses in the care, management, preservation, and settlement of the estate. *(Stats.1990, c. 79 (A.B.759), § 14, operative July 1, 1991.)*

Law Revision Commission Comments

1990 Enactment

Section 11004 continues Section 11004 of the repealed Probate Code without change. The section permits expenses such as insurance, gardening, pool maintenance, and maintenance of property pending sale or distribution to be paid from the estate.

Background on Section 11004 of Repealed Code

Section 11004 was added by 1988 Cal.Stat. ch. 1199 § 91. The section restated a provision formerly found in Probate Code Section 900 (as that section existed prior to its amendment by 1988 Cal.Stat. ch. 1199 § 54.3). The section generalized the former language that provided for allowance of expenses in the care, management, and settlement of the estate. The section was amended by 1989 Cal.Stat. ch. 21 § 27 to make clear that the phrase "necessary expenses in the

administration of the estate" includes the necessary expenses in the care, management, preservation, and settlement of the estate; this amendment did not make a substantive change in the section. See Communication from the California Law Revision Commission Concerning Assembly Bill 156, 20 Cal.L.Revision Comm'n Reports 227, 231–32 (1990). For background on the provisions of this part, see the Comment to this part under the part heading. [20 Cal.L.Rev.Comm.Reports 1001 (1990)].

§ 11005. Debt paid without claim filed

If a debt has been paid within the time prescribed in Section 9154 but without a claim having been filed and established in the manner prescribed by statute, in settling the account the court shall allow the amount paid if all of the following are proven:

(a) The debt was justly due.

(b) The debt was paid in good faith.

(c) The amount paid did not exceed the amount reasonably necessary to satisfy the indebtedness.

(d) The estate is solvent. *(Stats.1990, c. 79 (A.B.759), § 14, operative July 1, 1991.)*

Law Revision Commission Comments

1990 Enactment

Section 11005 continues Section 11005 of the repealed Probate Code without change.

Background on Section 11005 of Repealed Code

Section 11005 was added by 1988 Cal.Stat. ch. 1199 § 91. The section restated former Probate Code Section 929 (repealed by 1988 Cal.Stat. ch. 1199 § 54.5), substituting the phrase "did not exceed the amount reasonably necessary to satisfy the indebtedness" for the phrase "was the true amount of such indebtedness" in subdivision (c). The addition of the limitation that the debt shall have been paid within the time prescribed in Section 9154 (claim filing period plus 30 days) codified the effect of existing case law. Cf. Estate of Erwin, 117 Cal.App.2d 203, 255 P.2d 97 (1953) (claim not made within claim filing period). For background on the provisions of this part, see the Comment to this part under the part heading. [20 Cal.L.Rev.Comm.Reports 1001 (1990)].

Cross References

Affidavits, verification, see Code of Civil Procedure § 2009.
Allowance or rejection of claims, see Probate Code § 9250.
Claims, vouchers of proof, see Probate Code § 9151.
Judges at chambers, approval of claims, see Code of Civil Procedure § 166.
Order of payment of decedent's debts, see Probate Code § 11420.
Powers and duties of joint personal representatives, see Probate Code § 9630.
Presentation and payment of claims, see Probate Code § 9001 et seq.
Special administrator, verified account of, see Probate Code § 8546.

§ 11006. Repealed by Stats.1989, c. 544, § 17

Law Revision Commission Comments

Section 11006 of the repealed Probate Code is omitted from the new Probate Code because the effect of an order settling an account is now governed by Section 7250 (effect of order made pursuant to provisions of this code concerning the administration of the decedent's estate). [20 Cal.L.Rev.Comm.Reports 1001 (1990)].

CHAPTER 4. COMPELLING ACCOUNT

Cross References

Failure to file inventory and appraisal, compelled filing pursuant to this chapter, see Probate Code § 8804.

§ 11050. Failure to file account; contempt

Subject to the provisions of this chapter, if the personal representative does not file a required account, the court shall compel the account by punishment for contempt. *(Stats.1990, c. 79 (A.B.759), § 14, operative July 1, 1991.)*

Law Revision Commission Comments

1990 Enactment

Section 11050 continues Section 11050 of the repealed Probate Code without change. This chapter may also be used to compel an account by a personal representative whose authority is terminated. See Section 10952. See also Section 8804 (use of procedure in this chapter to compel filing of inventory and appraisal).

Background on Section 11050 of Repealed Code

Section 11050 was added by 1988 Cal.Stat. ch. 1199 § 91. The section restated the third sentence of former Probate Code Section 922 (repealed by 1988 Cal.Stat. ch. 1199 § 54.5) without substantive change. For background on the provisions of this part, see the Comment to this part under the part heading. [20 Cal.L.Rev.Comm.Reports 1001 (1990)].

§ 11051. Citation; appearance to show cause; avoiding service; removal from office

(a) A citation shall be issued, served, and returned, requiring a personal representative who does not file a required account to appear and show cause why the personal representative should not be punished for contempt.

(b) If the personal representative purposefully evades personal service of the citation, the personal representative shall be removed from office. *(Stats.1990, c. 79 (A.B.759), § 14, operative July 1, 1991.)*

Law Revision Commission Comments

1990 Enactment

Section 11051 continues Section 11051 of the repealed Probate Code without change. See also Sections 1240–1242 (citations).

Background on Section 11051 of Repealed Code

Section 11051 was added by 1988 Cal.Stat. ch. 1199 § 91. Subdivision (a) restated the last sentence of former Probate Code Section 922 (repealed by 1988 Cal.Stat. ch. 1199 § 54.5) without substantive change. Subdivision (b) restated a portion of former Probate Code Section 924 (repealed by 1988 Cal.Stat. ch. 1199 § 54.5) without substantive change. For background on the provisions of this part, see the Comment to this part under the part heading. [20 Cal.L.Rev.Comm.Reports 1001 (1990)].

Cross References

Removal from office,
  Generally, see Probate Code § 8500.
  Contempt, see Probate Code § 8505.

Embezzlement, waste or mismanagement, see Probate Code § 8502.

§ 11052. Failure to appear and file account; contempt; removal from office

If the personal representative does not appear and file a required account, after having been duly cited, the personal representative may be punished for contempt or removed from office, or both, in the discretion of the court. *(Stats. 1990, c. 79 (A.B.759), § 14, operative July 1, 1991.)*

Law Revision Commission Comments

1990 Enactment

Section 11052 continues Section 11052 of the repealed Probate Code without change. See also Section 8505 (removal from office for contempt).

Background on Section 11052 of Repealed Code

Section 11052 was added by 1988 Cal.Stat. ch. 1199 § 91. The section restated the last sentence of former Probate Code Section 921 and restated a portion of former Probate Code Section 924 (provisions repealed by 1988 Cal.Stat. ch. 1199 § 54.5) without substantive change. For background on the provisions of this part, see the Comment to this part under the part heading. [20 Cal.L.Rev.Comm.Reports 1001 (1990)].

Part 9

PAYMENT OF DEBTS

Application

Application of Part 9 to proceedings for the administration of decedents' estates commenced before July 1, 1988, see Probate Code § 11405.

Law Revision Commission Comments

1990 Enactment

This part supersedes Part 9 (commencing with Section 11400) of Division 7 of the repealed Probate Code. The superseded part was enacted upon recommendation of the California Law Revision Commission. See *Recommendation Relating to Creditor Claims Against Decedent's Estate,* 19 Cal.L.Revision Comm'n Reports 299 (1988). [20 Cal.L.Rev.Comm.Reports 1001 (1990)].

Cross References

Preferred claims for purposes of labor standards enforcement, work performed or personal services rendered under this part, see Labor Code § 100.5.

CHAPTER 1. DEFINITIONS AND PRELIMINARY PROVISIONS

Application

Application of Part 9 to proceedings for the admin-istration of decedents' estates commenced before July 1, 1988, see Probate Code § 11405.

ARTICLE 1.   DEFINITIONS

Section
11400.   Application of definitions.
11401.   Debt.
11402.   Wage claim.

Application

Application of Part 9 to proceedings for the admin-istration of decedents' estates commenced before July 1, 1988, see Probate Code § 11405.

§ 11400.   Application of definitions

Unless the provision or context otherwise requires, the definitions in this article govern the construction of this part. *(Stats.1990, c. 79 (A.B.759), § 14, operative July 1, 1991.)*

Application

Application of Part 9 to proceedings for the admin-istration of decedents' estates commenced before July 1, 1988, see Probate Code § 11405.

Law Revision Commission Comments

1990 Enactment

Section 11400 continues Section 11400 of the repealed Probate Code without change. This part does not apply in any proceeding for administration of a decedent's estate commenced before July 1, 1988. See Section 11405. As to the application of any amendments made after that date, see Section 3.

Background on Section 11400 of Repealed Code

Section 11400 was a new provision added by 1987 Cal.Stat. ch. 923 § 93. [20 Cal.L.Rev.Comm.Reports 1001 (1990)].

§ 11401.   Debt

"Debt" means:

(a) A claim that is established under Part 4 (commencing with Section 9000) or that is otherwise payable in the course of administration.

(b) An expense of administration.

(c) A charge against the estate including, but not limited to, taxes, expenses of last illness, and family allowance. *(Stats.1990, c. 79 (A.B.759), § 14, operative July 1, 1991.)*

Application

Application of Part 9 to proceedings for the admin-istration of decedents' estates commenced before July 1, 1988, see Probate Code § 11405.

Law Revision Commission Comments

1990 Enactment

Section 11401 continues Section 11401 of the repealed Probate Code without change. Subdivision (a) includes debts payable under the Independent Administration of Estates Act that are not estab-lished under Section 9000 et seq. (creditor claims), as well as other debts paid even though not presented through the formal claim procedure. See Sections 9154 (waiver of formal defects), 11005

(accounts), 11422 (payment of debts on court order). This part does not apply in any proceeding for administration of a decedent's estate commenced before July 1, 1988. See Section 11405. As to the application of any amendments made after that date, see Section 3.

Background on Section 11401 of Repealed Code

Section 11401 was added by 1987 Cal.Stat. ch. 923 § 93. The section superseded the introductory portion of former Probate Code Section 950 (repealed by 1987 Cal.Stat. ch. 923 § 48). [20 Cal.L.Rev.Comm.Reports 1001 (1990)].

§ 11402.   Wage claim

"Wage claim" means a claim for wages, not exceeding two thousand dollars ($2,000), of each employee of the decedent for work done or personal services rendered within 90 days before the death of the decedent. *(Stats.1990, c. 79 (A.B. 759), § 14, operative July 1, 1991.)*

Application

Application of Part 9 to proceedings for the admin-istration of decedents' estates commenced before July 1, 1988, see Probate Code § 11405.

Law Revision Commission Comments

1990 Enactment

Section 11402 continues Section 11402 of the repealed Probate Code without change. This part does not apply in any proceeding for administration of a decedent's estate commenced before July 1, 1988. See Section 11405. As to the application of any amendments made after that date, see Section 3.

Background on Section 11402 of Repealed Code

Section 11402 was added by 1987 Cal.Stat. ch. 923 § 93. The section restated the first sentence of paragraph (6) of former Probate Code Section 950 and a portion of former Probate Code Section 951 (provisions repealed by 1987 Cal.Stat. ch. 923 § 48) and increased the amount from $900 to $2,000. [20 Cal.L.Rev.Comm.Reports 1001 (1990)].

ARTICLE 2.   PROCEEDINGS COMMENCED BEFORE JULY 1, 1988

Section
11405.   Application of part; continued application of prior law.

§ 11405.   Application of part; continued application of prior law

(a) This part does not apply in any proceeding for the administration of a decedent's estate commenced before July 1, 1988.

(b) The applicable law in effect before July 1, 1988, governing the subject matter of this part continues to apply in any proceeding for administration of a decedent's estate commenced before July 1, 1988, notwithstanding its repeal by Chapter 923 of the Statutes of 1987. *(Stats.1990, c. 79 (A.B.759), § 14, operative July 1, 1991.)*

Law Revision Commission Comments

1990 Enactment

Section 11405 continues Section 11405 of the repealed Probate Code without substantive change.

Section 11405 was a new provision added by 1987 Cal.Stat. ch. 923 § 93. [20 Cal.L.Rev.Comm.Reports 1001 (1990)].

CHAPTER 2. GENERAL PROVISIONS

Application

Application of Part 9 to proceedings for the administration of decedents' estates commenced before July 1, 1988, see Probate Code § 11405.

§ 11420. Debt classes; priorities; priority within class; proportionate shares

(a) Debts shall be paid in the following order of priority among classes of debts, except that debts owed to the United States or to this state that have preference under the laws of the United States or of this state shall be given the preference required by such laws:

(1) Expenses of administration. With respect to obligations secured by mortgage, deed of trust, or other lien, including, but not limited to, a judgment lien, only those expenses of administration incurred that are reasonably related to the administration of that property by which obligations are secured shall be given priority over these obligations.

(2) Obligations secured by a mortgage, deed of trust, or other lien, including, but not limited to, a judgment lien, in the order of their priority, so far as they may be paid out of the proceeds of the property subject to the lien. If the proceeds are insufficient, the part of the obligation remaining unsatisfied shall be classed with general debts.

(3) Funeral expenses.

(4) Expenses of last illness.

(5) Family allowance.

(6) Wage claims.

(7) General debts, including judgments not secured by a lien and all other debts not included in a prior class.

(b) Except as otherwise provided by statute, the debts of each class are without preference or priority one over another. No debt of any class may be paid until all those of prior classes are paid in full. If property in the estate is insufficient to pay all debts of any class in full, each debt in that class shall be paid a proportionate share. *(Stats.1990, c.*

79 *(A.B.759), § 14, operative July 1, 1991. Amended by Stats.1996, c. 862 (A.B.2751), § 33.)*

Application

Application of Part 9 to proceedings for the administration of decedents' estates commenced before July 1, 1988, see Probate Code § 11405.

Law Revision Commission Comments

1990 Enactment

Section 11420 continues Section 11420 of the repealed Probate Code without change. See also Section 9807 (payment of established claim where resort to security insufficient to pay claim). This part does not apply in any proceeding for administration of a decedent's estate commenced before July 1, 1988. See Section 11405. As to the application of any amendments made after that date, see Section 3.

Background on Section 11420 of Repealed Code

Section 11420 was added by 1987 Cal.Stat. ch. 923 § 93. Subdivision (a) restated former Probate Code Section 950 (repealed by 1987 Cal.Stat. ch. 923 § 48), except that Section 11420 made clear that preferred debts owed to the United States and to California must be recognized to the extent required by law. See, e.g., Rev. & Tax.Code § 19265 (priority of claim for taxes under Personal Income Tax Law). Subdivision (b) restated the third sentence of former Probate Code Section 952 without substantive change and superseded the last sentence of former Probate Code Section 953 (provisions repealed by 1987 Cal.Stat. ch. 923 § 48). [20 Cal.L.Rev.Comm.Reports 1001 (1990)].

Cross References

Abatement of shares of beneficiaries, see Probate Code § 21401.
Family allowance, generally, see Probate Code § 6540 et seq.
Interest on debts to cease on payment, see Probate Code § 11423.
Notes and mortgages, generally, see Probate Code § 9800 et seq.
Preferred claims and liens, filing by Division of Labor Standards Enforcement, see Labor Code § 99 et seq.
Priority of liens, generally, see Civil Code § 2897 et seq.
Recordation of mortgages, generally, see Civil Code § 2952.
Rules as to payment of claims, see Probate Code § 9300 et seq.
Special administrators, payment of lien charges on property, see Probate Code § 8544.
Wage claims, priority of payment by guardian and conservator, see Probate Code § 2431.

§ 11421. Debts to be paid when there are sufficient funds after covering administration expenses

Subject to Section 11420, as soon as the personal representative has sufficient funds, after retaining sufficient funds to pay expenses of administration, the personal representative shall pay the following:

(a) Funeral expenses.

(b) Expenses of last illness.

(c) Family allowance.

(d) Wage claims. *(Stats.1990, c. 79 (A.B.759), § 14, operative July 1, 1991.)*

Application

Application of Part 9 to proceedings for the administration of decedents' estates commenced before July 1, 1988, see Probate Code § 11405.

Law Revision Commission Comments
1990 Enactment

Section 11421 continues Section 11421 of the repealed Probate Code without change. The introductory clause recognizes that the order of priority for payment of funeral expenses, expenses of last illness, family allowance, and wage claims is the basic order of priority provided in Section 11420. Section 11421 is an exception to the rule of Section 11422 (payment of debts on court order) in that payment under Section 11421 is required even though the court has not ordered payment. This part does not apply in any proceeding for administration of a decedent's estate commenced before July 1, 1988. See Section 11405. As to the application of any amendments made after that date, see Section 3.

Background on Section 11421 of Repealed Code

Section 11421 was added by 1987 Cal.Stat. ch. 923 § 93 and was amended by 1988 Cal.Stat. ch. 113 § 15.3. The section as enacted restated the first portion of former Probate Code Section 951 (repealed by 1987 Cal.Stat. ch. 923 § 48), but added a reference to "debts owed to the United States or to this state that have preference under the laws of the United States or of this state." The 1988 amendment deleted this addition. The amendment recognized that such debts are not given preference over expenses of administration or charges against the estate, but only over other debts due from the decedent. See, e.g., Estate of Muldoon, 128 Cal.App.2d 284, 275 P.2d 597 (1954) (federal preference); Estate of Jacobs, 61 Cal. App.2d 152, 142 P.2d 454 (1943) (state preference). See Section 11420 and the Comment thereto. See also Rev. & Tax.Code § 19265 (personal income tax priority over claims other than taxes, expenses of administration, funeral expenses, expenses of last illness, family allowance, and wage claims). The amendment also had the effect of reinstating the priority given wage claims by former Probate Code Section 951. For background on the 1988 amendment, see *Communication from the California Law Revision Commission Concerning Assembly Bill 2779*, 19 Cal.L.Revision Comm'n Reports 1191, 1194 (1988). [20 Cal.L.Rev.Comm.Reports 1001 (1990)].

Cross References

Borrowing money to pay debts, expenses and claims, see Probate Code § 9800.
Federal estate tax, payment, see Probate Code § 20100 et seq.
Funeral expense payment before grant of letters, see Probate Code § 8400.
Powers and duties of joint personal representatives, see Probate Code § 9630 et seq.
Rules as to payment of claims, see Probate Code § 9300 et seq.
Wage claims, payment by guardian or conservator, see Probate Code § 2431.

§ 11422. Payment of debt not required until ordered by court; exceptions; court order to pay debts; final account and hearing

(a) Except as provided in Section 11421, the personal representative is not required to pay a debt until payment has been ordered by the court.

(b) On the settlement of any account of the personal representative after the expiration of four months after the date letters are first issued to a general personal representative, the court shall order payment of debts, as the circumstances of the estate permit. If property in the estate is insufficient to pay all of the debts, the order shall specify the amount to be paid to each creditor.

(c) If the estate will be exhausted by the payment ordered, the account of the personal representative constitutes a final account, and notice of hearing shall be the notice given for the hearing of a final account. The personal representative is entitled to a discharge when the personal representative has complied with the terms of the order.

(d) Nothing in this section precludes settlement of an account of a personal representative for payment of a debt made without prior court authorization. *(Stats.1990, c. 79 (A.B.759), § 14, operative July 1, 1991.)*

Application

Application of Part 9 to proceedings for the administration of decedents' estates commenced before July 1, 1988, see Probate Code § 11405.

Law Revision Commission Comments
1990 Enactment

Section 11422 continues Section 11422 of the repealed Probate Code without change. This section makes clear that the notice of hearing of an account that will result in the estate being exhausted must comply with the requirements for notice of hearing of a final account. See Section 11000 (final account). Discharge may be obtained by court order. Section 12250 (order of discharge). For approval of the personal representative's account where payment is made without prior court order, see Section 11005 (accounts). See also Section 9154 (waiver of formal defects). This part does not apply in any proceeding for administration of a decedent's estate commenced before July 1, 1988. See Section 11405. As to the application of any amendments made after that date, see Section 3.

Background on Section 11422 of Repealed Code

Section 11422 was added by 1987 Cal.Stat. ch. 923 § 93. Subdivision (a) restated the last portion of former Probate Code Section 951 (repealed by 1987 Cal.Stat. ch. 923 § 48) without substantive change. Subdivisions (b) and (c) restated the first, second, and fourth sentences of former Probate Code Section 952 (repealed by 1987 Cal.Stat. ch. 923 § 48) without substantive change. Subdivision (d) was new. [20 Cal.L.Rev.Comm.Reports 1001 (1990)].

Cross References

Appeals, order for payment of debt, see Probate Code § 7240.
Borrowing money to pay claims, see Probate Code § 9800 et seq.
Discharge for want of property subject to administration, see Probate Code § 12251.
Final discharge after distribution, see Probate Code § 12250.
Final distribution, see Probate Code § 11600 et seq.
Orders, see Probate Code § 1047.
Powers and duties of joint personal representative, see Probate Code § 9630 et seq.
Preliminary distribution, see Probate Code § 11600 et seq.
Presentation of claims, see Probate Code § 9100 et seq.
Rules as to payment of claims, see Probate Code § 9300 et seq.

§ 11423. Interest on debt; accrual; rate

(a) Interest accrues on a debt from the date the court orders payment of the debt until the date the debt is paid. Interest accrues at the legal rate on judgments.

(b) Notwithstanding subdivision (a), in the case of a debt based on a written contract, interest accrues at the rate and in accordance with the terms of the contract. The personal representative may, by order of the court, pay all or part of the interest accumulated and unpaid at any time when there are sufficient funds, whether the debt is then due or not.

(c) Notwithstanding subdivision (a), in the case of a debt for unpaid taxes or any other debt for which interest is expressly provided by statute, interest accrues at the rate and in accordance with the terms of the statute. *(Stats.1990, c. 79 (A.B.759), § 14, operative July 1, 1991.)*

Application

Application of Part 9 to proceedings for the administration of decedents' estates commenced before July 1, 1988, see Probate Code § 11405.

Law Revision Commission Comments

1990 Enactment

Section 11423 continues Section 11423 of the repealed Probate Code without change. The legal rate of interest on judgments is provided in Code of Civil Procedure Section 685.010. For special statutory rates of interest, see, e.g., Rev. & Tax.Code §§ 19269 (adjusted annual rate under Personal Income Tax Law), 6591.5 (modified adjusted rate under Sales and Use Tax Law). In the case of a debt reduced to judgment, interest commences on entry of the judgment. Code Civ.Proc. § 685.020. This part does not apply in any proceeding for administration of a decedent's estate commenced before July 1, 1988. See Section 11405. As to the application of any amendments made after that date, see Section 3.

Background on Section 11423 of Repealed Code

Section 11423 was added by 1987 Cal.Stat. ch. 923 § 93. The section superseded former Probate Code Section 733 (repealed by 1987 Cal.Stat. ch. 923 § 37). [20 Cal.L.Rev.Comm.Reports 1001 (1990)].

§ 11424. Liability of personal representative for failure to pay debt

The personal representative shall pay a debt to the extent of the order for payment of the debt, and is liable personally and on the bond, if any, for failure to make the payment. *(Stats.1990, c. 79 (A.B.759), § 14, operative July 1, 1991.)*

Application

Application of Part 9 to proceedings for the administration of decedents' estates commenced before July 1, 1988, see Probate Code § 11405.

Law Revision Commission Comments

1990 Enactment

Section 11424 continues Section 11424 of the repealed Probate Code with the omission of subdivision (b). The omitted subdivision is unnecessary in view of Section 1049 (enforcement of orders). For provisions on abatement of devises, see Sections 21400–21406. This part does not apply in any proceeding for administration of a decedent's estate commenced before July 1, 1988. See Section 11405. As to the application of any amendments made after that date, see Section 3.

Background on Section 11424 of Repealed Code

Section 11424 was added by 1987 Cal.Stat. ch. 923 § 93. The section restated former Probate Code Section 954 (repealed by 1987 Cal.Stat. ch. 923 § 48) without substantive change. [20 Cal.L.Rev.Comm.Reports 1001 (1990)].

Cross References

Execution of judgments in civil actions, see Code of Civil Procedure § 683.010 et seq.
Nature of liability on bond, see Code of Civil Procedure § 996.460 et seq.
Notice,
  Generally, see Probate Code § 1200 et seq.
  Petition to administer estate, see Probate Code § 8121.

Promise of executor or administrator to pay claims to be in writing, see Probate Code § 9604.
Rules as to payments of claims, see Probate Code § 9300 et seq.

§§ 11425 to 11427. Repealed by Stats.1991, c. 1055 (S.B. 271), §§ 28 to 30

Law Revision Commission Comments

1991 Repeal

Former Section 11425 is not continued. It is superseded by Section 11462 (agreement of interested persons). [20 Cal.L.Rev.Comm.Reports 2707 (1990)].

Former Section 11426 is continued in Section 11465 (appointment of trustee) and broadened to apply to debts that are disputed or otherwise not due as well as debts that are contingent or payable in installments. [20 Cal.L.Rev.Comm.Reports 2707 (1990)].

Former Section 11427 is continued in Section 11463 (deposit in account withdrawable only on court order), except that the deposit in court is replaced by deposit in a blocked account. [20 Cal.L.Rev.Comm.Reports 2707 (1990)].

§ 11428. Debts unpayable because creditor cannot be found; deposit of payment with county treasurer; receipt; disposition of deposit

(a) If an estate is in all other respects ready to be closed, and it appears to the satisfaction of the court, on affidavit or evidence taken in open court, that a debt has not been and cannot be paid because the creditor cannot be found, the court or judge shall make an order fixing the amount of the payment and directing the personal representative to deposit the payment with the county treasurer of the county in which the proceeding is pending.

(b) The county treasurer shall give a receipt for the deposit, for which the county treasurer is liable on the official bond. The receipt shall be treated by the court or judge in favor of the personal representative with the same force and effect as if executed by the creditor.

(c) A deposit with the county treasurer under the provisions of this section shall be received, accounted for, and disposed of as provided by Section 1444 of the Code of Civil Procedure. A deposit in the State Treasury under the provisions of this section shall be deemed to be made under the provisions of Article 1 (commencing with Section 1440) of Chapter 6 of Title 10 of Part 3 of the Code of Civil Procedure. *(Stats.1990, c. 79 (A.B.759), § 14, operative July 1, 1991.)*

Application

Application of Part 9 to proceedings for the administration of decedents' estates commenced before July 1, 1988, see Probate Code § 11405.

Law Revision Commission Comments

1990 Enactment

Section 11428 continues Section 11428 of the repealed Probate Code without change. The amount of the deposit under this section includes interest on the debt from the date payment was ordered. See Section 11423 (interest). This part does not apply in any proceeding for administration of a decedent's estate commenced before July 1, 1988. See Section 11405. As to the application of any amendments made after that date, see Section 3.

Section 11428 was added by 1987 Cal.Stat. ch. 923 § 93. The section restated former Probate Code Section 738 (repealed by 1987 Cal.Stat. ch. 923 § 37) without substantive change. [20 Cal.L.Rev.Comm.Reports 1001 (1990)].

Cross References

Deposits with county treasurer, see Code of Civil Procedure § 573; Government Code § 68084; Probate Code § 11850 et seq.
Estates of deceased persons, payment to state, see Code of Civil Procedure § 1443.
Money or property delivered under this section, presumption, handling, see Code of Civil Procedure § 1443.
Unclaimed property act, see Code of Civil Procedure §§ 1300 et seq., 1500 et seq.; Financial Code §§ 3121, 3150, 3160 et seq.; Government Code § 13470; Penal Code § 5061 et seq.; Probate Code §§ 6800, 7643, 11854; Welfare and Institutions Code §§ 1015 et seq., 4126 et seq.

§ 11429. Right of contribution among creditors; liability of personal representative

(a) Where the accounts of the personal representative have been settled and an order made for the payment of debts and distribution of the estate, a creditor who is not paid, whether or not included in the order for payment, has no right to require contribution from creditors who are paid or from distributees, except to the extent provided in Section 9392.

(b) Nothing in this section precludes recovery against the personal representative personally or on the bond, if any, by a creditor who is not paid, subject to Section 9053. *(Stats.1990, c. 79 (A.B.759), § 14, operative July 1, 1991. Amended by Stats.1990, c. 140 (S.B.1855), § 14.1, operative July 1, 1991.)*

Application

Application of Part 9 to proceedings for the administration of decedents' estates commenced before July 1, 1988, see Probate Code § 11405.

Law Revision Commission Comments

1990 Enactment

Section 11429 continues Section 11429 of the repealed Probate Code without change. This part does not apply in any proceeding for administration of a decedent's estate commenced before July 1, 1988. See Section 11405. As to the application of any amendments made after that date, see Section 3.

1990 Amendment

Section 11429 (enacted as a part of the new Probate Code by 1990 Cal.Stat. ch. 79 § 14) was amended by 1990 Cal.Stat. ch. 140 § 14.1.

Subdivision (a) was amended to recognize the liability of distributees provided by Section 9392 (liability of distributee).

Subdivision (b) was amended to make specific reference to the statutory immunity of the personal representative for actions and omissions in notifying creditors. This amendment is not a change in law, but is intended for cross-referencing purposes only. The reference to the specific immunity provided in Section 9053 should not be construed to limit the availability of any other applicable defenses of the personal representative.

For background on the 1990 amendment, see Recommendation Relating to Notice to Creditors in Estate Administration, 20 Cal.L. Revision Comm'n Reports 507 (1990). [20 Cal.L.Rev.Comm.Reports 1001 (1990)].

Section 11429 was added by 1987 Cal.Stat. ch. 923 § 93. The section superseded former Probate Code Section 955 (repealed by 1987 Cal.Stat. ch. 923 § 48). [20 Cal.L.Rev.Comm.Reports 1001 (1990)].

Cross References

Oaths, see Probate Code § 8403.
Publication of notice to creditors, see Probate Code § 9001.

CHAPTER 3. ALLOCATION OF DEBTS BETWEEN ESTATE AND SURVIVING SPOUSE

Application

Application of Part 9 to proceedings for the administration of decedents' estates commenced before July 1, 1988, see Probate Code § 11405.

§ 11440. Petition to allocate debt

If it appears that a debt of the decedent has been paid or is payable in whole or in part by the surviving spouse, or that a debt of the surviving spouse has been paid or is payable in whole or in part from property in the decedent's estate, the personal representative, the surviving spouse, or a beneficiary may, at any time before an order for final distribution is made, petition for an order to allocate the debt. *(Stats.1990, c. 79 (A.B.759), § 14, operative July 1, 1991.)*

Application

Application of Part 9 to proceedings for the administration of decedents' estates commenced before July 1, 1988, see Probate Code § 11405.

Law Revision Commission Comments

1990 Enactment

Section 11440 continues Section 11440 of the repealed Probate Code without change. Under this section, a petition may be made for allocation of a debt of the decedent or of the surviving spouse even though the creditor has not made a claim and the debt has not been established under Part 4 (commencing with Section 9000). In this respect, the term "debt" is used in this section more broadly than the definition in Section 11401 ("debt" defined). For general provisions relating to petitions and other papers, see Sections 1020–1023. This part does not apply in any proceeding for administration of a decedent's estate commenced before July 1, 1988. See Section 11405. As to the application of any amendments made after that date, see Section 3.

Section 11440 was added by 1987 Cal.Stat. ch. 923 § 93. The section combined subdivision (a) of former Probate Code Section 980 (repealed by 1987 Cal.Stat. ch. 923 § 48.6) with portions of former Probate Code Sections 704.2 and 704.4 (claim by surviving spouse) (provisions repealed by 1987 Cal.Stat. ch. 923 § 37), but allowed the petition to be made at any time before the court order for final distribution. [20 Cal.L.Rev.Comm.Reports 1001 (1990)].

§ 11441. Contents of petition

The petition shall include a statement of all of the following:

(a) All debts of the decedent and surviving spouse known to the petitioner that are alleged to be subject to allocation and whether paid in whole or part or unpaid.

(b) The reason why the debts should be allocated.

(c) The proposed allocation and the basis for allocation alleged by the petitioner. *(Stats.1990, c. 79 (A.B.759), § 14, operative July 1, 1991.)*

Application

Application of Part 9 to proceedings for the administration of decedents' estates commenced before July 1, 1988, see Probate Code § 11405.

Law Revision Commission Comments

1990 Enactment

Section 11441 continues Section 11441 of the repealed Probate Code without change. The term "debt" is used in this section more broadly than the definition in Section 11401 ("debt" defined). See the Comment to Section 11440. For general provisions relating to petitions and other papers, see Sections 1020–1023. This part does not apply in any proceeding for administration of a decedent's estate commenced before July 1, 1988. See Section 11405. As to the application of any amendments made after that date, see Section 3.

Background on Section 11441 of Repealed Code

Section 11441 was added by 1987 Cal.Stat. ch. 923 § 93. The section combined subdivision (b) of former Probate Code Section 980 (repealed by 1987 Cal.Stat. ch. 923 § 48.6) and portions of former Probate Code Sections 704.2 and 704.4 (provisions repealed by 1987 Cal.Stat. ch. 923 § 37). [20 Cal.L.Rev.Comm.Reports 1001 (1990)].

§ 11442. Value of separate and community property affecting allocation where no inventory and appraisal provided; show cause order

If it appears from the petition that allocation would be affected by the value of the separate property of the surviving spouse and any community property and quasi-community property not administered in the estate and if an inventory and appraisal of the property has not been provided by the surviving spouse, the court shall make an order to show cause why the information should not be provided. *(Stats.1990, c. 79 (A.B.759), § 14, operative July 1, 1991.)*

Application

Application of Part 9 to proceedings for the administration of decedents' estates commenced before July 1, 1988, see Probate Code § 11405.

Law Revision Commission Comments

1990 Enactment

Section 11442 continues Section 11442 of the repealed Probate Code without change. For general provisions relating to hearings and orders, see Sections 1040–1050. This part does not apply in any proceeding for administration of a decedent's estate commenced before July 1, 1988. See Section 11405. As to the application of any amendments made after that date, see Section 3.

Background on Section 11442 of Repealed Code

Section 11442 was added by 1987 Cal.Stat. ch. 923 § 93. The section restated subdivision (c) of former Probate Code Section 980 (repealed by 1987 Cal.Stat. ch. 923 § 48.6) without substantive change and superseded portions of former Probate Code Sections 704.2 and 704.4 (provisions repealed by 1987 Cal.Stat. ch. 923 § 37). [20 Cal.L.Rev.Comm.Reports 1001 (1990)].

§ 11443. Notice of hearing on show cause order

The petitioner shall give notice of the hearing as provided in Section 1220, together with a copy of the petition and the order to show cause, if any. *(Stats.1990, c. 79 (A.B.759), § 14, operative July 1, 1991.)*

Application

Application of Part 9 to proceedings for the administration of decedents' estates commenced before July 1, 1988, see Probate Code § 11405.

Law Revision Commission Comments

1990 Enactment

Section 11443 continues Section 11443 of the repealed Probate Code without change. For general provisions, see Sections 1200–1230 (notice of hearing), 1250–1252 (request for special notice), 1260–1265 (proof of giving of notice). This part does not apply in any proceeding for administration of a decedent's estate commenced before July 1, 1988. See Section 11405. As to the application of any amendments made after that date, see Section 3.

Background on Section 11443 of Repealed Code

Section 11443 was added by 1987 Cal.Stat. ch. 923 § 93. The section superseded subdivision (d) of former Probate Code Section 980 (repealed by 1987 Cal.Stat. ch. 923 § 48.6) and incorporated general service of notice procedures. [20 Cal.L.Rev.Comm.Reports 1001 (1990)].

§ 11444. Allocation of debt

(a) The personal representative and the surviving spouse may provide for allocation by agreement and, on a determination by the court that the agreement substantially protects the rights of interested persons, the allocation provided in the agreement shall be ordered by the court.

(b) In the absence of an agreement, each debt subject to allocation shall first be characterized by the court as separate or community, in accordance with the laws of the state applicable to marital dissolution proceedings. Following that characterization, the debt or debts shall be allocated as follows:

(1) Separate debts of either spouse shall be allocated to that spouse's separate property assets, and community debts shall be allocated to the spouses' community property assets.

(2) If a separate property asset of either spouse is subject to a secured debt that is characterized as that spouse's separate debt, and the net equity in that asset available to satisfy that secured debt is less than that secured debt, the unsatisfied portion of that secured debt shall be treated as an unsecured separate debt of that spouse and allocated to the net value of that spouse's other separate property assets.

(3) If the net value of either spouse's separate property assets is less than that spouse's unsecured separate debt or debts, the unsatisfied portion of the debt or debts shall be allocated to the net value of that spouse's one-half share of

the community property assets. If the net value of that spouse's one-half share of the community property assets is less than that spouse's unsatisfied unsecured separate debt or debts, the remaining unsatisfied portion of the debt or debts shall be allocated to the net value of the other spouse's one-half share of the community property assets.

(4) If a community property asset is subject to a secured debt that is characterized as a community debt, and the net equity in that asset available to satisfy that secured debt is less than that secured debt, the unsatisfied portion of that secured debt shall be treated as an unsecured community debt and allocated to the net value of the other community property assets.

(5) If the net value of the community property assets is less than the unsecured community debt or debts, the unsatisfied portion of the debt or debts shall be allocated equally between the separate property assets of the decedent and the surviving spouse. If the net value of either spouse's separate property assets is less than that spouse's share of the unsatisfied portion of the unsecured community debt or debts, the remaining unsatisfied portion of the debt or debts shall be allocated to the net value of the other spouse's separate property assets.

(c) For purposes of this section:

(1) The net value of either spouse's separate property asset shall refer to its fair market value as of the date of the decedent's death, minus the date-of-death balance of any liens and encumbrances on that asset that have been characterized as that spouse's separate debts.

(2) The net value of a community property asset shall refer to its fair market value as of the date of the decedent's death, minus the date-of-death balance of any liens and encumbrances on that asset that have been characterized as community debts.

(3) In the case of a nonrecourse debt, the amount of that debt shall be limited to the net equity in the collateral, based on the fair market value of the collateral as of the date of the decedent's death, that is available to satisfy that debt. For the purposes of this paragraph, "nonrecourse debt" means a debt for which the debtor's obligation to repay is limited to the collateral securing the debt, and for which a deficiency judgment against the debtor is not permitted by law.

(d) Notwithstanding the foregoing provisions of this section, the court may order a different allocation of debts between the decedent's estate and the surviving spouse if the court finds a different allocation to be equitable under the circumstances.

(e) Nothing contained in this section is intended to impair or affect the rights of third parties. If a personal representative or the surviving spouse incurs any damages or expense, including attorney's fees, on account of the nonpayment of a debt that was allocated to the other party pursuant to subdivision (b), or as the result of a debt being misallocated due to fraud or intentional misrepresentation by the other party, the party incurring damages shall be entitled to recover from the other party for damages or expense deemed reasonable by the court that made the allocation. *(Stats. 1990, c. 79 (A.B.759), § 14, operative July 1, 1991. Amended by Stats.2001, c. 72 (S.B.668), § 1.)*

Application of Part 9 to proceedings for the administration of decedents' estates commenced before July 1, 1988, see Probate Code § 11405.

Law Revision Commission Comments

1990 Enactment

Section 11444 continues Section 11444 of the repealed Probate Code without change. This section makes clear that allocation of liability is to be based on rules applicable to liability of marital property for debts during marriage. See Civil Code Sections 5120.010–5122. This part does not apply in any proceeding for administration of a decedent's estate commenced before July 1, 1988. See Section 11405. As to the application of any amendments made after that date, see Section 3.

Background on Section 11444 of Repealed Code

Section 11444 was added by 1987 Cal.Stat. ch. 923 § 93. The section combined subdivision (e) of former Probate Code Section 980 (repealed by 1987 Cal.Stat. ch. 923 § 48.6) and a portion of former Probate Code Section 713.5 (repealed by 1987 Cal.Stat. ch. 923 § 37). [20 Cal.L.Rev.Comm.Reports 1001 (1990)].

§ 11445. Payment of allocated shares; court order

On making a determination as provided in this chapter, the court shall make an order that:

(a) Directs the personal representative to make payment of the amounts allocated to the estate by payment to the surviving spouse or creditors.

(b) Directs the personal representative to charge amounts allocated to the surviving spouse against any property or interests of the surviving spouse that are in the possession or control of the personal representative. To the extent that property or interests of the surviving spouse in the possession or control of the personal representative are insufficient to satisfy the allocation, the court order shall summarily direct the surviving spouse to pay the allocation to the personal representative. *(Stats.1990, c. 79 (A.B.759), § 14, operative July 1, 1991.)*

Application

Application of Part 9 to proceedings for the administration of decedents' estates commenced before July 1, 1988, see Probate Code § 11405.

Law Revision Commission Comments

1990 Enactment

Section 11445 continues Section 11445 of the repealed Probate Code without change. For general provisions relating to hearings and orders, see Sections 1040–1050. See also Section 7240 (order appealable). This part does not apply in any proceeding for administration of a decedent's estate commenced before July 1, 1988. See Section 11405. As to the application of any amendments made after that date, see Section 3.

Background on Section 11445 of Repealed Code

Section 11445 was added by 1987 Cal.Stat. ch. 923 § 93. The section combined subdivision (f) of former Probate Code Section 980 (repealed by 1987 Cal.Stat. ch. 923 § 48.6) and a portion of former Probate Code Section 713.5 (repealed by 1987 Cal.Stat. ch. 923 § 37). [20 Cal.L.Rev.Comm.Reports 1001 (1990)].

§ 11446. Last illness and funeral expenses

Notwithstanding any other statute, funeral expenses and expenses of last illness shall be charged against the estate of the decedent and shall not be allocated to, or charged against the community share of, the surviving spouse, whether or not the surviving spouse is financially able to pay the expenses and whether or not the surviving spouse or any other person is also liable for the expenses. *(Stats.1990, c. 79 (A.B.759), § 14, operative July 1, 1991.)*

Application

Application of Part 9 to proceedings for the administration of decedents' estates commenced before July 1, 1988, see Probate Code § 11405.

Law Revision Commission Comments

1990 Enactment

Section 11446 continues Section 11446 of the repealed Probate Code without change. This part does not apply in any proceeding for administration of a decedent's estate commenced before July 1, 1988. See Section 11405. As to the application of any amendments made after that date, see Section 3.

Background on Section 11446 of Repealed Code

Section 11446 was added by 1987 Cal.Stat. ch. 923 § 93. The section restated former Probate Code Section 951.1 (repealed by 1987 Cal.Stat. ch. 923 § 48) without substantive change. [20 Cal.L.Rev.Comm.Reports 1001 (1990)].

Cross References

Funeral expenses, payment before grant of letters, see Probate Code § 8400.
Public administrators, summary sale of decedent's property, see Probate Code § 7660 et seq.

CHAPTER 4.   DEBTS THAT ARE CONTINGENT, DISPUTED, OR NOT DUE

Section
11460. Definitions.
11461. Court order; petition; notice of hearing.
11462. Agreement of interested persons.
11463. Deposit in account withdrawable only on court order.
11464. Distribution subject to assumption of liability.
11465. Appointment of trustee.
11466. Distribution subject to bond.
11467. Continuation of administration.

Application

Application of Part 9 to proceedings for the administration of decedents' estates commenced before July 1, 1988, see Probate Code § 11405.

§ 11460. Definitions

As used in this chapter:

(a) A debt is "contingent" if it is established under Part 4 (commencing with Section 9000) in either a fixed or an uncertain amount and will become absolute on occurrence of a stated event other than the passage of time. The term includes a secured obligation for which there may be recourse against property in the estate, other than the property that is the security, if the security is insufficient.

(b) A debt is "disputed" if it is a claim rejected in whole or in part under Part 4 (commencing with Section 9000) and is not barred under Section 9353 as to the part rejected.

(c) A debt is "not due" if it is established under Part 4 (commencing with Section 9000) and will become due on the passage of time. The term includes a debt payable in installments. *(Added by Stats.1991, c. 1055 (S.B.271), § 31.)*

Application

Application of Part 9 to proceedings for the administration of decedents' estates commenced before July 1, 1988, see Probate Code § 11405.

Law Revision Commission Comments

1991 Addition

The definitions in Section 11460 vary the definition of "debt" in Section 11401. See Section 11400 (definition in 11401 does not govern if provision or context otherwise requires).

Subdivision (a) is new.

Under subdivision (b), a rejected claim is not barred if within three months after the notice of rejection is given or after the claim becomes due the creditor commences an action on the claim or the matter is referred to a referee or to arbitration.

Subdivision (c) incorporates the aspect of former Section 11426 that related to installment debts. [20 Cal.L.Rev.Comm.Reports 2707 (1990)].

§ 11461. Court order; petition; notice of hearing

When all other debts have been paid and the estate is otherwise in a condition to be closed, on petition by an interested person, the court may make or modify an order or a combination of orders under this chapter that the court in its discretion determines is appropriate to provide adequately for a debt that is contingent, disputed, or not due, if the debt becomes absolute, established, or due. Notice of the hearing on the petition shall be given as provided in Section 1220 to the creditor whose debt is contingent, disputed, or not due, as well as to the persons provided in Section 11601. *(Added by Stats.1991, c. 1055 (S.B.271), § 31.)*

Application

Application of Part 9 to proceedings for the administration of decedents' estates commenced before July 1, 1988, see Probate Code § 11405.

Law Revision Commission Comments

1991 Addition

Section 11461 is correlative with Section 11640 (order for final distribution when all debts have been paid or adequately provided for). The term "interested person" is defined in Section 48. [20 Cal.L.Rev.Comm.Reports 2707 (1990)].

§ 11462. Agreement of interested persons

Notwithstanding any other provision of this chapter, if the court determines that all interested persons agree to the manner of providing for a debt that is contingent, disputed, or not due and that the agreement reasonably protects all interested persons and will not extend administration of the estate unreasonably, the court shall approve the agreement. *(Added by Stats.1991, c. 1055 (S.B.271), § 31.)*

Application

*Application of Part 9 to proceedings for the admin-
istration of decedents' estates commenced before July
1, 1988, see Probate Code § 11405.*

Law Revision Commission Comments

1991 Addition

Section 11462 is new. Regardless of the other techniques provided in this chapter for securing payment, if all interested persons agree
and the agreement reasonably protects them, the court must ratify
the agreement (unless the agreement requires administration of the
estate to be continued for an unreasonable length of time). The
agreement may require, for example, immediate payment of a debt
that is disputed, contingent, or not due, if the interested persons are
able to work out a satisfactory discount, compromise, or settlement.
Cf. former Section 11425 (right of creditor to payment of debt not
due if interest is waived). The term "interested person" is defined in
Section 48. [20 Cal.L.Rev.Comm.Reports 2707 (1990)].

§ 11463. Deposit in account withdrawable only on court order

The court may order an amount deposited in a financial
institution, as provided in Chapter 3 (commencing with
Section 9700) of Part 5, that would be payable if a debt that is
contingent, disputed, or not due, were absolute, established,
or due. The order shall provide that the amount deposited is
subject to withdrawal only upon authorization of the court, to
be paid to the creditor when the debt becomes absolute,
established, or due, or to be distributed in the manner
provided in Section 11642 if the debt does not become
absolute or established. *(Added by Stats.1991, c. 1055
(S.B.271), § 31.)*

Application

*Application of Part 9 to proceedings for the admin-
istration of decedents' estates commenced before July
1, 1988, see Probate Code § 11405.*

Law Revision Commission Comments

1991 Addition

Section 11463 replaces the deposit in court of former Section
11427 with deposit in a blocked account. The reference to Section
11642 incorporates any omnibus order for final distribution or
subsequent court order for distribution. [20 Cal.L.Rev.Comm.Re-
ports 2707 (1990)].

§ 11464. Distribution subject to assumption of liability

(a) The court may order property in the estate distributed
to a person entitled to it under the final order for distribution, if the person files with the court an assumption of
liability for a contingent or disputed debt as provided in
subdivision (b). The court may impose any other conditions
the court in its discretion determines are just, including that
the distributee give a security interest in all or part of the
property distributed or that the distributee give a bond in an
amount determined by the court.

(b) As a condition for an order under subdivision (a), each
distributee shall file with the court a signed and acknowledged agreement assuming personal liability for the contingent or disputed debt and consenting to jurisdiction within
this state for the enforcement of the debt if it becomes
absolute or established. The personal liability of each
distributee shall not exceed the fair market value on the date

of distribution of the property received by the distributee, less
the amount of liens and encumbrances. If there is more than
one distributee, the personal liability of the distributees is
joint and several.

(c) If the debt becomes absolute or established, it may be
enforced against each distributee in the same manner as it
could have been enforced against the decedent if the
decedent had not died. In an action based on the debt, the
distributee may assert any defense, cross-complaint, or setoff
that would have been available to the decedent if the
decedent had not died.

(d) The statute of limitations applicable to a contingent
debt is tolled from the time the creditor's claim is filed until
30 days after the order for distribution becomes final. The
signing of an agreement under subdivision (b) neither extends
nor revives any limitation period. *(Added by Stats.1991, c.
1055 (S.B.271), § 31.)*

Application

*Application of Part 9 to proceedings for the admin-
istration of decedents' estates commenced before July
1, 1988, see Probate Code § 11405.*

Law Revision Commission Comments

1991 Addition

Section 11464 is new. It provides for assumption of personal
liability to the creditor and the right of the creditor to enforce the
liability against the distributee.

A bond requirement under subdivision (a) may be satisfied by a
cash deposit. Code Civ.Proc. § 995.710 (deposit in lieu of bond).

Tolling of the limitation period for contingent claims under
subdivision (d) supplements Section 9352 (tolling during administration). The limitation period applicable to a disputed claim is
governed by Sections 9353 and 9370. [20 Cal.L.Rev.Comm.Reports
2707 (1990)].

§ 11465. Appointment of trustee

(a) The court may order that a trustee be appointed to
receive payment for a debt that is contingent, disputed, or not
due. The court in determining the amount paid to the
trustee shall compute the present value of the debt, giving
consideration to a reasonable return on the amount to be
invested. The trustee shall invest the payment in investments
that would be proper for a personal representative or as
authorized in the order.

(b) The trustee shall pay the debt as provided in the order.
On completion of payment, any excess in possession of the
trustee shall be distributed in the manner provided in Section
11642. *(Added by Stats.1991, c. 1055 (S.B.271), § 31.)*

Application

*Application of Part 9 to proceedings for the admin-
istration of decedents' estates commenced before July
1, 1988, see Probate Code § 11405.*

Law Revision Commission Comments

1991 Addition

Section 11465 continues former Section 11426 without substantive
change and broadens it to apply to debts that are disputed or
otherwise not due as well as debts that are contingent or payable in
installments. The reference to Section 11642 incorporates any

omnibus order for final distribution or subsequent court order for distribution. [20 Cal.L.Rev.Comm.Reports 2707 (1990)].

§ 11466. Distribution subject to bond

The court may order property in the estate distributed to a person entitled to it under the final order for distribution, if the person gives a bond conditioned on payment by the person of the amount of a contingent or disputed debt that becomes absolute or established. The amount of the bond shall be determined by the court, not to exceed the fair market value on the date of distribution of the property received by the distributee, less the amount of liens and encumbrances. In the case of a disputed debt or in the case of a contingent debt where litigation is required to establish the contingency, the cost of the bond is recoverable from the unsuccessful party as a cost of litigation. *(Added by Stats. 1991, c. 1055 (S.B.271), § 31.)*

Application

Application of Part 9 to proceedings for the administration of decedents' estates commenced before July 1, 1988, see Probate Code § 11405.

Law Revision Commission Comments

1991 Addition

Section 11466 is new. [20 Cal.L.Rev.Comm.Reports 2707 (1990)].

§ 11467. Continuation of administration

The court may order that the administration of the estate continue until the contingency, dispute, or passage of time of a debt that is contingent, disputed, or not due is resolved. *(Added by Stats.1991, c. 1055 (S.B.271), § 31.)*

Application

Application of Part 9 to proceedings for the administration of decedents' estates commenced before July 1, 1988, see Probate Code § 11405.

Law Revision Commission Comments

1991 Addition

Section 11467 gives the court authority to order continuation of administration, if appropriate. This is a specific application of the general authority of the court to order continuation of administration for a reasonable time. Section 11640(c); see also Section 12201 (report of status of administration). [20 Cal.L.Rev.Comm.Reports 2707 (1990)].

Part 10

DISTRIBUTION OF ESTATE

Law Revision Commission Comments

1990 Enactment

This part supersedes Part 10 (commencing with Section 11600) of Division 7 of the repealed Probate Code. The superseded part was enacted upon recommendation of the California Law Revision Commission. See Recommendation Relating to Distribution and Discharge, 19 Cal.L.Revision Comm'n Reports 953 (1988). See also Communication from the California Law Revision Commission Concerning Assembly Bill 2841, 19 Cal.L.Revision Comm'n Reports 1201, 1243–48 (1988). [20 Cal.L.Rev.Comm.Reports 1001 (1990)].

CHAPTER 1. ORDER FOR DISTRIBUTION

Cross References

Order for distribution to sister state personal representative pursuant to this chapter, see Probate Code § 12540.

ARTICLE 1. GENERAL PROVISIONS

§ 11600. Preliminary or final distribution; order; petition

The personal representative or an interested person may petition the court under this chapter for an order for preliminary or final distribution of the decedent's estate to the persons entitled thereto. *(Stats.1990, c. 79 (A.B.759), § 14, operative July 1, 1991.)*

Law Revision Commission Comments

1990 Enactment

Section 11600 continues Section 11600 of the repealed Probate Code without change. For the time and manner prescribed for making a petition, see Sections 11620 (petition for preliminary distribution) and 11640 (petition for final distribution). See also Sections 12200–12206 (time for closing estate). For general provisions relating to petitions and other papers, See Sections 1020–1023.

Background on Section 11600 of Repealed Code

Section 11600 was added by 1988 Cal.Stat. ch. 1199 § 91.5. The section restated without substantive change a portion of subdivision (a) of former Probate Code Section 1000 (with the exception of the reference to distribution of "priorities") and a portion of subdivision (a) of former Probate Code Section 1020 (provisions repealed by 1988 Cal.Stat. ch. 1199 § 55.5). For background on the provisions of this part, see the Comment to this part under the part heading. [20 Cal.L.Rev.Comm.Reports 1001 (1990)].

§ 11601. Hearing; notice

Notice of the hearing on the petition shall be given as provided in Section 1220 to all of the following persons:

(a) Each person listed in Section 1220.

(b) Each known heir whose interest in the estate would be affected by the petition.

(c) Each known devisee whose interest in the estate would be affected by the petition.

(d) The Attorney General, at the office of the Attorney General in Sacramento, if any portion of the estate is to escheat to the state and its interest in the estate would be affected by the petition.

(e) The Controller, if property is to be distributed to the state because there is no known beneficiary or if property is to be distributed to a beneficiary whose whereabouts is unknown. A copy of the latest account filed with the court shall be served on the Controller with the notice. *(Stats. 1990, c. 79 (A.B.759), § 14, operative July 1, 1991.)*

Law Revision Commission Comments

1990 Enactment

Section 11601 continues Section 11601 of the repealed Probate Code without substantive change. For general provisions, see Sections 1200–1230 (notice of hearing), 1250–1252 (request for special notice), 1260–1265 (proof of giving of notice).

Background on Section 11601 of Repealed Code

Section 11601 was added by 1988 Cal.Stat. ch. 1199 § 91.5. With the exception of subdivision (b)(4), the section restated subdivisions (b) and (c) of former Probate Code Sections 1000, 1020, and 1027 (provisions repealed by 1988 Cal.Stat. ch. 1199 § 55.5). Subdivision (b)(4) restated subdivision (d) of former Probate Code Section 1027 (repealed by 1988 Cal.Stat. ch. 1199 § 55.5), except that the time of notice was reduced from 30 days to 15. For background on the provisions of this part, see the Comment to this part under the part heading. [20 Cal.L.Rev.Comm.Reports 1001 (1990)].

§ 11602. Opposing petition

The personal representative or any interested person may oppose the petition. *(Stats.1990, c. 79 (A.B.759), § 14, operative July 1, 1991.)*

Law Revision Commission Comments

1990 Enactment

Section 11602 continues Section 11602 of the repealed Probate Code without change. See also Section 1043 (objections).

Background on Section 11602 of Repealed Code

Section 11602 was added by 1988 Cal.Stat. ch. 1199 § 91.5. The section restated without substantive change subdivision (d) of former Probate Code Section 1000 and a portion of the second sentence of subdivision (a) of former Probate Code Section 1020 (provisions repealed by 1988 Cal.Stat. ch. 1199 § 55.5). For background on the provisions of this part, see the Comment to this part under the part heading. [20 Cal.L.Rev.Comm.Reports 1001 (1990)].

§ 11603. Order; issuance; contents; designation of alternate distributees

(a) If the court determines that the requirements for distribution are satisfied, the court shall order distribution of the decedent's estate, or such portion as the court directs, to the persons entitled thereto.

(b) The order shall:

(1) Name the distributees and the share to which each is entitled.

(2) Provide that property distributed subject to a limitation or condition, including, but not limited to, an option granted under Chapter 16 (commencing with Section 9960) of Part 5, is distributed to the distributees subject to the terms of the limitation or condition.

(c) If the whereabouts of a distributee named in the order is unknown, the order shall provide for alternate distributees and the share to which each is entitled. The alternate distributees shall be the persons, to the extent known or reasonably ascertainable, who would be entitled under the decedent's will or under the laws of intestate succession if the distributee named in the order had predeceased the decedent, or in the case of a devise for a charitable purpose, under the doctrine of cy pres. If the distributee named in the order does not claim the share to which the distributee is entitled within five years after the date of the order, the distributee is deemed to have predeceased the decedent for the purpose of this section and the alternate distributees are entitled to the share as provided in the order. *(Stats.1990, c. 79 (A.B.759), § 14, operative July 1, 1991. Amended by Stats.2000, c. 17 (A.B.1491), § 4.6.)*

Law Revision Commission Comments

1990 Enactment

Section 11603 continues Section 11603 of the repealed Probate Code without change. For the requirements for distribution, see Sections 11621 (preliminary distribution) and 11640 (final distribution). See also Sections 1040–1050 (hearings and orders).

2000 Amendment

Section 11603 is amended to add subdivision (c). In cases to which subdivision (c) applies, the personal representative may deposit the property with the county treasurer. Section 11850. For money, no court order is required for the deposit. For other personal property, a court order is required. Section 11851. A person may claim the money or other personal property on deposit in the county treasury by filing a petition with the court. Section 11854.

In a testate estate, the court determines the alternate distributees under the decedent's will and applicable statutes. If the primary distributee is kindred of the testator or kindred of a surviving, deceased, or former spouse of the testator, the antilapse statute applies (Section 21110), and the alternate distributees are the issue of the missing distributee. In an intestate estate, the court determines the alternate distributees under the laws of intestate succession. See Sections 6400–6414.

In the case of a devise for a charitable purpose without a designated trustee or identified beneficiary, the Attorney General should ensure that there is an appropriate alternate charitable distribution. *Cf.* Prob. Code §§8111 (notice to Attorney General of charitable devise), 11703 (Attorney General petition to determine persons entitled to distribution); Gov't Code §§12580–12599.5 (Uniform Supervision of Trustees for Charitable Purposes Act).

If a primary distributee's whereabouts is unknown, potential alternate distributees under subdivision (c) are entitled to notice pursuant to Section 11601 (known heir or devisee whose interest would be affected). Moreover, the personal representative, or a person claiming to be entitled as an alternate distributee under subdivision (c), may petition the court pursuant to Article 2

(commencing with Section 11700) for a determination of persons entitled to distribution. [29 Cal.L.Rev.Comm.Reports 743 (1999)].

Background on Section 11603 of Repealed Code

Section 11603 was added by 1988 Cal.Stat. ch. 1199 § 91.5. The section restated portions of subdivision (e) of former Probate Code Section 584.3 (repealed by 1987 Cal.Stat. ch. 923 § 35) and of former Probate Code Sections 1001 and 1021 (provisions repealed by 1988 Cal.Stat. ch. 1199 § 55.5) without substantive change. For background on the provisions of this part, see the Comment to this part under the part heading. [20 Cal.L.Rev.Comm.Reports 1001 (1990)].

Cross References

Appeal of order of distribution, see Probate Code § 7240.
Determination of persons entitled to distribution, generally, see Probate Code § 11700 et seq.
Orders, contents, see Probate Code § 1047 et seq.
Partition before distribution, see Probate Code § 11950 et seq.
Recordation, order of distribution of real property, see Probate Code § 7263.

§ 11604. Distribution to person other than beneficiary; court inquiry; refusal or change of distribution; grounds; notice of hearing

(a) This section applies where distribution is to be made to any of the following persons:

(1) The transferee of a beneficiary.

(2) Any person other than a beneficiary under an agreement, request, or instructions of a beneficiary or the attorney in fact of a beneficiary.

(b) The court on its own motion, or on motion of the personal representative or other interested person or of the public administrator, may inquire into the circumstances surrounding the execution of, and the consideration for, the transfer, agreement, request, or instructions, and the amount of any fees, charges, or consideration paid or agreed to be paid by the beneficiary.

(c) The court may refuse to order distribution, or may order distribution on any terms that the court deems just and equitable, if the court finds either of the following:

(1) The fees, charges, or consideration paid or agreed to be paid by a beneficiary are grossly unreasonable.

(2) The transfer, agreement, request, or instructions were obtained by duress, fraud, or undue influence.

(d) Notice of the hearing on the motion shall be served on the beneficiary and on the persons described in subdivision (a) at least 15 days before the hearing in the manner provided in Section 415.10 or 415.30 of the Code of Civil Procedure. *(Stats.1990, c. 79 (A.B.759), § 14, operative July 1, 1991.)*

Law Revision Commission Comments

1990 Enactment

Section 11604 continues Section 11604 of the repealed Probate Code without substantive change. For general provisions, see Sections 1000–1004 (rules of practice), 1020–1023 (petitions and other papers), 1040–1050 (hearings and orders), 1200–1230 (notice of hearing), 1250–1252 (request for special notice), 1260–1265 (proof of giving of notice).

Background on Section 11604 of Repealed Code

Section 11604 was added by 1988 Cal.Stat. ch. 1199 § 91.5. The section restated former Probate Code Section 1020.1 (repealed by

1988 Cal.Stat. ch. 1199 § 55.5), standardizing the manner of notice with other provisions in the code. For background on the provisions of this part, see the Comment to this part under the part heading. [20 Cal.L.Rev.Comm.Reports 1001 (1990)].

Cross References

Duress, see Civil Code § 1569.
Fraud, see Civil Code § 1571 et seq.
Fraudulent instruments and transfers, see Civil Code § 3439 et seq.
Notices, generally, see Probate Code § 1200 et seq.

§ 11604.5. Transfer of beneficiary's interest in estate for consideration; written agreement; compliance; violation of section

(a) This section applies when distribution from a decedent's estate is made to a transferee for value who acquires any interest of a beneficiary in exchange for cash or other consideration.

(b) For purposes of this section, a transferee for value is a person who satisfies both of the following criteria:

(1) He or she purchases the interest from a beneficiary for consideration pursuant to a written agreement.

(2) He or she, directly or indirectly, regularly engages in the purchase of beneficial interests in estates for consideration.

(c) This section does not apply to any of the following:

(1) A transferee who is a beneficiary of the estate or a person who has a claim to distribution from the estate under another instrument or by intestate succession.

(2) A transferee who is either the registered domestic partner of the beneficiary, or is related by blood, marriage, or adoption to the beneficiary or the decedent.

(3) A transaction made in conformity with the California Finance Lenders Law (Division 9 (commencing with Section 22000) of the Financial Code) and subject to regulation by the Department of Business Oversight.

(4) A transferee who is engaged in the business of locating missing or unknown heirs and who acquires an interest from a beneficiary solely in exchange for providing information or services associated with locating the heir or beneficiary.

(d) A written agreement is effective only if all of the following conditions are met:

(1) The executed written agreement is filed with the court not later than 30 days following the date of its execution or, if administration of the decedent's estate has not commenced, then within 30 days of issuance of the letters of administration or letters testamentary, but in no event later than 15 days prior to the hearing on the petition for final distribution. Prior to filing or serving that written agreement, the transferee for value shall redact any personally identifying information about the beneficiary, other than the name and address of the beneficiary, and any financial information provided by the beneficiary to the transferee for value on the application for cash or other consideration, from the agreement.

(2) If the negotiation or discussion between the beneficiary and the transferee for value leading to the execution of the written agreement by the beneficiary was conducted in a language other than English, the beneficiary shall receive the written agreement in English, together with a copy of the agreement translated into the language in which it was negotiated or discussed. The written agreement and the translated copy, if any, shall be provided to the beneficiary.

(3) The documents signed by, or provided to, the beneficiary are printed in at least 10–point type.

(4) The transferee for value executes a declaration or affidavit attesting that the requirements of this section have been satisfied, and the declaration or affidavit is filed with the court within 30 days of execution of the written agreement or, if administration of the decedent's estate has not commenced, then within 30 days of issuance of the letters of administration or letters testamentary, but in no event later than 15 days prior to the hearing on the petition for final distribution.

(5) Notice of the assignment is served on the personal representative or the attorney of record for the personal representative within 30 days of execution of the written agreement or, if general or special letters of administration or letters testamentary have not been issued, then within 30 days of issuance of the letters of administration or letters testamentary, but in no event later than 15 days prior to the hearing on the petition for final distribution.

(e) The written agreement shall include the following terms, in addition to any other terms:

(1) The amount of consideration paid to the beneficiary.

(2) A description of the transferred interest.

(3) If the written agreement so provides, the amount by which the transferee for value would have its distribution reduced if the beneficial interest assigned is distributed prior to a specified date.

(4) A statement of the total of all costs or fees charged to the beneficiary resulting from the transfer for value, including, but not limited to, transaction or processing fees, credit report costs, title search costs, due diligence fees, filing fees, bank or electronic transfer costs, or any other fees or costs. If all the costs and fees are paid by the transferee for value and are included in the amount of the transferred interest, then the statement of costs need not itemize any costs or fees. This subdivision shall not apply to costs, fees, or damages arising out of a material breach of the agreement or fraud by or on the part of the beneficiary.

(f) A written agreement shall not contain any of the following provisions and, if any such provision is included, that provision shall be null and void:

(1) A provision holding harmless the transferee for value, other than for liability arising out of fraud by the beneficiary.

(2) A provision granting to the transferee for value agency powers to represent the beneficiary's interest in the decedent's estate beyond the interest transferred.

(3) A provision requiring payment by the beneficiary to the transferee for value for services not related to the written agreement or services other than the transfer of interest under the written agreement.

(4) A provision permitting the transferee for value to have recourse against the beneficiary if the distribution from the estate in satisfaction of the beneficial interest is less than the beneficial interest assigned to the transferee for value, other than recourse for any expense or damage arising out of the material breach of the agreement or fraud by the beneficiary.

(g) The court on its own motion, or on the motion of the personal representative or other interested person, may inquire into the circumstances surrounding the execution of, and the consideration for, the written agreement to determine that the requirements of this section have been satisfied.

(h) The court may refuse to order distribution under the written agreement, or may order distribution on any terms that the court considers equitable, if the court finds that the transferee for value did not substantially comply with the requirements of this section, or if the court finds that any of the following conditions existed at the time of transfer:

(1) The fees, charges, or consideration paid or agreed to be paid by the beneficiary were grossly unreasonable.

(2) The transfer of the beneficial interest was obtained by duress, fraud, or undue influence.

(i) In addition to any remedy specified in this section, for any willful violation of the requirements of this section found to be committed in bad faith, the court may require the transferee for value to pay to the beneficiary up to twice the value paid for the assignment.

(j) Notice of the hearing on any motion brought under this section shall be served on the beneficiary and on the transferee for value at least 15 days before the hearing in the manner provided in Section 415.10 or 415.30 of the Code of Civil Procedure.

(k) If the decedent's estate is not subject to a pending court proceeding under the Probate Code in California, but is the subject of a probate proceeding in another state, the transferee for value shall not be required to submit to the court a copy of the written agreement as required under paragraph (1) of subdivision (d). If the written agreement is entered into in California or if the beneficiary is domiciled in California, that written agreement shall otherwise conform to the provisions of subdivisions (d), (e), and (f) in order to be effective. *(Added by Stats.2005, c. 438 (S.B.390), § 1. Amended by Stats.2015, c. 190 (A.B.1517), § 71, eff. Jan. 1, 2016.)*

§ 11605. Finality of order

When a court order made under this chapter becomes final, the order binds and is conclusive as to the rights of all interested persons. *(Stats.1990, c. 79 (A.B.759), § 14, operative July 1, 1991.)*

Law Revision Commission Comments
1990 Enactment

Section 11605 continues Section 11605 of the repealed Probate Code without change. The court may correct clerical errors in orders as entered. See Code Civ.Proc. § 473. See also Sections 7260–7263 (orders affecting property).

Background on Section 11605 of Repealed Code

Section 11605 was added by 1988 Cal.Stat. ch. 1199 § 91.5. The section restated portions of former Probate Code Sections 1003, 1021, and 1054 (provisions repealed by 1988 Cal.Stat. ch. 1199 § 55.5). For background on the provisions of this part, see the Comment to this part under the part heading. [20 Cal.L.Rev.Comm.Reports 1001 (1990)].

Cross References

Appeals, see Probate Code § 7240.

Conclusiveness of other matters,
    Determination of persons entitled to distribution, see Probate Code § 11705.
    Judgment or final order, see Code of Civil Procedure § 1908.
    Settlement of accounts, see Probate Code § 7250.
Decree of final discharge, see Probate Code § 12250.
Estates of nonresidents, delivery of property or proceeds to personal representative in state of decedent's residence, court order, see Probate Code § 12540.

ARTICLE 2. PRELIMINARY DISTRIBUTION

§ 11620. Petition; time

A petition for an order for preliminary distribution of all, or a portion of, the share of a decedent's estate to which a beneficiary is entitled may not be filed unless at least two months have elapsed after letters are first issued to a general personal representative. *(Stats.1990, c. 79 (A.B.759), § 14, operative July 1, 1991.)*

Law Revision Commission Comments
1990 Enactment

Section 11620 continues Section 11620 of the repealed Probate Code without substantive change. The petition may be made by the personal representative, a beneficiary, or other interested person. See Section 11600 (petition for distribution). If distribution is made before four months have elapsed, the distributee must give a bond in the amount of the distribution. See Section 11622(a) (bond). If distribution is made after four months have elapsed, the court may require the distributee to give a bond. See Section 11622(b) (bond). See also Section 58 ("general personal representative" includes a special administrator who has the powers, duties, and obligations of a general personal representative under Section 8545).

Background on Section 11620 of Repealed Code

Section 11620 was added by 1988 Cal.Stat. ch. 1199 § 91.5. The section restated a portion of subdivision (a) of former Probate Code Section 1000 (repealed by 1988 Cal.Stat. ch. 1199 § 55.5). For background on the provisions of this part, see the Comment to this part under the part heading. [20 Cal.L.Rev.Comm.Reports 1001 (1990)].

§ 11621. Injury to creditor, estate, or interested person; bond

(a) The court shall order distribution under this article if at the hearing it appears that the distribution may be made without loss to creditors or injury to the estate or any interested person.

(b) The order for distribution shall be stayed until any bond required by the court is filed. *(Stats.1990, c. 79 (A.B.759), § 14, operative July 1, 1991.)*

Law Revision Commission Comments
1990 Enactment

Section 11621 continues Section 11621 of the repealed Probate Code without change.

Background on Section 11621 of Repealed Code

Section 11621 was added by 1988 Cal.Stat. ch. 1199 § 91.5. The section superseded a portion of former Probate Code Section 1001 (repealed by 1988 Cal.Stat. ch. 1199 § 55.5). For background on the provisions of this part, see the Comment to this part under the part heading. [20 Cal.L.Rev.Comm.Reports 1001 (1990)].

§ 11622. Bond

(a) If the court orders distribution before four months have elapsed after letters are first issued to a general personal representative, the court shall require a bond. The bond shall be in the amount of the distribution.

(b) If the court orders distribution after four months have elapsed after letters are first issued to a general personal representative, the court may require a bond. The bond shall be in the amount the court orders.

(c) Any bond required by the court shall be given by the distributee and filed with the court. The bond shall be conditioned on payment of the distributee's proper share of the debts of the estate, not exceeding the amount distributed. *(Stats.1990, c. 79 (A.B.759), § 14, operative July 1, 1991.)*

Law Revision Commission Comments
1990 Enactment

Section 11622 continues Section 11622 of the repealed Probate Code without change.

Background on Section 11622 of Repealed Code

Section 11622 was added by 1988 Cal.Stat. ch. 1199 § 91.5. The section superseded a portion of former Probate Code Section 1001 (repealed by 1988 Cal.Stat. ch. 1199 § 55.5). For background on the provisions of this part, see the Comment to this part under the part heading. [20 Cal.L.Rev.Comm.Reports 1001 (1990)].

§ 11623. Independently administered estate; preliminary distribution on notice

(a) Notwithstanding Section 11601, if authority is granted to administer the estate without court supervision under the Independent Administration of Estates Act, Part 6 (commencing with Section 10400):

(1) The personal representative may petition the court for an order for preliminary distribution on notice as provided in Section 1220. Notwithstanding subdivision (c) of Section 1220, the court may not dispense with notice unless the time for filing creditor claims has expired.

(2) The aggregate of all property distributed under this section shall not exceed 50 percent of the net value of the estate. For the purpose of this subdivision, "net value of the estate" means the excess of the value of the property in the estate, as determined by all inventories and appraisals on file with the court, over the total amount of all creditor claims and of all liens and encumbrances recorded or known to the personal representative not included in a creditor claim, excluding any estate tax lien occasioned by the decedent's death.

(b) Nothing in this section limits the authority of the personal representative to make preliminary distribution under other provisions of this chapter, whether or not authority is granted to administer the estate under the Independent Administration of Estates Act, Part 6 (commencing with Section 10400). *(Stats.1990, c. 79 (A.B.759),*

§ 14, operative July 1, 1991. Amended by Stats.1990, c. 710 (S.B.1775), § 41, operative July 1, 1991; Stats.1991, c. 82 (S.B.896), § 30.5, eff. June 30, 1991, operative July 1, 1991.)

Law Revision Commission Comments
1990 Enactment

Section 11623 continues Section 11623 of the repealed Probate Code without substantive change. The court may order reduced notice (Section 1203) as well as prescribe an ex parte hearing in an appropriate case (Section 1220(c)). Subdivision (b) makes clear that the total of all distributions under this section may not exceed 50 percent of the net value of the estate. An account is not statutorily required for an order of preliminary distribution as it is for an order for final distribution. See Section 10951 (final account). However, the court may not make an order under this section unless it is satisfied from the information presented to it that distribution may be made without loss to creditors or injury to the estate or any interested person. See Section 11621 (order for distribution).

For general provisions, see Sections 1000–1004 (rules of practice), 1020–1023 (petitions and other papers), 1040–1050 (hearings and orders), 1200–1230 (notice of hearing), 1250–1252 (request for special notice), 1260–1265 (proof of giving of notice).

1990 Amendment

Section 11623 (enacted as a part of the new Probate Code by 1990 Cal.Stat. ch. 79 § 14) was amended by 1990 Cal.Stat. ch. 710 § 41 to add subdivision (b) to make clear that the section is not the exclusive means by which a personal representative with independent administration authority may make distribution. This is a clarification, not a change, of existing law. [20 Cal.L.Rev.Comm.Reports 1001 (1990)].

1991 Amendment

Section 11623 is amended to replace the former language "[n]otwithstanding any other provision of this chapter" with the language "[n]otwithstanding Section 11601." This makes clear that the provisions of Section 11623 allowing reduced notice (notice under Section 1220 instead of Section 11601) control over the notice provisions of Section 11601. Other provisions of this chapter do apply to proceedings under this section, including those relating to opposing the petition (Section 11602), contents of court order (Section 11603), requirements for distribution to a person other than an estate beneficiary (Section 11604), binding effect of order (Section 11605), time for petition (Section 11620), requirement of bond (Section 11622), and payment of costs (Section 11624). [21 Cal.L.Rev.Comm.Reports 67 (1991)].

Background on Section 11623 of Repealed Code

Section 11623 was added by 1988 Cal.Stat. ch. 1199 § 91.5. The section superseded former Probate Code Section 1004 (repealed by 1988 Cal.Stat. ch. 1199 § 55.5). The provision of former law relating to dispensing with an account was omitted. For background on the provisions of this part, see the Comment to this part under the part heading. [20 Cal.L.Rev.Comm.Reports 1001 (1990)].

§ 11624. Costs

The costs of a proceeding under this article shall be paid by the distributee or the estate in proportions determined by the court. *(Stats.1990, c. 79 (A.B.759), § 14, operative July 1, 1991.)*

Law Revision Commission Comments
1990 Enactment

Section 11624 continues Section 11624 of the repealed Probate Code without change. Under this section, the allocation of costs is left to the court, whether or not the personal representative is the petitioner. One factor in the exercise of the court's discretion could be whether the personal representative was negligent in failing to make prompt distribution, necessitating a petition under this chapter. For expenses of partition, see Section 11955.

Background on Section 11624 of Repealed Code

Section 11624 was added by 1988 Cal.Stat. ch. 1199 § 91.5. The section superseded former Probate Code Section 1002 (repealed by 1988 Cal.Stat. ch. 1199 § 55.5). For background on the provisions of this part, see the Comment to this part under the part heading. [20 Cal.L.Rev.Comm.Reports 1001 (1990)].

Cross References

Apportionment of expense, attorney's fees in partition before distribution, see Probate Code § 11955.
Costs,
Generally, see Probate Code § 1002.
Actions on claims, see Probate Code §§ 9252, 9255.
Appeals, see California Rules of Court, Rule 8.276.
Civil actions, see Code of Civil Procedure § 1021 et seq.
Contests after probate, see Probate Code § 1002.
Recovery of fraudulently conveyed property, see Probate Code § 9653.
Family allowance, costs to be paid by estate in actions for, see Probate Code § 6544.

ARTICLE 3. FINAL DISTRIBUTION

Section
11640. Debts; petition; order; ademption by satisfaction; advancements; continued administration.
11641. Distribution upon entry of order.
11642. Property acquired or discovered after order made.

§ 11640. Debts; petition; order; ademption by satisfaction; advancements; continued administration

(a) When all debts have been paid or adequately provided for, or if the estate is insolvent, and the estate is in a condition to be closed, the personal representative shall file a petition for, and the court shall make, an order for final distribution of the estate.

(b) The court shall hear and determine and resolve in the order all questions arising under Section 21135 (ademption by satisfaction) or Section 6409 (advancements).

(c) If debts remain unpaid or not adequately provided for or if, for other reasons, the estate is not in a condition to be closed, the administration may continue for a reasonable time, subject to Chapter 1 (commencing with Section 12200) of Part 11 (time for closing estate). *(Stats.1990, c. 79 (A.B.759), § 14, operative July 1, 1991. Amended by Stats. 2002, c. 138 (A.B.1784), § 9.)*

Law Revision Commission Comments

1990 Enactment

Section 11640 continues Section 11640 of the repealed Probate Code without substantive change. The petition may be made by the personal representative, a beneficiary, or other interested person. See Section 11600 (petition for distribution). Unless there has been a waiver of accounts, the estate is not in a condition to be closed until final settlement of the accounts of the personal representative. See also Sections 12201 (report of status of administration), 12205 (reduction of compensation of personal representative for delay in administration of estate).

For general provisions, see Sections 1000–1004 (rules of practice), 1020–1023 (petitions and other papers), 1040–1050 (hearings and orders), 1200–1230 (notice of hearing), 1250–1252 (request for special notice), 1260–1265 (proof of giving of notice).

2002 Amendment

Section 11640 is amended to correct a cross-reference.

Background on Section 11640 of Repealed Code

Section 11640 was added by 1988 Cal.Stat. ch. 1199 § 91.5. Subdivision (a) restated portions of former Probate Code Section 956 (reenacted without change by 1987 Cal.Stat. ch. 923 § 48.5 and repealed by 1988 Cal.Stat. ch. 1199 § 55) and subdivision (a) of former Probate Code Sections 1020 and 1027 (provisions repealed by 1988 Cal.Stat. ch. 1199 § 55.5) with the addition of a reference to the insolvency of the estate. Subdivision (b) restated a portion of former Probate Code Section 1054 (repealed by 1988 Cal.Stat. ch. 1199 § 55.5) without substantive change. Subdivision (c) restated a portion of former Probate Code Section 956 (reenacted without change by 1987 Cal.Stat. ch. 923 § 48.5 and repealed by 1988 Cal.Stat. ch. 1199 § 55), with the addition of a reference to the provisions governing the time for closing the estate. For background on the provisions of this part, see the Comment to this part under the part heading. [20 Cal.L.Rev.Comm.Reports 1001 (1990)].

Cross References

Final distribution, see Probate Code § 11600 et seq.

§ 11641. Distribution upon entry of order

When an order settling a final account and for final distribution is entered, the personal representative may immediately distribute the property in the estate to the persons entitled to distribution, without further notice or proceedings. *(Stats.1990, c. 79 (A.B.759), § 14, operative July 1, 1991.)*

Law Revision Commission Comments

1990 Enactment

Section 11641 continues Section 11641 of the repealed Probate Code without change. For a stay in case of an appeal, see Section 7241.

Background on Section 11641 of Repealed Code

Section 11641 was added by 1988 Cal.Stat. ch. 1199 § 91.5. The section superseded the last portion of the second sentence of former Probate Code Section 926 (repealed by 1988 Cal.Stat. ch. 1199 § 54.5). The section was amended by 1989 Cal.Stat. ch. 21 § 28 to permit distribution on entry of an order for final distribution. See Communication from the California Law Revision Commission Concerning Assembly Bill 156, 20 Cal.L.Revision Comm'n Reports 227, 232 (1990). For background on the provisions of this part, see the Comment to this part under the part heading. [20 Cal.L.Rev.Comm.Reports 1001 (1990)].

§ 11642. Property acquired or discovered after order made

Any property acquired or discovered after the court order for final distribution is made shall be distributed in the following manner:

(a) If the order disposes of the property, distribution shall be made in the manner provided in the order. The court may, in an appropriate case, require a supplemental account and make further instructions relating to the property.

(b) If the order does not dispose of the property, distribution shall be made either (1) in the manner ordered by the court on a petition for instructions or (2) under Section 12252 (administration after discharge) if the personal representative has been discharged. *(Stats.1990, c. 79 (A.B.759), § 14, operative July 1, 1991.)*

Law Revision Commission Comments

1990 Enactment

Section 11642 continues Section 11642 of the repealed Probate Code without substantive change.

Background on Section 11642 of Repealed Code

Section 11642 was added by 1988 Cal.Stat. ch. 1199 § 91.5. The section superseded former Probate Code Section 1020.5 (supplementary account) (repealed by 1988 Cal.Stat. ch. 1199 § 55.5). For background on the provisions of this part, see the Comment to this part under the part heading. [20 Cal.L.Rev.Comm.Reports 1001 (1990)].

Cross References

Certificate of tax payment, see Revenue and Taxation Code § 19513 et seq.
Final account, see Probate Code § 10951.
Notice, see Probate Code § 1200 et seq.
Setting matters for hearing, see Probate Code § 1041.

CHAPTER 2. DETERMINATION OF PERSONS ENTITLED TO DISTRIBUTION

Section
11700. Petition; time.
11701. Notice of hearing.
11702. Written statement of interest; failure to file; other pleadings.
11703. Attorney General entitled to distribution; charitable trust or devise without designated trustee or beneficiary; escheat.
11704. Evidence; late petition; personal representative petition to participate.
11705. Court order; finality.

§ 11700. Petition; time

At any time after letters are first issued to a general personal representative and before an order for final distribution is made, the personal representative, or any person claiming to be a beneficiary or otherwise entitled to distribution of a share of the estate, may file a petition for a court determination of the persons entitled to distribution of the decedent's estate. The petition shall include a statement of the basis for the petitioner's claim. *(Stats.1990, c. 79 (A.B.759), § 14, operative July 1, 1991.)*

Law Revision Commission Comments

1990 Enactment

Section 11700 continues Section 11700 of the repealed Probate Code without change. This section permits a petition until a final order for distribution is made. The time limit is jurisdictional. See Section 11704 (hearing); cf. Section 11605 (conclusiveness of order). For general provisions, see Sections 1000–1004 (rules of practice), 1020–1023 (petitions and other papers), 1040–1050 (hearings and orders).

Background on Section 11700 of Repealed Code

Section 11700 was added by 1988 Cal.Stat. ch. 1199 § 91.5. The section restated the first sentence of former Probate Code Section 1080 (repealed by 1988 Cal.Stat. ch. 1199 § 56.5), but permits a petition until a final order for distribution is made. That time limit, unlike the time limit of former Section 1080, is jurisdictional. For

background on the provisions of this part, see the Comment to this part under the part heading. [20 Cal.L.Rev.Comm.Reports 1001 (1990)].

Cross References

Appeal of orders or refusal to make orders determining heirship, see Probate Code § 7240.
Charitable trusts, distribution of income, unauthorized acts of trustee, see Probate Code § 16100 et seq.
Escheat, see Code of Civil Procedure § 1420 et seq.; Probate Code § 6800 et seq.
Final distribution, see Probate Code § 11600 et seq.
Intervention, see Code of Civil Procedure §§ 387, 388.
Publication of notice to creditors, see Probate Code § 9001 et seq.

§ 11701. Notice of hearing

Notice of the hearing on the petition shall be given as provided in Section 1220 to all of the following persons:

(a) Each person listed in Section 1220.

(b) Each known heir whose interest in the estate would be affected by the petition.

(c) Each known devisee whose interest in the estate would be affected by the petition.

(d) The Attorney General, at the office of the Attorney General in Sacramento, if any portion of the estate is to escheat to the state and its interest in the estate would be affected by the petition. *(Stats.1990, c. 79 (A.B.759), § 14, operative July 1, 1991.)*

Law Revision Commission Comments

1990 Enactment

Section 11701 continues Section 11701 of the repealed Probate Code without substantive change. For general provisions, see Sections 1200–1230 (notice of hearing), 1250–1252 (request for special notice), 1260–1265 (proof of giving of notice). See also Section 1285 (clerk to set matter for hearing).

Background on Section 11701 of Repealed Code

Section 11701 was added by 1988 Cal.Stat. ch. 1199 § 91.5. Subdivision (a) continued the second sentence of former Probate Code Section 1080 (repealed by 1988 Cal.Stat. ch. 1199 § 56.5) without substantive change. Subdivision (b) superseded the third sentence of former Probate Code Section 1080 (repealed by 1988 Cal.Stat. ch. 1199 § 56.5). For background on the provisions of this part, see the Comment to this part under the part heading. [20 Cal.L.Rev.Comm.Reports 1001 (1990)].

§ 11702. Written statement of interest; failure to file; other pleadings

(a) Any interested person may appear and, at or before the time of the hearing, file a written statement of the person's interest in the estate. The written statement may be in support of, or in opposition to, the petition. No other pleadings are necessary and the written statement of each claimant shall be deemed denied by each of the other claimants to the extent the written statements conflict.

(b) If a person fails timely to file a writen [1] statement:

(1) The case is at issue notwithstanding the failure and the case may proceed on the petition and written statements filed by the time of the hearing, and no further pleadings by other persons are necessary.

(2) The person may not participate further in the proceeding for determination of persons entitled to distribution, but the person's interest in the estate is not otherwise affected.

(3) The person is bound by the decision in the proceeding. *(Stats.1990, c. 79 (A.B.759), § 14, operative July 1, 1991.)*

¹ So in enrolled bill.

Law Revision Commission Comments
1990 Enactment

Section 11702 continues Section 11702 of the repealed Probate Code without change. Subdivision (b) is comparable to Section 8251(c) (will contest). For general provisions, see Sections 1000–1004 (rules of practice), 1020–1023 (petitions and other papers), 1040–1050 (hearings and orders).

Background on Section 11702 of Repealed Code

Section 11702 was added by 1988 Cal.Stat. ch. 1199 § 91.5. Subdivision (a) restated the fourth and fifth sentences of former Probate Code Section 1080 (repealed by 1988 Cal.Stat. ch. 1199 § 56.5) without substantive change, with the clarification that the written statement may be in support of or in opposition to the petition. Subdivision (b) was new. For background on the provisions of this part, see the Comment to this part under the part heading. [20 Cal.L.Rev.Comm.Reports 1001 (1990)].

§ 11703. Attorney General entitled to distribution; charitable trust or devise without designated trustee or beneficiary; escheat

The Attorney General shall be deemed to be a person entitled to distribution of the estate for purposes of this chapter if the estate involves or may involve any of the following:

(a) A charitable trust, other than a charitable trust with a designated trustee that may lawfully accept the trust.

(b) A devise for a charitable purpose without an identified beneficiary.

(c) An escheat to the State of California. *(Stats.1990, c. 79 (A.B.759), § 14, operative July 1, 1991.)*

Law Revision Commission Comments
1990 Enactment

Section 11703 continues Section 11703 of the repealed Probate Code without change.

Background on Section 11703 of Repealed Code

Section 11703 was added by 1988 Cal.Stat. ch. 1199 § 91.5. The section restated the last sentence of former Probate Code Section 1080 (repealed by 1988 Cal.Stat. ch. 1199 § 56.5) without substantive change. For background on the provisions of this part, see the Comment to this part under the part heading. [20 Cal.L.Rev.Comm.Reports 1001 (1990)].

§ 11704. Evidence; late petition; personal representative petition to participate

(a) The court shall consider as evidence in the proceeding any statement made in a petition filed under Section 11700 and any statement of interest filed under Section 11702. The court shall not hear or consider a petition filed after the time prescribed in Section 11700.

(b)(1) The personal representative may petition the court for authorization to participate, as necessary to assist the court, in the proceeding. Notice of the hearing on the

petition shall be given to the persons identified in Section 11701 in the manner provided in Section 1220.

(2) The court may grant or deny this petition, in whole or in part, on the pleadings, without an evidentiary hearing or further discovery. A petition filed pursuant to this subdivision may be granted only upon a showing of good cause. The court shall determine the manner and capacity in which the personal representative may provide assistance in the proceeding. The court may direct the personal representative to file papers as a party to the proceeding, or to take other specified action, if deemed by the court to be necessary to assist the court. *(Stats.1990, c. 79 (A.B.759), § 14, operative July 1, 1991. Amended by Stats.2013, c. 84 (A.B.1160), § 1.)*

Law Revision Commission Comments
1990 Enactment

Section 11704 restates Section 11704 of the repealed Probate Code without substantive change. The procedure applicable in a proceeding under this chapter is that applicable to civil actions generally. See Section 1000 (general rules of practice govern). In addition to evidence otherwise admissible in the proceeding, Section 11704 makes admissible the statements referred to in subdivision (a). For general provisions, see Sections 1000–1004 (rules of practice), 1020–1023 (petitions and other papers), 1040–1050 (hearings and orders).

Background on Section 11704 of Repealed Code

Section 11704 was added by 1988 Cal.Stat. ch. 1199 § 91.5. The section restated without substantive change the second sentence and the first portion of the third sentence of former Probate Code Section 1081 (repealed by 1988 Cal.Stat. ch. 1199 § 56.5), except that a prior court order is not required for participation of the personal representative. The provisions of former Section 1081 for jury trial and special rules of evidence were not continued. For background on the provisions of this part, see the Comment to this part under the part heading. [20 Cal.L.Rev.Comm.Reports 1001 (1990)].

§ 11705. Court order; finality

(a) The court shall make an order that determines the persons entitled to distribution of the decedent's estate and specifies their shares.

(b) When the court order becomes final it binds and is conclusive as to the rights of all interested persons. *(Stats. 1990, c. 79 (A.B.759), § 14, operative July 1, 1991.)*

Law Revision Commission Comments
1990 Enactment

Section 11705 continues Section 11705 of the repealed Probate Code without change. For general provisions relating to hearings and orders, see Sections 1040–1050. See also Section 11750 (good faith purchaser for value of distributed property).

Background on Section 11705 of Repealed Code

Section 11705 was added by 1988 Cal.Stat. ch. 1199 § 91.5. Subdivision (a) restated the last portion of the second sentence of former Probate Code Section 1081 (repealed by 1988 Cal.Stat. ch. 1199 § 56.5) without substantive change. Subdivision (b) restated former Probate Code Section 1082 (repealed by 1988 Cal.Stat. ch. 1199 § 56.5) without substantive change. For background on the provisions of this part, see the Comment to this part under the part heading. [20 Cal.L.Rev.Comm.Reports 1001 (1990)].

Cross References
Advancements, conclusiveness of decree regarding questions, see Probate Code § 11640.

Appealable orders, see Code of Civil Procedure § 904.1.; Probate Code § 7240 et seq.

Conclusiveness of judgment or final order, see Code of Civil Procedure § 1908.

Decree assigning small estate set-aside to surviving spouse or children, conclusiveness, see Probate Code § 6610.

Estates of nonresidents, court order, see Probate Code § 12540.

Final distribution orders, conclusiveness of, see Probate Code § 11605.

Order settling an account, conclusiveness of, see Probate Code § 7250.

Probate of will, conclusiveness of, see Probate Code § 8226.

Stay of enforcement, see Code of Civil Procedure § 916 et seq.

CHAPTER 3. DISTRIBUTION OF PROPERTY IN ESTATE

Cross References

Application of old and new law, see Probate Code § 3.

§ 11750. Personal representative responsibility; distributee demand and suit to recover; good faith purchaser for value

(a) The personal representative is responsible for distribution of the property in the estate in compliance with the terms of the court order for distribution.

(b) A distributee may demand, sue for, and recover from the personal representative or any person in possession, property to which the distributee is entitled.

(c) A distribution of property made in compliance with the terms of the court order for distribution is valid as to a person acting in good faith and for a valuable consideration. *(Stats.1990, c. 79 (A.B.759), § 14, operative July 1, 1991.)*

Law Revision Commission Comments

1990 Enactment

Section 11750 continues Section 11750 of the repealed Probate Code without change, except that subdivision (c) is revised to extend to any person who enters into a transaction in good faith and for a valuable consideration, not only purchasers. In the case of a distribution to a trust, the trustee is the distributee. See also Section 34 ("devisee" defined). With respect to after-discovered or after-acquired property, see Section 11642.

Background on Section 11750 of Repealed Code

Section 11750 was added by 1988 Cal.Stat. ch. 1199 § 91.5. Subdivisions (a) and (c) were new. Subdivision (b) restated a portion of former Probate Code Section 1021 (repealed by 1988 Cal.Stat. ch. 1199 § 55.5). For background on the provisions of this part, see the Comment to this part under the part heading. [20 Cal.L.Rev.Comm.Reports 1001 (1990)].

§ 11751. Receipt from distributee; recordation of order or deed

The personal representative shall obtain the receipt of the distributee for property in the estate distributed by the personal representative. In the case of real property, the personal representative shall record the court order for distribution or the personal representative's deed or both in the county in which the real property is located. Recordation of the order or deed is deemed to be a receipt of the distributee for the property. *(Stats.1990, c. 79 (A.B.759), § 14, operative July 1, 1991.)*

Law Revision Commission Comments

1990 Enactment

Section 11751 continues Section 11751 of the repealed Probate Code without change. Failure of the personal representative to record the court order for distribution of real property or the personal representative's deed does not affect title of the distributee. See also Section 7263 (recordation of order affecting title to real property).

Background on Section 11751 of Repealed Code

Section 11751 was a new provision added by 1988 Cal.Stat. ch. 1199 § 91.5. For background on the provisions of this part, see the Comment to this part under the part heading. [20 Cal.L.Rev.Comm.Reports 1001 (1990)].

§ 11752. Life estate in personal property; inventory

If personal property in the possession of a distributee is subject to possession by the distributee for life only, the personal representative shall demand an inventory of the property from the distributee. On receipt, the personal representative shall file the inventory with the court and deliver a copy to any distributee of the remainder. *(Stats. 1990, c. 79 (A.B.759), § 14, operative July 1, 1991.)*

Law Revision Commission Comments

1990 Enactment

Section 11752 continues Section 11752 of the repealed Probate Code without change.

Background on Section 11752 of Repealed Code

Section 11752 was added by 1988 Cal.Stat. ch. 1199 § 91.5. The section superseded former Probate Code Section 1065 (repealed by 1988 Cal.Stat. ch. 1199 § 55.5). For background on the provisions of this part, see the Comment to this part under the part heading. [20 Cal.L.Rev.Comm.Reports 1001 (1990)].

§ 11753. Discharge of personal representative; receipts; recordation statement

(a) Distribution in compliance with the court order entitles the personal representative to a full discharge with respect to property included in the order.

(b) The personal representative shall, before or at the time of the petition for discharge, file receipts for all property in the estate. In the case of real property, the personal representative shall file a statement that identifies the date and place of the recording and other appropriate recording information for the court order for distribution or the personal representative's deed.

(c) The court may excuse the filing of a receipt on a showing that the personal representative is unable, after reasonable effort, to obtain a receipt and that the property has been delivered to or is in the possession of the distributee. *(Stats.1990, c. 79 (A.B.759), § 14, operative July 1, 1991.)*

Law Revision Commission Comments

1990 Enactment

Section 11753 continues Section 11753 of the repealed Probate Code without substantive change. For provisions governing discharge of the personal representative, see Sections 12250–12252. Recording information under subdivision (b) may include an instrument number and a book and page number where appropriate.

Background on Section 11753 of Repealed Code

Section 11753 was added by 1988 Cal.Stat. ch. 1199 § 91.5. Subdivision (a) restated a portion of former Probate Code Section 1003 (repealed by 1988 Cal.Stat. ch. 1199 § 55.5), but eliminated the reference to a personal representative "in this State." Subdivisions (b) and (c) were new. For background on the provisions of this part, see the Comment to this part under the part heading. [20 Cal.L.Rev.Comm.Reports 1001 (1990)].

§ 11754. Expenses of estate administration

Expenses of administration of the estate shall include reasonable storage, delivery, and shipping costs for distribution of tangible personal property to a distributee. *(Added by Stats.1994, c. 806 (A.B.3686), § 34.)*

CHAPTER 4. DECEASED DISTRIBUTEE

Section
11801. Distribution as if living; exception by will.
11802. Personal representative of beneficiary's estate; minor issue of decedent; application for distribution without administration.

Cross References

Application of old and new law, see Probate Code § 3.

§ 11801. Distribution as if living; exception by will

(a) Except as provided in subdivision (b), the share in a decedent's estate of a beneficiary who survives the decedent but who dies before distribution shall be distributed under this chapter with the same effect as though the distribution were made to the beneficiary while living.

(b) Subject to Section 21525, distribution may not be made under this chapter if the decedent's will provides that the beneficiary is entitled to take under the will only if the beneficiary survives the date of distribution or other period stated in the will and the beneficiary fails to survive the date of distribution or other period. *(Stats.1990, c. 79 (A.B.759), § 14, operative July 1, 1991.)*

Law Revision Commission Comments

1990 Enactment

Section 11801 continues Section 11801 of the repealed Probate Code without change. A distribution made under court order is valid as to bona fide purchasers for value. See Section 11750 (responsibility for distribution). A provision in a will requiring survival to the date of distribution is satisfied by survival to the date distribution could and should have occurred. Estate of Taylor, 66 Cal.2d 855, 428 P.2d 301, 59 Cal.Rptr. 437 (1967).

Background on Section 11801 of Repealed Code

Section 11801 was added by 1988 Cal.Stat. ch. 1199 § 91.5. The section restated the second paragraph of former Probate Code Section 1023 (repealed by 1988 Cal.Stat. ch. 1199 § 55.5), omitting the reference to an improper distribution being void. The section was amended by 1989 Cal.Stat. ch. 21 § 29 to make clear that, in the case of a marital deduction gift, any survival requirement in the will that exceeds or may exceed six months is construed to be a six month limitation under Section 21525. See Communication from the California Law Revision Commission Concerning Assembly Bill 156, 20 Cal.L.Revision Comm'n Reports 227, 232 (1990). For background on the provisions of this part, see the Comment to this part under the part heading. [20 Cal.L.Rev.Comm.Reports 1001 (1990)].

§ 11802. Personal representative of beneficiary's estate; minor issue of decedent; application for distribution without administration

If a beneficiary satisfies the requirement of Section 11801, the beneficiary's share in the decedent's estate shall be distributed as follows:

(a) Except as otherwise provided in this section, distribution shall be made to the personal representative of the estate of the beneficiary for the purpose of administration in the estate of the beneficiary.

(b) If the beneficiary was issue of the decedent and died intestate while under the age of majority and not having been emancipated, distribution shall be made directly to the heirs of the beneficiary without administration in the estate of the beneficiary.

(c) If a person entitled to the beneficiary's share proceeds under Division 8 (commencing with Section 13000) (disposition of estate without administration), distribution shall be made under Division 8. *(Stats.1990, c. 79 (A.B.759), § 14, operative July 1, 1991.)*

Law Revision Commission Comments

1990 Enactment

Section 11802 continues Section 11802 of the repealed Probate Code without substantive change.

Background on Section 11802 of Repealed Code

Section 11802 was added by 1988 Cal.Stat. ch. 1199 § 91.5. Subdivision (a) restated the first paragraph of former Probate Code Section 1023 (repealed by 1988 Cal.Stat. ch. 1199 § 55.5) without substantive change. Subdivision (b) restated former Probate Code Section 1022 (repealed by 1988 Cal.Stat. ch. 1199 § 55.5), substituting emancipation for marriage. Subdivision (c) was new. For background on the provisions of this part, see the Comment to this part under the part heading. [20 Cal.L.Rev.Comm.Reports 1001 (1990)].

CHAPTER 5. DEPOSIT WITH COUNTY TREASURER

Section
11850. Cases in which property may be deposited with county treasurer.
11851. Money; personal property; sale; deposit with controller.
11852. Receipt; liability.
11853. Order for distribution; certified copy.
11854. Claim for deposited property; petition; contents; hearing; service on Attorney General; property deposited in State Treasury.

Application of old and new law, see Probate Code § 3.
Public administrators, payments pursuant to this chapter after final distribution of an estate, see Probate Code § 7624.

§ 11850. Cases in which property may be deposited with county treasurer

Subject to Section 11851, the personal representative may deposit property to be distributed with the county treasurer of the county in which the proceedings are pending in the name of the distributee in any of the following cases:

(a) The property remains in the possession of the personal representative unclaimed or the whereabouts of the distributee is unknown.

(b) The distributee refuses to give a receipt for the property.

(c) The distributee is a minor or incompetent person who has no guardian, conservator, or other fiduciary to receive the property or person authorized to give a receipt for the property.

(d) For any other reason the property cannot be distributed, and the personal representative desires discharge. Notwithstanding Section 11851, deposit may not be made under this subdivision except on court order. *(Stats.1990, c. 79 (A.B.759), § 14, operative July 1, 1991.)*

Law Revision Commission Comments
1990 Enactment

Section 11850 continues Section 11850 of the repealed Probate Code without change, except that subdivision (b) is revised to delete the reference to an acceptance by the distributee. The concept of an acceptance is not implemented in the statutes on distribution. Distribution is made to the named distributee or any known assignee of the named distributee, regardless of the place of residence of the distributee.

Distribution to the county treasurer under this section is permissive. Therefore, the personal representative may make distribution in any other manner that is appropriate. For example, distribution to a minor for whom no guardian has been appointed might be made under the Uniform Transfers to Minors Act (Sections 3905–3906) or other under another appropriate statute.

If the distributee is a nonresident minor or nonresident incompetent person who has a guardian, conservator, or other fiduciary of the estate legally appointed under the law of another jurisdiction, the distribution of the person's share should be made to the fiduciary.

Money deposited with the county treasurer does not bear interest for the benefit of the distributee. See Gov't Code § 53844 (interest on funds in county treasury credited to general fund of county).

Background on Section 11850 of Repealed Code

Section 11850 was added by 1988 Cal.Stat. ch. 1199 § 91.5. The section superseded portions of former Probate Code Sections 1060 and 1062 (provisions repealed by 1988 Cal.Stat. ch. 1199 § 55.5). For background on the provisions of this part, see the Comment to this part under the part heading. [20 Cal.L.Rev.Comm.Reports 1001 (1990)].

Administration by public administrators, generally, see Probate Code § 7600 et seq.
Conservatorship, establishment, see Probate Code § 1800 et seq.
Creditor not found, deposit in county treasury, see Probate Code § 11428.

Deposit of unclaimed property, generally, see Code of Civil Procedure § 1310 et seq.
Disposition of unclaimed property, estates of deceased persons, see Code of Civil Procedure § 1440 et seq.
Distribution to person other than beneficiary, generally, see Probate Code § 11604.
Guardians, appointment, see Probate Code § 1510 et seq.
Minors, defined, see Family Code § 6500.

§ 11851. Money; personal property; sale; deposit with controller

(a) If property authorized by Section 11850 to be deposited with the county treasurer consists of money, the personal representative may deposit the money.

(b) If property authorized by Section 11850 to be deposited with the county treasurer consists of personal property other than money, the personal representative may not deposit the personal property except on court order. If it appears to the court that sale is for the benefit of interested persons, the court shall order the personal property sold, and the proceeds of sale, less expenses of sale allowed by the court, shall be deposited in the county treasury. If it appears to the court that sale is not for the benefit of interested persons, the court shall order the personal property deposited with the Controller, to be held subject to the provisions of Chapter 6 (commencing with Section 11900). *(Stats.1990, c. 79 (A.B.759), § 14, operative July 1, 1991.)*

Law Revision Commission Comments
1990 Enactment

Section 11851 continues Section 11851 of the repealed Probate Code without change.

Background on Section 11851 of Repealed Code

Section 11851 was added by 1988 Cal.Stat. ch. 1199 § 91.5. The section superseded portions of former Probate Code Sections 1060 and 1062 (provisions repealed by 1988 Cal.Stat. ch. 1199 § 55.5). For background on the provisions of this part, see the Comment to this part under the part heading. [20 Cal.L.Rev.Comm.Reports 1001 (1990)].

Conservatorship, see Probate Code § 1800 et seq.
Deposit of funds, order of court, see Code of Civil Procedure § 574.
Disposition of unclaimed money or property, see Code of Civil Procedure § 1440 et seq.
Guardians, appointment,
  Generally, see Probate Code § 1510 et seq.
  Sale or disposal of unclaimed property, see Code of Civil Procedure § 1370 et seq.

§ 11852. Receipt; liability

The county treasurer shall give a receipt for a deposit made under this chapter and is liable on the official bond of the county treasurer for the money deposited. The receipt has the same effect as if executed by the distributee. *(Stats.1990, c. 79 (A.B.759), § 14, operative July 1, 1991.)*

Law Revision Commission Comments
1990 Enactment

Section 11852 continues Section 11852 of the repealed Probate Code without change. Personal property not ordered sold may be deposited with the State Controller. See Section 11851.

Background on Section 11852 of Repealed Code

Section 11852 was added by 1988 Cal.Stat. ch. 1199 § 91.5. The section restated the last portions of former Probate Code Sections 1060 and 1062 (repealed by 1988 Cal.Stat. ch. 1199 § 55.5), except that the provision for a receipt having the effect of a voucher is not continued. For background on the provisions of this part, see the Comment to this part under the part heading. [20 Cal.L.Rev.Comm.Reports 1001 (1990)].

Cross References

Official bonds, generally, see Government Code § 1450 et seq.

§ 11853. Order for distribution; certified copy

If money is deposited or is already on deposit with the county treasurer, the personal representative shall deliver to the county treasurer a certified copy of the order for distribution. *(Stats.1990, c. 79 (A.B.759), § 14, operative July 1, 1991.)*

Law Revision Commission Comments

1990 Enactment

Section 11853 continues Section 11853 of the repealed Probate Code without change. Personal property not ordered sold may be deposited with the State Controller. See Section 11851.

Background on Section 11853 of Repealed Code

Section 11853 was added by 1988 Cal.Stat. ch. 1199 § 91.5. The section restated former Probate Code Section 1060.1 (repealed by 1988 Cal.Stat. ch. 1199 § 55.5) without substantive change and superseded former Probate Code Section 1224 (repealed by 1987 Cal.Stat. ch. 923 § 59). For background on the provisions of this part, see the Comment to this part under the part heading. [20 Cal.L.Rev.Comm.Reports 1001 (1990)].

Cross References

Conclusiveness of order of distribution, see Probate Code § 11605.
Court order for distribution to sister state personal representative, see Probate Code § 12540.
Deposit of funds, order of court, see Code of Civil Procedure § 574.
Deposits with county treasurer,
 Estate moneys, by public administrator, see Probate Code § 7640.
 Payment of debts, where creditor not found, see Probate Code § 11428.
Distribution of estate, generally, see Probate Code § 11600 et seq.

§ 11854. Claim for deposited property; petition; contents; hearing; service on Attorney General; property deposited in State Treasury

(a) A person may claim money on deposit in the county treasury by filing a petition with the court that made the order for distribution. The petition shall show the person's claim or right to the property. Unless the petition is filed by the person named in the decree for distribution of a decedent's estate, or the legal representative of the person or the person's estate, the petition shall state the facts required to be stated in a petition for escheated property filed under Section 1355 of the Code of Civil Procedure. On the filing of the petition, the same proceedings shall be had as are required by that section, except that the hearing shall be ex parte unless the court orders otherwise.

(b) If so ordered by the court, a copy of the petition shall be served on the Attorney General. The Attorney General may answer the petition, at the Attorney General's discretion.

(c) If the court is satisfied that the claimant has a right to the property claimed, the court shall make an order establishing the right. On presentation of a certified copy of the order, the county auditor shall draw a warrant on the county treasurer for the amount of money covered by the order.

(d) A claim for money distributed in the estate of a deceased person made after the deposit of the property in the State Treasury is governed by the provisions of Chapter 3 (commencing with Section 1335) of Title 10 of Part 3 of the Code of Civil Procedure. *(Stats.1990, c. 79 (A.B.759), § 14, operative July 1, 1991. Amended by Stats.1994, c. 806 (A.B.3686), § 35.)*

Law Revision Commission Comments

1990 Enactment

Section 11854 continues Section 11854 of the repealed Probate Code without substantive change. See also Section 11850 (when deposit with county treasurer authorized). Personal property not ordered sold may be deposited with the State Controller. See Section 11851.

Background on Section 11854 of Repealed Code

Section 11854 was added by 1988 Cal.Stat. ch. 1199 § 91.5. The section restated subdivision (a) of former Probate Code Section 1064 (repealed by 1988 Cal.Stat. ch. 1199 § 55.5), but omitted the provisions relating to property other than money deposited with the county treasurer. Such property may be deposited with the State Controller. See Section 11850 (when deposit with county treasurer authorized). Unlike the former provision, Section 11854 provided for an ex parte order with notice to the Attorney General as the court determines, and substituted a court order for the certificate of right. For background on the provisions of this part, see the Comment to this part under the part heading. [20 Cal.L.Rev.Comm.Reports 1001 (1990)].

Cross References

Attorney general's proceedings on unclaimed property, escheat, see Code of Civil Procedure § 1410; Cal. Const. Art. 5, § 13; Government Code § 12540 et seq.
Unclaimed property,
 Generally, see Code of Civil Procedure § 1300 et seq.
 Claims to unclaimed property, see Code of Civil Procedure § 1350 et seq.
 Petition and jurisdiction as to determination of title to unclaimed property, see Code of Civil Procedure § 1353 et seq.
Unclaimed property law, escheat, see Code of Civil Procedure § 1500 et seq.

CHAPTER 6. DISTRIBUTION TO STATE

Cross References

Application of old and new law, see Probate Code § 3.

Estates of deceased persons, payment to state, see Code of Civil Procedure § 1443.

§ 11900. Property not ordered distributed to known beneficiaries; conversion of real or tangible personal property to money

(a) The court shall order property that is not ordered distributed to known beneficiaries to be distributed to the state.

(b) Insofar as practicable, any real property or tangible personal property shall be converted to money before distribution to the state. *(Stats.1990, c. 79 (A.B.759), § 14, operative July 1, 1991.)*

Law Revision Commission Comments

1990 Enactment

Section 11900 continues Section 11900 of the repealed Probate Code without change. See also Section 7663 (summary disposition of small estate by public administrator; deposit with county treasurer for use in general fund of the county where there are no beneficiaries).

Background on Section 11900 of Repealed Code

Section 11900 was added by 1988 Cal.Stat. ch. 1199 § 91.5. The section restated the last portion of subdivision (a) of former Probate Code Section 1027 (repealed by 1988 Cal.Stat. ch. 1199 § 55.5) without substantive change. For background on the provisions of this part, see the Comment to this part under the part heading. [20 Cal.L.Rev.Comm.Reports 1001 (1990)].

§ 11901. Court order including trust language; legal and equitable title in state

If the court orders distribution of property in the decedent's estate to the state, and the order includes words that otherwise create a trust in favor of unknown or unidentified persons as a class, the distribution shall vest in the state both legal and equitable title to the property. *(Stats.1990, c. 79 (A.B.759), § 14, operative July 1, 1991.)*

Law Revision Commission Comments

1990 Enactment

Section 11901 continues Section 11901 of the repealed Probate Code without change. The title of the state under this section is subject to the right of persons to claim the property as provided in this chapter. See Section 11903 (claims against property distributed to state).

Background on Section 11901 of Repealed Code

Section 11901 was added by 1988 Cal.Stat. ch. 1199 § 91.5. The section restated subdivision (e) of former Probate Code Section 1027 (repealed by 1988 Cal.Stat. ch. 1199 § 55.5) without substantive change. For background on the provisions of this part, see the Comment to this part under the part heading. [20 Cal.L.Rev.Comm.Reports 1001 (1990)].

§ 11902. Duties of personal representative; delivery of property; recordation of order; information to controller

(a) If the court orders distribution to the state, the personal representative shall promptly:

(1) Deliver any money to the State Treasurer.

(2) Deliver any personal property other than money to the Controller for deposit in the State Treasury.

(3) Cause a certified copy of the order to be recorded in the office of the county recorder of each county in which any real property is located.

(b) At the time of making a delivery of property or recordation under this section, the personal representative shall deliver to the Controller a certified copy of the order for distribution together with a statement of the date and place of each recording and other appropriate recording information. *(Stats.1990, c. 79 (A.B.759), § 14, operative July 1, 1991.)*

Law Revision Commission Comments

1990 Enactment

Section 11902 continues Section 11902 of the repealed Probate Code without substantive change.

Background on Section 11902 of Repealed Code

Section 11902 was added by 1988 Cal.Stat. ch. 1199 § 91.5. The section restated without substantive change subdivisions (f) and (g) of former Probate Code Section 1027 and former Probate Code Section 1028 (provisions repealed by 1988 Cal.Stat. ch. 1199 § 55.5). For background on the provisions of this part, see the Comment to this part under the part heading. [20 Cal.L.Rev.Comm.Reports 1001 (1990)].

Cross References

Assessment of real property distributed to state, see Revenue and Taxation Code § 982.1.

Escheat for failure to claim property, see Code of Civil Procedure § 1351.

Property deposited for benefit of known heirs, recordation of, see Code of Civil Procedure § 1316.

Recordation of order regarding title to real property, see Probate Code § 7263.

Recording of instruments affecting real property, see Civil Code § 1169 et seq.

§ 11903. Time to file claim; vesting of property in state

(a) Property distributed to the state shall be held by the Treasurer for a period of five years from the date of the order for distribution, within which time any person may claim the property in the manner provided by Title 10 (commencing with Section 1300) of Part 3 of the Code of Civil Procedure.

(b) A person who does not claim the property within the time prescribed in this section is forever barred, and the property vests absolutely in the state, subject to the provisions of Title 10 (commencing with Section 1300) of Part 3 of the Code of Civil Procedure. *(Stats.1990, c. 79 (A.B.759), § 14, operative July 1, 1991.)*

Law Revision Commission Comments

1990 Enactment

Section 11903 continues Section 11903 of the repealed Probate Code without change. Under the general claim procedures of the Code of Civil Procedure, the limitations bar may be tolled as to minors and incompetent persons in some situations. See, e.g., Code Civ.Proc. § 1441.

Background on Section 11903 of Repealed Code

Section 11903 was added by 1988 Cal.Stat. ch. 1199 § 91.5. The section restated subdivisions (i) and (j) of former Probate Code Section 1027 (repealed by 1988 Cal.Stat. ch. 1199 § 55.5) without substantive change. For background on the provisions of this part, see the Comment to this part under the part heading. [20 Cal.L.Rev.Comm.Reports 1001 (1990)].

§ 11904. Deposit in county treasury

No deposit of property in an estate shall be made in the county treasury by a personal representative if any other property in the estate is to be or has been distributed to the state under this chapter, but the property that would otherwise be deposited in the county treasury shall be transmitted promptly to the State Treasurer or Controller as provided in this chapter. *(Stats.1990, c. 79 (A.B.759), § 14, operative July 1, 1991.)*

Law Revision Commission Comments
1990 Enactment

Section 11904 continues Section 11904 of the repealed Probate Code without change. See also Section 7622 (general rules governing administration of estates apply to public administrator). Section 11904 is intended for the convenience of the claimant of property in only having to deal with one governmental agency. In the case of deposit of distribution of property to the state, money is delivered to the State Treasurer and personal property is delivered to the State Controller. See Section 11902 (disposition of property distributed to state).

Background on Section 11904 of Repealed Code

Section 11904 was added by 1988 Cal.Stat. ch. 1199 § 91.5. The section restated subdivision (h) of former Probate Code Section 1027 (repealed by 1988 Cal.Stat. ch. 1199 § 55.5) without substantive change. For background on the provisions of this part, see the Comment to this part under the part heading. [20 Cal.L.Rev.Comm.Reports 1001 (1990)].

CHAPTER 7. PARTITION OR ALLOTMENT OF PROPERTY

Section
11950. Two or more beneficiaries entitled to undivided interests; petition for partition, allotment or other division; property interests not subject to administration.
11951. Petition; time; contents.
11952. Hearing; notice; parties; objection to jurisdiction.
11953. Division proportionate to party's interest; sale instead of division; agreement to accept undivided interest.
11954. Referees for partition; number; powers and duties.
11955. Expenses of partition; attorney fees; unpaid expenses as lien.
11956. Distribution; weight of court-ordered division; modification; appeal.

Cross References
Application of old and new law, see Probate Code § 3.

§ 11950. Two or more beneficiaries entitled to undivided interests; petition for partition, allotment or other division; property interests not subject to administration

(a) If two or more beneficiaries are entitled to the distribution of undivided interests in property and have not agreed among themselves to a partition, allotment, or other division of the property, any of them, or the personal representative at the request of any of them, may petition the court to make a partition, allotment, or other division of the

property that will be equitable and will avoid the distribution of undivided interests.

(b) A proceeding under this chapter is limited to interests in the property that are subject to administration and does not include other interests except to the extent the owners of other interests in the property consent to be bound by the partition, allotment, or other division. *(Stats.1990, c. 79 (A.B.759), § 14, operative July 1, 1991.)*

Law Revision Commission Comments
1990 Enactment

Section 11950 continues Section 11950 of the repealed Probate Code without change. Both real and personal property are subject to division under this chapter. See Section 62 ("property" defined). The partition may affect only interests in the property that are subject to administration. It should be noted that partitioned property may not be distributed except under the general provisions for distribution.

Background on Section 11950 of Repealed Code

Section 11950 was added by 1988 Cal.Stat. ch. 1199 § 91.5. The section restated former Probate Code Section 1100 (repealed by 1988 Cal.Stat. ch. 1199 § 57), making clear that the partition may affect only interests in the property that are subject to administration. For background on the provisions of this part, see the Comment to this part under the part heading. [20 Cal.L.Rev.Comm.Reports 1001 (1990)].

Cross References

Authorization for partition actions when decedent leaves undivided interest in property, see Probate Code § 9823.
Distribution of estate, generally, see Probate Code § 11600 et seq.
Guardians or conservators, partition actions, see Probate Code § 2463.
Partition of real and personal property, see Code of Civil Procedure § 872.010 et seq.

§ 11951. Petition; time; contents

(a) A petition under this chapter may be filed at any time before an order for distribution of the affected property becomes final.

(b) The petition shall:

(1) Describe the property.

(2) State the names of the persons having or claiming undivided interests.

(3) Describe the undivided interests, so far as known to the petitioner. *(Stats.1990, c. 79 (A.B.759), § 14, operative July 1, 1991.)*

Law Revision Commission Comments
1990 Enactment

Section 11951 continues Section 11951 of the repealed Probate Code without substantive change. For general provisions relating to petitions and other papers, see Sections 1020–1023.

Background on Section 11951 of Repealed Code

Section 11951 was added by 1988 Cal.Stat. ch. 1199 § 91.5. The section restated the first and second sentences of former Probate Code Section 1101 (repealed by 1988 Cal.Stat. ch. 1199 § 57) without substantive change, except that the petition may be filed before the time to make claims has expired but may not be filed after an order for distribution has become final. For background on the provisions of this part, see the Comment to this part under the part heading. [20 Cal.L.Rev.Comm.Reports 1001 (1990)].

§ 11952. Hearing; notice; parties; objection to jurisdiction

(a) Notice of the hearing on the petition shall be given as provided in Section 1220 to the personal representative and to the persons entitled to distribution of the undivided interests.

(b) At the hearing the persons entitled to distribution of the undivided interests shall be considered the parties to the proceeding whether or not they have appeared or filed a responsive pleading. No one shall be considered as a plaintiff or as a defendant.

(c) Any objection to the jurisdiction of the court shall be made and resolved in the manner prescribed in Part 19 (commencing with Section 850) of Division 2. *(Stats.1990, c. 79 (A.B.759), § 14, operative July 1, 1991. Amended by Stats.2003, c. 32 (A.B.167), § 12.)*

Law Revision Commission Comments

1990 Enactment

Section 11952 continues Section 11952 of the repealed Probate Code without change. For general provisions, see Sections 1000–1004 (rules of practice), 1020–1023 (petitions and other papers), 1040–1050 (hearings and orders), 1200–1230 (notice of hearing), 1250–1252 (request for special notice), 1260–1265 (proof of giving of notice).

2003 Amendment

Section 11952 is amended to reflect relocation (from former Section 9860 *et seq.* to Section 850 *et seq.*) of the statutes relating to conveyance or transfer of property claimed to belong to the decedent or another person. See 2001 Cal. Stat. ch. 49, §§ 1, 4. [33 Cal.L.Rev.Comm. Reports 163 (2003)].

Background on Section 11952 of Repealed Code

Section 11952 was added by 1988 Cal.Stat. ch. 1199 § 91.5. The section superseded former Probate Code Section 1102 and the third, fourth, and fifth sentences of former Probate Code Section 1101 (provisions repealed by 1988 Cal.Stat. ch. 1199 § 57). For background on the provisions of this part, see the Comment to this part under the part heading. [20 Cal.L.Rev.Comm.Reports 1001 (1990)].

Cross References

Distribution of estate, generally, see Probate Code § 11600 et seq.
Parties, civil actions for partition, see Code of Civil Procedure § 872.510 et seq.

§ 11953. Division proportionate to party's interest; sale instead of division; agreement to accept undivided interest

(a) The court shall partition, allot, or otherwise divide the property so that each party receives property with a value proportionate to the value of the party's interest in the whole.

(b) The court may direct the personal representative to sell property where, under the circumstances, sale would be more equitable than partition and where the property cannot conveniently be allotted to any one party. The sale shall be conducted in the same manner as other sales made during administration of an estate.

(c) Any two or more parties may agree to accept undivided interests. *(Stats.1990, c. 79 (A.B.759), § 14, operative July 1, 1991.)*

Law Revision Commission Comments

1990 Enactment

Section 11953 continues Section 11953 of the repealed Probate Code without substantive change.

Background on Section 11953 of Repealed Code

Section 11953 was added by 1988 Cal.Stat. ch. 1199 § 91.5. The section restated former Probate Code Section 1103 (repealed by 1988 Cal.Stat. ch. 1199 § 57) without substantive change. For background on the provisions of this part, see the Comment to this part under the part heading. [20 Cal.L.Rev.Comm.Reports 1001 (1990)].

Cross References

Civil actions for partition, sale or division of property, see Code of Civil Procedure § 872.010 et seq.

§ 11954. Referees for partition; number; powers and duties

(a) The court, in its discretion, may appoint one or three referees to partition property capable of being partitioned, if requested to do so by a party. The number of referees appointed must conform to the request of at least one of the parties.

(b) The referees shall have the powers and perform the duties of referees in, and the court shall have the same powers with respect to their report as in, partition actions under Title 10.5 (commencing with Section 872.010) of Part 2 of the Code of Civil Procedure. *(Stats.1990, c. 79 (A.B.759), § 14, operative July 1, 1991.)*

Law Revision Commission Comments

1990 Enactment

Section 11954 continues Section 11954 of the repealed Probate Code without change.

Background on Section 11954 of Repealed Code

Section 11954 was added by 1988 Cal.Stat. ch. 1199 § 91.5. The section restated former Probate Code Section 1104 (repealed by 1988 Cal.Stat. ch. 1199 § 57) without substantive change. For background on the provisions of this part, see the Comment to this part under the part heading. [20 Cal.L.Rev.Comm.Reports 1001 (1990)].

Cross References

Referees in civil actions for partition, see Code of Civil Procedure § 873.010 et seq.
References and trial by referees, see Code of Civil Procedure § 638 et seq.

§ 11955. Expenses of partition; attorney fees; unpaid expenses as lien

The expenses of partition shall be equitably apportioned by the court among the parties, but each party must pay the party's own attorney's fees. The amount charged to each party shall be included and specified in the order and, to the extent unpaid, constitutes a lien on the property allotted to the party. *(Stats.1990, c. 79 (A.B.759), § 14, operative July 1, 1991.)*

Law Revision Commission Comments

1990 Enactment

Section 11955 continues Section 11955 of the repealed Probate Code without change.

Background on Section 11955 of Repealed Code

Section 11955 was added by 1988 Cal.Stat. ch. 1199 § 91.5. The section restated former Probate Code Section 1105 (repealed by 1988 Cal.Stat. ch. 1199 § 57), with the addition of the requirement that expenses be specified in the order before they may become a lien on the property. For background on the provisions of this part, see the Comment to this part under the part heading. [20 Cal.L.Rev.Comm.Reports 1001 (1990)].

Cross References

Civil actions for partition, costs, see Code of Civil Procedure § 874.010 et seq.
Costs in administration of estates, generally, see Probate Code § 1002.

§ 11956. Distribution; weight of court-ordered division; modification; appeal

(a) The partition, allotment, or other division made by the court shall control in proceedings for distribution, unless modified for good cause on reasonable notice.

(b) The proceedings leading to the partition, allotment, or other division may be reviewed on appeal from the order for distribution. *(Stats.1990, c. 79 (A.B.759), § 14, operative July 1, 1991.)*

Law Revision Commission Comments

1990 Enactment

Section 11956 continues Section 11956 of the repealed Probate Code without change.

Background on Section 11956 of Repealed Code

Section 11956 was added by 1988 Cal.Stat. ch. 1199 § 91.5. The section restated former Probate Code Section 1106 (repealed by 1988 Cal.Stat. ch. 1199 § 57) without substantive change. For background on the provisions of this part, see the Comment to this part under the part heading. [20 Cal.L.Rev.Comm.Reports 1001 (1990)].

Cross References

Appeals, see Code of Civil Procedure § 904.1.; Probate Code § 7240 et seq.
Conclusiveness of orders, see Probate Code §§ 11605, 11705.
Distribution of estate, generally, see Probate Code § 11600 et seq.

CHAPTER 8. INTEREST AND INCOME ACCRUING DURING ADMINISTRATION

Application

Application of chapter limited to cases where decedent died on or after July 1, 1989, see Probate Code § 12007.

Law Revision Commission Comments

1990 Enactment

This chapter supersedes Chapter 8 (commencing with Section 12000) of Division 7 of the repealed Probate Code. The superseded chapter was enacted upon recommendation of the California Law Revision Commission. See Recommendation Relating to Interest and Income During Administration, 19 Cal.L.Revision Comm'n Reports 1019 (1988). See also Communication from the California Law Revision Commission Concerning Assembly Bill 2841, 19 Cal.L.Revision Comm'n Reports 1201, 1246–48 (1988).

The rules of Chapter 8 are incorporated by reference in Section 16314 (interest and income on trust distributions). [20 Cal.L.Rev.Comm.Reports 1001 (1990)].

Cross References

Application of old and new law, see Probate Code § 3.
Rules applicable after decedent's death or termination of income interest, see Probate Code § 16340.

§ 12000. Intent of testator; application of chapter

The provisions of this chapter apply where the intention of the testator is not otherwise indicated by the will. *(Stats. 1990, c. 79 (A.B.759), § 14, operative July 1, 1991.)*

Application

Application of chapter limited to cases where decedent died on or after July 1, 1989, see Probate Code § 12007.

Law Revision Commission Comments

1990 Enactment

Section 12000 continues Section 12000 of the repealed Probate Code without change. The language of this section is comparable to that used in Sections 6140(b) and 6165 (rules of construction of wills). This chapter does not apply where the decedent died before July 1, 1989. See Section 12007. As to the application of any amendments made after that date, see Section 3.

Background on Section 12000 of Repealed Code

Section 12000 was added by 1988 Cal.Stat. ch. 1199 § 91.5. The section restated without substantive change former Probate Code Section 660 (added by 1983 Cal.Stat. ch. 842 § 40) and the introductory clause of subdivision (a) of former Probate Code Section 664 (added by 1983 Cal.Stat. ch. 842 § 40) (provisions repealed by 1988 Cal.Stat. ch. 1199 § 52). For background on the provisions of this chapter, see the Comment to this chapter under the chapter heading. [20 Cal.L.Rev.Comm.Reports 1001 (1990)].

§ 12001. Rate of interest

If interest is payable under this chapter, the rate of interest is three percentage points less than the legal rate on judgments in effect one year after the date of the testator's death and shall not be recomputed in the event of a change in the applicable rate thereafter. *(Stats.1990, c. 79 (A.B.759), § 14, operative July 1, 1991. Amended by Stats.1992, c. 871 (A.B.2975), § 14.)*

Application

Application of chapter limited to cases where decedent died on or after July 1, 1989, see Probate Code § 12007.

Law Revision Commission Comments

1990 Enactment

Section 12001 restates Section 12001 of the repealed Probate Code without substantive change. This section provides a fixed rate based on the minimum Series EE United States Savings Bond rate in effect one year after the decedent's death, regardless whether interest commences to accrue before, on, or after the one year anniversary. The minimum rate payable on a Series EE United States savings bond may be obtained from a financial institution or from the U.S. Savings Bond Division of the Department of Treasury (1–800–USBONDS). The rule of Section 12001 applies where the intention of the testator is not indicated by the will. See Section 12000. This chapter does not apply where the decedent died before July 1, 1989. See Section 12007. As to the application of any amendments made after that date, see Section 3.

Background on Section 12001 of Repealed Code

Section 12001 was added by 1988 Cal.Stat. ch. 1199 § 91.5. The section superseded portions of subdivisions (a) and (c) of former Probate Code Section 663 (added by 1983 Cal.Stat. ch. 842 § 40 and repealed by 1988 Cal.Stat. ch. 1199 § 52). Under former Section 663, the rate of interest was that payable on a money judgment entered in this state. Section 12001 provides a fixed rate based on the minimum Series EE United States Savings Bond rate in effect one year after the decedent's death, regardless whether interest commences to accrue before, on, or after the one year anniversary. For background on the provisions of this chapter, see the Comment to this chapter under the chapter heading. [20 Cal.L.Rev.Comm.Reports 1001 (1990)].

Cross References

Liability for breach of trust,
  Generally, see Probate Code § 16440.
  Amount of interest, see Probate Code § 16441.

§ 12002. Specific devise; expenses; payment of deficiency; charge against devisee's share; equitable lien; sale during administration

(a) Except as provided in this section, a specific devise does not bear interest.

(b) A specific devise carries with it income on the devised property from the date of death, less expenses attributable to the devised property during administration of the estate. For purposes of this section, expenses attributable to property are expenses that result directly from the use or ownership of the property, including property tax and tax on the income from the property, but excluding estate and generation-skipping transfer taxes.

(c) If income of specifically devised property is not sufficient to pay expenses attributable to the property, the deficiency shall be paid out of the estate until the property is distributed to the devisee or the devisee takes possession of or occupies the property, whichever occurs first. To the extent a deficiency paid out of the estate is attributable to the period that commences one year after the testator's death, whether paid during or after expiration of the one year period following the date of death, the amount paid is a charge against the share of the devisee, and the personal representa-

tive has an equitable lien on the specifically devised property as against the devisee in the amount paid.

(d) If specifically devised property is sold during administration of the estate, the devisee is entitled to the net income from the property until the date of sale, and to interest on the net sale proceeds thereafter, but no interest accrues during the first year after the testator's death. *(Stats.1990, c. 79 (A.B.759), § 14, operative July 1, 1991.)*

Application

Application of chapter limited to cases where decedent died on or after July 1, 1989, see Probate Code § 12007.

Law Revision Commission Comments

1990 Enactment

Section 12002 restates Section 12002 of the repealed Probate Code without substantive change. This section applies to specific devises of real and personal property. See Section 32 ("devise" defined). The expenses attributable to the property under subdivision (b) are those relating directly to the property, including maintenance, insurance, property taxes, and income taxes allocable to income from the property. The rule of Section 12002 applies where the intention of the testator is not indicated by the will. See Section 12000.

Subdivision (c) limits the burden on the estate to the first year after the decedent's death. Expenses paid out by the estate after the first year are ultimately borne by the distributee of the property. The equitable lien imposed by subdivision (c) is not good against a transferee of the property who gives fair consideration for the property without knowledge of the lien. See generally 1 J. Pomeroy, Equity Jurisprudence §§ 165, 168, 171(4) (5th ed. 1941); cf. Section 15685 and the Comment thereto (trustee's lien).

Subdivision (d) is a combination of the rules of subdivision (b) and Section 12003.

This chapter does not apply where the decedent died before July 1, 1989. See Section 12007. As to the application of any amendments made after that date, see Section 3.

Background on Section 12002 of Repealed Code

Section 12002 was a new provision added by 1988 Cal.Stat. ch. 1199 § 91.5. For background on the provisions of this chapter, see the Comment to this chapter under the chapter heading.

Subdivision (a) codified case law. See Estate of McKenzie, 199 Cal.App.2d 393, 399–400, 18 Cal.Rptr. 680 (1962) (inheritance from another estate).

Subdivision (b) codified case law. See, e.g., In re Estate of Daly, 202 Cal. 284, 287, 260 P. 296 (1927) (stock).

The first sentence of subdivision (c) was consistent with Estate of Reichel, 28 Cal.App.3d 156, 103 Cal.Rptr. 836 (1972) (where specifically devised real property produces no income but is occupied rent free by the devisee from testator's death, expenses on the property are chargeable to the devisee). [20 Cal.L.Rev.Comm.Reports 1001 (1990)].

Cross References

Abatement of shares of beneficiaries, see Probate Code § 21401.

§ 12003. General pecuniary devise

If a general pecuniary devise, including a general pecuniary devise in trust, is not distributed within one year after the testator's death, the devise bears interest thereafter. *(Stats. 1990, c. 79 (A.B.759), § 14, operative July 1, 1991.)*

Application

Application of chapter limited to cases where decedent died on or after July 1, 1989, see Probate Code § 12007.

Law Revision Commission Comments

1990 Enactment

Section 12003 continues Section 12003 of the repealed Probate Code without change. The rule of this section applies where the intention of the testator is not indicated by the will. See Section 12000. This chapter does not apply where the decedent died before July 1, 1989. See Section 12007. As to the application of any amendments made after that date, see Section 3.

Background on Section 12003 of Repealed Code

Section 12003 was added by 1988 Cal.Stat. ch. 1199 § 91.5. The section restated subdivision (a) of former Probate Code Section 663 (added by 1983 Cal.Stat. ch. 842 § 40 and repealed by 1988 Cal.Stat. ch. 1199 § 52), except that the rate of interest was specified in Section 12001. For background on the provisions of this chapter, see the Comment to this chapter under the chapter heading. [20 Cal.L.Rev.Comm.Reports 1001 (1990)].

Cross References

Administration of trusts, see Probate Code § 17300 et seq.
Distribution of estate, generally, see Probate Code § 11600 et seq.

§ 12004. Annuity

(a) An annuity commences at the testator's death and shall be paid at the end of the annual, monthly, or other specified period.

(b) If an annuity is not paid at the end of the specified period, it bears interest thereafter, but no interest accrues during the first year after the testator's death. *(Stats.1990, c. 79 (A.B.759), § 14, operative July 1, 1991.)*

Application

Application of chapter limited to cases where decedent died on or after July 1, 1989, see Probate Code § 12007.

Law Revision Commission Comments

1990 Enactment

Section 12004 continues Section 12004 of the repealed Probate Code without change. The rule of this section applies where the intention of the testator is not indicated by the will. See Section 12000. This chapter does not apply where the decedent died before July 1, 1989. See Section 12007. As to the application of any amendments made after that date, see Section 3.

Background on Section 12004 of Repealed Code

Section 12004 was added by 1988 Cal.Stat. ch. 1199 § 91.5. Subdivision (a) restated subdivision (b) of former Probate Code Section 663 (added by 1983 Cal.Stat. ch. 842 § 40 and repealed by 1988 Cal.Stat. ch. 1199 § 52) without substantive change. Subdivision (b) superseded the portion of subdivision (c) of former Probate Code Section 663 (added by 1983 Cal.Stat. ch. 842 § 40 and repealed by 1988 Cal.Stat. ch. 1199 § 52) that related to annuities. For background on the provisions of this chapter, see the Comment to this chapter under the chapter heading. [20 Cal.L.Rev.Comm.Reports 1001 (1990)].

§ 12005. Devise for maintenance

A devisee of a devise for maintenance is entitled to interest on the amount of any unpaid accumulations of the payments held by the personal representative on each anniversary of the testator's death, computed from the date of the anniversary. *(Stats.1990, c. 79 (A.B.759), § 14, operative July 1, 1991.)*

Application

Application of chapter limited to cases where decedent died on or after July 1, 1989, see Probate Code § 12007.

Law Revision Commission Comments

1990 Enactment

Section 12005 continues Section 12005 of the repealed Probate Code without change. A devise for maintenance, within the meaning of this section, includes a devise for support. The rule of Section 12005 applies where the intention of the testator is not indicated by the will. See Section 12000. This chapter does not apply where the decedent died before July 1, 1989. See Section 12007. As to the application of any amendments made after that date, see Section 3.

Background on Section 12005 of Repealed Code

Section 12005 was added by 1988 Cal.Stat. ch. 1199 § 91.5. The section restated the portion of subdivision (c) of former Probate Code Section 663 (added by 1983 Cal.Stat. ch. 842 § 40 and repealed by 1988 Cal.Stat. ch. 1199 § 52) that related to devises for maintenance. For background on the provisions of this chapter, see the Comment to this chapter under the chapter heading. [20 Cal.L.Rev.Comm.Reports 1001 (1990)].

§ 12006. Other income; pro rata distribution; tenancy for life or term of years

Net income received during administration not paid under other provisions of this chapter and not otherwise devised shall be distributed pro rata as income among all distributees who receive either residuary or intestate property. If a distributee takes for life or for a term of years, the pro rata share of income belongs to the tenant for life or for the term of years. *(Stats.1990, c. 79 (A.B.759), § 14, operative July 1, 1991.)*

Application

Application of chapter limited to cases where decedent died on or after July 1, 1989, see Probate Code § 12007.

Law Revision Commission Comments

1990 Enactment

Section 12006 continues Section 12006 of the repealed Probate Code without change. The rule of this section applies where the intention of the testator is not indicated by the will. See Section 12000. The rule of this section applies to a person who receives either testate or intestate property. Cf. Section 6148 (failed devise). This chapter does not apply where the decedent died before July 1, 1989. See Section 12007. As to the application of any amendments made after that date, see Section 3.

Background on Section 12006 of Repealed Code

Section 12006 was added by 1988 Cal.Stat. ch. 1199 § 91.5. The section superseded former Probate Code Section 664 (added by 1983 Cal.Stat. ch. 842 § 40 and repealed by 1988 Cal.Stat. ch. 1199 § 52). The former reference to a distribution to a beneficiary in trust as income to the trust was omitted; this matter is governed by Section 16305(a) (California Revised Uniform Principal and Income Act). The reference to intestate property was new and recognized that there may be a partial intestacy in a testate estate. For background on the provisions of this chapter, see the Comment to this chapter under the chapter heading. [20 Cal.L.Rev.Comm.Reports 1001 (1990)].

§ 12007. Application of chapter

This chapter does not apply in cases where the decedent died before July 1, 1989. In cases where the decedent died before July 1, 1989, the applicable law in effect before July 1, 1989, continues to apply. *(Stats.1990, c. 79 (A.B.759), § 14, operative July 1, 1991.)*

Law Revision Commission Comments

1990 Enactment

Section 12007 continues Section 12007 of the repealed Probate Code without substantive change.

Background on Section 12007 of Repealed Code

Section 12007 was a new provision added by 1988 Cal.Stat. ch. 1199 § 91.5. For background on the provisions of this chapter, see the Comment to this chapter under the chapter heading. [20 Cal.L.Rev.Comm.Reports 1001 (1990)].

Part 11

CLOSING ESTATE ADMINISTRATION

Law Revision Commission Comments

1990 Enactment

This part supersedes Part 11 (commencing with Section 12200) of Division 7 of the repealed Probate Code. The superseded part was enacted upon recommendation of the California Law Revision Commission. See Recommendation Relating to Distribution and Discharge, 19 Cal.L.Revision Comm'n Reports 953 (1988). See also Communication from the California Law Revision Commission Concerning Assembly Bill 2841, 19 Cal.L.Revision Comm'n Reports 1201, 1248 (1988). [20 Cal.L.Rev.Comm.Reports 1001 (1990)].

CHAPTER 1. TIME FOR CLOSING ESTATE

Cross References

Application of old and new law, see Probate Code § 3.

§ 12200. Petition for final distribution order; report of status of administration; time

The personal representative shall either petition for an order for final distribution of the estate or make a report of status of administration not later than the following times:

(a) In an estate for which a federal estate tax return is not required, within one year after the date of issuance of letters.

(b) In an estate for which a federal estate tax return is required, within 18 months after the date of issuance of letters. *(Stats.1990, c. 79 (A.B.759), § 14, operative July 1, 1991.)*

Law Revision Commission Comments

1990 Enactment

Section 12200 continues Section 12200 of the repealed Probate Code without change.

Background on Section 12200 of Repealed Code

Section 12200 was added by 1988 Cal.Stat. ch. 1199 § 93. The section restated the first sentence of former Probate Code Section 1025.5 (repealed by 1988 Cal.Stat. ch. 1199 § 55.5) without substantive change. For background on the provisions of this part, see the Comment to this part under the part heading. [20 Cal.L.Rev.Comm.Reports 1001 (1990)].

§ 12201. Report of status of administration; contents; filing; hearing; notice; continuation of administration; final distribution

If a report of status of administration is made under Section 12200:

(a) The report shall show the condition of the estate, the reasons why the estate cannot be distributed and closed, and an estimate of the time needed to close administration of the estate.

(b) The report shall be filed with the court. Notice of hearing of the report shall be given as provided in Section 1220 to persons then interested in the estate, and shall include a statement in not less than 10-point boldface type or a reasonable equivalent thereof if printed, or in all capital letters if not printed, in substantially the following words: "YOU HAVE THE RIGHT TO PETITION FOR AN ACCOUNT UNDER SECTION 10950 OF THE CALIFORNIA PROBATE CODE."

(c) On the hearing of the report, the court may order either of the following:

(1) That the administration of the estate continue for the time and on the terms and conditions that appear reasonable, including an account under Section 10950, if the court determines that continuation of administration is in the best interests of the estate or of interested persons.

(2) That the personal representative shall petition for final distribution. *(Stats.1990, c. 79 (A.B.759), § 14, operative July 1, 1991.)*

Law Revision Commission Comments

1990 Enactment

Section 12201 continues Section 12201 of the repealed Probate Code without change. This section makes specific reference to the availability of an account under Section 10950; however, the court may not order an account under Section 10950 if the waiver or satisfaction provisions of Section 10954 (when account is not required) are satisfied. The report of status of administration must be verified. See Section 1021. For general provisions, see Sections 1000–1004 (rules of practice), 1020–1023 (petitions and other papers), 1040–1050 (hearings and orders), 1200–1230 (notice of hearing), 1250–1252 (request for special notice), 1260–1265 (proof of giving of notice).

Background on Section 12201 of Repealed Code

Section 12201 was added by 1988 Cal.Stat. ch. 1199 § 93. The section restated the second, third, and fourth sentences of former Probate Code Section 1025.5 (repealed by 1988 Cal.Stat. ch. 1199 § 55.5), with the addition of an estimate of the time needed to close administration. The section also superseded a portion of former Probate Code Section 956 ("administration may continue for such time as may be reasonable") (reenacted without change by 1987 Cal.Stat. ch. 923 § 48.5 and repealed by 1988 Cal.Stat. ch. 1199 § 55). For background on the provisions of this part, see the Comment to this part under the part heading. [20 Cal.L.Rev.Comm.Reports 1001 (1990)].

§ 12202. Appearance to show condition of estate and reasons for failure to make distribution; petition; citation by court; hearing

(a) The court may, on petition of any interested person or on its own motion, for good cause shown on the record, cite the personal representative to appear before the court and show the condition of the estate and the reasons why the estate cannot be distributed and closed.

(b) On the hearing of the citation, the court may either order the administration of the estate to continue or order the personal representative to petition for final distribution, as provided in Section 12201. *(Stats.1990, c. 79 (A.B.759), § 14, operative July 1, 1991. Amended by Stats.1996, c. 563 (S.B.392), § 28.)*

Law Revision Commission Comments

1990 Enactment

Section 12202 restates Section 12202 of the repealed Probate Code without substantive change. See also Sections 1240–1242 (citations).

Background on Section 12202 of Repealed Code

Section 12202 was added by 1988 Cal.Stat. ch. 1199 § 93. The section restated the second paragraph of former Probate Code Section 1025.5 (repealed by 1988 Cal.Stat. ch. 1199 § 55.5) without substantive change. For background on the provisions of this part, see the Comment to this part under the part heading. [20 Cal.L.Rev.Comm.Reports 1001 (1990)].

§ 12203. Family allowance; continuation of administration to pay; determinations; preliminary distribution

(a) For purposes of this chapter, continuation of the administration of the estate in order to pay a family allowance is not in the best interests of the estate or interested persons unless the court determines both of the following:

(1) The family allowance is needed by the recipient to pay for necessaries of life, including education so long as pursued to advantage.

(2) The needs of the recipient for continued family allowance outweigh the needs of the decedent's beneficiaries whose interests would be adversely affected by continuing the administration of the estate for this purpose.

(b) Nothing in this section shall be construed to authorize continuation of a family allowance beyond the time prescribed in Section 6543.

(c) Nothing in this section limits the power of the court to order a preliminary distribution of the estate. *(Stats.1990, c. 79 (A.B.759), § 14, operative July 1, 1991.)*

Law Revision Commission Comments

1990 Enactment

Section 12203 continues Section 12203 of the repealed Probate Code without change. This section provides standards for the court in determining whether to continue administration of the estate to pay a family allowance. Subdivision (b) makes clear the interrelation between this section and Section 6543 (termination of family allowance).

Background on Section 12203 of Repealed Code

Section 12203 was added by 1988 Cal.Stat. ch. 1199 § 93. Subdivision (a) restated former Probate Code Section 1026 (added by 1983 Cal.Stat. ch. 842 § 43 and repealed by 1988 Cal.Stat. ch. 1199 § 55.5) without substantive change. Subdivisions (b) and (c) were new. For background on the provisions of this part, see the Comment to this part under the part heading. [20 Cal.L.Rev.Comm.Reports 1001 (1990)].

§ 12204. Noncompliance of personal representative with order; removal from office

Failure of the personal representative to comply with an order made under this chapter is grounds for removal from office. *(Stats.1990, c. 79 (A.B.759), § 14, operative July 1, 1991.)*

Law Revision Commission Comments

1990 Enactment

Section 12204 continues Section 12204 of the repealed Probate Code without change.

Background on Section 12204 of Repealed Code

Section 12204 was added by 1988 Cal.Stat. ch. 1199 § 93. The section restated the third paragraph of former Probate Code Section 1025.5 (repealed by 1988 Cal.Stat. ch. 1199 § 55.5) without substantive change. For background on the provisions of this part, see the Comment to this part under the part heading. [20 Cal.L.Rev.Comm.Reports 1001 (1990)].

§ 12205. Reduction of compensation; personal representative or attorney

(a) The court may reduce the compensation of the personal representative or the attorney for the personal representative by an amount the court determines to be appropriate if the court makes all of the following determinations:

(1) The time taken for administration of the estate exceeds the time required by this chapter or prescribed by the court.

(2) The time taken was within the control of the personal representative or attorney whose compensation is being reduced.

(3) The delay was not in the best interest of the estate or interested persons.

(b) An order under this section reducing compensation may be made regardless of whether the compensation otherwise allowable under Part 7 (commencing with Section 10800) would be reasonable compensation for the services rendered by the personal representative or attorney.

(c) An order under this section may be made at any of the following hearings:

(1) The hearing for final distribution.

(2) The hearing for an allowance on the compensation of the personal representative or attorney.

(d) In making a determination under this section, the court shall take into account any action taken under Section 12202 as a result of a previous delay. *(Stats.1990, c. 79 (A.B.759), § 14, operative July 1, 1991. Amended by Stats. 1990, c. 710 (S.B.1775), § 42, operative July 1, 1991.)*

Law Revision Commission Comments
1990 Enactment and Amendment

Section 12205 (enacted as a part of the new Probate Code by 1990 Cal.Stat. ch. 79 § 14) was amended by 1990 Cal.Stat. ch. 710 § 42. As originally enacted, Section 12205 of the new Probate Code revised Section 12205 of the repealed Probate Code to reflect the fact that Assembly Bill 831 of the 1989–1990 regular session would have substituted an agreed fee system for the statutory fee system for probate attorney fees. However, Assembly Bill 831 was not enacted, and Section 12205 was amended by 1990 Cal.Stat. ch. 710 § 42 to reflect this fact. See the Comment to Section 900.

Section 12205 as amended continues Section 12205 of the repealed Probate Code without substantive change.

Background on Section 12205 of Repealed Code

Section 12205 was added by 1988 Cal.Stat. ch. 1199 § 93. The section restated the fourth paragraph of former Probate Code Section 1025.5 (repealed by 1988 Cal.Stat. ch. 1199 § 55.5), with the addition of a direction to the court to consider prior delays in setting sanctions. For background on the provisions of this part, see the Comment to this part under the part heading. [20 Cal.L.Rev.Comm. Reports 1001 (1990)].

§ 12206. Time limit in will

A limitation in a will of the time for administration of an estate is directory only and does not limit the power of the personal representative or the court to continue administration of the estate beyond the time limitation in the will if the continuation is necessary. *(Stats.1990, c. 79 (A.B.759), § 14, operative July 1, 1991.)*

Law Revision Commission Comments
1990 Enactment

Section 12206 continues Section 12206 of the repealed Probate Code without change.

Background on Section 12206 of Repealed Code

Section 12206 was added by 1988 Cal.Stat. ch. 1199 § 93. The section restated former Probate Code Section 1025 (repealed by 1988 Cal.Stat. ch. 1199 § 55.5) without substantive change. For back-

ground on the provisions of this part, see the Comment to this part under the part heading. [20 Cal.L.Rev.Comm.Reports 1001 (1990)].

Cross References
Closing or continuing administration contingent upon payment of debts, see Probate Code § 11640.
Construction of wills, generally, see Probate Code § 21102 et seq.
Discharge on payment of debts or exhaustion of estate, see Probate Code § 11422.
Failure to commence administration within six months, direction to public administrator, see Code of Civil Procedure § 1420.

CHAPTER 2. DISCHARGE OF PERSONAL REPRESENTATIVE

Section
12250. Compliance with final distribution order; receipts filing; ex parte petition; discharge from liability.
12251. No property subject to administration; petition for termination of proceedings and discharge; notice of hearing.
12252. Subsequent administration; appointment of personal representative; priority; notice of hearing.

Cross References
Application of old and new law, see Probate Code § 3.

§ 12250. Compliance with final distribution order; receipts filing; ex parte petition; discharge from liability

(a) When the personal representative has complied with the terms of the order for final distribution and has filed the appropriate receipts or the court has excused the filing of a receipt as provided in Section 11753, the court shall, on ex parte petition, make an order discharging the personal representative from all liability incurred thereafter.

(b) Nothing in this section precludes discharge of the personal representative for distribution made without prior court order, so long as the terms of the order for final distribution are satisfied. *(Stats.1990, c. 79 (A.B.759), § 14, operative July 1, 1991.)*

Law Revision Commission Comments
1990 Enactment

Subdivision (a) of Section 12250 restates Section 12250 of the repealed Probate Code without substantive change. Subdivision (b) codifies existing practice. The estate is fully administered for purposes of this section when all sums of money due from the personal representative have been paid, all property of the estate has been distributed to the persons entitled under court order, and all the acts lawfully required of the personal representative have been performed. As to after-discovered property, see Section 11642.

Background on Section 12250 of Repealed Code

Section 12250 was added by 1988 Cal.Stat. ch. 1199 § 93. The section restated former Probate Code Section 1066 (repealed by 1988 Cal.Stat. ch. 1199 § 55.5), except that the provision for production of vouchers was not continued, and the petition is made ex parte under Section 12250. For background on the provisions of this part, see the Comment to this part under the part heading. [20 Cal.L.Rev.Comm.Reports 1001 (1990)].

Cross References
Discharge on exhaustion of assets of estate, see Probate Code § 11422.

Distribution of property in compliance with court order as discharge, see Probate Code § 11753.
Final distribution, order, see Probate Code §§ 11603, 11605, 11641.
Settlement of account, see Probate Code § 11000 et seq.

§ 12251. No property subject to administration; petition for termination of proceedings and discharge; notice of hearing

(a) At any time after appointment of a personal representative and whether or not letters have been issued, if it appears there is no property of any kind belonging to the estate and subject to administration, the personal representative may petition for the termination of further proceedings and for discharge of the personal representative. The petition shall state the facts required by this subdivision.

(b) Notice of the hearing on the petition shall be given as provided in Section 1220 to all interested persons.

(c) If it appears to the satisfaction of the court on the hearing that the facts stated in the petition are true, the court shall make an order terminating the proceeding and discharging the personal representative. (Stats.1990, c. 79 (A.B.759), § 14, operative July 1, 1991.)

Law Revision Commission Comments
1990 Enactment

Section 12251 continues Section 12251 of the repealed Probate Code without change. Proceedings may be taken under this section without the return of an inventory provided for by Part 3 (commencing with Section 8800). See subdivision (a) ("at any time"). For general provisions, see Sections 1000–1004 (rules of practice), 1020–1023 (petitions and other papers), 1040–1050 (hearings and orders), 1200–1230 (notice of hearing), 1250–1252 (request for special notice), 1260–1265 (proof of giving of notice).

Background on Section 12251 of Repealed Code

Section 12251 was added by 1988 Cal.Stat. ch. 1199 § 93. The section restated former Probate Code Section 1068 (repealed by 1988 Cal.Stat. ch. 1199 § 55.5), with the addition of subdivision (b). For background on the provisions of this part, see the Comment to this part under the part heading. [20 Cal.L.Rev.Comm.Reports 1001 (1990)].

Cross References

Discharge of personal representative on exhaustion of payments to creditors, see Probate Code § 11422.

§ 12252. Subsequent administration; appointment of personal representative; priority; notice of hearing

If subsequent administration of an estate is necessary after the personal representative has been discharged because other property is discovered or because it becomes necessary or proper for any other cause, both of the following shall apply:

(a) The court shall appoint as personal representative the person entitled to appointment in the same order as is directed in relation to an original appointment, except that the person who served as personal representative at the time of the order of discharge has priority.

(b) Notice of hearing of the appointment shall be given as provided in Section 1220 to the person who served as personal representative at the time of the order of discharge and to other interested persons. If property has been distributed to the State of California, a copy of any petition for subsequent appointment of a personal representative and the notice of hearing shall be given as provided in Section 1220 to the Controller. (Stats.1990, c. 79 (A.B.759), § 14, operative July 1, 1991. Amended by Stats.2007, c. 388 (A.B.403), § 1; Stats.2009, c. 8 (A.B.1163), § 3.)

Law Revision Commission Comments
1990 Enactment

Section 12252 restates Section 12252 of the repealed Probate Code without substantive change. As to after-discovered property, see Section 11642. For general provisions, see Sections 1040–1050 (hearings and orders), 1200–1230 (notice of hearing), 1250–1252 (request for special notice), 1260–1265 (proof of giving of notice).

2009 Amendment

Section 12252 is amended to remove language relating to a personal representative holding the attorney-client privilege. That issue is addressed in Evidence Code Section 953. [38 Cal.L.Rev. Comm. Reports 163 (2008)].

Background on Section 12252 of Repealed Code

Section 12252 was added by 1988 Cal.Stat. ch. 1199 § 93. The section restated former Probate Code Section 1067 (repealed by 1988 Cal.Stat. ch. 1199 § 55.5), conforming the notice provisions to Section 1220. For background on the provisions of this part, see the Comment to this part under the part heading. [20 Cal.L.Rev.Comm.Reports 1001 (1990)].

Cross References

Appointment of administrators with the will annexed, see Probate Code § 8440 et seq.
Appointment of personal representatives, generally, see Probate Code § 8400 et seq.
Powers and duties of successor personal representative, see Probate Code § 8524.
Property acquired or discovered after final distribution order made, see Probate Code § 11642.

Part 12

ADMINISTRATION OF ESTATES OF MISSING PERSONS PRESUMED DEAD

Law Revision Commission Comments

1990 Enactment

This part supersedes Part 12 (commencing with Section 12400) of Division 7 of the repealed Probate Code. The superseded part was enacted upon recommendation of the California Law Revision Commission. See Recommendation Relating to Administration of Estates of Missing Persons, 19 Cal.L.Revision Comm'n Reports 637 (1988). [20 Cal.L.Rev.Comm.Reports 1001 (1990)].

Cross References

Application of old and new law, see Probate Code § 3.

§ 12400. Missing person

Unless the provision or context otherwise requires, as used in this part, "missing person" means a person who is presumed to be dead under Section 12401. *(Stats.1990, c. 79 (A.B.759), § 14, operative July 1, 1991.)*

Law Revision Commission Comments

1990 Enactment

Section 12400 continues Section 12400 of the repealed Probate Code without change.

Background on Section 12400 of Repealed Code

Section 12400 was added by 1987 Cal.Stat. ch. 923 § 93. The section restated former Probate Code Section 1350 (repealed by 1987 Cal.Stat. ch. 923 § 60.7) without substantive change. For background on the provisions of this part, see the Comment to this part under the part heading. [20 Cal.L.Rev.Comm.Reports 1001 (1990)].

§ 12401. Presumption of death; presumed occurrence of death

In proceedings under this part, a person who has not been seen or heard from for a continuous period of five years by those who are likely to have seen or heard from that person, and whose absence is not satisfactorily explained after diligent search or inquiry, is presumed to be dead. The person's death is presumed to have occurred at the end of the period unless there is sufficient evidence to establish that death occurred earlier. *(Stats.1990, c. 79 (A.B.759), § 14, operative July 1, 1991.)*

Law Revision Commission Comments

1990 Enactment

Section 12401 continues Section 12401 of the repealed Probate Code without change. This section is the same in substance as Uniform Probate Code Section 1–107(4) (1987). As to the construction of provisions drawn from uniform acts, see Section 2. See also Evid.Code §§ 667 (general presumption of death), 1282 (finding of presumed death by federal employee).

Background on Section 12401 of Repealed Code

Section 12401 was added by 1987 Cal.Stat. ch. 923 § 93. The section restated former Probate Code Section 1351 (repealed by 1987 Cal.Stat. ch. 923 § 60.7) without substantive change. The language of the standard as stated in Section 12401 was revised for consistency with Section 12404. For background on the provisions of this part, see the Comment to this part under the part heading. [20 Cal.L.Rev.Comm.Reports 1001 (1990)].

§ 12402. Administration of missing person's estate

Subject to the provisions of this part, the estate of a missing person may be administered in the manner provided general-ly for the administration of estates of deceased persons. *(Stats.1990, c. 79 (A.B.759), § 14, operative July 1, 1991.)*

Law Revision Commission Comments

1990 Enactment

Section 12402 continues Section 12402 of the repealed Probate Code without change. The time limitations on preliminary and final distribution apply to distribution under this part. See also Section 12408 (recovery of property by missing person upon reappearance).

Background on Section 12402 of Repealed Code

Section 12402 was added by 1987 Cal.Stat. ch. 923 § 93. The section restated former Probate Code Section 1352 (repealed by 1987 Cal.Stat. ch. 923 § 60.7) without substantive change, except that the one-year delay of distribution was not continued. Under Section 12402, the general limitations on distribution of estates apply. The reference to distribution of the estate in former Section 1352 also was omitted from Section 12402; distribution is included in the process of administration under Section 12402. For background on the provisions of this part, see the Comment to this part under the part heading. [20 Cal.L.Rev.Comm.Reports 1001 (1990)].

Cross References

Administration of estates of decedents,
　Generally, see Probate Code § 7000 et seq.
　Collection or transfer of estate without administration, generally, see Probate Code § 13000 et seq.
　Independent administration, generally, see Probate Code § 10400 et seq.

§ 12403. Jurisdiction

(a) If the missing person was a resident of this state when last seen or heard from, the superior court of the county of the person's last known place of residence has jurisdiction for the purposes of this part.

(b) If the missing person was a nonresident of this state when last seen or heard from, the superior court of a county where real property of the missing person is located, or of a county where personal property is located if the missing person has no real property in this state, has jurisdiction for the purposes of this part. *(Stats.1990, c. 79 (A.B.759), § 14, operative July 1, 1991.)*

Law Revision Commission Comments

1990 Enactment

Section 12403 continues Section 12403 of the repealed Probate Code without change.

Background on Section 12403 of Repealed Code

Section 12403 was added by 1987 Cal.Stat. ch. 923 § 93. The section restated former Probate Code Section 1353 (repealed by 1987 Cal.Stat. ch. 923 § 60.7) without substantive change. For background on the provisions of this part, see the Comment to this part under the part heading. [20 Cal.L.Rev.Comm.Reports 1001 (1990)].

Cross References

Jurisdiction and venue, generally, see Probate Code § 7050 et seq.

§ 12404. Petition for administration of estate; persons who may file; contents of petition

(a) A petition may be filed in the court having jurisdiction under Section 12403 for the administration of the estate of a missing person.

(b) The petition may be filed by any person who may be appointed as a personal representative, other than a person described in subdivision (r) of Section 8461.

(c) In addition to the matters otherwise required in a petition for administration of the estate, the petition shall state all of the following:

(1) The last known place of residence and the last known address of the missing person.

(2) The time and circumstances when the missing person was last seen or heard from.

(3) That the missing person has not been seen or heard from for a continuous period of five years by the persons likely to have seen or heard from the missing person (naming them and their relationship to the missing person) and that the whereabouts of the missing person is unknown to those persons and to the petitioner.

(4) A description of the search or the inquiry made concerning the whereabouts of the missing person. *(Stats. 1990, c. 79 (A.B.759), § 14, operative July 1, 1991.)*

Law Revision Commission Comments

1990 Enactment

Section 12404 continues Section 12404 of the repealed Probate Code without substantive change. Subdivision (b) does not affect the order of priority of appointment of an administrator; this is controlled by provisions governing administration generally. However, a person who qualifies for appointment as a personal representative only as "[a]ny other person" under subdivision (r) of Section 8461 may not petition under Section 12404; only persons who fall into some other category listed in Section 8461 may petition. Pursuant to subdivision (c) of Section 12404 and Section 12402, the general requirements for a petition for administration of the estate apply to proceedings under this part. For general provisions relating to petitions, see Sections 1020–1023.

Background on Section 12404 of Repealed Code

Section 12404 was added by 1987 Cal.Stat. ch. 923 § 93 and was amended by 1988 Cal.Stat. ch. 1199 § 93.5. The section as enacted restated subdivisions (a) to (c) of former Probate Code Section 1354 (repealed by 1987 Cal.Stat. ch. 923 § 60.7) without substantive change, except as noted below:

(1) The reference to probate of the will in former Section 1354(a) was omitted from Section 12404 as surplus.

(2) The list of persons who could petition under former Section 1354(b) was revised in Section 12404 to incorporate the list of persons who may be appointed as personal representative. This revision made clear that a petition may be filed by persons such as the public administrator or a creditor. See Section 8461(p) (public administrator) and (q) (creditors). However, this revision did not permit a person who qualified for appointment as a personal representative only as a "person legally competent" under paragraph (12) of subdivision (a) of former Probate Code Section 422 (repealed by 1988 Cal.Stat. ch. 1199 § 45) (now "[a]ny other person" under subdivision (r) of Section 8461), to petition under Section 12404; only persons who fall into some other category could petition.

(3) The requirement of Section 12404 that the petitioner give the last known address of the missing person in subdivision (c)(1) was new. Subdivision (c)(2) of Section 12404 was revised for consistency with subdivision (c)(3). Subdivision (c)(3) of Section 12404 was revised to eliminate the need to identify the persons most likely to know the whereabouts of the missing person. The reference in Section 12404 to seeing the missing person was new, but made no substantive change.

For background on the provisions of this part, see the Comment to this part under the part heading.

The 1988 amendment corrected a reference to another statutory provision. [20 Cal.L.Rev.Comm.Reports 1001 (1990)].

Cross References

Administration of estates of decedents,
Generally, see Probate Code § 7000 et seq.
Commencement of proceedings, see Probate Code § 8000 et seq.
Independent administration, generally, see Probate Code § 10400 et seq.
Personal representative,
Appointment, see Probate Code § 8400 et seq.
Defined, see Probate Code § 58.
Petitions and other papers,
Generally, see Probate Code § 1020 et seq.
Contents, see Probate Code § 8002.

§ 12405. Notice of hearing; notice to missing person

Notice of hearing shall be served and published, and proof made, in the same manner as in proceedings for administration of the estate of a decedent, except that notice of hearing on the petition shall also be sent by registered mail to the missing person at his or her last known address. *(Stats.1990, c. 79 (A.B.759), § 14, operative July 1, 1991.)*

Law Revision Commission Comments

1990 Enactment

Section 12405 continues Section 12405 of the repealed Probate Code without change. See also Sections 5 (use of certified mail satisfies registered mail requirement), 1260–1265 (proof of giving of notice).

Background on Section 12405 of Repealed Code

Section 12405 was added by 1987 Cal.Stat. ch. 923 § 93. The section replaced former Probate Code Section 1355 (repealed by 1987 Cal.Stat. ch. 923 § 60.7). Under Section 12405, the hearing was no longer delayed for three months nor was publication required for 90 days before the hearing. For background on the provisions of this part, see the Comment to this part under the part heading. [20 Cal.L.Rev.Comm.Reports 1001 (1990)].

Cross References

Administration of estates of decedents, generally, see Probate Code § 7000 et seq.
Notice of hearing,
Generally, see Probate Code §§ 1200 et seq., 8000 et seq.
Contents, see Probate Code § 8100 et seq.
Mailing requirements, see Probate Code § 1220 et seq.
Posting requirements, see Probate Code § 1230.
Proof requirements, see Probate Code § 1260 et seq.
Publication requirements, see Probate Code §§ 8003, 8120 et seq.
Service requirements, see Probate Code §§ 8003, 8110 et seq.
Special notice requests, see Probate Code § 1250 et seq.

§ 12406. Determination if missing person should be presumed dead; order to conduct search; cost of search

(a) At the hearing, the court shall determine whether the alleged missing person is a person who is presumed to be dead under Section 12401. The court may receive evidence and consider the affidavits and depositions of persons likely to have seen or heard from or know the whereabouts of the alleged missing person.

(b) If the court is not satisfied that a diligent search or inquiry has been made for the missing person, the court may order the petitioner to conduct a diligent search or inquiry and to report the results. The court may order the search or inquiry to be made in any manner that the court determines to be advisable, including any or all of the following methods:

(1) Inserting in one or more suitable newspapers or other periodicals a notice requesting information from any person having knowledge of the whereabouts of the missing person.

(2) Notifying law enforcement officials and public welfare agencies in appropriate locations of the disappearance of the missing person.

(3) Engaging the services of an investigator.

(c) The costs of a search ordered by the court pursuant to subdivision (b) shall be paid by the estate of the missing person, but if there is no administration, the court in its discretion may order the petitioner to pay the costs. *(Stats. 1990, c. 79 (A.B.759), § 14, operative July 1, 1991.)*

Law Revision Commission Comments

1990 Enactment

Section 12406 continues Section 12406 of the repealed Probate Code without change. Subdivision (c) makes the estate presumptively liable for costs, but gives the court discretion to order the petitioner to pay costs if there is no administration. For general provisions, see Sections 1000–1004 (rules of practice), 1040–1050 (hearings and orders).

Background on Section 12406 of Repealed Code

Section 12406 was added by 1987 Cal.Stat. ch. 923 § 93. Subdivisions (a) and (b) restated subdivisions (a) and (b) of former Probate Code Section 1356 (repealed by 1987 Cal.Stat. ch. 923 § 60.7) without substantive change. The word "reasonably" which preceded "diligent search" under former Section 1356(b) was omitted, but this was not a substantive change. The court has the authority to order a search that is appropriate under the circumstances of the case. The reference in subdivision (b)(1) of Section 12406 to newspapers was new; this was not a substantive change.

Subdivision (c) gives the court discretion to order the petitioner to pay costs if there is no administration. Subdivision (c) of former Section 1356 required that costs be paid by the petitioner if there was no administration.

For background on the provisions of this part, see the Comment to this part under the part heading. [20 Cal.L.Rev.Comm.Reports 1001 (1990)].

Cross References

Administration of estates of decedents,
   Generally, see Probate Code § 7000 et seq.
   Collection or transfer of estate without administration, see Probate Code § 13000 et seq.
   Commencement of administration proceedings, generally, see Probate Code § 8000 et seq.
   Independent administration, generally, see Probate Code § 10400 et seq.
Hearings and orders, generally, see Probate Code § 1040 et seq.

§ 12407. Person presumed dead; appointment of personal representative to administer estate; date of death

(a) If the court finds that the alleged missing person is a person presumed to be dead under Section 12401, the court shall do both of the following:

(1) Appoint a personal representative for the estate of the missing person in the manner provided for the estates of deceased persons.

(2) Determine the date of the missing person's death.

(b) The personal representative shall administer the estate of the missing person in the same general manner and method of procedure, and with the same force and effect, as provided for the administration of the estates of deceased persons, except as otherwise provided in this part. *(Stats. 1990, c. 79 (A.B.759), § 14, operative July 1, 1991.)*

Law Revision Commission Comments

1990 Enactment

Section 12407 continues Section 12407 of the repealed Probate Code without change. See also Sections 12401 (death presumed at end of five-year period unless sufficient evidence of earlier death), 12402 (manner of administration and distribution).

Background on Section 12407 of Repealed Code

Section 12407 was added by 1987 Cal.Stat. ch. 923 § 93. The section restated former Probate Code Section 1357 (repealed by 1987 Cal.Stat. ch. 923 § 60.7) without substantive change. For background on the provisions of this part, see the Comment to this part under the part heading. [20 Cal.L.Rev.Comm.Reports 1001 (1990)].

Cross References

Administration of estates of decedents,
   Generally, see Probate Code § 7000 et seq.
   Collection or transfer of estate without administration, see Probate Code § 13000 et seq.
   Commencement of proceedings, see Probate Code § 8000 et seq.
   Independent administration, generally, see Probate Code § 10400 et seq.
Personal representative,
   Appointment, see Probate Code § 8400 et seq.
   Defined, see Probate Code § 58.

§ 12408. Reappearance of missing person; recovery of property; limitations of actions; order for final distribution conclusive as to parties; disputed identity of reappearing missing person

(a) If the missing person reappears:

(1) The missing person may recover property of the missing person's estate in the possession of the personal representative, less fees, costs, and expenses thus far incurred.

(2) The missing person may recover from distributees any property of the missing person's estate that is in their possession, or the value of distributions received by them, to the extent that recovery from distributees is equitable in view of all the circumstances, but an action under this paragraph is forever barred five years after the time the distribution was made.

(b) The remedies available to the missing person under subdivision (a) are exclusive, except for any remedy the missing person may have by reason of fraud or intentional wrongdoing.

(c) Except as provided in subdivisions (a) and (b), the order for final distribution, when it becomes final, is conclusive as to the rights of the missing person, the rights of the beneficiaries of the missing person, and the rights of all other persons interested in the estate.

(d) If a dispute arises as to the identity of a person claiming to be a reappearing missing person, the person making the claim or any other interested person may file a petition under Section 11700, notwithstanding the limitations of time prescribed in Section 11700, for the determination of the identity of the person claiming to be the reappearing missing person. *(Stats.1990, c. 79 (A.B.759), § 14, operative July 1, 1991.)*

Law Revision Commission Comments
1990 Enactment

Section 12408 continues Section 12408 of the repealed Probate Code without change.

Subdivisions (a) and (b) are drawn from the last paragraph of Section 3–412 of the Uniform Probate Code (1987), but a provision is added barring an action under paragraph (a)(2) five years after distribution under Section 12407(b). As to the construction of provisions drawn from uniform acts, see Section 2.

Subdivision (c) is consistent with Section 11605 (effect of an order for final distribution in probate proceedings generally). Subdivision (c) permits a distributee to convey good title to property of the missing person before the time an action by the missing person against the distributee would be barred under subdivision (a)(2). This is because subdivision (c) provides a rule that the order for final distribution, when it becomes final, is conclusive as to the rights of the missing person. The exception to this rule in subdivision (a)(2) is limited to property in the hands of the distributee or the value of distributions received by the distributee; subdivision (a)(2) does not permit an action against the person to whom the property has been transferred by the distributee. Where a distributee has encumbered property of the missing person, the lender likewise would be protected under subdivision (c); but, if the action of the missing person is not barred under subdivision (a)(2), the reappearing missing person might recover from the distributee the property, subject to the encumbrance.

Background on Section 12408 of Repealed Code

Section 12408 was added by 1987 Cal.Stat. ch. 923 § 93 and was amended by 1988 Cal.Stat. ch. 1199 § 94. The section restated former Probate Code Section 1358 (repealed by 1987 Cal.Stat. ch. 923 § 60.7) without substantive change, except that the five-year period under Section 12408 ran from the time of distribution rather than the time of the petition and the term "beneficiaries" was substituted for "heirs, devisees, and legatees." For background on the provisions of this part, see the Comment to this part under the part heading.

The provision barring an action under paragraph (a)(2) of Section 12408 five years after distribution under Section 12404 continued the general effect of the parts of former Probate Code Sections 287–292 (the statute in effect before former Sections 1350–1359 and which was repealed by 1983 Cal.Stat. ch. 201 § 3) that gave a distribution conclusive effect after the missing person had been missing 10 years.

Subdivision (d) of Section 12408 restated former Section 1358(d) without substantive change, but was revised to make clear that the restrictions on the time of filing a petition under Section 1080 do not apply under this part.

The 1988 amendment corrected references to other statutory provisions. [20 Cal.L.Rev.Comm.Reports 1001 (1990)].

Cross References

Administration of estates of decedents,
   Generally, see Probate Code § 7000 et seq.
   Distribution of estate, generally, see Probate Code § 11600 et seq.
   Final distribution of estate, see Probate Code § 11640 et seq.
   Persons entitled to distribution, see Probate Code § 11700 et seq.
Beneficiary, defined, see Probate Code § 24.
Personal representative, defined, see Probate Code § 58.

§ 12409. Repealed by Stats.1990, c. 79 (A.B.759), § 13, operative July 1, 1991

Law Revision Commission Comments
1990 Repeal

Section 12409 of the repealed Probate Code is omitted from the new Probate Code because it has served its purpose in the transition to the law that became operative on January 1, 1984. See 1987 Cal.Stat. ch. 923, § 93. See also Section 3 (general transitional provision). [20 Cal.L.Rev.Comm.Reports 1001 (1990)].

Part 13

NONDOMICILIARY DECEDENTS

Law Revision Commission Comments
1990 Enactment

This part supersedes Part 13 (commencing with Section 12500) of Division 7 of the repealed Probate Code. The superseded part was enacted upon recommendation of the California Law Revision Commission. See Recommendation Relating to Nondomiciliary Decedents, 19 Cal.L.Revision Comm'n Reports 993 (1988). [20 Cal.L.Rev.Comm.Reports 1001 (1990)].

CHAPTER 1. DEFINITIONS

Cross References

Application of old and new law, see Probate Code § 3.

§ 12500. Application of chapter

Unless the provision or context otherwise requires, the definitions in this chapter govern the construction of this part. *(Stats.1990, c. 79 (A.B.759), § 14, operative July 1, 1991.)*

Law Revision Commission Comments
1990 Enactment

Section 12500 continues Section 12500 of the repealed Probate Code without change. This section is comparable to Section 20.

Background on Section 12500 of Repealed Code

Section 12500 was a new provision added by 1988 Cal.Stat. ch. 1199 § 94.5. For background on the provisions of this part, see the Comment to this part under the part heading. [20 Cal.L.Rev.Comm.Reports 1001 (1990)].

§ 12501.   Ancillary administration

"Ancillary administration" means proceedings in this state for administration of the estate of a nondomiciliary decedent. *(Stats.1990, c. 79 (A.B.759), § 14, operative July 1, 1991.)*

Law Revision Commission Comments

1990 Enactment

Section 12501 continues Section 12501 of the repealed Probate Code without change.

Background on Section 12501 of Repealed Code

Section 12501 was a new provision added by 1988 Cal.Stat. ch. 1199 § 94.5. For background on the provisions of this part, see the Comment to this part under the part heading. [20 Cal.L.Rev.Comm.Reports 1001 (1990)].

§ 12502.   Foreign nation

"Foreign nation" means a jurisdiction other than a state of the United States. *(Stats.1990, c. 79 (A.B.759), § 14, operative July 1, 1991.)*

Law Revision Commission Comments

1990 Enactment

Section 12502 continues Section 12502 of the repealed Probate Code without change. "State" is defined in Section 74 as "any state of the United States, the District of Columbia, the Commonwealth of Puerto Rico, and any territory or possession subject to the legislative authority of the United States." See also 28 U.S.C. § 1738 (1982) (implementing the full faith and credit clause of the U.S. Constitution).

Background on Section 12502 of Repealed Code

Section 12502 was a new provision added by 1988 Cal.Stat. ch. 1199 § 94.5. For background on the provisions of this part, see the Comment to this part under the part heading. [20 Cal.L.Rev.Comm.Reports 1001 (1990)].

§ 12503.   Foreign nation personal representative

"Foreign nation personal representative" means a personal representative appointed in a jurisdiction other than a state of the United States. *(Stats.1990, c. 79 (A.B.759), § 14, operative July 1, 1991.)*

Law Revision Commission Comments

1990 Enactment

Section 12503 continues Section 12503 of the repealed Probate Code without change.

Background on Section 12503 of Repealed Code

Section 12503 was a new provision added by 1988 Cal.Stat. ch. 1199 § 94.5. For background on the provisions of this part, see the Comment to this part under the part heading. [20 Cal.L.Rev.Comm.Reports 1001 (1990)].

§ 12504.   Local personal representative

"Local personal representative" means a nondomiciliary decedent's personal representative appointed in this state. *(Stats.1990, c. 79 (A.B.759), § 14, operative July 1, 1991.)*

Law Revision Commission Comments

1990 Enactment

Section 12504 continues Section 12504 of the repealed Probate Code without change.

Background on Section 12504 of Repealed Code

Section 12504 was a new provision added by 1988 Cal.Stat. ch. 1199 § 94.5. For background on the provisions of this part, see the Comment to this part under the part heading. [20 Cal.L.Rev.Comm.Reports 1001 (1990)].

§ 12505.   Nondomiciliary decedent

"Nondomiciliary decedent" means a person who dies domiciled in a sister state or foreign nation. *(Stats.1990, c. 79 (A.B.759), § 14, operative July 1, 1991.)*

Law Revision Commission Comments·

1990 Enactment

Section 12505 continues Section 12505 of the repealed Probate Code without change. The term "nondomiciliary decedent" is not limited to a decedent who dies domiciled in a sister state (defined in Section 12506), but also includes a decedent who dies domiciled in a foreign nation (defined in Section 12502). However, some provisions of this part apply only to nondomiciliary decedents who die domiciled in a sister state. See Sections 12540–12541 (distribution of property to sister state personal representative), 12570–12572 (collection of personal property of small estate without ancillary administration).

Background on Section 12505 of Repealed Code

Section 12505 was a new provision added by 1988 Cal.Stat. ch. 1199 § 94.5. For background on the provisions of this part, see the Comment to this part under the part heading. [20 Cal.L.Rev.Comm.Reports 1001 (1990)].

§ 12506.   Sister state

"Sister state" means a state other than this state. *(Stats. 1990, c. 79 (A.B.759), § 14, operative July 1, 1991.)*

Law Revision Commission Comments

1990 Enactment

Section 12506 continues Section 12506 of the repealed Probate Code without change.

Background on Section 12506 of Repealed Code

Section 12506 was a new provision added by 1988 Cal.Stat. ch. 1199 § 94.5. For background on the provisions of this part, see the Comment to this part under the part heading. [20 Cal.L.Rev.Comm.Reports 1001 (1990)].

§ 12507.   Sister state personal representative

"Sister state personal representative" means a personal representative appointed in a sister state. *(Stats.1990, c. 79 (A.B.759), § 14, operative July 1, 1991.)*

Law Revision Commission Comments

1990 Enactment

Section 12507 continues Section 12507 of the repealed Probate Code without change.

Background on Section 12507 of Repealed Code

Section 12507 was a new provision added by 1988 Cal.Stat. ch. 1199 § 94.5. For background on the provisions of this part, see the Comment to this part under the part heading. [20 Cal.L.Rev.Comm.Reports 1001 (1990)].

CHAPTER 2. ANCILLARY ADMINISTRATION

ARTICLE 1. OPENING ANCILLARY ADMINISTRATION

Cross References

Application of old and new law, see Probate Code § 3.

§ 12510. Petition; probate of will; appointment of local personal representative

Any interested person, or a sister state or foreign nation personal representative, may commence an ancillary administration proceeding by a petition to the court for either or both of the following:

(a) Probate of the nondomiciliary decedent's will.

(b) Appointment of a local personal representative. *(Stats.1990, c. 79 (A.B.759), § 14, operative July 1, 1991.)*

Law Revision Commission Comments

1990 Enactment

Section 12510 continues Section 12510 of the repealed Probate Code without change. As used in Section 12510, "interested person" includes the person named as executor in the decedent's will. See Section 48. For the proper court, see Section 12511 (venue).

Background on Section 12510 of Repealed Code

Section 12510 was added by 1988 Cal.Stat. ch. 1199 § 94.5. The section superseded former Probate Code Section 360 and continued part of the first sentence of former Probate Code Section 361 without substantive change. Former Sections 360 and 361 were repealed by 1988 Cal.Stat. ch. 1199 § 40. For background on the provisions of this part, see the Comment to this part under the part heading. [20 Cal.L.Rev.Comm.Reports 1001 (1990)].

Cross References

Conditions of probate of foreign will, see Probate Code §§ 12522, 12523.

Hearing of petition for original probate, see Probate Code §§ 8003, 8110.

Persons who may petition for original probate, see Probate Code § 8000.

Petition for original probate, see Probate Code § 8002.

§ 12511. Venue

The proper county for an ancillary administration proceeding under this chapter is the county determined pursuant to Section 7052. *(Stats.1990, c. 79 (A.B.759), § 14, operative July 1, 1991.)*

Law Revision Commission Comments

1990 Enactment

Section 12511 continues Section 12511 of the repealed Probate Code without change. This section incorporates the nondomiciliary venue provision of Section 7052. See also Section 7050 (jurisdiction and authority of court or judge).

Background on Section 12511 of Repealed Code

Section 12511 was added by 1988 Cal.Stat. ch. 1199 § 94.5. The section restated the last part of former Probate Code Section 360 (repealed by 1988 Cal.Stat. ch. 1199 § 40) without substantive change. For background on the provisions of this part, see the Comment to this part under the part heading. [20 Cal.L.Rev.Comm.Reports 1001 (1990)].

§ 12512. Notice; procedure

Notice of an ancillary administration proceeding shall be given and, except as provided in Article 2 (commencing with Section 12520), the same proceedings had as in the case of a petition for probate of a will or appointment of a personal representative of a person who dies domiciled in this state. *(Stats.1990, c. 79 (A.B.759), § 14, operative July 1, 1991.)*

Law Revision Commission Comments

1990 Enactment

Section 12512 continues Section 12512 of the repealed Probate Code without change. See also Section 12530 (application of general provisions).

Background on Section 12512 of Repealed Code

Section 12512 was added by 1988 Cal.Stat. ch. 1199 § 94.5. The section restated the last sentence of former Probate Code Section 361 (repealed by 1988 Cal.Stat. ch. 1199 § 40) without substantive change. For background on the provisions of this part, see the Comment to this part under the part heading. [20 Cal.L.Rev.Comm.Reports 1001 (1990)].

§ 12513. Personal representative; sister state; priority; nominee

If the decedent dies while domiciled in a sister state, a personal representative appointed by a court of the decedent's domicile has priority over all other persons except where the decedent's will nominates a different person to be the personal representative in this state. The sister state personal representative may nominate another person as personal representative and the nominee has the same priority as the sister state personal representative. *(Stats. 1990, c. 79 (A.B.759), § 14, operative July 1, 1991.)*

Law Revision Commission Comments

1990 Enactment

Section 12513 continues Section 12513 of the repealed Probate Code without change. This section is drawn from Section 3–203(g) of the Uniform Probate Code (1987). As to the construction of provisions drawn from uniform acts, see Section 2. This section applies only where the nondomiciliary decedent has died while domiciled in a sister state, not where a person was domiciled in a foreign nation. Consequently, only sister state personal representatives, not foreign nation personal representatives, are entitled to the priority provided in this section. Section 12513 deals only with priority; the sister state personal representative must still qualify for appointment pursuant to Section 8400 et seq.

Background on Section 12513 of Repealed Code

Section 12513 was a new provision added by 1988 Cal.Stat. ch. 1199 § 94.5. For background on the provisions of this part, see the Comment to this part under the part heading. [20 Cal.L.Rev.Comm.Reports 1001 (1990)].

ARTICLE 2. PROBATE OF NONDOMICILIARY DECEDENT'S WILL ADMITTED TO PROBATE IN SISTER STATE OR FOREIGN NATION

Section

12520. Application of article; probate under other provisions.

12521. Petition; contents.

12522. Will established in sister state; admission to probate in this state; contest or revocation of probate; grounds.

12523. Will established in foreign nation; admission to probate in state; conditions.

12524. Effect of nondomiciliary decedent's will admitted to probate.

Cross References

Application of old and new law, see Probate Code § 3.

§ 12520. Application of article; probate under other provisions

(a) If a nondomiciliary decedent's will has been admitted to probate in a sister state or foreign nation and satisfies the requirements of this article, probate of the will in an ancillary administration proceeding is governed by this article.

(b) If a nondomiciliary decedent's will has been admitted to probate in a sister state or foreign nation, but does not satisfy the requirements of this article, the will may be probated in an ancillary administration proceeding pursuant to Part 2 (commencing with Section 8000). *(Stats.1990, c. 79 (A.B.759), § 14, operative July 1, 1991.)*

Law Revision Commission Comments

1990 Enactment

Section 12520 continues Section 12520 of the repealed Probate Code without change. Subdivision (a) makes clear that the procedure of this article applies only where a sister state or foreign nation order admitting a will to probate satisfies the requirements of Sections 12522 or 12523. As provided in subdivision (b), the general provisions concerning opening administration apply where the sister state or foreign nation order is not entitled to recognition. See Section 8000 et seq. The general provisions also apply in any case where admission has not been sought in the sister state or foreign nation. See also Section 6113 (choice of law as to execution of will).

Background on Section 12520 of Repealed Code

Section 12520 was a new provision added by 1988 Cal.Stat. ch. 1199 § 94.5. For background on the provisions of this part, see the Comment to this part under the part heading. [20 Cal.L.Rev.Comm.Reports 1001 (1990)].

§ 12521. Petition; contents

(a) A petition for probate of a nondomiciliary decedent's will under this article shall include both of the following:

(1) The will or an authenticated copy of the will.

(2) An authenticated copy of the order admitting the will to probate in the sister state or foreign nation or other evidence of the establishment or proof of the will in accordance with the law of the sister state or foreign nation.

(b) As used in this section, "authenticated copy" means a copy that satisfies the requirements of Article 2 (commencing with Section 1530) of Chapter 2 of Division 11 of the Evidence Code. *(Stats.1990, c. 79 (A.B.759), § 14, operative July 1, 1991.)*

Law Revision Commission Comments

1990 Enactment

Section 12521 continues Section 12521 of the repealed Probate Code without change. For the persons who may petition under Section 12521, see Section 12510. For general provisions relating to petitions, see Sections 1020–1023.

Background on Section 12521 of Repealed Code

Section 12521 was added by 1988 Cal.Stat. ch. 1199 § 94.5. The section superseded part of the first sentence of former Probate Code Section 361 (repealed by 1988 Cal.Stat. ch. 1199 § 40). For background on the provisions of this part, see the Comment to this part under the part heading. [20 Cal.L.Rev.Comm.Reports 1001 (1990)].

§ 12522. Will established in sister state; admission to probate in this state; contest or revocation of probate; grounds

If a will of a nondomiciliary decedent was admitted to probate, or established or proved, in accordance with the laws of a sister state, the court shall admit the will to probate in this state, and may not permit a contest or revocation of probate, unless one or more of the following are shown:

(a) The determination in the sister state is not based on a finding that at the time of death the decedent was domiciled in the sister state.

(b) One or more interested parties were not given notice and an opportunity for contest in the proceedings in the sister state.

(c) The determination in the sister state is not final. *(Stats.1990, c. 79 (A.B.759), § 14, operative July 1, 1991.)*

Law Revision Commission Comments

1990 Enactment

Section 12522 continues Section 12522 of the repealed Probate Code without substantive change. This section presumes a sister state order admitting a will to probate to be valid. The burden is on an opponent of the will to show that the order is not entitled to full faith and credit in this state.

Background on Section 12522 of Repealed Code

Section 12522 was added by 1988 Cal.Stat. ch. 1199 § 94.5. The section superseded former Probate Code Section 362 (repealed by 1988 Cal.Stat. ch. 1199 § 40) to the extent that former Section 362 applied to wills admitted to probate in sister states. The provision of former Section 362 that the will must be valid under the law of the testator's domicile at death or under the law of this state was not continued in Section 12522. For rules governing the validity of a will first offered for probate in this state, see Section 6113. For background on the provisions of this part, see the Comment to this part under the part heading. [20 Cal.L.Rev.Comm.Reports 1001 (1990)].

§ 12523. Will established in foreign nation; admission to probate in state; conditions

(a) Except as provided in subdivision (b), if a will of a nondomiciliary decedent was admitted to probate, or established or proved, in accordance with the laws of a foreign nation, the court shall admit the will to probate in this state, and may not permit a contest or revocation of probate, if it appears from the order admitting the will to probate in the foreign nation, or otherwise appears, that all of the following conditions are satisfied:

(1) The determination in the foreign nation is based on a finding that at the time of death the decedent was domiciled in the foreign nation.

(2) All interested parties were given notice and an opportunity for contest in the proceedings in the foreign nation.

(3) The determination in the foreign nation is final.

(b) The court may refuse to admit the will, even though it is shown to satisfy the conditions provided in subdivision (a), where the order admitting the will was made under a judicial system that does not provide impartial tribunals or procedures compatible with the requirements of due process of law. *(Stats.1990, c. 79 (A.B.759), § 14, operative July 1, 1991.)*

Law Revision Commission Comments

1990 Enactment

Section 12523 continues Section 12523 of the repealed Probate Code without change. Under subdivision (a), the proponent of the will admitted in the foreign nation has the burden of showing that the specified conditions are satisfied. Subdivision (b) is drawn from the Uniform Foreign Money–Judgments Recognition Act § 4(a)(1), 13 U.L.A. (1962 & Supp.1989). As to the construction of provisions drawn from uniform acts, see Section 2. See Code Civ.Proc. § 1713.4(a)(1) (recognition of foreign nation money judgments).

Background on Section 12523 of Repealed Code

Section 12523 was added by 1988 Cal.Stat. ch. 1199 § 94.5. The section superseded former Probate Code Section 362 (repealed by 1988 Cal.Stat. ch. 1199 § 40) to the extent that it applied to wills admitted to probate in foreign nations. The provision of former Section 362 that the will must be valid under the law of the testator's domicile at death or under the law of this state was not continued in Section 12523. For rules governing the validity of a will first offered for probate in this state, see Section 6113. For background on the provisions of this part, see the Comment to this part under the part heading. [20 Cal.L.Rev.Comm.Reports 1001 (1990)].

§ 12524. Effect of nondomiciliary decedent's will admitted to probate

A nondomiciliary decedent's will admitted to probate under this article has the same force and effect as the will of a person who dies while domiciled in this state that is admitted to probate in this state. *(Stats.1990, c. 79 (A.B.759), § 14, operative July 1, 1991.)*

Law Revision Commission Comments

1990 Enactment

Section 12524 continues Section 12524 of the repealed Probate Code without change.

Background on Section 12524 of Repealed Code

Section 12524 was added by 1988 Cal.Stat. ch. 1199 § 94.5. The section restated part of former Probate Code Section 362 (repealed

by 1988 Cal.Stat. ch. 1199 § 40) without substantive change. For background on the provisions of this part, see the Comment to this part under the part heading. [20 Cal.L.Rev.Comm.Reports 1001 (1990)].

ARTICLE 3. APPLICATION OF GENERAL PROVISIONS

Section
12530. Application of code provisions.

Cross References

Application of old and new law, see Probate Code § 3.

§ 12530. Application of code provisions

Except to the extent otherwise provided in this chapter, ancillary administration of a decedent's estate is subject to all other provisions of this code concerning the administration of the decedent's estate, including, but not limited to, opening estate administration, inventory and appraisal, creditor claims, estate management, independent administration, compensation, accounts, payment of debts, distribution, and closing estate administration. *(Stats.1990, c. 79 (A.B.759), § 14, operative July 1, 1991.)*

Law Revision Commission Comments

1990 Enactment

Section 12530 continues Section 12530 of the repealed Probate Code without change. This section makes clear that the general provisions relating to estate administration apply to administration under this chapter, except as otherwise provided. For exceptions, see, e.g., Section 12540 (conditions for distribution to sister state personal representative).

Background on Section 12530 of Repealed Code

Section 12530 was a new provision added by 1988 Cal.Stat. ch. 1199 § 94.5. The section was amended by 1989 Cal.Stat. ch. 21 § 30 to make clear that the section applies in estate administration proceedings throughout the code, whether pursuant to this division or any other division of the code. For background on the provisions of this part, see the Comment to this part under the part heading. [20 Cal.L.Rev.Comm.Reports 1001 (1990)].

ARTICLE 4. DISTRIBUTION OF PROPERTY TO SISTER STATE PERSONAL REPRESENTATIVE

Section
12540. Court order for distribution to sister state personal representative.
12541. Sale of real property.
12542. Insolvent estate.

Cross References

Application of old and new law, see Probate Code § 3.

§ 12540. Court order for distribution to sister state personal representative

(a) If a person dies while domiciled in a sister state, the court in an ancillary administration proceeding may make an order for preliminary or final distribution of all or part of the decedent's personal property in this state to the sister state personal representative if distribution is in the best interest of the estate or interested persons.

(b) The court order shall be made in the manner and pursuant to the procedure provided in, and is subject to the provisions of, Chapter 1 (commencing with Section 11600) of Part 10. *(Stats.1990, c. 79 (A.B.759), § 14, operative July 1, 1991.)*

Law Revision Commission Comments
1990 Enactment

Section 12540 continues Section 12540 of the repealed Probate Code without change. This procedure applies only where the nondomiciliary decedent has died while domiciled in a sister state, not where the decedent died domiciled in a foreign nation. Consequently, distribution may be made to a sister state personal representative under this article, but not to a foreign nation personal representative.

Under Section 12540 a petition may be made by the local personal representative, a beneficiary, or other interested person. See Section 11600. Notice of the hearing on the petition is given in the manner provided in Section 1220. Any interested person may oppose the petition. See Section 11602 (opposition to petition). Preliminary distribution may not be ordered unless two months have elapsed and distribution may be made without loss to creditors or injury to the estate or any interested person. See Sections 11620 (time for petition), 11621 (order for distribution). Final distribution may not be ordered unless the estate is in a condition to be closed. See Section 11640 (petition and order). For general provisions, see Sections 1000–1004 (rules of practice), 1040–1050 (hearings and orders). Distribution in compliance with the court order entitles the local personal representative to a full discharge, and when the order becomes final it is conclusive against all interested persons. See Sections 11753 (filing receipts and discharge), 11605 (conclusiveness of order).

It should be noted that distribution may be made to a sister state personal representative in ancillary administration only upon a court determination that the distribution is in the best interest of the estate or interested persons. In other cases, distribution is made directly to the beneficiaries. See In re Estate of Hudson, 63 Cal. 454 (1883); Durham, Ancillary Administration, in 3 California Decedent Estate Practice § 33.50 (Cal.Cont.Ed.Bar 1987 & rev. 1988).

Background on Section 12540 of Repealed Code

Section 12540 was added by 1988 Cal.Stat. ch. 1199 § 94.5. The section superseded parts of former Probate Code Section 1000, part of the first sentence of former Probate Code Section 1040, the last sentence of former Probate Code Section 1041, and former Probate Code Section 1042 (provisions repealed by 1988 Cal.Stat. ch. 1199 § 55.5). For background on the provisions of this part, see the Comment to this part under the part heading. [20 Cal.L.Rev.Comm.Reports 1001 (1990)].

Cross References
Conclusiveness of other matters,
 Advancements, see Probate Code § 11640.
 Determination of persons entitled to distribution, see Probate Code § 11705.
 Final distribution decree, see Probate Code § 11605.
 Preliminary distribution order, see Probate Code § 11605.
Discharge decree, see Probate Code § 12250.
Distribution of estate,
 Application for, see Probate Code § 11600.
 Time for, see Probate Code § 11640.
Order settling final account or for final distribution, see Probate Code § 11000.
Persons interested in the estate,
 Allowed claims, contest of validity, see Probate Code § 9254.
 Borrowing money and mortgaging of property, see Probate Code § 9802.

Contests before probate, see Probate Code §§ 8004, 8250.
Contests of petition for letters of administration, see Probate Code § 8004.
Distribution of decedent's estate, petition for, see Probate Code § 11600.
Final distribution, see Probate Code § 11640.
Lease of property, see Probate Code § 9943.
Petition for probate, see Probate Code § 8000.
Proration of federal estate taxes among, see Probate Code § 20110.
Removal of personal representative, see Probate Code § 8500.
Sale of property, petition for order requiring, see Probate Code § 10001.
Petition for distribution, see Probate Code §§ 11600, 11640.
Sale of real property generally, see Probate Code § 10300 et seq.
Trust administration of assets, transfer from another jurisdiction, see Probate Code § 17450.

§ 12541. Sale of real property

If necessary to make distribution pursuant to this article, real property in the nondomiciliary decedent's estate may be sold and the court may order the proceeds to be distributed to the sister state personal representative. The sale shall be made in the same manner as other sales of real property of a decedent. *(Stats.1990, c. 79 (A.B.759), § 14, operative July 1, 1991.)*

Law Revision Commission Comments
1990 Enactment

Section 12541 continues Section 12541 of the repealed Probate Code without change. This section is an exception to the normal rule where distribution is made to the beneficiaries. See Section 12530 (application of general provisions, including distribution rules). This section does not limit authority the sister state personal representative may have under the Independent Administration of Estates Act. See Sections 10400–10592.

Background on Section 12541 of Repealed Code

Section 12541 was added by 1988 Cal.Stat. ch. 1199 § 94.5. The section superseded the last part of the first sentence and all of the second sentence of former Probate Code Section 1040 (repealed by 1988 Cal.Stat. ch. 1199 § 55.5). Section 12541 broadened the former provisions so that the court may order a sale of real property of the estate in the course of either preliminary or final distribution. For background on the provisions of this part, see the Comment to this part under the part heading. [20 Cal.L.Rev.Comm.Reports 1001 (1990)].

§ 12542. Insolvent estate

If the nondomiciliary decedent's estate in the sister state where the decedent was domiciled is insolvent, distribution may be made only to the sister state personal representative and not to the beneficiaries. *(Stats.1990, c. 79 (A.B.759), § 14, operative July 1, 1991.)*

Law Revision Commission Comments
1990 Enactment

Section 12542 continues Section 12542 of the repealed Probate Code without change.

Background on Section 12542 of Repealed Code

Section 12542 was a new provision added by 1988 Cal.Stat. ch. 1199 § 94.5. For background on the provisions of this part, see the Comment to this part under the part heading. [20 Cal.L.Rev.Comm.Reports 1001 (1990)].

CHAPTER 3. COLLECTION OF PERSONAL PROPERTY OF SMALL ESTATE BY SISTER STATE PERSONAL REPRESENTATIVE WITHOUT ANCILLARY ADMINISTRATION

Section
12570. Affidavit procedure.
12571. Governing provisions.
12572. Action against holder of property; attorney fees.
12573. Liability of personal representative.
12574. Repealed.

Cross References

Application of old and new law, see Probate Code § 3.

§ 12570. Affidavit procedure

If a nondomiciliary decedent's property in this state satisfies the requirements of Section 13100, a sister state personal representative may, without petitioning for ancillary administration, use the affidavit procedure provided by Chapter 3 (commencing with Section 13100) of Part 1 of Division 8 to collect personal property of the decedent. *(Stats.1990, c. 79 (A.B.759), § 14, operative July 1, 1991.)*

Law Revision Commission Comments

1990 Enactment

Section 12570 continues Section 12570 of the repealed Probate Code without change. This section permits a sister state personal representative to collect personal property of a small estate by using the affidavit procedure set out in Sections 13100–13115. The sister state personal representative is a successor in interest for this purpose. See Section 13051(d). The affidavit procedure for collecting real property (Sections 13200–13208) is not available to the sister state personal representative. However, the beneficiaries may employ the affidavit procedure even though the sister state personal representative may not. Where the estate in California does not qualify for collection under Section 13100 or where real property is involved, the sister state personal representative must use other procedures. The simplified affidavit procedure under this chapter applies where the value of the property in this state does not exceed $60,000 (as determined pursuant to Sections 13050 and 13100). Transfer to the sister state personal representative under this procedure results in a transfer for the purposes of administration, whereas the general affidavit procedure results in transfer to the ultimate beneficiaries. This procedure is not available to foreign nation personal representatives. See Section 12507 ("sister state personal representative" defined).

Background on Section 12570 of Repealed Code

Section 12570 was a new provision added by 1988 Cal.Stat. ch. 1199 § 94.5. For background on the provisions of this part, see the Comment to this part under the part heading. [20 Cal.L.Rev.Comm.Reports 1001 (1990)].

Cross References

Affidavits, see Code of Civil Procedure §§ 2003, 2009 et seq.

§ 12571. Governing provisions

The effect of payment, delivery, or transfer of personal property to the sister state personal representative pursuant to this chapter, and the effect of failure to do so, are governed by Chapter 3 (commencing with Section 13100) of Part 1 of Division 8. *(Stats.1990, c. 79 (A.B.759), § 14, operative July 1, 1991.)*

Law Revision Commission Comments

1990 Enactment

Section 12571 continues Section 12571 of the repealed Probate Code without change. This section makes clear that the rules concerning the effect of compliance with the affidavit procedure or refusal to comply are the same where the procedure is used by a sister state personal representative.

Background on Section 12571 of Repealed Code

Section 12571 was a new provision added by 1988 Cal.Stat. ch. 1199 § 94.5. For background on the provisions of this part, see the Comment to this part under the part heading. [20 Cal.L.Rev.Comm.Reports 1001 (1990)].

Cross References

Notice, see Probate Code § 1200 et seq.

§ 12572. Action against holder of property; attorney fees

The sister state personal representative may bring an action against a holder of the decedent's property, and may be awarded attorney's fees, as provided in subdivision (b) of Section 13105. *(Stats.1990, c. 79 (A.B.759), § 14, operative July 1, 1991.)*

Law Revision Commission Comments

1990 Enactment

Section 12572 continues Section 12572 of the repealed Probate Code without change. This section provides an exception to the general rule that a sister state personal representative may not bring an action in this state. See Code Civ.Proc. § 1913. Where property has been transferred to a successor by affidavit, the sister state personal representative does not have the power to bring an action under Section 13111(d) unless the sister state personal representative is appointed as the local personal representative in ancillary administration.

Background on Section 12572 of Repealed Code

Section 12572 was a new provision added by 1988 Cal.Stat. ch. 1199 § 94.5. For background on the provisions of this part, see the Comment to this part under the part heading. [20 Cal.L.Rev.Comm.Reports 1001 (1990)].

§ 12573. Liability of personal representative

A sister state personal representative who takes property by affidavit under this chapter is not liable as a person to whom payment, delivery, or transfer of the decedent's property is made under Section 13109 or 13110 to the extent that the sister state personal representative restores the property to the nondomiciliary decedent's estate in the sister state in compliance with Section 13111. *(Stats.1990, c. 79 (A.B.759), § 14, operative July 1, 1991.)*

Law Revision Commission Comments

1990 Enactment

Section 12573 continues Section 12573 of the repealed Probate Code without change. This section provides a special rule governing the liability of a sister state personal representative who takes personal property by an affidavit under this chapter. Under this section, the sister state personal representative is liable to creditors under Section 13110 or to heirs or devisees under Section 13111 only if the property collected by affidavit is not put in the estate for purposes of administration in the sister state.

§ 12573

ADMINISTRATION OF ESTATES OF DECEDENTS

Background on Section 12573 of Repealed Code

Section 12573 was a new provision added by 1988 Cal.Stat. ch. 1199 § 94.5. For background on the provisions of this part, see the Comment to this part under the part heading. [20 Cal.L.Rev.Comm.Reports 1001 (1990)].

§ 12574. Repealed by Stats.1990, c. 79 (A.B.759), § 13, operative July 1, 1991

Law Revision Commission Comments

1990 Repeal

Section 12574 of the repealed Probate Code is omitted from the new Probate Code because it has served its purpose in the transition to the law that became operative on July 1, 1989. See 1989 Cal.Stat. ch. 1199, § 94.5. See also Section 3 (general transitional provision). [20 Cal.L.Rev.Comm.Reports 1001 (1990)].

CHAPTER 4. JURISDICTION OVER FOREIGN PERSONAL REPRESENTATIVE

Section
12590. Submission to jurisdiction; limit.
12591. Extent of jurisdiction.

Cross References

Application of old and new law, see Probate Code § 3.

§ 12590. Submission to jurisdiction; limit

A sister state personal representative or foreign nation personal representative submits personally in a representative capacity to the jurisdiction of the courts of this state in any proceeding relating to the estate by any of the following actions:

(a) Filing a petition for ancillary administration.

(b) Receiving money or other personal property pursuant to Chapter 3 (commencing with Section 12570). Jurisdiction under this subdivision is limited to the amount of money and the value of personal property received.

(c) Doing any act in this state as a personal representative that would have given this state jurisdiction over the personal representative as an individual. *(Stats.1990, c. 79 (A.B.759), § 14, operative July 1, 1991.)*

Law Revision Commission Comments

1990 Enactment

Section 12590 continues Section 12590 of the repealed Probate Code without change. This section is drawn from Section 4–301 of the Uniform Probate Code (1987). As to the construction of provisions drawn from uniform acts, see Section 2.

Background on Section 12590 of Repealed Code

Section 12590 was a new provision added by 1988 Cal.Stat. ch. 1199 § 94.5. For background on the provisions of this part, see the Comment to this part under the part heading. [20 Cal.L.Rev.Comm.Reports 1001 (1990)].

§ 12591. Extent of jurisdiction

A sister state personal representative or foreign nation personal representative is subject to the jurisdiction of the courts of this state in a representative capacity to the same extent that the nondomiciliary decedent was subject to jurisdiction at the time of death. *(Stats.1990, c. 79 (A.B.759), § 14, operative July 1, 1991.)*

Law Revision Commission Comments

1990 Enactment

Section 12591 continues Section 12591 of the repealed Probate Code without change. This section is drawn from Section 4–302 of the Uniform Probate Code (1987) and is consistent with Section 410.10 of the Code of Civil Procedure and with case law. See Mitsui Manufacturers Bank v. Tucker, 152 Cal.App.3d 428, 199 Cal.Rptr. 517 (1984). As to the construction of provisions drawn from uniform acts, see Section 2. Nothing in this section excuses a creditor from compliance with any applicable creditor claim requirements in ancillary administration proceedings.

Background on Section 12591 of Repealed Code

Section 12591 was a new provision added by 1988 Cal.Stat. ch. 1199 § 94.5. For background on the provisions of this part, see the Comment to this part under the part heading. [20 Cal.L.Rev.Comm.Reports 1001 (1990)].

862

Division 8

DISPOSITION OF ESTATE WITHOUT ADMINISTRATION

Cross References

Real property, "transfer fee" defined, see Civil Code § 1098.

Law Revision Commission Comments

1990 Enactment

This division supersedes Division 8 (commencing with Section 13000) of the repealed Probate Code. The superseded division was enacted upon recommendation of the California Law Revision Commission. See Recommendation Relating to Distribution of Estate Without Administration, 18 Cal.L.Revision Comm'n Reports 1005 (1986); Communication from California Law Revision Commission Concerning Assembly Bill 2625, 18 Cal.L.Revision Comm'n Reports 1743 (1986). The Commission, in cooperation with California Continuing Education of the Bar, published the recommended legislation as enacted with official comments. See Selected 1986 Trust and Probate Legislation, 18 Cal.L.Revision Comm'n Reports 1201, 1503–96 (1986).

Legislation enacted to effectuate an earlier Commission recommendation made significant improvements in the law relating to the distribution of estates without administration. See Recommendation Relating to Distribution of Estates Without Administration, 17 Cal.L.Revision Comm'n Reports 421 (1984). See also Report of Senate Committee on Judiciary on Assembly Bill 2270, 18 Cal.L.Revision Comm'n Reports 63, 64–65 (1986). [20 Cal.L.Rev.Comm.Reports 1001 (1990)].

Part 1

COLLECTION OR TRANSFER OF SMALL ESTATE WITHOUT ADMINISTRATION

Application

Application of Part 1, see Probate Code § 13053.

CHAPTER 1. DEFINITIONS

Application

Application of Part 1, see Probate Code § 13053.

Cross References

Application of old and new law, see Probate Code § 3.
Payment of lottery prizes upon death of prizewinner, see Government Code § 8880.32.

§ 13000. Construction of part

Unless the provision or context otherwise requires, the definitions in this chapter govern the construction of this part. *(Stats.1990, c. 79 (A.B.759), § 14, operative July 1, 1991.)*

Law Revision Commission Comments

1990 Enactment

Section 13000 continues Section 13000 of the repealed Probate Code without substantive change.

Background on Section 13000 of Repealed Code

Section 13000 was a new provision added by 1986 Cal.Stat. ch. 783 § 24. For background on the provisions of this division, see the Comment to this division under the division heading. [20 Cal.L.Rev.Comm.Reports 1001 (1990)].

§ 13002. Holder of the decedent's property

"Holder of the decedent's property" or "holder" means, with respect to any particular item of property of the decedent, the person owing money to the decedent, having custody of tangible personal property of the decedent, or acting as registrar or transfer agent of the evidences of a debt, obligation, interest, right, security, or chose in action belonging to the decedent. *(Stats.1990, c. 79 (A.B.759), § 14, operative July 1, 1991.)*

Law Revision Commission Comments

1990 Enactment

Section 13002 continues Section 13002 of the repealed Probate Code without change. A person owing money to the decedent includes a financial institution. See Section 56 (defining "person").

Background on Section 13002 of Repealed Code

Section 13002 was added by 1986 Cal.Stat. ch. 783 § 24. The section was drawn from language of a portion of subdivision (b) of former Probate Code Section 630 (repealed by 1986 Cal.Stat. ch. 783 § 9). For background on the provisions of this division, see the Comment to this division under the division heading. [20 Cal.L.Rev.Comm.Reports 1001 (1990)].

§ 13004. Particular item of property

(a) "Particular item of property" means:

(1) Particular personal property of the decedent which is sought to be collected, received, or transferred by the successor of the decedent under Chapter 3 (commencing with Section 13100).

(2) Particular real property of the decedent, or particular real and personal property of the decedent, for which the

successor of the decedent seeks a court order determining succession under Chapter 4 (commencing with Section 13150).

(3) Particular real property of the decedent with respect to which the successor of the decedent files an affidavit of succession under Chapter 5 (commencing with Section 13200).

(b) Subject to subdivision (a), "particular item of property" includes all interests specified in Section 62. *(Stats.1990, c. 79 (A.B.759), § 14, operative July 1, 1991. Amended by Stats.1991, c. 1055 (S.B.271), § 32.)*

Law Revision Commission Comments

1990 Enactment

Section 13004 continues Section 13004 of the repealed Probate Code without change. The definition provided by Section 13004, together with the definition of "successor of the decedent" in Section 13006, requires that an affidavit or declaration be executed by all of the persons who succeed to the particular property sought to be collected, received, or transferred (see Sections 13100, 13101, 13200) and that a petition be verified by all of the persons who succeed to the particular real property that is the subject of the petition (see Sections 13151–13152).

1991 Amendment

Section 13004 is amended to conform to the revision of Chapter 4 (commencing with Section 13150) which makes that chapter applicable to personal property of the decedent under some circumstances. [20 Cal.L.Rev.Comm.Reports 2737 (1990)].

Background on Section 13004 of Repealed Code

Section 13004 was a new provision added by 1986 Cal.Stat. ch. 783 § 24. For background on the provisions of this division, see the Comment to this division under the division heading. [20 Cal.L.Rev.Comm.Reports 1001 (1990)].

§ 13005. Property of the decedent

"Property of the decedent," "decedent's property," "money due the decedent," and similar phrases, include property that becomes part of the decedent's estate on the decedent's death, whether by designation of the estate as beneficiary under an insurance policy on the decedent's life or under the decedent's retirement plan, or otherwise. *(Added by Stats. 1991, c. 1055 (S.B.271), § 33.)*

Law Revision Commission Comments

1991 Addition

Section 13005 makes clear that the affidavit procedure under Chapter 3 (commencing with Section 13100) may be used by the successor of the decedent to collect insurance on the decedent's life payable to the estate of the decedent, and other property that becomes part of the decedent's estate on the decedent's death. Property that becomes part of the decedent's estate on the decedent's death also is included in determining whether the decedent's real and personal property in this state exceeds $60,000 for the purpose of Section 13100.

Property may become part of the decedent's estate from causes other than a designation of the estate as beneficiary, including failure of the primary and secondary beneficiaries of the decedent's life insurance or retirement plan to survive the decedent, and disclaimer of insurance or retirement benefits by the beneficiary. [20 Cal.L.Rev.Comm.Reports 2737 (1990)].

§ 13006. Successor of the decedent

"Successor of the decedent" means:

(a) If the decedent died leaving a will, the sole beneficiary or all of the beneficiaries who succeeded to a particular item of property of the decedent under the decedent's will. For the purposes of this part, a trust is a beneficiary under the decedent's will if the trust succeeds to the particular item of property under the decedent's will.

(b) If the decedent died without a will, the sole person or all of the persons who succeeded to the particular item of property of the decedent under Sections 6401 and 6402 or, if the law of a sister state or foreign nation governs succession to the particular item of property, under the law of the sister state or foreign nation. *(Stats.1990, c. 79 (A.B.759), § 14, operative July 1, 1991. Amended by Stats.1991, c. 1055 (S.B.271), § 34.)*

Law Revision Commission Comments

1990 Enactment

Section 13006 continues Section 13006 of the repealed Probate Code without change. A guardian, conservator, custodian, or attorney-in-fact may act on behalf of the person entitled to the property. See Section 13051. A trustee of a trust created by the will of the decedent is not a beneficiary under the decedent's will for the purposes of this part. Only the trustee of a trust created during the decedent's lifetime that is entitled to all or a portion of the decedent's property may act as a successor of the decedent under this part. See the Comment to Section 13051; see also the Comment to Section 13004. See also Sections 12570–12573 (collection of personal property of small estate by sister state personal representative without ancillary administration).

1991 Amendment

Section 13006 is amended to delete the language which precluded the trustee of a testamentary trust from using the procedures under this part. This deletion allows the trustee of a testamentary trust created in the decedent's will to act on behalf of the trust. This permits the trustee to use a small estate summary procedure where no proceeding is being or has been conducted in California for administration of the decedent's estate or where the decedent's personal representative has consented to use of the procedure. See Sections 13101(a)(4), 13108(a)(2), 13150(b), 13200(a)(7). [20 Cal.L.Rev.Comm.Reports 2737 (1990)].

Background on Section 13006 of Repealed Code

Section 13006 was added by 1986 Cal.Stat. ch. 783 § 24 and was amended by 1988 Cal.Stat. ch. 1199 § 95. Subdivision (a) was drawn from portions of subdivision (b) of former Probate Code Section 630 (repealed by 1986 Cal.Stat. ch. 783 § 9). Subdivision (b) expanded the provision of subdivision (b) of former Section 630 to include all persons who succeeded to a particular item of property of the decedent under Sections 6401 and 6402 (intestate succession). Former Section 630 limited the heirs who could use the former summary affidavit procedure to the following relatives of the decedent: surviving spouse, children, issue of deceased children, parents, brothers or sisters, issue of deceased brothers or sisters, and grandparents. Under subdivision (b) of Section 13006, the persons who can use the summary provisions of this part are not so limited. For background on the provisions of this division, see the Comment to this division under the division heading.

The 1988 amendment revised subdivision (b) to cover the situation where the succession to property is governed by the law of a jurisdiction other than California. See Sections 12502 ("foreign nation" defined), 12506 ("sister state" defined). For background on the 1988 amendment, see Comments to Conforming Revisions and

Repeals, 19 Cal.L.Revision Comm'n Reports 1031, 1094 (1988). [20 Cal.L.Rev.Comm.Reports 1001 (1990)].

Cross References

Succession, see Probate Code § 6400.

§ 13007. Proceeding

"Proceeding" means either that a petition is currently pending in this state for administration of a decedent's estate under Division 7 (commencing with Section 7000), a special administrator for the decedent's estate has been appointed in this state and is now serving, or a personal representative for the decedent's estate has been appointed in this state with general powers. "Proceeding" does not include a petition for administration which was dismissed without the appointment of a personal representative, any proceeding under Division 8 (commencing with Section 13000), or any action or proceeding in another state. *(Added by Stats.1992, c. 871 (A.B.2975), § 15.)*

CHAPTER 2. GENERAL PROVISIONS

Section
13050. Property excluded in determining property or estate of decedent or its value.
13051. Guardian or conservator; trustee; custodian; sister state personal representative; durable power of attorney.
13052. Date of valuation.
13053. Application of part.
13054. References to former provisions deemed references to comparable provisions of Chapter 3.

Application

Application of Part 1, see Probate Code § 13053.

Cross References

Application of old and new law, see Probate Code § 3.

§ 13050. Property excluded in determining property or estate of decedent or its value

(a) For the purposes of this part:

(1) Any property or interest or lien thereon which, at the time of the decedent's death, was held by the decedent as a joint tenant, or in which the decedent had a life or other interest terminable upon the decedent's death, or which was held by the decedent and passed to the decedent's surviving spouse pursuant to Section 13500, shall be excluded in determining the property or estate of the decedent or its value. This excluded property shall include, but not be limited to, property in a trust revocable by the decedent during his or her lifetime.

(2) A multiple-party account to which the decedent was a party at the time of the decedent's death shall be excluded in determining the property or estate of the decedent or its value, whether or not all or a portion of the sums on deposit are community property, to the extent that the sums on deposit belong after the death of the decedent to a surviving party, P.O.D. payee, or beneficiary. For the purposes of this paragraph, the terms " multiple-party account," "party," "P.O.D. payee," and "beneficiary" are defined in Article 2

(commencing with Section 5120) of Chapter 1 of Part 2 of Division 5.

(b) For the purposes of this part, all of the following property shall be excluded in determining the property or estate of the decedent or its value:

(1) Any vehicle registered under Division 3 (commencing with Section 4000) of the Vehicle Code or titled under Division 16.5 (commencing with Section 38000) of the Vehicle Code.

(2) Any vessel numbered under Division 3.5 (commencing with Section 9840) of the Vehicle Code.

(3) Any manufactured home, mobilehome, commercial coach, truck camper, or floating home registered under Part 2 (commencing with Section 18000) of Division 13 of the Health and Safety Code.

(c) For the purposes of this part, the value of the following property shall be excluded in determining the value of the decedent's property in this state:

(1) Any amounts due to the decedent for services in the Armed Forces of the United States.

(2) The amount, not exceeding fifteen thousand dollars ($15,000), of salary or other compensation, including compensation for unused vacation, owing to the decedent for personal services from any employment. *(Stats.1990, c. 79 (A.B.759), § 14, operative July 1, 1991. Amended by Stats. 1996, c. 563 (S.B.392), § 29; Stats.2011, c. 117 (A.B.1305), § 3.)*

Law Revision Commission Comments

1990 Enactment

Section 13050 continues Section 13050 of the repealed Probate Code without substantive change.

The exclusion for an interest that terminates at death under subdivision (a)(1) embraces life interests in trusts and contractual rights (such as insurance and employee retirement or death benefits) that terminate at death, as well as life interests in other property.

Paragraph (2) of subdivision (a) is a special application of paragraph (1) of subdivision (a). Paragraph (2) excludes multiple-party account funds, whether or not they are community property under Section 5305, to the extent that the funds pass to a surviving party, P.O.D. payee, or beneficiary. To the extent that the funds do not belong after the death of the decedent to a surviving party, P.O.D. payee, or beneficiary, the funds are includable in the decedent's estate for the purpose of this part.

The state registered property excluded under subdivision (b) can be transferred without probate under special statutory provisions. See Health & Safety Code § 18102 (manufactured homes, mobilehomes, commercial coaches, truck campers, and floating homes); Veh.Code §§ 5910 (vehicles), 9916 (vessels).

Although the salary exclusion under subdivision (c) does not prevent the use of the affidavit procedure under Sections 13100–13115 to collect salary owed to the decedent, other procedures for collection of the salary owed to the decedent may be available. See, e.g., Gov't Code §§ 12479 (designation by state employee of person to receive warrants upon employee's death), 53245 (designation by public employee of person to receive warrants upon employee's death). See also Prob.Code §§ 5000 (payment of money due to decedent to person designated by decedent), 13600 (collection by surviving spouse of compensation, not exceeding $5,000, owed by employer to decedent).

1996 Amendment

Subdivision (a)(1) of Section 13050 is amended to add the reference to a trust revocable by the decedent during lifetime. It is a specific application of the principle stated in subdivision (a)(1) that property in which the decedent had an interest terminable at death is excluded in determining the property or estate of the decedent for purposes of this part. This codifies case law. See Estate of Heigho, 186 Cal.App.2d 360, 364–65, 9 Cal.Rptr. 196 (1960). [26 Cal.L.Rev. Comm. Reports 21 (1996)].

Background on Section 13050 of Repealed Code

Section 13050 was added by 1986 Cal.Stat. ch. 783 § 24 and amended by 1989 Cal.Stat. ch. 397 § 39. Paragraph (1) of subdivision (a) continued former Probate Code Section 632 (repealed by 1986 Cal.Stat. ch. 783 § 9) without substantive change. Paragraph (2) of subdivision (a) was new and was the same in substance as subdivision (b) of former Probate Code Section 647 (repealed by 1986 Cal.Stat. ch. 783 § 9). Paragraph (2) made clear that funds in a multiple-party account as defined in Section 5101 were excluded in determining the property or estate of the decedent or its value to the extent that the funds belong after the death of the decedent to a surviving party, P.O.D. payee, or beneficiary. Under former Section 632 (repealed by 1986 Cal.Stat. ch. 783 § 9, now paragraph (1) of subdivision (a) of Section 13050), joint tenancy accounts were expressly excluded from the decedent's estate, and Totten trust accounts and P.O.D. accounts were presumably also excluded as an estate terminable upon the decedent's death.

Subdivision (b) continued the portion of subdivision (a) of former Probate Code Section 630 (repealed by 1986 Cal.Stat. ch. 783 § 9) that excluded certain state registered property in determining the estate or its value with the addition of "floating home" in paragraph (3). This addition reflected the 1985 amendment to Section 18102 of the Health and Safety Code which added "floating homes" to the kinds of property which can be transferred without administration under that section. See 1985 Cal.Stat. ch. 1467, § 27.

Subdivision (c) continued without substantive change the portion of subdivision (a) of former Section 630 (repealed by 1986 Cal.Stat. ch. 783 § 9) that provided a salary exclusion in determining the value of the decedent's property.

The 1989 amendment substituted a correct reference for the former reference to Section 5101. See Recommendation Relating to Multiple–Party Accounts in Financial Institutions, 20 Cal.L.Revision Comm'n Reports 95 (1990).

For background on the provisions of this division, see the Comment to this division under the division heading. [20 Cal.L.Rev.Comm.Reports 1001 (1990)].

§ 13051. Guardian or conservator; trustee; custodian; sister state personal representative; durable power of attorney

For the purposes of this part:

(a) The guardian or conservator of the estate of a person entitled to any of the decedent's property may act on behalf of the person without authorization or approval of the court in which the guardianship or conservatorship proceeding is pending.

(b) The trustee of a trust may act on behalf of the trust. In the case of a trust that is subject to continuing jurisdiction of the court pursuant to Chapter 4 (commencing with Section 17300) of Part 5 of Division 9, the trustee may act on behalf of the trust without the need to obtain approval of the court.

(c) If the decedent's will authorizes a custodian under the Uniform Gifts to Minors Act or the Uniform Transfers to Minors Act of any state to receive a devise to a beneficiary,

the custodian may act on behalf of the beneficiary until such time as the custodianship terminates.

(d) A sister state personal representative may act on behalf of the beneficiaries as provided in Chapter 3 (commencing with Section 12570) of Part 13 of Division 7.

(e) The attorney in fact authorized under a durable power of attorney may act on behalf of the beneficiary giving the power of attorney. *(Stats.1990, c. 79 (A.B.759), § 14, operative July 1, 1991. Amended by Stats.1991, c. 1055 (S.B.271), § 35.)*

Law Revision Commission Comments
1990 Enactment

Section 13051 continues Section 13051 of the repealed Probate Code with two additions:

(1) A sentence is added to subdivision (b) to make clear that a trustee may act without court approval, even though the trust is subject to the continuing jurisdiction of the court.

(2) Subdivision (e) has been added to make clear that an attorney in fact authorized under a durable power of attorney may act on behalf of the beneficiary giving the power of attorney.

Under subdivision (b), the trustee must be the trustee of a living trust created by the decedent or by another during the decedent's lifetime or the trustee of a testamentary trust created by another who died during the decedent's lifetime; the trustee of a trust created by the decedent's will is not included under subdivision (b).

Section 12570 limits the power of the sister state personal representative to collection of personal property. See also Section 12507 ("sister state personal representative" defined).

1991 Amendment

Subdivision (b) of Section 13051 is amended to eliminate the restriction that the trust must be created during the decedent's lifetime. This deletion allows the trustee of a testamentary trust by whomever created to act on behalf of the trust. This permits the trustee to use a small estate summary procedure where no proceeding is being or has been conducted in California for administration of the decedent's estate or where the decedent's personal representative has consented to use of the procedure. See Sections 13101(a)(4), 13108(a)(2), 13150(b), 13200(a)(7). See also Section 13006 ("successor of the decedent" defined). [20 Cal.L.Rev.Comm.Reports 2737 (1990)].

Background on Section 13051 of Repealed Code

Section 13051 was added by 1986 Cal.Stat. ch. 783 § 24 and was amended by 1988 Cal.Stat. ch. 1199 § 95.5. Subdivision (a) was drawn from subdivision (d) of former Probate Code Section 650 (repealed by 1986 Cal.Stat. ch. 783 § 9) and was consistent with the portion of subdivision (b) of former Probate Code Section 630 (repealed by 1986 Cal.Stat. ch. 783 § 9) which referred to the guardian or conservator of the estate. Subdivision (b) was new and superseded the portion of subdivision (b) of former Section 630 which referred to a trustee. Subdivision (c) was drawn from subdivision (c) of former Section 630. For background on the provisions of this division, see the Comment to this division under the division heading.

The 1988 amendment added subdivision (d). For background on the 1988 amendment, see Comments to Conforming Revisions and Repeals, 19 Cal.L.Revision Comm'n Reports 1031, 1094 (1988). [20 Cal.L.Rev.Comm.Reports 1001 (1990)].

§ 13052. Date of valuation

In making an appraisal for the purposes of this part, the probate referee shall use the date of the decedent's death as the date of valuation of the property. *(Stats.1990, c. 79 (A.B.759), § 14, operative July 1, 1991.)*

Law Revision Commission Comments

1990 Enactment

Section 13052 continues Section 13052 of the repealed Probate Code without change. This section makes clear that the probate referee is to use the date of the decedent's death as the date of valuation in making an inventory and appraisal for the purposes of this part. Thus, for example, record title to real property may be transferred by affidavit under Chapter 5 (commencing with Section 13200) even if the real property since the date of death has appreciated to a value in excess of $10,000. For provisions concerning inventory and appraisal, see Sections 13103 (affidavit procedure for collection or transfer of personal property), 13152(b) (petition for court order determining succession to real property), 13200(c) (affidavit procedure for real property of small value).

Background on Section 13052 of Repealed Code

Section 13052 was a new provision added by 1986 Cal.Stat. ch. 783 § 24 and was amended by 1988 Cal.Stat. ch. 1199 § 96. The 1988 amendment corrected terminology. See new Probate Code Sections 400–453 (probate referees). For background on the provisions of this division, see the Comment to this division under the division heading. For background on the 1988 amendment, see Comments to Conforming Revisions and Repeals, 19 Cal.L.Revision Comm'n Reports 1031, 1094 (1988). [20 Cal.L.Rev.Comm.Reports 1001 (1990)].

§ 13053. Application of part

(a) Except as provided in subdivision (b), this part applies whether the decedent died before, on, or after July 1, 1987.

(b) This part does not apply and the law in effect at the time of payment, delivery, or transfer shall apply if the payment, delivery, or transfer was made prior to July 1, 1987, pursuant to former Probate Code Sections 630 to 632, inclusive, repealed by Chapter 783 of the Statutes of 1986. *(Stats.1990, c. 79 (A.B.759), § 14, operative July 1, 1991.)*

Law Revision Commission Comments

1990 Enactment

Section 13053 continues Section 13053 of the repealed Probate Code without substantive change. This section makes clear that this part applies if the payment, delivery, or transfer is made on or after July 1, 1987, without regard to whether the decedent died before or after that date. Thus, where the decedent died before July 1, 1987, the provisions of this part may be used to require the payment, delivery, or transfer if the property was not paid, delivered, or transferred prior to July 1, 1987, pursuant to the provisions of former Probate Code Sections 630–632 (repealed by 1986 Cal.Stat. ch. 783 § 9). Section 13053 preserves prior law where a payment, delivery, or transfer was made under prior law before July 1, 1987. As to the application of any amendments made after that date, see Section 3.

Background on Section 13053 of Repealed Code

Section 13053 was a new provision added by 1986 Cal.Stat. ch. 783 § 24. For background on the provisions of this division, see the Comment to this division under the division heading. [20 Cal.L.Rev.Comm.Reports 1001 (1990)].

§ 13054. References to former provisions deemed references to comparable provisions of Chapter 3

A reference in any statute of this state or in a written instrument, including a will or trust, to a provision of former Sections 630 to 632, inclusive, repealed by Chapter 783,

Statutes of 1986, shall be deemed to be a reference to the comparable provisions of Chapter 3 (commencing with Section 13100). *(Stats.1990, c. 79 (A.B.759), § 14, operative July 1, 1991.)*

Law Revision Commission Comments

1990 Enactment

Section 13054 continues Section 13054 of the repealed Probate Code without substantive change. This section makes clear that a reference in a statute or written instrument to a provision of former law is deemed to be a reference to the comparable provision of Chapter 3 (commencing with Section 13100).

Background on Section 13054 of Repealed Code

Section 13054 was a new provision added by 1986 Cal.Stat. ch. 783 § 24. The clause in Section 13054 of the repealed Probate Code making the section apply on and after July 1, 1987, was omitted as obsolete. For background on the provisions of this division, see the Comment to this division under the division heading.

CHAPTER 3. AFFIDAVIT PROCEDURE FOR COLLECTION OR TRANSFER OF PERSONAL PROPERTY

Section

Application

Application of Part 1, see Probate Code § 13053.

Law Revision Commission Comments
1990 Enactment

The procedure provided by this chapter can be used only if all of the following conditions are satisfied:

(1) The gross value of the decedent's real and personal property in this state (excluding certain property) does not exceed $60,000. See Section 13100. See also Section 13050 (exclusions).

(2) No proceeding for the administration of the decedent's estate is pending or has been conducted in California. See Section 13108.

(3) Not less than 40 days have elapsed since the death of the decedent. See Section 13100. (Other provisions permit a surviving spouse to collect salary owing to the deceased spouse without waiting for a 40–day period to elapse. See Sections 13600–13606.)

(4) The person who seeks to collect the money, receive the property, or have the evidences transferred is the successor of the decedent. See Section 13101. The affidavit or declaration required by Section 13101 must be executed by all the successors who have an interest in the property sought to be collected, received, or transferred. See Sections 13004 (defining "particular item of property"), 13006 (defining "successor of the decedent").

The procedure under this chapter cannot be used for real property. See Section 13115. However, the phrase "whether or not secured by a lien on real property" in subdivision (c) of Section 13100 makes clear that evidence of a debt or obligation may be transferred under this chapter even though the debt or obligation is secured by a lien on real property. Where a particular item of property transferred under this chapter is an obligation secured by a lien on real property, Section 13106.5 requires that the affidavit or declaration be recorded in the office of the county recorder of the county where the real property is located. For a procedure for obtaining without probate a court order determining the persons who succeed to real property of a decedent (limited to a case where the gross value of decedent's real and personal property in this state does not exceed $60,000), see Sections 13150–13157. For an affidavit procedure for obtaining marketable title to real property of a decedent without probate (limited to a case where the gross value of decedent's real property in this state does not exceed $10,000), see Sections 13200–13208. For a procedure permitting a surviving spouse to obtain a court order that real property passed to the surviving spouse (without limit as to the value of the real property), see Sections 13650–13660. See also Sections 13540–13542 (right of surviving spouse to dispose of real property). [20 Cal.L.Rev.Comm.Reports 1001 (1990)].

Cross References

Application of old and new law, see Probate Code § 3.
Destruction of court records, notice, retention periods, see Government Code § 68152.
Nondomiciliary decedent, use of procedure provided by this chapter, see Probate Code § 12570 et seq.
Sale of tax-deeded property, claims for excess proceeds, heirs of deceased title-holder, see Revenue and Taxation Code § 4675.

§ 13100. Estates not exceeding $150,000; authorization to act without procuring letters of administration or awaiting probate

Excluding the property described in Section 13050, if the gross value of the decedent's real and personal property in this state does not exceed one hundred fifty thousand dollars ($150,000) and if 40 days have elapsed since the death of the decedent, the successor of the decedent may, without procuring letters of administration or awaiting probate of the will, do any of the following with respect to one or more particular items of property:

(a) Collect any particular item of property that is money due the decedent.

(b) Receive any particular item of property that is tangible personal property of the decedent.

(c) Have any particular item of property that is evidence of a debt, obligation, interest, right, security, or chose in action belonging to the decedent transferred, whether or not secured by a lien on real property. *(Stats.1990, c. 79 (A.B.759), § 14, operative July 1, 1991. Amended by Stats. 1996, c. 86 (A.B.2146), § 4; Stats.1996, c. 862 (A.B.2751), § 34; Stats.2011, c. 117 (A.B.1305), § 4.)*

Law Revision Commission Comments
1990 Enactment

Section 13100 continues Section 13100 of the repealed Probate Code without change. The requirement that not less than 40 days have elapsed since the death of the decedent is consistent with Section 13540 (surviving spouse has power to deal with and dispose of real property after 40 days from the death of other spouse). For similar requirements, see Health & Safety Code § 18102 (requirement that 40 days have elapsed from death of owner to permit transfer of registration of manufactured home, mobilehome, commercial coach, truck camper, or floating home using affidavit procedure); Veh.Code § 9916 (requirement that 40 days have elapsed from death of owner to permit transfer of ownership of vessel using affidavit procedure). But see Sections 330 (delivery of decedent's tangible personal property), 13600–13606 (surviving spouse may collect salary owing to the deceased spouse without waiting for a 40–day period to elapse).

The procedure under this chapter cannot be used for real property. See Section 13115. However, the phrase "whether or not secured by a lien on real property" in subdivision (c) of Section 13100 makes clear that evidence of a debt or obligation may be transferred under this chapter even though the debt or obligation is secured by a lien on real property. Where a particular item of property transferred under this chapter is an obligation secured by a lien on real property, Section 13106.5 requires that the affidavit or declaration be recorded in the office of the county recorder of the county where the real property is located if the instrument creating the lien on the real property has been recorded in that county. See also the Comment to this chapter under the chapter heading.

Background on Section 13100 of Repealed Code

Section 13100 was added by 1986 Cal.Stat. ch. 783 § 24. The section continued without substantive change a portion of former Probate Code Section 630 (repealed by 1986 Cal.Stat. ch. 783 § 9) with the addition of the requirement that 40 days have elapsed since the death of the decedent and the omission of the provision that precluded use of the affidavit procedure where the gross value of the decedent's real property in this state exceeded $10,000. For background on the provisions of this division, see the Comment to this division under the division heading. [20 Cal.L.Rev.Comm.Reports 1001 (1990)].

Cross References

Nondomiciliary decedent's property, see Probate Code § 12570.

§ 13101. Affidavit or declaration; contents; requirements; attachments

(a) To collect money, receive tangible personal property, or have evidences of a debt, obligation, interest, right, security, or chose in action transferred under this chapter, an affidavit or a declaration under penalty of perjury under the laws of this state shall be furnished to the holder of the decedent's property stating all of the following:

(1) The decedent's name.

(2) The date and place of the decedent's death.

(3) "At least 40 days have elapsed since the death of the decedent, as shown in a certified copy of the decedent's death certificate attached to this affidavit or declaration."

(4) Either of the following, as appropriate:

(A) "No proceeding is now being or has been conducted in California for administration of the decedent's estate."

(B) "The decedent's personal representative has consented in writing to the payment, transfer, or delivery to the affiant or declarant of the property described in the affidavit or declaration."

(5) "The current gross fair market value of the decedent's real and personal property in California, excluding the property described in Section 13050 of the California Probate Code, does not exceed one hundred fifty thousand dollars ($150,000)."

(6) A description of the property of the decedent that is to be paid, transferred, or delivered to the affiant or declarant.

(7) The name of the successor of the decedent (as defined in Section 13006 of the California Probate Code) to the described property.

(8) Either of the following, as appropriate:

(A) "The affiant or declarant is the successor of the decedent (as defined in Section 13006 of the California Probate Code) to the decedent's interest in the described property."

(B) "The affiant or declarant is authorized under Section 13051 of the California Probate Code to act on behalf of the successor of the decedent (as defined in Section 13006 of the California Probate Code) with respect to the decedent's interest in the described property."

(9) "No other person has a superior right to the interest of the decedent in the described property."

(10) "The affiant or declarant requests that the described property be paid, delivered, or transferred to the affiant or declarant."

(11) "The affiant or declarant affirms or declares under penalty of perjury under the laws of the State of California that the foregoing is true and correct."

(b) Where more than one person executes the affidavit or declaration under this section, the statements required by subdivision (a) shall be modified as appropriate to reflect that fact.

(c) If the particular item of property to be transferred under this chapter is a debt or other obligation secured by a lien on real property and the instrument creating the lien has been recorded in the office of the county recorder of the county where the real property is located, the affidavit or declaration shall satisfy the requirements both of this section and of Section 13106.5.

(d) A certified copy of the decedent's death certificate shall be attached to the affidavit or declaration.

(e) If the decedent's personal representative has consented to the payment, transfer, or delivery of the described property to the affiant or declarant, a copy of the consent and of the personal representative's letters shall be attached to the affidavit or declaration. *(Stats.1990, c. 79 (A.B.759), § 14,*

operative July 1, 1991. Amended by Stats.1991, c. 1055 (S.B.271), § 36; Stats.1996, c. 86 (A.B.2146), § 5; Stats.1996, c. 862 (A.B.2751), § 35; Stats.2011, c. 117 (A.B.1305), § 5.)

Law Revision Commission Comments
1990 Enactment

Section 13101 continues Section 13101 of the repealed Probate Code without change. See also the Comment to this chapter under the chapter heading.

The affidavit or declaration must be executed by all successors of the decedent who have an interest in the property sought to be collected, received, or transferred. See Sections 13004 (defining "particular item of property"), 13006 (defining "successor of the decedent").

1991 Amendment [Revised Comment]

Subdivision (a)(4) of Section 13101 is revised and subdivision (e) is added to reflect the new authorization for the decedent's personal representative to consent to use of the affidavit procedure, notwithstanding that an estate proceeding is pending or has been conducted in this state. See Section 13108(a)(2).

Subdivision (a)(9) is amended to change "a right" to "a superior right." This conforms Section 13101 to Section 13200(a)(9) (affidavit procedure for real property of small value), and is nonsubstantive. [21 Cal.L.Rev.Comm.Reports 71 (1991)].

Background on Section 13101 of Repealed Code

Section 13101 was added by 1986 Cal.Stat. ch. 783 § 24 and was amended by 1987 Cal.Stat. ch. 923 § 94 and by 1988 Cal.Stat. ch. 113 § 15.6. The section superseded portions of subdivision (b) of former Probate Code Section 630 (repealed by 1986 Cal.Stat. ch. 783 § 9). The portions of Section 13101 prescribing the contents of the affidavit or declaration were new provisions and replaced the provision of former Section 630 that required that the person or persons furnish an affidavit or declaration "showing the right of the person or persons to receive such money or property, or to have such evidences transferred." For background on the provisions of this division, see the Comment to this division under the division heading.

The 1987 amendment to Section 13101 was nonsubstantive; it added clarifying language to the introductory portion of subdivision (a). The 1988 amendment added subdivision (c) and relettered former subdivision (c) to be subdivision (d). Subdivision (c) was included to alert the person preparing or using the affidavit or declaration to the additional requirements of Section 13106.5. See also the Comment to Section 13105. For background on the 1988 amendment, see Communication from the California Law Revision Commission Concerning Assembly Bill 2779, 19 Cal.L.Revision Comm'n Reports 1191, 1194–95 (1988). [20 Cal.L.Rev.Comm.Reports 1001 (1990)].

Cross References
Affidavits, use of, see Code of Civil Procedure §§ 2003, 2009 et seq.

§ 13102. Evidence of ownership

(a) If the decedent had evidence of ownership of the property described in the affidavit or declaration and the holder of the property would have had the right to require presentation of the evidence of ownership before the duty of the holder to pay, deliver, or transfer the property to the decedent would have arisen, the evidence of ownership, if available, shall be presented with the affidavit or declaration to the holder of the decedent's property.

(b) If the evidence of ownership is not presented to the holder pursuant to subdivision (a), the holder may require, as a condition for the payment, delivery, or transfer of the property, that the person presenting the affidavit or declaration provide the holder with a bond or undertaking in a reasonable amount determined by the holder to be sufficient to indemnify the holder against all liability, claims, demands, loss, damages, costs, and expenses that the holder may incur or suffer by reason of the payment, delivery, or transfer of the property. Nothing in this subdivision precludes the holder and the person presenting the affidavit or declaration from dispensing with the requirement that a bond or undertaking be provided and instead entering into an agreement satisfactory to the holder concerning the duty of the person presenting the affidavit or declaration to indemnify the holder. *(Stats.1990, c. 79 (A.B.759), § 14, operative July 1, 1991.)*

Law Revision Commission Comments
1990 Enactment

Section 13102 continues Section 13102 of the repealed Probate Code without change. See also the Comment to this chapter under the chapter heading. Subdivision (a) is comparable to Health and Safety Code Section 18102 and Vehicle Code Sections 5910 and 9916 (transfer upon affidavit of manufactured home, mobilehome, commercial coach, truck camper, floating home, vehicle, or vessel upon furnishing affidavit and appropriate certificate of ownership or title and registration card, if available). See also Fin.Code § 6950 (payment of deposit account of nonresident decedent upon presentation of evidence of ownership of account, if any). Subdivision (b) protects the holder against the possible claim of another where there is outstanding evidence of ownership. The provision was drawn in part from Financial Code Section 6652 (issuance of new evidence of account by savings and loan association).

Background on Section 13102 of Repealed Code

Section 13102 was a new provision added by 1986 Cal.Stat. ch. 783 § 24. For background on the provisions of this division, see the Comment to this division under the division heading. See also the Comment to this chapter under the chapter heading. [20 Cal.L.Rev.Comm.Reports 1001 (1990)].

§ 13103. Real property; inventory and appraisal

If the estate of the decedent includes any real property in this state, the affidavit or declaration shall be accompanied by an inventory and appraisal of the real property. The inventory and appraisal of the real property shall be made as provided in Part 3 (commencing with Section 8800) of Division 7. The appraisal shall be made by a probate referee selected by the affiant or declarant from those probate referees appointed by the Controller under Section 400 to appraise property in the county where the real property is located. *(Stats.1990, c. 79 (A.B.759), § 14, operative July 1, 1991.)*

Law Revision Commission Comments
1990 Enactment

Section 13103 continues Section 13103 of the repealed Probate Code without substantive change. See also the Comment to this chapter under the chapter heading. This section requires an appraisal of real property by a probate referee. Even though the procedure provided in this chapter may be used to collect or transfer personal property only, the appraisal is required if the estate includes any real property in this state (excluding real property held in joint tenancy or other real property described in paragraph (1) of subdivision (a) of Section 13050). Even though an appraisal of the real property in this state is required, the inventory and appraisal

need not include an inventory and appraisal of the personal property in the decedent's estate or any real property that is not located in this state. If the decedent's estate does not include any real property in this state, no inventory and appraisal is required. For provisions relating to real property, see Chapter 4 (commencing with Section 13150) (court order determining succession to real property), Chapter 5 (commencing with Section 13200) (affidavit procedure for transfer of real property of small value).

Background on Section 13103 of Repealed Code

Section 13103 was a new provision added by 1986 Cal.Stat. ch. 783 § 24 and was amended by 1988 Cal.Stat. ch. 1199 § 96.5. Under former law, the affidavit or declaration alone was sufficient; no inventory and appraisal was required. For background on the provisions of this division, see the Comment to this division under the division heading.

The 1988 amendment corrected terminology and section references. The phrase "in this state" was added in the first clause of Section 13103 to conform to Section 13100. For background on the 1988 amendment, see Comments to Conforming Revisions and Repeals, 19 Cal.L.Revision Comm'n Reports 1031, 1094 (1988). [20 Cal.L.Rev.Comm.Reports 1001 (1990)].

§ 13104. Proof of identity

(a) Reasonable proof of the identity of each person executing the affidavit or declaration shall be provided to the holder of the decedent's property.

(b) Reasonable proof of identity is provided for the purposes of this section if both of the following requirements are satisfied:

(1) The person executing the affidavit or declaration is personally known to the holder.

(2) The person executes the affidavit or declaration in the presence of the holder.

(c) If the affidavit or declaration is executed in the presence of the holder, a written statement under penalty of perjury by a person personally known to the holder affirming the identity of the person executing the affidavit or declaration is reasonable proof of identity for the purposes of this section.

(d) If the affidavit or declaration is executed in the presence of the holder, the holder may reasonably rely on any of the following as reasonable proof of identity for the purposes of this section:

(1) An identification card or driver's license issued by the Department of Motor Vehicles of this state that is current or was issued during the preceding five years.

(2) A passport issued by the Department of State of the United States that is current or was issued during the preceding five years.

(3) Any of the following documents if the document is current or was issued during the preceding five years and contains a photograph and description of the person named on it, is signed by the person, and bears a serial or other identifying number:

(A) A passport issued by a foreign government that has been stamped by the United States Immigration and Naturalization Service.

(B) A driver's license issued by a state other than California.

(C) An identification card issued by a state other than California.

(D) An identification card issued by any branch of the armed forces of the United States.

(e) For the purposes of this section, a notary public's certificate of acknowledgment identifying the person executing the affidavit or declaration is reasonable proof of identity of the person executing the affidavit or declaration.

(f) Unless the affidavit or declaration contains a notary public's certificate of acknowledgment of the identity of the person, the holder shall note on the affidavit or declaration either that the person executing the affidavit or declaration is personally known or a description of the identification provided by the person executing the affidavit or declaration. *(Stats.1990, c. 79 (A.B.759), § 14, operative July 1, 1991.)*

Law Revision Commission Comments
1990 Enactment

Section 13104 continues Section 13104 of the repealed Probate Code without change. This section is designed to provide clear rules as to the type of identification that reasonably may be relied upon to establish the identity of a person executing an affidavit or declaration. This section is drawn from Civil Code Section 1185 (acknowledgment of instrument by notary public); but, unlike Civil Code Section 1185, Section 13104 does not permit a driver's license issued by a Canadian or Mexican public agency to be used as reasonable proof of identity.

Under subdivision (f), the holder must make a notation as required by subdivision (f) for each person executing the affidavit or declaration, but such a notation is not required for the person or persons for whom the affidavit or declaration contains a notary public's certificate of acknowledgment of identity. See also the Comment to this chapter under the chapter heading.

Background on Section 13104 of Repealed Code

Section 13104 was a new provision added by 1986 Cal.Stat. ch. 783 § 24. For background on the provisions of this division, see the Comment to this division under the division heading. [20 Cal.L.Rev.Comm.Reports 1001 (1990)].

§ 13105. Entitlement to property; transfer of ownership; refusal

(a) If the requirements of Sections 13100 to 13104, inclusive, are satisfied:

(1) The person or persons executing the affidavit or declaration as successor of the decedent are entitled to have the property described in the affidavit or declaration paid, delivered, or transferred to them.

(2) A transfer agent of a security described in the affidavit or declaration shall change the registered ownership on the books of the corporation from the decedent to the person or persons executing the affidavit or declaration as successor of the decedent.

(b) If the holder of the decedent's property refuses to pay, deliver, or transfer any personal property or evidence thereof to the successor of the decedent within a reasonable time, the successor may recover the property or compel its payment, delivery, or transfer in an action brought for that purpose against the holder of the property. If an action is brought against the holder under this section, the court shall award reasonable attorney's fees to the person or persons bringing the action if the court finds that the holder of the decedent's

property acted unreasonably in refusing to pay, deliver, or transfer the property to them as required by subdivision (a). *(Stats.1990, c. 79 (A.B.759), § 14, operative July 1, 1991.)*

Law Revision Commission Comments
1990 Enactment

Section 13105 continues Section 13105 of the repealed Probate Code without substantive change. See also the Comment to this chapter under the chapter heading.

Where the item of property transferred is an obligation secured by a lien on real property, Section 13106.5 requires that, in addition to the requirements of Section 13101, the affidavit or declaration include the recording reference to the instrument creating the lien and a notary public's certificate of acknowledgment identifying each person executing the affidavit or declaration.

Where the particular item of property transferred under this chapter is an obligation secured by a lien on real property, Section 13106.5 requires that the affidavit or declaration be recorded in the office of the county recorder of the county where the real property is located if the instrument creating the lien on the real property has been recorded in that county. Any duty of the obligor under Section 13105 to pay the successor of the decedent or otherwise to satisfy the obligation does not arise until the obligor has been furnished with satisfactory evidence that the affidavit or declaration has been recorded and satisfies the requirements of Section 13101 and subdivision (a) of Section 13106.5. Such evidence might be, for example, a certified copy of the recorded affidavit or declaration, but any other satisfactory evidence of the recorded affidavit or declaration would be sufficient. The reference to Civil Code Section 2935 in subdivision (b) of Section 13106.5 makes clear that the recording of the affidavit or declaration is not itself notice to the obligor so as to invalidate a payment made to the holder of the note secured by the lien on the real property.

Subdivision (b) makes clear that the duty imposed by subdivision (a) can be enforced by an action against the holder. This remedy is in addition to the remedies against the holder if the decedent's estate is probated. The holder does not act unreasonably in refusing to pay, deliver, or transfer the property if the refusal is based on the holder's good faith belief that there may be estate taxes payable.

The person paying, delivering, or transferring the property is protected from liability. See Section 13106. See also Section 13102(b) (providing bond to protect person paying, delivering, or transferring property). Payment or transfer pursuant to Section 13105 does not preclude later administration of the decedent's estate. See Section 13108. As to the liabilities of the person receiving the property, see Sections 13109–13113.

Background on Section 13105 of Repealed Code

Section 13105 was added by 1986 Cal.Stat. ch. 783 § 24. Subdivision (a) was drawn from portions of former Probate Code Section 630 (repealed by 1986 Cal.Stat. ch. 783 § 9). Subdivision (b) was new. For background on the provisions of this division, see the Comment to this division under the division heading. [20 Cal.L.Rev.Comm.Reports 1001 (1990)].

Cross References

Nondomiciliary decedent's property, sister state personal representative's action against holder of property, see Probate Code § 12572.

§ 13106. Discharge of liability; holder of decedent's property; taxes

(a) If the requirements of Sections 13100 to 13104, inclusive, are satisfied, receipt by the holder of the decedent's property of the affidavit or declaration constitutes sufficient acquittance for the payment of money, delivery of property, or changing registered ownership of property pursuant to this chapter and discharges the holder from any further liability with respect to the money or property. The holder may rely in good faith on the statements in the affidavit or declaration and has no duty to inquire into the truth of any statement in the affidavit or declaration.

(b) If the requirements of Sections 13100 to 13104, inclusive, are satisfied, the holder of the decedent's property is not liable for any taxes due to this state by reason of paying money, delivering property, or changing registered ownership of property pursuant to this chapter. *(Stats.1990, c. 79 (A.B.759), § 14, operative July 1, 1991.)*

Law Revision Commission Comments

1990 Enactment

Section 13106 continues Section 13106 of the repealed Probate Code without change. Subdivision (b) was drawn from Section 6855 of the Financial Code. See also Section 13102(b) (bond to protect person paying, delivering, or transferring property). See also the Comment to this chapter under the chapter heading.

Background on Section 13106 of Repealed Code

Section 13106 was added by 1986 Cal.Stat. ch. 783 § 24. Subdivision (a) continued the first sentence of former Probate Code Section 631 (repealed by 1986 Cal.Stat. ch. 783 § 9) without substantive change but with the addition of clarifying language. Subdivision (b) was new. For background on the provisions of this division, see the Comment to this division under the division heading. [20 Cal.L.Rev.Comm.Reports 1001 (1990)].

§ 13106.5. Transfer of obligation secured by lien on real property; recording affidavit or declaration; effect of transfer; deed of trust; reliance by trustee, purchaser

(a) If the particular item of property transferred under this chapter is a debt or other obligation secured by a lien on real property and the instrument creating the lien has been recorded in the office of the county recorder of the county where the real property is located, the affidavit or declaration described in Section 13101 shall be recorded in the office of the county recorder of that county and, in addition to the contents required by Section 13101, shall include both of the following:

(1) The recording reference of the instrument creating the lien.

(2) A notary public's certificate of acknowledgment identifying each person executing the affidavit or declaration.

(b) The transfer under this chapter of the debt or obligation secured by a lien on real property has the same effect as would be given to an assignment of the right to collect the debt or enforce the obligation. The recording of the affidavit or declaration under subdivision (a) shall be given the same effect as is given under Sections 2934 and 2935 of the Civil Code to recording an assignment of a mortgage and an assignment of the beneficial interest under a deed of trust.

(c) If a deed of trust upon the real property was given to secure the debt and the requirements of subdivision (a) and of Sections 13100 to 13103, inclusive, are satisfied:

(1) The trustee under the deed of trust may rely in good faith on the statements made in the affidavit or declaration and has no duty to inquire into the truth of any statement in the affidavit or declaration.

(2) A person acting in good faith and for a valuable consideration may rely upon a recorded reconveyance of the trustee under the deed of trust.

(d) If a mortgage upon the real property was given to secure the debt and the requirements of subdivision (a) and of Sections 13100 to 13103, inclusive, are satisfied, a person acting in good faith and for a valuable consideration may rely upon a recorded discharge of the mortgage executed by the person or persons executing the affidavit or declaration as successor of the decedent or by their successors in interest. *(Stats.1990, c. 79 (A.B.759), § 14, operative July 1, 1991.)*

Law Revision Commission Comments

1990 Enactment

Section 13106.5 continues Section 13106.5 of the repealed Probate Code without change, except that the section is revised to extend to any person who enters into a transaction in good faith and for a valuable consideration, not only purchasers, lessees, and lenders. This section covers the situation where the particular item of property transferred under this chapter is a debt (including a promissory note) secured by a lien on real property. See also the Comment to this chapter under the chapter heading.

Where the instrument (including a mortgage or deed of trust) creating the lien has been recorded, subdivision (a) requires that the affidavit or declaration be recorded in the office of the county recorder of the county where the real property is located instead of merely being furnished to the holder of the property as required by the introductory clause of subdivision (a) of Section 13101. Recording of the affidavit or declaration in the real property records is mandatory so that the title records will reflect the transfer of the debt and security interest under this chapter to the person or persons executing the affidavit or declaration as successor of the decedent and to establish of record their authority to execute a satisfaction or release of the mortgage where the debt is secured by a mortgage.

The affidavit or declaration must be in the form prescribed by Section 13101 and must also satisfy the requirements of paragraphs (1) and (2) of subdivision (a) of Section 13106.5. The affidavit or declaration must be executed under penalty of perjury under the laws of the State of California. See Section 13101(a)(11). A certified copy of the decedent's death certificate must be attached to the affidavit or declaration. Section 13101(d).

Subdivision (a)(1) requires that the recording reference of the instrument creating the lien be included in the affidavit or declaration. This information makes it easier to locate the recorded lien instrument. Additionally, the recording reference insures that the affidavit or declaration relates to an obligation secured by a lien on real property.

Subdivision (a)(2) requires that the affidavit or declaration include a notary public's certificate of acknowledgment identifying each person executing the affidavit or declaration. This is required because the affidavit or declaration is to be recorded in the real property records. The requirement also avoids the need to furnish the obligor on the debt with additional proof of the identity of each person executing the affidavit or declaration. See Section 13104(e).

Under subdivision (b), the transfer of the debt under this chapter is given the same effect as the assignment of the debt. It is a well established principle of law that the assignment of a debt carries with it the security for the payment of the debt. Thus, the assignment of a debt secured by a mortgage carries the mortgage with it (Civil Code § 2936); and, when a power to sell is given to a mortgagee or other encumbrancer in an instrument intended to secure the payment of money, the power is deemed a part of the security and vests in the person who by assignment becomes entitled to payment of the money, and the power of sale may be executed by that person if the assignment is acknowledged and recorded (Civil Code § 2932.5).

The person or persons executing the affidavit or declaration as successor of the decedent have the same rights and duties they would have if they were an assignee of the mortgage or an assignee of the beneficial interest under the deed of trust. See Civil Code § 2941. Giving these persons these rights permits, for example, a title insurer to rely upon the affidavit or declaration in case of the recording of a notice of default in a non-judicial foreclosure of the deed of trust or the mortgage (with a power of sale). The duties include, for example, the duty to execute a certificate of discharge of the mortgage if the lien is secured by a mortgage.

Under subdivision (b), the recording of the affidavit or declaration operates as constructive notice of its contents to all persons. See Civil Code § 2934. Any duty of the obligor under Section 13105 to pay the successor of the decedent or otherwise to satisfy the obligation does not arise until the obligor has been furnished with satisfactory evidence that the affidavit or declaration has been recorded and satisfies the requirements of subdivision (a). Such evidence might be, for example, a certified copy of the recorded affidavit or declaration, but any other satisfactory evidence of the recorded affidavit or declaration would be sufficient. The reference to Civil Code Section 2935 in subdivision (b) makes clear that the recording of the affidavit or declaration is not itself notice to the obligor so as to invalidate a payment made to the holder of the note secured by the lien on the real property.

Subdivision (c) makes clear that the trustee under the deed of trust can execute a reconveyance in reliance upon the statements made in the affidavit or declaration and protects a good faith purchaser, lessee, or lender who relies upon the recorded reconveyance. Subdivision (d) makes clear that a good faith purchaser, lessee, or lender may rely in good faith upon a recorded discharge of the mortgage executed by the person or persons executing the affidavit or declaration as successor of the decedent (or by the successor in interest of such a person). These protections are consistent with the protection given the holder of the decedent's property under Section 13106. They are necessary to protect the obligor on the debt who has paid the debt to the person or persons executing the affidavit or declaration and needs to have the property title records reflect the fact that the debt has been paid and the security released.

Except as specifically provided in Section 13106.5, the provisions of this chapter—including but not limited to Sections 13109–13113 (liability of persons to whom payment, delivery, or transfer of property is made under this chapter)—apply to money collected pursuant to Section 13106.5.

Section 13106.5 covers not only the right to payment of a debt secured by a lien on real property, but also the right to enforce an obligation the performance of which is secured by a lien on real property.

Background on Section 13106.5 of Repealed Code

Section 13106.5 was a new provision added by 1988 Cal.Stat. ch. 113 § 15.7. For background on this section, see Communication from the California Law Revision Commission Concerning Assembly Bill 2779, 19 Cal.L.Revision Comm'n Reports 1191, 1195–97 (1988). [20 Cal.L.Rev.Comm.Reports 1001 (1990)].

§ 13107. Payment of money or delivery of property to successors of decedent

Where the money or property claimed in an affidavit or declaration presented under this chapter is that of a deceased heir or devisee of a deceased person whose estate is being administered in this state, the personal representative of the person whose estate is being administered shall present the affidavit or declaration to the court in which the estate is being administered. The court shall direct the personal representative to pay the money or deliver the property to the person or persons identified by the affidavit or declaration as the successor of the decedent to the extent that the order for

distribution determines that the deceased heir or devisee was entitled to the money or property under the will or the laws of succession. *(Stats.1990, c. 79 (A.B.759), § 14, operative July 1, 1991.)*

Law Revision Commission Comments
1990 Enactment

Section 13107 continues Section 13107 of the repealed Probate Code without substantive change. See also the Comment to this chapter under the chapter heading.

Background on Section 13107 of Repealed Code

Section 13107 was added by 1986 Cal.Stat. ch. 783 § 24. The section continued former Probate Code Section 631.1 (repealed by 1986 Cal.Stat. ch. 783 § 9) without substantive change. For background on the provisions of this division, see the Comment to this division under the division heading. [20 Cal.L.Rev.Comm.Reports 1001 (1990)].

Cross References

Affidavit, use of, see Code of Civil Procedure §§ 2003, 2009 et seq. Succession, see Probate Code § 6400.

§ 13107.5. Pending action against decedent; substitution of parties without probate

Where the money or property claimed in an affidavit or declaration executed under this chapter is the subject of a pending action or proceeding in which the decedent was a party, the successor of the decedent shall, without procuring letters of administration or awaiting probate of the will, be substituted as a party in place of the decedent by making a motion under Article 3 (commencing with Section 377.30) of Chapter 4 of Title 2 of Part 2 of the Code of Civil Procedure. The successor of the decedent shall file the affidavit or declaration with the court when the motion is made. For the purpose of Article 3 (commencing with Section 377.30) of Chapter 4 of Title 2 of Part 2 of the Code of Civil Procedure, a successor of the decedent who complies with this chapter shall be considered as a successor in interest of the decedent. *(Added by Stats.1991, c. 1055 (S.B.271), § 37. Amended by Stats.1992, c. 178 (S.B.1496), § 39.)*

Law Revision Commission Comments
1991 Addition

Section 13107.5 is a new provision permitting the successor of the decedent (as defined in Section 13006) to be substituted for the decedent in an action or proceeding involving the money or property claimed by the successor that was pending when the decedent died. The right to be substituted for the decedent under this section exists only where the value of the estate, as determined pursuant to Section 13050, does not exceed $60,000. This right is consistent with the right of the successor under Section 13105(b) to bring an action to recover money or property that the holder refuses to pay or deliver to the successor.

The decedent's surviving spouse may use the procedure provided by this section if the surviving spouse is the successor in interest and the value of the estate, as determined pursuant to Section 13050, does not exceed $60,000. As provided in Section 13050(a)(1), the value of property passing to the surviving spouse pursuant to Section 13500 is excluded in determining the value of the estate.

Section 13107.5 will be replaced by the version of Section 13107.5 set out in the *Recommendation Relating to Litigation Involving Decedents*, 20 Cal.L.Revision Comm'n Reports 2785 (1990), if that recommendation is enacted. [20 Cal.L.Rev.Comm.Reports 2737 (1990)].

1992 Amendment

Section 13107.5 is amended to revise section references. This revision is a technical, nonsubstantive change. This section makes clear that the general procedure for substituting the decedent's successor in interest provided in the Code of Civil Procedure applies to disposition of small estates without probate under this part. For this purpose, a "successor of the decedent" as defined in Section 13006 is a "decedent's successor in interest" as defined in Code of Civil Procedure Section 377.11. [22 Cal.L.Rev.Comm.Reports 895 (1992)].

§ 13108. Use of procedure; effect on later proceedings

(a) The procedure provided by this chapter may be used only if one of the following requirements is satisfied:

(1) No proceeding for the administration of the decedent's estate is pending or has been conducted in this state.

(2) The decedent's personal representative consents in writing to the payment, transfer, or delivery of the property described in the affidavit or declaration pursuant to this chapter.

(b) Payment, delivery, or transfer of a decedent's property pursuant to this chapter does not preclude later proceedings for administration of the decedent's estate. *(Stats.1990, c. 79 (A.B.759), § 14, operative July 1, 1991. Amended by Stats. 1991, c. 1055 (S.B.271), § 38.)*

Law Revision Commission Comments
1990 Enactment

Section 13108 continues Section 13108 of the repealed Probate Code without change. See also the Comment to this chapter under the chapter heading.

1991 Amendment

Subdivision (a)(2) is added to Section 13108 to permit use of the procedure provided by this chapter, notwithstanding that an estate proceeding is pending or has been conducted in this state. [20 Cal.L.Rev.Comm.Reports 2737 (1990)].

Background on Section 13108 of Repealed Code

Section 13108 was added by 1986 Cal.Stat. ch. 783 § 24. Subdivision (a) was a new provision that was consistent with the last sentence of former Probate Code Section 631 (repealed by 1986 Cal.Stat. ch. 783 § 9). Subdivision (b) was drawn from the last sentence of former Probate Code Section 631. See generally Brezzo v. Brangero, 51 Cal.App. 79, 81, 196 P. 87 (1921); Evans, Comments on the Probate Code of California, 19 Calif.L.Rev. 602, 607 (1931). For background on the provisions of this division, see the Comment to this division under the division heading. [20 Cal.L.Rev.Comm.Reports 1001 (1990)].

§ 13109. Liability for unsecured debts

A person to whom payment, delivery, or transfer of the decedent's property is made under this chapter is personally liable, to the extent provided in Section 13112, for the unsecured debts of the decedent. Any such debt may be enforced against the person in the same manner as it could have been enforced against the decedent if the decedent had not died. In any action based upon the debt, the person may assert any defenses, cross-complaints, or setoffs that would have been available to the decedent if the decedent had not died. Nothing in this section permits enforcement of a claim that is barred under Part 4 (commencing with Section 9000) of Division 7. Section 366.2 of the Code of Civil Procedure applies in an action under this section. *(Stats.1990, c. 79 (A.B.759), § 14, operative July 1, 1991. Amended by Stats. 1990, c. 140 (S.B.1855), § 15.1, operative July 1, 1991; Stats.1992, c. 178 (S.B.1496), § 40.)*

Law Revision Commission Comments
1990 Enactment

Section 13109 continues Section 13109 of the repealed Probate Code without change. This section (by providing that any action based on the debt is subject to the same defenses that would have been available to the decedent if the decedent had not died) adopts the same statute of limitations that would have applied in an action against the decedent on the debt if the decedent had not died. The liability under this section is limited. See Section 13112. See also the Comment to this chapter under the chapter heading.

1990 Amendment

Section 13109 (enacted as a part of the new Probate Code by 1990 Cal.Stat. ch. 79 § 14) was amended by 1990 Cal.Stat. ch. 140 § 15.1 to make clear that the general one-year statute of limitations applicable to all causes of action against a decedent is applicable to liability for the decedent's debts under Section 13109. For background on the 1990 amendment, see Recommendation Relating to Notice to Creditors in Estate Administration, 20 Cal.L.Revision Comm'n Reports 507 (1990). [20 Cal.L.Rev.Comm.Reports 1001 (1990)].

1992 Amendment

Section 13109 is amended to revise a section reference. This revision is a technical, nonsubstantive change. [22 Cal.L.Rev.Comm.Reports 895 (1992)].

Background on Section 13109 of Repealed Code

Section 13109 was added by 1986 Cal.Stat. ch. 783 § 24 and was amended by 1988 Cal.Stat. ch. 113 § 16. Section 13109 was a new provision drawn from former Probate Code Section 645.3 (repealed by 1986 Cal.Stat. ch. 783 § 9, continued as Section 6611) (small estate set-aside), but Section 13109 did not include the one-year limitation on the duration of personal liability provided by Section 6611. Instead, Section 13109 followed Section 13554 (enforcement of liability of deceased spouse against surviving spouse) and Section 13156 (enforcement of debt against petitioners who receive low value real property under court order made in summary proceeding). For background on the provisions of this division, see the Comment to this division under the division heading.

The 1988 amendment revised Section 13109 to make clear that a person who takes personal property by affidavit is not liable to a creditor whose claim is barred. See, e.g., Sections 9002(b) (bar of claims not filed in accordance with statute), 9257 (bar of rejected claims). For background on this amendment, see Communication from the California Law Revision Commission Concerning Assembly Bill 2779, 19 Cal.L.Revision Comm'n Reports 1191, 1198 (1988). [20 Cal.L.Rev.Comm.Reports 1001 (1990)].

Cross References

Nondomiciliary decedent's property, liability of sister state personal representative under this section, see Probate Code § 12573.
Vessels transferred upon death of owner, application of this section, see Vehicle Code § 9916.

§ 13110. Liability to persons having superior rights; fraudulent transactions; limitations of actions

(a) Except as provided in subdivision (b), each person to whom payment, delivery, or transfer of the decedent's property is made under this chapter is personally liable to the extent provided in Section 13112 to any person having a superior right by testate or intestate succession from the decedent.

(b) In addition to any other liability the person has under this section and Sections 13109, 13111, and 13112, any person who fraudulently secures the payment, delivery, or transfer of the decedent's property under this chapter is liable to the person having such a superior right for three times the fair market value of the property. For the purposes of this subdivision, the "fair market value of the property" is the fair market value of the property paid, delivered, or transferred to the person liable under this subdivision, valued as of the time the person liable under this subdivision presents the affidavit or declaration under this chapter to the holder of the decedent's property, less any liens and encumbrances on that property at that time.

(c) An action to impose liability under this section is forever barred three years after the affidavit or declaration is presented under this chapter to the holder of the decedent's property, or three years after the discovery of the fraud, whichever is later. The three-year period specified in this subdivision is not tolled for any reason. *(Stats.1990, c. 79 (A.B.759), § 14, operative July 1, 1991. Amended by Stats. 1991, c. 1055 (S.B.271), § 39.)*

Law Revision Commission Comments

1990 Enactment

Section 13110 continues Section 13110 of the repealed Probate Code without change. This section makes clear that a person having a superior right to the property by testate or intestate succession can bring an action against the person who received the property. This remedy is an alternative to petitioning for the probate of the decedent's estate. See Section 13111. The liability under Section 13110 is limited. See Section 13112. See also the Comment to this chapter under the chapter heading.

1991 Amendment

Subdivision (b) of Section 13110 is amended to change "excluding" to "less" liens and encumbrances, to make clear that fair market value means net value. [20 Cal.L.Rev.Comm.Reports 2737 (1990)].

Background on Section 13110 of Repealed Code

Section 13110 was a new provision added by 1986 Cal.Stat. ch. 783 § 24. For background on the provisions of this division, see the Comment to this division under the division heading. [20 Cal.L.Rev.Comm.Reports 1001 (1990)].

Cross References

Nondomiciliary decedent's property, liability of sister state personal representative under this section, see Probate Code § 12573.
Vessels transferred upon death of owner, application of this section, see Vehicle Code § 9916.

§ 13111. Proceedings for administration, or personal representative's consent to disposition under this chapter and later request for restoration to estate; liability of persons who received property

(a) Subject to the provisions of this section, if proceedings for the administration of the decedent's estate are commenced in this state, or if the decedent's personal representative has consented to the payment, transfer, or delivery of the decedent's property under this chapter and the personal

representative later requests that the property be restored to the estate, each person to whom payment, delivery, or transfer of the decedent's property is made under this chapter is liable for:

(1) The restitution of the property to the estate if the person still has the property, together with (A) the net income the person received from the property and (B) if the person encumbered the property after it was delivered or transferred to the person, the amount necessary to satisfy the balance of the encumbrance as of the date the property is restored to the estate.

(2) The restitution to the estate of the fair market value of the property if the person no longer has the property, together with (A) the net income the person received from the property and (B) interest on the fair market value of the property from the date of disposition at the rate payable on a money judgment. For the purposes of this subdivision, the "fair market value of the property" is the fair market value, determined as of the time of the disposition of the property, of the property paid, delivered, or transferred to the person under this chapter, less any liens and encumbrances on the property at that time.

(b) Subject to subdivision (c) and subject to any additional liability the person has under Sections 13109 to 13112, inclusive, if the person fraudulently secured the payment, delivery, or transfer of the decedent's property under this chapter, the person is liable under this section for restitution to the decedent's estate of three times the fair market value of the property. For the purposes of this subdivision, the "fair market value of the property" is the fair market value, determined as of the time the person liable under this subdivision presents the affidavit or declaration under this chapter, of the property paid, delivered, or transferred to the person under this chapter, less the amount of any liens and encumbrances on the property at that time.

(c) The property and amount required to be restored to the estate under this section shall be reduced by any property or amount paid by the person to satisfy a liability under Section 13109 or 13110.

(d) An action to enforce the liability under this section may be brought only by the personal representative of the estate of the decedent. Whether or not the personal representative brings an action under this section, the personal representative may enforce the liability only to the extent necessary to protect the interests of the heirs, devisees, and creditors of the decedent.

(e) An action to enforce the liability under this section is forever barred three years after presentation of the affidavit or declaration under this chapter to the holder of the decedent's property, or three years after the discovery of the fraud, whichever is later. The three-year period specified in this subdivision is not tolled for any reason.

(f) In the case of a nondomiciliary decedent, restitution under this section shall be made to the estate in an ancillary administration proceeding. *(Stats.1990, c. 79 (A.B.759), § 14, operative July 1, 1991. Amended by Stats.1991, c. 1055 (S.B.271), § 40; Stats.2015, c. 293 (A.B.139), § 18, eff. Jan. 1, 2016.)*

Law Revision Commission Comments

1990 Enactment

Section 13111 continues Section 13111 of the repealed Probate Code without substantive change and adds the provision to paragraph (1) of subdivision (a) that, if the person encumbered the property after it was delivered or transferred, the person is liable for the amount necessary to satisfy the balance of the encumbrance as of the date the property is restored to the estate. This amount is in addition to the property and the net income the person received from the property. Section 13111 is comparable to Section 13206. See also the Comment to this chapter under the chapter heading.

1991 Amendment

Section 13111 is amended to reflect the authorization for the decedent's personal representative to consent to summary payment, transfer, or delivery of the decedent's property, notwithstanding that an estate proceeding is pending or has been conducted in this state. See Section 13108. [20 Cal.L.Rev.Comm.Reports 2737 (1990)].

Background on Section 13111 of Repealed Code

Section 13111 was a new provision added by 1986 Cal.Stat. ch. 783 § 24 and was amended by 1988 Cal.Stat. ch. 1199 § 97. For background on the provisions of this division, see the Comment to this division under the division heading.

The 1988 amendment revised subdivision (a) and added subdivision (f) to clarify the application of this section in the case of a nondomiciliary decedent. See Sections 12501 ("ancillary administration" defined), 12505 ("nondomiciliary decedent" defined). For background on the 1988 amendment, see Comments to Conforming Revisions and Repeals, 19 Cal.L.Revision Comm'n Reports 1031, 1095 (1988). [20 Cal.L.Rev.Comm.Reports 1001 (1990)].

2015 Amendment

Section 13111 is amended for parallelism with Section 5676 (revocable TOD deed). It makes clear that liability for restitution of property to the estate under this section is limited to satisfaction of creditor claims, regardless of whether restitution under this section is made voluntarily or pursuant to a court proceeding. Any surplus belongs to the successor of the decedent. [36 Cal.L.Rev.Comm. Reports 103 (2006)].

Cross References

Nondomiciliary decedent's property, sister state personal representative's restoration of property to estate in compliance with this section, see Probate Code § 12573.
Vessels transferred upon death of owner, application of this section, see Vehicle Code § 9916.

§ 13112. Exemption from liability; limitation on amount of liability

(a) A person to whom payment, delivery, or transfer of the decedent's property has been made under this chapter is not liable under Section 13109 or 13110 if proceedings for the administration of the decedent's estate are commenced in this state, and the person satisfies the requirements of Section 13111.

(b) Except as provided in subdivision (b) of Section 13110, the aggregate of the personal liability of a person under Sections 13109 and 13110 shall not exceed the fair market value, valued as of the time the affidavit or declaration is presented under this chapter, of the property paid, delivered, or transferred to the person under this chapter, less the amount of any liens and encumbrances on that property at that time, together with the net income the person received from the property and, if the property has been disposed of,

interest on the fair market value of the property accruing from the date of disposition at the rate payable on a money judgment. For the purposes of this subdivision, "fair market value of the property" has the same meaning as defined in paragraph (2) of subdivision (a) of Section 13111. *(Stats. 1990, c. 79 (A.B.759), § 14, operative July 1, 1991.)*

Law Revision Commission Comments

1990 Enactment

Section 13112 continues Section 13112 of the repealed Probate Code without change. This section limits the liability of a person to whom payment, delivery, or transfer of the decedent's property is made under this chapter. Proceedings in this state include ancillary administration. See the Section 13111(f) and the Comment thereto. See also the Comment to this chapter under the chapter heading.

Background on Section 13112 of Repealed Code

Section 13112 was a new provision added by 1986 Cal.Stat. ch. 783 § 24 and was amended by 1988 Cal.Stat. ch. 1199 § 97.5. For background on the provisions of this division, see the Comment to this division under the division heading. The 1988 amendment revised subdivision (a) to conform to the revision of Section 13111. See Section 13111(a). For background on the 1988 amendment, see Comments to Conforming Revisions and Repeals, 19 Cal.L.Revision Comm'n Reports 1031, 1095 (1988). [20 Cal.L.Rev.Comm.Reports 1001 (1990)].

Cross References

Vessels transferred upon death of owner, application of this section, see Vehicle Code § 9916.

§ 13113. Cumulative effect of remedies

The remedies available under Sections 13109 to 13112, inclusive, are in addition to any remedies available by reason of any fraud or intentional wrongdoing. *(Stats.1990, c. 79 (A.B.759), § 14, operative July 1, 1991.)*

Law Revision Commission Comments

1990 Enactment

Section 13113 continues Section 13113 of the repealed Probate Code without change. This section makes clear that the remedies provided in this chapter for decedent's estate, creditors, and persons having a superior right to the property do not limit any other remedies that are available by reason of fraud or intentional wrongdoing. See also the Comment to this chapter under the chapter heading.

Background on Section 13113 of Repealed Code

Section 13113 was a new provision added by 1986 Cal.Stat. ch. 783 § 24. For background on the provisions of this division, see the Comment to this division under the division heading. [20 Cal.L.Rev.Comm.Reports 1001 (1990)].

Cross References

Vessels transferred upon death of owner, application of this section, see Vehicle Code § 9916.

§ 13114. Payment of costs and fees; condition for paying money or delivery of property

(a) A public administrator who has taken possession or control of property of a decedent under Article 1 (commencing with Section 7600) of Chapter 4 of Part 1 of Division 7 may refuse to pay money or deliver property pursuant to this chapter if payment of the costs and fees described in Section

7604 has not first been made or adequately assured to the satisfaction of the public administrator.

(b) A coroner who has property found upon the body of a decedent, or who has taken charge of property of the decedent pursuant to Section 27491.3 of the Government Code, may refuse to pay or deliver the property pursuant to this chapter if payment of the reasonable costs of holding or safeguarding the property has not first been made or adequately assured to the satisfaction of the coroner. *(Stats. 1990, c. 79 (A.B.759), § 14, operative July 1, 1991.)*

Law Revision Commission Comments

1990 Enactment

Section 13114 continues Section 13114 of the repealed Probate Code without change. See also the Comment to this chapter under the chapter heading.

Background on Section 13114 of Repealed Code

Section 13114 was added by 1986 Cal.Stat. ch. 783 § 24 and was amended by 1987 Cal.Stat. ch. 923 § 94.1 and by 1988 Cal.Stat. ch. 1199 § 98. Subdivision (a) continued subdivision (e) of former Probate Code Section 630 (repealed by 1986 Cal.Stat. ch. 783 § 9) without substantive change. Subdivision (b) was a new provision added by the 1987 amendment. For background on the provisions of this division, see the Comment to this division under the division heading.

The 1988 amendment corrected terminology and section references. For background on the 1988 amendment, see Comments to Conforming Revisions and Repeals, 19 Cal.L.Revision Comm'n Reports 1031, 1095 (1988). [20 Cal.L.Rev.Comm.Reports 1001 (1990)].

§ 13115. Possession or transfer of real property; use of procedure not permitted

The procedure provided in this chapter may not be used to obtain possession or the transfer of real property. *(Stats. 1990, c. 79 (A.B.759), § 14, operative July 1, 1991.)*

Law Revision Commission Comments

1990 Enactment

Section 13115 continues Section 13115 of the repealed Probate Code without change. See also Section 13106.5 (recording of affidavit or declaration where property is obligation secured by lien on real property). For provisions relating to real property, see Chapter 4 (commencing with Section 13150) (court order determining succession to real property), Chapter 5 (commencing with Section 13200) (affidavit procedure for real property of small value). See also the Comment to this chapter under the chapter heading.

Background on Section 13115 of Repealed Code

Section 13115 was added by 1986 Cal.Stat. ch. 783 § 24. The section continued the last sentence of subdivision (b) of former Probate Code Section 630 (repealed by 1986 Cal.Stat. ch. 783 § 9) with language changes for clarification only and without substantive change. For background on the provisions of this division, see the Comment to this division under the division heading. [20 Cal.L.Rev.Comm.Reports 1001 (1990)].

§ 13116. Procedure provided in chapter as additional and supplemental to any other procedure

The procedure provided in this chapter is in addition to and supplemental to any other procedure for (1) collecting money due to a decedent, (2) receiving tangible personal property of a decedent, or (3) having evidence of ownership of property of a decedent transferred. Nothing in this chapter restricts or limits the release of tangible personal property of a decedent pursuant to any other provision of law. This section is declaratory of existing law. *(Stats.1990, c. 79 (A.B.759), § 14, operative July 1, 1991.)*

Law Revision Commission Comments

1990 Enactment

Section 13116 continues Section 13116 of the repealed Probate Code without change. This section makes clear that this chapter is supplemental and in addition to other procedures. Property may be delivered to a person under these other procedures without compliance with the requirements of this chapter. See, e.g., Sections 330 (delivery of decedent's tangible personal property), 13600–13606 (right of surviving spouse to collect salary owing to deceased spouse without waiting for a 40–day period to elapse). See also Fin.Code § 6950 (payment of deposit account of nonresident decedent); Gov't.Code § 27491.3 (property of deceased at scene of death; sealing of premises of deceased); Health & Safety Code § 18102 & Veh.Code §§ 5910, 9916 (transfer upon affidavit of manufactured home, mobilehome, commercial coach, truck camper, floating home, vehicle, or vessel). Section 13106, which protects the transferor from liability, does not apply where the property is released pursuant to other procedures. Other procedures may, however, protect the transferor from liability. See, e.g., Fin.Code § 6951 (protection of certain financial institutions); Veh.Code § 5910 (protection of Department of Motor Vehicles and its officers and employees). See also the Comment to this chapter under the chapter heading.

Background on Section 13116 of Repealed Code

Section 13116 was a new provision added by 1987 Cal.Stat. ch. 923 § 94.3. See Communication from California Law Revision Commission Concerning Assembly Bill 706, 19 Cal.L.Revision Comm'n Reports 545, 611 (1988). For background on the provisions of this division, see the Comment to this division under the division heading. [20 Cal.L.Rev.Comm.Reports 1001 (1990)].

CHAPTER 4. COURT ORDER DETERMINING SUCCESSION TO PROPERTY

Section

13150. When procedure provided by chapter may be used.
13151. Petition requesting court order; determination of succession.
13152. Contents of petition; inventory and appraisal; copy of will.
13153. Notice of hearing.
13154. Court order for transfer of property; determinations.
13155. Effect of order.
13156. Liability for decedent's unsecured debts; limitation; defenses, cross complaints, or setoffs.
13157. Attorneys' fees.
13158. Compliance with affidavit procedure for personal property collection or transfer.

Application

Application of Part 1, see Probate Code § 13053.

Law Revision Commission Comments

1990 Enactment

This chapter provides a procedure for obtaining, without the need for a probate proceeding, a court order determining that real property of the decedent passed to one or more persons by intestate succession or under the decedent's will. This procedure is compara-

DISPOSITION OF ESTATE WITHOUT ADMINISTRATION

ble to that provided by Sections 13650–13660 (order determining that property passed to surviving spouse).

The procedure provided by this chapter can be used only if all of the following conditions are satisfied:

(1) The gross value of the decedent's real and personal property in this state (excluding certain property) does not exceed $60,000. See Sections 13151, 13152. See also Section 13050 (excluded property).

(2) No proceeding is pending or has been conducted in this state for administration of the decedent's estate. See Section 13150.

(3) The decedent died leaving real property in this state and 40 days have elapsed since the death of the decedent. See Section 13151.

(4) The petition is joined in by all those who have succeeded to the real property by intestate succession or under the decedent's will. See Section 13151. See also Sections 13004 (defining "particular item of property"), 13006 (defining "successor of the decedent").

(5) The petition is accompanied by an inventory and appraisal by a probate referee. See Section 13152(b).

(6) Notice is given to each of the persons named in the petition. See Section 13153. See also Section 13152(a)(7) (persons required to be named in petition). [20 Cal.L.Rev.Comm.Reports 1001 (1990)].

Cross References

Application of old and new law, see Probate Code § 3.
Destruction of court records, notice, retention periods, see Government Code § 68152.

§ 13150. When procedure provided by chapter may be used

The procedure provided by this chapter may be used only if one of the following requirements is satisfied:

(a) No proceeding is being or has been conducted in this state for administration of the decedent's estate.

(b) The decedent's personal representative consents in writing to use of the procedure provided by this chapter to determine that real property of the decedent is property passing to the petitioners. *(Stats.1990, c. 79 (A.B.759), § 14, operative July 1, 1991. Amended by Stats.1991, c. 1055 (S.B.271), § 42.)*

Law Revision Commission Comments

1990 Enactment

Section 13150 continues Section 13150 of the repealed Probate Code without change. This section makes the procedure provided by this chapter an alternative to the probate of a small estate. See also the Comment to this chapter under the chapter heading.

1991 Amendment

Subdivision (b) is added to Section 13150 to permit the procedure provided by this chapter to be used if the decedent's personal representative consents, notwithstanding that an estate proceeding is pending or has been conducted in this state. [20 Cal.L.Rev.Comm.Reports 2737 (1990)].

Background on Section 13150 of Repealed Code

Section 13150 was a new provision added by 1986 Cal.Stat. ch. 783 § 24. For background on the provisions of this division, see the Comment to this division under the division heading. [20 Cal.L.Rev.Comm.Reports 1001 (1990)].

§ 13151. Petition requesting court order; determination of succession

Exclusive of the property described in Section 13050, if a decedent dies leaving real property in this state and the gross value of the decedent's real and personal property in this state does not exceed one hundred fifty thousand dollars ($150,000) and 40 days have elapsed since the death of the decedent, the successor of the decedent to an interest in a particular item of property that is real property, without procuring letters of administration or awaiting the probate of the will, may file a petition in the superior court of the county in which the estate of the decedent may be administered requesting a court order determining that the petitioner has succeeded to that real property. A petition under this chapter may include an additional request that the court make an order determining that the petitioner has succeeded to personal property described in the petition. *(Stats.1990, c. 79 (A.B.759), § 14, operative July 1, 1991. Amended by Stats.1991, c. 1055 (S.B.271), § 43; Stats.1996, c. 86 (A.B. 2146), § 6; Stats.1996, c. 862 (A.B.2751), § 36; Stats.2011, c. 117 (A.B.1305), § 6.)*

Law Revision Commission Comments

1990 Enactment

Section 13151 continues Section 13151 of the repealed Probate Code without change. See also the Comment to this chapter under the chapter heading.

1991 Amendment

Section 13151 is amended to delete the requirement that the petition request an order determining that administration of the decedent's estate is unnecessary. This requirement is no longer appropriate in view of the new authorization for the decedent's personal representative to consent to a court order determining succession to decedent's property pursuant to this chapter, notwithstanding that an estate proceeding is pending or has been conducted in this state. See Section 13150.

The last sentence is added to Section 13151 to permit a petition under this chapter to include a request that the court make an order determining that the petitioner has succeeded to personal property of the decedent. Such an order may be made only if the petition requests an order determining that the petitioner has succeeded to real property described in the petition. A petition requesting an order concerning personal property only is not permitted under this chapter. Where only personal property is involved, the affidavit procedure under Chapter 3 (commencing with Section 13100) is the appropriate summary procedure to use. [20 Cal.L.Rev.Comm.Reports 2737 (1990)].

Background on Section 13151 of Repealed Code

Section 13151 was a new provision added by 1986 Cal.Stat. ch. 783 § 24. For background on the provisions of this division, see the Comment to this division under the division heading. [20 Cal.L.Rev.Comm.Report 1001 (1990)].

Cross References

Fee for filing petition commencing or opposition papers concerning certain probate proceedings, see Government Code § 70655.
Filing fees, see Government Code § 26827.

§ 13152. Contents of petition; inventory and appraisal; copy of will

(a) The petition shall be verified by each petitioner, shall contain a request that the court make an order under this chapter determining that the property described in the petition is property passing to the petitioner, and shall state all of the following:

(1) The facts necessary to determine that the petition is filed in the proper county.

(2) The gross value of the decedent's real and personal property in this state, excluding the property described in Section 13050, as shown by the inventory and appraisal attached to the petition, does not exceed one hundred fifty thousand dollars ($150,000).

(3) A description of the particular item of real property in this state which the petitioner alleges is property of the decedent passing to the petitioner, and a description of the personal property which the petitioner alleges is property of the decedent passing to the petitioner if the requested order also is to include a determination that the described personal property is property passing to the petitioner.

(4) The facts upon which the petitioner bases the allegation that the described property is property passing to the petitioner.

(5) Either of the following, as appropriate:

(A) A statement that no proceeding is being or has been conducted in this state for administration of the decedent's estate.

(B) A statement that the decedent's personal representative has consented in writing to use of the procedure provided by this chapter.

(6) Whether estate proceedings for the decedent have been commenced in any other jurisdiction and, if so, where those proceedings are pending or were conducted.

(7) The name, age, address, and relation to the decedent of each heir and devisee of the decedent, the names and addresses of all persons named as executors of the will of the decedent, and, if the petitioner is the trustee of a trust that is a devisee under the will of the decedent, the names and addresses of all persons interested in the trust, as determined in cases of future interests pursuant to paragraph (1), (2), or (3) of subdivision (a) of Section 15804, so far as known to any petitioner.

(8) The name and address of each person serving as guardian or conservator of the estate of the decedent at the time of the decedent's death, so far as known to any petitioner.

(b) There shall be attached to the petition an inventory and appraisal in the form set forth in Section 8802 of the decedent's real and personal property in this state, excluding the property described in Section 13050. The appraisal shall be made by a probate referee selected by the petitioner from those probate referees appointed by the Controller under Section 400 to appraise property in the county where the real property is located. The appraisal shall be made as provided in Part 3 (commencing with Section 8800) of Division 7. The petitioner may appraise the assets which a personal representative could appraise under Section 8901.

(c) If the petitioner bases his or her claim to the described property upon the will of the decedent, a copy of the will shall be attached to the petition.

(d) If the decedent's personal representative has consented to use of the procedure provided by this chapter, a copy of the consent shall be attached to the petition. *(Stats.1990, c. 79 (A.B.759), § 14, operative July 1, 1991. Amended by*

Stats.1991, c. 1055 (S.B.271), § 44; Stats.1996, c. 86 (A.B. 2146), § 7; Stats.1996, c. 862 (A.B.2751), § 37; Stats.2011, c. 117 (A.B.1305), § 7.)

Law Revision Commission Comments
1990 Enactment

Section 13152 continues Section 13152 of the repealed Probate Code without substantive change. This section is comparable to Section 13651 (petition for order determining property is property passing to surviving spouse). See also the Comment to this chapter under the chapter heading. For general provisions relating to petitions, see Sections 1020–1023.

A guardian, conservator, trustee, custodian, or attorney-in-fact is authorized to act as petitioner on behalf of the person to whom the real property passes. See Section 13051.

The petitioner (rather than the court) selects the probate referee because the inventory and appraisal must be attached to the petition when filed. (Ordinarily, the court will not designate a probate referee until after a petition is filed.) The provision of subdivision (b) that makes this clear is the same as the last sentence of Section 13103 (affidavit procedure for collection or transfer of personal property) and the last sentence of subdivision (c) of Section 13200 (affidavit procedure for real property of less than $10,000 in value).

1991 Amendment

The introductory clause of Section 13152 is amended to delete the requirement that the petition request an order determining that administration of the decedent's estate is unnecessary. This requirement is no longer appropriate in view of the new authorization for the decedent's personal representative to consent to a court order determining succession to decedent's property pursuant to this chapter, notwithstanding that an estate proceeding is pending or has been conducted in this state. See Section 13150. Subdivision (d) is added to implement the new authorization. See also the Comment to Section 13151.

Section 13152 is also revised to reflect the fact that a petition under this chapter may include a request that the court make an order determining that the petitioner has succeeded to personal property of the decedent. See the Comment to Section 13151. [20 Cal.L.Rev.Comm.Reports 2737 (1990)].

Background on Section 13152 of Repealed Code

Section 13152 was a new provision added by 1986 Cal.Stat. ch. 783 § 24 and was amended by 1987 Cal.Stat. ch. 923 § 94.5, 1988 Cal.Stat. ch. 113 § 16.5, 1988 Cal.Stat. ch. 1199 § 98.5, and 1988 Cal.Stat. ch. 1447 § 5. For background on the provisions of this division, see the Comment to this division under the division heading.

The 1987 amendment revised Section 13152 to recognize that the petitioner (rather than the court) selects the probate referee. For background on this amendment, see Communication from California Law Revision Commission Concerning Assembly Bill 708, 19 Cal.L.Revision Comm'n Reports 545, 612 (1988).

The amendment made by 1988 Cal.Stat. ch. 113 § 16.5 revised subdivision (a)(7) to make a technical correction by substituting "petitioner" for "personal representative" as applicable to a trustee. This was a nonsubstantive revision. For background on this amendment, see Communication from the California Law Revision Commission Concerning Assembly Bill 2779, 19 Cal.L.Revision Comm'n Reports 1191, 1198 (1988).

The amendment made by 1988 Cal.Stat. ch. 1199 § 98.5 corrected terminology and section references. For background on this 1988 amendment, see Comments to Conforming Revisions and Repeals, 19 Cal.L.Revision Comm'n Reports 1031, 1095 (1988).

The amendment made by 1988 Cal.Stat. ch. 1447 § 5 made technical nonsubstantive revisions. [20 Cal.L.Rev.Comm.Reports 1001 (1990)].

§ 13153. Notice of hearing

Notice of the hearing shall be given as provided in Section 1220 to each of the persons named in the petition pursuant to Section 13152. *(Stats.1990, c. 79 (A.B.759), § 14, operative July 1, 1991.)*

Law Revision Commission Comments
1990 Enactment

Section 13153 continues Section 13153 of the repealed Probate Code without change. For general provisions relating to notice of hearing, see Sections 1200–1221. See also Sections 1250–1252 (request for special notice), 1260–1265 (proof of giving of notice). See also the Comment to this chapter under the chapter heading.

Background on Section 13153 of Repealed Code

Section 13153 was a new provision added by 1986 Cal.Stat. ch. 783 § 24 and was amended by 1987 Cal.Stat. ch. 923 § 95. For background on the provisions of this division, see the Comment to this division under the division heading.

The 1987 amendment deleted the provision requiring the clerk to set the matter for hearing, this provision being generalized in Section 1285. The former requirement that notice be given not less than 10 days before the hearing was replaced by a cross-reference to Section 1220 which provides for 15 days' notice. The former language relating to the manner of mailing notice was deleted and generalized in Sections 1215 (manner of mailing) and 1220 (manner of mailing notice of hearing). [20 Cal.L.Rev.Comm.Report 1001 (1990)].

§ 13154. Court order for transfer of property; determinations

(a) If the court makes the determinations required under subdivision (b), the court shall issue an order determining (1) that real property, to be described in the order, of the decedent is property passing to the petitioners and the specific property interest of each petitioner in the described property and (2) if the petition so requests, that personal property, to be described in the order, of the decedent is property passing to the petitioners and the specific property interest of each petitioner in the described property.

(b) The court may make an order under this section only if the court makes all of the following determinations:

(1) The gross value of the decedent's real and personal property in this state, excluding the property described in Section 13050, does not exceed one hundred fifty thousand dollars ($150,000).

(2) Not less than 40 days have elapsed since the death of the decedent.

(3) Whichever of the following is appropriate:

(A) No proceeding is being or has been conducted in this state for administration of the decedent's estate.

(B) The decedent's personal representative has consented in writing to use of the procedure provided by this chapter.

(4) The property described in the order is property of the decedent passing to the petitioner.

(c) If the petition has attached an inventory and appraisal that satisfies the requirements of subdivision (b) of Section 13152, the determination required by paragraph (1) of subdivision (b) of this section shall be made on the basis of the verified petition and the attached inventory and appraisal, unless evidence is offered by a person opposing the petition that the gross value of the decedent's real and personal property in this state, excluding the property described in Section 13050, exceeds one hundred fifty thousand dollars ($150,000). *(Stats.1990, c. 79 (A.B.759), § 14, operative July 1, 1991. Amended by Stats.1991, c. 1055 (S.B.271), § 45; Stats.1996, c. 86 (A.B.2146), § 8; Stats.2011, c. 117 (A.B. 1305), § 8.)*

Law Revision Commission Comments
1990 Enactment

Section 13154 continues Section 13154 of the repealed Probate Code without change. See also the Comment to this chapter under the chapter heading. This section states the determinations required for a court order determining that real property described in the order is property of the decedent passing to the petitioners. The court does not make a determination under Section 13154 as to the value of specific items or parcels of property; the court makes a determination only that "the gross value of the decedent's real and personal property in California, excluding the property described in Section 13050, does not exceed sixty thousand dollars ($60,000)."

For general provisions, see Sections 1000–1004 (rules of practice), 1040–1050 (hearings and orders), 7260–7263 (orders affecting property).

1991 Amendment

Section 13154 is amended to delete from subdivision (a) the requirement that the order include a determination that no administration of the decedent's estate is necessary and to revise subdivision (b)(3) to recognize the new authorization for the decedent's personal representative to consent to a court order determining succession to decedent's property pursuant to this chapter, notwithstanding that an estate proceeding is pending or has been conducted in this state. See Section 13150. See also the Comment to Section 13151.

Section 13154 also is amended to recognize that the court in a proceeding under this chapter may, if requested, include in its order a determination that the decedent's personal property is property passing to petitioners. See the Comment to Section 13151. [20 Cal.L.Rev.Comm.Reports 2737 (1990)].

Background on Section 13154 of Repealed Code

Section 13154 was a new provision added by 1986 Cal.Stat. ch. 783 § 24. For background on the provisions of this division, see the Comment to this division under the division heading. The section was amended by 1988 Cal.Stat. ch. 1199 § 99 to correct terminology. For background on the 1988 amendment, see Comments to Conforming Revisions and Repeals, 19 Cal.L.Revision Comm'n Reports 1031, 1095 (1988). [20 Cal.L.Rev.Comm.Reports 1001 (1990)].

§ 13155. Effect of order

Upon becoming final, an order under this chapter determining that property is property passing to the petitioner is conclusive on all persons, whether or not they are in being. *(Stats.1990, c. 79 (A.B.759), § 14, operative July 1, 1991. Amended by Stats.1991, c. 1055 (S.B.271), § 46.)*

Law Revision Commission Comments
1990 Enactment

Section 13155 continues Section 13155 of the repealed Probate Code without change. This section is comparable to Section 13657 (property passing to surviving spouse). See also the Comment to this chapter under the chapter heading.

1991 Amendment

Section 13155 is amended to reflect the expansion of the court's authority to include personal property in its order. See Section 13154. [20 Cal.L.Rev.Comm.Reports 2737 (1990)].

Section 13155 was a new provision added by 1986 Cal.Stat. ch. 783 § 24. For background on the provisions of this division, see the Comment to this division under the division heading. [20 Cal.L.Rev.Comm.Reports 1001 (1990)].

§ 13156. Liability for decedent's unsecured debts; limitation; defenses, cross complaints, or setoffs

(a) Subject to subdivisions (b), (c), and (d), the petitioner who receives the decedent's property pursuant to an order under this chapter is personally liable for the unsecured debts of the decedent.

(b) The personal liability of any petitioner shall not exceed the fair market value at the date of the decedent's death of the property received by that petitioner pursuant to an order under this chapter, less the amount of any liens and encumbrances on the property.

(c) In any action or proceeding based upon an unsecured debt of the decedent, the petitioner may assert any defense, cross-complaint, or setoff which would have been available to the decedent if the decedent had not died.

(d) Nothing in this section permits enforcement of a claim that is barred under Part 4 (commencing with Section 9000) of Division 7.

(e) Section 366.2 of the Code of Civil Procedure applies in an action under this section. *(Stats.1990, c. 79 (A.B.759), § 14, operative July 1, 1991. Amended by Stats.1990, c. 140 (S.B.1855), § 16.1, operative July 1, 1991; Stats.1992, c. 178 (S.B.1496), § 41.)*

Law Revision Commission Comments
1990 Enactment

Section 13156 continues Section 13156 of the repealed Probate Code without change. See also the Comment to this chapter under the chapter heading. This section is comparable to Section 6611 (small estate set-aside), but Section 13156 does not include the one-year limitation on the duration of personal liability provided by Section 6611. See the discussion in the Comment to Section 13109.

Subdivision (d) makes clear that a person who takes real property by court order under this chapter is not liable to a creditor whose claim is barred. See, e.g., Section 9002(b) (bar of claims not filed in accordance with statute).

1990 Amendment

Section 13156 (enacted as a part of the new Probate Code by 1990 Cal.Stat. ch. 79 § 14) was amended by 1990 Cal.Stat. ch. 140 § 16.1 to make clear that the general one-year statute of limitations applicable to all causes of action against a decedent is applicable to liability for the decedent's debts under Section 13156. For background on the 1990 amendment, see Recommendation Relating to Notice to Creditors in Estate Administration, 20 Cal.L.Revision Comm'n Reports 507 (1990). [20 Cal.L.Rev.Comm.Reports 1001 (1990)].

1992 Amendment

Section 13156 is amended to revise a section reference. This revision is a technical, nonsubstantive change. [22 Cal.L.Rev.Comm.Reports 895 (1992)].

Background on Section 13156 of Repealed Code

Section 13156 was a new provision added by 1986 Cal.Stat. ch. 783 § 24 and was amended by 1988 Cal.Stat. ch. 113 § 17. For background on the provisions of this division, see the Comment to this division under the division heading.

The 1988 amendment added subdivision (d). For background on the 1988 amendment, see Communication from the California Law Revision Commission Concerning Assembly Bill 2779, 19 Cal.L.Revision Comm'n Reports 1191, 1198 (1988). [20 Cal.L.Rev.Comm.Reports 1001 (1990)].

§ 13157. Attorneys' fees

The attorney's fees for services performed in connection with the filing of a petition and obtaining a court order under this chapter shall be determined by private agreement between the attorney and the client and are not subject to approval by the court. If there is no agreement between the attorney and the client concerning the attorney's fees for services performed in connection with the filing of a petition and obtaining of a court order under this chapter and there is a dispute concerning the reasonableness of the attorney's fees for those services, a petition may be filed with the court in the same proceeding requesting that the court determine the reasonableness of the attorney's fees for those services. If there is an agreement between the attorney and the client concerning the attorney's fees for services performed in connection with the filing of a petition and obtaining a court order under this chapter and there is a dispute concerning the meaning of the agreement, a petition may be filed with the court in the same proceeding requesting that the court determine the dispute. *(Stats.1990, c. 79 (A.B.759), § 14, operative July 1, 1991.)*

Law Revision Commission Comments
1990 Enactment

Section 13157 continues Section 13157 of the repealed Probate Code without substantive change. This section is comparable to Sections 6613 (small estate set-aside), 13660 (determination or confirmation of property passing or belonging to surviving spouse). See the Comment to Section 13660. See also the Comment to this chapter under the chapter heading.

Background on Section 13157 of Repealed Code

Section 13157 was a new provision added by 1986 Cal.Stat. ch. 783 § 24. For background on the provisions of this division, see the Comment to this division under the division heading. [20 Cal.L.Rev.Comm.Reports 1001 (1990)].

§ 13158. Compliance with affidavit procedure for personal property collection or transfer

Nothing in this chapter excuses compliance with Chapter 3 (commencing with Section 13100) by the holder of the decedent's personal property if an affidavit or declaration is furnished as provided in that chapter. *(Added by Stats.1991, c. 1055 (S.B.271), § 47.)*

Law Revision Commission Comments
1991 Addition

Section 13158 is added to ensure that the holder of decedent's personal property will not insist that the person seeking to collect the property by affidavit or declaration instead use the court procedure in this chapter. See Sections 13105, 13154. For the penalty for refusing to transfer the decedent's personal property to the person executing the affidavit or declaration, see Section 13105. [20 Cal.L.Rev.Comm.Reports 2737 (1990)].

CHAPTER 5. AFFIDAVIT PROCEDURE FOR REAL PROPERTY OF SMALL VALUE

Application

Application of Part 1, see Probate Code § 13053.

Law Revision Commission Comments
1990 Enactment

This chapter provides a procedure for obtaining marketable title to real property in which the decedent's interest is shown by a probate referee's appraisal not to exceed $10,000 gross value. The procedure was drawn in part from a statute enacted in Arizona in 1983. See Ariz.Rev.Stat.Ann. §§ 14–3971, 14–3972 (1988).

The procedure provided by this chapter can be used only if all of the following conditions are satisfied:

(1) The gross value of the decedent's real property in this state (excluding certain property) does not exceed $10,000. See Section 13200(a)(5). See also Section 13050 (exclusions).

(2) No proceeding for the administration of the decedent's estate is pending or has been conducted in California. See Section 13200(a)(7).

(3) Not less than six months have elapsed since the death of the decedent. See Section 13200(a) (introductory clause).

(4) The funeral expenses, expenses of last illness, and all unsecured debts of the decedent have been paid. See Section 13200(a)(8).

(5) The person executing the affidavit is the successor of the decedent. See Section 13200(a)(9). See also Section 13006 ("successor of the decedent" defined).

(6) The affidavit contains a notary public's certificate of acknowledgment identifying each person executing the affidavit. See Section 13200(b).

(7) An inventory and appraisal of the real property, made by a probate referee, is attached to the affidavit. See Section 13200(c).

(8) A copy of the decedent's will is attached to the affidavit if the successor of the decedent claims the property under the will of the decedent. See Section 13200(d).

(9) A certified copy of the decedent's death certificate is attached to the affidavit. See Section 13200(e).

Where the real property has a gross value in excess of $10,000 or where less than six months have elapsed since the death of the decedent, the affidavit procedure under this chapter may not be used; but there is another procedure available for obtaining a marketable title to the real property without the need for probate. See Sections 13150–13157 (where gross value of decedent's real and personal property in this state does not exceed $60,000, successor of decedent

may obtain court order determining succession to the real property). [20 Cal.L.Rev.Comm.Report 1001 (1990)].

Cross References

Application of old and new law, see Probate Code § 3.

§ 13200. Time for filing; contents of affidavit; service on guardian or conservator

(a) No sooner than six months from the death of a decedent, a person or persons claiming as successor of the decedent to a particular item of property that is real property may file in the superior court in the county in which the decedent was domiciled at the time of death, or if the decedent was not domiciled in this state at the time of death, then in any county in which real property of the decedent is located, an affidavit in the form prescribed by the Judicial Council pursuant to Section 1001 stating all of the following:

(1) The name of the decedent.

(2) The date and place of the decedent's death.

(3) A legal description of the real property and the interest of the decedent therein.

(4) The name and address of each person serving as guardian or conservator of the estate of the decedent at the time of the decedent's death, so far as known to the affiant.

(5) "The gross value of all real property in the decedent's estate located in California, as shown by the inventory and appraisal attached to this affidavit, excluding the real property described in Section 13050 of the California Probate Code, does not exceed fifty thousand dollars ($50,000)."

(6) "At least six months have elapsed since the death of the decedent as shown in a certified copy of decedent's death certificate attached to this affidavit."

(7) Either of the following, as appropriate:

(A) "No proceeding is now being or has been conducted in California for administration of the decedent's estate."

(B) "The decedent's personal representative has consented in writing to use of the procedure provided by this chapter."

(8) "Funeral expenses, expenses of last illness, and all unsecured debts of the decedent have been paid."

(9) "The affiant is the successor of the decedent (as defined in Section 13006 of the Probate Code) and to the decedent's interest in the described property, and no other person has a superior right to the interest of the decedent in the described property."

(10) "The affiant declares under penalty of perjury under the laws of the State of California that the foregoing is true and correct."

(b) For each person executing the affidavit, the affidavit shall contain a notary public's certificate of acknowledgment identifying the person.

(c) There shall be attached to the affidavit an inventory and appraisal of the decedent's real property in this state, excluding the real property described in Section 13050. The inventory and appraisal of the real property shall be made as provided in Part 3 (commencing with Section 8800) of Division 7. The appraisal shall be made by a probate referee selected by the affiant from those probate referees appointed by the Controller under Section 400 to appraise property in the county where the real property is located.

(d) If the affiant claims under the decedent's will and no estate proceeding is pending or has been conducted in California, a copy of the will shall be attached to the affidavit.

(e) A certified copy of the decedent's death certificate shall be attached to the affidavit. If the decedent's personal representative has consented to the use of the procedure provided by this chapter, a copy of the consent and of the personal representative's letters shall be attached to the affidavit.

(f) The affiant shall mail a copy of the affidavit and attachments to any person identified in paragraph (4) of subdivision (a). *(Stats.1990, c. 79 (A.B.759), § 14, operative July 1, 1991. Amended by Stats.1991, c. 1055 (S.B.271), § 48; Stats.1996, c. 86 (A.B.2146), § 9; Stats.2011, c. 117 (A.B. 1305), § 9.)*

Law Revision Commission Comments

1990 Enactment

Section 13200 continues Section 13200 of the repealed Probate Code without substantive change. The former reference to personal service has been omitted from subdivision (f) in view of Section 1216 (service by personal delivery satisfies a statutory requirement of service by mail). See also the Comment to this chapter under the chapter heading.

1991 Amendment

Section 13200 is amended to recognize that the decedent's personal representative may consent to use of the procedure provided by this chapter, notwithstanding that an estate proceeding is pending or has been conducted in this state. See Section 13210. [20 Cal.L.Rev.Comm.Reports 2737 (1990)].

Background on Section 13200 of Repealed Code

Section 13200 was a new provision added by 1986 Cal.Stat. ch. 783 § 24. For background on the provisions of this division, see the Comment to this division under the division heading. The section was amended by 1988 Cal.Stat. ch. 1199 § 99.5 to correct terminology and section references. [20 Cal.L.Rev.Comm.Reports 1001 (1990)].

Cross References

Fees for miscellaneous services, see Government Code § 70626.
Final distribution of estate by court and conclusiveness of decree, see Probate Code § 11600 et seq.
Passage of title to decedent's property, see Probate Code § 7000.
Recordation,
  Admission of will to probate, clerk to record in minutes, see Probate Code § 8225.
  Borrowing money and mortgaging property, see Probate Code § 9804.
  Certified copy of order establishing fact of death, see Probate Code § 210.
  Claim against real property under spouse's will, see Probate Code § 13541.
  Conveyances after confirmation, see Probate Code § 10314.
  Effect of recording or the want thereof, see Civil Code § 1213 et seq.
  Execution of conveyance or assignment of contract to purchase real property, see Probate Code § 10314.
  Real estate, judicial orders affecting title, see Probate Code § 7263.
  Recorder, see Government Code § 27201 et seq.

Unlawful transfers, see Civil Code § 1227 et seq.

§ 13201. Fee

Notwithstanding any other provision of law, the total fee for the filing of an affidavit under Section 13200 and the issuance of one certified copy of the affidavit under Section 13202 is as provided in subdivision (b) of Section 70626 of the Government Code. *(Stats.1990, c. 79 (A.B.759), § 14, operative July 1, 1991. Amended by Stats.2005, c. 75 (A.B.145), § 150, eff. July 19, 2005, operative Jan. 1, 2006.)*

Law Revision Commission Comments

1990 Enactment

Section 13201 continues Section 13201 of the repealed Probate Code without change. The fee provided by Section 13201 is the total filing fee. No additions to the $35 fee may be made for such fees as a law library fee, judges' retirement fee, reporter's fee, or the like. See also the Comment to this chapter under the chapter heading.

Background on Section 13201 of Repealed Code

Section 13201 was a new provision added by 1986 Cal.Stat. ch.783 § 24. For background on the provisions of this division, see the Comment to this division under the division heading. [20 Cal.L.Rv.Comm.Reports 1001 (1990)].

Cross References

Deposit of fees or fines collected pursuant to this section in the Trial Court Trust Fund, effect of prior agreements or practices, long-term revenue allocation schedule proposal, see Government Code § 68085.5.
Organization and government of courts, collection of fees and fines pursuant to this section, deposits, see Government Code § 68085.1.

§ 13202. Filing; certified copy; recording

Upon receipt of the affidavit and the required fee, the court clerk, upon determining that the affidavit is complete and has the required attachments, shall file the affidavit and attachments and shall issue a certified copy of the affidavit without the attachments. The certified copy shall be recorded in the office of the county recorder of the county where the real property is located. The county recorder shall index the certified copy in the index of grantors and grantees. The decedent shall be indexed as the grantor and each person designated as a successor to the property in the certified copy shall be indexed as a grantee. *(Stats.1990, c. 79 (A.B.759), § 14, operative July 1, 1991.)*

Law Revision Commission Comments

1990 Enactment

Section 13202 continues Section 13202 of the repealed Probate Code without change. See also the Comment to this chapter under the chapter heading.

Background on Section 13202 of Repealed Code

Section 13202 was a new provision added by 1986 Cal.Stat. ch. 783 § 24. For background on the provisions of this division, see the Comment to this division under the division heading. [20 Cal.L.Rv.Comm.Reports 1001 (1990)].

Cross References

Fees for miscellaneous services, see Government Code § 70626.

§ 13203. Good faith purchaser; rights and protections; later proceedings

(a) A person acting in good faith and for a valuable consideration with a person designated as a successor of the decedent to a particular item of property in a certified copy of an affidavit issued under Section 13202 and recorded in the county in which the real property is located has the same rights and protections as the person would have if each person designated as a successor in the recorded certified copy of the affidavit had been named as a distributee of the real property in an order for distribution that had become final.

(b) The issuance and recording of a certified copy of an affidavit under this chapter does not preclude later proceedings for administration of the decedent's estate. *(Stats.1990, c. 79 (A.B.759), § 14, operative July 1, 1991.)*

Law Revision Commission Comments

1990 Enactment

Section 13203 continues Section 13203 of the repealed Probate Code without change, except that the section is revised to extend to any person who enters into a transaction in good faith and for a valuable consideration, not only purchasers, lessees, and lenders. See also the Comment to this chapter under the chapter heading.

Subdivision (a) is designed to give the successors designated in the certified copy of the affidavit marketable title to the real property. Good faith purchasers, lessees, and lenders are protected to the same extent as they are protected when they deal with the distributee under an order for distribution that had become final. See Section 11605 (order for distribution binds and is conclusive as to the rights of all interested persons). Although Section 13203 protects good faith purchasers, lessees, and lenders, it does not preclude later probate proceedings. See subdivision (b). A subsequent probate proceeding will have no effect on good faith purchasers, lessees, and lenders. But the successor designated in the recorded affidavit has a duty to restore the property and its net income, or its value and interest on its proceeds if the property has been disposed of, to the estate if proceedings are later commenced for administration of the decedent's estate. See Section 13206. The successor also is liable to an unsecured creditor (Section 13204) or to a person having a superior right to the property (Section 13205). Liability under Sections 13204 and 13205 is limited. See Section 13207. If the person fraudulently executed or filed the affidavit, the person is liable to the decedent's estate or to a person having a superior right to the property for three times the fair market value of the property. See Sections 13205(b), 13206(b).

Background on Section 13203 of Repealed Code

Section 13203 was a new provision added by 1986 Cal.Stat. ch. 783 § 24. For background on the provisions of this division, see the Comment to this division under the division heading. The section was amended by 1988 Cal.Stat. ch. 1199 § 100 to correct terminology. [20 Cal.L.Rev.Comm.Reports 1001 (1990)].

§ 13204. Liability for decedent's unsecured debts

Each person who is designated as a successor of the decedent in a certified copy of an affidavit issued under Section 13202 is personally liable to the extent provided in Section 13207 for the unsecured debts of the decedent. Any such debt may be enforced against the person in the same manner as it could have been enforced against the decedent if the decedent had not died. In any action based upon the debt, the person may assert any defense, cross-complaint, or setoff that would have been available to the decedent if the decedent had not died. Nothing in this section permits enforcement of a claim that is barred under Part 4 (commencing with Section 9000) of Division 7. Section 366.2 of the Code of Civil Procedure applies in an action under this section. *(Stats.1990, c. 79 (A.B.759), § 14, operative July 1, 1991. Amended by Stats.1990, c. 140 (S.B.1855), § 17.1, operative July 1, 1991; Stats.1992, c. 178 (S.B.1496), § 42.)*

Law Revision Commission Comments

1990 Enactment

Section 13204 continues Section 13204 of the repealed Probate Code without change. See also the Comment to this chapter under the chapter heading. This section is comparable to Section 13109. See the Comment to Section 13109. The liability under Section 13204 is limited. See Section 13207. As to barred claims, see, e.g., Section 9002(b) (bar of claims not filed in accordance with statute).

1990 Amendment

Section 13204 (enacted as a part of the new Probate Code by 1990 Cal.Stat. ch. 79 § 14) was amended by 1990 Cal.Stat. ch. 140 § 17.1 to make clear that the general one-year statute of limitations applicable to all causes of action against a decedent is applicable to liability for the decedent's debts under Section 13204. For background on the 1990 amendment, see Recommendation Relating to Notice to Creditors in Estate Administration, 20 Cal.L.Revision Comm'n Reports 507 (1990). [20 Cal.L.Rev.Comm.Reports 1001 (1990)].

1992 Amendment

Section 13204 is amended to revise a section reference. This revision is a technical, nonsubstantive change. [22 Cal.L.Rev.Comm.Reports 895 (1992)].

Background on Section 13204 of Repealed Code

Section 13204 was a new provision added by 1986 Cal.Stat. ch. 783 § 24 and was amended by 1988 Cal.Stat. ch. 113 § 18. For background on the provisions of this division, see the Comment to this division under the division heading. The 1988 amendment added the last sentence to Section 13204 to make clear that a person who takes real property by affidavit is not liable to a creditor whose claim is barred. For background on the 1988 amendment, see Communication from the California Law Revision Commission Concerning Assembly Bill 2779, 19 Cal.L.Revision Comm'n Reports 1191, 1198 (1988). [20 Cal.L.Rev.Comm.Reports 1001 (1990)].

§ 13205. Liability to person having superior right by testate or intestate succession; fraudulent transactions; limitations of actions

(a) Except as provided in subdivision (b), each person who is designated as a successor of the decedent in a certified copy of any affidavit issued under Section 13202 is personally liable to the extent provided in Section 13207 to any person having a superior right by testate or intestate succession from the decedent.

(b) In addition to any other liability the person has under this section and Sections 13204, 13206, and 13207, if the person fraudulently executed or filed the affidavit under this chapter, the person is liable to the person having a superior right for three times the fair market value of the property. For the purposes of this subdivision, the "fair market value of the property" is the fair market value, determined as of the time the certified copy of the affidavit was issued under Section 13202, of the property the person liable took under the certified copy of the affidavit to which the other person has a superior right, less any liens and encumbrances on the property at that time.

(c) An action to impose liability under this section is forever barred three years after the certified copy of the affidavit is issued under Section 13202, or three years after the discovery of the fraud, whichever is later. The three-year period specified in this subdivision is not tolled for any reason. *(Stats.1990, c. 79 (A.B.759), § 14, operative July 1, 1991. Amended by Stats.1991, c. 1055 (S.B.271), § 49.)*

Law Revision Commission Comments
1990 Enactment

Section 13205 continues Section 13205 of the repealed Probate Code without change, except for the revision of subdivision (c) to conform it to Sections 13110(c) and 13206(f). The liability under Section 13205 is limited. See Section 13207. See also the Comment to this chapter under the chapter heading.

1991 Amendment

Subdivision (b) of Section 13205 is amended to change "excluding" to "less" liens and encumbrances, to make clear that fair market value means net value. [20 Cal.L.Rev.Comm.Reports 2737 (1990)].

Background on Section 13205 of Repealed Code

Section 13205 was a new provision added by 1986 Cal.Stat. ch. 783 § 24. For background on the provisions of this division, see the Comment to this division under the division heading. [20 Cal.L.Rev.Comm.Reports 1001 (1990)].

§ 13206. Later proceedings, or on request of personal representative; liability of successors; limitations of actions

(a) Subject to subdivisions (b), (c), (d), and (e), if proceedings for the administration of the decedent's estate are commenced, or if the decedent's personal representative has consented to use of the procedure provided by this chapter and the personal representative later requests that the property be restored to the estate, each person who is designated as a successor of the decedent in a certified copy of an affidavit issued under Section 13202 is liable for:

(1) The restitution to the decedent's estate of the property the person took under the certified copy of the affidavit if the person still has the property, together with (A) the net income the person received from the property and (B) if the person encumbered the property after the certified copy of the affidavit was issued, the amount necessary to satisfy the balance of the encumbrance as of the date the property is restored to the estate.

(2) The restitution to the decedent's estate of the fair market value of the property if the person no longer has the property, together with (A) the net income the person received from the property prior to disposing of it and (B) interest from the date of disposition at the rate payable on a money judgment on the fair market value of the property. For the purposes of this paragraph, the "fair market value of the property" is the fair market value, determined as of the time of the disposition of the property, of the property the person took under the certified copy of the affidavit, less the

amount of any liens and encumbrances on the property at the time the certified copy of the affidavit was issued.

(b) Subject to subdivision (d), if the person fraudulently executed or filed the affidavit under this chapter, the person is liable under this section for restitution to the decedent's estate of three times the fair market value of the property. For the purposes of this subdivision, the "fair market value of the property" is the fair market value, determined as of the time the certified copy of the affidavit was issued, of the property the person took under the certified copy of the affidavit, less the amount of any liens and encumbrances on the property at that time.

(c) Subject to subdivision (d), if proceedings for the administration of the decedent's estate are commenced and a person designated as a successor of the decedent in a certified copy of an affidavit issued under Section 13202 made a significant improvement to the property taken by the person under the certified copy of the affidavit in the good faith belief that the person was the successor of the decedent to that property, the person is liable for whichever of the following the decedent's estate elects:

(1) The restitution of the property, as improved, to the estate of the decedent upon the condition that the estate reimburse the person making restitution for (A) the amount by which the improvement increases the fair market value of the property restored, determined as of the time of restitution, and (B) the amount paid by the person for principal and interest on any liens or encumbrances that were on the property at the time the certified copy of the affidavit was issued.

(2) The restoration to the decedent's estate of the fair market value of the property, determined as of the time of the issuance of the certified copy of the affidavit under Section 13202, less the amount of any liens and encumbrances on the property at that time, together with interest on the net amount at the rate payable on a money judgment running from the date of the issuance of the certified copy of the affidavit.

(d) The property and amount required to be restored to the estate under this section shall be reduced by any property or amount paid by the person to satisfy a liability under Section 13204 or 13205.

(e) An action to enforce the liability under this section may be brought only by the personal representative of the estate of the decedent. Whether or not the personal representative brings an action under this section, the personal representative may enforce the liability only to the extent necessary to protect the interests of the heirs, devisees, and creditors of the decedent.

(f) An action to enforce the liability under this section is forever barred three years after the certified copy of the affidavit is issued under Section 13202, or three years after the discovery of the fraud, whichever is later. The three-year period specified in this subdivision is not tolled for any reason. *(Stats.1990, c. 79 (A.B.759), § 14, operative July 1, 1991. Amended by Stats.1991, c. 1055 (S.B.271), § 50; Stats.2015, c. 293 (A.B.139), § 19, eff. Jan. 1, 2016.)*

Law Revision Commission Comments

1990 Enactment

Section 13206 continues Section 13206 of the repealed Probate Code without change, except for the addition of the provision in paragraph (1) of subdivision (a) that, if the person encumbered the property after the certified copy of the affidavit was issued, the person is liable for the amount necessary to satisfy the balance of the encumbrance as of the date the property is restored to the estate. This amount is in addition to the property and the net income the person received from the property. Section 13206 is comparable to Section 13111. See the Comment to Section 13111. See also the Comment to this chapter under the chapter heading.

1991 Amendment

Section 13206 is amended to reflect the authorization for the decedent's personal representative to consent to use of the procedure provided by this chapter, notwithstanding that an estate proceeding is pending or has been conducted in this state. See Section 13210. [20 Cal.L.Rev.Comm.Reports 2737 (1990)].

Background on Section 13206 of Repealed Code

Section 13206 was a new provision added by 1986 Cal.Stat. ch. 783 § 24. For background on the provisions of this division, see the Comment to this division under the division heading. [20 Cal.L.Rev.Comm.Reports 1001 (1990)].

2015 Amendment

Section 13206 is amended for parallelism with Section 5676 (revocable TOD deed). It makes clear that liability for restitution of property to the estate under this section is limited to satisfaction of creditor claims, regardless of whether restitution under this section is made voluntarily or pursuant to a court proceeding. Any surplus belongs to the successor of the decedent. [36 Cal.L.Rev.Comm. Reports 103 (2006)].

§ 13207. Exemption from certain liability; limitation on liability

(a) A person designated as a successor of the decedent in a certified copy of an affidavit issued under Section 13202 is not liable under Section 13204 or 13205 if proceedings for the administration of the decedent's estate are commenced, or if the decedent's personal representative has consented to use of the procedure provided by this chapter and the personal representative later requests that the property be restored to the estate, and the person satisfies the requirements of Section 13206.

(b) Except as provided in subdivision (b) of Section 13205, the aggregate of the personal liability of a person under Sections 13204 and 13205 shall not exceed the sum of the following:

(1) The fair market value at the time of the issuance of the certified copy of the affidavit under Section 13202 of the decedent's property received by that person under this chapter, less the amount of any liens and encumbrances on the property at that time.

(2) The net income the person received from the property.

(3) If the property has been disposed of, interest on the fair market value of the property from the date of disposition at the rate payable on a money judgment. For the purposes of this paragraph, "fair market value of the property" has the same meaning as defined in paragraph (2) of subdivision (a) of Section 13206. *(Stats.1990, c. 79 (A.B.759), § 14, operative July 1, 1991. Amended by Stats.1991, c. 1055 (S.B.271), § 51.)*

Law Revision Commission Comments

1990 Enactment

Section 13207 continues Section 13207 of the repealed Probate Code without change. This section is comparable to Section 13112. See also the Comment to this chapter under the chapter heading.

1991 Amendment [Revised Comment]

Subdivision (a) of Section 13207 is amended to reflect the new authorization for the decedent's personal representative to consent to use of the procedure provided by this chapter, notwithstanding that an estate proceeding is pending or has been conducted in this state. See Section 13210.

Subdivision (b) is amended to make a technical, nonsubstantive clarification. [21 Cal.L.Rev.Comm.Reports 71 (1991)].

Background on Section 13207 of Repealed Code

Section 13207 was a new provision added by 1986 Cal.Stat. ch. 783 § 24. For background on the provisions of this division, see the Comment to this division under the division heading. [20 Cal.L.Rev.Comm.Reports 1001 (1990)].

§ 13208. Cumulative nature of remedies

The remedies available under Sections 13204 to 13207, inclusive, are in addition to any remedies available by reason of any fraud or intentional wrongdoing. *(Stats.1990, c. 79 (A.B.759), § 14, operative July 1, 1991.)*

Law Revision Commission Comments

1990 Enactment

Section 13208 continues Section 13208 of the repealed Probate Code without change. This section makes clear that the remedies provided in this chapter for the decedent's estate, creditors, and persons having a superior right to the property by testate or intestate succession do not limit any other remedies that are available by reason of fraud or intentional wrongdoing. See also the Comment to this chapter under the chapter heading.

Background on Section 13208 of Repealed Code

Section 13208 was a new provision added by 1986 Cal.Stat. ch. 783 § 24. For background on the provisions of this division, see the Comment to this division under the division heading. [20 Cal.L.Rev.Comm.Reports 1001 (1990)].

§ 13209. Repealed by Stats.1990, c. 79 (A.B.759), § 13, operative July 1, 1991

Law Revision Commission Comments

1990 Repeal

Section 13209 of the repealed Probate Code is omitted from the new Probate Code because it is unnecessary. See Section 1001(b) (Judicial Council forms). [20 Cal.L.Rev.Comm.Reports 1001 (1990)].

§ 13210. Procedure provided by this chapter; requirements for use

The procedure provided by this chapter may be used only if one of the following requirements is satisfied:

(a) No proceeding for the administration of the decedent's estate is pending or has been conducted in this state.

(b) The decedent's personal representative consents in writing to use of the procedure provided by this chapter. *(Added by Stats.1991, c. 1055 (S.B.271), § 52.)*

Section 13210 is a new provision. It expands the authorization to use the procedure provided by this chapter to cover the case where the decedent's personal representative consents to use of the procedure, notwithstanding that an estate proceeding is pending or has been conducted in this state. See also Section 13108 (summary collection of personal property). [20 Cal.L.Rev.Comm.Reports 2737 (1990)].

Part 2

PASSAGE OF PROPERTY TO SURVIVING SPOUSE WITHOUT ADMINISTRATION

Application

Application of Part 2 and construction of Probate Code references in written instruments, see Probate Code §§ 13505 and 13506.

CHAPTER 1. GENERAL PROVISIONS

Application

Application of Part 2 and construction of Probate Code references in written instruments, see Probate Code §§ 13505 and 13506.

Cross References

Application of old and new law, see Probate Code § 3.
Payment of lottery prizes upon death of prizewinner, see Government Code § 8880.32.

§ 13500. Spouse dying intestate; surviving spouse; administration not necessary

Except as provided in this chapter, when a * * * spouse dies intestate leaving property that passes to the surviving spouse under Section 6401, or dies testate and by his or her will devises all or a part of his or her property to the surviving spouse, the property passes to the survivor subject to the provisions of Chapter 2 (commencing with Section 13540)

and Chapter 3 (commencing with Section 13550), and no administration is necessary. *(Stats.1990, c. 79 (A.B.759), § 14, operative July 1, 1991. Amended by Stats.2016, c. 50 (S.B.1005), § 89, eff. Jan. 1, 2017.)*

Section 13500 continues Section 13500 of the repealed Probate Code without change. As to a surviving spouse's waiver of rights, see Sections 140–147.

Background on Section 13500 of Repealed Code

Section 13500 was added by 1986 Cal.Stat. ch. 783 § 24. The section restated subdivision (a) of former Probate Code Section 649.1 (repealed by 1986 Cal.Stat. ch. 783 § 9) without substantive change. For background on the provisions of this division, see the Comment to this division under the division heading. [20 Cal.L.Rev.Comm.Reports 1001 (1990)].

§ 13501. Property subject to administration

Except as provided in Chapter 6 (commencing with Section 6600) of Division 6 and in Part 1 (commencing with Section 13000) of this division, the following property of the decedent is subject to administration under this code:

(a) Property passing to someone other than the surviving spouse under the decedent's will or by intestate succession.

(b) Property disposed of in trust under the decedent's will.

(c) Property in which the decedent's will limits the surviving spouse to a qualified ownership. For the purposes of this subdivision, a devise to the surviving spouse that is conditioned on the spouse surviving the decedent by a specified period of time is not a "qualified ownership" interest if the specified period of time has expired. *(Stats.1990, c. 79 (A.B.759), § 14, operative July 1, 1991.)*

Section 13501 continues Section 13501 of the repealed Probate Code without substantive change. Administration of property described in Section 13501 may be avoided under Part 1 (commencing with Section 13000) (collection or transfer of small estate without administration) if the requirements of that part are satisfied. See also Chapter 6 (commencing with Section 6600) of Part 3 of Division 6 (small estate set-aside). As to a surviving spouse's waiver of rights, see Sections 140–147.

Background on Section 13501 of Repealed Code

Section 13501 was added by 1986 Cal.Stat. ch. 783 § 24. The section restated former Probate Code Section 649.3 (repealed by 1986 Cal.Stat. ch. 783 § 9) without substantive change. The section was amended by 1987 Cal.Stat. ch. 923 § 96 to revise a cross reference. The section was again amended by 1988 Cal.Stat. ch. 1199 § 100.5 to correct section references. For background on the provisions of this division, see the Comment to this division under the division heading. [20 Cal.L.Rev.Comm.Reports 1001 (1990)].

§ 13502. Property subject to administration upon election of surviving spouse

(a) Upon the election of the surviving spouse or the personal representative, guardian of the estate, or conservator of the estate of the surviving spouse, all or a portion of the following property may be administered under this code:

(1) The one-half of the community property that belongs to the decedent under Section 100, the one-half of the quasi-community property that belongs to the decedent under Section 101, and the separate property of the decedent.

(2) The one-half of the community property that belongs to the surviving spouse under Section 100 and the one-half of the quasi-community property that belongs to the surviving spouse under Section 101.

(b) The election shall be made by a writing specifically evidencing the election filed in the proceedings for the administration of the estate of the deceased spouse within four months after the issuance of letters, or within any further time that the court may allow upon a showing of good cause, and before entry of an order under Section 13656. *(Stats. 1990, c. 79 (A.B.759), § 14, operative July 1, 1991.)*

Law Revision Commission Comments

1990 Enactment

Section 13502 continues Section 13502 of the repealed Probate Code without substantive change. The surviving spouse may elect to probate only a portion of the surviving spouse's one-half of the community or quasi-community property. This permits, for example, probate of all of a block of stock that is community property without the need to probate the surviving spouse's one-half share of the other community property. As to a surviving spouse's waiver of rights, see Sections 140–147.

Background on Section 13502 of Repealed Code

Section 13502 was added by 1986 Cal.Stat. ch. 783 § 24 and was amended by 1988 Cal.Stat. ch. 1199 § 101. The section continued subdivisions (b) and (c) of former Probate Code Section 649.1 (repealed by 1986 Cal.Stat. ch. 783 § 9) with the addition of language in the introductory portion of subdivision (a) that makes clear that "all or a portion" of the described property of the deceased spouse or the surviving spouse may be administered. This language made clear that the surviving spouse may elect to have administered only a portion of the surviving spouse's one-half of the community or quasi-community property. This was consistent with the practice under prior law. The language also recognized the practice in some cases under former law of probating less than all of the property of the deceased spouse in the estate of the deceased spouse. The 1988 amendment corrected terminology and section references. For background on the provisions of this division, see the Comment to this division under the division heading. [20 Cal.L.Rev.Comm.Report 1001 (1990)].

Cross References

Allegations in petition for distribution concerning character of property, probate rules, see California Rules of Court, Rule 7.652.

§ 13502.5. Petition and order for administration; notice

(a) Upon a petition by the personal representative of a decedent and a showing of good cause, the court may order that a pecuniary devise to the surviving spouse, or a fractional interest passing to the surviving spouse in any property in which the remaining fraction is subject to the administration, may be administered under this code, except to the extent that it has passed by inheritance as determined by an order pursuant to Chapter 5 (commencing with Section 13650).

(b) Notice of this petition shall be given as provided in Section 1220 to the person designated in that section and to the surviving spouse. *(Added by Stats.1992, c. 871 (A.B. 2975), § 16.)*

§ 13503. Community property; election to transfer to trustee

(a) The surviving spouse or the personal representative, guardian of the estate, or conservator of the estate of the surviving spouse may file an election and agreement to have all or part of the one-half of the community property that belongs to the surviving spouse under Section 100 and the one-half of the quasi-community property that belongs to the surviving spouse under Section 101 transferred by the surviving spouse or the surviving spouse's personal representative, guardian, or conservator to the trustee under the will of the deceased spouse or the trustee of an existing trust identified by the will of the deceased spouse, to be administered and distributed by the trustee.

(b) The election and agreement shall be filed in the proceedings for the administration of the estate of the deceased spouse and before the entry of the order for final distribution in the proceedings. *(Stats.1990, c. 79 (A.B.759), § 14, operative July 1, 1991.)*

Law Revision Commission Comments

1990 Enactment

Section 13503 continues Section 13503 of the repealed Probate Code without change.

Background on Section 13503 of Repealed Code

Section 13503 was added by 1986 Cal.Stat. ch. 783 § 24 and was amended by 1988 Cal.Stat. ch. 1199 § 101.5. The section continued subdivision (d) of former Probate Code Section 649.1 (repealed by 1986 Cal.Stat. ch. 783 § 9) without substantive change. The 1988 amendment corrected terminology. For background on the provisions of this division, see the Comment to this division under the division heading. [20 Cal.L.Rev.Comm.Reports 1001 (1990)].

Cross References

Community and separate property in general, see Family Code § 751 et seq.; Probate Code §§ 3051, 3100 et seq.

§ 13504. Community property held in revocable trust

Notwithstanding the provisions of this part, community property held in a revocable trust described in Section 761 of the Family Code is governed by the provisions, if any, in the trust for disposition in the event of death. *(Stats.1990, c. 79 (A.B.759), § 14, operative July 1, 1991. Amended by Stats. 1994, c. 1269 (A.B.2208), § 61.6.)*

Law Revision Commission Comments

1990 Enactment

Section 13504 continues Section 13504 of the repealed Probate Code without change.

1994 Amendment

Section 13504 is amended to correct a cross-reference to former Civil Code Section 5110.150 which was superseded by Family Code Section 761. This is a technical, nonsubstantive change. [24 Cal.L.Rev.Comm.Reports 547 (1994), Annual Report for 1994, App. 5].

Background on Section 13504 of Repealed Code

Section 13504 was added by 1986 Cal.Stat. ch. 783 § 24 and amended by 1987 Cal.Stat. ch. 128 § 7. Section 13504 continued former Probate Code Section 649.5 (repealed by 1986 Cal.Stat. ch. 783 § 9) without substantive change. The 1987 amendment corrected a cross-reference. For background on the provisions of this division, see the Comment to this division under the division heading. [20 Cal.L.Rev.Comm.Reports 1001 (1990)].

§ 13505. Application of part

This part applies whether the deceased spouse died before, on, or after July 1, 1987. *(Stats.1990, c. 79 (A.B.759), § 14, operative July 1, 1991.)*

Law Revision Commission Comments
1990 Enactment

Section 13505 continues Section 13505 of the repealed Probate Code without change.

Background on Section 13505 of Repealed Code

Section 13505 was added by 1986 Cal.Stat. ch. 783 § 24. By making this part applicable whether the deceased spouse died before, on, or after the date this part became operative (July 1, 1987), the section eliminated the restrictive effect of former Section 658 (repealed by 1986 Cal.Stat. ch. 783 § 9) which preserved the law in effect prior to January 1, 1985, for cases where the deceased spouse died before that date. For background on the provisions of this division, see the Comment to this division under the division heading. [20 Cal.L.Rev.Comm.Reports 1001 (1990)].

§ 13506. References to former provisions deemed references to comparable provisions of this part

A reference in any statute of this state or in a written instrument, including a will or trust, to a provision of former Sections 202 to 206, inclusive, of the Probate Code (as repealed by Chapter 527 of the Statutes of 1984) or former Sections 649.1 to 649.5, inclusive, or Sections 650 to 658, inclusive, of the Probate Code (as repealed by Chapter 783 of the Statutes of 1986) shall be deemed to be a reference to the comparable provision of this part. *(Stats.1990, c. 79 (A.B. 759), § 14, operative July 1, 1991.)*

Law Revision Commission Comments
1990 Enactment

Section 13506 restates Section 13506 of the repealed Probate Code without substantive change. This section has been revised to delete the introductory clause which referred to the operative date of the section (July 1, 1987), this clause having become obsolete. Section 13506 makes clear that a reference in a statute or written instrument to a provision of former law is deemed to be a reference to the comparable provision of this part.

Background on Section 13506 of Repealed Code

Section 13506 was added by 1986 Cal.Stat. ch. 783 § 24. The section superseded former Probate Code Section 649.6 (repealed by 1986 Cal.Stat. ch. 783 § 9). For background on the provisions of this division, see the Comment to this division under the division heading. [20 Cal.L.Rev.Comm.Reports 1001 (1990)].

CHAPTER 2. RIGHT OF SURVIVING SPOUSE TO DISPOSE OF PROPERTY

Application

Application of Part 2 and construction of Probate Code references in written instruments, see Probate Code §§ 13505 and 13506.

Cross References

Community property of husband and wife, subject to express declaration in transfer documents, see Civil Code § 682.1.

§ 13540. Power to deal with and dispose of community or quasi-community real property

(a) Except as provided in Section 13541, after 40 days from the death of a spouse, the surviving spouse or the personal representative, guardian of the estate, or conservator of the estate of the surviving spouse has full power to sell, convey, lease, mortgage, or otherwise deal with and dispose of the community or quasi-community real property, and the right, title, and interest of any grantee, purchaser, encumbrancer, or lessee shall be free of rights of the estate of the deceased spouse or of devisees or creditors of the deceased spouse to the same extent as if the property had been owned as the separate property of the surviving spouse.

(b) The surviving spouse or the personal representative, guardian of the estate, or conservator of the estate of the surviving spouse may record, prior to or together with the instrument that makes a disposition of property under this section, an affidavit of the facts that establish the right of the surviving spouse to make the disposition.

(c) Nothing in this section affects or limits the liability of the surviving spouse under Sections 13550 to 13553, inclusive, and Chapter 3.5 (commencing with Section 13560). *(Stats. 1990, c. 79 (A.B.759), § 14, operative July 1, 1991. Amended by Stats.1991, c. 1055 (S.B.271), § 54; Stats.1994, c. 806 (A.B.3686), § 36.)*

Law Revision Commission Comments
1990 Enactment

Section 13540 continues Section 13540 of the repealed Probate Code without change. Subdivision (b) makes clear that this section does not affect or limit the liability of a surviving spouse under Sections 13550–13553. Although Section 13540 may preclude a devisee or creditor from enforcing his or her rights against a grantee, purchaser, encumbrancer, or lessee or against the property interest transferred to the grantee, purchaser, encumbrancer, or lessee, the section does not relieve the surviving spouse of any liability under Sections 13550–13553. If the surviving spouse is liable under those sections and the devisee or creditor obtains a judgment against the surviving spouse, the judgment may be enforced against any property of the surviving spouse (including the proceeds of the disposition described in Section 13540) that is subject to the enforcement of a judgment.

1991 Amendment

Subdivision (a) of Section 13540 is amended for completeness. Subdivision (b) is added to enable the surviving spouse to fill a gap in the chain of title. Subdivision (c) is amended to include a cross-reference to Sections 13560 to 13564 (liability for property of deceased spouse). [20 Cal.L.Rev.Comm.Reports 2769 (1990)].

Background on Section 13540 of Repealed Code

Section 13540 was added by 1986 Cal.Stat. ch. 783 § 24. The section continued the first portion of the first sentence and all of the last sentence of former Probate Code Section 649.2 (repealed by 1986 Cal.Stat. ch. 783 § 9). Subdivision (b) was a new provision.

For background on the provisions of this division, see the Comment to this division under the division heading. [20 Cal.L.Rev.Comm.Reports 1001 (1990)].

§ 13541. Exceptions; notice

(a) Section 13540 does not apply to a sale, conveyance, lease, mortgage, or other disposition that takes place after a notice that satisfies the requirements of this section is recorded in the office of the county recorder of the county in which real property is located.

(b) The notice shall contain all of the following:

(1) A description of the real property in which an interest is claimed.

(2) A statement that an interest in the property is claimed by a named person under the will of the deceased spouse.

(3) The name or names of the owner or owners of the record title to the property.

(c) There shall be endorsed on the notice instructions that it shall be indexed by the recorder in the name or names of the owner or owners of record title to the property, as grantor or grantors, and in the name of the person claiming an interest in the property, as grantee.

(d) A person shall not record a notice under this section for the purpose of slandering title to the property. If the court in an action or proceeding relating to the rights of the parties determines that a person recorded a notice under this section for the purpose of slandering title, the court shall award against the person the cost of the action or proceeding, including a reasonable attorney's fee, and the damages caused by the recording. *(Stats.1990, c. 79 (A.B.759), § 14, operative July 1, 1991. Amended by Stats.1991, c. 1055 (S.B.271), § 55.)*

Law Revision Commission Comments

1990 Enactment

Section 13541 continues Section 13541 of the repealed Probate Code without substantive change.

1991 Amendment

Subdivision (a) of Section 13541 is amended to make clear that the right provided in Section 13540 does not apply to a disposition made after a notice under this section is recorded, whether the notice is recorded before or after expiration of the 40–day waiting period provided in Section 13540.

Subdivision (d) is comparable to Civil Code Section 880.360 (marketable record title), and makes clear that recordation of notice under this section is not privileged. Subdivision (d) does not affect the elements of the cause of action for slander of title and codifies the measure of recovery for slander of title, with the addition of reasonable attorney's fees. See 5 B. Witkin, Summary of California Law, *Torts* § 572 (9th ed. 1988). [20 Cal.L.Rev.Comm.Reports 2769 (1990)].

Background on Section 13541 of Repealed Code

Section 13541 was added by 1986 Cal.Stat. ch. 783 § 24. The section restated a portion of former Probate Code Section 649.2 (repealed by 1986 Cal.Stat. ch. 783 § 9) without substantive change except that Section 13541 contained additional language to make clear that the notice must be recorded within 40 days from the death of the spouse. This clarification was consistent with language in Wilson v. Superior Court, 101 Cal.App.2d 592, 595, 225 P.2d 1002 (1951). For background on the provisions of this division, see the Comment to this division under the division heading. [20 Cal.L.Rev.Comm.Reports 1001 (1990)].

§ 13542. Application of former provisions

The repeal of former Section 649.2 by Chapter 783 of the Statutes of 1986 does not affect any sale, lease, mortgage, or other transaction or disposition of real property made prior to July 1, 1987, to which that section applied, and such a sale, lease, mortgage, or other transaction or disposition shall continue to be governed by the provisions of former Section 649.2 notwithstanding the repeal of that section. *(Stats.1990, c. 79 (A.B.759), § 14, operative July 1, 1991.)*

Law Revision Commission Comments

1990 Enactment

Section 13542 continues Section 13542 of the repealed Probate Code without substantive change. This section makes clear that dispositions made under repealed Probate Code Section 649.2 (repealed by 1986 Cal.Stat. ch. 783 § 9) are not affected.

Background on Section 13542 of Repealed Code

Section 13542 was a new provision added by 1986 Cal.Stat. ch. 783 § 24. For background on the provisions of this division, see the Comment to this division under the division heading. [20 Cal.L.Rev.Comm.Reports 1001 (1990)].

§ 13545. Securities

(a) After the death of a spouse, the surviving spouse, or the personal representative, guardian of the estate, or conservator of the estate of the surviving spouse has full power to sell, assign, pledge, or otherwise deal with and dispose of community or quasi-community property securities registered in the name of the surviving spouse alone, and the right, title, and interest of any purchaser, assignee, encumbrancer, or other transferee shall be free of the rights of the estate of the deceased spouse or of devisees or creditors of the deceased spouse to the same extent as if the deceased spouse had not died.

(b) Nothing in this section affects or limits the liability of a surviving spouse under Sections 13550 to 13553, inclusive, and Chapter 3.5 (commencing with Section 13560). *(Added by Stats.1991, c. 1055 (S.B.271), § 56.)*

Law Revision Commission Comments

1991 Addition

Section 13545 is drawn from Section 13540 (right of surviving spouse to dispose of real property).

Subdivision (a) makes clear that the right of a surviving spouse to deal with community and quasi-community property securities is not affected by the death of the other spouse. Thus, the fact that there may be a person having a superior right by testate succession to the decedent's share of securities does not impair the ability of the surviving spouse in whose name the securities are registered to make binding transactions affecting the securities just as if the deceased spouse had not died. See, e.g., Corp.Code § 420 (immunity of corporation and agents for executing properly endorsed securities transfer, including community property securities); Com.Code § 8302 (bona fide purchaser for value in good faith and without notice of adverse claim takes security free of adverse claim).

Subdivision (b) makes clear that this section does not affect or limit the liability of the surviving spouse under Sections 13550–13553 (liability for debts of deceased spouse) and 13560–13564 (liability for property of deceased spouse). Although Section 13545 may preclude a devisee or creditor from enforcing his or her rights against a purchaser, assignee, encumbrancer, or other transferee or against the property interest transferred to the purchaser, assignee, encumbrancer, or other transferee, the section does not relieve the surviving spouse of any liability under Sections 13550–13553 and 13560–13564. If the surviving spouse is liable under those sections and the devisee or creditor obtains a judgment against the surviving spouse, the judgment may be enforced against any property of the surviving spouse (including the proceeds of the disposition described in Section 13545) that is subject to the enforcement of a judgment. [20 Cal.L.Rev.Comm.Reports 2769 (1990)].

CHAPTER 3. LIABILITY FOR DEBTS OF DECEASED SPOUSE

Section
13550. Personal liability for debts chargeable against property.
13551. Limitation of liability.
13552. Limitation of actions.
13553. Exemption from liability.
13554. Enforcement of debt against surviving spouse.

Application

Application of Part 2 and construction of Probate Code references in written instruments, see Probate Code §§ 13505 and 13506.

Cross References

Community property of husband and wife, subject to express declaration in transfer documents, see Civil Code § 682.1.

§ 13550. Personal liability for debts chargeable against property

Except as provided in Sections 11446, 13552, 13553, and 13554, upon the death of a married person, the surviving spouse is personally liable for the debts of the deceased spouse chargeable against the property described in Section 13551 to the extent provided in Section 13551. *(Stats.1990, c. 79 (A.B.759), § 14, operative July 1, 1991.)*

Law Revision Commission Comments

1990 Enactment

Section 13550 continues Section 13550 of the repealed Probate Code without change.

Background on Section 13550 of Repealed Code

Section 13550 was added by 1986 Cal.Stat. ch. 783 § 24 and was amended by 1988 Cal.Stat. ch. 1199 § 102. The section continued subdivision (a) of former Probate Code Section 649.4 (repealed by 1986 Cal.Stat. ch. 783 § 9) without substantive change. The 1988 amendment corrected a section reference. For background on the provisions of this division, see the Comment to this division under the division heading. [20 Cal.L.Rev.Comm.Reports 1001 (1990)].

§ 13551. Limitation of liability

The liability imposed by Section 13550 shall not exceed the fair market value at the date of the decedent's death, less the amount of any liens and encumbrances, of the total of the following:

(a) The portion of the one-half of the community and quasi-community property belonging to the surviving spouse under Sections 100 and 101 that is not exempt from enforcement of a money judgment and is not administered in the estate of the deceased spouse.

(b) The portion of the one-half of the community and quasi-community property belonging to the decedent under Sections 100 and 101 that passes to the surviving spouse without administration.

(c) The separate property of the decedent that passes to the surviving spouse without administration. *(Stats.1990, c. 79 (A.B.759), § 14, operative July 1, 1991.)*

Law Revision Commission Comments

1990 Enactment

Section 13551 continues Section 13551 of the repealed Probate Code without change.

Background on Section 13551 of Repealed Code

Section 13551 was added by 1986 Cal.Stat. ch. 783 § 24. The section continued the substance of subdivision (b) of former Probate Code Section 649.4 (repealed by 1986 Cal.Stat. ch. 783 § 9) without substantive change but with the addition of language to make clear that (1) "value" means fair market value and (2) the value of property belonging to the surviving spouse that is administered in the estate of the deceased spouse is excluded in determining the extent of the liability of the surviving spouse. See Section 13502(a) (election to administer only a portion of the community and quasi-community property that belongs to the surviving spouse). For background on the provisions of this division, see the Comment to this division under the division heading. [20 Cal.L.Rev.Comm.Reports 1001 (1990)].

§ 13552. Limitation of actions

If proceedings are commenced in this state for the administration of the estate of the deceased spouse and the time for filing claims has commenced, any action upon the liability of the surviving spouse pursuant to Section 13550 is barred to the same extent as provided for claims under Part 4 (commencing with Section 9000) of Division 7, except as to the following:

(a) Creditors who commence judicial proceedings for the enforcement of the debt and serve the surviving spouse with the complaint therein prior to the expiration of the time for filing claims.

(b) Creditors who have or who secure the surviving spouse's acknowledgment in writing of the liability of the surviving spouse for the debts.

(c) Creditors who file a timely claim in the proceedings for the administration of the estate of the deceased spouse. *(Stats.1990, c. 79 (A.B.759), § 14, operative July 1, 1991.)*

Law Revision Commission Comments

1990 Enactment

Section 13552 continues Section 13552 of the repealed Probate Code without change.

Background on Section 13552 of Repealed Code

Section 13552 was added by 1986 Cal.Stat. ch. 783 § 24 and amended by 1987 Cal.Stat. ch. 923 § 97. Section 13552 continued subdivision (d) of former Probate Code Section 649.4 (repealed by 1986 Cal.Stat. ch. 783 § 9) without substantive change but added the clarifying phrase "who have or who secure" in subdivision (b). The 1987 amendment made technical, nonsubstantive revisions in the section. For background on the provisions of this division, see the Comment to this division under the division heading. [20 Cal.L.Rev.Comm.Reports 1001 (1990)].

§ 13553. Exemption from liability

The surviving spouse is not liable under this chapter if all the property described in paragraphs (1) and (2) of subdivision (a) of Section 13502 is administered under this code. *(Stats.1990, c. 79 (A.B.759), § 14, operative July 1, 1991.)*

Law Revision Commission Comments

1990 Enactment

Section 13553 continues Section 13553 of the repealed Probate Code without substantive change.

Background on Section 13553 of Repealed Code

Section 13553 was added by 1986 Cal.Stat. ch. 783 § 24 and was amended by 1988 Cal.Stat. ch. 1199 § 102.5. The section continued subdivision (c) of former Probate Code Section 649.4 (repealed by 1986 Cal.Stat. ch. 783 § 9) without substantive change. The 1988 amendment corrected a section reference. For background on the provisions of this division, see the Comment to this division under the division heading. [20 Cal.L.Rev.Comm.Reports 1001 (1990)].

§ 13554. Enforcement of debt against surviving spouse

(a) Except as otherwise provided in this chapter, any debt described in Section 13550 may be enforced against the surviving spouse in the same manner as it could have been enforced against the deceased spouse if the deceased spouse had not died.

(b) In any action or proceeding based upon the debt, the surviving spouse may assert any defense, cross-complaint, or setoff which would have been available to the deceased spouse if the deceased spouse had not died.

(c) Section 366.2 of the Code of Civil Procedure applies in an action under this section. *(Stats.1990, c. 79 (A.B.759), § 14, operative July 1, 1991. Amended by Stats.1990, c. 140, (S.B.1855), § 18.1, operative July 1, 1991; Stats.1992, c. 178 (S.B.1496), § 43.)*

Law Revision Commission Comments

Section 13554 (enacted as a part of the new Probate Code by 1990 Cal.Stat. ch. 79 § 14) was amended by 1990 Cal.Stat. ch. 140 § 18.1 to make clear that the general one-year statute of limitations applicable to all causes of action against a decedent is applicable to liability for the decedent's debts under Section 13554. Cf. former Code Civ.Proc. § 353.5 and Comment thereto. For background on the 1990 amendment, see Recommendation Relating to Notice to Creditors in Estate Administration, 20 Cal.L.Revision Comm'n Reports 507 (1990). [20 Cal.L.Rev.Comm.Reports 1001 (1990)].

1992 Amendment

Section 13554 is amended to revise a section reference. This revision is a technical, nonsubstantive change. [22 Cal.L.Rev.Comm.Reports 895 (1992)].

Background on Section 13554 of Repealed Code

Section 13554 was added by 1986 Cal.Stat. ch. 783 § 24. The section continued subdivision (e) of former Probate Code Section 649.4 (repealed by 1986 Cal.Stat. ch. 783 § 9) without substantive change. For background on the provisions of this division, see the Comment to this division under the division heading. [20 Cal.L.Rev.Comm.Reports 1001 (1990)].

CHAPTER 3.5. LIABILITY FOR DECEDENT'S PROPERTY

Application

Application of Part 2 and construction of Probate Code references in written instruments, see Probate Code §§ 13505 and 13506.

Cross References

Community property of husband and wife, subject to express declaration in transfer documents, see Civil Code § 682.1.

§ 13560. "Decedent's property" defined

For the purposes of this chapter, "decedent's property" means the one-half of the community property that belongs to the decedent under Section 100 and the one-half of the quasi-community property that belongs to the decedent under Section 101. *(Added by Stats.1991, c. 1055 (S.B.271), § 57.)*

Law Revision Commission Comments

1991 Addition

Section 13560 is included for drafting convenience. [20 Cal.L.Rev.Comm.Reports 2769 (1990)].

Cross References

Fee for filing papers in probate proceedings, see Government Code § 26827.

§ 13561. Liability to person having superior right; limitation of actions

(a) If the decedent's property is in the possession or control of the surviving spouse at the time of the decedent's death, the surviving spouse is personally liable to the extent provided in Section 13563 to any person having a superior right by testate succession from the decedent.

(b) An action to impose liability under this section is forever barred three years after the death of the decedent. The three-year period specified in this subdivision is not tolled for any reason. *(Added by Stats.1991, c. 1055 (S.B. 271), § 57.)*

Law Revision Commission Comments

1991 Addition

Section 13561 is drawn from subdivisions (a) and (c) of Section 13205 (affidavit procedure for real property of small value). [20 Cal.L.Rev.Comm.Reports 2769 (1990)].

§ 13562. Estate proceeding commenced; restitution; limitation of actions

(a) Subject to subdivisions (b), (c), and (d), if proceedings for the administration of the decedent's estate are commenced, the surviving spouse is liable for:

(1) The restitution to the decedent's estate of the decedent's property if the surviving spouse still has the decedent's property, together with (A) the net income the surviving spouse received from the decedent's property and (B) if the surviving spouse encumbered the decedent's property after the date of death, the amount necessary to satisfy the balance of the encumbrance as of the date the decedent's property is restored to the estate.

(2) The restitution to the decedent's estate of the fair market value of the decedent's property if the surviving spouse no longer has the decedent's property, together with (A) the net income the surviving spouse received from the decedent's property prior to disposing of it and (B) interest from the date of disposition at the rate payable on a money judgment on the fair market value of the decedent's property. For the purposes of this paragraph, the "fair market value of the decedent's property" is the fair market value of the decedent's property, determined as of the time of the disposition of the decedent's property, less the amount of any liens and encumbrances on the decedent's property at the time of the decedent's death.

(b) Subject to subdivision (c), if proceedings for the administration of the decedent's estate are commenced and the surviving spouse made a significant improvement to the decedent's property in the good faith belief that the surviving spouse was the successor of the decedent to the decedent's property, the surviving spouse is liable for whichever of the following the decedent's estate elects:

(1) The restitution of the decedent's property, as improved, to the estate of the decedent upon the condition that the estate reimburse the surviving spouse for (A) the amount by which the improvement increases the fair market value of the decedent's property restored, valued as of the time of restitution, and (B) the amount paid by the surviving spouse for principal and interest on any liens or encumbrances that were on the decedent's property at the time of the decedent's death.

(2) The restoration to the decedent's estate of the fair market value of the decedent's property, valued as of the time of the decedent's death, excluding the amount of any liens and encumbrances on the decedent's property at that time, together with interest on the net amount at the rate payable on a money judgment running from the date of the decedent's death.

(c) The property and amount required to be restored to the estate under this section shall be reduced by any property or amount paid by the surviving spouse to satisfy a liability under Chapter 3 (commencing with Section 13550).

(d) An action to enforce the liability under this section may be brought only by the personal representative of the estate of the decedent. Whether or not the personal representative brings an action under this section, the personal representative may enforce the liability only to the extent necessary to protect the interests of the heirs, devisees, and creditors of the decedent.

(e) An action to enforce the liability under this section is forever barred three years after the death of the decedent. The three-year period specified in this subdivision is not tolled for any reason. *(Added by Stats.1991, c. 1055 (S.B.*

271), § 57. Amended by Stats.2015, c. 293 (A.B.139), § 20, eff. Jan. 1, 2016.)

Law Revision Commission Comments

1991 Addition

Section 13562 is drawn from Section 13206 (affidavit procedure for real property of small value).

Under subdivision (a)(1), if the surviving spouse encumbered the property after the decedent's death, the surviving spouse is liable for the amount necessary to satisfy the balance of the encumbrance on the decedent's one-half interest as of the date the property is restored to the estate. This amount is in addition to the property and the net income the surviving spouse received from the property.

Restitution of property to the estate where the spouse still has the property may necessitate partition if the parties are unable to agree on possession or other matters. See Section 9823 (partition actions). [20 Cal.L.Rev.Comm.Reports 2769 (1990)].

2015 Amendment

Section 13562 is amended for parallelism with Section 5676 (revocable TOD deed). It makes clear that liability for restitution of property to the estate under this section is limited to satisfaction of creditor claims, regardless of whether restitution under this section is made voluntarily or pursuant to a court proceeding. Any surplus belongs to the surviving spouse. [36 Cal.L.Rev.Comm. Reports 103 (2006)].

§ 13563. Limitation on liability

(a) The surviving spouse is not liable under Section 13561 if proceedings for the administration of the decedent's estate are commenced and the surviving spouse satisfies the requirements of Section 13562.

(b) The aggregate of the personal liability of the surviving spouse under Section 13561 shall not exceed the sum of the following:

(1) The fair market value at the time of the decedent's death, less the amount of any liens and encumbrances on the decedent's property at that time, of the portion of the decedent's property that passes to any person having a superior right by testate succession from the decedent.

(2) The net income the surviving spouse received from the portion of the decedent's property that passes to any person having a superior right by testate succession from the decedent.

(3) If the decedent's property has been disposed of, interest on the fair market value of the portion of the decedent's property that passes to any person having a superior right by testate succession from the decedent from the date of disposition at the rate payable on a money judgment. For the purposes of this paragraph, "fair market value" is fair market value, determined as of the time of disposition of the decedent's property, less the amount of any liens and encumbrances on the decedent's property at the time of the decedent's death. *(Added by Stats.1991, c. 1055 (S.B.271), § 57.)*

Law Revision Commission Comments

1991 Addition

Section 13563 is drawn from Section 13207 (affidavit procedure for real property of small value). [20 Cal.L.Rev.Comm.Reports 2769 (1990)].

§ 13564. Other remedies not affected

The remedies available under Sections 13561 to 13563, inclusive, are in addition to any remedies available by reason of any fraud or intentional wrongdoing. *(Added by Stats. 1991, c. 1055 (S.B.271), § 57.)*

Law Revision Commission Comments

1991 Addition

Section 13564 is drawn from Section 13208 (affidavit procedure for real property of small value). This section makes clear that the remedies provided in this chapter for the decedent's estate and persons having a superior right to the property by testate succession do not limit any other remedies that are available by reason of fraud or intentional wrongdoing. [20 Cal.L.Rev.Comm.Reports 2769 (1990)].

CHAPTER 4. COLLECTION BY AFFIDAVIT OF COMPENSATION OWED TO DECEASED SPOUSE

Section
13600. Collection of salary or other compensation owed; maximum amount; cost-of-living adjustments.
13601. Affidavit or declaration; contents; proof of identity.
13602. Payment.
13603. Employers' discharge of liability.
13604. Refusal to pay; action; attorneys' fees.
13605. Effect of chapter on rights of heirs or devisees; liability for payment; fraudulent transactions.
13606. Cumulative nature of procedure.

Application

Application of Part 2 and construction of Probate Code references in written instruments, see Probate Code §§ 13505 and 13506.

Law Revision Commission Comments

1990 Enactment

This chapter provides a simple procedure that permits a surviving spouse immediately to collect not more than $5,000 of the earnings owed by an employer to the deceased spouse. Use of this procedure will provide funds for the surviving spouse until the probate proceeding is commenced and a family allowance may be obtained.

This chapter was drawn from Sections 13100–13115 (affidavit procedure for collection or transfer of property of small estate where death occurred not less than 40 days before affidavit presented to holder of property). However, use of the procedure under this chapter applies without regard to the amount of the decedent's estate; use of the procedure is not limited to cases where the estate is a small estate. Also, use of the procedure under this chapter is permitted without any delay after the death of the decedent; use of the procedure is not limited to cases where the decedent died not less than 40 days before the affidavit or declaration is presented to the employer. [20 Cal.L.Rev.Comm.Reports 1001 (1990)].

§ 13600. Collection of salary or other compensation owed; maximum amount; cost-of-living adjustments

(a) At any time after a * * * spouse dies, the surviving spouse or the guardian or conservator of the estate of the surviving spouse may, without procuring letters of administration or awaiting probate of the will, collect salary or other compensation owed by an employer for personal services of the deceased spouse, including compensation for unused vacation, not in excess of fifteen thousand dollars ($15,000) net.

(b) Not more than fifteen thousand dollars ($15,000) net in the aggregate may be collected by or for the surviving spouse under this chapter from all of the employers of the decedent.

(c) For the purposes of this chapter, a guardian or conservator of the estate of the surviving spouse may act on behalf of the surviving spouse without authorization or approval of the court in which the guardianship or conservatorship proceeding is pending.

(d) The fifteen-thousand-dollar ($15,000) net limitation set forth in subdivisions (a) and (b) does not apply to the surviving spouse or the guardian or conservator of the estate of the surviving spouse of a firefighter or peace officer described in subdivision (a) of Section 22820 of the Government Code.

(e) On January 1, 2003, and on January 1 of each year thereafter, the maximum net amount of salary or compensation payable under subdivisions (a) and (b) to the surviving spouse or the guardian or conservator of the estate of the surviving spouse may be adjusted to reflect any increase in the cost of living occurring after January 1 of the immediately preceding year. The United States city average of the "Consumer Price Index for All Urban Consumers," as published by the United States Bureau of Labor Statistics, shall be used as the basis for determining the changes in the cost of living. The cost-of-living increase shall equal or exceed 1 percent before any adjustment is made. The net amount payable may not be decreased as a result of the cost-of-living adjustment. *(Stats.1990, c. 79 (A.B.759), § 14, operative July 1, 1991. Amended by Stats.2002, c. 733 (A.B.2059), § 2, eff. Sept. 20, 2002; Stats.2004, c. 69 (S.B.626), § 35, eff. June 23, 2004; Stats.2011, c. 117 (A.B.1305), § 10; Stats.2012, c. 162 (S.B.1171), § 140; Stats.2016, c. 50 (S.B. 1005), § 90, eff. Jan. 1, 2017.)*

Law Revision Commission Comments

1990 Enactment

Section 13600 continues Section 13600 of the repealed Probate Code without change. See also the Comment to this chapter under the chapter heading.

This section permits the guardian or conservator of the estate of the surviving spouse to use the procedure under this chapter to collect compensation owing to the deceased spouse. See also Section 13601(d) (proof of appointment of person as guardian or conservator). Letters of the conservator of the estate of the surviving spouse would be reasonable proof of authority to act for the surviving spouse.

If the employer does not personally know the affiant or declarant, reasonable proof of identity must be provided to the employer. See Section 13601(c). The kinds of proof of identity that may be relied on are specified in Section 13104. See Section 13601(c).

Background on Section 13600 of Repealed Code

Section 13600 was a new provision added by 1986 Cal.Stat. ch. 783 § 24. For background on the provisions of this division, see the Comment to this division under the division heading. [20 Cal.L.Rev.Comm.Reports 1001 (1990)].

§13601. Affidavit or declaration; contents; proof of identity

(a) To collect salary or other compensation under this chapter, an affidavit or a declaration under penalty of perjury under the laws of this state shall be furnished to the employer of the deceased spouse stating all of the following:

(1) The name of the decedent.

(2) The date and place of the decedent's death.

(3) Either of the following, as appropriate:

(A) "The affiant or declarant is the surviving spouse of the decedent."

(B) "The affiant or declarant is the guardian or conservator of the estate of the surviving spouse of the decedent."

(4) "The surviving spouse of the decedent is entitled to the earnings of the decedent under the decedent's will or by intestate succession and no one else has a superior right to the earnings."

(5) "No proceeding is now being or has been conducted in California for administration of the decedent's estate."

(6) "Sections 13600 to 13605, inclusive, of the California Probate Code require that the earnings of the decedent, including compensation for unused vacation, not in excess of fifteen thousand dollars ($15,000) net, be paid promptly to the affiant or declarant."

(7) "Neither the surviving spouse, nor anyone acting on behalf of the surviving spouse, has a pending request to collect compensation owed by another employer for personal services of the decedent under Sections 13600 to 13605, inclusive, of the California Probate Code."

(8) "Neither the surviving spouse, nor anyone acting on behalf of the surviving spouse, has collected any compensation owed by an employer for personal services of the decedent under Sections 13600 to 13605, inclusive, of the California Probate Code except the sum of _____ dollars ($_____) which was collected from _____."

(9) "The affiant or declarant requests that he or she be paid the salary or other compensation owed by you for personal services of the decedent, including compensation for unused vacation, not to exceed fifteen thousand dollars ($15,000) net, less the amount of _____ dollars ($_____) which was previously collected."

(10) "The affiant or declarant affirms or declares under penalty of perjury under the laws of the State of California that the foregoing is true and correct."

(b) Reasonable proof of the identity of the surviving spouse shall be provided to the employer. If a guardian or conservator is acting for the surviving spouse, reasonable proof of the identity of the guardian or conservator shall also be provided to the employer. Proof of identity that is sufficient under Section 13104 is sufficient proof of identity for the purposes of this subdivision.

(c) If a person presenting the affidavit or declaration is a person claiming to be the guardian or conservator of the estate of the surviving spouse, the employer shall be provided with reasonable proof, satisfactory to the employer, of the appointment of the person to act as guardian or conservator of the estate of the surviving spouse. *(Stats.1990, c. 79*

(A.B.759), §14, operative July 1, 1991. Amended by Stats. 2003, c. 32 (A.B.167), §13; Stats.2011, c. 117 (A.B.1305), §11.)

Law Revision Commission Comments

1990 Enactment

Section 13601 continues Section 13601 of the repealed Probate Code without change. See also the Comment to this chapter under the chapter heading.

2003 Amendment

Section 13601 is amended to correct subdivision enumeration. It was incorrectly enumerated on enactment. See 1990 Cal. Stat. ch. 79, §14. [33 Cal.L.Rev.Comm. Reports 165 (2003)].

Background on Section 13601 of Repealed Code

Section 13601 was a new provision added by 1986 Cal.Stat. ch. 783 §24. For background on the provisions of this division, see the Comment to this division under the division heading. [20 Cal.L.Rev.Comm.Reports 1001 (1990)].

§13602. Payment

If the requirements of Section 13600 are satisfied, the employer to whom the affidavit or declaration is presented shall promptly pay the earnings of the decedent, including compensation for unused vacation, not in excess of fifteen thousand dollars ($15,000) net, to the person presenting the affidavit or declaration. *(Stats.1990, c. 79 (A.B.759), §14, operative July 1, 1991. Amended by Stats.2011, c. 117 (A.B.1305), §12.)*

Law Revision Commission Comments

1990 Enactment

Section 13602 continues Section 13602 of the repealed Probate Code without change. This section imposes a duty on the employer to pay promptly the decedent's earnings to the person presenting the affidavit or declaration. The employer who pays the decedent's earnings to the person presenting the affidavit or declaration is protected from liability. See Section 13603. Payment pursuant to Section 13602 does not preclude later administration of the decedent's estate. See Section 13605. As to the liability of the person receiving the payment, see Section 13605. See also the Comment to this chapter under the chapter heading.

Background on Section 13602 of Repealed Code

Section 13602 was a new provision added by 1986 Cal.Stat. ch. 783 §24. For background on the provisions of this division, see the Comment to this division under the division heading. [20 Cal.L.Rev.Comm.Reports 1001 (1990)].

§13603. Employers' discharge of liability

If the requirements of Section 13601 are satisfied, receipt by the employer of the affidavit or declaration constitutes sufficient acquittance for the compensation paid pursuant to this chapter and discharges the employer from any further liability with respect to the compensation paid. The employer may rely in good faith on the statements in the affidavit or declaration and has no duty to inquire into the truth of any statement in the affidavit or declaration. *(Stats.1990, c. 79 (A.B.759), §14, operative July 1, 1991.)*

1990 Enactment

Section 13603 continues Section 13603 of the repealed Probate Code without change. This section protects the employer who pays to the affiant or declarant compensation owing to the deceased spouse. To obtain this protection, the affidavit or declaration must satisfy the requirements of Section 13601 and must be accompanied by reasonable proof of the identity of the person presenting the affidavit as the surviving spouse or person acting for the surviving spouse and, if someone claims to be acting for the surviving spouse, must be accompanied by reasonable proof of the authority of the person to act for the surviving spouse. See Sections 13600 and 13601 and the Comment to Section 13600. Section 13603 is comparable to Section 13106. See also the Comment to this chapter under the chapter heading.

Background on Section 13603 of Repealed Code

Section 13603 was a new provision added by 1986 Cal.Stat. ch. 783 § 24. The section was drawn from the first sentence of former Probate Code Section 631 (repealed by 1986 Cal.Stat. ch. 783 § 9). For background on the provisions of this division, see the Comment to this division under the division heading. [20 Cal.L.Rev.Comm.Reports 1001 (1990)].

§ 13604. Refusal to pay; action; attorneys' fees

(a) If the employer refuses to pay as required by this chapter, the surviving spouse may recover the amount the surviving spouse is entitled to receive under this chapter in an action brought for that purpose against the employer.

(b) If an action is brought against the employer under this section, the court shall award reasonable attorney's fees to the surviving spouse if the court finds that the employer acted unreasonably in refusing to pay as required by this chapter. *(Stats.1990, c. 79 (A.B.759), § 14, operative July 1, 1991.)*

1990 Enactment

Section 13604 continues Section 13604 of the repealed Probate Code without substantive change. This section is comparable to subdivision (b) of Section 13105. Section 13604 makes clear that the duty imposed by Section 13602 may be enforced by an action against the employer. This remedy is in addition to the remedies against the employer if the estate of the deceased spouse is administered. See also Section 13656 (court order determining that property passed to surviving spouse made in proceeding to determine or confirm property passing or belonging to surviving spouse). See also the Comment to this chapter under the chapter heading.

Background on Section 13604 of Repealed Code

Section 13604 was a new provision added by 1986 Cal.Stat. ch. 783 § 24. For background on the provisions of this division, see the Comment to this division under the division heading. [20 Cal.L.Rev.Comm.Reports 1001 (1990)].

§ 13605. Effect of chapter on rights of heirs or devisees; liability for payment; fraudulent transactions

(a) Nothing in this chapter limits the rights of the heirs or devisees of the deceased spouse. Payment of a decedent's compensation pursuant to this chapter does not preclude later proceedings for administration of the decedent's estate.

(b) Any person to whom payment is made under this chapter is answerable and accountable therefor to the personal representative of the decedent's estate and is liable for the amount of the payment to any other person having a

superior right to the payment received. In addition to any other liability the person has under this section, a person who fraudulently secures a payment under this chapter is liable to a person having a superior right to the payment for three times the amount of the payment. *(Stats.1990, c. 79 (A.B. 759), § 14, operative July 1, 1991.)*

1990 Enactment

Section 13605 continues Section 13605 of the repealed Probate Code without change. This section makes clear that the surviving spouse takes under this chapter subject to the rights of any person having a superior right and has the duty to restore the payment received to the decedent's estate if the estate is administered. See also the Comment to this chapter under the chapter heading.

Background on Section 13605 of Repealed Code

Section 13605 was a new provision added by 1986 Cal.Stat. ch. 783 § 24. For background on the provisions of this division, see the Comment to this division under the division heading. [20 Cal.L.Rev.Comm.Reports 1001 (1990)].

§ 13606. Cumulative nature of procedure

The procedure provided in this chapter is in addition to, and not in lieu of, any other method of collecting compensation owed to a decedent. *(Stats.1990, c. 79 (A.B.759), § 14, operative July 1, 1991.)*

1990 Enactment

Section 13606 continues Section 13606 of the repealed Probate Code without change. This section makes clear that the procedure provided by this chapter is in addition to, and not in lieu of, any other method of collecting unpaid compensation owed to a decedent. See, e.g., Sections 5000 (payment of money due to decedent to person designated by decedent), 6600–6615 (small estate set-aside), 13100–13116 (affidavit procedure for collection or transfer of personal property of a small estate), 13650–13660 (court order determining that property passed to surviving spouse). See also Gov't Code §§ 12479 (designation by state employee of person to receive warrants upon employee's death), 53245 (designation by public employee of person to receive warrants upon employee's death). See also the Comment to this chapter under the chapter heading.

Background on Section 13606 of Repealed Code

Section 13606 was a new provision added by 1986 Cal.Stat. ch. 783 § 24. For background on the provisions of this division, see the Comment to this division under the division heading. [20 Cal.L.Rev.Comm.Reports 1001 (1990)].

CHAPTER 5. DETERMINATION OR CONFIRMATION OF PROPERTY PASSING OR BELONGING TO SURVIVING SPOUSE

Application

Application of Part 2 and construction of Probate Code references in written instruments, see Probate Code §§ 13505 and 13506.

Cross References

Destruction of court records, notice, retention periods, see Government Code § 68152.

§ 13650. Petition for order of administration not necessary

(a) A surviving spouse or the personal representative, guardian of the estate, or conservator of the estate of the surviving spouse may file a petition in the superior court of the county in which the estate of the deceased spouse may be administered requesting an order that administration of all or part of the estate is not necessary for the reason that all or part of the estate is property passing to the surviving spouse. The petition may also request an order confirming the ownership of the surviving spouse of property belonging to the surviving spouse under Section 100 or 101.

(b) To the extent of the election, this section does not apply to property that the petitioner has elected, as provided in Section 13502, to have administered under this code.

(c) A guardian or conservator may file a petition under this section without authorization or approval of the court in which the guardianship or conservatorship proceeding is pending. *(Stats.1990, c. 79 (A.B.759), § 14, operative July 1, 1991.)*

Law Revision Commission Comments

1990 Enactment

Section 13650 continues Section 13650 of the repealed Probate Code without substantive change. As to a surviving spouse's waiver of rights at death, see Sections 140–147.

Background on Section 13650 of Repealed Code

Section 13650 was added by 1986 Cal.Stat. ch. 783 § 24 and was amended by 1988 Cal.Stat. ch. 1199 § 103. Subdivision (a) continued the first sentence of subdivision (a) of former Probate Code Section 650 (repealed by 1986 Cal.Stat. ch. 783 § 9) without substantive change, but subdivision (a) of Section 13650 used language drawn from subdivision (c) of former Probate Code Section 655 (repealed by 1986 Cal.Stat. ch. 783 § 9) in place of the language of the first sentence of subdivision (a) of former Section 650 which referred to the allegation in the petition. Subdivision (b) continued subdivision (c) of former Section 650 (repealed by 1986 Cal.Stat. ch. 783 § 9) without substantive change. Subdivision (c) continued subdivision (d) of former Section 650 (repealed by 1986 Cal.Stat. ch. 783 § 9) without substantive change. The 1988 amendment corrected section references. For background on the provisions of this division, see the Comment to this division under the division heading. [20 Cal.L.Rev.Comm.Reports 1001 (1990)].

Cross References

Fee for filing petition commencing or opposition papers concerning certain probate proceedings, see Government Code § 70655.

Filing fees, see Government Code § 26827.

§ 13651. Contents of petition

(a) A petition filed pursuant to Section 13650 shall allege that administration of all or a part of the estate of the deceased spouse is not necessary for the reason that all or a part of the estate is property passing to the surviving spouse, and shall set forth all of the following information:

(1) If proceedings for the administration of the estate are not pending, the facts necessary to determine the county in which the estate of the deceased spouse may be administered.

(2) A description of the property of the deceased spouse which the petitioner alleges is property passing to the surviving spouse, including the trade or business name of any property passing to the surviving spouse that consists of an unincorporated business or an interest in an unincorporated business which the deceased spouse was operating or managing at the time of death, subject to any written agreement between the deceased spouse and the surviving spouse providing for a non pro rata division of the aggregate value of the community property assets or quasi-community assets, or both.

(3) The facts upon which the petitioner bases the allegation that all or a part of the estate of the deceased spouse is property passing to the surviving spouse.

(4) A description of any interest in the community property or quasi-community property, or both, which the petitioner requests the court to confirm to the surviving spouse as belonging to the surviving spouse pursuant to Section 100 or 101, subject to any written agreement between the deceased spouse and the surviving spouse providing for a non pro rata division of the aggregate value of the community property assets or quasi-community assets, or both.

(5) The name, age, address, and relation to the deceased spouse of each heir and devisee of the deceased spouse, the names and addresses of all persons named as executors of the will of the deceased spouse, and the names and addresses of all persons appointed as personal representatives of the deceased spouse, which are known to the petitioner.

Disclosure of any written agreement between the deceased spouse and the surviving spouse providing for a non pro rata division of the aggregate value of the community property assets or quasi-community property assets, or both, or the affirmative statement that this agreement does not exist. If a dispute arises as to the division of the community property assets or quasi-community property assets, or both, pursuant to this agreement, the court shall determine the division subject to terms and conditions or other remedies that appear equitable under the circumstances of the case, taking into account the rights of all interested persons.

(b) If the petitioner bases the allegation that all or part of the estate of the deceased spouse is property passing to the surviving spouse upon the will of the deceased spouse, a copy of the will shall be attached to the petition.

(c) If the petitioner bases the description of the property of the deceased spouse passing to the surviving spouse or the property to be confirmed to the surviving spouse, or both, upon a written agreement between the deceased spouse and the surviving spouse providing for a non pro rata division of the aggregate value of the community property assets or quasi-community assets, or both, a copy of the agreement shall be attached to the petition. *(Stats.1990, c. 79 (A.B.759), § 14, operative July 1, 1991. Amended by Stats.1998, c. 682 (A.B.2069), § 6.)*

Law Revision Commission Comments

1990 Enactment

Section 13651 continues Section 13651 of the repealed Probate Code without substantive change and adds the requirement that the petition state not only the name, age, and address of each heir or devisee of the deceased spouse but also the relation to the deceased spouse of each such heir or devisee. The requirement that the petition be verified has been omitted as unnecessary in view of Section 1021 which imposes a general requirement that petitions be verified. For general provisions, see Sections 1020–1023 (petitions and other papers).

Background on Section 13651 of Repealed Code

Section 13651 was added by 1986 Cal.Stat. ch. 783 § 24. The section continued a portion of subdivision (a) and all of subdivision (b) of former Probate Code Section 650 (repealed by 1986 Cal.Stat. ch. 783 § 9) without substantive change except that paragraph (2) of subdivision (a) of Section 13651 was revised to make clear that it was limited to an unincorporated business. For background on the provisions of this division, see the Comment to this division under the division heading.

§ 13652. Proceedings pending; additional fee not necessary

If proceedings for the administration of the estate of the deceased spouse are pending, a petition under this chapter shall be filed in those proceedings without the payment of an additional fee. *(Stats.1990, c. 79 (A.B.759), § 14, operative July 1, 1991.)*

Law Revision Commission Comments

1990 Enactment

Section 13652 continues Section 13652 of the repealed Probate Code without change.

Background on Section 13652 of Repealed Code

Section 13652 was added by 1986 Cal.Stat. ch. 783 § 24. The section continued the first sentence of former Probate Code Section 651 (repealed by 1986 Cal.Stat. ch. 783 § 9) without substantive change. For background on the provisions of this division, see the Comment to this division under the division heading. [20 Cal.L.Rev.Comm.Reports 1001 (1990)].

Cross References

Fee for filing petition commencing or opposition papers concerning certain probate proceedings, see Government Code § 70655. Filing fees, see Government Code § 26827.

§ 13653. Proceedings not pending; filing with petition for probate or administration

If proceedings for the administration of the estate of the deceased spouse are not pending, a petition under this chapter may, but need not, be filed with a petition for probate of the will of the deceased spouse or for administration of the estate of the deceased spouse. *(Stats.1990, c. 79 (A.B.759), § 14, operative July 1, 1991.)*

Law Revision Commission Comments

1990 Enactment

Section 13653 continues Section 13653 of the repealed Probate Code without substantive change. The word "verified" has been omitted as unnecessary in view of Section 1021 which imposes a general requirement that petitions be verified.

If proceedings for the administration of the estate of the deceased spouse are not pending, the petition may be filed with a petition for the probate of the will of the deceased spouse or for administration of the estate of the deceased spouse or the petition may be filed (without filing a petition for probate or administration) in the superior court of the county in which the estate of the deceased spouse may be administered. See Section 13650.

Background on Section 13653 of Repealed Code

Section 13653 was added by 1986 Cal.Stat. ch. 783 § 24. The section restated the second sentence of former Probate Code Section 651 (repealed by 1986 Cal.Stat. ch. 783 § 9) without substantive change. For background on the provisions of this division, see the Comment to this division under the division heading. [20 Cal.L.Rev.Comm.Reports 1001 (1990)].

§ 13654. Effect of petition

The filing of a petition under this chapter does not preclude the court from admitting the will of the deceased spouse to probate or appointing a personal representative of the estate of the deceased spouse upon the petition of any person legally entitled, including any petition for probate of the will or for administration of the estate which is filed with a petition filed under this chapter. *(Stats.1990, c. 79 (A.B. 759), § 14, operative July 1, 1991.)*

Law Revision Commission Comments

1990 Enactment

Section 13654 continues Section 13654 of the repealed Probate Code without change.

Background on Section 13654 of Repealed Code

Section 13654 was added by 1986 Cal.Stat. ch. 783 § 24. The section restated former Probate Code Section 652 (repealed by 1986 Cal.Stat. ch. 783 § 9) without substantive change. For background on the provisions of this division, see the Comment to this division under the division heading. [20 Cal.L.Rev.Comm.Reports 1001 (1990)].

§ 13655. Notice of hearing

(a) If proceedings for the administration of the estate of the deceased spouse are pending at the time a petition is filed under this chapter, or if the proceedings are not pending and if the petition filed under this chapter is not filed with a petition for probate of the deceased spouse's will or for administration of the estate of the deceased spouse, notice of the hearing on the petition filed under this chapter shall be given as provided in Section 1220 to all of the following persons:

(1) Each person listed in Section 1220 and each person named as executor in any will of the deceased spouse.

(2) All devisees and known heirs of the deceased spouse and, if the petitioner is the trustee of a trust that is a devisee under the will of the decedent, all persons interested in the trust, as determined in cases of future interests pursuant to paragraph (1), (2), or (3) of subdivision (a) of Section 15804.

(b) The notice specified in subdivision (a) shall also be mailed as provided in subdivision (a) to the Attorney General, addressed to the office of the Attorney General at Sacramento, if the petitioner bases the allegation that all or part of the estate of the deceased spouse is property passing to the surviving spouse upon the will of the deceased spouse and the will involves or may involve either of the following:

(1) A testamentary trust of property for charitable purposes other than a charitable trust with a designated trustee, resident in this state.

(2) A devise for a charitable purpose without an identified devisee or beneficiary. *(Stats.1990, c. 79 (A.B.759), § 14, operative July 1, 1991. Amended by Stats.1996, c. 563 (S.B.392), § 30.)*

Law Revision Commission Comments
1990 Enactment

Section 13655 continues Section 13655 of the repealed Probate Code without substantive change. The notice provisions in subdivision (b) have been revised to adopt the general notice provision of Section 1220. The requirement that the clerk set the petition for hearing has been omitted as unnecessary in view of Section 1041 which imposes this as a general requirement. For general provisions, see Sections 1200–1221 (notice of hearing), 1250–1252 (request for special notice), 1260–1265 (proof of giving notice).

Background on Section 13655 of Repealed Code

Section 13655 was added by 1986 Cal.Stat. ch. 783 § 24 and was amended by 1987 Cal.Stat. ch. 923 § 98, 1988 Cal.Stat. ch. 113 § 18.5, and 1988 Cal.Stat. ch. 1199 § 103.5. For background on the provisions of this division, see the Comment to this division under the division heading.

Subdivision (a) restated the substance of former Probate Code Section 654 (repealed by 1986 Cal.Stat. ch. 783 § 9) with two omissions:

(1) The last sentence of former Section 654, which required that a copy of the petition also be served, was not continued.

(2) The requirement of former Section 654 that notice of the hearing be given at least 20 days prior to the date of the hearing was superseded by the requirement that notice of hearing be given in the manner prescribed by the statute provisions referred to in subdivision (a) of Section 13655.

Subdivision (b) restated the substance of former Probate Code Section 653 (repealed by 1986 Cal.Stat. ch. 783 § 9) with the following changes:

(1) The requirement of former Section 653 that a copy of the petition be served was not continued.

(2) The requirement of former Section 653 that notice of hearing be given at least 20 days prior to the hearing was replaced by a requirement that notice of hearing be given at least 15 days before the hearing.

(3) The requirement of former Section 653 that notice of hearing be given to "[a]ll other persons who are named in the will of the deceased spouse, if the petitioner bases the allegation that all or part of the estate of the deceased spouse is property passing to the surviving spouse upon the will" was not continued. This requirement was replaced by the addition of language in paragraph (2) of subdivision (b) that required notice, if the personal representative is the trustee of a trust that is a devisee under the decedent's will, to all persons interested in the trust as determined in the case of future interests pursuant to the general statutory provision governing notice in future interests cases. Paragraphs (1) to (4), inclusive, of subdivision (b) of Section 13655 required notice to all persons who might be adversely affected by the order. The former requirement that notice be given to all persons named in the will, however,

apparently required notice to persons named in the will who were neither devisees nor named as executors of the will. Elimination of the requirement that notice be given to all persons named in the will avoided the need to give notice of hearing to persons who have no interest in the proceeding. For example, notice no longer needed to be given to a mortuary designated in the will to handle funeral arrangements, or to a former spouse where the will recites dissolution of a prior marriage.

The 1987 amendment (1) revised the second sentence of subdivision (b) of Section 13655 to conform to the general 15–day notice period provided in Section 1220, (2) revised the cross-reference in subdivision (b)(3) to the procedure for requesting special notice (see Sections 1250–1252), and (3) deleted the last paragraph of the section since had become obsolete. For background on the 1987 amendment, see Communication from California Law Revision Commission Concerning Assembly Bill 708, 19 Cal.L.Revision Comm'n Reports 545, 612–13 (1988). See also Recommendation Relating to Notice in Probate Proceedings, 19 Cal.L.Revision Comm'n Reports 357 (1988).

The amendment made by 1988 Cal.Stat. ch. 113 § 18.5 was a technical correction in subdivision (b)(2) by substituting "petitioner" for "personal representative" as applicable to a trustee. This was a nonsubstantive revision. For background on the 1988 amendment, see Communication from the California Law Revision Commission Concerning Assembly Bill 2779, 19 Cal.L.Revision Comm'n Reports 1191, 1198 (1988).

The amendment made by 1988 Cal.Stat. ch. 1199 § 103.5 corrected section references. [20 Cal.L.Rev.Comm.Reports 1001 (1990)].

§ 13656. Order; determination of property passing to surviving spouse

(a) If the court finds that all of the estate of the deceased spouse is property passing to the surviving spouse, the court shall issue an order describing the property, determining that the property is property passing to the surviving spouse, and determining that no administration is necessary. The court may issue any further orders which may be necessary to cause delivery of the property or its proceeds to the surviving spouse.

(b) If the court finds that all or part of the estate of the deceased spouse is not property passing to the surviving spouse, the court shall issue an order (1) describing any property which is not property passing to the surviving spouse, determining that that property does not pass to the surviving spouse and determining that that property is subject to administration under this code and (2) describing the property, if any, which is property passing to the surviving spouse, determining that that property passes to the surviving spouse, and determining that no administration of that property is necessary. If the court determines that property passes to the surviving spouse, the court may issue any further orders which may be necessary to cause delivery of that property or its proceeds to the surviving spouse.

(c) If the petition filed under this chapter includes a description of the interest of the surviving spouse in the community or quasi-community property, or both, which belongs to the surviving spouse pursuant to Section 100 or 101 and the court finds that the interest belongs to the surviving spouse, the court shall issue an order describing the property and confirming the ownership of the surviving spouse and may issue any further orders which may be necessary to cause ownership of the property to be confirmed in the surviving spouse. *(Stats.1990, c. 79 (A.B.759), § 14, operative July 1, 1991.)*

Law Revision Commission Comments

1990 Enactment

Section 13656 continues Section 13656 of the repealed Probate Code without substantive change. The order under subdivision (b) determines that property which is not property passing to the surviving spouse is subject to administration. But administration of this property may be avoided under Part 1 (commencing with Section 13000) (collection or transfer of small estate without administration) of this division if the requirements of that part are satisfied. See also Sections 6600–6614 (small estate set-aside). For general provisions relating to hearings and orders, see Sections 1040–1050. An order under Section 13656 is appealable. See Section 7240.

Background on Section 13656 of Repealed Code

Section 13656 was added by 1986 Cal.Stat. ch. 783 § 24 and was amended by 1988 Cal.Stat. ch. 1199 § 104. The section continued subdivisions (a) and (b) of former Probate Code Section 655 (repealed by 1986 Cal.Stat. ch. 783 § 9) without substantive change. The 1988 amendment corrected section references. For background on the provisions of this division, see the Comment to this division under the division heading. [20 Cal.L.Rev.Comm.Reports 1001 (1990)].

§ 13657. Conclusive nature of order

Upon becoming final, an order under Section 13656 (1) determining that property is property passing to the surviving spouse or (2) confirming the ownership of the surviving spouse of property belonging to the surviving spouse under Section 100 or 101 shall be conclusive on all persons, whether or not they are in being. *(Stats.1990, c. 79 (A.B.759), § 14, operative July 1, 1991.)*

Law Revision Commission Comments

1990 Enactment

Section 13657 continues Section 13657 of the repealed Probate Code without change. This section is comparable to Section 13155 (court order determining succession to real property in small estate).

Background on Section 13657 of Repealed Code

Section 13657 was added by 1986 Cal.Stat. ch. 783 § 24. The section continued subdivision (c) of former Probate Code Section 655 (repealed by 1986 Cal.Stat. ch. 783 § 9) without substantive change. For background on the provisions of this division, see the Comment to this division under the division heading. [20 Cal.L.Rev.Comm.Reports 1001 (1990)].

§ 13658. Unincorporated businesses; list of creditors; order to protect interests

If the court determines that all or a part of the property passing to the surviving spouse consists of an unincorporated business or an interest in an unincorporated business which the deceased spouse was operating or managing at the time of death, the court shall require the surviving spouse to file a list of all of the known creditors of the business and the amounts owing to each of them. The court may issue any order necessary to protect the interests of the creditors of the business, including, but not limited to, the filing of (1) an undertaking and (2) an inventory and appraisal in the form provided in Section 8802 and made as provided in Part 3 (commencing with Section 8800) of Division 7. *(Stats.1990, c. 79 (A.B.759), § 14, operative July 1, 1991.)*

Law Revision Commission Comments

1990 Enactment

Section 13658 continues Section 13658 of the repealed Probate Code without substantive change.

Background on Section 13658 of Repealed Code

Section 13658 was added by 1986 Cal.Stat. ch. 783 § 24 and was amended by 1988 Cal.Stat. ch. 1199 § 104.5. The section continued former Probate Code Section 656 (repealed by 1986 Cal.Stat. ch. 783 § 9) without substantive change except that (1) Section 13658 was limited to creditors of an "unincorporated" business and (2) language, drawn from former Probate Code Section 657 (repealed by 1986 Cal.Stat. ch. 783 § 9), was added to give the court specific authority to require the filing of an inventory and appraisal where necessary to protect the creditors of the business. The 1988 amendment corrected terminology and section references. For background on the provisions of this division, see the Comment to this division under the division heading. [20 Cal.L.Rev.Comm.Reports 1001 (1990)].

§ 13659. Inventory and appraisal

Except as provided in Section 13658, no inventory and appraisal of the estate of the deceased spouse is required in a proceeding under this chapter. However, within three months after the filing of a petition under this chapter, or within such further time as the court or judge for reasonable cause may allow, the petitioner may file with the clerk of the court an inventory and appraisal made as provided in Part 3 (commencing with Section 8800) of Division 7. The petitioner may appraise the assets which a personal representative could appraise under Section 8901. *(Stats.1990, c. 79 (A.B. 759), § 14, operative July 1, 1991.)*

Law Revision Commission Comments

1990 Enactment

Section 13659 continues Section 13659 of the repealed Probate Code without substantive change. An inventory and appraisal is not required to obtain an order under this chapter. However, Section 13659 gives the petitioner the option to file an inventory and appraisal in a proceeding under this chapter if the petitioner so desires. This option permits the petitioner to obtain an independent appraisal made by a probate referee if such an appraisal is desired by the petitioner. The petitioner may consider the independent appraisal useful for the purposes of capital gains taxes or other taxes. See also Section 13658 (authority of court to require the filing of an inventory and appraisal to protect creditors of unincorporated business of deceased spouse).

Background on Section 13659 of Repealed Code

Section 13659 was added by 1986 Cal.Stat. ch. 783 § 24 and was amended by 1988 Cal.Stat. ch. 1199 § 105. The first sentence of Section 13659 was drawn from former subdivision (a)(2)(A) of former Probate Code Section 605 (prior to its amendment by 1986 Cal.Stat. ch. 783 § 8). The remainder of Section 13659 was drawn from the first three sentences of former Section 657 (repealed by 1986 Cal.Stat. ch. 783 § 9). The 1988 amendment corrected terminology and section references. For background on the provisions of this division, see the Comment to this division under the division heading. [20 Cal.L.Rev.Comm.Reports 1001 (1990)].

§ 13660. Attorneys' fees

The attorney's fees for services performed in connection with the filing of a petition and obtaining of a court order under this chapter shall be determined by private agreement between the attorney and the client and are not subject to

PASSAGE OF PROPERTY TO SURVIVING SPOUSE

approval by the court. If there is no agreement between the attorney and the client concerning the attorney's fees for services performed in connection with the filing of a petition and obtaining of a court order under this chapter and there is a dispute concerning the reasonableness of the attorney's fees for those services, a petition may be filed with the court in the same proceeding requesting that the court determine the reasonableness of the attorney's fees for those services. If there is an agreement between the attorney and the client concerning the attorney's fees for services performed in connection with the filing of a petition and obtaining a court order under this chapter and there is a dispute concerning the meaning of the agreement, a petition may be filed with the court in the same proceeding requesting that the court determine the dispute. *(Stats.1990, c. 79 (A.B.759), § 14, operative July 1, 1991.)*

Law Revision Commission Comments
1990 Enactment

Section 13660 continues Section 13660 of the repealed Probate Code without change. In the case of a petition and order under this chapter, this section leaves the entire matter of the legal fees to private agreement between the attorney and the client. The last two sentences of Section 13660 make clear that the probate court has jurisdiction (1) to determine the reasonableness of the attorney's fees if there is a dispute and no agreement or (2) to determine the meaning of the agreement if there is a dispute concerning the meaning of an agreement concerning the attorney's fees for filing the petition and obtaining the order. The probate court has no jurisdiction with respect to attorney's fees for other legal work in connection with the decedent's property.

Background on Section 13660 of Repealed Code

Section 13660 was added by 1986 Cal.Stat. ch. 783 § 24. Section 13660 replaced the provision of prior law that provided for court approval of the attorney's fee for services performed in connection with the filing of a petition and obtaining a court order under former Probate Code Sections 650–658 (provisions repealed by 1986 Cal. Stat. ch. 783 § 9). See former subdivision (b) of former Probate Code Section 910 (prior to its amendment by 1975 Cal.Stat. ch. 173 § 11). No provision was made under former law for court approval of the attorney's fee for other legal work in connection with the estate of the deceased spouse (such as, for example, tax work, joint tenancy termination, or collection of insurance proceeds), and those matters were left to private agreement between the attorney and the client. For background on the provisions of this division, see the Comment to this division under the division heading. [20 Cal.L.Rev.Comm.Reports 1001 (1990)].

Division 9

TRUST LAW

Cross References

Real property, transfer fee defined, see Civil Code § 1098.

Law Revision Commission Comments

1990 Enactment

This division supersedes Division 9 (commencing with Section 15000) of the repealed Probate Code. The superseded division was enacted upon recommendation of the California Law Revision Commission. See Recommendation Proposing the Trust Law, 18 Cal.L.Revision Comm'n Reports 501 (1986). See also Communication from California Law Revision Commission Concerning Assembly Bill 2652, 18 Cal.L.Revision Comm'n Reports 1763 (1986). The Commission, in cooperation with California Continuing Education of the Bar, published the Trust Law as enacted with official comments. See Selected 1986 Trust and Probate Legislation, 18 Cal.L.Revision Comm'n Reports 1201, 1207–499 (1986).

After this division was enacted, revisions were made upon recommendation of the Law Revision Commission. See Recommendation Relating to Technical Revisions in the Trust Law, 18 Cal.L.Revision Comm'n Reports 1823 (1986); Communication from the California Law Revision Commission Concerning Assembly Bill 362, 19 Cal.L.Revision Comm'n Reports 541 (1988); Comments to Conforming Revisions and Repeals, 19 Cal.L.Revision Comm'n Reports 1031, 1097–98 (1988); Recommendation Relating to Trustees' Fees, 20 Cal.L.Revision Comm'n Reports 185 (1990). [20 Cal.L.Rev.Comm.Reports 1001 (1990)].

Cross References

Common law rules governing trusts, application, see Probate Code § 15002.

Construction of wills, trusts and other instruments, see Probate Code § 21101 et seq.

Relationships excluded from Code definition of trust, application of this Division, see Probate Code § 15003.

Trust for insurance or employee benefits, see Probate Code § 6320 et seq.

Uniform Testamentary Additions to Trusts Act, see Probate Code § 6300 et seq.

Part 1

GENERAL PROVISIONS

Application

Application of Division, see Probate Code § 15001.

§ 15000. Short title

This division shall be known and may be cited as the Trust Law. *(Stats.1990, c. 79 (A.B.759), § 14, operative July 1, 1991.)*

Law Revision Commission Comments

1990 Enactment

Section 15000 continues Section 15000 of the repealed Probate Code without change. This section provides a convenient means of referring to this division. While most important statutory provisions concerning trusts are included in this division, it should be noted that definitions and other general provisions applicable to this division are located elsewhere. See, e.g., Sections 24 ("beneficiary" defined), 56 ("person" defined), 62 ("property" defined), 82 ("trust" defined), 83 ("trust company" defined), 84 ("trustee" defined), 88 ("will" defined); see also Fin.Code §§ 1500–1591 (trust companies), 6515 (savings and loan associations as trustees); Gov't Code §§ 12580–12598 (Uniform Supervision of Trustees for Charitable Purposes Act).

Background on Section 15000 of Repealed Code

Section 15000 was a new provision added by 1986 Cal.Stat. ch. 820 § 40. For background on the provisions of this division, see the Comment to this division under the division heading. [20 Cal.L.Rev.Comm.Reports 1001 (1990)].

§ 15001. Application of division

Except as otherwise provided by statute:

(a) This division applies to all trusts regardless of whether they were created before, on, or after July 1, 1987.

(b) This division applies to all proceedings concerning trusts commenced on or after July 1, 1987.

(c) This division applies to all proceedings concerning trusts commenced before July 1, 1987, unless in the opinion of the court application of a particular provision of this division would substantially interfere with the effective conduct of the proceedings or the rights of the parties and other interested persons, in which case the particular provision of this division does not apply and prior law applies. *(Stats. 1990, c. 79 (A.B.759), § 14, operative July 1, 1991.)*

Law Revision Commission Comments

1990 Enactment [Revised Comment]

Section 15001 restates Section 15001 of the repealed Probate Code without substantive change. The language used in this section has been revised to reflect the fact that this division of the repealed Probate Code (the Trust Law) became operative on July 1, 1987.

Subdivision (a) provides the general rule that this division applies to all trusts, regardless of when created. Subdivision (a) is comparable to Section 8 of the Uniform Trustees' Powers Act (1964). As to the construction of provisions drawn from uniform acts, see Section 2. Subdivision (b), a specific application of the general rule stated in subdivision (a), makes clear that, except as otherwise provided by statute, this division applies to all proceedings commenced on or after July 1, 1987. Subdivision (c) is a special provision concerning the application of this division to proceedings concerning trusts commenced before July 1, 1987.

For special transitional provisions, see Sections 15401(d) (application of rules governing method of revocation by settlor), 16053 (language invoking standard of Uniform Prudent Investor Act), 16054 (application of Uniform Prudent Investor Act to existing relationships), 16062(b)-(d) (application of duty to account to beneficiaries), 16203 (application of rules governing trustee's powers), 16401(c) (application of rules governing trustee's liability to beneficiary for acts of agent), 16402(c) (application of rules governing trustee's liability to beneficiary for acts of cotrustee), 16403(c) (application of rules governing trustee's liability to beneficiary for acts of predecessor trustee), 18000(b) (application of rule governing personal liability of trustee to third persons on contracts). [25 Cal.L.Rev.Comm. Reports 673 (1995)].

1990 Enactment

Section 15001 restates Section 15001 of the repealed Probate Code without substantive change. The language used in this section has been revised to reflect the fact that this division of the repealed Probate Code (the Trust Law) became operative on July 1, 1987.

Subdivision (a) provides the general rule that this division applies to all trusts, regardless of when created. Subdivision (a) is comparable to Section 8 of the Uniform Trustees' Powers Act (1964). As to the construction of provisions drawn from uniform acts, see Section 2. Subdivision (b), a specific application of the general rule stated in subdivision (a), makes clear that, except as otherwise provided by statute, this division applies to all proceedings commenced on or after July 1, 1987. Subdivision (c) is a special provision concerning the application of this division to proceedings concerning trusts commenced before July 1, 1987.

For special transitional provisions, see Sections 15401(d) (application of rules governing method of revocation by settlor), 16042 (interpretation of trust terms concerning legal investments), 16062(b)-(d) (application of duty to account to beneficiaries), 16203 (application of rules governing trustee's powers), 16401(c) (application of rules governing trustee's liability to beneficiary for acts of agent), 16402(c) (application of rules governing trustee's liability to beneficiary for acts of cotrustee), 16403(c) (application of rules governing trustee's liability to beneficiary for acts of predecessor trustee), 16460(c) (application of limitations period in proceedings by beneficiaries against trustees), 18000(b) (application of rule governing personal liability of trustee to third persons on contracts).

Background on Section 15001 of Repealed Code

Section 15001 was added by 1986 Cal.Stat. ch. 820 § 40. For background on the provisions of this division, see the Comment to this division under the division heading.

Subdivision (a) continued without substantive change the second sentence of former Civil Code Section 2225 (repealed by 1986 Cal.Stat. ch. 820 § 7) (application of doctrine of merger), the first sentence of subdivision (e) of former Civil Code Section 2261 (repealed by 1986 Cal.Stat. ch. 820 § 7) (application of rules governing investments), and the first sentence of former Probate Code Section 1138.13 (repealed by 1986 Cal.Stat. ch. 820 § 31) (application of provisions governing court proceedings involving trusts), and superseded the second paragraph of former Probate Code Section 1120.2 (repealed by 1986 Cal.Stat. ch. 820 § 31).

Subdivision (b), which is subdivision (c) of the new Probate Code section, is drawn from Code of Civil Procedure Section 694.020 (application of Enforcement of Judgments Law). [20 Cal.L.Rev.Comm.Reports 1001 (1990)].

§ 15002. Common law as law of state

Except to the extent that the common law rules governing trusts are modified by statute, the common law as to trusts is the law of this state. *(Stats.1990, c. 79 (A.B.759), § 14, operative July 1, 1991.)*

Law Revision Commission Comments

1990 Enactment

Section 15002 continues Section 15002 of the repealed Probate Code without change. This section is a special application of the rule stated in Civil Code Section 22.2 (common law as rule of decision in California courts) and is drawn from Civil Code Section 1380.1 (common law applicable to powers of appointment). As used in this section, the "common law" does not refer to the common law as it existed in 1850 when the predecessor of Civil Code Section 22.2 was enacted; rather, the reference is to the contemporary and evolving rules of decision developed by the courts in exercise of their power to adapt the law to new situations and to changing conditions. See, e.g., Fletcher v. Los Angeles Trust & Sav. Bank, 182 Cal. 177, 187 P. 425 (1920). See also Section 15004 (application of division to charitable trusts).

Background on Section 15002 of Repealed Code

Section 15002 was added by 1986 Cal.Stat. ch. 820 § 40. The section superseded former Probate Code Section 1120.6(c) (preservation of power of court to permit modification or termination prior to enactment of statute) (repealed by 1986 Cal.Stat. ch. 820 § 31). For background on the provisions of this division, see the Comment to this division under the division heading. [20 Cal.L.Rev.Comm.Reports 1001 (1990)].

§ 15003. Constructive and resulting trusts; fiduciary and confidential relationships; entity or relationship excluded from trust definition

(a) Nothing in this division affects the substantive law relating to constructive or resulting trusts.

(b) The repeal of Title 8 (commencing with Section 2215) of Part 4 of Division 3 of the Civil Code by Chapter 820 of the Statutes of 1986 was not intended to alter the rules applied by the courts to fiduciary and confidential relationships, except as to express trusts governed by this division.

(c) Nothing in this division or in Section 82 is intended to prevent the application of all or part of the principles or procedures of this division to an entity or relationship that is excluded from the definition of "trust" provided by Section 82 where these principles or procedures are applied pursuant to statutory or common law principles, by court order or rule, or by contract. *(Stats.1990, c. 79 (A.B.759), § 14, operative July 1, 1991. Amended by Stats.1990, c. 710 (S.B.1775), § 43, operative July 1, 1991.)*

Law Revision Commission Comments

1990 Enactment

Section 15003 restates Section 15003 of the repealed Probate Code without substantive change. A reference to Chapter 820 of the Statutes of 1986 has been substituted in subdivision (b) for the phrase "the act that added this division to the Probate Code." This is a nonsubstantive change.

Subdivision (a) makes clear that the provisions in this division, relating as they do to express trusts, have no effect on the law relating to constructive and resulting trusts. See Section 82 ("trust" defined). Thus, Section 15003 supersedes various provisions of former law relating to "involuntary" trusts. See former Civil Code §§ 856 (repealed by 1986 Cal.Stat. ch. 820 § 5), 2215, 2217, 2275 (provisions repealed by 1986 Cal.Stat. ch. 820 § 7). For provisions relating to "involuntary trusts," see Civil Code Sections 2223–2225.

Subdivision (b) makes clear that the repeal in 1986 of the Civil Code provisions relating to trusts, particularly former Civil Code Sections 2215–2244 (provisions repealed by 1986 Cal.Stat. ch. 820 § 7), was not intended to affect the general fiduciary principles applicable to confidential relationships. Over the years, courts cited these provisions in cases involving different types of confidential and fiduciary relationships. See, e.g., Cooley v. Miller & Lux, 168 Cal. 120, 131, 142 P. 83 (1914) (attorney and client); Bone v. Hayes, 154 Cal. 759, 763, 99 P. 172 (1908) (agent and principal); Wickersham v. Crittenden, 93 Cal. 17, 29–30, 28 P. 788 (1892) (corporate officers); Baker v. Baker, 260 Cal.App.2d 583, 586, 67 Cal.Rptr. 523 (1968) (husband and wife); City of Fort Bragg v. Brandon, 41 Cal.App. 227, 229, 82 P. 454 (1919) (municipalities). On the other hand, courts also decided cases in this area on the basis of general equitable principles without citing the former Civil Code provisions. See, e.g., Estate of Kromrey, 98 Cal.App.2d 639, 645–46, 220 P.2d 805 (1950) (attorney and client); Committee of Missions v. Pacific Synod, 157 Cal. 105, 127, 106 P. 395 (1909) (church); Schwab v. Schwab–Wilson Machine Corp., 13 Cal.App.2d 1, 3, 55 P.2d 1268 (1936) (corporate directors). See also Civil Code §§ 2322 (authority of agent), 5103 (spouses' duty in transactions with each other); Corp.Code § 309 (performance of duties by corporate director).

Subdivision (b) also recognizes that the courts have the inherent power to fashion appropriate remedies under the circumstances and that this power in the area of confidential relationships does not depend upon the particular language of former Civil Code Sections 2215–2244. See Civil Code § 22.2 (common law as law of state); see also Prob.Code § 15002 (common law as law of state). Of course, trusts now governed by the new Trust Law are no longer subject to the repealed statutes. See Sections 3 (application of new law), 82 ("trust" defined).

Subdivision (c) is included to avoid the implication that the provisions of the Trust Law cannot be applied to entities and relationships that are excluded from the definition of "trust" as it is used in this division. The Trust Law, by its terms, governs trusts as defined in Section 82. Under Section 15003, the Trust Law is neutral on the question whether it may be applied to other types of entities and relationships, such as those excluded from the definition of "trust" by subdivision (b) of Section 82. The Trust Law is thus made available when it may appropriately be applied by statute, common law, court order or rule, or contract. See also Section 15002 (common law as law of state).

1990 Amendment

Section 15003 (enacted as a part of the new Probate Code by 1990 Cal.Stat. ch. 79 § 14) was amended by 1990 Cal.Stat. ch. 710 § 43. The 1990 amendment revised subdivision (a) to avoid any implication that this provision is a limitation on the jurisdiction of the superior court in proceedings under this division. This amendment is intended to reject dicta in Estate of Mullins, 206 Cal.App.3d 924, 931, 255 Cal.Rptr. 430 (1988). For provisions governing jurisdiction in proceedings under this division, see Sections 17000, 17001, and 17004. For background on the 1990 amendment, see Recommendation Relating to Jurisdiction of Superior Court in Trust Matters, 20 Cal.L.Revision Comm'n Reports 2253 (1990). [20 Cal.L.Rev.Comm.Reports 1001 (1990)].

Background on Section 15003 of Repealed Code

Section 15003 was a new provision that was added by 1986 Cal.Stat. ch. 820 § 40 and amended by 1987 Cal.Stat. ch. 128 § 8. For background on the provisions of this division, see the Comment to this division under the division heading. [20 Cal.L.Rev.Comm.Reports 1001 (1990)].

§ 15004. Application of division to charitable trusts

Unless otherwise provided by statute, this division applies to charitable trusts that are subject to the jurisdiction of the Attorney General to the extent that the application of the provision is not in conflict with the Uniform Supervision of Trustees for Charitable Purposes Act, Article 7 (commencing with Section 12580) of Chapter 6 of Part 2 of Division 3 of Title 2 of the Government Code. *(Stats.1990, c. 79 (A.B. 759), § 14, operative July 1, 1991.)*

Law Revision Commission Comments

1990 Enactment

Section 15004 continues Section 15004 of the repealed Probate Code without change. This section recognizes that special rules may apply to charitable trusts. See generally 7 B. Witkin, Summary of California Law Trusts §§ 37–55, at 5398–418 (8th ed. 1974); Restatement (Second) of Trusts §§ 348–403 (1957). Thus, the general rules of this division are subordinate to contrary provisions in this division and in the Uniform Supervision of Trustees for Charitable Purposes Act, Government Code Sections 12580–12598, as to trusts that are subject to the jurisdiction of the Attorney General. See Gov't Code §§ 12582 ("trustee" defined for purposes of uniform act), 12583 (charitable trustees excluded from coverage of uniform act); see also Sections 15205 (designation of beneficiary rule not applicable to charitable trusts), 16105 (Attorney General as party in proceedings involving certain private foundations), 17203(c) (notice to Attorney General of proceedings involving charitable trust), 17210 (enforcement of beneficiary's rights under charitable trust by Attorney General).

Background on Section 15004 of Repealed Code

Section 15004 was a new provision added by 1986 Cal.Stat. ch. 820 § 40. For background on the provisions of this division, see the Comment to this division under the division heading. [20 Cal.L.Rev.Comm.Reports 1001 (1990)].

Cross References

Charitable trusts, enforcement by Attorney General, see Government Code § 12598.

§ 15005. Repealed by Stats.1987, c. 923, § 99, operative Jan. 1, 1988

Law Revision Commission Comments

1987 Repeal

Section 15005 is omitted because it is no longer necessary. See Section 21101 (division applicable to wills, trusts, and other instruments). [19 Cal.L.Rev.Comm.Reports —— (1988)].

§ 15006. Repealed by Stats.1990, c. 79 (A.B.759), § 13, operative July 1, 1991

Law Revision Commission Comments

1990 Repeal

Section 15006 of the repealed Probate Code is omitted from the new Probate Code because it is unnecessary. See Section 1001(b) (Judicial Council forms). [20 Cal.L.Rev.Comm.Reports 1001 (1990)].

Part 2

CREATION, VALIDITY, MODIFICATION, AND TERMINATION OF TRUSTS

Application

Application of Division, see Probate Code § 15001.

Cross References

Common law rules governing trusts, application, see Probate Code § 15002.

Relationships excluded from Code definition of trust, application of this division, see Probate Code § 15003.

CHAPTER 1. CREATION AND VALIDITY OF TRUSTS

Application

Application of Division, see Probate Code § 15001.

Cross References

Common law rules governing trusts, application, see Probate Code § 15002.

Relationships excluded from Code definition of trust, application of this division, see Probate Code § 15003.

§ 15200. Methods of creating trusts

Subject to other provisions of this chapter, a trust may be created by any of the following methods:

(a) A declaration by the owner of property that the owner holds the property as trustee.

(b) A transfer of property by the owner during the owner's lifetime to another person as trustee.

(c) A transfer of property by the owner, by will or by other instrument taking effect upon the death of the owner, to another person as trustee.

(d) An exercise of a power of appointment to another person as trustee.

(e) An enforceable promise to create a trust. *(Stats.1990, c. 79 (A.B.759), § 14, operative July 1, 1991.)*

Law Revision Commission Comments

1990 Enactment

Section 15200 continues Section 15200 of the repealed Probate Code and expands the reference formerly made to a "testamentary" transfer in subdivision (c). This section is drawn from Section 17 of the Restatement (Second) of Trusts (1957).

A declaration under subdivision (a) must satisfy the requirements of Section 15206 (Statute of Frauds as applied to trust of real property) or 15207 (oral trust of personal property), if applicable. A trust may be created for the benefit of the settlor or of a third person (including the trustee). See Sections 15205 (designation of beneficiary), 15209 (exception to doctrine of merger). Consideration is not required to create a trust. See Section 15208. Subdivision (e) is worded differently from the corresponding provision in the Restatement to avoid the implication that it deals with the question of the time of creation of such a trust.

Background on Section 15200 of Repealed Code

Section 15200 was added by 1986 Cal.Stat. ch. 820 § 40. The section superseded parts of former Civil Code Sections 2221 and 2222 (provisions repealed by 1986 Cal.Stat. ch. 820 § 7). For background on the provisions of this division, see the Comment to this division under the division heading. [20 Cal.L.Rev.Comm.Reports 1001 (1990)].

Cross References

Powers of appointment, generally, see Probate Code § 600 et seq.

§ 15201. Intention to create trust

A trust is created only if the settlor properly manifests an intention to create a trust. *(Stats.1990, c. 79 (A.B.759), § 14, operative July 1, 1991.)*

Law Revision Commission Comments

1990 Enactment

Section 15201 continues Section 15201 of the repealed Probate Code without change. This section codifies Section 23 of the Restatement (Second) of Trusts (1957). Special requirements may apply to the manifestation of the settlor's intent. See Sections 15206 (Statute of Frauds as applied to trust of real property), 15207 (oral trust of personal property).

Background on Section 15201 of Repealed Code

Section 15201 was added by 1986 Cal.Stat. ch. 820 § 40. The section restated a requirement of former Civil Code Section 2221(1) (repealed by 1986 Cal.Stat. ch. 820 § 7) without substantive change. For background on the provisions of this division, see the Comment to this division under the division heading. [20 Cal.L.Rev.Comm.Reports 1001 (1990)].

§ 15202. Trust property

A trust is created only if there is trust property. *(Stats. 1990, c. 79 (A.B.759), § 14, operative July 1, 1991.)*

Law Revision Commission Comments

1990 Enactment

Section 15202 continues Section 15202 of the repealed Probate Code without change. This section is the same as Section 74 of the Restatement (Second) of Trusts (1957). See also Section 62 ("property" defined). For additional comments concerning the nature of property required to form a trust, see Restatement (Second) of Trusts §§ 75–86 (1957).

Background on Section 15202 of Repealed Code

Section 15202 was added by 1986 Cal.Stat. ch. 820 § 40. The section restated a requirement of former Civil Code Sections 2221 and 2222 (provisions repealed by 1986 Cal.Stat. ch. 820 § 7) without substantive change. For background on the provisions of this division, see the Comment to this division under the division heading. [20 Cal.L.Rev.Comm.Reports 1001 (1990)].

§ 15203. Trust purpose

A trust may be created for any purpose that is not illegal or against public policy. *(Stats.1990, c. 79 (A.B.759), § 14, operative July 1, 1991.)*

Law Revision Commission Comments

1990 Enactment

Section 15203 continues Section 15203 of the repealed Probate Code without change. See also Civil Code §§ 1667–1669 (unlawful contracts).

Background on Section 15203 of Repealed Code

Section 15203 was added by 1986 Cal.Stat. ch. 820 § 40. The section restated former Civil Code Section 2220 (repealed by 1986 Cal.Stat. ch. 820 § 7) without substantive change. For background on the provisions of this division, see the Comment to this division under the division heading. [20 Cal.L.Rev.Comm.Reports 1001 (1990)].

Cross References

Use of property, see Probate Code § 16004.

§ 15204. Trusts for indefinite or general purposes

A trust created for an indefinite or general purpose is not invalid for that reason if it can be determined with reasonable certainty that a particular use of the trust property comes within that purpose. *(Stats.1990, c. 79 (A.B.759), § 14, operative July 1, 1991.)*

Law Revision Commission Comments

1990 Enactment

Section 15204 continues Section 15204 of the repealed Probate Code without change. Under this section, a trust for indefinite or general purposes may be created and enforced, even though it is not limited to charitable purposes. This changes the rule applicable under cases such as In re Estate of Sutro, 155 Cal. 727, 730, 102 P. 920 (1909). This section is not intended to affect the law relating to the purposes for which a charitable trust may be created.

Background on Section 15204 of Repealed Code

Section 15204 was a new provision added by 1986 Cal.Stat. ch. 820 § 40. For background on the provisions of this division, see the Comment to this division under the division heading. [20 Cal.L.Rev.Comm.Reports 1001 (1990)].

§ 15205. Designation of beneficiary

(a) A trust, other than a charitable trust, is created only if there is a beneficiary.

(b) The requirement of subdivision (a) is satisfied if the trust instrument provides for either of the following:

(1) A beneficiary or class of beneficiaries that is ascertainable with reasonable certainty or that is sufficiently described so it can be determined that some person meets the description or is within the class.

(2) A grant of a power to the trustee or some other person to select the beneficiaries based on a standard or in the discretion of the trustee or other person. *(Stats.1990, c. 79 (A.B.759), § 14, operative July 1, 1991.)*

Law Revision Commission Comments

1990 Enactment

Section 15205 continues Section 15205 of the repealed Probate Code without change.

As provided in subdivision (a), this section does not govern the beneficiary designations in charitable trusts. This subject is left to case law. See Section 15002 (common law as law of state).

Under subdivision (b)(1), the determination of the class of beneficiaries can satisfy the requirements of this section if the class is ascertainable presently or in the future. Subdivision (b)(2) affords the settlor a greater degree of flexibility in creating a trust. Under subdivision (b)(2), a disposition that would be valid as a power of appointment will not fail just because it is made in trust. Cf. In re Estate of Davis, 13 Cal.App.2d 64, 69, 56 P.2d 584 (1936) (testamentary disposition in trust to distribute to sons and grandchildren as trustee upheld as power of appointment).

Background on Section 15205 of Repealed Code

Section 15205 was added by 1986 Cal.Stat. ch. 820 § 40. For background on the provisions of this division, see the Comment to this division under the division heading.

Subdivision (a) restated a requirement in former Civil Code Sections 2221 and 2222 (provisions repealed by 1986 Cal.Stat. ch. 820 § 7) as it applied to private (i.e., noncharitable) trusts.

Subdivision (b) continued the requirement of former Civil Code Sections 2221 and 2222 that the beneficiary be indicated with "reasonable certainty," but also permitted trusts to describe a beneficiary or class of beneficiaries in a less strict fashion so long as it can be determined that someone satisfies the criteria in the trust instrument. [20 Cal.L.Rev.Comm.Reports 1001 (1990)].

§ 15206. Statute of frauds

A trust in relation to real property is not valid unless evidenced by one of the following methods:

(a) By a written instrument signed by the trustee, or by the trustee's agent if authorized in writing to do so.

(b) By a written instrument conveying the trust property signed by the settlor, or by the settlor's agent if authorized in writing to do so.

(c) By operation of law. *(Stats.1990, c. 79 (A.B.759), § 14, operative July 1, 1991.)*

Law Revision Commission Comments

1990 Enactment

Section 15206 continues Section 15206 of the repealed Probate Code without change. See also Section 15003 (law relating to constructive and resulting trusts remains unaffected).

Background on Section 15206 of Repealed Code

Section 15206 was added by 1986 Cal.Stat. ch. 820 § 40. The section (1) restated former Civil Code Section 852 (repealed by 1986 Cal.Stat. ch. 820 § 5) without substantive change and (2) restated without substantive change the former part of Code of Civil Procedure Section 1971 (prior to its amendment by 1986 Cal.Stat. ch. 820 § 19) that related to trusts. For background on the provisions of this division, see the Comment to this division under the division heading. [20 Cal.L.Rev.Comm.Reports 1001 (1990)].

§ 15207.   Oral trusts of personal property

(a) The existence and terms of an oral trust of personal property may be established only by clear and convincing evidence.

(b) The oral declaration of the settlor, standing alone, is not sufficient evidence of the creation of a trust of personal property.

(c) In the case of an oral trust, a reference in this division or elsewhere to a trust instrument or declaration means the terms of the trust as established pursuant to subdivision (a). *(Stats.1990, c. 79 (A.B.759), § 14, operative July 1, 1991.)*

Law Revision Commission Comments

1990 Enactment

Section 15207 continues Section 15207 of the repealed Probate Code without change.

Subdivision (a) codifies the rule requiring clear and convincing evidence of the creation of an oral trust in personal property. See, e.g., Lefrooth v. Prentice, 202 Cal. 215, 227, 259 P. 947 (1927); Monell v. College of Physicians & Surgeons, 198 Cal.App.2d 38, 48, 17 Cal.Rptr. 744 (1961); Kobida v. Hinkelmann, 53 Cal.App.2d 186, 188–93, 127 P.2d 657 (1942). Under this rule, circumstantial evidence may be sufficient. See Fahrney v. Wilson, 180 Cal.App.2d 694, 697, 4 Cal.Rptr. 670 (1960).

Subdivision (b) states a requirement for the validity of oral trusts. Under subdivision (b), a delivery of personal property to another person accompanied by an oral declaration by the transferor that the transferee holds it in trust for a beneficiary creates a valid oral trust. Constructive delivery, such as by earmarking property or recording it in the name of the transferee, is also sufficient to comply with subdivision (b).

Subdivision (c) is designed to facilitate application of trust statutes to properly established oral trusts. Although Section 15400 provides that a trust is revocable unless the trust instrument expressly makes it irrevocable, an oral trust may be shown to be irrevocable pursuant to this section.

Nothing in this section affects the law concerning constructive trusts. See Section 15003 and the Comment thereto. Hence, in appropriate circumstances, an attempted disposition of property that fails to satisfy the requirements for an oral trust under Section 15207 may be remedied through the mechanism of a constructive trust.

Background on Section 15207 of Repealed Code

Section 15207 was a new provision added by 1986 Cal.Stat. ch. 820 § 40. For background on the provisions of this division, see the Comment to this division under the division heading. [20 Cal.L.Rev.Comm.Reports 1001 (1990)].

§ 15208.   Consideration

Consideration is not required to create a trust, but a promise to create a trust in the future is enforceable only if the requirements for an enforceable contract are satisfied. *(Stats.1990, c. 79 (A.B.759), § 14, operative July 1, 1991.)*

Law Revision Commission Comments

1990 Enactment

Section 15208 continues Section 15208 of the repealed Probate Code without change. This section is drawn from Section 112.003 of the Texas Trust Code. See Tex.Prop.Code Ann. § 112.003 (Vernon 1984). For a provision relating to an enforceable promise to create a trust, see Section 15200(e).

Background on Section 15208 of Repealed Code

Section 15208 was added by 1986 Cal.Stat. ch. 820 § 40. The section superseded the part of former Civil Code Section 2222(1) (repealed by 1986 Cal.Stat. ch. 820 § 7) which referred to consideration. For background on the provisions of this division, see the Comment to this division under the division heading. [20 Cal.L.Rev.Comm.Reports 1001 (1990)].

§ 15209.   Exception to doctrine of merger

If a trust provides for one or more successor beneficiaries after the death of the settlor, the trust is not invalid, merged, or terminated in either of the following circumstances:

(a) Where there is one settlor who is the sole trustee and the sole beneficiary during the settlor's lifetime.

(b) Where there are two or more settlors, one or more of whom are trustees, and the beneficial interest in the trust is in one or more of the settlors during the lifetime of the settlors. *(Stats.1990, c. 79 (A.B.759), § 14, operative July 1, 1991.)*

Law Revision Commission Comments

1990 Enactment

Section 15209 continues Section 15209 of the repealed Probate Code without change. See also In re Estate of Washburn, 11 Cal.App. 735, 746, 106 P. 415 (1909) (merger of legal and equitable estates).

Background on Section 15209 of Repealed Code

Section 15209 was added by 1986 Cal.Stat. ch. 820 § 40. The section restated the first sentence of former Civil Code Section 2225 (repealed by 1986 Cal.Stat. ch. 820 § 7) without substantive change. For background on the provisions of this division, see the Comment to this division under the division heading. [20 Cal.L.Rev.Comm.Reports 1001 (1990)].

§ 15210.   Trusts relating to real property; recordation

A trust created pursuant to this chapter which relates to real property may be recorded in the office of the county recorder in the county where all or a portion of the real property is located. *(Stats.1990, c. 79 (A.B.759), § 14, operative July 1, 1991.)*

Law Revision Commission Comments

1990 Enactment

Section 15210 continues Section 15210 of the repealed Probate Code without change.

Background on Section 15210 of Repealed Code

Section 15210 was a new provision added by 1987 Cal.Stats. ch. 1184 § 10. For background on the provisions of this division, see the Comment to this division under the division heading. [20 Cal.L.Rev.Comm.Reports 1001 (1990)].

§ 15211.   Trusts for noncharitable corporation, unincorporated society, or for lawful noncharitable purpose; duration

A trust for a noncharitable corporation or unincorporated society or for a lawful noncharitable purpose may be performed by the trustee for only 21 years, whether or not there is a beneficiary who can seek enforcement or termination of the trust and whether or not the terms of the trust contemplate a longer duration. *(Added by Stats.1991, c. 156 (A.B.1577), § 20.)*

Law Revision Commission Comments

1991 Addition

Section 15211 is a new provision that places a 21–year limit on trusts that were voidable under the rule against perpetuities provided in former Civil Code Section 715.2. Section 15211 is drawn from Section 2–907(a) of the Uniform Probate Code (Tent.Draft 1990). This section adopts a 21–year limitation in place of the 90–year period that would otherwise apply under the Uniform Statutory Rule Against Perpetuities. See Section 21205. [20 Cal.L.Rev.Comm.Reports 2501 (1990)].

§ 15212. Trusts for care of animals; duration; requirements; accountings; beneficiaries

(a) Subject to the requirements of this section, a trust for the care of an animal is a trust for a lawful noncharitable purpose. Unless expressly provided in the trust, the trust terminates when no animal living on the date of the settlor's death remains alive. The governing instrument of the animal trust shall be liberally construed to bring the trust within this section, to presume against the merely precatory or honorary nature of the disposition, and to carry out the general intent of the settlor. Extrinsic evidence is admissible in determining the settlor's intent.

(b) A trust for the care of an animal is subject to the following requirements:

(1) Except as expressly provided otherwise in the trust instrument, the principal or income shall not be converted to the use of the trustee or to any use other than for the benefit of the animal.

(2) Upon termination of the trust, the trustee shall distribute the unexpended trust property in the following order:

(A) As directed in the trust instrument.

(B) If the trust was created in a nonresiduary clause in the settlor's will or in a codicil to the settlor's will, under the residuary clause in the settlor's will.

(C) If the application of subparagraph (A) or (B) does not result in distribution of unexpended trust property, to the settlor's heirs under Section 21114.

(3) For the purposes of Section 21110, the residuary clause described in subparagraph (B) of paragraph (2) shall be treated as creating a future interest under the terms of a trust.

(c) The intended use of the principal or income may be enforced by a person designated for that purpose in the trust instrument or, if none is designated, by a person appointed by a court. In addition to a person identified in subdivision (a) of Section 17200, any person interested in the welfare of the animal or any nonprofit charitable organization that has as its principal activity the care of animals may petition the court regarding the trust as provided in Chapter 3 (commencing with Section 17200) of Part 5.

(d) If a trustee is not designated or no designated or successor trustee is willing or able to serve, a court shall name a trustee. A court may order the transfer of the trust property to a court-appointed trustee, if it is required to ensure that the intended use is carried out and if a successor trustee is not designated in the trust instrument or if no designated successor trustee agrees to serve or is able to serve. A court may also make all other orders and determinations as it shall deem advisable to carry out the intent of the settlor and the purpose of this section.

(e) The accountings required by Section 16062 shall be provided to the beneficiaries who would be entitled to distribution if the animal were then deceased and to any nonprofit charitable corporation that has as its principal activity the care of animals and that has requested these accountings in writing. However, if the value of the assets in the trust does not exceed forty thousand dollars ($40,000), no filing, report, registration, periodic accounting, separate maintenance of funds, appointment, or fee is required by reason of the existence of the fiduciary relationship of the trustee, unless ordered by the court or required by the trust instrument.

(f) Any beneficiary, any person designated by the trust instrument or the court to enforce the trust, or any nonprofit charitable corporation that has as its principal activity the care of animals may, upon reasonable request, inspect the animal, the premises where the animal is maintained, or the books and records of the trust.

(g) A trust governed by this section is not subject to termination pursuant to subdivision (b) of Section 15408.

(h) Section 15211 does not apply to a trust governed by this section.

(i) For purposes of this section, "animal" means a domestic or pet animal for the benefit of which a trust has been established. *(Added by Stats.2008, c. 168 (S.B.685), § 2.)*

CHAPTER 2. RESTRICTIONS ON VOLUNTARY AND INVOLUNTARY TRANSFERS

Application

Application of Division, see Probate Code § 15001.

Cross References

Common law rules governing trusts, application, see Probate Code § 15002.

Relationships excluded from Code definition of trust, application of this division, see Probate Code § 15003.

§ 15300. Restraint on transfer of income

Except as provided in Sections 15304 to 15307, inclusive, if the trust instrument provides that a beneficiary's interest in income is not subject to voluntary or involuntary transfer, the beneficiary's interest in income under the trust may not be transferred and is not subject to enforcement of a money judgment until paid to the beneficiary. *(Stats.1990, c. 79 (A.B.759), § 14, operative July 1, 1991.)*

Law Revision Commission Comments

1990 Enactment

Section 15300 continues Section 15300 of the repealed Probate Code without change. For qualifications of the protection provided by Section 15300, see Sections 15304 (settlor as beneficiary), 15305 (claim for child or spousal support), 15306 (claim for reimbursement of public support), 15306.5 (right of general creditors to reach maximum of one-fourth of payments due beneficiary), 15307 (amount of income in excess of amount needed for education and support subject to creditors' claims). Once the income is paid to the beneficiary, it is subject to claims of creditors. Kelly v. Kelly, 11 Cal.2d 356, 362–65, 79 P.2d 1059 (1938).

Background on Section 15300 of Repealed Code

Section 15300 was added by 1986 Cal.Stat. ch. 820 § 40. The section continued the power of a settlor to restrain transfer of the beneficiary's interest in income that was provided in former Civil Code Section 867 (repealed by 1986 Cal.Stat. ch. 820 § 5). The reference in former Civil Code Section 867 to restraints during the life of the beneficiary or for a term of years was not continued because it was unnecessary. The settlor was free to impose a restraint for a term of years under Section 15300. For background on the provisions of this division, see the Comment to this division under the division heading. [20 Cal.L.Rev.Comm.Reports 1001 (1990)].

Cross References

Accumulations,
  Generally, see Civil Code § 722 et seq.
  Income applied to support destitute beneficiaries, direction of court, see Civil Code § 726.
Interest as beneficiary of trust subject to satisfaction of money judgment, see Code of Civil Procedure § 709.010.

§ 15301. Restraint on transfer of principal

(a) Except as provided in subdivision (b) and in Sections 15304 to 15307, inclusive, if the trust instrument provides that a beneficiary's interest in principal is not subject to voluntary or involuntary transfer, the beneficiary's interest in principal may not be transferred and is not subject to enforcement of a money judgment until paid to the beneficiary.

(b) After an amount of principal has become due and payable to the beneficiary under the trust instrument, upon petition to the court under Section 709.010 of the Code of Civil Procedure by a judgment creditor, the court may make an order directing the trustee to satisfy the money judgment out of that principal amount. The court in its discretion may issue an order directing the trustee to satisfy all or part of the judgment out of that principal amount. *(Stats.1990, c. 79 (A.B.759), § 14, operative July 1, 1991.)*

Law Revision Commission Comments

1990 Enactment

Section 15301 continues Section 15301 of the repealed Probate Code without change.

Subdivision (a) makes clear that a restraint on voluntary or involuntary transfer of principal is valid. This rule is consistent with the result in several California cases. See Seymour v. McAvoy, 121

Cal. 438, 444, 53 P. 946 (1898) (creditor could not reach contingent remainder); San Diego Trust & Sav. Bank v. Heustis, 121 Cal.App. 675, 683–85, 694–97, 10 P.2d 158 (1932) (where husband was income and remainder beneficiary, estranged wife could not reach trust funds for support); Coughran v. First Nat'l Bank, 19 Cal.App.2d 152, 64 P.2d 1013 (1937) (in an action to quiet title, attachment levied against beneficiary's contingent fractional interest in trust property was held invalid). There was no clear holding under prior California law as to the validity of disabling restraints on transfer of trust principal by a vested remainder beneficiary.

Subdivision (b) permits a creditor to reach principal that is due or payable to the beneficiary, notwithstanding a spendthrift provision in the trust. Under prior California law, there was no decision determining whether a judgment creditor could reach principal held by the trustee that was due or payable where the beneficiary's interest was subject to a restraint on transfer.

For qualifications of the protection provided by Section 15301, see Sections 15304 (settlor as beneficiary), 15305 (claim for child or spousal support), 15306 (claim for reimbursement of public support), 15306.5 (right of general creditors to reach maximum of one-fourth of payments due beneficiary), 15307 (amount of income in excess of amount needed for education and support subject to creditors' claims). Where trust principal that was subject to a restraint on transfer has been paid to the beneficiary, it is subject to the claims against the beneficiary. See Kelly v. Kelly, 11 Cal.2d 356, 362–65, 79 P.2d 1059 (1938).

For general provisions relating to petitions and other papers, see Sections 1020–1023, 17201; see also Sections 1021 (petition to be verified), 1041 (clerk to set petition for hearing). For general provisions relating to notice of hearing, see Sections 1200–1221, 15802–15804, 17100–17105, 17203–17205; see also Sections 1260–1265 (proof of giving notice). For general provisions relating to hearings and orders, see Sections 1040–1050, 17000–17006, 17201–17202, 17206–17207.

Background on Section 15301 of Repealed Code

Section 15301 was a new provision added by 1986 Cal.Stat. ch. 820 § 40. For background on the provisions of this division, see the Comment to this division under the division heading. [20 Cal.L.Rev.Comm.Reports 1001 (1990)].

§ 15302. Trust for support

Except as provided in Sections 15304 to 15307, inclusive, if the trust instrument provides that the trustee shall pay income or principal or both for the education or support of a beneficiary, the beneficiary's interest in income or principal or both under the trust, to the extent the income or principal or both is necessary for the education or support of the beneficiary, may not be transferred and is not subject to the enforcement of a money judgment until paid to the beneficiary. *(Stats.1990, c. 79 (A.B.759), § 14, operative July 1, 1991.)*

Law Revision Commission Comments

1990 Enactment

Section 15302 continues Section 15302 of the repealed Probate Code without change.

This section is the same in substance as Section 154 of the Restatement (Second) of Trusts (1957), but is drafted to make clear that the protection applies to the extent that a trust provides for the education or support of the beneficiary and not only where the trust provides solely for the payment of an amount for education or support. Section 15302 is consistent with prior California law. See former Civil Code § 859 (repealed by 1986 Cal.Stat. ch. 820 § 5); Seymour v. McAvoy, 121 Cal. 438, 442–44, 53 P. 946 (1898).

For qualifications of the protection provided by Section 15302, see Sections 15304 (settlor as beneficiary), 15305 (claim for child or spousal support), 15306 (claim for reimbursement of public support), 15306.5 (right of general creditors to reach maximum of one-fourth of payments due beneficiary), 15307 (amount of income in excess of amount needed for education and support subject to creditors' claims).

Background on Section 15302 of Repealed Code

Section 15302 was a new provision added by 1986 Cal.Stat. ch. 820 § 40. For background on the provisions of this division, see the Comment to this division under the division heading. [20 Cal.L.Rev.Comm.Reports 1001 (1990)].

§ 15303. Discretion of trustee; transferee or creditor of beneficiary; power to compel trustee to pay any amount; liability of trustee to creditor

(a) If the trust instrument provides that the trustee shall pay to or for the benefit of a beneficiary so much of the income or principal or both as the trustee in the trustee's discretion sees fit to pay, a transferee or creditor of the beneficiary may not compel the trustee to pay any amount that may be paid only in the exercise of the trustee's discretion.

(b) If the trustee has knowledge of the transfer of the beneficiary's interest or has been served with process in a proceeding under Section 709.010 of the Code of Civil Procedure by a judgment creditor seeking to reach the beneficiary's interest, and the trustee pays to or for the benefit of the beneficiary any part of the income or principal that may be paid only in the exercise of the trustee's discretion, the trustee is liable to the transferee or creditor to the extent that the payment to or for the benefit of the beneficiary impairs the right of the transferee or creditor. This subdivision does not apply if the beneficiary's interest in the trust is subject to a restraint on transfer that is valid under Section 15300 or 15301.

(c) This section applies regardless of whether the trust instrument provides a standard for the exercise of the trustee's discretion.

(d) Nothing in this section limits any right the beneficiary may have to compel the trustee to pay to or for the benefit of the beneficiary all or part of the income or principal. *(Stats.1990, c. 79 (A.B.759), § 14, operative July 1, 1991.)*

Law Revision Commission Comments
1990 Enactment

Section 15303 continues Section 15303 of the repealed Probate Code without change.

Subdivisions (a) and (b) are drawn from Section 155 of the Restatement (Second) of Trusts (1957), and provide that a judgment creditor cannot compel the trustee of a discretionary trust to pay any part of the discretionary trust income or principal, although a judgment creditor may be able to reach any payment the trustee does decide to make. Subdivisions (a) and (b) are consistent with prior California law. See Canfield v. Security–First Nat'l Bank, 13 Cal.2d 1, 30–31, 87 P.2d 830 (1939) (citing Restatement of Trusts § 155); Alvis v. Bank of America, 95 Cal.App.2d 118, 124, 212 P.2d 608 (1949).

Unlike Section 155 of the Restatement, Section 15303 applies whether or not the trustee's discretion is subject to a standard. See Section 15303(c). The Restatement provision applies only where the trustee has "uncontrolled discretion." Accordingly, under Section 15303, even though the beneficiary of the trust could compel the trustee to make payment pursuant to the standard set out in the trust

instrument, the transferee or creditor has no similar right to compel the payment.

Subdivision (d) makes clear that this section does not affect or limit any right the beneficiary (as distinguished from a transferee or creditor of the beneficiary) may have to compel payment. See Estate of Ferrall, 41 Cal.2d 166, 258 P.2d 1009 (1953) (whether fraud, bad faith, or an abuse of discretion has been committed by trustees in refusing to make payments for the support of the beneficiary of a discretionary trust is subject to review by the court). See also In re Miller's Estate, 230 Cal.App.2d 888, 41 Cal.Rptr. 410 (1964) (court required trustee to make payments to beneficiary).

Background on Section 15303 of Repealed Code

Section 15303 was a new provision added by 1986 Cal.Stat. ch. 820 § 40. For background on the provisions of this division, see the Comment to this division under the division heading. [20 Cal.L.Rev.Comm.Reports 1001 (1990)].

Cross References

Enforcement of money judgment against interest in trust, see Code of Civil Procedure § 709.010.

§ 15304. Cases in which settlor is beneficiary

(a) If the settlor is a beneficiary of a trust created by the settlor and the settlor's interest is subject to a provision restraining the voluntary or involuntary transfer of the settlor's interest, the restraint is invalid against transferees or creditors of the settlor. The invalidity of the restraint on transfer does not affect the validity of the trust.

(b) If the settlor is the beneficiary of a trust created by the settlor and the trust instrument provides that the trustee shall pay income or principal or both for the education or support of the beneficiary or gives the trustee discretion to determine the amount of income or principal or both to be paid to or for the benefit of the settlor, a transferee or creditor of the settlor may reach the maximum amount that the trustee could pay to or for the benefit of the settlor under the trust instrument, not exceeding the amount of the settlor's proportionate contribution to the trust. *(Stats.1990, c. 79 (A.B.759), § 14, operative July 1, 1991.)*

Law Revision Commission Comments
1990 Enactment

Section 15304 continues Section 15304 of the repealed Probate Code without change.

The first sentence of subdivision (a) is the same in substance as Section 156(1) of the Restatement (Second) of Trusts (1957). See the comments to Restatement § 156. Subdivision (a) codifies the case-law rule applicable under prior law. See, e.g., Nelson v. California Trust Co., 33 Cal.2d 501, 202 P.2d 1021 (1949). This section does not affect the protection of certain pension trusts by Code of Civil Procedure Section 704.115. See Section 82 ("trusts" defined to exclude trusts for the primary purpose of paying pensions).

Subdivision (b) is drawn from Section 156(2) of the Restatement (Second) of Trusts (1957). The limitation on the amount that may be reached by transferees and creditors to the proportionate amount of the settlor's contribution is drawn from Wisconsin law. See Wis.Stat.Ann. § 701.06(6) (West 1981); see also the comments to Restatement § 156.

A person who furnishes the consideration for the creation of a trust is the settlor. McColgan v. Walter Magee, Inc., 172 Cal. 182, 155 P. 995 (1916) (beneficiary transferred assets into trust although certain other persons could have prevented transfer by refusal to consent); Parscal v. Parscal, 148 Cal.App.3d 1098, 1104–05, 196 Cal.Rptr. 462 (1983) (child support enforceable against beneficiary's interest in trust created by beneficiary's employers under a collective bargaining agreement with benefit credits according to the amount contributed by employers to employee's account).

Background on Section 15304 of Repealed Code

Section 15304 was a new provision added by 1986 Cal.Stat. ch. 820 § 40. For background on the provisions of this division, see the Comment to this division under the division heading. [20 Cal.L.Comm.Reports 1001 (1990)].

§ 15305. Claims for child or spousal support

(a) As used in this section, "support judgment" means a money judgment for support of the trust beneficiary's spouse or former spouse or minor child.

(b) If the beneficiary has the right under the trust to compel the trustee to pay income or principal or both to or for the benefit of the beneficiary, the court may, to the extent that the court determines it is equitable and reasonable under the circumstances of the particular case, order the trustee to satisfy all or part of the support judgment out of all or part of those payments as they become due and payable, presently or in the future.

(c) Whether or not the beneficiary has the right under the trust to compel the trustee to pay income or principal or both to or for the benefit of the beneficiary, the court may, to the extent that the court determines it is equitable and reasonable under the circumstances of the particular case, order the trustee to satisfy all or part of the support judgment out of all or part of future payments that the trustee, pursuant to the exercise of the trustee's discretion, determines to make to or for the benefit of the beneficiary.

(d) This section applies to a support judgment notwithstanding any provision in the trust instrument. *(Stats.1990, c. 79 (A.B.759), § 14, operative July 1, 1991.)*

Law Revision Commission Comments
1990 Enactment

Section 15305 continues Section 15305 of the repealed Probate Code without change.

This section is drawn in part from a provision of Wisconsin law relating to enforcement of child support. See Wis.Stat.Ann. § 701.06(4) (West 1981). Section 15305 reflects the same public policy as Section 157(a) of the Restatement (Second) of Trusts (1957). To obtain relief under Section 15305, the judgment creditor under the support judgment must file a petition with the court under Section 709.010 of the Code of Civil Procedure. For general provisions relating to petitions and other papers, see Sections 1020–1023, 17201; see also Sections 1021 (petition to be verified), 1041 (clerk to set petition for hearing). For general provisions relating to notice of hearing, see Sections 1200–1221, 15802–15804, 17100–17105, 17203–17205; see also Sections 1260–1265 (proof of giving notice). For general provisions relating to hearings and orders, see Sections 1040–1050, 17000–17006, 17201–17202, 17206–17207; see also Section 15308.

Although a trust is a spendthrift trust or a trust for support, the interest of the beneficiary can be reached in satisfaction of a money judgment against the beneficiary for child or spousal support. In some cases a spendthrift clause may be construed as not intended to exclude the beneficiary's dependents. Even if the clause is construed as applicable to claims of the dependents for support, it is against public policy to give full effect to the provision. A provision in the trust is not effective to exempt the trust from enforcement of a judgment for support of a minor child or support of a spouse or former spouse. See subdivision (b). As a general rule, the beneficiary should not be permitted to have the enjoyment of the interest under the trust while neglecting to support his or her dependents. It is a matter for the exercise of discretion by the court as to how much of the amount payable to the beneficiary under the trust should be applied for such support and how much the beneficiary should receive. Even though the beneficiary's spouse has obtained an order directing the beneficiary to pay a specified amount for support, the spouse cannot compel the trustee to pay the full amount ordered unless the court determines that it is equitable and reasonable under the circumstances of the particular case to compel the trustee to make the payment. The result is much the same as though the trust were created not solely for the benefit of the beneficiary, but also for the benefit of the beneficiary's dependents. Cf. Estate of Johnston, 252 Cal.App.2d 923, 927–30, 60 Cal.Rptr. 852 (1967) (discussion of public policy in light of former Civil Code § 859).

Background on Section 15305 of Repealed Code

Section 15305 was a new provision added by 1986 Cal.Stat. ch. 820 § 40. The section changed prior California law. Code of Civil Procedure Section 709.010 (prior to its amendment by 1986 Cal.Stat. ch. 820 § 18) included a provision giving the court discretion to divide periodic payments to a beneficiary from a trust (including a spendthrift trust) between the beneficiary and the person or persons entitled to child or spousal support from the beneficiary. The amount that could be applied to child or spousal support was limited to the amount that could have been applied to child or spousal support on a like amount of earnings. This provision was removed from Section 709.010, leaving Section 15305 to govern this situation. Apart from the provision in Code of Civil Procedure Section 709.010, under prior law child or spousal support was not a preferred claim against the interest of a trust beneficiary, and the support claimant was treated the same as any other creditor. See, e.g., In re Lawrence's Estate, 267 Cal.App.2d 77, 82–83, 72 Cal.Rptr. 851 (1968) (former wife); Canfield v. Security–First Nat'l Bank, 8 Cal.App.2d 277, 288–89, 48 P.2d 133 (1935) (former wife); San Diego Trust & Sav. Bank v. Heustis, 121 Cal.App. 675, 683–94, 10 P.2d 158 (1932) (estranged wife); Estate of Johnston, 252 Cal. App.2d 923, 928–29, 60 Cal.Rptr. 852 (1967) (minor child); but see Parscal v. Parscal, 148 Cal.App.3d 1098, 1104–05, 196 Cal.Rptr. 462 (1983) (child support enforceable against beneficiary's interest in trust created by beneficiary's employers under a collective bargaining agreement where employer's contributions based on employee's hours of work); cf. Estate of Lackmann, 156 Cal.App.2d 674, 678–83, 320 P.2d 186 (1958) (state institution in which beneficiary of a spendthrift trust was an inmate permitted to reach the beneficiary's interest). For background on the provisions of this division, see the Comment to this division under the division heading. [20 Cal.L.Rev.Comm.Reports 1001 (1990)].

§ 15305.5. Restitution judgment

(a) As used in this section, "restitution judgment" means a judgment awarding restitution for the commission of a felony or a money judgment for damages incurred as a result of conduct for which the defendant was convicted of a felony.

(b) If the beneficiary has the right under the trust to compel the trustee to pay income or principal or both to or for the benefit of the beneficiary, the court may, to the extent that the court determines it is equitable and reasonable under the circumstances of the particular case, order the trustee to satisfy all or part of the restitution judgment out of all or part of those payments as they become due and payable, presently or in the future.

(c) Whether or not the beneficiary has the right under the trust to compel the trustee to pay income or principal or both to or for the benefit of the beneficiary, the court may, to the extent that the court determines it is equitable and reasonable under the circumstances of the particular case, order the trustee to satisfy all or part of the restitution judgment out of all or part of future payments that the trustee, pursuant to the exercise of the trustee's discretion, determines to make to or for the benefit of the beneficiary.

(d) This section applies to a restitution judgment notwithstanding any provision in the trust instrument. *(Added by Stats.1991, c. 175 (A.B.534), § 1.)*

§ 15306. Liability for public support

(a) Notwithstanding any provision in the trust instrument, if a statute of this state makes the beneficiary liable for reimbursement of this state or a local public entity in this state for public support furnished to the beneficiary or to the beneficiary's spouse or minor child, upon petition to the court under Section 709.010 of the Code of Civil Procedure by the appropriate state or local public entity or public official, to the extent the court determines it is equitable and reasonable under the circumstances of the particular case, the court may do the following:

(1) If the beneficiary has the right under the trust to compel the trustee to pay income or principal or both to or for the benefit of the beneficiary, order the trustee to satisfy all or part of the liability out of all or part of the payments as they become due, presently or in the future.

(2) Whether or not the beneficiary has the right under the trust to compel the trustee to pay income or principal or both to or for the benefit of the beneficiary, order the trustee to satisfy all or part of the liability out of all or part of the future payments that the trustee, pursuant to the exercise of the trustee's discretion, determines to make to or for the benefit of the beneficiary.

(3) If the beneficiary is a settlor or the spouse or minor child of the settlor and the beneficiary does not have the right under the trust to compel the trustee to pay income or principal or both to or for the benefit of the beneficiary, to the extent that the trustee has the right to make payments of income or principal or both to or for the beneficiary pursuant to the exercise of the trustee's discretion, order the trustee to satisfy all or part of the liability without regard to whether the trustee has then exercised or may thereafter exercise the discretion in favor of the beneficiary.

(b) Subdivision (a) does not apply to any trust that is established for the benefit of an individual who has a disability that substantially impairs the individual's ability to provide for his or her own care or custody and constitutes a substantial handicap. If, however, the trust results in the individual being ineligible for needed public social services under Division 9 (commencing With Section 10000) of the Welfare and Institutions Code, this subdivision is not applicable and the provisions of subdivision (a) are to be applied. *(Stats.1990, c. 79 (A.B.759), § 14, operative July 1, 1991.)*

Law Revision Commission Comments
1990 Enactment

Section 15306 continues Section 15306 of the repealed Probate Code without substantive change. This section is drawn from Wisconsin law. See Wis.Stat.Ann. § 701.06(5)–(5m) (West 1981).

Subdivision (a) is generally consistent with prior California law which permitted a state institution in which the beneficiary of a spendthrift trust was an inmate to reach the beneficiary's interest. See Estate of Lackmann, 156 Cal.App.2d 674, 678–83, 320 P.2d 186 (1958) (citing Restatement of Trusts § 157). Section 15306 applies to reimbursement for public support provided in the form of aid furnished to an individual who is not in an institution as well as aid furnished while the individual is a resident of a state institution. See, e.g., Welf. & Inst. Code §§ 903 (liability for support of minor under order of juvenile court), 17403 (liability for support of indigent from public funds). However, subdivision (a) of Section 15306 makes clear that the state or local agency has the right to reach the beneficiary's interest for reimbursement of support provided to the spouse or minor child of the beneficiary.

Subdivision (b) limits the right of the state or a local agency to reach the beneficiary's interest in welfare cases where the trust was established to provide for the care of a disabled beneficiary who is unable to provide for his or her own care or custody. This limitation is intended to encourage potential settlors to provide in a trust for the care or support of a disabled person without the risk that the benefits of the trust will be taken to reimburse a public agency for a minimal level of support provided by the public agency. However, this rule is subject to the exception provided in the last sentence of subdivision (b).

For general provisions relating to petitions and other papers, see Sections 1020–1023, 17201; see also Sections 1021 (petition to be verified), 1041 (clerk to set petition for hearing). For general provisions relating to notice of hearing, see Sections 1200–1221, 15802–15804, 17100–17105, 17203–17205; see also Sections 1260–1265 (proof of giving notice). For general provisions relating to hearings and orders, see Sections 1040–1050, 17000–17006, 17201–17202, 17206–17207; see also Section 15308.

Background on Section 15306 of Repealed Code

Section 15306 was a new provision added by 1986 Cal.Stat. ch. 820 § 40. The section was amended by 1989 Cal.Stat. ch. 748 § 2 to add the last sentence to subdivision (b). For background on the provisions of this division, see the Comment to this division under the division heading. [20 Cal.L.Rev.Comm.Reports 1001 (1990)].

Cross References

Enforcement of money judgment against interest in trust, see Code of Civil Procedure § 709.010.

§ 15306.5. Court order directing trustee to satisfy judgments; payment to which beneficiary entitled; limitations

(a) Notwithstanding a restraint on transfer of the beneficiary's interest in the trust under Section 15300 or 15301, and subject to the limitations of this section, upon a judgment creditor's petition under Section 709.010 of the Code of Civil Procedure, the court may make an order directing the trustee to satisfy all or part of the judgment out of the payments to which the beneficiary is entitled under the trust instrument or that the trustee, in the exercise of the trustee's discretion, has determined or determines in the future to pay to the beneficiary.

(b) An order under this section may not require that the trustee pay in satisfaction of the judgment an amount exceeding 25 percent of the payment that otherwise would be made to, or for the benefit of, the beneficiary.

(c) An order under this section may not require that the trustee pay in satisfaction of the judgment any amount that the court determines is necessary for the support of the beneficiary and all the persons the beneficiary is required to support.

(d) An order for satisfaction of a support judgment, as defined in Section 15305, has priority over an order to satisfy a judgment under this section. Any amount ordered to be applied to the satisfaction of a judgment under this section shall be reduced by the amount of an order for satisfaction of a support judgment under Section 15305, regardless of whether the order for satisfaction of the support judgment was made before or after the order under this section.

(e) If the trust gives the trustee discretion over the payment of either principal or income of a trust, or both, nothing in this section affects or limits that discretion in any manner. The trustee has no duty to oppose a petition to satisfy a judgment under this section or to make any claim for exemption on behalf of the beneficiary. The trustee is not liable for any action taken, or omitted to be taken, in compliance with any court order made under this section.

(f) Subject to subdivision (d), the aggregate of all orders for satisfaction of money judgments against the beneficiary's interest in the trust may not exceed 25 percent of the payment that otherwise would be made to, or for the benefit of, the beneficiary. *(Stats.1990, c. 79 (A.B.759), § 14, operative July 1, 1991.)*

Law Revision Commission Comments
1990 Enactment

Section 15306.5 continues Section 15306.5 of the repealed Probate Code without change.

Subdivision (a) permits general creditors to seek to satisfy a money judgment from payments that are to be made to a trust beneficiary. This right applies to payments that are required by the terms of the trust or that are determined by the trustee in the exercise of the trustee's discretion under the trust. Subdivision (e), however, makes clear that the right of the creditor does not affect any discretion the trustee may have under the trust instrument to change the amount of the payment, or even to cease payment altogether. See also Section 15307 (creditor's right to reach income in excess of amount for education and support). As provided in the introductory clause, this creditor's right applies regardless of a restraint on transfer provided in the trust instrument.

The creditor's right under subdivision (a) is subject to important limitations provided in subdivisions (b) and (c). Subdivision (b) provides a maximum amount that the creditor can reach, equal to 25 percent of each payment. This provision is comparable to the rule that applied under former subdivision (c) of Code of Civil Procedure Section 709.010 (prior to its amendment by 1986 Cal.Stat. ch. 820 § 18) (incorporating the wage garnishment withholding standard of Code of Civil Procedure Section 706.050). See Code Civ.Proc. § 706.050 and the Comment thereto.

Subdivision (c) protects part or all of the payment that otherwise would be applied to the judgment where the amount is necessary for the support of the beneficiary and persons the beneficiary is required to support. This provision is comparable to Code of Civil Procedure Section 706.051 (wage garnishment exemption) which was incorporated by former subdivision (c) of Code of Civil Procedure Section 709.010 for purposes of enforcement of money judgments against trust payments.

Subdivision (d) makes clear that an order in favor of a creditor under this section is subject to the claim of a creditor who has obtained an order for enforcement of a support judgment, i.e., a minor child, spouse, or former spouse. The second sentence of subdivision (d) makes clear that the priority of support judgments does not depend on the time of issuance of the order for enforce-

ment. This scheme is comparable to the priority that applies to earnings withholding orders under the Wage Garnishment Law. See Code Civ.Proc. § 706.030(b)(2). It should also be noted that while a spouse, former spouse, or minor child enforcing a support judgment may use this section, in the normal case support creditors will apply under Section 15305. The limitations provided in this section do not apply to enforcement of a support judgment under Section 15305.

Subdivision (f) limits the aggregate amount of the beneficiary's interest in one trust that is subject to enforcement where several creditors have obtained orders. Thus, if one creditor is receiving 25 percent of the payment that otherwise would have been made to the beneficiary, a second general creditor will not be able to reach any of the payment in the hands of the trustee. If one creditor is receiving 15 percent, a second general creditor can reach only 10 percent of the original amount of the payment. Of course, the aggregate amount of all orders may be less than 25 percent if the court has determined under subdivision (c) that more than 75 percent of the original payment is necessary for the beneficiary's support. The introductory clause of subdivision (f) recognizes that the 25 percent limitation does not affect the amount that may be reached in satisfaction of a support judgment.

For general provisions relating to petitions and other papers, see Sections 1020–1023, 17201; see also Sections 1021 (petition to be verified), 1041 (clerk to set petition for hearing). For general provisions relating to notice of hearing, see Sections 1200–1221, 15802–15804, 17100–17105, 17203–17205; see also Sections 1260–1265 (proof of giving notice). For general provisions relating to hearings and orders, see Sections 1040–1050, 17000–17006, 17201–17202, 17206–17207; see also Section 15308.

Background on Section 15306.5 of Repealed Code

Section 15306.5 was added by 1986 Cal.Stat. ch. 820 § 40. The section restated the substance of former provisions of Code of Civil Procedure Section 709.010 (prior to its amendment by 1986 Cal.Stat. ch. 820 § 18). For background on the provisions of this division, see the Comment to this division under the division heading. [20 Cal.L.Rev.Comm.Reports 1001 (1990)].

§ 15307. Income in excess of amount for education and support; application to creditors' claim

Notwithstanding a restraint on transfer of a beneficiary's interest in the trust under Section 15300 or 15301, any amount to which the beneficiary is entitled under the trust instrument or that the trustee, in the exercise of the trustee's discretion, has determined to pay to the beneficiary in excess of the amount that is or will be necessary for the education and support of the beneficiary may be applied to the satisfaction of a money judgment against the beneficiary. Upon the judgment creditor's petition under Section 709.010 of the Code of Civil Procedure, the court may make an order directing the trustee to satisfy all or part of the judgment out of the beneficiary's interest in the trust. *(Stats.1990, c. 79 (A.B.759), § 14, operative July 1, 1991.)*

Law Revision Commission Comments
1990 Enactment

Section 15307 continues Section 15307 of the repealed Probate Code without change.

While Sections 15305 and 15306 permit only certain preferred creditors to reach the beneficiary's interest in the trust, Section 15307 permits an ordinary creditor to reach income under limited circumstances. To obtain relief under Section 15307, the judgment creditor must file a petition under Section 709.010 of the Code of Civil Procedure. See Code Civ.Proc. § 709.010(b). For general provisions relating to petitions and other papers, see Sections 1020–1023, 17201; see also Sections 1021 (petition to be verified), 1041 (clerk to set petition for hearing). For general provisions relating to notice of hearing, see Sections 1200–1221, 15802–15804, 17100–17105, 17203–17205; see also Sections 1260–1265 (proof of giving notice). For general provisions relating to hearings and orders, see Sections 1040–1050, 17000–17006, 17201–17202, 17206–17207; see also Section 15308.

Under Code of Civil Procedure Section 709.010, the court may make a continuing order for application of future payments to the satisfaction of the judgment. It should also be noted, however, that a creditor does not have the power to compel the trustee to exercise discretion. See Section 15303.

The introductory clause of Section 15307 makes clear that this section applies only to a trust in which transfer of the beneficiary's interest is restrained. Section 15307 does not apply to enforcement against a trust that does not restrain transfer of the beneficiary's interest; the entire interest of a beneficiary under such a trust may be applied to the satisfaction of a money judgment under Code of Civil Procedure Section 709.010.

A station-in-life test is used to determine the amount necessary for education and support under this section. See Canfield v. Security–First Nat'l Bank, 13 Cal.2d 1, 21–24, 87 P.2d 830 (1939); Magner v. Crooks, 139 Cal. 640, 642, 73 P. 585 (1903); Smith v. Smith, 51 Cal.App.2d 29, 35–38, 124 P.2d 117 (1942); cf. Alvis v. Bank of America, 95 Cal.App.2d 118, 122–24, 212 P.2d 608 (1949) (beneficiary who had disappeared). The California Supreme Court has rejected the more extreme New York cases, but has continued to embrace the station-in-life test which considers factors such as the social background of the beneficiary. See, e.g., Canfield v. Security–First Nat'l Bank, 13 Cal.2d 1, 24–28, 87 P.2d 830 (1939). If the trustee has discretion to determine the disposition of the trust income, the trustee may be able to defeat the creditor's attempt to reach the excess income under this section by reducing the amount to be paid to the beneficiary to the amount determined by the court to be necessary for the support and education of the beneficiary. See Estate of Canfield, 80 Cal.App.2d 443, 450–52, 181 P.2d 732 (1947); E. Griswold, Spendthrift Trusts § 428 (2d ed. 1947).

Other provisions may permit a creditor of the beneficiary to satisfy all or part of the creditor's claim out of all or part of the payments of the income or principal as they fall due, presently or in the future. See Sections 15305 (child or spousal support), 15306 (public support); see also Section 15304 (settlor as beneficiary).

Background on Section 15307 of Repealed Code

Section 15307 was added by 1986 Cal.Stat. ch. 820 § 40. The section replaced former Civil Code Section 859 (repealed by 1986 Cal.Stat. ch. 820 § 5). For background on the provisions of this division, see the Comment to this division under the division heading. [20 Cal.L.Rev.Comm.Reports 1001 (1990)].

Cross References

Income applied to support destitute beneficiary, see Civil Code § 726.
Restraining transfer of income, see Probate Code § 15300.

§ 15308. Subsequent modification of court order

Any order entered by a court under Section 15305, 15306, 15306.5, or 15307 is subject to modification upon petition of an interested person filed in the court where the order was made. *(Stats.1990, c. 79 (A.B.759), § 14, operative July 1, 1991.)*

Law Revision Commission Comments
1990 Enactment

Section 15308 continues Section 15308 of the repealed Probate Code without change. This section is drawn from Wisconsin law.

See Wis.Stat.Ann. § 701.06(7) (West 1981). See also Section 48 ("interested person" defined).

Background on Section 15308 of Repealed Code

Section 15308 was a new provision added by 1986 Cal.Stat. ch. 820 § 40. For background on the provisions of this division, see the Comment to this division under the division heading. [20 Cal.L.Rev.Comm.Reports 1001 (1990)].

§ 15309. Disclaimer not a transfer

A disclaimer or renunciation by a beneficiary of all or part of his or her interest under a trust shall not be considered a transfer under Section 15300 or 15301. *(Stats.1990, c. 79 (A.B.759), § 14, operative July 1, 1991.)*

Law Revision Commission Comments
1990 Enactment

Section 15309 continues Section 15309 of the repealed Probate Code without change. This section is drawn from Wisconsin law. See Wis.Stat.Ann. § 701.06(3) (West 1981).

Background on Section 15309 of Repealed Code

Section 15309 was a new provision added by 1986 Cal.Stat. ch. 820 § 40. For background on the provisions of this division, see the Comment to this division under the division heading. [20 Cal.L.Rev.Comm.Reports 1001 (1990)].

CHAPTER 3. MODIFICATION AND TERMINATION OF TRUSTS

Application

Application of Division, see Probate Code § 15001.

Cross References

Common law rules governing trusts, application, see Probate Code § 15002.
Relationships excluded from Code definition of trust, application of this division, see Probate Code § 15003.

§ 15400. Presumption of revocability

Unless a trust is expressly made irrevocable by the trust instrument, the trust is revocable by the settlor. This section applies only where the settlor is domiciled in this state when the trust is created, where the trust instrument is executed in this state, or where the trust instrument provides that the law of this state governs the trust. *(Stats.1990, c. 79 (A.B.759), § 14, operative July 1, 1991.)*

Law Revision Commission Comments

1990 Enactment

Section 15400 continues Section 15400 of the repealed Probate Code without change. For the procedure for revoking a trust, see Section 15401. See also Section 15402 (power to revoke includes power to modify).

Background on Section 15400 of Repealed Code

Section 15400 was added by 1986 Cal.Stat. ch. 820 § 40. The first sentence of Section 15400 restated part of the first sentence of former Civil Code Section 2280 (repealed by 1986 Cal.Stat. ch. 820 § 7) without substantive change. The second sentence was a new provision that limited the application of the California rule presuming revocability. For background on the provisions of this division, see the Comment to this division under the division heading. [20 Cal.L.Rev.Comm.Reports 1001 (1990)].

Cross References

Exclusion from law of state of rule of worthier title and presumption against intent of grantor to transfer interest by grant to heirs or next of kin, see Civil Code § 1073.
Power of appointment irrevocable unless power to revoke exists pursuant to this section,
Generally, see Probate Code § 695.

§ 15401. Revocable trusts; methods; multiple settlors; granting of power to revoke; modification or revocation by attorney in fact

(a) A trust that is revocable by the settlor or any other person may be revoked in whole or in part by any of the following methods:

(1) By compliance with any method of revocation provided in the trust instrument.

(2) By a writing, other than a will, signed by the settlor or any other person holding the power of revocation and delivered to the trustee during the lifetime of the settlor or the person holding the power of revocation. If the trust instrument explicitly makes the method of revocation provided in the trust instrument the exclusive method of revocation, the trust may not be revoked pursuant to this paragraph.

(b)(1) Unless otherwise provided in the instrument, if a trust is created by more than one settlor, each settlor may revoke the trust as to the portion of the trust contributed by that settlor, except as provided in Section 761 of the Family Code.

(2) Notwithstanding paragraph (1), a settlor may grant to another person, including, but not limited to, his or her spouse, a power to revoke all or part of that portion of the trust contributed by that settlor, regardless of whether that portion was separate property or community property of that settlor, and regardless of whether that power to revoke is exercisable during the lifetime of that settlor or continues after the death of that settlor, or both.

(c) A trust may not be modified or revoked by an attorney in fact under a power of attorney unless it is expressly permitted by the trust instrument.

(d) This section shall not limit the authority to modify or terminate a trust pursuant to Section 15403 or 15404 in an appropriate case.

(e) The manner of revocation of a trust revocable by the settlor or any other person that was created by an instrument executed before July 1, 1987, is governed by prior law and not by this section. *(Stats.1990, c. 79 (A.B.759), § 14, operative July 1, 1991. Amended by Stats.1994, c. 806 (A.B.3686), § 37; Stats.2012, c. 55 (A.B.1683), § 1.)*

Law Revision Commission Comments

1990 Enactment

Section 15401 continues Section 15401 of the repealed Probate Code without change.

The settlor may revoke a revocable trust in the manner provided in subdivision (a)(2), unless there is a contrary provision in the trust. This changes the rule under prior case law. See Rosenauer v. Title Ins. & Trust Co., 30 Cal.App.3d 300, 304, 106 Cal.Rptr. 321 (1973). The settlor may not revoke a trust by a will under subdivision (a)(2), even if the will purporting to revoke is delivered to the trustee during the lifetime of the settlor. However, the settlor may revoke by will if the trust so provides, pursuant to subdivision (a)(1). See Restatement (Second) of Trusts § 330 comment j (1957).

Under subdivision (b), a provision in the power of attorney permitting the attorney in fact to revoke or modify the trust is ineffective unless the trust instrument expressly authorizes revocation by the attorney in fact. See, e.g., Civil Code § 2467(a)(5) (provision in statutory power of attorney form permitting exercise of principal's power to revoke). See also Civil Code §§ 2400–2407 (Uniform Durable Power of Attorney Act), 2450–2473 (statutory short form power of attorney).

Subdivision (c) clarifies the relation of this section to other sections permitting modification and termination of trusts.

Subdivision (d) preserves the prior law governing the manner of revocation. Hence, if a trust created by an instrument executed before July 1, 1987, provides the manner of revocation, the statutory method provided in subdivision (a) is not available.

Background on Section 15401 of Repealed Code

Section 15401 was added by 1986 Cal.Stat. ch. 820 § 40 and was amended by 1988 Cal.Stat. ch. 113 § 19. Subdivision (a) superseded part of the first sentence of former Civil Code Section 2280 (repealed by 1986 Cal.Stat. ch. 820 § 7). The remainder of the section was new. For background on the provisions of this division, see the Comment to this division under the division heading.

The 1988 amendment revised subdivision (b) to make clear that the rule applicable to revocation by an attorney in fact applies to modification. This made subdivision (b) consistent with the rule provided in Section 15402. For background on the 1988 amendment, see *Communication from the California Law Revision Commission Concerning Assembly Bill 2779*, 19 Cal.L.Revision Comm'n Reports 1191, 1199 (1988). [20 Cal.L.Rev.Comm.Reports 1001 (1990)].

§ 15402. Modification of trust

Unless the trust instrument provides otherwise, if a trust is revocable by the settlor, the settlor may modify the trust by the procedure for revocation. *(Stats.1990, c. 79 (A.B.759), § 14, operative July 1, 1991.)*

Law Revision Commission Comments

1990 Enactment

Section 15402 continues Section 15402 of the repealed Probate Code without change. This section codifies the general rule that a power of revocation implies the power of modification. See Heifetz

v. Bank of America Nat'l Trust & Sav. Ass'n, 147 Cal.App.2d 776, 781–82, 305 P.2d 979 (1957); Restatement (Second) of Trusts § 331 comment g (1957). An unrestricted power to modify may also include the power to revoke a trust. See Heifetz v. Bank of America Nat'l Trust & Sav. Ass'n, supra, at 784; Restatement (Second) of Trusts § 331 comment h (1957). See also Sections 15600 (trustee's acceptance of modification of trust), 15601 (trustee's rejection of modification of trust).

Background on Section 15402 of Repealed Code

Section 15402 was a new provision added by 1986 Cal.Stat. ch. 820 § 40. For background on the provisions of this division, see the Comment to this division under the division heading. [20 Cal.L.Rev.Comm.Reports 1001 (1990)].

§ 15403. Modification or termination of irrevocable trust by all beneficiaries

(a) Except as provided in subdivision (b), if all beneficiaries of an irrevocable trust consent, they may compel modification or termination of the trust upon petition to the court.

(b) If the continuance of the trust is necessary to carry out a material purpose of the trust, the trust cannot be modified or terminated unless the court, in its discretion, determines that the reason for doing so under the circumstances outweighs the interest in accomplishing a material purpose of the trust. Under this section the court does not have discretion to permit termination of a trust that is subject to a valid restraint on transfer of the beneficiary's interest as provided in Chapter 2 (commencing with Section 15300). *(Stats.1990, c. 79 (A.B.759), § 14, operative July 1, 1991.)*

Law Revision Commission Comments

1990 Enactment

Section 15403 continues Section 15403 of the repealed Probate Code without change.

This section is drawn from Section 337 of the Restatement (Second) of Trusts (1957). Unlike the Restatement, however, subdivision (b) gives the court some discretion in applying the material purposes doctrine except in situations where transfer of the beneficiary's interest is restrained, such as by a spendthrift provision. See Section 15300 (restraint on transfer of beneficiary's interest). Section 15403 permits termination of an irrevocable trust with the consent of all beneficiaries where the trust provides for successive beneficiaries or postpones enjoyment of a beneficiary's interest. The discretionary power provided in subdivision (b) also represents a change in the prior California caselaw rule. See, e.g., Moxley v. Title Ins. & Trust Co., 27 Cal.2d 457, 462, 165 P.2d 15 (1946). Section 15403 is intended to provide some degree of flexibility in applying the material purposes doctrine in situations where transfer of the beneficiary's interest is not restrained. For provisions governing judicial proceedings, see Section 17200 et seq. For provisions relating to obtaining consent of persons under an incapacity, see, e.g., Civil Code §§ 2450, 2467 (statutory form of durable power of attorney); Prob.Code §§ 2580 (conservator), 1003 & 15405 (appointment of guardian ad litem). See also Section 15406 (rebuttable presumption of fertility). For provisions governing modification and termination of trusts where the consent of all beneficiaries cannot be obtained, see Sections 15408 (trust with uneconomically low principal) and 15409 (modification or termination by court order in changed circumstances).

Subdivision (a) limits the application of this section to irrevocable trusts since if the trust is revocable by the settlor, the method of revocation is governed by Section 15401. Compare Section 15404 (modification or termination by settlor and all beneficiaries).

For general provisions relating to petitions and other papers, see Sections 1020–1023, 17201; see also Sections 1021 (petition to be verified), 1041 (clerk to set petition for hearing). For general provisions relating to notice of hearing, see Sections 1200–1221, 15802–15804, 17100–17105, 17203–17205; see also Sections 1260–1265 (proof of giving notice). For general provisions relating to hearings and orders, see Sections 1040–1050, 17000–17006, 17201–17202, 17206–17207.

Background on Section 15403 of Repealed Code

Section 15403 was a new provision added by 1986 Cal.Stat. ch. 820 § 40. For background on the provisions of this division, see the Comment to this division under the division heading. [20 Cal.L.Rev.Comm.Reports 1001 (1990)].

§ 15404. Modification or termination by settlor and all beneficiaries

(a) If the settlor and all beneficiaries of a trust consent, they may compel the modification or termination of the trust.

(b) If any beneficiary does not consent to the modification or termination of the trust, upon petition to the court, the other beneficiaries, with the consent of the settlor, may compel a modification or a partial termination of the trust if the interests of the beneficiaries who do not consent are not substantially impaired.

(c) If the trust provides for the disposition of principal to a class of persons described only as "heirs" or "next of kin" of the settlor, or using other words that describe the class of all persons who would take under the rules of intestacy, the court may limit the class of beneficiaries whose consent is needed to compel the modification or termination of the trust to the beneficiaries who are reasonably likely to take under the circumstances. *(Stats.1990, c. 79 (A.B.759), § 14, operative July 1, 1991.)*

Law Revision Commission Comments

1990 Enactment

Section 15404 continues Section 15404 of the repealed Probate Code without change. Subdivisions (a) and (b) are drawn from Section 338 of the Restatement (Second) of Trusts (1957).

A trust may be modified or terminated pursuant to this section without court approval, but a court order may be sought by petition under Section 17200. A revocable trust may be modified or terminated pursuant to this section, as in a case where the method of modification or revocation specified in the trust is found to be overly restrictive. See Section 15401; compare Section 15801 (consent by beneficiary of revocable trust). However, nothing in this section affects the right of a settlor to revoke or modify a revocable trust under Section 15401. For provisions relating to obtaining consent of persons under an incapacity, see, e.g., Civil Code §§ 2450, 2467 (statutory form of durable power of attorney); Prob.Code §§ 2580 (conservator), 1003 & 15405 (appointment of guardian ad litem). See also Section 15406 (rebuttable presumption of fertility). A trust may be modified or terminated under this section regardless of any provision in the trust restraining transfer of the beneficiary's interest and regardless of whether its purposes have been achieved. See Restatement (Second) of Trusts § 338 comments b–d (1957).

Subdivision (c) reinstates a limited form of the doctrine of worthier title. The doctrine of worthier title was abolished in California in 1959 upon recommendation of the California Law Revision Commission. See 1959 Cal.Stat. ch. 122. See also Recommendation and Study Relating to The Doctrine of Worthier Title, 2 Cal.L.Revision Comm'n Reports D–1 (1959). Under subdivision (c), the need to obtain the consent of persons constituting the class of heirs or next of kin of the settlor may be excused by the court as to beneficiaries (typically unborn or remote beneficiaries) who are not reasonably likely to take principal under the trust. This limitation protects the interests of beneficiaries who are likely to take while permitting the settlor to modify or terminate an otherwise irrevocable trust in line with the probable intent of the settlor.

For general provisions relating to petitions and other papers, see Sections 1020–1023, 17201; see also Sections 1021 (petition to be verified), 1041 (clerk to set petition for hearing). For general provisions relating to notice of hearing, see Sections 1200–1221, 15802–15804, 17100–17105, 17203–17205; see also Sections 1260–1265 (proof of giving notice). For general provisions relating to hearings and orders, see Sections 1040–1050, 17000–17006, 17201–17202, 17206–17207.

Background on Section 15404 of Repealed Code

Section 15404 was added by 1986 Cal.Stat. ch. 820 § 40. Subdivision (a) restated the substance of the rule formerly provided by the second sentence of the second paragraph of Civil Code Section 771 (repealed by 1986 Cal.Stat. ch. 820 § 4) and superseded part of former Civil Code Section 2258(a) (repealed by 1986 Cal.Stat. ch. 820 § 7). Subdivisions (b) and (c) were new. For background on the provisions of this division, see the Comment to this division under the division heading. [20 Cal.L.Rev.Comm.Reports 1001 (1990)].

§ 15405. Guardian ad litem

For the purposes of Sections 15403 and 15404, the consent of a beneficiary who lacks legal capacity, including a minor, or who is an unascertained or unborn person may be given in proceedings before the court by a guardian ad litem, if it would be appropriate to do so. In determining whether to give consent, the guardian ad litem may rely on general family benefit accruing to living members of the beneficiary's family as a basis for approving a modification or termination of the trust. *(Stats.1990, c. 79 (A.B.759), § 14, operative July 1, 1991.)*

Law Revision Commission Comments
1990 Enactment

Section 15405 continues Section 15405 of the repealed Probate Code without change. This section recognizes that, where appropriate, a guardian ad litem may give consent to modification or termination on behalf of a beneficiary who lacks legal capacity (including a minor) or who is an unascertained or unborn person. The second sentence of the section permits a non-pecuniary quid pro quo as a basis for protecting the interests of the beneficiaries represented by the guardian ad litem. This provision is drawn from Wisconsin law. Wis.Stat.Ann. § 701.12(2) (West 1981). Under this rule, the guardian ad litem may rely on the assumption that a benefit conferred on potential parents will ultimately benefit a child who might be born into the family. On the quid pro quo doctrine generally, see Hatch v. Riggs Nat'l Bank, 361 F.2d 559 (D.C.Cir. 1966).

Background on Section 15405 of Repealed Code

Section 15405 was a new provision added by 1986 Cal.Stat. ch. 820 § 40 and amended by 1987 Cal.Stat. ch. 128 § 9. For background on the provisions of this division, see the Comment to this division under the division heading. [20 Cal.L.Rev.Comm.Reports 1001 (1990)].

§ 15406. Presumption of fertility rebuttable

In determining the class of beneficiaries whose consent is necessary to modify or terminate a trust pursuant to Section 15403 or 15404, the presumption of fertility is rebuttable. *(Stats.1990, c. 79 (A.B.759), § 14, operative July 1, 1991.)*

Law Revision Commission Comments
1990 Enactment

Section 15406 continues Section 15406 of the repealed Probate Code without change. This section abandons the "fertile octogenarian" doctrine as applied in the context of trust termination. Under this section, the way is open for the court to approve a termination where the possibility of the birth of additional beneficiaries is negligible. See Restatement (Second) of Trusts § 340 comment e (1957). Section 15406 thus adopts the modern view that fertility may not be a realistic issue or is subject to proof. See 4 A. Scott, The Law of Trusts § 340.1, at 513 (4th ed. 1987). This section rejects the prior California case-law rule. See Fletcher v. Los Angeles Trust & Sav. Bank, 182 Cal. 177, 184, 187 P. 425 (1920); Wogman v. Wells Fargo Bank & Union Trust Co., 123 Cal.App.2d 657, 665, 267 P.2d 423 (1954).

Background on Section 15406 of Repealed Code

Section 15406 was a new provision added by 1986 Cal.Stat. ch. 820 § 40. For background on the provisions of this division, see the Comment to this division under the division heading. [20 Cal.L.Rev.Comm.Reports 1001 (1990)].

§ 15407. Termination of trust

(a) A trust terminates when any of the following occurs:

(1) The term of the trust expires.

(2) The trust purpose is fulfilled.

(3) The trust purpose becomes unlawful.

(4) The trust purpose becomes impossible to fulfill.

(5) The trust is revoked.

(b) On termination of the trust, the trustee continues to have the powers reasonably necessary under the circumstances to wind up the affairs of the trust. *(Stats.1990, c. 79 (A.B.759), § 14, operative July 1, 1991.)*

Law Revision Commission Comments
1990 Enactment

Section 15407 continues Section 15407 of the repealed Probate Code without change. Subdivision (a) lists the ways in which trusts typically may terminate. Paragraph (1) codifies a prior case-law rule. See In re Estate of Hanson, 159 Cal. 401, 405, 114 P. 810 (1911); Restatement (Second) of Trusts § 334 (1957). Subdivision (b) makes clear that even though the trust has terminated, the trustee retains limited powers needed to wind up the affairs of the trust. For other provisions relating to trustees' powers, see Section 16200 et seq.

Background on Section 15407 of Repealed Code

Section 15407 was added by 1986 Cal.Stat. ch. 820 § 40. Paragraphs (1) and (5) of subdivision (a) were new. Paragraphs (2), (3), and (4) of subdivision (a) restated former Civil Code Section 2279 (repealed by 1986 Cal.Stat. ch. 820 § 7) without substantive change. Subdivision (b) was new. For background on the provisions of this division, see the Comment to this division under the division heading. [20 Cal.L.Rev.Comm.Reports 1001 (1990)].

Cross References

Account of trustee for minors or incompetents in workers' compensation proceedings, see Labor Code § 5307.5.
Application and order for accounting by testamentary trustee, see Probate Code § 17200.
Methods of revocation, see Probate Code § 15401.
Powers of trustees, see Probate Code § 16200 et seq.
Real estate, willful holding over by trustee, measure of damages, see Civil Code § 3335.

Written trust direction for accumulation of income of property beyond time limit as void and severable, see Civil Code § 725.

§ 15408. Trust with uneconomically low principal

(a) On petition by a trustee or beneficiary, if the court determines that the fair market value of the principal of a trust has become so low in relation to the cost of administration that continuation of the trust under its existing terms will defeat or substantially impair the accomplishment of its purposes, the court may, in its discretion and in a manner that conforms as nearly as possible to the intention of the settlor, order any of the following:

(1) Termination of the trust.

(2) Modification of the trust.

(3) Appointment of a new trustee.

(b) Notwithstanding subdivision (a), if the trust principal does not exceed forty thousand dollars ($40,000) in value, the trustee has the power to terminate the trust.

(c) The existence of a trust provision restraining transfer of the beneficiary's interest does not prevent application of this section. *(Stats.1990, c. 79 (A.B.759), § 14, operative July 1, 1991. Amended by Stats.2010, c. 621 (S.B.202), § 1.)*

Law Revision Commission Comments
1990 Enactment

Section 15408 continues Section 15408 of the repealed Probate Code without change. For general provisions relating to petitions and other papers, see Sections 1020–1023, 17201; see also Sections 1021 (petition to be verified), 1041 (clerk to set petition for hearing). For general provisions relating to notice of hearing, see Sections 1200–1221, 15802–15804, 17100–17105, 17203–17205; see also Sections 1260–1265 (proof of giving notice). For general provisions relating to hearings and orders, see Sections 1040–1050, 17000–17006, 17201–17202, 17206–17207. See also Section 15800 (limits on rights of beneficiary of revocable trust).

Subdivision (b) gives the trustee the power to terminate a trust with a principal value of $20,000 or less. In such case, the trustee need not seek court approval for termination of the trust; the presumption is established that a $20,000 trust is inherently uneconomical. A trustee has discretion, however, to seek court approval under Section 17200(b)(5) (approval of trustee's accounts), and even in a case where the trustee has determined to terminate the trust under subdivision (b), the trustee may seek instructions on the correct manner of distributing the trust property. See Sections 15410 (disposition of property upon termination), 17200(b)(4) (determining to whom property passes on termination).

Background on Section 15408 of Repealed Code

Section 15408 was added by 1986 Cal.Stat. ch. 820 § 40. Subdivisions (a) and (c) restated without substantive change subdivisions (a) and (d) of former Civil Code Section 2279.1 (repealed by 1986 Cal.Stat. ch. 820 § 7) and subdivisions (a) and (d) of former Probate Code Section 1120.6 (repealed by 1986 Cal.Stat. ch. 820 § 31). Subdivision (b) was new. For background on the provisions of this division, see the Comment to this division under the division heading. [20 Cal.L.Rev.Comm.Reports 1001 (1990)].

Cross References

Trust for care of animals, accountings and beneficiaries, see Probate Code § 15212.

§ 15409. Modification or termination in changed circumstances

(a) On petition by a trustee or beneficiary, the court may modify the administrative or dispositive provisions of the trust or terminate the trust if, owing to circumstances not known to the settlor and not anticipated by the settlor, the continuation of the trust under its terms would defeat or substantially impair the accomplishment of the purposes of the trust. In this case, if necessary to carry out the purposes of the trust, the court may order the trustee to do acts that are not authorized or are forbidden by the trust instrument.

(b) The court shall consider a trust provision restraining transfer of the beneficiary's interest as a factor in making its decision whether to modify or terminate the trust, but the court is not precluded from exercising its discretion to modify or terminate the trust solely because of a restraint on transfer. *(Stats.1990, c. 79 (A.B.759), § 14, operative July 1, 1991.)*

Law Revision Commission Comments
1990 Enactment

Section 15409 continues Section 15409 of the repealed Probate Code without change. Subdivision (a) is drawn from Sections 167 and 336 of the Restatement (Second) of Trusts (1957). Subdivision (b) is drawn from a provision of the Texas Trust Code. See Tex.Prop.Code Ann. § 112.054 (Vernon 1984). See also Sections 15800 (limits on rights of beneficiary of revocable trust), 16201 (power of court to relieve trustee from restrictions on powers). Modification of the dispositive provisions of a trust for the support of a beneficiary may be appropriate, for example, in a case where the beneficiary has become unable to support himself or herself due to poor health or serious injury. See, e.g., Whittingham v. California Trust Co., 214 Cal. 128, 4 P.2d 142 (1931). See also Civil Code § 726 (accelerated distribution of accumulations to destitute beneficiaries).

For general provisions relating to petitions and other papers, see Sections 1020–1023, 17201; see also Sections 1021 (petition to be verified), 1041 (clerk to set petition for hearing). For general provisions relating to notice of hearing, see Sections 1200–1221, 15802–15804, 17100–17105, 17203–17205; see also Sections 1260–1265 (proof of giving notice). For general provisions relating to hearings and orders, see Sections 1040–1050, 17000–17006, 17201–17202, 17206–17207.

Background on Section 15409 of Repealed Code

Section 15409 was a new provision added by 1986 Cal.Stat. ch. 820 § 40. For background on the provisions of this division, see the Comment to this division under the division heading. [20 Cal.L.Rev.Comm.Reports 1001 (1990)].

Cross References

Charitable trusts, enforcement by Attorney General, see Government Code § 12598.

Destitute beneficiaries, distribution of accumulations, see Civil Code § 726.

Power of court, relief from restrictions on powers of trustees, see Probate Code § 16201.

§ 15410. Disposition of property upon termination

At the termination of a trust, the trust property shall be disposed of as follows:

(a) In the case of a trust that is revoked by the settlor, the trust property shall be disposed of in the following order of priority:

(1) As directed by the settlor.

(2) As provided in the trust instrument.

(3) To the extent that there is no direction by the settlor or in the trust instrument, to the settlor, or his or her estate, as the case may be.

(b) In the case of a trust that is revoked by any person holding a power of revocation other than the settlor, the trust property shall be disposed of in the following order of priority:

(1) As provided in the trust instrument.

(2) As directed by the person exercising the power of revocation.

(3) To the extent that there is no direction in the trust instrument or by the person exercising the power of revocation, to the person exercising the power of revocation, or his or her estate, as the case may be.

(c) In the case of a trust that is terminated by the consent of the settlor and all beneficiaries, as agreed by the settlor and all beneficiaries.

(d) In any other case, as provided in the trust instrument or in a manner directed by the court that conforms as nearly as possible to the intention of the settlor as expressed in the trust instrument.

(e) If a trust is terminated by the trustee pursuant to subdivision (b) of Section 15408, the trust property may be distributed as determined by the trustee pursuant to the standard provided in subdivision (d) without the need for a court order. If the trust instrument does not provide a manner of distribution at termination and the settlor's intent is not adequately expressed in the trust instrument, the trustee may distribute the trust property to the living beneficiaries on an actuarial basis. *(Stats.1990, c. 79 (A.B. 759), § 14, operative July 1, 1991. Amended by Stats.2012, c. 55 (A.B.1683), § 2.)*

Law Revision Commission Comments
1990 Enactment

Section 15410 continues Section 15410 of the repealed Probate Code without change.

Subdivisions (a) and (b) recognize that the persons holding the power to modify a trust have the power to direct the manner of distribution of property upon termination. See Section 15402 (power to revoke includes power to modify), 15403 (termination by all beneficiaries), 15404 (termination by settlor and all beneficiaries).

Subdivision (c) applies to the cases not described in subdivisions (a) and (b). Subdivision (c) applies to cases where the trust terminates under its own terms, such as the expiration of a term of years or the occurrence of an event. See Section 15407(a)(1)–(2). Subdivision (c) also applies to cases where the trust is terminated pursuant to a court order without the consent of the settlor and beneficiaries. See, e.g., Sections 15407(a)(3) (termination where trust purpose becomes unlawful), 15407(a)(4) (termination where trust purpose becomes impossible to fulfill), 15408 (termination of trust with uneconomically low principal), 15409 (termination in changed circumstances).

Subdivision (d) provides for the application of subdivision (c) without the need for a court order in a case where a trustee has terminated a trust having a principal value of $20,000 or less pursuant to Section 15408(b). The second sentence of subdivision (d) provides a default rule for the disposition of trust property upon termination of a trust worth less than $20,000.

In appropriate circumstances, distributions on termination of a trust may be made to a custodian for a minor under the Uniform Transfers to Minors Act. See Sections 3905 (transfer authorized in trust), 3906 (other transfer by trustee).

Background on Section 15410 of Repealed Code

Section 15410 was a new provision that was added by 1986 Cal.Stat. ch. 820 § 40 and amended by 1987 Cal.Stat. ch. 128 § 10. Subdivision (a) superseded the part of former Civil Code Section 2280 (repealed by 1986 Cal.Stat. ch. 820 § 7) relating to disposition of property upon revocation. Subdivision (c) was drawn in part from subdivision (b) of former Civil Code Section 2279.1 (repealed by 1986 Cal.Stat. ch. 820 § 7) and subdivision (b) of former Probate Code Section 1120.6 (repealed by 1986 Cal.Stat. ch. 820 § 31), which applied to termination of trusts with uneconomically low principal. Subdivision (c) also superseded former Civil Code Section 864 (repealed by 1986 Cal.Stat. ch. 820 § 5) (disposition of real property upon failure or termination of trust). The 1987 amendment revised subdivision (d) to provide a default rule for disposition of trust property at termination of a trust worth less than $20,000. For background on the provisions of this division, see the Comment to this division under the division heading. [20 Cal.L.Rev.Comm.Reports 1001 (1990)].

§ 15411. Combinations of similar trusts

If the terms of two or more trusts are substantially similar, on petition by a trustee or beneficiary, the court, for good cause shown, may combine the trusts if the court determines that administration as a single trust will not defeat or substantially impair the accomplishment of the trust purposes or the interests of the beneficiaries. *(Stats.1990, c. 79 (A.B.759), § 14, operative July 1, 1991.)*

Law Revision Commission Comments
1990 Enactment

Section 15411 continues Section 15411 of the repealed Probate Code without change. This section applies to living trusts as well as testamentary trusts. In addition, a living trust and a testamentary trust may be combined under Section 15411. Trusts may be combined pursuant to Section 15411 only upon a petition pursuant to Section 17200(a) and (b)(14). See also Section 15800 (limits on rights of beneficiary of revocable trust).

For general provisions relating to petitions and other papers, see Sections 1020–1023, 17201; see also Sections 1021 (petition to be verified), 1041 (clerk to set petition for hearing). For general provisions relating to notice of hearing, see Sections 1200–1221, 15802–15804, 17100–17105, 17203–17205; see also Sections 1260–1265 (proof of giving notice). For general provisions relating to hearings and orders, see Sections 1040–1050, 17000–17006, 17201–17202, 17206–17207.

Background on Section 15411 of Repealed Code

Section 15411 was added by 1986 Cal.Stat. ch. 820 § 40. The section superseded former Probate Code Section 1133 (repealed by 1986 Cal.Stat. ch. 820 § 31). Unlike former Section 1133, Section 15411 was made applicable to living trusts as well as testamentary trusts. The requirement in former Section 1133 that the trusts be "substantially identical" was changed to "substantially similar." The reference to substantially impairing also was new; former Section 1133 referred only to "impairing" the interests of beneficiaries. The former requirement that the combination be consistent with the intent of the settlor and facilitate administration of the trust was superseded by the requirement that the combination may not defeat or substantially impair accomplishment of trust purposes. For background on the provisions of this division, see the Comment to this division under the division heading. [20 Cal.L.Rev.Comm.Reports 1001 (1990)].

§ 15412. Division of trusts

On petition by a trustee or beneficiary, the court, for good cause shown, may divide a trust into two or more separate trusts, if the court determines that dividing the trust will not defeat or substantially impair the accomplishment of the trust purposes or the interests of the beneficiaries. *(Stats.1990, c. 79 (A.B.759), § 14, operative July 1, 1991.)*

Law Revision Commission Comments

1990 Enactment

Section 15412 continues Section 15412 of the repealed Probate Code without change. This section provides a standard intended to protect the interests of beneficiaries without necessarily requiring their consent. Division of a trust may be appropriate, for example, in a situation where different members of a family desire their own separate trusts because of a disagreement or where a beneficiary has moved to a different part of the country.

For general provisions relating to petitions and other papers, see Sections 1020–1023, 17201; see also Sections 1021 (petition to be verified), 1041 (clerk to set petition for hearing). For general provisions relating to notice of hearing, see Sections 1200–1221, 15802–15804, 17100–17105, 17203–17205; see also Sections 1260–1265 (proof of giving notice). For general provisions relating to hearings and orders, see Sections 1040–1050, 17000–17006, 17201–17202, 17206–17207. See also Section 15800 (limits on rights of beneficiary of revocable trust).

Background on Section 15412 of Repealed Code

Section 15412 was added by 1986 Cal.Stat. ch. 820, § 40. The section superseded the authority to divide trusts in subdivision (a)(14) of former Probate Code Section 1138.1 (repealed by 1986 Cal.Stat. ch. 820 § 31). The former rule required the consent of all parties in interest, whereas Section 15412 provides a standard intended to protect the interests of beneficiaries without necessarily requiring their consent. For background on the provisions of this division, see the Comment to this division under the division heading. [20 Cal.L.Rev.Comm.Reports 1001 (1990)].

Cross References

Notice to attorney general, amending or conforming trust instrument to qualify estate for charitable estate tax deduction, see Probate Code § 17203.
Petition, see Probate Code § 17201.

§ 15413. Termination provisions; effectiveness

A trust provision, express or implied, that the trust may not be terminated is ineffective insofar as it purports to be applicable after the expiration of the longer of the periods provided by the statutory rule against perpetuities, Article 2 (commencing with Section 21205) of Chapter 1 of Part 2 of Division 11. *(Added by Stats.1991, c. 156 (A.B.1577), § 22.)*

Law Revision Commission Comments

1991 Addition

Section 15413 continues former Civil Code Section 716.5(b) without substantive change, and with modifications to reflect the enactment of the Uniform Statutory Rule Against Perpetuities. See Section 21200 *et seq.* This section applies the longer of the two time periods applicable under the statutory rule: (1) lives in being plus 21 years or (2) 90 years after creation of the interest. See Sections 21205–21207. See also Section 21225(d) (rule against perpetuities does not apply to discretionary power of trustee to distribute principal to beneficiary having indefeasibly vested interest). [20 Cal.L.Rev.Comm.Reports 2501 (1990)].

§ 15414. Continued existence after expiration; termination

Notwithstanding any other provision in this chapter, if a trust continues in existence after the expiration of the longer of the periods provided by the statutory rule against perpetuities, Article 2 (commencing with Section 21205) of Chapter 1 of Part 2 of Division 11, the trust may be terminated in either of the following manners:

(a) On petition by a majority of the beneficiaries.

(b) On petition by the Attorney General or by any person who would be affected by the termination, if the court finds that the termination would be in the public interest or in the best interest of a majority of the persons who would be affected by the termination. *(Added by Stats.1991, c. 156 (A.B.1577), § 23.)*

Law Revision Commission Comments

1991 Addition

Section 15414 restates former Civil Code Section 716.5(c) without substantive change, and with modifications to reflect the enactment of the Uniform Statutory Rule Against Perpetuities. See Section 21200 *et seq.* The introductory clause recognizes that this section is an exception to the general rules concerning trust termination provided in this chapter. Termination under this section is permissible after the expiration of the longer of the two time periods applicable under the statutory rule: (1) lives in being plus 21 years or (2) 90 years after creation of the interest. See Sections 21205–21207. As to judicial proceedings for termination, see Section 17200(b)(13). [20 Cal.L.Rev.Comm.Reports 2501 (1990)].

Part 3

TRUSTEES AND BENEFICIARIES

Application

Application of Division, see Probate Code § 15001.

CHAPTER 1. TRUSTEES

Application

Application of Division, see Probate Code § 15001.

Cross References

Common law rules governing trusts, application, see Probate Code § 15002.
Relationships excluded from Code definition of trust, application of this division, see Probate Code § 15003.

ARTICLE 1. GENERAL PROVISIONS

Application

Application of Division, see Probate Code § 15001.

Cross References

Common law rules governing trusts, application, see Probate Code § 15002.
Relationships excluded from Code definition of trust, application of this division, see Probate Code § 15003.

§ 15600. Acceptance of trust by trustee

(a) The person named as trustee may accept the trust, or a modification of the trust, by one of the following methods:

(1) Signing the trust instrument or the trust instrument as modified, or signing a separate written acceptance.

(2) Knowingly exercising powers or performing duties under the trust instrument or the trust instrument as modified, except as provided in subdivision (b).

(b) In a case where there is an immediate risk of damage to the trust property, the person named as trustee may act to preserve the trust property without accepting the trust or a modification of the trust, if within a reasonable time after acting the person delivers a written rejection of the trust or the modification of the trust to the settlor or, if the settlor is dead or incompetent, to a beneficiary. This subdivision does not impose a duty on the person named as trustee to act. *(Stats.1990, c. 79 (A.B.759), § 14, operative July 1, 1991.)*

Law Revision Commission Comments

1990 Enactment

Section 15600 continues Section 15600 of the repealed Probate Code without change.

Subdivision (a) is drawn from the Indiana Trust Code. See Ind.Code Ann. § 30–4–2–2(a)–(b) (West 1979). The provision in subdivision (a)(2) for acceptance of the trust by acts of the person named as trustee is consistent with prior case law. See, e.g., Heitman v. Cutting, 37 Cal.App. 236, 238, 174 P. 675 (1918).

Subdivision (b) also is drawn from the Indiana Trust Code. See Ind.Code Ann. § 30–4–2–2(d) (West 1979). The last sentence makes clear that the authority to act in an emergency does not impose a duty to act. The intention of this subdivision is to permit the person named as trustee to act in an emergency without being considered to have accepted the trust under the rule set out in subdivision (a)(2). See also Section 15601 (rejection of trust).

The rules governing acceptance of the trust at the commencement of the trust apply by analogy to acceptance of a modification of the trust. Thus, for example, a trustee is not subject to liability for breach of a new duty imposed through a modification of the trust unless the trustee signs the trust as modified or a separate acceptance under subdivision (a)(1) or performs the new duty under subdivision (a)(2).

Background on Section 15600 of Repealed Code

Section 15600 was a new provision added by 1986 Cal.Stat. ch. 820 § 40. Subdivision (a) superseded part of the introductory clause and subdivision (1) of former Civil Code Section 2222 and part of former Civil Code Section 2251 (provisions repealed by 1986 Cal.Stat. ch. 820 § 7). See also former Civil Code § 2258 (repealed by 1986 Cal.Stat. ch. 820 § 7) (trustee of revocable trust to follow directions

of settlor acceptable to trustee). For background on the provisions of this division, see the Comment to this division under the division heading. [20 Cal.L.Rev.Comm.Reports 1001 (1990)].

§ 15601. Rejection of trust; nonliability

(a) A person named as trustee may in writing reject the trust or a modification of the trust.

(b) If the person named as trustee does not accept the trust or a modification of the trust by a method provided in subdivision (a) of Section 15600 within a reasonable time after learning of being named as trustee or of the modification, the person has rejected the trust or the modification.

(c) A person named as trustee who rejects the trust or a modification of the trust is not liable with respect to the rejected trust or modification. *(Stats.1990, c. 79 (A.B.759), § 14, operative July 1, 1991.)*

Law Revision Commission Comments

1990 Enactment

Section 15601 continues Section 15601 of the repealed Probate Code without change. Section 15601 is drawn from the Indiana Trust Code. See Ind.Code Ann. § 30–4–2–2(c) (West 1979).

Under this section, a trustee may reject new duties without having to resign as trustee. However, if a modification is rejected, the trustee remains subject to the duties and liabilities under the trust as it existed before the modification. The provision in subdivision (c) that a trustee who rejects the trust is not liable is consistent with Sections 16000 (duty to administer trust upon acceptance) and 16400 (violation of duty is breach of trust). See also Sections 15660 (appointment of trustee to fill vacancy), 17200(b)(10) (petition to appoint trustee).

The appropriate recipient of the written rejection depends upon the circumstances of the case. Ordinarily, it would be appropriate to give the rejection to the person who informs the person of the proposed trusteeship. If proceedings involving the trust are pending, the rejection could be filed with the court clerk. In the case of a person named as trustee of a revocable living trust, it would be appropriate to give the rejection to the settlor. In any case it would be best to give notice of rejection to a beneficiary with a present interest in the trust since the beneficiary would be motivated to seek appointment of a new trustee.

Background on Section 15601 of Repealed Code

Section 15601 was a new provision added by 1986 Cal.Stat. ch. 820 § 40. The section superseded former Probate Code Section 1124 (repealed by 1986 Cal.Stat. ch. 820 § 31) which provided for rejection of certain testamentary trusts by filing a writing with the court clerk. For background on the provisions of this division, see the Comment to this division under the division heading. [20 Cal.L.Rev.Comm.Reports 1001 (1990)].

§ 15602. Trustee's bond

(a) A trustee is not required to give a bond to secure performance of the trustee's duties, unless any of the following circumstances occurs:

(1) A bond is required by the trust instrument.

(2) Notwithstanding a waiver of a bond in the trust instrument, a bond is found by the court to be necessary to protect the interests of beneficiaries or other persons having an interest in the trust.

(3) An individual who is not named as a trustee in the trust instrument is appointed as a trustee by the court.

(b) Notwithstanding paragraphs (1) and (3) of subdivision (a), the court may excuse a requirement of a bond, reduce or increase the amount of a bond, release a surety, or permit the substitution of another bond with the same or different sureties. The court may not, however, excuse the requirement of a bond for an individual described in paragraph (3) of subdivision (a), except under compelling circumstances. For the purposes of this section, a request by all the adult beneficiaries of a trust that bond be waived for an individual described in paragraph (3) of subdivision (a) for their trust is deemed to constitute a compelling circumstance.

(c) If a bond is required, it shall be filed or served and shall be in the amount and with sureties and liabilities ordered by the court.

(d) Except as otherwise provided in the trust instrument or ordered by the court, the cost of the bond shall be charged against the trust.

(e) A trust company may not be required to give a bond, notwithstanding a contrary provision in the trust instrument. *(Stats.1990, c. 79 (A.B.759), § 14, operative July 1, 1991. Amended by Stats.2004, c. 75 (A.B.1883), § 1.)*

Law Revision Commission Comments
1990 Enactment

Section 15602 continues Section 15602 of the repealed Probate Code without change.

Subdivisions (a)–(c) are drawn from Section 7–304 of the Uniform Probate Code (1987). As to the construction of provisions drawn from uniform acts, see Section 2. A nonprofit or charitable corporation that acts as trustee under a charitable trust is not a trust company, as defined in Section 83, and thus is subject to the provisions of paragraphs (1) and (2) of subdivision (a) of Section 15602 relating to when a bond is required. A bond is required if the trust instrument requires it (subject to the court's power to excuse the bond) or if the bond is found by the court to be necessary to protect the interests of beneficiaries. But a bond is not required of a nonprofit or charitable corporation that is appointed as trustee under a charitable trust merely because the corporation is not named as a trustee in the trust instrument. For provisions relating to nonprofit or charitable corporations acting as trustees, see, e.g., Corp.Code §§ 5140(k) (power of nonprofit public benefit corporation to act as trustee), 7140(k) (power of nonprofit mutual benefit corporation to act as trustee), 9140(k) (power of nonprofit religious corporation to act as trustee); Gov't Code § 12582.1 ("charitable corporation" defined for purposes of Uniform Supervision of Trustees for Charitable Purposes Act).

Subdivision (e) makes clear that a trust company may not be required to give a bond. See Section 83 ("trust company" defined).

For general provisions relating to petitions and other papers, see Sections 1020–1023, 17201; see also Sections 1021 (petition to be verified), 1041 (clerk to set petition for hearing). For general provisions relating to notice of hearing, see Sections 1200–1221, 15802–15804, 17100–17105, 17203–17205; see also Sections 1260–1265 (proof of giving notice). For general provisions relating to hearings and orders, see Sections 1040–1050, 17000–17006, 17201–17202, 17206–17207.

Background on Section 15602 of Repealed Code

Section 15602 was added by 1986 Cal.Stat. ch. 820 § 40. For background on the provisions of this division, see the Comment to this division under the division heading.

Subdivision (a)(3) restated part of former Probate Code Section 1127 (repealed by 1986 Cal.Stat. ch. 820 § 31) without substantive change, except that subdivision (a)(3) applies only to an individual

trustee who is not named or nominated as an original or successor trustee in the trust instrument. See also Sections 15643 (vacancy in office of trustee), 15660 (appointment of trustee to fill vacancy). In other respects, Section 15602 superseded former Probate Code Section 1127 (bond of trustee named by court) and former Probate Code Section 1127.5 (exception for substitute or successor trustee that is charitable corporation) (provisions repealed by 1986 Cal.Stat. ch. 820 § 31). Subdivision (d) superseded the second sentence of former Probate Code Section 1127 (repealed by 1986 Cal.Stat. ch. 820 § 31).

Subdivision (e) restated part of former Probate Code Sections 480 and 481 (provisions repealed by 1988 Cal.Stat. ch. 1199 § 47) without substantive change. [20 Cal.L.Rev.Comm.Reports 1001 (1990)].

Cross References

Official bonds, see Government Code § 1450 et seq.
Transfer of trust from another jurisdiction, requirement of bond, see Probate Code § 17455.

§ 15603. Certificate of trustee

On application by the trustee, the court clerk shall issue a certificate that the trustee is a duly appointed and acting trustee under the trust if the court file shows the incumbency of the trustee. *(Stats.1990, c. 79 (A.B.759), § 14, operative July 1, 1991.)*

Law Revision Commission Comments
1990 Enactment

Section 15603 continues Section 15603 of the repealed Probate Code without change.

Background on Section 15603 of Repealed Code

Section 15603 was added by 1986 Cal.Stat. ch. 820 § 40. The section restated former Probate Code Section 1130.1 (repealed by 1986 Cal.Stat. ch. 820 § 31) without substantive change and expanded the former provision to cover living trusts. For background on the provisions of this division, see the Comment to this division under the division heading. [20 Cal.L.Rev.Comm.Reports 1001 (1990)].

§ 15604. Nonprofit charitable corporation as trustee

(a) Notwithstanding any other provision of law, a nonprofit charitable corporation may be appointed as trustee of a trust created pursuant to this division, if all of the following conditions are met:

(1) The corporation is incorporated in this state.

(2) The articles of incorporation specifically authorize the corporation to accept appointments as trustee.

(3) For the three years prior to the filing of a petition under this section, the nonprofit charitable corporation has been exempt from payment of income taxes pursuant to Section 501(c)(3) of the Internal Revenue Code and has served as a private professional conservator in the state.

(4) The settlor or an existing trustee consents to the appointment of the nonprofit corporation as trustee or successor trustee, either in the petition or in a writing signed either before or after the petition is filed.

(5) The court determines the trust to be in the best interest of the settlor.

(6) The court determines that the appointment of the nonprofit corporation as trustee is in the best interest of the settlor and the trust estate.

(b) A petition for appointment of a nonprofit corporation as trustee under this section may be filed by any of the following:

(1) The settlor or the spouse of the settlor.

(2) The nonprofit charitable corporation.

(3) An existing trustee.

(c) The petition shall include in the caption the name of a responsible corporate officer who shall act for the corporation for purposes of this section. If, for any reason, the officer so named ceases to act as the responsible corporate officer for purposes of this section, the corporation shall file with the court a notice containing (1) the name of the successor responsible corporate officer and (2) the date the successor becomes the responsible corporate officer.

(d) The petition shall request that a trustee be appointed for the estate, shall specify the name, address, and telephone number of the proposed trustee and the name, address, and telephone number of the settlor or proposed settlor, and state the reasons why the appointment of the trustee is necessary.

(e) The petition shall set forth, so far as the information is known to the petitioner, the names and addresses of all persons entitled to notice of a conservatorship petition, as specified in subdivision (b) of Section 1821.

(f) Notice of the hearing on the petition shall be given in the same manner as provided in Sections 1822 and 1824.

(g) The trustee appointed by the court pursuant to this section shall do all of the following:

(1) File the required bond for the benefit of the trust estate in the same manner provided for conservators of the estate as set forth in Section 2320. This bond may not be waived, but the court may, in its discretion, permit the filing of a bond in an amount less than would otherwise be required under Section 2320.

(2) Comply with the requirements for registration and filing of annual statements pursuant to Article 4 (commencing with Section 2340) of Chapter 4 of Part 4 of Division 4.

(3) File with the court inventories and appraisals of the trust estate and present its accounts of the trust estate in the manner provided for conservators of the estate set forth in Chapter 7 (commencing with Section 2600) of Part 4 of Division 4.

(4) Be reimbursed for expenses and compensated as trustee in the manner provided for conservators of the estate as described in Chapter 8 (commencing with Section 2640) of Part 4 of Division 4. However, compensation as trustee appointed under this section shall be allowed only for services actually rendered.

(5) Be represented by counsel in all proceedings before the court. Any fee allowed for an attorney for the nonprofit charitable corporation shall be for services actually rendered.

(h) The trustee appointed by the court under this section may be removed by the court, or may resign in accordance with Chapter 9 (commencing with Section 2650) of Part 4 of Division 4. If the nonprofit charitable corporation resigns or is removed by the court, the settlor may appoint another person as successor trustee, or another nonprofit charitable corporation as trustee under this section.

(i) The trustee appointed by the court under this section is bound by the trust instrument created by the settlor, and shall be subject to the duties and responsibilities of a trustee as provided in this code. *(Added by Stats.1999, c. 424 (S.B. 1090), § 1. Amended by Stats.2001, c. 351 (A.B.479), § 2.)*

ARTICLE 2. COTRUSTEES

Application

Application of Division, see Probate Code § 15001.

Cross References

Common law rules governing trusts, application, see Probate Code § 15002.
Relationships excluded from Code definition of trust, application of this division, see Probate Code § 15003.

§ 15620. Actions by cotrustees

Unless otherwise provided in the trust instrument, a power vested in two or more trustees may only be exercised by their unanimous action. *(Stats.1990, c. 79 (A.B.759), § 14, operative July 1, 1991.)*

Law Revision Commission Comments

1990 Enactment

Section 15620 continues Section 15620 of the repealed Probate Code without change. See also Section 16402 (trustee's liability to beneficiary for acts of cotrustee).

Background on Section 15620 of Repealed Code

Section 15620 was added by 1986 Cal.Stat. ch. 820 § 40. The section restated former Civil Code Section 2268 (repealed by 1986 Cal.Stat. ch. 820 § 7) without substantive change and superseded the first part of former Civil Code Section 860 (repealed by 1986 Cal.Stat. ch. 820 § 5). Section 15620 also superseded the part of former Civil Code Section 2240 (repealed by 1986 Cal.Stat. ch. 820 § 7) relating to consent by cotrustees as to deposit of securities in a securities depository. For background on the provisions of this division, see the comment to this division under the division heading. [20 Cal.L.Rev.Comm.Reports 1001 (1990)].

Cross References

Joint authority, construction, see Civil Code § 12.
Joint personal representatives, validity of acts of majority, see Probate Code § 9630.
Liability of cotrustees for acts of others, see Probate Code § 16402.

§ 15621. Vacancy in office

Unless otherwise provided in the trust instrument, if a vacancy occurs in the office of a cotrustee, the remaining cotrustee or cotrustees may act for the trust as if they are the only trustees. *(Stats.1990, c. 79 (A.B.759), § 14, operative July 1, 1991.)*

Law Revision Commission Comments

1990 Enactment

Section 15621 continues Section 15621 of the repealed Probate Code without change. Under this section, a vacancy in the office of a cotrustee is disregarded in the operation of the trust so long as there is at least one trustee remaining. If the trust provides for majority rule, the remaining trustees act by majority vote of their number, even though the number of trustees constituting a majority is now less than before the vacancy occurred. In effect, the vacant positions are not counted in determining a quorum or in determining the number constituting a majority. This rule is subject to contrary provision in the trust instrument, as noted in the introductory clause. See also Sections 15643 (vacancy in office of trustee), 15660 (appointment of trustee to fill vacancy).

Background on Section 15621 of Repealed Code

Section 15621 was added by 1986 Cal.Stat. ch. 820 § 40. The section superseded the second part of former Civil Code Section 860 (repealed by 1986 Cal.Stat. ch. 820 § 5) and former Civil Code Section 2288 (repealed by 1986 Cal.Stat. ch. 820 § 7). For background on the provisions of this division, see the Comment to this division under the division heading. [20 Cal.L.Rev.Comm.Reports 1001 (1990)].

§ 15622. Temporary incapacity

Unless otherwise provided in the trust instrument, if a cotrustee is unavailable to perform the duties of the cotrustee because of absence, illness, or other temporary incapacity, the remaining cotrustee or cotrustees may act for the trust, as if they are the only trustees, where necessary to accomplish the purposes of the trust or to avoid irreparable injury to the trust property. *(Stats.1990, c. 79 (A.B.759), § 14, operative July 1, 1991.)*

Law Revision Commission Comments

1990 Enactment

Section 15622 continues Section 15622 of the repealed Probate Code with a technical, clarifying change. This section deals with the problem that may arise where a cotrustee is temporarily unable to fulfill its duties but the office of trustee is not vacant as under Section 15621. See also Section 17200(b)(2) (court determination of existence or nonexistence of power, duty, or right), (b)(6) (court instructions to trustee).

Background on Section 15622 of Repealed Code

Section 15622 is a new provision added by 1986 Cal.Stat. ch. 820 § 40. For background on the provisions of this division, see the Comment to this division under the division heading. [20 Cal.L.Rev.Comm.Reports 1001 (1990)].

ARTICLE 3. RESIGNATION AND REMOVAL OF TRUSTEES

Application

Application of Division, see Probate Code § 15001.

Cross References

Common law rules governing trusts, application, see Probate Code § 15002.

Relationships excluded from Code definition of trust, application of this division, see Probate Code § 15003.

§ 15640. Resignation

A trustee who has accepted the trust may resign only by one of the following methods:

(a) As provided in the trust instrument.

(b) In the case of a revocable trust, with the consent of the person holding the power to revoke the trust.

(c) In the case of a trust that is not revocable, with the consent of all adult beneficiaries who are receiving or are entitled to receive income under the trust or to receive a distribution of principal if the trust were terminated at the time consent is sought. If a beneficiary has a conservator, the conservator may consent to the trustee's resignation on behalf of the conservatee without obtaining court approval. Without limiting the power of the beneficiary to consent to the trustee's resignation, if the beneficiary has designated an attorney in fact who has the power under the power of attorney to consent to the trustee's resignation, the attorney in fact may consent to the resignation.

(d) Pursuant to a court order obtained on petition by the trustee under Section 17200. The court shall accept the trustee's resignation and may make any orders necessary for the preservation of the trust property, including the appointment of a receiver or a temporary trustee. *(Stats.1990, c. 79 (A.B.759), § 14, operative July 1, 1991.)*

Law Revision Commission Comments

1990 Enactment

Section 15640 continues Section 15640 of the repealed Probate Code with the following revisions:

(1) The section has been revised to make clear that court approval is not required to accomplish a resignation except under subdivision (d). This revision made explicit what was implicit under former law.

(2) The last two sentences have been added to subdivision (c) for consistency with Section 15660(c) (appointment of trustee to fill vacancy) and to make clear that a conservator may consent to the resignation without the need to obtain approval of the court in which the conservatorship is pending.

Subdivisions (a), (c), and (d) are similar to Section 106 of the Restatement (Second) of Trusts (1957), except that the class of persons whose consent is needed under subdivision (c) is more restricted. For a provision governing acceptance of the trust, see Section 15600. For provisions relating to consent by beneficiaries who lack capacity, see, e.g., Civil Code §§ 2450, 2467 (statutory form of durable power of attorney); Prob.Code §§ 1003 (guardian ad litem), 2580 (conservator).

Whether court approval is required under subdivision (a) depends on the terms of the trust. Subdivision (b) recognizes that the person holding the power to revoke a revocable trust has control over the trust rather than the beneficiaries. See Section 15800. Under subdivision (d), the court has authority to accept a resignation regardless of whether the trust provides a manner of resignation.

For general provisions relating to petitions and other papers, see Sections 1020–1023, 17201; see also Sections 1021 (petition to be verified), 1041 (clerk to set petition for hearing). For general provisions relating to notice of hearing, see Sections 1200–1221, 15802–15804, 17100–17105, 17203–17205; see also Sections 1260–1265 (proof of giving notice). For general provisions relating to hearings and orders, see Sections 1040–1050, 17000–17006, 17201–17202, 17206–17207. See also Section 17200(b)(11) (petition to accept resignation of trustee).

TRUST LAW

Background on Section 15640 of Repealed Code

Section 15640 was added by 1986 Cal.Stat. ch. 820 § 40. Subdivision (a)(1) continued part of the second sentence of former Probate Code Section 1138.8 (repealed by 1986 Cal.Stat. ch. 820 § 31) without substantive change. Subdivision (a)(3) superseded former Civil Code Section 2282(d) (repealed by 1986 Cal.Stat. ch. 820 § 7) which permitted discharge from the trust with the consent of "the beneficiary, if the beneficiary has capacity to contract."

Subdivision (a)(4) restated authority of the court under prior law. See former Civil Code §§ 2282(e), 2283 (provisions repealed by 1986 Cal.Stat. ch. 820 § 7); former Prob.Code §§ 1125.1, 1138.1(a)(9) (provisions repealed by 1986 Cal.Stat. ch. 820 § 31). Under subdivision (a)(4), the court had authority to accept a resignation regardless of whether the trust provides a manner of resignation. Former Probate Code Section 1138.8 permitted the court to act where the trust was silent.

The provision in subdivision (b) that the trustee's resignation shall be accepted by the court restated part of the fifth sentence of former Probate Code Section 1125.1 and part of the third sentence of former Probate Code Section 1138.8 (provisions repealed by 1986 Cal.Stat. ch. 820 § 31). The authority in subdivision (b) for protective orders restated part of the last sentence of the first paragraph of former Probate Code Section 1125.1 and part of the third sentence of former Probate Code Section 1138.8 (provisions repealed by 1986 Cal.Stat. ch. 820 § 31). See also Section 17206 (general authority to make necessary orders).

For background on the provisions of this division, see the Comment to this division under the division heading. For background on the 1990 revision of this section, see Recommendation Relating to Trustees' Fees, 20 Cal.L.Revision Comm'n Reports 185 (1990). [20 Cal.L.Rev.Comm.Reports 1001 (1990)].

Succession or appointment of trustees, see Probate Code § 15660.

§ 15641. Liability of resigning trustee

The liability for acts or omissions of a resigning trustee or of the sureties on the trustee's bond, if any, is not released or affected in any manner by the trustee's resignation. *(Stats. 1990, c. 79 (A.B.759), § 14, operative July 1, 1991.)*

Law Revision Commission Comments

Section 15641 continues Section 15641 of the repealed Probate Code without change. See also Sections 16460 (limitations on proceedings against trustee), 16461 (exculpation of trustee).

Background on Section 15641 of Repealed Code

Section 15641 was added by 1986 Cal.Stat. ch. 820 § 40. The section restated the second paragraph of former Probate Code Section 1125.1 and the first part of the last sentence of former Probate Code Section 1138.8 without substantive change (provisions repealed by 1986 Cal.Stat. ch. 820 § 31). Section 15641 also superseded the provisions of former Civil Code Section 2282 (repealed by 1986 Cal.Stat. ch. 820 § 7) relating to discharge of trustees from liability. For background on the provisions of this division, see the Comment to this division under the division heading. [20 Cal.L.Rev.Comm.Reports 1001 (1990)].

§ 15642. Removal of trustee; grounds; costs; surrender of property or suspension of powers

(a) A trustee may be removed in accordance with the trust instrument, by the court on its own motion, or on petition of a settlor, cotrustee, or beneficiary under Section 17200.

(b) The grounds for removal of a trustee by the court include the following:

(1) Where the trustee has committed a breach of the trust.

(2) Where the trustee is insolvent or otherwise unfit to administer the trust.

(3) Where hostility or lack of cooperation among cotrustees impairs the administration of the trust.

(4) Where the trustee fails or declines to act.

(5) Where the trustee's compensation is excessive under the circumstances.

(6) Where the sole trustee is a person described in subdivision (a) of Section 21350 or subdivision (a) of Section 21380, whether or not the person is the transferee of a donative transfer by the transferor, unless, based upon any evidence of the intent of the settlor and all other facts and circumstances, which shall be made known to the court, the court finds that it is consistent with the settlor's intent that the trustee continue to serve and that this intent was not the product of fraud or undue influence. Any waiver by the settlor of this provision is against public policy and shall be void. This paragraph shall not apply to instruments that became irrevocable on or before January 1, 1994. This paragraph shall not apply if any of the following conditions are met:

(A) The settlor is related by blood or marriage to, or is a cohabitant with, any one or more of the trustees, the person who drafted or transcribed the instrument, or the person who caused the instrument to be transcribed.

(B) The instrument is reviewed by an independent attorney who (1) counsels the settlor about the nature of his or her intended trustee designation and (2) signs and delivers to the settlor and the designated trustee a certificate in substantially the following form:

"CERTIFICATE OF INDEPENDENT REVIEW

I, _____, have reviewed
      (attorney's name)
_____ and have counseled my client,
    (name of instrument)
_____, fully and privately on the nature and
    (name of client)
legal effect of the designation as trustee of_____
                                (name of trustee)

contained in that instrument. I am so disassociated from the interest of the person named as trustee as to be in a position to advise my client impartially and confidentially as to the consequences of the designation. On the basis of this counsel, I conclude that the designation of a person who would otherwise be subject to removal under paragraph (6) of subdivision (b) of Section 15642 of the Probate Code is clearly the settlor's intent and that intent is not the product of fraud or undue influence.

_____   _____,"

  (Name of Attorney)   (Date)

This independent review and certification may occur either before or after the instrument has been executed, and if it occurs after the date of execution, the named trustee shall not be subject to removal under this paragraph. Any attorney whose written engagement signed by the client is expressly limited to the preparation of a certificate under this subdivision, including the prior counseling, shall not be considered to otherwise represent the client.

(C) After full disclosure of the relationships of the persons involved, the instrument is approved pursuant to an order under Article 10 (commencing with Section 2580) of Chapter 6 of Part 4 of Division 4.

(7) If, as determined under Part 17 (commencing with Section 810) of Division 2, the trustee is substantially unable to manage the trust's financial resources or is otherwise substantially unable to execute properly the duties of the office. When the trustee holds the power to revoke the trust, substantial inability to manage the trust's financial resources or otherwise execute properly the duties of the office may not be proved solely by isolated incidents of negligence or improvidence.

(8) If the trustee is substantially unable to resist fraud or undue influence. When the trustee holds the power to revoke the trust, substantial inability to resist fraud or undue influence may not be proved solely by isolated incidents of negligence or improvidence.

(9) For other good cause.

(c) If, pursuant to paragraph (6) of subdivision (b), the court finds that the designation of the trustee was not consistent with the intent of the settlor or was the product of fraud or undue influence, the person being removed as trustee shall bear all costs of the proceeding, including reasonable attorney's fees.

(d) If the court finds that the petition for removal of the trustee was filed in bad faith and that removal would be contrary to the settlor's intent, the court may order that the person or persons seeking the removal of the trustee bear all or any part of the costs of the proceeding, including reasonable attorney's fees.

(e) If it appears to the court that trust property or the interests of a beneficiary may suffer loss or injury pending a decision on a petition for removal of a trustee and any appellate review, the court may, on its own motion or on petition of a cotrustee or beneficiary, compel the trustee whose removal is sought to surrender trust property to a cotrustee or to a receiver or temporary trustee. The court may also suspend the powers of the trustee to the extent the court deems necessary.

(f) For purposes of this section, the term "related by blood or marriage" shall include persons within the seventh degree. (Stats.1990, c. 79 (A.B.759), § 14, operative July 1, 1991. Amended by Stats.1993, c. 293 (A.B.21), § 6; Stats.1995, c. 730 (A.B.1466), § 9; Stats.2006, c. 84 (A.B.2042), § 1; Stats.2010, c. 620 (S.B.105), § 3.)

Law Revision Commission Comments
1990 Enactment

Section 15642 continues Section 15642 of the repealed Probate Code with the following revisions:

(1) Subdivision (a) has been revised to give the settlor of an irrevocable living trust the right to petition for removal of a trustee.

(2) New paragraph (5) has been added to subdivision (b)—and former paragraph (5) has been redesignated to be paragraph (6)—to

make clear that a trustee may be removed in the court's discretion where the trustee's compensation is excessive under the circumstances. The addition of new paragraph (5) is a clarification of the law, rather than a new principle. For background on these revisions, see Recommendation Relating to Trustees' Fees, 20 Cal.L.Revision Comm'n Reports 185 (1990).

Subdivision (a) is the same in substance as Section 107 of the Restatement (Second) of Trusts (1957) except that it gives the settlor of an irrevocable living trust the right to petition for removal of a trustee. As to the rights of a settlor of a revocable trust, see Sections 15401 (revocation by settlor), 15402 (modification by settlor of revocable trust), 15800 (rights of person holding power of revocation). The right to petition for removal of a trustee does not give the settlor any other rights, such as the right to an account or to receive information concerning administration of the trust.

The statement of grounds for removal of the trustee by the court is drawn from the Texas Trust Code and the Restatement. See Tex.Prop.Code Ann. § 113.082(a) (Vernon 1984); Restatement (Second) of Trusts § 107 comments b–d (1957). As to the authority to remove as provided in the trust instrument, see Restatement (Second) of Trusts § 107 comment h (1957). If a trustee is removed, another trustee may be appointed to fill the vacancy as provided in Section 15660. See also Section 17206 (general authority to make necessary orders).

For general provisions relating to petitions and other papers, see Sections 1020–1023, 17201; see also Sections 1021 (petition to be verified), 1041 (clerk to set petition for hearing). For general provisions relating to notice of hearing, see Sections 1200–1221, 15802–15804, 17100–17105, 17203–17205; see also Sections 1260–1265 (proof of giving notice). For general provisions relating to hearings and orders, see Sections 1040–1050, 17000–17006, 17201–17202, 17206–17207. See also Section 17200(b)(10) (petition to remove trustee).

2010 Amendment

Section 15642(b)(6) is amended to correct a reference to former Section 21350 and to delete a superfluous word in the certificate form.

Subdivisions (b)(6) and (c) are amended to remove references to menace and duress. The references relate to the presumption of menace, duress, fraud, or undue influence that could arise under former Section 21350. Much of the substance of that provision is continued in Section 21380, but Section 21380 does not provide for a presumption of menace or duress. That change in the law makes the references to menace and duress in this section unnecessary. [38 Cal.L.Rev.Comm. Reports 107 (2008)].

Background on Section 15642 of Repealed Code

Section 15642 was added by 1986 Cal.Stat. ch. 820 § 40. The authority of the court under Section 15642 to remove trustees continued authority found in former law. See former Civil Code §§ 2233, 2283 (provisions repealed by 1986 Cal.Stat. ch. 820 § 7); former Prob.Code §§ 1123.5, 1138.1(a)(10) (Probate Code provisions repealed by 1986 Cal.Stat. ch. 820 § 31). The authority for removal on the court's own motion was drawn from the third sentence of former Probate Code Section 1123.5 (repealed by 1986 Cal.Stat. ch. 820 § 31). Paragraphs (1) and (2) of subdivision (b) of Section 15642 superseded parts of former Civil Code Sections 2233 and 2283 and part of the first sentence of former Probate Code Section 1123.5 (repealed by 1986 Cal.Stat. ch. 820 § 31). The general language relating to a trustee being otherwise unfit to administer the trust subsumed the reference in former Probate Code Section 1126 (repealed by 1986 Cal.Stat. ch. 820 § 31) to a trustee who is incapable of acting. Paragraph (3) of subdivision (b) continued part of the second sentence of former Probate Code Section 1123.5 (repealed by 1986 Cal.Stat. ch. 820 § 31) without substantive change, except that the reference to "ill feeling" was omitted as redundant with "hostility," and the word "continued" was omitted since the test is whether the administration of the trust is impaired. Paragraph (4) of subdivision (b) continued part of the first sentence of former Probate Code Section 1126 and part of the first sentence of former Probate Code Section 1138.9 (provisions repealed by 1986 Cal.Stat. ch. 820 § 31) without substantive change. Paragraph (5) of subdivision (b) continued authority found in former Probate Code Sections 1126 and 1138.9 (provisions repealed by 1986 Cal.Stat. ch. 820 § 31). Subdivision (c) continued former Probate Code Section 1138.2 (repealed by 1986 Cal.Stat. ch. 820 § 31) without substantive change and restated former Probate Code Section 1123.6 (repealed by 1986 Cal.Stat. ch. 820 § 31) without substantive change.

For background on the provisions of this division, see the Comment to this division under the division heading. [20 Cal.L.Rev.Comm.Reports 1001 (1990)].

Cross References

Filling vacancies in office of trustee, see Probate Code § 15660.
Presumption of fraud or undue influence with respect to wills and trusts, enumeration of certain donative transfers subject to the presumption, see Probate Code § 21380.
Prohibited transactions; exceptions, see Probate Code § 16004.
Violation of duties as breach of trust against beneficiary, see Probate Code § 16400.

§ 15643. Vacancies

There is a vacancy in the office of trustee in any of the following circumstances:

(a) The person named as trustee rejects the trust.

(b) The person named as trustee cannot be identified or does not exist.

(c) The trustee resigns or is removed.

(d) The trustee dies.

(e) A conservator or guardian of the person or estate of an individual trustee is appointed.

(f) The trustee is the subject of an order for relief in bankruptcy.

(g) A trust company's charter is revoked or powers are suspended, if the revocation or suspension is to be in effect for a period of 30 days or more.

(h) A receiver is appointed for a trust company if the appointment is not vacated within a period of 30 days. *(Stats.1990, c. 79 (A.B.759), § 14, operative July 1, 1991. Amended by Stats.2009, c. 500 (A.B.1059), § 57.)*

Law Revision Commission Comments
1990 Enactment

Section 15643 continues Section 15643 of the repealed Probate Code without change. For rules concerning filling a vacancy, see Section 15660. See also Sections 83 ("trust company" defined), 15601 (rejection of trust), 15640 (resignation of trustee), 15641 (liability of resigning trustee), 15642 (removal of trustee), 16460 (limitations on proceedings against trustee), 17200(b)(5) (petition to settle trustee's account), 18102 (protection of third person dealing with former trustee).

Background on Section 15643 of Repealed Code

Section 15643 was added by 1986 Cal.Stat. ch. 820 § 40. The section restated the first paragraph, including subdivisions (1) and (2), of former Civil Code Section 2281 (repealed by 1986 Cal.Stat. ch. 820 § 7) without substantive change, except that the reference in former law to discharge of the trustee was omitted as unnecessary. Section 15643 also restated part of the first sentence of former

Probate Code Section 1126 (repealed by 1986 Cal.Stat. ch. 820 § 31) without substantive change and restated part of the first sentence of former Probate Code Section 1138.9 (repealed by 1986 Cal.Stat. ch. 820 § 31) without substantive change. Section 15643 also superseded part of former Civil Code Section 860 (repealed by 1986 Cal.Stat. ch. 820 § 5) to the extent it related to the occurrence of a vacancy in the office of a trustee. For background on the provisions of this division, see the Comment to this division under the division heading. [20 Cal.L.Rev.Comm.Reports 1001 (1990)].

Cross References

Trustees under deeds of trust to secure obligations, application of this section, see Civil Code § 2934b.
Vacancy in office of cotrustee, see Probate Code § 15621.

§ 15644. Former trustees; delivery of property

When a vacancy has occurred in the office of trustee, the former trustee who holds property of the trust shall deliver the trust property to the successor trustee or a person appointed by the court to receive the property and remains responsible for the trust property until it is delivered. A trustee who has resigned or is removed has the powers reasonably necessary under the circumstances to preserve the trust property until it is delivered to the successor trustee and to perform actions necessary to complete the resigning or removed trustee's administration of the trust. *(Stats.1990, c. 79 (A.B.759), § 14, operative July 1, 1991.)*

Law Revision Commission Comments
1990 Enactment

Section 15644 continues Section 15644 of the repealed Probate Code without change. See Section 15643 (vacancy in office of trustee); see also Sections 16420(a)(4) (appointment of receiver or temporary trustee upon breach of trust), 17206 (authority to make necessary orders and appoint temporary trustee).

The second sentence of Section 15644 makes clear that a trustee who has resigned or is removed has the powers needed to complete the trustee's remaining duties. The trustee who has resigned remains liable for actions or omissions during his or her term as trustee even after the property is delivered to the successor until liability is barred. See Section 16460 (limitations on proceedings against trustee).

Background on Section 15644 of Repealed Code

Section 15644 was added by 1986 Cal.Stat. ch. 820 § 40. The first sentence of the section restated part of the fifth sentence of former Probate Code Section 1125.1 and part of the last sentence of former Probate Code Section 1138.8 (provisions repealed by 1986 Cal.Stat. ch. 820 § 31) without substantive change. For background on the provisions of this division, see the Comment to this division under the division heading. [20 Cal.L.Rev.Comm.Reports 1001 (1990)].

§ 15645. Nonrevocable trusts; trustee's refusal to transfer administration of trust

If the trustee of a trust that is not revocable has refused to transfer administration of the trust to a successor trust company on request of the beneficiaries described in subdivision (c) of Section 15640 and the court in subsequent proceedings under Section 17200 makes an order removing the existing trustee and appointing a trust company as successor trustee, the court may, in its discretion, award costs and reasonable attorney's fees incurred by the petitioner in the proceeding to be paid by the trustee or from the trust as ordered by the court. *(Stats.1990, c. 79 (A.B.759), § 14, operative July 1, 1991.)*

1990 Enactment

Section 15645 is a new provision intended to encourage an out of court solution where the beneficiaries of a trust want to transfer administration of the trust to a successor corporate trustee. For provisions concerning consent to transfer of the trust to a successor trust company, see Sections 15640 (resignation of trustee) and 15660 (appointment to fill vacancy in office of trustee). For background on the section, see Recommendation Relating to Trustees' Fees, 20 Cal.L.Revision Comm'n Reports 185 (1990). For background on the provisions of this division, see the Comment to this division under the division heading. [20 Cal.L.Rev.Comm.Reports 1001 (1990)].

ARTICLE 4. APPOINTMENT OF TRUSTEES

Section
15660. Vacancy; appointment.
15660.5. Public guardian or public administrator appointed as trustee by court; requirements.

Application

Application of Division, see Probate Code § 15001.

§ 15660. Vacancy; appointment

(a) If the trust has no trustee or if the trust instrument requires a vacancy in the office of a cotrustee to be filled, the vacancy shall be filled as provided in this section.

(b) If the trust instrument provides a practical method of appointing a trustee or names the person to fill the vacancy, the vacancy shall be filled as provided in the trust instrument.

(c) If the vacancy in the office of trustee is not filled as provided in subdivision (b), the vacancy may be filled by a trust company that has agreed to accept the trust on agreement of all adult beneficiaries who are receiving or are entitled to receive income under the trust or to receive a distribution of principal if the trust were terminated at the time the agreement is made. If a beneficiary has a conservator, the conservator may agree to the successor trustee on behalf of the conservatee without obtaining court approval. Without limiting the power of the beneficiary to agree to the successor trustee, if the beneficiary has designated an attorney in fact who has the power under the power of attorney to agree to the successor trustee, the attorney in fact may agree to the successor trustee.

(d) If the vacancy in the office of trustee is not filled as provided in subdivision (b) or (c), on petition of any interested person or any person named as trustee in the trust instrument, the court may, in its discretion, appoint a trustee to fill the vacancy. If the trust provides for more than one trustee, the court may, in its discretion, appoint the original number or any lesser number of trustees. In selecting a trustee, the court shall give consideration to any nomination by the beneficiaries who are 14 years of age or older. *(Stats.1990, c. 79 (A.B.759), § 14, operative July 1, 1991. Amended by Stats.1992, c. 871 (A.B.2975), § 17.)*

1990 Enactment

Section 15660 continues Section 15660 of the repealed Probate Code with the addition of new subdivision (c) and the redesignation of former subdivision (c) as subdivision (d). For a provision governing the occurrence of vacancies in the office of trustee, see Section 15643.

Subdivision (a) makes clear that the vacancy in the office of a cotrustee must be filled only if the trust so requires. If the vacancy in the office of cotrustee is not filled, the remaining cotrustees may continue to administer the trust under Section 15621, unless the trust instrument provides otherwise.

Subdivision (c) was added to permit a vacancy in the office of trustee to be filled, without the need for court approval, by a trust company selected by agreement of the adult beneficiaries of the trust. For background on subdivision (c), see Recommendation Relating to Trustees' Fees, 20 Cal.L.Revision Comm'n Reports 185 (1990). The persons who must agree to the new trustee under subdivision (c) are the same as those who must consent to a resignation under subdivision (c) of Section 15640. A vacancy may be filled under subdivision (c) whether or not the former trustee was a trust company. If the trustee resigns pursuant to subdivision (c) of Section 15640, the trust may be transferred to a trust company pursuant to subdivision (c) of Section 15660, all without court approval.

Subdivision (d) gives the court discretion to fill a vacancy in a case where the trust does not name a successor who is willing to accept the trust, where the trust does not provide a practical method of appointment, or where the trust does not require the vacancy to be filled. For a limitation on the rights of certain beneficiaries of revocable trusts, see Section 15800.

The provision in subdivision (d) requiring the court to give consideration to the wishes of the beneficiaries is consistent with the Restatement rule. See Restatement (Second) of Trusts § 108 comments d, i (1957).

For general provisions relating to petitions and other papers, see Sections 1020–1023, 17201; see also Sections 1021 (petition to be verified), 1041 (clerk to set petition for hearing). For general provisions relating to notice of hearing, see Sections 1200–1221, 15802–15804, 17100–17105, 17203–17205; see also Sections 1260–1265 (proof of giving notice). For general provisions relating to hearings and orders, see Sections 1040–1050, 17000–17006, 17201–17202, 17206–17207. See also Section 17200(b)(10) (petition to appoint trustee).

Background on Section 15660 of Repealed Code

Section 15660 was added by 1986 Cal.Stat. ch. 820 § 40.

Section 15660 superseded the following provisions:

(1) Former Civil Code Sections 2287 and 2289 (provisions repealed by 1986 Cal.Stat. ch. 820 § 7).

(2) Former Probate Code Sections 1125, 1126, and 1138.9 (provisions repealed by 1986 Cal.Stat. ch. 820 § 31).

The provision in subdivision (b) of Section 15660 relating to a "practical" method of appointing a trustee continued language found in former Civil Code Section 2287 and superseded part of former Probate Code Section 1138.9 (repealed by 1986 Cal.Stat. ch. 820 § 31).

The authority of the court to appoint the same or a lesser number of trustees in subdivision (d) of Section 15660 continued the second sentence of former Civil Code Section 2289 without substantive change. The provision in subdivision (d) requiring the court to give consideration to the wishes of the beneficiaries superseded the second sentence of former Civil Code Section 2287.

For background on the provisions of this division, see the Comment to this division under the division heading. [20 Cal.L.Rev.Comm.Reports 1001 (1990)].

Cross References

Appointment of trustee for minors or incompetents in workers' compensation proceedings, see Labor Code § 5307.5.
Declination of designated testamentary trustee to act; time; nonliability, see Probate Code § 15601.

Orders appointing, instructing and settling accounts of testamentary trustees as appealable, see Probate Code § 7240.

Running of limitation period tolled until appointment of trustee for minors or incompetents in workers' compensation proceedings, see Labor Code § 5408.

§ 15660.5. Public guardian or public administrator appointed as trustee by court; requirements

(a) The court may appoint as trustee of a trust the public guardian or public administrator of the county in which the matter is pending subject to the following requirements:

(1) Neither the public guardian nor the public administrator shall be appointed as trustee unless the court finds, after reasonable inquiry, that no other qualified person is willing to act as trustee or the public guardian, public administrator, or his or her representative consents.

(2) The public administrator shall not be appointed as trustee unless either of the following is true:

(A) At the time of the appointment and pursuant to the terms of the trust, the entire trust is then to be distributed outright. For purposes of this paragraph, a trust that is "then to be distributed outright" does not include a trust pursuant to which payments to, or on behalf of, a beneficiary or beneficiaries are to be made from the trust on an ongoing basis for more than six months after the date of distribution.

(B) The public administrator consents.

(3) Neither the public guardian nor the public administrator shall be appointed as a cotrustee unless the public guardian, public administrator, or his or her representative consents.

(4) Neither the public guardian nor the public administrator shall be appointed as general trustee without a hearing and notice to the public guardian or public administrator, or his or her representative, and other interested persons as provided in Section 17203.

(5) Neither the public guardian nor the public administrator shall be appointed as temporary trustee without receiving notice of hearing as provided in Section 1220. The court shall not waive this notice of hearing, but may shorten the time for notice upon a finding of good cause.

(b)(1) If the public guardian or the public administrator consents to the appointment as trustee under this section, he or she shall submit a written certification of the consent to the court no later than two court days after the noticed hearing date described in paragraph (4) or (5) of subdivision (a). The public administrator shall not be appointed as trustee under subparagraph (A) of paragraph (2) of subdivision (a) if, after receiving notice as required by this section, the public administrator files a written certification with the court that the public administrator is unable to provide the level of services needed to properly fulfill the obligations of a trustee of the trust.

(2) If the public administrator has been appointed as trustee without notice as required in paragraph (4) or (5) of subdivision (a), and the public administrator files a written certification with the court that he or she is unable to provide the level of services needed to properly fulfill the obligations of a trustee of the trust, this shall be good cause for the public administrator to be relieved as trustee.

(c) The order of appointment shall provide for an annual bond fee as described in Section 15688. *(Added by Stats. 2008, c. 237 (A.B.2343), § 5.)*

Cross References

Compensation of expenses, see Probate Code § 15688.

Standard of care, deposits and investments, see Probate Code § 16042.

ARTICLE 5. COMPENSATION AND INDEMNIFICATION OF TRUSTEES

Application

Application of Division, see Probate Code § 15001.

Cross References

Common law rules governing trusts, application, see Probate Code § 15002.

Relationships excluded from Code definition of trust, application of this division, see Probate Code § 15003.

§ 15680. Compensation; variance from terms of trust

(a) Subject to subdivision (b), and except as provided in Section 15688, if the trust instrument provides for the trustee's compensation, the trustee is entitled to be compensated in accordance with the trust instrument.

(b) Upon proper showing, the court may fix or allow greater or lesser compensation than could be allowed under the terms of the trust in any of the following circumstances:

(1) Where the duties of the trustee are substantially different from those contemplated when the trust was created.

(2) Where the compensation in accordance with the terms of the trust would be inequitable or unreasonably low or high.

(3) In extraordinary circumstances calling for equitable relief.

(c) An order fixing or allowing greater or lesser compensation under subdivision (b) applies only prospectively to actions taken in administration of the trust after the order is made. *(Stats.1990, c. 79 (A.B.759), § 14, operative July 1, 1991. Amended by Stats.2008, c. 237 (A.B.2343), § 6.)*

Law Revision Commission Comments
1990 Enactment

Section 15680 continues Section 15680 of the repealed Probate Code without change. See also Sections 15682 (court determination of prospective compensation), 17200(b)(9) (petition to fix compensation). Subdivision (c) makes clear that an order changing the amount of compensation cannot be applied retroactively to actions already taken.

For general provisions relating to petitions and other papers, see Sections 1020–1023, 17201; see also Sections 1021 (petition to be verified), 1041 (clerk to set petition for hearing). For general provisions relating to notice of hearing, see Sections 1200–1221, 15802–15804, 17100–17105, 17203–17205; see also Sections 1260–1265 (proof of giving notice). For general provisions relating to hearings and orders, see Sections 1040–1050, 17000–17006, 17201–17202, 17206–17207.

Background on Section 15680 of Repealed Code

Section 15680 was added by 1986 Cal.Stat. ch. 820 § 40. Subdivision (a) continued the first sentence of former Civil Code Section 2274 (repealed by 1986 Cal.Stat. ch. 820 § 7) without substantive change and restated the first sentence of former Probate Code Section 1122 (repealed by 1986 Cal.Stat. ch. 820 § 31) without substantive change. Subdivision (b) restated the second sentence of former Civil Code Section 2274 and the second sentence of former Probate Code Section 1122 (repealed by 1986 Cal.Stat. ch. 820 § 31) without substantive change, except that subdivision (b) made clear that the court could reduce the trustee's compensation when appropriate. For background on the provisions of this division, see the Comment to this division under the division heading. [20 Cal.L.Rev.Comm.Reports 1001 (1990)].

Cross References

Charitable trusts, enforcement by Attorney General, see Government Code § 12598.
Compensation of trustee for minors or incompetents in workers' compensation proceedings, see Labor Code § 5307.5.
Declaration of trust, see Probate Code §§ 15200, 15207.
Petition by trustee to superior court, grounds, see Probate Code § 16201.
Proceedings concerning trusts, petitions, see Probate Code § 17200.

§ 15681. Compensation not specified

If the trust instrument does not specify the trustee's compensation, the trustee is entitled to reasonable compensation under the circumstances. *(Stats.1990, c. 79 (A.B.759), § 14, operative July 1, 1991.)*

Law Revision Commission Comments

1990 Enactment

Section 15681 continues Section 15681 of the repealed Probate Code without change. The trustee has authority to fix and pay its compensation without the necessity of prior court review. See Section 16243 (power to pay compensation and other expenses). See also Sections 15682 (court determination of prospective compensation), 17200(b)(9) (petition to fix compensation).

Background on Section 15681 of Repealed Code

Section 15681 was added by 1986 Cal.Stat. ch. 820 § 40. The section continued the third sentence of former Civil Code Section 2274 (repealed by 1986 Cal.Stat. ch. 820 § 7) without substantive change and restated part of the third sentence of former Probate Code Section 1122 (repealed by 1986 Cal.Stat. ch. 820 § 31) without substantive change. For background on the provisions of this division, see the Comment to this division under the division heading. [20 Cal.L.Rev.Comm.Reports 1001 (1990)].

§ 15682. Periodic compensation

The court may fix an amount of periodic compensation under Sections 15680 and 15681 to continue for as long as the court determines is proper. *(Stats.1990, c. 79 (A.B.759), § 14, operative July 1, 1991.)*

Law Revision Commission Comments

1990 Enactment

Section 15682 continues Section 15682 of the repealed Probate Code without change. This section makes clear that the court may fix compensation prospectively. See also Section 17200(b)(9) (petition to fix compensation).

Background on Section 15682 of Repealed Code

Section 15682 was added by 1986 Cal.Stat. ch. 820 § 40. The section superseded the last part of the third sentence of former Probate Code Section 1122 (repealed by 1986 Cal.Stat. ch. 820 § 31). For background on the provisions of this division, see the Comment to this division under the division heading. [20 Cal.L.Rev.Comm.Reports 1001 (1990)].

§ 15683. Apportionment among cotrustees

Unless the trust instrument otherwise provides or the trustees otherwise agree, if the trust has two or more trustees, the compensation shall be apportioned among the cotrustees according to the services rendered by them. *(Stats.1990, c. 79 (A.B.759), § 14, operative July 1, 1991.)*

Law Revision Commission Comments

1990 Enactment

Section 15683 continues Section 15683 of the repealed Probate Code without change. See also Section 17200(b)(9) (petition to fix compensation).

Background on Section 15683 of Repealed Code

Section 15683 was added by 1986 Cal.Stat. ch. 820 § 40. The section restated the fourth sentence of former Civil Code Section 2274 (repealed by 1986 Cal.Stat. ch. 820 § 7) and the fourth sentence of former Probate Code Section 1122 (repealed by 1986 Cal.Stat. ch. 820 § 31) without substantive change. For background on the provisions of this division, see the Comment to this division under the division heading. [20 Cal.L.Rev.Comm.Reports 1001 (1990)].

§ 15684. Repayment for expenditures

A trustee is entitled to the repayment out of the trust property for the following:

(a) Expenditures that were properly incurred in the administration of the trust.

(b) To the extent that they benefited the trust, expenditures that were not properly incurred in the administration of the trust. *(Stats.1990, c. 79 (A.B.759), § 14, operative July 1, 1991.)*

Law Revision Commission Comments

1990 Enactment

Section 15684 continues Section 15684 of the repealed Probate Code without change. Under this section, a trustee is not entitled to attorney's fees and expenses of a proceeding where it is determined that the trustee breached the trust, unless the court otherwise orders as provided in subdivision (b). See, e.g., Estate of Gilmaker, 226 Cal.App.2d 658, 663–65, 38 Cal.Rptr. 270 (1964); Estate of Vokal, 121 Cal.App.2d 252, 258–61, 263 P.2d 64 (1953).

Background on Section 15684 of Repealed Code

Section 15684 was added by 1986 Cal.Stat. ch. 820 § 40. The section restated former Civil Code Section 2273 (repealed by 1986 Cal.Stat. ch. 820 § 7) without substantive change and superseded the part of the last sentence of former Probate Code Section 1122 (repealed by 1986 Cal.Stat. ch. 820 § 31) relating to proper expenses and the provisions relating to advancing the trustee's personal funds in subdivision (14) of former Probate Code Section 1120.2 (repealed by 1986 Cal.Stat. ch. 820 § 31). For background on the provisions of this division, see the Comment to this division under the division heading. [20 Cal.L.Rev.Comm.Reports 1001 (1990)].

Cross References

Assessment of trustee under representative designation for property taxation purposes, see Revenue and Taxation Code § 612.

Expenses and compensation of trustees, see Probate Code § 15680.

Fee for filing certificate of trustee respecting trustee assets of alien insurer, see Insurance Code § 1599.

Income tax credits, see Revenue and Taxation Code § 17733.

Payment of costs in action prosecuted or defended by trustee of express trust, see Code of Civil Procedure § 1026.

Payment of federal estate tax and California estate tax from corpus of trust or other temporary interest, without apportionment, see Probate Code § 20113.

Superior Court's discretion to dispense with or limit security required whenever trustee perfects an appeal, see Code of Civil Procedure § 919.

Trustee's bond, allowance for cost, see Probate Code § 15602.

§ 15685. Lien on trust property

The trustee has an equitable lien on the trust property as against the beneficiary in the amount of advances, with any interest, made for the protection of the trust, and for expenses, losses, and liabilities sustained in the administration of the trust or because of ownership or control of any trust property. *(Stats.1990, c. 79 (A.B.759), § 14, operative July 1, 1991.)*

Law Revision Commission Comments
1990 Enactment

Section 15685 continues Section 15685 of the repealed Probate Code without change. This section is the same in substance as part of Section 3(c)(18) of the Uniform Trustees' Powers Act (1964); however, the reference to the equitable nature of the lien is new. As to the construction of provisions drawn from uniform acts, see Section 2. An equitable lien is not good against a transferee of trust property who gives fair consideration for the property without knowledge of the lien. See generally 1 J. Pomeroy, Equity Jurisprudence §§ 165, 171(4) (5th ed. 1941); see also Restatement (Second) of Trusts § 244 comment c (1957). The reference in Section 15685 to liabilities because of ownership or control of trust property involves liability for taxes and assessments on trust property and tort liability arising out of trust property. See also Section 18001 (personal liability of trustee arising out of ownership or control of trust property).

Background on Section 15685 of Repealed Code

Section 15685 was added by 1986 Cal.Stat. ch. 820 § 40. The section restated part of subdivision (14) of former Probate Code Section 1120.2 (repealed by 1986 Cal.Stat. ch. 820 § 31) without substantive change. For background on the provisions of this division, see the Comment to this division under the division heading. [20 Cal.L.Rev.Comm.Reports 1001 (1990)].

§ 15686. Trustee's fee

(a) As used in this section, "trustee's fee" includes, but is not limited to, the trustee's periodic base fee, rate of percentage compensation, minimum fee, hourly rate, and transaction charge, but does not include fees for extraordinary services.

(b) A trustee may not charge an increased trustee's fee for administration of a particular trust unless the trustee first

gives at least 60 days' written notice of that increased fee to all of the following persons:

(1) Each beneficiary who is entitled to an account under Section 16062.

(2) Each beneficiary who was given the last preceding account.

(3) Each beneficiary who has made a written request to the trustee for notice of an increased trustee's fee and has given an address for receiving notice by mail.

(c) If a beneficiary files a petition under Section 17200 for review of the increased trustee's fee or for removal of the trustee and serves a copy of the petition on the trustee before the expiration of the 60-day period, the increased trustee's fee does not take effect as to that trust until otherwise ordered by the court or the petition is dismissed. *(Stats.1990, c. 79 (A.B.759), § 14, operative July 1, 1991. Amended by Stats.1992, c. 178 (S.B.1496), § 43.2.)*

Law Revision Commission Comments
1990 Enactment

Section 15686 is a new provision. For background on the section, see Recommendation Relating to Trustees' Fees, 20 Cal.L.Revision Comm'n Reports 185 (1990). See also Section 16060 (duty of the trustee to keep beneficiaries of trust reasonably informed of the trust and its administration). [20 Cal.L.Rev.Comm.Reports 1001 (1990)].

1992 Amendment

Subdivision (b) of Section 15686 is amended to specify the beneficiaries who are to be given notice of a proposed fee increase. The list of beneficiaries entitled to notice replaces the former standard requiring notice to beneficiaries whose interest may be affected by the fee increase. Under the new standard for giving notice of a fee increase, if a beneficiary is not receiving accounts under the trust (whether required by Section 16062 or given as a matter of practice), the beneficiary will need to give the trustee a written request for notice of a fee increase. Under subdivision (b)(3), it is the responsibility of the person requesting notice to provide an address. The trustee's duty to give notice is satisfied by sending notice to the address supplied by the person requesting the notice.

Subdivision (b) requires notice to be given only to "beneficiaries." Thus, if a person is no longer a beneficiary (as in a case where the person's interest has terminated), subdivision (b) does not require notice of an increased fee to be given the person, even if the person had given the trustee a written request for notice. See also Sections 15802 (notice to person holding power to revoke trust), 15804 (notice in case of future interest). [21 Cal.L.Rev.Comm.Reports 191 (1991)].

§ 15687. Attorney acting as trustee; dual compensation; disclosure

(a) Notwithstanding any provision of a trust to the contrary, a trustee who is an attorney may receive only (1) the trustee's compensation provided in the trust or otherwise provided in this article or (2) compensation for legal services performed for the trustee, unless the trustee obtains approval for the right to dual compensation as provided in subdivision (d).

(b) No parent, child, sibling, or spouse of a person who is a trustee, and no law partnership or corporation whose partner, shareholder, or employee is serving as a trustee shall receive any compensation for legal services performed for the trustee unless the trustee waives trustee compensation or unless the trustee obtains approval for the right to dual compensation as provided in subdivision (d).

(c) This section shall not apply if the trustee is related by blood or marriage to, or is a cohabitant with, the settlor.

(d) After full disclosure of the nature of the compensation and relationship of the trustee to all persons receiving compensation under this section, the trustee may obtain approval for dual compensation by either of the following:

(1) An order pursuant to paragraph (21) of subdivision (b) of Section 17200.

(2) Giving 30 days' advance written notice to the persons entitled to notice under Section 17203. Within that 30–day period, any person entitled to notice may object to the proposed action by written notice to the trustee or by filing a petition pursuant to paragraph (21) of subdivision (b) of Section 17200. If the trustee receives this objection during that 30–day period and if the trustee wishes dual compensation, the trustee shall file a petition for approval pursuant to paragraph (21) of subdivision (b) of Section 17200.

(e) Any waiver of the requirements of this section is against public policy and shall be void.

(f) This section applies to services rendered on or after January 1, 1994. *(Added by Stats.1993, c. 293 (A.B.21), § 6.3. Amended by Stats.1995, c. 730 (A.B.1466), § 10.)*

Cross References
Violation of this section as grounds for discipline, see Business and Professions Code § 6103.6.

§ 15688. Public guardian or public administrator appointed as trustee; compensation; authorized payments

Notwithstanding any other provision of this article and the terms of the trust, a public guardian or public administrator who is appointed as a trustee of a trust pursuant to Section 15660.5 shall be paid from the trust property for all of the following:

(a) Reasonable expenses incurred in the administration of the trust.

(b) Compensation for services of the public guardian or public administrator and the attorney of the public guardian or public administrator, as follows:

(1) If the public guardian or public administrator is appointed as trustee of a trust that provides for the outright distribution of the entire trust estate, compensation for the public guardian or public administrator, and any attorney for the public guardian or public administrator, shall be calculated as that provided to a personal representative and attorney pursuant to Part 7 (commencing with Section 10800) of Division 7, based on the fair market value of the assets as of the date of the appointment, provided that the minimum amount of compensation for the public guardian or the public administrator shall be one thousand dollars ($1,000). Additionally, the minimum amount of compensation for the attorney for the public guardian or the public administrator, if any, shall be one thousand dollars ($1,000).

(2) For a trust other than that described in paragraph (1), the public guardian or public administrator shall be compensated as provided in Section 15680. Compensation shall be consistent with compensation allowed for professional fiduciaries or corporate fiduciaries providing comparable services.

(3) Except as provided in paragraph (1), reasonable compensation for the attorney for the public guardian or public administrator.

(c) An annual bond fee in the amount of twenty-five dollars ($25) plus one-fourth of 1 percent of the amount of the trust assets greater than ten thousand dollars ($10,000). The amount charged shall be deposited in the county treasury. *(Added by Stats.1997, c. 93 (S.B.696), § 3. Amended by Stats.2002, c. 784 (S.B.1316), § 581; Stats.2008, c. 237 (A.B.2343), § 7.)*

Law Revision Commission Comments
2002 Amendment
Subdivision (b) of Section 15688 is amended to reflect elimination of the county clerk's role as ex officio clerk of the superior court. See former Gov't Code § 26800 (county clerk acting as clerk of superior court). The powers, duties, and responsibilities formerly exercised by the county clerk as ex officio clerk of the court are delegated to the court administrative or executive officer, and the county clerk is relieved of those powers, duties, and responsibilities. See Gov't Code §§ 69840 (powers, duties, and responsibilities of clerk of court and deputy clerk of court), 71620 (trial court personnel). [32 Cal.L.Rev. Comm. Reports 526 (2002)].

CHAPTER 2. BENEFICIARIES
Section
15800. Limitations on rights.
15801. Consent.
15802. Notice due beneficiary; person holding power to revoke.
15803. Rights of holder of power of appointment or withdrawal.
15804. Notice; future interest of beneficiary.
15805. Attorney General subject to limitations on beneficiary rights.

Application
Application of Division, see Probate Code § 15001.

Cross References
Common law rules governing trusts, application, see Probate Code § 15002.
Relationships excluded from Code definition of trust, application of this division, see Probate Code § 15003.

§ 15800. Limitations on rights

Except to the extent that the trust instrument otherwise provides or where the joint action of the settlor and all beneficiaries is required, during the time that a trust is revocable and the person holding the power to revoke the trust is competent:

(a) The person holding the power to revoke, and not the beneficiary, has the rights afforded beneficiaries under this division.

(b) The duties of the trustee are owed to the person holding the power to revoke. *(Stats.1990, c. 79 (A.B.759), § 14, operative July 1, 1991.)*

Section 15800 continues Section 15800 of the repealed Probate Code without change. This section has the effect of postponing the enjoyment of rights of beneficiaries of revocable trusts until the death or incompetence of the settlor or other person holding the power to revoke the trust. See also Section 15803 (holder of general power of appointment or power to withdraw property from trust treated as settlor). Section 15800 thus recognizes that the holder of a power of revocation is in control of the trust and should have the right to enforce the trust. See Section 17200 et seq. (judicial proceedings concerning trusts). A corollary principle is that the holder of the power of revocation may direct the actions of the trustee. See Section 16001 (duties of trustee of revocable trust); see also Sections 15401 (method of revocation by settlor), 15402 (power to revoke includes power to modify). Under this section, the duty to inform and account to beneficiaries is owed to the person holding the power to revoke during the time that the trust is presently revocable. See Section 16060 et seq. (trustee's duty to inform and account to beneficiaries). The introductory clause recognizes that the trust instrument may provide rights to beneficiaries of revocable trusts which must be honored until such time as the trust is modified to alter those rights. See Sections 16001 (duties of trustee of revocable trust), 16080–16081 (duties with regard to discretionary trusts). The introductory clause also makes clear that this section does not eliminate the rights of beneficiaries of revocable trusts in situations where the joint action of the settlor and all beneficiaries is required. See Sections 15404 (modification or termination by settlor and all beneficiaries), 15410(b) (disposition of property on termination of trust with consent of settlor and all beneficiaries).

Background on Section 15800 of Repealed Code

Section 15800 was a new provision added by 1986 Cal.Stat. ch. 820 § 40. For background on the provisions of this division, see the Comment to this division under the division heading. [20 Cal.L.Rev.Comm.Reports 1001 (1990)].

Cross References

Duty of trustees of revocable trusts, see Probate Code § 16001.
Exceptions to requirement to provide certain information to beneficiary, see Probate Code § 16069.
Method of revocation by settlor, see Probate Code § 15401.
Revocation power including power to modify trust, see Probate Code § 15402.

§ 15801. Consent

(a) In any case where the consent of a beneficiary may be given or is required to be given before an action may be taken, during the time that a trust is revocable and the person holding the power to revoke the trust is competent, the person holding the power to revoke, and not the beneficiary, has the power to consent or withhold consent.

(b) This section does not apply where the joint consent of the settlor and all beneficiaries is required by statute. *(Stats.1990, c. 79 (A.B.759), § 14, operative July 1, 1991.)*

Law Revision Commission Comments
1990 Enactment

Section 15801 continues Section 15801 of the repealed Probate Code without change.

Subdivision (a) recognizes the principle that the consent of a beneficiary of a revocable trust should not have any effect during the time that the trust is presently revocable, since the power over the trust is held by the settlor or other person holding the power to revoke. See the Comment to Section 15800. See also Section 15803

(holder of general power of appointment or power to withdraw property from trust treated as settlor). Under the rule provided in Section 15801, the consent of the person holding the power to revoke, rather than the beneficiaries, excuses the trustee from liability as provided in Section 16460(a) (limitations on proceedings against trustee). For provisions permitting a trustee to be relieved of liability by the beneficiaries, see Sections 16463 (consent), 16464 (release), 16465 (affirmance).

Subdivision (b) makes clear that this section does not eliminate the requirement of obtaining the consent of beneficiaries in cases where the consent of the settlor and all beneficiaries is required. See Section 15404 (modification or termination by settlor and all beneficiaries).

Background on Section 15801 of Repealed Code

Section 15801 was a new provision added by 1986 Cal.Stat. ch. 820 § 40. For background on the provisions of this division, see the Comment to this division under the division heading. [20 Cal.L.Rev.Comm.Reports 1001 (1990)].

Cross References

Limitation of actions, consent barring claims, see Probate Code § 16460.

§ 15802. Notice due beneficiary; person holding power to revoke

Notwithstanding any other statute, during the time that a trust is revocable and the person holding the power to revoke the trust is competent, a notice that is to be given to a beneficiary shall be given to the person holding the power to revoke and not to the beneficiary. *(Stats.1990, c. 79 (A.B. 759), § 14, operative July 1, 1991.)*

Law Revision Commission Comments
1990 Enactment

Section 15802 continues Section 15802 of the repealed Probate Code without change. This section recognizes that notice to the beneficiary of a revocable trust would be an idle act in the case of a revocable trust since the beneficiary is powerless to act. See Section 15800 (limits on rights of beneficiary of revocable trust). See also Section 15803 (holder of general power of appointment or power to withdraw property from trust treated as settlor). For notice provisions, see Sections 17100–17105, 17203, 17403, 17454.

Background on Section 15802 of Repealed Code

Section 15802 was a new provision added by 1986 Cal.Stat. ch. 820 § 40. For background on the provisions of this division, see the Comment to this division under the division heading. [20 Cal.L.Rev.Comm.Reports 1001 (1990)].

§ 15803. Rights of holder of power of appointment or withdrawal

The holder of a presently exercisable general power of appointment or power to withdraw property from the trust has the rights of a person holding the power to revoke the trust that are provided by Sections 15800 to 15802, inclusive, to the extent of the holder's power over the trust property. *(Stats.1990, c. 79 (A.B.759), § 14, operative July 1, 1991.)*

Law Revision Commission Comments
1990 Enactment

Section 15803 continues Section 15803 of the repealed Probate Code without change. This section makes clear that a holder of a power of appointment or a power of withdrawal is treated as a person holding the power to revoke the trust for purposes of Sections 15800–

15802 in recognition of the fact that the holder of such power is in an equivalent position to control the trust as it relates to the property covered by the power.

Background on Section 15803 of Repealed Code

Section 15803 was a new provision added by 1986 Cal.Stat. ch. 820 § 40 and amended by 1987 Cal.Stat. ch. 128 § 11. For background on the provisions of this division, see the Comment to this division under the division heading. [20 Cal.L.Rev.Comm.Reports 1001 (1990)].

Cross References

Powers of appointment, generally, see Probate Code § 600 et seq.

§ 15804. Notice; future interest of beneficiary

(a) Subject to subdivisions (b) and (c), it is sufficient compliance with a requirement in this division that notice be given to a beneficiary, or to a person interested in the trust, if notice is given as follows:

(1) Where an interest has been limited on any future contingency to persons who will compose a certain class upon the happening of a certain event without further limitation, notice shall be given to the persons in being who would constitute the class if the event had happened immediately before the commencement of the proceeding or if there is no proceeding, if the event had happened immediately before notice is given.

(2) Where an interest has been limited to a living person and the same interest, or a share therein, has been further limited upon the happening of a future event to the surviving spouse or to persons who are or may be the distributees, heirs, issue, or other kindred of the living person, notice shall be given to the living person.

(3) Where an interest has been limited upon the happening of any future event to a person, or a class of persons, or both, and the interest, or a share of the interest, has been further limited upon the happening of an additional future event to another person, or a class of persons, or both, notice shall be given to the person or persons in being who would take the interest upon the happening of the first of these events.

(b) If a conflict of interest involving the subject matter of the trust proceeding exists between a person to whom notice is required to be given and a person to whom notice is not otherwise required to be given under subdivision (a), notice shall also be given to persons not otherwise entitled to notice under subdivision (a) with respect to whom the conflict of interest exists.

(c) Nothing in this section affects any of the following:

(1) Requirements for notice to a person who has requested special notice, a person who has filed notice of appearance, or a particular person or entity required by statute to be given notice.

(2) Availability of a guardian ad litem pursuant to Section 1003.

(d) As used in this section, "notice" includes other papers. *(Stats.1990, c. 79 (A.B.759), § 14, operative July 1, 1991. Amended by Stats.1992, c. 178 (S.B.1496), § 43.4.)*

Law Revision Commission Comments

1990 Enactment

Section 15804 continues Section 15804 of the repealed Probate Code without change. For provisions where this section applies, see Sections 17203 (notice of hearing on petitions generally), 17351 (provisions for removal of certain testamentary trusts from continuing jurisdiction), 17403 (notice of petition for transfer to another jurisdiction), 17454 (notice of petition for transfer to California). See Section 17204 (request for special notice). See also Section 24 ("beneficiary" defined).

1992 Amendment

Subdivision (a)(1) of Section 15804 is amended to clarify its application to notices given under this division outside of judicial proceedings. See, e.g., Section 15686 (notice of trustee's fee).

Subdivision (d) has been added to make clear that other papers, such as accounts to beneficiaries under Section 16062, are covered by the rules governing notice in this section. [21 Cal.L.Rev.Comm.Reports 191 (1991)].

Background on Section 15804 of Repealed Code

Section 15804 was added by 1986 Cal.Stat. ch. 820 § 40 and was amended by 1988 Cal.Stat. ch. 1199 § 105.3. Subdivision (a) restated former Probate Code Section 1215.1 (repealed by 1986 Cal.Stat. ch. 820 § 35) without substantive change. Subdivision (b) restated former Probate Code Section 1215.2 (repealed by 1986 Cal.Stat. ch. 820 § 35) without substantive change. Subdivision (c) restated the first sentence of former Probate Code Section 1215.4 (repealed by 1986 Cal.Stat. ch. 820 § 35) without substantive change. The 1988 amendment corrected a cross-reference. For background on the provisions of this division, see the Comment to this division under the division heading. [20 Cal.L.Rev.Comm.Reports 1001 (1990)].

§ 15805. Attorney General subject to limitations on beneficiary rights

Notwithstanding any other provision of law, the Attorney General is subject to the limitations on the rights of beneficiaries of revocable trusts provided by Sections 15800 to 15802, inclusive. *(Stats.1990, c. 79 (A.B.759), § 14, operative July 1, 1991.)*

Law Revision Commission Comments

1990 Enactment

Section 15805 continues Section 15805 of the repealed Probate Code without change. This section makes clear that the Attorney General is treated the same as a beneficiary of a revocable living trust for purposes of the provisions limiting such beneficiaries' rights. This section is consistent with Section 24 which defines beneficiary to include any person entitled to enforce a charitable trust, taking into account the provision of Section 15800 that beneficiaries of revocable trusts do not have the rights normally afforded beneficiaries so long as the charitable trust is revocable and the person holding the power to revoke remains competent. This section recognizes that the Attorney General's rights to receive notice under Section 17203(c) and to petition under Section 17210 are limited just as in the case of individual beneficiaries.

Background on Section 15805 of Repealed Code

Section 15805 was a new provision added by 1987 Cal.Stat. ch. 128 § 12. For background on the provisions of this division, see the Comment to this division under the division heading. [20 Cal.L.Rev.Comm.Reports 1001 (1990)].

Part 4

TRUST ADMINISTRATION

Application

Application of Division, see Probate Code § 15001.

CHAPTER 1. DUTIES OF TRUSTEES

Application

Application of Division, see Probate Code § 15001.

Cross References

Common law rules governing trusts, application, see Probate Code § 15002.
Relationships excluded from Code definition of trust, application of this Division, see Probate Code § 15003.

ARTICLE 1. TRUSTEE'S DUTIES IN GENERAL

Application

Application of Division, see Probate Code § 15001.

Cross References

Applicability, directors of a corporation, see Corporations Code § 9240.
Authorized investments, cemetery endowments, see Health and Safety Code § 8751.1.
Breach of trust, liability of trustee, see Probate Code § 16400 et seq.
Common law rules governing trusts, application, see Probate Code § 15002.
Duties and liabilities, director of a corporation, see Corporations Code § 7230.
Duties of trustees, directors of a corporation, see Corporations Code § 5230.
Relationships excluded from Code definition of trust, application of this Division, see Probate Code § 15003.
Trustees report requirements, cemeteries, see Health and Safety Code § 8731.

§ 16000. Duty to administer trust

On acceptance of the trust, the trustee has a duty to administer the trust according to the trust instrument and, except to the extent the trust instrument provides otherwise, according to this division. *(Stats.1990, c. 79 (A.B.759), § 14, operative July 1, 1991.)*

Law Revision Commission Comments

1990 Enactment [Revised Comment]

Section 16000 continues Section 16000 of the repealed Probate Code without change. This section is drawn in part from Sections 164 and 169 of the Restatement (Second) of Trusts (1957). See also Sections 15600 (acceptance of trust by trustee), 15800 (duties owed to person holding power to revoke), 15803 (duties owed to person with general power of appointment or power to withdraw trust property), 16001 (duties of trustee of revocable trust), 16040 (trustee's general standard of care in performing duties), 16046 (prudent investor rule), 16047 (standard of care, portfolio strategy, risk and return objectives), 16049 (duties at inception of trusteeship). For provisions permitting the beneficiaries to relieve the trustee from liability, see Sections 16463 (consent), 16464 (release), 16465 (affirmance). [25 Cal.L.Rev.Comm. Reports 673 (1995)].

Background on Section 16000 of Repealed Code

Section 16000 was added by 1986 Cal.Stat. ch. 820 § 40. The section restated the part of former Civil Code Section 2258 (repealed by 1986 Cal.Stat. ch. 820 § 7) requiring the trustee to "fulfill the purpose of the trust" and also superseded former Civil Code Section 2253 (repealed by 1986 Cal.Stat. ch. 820 § 7) insofar as it related to control of the trustee's duties by the trust instrument. For background on the provisions of this division, see the Comment to this division under the division heading. [20 Cal.L.Rev.Comm.Reports 1001 (1990)].

Cross References

Agent's authority not to include violation of statutory duty, see Civil Code § 2322.
Applicability, directors of a corporation, see Corporations Code § 9240.
Authorized investments, cemetery endowments, see Health and Safety Code § 8751.1.
Duties and liabilities, director of a corporation, see Corporations Code § 7230.
Duties of trustees, directors of a corporation, see Corporations Code § 5230.
Investment of trust funds, application of this Part, see Financial Code § 1561.
Obligations of trustees, see Probate Code § 16002.

Trustees report requirements, cemeteries, see Health and Safety Code § 8731.

§ 16001. Revocable trusts

(a) Except as provided in subdivision (b), the trustee of a revocable trust shall follow any written direction acceptable to the trustee given from time to time (1) by the person then having the power to revoke the trust or the part thereof with respect to which the direction is given or (2) by the person to whom the settlor delegates the right to direct the trustee.

(b) If a written direction given under subdivision (a) would have the effect of modifying the trust, the trustee has no duty to follow the direction unless it complies with the requirements for modifying the trust. *(Stats.1990, c. 79 (A.B.759), § 14, operative July 1, 1991.)*

Law Revision Commission Comments
1990 Enactment [Revised Comment]

Section 16001 continues Section 16001 of the repealed Probate Code without change. The qualification in subdivision (a) that a direction be acceptable to the trustee does not mean that the trustee is required to determine the propriety of the direction. For the rule protecting the trustee from liability for following directions under this section, see Section 16462. See also Sections 15800 (duties owed to person holding power to revoke), 16000 (duties subject to control in trust instrument), 16040 (trustee's general standard of care in performing duties), 16046 (prudent investor rule), 16047 (standard of care, portfolio strategy, risk and return objectives).

Subdivision (b) clarifies the relationship between the duty to follow directions provided in subdivision (a) and the rules governing modification of trusts. See Sections 15401 (method of revocation by settlor), 15402 (power to revoke includes power to modify). [25 Cal.L.Rev.Comm. Reports 673 (1995)].

Background on Section 16001 of Repealed Code

Section 16001 was added by 1986 Cal.Stat. ch. 820 § 40. Subdivision (a) continued the first sentence of former Civil Code Section 2258(b) (repealed by 1986 Cal.Stat. ch. 820 § 7) without substantive change. Subdivision (b) was a new provision. For background on the provisions of this division, see the Comment to this division under the division heading. [20 Cal.L.Rev.Comm.Reports 1001 (1990)].

§ 16002. Duty of loyalty

(a) The trustee has a duty to administer the trust solely in the interest of the beneficiaries.

(b) It is not a violation of the duty provided in subdivision (a) for a trustee who administers two trusts to sell, exchange, or participate in the sale or exchange of trust property between the trusts, if both of the following requirements are met:

(1) The sale or exchange is fair and reasonable with respect to the beneficiaries of both trusts.

(2) The trustee gives to the beneficiaries of both trusts notice of all material facts related to the sale or exchange that the trustee knows or should know. *(Stats.1990, c. 79 (A.B.759), § 14, operative July 1, 1991.)*

Law Revision Commission Comments
1990 Enactment [Revised Comment]

Section 16002 continues Section 16002 of the repealed Probate Code without change. Subdivision (a) codifies the substance of Section 170(1) of the Restatement (Second) of Trusts (1957). Subdivision (a) is also included within the Uniform Prudent Investor

Act (1994). See Section 16045 & Comment. See also Sections 16000 (duties subject to control by trust instrument), 16040 (trustee's general standard of care in performing duties), 16046 (prudent investor rule), 16047 (standard of care, portfolio strategy, risk and return objectives). This article does not attempt to state all aspects of the trustee's duty of loyalty, nor does this article seek to cover all duties that may exist. See Section 15002 (common law as law of state). See also Section 16015 (certain actions not violations of duties). For provisions permitting the beneficiaries to relieve the trustee from liability, see Sections 16463 (consent), 16464 (release), 16465 (affirmance).

Subdivision (b) is drawn from Indiana law. See Ind. Code Ann. § 30–4–3–7(d) (West Supp. 1988). This subdivision permits sales or exchanges between two or more trusts that have the same trustee without running afoul of the duty of loyalty. See Restatement (Second) of Trusts § 170 comment r (1957). Subdivision (b) does not require the trustee to give notice to all beneficiaries of both trusts; for limitations on the need to give notice, see Sections 15802 (notice to beneficiary of revocable trust) and 15804 (notice in case involving future interest of beneficiary). See also Sections 15800 (limits on rights of beneficiary of revocable trust), 15801 (consent of beneficiary of revocable trust). [25 Cal.L.Rev.Comm. Reports 673 (1995)].

Background on Section 16002 of Repealed Code

Section 16002 was added by 1986 Cal.Stat. ch. 820 § 40. The section restated the general duty of loyalty expressed in former Civil Code Sections 2228 (trustee to act in "highest good faith"), 2229 (not to use property for trustee's profit), 2231 (influence not to be used for trustee's advantage), 2232 (trustee not to undertake adverse trust), 2233 (trustee to disclose adverse interest), 2235 (transactions between trustee and beneficiary presumed under undue influence), and 2263 (trustee cannot enforce claim against trust purchased after becoming trustee) (provisions repealed by 1986 Cal.Stat. ch. 820 § 7). Subdivision (b) was a new provision. For background on the provisions of this division, see the Comment to this division under the division heading. [20 Cal.L.Rev.Comm.Reports 1001 (1990)].

Cross References

Authority of agent, violation of duty, see Civil Code § 2322.
Embezzlement by trustee, see Penal Code §§ 504, 506.
Uniform Prudent Investor Act, provisions of this section included, see Probate Code § 16045 et seq.
Violation of duties as breach of trust against beneficiary, see Probate Code § 16400.
Violation of or unfitness to execute trust as warranting removal of trustee, see Probate Code § 15642.

§ 16003. Multiple beneficiaries; impartiality

If a trust has two or more beneficiaries, the trustee has a duty to deal impartially with them and shall act impartially in investing and managing the trust property, taking into account any differing interests of the beneficiaries. *(Stats. 1990, c. 79 (A.B.759), § 14, operative July 1, 1991. Amended by Stats.1995, c. 63 (S.B.222), § 1.)*

Law Revision Commission Comments
1990 Enactment

Section 16003 continues Section 16003 of the repealed Probate Code without change. This section codifies the substance of Section 183 of the Restatement (Second) of Trusts (1957). This section is in accord with prior case law. See Estate of Miller, 107 Cal.App. 438, 290 P. 528 (1930). For provisions permitting the beneficiaries to relieve the trustee from liability, see Sections 16463 (consent), 16464 (release), 16465 (affirmance). See also Sections 16000 (duties subject to control by trust instrument), 16040 (trustee's standard of care in performing duties).

1995 Amendment

Section 16003 is amended to provide additional detail drawn from Section 6 of the Uniform Prudent Investor Act (1994).

This section codifies the substance of Section 183 of the Restatement (Second) of Trusts (1957) and is in accord with prior case law. See Estate of Miller, 107 Cal.App. 438, 290 P. 528 (1930). For provisions permitting the beneficiaries to relieve the trustee from liability, see Sections 16463 (consent), 16464 (release), 16465 (affirmance). See also Sections 16000 (duties subject to control by trust instrument), 16040 (trustee's general standard of care in performing duties), 16046 (prudent investor rule), 16047 (standard of care, portfolio strategy, risk and return objectives). [25 Cal.L.Rev.Comm. Reports 543, 673 (1995)].

Background on Section 16003 of Repealed Code

Section 16003 was a new provision added by 1986 Cal.Stat. ch. 820 § 40. For background on the provisions of this division, see the Comment to this division under the division heading. [20 Cal.L.Rev.Comm.Reports 1001 (1990)].

Cross References

Uniform Prudent Investor Act, provisions of this section included, see Probate Code § 16045 et seq.

§ 16004. Conflicts of interest

(a) The trustee has a duty not to use or deal with trust property for the trustee's own profit or for any other purpose unconnected with the trust, nor to take part in any transaction in which the trustee has an interest adverse to the beneficiary.

(b) The trustee may not enforce any claim against the trust property that the trustee purchased after or in contemplation of appointment as trustee, but the court may allow the trustee to be reimbursed from trust property the amount that the trustee paid in good faith for the claim.

(c) A transaction between the trustee and a beneficiary which occurs during the existence of the trust or while the trustee's influence with the beneficiary remains and by which the trustee obtains an advantage from the beneficiary is presumed to be a violation of the trustee's fiduciary duties. This presumption is a presumption affecting the burden of proof. This subdivision does not apply to the provisions of an agreement between a trustee and a beneficiary relating to the hiring or compensation of the trustee. *(Stats.1990, c. 79 (A.B.759), § 14, operative July 1, 1991.)*

Law Revision Commission Comments

1990 Enactment [Revised Comment]

Section 16004 continues Section 16004 of the repealed Probate Code without change. For provisions permitting the beneficiaries to relieve the trustee from liability, see Sections 16463 (consent), 16464 (release), 16465 (affirmance). See also Sections 16000 (duties subject to control by trust instrument), 16015 (certain actions not violations of duties), 16040 (trustee's general standard of care in performing duties), 16046 (prudent investor rule), 16047 (standard of care, portfolio strategy, risk and return objectives).

The court referred to in subdivision (b) may be the court where the trust is administered, such as where the trustee seeks reimbursement for the claim under Section 17200(b), or the court where enforcement of the claim is sought, such as where the trustee seeks to foreclose a lien or seeks recognition of the claim in proceedings commenced by some other creditor. [25 Cal.L.Rev.Comm. Reports 673 (1995)].

Background on Section 16004 of Repealed Code

Section 16004 was added by 1986 Cal.Stat. ch. 820 § 40. Subdivision (a) restated former Civil Code Section 2229 and part of the introductory provision of former Civil Code Section 2230 (provisions repealed by 1986 Cal.Stat. ch. 820 § 7) without substantive change. Subdivision (b) restated former Civil Code Section 2263 (repealed by 1986 Cal.Stat. ch. 820 § 7) without substantive change. The first sentence of subdivision (c) restated the presumption of former Civil Code Section 2235 (repealed by 1986 Cal.Stat. ch. 820 § 7), but the presumption in Section 16004 was phrased in terms of a violation of the trustee's fiduciary duties, rather than a presumption of insufficient consideration and undue influence. The second sentence relating to the nature of the presumption was consistent with prior case law. See, e.g., McDonald v. Hewlett, 102 Cal.App.2d 680, 687–88, 228 P.2d 83 (1951); see also Evid.Code §§ 605 (presumption affecting burden of proof defined), 606 (effect of presumption affecting burden of proof). The exception to the burden of proof provided in the last sentence of subdivision (c) restated the second sentence of former Civil Code Section 2235 without substantive change. For background on the provisions of this division, see the Comment to this division under the division heading. [20 Cal.L.Rev.Comm.Reports 1001 (1990)].

Cross References

Authority of agent, violation of duty, see Civil Code § 2322.
Burden of proof, generally, see Evidence Code § 500 et seq.
Embezzlement by trustee, see Penal Code §§ 504, 506.
Measure of liability for breach of trust, see Probate Code § 16440.
Presumption of trustee's conveyance of realty when necessary to perfect title, see Evidence Code § 642.
Removal of trustee, grounds, see Probate Code § 15642.
Violation of duties as breach of trust against beneficiary, see Probate Code § 16400.

§ 16004.5. Trustee requiring beneficiary to relieve trustee of liability as condition for making distribution or payment to, or for benefit of, beneficiary; prohibition; trustee's rights

(a) A trustee may not require a beneficiary to relieve the trustee of liability as a condition for making a distribution or payment to, or for the benefit of, the beneficiary, if the distribution or payment is required by the trust instrument.

(b) This section may not be construed as affecting the trustee's right to:

(1) Maintain a reserve for reasonably anticipated expenses, including, but not limited to, taxes, debts, trustee and accounting fees, and costs and expenses of administration.

(2) Seek a voluntary release or discharge of a trustee's liability from the beneficiary.

(3) Require indemnification against a claim by a person or entity, other than a beneficiary referred to in subdivision (a), which may reasonably arise as a result of the distribution.

(4) Withhold any portion of an otherwise required distribution that is reasonably in dispute.

(5) Seek court or beneficiary approval of an accounting of trust activities. *(Added by Stats.2003, c. 585 (A.B.1705), § 1.)*

§ 16005. Adverse trusts

The trustee of one trust has a duty not to knowingly become a trustee of another trust adverse in its nature to the interest of the beneficiary of the first trust, and a duty to eliminate the conflict or resign as trustee when the conflict is discovered. *(Stats.1990, c. 79 (A.B.759), § 14, operative July 1, 1991.)*

Law Revision Commission Comments
1990 Enactment [Revised Comment]

Section 16005 continues Section 16005 of the repealed Probate Code without change. For provisions permitting the beneficiaries to relieve the trustee from liability, see Sections 16463 (consent), 16464 (release), 16465 (affirmance). See also Sections 16000 (duties subject to control by trust instrument), 16040 (trustee's general standard of care in performing duties), 16046 (prudent investor rule), 16047 (standard of care, portfolio strategy, risk and return objectives). [25 Cal.L.Rev.Comm. Reports 673 (1995)].

Background on Section 16005 of Repealed Code

Section 16005 was added by 1986 Cal.Stat. ch. 820 § 40. The section superseded former Civil Code Section 2232 (repealed by 1986 Cal.Stat. ch. 820 § 7). For background on the provisions of this division, see the Comment to this division under the division heading. [20 Cal.L.Rev.Comm.Reports 1001 (1990)].

Cross References

Authority of agent, violation of duty, see Civil Code § 2322.
Violation of duty as breach of trust against beneficiary, see Probate Code § 16400.

§ 16006. Control and preservation of trust property

The trustee has a duty to take reasonable steps under the circumstances to take and keep control of and to preserve the trust property. *(Stats.1990, c. 79 (A.B.759), § 14, operative July 1, 1991.)*

Law Revision Commission Comments
1990 Enactment [Revised Comment]

Section 16006 continues Section 16006 of the repealed Probate Code without change. This section codifies the substance of Sections 175 and 176 of the Restatement (Second) of Trusts (1957). The section is in accord with prior case law. See, e.g., Purdy v. Bank of America Nat'l Tr. & Sav. Ass'n, 2 Cal.2d 298, 302–04, 40 P.2d 481 (1935); Estate of Duffill, 188 Cal. 536, 547, 206 P. 42 (1922); Martin v. Bank of America Nat'l Tr. & Sav. Ass'n, 4 Cal.App.2d 431, 436, 41 P.2d 200 (1935). For provisions permitting the beneficiaries to relieve the trustee from liability, see Sections 16463 (consent), 16464 (release), 16465 (affirmance). See also Sections 16000 (duties subject to control by trust instrument), 16040 (trustee's general standard of care in performing duties), 16046 (prudent investor rule), 16047 (standard of care, portfolio strategy, risk and return objectives). [25 Cal.L.Rev.Comm. Reports 673 (1995)].

Background on Section 16006 of Repealed Code

Section 16006 was a new provision added by 1986 Cal.Stat. ch. 820 § 40. For background on the provisions of this division, see the Comment to this division under the division heading. [20 Cal.L.Rev.Comm.Reports 1001 (1990)].

§ 16007. Productivity of trust property

The trustee has a duty to make the trust property productive under the circumstances and in furtherance of the purposes of the trust. *(Stats.1990, c. 79 (A.B.759), § 14, operative July 1, 1991.)*

Law Revision Commission Comments
1990 Enactment [Revised Comment]

Section 16007 continues Section 16007 of the repealed Probate Code without change. The section codifies the substance of Section 181 of the Restatement (Second) of Trusts (1957). For the trustee's standard of care governing investments and management of trust property, see Section 16047. In appropriate circumstances under Section 16007, property may be made productive by appreciation in value rather than by production of income. If the trust instrument imposes a duty on the trustee to hold property and give possession of it to a beneficiary at a later date, this duty would override the general duty to make the property productive. See Restatement (Second) of Trusts § 181 comment a (1957). Similarly, if a beneficiary has the right under the trust instrument to occupy a home, the trustee would have no duty to make the property productive of income. For provisions permitting the beneficiaries to relieve the trustee from liability, see Sections 16463 (consent), 16464 (release), 16465 (affirmance). See also Sections 16000 (duties subject to control by trust instrument), 16046(b) (prudent investor rule subject to control by trust instrument). [25 Cal.L.Rev.Comm. Reports 673 (1995)].

Background on Section 16007 of Repealed Code

Section 16007 was a new provision added by 1986 Cal.Stat. ch. 820 § 40. For background on the provisions of this division, see the Comment to this division under the division heading. [20 Cal.L.Rev.Comm.Reports 1001 (1990)].

§ 16008. Repealed by Stats.1995, c. 63 (S.B.222), § 2
Law Revision Commission Comments
1995 Repeal

Section 16008 is superseded by the rules in Section 16048 (diversification) and 16049 (duties at inception of trusteeship). [25 Cal.L.Rev.Comm. Reports 673 (1995)].

§ 16009. Separation and identification of trust property

The trustee has a duty to do the following:

(a) To keep the trust property separate from other property not subject to the trust.

(b) To see that the trust property is designated as property of the trust. *(Stats.1990, c. 79 (A.B.759), § 14, operative July 1, 1991.)*

Law Revision Commission Comments
1990 Enactment [Revised Comment]

Section 16009 continues Section 16009 of the repealed Probate Code without change. This section codifies the substance of Section 179 of the Restatement (Second) of Trusts (1957), but the Restatement provision for keeping trust property separate from the trustee's individual property is omitted since it is redundant with subdivision (a). For exceptions to this general duty, see, e.g., Fin. Code §§ 1563 (securities registered in name of nominee), 1564 (Uniform Common Trust Fund Act). For provisions permitting the beneficiaries to relieve the trustee from liability, see Sections 16463 (consent), 16464 (release), 16465 (affirmance). See also Sections 16000 (duties subject to control by trust instrument), 16040 (trustee's general standard of care in performing duties), 16046 (prudent investor rule), 16047 (standard of care, portfolio strategy, risk and return objectives). [25 Cal.L.Rev.Comm. Reports 673 (1995)].

Background on Section 16009 of Repealed Code

Section 16009 was added by 1986 Cal.Stat. ch. 820 § 40. The section superseded the rule against commingling provided in former Civil Code Section 2236 (repealed by 1986 Cal.Stat. ch. 820 § 7). For background on the provisions of this division, see the Comment to this division under the division heading. [20 Cal.L.Rev.Comm.Reports 1001 (1990)].

Cross References

Authority of agent, violation of duty, see Civil Code § 2322.

Measure of liability for breach of trust, see Probate Code § 16440.

Redress of breach by compelling payment of money, see Probate Code § 16420.

Trust funds not to be mingled or used in conduct of bank or trust company business, see Financial Code § 1591.

§ 16010. Enforcement of claims

The trustee has a duty to take reasonable steps to enforce claims that are part of the trust property. *(Stats.1990, c. 79 (A.B.759), § 14, operative July 1, 1991.)*

Law Revision Commission Comments
1990 Enactment [Revised Comment]

Section 16010 continues Section 16010 of the repealed Probate Code without change. This section codifies the substance of Section 177 of the Restatement (Second) of Trusts (1957) and is in accord with prior case law. See Ellig v. Naglee, 9 Cal. 683, 695–96 (1858). Depending upon the circumstances of the case, it might not be reasonable to enforce a claim in view of the likelihood of recovery and the cost of suit and enforcement. For provisions permitting the beneficiaries to relieve the trustee from liability, see Sections 16463 (consent), 16464 (release), 16465 (affirmance). See also Sections 16000 (duties subject to control by trust instrument), 16040 (trustee's general standard of care in performing duties), 16046 (prudent investor rule), 16047 (standard of care, portfolio strategy, risk and return objectives). [25 Cal.L.Rev.Comm. Reports 673 (1995)].

Background on Section 16010 of Repealed Code

Section 16010 was a new provision added by 1986 Cal.Stat. ch. 820 § 40. For background on the provisions of this division, see the Comment to this division under the division heading. [20 Cal.L.Rev.Comm.Reports 1001 (1990)].

§ 16011. Defense of actions

The trustee has a duty to take reasonable steps to defend actions that may result in a loss to the trust. *(Stats.1990, c. 79 (A.B.759), § 14, operative July 1, 1991.)*

Law Revision Commission Comments
1990 Enactment [Revised Comment]

Section 16011 continues Section 16011 of the repealed Probate Code without change. This section codifies the substance of the first part of Section 178 of the Restatement (Second) of Trusts (1957) and is in accord with prior case law. See, e.g., Estate of Duffill, 188 Cal. 536, 554–55, 206 P. 42 (1922). Depending on the circumstances of the case, it might be reasonable to settle an action or suffer a default rather than to defend an action. For provisions permitting the beneficiaries to relieve the trustee from liability, see Sections 16463 (consent), 16464 (release), 16465 (affirmance). See also Sections 16000 (duties subject to control by trust instrument), 16040 (trustee's general standard of care in performing duties), 16046 (prudent investor rule), 16047 (standard of care, portfolio strategy, risk and return objectives). [25 Cal.L.Rev.Comm. Reports 673 (1995)].

Background on Section 16011 of Repealed Code

Section 16011 was a new provision added by 1986 Cal.Stat. ch. 820 § 40. For background on the provisions of this division, see the Comment to this division under the division heading. [20 Cal.L.Rev.Comm.Reports 1001 (1990)].

§ 16012. Delegation of duties; prohibitions; exceptions

(a) The trustee has a duty not to delegate to others the performance of acts that the trustee can reasonably be required personally to perform and may not transfer the office of trustee to another person nor delegate the entire administration of the trust to a cotrustee or other person.

(b) In a case where a trustee has properly delegated a matter to an agent, cotrustee, or other person, the trustee has a duty to exercise general supervision over the person performing the delegated matter.

(c) This section does not apply to investment and management functions under Section 16052. *(Stats.1990, c. 79 (A.B.759), § 14, operative July 1, 1991. Amended by Stats. 1995, c. 63 (S.B.222), § 3.)*

Law Revision Commission Comments
1990 Enactment

Section 16012 continues Section 16012 of the repealed Probate Code without change.

The first part of subdivision (a) codifies the substance of Section 171 of the Restatement (Second) of Trusts (1957). The second part of subdivision (a) codifies the substance of Section 4 of the Uniform Trustees' Powers Act (1964). As to the construction of provisions drawn from uniform acts, see Section 2. The duty not to delegate administration of the trust does not preclude employment of an agent in a proper case. A trust company may delegate matters involved in trust administration to its affiliates. For provisions permitting the beneficiaries to relieve the trustee from liability, see Sections 16463 (consent), 16464 (release), 16465 (affirmance). See also Sections 15620 (actions by cotrustees), 15621 (vacancy in office of cotrustee), 15622 (temporary incapacity of cotrustee), 16000 (duties subject to control by trust instrument), 16040 (trustee's standard of care in performing duties), 16247 (power to hire agents of trust).

Subdivision (b) is drawn from comment k to Section 171 of the Restatement (Second) of Trusts (1957).

1995 Amendment

Section 16012 is amended to recognize the special rule in Section 16052 applicable under the Uniform Prudent Investor Act (1994).

Subdivisions (a) and (b) continue Section 16012 of the repealed Probate Code without change. The first part of subdivision (a) codifies the substance of Section 171 of the Restatement (Second) of Trusts (1957). The second part of subdivision (a) codifies the substance of Section 4 of the Uniform Trustees' Powers Act (1964). As to the construction of provisions drawn from uniform acts, see Section 2. The duty not to delegate administration of the trust does not preclude employment of an agent in a proper case. A trust company may delegate matters involved in trust administration to its affiliates. For provisions permitting the beneficiaries to relieve the trustee from liability, see Sections 16463 (consent), 16464 (release), 16465 (affirmance). See also Sections 15620 (actions by cotrustees), 15621 (vacancy in office of cotrustee), 15622 (temporary incapacity of cotrustee), 16000 (duties subject to control by trust instrument), 16040 (trustee's general standard of care in performing duties), 16247 (power to hire agents of trust).

Subdivision (b) is drawn from comment k to Section 171 of the Restatement (Second) of Trusts (1957). [25 Cal.L.Rev.Comm. Reports 543, 673 (1995)].

Background on Section 16012 of Repealed Code

Section 16012 was a new provision added by 1986 Cal.Stat. ch. 820 § 40. For background on the provisions of this division, see the Comment to this division under the division heading. [20 Cal.L.Rev.Comm.Reports 1001 (1990)].

§ 16013. Cotrustees

If a trust has more than one trustee, each trustee has a duty to do the following:

(a) To participate in the administration of the trust.

(b) To take reasonable steps to prevent a cotrustee from committing a breach of trust or to compel a cotrustee to redress a breach of trust. *(Stats.1990, c. 79 (A.B.759), § 14, operative July 1, 1991.)*

Law Revision Commission Comments

1990 Enactment [Revised Comment]

Section 16013 continues Section 16013 of the repealed Probate Code without change. This section codifies the substance of Section 184 of the Restatement (Second) of Trusts (1957) and is in accord with prior case law. See Bermingham v. Wilcox, 120 Cal. 467, 471–73, 52 P. 822 (1898). For provisions permitting the beneficiaries to relieve the trustee from liability, see Sections 16463 (consent), 16464 (release), 16465 (affirmance). See also Sections 16000 (duties subject to control by trust instrument), 16040 (trustee's general standard of care in performing duties), 16402 (trustee's liability to beneficiary for acts of cotrustee), 16046 (prudent investor rule), 16047 (standard of care, portfolio strategy, risk and return objectives). If one cotrustee is also a settlor under a revocable trust, another cotrustee who is not a settlor has a duty to follow the directions of the settlor-cotrustee pursuant to Section 16001. That duty supersedes the general duty under this section. [25 Cal.L.Rev.Comm. Reports 673 (1995)].

Background on Section 16013 of Repealed Code

Section 16013 was a new provision added by 1986 Cal.Stat. ch. 820 § 40. For background on the provisions of this division, see the Comment to this division under the division heading. [20 Cal.L.Rev.Comm.Reports 1001 (1990)].

Cross References

Liability for acts of co-trustees, see Probate Code § 16402.

§ 16014. Special skills

(a) The trustee has a duty to apply the full extent of the trustee's skills.

(b) If the settlor, in selecting the trustee, has relied on the trustee's representation of having special skills, the trustee is held to the standard of the skills represented. *(Stats.1990, c. 79 (A.B.759), § 14, operative July 1, 1991.)*

Law Revision Commission Comments

1990 Enactment [Revised Comment]

Section 16014 continues Section 16014 of the repealed Probate Code without change. Subdivision (a) codifies a duty set forth in Coberly v. Superior Court, 231 Cal.App.2d 685, 689, 42 Cal.Rptr. 64 (1965).

Subdivision (b) is similar to the last part of Section 7–302 of the Uniform Probate Code (1987) and the last part of Section 174 of the Restatement (Second) of Trusts (1957). As to the construction of provisions drawn from uniform acts, see Section 2. Subdivision (b) does not limit the duty provided in subdivision (a). Thus, the nature of the trustee's representations to the settlor leading up to the selection of the trustee does not affect the trustee's duty to use the full extent of his or her skills.

For provisions permitting the beneficiaries to relieve the trustee from liability, see Sections 16463 (consent), 16464 (release), 16465 (affirmance). See also Sections 16000 (duties subject to control by trust instrument), 16040 (trustee's general standard of care in performing duties), 16046 (prudent investor rule), 16047 (standard of care, portfolio strategy, risk and return objectives). [25 Cal.L.Rev. Comm. Reports 673 (1995)].

Background on Section 16014 of Repealed Code

Section 16014 was a new provision added by 1986 Cal.Stat. ch. 820 § 40. For background on the provisions of this division, see the Comment to this division under the division heading. [20 Cal.L.Rev.Comm.Reports 1001 (1990)].

§ 16015. Provision of services in ordinary course of business

The provision of services for compensation by a regulated financial institution or its affiliates in the ordinary course of business either to a trust of which it also acts as trustee or to a person dealing with the trust is not a violation of the duty provided in Section 16002 or 16004. For the purposes of this section, "affiliate" means a corporation that directly or indirectly through one or more intermediaries controls, is controlled by, or is under common control with another domestic or foreign corporation. *(Stats.1990, c. 79 (A.B.759), § 14, operative July 1, 1991.)*

Law Revision Commission Comments

1990 Enactment

Section 16015 continues Section 16015 of the repealed Probate Code without change. This section is consistent with the rule stated in Estate of Pitzer, 155 Cal.App.3d 979, 988, 202 Cal.Rptr. 855 (1984). The definition of "affiliate" is the same as that provided in Corporations Code Section 150, with the addition of the reference to "domestic or foreign" corporations.

Background on Section 16015 of Repealed Code

Section 16015 was a new provision added by 1986 Cal.Stat. ch. 820 § 40. For background on the provisions of this division, see the Comment to this division under the division heading. [20 Cal.L.Rev.Comm.Reports 1001 (1990)].

ARTICLE 2. TRUSTEE'S STANDARD OF CARE

Application

Application of Division, see Probate Code § 15001.

Cross References

Application of old and new law, see Probate Code § 3.
Common law rules governing trusts, application, see Probate Code § 15002.
Relationships excluded from Code definition of trust, application of this Division, see Probate Code § 15003.
Trust powers, investment plans, see Financial Code § 14860.

§ 16040. Standard of care; modification by trust instrument; exceptions

(a) The trustee shall administer the trust with reasonable care, skill, and caution under the circumstances then prevailing that a prudent person acting in a like capacity would use in the conduct of an enterprise of like character and with like aims to accomplish the purposes of the trust as determined from the trust instrument.

(b) The settlor may expand or restrict the standard provided in subdivision (a) by express provisions in the trust instrument. A trustee is not liable to a beneficiary for the trustee's good faith reliance on these express provisions.

(c) This section does not apply to investment and management functions governed by the Uniform Prudent Investor Act, Article 2.5 (commencing with Section 16045). *(Stats. 1990, c. 79 (A.B.759), § 14, operative July 1, 1991. Amended by Stats.1995, c. 63 (S.B.222), § 4.)*

Law Revision Commission Comments

1990 Enactment

Section 16040 continues Section 16040 of the repealed Probate Code without change. Subdivision (a) provides a general standard of care for administration of the trust; subdivision (b) provides the standard of care applicable to investment and management of trust property.

An expert trustee is held to the standard of care of other experts. See the discussions in Estate of Collins, 72 Cal.App.3d 663, 673, 139 Cal.Rptr. 644 (1977); Coberly v. Superior Court, 231 Cal.App.2d 685, 689, 42 Cal.Rptr. 64 (1965); Estate of Beach, 15 Cal.3d 623, 635, 542 P.2d 994, 125 Cal.Rptr. 570 (1975) (bank as executor); see also Section 16014 (duty to use special skills); Comment to Section 2401 (standard of care applicable to professional guardian or conservator of estate); Comment to Section 3912 (standard of care applicable to professional fiduciary acting as custodian under California Uniform Transfers to Minors Act). The last sentence of subdivision (b) reflects the portfolio approach for judging investment decisions.

1995 Amendment

Section 16040 is amended for harmony with the new Uniform Prudent Investor Act, Article 2.5 (commencing with Section 16045). This section provides a general standard of care that applies where the special, more detailed rule applicable to investments and management of trust property does not apply, such as determining whether to make discretionary distributions, communicating with beneficiaries, and relations with creditors. See subdivision (c).

The portfolio rule formerly provided by subdivision (b) is restated in Section 16047. Former subdivision (c) has been redesignated as subdivision (b) and revised to delete the reference to former subdivision (b). For a special rule protecting the trustee's good-faith reliance on trust provisions concerning investments, see Section 16046 (prudent investor rule). [25 Cal.L.Rev.Comm. Reports 543, 673 (1995)].

Background on Section 16040 of Repealed Code

Section 16040 was added by 1986 Cal.Stat. ch. 820 § 40. For background on the provisions of this division, see the Comment to this division under the division heading.

Subdivision (a) is drawn from subdivision (a)(1) of former Civil Code Section 2261 (repealed by 1986 Cal.Stat. ch. 820 § 7) which applied to investment and management decisions. This subdivision superseded the "ordinary care and diligence" standard that was provided in former Civil Code Section 2259 (repealed by 1986 Cal.Stat. ch. 820 § 7).

Subdivision (b) restated subdivision (a)(1) of former Civil Code Section 2261 without substantive change. The former reference to attaining the goals of the trustor was changed to refer to accomplishing the purposes of the trust.

Subdivision (c) restated subdivision (a)(2) of former Civil Code Section 2261 without substantive change. [20 Cal.L.Rev.Comm.Reports 1001 (1990)].

Cross References

Absolute, sole, or uncontrolled discretion conferred on trustee by instrument, see Probate Code § 16081.
Boxers' Pension Fund, investor standard of care, see Business and Professions Code § 18882.
Breach of trust actions, see Probate Code § 16420 et seq.
Deposit of funds awaiting investment, see Financial Code § 1562.

Duty not to delegate trustee responsibilities, see Probate Code § 16012.
Holding of amounts set aside as cash on hand, deposits, investments, see Insurance Code § 12383.
Investment of monies for minors or incompetents, see Probate Code § 3602 et seq.
Investments by commercial banks, see Financial Code § 1002
Liability of trustee to third persons, see Probate Code § 18000 et seq.
Ordinary care and diligence of depositary for hire, see Civil Code § 1852.
Powers of trust companies, see Financial Code § 1580.
Powers of trustees,
　　Generally, see Probate Code § 16200 et seq.
　　Investment powers, see Probate Code § 16047.
Slight care of gratuitous depositary, see Civil Code § 1846.
Trust powers, investment of funds, see Financial Code § 14860.
Trust proceedings, see Probate Code § 17200 et seq.

§ 16041.　　Effect of compensation

A trustee's standard of care and performance in administering the trust is not affected by whether or not the trustee receives any compensation. *(Stats.1990, c. 79 (A.B.759), § 14, operative July 1, 1991.)*

Law Revision Commission Comments

1990 Enactment

Section 16041 continues Section 16041 of the repealed Probate Code without change. A different rule applies to a custodian under the California Uniform Transfers to Minors Act. See Section 3912(b)(1).

Background on Section 16041 of Repealed Code

Section 16041 was added by 1986 Cal.Stat. ch. 820 § 40. The section restated without substantive change the part of former Civil Code Section 2259 (repealed by 1986 Cal.Stat. ch. 820 § 7) relating to the effect of compensation on the standard of care. For background on the provisions of this division, see the Comment to this division under the division heading. [20 Cal.L.Rev.Comm.Reports 1001 (1990)].

§ 16042.　　Public guardian; deposits and investments

(a) Notwithstanding the requirements of this article, Article 2.5 (commencing with Section 16045), and the terms of the trust, all trust funds that come within the custody of the public guardian who is appointed as trustee of the trust pursuant to Section 15660.5 may be deposited or invested in the same manner, and would be subject to the same terms and conditions, as a deposit or investment by the public administrator of funds in the estate of a decedent pursuant to Article 3 (commencing with Section 7640) of Chapter 4 of Part 1 of Division 7.

(b) Upon the deposit or investment of trust property pursuant to subdivision (a), the public guardian shall be deemed to have met the standard of care specified in this article and Article 2.5 (commencing with Section 16045) with respect to this trust property. *(Added by Stats.1997, c. 93 (S.B.696), § 4.)*

ARTICLE 2.5.　UNIFORM PRUDENT INVESTOR ACT

Cross References

California Endowment for Marine Preservation to have investment policies consistent with this Act, see Public Resources Code § 71561.

Reasonably prudent investor standards, accounting practices, investment policies, see Public Resources Code § 71561.

§ 16045.   Short title

This article, together with subdivision (a) of Section 16002 and Section 16003, constitutes the prudent investor rule and may be cited as the Uniform Prudent Investor Act. *(Added by Stats.1995, c. 63 (S.B.222), § 6.)*

Law Revision Commission Comments

1995 Addition

Section 16045 has the same purpose as Section 12 of the Uniform Prudent Investor Act (1994) promulgated by the National Conference of Commissioners on Uniform State Laws. Most of the substance of the uniform act is set forth in this article, but some rules already exist in other parts of the Trust Law and are included within the short title by specific reference. See Sections 16002(a) (duty of loyalty), 16003 (duty to deal impartially with beneficiaries).

See also Section 2 (construction of provisions drawn from uniform acts), which is the same in substance as Section 11 of the Uniform Prudent Investor Act (1994), and Section 13 (severability), which is the same in substance as Section 14 of the Uniform Prudent Investor Act (1994). For a list of uniform acts in the Probate Code, see Section 2 Comment. [25 Cal.L.Rev.Comm. Reports 543, 673 (1995)].

Cross References

Reasonably prudent investor standards, accounting practices, investment policies, see Public Resources Code § 71561.

§ 16046.   Compliance; duty of trustee; exception; liability

(a) Except as provided in subdivision (b), a trustee who invests and manages trust assets owes a duty to the beneficiaries of the trust to comply with the prudent investor rule.

(b) The settlor may expand or restrict the prudent investor rule by express provisions in the trust instrument. A trustee is not liable to a beneficiary for the trustee's good faith reliance on these express provisions. *(Added by Stats.1995, c. 63 (S.B.222), § 6.)*

Law Revision Commission Comments

1995 Addition

Section 16046 is similar to Section 1 of the Uniform Prudent Investor Act (1994). See also Section 16045 (prudent investor rule defined). Subdivision (a) and the first sentence of subdivision (b) are a special application of the general duty provided in Section 16000 (duty to administer trust according to statute, subject to control in trust).

Subdivision (b) continues the rule in former subdivision (c) (now subdivision (b)) of Section 16040, insofar as it applied to matters now governed by this article. The first sentence of subdivision (b) is the same in substance as the first sentence Section 1(b) of the Uniform Prudent Investor Act (1994). The second sentence continues the good-faith standard of Section 16040 in place of the reasonable reliance rule of the Uniform Prudent Investor Act (1994). [25 Cal.L.Rev.Comm. Reports 673 (1995)].

§ 16047.   Standard of care; investments and management; considerations

(a) A trustee shall invest and manage trust assets as a prudent investor would, by considering the purposes, terms, distribution requirements, and other circumstances of the trust. In satisfying this standard, the trustee shall exercise reasonable care, skill, and caution.

(b) A trustee's investment and management decisions respecting individual assets and courses of action must be evaluated not in isolation, but in the context of the trust portfolio as a whole and as a part of an overall investment strategy having risk and return objectives reasonably suited to the trust.

(c) Among circumstances that are appropriate to consider in investing and managing trust assets are the following, to the extent relevant to the trust or its beneficiaries:

(1) General economic conditions.

(2) The possible effect of inflation or deflation.

(3) The expected tax consequences of investment decisions or strategies.

(4) The role that each investment or course of action plays within the overall trust portfolio.

(5) The expected total return from income and the appreciation of capital.

(6) Other resources of the beneficiaries known to the trustee as determined from information provided by the beneficiaries.

(7) Needs for liquidity, regularity of income, and preservation or appreciation of capital.

(8) An asset's special relationship or special value, if any, to the purposes of the trust or to one or more of the beneficiaries.

(d) A trustee shall make a reasonable effort to ascertain facts relevant to the investment and management of trust assets.

(e) A trustee may invest in any kind of property or type of investment or engage in any course of action or investment strategy consistent with the standards of this chapter. *(Added by Stats.1995, c. 63 (S.B.222), § 6.)*

Law Revision Commission Comments

1995 Addition

Section 16047 is generally the same in substance as Section 2(a)-(e) of the Uniform Prudent Investor Act (1994). Subdivisions (a)-(c) of Section 16047 replace the portfolio investment rule of former subdivision (b) of Section 16040. Subdivision (a) is also the same in substance as the first paragraph and subsection (a) of Section 227 of Restatement (Third) of Trusts: Prudent Investor Rule (1992).

The second sentence of subdivision (a) states the basic elements of prudence. Thus, where "prudence" is used in this article, it includes "reasonable care, skill, and caution." These elements are delineated in the Restatement:

[Care]

The duty of care requires the trustee to exercise reasonable effort and diligence in making and monitoring investments for the trust, with attention to the trust's objectives. The trustee has a related duty of care in keeping informed of rights and opportunities associated with those investments....

[Skill]

The exercise of care alone is not sufficient, however, because a trustee is liable for losses resulting from failure to use the skill of an individual of ordinary intelligence. This is so despite the careful use of all the skill of which the particular trustee is capable.

On the other hand, if follows from the requirement of care as well as from sound policy that, if the trustee possesses a degree of skill greater than that of an individual of ordinary intelligence, the trustee is liable for a loss that results from failure to make reasonably diligent use of that skill....

[Caution]

In addition to the duty to use care and skill, the trustee must exercise the caution of a prudent investor managing similar funds for similar purposes. In the absence of contrary provisions in the terms of the trust, this requirement of caution requires the trustee to invest with a view both to safety of the capital and to securing a reasonable return....

Restatement (Third) of Trusts: Prudent Investor Rule § 227 comments d & e (1992). For a full discussion, see *id.* § 227, comments & Reporter's Notes (1992).

Subdivision (d) is new to the code. Subdivision (e) replaces former Section 16223 ("The trustee has the power to invest in any kind of property, whether real, personal, or mixed."). This subdivision, like its predecessor, makes clear that there are no categorical restrictions on proper investments. Any form of investment is permissible in the absence of a prohibition in the trust instrument or an overriding duty. This subdivision is intended to permit investment in investment company shares, mutual funds, index funds, and other modern vehicles for collective investments. While investment in these funds is not forbidden merely because discretion over the fund is delegated to others, the trustee is ultimately subject to fiduciary standards under this chapter in making the investment. See also Sections 62 ("property" defined), 16053 (language invoking standard of Uniform Prudent Investor Act), 16202 (exercise of powers is subject to duties), 16203 (trust instrument that incorporates the powers provided in former Section 1120.2 of the repealed Probate Code).

Statutes pertaining to legal investments appear in other codes. See, e.g., Fin. Code §§ 1561.1 (funds provided services by trust company or affiliate), 1564 (common trust funds); Gov't Code §§ 971.2, 17202, 61673; Harb. & Nav. Code §§ 6331, 6931; Health and Safety Code §§ 33663, 34369, 37649, 52040, 52053.5; Pub. Res. Code § 26026; Sts. & Hy. Code §§ 8210, 25371, 30241, 30242, 31173; Water Code §§ 9526, 20064.

Section 2(f) of the Uniform Prudent Investor Act (1994) has been omitted from Section 16047 because it is unnecessary. The same general rule is provided by Section 16014 (duty to use special skills). An expert trustee is held to the standard of care of other experts. See the discussions in Estate of Collins, 72 Cal.App.3d 663, 673, 139 Cal.Rptr. 644 (1977); Coberly v. Superior Court, 231 Cal.App.2d 685, 689, 42 Cal.Rptr. 64 (1965); Estate of Beach, 15 Cal.3d 623, 635, 542 P.2d 994, 125 Cal.Rptr. 570 (1975) (bank as executor); see also Section 2401 Comment (standard of care applicable to professional guardian or conservator of estate); Section 3912 Comment (standard of care applicable to professional fiduciary acting as custodian under California Uniform Transfers to Minors Act). [25 Cal.L.Rev.Comm. Reports 673 (1995)].

Cross References

Marriage rights and obligations, contracts with each other and third parties, fiduciary relationship, see Family Code § 721.

§ 16048. Diversification; duty of trustee; exception

In making and implementing investment decisions, the trustee has a duty to diversify the investments of the trust unless, under the circumstances, it is prudent not to do so. *(Added by Stats.1995, c. 63 (S.B.222), § 6.)*

Law Revision Commission Comments
1995 Addition

Section 16048 is drawn from Section 227(b) of the Restatement (Third) of Trusts: Prudent Investor Rule (1992), and is similar to Section 3 of the Uniform Prudent Investor Act (1994). This section is new to the Trust Law, but is consistent with case law. See, e.g., Estate of Collins, 72 Cal.App.3d 663, 669–72, 139 Cal.Rptr. 644, 648–49 (1977). This section, along with Section 16049, supersedes the rule in former Section 16008 (disposition of improper investments and retention of property in furtherance of trust purposes). See the comments to Restatement (Third) of Trusts: Prudent Investor Rule § 227 (1992). [25 Cal.L.Rev.Comm. Reports 673 (1995)].

§ 16049. Review of assets; time for compliance

Within a reasonable time after accepting a trusteeship or receiving trust assets, a trustee shall review the trust assets and make and implement decisions concerning the retention and disposition of assets, in order to bring the trust portfolio into compliance with the purposes, terms, distribution requirements, and other circumstances of the trust, and with the requirements of this chapter. *(Added by Stats.1995, c. 63 (S.B.222), § 6.)*

Law Revision Commission Comments
1995 Addition

Section 16049 is the same as Section 4 of the Uniform Prudent Investor Act (1994). For related duties, see Sections 16000 (duty to administer trust on acceptance), 16006 (duty to take control of and preserve trust property). This section, along with Section 16048, supersedes the rule in former Section 16008 (disposition of improper investments and retention of property in furtherance of trust purposes). [25 Cal.L.Rev.Comm. Reports 543, 673 (1995)].

§ 16050. Costs; incurrence

In investing and managing trust assets, a trustee may only incur costs that are appropriate and reasonable in relation to the assets, overall investment strategy, purposes, and other circumstances of the trust. *(Added by Stats.1995, c. 63 (S.B.222), § 6.)*

Law Revision Commission Comments
1995 Addition

Section 16050 is similar to Section 7 of the Uniform Prudent Investor Act (1994). This section is consistent with the rules concerning costs in Section 227(c)(3) of the Restatement (Third) of Trusts: Prudent Investor Rule (1992). For related rules concerning reimbursement and compensation of trustees, see Sections 15680–15685. The duty to minimize costs applies to delegation to agents and hiring advisers as well as to other aspects of fiduciary investing. In deciding whether to delegate, the trustee must balance the projected benefits against the likely costs. Similarly, in deciding how to delegate, the trustee must take costs into account. The trustee must be alert to protect the beneficiary from "double dipping." If, for example, the trustee's regular compensation schedule presupposes that the trustee will conduct the investment management function, it should ordinarily follow that the trustee will lower its fee if delegating the investment function to an outside manager. [25 Cal.L.Rev. Comm. Reports 673 (1995)].

§ 16051.   Compliance determinations; standards

Compliance with the prudent investor rule is determined in light of the facts and circumstances existing at the time of a trustee's decision or action and not by hindsight. *(Added by Stats.1995, c. 63 (S.B.222), § 6.)*

Law Revision Commission Comments

1995 Addition

Section 16051 is the same as Section 8 of the Uniform Prudent Investor Act (1994). See also Section 16045 (prudent investor rule defined). For related rules governing trustee liability, see Sections 16440–16465. [25 Cal.L.Rev.Comm. Reports 543, 673 (1995)].

§ 16052.   Delegation of investment and management functions; standards of care; trustees and agents; liability; jurisdiction

(a) A trustee may delegate investment and management functions as prudent under the circumstances. The trustee shall exercise prudence in the following:

(1) Selecting an agent.

(2) Establishing the scope and terms of the delegation, consistent with the purposes and terms of the trust.

(3) Periodically reviewing the agent's overall performance and compliance with the terms of the delegation.

(b) In performing a delegated function, an agent has a duty to exercise reasonable care to comply with the terms of the delegation.

(c) Except as otherwise provided in Section 16401, a trustee who complies with the requirements of subdivision (a) is not liable to the beneficiaries or to the trust for the decisions or actions of the agent to whom the function was delegated.

(d) By accepting the delegation of a trust function from the trustee of a trust that is subject to the law of this state, an agent submits to the jurisdiction of the courts of this state. *(Added by Stats.1995, c. 63 (S.B.222), § 6.)*

Law Revision Commission Comments

1995 Addition

Section 16052 is the same in substance as Section 9 of the Uniform Prudent Investor Act (1994), except that subdivision (c) has been revised for coordination with the basic rule on liability for acts of agents in Section 16401. Unlike the uniform act, the second sentence of subdivision (a) refers to the exercise of "prudence" rather than "reasonable care, skill, and caution." This is not a substantive change, however, since "prudence" means "reasonable care, skill, and caution" as provided in Section 16047(a). See Section 16047 Comment.

The duty to review the agent's overall performance under subdivision (a)(3) would include the periodic evaluation of the continued need for and appropriateness of the delegation of authority. In particular circumstances, the trustee may need to terminate the delegation to comply with the duty under Section 16401(b)(3) (duty to use prudence in retaining agent). Section 16052 provides special exceptions to the general rule concerning delegation (Section 16012) and the trustee's liability for acts of agents (Section 16401). See also

Section 16247 (power to hire accountants, auditors, investment advisors, etc.). [25 Cal.L.Rev.Comm. Reports 673 (1995)].

§ 16053.   Terms or language authorizing application of chapter

The following terms or comparable language in the provisions of a trust, unless otherwise limited or modified, authorizes any investment or strategy permitted under this chapter: "investments permissible by law for investment of trust funds," "legal investments," "authorized investments," "using the judgment and care under the circumstances then prevailing that persons of prudence, discretion, and intelligence exercise in the management of their own affairs, not in regard to speculation but in regard to the permanent disposition of their funds, considering the probable income as well as the probable safety of their capital," "prudent man rule," "prudent trustee rule," "prudent person rule," and "prudent investor rule." *(Added by Stats.1995, c. 63 (S.B. 222), § 6.)*

Law Revision Commission Comments

1995 Addition

Section 16053 is the same as Section 10 of the Uniform Prudent Investor Act (1994) and restates former Section 16042 without substantive change. See also Section 16045 (prudent investor rule defined). [25 Cal.L.Rev.Comm. Reports 543, 673 (1995)].

§ 16054.   Application of article; retroactivity

This article applies to trusts existing on and created after its effective date. As applied to trusts existing on its effective date, this article governs only decisions or actions occurring after that date. *(Added by Stats.1995, c. 63 (S.B.222), § 6.)*

Law Revision Commission Comments

1995 Addition

Section 16054 is the same as Section 11 of the Uniform Prudent Investor Act (1994) and is a specific application of the general transitional provisions in Section 3. [25 Cal.L.Rev.Comm. Reports 543, 673 (1995)].

ARTICLE 3.   TRUSTEE'S DUTY TO REPORT INFORMATION AND ACCOUNT TO BENEFICIARIES

TRUST LAW

Section

16069. Exceptions to requirement to provide certain information to beneficiary.

Application

Application of Division, see Probate Code § 15001.

Cross References

Application of old and new law, see Probate Code § 3.
Common law rules governing trusts, application, see Probate Code § 15002.
Relationships excluded from Code definition of trust, application of this Division, see Probate Code § 15003.

§ 16060. Duty to inform

The trustee has a duty to keep the beneficiaries of the trust reasonably informed of the trust and its administration. *(Stats.1990, c. 79 (A.B.759), § 14, operative July 1, 1991.)*

Law Revision Commission Comments

1990 Enactment

Section 16060 continues Section 16060 of the repealed Probate Code without change. The section is drawn from the first sentence of Section 7–303 of the Uniform Probate Code (1987) and is consistent with the duty stated in prior California case law to give beneficiaries complete and accurate information relative to the administration of a trust when requested at reasonable times. See Strauss v. Superior Court, 36 Cal.2d 396, 401, 224 P.2d 726 (1950). As to the construction of provisions drawn from uniform acts, see Section 2. The trustee is under a duty to communicate to the beneficiary information that is reasonably necessary to enable the beneficiary to enforce the beneficiary's rights under the trust or to prevent or redress a breach of trust. See Restatement (Second) of Trusts § 173 comment c (1957). Ordinarily, the trustee is not under a duty to furnish information to the beneficiary in the absence of a request for the information. See id. comment d. Thus, the general duty provided in this section is ordinarily satisfied by compliance with Sections 16061 and 16062 unless there are special circumstances requiring particular information to be reported to beneficiaries. However, if the trustee is dealing with the beneficiary on the trustee's own account, the trustee has a duty to communicate material facts in connection with the transaction that the trustee knows or should know. The trustee also has a duty to communicate material facts affecting the beneficiary's interest that the trustee knows the beneficiary does not know and that the beneficiary needs to know for protection in dealing with a third person. See id. During the time that a revocable trust can be revoked, the duty provided by this section is not owed to the beneficiaries but only to the settlor or other person having the power to revoke. See Section 15800. See also Sections 24 ("beneficiary" defined), 16000 (duties subject to control in trust instrument), 16001 (duties of trustee of revocable trust), 16460 (limitations on proceedings against trustee).

Background on Section 16060 of Repealed Code

Section 16060 was a new provision added by 1986 Cal.Stat. ch. 820 § 40. For background on the provisions of this division, see the Comment to this division under the division heading. [20 Cal.L.Rev.Comm.Reports 1001 (1990)].

§ 16060.5. Terms of the trust

As used in this article, "terms of the trust" means the written trust instrument of an irrevocable trust or those provisions of a written trust instrument in effect at the settlor's death that describe or affect that portion of a trust that has become irrevocable at the death of the settlor. In addition, "terms of the trust" includes, but is not limited to, signatures, amendments, disclaimers, and any directions or instructions to the trustee that affect the disposition of the trust. "Terms of the trust" does not include documents which were intended to affect disposition only while the trust was revocable. If a trust has been completely restated, "terms of the trust" does not include trust instruments or amendments which are superseded by the last restatement before the settlor's death, but it does include amendments executed after the restatement. "Terms of the trust" also includes any document irrevocably exercising a power of appointment over the trust or over any portion of the trust which has become irrevocable. *(Added by Stats.1997, c. 724 (A.B.1172), § 21. Amended by Stats.1998, c. 682 (A.B.2069), § 7; Stats.2000, c. 34 (A.B.460), § 2.)*

§ 16060.7. Trustee to provide terms of trust to beneficiary

On the request of a beneficiary, the trustee shall provide the terms of the trust to the beneficiary unless the trustee is not required to provide the terms of the trust to the beneficiary in accordance with Section 16069. *(Added by Stats.2010, c. 621 (S.B.202), § 2.)*

§ 16061. Request by beneficiary

Except as provided in Section 16069, on reasonable request by a beneficiary, the trustee shall report to the beneficiary by providing requested information to the beneficiary relating to the administration of the trust relevant to the beneficiary's interest. *(Stats.1990, c. 79 (A.B.759), § 14, operative July 1, 1991. Amended by Stats.1998, c. 682 (A.B.2069), § 8; Stats. 2010, c. 621 (S.B.202), § 3.)*

Law Revision Commission Comments

1990 Enactment

Section 16061 continues Section 16061 of the repealed Probate Code without change. The section is drawn from Section 7–303(b) of the Uniform Probate Code (1987). As to the construction of provisions drawn from uniform acts, see Section 2. The reference to the acts of the trustee is drawn from former Probate Code Section 1138.1(a)(5) (repealed by 1986 Cal.Stat. ch. 820, § 31). If the trustee does not comply with the reasonable request of the beneficiary, information may be sought on petition pursuant to Section 17200(b)(7). Note that the right to petition for a report or account under Section 17200(b)(7) is limited to one report or account every six months and after a trustee has failed to furnish the report or account within 60 days after a written request. A beneficiary who is not entitled to an annual account under Section 16062 may be entitled to information or a particular account under this section. The availability of information on request under this section does not negate the affirmative duty of the trustee to provide information under Section 16060. During the time that a revocable trust can be revoked, the right to request information pursuant to this section does not belong to the beneficiaries but only to the settlor or other person having the power to revoke. See Section 15800. See also Sections 24 ("beneficiary" defined), 16064 (exceptions to duty to report and account). In an appropriate case, more or different information may be required under this section than through the duty to account annually. See Section 16063 (contents of annual account).

Background on Section 16061 of Repealed Code

Section 16061 was a new provision added by 1986 Cal.Stat. ch. 820 § 40. For background on the provisions of this division, see the Comment to this division under the division heading. [20 Cal.L.Rev.Comm.Reports 1001 (1990)].

946

Compelling trustee to provide information about the trust pursuant to this section, see Probate Code § 17200.
Information about voting shares in a trust, see Corporations Code § 711.

§ 16061.5. Irrevocable trusts; copies of terms to beneficiaries and heirs; determinations of heirship

(a) A trustee shall provide a true and complete copy of the terms of the irrevocable trust, or irrevocable portion of the trust, to each of the following:

(1) Any beneficiary of the trust who requests it, and to any heir of a deceased settlor who requests it, when a revocable trust or any portion of a revocable trust becomes irrevocable because of the death of one or more of the settlors of the trust, when a power of appointment is effective or lapses upon the death of a settlor under the circumstances described in paragraph (3) of subdivision (a) of Section 16061.7, or because, by the express terms of the trust, the trust becomes irrevocable within one year of the death of a settlor because of a contingency related to the death of one or more of the settlors of the trust.

(2) Any beneficiary of the trust who requests it, whenever there is a change of trustee of an irrevocable trust.

(3) If the trust is a charitable trust subject to the supervision of the Attorney General, to the Attorney General, if requested, when a revocable trust or any portion of a revocable trust becomes irrevocable because of the death of one or more of the settlors of the trust, when a power of appointment is effective or lapses upon the death of a settlor under the circumstances described in paragraph (3) of subdivision (a) of Section 16061.7, or because, by the express terms of the trust, the trust becomes irrevocable within one year of the death of a settlor because of a contingency related to the death of one or more of the settlors of the trust, and whenever there is a change of trustee of an irrevocable trust.

(b) The trustee shall, for purposes of this section, rely upon any final judicial determination of heirship. However, the trustee shall have discretion to make a good faith determination by any reasonable means of the heirs of a deceased settlor in the absence of a final judicial determination of heirship known to the trustee. *(Added by Stats.1997, c. 724 (A.B.1172), § 22. Amended by Stats.1998, c. 682 (A.B.2069), § 9; Stats.2000, c. 34 (A.B.460), § 3; Stats.2010, c. 621 (S.B.202), § 4.)*

Attorney General, generally, see Government Code § 12500 et seq.

§ 16061.7. Status of trust changing to irrevocable, change of trustee of irrevocable trust, or power of appointment of irrevocable trust becoming effective or lapsing; notification; final judicial determination of heirship

(a) A trustee shall serve a notification by the trustee as described in this section in the following events:

(1) When a revocable trust or any portion thereof becomes irrevocable because of the death of one or more of the settlors of the trust, or because, by the express terms of the trust, the trust becomes irrevocable within one year of the death of a settlor because of a contingency related to the death of one or more of the settlors of the trust.

(2) Whenever there is a change of trustee of an irrevocable trust.

(3) Whenever a power of appointment retained by a settlor is effective or lapses upon death of the settlor with respect to an inter vivos trust which was, or was purported to be, irrevocable upon its creation. This paragraph shall not apply to a charitable remainder trust. For purposes of this paragraph, "charitable remainder trust" means a charitable remainder annuity trust or charitable remainder unitrust as defined in Section 664(d) of the Internal Revenue Code.[1]

(4) The duty to serve the notification by the trustee pursuant to this subdivision is the duty of the continuing or successor trustee, and any one cotrustee may serve the notification.

(b) The notification by the trustee required by subdivision (a) shall be served on each of the following:

(1) Each beneficiary of the irrevocable trust or irrevocable portion of the trust, subject to the limitations of Section 15804.

(2) Each heir of the deceased settlor, if the event that requires notification is the death of a settlor or irrevocability within one year of the death of the settlor of the trust by the express terms of the trust because of a contingency related to the death of a settlor.

(3) If the trust is a charitable trust subject to the supervision of the Attorney General, to the Attorney General.

(c) A trustee shall, for purposes of this section, rely upon any final judicial determination of heirship, known to the trustee, but the trustee shall have discretion to make a good faith determination by any reasonable means of the heirs of a deceased settlor in the absence of a final judicial determination of heirship known to the trustee.

(d) The trustee need not provide a copy of the notification by trustee to any beneficiary or heir (1) known to the trustee but who cannot be located by the trustee after reasonable diligence or (2) unknown to the trustee.

(e) The notification by trustee shall be served by mail to the last known address, pursuant to Section 1215, or by personal delivery.

(f) The notification by trustee shall be served not later than 60 days following the occurrence of the event requiring service of the notification by trustee, or 60 days after the trustee became aware of the existence of a person entitled to receive notification by trustee, if that person was not known to the trustee on the occurrence of the event requiring service of the notification. If there is a vacancy in the office of the trustee on the date of the occurrence of the event requiring service of the notification by trustee, or if that event causes a vacancy, then the 60-day period for service of the notification by trustee commences on the date the new trustee commences to serve as trustee.

(g) The notification by trustee shall contain the following information:

(1) The identity of the settlor or settlors of the trust and the date of execution of the trust instrument.

(2) The name, mailing address and telephone number of each trustee of the trust.

(3) The address of the physical location where the principal place of administration of the trust is located, pursuant to Section 17002.

(4) Any additional information that may be expressly required by the terms of the trust instrument.

(5) A notification that the recipient is entitled, upon reasonable request to the trustee, to receive from the trustee a true and complete copy of the terms of the trust.

(h) If the notification by the trustee is served because a revocable trust or any portion of it has become irrevocable because of the death of one or more settlors of the trust, or because, by the express terms of the trust, the trust becomes irrevocable within one year of the death of a settlor because of a contingency related to the death of one or more of the settlors of the trust, the notification by the trustee shall also include a warning, set out in a separate paragraph in not less than 10-point boldface type, or a reasonable equivalent thereof, that states as follows:

"You may not bring an action to contest the trust more than 120 days from the date this notification by the trustee is served upon you or 60 days from the date on which a copy of the terms of the trust is mailed or personally delivered to you during that 120-day period, whichever is later."

(i) Any waiver by a settlor of the requirement of serving the notification by trustee required by this section is against public policy and shall be void.

(j) A trustee may serve a notification by trustee in the form required by this section on any person in addition to those on whom the notification by trustee is required to be served. A trustee is not liable to any person for serving or for not serving the notice on any person in addition to those on whom the notice is required to be served. A trustee is not required to serve a notification by trustee if the event that otherwise requires service of the notification by trustee occurs before January 1, 1998. *(Added by Stats.1997, c. 724 (A.B.1172), § 23. Amended by Stats.1998, c. 682 (A.B.2069), § 10; Stats.2000, c. 34 (A.B.460), § 4; Stats.2000, c. 592 (A.B.1628), § 1; Stats.2010, c. 621 (S.B.202), § 5.)*

¹ Internal Revenue Code sections are in Title 26 of the U.S.C.A.

Cross References

Attorney General, generally, see Government Code § 12500 et seq.

§ 16061.8. Limitations of actions to contest trust

No person upon whom the notification by the trustee is served pursuant to this chapter, whether the notice is served on him or her within or after the time period set forth in subdivision (f) of Section 16061.7, may bring an action to contest the trust more than 120 days from the date the notification by the trustee is served upon him or her, or 60 days from the day on which a copy of the terms of the trust is mailed or personally delivered to him or her during that 120-day period, whichever is later. *(Added by Stats.1997, c. 724 (A.B.1172), § 24. Amended by Stats.2000, c. 34 (A.B.460), § 5; Stats.2000, c. 592 (A.B.1628), § 2; Stats.2010, c. 621 (S.B.202), § 6.)*

§ 16061.9. Notification service by trustee; liability of trustee

(a) A trustee who fails to serve the notification by trustee as required by Section 16061.7 on a beneficiary shall be responsible for all damages, attorney's fees, and costs caused by the failure unless the trustee makes a reasonably diligent effort to comply with that section.

(b) A trustee who fails to serve the notification by trustee as required by Section 16061.7 on an heir who is not a beneficiary and whose identity is known to the trustee shall be responsible for all damages caused to the heir by the failure unless the trustee shows that the trustee made a reasonably diligent effort to comply with that section. For purposes of this subdivision, "reasonably diligent effort" means that the trustee has sent notice by first-class mail to the heir at the heir's last mailing address actually known to the trustee.

(c) A trustee, in exercising discretion with respect to the timing and nature of distributions of trust assets, may consider the fact that the period in which a beneficiary or heir could bring an action to contest the trust has not expired. *(Added by Stats.2000, c. 34 (A.B.460), § 6.)*

§ 16062. Accounting; limitations or waivers in trust instrument

(a) Except as otherwise provided in this section and in Section 16064, the trustee shall account at least annually, at the termination of the trust, and upon a change of trustee, to each beneficiary to whom income or principal is required or authorized in the trustee's discretion to be currently distributed.

(b) A trustee of a living trust created by an instrument executed before July 1, 1987, is not subject to the duty to account provided by subdivision (a).

(c) A trustee of a trust created by a will executed before July 1, 1987, is not subject to the duty to account provided by subdivision (a), except that if the trust is removed from continuing court jurisdiction pursuant to Article 2 (commencing with Section 17350) of Chapter 4 of Part 5, the duty to account provided by subdivision (a) applies to the trustee.

(d) Except as provided in Section 16064, the duty of a trustee to account pursuant to former Section 1120.1a of the Probate Code (as repealed by Chapter 820 of the Statutes of 1986), under a trust created by a will executed before July 1, 1977, which has been removed from continuing court jurisdiction pursuant to former Section 1120.1a, continues to apply after July 1, 1987. The duty to account under former Section 1120.1a may be satisfied by furnishing an account that satisfies the requirements of Section 16063.

(e) Any limitation or waiver in a trust instrument of the obligation to account is against public policy and shall be void as to any sole trustee who is either of the following:

(1) A disqualified person as defined in former Section 21350.5 (as repealed by Chapter 620 of the Statutes of 2010).

(2) Described in subdivision (a) of Section 21380, but not described in Section 21382. *(Stats.1990, c. 79 (A.B.759), § 14, operative July 1, 1991. Amended by Stats.1993, c. 293 (A.B.21), § 6.5; Stats.1998, c. 682 (A.B.2069), § 11; Stats. 2001, c. 159 (S.B.662), § 165.5; Stats.2010, c. 620 (S.B.105),*

§ 4; Stats.2011, c. 296 (A.B.1023), § 244; Stats.2016, c. 86 (S.B.1171), § 250, eff. Jan. 1, 2017.)

Law Revision Commission Comments

1990 Enactment

Section 16062 continues Section 16062 of the repealed Probate Code without change.

Subdivision (a) imposes the general duty to account at least annually and at the termination of the trust and upon a change of trustees. This duty is subject to the exceptions provided in this section and in Section 16064. The duty to provide information under Section 16060 is not necessarily satisfied by compliance with Section 16062.

Subdivision (b) makes clear that the requirement of furnishing an account under subdivision (a) does not apply to a living trust created by an instrument executed before July 1, 1987. As to the application of any amendments made after that date, see Section 3.

Subdivision (c) provides as a general rule that testamentary trusts that were not subject to continuing court jurisdiction under former law—i.e., trusts created by wills executed between July 1, 1977, and June 30, 1987, and trusts created by earlier wills that were republished during that time—are not subject to the accounting requirements of subdivision (a). However, subdivision (c) makes the accounting requirement of subdivision (a) applicable to testamentary trusts that are removed from continuing jurisdiction under Sections 17350–17354 after July 1, 1987.

Subdivision (d) makes clear that, where a trust was removed from continuing jurisdiction under former law, the annual accounting required by former Probate Code Section 1120.1a(b) (repealed by 1986 Cal.Stat. ch. 820, § 31) is still required, notwithstanding the repeal of Section 1120.1a. For the sake of administrative simplicity, however, this requirement may be satisfied by compliance with Section 16063 (contents of accounting). The introductory clause of subdivision (d) also makes clear that the accounting requirement is subject to relevant exceptions in Section 16064, such as where the beneficiary waives the right to account.

Notwithstanding being excused from the duty to report information or account, the trustee may want to provide information or account to the beneficiaries in order to start the running of the statute of limitations pursuant to Section 16460.

2010 Amendment

Section 16062(e) is amended to correct a reference to former Section 21350.5. [38 Cal.L.Rev.Comm. Reports 107 (2008)].

Background on Section 16062 of Repealed Code

Section 16062 was added by 1986 Cal.Stat. ch. 820 § 40 and amended by 1987 Cal.Stat. ch. 128 § 13. Subdivision (a) superseded parts of subdivisions (b) and (c) of former Probate Code Section 1120.1a and parts of former Probate Code Sections 1121 and 1138.1(a)(5) (provisions repealed by 1986 Cal.Stat. ch. 820 § 31). The requirement of an annual account is drawn from the statute formerly applicable to testamentary trusts created before July 1, 1977. See former Prob.Code § 1120.1a (repealed by 1986 Cal.Stat. ch. 820 § 31). For background on the provisions of this division, see the Comment to this division under the division heading. [20 Cal.L.Rev.Comm.Reports 1001 (1990)].

Cross References

Minor's gross earnings set aside in trust for the benefit of the minor, see Family Code § 6752.
Presumption of fraud or undue influence with respect to wills and trusts, enumeration of certain donative transfers subject to the presumption, see Probate Code § 21380.

Trust for care of animals, accountings and beneficiaries, see Probate Code § 15212.

§ 16063.   Contents of account; manner of presentation

(a) An account furnished pursuant to Section 16062 shall contain the following information:

(1) A statement of receipts and disbursements of principal and income that have occurred during the last complete fiscal year of the trust or since the last account.

(2) A statement of the assets and liabilities of the trust as of the end of the last complete fiscal year of the trust or as of the end of the period covered by the account.

(3) The trustee's compensation for the last complete fiscal year of the trust or since the last account.

(4) The agents hired by the trustee, their relationship to the trustee, if any, and their compensation, for the last complete fiscal year of the trust or since the last account.

(5) A statement that the recipient of the account may petition the court pursuant to Section 17200 to obtain a court review of the account and of the acts of the trustee.

(6) A statement that claims against the trustee for breach of trust may not be made after the expiration of three years from the date the beneficiary receives an account or report disclosing facts giving rise to the claim.

(b) All accounts filed to be approved by a court shall be presented in the manner provided in Chapter 4 (commencing with Section 1060) of Part 1 of Division 3. *(Added by Stats.1997, c. 724 (A.B.1172), § 26.)*

Cross References

Compliance excused for three year limitation of actions against trustee, see Probate Code § 16461.
Minor's gross earnings set aside in trust for the benefit of the minor, see Family Code § 6752.

§ 16064.   Accounting requirement; exceptions

The trustee is not required to account to a beneficiary as described in subdivision (a) of Section 16062, in any of the following circumstances:

(a) To the extent the trust instrument waives the account, except that no waiver described in subdivision (e) of Section 16062 shall be valid or enforceable. Regardless of a waiver of accounting in the trust instrument, upon a showing that it is reasonably likely that a material breach of the trust has occurred, the court may compel the trustee to account.

(b) As to a beneficiary who has waived in writing the right to an account. A waiver of rights under this subdivision may be withdrawn in writing at any time as to accounts for transactions occurring after the date of the written withdrawal. Regardless of a waiver of accounting by a beneficiary, upon a showing that is reasonably likely that a material breach of the trust has occurred, the court may compel the trustee to account.

(c) In any of the circumstances set forth in Section 16069. *(Stats.1990, c. 79 (A.B.759), § 14, operative July 1, 1991. Amended by Stats.1992, c. 871 (A.B.2975), § 18; Stats.1993, c. 293 (A.B.21), § 6.7; Stats.2010, c. 621 (S.B.202), § 7.)*

Law Revision Commission Comments
1990 Enactment

Section 16064 continues Section 16064 of the repealed Probate Code without change. This section provides several limitations on the duty to report under Section 16061 and the duty to account under Section 16062. See also Sections 24 ("beneficiary" defined), 15800 (limits on rights of beneficiary of revocable trust). Notwithstanding being excused from the duty to report information, the trustee may want to provide information to the beneficiaries in order to start the running of the statute of limitations pursuant to Section 16460. See also Section 17200 (right of trustee or beneficiary to petition the court concerning the internal affairs of the trust).

Background on Section 16064 of Repealed Code

Section 16064 was a new provision added by 1986 Cal.Stat. ch. 820 § 40. For background on the provisions of this division, see the Comment to this division under the division heading. [20 Cal.L.Rev.Comm.Reports 1001 (1990)].

Cross References

Compelling trustee to account to beneficiary subject to provisions of this section, see Probate Code § 17200.

§ 16068. Waiver of certain obligations of trustee against public policy

Any waiver by a settlor of the obligation of the trustee of either of the following is against public policy and shall be void:

(a) To provide the terms of the trust to the beneficiary as required by Sections 16060.7 and 16061.5.

(b) To provide requested information to the beneficiary as required by Section 16061. *(Added by Stats.2010, c. 621 (S.B.202), § 8.)*

§ 16069. Exceptions to requirement to provide certain information to beneficiary

The trustee is not required to account to the beneficiary, provide the terms of the trust to a beneficiary, or provide requested information to the beneficiary pursuant to Section 16061, in any of the following circumstances:

(a) In the case of a beneficiary of a revocable trust, as provided in Section 15800, for the period when the trust may be revoked.

(b) If the beneficiary and the trustee are the same person. *(Added by Stats.2010, c. 621 (S.B.202), § 9.)*

ARTICLE 4. DUTIES WITH REGARD TO DISCRETIONARY POWERS

Section
16080. Discretionary power; reasonable exercise.
16081. Fiduciary principles; discretion; trustees; exceptions.
16082. Use of power held for benefit of others to discharge obligation of person holding power.

Application

Application of Division, see Probate Code § 15001.

Cross References

Application of old and new law, see Probate Code § 3.
Common law rules governing trusts, application, see Probate Code § 15002.

Relationships excluded from Code definition of trust, application of this Division, see Probate Code § 15003.

§ 16080. Discretionary power; reasonable exercise

Except as provided in Section 16081, a discretionary power conferred upon a trustee is not left to the trustee's arbitrary discretion, but shall be exercised reasonably. *(Stats.1990, c. 79 (A.B.759), § 14, operative July 1, 1991.)*

Law Revision Commission Comments
1990 Enactment

Section 16080 continues Section 16080 of the repealed Probate Code without change.

Background on Section 16080 of Repealed Code

Section 16080 was added by 1986 Cal.Stat. ch. 820 § 40. The section continued former Civil Code Section 2269(a) (repealed by 1986 Cal.Stat. ch. 820 § 7) without substantive change. For background on the provisions of this division, see the Comment to this division under the division heading. [20 Cal.L.Rev.Comm.Reports 1001 (1990)].

Cross References

Review of exercise of discretionary powers, see Probate Code § 17200.

§ 16081. Fiduciary principles; discretion; trustees; exceptions

(a) Subject to the additional requirements of subdivisions (b), (c), and (d), if a trust instrument confers "absolute," "sole," or "uncontrolled" discretion on a trustee, the trustee shall act in accordance with fiduciary principles and shall not act in bad faith or in disregard of the purposes of the trust.

(b) Notwithstanding the use of terms like "absolute," "sole," or "uncontrolled" by a settlor or a testator, a person who is a beneficiary of a trust that permits the person, either individually or as trustee or cotrustee, to make discretionary distributions of income or principal to or for the benefit of himself or herself pursuant to a standard, shall exercise that power reasonably and in accordance with the standard.

(c) Unless a settlor or a testator clearly indicates that a broader power is intended by express reference to this subdivision, a person who is a beneficiary of a trust that permits the person, as trustee or cotrustee, to make discretionary distributions of income or principal to or for the benefit of himself or herself may exercise that power in his or her favor only for his or her health, education, support, or maintenance within the meaning of Sections 2041 and 2514 of the Internal Revenue Code. Notwithstanding the foregoing and the provisions of Section 15620, if a power to make discretionary distributions of income or principal is conferred upon two or more trustees, the power may be exercised by any trustee who is not a current permissible beneficiary of that power; and provided further that if there is no trustee who is not a current permissible beneficiary of that power, any party in interest may apply to a court of competent jurisdiction to appoint a trustee who is not a current permissible beneficiary of that power, and the power may be exercised by the trustee appointed by the court.

(d) Subdivision (c) does not apply to either of the following:

(1) Any power held by the settlor of a revocable or amendable trust.

(2) Any power held by a settlor's spouse or a testator's spouse who is the trustee of a trust for which a marital deduction, as defined in Section 21520, has been allowed.

(e) Subdivision (c) applies to any of the following:

(1) Any trust executed on or after January 1, 1997.

(2) Any testamentary trust created under a will executed on or after January 1, 1997.

(3) Any irrevocable trust created under a document executed before January 1, 1997, or any revocable trust executed before that date if the settlor was incapacitated as of that date, unless all parties in interest elect affirmatively not to be subject to the application of subdivision (c) through a written instrument delivered to the trustee. That election shall be made on or before the latest of January 1, 1998, three years after the date on which the trust became irrevocable, or, in the case of a revocable trust where the settlor was incapacitated, three years after the date on which the settlor became incapacitated.

(f) Notwithstanding the foregoing, the provisions of subdivision (c) neither create a new cause of action nor impair an existing cause of action that, in either case, relates to any power limited by subdivision (c) that was exercised before January 1, 1997.

(g) For purposes of this section, the term "party in interest" means any of the following persons:

(1) If the trust is revocable and the settlor is incapacitated, the settlor's legal representative under applicable law, or the settlor's attorney-in-fact under a durable power of attorney that is sufficient to grant the authority required under subdivision (c) or (e), as applicable.

(2) If the trust is irrevocable, each trustee, each beneficiary then entitled or authorized to receive income distributions from the trust, or each remainder beneficiary who would be entitled to receive notice of a trust proceeding under Section 15804. Any beneficiary who lacks legal capacity may be represented by the beneficiary's legal representative, attorney-in-fact under a durable power of attorney that is sufficient to grant the authority required under subdivision (c) or (e), as applicable, or in the absence of a legal representative or attorney-in-fact, a guardian ad litem appointed for that purpose. *(Stats.1990, c. 79 (A.B.759), § 14, operative July 1, 1991. Amended by Stats.1996, c. 410 (S.B.1907), § 1.)*

Law Revision Commission Comments

1990 Enactment

Section 16081 continues Section 16081 of the repealed Probate Code without change. See also Section 17200(b)(5) (court review of exercise of discretionary powers).

Background on Section 16081 of Repealed Code

Section 16081 was added by 1986 Cal.Stat. ch. 820 § 40. The section continued subdivision (c) and most of subdivision (d) of former Civil Code Section 2269 (repealed by 1986 Cal.Stat. ch. 820 § 7) without change. For background on the provisions of this division, see the Comment to this division under the division heading. [20 Cal.L.Rev.Comm.Reports 1001 (1990)].

Cross References

Standard of care, see Probate Code § 16040.

§ 16082. Use of power held for benefit of others to discharge obligation of person holding power

Except as otherwise specifically provided in the trust instrument, a person who holds a power to appoint or distribute income or principal to or for the benefit of others, either as an individual or as trustee, may not use the power to discharge the legal obligations of the person holding the power. *(Stats.1990, c. 79 (A.B.759), § 14, operative July 1, 1991.)*

Law Revision Commission Comments

1990 Enactment

Section 16082 continues Section 16082 of the repealed Probate Code without change. This section is intended to deal with problems that may arise under federal tax law. See I.R.C. §§ 674(a), 678(c), 2036.

Background on Section 16082 of Repealed Code

Section 16082 was added by 1987 Cal.Stat. ch. 128 § 15. The section restated former Civil Code Section 2269(e) (repealed by 1986 Cal.Stat. ch. 820 § 7) without substantive change, as applied to trusts. For background on the provisions of this division, see the Comment to this division under the division heading. [20 Cal.L.Rev.Comm.Reports 1001 (1990)].

ARTICLE 5. DUTIES OF TRUSTEES OF PRIVATE FOUNDATIONS, CHARITABLE TRUSTS, AND SPLIT–INTEREST TRUSTS

Application

Application of Division, see Probate Code § 15001.

Cross References

Application of old and new law, see Probate Code § 3.
Common law rules governing trusts, application, see Probate Code § 15002.
Relationships excluded from Code definition of trust, application of this Division, see Probate Code § 15003.

§ 16100. Definitions

As used in this article, the following definitions shall control:

(a) "Charitable trust" means a charitable trust as described in Section 4947(a)(1) of the Internal Revenue Code.

(b) "Private foundation" means a private foundation as defined in Section 509 of the Internal Revenue Code.

(c) "Split-interest trust" means a split-interest trust as described in Section 4947(a)(2) of the Internal Revenue Code. *(Stats.1990, c. 79 (A.B.759), § 14, operative July 1, 1991.)*

Section 16100 continues Section 16100 of the repealed Probate Code without change. This section defines terms for purposes of this article.

Background on Section 16100 of Repealed Code

Section 16100 was added by 1986 Cal.Stat. ch. 820 § 40. Subdivisions (a) and (b) restated parts of former Civil Code Section 2271 (repealed by 1986 Cal.Stat. ch. 820 § 7) without substantive change. Subdivision (c) restated part of subdivision (a) of former Civil Code Section 2271.1 (repealed by 1986 Cal.Stat. ch. 820 § 7) without substantive change. The references in these former sections to the Tax Reform Act of 1969 were omitted because they were superfluous. See Section 7 (reference to law includes later amendments or additions). For background on the provisions of this division, see the Comment to this division under the division heading. [20 Cal.L.Rev.Comm.Reports 1001 (1990)].

§ 16101. Charitable trust or private foundation; distribution of income

During any period when a trust is deemed to be a charitable trust or a private foundation, the trustee shall distribute its income for each taxable year (and principal if necessary) at a time and in a manner that will not subject the property of the trust to tax under Section 4942 of the Internal Revenue Code. *(Stats.1990, c. 79 (A.B.759), § 14, operative July 1, 1991.)*

Section 16101 continues Section 16101 of the repealed Probate Code without change. See Section 16100 ("charitable trust" and "private foundation" defined).

Background on Section 16101 of Repealed Code

Section 16101 was added by 1986 Cal.Stat. ch. 820 § 40. The section restated part of the first paragraph of former Civil Code Section 2271 (repealed by 1986 Cal.Stat. ch. 820 § 7) without substantive change. See also Section 10 (singular includes plural). For background on the provisions of this division, see the Comment to this division under the division heading. [20 Cal.L.Rev.Comm.Reports 1001 (1990)].

§ 16102. Restrictions

During any period when a trust is deemed to be a charitable trust, a private foundation, or a split-interest trust, the trustee shall not do any of the following:

(a) Engage in any act of self-dealing as defined in Section 4941(d) of the Internal Revenue Code.

(b) Retain any excess business holdings as defined in Section 4943(c) of the Internal Revenue Code.

(c) Make any investments in such manner as to subject the property of the trust to tax under Section 4944 of the Internal Revenue Code.

(d) Make any taxable expenditure as defined in Section 4945(d) of the Internal Revenue Code. *(Stats.1990, c. 79 (A.B.759), § 14, operative July 1, 1991.)*

Section 16102 continues Section 16102 of the repealed Probate Code without change.

Background on Section 16102 of Repealed Code

Section 16102 was added by 1986 Cal.Stat. ch. 820 § 40. The section restated part of the first paragraph of former Civil Code Section 2271 (applicable to charitable trusts and private foundations) and part of subdivision (a) of former Civil Code Section 2271.1 (applicable to split-interest trusts) (provisions repealed by 1986 Cal.Stat. ch. 820 § 7) without substantive change. The references in former law to specific amendatory sections of the Tax Reform Act of 1969 were omitted because they were unnecessary in view of Section 16100(b). See also Section 10 (singular includes plural). For background on the provisions of this division, see the Comment to this division under the division heading. [20 Cal.L.Rev.Comm.Reports 1001 (1990)].

§ 16103. Split-interest trusts; exemptions from provisions

With respect to split-interest trusts:

(a) Subdivisions (b) and (c) of Section 16102 do not apply to any trust described in Section 4947(b)(3) of the Internal Revenue Code.

(b) Section 16102 does not apply with respect to any of the following:

(1) Any amounts payable under the terms of such trust to income beneficiaries, unless a deduction was allowed under Section 170(f)(2)(B), 2055(e)(2)(B), or 2522(c)(2)(B) of the Internal Revenue Code.

(2) Any amounts in trust other than amounts for which a deduction was allowed under Section 170, 545(b)(2), 556(b)(2), 642(c), 2055, 2106(a)(2), or 2522 of the Internal Revenue Code, if the amounts are segregated, as that term is defined in Section 4947(a)(3) of the Internal Revenue Code, from amounts for which no deduction was allowable.

(3) Any amounts irrevocably transferred in trust before May 27, 1969. *(Stats.1990, c. 79 (A.B.759), § 14, operative July 1, 1991.)*

Section 16103 continues Section 16103 of the repealed Probate Code without change. See also Section 16100 ("split-interest trust" defined).

Background on Section 16103 of Repealed Code

Section 16103 was added by 1986 Cal.Stat. ch. 820 § 40. The section restated subdivisions (b) and (c) of former Civil Code Section 2271.1 (repealed by 1986 Cal.Stat. ch. 820 § 7) without substantive change, but the word "irrevocably" in subdivision (b)(3) was added for conformity with federal law. For background on the provisions of this division, see the Comment to this division under the division heading. [20 Cal.L.Rev.Comm.Reports 1001 (1990)].

§ 16104. Incorporation of statutes in trust instruments

The provisions of Sections 16101, 16102, and 16103 shall be deemed to be contained in the instrument creating every trust to which this article applies. Any provision of the instrument inconsistent with or contrary to this article is without effect. *(Stats.1990, c. 79 (A.B.759), § 14, operative July 1, 1991.)*

Section 16104 continues Section 16104 of the repealed Probate Code without change.

Background on Section 16104 of Repealed Code

Section 16104 was added by 1986 Cal.Stat. ch. 820 § 40. The section restated the second paragraph of former Civil Code Section 2271 and subdivision (d) of former Civil Code Section 2271.1 (provisions repealed by 1986 Cal.Stat. ch. 820 § 7) without substantive change. For background on the provisions of this division, see the Comment to this division under the division heading. [20 Cal.L.Rev.Comm.Reports 1001 (1990)].

§ 16105. Proceedings

(a) A proceeding contemplated by Section 101(*l*)(3) of the federal Tax Reform Act of 1969 (Public Law 91–172)[1] may be commenced pursuant to Section 17200 by the organization involved. All specifically named beneficiaries of the organization and the Attorney General shall be parties to the proceedings. Notwithstanding Section 17000, this provision is not exclusive and does not limit any jurisdiction that otherwise exists.

(b) If an instrument creating a trust affected by this section has been recorded, a notice of pendency of judicial proceedings under this section shall be recorded in a similar manner within 10 days from the commencement of the proceedings. A duly certified copy of any final judgment or decree in the proceedings shall be similarly recorded. *(Stats.1990, c. 79 (A.B.759), § 14, operative July 1, 1991.)*

[1] See 26 U.S.C.A. § 4940 note.

Law Revision Commission Comments
1990 Enactment

Section 16105 continues Section 16105 of the repealed Probate Code without change. See also Sections 17200(b)(19) (petition for purpose of Section 16105), 17203(c) (notice to Attorney General). For the text of Section 101(*l*)(3) of the Tax Reform Act of 1969, relating to judicial proceedings by a private foundation that are necessary to reform or excuse compliance with its governing instrument to comply with 26 U.S.C. § 4942, see the note following 26 U.S.C.A. § 4940.

Background on Section 16105 of Repealed Code

Section 16105 was added by 1986 Cal.Stat. ch. 820 § 40. The section restated former Civil Code Section 2271.2 (repealed by 1986 Cal.Stat. ch. 820 § 7) without substantive change. The reference to the procedure applicable to the internal affairs of trusts in Section 17200 was new. For background on the provisions of this division, see the Comment to this division under the division heading. [20 Cal.L.Rev.Comm.Reports 1001 (1990)].

Cross References

Attorney General, generally, see Government Code § 12500 et seq.

CHAPTER 2. POWERS OF TRUSTEES

Application

Application of Division, see Probate Code § 15001.

Cross References

Common law rules governing trusts, application, see Probate Code § 15002.
Notice of proposed actions, application or assertion of other rights and remedies, see Probate Code § 16500.
Relationships excluded from Code definition of trust, application of this Division, see Probate Code § 15003.

ARTICLE 1. GENERAL PROVISIONS

Application

Application of Division, see Probate Code § 15001.

Cross References

Application of old and new law, see Probate Code § 3.
Common law rules governing trusts, application, see Probate Code § 15002.
Relationships excluded from Code definition of trust, application of this Division, see Probate Code § 15003.

§ 16200. General powers

A trustee has the following powers without the need to obtain court authorization:

(a) The powers conferred by the trust instrument.

(b) Except as limited in the trust instrument, the powers conferred by statute.

(c) Except as limited in the trust instrument, the power to perform any act that a trustee would perform for the purposes of the trust under the standard of care provided in Section 16040 or 16047. *(Stats.1990, c. 79 (A.B.759), § 14, operative July 1, 1991. Amended by Stats.1995, c. 63 (S.B.222), § 7.)*

Law Revision Commission Comments
1990 Enactment [Revised Comment]

Section 16200 continues Section 16200 of the repealed Probate Code without change. This section is drawn from Sections 2(a) and 3(a) of the Uniform Trustees' Powers Act (1964) and from various California statutes that existed before the enactment of Section 16200 of the repealed Probate Code. As to the construction of provisions drawn from uniform acts, see Section 2.

The introductory clause of Section 16200 makes clear that the trustee has the powers as provided in this section without the need to obtain court authorization. See also Section 16201 (power of court to relieve trustee from restrictions on powers).

Subdivision (b) gives the trustee the statutory powers without the need to incorporate them. The main list of powers is provided in Article 2 (commencing with Section 16220). Additional powers are provided by statutes outside this chapter. See, e.g., Section 16300 *et seq.* (Revised Uniform Principal and Income Act).

Under subdivision (c), the trustee has the powers of a prudent person, without the need to obtain prior court approval. However, if the trustee desires court approval before exercising a power or desires court review after exercise of a power, the procedure provided in Section 17200 *et seq.* is available. This subdivision is drawn from Section 3(a) of the Uniform Trustees' Powers Act (1964). As to the construction of provisions drawn from uniform acts, see Section 2.

The exercise of powers by the trustee is subject to various important limitations as recognized in this section and as provided elsewhere. Subdivisions (b) and (c) make clear that the exercise of statutory or "prudent person" powers is subject to limitations provided in the trust. Section 16202 makes clear that the exercise of powers by the trustee is subject to the fiduciary duties owed to the beneficiaries. See the Comment to Section 16202; see also Section 16201 (power of court to relieve trustee from restrictions on powers). As to the construction of trust language that refers to "investments permissible by law for investment of trust funds," "authorized by law for investment of trust funds," "legal investments," "authorized investments," or "investments acquired using the judgment and care which men of prudence, discretion, and intelligence exercise in the management of their own affairs," or other words of similar meaning in defining the powers of the trustee relative to investments, see Section 16053. [25 Cal.L.Rev.Comm. Reports 543, 673 (1995)].

Background on Section 16200 of Repealed Code

Section 16200 was added by 1986 Cal.Stat. ch. 820 § 40. For background on the provisions of this division, see the Comment to this division under the division heading.

Subdivisions (a) and (b) superseded part of former Civil Code Section 2240 (power to deposit securities subject to contrary provision in trust instrument) and restated the second sentence of former Civil Code Section 2267 (trustee has authority conferred by trust instrument and statute) (provisions repealed by 1986 Cal.Stat. ch. 820 § 7) without substantive change. Subdivision (b) also superseded the authority to make deposits provided in subdivision (c) of former Civil Code Section 2261 (repealed by 1986 Cal.Stat. ch. 820 § 7). Subdivision (a) was consistent with the part of subdivision (a) of former Civil Code Section 2258 (repealed by 1986 Cal.Stat. ch. 820 § 7) that required the trustee to fulfill the purposes of the trust.

The introductory clause of Section 16200 superseded the first paragraph of former Probate Code Section 1120.2 which required court approval to exercise powers not expressed in the trust and subdivision (18) of former Probate Code Section 1120.2 (repealed by 1986 Cal.Stat. ch. 820 § 31) which gave the court authority to grant necessary or desirable powers.

Subdivision (b) gave the trustee the statutory powers without the need to incorporate them, as was required under former Probate Code Section 1120.2. [20 Cal.L.Rev.Comm.Reports 1001 (1990)].

Cross References

Cotrustees, power exercised through unanimous action, see Probate Code § 15620.
Notice of proposed actions, application or assertion of other rights and remedies, see Probate Code § 16500.
Proceedings concerning trusts, petition, see Probate Code § 17200.
Standard of care of trustee, see Probate Code § 16040 et seq.

§ 16201. Power of court; relief from restrictions on powers

This chapter does not affect the power of a court to relieve a trustee from restrictions on the exercise of powers under the trust instrument. *(Stats.1990, c. 79 (A.B.759), § 14, operative July 1, 1991.)*

Law Revision Commission Comments
1990 Enactment [Revised Comment]

Section 16201 continues Section 16201 of the repealed Probate Code without change. This section did not change the prior case law rule permitting deviation from trust restrictions as necessary in unforeseen circumstances. See, e.g., Estate of Loring, 29 Cal.2d 423, 436–37, 175 P.2d 524 (1946); Adams v. Cook, 15 Cal.2d 352, 359, 101 P.2d 484 (1940); Estate of Mabury, 54 Cal.App.3d 969, 984–85, 127 Cal.Rptr. 233 (1976); see also Restatement (Second) of Trusts § 167 (1957). For a provision permitting the court to modify a trust where there has been a material change of circumstances, see Section

15409. As to the construction of trust language that refers to "investments permissible by law for investment of trust funds," "authorized by law for investment of trust funds," "legal investments," "authorized investments," or "investments acquired using the judgment and care which men of prudence, discretion, and intelligence exercise in the management of their own affairs," or other words of similar meaning in defining the powers of the trustee relative to investments, see Section 16053. [25 Cal.L.Rev.Comm. Reports 673 (1995)].

Background on Section 16201 of Repealed Code

Section 16201 was added by 1986 Cal.Stat. ch. 820 § 40. The section restated subdivision (d) of former Civil Code Section 2261 (repealed by 1986 Cal.Stat. ch. 820 § 7) without substantive change, except that the rule was made general and was not restricted to the making or retention of investments as under former Civil Code Section 2261(d). Section 16201 also superseded subdivision (18) of former Probate Code Section 1120.2 (repealed by 1986 Cal.Stat. ch. 820 § 31). For background on the provisions of this division, see the Comment to this division under the division heading. [20 Cal.L.Rev.Comm.Reports 1001 (1990)].

§ 16202. Exercise of powers; fiduciary duties

The grant of a power to a trustee, whether by the trust instrument, by statute, or by the court, does not in itself require or permit the exercise of the power. The exercise of a power by a trustee is subject to the trustee's fiduciary duties. *(Stats.1990, c. 79 (A.B.759), § 14, operative July 1, 1991.)*

Law Revision Commission Comments
1990 Enactment [Revised Comment]

Section 16202 continues Section 16202 of the repealed Probate Code without change. This section recognizes that a power granted to the trustee from any source does not necessarily permit the exercise of the power, nor does it prevent the exercise of a power in a manner that conflicts with a general duty where the trust instrument so directs (see Section 16000) or where the trustee is directed so to act by a person holding the power to revoke the trust (see Section 16001). For example, the trust instrument may give the trustee discretion to favor one beneficiary over others, in apparent conflict with the general duty to deal with beneficiaries impartially under Section 16003. See also Section 16000 *et seq.* (trustee's fiduciary duties). As to the construction of trust language that refers to "investments permissible by law for investment of trust funds," "authorized by law for investment of trust funds," "legal investments," "authorized investments," or "investments acquired using the judgment and care which men of prudence, discretion, and intelligence exercise in the management of their own affairs," or other words of similar meaning in defining the powers of the trustee relative to investments, see Section 16053. [25 Cal.L.Rev.Comm. Reports 673 (1995)].

Background on Section 16202 of Repealed Code

Section 16202 was a new provision added by 1986 Cal.Stat. ch. 820 § 40. For background on the provisions of this division, see the Comment to this division under the division heading. [20 Cal.L.Rev.Comm.Reports 1001 (1990)].

§ 16203. References to former provisions

An instrument that incorporates the powers provided in former Section 1120.2 (repealed by Chapter 820 of the Statutes of 1986) shall be deemed to refer to the powers provided in Article 2 (commencing with Section 16220). For this purpose, the trustee's powers under former Section 1120.2 are not diminished and the trustee is not required to obtain court approval for exercise of a power for which court approval was not required by former law. *(Stats.1990, c. 79 (A.B.759), § 14, operative July 1, 1991.)*

Law Revision Commission Comments
1990 Enactment [Revised Comment]

Section 16203 continues Section 16203 of the repealed Probate Code with technical changes. This section makes clear the effect of references in instruments to the former provisions listing trustees' powers. As to the construction of trust language that refers to "investments permissible by law for investment of trust funds," "authorized by law for investment of trust funds," "legal investments," "authorized investments," or "investments acquired using the judgment and care which men of prudence, discretion, and intelligence exercise in the management of their own affairs," or other words of similar meaning in defining the powers of the trustee relative to investments, see Section 16053. [25 Cal.L.Rev.Comm. Reports 673 (1995)].

Background on Section 16203 of Repealed Code

Section 16203 was a new provision added by 1986 Cal.Stat. ch. 820 § 40. For background on the provisions of this division, see the Comment to this division under the division heading. [20 Cal.L.Rev.Comm.Reports 1001 (1990)].

ARTICLE 2. SPECIFIC POWERS OF TRUSTEES

Application

Application of Division, see Probate Code § 15001.

Cross References

Application of old and new law, see Probate Code § 3.

Common law rules governing trusts, application, see Probate Code § 15002.
Conveyances or transfers of property claimed to belong to decedent or other person, see Probate Code § 850 et seq.
Instrument incorporating powers in former § 1120.2 deemed to refer to powers in this Article, see Probate Code § 16203.
Relationships excluded from Code definition of trust, application of this Division, see Probate Code § 15003.

§ 16220. Collecting and holding property

The trustee has the power to collect, hold, and retain trust property received from a settlor or any other person until, in the judgment of the trustee, disposition of the property should be made. The property may be retained even though it includes property in which the trustee is personally interested. *(Stats.1990, c. 79 (A.B.759), § 14, operative July 1, 1991.)*

Law Revision Commission Comments
1990 Enactment [Revised Comment]

Section 16220 continues Section 16220 of the repealed Probate Code without change. This section is the same in substance as Section 3(c)(1) of the Uniform Trustees' Powers Act (1964). As to the construction of provisions drawn from uniform acts, see Section 2. The exercise of the power to hold property under this section is subject to the limitation provided in Section 21524(c) in the case of a marital deduction trust. See also Sections 62 ("property" defined), 16053 (language invoking standard of Uniform Prudent Investor Act), 16202 (exercise of powers is subject to duties), 16203 (trust instrument that incorporates the powers provided in former Section 1120.2 of the repealed Probate Code). [25 Cal.L.Rev.Comm. Reports 673 (1995)].

Background on Section 16220 of Repealed Code

Section 16220 was added by 1986 Cal.Stat. ch. 820 § 40. The section superseded part of subdivision (b) of former Civil Code Section 2261 (repealed by 1986 Cal.Stat. ch. 820 § 7) and part of subdivision (2) of former Probate Code Section 1120.2 (repealed by 1986 Cal.Stat. ch. 820 § 31). The specific references to stock in the trustee or in a corporation controlling or controlled by the trustee in former Civil Code Section 2261(b) and in former Probate Code Section 1120.2(2) were omitted from Section 16220 because they were unnecessary; however, the substance of the law was not changed by Section 16220 since stock of the type described by the former provisions is within the general language of the new law. See Section 62 ("property" defined). For background on the provisions of this division, see the Comment to this division under the division heading. [20 Cal.L.Rev.Comm.Reports 1001 (1990)].

Cross References
Powers of trustees, generally, see Probate Code § 16200.

§ 16221. Additions to trust

The trustee has the power to accept additions to the property of the trust from a settlor or any other person. *(Stats.1990, c. 79 (A.B.759), § 14, operative July 1, 1991.)*

Law Revision Commission Comments
1990 Enactment

Section 16221 continues Section 16221 of the repealed Probate Code without change. This section is the same in substance as Section 3(c)(2) of the Uniform Trustees' Powers Act (1964). As to the construction of provisions drawn from uniform acts, see Section 2. See also Sections 62 ("property" defined), 16202 (exercise of powers is subject to duties), 16203 (trust instrument that incorporates the powers provided in former Section 1120.2 of the repealed Probate Code).

Background on Section 16221 of Repealed Code

Section 16221 was added by 1986 Cal.Stat. ch. 820 § 40. The section superseded part of the first sentence of subdivision (b) of former Probate Code Section 1120 and paragraph (3) of subdivision (a) of former Probate Code Section 1138.1 (provisions repealed by 1986 Cal.Stat. ch. 820 § 31). For background on the provisions of this division, see the Comment to this division under the division heading. [20 Cal.L.Rev.Comm.Reports 1001 (1990)].

§ 16222. Continuation of business

(a) Subject to subdivision (b), the trustee has the power to continue or participate in the operation of any business or other enterprise that is part of the trust property and may effect incorporation, dissolution, or other change in the form of the organization of the business or enterprise.

(b) Except as provided in subdivision (c), the trustee may continue the operation of a business or other enterprise only as authorized by the trust instrument or by the court. For the purpose of this subdivision, the lease of four or fewer residential units is not considered to be the operation of a business or other enterprise.

(c) The trustee may continue the operation of a business or other enterprise for a reasonable time pending a court hearing on the matter or pending a sale of the business or other enterprise.

(d) The limitation provided in subdivision (b) does not affect any power to continue or participate in the operation of a business or other enterprise that the trustee has under a trust created by an instrument executed before July 1, 1987. *(Stats.1990, c. 79 (A.B.759), § 14, operative July 1, 1991.)*

Law Revision Commission Comments
1990 Enactment [Revised Comment]

Section 16222 continues Section 16222 of the repealed Probate Code without change. Subdivision (a) is similar to Section 3(c)(3) of the Uniform Trustees' Powers Act (1964). As to the construction of provisions drawn from uniform acts, see Section 2. Under Section 16222, the trustee may have the power to continue a business that is made part of the trust, but may not enter into a new business. See also 16053 (language invoking standard of Uniform Prudent Investor Act), 16202 (exercise of powers is subject to duties), 16203 (trust instrument that incorporates the powers provided in former Section 1120.2 of the repealed Probate Code).

Subdivision (b) excludes the lease of four or fewer residential units from the requirement that the trustee obtain court approval to continue operation of a business or other enterprise that is a part of trust property. It is irrelevant whether the residential units are located in one or more buildings or on one or more lots.

Subdivision (d) limits the rule in subdivision (b) requiring court authorization for the trustee to operate a business or other enterprise that is a part of trust property. This is a special application of the rule stated in Section 16203. [25 Cal.L.Rev.Comm. Reports 673 (1995)].

Background on Section 16222 of Repealed Code

Section 16222 was added by 1986 Cal.Stat. ch. 820 § 40 and amended by 1987 Cal.Stat. ch. 128 § 16. Subdivision (a) continued subdivision (17) of former Probate Code Section 1120.2 (repealed by 1986 Cal.Stat. ch. 820 § 31) without substantive change. Subdivisions (b) and (c) were new. For background on the provisions of this division, see the Comment to this division under the division heading. [20 Cal.L.Rev.Comm.Reports 1001 (1990)].

§ 16223. Repealed by Stats.1995, c. 63 (S.B.222), § 8
Law Revision Commission Comments
1995 Repeal

Section 16223 is replaced by Section 16047(e), which provides the same unrestricted power of investment under the Uniform Prudent Investor Act. [25 Cal.L.Rev.Comm. Reports 688 (1995)].

§ 16224. Investments and obligations of United States government

(a) In the absence of an express provision to the contrary in a trust instrument, where the instrument directs or permits investment in obligations of the United States government, the trustee has the power to invest in those obligations directly or in the form of an interest in a money market mutual fund registered under the Investment Company Act of 1940 (15 U.S.C. Sec. 80a–1 et seq.) or an investment vehicle authorized for the collective investment of trust funds pursuant to Section 9.18 of Part 9 of Title 12 of the Code of Federal Regulations, the portfolios of which are limited to United States government obligations maturing not later than five years from the date of investment or reinvestment and to repurchase agreements fully collateralized by United States government obligations.

(b) This section applies only to trusts created on or after January 1, 1985. *(Stats.1990, c. 79 (A.B.759), § 14, operative July 1, 1991.)*

Law Revision Commission Comments
1990 Enactment [Revised Comment]

Section 16224 continues Section 16224 of the repealed Probate Code without change. See also Sections 16053 (language invoking standard of Uniform Prudent Investor Act), 16202 (exercise of powers is subject to duties), 16203 (trust instrument that incorporates the powers provided in former Section 1120.2 of the repealed Probate Code). [25 Cal.L.Rev.Comm. Reports 673 (1995)].

Background on Section 16224 of Repealed Code

Section 16224 was added by 1986 Cal.Stat. ch. 820 § 40. The section continued the first sentence of subdivision (a) and subdivision (b) of former Civil Code Section 2269.1 (repealed by 1986 Cal.Stat. ch. 820 § 7) with some technical changes to eliminate surplus language. For background on the provisions of this division, see the Comment to this division under the division heading. [20 Cal.L.Rev.Comm.Reports 1001 (1990)].

§ 16225. Deposits

(a) The trustee has the power to deposit trust funds at reasonable interest in any of the following accounts:

(1) An insured account in a financial institution.

(2) To the extent that the account is collateralized, an account in a bank, an account in an insured savings and loan association, or an account in an insured credit union.

(b) A trustee may deposit trust funds pursuant to subdivision (a) in a financial institution operated by, or that is an affiliate of, the trustee. For the purpose of this subdivision, "affiliate" means a corporation that directly or indirectly through one or more intermediaries controls, is controlled by, or is under common control with another domestic or foreign corporation.

(c) This section does not limit the power of a trustee in a proper case to deposit trust funds in an account described in subdivision (a) that is subject to notice or other conditions respecting withdrawal prescribed by law or governmental regulation.

(d) The court may authorize the deposit of trust funds in an account described in subdivision (a) in an amount greater than the maximum insured or collateralized amount.

(e) Nothing in this section prevents the trustee from holding an amount of trust property reasonably necessary for the orderly administration of the trust in the form of cash or in a checking account without interest. *(Stats.1990, c. 79 (A.B.759), § 14, operative July 1, 1991.)*

Law Revision Commission Comments

1990 Enactment

Section 16225 continues Section 16225 of the repealed Probate Code without change. See Section 21 ("account" defined). See also Section 16202 (exercise of powers is subject to duties). See also Fin.Code § 764 (fiduciaries' deposits in banks). For other provisions relating to deposits by trustees, see Fin.Code §§ 7000–7002. See also Uniform Trustees' Powers Act § 3(c)(6) (1964). The definition of "affiliated" in second sentence of subdivision (b) is the same as that provided in Corporations Code Section 150. Court authorization under subdivision (d) may be obtained as provided in Section 17200(b)(2), (5), and (6). Section 16225 is comparable to Sections 2453 and 2453.5 (deposits by guardians and conservators).

Subdivision (e) recognizes that the limitation of the power to make deposits to accounts affording reasonable interest provided in subdivision (a) is not absolute but is subject to reasonable requirements of trust administration. Subdivision (e) is consistent with Section 9705(b) (administration of decedent's estate).

Background on Section 16225 of Repealed Code

Section 16225 was added by 1986 Cal.Stat. ch. 820 § 40 and was amended by 1988 Cal.Stat. ch. 1199 § 105.5. The section restated the part of subdivision (c) of former Civil Code Section 2261 (repealed by 1986 Cal.Stat. ch. 820 § 7) relating to deposits in banks. The requirement that funds be deposited at reasonable interest was new. The limitation on bank deposits in subdivision (a)(1) was the same as that provided in former Civil Code Section 2261(c), except that the reference to present or future laws of the United States was omitted as unnecessary. Subdivisions (a)(2) and (a)(3) incorporated limitations applicable under the guardianship and conservatorship statute; the language relating to the extent to which trust funds may be deposited in such accounts was new. Subdivisions (b)–(d) of Section 16225 restated part of subdivision (c) of former Civil Code Section 2261 without substantive change. Subdivision (e) was new. For background on the provisions of this division, see the Comment to this division under the division heading.

The 1988 amendment conformed the terminology of subdivision (a) of Section 16225 to the general definitions. See Sections 22 (account in an insured credit union), 23 (account in an insured savings and loan association), 40 (financial institution), 46 (insured account in a financial institution). The 1988 amendment was technical and nonsubstantive. [20 Cal.L.Rev.Comm.Reports 1001 (1990)].

Cross References

Common trust funds of trust companies, see Financial Code § 1564. Deposit of trust company funds awaiting investment, see Financial Code § 1562.

Savings accounts of savings associations as legal investments for funds of trustees, see Financial Code § 7000.

§ 16226.   Acquisition and disposition of property

The trustee has the power to acquire or dispose of property, for cash or on credit, at public or private sale, or by exchange. *(Stats.1990, c. 79 (A.B.759), § 14, operative July 1, 1991.)*

Law Revision Commission Comments

1990 Enactment [Revised Comment]

Section 16226 continues Section 16226 of the repealed Probate Code without change. This section is the same in substance as part of Section 3(c)(7) of the Uniform Trustees' Powers Act (1964). As to the construction of provisions drawn from uniform acts, see Section 2. See also Sections 62 ("property" defined), 16053 (language invoking standard of Uniform Prudent Investor Act), 16202 (exercise of powers is subject to duties), 16203 (trust instrument that incorporates the powers provided in former Section 1120.2 of the repealed Probate Code). [25 Cal.L.Rev.Comm. Reports 673 (1995)].

Background on Section 16226 of Repealed Code

Section 16226 was added by 1986 Cal.Stat. ch. 820 § 40. The section restated part of the second sentence of paragraph (1) of subdivision (a) of former Civil Code Section 2261 (repealed by 1986 Cal.Stat. ch. 820 § 7) and part of subdivision (5) of former Probate Code Section 1120.2 (repealed by 1986 Cal.Stat. ch. 820 § 31) without substantive change. Section 16226 also superseded the part of subdivision (1) of former Probate Code Section 1120.2 pertaining to sale of trust assets on deferred payments. For background on the provisions of this division, see the Comment to this division under the division heading. [20 Cal.L.Rev.Comm.Reports 1001 (1990)].

Cross References

Trustee to manage proceeds of sale of property subject to life estate upon partition, see Code of Civil Procedure § 873.840.

§ 16227.   Management of property

The trustee has the power to manage, control, divide, develop, improve, exchange, partition, change the character of, or abandon trust property or any interest therein. *(Stats.1990, c. 79 (A.B.759), § 14, operative July 1, 1991.)*

Law Revision Commission Comments

1990 Enactment [Revised Comment]

Section 16227 continues Section 16227 of the repealed Probate Code without change. This section is the same in substance as part of Section 3(c)(7) of the Uniform Trustees' Powers Act (1964). As to the construction of provisions drawn from uniform acts, see Section 2. See also Sections 62 ("property" defined), 16053 (language invoking standard of Uniform Prudent Investor Act), 16202 (exercise of powers is subject to duties), 16203 (trust instrument that incorporates the powers provided in former Section 1120.2 of the repealed Probate Code). [25 Cal.L.Rev.Comm. Reports 673 (1995)].

Background on Section 16227 of Repealed Code

Section 16227 was added by 1986 Cal.Stat. ch. 820 § 40. The section continued the authority to manage, control, or divide property provided in subdivision (1) of former Probate Code Section 1120.2 (repealed by 1986 Cal.Stat. ch. 820 § 31) and part of subdivision (5) of former Probate Code Section 1120.2 without change, except that "property" was used in place of "asset." For background on the provisions of this division, see the Comment to this division under the division heading. [20 Cal.L.Rev.Comm.Reports 1001 (1990)].

§ 16228. Encumbrance, mortgage, or pledge

The trustee has the power to encumber, mortgage, or pledge trust property for a term within or extending beyond the term of the trust in connection with the exercise of any power vested in the trustee. *(Stats.1990, c. 79 (A.B.759), § 14, operative July 1, 1991.)*

Law Revision Commission Comments
1990 Enactment [Revised Comment]

Section 16228 continues Section 16228 of the repealed Probate Code without change. This section is the same in substance as part of Section 3(c)(7) of the Uniform Trustees' Powers Act (1964). As to the construction of provisions drawn from uniform acts, see Section 2. See also Sections 62 ("property" defined), 16053 (language invoking standard of Uniform Prudent Investor Act), 16202 (exercise of powers is subject to duties), 16203 (trust instrument that incorporates the powers provided in former Section 1120.2 of the repealed Probate Code). [25 Cal.L.Rev.Comm. Reports 673 (1995)].

Background on Section 16228 of Repealed Code

Section 16228 was added by 1986 Cal.Stat. ch. 820 § 40. The section superseded part of subdivision (3) of former Probate Code Section 1120.2 (repealed by 1986 Cal.Stat. ch. 820 § 31). For background on the provisions of this division, see the Comment to this division under the division heading. [20 Cal.L.Rev.Comm.Reports 1001 (1990)].

§ 16229. Repairs and alterations

The trustee has the power to do any of the following:

(a) Make ordinary or extraordinary repairs, alterations, or improvements in buildings or other trust property.

(b) Demolish any improvements.

(c) Raze existing or erect new party walls or buildings. *(Stats.1990, c. 79 (A.B.759), § 14, operative July 1, 1991.)*

Law Revision Commission Comments
1990 Enactment [Revised Comment]

Section 16229 continues Section 16229 of the repealed Probate Code without substantive change. This section is the same in substance as Section 3(c)(8) of the Uniform Trustees' Powers Act (1964). As to the construction of provisions drawn from uniform acts, see Section 2. See also Sections 16053 (language invoking standard of Uniform Prudent Investor Act), 16202 (exercise of powers is subject to duties), 16203 (trust instrument that incorporates the powers provided in former Section 1120.2 of the repealed Probate Code). [25 Cal.L.Rev.Comm. Reports 673 (1995)].

Background on Section 16229 of Repealed Code

Section 16229 was added by 1986 Cal.Stat. ch. 820 § 40. The section continued subdivision (6) of former Probate Code Section 1120.2 (repealed by 1986 Cal.Stat. ch. 820 § 31) without substantive change but the reference to improvements was new. For background on the provisions of this division, see the Comment to this division under the division heading. [20 Cal.L.Rev.Comm.Reports 1001 (1990)].

§ 16230. Development of land

The trustee has the power to do any of the following:

(a) Subdivide or develop land.

(b) Dedicate land to public use.

(c) Make or obtain the vacation of plats and adjust boundaries.

(d) Adjust differences in valuation on exchange or partition by giving or receiving consideration.

(e) Dedicate easements to public use without consideration. *(Stats.1990, c. 79 (A.B.759), § 14, operative July 1, 1991.)*

Law Revision Commission Comments
1990 Enactment [Revised Comment]

Section 16230 continues Section 16230 of the repealed Probate Code without change. This section is the same in substance as Section 3(c)(9) of the Uniform Trustees' Powers Act (1964). As to the construction of provisions drawn from uniform acts, see Section 2. See also Sections 16053 (language invoking standard of Uniform Prudent Investor Act), 16202 (exercise of powers is subject to duties), 16203 (trust instrument that incorporates the powers provided in former Section 1120.2 of the repealed Probate Code). [25 Cal. L.Rev.Comm. Reports 673 (1995)].

Background on Section 16230 of Repealed Code

Section 16230 was added by 1986 Cal.Stat. ch. 820 § 40. The section continued subdivision (7) of former Probate Code Section 1120.2 (repealed by 1986 Cal.Stat. ch. 820 § 31) without substantive change. For background on the provisions of this division, see the Comment to this division under the division heading. [20 Cal.L.Rev.Comm.Reports 1001 (1990)].

§ 16231. Leases

The trustee has the power to enter into a lease for any purpose as lessor or lessee with or without the option to purchase or renew and for a term within or extending beyond the term of the trust. *(Stats.1990, c. 79 (A.B.759), § 14, operative July 1, 1991.)*

Law Revision Commission Comments
1990 Enactment [Revised Comment]

Section 16231 continues Section 16231 of the repealed Probate Code without change. This section is the same in substance as Section 3(c)(10) of the Uniform Trustees' Powers Act (1964). As to the construction of provisions drawn from uniform acts, see Section 2. See also Sections 16053 (language invoking standard of Uniform Prudent Investor Act), 16202 (exercise of powers is subject to duties), 16203 (trust instrument that incorporates the powers provided in former Section 1120.2 of the repealed Probate Code). [25 Cal. L.Rev.Comm. Reports 673 (1995)].

Background on Section 16231 of Repealed Code

Section 16231 was added by 1986 Cal.Stat. ch. 820 § 40. The section restated part of subdivision (1) of former Probate Code Section 1120.2 (repealed by 1986 Cal.Stat. ch. 820 § 31) without substantive change and superseded former Civil Code Section 2272 (repealed by 1986 Cal.Stat. ch. 820 § 7). For background on the provisions of this division, see the Comment to this division under the division heading. [20 Cal.L.Rev.Comm.Reports 1001 (1990)].

Cross References
Termination of the trust, see Probate Code § 15407.

§ 16232. Mineral leases

The trustee has the power to enter into a lease or arrangement for exploration and removal of gas, oil, or other minerals or geothermal energy, and to enter into a community oil lease or a pooling or unitization agreement, and for a term within or extending beyond the term of the trust. *(Stats.1990, c. 79 (A.B.759), § 14, operative July 1, 1991.)*

Law Revision Commission Comments

1990 Enactment [Revised Comment]

Section 16232 continues Section 16232 of the repealed Probate Code with the addition of a reference to geothermal energy. The reference to a pooling or unitization agreement is drawn from Section 3(c)(11) of the Uniform Trustees' Powers Act (1964). As to the construction of provisions drawn from uniform acts, see Section 2. The authority to make leases or agreements extending beyond the term of the trust is consistent with Section 16231 (general power to lease). See also Sections 16053 (language invoking standard of Uniform Prudent Investor Act), 16202 (exercise of powers is subject to duties), 16203 (trust instrument that incorporates the powers provided in former Section 1120.2 of the repealed Probate Code). [25 Cal.L.Rev.Comm. Reports 673 (1995)].

Background on Section 16232 of Repealed Code

Section 16232 was added by 1986 Cal.Stat. ch. 820 § 40. The section restated part of subdivision (1) of former Probate Code Section 1120.2 (repealed by 1986 Cal.Stat. ch. 820 § 31) without substantive change and added the reference to a pooling or unitization agreement drawn from Section 3(c)(11) of the Uniform Trustees' Powers Act (1964). As to the construction of provisions drawn from uniform acts, see Section 2. For background on the provisions of this division, see the Comment to this division under the division heading. [20 Cal.L.Rev.Comm.Reports 1001 (1990)].

§ 16233. Options

The trustee has the power to grant an option involving disposition of trust property or to take an option for the acquisition of any property, and an option may be granted or taken that is exercisable beyond the term of the trust. *(Stats.1990, c. 79 (A.B.759), § 14, operative July 1, 1991.)*

Law Revision Commission Comments

1990 Enactment [Revised Comment]

Section 16233 continues Section 16233 of the repealed Probate Code without change. This section is the same in substance as Section 3(c)(12) of the Uniform Trustees' Powers Act (1964). As to the construction of provisions drawn from uniform acts, see Section 2. The authority to grant or take options exercisable beyond the term of the trust is consistent with Section 16231 (general power to lease). An option under this section includes a right of first refusal. See also Sections 62 ("property" defined), 16053 (language invoking standard of Uniform Prudent Investor Act), 16202 (exercise of powers is subject to duties), 16203 (trust instrument that incorporates the powers provided in former Section 1120.2 of the repealed Probate Code). [25 Cal.L.Rev.Comm. Reports 673 (1995)].

Background on Section 16233 of Repealed Code

Section 16233 was added by 1986 Cal.Stat. ch. 820 § 40. The first half of Section 16233 continued subdivision (8) of former Probate Code Section 1120.2 (repealed by 1986 Cal.Stat. ch. 820 § 31) without substantive change, but the word "property" was used in place of "asset." The authority to grant or take options exercisable beyond the term of the trust was new. For background on the provisions of this division, see the Comment to this division under the division heading. [20 Cal.L.Rev.Comm.Reports 1001 (1990)].

§ 16234. Voting rights, etc.; corporate shares, memberships, or property

With respect to any shares of stock of a domestic or foreign corporation, any membership in a nonprofit corporation, or any other property, a trustee has the power to do any of the following:

(a) Vote in person, and give proxies to exercise, any voting rights with respect to the shares, memberships, or property.

(b) Waive notice of a meeting or give consent to the holding of a meeting.

(c) Authorize, ratify, approve, or confirm any action that could be taken by shareholders, members, or property owners. *(Stats.1990, c. 79 (A.B.759), § 14, operative July 1, 1991.)*

Law Revision Commission Comments

1990 Enactment [Revised Comment]

Section 16234 continues Section 16234 of the repealed Probate Code without change. This section is comparable to Section 2458 (voting rights under guardianship and conservatorship statute). See also Corp. Code §§ 702(a) (voting of shares by trustee), 703(c) (voting of shares in corporate trustee), 705 (proxies); Prob. Code §§ 16053 (language invoking standard of Uniform Prudent Investor Act), 16202 (exercise of powers is subject to duties), 16203 (trust instrument that incorporates the powers provided in former Section 1120.2 of the repealed Probate Code). [25 Cal.L.Rev.Comm. Reports 673 (1995)].

Background on Section 16234 of Repealed Code

Section 16234 was added by 1986 Cal.Stat. ch. 820 § 40. The section restated without substantive change subdivision (9) of former Probate Code Section 1120.2 (repealed by 1986 Cal.Stat. ch. 820 § 31) and former Civil Code Section 2270 (repealed by 1986 Cal.Stat. ch. 820 § 7), except that the requirement in former Civil Code Section 2270 that authorizations be in writing was omitted. For background on the provisions of this division, see the Comment to this division under the division heading. [20 Cal.L.Rev.Comm.Reports 1001 (1990)].

Cross References

Personal nonliability of trustee for subscription price of shares, see Corporations Code § 413.
Power of trustee to make endorsement, see Commercial Code § 8315.
Registration of stock held in trust in name of nominee of trust company, see Financial Code § 1563.
Termination of trust, see Probate Code § 15407.
Trustee permitted to give proxies, see Corporations Code § 705.
Voting of shares standing in name of trustee, see Corporations Code § 702.

§ 16235. Payment of calls and assessments

The trustee has the power to pay calls, assessments, and any other sums chargeable or accruing against or on account of securities. *(Stats.1990, c. 79 (A.B.759), § 14, operative July 1, 1991.)*

Law Revision Commission Comments

1990 Enactment [Revised Comment]

Section 16235 continues Section 16235 of the repealed Probate Code without change. This section is the same as Section 3(c)(14) of the Uniform Trustees' Powers Act (1964). As to the construction of provisions drawn from uniform acts, see Section 2. See also Sections 16053 (language invoking standard of Uniform Prudent Investor Act), 16202 (exercise of powers is subject to duties), 16203 (trust instrument that incorporates the powers provided in former Section 1120.2 of the repealed Probate Code). [25 Cal.L.Rev.Comm. Reports 673 (1995)].

Background on Section 16235 of Repealed Code

Section 16235 was added by 1986 Cal.Stat. ch. 820 § 40. The section continued subdivision (10) of former Probate Code Section 1120.2 (repealed by 1986 Cal.Stat. ch. 820 § 31) without substantive change. For background on the provisions of this division, see the Comment to this division under the division heading. [20 Cal.L.Rev.Comm.Reports 1001 (1990)].

§ 16236. Stock subscriptions and conversions

The trustee has the power to sell or exercise stock subscription or conversion rights. *(Stats.1990, c. 79 (A.B. 759), § 14, operative July 1, 1991.)*

Law Revision Commission Comments

1990 Enactment [Revised Comment]

Section 16236 continues Section 16236 of the repealed Probate Code without change. This section is the same as the first part of Section 3(c)(15) of the Uniform Trustees' Powers Act (1964). As to the construction of provisions drawn from uniform acts, see Section 2. See also Sections 16053 (language invoking standard of Uniform Prudent Investor Act), 16202 (exercise of powers is subject to duties), 16203 (trust instrument that incorporates the powers provided in former Section 1120.2 of the repealed Probate Code). [25 Cal. L.Rev.Comm. Reports 673 (1995)].

Background on Section 16236 of Repealed Code

Section 16236 was added by 1986 Cal.Stat. ch. 820 § 40. The section continued subdivision (11) of former Probate Code Section 1120.2 (repealed by 1986 Cal.Stat. ch. 820 § 31) without substantive change. For background on the provisions of this division, see the Comment to this division under the division heading. [20 Cal.L.Rev.Comm.Reports 1001 (1990)].

Cross References

Corporate shares, liability of fiduciary for subscription price, see Corporations Code § 413.

§ 16237. Consent to change in form of business; voting trusts

The trustee has the power to consent, directly or through a committee or other agent, to the reorganization, consolidation, merger, dissolution, or liquidation of a corporation or other business enterprise, and to participate in voting trusts, pooling arrangements, and foreclosures, and in connection therewith, to deposit securities with and transfer title and delegate discretion to any protective or other committee as the trustee may deem advisable. *(Stats.1990, c. 79 (A.B.759), § 14, operative July 1, 1991.)*

Law Revision Commission Comments

1990 Enactment [Revised Comment]

Section 16237 continues Section 16237 of the repealed Probate Code without substantive change. This section, in part, is similar to the second part of Section 3(c)(15) of the Uniform Trustees' Powers Act (1964). As to the construction of provisions drawn from uniform acts, see Section 2. See also Sections 16053 (language invoking standard of Uniform Prudent Investor Act), 16202 (exercise of powers is subject to duties), 16203 (trust instrument that incorporates the powers provided in former Section 1120.2 of the repealed Probate Code). [25 Cal.L.Rev.Comm. Reports 673 (1995)].

Background on Section 16237 of Repealed Code

Section 16237 was added by 1986 Cal.Stat. ch. 820 § 40. The section continued subdivision (4) of former Probate Code Section 1120.2 (repealed by 1986 Cal.Stat. ch. 820 § 31) without substantive

change. For background on the provisions of this division, see the Comment to this division under the division heading. [20 Cal.L.Rev.Comm.Reports 1001 (1990)].

§ 16238. Holding securities

The trustee has the power to hold a security in the name of a nominee or in other form without disclosure of the trust so that title to the security may pass by delivery. *(Stats.1990, c. 79 (A.B.759), § 14, operative July 1, 1991.)*

Law Revision Commission Comments

1990 Enactment [Revised Comment]

Section 16238 continues Section 16238 of the repealed Probate Code, but deletes the reference to the liability of the trustee for an act of the nominee for consistency with Section 9736 (decedent's estate management). This matter is governed by general provisions on liability of a trustee. See, e.g., Section 16401. This section is comparable to Section 3(c)(16) of the Uniform Trustees' Powers Act (1964). As to the construction of provisions drawn from uniform acts, see Section 2. See also Corp. Code § 702(a) (trustee not entitled to vote shares without transfer into trustee's name); Fin. Code § 1563 (trust company may register securities in name of nominee); Prob. Code §§ 16053 (language invoking standard of Uniform Prudent Investor Act), 16202 (exercise of powers is subject to duties), 16203 (trust instrument that incorporates the powers provided in former Section 1120.2 of the repealed Probate Code). [25 Cal.L.Rev. Comm. Reports 673 (1995)].

Background on Section 16238 of Repealed Code

Section 16238 was added by 1986 Cal.Stat. ch. 820 § 40. The section continued subdivision (12) of former Probate Code Section 1120.2 (repealed by 1986 Cal.Stat. ch. 820 § 31) without substantive change. For background on the provisions of this division, see the Comment to this division under the division heading. [20 Cal.L.Rev.Comm.Reports 1001 (1990)].

§ 16239. Deposit of securities in securities depository

The trustee has the power to deposit securities in a securities depository, as defined in Section 30004 of the Financial Code, which is licensed under Section 30200 of the Financial Code or is exempt from licensing by Section 30005 or 30006 of the Financial Code. The securities may be held by the securities depository in the manner authorized by Section 775 of the Financial Code. *(Stats.1990, c. 79 (A.B.759), § 14, operative July 1, 1991.)*

Law Revision Commission Comments

1990 Enactment [Revised Comment]

Section 16239 continues Section 16239 of the repealed Probate Code without change. See also Sections 16053 (language invoking standard of Uniform Prudent Investor Act), 16200 (powers subject to control by trust instrument), 16202 (exercise of powers is subject to duties), 16203 (trust instrument that incorporates the powers provided in former Section 1120.2 of the repealed Probate Code). [25 Cal.L.Rev.Comm. Reports 673 (1995)].

Background on Section 16239 of Repealed Code

Section 16239 was added by 1986 Cal.Stat. ch. 820 § 40. The section continued part of former Civil Code Section 2240 (repealed by 1986 Cal.Stat. ch. 820 § 7) without substantive change. Section 16239 did not continue the provision in former Civil Code Section 2240 relating to consent by cofiduciaries. See Section 15620 (actions by cotrustees). For background on the provisions of this division, see the Comment to this division under the division heading. [20 Cal.L.Rev.Comm.Reports 1001 (1990)].

§ 16240. Insurance

The trustee has the power to insure the property of the trust against damage or loss and to insure the trustee against liability with respect to third persons. *(Stats.1990, c. 79 (A.B.759), § 14, operative July 1, 1991.)*

Law Revision Commission Comments

1990 Enactment [Revised Comment]

Section 16240 continues Section 16240 of the repealed Probate Code without change. This section is the same in substance as Section 3(c)(17) of the Uniform Trustees' Powers Act (1964). As to the construction of provisions drawn from uniform acts, see Section 2. See also Sections 62 ("property" defined), 16053 (language invoking standard of Uniform Prudent Investor Act), 16202 (exercise of powers is subject to duties), 16203 (trust instrument that incorporates the powers provided in former Section 1120.2 of the repealed Probate Code). [25 Cal.L.Rev.Comm. Reports 673 (1995)].

Background on Section 16240 of Repealed Code

Section 16240 was added by 1986 Cal.Stat. ch. 820 § 40. The section restated subdivision (13) of former Probate Code Section 1120.2 (repealed by 1986 Cal.Stat. ch. 820 § 31) without substantive change. For background on the provisions of this division, see the Comment to this division under the division heading. [20 Cal.L.Rev.Comm.Reports 1001 (1990)].

§ 16241. Borrowing money

The trustee has the power to borrow money for any trust purpose to be repaid from trust property. The lender may include, but is not limited to, a bank holding company, affiliate, or subsidiary of the trustee. *(Stats.1990, c. 79 (A.B.759), § 14, operative July 1, 1991.)*

Law Revision Commission Comments

1990 Enactment [Revised Comment]

Section 16241 continues Section 16241 of the repealed Probate Code without change. The first sentence of this section is similar to part of Section 3(c)(18) of the Uniform Trustees' Powers Act (1964). As to the construction of provisions drawn from uniform acts, see Section 2. See also Sections 62 ("property" defined), 16053 (language invoking standard of Uniform Prudent Investor Act), 16202 (exercise of powers is subject to duties), 16203 (trust instrument that incorporates the powers provided in former Section 1120.2 of the repealed Probate Code). [25 Cal.L.Rev.Comm. Reports 673 (1995)].

Background on Section 16241 of Repealed Code

Section 16241 was added by 1986 Cal.Stat. ch. 820 § 40 and amended by 1988 Cal.Stat. ch. 1341 § 1. As enacted, the section superseded the authority to borrow provided in subdivision (3) of former Probate Code Section 1120.2 (repealed by 1986 Cal.Stat. ch. 820 § 31). For background on the provisions of this division, see the Comment to this division under the division heading. The 1988 amendment added the second sentence. [20 Cal.L.Rev.Comm.Reports 1001 (1990)].

§ 16242. Payment and settlement of claims

The trustee has the power to do any of the following:

(a) Pay or contest any claim.

(b) Settle a claim by or against the trust by compromise, arbitration, or otherwise.

(c) Release, in whole or in part, any claim belonging to the trust. *(Stats.1990, c. 79 (A.B.759), § 14, operative July 1, 1991.)*

Law Revision Commission Comments

1990 Enactment [Revised Comment]

Section 16242 continues Section 16242 of the repealed Probate Code without change. This section is substantially the same as Section 3(c)(19) of the Uniform Trustees' Powers Act (1964). As to the construction of provisions drawn from uniform acts, see Section 2. The trustee has the power to release a claim; the determination of when to release a claim depends upon the duties imposed on the trustee. As a general matter, the trustee should be able to release a claim not only when it is uncollectible, but also when it is uneconomical to attempt to collect it. See also Sections 16010 (duty to enforce claims), 16011 (duty to defend actions), 16053 (language invoking standard of Uniform Prudent Investor Act), 16202 (exercise of powers is subject to duties), 16203 (trust instrument that incorporates the powers provided in former Section 1120.2 of the repealed Probate Code). [25 Cal.L.Rev.Comm. Reports 673 (1995)].

Background on Section 16242 of Repealed Code

Section 16242 was added by 1986 Cal.Stat. ch. 820 § 40. Subdivisions (a) and (b) continued the first and second clauses of subdivision (15) of former Probate Code Section 1120.2 (repealed by 1986 Cal.Stat. ch. 820 § 31) without substantive change. Subdivision (c) continued the third clause of subdivision (15) of former Probate Code Section 1120.2 without substantive change, except that the limitation on releasing claims only to the extent that they were uncollectible was not continued. For background on the provisions of this division, see the Comment to this division under the division heading. [20 Cal.L.Rev.Comm.Reports 1001 (1990)].

§ 16243. Payment of trust expenses

The trustee has the power to pay taxes, assessments, reasonable compensation of the trustee and of employees and agents of the trust, and other expenses incurred in the collection, care, administration, and protection of the trust. *(Stats.1990, c. 79 (A.B.759), § 14, operative July 1, 1991.)*

Law Revision Commission Comments

1990 Enactment

Section 16243 continues Section 16243 of the repealed Probate Code without change. The section is the same in substance as Section 3(c)(20) of the Uniform Trustees' Powers Act (1964). As to the construction of provisions drawn from uniform acts, see Section 2. For other provisions relating to trustees' compensation, see Sections 15680–15683. See also Section 16202 (exercise of powers is subject to duties).

Background on Section 16243 of Repealed Code

Section 16243 was added by 1986 Cal.Stat. ch. 820 § 40. The section continued subdivision (16) of former Probate Code Section 1120.2 (repealed by 1986 Cal.Stat. ch. 820 § 31) without substantive change, except that the references to reasonable compensation and compensation of employees and agents were new. For background on the provisions of this division, see the Comment to this division under the division heading. [20 Cal.L.Rev.Comm.Reports 1001 (1990)].

§ 16244. Loans to beneficiary

The trustee has the following powers:

(a) To make loans out of trust property to the beneficiary on terms and conditions that the trustee determines are fair and reasonable under the circumstances.

(b) To guarantee loans to the beneficiary by encumbrances on trust property. *(Stats.1990, c. 79 (A.B.759), § 14, operative July 1, 1991.)*

1990 Enactment

Section 16244 continues Section 16244 of the repealed Probate Code without change. The determination of what is fair and reasonable is subject to the fiduciary duties of the trustee and must be made in light of the purposes of the trust. If the trustee requires security for the loan to the beneficiary, adequate security under this section may consist of a charge on the beneficiary's interest in the trust. See Restatement (Second) of Trusts § 255 (1957). The interest of a beneficiary that is subject to a spendthrift restraint may not be used for security for a loan under this section. See Section 15300 et seq. (restraints on transfer). See also Section 16202 (exercise of powers is subject to duties).

Background on Section 16244 of Repealed Code

Section 16244 was a new provision added by 1986 Cal.Stat. ch. 820 § 40. For background on the provisions of this division, see the Comment to this division under the division heading. [20 Cal.L.Rev.Comm.Reports 1001 (1990)].

§ 16245. Distributions

The trustee has the power to pay any sum of principal or income distributable to a beneficiary, without regard to whether the beneficiary is under a legal disability, by paying the sum to the beneficiary or by paying the sum to another person for the use or benefit of the beneficiary. Any sum distributable under this section to a custodian under the California Uniform Transfers to Minors Act (Part 9 (commencing with Section 3900)) shall be subject to Section 3906. *(Stats.1990, c. 79 (A.B.759), § 14, operative July 1, 1991. Amended by Stats.1996, c. 862 (A.B.2751), § 39.)*

1990 Enactment

Section 16245 continues Section 16245 of the repealed Probate Code without change. This section is drawn from Section 3(c)(22) of the Uniform Trustees' Powers Act (1964). As to the construction of provisions drawn from uniform acts, see Section 2. The exercise of the power to distribute property under this section is subject to the limitation provided in Section 21524(b) in the case of a marital deduction trust. See also Section 16202 (exercise of powers is subject to duties). In an appropriate case, a distribution may be made to a custodian under the California Uniform Transfers to Minors Act. See Sections 3905 (transfer authorized by trust), 3906 (other transfer by trustee).

Background on Section 16245 of Repealed Code

Section 16245 was a new provision added by 1986 Cal.Stat. ch. 820 § 40. For background on the provisions of this division, see the Comment to this division under the division heading. [20 Cal.L.Rev.Comm.Reports 1001 (1990)].

§ 16246. Nature and value of distributions

The trustee has the power to effect distribution of property and money in divided or undivided interests and to adjust resulting differences in valuation. A distribution in kind may be made pro rata or non pro rata, and may be made pursuant to any written agreement providing for a non pro rata division of the aggregate value of the community property assets or quasi-community property assets, or both. *(Stats.1990, c. 79 (A.B.759), § 14, operative July 1, 1991. Amended by Stats.1998, c. 682 (A.B.2069), § 12.)*

1990 Enactment

Section 16246 continues Section 16246 of the repealed Probate Code without change. The first sentence is the same as Section 3(c)(23) of the Uniform Trustees' Powers Act (1964). As to the construction of provisions drawn from uniform acts, see Section 2. The trustee also has the power to sell property in order to make the distribution. The second sentence recognizes the authority to take gains and losses into account for tax purposes when making distributions. This power provides needed flexibility and avoids the possibility of a taxable event arising from a non-pro rata distribution. See also Section 16202 (exercise of powers is subject to duties).

Background on Section 16246 of Repealed Code

Section 16246 was a new provision added by 1986 Cal.Stat. ch. 820 § 40. For background on the provisions of this division, see the Comment to this division under the division heading. [20 Cal.L.Rev.Comm.Reports 1001 (1990)].

§ 16247. Hiring persons

The trustee has the power to hire persons, including accountants, attorneys, auditors, investment advisers, appraisers (including probate referees appointed pursuant to Section 400), or other agents, even if they are associated or affiliated with the trustee, to advise or assist the trustee in the performance of administrative duties. *(Stats.1990, c. 79 (A.B.759), § 14, operative July 1, 1991. Amended by Stats.1994, c. 806 (A.B.3686), § 38.)*

1990 Enactment [Revised Comment]

Section 16247 is the same in substance as part of Section 3(c)(24) of the Uniform Trustees' Powers Act (1964). As to the construction of provisions drawn from uniform acts, see Section 2. If the trustee is in doubt concerning the propriety of hiring an agent, the judicial procedure for obtaining instructions is available. See Section 17200(b)(6). An agent with a close relationship with the trustee or an insider may be hired when it is in the best interests of the trust, taking into account the duty of loyalty (see Section 16002) and the duty to avoid conflicts of interest (see Section 16004), and particularly as to routine matters; but in situations involving substantial matters, it is best to hire outside agents. The trustee has a duty to inform certain beneficiaries of agents hired, their relationship to the trustee, if any, and their compensation. See Section 16063(d).

See also Sections 16012 (general duty not to delegate), 16014 (duty to use special skills), 16052 (delegation of investment and management functions), 16202 (exercise of powers is subject to duties), 16401 (trustee's liability to beneficiary for acts of agent). [25 Cal.L.Rev.Comm. Reports 673 (1995)].

Background on Section 16247 of Repealed Code

Section 16247 was a new provision added by 1986 Cal.Stat. ch. 820 § 40. For background on the provisions of this division, see the Comment to this division under the division heading. [20 Cal.L.Rev.Comm.Reports 1001 (1990)].

§ 16248. Execution and delivery of instruments

The trustee has the power to execute and deliver all instruments which are needed to accomplish or facilitate the exercise of the powers vested in the trustee. *(Stats.1990, c. 79 (A.B.759), § 14, operative July 1, 1991.)*

Law Revision Commission Comments

1990 Enactment

Section 16248 continues Section 16248 of the repealed Probate Code without change. This section is the same in substance as Section 3(c)(26) of the Uniform Trustees' Powers Act (1964). As to the construction of provisions drawn from uniform acts, see Section 2. See also Section 16202 (exercise of powers is subject to duties).

Background on Section 16248 of Repealed Code

Section 16248 was a new provision added by 1986 Cal.Stat. ch. 820 § 40. For background on the provisions of this division, see the Comment to this division under the division heading. [20 Cal.L.Rev.Comm.Reports 1001 (1990)].

§ 16249. Actions and proceedings

The trustee has the power to prosecute or defend actions, claims, or proceedings for the protection of trust property and of the trustee in the performance of the trustee's duties. *(Stats.1990, c. 79 (A.B.759), § 14, operative July 1, 1991. Amended by Stats.1992, c. 871 (A.B.2975), § 19; Stats.2001, c. 49 (S.B.669), § 5.)*

Law Revision Commission Comments

1990 Enactment

Section 16249 continues Section 16249 of the repealed Probate Code without change. This section is the same in substance as Section 3(c)(25) of the Uniform Trustees' Powers Act (1964). As to the construction of provisions drawn from uniform acts, see Section 2. As to the propriety of reimbursement for attorney's fees and other expenses of an action or proceeding, see Section 15684 and the Comment thereto. See also Sections 62 ("property" defined), 16010 (duty to enforce claims), 16011 (duty to defend actions), 16202 (exercise of powers is subject to duties).

Background on Section 16249 of Repealed Code

Section 16249 was added by 1986 Cal.Stat. ch. 820 § 40. The section superseded the last clause of subdivision (15) of former Probate Code Section 1120.2 (repealed by 1986 Cal.Stat. ch. 820 § 31). For background on the provisions of this division, see the Comment to this division under the division heading. [20 Cal.L.Rev.Comm.Reports 1001 (1990)].

Cross References

Conveyances or transfers of property claimed to belong to decedent or other person,
   Generally, see Probate Code § 850 et seq.
  Wrongful taking, concealment or disposition of trust property, liability, see Probate Code § 859.
Suits by trustee of express trust without joining persons beneficially interested, see Code of Civil Procedure § 369.

§§ 16300 to 16315. Repealed by Stats.1999, c. 145 (A.B. 846), § 4

Law Revision Commission Comments

1999 Repeal

Former Section 16300 is superseded by Section 16320 (short title of new Uniform Principal and Income Act). [29 Cal.L.Rev.Comm. Reports 245 (1999)].

The substance of the introductory clause of former Section 16301 is continued in Section 16321 (application of definitions).

Subdivision (a) is superseded by Section 16325 ("income beneficiary" defined).

Subdivision (b) is not continued. See the "Background from Uniform Act" comment below.

Subdivision (c) is not continued. [29 Cal.L.Rev.Comm. Reports 245 (1999)].

Former Section 16302 is superseded by Section 16335 (general fiduciary duties). [29 Cal.L.Rev.Comm. Reports 245 (1999)].

Former Section 16303 is not continued. The new Uniform Principal and Income Act (Prob. Code §§ 16320–16375) does not include a catalog provision like former Section 16303. What is included in income and principal is determined by application of all relevant rules. See also Section 16324 ('income' defined). [29 Cal.L.Rev.Comm. Reports 245 (1999)].

Former Section 16304 is superseded by Sections 16340–16341 (decedent's estate or terminating income interest) and 16345–16347 (apportionment at beginning and end of income interest). [29 Cal.L.Rev.Comm. Reports 245 (1999)].

Former Section 16305 is superseded by Section 16340 (determination and distribution of net income and principal). [29 Cal.L.Rev. Comm. Reports 245 (1999)].

Former Section 16306 is superseded by Section 16350 (character of receipts). [29 Cal.L.Rev.Comm. Reports 245 (1999)].

Former Section 16307 is superseded by Section 16357 (obligation to pay money). [29 Cal.L.Rev.Comm. Reports 245 (1999)].

Former Section 16308 is superseded by Section 16350 (character of receipts) and 16352 (business and other activities conducted by trustee). [29 Cal.L.Rev.Comm. Reports 245 (1999)].

Former Section 16309 is superseded by Sections 16363 (minerals, water, and other natural resources) and 16364 (timber). [29 Cal.L.Rev.Comm. Reports 245 (1999)].

Former Section 16310 is superseded by Sections 16361 (deferred compensation, annuities, and similar payments), 16362 (liquidating asset), and 16364 (timber). [29 Cal.L.Rev.Comm. Reports 245 (1999)].

Former Section 16311 is not continued. See Section 16365 (property not productive of income). [29 Cal.L.Rev.Comm. Reports 245 (1999)].

Former Section 16312 is superseded by Sections 16371 (disbursements from principal, 16372 (transfers from income to principal for depreciation), and 16373 (transfers from income to reimburse principal). [29 Cal.L.Rev.Comm. Reports 245 (1999)].

Former Section 16313 is superseded by Section 16372 (transfers from income to principal for depreciation). [29 Cal.L.Rev.Comm. Reports 245 (1999)].

The substance of former Section 16314 is continued in Section 16340. See Section 16340 Comment. [29 Cal.L.Rev.Comm. Reports 245 (1999)].

Former Section 16315 is not continued. See Section 16339 (application of chapter to existing trusts and estates). [29 Cal.L.Rev. Comm. Reports 245 (1999)].

CHAPTER 3. UNIFORM PRINCIPAL AND INCOME ACT

Application

Application of Division, see Probate Code § 15001.

Law Revision Commission Comments

1999 Addition

This chapter contains the California version of the Uniform Principal and Income Act of 1997 (UPAIA). It supersedes the California version of the Revised Uniform Principal and Income Act of 1962 (RUPIA) in former Sections 16300–16315. Many provisions in this chapter are the same as or drawn from the Uniform Principal and Income Act of 1997. In Comments to sections in this chapter, a reference to the "Uniform Principal and Income Act (1997)," the "uniform act," or "UPAIA" means the official text of the uniform act approved by the National Conference of Commissioners on Uniform State Laws. Variations from the official text of the uniform act are noted in the Comments to sections in this chapter. [29 Cal.L.Rev. Comm. Reports 245 (1999)].

Cross References

Notice of proposed actions, application or assertion of other rights and remedies, see Probate Code § 16500.

ARTICLE 1. SHORT TITLE AND DEFINITIONS

Section
16320. Short title.
16321. Application of definitions.
16322. Accounting period.
16323. Fiduciary.
16324. Income.
16325. Income beneficiary.
16326. Income interest.
16327. Mandatory income interest.
16328. Net income.

Application

Application of Division, see Probate Code § 15001.

Cross References

Common trust funds, educational institutions, distributions, see Corporations Code § 10251.

§ 16320. Short title

This chapter may be cited as the Uniform Principal and Income Act. *(Added by Stats.1999, c. 145 (A.B.846), § 5.)*

Law Revision Commission Comments

1999 Addition

Section 16320 replaces former Section 16300 (short title of Revised Uniform Principal and Income Act of 1962). Some provisions included in the Uniform Principal and Income Act (1997) are generalized elsewhere in this code. See Sections 2(b) construction of provisions drawn from uniform acts (*cf.* UPAIA § 601), 11 (severability) (*cf.* UPAIA § 602). [29 Cal.L.Rev.Comm. Reports 245 (1999)].

Cross References

Common trust funds, educational institutions, distributions, see Corporations Code § 10251.
Notice of proposed actions, application or assertion of other rights and remedies, see Probate Code § 16500.

§ 16321. Application of definitions

The definitions in this article govern the construction of this chapter. *(Added by Stats.1999, c. 145 (A.B.846), § 5.)*

Law Revision Commission Comments

1999 Addition

Section 16321 continues the introductory clause of former Section 16301. For other definitions applicable to this chapter, see Part 2 (commencing with Section 20) of Division 1. Several definitions in the Uniform Principal and Income Act (1997) are not included in this chapter because they are provided in the general Probate Code definitions. See Sections 24 ("beneficiary" defined), 56 ("person" defined), 84 ("trustee" defined). [29 Cal.L.Rev.Comm. Reports 245 (1999)].

§ 16322. Accounting period

"Accounting period" means a calendar year unless another 12–month period is selected by a fiduciary. The term includes a portion of a calendar year or other 12–month period that begins when an income interest begins or ends when an income interest ends. *(Added by Stats.1999, c. 145 (A.B.846), § 5.)*

Law Revision Commission Comments

1999 Addition

Section 16322 is the same as Section 102(1) of the Uniform Principal and Income Act (1997).
See also Sections 16323 ("fiduciary" defined), 16326 ("income interest" defined). [29 Cal.L.Rev.Comm. Reports 245 (1999)].

Cross References

Fiduciary defined for purposes of this Chapter, see Probate Code § 16323.
Income defined for purposes of this Chapter, see Probate Code § 16324.
Income interest defined for purposes of this Chapter, see Probate Code § 16326.

§ 16323. Fiduciary

"Fiduciary" means a personal representative or a trustee. *(Added by Stats.1999, c. 145 (A.B.846), § 5.)*

Law Revision Commission Comments

1999 Addition

Section 16323 is the same in substance as Section 102(3) of the Uniform Principal and Income Act (1997). This chapter applies to wills and trusts, unlike the former principal and income law, which applied only to trusts. Compare Section 16335 (general fiduciary duties) with former Section 16302 (duty of trustee as to receipts and expenditures). See also Section 10531(a) (principal and income allocations and determinations by personal representative under the Independent Administration of Estates Act). For the purposes of this chapter, the definition of fiduciary in this section is used instead of the general definition in Section 39. See also Sections 58 ("personal representative" defined), 84 ("trustee" defined). The second sentence of UPAIA Section 102(3) is omitted as surplus, since the definition of personal representative in Section 58 covers the same persons. [29 Cal.L.Rev.Comm. Reports 245 (1999)].

§ 16324. Income

"Income" means money or property that a fiduciary receives as current return from a principal asset. The term includes a portion of receipts from a sale, exchange, or liquidation of a principal asset, to the extent provided in Article 5.1 (commencing with Section 16350), 5.2 (commencing with Section 16355), or 5.3 (commencing with Section 16360). *(Added by Stats.1999, c. 145 (A.B.846), § 5.)*

Law Revision Commission Comments

1999 Addition

Section 16324 is the same as Section 102(4) of the Uniform Principal and Income Act (1997). The definition of "principal" in the uniform act is not included in this chapter because it is not needed.

See also Sections 62 ("property" defined), 16323 ("fiduciary" defined). [29 Cal.L.Rev.Comm. Reports 245 (1999)].

Cross References

Fiduciary defined for purposes of this Chapter, see Probate Code § 16323.

§ 16325. Income beneficiary

"Income beneficiary" means a person to whom net income of a trust is or may be payable. *(Added by Stats.1999, c. 145 (A.B.846), § 5.)*

Law Revision Commission Comments

1999 Addition

Section 16325 supersedes former Section 16301(a) and is the same as Section 102(5) of the Uniform Principal and Income Act (1997). The definition of "remainder beneficiary" in the uniform act is not included in this chapter because it is not needed.

See also Section 16328 ("net income" defined). [29 Cal.L.Rev. Comm. Reports 245 (1999)].

Background from Uniform Act

The definitions of income beneficiary (Section 102(5)) and income interest (Section 102(6)) cover both mandatory and discretionary beneficiaries and interests. There are no definitions for 'discretionary income beneficiary' or 'discretionary income interest' because those terms are not used in the Act.

[Adapted from Unif. Principal and Income Act § 102(5) comment (1997)].

Cross References

Income defined for purposes of this Chapter, see Probate Code § 16324.
Net income defined for purposes of this Chapter, see Probate Code § 16328.

§ 16326. Income interest

"Income interest" means the right of an income beneficiary to receive all or part of net income, whether the trust requires it to be distributed or authorizes it to be distributed in the trustee's discretion. *(Added by Stats.1999, c. 145 (A.B.846), § 5.)*

Law Revision Commission Comments

1999 Addition

Section 16326 is the same as Section 102(6) of the Uniform Principal and Income Act (1997), except that "trust" is used in place of "terms of the trust."

See also Sections 16325 ("income beneficiary" defined), 16328 ("net income" defined). [29 Cal.L.Rev.Comm. Reports 245 (1999)].

Cross References

Income defined for purposes of this Chapter, see Probate Code § 16324.
Net income defined for purposes of this Chapter, see Probate Code § 16328.

§ 16327. Mandatory income interest

"Mandatory income interest" means the right of an income beneficiary to receive net income that the trust requires the fiduciary to distribute. *(Added by Stats.1999, c. 145 (A.B. 846), § 5.)*

Law Revision Commission Comments

1999 Addition

Section 16327 is the same as Section 102(7) of the Uniform Principal and Income Act (1997), except that "trust" is used in place of "terms of the trust."

See also Sections 16323 ("fiduciary" defined), 16325 ("income beneficiary" defined), 16328 ("net income" defined). [29 Cal.L.Rev. Comm. Reports 245 (1999)].

Cross References

Fiduciary defined for purposes of this Chapter, see Probate Code § 16323.
Income defined for purposes of this Chapter, see Probate Code § 16324.
Income interest defined for purposes of this Chapter, see Probate Code § 16326.
Net income defined for purposes of this Chapter, see Probate Code § 16328.

§ 16328. Net income

"Net income" means the total receipts allocated to income during an accounting period minus the disbursements made from income during the accounting period, plus or minus transfers under this chapter to or from income during the accounting period. During any period in which the trust is being administered as a unitrust, either pursuant to the powers conferred by Sections 16336.4 to 16336.6, inclusive, or pursuant to the terms of the governing instrument, "net income" means the unitrust amount, if the unitrust amount is no less than 3 percent and no more than 5 percent of the fair market value of the trust assets, whether determined annually or averaged on a multiple year basis. *(Added by Stats.1999, c. 145 (A.B.846), § 5. Amended by Stats.2005, c. 100 (S.B.754), § 1.)*

Law Revision Commission Comments

1999 Addition

Section 16328 is the same as Section 102(8) of the Uniform Principal and Income Act (1997).

See also Section 16322 ("accounting period" defined), 16324 ("income" defined). [29 Cal.L.Rev.Comm. Reports 245 (1999)].

Background from Uniform Act

The reference to "transfers under this Act to or from income" means transfers made under Sections 104(a), 412(b), 502(b), 503(b), 504(a), and 506 [Prob. Code §§ 16336(a), 16364(b), 16371(b), 16372(b), 16373(a) & 16375(a)].

[Adapted from Unif. Principal and Income Act § 102(8) comment (1997)].

Accounting period defined for purposes of this Chapter, see Probate Code § 16322.

Income defined for purposes of this Chapter, see Probate Code § 16324.

ARTICLE 2. GENERAL PROVISIONS AND FIDUCIARY DUTIES

Section

16335.   Allocation between principal and income; impartial exercise of discretion.

16336.   Adjustments between principal and income.

16336.4. Conversion of trust into unitrust.

16336.5. Conversion of trust to a unitrust; other circumstances when authorized without court order; court ordered conversion.

16336.6. Reconversion of trust from unitrust or change in payout percentage of unitrust.

16336.7. No duty imposed on trustee to convert or reconvert trust or to consider conversion or reconversion; application of § 16503.

16337.   Notice of proposed action by trustee.

16338.   Proceedings relating to § 16336 and §§ 16336.4 to 16336.6; remedy.

16339.   Application of chapter.

Application

Application of Division, see Probate Code § 15001.

§ 16335. Allocation between principal and income; impartial exercise of discretion

(a) In allocating receipts and disbursements to or between principal and income, and with respect to any other matter within the scope of this chapter, a fiduciary:

(1) Shall administer a trust or decedent's estate in accordance with the trust or the will, even if there is a different provision in this chapter.

(2) May administer a trust or decedent's estate by the exercise of a discretionary power of administration given to the fiduciary by the trust or the will, even if the exercise of the power produces a result different from a result required or permitted by this chapter, and no inference that the fiduciary has improperly exercised the discretion arises from the fact that the fiduciary has made an allocation contrary to a provision of this chapter.

(3) Shall administer a trust or decedent's estate in accordance with this chapter if the trust or the will does not contain a different provision or does not give the fiduciary a discretionary power of administration.

(4) Shall add a receipt or charge a disbursement to principal to the extent that the trust or the will and this chapter do not provide a rule for allocating the receipt or disbursement to or between principal and income.

(b) In exercising a discretionary power of administration regarding a matter within the scope of this chapter, whether granted by a trust, a will, or this chapter, including the trustee's power to adjust under subdivision (a) of Section 16336, and the trustee's power to convert into a unitrust or reconvert or change the unitrust payout percentage pursuant to Sections 16336.4 to 16336.6, inclusive, the fiduciary shall administer the trust or decedent's estate impartially, except to the extent that the trust or the will expresses an intention that the fiduciary shall or may favor one or more of the beneficiaries. The exercise of discretion in accordance with this chapter is presumed to be fair and reasonable to all beneficiaries. *(Added by Stats.1999, c. 145 (A.B.846), § 5. Amended by Stats.2005, c. 100 (S.B.754), § 2.)*

Law Revision Commission Comments

1999 Addition

Section 16335 supersedes former Section 16302 and is generally the same as Section 103 of the Uniform Principal and Income Act (1997), with a number of changes. The last clause in subdivision (a)(2) has been added to preserve and generalize the "no inference" rule in former Section 16302(b). "Trust" is used in place of "terms of the trust" throughout. As provided in the introductory clause of subdivision (a), its rules apply to allocation between principal and income (Sections 16350–16375), as under former Section 16302, but in addition, these rules apply to matters within the scope of Sections 16335–16341.

The rule in the first sentence of subdivision (b) is a special expression of the general fiduciary duty in Section 16003. The wording in the second sentence has been revised to make clear that the presumption applies to exercise of discretion under this chapter.

See also Sections 82 ("trust" defined), 16323 ("fiduciary" defined), 16324 ("income" defined). [29 Cal.L.Rev.Comm. Reports apx. 4 (1999)].

Background from Uniform Act

Prior Act. The rule in Section 2(a) of the 1962 Act [former Prob. Code § 16302] is restated in Section 103(a) [Prob. Code § 16335(a)], without changing its substance, to emphasize that the Act contains only default rules and that provisions in the terms of the trust are paramount. However, Section 2(a) of the 1962 Act [former Prob. Code § 16302] applies only to the allocation of receipts and disbursements to or between principal and income. In this Act, the first sentence of Section 103(a) [Prob. Code § 16335(a)] states that it also applies to matters within the scope of Articles [3 (commencing with Prob. Code § 16340)] and 4 (commencing with Prob. Code § 16345)]. Section 103(a)(2) [Prob. Code § 16335(a)(2)] incorporates the rule in Section 2(b) of the 1962 Act [former Prob. Code § 16302(b)] that a discretionary allocation made by the trustee that is contrary to a rule in the Act should not give rise to an inference of imprudence or partiality by the trustee.

Fiduciary discretion. The general rule is that if a discretionary power is conferred upon a trustee, the exercise of that power is not subject to control by a court except to prevent an abuse of discretion. Restatement (Second) of Trusts § 187. The situations in which a court will control the exercise of a trustee's discretion are discussed in the comments to § 187. See also *id.* § 233 comment *p.*

Questions for which there is no provision. Section 103(a)(4) [Prob. Code § 16335(a)(4)] allocates receipts and disbursements to principal when there is no provision for a different allocation in the terms of the trust, the will, or the Act. This may occur because money is received from a financial instrument not available at the present time (inflation-indexed bonds might have fallen into this category had they been announced after this Act was approved by the Commissioners on Uniform State Laws) or because a transaction is of a type or occurs in a manner not anticipated by the Drafting Committee for this Act or the drafter of the trust instrument.

Allocating to principal a disbursement for which there is no provision in the Act or the terms of the trust preserves the income beneficiary's level of income in the year it is allocated to principal, but thereafter will reduce the amount of income produced by the principal. Allocating to principal a receipt for which there is no provision will increase the income received by the income beneficiary in subsequent years, and will eventually, upon termination of the trust, also favor the remainder beneficiary. Allocating these items to principal implements the rule that requires a trustee to administer the trust impartially .... However, if the trustee decides that an adjustment between principal and income is needed to enable the trustee to comply with Section 103(b) [Prob. Code § 16335(b)], after considering the return from the portfolio as a whole, the trustee may make an appropriate adjustment under Section 104(a) [Prob. Code § 16336(a)].

Duty of impartiality. Whenever there are two or more beneficiaries, a trustee is under a duty to deal impartially with them. Restatement of Trusts 3d: Prudent Investor Rule § 183 (1992). [See Prob. Code § 16003.] This rule applies whether the beneficiaries' interests in the trust are concurrent or successive. If the terms of the trust give the trustee discretion to favor one beneficiary over another, a court will not control the exercise of such discretion except to prevent the trustee from abusing it. *Id.* § 183, comment *a.* "The precise meaning of the trustee's duty of impartiality and the balancing of competing interests and objectives inevitably are matters of judgment and interpretation. Thus, the duty and balancing are affected by the purposes, terms, distribution requirements, and other circumstances of the trust, not only at the outset but as they may change from time to time." *Id.* § 232, comment *c.*

The terms of a trust may provide that the trustee, or an accountant engaged by the trustee, or a committee of persons who may be family members or business associates, shall have the power to determine what is income and what is principal. If the terms of a trust provide that this Act specifically or principal and income legislation in general does not apply to the trust but fail to provide a rule to deal with a matter provided for in this Act, the trustee has an implied grant of discretion to decide the question. Section 103(b) [Prob. Code § 16335(b)] provides that the rule of impartiality applies in the exercise of such a discretionary power to the extent that the terms of the trust do not provide that one or more of the beneficiaries are to be favored. The fact that a person is named an income beneficiary or a remainder beneficiary is not by itself an indication of partiality for that beneficiary.

[Adapted from Unif. Principal and Income Act § 103 comment (1997)].

Cross References
Fiduciary defined for purposes of this Chapter, see Probate Code § 16323.
Income defined for purposes of this Chapter, see Probate Code § 16324.

§ 16336. Adjustments between principal and income

(a) Subject to subdivision (b), a trustee may make an adjustment between principal and income to the extent the trustee considers necessary if all of the following conditions are satisfied:

(1) The trustee invests and manages trust assets under the prudent investor rule.

(2) The trust describes the amount that shall or may be distributed to a beneficiary by referring to the trust's income.

(3) The trustee determines, after applying the rules in subdivision (a) of Section 16335, and considering any power the trustee may have under the trust to invade principal or accumulate income, that the trustee is unable to comply with subdivision (b) of Section 16335.

(b) A trustee may not make an adjustment between principal and income in any of the following circumstances:

(1) Where it would diminish the income interest in a trust (A) that requires all of the income to be paid at least annually to a spouse and (B) for which, if the trustee did not have the power to make the adjustment, an estate tax or gift tax marital deduction would be allowed, in whole or in part.

(2) Where it would reduce the actuarial value of the income interest in a trust to which a person transfers property with the intent to qualify for a gift tax exclusion.

(3) Where it would change the amount payable to a beneficiary as a fixed annuity or a fixed fraction of the value of the trust assets.

(4) Where it would be made from any amount that is permanently set aside for charitable purposes under a will or trust, unless both income and principal are so set aside.

(5) Where possessing or exercising the power to make an adjustment would cause an individual to be treated as the owner of all or part of the trust for income tax purposes, and the individual would not be treated as the owner if the trustee did not possess the power to make an adjustment.

(6) Where possessing or exercising the power to make an adjustment would cause all or part of the trust assets to be included for estate tax purposes in the estate of an individual who has the power to remove a trustee or appoint a trustee, or both, and the assets would not be included in the estate of the individual if the trustee did not possess the power to make an adjustment.

(7) Where the trustee is a beneficiary of the trust.

(8) During any period in which the trust is being administered as a unitrust pursuant to the trustee's exercise of the power to convert provided in Section 16336.4 or 16336.5, or pursuant to the terms of the governing instrument.

(c) Notwithstanding Section 15620, if paragraph (5), (6), or (7) of subdivision (b) applies to a trustee and there is more than one trustee, a cotrustee to whom the provision does not apply may make the adjustment unless the exercise of the power by the remaining trustee or trustees is not permitted by the trust.

(d) A trustee may release the entire power conferred by subdivision (a) or may release only the power to adjust from income to principal or the power to adjust from principal to income in either of the following circumstances:

(1) If the trustee is uncertain about whether possessing or exercising the power will cause a result described in paragraphs (1) to (6), inclusive, of subdivision (b).

(2) If the trustee determines that possessing or exercising the power will or may deprive the trust of a tax benefit or impose a tax burden not described in subdivision (b).

(e) A release under subdivision (d) may be permanent or for a specified period, including a period measured by the life of an individual.

(f) A trust that limits the power of a trustee to make an adjustment between principal and income does not affect the application of this section unless it is clear from the trust that it is intended to deny the trustee the power of adjustment provided by subdivision (a).

(g) In deciding whether and to what extent to exercise the power to make adjustments under this section, the trustee may consider, but is not limited to, any of the following:

(1) The nature, purpose, and expected duration of the trust.

(2) The intent of the settlor.

(3) The identity and circumstances of the beneficiaries.

(4) The needs for liquidity, regularity of income, and preservation and appreciation of capital.

(5) The assets held in the trust; the extent to which they consist of financial assets, interests in closely held enterprises, tangible and intangible personal property, or real property; the extent to which an asset is used by a beneficiary; and whether an asset was purchased by the trustee or received from the settlor.

(6) The net amount allocated to income under other statutes and the increase or decrease in the value of the principal assets, which the trustee may estimate as to assets for which market values are not readily available.

(7) Whether and to what extent the trust gives the trustee the power to invade principal or accumulate income or prohibit the trustee from invading principal or accumulating income, and the extent to which the trustee has exercised a power from time to time to invade principal or accumulate income.

(8) The actual and anticipated effect of economic conditions on principal and income and effects of inflation and deflation.

(9) The anticipated tax consequences of an adjustment.

(h) Nothing in this section or in this chapter is intended to create or imply a duty to make an adjustment, and a trustee is not liable for not considering whether to make an adjustment or for choosing not to make an adjustment. *(Added by Stats.1999, c. 145 (A.B.846), § 5. Amended by Stats.2005, c. 100 (S.B.754), § 3.)*

Law Revision Commission Comments

1999 Addition

Section 16336 is drawn in large part from Section 104 of the Uniform Principal and Income Act (1997). The purpose of this section is to provide a way to reconcile the tension that may exist between the duties under the Uniform Prudent Investor Act (Section 16045 *et seq.*) and the technical trust accounting rules governing allocations between principal and income provided in other parts of this chapter, the Uniform Principal and Income Act. The power to adjust is a discretionary power and is subject to rules governing exercise of discretionary powers, both under the trust terms and the law of trusts. If a trustee decides to exercise the power to adjust, the trustee may exercise the power under the authority of this section and related rules, or may prefer to seek the agreement of beneficiaries before making the adjustment. A procedure for giving notice of proposed action is provided in Section 16337. The trustee may also seek court approval under Section 17200(b)(5) of a decision to make an adjustment. Subdivision (h) reaffirms and expands on the portion of subdivision (a) providing that the trustee *may* make an adjustment *to the extent the trustee considers necessary.* Subdivision (h) makes clear that the existence of the adjustment power does not create or imply a duty to consider its use or to use it. The *existence* of the power to adjust is a neutral factor. The trustee may, without liability, decide as an institutional policy or with respect to individual trusts or classes of trusts, whether and under what conditions it will use the adjustment power. This rule is a corollary of the principle stated in Section 16202 that the grant of a power does not authorize its use and that exercise of a power is subject to fiduciary duties. Subdivision (h) does not, however, affect any liability that may result from breach of a duty under other trust law.

The condition expressed in subdivision (a)(1)—that the trustee invests and manages trust assets under the prudent investor rule—will almost always be met. The Uniform Prudent Investor Act (Sections 16045–16054) applies to all California trusts, except to the extent a trust provides otherwise. See Sections 16046(b) (control by trust instrument), 16054 (application of prudent investor rule to all trusts). Under Section 16046, even where the trust provides special rules, to the extent the rules can be classed as a prudent investor rule, the condition of subdivision (a)(1) is satisfied.

The trustee's determination of whether to make an adjustment under this section, and how to implement the adjustment, are subject to the trustee's fiduciary duties. See Sections 16003, 16335(b). Unlike Section 104(b) of the Uniform Principal and Income Act (1997), this section does not mandate consideration of particular factors, but the UPAIA factors provide useful guidance, and are set out in subdivision (g) by way of illustration. Consideration of the factors in the course of determining whether or how to make an adjustment is discretionary, as is clear from the introductory language of subdivision (g) ("trustee may consider ... any of the following"). See also subdivision (h).

The introductory clause in subdivision (c) recognizes that this subdivision is an exception to the default rule requiring trustees to act unanimously.

See also Sections 24 ("beneficiary" defined), 84 ("trustee" defined), 16324 ("income" defined). [29 Cal.L.Rev.Comm. Reports apx. 4 (1999)].

Background from Uniform Act

Purpose and Scope of Provision. The purpose of Section 104 [Prob. Code § 16336] is to enable a trustee to select investments using the standards of a prudent investor without having to realize a particular portion of the portfolio's total return in the form of traditional trust accounting income such as interest, dividends, and rents. Section 104(a) [Prob. Code § 16336(a)] authorizes a trustee to make adjustments between principal and income if three conditions are met: (1) the trustee must be managing the trust assets under the prudent investor rule; (2) the terms of the trust must express the income beneficiary's distribution rights in terms of the right to receive "income" in the sense of traditional trust accounting income; and (3) the trustee must determine, after applying the rules in Section 103(a) [Prob. Code § 16335(a)], that he is unable to comply with Section 103(b) [Prob. Code § 16335(b)].... [The] trustee may not make an adjustment in circumstances described in Section 104(c) [Prob. Code § 16336(b)].

Section 104 [Prob. Code § 16336] does not empower a trustee to increase or decrease the degree of beneficial enjoyment to which a beneficiary is entitled under the terms of the trust; rather, it authorizes the trustee to make adjustments between principal and income that may be necessary if the income component of a portfolio's total return is too small or too large because of investment decisions made by the trustee under the prudent investor rule. The paramount consideration in applying Section 104(a) [Prob. Code § 16336(a)] is the requirement in Section 103(b) [Prob. Code § 16335(b)] that "the fiduciary shall administer the trust or decedent's estate impartially, except to the extent that the trust or the will expresses an intention that the fiduciary shall or may favor one or more of the beneficiaries]." The power to adjust is subject to control by the court to prevent an abuse of discretion. Restatement (Second) of Trusts § 187 (1959). See also *id.* §§ 183, 232, 233, Comment *p* (1959).

Section 104 [Prob. Code § 16336] will be important for trusts that are irrevocable when a State adopts the prudent investor rule by statute [see Prob. Code § 16045 *et seq.*] or judicial approval of the rule in Restatement of Trusts 3d: Prudent Investor Rule. Wills and trust instruments executed after the rule is adopted can be drafted to describe a beneficiary's distribution rights in terms that do not depend upon the amount of trust accounting income, but to the extent that drafters of trust documents continue to describe an income beneficiary's distribution rights by referring to trust accounting income, Section 104 [Prob. Code § 16336] will be an important tool in trust administration.

Three conditions to the exercise of the power to adjust. The first of the three conditions [Prob. Code § 16336(a)(1)] that must be met before a trustee can exercise the power to adjust—that the trustee invest and manage trust assets as a prudent investor—is expressed in this Act by language derived from the Uniform Prudent Investor Act, but the condition will be met whether the prudent investor rule applies because the Uniform Act or other prudent investor legislation has been enacted, the prudent investor rule has been approved by the courts, or the terms of the trust require it. [See California Uniform Prudent Investor Act, Prob. Code §§ 16045–16054.] Even if a State's legislature or courts have not formally adopted the rule, the Restatement establishes the prudent investor rule as an authoritative interpretation of the common law prudent man rule, referring to the prudent investor rule as a "modest reformulation of the Harvard College dictum and the basic rule of prior Restatements." Restatement of Trusts 3d: Prudent Investor Rule, Introduction, at 5. As a result, there is a basis for concluding that the first condition is satisfied in virtually all States except those in which a trustee is permitted to invest only in assets set forth in a statutory "legal list."

The second condition [Prob. Code § 16336(a)(2)] will be met when the terms of the trust require all of the "income" to be distributed at regular intervals; or when the terms of the trust require a trustee to distribute all of the income, but permit the trustee to decide how much to distribute to each member of a class of beneficiaries; or when the terms of a trust provide that the beneficiary shall receive the greater of the trust accounting income and a fixed dollar amount (an annuity), or of trust accounting income and a fractional share of the value of the trust assets (a unitrust amount). If the trust authorizes the trustee in its discretion to distribute the trust's income to the beneficiary or to accumulate some or all of the income, the condition will be met because the terms of the trust do not permit the trustee to distribute more than the trust accounting income.

To meet the third condition [Prob. Code § 16336(a)(3)], the trustee must first meet the requirements of Section 103(a) [Prob. Code § 16335(a)], i.e., she must apply the terms of the trust, decide whether to exercise the discretionary powers given to the trustee under the terms of the trust, and must apply the provisions of the Act if the terms of the trust do not contain a different provision or give the trustee discretion. Second, the trustee must determine the extent to which the terms of the trust clearly manifest an intention by the settlor that the trustee may or must favor one or more of the beneficiaries. To the extent that the terms of the trust do not require partiality, the trustee must conclude that she is unable to comply with the duty to administer the trust impartially. To the extent that the terms of the trust do require or permit the trustee to favor the income beneficiary or the remainder beneficiary, the trustee must conclude that she is unable to achieve the degree of partiality required or permitted. If the trustee comes to either conclusion—that she is unable to administer the trust impartially or that she is unable to achieve the degree of partiality required or permitted C she may exercise the power to adjust under Section 104(a) [Prob. Code § 16336(a)].

Impartiality and productivity of income. The duty of impartiality between income and remainder beneficiaries is linked to the trustee's duty to make the portfolio productive of trust accounting income whenever the distribution requirements are expressed in terms of distributing the trust's "income." The 1962 Act implies that the duty to produce income applies on an asset by asset basis because the right of an income beneficiary to receive "delayed income" from the sale proceeds of underproductive property under Section 12 of that Act arises if "any part of principal ... has not produced an average net income of at least 1% per year of its inventory value for more than a year ...." Under the prudent investor rule, "[t]o whatever extent a requirement of income productivity exists, ... the requirement applies not investment by investment but to the portfolio as a whole." Restatement of Trusts 3d: Prudent Investor Rule § 227, Comment *i*, at 34. [See Prob. Code § 16047.] The power to adjust under Section 104(a) [Prob. Code § 16336(a)] is also to be exercised by considering net income from the portfolio as a whole and not investment by investment. Section 413(b) of this Act [Prob. Code § 16365(b)] eliminates the underproductive property rule in all cases other than trusts for which a marital deduction is allowed; the rule applies to a marital deduction trust if the trust's assets "consist substantially of property that does not provide the spouse with sufficient income from or use of the trust assets ..." — in other words, the section applies by reference to the portfolio as a whole.

While the purpose of the power to adjust in Section 104(a) [Prob. Code § 16336(a)] is to eliminate the need for a trustee who operates under the prudent investor rule to be concerned about the income component of the portfolio's total return, the trustee must still determine the extent to which a distribution must be made to an income beneficiary and the adequacy of the portfolio's liquidity as a whole to make that distribution.

For a discussion of investment considerations involving specific investments and techniques under the prudent investor rule, see Restatement of Trusts 3d: Prudent Investor Rule § 227, Comments *k-p.* [See also Prob. Code §§ 16045–16054, California Uniform Prudent Investor Act].

Factors to consider in exercising the power to adjust. Section 104(b) requires [not required in Prob. Code § 16336—subdivision (g) of the California section lists discretionary factors by way of illustration] a trustee to consider factors relevant to the trust and its beneficiaries in deciding whether and to what extent the power to adjust should be exercised. Section 2(c) of the Uniform Prudent Investor Act [see Prob. Code § 16047(c)] sets forth circumstances that a trustee is to consider in investing and managing trust assets. The circumstances in Section 2(c) of the Uniform Prudent Investor Act are the source of the factors in paragraphs (3) through (6) and (8) of Section 104(b) (modified where necessary to adapt them to the purposes of this Act) so that, to the extent possible, comparable factors will apply to investment decisions and decisions involving the power to adjust. [See Prob. Code §§ 16047(c)(3)-(6) & (8), 16336(g)]. If a trustee who is operating under the prudent investor rule decides that the portfolio should be composed of financial assets whose total return will result primarily from capital appreciation rather than dividends, interest, and rents, the trustee can decide at the same time the extent to which an adjustment from principal to income may be necessary under Section 104. On the other hand, if a trustee decides that the risk and return objectives for the trust are best achieved by a portfolio whose total return includes interest and dividend income that is sufficient to provide the income beneficiary with the beneficial interest to which the beneficiary is entitled under the terms of the trust, the trustee can decide that it is unnecessary to exercise the power to adjust.

Assets received from the settlor. Section 3 of the Uniform Prudent Investor Act provides that "[a] trustee shall diversify the investments of the trust unless the trustee reasonably determines that, because of special circumstances, the purposes of the trust are better served without diversifying." [For a comparable rule, see Prob. Code § 16048.] The special circumstances may include the wish to retain a family business, the benefit derived from deferring liquidation of the asset in order to defer payment of income taxes, or the anticipated capital appreciation from retaining an asset such as undeveloped real estate for a long period. To the extent the trustee retains assets received from the settlor because of special circumstances that overcome the duty to diversify, the trustee may take these circumstances into account in determining whether and to what extent the power to adjust should be exercised to change the results produced by other provisions of this Act that apply to the retained assets. See Section 104(b)(5) [Prob. Code § 16336(g)(5)]; Uniform Prudent Investor Act § 3, Comment, 7B U.L.A. 18, at 25–26 (Supp. 1997); Restatement of Trusts 3d: Prudent Investor Rule § 229 and Comments *a-e.*

Limitations on the power to adjust. The purpose of subsections (c)(1) through (4) [Prob. Code § 16336(b)(1)-(4)] is to preserve tax benefits that may have been an important purpose for creating the trust. Subsections (c)(5), (6), and (8) [Prob. Code § 16336(b)(5)-(6); UPAIA subsection (c)(8) is omitted in California] deny the power to adjust in the circumstances described in those subsections in order to prevent adverse tax consequences, and subsection (c)(7) [Prob. Code § 16336(b)(7)] denies the power to adjust to any beneficiary, whether or not possession of the power may have adverse tax consequences.

Under subsection (c)(1) [Prob. Code § 16336(b)(1)], a trustee cannot make an adjustment that diminishes the income interest in a trust that requires all of the income to be paid at least annually to a spouse and for which an estate tax or gift tax marital deduction is allowed; but this subsection does not prevent the trustee from making an adjustment that increases the amount of income paid from a marital deduction trust to the spouse. Subsection (c)(1) [Prob. Code § 16336(b)(1)] applies to a trust that qualifies for the marital deduction because the spouse has a general power of appointment over the trust, but it applies to a qualified terminable interest property (QTIP) trust only if and to the extent that the fiduciary makes the election required to obtain the tax deduction. Subsection (c)(1) [Prob. Code § 16336(b)(1)] does not apply to a so-called 'estate' trust. This type of trust qualifies for the marital deduction because the terms of the trust require the principal and undistributed income to be paid to the surviving spouse's estate when the spouse dies; it is not necessary for the terms of an estate trust to require the income to be distributed annually. Reg. § 20.2056(c)–2(b)(1)(iii).

Subsection (c)(3) [Prob. Code § 16336(b)(3)] applies to annuity trusts and unitrusts with no charitable beneficiaries as well as to trusts with charitable income or remainder beneficiaries; its purpose is to make it clear that a beneficiary's right to receive a fixed annuity or a fixed fraction of the value of a trust's assets is not subject to adjustment under Section 104(a) [Prob. Code § 16336(a)]. Subsection (c)(3) [Prob. Code § 16336(b)(3)] does not apply to any additional amount to which the beneficiary may be entitled that is expressed in terms of a right to receive income from the trust. For example, if a beneficiary is to receive a fixed annuity or the trust's income, whichever is greater, subsection (c)(3) [Prob. Code § 16336(b)(3)] does not prevent a trustee from making an adjustment under Section 104(a) [Prob. Code § 16336(a)] in determining the amount of the trust's income.

If subsection (c)(5), (6), (7), or (8) [Prob. Code § 16336(b)(5)-(7); UPAIA subsection (c)(8) is omitted in California], prevents a trustee from exercising the power to adjust, subsection (d) [Prob. Code § 16336(c)] permits a cotrustee who is not subject to the provision to exercise the power unless the terms of the trust do not permit the cotrustee to do so.

Release of the power to adjust. Section 104(e) [Prob. Code § 16336(d)-(e)] permits a trustee to release all or part of the power to adjust in circumstances in which the possession or exercise of the power might deprive the trust of a tax benefit or impose a tax burden. For example, if possessing the power would diminish the actuarial value of the income interest in a trust for which the income beneficiary's estate may be eligible to claim a credit for property previously taxed if the beneficiary dies within ten years after the death of the person creating the trust, the trustee is permitted under subsection (e) [Prob. Code § 16336(d)] to release just the power to adjust from income to principal.

Trust terms that limit a power to adjust. Section 104(f) [Prob. Code § 16336(f)] applies to trust provisions that limit a trustee's power to adjust. Since the power is intended to enable trustees to employ the prudent investor rule without being constrained by traditional principal and income rules, an instrument executed before the adoption of this Act whose terms describe the amount that may or must be distributed to a beneficiary by referring to the trust's income or that prohibit the invasion of principal or that prohibit equitable adjustments in general should not be construed as forbidding the use of the power to adjust under Section 104(a) [Prob. Code § 16336(a)] if the need for adjustment arises because the trustee is operating under the prudent investor rule. Instruments containing such provisions that are executed after the adoption of this Act should specifically refer to the power to adjust if the settlor intends to forbid its use. See generally, Joel C. Dobris, *Limits on the Doctrine of Equitable Adjustment in Sophisticated Postmortem Tax Planning*, 66 Iowa L. Rev. 273 (1981).

Examples. The following examples illustrate the application of Section 104 [Prob. Code § 16336]:

Example (1) — T is the successor trustee of a trust that provides income to A for life, remainder to B. T has received from the prior trustee a portfolio of financial assets invested 20% in stocks and 80% in bonds. Following the prudent investor rule, T determines that a strategy of investing the portfolio 50% in stocks and 50% in bonds has risk and return objectives that are reasonably suited to the trust, but T also determines that adopting this approach will cause the trust to receive a smaller amount of dividend and interest income. After considering the [relevant] factors ..., T may transfer cash from principal to income to the extent T considers it necessary to increase the amount distributed to the income beneficiary.

Example (2) — T is the trustee of a trust that requires the income to be paid to the settlor's son C for life, remainder to C's daughter D. In a period of very high inflation, T purchases bonds that pay double-digit interest and determines that a portion of the interest, which is allocated to income under Section 406 of this Act [Prob. Code § 16357], is a return of capital. In consideration of the loss of value of principal due to inflation and other factors that T considers relevant, T may transfer part of the interest to principal.

Example (3) — T is the trustee of a trust that requires the income to be paid to the settlor's sister E for life, remainder to charity F. E is a retired schoolteacher who is single and has no children. E's income from her social security, pension, and savings exceeds the amount required to provide for her accustomed standard of living. The terms of the trust permit T to invade principal to provide for E's health and to support her in her accustomed manner of living, but do not otherwise indicate that T should favor E or F. Applying the prudent investor rule, T determines that the trust assets should be invested entirely in growth stocks that produce very little dividend income. Even though it is not necessary to invade principal to maintain E's accustomed standard of living, she is entitled to receive from the trust the degree of beneficial enjoyment normally accorded a person who is the sole income beneficiary of a trust, and T may transfer cash from principal to income to provide her with that degree of enjoyment.

Example (4) — T is the trustee of a trust that is governed by the law of State X. The trust became irrevocable before State X adopted the prudent investor rule. The terms of the trust require all of the income to be paid to G for life, remainder to H, and also give T the power to invade principal for the benefit of G for 'dire emergencies only.' The terms of the trust limit the aggregate amount that T can distribute to G from principal during G's life to 6% of the trust's value at its inception. The trust's portfolio is invested initially 50% in stocks and 50% in bonds, but after State X adopts the prudent investor rule T determines that, to achieve suitable risk and return objectives for the trust, the assets should be invested 90% in stocks and 10% in bonds. This change increases the total return from the portfolio and decreases the dividend and interest income. Thereafter, even though G does not experience a dire emergency, T may exercise the power to adjust under Section 104(a) [Prob. Code § 16336(a)] to the extent that T determines that the adjustment is from only the capital appreciation resulting from the change in the portfolio's asset allocation. If T is unable to determine the extent to which capital appreciation resulted from the change in asset allocation or is unable to maintain adequate records to determine the extent to which principal distributions to G for dire emergencies do not exceed the 6% limitation, T may not exercise the power to adjust. See Joel C. Dobris, *Limits on the Doctrine of Equitable Adjustment in Sophisticated Postmortem Tax Planning*, 66 Iowa L. Rev. 273 (1981).

Example (5) — *T* is the trustee of a trust for the settlor's child. The trust owns a diversified portfolio of marketable financial assets with a value of $600,000, and is also the sole beneficiary of the settlor's IRA, which holds a diversified portfolio of marketable financial assets with a value of $900,000. The trust receives a distribution from the IRA that is the minimum amount required to be distributed under the Internal Revenue Code, and *T* allocates 10% of the distribution to income under Section 409(c) of this Act [Prob. Code § 16361(c)]. The total return on the IRA's assets exceeds the amount distributed to the trust, and the value of the IRA at the end of the year is more than its value at the beginning of the year. Relevant factors that *T* may consider in determining whether to exercise the power to adjust and the extent to which an adjustment should be made to comply with Section 103(b) [Prob. Code § 16335(b)] include the total return from all of the trust's assets, those owned directly as well as its interest in the IRA, the extent to which the trust will be subject to income tax on the portion of the IRA distribution that is allocated to principal, and the extent to which the income beneficiary will be subject to income tax on the amount that *T* distributes to the income beneficiary.

Example (6) — *T* is the trustee of a trust whose portfolio includes a large parcel of undeveloped real estate. *T* pays real property taxes on the undeveloped parcel from income each year pursuant to Section 501(3) [Prob. Code § 16370(c)]. After considering the return from the trust's portfolio as a whole and other relevant factors ..., *T* may exercise the power to adjust under Section 104(a) [Prob. Code § 16336(a)] to transfer cash from principal to income in order to distribute to the income beneficiary an amount that *T* considers necessary to comply with Section 103(b) [Prob. Code § 16335(b)].

Example (7) — *T* is the trustee of a trust whose portfolio includes an interest in a mutual fund that is sponsored by *T*. As the manager of the mutual fund, *T* charges the fund a management fee that reduces the amount available to distribute to the trust by $2,000. If the fee had been paid directly by the trust, one-half of the fee would have been paid from income under Section 501(1) [Prob. Code § 16370(a)] and the other one-half would have been paid from principal under Section 502(a)(1) [Prob. Code § 16371(a)(1)]. After considering the total return from the portfolio as a whole and other relevant factors ..., *T* may exercise its power to adjust under Section 104(a) [Prob. Code § 16336(a)] by transferring $1,000, or half of the trust's proportionate share of the fee, from principal to income.

[Adapted from Unif. Principal and Income Act § 104 comment (1997)].

Cross References

Income defined for purposes of this Chapter, see Probate Code § 16324.
Income interest defined for purposes of this Chapter, see Probate Code § 16326.

§ 16336.4. Conversion of trust into unitrust

(a) Unless expressly prohibited by the governing instrument, a trustee may convert a trust into a unitrust, as described in this section. A trust that limits the power of the trustee to make an adjustment between principal and income or modify the trust does not affect the application of this section unless it is clear from the governing instrument that it is intended to deny the trustee the power to convert into a unitrust.

(b) The trustee may convert a trust into a unitrust without a court order if all of the following apply:

(1) The conditions set forth in subdivision (a) of Section 16336 are satisfied.

(2) The unitrust proposed by the trustee conforms to the provisions of paragraphs (1) to (8), inclusive, of subdivision (e).

(3) The trustee gives written notice of the trustee's intention to convert the trust into a unitrust and furnishes the information required by subdivision (c). The notice shall comply with the requirements of Chapter 5 (commencing with Section 16500), including notice to a beneficiary who is a minor and to the minor's guardian, if any.

(4) No beneficiary objects to the proposed action in a writing delivered to the trustee within the period prescribed by subdivision (d) of Section 16502 or a longer period as is specified in the notice described in subdivision (c).

(c) The notice described in paragraph (3) of subdivision (b) shall include a copy of Sections 16336.4 to 16336.7, inclusive, and all of the following additional information:

(1) A statement that the trust shall be administered in accordance with the provisions of subdivision (e) and the effective date of the conversion.

(2) A description of the method to be used for determining the fair market value of trust assets.

(3) The amount actually distributed to the income beneficiary during the previous accounting year of the trust.

(4) The amount that would have been distributed to the income beneficiary during the previous accounting year of the trust had the trustee's proposed changes been in effect during that entire year.

(5) The discretionary decisions the trustee proposes to make as of the conversion date pursuant to subdivision (f).

(d) In deciding whether to exercise the power conferred by this section, a trustee may consider, among other things, the factors set forth in subdivision (g) of Section 16336.

(e) Except to the extent that the court orders otherwise or the parties agree otherwise pursuant to Section 16336.5 after a trust is converted to a unitrust, all of the following shall apply:

(1) The trustee shall make regular distributions in accordance with the governing instrument construed in accordance with the provisions of this section.

(2) The term "income" in the governing instrument shall mean an annual distribution, the unitrust amount, equal to 4 percent, which is the payout percentage, of the net fair market value of the trust's assets, whether those assets would be considered income or principal under other provisions of this chapter, averaged over the lesser of the following:

(A) The three preceding years.

(B) The period during which the trust has been in existence.

(3) During each accounting year of the trust following its conversion into a unitrust, the trustee shall, as early in the year as is practicable, furnish each income beneficiary with a statement describing the computation of the unitrust amount for that accounting year.

(4) The trustee shall determine the net fair market value of each asset held in the trust no less often than annually. However, the following property shall not be included in determining the unitrust amount:

971

(A) Any residential property or any tangible personal property that, as of the first business day of the current accounting year, one or more current beneficiaries of the trust have or have had the right to occupy, or have or have had the right to possess or control, other than in his or her capacity as trustee of the trust, which property shall be administered according to other provisions of this chapter as though no conversion to a unitrust had occurred.

(B) Any asset specifically devised to a beneficiary to the extent necessary, in the trustee's reasonable judgment, to avoid a material risk of exhausting other trust assets prior to termination of the trust. All net income generated by a specifically devised asset excluded from the unitrust computation pursuant to this subdivision shall be accumulated or distributed by the trustee according to the rules otherwise applicable to that net income pursuant to other provisions of this chapter.

(C) Any asset while held in a testator's estate or a terminating trust.

(5) The unitrust amount, as otherwise computed pursuant to this subdivision, shall be reduced proportionately for any material distribution made to accomplish a partial termination of the trust required by the governing instrument or made as a result of the exercise of a power of appointment or withdrawal, other than distributions of the unitrust amount, and shall be increased proportionately for the receipt of any material addition to the trust, other than a receipt that represents a return on investment, during the period considered in paragraph (2) in computing the unitrust amount. For the purpose of this paragraph, a distribution or an addition shall be "material" if the net value of the distribution or addition, when combined with all prior distributions made or additions received during the same accounting year, exceeds 10 percent of the value of the assets used to compute the unitrust amount as of the most recent prior valuation date. The trustee may, in the reasonable exercise of his or her discretion, adjust the unitrust amount pursuant to this subdivision even if the distributions or additions are not sufficient to meet the definition of materiality set forth in the preceding sentence.

(6) In the case of a short year in which a beneficiary's right to payments commences or ceases, the trustee shall prorate the unitrust amount on a daily basis.

(7) Unless otherwise provided by the governing instrument or determined by the trustee, the unitrust amount shall be considered paid in the following order from the following sources:

(A) From the net taxable income, other than capital gains, determined as if the trust were other than a unitrust.

(B) From net realized short-term capital gains.

(C) From net realized long-term capital gains.

(D) From tax-exempt and other income.

(E) From principal of the trust.

(8) Expenses that would be deducted from income if the trust were not a unitrust may not be deducted from the unitrust amount.

(f) The trustee shall determine, in the trustee's discretion, all of the following matters relating to administration of a unitrust created pursuant to this section:

(1) The effective date of a conversion to a unitrust.

(2) The frequency of payments in satisfaction of the unitrust amount.

(3) Whether to value the trust's assets annually or more frequently.

(4) What valuation dates to use.

(5) How to value nonliquid assets.

(6) The characterization of the unitrust payout for income tax reporting purposes. However, the trustee's characterization shall be consistent.

(7) Any other matters that the trustee deems appropriate for the proper functioning of the unitrust.

(g) A conversion into a unitrust does not affect a provision in the governing instrument directing or authorizing the trustee to distribute principal or authorizing the exercise of a power of appointment over or withdrawal of all or a portion of the principal.

(h) A trustee may not convert a trust into a unitrust in any of the following circumstances:

(1) If payment of the unitrust amount would change the amount payable to a beneficiary as a fixed annuity or a fixed fraction of the value of the trust assets.

(2) If the unitrust distribution would be made from any amount that is permanently set aside for charitable purposes under the governing instrument and for which a federal estate or gift tax deduction has been taken, unless both income and principal are set aside.

(3) If possessing or exercising the power to convert would cause an individual to be treated as the owner of all or part of the trust for federal income tax purposes, and the individual would not be treated as the owner if the trustee did not possess the power to convert.

(4) If possessing or exercising the power to convert would cause all or part of the trust assets to be subject to federal estate or gift tax with respect to an individual, and the assets would not be subject to federal estate or gift tax with respect to the individual if the trustee did not possess the power to convert.

(5) If the conversion would result in the disallowance of a federal estate tax or gift tax marital deduction that would be allowed if the trustee did not have the power to convert.

(i) If paragraph (3) or (4) of subdivision (h) applies to a trustee and there is more than one trustee, a cotrustee to whom the provision does not apply may convert the trust unless the exercise of the power by the remaining trustee or trustees is prohibited by the governing instrument. If paragraph (3) or (4) of subdivision (h) applies to all of the trustees, the court may order the conversion as provided in subdivision (b) of Section 16336.5.

(j)(1) A trustee may release the power conferred by this section to convert to a unitrust if either of the following circumstances exist:

(A) The trustee is uncertain about whether possessing or experiencing the power will cause a result described in paragraph (3), (4), or (5) of subdivision (h).

(B) The trustee determines that possessing or exercising the power will or may deprive the trust of a tax benefit or impose a tax burden not described in subdivision (h).

(2) A release pursuant to paragraph (1) may be permanent or for a specified period, including a period measured by the life of an individual. *(Added by Stats.2005, c. 100 (S.B.754), § 4. Amended by Stats.2010, c. 621 (S.B.202), § 10.)*

Cross References

Income defined for purposes of this Chapter, see Probate Code § 16324.

Net income defined for purposes of this Chapter, see Probate Code § 16328.

§ 16336.5. Conversion of trust to a unitrust; other circumstances when authorized without court order; court ordered conversion

(a) The trustee may convert a trust into a unitrust upon terms other than those set forth in subdivision (e) of Section 16336.4, without court order, if all of the following apply:

(1) The conditions set forth in subdivision (a) of Section 16336 are satisfied.

(2) The trustee gives written notice of the trustee's intention to convert the trust into a unitrust and furnishes the information required by subdivision (c) of Section 16336.4. The notice shall comply with the requirements of Chapter 5 (commencing with Section 16500), including notice to a beneficiary who is a minor and to the minor's guardian, if any.

(3) The payout percentage to be adopted is at least 3 percent and no greater than 5 percent.

(4) All beneficiaries entitled to notice under Section 16501 consent in writing to the proposed action after having been furnished with the notice described in subdivision (c) of Section 16336.4.

(b) The court may order the conversion of a trust into a unitrust as provided in this subdivision.

(1)(A) The trustee may petition the court to approve the conversion to a unitrust for any one of the following reasons:

(i) A beneficiary timely objects to a proposed conversion to a unitrust.

(ii) The trustee proposes to make the conversion upon terms other than those described in subdivision (e) of Section 16336.4.

(iii) Paragraph (3) or (4) of subdivision (h) of Section 16336.4 applies to all currently acting trustees.

(iv) If the trustee determines, in its discretion, that a petition is advisable.

(B) In no event, however, may the court authorize conversion to a unitrust with a payout percentage of less than 3 percent or greater than 5 percent of the fair market value of the trust assets.

(2) A beneficiary may petition the court to order the conversion.

(3) The court shall approve the conversion proposed by the trustee or direct the conversion requested by the benefi-

ciary if the conditions set forth in subdivision (a) of Section 16336 are satisfied and the court concludes that conversion of the trust on the terms proposed will enable the trustee to better comply with the provisions of subdivision (b) of Section 16335.

(4) In deciding whether to approve a proposed conversion or direct a requested conversion, the court may consider, among other factors, those described in subdivision (g) of Section 16336. *(Added by Stats.2005, c. 100 (S.B.754), § 5.)*

§ 16336.6. Reconversion of trust from unitrust or change in payout percentage of unitrust

Unless expressly prohibited by the governing instrument, a trustee may reconvert the trust from a unitrust or change the payout percentage of a unitrust.

(a) The trustee may make the reconversion or change in payout percentage without a court order if all of the following conditions are satisfied:

(1) At least three years have elapsed since the most recent conversion to a unitrust.

(2) The trustee determines that reconversion or change in payout percentage would enable the trustee to better comply with the provisions of subdivision (b) of Section 16335.

(3) One of the following notice requirements is satisfied:

(A) In the case of a proposed reconversion, the trustee gives written notice of the trustee's intention to convert that complies with the requirements of Chapter 5 (commencing with Section 16500) and no beneficiary objects to the proposed action in a writing delivered to the trustee within the period prescribed by subdivision (d) of Section 16502. The trustee's notice shall include the information described in subdivision (3) and (4) of subdivision (c) of Section 16336.4.

(B) In the case of a proposed change in payout percentage, the trustee gives written notice stating the new payout percentage that the trustee proposes to adopt, which notice shall comply with the requirements of Chapter 5 (commencing with Section 16500), and no beneficiary objects to the proposed action in a writing delivered to the trustee within the period prescribed by subdivision (d) of Section 16502.

(b) The trustee may make the reconversion or change in payout percentage at any time pursuant to court order provided that: (1) the court determines that reconversion or change in payout percentage will enable the trustee to better comply with the provisions of subdivision (b) of Section 16335, and (2) in the case of a change in payout percentage, the new payout percentage is at least 3 percent and no greater than 5 percent. The court may enter an order pursuant to this subdivision upon the petition of the trustee or any beneficiary. *(Added by Stats.2005, c. 100 (S.B.754), § 6.)*

§ 16336.7. No duty imposed on trustee to convert or reconvert trust or to consider conversion or reconversion; application of § 16503

(a) Sections 16336.4 to 16336.6, inclusive, shall not impose any duty on the trustee to convert or reconvert a trust or to consider a conversion or reconversion.

(b) Subdivision (b) of Section 16503 applies to all actions pursuant to Sections 16336.4 to 16336.6, inclusive, for which notice of proposed action is given in compliance with Chapter 5 (commencing with Section 16500), including notice to a beneficiary who is a minor and to the minor's guardian, if any. *(Added by Stats.2005, c. 100 (S.B.754), § 7.)*

§ 16337.   Notice of proposed action by trustee

A trustee may give a notice of proposed action regarding a matter governed by this chapter as provided in Chapter 5 (commencing with Section 16500). For the purpose of this section, a proposed action includes a course of action and a decision not to take action. *(Added by Stats.1999, c. 145 (A.B.846), § 5. Amended by Stats.2004, c. 54 (S.B.1021), § 1.)*

Law Revision Commission Comments

1999 Addition

Section 16337 is new. This section provides a special notice of proposed action procedure applicable to principal and income allocation matters governed by this chapter. This procedure does not apply generally to trust administration. Some features of this procedure are drawn from the notice of proposed action procedure (see, e.g., Sections 10582, 10585–10587) under the Independent Administration of Estates Act (Section 10400 *et seq.*). This section applies only to notice of proposed action given by trustees. Personal representatives with authority under the Independent Administration of Estates Act have the option of using the notice of proposed action procedure under that act. See Sections 10531(a) (principal and income allocations and determinations), 10580(b) (optional use of notice of proposed action procedure).

See also Section 1215 (manner of giving notice). For judicial proceedings concerning trusts, see, e.g., Section 17200. [29 Cal. L.Rev.Comm. Reports 245 (1999)].

§ 16338.   Proceedings relating to § 16336 and §§ 16336.4 to 16336.6; remedy

In a proceeding with respect to a trustee's exercise or nonexercise of the power to make an adjustment under Section 16336, the sole remedy is to direct, deny, or revise an adjustment between principal and income. In a proceeding with respect to a trustee's exercise or nonexercise of a power conferred by Sections 16336.4 to 16336.6, inclusive, the sole remedy is to obtain an order directing the trustee to convert the trust to a unitrust, to reconvert from a unitrust, to change the distribution percentage, or to order any administrative procedures the court determines to be necessary or helpful for the proper functioning of the trust. *(Added by Stats.1999, c. 145 (A.B.846), § 5. Amended by Stats.2005, c. 100 (S.B.754), § 8.)*

Law Revision Commission Comments

1999 Addition

Section 16338 limits the remedy in proceedings concerning adjustments under Section 16336 to correcting the adjustment. This rule recognizes that if there is a dispute concerning exercise of the adjustment power, it is between the affected beneficiaries, and not between the trustee and beneficiaries. Accordingly, the trustee is not liable for a surcharge or denial of fees where the dispute relates to the exercise or nonexercise of the power to adjust or the proper level of an adjustment, if any. [29 Cal.L.Rev.Comm. Reports apx. 4 (1999)].

Cross References

Income defined for purposes of this Chapter, see Probate Code § 16324.

§ 16339.   Application of chapter

This chapter applies to every trust or decedent's estate existing on or after January 1, 2000, except as otherwise expressly provided in the trust or will or in this chapter. *(Added by Stats.1999, c. 145 (A.B.846), § 5.)*

Law Revision Commission Comments

1999 Addition

Section 16339 is the same in substance as Section 605 of the Uniform Principal and Income Act (1997).

See also Section 3 (general transitional provisions). [29 Cal. L.Rev.Comm. Reports apx. 4 (1999)].

ARTICLE 3.   DECEDENT'S ESTATE OR TERMINATING INCOME INTEREST

Section
16340.   Rules applicable after decedent's death or termination of income interest.
16341.   Beneficiary's portion of net income; maintenance of records; distribution date.

Application

Application of Division, see Probate Code § 15001.

§ 16340.   Rules applicable after decedent's death or termination of income interest

After the decedent's death, in the case of a decedent's estate, or after an income interest in a trust ends, the following rules apply:

(a) If property is specifically given to a beneficiary, by will or trust, the fiduciary of the estate or of the terminating income interest shall distribute the net income and principal receipts to the beneficiary who is to receive the property, subject to the following rules:

(1) The net income and principal receipts from the specifically given property are determined by including all of the amounts the fiduciary receives or pays with respect to the property, whether the amounts accrued or became due before, on, or after the decedent's death or an income interest in a trust ends, and by making a reasonable provision for amounts the fiduciary believes the estate or terminating income interest may become obligated to pay after the property is distributed.

(2) The fiduciary may not reduce income and principal receipts from the specifically given property on account of a payment described in Section 16370 or 16371, to the extent that the will, the trust, or Section 12002 requires payment from other property or to the extent that the fiduciary recovers the payment from a third person.

(3) A specific gift distributable under a trust shall carry with it the same benefits and burdens as a specific devise under a will, as set forth in Chapter 8 (commencing with Section 12000) of Part 10 of Division 7.

(b) A general pecuniary gift, an annuity, or a gift of maintenance distributable under a trust carries with it income and bears interest in the same manner as a general pecuniary devise, an annuity, or a gift of maintenance under a will, as set forth in Chapter 8 (commencing with Section 12000) of Part 10 of Division 7. The fiduciary shall distribute to a beneficiary who receives a pecuniary amount, whether outright or in trust, the interest or any other amount provided by the will, the trust, this subdivision, or Chapter 8 (commencing with Section 12000) of Part 10 of Division 7, from the remaining net income determined under subdivision (c) or from principal to the extent that net income is insufficient.

(c) The fiduciary shall determine the remaining net income of the decedent's estate or terminating income interest as provided in this chapter and by doing the following:

(1) Including in net income all income from property used to discharge liabilities.

(2) Paying from income or principal, in the fiduciary's discretion, fees of attorneys, accountants, and fiduciaries, court costs and other expenses of administration, and interest on death taxes, except that the fiduciary may pay these expenses from income of property passing to a trust for which the fiduciary claims an estate tax marital or charitable deduction only to the extent that the payment of these expenses from income will not cause the reduction or loss of the deduction.

(3) Paying from principal all other disbursements made or incurred in connection with the settlement of a decedent's estate or the winding up of a terminating income interest, including debts, funeral expenses, disposition of remains, family allowances, and death taxes and related penalties that are apportioned to the estate or terminating income interest by the will, the trust, or Division 10 (commencing with Section 20100).

(d) After distributions required by subdivision (b), the fiduciary shall distribute the remaining net income determined under subdivision (c) in the manner provided in Section 16341 to all other beneficiaries.

(e) For purposes of this section, a reference in Chapter 8 (commencing with Section 12000) of Part 10 of Division 7 to the date of the testator's death means the date of the settlor's death or of the occurrence of some other event on which the distributee's right to receive the gift depends.

(f) If a trustee has distributed a specific gift or a general pecuniary gift before January 1, 2007, the trustee may allocate income and principal as set forth in this chapter or in any other manner permissible under the law in effect at the time of the distribution. If the trustee distributes a specific gift or a general pecuniary gift after December 31, 2006, then the trustee shall allocate income and principal as provided in this chapter. *(Added by Stats.1999, c. 145 (A.B.846), § 5. Amended by Stats.2006, c. 569 (A.B.2347), § 1.)*

Law Revision Commission Comments
1999 Addition

Section 16340 is drawn from Section 201 of the Uniform Principal and Income Act (1997), with a number of modifications to conform with the California rule on specific gifts and to improve readability. The revised language is intended to set out the rules in logical order, the order in which the fiduciary would make determinations and allocations. This section supersedes former Sections 16305 and 16314.

This section invokes rules provided elsewhere in this chapter that apply to trustees. In places, the uniform act refers specifically to rules "which apply to trustees." See UPAIA Section 201(1)-(2). This language has been omitted to simplify this section, but the concept is the same: the rules applicable to trustees (and fiduciaries generally) in this chapter are to be applied both in cases of decedent's estates and terminating income interests in trusts under this section.

Subdivision (a) is drawn from UPAIA Section 201(1) and (5). The introductory clause is drawn from UPAIA Section 201(1). Subdivision (a)(1) is the same in substance as the second sentence of UPAIA Section 201(5). Subdivision (a)(2) is the same in substance as the first sentence of UPAIA Section 201(5).

Subdivisions (a) and (b) continue former Section 16314(a) without substantive change. This rule substitutes for UPAIA Section 201(3).

Subdivision (c) is the same in substance as UPAIA Section 201(2).

Subdivision (d) is the same in substance as UPAIA Section 201(4).

Subdivision (e) continues former Section 16314(b).

See also Sections 62 ("property" defined), 16323 ("fiduciary" defined), 16324 ("income" defined), 16326 ("income interest" defined), 16328 ("net income" defined). [29 Cal.L.Rev.Comm. Reports 245 (1999)].

Background from Uniform Act

Terminating income interests and successive income interests. A trust that provides for a single income beneficiary and an outright distribution of the remainder ends when the income interest ends. A more complex trust may have a number of income interests, either concurrent or successive, and the trust will not necessarily end when one of the income interests ends. For that reason, the Act speaks in terms of income interests ending and beginning rather than trusts ending and beginning. When an income interest in a trust ends, the trustee's powers continue during the winding up period required to complete its administration. A terminating income interest is one that has ended but whose administration is not complete.

If two or more people are given the right to receive specified percentages or fractions of the income from a trust concurrently and one of the concurrent interests ends, e.g., when a beneficiary dies, the beneficiary's income interest ends but the trust does not. Similarly, when a trust with only one income beneficiary ends upon the beneficiary's death, the trust instrument may provide that part or all of the trust assets shall continue in trust for another income beneficiary. While it is common to think and speak of this (and even to characterize it in a trust instrument) as a 'new' trust, it is a continuation of the original trust for a remainder beneficiary who has an income interest in the trust assets instead of the right to receive them outright. For purposes of this Act, this is a successive income interest in the same trust. The fact that a trust may or may not end when an income interest ends is not significant for purposes of this Act.

If the assets that are subject to a terminating income interest pass to another trust because the income beneficiary exercises a general power of appointment over the trust assets, the recipient trust would be a new trust; and if they pass to another trust because the beneficiary exercises a nongeneral power of appointment over the trust assets, the recipient trust might be a new trust in some States (see 5A Austin W. Scott & William F. Fratcher, The Law of Trusts § 640, at 483 (4th ed. 1989)); but for purposes of this Act a new trust created in these circumstances is also a successive income interest.

Administration expenses and interest on death taxes. Under Section 201(2)(B) [Prob. Code § 16340(c)(2)] a fiduciary may pay administration expenses and interest on death taxes from either income or principal. An advantage of permitting the fiduciary to choose the source of the payment is that, if the fiduciary's decision is consistent with the decision to deduct these expenses for income tax purposes or estate tax purposes, it eliminates the need to adjust between principal and income that may arise when, for example, an expense that is paid from principal is deducted for income tax purposes or an expense that is paid from income is deducted for estate tax purposes.

The United States Supreme Court has considered the question of whether an estate tax marital deduction or charitable deduction should be reduced when administration expenses are paid from income produced by property passing in trust for a surviving spouse or for charity and deducted for income tax purposes. The Court rejected the IRS position that administration expenses properly paid from income under the terms of the trust or state law must reduce the amount of a marital or charitable transfer, and held that the value of the transferred property is not reduced for estate tax purposes unless the administration expenses are material in light of the income the trust corpus could have been expected to generate. Commissioner v. Estate of Otis C. Hubert, 117 S. Ct. 1124 (1997). The provision in Section 201(2)(B) [Prob. Code § 16340(c)(2)] permits a fiduciary to pay and deduct administration expenses from income only to the extent that it will not cause the reduction or loss of an estate tax marital or charitable contributions deduction, which means that the limit on the amount payable from income will be established eventually by Treasury Regulations.

Interest on estate taxes. The IRS agrees that interest on estate and inheritance taxes may be deducted for income tax purposes without having to reduce the estate tax deduction for amounts passing to a charity or surviving spouse, whether the interest is paid from principal or income. Rev. Rul. 93–48, 93–2 C.B. 270. For estates of persons who died before 1998, a fiduciary may not want to deduct for income tax purposes interest on estate tax that is deferred under Section 6166 or 6163 because deducting that interest for estate tax purposes may produce more beneficial results, especially if the estate has little or no income or the income tax bracket is significantly lower than the estate tax bracket. For estates of persons who die after 1997, no estate tax or income tax deduction will be allowed for interest paid on estate tax that is deferred under Section 6166. However, interest on estate tax deferred under Section 6163 will continue to be deductible for both purposes, and interest on estate tax deficiencies will continue to be deductible for estate tax purposes if an election under Section 6166 is not in effect.

Under the 1962 Act, Section 13(c)(5) charges interest on estate and inheritance taxes to principal. The 1931 Act has no provision. Section 501(3) of this Act [Prob. Code § 16370(c)] provides that, except to the extent provided in Section 201(2)(B) or (C) [Prob. Code § 16340(c)(2) or (c)(3)], all interest must be paid from income. [Adapted from Unif. Principal and Income Act § 201 comment (1997)].

Cross References

Fiduciary defined for purposes of this Chapter, see Probate Code § 16323.

Income defined for purposes of this Chapter, see Probate Code § 16324.

Income interest defined for purposes of this Chapter, see Probate Code § 16326.

Net income defined for purposes of this Chapter, see Probate Code § 16328.

§ 16341.　Beneficiary's portion of net income; maintenance of records; distribution date

(a) Each beneficiary described in subdivision (d) of Section 16340 is entitled to receive a portion of the net income equal to the beneficiary's fractional interest in undistributed principal assets, using values as of the distribution dates and without reducing the values by any unpaid principal obligations.

(b) If a fiduciary does not distribute all of the collected but undistributed net income to each beneficiary as of a distribu-

tion date, the fiduciary shall maintain appropriate records showing the interest of each beneficiary in that net income.

(c) The distribution date for purposes of this section may be the date as of which the fiduciary calculates the value of the assets if that date is reasonably near the date on which assets are actually distributed. *(Added by Stats.1999, c. 145 (A.B.846), § 5.)*

Law Revision Commission Comments

1999 Addition

Section 16341 is drawn from parts of Section 202 of the Uniform Principal and Income Act (1997). This section retains the basic rules of the UPAIA section, but omits some unnecessary detail. This section supersedes parts of former Section 16304.

Subdivision (a) is the same in substance as the first sentence of UPAIA Section 202(a), and includes the 'unpaid principal obligation' rule from UPAIA Section 202(b)(3). The second sentence of Section 202(a) is not needed because it simply reaffirms that the rule in the first sentence is to be applied when there are more than one distributions:

If a fiduciary makes more than one distribution of assets to beneficiaries to whom this section applies, each beneficiary, including one who does not receive part of the distribution, is entitled, as of each distribution date, to the net income the fiduciary has received after the date of death or terminating event or earlier distribution date but has not distributed as of the current distribution date. [UPAIA § 202(a) 2d sent.].

Subdivision (b) is the same as UPAIA Section 202(c), except that the reference to "person" in the uniform act has been changed to "beneficiary."

Subdivision (c) is the same as UPAIA Section 202(b)(4).

The following UPAIA rules are not included in Section 16341 because they are already stated in the general rule as set out in subdivision (a):

The beneficiary is entitled to receive a portion of the net income equal to the beneficiary's fractional interest in the undistributed principal assets immediately before the distribution date, including assets that later may be sold to meet principal obligations. [UPAIA § 202(b)(1)].

The beneficiary's fractional interest in the undistributed principal assets must be calculated on the basis of the aggregate value of those assets as of the distribution date without reducing the value by any unpaid principal obligation. [UPAIA § 202(b)(3)].

Subdivisions (b)(2) and (d) of UPAIA Section 202 are omitted as unnecessary in view of the special California rules on interest and income accruing during administration. See Sections 12000–12006, 16305. The uniform act provision was added to fill a gap noted by several commentators (see UPAIA § 202 comment) — a gap that had been filled by earlier California legislation, which is unaffected by enactment of this chapter. For background on former law, see *Recommendation Relating to Interest and Income During Administration*, 19 Cal. L. Revision Comm'n Reports 1019 (1988). [29 Cal.L.Rev.Comm. Reports 245 (1999)].

Background from Uniform Act

Relationship to prior Acts. Section 202 [Prob. Code § 16341] retains the concept in Section 5(b)(2) of the 1962 Act [see former Prob. Code § 16305] that the residuary legatees of estates are to receive net income earned during the period of administration on the basis of their proportionate interests in the undistributed assets when distributions are made. It changes the basis for determining their proportionate interests by using asset values as of a date reasonably near the time of distribution instead of inventory values....

[Adapted from Unif. Principal and Income Act § 202 comment (1997)].

Fiduciary defined for purposes of this Chapter, see Probate Code § 16323.

Income defined for purposes of this Chapter, see Probate Code § 16324.

Net income defined for purposes of this Chapter, see Probate Code § 16328.

ARTICLE 4.   APPORTIONMENT AT BEGINNING AND END OF INCOME INTEREST

Section

16345.   Beneficiary's entitlement to net income; assets subject to trust; assets subject to successive income interest; termination of income interest.

16346.   Allocation of income receipt or disbursement.

16347.   Undistributed income; payment to beneficiary.

Application

Application of Division, see Probate Code § 15001.

§ 16345.   Beneficiary's entitlement to net income; assets subject to trust; assets subject to successive income interest; termination of income interest

(a) An income beneficiary is entitled to net income from the date on which the income interest begins. An income interest begins on the date specified in the trust or, if no date is specified, on the date an asset becomes subject to a trust or successive income interest.

(b) An asset becomes subject to a trust at the following times:

(1) In the case of an asset that is transferred to a trust during the transferor's life, on the date it is transferred to the trust.

(2) In the case of an asset that becomes subject to a trust by reason of a will, even if there is an intervening period of administration of the testator's estate, on the date of the testator's death.

(3) In the case of an asset that is transferred to a fiduciary by a third party because of the individual's death, on the date of the individual's death.

(c) An asset becomes subject to a successive income interest on the day after the preceding income interest ends, as determined under subdivision (d), even if there is an intervening period of administration to wind up the preceding income interest.

(d) An income interest ends on the day before an income beneficiary dies, or another terminating event occurs, or on the last day of a period during which there is no beneficiary to whom a trustee may distribute income. *(Added by Stats.1999, c. 145 (A.B.846), § 5.)*

Law Revision Commission Comments

1999 Addition

Section 16345 is the same in substance as Section 301 of the Uniform Principal and Income Act (1997). This section supersedes parts of former Section 16304.

See also Sections 24 ("beneficiary" defined), 84 ("trustee" defined), 16324 ("income" defined), 16325 ("income beneficiary" defined), 16326 ("income interest" defined), 16328 ("net income" defined). [29 Cal.L.Rev.Comm. Reports 245 (1999)].

Background from Uniform Act

Period during which there is no beneficiary. The purpose of the second part of subsection (d) is to provide that, at the end of a period during which there is no beneficiary to whom a trustee may distribute income, the trustee must apply the same apportionment rules that apply when a mandatory income interest ends. This provision would apply, for example, if a settlor creates a trust for grandchildren before any grandchildren are born. When the first grandchild is born, the period preceding the date of birth is treated as having ended, followed by a successive income interest, and the apportionment rules in Sections 302 and 303 [Prob. Code §§ 16346–16347] apply accordingly if the terms of the trust do not contain different provisions.

[Adapted from Unif. Principal and Income Act § 301 comment (1997)].

Fiduciary defined for purposes of this Chapter, see Probate Code § 16323.

Income defined for purposes of this Chapter, see Probate Code § 16324.

Income interest defined for purposes of this Chapter, see Probate Code § 16326.

Net income defined for purposes of this Chapter, see Probate Code § 16328.

§ 16346.   Allocation of income receipt or disbursement

(a) A trustee shall allocate an income receipt or disbursement other than one to which subdivision (a) of Section 16340 applies to principal if its due date occurs before a decedent dies in the case of an estate or before an income interest begins in the case of a trust or successive income interest.

(b) A trustee shall allocate an income receipt or disbursement to income if its due date occurs on or after the date on which a decedent dies or an income interest begins and it is a periodic due date. An income receipt or disbursement shall be treated as accruing from day to day if its due date is not periodic or it has no due date. The portion of the receipt or disbursement accruing before the date on which a decedent dies or an income interest begins shall be allocated to principal and the balance shall be allocated to income.

(c) An item of income or an obligation is due on the date the payer is required to make a payment. If a payment date is not stated, there is no due date for the purposes of this chapter. Distributions to shareholders or other owners from an entity to which Section 16350 applies are deemed to be due on the date fixed by the entity for determining who is entitled to receive the distribution or, if no date is fixed, on the declaration date for the distribution. A due date is periodic for receipts or disbursements that must be paid at regular intervals under a lease or an obligation to pay interest or if an entity customarily makes distributions at regular intervals. *(Added by Stats.1999, c. 145 (A.B.846), § 5.)*

Law Revision Commission Comments

1999 Addition

Section 16346 is the same in substance as Section 302 of the Uniform Principal and Income Act (1997). This section supersedes parts of former Section 16304.

See also Sections 84 ("trustee" defined), 16324 ("income" defined), 16326 ("income interest" defined). [29 Cal.L.Rev.Comm. Reports 245 (1999)].

Background from Uniform Act

Prior Acts. Professor Bogert stated that "Section 4 of the [1962] Act makes a change with respect to the apportionment of the income of trust property not due until after the trust began but which accrued in part before the commencement of the trust. It treats such income as to be credited entirely to the income account in the case of a living trust, but to be apportioned between capital and income in the case of a testamentary trust. The [1931] Act apportions such income in the case of both types of trusts, except in the case of corporate dividends." George G. Bogert, *The Revised Uniform Principal and Income Act*, 38 Notre Dame Law. 50, 52 (1962). The 1962 Act also provides that an asset passing to an inter vivos trust by a bequest in the settlor's will is governed by the rule that applies to a testamentary trust, so that different rules apply to assets passing to an inter vivos trust depending upon whether they were transferred to the trust during the settlor's life or by his will.

Having several different rules that apply to similar transactions is confusing. In order to simplify administration, Section 302 [Prob. Code § 16346] applies the same rule to inter vivos trusts (revocable and irrevocable), testamentary trusts, and assets that become subject to an inter vivos trust by a testamentary bequest.

Periodic payments. Under Section 302 [Prob. Code § 16346], a periodic payment is principal if it is due but unpaid before a decedent dies or before an asset becomes subject to a trust, but the next payment is allocated entirely to income and is not apportioned. Thus, periodic receipts such as rents, dividends, interest, and annuities, and disbursements such as the interest portion of a mortgage payment, are not apportioned. This is the original common law rule. Edwin A. Howes, Jr., The American Law Relating to Income and Principal 70 (1905). In trusts in which a surviving spouse is dependent upon a regular flow of cash from the decedent's securities portfolio, this rule will help to maintain payments to the spouse at the same level as before the settlor's death. Under the 1962 Act, the pre-death portion of the first periodic payment due after death is apportioned to principal in the case of a testamentary trust or securities bequeathed by will to an inter vivos trust.

Nonperiodic payments. Under the second sentence of Section 302(b) [Prob. Code § 16346(b)], interest on an obligation that does not provide a due date for the interest payment, such as interest on an income tax refund, would be apportioned to principal to the extent it accrues before a person dies or an income interest begins unless the obligation is specifically given to a devisee or remainder beneficiary, in which case all of the accrued interest passes under Section 201(1) [Prob. Code § 16340(a)] to the person who receives the obligation. The same rule applies to interest on an obligation that has a due date but does not provide for periodic payments. If there is no stated interest on the obligation, such as a zero coupon bond, and the proceeds from the obligation are received more than one year after it is purchased or acquired by the trustee, the entire amount received is principal under Section 406 [Prob. Code § 16357].

[Adapted from Unif. Principal and Income Act § 302 comment (1997)].

Cross References

Income defined for purposes of this Chapter, see Probate Code § 16324.
Income interest defined for purposes of this Chapter, see Probate Code § 16326.

§ 16347. Undistributed income; payment to beneficiary

(a) For the purposes of this section, "undistributed income" means net income received before the date on which an income interest ends. The term does not include an item of income or expense that is due or accrued or net income that has been added or is required to be added to principal by the trust.

(b) Except as provided in subdivision (c), on the date when a mandatory income interest ends, the trustee shall pay to a mandatory income beneficiary who survives that date, or to the estate of a deceased mandatory income beneficiary whose death causes the interest to end, the beneficiary's share of the undistributed income that is not disposed of under the trust.

(c) If immediately before the income interest ends, the beneficiary under subdivision (b) has an unqualified power to revoke more than 5 percent of the trust, the undistributed income from the portion of the trust that may be revoked shall be added to principal.

(d) When a trustee's obligation to pay a fixed annuity or a fixed fraction of the value of the trust's assets ends, the trustee shall prorate the final payment. *(Added by Stats.1999, c. 145 (A.B.846), § 5.)*

Law Revision Commission Comments

1999 Addition

Section 16347 is the same in substance as Section 303 of the Uniform Principal and Income Act (1997). This section supersedes parts of former Section 16304.

Subdivision (a) is the same as UPAIA Section 303(a).

Subdivisions (b) and (c) are the same in substance as UPAIA Section 303(b). The provision has been restructured for clarity and some minor wording changes have been made. The "unless" clause in the uniform act provision is stated as an exception in subdivision (c), as recognized in the introductory clause of subdivision (b).

Subdivision (d) is the same as the first part of UPAIA Section 303(c). The last clause of UPAIA Section 303(c) ("if and to the extent required by applicable law to accomplish a purpose of the trust or its settlor relating to income, gift, estate, or other tax requirements") is omitted as being repetitive of general principles.

See also Sections 84 ("trustee" defined), 16324 ("income" defined), 16325 ("income beneficiary" defined), 16326 ("income interest" defined), 16327 ("mandatory income interest" defined), 16328 ("net income" defined). [29 Cal.L.Rev.Comm. Reports 245 (1999)].

Background from Uniform Act

Prior Acts. Both the 1931 Act (Section 4) and the 1962 Act (Section 4(d) [see former Prob. Code § 16304]) provide that a deceased income beneficiary's estate is entitled to the undistributed income. The Drafting Committee concluded that this is probably not what most settlors would want, and that, with respect to undistributed income, most settlors would favor the income beneficiary first, the remainder beneficiaries second, and the income beneficiary's heirs last, if at all. However, it decided not to eliminate this provision to avoid causing disputes about whether the trustee should have distributed collected cash before the income beneficiary died.

Accrued periodic payments. Under the prior Acts, an income beneficiary or his estate is entitled to receive a portion of any payments, other than dividends, that are due or that have accrued when the income interest terminates. The last sentence of subsection (a) changes that rule by providing that such items are not included in undistributed income. The items affected include periodic payments of interest, rent, and dividends, as well as items of income that accrue over a longer period of time; the rule also applies to expenses that are due or accrued.

Example—accrued periodic payments. The rules in Section 302 and Section 303 [Prob. Code §§ 16346 & 16347] work in the following manner: Assume that a periodic payment of rent that is due on July 20 has not been paid when an income interest ends on July 30; the successive income interest begins on July 31, and the rent payment that was due on July 20 is paid on August 3. Under Section 302(a) [Prob. Code § 16346(a)], the July 20 payment is added to the principal of the successive income interest when received. Under

Section 302(b) [Prob. Code § 16346(b)], the entire periodic payment of rent that is due on August 20 is income when received by the successive income interest. Under Section 303 [Prob. Code § 16347], neither the income beneficiary of the terminated income interest nor the beneficiary's estate is entitled to any part of either the July 20 or the August 20 payments because neither one was received before the income interest ended on July 30. The same principles apply to expenses of the trust.

Beneficiary with an unqualified power to revoke. The requirement in subsection (b) to pay undistributed income to a mandatory income beneficiary or her estate does not apply to the extent the beneficiary has an unqualified power to revoke more than five percent of the trust immediately before the income interest ends. Without this exception, subsection (b) would apply to a revocable living trust whose settlor is the mandatory income beneficiary during her lifetime, even if her will provides that all of the assets in the probate estate are to be distributed to the trust.

If a trust permits the beneficiary to withdraw all or a part of the trust principal after attaining a specified age and the beneficiary attains that age but fails to withdraw all of the principal that she is permitted to withdraw, a trustee is not required to pay her or her estate the undistributed income attributable to the portion of the principal that she left in the trust. The assumption underlying this rule is that the beneficiary has either provided for the disposition of the trust assets (including the undistributed income) by exercising a power of appointment that she has been given or has not withdrawn the assets because she is willing to have the principal and undistributed income be distributed under the terms of the trust. If the beneficiary has the power to withdraw 25% of the trust principal, the trustee must pay to her or her estate the undistributed income from the 75% that she cannot withdraw.

[Adapted from Unif. Principal and Income Act § 303 comment (1997)].

Cross References

Income defined for purposes of this Chapter, see Probate Code § 16324.

Income interest defined for purposes of this Chapter, see Probate Code § 16326.

ARTICLE 5.1. ALLOCATION OF RECEIPTS DURING ADMINISTRATION OF TRUST: RECEIPTS FROM ENTITIES

Section
16350. Allocation of receipts to income or principal; partial liquidation determination.
16351. Allocation of amounts received from specified trusts or estates.
16352. Separate accounting records for business or other activity.

Application

Application of Division, see Probate Code § 15001.

§ 16350. Allocation of receipts to income or principal; partial liquidation determination

(a) For the purposes of this section:

(1) "Entity" means a corporation, partnership, limited liability company, regulated investment company, real estate investment trust, common trust fund, or any other organization in which a trustee has an interest other than a trust or decedent's estate to which Section 16351 applies, a business or activity to which Section 16352 applies, or an asset-backed security to which Section 16367 applies.

(2) "Capital asset" means a capital asset as defined in Section 1221 of the Internal Revenue Code.[1]

(b) Except as otherwise provided in this section, a trustee shall allocate to income money received from an entity.

(c) A trustee shall allocate to principal the following receipts from an entity:

(1) Property other than money.

(2) Money received in one distribution or a series of related distributions in exchange for part or all of a trust's interest in the entity.

(3) Money received in total liquidation of the entity or in partial liquidation of the entity, as defined in subdivision (d), except for money received from an entity that is a regulated investment company or a real estate investment trust if the money distributed is a net short-term capital gain distribution.

(4) Money received from an entity that is a regulated investment company or a real estate investment trust if the money distributed is a capital gain dividend for federal income tax purposes. A capital gain dividend shall not include money received as a net short-term capital gain distribution from a regulated investment company or real estate investment trust.

(d) For purposes of paragraph (3) of subdivision (c), money shall be treated as received in partial liquidation to the extent the amount received from the distributing entity is attributable to the proceeds from a sale by the distributing entity, or by the distributing entity's subsidiary or affiliate, of a capital asset. The following shall apply to determine whether money is received in partial liquidation:

(1) A trustee may rely without investigation on a written statement made by the distributing entity regarding the receipt.

(2) A trustee may rely without investigation on other information actually known by the trustee regarding whether the receipt is attributable to the proceeds from a sale by the distributing entity, or by the distributing entity's subsidiary or affiliate, of a capital asset.

(3) With regard to each receipt from a distributing entity, if within 30 days from the date of the receipt the distributing entity provides no written statement to the trustee that the receipt is a distribution attributable to the proceeds from a sale of a capital asset by the distributing entity or by the distributing entity's subsidiary or affiliate and the trustee has no actual knowledge that the receipt is a distribution attributable to the proceeds from a sale of a capital asset by the distributing entity or by the distributing entity's subsidiary or affiliate, then the following shall apply:

(A) The trustee shall have no duty to investigate whether the receipt from the distributing entity is in partial liquidation of the entity.

(B) If, on the date of receipt, the receipt from the distributing entity is in excess of 10 percent of the value of the trust's interest in the distributing entity, then the receipt shall be deemed to be received in partial liquidation of the distributing entity, and the trustee shall allocate all of the receipt to principal. For purposes of this subparagraph, the value of the trust's interest in the distributing entity shall be determined as follows:

(i) In the case of an interest that is a security regularly traded on a public exchange or market, the closing price of the security on the public exchange or market occurring on the last business day before the date of the receipt.

(ii) In the case of an interest that is not a security regularly traded on a public exchange or market, the trust's proportionate share of the value of the distributing entity as set forth in the most recent appraisal, if any, actually received by the trustee and prepared by a professional appraiser with a valuation date within three years of the date of the receipt. The trustee shall have no duty to investigate the existence of the appraisal or to obtain an appraisal nor shall the trustee have any liability for relying upon an appraisal prepared by a professional appraiser. The term "professional appraiser" shall refer to an appraiser who has earned an appraisal designation for valuing the type of property subject to the appraisal from a recognized professional appraiser organization.

(iii) If the trust's interest in the distributing entity cannot be valued under clause (i) or clause (ii), the trust's proportionate share of the distributing entity's net assets, to be calculated as gross assets minus liabilities, as shown in the distributing entity's yearend financial statements immediately preceding the receipt.

(iv) If the trust's interest in the distributing entity cannot be valued under clause (i), (ii), or (iii), the federal cost basis of the trust's interest in the distributing entity on the date immediately before the date of the receipt.

(e) If a trustee allocates a receipt to principal in accordance with subdivision (d), or allocates a receipt to income because the receipt is not determined to be in partial liquidation under subdivision (d), the trustee shall not be liable for any claim of improper allocation of the receipt that is based on information that was not received or actually known by the trustee as of the date of allocation.

(f)(1) Notwithstanding anything to the contrary in subdivision (d), if the receipt was allocated between December 2, 2004, and July 18, 2005, a trustee shall not be liable for allocating the receipt to income if the amount received by the trustee, when considered together with the amount received by all owners, collectively, exceeded 20 percent of the entity's gross assets, but the amount received by the trustee did not exceed 20 percent of the entity's gross assets.

(2) Money is not received in partial liquidation, nor may it be taken into account under subdivision (d), to the extent that it does not exceed the amount of income tax that a trustee or beneficiary is required to pay on taxable income of the entity that distributes the money. *(Added by Stats.1999, c. 145 (A.B.846), § 5. Amended by Stats.2005, c. 51 (S.B.296), § 1, eff. July 18, 2005; Stats.2013, c. 105 (A.B.1029), § 1; Stats. 2014, c. 867 (A.B.296), § 1, eff. Sept. 30, 2014.)*

1 Internal Revenue Code sections are in Title 26 of the U.S.C.A.

Law Revision Commission Comments
1999 Addition

Section 16350 is the same in substance as Section 401 of the Uniform Principal and Income Act (1997), with several minor changes. This section supersedes former law concerning corporate distributions (former Section 16306) and business and partnership distributions (former Section 16308).

Subdivision (d) combines the substance of subdivisions (d) and (e) of the uniform act and makes clear that the rules relate to partial liquidations covered by subdivision (c)(3). In subdivision (e), the uniform act limitation that the statement must be made "at or near the time of distribution" has been omitted. This is consistent with the rule under former Section 16306(e).

See also Sections 24 ("beneficiary" defined), 62 ("property" defined), 84 ("trustee" defined). [29 Cal.L.Rev.Comm. Reports 245 (1999)].

Background from Uniform Act

Entities to which Section 401 [Prob. Code § 16350] applies. The reference to partnerships in Section 401(a) [Prob. Code § 16350(a)] is intended to include all forms of partnerships, including limited partnerships, limited liability partnerships, and variants that have slightly different names and characteristics from State to State. The section does not apply, however, to receipts from an interest in property that a trust owns as a tenant in common with one or more co-owners, nor would it apply to an interest in a joint venture if, under applicable law, the trust's interest is regarded as that of a tenant in common.

Capital gain dividends. Under the Internal Revenue Code and the Income Tax Regulations, a "capital gain dividend" from a mutual fund or real estate investment trust is the excess of the fund's or trust's net long-term capital gain over its net short-term capital loss. As a result, a capital gain dividend does not include any net short-term capital gain, and cash received by a trust because of a net short-term capital gain is income under this Act.

Reinvested dividends. If a trustee elects (or continues an election made by its predecessor) to reinvest dividends in shares of stock of a distributing corporation or fund, whether evidenced by new certificates or entries on the books of the distributing entity, the new shares would be principal. Making or continuing such an election would be equivalent to deciding under Section 104 [Prob. Code § 16336] to transfer income to principal in order to comply with Section 103(b) [Prob. Code § 16335(b)]. However, if the trustee makes or continues the election for a reason other than to comply with Section 103(b) [Prob. Code § 16335(b)], e.g., to make an investment without incurring brokerage commissions, the trustee should transfer cash from principal to income in an amount equal to the reinvested dividends.

Distribution of property. The 1962 Act describes a number of types of property that would be principal if distributed by a corporation. This becomes unwieldy in a section that applies to both corporations and all other entities. By stating that principal includes the distribution of any property other than money, Section 401 [Prob. Code § 16350] embraces all of the items enumerated in Section 6 of the 1962 Act [former Prob. Code § 16306] as well as any other form of nonmonetary distribution not specifically mentioned in that Act.

Partial liquidations. Under subsection (d)(1) [subdivision (d)(1)(A)], any distribution designated by the entity as a partial liquidating distribution is principal regardless of the percentage of total assets that it represents. If a distribution exceeds 20% of the entity's gross assets, the entire distribution is a partial liquidation under subsection (d)(2) [subdivision (d)(1)(B)] whether or not the entity describes it as a partial liquidation. In determining whether a distribution is greater than 20% of the gross assets, the portion of the distribution that does not exceed the amount of income tax that the trustee or a beneficiary must pay on the entity's taxable income is ignored.

Other large distributions. A cash distribution may be quite large (for example, more than 10% but not more than 20% of the entity's gross assets) and have characteristics that suggest it should be treated as principal rather than income. For example, an entity may have received cash from a source other than the conduct of its normal business operations because it sold an investment asset; or because it sold a business asset other than one held for sale to customers in the normal course of its business and did not replace it; or it borrowed a large sum of money and secured the repayment of the loan with a substantial asset; or a principal source of its cash was from assets such as mineral interests, 90% of which would have been allocated to principal if the trust had owned the assets directly. In such a case the trustee, after considering the total return from the portfolio as a whole and the income component of that return, may decide to exercise the power under Section 104(a) [Prob. Code § 16336(a)] to make an adjustment between income and principal, subject to the limitations in Section 104(c) [Prob. Code § 16336(b)].

[Adapted from Unif. Principal and Income Act § 401 comment (1997)].

Cross References

Income defined for purposes of this Chapter, see Probate Code § 16324.

§ 16351. Allocation of amounts received from specified trusts or estates

A trustee shall allocate to income an amount received as a distribution of income from a trust or a decedent's estate (other than an interest in an investment entity) in which the trust has an interest other than a purchased interest, and shall allocate to principal an amount received as a distribution of principal from the trust or estate. *(Added by Stats.1999, c. 145 (A.B.846), § 5.)*

Law Revision Commission Comments

1999 Addition

Section 16351 is drawn from the first sentence of Section 402 of the Uniform Principal and Income Act (1997). This section applies to interests that have not been purchased—if the trustee purchases an interest in a trust that is an investment entity, or a decedent or donor transfers an interest in such a trust to a trustee, Section 16350 applies to a receipt from the trust.

See also Sections 84 ("trustee" defined), 16324 ("income" defined). [29 Cal.L.Rev.Comm. Reports 245 (1999)].

Background from Uniform Act

Terms of the distributing trust or estate. Under Section 103(a) [Prob. Code § 16335(a)], a trustee is to allocate receipts in accordance with the terms of the recipient trust or, if there is no provision, in accordance with this Act. However, in determining whether a distribution from another trust or an estate is income or principal, the trustee should also determine what the terms of the distributing trust or estate say about the distribution—for example, whether they direct that the distribution, even though made from the income of the distributing trust or estate, is to be added to principal of the recipient trust. Such a provision should override the terms of this Act, but if the terms of the recipient trust contain a provision requiring such a distribution to be allocated to income, the trustee may have to obtain a judicial resolution of the conflict between the terms of the two documents.

Investment trusts. An investment entity to which the second sentence of this section applies includes a mutual fund, a common trust fund, a business trust or other entity organized as a trust for the purpose of receiving capital contributed by investors, investing that capital, and managing investment assets, including asset-backed security arrangements to which Section 415 applies. See John H. Langbein, *The Secret Life of the Trust: The Trust as an Instrument of Commerce*, 107 Yale L.J. 165 (1997).

[Adapted from Unif. Principal and Income Act § 402 comment (1997)].

Cross References

Income defined for purposes of this Chapter, see Probate Code § 16324.

§ 16352. Separate accounting records for business or other activity

(a) If a trustee who conducts a business or other activity determines that it is in the best interest of all the beneficiaries to account separately for the business or other activity instead of accounting for it as part of the trust's general accounting records, the trustee may maintain separate accounting records for its transactions, whether or not its assets are segregated from other trust assets.

(b) A trustee who accounts separately for a business or other activity may determine the extent to which its net cash receipts must be retained for working capital, the acquisition or replacement of fixed assets, and its other reasonably foreseeable needs, and the extent to which the remaining net cash receipts are accounted for as principal or income in the trust's general accounting records. If a trustee sells assets of the business or other activity, other than in the ordinary course of the business or other activity, the trustee shall account for the net amount received as principal in the trust's general accounting records to the extent the trustee determines that the amount received is no longer required in the conduct of the business or other activity.

(c) Businesses and other activities for which a trustee may maintain separate accounting records include the following:

(1) Retail, manufacturing, service, and other traditional business activities.

(2) Farming.

(3) Raising and selling livestock and other animals.

(4) Managing rental properties.

(5) Extracting minerals and other natural resources.

(6) Timber operations.

(7) Activities to which Section 16366 applies. *(Added by Stats.1999, c. 145 (A.B.846), § 5.)*

Law Revision Commission Comments

1999 Addition

Section 16352 is the same in substance as Section 403 of the Uniform Principal and Income Act (1997), with some minor technical revisions. This section supersedes parts of former Section 16308.

See also Sections 24 ("beneficiary" defined), 84 ("trustee" defined), 16324 ("income" defined). [29 Cal.L.Rev.Comm. Reports 245 (1999)].

Background from Uniform Act

Purpose and scope. The provisions in Section 403 [Prob. Code § 16352] are intended to give greater flexibility to a trustee who operates a business or other activity in proprietorship form rather than in a wholly-owned corporation (or, where permitted by state law, a single-member limited liability company), and to facilitate the trustee's ability to decide the extent to which the net receipts from the activity should be allocated to income, just as the board of directors of a corporation owned entirely by the trust would decide the amount of the annual dividend to be paid to the trust. It permits a trustee to account for farming or livestock operations, rental properties, oil and gas properties, timber operations, and activities in derivatives and options as though they were held by a separate entity.

It is not intended, however, to permit a trustee to account separately for a traditional securities portfolio to avoid the provisions of this Act that apply to such securities.

Section 403 [Prob. Code § 16352] permits the trustee to account separately for each business or activity for which the trustee determines separate accounting is appropriate. A trustee with a computerized accounting system may account for these activities in a "subtrust"; an individual trustee may continue to use the business and record-keeping methods employed by the decedent or transferor who may have conducted the business under an assumed name. The intent of this section is to give the trustee broad authority to select business record-keeping methods that best suit the activity in which the trustee is engaged.

If a fiduciary liquidates a sole proprietorship or other activity to which Section 403 [Prob. Code § 16352] applies, the proceeds would be added to principal, even though derived from the liquidation of accounts receivable, because the proceeds would no longer be needed in the conduct of the business. If the liquidation occurs during probate or during an income interest's winding up period, none of the proceeds would be income for purposes of Section 201 [Prob. Code § 16340].

Separate accounts. A trustee may or may not maintain separate bank accounts for business activities that are accounted for under Section 403 [Prob. Code § 16352]. A professional trustee may decide not to maintain separate bank accounts, but an individual trustee, especially one who has continued a decedent's business practices, may continue the same banking arrangements that were used during the decedent's lifetime. In either case, the trustee is authorized to decide to what extent cash is to be retained as part of the business assets and to what extent it is to be transferred to the trust's general accounts, either as income or principal.

[Adapted from Unif. Principal and Income Act § 403 comment (1997)].

Cross References

Income defined for purposes of this Chapter, see Probate Code § 16324.

ARTICLE 5.2. ALLOCATION OF RECEIPTS DURING ADMINISTRATION OF TRUST: RECEIPTS NOT NORMALLY APPORTIONED

Application

Application of Division, see Probate Code § 15001.

§ 16355. Amounts allocated to principal

A trustee shall allocate to principal:

(a) To the extent not allocated to income under this chapter, assets received from a transferor during the transferor's lifetime, a decedent's estate, a trust with a terminating income interest, or a payer under a contract naming the trust or its trustee as beneficiary.

(b) Subject to any contrary rules in this article and in Articles 5.1 (commencing with Section 16350) and 5.3 (commencing with Section 16360), money or other property received from the sale, exchange, liquidation, or change in form of a principal asset, including realized profit.

(c) Amounts recovered from third parties to reimburse the trust because of disbursements described in paragraph (7) of subdivision (a) of Section 16371 or for other reasons to the extent not based on the loss of income.

(d) Proceeds of property taken by eminent domain, but a separate award made for the loss of income with respect to an accounting period during which a current income beneficiary had a mandatory income interest is income.

(e) Net income received in an accounting period during which there is no beneficiary to whom a trustee may or must distribute income.

(f) Other receipts allocated to principal as provided in Article 5.3 (commencing with Section 16360). *(Added by Stats.1999, c. 145 (A.B.846), § 5.)*

Law Revision Commission Comments

1999 Addition

Section 16355 is the same in substance as Section 404 of the Uniform Principal and Income Act (1997), with some minor editorial changes. This section supersedes parts of former Section 16303(b) (inclusions in principal). Subdivision (b) makes clear that the general rule allocating receipts from the sale, exchange, liquidation, or change in form of principal assets is subject to special rules in other sections. See, e.g., Section 16362 (liquidating assets).

See also Sections 62 ("property" defined), 84 ("trustee" defined), 16322 ("accounting period" defined), 16324 ("income" defined), 16325 ("income beneficiary" defined). [29 Cal.L.Rev.Comm. Reports 245 (1999)].

Background from Uniform Act

Eminent domain awards. Even though the award in an eminent domain proceeding may include an amount for the loss of future rent on a lease, if that amount is not separately stated the entire award is principal. The rule is the same in the 1931 and 1962 Acts.

[Adapted from Unif. Principal and Income Act § 404 comment (1997)].

Cross References

Accounting period defined for purposes of this Chapter, see Probate Code § 16322.
Income defined for purposes of this Chapter, see Probate Code § 16324.
Income interest defined for purposes of this Chapter, see Probate Code § 16326.
Net income defined for purposes of this Chapter, see Probate Code § 16328.

§ 16356. Amounts received from rental property; allocation

Unless the trustee accounts for receipts from rental property pursuant to Section 16352, the trustee shall allocate to income an amount received as rent of real or personal property, including an amount received for cancellation or renewal of a lease. An amount received as a refundable deposit, including a security deposit or a deposit that is to be applied as rent for future periods, shall be added to principal and held subject to the terms of the lease, and is not available for distribution to a beneficiary until the trustee's contractual obligations have been satisfied with respect to that amount. *(Added by Stats.1999, c. 145 (A.B.846), § 5.)*

Section 16356 is the same in substance as Section 405 of the Uniform Principal and Income Act (1997), with some technical changes in the introductory clause to clarify the relation of this section to Section 16352.

See also Sections 62 ("property" defined), 84 ("trustee" defined). [29 Cal.L.Rev.Comm. Reports apx. 4 (1999)].

Background from Uniform Act

Application of Section 403 [Prob. Code § 16352]. This section applies to the extent that the trustee does not account separately under Section 403 [Prob. Code § 16352] for the management of rental properties owned by the trust.

Receipts that are capital in nature. A portion of the payment under a lease may be a reimbursement of principal expenditures for improvements to the leased property that is characterized as rent for purposes of invoking contractual or statutory remedies for nonpayment. If the trustee is accounting for rental income under Section 405 [Prob. Code § 16356], a transfer from income to reimburse principal may be appropriate under Section 504 [Prob. Code § 16373] to the extent that some of the 'rent' is really a reimbursement for improvements. [This set of facts could also be a relevant factor for a trustee to consider under Section 104(b) [see Prob. Code § 16336(g) & Comment] in deciding whether and to what extent to make an adjustment between principal and income under Section 104(a) [Prob. Code § 16336(a)] after considering the return from the portfolio as a whole.]

[Adapted from Unif. Principal and Income Act § 405 comment (1997)].

Cross References

Income defined for purposes of this Chapter, see Probate Code § 16324.

§ 16357. Interest on obligation to pay money; allocation

(a) An amount received as interest, whether determined at a fixed, variable, or floating rate, on an obligation to pay money to the trustee, including an amount received as consideration for prepaying principal, shall be allocated to income without any provision for amortization of premium.

(b) An amount received from the sale, redemption, or other disposition of an obligation to pay money to the trustee more than one year after it is purchased or acquired by the trustee, including an obligation whose purchase price, or its value when it is otherwise acquired, is less than its value at maturity, shall be allocated to principal. If the obligation matures within one year after it is purchased or acquired by the trustee, an amount received in excess of its purchase price, or its value when it is otherwise acquired, shall be allocated to income.

(c) This section does not apply to an obligation to which Section 16361, 16362, 16363, 16364, 16366, or 16367 applies. *(Added by Stats.1999, c. 145 (A.B.846), § 5.)*

Section 16357 is the same in substance as Section 406 of the Uniform Principal and Income Act (1997), with some minor editorial revisions. Subdivision (b) has been redrafted for clarity and parallelism with subdivision (a). This section supersedes former Section 16307.

See also Sections 84 ("trustee" defined), 16324 ("income" defined). [29 Cal.L.Rev.Comm. Reports 245 (1999)].

Background from Uniform Act

Variable or floating interest rates. The reference in subsection (a) to variable or floating interest rate obligations is intended to clarify that, even though an obligation's interest rate may change from time to time based upon changes in an index or other market indicator, an obligation to pay money containing a variable or floating rate provision is subject to this section and is not to be treated as a derivative financial instrument under Section 414 [Prob. Code § 16366].

Discount obligations. Subsection (b) applies to all obligations acquired at a discount, including short-term obligations such as U.S. Treasury Bills, long-term obligations such as U.S. Savings Bonds, zero-coupon bonds, and discount bonds that pay interest during part, but not all, of the period before maturity. Under subsection (b), the entire increase in value of these obligations is principal when the trustee receives the proceeds from the disposition unless the obligation, when acquired, has a maturity of less than one year. In order to have one rule that applies to all discount obligations, the Act eliminates the provision in the 1962 Act for the payment from principal of an amount equal to the increase in the value of U.S. Series E bonds. The provision for bonds that mature within one year after acquisition by the trustee is derived from the Illinois act. 760 ILCS 15/8 (1996).

Subsection (b) also applies to inflation-indexed bonds—any increase in principal due to inflation after issuance is principal upon redemption if the bond matures more than one year after the trustee acquires it; if it matures within one year, all of the increase, including any attributable to an inflation adjustment, is income.

Effect of Section 104 [Prob. Code § 16336]. In deciding whether and to what extent to exercise the power to adjust between principal and income granted by Section 104(a) [Prob. Code § 16336(a)], a relevant factor for the trustee to consider is the effect on the portfolio as a whole of having a portion of the assets invested in bonds that do not pay interest currently.

[Adapted from Unif. Principal and Income Act § 406 comment (1997)].

Cross References

Income defined for purposes of this Chapter, see Probate Code § 16324.

§ 16358. Life insurance policy proceeds; proceeds of contracts insuring against certain losses; allocation

(a) Except as otherwise provided in subdivision (b), a trustee shall allocate to principal the proceeds of a life insurance policy or other contract in which the trust or its trustee is named as beneficiary, including a contract that insures the trust or its trustee against loss for damage to, destruction of, or loss of title to a trust asset. The trustee shall allocate dividends on an insurance policy to income if the premiums on the policy are paid from income, and to principal if the premiums are paid from principal.

(b) A trustee shall allocate to income proceeds of a contract that insures the trustee against loss of occupancy or other use by an income beneficiary, loss of income, or, subject to Section 16352, loss of profits from a business.

(c) This section does not apply to a contract to which Section 16361 applies. *(Added by Stats.1999, c. 145 (A.B. 846), § 5.)*

Section 16358 is the same as Section 407 of the Uniform Principal and Income Act (1997). This section supersedes former Section 16303(b)(3) (insurance proceeds on property). Life insurance was not covered by prior law.

See also Sections 24 ("beneficiary" defined), 84 ("trustee" defined), 16324 ("income" defined). [29 Cal.L.Rev.Comm. Reports 245 (1999)].

Cross References

Income defined for purposes of this Chapter, see Probate Code § 16324.

ARTICLE 5.3. ALLOCATION OF RECEIPTS DURING ADMINISTRATION OF TRUST: RECEIPTS NORMALLY APPORTIONED

Application

Application of Division, see Probate Code § 15001.

§ 16360. Insubstantial allocation; allocation of entire amount to principal; exceptions

(a) If a trustee determines that an allocation between principal and income required by Section 16361, 16362, 16363, 16364, or 16367 is insubstantial, the trustee may allocate the entire amount to principal unless one of the circumstances described in subdivision (b) of Section 16336 applies to the allocation. This power may be exercised by a cotrustee in the circumstances described in subdivision (c) of Section 16336 and may be released for the reasons and in the manner provided in subdivisions (d) and (e) of Section 16336.

(b) An allocation is presumed to be insubstantial in either of the following cases:

(1) Where the amount of the allocation would increase or decrease net income in an accounting period, as determined before the allocation, by less than 10 percent.

(2) Where the value of the asset producing the receipt for which the allocation would be made is less than 10 percent of the total value of the trust's assets at the beginning of the accounting period.

(c) Nothing in this section imposes a duty on the trustee to make an allocation under this section, and the trustee is not liable for failure to make an allocation under this section. *(Added by Stats.1999, c. 145 (A.B.846), § 5.)*

Subdivisions (a) and (b) of Section 16360 are drawn from Section 408 of the Uniform Principal and Income Act (1997). Subdivision (c) is added to make clear that exercise of the power under this section is wholly discretionary with the trustee.

See also Sections 84 ("trustee" defined), 16322 ("accounting period" defined), 16324 ("income" defined). [29 Cal.L.Rev.Comm. Reports 245 (1999)].

Background from Uniform Act

This section is intended to relieve a trustee from making relatively small allocations while preserving the trustee's right to do so if an allocation is large in terms of absolute dollars.

For example, assume that a trust's assets, which include a working interest in an oil well, have a value of $1,000,000; the net income from the assets other than the working interest is $40,000; and the net receipts from the working interest are $400. The trustee may allocate all of the net receipts from the working interest to principal instead of allocating 10%, or $40, to income under Section 411 [Prob. Code § 16363]. If the net receipts from the working interest are $35,000, so that the amount allocated to income under Section 411 [Prob. Code § 16363] would be $3,500, the trustee may decide that this amount is sufficiently significant to the income beneficiary that the allocation provided for by Section 411 [Prob. Code § 16363] should be made, even though the trustee is still permitted under Section 408 [Prob. Code § 16360] to allocate all of the net receipts to principal because the $3,500 would increase the net income of $40,000, as determined before making an allocation under Section 411 [Prob. Code § 16363], by less than 10%. Section 408 [Prob. Code § 16360] will also relieve a trustee from having to allocate net receipts from the sale of trees in a small woodlot between principal and income.

While the allocation to principal of small amounts under this section should not be a cause for concern for tax purposes, allocations are not permitted under this section in circumstances described in Section 104(c) [Prob. Code § 16336(b)] to eliminate claims that the power in this section has adverse tax consequences.

[Adapted from Unif. Principal and Income Act § 408 comment (1997)].

Cross References

Accounting period defined for purposes of this Chapter, see Probate Code § 16322.
Income defined for purposes of this Chapter, see Probate Code § 16324.
Net income defined for purposes of this Chapter, see Probate Code § 16328.

§ 16361. Payments characterized by payer as interest or dividend or payment in lieu of interest or dividend; trustee allocation; other payments; applicability

(a) For purposes of this section, the following terms have the following meanings:

(1) "Payment" means a payment that a trustee may receive over a fixed number of years or during the life of an individual because of services rendered or property transferred to the payer in exchange for future payments. The term also includes a payment made in money or property from the payer's general assets or from a separate fund created by the payer. For purposes of subdivisions (d), (e),

(f), and (g), "payment" also includes any payment from a separate fund, regardless of the reason for the payment.

(2) "Separate fund" includes a private or commercial annuity, an individual retirement account, and a pension, profit-sharing, stock bonus, or stock ownership plan.

(b) To the extent that any portion of the payment is characterized by the payer as interest, a dividend, or a payment made in lieu of interest or a dividend, a trustee shall allocate that portion of the payment to income. The trustee shall allocate to principal the balance of the payment.

(c) If no part of a payment is characterized as interest, a dividend, or an equivalent payment, and all or part of the payment is required to be made, a trustee shall allocate to income 10 percent of the part that is required to be made during the accounting period and the balance to principal. If no part of a payment is required to be made or the payment received is the entire amount to which the trustee is entitled, the trustee shall allocate the entire payment to principal. For purposes of this subdivision, a payment is not "required to be made" to the extent that it is made because the trustee exercises a right of withdrawal.

(d) Subdivisions (f) and (g) shall apply, except as provided in subdivision (e), and subdivisions (b) and (c) shall not apply, in determining the allocation of a payment made from a separate fund to either of the following:

(1) A trust to which an election to qualify for a marital deduction is made under Section 2056(b)(7) of the Internal Revenue Code. [1]

(2) A trust that qualifies for the marital deduction under Section 2056(b)(5) of the Internal Revenue Code.

(e) Subdivisions (d), (f), and (g) shall not apply if the series of payments would, without the application of subdivision (d), qualify for the marital deduction under Section 2056(b)(7)(C) of the Internal Revenue Code.

(f) If the separate fund payer provides documentation reflecting the internal income of the separate fund to the trustee, the trustee shall allocate the internal income of each separate fund for the accounting period as if the separate fund were a trust subject to this act. Upon request of the surviving spouse, the trustee shall require that the person administering the separate fund distribute this internal income to the trust. The trustee shall allocate a payment from the separate fund to income to the extent of the internal income of the separate fund and distribute that amount to the surviving spouse. The trustee shall allocate the balance to principal. Upon request of the surviving spouse, the trustee shall allocate principal to income to the extent the internal income of the separate fund exceeds payments made from the separate fund to the trust during the accounting period.

(g) If the separate fund payer does not provide documentation reflecting the internal income of the separate fund to the trustee, but the trustee can determine the value of the separate fund, the internal income of the separate fund is deemed to equal 4 percent of the fund's value, according to the most recent statement of value preceding the beginning of the accounting period. If the separate fund payer does not provide documentation reflecting the internal income of the separate fund to the trustee and the trustee cannot determine the value of the separate fund, the internal income of the fund is deemed to equal the product of the interest rate and the present value of the expected future payments, as determined under Section 7520 of the Internal Revenue Code for the month preceding the accounting period for which the computation is made.

(h) This section does not apply to a payment to which Section 16362 applies. *(Added by Stats.2006, c. 569 (A.B. 2347), § 3. Amended by Stats.2009, c. 152 (A.B.1545), § 1; Stats.2010, c. 71 (A.B.229), § 1.)*

[1] Internal Revenue Code sections are in Title 26 of the U.S.C.A.

Application

For application of this section, see Probate Code § 16361.1.

Cross References

Accounting period defined for purposes of this Chapter, see Probate Code § 16322.

Income defined for purposes of this Chapter, see Probate Code § 16324.

§ 16361.1. Application of Section 16361

Section 16361, as amended by the act adding this section, applies to a trust described in subdivision (d) of Section 16361, on and after the following dates:

(a) If the trust is not funded as of January 1, 2010, the date of the decedent's death.

(b) If the trust is initially funded in the calendar year beginning January 1, 2010, the date of the decedent's death.

(c) If the trust is not described in subdivision (a) or (b), on January 1, 2010. *(Added by Stats.2009, c. 152 (A.B.1545), § 2.)*

§ 16362. Receipts from liquidating assets; allocation

(a) In this section, "liquidating asset" means an asset whose value will diminish or terminate because the asset is expected to produce receipts for a period of limited duration. The term includes a leasehold, patent, copyright, royalty right, and right to receive payments under an arrangement that does not provide for the payment of interest on the unpaid balance. The term does not include a payment subject to Section 16361, resources subject to Section 16363, timber subject to Section 16364, an activity subject to Section 16366, an asset subject to Section 16367, or any asset for which the trustee establishes a reserve for depreciation under Section 16372.

(b) A trustee shall allocate to income 10 percent of the receipts from a liquidating asset and the balance to principal. *(Added by Stats.1999, c. 145 (A.B.846), § 5.)*

Law Revision Commission Comments
1999 Addition

Section 16362 is the same as Section 410 of the Uniform Principal and Income Act (1997), except that the limitation on rights to receive payments "during a period of more than one year" is omitted. This section supersedes part of former Section 16310.

See also Sections 84 ("trustee" defined), 16324 ("income" defined). [29 Cal.L.Rev.Comm. Reports 245 (1999)].

Background from Uniform Act

Prior Acts. Section 11 of the 1962 Act [former Prob. Code § 16310] allocates receipts from "property subject to depletion" to income in an amount "not in excess of 5%" of the asset's inventory value. The 1931 Act has a similar 5% rule that applies when the trustee is under a duty to change the form of the investment. The 5% rule imposes on a trust the obligation to pay a fixed annuity to the income beneficiary until the asset is exhausted. Under both the 1931 and 1962 Acts the balance of each year's receipts is added to principal. A fixed payment can produce unfair results. The remainder beneficiary receives all of the receipts from unexpected growth in the asset, e.g., if royalties on a patent or copyright increase significantly. Conversely, if the receipts diminish more rapidly than expected, most of the amount received by the trust will be allocated to income and little to principal. Moreover, if the annual payments remain the same for the life of the asset, the amount allocated to principal will usually be less than the original inventory value. For these reasons, Section 410 [Prob. Code § 16362] abandons the annuity approach under the 5% rule.

Lottery payments. The reference in subsection (a) to rights to receive payments under an arrangement that does not provide for the payment of interest includes state lottery prizes and similar fixed amounts payable over time that are not deferred compensation arrangements covered by Section 409 [Prob. Code § 16361].

[Adapted from Unif. Principal and Income Act § 410 comment (1997)].

Cross References

Income defined for purposes of this Chapter, see Probate Code § 16324.

§ 16363. Receipts from mineral or water interests or other natural resources; allocation

(a) To the extent that a trustee accounts for receipts from an interest in minerals, water, or other natural resources pursuant to this section, the trustee shall allocate them as follows:

(1) If received as a nominal bonus, nominal delay rental, or nominal annual rent on a lease, a receipt shall be allocated to income.

(2) If received from a production payment, a receipt shall be allocated to income if and to the extent that the agreement creating the production payment provides a factor for interest or its equivalent. The balance shall be allocated to principal.

(3) If an amount received as a royalty, shut-in-well payment, take-or-pay payment, bonus, or delay rental is more than nominal, 90 percent shall be allocated to principal and the balance to income.

(4) If an amount is received from a working interest or any other interest in mineral or other natural resources not described in paragraph (1), (2), or (3), 90 percent of the net amount received shall be allocated to principal and the balance to income.

(b) An amount received on account of an interest in water that is renewable shall be allocated to income. If the water is not renewable, 90 percent of the amount shall be allocated to principal and the balance to income.

(c) This chapter applies whether or not a decedent or donor was extracting minerals, water, or other natural resources before the interest became subject to the trust.

(d) If a trust owned an interest in minerals, water, or other natural resources on January 1, 2000, the trustee may at all times allocate receipts from the interest as provided in this chapter or in the manner reasonably used by the trustee prior to that date. Receipts from an interest in minerals, water, or other natural resources acquired after January 1, 2000, shall

be allocated by the trustee as provided in this chapter. If the interest was owned by the trust on January 1, 2000, a trustee that allocated receipts from the interest between January 1, 2000, and December 31, 2006, as provided in this chapter shall not have a duty to review that allocation and shall not have liability arising from the allocation. Nothing in this section is intended to create or imply a duty to allocate in a manner used by the trustee prior to January 1, 2000, and a trustee is not liable for not considering whether to make such an allocation or for choosing not to make such an allocation. *(Added by Stats.1999, c. 145 (A.B.846), § 5. Amended by Stats.2006, c. 569 (A.B.2347), § 4.)*

Law Revision Commission Comments
1999 Addition

Section 16363 is the same as Section 411(a)-(c) of the Uniform Principal and Income Act (1997), with the addition of the reference to "nominal bonus" in subdivision (a)(1). This section supersedes parts of former Section 16309.

See also Sections 84 ("trustee" defined), 16324 ("income" defined). [29 Cal.L.Rev.Comm. Reports 245 (1999)].

Background from Uniform Act

... Section 411 [Prob. Code § 16363] allocates 90% of the net receipts to principal and 10% to income. A depletion provision that is tied to past or present Code provisions is undesirable because it causes a large portion of the oil and gas receipts to be paid out as income. As wells are depleted, the amount received by the income beneficiary falls drastically. Allocating a larger portion of the receipts to principal enables the trustee to acquire other income producing assets that will continue to produce income when the mineral reserves are exhausted.

Application of Sections 403 [Prob. Code § 16352] and 408 [Prob. Code § 16360]. This section applies to the extent that the trustee does not account separately for receipts from minerals and other natural resources under Section 403 or allocate all of the receipts to principal under Section 408 [Prob. Code § 16360].

Open mine doctrine. The purpose of Section 411(c) [Prob. Code § 16363(c)] is to abolish the "open mine doctrine" as it may apply to the rights of an income beneficiary and a remainder beneficiary in receipts from the production of minerals from land owned or leased by a trust. Instead, such receipts are to be allocated to or between principal and income in accordance with the provisions of this Act. For a discussion of the open mine doctrine, see generally 3A Austin W. Scott & William F. Fratcher, The Law of Trusts § 239.3 (4th ed. 1988), and Nutter v. Stockton, 626 P.2d 861 (Okla. 1981).

[Adapted from Unif. Principal and Income Act § 411 comment (1997)].

Cross References

Income defined for purposes of this Chapter, see Probate Code § 16324.

§ 16364. Receipts from sale of timber and related products; allocation

(a) To the extent that a trustee accounts for receipts from the sale of timber and related products pursuant to this section, the trustee shall allocate the net receipts as follows:

(1) To income to the extent that the amount of timber removed from the land does not exceed the rate of growth of the timber during the accounting periods in which a beneficiary has a mandatory income interest.

(2) To principal to the extent that the amount of timber removed from the land exceeds the rate of growth of the

timber or the net receipts are from the sale of standing timber.

(3) To or between income and principal if the net receipts are from the lease of timberland or from a contract to cut timber from land owned by a trust, by determining the amount of timber removed from the land under the lease or contract and applying the rules in paragraphs (1) and (2).

(4) To principal to the extent that advance payments, bonuses, and other payments are not allocated pursuant to paragraph (1), (2), or (3).

(b) In determining net receipts to be allocated under subdivision (a), a trustee shall deduct and transfer to principal a reasonable amount for depletion.

(c) This chapter applies whether or not a decedent or transferor was harvesting timber from the property before it became subject to the trust.

(d) If a trust owned an interest in timberland on January 1, 2000, the trustee may at all times allocate net receipts from the sale of timber and related products as provided in this chapter or in the manner reasonably used by the trustee prior to that date. Net receipts from an interest in timberland acquired after January 1, 2000, shall be allocated by the trustee as provided in this chapter. If the interest was owned by the trust on January 1, 2000, a trustee that allocated net receipts from the interest between January 1, 2000, and December 31, 2006, as provided in this chapter shall not have a duty to review that allocation and shall not have liability arising from the allocation. Nothing in this section is intended to create or imply a duty to allocate in a manner used by the trustee prior to January 1, 2000, and a trustee is not liable for not considering whether to make such an allocation or for choosing not to make such an allocation. *(Added by Stats.1999, c. 145 (A.B.846), § 5. Amended by Stats.2006, c. 569 (A.B.2347), § 5.)*

Law Revision Commission Comments
1999 Addition

Section 16364 is the same in substance as Section 412(a)-(c) of the Uniform Principal and Income Act (1997), with some minor editorial revisions. This section supersedes former Section 16310 to the extent it applied to timber.

See also Sections 84 ("trustee" defined), 16322 ("accounting period" defined), 16324 ("income" defined). [29 Cal.L.Rev.Comm. Reports 245 (1999)].

Background from Uniform Act

Scope of section. The rules in Section 412 [Prob. Code § 16364] are intended to apply to net receipts from the sale of trees and by-products from harvesting and processing trees without regard to the kind of trees that are cut or whether the trees are cut before or after a particular number of years of growth. The rules apply to the sale of trees that are expected to produce lumber for building purposes, trees sold as pulpwood, and Christmas and other ornamental trees. Subsection (a) applies to net receipts from property owned by the trustee and property leased by the trustee. The Act is not intended to prevent a tenant in possession of the property from using wood that he cuts on the property for personal, noncommercial purposes, such as a Christmas tree, firewood, mending old fences or building new fences, or making repairs to structures on the property.

Under subsection (a), the amount of net receipts allocated to income depends upon whether the amount of timber removed is more or less than the rate of growth. The method of determining the amount of timber removed and the rate of growth is up to the trustee, based on methods customarily used for the kind of timber involved.

Application of Sections 403 and 408 [Prob. Code §§ 16352 & 16360]. This section applies to the extent that the trustee does not account separately for net receipts from the sale of timber and related products under Section 403 [Prob. Code § 16352]or allocate all of the receipts to principal under Section 408 [Prob. Code § 16360]. The option to account for net receipts separately under Section 403 [Prob. Code § 16352] takes into consideration the possibility that timber harvesting operations may have been conducted before the timber property became subject to the trust, and that it may make sense to continue using accounting methods previously established for the property. It also permits a trustee to use customary accounting practices for timber operations even if no harvesting occurred on the property before it became subject to the trust.

[Adapted from Unif. Principal and Income Act § 412 comment (1997)].

Cross References

Accounting period defined for purposes of this Chapter, see Probate Code § 16322.
Income defined for purposes of this Chapter, see Probate Code § 16324.
Income interest defined for purposes of this Chapter, see Probate Code § 16326.

§ 16365. Increasing income in order to obtain marital deduction

(a) If a marital deduction is allowed for all or part of a trust whose assets consist substantially of property that does not provide the spouse with sufficient income from or use of the trust assets, and if the amounts that the trustee transfers from principal to income under Section 16336 and distributes to the spouse from principal pursuant to the terms of the trust are insufficient to provide the spouse with the beneficial enjoyment required to obtain the marital deduction, the spouse may require the trustee to make property productive of income or convert it into productive property or exercise the power under subdivision (a) of Section 16336 within a reasonable time. The trustee may decide which action or combination of actions to take.

(b) In cases not governed by subdivision (a), proceeds from the sale or other disposition of a trust asset are principal without regard to the amount of income the asset produces during any accounting period. *(Added by Stats.1999, c. 145 (A.B.846), § 5.)*

Law Revision Commission Comments
1999 Addition

Section 16365 is the same as Section 413 of the Uniform Principal and Income Act (1997), with the addition of the reasonable time standard drawn from the former version of Section 21524(c).This section continues the former rule provided in Section 21524(c). This section supersedes part of former Section 16311 (underproductive property).

See also Sections 16322 ("accounting period" defined), 16324 ("income" defined). [29 Cal.L.Rev.Comm. Reports 245 (1999)].

Background from Uniform Act

Prior Acts' Conflict with Uniform Prudent Investor Act. Section 2(b) of the Uniform Prudent Investor Act provides that "[a] trustee's investment and management decisions respecting individual assets

987

must be evaluated not in isolation but in the context of the trust portfolio as a whole ...." [See Prob. Code § 16047(b)]. The underproductive property provisions in Section 12 of the 1962 Act [former Prob. Code § 16311] and Section 11 of the 1931 Act give the income beneficiary a right to receive a portion of the proceeds from the sale of underproductive property as "delayed income." In each Act the provision applies on an asset by asset basis and not by taking into consideration the trust portfolio as a whole, which conflicts with the basic precept in Section 2(b) of the Prudent Investor Act [Prob. Code § 16047(b)]. Moreover, in determining the amount of delayed income, the prior Acts do not permit a trustee to take into account the extent to which the trustee may have distributed principal to the income beneficiary, under principal invasion provisions in the terms of the trust, to compensate for insufficient income from the unproductive asset....

Duty to make property productive of income. In order to implement the Uniform Prudent Investor Act, this Act abolishes the right to receive delayed income from the sale proceeds of an asset that produces little or no income, but it does not alter existing state law regarding the income beneficiary's right to compel the trustee to make property productive of income. As the law continues to develop in this area, the duty to make property productive of current income in a particular situation should be determined by taking into consideration the performance of the portfolio as a whole and the extent to which a trustee makes principal distributions to the income beneficiary under the terms of the trust ....

Trusts for which the value of the right to receive income is important for tax reasons may be affected by Reg. § 1.7520–3(b)(2)(v) *Example (1)*, § 20.7520–3(b)(2)(v) *Examples (1)* and *(2)*, and § 25.7520–3(b)(2)(v) *Examples (1)* and *(2)*, which provide that if the income beneficiary does not have the right to compel the trustee to make the property productive, the income interest is considered unproductive and may not be valued actuarially under those sections.

Marital deduction trusts. Subsection (a) draws on language in Reg. § 20.2056(b)–5(f)(4) and (5) to enable a trust for a spouse to qualify for a marital deduction if applicable state law is unclear about the spouse's right to compel the trustee to make property productive of income. [See Prob. Code § 21524(c)]. The trustee should also consider the application of Section 104 of this Act [Prob. Code § 16336] and the provisions of Restatement of Trusts 3d: Prudent Investor Rule § 240, at 186, app. § 240, at 252 (1992). Example (6) in the Comment to Section 104 [Prob. Code § 16336] describes a situation involving the payment from income of carrying charges on unproductive real estate in which Section 104 [Prob. Code § 16336] may apply.

Once the two conditions have occurred—insufficient beneficial enjoyment from the property and the spouse's demand that the trustee take action under this section—the trustee must act; but instead of the formulaic approach of the 1962 Act, which is triggered only if the trustee sells the property, this Act permits the trustee to decide whether to make the property productive of income, convert it, transfer funds from principal to income, or to take some combination of those actions. The trustee may rely on the power conferred by Section 104(a) [Prob. Code § 16336(a)] to adjust from principal to income if the trustee decides that it is not feasible or appropriate to make the property productive of income or to convert the property. Given the purpose of Section 413 [Prob. Code § 16365], the power under Section 104(a) [Prob. Code § 16336(a)] would be exercised to transfer principal to income and not to transfer income to principal.

Section 413 [Prob. Code § 16365] does not apply to a so-called 'estate' trust, which will qualify for the marital deduction, even though the income may be accumulated for a term of years or for the life of the surviving spouse, if the terms of the trust require the principal and undistributed income to be paid to the surviving spouse's estate when the spouse dies. Reg. § 20.2056(c)–2(b)(1)(iii).

[Adapted from Unif. Principal and Income Act § 413 comment (1997)].

Cross References

Accounting period defined for purposes of this Chapter, see Probate Code § 16322.

Income defined for purposes of this Chapter, see Probate Code § 16324.

§ 16366. Transactions in derivatives; allocation of receipts and disbursements; options to buy or sell property; allocation of amounts received or paid

(a) In this section, "derivative" means a contract or financial instrument or a combination of contracts and financial instruments that gives a trust the right or obligation to participate in some or all changes in the price of a tangible or intangible asset or group of assets, or changes in a rate, an index of prices or rates, or other market indicator for an asset or a group of assets.

(b) To the extent that a trustee does not account under Section 16352 for transactions in derivatives, the trustee shall allocate to principal receipts from and disbursements made in connection with those transactions.

(c) If a trustee grants an option to buy property from the trust, whether or not the trust owns the property when the option is granted, grants an option that permits another person to sell property to the trust, or acquires an option to buy property for the trust or an option to sell an asset owned by the trust, and the trustee or other owner of the asset is required to deliver the asset if the option is exercised, an amount received for granting the option shall be allocated to principal. An amount paid to acquire the option shall be paid from principal. A gain or loss realized upon the exercise of an option, including an option granted to a settlor of the trust for services rendered, shall be allocated to principal. *(Added by Stats.1999, c. 145 (A.B.846), § 5.)*

Law Revision Commission Comments

1999 Addition

Section 16366 is the same as Section 414 of the Uniform Principal and Income Act (1997). The subject of this section was not covered by the former principal and income act.

See also Sections 62 ("property" defined), 84 ("trustee" defined). [29 Cal.L.Rev.Comm. Reports 245 (1999)].

Background from Uniform Act

Scope and application. It is difficult to predict how frequently and to what extent trustees will invest directly in derivative financial instruments rather than participating indirectly through investment entities that may utilize these instruments in varying degrees. If the trust participates in derivatives indirectly through an entity, an amount received from the entity will be allocated under Section 401 [Prob. Code § 16350] and not Section 414 [Prob. Code § 16366]. If a trustee invests directly in derivatives to a significant extent, the expectation is that receipts and disbursements related to derivatives will be accounted for under Section 403 [Prob. Code § 16352]; if a trustee chooses not to account under Section 403 [Prob. Code § 16352], Section 414(b) [Prob. Code § 16366(b)] provides the default rule. Certain types of option transactions in which trustees may engage are dealt with in subsection (c) to distinguish those transactions from ones involving options that are embedded in derivative financial instruments.

Definition of "derivative." "Derivative" is a difficult term to define because new derivatives are invented daily as dealers tailor their terms to achieve specific financial objectives for particular clients. Since derivatives are typically contract-based, a derivative can probably be devised for almost any set of objectives if another party can be found who is willing to assume the obligations required to meet those objectives.

The most comprehensive definition of derivative is in the Exposure Draft of a Proposed Statement of Financial Accounting Standards titled "Accounting for Derivative and Similar Financial Instruments and for Hedging Activities," which was released by the Financial Accounting Standards Board (FASB) on June 20, 1996 (No. 162–B). The definition in Section 414(a) [Prob. Code § 16366(a)] is derived in part from the FASB definition. The purpose of the definition in subsection (a) is to implement the substantive rule in subsection (b) that provides for all receipts and disbursements to be allocated to principal to the extent the trustee elects not to account for transactions in derivatives under Section 403 [Prob. Code § 16352]. As a result, it is much shorter than the FASB definition, which serves much more ambitious objectives.

A derivative is frequently described as including futures, forwards, swaps and options, terms that also require definition, and the definition in this Act avoids these terms. FASB used the same approach, explaining in paragraph 65 of the Exposure Draft:

The definition of *derivative financial instrument* in this Statement includes those financial instruments generally considered to be derivatives, such as forwards, futures, swaps, options, and similar instruments. The Board considered defining a derivative financial instrument by merely referencing those commonly understood instruments, similar to paragraph 5 of Statement 119, which says that "... a derivative financial instrument is a futures, forward, swap, or option contract, or other financial instrument with similar characteristics." However, the continued development of financial markets and innovative financial instruments could ultimately render a definition based on examples inadequate and obsolete. The Board, therefore, decided to base the definition of a derivative financial instrument on a description of the common characteristics of those instruments in order to accommodate the accounting for newly developed derivatives. (Footnote omitted).

Marking to market. A gain or loss that occurs because the trustee marks securities to market or to another value during an accounting period is not a transaction in a derivative financial instrument that is income or principal under the Act C only cash receipts and disbursements, and the receipt of property in exchange for a principal asset, affect a trust's principal and income accounts.

Receipt of property other than cash. If a trustee receives property other than cash upon the settlement of a derivatives transaction, that property would be principal under Section 404(2) [Prob. Code § 16355(b)].

Options. Options to which subsection (c) applies include an option to purchase real estate owned by the trustee and a put option purchased by a trustee to guard against a drop in value of a large block of marketable stock that must be liquidated to pay estate taxes. Subsection (c) would also apply to a continuing and regular practice of selling call options on securities owned by the trust if the terms of the option require delivery of the securities. It does not apply if the consideration received or given for the option is something other than cash or property, such as cross-options granted in a buy-sell agreement between owners of an entity.

[Adapted from Unif. Principal and Income Act § 414 comment (1997)].

§ 16367. Payments from collateral financial assets and payments in exchange for interest in asset-backed security; allocation

(a) In this section, "asset-backed security" means an asset whose value is based upon the right it gives the owner to receive distributions from the proceeds of financial assets that provide collateral for the security. The term includes an asset that gives the owner the right to receive from the collateral financial assets only the interest or other current return or only the proceeds other than interest or current return. The term does not include an asset to which Section 16350 or 16361 applies.

(b) If a trust receives a payment from interest or other current return and from other proceeds of the collateral financial assets, the trustee shall allocate to income the portion of the payment which the payer identifies as being from interest or other current return and shall allocate the balance of the payment to principal.

(c) If a trust receives one or more payments in exchange for the trust's entire interest in an asset-backed security in one accounting period, the trustee shall allocate the payments to principal. If a payment is one of a series of payments that will result in the liquidation of the trust's interest in the security over more than one accounting period, the trustee shall allocate 10 percent of the payment to income and the balance to principal. *(Added by Stats.1999, c. 145 (A.B.846), § 5.)*

Law Revision Commission Comments

1999 Addition

Section 16367 is the same as Section 415 of the Uniform Principal and Income Act (1997).

See also Sections 84 ("trustee" defined), 16322 ("accounting period" defined), 16324 ("income" defined). [29 Cal.L.Rev.Comm. Reports 245 (1999)].

Background from Uniform Act

Scope of section. Typical asset-backed securities include arrangements in which debt obligations such as real estate mortgages, credit card receivables and auto loans are acquired by an investment trust and interests in the trust are sold to investors. The source for payments to an investor is the money received from principal and interest payments on the underlying debt. An asset-backed security includes an "interest only" or a "principal only" security that permits the investor to receive only the interest payments received from the bonds, mortgages or other assets that are the collateral for the asset-backed security, or only the principal payments made on those collateral assets. An asset-backed security also includes a security that permits the investor to participate in either the capital appreciation of an underlying security or in the interest or dividend return from such a security, such as the "Primes" and "Scores" issued by Americus Trust. An asset-backed security does not include an interest in a corporation, partnership, or an investment trust described in the Comment to Section 402 [Prob. Code § 16351], whose assets consist significantly or entirely of investment assets. Receipts from an instrument that do not come within the scope of this section or any other section of the Act would be allocated entirely to principal under the rule in Section 103(a)(4) [Prob. Code § 16335(a)(4)], and the trustee may then consider whether and to what extent to exercise the power to adjust in Section 104 [Prob. Code § 16336], taking into account the return from the portfolio as whole and other relevant factors.

[Adapted from Unif. Principal and Income Act § 415 comment (1997)].

Cross References

Accounting period defined for purposes of this Chapter, see Probate Code § 16322.

Income defined for purposes of this Chapter, see Probate Code § 16324.

ARTICLE 6. ALLOCATION OF DISBURSEMENTS DURING ADMINISTRATION OF TRUST

Section

Application

Application of Division, see Probate Code § 15001.

§ 16370. Disbursements from income

A trustee shall make the following disbursements from income to the extent that they are not disbursements to which paragraph (2) or (3) of subdivision (c) of Section 16340 applies:

(a) Except as otherwise ordered by the court, one-half of the regular compensation of the trustee and of any person providing investment advisory or custodial services to the trustee.

(b) Except as otherwise ordered by the court, one-half of all expenses for accountings, judicial proceedings, or other matters that involve both the income and remainder interests.

(c) All of the other ordinary expenses incurred in connection with the administration, management, or preservation of trust property and the distribution of income, including interest, ordinary repairs, regularly recurring taxes assessed against principal, and expenses of a proceeding or other matter that concerns primarily the income interest.

(d) All recurring premiums on insurance covering the loss of a principal asset or the loss of income from or use of the asset. *(Added by Stats.1999, c. 145 (A.B.846), § 5.)*

Law Revision Commission Comments

1999 Addition

Section 16370 is the same as Section 501 of the Uniform Principal and Income Act (1997), with the addition of the recognition of court orders in subdivisions (a) and (b).

See also Sections 62 ("property" defined), 84 ("trustee" defined), 16324 ("income" defined), 16326 ("income interest" defined). [29 Cal.L.Rev.Comm. Reports 245 (1999)].

Background from Uniform Act

Trustee fees. The regular compensation of a trustee or the trustee's agent includes compensation based on a percentage of either principal or income or both.

Insurance premiums. The reference in [subdivision (d)] to "recurring" premiums is intended to distinguish premiums paid annually for fire insurance from premiums on title insurance, each of which covers the loss of a principal asset. Title insurance premiums would be a principal disbursement under Section 502(a)(5) [Prob. Code § 16371(a)(5)].

Regularly recurring taxes. The reference to "regularly recurring taxes assessed against principal" includes all taxes regularly imposed on real property and tangible and intangible personal property.

[Adapted from Unif. Principal and Income Act § 501 comment (1997)].

Cross References

Income defined for purposes of this Chapter, see Probate Code § 16324.
Income interest defined for purposes of this Chapter, see Probate Code § 16326.

§ 16371. Disbursements from principal

(a) A trustee shall make the following disbursements from principal:

(1) Except as otherwise ordered by the court, the remaining one-half of the disbursements described in subdivisions (a) and (b) of Section 16370.

(2) Except as otherwise ordered by the court, all of the trustee's compensation calculated on principal as a fee for acceptance, distribution, or termination, and disbursements made to prepare property for sale.

(3) Payments on the principal of a trust debt.

(4) Expenses of a proceeding that concerns primarily principal, including a proceeding to construe the trust or to protect the trust or its property.

(5) Premiums paid on a policy of insurance not described in subdivision (d) of Section 16370 of which the trust is the owner and beneficiary.

(6) Estate, inheritance, and other transfer taxes, including penalties, apportioned to the trust.

(7) Disbursements related to environmental matters, including reclamation, assessing environmental conditions, remedying and removing environmental contamination, monitoring remedial activities and the release of substances, preventing future releases of substances, collecting amounts from persons liable or potentially liable for the costs of those activities, penalties imposed under environmental laws or regulations and other payments made to comply with those laws or regulations, statutory or common law claims by third parties, and defending claims based on environmental matters.

(b) If a principal asset is encumbered with an obligation that requires income from that asset to be paid directly to the creditor, the trustee shall transfer from principal to income an amount equal to the income paid to the creditor in reduction of the principal balance of the obligation. *(Added by Stats.1999, c. 145 (A.B.846), § 5.)*

Law Revision Commission Comments

1999 Addition

Section 16371 is the same as Section 502 of the Uniform Principal and Income Act (1997), with the addition of the recognition of court orders in subdivisions (a)(1) and (a)(2).

See also Sections 62 ("property" defined), 84 ("trustee" defined), 16324 ("income" defined). [29 Cal.L.Rev.Comm. Reports 245 (1999)].

Background from Uniform Act

Environmental expenses. All environmental expenses are payable from principal, subject to the power of the trustee to transfer funds to principal from income under Section 504 [Prob. Code § 16373]. However, the Drafting Committee decided that it was not necessary to broaden this provision to cover other expenditures made under compulsion of governmental authority. See generally the annotation at 43 A.L.R.4th 1012 (Duty as Between Life Tenant and Remainderman with Respect to Cost of Improvements or Repairs Made Under Compulsion of Governmental Authority).

Environmental expenses paid by a trust are to be paid from principal under Section 502(a)(7) [Prob. Code § 16371(a)(7)] on the assumption that they will usually be extraordinary in nature. Environmental expenses might be paid from income if the trustee is carrying on a business that uses or sells toxic substances, in which case environmental cleanup costs would be a normal cost of doing business and would be accounted for under Section 403 [Prob. Code § 16352]. In accounting under that Section, environmental costs will be a factor in determining how much of the net receipts from the business is trust income. Paying all other environmental expenses from principal is consistent with this Act's approach regarding receipts—when a receipt is not clearly a current return on a principal asset, it should be added to principal because over time both the income and remainder beneficiaries benefit from this treatment. Here, allocating payments required by environmental laws to principal imposes the detriment of those payments over time on both the income and remainder beneficiaries.

Under Sections 504(a) and 504(b)(5) [Prob. Code § 16373(a) & (b)(5)], a trustee who makes or expects to make a principal disbursement for an environmental expense described in Section 502(a)(7) [Prob. Code § 16371(a)(7)] is authorized to transfer an appropriate amount from income to principal to reimburse principal for disbursements made or to provide a reserve for future principal disbursements.

The first part of Section 502(a)(7) [Prob. Code § 16371(a)(7)] is based upon the definition of an 'environmental remediation trust' in Treas. Reg. § 301.7701–4(e) (as amended in 1996). This is not because the Act applies to a environmental remediation trust, but because the definition is a useful and thoroughly vetted description of the kinds of expenses that a trustee owning contaminated property might incur. Expenses incurred to comply with environmental laws include the cost of environmental consultants, administrative proceedings and burdens of every kind imposed as the result of an administrative or judicial proceeding, even though the burden is not formally characterized as a penalty.

Title proceedings. Disbursements that are made to protect a trust's property, referred to in Section 502(a)(4) [Prob. Code § 16371(a)(4)], include an 'action to assure title' that is mentioned in Section 13(c)(2) of the 1962 Act [former Prob. Code § 16312(d)(2)].

Insurance premiums. Insurance premiums referred to in Section 502(a)(5) [Prob. Code § 16371(a)(5)] include title insurance premiums. They also include premiums on life insurance policies owned by the trust, which represent the trust's periodic investment in the insurance policy. There is no provision in the 1962 Act for life insurance premiums.

Taxes. Generation-skipping transfer taxes are payable from principal under subsection (a)(6).

[Adapted from Unif. Principal and Income Act § 502 comment (1997)].

Cross References

Income defined for purposes of this Chapter, see Probate Code § 16324.

§ 16372. Assets subject to depreciation; transfer from income to principal of portion of net cash receipts

(a) For purposes of this section, "depreciation" means a reduction in value due to wear, tear, decay, corrosion, or gradual obsolescence of a fixed asset having a useful life of more than one year.

(b) A trustee may transfer from income to principal a reasonable amount of the net cash receipts from a principal asset that is subject to depreciation, under generally accepted accounting principles, but may not transfer any amount for depreciation under this section in any of the following circumstances:

(1) As to the portion of real property used or available for use by a beneficiary as a residence or of tangible personal property held or made available for the personal use or enjoyment of a beneficiary.

(2) During the administration of a decedent's estate.

(3) If the trustee is accounting under Section 16352 for the business or activity in which the asset is used.

(c) An amount transferred from income to principal need not be held as a separate fund. *(Added by Stats.1999, c. 145 (A.B.846), § 5.)*

Law Revision Commission Comments

1999 Addition

Section 16372 supersedes former Section 16313 and is the same as Section 503 of the Uniform Principal and Income Act (1997), with some clarifying language and the addition of the generally accepted accounting principles standard in subdivision (b). This addition continues the substance of former Section 16312(b)(2). Section 16372 also supersedes the last part of former Section 16312(d)(3). The word "may" in subdivision (b) has the same meaning as the phrase "is not required to" in former Section 16313.

See also Sections 84 ("trustee" defined), 16324 ("income" defined). [29 Cal.L.Rev.Comm. Reports apx. 4 (1999)].

Background from Uniform Act

Prior Acts. The 1931 Act has no provision for depreciation. Section 13(a)(2) of the 1962 Act [former Prob. Code § 16312(b)(2)] provides that a charge shall be made against income for "... a reasonable allowance for depreciation on property subject to depreciation under generally accepted accounting principles ...." That provision has been resisted by many trustees, who do not provide for any depreciation for a variety of reasons. One reason relied upon is that a charge for depreciation is not needed to protect the remainder beneficiaries if the value of the land is increasing; another is that generally accepted accounting principles may not require depreciation to be taken if the property is not part of a business. The Drafting Committee concluded that the decision to provide for depreciation should be discretionary with the trustee. The power to transfer funds from income to principal that is granted by this section is a discretionary power of administration referred to in Section 103(b) [Prob. Code § 16335(b)], and in exercising the power a trustee must comply with Section 103(b) [Prob. Code § 16335(b)].

One purpose served by transferring cash from income to principal for depreciation is to provide funds to pay the principal of an indebtedness secured by the depreciable property. Section 504(b)(4) [Prob. Code § 16373(b)(4)] permits the trustee to transfer additional cash from income to principal for this purpose to the extent that the amount transferred from income to principal for depreciation is less than the amount of the principal payments.

[Adapted from Unif. Principal and Income Act § 503 comment (1997)].

Cross References

Income defined for purposes of this Chapter, see Probate Code
§ 16324.

§ 16373. Transfer from income to principal in anticipation of principal disbursement

(a) If a trustee makes or expects to make a principal disbursement described in this section, the trustee may transfer an appropriate amount from income to principal in one or more accounting periods to reimburse principal or to provide a reserve for future principal disbursements.

(b) Principal disbursements to which subdivision (a) applies include the following, but only to the extent that the trustee has not been and does not expect to be reimbursed by a third party:

(1) An amount chargeable to income but paid from principal because it is unusually large, including extraordinary repairs.

(2) A capital improvement to a principal asset, whether in the form of changes to an existing asset or the construction of a new asset, including special assessments.

(3) Disbursements made to prepare property for rental, including tenant allowances, leasehold improvements, and broker's commissions.

(4) Periodic payments on an obligation secured by a principal asset to the extent that the amount transferred from income to principal for depreciation is less than the periodic payments.

(5) Disbursements described in paragraph (7) of subdivision (a) of Section 16371.

(c) If the asset whose ownership gives rise to the disbursements becomes subject to a successive income interest after an income interest ends, a trustee may continue to transfer amounts from income to principal as provided in subdivision (a). *(Added by Stats.1999, c. 145 (A.B.846), § 5.)*

Law Revision Commission Comments

1999 Addition

Section 16373 is the same in substance as Section 504 of the Uniform Principal and Income Act (1997), with some minor editorial changes. This section supersedes the first part of former Section 16312(d)(3).

See also Sections 62 ("property" defined), 84 ("trustee" defined), 16322 ("accounting period" defined), 16324 ("income" defined), 16326 ("income interest" defined). [29 Cal.L.Rev.Comm. Reports 245 (1999)].

Background from Uniform Act

Prior Acts. The sources of Section 504 [Prob. Code § 16373] are Section 13(b) of the 1962 Act [former Prob. Code § 16312(c)], which permits a trustee to "regularize distributions," if charges against income are unusually large, by using "reserves or other reasonable means" to withhold sums from income distributions; Section 13(c)(3) of the 1962 Act [former Prob. Code § 16312(d)(3)], which authorizes a trustee to establish an allowance for depreciation out of income if principal is used for extraordinary repairs, capital improvements and special assessments; and Section 12(3) of the 1931 Act, which permits the trustee to spread income expenses of unusual amount "throughout a series of years." Section 504 [Prob. Code § 16373] contains a more detailed enumeration of the circumstances in which this authority may be used, and includes in subsection (b)(4) the express

authority to use income to make principal payments on a mortgage if the depreciation charge against income is less than the principal payments on the mortgage.

[Adapted from Unif. Principal and Income Act § 504 comment (1997)].

Cross References

Accounting period defined for purposes of this Chapter, see Probate Code § 16322.

Income defined for purposes of this Chapter, see Probate Code § 16324.

Income interest defined for purposes of this Chapter, see Probate Code § 16326.

§ 16374. Payment of taxes

(a) A tax required to be paid by a trustee based on receipts allocated to income shall be paid from income.

(b) A tax required to be paid by a trustee based on receipts allocated to principal shall be paid from principal, even if the tax is called an income tax by the taxing authority.

(c) A tax required to be paid by a trustee on the trust's share of an entity's taxable income shall be paid as follows:

(1) From income to the extent that receipts from the entity are allocated only to income.

(2) From principal to the extent that receipts from the entity are allocated only to principal.

(3) Proportionately from principal and income to the extent that receipts from the entity are allocated to both income and principal.

(4) From principal to the extent that the tax exceeds the total receipts from the entity.

(d) After applying subdivisions (a), (b), and (c), the trustee shall adjust income or principal receipts to the extent that the trust's taxes are reduced because the trust receives a deduction for payments made to a beneficiary. *(Added by Stats. 1999, c. 145 (A.B.846), § 5. Amended by Stats.2009, c. 152 (A.B.1545), § 3.)*

Law Revision Commission Comments

1999 Addition

Section 16374 is the same as Section 505 of the Uniform Principal and Income Act (1997), with some minor editorial changes.

See also Sections 84 ("trustee" defined), 16324 ("income" defined). [29 Cal.L.Rev.Comm. Reports 245 (1999)].

Background from Uniform Act

Electing Small Business Trusts. An Electing Small Business Trust (ESBT) is a creature created by Congress in the Small Business Job Protection Act of 1996 (P.L. 104–188). For years beginning after 1996, an ESBT may qualify as an S corporation stockholder even if the trustee does not distribute all of the trust's income annually to its beneficiaries. The portion of an ESBT that consists of the S corporation stock is treated as a separate trust for tax purposes (but not for trust accounting purposes), and the S corporation income is taxed directly to that portion of the trust even if some or all of that income is distributed to the beneficiaries.

A trust normally receives a deduction for distributions it makes to its beneficiaries. Subsection (d) takes into account the possibility that an ESBT may not receive a deduction for trust accounting income that is distributed to the beneficiaries. Only limited guidance has been issued by the Internal Revenue Service, and it is too early to anticipate all of the technical questions that may arise, but the powers granted to a trustee in Sections 506 [Prob. Code § 16375] and 104 [Prob. Code § 16336] to make adjustments are probably sufficient to enable a trustee to correct inequities that may arise because of technical problems.

[Adapted from Unif. Principal and Income Act § 505 comment (1997)].

Cross References

Income defined for purposes of this Chapter, see Probate Code § 16324.

§ 16374.5. Distributions to beneficiaries

Unless otherwise provided by the governing instrument, determined by the trustee, or ordered by the court, distributions to beneficiaries shall be considered paid in the following order from the following sources:

(a) From net taxable income other than capital gains.

(b) From net realized short-term capital gains.

(c) From net realized long-term capitalized gains.

(d) From tax-exempt and other income.

(e) From principal of the trust. *(Added by Stats.2006, c. 569 (A.B.2347), § 6.)*

Cross References

Income defined for purposes of this Chapter, see Probate Code § 16324.

§ 16375. Adjustments between principal and interest in certain cases

(a) A fiduciary may make adjustments between principal and income to offset the shifting of economic interests or tax benefits between income beneficiaries and remainder beneficiaries that arise from any of the following:

(1) Elections and decisions, other than those described in subdivision (b), that the fiduciary makes from time to time regarding tax matters.

(2) An income tax or any other tax that is imposed upon the fiduciary or a beneficiary as a result of a transaction involving or a distribution from the estate or trust.

(3) The ownership by a decedent's estate or trust of an interest in an entity whose taxable income, whether or not distributed, is includable in the taxable income of the estate, trust, or a beneficiary.

(b) If the amount of an estate tax marital deduction or charitable contribution deduction is reduced because a fiduciary deducts an amount paid from principal for income tax purposes instead of deducting it for estate tax purposes, and as a result estate taxes paid from principal are increased and income taxes paid by a decedent's estate, trust, or beneficiary are decreased, each estate, trust, or beneficiary that benefits from the decrease in income tax shall reimburse the principal from which the increase in estate tax is paid. The total reimbursement must equal the increase in the estate tax to the extent that the principal used to pay the increase would have qualified for a marital deduction or charitable contribution deduction but for the payment. The proportionate share of the reimbursement for each estate, trust, or beneficiary whose income taxes are reduced must be the same as its proportionate share of the total decrease in income tax. An

estate or trust shall reimburse principal from income. *(Added by Stats.1999, c. 145 (A.B.846), § 5.)*

Law Revision Commission Comments
1999 Addition

Section 16375 is the same as Section 506 of the Uniform Principal and Income Act (1997), with some minor editorial changes.

See also Sections 16323 ("fiduciary" defined), 16324 ("income" defined), 16325 ("income beneficiary" defined). [29 Cal.L.Rev. Comm. Reports 245 (1999)].

Background from Uniform Act

Discretionary adjustments. Section 506(a) [Prob. Code § 16375(a)] permits the fiduciary to make adjustments between income and principal because of tax law provisions. It would permit discretionary adjustments in situations like these: (1) A fiduciary elects to deduct administration expenses that are paid from principal on an income tax return instead of on the estate tax return; (2) a distribution of a principal asset to a trust or other beneficiary causes the taxable income of an estate or trust to be carried out to the distributee and relieves the persons who receive the income of any obligation to pay income tax on the income; or (3) a trustee realizes a capital gain on the sale of a principal asset and pays a large state income tax on the gain, but under applicable federal income tax rules the trustee may not deduct the state income tax payment from the capital gain in calculating the trust's federal capital gain tax, and the income beneficiary receives the benefit of the deduction for state income tax paid on the capital gain. See generally Joel C. Dobris, *Limits on the Doctrine of Equitable Adjustment in Sophisticated Postmortem Tax Planning*, 66 Iowa L. Rev. 273 (1981).

Section 506(a)(3) [Prob. Code § 16375(a)(3)] applies to a qualified Subchapter S trust (QSST) whose income beneficiary is required to include a pro rata share of the S corporation's taxable income in his return. If the QSST does not receive a cash distribution from the corporation that is large enough to cover the income beneficiary's tax liability, the trustee may distribute additional cash from principal to the income beneficiary. In this case the retention of cash by the corporation benefits the trust principal. This situation could occur if the corporation's taxable income includes capital gain from the sale of a business asset and the sale proceeds are reinvested in the business instead of being distributed to shareholders.

Mandatory adjustment. Subsection (b) provides for a mandatory adjustment from income to principal to the extent needed to preserve an estate tax marital deduction or charitable contributions deduction. It is derived from New York's EPTL § 11–1.2(A), which requires principal to be reimbursed by those who benefit when a fiduciary elects to deduct administration expenses on an income tax return instead of the estate tax return. Unlike the New York provision, subsection (b) limits a mandatory reimbursement to cases in which a marital deduction or a charitable contributions deduction is reduced by the payment of additional estate taxes because of the fiduciary's income tax election. It is intended to preserve the result reached in *Estate of Britenstool v. Commissioner*, 46 T.C. 711 (1966), in which the Tax Court held that a reimbursement required by the predecessor of EPTL § 11–1.2(A) resulted in the estate receiving the same charitable contributions deduction it would have received if the administration expenses had been deducted for estate tax purposes instead of for income tax purposes. Because a fiduciary will elect to deduct administration expenses for income tax purposes only when the income tax reduction exceeds the estate tax reduction, the effect of this adjustment is that the principal is placed in the same position it would have occupied if the fiduciary had deducted the expenses for estate tax purposes, but the income beneficiaries receive an additional benefit. For example, if the income tax benefit from the deduction is $30,000 and the estate tax benefit would have been $20,000, principal will be reimbursed $20,000 and the net benefit to the income beneficiaries will be $10,000.

Irrevocable grantor trusts. Under Sections 671–679 of the Internal Revenue Code (the "grantor trust" provisions), a person who creates an irrevocable trust for the benefit of another person may be subject to tax on the trust's income or capital gains, or both, even though the settlor is not entitled to receive any income or principal from the trust. Because this is now a well-known tax result, many trusts have been created to produce this result, but there are also trusts that are unintentionally subject to this rule. The Act does not require or authorize a trustee to distribute funds from the trust to the settlor in these cases because it is difficult to establish a rule that applies only to trusts where this tax result is unintended and does not apply to trusts where the tax result is intended. Settlors who intend this tax result rarely state it as an objective in the terms of the trust, but instead rely on the operation of the tax law to produce the desired result. As a result it may not be possible to determine from the terms of the trust if the result was intentional or unintentional. If the drafter of such a trust wants the trustee to have the authority to distribute principal or income to the settlor to reimburse the settlor for taxes paid on the trust's income or capital gains, such a provision should be placed in the terms of the trust. In some situations the Internal Revenue Service may require that such a provision be placed in the terms of the trust as a condition to issuing a private letter ruling.

[Adapted from Unif. Principal and Income Act § 506 comment (1997)].

CHAPTER 4. LIABILITY OF TRUSTEES TO BENEFICIARIES

Application

Application of Division, see Probate Code § 15001.

Cross References

Common law rules governing trusts, application, see Probate Code § 15002.
Relationships excluded from Code definition of trust, application of this division, see Probate Code § 15003.

ARTICLE 1. LIABILITY FOR BREACH OF TRUST

Application

Application of Division, see Probate Code § 15001.

Cross References

Application of old and new law, see Probate Code § 3.
Common law rules governing trusts, application, see Probate Code § 15002.
Liability of fiduciaries, limitations, see Health and Safety Code § 25548.4.

Relationships excluded from Code definition of trust, application of this Division, see Probate Code § 15003.

§ 16400. Violations of duties; breach of trust

A violation by the trustee of any duty that the trustee owes the beneficiary is a breach of trust. *(Stats.1990, c. 79 (A.B.759), § 14, operative July 1, 1991.)*

Law Revision Commission Comments

1990 Enactment

Section 16400 continues Section 16400 of the repealed Probate Code without change. This section is drawn from Section 201 of the Restatement (Second) of Trusts (1957). While a trust is revocable, the trustee owes duties to the person holding the power to revoke and not to the named beneficiaries. See Section 15800; see also Section 15803 (holder of general power of appointment or power to withdraw property from trust treated as settlor).

Background on Section 16400 of Repealed Code

Section 16400 was a new provision added by 1986 Cal.Stat. ch. 820 § 40. The section superseded former Civil Code Section 2234 (repealed by 1986 Cal.Stat. ch. 820 § 7). For background on the provisions of this division, see the Comment to this division under the division heading. [20 Cal.L.Rev.Comm.Reports 1001 (1990)].

Cross References

Duties of trustees, see Probate Code § 16000 et seq.
Liability of fiduciaries, limitations, see Health and Safety Code § 25548.4.

§ 16401. Liability for acts of agents

(a) Except as provided in subdivision (b), the trustee is not liable to the beneficiary for the acts or omissions of an agent.

(b) Under any of the circumstances described in this subdivision, the trustee is liable to the beneficiary for an act or omission of an agent employed by the trustee in the administration of the trust that would be a breach of the trust if committed by the trustee:

(1) Where the trustee directs the act of the agent.

(2) Where the trustee delegates to the agent the authority to perform an act that the trustee is under a duty not to delegate.

(3) Where the trustee does not use reasonable prudence in the selection of the agent or the retention of the agent selected by the trustee.

(4) Where the trustee does not periodically review the agent's overall performance and compliance with the terms of the delegation.

(5) Where the trustee conceals the act of the agent.

(6) Where the trustee neglects to take reasonable steps to compel the agent to redress the wrong in a case where the trustee knows of the agent's acts or omissions.

(c) The liability of a trustee for acts or omissions of agents that occurred before July 1, 1987, is governed by prior law and not by this section. *(Stats.1990, c. 79 (A.B.759), § 14, operative July 1, 1991. Amended by Stats.1995, c. 63 (S.B.222), § 9.)*

Law Revision Commission Comments
1990 Enactment

Section 16401 continues Section 16401 of the repealed Probate Code without change.

Subdivisions (a) and (b) are drawn from Section 225 of the Restatement (Second) of Trusts (1957). Whether a trustee has acted reasonably under this section depends upon application of the standard of care provided in Section 16040. The trustee of a revocable trust is not liable where the agent's act is performed or omitted pursuant to the written instructions of the person having the power to revoke the trust. See Section 16462. Similarly, the trustee of a revocable trust is not liable for hiring an agent where the trustee is directed to do so in writing by the person having the power to revoke. See Section 16462. It should also be noted that the liability to beneficiaries does not include beneficiaries under a revocable trust during the time that the trust can be revoked. See Section 15800; see also Sections 15803 (holder of general power of appointment or power to withdraw property from trust treated as settlor), 16000 (duty to administer trust).

The six paragraphs of subdivision (b) state independent bases for imposition of liability on the trustee. For example, if the trustee has not used reasonable care in selecting or retaining an agent, the trustee may be held liable for the agent's breach under paragraph (3); but even if the trustee has no control over selection or retention of the agent, the trustee may still be held liable for the agent's breach under paragraph (1) if the trustee has the power to direct the agent's actions. It should also be noted that paragraphs (2), (5), and (6) of subdivision (b) apply regardless of whether the trustee has any control over the agent.

Subdivision (c) preserves the prior law governing the trustee's liability for acts or omissions of agents occurring before July 1, 1987.

1995 Amendment

Subdivision (b) of Section 16401 is amended for consistency with Section 16052 (delegation of investment and management functions), part of the Uniform Prudent Investor Act (1994). See Section 16052 & Comment. Subdivision (b)(1) is also revised in light of language in Section 225(2)(a) of the Restatement (Second) of Trusts (1957). Subdivision (b)(3) is amended to refer to the use of "prudence" which includes the elements of reasonable care, skill, and caution under Section 16040 (standard of care in non-investment functions) or Section 16047(a) (standard of care in investment and management functions under Uniform Prudent Investor Act). This is not intended to be a substantive change. Subdivision (b)(4) is amended to state a more concrete standard and to be consistent with the delegation rules governing investment and management under the Uniform Prudent Investor Act. See Section 16052(a).

Subdivisions (a) and (b) are drawn from Section 225 of the Restatement (Second) of Trusts (1957). Whether a trustee has acted reasonably under this section depends upon application of the standard of care provided in Section 16040. The trustee of a revocable trust is not liable where the agent's act is performed or omitted pursuant to the written instructions of the person having the power to revoke the trust. See Section 16462. Similarly, the trustee of a revocable trust is not liable for hiring an agent where the trustee is directed to do so in writing by the person having the power to revoke. See Section 16462. It should also be noted that the liability to beneficiaries does not include beneficiaries under a revocable trust during the time that the trust can be revoked. See Section 15800; see also Sections 15803 (holder of general power of appointment or power to withdraw property from trust treated as settlor), 16000 (duty to administer trust).

The six paragraphs of subdivision (b) state independent bases for imposition of liability on the trustee. For example, if the trustee has not used reasonable care in selecting or retaining an agent, the trustee may be held liable for the agent's breach under paragraph (3); but even if the trustee has no control over selection or retention of

the agent, the trustee may still be held liable for the agent's breach under paragraph (1) if the trustee directed or permitted the agent's actions. It should also be noted that paragraphs (2), (5), and (6) of subdivision (b) apply regardless of whether the trustee has any control over the agent. [25 Cal.L.Rev.Comm. Reports 673 (1995)].

Background on Section 16401 of Repealed Code

Section 16401 was a new provision added by 1986 Cal.Stat. ch. 820 § 40. The former statutes did not provide a rule governing the trustee's liability for the acts or omissions of agents of the trust. For background on the provisions of this division, see the Comment to this division under the division heading. [20 Cal.L.Rev.Comm.Reports 1001 (1990)].

§ 16402.   Liability for acts of cotrustees

(a) Except as provided in subdivision (b), a trustee is not liable to the beneficiary for a breach of trust committed by a cotrustee.

(b) A trustee is liable to the beneficiary for a breach committed by a cotrustee under any of the following circumstances:

(1) Where the trustee participates in a breach of trust committed by the cotrustee.

(2) Where the trustee improperly delegates the administration of the trust to the cotrustee.

(3) Where the trustee approves, knowingly acquiesces in, or conceals a breach of trust committed by the cotrustee.

(4) Where the trustee negligently enables the cotrustee to commit a breach of trust.

(5) Where the trustee neglects to take reasonable steps to compel the cotrustee to redress a breach of trust in a case where the trustee knows or has information from which the trustee reasonably should have known of the breach.

(c) The liability of a trustee for acts or omissions of a cotrustee that occurred before July 1, 1987, is governed by prior law and not by this section. *(Stats.1990, c. 79 (A.B.759), § 14, operative July 1, 1991.)*

Law Revision Commission Comments
1990 Enactment

Section 16402 continues Section 16402 of the repealed Probate Code without change. Subdivisions (a) and (b) are drawn from Section 224 of the Restatement (Second) of Trusts (1957).

Subdivision (b)(5) is consistent with the prior case-law rule. See Estate of Hensel, 144 Cal.App.2d 429, 438, 301 P.2d 105 (1956) (citing the rule from the first Restatement). See also Blackmon v. Hale, 1 Cal.3d 548, 559, 463 P.2d 418, 83 Cal.Rptr. 194 (1970) (negligent inattention to duties).

For the duty of a trustee with respect to cotrustees, see Section 16013. It should also be noted that the liability to beneficiaries does not include beneficiaries under revocable trusts during the time that the trust can be revoked. See Section 15800; see also Sections 15803 (holder of general power of appointment or power to withdraw property from trust treated as settlor), 16000 (duty to administer trust).

Subdivision (c) preserves the prior law governing the trustee's liability for acts or omissions of cotrustees occurring before July 1, 1987.

Background on Section 16402 of Repealed Code

Section 16402 was added by 1986 Cal.Stat. ch. 820 § 40. For background on the provisions of this division, see the Comment to this division under the division heading.

Section 16402 restated the substance of former Civil Code Section 2239 (repealed by 1986 Cal.Stat. ch. 820 § 7) as follows:

(1) The substance of the former liability for consenting to wrongful acts of the cotrustee was restated in subdivision (b)(3).

(2) The substance of the former liability for negligently enabling the cotrustee to commit a breach was restated in subdivision (b)(4).

(3) The substance of the former statement that the trustee was liable "for no others" was restated in subdivision (a). [20 Cal.L.Rev.Comm.Reports 1001 (1990)].

Cross References

Duties of cotrustees, see Probate Code § 16013.
Unity of action by cotrustees, see Probate Code § 15620.

§ 16403. Liability for acts of predecessors

(a) Except as provided in subdivision (b), a successor trustee is not liable to the beneficiary for a breach of trust committed by a predecessor trustee.

(b) A successor trustee is liable to the beneficiary for breach of trust involving acts or omissions of a predecessor trustee in any of the following circumstances:

(1) Where the successor trustee knows or has information from which the successor trustee reasonably should have known of a situation constituting a breach of trust committed by the predecessor trustee and the successor trustee improperly permits it to continue.

(2) Where the successor trustee neglects to take reasonable steps to compel the predecessor trustee to deliver the trust property to the successor trustee.

(3) Where the successor trustee neglects to take reasonable steps to redress a breach of trust committed by the predecessor trustee in a case where the successor trustee knows or has information from which the successor trustee reasonably should have known of the predecessor trustee's breach.

(c) The liability of a trustee for acts or omissions of a predecessor trustee that occurred before July 1, 1987, is governed by prior law and not by this section. *(Stats.1990, c. 79 (A.B.759), § 14, operative July 1, 1991.)*

Law Revision Commission Comments

1990 Enactment

Section 16403 continues Section 16403 of the repealed Probate Code without change. Subdivisions (a) and (b) are the same in substance as Section 223 of the Restatement (Second) of Trusts (1957), except that the language relating to what the trustee should have known in subdivisions (b)(1) and (b)(3) differs from the Restatement. In certain circumstances it may not be reasonable to enforce a claim against a former trustee, depending upon the likelihood of recovery and the cost of suit and enforcement. It should also be noted that the liability to beneficiaries does not include beneficiaries under revocable trusts during the time that the trust can be revoked. See Section 15800; see also Section 15803 (holder of general power of appointment or power to withdraw property from trust treated as settlor). For provisions permitting a trustee to be relieved of liability for acts of a predecessor trustee, see Sections 16463 (consent), 16464 (release), 16465 (affirmance).

Subdivision (c) preserves the prior law governing the trustee's liability for acts or omissions of a predecessor trustee occurring before July 1, 1987.

Background on Section 16403 of Repealed Code

Section 16403 is a new provision added by 1986 Cal.Stat. ch. 820 § 40. For background on the provisions of this division, see the Comment to this division under the division heading. [20 Cal.L.Rev.Comm.Reports 1001 (1990)].

ARTICLE 2.   REMEDIES FOR BREACH OF TRUST

Application

Application of Division, see Probate Code § 15001.

Cross References

Application of old and new law, see Probate Code § 3.
Common law rules governing trusts, application, see Probate Code § 15002.
Relationships excluded from Code definition of trust, application of this Division, see Probate Code § 15003.

§ 16420.   Breach of trust; actions

(a) If a trustee commits a breach of trust, or threatens to commit a breach of trust, a beneficiary or cotrustee of the trust may commence a proceeding for any of the following purposes that is appropriate:

(1) To compel the trustee to perform the trustee's duties.

(2) To enjoin the trustee from committing a breach of trust.

(3) To compel the trustee to redress a breach of trust by payment of money or otherwise.

(4) To appoint a receiver or temporary trustee to take possession of the trust property and administer the trust.

(5) To remove the trustee.

(6) Subject to Section 18100, to set aside acts of the trustee.

(7) To reduce or deny compensation of the trustee.

(8) Subject to Section 18100, to impose an equitable lien or a constructive trust on trust property.

(9) Subject to Section 18100, to trace trust property that has been wrongfully disposed of and recover the property or its proceeds.

(b) The provision of remedies for breach of trust in subdivision (a) does not prevent resort to any other appropriate remedy provided by statute or the common law. *(Stats. 1990, c. 79 (A.B.759), § 14, operative July 1, 1991.)*

Law Revision Commission Comments

1990 Enactment

Section 16420 continues Section 16420 of the repealed Probate Code without change.

Subdivision (a) codifies in general terms the remedies available to a beneficiary or cotrustee where a trustee has committed a breach of trust or threatens to do so. For the applicable procedure, see Section 17200 et seq. (judicial proceedings concerning trusts). As provided in subdivision (b), the list of remedies in subdivision (a) is not necessarily exclusive and is not intended to prevent resort to any other appropriate remedy. See Section 15002 (common law as law of state); Penal Code § 506 (embezzlement by trustee); People v.

Stanford, 16 Cal.2d 247, 105 P.2d 969 (1940) (embezzlement); see also Section 16421 (remedies are exclusively equitable). The petitioner may seek any one or more of the remedies as is appropriate in the circumstances of the case. Section 16420 provides a general list of remedies and does not attempt to set out the refinements and exceptions developed over many years by the common law. The availability of a particular remedy listed in Section 16420, and its application under the circumstances, are governed by the common law. See Section 15002 (common law as law of state).

As to paragraph (1) of subdivision (a) of Section 16420, see Bacon v. Grosse, 165 Cal. 481, 132 P. 1027 (1913); Restatement (Second) of Trusts § 199(a) (1957).

Paragraph (2) is consistent with other statutes. See Civil Code § 3422; Code Civ.Proc. § 526; see also Quist v. Empire Water Co., 204 Cal. 646, 269 P. 533 (1928); St. James Church of Christ Holiness v. Superior Court, 135 Cal.App.2d 352, 359–62, 287 P.2d 387 (1955); Restatement (Second) of Trusts § 199(b) (1957).

The reference to payment of money in paragraph (3) is comprehensive and includes liability that might be characterized as damages, restitution, or surcharge. For the measure of liability, see Article 3 (commencing with Section 16440). The characterization of monetary liability does not affect the fact that the remedies for breach of trust are exclusively equitable, as provided in Section 16421. In certain circumstances, rather than ordering the payment of money, it may be appropriate for the court to order the trustee to transfer tangible property as a remedy for breach of trust. See also Restatement (Second) of Trusts § 199(c) (1957).

Paragraph (4) provides explicit authority for the appointment of a receiver. See Code Civ.Proc. § 564(1), (8); Bowles v. Superior Court, 44 Cal.2d 574, 583–84, 283 P.2d 704 (1955) (appointment of receiver pending removal of trustees and as temporary trustee); see also Restatement (Second) of Trusts § 199(d) (1957). Paragraph (4) also permits appointment of a temporary trustee where appointment of a receiver would be appropriate. See Sections 15660 (appointment of trustee to fill vacancy), 17206 (authority to make necessary orders and appoint temporary trustee).

As to paragraph (5), see Restatement (Second) of Trusts § 199(e) (1957). For provisions governing removal of trustees, see Sections 15642 (grounds for removal), 15644 (delivery of property by removed trustee), 17200(b)(10) (petition for removal).

The authority under paragraph (6) to set aside wrongful acts of the trustee is a corollary of the power to enjoin a threatened breach as provided in paragraph (2). As recognized in the introductory clause of paragraph (6), the wrongful acts of the trustee may not be set aside if to do so would impair the rights of bona fide purchasers. See also G. Bogert, The Law of Trusts and Trustees § 861, at 16–17 (rev. 2d ed. 1982).

Paragraph (7) is drawn from Section 243 of the Restatement (Second) of Trusts (1957). Prior California statutes provided only for the determination of reasonable compensation and for the allowance of greater compensation under appropriate circumstances. See former Civil Code § 2274 (repealed by 1986 Cal.Stat. ch. 820 § 7); former Prob.Code §§ 1122, 1138.1(a)(7) (provisions repealed by 1986 Cal.Stat. ch. 820 § 31).

Paragraph (8) states a general rule recognized in California cases. See, e.g., Citizens' Bank v. Rucker, 138 Cal. 606, 609–10, 72 P. 46 (1903); see also Restatement (Second) of Trusts § 202 (1957). The introductory clause recognizes that this remedy is limited by the rights of bona fide purchasers as provided in Section 18100.

Paragraph (9) is consistent with California case law. See Noble v. Noble, 198 Cal. 129, 135, 243 P. 439 (1926); Keeney v. Bank of Italy, 33 Cal.App. 515, 517, 165 P. 735 (1917); People v. California Safe Deposit & Trust Co., 175 Cal. 756, 759–60, 167 P. 388 (1917); Church v. Bailey, 90 Cal.App.2d 501, 504, 203 P.2d 547 (1949); Carlin v. Masten, 118 Cal.App. 373, 376–77, 5 P.2d 65 (1931). The introductory clause recognizes that this remedy is limited by the rights of bona fide purchasers as provided in Section 18100.

Background on Section 16420 of Repealed Code

Section 16420 was added by 1986 Cal.Stat. ch. 820 § 40. Paragraph (1) of subdivision (a) superseded a part of former Civil Code Sections 863 (repealed by 1986 Cal.Stat. eh. 820 § 5) (beneficiary may "enforce the performance of the trust") and 2251 (repealed by 1986 Cal.Stat. ch. 820 § 7) (beneficiary may "take advantage" of trust). Paragraph (2) was new. Paragraph (3) restated the general liability provided in former Civil Code Sections 2236–2238 and 2262 (provisions repealed by 1986 Cal.Stat. ch. 820 § 7). Paragraph (4) was new. Paragraph (5) restated in general terms the authority to remove a trustee for breach of trust provided by former Civil Code Section 2283 (repealed by 1986 Cal.Stat. ch. 820 § 7) and former Probate Code Section 1123.5 (repealed by 1986 Cal.Stat. ch. 820 § 31). Paragraphs (6)–(9) were new. For background on the provisions of this division, see the Comment to this division under the division heading. [20 Cal.L.Rev.Comm.Reports 1001 (1990)].

Cross References

Adverse interest as warranting removal of trustee, see Probate Code § 15642.

Final injunction to prevent breach of obligation arising from a trust, grant, see Civil Code § 3422.

Limitation of actions to enforce trust, see Probate Code § 16460.

Protection of obligations to third persons, see Probate Code § 18100.

Removal of testamentary trustee, notice, see Probate Code § 15642.

§ 16421. Exclusivity of remedies

The remedies of a beneficiary against the trustee are exclusively in equity. *(Stats.1990, c. 79 (A.B.759), § 14, operative July 1, 1991.)*

Law Revision Commission Comments
1990 Enactment

Section 16421 continues Section 16421 of the repealed Probate Code without change. This section is drawn from Section 197 of the Restatement (Second) of Trusts (1957). For a list of remedies, see Section 16420. Under this section, for example, the beneficiary may not commence an action against the trustee for breach of contract. See Restatement (Second) of Trusts § 197 comment b (1957). However, the trustee may be found liable for the payment of money on account of the breach. See Sections 16420(a)(3) (compelling payment of money for breach of trust), 16440–16441 (measure of liability for breach of trust).

Background on Section 16421 of Repealed Code

Section 16421 was a new provision added by 1986 Cal.Stat. ch. 820 § 40. For background on the provisions of this division, see the Comment to this division under the division heading. [20 Cal.L.Rev.Comm.Reports 1001 (1990)].

Cross References

Statutory or common law remedies for breach of trust, see Probate Code § 16442.

ARTICLE 3. MEASURE OF LIABILITY FOR BREACH OF TRUST

Application

Application of Division, see Probate Code § 15001.

Application of old and new law, see Probate Code § 3.
Common law rules governing trusts, application, see Probate Code
§ 15002.
Relationships excluded from Code definition of trust, application of
this Division, see Probate Code § 15003.

§ 16440. Breach of trust; liability; good faith actions

(a) If the trustee commits a breach of trust, the trustee is chargeable with any of the following that is appropriate under the circumstances:

(1) Any loss or depreciation in value of the trust estate resulting from the breach of trust, with interest.

(2) Any profit made by the trustee through the breach of trust, with interest.

(3) Any profit that would have accrued to the trust estate if the loss of profit is the result of the breach of trust.

(b) If the trustee has acted reasonably and in good faith under the circumstances as known to the trustee, the court, in its discretion, may excuse the trustee in whole or in part from liability under subdivision (a) if it would be equitable to do so. *(Stats.1990, c. 79 (A.B.759), § 14, operative July 1, 1991.)*

Law Revision Commission Comments
1990 Enactment [Revised Comment]

Section 16440 continues Section 16440 of the repealed Probate Code without change. Subdivision (a) is drawn from Section 205 of the Restatement (Second) of Trusts (1957). See also Section 16047 (duty to consider investments as part of an overall investment strategy under Uniform Prudent Investor Act).

Subdivision (b) codifies the good-faith exception to the general liability rules found in the Restatement. See Restatement (Second) of Trusts § 205 comment g (1957). This rule supersedes subdivision (a) of former Civil Code Section 2238 and represents an expansion of the rule in Estate of Talbot, 141 Cal.App.2d 309, 320–27, 296 P.2d 848 (1956). In *Talbot,* liability for appreciation damages was excused on the grounds of good faith, but the trustee was liable for the breach in the amount of the loss to the corpus plus interest. [25 Cal.L.Rev.Comm. Reports 673 (1995)].

Background on Section 16440 of Repealed Code

Section 16440 was added by 1986 Cal.Stat. ch. 820 § 40. Subdivision (a) superseded former Civil Code Sections 2237 and 2238 (provisions repealed by 1986 Cal.Stat. ch. 820 § 7). Subdivision (b) superseded subdivision (a) of former Civil Code Section 2238. For background on the provisions of this division, see the Comment to this division under the division heading. [20 Cal.L.Rev.Reports 1001 (1990)].

Limitations of actions, see Probate Code § 16460.

§ 16441. Interest; amount; excuse from liability

(a) If the trustee is liable for interest pursuant to Section 16440, the trustee is liable for the greater of the following amounts:

(1) The amount of interest that accrues at the legal rate on judgments in effect during the period when the interest accrued.

(2) The amount of interest actually received.

(b) If the trustee has acted reasonably and in good faith under the circumstances as known to the trustee, the court, in its discretion, may excuse the trustee in whole or in part from liability under subdivision (a) if it would be equitable to do so. *(Stats.1990, c. 79 (A.B.759), § 14, operative July 1, 1991. Amended by Stats.1998, c. 77 (S.B.1841), § 5.)*

Law Revision Commission Comments
1990 Enactment

Section 16441 continues Section 16441 of the repealed Probate Code without change. Under subdivision (a), the legal rate of interest on judgments in effect when the liability accrued is applied. Thus, the rate is 7 percent per year until January 1, 1983, when the interest rate on judgments was raised to 10 percent per year. See Code Civ.Proc. § 685.010; American Nat'l Bank v. Peacock, 165 Cal.App.3d 1206, 1210–12, 212 Cal.Rptr. 97 (1985). Notwithstanding Section 16442, interest is not compounded under the Trust Law as it was under former Civil Code Section 2262. For example, if a trustee is found liable for a breach of trust that occurred in 1980 and is charged with interest at the rate provided in subdivision (a) of Section 16441, interest is determined at the rate of 7 percent from 1980 until December 31, 1982, and then at the rate of 10 percent from January 1, 1983, until the date of judgment. After judgment, interest accrues at the rate of 10 percent pursuant to Code of Civil Procedure Section 685.010.

Background on Section 16441 of Repealed Code

Section 16441 was added by 1986 Cal.Stat. ch. 820 § 40 and was amended by 1987 Cal.Stat. ch. 128 § 18. The section superseded former Civil Code Section 2262 (liability for interest upon failure to properly invest trust funds) and part of former Civil Code Section 2237 (liability for interest on proceeds) (provisions repealed by 1986 Cal.Stat. ch. 820 § 7).

The 1987 amendment clarified the interest rate applicable to a determination of liability for a breach occurring before the operative date of this division.

For background on the provisions of this division, see the Comment to this division under the division heading. [20 Cal.L.Rev.Comm.Reports 1001 (1990)].

Judgments, rates of interest, see Cal. Const. Art. 15, § 1; Code of
Civil Procedure § 685.010 et seq.

§ 16442. Availability of other remedies

The provisions in this article for liability of a trustee for breach of trust do not prevent resort to any other remedy available under the statutory or common law. *(Stats.1990, c. 79 (A.B.759), § 14, operative July 1, 1991.)*

Law Revision Commission Comments
1990 Enactment

Section 16442 continues Section 16442 of the repealed Probate Code without change. This section makes clear that Sections 16440 and 16441 do not prevent resort to any other remedy available against the trustee under the statutory or common law. See Section 15002 (common law as law of state); see also Section 16420 (remedies for breach of trust).

Background on Section 16442 of Repealed Code

Section 16442 was a new provision added by 1986 Cal.Stat. ch. 820 § 40. For background on the provisions of this division, see the Comment to this division under the division heading. [20 Cal.L.Rev.Comm.Reports 1001 (1990)].

Cross References

Equitable remedies, exclusivity, see Probate Code § 16421.

ARTICLE 4. LIMITATIONS AND EXCULPATION

Section
16460. Existence of claims; adequate disclosure; account or report.
16461. Exculpation of trustee; trust provisions; objections.
16462. Revocable trusts; liability for acts performed pursuant to written directions.
16463. Beneficiary's consent; nonliability of trustee.
16464. Beneficiary's release or contract; discharge of trustee's liability.
16465. Affirmation by beneficiary; nonliability of trustee.

Application

Application of Division, see Probate Code § 15001.

Cross References

Application of old and new law, see Probate Code § 3.
Common law rules governing trusts, application, see Probate Code § 15002.
Relationships excluded from Code definition of trust, application of this Division, see Probate Code § 15003.

§ 16460. Existence of claims; adequate disclosure; account or report

(a) Unless a claim is previously barred by adjudication, consent, limitation, or otherwise:

(1) If a beneficiary has received an interim or final account in writing, or other written report, that adequately discloses the existence of a claim against the trustee for breach of trust, the claim is barred as to that beneficiary unless a proceeding to assert the claim is commenced within three years after receipt of the account or report. An account or report adequately discloses existence of a claim if it provides sufficient information so that the beneficiary knows of the claim or reasonably should have inquired into the existence of the claim.

(2) If an interim or final account in writing or other written report does not adequately disclose the existence of a claim against the trustee for breach of trust or if a beneficiary does not receive any written account or report, the claim is barred as to that beneficiary unless a proceeding to assert the claim is commenced within three years after the beneficiary discovered, or reasonably should have discovered, the subject of the claim.

(b) For the purpose of subdivision (a), a beneficiary is deemed to have received an account or report, as follows:

(1) In the case of an adult who is reasonably capable of understanding the account or report, if it is received by the adult personally.

(2) In the case of an adult who is not reasonably capable of understanding the account or report, if it is received by the person's legal representative, including a guardian ad litem or other person appointed for this purpose.

(3) In the case of a minor, if it is received by the minor's guardian or, if the minor does not have a guardian, if it is received by the minor's parent so long as the parent does not have a conflict of interest.

(c) A written account or report under this section may, but need not, satisfy the requirements of Section 16061 or 16063 or any other provision. *(Stats.1990, c. 79 (A.B.759), § 14, operative July 1, 1991. Amended by Stats.1996, c. 862 (A.B.2751), § 40.)*

Law Revision Commission Comments
1990 Enactment

Section 16460 continues Section 16460 of the repealed Probate Code with the omission of subdivision (c). The omitted subdivision (which provided that a claim arising before July 1, 1987, was not barred by Section 16460 until July 1, 1988) has been omitted as obsolete.

Section 16460 is drawn in part from Section 7–307 of the Uniform Probate Code (1987). As to the construction of provisions drawn from uniform acts, see Section 2. For provisions governing consent, release, and affirmance by beneficiaries to relieve the trustee of liability, see Sections 16463–16465. The reference in the introductory clause to claims "otherwise" barred also includes principles such as estoppel and laches that apply under the common law. See Section 15002 (common law as law of state). See also Sections 16461 (exculpation of trustee by provision in trust instrument), 16462 (nonliability for following instructions under revocable trust). During the time that a trust is revocable, the person holding the power to revoke is the one who must receive the account or report in order to commence the running of the limitations period provided in this section. See Sections 15800 (limits on rights of beneficiary of revocable trust), 16064(b) (exception to duty to account). Under prior law, the four-year limitations period provided in Code of Civil Procedure Section 343 was applied to actions for breach of express trusts. See Cortelyou v. Imperial Land Co., 166 Cal. 14, 20, 134 P. 981 (1913); Oeth v. Mason, 247 Cal.App.2d 805, 811–12, 56 Cal.Rptr. 69 (1967). Section 16460 is an exception to the four-year rule provided in Code of Civil Procedure Section 343.

Subdivision (b) provides special rules concerning who must receive the account or report for it to have the effect of barring claims based on the information disclosed. Under subdivision (b)(2) it may be appropriate to seek the appointment of a guardian ad litem or some other person to receive accounts and reports where no conservator has been appointed for the person and there is serious doubt that the beneficiary can understand the account or report. See Section 1003 (guardian ad litem).

For provisions relating to the duty to report information and account to beneficiaries, see Sections 16060–16064.

1996 Amendment

Subdivision (a)(2) of Section 16460 is amended to make clear that it applies both where an insufficient account or report is given the beneficiary as well as where the beneficiary has not received any written account or report. This revision is consistent with the original intent of this section, and rejects the contrary conclusion reached by the court in DiGrazia v. Anderlini, 22 Cal.App.4th 1337, 1346-48, 28 Cal.Rptr.2d 37, 42-44 (1994). The three-year statute of limitations under subdivision (a) is applicable to all claims for breach of trust and the four-year statute of Code of Civil Procedure Section 343 is inapplicable. See Comment to Section 16460 as enacted by 1986 Cal. Stat. ch. 820, *Selected 1986 Trust and Probate Legislation,* 18 Cal. L. Revision Comm'n Reports 1201, 1424-25 (1986), and as re-enacted by 1990 Cal. Stat. ch. 79, *Recommendation Proposing New Probate Code,* 20 Cal. L. Revision Comm'n Reports 1001, 1940-41 (1990).

Subdivision (c) is added to make clear that the requirements for a written account or report under this section are independent of other statutes. The governing rule determining whether paragraph (1) or paragraph (2) of subdivision (a) applies is whether the account or report "adequately discloses the existence of a claim." Subdivision (c) rejects the holding in DiGrazia v. Anderlini, 22 Cal.App.4th 1337,

1348-49, 28 Cal.Rptr.2d 37, 44-45 (1994), that an account or report under this section must satisfy the minimum standards set out in Section 16061 or 16063. [26 Cal.L.Rev.Comm. Reports 1 (1996)].

Background on Section 16460 of Repealed Code

Section 16460 was added by 1986 Cal.Stat. ch. 820 § 40. The section superseded the provisions of former Civil Code Section 2282 (repealed by 1986 Cal.Stat. ch. 820 § 7) relating to discharge of trustees. For background on the provisions of this division, see the Comment to this division under the division heading. [20 Cal.L.Rev.Comm.Reports 1001 (1990)].

§ 16461. Exculpation of trustee; trust provisions; objections

(a) Except as provided in subdivision (b), (c), or (d), the trustee can be relieved of liability for breach of trust by provisions in the trust instrument.

(b) A provision in the trust instrument is not effective to relieve the trustee of liability (1) for breach of trust committed intentionally, with gross negligence, in bad faith, or with reckless indifference to the interest of the beneficiary, or (2) for any profit that the trustee derives from a breach of trust.

(c) Subject to subdivision (b), a provision in a trust instrument that releases the trustee from liability if a beneficiary fails to object to an item in an interim or final account or other written report within a specified time period is effective only if all of the following conditions are met:

(1) The account or report sets forth the item.

(2) The period specified in the trust instrument for the beneficiary to object is not less than 180 days, or the trustee elects to follow the procedure provided in subdivision (d).

(3) Written notice in 12–point boldface type is provided to a beneficiary with the account or report in the following form:

NOTICE TO BENEFICIARIES

YOU HAVE [insert "180 days" or the period specified in the trust instrument, whichever is longer] FROM YOUR RECEIPT OF THIS ACCOUNT OR REPORT TO MAKE AN OBJECTION TO ANY ITEM SET FORTH IN THIS ACCOUNT OR REPORT. ANY OBJECTION YOU MAKE MUST BE IN WRITING; IT MUST BE DELIVERED TO THE TRUSTEE WITHIN THE PERIOD STATED ABOVE; AND IT MUST STATE YOUR OBJECTION. YOUR FAILURE TO DELIVER A WRITTEN OBJECTION TO THE TRUSTEE WITHIN THE PERIOD STATED ABOVE WILL PERMANENTLY PREVENT YOU FROM LATER ASSERTING THIS OBJECTION AGAINST THE TRUSTEE. IF YOU DO MAKE AN OBJECTION TO THE TRUSTEE, THE THREE–YEAR PERIOD PROVIDED IN SECTION 16460 OF THE PROBATE CODE FOR COMMENCEMENT OF LITIGATION WILL APPLY TO CLAIMS BASED ON YOUR OBJECTION AND WILL BEGIN TO RUN ON THE DATE THAT YOU RECEIVE THIS ACCOUNT OR REPORT.

(d) A provision in a trust instrument that provides for a period less than 180 days to object to an item in an account or report shall be ineffective to release the trustee from liability. A trustee of a trust created by an instrument with an ineffective period may elect to be governed by the provisions of subdivision (c) by complying with the requirements of

subdivision (c), except that "180 days" shall be substituted in the notice form for the ineffective period.

(e) Subject to subdivision (b), a beneficiary who fails to object in writing to an account or report that complies with the requirements of subdivision (c) within the specified, valid period shall be barred from asserting any claim against the trustee regarding an item that is adequately disclosed in the account or report. An item is adequately disclosed if the disclosure regarding the item meets the requirements of paragraph (1) of subdivision (a) of Section 16460.

(f) Except as provided in subdivision (a) of Section 16460, the trustee may not be released from liability as to any claim based on a written objection made by a beneficiary if the objection is delivered to the trustee within the specified, effective period. If a beneficiary has filed a written objection to an account or report that complies with the requirements of subdivision (c) within the specified, valid period that concerns an item that affects any other beneficiary of the trust, any affected beneficiary may join in the objection anytime within the specified, valid period or while the resolution of the objection is pending, whichever is later. This section is not intended to establish a class of beneficiaries for actions on an account and report or provide that the action of one beneficiary is for the benefit of all beneficiaries. This section does not create a duty for any trustee to notify beneficiaries of objections or resolution of objections.

(g) Provided that a beneficiary has filed a written objection to an account or report that complies with the requirements of subdivision (c) within the specified, valid period, a supplemental written objection may be delivered in the same manner as the objection not later than 180 days after the receipt of the account or report or no later than the period specified in the trust instrument, whichever is longer.

(h) Compliance with subdivision (c) excuses compliance with paragraph (6) of subdivision (a) of Section 16063 for the account or report to which that notice relates.

(i) Subject to subdivision (b), if proper notice has been given and a beneficiary has not made a timely objection, the trustee is not liable for any other claims adequately disclosed by any item in the account or report.

(j) Subdivisions (c) to (i), inclusive, apply to all accounts and reports submitted after the effective date of the act adding these subdivisions. *(Stats.1990, c. 79 (A.B.759), § 14, operative July 1, 1991. Amended by Stats.2004, c. 538 (A.B.1990), § 1.)*

Law Revision Commission Comments

1990 Enactment

Section 16461 continues Section 16461 of the repealed Probate Code without change. This section is the same in substance as part of Section 222 of the Restatement (Second) of Trusts (1957), except that the reference to gross negligence does not appear in the Restatement. For special provisions applicable to revocable trusts, see Section 16462. Although a trust may not exculpate a trustee from liability for a profit from a breach, as provided in clause (2) of subdivision (b), the trust may limit the trustee's duties with the effect that the trustee does not commit a breach in that area. However, it is against public policy to attempt to eliminate liability for profits derived from a breach of a duty that the trustee does have. See Restatement (Second) of Trusts § 222 comments b & c (1957).

Section 16461 was a new provision added by 1986 Cal.Stat. ch. 820 § 40. For background on the provisions of this division, see the Comment to this division under the division heading. [20 Cal.L.Rev.Comm.Reports 1001 (1990)].

§ 16462. Revocable trusts; liability for acts performed pursuant to written directions

(a) Notwithstanding Section 16461, a trustee of a revocable trust is not liable to a beneficiary for any act performed or omitted pursuant to written directions from the person holding the power to revoke, including a person to whom the power to direct the trustee is delegated.

(b) Subdivision (a) applies to a trust that is revocable in part with respect to the interest of the beneficiary in that part of the trust property. *(Stats.1990, c. 79 (A.B.759), § 14, operative July 1, 1991.)*

Law Revision Commission Comments

1990 Enactment

Section 16462 continues Section 16462 of the repealed Probate Code without change. See also Section 16001 (trustee's duty to follow written directions under revocable trust).

Background on Section 16462 of Repealed Code

Section 16462 was added by 1986 Cal.Stat. ch. 820 § 40. The section restated subdivision (b) of former Civil Code Section 2258 (repealed by 1986 Cal.Stats. ch. 820 § 7), insofar as it concerned the trustee's liability under a revocable trust, without substantive change. Section 16462 also restated subdivision (b) of former Civil Code Section 2238 (repealed by 1986 Cal.Stats. ch. 820 § 7) without substantive change. For background on the provisions of this division, see the Comment to this division under the division heading.

§ 16463. Beneficiary's consent; nonliability of trustee

(a) Except as provided in subdivisions (b) and (c), a beneficiary may not hold the trustee liable for an act or omission of the trustee as a breach of trust if the beneficiary consented to the act or omission before or at the time of the act or omission.

(b) The consent of the beneficiary does not preclude the beneficiary from holding the trustee liable for a breach of trust in any of the following circumstances:

(1) Where the beneficiary was under an incapacity at the time of the consent or of the act or omission.

(2) Where the beneficiary at the time consent was given did not know of his or her rights and of the material facts (A) that the trustee knew or should have known and (B) that the trustee did not reasonably believe that the beneficiary knew.

(3) Where the consent of the beneficiary was induced by improper conduct of the trustee.

(c) Where the trustee has an interest in the transaction adverse to the interest of the beneficiary, the consent of the beneficiary does not preclude the beneficiary from holding the trustee liable for a breach of trust under any of the circumstances described in subdivision (b) or where the transaction to which the beneficiary consented was not fair and reasonable to the beneficiary. *(Stats.1990, c. 79 (A.B. 759), § 14, operative July 1, 1991.)*

Law Revision Commission Comments

1990 Enactment

Section 16463 continues Section 16463 of the repealed Probate Code without substantive change. This section is the same in substance as Section 216 of the Restatement (Second) of Trusts (1957). See also Sections 16460 (limitations on proceedings against trustee), 16464 (release), 16465 (affirmance). As to other rules that may limit the trustee's liability, see the Comment to Section 16460.

Background on Section 16463 of Repealed Code

Section 16463 was a new provision added by 1986 Cal.Stat. ch. 820 § 40. The section superseded provisions relating to beneficiaries' consent to relieve a trustee of liability that appeared in former Civil Code Sections 2230, 2232, and 2282(d) (provisions repealed by 1986 Cal.Stats. ch. 820 § 7). For background on the provisions of this division, see the Comment to this division under the division heading. [20 Cal.L.Rev.Comm.Reports 1001 (1990)].

Cross References

Presumption against trustees in transactions with beneficiaries, see Probate Code § 16004.
Undertaking trust adverse to interest of beneficiary, see Probate Code § 16005.
Violation of duties as breach of trust against beneficiary, see Probate Code § 16400.

§ 16464. Beneficiary's release or contract; discharge of trustee's liability

(a) Except as provided in subdivision (b), a beneficiary may be precluded from holding the trustee liable for a breach of trust by the beneficiary's release or contract effective to discharge the trustee's liability to the beneficiary for that breach.

(b) A release or contract is not effective to discharge the trustee's liability for a breach of trust in any of the following circumstances:

(1) Where the beneficiary was under an incapacity at the time of making the release or contract.

(2) Where the beneficiary did not know of his or her rights and of the material facts (A) that the trustee knew or reasonably should have known and (B) that the trustee did not reasonably believe that the beneficiary knew.

(3) Where the release or contract of the beneficiary was induced by improper conduct of the trustee.

(4) Where the transaction involved a bargain with the trustee that was not fair and reasonable. *(Stats.1990, c. 79 (A.B.759), § 14, operative July 1, 1991.)*

Law Revision Commission Comments

1990 Enactment

Section 16464 continues Section 16464 of the repealed Probate Code without change. This section is the same in substance as Section 217 of the Restatement (Second) of Trusts (1957). See also Sections 16460 (limitations on proceedings against trustee), 16463 (consent), 16465 (affirmance). As to other rules that may limit the trustee's liability, see the Comment to Section 16460.

Background on Section 16464 of Repealed Code

Section 16464 was a new provision added by 1986 Cal.Stat. ch. 820 § 40. The section superseded former Civil Code Section 2230 (repealed by 1986 Cal.Stats. ch. 820 § 7) to the extent that section governed release. For background on the provisions of this division, see the Comment to this division under the division heading. [20 Cal.L.Rev.Comm.Reports 1001 (1990)].

§ 16465. Affirmation by beneficiary; nonliability of trustee

(a) Except as provided in subdivision (b), if the trustee, in breach of trust, enters into a transaction that the beneficiary may at his or her option reject or affirm, and the beneficiary affirms the transaction, the beneficiary shall not thereafter reject it and hold the trustee liable for any loss occurring after the trustee entered into the transaction.

(b) The affirmation of a transaction by the beneficiary does not preclude the beneficiary from holding a trustee liable for a breach of trust if, at the time of the affirmation, any of the following circumstances existed:

(1) The beneficiary was under an incapacity.

(2) The beneficiary did not know of his or her rights and of the material facts (A) that the trustee knew or reasonably should have known and (B) that the trustee did not reasonably believe that the beneficiary knew.

(3) The affirmation was induced by improper conduct of the trustee.

(4) The transaction involved a bargain with the trustee that was not fair and reasonable. *(Stats.1990, c. 79 (A.B.759), § 14, operative July 1, 1991.)*

Law Revision Commission Comments
1990 Enactment

Section 16465 continues Section 16465 of the repealed Probate Code without change. This section is the same in substance as Section 218 of the Restatement (Second) of Trusts (1957). See also Sections 16460 (limitations on proceedings against trustee), 16463 (consent), 16464 (release). As to other rules that may limit the trustee's liability, see the Comment to Section 16460.

Background on Section 16465 of Repealed Code

Section 16465 was a new provision added by 1986 Cal.Stat. ch. 820 § 40. For background on the provisions of this division, see the Comment to this division under the division heading. [20 Cal.L.Rev.Comm.Reports 1001 (1990)].

CHAPTER 5. NOTICE OF PROPOSED ACTION BY TRUSTEE

Cross References

Uniform Principal and Income Act, fiduciary duties, notice of proposed action, see Probate Code § 16337.

§ 16500. Notice of proposed action by trustee; application or assertion of other rights or remedies

Subject to subdivision (d) of Section 16501, a trustee may give a notice of proposed action regarding a matter governed by Chapter 2 (commencing with Section 16200) or Chapter 3 (commencing with Section 16320) as provided in this chapter. For the purpose of this chapter, a proposed action includes a course of action or a decision not to take action. This chapter does not preclude an application or assertion of any other rights or remedies available to an interested party as otherwise provided in this part regarding an action to be taken or not to be taken by the trustee. *(Added by Stats.2004, c. 54 (S.B.1021), § 2.)*

§ 16501. Mailing notice of proposed action by trustee; consent to proposed action; copies of notice; actions in which notice prohibited

(a) The trustee who elects to provide notice pursuant to this chapter shall mail notice of the proposed action to each of the following:

(1) A beneficiary who is receiving, or is entitled to receive, income under the trust, including a beneficiary who is entitled to receive income at the discretion of the trustee.

(2) A beneficiary who would receive a distribution of principal if the trust were terminated at the time the notice is given.

(b) Notice of proposed action is not required to be given to a person who consents in writing to the proposed action. The consent may be executed at any time before or after the proposed action is taken.

(c) A trustee is not required to provide a copy of the notice of proposed action to a beneficiary who is known to the trustee but who cannot be located by the trustee after reasonable diligence or who is unknown to the trustee.

(d) Notwithstanding any other provision of this chapter, the trustee may not use a notice of proposed action in any of the following actions:

(1) Allowance of the trustee's compensation.

(2) Allowance of compensation of the attorney for the trustee.

(3) Settlement of accounts.

* * *

(4) Discharge of the trustee.

(5) Sale of property of the trust to the trustee or to the attorney for the trustee.

(6) Exchange of property of the trust for property of the trustee or for property of the attorney for the trustee.

(7) Grant of an option to purchase property of the trust to the trustee or to the attorney for the trustee.

(8) Allowance, payment, or compromise of a claim of the trustee, or the attorney for the trustee, against the trust.

(9) Compromise or settlement of a claim, action, or proceeding by the trust against the trustee or against the attorney for the trust.

(10) Extension, renewal, or modification of the terms of a debt or other obligation of the trustee, or the attorney for the trustee, owing to or in favor of the trust. *(Added by Stats.2004, c. 54 (S.B.1021), § 2. Amended by Stats.2016, c. 64 (A.B.1700), § 1, eff. Jan. 1, 2017.)*

§ 16502. Contents of notice

The notice of proposed action shall state that it is given pursuant to this section and shall include all of the following:

(a) The name and mailing address of the trustee.

(b) The name and telephone number of a person who may be contacted for additional information.

(c) A description of the action proposed to be taken and an explanation of the reasons for the action.

(d) The time within which objections to the proposed action can be made, which shall be at least 45 days from the mailing of the notice of proposed action.

(e) The date on or after which the proposed action may be taken or is effective. *(Added by Stats.2004, c. 54 (S.B.1021), § 2.)*

§ 16503. Objections to proposed actions by beneficiary; failure to object; petitions

(a) A beneficiary may object to the proposed action by mailing a written objection to the trustee at the address stated in the notice of proposed action within the time period specified in the notice of proposed action.

(b) A trustee is not liable to a beneficiary for an action regarding a matter governed by this part if the trustee does not receive a written objection to the proposed action from a beneficiary within the applicable period and the other requirements of this section are satisfied. If no beneficiary entitled to notice objects under this section, the trustee is not liable to any current or future beneficiary with respect to the proposed action. This subdivision does not apply to a person who is a minor or an incompetent adult at the time of receiving the notice of proposed action unless the notice is served on a guardian or conservator of the estate of the person.

(c) If the trustee receives a written objection within the applicable period, either the trustee or a beneficiary may petition the court to have the proposed action taken as proposed, taken with modifications, or denied. In the proceeding, a beneficiary objecting to the proposed action has the burden of proving that the trustee's proposed action should not be taken. A beneficiary who has not objected is not estopped from opposing the proposed action in the proceeding.

(d) If the trustee decides not to implement the proposed action, the trustee shall notify the beneficiaries of the decision not to take the action and the reasons for the decision, and the trustee's decision not to implement the proposed action does not itself give rise to liability to any current or future beneficiary. A beneficiary may petition the court to have the action taken, and has the burden of proving that it should be taken. *(Added by Stats.2004, c. 54 (S.B. 1021), § 2.)*

Cross References

Conversion of trust to unitrust, duties of trustee, see Probate Code § 16336.7.

§ 16504. Use of procedures by trustee prior to action

This chapter does not require a trustee to use these procedures prior to taking any action. *(Added by Stats.2004, c. 54 (S.B.1021), § 2.)*

Part 5

JUDICIAL PROCEEDINGS CONCERNING TRUSTS

Application

Application of Division, see Probate Code § 15001.

Cross References

Common law rules governing trusts, application, see Probate Code § 15002.

Destruction of court records, notice, retention periods, see Government Code § 68152.

Relationships excluded from Code definition of trust, application of this Division, see Probate Code § 15003.

CHAPTER 1. JURISDICTION AND VENUE

Application

Application of Division, see Probate Code § 15001.

Cross References

Application of old and new law, see Probate Code § 3.

Common law rules governing trusts, application, see Probate Code § 15002.

Relationships excluded from Code definition of trust, application of this division, see Probate Code § 15003.

§ 17000. Exclusive and concurrent jurisdiction

(a) The superior court having jurisdiction over the trust pursuant to this part has exclusive jurisdiction of proceedings concerning the internal affairs of trusts.

(b) The superior court having jurisdiction over the trust pursuant to this part has concurrent jurisdiction of the following:

(1) Actions and proceedings to determine the existence of trusts.

(2) Actions and proceedings by or against creditors or debtors of trusts.

(3) Other actions and proceedings involving trustees and third persons. *(Stats.1990, c. 79 (A.B.759), § 14, operative July 1, 1991.)*

Law Revision Commission Comments
1990 Enactment

Section 17000 continues Section 17000 of the repealed Probate Code without change. Subdivision (a) is drawn from the first sentence of Section 7–201(a) of the Uniform Probate Code (1987). Subdivision (a) provides for exclusive jurisdiction in the superior court in matters involving the internal affairs of trusts. See Chapter 3 (commencing with Section 17200). It is intended that the department of the superior court that customarily deals with probate matters will exercise the exclusive jurisdiction relating to internal trust affairs provided by subdivision (a). This department of the superior court is not a court of limited power. See Section 17001 (superior court sitting in probate is full-power court). Subdivision (b) is drawn from Section 7–204 of the Uniform Probate Code (1987). As to the construction of provisions drawn from uniform acts, see Section 2.

Background on Section 17000 of Repealed Code

Section 17000 was added by 1986 Cal.Stat. ch. 820 § 40. Subdivision (a) superseded former Probate Code Section 1123.7 (repealed by 1986 Cal.Stat. ch. 820 § 31). Jurisdiction was in the superior court under former Probate Code Section 1138.3 (repealed by 1986 Cal.Stat. ch. 820 § 31). Subdivision (b) was new. For background on the provisions of this division, see the Comment to this division under the division heading. [20 Cal.L.Rev.Comm.Reports 1001 (1990)].

Cross References

Interest as beneficiary of trust subject to satisfaction of money judgment, see Code of Civil Procedure § 709.010.

§ 17001. Powers of court

In proceedings commenced pursuant to this division, the court is a court of general jurisdiction and has all the powers of the superior court. *(Stats.1990, c. 79 (A.B.759), § 14, operative July 1, 1991. Amended by Stats.1990, c. 710 (S.B.1775), § 44, operative July 1, 1991.)*

Law Revision Commission Comments
1990 Enactment

Section 17001 continues Section 17001 of the repealed Probate Code without change. This section makes clear that the department of the superior court exercising the exclusive jurisdiction to determine internal trust affairs provided by Section 17000(a) has all the powers of the superior court when exercising its general jurisdiction. Hence, while not intending to disrupt the traditional division of business among different departments of the superior court, this section rejects the limitation on the powers of the probate court that has been cited in appellate decisions. See, e.g., Copley v. Copley, 80 Cal.App.3d 97, 106–07, 145 Cal.Rptr. 437 (1978).

1990 Amendment

Section 17001 (enacted as a part of the new Probate Code by 1990 Cal.Stat. ch. 79 § 14) was amended by 1990 Cal.Stat. ch. 710 § 44. The 1990 amendment deletes unnecessary language from which a negative implication could be drawn, i.e., that the court would not have "all the powers of the superior court" when exercising concurrent jurisdiction, as well as exclusive jurisdiction. This amendment is needed to reject dicta in recent cases as to limitations on the power and jurisdiction of the court in proceedings properly commenced under this division. See Estate of Mullins, 206 Cal. App.3d 924, 930–31, 255 Cal.Rptr. 430 (1988); Johnson v. Tate, 215 Cal.App.3d 1282, 1285–87, 264 Cal.Rptr. 68 (1989). This amendment also reaffirms the original intent of this section, along with Sections 17000 and 17004, to eliminate any limitations on the power of the court hearing matters under this division, whether or not it is

called the "probate court," to exercise jurisdiction over all parties constitutionally before it and completely dispose of the dispute. This section, along with Sections 17000 and 17004, is intended to eliminate any notion that the "probate court" is one of limited power or that it cannot dispose of matters properly brought before it, while preserving the power of the superior court in a particular county to organize itself into divisions for the efficient conduct of judicial business. If a court determines that it is not the appropriate forum or division of the court to hear a case, the court should transfer the matter to the appropriate court or division. See Code Civ.Proc. § 396. For background on the 1990 amendment, see Recommendation Relating to Jurisdiction of Superior Court in Trust Matters, 20 Cal.L.Revision Comm'n Reports 2253 (1990). [20 Cal.L.Rev.Comm.Reports 1001 (1990)].

Background on Section 17001 of Repealed Code

Section 17001 was a new provision added by 1986 Cal.Stat. ch. 820 § 40. For background on the provisions of this division, see the Comment to this division under the division heading. [20 Cal.L.Rev.Comm.Reports 1001 (1990)].

§ 17002. Principal place of administration of trust

(a) The principal place of administration of the trust is the usual place where the day-to-day activity of the trust is carried on by the trustee or its representative who is primarily responsible for the administration of the trust.

(b) If the principal place of administration of the trust cannot be determined under subdivision (a), it shall be determined as follows:

(1) If the trust has a single trustee, the principal place of administration of the trust is the trustee's residence or usual place of business.

(2) If the trust has more than one trustee, the principal place of administration of the trust is the residence or usual place of business of any of the cotrustees as agreed upon by them or, if not, the residence or usual place of business of any of the cotrustees. *(Stats.1990, c. 79 (A.B.759), § 14, operative July 1, 1991.)*

Law Revision Commission Comments
1990 Enactment

Section 17002 continues Section 17002 of the repealed Probate Code without change.

Background on Section 17002 of Repealed Code

Section 17002 was added by 1986 Cal.Stat. ch. 820 § 40. The section superseded the second and third sentences of subdivision (a) of former Probate Code Section 1138.3 (repealed by 1986 Cal.Stat. ch. 820 § 31). Subdivision (a) of Section 17002 substituted a criterion of day-to-day activity for the former reference to the location of the day-to-day records of the trust. For background on the provisions of this division, see the Comment to this division under the division heading. [20 Cal.L.Rev.Comm.Reports 1001 (1990)].

§ 17003. Jurisdiction over trustees and beneficiaries

Subject to Section 17004:

(a) By accepting the trusteeship of a trust having its principal place of administration in this state the trustee submits personally to the jurisdiction of the court under this division.

(b) To the extent of their interests in the trust, all beneficiaries of a trust having its principal place of administration in this state are subject to the jurisdiction of the court under this division. *(Stats.1990, c. 79 (A.B.759), § 14, operative July 1, 1991.)*

Law Revision Commission Comments

1990 Enactment

Section 17003 continues Section 17003 of the repealed Probate Code without change. This section is drawn from Section 7–103 of the Uniform Probate Code (1987) and is intended to facilitate the exercise of the court's power under this chapter. As to the construction of provisions drawn from uniform acts, see Section 2. As recognized by the introductory clause, constitutional limitations on assertion of jurisdiction apply to the exercise of jurisdiction under Section 17003. Consequently, appropriate notice must be given to a trustee or beneficiary as a condition of jurisdiction under this section. See, e.g., Mullane v. Central Hanover Bank & Trust Co., 339 U.S. 306 (1950). Section 17003 is not a limitation on the jurisdiction of the court over the trust, trust property, or parties to the trust. See Section 17004 (general basis of jurisdiction). See also Section 15800 (limits on rights of beneficiary of revocable trust).

Background on Section 17003 of Repealed Code

Section 17003 was a new provision added by 1986 Cal.Stat. ch. 820 § 40. For background on the provisions of this division, see the Comment to this division under the division heading. [20 Cal.L.Rev.Comm.Reports 1001 (1990)].

§ 17004. Basis of jurisdiction

The court may exercise jurisdiction in proceedings under this division on any basis permitted by Section 410.10 of the Code of Civil Procedure. *(Stats.1990, c. 79 (A.B.759), § 14, operative July 1, 1991.)*

Law Revision Commission Comments

1990 Enactment

Section 17004 continues Section 17004 of the repealed Probate Code without change.

Section 17004 recognizes that the court, in proceedings relating to internal trust affairs or other purposes described in Section 17000, may exercise jurisdiction on any basis that is not inconsistent with the California or United States Constitutions, as provided in Code of Civil Procedure Section 410.10. See generally Judicial Council Comment to Code Civ.Proc. § 410.10. In addition, Section 17003 codifies a basis of personal jurisdiction derived from concepts of presence in the state and consent to jurisdiction. However, personal jurisdiction over a trustee may be exercised where the trustee is found, regardless of the location of the trust property. See Estate of Knox, 52 Cal.App.2d 338, 348, 126 P.2d 108 (1942). Similarly, jurisdiction may be exercised to determine matters concerning trust property, particularly land, located in California even if the principal place of administration of the trust is not in California. See Restatement (Second) of Conflict of Laws § 276 & comments (1969); 5 A. Scott, The Law of Trusts §§ 644–47, at 4074–83 (3d ed.1967).

A determination that a California court may exercise jurisdiction is not decisive if the exercise would be an undue interference with the jurisdiction of a court of another state which has primary supervision over the administration of the trust. See Estate of Knox, 52 Cal.App.2d 338, 344–48, 126 P.2d 108 (1942); Schuster v. Superior Court, 98 Cal.App. 619, 623–28, 277 P. 509 (1929); Restatement (Second) of Conflict of Laws § 267 & comments (1969). This concept of primary supervision in the context of trust administration is a special application of the doctrine of forum non conveniens, which is recognized generally in Code of Civil Procedure Section 410.30.

Where the court has acquired jurisdiction over parties to a trust, jurisdiction continues over the parties and the subject of the proceeding, notwithstanding the removal from the state of a person or trust property, until the conclusion of the action or proceeding concerning the trust. See Code Civ.Proc. § 410.50(b); cf. Maloney v. Maloney, 67 Cal.App.2d 278, 280, 154 P.2d 426 (1944) (jurisdiction over child custody issue).

Background on Section 17004 of Repealed Code

Section 17004 was a new provision added by 1986 Cal.Stat. ch. 820 § 40. For background on the provisions of this division, see the Comment to this division under the division heading. [20 Cal.L.Rev.Comm.Reports 1001 (1990)].

§ 17005. Venue

(a) The proper county for commencement of a proceeding pursuant to this division is either of the following:

(1) In the case of a living trust, the county where the principal place of administration of the trust is located.

(2) In the case of a testamentary trust, either the county where the decedent's estate is administered or where the principal place of administration of the trust is located.

(b) If a living trust has no trustee, the proper county for commencement of a proceeding for appointing a trustee is the county where the trust property, or some portion of the trust property, is located.

(c) Except as otherwise provided in subdivisions (a) and (b), the proper county for commencement of a proceeding pursuant to this division is determined by the rules applicable to civil actions generally. *(Stats.1990, c. 79 (A.B.759), § 14, operative July 1, 1991.)*

Law Revision Commission Comments

1990 Enactment

Section 17005 continues Section 17005 of the repealed Probate Code without change. See also Section 17002 (principal place of administration of trust).

Subdivision (b) applies only to appointment of a trustee for a living trust that has no trustee. Proceedings to appoint a trustee for a testamentary trust that has no trustee are commenced in the county where the decedent's estate is administered. See subdivision (a)(2).

Subdivision (c) provides venue rules applicable in cases not covered by subdivisions (a) and (b), such as where jurisdiction over a trust, trust property, or parties to a trust is based on a factor other than the presence of the principal place of administration in this state. See Section 17004 (general basis of jurisdiction). Thus, for example, when the principal place of administration of a trust is in another state, but jurisdiction is proper in California, the general rules governing venue apply. See, e.g., Code Civ.Proc. §§ 392 (real property), 395 (county of defendant's residence). This subdivision is drawn from Section 7–204 of the Uniform Probate Code (1987). As to the construction of provisions drawn from uniform acts, see Section 2.

Background on Section 17005 of Repealed Code

Section 17005 was added by 1986 Cal.Stat. ch. 820 § 40. Subdivision (a)(1) restated part of the first sentence of subdivision (a) of former Probate Code Section 1138.3 (repealed by 1986 Cal.Stat. ch. 820 § 31) without substantive change. Subdivision (a)(2) restated former Probate Code Section 1138.3(b) without substantive change and extended the former provision to all testamentary trusts. Subdivision (b) restated part of the first sentence of former Civil Code Section 2289 (repealed by 1986 Cal.Stat. ch. 820 § 7) without substantive change, except that it made clear that it applied only to appointment of a trustee for a living trust that has no trustee. For background on the provisions of this division, see the Comment to this division under the division heading. [20 Cal.L.Rev.Comm.Reports 1001 (1990)].

Cross References

Administration of trust transferred from another jurisdiction, see Probate Code § 17457.

Executor, administrator, guardian, conservator, or trustee in official or representative capacity, venue, see Code of Civil Procedure § 395.1.

Petition for appointment of trustee upon transfer from another jurisdiction, venue, see Probate Code § 17452.

§ 17006. Jury trial

There is no right to a jury trial in proceedings under this division concerning the internal affairs of trusts. *(Stats.1990, c. 79 (A.B.759), § 14, operative July 1, 1991.)*

Law Revision Commission Comments

1990 Enactment

Section 17006 continues Section 17006 of the repealed Probate Code without change. This section codifies the case law rule. See People v. One 1941 Chevrolet Coupe, 37 Cal.2d 283, 286–87, 231 P.2d 832 (1951); C & K Engineering Contractors v. Amber Steel Co., 23 Cal.3d 1, 8, 587 P.2d 1136, 151 Cal.Rptr. 323 (1978); Estate of Beach, 15 Cal.3d 623, 642, 542 P.2d 994, 125 Cal.Rptr. 570 (1975).

Background on Section 17006 of Repealed Code

Section 17006 was a new provision added by 1986 Cal.Stat. ch. 820 § 40. For background on the provisions of this division, see the Comment to this division under the division heading. [20 Cal.L.Rev.Comm.Reports 1001 (1990)].

CHAPTER 2. NOTICE

Application

Application of Division, see Probate Code § 15001.

Cross References

Application of old and new law, see Probate Code § 3.
Common law rules governing trusts, application, see Probate Code § 15002.
Relationships excluded from Code definition of trust, application of this Division, see Probate Code § 15003.

§ 17100. Notice governed by Part 2

Except as otherwise provided in this division, notice in proceedings commenced pursuant to this division, or notice otherwise required by this division, is governed by Part 2 (commencing with Section 1200) of Division 3. *(Stats.1990, c. 79 (A.B.759), § 14, operative July 1, 1991.)*

Law Revision Commission Comments

1990 Enactment

Section 17100 is new. It supersedes Sections 17100–17107 of the repealed Probate Code.

Background on Sections 17100–17107 of Repealed Code

Sections 17100–17107 were added by 1986 Cal.Stat. ch. 820 § 40. [20 Cal.L.Rev.Comm.Reports 1001 (1990)].

§ 17101. Repealed by Stats.1990, c. 79 (A.B.759), § 13, operative July 1, 1991

Law Revision Commission Comments

1990 Repeal

Section 17101 of the repealed Probate Code is omitted from the new Probate Code because it is unnecessary. See Sections 1001(b) (Judicial Council forms), 17100 (general notice provisions apply). [20 Cal.L.Rev.Comm.Reports 1001 (1990)].

§ 17102. Repealed by Stats.1990, c. 710 (S.B.1775), § 45

Law Revision Commission Comments

1990 Enactment and Repeal

Former Section 17102 enacted as a part of the new Probate Code by 1990 Cal.Stat. ch. 79 § 14) was repealed by 1990 Cal.Stat. ch. 710 § 45. The repealed section is generalized in Section 1212 (manner of mailing notice where address is unknown). See Section 17100 (general notice provision apply to Trust Law). For background on this repeal, see Recommendation Relating to Notice in Probate Where Address Unknown, 20 Cal.L. Revision Comm'n Reports 2245 (1990). [20 Cal.L.Rev.Comm.Reports 1001 (1990)].

§§ 17103, 17104. Repealed by Stats.1990, c. 79 (A.B.759), § 13, operative July 1, 1991

Law Revision Commission Comments

1990 Repeal

Section 17103 of the repealed Probate Code is omitted from the new Probate Code because it is unnecessary. See Section 1216(a) (personal delivery instead of mailing). See also 17100 (general notice provisions apply). [20 Cal.L.Rev.Comm.Reports 1001 (1990)].

Section 17104 of the repealed Probate Code is superseded by Section 1260 (proof of giving notice). See also 17100 (general notice provisions apply). [20 Cal.L.Rev.Comm.Reports 1001 (1990)].

§ 17105. Notice to persons interested in trust without court order

A petitioner or other person required to give notice may cause notice to be given to any person interested in the trust without the need for a court order. *(Stats.1990, c. 79 (A.B.759), § 14, operative July 1, 1991.)*

Law Revision Commission Comments

1990 Enactment

Section 17105 continues Section 17105(b) of the repealed Probate Code without change.

Background on Subdivision (b) of Section 17105 of Repealed Code

Section 17105 was added by 1986 Cal.Stat. ch. 820 § 40. Subdivision (b) restated the second sentence of former Probate Code Section 1215.4 (repealed by 1986 Cal.Stat. ch. 820 § 35) without substantive change. For background on the provisions of this division, see the Comment to this division under the division heading. [20 Cal.L.Rev.Comm.Reports 1001 (1990)].

§§ 17106, 17107. Repealed by Stats.1990, c. 79 (A.B.759), § 13, operative July 1, 1991

Section 17106 of the repealed Probate Code is omitted from the new Probate Code because it is unnecessary. See Section 1203 (order shortening time). See also 17100 (general notice provisions apply). [20 Cal.L.Rev.Comm.Reports 1001 (1990)].

Section 17107 of the repealed Probate Code is omitted from the new Probate Code because it is unnecessary. See Section 1045 (continuance and postponement of hearings), 1205 (notice of continued or postponed hearings). See also 17100 (general notice provisions apply). [20 Cal.L.Rev.Comm.Reports 1001 (1990)].

CHAPTER 3. PROCEEDINGS CONCERNING TRUSTS

Application

Application of Division, see Probate Code § 15001.

Cross References

Application of old and new law, see Probate Code § 3.
Common law rules governing trusts, application, see Probate Code § 15002.
Fee for filing petition and opposition papers concerning internal affairs of certain trusts or first accounts of trustees of certain testamentary trusts, see Government Code § 70652.
Relationships excluded from Code definition of trust, application of this Division, see Probate Code § 15003.
Trust for care of animals, accountings and beneficiaries, see Probate Code § 15212.

§ 17200. Internal affairs; existence of trust; petition by trustee or beneficiary; purposes

(a) Except as provided in Section 15800, a trustee or beneficiary of a trust may petition the court under this chapter concerning the internal affairs of the trust or to determine the existence of the trust.

(b) Proceedings concerning the internal affairs of a trust include, but are not limited to, proceedings for any of the following purposes:

(1) Determining questions of construction of a trust instrument.

(2) Determining the existence or nonexistence of any immunity, power, privilege, duty, or right.

(3) Determining the validity of a trust provision.

(4) Ascertaining beneficiaries and determining to whom property shall pass or be delivered upon final or partial termination of the trust, to the extent the determination is not made by the trust instrument.

(5) Settling the accounts and passing upon the acts of the trustee, including the exercise of discretionary powers.

(6) Instructing the trustee.

(7) Compelling the trustee to do any of the following:

(A) Provide a copy of the terms of the trust.

(B) Provide information about the trust under Section 16061 if the trustee has failed to provide the requested information within 60 days after the beneficiary's reasonable written request, and the beneficiary has not received the requested information from the trustee within the six months preceding the request.

(C) Account to the beneficiary, subject to the provisions of Section 16064, if the trustee has failed to submit a requested account within 60 days after written request of the beneficiary and no account has been made within six months preceding the request.

(8) Granting powers to the trustee.

(9) Fixing or allowing payment of the trustee's compensation or reviewing the reasonableness of the trustee's compensation.

(10) Appointing or removing a trustee.

(11) Accepting the resignation of a trustee.

(12) Compelling redress of a breach of the trust by any available remedy.

(13) Approving or directing the modification or termination of the trust.

(14) Approving or directing the combination or division of trusts.

(15) Amending or conforming the trust instrument in the manner required to qualify a decedent's estate for the charitable estate tax deduction under federal law, including the addition of mandatory governing instrument requirements for a charitable remainder trust as required by final regulations and rulings of the United States Internal Revenue Service.

(16) Authorizing or directing transfer of a trust or trust property to or from another jurisdiction.

(17) Directing transfer of a testamentary trust subject to continuing court jurisdiction from one county to another.

(18) Approving removal of a testamentary trust from continuing court jurisdiction.

(19) Reforming or excusing compliance with the governing instrument of an organization pursuant to Section 16105.

(20) Determining the liability of the trust for any debts of a deceased settlor. However, nothing in this paragraph shall provide standing to bring an action concerning the internal affairs of the trust to a person whose only claim to the assets of the decedent is as a creditor.

(21) Determining petitions filed pursuant to Section 15687 and reviewing the reasonableness of compensation for legal

services authorized under that section. In determining the reasonableness of compensation under this paragraph, the court may consider, together with all other relevant circumstances, whether prior approval was obtained pursuant to Section 15687.

(22) If a member of the State Bar of California has transferred the economic interest of his or her practice to a trustee and if the member is a deceased member under Section 9764, a petition may be brought to appoint a practice administrator. The procedures, including, but not limited to, notice requirements, that apply to the appointment of a practice administrator for a deceased member shall apply to the petition brought under this section.

(23) If a member of the State Bar of California has transferred the economic interest of his or her practice to a trustee and if the member is a disabled member under Section 2468, a petition may be brought to appoint a practice administrator. The procedures, including, but not limited to, notice requirements, that apply to the appointment of a practice administrator for a disabled member shall apply to the petition brought under this section.

(c) The court may, on its own motion, set and give notice of an order to show cause why a trustee who is a professional fiduciary, and who is required to be licensed under Chapter 6 (commencing with Section 6500) of Division 3 of the Business and Professions Code, should not be removed for failing to hold a valid, unexpired, unsuspended license. *(Stats.1990, c. 79 (A.B.759), § 14, operative July 1, 1991. Amended by Stats.1991, c. 992 (S.B.727), § 1; Stats.1993, c. 293 (A.B.21), § 7; Stats.1996, c. 862 (A.B.2751), § 41; Stats.1997, c. 724 (A.B.1172), § 27; Stats.1998, c. 682 (A.B.2069), § 13; Stats. 1999, c. 175 (A.B.239), § 5; Stats.2003, c. 629 (S.B.294), § 8; Stats.2010, c. 621 (S.B.202), § 11.)*

Law Revision Commission Comments
1990 Enactment

Section 17200 continues Section 17200 of the repealed Probate Code with the revision of subdivision (b)(9) to make clear that the reasonableness of the trustee's compensation is subject to review on petition under this section. This revision is a clarification of prior law and not a substantive change. For background on this revision, see Recommendation Relating to Trustees' Fees, 20 Cal.L. Revision Comm'n Reports 185 (1990).

The introductory clause of subdivision (a) has the effect of giving the right to petition concerning the internal affairs of a revocable living trust to the settlor (or other person holding the power to revoke) instead of the beneficiaries during the time that the settlor (or other person holding the power to revoke) is competent. See Section 15800 and the Comment thereto.

The list of grounds for a petition concerning the internal affairs of a trust under subdivision (b) is not exclusive and is not intended to preclude a petition for any other purpose that can be characterized as an internal affair of the trust. Paragraphs (1) and (2) of subdivision (b) are drawn from Section 7–201(a) of the Uniform Probate Code (1987). As to the construction of provisions drawn from uniform acts, see Section 2.

Various provisions elsewhere in this division relate to proceedings under this chapter. For limitations on the right of a beneficiary to compel the trustee to account or report under paragraph (7), see Sections 15800 and 16060–16064. As to granting powers to the trustee under paragraph (8), see Section 16201. As to the trustee's compensation under paragraph (9), see Sections 15680–15683; see also Section 15645 (costs and attorney's fees in proceedings for

transfer of trust to successor trust company). As to breaches of trust involved in paragraph (12), see Sections 16400–16462. As to modification and termination of trusts under paragraph (13), see Sections 15400–15410. As to combining or dividing trusts under paragraph (14), see Sections 15411 and 15412. As to transfers of trusts under paragraph (16), see Sections 17400–17405 and 17450– 17457. As to transfers of certain testamentary trusts within California under paragraph (17), see Section 17304. As to removal of certain testamentary trusts from continuing court jurisdiction under paragraph (18), see Section 17352.

The procedure provided in this chapter is available to determine matters concerning the administration of trusts notwithstanding a purported limitation or exclusion in the trust instrument. The provision in subdivision (b) of former Section 1138.1 of the repealed Probate Code (repealed by 1986 Cal.Stat. ch. 820 § 31) to the effect that the trust could restrict the availability of remedies is not continued.

See also Sections 24 ("beneficiary" defined), 82 ("trust" defined), 17005 (venue).

Background on Section 17200 of Repealed Code

Section 17200 was added by 1986 Cal.Stat. ch. 820 § 40. The section restated the substance of subdivision (a) of former Probate Code Section 1138.1 and superseded parts of former Probate Code Section 1120 (provisions repealed by 1986 Cal.Stat. ch. 820 § 31). The reference to determining the existence of a trust in subdivision (a) was new. Subdivision (a) also restated without substantive change part of former Probate Code Section 1139.1 and the first sentence of former Probate Code Section 1139.2 (petition for transfer of trust to another jurisdiction) and part of former Probate Code Section 1139.12 (petition for transfer to California) (provisions repealed by 1986 Cal.Stat. ch. 820 § 31). The introductory clause of subdivision (a) (referring to Section 15800) was new.

Paragraphs (1), (2), and (3) of subdivision (b) were new. Paragraph (5) restated parts of subdivisions (b) and (d) of former Civil Code Section 2269 (repealed by 1986 Cal.Stat. ch. 820 § 7) (review of exercise of discretionary powers) without substantive change. See Sections 16080–16081 (duties with regard to discretionary powers). Paragraph (9) superseded the last sentence of former Civil Code Section 2274 (repealed by 1986 Cal.Stat. ch. 820 § 7).

For background on the provisions of this division, see the Comment to this division under the division heading. [20 Cal.L.Rev.Comm.Reports 1001 (1990)].

Cross References

Charitable trusts, enforcement by Attorney General, see Government Code § 12598.

Delayed distribution of decedent's property or death benefits, petition requesting distribution, see Probate Code § 249.8.

Fee for filing petition and opposition papers concerning internal affairs of certain trusts or first accounts of trustees of certain testamentary trusts, see Government Code § 70652.

Practice administrator, powers, deceased or disabled members, see Business and Professions Code § 6185.

Trust for care of animals, accountings and beneficiaries, see Probate Code § 15212.

Trust law and judicial proceedings, beneficiaries and interested persons, special notice, see Probate Code § 17204.

Trustee's standard of care, see Probate Code § 16040.

§ 17200.1. Transfer of property of trust; conduct of proceedings

All proceedings concerning the transfer of property of the trust shall be conducted pursuant to the provisions of Part 19 (commencing with Section 850) of Division 2. *(Added by Stats.2001, c. 49 (S.B.669), § 7.)*

§ 17200.2. Repealed by Stats.2001, c. 49 (S.B.669), § 8

§ 17201. Filing petition; commencement of proceeding

A proceeding under this chapter is commenced by filing a petition stating facts showing that the petition is authorized under this chapter. The petition shall also state the grounds of the petition and the names and addresses of each person entitled to notice of the petition. *(Stats.1990, c. 79 (A.B.759), § 14, operative July 1, 1991. Amended by Stats.1996, c. 862 (A.B.2751), § 44.)*

Law Revision Commission Comments

1990 Enactment

Section 17201 continues subdivision (a) of Section 17201 of the repealed Probate Code without change, except that the reference to verification is omitted as unnecessary. See Section 1021 (verification required). Subdivision (b) of repealed Section 17201 is not continued because this matter is governed by Section 1041 (clerk to set matter for hearing).

Background on Section 17201 of Repealed Code

Section 17201 was added by 1986 Cal.Stat. ch. 820 § 40. Subdivision (a) restated the first sentence of former Probate Code Section 1138.4 (repealed by 1986 Cal.Stat. ch. 820 § 31), except for the former provision relating to authorization by the terms of the trust. The provision of Section 17201 relating to the grounds of the petition superseded part of former Probate Code Section 1138.7 (repealed by 1986 Cal.Stat. ch. 820 § 31). Subdivision (a) also superseded parts of former Probate Code Sections 1123.5, 1123.6, 1128, 1139.2, and 1139.14 (provisions repealed by 1986 Cal.Stat. ch. 820 § 31). Subdivision (b) restated parts of former Probate Code Sections 1120(b), 1120.1a(d), 1123.5, 1125.1, 1129, 1138.6(a), 1139.3, and 1139.15 (provisions repealed by 1986 Cal.Stat. ch. 820 § 31) without substantive change. For background on the provisions of this division, see the Comment to this division under the division heading. [20 Cal.L.Rev.Comm.Reports 1001 (1990)].

§ 17202. Dismissal of petition

The court may dismiss a petition if it appears that the proceeding is not reasonably necessary for the protection of the interests of the trustee or beneficiary. *(Stats.1990, c. 79 (A.B.759), § 14, operative July 1, 1991.)*

Law Revision Commission Comments

1990 Enactment

Section 17202 continues Section 17202 of the repealed Probate Code without change. See also Section 17200(a) (who may petition).

Background on Section 17202 of Repealed Code

Section 17202 was added by 1986 Cal.Stat. ch. 820 § 40. The section restated subdivision (a) of former Probate Code Section 1138.5 (repealed by 1986 Cal.Stat. ch. 820 § 31) without substantive change. For background on the provisions of this division, see the Comment to this division under the division heading. [20 Cal.L.Rev.Comm.Reports 1001 (1990)].

§ 17203. Notice

(a) At least 30 days before the time set for the hearing on the petition, the petitioner shall cause notice of hearing to be mailed to all of the following persons:

(1) All trustees.

(2) All beneficiaries, subject to Chapter 2 (commencing with Section 15800) of Part 3.

(3) The Attorney General, if the petition relates to a charitable trust subject to the jurisdiction of the Attorney General.

(b) At least 30 days before the time set for hearing on the petition, the petitioner shall cause notice of the hearing and a copy of the petition to be served in the manner provided in Chapter 4 (commencing with Section 413.10) of Title 5 of Part 2 of the Code of Civil Procedure on any person, other than a trustee or beneficiary, whose right, title, or interest would be affected by the petition and who does not receive notice pursuant to subdivision (a). The court may not shorten the time for giving notice under this subdivision.

(c) If a person to whom notice otherwise would be given has been deceased for at least 40 days, and no personal representative has been appointed for the estate of that person, and the deceased person's right, title, or interest has not passed to any other person pursuant to Division 8 (commencing with Section 13000) or otherwise, notice may instead be given to the following persons:

(1) Each heir and devisee of the decedent, and all persons named as executors of the will of the decedent, so far as known to the petitioner.

(2) Each person serving as guardian or conservator of the decedent at the time of the decedent's death, so far as known to the petitioner. *(Stats.1990, c. 79 (A.B.759), § 14, operative July 1, 1991. Amended by Stats.1992, c. 871 (A.B.2975), § 20; Stats.1994, c. 806 (A.B.3686), § 39; Stats.1996, c. 862 (A.B.2751), § 45; Stats.1997, c. 724 (A.B.1172), § 28.)*

Law Revision Commission Comments

1990 Enactment

Section 17203 continues Section 17203 of the repealed Probate Code without change, except that the reference to notice to persons who are not petitioners is omitted. This matter is governed by Section 1201 (notice not required to person giving notice). See also Sections 17100–17105 (manner of notice).

Subdivision (b) recognizes that there are other rules governing which beneficiaries are entitled to notice. Under Section 15802, beneficiaries of revocable trusts are not entitled to notice during the time that the trust may be revoked, nor are such beneficiaries entitled to get notice even if they have requested special notice pursuant to Section 17204. Under Section 15804, the need to give notice is limited in the case of certain beneficiaries having future interests, but this limitation does not apply to beneficiaries who have requested special notice. See Section 15804(c)(1). These rules limit the requirement of notice whether the interest involved is that of a beneficiary of a private trust or that of a beneficiary of a charitable trust subject to jurisdiction of the Attorney General.

Subdivision (c) reflects the notice requirements of Government Code Section 12591. See also Section 24 ("beneficiary" defined).

Background on Section 17203 of Repealed Code

Section 17203 was added by 1986 Cal.Stat. ch. 820 § 40. The introductory paragraph and subdivisions (a) and (b) restated the first part of the second paragraph of subdivision (a) of former Probate Code Section 1138.6 (repealed by 1986 Cal.Stat. ch. 820 § 31) without substantive change. Subdivision (c) superseded part of subdivision (f) of former Probate Code Section 1120.1a, subdivision (d) of former Probate Code Section 1138.6, and the third sentence of former Probate Code Section 1139.3 (provisions repealed by 1986 Cal.Stat. ch. 820 § 31). Section 17203 also superseded parts of former Probate Code Section 1125.1 and 1126 (provisions repealed by 1986 Cal.Stat. ch. 820 § 31). For background on the provisions of this division, see the Comment to this division under the division heading. [20 Cal.L.Rev.Comm.Reports 1001 (1990)].

Cross References

Attorney General, generally, see Government Code § 12500 et seq. Sufficient notice in future interest cases, see Probate Code § 15804. Trust law and judicial proceedings, beneficiaries and interested persons, special notice, see Probate Code § 17204.

§ 17204. Beneficiaries' interested persons; verified statements; definitions; request for special notice

(a) If proceedings involving a trust are pending, a beneficiary of the trust may, in person or by attorney, file with the court clerk where the proceedings are pending a written request stating that the beneficiary desires special notice of the filing of petitions in the proceeding relating to any or all of the purposes described in Section 17200 and giving an address for receiving notice by mail. A copy of the request shall be personally delivered or mailed to the trustee or the trustee's attorney. If personally delivered, the request is effective when it is delivered. If mailed, the request is effective when it is received. When the original of the request is filed with the court clerk, it shall be accompanied by a written admission or proof of service. A request for special notice may be modified or withdrawn in the same manner as provided for the making of the initial request.

(b)(1) An interested person may request special notice in the same manner as a beneficiary under subdivision (a), for the purpose set forth in paragraph (9) of subdivision (b) of Section 17200. The request for special notice shall be accompanied by a verified statement of the person's interest.

(2) For purposes set forth in paragraphs (2), (4) to (6), inclusive, (8), (12), (16), (20), and (21) of subdivision (b) of Section 17200, an interested person may petition the court for an order for special notice of proceedings involving a trust. The petition shall include a verified statement of the creditor's interest and may be served on the trustee or the trustee's attorney by personal delivery or in the manner required by Section 1215. The petition may be made by ex parte application.

(3) For purposes of this subdivision, an "interested person" means only a creditor of a trust or, if the trust has become irrevocable upon the death of a trustor, a creditor of the trustor.

(4) This section does not confer standing on an interested person if standing does not otherwise exist.

(c) Except as provided in subdivision (d), after serving and filing a request and proof of service pursuant to subdivision (a) or paragraph (1) of subdivision (b), the beneficiary or the interested person is entitled to notice pursuant to Section 17203. If the petition of an interested person filed pursuant to paragraph (2) of subdivision (b) is granted by the court, the interested person is entitled to notice pursuant to Section 17203.

(d) A request for special notice made by a beneficiary whose right to notice is restricted by Section 15802 is not effective. *(Stats.1990, c. 79 (A.B.759), § 14, operative July 1, 1991. Amended by Stats.2004, c. 334 (A.B.2872), § 1.)*

Law Revision Commission Comments

1990 Enactment

Section 17204 restates Section 17204 of the repealed Probate Code without substantive change. The last five sentences are added to subdivision (a) for consistency with the general provisions relating to requests for special notice in Section 1250(e)–(f). Subdivision (c) makes clear that the restrictions on rights of beneficiaries of revocable trusts apply to the right to request special notice. Section 15804 limits the need to give notice to certain beneficiaries with future interests, but does not restrict the right of such beneficiaries to request special notice. See Section 15804(c)(1). See also Sections 1260–1265 (proof of notice).

Background on Section 17204 of Repealed Code

Section 17204 was added by 1986 Cal.Stat. ch. 820 § 40. The section superseded the former provisions relating to requests for special notice with regard to testamentary trusts in former Probate Code Sections 1120.5 (repealed by 1986 Cal.Stat. ch. 820 § 31) and Sections 1202 and 1202.5 (provisions repealed by 1987 Cal.Stat. ch. 923 § 59) and the former provisions relating to trusts in former Probate Code Sections 1200 and 1200.5 (provisions repealed by 1987 Cal.Stat. ch. 923 § 59). [20 Cal.L.Rev.Comm.Reports 1001 (1990)].

Cross References

Request for special notice pursuant to this section, superior court filing fees, see Government Code § 70662.

§ 17205. Request for copy of petition

If a trustee or beneficiary has served and filed either a notice of appearance, in person or by counsel, directed to the petitioner or the petitioner's counsel in connection with a particular petition and proceeding or a written request for a copy of the petition, and has given an address to which notice or a copy of the petition may be mailed or delivered, the petitioner shall cause a copy of the petition to be mailed to that person within five days after service of the notice of appearance or receipt of the request. *(Stats.1990, c. 79 (A.B.759), § 14, operative July 1, 1991.)*

Law Revision Commission Comments

1990 Enactment

Section 17205 continues Section 17205 of the repealed Probate Code without change. This section provides the manner of determining to whom a copy of a petition in a particular proceeding should be sent.

Background on Section 17205 of Repealed Code

Section 17205 was added by 1986 Cal.Stat. ch. 820 § 40. The section restated the third paragraph of subdivision (a) of former Probate Code Section 1138.6 (repealed by 1986 Cal.Stat. ch. 820 § 31) without substantive change. For background on the provisions of this division, see the Comment to this division under the division heading. [20 Cal.L.Rev.Comm.Reports 1001 (1990)].

§ 17206. Power of court

The court in its discretion may make any orders and take any other action necessary or proper to dispose of the matters presented by the petition, including appointment of a temporary trustee to administer the trust in whole or in part. *(Stats.1990, c. 79 (A.B.759), § 14, operative July 1, 1991.)*

Law Revision Commission Comments
1990 Enactment

Section 17206 continues Section 17206 of the repealed Probate Code without change.

Background on Section 17206 of Repealed Code

Section 17206 was added by 1986 Cal.Stat. ch. 820 § 40. The first part of the section continued former Probate Code Section 1138.2 and part of former Probate Code Section 1121 (provisions repealed by 1986 Cal.Stat. ch. 820 § 31) without substantive change. This section also superseded the last clause of subdivision (b) of former Probate Code Section 1120.6 (repealed by 1986 Cal.Stat. ch. 820 § 31). The authority to appoint a temporary trustee was new. For background on the provisions of this division, see the Comment to this division under the division heading. [20 Cal.L.Rev.Comm.Reports 1001 (1990)].

§ 17207. Repealed by Stats.1997, c. 724 (A.B.1172), § 29

§ 17208. Repealed by Stats.1988, c. 1199, § 107.5, operative July 1, 1989

Law Revision Commission Comments
1988 Repeal

Section 17208 is restated without substantive change and generalized in Section 1003 which applies to the entire Probate Code [19 Cal.L.Rev.Comm. Reports 1098 (1988)].

§ 17209. Administration of trusts; judicial intervention intermittent

The administration of trusts is intended to proceed expeditiously and free of judicial intervention, subject to the jurisdiction of the court. *(Stats.1990, c. 79 (A.B.759), § 14, operative July 1, 1991.)*

Law Revision Commission Comments
1990 Enactment

Section 17209 continues Section 17209 of the repealed Probate Code without change.

Background on Section 17209 of Repealed Code

Section 17209 was added by 1986 Cal.Stat. ch. 820 § 40. The section restated former Probate Code Section 1138.12 (repealed by 1986 Cal.Stat. ch. 820 § 31) without substantive change. For background on the provisions of this division, see the Comment to this division under the division heading. [20 Cal.L.Rev.Comm.Reports 1001 (1990)].

§ 17210. Charitable trusts; petition by Attorney General

In a case involving a charitable trust subject to the jurisdiction of the Attorney General, the Attorney General may petition under this chapter. *(Stats.1990, c. 79 (A.B.759), § 14, operative July 1, 1991.)*

Law Revision Commission Comments
1990 Enactment

Section 17210 continues Section 17210 of the repealed Probate Code without change. This section codifies the general rule that the Attorney General stands in the place of the beneficiaries of a charitable trust for purposes of enforcement of the trust. See Section 24 ("beneficiary" defined to include any person entitled to enforce the trust in the case of a charitable trust); see, e.g., People v. Cogswell, 113 Cal. 129, 136, 45 P. 270 (1896); Estate of Schloss, 56 Cal.2d 248, 257, 363 P.2d 875, 14 Cal.Rptr. 643 (1961); see also Restatement (Second) of Trusts § 391 (1957).

Background on Section 17210 of Repealed Code

Section 17210 was a new provision added by 1986 Cal.Stat. ch. 820 § 40. For background on the provisions of this division, see the Comment to this division under the division heading. [20 Cal.L.Rev.Comm.Reports 1001 (1990)].

Cross References

Attorney General, generally, see Government Code § 12500 et seq.
Charitable trusts, enforcement by Attorney General, see Government Code § 12598.

§ 17211. Contests of accounts and opposition to contests without reasonable cause or in bad faith; payment of costs and expenses; personal liability

(a) If a beneficiary contests the trustee's account and the court determines that the contest was without reasonable cause and in bad faith, the court may award against the contestant the compensation and costs of the trustee and other expenses and costs of litigation, including attorney's fees, incurred to defend the account. The amount awarded shall be a charge against any interest of the beneficiary in the trust. The contestant shall be personally liable for any amount that remains unsatisfied.

(b) If a beneficiary contests the trustee's account and the court determines that the trustee's opposition to the contest was without reasonable cause and in bad faith, the court may award the contestant the costs of the contestant and other expenses and costs of litigation, including attorney's fees, incurred to contest the account. The amount awarded shall be a charge against the compensation or other interest of the trustee in the trust. The trustee shall be personally liable and on the bond, if any, for any amount that remains unsatisfied. *(Added by Stats.1996, c. 563 (S.B.392), § 31.)*

CHAPTER 4. TESTAMENTARY TRUSTS SUBJECT TO CONTINUING COURT JURISDICTION

Application

Application of Division, see Probate Code § 15001.

Cross References

Common law rules governing trusts, application, see Probate Code § 15002.
Fees for filing papers in probate proceedings, see Government Code § 70650.
Relationships excluded from Code definition of trust, application of this Division, see Probate Code § 15003.
Uniform filing fees, first account of a trustee of a testamentary trust subject to provisions of this Chapter, see Government Code § 70652.

ARTICLE 1. ADMINISTRATION OF TESTAMENTARY TRUSTS SUBJECT TO CONTINUING COURT JURISDICTION

Application

Application of Division, see Probate Code § 15001.

Cross References

Application of old and new law, see Probate Code § 3.
Common law rules governing trusts, application, see Probate Code § 15002.
Fee for filing petition and opposition papers concerning internal affairs of certain trusts or first accounts of trustees of certain testamentary trusts, see Government Code § 70652.
Filing fees for first account of a testamentary trustee of a trust subject to continuing jurisdiction of court under this Chapter, see Government Code § 70650.
Relationships excluded from Code definition of trust, application of this Division, see Probate Code § 15003.

§ 17300. Application of article

This article applies only to the following:

(a) A trust created by a will executed before July 1, 1977, and not incorporated by reference in a will on or after July 1, 1977.

(b) A trust created by a will which provides that the trust is subject to the continuing jurisdiction of the superior court. *(Stats.1990, c. 79 (A.B.759), § 14, operative July 1, 1991.)*

Law Revision Commission Comments

1990 Enactment

Section 17300 continues Section 17300 of the repealed Probate Code without change. The effect of this section is to limit the application of provisions for continuing jurisdiction of the court to two classes of trusts: (1) trusts created by a will executed before July 1, 1977, when trusts were no longer required to be subject to continuing jurisdiction (see 1976 Cal.Stat. ch. 860 § 3), and not incorporated by reference thereafter, and (2) trusts that are specifically made subject to the continuing jurisdiction of the court by a provision in the trust instrument. A trust created by a will executed before July 1, 1977, which is incorporated by reference in a will thereafter, but that contains a provision making it subject to the continuing jurisdiction of the court, falls into the second class. See also Section 6130 (incorporation by reference in a will).

Background on Section 17300 of Repealed Code

Section 17300 was added by 1986 Cal.Stat. ch. 820 § 40. The section restated without substantive change a part of subdivision (a) of former Probate Code Section 1120, and the exception to former Section 1120 provided in the first sentence of subdivision (d) of former Probate Code Section 1120.1a (provisions repealed by 1986 Cal.Stat. ch. 820 § 31). For background on the provisions of this division, see the Comment to this division under the division heading. [20 Cal.L.Rev.Comm.Reports 1001 (1990)].

Cross References

Fee for filing papers in probate proceedings, see Government Code § 70650.
Fee for filing petition and opposition papers concerning internal affairs of certain trusts or first accounts of trustees of certain testamentary trusts, see Government Code § 70652.

§ 17301. Continuing trust; retention of jurisdiction

If a trust described in Section 17300 continues after distribution of the decedent's estate, the court in which the decedent's estate was administered retains jurisdiction over the trust for any of the purposes specified in Section 17200. *(Stats.1990, c. 79 (A.B.759), § 14, operative July 1, 1991.)*

Law Revision Commission Comments

1990 Enactment

Section 17301 continues Section 17301 of the repealed Probate Code without change.

Background on Section 17301 of Repealed Code

Section 17301 was added by 1986 Cal.Stat. ch. 820 § 40. The section preserved the continuing jurisdiction over testamentary trusts of the superior court where the decedent's estate was administered which was provided in subdivision (b) of former Probate Code Section 1120 (repealed by 1986 Cal.Stat. ch. 820 § 31). The incorporation of the grounds for a petition under Section 17200 continued the various grounds for invoking the court's continuing jurisdiction provided in subdivision (b) of former Probate Code Section 1120. For background on the provisions of this division, see the Comment to this division under the division heading. [20 Cal.L.Rev.Comm.Reports 1001 (1990)].

§ 17302. Application of law

Except as otherwise provided in this article, proceedings relating to trusts under continuing court jurisdiction are governed by this part. *(Stats.1990, c. 79 (A.B.759), § 14, operative July 1, 1991.)*

Law Revision Commission Comments

1990 Enactment

Section 17302 continues Section 17302 of the repealed Probate Code without change. This section makes clear that the general procedures governing judicial proceedings relating to trusts apply to proceedings involving trusts that remain subject to continuing court jurisdiction. See Sections 17000–17210. This incorporation of the general provisions continues the substance of much of the law relating to trusts subject to continuing court jurisdiction because the general procedures are drawn in part from former Probate Code Section 1120 et seq. (provisions repealed by 1986 Cal.Stat. ch. 820, § 31). See the Comments to Sections 17000–17210. This article has the effect of making inapplicable the alternative venue over testamentary trusts provided in Section 17005. The other distinction between proceedings under this article and those under Section 17200 et seq. is that no filing fee is required when a petition relating to an account is filed under the continuing jurisdiction provided in this article. See Gov't Code § 26827.4(b). In other respects, the procedures are the same.

Background on Section 17302 of Repealed Code

Section 17302 was a new provision added by 1986 Cal.Stat. ch. 820 § 40. For background on the provisions of this division, see the Comment to this division under the division heading. [20 Cal.L.Rev.Comm.Reports 1001 (1990)].

§ 17303. Removal from continuing jurisdiction

This article does not apply to a trust described in Section 17300 that has been removed from continuing court jurisdiction. *(Stats.1990, c. 79 (A.B.759), § 14, operative July 1, 1991.)*

1990 Enactment

Section 17303 continues Section 17303 of the repealed Probate Code without change. This section makes clear the relation between this article and Article 2 (commencing with Section 17350). After a trust is removed from continuing court jurisdiction, the general provisions of this part apply to the trust.

Background on Section 17303 of Repealed Code

Section 17303 was a new provision added by 1986 Cal.Stat. ch. 820 § 40. For background on the provisions of this division, see the Comment to this division under the division heading. [20 Cal.L.Rev.Comm.Reports 1001 (1990)].

§ 17304. Transfer of jurisdiction

(a) At any time after final distribution of the decedent's estate, a trust described in Section 17300 may be transferred to a different county in this state as provided in this section.

(b) The petition for transfer shall set forth all of the following:

(1) The name of the county to which jurisdiction over the trust is sought to be transferred.

(2) The names, ages, and places of residence of the trustees and all beneficiaries of the trust, so far as known to the petitioner.

(3) A brief description of the character, condition, value, and location of property of the trust.

(4) A brief statement of the reasons for transfer.

(c) If, after hearing, it appears to the court that the transfer of jurisdiction to the county designated in the petition or to any other county in this state will be in the best interests of the estate, or that economical and convenient administration of the trust will be facilitated by the transfer, the court shall make an order transferring jurisdiction over the trust. Upon such order, the court clerk shall certify a copy of the order of transfer to the clerk of the court to which jurisdiction is transferred, together with copies of the instrument creating the trust, the decree of distribution, and any other documents or matters of record the court determines by order to be necessary to define the powers and duties of the trustee, or otherwise to be necessary in connection with further administration of the trust.

(d) The court to which jurisdiction is transferred may from time to time require by order the filing of certified copies of additional papers or matters of record from the court in which the decedent's estate was administered as are required.

(e) Upon the filing of a certified copy of the order of transfer, together with supporting documents, the court to which jurisdiction is transferred has the same jurisdiction over the trust as the court in which the decedent's estate was administered but for the transfer. *(Stats.1990, c. 79 (A.B. 759), § 14, operative July 1, 1991.)*

1990 Enactment

Section 17304 continues Section 17304 of the repealed Probate Code without change. For general provisions relating to petitions and other papers, see Sections 1020–1023, 17201; see also Sections 1021 (petition to be verified), 1041 (clerk to set petition for hearing). For general provisions relating to notice of hearing, see Sections 1200–1221, 15802, 17100–17105, 17203–17205; see also Sections 1260–1265 (proof of giving notice). For general provisions relating to hearings and orders, see Sections 1040–1050, 17000–17006, 17201–17202, 17206–17207.

Background on Section 17304 of Repealed Code

Section 17304 was added by 1986 Cal.Stat. ch. 820 § 40. The section restated the transfer provisions of former Probate Code Sections 1128 and 1129 (provisions repealed by 1986 Cal.Stat. ch. 820 § 31). Subdivision (a) continued the authority provided by the first sentence of former Probate Code Section 1128. Subdivision (b) restated the contents of the petition set forth in former Probate Code Section 1128 without substantive change. Subdivision (c) restated the fourth and fifth sentences of the first paragraph of former Probate Code Section 1129 without substantive change. Subdivision (d) continued the last sentence of the first paragraph of former Probate Code Section 1129 without substantive change. Subdivision (e) continued the second paragraph of former Probate Code Section 1129 without substantive change. For background on the provisions of this division, see the Comment to this division under the division heading. [20 Cal.L.Rev.Comm.Reports 1001 (1990)].

Cross References

Court order, transfer of place of administration or assets to another jurisdiction outside state, see Probate Code § 17401.

Transfer of proceedings in probate, see Probate Code § 7070.

ARTICLE 2. REMOVAL OF TRUSTS FROM CONTINUING COURT JURISDICTION

Application

Application of Division, see Probate Code § 15001.

Cross References

Application of old and new law, see Probate Code § 3.

Common law rules governing trusts, application, see Probate Code § 15002.

Relationships excluded from Code definition of trust, application of this Division, see Probate Code § 15003.

Trustee of trust created before July 1, 1987, duty to account if trust removed from continuing court jurisdiction, see Probate Code § 16062.

§ 17350. Application of article

This article applies only to trusts created by will executed before July 1, 1977, and not incorporated by reference in a will on or after July 1, 1977. *(Stats.1990, c. 79 (A.B.759), § 14, operative July 1, 1991.)*

1990 Enactment

Section 17350 continues Section 17350 of the repealed Probate Code without change. See also Section 6130 (incorporation by reference in wills).

Background on Section 17350 of Repealed Code

Section 17350 was added by 1986 Cal.Stat. ch. 820 § 40. The section restated the first sentence of former Probate Code Section

1120.1a (repealed by 1986 Cal.Stat. ch. 820 § 31) without substantive change insofar as it provided an operative date for provisions relating to removal of trusts from continuing court jurisdiction. For background on the provisions of this division, see the Comment to this division under the division heading. [20 Cal.L.Rev.Comm.Reports 1001 (1990)].

§ 17351. Trust companies; removal of trust from continuing jurisdiction

(a) If any of the trustees of a trust described in Section 17350 is a trust company, the trust shall be removed from continuing court jurisdiction as provided in this section. Within six months after the initial funding of the trust, the trustee shall give a notice of removal of the trust from continuing court jurisdiction to each beneficiary. Notice of removal shall be sent by registered or certified mail or by first-class mail, but notice sent by first-class mail is effective only if an acknowledgment of receipt of notice is signed by the beneficiary and returned to the trustee.

(b) The notice of removal of the trust from continuing court jurisdiction shall contain the following:

(1) A statement that as of January 1, 1983, the law was changed to remove the necessity for continuing court jurisdiction over the trust.

(2) A statement that Section 17200 of the Probate Code gives any beneficiary the right to petition a court to determine important matters relating to the administration of the trust.

(3) A copy of the text of Sections 17200 and 17201.

(4) A statement that each income beneficiary, as defined in Section 16325, is entitled to an annual statement of the principal and income receipts and disbursements of the trust and that any other beneficiary is entitled to such information upon written request to the trustee.

(5) The name and location of the court in the county in which it is appropriate to file a petition pursuant to Section 17200, the name and location of the court that had jurisdiction over the administration of the decedent's estate, and a statement that it is appropriate to file a petition pursuant to Section 17200 with either court.

(c) The trustee shall file with the court that had jurisdiction over the administration of the decedent's estate proof of giving notice under this section within seven months after the initial funding of the trust. *(Stats.1990, c. 79 (A.B.759), § 14, operative July 1, 1991. Amended by Stats.1999, c. 145 (A.B.846), § 6.)*

Law Revision Commission Comments

1990 Enactment

Section 17351 continues Section 17351 of the repealed Probate Code without change. See Sections 1215 (notice sent to person's address), 1216 (personal delivery instead of mailing), 1260–1265 (proof of giving notice); see also Sections 24 ("beneficiary" defined), 83 ("trust company" defined).

1999 Amendment

Subdivision (b)(4) of Section 17351 is amended to correct a cross-reference. The definition in former Section 16301(a) is superseded by Section 16325. This is a technical, nonsubstantive change. [29 Cal.L.Rev.Comm. Reports 245 (1999)].

Background on Section 17351 of Repealed Code

Section 17351 was added by 1986 Cal.Stat. ch. 820 § 40. The section restated subdivision (a) of former Probate Code Section 1120.1a (repealed by 1986 Cal.Stat. ch. 820 § 31) with some technical changes. For background on the provisions of this division, see the Comment to this division under the division heading. [20 Cal.L.Rev.Comm.Reports 1001 (1990)].

§ 17352. Trustees not trust companies

(a) If none of the trustees of a trust described in Section 17350 is a trust company, the trust may be removed from continuing court jurisdiction only with approval of the court. The trustee may petition for court approval at any time, and from time to time, in the trustee's discretion.

(b) The petition for removal shall set forth the trust accounts in detail, report the trustee's acts, and show the condition of the trust estate. A copy of the trust instrument shall be attached to the petition.

(c) At the hearing the court may receive testimony from any interested person and may grant or deny the petition, or may grant the petition on such conditions as the court in its discretion deems proper.

(d) If the petition is granted, the trustee shall send the notice of removal of the trust provided in subdivision (b) of Section 17351 and file proof of service as required by subdivision (c) of Section 17351 within six months and seven months, respectively, from the date the petition is granted. A copy of the court order granting the petition shall be attached to the notice.

(e) If the petition is not granted, the trust shall continue to be administered under Article 1 (commencing with Section 17300) as if the settlor had provided in the will that the court does not lose jurisdiction of the estate by final distribution. *(Stats.1990, c. 79 (A.B.759), § 14, operative July 1, 1991.)*

Law Revision Commission Comments

1990 Enactment

Section 17352 continues Section 17352 of the repealed Probate Code without change. See Section 17000 (subject-matter jurisdiction of court). For general provisions relating to petitions and other papers, see Sections 1020–1023, 17201; see also Sections 1021 (petition to be verified), 1041 (clerk to set petition for hearing). For general provisions relating to notice of hearing, see Sections 1200–1221, 15802, 17100–17105, 17203–17205; see also Sections 1260–1265 (proof of giving notice). For general provisions relating to hearings and orders, see Sections 1040–1050, 17000–17006, 17201–17202, 17206–17207. See also Section 83 ("trust company" defined).

Background on Section 17352 of Repealed Code

Section 17352 was added by 1986 Cal.Stat. ch. 820 § 40. The section restated part of subdivision (d) of former Probate Code Section 1120.1a (repealed by 1986 Cal.Stat. ch. 820 § 31) with some technical changes. For background on the provisions of this division, see the Comment to this division under the division heading. [20 Cal.L.Rev.Comm.Reports 1001 (1990)].

§ 17353. Trust companies appointed as successor trustees

If a trust company is appointed as a successor trustee of a trust which, at the time of the appointment, is subject to continuing court jurisdiction because it was not removed pursuant to Section 17352, the successor trustee shall comply with Section 17351. For the purpose of complying with

Section 17351, the date of appointment of the successor trustee shall be treated as the date of initial funding of the trust. *(Stats.1990, c. 79 (A.B.759), § 14, operative July 1, 1991.)*

Law Revision Commission Comments

1990 Enactment

Section 17353 continues Section 17353 of the repealed Probate Code without change. See also Section 83 ("trust company" defined).

Background on Section 17353 of Repealed Code

Section 17353 was added by 1986 Cal.Stat. ch. 820 § 40. The section restated the first sentence of subdivision (g) of former Probate Code Section 1120.1a (repealed by 1986 Cal.Stat. ch. 820 § 31) without substantive change. For background on the provisions of this division, see the Comment to this division under the division heading. [20 Cal.L.Rev.Comm.Reports 1001 (1990)].

§ 17354. Effect of change in trustees

After a trust is removed from continuing court jurisdiction pursuant to this article, neither a change in trustees nor any other event causes the trust to be subject to continuing court jurisdiction under Article 1 (commencing with Section 17300). *(Stats.1990, c. 79 (A.B.759), § 14, operative July 1, 1991.)*

Law Revision Commission Comments

1990 Enactment

Section 17354 continues Section 17354 of the repealed Probate Code without change.

Background on Section 17354 of Repealed Code

Section 17354 was added by 1986 Cal.Stat. ch. 820 § 40. The section restated the second sentence of subdivision (g) of former Probate Code Section 1120.1a (repealed by 1986 Cal.Stat. ch. 820 § 31) without substantive change. For background on the provisions of this division, see the Comment to this division under the division heading. [20 Cal.L.Rev.Comm.Reports 1001 (1990)].

CHAPTER 5. TRANSFER OF TRUST TO ANOTHER JURISDICTION

Application

Application of Division, see Probate Code § 15001.

Cross References

Application of old and new law, see Probate Code § 3.
Common law rules governing trusts, application, see Probate Code § 15002.
Relationships excluded from Code definition of trust, application of this Division, see Probate Code § 15003.

§ 17400. Application of chapter

(a) This chapter applies to all of the following:

(1) A trust that is subject to this division.

(2) A trust subject to Chapter 8 (commencing with Section 6320) of Part 1 of Division 6.

(3) Any other trust to which the provisions of this chapter are made applicable by statute or trust instrument.

(b) This chapter does not prevent the transfer of the place of administration of a trust or of trust property to another jurisdiction by any other available means. *(Stats.1990, c. 79 (A.B.759), § 14, operative July 1, 1991.)*

Law Revision Commission Comments

1990 Enactment

Section 17400 continues Section 17400 of the repealed Probate Code without change. Subdivision (a)(1) permits the transfer of oral trusts. See 15207 (oral trusts of personal property). Under the definition of "trust" in Section 82, this chapter also applies to charitable trusts. See 15004 (application of division to charitable trusts). See also Sections 17005 (venue), 17200(b)(16) (proceedings for transfer of trust).

Background on Section 17400 of Repealed Code

Section 17400 was added by 1986 Cal.Stat. ch. 820 § 40. Subdivision (a) restated subdivision (a) of former Probate Code Section 1139 (repealed by 1986 Cal.Stat. ch. 820 § 31) without substantive change, but subdivision (a)(1) of Section 17400 also permitted the transfer of oral trusts. Subdivision (b) superseded subdivision (b) of former Probate Code Section 1139 (repealed by 1986 Cal.Stat. ch. 820 § 31). For background on the provisions of this division, see the Comment to this division under the division heading. [20 Cal.L.Rev.Comm.Reports 1001 (1990)].

§ 17401. Transfer to jurisdiction outside state

(a) The court may make an order for the transfer of the place of administration of a trust or the transfer of some or all of the trust property to a jurisdiction outside this state as provided in this chapter.

(b) Except as otherwise provided in this chapter, proceedings under this chapter are governed by this part. *(Stats. 1990, c. 79 (A.B.759), § 14, operative July 1, 1991.)*

Law Revision Commission Comments

1990 Enactment

Section 17401 continues Section 17401 of the repealed Probate Code without change. See also Sections 62 ("property" defined), 17000 (subject-matter jurisdiction of superior court). Subdivision (b) makes clear that the general rules applicable under this part apply unless this chapter provides a different rule. See, e.g., Sections 17006 (jury trial), 17100–17105 (notice), 17200–17210 (proceedings).

Background on Section 17401 of Repealed Code

Section 17401 was added by 1986 Cal.Stat. ch. 820 § 40. Subdivision (a) restated the first part of former Probate Code Section 1139.1 without substantive change and superseded former Probate Code Section 1132 (provisions repealed by 1986 Cal.Stat. ch. 820 § 31). Subdivision (b) was new. For background on the provisions of this division, see the Comment to this division under the division heading. [20 Cal.L.Rev.Comm.Reports 1001 (1990)].

§ 17402. Petition; contents

The petition for transfer shall set forth all of the following:

(a) The names and places of residence of the following:

(1) The trustee administering the trust in this state.

(2) The trustee, including any domiciliary trustee, who will administer the trust or trust property in the other jurisdiction.

(b) The names, ages, and places of residence of the living beneficiaries, as far as known to the petitioner.

(c) Whether the trustee who will administer the trust in the other jurisdiction has agreed to accept the trust. If so, the acceptance or a copy shall be attached as an exhibit to the petition or otherwise filed with the court.

(d) A general statement of the qualifications of the trustee who will administer the trust in the other jurisdiction and the amount of fiduciary bond, if any. If the trustee is an individual, the statement shall include the trustee's age.

(e) A general statement of the nature and value of the property of any trust of the same settlor being administered in the other jurisdiction by the trustee who will administer the trust in the other jurisdiction.

(f) The name of the court, if any, having jurisdiction of the trustee in the other jurisdiction or of its accounts or in which a proceeding may be had with respect to administration of the trust or the trustee's accounts.

(g) A statement of the character, condition, location, and value of the trust property sought to be transferred.

(h) Whether there is any pending civil action in this state against the trustee arising out of the administration of the trust sought to be transferred.

(i) A statement of the reasons for the transfer. *(Stats. 1990, c. 79 (A.B.759), § 14, operative July 1, 1991.)*

Law Revision Commission Comments
1990 Enactment

Section 17402 continues Section 17402 of the repealed Probate Code without change. For general provisions relating to petitions and other papers, see Sections 1020–1023, 17201; see also Sections 1021 (petition to be verified), 1041 (clerk to set petition for hearing). See also Sections 24 ("beneficiary" defined), 17200(a) (petition by trustee or beneficiary).

Background on Section 17402 of Repealed Code

Section 17402 was added by 1986 Cal.Stat. ch. 820 § 40. The section restated the part of former Probate Code Section 1139.2 (repealed by 1986 Cal.Stat. ch. 820 § 31) providing for the contents of the petition for transfer without substantive change. The reference in subdivision (b) to living beneficiaries restated part of former Probate Code Section 1139.7 (repealed by 1986 Cal.Stat. ch. 820 § 31) without substantive change. For background on the provisions of this division, see the Comment to this division under the division heading. [20 Cal.L.Rev.Comm.Reports 1001 (1990)].

§ 17403. Notice

(a) At least 30 days before the time set for the hearing on the petition, the petitioner shall cause notice of the time and place of the hearing to be mailed to each of the persons named in the petition at their respective addresses as stated in the petition.

(b) Any person interested in the trust, as trustee, beneficiary, or otherwise, may appear and file written grounds in opposition to the petition. *(Stats.1990, c. 79 (A.B.759), § 14, operative July 1, 1991.)*

Law Revision Commission Comments
1990 Enactment

Section 17403 continues Section 17403 of the repealed Probate Code without change. See Section 17402 (places of residence listed in petition). For general provisions relating to notice of hearing, see Sections 1200–1221, 15802–15804, 17100–17105, 17203–17205; see also Sections 1260–1265 (proof of giving notice). For a provision governing notice to the Attorney General in a case involving a charitable trust, see Section 17203(c).

Background on Section 17403 of Repealed Code

Section 17403 was added by 1986 Cal.Stat. ch. 820 § 40. Subdivision (a) restated the second sentence of former Probate Code Section 1139.3 (repealed by 1986 Cal.Stat. ch. 820 § 31) without substantive change. Subdivision (b) continued the fourth sentence of former Probate Code Section 1139.3 without substantive change. For background on the provisions of this division, see the Comment to this division under the division heading. [20 Cal.L.Rev.Comm.Report 1001 (1990)].

§ 17404. Order granting transfer

The court may, in its discretion, grant the petition and order the trustee to transfer the trust property or to transfer the place of administration of the trust to the other jurisdiction if, after hearing, all of the following appear to the court:

(a) The transfer of the trust property to a trustee in another jurisdiction, or the transfer of the place of administration of the trust to another jurisdiction, will promote the best interests of the trust and those interested in it, taking into account the interest in the economical and convenient administration of the trust.

(b) The transfer will not violate the trust instrument.

(c) Any new trustee to whom the trust property is to be transferred is qualified, willing, and able to administer the trust or trust property under the trust instrument. *(Stats. 1990, c. 79 (A.B.759), § 14, operative July 1, 1991.)*

Law Revision Commission Comments
1990 Enactment

Section 17404 continues Section 17404 of the repealed Probate Code without change. For general provisions relating to hearings and orders, see Sections 1040–1050, 17000–17006, 17201–17202, 17206–17207.

Background on Section 17404 of Repealed Code

Section 17404 was added by 1986 Cal.Stat. ch. 820 § 40. The section restated without substantive change the introductory clause and subdivisions (1), (3), and (4) of former Probate Code Section 1139.4 (prerequisites for transfer) and part of former Probate Code Section 1139.1 (subject to limitation in trust) (provisions repealed by 1986 Cal.Stat. ch. 820 § 31), except that Section 17404 required the court to take into account the interest in economical and convenient administration rather than to find that it would necessarily result from the transfer. The requirement in subdivision (c) that the new trustee be willing was included for consistency with Section 17455(a)(3).

The discontinuation of subdivision (2) of former Probate Code Section 1139.4 (repealed by 1986 Cal.Stat. ch. 820 § 31) relating to "substantial rights of residents" was not intended to have any effect on the court's discretion to approve or disapprove a transfer.

For background on the provisions of this division, see the Comment to this division under the division heading. [20 Cal.L.Rev.Comm.Report 1001 (1990)].

§ 17405. Manner of transfer; discharge of trustee

If a transfer is ordered under this chapter, the court may direct the manner of transfer and impose terms and conditions as may be just, including, but not limited to, a requirement for the substitution of a successor trustee in any pending litigation in this state. The delivery of property in accordance with the order of the court is a full discharge of the trustee in relation to all property embraced in the order. *(Stats.1990, c. 79 (A.B.759), § 14, operative July 1, 1991.)*

Law Revision Commission Comments

1990 Enactment

Section 17405 continues Section 17405 of the repealed Probate Code without change. For general provisions relating to hearings and orders, see Sections 1040–1050, 17000–17006, 17201–17202, 17206–17207.

Background on Section 17405 of Repealed Code

Section 17405 was added by 1986 Cal.Stat. ch. 820 § 40. The section continued former Probate Code Section 1139.5 (repealed by 1986 Cal.Stat. ch. 820 § 31) without substantive change. For background on the provisions of this division, see the Comment to this division under the division heading. [20 Cal.L.Rev.Comm.Report 1001 (1990)].

CHAPTER 6. TRANSFER OF TRUST FROM ANOTHER JURISDICTION

Application

Application of Division, see Probate Code § 15001.

Cross References

Application of old and new law, see Probate Code § 3.
Common law rules governing trusts, application, see Probate Code § 15002.
Relationships excluded from Code definition of trust, application of this Division, see Probate Code § 15003.

§ 17450. Application of chapter

(a) This chapter applies to a trust, or portion thereof, administered in a jurisdiction outside this state.

(b) This chapter does not prevent the transfer of the place of administration of a trust or of trust property to this state by any other available means. *(Stats.1990, c. 79 (A.B.759), § 14, operative July 1, 1991.)*

Law Revision Commission Comments

1990 Enactment

Section 17450 continues Section 17450 of the repealed Probate Code without change. Section 17450 makes this chapter applicable to the transfer to California of the place of administration of trusts or trust property administered in a jurisdiction outside California. Hence, this chapter applies to trusts administered in foreign countries as well as those administered in other states. See Section 82 ("trust" defined). See also Section 17200(b)(16) (proceedings for transfer of trust).

Background on Section 17450 of Repealed Code

Section 17450 was added by 1986 Cal.Stat. ch. 820 § 40. Subdivision (a) restated subdivision (a) of former Probate Code Section 1139.10 (repealed by 1986 Cal.Stat. ch. 820 § 31) without substantive change, except that subdivision (a) of Section 17450 also permitted the transfer of oral trusts to California. See Section 15207 (oral trusts of personal property). See Section 82 ("trust" defined). Subdivision (b) superseded subdivision (b) of former Probate Code Section 1139.10 (repealed by 1986 Cal.Stat. ch. 820 § 31). For background on the provisions of this division, see the Comment to this division under the division heading. [20 Cal.L.Rev.Comm.Reports 1001 (1990)].

Cross References

Testamentary trusts, transfer to different county, see Probate Code § 17304.
Transfer of place of administration or property to another jurisdiction outside of California, see Probate Code § 17401.

§ 17451. Order accepting transfer

(a) The court may make an order accepting the transfer of the place of administration of a trust from another jurisdiction to this state or the transfer of some or all of the trust property in another jurisdiction to a trustee in this state as provided in this chapter.

(b) Except as otherwise provided in this chapter, proceedings under this chapter are governed by this part. *(Stats. 1990, c. 79 (A.B.759), § 14, operative July 1, 1991.)*

Law Revision Commission Comments

1990 Enactment

Section 17451 continues Section 17451 of the repealed Probate Code without change. Subdivision (a) is comparable to Section 17401(a). See also Sections 62 ("property" defined), 17000 (subject matter jurisdiction in superior court). Subdivision (b) makes clear that the general rules applicable under this part apply unless this chapter provides a different rule.

Background on Section 17451 of Repealed Code

Section 17451 was added by 1986 Cal.Stat. ch. 820 § 40. Subdivision (a) restated former Probate Code Section 1139.11 (repealed by 1986 Cal.Stat. ch. 820 § 31) without substantive change. Subdivision (b) was new. For background on the provisions of this division, see the Comment to this division under the division heading. [20 Cal.L.Rev.Comm.Reports 1001 (1990)].

§ 17452. Venue

(a) If the petition requests that a resident of this state be appointed trustee, the petition shall be filed in the court of the county where the proposed principal place of administration of the trust pursuant to Section 17002 is located.

(b) If the petition requests that only a nonresident of this state be appointed trustee, the petition shall be filed in the court of the county where either (1) any beneficiary resides or (2) a substantial portion of the trust property to be transferred is located or will be located. *(Stats.1990, c. 79 (A.B.759), § 14, operative July 1, 1991.)*

Law Revision Commission Comments

1990 Enactment

Section 17452 continues Section 17452 of the repealed Probate Code without change. See also Section 17000 (subject matter jurisdiction of superior court).

Background on Section 17452 of Repealed Code

Section 17452 was added by 1986 Cal.Stat. ch. 820 § 40. The section restated former Probate Code Section 1139.13 (repealed by 1986 Cal.Stat. ch. 820 § 31) without substantive change. For background on the provisions of this division, see the Comment to this division under the division heading. [20 Cal.L.Rev.Comm.Reports 1001 (1990)].

§ 17453. Petition; contents

The petition for transfer shall set forth all of the following:

(a) The names and places of residence of the following:

(1) The trustee administering the trust in the other jurisdiction.

(2) The proposed trustee to whom administration of the trust or trust property will be transferred.

(b) The names, ages, and places of residence of all living beneficiaries, as far as known to the petitioner.

(c) Whether administration of the trust has been subject to supervision in a jurisdiction outside this state. If so, the petition shall state whether a petition or appropriate request for transfer of place of administration of the trust or trust property to this state has been filed, if necessary, with the court in the other jurisdiction, and the status of the petition or request.

(d) Whether the trustee proposed to administer the trust in this state has agreed to accept the trust in this state. If the trustee has agreed, the acceptance shall be attached as an exhibit to the petition or otherwise filed with the court.

(e) A general statement of the qualifications of the trustee proposed to administer the trust in this state and the amount of any bond to be requested. If the trustee is an individual, the statement shall include the trustee's age.

(f) A copy of the trust instrument or a statement of the terms of the trust instrument in effect at the time the petition is filed, including all amendments thereto.

(g) A statement of the character, condition, location, and value of the trust property sought to be transferred.

(h) A statement of the reasons for the transfer. *(Stats. 1990, c. 79 (A.B.759), § 14, operative July 1, 1991.)*

Law Revision Commission Comments
1990 Enactment

Section 17453 continues Section 17453 of the repealed Probate Code without change. This section is comparable to Section 17402. For general provisions relating to petitions and other papers, see Sections 1020–1023, 17201; see also Sections 1021 (petition to be verified), 1041 (clerk to set petition for hearing). See also Sections 24 ("beneficiary" defined), 17200(a) (petition by trustee or beneficiary).

Background on Section 17453 of Repealed Code

Section 17453 was added by 1986 Cal.Stat. ch. 820 § 40. The section continued former Probate Code Section 1139.14 (repealed by 1986 Cal.Stat. ch. 820 § 31) without substantive change, except that the statement of the age of the trustee is now required only of individual trustees. The reference in subdivision (b) to living beneficiaries restated part of former Probate Code Section 1139.19 (repealed by 1986 Cal.Stat. ch. 820 § 31) without substantive change. For background on the provisions of this division, see the Comment to this division under the division heading. [20 Cal.L.Rev.Comm.Reports 1001 (1990)].

§ 17454. Notice

(a) At least 30 days before the time set for the hearing on the petition, the petitioner shall cause notice of the time and place of the hearing to be mailed to each of the persons named in the petition at their respective addresses as stated in the petition.

(b) Any person interested in the trust, as trustee, beneficiary, or otherwise, may appear and file written grounds in opposition to the petition. *(Stats.1990, c. 79 (A.B.759), § 14, operative July 1, 1991.)*

Law Revision Commission Comments
1990 Enactment

Section 17454 continues Section 17454 of the repealed Probate Code without change. See Section 17453 (places of residence listed in petition). Section 17454 is comparable to Section 17403. For general provisions relating to notice of hearing, see Sections 1200–1221, 15802–15804, 17100–17105, 17203–17205; see also Sections 1260–1265 (proof of giving notice). For a provision governing notice to the Attorney General in a case involving a charitable trust, see Section 17203(c).

Background on Section 17454 of Repealed Code

Section 17454 was added by 1986 Cal.Stat. ch. 820 § 40. Subdivision (a) restated the second sentence of subdivision (a) of former Probate Code Section 1139.15 (repealed by 1986 Cal.Stat. ch. 820 § 31) without substantive change. Subdivision (b) continued subdivision (b) of former Probate Code Section 1139.15 without change. For background on the provisions of this division, see the Comment to this division under the division heading. [20 Cal.L.Rev.Comm.Reports 1001 (1990)].

§ 17455. Order accepting transfer and appointing trustee

(a) The court may, in its discretion, grant the petition and issue an order accepting transfer of trust property or the place of administration of the trust to this state and appoint a trustee to administer the trust in this state, if, after hearing, all of the following appear to the court:

(1) The transfer of the trust property to a trustee in this state, or the transfer of the place of administration of the trust to this state, will promote the best interests of the trust and those interested in it, taking into account the interest in the economical and convenient administration of the trust.

(2) The transfer will not violate the trust instrument.

(3) The trustee appointed by the court to administer the trust in this state, and to whom the trust property is to be transferred, is qualified, willing, and able to administer the trust or trust property under the trust instrument.

(4) The proper court in the other jurisdiction has approved the transfer if approval is necessary under the law of the other jurisdiction.

(b) If the court grants the petition under subdivision (a), the court shall require the trustee to give a bond, if necessary under the law of the other jurisdiction or of this state, and may require bond as provided in Section 15602. *(Stats.1990, c. 79 (A.B.759), § 14, operative July 1, 1991.)*

Law Revision Commission Comments
1990 Enactment

Section 17455 continues Section 17455 of the repealed Probate Code without change. For general provisions relating to hearings and orders, see Sections 1040–1050, 17000–17006, 17201–17202, 17206–17207.

Background on Section 17455 of Repealed Code

Section 17455 was added by 1986 Cal.Stat. ch. 820 § 40. The section restated former Probate Code Section 1139.16 (repealed by 1986 Cal.Stat. ch. 820 § 31) without substantive change, except that (1) the court was required to take into account the interest in economical and convenient administration rather than to find that it would necessarily result from the transfer, (2) a bond was required only if the law of the other jurisdiction or California so provided, and (3) the court's authority to require bond under general provisions was recognized. See, e.g., Section 15602(a)(3) (bond required of trustee appointed by court). The reference to "assets" in former Probate Code Section 1139.16 was replaced with a reference to "property"; this was a non-substantive change. See Section 62 ("property" defined). For background on the provisions of this division, see the Comment to this division under the division heading. [20 Cal.L.Rev.Comm.Reports 1001 (1990)].

§ 17456. Conditional order accepting transfer

If appropriate to facilitate transfer of the trust property or the place of administration of a trust to this state, the court may issue a conditional order appointing a trustee to administer the trust in this state and indicating that transfer to this state will be accepted if transfer is approved by the proper court of the other jurisdiction. *(Stats.1990, c. 79 (A.B.759), § 14, operative July 1, 1991.)*

Law Revision Commission Comments
1990 Enactment

Section 17456 continues Section 17456 of the repealed Probate Code without change. This section provides a method whereby the California court can indicate its willingness to accept jurisdiction over a trust administered in another jurisdiction where the law of the other jurisdiction requires appointment of a trustee in the proposed new place of administration before approving transfer. See, e.g., Mass.Gen.Laws Ann. ch. 206, § 29 (West 1958). For general provisions relating to hearings and orders, see Sections 1040–1050, 17000–17006, 17201–17202, 17206–17207.

Background on Section 17456 of Repealed Code

Section 17456 was added by 1986 Cal.Stat. ch. 820 § 40. The section continued former Probate Code Section 1139.17 (repealed by 1986 Cal.Stat. ch. 820 § 31) without substantive change. The reference to "assets" in former Probate Code Section 1139.17 was replaced with a reference to "property"; this was a non-substantive change. See Section 62 ("property" defined). For background on the provisions of this division, see the Comment to this division under the division heading. [20 Cal.L.Rev.Comm.Reports 1001 (1990)].

§ 17457. Administration; validity; construction

A trust transferred to this state pursuant to this chapter shall be administered in the same manner as a trust of that type created in this state. The validity of a trust and the construction of the beneficial provisions of a trust transferred to this state are not affected by this section. *(Stats.1990, c. 79 (A.B.759), § 14, operative July 1, 1991.)*

Law Revision Commission Comments
1990 Enactment

Section 17457 continues Section 17457 of the repealed Probate Code without change. Under this section, a transferred trust is treated the same as a trust that was created in California, and so is governed by this division. See also Section 15004 (application of

division to charitable trusts); Gov't Code §§ 12580–12598 (supervision of certain charitable trusts). This section is not intended to provide choice of law rules. A trust that was subject to judicial supervision in another state will not be subject to continuing court jurisdiction under Sections 17300–17304 unless the trust instrument so provides and the court so determines in the order accepting transfer to California.

The validity of the trust and the construction of its beneficial provisions are not affected by this section; the procedural and administrative provisions are covered by this section. See also Section 15400 (limitation on California rule that trust is revocable unless it provides otherwise).

Background on Section 17457 of Repealed Code

Section 17457 was added by 1986 Cal.Stat. ch. 820 § 40 and amended by 1987 Cal.Stat. ch. 128 § 19. The first sentence superseded former Probate Code Section 1139.18 (repealed by 1986 Cal.Stat. ch. 820 § 31). The second sentence was added by the 1987 amendment to make clear that the validity of the trust and the construction of its beneficial provisions are not affected by this section. For background on the provisions of this division, see the Comment to this division under the division heading. [20 Cal.L.Rev.Comm.Reports 1001 (1990)].

Part 6

RIGHTS OF THIRD PERSONS

Application

Application of Division, see Probate Code § 15001.

Cross References

Common law rules governing trusts, application, see Probate Code § 15002.
Relationships excluded from Code definition of trust, application of this Division, see Probate Code § 15003.

CHAPTER 1. LIABILITY OF TRUSTEE TO THIRD PERSONS

Application

Application of Division, see Probate Code § 15001.

Cross References

Application of old and new law, see Probate Code § 3.
Common law rules governing trusts, application, see Probate Code § 15002.

Relationships excluded from Code definition of trust, application of this Division, see Probate Code § 15003.

§ 18000. Personal liability; limitations

(a) Unless otherwise provided in the contract or in this chapter, a trustee is not personally liable on a contract properly entered into in the trustee's fiduciary capacity in the course of administration of the trust unless the trustee fails to reveal the trustee's representative capacity or identify the trust in the contract.

(b) The personal liability of a trustee on a contract entered into before July 1, 1987, is governed by prior law and not by this section. *(Stats.1990, c. 79 (A.B.759), § 14, operative July 1, 1991.)*

Law Revision Commission Comments

1990 Enactment

Section 18000 continues Section 18000 of the repealed Probate Code without change. Subdivision (a) is drawn from Section 7–306(a) of the Uniform Probate Code (1987). However, unlike the Uniform Probate Code, this section excuses the trustee from personal liability on a contract where *either* the trustee's representative capacity *or* the identity of the trust is revealed in the contract. Under Section 18000, it is assumed that either one of these statements in a contract puts the person contracted with on notice of the fact that the other person is a trustee. As to the construction of provisions drawn from uniform acts, see Section 2. The protection afforded the trustee by this section applies only to contracts that are properly entered into in the trustee's fiduciary capacity, meaning that the trustee is exercising an available power and is not violating a duty. This section does not excuse any liability the trustee may have for breach of trust. See Section 18005 (liability as between trustee and trust estate).

The rule provided in subdivision (a) is the reverse of the prior case-law rule in California that a trustee was personally liable on a contract unless the contract stipulated that the trustee was not liable. See Hall v. Jameson, 151 Cal. 606, 611–12, 91 P. 518 (1907); Duncan v. Dormer, 94 Cal.App. 218, 221, 270 P. 1003 (1928); but cf. Purdy v. Bank of America Nat'l Tr. & S. Ass'n, 2 Cal.2d 298, 301–02, 40 P.2d 481 (1935) (trust estate also liable when properly bound by acts of trustee). However, to fall within the rule of subdivision (a) of Section 18000, either the trustee's status or the identity of the trust must be revealed. This was not sufficient under prior case law. See Hall v. Jameson, supra. Subdivision (b) preserves the case-law rule governing a trustee's personal liability for pre-operative date contracts.

Background on Section 18000 of Repealed Code

Section 18000 was a new provision added by 1986 Cal.Stat. ch. 820 § 40. Subdivision (a) superseded former Civil Code Section 2267 (repealed by 1986 Cal.Stats. ch. 820 § 7) to the extent it affected liability. For background on the provisions of this division, see the Comment to this division under the division heading. [20 Cal.L.Rev.Comm.Reports 1001 (1990)].

Cross References

Mutual obligations of principals and third persons, see Civil Code § 2330 et seq.

§ 18001. Obligations arising from ownership or control of trust property

A trustee is personally liable for obligations arising from ownership or control of trust property only if the trustee is personally at fault. *(Stats.1990, c. 79 (A.B.759), § 14, operative July 1, 1991.)*

Law Revision Commission Comments

1990 Enactment

Section 18001 continues Section 18001 of the repealed Probate Code without change. This section is the same in substance as part of Section 7–306(b) of the Uniform Probate Code (1987). As to the construction of provisions drawn from uniform acts, see Section 2. A trustee is "personally at fault" when the trustee either intentionally or negligently, acts or fails to act. For rules governing the assertion of claims, see Section 18004. The question of ultimate liability as between the trust and the trustee is governed by Section 18005.

Background on Section 18001 of Repealed Code

Section 18001 was a new provision added by 1986 Cal.Stat. ch. 820 § 40. For background on the provisions of this division, see the Comment to this division under the division heading. [20 Cal.L.Rev.Comm.Reports 1001 (1990)].

Cross References

Liability of fiduciaries, limitations, see Health and Safety Code § 25548.3.

§ 18002. Torts

A trustee is personally liable for torts committed in the course of administration of the trust only if the trustee is personally at fault. *(Stats.1990, c. 79 (A.B.759), § 14, operative July 1, 1991.)*

Law Revision Commission Comments

1990 Enactment

Section 18002 continues Section 18002 of the repealed Probate Code without change. This section is the same in substance as part of Section 7–306(b) of the Uniform Probate Code (1987). As to the construction of provisions drawn from uniform acts, see Section 2. A trustee is "personally at fault" when the trustee commits a tort either intentionally or negligently. Cf. Johnston v. Long, 30 Cal.2d 54, 62–63, 181 P.2d 645 (1947) (liability of fiduciaries for torts committed by agents depends on personal fault). For rules governing the assertion of claims, see Section 18004. The question of ultimate liability as between the trust and the trustee is governed by Section 18005.

Background on Section 18002 of Repealed Code

Section 18002 was a new provision added by 1986 Cal.Stat. ch. 820 § 40. For background on the provisions of this division, see the Comment to this division under the division heading. [20 Cal.L.Rev.Comm.Reports 1001 (1990)].

Cross References

Liability of fiduciaries, limitations, see Health and Safety Code § 25548.3.

§ 18003. Dissenting cotrustees

(a) A cotrustee who does not join in exercising a power held by three or more cotrustees is not liable to third persons for the consequences of the exercise of the power.

(b) A dissenting cotrustee who joins in an action at the direction of the majority cotrustees is not liable to third persons for the action if the dissenting cotrustee expresses the dissent in writing to any other cotrustee at or before the time the action is taken.

(c) This section does not excuse a cotrustee from liability for failure to discharge the cotrustee's duties as a trustee. *(Stats.1990, c. 79 (A.B.759), § 14, operative July 1, 1991.)*

Law Revision Commission Comments
1990 Enactment

Section 18003 continues Section 18003 of the repealed Probate Code without change. This section is drawn from the Texas Trust Code. See Tex.Prop.Code Ann. § 114.006 (Vernon 1984).

Background on Section 18003 of Repealed Code

Section 18003 was a new provision added by 1986 Cal.Stat. ch. 820 § 40. For background on the provisions of this division, see the Comment to this division under the division heading. [20 Cal.L.Rev.Comm.Reports 1001 (1990)].

§ 18004. Contract claims

A claim based on a contract entered into by a trustee in the trustee's representative capacity, on an obligation arising from ownership or control of trust property, or on a tort committed in the course of administration of the trust may be asserted against the trust by proceeding against the trustee in the trustee's representative capacity, whether or not the trustee is personally liable on the claim. *(Stats.1990, c. 79 (A.B.759), § 14, operative July 1, 1991.)*

Law Revision Commission Comments
1990 Enactment

Section 18004 continues Section 18004 of the repealed Probate Code without change. This section is the same in substance as Section 7–306(c) of the Uniform Probate Code (1987). As to the construction of provisions drawn from uniform acts, see Section 2. Section 18004 alters the prior case law rule that the trustee could not be sued in a representative capacity where the trust estate was not liable. See Purdy v. Bank of America Nat'l Tr. & S. Ass'n, 2 Cal.2d 298, 301, 40 P.2d 481 (1935); Rapaport v. Forer, 20 Cal.App.2d 271, 278, 66 P.2d 1242 (1937). See also Sections 18000 (personal liability on contract), 18005 (liability as between trustee and trust estate).

Background on Section 18004 of Repealed Code

Section 18004 was added by 1986 Cal.Stat. ch. 820 § 40. The section superseded the first and last sentences of former Civil Code Section 2267 (repealed by 1986 Cal.Stats. ch. 820 § 7) (acts of trustee within scope of authority bind trust property). For background on the provisions of this division, see the Comment to this division under the division heading. [20 Cal.L.Rev.Comm.Reports 1001 (1990)].

§ 18005. Proceedings for determination

The question of liability as between the trust estate and the trustee personally may be determined in a proceeding under Section 17200. *(Stats.1990, c. 79 (A.B.759), § 14, operative July 1, 1991.)*

Law Revision Commission Comments
1990 Enactment

Section 18005 continues Section 18005 of the repealed Probate Code without change. This section is drawn from Section 7–306(d) of the Uniform Probate Code (1987). As to the construction of provisions drawn from uniform acts, see Section 2. Under this section, ultimate liability as between the estate and the trustee need not be determined before the third person's claim can be satisfied. It is permissible, and may be preferable, for judgment to be entered against the trust without determining the trustee's ultimate liability until later. Where judgment is entered against the trustee individually, the question of the trustee's right to reimbursement may be settled informally with the beneficiaries or in a separate proceeding in the probate court. For rules governing indemnification of trustees, see Section 15684. See also Section 17200 et seq. (proceedings against trustee by beneficiary).

Background on Section 18005 of Repealed Code

Section 18005 was a new provision added by 1986 Cal.Stat. ch. 820 § 40. For background on the provisions of this division, see the Comment to this division under the division heading. [20 Cal.L.Rev.Comm.Reports 1001 (1990)].

CHAPTER 2. PROTECTION OF THIRD PERSONS

Application

Application of Division, see Probate Code § 15001.

Cross References

Common law rules governing trusts, application, see Probate Code § 15002.
Relationships excluded from Code definition of trust, application of this Division, see Probate Code § 15003.

§ 18100. Obligations of third persons

With respect to a third person dealing with a trustee or assisting a trustee in the conduct of a transaction, if the third person acts in good faith and for a valuable consideration and without actual knowledge that the trustee is exceeding the trustee's powers or improperly exercising them:

(a) The third person is not bound to inquire whether the trustee has power to act or is properly exercising a power and may assume without inquiry the existence of a trust power and its proper exercise.

(b) The third person is fully protected in dealing with or assisting the trustee just as if the trustee has and is properly exercising the power the trustee purports to exercise. *(Stats. 1990, c. 79 (A.B.759), § 14, operative July 1, 1991.)*

Law Revision Commission Comments
1990 Enactment

Section 18100 continues Section 18100 of the repealed Probate Code without change. This section is drawn from Section 7 of the Uniform Trustees' Powers Act (1964). As to the construction of provisions drawn from uniform acts, see Section 2.

Section 18100 was added by 1986 Cal.Stat. ch. 820 § 40. The section superseded former Civil Code Section 2243 (repealed by 1986 Cal.Stats. ch. 820 § 7). For background on the provisions of this division, see the Comment to this division under the division heading. [20 Cal.L.Rev.Comm.Reports 1001 (1990)].

Cross References

Proceedings against trustees for breach of trust subject to this section, see Probate Code § 16420.

Trustee defined, see Probate Code § 84.

§ 18100.5. Certification of trust; contents; trust document excerpt copies; certification reliance; liability; recordation

(a) The trustee may present a certification of trust to any person in lieu of providing a copy of the trust instrument to establish the existence or terms of the trust. A certification of trust may be executed by the trustee voluntarily or at the request of the person with whom the trustee is dealing.

(b) The certification of trust may confirm the following facts or contain the following information:

(1) The existence of the trust and date of execution of the trust instrument.

(2) The identity of the settlor or settlors and the currently acting trustee or trustees of the trust.

(3) The powers of the trustee.

(4) The revocability or irrevocability of the trust and the identity of any person holding any power to revoke the trust.

(5) When there are multiple trustees, the signature authority of the trustees, indicating whether all, or less than all, of the currently acting trustees are required to sign in order to exercise various powers of the trustee.

(6) The trust identification number, whether a social security number or an employer identification number.

(7) The manner in which title to trust assets should be taken.

(8) The legal description of any interest in real property held in the trust.

(c) The certification shall contain a statement that the trust has not been revoked, modified, or amended in any manner which would cause the representations contained in the certification of trust to be incorrect and shall contain a statement that it is being signed by all of the currently acting trustees of the trust. The certification shall be in the form of an acknowledged declaration signed by all currently acting trustees of the trust. The certification signed by the currently acting trustee may be recorded in the office of the county recorder in the county where all or a portion of the real property is located.

(d) The certification of trust may, but is not required to, include excerpts from the original trust documents, any amendments thereto, and any other documents evidencing or pertaining to the succession of successor trustees. The certification of trust shall not be required to contain the dispositive provisions of the trust which set forth the distribution of the trust estate.

(e) A person whose interest is, or may be, affected by the certification of trust may require that the trustee offering or recording the certification of trust provide copies of those excerpts from the original trust documents, any amendments thereto, and any other documents which designate, evidence, or pertain to the succession of the trustee or confer upon the trustee the power to act in the pending transaction, or both. Nothing in this section is intended to require or imply an obligation to provide the dispositive provisions of the trust or the entire trust and amendments thereto.

(f) A person who acts in reliance upon a certification of trust without actual knowledge that the representations contained therein are incorrect is not liable to any person for so acting. A person who does not have actual knowledge that the facts contained in the certification of trust are incorrect may assume without inquiry the existence of the facts contained in the certification of trust. Actual knowledge shall not be inferred solely from the fact that a copy of all or part of the trust instrument is held by the person relying upon the trust certification. Any transaction, and any lien created thereby, entered into by the trustee and a person acting in reliance upon a certification of trust shall be enforceable against the trust assets. However, if the person has actual knowledge that the trustee is acting outside the scope of the trust, then the transaction is not enforceable against the trust assets. Nothing contained herein shall limit the rights of the beneficiaries of the trust against the trustee.

(g) A person's failure to demand a certification of trust does not affect the protection provided that person by Section 18100, and no inference as to whether that person has acted in good faith may be drawn from the failure to demand a certification of trust. Nothing in this section is intended to create an implication that a person is liable for acting in reliance upon a certification of trust under circumstances where the requirements of this section are not satisfied.

(h) Except when requested by a beneficiary or in the context of litigation concerning a trust and subject to the provisions of subdivision (e), any person making a demand for the trust documents in addition to a certification of trust to prove facts set forth in the certification of trust acceptable to the third party shall be liable for damages, including attorney's fees, incurred as a result of the refusal to accept the certification of trust in lieu of the requested documents if the court determines that the person acted in bad faith in requesting the trust documents.

(i) Any person may record a certification of trust that relates to an interest in real property in the office of the county recorder in any county in which all or a portion of the real property is located. The county recorder shall impose any fee prescribed by law for recording that document sufficient to cover all costs incurred by the county in recording the document. The recorded certification of trust shall be a public record of the real property involved. This subdivision does not create a requirement to record a certification of trust in conjunction with the recordation of a transfer of title of real property involving a trust. (*Added by Stats.1993, c. 530 (A.B.1249), § 2. Amended by Stats.2004, c. 136 (A.B.1848), § 1.*)

§ 18101. Application of property delivered to trustee

A third person who acts in good faith is not bound to ensure the proper application of trust property paid or delivered to the trustee. *(Stats.1990, c. 79 (A.B.759), § 14, operative July 1, 1991.)*

Law Revision Commission Comments

1990 Enactment

Section 18101 continues Section 18101 of the repealed Probate Code without change. This section is essentially the same as the last sentence of Section 7 of the Uniform Trustees' Powers Act (1964). As to the construction of provisions drawn from uniform acts, see Section 2.

Background on Section 18101 of Repealed Code

Section 18101 was added by 1986 Cal.Stat. ch. 820 § 40. The section superseded former Civil Code Section 2244 (repealed by 1986 Cal.Stats. ch. 820 § 7). For background on the provisions of this division, see the Comment to this division under the division heading. [Cal.L.Rev.Comm.Reports 1001 (1990)].

§ 18102. Transactions with former trustees

If a third person acting in good faith and for a valuable consideration enters into a transaction with a former trustee without knowledge that the person is no longer a trustee, the third person is fully protected just as if the former trustee were still a trustee. *(Stats.1990, c. 79 (A.B.759), § 14, operative July 1, 1991.)*

Law Revision Commission Comments

1990 Enactment

Section 18102 continues Section 18102 of the repealed Probate Code without change. See also Section 15643 (vacancy in office of trustee).

Background on Section 18102 of Repealed Code

Section 18102 was added by 1986 Cal.Stat. ch. 820 § 40. The section restated the second paragraph of former Civil Code Section 2281 (repealed by 1986 Cal.Stats. ch. 820 § 7) without substantive change, but was drafted for consistency with Section 18100. For background on the provisions of this division, see the Comment to this division under the division heading. [Cal.L.Rev.Comm.Reports 1001 (1990)].

Cross References

Trustees under deeds of trust to secure obligations, application of this section, see Civil Code § 2934b.

§ 18103. Effect on purchaser of omission of trust from grant of real property

If an express trust relating to real property is not contained or declared in the grant to the trustee, or in an instrument signed by the trustee and recorded in the same office with the grant to the trustee, the grant shall be deemed absolute in favor of a person dealing with the trustee in good faith and for a valuable consideration. *(Stats.1990, c. 79 (A.B.759), § 14, operative July 1, 1991.)*

Law Revision Commission Comments

1990 Enactment

Section 18103 continues Section 18103 of the repealed Probate Code without change, except that the section is revised to extend to any person who enters into a transaction in good faith and for a valuable consideration, not only purchasers. See also Civil Code § 1214 (prior recording of subsequent conveyances).

Background on Section 18103 of Repealed Code

Section 18103 was added by 1986 Cal.Stat. ch. 820 § 40. The section continued former Civil Code Section 869 (repealed by 1986 Cal.Stats. ch. 820 § 5) without substantive change. For background on the provisions of this division, see the Comment to this division under the division heading. [Cal.L.Rev.Comm.Reports 1001 (1990)].

§ 18104. Effect on real property transactions where beneficiary undisclosed

(a) If an interest in or lien or encumbrance on real property is conveyed, created, or affected by an instrument in favor of a person in trust but no beneficiary is indicated in the instrument, it is presumed that the person holds the interest, lien, or encumbrance absolutely and free of the trust. This is a presumption affecting the burden of proof. In an action or proceeding involving the interest, lien, or encumbrance instituted against the person, the person shall be deemed the only necessary representative of the undisclosed beneficiary and of the original grantor or settlor and anyone claiming under them. A judgment is binding upon and conclusive against these persons as to all matters finally adjudicated in the judgment.

(b) An instrument executed by the person holding an interest, lien, or encumbrance described in subdivision (a), whether purporting to be the act of that person in his or her own right or in the capacity of a trustee, is presumed to affect the interest, lien, or encumbrance according to the tenor of the instrument. This is a presumption affecting the burden of proof. Upon the recording of the instrument in the county where the land affected by the instrument is located, the presumption is conclusive in favor of a person acting in good faith and for valuable consideration. *(Stats.1990, c. 79 (A.B.759), § 14, operative July 1, 1991.)*

Law Revision Commission Comments

1990 Enactment

Section 18104 continues Section 18104 of the repealed Probate Code without substantive change, except that the presumption in subdivision (b) is revised to extend to any person who enters into a transaction in good faith and for a valuable consideration, not only purchasers and encumbrancers. The language relating to the presumptions affecting the burden of proof in both subdivisions (a) and (b) is consistent with Evidence Code Section 605.

Background on Section 18104 of Repealed Code

Section 18104 was added by 1986 Cal.Stat. ch. 820 § 40. The section restated the first two paragraphs of former Civil Code Section 869a (repealed by 1986 Cal.Stats. ch. 820 § 5) without substantive change. See Hansen v. G & G Trucking Co., 236 Cal.App.2d 481, 491–94, 46 Cal.Rptr. 186 (1965) (presumption rebuttable, not conclusive). For background on the provisions of this division, see the Comment to this division under the division heading. [20 Cal.L.Rev.Comm.Reports 1001 (1990)].

Cross References

Burden of proof, generally, see Evidence Code § 500 et seq.

§ 18105. Change of trustee affecting title or interest in real property; execution and recordation of affidavit of change of trustee; fees; contents

If title to an interest in real property is affected by a change of trustee, the successor trustee may execute and record in the county in which the property is located an affidavit of change of trustee. The county recorder shall impose any fee prescribed by law for recording that document in an amount sufficient to cover all costs incurred by the county in recording the document. The affidavit shall include the legal description of the real property, the name of the former trustee or trustees and the name of the successor trustee or trustees. The affidavit may also, but is not required to, include excerpts from the original trust documents, any amendments thereto, and any other documents evidencing or pertaining to the succession of the successor trustee or trustees. *(Added by Stats.2004, c. 136 (A.B.1848), § 2.)*

§ 18106. Recordation of document establishing change of trustee; applicability of statutory requirements for recorded documents; indexing of document; indexing fees

(a) A document establishing the fact of change of trustee recorded pursuant to this chapter is subject to all statutory requirements for recorded documents.

(b) The county recorder shall index a document establishing the fact of change of a trustee recorded pursuant to this section in the index of grantors and grantees. The index entry shall be for the grantor, and for the purpose of this index, the person who has been succeeded as trustee shall be deemed to be the grantor. The county recorder shall impose any fee prescribed by law for indexing that document in an amount sufficient to cover all costs incurred by the county in indexing the document. *(Added by Stats.2004, c. 136 (A.B. 1848), § 3.)*

§ 18107. Recordation of document establishing change of trustee as prima facie evidence of change of trustee; nature of presumption

A document establishing the change of a trustee recorded pursuant to this chapter is prima facie evidence of the change of trustee insofar as the document identifies an interest in real property located in the county, title to which is affected by the change of trustee. The presumption established by this section is a presumption affecting the burden of producing evidence. *(Added by Stats.2004, c. 136 (A.B.1848), § 4.)*

Cross References

Prima facie evidence, see Evidence Code § 602.

§ 18108. Interests affected by recordation of change of trustee affidavit; provision by successor trustee of copies of original trust document excerpts evidencing succession of trustee or trustees

Any person whose interest is, or may be, affected by the recordation of an affidavit of change of trustee pursuant to this chapter may require that the successor trustee provide copies of those excerpts from the original trust documents, any amendments thereto, and any other documents which evidence or pertain to the succession of the successor trustee or trustees. Nothing in this section is intended to require or imply an obligation to provide the dispositive provisions of the trust or the entire trust and any amendments thereto. *(Added by Stats.2004, c. 136 (A.B.1848), § 5.)*

CHAPTER 3. RIGHTS OF CREDITORS OF SETTLOR

Application

Application of Division, see Probate Code § 15001.

Cross References

Common law rules governing trusts, application, see Probate Code § 15002.
Relationships excluded from Code definition of trust, application of this Division, see Probate Code § 15003.

§ 18200. Revocable trusts; creditors' rights during settlor's lifetime

If the settlor retains the power to revoke the trust in whole or in part, the trust property is subject to the claims of creditors of the settlor to the extent of the power of revocation during the lifetime of the settlor. *(Stats.1990, c. 79 (A.B.759), § 14, operative July 1, 1991.)*

Law Revision Commission Comments

1990 Enactment

Section 18200 continues Section 18200 of the repealed Probate Code without change. This section is analogous to the rule applicable to property subject to an unexercised power of appointment created by a donor in favor of himself or herself. See Civil Code § 1390.4. Section 18200 permits the creditor to ignore the trust to the extent that it is revocable.

Background on Section 18200 of Repealed Code

Section 18200 was a new provision added by 1986 Cal.Stat. ch. 820 § 40. For background on the provisions of this division, see the Comment to this division under the division heading. [20 Cal.L.Rev.Comm.Reports 1001 (1990)].

§ 18201. Trust property subject to claims of creditors

Any settlor whose trust property is subject to the claims of creditors pursuant to Section 18200 shall be entitled to all exemptions as provided in Chapter 4 (commencing with Section 703.010) of Division 2 of Title 9 of Part 2 of the Code of Civil Procedure. *(Added by Stats.1998, c. 682 (A.B.2069), § 14.)*

§ 18500. Repealed by Stats.2008, c. 715 (S.B.1329), § 3

Part 7

UNIFORM PRUDENT MANAGEMENT OF INSTITUTIONAL FUNDS ACT

Application

Application of Division, see Probate Code § 15001.

Cross References

Application of Uniform Prudent Management of Institutional Funds Act, see Corporations Code § 5240.
California Endowment for Marine Preservation to have investment policies consistent with this Act, see Public Resources Code § 71561.
Eligible holders of endowments, requirements imposed upon holders of endowments, mitigation agreement additional requirements, see Government Code § 65968.
Mitigation lands, requirements imposed upon holders of accompanying funds relative to experience, capacity, and knowledge to manage property for mitigation purposes and any accompanying funds, see Government Code § 65965 et seq.
Nonprofit religious corporations, investment standards, application of Uniform Prudent Management of Institutional Funds Act, see Corporations Code § 9250.

§ 18501. Short title

This part may be cited as the Uniform Prudent Management of Institutional Funds Act. *(Added by Stats.2008, c. 715 (S.B.1329), § 4.)*

Cross References

Application of Uniform Prudent Management of Institutional Funds Act, see Corporations Code § 5240.
Mitigation lands, requirements imposed upon holders of accompanying funds relative to experience, capacity, and knowledge to manage property for mitigation purposes and any accompanying funds, see Government Code § 65965 et seq.
Reasonably prudent investor standards, accounting practices, investment policies, see Public Resources Code § 71561.

§ 18502. Definitions

As used in this part, the following terms shall have the following meanings:

(a) "Charitable purpose" means the relief of poverty, the advancement of education or religion, the promotion of health, the promotion of a governmental purpose, or any other purpose the achievement of which is beneficial to the community.

(b) "Endowment fund" means an institutional fund or part thereof that, under the terms of a gift instrument, is not wholly expendable by the institution on a current basis. The term does not include assets that an institution designates as an endowment fund for its own use.

(c) "Gift instrument" means a record or records, including an institutional solicitation, under which property is granted to, transferred to, or held by an institution as an institutional fund.

(d) "Institution" means any of the following:

(1) A person, other than an individual, organized and operated exclusively for charitable purposes.

(2) A government or governmental subdivision, agency, or instrumentality, to the extent that it holds funds exclusively for a charitable purpose.

(3) A trust that had both charitable and noncharitable interests, after all noncharitable interests have terminated.

(e) "Institutional fund" means a fund held by an institution exclusively for charitable purposes. The term does not include any of the following:

(1) Program-related assets.

(2) A fund held for an institution by a trustee that is not an institution.

(3) A fund in which a beneficiary that is not an institution has an interest, other than an interest that could arise upon violation or failure of the purposes of the fund.

(f) "Person" means an individual, corporation, business trust, estate, trust, partnership, limited liability company, association, joint venture, public corporation, government or governmental subdivision, agency, or instrumentality, or any other legal or commercial entity.

(g) "Program-related asset" means an asset held by an institution primarily to accomplish a charitable purpose of the institution and not primarily for investment.

(h) "Record" means information that is inscribed on a tangible medium or that is stored in an electronic or other medium and is retrievable in perceivable form. *(Added by Stats.2008, c. 715 (S.B.1329), § 4.)*

§ 18502.5. Repealed by Stats.1990, c. 1307 (S.B.2649), § 4, operative Jan. 1, 1994

§ 18503. Managing and investing an institutional fund; requirements

(a) Subject to the intent of a donor expressed in a gift instrument, an institution, in managing and investing an institutional fund, shall consider the charitable purposes of the institution and the purposes of the institutional fund.

(b) In addition to complying with the duty of loyalty imposed by law other than this part, each person responsible for managing and investing an institutional fund shall manage and invest the fund in good faith and with the care an ordinarily prudent person in a like position would exercise under similar circumstances.

(c) In managing and investing an institutional fund, an institution is subject to both of the following:

(1) It may incur only costs that are appropriate and reasonable in relation to the assets, the purposes of the institution, and the skills available to the institution.

(2) It shall make a reasonable effort to verify facts relevant to the management and investment of the fund.

(d) An institution may pool two or more institutional funds for purposes of management and investment.

(e) Except as otherwise provided by a gift instrument, the following rules apply:

(1) In managing and investing an institutional fund, all of the following factors, if relevant, must be considered:

(A) General economic conditions.

(B) The possible effect of inflation or deflation.

(C) The expected tax consequences, if any, of investment decisions or strategies.

(D) The role that each investment or course of action plays within the overall investment portfolio of the fund.

(E) The expected total return from income and the appreciation of investments.

(F) Other resources of the institution.

(G) The needs of the institution and the fund to make distributions and to preserve capital.

(H) An asset's special relationship or special value, if any, to the charitable purposes of the institution.

(2) Management and investment decisions about an individual asset must be made not in isolation but rather in the context of the institutional fund's portfolio of investments as a whole and as a part of an overall investment strategy having risk and return objectives reasonably suited to the fund and to the institution.

(3) Except as otherwise provided by law other than this part, an institution may invest in any kind of property or type of investment consistent with this section.

(4) An institution shall diversify the investments of an institutional fund unless the institution reasonably determines that, because of special circumstances, the purposes of the fund are better served without diversification.

(5) Within a reasonable time after receiving property, an institution shall make and carry out decisions concerning the retention or disposition of the property or to rebalance a portfolio, in order to bring the institutional fund into compliance with the purposes, terms, and distribution requirements of the institution as necessary to meet other circumstances of the institution and the requirements of this part.

(6) A person that has special skills or expertise, or is selected in reliance upon the person's representation that the person has special skills or expertise, has a duty to use those skills or that expertise in managing and investing institutional funds.

(f) Nothing in this section alters the duties and liabilities of a director of a nonprofit public benefit corporation under Section 5240 of the Corporations Code. *(Added by Stats. 2008, c. 715 (S.B.1329), § 4.)*

Cross References

Charitable purpose defined for purposes of this Part, see Probate Code § 18502.
Gift instrument defined for purposes of this Part, see Probate Code § 18502.
Institution defined for purposes of this Part, see Probate Code § 18502.
Institutional fund defined for purposes of this Part, see Probate Code § 18502.
Person defined for purposes of this Part, see Probate Code § 18502.

§ 18504. Appropriation; expenditures; endowment fund

(a) Subject to the intent of a donor expressed in the gift instrument, an institution may appropriate for expenditure or accumulate so much of an endowment fund as the institution determines is prudent for the uses, benefits, purposes, and duration for which the endowment fund is established. Unless stated otherwise in the gift instrument, the assets in an endowment fund are donor-restricted assets until appropriated for expenditure by the institution. In making a determination to appropriate or accumulate, the institution shall act in good faith, with the care that an ordinarily prudent person in a like position would exercise under similar circumstances, and shall consider, if relevant, all of the following factors:

(1) The duration and preservation of the endowment fund.

(2) The purposes of the institution and the endowment fund.

(3) General economic conditions.

(4) The possible effect of inflation or deflation.

(5) The expected total return from income and the appreciation of investments.

(6) Other resources of the institution.

(7) The investment policy of the institution.

(b) To limit the authority to appropriate for expenditure or accumulate under subdivision (a), a gift instrument must specifically state the limitation.

(c) Terms in a gift instrument designating a gift as an endowment, or a direction or authorization in the gift instrument to use only "income," "interest," "dividends," or "rents, issues, or profits," or "to preserve the principal intact," or words of similar import have both of the following effects:

(1) To create an endowment fund of permanent duration unless other language in the gift instrument limits the duration or purpose of the fund.

(2) To not otherwise limit the authority to appropriate for expenditure or accumulate under subdivision (a).

(d) The appropriation for expenditure in any year of an amount greater than 7 percent of the fair market value of an endowment fund, calculated on the basis of market values determined at least quarterly and averaged over a period of not less than three years immediately preceding the year in which the appropriation for expenditure is made, creates a rebuttable presumption of imprudence. For an endowment fund in existence for fewer than three years, the fair market value of the endowment fund shall be calculated for the period the endowment fund has been in existence. This subdivision does not do any of the following:

(1) Apply to an appropriation for expenditure permitted under law other than this part or by the gift instrument.

(2) Apply to a private or public postsecondary educational institution, or to a campus foundation established by and operated under the auspices of such an educational institution.

(3) Create a presumption of prudence for an appropriation for expenditure of an amount less than or equal to 7 percent of the fair market value of the endowment fund. *(Added by Stats.2008, c. 715 (S.B.1329), § 4.)*

Cross References

Endowment fund defined for purposes of this Part, see Probate Code § 18502.

Gift instrument defined for purposes of this Part, see Probate Code § 18502.

Institution defined for purposes of this Part, see Probate Code § 18502.

Person defined for purposes of this Part, see Probate Code § 18502.

§ 18505. Delegation of management and investment; liability

(a) Subject to any specific limitation set forth in a gift instrument or in law other than this part, an institution may delegate to an external agent the management and investment of an institutional fund to the extent that an institution could prudently delegate under the circumstances. An institution shall act in good faith, with the care that an ordinarily prudent person in a like position would exercise under similar circumstances, in all of the following:

(1) Selecting an agent.

(2) Establishing the scope and terms of the delegation, consistent with the purposes of the institution and the institutional fund.

(3) Periodically reviewing the agent's actions in order to monitor the agent's performance and compliance with the scope and terms of the delegation.

(b) In performing a delegated function, an agent owes a duty to the institution to exercise reasonable care to comply with the scope and terms of the delegation.

(c) An institution that complies with subdivision (a) is not liable for the decisions or actions of an agent to which the function was delegated except to the extent a trustee would be liable for those actions or decisions under Sections 16052 and 16401.

(d) By accepting delegation of a management or investment function from an institution that is subject to the laws of this state, an agent submits to the jurisdiction of the courts of this state in all proceedings arising from or related to the delegation or the performance of the delegated function.

(e) An institution may delegate management and investment functions to its committees, officers, or employees as authorized by law of this state other than this part. (*Added by Stats.2008, c. 715 (S.B.1329), § 4.*)

Cross References

Gift instrument defined for purposes of this Part, see Probate Code § 18502.

Institution defined for purposes of this Part, see Probate Code § 18502.

Institutional fund defined for purposes of this Part, see Probate Code § 18502.

Person defined for purposes of this Part, see Probate Code § 18502.

§ 18506. Release or modification of restriction contained in a gift instrument

(a) If the donor consents in a record, an institution may release or modify, in whole or in part, a restriction contained in a gift instrument on the management, investment, or purpose of an institutional fund. A release or modification may not allow a fund to be used for a purpose other than a charitable purpose of the institution.

(b) The court, upon application of an institution, may modify a restriction contained in a gift instrument regarding the management or investment of an institutional fund if the restriction has become impracticable or wasteful, if it impairs the management or investment of the fund, or if, because of circumstances not anticipated by the donor, a modification of a restriction will further the purposes of the fund. The institution shall notify the Attorney General of the application, and the Attorney General must be given an opportunity to be heard. To the extent practicable, any modification must be made in accordance with the donor's probable intention.

(c) If a particular charitable purpose or a restriction contained in a gift instrument on the use of an institutional fund becomes unlawful, impracticable, impossible to achieve, or wasteful, the court, upon application of an institution, may modify the purpose of the fund or the restriction on the use of the fund in a manner consistent with the charitable purposes expressed in the gift instrument. The institution shall notify the Attorney General of the application, and the Attorney General must be given an opportunity to be heard.

(d) If an institution determines that a restriction contained in a gift instrument on the management, investment, or purpose of an institutional fund is unlawful, impracticable, impossible to achieve, or wasteful, the institution, 60 days after notification to the Attorney General and to the donor at the donor's last known address in the records of the institution, may release or modify the restriction, in whole or part, if all of the following apply:

(1) The institutional fund subject to the restriction has a total value of less than one hundred thousand dollars ($100,000).

(2) More than 20 years have elapsed since the fund was established.

(3) The institution uses the property in a manner consistent with the charitable purposes expressed in the gift instrument. An institution that releases or modifies a restriction under this subdivision may, if appropriate circumstances arise thereafter, use the property in accordance with the restriction notwithstanding its release or modification, and that use is deemed to satisfy the consistency requirement of this paragraph. (*Added by Stats.2008, c. 715 (S.B.1329), § 4.*)

Cross References

Attorney General, generally, see Government Code § 12500 et seq.

Charitable purpose defined for purposes of this Part, see Probate Code § 18502.

Gift instrument defined for purposes of this Part, see Probate Code § 18502.

Institution defined for purposes of this Part, see Probate Code § 18502.

Institutional fund defined for purposes of this Part, see Probate Code § 18502.

Record defined for purposes of this Part, see Probate Code § 18502.

§ 18507. Compliance

Compliance with this part is determined in light of the facts and circumstances existing at the time a decision is made or action is taken, and not by hindsight. (*Added by Stats.2008, c. 715 (S.B.1329), § 4.*)

§ 18508. Application of part

This part applies to institutional funds existing on or established after January 1, 2009. As applied to institutional funds existing on January 1, 2009, this part governs only decisions made or actions taken on or after that date. *(Added by Stats.2008, c. 715 (S.B.1329), § 4.)*

Cross References

Institutional fund defined for purposes of this Part, see Probate Code § 18502.

§ 18509. Applicability with respect to the Electronic Signatures in Global and National Commerce Act

This part modifies, limits, and supersedes the Electronic Signatures in Global and National Commerce Act (15 U.S.C. Sec. 7001 et seq.), but does not modify, limit, or supersede Section 101 of that act (15 U.S.C. Sec. 7001(a)), or authorize electronic delivery of any of the notices described in Section 103 of that act (15 U.S.C. Sec. 7003(b)). *(Added by Stats.2008, c. 715 (S.B.1329), § 4.)*

§ 18510. Uniformity

In applying and construing this uniform act, consideration must be given to the need to promote uniformity of the law with respect to its subject matter among states that enact it. *(Added by Stats.2008, c. 715 (S.B.1329), § 4.)*

Part 8

PAYMENT OF CLAIMS, DEBTS, AND EXPENSES FROM REVOCABLE TRUST OF DECEASED SETTLOR

Application

Application of Part 8 to claims against deceased settlors who die on or after January 1, 1992, see Probate Code § 19012.

Application of Division, see Probate Code § 15001.

CHAPTER 1. GENERAL PROVISIONS

Application

Application of Part 8 to claims against settlors who died before January 1, 1992, see Probate Code § 19012.

Application of Division, see Probate Code § 15001.

Cross References

Death of person against whom action may be brought, limitation period, see Code of Civil Procedure § 366.2.

§ 19000. Definitions

As used in this part:

(a) "Claim" means a demand for payment for any of the following, whether due, not due, accrued or not accrued, or contingent, and whether liquidated or unliquidated:

(1) Liability of the deceased settlor, whether arising in contract, tort, or otherwise.

(2) Liability for taxes incurred before the deceased settlor's death, whether assessed before or after the deceased settlor's death, other than property taxes and assessments secured by real property liens.

(3) Liability for the funeral expenses of the deceased settlor.

(b) "Claim" does not include a dispute regarding title to specific property alleged to be included in the trust estate.

(c) "Creditor" means a person who may have a claim against the trust property.

(d) "Trust" means a trust described in Section 18200, or, if a portion of a trust, that portion that remained subject to the power of revocation at the deceased settlor's death.

(e) "Deceased settlor" means a deceased person who, at the time of his or her death, held the power to revoke the trust in whole or in part.

(f) "Debts" means all claims, as defined in subdivision (a), all expenses of administration, and all other proper charges against the trust estate, including taxes.

(g) "Probate estate" means a decedent's estate subject to administration pursuant to Division 7 (commencing with Section 7000).

(h) "Trust estate" means a decedent's property, real and personal, that is titled in the name of the trustee of the deceased settlor's trust or confirmed by order of the court to the trustee of the deceased settlor's trust. *(Added by Stats.1991, c. 992 (S.B.727), § 3. Amended by Stats.1996, c. 862 (A.B.2751), § 46; Stats.2007, c. 159 (A.B.341), § 8; Stats.2015, c. 48 (S.B.785), § 1, eff. Jan. 1, 2016.)*

Cross References

Death of person against whom action may be brought, limitation period, see Code of Civil Procedure § 366.2.

§ 19001. Property subject to claims of creditors; priority of payment

(a) Upon the death of a settlor, the property of the deceased settlor that was subject to the power of revocation at the time of the settlor's death is subject to the claims of creditors of the deceased settlor's probate estate and to the expenses of administration of the probate estate to the extent that the deceased settlor's probate estate is inadequate to satisfy those claims and expenses.

(b) The deceased settlor, by appropriate direction in the trust instrument, may direct the priority of sources of payment of debts among subtrusts or other gifts established by the trust at the deceased settlor's death. Notwithstanding this subdivision, no direction by the settlor shall alter the priority of payment, from whatever source, of the matters set forth in Section 11420 which shall be applied to the trust as it applies to a probate estate. *(Added by Stats.1991, c. 992 (S.B.727), § 3. Amended by Stats.2015, c. 48 (S.B.785), § 2, eff. Jan. 1, 2016.)*

Cross References

Claim defined for purposes of this Part, see Probate Code § 19000.
Creditor defined for purposes of this Part, see Probate Code § 19000.
Debts defined for purposes of this Part, see Probate Code § 19000.
Deceased settlor defined for purposes of this Part, see Probate Code § 19000.
Trust defined for purposes of this Part, see Probate Code § 19000.

§ 19002. Construction of part

(a) Except as expressly provided, this part shall not be construed to affect the right of any creditor to recover from any revocable trust established by the deceased settlor.

(b) Nothing in this part shall be construed as a construction or alteration of any claims procedure set forth under Part 4 (commencing with Section 9000) of Division 7. *(Added by Stats.1991, c. 992 (S.B.727), § 3.)*

Cross References

Claim defined for purposes of this Part, see Probate Code § 19000.
Creditor defined for purposes of this Part, see Probate Code § 19000.
Deceased settlor defined for purposes of this Part, see Probate Code § 19000.
Trust defined for purposes of this Part, see Probate Code § 19000.

§ 19003. Notice to creditors; publication and service; filing; notice or request to public entities

(a) At any time following the death of the settlor, and during the time that there has been no filing of a petition to administer the probate estate of the deceased settlor in this state of which the trustee has actual knowledge, the trustee may file with the court a proposed notice to creditors. Upon the court's assignment of a proceeding number to the proposed notice, the trustee shall publish and serve notice to creditors of the deceased settlor in the form and within the time prescribed in Chapters 3 (commencing with Section 19040) and 4 (commencing with Section 19050). That action shall constitute notice to creditors of the requirements of this part.

(b) The filing shall be made with the superior court for the county in this state where the deceased settlor resided at the time of death, or if none, in any county in this state in which trust property was located at the time of the settlor's death, or if none, in the county in this state that was the principal place of administration of the trust at the time of the settlor's death.

(c) Nothing in subdivision (a) affects a notice or request to a public entity required by Chapter 7 (commencing with Section 19200). *(Added by Stats.1991, c. 992 (S.B.727), § 3. Amended by Stats.2015, c. 48 (S.B.785), § 3, eff. Jan. 1, 2016.)*

Cross References

Creditor defined for purposes of this Part, see Probate Code § 19000.
Deceased settlor defined for purposes of this Part, see Probate Code § 19000.
Trust defined for purposes of this Part, see Probate Code § 19000.

§ 19004. Effect of filing, publishing, and serving notice

If the trustee files, publishes, and serves notice as set forth in Section 19003, then:

(a) All claims against the trust shall be filed in the manner and within the time provided in this part.

(b) A claim that is not filed as provided in this part is barred from collection from trust assets.

(c) The holder of a claim may not maintain an action on the claim against the trust unless the claim is first filed as provided in this part. *(Added by Stats.1991, c. 992 (S.B.727), § 3.)*

Cross References

Claim defined for purposes of this Part, see Probate Code § 19000.
Trust defined for purposes of this Part, see Probate Code § 19000.

§ 19005. Payment, rejection, contest, or settlement of claims

The trustee may at any time pay, reject, or contest any claim against the deceased settlor or settle any claim by compromise, arbitration, or otherwise. The trustee may also file a petition in the manner set forth in Chapter 2 (commencing with Section 19020) to settle any claim. *(Added by Stats.1991, c. 992 (S.B.727), § 3.)*

Cross References

Claim defined for purposes of this Part, see Probate Code § 19000.
Deceased settlor defined for purposes of this Part, see Probate Code § 19000.

§ 19006. Protection from creditors; trustees, beneficiaries, and personal representatives; recovery of trust assets

(a) If a trustee of a trust established by the deceased settlor files, publishes, and serves notice as provided in

Section 19003 the protection from creditors afforded that trustee and trust shall also be afforded to any other trusts established by the deceased settlor and the trustees and beneficiaries of those trusts.

(b) If the personal representative of the deceased settlor's probate estate has published notice under Section 8120 and given notice of administration of the probate estate of the deceased settlor under Chapter 2 (commencing with Section 9050) of Part 4 of Division 7, the protection from creditors afforded the personal representative of the deceased settlor's probate estate shall be afforded to the trustee and to the beneficiaries of the trust.

(c) In the event that, following the filing and publication of the notice set forth in Section 19003, there shall be commenced any proceeding under which a notice pursuant to Section 8120 is required to be published, then the trustee shall have a right of collection against that probate estate to recover the amount of any debts paid from trust assets that would otherwise have been satisfied (whether by law or by direction in the deceased settlor's will or trust) by the property subject to probate proceedings. *(Added by Stats. 1991, c. 992 (S.B.727), § 3. Amended by Stats.2015, c. 48 (S.B.785), § 4, eff. Jan. 1, 2016.)*

Cross References

Creditor defined for purposes of this Part, see Probate Code § 19000.
Debts defined for purposes of this Part, see Probate Code § 19000.
Deceased settlor defined for purposes of this Part, see Probate Code § 19000.
Trust defined for purposes of this Part, see Probate Code § 19000.

§ 19007. Liability of one trust as against any other established by settlor

Nothing in this part shall determine the liability of any trust established by the deceased settlor as against any other trust established by that settlor, except to the extent that the trustee of the other trust shall file, publish, and serve the notice specified in Section 19003 and thereafter seek a determination of relative liability pursuant to Chapter 2 (commencing with Section 19020). *(Added by Stats.1991, c. 992 (S.B.727), § 3.)*

Cross References

Deceased settlor defined for purposes of this Part, see Probate Code § 19000.
Trust defined for purposes of this Part, see Probate Code § 19000.

§ 19008. Absence of proceeding to administer probate estate and failure to file proposed notice to creditors; liability of trust

If there is no proceeding to administer the probate estate of the deceased settlor, and if the trustee does not file a proposed notice to creditors pursuant to Section 19003 and does not publish notice to creditors pursuant to Chapter 3 (commencing with Section 19040), then the liability of the trust to any creditor of the deceased settlor shall be as otherwise provided by law. *(Added by Stats.1991, c. 992 (S.B.727), § 3. Amended by Stats.2015, c. 48 (S.B.785), § 5, eff. Jan. 1, 2016.)*

Cross References

Creditor defined for purposes of this Part, see Probate Code § 19000.
Deceased settlor defined for purposes of this Part, see Probate Code § 19000.
Trust defined for purposes of this Part, see Probate Code § 19000.

§ 19009. Disclosure of existence of trust or contents of provisions to creditor or beneficiary

Nothing in this part shall be construed to permit or require disclosure of the existence of the trust or the contents of any of its provisions to any creditor or beneficiary except as that creditor or beneficiary may otherwise be entitled to that information. *(Added by Stats.1991, c. 992 (S.B.727), § 3.)*

Cross References

Creditor defined for purposes of this Part, see Probate Code § 19000.
Trust defined for purposes of this Part, see Probate Code § 19000.

§ 19010. Trustee's duty to initiate notice proceeding; liability for failure to initiate proceeding

Nothing in this part imposes any duty on the trustee to initiate the notice proceeding set forth in Section 19003, and the trustee is not liable for failure to initiate the proceeding under this part. *(Added by Stats.1991, c. 992 (S.B.727), § 3.)*

§ 19011. Petition, notice, claim form, and allowance or rejection form; form and contents; mailing or delivery of copy of claim form

(a) The Judicial Council may prescribe the form and contents of the petition, notice, claim form, and allowance or rejection form to be used pursuant to this part. The allowance or rejection form may be part of the claim form.

(b) Any claim form adopted by the Judicial Council shall inform the creditor that the claim must be filed with the court and a copy mailed or delivered to the trustee. The claim form shall include a proof of mailing or delivery of a copy of the claim to the trustee, which may be completed by the claimant. *(Added by Stats.1991, c. 992 (S.B.727), § 3. Amended by Stats.2007, c. 159 (A.B.341), § 9.)*

Cross References

Claim defined for purposes of this Part, see Probate Code § 19000.
Creditor defined for purposes of this Part, see Probate Code § 19000.

§ 19012. Application of part; continuing effect of prior law

(a) This part applies to claims against any deceased settlor who dies on or after January 1, 1992.

(b) The applicable law in effect before January 1, 1992, continues to apply to claims against any deceased settlor who dies before January 1, 1992. *(Added by Stats.1991, c. 992 (S.B.727), § 3.)*

Cross References

Claim defined for purposes of this Part, see Probate Code § 19000.

Deceased settlor defined for purposes of this Part, see Probate Code § 19000.

CHAPTER 2. PETITION FOR APPROVAL AND SETTLEMENT OF CLAIMS AGAINST DECEASED SETTLOR

Application

Application of Part 8 to claims against settlors who died before January 1, 1992, see Probate Code § 19012.

Application of Division, see Probate Code § 15001.

§ 19020. Allowance, compromise or settlement of claims; allocation of amounts due to two or more trusts; petition

At any time after the filing and first publication of notice pursuant to Chapter 3 (commencing with Section 19040), and after expiration of the time to file claims provided in that chapter, a trustee or beneficiary may petition the court under this chapter to approve either of the following:

(a) Allowance, compromise, or settlement of any claims that have not been rejected by the trustee under the procedure provided in this part and for which trust property may be liable.

(b) An allocation of any amounts due by reason of an action described in subdivision (a) to two or more trusts which may be liable for the claims. *(Added by Stats.1991, c. 992 (S.B.727), § 3.)*

Cross References

Claim defined for purposes of this Part, see Probate Code § 19000.
Fee for filing petition commencing or opposition papers concerning certain probate proceedings, see Government Code § 70655.
Trust defined for purposes of this Part, see Probate Code § 19000.

§ 19021. Filing of petition; jurisdiction

The petition shall be filed in that county as may be determined pursuant to Section 19003. In the event this action seeks approval of allocation to two or more trusts for which the notice proceeding in Section 19003 would prescribe superior courts for more than one county, the court located in the county so prescribed for the trustee initiating the proceeding under this chapter shall have jurisdiction. *(Added by Stats.1991, c. 992 (S.B.727), § 3.)*

Cross References

Trust defined for purposes of this Part, see Probate Code § 19000.

§ 19022. Commencement of proceedings; petition; filing and contents; hearing

(a) A proceeding under this chapter is commenced by filing a verified petition stating facts showing that the petition is authorized under this chapter and the grounds of the petition.

(b) The petition shall set forth a description of the trust and the names of creditors with respect to which action is requested and a description of each claim, together with the requested determination by the court with respect to the claims, provided, however, that this section does not require the filing of a copy of the trust or disclosure of the beneficial interests of the trust. That petition shall also set forth the beneficiaries of the trust, those claimants whose interest in the trust may be affected by the petition, and the trustees of any other trust to which an allocation of liability may be approved by the court pursuant to the petition.

(c) The clerk shall set the matter for hearing. *(Added by Stats.1991, c. 992 (S.B.727), § 3. Amended by Stats.2007, c. 159 (A.B.341), § 10.)*

Cross References

Claim defined for purposes of this Part, see Probate Code § 19000.
Creditor defined for purposes of this Part, see Probate Code § 19000.
Trust defined for purposes of this Part, see Probate Code § 19000.

§ 19023. Notice of hearing; service on interested creditors

At least 30 days before the time set for the hearing on the petition, the petitioner shall cause notice of the time and place of the hearing and a copy of the petition to be served on each of the creditors whose interests in the estate may be affected by the petition in the manner provided in Chapter 4 (commencing with Section 413.10) of Title 5 of Part 2 of the Code of Civil Procedure. *(Added by Stats.1991, c. 992 (S.B.727), § 3. Amended by Stats.2007, c. 159 (A.B.341), § 11.)*

Cross References

Creditor defined for purposes of this Part, see Probate Code § 19000.

§ 19024. Notice of hearing; persons not petitioners

At least 30 days before the time set for the hearing on the petition, the petitioner shall cause notice of the time and place of the hearing, together with a copy of the petition, to be mailed to each of the following persons who is not a petitioner:

(a) All trustees of the trust and of any other trusts to which an allocation of liability may be approved by the court pursuant to the petition.

(b) All beneficiaries affected.

(c) The personal representative of the deceased settlor's probate estate, if any is known to the trustee.

(d) The Attorney General, if the petition relates to a charitable trust subject to the jurisdiction of the Attorney General, unless the Attorney General waives notice. *(Added by Stats.1991, c. 992 (S.B.727), § 3. Amended by Stats.2015, c. 48 (S.B.785), § 6, eff. Jan. 1, 2016.)*

Cross References

Attorney General, generally, see Government Code § 12500 et seq.
Deceased settlor defined for purposes of this Part, see Probate Code § 19000.
Trust defined for purposes of this Part, see Probate Code § 19000.

§ 19025. Failure to file written pleading upon notice; effect of court order

(a) If any creditor, beneficiary, or trustee fails timely to file a written pleading upon notice, then the case is at issue, notwithstanding the failure. The case may proceed on the petition and written statements filed by the time of the hearing, and no further pleadings by other persons are necessary. The creditor, beneficiary, or trustee who failed timely to file a written pleading upon notice may not participate further in the proceeding for the determination requested, and that creditor, beneficiary, or trustee shall be bound by the decision in the proceeding.

(b) The court's order, when final, shall be conclusive as to the liability of the trust property with respect to the claims at issue in the petition. In the event of a subsequent administration of the probate estate of the deceased settlor, that order shall be binding on the personal representative of the probate estate of the deceased settlor as well as all creditors and beneficiaries who had notice of the petition. *(Added by Stats.1991, c. 992 (S.B.727), § 3. Amended by Stats.2007, c. 159 (A.B.341), § 12; Stats.2015, c. 48 (S.B.785), § 7, eff. Jan. 1, 2016.)*

Cross References

Claim defined for purposes of this Part, see Probate Code § 19000.
Creditor defined for purposes of this Part, see Probate Code § 19000.
Deceased settlor defined for purposes of this Part, see Probate Code § 19000.
Trust defined for purposes of this Part, see Probate Code § 19000.

§ 19026. Dismissal of petition

The court may dismiss a petition if it appears that the proceeding is not reasonably necessary for the protection of the interests of the trustee or any beneficiary of the trust. *(Added by Stats.1991, c. 992 (S.B.727), § 3.)*

Cross References

Trust defined for purposes of this Part, see Probate Code § 19000.

§ 19027. Court's discretion; orders and other actions

(a) The court in its discretion may make any orders and take any other action necessary or proper to dispose of the matters presented by the petition.

(b) If the court determines that the assets of the trust estate are insufficient to pay all debts, then the court shall order payment in the manner specified by Section 11420. *(Added by Stats.1991, c. 992 (S.B.727), § 3.)*

Cross References

Debts defined for purposes of this Part, see Probate Code § 19000.
Trust defined for purposes of this Part, see Probate Code § 19000.

§ 19028. Repealed by Stats.1997, c. 724 (A.B.1172), § 30

§ 19029. Guardian ad litem; appointment

The court may, on its own motion or on request of a trustee or other person interested in the trust, appoint a guardian ad litem in accordance with Section 1003. *(Added by Stats.1991, c. 992 (S.B.727), § 3.)*

Cross References

Trust defined for purposes of this Part, see Probate Code § 19000.

§ 19030. Charitable trusts; petition by Attorney General

In a case involving a charitable trust subject to the jurisdiction of the Attorney General, the Attorney General may petition under this chapter. *(Added by Stats.1991, c. 992 (S.B.727), § 3.)*

Cross References

Attorney General, generally, see Government Code § 12500 et seq.
Trust defined for purposes of this Part, see Probate Code § 19000.

CHAPTER 3. PUBLICATION OF NOTICE

Section
19040. Publication; period; number of publications; type of newspaper; posting; form.
19041. Legislative findings and declarations.

Application

Application of Part 8 to claims against settlors who died before January 1, 1992, see Probate Code § 19012.

Application of Division, see Probate Code § 15001.

§ 19040. Publication; period; number of publications; type of newspaper; posting; form

(a) Publication of notice pursuant to this section shall be for at least 15 days. Three publications in a newspaper published once a week or more often, with at least five days intervening between the first and last publication dates, not counting the first and last publication dates as part of the five-day period, are sufficient. Notice shall be published in a newspaper of general circulation in the city, county, or city and county in this state where the deceased settlor resided at the time of death, or if none, in the city, county, or city and county in this state wherein trust property was located at the time of the settlor's death, or if none, in the city, county, or city and county in this state wherein the principal place of administration of the trust was located at the time of the settlor's death. If there is no newspaper of general circulation published in the applicable city, county, or city and county, notice shall be published in a newspaper of general circulation published in this state nearest to the applicable city, county, or city and county seat, and which is circulated within the applicable city, county, or city and county. If there is no such newspaper, notice shall be given in written or printed form, posted at three of the most public places within the community. For purposes of this section, "city" means a charter city as defined in Section 34101 of the Government Code or a general law city as defined in Section 34102 of the Government Code.

(b) The caption of the notice, the deceased settlor's name, and the name of the trustee shall be in at least 8–point type, the text of the notice shall be in at least 7–point type, and the notice shall state substantially as follows:

NOTICE TO CREDITORS

OF _____

#_____

SUPERIOR COURT OF CALIFORNIA

COUNTY OF _____

Notice is hereby given to the creditors and contingent creditors of the above-named decedent, that all persons having claims against the decedent are required to file them with the Superior Court, at ___, and mail a copy to ___, as trustee of the trust dated ___ wherein the decedent was the settlor, at ___, within the later of four months after ___ (the date of the first publication of notice to creditors) or, if notice is mailed or personally delivered to you, 60 days after the date this notice is mailed or personally delivered to you. A claim form may be obtained from the court clerk. For your protection, you are encouraged to file your claim by certified mail, with return receipt requested.

(name and address of trustee or attorney)

(c) An affidavit showing due publication of notice shall be filed with the clerk upon completion of the publication. The affidavit shall contain a copy of the notice, and state the date of its first publication. *(Added by Stats.1991, c. 992 (S.B.727), § 3. Amended by Stats.2007, c. 159 (A.B.341), § 13.)*

Cross References

Claim defined for purposes of this Part, see Probate Code § 19000.
Creditor defined for purposes of this Part, see Probate Code § 19000.
Deceased settlor defined for purposes of this Part, see Probate Code § 19000.
Trust defined for purposes of this Part, see Probate Code § 19000.

§ 19041. Legislative findings and declarations

The Legislature finds and declares that to be most effective, notice to creditors should be published in compliance with the procedures specified in Section 19040. However, the Legislature recognizes the possibility that in unusual cases due to confusion over jurisdictional boundaries or oversights the notice may inadvertently be published in a newspaper which does not meet these requirements. Therefore, to prevent a minor error in publication from invalidating what would otherwise be a proper proceeding, the Legislature further finds and declares that notice published in a good faith attempt to comply with Section 19040 shall be sufficient to provide notice to creditors and establish jurisdiction if the court expressly finds that the notice was published in a newspaper of general circulation published within the city, county, or city and county and widely circulated within a true cross section of the community in which the deceased settlor resided or wherein the principal place of administration of the trust was located or the property was located in substantial compliance with Section 19040. *(Added by Stats.1991, c. 992 (S.B.727), § 3.)*

Cross References

Creditor defined for purposes of this Part, see Probate Code § 19000.
Deceased settlor defined for purposes of this Part, see Probate Code § 19000.
Trust defined for purposes of this Part, see Probate Code § 19000.

CHAPTER 4. ACTUAL NOTICE TO CREDITORS

Application

Application of Part 8 to claims against settlors who died before January 1, 1992, see Probate Code § 19012.

Application of Division, see Probate Code § 15001.

§ 19050. Known creditors; notice

Except as provided in Section 19054, if the trustee has knowledge of a creditor of the deceased settlor, the trustee shall give notice to the creditor. The notice shall be given as provided in Section 1215. For the purpose of this section, a trustee has knowledge of a creditor of the deceased settlor if the trustee is aware that the creditor has demanded payment from the deceased settlor or the trust estate. *(Added by Stats.1991, c. 992 (S.B.727), § 3. Amended by Stats.2007, c. 159 (A.B.341), § 14.)*

Cross References

Creditor defined for purposes of this Part, see Probate Code § 19000.
Deceased settlor defined for purposes of this Part, see Probate Code § 19000.
Trust defined for purposes of this Part, see Probate Code § 19000.

§ 19051. Time limitations

The notice shall be given before expiration of the later of the following times:

(a) Four months after the first publication of notice under Section 19040.

(b) Thirty days after the trustee first has knowledge of the creditor. *(Added by Stats.1991, c. 992 (S.B.727), § 3. Amended by Stats.2007, c. 159 (A.B.341), § 15.)*

Cross References

Creditor defined for purposes of this Part, see Probate Code § 19000.

§ 19052. Form of notice

The notice shall be in substantially the following form:

NOTICE TO CREDITORS

OF _____

#_____

SUPERIOR COURT OF CALIFORNIA

COUNTY OF _____

Notice is hereby given to the creditors and contingent creditors of the above-named decedent, that all persons having claims against the decedent are required to file them with the Superior Court, at ___, and mail or deliver a copy to ___, as trustee of the trust dated ___ wherein the decedent was the settlor, at ___, within the later of four months after ___ (the date of the first publication of notice to creditors) or, if notice is mailed or personally delivered to you, 60 days after the date this notice is mailed or personally delivered to you, or you must petition to file a late claim as provided in Section 19103 of the Probate Code. A claim form may be obtained from the court clerk. For your protection, you are encouraged to file your claim by certified mail, with return receipt requested.

| (Date of mailing this notice if applicable) | (name and address of trustee or attorney) |

(Added by Stats.1991, c. 992 (S.B.727), § 3. Amended by Stats.2007, c. 159 (A.B.341), § 16.)

Cross References

Claim defined for purposes of this Part, see Probate Code § 19000.
Creditor defined for purposes of this Part, see Probate Code § 19000.
Trust defined for purposes of this Part, see Probate Code § 19000.

§ 19053. Liability of trustee for giving and failing to give notice; liability of trust estate; duty of trustee to search for creditors

(a) If the trustee believes that notice to a particular creditor is or may be required by this chapter and gives notice based on that belief, the trustee is not liable to any person for giving the notice, whether or not required by this chapter.

(b) If the trustee fails to give notice required by this chapter, the trustee is not liable to any person for that failure, unless a creditor establishes all of the following:

(1) The failure was in bad faith.

(2) The creditor did not have actual knowledge of the proceedings under Chapter 1 (commencing with Section 19000) sooner than one year after publication of notice to creditors under Section 19040, and payment would have been made on the creditor's claim if the claim had been properly filed.

(3) Within 16 months after the first publication of notice under Section 19040, the creditor did both of the following:

(A) Filed a petition requesting that the court in which the proceedings under Chapter 1 (commencing with Section 19000) were initiated make an order determining the liability of the trustee under this subdivision.

(B) At least 30 days before the hearing on the petition, caused notice of the hearing and a copy of the petition to be served on the trustee in the manner provided in Chapter 4 (commencing with Section 413.10) of Title 5 of Part 2 of the Code of Civil Procedure.

(c) Nothing in this section affects the liability of the trust estate, if any, for the claim of a creditor, and the trustee is not liable to the extent the claim is paid out of the trust estate.

(d) Nothing in this chapter imposes a duty on the trustee to make a search for creditors of the deceased settlor. *(Added by Stats.1991, c. 992 (S.B.727), § 3. Amended by Stats.2007, c. 159 (A.B.341), § 17.)*

§ 19054. Known creditors; situations where notice not needed

Notwithstanding Section 19050, the trustee need not give notice to a creditor even though the trustee has knowledge of the creditor if either of the following conditions is satisfied:

(a) The creditor has filed a claim as provided in this part.

(b) The creditor has demanded payment and the trustee elects to treat the demand as a claim under Section 19154. *(Added by Stats.1991, c. 992 (S.B.727), § 3. Amended by Stats.2003, c. 32 (A.B.167), § 14.)*

Law Revision Commission Comments

2003 Amendment

Section 19054 is amended to correct an incorrect cross-reference. See Section 19154 (election to treat demand as claim). [33 Cal.L.Rev. Comm. Reports 165 (2003)].

Cross References

Claim defined for purposes of this Part, see Probate Code § 19000.
Creditor defined for purposes of this Part, see Probate Code § 19000.

CHAPTER 5. TIME FOR FILING CLAIMS

Section

Application

Application of Part 8 to claims against settlors who died before January 1, 1992, see Probate Code § 19012.

Application of Division, see Probate Code § 15001.

§ 19100. Claims; time for filing; statute of limitations

(a) A creditor shall file a claim before expiration of the later of the following times:

(1) Four months after the first publication of notice to creditors under Section 19040.

(2) Sixty days after the date actual notice is mailed or personally delivered to the creditor. This paragraph does not extend the time provided in Section 366.2 of the Code of Civil Procedure.

(b) A reference in another statute to the time for filing a claim means the time provided in paragraph (1) of subdivision (a).

(c) This section shall not be interpreted to extend or toll any other statute of limitations, including that provided by Section 366.2 of the Code of Civil Procedure. *(Added by*

Stats.1991, c. 992 (S.B.727), § 3. Amended by Stats.2007, c. 159 (A.B.341), § 18.)

Cross References

Claim defined for purposes of this Part, see Probate Code § 19000. Creditor defined for purposes of this Part, see Probate Code § 19000.

§ 19101. Vacancy in office of trustee; time for filing claim

A vacancy in the office of the trustee that occurs before expiration of the time for filing a claim does not extend the time. *(Added by Stats.1991, c. 992 (S.B.727), § 3.)*

Cross References

Claim defined for purposes of this Part, see Probate Code § 19000.

§ 19102. Timely filing; actions by trustee or court after expiration of time for filing

A claim that is filed before expiration of the time for filing the claim is timely even if acted on by the trustee or the court after expiration of the time for filing claims. *(Added by Stats.1991, c. 992 (S.B.727), § 3.)*

Cross References

Claim defined for purposes of this Part, see Probate Code § 19000.

§ 19103. Claims filed after expiration of time for filing; conditions; time limitation; property subject to claim

(a) Except as provided in subdivision (b), upon petition by a creditor or a trustee, the court may allow a claim to be filed after expiration of the time for filing a claim provided in Section 19100 if either of the following conditions are satisfied:

(1) The trustee failed to send proper and timely notice to the creditor and the petition is filed within 60 days after the creditor has actual knowledge of the administration of the trust.

(2) The creditor did not have knowledge of the facts giving rise to the existence of the claim more than 30 days prior to the time for filing a claim as provided in Section 19100, and the petition is filed within 60 days after the creditor has actual knowledge of both of the following:

(A) The existence of the facts reasonably giving rise to the existence of the claim.

(B) The administration of the trust.

(b) Notwithstanding subdivision (a), the court shall not allow a claim to be filed under this section more than one year after the date of first publication of notice to creditors under Section 19040. Nothing in this subdivision authorizes allowance or approval of a claim barred by, or extends the time provided in, Section 366.2 of the Code of Civil Procedure.

(c) The court may condition the claim on terms that are just and equitable. The court may deny the claimant's petition if a distribution to trust beneficiaries or payment to general creditors has been made and it appears the filing or establishment of the claim would cause or tend to cause unequal treatment among beneficiaries or creditors.

(d) Regardless of whether the claim is later established in whole or in part, property distributed under the terms of the trust subsequent to an order settling claims under Chapter 2 (commencing with Section 19020) and payments otherwise properly made before a claim is filed under this section are not subject to the claim. Except to the extent provided in Chapter 12 (commencing with Section 19400) and subject to Section 19053, the trustee, distributee, or payee is not liable on account of the prior distribution or payment. This subdivision does not limit the liability of a person who receives a preliminary distribution of property to restore to the trust an amount sufficient for payment of the beneficiary's proper share of the claim, not exceeding the amount distributed. *(Added by Stats.1991, c. 992 (S.B.727), § 3. Amended by Stats.1992, c. 178 (S.B.1496), § 44; Stats.2007, c. 159 (A.B.341), § 19.)*

Law Revision Commission Comments

1992 Amendment

Section 19103 is amended to revise a section reference. This revision is a technical, nonsubstantive change. [22 Cal.L.Rev.Comm.Reports 895 (1992)].

Cross References

Claim defined for purposes of this Part, see Probate Code § 19000. Creditor defined for purposes of this Part, see Probate Code § 19000. Trust defined for purposes of this Part, see Probate Code § 19000.

§ 19104. Amendment or revision of claim; filing; restrictions

(a) Subject to subdivision (b), if a claim is filed within the time provided in this chapter, the creditor may later amend or revise the claim. The amendment or revision shall be filed in the same manner as the claim.

(b) An amendment or revision may not be made to increase the amount of the claim after the time for filing a claim has expired. An amendment or revision to specify the amount of a claim that, at the time of filing, was not due, was contingent, or was not yet ascertainable, is not an increase in the amount of the claim within the meaning of this subdivision. An amendment or revision of a claim may not be made for any purpose after the earlier of the following times:

(1) The time the court makes an order approving settlement of the claim against the deceased settlor under Chapter 2 (commencing with Section 19020).

(2) One year after the date of the first publication of notice to creditors under Section 19040. Nothing in this paragraph authorizes allowance or approval of a claim barred by, or extends the time provided in, Section 366.2 of the Code of Civil Procedure. *(Added by Stats.1991, c. 992 (S.B.727), § 3. Amended by Stats.1992, c. 178 (S.B.1496), § 45; Stats. 2007, c. 159 (A.B.341), § 20.)*

Law Revision Commission Comments

1992 Amendment

Section 19104 is amended to revise a section reference. This revision is a technical, nonsubstantive change. [22 Cal.L.Rev.Comm.Reports 895 (1992)].

Cross References

Claim defined for purposes of this Part, see Probate Code § 19000.

Creditor defined for purposes of this Part, see Probate Code § 19000.

Deceased settlor defined for purposes of this Part, see Probate Code § 19000.

CHAPTER 6. FILING OF CLAIMS

Application

Application of Part 8 to claims against settlors who died before January 1, 1992, see Probate Code § 19012.

Application of Division, see Probate Code § 15001.

§ 19150. Persons authorized to file claim; trustee's copy; failure to mail copy

(a) A claim may be filed by the creditor or a person acting on behalf of the claimant.

(b) A claim shall be filed with the court and a copy shall be mailed to the trustee. Failure to mail a copy to the trustee does not invalidate a properly filed claim, but any loss that results from the failure shall be borne by the creditor. *(Added by Stats.1991, c. 992 (S.B.727), § 3. Amended by Stats.2007, c. 159 (A.B.341), § 21.)*

Cross References

Claim defined for purposes of this Part, see Probate Code § 19000.
Creditor defined for purposes of this Part, see Probate Code § 19000.

§ 19151. Affidavit of claimant or person on behalf of creditor; contents; vouchers or proof to be produced

(a) A claim shall be supported by the affidavit of the creditor or the person on behalf of the claimant stating:

(1) The claim is a just claim.

(2) If the claim is due, the facts supporting the claim, the amount of the claim, and that all payments on and offsets to the claim have been credited.

(3) If the claim is not due or contingent, or the amount is not yet ascertainable, the facts supporting the claim.

(4) If the affidavit is made by a person other than the creditor, the reason it is not made by the creditor.

(b) The trustee may require satisfactory vouchers or proof to be produced to support the claim. An original voucher may be withdrawn after a copy is provided. If a copy is provided, the copy shall be attached to the claim. *(Added by Stats.1991, c. 992 (S.B.727), § 3. Amended by Stats.2007, c. 159 (A.B.341), § 22.)*

Cross References

Claim defined for purposes of this Part, see Probate Code § 19000.
Creditor defined for purposes of this Part, see Probate Code § 19000.

§ 19152. Claims based on written instrument; attachment of original or copy; claims secured by mortgage, deed of trust, or other lien description

(a) If a claim is based on a written instrument, either the original or a copy of the original with all endorsements shall be attached to the claim. If a copy is attached, the original instrument shall be exhibited to the trustee on demand unless it is lost or destroyed, in which case the fact that it is lost or destroyed shall be stated in the claim.

(b) If the claim or a part of the claim is secured by a mortgage, deed of trust, or other lien that is recorded in the office of the recorder of the county in which the property subject to the lien is located, it is sufficient to describe the mortgage, deed of trust, or lien and the recording reference for the instrument that created the mortgage, deed of trust, or other lien. *(Added by Stats.1991, c. 992 (S.B.727), § 3.)*

Cross References

Claim defined for purposes of this Part, see Probate Code § 19000.
Trust defined for purposes of this Part, see Probate Code § 19000.

§ 19153. Claim form; adoption by Judicial Council; contents

The Judicial Council may adopt a claim form which shall inform the creditor that the claim must be filed with the court and a copy mailed or delivered to the trustee. Any such claim form shall include a proof of mailing or delivery of a copy of the claim to the trustee which may be completed by the creditor. *(Added by Stats.1991, c. 992 (S.B.727), § 3.)*

Cross References

Claim defined for purposes of this Part, see Probate Code § 19000.
Creditor defined for purposes of this Part, see Probate Code § 19000.

§ 19154. Written demand for payment; waiver of formal defects and election to treat as claim; application of equitable principles

(a) Notwithstanding any other provision of this part, if a creditor makes a written demand for payment within the time specified in Section 19100, the trustee may waive formal defects and elect to treat the demand as a claim that is filed and established under this part by paying the amount demanded.

(b) Nothing in this section limits application of the doctrines of waiver, estoppel, laches, or detrimental reliance or any other equitable principle. *(Added by Stats.1991, c. 992 (S.B.727), § 3. Amended by Stats.2007, c. 159 (A.B.341), § 23.)*

Cross References

Claim defined for purposes of this Part, see Probate Code § 19000.
Creditor defined for purposes of this Part, see Probate Code § 19000.
Notice to creditors, necessity of notice if trustee elects to treat payment demand as claim under this section, see Probate Code § 19054.

CHAPTER 7. CLAIMS BY PUBLIC ENTITIES

Application

Application of Part 8 to claims against settlors who died before January 1, 1992, see Probate Code § 19012.

Application of Division, see Probate Code § 15001.

§ 19200. Public entity; filing of claim; time limitation

(a) Except as provided in this chapter, a claim by a public entity shall be filed within the time otherwise provided in this part. A claim not so filed is barred, including any lien imposed for the claim.

(b) As used in this chapter, "public entity" has the meaning provided in Section 811.2 of the Government Code, and includes an officer authorized to act on behalf of the public entity. *(Added by Stats.1991, c. 992 (S.B.727), § 3.)*

Cross References

Claim defined for purposes of this Part, see Probate Code § 19000.

§ 19201. Claims arising under certain laws, acts, or codes; form for written notice or request; barred claims

(a) Notwithstanding any other statute, if a claim of a public entity arises under a law, act, or code listed in subdivision (b):

(1) The public entity may provide a form to be used for the written notice or request to the public entity required by this chapter. Where appropriate, the form may require the decedent's social security number, if known.

(2) The claim is barred only after written notice or request to the public entity and expiration of the period provided in the applicable section. If no written notice or request is made, the claim is enforceable by the remedies, and is barred at the time, otherwise provided in the law, act, or code.

(b)

Law, Act, or Code	Applicable Section
Sales and Use Tax Law (commencing with Section 6001 of the Revenue and Taxation Code)	Section 6487.1 of the Revenue and Taxation Code
Bradley–Burns Uniform Local Sales and Use Tax Law (commencing with Section 7200 of the Revenue and Taxation Code)	Section 6487.1 of the Revenue and Taxation Code
Transactions and Use Tax Law (commencing with	Section 6487.1 of the Revenue and Taxation Code
Section 7251 of the Revenue and Taxation Code)	Applicable Section
Motor Vehicle Fuel License Tax Law (commencing with Section 7301 of the Revenue and Taxation Code)	Section 7675.1 of the Revenue and Taxation Code
Use Fuel Tax Law (commencing with Section 8601 of the Revenue and Taxation Code)	Section 8782.1 of the Revenue and Taxation Code
Administration of Franchise and Income Tax Law (commencing with Section 18401 of the Revenue and Taxation Code)	Section 19517 of the Revenue and Taxation Code
Cigarette Tax Law (commencing with Section 30001 of the Revenue and Taxation Code)	Section 30207.1 of the Revenue and Taxation Code
Alcoholic Beverage Tax Law (commencing with Section 32001 of the Revenue and Taxation Code)	Section 32272.1 of the Revenue and Taxation Code
Unemployment Insurance Code	Section 1090 of the Unemployment Insurance Code
State Hospitals (commencing with Section 7200 of the Welfare andInstitutions[1] Code)	Section 7277.1 of the Welfare and Institutions Code
Medi–Cal Act (commencing with Section 14000 of the Welfare and Institutions Code)	Section 9202 of the Probate Code
Waxman–Duffy Prepaid Health Plan Act (commencing with Section 14200 of the Welfare and Institutions Code)	Section 9202 of the Probate Code

[1] So in enrolled bill.

(Added by Stats.1991, c. 992 (S.B.727), § 3. Amended by Stats.2007, c. 159 (A.B.341), § 24; Stats.2014, c. 144 (A.B. 1847), § 50, eff. Jan. 1, 2015.)

Cross References

Claim defined for purposes of this Part, see Probate Code § 19000.

§ 19202. Health care received by deceased; notice of death to State Director of Health Services

(a) If the trustee knows or has reason to believe that the deceased settlor received health care under Chapter 7 (commencing with Section 14000) or Chapter 8 (commencing with Section 14200) of Part 3 of Division 9 of the Welfare and Institutions Code, or was the surviving spouse of a person who received that health care, the trustee shall give the State Director of Health Services notice of the death of the deceased settlor or surviving spouse in the manner provided in Section 215.

(b) The director has four months after notice is given in which to file a claim. *(Added by Stats.1991, c. 992 (S.B.727), § 3. Amended by Stats.2007, c. 159 (A.B.341), § 25.)*

Cross References

Claim defined for purposes of this Part, see Probate Code § 19000.
Deceased settlor defined for purposes of this Part, see Probate Code § 19000.

§ 19203. Property distributed before expiration of filing time; claim against distributees; interests and other costs

If property in the trust is distributed before expiration of the time allowed a public entity to file a claim, the public entity has a claim against the distributees to the full extent of the public entity's claim or each distributee's share of the distributed property, as set forth in Section 19402, whichever is less. The public entity's claim against distributees includes interest at a rate equal to that specified in Section 19521 of the Revenue and Taxation Code, from the date of distribution or the date of filing the claim by the public entity, whichever is later, plus other accruing costs as in the case of enforcement of a money judgment. *(Added by Stats.1991, c. 992 (S.B.727), § 3. Amended by Stats.2007, c. 159 (A.B.341), § 26.)*

Cross References

Claim defined for purposes of this Part, see Probate Code § 19000.
Trust defined for purposes of this Part, see Probate Code § 19000.

§ 19204. Priority of debts; construction of chapter

Nothing in this chapter shall be construed to affect the order of priority of debts provided for under other provisions of law. *(Added by Stats.1991, c. 992 (S.B.727), § 3.)*

Cross References

Debts defined for purposes of this Part, see Probate Code § 19000.

§ 19205. Liability for restitution of amounts illegally acquired; application of chapter

This chapter does not apply to liability for the restitution of amounts illegally acquired through the means of a fraudulent, false, or incorrect representation, or a forged or unauthorized endorsement. *(Added by Stats.1991, c. 992 (S.B.727), § 3.)*

CHAPTER 8. ALLOWANCE AND REJECTION OF CLAIMS

Application

Application of Part 8 to claims against settlors who died before January 1, 1992, see Probate Code § 19012.

Application of Division, see Probate Code § 15001.

§ 19250. Allowance or rejection of claim by trustee

When a claim is filed, the trustee shall allow or reject the claim in whole or in part. *(Added by Stats.1991, c. 992 (S.B.727), § 3.)*

Cross References

Claim defined for purposes of this Part, see Probate Code § 19000.

§ 19251. Allowance or rejection; filing with court clerk; notice to claimant; contents and form; application of section

(a) Any allowance or rejection shall be in writing. The trustee shall file the allowance or rejection with the court clerk and give notice to the claimant, together with a copy of the allowance or rejection, as provided in Section 1215.

(b) The allowance or rejection shall contain the following information:

(1) The name of the claimant.

(2) The date of the settlor's death.

(3) The total amount of the claim.

(4) The amount allowed or rejected by the trustee.

(5) A statement that the claimant has 90 days from the time the notice of rejection is given, or 90 days after the claim becomes due, whichever is later, in which to bring an action on a claim rejected in whole or in part.

(c) The Judicial Council shall prescribe an allowance or rejection form, which may be part of the claim form. Use of a form prescribed by the Judicial Council is deemed to satisfy the requirements.

(d) This section does not apply to a demand the trustee elects to treat as a claim under Section 19154. *(Added by Stats.1991, c. 992 (S.B.727), § 3.)*

Cross References

Claim defined for purposes of this Part, see Probate Code § 19000.

§ 19252. Powers of trustee or attorney for trustee; allowance, rejection, payment or compromise

The trustee shall have the power to pay any claim or portion of a claim and payment shall constitute allowance of the claim to the extent of the payment. The trustee shall have the power to compromise any claim or portion of a claim. If the trustee or the attorney for the trustee is a creditor of the deceased settlor, the trustee shall have the same powers regarding allowance, rejection, payment, or compromise set forth in this chapter. *(Added by Stats.1991, c. 992 (S.B.727), § 3. Amended by Stats.2007, c. 159 (A.B.341), § 27.)*

§ 19253. Barred claims; tolling of statute of limitations

(a) A claim barred by the statute of limitations may not be allowed by the trustee.

(b) The filing of a claim tolls the statute of limitations otherwise applicable to the claim until the trustee gives notice of allowance or rejection.

(c) The allowance of a claim further tolls the statute of limitations as to the part of the claim allowed until the allowed portion of the claim is paid.

(d) Notwithstanding the statute of limitations otherwise applicable to a claim, if an action on a rejected claim is not commenced or if the matter is not referred to a referee or to arbitration within the time prescribed in Section 19255, it is forever barred. *(Added by Stats.1991, c. 992 (S.B.727), § 3.)*

§ 19254. Refusal or neglect of trustee to act on claim; equivalent to giving notice of rejection

If within 30 days after a claim is filed the trustee has refused or neglected to act on the claim, the refusal or neglect may, at the option of the claimant, be deemed equivalent to the giving of a notice of rejection on the 30th day. *(Added by Stats.1991, c. 992 (S.B.727), § 3.)*

§ 19255. Rejected claims; actions on claim for referral to referee or arbitration; commencement of action; notice; property distributed; court costs and litigation expenses

(a) A rejected claim is barred as to the part rejected unless the creditor brings an action on the claim or the matter is referred to a referee or to arbitration within the following times, excluding any time during which there is a vacancy in the office of the trustee:

(1) If the claim is due at the time of giving the notice of rejection, 90 days after the notice is given.

(2) If the claim is not due at the time of giving the notice of rejection, 90 days after the claim becomes due.

(b) In addition to any other county in which an action on a rejected claim may be commenced, the action may be commenced in the county or city and county wherein the principal place of administration of the trust is located.

(c) The creditor shall file a notice of the pendency of the action or the referral to a referee or to arbitration with the court clerk in the trust proceeding, together with proof of giving a copy of the notice to the trustee as provided in Section 1215. Personal service of a copy of the summons and complaint on the trustee is equivalent to the filing and giving of the notice.

(d) Any property distributed by the trustee under the terms of the trust after 120 days from the later of the time the notice of rejection is given or the claim is due and before the notice of pendency of action or referral or arbitration is filed and given, excluding therefrom any time during which there is a vacancy in the office of the trustee, is not subject to the claim. Neither the trustee nor the distributee is liable on account of the distribution.

(e) The prevailing party in the action shall be awarded court costs and, if the court determines that the prosecution or defense of the action against the prevailing party was unreasonable, the prevailing party shall be awarded reasonable litigation expenses, including attorney's fees. For the purpose of this subdivision, the prevailing party shall be the trustee if the creditor recovers an amount equal to or less than the amount of the claim allowed by the trustee, and shall be the creditor if the creditor recovers an amount greater than the amount of the claim allowed by the trustee. *(Added by Stats.1991, c. 992 (S.B.727), § 3. Amended by Stats.1994, c. 40 (A.B.797), § 2, eff. April 19, 1994, operative Jan. 1, 1995; Stats.2007, c. 159 (A.B.341), § 28.)*

CHAPTER 9. CLAIMS ESTABLISHED BY JUDGMENT

§ 19300. Money judgments against deceased settlor, trustee, or trust estate; property subject to enforcement of judgments; filing of claim

(a) Except as provided in Section 19303, after the death of the settlor all money judgments against the deceased settlor on a claim against the deceased settlor or against the trustee on a claim against the decedent or the trust estate are payable in the course of administration and are not enforceable against property in the trust estate of the deceased settlor under the Enforcement of Judgments Law (Title 9 (commencing with Section 680.010) of Part 2 of the Code of Civil Procedure).

(b) Subject to Section 19301, a judgment referred to in subdivision (a) shall be filed in the same manner as other claims. *(Added by Stats.1991, c. 992 (S.B.727), § 3.)*

Cross References

Claim defined for purposes of this Part, see Probate Code § 19000.
Deceased settlor defined for purposes of this Part, see Probate Code § 19000.
Trust defined for purposes of this Part, see Probate Code § 19000.

§ 19301.   Final money judgments

When a money judgment against a trustee in a representative capacity becomes final, it conclusively establishes the validity of the claim for the amount of the judgment. The judgment shall provide that it is payable out of property in the deceased settlor's trust estate in the course of administration. An abstract of the judgment shall be filed in the trust administration proceedings. *(Added by Stats.1991, c. 992 (S.B.727), § 3.)*

Cross References

Claim defined for purposes of this Part, see Probate Code § 19000.
Deceased settlor defined for purposes of this Part, see Probate Code § 19000.
Trust defined for purposes of this Part, see Probate Code § 19000.

§ 19302.   Judgment for possession of trust property or for sale of trust property; enforcement; property subject to enforcement; demand for money not satisfied from trust property; filing of claim

(a) Notwithstanding the death of the settlor, a judgment for possession of trust property or a judgment for sale of trust property may be enforced under the Enforcement of Judgments Law (Title 9 (commencing with Section 680.010) of Part 2 of the Code of Civil Procedure). Nothing in this subdivision authorizes enforcement under the Enforcement of Judgments Law against any property in the trust estate of the deceased settlor other than the property described in the judgment for possession or sale.

(b) After the death of the settlor, a demand for money that is not satisfied from the trust property described in a judgment for sale of property shall be filed as a claim in the same manner as other claims and is payable in the course of administration. *(Added by Stats.1991, c. 992 (S.B.727), § 3.)*

Cross References

Claim defined for purposes of this Part, see Probate Code § 19000.
Deceased settlor defined for purposes of this Part, see Probate Code § 19000.
Trust defined for purposes of this Part, see Probate Code § 19000.

§ 19303.   Trust property subject to execution lien; enforcement of judgment; payment of balance of judgment remaining unsatisfied

If trust property of the deceased settlor is subject to an execution lien at the time of the settlor's death, enforcement against the property may proceed under the Enforcement of Judgments Law (Title 9 (commencing with Section 680.010) of Part 2 of the Code of Civil Procedure) to satisfy the judgment. The levying officer, as defined in Section 680.260

of the Code of Civil Procedure, shall account to the trustee for any surplus. If the judgment is not satisfied, the balance of the judgment remaining unsatisfied is payable in the course of administration. *(Added by Stats.1991, c. 992 (S.B.727), § 3.)*

Cross References

Deceased settlor defined for purposes of this Part, see Probate Code § 19000.
Trust defined for purposes of this Part, see Probate Code § 19000.

§ 19304.   Attachment liens; conversion into judgment lien; family's exemption for property levied on under writ of attachment

(a) An attachment lien may be converted into a judgment lien on property in the trust estate subject to the attachment lien, with the same priority as the attachment lien, in either of the following cases:

(1) Where the judgment debtor dies after entry of judgment in an action in which the property was attached.

(2) Where a judgment is entered after the death of the defendant in an action in which the property was attached.

(b) To convert the attachment lien into a judgment lien, the levying officer shall, after entry of judgment in the action in which the property was attached and before the expiration of the attachment lien, do one of the following:

(1) Serve an abstract of the judgment, and a notice that the attachment lien has become a judgment lien, on the trustee or other person holding property subject to the attachment lien.

(2) Record or file in any office where the writ of attachment and notice of attachment are recorded or filed an abstract of the judgment and a notice that the attachment lien has become a judgment lien. If the attached property is real property, the plaintiff or the plaintiff's attorney may record the required abstract and notice with the same effect as if recorded by the levying officer.

(c) After the death of the settlor, any members of the deceased settlor's family who were supported in whole or in part by the deceased settlor may claim an exemption provided in Section 487.020 of the Code of Civil Procedure for property levied on under the writ of attachment if the right to the exemption exists at the time the exemption is claimed. The trustee may claim the exemption on behalf of members of the deceased settlor's family. The claim of exemption may be made at any time before the time the abstract and notice are served, recorded, or filed under subdivision (b) with respect to the property claimed to be exempt. The claim of exemption shall be made in the same manner as an exemption is claimed under Section 482.100 of the Code of Civil Procedure. *(Added by Stats.1991, c. 992 (S.B.727), § 3. Amended by Stats.2007, c. 159 (A.B.341), § 29.)*

Cross References

Claim defined for purposes of this Part, see Probate Code § 19000.
Deceased settlor defined for purposes of this Part, see Probate Code § 19000.

Trust defined for purposes of this Part, see Probate Code § 19000.

CHAPTER 10.   ALLOCATION OF DEBTS BETWEEN TRUST AND SURVIVING SPOUSE

Application

Application of Part 8 to claims against settlors who died before January 1, 1992, see Probate Code § 19012.

Application of Division, see Probate Code § 15001.

§ 19320.   Debt paid or payable from property in settlor's trust; petition for order to allocate debt

If it appears that a debt of the deceased settlor has been paid or is payable in whole or in part from property in the deceased settlor's trust, then the trustee, the surviving spouse, the personal representative, if any, of a deceased settlor's probate estate, or a beneficiary may petition for an order to allocate the debt. *(Added by Stats.1991, c. 992 (S.B.727), § 3. Amended by Stats.2015, c. 48 (S.B.785), § 8, eff. Jan. 1, 2016.)*

Cross References

Deceased settlor defined for purposes of this Part, see Probate Code § 19000.
Trust defined for purposes of this Part, see Probate Code § 19000.

§ 19321.   Petition for order to allocate debt; contents

A petition under Section 19320 shall include a statement of all of the following:

(a) All debts of the deceased settlor and surviving spouse known to the petitioner that are alleged to be subject to allocation and whether paid in whole or in part or unpaid.

(b) The reason why the debts should be allocated.

(c) The proposed allocation and the basis for allocation alleged by the petitioner. *(Added by Stats.1991, c. 992 (S.B.727), § 3.)*

Cross References

Debts defined for purposes of this Part, see Probate Code § 19000.
Deceased settlor defined for purposes of this Part, see Probate Code § 19000.

§ 19322.   Allocations affected by value of spousal property, community property and quasi-community property; court orders to show cause why information should not be provided

If it appears from the petition under Section 19320 that allocation would be affected by the value of the separate property of the surviving spouse and any community property and quasi-community property not administered in the trust, and if an inventory and appraisal of the property has not been provided by the surviving spouse, the court shall make an order to show cause why the information should not be provided. *(Added by Stats.1991, c. 992 (S.B.727), § 3.)*

Cross References

Trust defined for purposes of this Part, see Probate Code § 19000.

§ 19323.   Hearing; notice to surviving spouse; notice to certain other persons who are not petitioners

(a) At least 30 days before the time set for the hearing on the petition, the petitioner shall cause notice of the time and place of the hearing and a copy of the petition to be served on the surviving spouse in the manner provided in Chapter 4 (commencing with Section 413.10) of Title 5 of Part 2 of the Code of Civil Procedure.

(b) At least 30 days before the time set for the hearing on the petition, the petitioner shall cause notice of the time and place of hearing, together with a copy of the petition, to be mailed to each of the following persons who are not petitioners:

(1) All trustees of the trust and of any trusts to which an allocation of liability may be approved by the court pursuant to the petition.

(2) All beneficiaries affected.

(3) The personal representative of the deceased settlor's probate estate, if any is known to the trustee.

(4) The Attorney General, if the petition relates to a charitable trust subject to the jurisdiction of the Attorney General, unless the Attorney General waives notice. *(Added by Stats.1991, c. 992 (S.B.727), § 3. Amended by Stats.2015, c. 48 (S.B.785), § 9, eff. Jan. 1, 2016.)*

Cross References

Attorney General, generally, see Government Code § 12500 et seq.
Deceased settlor defined for purposes of this Part, see Probate Code § 19000.
Trust defined for purposes of this Part, see Probate Code § 19000.

§ 19324.   Allocation of debt

(a) The trustee, the personal representative, if any, of a deceased settlor's probate estate, and the surviving spouse may provide for allocation of debts by agreement so long as the agreement substantially protects the rights of other interested persons. The trustee, the personal representative, or the spouse may request and obtain court approval of the allocation provided in the agreement.

(b) In the absence of an agreement, each debt subject to allocation shall first be characterized by the court as separate or community, in accordance with the laws of the state applicable to marital dissolution proceedings. Following that characterization, the debt or debts shall be allocated as follows:

(1) Separate debts of either spouse shall be allocated to that spouse's separate property assets, and community debts shall be allocated to the spouses' community property assets.

(2) If a separate property asset of either spouse is subject to a secured debt that is characterized as that spouse's

separate debt, and the net equity in that asset available to satisfy that secured debt is less than that secured debt, the unsatisfied portion of that secured debt shall be treated as an unsecured separate debt of that spouse and allocated to the net value of that spouse's other separate property assets.

(3) If the net value of either spouse's separate property assets is less than that spouse's unsecured separate debt or debts, the unsatisfied portion of the debt or debts shall be allocated to the net value of that spouse's one-half share of the community property assets. If the net value of that spouse's one-half share of the community property assets is less than that spouse's unsatisfied unsecured separate debt or debts, the remaining unsatisfied portion of the debt or debts shall be allocated to the net value of the other spouse's one-half share of the community property assets.

(4) If a community property asset is subject to a secured debt that is characterized as a community debt, and the net equity in that asset available to satisfy that secured debt is less than that secured debt, the unsatisfied portion of that secured debt shall be treated as an unsecured community debt and allocated to the net value of the other community property assets.

(5) If the net value of the community property assets is less than the unsecured community debt or debts, the unsatisfied portion of the debt or debts shall be allocated equally between the separate property assets of the deceased settlor and the surviving spouse. If the net value of either spouse's separate property assets is less than that spouse's share of the unsatisfied portion of the unsecured community debt or debts, the remaining unsatisfied portion of the debt or debts shall be allocated to the net value of the other spouse's separate property assets.

(c) For purposes of this section:

(1) The net value of either spouse's separate property asset shall refer to its fair market value as of the date of the deceased settlor's death, minus the date-of-death balance of any liens and encumbrances on that asset that have been characterized as that spouse's separate debts.

(2) The net value of a community property asset shall refer to its fair market value as of the date of the deceased settlor's death, minus the date-of-death balance of any liens and encumbrances on that asset that have been characterized as community debts.

(3) In the case of a nonrecourse debt, the amount of that debt shall be limited to the net equity in the collateral, based on the fair market value of the collateral as of the date of the decedent's death, that is available to satisfy that debt. For the purposes of this paragraph, "nonrecourse debt" means a debt for which the debtor's obligation to repay is limited to the collateral securing the debt, and for which a deficiency judgment against the debtor is not permitted by law.

(d) Notwithstanding the foregoing provisions of this section, the court may order a different allocation of debts between the deceased settlor's probate estate, trust, and the surviving spouse if the court finds a different allocation to be equitable under the circumstances.

(e) Nothing contained in this section is intended to impair or affect the rights of third parties. If a trustee, a personal representative, if any, of a deceased settlor's probate estate, or the surviving spouse incurs any damages or expense, including attorney's fees, on account of the nonpayment of a debt that was allocated to the other party pursuant to subdivision (b), or as the result of a debt being misallocated due to fraud or intentional misrepresentation by the other party, the party incurring damages shall be entitled to recover from the other party for damages or expense deemed reasonable by the court that made the allocation. *(Added by Stats.1991, c. 992 (S.B.727), § 3. Amended by Stats.2001, c. 72 (S.B.668), § 2.)*

Debts defined for purposes of this Part, see Probate Code § 19000.
Deceased settlor defined for purposes of this Part, see Probate Code § 19000.
Trust defined for purposes of this Part, see Probate Code § 19000.

§ 19325. Court orders; allocated amounts

On making a determination as provided in this chapter, the court shall make an order that:

(a) Directs the trustee to make payment of the amounts allocated to the trust by payment to the surviving spouse or creditors.

(b) Directs the trustee to charge amounts allocated to the surviving spouse against any property or interests of the surviving spouse that are in the possession or control of the trustee. To the extent that property or interests of the surviving spouse in the possession or control of the trustee are insufficient to satisfy the allocation, the court order shall summarily direct the surviving spouse to pay the allocation to the trustee. *(Added by Stats.1991, c. 992 (S.B.727), § 3.)*

Creditor defined for purposes of this Part, see Probate Code § 19000.
Trust defined for purposes of this Part, see Probate Code § 19000.

§ 19326. Funeral expenses and expenses of last illness

Notwithstanding any other statute, funeral expenses and expenses of last illness, in the absence of specific provisions in a will or trust to the contrary, shall be charged against the deceased settlor's probate estate and thereafter, against the deceased settlor's share of the trust and shall not be allocated to or charged against, the community share of the surviving spouse, whether or not the surviving spouse is financially able to pay the expenses and whether or not the surviving spouse or any other person is also liable for the expenses. *(Added by Stats.1991, c. 992 (S.B.727), § 3.)*

Deceased settlor defined for purposes of this Part, see Probate Code § 19000.
Trust defined for purposes of this Part, see Probate Code § 19000.

CHAPTER 11. LIABILITY OF SETTLOR'S SURVIVING SPOUSE

Application of Part 8 to claims against settlors who died before January 1, 1992, see Probate Code § 19012.

Application of Division, see Probate Code § 15001.

§ 19330. Barred claims

If proceedings are commenced under this part for the settlement of claims against the trust, and the time for filing claims has commenced, any action upon the liability of the surviving spouse under Chapter 3 (commencing with Section 13550) is barred to the same extent as provided for claims under this part, except as to the following:

(a) Any creditor who commences judicial proceedings to enforce a claim and serves the surviving spouse with the complaint prior to the expiration of the time for filing claims.

(b) Any creditor who has or who secures the surviving spouse's acknowledgment in writing of the liability of the surviving spouse for the claim.

(c) Any creditor who files a timely claim in the proceedings for the administration of the estate of the deceased spouse. *(Added by Stats.1991, c. 992 (S.B.727), § 3.)*

Cross References

Claim defined for purposes of this Part, see Probate Code § 19000.
Creditor defined for purposes of this Part, see Probate Code § 19000.
Trust defined for purposes of this Part, see Probate Code § 19000.

CHAPTER 12. DISTRIBUTEE LIABILITY

Section
19400. Beneficiary of trust; liability for unsecured claims.
19401. Creditor claim not filed; distributee liability; conditions.
19402. Defenses, cross-complaints, or setoffs; applicability of personal liability under chapter; limit of liability; value of property.
19403. Rights of purchaser or encumbrancer in good faith and for value.

Application

Application of Part 8 to claims against settlors who died before January 1, 1992, see Probate Code § 19012.

Application of Division, see Probate Code § 15001.

§ 19400. Beneficiary of trust; liability for unsecured claims

Subject to Section 366.2 of the Code of Civil Procedure, if there is no proceeding to administer the probate estate of the deceased settlor, and if the trustee does not file a proposed notice to creditors pursuant to Section 19003 and does not publish notice to creditors pursuant to Chapter 3 (commencing with Section 19040), then a beneficiary of the trust to whom payment, delivery, or transfer of the deceased settlor's property is made pursuant to the terms of the trust is personally liable, to the extent provided in Section 19402, for the unsecured claims of the creditors of the deceased settlor's probate estate. *(Added by Stats.1991, c. 992 (S.B.727), § 3. Amended by Stats.1992, c. 178 (S.B.1496), § 46; Stats.2015, c. 48 (S.B.785), § 10, eff. Jan. 1, 2016.)*

Law Revision Commission Comments
1992 Amendment

Section 19400 is amended to revise a section reference. This revision is a technical, nonsubstantive change. [22 Cal.L.Rev.Comm.Reports 895 (1992)].

Cross References

Claim defined for purposes of this Part, see Probate Code § 19000.
Creditor defined for purposes of this Part, see Probate Code § 19000.
Deceased settlor defined for purposes of this Part, see Probate Code § 19000.
Trust defined for purposes of this Part, see Probate Code § 19000.

§ 19401. Creditor claim not filed; distributee liability; conditions

Subject to Section 19402, if the trustee filed a proposed notice to creditors pursuant to Section 19003 and published notice to creditors pursuant to Section 19040, and if the identity of the creditor was known to, or reasonably ascertainable by, the trustee within four months of the first publication of notice pursuant to Section 19040, then a person to whom property is distributed is personally liable for the claim of the creditor, without a claim first having been filed, if all of the following conditions are satisfied:

(a) The claim of the creditor was not merely conjectural.

(b) Notice to the creditor was not given to the creditor under Chapter 4 (commencing with Section 19050) and neither the creditor nor the attorney representing the creditor in the matter had actual knowledge of the administration of the trust estate sooner than one year after the date of first publication of notice pursuant to Section 19040.

(c) The statute of limitations applicable to the claim under Section 366.2 of the Code of Civil Procedure has not expired at the time of commencement of an action under this section. *(Added by Stats.1991, c. 992 (S.B.727), § 3. Amended by Stats.1992, c. 178 (S.B.1496), § 47.)*

Law Revision Commission Comments
1992 Amendment

Section 19401 is amended to revise a section reference. This revision is a technical, nonsubstantive change. [22 Cal.L.Rev.Comm.Reports 895 (1992)].

Cross References

Claim defined for purposes of this Part, see Probate Code § 19000.
Creditor defined for purposes of this Part, see Probate Code § 19000.
Trust defined for purposes of this Part, see Probate Code § 19000.

§ 19402. Defenses, cross-complaints, or setoffs; applicability of personal liability under chapter; limit of liability; value of property

(a) In any action under this chapter, subject to Section 366.2 of the Code of Civil Procedure, the distributee may assert any defenses, cross-complaints, or setoffs that would have been available to the deceased settlor if the settlor had not died.

(b) Personal liability under this chapter is applicable only to the extent the claim of the creditor cannot be satisfied out of the trust estate of the deceased settlor and is limited to a pro rata portion of the claim of the creditor, based on the proportion that the value of the property distributed to the person out of the trust estate bears to the total value of all property distributed to all persons out of the trust estate. Personal liability under this chapter for all claims of all creditors shall not exceed the value of the property distributed to the person out of the trust estate. As used in this chapter, the value of the property is the fair market value of the property on the date of its distribution, less the amount of any liens and encumbrances on the property at that time. *(Added by Stats.1991, c. 992 (S.B.727), § 3. Amended by Stats.1992, c. 178 (S.B.1496), § 48.)*

Law Revision Commission Comments
1992 Amendment

Section 19402 is amended to revise a section reference. This revision is a technical, nonsubstantive change. [22 Cal.L.Rev.Comm.Reports 895 (1992)].

Cross References

Claim defined for purposes of this Part, see Probate Code § 19000.
Creditor defined for purposes of this Part, see Probate Code § 19000.
Deceased settlor defined for purposes of this Part, see Probate Code § 19000.
Trust defined for purposes of this Part, see Probate Code § 19000.

§ 19403. Rights of purchaser or encumbrancer in good faith and for value

Nothing in this chapter affects the rights of a purchaser or encumbrancer of property in good faith and for value from a person who is personally liable under this section. *(Added by Stats.1991, c. 992 (S.B.727), § 3. Amended by Stats.2004, c. 183 (A.B.3082), § 280.)*

Division 10

PRORATION OF TAXES

Law Revision Commission Comments

1990 Enactment

This division supersedes Division 10 (commencing with 20100) of the repealed Probate Code. The superseded division was enacted upon recommendation of the California Law Revision Commission. See *Recommendation Relating to Proration of Estate Taxes*, 18 Cal.L.Revision Comm'n Reports 1127 (1986); *Communication from California Law Revision Commission Concerning Assembly Bill 2625*, 18 Cal.L.Revision Comm'n Reports 1743, 1758–59 (1986). The Commission, in cooperation with California Continuing Education of the Bar, published the recommended legislation as enacted with official comments. See Selected 1986 Trust and Probate Legislation, 18 Cal.L.Revision Comm'n Reports 1201, 1623–46 (1986). [20 Cal.L.Rev.Comm.Reports 1001 (1990)].

Cross References

Abatement of shares of beneficiaries except as provided in this Division, see Probate Code § 21401.

CHAPTER 1. PRORATION OF ESTATE TAXES

Application

Application of chapter, see Probate Code § 20101.

Cross References

Decedent's estate, grounds for appeal, final orders under this Chapter, see Probate Code § 1303.

ARTICLE 1. GENERAL PROVISIONS

Application

Application of chapter, see Probate Code § 20101.

§ 20100. Definitions

Except where the context otherwise requires, the following definitions shall govern the construction of this chapter:

(a) "Estate tax" means a tax imposed by any federal or California estate tax law, now existing or hereafter enacted, and includes interest and penalties on any deficiency.

(b) "Person interested in the estate" means any person, including a personal representative, entitled to receive, or who has received, from a decedent while alive or by reason of the death of the decedent any property or interest therein.

(c) "Personal representative" includes a guardian, conservator, trustee, or other person charged with the responsibility of paying the estate tax.

(d) "Property" means property included in the gross estate for federal estate tax purposes.

(e) "Value" means fair market value as determined for federal estate tax purposes. *(Stats.1990, c. 79 (A.B.759), § 14, operative July 1, 1991.)*

Law Revision Commission Comments

1990 Enactment

Section 20100 continues Section 20100 of the repealed Probate Code without change.

The definition of "person interested in the estate" in subdivision (b) includes but is not limited to persons who receive property by nonprobate transfer, such as a joint tenant or the beneficiary of a trust.

Subdivision (c) defines "personal representative" broadly to include more than an executor, administrator, administrator with the will annexed, or special administrator.

The definition of "property" in subdivision (d) makes clear that the term includes property transferred by the decedent during life if included in the gross estate for federal estate tax purposes. See, e.g., I.R.C. § 2035. Cf. subdivision (b) ("person interested in estate" includes person who received property from a decedent while alive).

Subdivision (e) defines the term "value" to mean fair market value as determined for federal estate tax purposes. Thus, where an alternate valuation is elected pursuant to Section 2032 of the Internal Revenue Code, "value" means the fair market value determined as of the alternate valuation date for federal estate tax purposes. See Treas.Reg. § 20.2031–1(b), 26 C.F.R. § 20.2031–1(b) (1988).

This chapter does not apply to persons interested in the estate of a decedent who died before January 1, 1987. Prior law continues to apply where the decedent died before January 1, 1987. See Section 20101. As to the application of any amendments made after that date, see Section 3.

Background on Section 20100 of Repealed Code

Section 20100 was added by 1986 Cal.Stat. ch. 783 § 25. The section superseded former Probate Code Section 977 (repealed by 1986 Cal.Stat. ch. 783 § 16). The definition of "gross estate" in former Section 977(b) erroneously had the effect of prorating taxes to adjusted taxable gifts. For background on the provisions of this division, see the Comment to this division under the division heading. [20 Cal.L.Rev.Comm.Reports 1001 (1990)].

§ 20101. Application of chapter

(a) This chapter does not apply to persons interested in the estate of a decedent who died before January 1, 1987.

(b) Notwithstanding the repeal of former Article 4a (commencing with Section 970) of Chapter 15 of Division 3 of the Probate Code by Chapter 783 of the Statutes of 1986, the provisions of that former article remain applicable where the decedent died before January 1, 1987. No inference as to the applicable law in effect before January 1, 1987, shall be drawn from the enactment of this chapter. *(Stats.1990, c. 79 (A.B.759), § 14, operative July 1, 1991.)*

Section 20101 continues Section 20101 of the repealed Probate Code without substantive change.

Background on Section 20101 of Repealed Code

Section 20101 was a new provision added by 1986 Cal.Stat. ch. 783 § 25. For background on the provisions of this division, see the Comment to this division under the division heading. [20 Cal.L.Rev.Comm.Reports 1001 (1990)].

Cross References

Person interested in the estate defined for purposes of this Chapter, see Probate Code § 20100.

ARTICLE 2.   PRORATION

Section
20110. Exemptions.
20111. Proportion to total value of property.
20112. Allowances for credits, exemptions, and deductions; interest and penalties.
20113. Temporary interest and remainder.
20114. Qualified real property; election pursuant to federal Internal Revenue Code.
20114.5. Increase in federal estate tax; charge against persons receiving excess retirement accumulation.
20115. Extended tax under federal estate tax law.
20116. Recovery from persons interested where property does not come into possession of personal representative; amounts not recoverable.
20117. Right of reimbursement.

Application

Application of chapter, see Probate Code § 20101.

§ 20110.   Exemptions

(a) Except as provided in subdivision (b), any estate tax shall be equitably prorated among the persons interested in the estate in the manner prescribed in this article.

(b) This section does not apply:

(1) To the extent the decedent in a written inter vivos or testamentary instrument disposing of property specifically directs that the property be applied to the satisfaction of an estate tax or that an estate tax be prorated to the property in the manner provided in the instrument. As used in this paragraph, an "instrument disposing of property" includes an instrument that creates an interest in property or an amendment to an instrument that disposes of property or creates an interest in property.

(2) Where federal law directs otherwise. If federal law directs the manner of proration of the federal estate tax, the California estate tax shall be prorated in the same manner. *(Stats.1990, c. 79 (A.B.759), § 14, operative July 1, 1991.)*

Law Revision Commission Comments

1990 Enactment

Section 20110 continues Section 20110 of the repealed Probate Code without change. The section recognizes that federal law may provide for a different manner of proration. See, e.g., I.R.C. § 2207A. In such a situation, proration of the California estate tax must conform to the federal proration.

Section 20110 allows proration of an extended estate tax prior to actual payment of the tax. See Section 20115 (proration of extended estate tax). Penalties and interest on an estate tax are prorated pursuant to Section 20112 (allowance and charges for credits, deductions, interest, and other adjustments).

This chapter does not apply to persons interested in the estate of a decedent who died before 1, 1987. Prior law continues to apply where the decedent died before January 1, 1987. See Section 20101. As to the application of any amendments made after that date, see Section 3.

Background on Section 20110 of Repealed Code

Section 20110 was added by 1986 Cal.Stat. ch. 783 § 25. The section restated former Probate Code Section 970 (repealed by 1986 Cal.Stat. ch. 783 § 16) without substantive change, but recognized that federal law may provide for a different manner of proration. See, e.g., I.R.C. § 2207A. In such a situation, proration of the California estate tax must conform to the federal proration. For background on the provisions of this division, see the Comment to this division under the division heading. [20 Cal.L.Rev.Comm.Reports 1001 (1990)].

Cross References

Estate tax defined for purposes of this Chapter, see Probate Code § 20100.
Person interested in the estate defined for purposes of this Chapter, see Probate Code § 20100.
Property defined for purposes of this Chapter, see Probate Code § 20100.

§ 20111.   Proportion to total value of property

The proration required by this article shall be made in the proportion that the value of the property received by each person interested in the estate bears to the total value of all property received by all persons interested in the estate, subject to the provisions of this article. *(Stats.1990, c. 79 (A.B.759), § 14, operative July 1, 1991.)*

Law Revision Commission Comments

1990 Enactment

Section 20111 continues Section 20111 of the repealed Probate Code without change. The section does not require a court order to make the proration. Cf. Sections 20120–20125 for optional court procedure to determine proration.

The proration is made against all property included in the decedent's gross estate for federal estate tax purposes, including gifts includible in the estate pursuant to Section 2035 of the Internal Revenue Code. See Sections 20100 (definitions) and 20110 (proration among persons interested in estate) and the Comments thereto. The proration is based on fair market value as determined for federal estate tax purposes, even though the estate tax may be based on a special value. Adjustments for interest and penalties may be made on an equitable basis. See Section 20112 (allowance and charges for credits, deductions, interest, and other adjustments).

This chapter does not apply to persons interested in the estate of a decedent who died before January 1, 1987. Prior law continues to apply where the decedent died before January 1, 1987. See Section 20101. As to the application of any amendments made after that date, see Section 3.

Background on Section 20111 of Repealed Code

Section 20111 was added by 1986 Cal.Stat. ch. 783 § 25. The section continued former Probate Code Section 971 (repealed by 1986 Cal.Stat. ch. 783 § 16) without substantive change, but Section 20111 did not require a court order to make the proration as was required under former Section 971. For background on the provisions of this division, see the Comment to this division under the division heading. [20 Cal.L.Rev.Comm.Reports 1001 (1990)].

Person interested in the estate defined for purposes of this Chapter, see Probate Code § 20100.

Property defined for purposes of this Chapter, see Probate Code § 20100.

Value defined for purposes of this Chapter, see Probate Code § 20100.

§ 20112. Allowances for credits, exemptions, and deductions; interest and penalties

(a) In making a proration of the federal estate tax, allowances shall be made for credits allowed for state or foreign death taxes in determining the federal tax payable and for exemptions and deductions allowed for the purpose of determining the taxable estate.

(b) In making a proration of the California estate tax, allowances shall be made for (1) credits (other than the credit for state death taxes paid) allowed by the federal estate tax law and attributable to property located in this state, and (2) exemptions and deductions allowed by the federal estate tax law for the purpose of determining the taxable estate attributable to property located in this state.

(c) In making a proration of an estate tax, interest on extension of taxes and interest and penalties on any deficiency shall be charged to equitably reflect the benefits and burdens of the extension or deficiency and of any tax deductions associated with the interest and penalties. *(Stats. 1990, c. 79 (A.B.759), § 14, operative July 1, 1991.)*

Section 20112 continues Section 20112 of the repealed Probate Code without change. Subdivision (a) refers to exemptions in anticipation of future enactment of exemptions. This chapter does not apply to persons interested in the estate of a decedent who died before January 1, 1987. Prior law continues to apply where the decedent died before January 1, 1987. See Section 20101. As to the application of any amendments made after that date, see Section 3.

Section 20112 was added by 1986 Cal.Stat. ch. 783 § 25. Subdivisions (a) and (b) continued former Probate Code Section 972 (repealed by 1986 Cal.Stat. ch. 783 § 16) without substantive change. Although the federal estate tax exemption was replaced by a unified tax credit and other credits were allowed, subdivision (a) also referred to exemptions in anticipation of future enactment of exemptions. Subdivision (c) was new. For background on the provisions of this division, see the Comment to this division under the division heading. [20 Cal.L.Rev.Comm.Reports 1001 (1990)].

Estate tax defined for purposes of this Chapter, see Probate Code § 20100.

Property defined for purposes of this Chapter, see Probate Code § 20100.

§ 20113. Temporary interest and remainder

If a trust is created, or other provision made whereby a person is given an interest in the income of, an estate for years or for life in, or other temporary interest in, any property, the estate tax on both the temporary interest and on the remainder thereafter shall be charged against and paid out of the corpus of the property without apportionment between remainders and temporary estates. *(Stats.1990, c. 79 (A.B.759), § 14, operative July 1, 1991.)*

Section 20113 continues Section 20113 of the repealed Probate Code without change. This chapter does not apply to persons interested in the estate of a decedent who died before January 1, 1987. Prior law continues to apply where the decedent died before January 1, 1987. See Section 20101. As to the application of any amendments made after that date, see Section 3.

Section 20113 was added by 1986 Cal.Stat. ch. 783 § 25. The section continued former Probate Code Section 973 (repealed by 1986 Cal.Stat. ch. 783 § 16) without substantive change. For background on the provisions of this division, see the Comment to this division under the division heading. [20 Cal.L.Rev.Comm.Reports 1001 (1990)].

Estate tax defined for purposes of this Chapter, see Probate Code § 20100.

Property defined for purposes of this Chapter, see Probate Code § 20100.

§ 20114. Qualified real property; election pursuant to federal Internal Revenue Code

(a) As used in this section, "qualified real property" means qualified real property as defined in Section 2032A of the Internal Revenue Code (26 U.S.C. Sec. 2032A).

(b) If an election is made pursuant to Section 2032A of the Internal Revenue Code (26 U.S.C. Sec. 2032A), the proration shall be based upon the amount of federal estate tax that would be payable but for the election. The amount of the reduction in federal estate tax resulting from an election pursuant to Section 2032A of the Internal Revenue Code (26 U.S.C. Sec. 2032A) shall reduce the tax that is otherwise attributable to the qualified real property that is the subject of the election. If the tax that is otherwise attributable to the qualified real property is reduced to zero pursuant to this subdivision, any excess amount of reduction shall reduce the tax otherwise payable with respect to the other property, this amount to be equitably prorated in accordance with Section 20111.

(c) If additional federal estate tax is imposed under subsection (c) of Section 2032A of the Internal Revenue Code (26 U.S.C. Sec. 2032A) by reason of early disposition or cessation of qualified use, the additional tax shall be a charge against the portion of the qualified real property to which the additional tax is attributable, and shall be equitably prorated among the persons interested in that portion of the qualified real property in proportion to their interests. *(Stats.1990, c. 79 (A.B.759), § 14, operative July 1, 1991.)*

Section 20114 continues Section 20114 of the repealed Probate Code without change. This section deals with specially valued real property. Where an election is made to specially value qualified real property under Internal Revenue Code Section 2032A, the qualified heirs who receive the qualified real property receive the entire benefit of the estate tax reduction resulting from the election and are likewise liable for the entire amount of any additional tax subsequently imposed on the property. For example, assume an estate in which, absent a special valuation election, each beneficiary receives property of equal value and shares equally in the prorated estate taxes. If one beneficiary makes a special valuation election that reduces the total estate tax, the amount of the reduction must be allocated entirely to that beneficiary, and the others must pay the amount they would have been liable for absent the special valuation election.

To illustrate the operation of Section 20114, assume the decedent dies in 1987, leaving an estate consisting of $500,000 cash and real property having a fair market value of $500,000 (and a value under Internal Revenue Code Section 2032A of $250,000). The decedent's will leaves the real property to A and the cash to B.

(1) If no election is made under Section 2032A, the taxable estate is $1,000,000. The estate tax is $153,000, which is prorated $76,500 to A and $76,500 to B.

(2) If an election is made under Section 2032A, the taxable estate is $750,000. The estate tax is $55,500; the reduction in estate tax is $97,500. A is credited with $76,500 against the fair market value proration. (This represents the amount of the reduction in tax resulting from the election, to the extent of the tax that would be attributable to the qualified real property but for the election.) A pays no tax and B pays the full tax of $55,500, which represents a reduction of B's tax liability by $21,000.

Subdivision (b) ensures that A receives the benefit of the tax relief under Section 2032A, up to the amount of tax that would have been prorated to the fair market value of the qualified real property. B also benefits from the election, but no further compensating adjustment is required, except that if B shares the devise with other persons, the tax obligation of each of the others is reduced by a proportionate share of the $21,000 savings.

Subdivision (c) provides that any additional tax under Internal Revenue Code Section 2032A(c) will be imposed only upon those who received the qualified real property and benefited from the election. If A causes the full additional tax to be assessed under Internal Revenue Code Section 2032A(c), the entire additional tax of $97,500 will be prorated to A. This is true even though B also benefited from the election under Section 2032A.

This chapter does not apply to persons interested in the estate of a decedent who died before January 1, 1987. Prior law continues to apply where the decedent died before January 1, 1987. See Section 20101. As to the application of any amendments made after that date, see Section 3.

Background on Section 20114 of Repealed Code

Section 20114 was a new provision added by 1986 Cal.Stat. ch. 783 § 25. For background on the provisions of this division, see the Comment to this division under the division heading. [20 Cal.L.Rev.Comm.Reports 1001 (1990)].

Cross References

Estate tax defined for purposes of this Chapter, see Probate Code § 20100.
Property defined for purposes of this Chapter, see Probate Code § 20100.

§ 20114.5. Increase in federal estate tax; charge against persons receiving excess retirement accumulation

(a) As used in this section:

(1) A reference to Section 4980A of the Internal Revenue Code means Section 4980A of the federal Internal Revenue Code of 1986 as amended (26 U.S.C. Sec. 4980A) and also means former Section 4981A of the federal Internal Revenue Code of 1986.

(2) "Excess retirement accumulation" has the meaning given it in paragraph (3) of subsection (d) of Section 4980A.

(b) If the federal estate tax is increased under subsection (d) of Section 4980A of the Internal Revenue Code, the amount of the increase shall be a charge against the persons who receive the excess retirement accumulation that gives rise to the increase, and shall be equitably prorated among all persons who receive interests in qualified employer plans and individual retirement plans to which the excess retirement accumulation is attributable. *(Stats.1990, c. 79 (A.B.759), § 14, operative July 1, 1991. Amended by Stats.2004, c. 183 (A.B.3082), § 281.)*

Law Revision Commission Comments

1990 Enactment [Revised Comment]

Section 20114.5 continues Section 20114.5 of the repealed Probate Code without substantive change. This section specifies the manner of proration of the 15 percent tax on excess retirement accumulations imposed by the Tax Reform Act of 1986, Pub.L. No. 99–514, § 1133(a). This chapter does not apply to persons interested in the estate of a decedent who died before January 1, 1987. Prior law continues to apply where the decedent died before January 1, 1987. See Section 20101. As to the application of any amendments made after that date, see Section 3.

Background on Section 20114.5 of Repealed Code

Section 20114.5 was a new provision added by 1987 Cal.Stat. ch. 128 § 20 and amended by 1987 Cal.Stat. ch. 923 § 100.5. It was also amended by 1989 Cal.Stat. ch. 544 § 18 to correct references to the Internal Revenue Code. For background on Section 20114.5, see *Communication from the California Law Revision Commission Concerning Assembly Bill 362*, 19 Cal.L.Revision Comm'n Reports 541, 543 (1988); see also *Communication from the California Law Revision Commission Concerning Assembly Bill 158*, 20 Cal.L.Revision Comm'n Reports 235, 242 (1990). [21 Cal.L.Rev.Comm.Reports 75 (1991)].

Cross References

Estate tax defined for purposes of this Chapter, see Probate Code § 20100.

§ 20115. Extended tax under federal estate tax law

Where the payment of any portion of the federal estate tax is extended under the provisions of the federal estate tax law, the amount of extended tax shall be a charge against the persons who receive the specific property that gives rise to the extension. *(Stats.1990, c. 79 (A.B.759), § 14, operative July 1, 1991.)*

Law Revision Commission Comments

1990 Enactment

Section 20115 continues Section 20115 of the repealed Probate Code without change. This section ensures that the persons who receive property that gives rise to the extension of estate tax are the persons who benefit from the extension privilege. With respect to allocation of any interest on the extension, see Section 20112 (allowance and charges for credits, deductions, interest, and other adjustments).

Section 20115 makes clear that where a decedent's estate consists of a closely held business with respect to which estate taxes may be extended, the deferred tax and interest thereon follow the business. If the persons who receive the property fail to pay the tax when due and the tax is collected from persons other than the persons to whom the tax is prorated, the persons from whom the tax is collected have a right of reimbursement against the persons to whom the tax is prorated. See Section 20117 (reimbursement for overpayment).

This chapter does not apply to persons interested in the estate of a decedent who died before January 1, 1987. Prior law continues to apply where the decedent died before January 1, 1987. See Section 20101. As to the application of any amendments made after that date, see Section 3.

Background on Section 20115 of Repealed Code

Section 20115 was a new provision added by 1986 Cal.Stat. ch. 783 § 25. For background on the provisions of this division, see the Comment to this division under the division heading. [20 Cal.L.Rev.Comm.Reports 1001 (1990)].

Cross References

Estate tax defined for purposes of this Chapter, see Probate Code § 20100.
Property defined for purposes of this Chapter, see Probate Code § 20100.

§ 20116. Recovery from persons interested where property does not come into possession of personal representative; amounts not recoverable

(a) If all property does not come into the possession of the personal representative, the personal representative is entitled, and has the duty, to recover from the persons interested in the estate the proportionate amount of the estate tax with which the persons are chargeable under this chapter.

(b) If the personal representative cannot collect from any person interested in the estate the amount of an estate tax apportioned to the person, the amount not recoverable shall be equitably prorated among the other persons interested in the estate who are subject to proration. *(Stats.1990, c. 79 (A.B.759), § 14, operative July 1, 1991.)*

Law Revision Commission Comments
1990 Enactment

Section 20116 continues Section 20116 of the repealed Probate Code without change. Recovery of estate taxes pursuant to this section includes prorated interest and penalties. See Sections 20112 (allowance and charges for credits, deductions, interest, and other adjustments) and 20100(a) ("estate tax" defined).

The court may by order direct payment of the amount of taxes owed by a person to the personal representative. Section 20123 (court order to effectuate proration). As to costs incurred in enforcing a proration order, see Code Civ.Proc. § 685.040. Failure of the personal representative to make a good faith effort to collect taxes prorated against a person is a breach of the fiduciary obligation of the personal representative, for which the personal representative is liable personally and on the bond, if any.

This chapter does not apply to persons interested in the estate of a decedent who died before January 1, 1987. Prior law continues to apply where the decedent died before January 1, 1987. See Section 20101. As to the application of any amendments made after that date, see Section 3.

Background on Section 20116 of Repealed Code

Section 20116 was added by 1986 Cal.Stat. ch. 783 § 25. Subdivision (a) continued former Probate Code Section 975 (repealed by 1986 Cal.Stat. ch. 783 § 16) without substantive change. Subdivision (b) was new. For background on the provisions of this division, see the Comment to this division under the division heading. [20 Cal.L.Rev.Comm.Reports 1001 (1990)].

Cross References

Estate tax defined for purposes of this Chapter, see Probate Code § 20100.
Person interested in the estate defined for purposes of this Chapter, see Probate Code § 20100.
Personal representative defined for purposes of this Chapter, see Probate Code § 20100.
Property defined for purposes of this Chapter, see Probate Code § 20100.

§ 20117. Right of reimbursement

(a) If a person is charged with or required to pay an estate tax greater than the amount prorated to that person because another person does not pay the amount of estate tax prorated to the other person, the person charged with or required to pay the greater amount has a right of reimbursement against the other person.

(b) The right of reimbursement may be enforced through the personal representative in the discretion of the personal representative, or may be enforced directly by the person charged with or required to pay the greater amount, and for the purpose of direct enforcement the person is subrogated to the position of the personal representative.

(c) The personal representative or person who has a right of reimbursement may commence a proceeding to have a court determine the right of reimbursement. The provisions of Article 3 (commencing with Section 20120) shall govern the proceeding, with changes necessary to make the provisions appropriate for application to the proceeding, and the court order determining the right of reimbursement is an enforceable judgment. *(Stats.1990, c. 79 (A.B.759), § 14, operative July 1, 1991.)*

Law Revision Commission Comments
1990 Enactment

Section 20117 continues Section 20117 of the repealed Probate Code without change. Subdivision (c) incorporates the judicial proration procedure, mutatis mutandis. This chapter does not apply to persons interested in the estate of a decedent who died before January 1, 1987. Prior law continues to apply where the decedent died before January 1, 1987. See Section 20101. As to the application of any amendments made after that date, see Section 3.

Background on Section 20117 of Repealed Code

Section 20117 was a new provision added by 1986 Cal.Stat. ch. 783 § 25. For background on the provisions of this division, see the Comment to this division under the division heading. [20 Cal.L.Rev.Comm.Reports 1001 (1990)].

Cross References

Estate tax defined for purposes of this Chapter, see Probate Code § 20100.
Personal representative defined for purposes of this Chapter, see Probate Code § 20100.

ARTICLE 3. JUDICIAL PROCEEDINGS

1049

Application

Application of chapter, see Probate Code § 20101.

§ 20120. Commencement of proceeding

(a) The personal representative or any person interested in the estate may commence a proceeding to have a court determine the proration pursuant to this chapter.

(b) A proceeding under this article shall be commenced in the court in which the estate of the decedent was administered or, if no administration proceedings have been commmenced,[1] in the superior court of any county in which the estate of the decedent may be administered.

(c) If proceedings for the administration of the decedent's estate are pending, a proceeding under this article shall be combined with the administration proceedings. If a proceeding is commenced at any time before final distribution, there shall be no additional filing fee. *(Stats.1990, c. 79 (A.B.759), § 14, operative July 1, 1991.)*

[1] So in enrolled bill.

Law Revision Commission Comments

1990 Enactment

Section 20120 continues Section 20120 of the repealed Probate Code without change. The general rules applicable to civil actions and proceedings, including the rules applicable to parties and pleadings, govern proceedings under this article. See Section 1000 (general rules of practice govern). This chapter does not apply to persons interested in the estate of a decedent who died before January 1, 1987. Prior law continues to apply where the decedent died before January 1, 1987. See Section 20101. As to the application of any amendments made after that date, see Section 3.

Background on Section 20120 of Repealed Code

Section 20120 was added by 1986 Cal.Stat. ch. 783 § 25. Sections 20120–20125 superseded (1) a portion of former Probate Code Section 971 (repealed by 1986 Cal.Stat. ch. 783 § 16), requiring court proration, and (2) a portion of former Probate Code Section 975 (repealed by 1986 Cal.Stat. ch. 783 § 16), providing for a court order for payment. For background on the provisions of this division, see the Comment to this division under the division heading. [20 Cal.L.Rev.Comm.Reports 1001 (1990)].

Cross References

Person interested in the estate defined for purposes of this Chapter, see Probate Code § 20100.
Personal representative defined for purposes of this Chapter, see Probate Code § 20100.

§ 20121. Petition

A proceeding under this article shall be commenced by filing a petition that sets forth all of the following information:

(a) The jurisdictional facts.

(b) Other facts necessary for the court to determine the proration of estate taxes. *(Stats.1990, c. 79 (A.B.759), § 14, operative July 1, 1991.)*

Law Revision Commission Comments

1990 Enactment

Section 20121 continues Section 20121 of the repealed Probate Code without substantive change. See the Comment to Section 20120. The requirement that the petition be verified has been omitted in view of Section 1021 which imposes this as a general requirement. For general provisions, see Sections 1020–1023 (petitions and other papers).

Background on Section 20121 of Repealed Code

Section 20121 was added by 1986 Cal.Stat. ch. 783 § 25. Sections 20120–20125 superseded (1) a portion of former Probate Code Section 971 (repealed by 1986 Cal.Stat. ch. 783 § 16), requiring court proration, and (2) a portion of former Probate Code Section 975 (repealed by 1986 Cal.Stat. ch. 783 § 16), providing for a court order for payment. For background on the provisions of this division, see the Comment to this division under the division heading. [20 Cal.L.Rev.Comm.Reports 1001 (1990)].

Cross References

Estate tax defined for purposes of this Chapter, see Probate Code § 20100.

§ 20122. Notice of hearing; summons and copy of petition to persons interested

Not less than 30 days before the hearing, the petitioner shall do both of the following:

(a) Cause notice of the hearing and a copy of the petition to be mailed to the personal representative and to each person interested in the estate against whom prorated amounts may be charged pursuant to paragraph (1) of subdivision (a) of Section 20123.

(b) Cause a summons and a copy of the petition to be served on each person interested in the estate who may be directed to make payment of prorated amounts pursuant to paragraph (2) of subdivision (a) of Section 20123. The summons shall be in the form and shall be served in the manner prescribed in Title 5 (commencing with Section 410.10) of Part 2 of the Code of Civil Procedure. *(Stats.1990, c. 79 (A.B.759), § 14, operative July 1, 1991.)*

Law Revision Commission Comments

1990 Enactment

Section 20122 continues Section 20122 of the repealed Probate Code without change. See the Comment to Section 20120. For general provisions, see Sections 1200–1230 (notice of hearing), 1250–1252 (request for special notice), 1260–1265 (proof of giving of notice).

Background on Section 20122 of Repealed Code

Section 20122 was added by 1986 Cal.Stat. ch. 783 § 25. Sections 20120–20125 superseded (1) a portion of former Probate Code Section 971 (repealed by 1986 Cal.Stat. ch. 783 § 16), requiring court proration, and (2) a portion of former Probate Code Section 975 (repealed by 1986 Cal.Stat. ch. 783 § 16), providing for a court order for payment. For background on the provisions of this division, see the Comment to this division under the division heading. [20 Cal.L.Rev.Comm.Reports 1001 (1990)].

Cross References

Person interested in the estate defined for purposes of this Chapter, see Probate Code § 20100.

Personal representative defined for purposes of this Chapter, see Probate Code § 20100.

§ 20123. Order

(a) The court, upon making a determination as provided in this article, shall make an order:

(1) Directing the personal representative to charge the prorated amounts against the persons against whom an estate tax has been prorated insofar as the personal representative is in possession of any property or interests of the persons against whom the charge may be made.

(2) Summarily directing all other persons against whom an estate tax has been prorated to make payment of the prorated amounts to the personal representative.

(b) A court order made under this section is a judgment that may be enforced against the persons against whom an estate tax has been prorated. *(Stats.1990, c. 79 (A.B.759), § 14, operative July 1, 1991. Amended by Stats.1997, c. 724 (A.B.1172), § 31.)*

Law Revision Commission Comments

1990 Enactment

Section 20123 continues Section 20123 of the repealed Probate Code without change. The court order prorating an estate tax includes interest and penalties. See Section 20112 (allowance and charges for credits, deductions, interest, and other adjustments); see also Section 20100(a) ("estate tax" defined). For general provisions relating to hearings and orders, see Sections 1040–1049. This chapter does not apply to persons interested in the estate of a decedent who died before January 1, 1987. Prior law continues to apply where the decedent died before January 1, 1987. See Section 20101. As to the application of any amendments made after that date, see Section 3.

Background on Section 20123 of Repealed Code

Section 20123 was added by 1986 Cal.Stat. ch. 783 § 25. Subdivision (a) restated former Probate Code Section 976 (repealed by 1986 Cal.Stat. ch. 783 § 16) without substantive change. Subdivisions (b) and (c) were new. Sections 20120–20125 superseded (1) a portion of former Probate Code Section 971 (repealed by 1986 Cal.Stat. ch. 783 § 16), requiring court proration, and (2) a portion of former Probate Code Section 975 (repealed by 1986 Cal.Stat. ch. 783 § 16), providing for a court order for payment. For background on the provisions of this division, see the Comment to this division under the division heading. [20 Cal.L.Rev.Comm.Reports 1001 (1990)].

Cross References

Estate tax defined for purposes of this Chapter, see Probate Code § 20100.
Personal representative defined for purposes of this Chapter, see Probate Code § 20100.
Property defined for purposes of this Chapter, see Probate Code § 20100.

§ 20124. Modification of order

Upon petition by the personal representative or any person interested in the estate, the court shall modify an order made pursuant to this article whenever it appears that the amount of estate tax as actually determined is different from the amount of estate tax on which the court based the order. *(Stats.1990, c. 79 (A.B.759), § 14, operative July 1, 1991.)*

Law Revision Commission Comments

1990 Enactment

Section 20124 continues Section 20124 of the repealed Probate Code without change. This section provides for the possibility that subsequent to the making of an order, the taxes may be adjusted as a result of audit or the filing of an amended return. For general provisions relating to petitions, see Sections 1020–1023. The section does not apply to any additional tax under Internal Revenue Code Section 2032A(c) resulting from a disposition or cessation of qualified use of specially valued property. See Section 20114 (proration of additional tax on certain qualified real property). Section 20124 does not provide a limitation period for modification of a proration order; the matter is left to laches and other equitable doctrines within the discretion of the court.

This chapter does not apply to persons interested in the estate of a decedent who died before January 1, 1987. Prior law continues to apply where the decedent died before January 1, 1987. See Section 20101. As to the application of any amendments made after that date, see Section 3.

Background on Section 20124 of Repealed Code

Section 20124 was added by 1986 Cal.Stat. ch. 783 § 25. Sections 20120–20125 superseded (1) a portion of former Probate Code Section 971 (repealed by 1986 Cal.Stat. ch. 783 § 16), requiring court proration, and (2) a portion of former Probate Code Section 975 (repealed by 1986 Cal.Stat. ch. 783 § 16), providing for a court order for payment. For background on the provisions of this division, see the Comment to this division under the division heading. [20 Cal.L.Rev.Comm.Reports 1001 (1990)].

Cross References

Estate tax defined for purposes of this Chapter, see Probate Code § 20100.
Person interested in the estate defined for purposes of this Chapter, see Probate Code § 20100.
Personal representative defined for purposes of this Chapter, see Probate Code § 20100.

§ 20125. Personal representative in another state; actions

(a) A personal representative acting or resident in another state may commence an action in this state to recover from a person interested in the estate, who either is resident in this state or owns property in this state, the amount of the federal estate tax, or an estate tax or death duty payable to another state, apportioned to the person.

(b) The action shall be commenced in the superior court of any county in which administration of the estate of the decedent would be proper or, if none, in which any defendant resides.

(c) For purposes of the action the apportionment by the court having jurisdiction of the administration of the decedent's estate in the other state is prima facie correct. *(Stats.1990, c. 79 (A.B.759), § 14, operative July 1, 1991.)*

Law Revision Commission Comments

1990 Enactment

Section 20125 continues Section 20125 of the repealed Probate Code without change. See also Code Civ.Proc. §§ 1710.10–1710.65 (sister state money-judgments). This chapter does not apply to persons interested in the estate of a decedent who died before January 1, 1987. Prior law continues to apply where the decedent died before January 1, 1987. See Section 20101. As to the application of any amendments made after that date, see Section 3.

Background on Section 20125 of Repealed Code

Section 20125 was a new provision added by 1986 Cal.Stat. ch. 783 § 25. Sections 20120–20125 superseded (1) a portion of former Probate Code Section 971 (repealed by 1986 Cal.Stat. ch. 783 § 16), requiring court proration, and (2) a portion of former Probate Code Section 975 (repealed by 1986 Cal.Stat. ch. 783 § 16), providing for a court order for payment. For background on the provisions of this division, see the Comment to this division under the division heading. [20 Cal.L.Rev.Comm.Reports 1001 (1990)].

Cross References

Estate tax defined for purposes of this Chapter, see Probate Code § 20100.

Person interested in the estate defined for purposes of this Chapter, see Probate Code § 20100.

Personal representative defined for purposes of this Chapter, see Probate Code § 20100.

Property defined for purposes of this Chapter, see Probate Code § 20100.

CHAPTER 2. PRORATION OF TAXES ON GENERATION–SKIPPING TRANSFER

Application

Application of chapter, see Probate Code § 20201.

Law Revision Commission Comments

1990 Enactment

Sections 20200–20225 parallel comparable provisions of Chapter 1 (commencing with Section 20100) (proration of estate taxes). This chapter does not apply to transferees of property of a decedent who died before January 1, 1987. No inference as to the applicable law in effect before January 1, 1987, shall be drawn from the enactment of this chapter. See Section 20201. As to the application of any amendments made after that date, see Section 3. [20 Cal.L.Rev.Comm.Reports 1001 (1990)].

Cross References

Decedent's estate, grounds for appeal, final orders under this Chapter, see Probate Code § 1303.

ARTICLE 1.   GENERAL PROVISIONS

Section
20200. Definitions.
20201. Application of chapter.

Application

Application of chapter, see Probate Code § 20201.

§ 20200. Definitions

Except where the context otherwise requires, the following definitions shall govern the construction of this chapter:

(a) "Generation-skipping transfer tax" means a tax imposed by any federal or California generation-skipping transfer tax law, now existing or hereafter enacted, and includes interest and penalties on any deficiency.

(b) "Property" means property on which a generation-skipping transfer tax is imposed.

(c) "Transferee" means any person who receives, who is deemed to receive, or who is the beneficiary of, any property.

(d) "Trustee" means any person who is a trustee within the meaning of the federal generation-skipping transfer tax law, or who is otherwise required to pay a generation-skipping transfer tax.

(e) "Value" means fair market value as determined for generation-skipping transfer tax purposes. *(Stats.1990, c. 79 (A.B.759), § 14, operative July 1, 1991.)*

Law Revision Commission Comments

1990 Enactment

Section 20200 continues Section 20200 of the repealed Probate Code without change.

Background on Section 20200 of Repealed Code

Section 20200 was a new provision added by 1986 Cal.Stat. ch. 783 § 25. For background on the provisions of this division, see the Comment to this division under the division heading. [20 Cal.L.Rev.Comm.Reports 1001 (1990)].

§ 20201. Application of chapter

(a) This chapter does not apply to transferees of property of a decedent who died before January 1, 1987.

(b) No inference as to the applicable law in effect before January 1, 1987, shall be drawn from the enactment of this chapter. *(Stats.1990, c. 79 (A.B.759), § 14, operative July 1, 1991.)*

Law Revision Commission Comments

1990 Enactment

Section 20201 continues Section 20201 of the repealed Probate Code without substantive change.

Background on Section 20201 of Repealed Code

Section 20201 was a new provision added by 1986 Cal.Stat. ch. 783 § 25. For background on the provisions of this division, see the Comment to this division under the division heading. [20 Cal.L.Rev.Comm.Reports 1001 (1990)].

Cross References

Property defined for purposes of this Chapter, see Probate Code § 20200.

Transferee defined for purposes of this Chapter, see Probate Code § 20200.

ARTICLE 2.   PRORATION

Application

Application of chapter, see Probate Code § 20201.

§ 20210. Equitable proration; exemption from article

(a) Except as provided in subdivision (b), any generation-skipping transfer tax shall be equitably prorated among the transferees in the manner prescribed in this article.

(b) This section does not apply:

(1) To the extent the transferor in a written instrument transferring property specifically directs that the property be applied to the satisfaction of a generation-skipping transfer tax or that a generation-skipping transfer tax be prorated to the property in the manner provided in the instrument.

(2) Where federal law directs otherwise. If federal law directs the manner of proration of the federal generation-skipping transfer tax, the California generation-skipping transfer tax shall be prorated in the same manner. *(Stats. 1990, c. 79 (A.B.759), § 14, operative July 1, 1991.)*

Law Revision Commission Comments

1990 Enactment

Section 20210 continues Section 20210 of the repealed Probate Code without change. Proration of a generation-skipping transfer tax includes proration of interest and penalties on any deficiency. See Sections 20200(a) ("generation-skipping transfer tax" defined) and 20212 (allowance and charges for credits, deductions, and interest).

This chapter does not apply to transferees of property of a decedent who died before January 1, 1987. No inference as to the applicable law in effect before January 1, 1987, shall be drawn from the enactment of this chapter. See Section 20201. As to the application of any amendments made after that date, see Section 3.

Background on Section 20210 of Repealed Code

Section 20210 was a new provision added by 1986 Cal.Stat. ch. 783 § 25. For background on the provisions of this division, see the Comment to this division under the division heading. [20 Cal.L.Rev.Comm.Reports 1001 (1990)].

Cross References

Generation-skipping transfer tax defined for purposes of this Chapter, see Probate Code § 20200.
Property defined for purposes of this Chapter, see Probate Code § 20200.
Transferee defined for purposes of this Chapter, see Probate Code § 20200.

§ 20211. Proration proportional to value of property

The proration required by this article shall be made in the proportion that the value of the property received by each transferee bears to the total value of all property received by all transferees, subject to the provisions of this article. *(Stats.1990, c. 79 (A.B.759), § 14, operative July 1, 1991.)*

Law Revision Commission Comments

1990 Enactment

Section 20211 continues Section 20211 of the repealed Probate Code without change. See the Comment to this chapter under the chapter heading.

Background on Section 20211 of Repealed Code

Section 20211 was a new provision added by 1986 Cal.Stat. ch. 783 § 25. For background on the provisions of this division, see the Comment to this division under the division heading. [20 Cal.L.Rev.Comm.Reports 1001 (1990)].

Cross References

Property defined for purposes of this Chapter, see Probate Code § 20200.
Transferee defined for purposes of this Chapter, see Probate Code § 20200.
Value defined for purposes of this Chapter, see Probate Code § 20200.

§ 20212. Allowances for credits, exemptions, and deductions; interest and penalties

In making a proration required by this article:

(a) Allowances shall be made for credits, exemptions, and deductions allowed for the purpose of determining the tax payable.

(b) Interest and penalties on any deficiency shall be charged to equitably reflect the benefits and burdens of the deficiency and of any tax deductions associated with the interest and penalties. *(Stats.1990, c. 79 (A.B.759), § 14, operative July 1, 1991.)*

Law Revision Commission Comments

1990 Enactment

Section 20212 continues Section 20212 of the repealed Probate Code without change. See the Comment to this chapter under the chapter heading.

Background on Section 20212 of Repealed Code

Section 20212 was a new provision added by 1986 Cal.Stat. ch. 783 § 25. For background on the provisions of this division, see the Comment to this division under the division heading. [20 Cal.L.Rev.Comm.Reports 1001 (1990)].

§ 20213. Trusts; tax on interest

If a trust is created or other provision made whereby a transferee is given an interest in income, or an estate for years or for life, or another temporary interest in property, the tax on both the temporary interest and other interests in the property shall be charged against, and paid out of, the corpus of the property without apportionment between the temporary and other interests. *(Stats.1990, c. 79 (A.B.759), § 14, operative July 1, 1991.)*

Law Revision Commission Comments

1990 Enactment

Section 20213 continues Section 20213 of the repealed Probate Code without change. See the Comment to this chapter under the chapter heading.

Background on Section 20213 of Repealed Code

Section 20213 was a new provision added by 1986 Cal.Stat. ch. 783 § 25. For background on the provisions of this division, see the Comment to this division under the division heading. [20 Cal.L.Rev.Comm.Reports 1001 (1990)].

Cross References

Property defined for purposes of this Chapter, see Probate Code § 20200.

Transferee defined for purposes of this Chapter, see Probate Code § 20200.

§ 20214. Recovery of tax from transferees; property not coming into possession of trustees; amount not recoverable

(a) If all property does not come into the possession of the trustee, the trustee is entitled, and has the duty, to recover from the transferees, the proportionate amount of the tax with which the transferees are chargeable under this chapter.

(b) If the trustee cannot collect from any transferee the amount of tax apportioned to the transferee, the amount not recoverable shall be equitably prorated among the other transferees who are subject to proration. *(Stats.1990, c. 79 (A.B.759), § 14, operative July 1, 1991.)*

Law Revision Commission Comments

1990 Enactment

Section 20214 continues Section 20214 of the repealed Probate Code without change. See the Comment to this chapter under the chapter heading.

Background on Section 20214 of Repealed Code

Section 20214 was a new provision added by 1986 Cal.Stat. ch. 783 § 25. For background on the provisions of this division, see the Comment to this division under the division heading. [20 Cal.L.Rev.Reports 1001 (1990)].

Cross References

Property defined for purposes of this Chapter, see Probate Code § 20200.
Transferee defined for purposes of this Chapter, see Probate Code § 20200.
Trustee defined for purposes of this Chapter, see Probate Code § 20200.

§ 20215. Right of reimbursement

(a) If a person is charged with, or required to pay, a generation-skipping transfer tax greater than the amount prorated to that person because another person does not pay the amount of generation-skipping transfer tax prorated to the other person, the person charged with or required to pay the greater amount has a right of reimbursement against the other person.

(b) The right of reimbursement may be enforced through the trustee in the discretion of the trustee, or may be enforced directly by the person charged with, or required to pay, the greater amount and, for the purpose of direct enforcement, the person is subrogated to the position of the trustee.

(c) The trustee or person who has a right of reimbursement may commence a proceeding to have a court determine the right of reimbursement. The provisions of Article 3 (commencing with Section 20220) shall govern the proceeding, with changes necessary to make the provisions appropriate for application to the proceeding, and the court order determining the right of reimbursement is an enforceable judgment. *(Stats.1990, c. 79 (A.B.759), § 14, operative July 1, 1991.)*

Law Revision Commission Comments

1990 Enactment

Section 20215 continues Section 20215 of the repealed Probate Code without change. See the Comment to this chapter under the chapter heading.

Background on Section 20215 of Repealed Code

Section 20215 was a new provision added by 1986 Cal.Stat. ch. 783 § 25. For background on the provisions of this division, see the Comment to this division under the division heading. [20 Cal.L.Rev.Reports 1001 (1990)].

Cross References

Generation-skipping transfer tax defined for purposes of this Chapter, see Probate Code § 20200.
Trustee defined for purposes of this Chapter, see Probate Code § 20200.

ARTICLE 3.   JUDICIAL PROCEEDINGS

Application

Application of chapter, see Probate Code § 20201.

§ 20220. Commencement of proceedings

(a) The trustee or any transferee may commence a proceeding to have a court determine the proration pursuant to this chapter.

(b) A proceeding under this article shall be commenced in the court in which the estate of the decedent was administered or, if no administration proceedings have been commenced, in the superior court of any county in which the estate of the decedent may be administered.

(c) If proceedings for the administration of the decedent's estate are pending, a proceeding under this article shall be combined with the administration proceedings. If a proceeding is commenced at any time before final distribution, there shall be no additional filing fee. *(Stats.1990, c. 79 (A.B.759), § 14, operative July 1, 1991.)*

Law Revision Commission Comments

1990 Enactment

Section 20220 continues Section 20220 of the repealed Probate Code without change. See the Comment to this chapter under the chapter heading.

Background on Section 20220 of Repealed Code

Section 20220 was a new provision added by 1986 Cal.Stat. ch. 783 § 25. For background on the provisions of this division, see the Comment to this division under the division heading. [20 Cal.L.Rev.Reports 1001 (1990)].

Transferee defined for purposes of this Chapter, see Probate Code § 20200.

Trustee defined for purposes of this Chapter, see Probate Code § 20200.

§ 20221. Petition

A proceeding under this article shall be commenced by filing a petition that sets forth all of the following information:

(a) The jurisdictional facts.

(b) Other facts necessary for the court to determine the proration of the generation-skipping transfer tax. *(Stats. 1990, c. 79 (A.B.759), § 14, operative July 1, 1991.)*

Law Revision Commission Comments
1990 Enactment

Section 20221 continues Section 20221 of the repealed Probate Code without substantive change. See the Comment to this chapter under the chapter heading. The requirement that the petition be verified has been omitted in view of Section 1021 which imposes this as a general requirement. For general provisions relating to petitions, see Sections 1020–1023.

Background on Section 20221 of Repealed Code

Section 20221 was a new provision added by 1986 Cal.Stat. ch. 783 § 25. For background on the provisions of this division, see the Comment to this division under the division heading. [20 Cal.L.Rev.Reports 1001 (1990)].

Cross References

Generation-skipping transfer tax defined for purposes of this Chapter, see Probate Code § 20200.

§ 20222. Notice; summons and copy of petition to persons who may be directed to make payments

Not less than 30 days before the hearing the petitioner shall do both of the following:

(a) Cause notice of the hearing and a copy of the petition to be mailed to the trustee and each transferee against whom prorated amounts may be charged pursuant to paragraph (1) of subdivision (a) of Section 20223.

(b) Cause a summons and a copy of the petition to be served on each transferee who may be directed to make payment of prorated amounts pursuant to paragraph (2) of subdivision (a) of Section 20223. The summons shall be in the form and shall be served in the manner prescribed in Title 5 (commencing with Section 410.10) of Part 2 of the Code of Civil Procedure. *(Stats.1990, c. 79 (A.B.759), § 14, operative July 1, 1991.)*

Law Revision Commission Comments
1990 Enactment

Section 20222 continues Section 20222 of the repealed Probate Code without change. See the Comment to this chapter under the chapter heading. For general provisions, see Sections 1200–1230 (notice of hearing), 1250–1252 (request for special notice), 1260–1265 (proof of giving of notice).

Background on Section 20222 of Repealed Code

Section 20222 was a new provision added by 1986 Cal.Stat. ch. 783 § 25. For background on the provisions of this division, see the

Comment to this division under the division heading. [20 Cal.L.Rev.Comm.Reports 1001 (1990)].

Cross References

Transferee defined for purposes of this Chapter, see Probate Code § 20200.

Trustee defined for purposes of this Chapter, see Probate Code § 20200.

§ 20223. Court order

(a) The court, upon making a determination as provided in this article, shall make an order:

(1) Directing the trustee to charge the prorated amounts against the transferees against whom the generation-skipping transfer tax has been prorated insofar as the trustee is in possession of any property or interests of the transferees against whom the charge may be made.

(2) Summarily directing all other transferees against whom the generation-skipping transfer tax has been prorated to make payment of the prorated amounts to the trustee.

(b) A court order made under this section is a judgment that may be enforced against the persons against whom a generation-skipping transfer tax has been prorated. *(Stats. 1990, c. 79 (A.B.759), § 14, operative July 1, 1991. Amended by Stats.1997, c. 724 (A.B.1172), § 32.)*

Law Revision Commission Comments
1990 Enactment

Section 20223 continues Section 20223 of the repealed Probate Code without change. See the Comment to this chapter under the chapter heading. For general provisions relating to hearings and orders, see Sections 1040–1049.

Background on Section 20223 of Repealed Code

Section 20223 was a new provision added by 1986 Cal.Stat. ch. 783 § 25. For background on the provisions of this division, see the Comment to this division under the division heading. [20 Cal.L.Rev.Comm.Reports 1001 (1990)].

Cross References

Generation-skipping transfer tax defined for purposes of this Chapter, see Probate Code § 20200.

Property defined for purposes of this Chapter, see Probate Code § 20200.

Transferee defined for purposes of this Chapter, see Probate Code § 20200.

Trustee defined for purposes of this Chapter, see Probate Code § 20200.

§ 20224. Modification of order

Upon petition by the trustee or any transferee, the court shall modify an order made pursuant to this article whenever it appears that the amount of generation-skipping transfer tax as actually determined is different from the amount of tax on which the court based the order. *(Stats.1990, c. 79 (A.B.759), § 14, operative July 1, 1991.)*

Law Revision Commission Comments
1990 Enactment

Section 20224 continues Section 20224 of the repealed Probate Code without change. See the Comment to this chapter under the chapter heading. For general provisions relating to petitions, see Sections 1020–1023.

Background on Section 20224 of Repealed Code

Section 20224 was a new provision added by 1986 Cal.Stat. ch. 783 § 25. For background on the provisions of this division, see the Comment to this division under the division heading. [20 Cal.L.Rev.Comm.Reports 1001 (1990)].

Cross References

Generation-skipping transfer tax defined for purposes of this Chapter, see Probate Code § 20200.

Trustee defined for purposes of this Chapter, see Probate Code § 20200.

§ 20225. Actions by nonresidents

(a) A trustee acting or resident in another state may commence an action in this state to recover from a transferee, who either is resident in this state or owns property in this state, the amount of the federal generation-skipping transfer tax, or a generation-skipping transfer tax payable to another state, apportioned to the person.

(b) The action shall be commenced in the superior court of any county in which administration of the estate of the decedent would be proper or, if none, in which any defendant resides.

(c) For purposes of the action an apportionment by the court having jurisdiction of the administration of the decedent's estate in the other state is prima facie correct. *(Stats.1990, c. 79 (A.B.759), § 14, operative July 1, 1991.)*

Law Revision Commission Comments

1990 Enactment

Section 20225 continues Section 20225 of the repealed Probate Code without change. See also Code Civ.Proc. §§ 1710.10–1710.65 (sister state money-judgments). This chapter applies to transferees of property of a decedent who dies on or after January 1, 1987; no inference as to the applicable law in effect before January 1, 1987, shall be drawn from the enactment of this chapter. See Section 20201. As to the application of any amendments made after that date, see Section 3.

Background on Section 20225 of Repealed Code

Section 20225 was a new provision added by 1986 Cal.Stat. ch. 783 § 25. For background on the provisions of this division, see the Comment to this division under the division heading. [20 Cal.L.Rev.Comm.Reports 1001 (1990)].

Cross References

Generation-skipping transfer tax defined for purposes of this Chapter, see Probate Code § 20200.

Property defined for purposes of this Chapter, see Probate Code § 20200.

Transferee defined for purposes of this Chapter, see Probate Code § 20200.

Trustee defined for purposes of this Chapter, see Probate Code § 20200.

§ 21100. Repealed by Stats.1988, c. 1199, § 107.8, operative July 1, 1989

Law Revision Commission Comments

1988 Repeal

Subdivision (a) of former Section 21100 is continued in Section 39 without change. Subdivision (b) is continued in Section 45 without change. Subdivision (c) is continued in Section 81 without change. [19 Cal.L.Rev.Comm. Reports 1249 (1988)].

Division 11

CONSTRUCTION OF WILLS, TRUSTS, AND OTHER INSTRUMENTS

Part 1

RULES FOR INTERPRETATION OF INSTRUMENTS

Cross References

Wills and intestate succession, application of certain chapters when testator died prior to January 1, 1985, see Probate Code § 6103.

CHAPTER 1.   GENERAL PROVISIONS

§ 21101.   Application of part

Unless the provision or context otherwise requires, this part applies to a will, trust, deed, and any other instrument. *(Added by Stats.1994, c. 806 (A.B.3686), § 41.   Amended by Stats.2002, c. 138 (A.B.1784), § 10.)*

Law Revision Commission Comments

1990 Enactment

Section 21101 continues Section 21101 of the repealed Probate Code without change.   See also Section 45 (defining "instrument").

This division does not apply to an instrument if its terms expressly or by necessary implication make this division inapplicable.

2002 Amendment

The amendment to Section 21101 is technical.

Section 21101 makes the rules of construction in this part applicable to a governing instrument of any type, except to the extent the application of a particular provision is limited by its terms to a specific type of donative disposition or governing instrument. See, e.g., Sections 21105 (will passes all property including after-acquired property), 21109 (requirement for at-death transfer that transferee survive transferor), 21132 (change in form of securities disposed of by at-death transfer), 21135 (ademption of at-death transfer by satisfaction). See also Section 45 ("instrument" defined). [31 Cal.L.Rev. Comm. Reports 191 (2001)].

Background on Section 21101 of Repealed Code

Section 21101 was a new provision added by 1987 Cal.Stat. ch. 923 § 101.   For background on the provisions of this part, see the Comment to this part under the part heading.   [20 Cal.L.Rev.Comm.Reports 1001 (1990)].

§ 21102.   Intention of transferor as controlling; rules of construction; use of extrinsic evidence

(a) The intention of the transferor as expressed in the instrument controls the legal effect of the dispositions made in the instrument.

(b) The rules of construction in this part apply where the intention of the transferor is not indicated by the instrument.

(c) Nothing in this section limits the use of extrinsic evidence, to the extent otherwise authorized by law, to determine the intention of the transferor. *(Added by Stats. 1994, c. 806 (A.B.3686), § 41.   Amended by Stats.2002, c. 138 (A.B.1784), § 11.)*

Law Revision Commission Comments

2002 Amendment

The amendment to subdivision (b) of Section 21102 is technical.

The 1994 enactment of Section 21102 extended former Section 6140 (wills) to trusts and other instruments. See also Section 21101 (application of part). The section is drawn from Section 2–603 of the Uniform Probate Code (1987). As to the construction of provisions drawn from uniform acts, see Section 2.

Subdivision (c) is added to make clear the admissibility of extrinsic evidence under this section, including for the purpose of rebutting the presumed intention attributed to a transferor by a rule of construction. Subdivision (c) neither expands nor limits the extent to which extrinsic evidence admissible under former law may be used to determine the transferor's intent as expressed in the instrument. See e.g., Estate of Russell, 69 Cal.2d 200, 215–16, 444 P.2d 353, 70 Cal.Rptr. 561 (1968). See generally 12 B. Witkin, Summary of California Law *Wills and Probate* §§ 245–47, at 280–84 (9th ed. 1990). *Cf.* Section 6111.5 (will); Estate of Anderson, 56 Cal.App.4th 235, 65 Cal.Rptr.2d 307 (1997) (extrinsic evidence admissible); Estate of Guidotti, 90 Cal.App.4th 1403, 109 Cal.Rptr.2d 674 (2001) (use of extrinsic evidence). See also Section 12206 (limitation in will of time for administration of estate is directory only). Likewise, under the parol evidence rule, extrinsic evidence may be available to explain, interpret, or supplement an expressed intention of the transferor. Code Civ. Proc. § 1856.

Nothing in this section affects the law governing reformation of an instrument to effectuate the intention of the transferor in case of mistake or for other cause. [31 Cal.L.Rev.Comm. Reports 191 (2001)].

§ 21103.   Local law of state

The meaning and legal effect of a disposition in an instrument is determined by the local law of a particular state selected by the transferor in the instrument unless the application of that law is contrary to the rights of the surviving spouse to community and quasi-community property, to any other public policy of this state applicable to the disposition, or, in the case of a will, to Part 3 (commencing with Section 6500) of Division 6. *(Added by Stats.1994, c. 806 (A.B.3686), § 41. Amended by Stats.2002, c. 138 (A.B.1784), § 12.)*

Law Revision Commission Comments
2002 Amendment

The amendments to Section 21103 are technical. The 1994 enactment of Section 21103 extended former Section 6141 (wills) to trusts and other instruments. See also Section 21101 (application of part).

This section is consistent with Section 2–602 of the Uniform Probate Code (1987). The reference in Section 2–602 of the Uniform Probate Code to an elective share is replaced by a reference to the rights of the surviving spouse to community and quasi-community property. The reference to Part 3 (commencing with Section 6500) of Division 6 is drawn from the reference in Section 2–602 of the Uniform Probate Code to provisions relating to elective share, exempt property, and allowances. As to the construction of provisions drawn from uniform acts, see Section 2. See also Section 78 (definition of "surviving spouse"). [31 Cal.L.Rev.Comm. Reports 192 (2001)].

§ 21104.   At-death transfer defined

As used in this part, "at-death transfer" means a transfer that is revocable during the lifetime of the transferor, but does not include a joint tenancy or joint account with right of survivorship. *(Added by Stats.1994, c. 806 (A.B.3686), § 41. Amended by Stats.2002, c. 138 (A.B.1784), § 13.)*

Law Revision Commission Comments
2002 Amendment

Section 21104 is amended to replace the former definition of "testamentary gift." As used in this part, an at-death transfer does not include an irrevocable lifetime transfer, such as an outright gift or an irrevocable trust. An at-death transfer does include a will and a revocable trust, as well as a pay-on-death account, "Totten" (or bank account) trust, beneficiary designation under an insurance policy or pension plan, and the like. An irrevocable beneficiary designation is usually subject to a survival requirement pursuant to the terms of its

governing instrument for purposes of Section 21109 (requirement that transferee survive transferor).

The term is used in Sections 21109 (requirement that transferee survive transferor), 21110 (anti-lapse), 21117 (classification of at-death transfer), 21132 (change in form of securities), 21133 (proceeds of specific gift), and 21135 (ademption by satisfaction) [31 Cal.L.Rev. Comm. Reports 193 (2001)].

§ 21105.   Transfer of property by will; after-acquired property

Except as otherwise provided in Sections 641 and 642, a will passes all property the testator owns at death, including property acquired after execution of the will. *(Added by Stats.1994, c. 806 (A.B.3686), § 41. Amended by Stats.2002, c. 138 (A.B.1784), § 14.)*

Law Revision Commission Comments
2002 Amendment

The amendment to Section 21105 is technical. The 1994 enactment of Section 21105 continued former Section 6142.

The section is drawn from Section 2–603 of the Uniform Probate Code (1987). As to the construction of provisions drawn from uniform acts, see Section 2. Nothing in the section limits the extent to which extrinsic evidence admissible under former law may be used to determine the testator's intent as expressed in the will. See Section 21102 (intention of transferor). [31 Cal.L.Rev.Comm. Reports 194 (2001)].

§ 21106.   Repealed by Stats.2002, c. 138 (A.B.1784), § 15
Law Revision Commission Comments
2002 Repeal

Section 21106 is repealed as incomplete and unnecessary. *Cf.* Civil Code § 686 (what interests are in common). [31 Cal.L.Rev.Comm. Reports 194 (2001)].

§ 21107.   Conversion of real property into money; personal property

If an instrument directs the conversion of real property into money at the transferor's death, the real property and its proceeds shall be deemed personal property from the time of the transferor's death. *(Added by Stats.1994, c. 806 (A.B. 3686), § 41. Amended by Stats.2002, c. 138 (A.B.1784), § 16.)*

Law Revision Commission Comments
2002 Amendment

The amendment to Section 21107 is technical. The 1994 enactment of Section 21107 extended former Section 6144 (wills) to trusts and other instruments. See also Section 21101 (application of part).

This section is declaratory of the common law doctrine of equitable conversion. See *In re* Estate of Gracey, 200 Cal. 482, 488–89, 253 P. 921 (1927). See generally 11 B. Witkin, Summary of California Law *Equity* §§ 163–66, at 842–47 (9th ed. 1990). Nothing in the section limits the extent to which extrinsic evidence admissible under former law may be used to determine the transferor's intent as expressed in the instrument. See generally Witkin, *id*; Section 21102 (intention of transferor). [31 Cal.L.Rev.Comm. Reports 194 (2001)].

§ 21108.   Common law rule of worthier title; interest transferred to transferor's own heirs or next of kin

The law of this state does not include (a) the common law rule of worthier title that a transferor cannot devise an interest to his or her own heirs or (b) a presumption or rule of interpretation that a transferor does not intend, by a transfer to his or her own heirs or next of kin, to transfer an interest to them. The meaning of a transfer of a legal or equitable interest to a transferor's own heirs or next of kin, however designated, shall be determined by the general rules applicable to the interpretation of instruments. *(Added by Stats.1994, c. 806 (A.B.3686), § 41. Amended by Stats.2002, c. 138 (A.B.1784), § 17.)*

Law Revision Commission Comments

2002 Amendment

Section 21108 is amended to remove an obsolete transitional provision.

The 1994 enactment of Section 21108 extended former Section 6145 (wills) to trusts and other instruments. See also Sections 21101 (application of part), 21114 (class gift to heirs, next of kin, relatives, and the like). For background on this section, see *Recommendation and Study Relating to the Doctrine of Worthier Title*, 2 Cal. L. Revision Comm'n Reports D–1 (1959). [31 Cal.L.Rev.Comm. Reports 195 (2001)].

§ 21109. Transferees; failure to survive

(a) A transferee who fails to survive the transferor of an at-death transfer or until any future time required by the instrument does not take under the instrument.

(b) If it cannot be determined by clear and convincing evidence that the transferee survived until a future time required by the instrument, it is deemed that the transferee did not survive until the required future time. *(Added by Stats.1994, c. 806 (A.B.3686), § 41. Amended by Stats.2002, c. 138 (A.B.1784), § 18.)*

Law Revision Commission Comments

2002 Amendment

Subdivision (a) of Section 21109 is amended to clarify and limit its application. See Section 21104 ("at-death transfer" defined).

Former subdivision (b) is deleted as unnecessary. The general "clear and convincing evidence" standard of Section 220 applies.

The 1994 enactment of Section 21109 extended former Section 6146 (wills) to at-death transfers. See Section 21104 ("at-death transfer" defined). The question of whether or not survival is required in other cases is determined according to general rules of interpretation and construction. See, e.g., Section 21102 (intention of transferor).

The at-death transfer provision of Section 21109 changes the traditional common law and California rule illustrated by Randall v. Bank of America, 48 Cal.App.2d 249, 119 P.2d 754 (1941) (remainder interest in revocable trust held not divested by beneficiary's failure to survive settlor; upon settlor's death the trust property passed to deceased beneficiary's estate). However, language of this section referring to survival "until a future time required by the instrument" does not change the result of other future interest cases that have generally refused to find an implied condition of survival where the instrument fails expressly to impose such a condition, such as Estate of Stanford, 49 Cal.2d 120, 315 P.2d 681 (1957) (testamentary trust for *A* for life, remainder to *A*'s "children"; despite class gift form, remainder passed to estate of child who predeceased *A*), and Estate of Ferry, 55 Cal.2d 776, 361 P.2d 900, 13 Cal.Rptr. 180 (1961) (even though the interest in question was subject to another condition precedent, court refused to find an implied condition of survival). See also Restatement (Second) of Property (Donative Transfers) § 27.3 (1987).

With respect to a class gift of a future interest, Section 21109 must be read together with Section 21114. If the transferee fails to survive but is properly related to the transferor or the transferor's spouse, the

antilapse statute may substitute the transferee's issue. See Section 21110. See also Section 21112 (conditions referring to "issue").

For a provision governing the administration and disposition of community property and quasi-community property where one spouse does not survive the other, see Section 103. See also Sections 230–234 (proceeding to determine whether devisee survived testator). [31 Cal.L.Rev.Comm. Reports 195 (2001)].

Cross References

At-death transfer defined for purposes of this Part, see Probate Code § 21104.

Simultaneous death, determination of survival, petitions and purposes, see Probate Code § 230.

§ 21110. Transferee's death; taking by representation; contrary intent in instrument

(a) Subject to subdivision (b), if a transferee is dead when the instrument is executed, or fails or is treated as failing to survive the transferor or until a future time required by the instrument, the issue of the deceased transferee take in the transferee's place in the manner provided in Section 240. A transferee under a class gift shall be a transferee for the purpose of this subdivision unless the transferee's death occurred before the execution of the instrument and that fact was known to the transferor when the instrument was executed.

(b) The issue of a deceased transferee do not take in the transferee's place if the instrument expresses a contrary intention or a substitute disposition. A requirement that the initial transferee survive the transferor or survive for a specified period of time after the death of the transferor constitutes a contrary intention. A requirement that the initial transferee survive until a future time that is related to the probate of the transferor's will or administration of the estate of the transferor constitutes a contrary intention.

(c) As used in this section, "transferee" means a person who is kindred of the transferor or kindred of a surviving, deceased, or former spouse of the transferor. *(Added by Stats.1994, c. 806 (A.B.3686), § 41. Amended by Stats.2002, c. 138 (A.B.1784), § 19.)*

Law Revision Commission Comments

2002 Amendment

Subdivision (b) of Section 21110 is amended to avoid the implication that a specific period of time is the only expression of survival that constitutes a contrary intention. While an expression of that type may well indicate an intention that the antilapse statute not apply, other survival requirements in an instrument may also be sufficient to override the antilapse statute.

In applying the provision of subdivision (b) relating to a substitute gift, care must be taken not to ascribe to the transferor too readily or too broadly an intention to override the antilapse statute, the purpose of which is to lessen the risk of serious oversight by the transferor. For example, by providing a substitute taker, the transferor may very well intend to override the antilapse statute in the ordinary case. If, however, the substitute taker has also predeceased the transferor, the transferor may have intended that the antilapse statute should apply to the first taker.

Section 21110 does not make a substitute gift in the case of a class gift where a person otherwise answering the description of the class was dead when the instrument was executed and that fact was known to the transferor. It is consistent with Estate of Steidl, 89 Cal.App.2d 488, 201 P.2d 58 (1948) (antilapse statute applied where class member died before testator but after execution of will).

Subdivision (c) makes the antilapse statute apply not only to kindred of the transferor but also to kindred of a surviving, deceased, or former spouse of the transferor. Thus, if the transferor were to make a transfer to a stepchild who predeceased the transferor, Section 21110 will make a substitute gift to issue of the predeceased stepchild. The term "kindred" was taken from former Section 92 (repealed by 1983 Cal. Stat. ch. 842, § 18) and refers to persons related by blood. In re Estate of Sowash, 62 Cal.App. 512, 516, 217 P. 123 (1923). In addition, an adoptee is generally kindred of the adoptive family and not of the natural relatives. See Section 21115 (halfbloods, adopted persons, persons born out of wedlock, stepchildren, and foster children, plus issue of such persons, as "kindred" or "issue"). See also Estate of Goulart, 222 Cal.App.2d 808, 35 Cal.Rptr. 465 (1963).

As to when a transferee is treated as having predeceased the transferor, see Sections 220 (simultaneous death), 282 (effect of disclaimer), 250 (effect of feloniously and intentionally killing decedent), 6122 & 5600 (effect of dissolution of marriage), See also Sections 230–234 (proceeding to determine survival), 240 (manner of taking by representation). [31 Cal.L.Rev.Comm. Reports 197 (2001)].

Cross References

Construction of instruments, lifetime gifts, satisfaction of at-death transfer, see Probate Code § 21135.

Simultaneous death, determination of survival, petitions and purposes, see Probate Code § 230.

Trust for care of animals, accountings and beneficiaries, see Probate Code § 15212.

§ 21111. Failed transfers

(a) Except as provided in subdivision (b) and subject to Section 21110, if a transfer fails for any reason, the property is transferred as follows:

(1) If the transferring instrument provides for an alternative disposition in the event the transfer fails, the property is transferred according to the terms of the instrument.

(2) If the transferring instrument does not provide for an alternative disposition but does provide for the transfer of a residue, the property becomes a part of the residue transferred under the instrument.

(3) If the transferring instrument does not provide for an alternative disposition and does not provide for the transfer of a residue, or if the transfer is itself a residuary gift, the property is transferred to the decedent's estate.

(b) Subject to Section 21110, if a residuary gift or a future interest is transferred to two or more persons and the share of a transferee fails for any reason, and no alternative disposition is provided, the share passes to the other transferees in proportion to their other interest in the residuary gift or the future interest.

(c) A transfer of "all my estate" or words of similar import is a residuary gift for purposes of this section.

(d) If failure of a future interest results in an intestacy, the property passes to the heirs of the transferor determined pursuant to Section 21114. *(Added by Stats.1994, c. 806 (A.B.3686), § 41. Amended by Stats.1996, c. 563 (S.B.392), § 32; Stats.2001, c. 417 (A.B.873), § 11; Stats.2002, c. 138 (A.B.1784), § 20.)*

Law Revision Commission Comments
2001 Amendment

Section 21111 is amended to clarify the treatment of a failed transfer by will, trust, life insurance policy, or other instrument transferring property at death, where the transferring instrument does not provide for the transfer of a residue. [28 Cal.L.Rev.Comm. Reports 599 (1998)].

2002 Amendment

Section 21111 is amended to clarify the treatment of a failed residuary gift.

Under subdivision (a)(1), an alternative disposition may take the form of a transfer of specifically identifiable property (specific gift) or a transfer from general assets of the transferor (general gift) that includes the specific property.

The 1994 enactment of Section 21111 extended former Section 6148 (wills) to trusts and other instruments. See also Section 21101 (application of part). This section is drawn from Section 2–606 of the Uniform Probate Code (1987). As to the construction of provisions drawn from uniform acts, see Section 2.

With respect to a residuary devise, subdivision (b) abolishes the "no residue of a residue" rule, illustrated by Estate of Murphy, 157 Cal. 63, 106 P. 230 (1910). It preserves the change made by former Section 6148 in the California case law rule that if the share of one of several residuary devisees fails, the share passed by intestacy. See, e.g., Estate of Russell, 69 Cal.2d 200, 215–16, 444 P.2d 353, 70 Cal.Rptr. 561 (1968); *In re* Estate of Kelleher, 205 Cal. 757, 760–61, 272 P. 1060 (1928); Estate of Anderson, 166 Cal.App.2d 39, 42, 332 P.2d 785 (1985).

For purposes of this section, a gift of "my estate" is a residuary gift rather than a general gift. Subdivision (c). In the case of a failed gift of a portion of an estate or residue, this section may be applied in appropriate circumstances so as to prevent an intestacy or a distorted disposition.

Where a failed gift is transferred to the decedent's estate under this section, it will often result in an intestacy. *Cf.* Section 21114 (class gift to heirs, next of kin, relatives, and the like). [31 Cal.L.Rev. Comm. Reports 198 (2001)].

Cross References

Construction of instruments, lifetime gifts, satisfaction of at-death transfer, see Probate Code § 21135.

§ 21112. Issue; conditions

A condition in a transfer of a present or future interest that refers to a person's death "with" or "without" issue, or to a person's "having" or "leaving" issue or no issue, or a condition based on words of similar import, is construed to refer to that person's being dead at the time the transfer takes effect in enjoyment and to that person either having or not having, as the case may be, issue who are alive at the time of enjoyment. *(Added by Stats.1994, c. 806 (A.B.3686), § 41. Amended by Stats.2002, c. 138 (A.B.1784), § 21.)*

Law Revision Commission Comments
2002 Amendment

The amendment to Section 21112 is technical. The 1994 enactment of Section 21112 extended former Section 6149 (wills) to trusts and other instruments. See also Section 21101 (application of part).

The section overrules California's much criticized theory of indefinite failure of issue established by *In re* Estate of Carothers, 161 Cal. 588, 119 P. 926 (1911). See generally 12 B. Witkin, Summary of California Law *Wills and Probate* §§ 279–80, at 310–12 (9th ed. 1990). Section 6149 adopts the majority view of the Restatement of Property. See Witkin, *id.* § 280, at 310–12; Annot., 26 A.L.R.3d 407

(1969); Restatement of Property § 269 (1940). Under Section 21112, if the transfer is "to *A* for life, remainder to *B* and *B*'s heirs, but if *B* dies without issue, then to *C*," the transfer is read as meaning "if *B* dies before *A* without issue living at the death of *A*." If *B* survives *A*, whether or not *B* then has living issue, *B* takes the transfer absolutely. If *B* predeceases *A* with issue then living but at the time of *A*'s subsequent death *B* does not have living issue, the transfer goes to *C*. [31 Cal.L.Rev.Comm. Reports 200 (2001)].

§ 21113. Repealed by Stats.2002, c. 138 (A.B.1784), § 22

Law Revision Commission Comments

2002 Repeal

Section 21113 is repealed as unnecessary. It inadequately codified the common law "rule of convenience," failing to include its common law exceptions. See Restatement (Second) of Property §§ 26.1–26.2 (1987). Repeal of this section does not reject existing law on this subject, but is intended to eliminate any implication that the section is a complete statement of the existing law. [31 Cal.L.Rev.Comm. Reports 201 (2001)].

§ 21114. Transfers to heirs; designated persons

(a) If a statute or an instrument provides for transfer of a present or future interest to, or creates a present or future interest in, a designated person's "heirs," "heirs at law," "next of kin," "relatives," or "family," or words of similar import, the transfer is to the persons, including the state under Section 6800, and in the shares that would succeed to the designated person's intestate estate under the intestate succession law of the transferor's domicile, if the designated person died when the transfer is to take effect in enjoyment. If the designated person's surviving spouse is living but is remarried at the time the transfer is to take effect in enjoyment, the surviving spouse is not an heir of the designated person for purposes of this section.

(b) As used in this section, "designated person" includes the transferor. *(Added by Stats.1994, c. 806 (A.B.3686), § 41. Amended by Stats.2002, c. 138 (A.B.1784), § 23.)*

Law Revision Commission Comments

2002 Amendment

Section 21114 is amended to conform to Uniform Probate Code Section 2–711 (1993). The amendment clarifies a number of issues:

(1) Application of the section to interests acquired by operation of law.

(2) Application of escheat principles.

(3) Application of the law of another state, based on the transferor's domicile.

(4) Elimination of the special rule for ancestral property.

The 1994 enactment of Section 21114 extended former Section 6151 (wills) to trusts and other instruments. See also Section 21101 (application of part). The former section was drawn from Section 2514 of the Pennsylvania Consolidated Statutes, Title 20, and established a special rule for a class gift to an indefinite class such as the transferor's or another designated person's "heirs," "next of kin," "relative," "family," and the like. As Section 21114 applies to a transfer of a future interest, the section is consistent with Section 21109 in that Section 21114 establishes a constructional preference against early vesting. However, Section 21114 differs from Section 21109 in that one who does not survive until the future interest takes effect in enjoyment is not deemed a member of the indefinite class described in Section 21114 (such as "heirs"), is therefore not a "transferee" under the class gift, and no substitute gift will be made by the antilapse statute (Section 21110). If the transfer of a future interest is to a more definite class such as "children," one coming

within that description who fails to survive until the transfer takes effect in enjoyment does not take under the instrument (Section 21109) but may nonetheless be a "deceased transferee" under the antilapse statute (Section 21110) permitting substitution of the deceased transferee's issue. See Sections 21109 & 21110 Comments. See also Section 21115(c)(3) (rules for determining persons who would be heirs of transferor or other person).

By postponing the determination of class membership until the gift takes effect in enjoyment where the class is indefinite (e.g., to "heirs"), Section 21114 should reduce the uncertainty of result under prior law. See Halbach, *Future Interests: Express and Implied Conditions of Survival*, 49 Cal. L. Rev. 297, 317–20 (1961). Section 21114 is consistent with *Estate of Easter*, 24 Cal.2d 191, 148 P.2d 601 (1944). [31 Cal.L.Rev.Comm. Reports 201 (2001)].

Cross References

Trust for care of animals, accountings and beneficiaries, see Probate Code § 15212.

§ 21115. Halfbloods, adoptees, persons born out of wedlock, stepchildren and foster children; inclusion; intestate succession

(a) Except as provided in subdivision (b), halfbloods, adopted persons, persons born out of wedlock, stepchildren, foster children, and the issue of these persons when appropriate to the class, are included in terms of class gift or relationship in accordance with the rules for determining relationship and inheritance rights for purposes of intestate succession.

(b) In construing a transfer by a transferor who is not the natural parent, a person born to the natural parent shall not be considered the child of that parent unless the person lived while a minor as a regular member of the household of the natural parent or of that parent's parent, brother, sister, spouse, or surviving spouse. In construing a transfer by a transferor who is not the adoptive parent, a person adopted by the adoptive parent shall not be considered the child of that parent unless the person lived while a minor (either before or after the adoption) as a regular member of the household of the adopting parent or of that parent's parent, brother, sister, or surviving spouse.

(c) Subdivisions (a) and (b) shall also apply in determining:

(1) Persons who would be kindred of the transferor or kindred of a surviving, deceased, or former spouse of the transferor under Section 21110.

(2) Persons to be included as issue of a deceased transferee under Section 21110.

(3) Persons who would be the transferor's or other designated person's heirs under Section 21114.

(d) The rules for determining intestate succession under this section are those in effect at the time the transfer is to take effect in enjoyment. *(Added by Stats.1994, c. 806 (A.B.3686), § 41. Amended by Stats.2002, c. 138 (A.B.1784), § 24.)*

Law Revision Commission Comments

2002 Amendment

Subdivision (d) is added to Section 21115 for consistency with the choice of law rules of Section 21114. The 1994 enactment of Section

21115 extended former Section 6152 (wills) to trusts and other instruments. See also Section 21101 (application of part).

Subdivision (a) is drawn from Section 2–611 of the Uniform Probate Code (1987). As to the construction of provisions drawn from uniform acts, see Section 2. To the extent that California cases had addressed the matter, subdivision (a) is consistent with prior California law. See 12 B. Witkin, Summary of California Law *Wills and Probate* §§ 287–90, at 320–23 (9th ed. 1990). For the rules for determining relationship and inheritance rights for purposes of intestate succession, see Sections 6406, 6408. Under some circumstances stepchildren and foster children are included in terms of class gift or relationship pursuant to the rules for intestate succession. See Section 6408 (when stepchild or foster child treated the same as adopted child).

Subdivision (b) precludes the adoption of a person (often an adult) solely for the purpose of permitting the adoptee to take under the testamentary instrument of another. Subdivision (b) also construes a transfer to exclude a child born out of wedlock (where the transferor is not the parent) if the child never lives while a minor as a regular member of the parent's household. A child is included in class gift terminology in the transferor's instrument if the child lived while a minor or as a regular member of the household of the parent's spouse or surviving spouse. As a result, a child born of a marital relationship will almost always be included in the class, consistent with the transferor's likely intent.

Subdivision (c) makes clear that the rules stated in subdivisions (a) and (b) apply for the purposes of the antilapse statute (Section 21110) and in construing transfers (Section 21114). [31 Cal.L.Rev. Comm. Reports 203 (2001)].

§ 21116. Repealed by Stats.2002, c. 138 (A.B.1784), § 25

Law Revision Commission Comments

2002 Repeal

Section 21116 is not continued. It codified a presumption in favor of early vesting that is overbroad and inconsistent with the rule of deferred vesting applicable in some circumstances. See, e.g., Section 21114 (class gift to heirs, next of kin, relatives, and the like). Repeal of this section does not reject existing law on this subject, but is intended to eliminate any implication that the section is a complete statement of the existing law. [31 Cal.L.Rev. Comm. Reports 205 (2001)].

§ 21117. Classification of at-death transfers

At-death transfers are classified as follows:

(a) A specific gift is a transfer of specifically identifiable property.

(b) A general gift is a transfer from the general assets of the transferor that does not give specific property.

(c) A demonstrative gift is a general gift that specifies the fund or property from which the transfer is primarily to be made.

(d) A general pecuniary gift is a pecuniary gift within the meaning of Section 21118.

(e) An annuity is a general pecuniary gift that is payable periodically.

(f) A residuary gift is a transfer of property that remains after all specific and general gifts have been satisfied. *(Added by Stats.1994, c. 806 (A.B.3686), § 41. Amended by Stats.2002, c. 138 (A.B.1784), § 26.)*

Law Revision Commission Comments

2002 Amendment

Section 21117 is amended to correct terminology. See Section 21104 ("at-death transfer" defined). The 1994 enactment of Section 21117 extended former Section 6154 (wills) to trusts and other instruments. See also Section 21101 (application of part).

For the priority that a demonstrative gift has over other general gifts and the priority that an annuity has over other general gifts, see Section 21403(b). See also *Recommendation Relating to Interest and Income During Administration*, 19 Cal. L. Revision Comm'n Reports 1019 (1988); *Comments to Conforming Revisions and Repeals*, 19 Cal. L. Revision Comm'n Reports 1031, 1089–90 (1988); *Communication from the California Law Revision Commission Concerning Assembly Bill 2841*, 19 Cal. L. Revision Comm'n Reports 1201, 1228–29 (1988). [31 Cal.L.Rev.Comm. Reports 205 (2001)].

Cross References

At-death transfer defined for purposes of this Part, see Probate Code § 21104.

§ 21118. Satisfaction of pecuniary gift by distribution of property other than money; valuation of property

(a) If an instrument authorizes a fiduciary to satisfy a pecuniary gift wholly or partly by distribution of property other than money, property selected for that purpose shall be valued at its fair market value on the date of distribution, unless the instrument expressly provides otherwise. If the instrument permits the fiduciary to value the property selected for distribution as of a date other than the date of distribution, then, unless the instrument expressly provides otherwise, the property selected by the fiduciary for that purpose shall fairly reflect net appreciation and depreciation (occurring between the valuation date and the date of distribution) in all of the assets from which the distribution could have been made.

(b) As used in this section, "pecuniary gift" means a transfer of property made in an instrument that either is expressly stated as a fixed dollar amount or is a dollar amount determinable by the provisions of the instrument. *(Added by Stats.1994, c. 806 (A.B.3686), § 41. Amended by Stats.2002, c. 138 (A.B.1784), § 27.)*

Law Revision Commission Comments

2002 Amendment

Section 21118 is amended to incorporate the standard of Treasury Regulations Section 26.2642–2(b)(2) (1996) (valuation). [31 Cal. L.Rev.Comm. Reports 206 (2001)].

CHAPTER 2. ASCERTAINING MEANING OF LANGUAGE USED IN THE INSTRUMENT

§ 21120. Interpretation of words to give every expression some effect; preference given to avoid intestacy or failure of a transfer

The words of an instrument are to receive an interpretation that will give every expression some effect, rather than one that will render any of the expressions inoperative. Preference is to be given to an interpretation of an instrument that will prevent intestacy or failure of a transfer, rather than one that will result in an intestacy or failure of a transfer. *(Added by Stats.1994, c. 806 (A.B.3686), § 41. Amended by Stats. 2002, c. 138 (A.B.1784), § 28.)*

Law Revision Commission Comments

2002 Amendment

Section 21120 is amended to more fully implement its application to trusts and other instruments. The 1994 enactment of Section 21120 extended former Section 6160 (wills) to trusts and other instruments. See also Section 21101 (application of part).

This part does not apply to an instrument if its terms expressly or by necessary implication make this part inapplicable. See Section 21101 (application of part). [31 Cal.L.Rev.Comm. Reports 207 (2001)].

§ 21121. Construction of parts in relation to each other; consistent whole; ambiguity

All parts of an instrument are to be construed in relation to each other and so as, if possible, to form a consistent whole. If the meaning of any part of an instrument is ambiguous or doubtful, it may be explained by any reference to or recital of that part in another part of the instrument. *(Added by Stats.1994, c. 806 (A.B.3686), § 41. Amended by Stats.2002, c. 138 (A.B.1784), § 29.)*

Law Revision Commission Comments

2002 Amendment

The amendment to Section 21121 is technical. The 1994 enactment of Section 21121 extended former Section 6161 (wills) to trusts and other instruments. See also Section 21101 (application of part). [31 Cal.L.Rev.Comm. Reports 207 (2001)].

§ 21122. Ordinary grammatical meaning; technical words

The words of an instrument are to be given their ordinary and grammatical meaning unless the intention to use them in another sense is clear and their intended meaning can be ascertained. Technical words are not necessary to give effect to a disposition in an instrument. Technical words are to be considered as having been used in their technical sense unless (a) the context clearly indicates a contrary intention or (b) it satisfactorily appears that the instrument was drawn solely by the transferor and that the transferor was unacquainted with the technical sense. *(Added by Stats.1994, c. 806 (A.B.3686), § 41. Amended by Stats.2002, c. 138 (A.B.1784), § 30.)*

Law Revision Commission Comments

2002 Amendment

The amendment to Section 21122 is technical. The 1994 enactment of Section 21122 extended former Section 6162 (wills) to trusts and other instruments. See also Section 21101 (application of part). [31 Cal.L.Rev.Comm. Reports 208 (2001)].

CHAPTER 3. EXONERATION; ADEMPTION

§ 21131. Specific gifts; right of exoneration

A specific gift passes the property transferred subject to any mortgage, deed of trust, or other lien existing at the date of death, without right of exoneration, regardless of a general directive to pay debts contained in the instrument. *(Added by Stats.1994, c. 806 (A.B.3686), § 41. Amended by Stats. 2002, c. 138 (A.B.1784), § 31.)*

Law Revision Commission Comments

2002 Amendment

The amendment to Section 21131 is technical. See Section 45 ("instrument" defined). The 1994 enactment of Section 21131 extended former Section 6170 (wills) to trusts and other instruments. See also Section 21101 (application of part). See also Section 21117(a) ("specific gift" defined).

This section expands the rule stated in Section 2–609 of the Uniform Probate Code (1987) to cover any lien. This expansion makes Section 21131 consistent with Section 21404. As to the construction of provisions drawn from uniform acts, see Section 2. Former Section 6170 reversed the prior California case law rule that, in the absence of an expressed intention of the testator to the contrary, if the debt which encumbers the devised property is one for which the testator was personally liable, the devisee was entitled to "exoneration," that is, to receive the property free of the encumbrance by having the debt paid out of other assets of the estate. See 12 B. Witkin, Summary of California Law *Wills and Probate* § 624, at 654–55 (9th ed. 1990). The rule stated in Section 21131 applies in the absence of a contrary intention of the transferor. See Section 21102. See also Sections 32 ("devise" means a disposition of real or personal property by will), 62 ("property" defined). [31 Cal.L.Rev.Comm. Reports 208 (2001)].

§ 21132. At-death transfer of securities

(a) If a transferor executes an instrument that makes an at-death transfer of securities and the transferor then owned securities that meet the description in the instrument, the transfer includes additional securities owned by the transferor at death to the extent the additional securities were acquired by the transferor after the instrument was executed as a result of the transferor's ownership of the described securities and are securities of any of the following types:

(1) Securities of the same organization acquired by reason of action initiated by the organization or any successor, related, or acquiring organization, excluding any acquired by exercise of purchase options.

(2) Securities of another organization acquired as a result of a merger, consolidation, reorganization, or other distribution by the organization or any successor, related, or acquiring organization.

(3) Securities of the same organization acquired as a result of a plan of reinvestment.

(b) Distributions in cash before death with respect to a described security are not part of the transfer. *(Added by Stats.2002, c. 138 (A.B.1784), § 33.)*

Law Revision Commission Comments

2002 Addition

New Section 21132 supersedes former Section 21132 (change in form of securities). The 1994 enactment of Section 21132 extended former Section 6171 (wills) to other at-death transfers. See also Section 21101 (application of part). The new section is based on Uniform Probate Code Section 2–605 (1990); the former section was based on Uniform Probate Code Section 2–605 (1987). As to the construction of provisions drawn from uniform acts, see Section 2.

This section is generally consistent with prior California case law. See 12 B. Witkin, Summary of California Law *Wills and Probate* §§ 317–18, at 350–51 (9th ed. 1990). The rules stated in Section 21132 apply in the absence of a contrary intention of the transferor. See Section 21102.

Under Section 21132, if the transferor makes a specific gift of only a portion of the stock the transferor owns in a particular company and there is a stock split or stock dividend, the specific transferee is entitled only to a proportionate share of the additional stock received. For example, if the transferor owns 500 shares of stock, transfers 100 shares to a child, and the stock splits two for one, the child is entitled to 200 shares, not 600. [31 Cal.L.Rev.Comm. Reports 209 (2001)].

2002 Repeal

Former Section 21132 is superseded by new Section 21132 (change in form of securities). [31 Cal.L.Rev.Comm. Reports 209 (2001)].

Cross References

At-death transfer defined for purposes of this Part, see Probate Code § 21104.

§ 21133.   Receipt of at-death transfers of specific gifts; recipient's rights

A recipient of an at-death transfer of a specific gift has a right to the property specifically given, to the extent the property is owned by the transferor at the time the gift takes effect in possession or enjoyment, and all of the following:

(a) Any balance of the purchase price (together with any security agreement) owing from a purchaser to the transferor at the time the gift takes effect in possession or enjoyment by reason of sale of the property.

(b) Any amount of an eminent domain award for the taking of the property unpaid at the time the gift takes effect in possession or enjoyment.

(c) Any proceeds unpaid at the time the gift takes effect in possession or enjoyment on fire or casualty insurance on or other recovery for injury to the property.

(d) Property owned by the transferor at the time the gift takes effect in possession or enjoyment and acquired as a result of foreclosure, or obtained in lieu of foreclosure, of the security interest for a specifically given obligation. *(Added by*

Stats.1994, c. 806 (A.B.3686), § 41.   Amended by Stats.2002, c. 138 (A.B.1784), § 34.)

Law Revision Commission Comments

2002 Amendment

The 1994 enactment of Section 21133 extended former Section 6172 (wills) to trusts and other instruments. See also Section 21101 (application of part). The section is limited in its application to at-death transfers—transfers that are revocable during the transferor's lifetime but become effective on the transferor's death. See Section 21104 ("at-death transfer" defined). See also Section 21117(a) ("specific gift" defined).

Section 21133 is amended for conformity with Uniform Probate Code Section 2–606(a) (1990). (Section 21133 is based on former Uniform Probate Code Section 2–608(a) (1987), which is superseded by Uniform Probate Code Section 2–606(a) (1990).) As to the construction of provisions drawn from uniform acts, see Section 2.

This section is generally similar to prior California case law. See, e.g. Estate of Shubin, 252 Cal.App.2d 588, 60 Cal.Rptr. 678 (1967); *cf.* Estate of Newsome, 248 Cal.App.2d 712, 56 Cal.Rptr. 874 (1967). See also Sections 32 ("devise" defined), 62 ("property" defined). The rules stated in Section 21133 apply in the absence of a contrary intention of the transferor. See Section 21102.

The rules of nonademption in Sections 21133–21135 are not exclusive, and nothing in these provisions is intended to increase the incidence of ademption in California. See Section 21139. [31 Cal.L.Rev.Comm. Reports 211 (2001)].

Cross References

At-death transfer defined for purposes of this Part, see Probate Code § 21104.

§ 21134.   Specifically given property sold or encumbered by a deed of trust, mortgage, or other instrument by a conservator, agent, or trustee; transferee's rights; eminent domain awards, insurance proceeds, or recovery for injury; application of section

(a) Except as otherwise provided in this section, if, after the execution of the instrument of gift, specifically given property is sold, or encumbered by a deed of trust, mortgage, or other instrument, by a conservator, by an agent acting within the authority of a durable power of attorney for an incapacitated principal, or by a trustee acting for an incapacitated settlor of a trust established by the settlor as a revocable trust, the transferee of the specific gift has the right to a general pecuniary gift equal to the net sale price of the property unreduced by the payoff of any such encumbrance, or the amount of the unpaid encumbrance on the property as well as the property itself.

(b) Except as otherwise provided in this section, if an eminent domain award for the taking of specifically given property is paid to a conservator, to an agent acting within the authority of a durable power of attorney for an incapacitated principal, or to a trustee acting for an incapacitated settlor of a trust established by the settlor as a revocable trust, or if the proceeds on fire or casualty insurance on, or recovery for injury to, specifically gifted property are paid to a conservator, to an agent acting within the authority of a durable power of attorney for an incapacitated principal, or to a trustee acting for an incapacitated settlor of a trust established by the settlor as a revocable trust, the recipient of the specific gift has the right to a general pecuniary gift equal to the eminent domain award or the insurance proceeds or

1064

recovery unreduced by the payoff of any encumbrance placed on the property by the conservator, agent, or trustee, after the execution of the instrument of gift.

(c) For the purpose of the references in this section to a conservator, this section does not apply if, after the sale, mortgage, condemnation, fire, or casualty, or recovery, the conservatorship is terminated and the transferor survives the termination by one year.

(d) For the purpose of the references in this section to an agent acting with the authority of a durable power of attorney for an incapacitated principal, or to a trustee acting for an incapacitated settlor of a trust established by the settlor as a revocable trust, (1) "incapacitated principal" or "incapacitated settlor" means a principal or settlor who is an incapacitated person, (2) no adjudication of incapacity before death is necessary, and (3) the acts of an agent within the authority of a durable power of attorney are presumed to be for an incapacitated principal. However, there shall be no presumption of a settlor's incapacity concerning the acts of a trustee.

(e) The right of the transferee of the specific gift under this section shall be reduced by any right the transferee has under Section 21133. *(Added by Stats.1994, c. 806 (A.B. 3686), § 41. Amended by Stats.2002, c. 138 (A.B.1784), § 35; Stats.2012, c. 195 (A.B.1985), § 1.)*

Law Revision Commission Comments

2002 Amendment

The 1994 enactment of Section 21134 extended former Section 6173 (wills) to trusts and other instruments. See also Sections 21101 (application of part), 21117(a) ("specific gift" defined).

Section 21134 is amended for conformity with Uniform Probate Code Section 2–606(b) (1990). (Section 21134 is based on former Uniform Probate Code Section 2–608(b) (1987), which is superseded by Uniform Probate Code Section 2–606(b) (1990).) As to the construction of provisions drawn from uniform acts, see Section 2.

Subdivisions (a) and (b) are consistent with prior California case law. See Estate of Packham, 232 Cal.App.2d 847, 43 Cal.Rptr. 318 (1965). See also Section 62 ("property" defined). The rules stated in Section 21134 apply in the absence of a contrary intention of the transferor. See Section 21102. See also Section 21139 (rules stated in Sections 21133–21135 not exhaustive).

Subdivision (c) revises the corresponding Uniform Probate Code language to refer to the conservatorship being terminated rather than to it being "adjudicated that the disability of the testator has ceased." The application of subdivision (c) turns on whether a conservatorship has been terminated, and not on whether the transferor has regained the capacity to make an instrument of transfer. Thus subdivision (c) provides a rule of administrative convenience and avoids the need to litigate the question of whether the conservatee had capacity to make an instrument of transfer after the time of the sale, condemnation, fire, or casualty.

It should be noted that the presumption provided in subdivision (d) applies only for the purpose of the references in this section to an agent acting with the authority of a durable power of attorney for an incapacitated principal. [31 Cal.L.Rev.Comm. Reports 212 (2001)].

§ 21135. Lifetime gifts; satisfaction of at-death transfer; conditions

(a) Property given by a transferor during his or her lifetime to a person is treated as a satisfaction of an at-death transfer to that person in whole or in part only if one of the following conditions is satisfied:

(1) The instrument provides for deduction of the lifetime gift from the at-death transfer.

(2) The transferor declares in a contemporaneous writing that the gift is in satisfaction of the at-death transfer or that its value is to be deducted from the value of the at-death transfer.

(3) The transferee acknowledges in writing that the gift is in satisfaction of the at-death transfer or that its value is to be deducted from the value of the at-death transfer.

(4) The property given is the same property that is the subject of a specific gift to that person.

(b) Subject to subdivision (c), for the purpose of partial satisfaction, property given during lifetime is valued as of the time the transferee came into possession or enjoyment of the property or as of the time of death of the transferor, whichever occurs first.

(c) If the value of the gift is expressed in the contemporaneous writing of the transferor, or in an acknowledgment of the transferee made contemporaneously with the gift, that value is conclusive in the division and distribution of the estate.

(d) If the transferee fails to survive the transferor, the gift is treated as a full or partial satisfaction of the gift, as the case may be, in applying Sections 21110 and 21111 unless the transferor's contemporaneous writing provides otherwise. *(Added by Stats.1994, c. 806 (A.B.3686), § 41. Amended by Stats.2002, c. 138 (A.B.1784), § 36.)*

Law Revision Commission Comments

2002 Amendment

The 1994 enactment of Section 21135 extended former Section 6174 (wills) to trusts and other instruments. See also Section 21101 (application of part).

Section 21135 is amended for conformity with Uniform Probate Code Section 2–609 (1990). (Section 21135 is based on former Uniform Probate Code Section 2–612 (1987), which is superseded by Uniform Probate Code Section 2–609 (1990).) As to the construction of provisions drawn from uniform acts, see Section 2.

Section 21135 is also amended to fill gaps and correct terminology. See Sections 21104 ("at-death transfer" defined), 21117 (classification of at-death transfer). See also Section 11640 (hearing and order resolving questions arising under Section 21135). For a comparable intestate succession rule concerning advancements, see Section 6409. [31 Cal.L.Rev.Comm. Reports 213 (2001)].

Cross References

Administration of estates, petitions for distribution by the personal representative, court hearings, see Probate Code § 11640.
At-death transfer defined for purposes of this Part, see Probate Code § 21104.

§ 21136. Repealed by Stats.2002, c. 138 (A.B.1784), § 37

Law Revision Commission Comments

2002 Repeal

Section 21136 is not continued. The matter is governed by case law. See, e.g., 12 B. Witkin, Summary of California Law *Wills and Probate* § 314 *et seq.*, at 347–50 (9th ed. 1990). Repeal of this section does not reject existing law on this subject, but is intended to eliminate any implication that the section is a complete statement of the existing law. [31 Cal. L.Rev.Comm. Reports 215 (2001)].

§ 21137. Repealed by Stats.2002, c. 138 (A.B.1784), § 38

Law Revision Commission Comments

2002 Repeal

Section 21137 is not continued. The matter is governed by case law. See, e.g., 12 B. Witkin, Summary of California Law *Wills and Probate* § 314 *et seq.*, at 347–50 (9th ed. 1990). Repeal of this section does not reject existing law on this subject, but is intended to eliminate any implication that the section is a complete statement of the existing law. [31 Cal. L.Rev.Comm. Reports 215 (2001)].

§ 21138. Repealed by Stats.2002, c. 138 (A.B.1784), § 39

Law Revision Commission Comments

2002 Repeal

Section 21138 is not continued. The matter is governed by case law. See, e.g., 12 B. Witkin, Summary of California Law *Wills and Probate* § 314 *et seq.*, at 347–50 (9th ed. 1990). Repeal of this section does not reject existing law on this subject, but is intended to eliminate any implication that the section is a complete statement of the existing law. [31 Cal. L.Rev.Comm. Reports 216 (2001)].

§ 21139. Rules not exhaustive; ademption

The rules stated in Sections 21133 to 21135, inclusive, are not exhaustive, and nothing in those sections is intended to increase the incidence of ademption under the law of this state. *(Added by Stats.1994, c. 806 (A.B.3686), § 41. Amended by Stats.2002, c. 138 (A.B.1784), § 40.)*

Law Revision Commission Comments

2002 Amendment

The 1994 enactment of Section 21139 extended former Section 6178 (wills) to trusts and other instruments. See also Section 21101 (application of part). Section 21139 is amended to reflect repeal of Sections 21136–21138.

This section recognizes that the rules stated in Sections 21133–21135 cover a number of special situations where a specific gift is not adeemed but do not cover all situations where a specific gift is not adeemed. This section also makes clear that the inclusion of these specific statutory rules is not intended to increase the incidence of ademption in California. [31 Cal.L.Rev.Comm. Reports 216 (2001)].

CHAPTER 4. EFFECTIVE DATES

§ 21140. Application of part

This part applies to all instruments, regardless of when they were executed. *(Added by Stats.1994, c. 806 (A.B.3686), § 41. Amended by Stats.2002, c. 138 (A.B.1784), § 41.)*

Law Revision Commission Comments

2002 Amendment

Section 21140 is amended to delete the transitional provision in subdivision (b). [31 Cal.L.Rev.Comm. Reports 216 (2001)].

Part 2

PERPETUITIES

Application

Application of Part 2, see Probate Code § 21202.

CHAPTER 1. UNIFORM STATUTORY RULE AGAINST PERPETUITIES

Application

Application of Part 2, see Probate Code § 21202.

ARTICLE 1. GENERAL PROVISIONS

Application

Application of Part 2, see Probate Code § 21202.

Cross References

Powers of appointment, generally, see Probate Code § 600 et seq.

§ 21200. Short title

This chapter shall be known and may be cited as the Uniform Statutory Rule Against Perpetuities. *(Added by Stats.1991, c. 156 (A.B.1577), § 24.)*

Law Revision Commission Comments

1991 Addition

Section 21200 provides a short title for this chapter and is the same as Section 6 of the Uniform Statutory Rule Against Perpetuities (1990). As to the construction of uniform acts, see Section 2(b). This part applies to nonvested property interests regardless of whether they were created before or after January 1, 1992. See Section 21202. [20 Cal.L.Rev.Comm.Reports 2501 (1990)].

§ 21201. Common law rule superseded

This chapter supersedes the common law rule against perpetuities. *(Added by Stats.1991, c. 156 (A.B.1577), § 24.)*

Law Revision Commission Comments

1991 Addition

Section 21201 is the same in substance as part of Section 9 of the Uniform Statutory Rule Against Perpetuities (1990). This chapter supersedes the common law rule against perpetuities, which was specifically incorporated into California law by former Civil Code Section 715.2 and related sections. See Section 21202 (application of part). [20 Cal.L.Rev.Comm.Reports 2501 (1990)].

Background (adapted from official comments to Uniform Statutory Rule Against Perpetuities)

As provided in Section 21201, this chapter supersedes the common law rule against perpetuities (common law rule) and the statutory provisions previously in effect, replacing them with the statutory rule against perpetuities (statutory rule) set forth in Article 2 (commencing with Section 21205) and by the other provisions in this chapter.

Unless excluded by Section 21225, the statutory rule applies to nonvested property interests and to powers of appointment over property or property interests that are nongeneral powers, general testamentary powers, or general powers not presently exercisable because of a condition precedent. The statutory rule does not apply to vested property interests. See, e.g., X's interest in Example (23) in the Background to this section. Nor does the statutory rule apply to presently exercisable general powers of appointment. See, e.g., G's power in Example (19) in the Background to Section 21206; G's power in Example (1) in the Background to Section 21211; A's power in Example (2) in the Background to Section 21211; X's power in Example (3) in the Background to Section 21211; A's noncumulative power of withdrawal in Example (4) in the Background to Section 21211.

G. Subsidiary Common Law Doctrines: Whether Superseded by This Chapter

The courts, in interpreting the common law rule, developed several subsidiary doctrines. This chapter does not supersede those subsidiary doctrines except to the extent the provisions of this chapter conflict with them. As explained below, most of these common law doctrines remain in full force or in force in modified form.

1. Constructional Preference for Validity

Professor Gray in his treatise on the common law rule against perpetuities declared that a will or deed is to be construed without regard to the rule, and then the rule is to be "remorselessly" applied to the provisions so construed. J. Gray, The Rule Against Perpetuities § 629 (4th ed. 1942). Some courts may still adhere to this proposition. Colorado Nat'l Bank v. McCabe, 143 Colo. 21, 353 P.2d 385 (1960). Most courts, it is believed, would today be inclined to adopt the proposition put by the Restatement of Property § 375 (1944), which is that where an instrument is ambiguous—that is, where it is fairly susceptible to two or more constructions, one of which causes a rule violation and the other of which does not—the construction that does not result in a rule violation should be adopted. The California rule favors construction for validity. See, e.g., Civil Code § 3541; Wong v. Di Grazia, 60 Cal.2d 525, 539–40, 386 P.2d 817, 35 Cal.Rptr. 241 (1963); Estate of Phelps, 182 Cal. 752, 761, 190 P. 17 (1920); Estate of Grove, 70 Cal.App.3d 355, 362–63, 138 Cal.Rptr. 684 (1977). Other cases supporting this view include: Southern Bank & Trust Co. v. Brown, 271 S.C. 260, 246 S.E.2d 598 (1978); Davis v. Rossi, 326 Mo. 911, 34 S.W.2d 8 (1930); Watson v. Goldthwaite, 345 Mass. 29, 34–35, 184 N.E.2d 340 (1962); Walker v. Bogle, 244 Ga. 439, 260 S.E.2d 338 (1979); Drach v. Ely, 237 Kan. 654, 703 P.2d 746 (1985).

The constructional preference for validity is not superseded by this chapter, but its role is likely to be different. The situation is likely to be that one of the constructions to which the ambiguous instrument is fairly susceptible would result in validity under Section 21205(a), 21206(a), or 21207(a), but the other construction does not necessarily result in invalidity; rather it results in the interest's validity being governed by Section 21205(b), 21206(b), or 21207(b). Nevertheless, even though the result of adopting the other construction is not as harsh as it is at common law, it is expected that the courts will incline toward the construction that validates the disposition under Section 21205(a), 21206(a), or 21207(a).

2. Conclusive Presumption of Lifetime Fertility

At common law, all individuals—regardless of age, sex, or physical condition—are conclusively presumed to be able to have children throughout their entire lifetimes. This principle is not superseded by this chapter, and in view of the widely accepted rule of construction that adopted children are presumably included in class gifts, the conclusive presumption of lifetime fertility is not unrealistic. Since even elderly individuals probably cannot be excluded from adopting children based on their ages alone, the possibility of having children by adoption is seldom extinct. See, generally, Waggoner, In re

Lattouf's Will and the Presumption of Lifetime Fertility in Perpetuity Law, 20 San Diego L.Rev. 763 (1983). Under this chapter, the main force of this principle is felt as in Example (7) in the Background to Section 21205, where it prevents a nonvested property interest from passing the test for initial validity under Section 21205(a).

For a California case approving the common law rule, see Fletcher v. Los Angeles Trust & Sav. Bank, 182 Cal. 177, 184–85, 187 P. 425 (1920).

3. Act Supersedes Doctrine of Infectious Invalidity

At common law, the invalidity of an interest can, under the doctrine of infectious invalidity, be held to invalidate one or more otherwise valid interests created by the disposition or even invalidate the entire disposition. The question turns on whether the general dispositive scheme of the transferor will be better carried out by eliminating only the invalid interest or by eliminating other interests as well. This is a question that is answered on a case-by-case basis. Several items are relevant to the question, including who takes the stricken interests in place of those the transferor designated to take. For the rule applied in California, see, e.g., Estate of Willey, 128 Cal. 1, 11, 60 P. 471 (1900) (severance allowed); Estate of Troy, 214 Cal. 53, 59–65, 3 P.2d 930 (1931) (severance allowed); Estate of Gump, 16 Cal.2d 535, 547, 107 P.2d 17 (1940) (severance allowed); Estate of Van Wyck, 185 Cal. 49, 63, 196 P. 50 (1921) (severance denied); Sheean v. Michel, 6 Cal.2d 324, 329, 57 P.2d 127 (1936) (severance denied).

The doctrine of infectious invalidity is superseded by Section 21220, under which the court, on petition of an interested person, is required to reform the disposition to approximate as closely as possible the transferor's manifested plan of distribution when an invalidity under the statutory rule occurs.

4. Separability

The common law's separability doctrine is that when an interest is expressly subject to alternative contingencies, the situation is treated as if two interests were created in the same person or class. Each interest is judged separately; the invalidity of one of the interests does not necessarily cause the other one to be invalid. This common law principle was established in Longhead v. Phelps, 2 Wm.Bl. 704, 96 Eng.Rep. 414 (K.B. 1770), and is followed in this country. L. Simes & A. Smith, The Law of Future Interests § 1257 (2d ed. 1956); 6 American Law of Property § 24.54 (A. Casner ed. 1952); Restatement of Property § 376 (1944). Under this doctrine, if property is devised "to B if X-event or Y-event happens," B in effect has two interests, one contingent on X-event happening and the other contingent on Y-event happening. If the interest contingent on X-event but not the one contingent on Y-event is invalid, the consequence of separating B's interest into two is that only one of them, the one contingent on X-event, is invalid. B still has a valid interest—the one contingent on the occurrence of Y-event.

The separability principle is not superseded by this chapter. As illustrated in the following example, its invocation will usually result in one of the interests being initially validated by Section 21205(a) and the validity of the other interest being governed by Section 21205(b).

Example (22)—Separability case. G devised real property "to A for life, then to A's children who survive A and reach 25, but if none of A's children survives A or if none of A's children who survives A reaches 25, then to B." G was survived by his brother (B), by his daughter (A), by A's husband (H), and by A's two minor children (X and Y).

The remainder interest in favor of A's children who reach 25 fails the test of Section 21205(a) for initial validity. Its validity is, therefore, governed by Section 21205(b) and depends on each of A's children doing any one of the following things within 90 years after G's death: predeceasing A, surviving A and failing to reach 25, or surviving A and reaching 25.

Under the separability doctrine, B has two interests. One of them is contingent on none of A's children surviving A. That interest passes the test for initial validity under Section 21205(a); the validating life is A. B's other interest, which is contingent on none of A's surviving children reaching 25, fails the test for initial validity under Section 21205(a). Its validity is governed by Section 21205(b) and depends on each of A's surviving children either reaching 25 or dying under 25 within 90 years after G's death.

Suppose that after G's death, A has a third child (Z). A subsequently dies, survived by her husband (H) and by X, Y, and Z. This, of course, causes B's interest that was contingent on none of A's children surviving A to terminate. If X, Y, and Z had all reached the age of 25 by the time of A's death, their interest would vest at A's death, and that would end the matter. If one or two, but not all three of them, had reached the age of 25 at A's death, B's other interest—the one that was contingent on none of A's surviving children reaching 25—would also terminate. As for the children's interest, if the after-born child Z's age was such at A's death that Z could not be alive and under the age of 25 at the expiration of the allowable waiting period, the class gift in favor of the children would be valid under Section 21205(b), because none of those then under 25 could fail either to reach 25 or die under 25 after the expiration of the allowable 90–year waiting period. If, however, Z's age at A's death was such that Z could be alive and under the age of 25 at the expiration of the allowable 90–year waiting period, the circumstances requisite to reformation under Section 21220(b) would arise, and the court would be justified in reforming G's disposition by reducing the age contingency with respect to Z to the age he would reach on the date when the allowable waiting period is due to expire. See Example (3) in the Background to Section 21220. So reformed, the class gift in favor of A's children could not become invalid under Section 21205(b), and the children of A who had already reached 25 by the time of A's death could receive their shares immediately.

5. The "All-or-Nothing" Rule with Respect to Class Gifts

The common law applies an "all-or-nothing" rule with respect to class gifts, under which a class gift stands or falls as a whole. The all-or-nothing rule, usually attributed to Leake v. Robinson, 2 Mer. 363, 35 Eng.Rep. 979 (Ch.1817), is commonly stated as follows: If the interest of any potential class member might vest too remotely, the entire class gift violates the rule. Although this chapter does not supersede the basic idea of the much-maligned "all-or-nothing" rule, the evils sometimes attributed to it are substantially if not entirely eliminated by the wait-and-see feature of the statutory rule and by the availability of reformation under Section 21220, especially in the circumstances described in Section 21220(b)–(c). For illustrations of the application of the all-or-nothing rule under this chapter, see Examples (3), (4), and (6) in the Background to Section 21220.

For application and interpretation of the all-or-nothing rule California, see, e.g., Estate of Troy, 214 Cal. 53, 56–58, 3 P.2d 930 (1931); Estate of Grove, 70 Cal.App.3d 355, 361–62, 138 Cal.Rptr. 684 (1977); Estate of Ghiglia, 42 Cal.App.3d 433, 438–41, 116 Cal.Rptr. 827 (1974).

6. The Specific Sum Doctrine

The common law recognizes a doctrine called the specific sum doctrine, which is derived from Storrs v. Benbow, 3 De G.M. & G. 390, 43 Eng.Rep. 153 (Ch.1853), and states: If a specified sum of money is to be paid to each member of a class, the interest of each class member is entitled to separate treatment and is valid or invalid under the rule on its own. The specific sum doctrine is not superseded by this chapter.

The operation of the specific sum doctrine under this chapter is illustrated in the following example.

Example (23)—Specific sum case. G bequeathed "$10,000 to each child of A, born before or after my death, who attains 25." G was survived by A and by A's two children (X and Y). X but

not Y had already reached 25 at G's death. After G's death a third child (Z) was born to A..

If the phrase "born before or after my death" had been omitted, the class would close as of G's death under the common law rule of construction known as the rule of convenience: The after-born child, Z, would not be entitled to a $10,000 bequest, and the interests of both X and Y would be valid upon their creation at G's death. X's interest would be valid because it was initially vested; neither the common law rule nor the statutory rule applies to interests that are vested upon their creation. Although the interest of Y was not vested upon its creation, it would be initially valid under Section 21205(a) because Y would be his own validating life; Y will either reach 25 or die under 25 within his own lifetime.

The inclusion of the phrase "before or after my death," however, would probably be construed to mean that G intended after-born children to receive a $10,000 bequest. See Earle Estate, 369 Pa. 52, 85 A.2d 90 (1951). Assuming that this construction were adopted, the specific sum doctrine allows the interest of each child of A to be treated separately from the others for purposes of the statutory rule. For the reasons cited above, the interests of X and Y are initially valid under Section 21205(a). The nonvested interest of Z, however, fails the test for initial validity under Section 21205(a); there is no validating life because Z, who was not alive when the interest was created, could reach 25 or die under 25 more than 21 years after the death of the survivor of A, X, and Y. Under Section 21205(b), the validity of Z's interest depends on Z's reaching (or failing to reach) 25 within 90 years after G's death.

7. The Sub–Class Doctrine

The common law recognizes a doctrine called the sub-class doctrine, which is derived from Cattlin v. Brown, 11 Hare 372, 68 Eng.Rep. 1318 (Ch. 1853), and states: If the ultimate takers are not described as a single class but rather as a group of subclasses, and if the share to which each separate subclass is entitled will finally be determined within the period of the rule, the gifts to the different subclasses are separable for the purpose of the rule. American Security & Trust Co. v. Cramer, 175 F.Supp. 367 (D.D.C.1959); Restatement of Property § 389 (1944). The sub-class doctrine is not superseded by this chapter.

The operation of the sub-class doctrine under this chapter is illustrated in the following example.

Example (24)—Sub-class case. G devised property in trust, directing the trustee to pay the income "to A for life, then in equal shares to A's children for their respective lives; on the death of each child, the proportionate share of corpus of the one so dying shall go to the children of such child." G was survived by A and by A's two children (X and Y). After G's death, another child (Z) was born to A. A now has died, survived by X, Y, and Z.

Under the sub-class doctrine, each remainder interest in favor of the children of a child of A is treated separately from the others. This allows the remainder interest in favor of X's children and the remainder interest in favor of Y's children to be validated under Section 21205(a). X is the validating life for the one, and Y is the validating life for the other.

The remainder interest in favor of the children of Z fails the test for initial validity under Section 21205(a); there is no validating life because Z, who was not alive when the interest was created, could have children more than 21 years after the death of the survivor of A, X, and Y. Under Section 21205(b), the validity of the remainder interest in favor of Z's children depends on Z's dying within 90 years after G's death.

Note why both of the requirements of the sub-class rule are met. The ultimate takers are described as a group of sub-classes rather than as a single class: "children of the child so dying," as opposed to "grandchildren." The share to which each separate sub-class is entitled is certain to be finally determined within a life in being plus 21 years: As of A's death, who is a life in being, it is certain to be known how many children he had surviving him; since in fact there were three, we know that each sub-class will ultimately be entitled to one-third of the corpus, neither more nor less. The possible failure of the one-third share of Z's children does not increase to one-half the share going to X's and Y's children; they still are entitled to only one-third shares. Indeed, should it turn out that X has children but Y does not, this would not increase the one-third share to which X's children are entitled.

Example (25)—General testamentary powers—sub-class case. G devised property in trust, directing the trustee to pay income "to A for life, then in equal shares to A's children for their respective lives; on the death of each child, the proportionate share of corpus of the one so dying shall go to such persons as the one so dying shall by will appoint; in default of appointment, to G's grandchildren in equal shares." G was survived by A and by A's two children (X and Y). After G's death, another child (Z) was born to A

The general testamentary powers conferred on each of A's children are entitled to separate treatment under the principles of the sub-class doctrine. See above. Consequently, the powers conferred on X and Y, A's children who were living at G's death, are initially valid under Section 21207(a). But the general testamentary power conferred on Z, A's child who was born after G's death, fails the test of Section 21207(a) for initial validity. The validity of Z's power is governed by Section 21207(b). Z's death must occur within 90 years after G's death if any provision in Z's will purporting to exercise his power is to be valid.

8. Duration of Indestructible Trusts—Termination of Trusts by Beneficiaries

The widely accepted view in American law is that the beneficiaries of a trust other than a charitable trust can compel its premature termination if all beneficiaries consent and if such termination is not expressly restrained or impliedly restrained by the existence of a "material purpose" of the settlor in establishing the trust. Restatement (Second) of Trusts § 337 (1959); 4 A. Scott, The Law of Trusts § 337 (3d ed. 1967). California law varies this rule by giving the court discretion in applying the material purposes doctrine, except as to a restraint on disposition of the beneficiaries' interests. See Section 15403.

A trust that cannot be terminated by its beneficiaries is called an indestructible trust. It is generally accepted that the duration of the indestructibility of a trust, other than a charitable trust, is limited to the applicable perpetuity period. See Restatement (Second) of Trusts § 62 comment o (1959); Restatement (Second) of Property (Donative Transfers) § 2.1 & Legislative Note & Reporter's Note (1983); 1 A. Scott, The Law of Trusts § 62.10(2) (3d ed. 1967); J. Gray, The Rule Against Perpetuities § 121 (4th ed. 1942); L. Simes & A. Smith, The Law of Future Interests §§ 1391–93 (2d ed. 1956). In California this rule is provided by statute. See Prob.Code § 15414 (continuing substance of former Civil Code § 716.5). Nothing in this chapter supersedes this principle. One modification, however, is necessary: As to trusts that contain a nonvested property interest or power of appointment whose validity is governed by the wait-and-see element adopted in Section 21205(b), 21206(b), or 21207(b), the courts can be expected to determine that the applicable perpetuity period is 90 years. [20 Cal.L.Rev.Comm.Reports 2543 (1990)].

§ 21202. Application of part

(a) Except as provided in subdivision (b), this part applies to nonvested property interests and unexercised powers of appointment regardless of whether they were created before, on, or after January 1, 1992.

(b) This part does not apply to any property interest or power of appointment the validity of which has been determined in a judicial proceeding or by a settlement among interested persons. *(Added by Stats.1991, c. 156 (A.B.1577), § 24.)*

Law Revision Commission Comments

1991 Addition

Subdivision (a) of Section 21202 applies the new statutory rule against perpetuities to nonvested property interests and unexercised powers of appointment whether created before, on, or after January 1, 1992, except as provided in subdivision (b). This rule differs from Section 5 of the Uniform Statutory Rule Against Perpetuities (1990). [20 Cal.L.Rev.Comm.Reports 2501 (1990)].

ARTICLE 2. STATUTORY RULE AGAINST PERPETUITIES

Application

Application of Part 2, see Probate Code § 21202.

Application of this article, see Probate Code § 21225.

§ 21205. Nonvested property interests; validity; conditions

A nonvested property interest is invalid unless one of the following conditions is satisfied:

(a) When the interest is created, it is certain to vest or terminate no later than 21 years after the death of an individual then alive.

(b) The interest either vests or terminates within 90 years after its creation. *(Added by Stats.1991, c. 156 (A.B.1577), § 24.)*

Law Revision Commission Comments

1991 Addition

Section 21205 is the same in substance as Section 1(a) of the Uniform Statutory Rule Against Perpetuities (1990). This section, along with Sections 21206–21208, supersedes former Civil Code Section 715.2. See also Sections 21230 (validating lives), 21231 (spouse as life in being).

Background (adapted from Prefatory Note to Uniform Statute). This article sets forth the statutory rule against perpetuities (statutory rule). The statutory rule and the other provisions of this part supersede the common law rule against perpetuities (common law rule) and replace the former statutory version. See Section 21201. Section 21205 deals with nonvested property interests; Sections 21206 and 21207 deal with powers of appointment.

Subdivision (a) of Section 21205 codifies the validating side of the common law rule. In effect, subdivision (a) provides that a nonvested property interest that is valid under the common law rule is valid under the statutory rule and can be declared so at its inception. In such a case, nothing would be gained and much would be lost by invoking a waiting period during which the validity of the interest or power is in abeyance.

Subdivision (b) establishes the wait-and-see rule by providing that an interest or a power of appointment that is not validated by subdivision (a), and hence would have been invalid under the common law rule, is nevertheless valid if it does not actually remain nonvested when the allowable 90–year waiting period expires. [20 Cal.L.Rev.Comm.Reports 2501 (1990)].

Background (adapted from official comments to Uniform Statutory Rule Against Perpetuities)

A. General Purpose

Sections 21205–21207 set forth the statutory rule against perpetuities (statutory rule). As provided in Section 21201, the statutory rule supersedes the common law rule against perpetuities (common law rule) and prior statutes. See the Comment to Section 21201.

1. The Common Law Rule's Validating and Invalidating Sides

The common law rule against perpetuities is a rule of initial validity or invalidity. At common law, a nonvested property interest is either valid or invalid as of its creation. Like most rules of property law, the common law rule has both a validating and an invalidating side. Both sides are derived from John Chipman Gray's formulation of the common law rule:

No [nonvested property] interest is good unless it must vest, if at all, not later than 21 years after some life in being at the creation of the interest.

J. Gray, The Rule Against Perpetuities § 201 (4th ed. 1942). From this formulation, the validating and invalidating sides of the common law rule are derived as follows:

Validating Side of the Common Law Rule. A nonvested property interest is valid when it is created (initially valid) if it is then certain to vest or terminate (fail to vest)—one or the other—no later than 21 years after the death of an individual then alive.
Invalidating Side of the Common Law Rule. A nonvested property interest is invalid when it is created (initially invalid) if there is no such certainty.

Notice that the invalidating side focuses on a lack of certainty, which means that invalidity under the common law rule is not dependent on actual post-creation events but only on possible post-creation events. Actual post-creation events are irrelevant, even those that are known at the time of the lawsuit. It is generally recognized that the invalidating side of the common law rule is harsh because it can invalidate interests on the ground of possible post-creation events that are extremely unlikely to happen and that in actuality almost never do happen, if ever.

2. The Statutory Rule Against Perpetuities

The essential difference between the common law rule and its statutory replacement is that the statutory rule preserves the common law rule's overall policy of preventing property from being tied up in unreasonably long or even perpetual family trusts or other property arrangements, while eliminating the harsh potential of the common law rule. The statutory rule achieves this result by codifying (in slightly revised form) the validating side of the common law rule and modifying the invalidating side by adopting a wait-and-see element. Under the statutory rule, interests that would have been initially valid at common law continue to be initially valid, but interests that would have been initially invalid at common law are invalid only if they do not actually vest or terminate within the allowable waiting period set forth in Section 21205(b). Thus, the Uniform Act recasts the validating and invalidating sides of the rule against perpetuities as follows:

Validating Side of the Statutory Rule: A nonvested property interest is initially valid if, when it is created, it is then certain to vest or terminate (fail to vest)—one or the other—no later than 21 years after the death of an individual then alive. The validity of a nonvested property interest that is not initially valid is in abeyance.

Such an interest is valid if it vests within the allowable waiting period after its creation.
Invalidating Side of the Statutory Rule: A nonvested property interest that is not initially valid becomes invalid (and subject to reformation under Section 21220) if it neither vests nor terminates within the allowable waiting period after its creation.

As indicated, this modification of the invalidating side of the common law rule is generally known as the wait-and-see method of perpetuity reform. The wait-and-see method of perpetuity reform was approved by the American Law Institute as part of the Restatement (Second) of Property (Donative Transfers) §§ 1.1–1.6 (1983). For a discussion of the various methods of perpetuity reform, including the wait-and-see method and the Restatement (Second)'s version of wait-and-see, see Waggoner, Perpetuity Reform, 81 Mich.L.Rev. 1718 (1983).

B. Section 21205(a): Nonvested Property Interests That Are Initially Valid

1. Nonvested Property Interest

Section 21205 sets forth the statutory rule against perpetuities with respect to nonvested property interests. A nonvested property interest (also called a contingent property interest) is a future interest in property that is subject to an unsatisfied condition precedent. In the case of a class gift, the interests of all the unborn members of the class are nonvested because they are subject to the unsatisfied condition precedent of being born. At common law, the interests of all potential class members must be valid or the class gift is invalid. As pointed out in the Background to Section 21201, this so-called all-or-nothing rule with respect to class gifts is not superseded by this chapter, and so remains in effect under the statutory rule. Consequently, all class gifts that are subject to open are to be regarded as nonvested property interests for the purposes of this chapter.

2. Section 21205(a) Codifies the Validating Side of the Common Law Rule

The validating side of the common law rule is codified in Section 21205(a) and, with respect to powers of appointment, in Sections 21206(a) and 21207(a).

A nonvested property interest that satisfies the requirement of Section 21205(a) is initially valid. That is, it is valid as of the time of its creation. There is no need to subject such an interest to the waiting period set forth in Section 21205(b), nor would it be desirable to do so.

For a nonvested property interest to be valid as of the time of its creation under Section 21205(a), there must then be a certainty that the interest will either vest or terminate—an interest terminates when vesting becomes impossible—no later than 21 years after the death of an individual then alive. To satisfy this requirement, it must be established that there is no possible chain of events that might arise after the interest was created that would allow the interest to vest or terminate after the expiration of the 21–year period following the death of an individual in being at the creation of the interest. Consequently, initial validity under Section 21205(a) can be established only if there is an individual for whom there is a causal connection between the individual's death and the interest's vesting or terminating no later than 21 years thereafter.

The individual described in Sections 21205(a), 21206(a), and 21207(a) is often referred to as the "validating life," the term used throughout the Background Comments to this chapter.

3. Determining Whether There Is a Validating Life

The process for determining whether a validating life exists is to postulate the death of each individual connected in some way to the transaction, and ask the question: Is there with respect to this individual an invalidating chain of possible events? If one individual can be found for whom the answer is No, that individual can serve as the validating life. As to that individual there will be the requisite causal connection between his or her death and the questioned interest's vesting or terminating no later than 21 years thereafter.

In searching for a validating life, only individuals who are connected in some way to the transaction need to be considered, for they are the only ones who have a chance of supplying the requisite causal connection. Such individuals vary from situation to situation, but typically include the beneficiaries of the disposition, including the taker or takers of the nonvested property interest, and individuals related to them by blood or adoption, especially in the ascending and descending lines. There is no point in even considering the life of an individual unconnected to the transaction—an individual from the world at large who happens to be in being at the creation of the interest. See Section 21230 (validating lives). No such individual can be a validating life because there will be an invalidating chain of possible events as to every unconnected individual who might be proposed: Any such individual can immediately die after the creation of the nonvested property interest without causing any acceleration of the interest's vesting or termination. (The life expectancy of any unconnected individual, or even the probability that one of a number of new-born babies will live a long life, is irrelevant.)

Example (1)—Parent of devisees as the validating life. G devised property "to A for life, remainder to A's children who attain 21." G was survived by his son (A), by his daughter (B), by A's wife (W), and by A's two children (X and Y).

The nonvested property interest in favor of A's children who reach 21 satisfies the requirement of Section 21205(a), and the interest is initially valid. When the interest was created (at G's death), the interest was then certain to vest or terminate no later than 21 years after A's death.

The process by which A is determined to be the validating life is one of testing various candidates to see if any of them have the requisite causal connection. As noted above, no one from the world at large can have the requisite causal connection, and so such individuals are disregarded. Once the inquiry is narrowed to the appropriate candidates, the first possible validating life that comes to mind is A, who does in fact fulfill the requirement: Since A's death cuts off the possibility of any more children being born to him, it is impossible, no matter when A dies, for any of A's children to be alive and under the age of 21 beyond 21 years after A's death. (See the Background to Section 21208).

A is therefore the validating life for the nonvested property interest in favor of A's children who attain 21. None of the other individuals who is connected to this transaction could serve as the validating life because an invalidating chain of possible post-creation events exists as to each one of them. The other individuals who might be considered include W, X, Y, and B. In the case of W, an invalidating chain of events is that she might predecease A, A might remarry and have a child by his new wife, and such child might be alive and under the age of 21 beyond the 21–year period following W's death. With respect to X and Y, an invalidating chain of events is that they might predecease A, A might later have another child, and that child might be alive and under 21 beyond the 21–year period following the death of the survivor of X and Y. As to B, she suffers from the same invalidating chain of events as exists with respect to X and Y. The fact that none of these other individuals can serve as the validating life is of no consequence, however, because only one such individual is required for the validity of a nonvested interest to be established, and that individual is A.

4. Rule of Section 21208 (Posthumous Birth)

See the Background to Section 21208.

5. Recipients as Their Own Validating Lives

It is well established at common law that, in appropriate cases, the recipient of an interest can be his or her own validating life. See, e.g., Rand v. Bank of California, 236 Or. 619, 388 P.2d 437 (1964). Given the right circumstances, this principle can validate interests that are contingent on the recipient's reaching an age in excess of 21, or are contingent on the recipient's surviving a particular point in time that is or might turn out to be in excess of 21 years after the

interest was created or after the death of a person in being at the date of creation.

Example (2)—Devisees as their own validating lives. G devised real property "to A's children who attain 25." A predeceased G. At G's death, A had three living children, all of whom were under 25.

The nonvested property interest in favor of A's children who attain 25 is validated by Section 21205(a). Under Section 21208, the possibility that A will have a child born to him after his death (and since A predeceased G, after G's death) must be disregarded. Consequently, even if A's wife survived G, and even if she was pregnant at G's death or even if A had deposited sperm in a sperm bank prior to his death, it must be assumed that all of A's children are in being at G's death. A's children are, therefore, their own validating lives. (Note that Section 21208 requires that in determining whether an individual is a validating life, the possibility that a child will be born to "an" individual after the individual's death must be disregarded. The validating life and the individual whose having a post-death child is disregarded need not be the same individual.) Each one of A's children, all of whom under Section 21208 are regarded as alive at G's death, will either reach the age of 25 or fail to do so within his or her own lifetime. To say this another way, it is certain to be known no later than at the time of the death of each child whether or not that child survived to the required age.

6. Validating Life Can Be Survivor of Group

In appropriate cases, the validating life need not be individualized at first. Rather the validating life can initially (i.e., when the interest was created) be the unidentified survivor of a group of individuals. It is common in such cases to say that the members of the group are the validating lives, but the true meaning of the statement is that the validating life is the member of the group who turns out to live the longest. As the court said in Skatterwood v. Edge, 1 Salk. 229, 91 Eng.Rep. 203 (K.B.1697), "for let the lives be never so many, there must be a survivor, and so it is but the length of that life; for Twisden used to say, the candles were all lighted at once."

Example (3)—Case of validating life being the survivor of a group. G devised real property "to such of my grandchildren as attain 21." Some of G's children are living at G's death.

The nonvested property interest in favor of G's grandchildren who attain 21 is valid under Section 21205(a). The validating life is that one of G's children who turns out to live the longest. Since under Section 21208, it must be assumed that none of G's children will have post-death children, it is regarded as impossible for any of G's grandchildren to be alive and under 21 beyond the 21–year period following the death of G's last surviving child.

Example (4)—Sperm bank case. G devised property in trust, directing the income to be paid to G's children for the life of the survivor, then to G's grandchildren for the life of the survivor, and on the death of G's last surviving grandchild, to pay the corpus to G's great-grandchildren then living. G's children all predeceased him, but several grandchildren were living at G's death. One of G's predeceased children (his son, A) had deposited sperm in a sperm bank. A's widow was living at G's death.

The nonvested property interest in favor of G's great-grandchildren is valid under Section 21205(a). The validating life is the last surviving grandchild among the grandchildren living at G's death. Under Section 21208, the possibility that A will have a child conceived after G's death must be disregarded. Note that Section 21208 requires that in determining whether an individual is a validating life, the possibility that a child will be born to "an" individual after the individual's death is disregarded. The validating life and the individual whose having a post-death child is disregarded need not be the same individual. Thus in this example, by disregarding the possibility that A will have a conceived-after-death child, G's last surviving grandchild becomes the validating life because G's last surviving grandchild is deemed to have been alive at G's death, when the great-grandchildren's interests were created.

Example (5)—Child in gestation case. G devised property in trust, to pay the income equally among G's living children; on the death of G's last surviving child, to accumulate the income for 21 years; on the 21st anniversary of the death of G's last surviving child, to pay the corpus and accumulated income to G's then-living descendants, per stirpes; if none, to X Charity. At G's death his child (A) was 6 years old, and G's wife (W) was pregnant. After G's death, W gave birth to their second child (B).

The nonvested property interests in favor of G's descendants and in favor of X Charity are valid under Section 21205(a). The validating life is A. Under Section 21208, the possibility that a child will be born to an individual after the individual's death must be disregarded for the purposes of determining validity under Section 21205(a). Consequently, the possibility that a child will be born to G after his death must be disregarded; and the possibility that a child will be born to any of G's descendants after their deaths must also be disregarded.

Note, however, that the rule of Section 21208 does not apply to the question of the entitlement of an after-born child to take a beneficial interest in the trust. The common law rule (sometimes codified) that a child in gestation is treated as alive, if the child is subsequently born viable, applies to this question. Thus, Section 21208 does not prevent B from being an income beneficiary under G's trust, nor does it prevent a descendant in gestation on the 21st anniversary of the death of G's last surviving child from being a member of the class of G's "then-living descendants," as long as such descendant has no then-living ancestor who takes instead.

7. Different Validating Lives Can and in Some Cases Must Be Used

Dispositions of property sometimes create more than one nonvested property interest. In such cases, the validity of each interest is treated individually. A validating life that validates one interest might or might not validate the other interests. Since it is not necessary that the same validating life be used for all interests created by a disposition, the search for a validating life for each of the other interests must be undertaken separately.

8. Perpetuity Saving Clauses and Similar Provisions

Knowledgeable lawyers almost routinely insert perpetuity saving clauses into instruments they draft. (For additional discussion of perpetuity saving clauses, see the Background to Section 21209.) Saving clauses contain two components, the first of which is the perpetuity-period component. This component typically requires the trust or other arrangement to terminate no later than 21 years after the death of the last survivor of a group of individuals designated therein by name or class. (The lives of corporations, animals, or sequoia trees cannot be used.) The second component of saving clauses is the gift-over component. This component expressly creates a gift over that is guaranteed to vest at the termination of the period set forth in the perpetuity-period component, but only if the trust or other arrangement has not terminated earlier in accordance with its other terms.

It is important to note that regardless of what group of individuals is designated in the perpetuity-period component of a saving clause, the surviving member of the group is not necessarily the individual who would be the validating life for the nonvested property interest or power of appointment in the absence of the saving clause. Without the saving clause, one or more interests or powers may in fact fail to satisfy the requirement of Section 21205(a), 21206(a), or 21207(a) for initial validity. By being designated in the saving clause, however, the survivor of the group becomes the validating life for all interests and powers in the trust or other arrangement: The saving clause confers on the last surviving member of the designated group the requisite causal connection between his or her death and the impossibility of any interest or power in the trust or other arrange-

ment remaining in existence beyond the 21-year period following such individual's death.

Example (6)—Valid saving clause case. A testamentary trust directs income to be paid to the testator's children for the life of the survivor, then to the testator's grandchildren for the life of the survivor, corpus on the death of the testator's last living grandchild to such of the testator's descendants as the last living grandchild shall by will appoint; in default of appointment, to the testator's then-living descendants, per stirpes. A saving clause in the will terminates the trust, if it has not previously terminated, 21 years after the death of the testator's last surviving descendant who was living at the testator's death. The testator was survived by children.

In the absence of the saving clause, the nongeneral power of appointment in the last living grandchild and the nonvested property interest in the gift-in-default clause in favor of the testator's descendants fail the test of Sections 21205(a) and 21207(a) for initial validity. That is, were it not for the saving clause, there is no validating life. However, the surviving member of the designated group becomes the validating life, so that the saving clause does confer initial validity on the nongeneral power of appointment and on the nonvested property interest under Sections 21205(a) and 21207(a).

If the governing instrument designates a group of individuals that would cause it to be impracticable to determine the death of the survivor, the common law courts have developed the doctrine that the validity of the nonvested property interest or power of appointment is determined as if the provision in the governing instrument did not exist. See cases cited in Restatement (Second) of Property (Donative Transfers) Reporter's Note No. 3, at 45 (1983). See also Restatement (Second) of Property (Donative Transfers) § 1.3(1) comment a (1983); Restatement of Property § 374 & comment 1 (1944); 6 American Law of Property § 24.13 (A. Casner ed. 1952); 5A R. Powell, The Law of Real Property ¶ 766[5] (1985); L. Simes & A. Smith, The Law of Future Interests § 1223 (2d ed. 1956). If, for example, the designated group in Example (6) were the residents of X City (or the members of Y Country Club) living at the time of the testator's death, the saving clause would not validate the power of appointment or the nonvested property interest. Instead, the validity of the power of appointment and the nonvested property interest would be determined as if the provision in the governing instrument did not exist. Since without the saving clause the power of appointment and the nonvested property interest would fail to satisfy the requirements of Sections 21205(a) and 21207(a) for initial validity, their validity would be governed by Sections 21205(b) and 21207(b).

The application of the above common law doctrine, which is not superseded by this chapter and so remains in full force, is not limited to saving clauses. It also applies to trusts or other arrangements where the period thereof is directly linked to the life of the survivor of a designated group of individuals. An example is a trust to pay the income to the grantor's descendants from time to time living, per stirpes, for the period of the life of the survivor of a designated group of individuals living when the nonvested property interest or power of appointment in question was created, plus the 21-year period following the survivor's death; at the end of the 21-year period, the corpus is to be divided among the grantor's then-living descendants, per stirpes, and if none, to the XYZ Charity. If the group of individuals so designated is such that it would be impracticable to determine the death of the survivor, the validity of the disposition is determined as if the provision in the governing instrument did not exist. The term of the trust is therefore governed by the allowable 90-year period of Section 21205(b), 21206(b), or 21207(b) of the statutory rule.

9. Additional references

Restatement (Second) of Property (Donative Transfers) § 1.3(1) & comments (1983); Waggoner, Perpetuity Reform, 81 Mich.L.Rev. 1718, 1720–26 (1983).

C. Section 21205(b): Wait-and-See—Nonvested Property Interests Whose Validity is Initially in Abeyance

Unlike the common law rule, the statutory rule against perpetuities does not automatically invalidate nonvested property interests for which there is no validating life. A nonvested property interest that does not meet the requirements for validity under Section 21205(a) might still be valid under the wait-and-see provisions of Section 21205(b). Such an interest is invalid under Section 21205(b) only if in actuality it does not vest (or terminate) during the allowable waiting period. Such an interest becomes invalid, in other words, only if it is still in existence and nonvested when the allowable waiting period expires.

1. The 90–Year Allowable Waiting Period

Since a wait-and-see rule against perpetuities, unlike the common law rule, makes validity or invalidity turn on actual post-creation events, it requires that an actual period of time be measured off during which the contingencies attached to an interest are allowed to work themselves out to a final resolution. The statutory rule against perpetuities establishes an allowable waiting period of 90 years. Nonvested property interests that have neither vested nor terminated at the expiration of the 90–year allowable waiting period become invalid.

As explained in the Prefatory Note to the Uniform Statutory Rule Against Perpetuities (1986), the allowable period of 90 years is not an arbitrarily selected period of time. On the contrary, the 90–year period represents a reasonable approximation of—a proxy for—the period of time that would, on average, be produced through the use of an actual set of measuring lives identified by statute and then adding the traditional 21–year tack-on period after the death of the survivor.

2. Technical Violations of the Common Law Rule

One of the harsh aspects of the invalidating side of the common law rule, against which the adoption of the wait-and-see element in Section 21205(b) is designed to relieve, is that nonvested property interests at common law are invalid even though the invalidating chain of possible events almost certainly will not happen. In such cases, the violation of the common law rule could be said to be merely technical. Nevertheless, at common law, the nonvested property interest is invalid.

Cases of technical violation fall generally into discrete categories, identified and named by Professor Leach in Perpetuities in a Nutshell, 51 Harv.L.Rev. 638 (1938), as the fertile octogenarian, the administrative contingency, and the unborn widow. The following three examples illustrate how Section 21205(b) affects these categories.

Example (7)—Fertile octogenarian case. G devised property in trust, directing the trustee to pay the net income therefrom "to A for life, then to A's children for the life of the survivor, and upon the death of A's last surviving child to pay the corpus of the trust to A's grandchildren." G was survived by A (a female who had passed the menopause) and by A's two adult children (X and Y).

The remainder interest in favor of G's grandchildren would be invalid at common law, and consequently is not validated by Section 21205(a). There is no validating life because, under the common law's conclusive presumption of lifetime fertility, which is not superseded by this chapter (see the Background to Section 21201), A might have a third child (Z), conceived and born after G's death, who will have a child conceived and born more than 21 years after the death of the survivor of A, X, and Y.

Under Section 21205(b), however, the remote possibility of the occurrence of this chain of events does not invalidate the grandchildren's interest. The interest becomes invalid only if it remains in existence and nonvested 90 years after G's death. The chance that the grandchildren's remainder interest will become invalid under Section 21205(b) is negligible.

Example (8)—Administrative contingency case. G devised property "to such of my grandchildren, born before or after my death, as may be living upon final distribution of my estate." G was survived by children and grandchildren.

The remainder interest in favor of A's grandchildren would be invalid at common law, and consequently is not validated by Section 21205(a). The final distribution of G's estate might not occur within 21 years of G's death, and after G's death grandchildren might be conceived and born who might survive or fail to survive the final distribution of G's estate more than 21 years after the death of the survivor of G's children and grandchildren who were living at G's death.

Under Section 21205(b), however, the remote possibility of the occurrence of this chain of events does not invalidate the grandchildren's remainder interest. The interest becomes invalid only if it remains in existence and nonvested 90 years after G's death. Since it is almost certain that the final distribution of G's estate will occur pbwell within this 90–year period, the chance that the grandchildren's interest will be invalid is negligible.

Example (9)—Unborn widow case. G devised property in trust, the income to be paid "to my son A for life, then to A's spouse for her life, and upon the death of the survivor of A and his spouse, the corpus to be delivered to A's then living descendants." G was survived by A, by A's wife (W), and by their adult children (X and Y).

Unless the interest in favor of A's "spouse" is construed to refer only to W, rather than to whoever is A's spouse when he dies, if anyone, the remainder interest in favor of A's descendants would be invalid at common law, and consequently is not validated by Section 21205(a). There is no validating life because A's spouse might not be W; A's spouse might be someone who was conceived and born after G's death; she might outlive the death of the survivor of A, W, X, and Y by more than 21 years; and descendants of A might be born or die before the death of A's spouse but after the 21–year period following the death of the survivor of A, W, X, and Y.

Under Section 21205(b), however, the remote possibility of the occurrence of this chain of events does not invalidate the descendants remainder interest. The interest becomes invalid only if it remains in existence and nonvested 90 years after G's death. The chance that the descendants remainder interest will become invalid under the statutory rule is small.

3. Age Contingencies in Excess of 21

Another category of technical violation of the common law rule arises in cases of age contingencies in excess of 21 where the takers cannot be their own validating lives (unlike Example (2), above). The violation of the common law rule falls into the technical category because the insertion of a saving clause would in almost all cases allow the disposition to be carried out as written. In effect, the statutory rule operates like the perpetuity-period component of a saving clause.

Example (10)—Age contingency in excess of 21 case. G devised property in trust, directing the trustee to pay the income "to A for life, then to A's children; the corpus of the trust is to be equally divided among A's children who reach the age of 30." G was survived by A, by A's spouse (H), and by A's two children (X and Y), both of whom were under the age of 30 when G died.

The remainder interest in favor of A's children who reach 30 is a class gift. At common law, the interests of all potential class members must be valid or the class gift is totally invalid. Leake v. Robinson, 2 Mer. 363, 35 Eng.Rep. 979 (Ch. 1817). This chapter does not supersede the all-or-nothing rule for class gifts (see the Background to Section 21201), and so the all-or-nothing rule continues to apply under this chapter. Although X and Y will either reach 30 or die under 30 within their own lifetimes, there is at G's death the possibility that A will have an afterborn child (Z) who will reach 30 or die under 30 more than 21 years after the death of the survivor of A, H, X, and Y. The class gift would be invalid at common law and consequently is not validated by Section 21205(a).

Under Section 21205(b), however, the possibility of the occurrence of this chain of events does not invalidate the children's remainder interest. The interest becomes invalid only if an interest of a class member remains nonvested 90 years after G's death.

Although unlikely, suppose that at A's death Z's age is such that he could be alive and under the age of 30 at the expiration of the allowable waiting period. Suppose further that at A's death X or Y or both is over the age of 30. The court, upon the petition of an interested person, must under Section 21220 reform G's disposition. See Example (3) in the Background to Section 21220. [20 Cal.L.Rev.Comm.Reports 2543 (1990)].

§ 21206. General power of appointment; condition precedent; validity; conditions

A general power of appointment not presently exercisable because of a condition precedent is invalid unless one of the following conditions is satisfied:

(a) When the power is created, the condition precedent is certain to be satisfied or become impossible to satisfy no later than 21 years after the death of an individual then alive.

(b) The condition precedent either is satisfied or becomes impossible to satisfy within 90 years after its creation. *(Added by Stats.1991, c. 156 (A.B.1577), § 24.)*

Law Revision Commission Comments

1991 Addition

Section 21206 is the same in substance as Section 1(b) of the Uniform Statutory Rule Against Perpetuities (1990). See Comment to Section 21205. See also Sections 21230 (validating lives), 21231 (spouse as life in being).

Background (adapted from Prefatory Note to Uniform Statute). This article sets forth the statutory rule against perpetuities (statutory rule). The statutory rule and the other provisions of this part supersede the common law rule against perpetuities (common law rule) and replace the former statutory version. See Section 21201. Section 21205 deals with nonvested property interests; Sections 21206 and 21207 deal with powers of appointment.

Subdivision (a) of Section 21206 codifies the validating side of the common law rule. In effect, subdivision (a) provides that a power of appointment that is valid under the common law rule is valid under the statutory rule and can be declared so at its inception. In such a case, nothing would be gained and much would be lost by invoking a waiting period during which the validity of the interest or power is in abeyance.

Subdivision (b) establishes the wait-and-see rule by providing that an interest or a power of appointment that is not validated by subdivision (a), and hence would have been invalid under the common law rule, is nevertheless valid if the power ceases to be subject to a condition precedent or is no longer exercisable when the allowable 90–year waiting period expires. [20 Cal.L.Rev.Comm.Reports 2501 (1990)].

Background (adapted from official comments to Uniform Statutory Rule Against Perpetuities)

D. Sections 21206(a) and 21207(a): Powers of Appointment That Are Initially Valid

Sections 21206 and 21207 set forth the statutory rule against perpetuities with respect to powers of appointment. A power of appointment is the authority, other than as an incident of the beneficial ownership of property, to designate recipients of beneficial interests in or powers of appointment over property. Restatement (Second) of Property (Donative Transfers) § 11.1 (1986). The property or property interest subject to a power of appointment is called the "appointive property."

The various persons connected to a power of appointment are identified by a special terminology. The "donor" is the person who created the power of appointment. The "donee" is the person who holds the power of appointment, i.e., the powerholder. The "objects" are the persons to whom an appointment can be made. The "appointees" are the persons to whom an appointment has been made. The "takers in default" are the persons whose property interests are subject to being defeated by the exercise of the power of appointment and who take the property to the extent the power is not effectively exercised. Restatement (Second) of Property (Donative Transfers) § 11.2 (1986).

A power of appointment is "general" if it is exercisable in favor of the donee of the power, the donee's creditors, the donee's estate, or the creditors of the donee's estate. A power of appointment that is not general is a "nongeneral" power of appointment. Restatement (Second) of Property (Donative Transfers) § 11.4 (1986).

A power of appointment is "presently exercisable" if, at the time in question, the donee can by an exercise of the power create an interest in or a power of appointment over the appointive property. Restatement (Second) of Property (Donative Transfers) § 11.5 (1986). A power of appointment is "testamentary" if the donee can exercise it only in the donee's will. Restatement of Property § 321 (1940). A power of appointment is "not presently exercisable because of a condition precedent" if the only impediment to its present exercisability is a condition precedent, i.e., the occurrence of some uncertain event. Since a power of appointment terminates on the donee's death, a deferral of a power's present exercisability until a future time (even a time certain) imposes a condition precedent that the donee be alive at that future time.

A power of appointment is a "fiduciary" power if it is held by a fiduciary and is exercisable by the fiduciary in a fiduciary capacity. A power of appointment that is exercisable in an individual capacity is a "nonfiduciary" power. As used in this chapter, the term "power of appointment" refers to "fiduciary" and to "nonfiduciary" powers, unless the context indicates otherwise.

Although Gray's formulation of the common law rule against perpetuities (see the Background to Section 21205) does not speak directly of powers of appointment, the common law rule is applicable to powers of appointment (other than presently exercisable general powers of appointment). The principle of Sections 21206(a) and 21207(a) is that a power of appointment that satisfies the common law rule against perpetuities is valid under the statutory rule against perpetuities, and consequently it can be validly exercised, without being subjected to a waiting period during which the power's validity is in abeyance.

Two different tests for validity are employed at common law, depending on what type of power is at issue. In the case of a nongeneral power (whether or not presently exercisable) and in the case of a general testamentary power, the power is initially valid if, when the power was created, it is certain that the latest possible time that the power can be exercised is no later than 21 years after the death of an individual then in being. In the case of a general power not presently exercisable because of a condition precedent, the power is initially valid if it is then certain that the condition precedent to its exercise will either be satisfied or become impossible to satisfy no later than 21 years after the death of an individual then in being. Sections 21206(a) and 21207(a) codify these rules. Under either test, initial validity depends on the existence of a validating life. The procedure for determining whether a validating life exists is essentially the same procedure explained in Part B, above, pertaining to nonvested property interests.

Example (11)—Initially valid general testamentary power case. G devised property "to A for life, remainder to such persons, including A's estate or the creditors of A's estate, as A shall by will appoint." G was survived by his daughter (A).

A's power, which is a general testamentary power, is valid as of its creation under Section 21207(a). The test is whether or not the power can be exercised beyond 21 years after the death of an individual in being when the power was created (G's death). Since A's power cannot be exercised after A's death, the validating life is A, who was in being at G's death.

Example (12)—Initially valid nongeneral power case. G devised property "to A for life, remainder to such of A's descendants as A shall appoint." G was survived by his daughter (A).

A's power, which is a nongeneral power, is valid as of its creation under Section 21207(a). The validating life is A; the analysis leading to validity is the same as applied in Example (11), above.

Example (13)—Case of initially valid general power not presently exercisable because of a condition precedent. G devised property "to A for life, then to A's first born child for life, then to such persons, including A's first born child or such child's estate or creditors, as A's first born child shall appoint." G was survived by his daughter (A), who was then childless.

The power in A's first born child, which is a general power not presently exercisable because of a condition precedent, is valid as of its creation under Section 21206(a). The power is subject to a condition precedent—that A have a child—but this is a contingency that under Section 21208 is deemed certain to be resolved one way or the other within A's lifetime. A is therefore the validating life: The power cannot remain subject to the condition precedent after A's death. Note that the latest possible time that the power can be exercised is at the death of A's first born child, which might occur beyond 21 years after the death of A (and anyone else who was alive when G died). Consequently, if the power conferred on A's first born child had been a nongeneral power or a general testamentary power, the power could not be validated by Section 21207(a); instead, the power's validity would be governed by Section 21207(b).

E. Sections 21206(b) and 21207(b): Wait-and-See—Powers of Appointment Whose Validity Is Initially in Abeyance

1. Powers of Appointment

Under the common law rule, a general power not presently exercisable because of a condition precedent is invalid as of the time of its creation if the condition might neither be satisfied nor become impossible to satisfy within a life in being plus 21 years. A nongeneral power (whether or not presently exercisable) or a general testamentary power is invalid as of the time of its creation if it might not terminate (by irrevocable exercise or otherwise) within a life in being plus 21 years.

Sections 21206(b) and 21207(b), by adopting the wait-and-see method of perpetuity reform, shift the ground of invalidity from possible to actual post-creation events. Under these subdivisions, a power of appointment that would have violated the common law rule, and therefore fails the tests in Section 21206(a) or 21207(a) for initial validity, is nevertheless not invalid as of the time of its creation. Instead, its validity is in abeyance. A general power not presently exercisable because of a condition precedent is invalid only if in actuality the condition neither is satisfied nor becomes impossible to satisfy within the allowable 90–year waiting period. A nongeneral power or a general testamentary power is invalid only if in actuality it does not terminate (by irrevocable exercise or otherwise) within the allowable 90–year waiting period.

Example (14)—General testamentary power case. G devised property "to A for life, then to A's first born child for life, then to such persons, including the estate or the creditors of the estate of A's first born child, as A's first born child shall by will appoint; in default of appointment, to G's grandchildren in equal shares." G was survived by his daughter (A), who was then childless, and by his son (B), who had two children (X and Y).

Since the general testamentary power conferred on A's first born child fails the test of Section 21207(a) for initial validity, its validity is governed by Section 21207(b). If A has a child, such child's death must occur within 90 years of G's death for any provision in the child's will purporting to exercise the power to be valid.

Example (15)—Nongeneral power case. G devised property "to A for life, then to A's first born child for life, then to such of G's grandchildren as A's first born child shall appoint; in default of appointment, to the children of G's late nephew, Q." G was survived by his daughter (A), who was then childless, by his son (B), who had two children (X and Y), and by Q's two children (R and S).

Since the nongeneral power conferred on A's first born child fails the test of Section 21207(a) for initial validity, its validity is governed by Section 21207(b). If A has a child, such child must exercise the power within 90 years after G's death or the power becomes invalid.

Example (16)—General power not presently exercisable because of a condition precedent. G devised property "to A for life, then to A's first born child for life, then to such persons, including A's first born child or such child's estate or creditors, as A's first born child shall appoint after reaching the age of 25; in default of appointment, to G's grandchildren." G was survived by his daughter (A), who was then childless, and by his son (B), who had two children (X and Y).

The power conferred on A's first born child is a general power not presently exercisable because of a condition precedent. Since the power fails the test of Section 21206(a) for initial validity, its validity is governed by Section 21206(b). If A has a child, such child must reach the age of 25 (or die under 25) within 90 years after G's death or the power is invalid.

2. Fiduciary Powers

Purely administrative fiduciary powers are excluded from the statutory rule under Section 21225(b)–(c), but the only distributive fiduciary power that is excluded is the power described in Section 21225(d). Otherwise, distributive fiduciary powers are subject to the statutory rule. Such powers are usually nongeneral powers.

Example (17)—Trustee's discretionary powers over income and corpus. G devised property in trust, the terms of which were that the trustee was authorized to accumulate the income or pay it or a portion of it out to A during A's lifetime; after A's death, the trustee was authorized to accumulate the income or to distribute it in equal or unequal shares among A's children until the death of the survivor; and on the death of A's last surviving child to pay the corpus and accumulated income (if any) to B. The trustee was also granted the discretionary power to invade the corpus on behalf of the permissible recipient or recipients of the income.

The trustee's nongeneral powers to invade corpus and to accumulate or spray income among A's children are not excluded by Section 21225(d), nor are they initially valid under Section 21207(a). Their validity is, therefore, governed by Section 21207(b). Both powers become invalid thereunder, and hence no longer exercisable, 90 years after G's death.

It is doubtful that the powers will become invalid, because the trust will probably terminate by its own terms earlier than the expiration of the allowable 90–year period. But if the powers do become invalid, and hence no longer exercisable, they become invalid as of the time the allowable 90–year period expires. Any exercises of either power that took place before the expiration of the allowable 90–year period are not invalidated retroactively. In addition, if the powers do become invalid, a court in an appropriate proceeding must reform the instrument in accordance with the provisions of Section 21220.

F. The Validity of the Donee's Exercise of a Valid Power

1. Donee's Exercise of Power

The fact that a power of appointment is valid, either because it (1) was not subject to the statutory rule to begin with, (2) is initially valid under Sections 21206(a) or 21207(a), or (3) becomes valid under Sections 21206(b) or 21207(b), means merely that the power can be validly exercised. It does not mean that any exercise that the donee decides to make is valid. The validity of the interests or powers created by the exercise of a valid power is a separate matter, governed by the provisions of this chapter. A key factor in deciding the validity of such appointed interests or appointed powers is determining when they were created for purposes of this chapter. Under Sections 21211 and 21212, as explained in the Background to those sections, the time of creation is when the power was exercised if it was a presently exercisable general power; and if it was a nongeneral power or a general testamentary power, the time of creation is when the power was created. This is the rule generally accepted at common law (see Restatement (Second) of Property (Donative Transfers) § 1.2, comment d (1983); Restatement of Property § 392 (1944)), and it is the rule adopted under this chapter.

Example (18)—Exercise of a nongeneral power of appointment. G was the life income beneficiary of a trust and the donee of a nongeneral power of appointment over the succeeding remainder interest, exercisable in favor of M's descendants (except G). The trust was created by the will of G's mother, M, who predeceased him. G exercised his power by his will, directing the income to be paid after his death to his brother B's children for the life of the survivor, and upon the death of B's last surviving child, to pay the corpus of the trust to B's grandchildren. B predeceased M; B was survived by his two children, X and Y, who also survived M and G.

G's power and his appointment are valid. The power and the appointed interests were created at M's death when the power was created, not on G's death when it was exercised. See Sections 21210–21211. G's power passes the test for initial validity under Section 21207(a): G himself is the validating life. G's appointment also passes the test for initial validity under Section 21205(a): Since B was dead at M's death, the validating life is the survivor of B's children, X and Y.

Suppose that G's power was exercisable only in favor of G's own descendants, and that G appointed the identical interests in favor of his own children and grandchildren. Suppose further that at M's death, G had two children, X and Y, and that a third child, Z, was born later. X, Y, and Z survived G. In this case, the remainder interest in favor of G's grandchildren would not pass the test for initial validity under Section 21205(a). Its validity would be governed by Section 21205(b), under which it would be valid if G's last surviving child died within 90 years after M's death.

If G's power were a general testamentary power of appointment, rather than a nongeneral power, the solution would be the same. The period of the statutory rule with respect to interests created by the exercise of a general testamentary power starts to run when the power was created (at M's death, in this example), not when the power was exercised (at G's death).

Example (19)—Exercise of a presently exercisable general power of appointment. G was the life income beneficiary of a trust and the donee of a presently exercisable general power of appointment over the succeeding remainder interest. G exercised the power by deed, directing the trustee after his death to pay the income to G's children in equal shares for the life of the survivor, and upon the death of his last surviving child to pay the corpus of the trust to his grandchildren.

The validity of G's power is not in question. A presently exercisable general power of appointment is not subject to the statutory rule against perpetuities. G's appointment, however, is subject to the statutory rule. If G reserved a power to revoke his appointment, the remainder interest in favor of G's grandchildren passes the test for initial validity under Section 21205(a). Under Sections 21210–21211, the appointed remainder interest was created at G's death. The validating life for his grandchildren's remainder interest is G's last surviving child.

If G's appointment were irrevocable, however, the grandchildren's remainder interest fails the test of Section 21205(a) for initial validity. Under Sections 21210–21211, the appointed remainder interest was created upon delivery of the deed exercising G's power (or when the exercise otherwise became effective). Since the validity of the grandchildren's remainder interest is governed by Section 21205(b), the remainder interest becomes invalid, and the disposition becomes subject to reformation under Section 21220, if G's last surviving child lives beyond 90 years after the effective date of G's appointment.

Example (20)—Exercises of successively created nongeneral powers of appointment. G devised property to A for life, remainder to such of A's descendants as A shall appoint. At his death, A exercised his nongeneral power by appointing to his child B for life, remainder to such of B's descendants as B shall appoint. At his death, B exercised his nongeneral power by appointing to his child C for life, remainder to C's children. A and B were living at G's death. Thereafter, C was born. A later died, survived by B and C. B then died survived by C.

A's nongeneral power passes the test for initial validity under Section 21207(a). A is the validating life. B's nongeneral power, created by A's appointment, also passes the test for initial validity under Section 21207(a). Since under Sections 21210–21211 the appointed interests and powers are created at G's death, and since B was then alive, B is the validating life for his nongeneral power. (If B had been born after G's death, however, his power would have failed the test for initial validity under Section 21207(a); its validity would be governed by Section 21207(b), and would turn on whether or not it was exercised by B within 90 years after G's death.)

Although B's power is valid, his exercise may be partly invalid. The remainder interest in favor of C's children fails the test of Section 21205(a) for initial validity. The period of the statutory rule begins to run at G's death, under Sections 21210–21212. (Since B's power was a nongeneral power, B's appointment under the common law relation back doctrine of powers of appointment is treated as having been made by A. If B's appointment related back no further than that, of course, it would have been validated by Section 21205(a) because C was alive at A's death. However, A's power was also a nongeneral power, so relation back goes another step. A's appointment—which now includes B's appointment—is treated as having been made by G.) Since C was not alive at G's death, he cannot be the validating life. And, since C might have more children more than 21 years after the deaths of A and B and any other individual who was alive at G's death, the remainder interest in favor of his children is not initially validated by Section 21205(a). Instead, its validity is governed by Section 21205(b), and turns on whether or not C dies within 90 years after G's death.

Note that if either A's power or B's power (or both) had been a general testamentary power rather than a nongeneral power, the above solution would not change. However, if either A's power or B's power (or both) had been a presently exercisable general power, B's appointment would have passed the test for initial validity under Section 21205(a). (If A had the presently exercisable general power, the appointed interests and power would be created at A's death, not G's; and if the presently exercisable general power were held by B, the appointed interests and power would be created at B's death.)

2. Common Law "Second–Look" Doctrine

As indicated above, both at common law and under this chapter, appointed interests and powers established by the exercise of a general testamentary power or a nongeneral power are created when the power was created, not when the power was exercised. In applying this principle, the common law recognizes a so-called doctrine of second-look, under which the facts existing on the date of the exercise are taken into account in determining the validity of appointed interests and appointed powers. E.g., Warren's Estate, 320 Pa. 112, 182 A. 396 (1930); In re Bird's Estate, 225 Cal.App.2d 196, 37 Cal.Rptr. 288 (1964). The common law's second-look doctrine in effect constitutes a limited wait-and-see doctrine, and is therefore subsumed under but not totally superseded by this chapter. The following example, which is a variation of Example (18) above, illustrates how the second-look doctrine operates at common law and how the situation would be analyzed under this chapter.

Example (21)—Second-look case. G was the life income beneficiary of a trust and the donee of a nongeneral power of appointment over the succeeding remainder interest, exercisable in favor of G's descendants. The trust was created by the will of his mother, M, who predeceased him. G exercised his power by his will, directing the income to be paid after his death to his children for the life of the survivor, and upon the death of his last surviving child, to pay the corpus of the trust to his grandchildren. At M's death, G had two children, X and Y. No further children were born to G, and at his death X and Y were still living.

The common law solution of this example is as follows: G's appointment is valid under the common law rule. Although the period of the rule begins to run at M's death, the facts existing at G's death can be taken into account. This second look at the facts discloses that G had no additional children. Thus the possibility of additional children, which existed at M's death when the period of the rule began to run, is disregarded. The survivor of X and Y, therefore, becomes the validating life for the remainder interest in favor of G's grandchildren, and G's appointment is valid. The common law's second-look doctrine would not, however, save G's appointment if he actually had one or more children after M's death and if at least one of these after-born children survived G.

Under this chapter, if no additional children are born to G after M's death, the common law second-look doctrine can be invoked as of G's death to declare G's appointment then to be valid under Section 21205(a); no further waiting is necessary. However, if additional children are born to G and one or more of them survives G, Section 21205(b) applies and the validity of G's appointment depends on G's last surviving child dying within 90 years after M's death.

3. Additional References

Restatement (Second) of Property (Donative Transfers) § 1.2 comments d, f, g, & h; § 1.3 comment g; § 1.4 comment 1 (1983). [20 Cal.L.Rev.Comm.Reports 2543 (1990)].

§ 21207. Nongeneral power of appointment; general testamentary power of appointment; validity; conditions

A nongeneral power of appointment or a general testamentary power of appointment is invalid unless one of the following conditions is satisfied:

(a) When the power is created, it is certain to be irrevocably exercised or otherwise to terminate no later than 21 years after the death of an individual then alive.

(b) The power is irrevocably exercised or otherwise terminates within 90 years after its creation. *(Added by Stats.1991, c. 156 (A.B.1577), § 24.)*

Law Revision Commission Comments

1991 Addition

Section 21207 is the same in substance as Section 1(c) of the Uniform Statutory Rule Against Perpetuities (1990). See Comment to Section 21205. See also Sections 21230 (validating lives), 21231 (spouse as life in being).

Background (adapted from Prefatory Note to Uniform Statute). This article sets forth the statutory rule against perpetuities (statutory rule). The statutory rule and the other provisions of this part supersede the common law rule against perpetuities (common law rule) and replace the former statutory version. See Section 21201. Section 21205 deals with nonvested property interests; Sections 21206 and 21207 deal with powers of appointment.

Subdivision (a) of Section 21207 codifies the validating side of the common law rule. In effect, subdivision (a) provides that a power of appointment that is valid under the common law rule is valid under the statutory rule and can be declared so at its inception. In such a case, nothing would be gained and much would be lost by invoking a waiting period during which the validity of the interest or power is in abeyance.

Subdivision (b) establishes the wait-and-see rule by providing that an interest or a power of appointment that is not validated by subdivision (a), and hence would have been invalid under the common law rule, is nevertheless valid if the power ceases to be subject to a condition precedent or is no longer exercisable when the allowable 90–year waiting period expires. [20 Cal.L.Rev.Comm.Reports 2501 (1990)].

Background (adapted from official comments to Uniform Statutory Rule Against Perpetuities)

For additional background on Probate Code § 21207, adapted from the official comments to the Uniform Statutory Rule Against Perpetuities, see background comments under Probate Code § 21206.

§ 21208. Posthumous births

In determining whether a nonvested property interest or a power of appointment is valid under this article, the possibility that a child will be born to an individual after the individual's death is disregarded. *(Added by Stats.1991, c. 156 (A.B.1577), § 24.)*

Law Revision Commission Comments

1991 Addition

Section 21208 is the same in substance as Section 1(d) of the Uniform Statutory Rule Against Perpetuities (1990). This section supersedes part of the first sentence of former Civil Code Section 715.2 which served the same purpose as to a period of gestation. [20 Cal.L.Rev.Comm.Reports 2501 (1990)].

Background (adapted from official comments to Uniform Statutory Rule Against Perpetuities).

The rule established in Section 21208 plays a significant role in the search for a validating life. Section 21208 declares that the possibility that a child will be born to an individual after the individual's death is to be disregarded. It is important to note that this rule applies only for the purposes of determining the validity of an interest (or power of appointment) under Section 21205(a), 21206(a) or 21207(a). The rule of Section 21208 does not apply, for example, to questions such as whether or not a child who is born to an individual after the individual's death qualifies as a taker of a beneficial interest—as a member of a class or otherwise. Neither Section 21208, nor any other provision of this chapter, supersedes the widely accepted common law principle, sometimes codified, that a child in gestation (a child sometimes described as a child en ventre sa mere) who is later born alive is regarded as alive at the commencement of gestation.

The limited purpose of Section 21208 is to solve a perpetuity problem caused by advances in medical science. The problem is illustrated by a case such as Example (1) in the Background to Section 21205—"to A for life, remainder to A's children who reach 21." When the common law rule was developing, the possibility was recognized, strictly speaking, that one or more of A's children might reach 21 more than 21 years after A's death. The possibility existed because A's wife (who might not be a life in being) might be pregnant when A died. If she was, and if the child was born viable a few months after A's death, the child could not reach his or her 21st birthday within 21 years after A's death. The device then invented to validate the interest of A's children was to "extend" the allowable perpetuity period by tacking on a period of gestation, if needed. As a result, the common law perpetuity period was comprised of three components: (1) a life in being (2) plus 21 years (3) plus a period of gestation, when needed. Today, thanks to sperm banks, frozen embryos, and even the possibility of artificially maintaining the body functions of deceased pregnant women long enough to develop the fetus to viability—advances in medical science unanticipated when the common law rule was in its developmental stages—having a pregnant wife at death is no longer the only way of having children after death. These medical developments, and undoubtedly others to come, make the mere addition of a period of gestation inadequate as a device to confer initial validity under Section 21205(a) on the interest of A's children in the above example. The rule of Section 21208, however, does ensure the initial validity of the children's interest. Disregarding the possibility that children of A will be born after his death allows A to be the validating life. None of his children, under this assumption, can reach 21 more than 21 years after his death.

Note that Section 21208 subsumes not only the case of children conceived after death, but also the more conventional case of children in gestation at death. With Section 21208 in place, the third component of the common law perpetuity period is unnecessary and has been jettisoned. The perpetuity period recognized in Section 21205(a), 21206(a), or 21207(a) has only two components: (1) a life in being (2) plus 21 years.

As to the legal status of conceived-after-death children, that question has not yet been resolved. For example, if in Example (1) in the Background to Section 21205 it in fact turns out that A does leave sperm on deposit at a sperm bank and if in fact A's wife does become pregnant as a result of artificial insemination, the child or children produced thereby might not be included at all in the class gift. Cf. Restatement (Second) of Property (Donative Transfers) Introductory Note to Ch. 26, at 2–3 (Tent. Draft No. 9, 1986). Without trying to predict how that matter will be settled in the future, the best way to handle the problem from the perpetuity perspective is Section 21208's rule requiring the possibility of post-death children to be disregarded. [20 Cal.L.Rev.Comm.Reports 2543 (1990)].

§ 21209. Construction of "later of" language in perpetuity saving clause; application of section

(a) If, in measuring a period from the creation of a trust or other property arrangement, language in a governing instrument (1) seeks to disallow the vesting or termination of any interest or trust beyond, (2) seeks to postpone the vesting or termination of any interest or trust until, or (3) seeks to operate in effect in any similar fashion upon, the later of (A) the expiration of a period of time not exceeding 21 years after the death of the survivor of specified lives in being at the creation of the trust or other property arrangement or (B) the

expiration of a period of time that exceeds or might exceed 21 years after the death of the survivor of lives in being at the creation of the trust or other property arrangement, that language is inoperative to the extent it produces a period that exceeds 21 years after the death of the survivor of the specified lives.

(b) Notwithstanding Section 21202, this section applies only to governing instruments, including instruments exercising powers of appointment, executed on or after January 1, 1992. *(Added by Stats.1991, c. 156 (A.B.1577), § 24.)*

Law Revision Commission Comments
1991 Addition [Revised Comment]

Subdivision (a) of Section 21209 is the same in substance as Section 1(e) of the Uniform Statutory Rule Against Perpetuities. This section is intended to invalidate a two-pronged perpetuity saving clause to the extent that it attempts to employ a period of time extending beyond the traditional perpetuities period of lives in being plus 21 years. The effect of this rule is that there is no advantage to be gained by inserting such a "later of" clause in an instrument. A standard perpetuity saving clause in use before enactment of USRAP continues to be appropriate. Consequently, instruments should not be redrafted in an attempt to apply a "later of" 90 years or lives–in–being–plus–21–years test. This section also prevents the loss of grandfathered status under the federal generation-skipping transfer tax involving exercise of a nongeneral power of appointment under a pre–1986 irrevocable trust. See Temp.Treas.Reg. § 26.2601–1(b)(1)(v)(B)(2) (1988) (as agreed to be amended); see also Appendix to *Recommendation Relating to Uniform Statutory Rule Against Perpetuities*, 20 Cal.L.Revision Comm'n Reports 2501, 2577–79 (1990); Unif.Prob.Code § 2–901(e) comment (9th ed. 1990).

Subdivision (b) makes clear that subdivision (a) applies only prospectively. [21 Cal.L.Rev.Comm.Reports 69 (1991)].

Background (adapted from official comments to Uniform Statutory Rule Against Perpetuities)

1. Effect of Certain "Later-of" Type Language

The provision set out in Section 21209 was added to the Uniform Statutory Rule Against Perpetuities in 1990 (USRAP § 1(e)). It primarily applies to a non-traditional type of "later of" clause (described below). Use of that type of clause might have produced unintended consequences, which are now rectified by the addition of Section 21209.

In general, perpetuity saving or termination clauses can be used in either of two ways. The predominant use of such clauses is as an override clause. That is, the clause is not an integral part of the dispositive terms of the trust, but operates independently of the dispositive terms; the clause provides that all interests must vest no later than at a specified time in the future, and sometimes also provides that the trust must then terminate, but only if any interest has not previously vested or if the trust has not previously terminated. The other use of such a clause is as an integral part of the dispositive terms of the trust; that is, the clause is the provision that directly regulates the duration of the trust. Traditional perpetuity saving or termination clauses do not use a "later of" approach; they mark off the maximum time of vesting or termination only by reference to a 21–year period following the death of the survivor of specified lives in being at the creation of the trust.

Section 21209 applies to a non-traditional clause called a "later of" (or "longer of") clause. Such a clause might provide that the maximum time of vesting or termination of any interest or trust must occur no later than the later of (A) 21 years after the death of the survivor of specified lives in being at the creation of the trust or (B) 90 years after the creation of the trust.

Under Section 21205, this type of "later of" clause would not achieve a "later of" result. Section 21205 provides:

21205. A nonvested property interest is invalid unless one of the following conditions is satisfied:

(a) When the interest is created, it is certain to vest or terminate no later than 21 years after the death of an individual then alive.

(b) The interest either vests or terminates within 90 years after its creation.

If used as an override clause in conjunction with a trust whose terms were, by themselves, valid under the common law rule against perpetuities (common law rule), the "later of" clause would do no harm. The trust would be valid under the common law rule as codified in Section 21205(a) because the clause itself would neither postpone the vesting of any interest nor extend the duration of the trust. But, if used either (1) as an override clause in conjunction with a trust whose terms were not valid under the common law rule or (2) as the provision that directly regulated the duration of the trust, the "later of" clause would not cure the perpetuity violation in case (1) and would create a perpetuity violation in case (2). In neither case would the clause qualify the trust for validity at common law under Section 21205(a) because the clause would not guarantee that all interests will be certain to vest or terminate no later than 21 years after the death of an individual then alive. In any given case, 90 years can turn out to be longer than the period produced by the language relating to specified lives in being plus 21 years.

Because the clause would fail to qualify the trust for validity under the common law rule of Section 21205(a), the nonvested interests in the trust would be subject to the wait-and-see element of Section 21205(b) and vulnerable to a reformation suit under Section 21220. Under Section 21205(b), an interest that is not valid at common law is invalid unless it actually vests or terminates within 90 years after its creation. Section 21205(b) does not grant such nonvested interests a permissible vesting period of either 90 years or a period of 21 years after the death of the survivor of specified lives in being. Section 21205(b) only grants such interests a period of 90 years in which to vest.

The operation of Section 21205, as outlined above, is also supported by perpetuity policy. If Section 21205 allowed a "later of" clause to achieve a "later of" result, it would authorize an improper use of the 90–year permissible vesting period of Section 21205(b). The 90–year period of Section 21205(b) is designed to approximate the period that, on average, would be produced by using actual lives in being plus 21 years. Because in any given case the period actually produced by lives in being plus 21 years can be shorter or longer than 90 years, an attempt to utilize a 90–year period in a "later of" clause improperly seeks to turn the 90–year average into a minimum.

Set against this background, the addition of Section 21209 is quite beneficial. Section 21209 limits the effect of this type of "later of" language to 21 years after the death of the survivor of the specified lives, in effect transforming the clause into a traditional perpetuity saving or termination clause. By doing so, Section 21209 grants initial validity to the trust under the common law rule as codified in Section 21205(a) and precludes a reformation suit under Section 21220.

Note that Section 21209 covers variations of the "later of" clause described above, such as a clause that postpones vesting until the later of (A) 20 years after the death of the survivor of specified lives in being or (B) 89 years. Section 21209 does not, however, apply to all dispositions that incorporate a "later of" approach. To come under Section 21209, the specified-lives prong must include a tack-on period of up to 21 years. Without a tack-on period, a "later of" disposition, unless valid at common law, comes under Section 21205(b) and is given 90 years in which to vest. An example would be a disposition that creates an interest that is to vest upon "the later of the death of my widow or 30 years after my death."

2. Coordination of the Federal Generation–Skipping Transfer Tax with the Uniform Statutory Rule.

Section 1433(b)(2) of the Tax Reform Act of 1986 generally exempts (or "grandfathers") trusts from the federal generation-skipping transfer tax that were irrevocable on September 25, 1985. This section adds, however, that the exemption applies "only to the extent that such transfer is not made out of corpus added to the trust after September 25, 1985." The provisions of Section 1433(b)(2) were first implemented by Temp.Treas.Reg. § 26.2601–1, promulgated by T.D. 8187 on March 14, 1988. Insofar as the statutory rule is concerned, a key feature of that temporary regulation is the concept that the statutory reference to "corpus added to the trust after September 25, 1985" not only covers actual post-September 25, 1985, transfers of new property or corpus to a grandfathered trust, but "constructive" additions as well. Under the temporary regulation as first promulgated, a "constructive" addition occurs if, after September 25, 1985, the donee of a nongeneral power of appointment exercises that power

in a manner that may postpone or suspend the vesting, absolute ownership or power of alienation of an interest in property for a period, measured from the date of creation of the trust, extending beyond any life in being at the date of creation of the trust plus a period of 21 years. If a power is exercised by creating another power it will be deemed to be exercised to whatever extent the second power may be exercised.

Temp.Treas.Reg. § 26.2601–1(b)(1)(v)(B)(2) (1988). The literal wording of this regulation, as first promulgated, could have jeopardized the grandfathered status of an exempt trust if (1) the trust created a nongeneral power of appointment, (2) the donee exercised that nongeneral power, and (3) the statutory rule is the perpetuity law applicable to the donee's exercise. This possibility arose not only because the donee's exercise itself might come under the 90–year permissible vesting period of Section 21205(b) if it otherwise violated the common law rule and hence was not validated under Section 21205(a). The possibility also arose in a less obvious way if the donee's exercise created another nongeneral power. The last sentence of the temporary regulation states that "if a power is exercised by creating another power it will be deemed to be exercised to whatever extent the second power may be exercised." [Emphasis added].

In late March 1990, the National Conference of Commissioners on Uniform State Laws (NCCUSL) filed a formal request with the Treasury Department asking that measures be taken to coordinate the regulation with USRAP. In November 1990, the Treasury Department responded by stating that it "will amend the temporary regulations to accommodate the 90–year period under USRAP as originally promulgated [in 1986] or as amended [in 1990 by the addition of USRAP § 1(e)]." Letter of intent from Michael J. Graetz, Deputy Assistant Secretary of the Treasury (Tax Policy), to Lawrence J. Bugge, President, National Conference of Commissioners on Uniform State Laws (Nov. 16, 1990) (hereinafter cited as "Treasury Letter"). This should effectively remove the possibility of loss of grandfathered status under the statutory rule merely because the donee of a nongeneral power created in a grandfathered trust inadvertently exercises that power in violation of the common law rule or merely because the donee exercises that power by creating a second nongeneral power that might, in the future, be inadvertently exercised in violation of the common law rule.

The Treasury Letter states, however, that any effort by the donee of a nongeneral power in a grandfathered trust to obtain a "later of" specified-lives-in-being-plus–21–years or 90–years result will be treated as a constructive addition, unless that effort is nullified by state law. As explained above, the statutory rule, as originally promulgated in 1986 or as amended in 1990 by the addition of Section 1(e) (Section 21209 in California), nullifies any direct effort to obtain a "later of" result by the use of a "later of" clause.

The Treasury Letter states that an indirect effort to obtain a "later of" result would also be treated as a constructive addition that would bring grandfathered status to an end, unless the attempt to obtain the "later-of" result is nullified by state law. The Treasury Letter indicates that an indirect effort to obtain a "later of" result could arise if the donee of a nongeneral power successfully attempts to prolong the duration of a grandfathered trust by switching from a specified-lives-in-being-plus–21–years perpetuity period to a 90–year perpetuity period, or vice versa. This is a highly unlikely chain of events, and donees and their attorneys should be warned of the consequences of engaging in such manipulation. Nevertheless, should a donee attempt to make a switch from a specified-lives-in-being-plus–21–years perpetuity period to a 90–year perpetuity period, Section 21209 can play an important role in preserving grandfathered status by nullifying the attempt. For example, suppose that the original grandfathered trust contained a standard perpetuity saving clause declaring that all interests in the trust must vest no later than 21 years after the death of the survivor of specified lives in being. In exercising a nongeneral power created in that trust, any indirect effort by the donee to obtain a "later of" result by adopting a 90–year perpetuity saving clause will likely be nullified by Section 21209. If that exercise occurs at a time when it has become clear or reasonably predictable that the 90–year period will prove longer, the donee's exercise would constitute language in a governing instrument that seeks to operate in effect to postpone the vesting of any interest until the later of the specified-lives-in-being-plus–21–years period or 90 years. Section 21209 makes that language inoperative to the extent it produces a period of time that exceeds 21 years after the death of the survivor of the specified lives.

Although Section 21209 would not nullify a switch from a 90–year period to a specified-lives-in-being-plus–21–years period, the relation-back doctrine generally recognized in the exercise of nongeneral powers stands as a state-law doctrine that could potentially be invoked to nullify such an attempted switch (and one going in the other direction as well). Under that doctrine, interests created by the exercise of a nongeneral power are considered created by the donor of that power. See, e.g., Restatement (Second) of Property, Donative Transfers § 11.1 comment b (1986). As such, the maximum vesting period applicable to interests created by the exercise of a nongeneral power would apparently be covered by the perpetuity saving clause in the document that created the power, notwithstanding any different period the donee seeks to adopt. [20 Cal.L.Rev.Comm.Reports 2543 (1990)].

ARTICLE 3. TIME OF CREATION OF INTEREST

Section

21210. Nonvested property interests or powers of appointment.
21211. Powers exercisable by one person alone.
21212. Interests or powers arising from transfer of property; previously funded trusts; other existing property arrangement.

Application

Application of Part 2, see Probate Code § 21202.

§ 21210. Nonvested property interests or powers of appointment

Except as provided in Sections 21211 and 21212, the time of creation of a nonvested property interest or a power of appointment is determined by other applicable statutes or, if none, under general principles of property law. *(Added by Stats.1991, c. 156 (A.B.1577), § 24.)*

Law Revision Commission Comments
1991 Addition

Section 21210 is the same in substance as Section 2(a) of the Uniform Statutory Rule Against Perpetuities (1990), with the addition of the reference to other statutory provisions. The cross-reference in Section 2(a) of the uniform statute to the prospective application provision (§ 5(a)) is omitted because this part applies to all interests regardless of their date of creation. See Section 21202. This section supersedes Civil Code Section 1391.1(a)(2).

Background (adapted from Prefatory Note to Uniform Statute). This article defines the time when, for purposes of this chapter, a nonvested property interest or a power of appointment is created. The period of time allowed by Article 2 (commencing with Section 21205) (statutory rule against perpetuities) is marked off from the time of creation of the nonvested property interest or power of appointment in question. Section 21202, with certain exceptions, provides that this chapter applies to nonvested property interests and powers of appointment regardless of whether they were created before, on, or after January 1, 1992. [20 Cal.L.Rev.Comm.Reports 2501 (1990)].

Background (adapted from official comments to Uniform Statutory Rule Against Perpetuities)

General Principles of Property Law; When Nonvested Property Interests and Powers of Appointment Are Created

Under Sections 21205–21207, the period of time allowed by the statutory rule against perpetuities is marked off from the time of creation of the nonvested property interest or power of appointment in question. Except as provided in Sections 21211 and 21212, the time of creation of nonvested property interests and powers of appointment is determined under general principles of property law.

Since a will becomes effective as a dispositive instrument upon the decedent's death, not upon the execution of the will, general principles of property law determine that the time when a nonvested property interest or a power of appointment created by will is created is at the decedent's death.

With respect to a nonvested property interest or a power of appointment created by inter vivos transfer, the time when the interest or power is created is the date the transfer becomes effective for purposes of property law generally, normally the date of delivery of the deed.

With respect to a nonvested property interest or a power of appointment created by the testamentary or inter vivos exercise of a power of appointment, general principles of property law adopt the "relation back" doctrine. Under that doctrine, the appointed interests or powers are created when the power was created not when it was exercised, if the exercised power was a nongeneral power or a general testamentary power. If the exercised power was a general power presently exercisable, the relation back doctrine is not followed; the time of creation of the appointed property interests or appointed powers is regarded as the time when the power was irrevocably exercised, not when the power was created. [20 Cal.L.Rev.Comm.Reports 2543 (1990)].

§ 21211. Powers exercisable by one person alone

For purposes of this chapter:

(a) If there is a person who alone can exercise a power created by a governing instrument to become the unqualified beneficial owner of (1) a nonvested property interest or (2) a property interest subject to a power of appointment described in Section 21206 or 21207, the nonvested property interest or power of appointment is created when the power to become the unqualified beneficial owner terminates.

(b) A joint power with respect to community property held by individuals married to each other is a power exercisable by one person alone. *(Added by Stats.1991, c. 156 (A.B.1577), § 24.)*

Law Revision Commission Comments
1991 Addition

Section 21211 is the same in substance as Section 2(b) of the Uniform Statutory Rule Against Perpetuities (1990). Section 21211(a) supersedes Civil Code Sections 716 and 1391.1(a). The reference to the Uniform Marital Property Act in Section 2(b) of the Uniform Statutory Rule Against Perpetuities is not included in Section 21211(b) because it is unnecessary in light of the definition of community property in Section 28. See Comment to Section 28.

Background (adapted from Prefatory Note to Uniform Statute). Section 21211 provides that, if one person can exercise a power to become the unqualified beneficial owner of a nonvested property interest (or a property interest subject to a power of appointment described in Section 21206 or 21207), the time of creation of the nonvested property interest or the power of appointment is postponed until the power to become unqualified beneficial owner ceases to exist. This is in accord with existing common law. [20 Cal.L.Rev.Comm.Reports 2501 (1990)].

Background (adapted from official comments to Uniform Statutory Rule Against Perpetuities)

1. Postponement, for Purposes of This Chapter, of the Time When a Nonvested Property Interest or a Power of Appointment Is Created in Certain Cases

The reason that the significant date for purposes of this chapter is the date of creation is that the unilateral control of the interest (or the interest subject to the power) by one person is then relinquished. In certain cases, all beneficial rights in a property interest (including an interest subject to a power of appointment) remain under the unilateral control of one person even after the delivery of the deed or even after the decedent's death. In such cases, under Section 21211, the interest or power is created, for purposes of this chapter, when no person, acting alone, has a power presently exercisable to become the unqualified beneficial owner of the property interest (or the property interest subject to the power of appointment).

Example (1)—Revocable inter vivos trust case. G conveyed property to a trustee, directing the trustee to pay the net income therefrom to himself (G) for life, then to G's son A for his life, then to A's children for the life of the survivor of A's children who are living at G's death, and upon the death of such last surviving child, the corpus of the trust is to be distributed among A's then-living descendants, per stirpes. G retained the power to revoke the trust.

Because of G's reservation of the power to revoke the trust, the creation for purposes of this chapter of the nonvested property interests in this case occurs at G's death, not when the trust was established. This is in accordance with common law, for purposes of the common law rule against perpetuities. Cook v. Horn, 214 Ga. 289, 104 S.E.2d 461 (1958).

The rationale that justifies the postponement of the time of creation in such cases is as follows. A person, such as G in the above example, who alone can exercise a power to become the unqualified beneficial owner of a nonvested property interest is in effect the owner of that property interest. Thus, any nonvested property interest subject to such a power is not created for purposes of this chapter until the power terminates (by release, expiration at the death of the donee, or otherwise). Similarly, as noted above, any property interest or power of appointment created in an appointee by the irrevocable exercise of such a power is created at the time of the donee's irrevocable exercise.

For the date of creation to be postponed under Section 21211, the power need not be a power to revoke, and it need not be held by the settlor or transferor. A presently exercisable power held by any person acting alone to make himself the unqualified beneficial owner of the nonvested property interest or the property interest subject to a power of appointment is sufficient. If such a power exists, the time when the interest or power is created, for purposes of this chapter, is postponed until the termination of the power (by irrevocable exercise, release, contract to exercise or not to exercise, expiration at the death of the donee, or otherwise). An example of such a power that might not be held by the settlor or transferor is a power, held by any person who can act alone, fully to invade the corpus of a trust.

An important consequence of the idea that a power need not be held by the settlor for the time of creation to be postponed under this section is that it makes postponement possible even in cases of testamentary transfers.

Example (2)—Testamentary trust case. G devised property in trust, directing the trustee to pay the income "to A for life, remainder to such persons (including A, his creditors, his estate, and the creditors of his estate) as A shall appoint; in default of appointment, the property to remain in trust to pay the income to A's children for the life of the survivor, and upon the death of A's last surviving child, to pay the corpus to A's grandchildren." A survived G.

If A exercises his presently exercisable general power, any nonvested property interest or power of appointment created by A's appointment is created for purposes of this chapter when the power is exercised. If A does not exercise the power, the nonvested property interests in G's gift-in-default clause are created when A's power terminates (at A's death). In either case, the postponement is justified because the transaction is the equivalent of G's having devised the full remainder interest (following A's income interest) to A and of A's having in turn transferred that interest in accordance with his exercise of the power or, in the event the power is not exercised, devised that interest at his death in accordance with G's gift-in-default clause. Note, however, that if G had conferred on A a nongeneral power or a general testamentary power, A's power of appointment, any nonvested property interest or power of appointment created by A's appointment, if any, and the nonvested property interests in G's gift-in-default clause would be created at G's death.

2. Unqualified Beneficial Owner of the Nonvested Property Interest or the Property Interest Subject to a Power of Appointment

For the date of creation to be postponed under Section 21211, the presently exercisable power must be one that entitles the donee of the power to become the unqualified beneficial owner of the nonvested property interest (or the property interest subject to a nongeneral power of appointment, a general testamentary power of appointment, or a general power of appointment not presently exercisable because of a condition precedent). This requirement was met in Example (2), above, because A could by appointing the remainder interest to himself become the unqualified beneficial owner of all the nonvested property interests in G's gift-in-default clause. In Example (2) it is not revealed whether A, if he exercised the power in his own favor, also had the right as sole beneficiary of the trust to compel the termination of the trust and possess himself as unqualified beneficial owner of the property that was the subject of the trust. Having the power to compel termination of the trust is not necessary. If, for example, the trust in Example (2) was a spendthrift trust or contained any other feature that under Section 15403 would prevent A as sole beneficiary from compelling termination of the trust, A's presently exercisable general power over the remainder interest would still postpone the time of creation of the nonvested property interests in G's gift-in-default clause because the power enables A to become the unqualified beneficial owner of such interests.

Furthermore, it is not necessary that the donee of the power have the power to become the unqualified beneficial owner of all beneficial rights in the trust. In Example (2), the property interests in G's gift-in-default clause are not created for purposes of this chapter until A's power expires (or on A's appointment, until the power's exercise) even if someone other than A was the income beneficiary of the trust.

3. Presently Exercisable Power

For the date of creation to be postponed under Section 21211, the power must be presently exercisable. A testamentary power does not qualify. A power not presently exercisable because of a condition precedent does not qualify. If the condition precedent later becomes satisfied, however, so that the power becomes presently exercisable, the interests or powers subject thereto are not created, for purposes of this chapter, until the termination of the power. The common law decision of Fitzpatrick v. Mercantile Safe Deposit Co., 220 Md. 534, 155 A.2d 702 (1959), appears to be in accord with this proposition.

Example (3)—General power in unborn child case. G devised property "to A for life, then to A's first-born child for life, then to such persons, including A's first-born child or such child's estate or creditors, as A's first-born child shall appoint." There was a further provision that in default of appointment, the trust would continue for the benefit of G's descendants. G was survived by his daughter (A), who was then childless. After G's death, A had a child, X. A then died, survived by X.

As of G's death, the power of appointment in favor of A's first-born child and the property interests in G's gift-in-default clause would be regarded as having been created at G's death because the power in A's first-born child was then a general power not presently exercisable because of a condition precedent.

At X's birth, X's general power became presently exercisable and excluded from the statutory rule. X's power also qualifies as a power exercisable by one person alone to become the unqualified beneficial owner of the property interests in G's gift-in-default clause. Consequently, the nonvested property interests in G's gift-in-default clause are not created, for purposes of this chapter, until the termination of X's power. If X exercises his presently exercisable general power, before or after A's death, the appointed interests or powers are created, for purposes of this chapter, as of X's exercise of the power.

4. Partial Powers

For the date of creation to be postponed under Section 21211, the person must have a presently exercisable power to become the unqualified beneficial owner of the full nonvested property interest or the property interest subject to a power of appointment described in Section 21206 or 21207. If, for example, the subject of the transfer was an undivided interest such as a one-third tenancy in common, the power qualifies even though it relates only to the undivided one-third interest in the tenancy in common; it need not relate to the whole property. A power to become the unqualified beneficial owner of only part of the nonvested property interest or the property interest subject to a power of appointment, however, does not postpone the time of creation of the interests or powers subject thereto, unless the power is actually exercised.

Example (4)—"5 and 5" power case. G devised property in trust, directing the trustee to pay the income "to A for life, remainder to such persons (including A, his creditors, his estate, and the creditors of his estate) as A shall by will appoint;" in default of appointment, the governing instrument provided for the property to continue in trust. A was given a noncumulative power to withdraw the greater of $5,000 or 5% of the corpus of the trust annually. A survived G. A never exercised his noncumulative power of withdrawal.

G's death marks the time of creation of: A's testamentary power of appointment; any nonvested property interest or power of appointment created in G's gift-in-default clause; and any appointed interest or power created by a testamentary exercise of A's power of appointment over the remainder interest. A's general power of appointment over the remainder interest does not postpone the time of creation because it is not a presently exercisable power. A's noncumulative power to

withdraw a portion of the trust each year does not postpone the time of creation as to all or the portion of the trust with respect to which A allowed his power to lapse each year because A's power is a power over only part of any nonvested property interest or property interest subject to a power of appointment in G's gift-in-default clause and over only part of any appointed interest or power created by a testamentary exercise of A's general power of appointment over the remainder interest. The same conclusion has been reached at common law. See Ryan v. Ward, 192 Md. 342, 64 A.2d 258 (1949).

If, however, in any year A exercised his noncumulative power of withdrawal in a way that created a nonvested property interest (or power of appointment) in the withdrawn amount (for example, if A directed the trustee to transfer the amount withdrawn directly into a trust created by A), the appointed interests (or powers) would be created when the power was exercised, not when G died.

5. Incapacity of the Donee of the Power

The fact that the donee of a power lacks the capacity to exercise it, by reason of minority, mental incompetency, or any other reason, does not prevent the power held by such person from postponing the time of creation under Section 21211, unless the governing instrument extinguishes the power (or prevents it from coming into existence) for that reason.

6. Joint Powers—Community Property; Marital Property

For the date of creation to be postponed under Section 21211, the power must be exercisable by one person alone. A joint power does not qualify, except that, under Section 21211(b), a joint power over community property (or over marital property under a Uniform Marital Property Act held by individuals married to each other, pursuant to the definition of community property in Section 28) is, for purposes of this chapter, treated as a power exercisable by one person acting alone. See Restatement (Second) of Property (Donative Transfers) § 1.2 comment b & illustrations 5, 6, & 7 (1983) for the rationale supporting the enactment of the bracketed sentence and examples illustrating its principle. [20 Cal.L.Rev.Comm.Reports 2543 (1990)].

§ 21212. Interests or powers arising from transfer of property; previously funded trusts; other existing property arrangement

For purposes of this chapter, a nonvested property interest or a power of appointment arising from a transfer of property to a previously funded trust or other existing property arrangement is created when the nonvested property interest or power of appointment in the original contribution was created. *(Added by Stats.1991, c. 156 (A.B.1577), § 24.)*

Law Revision Commission Comments

1991 Addition

Section 21212 is the same in substance as Section 2(c) of the Uniform Statutory Rule Against Perpetuities (1990).

Background (adapted from Prefatory Note to Uniform Statute). Section 21212 provides that nonvested property interests and powers of appointment arising out of transfers to a previously funded trust or other existing property arrangement are created when the nonvested property interest or power of appointment arising out of the original contribution was created. This avoids an administrative difficulty that can arise at common law when subsequent transfers are made to an existing irrevocable trust. Arguably, at common law, each transfer starts the period of the rule running anew as to that transfer. This difficulty is avoided by Section 21212. [20 Cal.L.Rev.Comm.Reports 2501 (1990)].

Background (adapted from official comments to Uniform Statutory Rule Against Perpetuities)

No Staggered Periods

For purposes of this chapter, Section 21212 in effect treats a transfer of property to a previously funded trust or other existing property arrangement as having been made when the nonvested property interest or power of appointment in the original contribution was created. The purpose of Section 21212 is to avoid the administrative difficulties that would otherwise result where subsequent transfers are made to an existing irrevocable trust. Without Section 21212, the allowable period under the statutory rule would be marked off in such cases from different times with respect to different portions of the same trust.

Example (5)—Series of transfers case. In Year One, G created an irrevocable inter vivos trust, funding it with $20,000 cash. In Year Five, when the value of the investments in which the original $20,000 contribution was placed had risen to a value of $30,000, G added $10,000 cash to the trust. G died in Year Ten. G's will poured the residuary of his estate into the trust. G's residuary estate consisted of Blackacre (worth $20,000) and securities (worth $80,000). At G's death, the value of the investments in which the original $20,000 contribution and the subsequent $10,000 contribution were placed had risen to a value of $50,000.

Were it not for Section 21212, the allowable period under the statutory rule would be marked off from three different times: Year One, Year Five, and Year Ten. The effect of Section 21212 is that the allowable period under the statutory rule starts running only once—in Year One—with respect to the entire trust. This result is defensible not only to prevent the administrative difficulties inherent in recognizing staggered periods. It also is defensible because if G's inter vivos trust had contained a perpetuity saving clause, the perpetuity-period component of the clause would be geared to the time when the original contribution to the trust was made; this clause would cover the subsequent contributions as well. Since the major justification for the adoption by this chapter of the wait-and-see method of perpetuity reform is that it amounts to a statutory insertion of a saving clause, Section 21212 is consistent with the theory of this chapter. [20 Cal.L.Rev.Comm.Reports 2543 (1990)].

ARTICLE 4.   REFORMATION

Section
21220.   Petition; conditions.

Application

Application of Part 2, see Probate Code § 21202.

§ 21220.   Petition; conditions

On petition of an interested person, a court shall reform a disposition in the manner that most closely approximates the transferor's manifested plan of distribution and is within the 90 years allowed by the applicable provision in Article 2 (commencing with Section 21205), if any of the following conditions is satisfied:

(a) A nonvested property interest or a power of appointment becomes invalid under the statutory rule against perpetuities provided in Article 2 (commencing with Section 21205).

(b) A class gift is not but might become invalid under the statutory rule against perpetuities provided in Article 2 (commencing with Section 21205), and the time has arrived when the share of any class member is to take effect in possession or enjoyment.

(c) A nonvested property interest that is not validated by subdivision (a) of Section 21205 can vest but not within 90 years after its creation. *(Added by Stats.1991, c. 156 (A.B. 1577), § 24.)*

Law Revision Commission Comments
1991 Addition

Section 21220 is the same in substance as Section 3 of the Uniform Statutory Rule Against Perpetuities (1990). Section 21220 supersedes Civil Code Section 715.5 (reformation or construction to avoid violation of rule against perpetuities).

Background (adapted from Prefatory Note to Uniform Statute). Section 21220 directs a court, on petition of an interested person, to reform a disposition within the limits of the allowable 90–year period, in the manner deemed by the court most closely to approximate the transferor's manifested plan of distribution, in three circumstances: (1) when a nonvested property interest or a power of appointment becomes invalid under the statutory rule; (2) when a class gift has not but still might become invalid under the statutory rule and the time has arrived when the share of a class member is to take effect in possession or enjoyment; and (3) when a nonvested property interest can vest, but cannot do so within the allowable 90–year waiting period. It is anticipated that the circumstances requisite to reformation under this section will rarely arise, and consequently that this section will seldom need to be applied. [20 Cal.L.Rev.Comm.Reports 2501 (1990)].

Background (adapted from official comments to Uniform Statutory Rule Against Perpetuities)
1.   Reformation

This section requires a court, on petition of an interested person, to reform a disposition whose validity is governed by the wait-and-see element of Section 21205(b), 21206(b), or 21207(b) so that the reformed disposition is within the limits of the 90–year period allowed by those sections, in the manner deemed by the court most closely to approximate the transferor's manifested plan of distribution, in three circumstances: First, when (after the application of the statutory rule) a nonvested property interest or a power of appointment becomes invalid under the statutory rule; second, when a class gift has not but still might become invalid under the statutory rule and the time has arrived when the share of one or more class members is to take effect in possession or enjoyment; and third, when a nonvested property interest can vest, but cannot do so within the allowable 90–year period under the statutory rule.

It is anticipated that the circumstances requisite to reformation will seldom arise, and consequently that this section will be applied infrequently. If, however, one of the three circumstances arises, the court in reforming is authorized to alter existing interests or powers and to create new interests or powers by implication or construction based on the transferor's manifested plan of distribution as a whole. In reforming, the court is urged not to invalidate any vested interest retroactively (the doctrine of infectious invalidity having been superseded by this chapter, as indicated in the Background to Section 21201). The court is also urged not to reduce an age contingency in excess of 21 unless it is absolutely necessary, and if it is deemed necessary to reduce such an age contingency, not to reduce it automatically to 21 but rather to reduce it no lower than absolutely necessary. See Example (3) below; Waggoner, Perpetuity Reform, 81 Mich.L.Rev. 1718, 1755–59 (1983); Langbein & Waggoner, Reformation of Wills on the Ground of Mistake: Change of Direction in American Law?, 130 U.Pa.L.Rev. 521, 546–49 (1982).

2.   Judicial Sale of Land Affected by Future Interests

Although this section—except for cases that fall under subdivisions (b) or (c)—defers the time when a court is directed to reform a disposition until the expiration of the allowable 90–year waiting period, this section is not to be understood as preventing an earlier application of other remedies. In particular, in the case of interests in land not in trust, the principle, codified in many states, is widely recognized that there is judicial authority, under specified circumstances, to order a sale of land in which there are future interests. See 1 American Law of Property §§ 4.98–4.99 (A. Casner ed. 1952); L. Simes & A. Smith, The Law of Future Interests §§ 1941–46 (2d ed. 1956); see also Restatement of Property § 179, at 485–95 (1936); L. Simes & C. Taylor, Improvement of Conveyancing by Legislation 235–38 (1960). Nothing in Section 21220 should be taken as precluding this type of remedy, if appropriate, before the expiration of the allowable 90–year waiting period.

3. Duration of the Indestructibility of Trusts—Termination of Trusts by Beneficiaries

As noted in the Background to Section 21201, it is generally accepted that a trust cannot remain indestructible beyond the period of the rule against perpetuities. Under this chapter, the period of the rule against perpetuities applicable to a trust whose validity is governed by the wait-and-see element of Section 21205(b), 21206(b), or 21207(b) is 90 years. The result of any reformation under Section 21220 is that all nonvested property interests in the trust will vest in interest (or terminate) no later than the 90th anniversary of their creation. In the case of trusts containing a nonvested property interest or a power of appointment whose validity is governed by Section 21205(b), 21206(b), or 21207(b), courts can therefore be expected to adopt the rule that no purpose of the settlor, expressed in or implied from the governing instrument, can prevent the beneficiaries of a trust other than a charitable trust from compelling its termination after 90 years after every nonvested property interest and power of appointment in the trust was created. See Section 15414 (termination of trust after perpetuity period).

4. Subdivision (a): Invalid Property Interest or Power of Appointment

Subdivision (a) is illustrated by the following examples.

Example (1)—Multiple generation trust. G devised property in trust, directing the trustee to pay the income "to A for life, then to A's children for the life of the survivor, then to A's grandchildren for the life of the survivor, and on the death of A's last surviving grandchild, the corpus of the trust is to be divided among A's then living descendants per stirpes; if none, to" a specified charity. G was survived by his child (A) and by A's two minor children (X and Y). After G's death, another child (Z) was born to A. Subsequently, A died, survived by his children (X, Y, and Z) and by three grandchildren (M, N, and O).

There are four interests subject to the statutory rule in this example: (1) the income interest in favor of A's children, (2) the income interest in favor of A's grandchildren, (3) the remainder interest in the corpus in favor of A's descendants who survive the death of A's last surviving grandchild, and (4) the alternative remainder interest in the corpus in favor of the specified charity. The first interest is initially valid under Section 21205(a); A is the validating life for that interest. There is no validating life for the other three interests, and so their validity is governed by Section 21205(b).

If, as is likely, A and A's children all die before the 90th anniversary of G's death, the income interest in favor of A's grandchildren is valid under Section 21205(b).

If, as is also likely, some of A's grandchildren are alive on the 90th anniversary of G's death, the alternative remainder interests in the corpus of the trust then become invalid under Section 21205(b), giving rise to the prerequisite to reformation under Section 21220(a). A court would be justified in reforming G's disposition by closing the class in favor of G's descendants as of the 90th anniversary of G's death (precluding new entrants thereafter), by moving back the condition of survivorship on the class so that the remainder interest is in favor of G's descendants who survive the 90th anniversary of G's death (rather than in favor of those who survive the death of A's last surviving grandchild), and by redefining the class so that its makeup is

formed as if A's last surviving grandchild died on the 90th anniversary of G's death.

Example (2)—Sub–class case. G devised property in trust, directing the trustee to pay the income "to A for life, then in equal shares to A's children for their respective lives; on the death of each child the proportionate share of corpus of the one so dying shall go to the descendants of such child surviving at such child's death, per stirpes." G was survived by A and by A's two children (X and Y). After G's death, another child (Z) was born to A. Subsequently, A died, survived by X, Y, and Z.

Under the sub-class doctrine, each remainder interest in favor of the descendants of a child of A is treated separately from the others. Consequently, the remainder interest in favor of X's descendants and the remainder interest in favor of Y's descendants are valid under Section 21205(a): X is the validating life for the one, and Y is the validating life for the other.

The remainder interest in favor of the descendants of Z is not validated by Section 21205(a) because Z, who was not alive when the interest was created, could have descendants more than 21 years after the death of the survivor of A, X, and Y. Instead, the validity of the remainder interest in favor of Z's descendants is governed by Section 21205(b), under which its validity depends on Z's dying within 90 years after G's death.

Although unlikely, suppose that Z is still living 90 years after G's death. The remainder interest in favor of Z's descendants will then become invalid under the statutory rule, giving rise to the prerequisite to reformation under Section 21220(a). In such circumstances, a court would be justified in reforming the remainder interest in favor of Z's descendants by making it indefeasibly vested as of the 90th anniversary of G's death. To do this, the court would reform the disposition by eliminating the condition of survivorship of Z and closing the class to new entrants after the 90th anniversary of G's death.

5. Subdivision (b): Class Gifts Not Yet Invalid

Subdivision (b), which, upon the petition of an interested person, requires reformation in certain cases where a class gift has not but still might become invalid under the statutory rule, is illustrated by the following examples.

Example (3)—Age contingency in excess of 21. G devised property in trust, directing the trustee to pay the income "to A for life, then to A's children; the corpus of the trust is to be equally divided among A's children who reach the age of 30." G was survived by A, by A's spouse (H), and by A's two children (X and Y), both of whom were under the age of 30 when G died.

Since the remainder interest in favor of A's children who reach 30 is a class gift, at common law (Leake v. Robinson, 2 Mer. 363, 35 Eng.Rep. 979 (Ch. 1817)) and under this chapter (see the Background to Section 21201) the interests of all potential class members must be valid or the class gift is totally invalid. Although X and Y will either reach 30 or die under 30 within their own lifetimes, there is at G's death the possibility that A will have an afterborn child (Z) who will reach 30 or die under 30 more than 21 years after the death of the survivor of A, H, X, and Y. There is no validating life, and the class gift is therefore not validated by Section 21205(a).

Under Section 21205(b), the children's remainder interest becomes invalid only if an interest of a class member neither vests nor terminates within 90 years after G's death. If in fact there is an afterborn child (Z), and if upon A's death, Z has at least reached an age such that he cannot be alive and under the age of 30 on the 90th anniversary of G's death, the class gift is valid. (Note that at Z's birth it would have been known whether or not Z could be alive and under the age of 30 on the 90th anniversary of G's death; nevertheless, even if it was then certain that Z could not be alive and under the age of 30 on the 90th anniversary of G's death, the class gift could not then have been declared valid because, A being alive, it was then possible for one or more additional children to have later been born to or adopted by A.)

Although unlikely, suppose that at A's death (prior to the expiration of the 90–year period), Z's age was such that he could be alive and under the age of 30 on the 90th anniversary of G's death. Suppose further that at A's death X and Y were over the age of 30. Z's interest and hence the class gift as a whole is not yet invalid under the statutory rule because Z might die under the age of 30 within the remaining part of the 90–year period following G's death; but the class gift might become invalid because Z might be alive and under the age of 30, 90 years after G's death. Consequently, the prerequisites to reformation set forth in subdivision (b) are satisfied, and a court would be justified in reforming G's disposition to provide that Z's interest is contingent on reaching the age he can reach if he lives to the 90th anniversary of G's death. This would render Z's interest valid so far as the statutory rule against perpetuities is concerned, and allow the class gift as a whole to be declared valid. X and Y would thus be entitled immediately to their one-third shares each. If Z's interest later vested, Z would receive the remaining one-third share. If Z failed to reach the required age under the reformed disposition, the remaining one-third share would be divided equally between X and Y or their successors in interest.

Example (4)—Case where subdivision (b) applies, not involving an age contingency in excess of 21. G devised property in trust, directing the trustee to pay the income "to A for life, then to A's children; the corpus of the trust is to be equally divided among A's children who graduate from an accredited medical school or law school." G was survived by A, by A's spouse (H), and by A's two minor children (X and Y).

As in Example (3), the remainder interest in favor of A's children is a class gift, and the common law principle is not superseded by this chapter by which the interests of all potential class members must be valid or the class gift is totally invalid. Although X and Y will either graduate from an accredited medical or law school, or fail to do so, within their own lifetimes, there is at G's death the possibility that A will have an after-born child (Z), who will graduate from an accredited medical or law school (or die without having done either) more than 21 years after the death of the survivor of A, H, X, and Y. The class gift would not be valid under the common law rule and is, therefore, not validated by Section 21205(a).

Under Section 21205(b), the children's remainder interest becomes invalid only if an interest of a class member neither vests nor terminates within 90 years after G's death.

Suppose in fact that there is an afterborn child (Z), and that at A's death Z was a freshman in college. Suppose further that at A's death X had graduated from an accredited law school and that Y had graduated from an accredited medical school. Z's interest and hence the class gift as a whole is not yet invalid under Section 21205(b) because the 90–year period following G's death has not yet expired; but the class gift might become invalid because Z might be alive but not a graduate of an accredited medical or law school 90 years after G's death. Consequently, the prerequisites to reformation set forth in Section 21220(b) are satisfied, and a court would be justified in reforming G's disposition to provide that Z's interest is contingent on graduating from an accredited medical or law school within 90 years after G's death. This would render Z's interest valid so far as the Section 21205(b) is concerned and allow the class gift as a whole to be declared valid. X and Y would thus be entitled immediately to their one-third shares each. If Z's interest later vested, Z would receive the remaining one-third share. If Z failed to graduate from an accredited medical or law school within the allowed time under the disposition as so

reformed, the remaining one-third share would be divided equally between X and Y or their successors in interest.

6. Subdivision (c): Interests That Can Vest But Not Within the Allowable 90–Year Period

In exceedingly rare cases, an interest might be created that can vest, but not within the allowable 90–year period of the statutory rule. This may be the situation when the interest was created (see Example (5)), or it may become the situation at some time thereafter (see Example (6)). Whenever the situation occurs, the court, upon the petition of an interested person, is required by subdivision (c) to reform the disposition within the limits of the allowable 90–year period.

Example (5)—Case of an interest, as of its creation, being impossible to vest within the allowable 90–year period. G devised property in trust, directing the trustee to divide the income, per stirpes, among G's descendants from time to time living, for 100 years. At the end of the 100–year period following G's death, the trustee is to distribute the corpus and accumulated income to G's then-living descendants, per stirpes; if none, to the XYZ Charity.

The nonvested property interest in favor of G's descendants who are living 100 years after G's death can vest, but not within the allowable 90–year period of Section 21205(b). The interest would violate the common law rule, and hence is not validated by Section 21205(a), because there is no validating life. In these circumstances, a court is required by Section 21220(c) to reform G's disposition within the limits of the allowable 90–year period. An appropriate result would be for the court to lower the period following G's death from a 100–year period to a 90–year period.

Note that the circumstance that triggers the direction to reform the disposition under this subdivision is that the nonvested property interest still can vest, but cannot vest within the allowable 90–year period of Section 21205(b). It is not necessary that the interest be certain to become invalid under that subdivision. For the interest to be certain to become invalid under Section 21205(b), it would have to be certain that it can neither vest nor terminate within the allowable 90–year period. In this example, the interest of G's descendants might terminate within the allowable period (by all of G's descendants dying within 90 years of G's death). If this were to happen, the interest of XYZ Charity would be valid because it would have vested within the allowable period. However, it was thought desirable to require reformation without waiting to see if this would happen: The only way that G's descendants, who are G's primary set of beneficiaries, would have a chance to take the property is to reform the disposition within the limits of the allowable 90–year period on the ground that their interest cannot vest within the allowable period and subdivision (c) so provides.

Example (6)—Case of an interest after its creation becoming impossible to vest within the allowable 90–year period. G devised property in trust, with the income to be paid to A. The corpus of the trust was to be divided among A's children who reach 30, each child's share to be paid on the child's 30th birthday; if none reaches 30, to the XYZ Charity. G was survived by A and by A's two children (X and Y). Neither X nor Y had reached 30 at G's death.

The class gift in favor of A's children who reach 30 would violate the common law rule against perpetuities and, thus, is not validated by Section 21205(a). Its validity is therefore governed by Section 21205(b).

Suppose that after G's death, and during A's lifetime, X and Y die and a third child (Z) is born to or adopted by A. At A's death, Z is living but her age is such that she cannot reach 30 within the remaining part of the 90–year period following G's death. As of A's death, it has become the situation that Z's interest cannot vest within the allowable period. The circumstances requisite to reformation under subdivision (c) have arisen. An appropriate result would be for the court to lower the age contingency to the age Z can reach 90 years after G's death.

7. Additional References

For additional discussion and illustrations of the application of some of the principles of this section, see the comments to Restatement (Second) of Property (Donative Transfers) § 1.5 (1983). [20 Cal.L.Rev.Comm.Reports 2543 (1990)].

ARTICLE 5. EXCLUSIONS FROM STATUTORY RULE AGAINST PERPETUITIES

Section
21225. Application of Article 2.

Application

Application of Part 2, see Probate Code § 21202.

§ 21225. Application of Article 2

Article 2 (commencing with Section 21205) does not apply to any of the following:

(a) A nonvested property interest or a power of appointment arising out of a nondonative transfer, except a nonvested property interest or a power of appointment arising out of (1) a premarital or postmarital agreement, (2) a separation or divorce settlement, (3) a spouse's election, (4) or a similar arrangement arising out of a prospective, existing, or previous marital relationship between the parties, (5) a contract to make or not to revoke a will or trust, (6) a contract to exercise or not to exercise a power of appointment, (7) a transfer in satisfaction of a duty of support, or (8) a reciprocal transfer.

(b) A fiduciary's power relating to the administration or management of assets, including the power of a fiduciary to sell, lease, or mortgage property, and the power of a fiduciary to determine principal and income.

(c) A power to appoint a fiduciary.

(d) A discretionary power of a trustee to distribute principal before termination of a trust to a beneficiary having an indefeasibly vested interest in the income and principal.

(e) A nonvested property interest held by a charity, government, or governmental agency or subdivision, if the nonvested property interest is preceded by an interest held by another charity, government, or governmental agency or subdivision.

(f) A nonvested property interest in or a power of appointment with respect to a trust or other property arrangement forming part of a pension, profit-sharing, stock bonus, health, disability, death benefit, income deferral, or other current or deferred benefit plan for one or more employees, independent contractors, or their beneficiaries or spouses, to which contributions are made for the purpose of distributing to or for the benefit of the participants or their beneficiaries or spouses the property, income, or principal in the trust or other property arrangement, except a nonvested property interest or a power of appointment that is created by an election of a participant or a beneficiary or spouse.

(g) A property interest, power of appointment, or arrangement that was not subject to the common law rule against perpetuities or is excluded by another statute of this state.

(h) A trust created for the purpose of providing for its beneficiaries under hospital service contracts, group life insurance, group disability insurance, group annuities, or any combination of such insurance, as defined in the Insurance Code. *(Added by Stats.1991, c. 156 (A.B.1577), § 24. Amended by Stats.1996, c. 563 (S.B.392), § 33.)*

Law Revision Commission Comments

1991 Addition

Subdivisions (a)–(g) of Section 21225 are the same in substance as Section 4 of the Uniform Statutory Rule Against Perpetuities (1990). Subdivision (e) supersedes former Civil Code Section 715 (no perpetuities allowed except for eleemosynary purposes). For a statutory exclusion under (g), see Health and Safety Code § 8559 (cemeteries). Subdivision (h) restates former Civil Code Section 715.4 without substantive change. For other limitations on interests not subject to the statutory rule against perpetuities, see, e.g., Civil Code §§ 715 (leases to commence in future), 883.010–883.270 (mineral rights), 884.010–884.030 (unexercised options), 885.010–885.070 (powers of termination), 887.010–887.090 (abandoned easements).

Background (adapted from Prefatory Note to Uniform Statute). Section 21225 identifies the interests and powers that are excluded from the Statutory Rule Against Perpetuities. This section is in part declaratory of existing common law. All the exclusions from the common law rule recognized at common law and by statute in this state are preserved. In line with long-standing scholarly commentary, Section 21225(a) excludes nondonative transfers from the statutory rule. The rule against perpetuities is an inappropriate instrument of social policy to use as a control on such arrangements. The period of the rule—a life in being plus 21 years—is suitable for donative transfers only. [20 Cal.L.Rev.Comm.Reports 2501 (1990)].

Background (adapted from official comments to Uniform Statutory Rule Against Perpetuities)

Section 21225 lists several exclusions from the statutory rule against perpetuities (statutory rule). Some are declaratory of existing law; others are contrary to existing law. Since the common law rule against perpetuities and the Civil Code perpetuities provisions are superseded by this chapter, a nonvested property interest, power of appointment, or other arrangement excluded from the statutory rule by this section is not subject to the rule against perpetuities, statutory or otherwise.

A. Subdivision (a): Nondonative Transfers Excluded

1. Rationale

In line with long-standing scholarly commentary, subdivision (a) excludes (with certain enumerated exceptions) nonvested property interests and powers of appointment arising out of a nondonative transfer. The rationale for this exclusion is that the rule against perpetuities is a wholly inappropriate instrument of social policy to use as a control over such arrangements. The period of the rule—a life in being plus 21 years—is not suitable for nondonative transfers, and this point applies with equal force to the 90–year allowable waiting period under the wait-and-see element of Sections 21205–21207 because that period represents an approximation of the period of time that would be produced, on average, by using a statutory list identifying actual measuring lives and adding a 21–year period following the death of the survivor.

No general exclusion from the common law rule against perpetuities is recognized for nondonative transfers, and so subdivision (a) is contrary to existing common law. (But see Metropolitan Transportation Authority v. Bruken Realty Corp., 67 N.Y.2d 156, 165–66, 492 N.E.2d 379, 501 N.Y.S.2d 306 (1986), pointing out the inappropriateness of the period of a life in being plus 21 years to cases of commercial and governmental transactions and noting that the rule against perpetuities can invalidate legitimate transactions in such cases.)

Subdivision (a) is therefore inconsistent with decisions holding the common law rule to be applicable to the following types of property interests or arrangements when created in a nondonative, commercial-type transaction, as they almost always are: options (e.g., Milner v. Bivens, 255 Ga. 49, 335 S.E.2d 288 (1985)); preemptive rights in the nature of a right of first refusal (e.g., Atchison v. City of Englewood, 170 Colo. 295, 463 P.2d 297 (1969); Robroy Land Co., Inc. v. Prather, 24 Wash.App. 511, 601 P.2d 297 (1969)); leases to commence in the future, at a time certain or on the happening of a future event such as the completion of a building (e.g., Southern Airways Co. v. DeKalb County, 101 Ga.App. 689, 115 S.E.2d 207 (1960)); nonvested easements; top leases and top deeds with respect to interests in minerals (e.g., Peveto v. Starkey, 645 S.W.2d 770 (Tex.1982)); and so on.

2. Consideration Does Not Necessarily Make the Transfer Nondonative

A transfer can be supported by consideration and still be donative in character and hence not excluded from the statutory rule. A transaction that is essentially gratuitous in nature, accompanied by donative intent on the part of at least one party to the transaction, is not to be regarded as nondonative simply because it is for consideration. Thus, for example, the exclusion would not apply if a parent purchases a parcel of land for full and adequate consideration, and directs the seller to make out the deed in favor of the purchaser's daughter for life, remainder to such of the daughter's children as reach 25. The nonvested property interest of the daughter's children is subject to the statutory rule.

3. Some Transactions Not Excluded Even If Considered Nondonative

Some types of transactions—although in some sense supported by consideration and hence arguably nondonative—arise out of a domestic situation, and should not be excluded from the statutory rule. To avoid uncertainty with respect to such transactions, subdivision (a) specifies that nonvested property interests or powers of appointment arising out of any of the following transactions are not excluded by the nondonative-transfers exclusion in subdivision (a): a premarital or postmarital agreement; a separation or divorce settlement; a spouse's election, such as the "widow's election" in community property states; an arrangement similar to any of the foregoing arising out of a prospective, existing, or previous marital relationship between the parties; a contract to make or not to revoke a will or trust; a contract to exercise or not to exercise a power of appointment; a transfer in full or partial satisfaction of a duty of support; or a reciprocal transfer. The term "reciprocal transfer" is to be interpreted in accordance with the reciprocal transfer doctrine in the tax law (see United States v. Estate of Grace, 395 U.S. 316 (1969)).

4. Other Means of Controlling Some Nondonative Transfers

Some commercial transactions respecting land or mineral interests, such as options in gross (including rights of first refusal), leases to commence in the future, nonvested easements, and top leases and top deeds in commercial use in the oil and gas industry, directly or indirectly restrain the alienability of property or provide a disincentive to improve the property. Although controlling the duration of such interests is desirable, they are excluded by subdivision (a) from the statutory rule because, as noted above, the period of a life in being plus 21 years—actual or by the 90–year proxy—is inappropriate for them; that period is appropriate for family-oriented, donative transfers. Other provisions limit these types of interests. See, e.g., Civil Code §§ 715 (lease to commence in future), 883.110–883.270 (mineral rights), 884.010–884.030 (unexercised options), 887.010–887.090 (abandoned easements).

B. Subdivisions (b)–(g): Other Exclusions

1. Subdivision (b)—Administrative Fiduciary Powers

Fiduciary powers are subject to the statutory rule against perpetuities, unless specifically excluded. Purely administrative fiduciary powers are excluded by subdivisions (b) and (c), but distributive fiduciary powers are generally speaking not excluded. The only distributive fiduciary power excluded is the one described in subdivision (d).

The application of subdivision (b) to fiduciary powers can be illustrated by the following example.

Example (1). G devised property in trust, directing the trustee (a bank) to pay the income to A for life, then to A's children for the life of the survivor, and on the death of A's last surviving child to pay the corpus to B. The trustee is granted the discretionary power to sell and to reinvest the trust assets and to invade the corpus on behalf of the income beneficiary or beneficiaries.

The trustee's fiduciary power to sell and reinvest the trust assets is a purely administrative power, and under subdivision (b) of this section is not subject to the statutory rule.

The trustee's fiduciary power to invade corpus, however, is a nongeneral power of appointment that is not excluded from the statutory rule. Its validity, and hence its exercisability, is governed by Section 21207. Since the power is not initially valid under Section 21207(a), Section 21207(b) applies and the power ceases to be exercisable 90 years after G's death.

2. Subdivision (c)—Powers to Appoint a Fiduciary

Subdivision (c) excludes from the statutory rule against perpetuities powers to appoint a fiduciary (a trustee, successor trustee, or co-trustee, a personal representative, successor personal representative, or co-personal representative, an executor, successor executor, or co-executor, etc.). Sometimes such a power is held by a fiduciary and sometimes not. In either case, the power is excluded from the statutory rule.

3. Subdivision (d)—Certain Distributive Fiduciary Power

The only distributive fiduciary power excluded from the statutory rule against perpetuities is the one described in subdivision (d); the excluded power is a discretionary power of a trustee to distribute principal before the termination of a trust to a beneficiary who has an indefeasibly vested interest in the income and principal.

Example (2). G devised property in trust, directing the trustee (a bank) to pay the income to A for life, then to A's children; each child's share of principal is to be paid to the child when he or she reaches 40; if any child dies under 40, the child's share is to be paid to the child's estate as a property interest owned by such child. The trustee is given the discretionary power to advance all or a portion of a child's share before the child reaches 40. G was survived by A, who was then childless.

The trustee's discretionary power to distribute principal to a child before the child's 40th birthday is excluded from the statutory rule against perpetuities. (The trustee's duty to pay the income to A and after A's death to A's children is not subject to the statutory rule because it is a duty, not a power.)

4. Subdivision (e)—Charitable or Governmental Gifts

Subdivision (e) codifies the common law principle that a nonvested property interest held by a charity, a government, or a governmental agency or subdivision is excluded from the rule against perpetuities if the interest was preceded by an interest that is held by another charity, government, or governmental agency or subdivision. See L. Simes & A. Smith, The Law of Future Interests §§ 1278–87 (2d ed. 1956); Restatement (Second) of Property (Donative Transfers) § 1.6 (1983); Restatement of Property § 397 (1944).

Example (3). G devised real property "to the X School District so long as the premises are used for school purposes, and upon the cessation of such use, to Y City."

The nonvested property interest held by Y City (an executory interest) is excluded from the statutory rule under subdivision (e) because it was preceded by a property interest (a fee simple determinable) held by a governmental subdivision, X School District.

The exclusion of charitable and governmental gifts applies only in the circumstances described. If a nonvested property interest held by a charity is preceded by a property interest that is held by a noncharity, the exclusion does not apply; rather, the validity of the nonvested property interest held by the charity is governed by the other sections of this chapter.

Example (4). G devised real property "to A for life, then to such of A's children as reach 25, but if none of A's children reaches 25, to X Charity."

The nonvested property interest held by X Charity is not excluded from the statutory rule.

If a nonvested property interest held by a noncharity is preceded by a property interest that is held by a charity, the exclusion does not apply; rather, the validity of the nonvested property interest in favor of the noncharity is governed by the other sections of this chapter.

Example (5). G devised real property "to the City of Sidney so long as the premises are used for a public park, and upon the cessation of such use, to my brother, B."

The nonvested property interest held by B is not excluded from the statutory rule by subdivision (e).

5. Subdivision (f)—Trusts for Employees and Others; Trusts for Self–Employed Individuals

Subdivision (f) excludes from the statutory rule against perpetuities nonvested property interests and powers of appointment with respect to a trust or other property arrangement, whether part of a "qualified" or "unqualified" plan under the federal income tax law, forming part of a bona fide benefit plan for employees (including owner-employees), independent contractors, or their beneficiaries or spouses. The exclusion granted by this subdivision does not, however, extend to a nonvested property interest or a power of appointment created by an election of a participant or beneficiary or spouse.

6. Subdivision (g)—Pre-existing Exclusions from the Common Law Rule Against Perpetuities

Subdivision (g) ensures that all property interests, powers of appointment, or arrangements that were excluded from the common law rule against perpetuities or are excluded by another statute of this state are also excluded from the statutory rule against perpetuities. Possibilities of reverter and rights of entry (also known as rights of re-entry, rights of entry for condition broken, and powers of termination) are not subject to the common law rule against perpetuities, and so are excluded from the statutory rule. [20 Cal.L.Rev.Comm.Reports 2543 (1990)].

CHAPTER 2. RELATED PROVISIONS

Application

Application of Part 2, see Probate Code § 21202.

§ 21230. Validating lives

The lives of individuals selected to govern the time of vesting pursuant to Article 2 (commencing with Section 21205) of Chapter 1 may not be so numerous or so situated that evidence of their deaths is likely to be unreasonably difficult to obtain. *(Added by Stats.1991, c. 156 (A.B.1577), § 24.)*

Law Revision Commission Comments

1991 Addition

Section 21230 restates the second sentence of former Civil Code Section 715.2 without substantive change. This collateral rule applies in determining validity under Sections 21205(a), 21206(a), and 21207(a). [20 Cal.L.Rev.Comm.Reports 2501 (1990)].

§ 21231. Spouse as life in being

In determining the validity of a nonvested property interest pursuant to Article 2 (commencing with Section 21205) of Chapter 1, an individual described as the spouse of an individual alive at the commencement of the perpetuities period shall be deemed to be an individual alive when the interest is created, whether or not the individual so described was then alive. *(Added by Stats.1991, c. 156 (A.B.1577), § 24.)*

Law Revision Commission Comments

1991 Addition

Section 21231 restates former Civil Code Section 715.7 without substantive change. This rule of construction applies in determining validity under Sections 21205(a), 21206(a), and 21207(a). [20 Cal.L.Rev.Comm.Reports 2501 (1990)].

§§ 21300 to 21308. Repealed by Stats.2008, c. 174 (S.B. 1264), § 1, operative Jan. 1, 2010

Part 3

NO CONTEST CLAUSE

§ 21310. Definitions

As used in this part:

(a) "Contest" means a pleading filed with the court by a beneficiary that would result in a penalty under a no contest clause, if the no contest clause is enforced.

(b) "Direct contest" means a contest that alleges the invalidity of a protected instrument or one or more of its terms, based on one or more of the following grounds:

(1) Forgery.

(2) Lack of due execution.

(3) Lack of capacity.

(4) Menace, duress, fraud, or undue influence.

(5) Revocation of a will pursuant to Section 6120, revocation of a trust pursuant to Section 15401, or revocation of an instrument other than a will or trust pursuant to the procedure for revocation that is provided by statute or by the instrument.

(6) Disqualification of a beneficiary under Section 6112, 21350, or 21380.

(c) "No contest clause" means a provision in an otherwise valid instrument that, if enforced, would penalize a beneficiary for filing a pleading in any court.

(d) "Pleading" means a petition, complaint, cross-complaint, objection, answer, response, or claim.

(e) "Protected instrument" means all of the following instruments:

(1) The instrument that contains the no contest clause.

(2) An instrument that is in existence on the date that the instrument containing the no contest clause is executed and is expressly identified in the no contest clause, either individually or as part of an identifiable class of instruments, as being governed by the no contest clause. *(Added by Stats.2008, c. 174 (S.B.1264), § 2, operative Jan. 1, 2010. Amended by Stats.2010, c. 620 (S.B.105), § 5.)*

Law Revision Commission Comments
2008 Addition

Section 21310 is new. Subdivision (a) continues part of the substance of former Section 21300(b).

Subdivision (b)(1)–(5) continues the substance of former Section 21300(b), except that mistake and misrepresentation are no longer included as separate grounds for a direct contest.

Subdivision (b)(6) is consistent with former Sections 21306(a)(3) and 21307(c).

Subdivision (c) continues the substance of former Section 21300(d).

Subdivision (d) restates the substance of former Section 21305(f).

Subdivision (e) is new. Subdivision (e)(1) provides that a protected instrument includes an instrument that contains a no contest clause. That may include an instrument that expressly incorporates or republishes a no contest clause in another instrument. Subdivision (e)(2) is similar to former Section 21305(a)(3). [38 Cal.L.Rev. Comm. Reports apx 5 (2008)].

2010 Amendment

Section 21310 is amended to correct a reference to former Section 21350. [38 Cal.L.Rev.Comm. Reports 107 (2008)].

Cross References

Presumption of fraud or undue influence with respect to wills and trusts, enumeration of certain donative transfers subject to the presumption, see Probate Code § 21380.

§ 21311. Enforcement of clause

(a) A no contest clause shall only be enforced against the following types of contests:

(1) A direct contest that is brought without probable cause.

(2) A pleading to challenge a transfer of property on the grounds that it was not the transferor's property at the time of the transfer. A no contest clause shall only be enforced under this paragraph if the no contest clause expressly provides for that application.

(3) The filing of a creditor's claim or prosecution of an action based on it. A no contest clause shall only be enforced under this paragraph if the no contest clause expressly provides for that application.

(b) For the purposes of this section, probable cause exists if, at the time of filing a contest, the facts known to the contestant would cause a reasonable person to believe that there is a reasonable likelihood that the requested relief will be granted after an opportunity for further investigation or discovery. *(Added by Stats.2008, c. 174 (S.B.1264), § 2, operative Jan. 1, 2010.)*

Law Revision Commission Comments
2008 Addition

Section 21311 is new.

Subdivision (a)(1) generalizes the probable cause exception provided in former Sections 21306 and 21307, so that it applies to all direct contests.

For a direct contest based on Section 6112 or 21350, the probable cause exception requires only that the contestant show probable cause that a beneficiary is a witness described in Section 6112(c) or a "disqualified person" under Section 21350.5.

Subdivision (a)(2) restates the substance of former Section 21305(a)(2). It provides for enforcement of a no contest clause in response to a pleading that contests a transfer of property on the ground that the property was not subject to the transferor's dispositional control at the time of the transfer. Probable cause is not a defense to the enforcement of a no contest clause under this provision.

Subdivision (a)(3) continues former Section 21305(a)(1) without substantive change. Probable cause is not a defense to the enforcement of a no contest clause under this provision.

Subdivision (b) restates the reasonable cause exception provided in former Sections 21306, with two exceptions:

(1) The former standard referred only to the contestant's factual contentions. By contrast, subdivision (b) refers to the granting of relief, which requires not only the proof of factual contentions but also a legally sufficient ground for the requested relief.

(2) The former standard required only that success be "likely." One court interpreted that standard as requiring only that a contest be "legally tenable.'" In re Estate of Gonzalez, 102 Cal.App.4th 1296, 1304, 126 Cal.Rptr.2d 332 (2002). Subdivision (a) imposes a higher standard. There must be a "reasonable likelihood" that the requested relief will be granted. The term "reasonable likelihood" has been interpreted to mean more than merely possible, but less than "more probable than not." See Alvarez v. Superior Ct., 154 Cal.App.4th 642, 653 n.4, 64 Cal.Rptr.3d 854 (2007) (construing Penal Code § 938.1); People v. Proctor, 4 Cal.4th 499, 523, 15 Cal.Rptr.2d 340 (1992) (construing Penal Code § 1033). See Section 21310(b) ("direct contest" defined). [38 Cal.L.Rev.Comm. Reports apx 5 (2008)].

Cross References

Beneficiary defined, see Probate Code § 24.
Contest defined for purposes of this Part, see Probate Code § 21310.
Direct contest defined for purposes of this Part, see Probate Code § 21310.
No contest clause defined for purposes of this Part, see Probate Code § 21310.
Pleading defined for purposes of this Part, see Probate Code § 21310.

§ 21312. Construction of clause

In determining the intent of the transferor, a no contest clause shall be strictly construed. *(Added by Stats.2008, c. 174 (S.B.1264), § 2, operative Jan. 1, 2010.)*

Law Revision Commission Comments
2008 Addition

Section 21312 continues former Section 21304 without change. [37 Cal.L.Rev.Comm. Reports 359 (2007)].

§ 21313. Legislative intent; codification; common law

This part is not intended as a complete codification of the law governing enforcement of a no contest clause. The common law governs enforcement of a no contest clause to the extent this part does not apply. *(Added by Stats.2008, c. 174 (S.B.1264), § 2, operative Jan. 1, 2010.)*

Law Revision Commission Comments

2008 Addition

Section 21313 continues former Section 21301 without change. [37 Cal.L.Rev.Comm. Reports 359 (2007)].

§ 21314. Contrary provision in instrument; application of part

This part applies notwithstanding a contrary provision in the instrument. *(Added by Stats.2008, c. 174 (S.B.1264), § 2, operative Jan. 1, 2010.)*

Law Revision Commission Comments

2008 Addition

Section 21314 continues former Section 21302 without change. [37 Cal.L.Rev.Comm. Reports 359 (2007)].

§ 21315. Application of part to any instrument executed

(a) This part applies to any instrument, whenever executed, that became irrevocable on or after January 1, 2001.

(b) This part does not apply to an instrument that became irrevocable before January 1, 2001. *(Added by Stats.2008, c. 174 (S.B.1264), § 2, operative Jan. 1, 2010.)*

Law Revision Commission Comments

2008 Addition

Section 21315 is new. It is similar in effect to the application date provisions of former Section 21305. Section 3 may further limit the application of this chapter to an instrument that became irrevocable prior to the operative date of the chapter. See Section 3(d)–(f), (h). An instrument that is not governed by this chapter would be governed by the law that applied to the instrument prior to the operative date of this chapter. See Section 3(g). [37 Cal.L.Rev. Comm. Reports 359 (2007)].

§§ 21320 to 21322. Repealed by Stats.2008, c. 174 (S.B. 1264), § 1, operative Jan. 1, 2010

Part 3.5

LIMITATIONS ON TRANSFERS TO DRAFTERS AND OTHERS [REPEALED]

§§ 21350 to 21356. Repealed by Stats.2011, c. 296 (A.B. 1023), § 245, operative Jan. 1, 2014

Part 3.7

PRESUMPTION OF FRAUD OR UNDUE INFLUENCE

Application

For application of Part 3.7, see Probate Code § 21392.

CHAPTER 1. DEFINITIONS

Application

For application of Part 3.7, see Probate Code § 21392.

§ 21360. Application of definitions

The definitions in this chapter govern the construction of this part. *(Added by Stats.2010, c. 620 (S.B.105), § 7.)*

Law Revision Commission Comments

2010 Addition

Section 21360 is new. [38 Cal.L.Rev.Comm. Reports 107 (2008)].

§ 21362. "Care custodian" and "health and social services" defined

(a) "Care custodian" means a person who provides health or social services to a dependent adult, except that "care custodian" does not include a person who provided services without remuneration if the person had a personal relationship with the dependent adult (1) at least 90 days before providing those services, (2) at least six months before the dependent adult's death, and (3) before the dependant adult was admitted to hospice care, if the dependent adult was admitted to hospice care. As used in this subdivision, "remuneration" does not include the donative transfer at issue under this chapter or the reimbursement of expenses.

(b) For the purposes of this section, "health and social services" means services provided to a dependent adult because of the person's dependent condition, including, but not limited to, the administration of medicine, medical testing, wound care, assistance with hygiene, companionship, housekeeping, shopping, cooking, and assistance with finances. *(Added by Stats.2010, c. 620 (S.B.105), § 7.)*

Law Revision Commission Comments

2010 Addition

Section 21362 is similar to the last sentence of former Section 21350(c), with two substantive exceptions:

(1) The definition of "care custodian" does not include a person who provides health and social services without remuneration and who had a personal relationship with the dependent adult a specified period of time prior to the provision of services, the death of the dependent adult, and the admission of the dependent adult to hospice care.

(2) The definition of "care custodian" does not incorporate the list of persons from Welfare and Institutions Code Section 15610.17.

Subdivision (b) provides an illustrative list of the sorts of services that are included in the term "health and social services".

See also Section 56 ("person" defined). [40 Cal.L.Rev.Comm. Reports 45 (2010)].

Cross References

Dependent adult defined for purposes of this Part, see Probate Code § 21366.

§ 21364. "Cohabitant" defined

"Cohabitant" has the meaning provided in Section 13700 of the Penal Code. *(Added by Stats.2010, c. 620 (S.B.105), § 7.)*

Law Revision Commission Comments

2010 Addition

Section 21364 continues the second sentence of former Section 21351(a) without substantive change, except that the definition is generalized so that it applies to every use of the term "cohabitant" in this part. Under former law, the definition of "cohabitant" applied to former Section 21351, but not to former Section 21350. [38 Cal.L.Rev.Comm. Reports 107 (2008)].

§ 21366. "Dependent adult" defined

"Dependent adult" means a person who, at the time of executing the instrument at issue under this part, was a person described in either of the following:

(a) The person was 65 years of age or older and satisfied one or both of the following criteria:

(1) The person was unable to provide properly for his or her personal needs for physical health, food, clothing, or shelter.

(2) Due to one or more deficits in the mental functions listed in paragraphs (1) to (4), inclusive, of subdivision (a) of Section 811, the person had difficulty managing his or her own financial resources or resisting fraud or undue influence.

(b) The person was 18 years of age or older and satisfied one or both of the following criteria:

(1) The person was unable to provide properly for his or her personal needs for physical health, food, clothing, or shelter.

(2) Due to one or more deficits in the mental functions listed in paragraphs (1) to (4), inclusive, of subdivision (a) of Section 811, the person had substantial difficulty managing his or her own financial resources or resisting fraud or undue influence. *(Added by Stats.2010, c. 620 (S.B.105), § 7.)*

Law Revision Commission Comments

2010 Addition

Section 21366 is new.
See also Section 45 "instrument". [40 Cal.L.Rev.Comm. Reports 45 (2010)].

§ 21368. "Domestic partner" defined

"Domestic partner" has the meaning provided in Section 297 of the Family Code. *(Added by Stats.2010, c. 620 (S.B.105), § 7.)*

Law Revision Commission Comments

2010 Addition

Section 21368 continues former Section 21350(d) and part of the first sentence of former Section 21351(a), without substantive change. [38 Cal.L.Rev.Comm. Reports 107 (2008)].

§ 21370. "Independent attorney" defined

"Independent attorney" means an attorney who has no legal, business, financial, professional, or personal relationship with the beneficiary of a donative transfer at issue under this part, and who would not be appointed as a fiduciary or receive any pecuniary benefit as a result of the operation of the instrument containing the donative transfer at issue under this part. *(Added by Stats.2010, c. 620 (S.B.105), § 7.)*

Law Revision Commission Comments

2010 Addition

Section 21370 is new. The standard provided in this section is similar to California Rules of Professional Conduct 3–310(B)(1) and (3), except that there is an exclusion for an attorney who would be appointed as fiduciary or receive a pecuniary benefit by operation of the instrument to be reviewed. See also Section 21384 (independent attorney review). [40 Cal.L.Rev.Comm. Reports 45 (2010)].

§ 21374. "Related by blood or affinity" and "spouse or domestic partner" defined

(a) A person who is "related by blood or affinity" to a specified person means any of the following persons:

(1) A spouse or domestic partner of the specified person.

(2) A relative within a specified degree of kinship to the specified person or within a specified degree of kinship to the spouse or domestic partner of the specified person.

(3) The spouse or domestic partner of a person described in paragraph (2).

(b) For the purposes of this section, "spouse or domestic partner" includes a predeceased spouse or predeceased domestic partner.

(c) In determining a relationship under this section, Sections 6406 and 6407, and Chapter 2 (commencing with Section 6450) of Part 2 of Division 6, are applicable. *(Added by Stats.2010, c. 620 (S.B.105), § 7.)*

Law Revision Commission Comments

2010 Addition

Section 21374 restates the substance of former Section 21350(b) to make clear that a spouse and domestic partner are treated in the same way under this provision.

Subdivision (a)(3) applies to the spouse or domestic partner of a relative regardless of whether that relative is living or deceased.

See also Section 21368 ("domestic partner"). [38 Cal.L.Rev. Comm. Reports 107 (2008)].

Application

For application of Part 3.7, see Probate Code § 21392.

§ 21380. Presumption of fraud or undue influence for certain enumerated transfers; burden of proof; costs and attorney's fees

(a) A provision of an instrument making a donative transfer to any of the following persons is presumed to be the product of fraud or undue influence:

(1) The person who drafted the instrument.

(2) A person in a fiduciary relationship with the transferor who transcribed the instrument or caused it to be transcribed.

(3) A care custodian of a transferor who is a dependent adult, but only if the instrument was executed during the period in which the care custodian provided services to the transferor, or within 90 days before or after that period.

(4) A person who is related by blood or affinity, within the third degree, to any person described in paragraphs (1) to (3), inclusive.

(5) A cohabitant or employee of any person described in paragraphs (1) to (3), inclusive.

(6) A partner, shareholder, or employee of a law firm in which a person described in paragraph (1) or (2) has an ownership interest.

(b) The presumption created by this section is a presumption affecting the burden of proof. The presumption may be rebutted by proving, by clear and convincing evidence, that the donative transfer was not the product of fraud or undue influence.

(c) Notwithstanding subdivision (b), with respect to a donative transfer to the person who drafted the donative instrument, or to a person who is related to, or associated with, the drafter as described in paragraph (4), (5), or (6) of subdivision (a), the presumption created by this section is conclusive.

(d) If a beneficiary is unsuccessful in rebutting the presumption, the beneficiary shall bear all costs of the proceeding, including reasonable attorney's fees. *(Added by Stats. 2010, c. 620 (S.B.105), § 7.)*

Law Revision Commission Comments

2010 Addition

Subdivision (a) of Section 21380 restates the substance of former Section 21350(a), with three exceptions:

(1) Subdivision (a)(3) limits the care custodian presumption to gifts made during the period in which the care custodian provided services to the transferor, or within 90 days before or after that period.

(2) Subdivision (a)(6) generalizes the reference to a "law partnership or law corporation" in former Section 21350(a)(3), to include any law firm, regardless of how it is organized.

(3) Subdivision (a)(6) generalizes the rule creating a presumption of fraud or undue influence when a gift is made to the law firm of the drafter of a donative instrument, so that it also applies to a fiduciary of the transferor who transcribes an instrument or causes it to be transcribed.

Subdivision (b) restates the substance of the first sentence of former Section 21351(d), with two exceptions:

(1) The former limitation on proof by the testimony of the beneficiary is not continued.

(2) The presumption of menace and duress is not continued.

Subdivision (c) continues the substance of former Section 21351(e)(1), and expands the rule to apply to gifts to specified relatives and associates of the drafter of a donative instrument.

Subdivision (d) restates the substance of the second sentence of former Section 21351(d).

The burden of establishing the facts that give rise to the presumption under subdivision (a) is borne by the person who contests the validity of a donative transfer under this section. See Evid. Code § 500 (general rule on burden of proof).

See also Sections 45 ("instrument"), 21362 ("care custodian"), 21364 ("cohabitant"), 21366 ("dependent adult"), 21368 ("domestic partner"), 21372 ("interested witness"), 21374 ("related by blood or affinity"). [40 Cal.L.Rev.Comm. Reports 45 (2010)].

§ 21382. Exclusion from presumption for certain documents or transfers

Section 21380 does not apply to any of the following instruments or transfers:

(a) A donative transfer to a person who is related by blood or affinity, within the fourth degree, to the transferor or is the cohabitant of the transferor.

(b) An instrument that is drafted or transcribed by a person who is related by blood or affinity, within the fourth degree, to the transferor or is the cohabitant of the transferor.

(c) An instrument that is approved pursuant to an order under Article 10 (commencing with Section 2580) of Chapter 6 of Part 4 of Division 4, after full disclosure of the relationships of the persons involved.

(d) A donative transfer to a federal, state, or local public entity, an entity that qualifies for an exemption from taxation under Section 501(c)(3) or 501(c)(19) of the Internal Revenue Code,[1] or a trust holding the transferred property for the entity.

(e) A donative transfer of property valued at five thousand dollars ($5,000) or less, if the total value of the transferor's estate equals or exceeds the amount stated in Section 13100.

(f) An instrument executed outside of California by a transferor who was not a resident of California when the instrument was executed. *(Added by Stats.2010, c. 620 (S.B.105), § 7.)*

[1] Internal Revenue Code sections are in Title 26 of U.S.C.A.

Law Revision Commission Comments
2010 Addition

Subdivisions (a) and (b) of Section 21382 restate the substance of former Section 21351(a) and (g), with the following exceptions:

(1) The scope of the exemption is narrowed from the fifth degree of relation to the fourth.

(2) "Heirs of the transferor" are no longer included in the exemption.

(3) The former exemption of an instrument drafted by an exempt person has been generalized to include an instrument that is transcribed by an exempt person.

Subdivision (c) continues former Section 21351(c) without substantive change.

Subdivision (d) continues former Section 21351(f) without substantive change.

Subdivision (e) continues former Section 21351(h) without substantive change, except that the $3,000 amount for a small gift has been increased to $5,000.

Subdivision (f) continues former Section 21351(i) without substantive change.

See also Sections 45 ("instrument"), 21364 ("cohabitant"), 21374 ("related by blood or affinity"). [40 Cal.L.Rev.Comm. Reports 45 (2010)].

Cross References

Cohabitant defined for purposes of this Part, see Probate Code § 21364.

Related by blood or affinity defined for purposes of this Part, see Probate Code § 21374.

§ 21384. Gifts excluded from presumption; certificate of independent review

(a) A gift is not subject to Section 21380 if the instrument is reviewed by an independent attorney who counsels the transferor, out of the presence of any heir or proposed beneficiary, about the nature and consequences of the intended transfer, including the effect of the intended transfer on the transferor's heirs and on any beneficiary of a prior donative instrument, attempts to determine if the intended transfer is the result of fraud or undue influence, and signs and delivers to the transferor an original certificate in substantially the following form:

"CERTIFICATE OF INDEPENDENT REVIEW

I, _____, have reviewed
　　　　　(attorney's name)
_____and have counseled the transferor,
　(name of instrument)
_____, on the nature and consequences of any
　(name of transferor)
transfers of property to _____
　　　　　　　　　　　　　　　(name of person described in
　　　　　　　　　　　　　　　Section 21380 of the Probate Code)
that would be made by the instrument.

I am an "independent attorney" as defined in Section 21370 of the Probate Code and am in a position to advise the transferor independently, impartially, and confidentially as to the consequences of the transfer.

On the basis of this counsel, I conclude that the transfers to _____that would
(name of person described in Section 21380 of the
　　　　　　　　Probate Code)
be made by the instrument are not the product of fraud or undue influence.

_____   _____ "
　(Name of Attorney)   (Date)

(b) An attorney whose written engagement, signed by the transferor, is expressly limited solely to compliance with the requirements of this section, shall not be considered to otherwise represent the transferor as a client.

(c) An attorney who drafts an instrument can review and certify the same instrument pursuant to this section, but only as to a gift to a care custodian. In all other circumstances, an attorney who drafts an instrument may not review and certify the instrument.

(d) If the certificate is prepared by an attorney other than the attorney who drafted the instrument that is under review, a copy of the signed certification shall be provided to the drafting attorney. *(Added by Stats.2010, c. 620 (S.B.105), § 7.)*

Law Revision Commission Comments
2010 Addition

Section 21384 restates the substance of former Section 21351(b), with the following exceptions:

(1) The counseling must be conducted out of the presence of any heir or proposed beneficiary.

(2) The counseling must address the effect of the intended transfer on the transferor's heirs and other beneficiaries.

(3) A drafting attorney may conduct the review and certification of a gift to a care custodian.

See also Sections 45 ("instrument"), 21362 ("care custodian"), 21370 ("independent attorney"). [40 Cal.L.Rev.Comm. Reports 45 (2010)].

Cross References

Care custodian defined for purposes of this Part, see Probate Code § 21362.

§ 21386. Presumption for gifts that failed under this part

If a gift fails under this part, the instrument making the gift shall operate as if the beneficiary had predeceased the transferor without spouse, domestic partner, or issue. *(Added by Stats.2010, c. 620 (S.B.105), § 7.)*

Law Revision Commission Comments

2010 Addition

Section 21386 restates the substance of former Section 21353. Language purporting to guarantee the beneficiary of a failed gift an amount equal to the intestate share of that beneficiary, had the transferor died intestate, is not continued. That language had no substantive effect. Under former Section 21351(a) & (g), a gift to an "heir" of the transferor was exempt from the presumption of invalidity established in former Section 21350. Thus, the beneficiary of a gift that failed under former Section 21350 could only be a non-heir. A non-heir, by definition, is not entitled to an intestate share of the transferor's estate. See Section 44 ("heir" defined).

See also Sections 45 ("instrument"), 21368 ("domestic partner"). [38 Cal.L.Rev.Comm. Reports 107 (2008)].

Cross References

Domestic partner defined for purposes of this Part, see Probate Code § 21368.

§ 21388. Personal liability for certain property transfers

(a) A person is not liable for transferring property pursuant to an instrument that is subject to the presumption created under this part, unless the person is served with notice, prior to transferring the property, that the instrument has been contested under this part.

(b) A person who is served with notice that an instrument has been contested under this part is not liable for failing to transfer property pursuant to the instrument, unless the person is served with notice that the validity of the transfer has been conclusively determined by a court. *(Added by Stats.2010, c. 620 (S.B.105), § 7.)*

Law Revision Commission Comments

2010 Addition

Section 21388 restates the substance of former Section 21352, except that the provisions are now conditioned on service of notice that a contest has been filed or that the validity of a contested transfer has been conclusively determined by a court.

See also Section 45 ("instrument"). [38 Cal.L.Rev.Comm. Reports 107 (2008)].

§ 21390. Contrary provision in instrument; application of part

This part applies notwithstanding a contrary provision in an instrument. *(Added by Stats.2010, c. 620 (S.B.105), § 7.)*

Law Revision Commission Comments

2010 Addition

Section 21390 continues former Section 21354 without substantive change.

See also Section 45 "instrument". [38 Cal.L.Rev.Comm. Reports 107 (2008)].

§ 21392. Application of part; application of common law

(a) This part shall apply to instruments that become irrevocable on or after January 1, 2011. For the purposes of this section, an instrument that is otherwise revocable or amendable shall be deemed to be irrevocable if, on or after January 1, 2011, the transferor by reason of incapacity was unable to change the disposition of the transferor's property and did not regain capacity before the date of the transferor's death.

(b) It is the intent of the Legislature that this part supplement the common law on undue influence, without superseding or interfering in the operation of that law. Nothing in this part precludes an action to contest a donative transfer under the common law or under any other applicable law. This subdivision is declarative of existing law. *(Added by Stats.2010, c. 620 (S.B.105), § 7.)*

Law Revision Commission Comments

2010 Addition

Subdivision (a) of Section 21392 limits the application of this part to instruments that become irrevocable on or after January 1, 2011. Instruments that became irrevocable before that date are governed by the former law. See Sections 3(g), 21355.

Subdivision (b) is new. It makes clear that this part supplements and does not supersede the common law governing menace, duress, fraud, and undue influence. See Bernard v. Foley, 39 Cal.4th 794, 800, 139 P.3d 1196, 47 Cal.Rptr.3d 248 (2006); Rice v. Clark, 28 Cal.4th 89, 97, 47 P.3d 300, 120 Cal.Rptr.2d 522 (2002).

See also Section 45 ("instrument"). [40 Cal.L.Rev.Comm. Reports 45 (2010)].

Part 4

ABATEMENT

Application

Part 4 not applicable to gifts made before July 1, 1989, see Probate Code § 21406.

Law Revision Commission Comments

1990 Enactment

The provisions of this part apply to trusts and other instruments as well as to wills. See Section 21101.

This part supersedes Part 4 (commencing with Section 21400) of Division 11 of the repealed Probate Code. The superseded part was enacted upon recommendation of the California Law Revision Commission. See Recommendation Relating to Abatement, 19 Cal.L.Revision Comm'n Reports 865 (1988). See also Communication from the California Law Revision Commission Concerning Assembly Bill 2841, 19 Cal.L.Revision Comm'n Reports 1201, 1249 (1988). [20 Cal.L.Rev.Comm.Reports 1001 (1990)].

§ 21400. Effectuation of instrument, transferor's plan, or purpose of transfer

Notwithstanding any other provision of this part, if the instrument provides for abatement, or if the transferor's plan or if the purpose of the transfer would be defeated by abatement as provided in this part, the shares of beneficiaries abate as is necessary to effectuate the instrument, plan, or purpose. *(Stats.1990, c. 79 (A.B.759), § 14, operative July 1, 1991.)*

Law Revision Commission Comments

1990 Enactment

Section 21400 continues Section 21400 of the repealed Probate Code without change. This section is drawn from subsection (b) of Section 3–902 of the Uniform Probate Code (1987). As to the construction of provisions drawn from uniform acts, see Section 2. See also Section 21101 (division applicable to wills, trusts, and other instruments). Section 21400 does not apply to a gift made before July 1, 1989. See Section 21406. As to the application of any amendments made after that date, see Section 3.

Background on Section 21400 of Repealed Code

Section 21400 was added by 1988 Cal.Stat. ch. 1199 § 108. The section generalized a number of provisions in then existing statutes. See former Prob.Code §§ 736 (repealed by 1988 Cal.Stat. ch. 1199 § 53), 750–752 (repealed by 1988 Cal.Stat. ch. 1199 § 53.5). The section was consistent with prior case law. See Estate of Jenanyan, 31 Cal.3d 703, 646 P.2d 196, 183 Cal.Rptr. 525 (1982). For background on the provisions of this part, see the Comment to this part under the part heading. [20 Cal.L.Rev.Comm.Reports 1001 (1990)].

Cross References

Advancements and ademptions, see Probate Code §§ 6409, 21135.
Beneficiary, defined, see Probate Code § 24.
Construction of wills,
   Generally, see Probate Code § 21102 et seq.
   Failed transfers, see Probate Code § 21111.
   Intention of testator, see Probate Code § 21102.
   Meaning of language used in will, see Probate Code § 21120 et seq.
Gifts in view of death, treatment as legacies, see Probate Code § 5705.
Instrument, defined, see Probate Code § 45.
Intention of testator not otherwise indicated by will, see Probate Code § 12000.
Interested persons as competent witnesses to will, see Probate Code § 6112.
Intestacy avoided, see Probate Code § 21120.
Legacies, distinctions and designations, see Probate Code § 21402.
Sales under direction of will, see Probate Code § 10000.
Transfer of property by will, see Probate Code § 21105.
Transferor, defined, see Probate Code § 81.

§ 21401. Purpose for abatement; priority between real and personal property

Except as provided in Sections 21612 (omitted spouse) and 21623 (omitted children) and in Division 10 (commencing with Section 20100) (proration of taxes), shares of beneficiaries abate as provided in this part for all purposes, including payment of the debts, expenses, and charges specified in Section 11420, satisfaction of gifts, and payment of expenses on specifically devised property pursuant to Section 12002, and without any priority as between real and personal property. *(Stats.1990, c. 79 (A.B.759), § 14, operative July 1, 1991. Amended by Stats.2003, c. 32 (A.B.167), § 15.)*

Law Revision Commission Comments

1990 Enactment

Section 21401 continues Section 21401 of the repealed Probate Code without change. See also Section 3–902 of the Uniform Probate Code (1987). As to the construction of provisions drawn from uniform acts, see Section 2. This section is subject to Section 21400 (abatement subject to transferor's intent). See also Section 21101 (division applicable to wills, trusts, and other instruments). Section 21401 does not apply to a gift made before July 1, 1989. See Section 21406. As to the application of any amendments made after that date, see Section 3.

2003 Amendment

Section 21401 is amended to reflect relocation of former Section 6562 to Section 21612 (via former Section 26112) (share of omitted spouse) and of former Section 6573 to Section 21623 (share of omitted child). See 1997 Cal. Stat. ch. 724, §§ 17, 34. [33 Cal.L.Rev. Comm. Reports 165 (2003)].

Background on Section 21401 of Repealed Code

Section 21401 was added by 1988 Cal.Stat. ch. 1199 § 108. The section superseded a portion of the first sentence of former Probate Code Section 750 and a portion of the introductory clause of former Probate Code Section 751 (provisions repealed by 1988 Cal.Stat. ch. 1199 § 53.5). The provision that there is no priority as between real and personal property restated a provision formerly found in the California statutes. See former Probate Code Section 754 (first sentence) (repealed by 1988 Cal.Stat. ch. 1199 § 53.5). The provision was consistent with prior case law. See, e.g., In re Estate of Woodworth, 31 Cal. 595, 614 (1867). For background on the provisions of this part, see the Comment to this part under the part heading. [20 Cal.L.Rev.Comm.Reports 1001 (1990)].

Cross References

Advancements and ademptions, see Probate Code §§ 6409, 21135.
Beneficiary, defined, see Probate Code § 24.
Borrowing money and mortgaging property, see Probate Code §§ 9800, 9804.
Claims against estate,
   Acquisition by representatives, see Probate Code § 9880 et seq.
   Application to payment of debts of specific devise of debt, see Probate Code § 8851.
   Presentation and payment, see Probate Code § 9100 et seq.
   Special relations of debtor and creditor, see Civil Code § 3429 et seq.
Community property, see Probate Code § 13500 et seq.
Debt payment,
   Generally, see Probate Code § 11400 et seq.
   Allocation between estate and surviving spouse, see Probate Code § 11440 et seq.
   Classes of debts, see Probate Code § 11420.
   Definition of debt, see Probate Code § 11401
Decedent's property as subject to debts, expenses and allowances, see Probate Code §§ 7000, 7001.
Devise, defined, see Probate Code § 32.
Distribution and payment of legacies, see Probate Code § 11600 et seq.
Family allowance,
   Generally, see Probate Code § 6540 et seq.
   Defined, see Probate Code § 38.
   Persons entitled, see Probate Code § 6540.
Federal estate tax, see Probate Code § 20110 et seq.
Intestacy avoided, see Probate Code § 21120.
Orders,
   Generally, see Probate Code § 11422.
   Priorities, see Probate Code § 11420.
Proration of taxes,
   Generally, see Probate Code § 20100 et seq.
   Estate taxes, see Probate Code § 20100 et seq.
   Taxes on generation-skipping transfer, see Probate Code § 20200 et seq.
Real property, defined, see Probate Code § 68.

Sale of encumbered property,
     Application of purchase money, see Probate Code § 10361.
     Discharge upon payment, see Probate Code § 10362.
     Purchase by lienholder, see Probate Code § 10363.
Specific devise, expenses, see Probate Code § 12002.
Transfer of property by will, see Probate Code § 21105.

§ 21402. Order of abatement

(a) Shares of beneficiaries abate in the following order:

(1) Property not disposed of by the instrument.

(2) Residuary gifts.

(3) General gifts to persons other than the transferor's relatives.

(4) General gifts to the transferor's relatives.

(5) Specific gifts to persons other than the transferor's relatives.

(6) Specific gifts to the transferor's relatives.

(b) For purposes of this section, a "relative" of the transferor is a person to whom property would pass from the transferor under Section 6401 or 6402 (intestate succession) if the transferor died intestate and there were no other person having priority. *(Stats.1990, c. 79 (A.B.759), § 14, operative July 1, 1991.)*

Law Revision Commission Comments

1990 Enactment

Section 21402 continues Section 21402 of the repealed Probate Code without change. Under subdivision (b), "relatives" includes the transferor's blood relatives other than those who may not take from the transferor by intestate succession because of an adoption. See Section 6408 (adoption). "Relatives" also includes a spouse, as well as other persons who are not blood relatives but who are considered to be children or parents of the transferor for purposes of Sections 6401 and 6402 by virtue of provisions such as Section 6408 (adoptive, foster parent, and stepparent relationships). This section is subject to Section 21400 (abatement subject to transferor's intent). See also Section 21101 (division applicable to wills, trusts, and other instruments). Section 21402 does not apply to a gift made before July 1, 1989. See Section 21406. As to the application of any amendments made after that date, see Section 3.

Background on Section 21402 of Repealed Code

Section 21402 was added by 1988 Cal.Stat. ch. 1199 § 108. Paragraphs (1) and (2) of subdivision (a) of Section 21402 restated the first portion of the second sentence of former Probate Code Section 750 and all of former Probate Code Section 751 (provisions repealed by 1988 Cal.Stat. ch. 1199 § 53.5), and generalized those provisions to apply to other gifts as well as devises. The preference in subdivision (a) of Section 21402 for specific gifts in paragraphs (5) and (6) over general gifts in paragraphs (3) and (4) continued the rule of Estate of Jenanyan, 31 Cal.3d 703, 711–12, 646 P.2d 196, 183 Cal.Rptr. 525 (1982). The preference in subdivision (a) of Section 21402 for relatives in paragraphs (4) and (6) over nonrelatives in paragraphs (3) and (5) continued the last portion of former Probate Code Section 752 (repealed by 1988 Cal.Stat. ch. 1199 § 53.5). See also Estate of Buck, 32 Cal.2d 372, 376, 196 P.2d 769 (1948); Estate of De Santi, 53 Cal.App.2d 716, 719–21, 128 P.2d 434 (1942). For background on the provisions of this part, see the Comment to this part under the part heading. [20 Cal.L.Rev.Comm.Reports 1001 (1990)].

Cross References

Adoption, parent and child relationship, see Probate Code § 6451.

Advancements and ademptions, see Probate Code §§ 21135, 6409.
Beneficiary, defined, see Probate Code § 24.
Foster parent and child relationships, see Probate Code § 6454.
Gifts in view of death, treatment as legacies, see Probate Code § 5705.
Half blood relatives, share of estate, see Probate Code § 6406.
Instrument, defined, see Probate Code § 45.
Intestate estate, share of surviving spouse, see Probate Code §§ 6401, 6402.
Parent and child relationship, establishment, see Probate Code § 6450 et seq.
Property, defined, see Probate Code § 62.
Stepparent and child relationships, see Probate Code § 6454.
Transfer of property by will, see Probate Code § 21105.
Transferor, defined, see Probate Code § 81.

§ 21403. Pro rata abatement; annuities and demonstrative gifts as specific or general gifts

(a) Subject to subdivision (b), shares of beneficiaries abate pro rata within each class specified in Section 21402.

(b) Gifts of annuities and demonstrative gifts are treated as specific gifts to the extent they are satisfied out of the fund or property specified in the gift and as general gifts to the extent they are satisfied out of property other than the fund or property specified in the gift. *(Stats.1990, c. 79 (A.B.759), § 14, operative July 1, 1991.)*

Law Revision Commission Comments

1990 Enactment

Section 21403 continues Section 21403 of the repealed Probate Code without change. This section is subject to Section 21400 (abatement subject to transferor's intent). See also Section 21101 (division applicable to wills, trusts, and other instruments). Section 21403 does not apply to a gift made before July 1, 1989. See Section 21406. As to the application of any amendments made after that date, see Section 3.

Background on Section 21403 of Repealed Code

Section 21403 was added by 1988 Cal.Stat. ch. 1199 § 108. Subdivision (a) of Section 21403 restated a portion of the second sentence of former Probate Code Section 750 and a portion of former Probate Code Section 752 (provisions repealed by 1988 Cal.Stat. ch. 1199 § 53.5), superseded the first portion of former Probate Code Section 753 (repealed by 1988 Cal.Stat. ch. 1199 § 53.5) (if preferred devise sold, all devisees must contribute), and generalized those provisions to apply to other gifts as well as devises. Subdivision (b) of Section 21403 superseded the last portion of subdivision (c) of former Probate Code Section 662 (repealed by 1988 Cal.Stat. ch. 1199 § 52), and generalized it to apply to other gifts as well as devises. For background on the provisions of this part, see the Comment to this part under the part heading. [20 Cal.L.Rev.Comm.Reports 1001 (1990)].

Cross References

Beneficiary, defined, see Probate Code § 24.

§ 21404. Specific gift to be exonerated from lien; abatement of other specific gift

If an instrument requires property that is the subject of a specific gift to be exonerated from a mortgage, deed of trust, or other lien, a specific gift of other property does not abate for the purpose of exonerating the encumbered property. *(Stats.1990, c. 79 (A.B.759), § 14, operative July 1, 1991.)*

Law Revision Commission Comments

1990 Enactment

Section 21404 continues Section 21404 of the repealed Probate Code without change. This section is subject to Section 21400 (abatement subject to transferor's intent). See also Section 21101 (division applicable to wills, trusts, and other instruments). Section 21404 does not apply to a gift made before July 1, 1989. See Section 21406. As to the application of any amendments made after that date, see Section 3.

Background on Section 21404 of Repealed Code

Section 21404 was added by 1988 Cal.Stat. ch. 1199 § 108. The section restated former Probate Code Section 736 (repealed by 1988 Cal.Stat. ch. 1199 § 53) and generalized it to apply to exoneration of personal as well as real property and to apply to other gifts as well as devises. For background on the provisions of this part, see the Comment to this part under the part heading. [20 Cal.L.Rev.Comm.Reports 1001 (1990)].

Cross References

Instrument, defined, see Probate Code § 45.

§ 21405. Distributee's contribution for abatement

(a) In any case in which there is abatement when a distribution is made during estate administration, the court shall fix the amount each distributee must contribute for abatement. The personal representative shall reduce the distributee's share by that amount.

(b) If a specific gift must be abated, the beneficiary of the specific gift may satisfy the contribution for abatement out of the beneficiary's property other than the property that is the subject of the specific gift. *(Stats.1990, c. 79 (A.B.759), § 14, operative July 1, 1991.)*

Law Revision Commission Comments

1990 Enactment

Section 21405 continues Section 21405 of the repealed Probate Code without change. Contribution may be required for abatement for any purpose, including sale of property for payment of debts or expenses or family allowance. See Section 21401 (purposes for which abatement made). See also Section 21101 (division applicable to wills, trusts, and other instruments). Section 21405 does not apply to a gift made before July 1, 1989. See Section 21406. As to the application of any amendments made after that date, see Section 3.

Background on Section 21405 of Repealed Code

Section 21405 was added by 1988 Cal.Stat. ch. 1199 § 108. Subdivision (a) of Section 21405 restated the last portion of former Probate Code Section 753 (repealed by 1988 Cal.Stat. ch. 1199 § 53.5) without substantive change. Subdivision (b) was new. For background on the provisions of this part, see the Comment to this part under the part heading. [20 Cal.L.Rev.Comm.Reports 1001 (1990)].

Cross References

Administration of estates, generally, see Probate Code § 7000 et seq.
Beneficiary, defined, see Probate Code § 24.
Distribution of estate, generally, see Probate Code § 11600 et seq.
Personal representative, defined, see Probate Code § 58.
Property, defined, see Probate Code § 62.

§ 21406. Application of part

(a) This part does not apply to a gift made before July 1, 1989. In the case of a gift made before July 1, 1989, the law

that would have applied had this part not been enacted shall apply.

(b) For purposes of this section a gift by will is made on the date of the decedent's death. *(Stats.1990, c. 79 (A.B.759), § 14, operative July 1, 1991.)*

Law Revision Commission Comments

1990 Enactment

Section 21406 continues Section 21406 of the repealed Probate Code without substantive change. See also Section 21101 (division applicable to wills, trusts, and other instruments).

Background on Section 21406 of Repealed Code

Section 21406 was a new provision added by 1988 Cal.Stat. ch. 1199 § 108. For background on the provisions of this part, see the Comment to this part under the part heading. [20 Cal.L.Rev.Comm.Reports 1001 (1990)].

Part 5

COMPLIANCE WITH INTERNAL REVENUE CODE

Application

Part 5 is applicable to distributions made on or after Jan. 1, 1988. For provisions applicable to distributions made on or after Jan. 1, 1983, and before Jan. 1, 1988, see Probate Code § 21501.

Law Revision Commission Comments

1990 Enactment

This part supersedes Part 5 (commencing with Section 21500) of Division 11 of the repealed Probate Code. The superseded part was enacted upon recommendation of the California Law Revision Commission. See Recommendation Relating to Marital Deduction Gifts, 19 Cal.L.Revision Comm'n Reports 615, 625–32 (1988). [20 Cal.L.Rev.Comm.Reports 1001 (1990)].

CHAPTER 1. GENERAL PROVISIONS

Application

Part 5 is applicable to distributions made on or after Jan. 1, 1988. For provisions applicable to distributions made on or after Jan. 1, 1983, and before Jan. 1, 1988, see Probate Code § 21501.

§ 21500. "Internal Revenue Code" defined

As used in this part, "Internal Revenue Code" means the Internal Revenue Code of 1986, as amended from time to time. A reference to a provision of the Internal Revenue

Code includes any subsequent provision of law enacted in its place. *(Stats.1990, c. 79 (A.B.759), § 14, operative July 1, 1991.)*

Law Revision Commission Comments

1990 Enactment

Section 21500 continues Section 21500 of the repealed Probate Code without change. See also Section 7 (amendments and additions).

Background on Section 21500 of Repealed Code

Section 21500 was added by 1987 Cal.Stat. ch. 923 § 101. Section 21500 restated subdivision (g) of former Section 1030 (repealed by 1987 Cal.Stat. ch. 923 § 54.5) without substantive change. [20 Cal.L.Rev.Comm.Reports 1001 (1990)].

§ 21501.   Application of law to distributions

(a) This part applies to a distribution made on or after January 1, 1988, whether the transferor died before, on, or after that date.

(b) A distribution made on or after January 1, 1983, and before January 1, 1988, is governed by the applicable law in effect before January 1, 1988. *(Stats.1990, c. 79 (A.B.759), § 14, operative July 1, 1991.)*

Law Revision Commission Comments

1990 Enactment

Section 21501 continues Section 21501 of the repealed Probate Code without change.

Background on Section 21501 of Repealed Code

Section 21501 was added by 1987 Cal.Stat. ch. 923 § 101. Subdivision (a) was new. Subdivision (b) preserved the effect of the first sentence of subdivision (a) of former Section 1031 (repealed by 1987 Cal.Stat. ch. 923 § 54.5). [20 Cal.L.Rev.Comm.Reports 1001 (1990)].

§ 21502.   Instruments making part inapplicable; incorporation by reference of part provisions

(a) This part does not apply to an instrument the terms of which expressly or by necessary implication make this part inapplicable.

(b) By an appropriate statement made in an instrument, the transferor may incorporate by reference any or all of the provisions of this part. The effect of incorporating a provision of this part in an instrument is to make the incorporated provision a part of the instrument as though the language of the incorporated provision were set forth verbatim in the instrument. Unless an instrument incorporating a provision of this part provides otherwise, the instrument automatically incorporates the provision's amendments. *(Stats.1990, c. 79 (A.B.759), § 14, operative July 1, 1991.)*

Law Revision Commission Comments

1990 Enactment

Section 21502 continues Section 21502 of the repealed Probate Code without change. This part applies to trusts as well as wills. See Section 21101 (division applicable to wills, trusts, and other instruments). Cf. former Section 15005 (repealed by 1987 Cal.Stat. ch. 923 § 99) (law applicable to marital deduction gifts in trust).

Background on Section 21502 of Repealed Code

Section 21502 was added by 1987 Cal.Stat. ch. 923 § 101. Subdivision (a) restated the second sentence of subdivision (a) of former Section 1031 (repealed by 1987 Cal.Stat. ch. 923 § 54.5) without substantive change. Subdivision (b) restated subdivision (b) of former Section 1031 without substantive change. [20 Cal.L.Rev.Comm.Reports 1001 (1990)].

Cross References

Instrument, defined, see Probate Code § 45.
Transferor, defined, see Probate Code § 81.

§ 21503.   Formulas to eliminate or reduce federal estate tax; maximum fraction or amount

(a) If an instrument includes a formula intended to eliminate the federal estate tax, the formula shall be applied to eliminate or to reduce to the maximum extent possible the federal estate tax.

(b) If an instrument includes a formula that refers to a maximum fraction or amount that will not result in a federal estate tax, the formula shall be construed to refer to the maximum fraction or amount that will not result in or increase the federal estate tax. *(Stats.1990, c. 79 (A.B.759), § 14, operative July 1, 1991.)*

Law Revision Commission Comments

1990 Enactment

Section 21503 continues Section 21503 of the repealed Probate Code without change. This section establishes rules of construction that apply formula clauses to the maximum extent possible, consistent with their intent. One effect of these rules is that a formula clause applies to the tax imposed by chapter 11 (commencing with Section 2001) of Subtitle B of the Internal Revenue Code and not to the tax imposed by Section 4980A of the Internal Revenue Code, which the formula clause cannot affect.

Background on Section 21503 of Repealed Code

Section 21503 was a new provision added by 1987 Cal.Stat. ch. 923 § 101. [20 Cal.L.Rev.Comm.Reports 1001 (1990)].

Cross References

Instrument, defined, see Probate Code § 45.

CHAPTER 2.   MARITAL DEDUCTION GIFTS

Application

Part 5 is applicable to distributions made on or after Jan. 1, 1988. For provisions applicable to distributions made on or after Jan. 1, 1983, and before Jan. 1, 1988, see Probate Code § 21501.

§ 21520. Definitions

As used in this chapter:

(a) "Marital deduction" means the federal estate tax deduction allowed for transfers under Section 2056 of the Internal Revenue Code or the federal gift tax deduction allowed for transfers under Section 2523 of the Internal Revenue Code.

(b) "Marital deduction gift" means a transfer of property that is intended to qualify for the marital deduction. *(Stats. 1990, c. 79 (A.B.759), § 14, operative July 1, 1991.)*

Law Revision Commission Comments

1990 Enactment

Section 21520 continues Section 21520 of the repealed Probate Code without change. Whether an instrument contains a marital deduction gift depends upon the intention of the transferor at the time the instrument is executed.

Background on Section 21520 of Repealed Code

Section 21520 was added by 1987 Cal.Stat. ch. 923 § 101 and was amended by 1988 Cal.Stat. ch. 113 § 20. The section restated subdivisions (b) and (d) of former Section 1030 (repealed by 1987 Cal.Stat. ch. 923 § 54.5), and expanded them to apply to the gift tax as well as the estate tax. The 1988 amendment restored a missing word in subdivision (a). [20 Cal.L.Rev.Comm.Reports 1001 (1990)].

Cross References

Internal Revenue Code defined for purposes of this Part, see Probate Code § 21500.

§ 21521. Sections 21524 and 21526 not to apply to estate trusts

Sections 21524 and 21526 do not apply to a trust that qualifies for the marital deduction under Section 20.2056(e)-2(b) of the Code of Federal Regulations (commonly referred to as the "estate trust"). *(Stats.1990, c. 79 (A.B.759), § 14, operative July 1, 1991.)*

Law Revision Commission Comments

1990 Enactment

Section 21521 continues Section 21521 of the repealed Probate Code without change.

Background on Section 21521 of Repealed Code

Section 21521 was added by 1987 Cal.Stat. ch. 923 § 101 and was amended by 1988 Cal.Stat. ch. 113 § 21. The section restated the fourth sentence of subdivision (a) of former Section 1032 (repealed by 1987 Cal.Stat. ch. 923 § 54.5) without substantive change and was amended in 1988 to make its application more precise. [20 Cal.L.Rev.Comm.Reports 1001 (1990)].

Cross References

Marital deduction defined for purposes of this Chapter, see Probate Code § 21520.

§ 21522. Instruments containing marital deduction gifts; construction; acts of fiduciary

If an instrument contains a marital deduction gift:

(a) The provisions of the instrument, including any power, duty, or discretionary authority given to a fiduciary, shall be construed to comply with the marital deduction provisions of the Internal Revenue Code.

(b) The fiduciary shall not take any action or have any power that impairs the deduction as applied to the marital deduction gift.

(c) The marital deduction gift may be satisfied only with property that qualifies for the marital deduction. *(Stats.1990, c. 79 (A.B.759), § 14, operative July 1, 1991.)*

Law Revision Commission Comments

1990 Enactment

Section 21522 continues Section 21522 of the repealed Probate Code without change.

Background on Section 21522 of Repealed Code

Section 21522 was added by 1987 Cal.Stat. ch. 923 § 101. Subdivisions (a) and (b) of Section 21522 restated the first three sentences of subdivision (a) of former Section 1032 (repealed by 1987 Cal.Stat. ch. 923 § 54.5) without substantive change. See Sections 21500 ("Internal Revenue Code" defined) and 21520 ("marital deduction gift" defined). Subdivision (c) restated subdivision (b) of former Section 1033 (repealed by 1987 Cal.Stat. ch. 923 § 54.5) without substantive change. [20 Cal.L.Rev.Comm.Reports 1001 (1990)].

Cross References

Fiduciary, defined, see Probate Code § 39.
Instrument, defined, see Probate Code § 45.
Internal Revenue Code, defined, see Probate Code § 21500.
Marital deduction defined for purposes of this Chapter, see Probate Code § 21520.
Marital deduction gift, defined, see Probate Code § 21520.

§ 21523. Economic Recovery Act of 1981; instruments intending to maximize allowable marital deduction

(a) The Economic Recovery Tax Act of 1981 was enacted August 13, 1981. This section applies to an instrument executed before September 12, 1981 (before 30 days after enactment of the Economic Recovery Tax Act of 1981).

(b) If an instrument described in subdivision (a) indicates the transferor's intention to make a gift that will provide the maximum allowable marital deduction, the instrument passes to the recipient an amount equal to the maximum amount of the marital deduction that would have been allowed as of the date of the gift under federal law as it existed before enactment of the Economic Recovery Tax Act of 1981, with adjustments for the following, if applicable:

(1) The provisions of Section 2056(c)(1)(B) and (C) of the Internal Revenue Code in effect immediately before enactment of the Economic Recovery Tax Act of 1981.

(2) To reduce the amount passing under the gift by the final federal estate tax values of any other property that passes under or outside of the instrument and qualifies for the marital deduction. This subdivision does not apply to qualified terminable interest property under Section 2056(b)(7) of the Internal Revenue Code. *(Stats.1990, c. 79 (A.B.759), § 14, operative July 1, 1991.)*

Law Revision Commission Comments

1990 Enactment

Section 21523 continues Section 21523 of the repealed Probate Code without substantive change. Subdivision (b) makes it possible to make a "QTIP" trust election in a pre-September 13, 1981, instrument under Internal Revenue Code Section 2056(b)(7) without thereby reducing the formula marital deduction gift on a dollar-for-dollar basis.

Background on Section 21523 of Repealed Code

Section 21523 was added by 1987 Cal.Stat. ch. 923 § 1001. The section restated subdivision (c) of former Section 1030 and subdivisions (a) and (c) of former Section 1034 (provisions repealed by 1987 Cal.Stat. ch. 923 § 54.5) with the addition of a provision in subdivision (b) of Section 21523 to make it possible to make a "QTIP" trust election in a pre-September 13, 1981, instrument under Internal Revenue Code Section 2056(b)(7) without thereby reducing the formula marital deduction gift on a dollar-for-dollar basis. Subdivision (b) of former Section 1034 was omitted in conformity with the change in the generation-skipping transfer tax made by the Tax Reform Act of 1986, Pub.L. No. 99–514. [20 Cal.L.Rev.Comm.Reports 1001 (1990)].

Cross References

Instrument, defined, see Probate Code § 45.
Internal Revenue Code, defined, see Probate Code § 21500.
Marital deduction defined for purposes of this Chapter, see Probate Code § 21520.
Marital deduction gift defined for purposes of this Chapter, see Probate Code § 21520.
Transferor, defined, see Probate Code § 81.

§ 21524. Marital deduction trusts

If a marital deduction gift is made in trust, in addition to the other provisions of this chapter, each of the following provisions also applies to the marital deduction trust:

(a) The transferor's spouse is the only beneficiary of income or principal of the marital deduction property as long as the spouse is alive. Nothing in this subdivision precludes exercise by the transferor's spouse of a power of appointment included in a trust that qualifies as a general power of appointment marital deduction trust.

(b) * * * The transferor's spouse is entitled to all of the income of the marital deduction property not less frequently than annually, as long as the spouse is alive. For purposes of this subdivision, income shall be construed in a manner consistent with subdivision (b) of Section 2056 and subdivision (f) of Section 2523 of the Internal Revenue Code [1] and shall include a unitrust payment or other allocation of income determined pursuant to a reasonable apportionment of total investment return that meets the requirements of Section 643 of the Internal Revenue Code and the regulations adopted pursuant to that statute.

(c) The transferor's spouse has the right to require that the trustee of the trust make unproductive marital deduction property productive or to convert it into productive property within a reasonable time.

* * * (Stats.1990, c. 79 (A.B.759), § 14, operative July 1, 1991. Amended by Stats.1999, c. 145 (A.B.846), § 7; Stats. 2016, c. 140 (S.B.1265), § 1, eff. Jan. 1, 2017.)

[1] Internal Revenue Code sections are in Title 26 of the U.S.C.A.

Law Revision Commission Comments
1990 Enactment

Section 21524 continues Section 21524 of the repealed Probate Code without change. Subdivision (d) provides for qualification of a QTIP trust that is silent about the payment of income between the last distribution date of the trust and the date of the spouse's death and also provides for qualification of a QTIP trust that mandates payment of income to the remaindermen. It should be noted that the limitations provided in this section do not apply to an "estate trust." See Section 21521 (section inapplicable to estate trust).

1999 Amendment

Subdivision (d) of Section 21524 is amended to revise a cross-reference, in light of the replacement of the former Revised Uniform Principal and Income Act (Sections 16300–16315) by a new Uniform Principal and Income Act (Sections 16320–16375). [29 Cal.L.Rev. Comm. Reports 245 (1999)].

Background on Section 21524 of Repealed Code

Section 21524 was added by 1987 Cal.Stat. ch. 923 § 101. The section restated former Section 1035 (repealed by 1987 Cal.Stat. ch. 923 § 54.5), combining the concepts of former subdivisions (b) and (c) and revising subdivision (d) to provide for qualification of a QTIP trust that is silent about the payment of income between the last distribution date of the trust and the date of the spouse's death and, beyond that, to provide for qualification of a QTIP trust that mandates payment of income to the remaindermen. [20 Cal.L.Rev.Comm.Reports 1001 (1990)].

Cross References

Beneficiary, defined, see Probate Code § 24.
Estate trust, application of this section, see Probate Code § 21521.
Internal Revenue Code defined for purposes of this Part, see Probate Code § 21500.
Marital deduction defined for purposes of this Chapter, see Probate Code § 21520.
Marital deduction gift defined for purposes of this Chapter, see Probate Code § 21520.
Powers of appointment, generally, see Probate Code § 600 et seq.
Transferor, defined, see Probate Code § 81.
Trust, defined, see Probate Code § 82.

§ 21525. Condition in instrument that spouse survive transferor; time limitations

(a) If an instrument that makes a marital deduction gift includes a condition that the transferor's spouse survive the transferor by a period that exceeds or may exceed six months, other than a condition described in subdivision (b), the condition shall be limited to six months as applied to the marital deduction gift.

(b) If an instrument that makes a marital deduction gift includes a condition that the transferor's spouse survive a common disaster that results in the death of the transferor, the condition shall be limited to the time of the final audit of the federal estate tax return for the transferor's estate, if any, as applied to the marital deduction gift.

(c) The amendment of subdivision (a) made by Chapter 113 of the Statutes of 1988 is declaratory of, and not a change in, either existing law or former Section 1036 (repealed by Chapter 923 of the Statutes of 1987). (Stats.1990, c. 79 (A.B.759), § 14, operative July 1, 1991.)

Law Revision Commission Comments
1990 Enactment

Section 21525 continues Section 21525 of the repealed Probate Code without substantive change. See I.R.C. § 2056(b)(3); 26 C.F.R. § 20.2056(b)–3.

Background on Section 21525 of Repealed Code

Section 21525 was added by 1987 Cal.Stat. ch. 923 § 101 and was amended by 1988 Cal.Stat. ch. 113 § 21.5. Subdivision (a) of Section 21525 restated former Probate Code Section 1036 (repealed by 1987

Cal.Stat. ch. 923 § 54.5) without substantive change. Subdivision (b) was new. Subdivision (c) was added by the 1988 amendment. [20 Cal.L.Rev.Comm.Reports 1001 (1990)].

Cross References

Instrument, defined, see Probate Code § 45.
Marital deduction defined for purposes of this Chapter, see Probate Code § 21520.
Marital deduction gift defined for purposes of this Chapter, see Probate Code § 21520.
Transferor, defined, see Probate Code § 81.

§ 21526. Liability of fiduciary

A fiduciary is not liable for a good faith decision to make any election, or not to make any election, referred to in Section 2056(b)(7) or Section 2523(f) of the Internal Revenue Code. *(Stats.1990, c. 79 (A.B.759), § 14, operative July 1, 1991.)*

Law Revision Commission Comments

1990 Enactment

Section 21526 continues Section 21526 of the repealed Probate Code without change. This section is analogous to a portion of Section 1537d of 79 Kansas Statutes Annotated (1984). It provides protection for a partial, as well as a full, election.

Background on Section 21526 of Repealed Code

Section 21526 was added by 1987 Cal.Stat. ch. 923 § 101. The section superseded the fifth sentence of subdivision (a) of former Section 1032 (repealed by 1987 Cal.Stat. ch. 923 § 54.5). [20 Cal.L.Rev.Comm.Reports 1001 (1990)].

Cross References

Estate trust, this section inapplicable, see Probate Code § 21521.
Fiduciary, defined, see Probate Code § 39.
Internal Revenue Code defined for purposes of this Part, see Probate Code § 21500.

CHAPTER 3. CHARITABLE GIFTS

Section
21540. Charitable remainder unitrusts; charitable remainder annuity trusts.
21541. Charitable lead trusts.

Application

Part 5 is applicable to distributions made on or after Jan. 1, 1988. For provisions applicable to distributions made on or after Jan. 1, 1983, and before Jan. 1, 1988, see Probate Code § 21501.

§ 21540. Charitable remainder unitrusts; charitable remainder annuity trusts

If an instrument indicates the transferor's intention to comply with the Internal Revenue Code requirements for a charitable remainder unitrust or a charitable remainder annuity trust as each is defined in Section 664 of the Internal Revenue Code, the provisions of the instrument, including any power, duty, or discretionary authority given to a fiduciary, shall be construed to comply with the charitable deduction provisions of Section 2055 or Section 2522 of the Internal Revenue Code and the charitable remainder trust provisions of Section 664 of the Internal Revenue Code in order to conform to that intent. In no event shall the

fiduciary take an action or have a power that impairs the charitable deduction. The provisions of the instrument may be augmented in any manner consistent with Section 2055(e) or Section 2522(c) of the Internal Revenue Code on a petition provided for in Section 17200. *(Stats.1990, c. 79 (A.B.759), § 14, operative July 1, 1991.)*

Law Revision Commission Comments

1990 Enactment

Section 21540 continues Section 21540 of the repealed Probate Code without change. Whether an instrument contains a gift under this section depends upon the intention of the transferor at the time the instrument is executed.

Background on Section 21540 of Repealed Code

Section 21540 was added by 1987 Cal.Stat. ch. 923 § 101. The section restated subdivision (b) of former Probate Code Section 1032 (repealed by 1987 Cal.Stat. ch. 923 § 54.5) and applied it to living as well as testamentary trusts. [20 Cal.L.Rev.Comm.Reports 1001 (1990)].

Cross References

Instrument, defined, see Probate Code § 45.
Internal Revenue Code defined for purposes of this Part, see Probate Code § 21500.
Petitions, proceedings concerning trusts, see Probate Code § 17200 et seq.
Transferor, defined, see Probate Code § 81.

§ 21541. Charitable lead trusts

If an instrument indicates the transferor's intention to comply with the requirements for a charitable lead trust as described in Section 170(f)(2)(B) and Section 2055(e)(2) or Section 2522(c)(2) of the Internal Revenue Code, the provisions of the instrument, including any power, duty, or discretionary authority given to a fiduciary, shall be construed to comply with the provisions of that section in order to conform to that intent. In no event shall the fiduciary take any action or have any power that impairs the charitable deduction. The provisions of the instrument may be augmented in any manner consistent with that intent upon a petition provided for in Section 17200. *(Stats.1990, c. 79 (A.B.759), § 14, operative July 1, 1991.)*

Law Revision Commission Comments

1990 Enactment

Section 21541 continues Section 21541 of the repealed Probate Code without change. This section extends the general approach of Section 21540 (charitable remainder unitrusts and annuity trusts) to include charitable lead trusts.

Background on Section 21541 of Repealed Code

Section 21541 was a new provision added by 1987 Cal.Stat. ch. 923 § 101. [20 Cal.L.Rev.Comm.Reports 1001 (1990)].

Cross References

Fiduciary, defined, see Probate Code § 39.
Instrument, defined, see Probate Code § 45.
Internal Revenue Code defined for purposes of this Part, see Probate Code § 21500.
Petitions, proceedings concerning trusts, see Probate Code § 17200 et seq.

Transferor, defined, see Probate Code § 81.

Part 6

FAMILY PROTECTION: OMITTED SPOUSES AND CHILDREN

Application

Part 6 is not applicable where decedent died before Jan. 1, 1998, see Probate Code § 21630. For provisions applicable to estates of decedents who died before Jan. 1, 1998, see Chapter 5, Probate Code § 6560 et seq.

CHAPTER 1. GENERAL PROVISIONS

Application

Part 6 is not applicable where decedent died before Jan. 1, 1998, see Probate Code § 21630. For provisions applicable to estates of decedents who died before Jan. 1, 1998, see Chapter 5, Probate Code § 6560 et seq.

§ 21600. Application of part

This part shall apply to property passing by will through a decedent's estate or by a trust, as defined in Section 82, that becomes irrevocable only on the death of the settlor. *(Added by Stats.1997, c. 724 (A.B.1172), § 34.)*

Application

Part 6 is not applicable where decedent died before Jan. 1, 1998, see Probate Code § 21630. For provisions applicable to estates of decedents who died before Jan. 1, 1998, see Chapter 5, Probate Code § 6560 et seq.

Cross References

Estate defined for purposes of this Part, see Probate Code § 21601.

§ 21601. Definitions

(a) For purposes of this part, "decedent's testamentary instruments" means the decedent's will or revocable trust.

(b) "Estate" as used in this part shall include a decedent's probate estate and all property held in any revocable trust that becomes irrevocable on the death of the decedent. *(Added by Stats.1997, c. 724 (A.B.1172), § 34.)*

Application

Part 6 is not applicable where decedent died before Jan. 1, 1998, see Probate Code § 21630. For provisions applicable to estates of decedents who died

before Jan. 1, 1998, see Chapter 5, Probate Code § 6560 et seq.

CHAPTER 2. OMITTED SPOUSES

Application

Part 6 is not applicable where decedent died before Jan. 1, 1998, see Probate Code § 21630. For provisions applicable to estates of decedents who died before Jan. 1, 1998, see Chapter 5, Probate Code § 6560 et seq.

§ 21610. Share of omitted spouse

Except as provided in Section 21611, if a decedent fails to provide in a testamentary instrument for the decedent's surviving spouse who married the decedent after the execution of all of the decedent's testamentary instruments, the omitted spouse shall receive a share in the decedent's estate, consisting of the following property in said estate:

(a) The one-half of the community property that belongs to the decedent under Section 100.

(b) The one-half of the quasi-community property that belongs to the decedent under Section 101.

(c) A share of the separate property of the decedent equal in value to that which the spouse would have received if the decedent had died without having executed a testamentary instrument, but in no event is the share to be more than one-half the value of the separate property in the estate. *(Added by Stats.1997, c. 724 (A.B.1172), § 34.)*

Application

Part 6 is not applicable where decedent died before Jan. 1, 1998, see Probate Code § 21630. For provisions applicable to estates of decedents who died before Jan. 1, 1998, see Chapter 5, Probate Code § 6560 et seq.

Cross References

Decedent's testamentary instruments defined for purposes of this Part, see Probate Code § 21601.
Estate defined for purposes of this Part, see Probate Code § 21601.

§ 21611. Spouse not to receive share; circumstances

The spouse shall not receive a share of the estate under Section 21610 if any of the following is established:

(a) The decedent's failure to provide for the spouse in the decedent's testamentary instruments was intentional and that intention appears from the testamentary instruments.

(b) The decedent provided for the spouse by transfer outside of the estate passing by the decedent's testamentary instruments and the intention that the transfer be in lieu of a provision in said instruments is shown by statements of the decedent or from the amount of the transfer or by other evidence.

(c) The spouse made a valid agreement waiving the right to share in the decedent's estate. *(Added by Stats.1997, c. 724 (A.B.1172), § 34.)*

Application

Part 6 is not applicable where decedent died before Jan. 1, 1998, see Probate Code § 21630. For provisions applicable to estates of decedents who died before Jan. 1, 1998, see Chapter 5, Probate Code § 6560 et seq.

Cross References

Decedent's testamentary instruments defined for purposes of this Part, see Probate Code § 21601.
Estate defined for purposes of this Part, see Probate Code § 21601.

§ 21612. Manner of satisfying share of omitted spouse; intention of decedent

(a) Except as provided in subdivision (b), in satisfying a share provided by this chapter:

(1) The share will first be taken from the decedent's estate not disposed of by will or trust, if any.

(2) If that is not sufficient, so much as may be necessary to satisfy the share shall be taken from all beneficiaries of decedent's testamentary instruments in proportion to the value they may respectively receive. The proportion of each beneficiary's share that may be taken pursuant to this subdivision shall be determined based on values as of the date of the decedent's death.

(b) If the obvious intention of the decedent in relation to some specific gift or devise or other provision of a testamentary instrument would be defeated by the application of subdivision (a), the specific devise or gift or provision may be exempted from the apportionment under subdivision (a), and a different apportionment, consistent with the intention of the decedent, may be adopted. *(Formerly § 26112, added by Stats.1997, c. 724 (A.B.1172), § 34. Renumbered § 21612 and amended by Stats.2003, c. 32 (A.B.167), § 17.)*

Application

Part 6 is not applicable where decedent died before Jan. 1, 1998, see Probate Code § 21630. For provisions applicable to estates of decedents who died before Jan. 1, 1998, see Chapter 5, Probate Code § 6560 et seq.

Law Revision Commission Comments
2003 Renumbered and Amended

Former Section 26112 is renumbered as 21612. It was incorrectly numbered on enactment. See 1997 Cal. Stat. ch. 724, § 34.

Subdivision (a)(2) of Section 21612 is amended to make clear that it is the proportionate obligation of each beneficiary, rather than the total amount of the obligation, that is determined based on the date of death valuation. Thus for example if there are two beneficiaries entitled to receive property valued equally as of the date of death, the proportionate amount that will be taken from each is one-half the value of property distributed to each, regardless of the relative value of the property on the date of the distribution.

In a case where the share of the omitted spouse is partially satisfied pursuant to subdivision (a)(1), the obligation of the beneficiaries for the remainder abates proportionately. Thus if half the share of the omitted spouse is satisfied pursuant to subdivision (a)(1), the amount for which each of the beneficiaries is otherwise responsible pursuant

to subdivision (a)(2) is reduced by half. [33 Cal.L.Rev.Comm. Reports 150 (2003)].

Cross References

Abatement of shares of beneficiaries, exception to abatement requirements for omitted spouse or omitted children, see Probate Code § 21401.
Decedent's testamentary instruments defined for purposes of this Part, see Probate Code § 21601.
Estate defined for purposes of this Part, see Probate Code § 21601.

CHAPTER 3.   OMITTED CHILDREN

Application

Part 6 is not applicable where decedent died before Jan. 1, 1998, see Probate Code § 21630. For provisions applicable to estates of decedents who died before Jan. 1, 1998, see Chapter 5, Probate Code § 6560 et seq.

§ 21620. Child born or adopted after execution of will; share in estate

Except as provided in Section 21621, if a decedent fails to provide in a testamentary instrument for a child of decedent born or adopted after the execution of all of the decedent's testamentary instruments, the omitted child shall receive a share in the decedent's estate equal in value to that which the child would have received if the decedent had died without having executed any testamentary instrument. *(Added by Stats.1997, c. 724 (A.B.1172), § 34.)*

Application

Part 6 is not applicable where decedent died before Jan. 1, 1998, see Probate Code § 21630. For provisions applicable to estates of decedents who died before Jan. 1, 1998, see Chapter 5, Probate Code § 6560 et seq.

Cross References

Decedent's testamentary instruments defined for purposes of this Part, see Probate Code § 21601.
Estate defined for purposes of this Part, see Probate Code § 21601.

§ 21621. Child not to receive share; circumstances

A child shall not receive a share of the estate under Section 21620 if any of the following is established:

(a) The decedent's failure to provide for the child in the decedent's testamentary instruments was intentional and that intention appears from the testamentary instruments.

(b) The decedent had one or more children and devised or otherwise directed the disposition of substantially all the estate to the other parent of the omitted child.

(c) The decedent provided for the child by transfer outside of the estate passing by the decedent's testamentary instruments and the intention that the transfer be in lieu of a provision in said instruments is show by statements of the decedent or from the amount of the transfer or by other evidence. *(Added by Stats.1997, c. 724 (A.B.1172), § 34.)*

Application

Part 6 is not applicable where decedent died before Jan. 1, 1998, see Probate Code § 21630. For provisions applicable to estates of decedents who died before Jan. 1, 1998, see Chapter 5, Probate Code § 6560 et seq.

Cross References

Decedent's testamentary instruments defined for purposes of this Part, see Probate Code § 21601.
Estate defined for purposes of this Part, see Probate Code § 21601.

§ 21622. Decedent's erroneous belief or lack of knowledge; child's share of estate

If, at the time of the execution of all of decedent's testamentary instruments effective at the time of decedent's death, the decedent failed to provide for a living child solely because the decedent believed the child to be dead or was unaware of the birth of the child, the child shall receive a share in the estate equal in value to that which the child would have received if the decedent had died without having executed any testamentary instruments. *(Added by Stats. 1997, c. 724 (A.B.1172), § 34.)*

Application

Part 6 is not applicable where decedent died before Jan. 1, 1998, see Probate Code § 21630. For provisions applicable to estates of decedents who died before Jan. 1, 1998, see Chapter 5, Probate Code § 6560 et seq.

Cross References

Decedent's testamentary instruments defined for purposes of this Part, see Probate Code § 21601.
Estate defined for purposes of this Part, see Probate Code § 21601.

§ 21623. Manner of satisfying share of omitted child; intention of decedent

(a) Except as provided in subdivision (b), in satisfying a share provided by this chapter:

(1) The share will first be taken from the decedent's estate not disposed of by will or trust, if any.

(2) If that is not sufficient, so much as may be necessary to satisfy the share shall be taken from all beneficiaries of decedent's testamentary instruments in proportion to the value they may respectively receive. The proportion of each beneficiary's share that may be taken pursuant to this subdivision shall be determined based on values as of the date of the decedent's death.

(b) If the obvious intention of the decedent in relation to some specific gift or devise or other provision of a testamentary instrument would be defeated by the application of subdivision (a), the specific devise or gift or provision of a testamentary instrument may be exempted from the apportionment under subdivision (a), and a different apportionment, consistent with the intention of the decedent, may be

adopted. *(Added by Stats.1997, c. 724 (A.B.1172), § 34. Amended by Stats.2003, c. 32 (A.B.167), § 16.)*

Application

Part 6 is not applicable where decedent died before Jan. 1, 1998, see Probate Code § 21630. For provisions applicable to estates of decedents who died before Jan. 1, 1998, see Chapter 5, Probate Code § 6560 et seq.

Law Revision Commission Comments

2003 Amendment

Subdivision (a)(2) of Section 21623 is amended to make clear that it is the proportionate obligation of each beneficiary, rather than the total amount of the obligation, that is determined based on the date of death valuation. Thus for example if there are two beneficiaries entitled to receive property valued equally as of the date of death, the proportionate amount that will be taken from each is one-half the value of property distributed to each, regardless of the relative value of the property on the date of the distribution.

In a case where the share of the omitted child is partially satisfied pursuant to subdivision (a)(1), the obligation of the beneficiaries for the remainder abates proportionately. Thus if half the share of the omitted child is satisfied pursuant to subdivision (a)(1), the amount for which each of the beneficiaries is otherwise responsible pursuant to subdivision (a)(2) is reduced by half. [33 Cal.L.Rev.Comm. Reports 167 (2003)].

Cross References

Abatement of shares of beneficiaries, exception to abatement requirements for omitted spouse or omitted children, see Probate Code § 21401.
Decedent's testamentary instruments defined for purposes of this Part, see Probate Code § 21601.
Estate defined for purposes of this Part, see Probate Code § 21601.

CHAPTER 4. APPLICABILITY

Section
21630. Decedent's death before January 1, 1998; application of part.

Application

For provisions applicable to estates of decedents who died before Jan. 1, 1998, see Chapter 5, Probate Code § 6560 et seq.

§ 21630. Decedent's death before January 1, 1998; application of part

This part does not apply if the decedent died before January 1, 1998. The law applicable prior to January 1, 1998, applies if the decedent died before January 1, 1998. *(Added by Stats.1997, c. 724 (A.B.1172), § 34.)*

Application

For provisions applicable to estates of decedents who died before Jan. 1, 1998, see Chapter 5, Probate Code § 6560 et seq.

Part 7

CONTRACTS REGARDING TESTAMENTARY OR INTESTATE SUCCESSION

Section

21700. Contract to make will or devise; establishment; effect of execution of joint will or mutual wills; applicable law.

26112. Renumbered.

§ 21700. Contract to make will or devise; establishment; effect of execution of joint will or mutual wills; applicable law

(a) A contract to make a will or devise or other instrument, or not to revoke a will or devise or other instrument, or to die intestate, if made after the effective date of this statute, can be established only by one of the following:

(1) Provisions of a will or other instrument stating the material provisions of the contract.

(2) An expressed reference in a will or other instrument to a contract and extrinsic evidence proving the terms of the contract.

(3) A writing signed by the decedent evidencing the contract.

(4) Clear and convincing evidence of an agreement between the decedent and the claimant or a promise by the decedent to the claimant that is enforceable in equity.

(5) Clear and convincing evidence of an agreement between the decedent and another person for the benefit of the claimant or a promise by the decedent to another person for the benefit of the claimant that is enforceable in equity.

(b) The execution of a joint will or mutual wills does not create a presumption of a contract not to revoke the will or wills.

(c) A contract to make a will or devise or other instrument, or not to revoke a will or devise or other instrument, or to die intestate, if made prior to the effective date of this section, shall be construed under the law applicable to the contract prior to the effective date of this section. *(Added by Stats.2000, c. 17 (A.B.1491), § 8.)*

§ 26112. Renumbered § 21612 and amended by Stats.2003, c. 32 (A.B.167), § 17

Law Revision Commission Comments

2003 Renumbered and Amended

Former Section 26112 is renumbered as 21612. It was incorrectly numbered on enactment. See 1997 Cal. Stat. ch. 724, § 34.

Subdivision (a)(2) of Section 21612 is amended to make clear that it is the proportionate obligation of each beneficiary, rather than the total amount of the obligation, that is determined based on the date of death valuation. Thus for example if there are two beneficiaries entitled to receive property valued equally as of the date of death, the proportionate amount that will be taken from each is one-half the value of property distributed to each, regardless of the relative value of the property on the date of the distribution.

In a case where the share of the omitted spouse is partially satisfied pursuant to subdivision (a)(1), the obligation of the beneficiaries for the remainder abates proportionately. Thus if half the share of the omitted spouse is satisfied pursuant to subdivision (a)(1), the amount for which each of the beneficiaries is otherwise responsible pursuant to subdivision (a)(2) is reduced by half. [33 Cal.L.Rev.Comm. Reports 166 (2003)].

CODE OF CIVIL PROCEDURE

Part 2

OF CIVIL ACTIONS

Cross References

Arbitration of attorneys' fees, agreement to be bound by award of arbitrator, trial after arbitration in absence of agreement, see Business and Professions Code § 6204.
Eminent domain, rules of practice, see Code of Civil Procedure § 1230.040.
Forcible entry and detainer proceedings, applicability of this Part, see Code of Civil Procedure § 1177.
Produce dealers, rules of practice applicable, see Food and Agricultural Code § 56134.75.

Title 3

OF THE PARTIES TO CIVIL ACTIONS

CHAPTER 4. EFFECT OF DEATH

Cross References

Administrative subpoena or summons, see Government Code § 7474.
Exemplary damages, generally, see Civil Code § 3294.
Involuntary trusts, beneficiaries, construction with this chapter, see Civil Code § 2225.
State departments and agencies, investigations and hearings, service of process, see Government Code § 11184.

ARTICLE 1.   DEFINITIONS

Section
377.10.   Beneficiary of the decedent's estate.
377.11.   Decedent's successor in interest.

§ 377.10.   Beneficiary of the decedent's estate

For the purposes of this chapter, "beneficiary of the decedent's estate" means:

(a) If the decedent died leaving a will, the sole beneficiary or all of the beneficiaries who succeed to a cause of action, or to a particular item of property that is the subject of a cause of action, under the decedent's will.

(b) If the decedent died without leaving a will, the sole person or all of the persons who succeed to a cause of action, or to a particular item of property that is the subject of a cause of action, under Sections 6401 and 6402 of the Probate Code or, if the law of a sister state or foreign nation governs succession to the cause of action or particular item of property, under the law of the sister state or foreign nation. *(Added by Stats.1992, c. 178 (S.B.1496), § 20.)*

Law Revision Commission Comments

1992 Addition

Section 377.10 is a new provision drawn from Probate Code Section 13006. See also Section 377.11 ("decedent's successor in interest" defined). [22 Cal.L.Rev.Comm.Reports 895 (1992)].

Cross References

Damages based upon death resulting from homicide, see Civil Code § 3294.

§ 377.11.   Decedent's successor in interest

For the purposes of this chapter, "decedent's successor in interest" means the beneficiary of the decedent's estate or other successor in interest who succeeds to a cause of action or to a particular item of the property that is the subject of a cause of action. *(Added by Stats.1992, c. 178 (S.B.1496), § 20.)*

Law Revision Commission Comments

1992 Addition

Section 377.11 is new. The term "successor in interest" is derived from the second sentence of former Section 385. "Beneficiary of the decedent's estate" is defined in Section 377.10, and refers to takers of assets that are or would be subject to probate. Other successors in interest include persons who take property at the decedent's death by operation of law or a contract or account agreement.

The decedent's successor in interest does not include a person to whom the cause of action or property was assigned during the decedent's lifetime. [22 Cal.L.Rev.Comm.Reports 895 (1992)].

Cross References

Civil actions for abuse of elderly or dependent adults, jurisdiction, right to maintain action, see Welfare and Institutions Code § 15657.3.
Decedent's cause of action, statement from successor in interest, see Code of Civil Procedure § 377.32.

ARTICLE 2.   SURVIVAL AND CONTINUATION

Section
377.20.   Cause of action survives; limitations; loss or damage simultaneous with death.
377.21.   Pending actions.
377.22.   Assignment of cause of action.

§ 377.20.   Cause of action survives; limitations; loss or damage simultaneous with death

(a) Except as otherwise provided by statute, a cause of action for or against a person is not lost by reason of the person's death, but survives subject to the applicable limitations period.

(b) This section applies even though a loss or damage occurs simultaneously with or after the death of a person who would have been liable if the person's death had not preceded or occurred simultaneously with the loss or damage. *(Added by Stats.1992, c. 178 (S.B.1496), § 20.)*

Law Revision Commission Comments

1992 Addition

Subdivision (a) of Section 377.20 restates the first part of former Probate Code Section 573(a) without substantive change. Subdivision (b) restates former Probate Code Section 573(d) without substantive change. The applicable limitations period may be affected by the death of a person. See Sections 366.1–366.2 (time of commencement of action after death of person). [22 Cal.L.Rev.Comm.Reports 895 (1992)].

§ 377.21. Pending actions

A pending action or proceeding does not abate by the death of a party if the cause of action survives. *(Added by Stats.1992, c. 178 (S.B.1496), § 20.)*

Law Revision Commission Comments

1992 Addition

Section 377.21 restates part of the first sentence of former Section 385 without substantive change. [22 Cal.L.Rev.Comm.Reports 895 (1992)].

§ 377.22. Assignment of cause of action

Nothing in this chapter shall be construed as affecting the assignability of causes of action. *(Added by Stats.1992, c. 178 (S.B.1496), § 20.)*

Law Revision Commission Comments

1992 Addition

Section 377.22 restates former Probate Code Section 573(e) without substantive change. [22 Cal.L.Rev.Comm.Reports 895 (1992)].

ARTICLE 3.   DECEDENT'S CAUSE OF ACTION

Section
377.30. Surviving cause of action; person to whom passes; commencement of action.
377.31. Pending action or proceeding; continuance.
377.32. Statement from successor in interest; information required.
377.33. Court orders.
377.34. Damages recoverable.
377.35. Application of article.

Cross References

Disposition of small estate without administration, substitution of parties without probate, see Probate Code § 13107.5.

§ 377.30. Surviving cause of action; person to whom passes; commencement of action

A cause of action that survives the death of the person entitled to commence an action or proceeding passes to the decedent's successor in interest, subject to Chapter 1 (commencing with Section 7000) of Part 1 of Division 7 of the Probate Code, and an action may be commenced by the decedent's personal representative or, if none, by the decedent's successor in interest. *(Added by Stats.1992, c. 178 (S.B.1496), § 20.)*

Law Revision Commission Comments

1992 Addition

Section 377.30 restates the first part of former Code of Civil Procedure Section 353(a) and part of former Probate Code Section

573(a) without substantive change, but adds the reference to the successor in interest drawn from former Code of Civil Procedure Section 385. Under this section, an action or proceeding may be commenced by the decedent's successor in interest only if there is no personal representative. The distributee of the cause of action in probate is the successor in interest or, if there is no distribution, the heir, devisee, trustee, or other successor has the right to proceed under this article. See Section 377.11 ("decedent's successor in interest" defined). See also Prob. Code § 58 ("personal representative" defined). The addition of the reference to the successor in interest makes the rules applicable to commencement of an action consistent with the rules applicable to continuation of a pending action. Thus, the distinction between commencing and continuing the decedent's action drawn in Everett v. Commissioner, T.C.M. (P–H) ¶ 89,124 (Mar. 27, 1989), is not applicable under Sections 377.30 and 377.31. [22 Cal.L.Rev.Comm.Reports 895 (1992)].

Cross References

"Action" as including "special proceeding", see Code of Civil Procedure § 363.
Joinder with wrongful death actions, see Code of Civil Procedure § 377.62.
Personal representatives, actions by and against, see Probate Code § 9820 et seq.
Probate proceedings, claims against estates, see Probate Code § 9000 et seq.
Survival or continuation of action, see Code of Civil Procedure §§ 377.20 et seq., 377.41.

§ 377.31. Pending action or proceeding; continuance

On motion after the death of a person who commenced an action or proceeding, the court shall allow a pending action or proceeding that does not abate to be continued by the decedent's personal representative or, if none, by the decedent's successor in interest. *(Added by Stats.1992, c. 178 (S.B.1496), § 20.)*

Law Revision Commission Comments

1992 Addition

Section 377.31 restates part of former Section 385, but recognizes that the personal representative or successor in interest has an absolute right to be substituted for the decedent; substitution in this situation is not discretionary with the court. See, e.g., Pepper v. Superior Court, 76 Cal.App.3d 252, 260–61, 142 Cal.Rptr. 759 (1977). See also Section 377.11 ("decedent's successor in interest" defined); Prob.Code § 58 ("personal representative" defined).

This section is consistent with the application of former Section 385 in a federal Tax Court. See Everett v. Commissioner, T.C.M. (P–H) ¶ 89,124 (Mar. 27, 1989) (daughter of decedent petitioner substituted as party under federal rules adopting local law as to proper parties). [22 Cal.L.Rev.Comm.Reports 895 (1992)].

Cross References

Joinder with wrongful death actions, see Code of Civil Procedure § 377.62.

§ 377.32. Statement from successor in interest; information required

(a) The person who seeks to commence an action or proceeding or to continue a pending action or proceeding as the decedent's successor in interest under this article, shall execute and file an affidavit or a declaration under penalty of perjury under the laws of this state stating all of the following:

(1) The decedent's name.

(2) The date and place of the decedent's death.

(3) "No proceeding is now pending in California for administration of the decedent's estate."

(4) If the decedent's estate was administered, a copy of the final order showing the distribution of the decedent's cause of action to the successor in interest.

(5) Either of the following, as appropriate, with facts in support thereof:

(A) "The affiant or declarant is the decedent's successor in interest (as defined in Section 377.11 of the California Code of Civil Procedure) and succeeds to the decedent's interest in the action or proceeding."

(B) "The affiant or declarant is authorized to act on behalf of the decedent's successor in interest (as defined in Section 377.11 of the California Code of Civil Procedure) with respect to the decedent's interest in the action or proceeding."

(6) "No other person has a superior right to commence the action or proceeding or to be substituted for the decedent in the pending action or proceeding."

(7) "The affiant or declarant affirms or declares under penalty of perjury under the laws of the State of California that the foregoing is true and correct."

(b) Where more than one person executes the affidavit or declaration under this section, the statements required by subdivision (a) shall be modified as appropriate to reflect that fact.

(c) A certified copy of the decedent's death certificate shall be attached to the affidavit or declaration. *(Added by Stats.1992, c. 178 (S.B.1496), § 20.)*

Law Revision Commission Comments
1992 Addition

Section 337.330 [sic] is new. The affidavit provided in this section is drawn from the affidavit provided in Probate Code Section 13101. [22 Cal.L.Rev.Comm.Reports 895 (1992)].

Cross References

Civil actions for abuse of elderly or dependent adults, jurisdiction, right to maintain action, see Welfare and Institutions Code § 15657.3.

§ 377.33. Court orders

The court in which an action is commenced or continued under this article may make any order concerning parties that is appropriate to ensure proper administration of justice in the case, including appointment of the decedent's successor in interest as a special administrator or guardian ad litem. *(Added by Stats.1992, c. 178 (S.B.1496), § 20.)*

Law Revision Commission Comments
1992 Addition

Section 377.33 is new. The court in which the action or proceeding is pending has authority to resolve questions concerning the proper parties to the litigation and to make conclusive and binding orders, including determinations of the right of a successor in interest to commence or continue an action or proceeding. The references to appointment of the successor in interest as a special administrator or guardian ad litem are intended to recognize that there may be a need to impose fiduciary duties on the successor to protect the interests of other potential beneficiaries. See Code

Civ.Proc. §§ 372–373.5 (guardian ad litem); Prob. Code §§ 8540–8547 (special administrator). [22 Cal.L.Rev.Comm.Reports 895 (1992)].

Cross References

Civil actions for abuse of elderly or dependent adults, jurisdiction, right to maintain action, see Welfare and Institutions Code § 15657.3.

§ 377.34. Damages recoverable

In an action or proceeding by a decedent's personal representative or successor in interest on the decedent's cause of action, the damages recoverable are limited to the loss or damage that the decedent sustained or incurred before death, including any penalties or punitive or exemplary damages that the decedent would have been entitled to recover had the decedent lived, and do not include damages for pain, suffering, or disfigurement. *(Added by Stats.1992, c. 178 (S.B.1496), § 20.)*

Law Revision Commission Comments
1992 Addition

Section 377.34 restates former Probate Code Section 573(c) without substantive change, and adds the reference to the successor in interest. See Section 377.11 ("decedent's successor in interest" defined); Prob. Code § 58 ("personal representative" defined). The limitations in this section apply to the decedent's cause of action and not to a cause of action that others may have for the wrongful death of the decedent. See Sections 377.60–377.62 (wrongful death). [22 Cal.L.Rev.Comm.Reports 895 (1992)].

Cross References

Civil actions for abuse of elderly or dependent adults, applicability of limits on damages, see Welfare and Institutions Code § 15657.05.
Wrongful death actions, recovery of damages recoverable under this section, see Code of Civil Procedure § 377.61.

§ 377.35. Application of article

On or after January 1, 1993, this article applies to the commencement of an action or proceeding the decedent was entitled to commence, and to the continuation of an action or proceeding commenced by the decedent, regardless of whether the decedent died before, on, or after January 1, 1993. *(Added by Stats.1992, c. 178 (S.B.1496), § 20.)*

Law Revision Commission Comments
1992 Addition

Section 377.35 makes clear that, as of the operative date, the procedures provided by this article apply regardless of the date of the decedent's death. Thus, for example, if the limitations period provided in Section 366.1 has not run, a successor in interest of a decedent who died before January 1, 1993, may proceed under this article, assuming that a personal representative has not been appointed. See, e.g., Section 377.30 (commencement of action by personal representative or, if none, by successor in interest). However, if the limitations period under Section 366.1 has run before January 1, 1993, this article cannot be applied to revive the cause of action. Similarly, an action commenced by a decedent who died before January 1, 1993, may be continued by a successor in interest or personal representative as provided in this article. [22 Cal.L.Rev.Comm.Reports 895 (1992)].

ARTICLE 4. CAUSE OF ACTION AGAINST DECEDENT

Section
377.40. Persons subject to suit.
377.41. Pending actions; continuance; restrictions.
377.42. Damages recoverable.
377.43. Application of article.

§ 377.40. Persons subject to suit

Subject to Part 4 (commencing with Section 9000) of Division 7 of the Probate Code governing creditor claims, a cause of action against a decedent that survives may be asserted against the decedent's personal representative or, to the extent provided by statute, against the decedent's successor in interest. *(Added by Stats.1992, c. 178 (S.B.1496), § 20.)*

Law Revision Commission Comments

1992 Addition

Section 377.40 restates a portion of the first sentence of former Code of Civil Procedure Section 353(b) and part of former Probate Code Section 573(a) without substantive change. For special rules providing direct liability of successors in interest, see, e.g., Prob. Code §§ 13109 (transferee of property by affidavit), 13550 (surviving spouse who takes property without administration).

The introductory portion of Section 377.40, referring to Part 4 (creditor claims) of Division 7 of the Probate Code, is intended for cross-referencing purposes. See Prob. Code §§ 9350–9399 (claims in litigation). For special rules governing liability covered by insurance, see Code Civ.Proc. § 377.50; Prob. Code §§ 550–555.

See also Code Civ.Proc. § 377.11 ("decedent's successor in interest" defined); Prob. Code § 58 ("personal representative" defined). [22 Cal.L.Rev.Comm.Reports 895 (1992)].

Cross References

"Action" as including "special proceeding", see Code of Civil Procedure § 363.
Personal representatives, actions by and against, see Probate Code § 9820 et seq.
Probate proceedings, claims against estates, see Probate Code § 9000 et seq.
Survival or continuation of action, see Code of Civil Procedure §§ 377.20 et seq., 377.41.

§ 377.41. Pending actions; continuance; restrictions

On motion, the court shall allow a pending action or proceeding against the decedent that does not abate to be continued against the decedent's personal representative or, to the extent provided by statute, against the decedent's successor in interest, except that the court may not permit an action or proceeding to be continued against the personal representative unless proof of compliance with Part 4 (commencing with Section 9000) of Division 7 of the Probate Code governing creditor claims is first made. *(Added by Stats.1992, c. 178 (S.B.1496), § 20.)*

Law Revision Commission Comments

1992 Addition

Section 377.41 supersedes part of former Section 385. An action or proceeding may be continued against the decedent's successor in interest only if a statute provides for liability in such cases. For special rules providing direct liability of successors in interest, see, e.g., Prob.Code §§ 13109 (transferee of property by affidavit), 13550

(surviving spouse who takes property without administration), 18201 (trust assets). See also Section 377.11 ("decedent's successor in interest" defined); Prob. Code § 58 ("personal representative" defined); Veh. Code § 17452 (continuation of action against personal representative of nonresident defendant involved in motor vehicle accident). [22 Cal.L.Rev.Comm.Reports 895 (1992)].

Cross References

Estate administration, nonresident personal representatives, appointment of secretary of state as attorney, see Probate Code § 8572.
Estate administration, nonresident personal representatives, service of process or notice in civil action, see Probate Code § 8574.

§ 377.42. Damages recoverable

In an action or proceeding against a decedent's personal representative or, to the extent provided by statute, against the decedent's successor in interest, on a cause of action against the decedent, all damages are recoverable that might have been recovered against the decedent had the decedent lived except damages recoverable under Section 3294 of the Civil Code or other punitive or exemplary damages. *(Added by Stats.1992, c. 178 (S.B.1496), § 20.)*

Law Revision Commission Comments

1992 Addition

Section 377.42 restates former Probate Code Section 573(b) without substantive change, and applies the rule to successors in interest, to the extent they are liable. See Comments to Sections 377.40 & 377.41. See also Code Civ.Proc. § 377.11 ("decedent's successor in interest" defined); Prob. Code § 58 ("personal representative" defined). [22 Cal.L.Rev.Comm.Reports 895 (1992)].

§ 377.43. Application of article

This article applies to the commencement on or after January 1, 1993, of an action or proceeding against the decedent's personal representative or successor in interest, or to the making of a motion on or after January 1, 1993, to continue a pending action or proceeding against the decedent's personal representative or successor in interest, regardless of whether the decedent died before, on, or after January 1, 1993. *(Added by Stats.1992, c. 178 (S.B.1496), § 20.)*

Law Revision Commission Comments

1992 Addition

Section 377.43 makes clear that, as of the operative date, the procedures provided by this article apply to commencing an action, or making a motion to continue an action, against a personal representative or successor in interest regardless of the date of the decedent's death. Thus, for example, if a motion to substitute a successor in interest as a defendant has been made before January 1, 1993, this article would not apply to the case. A motion made after January 1, 1993, would be governed by this article even though the decedent died before that date. See, e.g., Section 377.41 (continuation of pending action against personal representative or successor in interest). [22 Cal.L.Rev.Comm.Reports 895 (1992)].

ARTICLE 5. INSURED CLAIMS

Section
377.50. Commencement or continuance of action.

§ 377.50. Commencement or continuance of action

An action to establish the decedent's liability for which the decedent was protected by insurance may be commenced or continued against the decedent's estate as provided in Chapter 1 (commencing with Section 550) of Part 13 of Division 2 of the Probate Code. *(Added by Stats.1992, c. 178 (S.B.1496), § 20.)*

Law Revision Commission Comments

1992 Addition

Section 377.50 is a new provision that provides a cross-reference to the special provisions in the Probate Code concerning insured claims against the decedent. [22 Cal.L.Rev.Comm.Reports 895 (1992)].

ARTICLE 6. WRONGFUL DEATH

Section
377.60. Persons with standing.
377.61. Damages recoverable.
377.62. Joinder with decedent's cause of action.

§ 377.60. Persons with standing

A cause of action for the death of a person caused by the wrongful act or neglect of another may be asserted by any of the following persons or by the decedent's personal representative on their behalf:

(a) The decedent's surviving spouse, domestic partner, children, and issue of deceased children, or, if there is no surviving issue of the decedent, the persons, including the surviving spouse or domestic partner, who would be entitled to the property of the decedent by intestate succession.

(b) Whether or not qualified under subdivision (a), if they were dependent on the decedent, the putative spouse, children of the putative spouse, stepchildren, or parents. As used in this subdivision, "putative spouse" means the surviving spouse of a void or voidable marriage who is found by the court to have believed in good faith that the marriage to the decedent was valid.

(c) A minor, whether or not qualified under subdivision (a) or (b), if, at the time of the decedent's death, the minor resided for the previous 180 days in the decedent's household and was dependent on the decedent for one-half or more of the minor's support.

(d) This section applies to any cause of action arising on or after January 1, 1993.

(e) The addition of this section by Chapter 178 of the Statutes of 1992 was not intended to adversely affect the standing of any party having standing under prior law, and the standing of parties governed by that version of this section as added by Chapter 178 of the Statutes of 1992 shall be the same as specified herein as amended by Chapter 563 of the Statutes of 1996.

(f)(1) For the purpose of this section, "domestic partner" means a person who, at the time of the decedent's death, was the domestic partner of the decedent in a registered domestic partnership established in accordance with subdivision (b) of Section 297 of the Family Code.

(2) Notwithstanding paragraph (1), for a death occurring prior to January 1, 2002, a person may maintain a cause of action pursuant to this section as a domestic partner of the decedent by establishing the factors listed in paragraphs (1) to (6), inclusive, of subdivision (b) of Section 297 of the Family Code, as it read pursuant to Section 3 of Chapter 893 of the Statutes of 2001, prior to its becoming inoperative on January 1, 2005.

(3) The amendments made to this subdivision during the 2003–04 Regular Session of the Legislature are not intended to revive any cause of action that has been fully and finally adjudicated by the courts, or that has been settled, or as to which the applicable limitations period has run. *(Added by Stats.1992, c. 178 (S.B.1496), § 20. Amended by Stats.1996, c. 563 (S.B.392), § 1; Stats.1997, c. 13 (S.B.449), § 1, eff. May 23, 1997; Stats.2001, c. 893 (A.B.25), § 2; Stats.2004, c. 947 (A.B.2580), § 1.)*

Law Revision Commission Comments

1992 Addition

Section 377.60 restates subdivision (b) and the first part of the first sentence of subdivision (a) of former Section 377 without substantive change, except as discussed below. If the wrongdoer dies before or after the decedent, the cause of action provided in this section may be asserted against the personal representative of the wrongdoer. See Sections 377.20 (survival of cause of action), 377.40 (assertion of cause of action against decedent). See also Prob.Code § 6400 *et seq.* (intestate succession). Unlike other provisions of this chapter that relate to causes of action belonging to the decedent, this article relates to a cause of action for the decedent's wrongful death, which belongs not to the decedent, but to the persons specified in this section. Thus, the cause of action is not property in the estate of the decedent, and the authority of the personal representative to assert the cause of action is for administrative convenience only and is not for the benefit of creditors or other persons interested in the decedent's estate.

Subdivision (a) revises the language of former Section 377(b)(1) to refer specifically to the decedent's surviving spouse, children, and issue of deceased children, as proper parties plaintiff in a wrongful death action. This makes clear that, even if the decedent's estate is entirely community property, the decedent's children and issue of deceased children are proper parties plaintiff, along with the decedent's surviving spouse. This codifies Fiske v. Wilkie, 67 Cal.App.2d 440, 444, 154 P.2d 725 (1945). Under Probate Code Section 258, Section 377.60 is subject to the rules relating to the effect of homicide. This changes the rule of Marks v. Lyerla, 1 Cal.App.4th 556, 2 Cal.Rptr.2d 63 (1991).

For background, see *Standing To Sue for Wrongful Death*, 22 Cal.L.Revision Comm'n Reports 955 (1992). [22 Cal.L.Rev.Comm.Reports 895 (1992)].

Cross References

Computation of time, see Code of Civil Procedure §§ 12 and 12a; Government Code § 6800 et seq.
Involuntary trusts, beneficiaries, construction with this chapter, see Civil Code § 2225.
Workers' compensation and insurance, action against third person, rights of employee and employer, see Labor Code § 3852.

§ 377.61. Damages recoverable

In an action under this article, damages may be awarded that, under all the circumstances of the case, may be just, but may not include damages recoverable under Section 377.34. The court shall determine the respective rights in an award of the persons entitled to assert the cause of action. *(Added by Stats.1992, c. 178 (S.B.1496), § 20.)*

Law Revision Commission Comments
1992 Addition

Section 377.61 restates the third and fourth sentences of former Section 377(a) without substantive change. [22 Cal.L.Rev.Comm.Reports 895 (1992)].

§ 377.62. Joinder with decedent's cause of action

(a) An action under Section 377.30 may be joined with an action under Section 377.60 arising out of the same wrongful act or neglect.

(b) An action under Section 377.60 and an action under Section 377.31 arising out of the same wrongful act or neglect may be consolidated for trial as provided in Section 1048. *(Added by Stats.1992, c. 178 (S.B.1496), § 20.)*

Law Revision Commission Comments
1992 Addition

Subdivision (a) of Section 377.62 restates and generalizes the fifth sentence of former Section 377(a).

Subdivision (b) replaces the last sentence of former Section 377(a). This subdivision incorporates the general provision governing consolidation of actions which recognizes the court's discretion to order consolidation. Former Section 377(a) provided that the court "shall" order consolidation on motion of an interested party. [22 Cal.L.Rev.Comm.Reports 895 (1992)].

Cross References

Exemplary damages, generally, see Civil Code § 3294.

Part 3

OF SPECIAL PROCEEDINGS OF A CIVIL NATURE

Cross References

Arbitration of attorneys' fees, see Business and Professions Code § 6203.
Regional centers for persons with developmental disabilities, actions against third parties, disputes regarding amount of regional center or department's lien to recover costs of services provided, see Welfare and Institutions Code § 4659.16.

Title 10

UNCLAIMED PROPERTY

Cross References

Abandoned animals, see Civil Code §§ 1834.5, 1834.6.
Authority to remove vehicles, local ordinances, see Vehicle Code § 22660.
Bail money, unclaimed, deposit in general fund of county, see Penal Code § 1463 et seq.
Bailee, unclaimed property, see Civil Code § 2081 et seq.
Bank liquidation,
    Unclaimed dividends and deposits, see Financial Code §§ 3121, 3121.5, 3150, 3160 et seq.
    Unpaid dividends and unclaimed deposits, see Financial Code §§ 3121, 3150.
Corporations, unclaimed distributive shares, dividends, etc., see Corporations Code § 2008 et seq.
Decedent leaving no heirs or devisees, applicability of this title, see Probate Code § 6800 et seq.
Decedent's property, escheat, see Probate Code § 6800 et seq.
Definitions applicable to this Title, see Code of Civil Procedure § 1300.
Department of mental health, unclaimed personalty of deceased or escaped inmate, see Welfare and Institutions Code §§ 4126, 4127.
Final distribution of estate property to state, applicability of this title, see Probate Code § 11903.
Grand jury, inquiry as to land which might escheat, see Penal Code § 920.
Insolvent insurers, disposition of unclaimed funds, see Insurance Code § 1056.5.
Investment, trust property, unclaimed, see Government Code § 13470.
Investment of Unclaimed Property Fund, see Government Code § 13470.

Location of owners of unclaimed property, disclosure of information contained in tax returns to state controller, see Revenue and Taxation Code § 19554.
Lost and unclaimed property, see Civil Code § 2080 et seq.
Missing claimant in liquidation of real property securities business, deposits of funds, see Business and Professions Code § 10239.30.
Personal property on premises at termination of tenancy, see Civil Code § 1980 et seq.
Persons who may file petitions to determine survival in cases of simultaneous death, see Probate Code § 231.
Petition for approval of account, see Probate Code § 1064.
Prisoner in state institution, unclaimed property of, disposition, see Penal Code §§ 5061, 5062.
Property, title to which fails for want of heirs or next of kin, see Government Code § 182.
Property in custody of federal officers, agencies and departments, see Code of Civil Procedure § 1600 et seq.
Property within state not belonging to any person as belonging to the people, see Government Code § 182.
Public administrator, unclaimed property, applicability of this title, see Probate Code § 7644.
Receivers having unclaimed funds, see Code of Civil Procedure § 570.
Role of Attorney General with escheated property, see Government Code §§ 12540 to 12544.
Trust property, unclaimed, disposal of, see Financial Code § 3160 et seq.
Unclaimed property,
    Generally, see Code of Civil Procedure § 1500 et seq.
    Fund, see Code of Civil Procedure § 1313 et seq.
    In hospitals, see Civil Code § 1862.5.
Unclaimed stolen or embezzled property delivered to county officer, see Penal Code § 1411.
Youth authority, disposition of unclaimed personalty, see Welfare and Institutions Code § 1015.

CHAPTER 6. DISPOSITION OF UNCLAIMED PROPERTY

Cross References

Definitions applicable to this Title, see Code of Civil Procedure § 1300.
Delivery of unclaimed property in estates to state treasurer or state controller, see Probate Code § 7643.

Property over which county public administrator shall take prompt possession or control, see Probate Code § 7601.

ARTICLE 1. ESTATES OF DECEASED PERSONS

Section
1440. Payment to state of unclaimed property from decedent's estate; presumption of payment under article.
1441. Money or property distributed to state; permanent escheat for failure to claim; rights of persons under disability; presumption in favor of bona fide purchasers.
1442. Right to claim; exception.
1443. Payment to state; presumption as to applicable law.
1444. Money or property deposited in county treasury for known heirs, etc.; payment to state treasurer or controller.
1444.5. Money on deposit with county treasurer received from public administrator or coroner.
1445. Undistributed money or property of estate; county treasurer's petition to pay into state treasury; order; payment.
1446. Money or property of person who died while confined in state penal institution; delivery to state; presumption.
1447. Money or property of person who died while confined in state institution; delivery to state; presumption.
1448. Money or property of person who died while confined in state youth institution; delivery to state; presumption.
1449. Presumption of payment or delivery under article; transmittal, receipt, accounting, and disposal.

Cross References

Claim against estate, deposit under this article when claimant not found, see Probate Code § 11428.
Credit to estate from which property received, see Code of Civil Procedure § 1392.
Credit to unlocated heirs, devisees, or legatees, see Code of Civil Procedure § 1393.
Deceased mental patient, applicability of this chapter to unclaimed property, see Welfare and Institutions Code § 4126.
Deceased prisoner, applicability of this chapter to unclaimed property, see Penal Code § 5061.
Definitions applicable to this Title, see Code of Civil Procedure § 1300.
Delivery of unclaimed property in estates to state treasurer or state controller under this article, see Probate Code § 7643.
Petition for escheated property received by state under this article, see Code of Civil Procedure § 1355.
Property over which county public administrator shall take prompt possession or control, see Probate Code § 7601.
Public administrator, unclaimed property, applicability of this Article, see Probate Code § 7644.
Separate accounts in unclaimed property fund for money deposited under each article of this chapter, see Code of Civil Procedure § 1314.
Youth authority, deceased prisoner, applicability of this chapter to unclaimed property, see Welfare and Institutions Code § 1015.

§ 1440. Payment to state of unclaimed property from decedent's estate; presumption of payment under article

Whenever, under the provisions of this title or under any other provision of law, any unclaimed money or other property in an estate of a deceased person, or any unclaimed amount payable pursuant to an allowed and approved claim against such an estate, is paid to the State or any officer or employee thereof for deposit in the State Treasury, it shall be deemed to have been so paid under the provisions of this article. *(Added by Stats.1951, c. 1708, p. 3952, § 5.)*

Cross References

Claim to proceeds of sale of unclaimed property of estate, see Probate Code § 11854.
Deceased developmentally disabled patients funds, see Welfare and Institutions Code § 4466.
Deceased prisoners, disposition of personal property, see Penal Code § 5061.
Distribution to state of decedent's unclaimed property, see Probate Code § 11900 et seq.
Escheat of decedent's property, see Probate Code § 6800 et seq.
Personal property of deceased inmate of state institution, see Welfare and Institutions Code § 4126.
Personal property on premises at termination of tenancy, see Civil Code § 1980 et seq.
Proceedings to determine rights of state, see Code of Civil Procedure § 1420.
Property of deceased juvenile delinquent, see Welfare and Institutions Code § 1015.
Purpose of title, see Code of Civil Procedure § 1305.
Unclaimed property, see Code of Civil Procedure §§ 1300, 1601.

§ 1441. Money or property distributed to state; permanent escheat for failure to claim; rights of persons under disability; presumption in favor of bona fide purchasers

Money or other property distributed to the state under Chapter 6 (commencing with Section 11900) of Part 10 of Division 7 of the Probate Code, if not claimed within five years from the date of the order for distribution, as provided in Chapter 3 [1], is permanently escheated to the state without further proceeding; saving, however, to infants and persons of unsound mind, the right to appear and file their claims within the time limited pursuant to Section 1430, or within one year after their respective disabilities cease; provided, however, that any such property shall be conclusively presumed to be permanently escheated to the state as to all persons in favor of a purchaser in good faith and for a valuable consideration from the state and anyone subsequently claiming under that purchaser, saving however, to infants and persons of unsound mind the right of recourse to the proceeds of any sale or other disposition of that property by the state and as herein provided. *(Added by Stats.1951, c. 1708, p. 3952, § 5. Amended by Stats.1951, c. 1738, p. 4148, § 4; Stats.1988, c. 1199, § 10, operative July 1, 1989; Stats. 1995, c. 105 (S.B.481), § 1.)*

[1] Code of Civil Procedure § 1335 et seq.

Law Revision Commission Comments

1988 Amendment

Section 1441 is amended to reflect the repeal of Probate Code Section 1144 and its replacement, in part, by Probate Code Section 7663 (distribution of property), which provides for escheat to the county, and to reflect the repeal of Probate Code Section 1027 and its replacement, in part, by Probate Code Section 11900 (distribution to State of California). [19 Cal.L.Rev.Comm. Reports 1036 (1988)].

Cross References

Cancellation of taxes, see Revenue and Taxation Code § 4986.5.

Permanent escheat,
  Generally, see Code of Civil Procedure §§ 1300, 1430, 1431.
  Defined, see Code of Civil Procedure § 1300.
Powers and duties common to cities and counties, unclaimed money,
  publication of notice, restitution money, see Government Code
  § 50050.
Presumptions, see Evidence Code § 600 et seq.
Proceedings to determine rights of state, see Code of Civil Procedure
  § 1420.

§ 1442. Right to claim; exception

Except as otherwise provided in Section 1441, any money
or other property paid into the State Treasury under the
provisions of this article may be claimed by the person
entitled thereto, as provided in Chapter 3.[1] *(Added by
Stats.1951, c. 1708, p. 3952, § 5.)*

[1] Code of Civil Procedure § 1335 et seq.

§ 1443. Payment to state; presumption as to applicable law

Notwithstanding any other provision of law, all money or
other property paid or delivered to the state or any officer or
employee thereof under the provisions of Section 7643 or
11428, Chapter 6 (commencing with Section 11900) of Part
10 of Division 7, or Section 6800, of the Probate Code, or
under any other section of the Probate Code, or any
amendment thereof adopted after the effective date of this
section, shall be deemed to be paid or delivered for deposit in
the State Treasury under the provisions of this article, and
shall be transmitted, received, accounted for, and disposed of,
as provided in this title. *(Added by Stats.1951, c. 1708, p.
3952, § 5. Amended by Stats.1953, c. 1758, p. 3517, § 3;
Stats.1983, c. 842, § 13, operative Jan. 1, 1985; Stats.1988, c.
1199, § 11, operative July 1, 1989.)*

Law Revision Commission Comments

1983 Amendment

Section 1443 is amended to substitute a reference to the provision
that supersedes former Section 231 which was formerly referred to in
Section 1443. [16 Cal.L.Rev.Comm. Reports 183 (1982)].

1988 Amendment

Section 1443 is amended to reflect the repeal of Probate Code
Section 738 and its replacement by Probate Code Section 11428
(deposit for missing creditor), the repeal of Probate Code Section
1027 and its replacement, in part, by Probate Code Section 11900
(distribution to State of California), the repeal of Probate Code
Section 1148 and its replacement by Probate Code Section 7643
(deposit with county treasurer), and the repeal of Probate Code
Section 1144 and its replacement, in part, by Probate Code Section
7663 (distribution of property), which provides for escheat to the
county. [19 Cal.L.Rev.Comm. Reports 1202 (1988)].

§ 1444. Money or property deposited in county treasury for known heirs, etc.; payment to state treasurer or controller

At the time of the next county settlement following the
expiration of one year from the date of its deposit in the
county treasury, all money or other property distributed in
the administration of an estate of a deceased person and
heretofore or hereafter deposited in the county treasury to
the credit of known heirs, legatees, or devisees, and any
money or other property remaining on deposit to the credit of

an estate after final distribution to such known heirs, legatees
or devisees, shall be paid to the Treasurer or Controller as
provided in Chapter 2.[1] *(Added by Stats.1951, c. 1708, p.
3952, § 5.)*

[1] Code of Civil Procedure § 1310 et seq.

Cross References

Claim against estate, claimant not found, applicability of this section,
  see Probate Code § 11428.
Decedent's estates, deposit of debt payment with county treasurer
  where creditor cannot be found, disposition pursuant to this
  section, see Probate Code § 11428.
State controller, see Code of Civil Procedure § 1300; Government
  Code § 12400 et seq.; Const. Art. 5, § 11.
State treasurer, see Code of Civil Procedure § 1300; Const. Art. 5,
  § 11; Government Code § 12300 et seq.

§ 1444.5. Money on deposit with county treasurer received from public administrator or coroner

Notwithstanding any other provision of law, any money on
deposit with the county treasurer of a county received from a
public administrator of the county in trust and to the account
of the estate of a deceased person or the creditor of a
deceased person, in an amount of fifty dollars ($50) or less as
to any one estate or creditor, and not covered by a decree of
distribution, which was received or remained on hand after
the final accounting in such deceased person's estate and the
discharge of such public administrator as representative of
the estate, and where the money has so remained on deposit
in trust for a period of 15 years or more unclaimed by any
heir, devisee or legatee of such deceased person, or by any
creditor having an allowed and approved claim against the
deceased person's estate remaining unpaid, shall be deemed
permanently escheated to the State of California. The total
of any such moneys so held in trust unclaimed for such period
may be paid in a lump sum by the county treasurer, from such
funds as he may have on hand for the purpose, to the State
Treasurer, at the time of the next county settlement after the
effective date of this section, or at any county settlement
thereafter. Such lump sum payment may be made by
designating it to have been made under this section, without
the necessity of any further report or statement of the estates
or claimants concerned, without the necessity of any order of
court, and without being subject to the provisions of Section
1311 or 1312. Upon receipt by the State Treasurer, any
permanently escheated money received by him under this
section shall forthwith be deposited in the School Land Fund,
subject only to the rights of minors and persons of unsound
mind saved to them by Section 1430.

This section shall also apply in all respects to any money on
deposit with a county treasurer received from the coroner of
the county in trust and to the account of a deceased person,
and any such money shall be held, deemed permanently
escheated, reported and paid over in like manner as herein-
above set forth. *(Added by Stats.1957, c. 1375, p. 2708 § 1.)*

Cross References

Permanent escheat, see Code of Civil Procedure §§ 1300, 1430, 1431,
  1441.
Public administrator, see Government Code § 27440 et seq.; Probate Code § 7600 et seq.

State Treasurer, generally, see Government Code § 12300 et seq.

§ 1445. Undistributed money or property of estate; county treasurer's petition to pay into state treasury; order; payment

If money or other property is deposited in a county treasury, and if the deposits belong (1) to known decedents' estates on which letters testamentary or letters of administration have never been issued or (2) to known decedents' estates on which letters testamentary or letters of administration have been issued but no decree of distribution has been rendered, due to the absence of any parties interested in the estate or the failure of such parties diligently to protect their interests by taking reasonable steps for the purpose of securing a distribution of the estate, the county treasurer shall, within one year following the expiration of five years from the date of such deposit, file a petition in the superior court of the county in which the deposit is held, setting forth the fact that the money or other personal property has remained in the county treasury under such circumstances for such five-year period, and petitioning the court for an order directing him to pay such money or other property into the State Treasury.

At the time of the next county settlement following the date of the making of the order by the court, unless earlier payment is required by the Controller, the county treasurer shall pay such money or other property to the Treasurer or Controller as provided in Chapter 2. *(Added by Stats.1951, c. 1708, p. 3953, § 5.)*

Cross References

State Controller, generally, see Government Code § 12400 et seq.
Superior court, generally, see Cal. Const. Art. 6 § 15.

§ 1446. Money or property of person who died while confined in state penal institution; delivery to state; presumption

Notwithstanding any other provision of law, all unclaimed money or other property belonging to any person who dies while confined in any state institution subject to the jurisdiction of the Director of Corrections, which is paid or delivered to the State or any officer or employee thereof under the provisions of Section 5061 of the Penal Code, or under any amendment thereof adopted after the effective date of this section, shall be deemed to be paid or delivered for deposit in the State Treasury under the provisions of this article, and shall be transmitted, received, accounted for, and disposed of, as provided in this part. *(Added by Stats.1951, c. 1708, p. 3953, § 5.)*

§ 1447. Money or property of person who died while confined in state institution; delivery to state; presumption

Notwithstanding any other law, all unclaimed money or other property belonging to a person who dies while confined in a state institution subject to the jurisdiction of the State Department of State Hospitals, which is paid or delivered to the state or an officer or employee thereof under the provisions of Section 166 of the Welfare and Institutions Code, or under any amendment thereof adopted after the effective date of Chapter 1708 of the Statutes of 1951 shall be deemed to be paid or delivered for deposit in the State Treasury under the provisions of this article, and shall be transmitted, received, accounted for, and disposed of, as provided in this part. *(Added by Stats.1951, c. 1708, p. 3953, § 5. Amended by Stats.2014, c. 144 (A.B.1847), § 7, eff. Jan. 1, 2015.)*

§ 1448. Money or property of person who died while confined in state youth institution; delivery to state; presumption

Notwithstanding any other provision of law, all unclaimed money or other property belonging to any person who dies while confined in any state institution subject to the jurisdiction of the Youth Authority, which is paid or delivered to the State or any officer thereof under the provisions of Section 1015 of the Welfare and Institutions Code or under any amendment thereof adopted after the effective date of this section, shall be deemed to be paid or delivered for deposit in the State Treasury under the provisions of this article, and shall be transmitted, received, accounted for, and disposed of, as provided in this part. *(Added by Stats.1951, c. 1708, p. 3953, § 5.)*

§ 1449. Presumption of payment or delivery under article; transmittal, receipt, accounting, and disposal

Notwithstanding any other provision of law, all presumptively abandoned money or other property paid or delivered to the Treasurer or Controller under the provisions of Section 7644 of the Probate Code shall be deemed to be paid or delivered for deposit in the State Treasury under the provisions of this article, and shall be transmitted, received, accounted for, and disposed of as provided in this title. *(Added by Stats.1953, c. 219, p. 1360, § 2. Amended by Stats.1988, c. 1199, § 12, operative July 1, 1989.)*

Law Revision Commission Comments

1988 Amendment

Section 1449 is amended to reflect the repeal of Probate Code Section 1147.5 and its replacement by Probate Code Section 7644 (deposit unclaimed in financial institution). [19 Cal.L.Rev.Comm. Reports 1036 (1988)].

Cross References

Presumption, see Evidence Code § 600 et seq.
State Controller, generally, see Government Code § 12400 et seq.

REVENUE AND TAXATION CODE

Division 2

OTHER TAXES

Part 8

PROHIBITION OF GIFT AND DEATH TAXES

CHAPTER 1. IMPOSITION OF TAX

§ 13301. Prohibition of tax

Neither the state nor any political subdivision of the state shall impose any gift, inheritance, succession, legacy, income, or estate tax, or any other tax, on gifts or on the estate or inheritance of any person or on or by reason of any transfer occurring by reason of a death. *(Added by Initiative Measure (Prop. 6, § 3, approved June 8, 1982, eff. June 8, 1982); Stats.1982, c. 1535, p. 5974, § 15.)*

Cross References

Estate or property defined for purposes of this Part, see Revenue and Taxation Code § 13402.
Transfer defined for purposes of this Part, see Revenue and Taxation Code § 13404.

§ 13302. State estate tax; imposition; amount

Notwithstanding the provisions of Section 13301, whenever a federal estate tax is payable to the United States, there is hereby imposed a California estate tax equal to the portion, if any, of the maximum allowable amount of the credit for state death taxes, allowable under the applicable federal estate tax law, which is attributable to property located in the State of California. However, in no event shall the estate tax hereby imposed result in a total death tax liability to the State of California and the United States in excess of the death tax liability to the United States which would result if this section were not in effect. *(Added by Initiative Measure (Prop. 6, § 3, approved June 8, 1982, eff. June 8, 1982); Stats.1982, c. 1535, p. 5974, § 15.)*

Cross References

Estate or property defined for purposes of this Part, see Revenue and Taxation Code § 13402.

§ 13303. Collection and administration

Section as added by Initiative Measure (Prop. 6, § 3, approved June 8, 1982, eff. June 8, 1982). See,

also, another section of the same number, added by Stats.1982, c. 1535, p. 5975, § 15.

The Legislature shall provide for the collection and administration of the tax imposed by Section 13302. *(Added by Initiative Measure (Prop. 6, § 3, approved June 8, 1982, eff. June 8, 1982).)*

Cross References

Decedent or transferor defined for purposes of this Part, see Revenue and Taxation Code § 13405.
Estate or property defined for purposes of this Part, see Revenue and Taxation Code § 13402.

§ 13303. Estate having property in this state, and other states; computation of state death tax credit attributable to California property

Section as added by Stats.1982, c. 1535, p. 5975, § 15. See, also, another section of the same number, added by Initiative Measure (Prop. 6, § 3, approved June 8, 1982, eff. June 8, 1982).

In a case where a decedent leaves property having a situs in this state, and leaves other property having a situs in another state, or other states, the portion of the maximum state death tax credit allowable against the federal estate tax on the total estate by the federal estate tax law which is attributable to the property having a situs in California shall be determined in the following manner:

(a) For the purpose of apportioning the maximum state death tax credit, the gross value of the property shall be that value finally determined for federal estate tax purposes.

(b) The maximum state death tax credit allowable shall be multiplied by the percentage which the gross value of property having a situs in California bears to the gross value of the entire estate subject to federal estate tax.

(c) The product determined pursuant to subdivision (b) shall be the portion of the maximum state death tax credit allowable which is attributable to property having a situs in California. *(Added by Stats.1982, c. 1535, p. 5975, § 15.)*

Cross References

Decedent or transferor defined for purposes of this Part, see Revenue and Taxation Code § 13405.
Estate or property defined for purposes of this Part, see Revenue and Taxation Code § 13402.

§ 13304. State death tax credit allowable against federal estate tax; property with situs in California; determination

In a case where the gross estate of a decedent includes property having a situs in this state, and includes other property having a situs in another state, or other states, the portion of the maximum state death tax credit allowable against the federal estate tax on the total estate by the federal estate tax law that is attributable to the property having a situs in California shall be determined in the following manner:

(a) For the purpose of apportioning the maximum state death tax credit, the gross value of the property shall be that value finally determined for federal estate tax purposes.

(b) The maximum state death tax credit allowable shall be multiplied by the percentage which the gross value of property having a situs in California bears to the gross value of the entire estate subject to federal estate tax.

(c) The product determined pursuant to subdivision (b) shall be the portion of the maximum state death tax credit allowable that is attributable to property having a situs in California. *(Added by Stats.1982, c. 327, p. 1490, § 169, eff. June 30, 1982. Amended by Stats.2000, c. 363 (A.B.2818), § 2, eff. July 21, 2000.)*

Cross References

Decedent or transferor defined for purposes of this Part, see Revenue and Taxation Code § 13405.
Estate or property defined for purposes of this Part, see Revenue and Taxation Code § 13402.
Gross estate defined for purposes of this Part, see Revenue and Taxation Code § 13409.

CHAPTER 2. DEFINITIONS

Section
13401. Definitions to govern construction.
13402. Estate or property.
13403. Personal representative.
13404. Transfer.
13405. Decedent or transferor.
13406. Transferee.
13407. Resident or resident decedent.
13408. Nonresident or nonresident decedent.
13409. Gross estate.
13410. Taxable estate.
13411. Federal credit.

§ 13401. Definitions to govern construction

Except where the context otherwise requires, the definitions given in this chapter govern construction of this part. *(Added by Stats.1982, c. 327, p. 1490, § 170, eff. June 30, 1982; Stats.1982, c. 1535, p. 5975, § 15.)*

§ 13402. Estate or property

"Estate" or "property" means the real or personal property or interest therein included in the gross estate of a decedent or transferor, and includes all of the following:

(a) All intangible personal property included in the gross estate of a resident decedent within or without the state or subject to the jurisdiction thereof.

(b) All intangible personal property in California included in the gross estate of a nonresident decedent of the United States, including all stock of a corporation organized under the laws of California or which has its principal place of business or does the major part of its business in California or of a federal corporation or national bank which has its principal place of business or does the major part of its business in California, excluding, however, savings accounts in savings and loan associations operating under the authority of the Division of Savings and Loan or the Federal Home Loan Bank board and bank deposits, unless those deposits are held and used in connection with a business conducted or operated, in whole or in part, in California. *(Added by Stats.1982, c. 327, p. 1490, § 170, eff. June 30, 1982; Stats. 1982, c. 1535, p. 5975, § 15. Amended by Stats.2000, c. 363 (A.B.2818), § 3, eff. July 21, 2000.)*

Cross References

Decedent or transferor defined for purposes of this Part, see Revenue and Taxation Code § 13405.
Gross estate defined for purposes of this Part, see Revenue and Taxation Code § 13409.
Nonresident or nonresident decedent defined for purposes of this Part, see Revenue and Taxation Code § 13408.
Resident or resident decedent defined for purposes of this Part, see Revenue and Taxation Code § 13407.

§ 13403. Personal representative

"Personal representative" means the personal representative of the decedent or, if there is no personal representative appointed, qualified and acting within this state, any person who is in actual or constructive possession of any property included in the gross estate of the decedent. *(Added by Stats.1982, c. 327, p. 1490, § 170, eff. June 30, 1982; Stats. 1982, c. 1535, p. 5975, § 15.)*

Cross References

Decedent or transferor defined for purposes of this Part, see Revenue and Taxation Code § 13405.
Estate or property defined for purposes of this Part, see Revenue and Taxation Code § 13402.
Gross estate defined for purposes of this Part, see Revenue and Taxation Code § 13409.

§ 13404. Transfer

"Transfer" means the inclusion of any property or other interest included in the gross estate of a decedent. *(Added by Stats.1982, c. 327, p. 1491, § 170, eff. June 30, 1982; Stats. 1982, c. 1535, p. 5975, § 15. Amended by Stats.2000, c. 363 (A.B.2818), § 4, eff. July 21, 2000.)*

Cross References

Decedent or transferor defined for purposes of this Part, see Revenue and Taxation Code § 13405.
Estate or property defined for purposes of this Part, see Revenue and Taxation Code § 13402.
Gross estate defined for purposes of this Part, see Revenue and Taxation Code § 13409.

§ 13405. Decedent or transferor

"Decedent" or "transferor" means any person whose death gives rise to a transfer. *(Added by Stats.1982, c. 327, p. 1491, § 170, eff. June 30, 1982; Stats.1982, c. 1535, p. 5976, § 15. Amended by Stats.2000, c. 363 (A.B.2818), § 5, eff. July 21, 2000.)*

Cross References

Transfer defined for purposes of this Part, see Revenue and Taxation Code § 13404.

§ 13406. Transferee

"Transferee" means any person to whom a transfer is made, and includes any legatee, devisee, heir, next of kin, grantee, donee, vendee, assignee, successor, survivor, or beneficiary. *(Added by Stats.1982, c. 327, p. 1491, § 170, eff. June 30, 1982; Stats.1982, c. 1535, p. 5976, § 15.)*

Cross References

Transfer defined for purposes of this Part, see Revenue and Taxation Code § 13404.

§ 13407. Resident or resident decedent

"Resident" or "resident decedent" means a decedent who was domiciled in California at his or her death. *(Added by Stats.1982, c. 327, p. 1491, § 170, eff. June 30, 1982; Stats. 1982, c. 1535, p. 5976, § 15.)*

Cross References

Decedent or transferor defined for purposes of this Part, see Revenue and Taxation Code § 13405.

§ 13408. Nonresident or nonresident decedent

"Nonresident" or "nonresident decedent" means a decedent who was domiciled outside of California at his or her death. *(Added by Stats.1982, c. 327, p. 1491, § 170, eff. June 30, 1982; Stats.1982, c. 1535, p. 5976, § 15.)*

Cross References

Decedent or transferor defined for purposes of this Part, see Revenue and Taxation Code § 13405.

§ 13409. Gross estate

"Gross estate" means "gross estate" as defined in Section 2031 of the United States Internal Revenue Code of 1954,[1] as amended or renumbered. *(Added by Stats.1982, c. 327, p. 1491, § 170, eff. June 30, 1982; Stats.1982, c. 1535, p. 5976, § 15.)*

[1] 26 U.S.C.A. § 2031.

Cross References

Estate or property defined for purposes of this Part, see Revenue and Taxation Code § 13402.

§ 13410. Taxable estate

"Taxable estate" means the "taxable estate" as defined in Section 2051 of the United States Internal Revenue Code of 1954,[1] as amended or renumbered. *(Added by Stats.1982, c. 327, p. 1491, § 170, eff. June 30, 1982; Stats.1982, c. 1535, p. 5976, § 15.)*

[1] 26 U.S.C.A. § 2051.

Cross References

Estate or property defined for purposes of this Part, see Revenue and Taxation Code § 13402.

§ 13411. Federal credit

"Federal credit" means the maximum amount of the credit for state death taxes allowed by Section 2011 of the United States Internal Revenue Code of 1954,[1] as amended or renumbered in respect to a decedent's taxable estate. *(Added by Stats.1982, c. 327, p. 1491, § 170, eff. June 30, 1982; Stats.1982, c. 1535, p. 5976, § 15.)*

[1] 26 U.S.C.A. § 2011.

Cross References

Decedent or transferor defined for purposes of this Part, see Revenue and Taxation Code § 13405.
Estate or property defined for purposes of this Part, see Revenue and Taxation Code § 13402.
Taxable estate defined for purposes of this Part, see Revenue and Taxation Code § 13410.

CHAPTER 3. RETURNS

ARTICLE 1. ESTATE TAX RETURN

§ 13501. Filing returns and copies; state tax and federal estate tax

The personal representative of every estate subject to the tax imposed by this part who is required to file a federal estate tax return shall file with the Controller on or before the federal estate tax return is required to be filed both of the following:

(a) A return for the tax due under this part.

(b) A true copy of the federal estate tax return. *(Added by Stats.1982, c. 327, p. 1491, § 171, eff. June 30, 1982; Stats. 1982, c. 1535, p. 5976, § 15.)*

Cross References

Estate or property defined for purposes of this Part, see Revenue and Taxation Code § 13402.
Personal representative defined for purposes of this Part, see Revenue and Taxation Code § 13403.
State Controller, generally, see Government Code § 12402 et seq.

§ 13502. Extension of time for filing

If the personal representative has obtained an extension of time for filing the federal estate tax return, the filing required by Section 13501 shall be similarly extended until the end of the time period granted in the extension of time for the federal estate tax return. A true copy of the federal extension shall be filed with the Controller. *(Added by Stats.1982, c. 327, p. 1491, § 171, eff. June 30, 1982; Stats. 1982, c. 1535, p. 5976, § 15.)*

Cross References

Estate or property defined for purposes of this Part, see Revenue and Taxation Code § 13402.
Personal representative defined for purposes of this Part, see Revenue and Taxation Code § 13403.
State Controller, generally, see Government Code § 12402 et seq.

§ 13503. Amended returns; payment of additional tax

If the personal representative files an amended federal estate tax return, he or she shall immediately file with the Controller an amended return with a true copy of the amended federal estate tax return. If the personal representative is required to pay an additional tax under this part pursuant to the amended return, he or she shall pay that additional tax, together with any interest as provided in Section 13550 at the same time the amended return is filed. *(Added by Stats.1982, c. 327, p. 1491, § 171, eff. June 30, 1982; Stats.1982, c. 1535, p. 5976, § 15.)*

Cross References

Estate or property defined for purposes of this Part, see Revenue and Taxation Code § 13402.

Personal representative defined for purposes of this Part, see Revenue and Taxation Code § 13403.

State Controller, generally, see Government Code § 12402 et seq.

§ 13504. Notice; final determination of federal estate tax due; payment of additional tax and interest

Upon final determination of the federal estate tax due, the personal representative shall, within 60 days after that determination, give written notice of it to the Controller. If any additional tax is due under this part by reason of this determination, the personal representative shall pay the same, together with interest as provided in Section 13550, at the same time he or she files the notice. *(Added by Stats.1982, c. 327, p. 1492, § 171, eff. June 30, 1982; Stats. 1982, c. 1535, p. 5976, § 15.)*

Cross References

Estate or property defined for purposes of this Part, see Revenue and Taxation Code § 13402.

Personal representative defined for purposes of this Part, see Revenue and Taxation Code § 13403.

State Controller, generally, see Government Code § 12402 et seq.

ARTICLE 2. PENALTIES

Section
13510. Failure to timely file; penalty; waiver.

§ 13510. Failure to timely file; penalty; waiver

If the return provided for in Section 13501 is not filed within the time period specified therein or the extension specified in Section 13502, then the personal representative shall pay, in addition to the interest provided in Section 13550, a penalty equal to 5 percent of the tax due pursuant to this part, as finally determined, for each month, or portion thereof, during which that failure to file continues, not exceeding 25 percent in the aggregate, unless it is shown that such failure is due to reasonable cause. If a similar penalty for failure to timely file the federal estate tax return is waived, that waiver shall be deemed to constitute reasonable cause for purposes of this section. *(Added by Stats.1982, c. 327, p. 1492, § 171, eff. June 30, 1982; Stats.1982, c. 1535, p. 5977, § 15.)*

Cross References

Estate or property defined for purposes of this Part, see Revenue and Taxation Code § 13402.

Personal representative defined for purposes of this Part, see Revenue and Taxation Code § 13403.

CHAPTER 4. DEFICIENCY DETERMINATION

Section
13516. Determination of deficiency; time.
13517. False, fraudulent or unfiled returns.

Section
13518. Erroneous determination; set aside; issuance of amended determination.
13519. Notice of deficiency.
13520. Erroneous determination; action to modify.

§ 13516. Determination of deficiency; time

In a case not involving a false or fraudulent return or failure to file a return, if the Controller determines at any time after the tax is due, but not later than four years after the return is filed, that the tax disclosed in any return required to be filed by this part is less than the tax disclosed by his or her examination, a deficiency shall be determined. That determination may also be made within such time after the expiration of that four-year period as may be agreed upon in writing between the Controller and the personal representative.

For purposes of this section, a return filed before the last day prescribed by law for filing that return shall be considered as filed on that last day. *(Added by Stats.1982, c. 327, p. 1492, § 172, eff. June 30, 1982; Stats.1982, c. 1535, p. 5977, § 15.)*

Cross References

Personal representative defined for purposes of this Part, see Revenue and Taxation Code § 13403.

State Controller, generally, see Government Code § 12402 et seq.

§ 13517. False, fraudulent or unfiled returns

In the case of a false or fraudulent return or failure to file a return, the Controller may determine the tax at any time. *(Added by Stats.1982, c. 327, p. 1492, § 172, eff. June 30, 1982; Stats.1982, c. 1535, p. 5977, § 15.)*

Cross References

State Controller, generally, see Government Code § 12402 et seq.

§ 13518. Erroneous determination; set aside; issuance of amended determination

In any case in which a deficiency has been determined in an erroneous amount, the Controller may, within three years after the erroneous determination was made, set aside the determination or issue an amended determination in the correct amount. *(Added by Stats.1982, c. 327, p. 1492, § 172, eff. June 30, 1982; Stats.1982, c. 1535, p. 5977, § 15.)*

Cross References

State Controller, generally, see Government Code § 12402 et seq.

§ 13519. Notice of deficiency

The Controller shall give notice of the deficiency determined, together with any penalty for failure to file a return, by personal service or by mail to the person filing the return at the address stated in the return, or, if no return is filed, to the person liable for the tax. Copies of the notice of deficiency may in like manner be given to such other persons as the Controller deems advisable. *(Added by Stats.1982, c. 327, p. 1492, § 172, eff. June 30, 1982; Stats.1982, c. 1535, p. 5977, § 15.)*

Cross References

State Controller, generally, see Government Code § 12402 et seq.

§ 13520. Erroneous determination; action to modify

In any case in which it is claimed that a deficiency has been determined in an erroneous amount, any person who is liable for the tax may, within three years after the determination was made, bring an action against the state in the superior court having jurisdiction to have the tax modified in whole or in part. *(Added by Stats.1982, c. 327, p. 1493, § 172, eff. June 30, 1982; Stats.1982, c. 1535, p. 5977, § 15.)*

CHAPTER 5. PAYMENT OF TAX

ARTICLE 1. GENERALLY

§ 13530. Payment by personal representative; duration of liability

The tax imposed by this part shall be paid by the personal representative to the extent of assets subject to his or her control. Liability for payment of the tax continues until the tax is paid. *(Added by Stats.1982, c. 327, p. 1493, § 173, eff. June 30, 1982; Stats.1982, c. 1535, p. 5978, § 15.)*

Cross References

Personal representative defined for purposes of this Part, see Revenue and Taxation Code § 13403.

§ 13531. Due date

The tax imposed by this part is due and payable at the date of the decedent's death. *(Added by Stats.1982, c. 327, p. 1493, § 173, eff. June 30, 1982; Stats.1982, c. 1535, p. 5978, § 15.)*

Cross References

Decedent or transferor defined for purposes of this Part, see Revenue and Taxation Code § 13405.

§ 13532. Delinquency date

The tax imposed by this part is delinquent at the expiration of nine months from the date on which it becomes due and payable, if not paid within that time. *(Added by Stats.1982, c. 327, p. 1493, § 173, eff. June 30, 1982; Stats.1982, c. 1535, p. 5978, § 15.)*

§ 13533. Payee; remittance

The tax imposed by this part shall be paid to the Controller by remittance to the Treasurer. *(Added by Stats.1982, c. 327, p. 1493, § 173, eff. June 30, 1982; Stats.1982, c. 1535, p. 5978, § 15.)*

Cross References

State Controller, generally, see Government Code § 12402 et seq.

§ 13534. Application of Internal Revenue Code provisions

In the case of any decedent dying on or after January 1, 1999, Section 6166 of the Internal Revenue Code, [1] enacted as of January 1, 1998, shall apply to any tax due, and the interest rate on amounts due, as provided in Section 6601(j) of the Internal Revenue Code, [2] enacted as of January 1, 1998, shall apply in lieu of the rate provided in Section 13550. *(Added by Stats.1998, c. 323 (A.B.2798), § 8, eff. Aug. 20, 1998.)*

[1] See 26 U.S.C.A. § 6166.
[2] See 26 U.S.C.A. § 6601.

Cross References

Decedent or transferor defined for purposes of this Part, see Revenue and Taxation Code § 13405.

ARTICLE 2. INTEREST

§ 13550. Imposition; rate

(a) The tax imposed by this part does not bear interest if it is paid prior to the date on which it otherwise becomes delinquent. However, if the tax is paid after that date, the tax bears interest at the rate for underpayment of estate tax provided in Section 6621(a)(2) of the Internal Revenue Code from the date it became delinquent and until it is paid. Interest under this section shall be compounded daily.

(b) The amendments made by Chapter 323 of the Statutes of 1998 shall apply to delinquent amounts unpaid on or after January 1, 1999, to December 31, 2000, inclusive. *(Added by Stats.1982, c. 327, p. 1493, § 173, eff. June 30, 1982; Stats. 1982, c. 1535, p. 5978, § 15. Amended by Stats.1998, c. 323 (A.B.2798), § 9, eff. Aug. 20, 1998; Stats.2000, c. 363 (A.B. 2818), § 6, eff. July 21, 2000, operative Jan. 1, 2001.)*

Cross References

Estate or property defined for purposes of this Part, see Revenue and Taxation Code § 13402.

§ 13551. Application of payments

Every payment on the tax imposed by this part is applied, first, to any interest due on the tax, secondly, to any penalty imposed by this part, and then, if there is any balance, to the tax itself. *(Added by Stats.2003, c. 221 (A.B.1556), § 1.)*

§ 13552. Treatment and collection of interest and penalties

All interest and penalties provided in this chapter shall be treated and collected in the same manner as taxes. *(Added by Stats.2003, c. 221 (A.B.1556), § 2.)*

ARTICLE 3. DELINQUENT TAX BOND

§ 13555. Delinquent tax; personal representative's bond; amount

If any personal representative fails to pay any tax imposed by this part for which he or she is liable prior to the delinquent date of the tax, he or she shall, on motion of the Controller, in his or her discretion, be required by the superior court having jurisdiction to execute a bond to the people of the State of California in a penalty of twice the amount of the tax with those sureties as the court may approve, conditioned for the payment of the tax, plus interest on the tax at the rate of 12 percent per annum commencing on the date that tax became delinquent, within a certain time to be fixed by the court and specified in the bond. *(Added by Stats.1982, c. 327, p. 1493, § 173, eff. June 30, 1982; Stats. 1982, c. 1535, p. 5978, § 15.)*

Cross References

Personal representative defined for purposes of this Part, see Revenue and Taxation Code § 13403.
State Controller, generally, see Government Code § 12402 et seq.

§ 13556. Filing bond and copy

The bond shall be filed in the office of the clerk of the court, and a certified copy shall be immediately transmitted to the Controller. *(Added by Stats.1982, c. 327, p. 1494, § 173, eff. June 30, 1982; Stats.1982, c. 1535, p. 5978, § 15.)*

Cross References

State Controller, generally, see Government Code § 12402 et seq.

§ 13557. Failure to file bond; revocation of letters of personal representative

If the bond is not filed within 20 days after the date of the filing of the order requiring it, the letters of the personal representative affected shall be revoked upon motion of the Controller. *(Added by Stats.1982, c. 327, p. 1494, § 173, eff. June 30, 1982; Stats.1982, c. 1535, p. 5978, § 15.)*

Cross References

Personal representative defined for purposes of this Part, see Revenue and Taxation Code § 13403.
State Controller, generally, see Government Code § 12402 et seq.

CHAPTER 6. REFUNDS

§ 13560. Entitlement to refund

Whenever the Controller determines that the tax due under this part has been over paid, the person making payment shall be entitled to a refund of the amount erroneously paid on presentation of proof satisfactory to the Controller that he or she is entitled to a refund. *(Added by Stats.1982, c. 327, p. 1494, § 174, eff. June 30, 1982; Stats. 1982, c. 1535, p. 5979, § 15.)*

Cross References

State Controller, generally, see Government Code § 12402 et seq.

§ 13561. Application; time

An application for the refund shall be made to the Controller within one year after the date the federal estate tax has been finally determined. *(Added by Stats.1982, c. 327, p. 1494, § 174, eff. June 30, 1982; Stats.1982, c. 1535, p. 5979, § 15.)*

Cross References

Estate or property defined for purposes of this Part, see Revenue and Taxation Code § 13402.
State Controller, generally, see Government Code § 12402 et seq.

§ 13562. Warrant

On proof satisfactory that the applicant is entitled to a refund, the Controller shall draw his or her warrant upon the Treasurer in favor of the person who paid the tax in the amount erroneously paid, and the Treasurer shall refund that amount. *(Added by Stats.1982, c. 327, p. 1494, § 174, eff. June 30, 1982; Stats.1982, c. 1535, p. 5979, § 15.)*

Cross References

State Controller, generally, see Government Code § 12402 et seq.

§ 13563. Interest

(a) For purposes of determining interest on overpayments for periods beginning before July 1, 2002, interest shall be allowed and paid upon any overpayment of tax due under this part in the same manner as provided in Sections 6621(a)(1) and 6622 of the Internal Revenue Code.

(b) For purposes of determining interest on overpayments for periods beginning on or after July 1, 2002, interest shall be allowed and paid upon any overpayment of tax due under this part at the lesser of the following:

(1) Five percent.

(2) The bond equivalent rate of 13–week United States Treasury bills, determined as follows:

(A) The bond equivalent rate of 13–week United States Treasury bills established at the first auction held during the month of January shall be utilized for determining the appropriate rate for the following July 1 to December 31, inclusive.

(B) The bond equivalent rate of 13–week United States Treasury bills established at the first auction held during the month of July shall be utilized for determining the appropriate rate for the following January 1 to June 30, inclusive.

(c) For purposes of subdivision (b), in computing the amount of any interest required to be paid by the state, that interest shall be computed as simple interest, not compound interest. That interest shall be allowed from the date on which payment would have become delinquent, if not paid, or the date of actual payment, whichever is later in time, to the date preceding the date of the refund warrant by not more than 30 days, the date to be determined by the Controller. *(Added by Stats.1982, c. 327, p. 1494, § 174, eff. June 30, 1982;*

Stats.1982, c. 1535, p. 5979, § 15. Amended by Stats.2000, c. 363 (A.B.2818), § 7, eff. July 21, 2000, operative Jan. 1, 2001; Stats.2002, c. 1124 (A.B.3000), § 52, eff. Sept. 30, 2002; Stats.2003, c. 697 (A.B.1741), § 5.)

Cross References

State Controller, generally, see Government Code § 12402 et seq.

CHAPTER 7. COLLECTION OF TAX

ARTICLE 1. SUIT FOR TAX

Section
13601. Action by state.

§ 13601. Action by state

The state may enforce its claim for any tax imposed by this part and enforce the lien of the tax by a civil action in any court of competent jurisdiction against any person liable for the tax or against any property subject to the lien. *(Added by Stats.1982, c. 327, p. 1494, § 175, eff. June 30, 1982; Stats. 1982, c. 1535, p. 5979, § 15.)*

Cross References

Estate or property defined for purposes of this Part, see Revenue and Taxation Code § 13402.

ARTICLE 2. LIEN OF TAX

Section
13610. State tax lien; law governing; extinguishment; duration; conditions.

§ 13610. State tax lien; law governing; extinguishment; duration; conditions

(a) If any personal representative fails to pay any tax, interest, or penalty imposed under this part at the time that it becomes due and payable, the amount thereof, including penalties and interest, together with any costs in addition thereto, shall thereupon be a perfected and enforceable state tax lien. Except as otherwise provided in subdivision (b), the lien is subject to Chapter 14 (commencing with Section 7150) of Division 7 of Title 1 of the Government Code.

(b) Notwithstanding subdivision (a) of Section 7172 of the Government Code, all of the following apply to a state tax lien created pursuant to subdivision (a):

(1) If the lien is not extinguished as in paragraph (2), (3), or (4), or otherwise released or discharged, it expires 10 years from the time a deficiency determination is issued pursuant to this part if, within that 10 years, no notice of the lien has been recorded or filed as provided in Section 7171 of the Government Code.

(2) If suit or a proceeding for collection of the tax has not been instituted within 5 years after the tax becomes due and payable, the lien ceases as to any bona fide purchaser, mortgagee, or lessee of, or beneficiary under a deed of trust on, the property subject to the lien.

(3) If property subject to the lien is sold, exchanged, or otherwise transferred pursuant to the Probate Code the lien ceases as to the property and attaches to the proceeds or other consideration received.

(4) If property subject to the lien is mortgaged, hypothecated or leased pursuant to the Probate Code, the lien becomes subject to and subordinate to the rights and interests of the mortgagee, lessee, or other person so secured or created, and attaches to the proceeds of the mortgage, hypothecation, or lease. *(Added by Stats.1982, c. 327, p. 1495, § 175, eff. June 30, 1982; Stats.1982, c. 1535, p. 5979, § 15. Amended by Stats.1983, c. 645, § 2.)*

Cross References

Definition of state tax lien for purposes of Government Code state tax lien provisions, lien created pursuant to this section, see Government Code § 7162.
Estate or property defined for purposes of this Part, see Revenue and Taxation Code § 13402.
Personal representative defined for purposes of this Part, see Revenue and Taxation Code § 13403.

ARTICLE 3. WARRANT FOR COLLECTION OF TAX

Section
13615. Warrant; enforcement of lien and collection of tax.
13616. Fees, commissions and expenses; payment.
13617. Liability for fees, commissions and expenses; collection.

§ 13615. Warrant; enforcement of lien and collection of tax

At any time within 10 years after any person is delinquent in the payment of any amount herein required to be paid, or within 10 years after the last recording or filing of a notice of state tax lien under Section 7171 of the Government Code, the Controller or his or her authorized representative may issue a warrant for the enforcement of any liens and for the collection of any amount required to be paid to the state under this part. The warrant shall be directed to any sheriff or marshal and shall have the same effect as a writ of execution. The warrant shall be levied and sale made pursuant to it in the same manner and with the same effect as a levy of and sale pursuant to a writ of execution. *(Added by Stats.1982, c. 327, p. 1495, § 175, eff. June 30, 1982; Stats. 1982, c. 1535, p. 5980, § 15. Amended by Stats.1996, c. 872 (A.B.3472), § 149.)*

Cross References

State Controller, generally, see Government Code § 12402 et seq.

§ 13616. Fees, commissions and expenses; payment

The Controller may pay or advance to the sheriff or marshal, the same fees, commissions, and expenses for his or her services as are provided by law for similar services pursuant to a writ of execution. The Controller, and not the court, shall approve the fees for publication in a newspaper. *(Added by Stats.1982, c. 327, p. 1495, § 175, eff. June 30, 1982; Stats.1982, c. 1535, p. 5980, § 15. Amended by Stats.1996, c. 872 (A.B.3472), § 150.)*

Cross References

State Controller, generally, see Government Code § 12402 et seq.

§ 13617. Liability for fees, commissions and expenses; collection

The fees, commissions, and expenses are obligations of the person required to pay any amount under this part and may be collected from him or her by virtue of the warrant or in any manner provided in this part for the collection of the tax. *(Added by Stats.1982, c. 327, p. 1495, § 175, eff. June 30, 1982; Stats.1982, c. 1535, p. 5980, § 15.)*

ARTICLE 4.   WRIT OF EXECUTION

Section
13620.   Issuance.
13621.   Property subject to writ.
13622.   Fee.

§ 13620.   Issuance

At any time after a tax imposed by this part is delinquent, the Controller may have a writ of execution issued for the enforcement of any judgment rendered pursuant to this part in respect to the tax. *(Added by Stats.1982, c. 327, p. 1495, § 175, eff. June 30, 1982; Stats.1982, c. 1535, p. 5980, § 15.)*

Cross References

State Controller, generally, see Government Code § 12402 et seq.

§ 13621.   Property subject to writ

The writ shall be executed against any property of the person liable for payment of the tax, or against any property subject to the lien of the tax. *(Added by Stats.1982, c. 327, p. 1496, § 175, eff. June 30, 1982; Stats.1982, c. 1535, p. 5980, § 15.)*

Cross References

Estate or property defined for purposes of this Part, see Revenue and Taxation Code § 13402.

§ 13622.   Fee

No fee shall be exacted from the Controller for the issuance of execution of the writ. *(Added by Stats.1982, c. 327, p. 1496, § 175, eff. June 30, 1982; Stats.1982, c. 1535, p. 5980, § 15.)*

Cross References

State Controller, generally, see Government Code § 12402 et seq.

ARTICLE 5.   MISCELLANEOUS

Section
13680.   Commencement of collection proceedings; time limi-
            tations.
13681.   Certificate of amount due; evidentiary effect.
13682.   Prevention or injunction of collection prohibited.
13683.   Actions in other states; comity; certificate of authori-
            ty of officials; evidentiary effect.
13684.   Cumulative effect of remedies.

§ 13680.   Commencement of collection proceedings; time limitations

Proceedings for the collection of any tax imposed by this part may be commenced at any time after the tax is due and within 10 years from and after the time a delinquency determination is issued pursuant to the provisions of this part. *(Added by Stats.1982, c. 327, p. 1496, § 175, eff. June 30, 1982; Stats.1982, c. 1535, p. 5980, § 15.)*

§ 13681.   Certificate of amount due; evidentiary effect

In any proceeding for the enforcement of the estate tax a certificate by the Controller showing the amount due is prima facie evidence of the imposition of the tax, of the fact that it is due, and of compliance by the Controller with all the provisions of this part in relation to the computation and determination of the tax. *(Added by Stats.1982, c. 327, p. 1496, § 175, eff. June 30, 1982; Stats.1982, c. 1535, p. 5980, § 15.)*

Cross References

Estate or property defined for purposes of this Part, see Revenue and
   Taxation Code § 13402.
Prima facie evidence, see Evidence Code § 602.
State Controller, generally, see Government Code § 12402 et seq.

§ 13682.   Prevention or injunction of collection prohibited

No injunction, writ of mandate, or other legal or equitable process shall ever issue in any suit, action, or proceeding in any court against this state or any officer of this state to prevent or enjoin the collection of any tax imposed by this part. *(Added by Stats.1982, c. 327, p. 1496, § 175, eff. June 30, 1982; Stats.1882, c. 1535, p. 5981, § 15.)*

Cross References

Mandamus, purpose of writ of mandate, courts which may issue writ
   and parties to whom issued, see Code of Civil Procedure § 1085.

§ 13683.   Actions in other states; comity; certificate of authority of officials; evidentiary effect

The Controller may bring suits in the courts of other states to collect estate taxes payable under this part.   An official of another state which extends a like comity to this state may sue for the collection of similar taxes in the courts of this state. A certificate by the secretary of state of another state, under the great seal of that state, that an official thereof has authority to collect its estate or other transfer taxes is conclusive evidence of the authority of that official in any suit for the collection of those taxes in any court of this state. *(Added by Stats.1982, c. 327, p. 1496, § 175, eff. June 30, 1982; Stats.1982, c. 1535, p. 5981, § 15.)*

Cross References

Estate or property defined for purposes of this Part, see Revenue and
   Taxation Code § 13402.
State Controller, generally, see Government Code § 12402 et seq.
Transfer defined for purposes of this Part, see Revenue and Taxation
   Code § 13404.

§ 13684.   Cumulative effect of remedies

The remedies of the state for the enforcement of the tax imposed by this part are cumulative, and no action taken by the Controller or any other state official constitutes an election by the state or any of its officers to pursue any remedy to the exclusion of any other remedy for which provision is made by this part. *(Added by Stats.1982, c. 327, p. 1496, § 175, eff. June 30, 1982; Stats.1982, c. 1535, p. 5981, § 15.)*

ARTICLE 6. TAX COMPROMISE

§ 13801. Compromise with personal representative of claimed nonresident decedent

The Controller may compromise with the personal representative the tax, including interest and penalty thereon, payable on the estate of any decedent who it is claimed was not a resident of this state at the time of his or her death. *(Added by Stats.1982, c. 327, p. 1496, § 175, eff. June 30, 1982; Stats.1982, c. 1535, p. 5981, § 15.)*

§ 13810. Dispute as to decedent's domicile; agreement as to amount of taxes; parties; filing; interest

When the Controller claims that a decedent was domiciled in this state at the time of his or her death and the taxing authorities of another state or states make a like claim on behalf of their state or states, the Controller may make a written agreement of compromise with the other taxing authorities and the executor or administrator that a certain sum shall be accepted in full satisfaction of any and all death taxes imposed by this state, including any interest to the date of filing the agreement. The agreement shall also fix the amount to be accepted by the other states in full satisfaction of death taxes. The executor or administrator is hereby authorized to make that agreement. Either the Controller or the executor or administrator shall file the agreement, or a duplicate, with the authority that would be empowered to determine death taxes for this state if there had been no agreement; and thereupon the tax shall be deemed conclusively fixed as therein provided. Unless the tax is paid within 90 days after filing the agreement, interest shall thereafter accrue upon the amount fixed in the agreement but the time between the decedent's death and the filing shall not be included in computing the interest. *(Added by Stats.1982, c. 327, p. 1496, § 175, eff. June 30, 1982; Stats.1982, c. 1535, p. 5981, § 15.)*

§ 13810.1. "State" defined

As used in this article, "state" means any state, territory, or possession of the United States, and the District of Columbia. *(Added by Stats.1982, c. 327, p. 1497, § 175, eff. June 30, 1982; Stats.1982, c. 1535, p. 5981, § 15.)*

§ 13810.2. Construction to effect uniformity

This article shall be so interpreted and construed as to effectuate its general purpose to make uniform the law of those states which enact it. *(Added by Stats.1982, c. 327, p. 1497, § 175, eff. June 30, 1982; Stats.1982, c. 1535, p. 5981, § 15.)*

§ 13810.3. Short title

This article may be cited as the "Uniform Act on Interstate Compromise of Death Taxes." *(Added by Stats.1982, c. 327, p. 1497, § 175, eff. June 30, 1982; Stats.1982, c. 1535, p. 5981, § 15.)*

§ 13810.4. Applicability of article

This article shall apply to estates of decedents dying before or after its enactment. *(Added by Stats.1982, c. 327, p. 1497, § 175, eff. June 30, 1982; Stats.1982, c. 1535, p. 5982, § 15.)*

ARTICLE 7. UNIFORM ACT ON INTERSTATE ARBITRATION OF DEATH TAXES

Alternative method for determination of domicile by arbitration, see Revenue and Taxation Code § 13830 et seq.

Tax compromise, see Revenue and Taxation Code § 13801.

§ 13820. Dispute as to decedent's domicile; agreement to arbitrate; board of arbitrators

When the Controller claims that a decedent was domiciled in this state at the time of his or her death and the taxing authorities of another state or states make a like claim on behalf of their state or states, the Controller may make a written agreement with the other taxing authorities and with the executor or administrator to submit the controversy to the decision of a board consisting of one or any uneven number of arbitrators (hereafter referred to in this article as "board"). The executor or administrator is hereby authorized to make the agreement. The parties to the agreement shall select the arbitrator or arbitrators. *(Added by Stats. 1982, c. 327, p. 1497, § 175, eff. June 30, 1982; Stats.1982, c. 1535, p. 5982, § 15.)*

Decedent or transferor defined for purposes of this Part, see Revenue and Taxation Code § 13405.

State Controller, generally, see Government Code § 12402 et seq.

§ 13820.1. Hearings

The board shall hold hearings at such times and places as it may determine, upon reasonable notice to the parties to the agreement, all of whom shall be entitled to be heard, to present evidence and to examine and cross-examine witnesses. *(Added by Stats.1982, c. 327, p. 1497, § 175, eff. June 30, 1982; Stats.1982, c. 1535, p. 5982, § 15.)*

§ 13820.2. Powers of board; enforcement of subpoenas

The board shall have power to administer oaths, take testimony, subpoena and require the attendance of witnesses and the production of books, papers and documents, and issue commissions to take testimony. Subpoenas may be signed by any member of the board. In case of failure to obey a subpoena, any judge of a court of record of this state, upon application by the board, may make an order requiring compliance with the subpoena, and the court may punish failure to obey the order as a contempt. *(Added by Stats. 1982, c. 327, p. 1497, § 175, eff. June 30, 1982; Stats.1982, c. 1535, p. 5982, § 15.)*

§ 13820.3. Determination; finality

The board shall, by majority vote, determine the domicile of the decedent at the time of his or her death. This determination shall be final for purposes of imposing and collecting death taxes but for no other purpose. *(Added by Stats.1982, c. 327, p. 1497, § 175, eff. June 30, 1982; Stats. 1982, c. 1535, p. 5982, § 15.)*

Decedent or transferor defined for purposes of this Part, see Revenue and Taxation Code § 13405.

§ 13820.4. Majority vote

Except as provided in Section 13820.2 in respect of the issuance of subpoenas, all questions arising in the course of the proceeding shall be determined by majority vote of the board. *(Added by Stats.1982, c. 327, p. 1498, § 175, eff. June 30, 1982; Stats.1982, c. 1535, p. 5982, § 15.)*

§ 13820.5. Determination; filing

The Controller, the board, or the executor or administrator shall file the determination of the board as to domicile, the record of the board's proceedings, and the agreement, or a duplicate, made pursuant to Section 13820, with the authority having jurisdiction to determine the death taxes in the state determined to be the domicile and shall file copies of all such documents with the authorities that would have been empowered to determine the death taxes in each of the other states involved. *(Added by Stats.1982, c. 327, p. 1498, § 175, eff. June 30, 1982; Stats.1982, c. 1535, p. 5982, § 15.)*

State Controller, generally, see Government Code § 12402 et seq.

§ 13820.6. Interest; maximum rate

In any case where it is determined by the board that the decedent died domiciled in this state, interest, if otherwise imposed by law, for nonpayment of death taxes between the date of the agreement and of filing of the determination of the board as to domicile, shall not exceed 10 percent per annum. *(Added by Stats.1982, c. 327, p. 1498, § 175, eff. June 30, 1982; Stats.1982, c. 1535, p. 5982, § 15.)*

Decedent or transferor defined for purposes of this Part, see Revenue and Taxation Code § 13405.

§ 13820.7. Written compromise

Nothing contained herein shall prevent at any time a written compromise, if otherwise lawful, by all parties to the agreement made pursuant to Section 13820, fixing the amounts to be accepted by this and any other state involved in full satisfaction of death taxes. *(Added by Stats.1982, c. 327, p. 1498, § 175, eff. June 30, 1982; Stats.1982, c. 1535, p. 5983, § 15.)*

§ 13820.8. Compensation and expenses; determination; administration expense

The compensation and expenses of the members of the board and its employees may be agreed upon among those members and the executor or administrator and if they cannot agree shall be fixed by the superior court of the state determined by the board to be the domicile of the decedent. The amounts so agreed upon or fixed shall be deemed an administration expense and shall be payable by the executor or administrator. *(Added by Stats.1982, c. 327, p. 1498, § 175, eff. June 30, 1982; Stats.1982, c. 1535, p. 5983, § 15.)*

Decedent or transferor defined for purposes of this Part, see Revenue and Taxation Code § 13405.

§ 13820.9. Applicability of article; states with similar laws

This article shall apply only to cases in which each of the states involved has a law identical with or substantially similar to this act. *(Added by Stats.1982, c. 327, p. 1498, § 175, eff. June 30, 1982; Stats.1982, c. 1535, p. 5983, § 15.)*

§ 13820.10.   State

As used in this article, the word "state" means any state, territory, or possession of the United States, and the District of Columbia.   *(Added by Stats.1982, c. 327, p. 1498, § 175, eff. June 30, 1982; Stats.1982, c. 1535, p. 5983, § 15.)*

§ 13820.11.   Construction to effect uniformity

This article shall be so interpreted and construed as to effectuate its general purpose to make uniform the law of those states which enact it.   *(Added by Stats.1982, c. 327, p. 1498, § 175, eff. June 30, 1982; Stats.1982, c. 1535, p. 5983, § 15.)*

§ 13820.12.   Short title

This article may be cited as the "Uniform Act on Interstate Arbitration of Death Taxes."   *(Added by Stats.1982, c. 327, p. 1498, § 175, eff. June 30, 1982; Stats.1982, c. 1535, p. 5983, § 15.)*

§ 13820.13.   Application of article to estates of decedents

This article shall apply to estates of decedents dying before or after its enactment.   *(Added by Stats.1982, c. 327, p. 1498, § 175, eff. June 30, 1982; Stats.1982, c. 1535, p. 5983, § 15.)*

Cross References

Decedent or transferor defined for purposes of this Part, see Revenue and Taxation Code § 13405.

Estate or property defined for purposes of this Part, see Revenue and Taxation Code § 13402.

ARTICLE 8.   DETERMINATION OF DOMICILE BY ARBITRATION: ALTERNATIVE METHOD

Cross References

Tax compromise, see Revenue and Taxation Code § 13801.
Uniform Act on Interstate Arbitration of Death Taxes, see Revenue and Taxation Code § 13820 et seq.

§ 13830.   Definitions

For the purposes of this article:

(a) "Executor" means an executor of the will or administrator of the estate of the decedent, but does not include an ancillary administrator nor an administrator with the will annexed if an executor named in the will has been appointed and has qualified in another state.

(b) "Taxing official" means the Controller of the State of California and the designated authority of a reciprocal state.

(c) "Death tax" means any tax levied by a state on account of the transfer or shifting of economic benefits in property at death, or in contemplation thereof, or intended to take effect in possession or enjoyment at or after death, whether denominated an "inheritance tax," "transfer tax," "succession tax," "estate tax," "death duty," "death dues," or otherwise.

(d) "Interested person" means any person who may be entitled to receive, or who has received, any property or interest which may be required to be considered in computing the death tax of any state involved.

(e) "State" means any state, territory, or possession of the United States, or the District of Columbia.   "This state" means the State of California.

(f) "Board" means board of arbitration.   *(Added by Stats. 1982, c. 327, p. 1498, § 175, eff. June 30, 1982; Stats.1982, c. 1535, p. 5983, § 15.)*

Cross References

Decedent or transferor defined for purposes of this Part, see Revenue and Taxation Code § 13405.

Estate or property defined for purposes of this Part, see Revenue and Taxation Code § 13402.

State Controller, generally, see Government Code § 12402 et seq.

Transfer defined for purposes of this Part, see Revenue and Taxation Code § 13404.

§ 13830.1.   Authorization; notice of election; effect of rejection

In any case in which this state and one or more other states each claims that it was the domicile of a decedent at his or her death, at any time prior to the commencement of legal action for determination of domicile within this state or within 60 days thereafter, any executor, or the taxing official of any such state, may elect to invoke the provisions of this article.   That executor or taxing official shall send a notice of that election by registered mail, receipt requested, to the taxing official of each such state and to each executor, ancillary administrator, and interested person.   Within 40 days after the receipt of that notice of election, any executor may reject that election by sending a notice, by registered mail, receipt requested, to all persons originally required to be sent a notice of election.   When an election has been rejected by an executor, no further proceedings shall be had under this article.   If that election is not rejected within the 40-day period, the dispute as to death taxes shall be determined solely as provided in this article.   No other proceedings to determine or assess those death taxes shall thereafter be prosecuted in any court of this state or otherwise.   *(Added by Stats.1982, c. 327, p. 1499, § 175, eff. June 30, 1982; Stats.1982, c. 1535, p. 5984, § 15.)*

Cross References

Death tax defined for purposes of this Article, see Revenue and Taxation Code § 13830.

Decedent or transferor defined for purposes of this Part, see Revenue and Taxation Code § 13405.

Executor defined for purposes of this Article, see Revenue and Taxation Code § 13830.
Interested person defined for purposes of this Article, see Revenue and Taxation Code § 13830.
State defined for purposes of this Article, see Revenue and Taxation Code § 13830.
Taxing official defined for purposes of this Article, see Revenue and Taxation Code § 13830.

§ 13830.2. Agreement accepting sum in full payment

In any case in which an election is made and not rejected the Controller may enter into a written agreement with the other taxing officials involved and with the executors to accept a certain sum in full payment of any death taxes, together with interest and penalties, that may be due this state; provided, this agreement fixes the amount to be paid the other states involved in the dispute. *(Added by Stats. 1982, c. 327, p. 1499, § 175, eff. June 30, 1982; Stats.1982, c. 1535, p. 5984, § 15.)*

Cross References

Death tax defined for purposes of this Article, see Revenue and Taxation Code § 13830.
Executor defined for purposes of this Article, see Revenue and Taxation Code § 13830.
State Controller, generally, see Government Code § 12402 et seq.
State defined for purposes of this Article, see Revenue and Taxation Code § 13830.
Taxing official defined for purposes of this Article, see Revenue and Taxation Code § 13830.

§ 13830.3. Failure to agree or lapse of time; effect

If in any case it appears that an agreement cannot be reached, as provided in Section 13830.2, or if one year shall have elapsed from the date of the election without an agreement having been reached, the domicile of the decedent at the time of his or her death shall be determined solely for death tax purposes as provided for in this article. *(Added by Stats.1982, c. 327, p. 1499, § 175, eff. June 30, 1982; Stats. 1982, c. 1535, p. 5984, § 15.)*

Cross References

Death tax defined for purposes of this Article, see Revenue and Taxation Code § 13830.
Decedent or transferor defined for purposes of this Part, see Revenue and Taxation Code § 13405.

§ 13830.4. Appointment of arbitration board members; chairman

Where only this state and one other state are involved, the Controller and the taxing official of the other state shall each appoint a member of a board of arbitration, and these members shall appoint the third member of the board. If this state and more than one other state are involved, the taxing officials thereof shall agree upon the authorities charged with the duty of administering death tax laws in three states not involved in the dispute and each of these authorities shall appoint a member of the board of arbitration. The board shall select one of its members as chairman. *(Added by Stats.1982, c. 327, p. 1499, § 175, eff. June 30, 1982; Stats.1982, c. 1535, p. 5984, § 15.)*

Cross References

Board defined for purposes of this Article, see Revenue and Taxation Code § 13830.
Death tax defined for purposes of this Article, see Revenue and Taxation Code § 13830.
State Controller, generally, see Government Code § 12402 et seq.
State defined for purposes of this Article, see Revenue and Taxation Code § 13830.
Taxing official defined for purposes of this Article, see Revenue and Taxation Code § 13830.

§ 13830.5. Hearings; notice

The board shall hold hearings at such places as are deemed necessary, upon reasonable notice to the executors, ancillary administrators, all other interested persons, and to the taxing officials of the states involved, all of whom are entitled to be heard. *(Added by Stats.1982, c. 327, p. 1500, § 175, eff. June 30, 1982; Stats.1982, c. 1535, p. 5984, § 15.)*

Cross References

Board defined for purposes of this Article, see Revenue and Taxation Code § 13830.
Executor defined for purposes of this Article, see Revenue and Taxation Code § 13830.
Interested person defined for purposes of this Article, see Revenue and Taxation Code § 13830.
State defined for purposes of this Article, see Revenue and Taxation Code § 13830.
Taxing official defined for purposes of this Article, see Revenue and Taxation Code § 13830.

§ 13830.6. Powers of arbitration board; subpoenas; punishment for failure to obey

The board may administer oaths, take testimony, subpoena witnesses and require their attendance, require the production of books, papers and documents, and issue commissions to take testimony. Subpoenas may be issued by any member of the board. Failure to obey a subpoena may be punished by any court of record in the same manner as if the subpoena had been issued by that court. *(Added by Stats.1982, c. 327, p. 1500, § 175, eff. June 30, 1982; Stats.1982, c. 1535, p. 5984, § 15.)*

Cross References

Board defined for purposes of this Article, see Revenue and Taxation Code § 13830.

§ 13830.7. Rules of evidence

Whenever practicable the board shall apply the rules of evidence then prevailing in the federal courts under the federal rules of civil procedure. *(Added by Stats.1982, c. 327, p. 1500, § 175, eff. June 30, 1982; Stats.1982, c. 1535, p. 5985, § 15.)*

Cross References

Board defined for purposes of this Article, see Revenue and Taxation Code § 13830.

§ 13830.8. Determination of domicile; effect; failure to render determination

The board shall determine the domicile of the decedent at the time of his or her death. This determination is final and conclusive and binds this state, and all of its judicial and administrative officials on all questions concerning the domicile of the decedent for death tax purposes. If the board does not render a determination within one year from the time that it is fully constituted, all authority of the board shall cease and the bar to court proceedings set forth in Section 13830.1 shall no longer exist. *(Added by Stats.1982, c. 327, p. 1500, § 175, eff. June 30, 1982; Stats.1982, c. 1535, p. 5985, § 15.)*

Cross References

Board defined for purposes of this Article, see Revenue and Taxation Code § 13830.
Death tax defined for purposes of this Article, see Revenue and Taxation Code § 13830.
Decedent or transferor defined for purposes of this Part, see Revenue and Taxation Code § 13405.
State defined for purposes of this Article, see Revenue and Taxation Code § 13830.

§ 13830.9. Compensation and expenses

The reasonable compensation and expenses of the members of the board and its employees shall be agreed upon among those members, the taxing officials involved, and the executors. If an agreement cannot be reached, compensation and expenses shall be determined by those taxing officials; and, if they cannot agree, by the appropriate probate court of the state determined to be the domicile. That amount shall be borne by the estate and shall be deemed an administration expense. *(Added by Stats.1982, c. 327, p. 1500, § 175, eff. June 30, 1982; Stats.1982, c. 1535, p. 5985, § 15.)*

Cross References

Board defined for purposes of this Article, see Revenue and Taxation Code § 13830.
Estate or property defined for purposes of this Part, see Revenue and Taxation Code § 13402.
Executor defined for purposes of this Article, see Revenue and Taxation Code § 13830.
State defined for purposes of this Article, see Revenue and Taxation Code § 13830.
Taxing official defined for purposes of this Article, see Revenue and Taxation Code § 13830.

§ 13830.10. Filing determination and record

The determination of the board and the record of its proceedings shall be filed with the authority having jurisdiction to assess the death tax in the state determined to be the domicile of the decedent and with the authorities which would have had jurisdiction to assess the death tax in each of the other states involved if the decedent had been found to be domiciled therein. *(Added by Stats.1982, c. 327, p. 1500, § 175, eff. June 30, 1982; Stats.1982, c. 1535, p. 5985, § 15.)*

Cross References

Board defined for purposes of this Article, see Revenue and Taxation Code § 13830.
Death tax defined for purposes of this Article, see Revenue and Taxation Code § 13830.
Decedent or transferor defined for purposes of this Part, see Revenue and Taxation Code § 13405.

State defined for purposes of this Article, see Revenue and Taxation Code § 13830.

§ 13830.11. Written agreement for sum in payment of tax; contents; assessment; coordination with federal estate tax credit

Notwithstanding the commencement of a legal action for determination of domicile within this state or the commencement of an arbitration proceeding, as provided in Section 13830.3, the Controller may in any case enter into a written agreement with the other taxing officials involved and with the executors to accept a certain sum in full payment of any death tax, together with interest and penalties, that may be due this state; provided, this agreement fixes the amount to be paid the other states involved in the dispute, at any time before that proceeding is concluded. Upon the filing of this agreement with the authority which would have jurisdiction to assess the death tax of this state, if the decedent died domiciled in this state, an assessment shall be made as provided in that agreement, and this assessment finally and conclusively fixes the amount of death tax due this state. If the aggregate amount payable under that agreement or under an agreement made in accordance with the provisions of Section 13830.2 to the states involved is less than the minimum credit allowable to the estate against the United States estate tax imposed with respect thereto, the executor forthwith shall also pay to this state the same percentage of the difference between that aggregate amount and the amount of that credit as the amount payable to this state under that agreement bears to that aggregate amount. *(Added by Stats.1982, c. 327, p. 1500, § 175, eff. June 30, 1982; Stats.1982, c. 1535, p. 5985, § 15.)*

Cross References

Death tax defined for purposes of this Article, see Revenue and Taxation Code § 13830.
Decedent or transferor defined for purposes of this Part, see Revenue and Taxation Code § 13405.
Estate or property defined for purposes of this Part, see Revenue and Taxation Code § 13402.
Executor defined for purposes of this Article, see Revenue and Taxation Code § 13830.
State Controller, generally, see Government Code § 12402 et seq.
State defined for purposes of this Article, see Revenue and Taxation Code § 13830.
Taxing official defined for purposes of this Article, see Revenue and Taxation Code § 13830.

§ 13830.12. Interest and penalties on unpaid taxes; limitation

When in any case the board of arbitration determines that a decedent dies domiciled in this state, the total amount of interest and penalties for nonpayment of the tax, between the date of the election and the final determination of the board, shall not exceed 12 percent of the amount of the taxes per annum. *(Added by Stats.1982, c. 327, p. 1501, § 175, eff. June 30, 1982; Stats.1982, c. 1535, p. 5986, § 15.)*

Cross References

Board defined for purposes of this Article, see Revenue and Taxation Code § 13830.
Decedent or transferor defined for purposes of this Part, see Revenue and Taxation Code § 13405.

State defined for purposes of this Article, see Revenue and Taxation Code § 13830.

§ 13830.13.   Application of article

This article shall be applicable only to cases in which each of the states involved in the dispute has in effect therein a law substantially similar hereto. However, nothing contained in this section shall prohibit the application of this article or any part hereof where any of the other states involved in the dispute have in effect therein a law empowering the tax authority to voluntarily enter into a binding arbitration or compromise agreement and such an agreement is so entered into. *(Added by Stats.1982, c. 327, p. 1501, § 175, eff. June 30, 1982; Stats.1982, c. 1535, p. 5986, § 15.)*

Cross References

State defined for purposes of this Article, see Revenue and Taxation Code § 13830.

CHAPTER 8.   COURT JURISDICTION AND PROCEDURE GENERALLY

ARTICLE 1.   COURT JURISDICTION

Section
14000.   Jurisdiction generally.
14001.   Jurisdiction; no estate subject to probate.
14002.   Jurisdiction; nonresident decedent.

§ 14000.   Jurisdiction generally

The superior court which has jurisdiction in probate of the estate of any decedent shall hear and determine all questions relative to any tax imposed by this part, whether the property listed in the estate tax return, or any portion thereof, is in the estate or not. *(Added by Stats.1982, c. 327, p. 1501, § 176, eff. June 30, 1982; Stats.1982, c. 1535, p. 5986, § 15.)*

Cross References

Decedent or transferor defined for purposes of this Part, see Revenue and Taxation Code § 13405.
Estate or property defined for purposes of this Part, see Revenue and Taxation Code § 13402.

§ 14001.   Jurisdiction; no estate subject to probate

In a case where a deceased resident of this state leaves no estate subject to probate administration, the superior court in which the decedent resided at the date of death shall hear and determine all questions relative to any tax imposed by this part. *(Added by Stats.1982, c. 327, p. 1501, § 176, eff. June 30, 1982; Stats.1982, c. 1535, p. 5986, § 15.)*

Cross References

Decedent or transferor defined for purposes of this Part, see Revenue and Taxation Code § 13405.
Estate or property defined for purposes of this Part, see Revenue and Taxation Code § 13402.
Resident or resident decedent defined for purposes of this Part, see Revenue and Taxation Code § 13407.

§ 14002.   Jurisdiction; nonresident decedent

In the case of a decedent who was not a resident of this state at the time of his or her death, the superior court of the county in which the decedent's real property is situated, or, if he or she had no real property in this state, the superior court of the county in which any of his or her personal property is situated, has jurisdiction to hear and determine all questions relative to any tax imposed by this part. If the decedent leaves property in more than one county, the superior court of any such county whose jurisdiction is first invoked has exclusive jurisdiction. *(Added by Stats.1982, c. 327, p. 1501, § 176, eff. June 30, 1982; Stats.1982, c. 1535, p. 5986, § 15.)*

Cross References

Decedent or transferor defined for purposes of this Part, see Revenue and Taxation Code § 13405.
Estate or property defined for purposes of this Part, see Revenue and Taxation Code § 13402.
Resident or resident decedent defined for purposes of this Part, see Revenue and Taxation Code § 13407.

ARTICLE 2.   COURT PROCEDURE GENERALLY

Section
14010.   Law governing procedure.
14011.   Relief inconsistent with law governing procedure not precluded.
14012.   Applicability of limitations provisions.
14013.   Charging fees to Controller prohibited.

§ 14010.   Law governing procedure

Except as otherwise provided in this part, the provisions of the Code of Civil Procedure relative to judgments, new trials, appeals, attachments, and execution of judgments, so far as applicable, govern all proceedings under this part. *(Added by Stats.1982, c. 327, p. 1502, § 176, eff. June 30, 1982; Stats. 1982, c. 1535, p. 5986, § 15.)*

§ 14011.   Relief inconsistent with law governing procedure not precluded

Nothing in this article precludes the state from any relief provided for in this part which may be inconsistent with the provisions of the Code of Civil Procedure. *(Added by Stats.1982, c. 327, p. 1502, § 176, eff. June 30, 1982; Stats. 1982, c. 1535, p. 5986, § 15.)*

§ 14012.   Applicability of limitations provisions

The provisions of the Code of Civil Procedure relative to the time of commencing civil actions do not apply to any action or proceeding under this part to levy, appraise, assess, determine, or enforce the collection of any tax, interest, or penalty imposed by this part. *(Added by Stats.1982, c. 327, p. 1502, § 176, eff. June 30, 1982; Stats.1982, c. 1535, p. 5986, § 15.)*

§ 14013.   Charging fees to Controller prohibited

No fee shall be charged the Controller for filing, recording, or certifying any petition, lis pendens, decree, or order for taking any oath or acknowledgement, in any proceedings under this part; nor shall any undertaking be required from the Controller or the state in any such proceeding. *(Added by Stats.1982, c. 327, p. 1502, § 176, eff. June 30, 1982; Stats.1982, c. 1535, p. 5987, § 15.)*

CHAPTER 9. ADMINISTRATION

ARTICLE 1. GENERALLY

§ 14101. Administration by Controller

This part shall be administered by the Controller. *(Added by Stats.1982, c. 327, p. 1502, § 177, eff. June 30, 1982; Stats.1982, c. 1535, p. 5987, § 15.)*

§ 14102. Employment of assistants

The Controller may employ those assistants, including attorneys, as may from time to time be necessary for the proper administration of this part. *(Added by Stats.1982, c. 327, p. 1502, § 177, eff. June 30, 1982; Stats.1982, c. 1535, p. 5987, § 15.)*

§ 14103. Rules and regulations

The Controller may make and enforce rules and regulations relating to the administration and enforcement of this part, and may prescribe the extent, if any, to which any ruling or regulation shall be applied without retroactive effect. *(Added by Stats.1982, c. 327, p. 1502, § 177, eff. June 30, 1982; Stats.1982, c. 1535, p. 5987, § 15.)*

§ 14104. Distribution of copies of part

The Controller shall, without charge, distribute a copy of this part to any person who requests it. *(Added by Stats.1982, c. 327, p. 1502, § 177, eff. June 30, 1982; Stats.1982, c. 1535, p. 5987, § 15.)*

ARTICLE 2. SPECIAL EMPLOYMENT

§ 14151. Attorney or representative

Whenever he or she is cited as a party to any proceeding or action to determine any tax imposed by this part, or whenever he or she deems it necessary for the better enforcement of this part to secure evidence of the evasion of, or to commence or appear in any proceeding or action to determine, any such tax, the Controller may, with the consent and approval of the Attorney General:

(a) Specially employ any attorney or other person in or out of the state to act for or represent him or her on the state's behalf.

(b) Incur any reasonable and necessary expense for and incident to the employment. *(Added by Stats.1982, c. 327, p. 1502, § 177, eff. June 30, 1982; Stats.1982, c. 1535, p. 5987, § 15.)*

ARTICLE 3. HEARINGS

§ 14201. Time or place; purpose

The Controller may conduct a hearing at any time or place for the purpose of determining whether a tax is due under this part. *(Added by Stats.1982, c. 327, p. 1503, § 177, eff. June 30, 1982; Stats.1982, c. 1535, p. 5987, § 15.)*

§ 14202. Jurisdiction and powers of Controller

For purposes of the hearing referred to in Section 14201, the Controller has all of the following:

(a) Jurisdiction to require the attendance before him or her of any person who he or she may have reason to believe possesses knowledge of any facts that will aid the Controller in the determination of the tax.

(b) All the powers of a referee of the superior court. *(Added by Stats.1982, c. 327, p. 1503, § 177, eff. June 30, 1982; Stats.1982, c. 1535, p. 5987, § 15.)*

§ 14203. Subpoenas; purposes

The Controller may issue subpoenas for any of the following purposes:

(a) Compelling the attendance of any person before him or her or the production of books and papers.

(b) Determining the amount of any tax due. *(Added by Stats.1982, c. 327, p. 1503, § 177, eff. June 30, 1982; Stats. 1982, c. 1535, p. 5987, § 15.)*

State Controller, generally, see Government Code § 12402 et seq.

§ 14204. Enforcement of subpoenas

On the filing by the Controller of a petition asking the court to do so, the superior court of the county in which a hearing is held may compel compliance with any subpoena issued by the Controller. *(Added by Stats.1982, c. 327, p. 1503, § 177, eff. June 30, 1982; Stats.1982, c. 1535, p. 5988, § 15.)*

Cross References

State Controller, generally, see Government Code § 12402 et seq.

§ 14205. Examination and taking testimony

The Controller may examine and take the testimony under oath of any person appearing before him or her concerning the determination of any tax due under this part. *(Added by Stats.1982, c. 327, p. 1503, § 177, eff. June 30, 1982; Stats. 1982, c. 1535, p. 5988, § 15.)*

Cross References

State Controller, generally, see Government Code § 12402 et seq.

§ 14206. Fees and expenses of persons attending hearings

Any person compelled to attend a hearing before the Controller is entitled to fees for attendance in an amount to be determined by the Controller, and to his or her expenses of attendance. The fees and expenses are a part of the cost of administering this part. *(Added by Stats.1982, c. 327, p. 1503, § 177, eff. June 30, 1982; Stats.1982, c. 1535, p. 5988, § 15.)*

Cross References

State Controller, generally, see Government Code § 12402 et seq.

ARTICLE 4.   INFORMATION CONFIDENTIAL

Section
14251. Confidential information and records; disclosure; offense; punishment.
14252. Examination of records by government officials.

§ 14251. Confidential information and records; disclosure; offense; punishment

All information and records acquired by the Controller or any of his or her employees are confidential in nature, and except insofar as may be necessary for the enforcement of this part or as may be permitted by this article, shall not be disclosed by any of them.

Except insofar as may be necessary for the enforcement of this part or as may be permitted by this article, any former or incumbent Controller or employee of the Controller who discloses any information acquired by any inspection or examination made pursuant to this article is guilty of a felony, and upon conviction shall be imprisoned pursuant to subdivision (h) of Section 1170 of the Penal Code. *(Added by Stats.1982, c. 327, p. 1503, § 177, eff. June 30, 1982; Stats. 1982, c. 1535, p. 5988, § 15. Amended by Stats.2011, c. 15 (A.B.109), § 569, eff. April 4, 2011, operative Oct. 1, 2011.)*

Cross References

Felonies, definition and penalties, see Penal Code §§ 17, 18.
State Controller, generally, see Government Code § 12402 et seq.

§ 14252. Examination of records by government officials

The Controller may allow any local, state, or federal official charged with the administration of any tax law to examine his or her estate tax records under those rules and regulations as he or she may prescribe. *(Added by Stats.1982, c. 327, p. 1504, § 177, eff. June 30, 1982; Stats.1982, c. 1535, p. 5988, § 15.)*

Cross References

Estate or property defined for purposes of this Part, see Revenue and Taxation Code § 13402.
State Controller, generally, see Government Code § 12402 et seq.

CHAPTER 10.   DISPOSITION OF PROCEEDS

Section
14301. Estate Tax Fund; deposits.
14302. Appropriation; Estate Tax Fund money.

§ 14301. Estate Tax Fund; deposits

All taxes and other money collected under this part and received by the Treasurer shall be deposited in the State Treasury to the credit of the Estate Tax Fund, which fund is hereby created. *(Added by Stats.1982, c. 327, p. 1504, § 178, eff. June 30, 1982; Stats.1982, c. 1535, p. 5988, § 15.)*

Cross References

Estate or property defined for purposes of this Part, see Revenue and Taxation Code § 13402.

§ 14302. Appropriation; Estate Tax Fund money

The money in the Estate Tax Fund is hereby appropriated as follows:

(a) To pay the refunds authorized by this part and by Part 9.5 (commencing with Section 16700).

(b) The balance of the money in the fund shall, on order of the Controller, be transferred to the unappropriated surplus in the State General Fund. *(Added by Stats.1982, c. 327, p. 1504, § 178, eff. June 30, 1982; Stats.1982, c. 1535, p. 5988, § 15.)*

Cross References

Estate or property defined for purposes of this Part, see Revenue and Taxation Code § 13402.
State Controller, generally, see Government Code § 12402 et seq.

Part 9.5

GENERATION SKIPPING TRANSFER TAX

CHAPTER 1.   DEFINITIONS

Section
16700. Short title.
16701. Definitions governing construction.
16702. "Generation-skipping transfer" defined.
16703. "Original transferor" defined.
16704. "Federal generation-skipping transfer tax" defined.

§ 16700. Short title

This part is known as the "Generation Skipping Transfer Tax Law." *(Added by Stats.1977, c. 1079, p. 3293, § 12, eff. Sept. 26, 1977.)*

Cross References

Generation-skipping transfer defined for purposes of this Part, see Revenue and Taxation Code § 16702.

§ 16701. Definitions governing construction

Except where the context otherwise requires, the definitions given in this chapter govern the construction of this part. *(Added by Stats.1977, c. 1079, p. 3293, § 12, eff. Sept. 26, 1977.)*

§ 16702. "Generation-skipping transfer" defined

"Generation-skipping transfer" includes every transfer subject to the tax imposed under Chapter 13 of Subtitle B of the Internal Revenue Code of 1986,[1] as amended, where the original transferor is a resident of the State of California at the date of original transfer, or the property transferred is real or personal property in California. *(Added by Stats.1977, c. 1079, p. 3293, § 12, eff. Sept. 26, 1977. Amended by Stats.1987, c. 1138, § 2, eff. Sept. 25, 1987.)*

[1] 26 U.S.C.A. § 2601 et seq.

Cross References

Original transferor defined for purposes of this Part, see Revenue and Taxation Code § 16703.

§ 16703. "Original transferor" defined

"Original transferor" means any grantor, donor, trustor or testator who by grant, gift, trust or will makes a transfer of real or personal property that results in a federal generation skipping transfer tax under applicable provisions of the Internal Revenue Code. *(Added by Stats.1977, c. 1079, p. 3293, § 12, eff. Sept. 26, 1977.)*

Cross References

Federal generation-skipping transfer tax defined for purposes of this Part, see Revenue and Taxation Code § 16704.
Generation-skipping transfer defined for purposes of this Part, see Revenue and Taxation Code § 16702.

§ 16704. "Federal generation-skipping transfer tax" defined

"Federal generation-skipping transfer tax" means the tax imposed by Chapter 13 of Subtitle B of the Internal Revenue Code of 1986,[1] as amended. *(Added by Stats.1977, c. 1079, p. 3294, § 12, eff. Sept. 26, 1977. Amended by Stats.1987, c. 1138, § 3, eff. Sept. 25, 1987.)*

[1] 26 U.S.C.A. § 2601 et seq.

Cross References

Generation-skipping transfer defined for purposes of this Part, see Revenue and Taxation Code § 16702.

CHAPTER 2. IMPOSITION OF THE TAX

ARTICLE 1. TAX IMPOSED

Section
16710. Imposition; amount; property in another state.

§ 16710. Imposition; amount; property in another state

(a) A tax is hereby imposed upon every generation-skipping transfer in an amount equal to the amount allowable as a credit for state generation-skipping transfer taxes under Section 2604 of the Internal Revenue Code.[1]

(b) If any of the property transferred is real property in another state or personal property having a business situs in another state which requires the payment of a tax for which credit is received against the federal generation-skipping transfer tax, any tax due pursuant to subdivision (a) of this section shall be reduced by an amount which bears the same ratio to the total state tax credit allowable for federal generation-skipping transfer tax purposes as the value of such property taxable in such other state bears to the value of the gross generation-skipping transfer for federal generation skipping transfer tax purposes. *(Added by Stats.1977, c. 1079, p. 3294, § 12, eff. Sept. 26, 1977. Amended by Stats.1987, c. 1138, § 4, eff. Sept. 25, 1987.)*

[1] Internal Revenue Code sections are in Title 26 of U.S.C.A.

Cross References

Federal generation-skipping transfer tax defined for purposes of this Part, see Revenue and Taxation Code § 16704.
Generation-skipping transfer defined for purposes of this Part, see Revenue and Taxation Code § 16702.

ARTICLE 2. RETURNS

Section
16720. Time for filing; filing copy of federal return.
16721. Contents of return.
16722. Amended return; filing; increase or decrease.

§ 16720. Time for filing; filing copy of federal return

Every person required to file a return reporting a generation skipping transfer under applicable federal statute and regulations shall file a return with the State Controller on or before the last day prescribed for filing the federal return.

There shall be attached to the return filed with the Controller a duplicate copy of the federal return. *(Added by Stats.1977, c. 1079, p. 3294, § 12, eff. Sept. 26, 1977.)*

Cross References

Generation-skipping transfer defined for purposes of this Part, see Revenue and Taxation Code § 16702.
State Controller, generally, see Government Code § 12402 et seq.

§ 16721. Contents of return

The return shall contain such information and be in such form as the Controller may prescribe and shall state the amount of tax due under the provisions of this part.

The return shall contain, or be verified by, a written declaration that it is made under the penalties of perjury. *(Added by Stats.1977, c. 1079, p. 3294, § 12, eff. Sept. 26, 1977.)*

Cross References

State Controller, generally, see Government Code § 12402 et seq.

§ 16722. Amended return; filing; increase or decrease

If, after the filing of a duplicate return, the federal authorities shall increase or decrease the amount of the federal generation skipping transfer tax, an amended return shall be filed with the State Controller showing all changes made in the original return and the amount of increase or decrease in the federal generation skipping transfer tax. *(Added by Stats.1977, c. 1079, p. 3294, § 12, eff. Sept. 26, 1977.)*

ARTICLE 3. DEFICIENCY DETERMINATION

§ 16730. Cases not involving false or fraudulent return; determination; limitation of actions; filing

In a case not involving a false or fraudulent return or failure to file a return, if the Controller determines at any time after the tax is due, but not later than four years after the return is filed, that the tax disclosed in any return required to be filed by this part is less than the tax disclosed by his examination, a deficiency shall be determined; provided that in a case where the federal generation skipping transfer tax has been increased upon audit of the federal return, the determination may be made at any time within one year after the federal generation skipping transfer tax becomes final.

For the purposes of this section, a return filed before the last day prescribed by law for filing such return shall be considered as filed on such last day. *(Added by Stats.1977, c. 1079, p. 3295, § 12, eff. Sept. 26, 1977.)*

§ 16731. False or fraudulent return; determination by Controller at any time

In the case of a false or fraudulent return or failure to file a return, the Controller may determine the tax at any time. *(Added by Stats.1977, c. 1079, p. 3295, § 12, eff. Sept. 26, 1977.)*

§ 16732. Setting aside or correcting an erroneous determination

In any case in which a deficiency has been determined in an erroneous amount, the Controller may, within three years after the erroneous determination was made, set aside the determination or issue an amended determination in the correct amount. *(Added by Stats.1977, c. 1079, p. 3295, § 12, eff. Sept. 26, 1977.)*

§ 16733. Notice of deficiency and penalty; copies

The Controller shall give notice of the deficiency determined, together with any penalty for failure to file a return or to show any transfer in the return filed, by personal service or by mail to the person filing the return at the address stated in the return, or, if no return is filed, to the person liable for the tax. Copies of the notice of deficiency may in like manner be given to such other persons as the Controller deems advisable. *(Added by Stats.1977, c. 1079, p. 3295, § 12, eff. Sept. 26, 1977.)*

§ 16734. Claim of erroneous deficiency; action; time for bringing

In any case in which it is claimed that a deficiency has been determined in an erroneous amount, any person who is liable for the tax may, within three years after the determination was made, bring an action against the state in the superior court having jurisdiction to have the tax modified in whole or in part. *(Added by Stats.1977, c. 1079, p. 3295, § 12, eff. Sept. 26, 1977.)*

CHAPTER 3. PAYMENT OF TAX

ARTICLE 1. GENERALLY

§ 16750. Person liable

The person liable for payment of the federal generation skipping transfer tax shall be liable for the tax imposed by this part. *(Added by Stats.1977, c. 1079, p. 3295, § 12, eff. Sept. 26, 1977.)*

§ 16751. Tax due upon taxable distribution or taxable termination as determined by federal law

The tax imposed by this part is due upon a taxable distribution or a taxable termination as determined under applicable provisions of the federal generation skipping transfer tax. *(Added by Stats.1977, c. 1079, p. 3295, § 12, eff. Sept. 26, 1977.)*

Federal generation-skipping transfer tax defined for purposes of this Part, see Revenue and Taxation Code § 16704.
Generation-skipping transfer defined for purposes of this Part, see Revenue and Taxation Code § 16702.

§ 16752. Time of delinquency

The tax becomes delinquent from and after the last day allowed for filing a return for the generation skipping transfer. *(Added by Stats.1977, c. 1079, p. 3295, § 12, eff. Sept. 26, 1977.)*

Generation-skipping transfer defined for purposes of this Part, see Revenue and Taxation Code § 16702.

§ 16753. Payment to State Controller; payee

The tax shall be paid to the State Controller by remittance payable to the State Treasurer. *(Added by Stats.1977, c. 1079, p. 3295, § 12, eff. Sept. 26, 1977.)*

State Controller, generally, see Government Code § 12402 et seq.
State Treasurer, generally, see Government Code § 12302 et seq.

ARTICLE 2. INTEREST AND PENALTIES

Section
16760. Interest on delinquency; rate.
16761. Applicability of payments.

§ 16760. Interest on delinquency; rate

If the tax is not paid before it becomes delinquent, it bears interest thereafter and until it is paid at the same rate per annum as provided in Section 6621(a)(2) of the Internal Revenue Code, compounded daily. *(Added by Stats.1977, c. 1079, p. 3296, § 12, eff. Sept. 26, 1977. Amended by Stats.2000, c. 363 (A.B.2818), § 8, eff. July 21, 2000, operative Jan. 1, 2001.)*

§ 16761. Applicability of payments

Every payment on the tax imposed by this part is applied, first, to any interest due on the tax, and then, if there is any balance, to the tax itself. *(Added by Stats.1977, c. 1079, p. 3296, § 12, eff. Sept. 26, 1977.)*

CHAPTER 4. COLLECTION OF TAX

ARTICLE 1. SUIT FOR TAX

Section
16800. Enforcement of tax lien by civil action.

§ 16800. Enforcement of tax lien by civil action

The state may enforce its claim for any tax imposed by this part and enforce the lien of the tax by a civil action in any court of competent jurisdiction against any person liable for the tax or against any property subject to the lien. *(Added by Stats.1977, c. 1079, p. 3296, § 12, eff. Sept. 26, 1977.)*

ARTICLE 2. LIEN OF TAX

Section
16810. Duration.

§ 16810. Duration

The tax imposed by this part is a lien in the manner prescribed in Section 13610 upon the property transferred from the time the generation skipping transfer is made and until the expiration of 10 years from and after the time a deficiency determination is issued pursuant to the provisions of this part or until the tax is paid, whichever is earlier. *(Added by Stats.1977, c. 1079, p. 3296, § 12, eff. Sept. 26, 1977. Amended by Stats.1987, c. 894, § 2.)*

Definition of state tax lien for purposes of Government Code state tax lien provisions, lien created pursuant to this section, see Government Code § 7162.
Generation-skipping transfer defined for purposes of this Part, see Revenue and Taxation Code § 16702.

ARTICLE 3. WRIT OF EXECUTION

Section
16820. Issuance to controller to enforce judgment.
16821. Manner of execution.

§ 16820. Issuance to controller to enforce judgment

At any time after a tax imposed by this part is delinquent, the Controller may have a writ of execution issued for the enforcement of any judgment rendered pursuant to this part in respect to the tax. *(Added by Stats.1977, c. 1079, p. 3296, § 12, eff. Sept. 26, 1977.)*

State Controller, generally, see Government Code § 12402 et seq.

§ 16821. Manner of execution

The writ shall be executed against any property of any person liable for the tax, or against any property subject to the lien of the tax. *(Added by Stats.1977, c. 1079, p. 3296, § 12, eff. Sept. 26, 1977.)*

ARTICLE 4. MISCELLANEOUS

Section
16830. Proceedings for collection of tax; time for commencement.

§ 16830. Proceedings for collection of tax; time for commencement

Proceedings for the collection of any tax imposed by this part may be commenced at any time after the tax is due and within 10 years from and after the time a deficiency determination is issued pursuant to the provisions of this part. *(Added by Stats.1977, c. 1079, p. 3296, § 12, eff. Sept. 26, 1977.)*

CHAPTER 5. REFUNDS

ARTICLE 1. WHEN ALLOWABLE

Section
16850. Finding of overpayment by Controller; refund.
16851. Time for refund; claim; allowance or denial.
16852. Persons entitled to refund.

§ 16850. Finding of overpayment by Controller; refund

If the Controller finds that there has been an overpayment of tax by a taxpayer for any reason, the amount of the overpayment shall be refunded to the taxpayer. *(Added by Stats.1977, c. 1079, p. 3297, § 12, eff. Sept. 26, 1977.)*

Cross References

State Controller, generally, see Government Code § 12402 et seq.

§ 16851. Time for refund; claim; allowance or denial

No refund shall be allowed or made after four years from the last day prescribed for filing the return or after one year from the date of the overpayment, whichever period expires the later, unless before the expiration of such period a claim therefor is filed by the taxpayer, or unless before the expiration of such period the Controller makes a refund. A claim for refund may be filed in such form as the Controller may prescribe, and the Controller shall allow or deny the claim, in whole or in part, and mail a notice of such determination to the claimant at the address stated on the claim. *(Added by Stats.1977, c. 1079, p. 3297, § 12, eff. Sept. 26, 1977.)*

Cross References

State Controller, generally, see Government Code § 12402 et seq.

§ 16852. Persons entitled to refund

Any person who has paid any tax imposed by this part which later is determined by judgment to have been in excess of the amount legally due, or an heir, the executor of the will, or the administrator of the estate of any such person, but not his assignee, is entitled to a refund in the amount of the excess paid within one year after the judgment becomes final. *(Added by Stats.1977, c. 1079, p. 3297, § 12, eff. Sept. 26, 1977.)*

ARTICLE 2. SUIT FOR REFUND

Section
16860. Time for action; persons entitled to bring action.
16861. Process; service.
16862. Hearing; judgment.

§ 16860. Time for action; persons entitled to bring action

Within four years from the last date prescribed for filing the return or within one year from the date the tax was paid, or within 90 days after a determination under Section 16851 is issued, whichever is later, any person who has paid the tax may bring an action against the state in the superior court having jurisdiction to have the tax refunded, in whole or in part. *(Added by Stats.1977, c. 1079, p. 3297, § 12, eff. Sept. 26, 1977.)*

§ 16861. Process; service

Process in the action directed to the state shall be served on the Controller. *(Added by Stats.1977, c. 1079, p. 3297, § 12, eff. Sept. 26, 1977.)*

Cross References

State Controller, generally, see Government Code § 12402 et seq.

§ 16862. Hearing; judgment

After a hearing in which the Controller shall represent the state, the court shall review the Controller's appraisement and determination of tax, and, as the case may require, shall by judgment modify or confirm the appraisement or determination in whole or in part. *(Added by Stats.1977, c. 1079, p. 3297, § 12, eff. Sept. 26, 1977.)*

Cross References

State Controller, generally, see Government Code § 12402 et seq.

ARTICLE 3. INTEREST ON REFUNDS

Section
16870. Allowance and payment.

§ 16870. Allowance and payment

Interest shall be allowed and paid upon any overpayment of tax due under this part in the same manner as provided in Section 6621(a)(1) and 6622 of the Internal Revenue Code. *(Added by Stats.1977, c. 1079, p. 3297, § 12, eff. Sept. 26, 1977. Amended by Stats.2000, c. 363 (A.B.2818), § 9, eff. July 21, 2000, operative Jan. 1, 2001.)*

CHAPTER 6. COURT JURISDICTION AND PROCEDURE GENERALLY

ARTICLE 1. COURT JURISDICTION

Section
16880. Transferor resident of state.
16881. Transferor not a resident of state.

§ 16880. Transferor resident of state

The superior court of the county in which a transferor resident of this state resided at the date of any generation skipping transfer made by him has jurisdiction to hear and determine all questions relative to any tax imposed by this part on the gift. *(Added by Stats.1977, c. 1079, p. 3298, § 12, eff. Sept. 26, 1977.)*

Cross References

Generation-skipping transfer defined for purposes of this Part, see Revenue and Taxation Code § 16702.

§ 16881. Transferor not a resident of state

In the case of a transferor who was not a resident of this state at the date of any generation skipping transfer made by him, the superior court of the county in which any of the transferor's real property is situated, or, if he has no real property in this state, the superior court of the county in which any of his personal property is situated, has jurisdiction to hear and determine all questions relative to any tax imposed by this part. If the transferor has property in more than one county, the superior court of any such county whose jurisdiction is first invoked has exclusive jurisdiction. *(Added by Stats.1977, c. 1079, p. 3298, § 12, eff. Sept. 26, 1977.)*

Generation-skipping transfer defined for purposes of this Part, see Revenue and Taxation Code § 16702.

ARTICLE 2.   COURT PROCEDURE GENERALLY

Section
16890.   Applicability of Code of Civil Procedure.

§ 16890.   Applicability of Code of Civil Procedure

Except as otherwise provided in this part, the provisions of the Code of Civil Procedure relative to judgments, new trials, appeals, attachments and execution of judgments, so far as applicable, govern all proceedings under this part. *(Added by Stats.1977, c. 1079, p. 3298, § 12, eff. Sept. 26, 1977.)*

CHAPTER 7.   ADMINISTRATION

ARTICLE 1.   GENERALLY

Section
16900.   Administration by Controller.
16901.   Employment of assistants.
16902.   Rules and regulations.
16903.   Cooperation of Franchise Tax Board.
16904.   Cooperation of State Board of Equalization.
16905.   Appearance by Controller.

§ 16900.   Administration by Controller

This part is administered by the Controller. *(Added by Stats.1977, c. 1079, p. 3298, § 12, eff. Sept. 26, 1977. Amended by Stats.1983, c. 407, § 5.)*

Cross References

State Controller, generally, see Government Code § 12402 et seq.

§ 16901.   Employment of assistants

The Controller may employ such assistants, including attorneys, as may from time to time be necessary for the proper administration of this part. *(Added by Stats.1977, c. 1079, p. 3298, § 12, eff. Sept. 26, 1977.)*

Cross References

State Controller, generally, see Government Code § 12402 et seq.

§ 16902.   Rules and regulations

The Controller may make and enforce rules and regulations relating to the administration and enforcement of this part, and may prescribe the extent, if any, to which any ruling or regulation shall be applied without retroactive effect. *(Added by Stats.1977, c. 1079, p. 3298, § 12, eff. Sept. 26, 1977.)*

Cross References

State Controller, generally, see Government Code § 12402 et seq.

§ 16903.   Cooperation of Franchise Tax Board

Under rules and regulations upon which the Controller and Franchise Tax Board may agree, the Franchise Tax Board shall cooperate in the enforcement of this part by reporting to the Controller any changes in the gross or net income of any person, or any other information obtained in the enforcement of any act administered by the Franchise Tax Board which may in any way indicate that a transfer has been made which is taxable under this part. *(Added by Stats.1977, c. 1079, p. 3298, § 12, eff. Sept. 26, 1977.)*

Cross References

State Controller, generally, see Government Code § 12402 et seq.

§ 16904.   Cooperation of State Board of Equalization

Under rules and regulations upon which the Controller and State Board of Equalization may agree, the State Board of Equalization shall cooperate in the enforcement of this part by reporting to the Controller any information obtained in the enforcement of any act administered by the State Board of Equalization which may in any way indicate that a transfer has been made which is taxable under this part. *(Added by Stats.1977, c. 1079, p. 3299, § 12, eff. Sept. 26, 1977.)*

Cross References

State Controller, generally, see Government Code § 12402 et seq.

§ 16905.   Appearance by Controller

The Controller on his own motion may appear in behalf of the state in any and all generation skipping transfer tax matters before any court. *(Added by Stats.1977, c. 1079, p. 3299, § 12, eff. Sept. 26, 1977.)*

Cross References

Generation-skipping transfer defined for purposes of this Part, see Revenue and Taxation Code § 16702.
State Controller, generally, see Government Code § 12402 et seq.

ARTICLE 2.   INSPECTION OF RECORDS

Section
16910.   Confidential nature of information and records; punishment for disclosure.
16911.   Inspection of Controller's records by local, state, or federal officials.

§ 16910.   Confidential nature of information and records; punishment for disclosure

All information and records acquired by the Controller or any of his employees are confidential in nature, and, except insofar as may be necessary for the enforcement of this part or as may be permitted by this article, shall not be disclosed by any of them.

Except insofar as may be necessary for the enforcement of this part or as may be permitted by this article, any former or incumbent Controller or employee of the Controller who discloses any information acquired by any inspection or examination made pursuant to this article is guilty of a felony, and upon conviction shall be imprisoned pursuant to subdivision (h) of Section 1170 of the Penal Code. *(Added by Stats.1977, c. 1079, p. 3299, § 12, eff. Sept. 26, 1977. Amended by Stats.2011, c. 15 (A.B.109), § 570, eff. April 4, 2011, operative Oct. 1, 2011.)*

§ 16911. Inspection of Controller's records by local, state, or federal officials

The Controller may allow any local, state, or federal official charged with the administration of any tax law to examine his generation skipping transfer tax records under such rules and regulations as he may prescribe. *(Added by Stats.1977, c. 1079, p. 3299, § 12, eff. Sept. 26, 1977.)*

CHAPTER 8. DISPOSITION OF PROCEEDS

Section
16950. Payment of moneys to Controller; deposit of funds.

§ 16950. Payment of moneys to Controller; deposit of funds

All money due under this part shall be paid to the Controller by remittance payable to the State Treasurer. The amounts received shall be deposited, after clearance of remittance, in the State Treasury to the credit of the Estate Tax Fund. *(Added by Stats.1977, c. 1079, p. 3299, § 12, eff. Sept. 26, 1977. Amended by Stats.1983, c. 407, § 6.)*

Part 10

PERSONAL INCOME TAX

Real estate investment trusts, treatment of election of under Internal Revenue Code §856, see Revenue and Taxation Code §24872.6.

References to United States mail treated as including references to any designated delivery service, see Revenue and Taxation Code §21027.

Restitution orders or other amounts imposed for criminal offenses due and payable to Franchise Tax Board, collection, application of these provisions to amounts collected, see Revenue and Taxation Code §19722.

S corporations,

Election by corporation to be treated as an S corporation and tax treatment of S corporations and their shareholders, application of election for purposes of this part, see Revenue and Taxation Code §23801.

Passive investment income tax, application of election for purposes of this part, see Revenue and Taxation Code §23811.

S corporations and shareholders, modification of amount of tax imposed on built-in gains, application, see Revenue and Taxation Code §23809.

San Joaquin Valley Unified Air Pollution Control District, mitigation of air contaminant emissions, F–35 Joint Strike Fighter program, see Health and Safety Code §40608.

Tangible personal property, qualified use tax, see Revenue and Taxation Code §6452.1.

Tax returns, revision of forms to allow reporting and payment of qualified use tax, see Revenue and Taxation Code §18510.

Taxpayers' rights advocate, availability of relief, see Revenue and Taxation Code §21004.

Verification, form and filing requirements for returns, see Revenue and Taxation Code §18621.

Voluntary compliance initiative for taxpayers subject to Part 10 and Part 11, see Revenue and Taxation Code §19751 et seq.

Voluntary Compliance Initiative Two, development of initiative for taxpayers subject to this Part, see Revenue and Taxation Code §19761.

CHAPTER 9. ESTATES, TRUSTS, BENEFICIARIES, AND DECEDENTS

§17731. Application of federal law

(a) Subchapter J of Chapter 1 of Subtitle A of the Internal Revenue Code, [1] relating to estates, trusts, beneficiaries, and decedents, shall apply, except as otherwise provided.

(b) Section 692(d)(2) of the Internal Revenue Code, relating to the ten thousand-dollar ($10,000) minimum benefit, does not apply. *(Added by Stats.1983, c. 488, § 59, eff. July 28, 1983. Amended by Stats.1993, c. 873 (A.B.35), § 23, eff. Oct. 6, 1993; Stats.2002, c. 690 (A.B.2670), § 3, eff. Sept. 18, 2002; Stats.2002, c. 807 (S.B.219), § 9, eff. Sept. 23, 2002; Stats.2003, c. 268 (A.B.967), § 1; Stats.2004, c. 552 (S.B. 1713), § 8, eff. Sept. 16, 2004; Stats.2005, c. 691 (A.B.115), § 37, eff. Oct. 7, 2005.)*

[1] Internal Revenue Code sections are in Title 26 of the U.S.C.A.

Cross References

Internal Revenue Code defined for purposes of this Part, see Revenue and Taxation Code § 17024.5.

§17731.5. Special rules for taxation of electing small business trusts

(a) Section 641(c)(2)(A) of the Internal Revenue Code [1] is modified to read: "The amount of the tax imposed by subdivision (e) of Section 17041 shall be determined by using the highest rate of tax applicable to an individual under subdivision (a) of Section 17041."

(b) Section 641(c)(2)(B) of the Internal Revenue Code is modified to read: "The credit allowed under subdivision (b) of Section 17733 shall be zero." *(Added by Stats.1997, c. 611 (S.B.455), § 41, eff. Oct. 3, 1997. Amended by Stats.2002, c. 34 (S.B.657), § 26, eff. May 8, 2002; Stats.2002, c. 35 (A.B.1122), § 26, eff. May 8, 2002.)*

[1] Internal Revenue Code sections appear in Title 26 of the U.S.C.A.

Application

Application, urgency and operative effect of Stats. 2002, c. 34 (S.B.657) and Stats.2002, c. 35 (A.B. 1122), see §§ 61 to 78 of those Acts.

Cross References

Individual defined for purposes of this Part, see Revenue and Taxation Code § 17005.

Internal Revenue Code defined for purposes of this Part, see Revenue and Taxation Code § 17024.5.

§17732. Personal exemption deduction

Section 642(b) of the Internal Revenue Code [1], relating to deduction for personal exemption, shall not apply. *(Added* by Stats.1983, c. 488, § 59, eff. July 28, 1983. Amended by Stats.1999, c. 987 (S.B.1229), § 46, eff. Oct. 10, 1999.)

[1] See 26 U.S.C.A. § 642(b).

§ 17733. Credit against tax in lieu of credit for personal exemption; disability trusts; credit

(a) An estate shall be allowed a credit of ten dollars ($10) against the tax imposed under Section 17041, less any amounts imposed under paragraph (1) of subdivision (d) or paragraph (1) of subdivision (e), or both, of Section 17560.

(b)(1) Except as provided in paragraph (2), a trust shall be allowed a credit of one dollar ($1) against the tax imposed under Section 17041, less any amounts imposed under paragraph (1) of subdivision (d) or paragraph (1) of subdivision (e), or both, of Section 17560.

(2)(A) A disability trust, as defined in Section 642(b)(2)(C) of the Internal Revenue Code,[1] shall be allowed a credit in an amount equal to the personal exemption credit authorized for a single individual pursuant to subdivision (a) of Section 17054.

(B) The credit authorized by subparagraph (A) shall be subject to the credit reduction provisions of Section 17054.1. For purposes of making the adjustments required by Section 17054.1, the adjusted gross income of the disability trust shall be computed in accordance with Section 67(e) of the Internal Revenue Code, relating to determination of adjusted gross income in case of estates and trusts.

(C) This paragraph applies to taxable years beginning on or after January 1, 2004.

(c) The credits allowed by this section shall be in lieu of the credits allowed under Section 17054 (relating to credit for personal exemption). (Added by Stats.1983, c. 488, § 59, eff. July 28, 1983. Amended by Stats.1991, c. 472 (S.B.426), § 17, eff. Oct. 2, 1991; Stats.2003, c. 268 (A.B.967), § 2; Stats.2005, c. 691 (A.B.115), § 37.5, eff. Oct. 7, 2005.)

[1] Internal Revenue Code sections are in Title 26 of the U.S.C.A.

§ 17734. Nonresident beneficiary; income and deductions derived through estate or trust

For purposes of computing "taxable income of a nonresident or part-year resident" under paragraph (1) of subdivision (i) of Section 17041, in the case of a nonresident beneficiary, income and deduction derived through an estate or trust shall be included in that computation only to the extent that the income or deduction is derived by the estate or trust from sources within this state. (Added by Stats.1983,

c. 488, § 59, eff. July 28, 1983. Amended by Stats.2001, c. 920 (A.B.1115), § 16, eff. Oct. 14, 2001.)

§ 17734.6. Alaska Native Settlement Trusts

Section 646 of the Internal Revenue Code,[1] relating to tax treatment of electing Alaska Native Settlement Trusts, shall not apply. (Added by Stats.2005, c. 691 (A.B.115), § 37.6, eff. Oct. 7, 2005.)

[1] Internal Revenue Code sections are in Title 26 of the U.S.C.A.

§ 17735. Estates; deductions under I.R.C. § 661(a) for amounts attributable and taxable to nonresident beneficiaries; certificate

(a) In the case of an estate, for taxable years beginning before January 1, 2014, no deductions shall be allowed under Section 661(a) of the Internal Revenue Code[1] with respect to amounts attributable and taxable to nonresident beneficiaries if the fiduciary failed to obtain a certificate as provided by former Section 19513.

(b) This section shall remain in effect only until December 1, 2018, and as of that date is repealed. (Added by Stats.1983, c. 795, § 2, eff. Sept. 14, 1983. Amended by Stats.1993, c. 31 (S.B.3), § 14, eff. June 16, 1993, operative Jan. 1, 1994; Stats.2013, c. 239 (A.B.672), § 1.)

[1] 26 U.S.C.A. § 661(a).

Repeal

For repeal of this section, see its terms.

§ 17736. Amounts permanently set aside; modification for purposes of this part; adjustment to deduction

(a) Section 642(c)(2) of the Internal Revenue Code[1] is modified for purposes of this part by substituting "December 31, 1970" for "October 9, 1969" throughout that paragraph.

(b) In lieu of Section 642(c)(4) of the Internal Revenue Code,[1] relating to adjustments, to the extent that the amount otherwise allowable as a deduction under Section 642(c) of the Internal Revenue Code, relating to deduction for amounts paid or permanently set aside for a charitable purpose, consists of gain described in Section 18152.5, proper adjustment shall be made for any exclusion allowable to the estate or trust under Section 18152.5. In the case of a trust, the deduction allowed by Section 642(c) of the Internal Revenue Code shall be subject to Section 681 of the Internal Revenue Code, relating to limitation on charitable deduction. *(Added by Stats.1984, c. 938, § 19, eff. Sept. 7, 1984. Amended by Stats.1993, c. 881 (S.B.671), § 10, eff. Oct. 6, 1993, operative Jan. 1, 1994.)*

[1] Internal Revenue Code sections are in Title 26 of U.S.C.A.

Cross References

Internal Revenue Code defined for purposes of this Part, see Revenue and Taxation Code § 17024.5.

§ 17737. Beneficiary; income of spouse

For purposes of computing the taxable income of the estate or trust and the taxable income of a spouse to whom Section 682(a) of the Internal Revenue Code [1] (relating to income of an estate or trust in the case of divorce, etc.) applies, that spouse shall be considered as the beneficiary for purposes of this chapter. *(Added by Stats.1985, c. 1461, § 34.5, eff. Oct. 1, 1985. Amended by Stats.1987, c. 1138, § 113, eff. Sept. 25, 1987.)*

[1] 26 U.S.C.A. § 682(a).

Cross References

Internal Revenue Code defined for purposes of this Part, see Revenue and Taxation Code § 17024.5.

§ 17742. Income taxable to estate or trust; residence of decedent, fiduciary or beneficiary

(a) Except as otherwise provided in this chapter, the income of an estate or trust is taxable to the estate or trust. The tax applies to the entire taxable income of an estate, if the decedent was a resident, regardless of the residence of the fiduciary or beneficiary, and to the entire taxable income of a trust, if the fiduciary or beneficiary (other than a beneficiary whose interest in such trust is contingent) is a resident, regardless of the residence of the settlor.

(b) For purposes of this article the residence of a corporate fiduciary of a trust means the place where the corporation transacts the major portion of its administration of the trust. *(Added by Stats.1983, c. 488, § 59, eff. July 28, 1983.)*

Cross References

Corporation defined for purposes of this Part, see Revenue and Taxation Code § 17009.
Credit for taxes paid in another state, see Revenue and Taxation Code § 18001 et seq.
Fiduciary defined for purposes of this Part, see Revenue and Taxation Code § 17006.
Resident defined for purposes of this Part, see Revenue and Taxation Code § 17014.

§ 17743. Residence of fiduciary; multiple fiduciaries; apportionment of income

Where the taxability of income under this chapter depends on the residence of the fiduciary and there are two or more fiduciaries for the trust, the income taxable under Section 17742 shall be apportioned according to the number of fiduciaries resident in this state pursuant to rules and regulations prescribed by the Franchise Tax Board. *(Added by Stats.1983, c. 488, § 59, eff. July 28, 1983.)*

Cross References

Fiduciary defined for purposes of this Part, see Revenue and Taxation Code § 17006.
Franchise Tax Board,
  Generally, see Government Code § 15700 et seq.
  Powers and duties, see Revenue and Taxation Code § 19501 et seq.
Franchise Tax Board and board defined for purposes of this Part, see Revenue and Taxation Code § 17003.
Resident defined for purposes of this Part, see Revenue and Taxation Code § 17014.
State defined for purposes of this Part, see Revenue and Taxation Code § 17018.

§ 17744. Residence of beneficiary; multiple beneficiaries; apportionment of income

Where the taxability of income under this chapter depends on the residence of the beneficiary and there are two or more beneficiaries of the trust, the income taxable under Section 17742 shall be apportioned according to the number and interest of beneficiaries resident in this state pursuant to rules and regulations prescribed by the Franchise Tax Board. *(Added by Stats.1983, c. 488, § 59, eff. July 28, 1983.)*

Cross References

Credit for taxes paid in another state or county, resident beneficiary, see Revenue and Taxation Code § 18005.
Franchise Tax Board,
  Generally, see Government Code § 15700 et seq.
  Powers and duties, see Revenue and Taxation Code § 19501 et seq.
Franchise Tax Board and board defined for purposes of this Part, see Revenue and Taxation Code § 17003.
Resident defined for purposes of this Part, see Revenue and Taxation Code § 17014.
State defined for purposes of this Part, see Revenue and Taxation Code § 17018.

§ 17745. Income taxable to beneficiaries

(a) If, for any reason, the taxes imposed on income of a trust which is taxable to the trust because the fiduciary or beneficiary is a resident of this state are not paid when due and remain unpaid when that income is distributable to the beneficiary, or in case the income is distributable to the beneficiary before the taxes are due, if the taxes are not paid when due, such income shall be taxable to the beneficiary when distributable to him except that in the case of a nonresident beneficiary such income shall be taxable only to the extent it is derived from sources within this state.

(b) If no taxes have been paid on the current or accumulated income of the trust because the resident beneficiary's interest in the trust was contingent such income shall be taxable to the beneficiary when distributed or distributable to him or her.

(c) The tax on that income which is taxable to the beneficiary under subdivisions (a) or (b) is a tax on the receipt of that income distributed or on the constructive receipt of that distributable income. For purposes of this section income accumulated by a trust continues to be income even though the trust provides that the income (ordinary or capital) shall become a part of the corpus.

(d) The tax attributable to the inclusion of that income in the gross income of that beneficiary for the year that income is distributed or distributable under subdivision (b) shall be the aggregate of the taxes which would have been attributable to that income had it been included in the gross income of that beneficiary ratably for the year of distribution and the five preceding taxable years, or for the period that the trust accumulated or acquired income for that contingent beneficiary, whichever period is the shorter.

(e) In the event that a person is a resident beneficiary during the period of accumulation, and leaves this state within 12 months prior to the date of distribution of accumulated income and returns to the state within 12 months after distribution, it shall be presumed that the beneficiary continued to be a resident of this state throughout the time of distribution.

(f) The Franchise Tax Board shall prescribe such regulations as it deems necessary for the application of this section. *(Added by Stats.1983, c. 488, § 59, eff. July 28, 1983.)*

Cross References

Credit for taxes paid in another state or country, "resident beneficiary" defined, see Revenue and Taxation Code § 18005.
Fiduciary defined for purposes of this Part, see Revenue and Taxation Code § 17006.
Franchise Tax Board,
  Generally, see Government Code § 15700 et seq.
  Powers and duties, see Revenue and Taxation Code § 19501 et seq.
Franchise Tax Board and board defined for purposes of this Part, see Revenue and Taxation Code § 17003.
Nonresident defined for purposes of this Part, see Revenue and Taxation Code § 17015.
Person defined for purposes of this Part, see Revenue and Taxation Code § 17007.
Resident defined for purposes of this Part, see Revenue and Taxation Code § 17014.
State defined for purposes of this Part, see Revenue and Taxation Code § 17018.
Taxable year defined for purposes of this Part, see Revenue and Taxation Code § 17010.

§ 17745.1. Application of 1963 amendments of former Sections 17742, 17745

The amendments of Sections 17742 and 17745 made at the 1963 Regular Session of the Legislature shall be applicable only with respect to taxable years beginning after December 31, 1962. Whether or not the income of a trust which is or was accumulated or is or was accumulated and distributed or accumulated and distributable is taxable by California for the years prior to 1963 shall be determined as if Sections 17742 and 17745 had not been amended at the 1963 Regular Session of the Legislature and without inferences drawn from the fact that such amendments were not made applicable with respect to taxable years beginning before January 1, 1963. *(Added by Stats.1983, c. 488, § 59, eff. July 28, 1983.)*

Cross References

Taxable year defined for purposes of this Part, see Revenue and Taxation Code § 17010.

§ 17750. Distributable net income

Section 643(a) of the Internal Revenue Code,[1] relating to distributable net income, is modified to provide that the exclusion under Section 18152.5 shall not be taken into account. *(Added by Stats.1985, c. 1461, § 35, eff. Oct. 1, 1985. Amended by Stats.1993, c. 881 (S.B.671), § 11, eff. Oct. 6, 1993, operative Jan. 1, 1994; Stats.1997, c. 611 (S.B.455), § 43, eff. Oct. 3, 1997.)*

[1] Internal Revenue Code sections are in Title 26 of U.S.C.A.

Cross References

Internal Revenue Code defined for purposes of this Part, see Revenue and Taxation Code § 17024.5.

§ 17751. Revocable trusts; modification of Internal Revenue Code provisions

Section 645 of the Internal Revenue Code,[1] relating to certain revocable trusts treated as part of estate, is modified as follows:

(a) An election under Section 645(a) of the Internal Revenue Code for federal purposes shall be treated for purposes of this part as an election made by the executor, if any, of the estate and the trustee of the qualified revocable trust under Section 645(a) of the Internal Revenue Code for state purposes and a separate election under paragraph (3) of subdivision (e) of Section 17024.5 shall not be allowed.

(b) If the executor, if any, of the estate and the trustee of a qualified revocable trust fail to make an election under Section 645(a) of the Internal Revenue Code for federal purposes with respect to that qualified revocable trust, that trust shall be treated and taxed for purposes of this part as a separate trust, an election under Section 645(a) of the Internal Revenue Code for state purposes with respect to that trust shall not be allowed, and a separate election under paragraph (3) of subdivision (e) of Section 17024.5 shall not be allowed with respect to that trust. *(Added by Stats.1998, c. 322 (A.B.2797), § 33, eff. Aug. 20, 1998. Amended by Stats.2002, c. 34 (S.B.657), § 27, eff. May 8, 2002; Stats.2002, c. 35 (A.B.1122), § 27, eff. May 8, 2002.)*

[1] Internal Revenue Code sections appear in Title 26 of the U.S.C.A.

Application

Application, urgency and operative effect of Stats. 2002, c. 34 (S.B.657) and Stats.2002, c. 35 (A.B. 1122), see §§ 61 to 78 of those Acts.

Cross References

State defined for purposes of this Part, see Revenue and Taxation Code § 17018.

§ 17752. Special Internal Revenue Code rules applicable to Internal Revenue Code §§ 661 and 662; modification of Internal Revenue Code provisions

Section 663 of the Internal Revenue Code,[1] relating to special rules applicable to Sections 661 and 662,[2] is modified as follows:

(a) Section 663(b) of the Internal Revenue Code, relating to distributions in the first 65 days of the taxable year, is modified as follows:

(1) An election under Section 663(b) of the Internal Revenue Code for federal purposes shall be treated for purposes of this part as an election made by the executor of the estate or the fiduciary of the trust, as the case may be,

under Section 663(b) of the Internal Revenue Code for state purposes and a separate election under paragraph (3) of subdivision (e) of Section 17024.5 shall not be allowed.

(2) If the executor of the estate or the fiduciary of the trust, as the case may be, fails to make an election under Section 663(b) of the Internal Revenue Code for federal purposes with respect to an amount properly paid or credited within 65 days of the taxable year, that amount shall not be considered for purposes of this part as having been paid or credited on the last day of the preceding taxable year, an election under Section 663(b) of the Internal Revenue Code for state purposes with respect to that amount shall not be allowed, and a separate election under paragraph (3) of subdivision (e) of Section 17024.5 shall not be allowed with respect to that amount.

(b) Section 663(c) of the Internal Revenue Code, relating to separate shares treated as separate estates or trusts, is modified as follows:

(1) An election under Section 663(c) of the Internal Revenue Code for federal purposes shall be treated for purposes of this part as an election made by the executor of the estate or the fiduciary of the trust, as the case may be, under Section 663(c) of the Internal Revenue Code for state purposes and a separate election under paragraph (3) of subdivision (e) of Section 17024.5 shall not be allowed.

(2) If the executor of the estate or the fiduciary of the trust, as the case may be, fails to make an election under Section 663(c) of the Internal Revenue Code for federal purposes with respect to separate shares treated as separate estates or trusts, an election under Section 663(c) of the Internal Revenue Code for state purposes shall not be allowed, and a separate election under paragraph (3) of subdivision (e) of Section 17024.5 shall not be allowed. *(Added by Stats.1998, c. 322 (A.B.2797), § 34, eff. Aug. 20, 1998.)*

[1] See 26 U.S.C.A. § 663.

[2] See 26 U.S.C.A. §§ 661 and 662.

Cross References

Computation of time, see Code of Civil Procedure §§ 12, 12a; Government Code § 6800 et seq.

Fiduciary defined for purposes of this Part, see Revenue and Taxation Code § 17006.

State defined for purposes of this Part, see Revenue and Taxation Code § 17018.

Taxable year defined for purposes of this Part, see Revenue and Taxation Code § 17010.

§ 17755. Charitable remainder annuity trusts or charitable remainder unitrusts; taxation of unrelated business taxable income

For taxable years beginning on or after January 1, 2014, Section 664(c)(2) of the Internal Revenue Code, [1] relating to excise tax, shall not apply and, in lieu thereof, the unrelated business taxable income, as defined in Section 23732, of every charitable remainder annuity trust or charitable remainder unitrust shall be subject to tax under Section 17651. *(Added by Stats.2014, c. 478 (A.B.2754), § 4, eff. Jan. 1, 2015.)*

[1] Internal Revenue Code sections are in Title 26 of the U.S.C.A.

§ 17760. Gain on certain transfers to foreign trusts and estates; application of federal provisions

Section 684 of the Internal Revenue Code, [1] relating to recognition of gain on certain transfers to certain foreign trusts and estates, shall not apply. *(Added by Stats.2005, c. 691 (A.B.115), § 38, eff. Oct. 7, 2005.)*

[1] Internal Revenue Code sections are in Title 26 of the U.S.C.A.

Cross References

Internal Revenue Code defined for purposes of this Part, see Revenue and Taxation Code § 17024.5.

§ 17760.5. Qualified funeral trusts; modification of Internal Revenue Code provisions

Section 685 of the Internal Revenue Code, [1] relating to treatment of funeral trusts, is modified as follows:

(a) Section 685(a) of the Internal Revenue Code is modified to read: In the case of a qualified funeral trust—

(1) Subparts B, C, D, and E of Subchapter J of Chapter 1 of Subtitle A of the Internal Revenue Code shall not apply.

(2) No credit for personal exemption shall be allowed under Section 17054 or Section 17733.

(b) Section 685(b) of the Internal Revenue Code is modified as follows:

(1) An election under Section 685(b)(5) of the Internal Revenue Code for federal purposes shall be treated for purposes of this part as an election made by the trustee of the qualified funeral trust under Section 685(b)(5) of the Internal Revenue Code for state purposes and a separate election under paragraph (3) of subdivision (e) of Section 17024.5 shall not be allowed.

(2) If the trustee of a qualified funeral trust fails to make an election under Section 685(b)(5) of the Internal Revenue Code for federal purposes with respect to a qualified funeral trust, that trust shall be treated for purposes of this part as owned under Subpart E of the Internal Revenue Code by the purchasers of the contracts described in Section 685(b)(1) of the Internal Revenue Code, an election under Section 685(b)(5) of the Internal Revenue Code for state purposes with respect to that trust shall not be allowed, and a separate election under paragraph (3) of subdivision (e) of Section 17024.5 shall not be allowed with respect to that trust.

(c) Section 685(d) of the Internal Revenue Code is modified to read: Subdivision (e) of Section 17041 shall be applied to each qualified funeral trust by treating each beneficiary's interest in each qualified funeral trust as a separate trust.

(d) The Franchise Tax Board may, by forms and instructions, provide rules for simplified reporting of all trusts having a single trustee consistent with the rules prescribed by the Secretary of the Treasury under Section 685 of the Internal Revenue Code.

(e) This section shall apply to taxable years ending after August 5, 1997.

(f) The amendments made to this section by the act adding this subdivision [2] shall apply to taxable years beginning on or after January 1, 1998. *(Added by Stats.1998, c. 7 (S.B.519),*

§ 10, eff. March 14, 1998. Amended by Stats.1998, c. 322 (A.B.2797), § 35, eff. Aug. 20, 1998.)

[1] See 26 U.S.C.A. § 685.

[2] Stats.1998, c. 322 (A.B.2797), eff. August 20, 1998.

Application

Under the terms of Stats.1998, c. 322, § 107, the section as added by Stats.1998, c. 7 (S.B.519), shall apply for taxable and income years beginning before January 1, 1998, and the section as amended by Stats.1998, c. 322 (A.B.2797), shall apply for taxable and income years beginning on or after January 1, 1998.

Cross References

Contracts, generally, see Civil Code § 1549 et seq.

Franchise Tax Board,
   Generally, see Government Code § 15700 et seq.
   Powers and duties, see Revenue and Taxation Code § 19501 et seq.

Franchise Tax Board and board defined for purposes of this Part, see Revenue and Taxation Code § 17003.

Pre-need funeral arrangements, trust agreements, election to pay taxes on the earnings on any trust, authority of trustee, see Business and Professions Code § 7735.

State defined for purposes of this Part, see Revenue and Taxation Code § 17018.

Taxable year defined for purposes of this Part, see Revenue and Taxation Code § 17010.

§ 17779. Excess distributions by trusts; application of federal provisions

Sections 665 to 668[1], inclusive, of the Internal Revenue Code shall not apply to distributions described in subdivision (b) of Section 17745. *(Added by Stats.1983, c. 488, § 59, eff. July 28, 1983.)*

[1] 26 U.S.C.A. §§ 665 to 668.

Cross References

Internal Revenue Code defined for purposes of this Part, see Revenue and Taxation Code § 17024.5.

WELFARE AND INSTITUTIONS CODE

Division 5

COMMUNITY MENTAL HEALTH SERVICES

Cross References

Authorized disclosure of confidential information and records, see Welfare and Institutions Code § 5328.15.

Confidentiality of information and records obtained in providing services to voluntary or involuntary recipients, see Welfare and Institutions Code § 5328.

Death of patient in state mental hospital, release of information to coroner, see Welfare and Institutions Code § 5328.8.

Dependent children, initial petition hearing, limitations upon right of parent or guardian to make educational or developmental services decisions for the child, see Welfare and Institutions Code §§ 319, 361.

Protective social services, developmentally disabled persons, see Welfare and Institutions Code § 4418.5.

Release of mentally disordered or developmentally disabled persons committed to youth authority, see Welfare and Institutions Code § 1756.

Part 1

THE LANTERMAN—PETRIS—SHORT ACT

Cross References

Emergency medical services and care, exclusion of psychiatric emergency medical condition from definition under certain contracts, see Health and Safety Code § 1317.1.

Fees in the Supreme Court and Courts of Appeal,

Filing record on appeal or petition for writ, rules governing time and method of payment, see Government Code § 68926.

Petition for hearing in the Supreme Court, see Government Code § 68927.

CHAPTER 3. CONSERVATORSHIP FOR GRAVELY DISABLED PERSONS

Cross References

Certification for intensive treatment, limitation on involuntary detention, see Welfare and Institutions Code § 5257.

Conservatorship, see Probate Code § 1800 et seq.

Costs of proceedings in superior court, see Welfare and Institutions Code § 5110.

Gravely disabled defined, see Welfare and Institutions Code § 5008.

Guardians, appointment, see Probate Code § 2250 et seq.

Historical course of mental disorder, consideration when applying definition of mental disorder for purposes of this Chapter, see Welfare and Institutions Code § 5008.2.

Person previously committed, new evaluation, proceedings under this chapter, see Welfare and Institutions Code § 5366.1.

Placement agency defined to include conservator,
Community care facilities, see Health and Safety Code § 1536.1.
Residential care facilities for the elderly, see Health and Safety Code § 1569.47.

Public guardian, generally, see Government Code § 27430 et seq.

Release of involuntary patients, exceptions, see Welfare and Institutions Code §§ 5257, 5264.

Rules on appeal from order establishing conservatorship under these provisions, see California Rules of Court, Rules 8.304 to 8.368, 8.508, 8.480.

§ 5350. Appointment; procedure

A conservator of the person, of the estate, or of the person and the estate may be appointed for a person who is gravely disabled as a result of a mental health disorder or impairment by chronic alcoholism.

The procedure for establishing, administering, and terminating a conservatorship under this chapter shall be the same as that provided in Division 4 (commencing with Section 1400) of the Probate Code, except as follows:

(a) A conservator may be appointed for a gravely disabled minor.

(b)(1) Appointment of a conservator under this part, including the appointment of a conservator for a person who is gravely disabled, as defined in subparagraph (A) of paragraph (1) of subdivision (h) of Section 5008, shall be subject to the list of priorities in Section 1812 of the Probate Code unless the officer providing conservatorship investigation recommends otherwise to the superior court.

(2) In appointing a conservator, as defined in subparagraph (B) of paragraph (1) of subdivision (h) of Section 5008, the court shall consider the purposes of protection of the public and the treatment of the conservatee. Notwithstanding any other provision of this section, the court shall not appoint the proposed conservator if the court determines that appointment of the proposed conservator will not result in adequate protection of the public.

(c) No conservatorship of the estate pursuant to this chapter shall be established if a conservatorship or guardianship of the estate exists under the Probate Code. When a gravely disabled person already has a guardian or conservator of the person appointed under the Probate Code, the proceedings under this chapter shall not terminate the prior proceedings but shall be concurrent with and superior thereto. The superior court may appoint the existing guardian or conservator of the person or another person as conservator of the person under this chapter.

(d)(1) The person for whom conservatorship is sought shall have the right to demand a court or jury trial on the issue of whether he or she is gravely disabled. Demand for court or jury trial shall be made within five days following the hearing on the conservatorship petition. If the proposed conservatee demands a court or jury trial before the date of the hearing as provided for in Section 5365, the demand shall constitute a waiver of the hearing.

(2) Court or jury trial shall commence within 10 days of the date of the demand, except that the court shall continue the trial date for a period not to exceed 15 days upon the request of counsel for the proposed conservatee.

(3) This right shall also apply in subsequent proceedings to reestablish conservatorship.

(e)(1) Notwithstanding subparagraph (A) of paragraph (1) of subdivision (h) of Section 5008, a person is not "gravely disabled" if that person can survive safely without involuntary detention with the help of responsible family, friends, or others who are both willing and able to help provide for the person's basic personal needs for food, clothing, or shelter.

(2) However, unless they specifically indicate in writing their willingness and ability to help, family, friends, or others shall not be considered willing or able to provide this help.

(3) The purpose of this subdivision is to avoid the necessity for, and the harmful effects of, requiring family, friends, and others to publicly state, and requiring the court to publicly find, that no one is willing or able to assist a person with a mental health disorder in providing for the person's basic needs for food, clothing, or shelter.

(4) This subdivision does not apply to a person who is gravely disabled, as defined in subparagraph (B) of paragraph (1) of subdivision (h) of Section 5008.

(f) Conservatorship investigation shall be conducted pursuant to this part and shall not be subject to Section 1826 or Chapter 2 (commencing with Section 1850) of Part 3 of Division 4 of the Probate Code.

(g) Notice of proceedings under this chapter shall be given to a guardian or conservator of the person or estate of the proposed conservatee appointed under the Probate Code.

(h) As otherwise provided in this chapter. *(Added by Stats.1967, c. 1667, p. 4074, § 36, operative July 1, 1969. Amended by Stats.1969, c. 722, p. 1430, § 23, eff. Aug. 8, 1969, operative July 1, 1969; Stats.1970, c. 68, p. 82, § 1; Stats.1970, c. 1627, p. 3448, § 24; Stats.1971, c. 776, p. 1529, § 4; Stats.1972, c. 574, p. 981, § 1; Stats.1978, c. 1294, p. 4244, § 4; Stats.1979, c. 730, p. 2533, § 145, operative Jan. 1, 1981; Stats.1986, c. 322, § 1; Stats.1989, c. 999, § 2; Stats.1995, c. 593 (A.B.145), § 3; Stats.2006, c. 799 (A.B.2858), § 2; Stats.2014, c. 144 (A.B.1847), § 94, eff. Jan. 1, 2015.)*

1979 Amendment

Section 5350 is amended to correct the references to the Probate Code in view of the guardianship-conservatorship revision. [14 Cal.L.Rev.Comm.Reports 958 (1978)].

Cross References

Conservatorship investigation defined for purposes of this Part, see Welfare and Institutions Code § 5008.

Court defined for purposes of this Part, see Welfare and Institutions Code § 5008.

Gravely disabled defined for purposes of this Chapter, see Welfare and Institutions Code § 5008.

Gravely disabled minor defined, see Welfare and Institutions Code § 5585.25.

Procedure for confinement of outpatient pending proceeding for revocation of outpatient status as not preventing hospitalization under other sections, see Welfare and Institutions Code § 5308.

§ 5350.1. Purpose

The purpose of conservatorship, as provided for in this article, is to provide individualized treatment, supervision, and placement. *(Added by Stats.1978, c. 1294, p. 4244, § 5.)*

§ 5350.2. Notification of family members or other designated persons; time and place of hearing

Reasonable attempts shall be made by the county mental health program to notify family members or any other person designated by the person for whom conservatorship is sought, of the time and place of the conservatorship hearing. The person for whom the conservatorship is sought shall be advised by the facility treating the person that he or she may request that information about the time and place of the conservatorship hearing not be given to family members, in those circumstances where the proposed conservator is not a family member. The request shall be honored by the mental health program. Neither this section nor Section 5350 shall be interpreted to allow the proposed conservatee to request that any proposed conservator not be advised of the time and place of the conservatorship hearing. *(Added by Stats.1986, c. 872, § 5. Amended by Stats.1987, c. 56, § 183.)*

§ 5350.5. Referral of conservatee for assessment to determine if conservatee has treatable mental illness and is unwilling or unable to accept voluntary treatment; counsel; filing of copy with court

(a) If a conservatorship has already been established under the Probate Code, the court, in a proceeding under the Probate Code, after an evidentiary hearing attended by the conservatee, unless the conservatee waives presence, and the conservatee's counsel, may refer the conservatee, in consultation with a licensed physician or licensed psychologist satisfying the conditions of subdivision (c) of Section 2032.020 of the Code of Civil Procedure providing assessment or treatment to the conservatee, for an assessment by the local mental health system or plan to determine if the conservatee has a treatable mental illness, including whether the conservatee is gravely disabled as a result of a mental disorder or impairment by chronic alcoholism, and is unwilling to accept, or is incapable of accepting, treatment voluntarily. If the conservatee cannot afford counsel, the court shall appoint counsel for him or her pursuant to Section 1471 of the Probate Code.

(b) The local mental health system or plan shall file a copy of the assessment with the court that made the referral for assessment in a proceeding under the Probate Code. *(Added by Stats.2016, c. 819 (A.B.1836), § 1, eff. Jan. 1, 2017.)*

§ 5351. Investigating agencies; provision of services

In each county or counties acting jointly under the provisions of Article 1 (commencing with Section 6500) of Chapter 5 of Division 7 of Title 1 of the Government Code, the governing board shall designate the agency or agencies to provide conservatorship investigation as set forth in this chapter. The governing board may designate that conservatorship services be provided by the public guardian or agency providing public guardian services. *(Added by Stats.1967, c. 1667, p. 4074, § 36, operative July 1, 1969. Amended by Stats.1968, c. 1374, p. 2660, § 51.5, operative July 1, 1969; Stats.1986, c. 335, § 1.)*

Cross References

Conservatorship investigation defined for purposes of this Part, see Welfare and Institutions Code § 5008.

§ 5352. Recommendation; petition; temporary conservator; procedure

When the professional person in charge of an agency providing comprehensive evaluation or a facility providing intensive treatment determines that a person in his care is gravely disabled as a result of mental disorder or impairment by chronic alcoholism and is unwilling to accept, or incapable of accepting, treatment voluntarily, he may recommend conservatorship to the officer providing conservatorship investigation of the county of residence of the person prior to his admission as a patient in such facility.

The professional person in charge of an agency providing comprehensive evaluation or a facility providing intensive treatment may recommend conservatorship for a person without the person being an inpatient in such facility, if both of the following conditions are met: (a) the professional person or another professional person designated by him has examined and evaluated the person and determined that he is gravely disabled; (b) the professional person or another professional person designated by him has determined that future examination on an inpatient basis is not necessary for a determination that the person is gravely disabled.

If the officer providing conservatorship investigation concurs with the recommendation, he shall petition the superior court in the county of residence of the patient to establish conservatorship.

Where temporary conservatorship is indicated, the fact shall be alternatively pleaded in the petition. The officer providing conservatorship investigation or other county officer or employee designated by the county shall act as the temporary conservator. *(Added by Stats.1967, c. 1667, p. 4074, § 36, operative July 1, 1969. Amended by Stats.1968, c. 1374, p. 2661, § 52, operative July 1, 1969; Stats.1969, c. 722, p. 1430, § 24, eff. Aug. 8, 1969, operative July 1, 1969; Stats.1970, c. 35, p. 56, § 1; Stats.1970, c. 1627, p. 3449, § 24.1; Stats.1972, c. 692, p. 1274, § 1; Stats.1979, c. 730, p. 2534, § 146, operative Jan. 1, 1981.)*

1979 Amendment

Section 5352 is amended to delete the references to the Probate Code in view of the revision of guardianship–conservatorship law. Under Section 5350 of the Welfare and Institutions Code, the procedure for establishing, administering, and terminating conservatorship under this chapter is the same as that provided in Division 4 (commencing with Section 1400) of the Probate Code. [14 Cal. L.Rev.Comm. Reports 958 (1978)].

Cross References

Conservatorship investigation defined for purposes of this Part, see Welfare and Institutions Code § 5008.
Court defined for purposes of this Part, see Welfare and Institutions Code § 5008.
Evaluation defined for purposes of this Part, see Welfare and Institutions Code § 5008.
Gravely disabled defined for purposes of this Chapter, see Welfare and Institutions Code § 5008.
Intensive treatment defined for purposes of this Part, see Welfare and Institutions Code § 5008.

§ 5352.1. Temporary conservatorship

(a) The court may establish a temporary conservatorship for a period not to exceed 30 days and appoint a temporary conservator on the basis of the comprehensive report of the officer providing conservatorship investigation filed pursuant to Section 5354, or on the basis of an affidavit of the professional person who recommended conservatorship stating the reasons for his or her recommendation, if the court is satisfied that the comprehensive report or affidavit shows the necessity for a temporary conservatorship.

(b) Except as provided in this section, all temporary conservatorships shall expire automatically at the conclusion of 30 days, unless prior to that date the court shall conduct a hearing on the issue of whether or not the proposed conservatee is gravely disabled as defined in subdivision (h) of Section 5008.

(c) If the proposed conservatee demands a court or jury trial on the issue whether he or she is gravely disabled, the court may extend the temporary conservatorship until the date of the disposition of the issue by the court or jury trial, provided that the extension shall in no event exceed a period of six months. *(Added by Stats.1969, c. 722, p. 1431, § 24.05, eff. Aug. 8, 1969, operative July 1, 1969. Amended by Stats.1971, c. 776, p. 1530, § 5; Stats.1972, c. 574, p. 981, § 2; Stats.2008, c. 179 (S.B.1498), § 238.)*

Cross References

Conservatorship investigation defined for purposes of this Part, see Welfare and Institutions Code § 5008.
Court defined for purposes of this Part, see Welfare and Institutions Code § 5008.
Gravely disabled defined for purposes of this Chapter, see Welfare and Institutions Code § 5008.

§ 5352.2. Public guardian; bond and oath

Where the duly designated officer providing conservatorship investigation is a public guardian, his official oath and bond as public guardian are in lieu of any other bond or oath on the grant of temporary letters of conservatorship to him. *(Added by Stats.1970, c. 566, p. 1138, § 1.)*

Cross References

Conservatorship investigation defined for purposes of this Part, see Welfare and Institutions Code § 5008.
Public guardian, see Government Code § 27430 et seq.

§ 5352.3. Additional detention pending filing petition; maximum involuntary detention for gravely disabled

If the professional person in charge of the facility providing intensive treatment recommends conservatorship pursuant to Section 5352, the proposed conservatee may be held in that facility for a period not to exceed three days beyond the designated period for intensive treatment if the additional time period is necessary for a filing of the petition for temporary conservatorship and the establishment of the temporary conservatorship by the court. The involuntary detention period for gravely disabled persons pursuant to Sections 5150, 5250, and 5170.15 shall not exceed 47 days unless continuance is granted. *(Added by Stats.1970, c. 1627, p. 3449, § 24.5. Amended by Stats.1988, c. 1517, § 13.)*

Cross References

Certification for fourteen days of intensive treatment, see Welfare and Institutions Code § 5250 et seq.
Court defined for purposes of this Part, see Welfare and Institutions Code § 5008.
Gravely disabled defined for purposes of this Chapter, see Welfare and Institutions Code § 5008.
Intensive treatment defined for purposes of this Part, see Welfare and Institutions Code § 5008.

§ 5352.4. Appeal of judgment establishing conservatorship; continuation of conservatorship; exception

If a conservatee appeals the court's decision to establish conservatorship, the conservatorship shall continue unless execution of judgment is stayed by the appellate court. *(Added by Stats.1972, c. 574, p. 982, § 4.)*

Cross References

Court defined for purposes of this Part, see Welfare and Institutions Code § 5008.

§ 5352.5. Initiation of proceedings; reimbursement

Conservatorship proceedings may be initiated for any person committed to a state hospital or local mental health facility or placed on outpatient treatment pursuant to Section 1026 or 1370 of the Penal Code or transferred pursuant to Section 4011.6 of the Penal Code upon recommendation of the medical director of the state hospital, or a designee, or professional person in charge of the local mental health facility, or a designee, or the local mental health director, or a designee, to the conservatorship investigator of the county of residence of the person prior to his or her admission to the hospital or facility or of the county in which the hospital or facility is located. The initiation of conservatorship proceedings or the existence of a conservatorship shall not affect any pending criminal proceedings.

Subject to the provisions of Sections 5150 and 5250, conservatorship proceedings may be initiated for any person convicted of a felony who has been transferred to a state hospital under the jurisdiction of the State Department of State Hospitals pursuant to Section 2684 of the Penal Code by the recommendation of the medical director of the state hospital to the conservatorship investigator of the county of residence of the person or of the county in which the state hospital is located.

Subject to the provisions of Sections 5150 and 5250, conservatorship proceedings may be initiated for any person committed to the Department of Corrections and Rehabilitation, Division of Juvenile Justice, or on parole from a facility of the Department of Corrections and Rehabilitation, Division of Juvenile Justice, by the Chief Deputy Secretary for Juvenile Justice or a designee, to the conservatorship investigator of the county of residence of the person or of the county in which the facility is situated.

The county mental health program providing conservatorship investigation services and conservatorship case management services for any persons except those transferred pursuant to Section 4011.6 of the Penal Code shall be reimbursed for the expenditures made by it for the services pursuant to the Short–Doyle Act (commencing with Section 5600) at 100 percent of the expenditures. Each county Short–Doyle plan shall include provision for the services in the plan. *(Added by Stats.1975, c. 1258, p. 3302, § 7. Amended by Stats.1977, c. 1252, p. 4572, § 572, operative July 1, 1978; Stats.1977, c. 691, p. 2231, § 5; Stats.1978, c. 429, p. 1455, § 209.5, eff. July 17, 1978, operative July 1, 1978; Stats.1986, c. 933, § 2; Stats.2012, c. 24 (A.B.1470), § 130, eff. June 27, 2012.)*

§ 5352.6. Individualized treatment plan; development; goals; progress review; termination of conservatorship by court

Within 10 days after conservatorship of the person has been established under the provisions of this article, there shall be an individualized treatment plan unless treatment is specifically found not to be appropriate by the court. The treatment plan shall be developed by the Short–Doyle Act community mental health service, the staff of a facility operating under a contract to provide such services in the individual's county of residence, or the staff of a health facility licensed pursuant to Chapter 2 (commencing with Section 1250) of Division 2 of the Health and Safety Code to provide inpatient psychiatric treatment. The person responsible for developing the treatment plan shall encourage the participation of the client and the client's family members, when appropriate, in the development, implementation, revision, and review of the treatment plan. The individualized treatment plan shall specify goals for the individual's treatment, the criteria by which accomplishment of the goals can be judged, and a plan for review of the progress of treatment. The goals of the treatment plan shall be equivalent to reducing or eliminating the behavioral manifestations of grave disability. If a treatment plan is not developed as provided herein then the matter shall be referred to the court by the Short–Doyle Act community mental health service, or the staff of a facility operating under a contract to provide such services, or the conservator, or the attorney of record for the conservatee.

When the progress review determines that the goals have been reached and the person is no longer gravely disabled, a person designated by the county shall so report to the court and the conservatorship shall be terminated by the court.

If the conservator fails to report to the court that the person is no longer gravely disabled as provided herein, then the matter shall be referred to the court by the Short–Doyle Act community mental health service, or the staff of a facility operating under a contract to provide such services, or the attorney of record for the conservatee. *(Added by Stats.1978, c. 1294, p. 4244, § 6. Amended by Stats.1986, c. 872, § 6.)*

§ 5353. Temporary conservator; arrangements pending determination of conservatorship; powers; residence of conservatee; sale or relinquishment of property

A temporary conservator under this chapter shall determine what arrangements are necessary to provide the person with food, shelter, and care pending the determination of conservatorship. He shall give preference to arrangements which allow the person to return to his home, family or friends. If necessary, the temporary conservator may require the person to be detained in a facility providing intensive treatment or in a facility specified in Section 5358 pending the determination of conservatorship. Any person so detained shall have the same right to judicial review set forth in Article 5 (commencing with Section 5275) of Chapter 2 of this part.

The powers of the temporary conservator shall be those granted in the decree, but in no event may they be broader than the powers which may be granted a conservator.

The court shall order the temporary conservator to take all reasonable steps to preserve the status quo concerning the conservatee's previous place of residence. The temporary conservator shall not be permitted to sell or relinquish on the conservatee's behalf any estate or interest in any real or personal property, including any lease or estate in real or personal property used as or within the conservatee's place of residence, without specific approval of the court, which may be granted only upon a finding based on a preponderance of the evidence that such action is necessary to avert irreparable harm to the conservatee. A finding of irreparable harm as to real property may be based upon a reasonable showing that such real property is vacant, that it cannot reasonably be rented, and that it is impossible or impractical to obtain fire or liability insurance on such property. *(Added by Stats.1967, c. 1667, p. 4074, § 36, operative July 1, 1969. Amended by Stats.1968, c. 1374, p. 2661, § 53, operative July 1, 1969; Stats.1969, c. 722, p. 1431, § 24.1, eff. Aug. 8, 1969, operative July 1, 1969; Stats.1971, c. 776, p. 1530, § 6; Stats.1972, c. 574, p. 982, § 3; Stats.1977, c. 1237, p. 4157, § 5; Stats.1978, c. 1268, p. 4116, § 2.)*

Court defined for purposes of this Part, see Welfare and Institutions Code § 5008.

Intensive treatment defined for purposes of this Part, see Welfare and Institutions Code § 5008.

Procedure for confinement of outpatient pending proceeding for revocation of outpatient status as not preventing hospitalization under other sections, see Welfare and Institutions Code § 5308.

§ 5354. Investigation of alternatives to conservatorship; recommendations of conservatorship; report of investigation, necessity, contents, transmittal, use; service of report

(a) The officer providing conservatorship investigation shall investigate all available alternatives to conservatorship and shall recommend conservatorship to the court only if no suitable alternatives are available. This officer shall render to the court a written report of investigation prior to the hearing. The report to the court shall be comprehensive and shall contain all relevant aspects of the person's medical, psychological, financial, family, vocational, and social condition, and information obtained from the person's family members, close friends, social worker, or principal therapist. The report shall also contain all available information concerning the person's real and personal property. The facilities providing intensive treatment or comprehensive evaluation shall disclose any records or information which may facilitate the investigation. If the officer providing conservatorship investigation recommends against conservatorship, he or she shall set forth all alternatives available. A copy of the report shall be transmitted to the individual who originally recommended conservatorship, to the person or agency, if any, recommended to serve as conservator, and to the person recommended for conservatorship. The court may receive the report in evidence and may read and consider the contents thereof in rendering its judgment.

(b) Notwithstanding Section 5328, when a court with jurisdiction over a person in a criminal case orders an evaluation of the person's mental condition pursuant to Section 5200, and that evaluation leads to a conservatorship investigation, the officer providing the conservatorship investigation shall serve a copy of the report required under subdivision (a) upon the defendant or the defendant's counsel. Upon the prior written request of the defendant or the defendant's counsel, the officer providing the conservatorship investigation shall also submit a copy of the report to the court hearing the criminal case, the district attorney, and the county probation department. The conservatorship investigation report and the information contained in that report, shall be kept confidential and shall not be further disclosed to anyone without the prior written consent of the defendant. After disposition of the criminal case, the court shall place all copies of the report in a sealed file, except as follows:

(1) The defendant and the defendant's counsel may retain their copy.

(2) If the defendant is placed on probation status, the county probation department may retain a copy of the report for the purpose of supervision of the defendant until the probation is terminated, at which time the probation department shall return its copy of the report to the court for

placement into the sealed file. *(Added by Stats.1967, c. 1667, p. 4074, § 36, operative July 1, 1969. Amended by Stats.1974, c. 833, p. 1795, § 1; Stats.1978, c. 1294, p. 4245, § 7; Stats.1982, c. 1598, § 7; Stats.2014, c. 734 (A.B.2190), § 4, eff. Jan. 1, 2015.)*

Conservatorship investigation defined for purposes of this Part, see Welfare and Institutions Code § 5008.

Court defined for purposes of this Part, see Welfare and Institutions Code § 5008.

Evaluation defined for purposes of this Part, see Welfare and Institutions Code § 5008.

Intensive treatment defined for purposes of this Part, see Welfare and Institutions Code § 5008.

State summary criminal history information, persons entitled to receive, restrictions on use, see Penal Code § 11105.1.

§ 5354.5. Acceptance or rejection of position as conservator; recommendation of substitute; public guardian

Except as otherwise provided in this section, the person recommended to serve as conservator shall promptly notify the officer providing conservatorship investigation whether he or she will accept the position if appointed. If notified that the person or agency recommended will not accept the position if appointed, the officer providing conservatorship investigation shall promptly recommend another person to serve as conservator.

The public guardian shall serve as conservator of any person found by a court under this chapter to be gravely disabled, if the court recommends the conservatorship after a conservatorship investigation, and if the court finds that no other person or entity is willing and able to serve as conservator. *(Added by Stats.1967, c. 1667, p. 4074, § 36, operative July 1, 1969. Amended by Stats.1986, c. 872, § 6.5.)*

Conservatorship investigation defined for purposes of this Part, see Welfare and Institutions Code § 5008.

Court defined for purposes of this Part, see Welfare and Institutions Code § 5008.

Gravely disabled defined for purposes of this Chapter, see Welfare and Institutions Code § 5008.

§ 5355. Designation of conservator; conflicts of interest; public guardian

If the conservatorship investigation results in a recommendation for conservatorship, the recommendation shall designate the most suitable person, corporation, state or local agency or county officer, or employee designated by the county to serve as conservator. No person, corporation, or agency shall be designated as conservator whose interests, activities, obligations or responsibilities are such as to compromise his or her or their ability to represent and safeguard the interests of the conservatee. Nothing in this section shall be construed to prevent the State Department of State Hospitals from serving as guardian pursuant to Section 7284, or the function of the conservatorship investigator and conservator being exercised by the same public officer or employee.

When a public guardian is appointed conservator, his or her official bond and oath as public guardian are in lieu of the conservator's bond and oath on the grant of letters of conservatorship. No bond shall be required of any other public officer or employee appointed to serve as conservator. *(Added by Stats.1967, c. 1667, p. 4074, § 36, operative July 1, 1969. Amended by Stats.1970, c. 566, p. 1138, § 2; Stats.1971, c. 1593, p. 3343, § 378.5; Stats.1971, c. 955, p. 1861, § 10; Stats.1973, c. 142, p. 417, § 71, eff. June 30, 1973, operative July 1, 1973; Stats.1974, c. 1060, p. 2284, § 9; Stats.1977, c. 1252, p. 4577, § 574, operative July 1, 1978; Stats.2012, c. 24 (A.B.1470), § 131, eff. June 27, 2012.)*

Cross References

Conservatorship investigation defined for purposes of this Part, see Welfare and Institutions Code § 5008.
Public guardian, see Government Code § 27430 et seq.

§ 5356. Investigation report; recommendations; agreement to serve as conservator

The report of the officer providing conservatorship investigation shall contain his or her recommendations concerning the powers to be granted to, and the duties to be imposed upon the conservator, the legal disabilities to be imposed upon the conservatee, and the proper placement for the conservatee pursuant to Section 5358. Except as provided in this section, the report to the court shall also contain an agreement signed by the person or agency recommended to serve as conservator certifying that the person or agency is able and willing to serve as conservator. The public guardian shall serve as conservator of any person found by a court under this chapter to be gravely disabled, if the court recommends the conservatorship after a conservatorship investigation, and if the court finds that no other person or entity is willing and able to serve as conservator. *(Added by Stats.1967, c. 1667, p. 4074, § 36, operative July 1, 1969. Amended by Stats.1980, c. 681, p. 2066, § 1; Stats.1986, c. 872, § 7.)*

Cross References

Conservatorship investigation defined for purposes of this Part, see Welfare and Institutions Code § 5008.
Court defined for purposes of this Part, see Welfare and Institutions Code § 5008.
Gravely disabled defined for purposes of this Chapter, see Welfare and Institutions Code § 5008.

§ 5357. Conservator; general and special powers; disability of conservatee

All conservators of the estate shall have the general powers specified in Chapter 6 (commencing with Section 2400) of Part 4 of Division 4 of the Probate Code and shall have the additional powers specified in Article 11 (commencing with Section 2590) of Chapter 6 of Part 4 of Division 4 of the Probate Code as the court may designate. The report shall set forth which, if any, of the additional powers it recommends. The report shall also recommend for or against the imposition of each of the following disabilities on the proposed conservatee:

(a) The privilege of possessing a license to operate a motor vehicle. If the report recommends against this right and if the court follows the recommendation, the agency providing conservatorship investigation shall, upon the appointment of the conservator, so notify the Department of Motor Vehicles.

(b) The right to enter into contracts. The officer may recommend against the person having the right to enter specified types of transactions or transactions in excess of specified money amounts.

(c) The disqualification of the person from voting pursuant to Section 2208 of the Elections Code.

(d) The right to refuse or consent to treatment related specifically to the conservatee's being gravely disabled. The conservatee shall retain all rights specified in Section 5325.

(e) The right to refuse or consent to routine medical treatment unrelated to remedying or preventing the recurrence of the conservatee's being gravely disabled. The court shall make a specific determination regarding imposition of this disability.

(f) The disqualification of the person from possessing a firearm pursuant to subdivision (e) of Section 8103. *(Added by Stats.1967, c. 1667, p. 4074, § 36, operative July 1, 1969. Amended by Stats.1969, c. 722, p. 1431, § 25, eff. Aug. 8, 1969, operative July 1, 1969; Stats.1976, c. 905, p. 2078, § 1; Stats.1978, c. 1363, p. 4531, § 14; Stats.1979, c. 730, p. 2535, § 147, operative Jan. 1, 1981; Stats.1984, c. 1562, § 3; Stats.1990, c. 180 (S.B.2138), § 1; Stats.1994, c. 923 (S.B. 1546), § 268.)*

Law Revision Commission Comments

1979 Amendment

Section 5357 is amended to revise the cross-references to the Probate Code in view of the revision of guardianship–conservatorship law in the Probate Code. [14 Cal.L.Rev.Comm. Reports 958 (1978)].

Cross References

Competence of former conservatee, see Welfare and Institutions Code § 5368.
Conservatorship investigation defined for purposes of this Part, see Welfare and Institutions Code § 5008.
Contract powers, loss by person whose incapacity judicially determined, see Civil Code § 40.
Court defined for purposes of this Part, see Welfare and Institutions Code § 5008.
Drivers' license,
  Mental defect, effect, see Vehicle Code § 12805 et seq.
  Statement in application, see Vehicle Code § 12800.
Firearms,
  Certificate for possession, see Welfare and Institutions Code § 8103.
  Mental patient, see Welfare and Institutions Code § 8100 et seq.
Gravely disabled defined for purposes of this Chapter, see Welfare and Institutions Code § 5008.
Restriction on disabilities imposed upon person complained against, see Welfare and Institutions Code § 5005.

§ 5358. Placement of conservatee; treatment

(a)(1) When ordered by the court after the hearing required by this section, a conservator appointed pursuant to this chapter shall place his or her conservatee as follows:

(A) For a conservatee who is gravely disabled, as defined in subparagraph (A) of paragraph (1) of subdivision (h) of Section 5008, in the least restrictive alternative placement, as designated by the court.

(B) For a conservatee who is gravely disabled, as defined in subparagraph (B) of paragraph (1) of subdivision (h) of

Section 5008, in a placement that achieves the purposes of treatment of the conservatee and protection of the public.

(2) The placement may include a medical, psychiatric, nursing, or other state-licensed facility, or a state hospital, county hospital, hospital operated by the Regents of the University of California, a United States government hospital, or other nonmedical facility approved by the State Department of Health Care Services or an agency accredited by the State Department of Health Care Services, or in addition to any of the foregoing, in cases of chronic alcoholism, to a county alcoholic treatment center.

(b) A conservator shall also have the right, if specified in the court order, to require his or her conservatee to receive treatment related specifically to remedying or preventing the recurrence of the conservatee's being gravely disabled, or to require his or her conservatee to receive routine medical treatment unrelated to remedying or preventing the recurrence of the conservatee's being gravely disabled. Except in emergency cases in which the conservatee faces loss of life or serious bodily injury, no surgery shall be performed upon the conservatee without the conservatee's prior consent or a court order obtained pursuant to Section 5358.2 specifically authorizing that surgery.

(c)(1) For a conservatee who is gravely disabled, as defined in subparagraph (A) of paragraph (1) of subdivision (h) of Section 5008, if the conservatee is not to be placed in his or her own home or the home of a relative, first priority shall be to placement in a suitable facility as close as possible to his or her home or the home of a relative. For the purposes of this section, suitable facility means the least restrictive residential placement available and necessary to achieve the purpose of treatment. At the time that the court considers the report of the officer providing conservatorship investigation specified in Section 5356, the court shall consider available placement alternatives. After considering all the evidence the court shall determine the least restrictive and most appropriate alternative placement for the conservatee. The court shall also determine those persons to be notified of a change of placement. The fact that a person for whom conservatorship is recommended is not an inpatient shall not be construed by the court as an indication that the person does not meet the criteria of grave disability.

(2) For a conservatee who is gravely disabled, as defined in subparagraph (B) of paragraph (1) of subdivision (h) of Section 5008, first priority shall be placement in a facility that achieves the purposes of treatment of the conservatee and protection of the public. The court shall determine the most appropriate placement for the conservatee. The court shall also determine those persons to be notified of a change of placement, and additionally require the conservator to notify the district attorney or attorney representing the originating county prior to any change of placement.

(3) For any conservatee, if requested, the local mental health director shall assist the conservator or the court in selecting a placement facility for the conservatee. When a conservatee who is receiving services from the local mental health program is placed, the conservator shall inform the local mental health director of the facility's location and any movement of the conservatee to another facility.

(d)(1) Except for a conservatee who is gravely disabled, as defined in subparagraph (B) of paragraph (1) of subdivision (h) of Section 5008, the conservator may transfer his or her conservatee to a less restrictive alternative placement without a further hearing and court approval. In any case in which a conservator has reasonable cause to believe that his or her conservatee is in need of immediate more restrictive placement because the condition of the conservatee has so changed that the conservatee poses an immediate and substantial danger to himself or herself or others, the conservator shall have the right to place his or her conservatee in a more restrictive facility or hospital. Notwithstanding Section 5328, if the change of placement is to a placement more restrictive than the court-determined placement, the conservator shall provide written notice of the change of placement and the reason therefor to the court, the conservatee's attorney, the county patient's rights advocate and any other persons designated by the court pursuant to subdivision (c).

(2) For a conservatee who is gravely disabled, as defined in subparagraph (B) of paragraph (1) of subdivision (h) of Section 5008, the conservator may not transfer his or her conservatee without providing written notice of the proposed change of placement and the reason therefor to the court, the conservatee's attorney, the county patient's rights advocate, the district attorney of the county that made the commitment, and any other persons designated by the court to receive notice. If any person designated to receive notice objects to the proposed transfer within 10 days after receiving notice, the matter shall be set for a further hearing and court approval. The notification and hearing is not required for the transfer of persons between state hospitals.

(3) At a hearing where the conservator is seeking placement to a less restrictive alternative placement pursuant to paragraph (2), the placement shall not be approved where it is determined by a preponderance of the evidence that the placement poses a threat to the safety of the public, the conservatee, or any other individual.

(4) A hearing as to placement to a less restrictive alternative placement, whether requested pursuant to paragraph (2) or pursuant to Section 5358.3, shall be granted no more frequently than is provided for in Section 5358.3. *(Added by Stats.1967, c. 1667, p. 4074, § 36, operative July 1, 1969. Amended by Stats.1968, c. 1374, p. 2661, § 54, operative July 1, 1969; Stats.1971, c. 1593, p. 3343, § 379, operative July 1, 1973; Stats.1973, c. 523, p. 1011, § 1; Stats.1976, c. 905, p. 2078, § 2; Stats.1977, c. 1252, p. 4576, § 575, operative July 1, 1978; Stats.1980, c. 681, p. 2067, § 2; Stats.1986, c. 872, § 8; Stats.1990, c. 180 (S.B.2138), § 2; Stats.1995, c. 593 (A.B. 145), § 4; Stats.2012, c. 34 (S.B.1009), § 98, eff. June 27, 2012; Stats.2013, c. 23 (A.B.82), § 36, eff. June 27, 2013.)*

Cross References

Conservatorship investigation defined for purposes of this Part, see Welfare and Institutions Code § 5008.

Court defined for purposes of this Part, see Welfare and Institutions Code § 5008.

Emergency defined for purposes of this Part, see Welfare and Institutions Code § 5008.

Evaluation defined for purposes of this Part, see Welfare and Institutions Code § 5008.

Gravely disabled defined for purposes of this Chapter, see Welfare and Institutions Code § 5008.

Voluntary admission to,

County hospital upon application of conservator, see Welfare and Institutions Code § 6004.

State hospital upon application of conservator, see Welfare and Institutions Code § 6002.

State mental hospital or institution, see Welfare and Institutions Code § 6000.

§ 5358.1. Nonliability of conservator, public guardian or peace officer for action by conservatee

Neither a conservator, temporary conservator, or public guardian appointed pursuant to this chapter, nor a peace officer acting pursuant to Section 5358.5, shall be held civilly or criminally liable for any action by a conservatee. (Added by Stats.1972, c. 574, p. 982, § 5.)

Cross References

Peace officer defined for purposes of this Part, see Welfare and Institutions Code § 5008.

§ 5358.2. Medical treatment of conservatee; court order; emergencies

If a conservatee requires medical treatment and the conservator has not been specifically authorized by the court to require the conservatee to receive medical treatment, the conservator shall, after notice to the conservatee, obtain a court order for that medical treatment, except in emergency cases in which the conservatee faces loss of life or serious bodily injury. The conservatee, if he or she chooses to contest the request for a court order, may petition the court for hearing which shall be held prior to granting the order. (Added by Stats.1976, c. 905, p. 2079, § 3. Amended by Stats.1990, c. 180 (S.B.2138), § 3.)

Cross References

Court defined for purposes of this Part, see Welfare and Institutions Code § 5008.

Emergency defined for purposes of this Part, see Welfare and Institutions Code § 5008.

§ 5358.3. Petition to contest rights denied conservatee or powers granted conservator; subsequent petitions; voting rights

At any time, a conservatee or any person on his behalf with the consent of the conservatee or his counsel, may petition the court for a hearing to contest the rights denied under Section 5357 or the powers granted to the conservator under Section 5358. However, after the filing of the first petition for hearing pursuant to this section, no further petition for rehearing shall be submitted for a period of six months.

A request for hearing pursuant to this section shall not affect the right of a conservatee to petition the court for a rehearing as to his status as a conservatee pursuant to Section 5364. A hearing pursuant to this section shall not include trial by jury. If a person's right to vote is restored, the court shall so notify the county elections official pursuant to subdivision (c) of Section 2210 of the Elections Code. (Added by Stats.1976, c. 905, p. 2079, § 4. Amended by Stats.1978, c. 1363, p. 4531, § 15; Stats.1994, c. 923 (S.B. 1546), § 269.)

Cross References

Court defined for purposes of this Part, see Welfare and Institutions Code § 5008.

§ 5358.5. Conservatee leaving facility without approval; return to facility or removal to county designated treatment facility; request to peace officer

When any conservatee placed into a facility pursuant to this chapter leaves the facility without the approval of the conservator or the person in charge of the facility, or when the conservator appointed pursuant to this chapter deems it necessary to remove his conservatee to the county designated treatment facility, the conservator may take the conservatee into custody and return him to the facility or remove him to the county designated treatment facility. A conservator, at his discretion, may request a peace officer to detain the conservatee and return such person to the facility in which he was placed or to transfer such person to the county designated treatment facility, pursuant to Section 7325 of the Welfare and Institutions Code. Such request shall be in writing and accompanied by a certified copy of the letters of conservatorship showing the person requesting detention and transfer to be the conservator appointed pursuant to this chapter as conservator of the person sought to be detained. Either the conservator or his assistant or deputy may request detention under this section. Whenever possible, persons charged with apprehension of persons pursuant to this section shall dress in plain clothes and shall travel in unmarked vehicles. (Added by Stats.1972, c. 574, p. 982, § 6. Amended by Stats.1974, c. 833, p. 1796, § 2.)

Cross References

Peace officer defined for purposes of this Part, see Welfare and Institutions Code § 5008.

§ 5358.6. Outpatient treatment for conservatee; agreement of person in charge of facility; progress report

Any conservator who places his or her conservatee in an inpatient facility pursuant to Section 5358, may also require the conservatee to undergo outpatient treatment. Before doing so, the conservator shall obtain the agreement of the person in charge of a mental health facility that the conservatee will receive outpatient treatment and that the person in charge of the facility will designate a person to be the outpatient supervisor of the conservatee. The person in charge of these facilities shall notify the county mental health director or his or her designee of such agreement. At 90-day intervals following the commencement of the outpatient treatment, the outpatient supervisor shall make a report in writing to the conservator and to the person in charge of the mental health facility setting forth the status and progress of the conservatee. (Added by Stats.1975, c. 960, p. 2244, § 6. Amended by Stats.1980, c. 681, p. 2067, § 3.)

§ 5358.7. Challenge by conservatee of placement or conditions of confinement; place of judicial review; place of return upon release

When any conservatee challenges his or her placement or conditions of confinement pursuant to Section 1473 of the Penal Code or Section 7250 of the Welfare and Institutions Code, notwithstanding the continuing jurisdiction of the court which appointed the conservators, judicial review shall be in the county where the conservatorship was established or in the county in which the conservatee is placed or confined. If the conservatee is released as a result of the hearing, he or she shall be returned to the county where the conservatorship originated. *(Added by Stats.1986, c. 226, § 1.)*

§ 5359. Alternative placement

A conservator appointed under this chapter shall find alternative placement for his conservatee within seven days after he is notified by the person in charge of the facility serving the conservatee that the conservatee no longer needs the care or treatment offered by that facility.

If unusual conditions or circumstances preclude alternative placement of the conservatee within seven days, the conservator shall find such placement within 30 days.

If alternative placement cannot be found at the end of the 30-day period the conservator shall confer with the professional person in charge of the facility and they shall then determine the earliest practicable date when such alternative placement may be obtained. *(Added by Stats.1967, c. 1667, p. 4074, § 36, operative July 1, 1969. Amended by Stats.1968, c. 1374, p. 2662, § 55, operative July 1, 1969; Stats.1980, c. 676, p. 2039, § 336.)*

§ 5360. Recommendations of officer providing conservatorship investigation

The officer providing conservatorship investigation shall recommend, in his report to the court, for or against imposition of a disability set forth in Section 5357 on the basis of the determination of the professional person who recommended conservatorship pursuant to Section 5352.

The officer providing conservatorship investigation shall recommend in his report any of the additional powers of a conservator set forth in Section 2591 of the Probate Code if the needs of the individual patient or his estate require such powers. In making such determination, the officer providing conservatorship investigation shall consult with the professional person who recommended conservatorship pursuant to Section 5352. *(Added by Stats.1967, c. 1667, p. 4074, § 36, operative July 1, 1969. Amended by Stats.1969, c. 722, p. 1432, § 27, eff. Aug. 8, 1969, operative July 1, 1969; Stats.1979, c. 730, p. 2535, § 148, operative Jan. 1, 1981.)*

Law Revision Commission Comments

1979 Amendment

Section 5360 is amended to correct the cross-reference to the Probate Code in view of the revision of guardianship-conservatorship law. [14 Cal.L.Rev.Comm. Reports 958 (1978)].

§ 5361. Termination; power and authority over estate; reappointment; opinion of physicians or psychologists; release or detention of conservatee

Conservatorship initiated pursuant to this chapter shall automatically terminate one year after the appointment of the conservator by the superior court. The period of service of a temporary conservator shall not be included in the one-year period. Where the conservator has been appointed as conservator of the estate, the conservator shall, for a reasonable time, continue to have such power and authority over the estate as the superior court, on petition by the conservator, may deem necessary for (1) the collection of assets or income which accrued during the period of conservatorship, but were uncollected before the date of termination, (2) the payment of expenses which accrued during period of conservatorship and of which the conservator was notified prior to termination, but were unpaid before the date of termination, and (3) the completion of sales of real property where the only act remaining at the date of termination is the actual transfer of title. If upon the termination of an initial or a succeeding period of conservatorship the conservator determines that conservatorship is still required, he may petition the superior court for his reappointment as conservator for a succeeding one-year period. The petition must include the opinion of two physicians or licensed psychologists who have a doctoral degree in psychology and at least five years of postgraduate experience in the diagnosis and treatment of emotional and mental disorders that the conservatee is still gravely disabled as a result of mental disorder or impairment by chronic alcoholism. In the event that the conservator is unable to obtain the opinion of two physicians or psychologists, he shall request that the court appoint them.

Any facility in which a conservatee is placed must release the conservatee at his request when the conservatorship terminates. A petition for reappointment filed by the conservator or a petition for appointment filed by a public guardian shall be transmitted to the facility at least 30 days before the automatic termination date. The facility may detain the conservatee after the end of the termination date only if the conservatorship proceedings have not been completed and the court orders the conservatee to be held until the proceedings have been completed. *(Added by Stats.1967, c. 1667, p. 4074, § 36, operative July 1, 1969. Amended by Stats.1968, c. 1374, p. 2662, § 56, operative July 1, 1969; Stats.1969, c. 722, p. 1432, § 28, eff. Aug. 8, 1969, operative July 1, 1969; Stats.1976, c. 110, p. 171, § 1, eff. April 9, 1976; Stats.1978, c. 1294, p. 4246, § 8; Stats.1979, c. 245, p. 534, § 2.)*

§ 5362. Notice of impending termination; petition for reappointment; court hearing or jury trial; decree of termination

(a) The clerk of the superior court shall notify each conservator, his or her conservatee and the person in charge of the facility in which the person resides, and the conservatee's attorney, at least 60 days before the termination of the one-year period. If the conservator is a private party, the clerk of the superior court shall also notify the mental health director and the county officer providing conservatorship investigation pursuant to Section 5355, at least 60 days before the termination of the one-year period. Notification shall be given in person or by first-class mail. The notification shall be in substantially the following form:

In the Superior Court of the State of California
for the County of _____

The people of the state of California
Concerning
_____

No. _____

Notice of Termination
of Conservatorship

The people of the State of California to _____
_____:
(conservatee, conservatee's attorney, conservator, and professional person in charge of the facility in which the conservatee resides, county mental health director, and county officer providing conservatorship investigation.)

The one-year conservatorship established for _____ pursuant to Welfare and Institutions Code Section _____ on _____ will terminate on _____. If the conservator, _____, wishes to reestablish conservatorship for another year he or she must petition the court by _____. Subject to a request for a court hearing by jury trial the judge may, on his or her own motion, accept or reject the conservator's petition.

If the conservator petitions to reestablish conservatorship the conservatee, the professional person in charge of the facility in which he or she resides, the conservatee's attorney, and, if the conservator is a private party, the county mental health director and the county officer providing conservatorship investigation shall be notified. If any of them request it, there shall be a court hearing or a jury trial, whichever is requested, on the issue of whether the conservatee is still gravely disabled and in need of conservatorship. If the private conservator does not petition for reappointment, the county officer providing conservatorship investigation may recommend another conservator. Such a petition shall be considered a petition for reappointment as conservator.

Clerk of the Superior Court by
_____
Deputy

(b) Subject to a request for a court hearing or jury trial, the judge may, on his or her own motion, accept or reject the conservator's petition.

If the conservator does not petition to reestablish conservatorship at or before the termination of the one-year period, the court shall issue a decree terminating conservatorship. The decree shall be sent to the conservator and his or her conservatee by first-class mail and shall be accompanied by a statement of California law as set forth in Section 5368. *(Added by Stats.1967, c. 1667, p. 4074, § 36, operative July 1, 1969. Amended by Stats.1968, c. 1374, p. 2662, § 56.5, operative July 1, 1969; Stats.1969, c. 722, p. 1432, § 28.1, eff. Aug. 8, 1969, operative July 1, 1969; Stats.1978, c. 1294, p.*

4246, § 9; Stats.1982, c. 1598, § 8; Stats.1983, c. 464, § 4; Stats.1985, c. 1239, § 5.)

Cross References

Conservatorship investigation defined for purposes of this Part, see Welfare and Institutions Code § 5008.
Court defined for purposes of this Part, see Welfare and Institutions Code § 5008.
Gravely disabled defined for purposes of this Chapter, see Welfare and Institutions Code § 5008.

§ 5363. Ratification of acts beyond term

In the event the conservator continues in good faith to act within the powers granted him in the original decree of conservatorship beyond the one-year period, he may petition for and shall be granted a decree ratifying his acts as conservator beyond the one-year period. The decree shall provide for a retroactive appointment of the conservator to provide continuity of authority in those cases where the conservator did not apply in time for reappointment. *(Added by Stats.1967, c. 1667, p. 4074, § 36, operative July 1, 1969.)*

§ 5364. Petition for rehearing on status as conservatee; notice of voter registration right

At any time, the conservatee may petition the superior court for a rehearing as to his status as a conservatee. However, after the filing of the first petition for rehearing pursuant to this section, no further petition for rehearing shall be submitted for a period of six months. If the conservatorship is terminated pursuant to this section, the court shall, in accordance with subdivision (c) of Section 2210 of the Elections Code, notify the county elections official that the person's right to register to vote is restored. *(Added by Stats.1967, c. 1667, p. 4074, § 36, operative July 1, 1969. Amended by Stats.1976, c. 905, p. 2080, § 5; Stats.1978, c. 1363, p. 4532, § 16; Stats.1994, c. 923 (S.B.1546), § 270.)*

Cross References

Court defined for purposes of this Part, see Welfare and Institutions Code § 5008.

§ 5365. Time for hearing petitions; attorney

A hearing shall be held on all petitions under this chapter within 30 days of the date of the petition. The court shall appoint the public defender or other attorney for the conservatee or proposed conservatee within five days after the date of the petition. *(Added by Stats.1967, c. 1667, p. 4074, § 36, operative July 1, 1969. Amended by Stats.1970, c. 509, p. 997, § 1; Stats.1970, c. 1627, p. 3449, § 25; Stats.1971, c. 776, p. 1530, § 7; Stats.1972, c. 574, p. 983, § 7.)*

Cross References

Advice as to right of counsel, see Welfare and Institutions Code §§ 5226, 5254.1, 5276, 5302.
Appointment of public defender or other attorney, see Welfare and Institutions Code §§ 5276, 5302.
Conservatorship for gravely disabled persons, appointment, demand for trial as waiver of hearing, see Welfare and Institutions Code § 5350.

Court defined for purposes of this Part, see Welfare and Institutions Code § 5008.

§ 5365.1. Waiver of presence of professionals and physicians; reception of documents

The conservatee or proposed conservatee may, upon advice of counsel, waive the presence at any hearing under this chapter of the physician or other professional person who recommended conservatorship pursuant to Section 5352 and of the physician providing evaluation or intensive treatment. In the event of such a waiver, such physician and professional persons shall not be required to be present at the hearing if it is stipulated that the recommendation and records of such physician or other professional person concerning the mental condition and treatment of the conservatee or proposed conservatee will be received in evidence. *(Added by Stats. 1971, c. 1162, p. 2221, § 4.)*

Cross References

Evaluation defined for purposes of this Part, see Welfare and Institutions Code § 5008.
Intensive treatment defined for purposes of this Part, see Welfare and Institutions Code § 5008.

§ 5366.1. Detention for evaluation; persons detained under court commitment or upon application of local health officer; disposition

(a) Any person detained as of June 30, 1969, under court commitment, in a private institution, a county psychiatric hospital, facility of the Veterans Administration, or other agency of the United States government, community mental health service, or detained in a state hospital or facility of the Veterans Administration upon application of a local health officer, pursuant to former Section 5567 or Sections 6000 to 6019, inclusive, as they read immediately preceding July 1, 1969, may be detained, after January 1, 1972, for a period no longer than 180 days, except as provided in this section.

(b) Any person detained pursuant to this section on the effective date of this section shall be evaluated by the facility designated by the county and approved by the State Department of Health Care Services pursuant to Section 5150 as a facility for 72–hour treatment and evaluation. The evaluation shall be made at the request of the person in charge of the institution in which the person is detained. If in the opinion of the professional person in charge of the evaluation and treatment facility or his or her designee, the evaluation of the person can be made by the professional person or his or her designee at the institution in which the person is detained, the person shall not be required to be evaluated at the evaluation and treatment facility, but shall be evaluated at the institution where he or she is detained, or other place to determine if the person is a danger to others, himself or herself, or gravely disabled as a result of mental disorder.

(c) Any person evaluated under this section shall be released from the institution in which he or she is detained immediately upon completion of the evaluation if in the opinion of the professional person in charge of the evaluation and treatment facility, or his or her designee, the person evaluated is not a danger to others, or to himself or herself, or gravely disabled as a result of mental disorder, unless the person agrees voluntarily to remain in the institution in which he or she has been detained.

(d) If in the opinion of the professional person in charge of the facility or his or her designee, the person evaluated requires intensive treatment or recommendation for conservatorship, the professional person or his or her designee shall proceed under Article 4 (commencing with Section 5250) of Chapter 2, or under Chapter 3 (commencing with Section 5350), of Part 1 of Division 5.

(e) If it is determined from the evaluation that the person is gravely disabled and a recommendation for conservatorship is made, and if the petition for conservatorship for the person is not filed by June 30, 1972, the court commitment or detention under a local health officer application for the person shall terminate and the patient shall be released unless he or she agrees to accept treatment on a voluntary basis. *(Added by Stats.1971, c. 1459, p. 2875, § 2. Amended by Stats.1973, c. 142, p. 418, § 72.5, eff. June 30, 1973, operative July 1, 1973; Stats.1977, c. 1252, p. 4578, § 577, operative July 1, 1978; Stats.2012, c. 34 (S.B.1009), § 99, eff. June 27, 2012; Stats.2013, c. 23 (A.B.82), § 37, eff. June 27, 2013.)*

Cross References

Court defined for purposes of this Part, see Welfare and Institutions Code § 5008.
Detention in private institution, see Welfare and Institutions Code § 6007.
Evaluation defined for purposes of this Part, see Welfare and Institutions Code § 5008.
Gravely disabled defined for purposes of this Chapter, see Welfare and Institutions Code § 5008.
Intensive treatment defined for purposes of this Part, see Welfare and Institutions Code § 5008.

§ 5367. Effect of conservatorship on prior commitment

Conservatorship established under this chapter shall supersede any commitment under former provisions of this code relating to inebriates or the mentally ill. *(Added by Stats. 1967, c. 1667, p. 4075, § 36, operative July 1, 1969. Amended by Stats.1968, c. 1374, p. 2664, § 58, operative July 1, 1969.)*

§ 5368. Effect of conservatorship on presumption of competence

A person who is no longer a conservatee shall not be presumed to be incompetent by virtue of his having been a conservatee under the provisions of this part. *(Added by Stats.1967, c. 1667, p. 4074, § 36, operative July 1, 1969.)*

Cross References

Burden of proof of insanity, see Evidence Code § 522.
Disabilities of conservatee, see Welfare and Institutions Code §§ 5356, 5357.
Drivers' license, statement in application, see Vehicle Code § 12800.
Firearms, possession by mental patients, see Welfare and Institutions Code § 8100 et seq.
Legal disability not imposed by evaluation proceedings, see Welfare and Institutions Code § 5005.
Public guardian, see Government Code § 27430 et seq.

§ 5369. Conservatee with criminal charges pending; recovery of competence

When a conservatee who has criminal charges pending against him and has been found mentally incompetent under Section 1370 of the Penal Code recovers his mental competence, the conservator shall certify that fact to the court, sheriff, and district attorney of the county in which the criminal charges are pending and to the defendant's attorney of record.

The court shall order the sheriff to immediately return the defendant to the court in which the criminal charges are pending. Within two judicial days of the defendant's return, the court shall hold a hearing to determine whether the defendant is entitled to be admitted to bail or released upon his own recognizance pending conclusion of criminal proceedings. *(Added by Stats.1974, c. 1511, p. 3323, § 13, eff. Sept. 27, 1974.)*

Cross References

Court defined for purposes of this Part, see Welfare and Institutions Code § 5008.

§ 5370. Conservatorship proceeding for one charged with offense

Notwithstanding any other provision of law, a conservatorship proceeding may be initiated pursuant to this chapter for any person who has been charged with an offense, regardless of whether action is pending or has been initiated pursuant to Section 1370 of the Penal Code. *(Added by Stats.1974, c. 1511, p. 3323, § 14, eff. Sept. 27, 1974.)*

§ 5370.1. Appointment of counsel for private conservator with insufficient funds

The court in which a petition to establish a conservatorship is filed may appoint the county counsel or a private attorney to represent a private conservator in all proceedings connected with the conservatorship, if it appears that the conservator has insufficient funds to obtain the services of a private attorney. Such appointments of the county counsel, however, may be made only if the board of supervisors have, by ordinance or resolution, authorized the county counsel to accept them. *(Added by Stats.1975, c. 960, p. 2245, § 8. Amended by Stats.1980, c. 415, p. 818, § 1.)*

Cross References

County counsel, duty to represent county in mental health proceedings, see Government Code § 27646.

Court defined for purposes of this Part, see Welfare and Institutions Code § 5008.

§ 5370.2. Protection and advocacy agency; services to be provided under contract; coordination with the advocates; plan to provide patients' rights advocacy services; reviews and investigations

(a) The State Department of State Hospitals and the State Department of Health Care Services shall contract with a single nonprofit agency that meets the criteria specified in subdivision (b) of Section 5510 to conduct the activities specified in paragraphs (1) to (4), inclusive. These two state departments shall enter into a memorandum of understanding to ensure the effective management of the contract and the required activities affecting county patients' rights programs:

(1) Provide patients' rights advocacy services for, and conduct investigations of alleged or suspected abuse and neglect of, including deaths of, persons with mental disabilities residing in state hospitals.

(2) Investigate and take action as appropriate and necessary to resolve complaints from or concerning recipients of mental health services residing in licensed health or community care facilities regarding abuse, and unreasonable denial, or punitive withholding of rights guaranteed under this division that cannot be resolved by county patients' rights advocates.

(3) Provide consultation, technical assistance, and support to county patients' rights advocates in accordance with their duties under Section 5520.

(4) Conduct program review of patients' rights programs.

(b) The services shall be provided in coordination with the appropriate mental health patients' rights advocates.

(c)(1) The contractor shall develop a plan to provide patients' rights advocacy services for, and conduct investigations of alleged or suspected abuse and neglect of, including the deaths of, persons with mental disabilities residing in state hospitals.

(2) The contractor shall develop the plan in consultation with the statewide organization of mental health patients' rights advocates, the statewide organization of mental health clients, and the statewide organization of family members of persons with mental disabilities, and the statewide organization of county mental health directors.

(3) In order to ensure that persons with mental disabilities have access to high quality advocacy services, the contractor shall establish a grievance procedure and shall advise persons receiving services under the contract of the availability of other advocacy services, including services provided by the protection and advocacy agency specified in Section 4901 and the county patients' rights advocates specified in Section 5520.

(d) Nothing contained in this section shall be construed to restrict or limit the authority of the department to conduct the reviews and investigations it deems necessary for personnel, criminal, and litigation purposes.

(e) The State Department of State Hospitals and the State Department of Health Care Services shall jointly contract on a multiyear basis for a contract term of up to five years. *(Added by Stats.1992, c. 722 (S.B.485), § 25, eff. Sept. 15, 1992. Amended by Stats.1995, c. 546 (S.B.361), § 2; Stats. 2010, c. 717 (S.B.853), § 138, eff. Oct. 19, 2010; Stats.2012, c. 34 (S.B.1009), § 100, eff. June 27, 2012.)*

§ 5371. Conflict of interest in evaluation of conservatee; independent conduct of investigation and administration of conservatorship

No person upon whom a duty is placed to evaluate, or who, in fact, does evaluate a conservatee for any purpose under this chapter shall have a financial or other beneficial interest in the facility where the conservatee is to be, or has been placed.

Conservatorship investigation and administration shall be conducted independently from any person or agency which provides mental health treatment for conservatees, if it has been demonstrated that the existing arrangement creates a conflict of interest between the treatment needs of the conservatee and the investigation or administration of the conservatorship. The person or agency responsible for the mental health treatment of conservatees shall execute a written agreement or protocol with the conservatorship investigator and administrator for the provision of services to conservatees. The agreement or protocol shall specify the responsibilities of each person or agency who is a party to the agreement or protocol, and shall specify a procedure to resolve disputes or conflicts of interest between agencies or persons. *(Added by Stats.1975, c. 960, p. 2245, § 9. Amended by Stats.1986, c. 335, § 2.)*

Cross References

Conservatorship investigation defined for purposes of this Part, see Welfare and Institutions Code § 5008.

§ 5372. Ex parte communications; prohibitions; exemption

(a) The provisions of Section 1051 of the Probate Code shall apply to conservatorships established pursuant to this chapter.

(b) The Judicial Council shall, on or before January 1, 2008, adopt a rule of court to implement this section.

(c) Subdivision (a) of this section shall become operative on January 1, 2008. *(Added by Stats.2006, c. 492 (S.B.1716), § 5.)*

Cross References

Court defined for purposes of this Part, see Welfare and Institutions Code § 5008.

Ex parte communications in proceedings under the Probate Code and certain other proceedings, see California Rules of Court, Rule 7.10.

CALIFORNIA RULES OF COURT

Title 7

PROBATE RULES

Chapter 1

GENERAL PROVISIONS

Rule 7.1.   Probate Rules

The rules in this title may be referred to as the Probate Rules. *(Adopted, eff. Jan. 1, 2007.)*

Rule 7.2.   Preliminary provisions

(a) Application of rules

The rules in this title apply to every action and proceeding to which the Probate Code applies and, unless they are elsewhere explicitly made applicable, do not apply to any other action or proceeding.

(b) Purpose of rules

The rules in this title are designed to implement the purposes of the probate law by promoting uniformity in practice and procedure.

(c) Rules of construction

Unless the context otherwise requires, these preliminary provisions and the following rules of construction govern the construction of the rules in this title:

(1) To the extent that the rules in this title are substantially the same as existing statutory provisions relating to the same subject matter, they must be construed as a restatement and a continuation of those statutes; and

(2) To the extent that the rules in this title may add to existing statutory provisions relating to the same subject matter, they must be construed so as to implement the purposes of the probate law.

(d) Jurisdiction

The rules in this title are not intended to expand, limit, or restrict the jurisdiction of the court in proceedings under the Probate Code. *(Formerly Rule 7.1, adopted, eff. Jan. 1, 2000. As amended, eff. Jan. 1, 2003. Renumbered Rule 7.2 and amended, eff. Jan. 1, 2007.)*

Rule 7.3.   Definitions and use of terms

As used in the rules in this title, unless the context or subject matter otherwise requires:

(1) The definitions in division 1, part 2 of the Probate Code [1] apply.

(2) "Pleading" means a contest, answer, petition, application, objection, response, statement of interest, report, or account filed in proceedings under the Probate Code.

(3) "Amended pleading" means a pleading that completely restates and supersedes the pleading it amends for all purposes.

(4) "Amendment to a pleading" means a pleading that modifies another pleading and alleges facts or requests relief materially different from the facts alleged or the relief requested in the modified pleading. An amendment to a pleading does not restate or supersede the modified pleading but must be read together with that pleading.

(5) "Supplement to a pleading" and "supplement" mean a pleading that modifies another pleading but does not allege facts or request relief materially different from the facts alleged or the relief requested in the supplemented pleading. A supplement to a pleading may add information to or may correct omissions in the modified pleading. *(Formerly Rule 7.2, adopted, eff. Jan. 1, 2000. As amended, eff. Jan. 1, 2002; Jan. 1, 2003. Renumbered Rule 7.3 and amended, eff. Jan. 1, 2007.)*

[1] See Probate Code § 20 et seq.

Rule 7.4.   Waiver of rules in probate proceedings

The court for good cause may waive the application of the rules in this title in an individual case. *(Formerly Rule 7.3, adopted, eff. Jan. 1, 2000. As amended, eff. Jan. 1, 2003. Renumbered Rule 7.4, eff. Jan. 1, 2007.)*

Rule 7.5.   Waivers of court fees in decedents' estates, conservatorships, and guardianships

(a) Scope of rule

This rule governs initial fee waivers, as defined in rule 3.50(b), that are requested by petitioners for the appointment of fiduciaries, or by fiduciaries after their appointment, in decedents' estates, conservatorships, and guardianships under the Probate Code. The rule also governs initial fee waivers in other civil actions or proceedings in which conservators or guardians are parties representing the interests of their conservatees or wards.

(b) Court fee waiver requested by a petitioner for the appointment of a conservator or guardian of the person, estate, or person and estate of a conservatee or ward

A petitioner for the appointment of a conservator or guardian of the person, estate, or person and estate of a conservatee or ward must base an application for an initial fee waiver on the personal financial condition of the proposed conservatee or ward.

(c) Court fee waiver requested by a petitioner for the appointment of a personal representative of a decedent's estate

A petitioner for the appointment of a personal representative of a decedent's estate must base an application for an initial fee waiver on the petitioner's personal financial condition.

(d) Effect of appointment of a personal representative of a decedent's estate on a court fee waiver

The appointment of a personal representative of a decedent's estate may be a change of financial condition for fee waiver purposes under Government Code section 68636 in accordance with the following:

(1) If the successful petitioner is an appointed personal representative:

(A) The petitioner's continued eligibility for an initial fee waiver must be based on the combined financial condition of the petitioner and the decedent's estate.

(B) Upon marshaling or collecting assets of the decedent's estate following the petitioner's appointment and qualification as personal representative, the petitioner must notify the court of a change in financial condition under Government Code section 68636(a) that may affect his or her ability to pay all or a portion of the waived court fees and costs.

(C) The court may make a preliminary determination under Government Code section 68636(b) that the petitioner's appointment as fiduciary is a change of financial condition that makes the petitioner no longer eligible for an initial fee waiver based, in whole or in part, on the estimates of estate value and income contained in the petitioner's *Petition for Probate*. In that event, the court must give notice and conduct the hearing required by section 68636(b).

(2) If the successful petitioner is not an appointed personal representative:

(A) An initial fee waiver for that petitioner continues in effect according to its terms for subsequent fees incurred by that petitioner in the proceeding solely in his or her individual capacity.

(B) The appointed personal representative may apply for an initial fee waiver. The application must be based on the combined financial condition of the personal representative and the decedent's estate.

(e) Financial condition of the conservatee or ward

(1) The financial condition of the conservatee or ward for purposes of this rule includes:

(A) The financial condition—to the extent of the information known or reasonably available to the conservator or guardian, or the petitioner for the conservator's or guardian's appointment, upon reasonable inquiry—of any person who has a duty to support the conservatee or ward, including a spouse, registered domestic partner, or parent. A divorced spouse's or divorced registered domestic partner's duty to support a conservatee and a parent's duty to support a ward under this subparagraph is limited to the

amount of support ordered by a court. Consideration of a support order as an element of the conservatee's or ward's financial condition under this rule is subject to the provisions of Government Code sections 68637(d) and (e), concerning the likelihood that the obligated person will pay all or any portion of the support ordered by the court;

(B) A conservatee's interest in community property that is outside the conservatorship estate and under the management or control of the conservatee's spouse or registered domestic partner; and

(C) The right to receive support, income, or other distributions from a trust or under a contract.

(2) Following the appointment of a conservator or guardian and the grant of an initial fee waiver based on the financial condition of the conservatee or ward, the conservator or guardian is the "person who received the initial fee waiver" for purposes of Government Code section 68636(a), whether or not he or she was the successful applicant for the initial waiver. The conservator or guardian must report to the court any changes in the financial condition of the conservatee or ward that affects his or her ability to pay all or a portion of the court fees and costs that were initially waived, including any changes in the financial condition of the persons or property mentioned in subparagraphs (1)(A) and (1)(B) of this subdivision of which the conservator or guardian becomes aware after reasonable investigation.

(f) Additional discretionary factors in the financial condition or circumstances of a decedent's, conservatee's, or ward's estate

(1) The financial condition of the decedent's, conservatee's, or ward's estate for purposes of this rule may, in the court's discretion, include consideration of:

(A) The estate's liquidity;

(B) Whether estate property or income is necessary for the support of a person entitled to a family allowance from the estate of a decedent, the conservatee or a person entitled to support from the conservatee, or the ward; or

(C) Whether property in a decedent's estate is specifically devised.

(2) If property of the estate is eliminated from consideration for initial court fee waiver purposes because of one or more of the factors listed in (1), the court may determine that the estate can pay a portion of court fees, can pay court fees over time, or can pay court fees at a later time, under an equitable arrangement within the meaning of Government Code sections 68632(c) and 68634(e)(5). An equitable arrangement under this paragraph may include establishment of a lien for initially waived court fees against property distributable from a decedent's estate or payable to the conservatee or ward or other successor in interest at the termination of a conservatorship or guardianship.

(g) Payment of previously waived court fees by a decedent's estate

If the financial condition of a decedent's estate is a change of financial condition of a fee waiver applicant under this rule that results in withdrawal of a previously granted initial waiver of fees in favor of a petitioner for the appointment of a personal representative, the estate must pay to the court, as an allowable expense of administration, the fees and costs previously waived.

(h) Termination or modification of previously granted initial fee waivers

(1) *Conservatorships and guardianships of the estate or person and estate*

Upon establishment of a conservatorship or guardianship of the estate or person and estate, the court may collect all or a portion of court fees previously waived from the estate of the conservatee or ward if the court finds that the estate has the ability to pay the fees, or a portion thereof, immediately, over a period of time, or under some other equitable agreement, without using moneys that normally would pay for the common necessaries of life for the conservatee or ward and his or her family. The court must comply with the notice and hearing requirements of the second paragraph of Government Code section 68634(e)(5) to make the findings authorized in this paragraph.

(2) *Conservatorships and guardianships of the person*

In a conservatorship or guardianship of the person, if the court seeks to reconsider or modify a court fee waiver previously granted based on collection, application, or consideration of support, assets, or income described in (e), it must proceed as provided in Government Code section 68636 and comply with the notice and hearing requirements of the second paragraph of Government Code section 68634(e)(5), including notice to the conservator or guardian, any support obligor, and any person in possession of the assets or income. The conservator or guardian must appear at the hearing on behalf of the conservatee or ward, and the court may also appoint counsel for the conservatee or ward under Probate Code section 1470.

(i) Civil actions in which a conservator or guardian is a party representing the interests of a conservatee or ward

In a civil action in which a conservator or guardian is a party representing the interests of a conservatee or ward against another party or parties, for purposes of Government Code sections 68631.5, 68636, and 68637:

(1) The conservator or guardian is the person with a duty to notify the court of a change of financial condition under section 68636(a) and the person the court may require to appear at a court hearing under sections 68636(b) and (c);

(2) The conservatee or ward and the persons identified in subparagraphs (1)(A) and (B) of subdivision (e) of this rule is the person or persons whose change of financial condition or circumstances of which the court is to be notified under section 68636(a); and

(3) The conservatee or ward is the person or party whose initial fees and costs were initially waived under sections 68636(c) and 68637.

(j) Advances of court fees and costs by legal counsel

(1) Government Code section 68633(g)—concerning agreements between applicants for initial court fee waivers and their legal counsel for counsel to advance court fees and costs and court hearings to determine the effect of the presence or absence of such agreements on the applications—applies to proceedings described in this rule.

(2) Conservators, guardians, and petitioners for their appointment applying for initial fee waivers under this rule represented by legal counsel, and their counsel, must complete the *Request to Waive Court Fees (Ward or Conservatee)* (form FW–001–GC), including items 2a and 2b, and, if a request to waive additional court fees is made, the *Request to Waive Additional Court Fees (Superior Court) (Ward or Conservatee)* (form FW–002–GC), including items 2a and 2b. The reference to "legal-aid type services" in these forms refers to legal services provided to an applicant by counsel for or affiliated with a qualified legal services project defined in Business and Professions Code section 6213.

(k) Expiration of initial court fee waivers in decedents' estates, conservatorships, and guardianships

"Final disposition of the case" in decedent's estate, conservatorship, and guardianship proceedings for purposes of determining the expiration of fee waivers under Government Code section 68639 occurs on the later of the following events:

(1) Termination of the proceedings by order of court or under operation of law in conservatorships and guardianships of the person; or

(2) Discharge of personal representatives of decedents' estates and discharge of conservators or guardians of estates. *(Adopted, eff. Sept. 1, 2015.)*

Rule 7.10. Ex parte communications in proceedings under the Probate Code and certain other proceedings

(a) Definitions

As used in this rule, the following terms have the meanings stated below:

(1) "Fiduciary" has the meaning specified in Probate Code section 39, and includes LPS conservators.

(2) "Person" has the meaning specified in Probate Code section 56.

(3) "Pleading" has the meaning specified in rule 7.3, but also includes petitions and objections or other opposition filed in LPS conservatorships. The term does not include creditors' claims and requests for special notice.

(4) A "party" is a fiduciary appointed in a proceeding under the Probate Code or an LPS conservatorship proceeding, and any other person who has filed a pleading in the proceeding concerning a matter then pending in the court.

(5) A "ward" is a minor subject to a guardianship under Division 4 of the Probate Code, including a proposed ward concerning whom a petition for appointment of a guardian has been filed.

(6) "Ex parte communication" is a communication between any party, attorney, or person in a proceeding under the Probate Code or an LPS conservatorship proceeding and the court outside the presence of all parties and attorneys, including written communications sent to the court without copies having been provided to other interested persons.

(7) "LPS Act" is the Lanterman–Petris–Short Act, part 1 of division 5 of the Welfare and Institutions Code, commencing with section 5000.

(8) "LPS Conservatorship" is a conservatorship proceeding under chapter 3 of the LPS Act, commencing with section

5350 of the Welfare and Institutions Code, for persons gravely disabled as the result of a mental disorder or impairment by chronic alcoholism.

(9) A "conservatee" is a person subject to a conservatorship under division 4 of the Probate Code or chapter 3 of the LPS Act, including a proposed conservatee concerning whom a petition for appointment of a conservator has been filed.

(10) A "matter then pending in the court" in proceedings under the Probate Code or in an LPS conservatorship proceeding refers to a request for relief or opposition in pleadings filed in the proceeding that has not yet been resolved by a decision of the court or an agreement of the parties.

(11) Concerning a proceeding under the Probate Code or an LPS conservatorship proceeding, the term "open proceeding" refers to a proceeding that has been commenced and has not been concluded by the final discharge of all fiduciaries or otherwise terminated as provided by law, whether or not there is a matter then pending in the court in the proceeding at any point in time.

(b) Ex parte communications by parties and attorneys prohibited

(1) Except under a stipulation of all parties to the contrary, no ex parte communications may be made by a party or an attorney for a party and the court concerning a matter then pending in the court in proceedings under the Probate Code or in an LPS conservatorship proceeding.

(2) Except as provided in (c)(1), the court must treat an ex parte communication to the court described in (1) in the same way that an ex parte communication from a party or attorney for a party must be treated in other civil actions or proceedings or in criminal actions.

(c) Ex parte communications received and considered

(1) Notwithstanding (b)(2), a judicial officer or court staff may receive an ex parte communication concerning an open proceeding under the Probate Code or an open LPS conservatorship proceeding for the limited purpose of ascertaining whether it is a communication described in (b) or a communication described in (c)(2).

(2) Subject to the requirements of (c)(3), a judicial officer may consider an ex parte communication from a person about a fiduciary's performance of his or her duties and responsibilities or regarding a conservatee or ward in an open proceeding under the Probate Code or an open LPS conservatorship proceeding. The court may decline to take further action on the communication, with or without replying to the person or returning any written communication received from the person. The court may also take appropriate action, consistent with due process and California law, including one or any combination of the following:

(A) Review the court file and take any action that is supported by the record, including ordering a status report or accounting if it appears that a status report or accounting should have been filed by a fiduciary but is delinquent.

(B) Refer the communication to a court investigator for further action, and receive, consider, and respond to any report from the investigator concerning it;

(C) If the communication discloses possible criminal activity, refer the matter to the appropriate law enforcement agency or prosecutor's office;

(D) If the communication discloses conduct that might subject a person or organization to disciplinary action on a license, refer the matter to the appropriate licensing agency;

(E) If the communication discloses possible elder or dependent adult abuse, or child abuse, refer the matter to appropriate state or local governmental agencies, including adult protective or child protective service departments; and

(F) Set a hearing regarding the communication, compel the fiduciary's attendance, and require a response from the fiduciary concerning the issues raised by the communication.

(3) The court must fully disclose communications described in (c)(2) and any response made by the court to the fiduciary and all other parties to any matter then pending in the court, and their attorneys, unless the court finds good cause to dispense with the disclosure if necessary to protect a conservatee or ward from harm. If the court dispenses with disclosure to any party or attorney, it must make written findings in support of its determination of good cause, and preserve the communication received and any response made by the court. The court may place its findings and the preserved communication under seal or otherwise secure their confidentiality. *(Adopted, eff. Jan. 1, 2008.)*

Chapter 2

NOTICES, PUBLICATION, AND SERVICE

Cross References

General notice provisions, see Probate Code § 1200 et seq.
Service of process,
  Generally, see Code of Civil Procedure § 413.10 et seq.
  Mail, see Code of Civil Procedure §§ 415.30 and 1012 et seq.
  Personal delivery, see Code of Civil Procedure § 415.10.
  Proof of service, see Code of Civil Procedure § 417.10 et seq.
  Publication, see Code of Civil Procedure § 415.50.

Rule 7.50. Description of pleading in notice of hearing

The notice of hearing on a pleading filed in a proceeding under the Probate Code must state the complete title of the pleading to which the notice relates. *(Adopted, eff. Jan. 1, 2003.)*

Cross References

General notice provisions, see Probate Code § 1200 et seq.

Rule 7.51. Service of notice of hearing

(a) Direct notice required

(1) Except as otherwise permitted in the Probate Code, a notice sent by mail under Probate Code section 1220 must be mailed individually and directly to the person entitled to notice.

(2) A notice mailed to a person in care of another person is insufficient unless the person entitled to notice is an adult and has directed the party giving notice in writing to send the notice in care of the second person.

(3) Notices mailed to more than one person in the same household must be sent separately to each person.

(b) Notice to attorney

If a notice is required or permitted to be given to a person who is represented by an attorney of record in the proceeding, the notice must be sent as required in Probate Code section 1214.

(c) Notice to guardian or conservator

(1) When a guardian or conservator has been appointed for a person entitled to notice, the notice must be sent to the guardian or conservator.

(2) A copy of the notice must also be sent to the ward or conservatee unless:

(A) The court dispenses with such notice; or

(B) Under Probate Code section 1210 in a decedent's estate proceeding, the notice is personally served on a California-resident guardian or conservator of the estate of the ward or conservatee.

(d) Notice to minor

Except as permitted in Probate Code section 1460.1 for guardianships, conservatorships, and certain protective proceedings under division 4 of the Probate Code, notice to a minor must be sent directly to the minor. A separate copy of the notice must be sent to the person or persons having legal custody of the minor, with whom the minor resides.

(e) Notice required in a decedent's estate when a beneficiary has died

(1) *Notice when a beneficiary dies after the decedent*

Notice must be sent to the personal representative of a beneficiary who died after the decedent and survived for a period required by the decedent's will. If no personal representative has been appointed for the postdeceased beneficiary, notice must be sent to his or her beneficiaries or other persons entitled to succeed to his or her interest in the decedent's estate.

(2) *Notice when a beneficiary of the decedent's will dies before the decedent*

When a beneficiary under the will of the decedent died before the decedent or fails to survive the decedent for a period required by the decedent's will, notice must be sent to the persons named in the decedent's will as substitute beneficiaries of the gift to the predeceased beneficiary. If the decedent's will does not make a substitute disposition of that gift, notice must be sent as follows:

(A) If the predeceased beneficiary is a "transferee" under Probate Code section 21110(c), to the issue of the predeceased beneficiary determined under Probate Code section 240 and to the residuary beneficiaries of the

decedent or to the decedent's heirs if decedent's will does not provide for distribution of the residue of the estate.

(B) If the predeceased beneficiary is not a "transferee" under Probate Code section 21110(c), to the residuary beneficiaries of the decedent or to the decedent's heirs if decedent's will does not provide for distribution of the residue of the estate.

(Adopted, eff. Jan. 1, 2003. As amended, eff. Jan. 1, 2004.)

Cross References

General notice provisions, see Probate Code § 1200 et seq.

Rule 7.52. Service of notice when recipient's address unknown

(a) Declaration of diligent search

Petitioner must file a declaration describing efforts made to locate a person entitled to notice in a proceeding under the Probate Code, but whose address is unknown, before the court will prescribe an alternate form of notice or dispense with notice under (c). The declaration must state the name of the person whose address is unknown, the last known address of the person, the approximate date when the person was last known to reside there, the efforts made to locate the person, and any facts that explain why the person's address cannot be obtained. The declaration must include a description of the attempts to learn of the person's business and residence addresses by:

(1) Inquiry of the relatives, friends, acquaintances, and employers of the person entitled to notice and of the person who is the subject of the proceeding;

(2) Review of appropriate city telephone directories and directory assistance; and

(3) Search of the real and personal property indexes in the recorder's and assessor's offices for the county where the person was last known or believed to reside.

(b) Mailed notice to county seat

Mailing notice to a person at a county seat is not a manner of giving notice reasonably calculated to give actual notice.

(c) The court may prescribe or dispense with notice

If a person entitled to notice cannot be located after diligent search, the court may prescribe the manner of giving notice to that person or may dispense with notice to that person. *(Adopted, eff. Jan. 1, 2003.)*

Cross References

General notice provisions, see Probate Code § 1200 et seq.

Rule 7.53. Notice of hearing of amended or supplemented pleadings

(a) Amended pleading and amendment to a pleading

An amended pleading or an amendment to a pleading requires the same notice of hearing (including publication) as the pleading it amends.

(b) Supplement to a pleading

A supplement to a pleading does not require additional notice of hearing, but a copy of a supplement to a pleading must be served if service of a copy of the pleading was required, unless waived by the court. *(Adopted, eff. Jan. 1, 2003.)*

General notice provisions, see Probate Code § 1200 et seq.

Rule 7.54. Publication of *Notice of Petition to Administer Estate*

Publication and service of a *Notice of Petition to Administer Estate* (form DE–121) under Probate Code sections 8110–8125 is sufficient notice of any instrument offered for probate that is filed with, and specifically referred to in, the petition for which notice is given. Any other instrument must be presented in an amended petition, and a new notice must be published and served. *(Adopted, eff. Jan. 1, 2003. As amended, eff. Jan. 1, 2007.)*

Proof of notice by publication, see Probate Code § 1262.

Rule 7.55. Ex parte application for order

(a) Special notice allegation

An ex parte application for an order must allege whether special notice has been requested.

(b) Allegation if special notice requested

If special notice has been requested, the application must identify each person who has requested special notice and must allege that special notice has been given to or waived by each person who has requested it.

(c) Proof of service or waiver of special notice

Proofs of service of special notice or written waivers of special notice must be filed with the application. *(Adopted, eff. Jan. 1, 2003. As amended, eff. Jan. 1, 2007.)*

Proof of giving notice, see Probate Code § 1260 et seq.
Request for special notice, see Probate Code § 1250.

Chapter 3

PLEADINGS

Rule 7.101. Use of Judicial Council forms

(a) Use of mandatory forms

If a petition, an order, or another document to be submitted to the court is one for which the Judicial Council has adopted a mandatory form, that form must be used. Except as provided in this rule, if the Judicial Council has adopted a mandatory form in more than one alternative version, one of the alternative versions must be used. If that form is inadequate in a particular situation, an addendum may be attached to it.

(b) Alternative mandatory forms

The following forms have been adopted by the Judicial Council as alternative mandatory forms for use in probate proceedings or other proceedings governed by provisions of the Probate Code:

(1) Petition for Appointment of Guardian of Minor (form GC–210) and Petition for Appointment of Guardian of the Person (form GC–210(P));

(2) *Petition for Appointment of Temporary Guardian* (form GC–110) and *Petition for Appointment of Temporary Guardian of the Person* (form GC–110(P));

(3) *Petition to Approve Compromise of Disputed Claim or Pending Action or Disposition of Proceeds of Judgment for Minor or Person With a Disability* (form MC–350) and *Expedited Petition to Approve Compromise of Disputed Claim or Pending Action or Disposition of Proceeds of Judgment for Minor or Person With a Disability* (form MC–350EX).

(c) Use of guardianship petitions

Notwithstanding any other provision of this rule, a party petitioning for appointment of a temporary guardian of the person of a minor may file either form GC–110 or form GC–110(P). A party petitioning for appointment of a general guardian of the person of a minor may file either form GC–210 or form GC–210(P). A party petitioning for appointment of a temporary guardian of the estate or the person and estate of a minor must file form GC–110. A party petitioning for appointment of a general guardian of the estate or the person and estate of a minor must file form GC–210. *(Adopted, eff. Jan. 1, 2001. As amended, eff. Jan. 1, 2002; Jan. 1, 2007; Jan. 1, 2010; Jan. 1, 2014.)*

Rule 7.102. Titles of pleadings and orders

The title of each pleading and of each proposed order must clearly and completely identify the nature of the relief sought or granted. *(Adopted, eff. Jan. 1, 2001. As amended, eff. Jan. 1, 2002; Jan. 1, 2003.)*

Rule 7.103. Signature and verification of pleadings

(a) Signature of parties

A pleading must be in writing and must be signed by all persons joining in it.

(b) Verification by parties

All pleadings filed in proceedings under the Probate Code must be verified. If two or more persons join in a pleading, it may be verified by any of them.

(c) Signature and verification by attorney

If a person is absent from the county where his or her attorney's office is located, or for some other cause is unable to sign or verify a pleading, the attorney may sign or verify it, unless the person is, or is seeking to become, a fiduciary appointed in the proceeding. *(Adopted, eff. Jan. 1, 2003.)*

Rule 7.104. Execution and verification of amended pleadings, amendments to pleadings, and supplements to pleadings; use of Judicial Council forms

(a) Amended pleading and amendment to a pleading

(1) All persons required to sign a pleading must sign an amended pleading. One of the persons required to verify a pleading must verify an amended pleading.

(2) All persons required to sign a pleading must sign an amendment to that pleading. One of the persons required to verify a pleading must verify an amendment to that pleading.

(3) A Judicial Council form must be used for an amended pleading, with the word "Amended" added to its caption, if the form was used for the pleading that is amended. A Judicial Council form must not be used for an amendment to a pleading.

(b) Supplement to a pleading

(1) A supplement to a pleading must be signed and verified by one of the persons who were required to sign and verify the pleading that is supplemented. However, the court may, in the exercise of its discretion, accept for filing and consider a supplement to a pleading signed under penalty of perjury by an attorney for the party offering it, where the information contained in the supplement is particularly within the knowledge of the attorney.

(2) A Judicial Council form must not be used for a supplement to a pleading. *(Adopted, eff. Jan. 1, 2003.)*

Chapter 4

APPOINTMENT OF EXECUTORS AND ADMINISTRATORS

Cross References

Appointment of personal representative, administrators, see Probate Code § 8460 et seq.

Rule 7.150. Acknowledgment of receipt of statement of duties and liabilities of personal representative

Before the court issues letters, each personal representative of a decedent's estate (other than a company authorized to conduct a trust business in California) must execute and file an acknowledgment of receipt of *Duties and Liabilities of Personal Representative* (form DE–147). *(Adopted, eff. Jan. 1, 2000. As amended, eff. Jan. 1, 2002; Jan. 1, 2007.)*

Rule 7.151. Reimbursement of graduated filing fee by successful subsequent petitioner

(a) Duty to reimburse

In decedents' estates commenced on or after August 18, 2003, and before January 1, 2008, a general personal representative appointed on a *Petition for Probate* (form DE–111) that was not the first-filed petition for appointment of a general personal representative in the proceeding must reimburse the unsuccessful petitioner on the first-filed petition for a portion of the filing fee paid by the unsuccessful petitioner.

(b) Amount of reimbursement

The reimbursement required under this rule is in the amount of:

(1) The filing fee paid by the unsuccessful petitioner in excess of the filing fee that would have been payable on that date for a *Petition for Probate* filed to commence administration of an estate valued at less than $250,000, less

(2) The unpaid amount of any costs or sanctions awarded against the unsuccessful petitioner in favor of the party that sought the personal representative's appointment in the proceeding.

(c) When reimbursement payable

The personal representative must make the reimbursement payment required under this rule in cash and in full no later than the date the *Inventory and Appraisal* (form DE–160/GC–040) is due under Probate Code section 8800(b), including additional time allowed by the court under that provision.

(d) Payment from estate funds

The reimbursement payment under this rule is an authorized expense of administration and may be made from estate funds without a prior court order.

(e) Receipt from unsuccessful petitioner

The unsuccessful petitioner must give a signed receipt for the reimbursement payment made under this rule.

(f) Personal representative's right to claim refund

A personal representative that is required to but fails to make the reimbursement payment under this rule may not claim a refund of the difference between the estimated filing fee and the corrected filing fee under rule 7.552(c).

(g) Petitioner on dismissed *Petition for Probate*

A petitioner that is eligible to receive a refund of filing fee for a dismissed *Petition for Probate* under rule 7.552(d) is not an unsuccessful petitioner within the meaning of this rule. *(Adopted, eff. Jan. 1, 2004. As amended, eff. Jan. 1, 2007; March 1, 2008.)*

Chapter 5

BONDING OF PERSONAL REPRESENTATIVES, GUARDIANS, CONSERVATORS, AND TRUSTEES

Cross References

Appointment of personal representative, bond required, see Probate Code § 8480 et seq.

Rule 7.201. Waiver of bond in will

(a) Statement of waiver in petition

If the will waives bond, the Petition for Probate must so state.

(b) Court's discretion to require bond

The court may require bond if the proposed personal representative resides outside California or for other good cause, even if the will waives bond. *(Adopted, eff. Jan. 1, 2000. As amended, eff. Jan. 1, 2001; Jan. 1, 2002; Jan. 1, 2007.)*

Rule 7.202.   Two or more personal representatives

If a will admitted to probate names two or more persons to serve as executors but not all serve and the will does not expressly waive bond if fewer than all of the named persons serve, the court must require each executor to give a bond unless the court waives this requirement under Probate Code section 8481(a)(2). *(Adopted, eff. Jan. 1, 2000. As amended, eff. Jan. 1, 2002.)*

Rule 7.203.   Separate bonds for individuals

Because a corporate fiduciary (whether personal representative, guardian, conservator, or trustee) cannot assume responsibility for the acts of an individual cofiduciary, an individual cofiduciary who is required to give a bond must provide a separate bond, except to the extent that the court orders the assets to be held solely by the corporate cofiduciary. *(Adopted, eff. Jan. 1, 2000. As amended, eff. Jan. 1, 2002.)*

Rule 7.204.   Duty to apply for order increasing bond

(a) Ex parte application for order

Immediately upon the occurrence of facts making it necessary or appropriate to increase the amount of the bond, the personal representative, or the guardian or conservator of the estate, must make an ex parte application for an order increasing the bond.

(b) Attorney's duty

If the personal representative, or the guardian or conservator of the estate, has not already made application under (a), the attorney for the personal representative, or the attorney for the guardian or conservator of the estate, must make the ex parte application immediately upon becoming aware of the need to increase bond.

(c) Amount

(1) The application by a personal representative under (a) or by the attorney for a personal representative under (b) must show the value of the estate's personal property and the probable annual gross income of the estate.

(2) The application by a guardian or conservator of the estate under (a) or by the attorney for a guardian or conservator of the estate under (b) must show the value of the estate's personal property, the probable annual gross income of all of the property of the estate, and the sum of the probable annual gross payments of the public benefits of the ward or conservatee identified in Probate Code section 2320(c)(3).

(3) If the personal representative has full Independent Administration of Estates Act (IAEA)[1] authority or the guardian or conservator of the estate has authority to sell estate real property without court confirmation, the application must also show the amount of the equity in estate real property. *(Adopted, eff. Jan. 1, 2000. As amended, eff. Jan. 1, 2002; Jan. 1, 2003.)*

[1] See Probate Code § 10400 et seq.

Rule 7.205.   Independent power to sell real property

If the personal representative requests or has been granted an independent power to sell or hypothecate real estate or to lease it for a term of more than one year, the personal representative must state in the request to fix the amount of the bond the value of the real property less encumbrances. *(Adopted, eff. Jan. 1, 2000. As amended, eff. Jan. 1, 2002.)*

Rule 7.206.   Bond upon sale of real property

If a bond or additional bond is required in an order confirming sale of real estate, the court must not file the order until the additional bond is filed. *(Adopted, eff. Jan. 1, 2000. As amended, eff. Jan. 1, 2002.)*

Rule 7.207.   Bonds of conservators and guardians

(a) Bond includes reasonable amount for recovery on the bond

Except as otherwise provided by statute, every conservator or guardian of the estate must furnish a bond that includes an amount determined under (b) as a reasonable amount for the cost of recovery to collect on the bond under Probate Code section 2320(c)(4).

(b) Amount of bond for the cost of recovery on the bond

The reasonable amount of bond for the cost of recovery to collect on the bond, including attorney's fees and costs, under Probate Code section 2320(c)(4) is:

(1) Ten percent (10%) of the value up to and including $500,000 of the following:

(A) The value of personal property of the estate;

(B) The value, less encumbrances, of real property of the estate that the guardian or conservator has the independent power to sell without approval or confirmation of the court under Probate Code sections 2590 and 2591(d);

(C) The probable annual income from all assets of the estate; and

(D) The probable annual gross payments described in Probate Code section 2320(c)(3); and

(2) Twelve percent (12%) of the value above $500,000 up to and including $1,000,000 of the property, income, and payments described in (1); and

(3) Two percent (2%) of the value above $1,000,000 of the property, income, and payments described in (1). *(Adopted, eff. Jan. 1, 2008. As amended, eff. Jan. 1, 2010.)*

Chapter 6

INDEPENDENT ADMINISTRATION OF ESTATES

Independent Administration of Estates Act, see Probate Code § 10400 et seq.

Rule 7.250. Report of actions taken under the Independent Administration of Estates Act [1]

(a) Report required

In any accounting, report, petition for preliminary distribution, or petition for final distribution, the petitioner must list and describe all actions taken without prior court approval under the Independent Administration of Estates Act (IAEA) if notice of the proposed action was required. The description of the action must include the following:

(1) The nature of the action;

(2) When the action was taken;

(3) A statement of when and to whom notice was given;

(4) Whether notice was waived, and if so, by whom; and

(5) Whether any objections were received.

(b) Actions reported in previous reports

An action taken under the IAEA that was (1) properly listed and described in a prior accounting, report, or petition for distribution, and (2) approved by the court, need not be listed and described in a subsequent account, report, or petition for distribution. *(Adopted, eff. Jan. 1, 2000. As amended, eff. Jan. 1, 2002; Jan. 1, 2007.)*

[1] See Probate Code § 10400 et seq.

Chapter 7

SPOUSAL OR DOMESTIC PARTNER PROPERTY PETITIONS

Rule
7.301. Spousal or domestic partner property petition filed with petition for probate.

Rule 7.301. Spousal or domestic partner property petition filed with petition for probate

A petition for spousal or domestic partner property determination or confirmation must be filed separately from a petition for probate of will or for letters of administration, even if both petitions are filed at the same time. The two petitions must be filed under the same case number. *(Adopted, eff. Jan. 1, 2000. As amended, eff. Jan. 1, 2002; Jan. 1, 2007.)*

Chapter 9

CREDITORS' CLAIMS

Rule
7.401. Personal representative's action on the claim.
7.402. Court's action on the claim.
7.403. Listing all claims in the final report.

Administration of estates of decedents, creditor claims, see Probate Code § 9000 et seq.

Rule 7.401. Personal representative's action on the claim

For each creditor's claim filed with the court, the personal representative (whether or not acting under the Independent Administration of Estates Act (IAEA)) [1] must:

(1) Allow or reject in whole or in part the claim in writing;

(2) Serve a copy of the allowance or rejection on the creditor and the creditor's attorney; and

(3) File a copy of the allowance or rejection with proof of service with the court. *(Adopted, eff. Jan. 1, 2000. As amended, eff. Jan. 1, 2002.)*

[1] See Probate Code § 10400 et seq.

Rule 7.402. Court's action on the claim

Except as to claims of the personal representative or the attorney, if the personal representative has authority to act under the Independent Administration of Estates Act (IAEA), [1] the court must not act on the personal representative's allowance or rejection of a creditor's claim unless good cause is shown. *(Adopted, eff. Jan. 1, 2000. As amended, eff. Jan. 1, 2002.)*

[1] See Probate Code § 10400 et seq.

Rule 7.403. Listing all claims in the final report

For each claim presented, the personal representative must state in the final report or petition for final distribution:

(1) The claimant's name;

(2) The date of filing of the claim;

(3) The nature of the claim;

(4) The amount claimed;

(5) The disposition of the claim; and

(6) If the claim was rejected, the date of service of the rejection and whether or not a lawsuit was filed. *(Adopted, eff. Jan. 1, 2000. As amended, eff. Jan. 1, 2002.)*

Chapter 10

SALES OF REAL AND PERSONAL PROPERTY

Rule
7.451. Refusal to show property to prospective buyers.
7.452. Petitioner or attorney required at hearing.
7.453. Petition for exclusive listing.
7.454. Ex parte application for order authorizing sale of securities or other personal property.

Sale of personal property, see Probate Code § 10250 et seq.
Sale of real property, see Probate Code § 10300 et seq.

Rule 7.451. Refusal to show property to prospective buyers

Upon a showing that the fiduciary has denied any bona fide prospective buyer or his or her broker a reasonable opportunity to inspect the property, the court must not confirm the sale but must continue the sale to allow inspection unless good cause is shown for the court to confirm the sale. *(Adopted, eff. Jan. 1, 2000. As amended, eff. Jan. 1, 2002.)*

Rule 7.452. Petitioner or attorney required at hearing

The court must not proceed with the hearing on a petition to confirm a sale of property unless the petitioner's attorney or petitioner, if unrepresented, is present. *(Adopted, eff. Jan. 1, 2000. As amended, eff. Jan. 1, 2002.)*

Cross References

Sale of personal property, sales to be reported and confirmed by court, see Probate Code § 10260.
Sale of real property, sales to be reported and confirmed by court, see Probate Code § 10308.

Rule 7.453. Petition for exclusive listing

A petition for approval of an exclusive listing under Probate Code section 10150(c) must state the following:

(1) A description of the property to be sold;

(2) The name of the broker to be employed;

(3) A summary of the terms of the exclusive listing agreement or include a copy of the listing agreement; and

(4) A detailed statement of the facts supporting the "necessity and the advantage" to the estate of having the exclusive listing. *(Adopted, eff. Jan. 1, 2000. As amended, eff. Jan. 1, 2002.)*

Rule 7.454. Ex parte application for order authorizing sale of securities or other personal property

An ex parte application for authority to sell or to surrender tangible or intangible personal property must state whether or not the property is specifically devised. If it is specifically devised, the written consent of the specific devisee to the sale or surrender must be filed. *(Adopted, eff. Jan. 1, 2003.)*

Cross References

Sale of securities, see Probate Code § 10200.

Chapter 11

INVENTORY AND APPRAISAL

Rule
7.501. Inventory and Appraisal to show sufficiency of bond.

Rule 7.501. Inventory and Appraisal to show sufficiency of bond

(a) Statement required

Every Inventory and Appraisal must contain one of the following statements:

(1) "Bond is waived";

(2) "Bond has been filed in the amount of $ *(specify amount)* and is insufficient"; or

(3) "Bond has been filed in the amount of $ *(specify amount)* and is sufficient."

(b) Insufficient bond

If the bond is insufficient, the fiduciary (the personal representative, or the guardian or conservator of the estate), or the attorney for the fiduciary, must immediately make ex parte application as provided in rule 7.204 for an order increasing the amount of the bond.

(c) Statement signed by attorney

The statement required by (a) must be signed by the attorney of record for each fiduciary who has an attorney of record and by each fiduciary who does not. *(Adopted, eff. Jan. 1, 2000. As amended, eff. Jan. 1, 2002; Jan. 1, 2003; Jan. 1, 2007.)*

Chapter 12

ACCOUNTS AND REPORTS OF EXECUTORS, ADMINISTRATORS, CONSERVATORS, AND GUARDIANS

Rule
7.550. Effect of waiver of account.
7.575. Accounts of conservators and guardians.

Cross References

Administration of estates of decedents, accounts, see Probate Code § 10900 et seq.

Rule 7.550. Effect of waiver of account

(a) Waiver of account

Except as provided in (b), if an accounting is waived under Probate Code section 10954, the details of receipts and disbursements need not be listed in the report required under section 10954(c)(1).

(b) Information required in report on waiver of account

The report required when an account has been waived must list the information required by law, including information as to:

(1) Creditors' claims;

(2) Sales, purchases, or exchanges of assets;

(3) Changes in the form of assets;

(4) Assets on hand;

(5) Whether the estate is solvent;

(6) Detailed schedules of receipts and gains or losses on sale (where an amount other than the amount of the Inventory and Appraisal is used as a basis for calculating fees or commissions);

(7) Costs of administration (if reimbursement of these costs is requested);

(8) The amount of any fees or commissions paid or to be paid;

(9) The calculation of such fees or commissions as described in rule 7.705; and

(10) For decedent's estate proceedings commenced on or after August 18, 2003, the information required by rule 7.552(a) and (b). *(Adopted, eff. Jan. 1, 2003. As amended, eff. Jan. 1, 2004; Jan. 1, 2007.)*

Cross References

Compensation of personal representatives and attorneys, calculation of statutory compensation, see California Rules of Court, Rule 7.705.

Rule 7.575.   Accounts of conservators and guardians

This rule defines standard and simplified accountings filed by conservators and guardians under Probate Code section 2620(a), provides when each type of accounting must or may be filed, and prescribes the use of Judicial Council accounting forms in both types of accountings.

(a) Standard and simplified accountings

A standard accounting lists receipts and disbursements in subject-matter categories, with each receipt and disbursement category subtotaled. A simplified accounting lists receipts and disbursements chronologically, by receipt or payment date, without subject-matter categories.

(b) Standard accounting authorized or required

A conservator or guardian may file any accounting required or authorized by Probate Code section 2620 as a standard accounting under this rule and must file a standard accounting if:

(1) The estate contains income real property;

(2) The estate contains a whole or partial interest in a trade or business;

(3) The appraised value of the estate is $500,000 or more, exclusive of the conservatee's or ward's personal residence;

(4) Except as provided in (c), Schedule A (receipts) or Schedule C (disbursements) prepared in a simplified accounting format exceeds five pages in length; or

(5) The court directs that a standard accounting be filed.

(c) Simplified accounting authorized

A conservator or guardian may file a simplified accounting in all cases not listed in (b). If required by this rule to file a standard accounting only because a receipts or disbursements schedule is longer than five pages under (b)(4), a conservator or guardian may file a simplified accounting, except for that schedule, which must be prepared in a standard accounting format.

(d) Standard and simplified accounting forms

Judicial Council forms designated as GC–400 are standard accounting forms. Forms designated as GC–405 are simplified accounting forms. Forms designated as GC–400/GC–405 are forms for both standard and simplified accountings. Each form is also designated by a suffix following its accounting designator that identifies the form's intended use, based either on the form's schedule letter as shown in the Summary of Account (form GC–400(SUM)/GC–405(SUM)) or the form's subject matter.

(e) Mandatory and optional forms

(1) Judicial Council accounting forms adopted as mandatory forms must be used by standard and simplified accounting filers. Judicial Council accounting forms approved as optional forms may be used by all accounting filers. Judicial Council accounting forms designated as GC–400/GC–405 that are approved as optional forms may be used by standard accounting filers but must be used by simplified accounting filers.

(2) Standard accounting filers electing not to use optional Judicial Council accounting forms must:

(A) State receipts and disbursements in the subject-matter categories specified in the optional Judicial Council forms for receipts and disbursements schedules;

(B) Provide the same information about any asset, property, transaction, receipt, disbursement, or other matter that is required by the applicable Judicial Council accounting form; and

(C) Provide the information in the same general layout as the applicable Judicial Council accounting form, but instructional material contained in the form and material contained or requested in the form's header and footer need not be provided.

(f) Required information in all accounts

Notwithstanding any other provision of this rule and the Judicial Council accounting forms, all standard and simplified accounting filers must provide all information in their accounting schedules or their Summary of Account that is required by Probate Code sections 1060–1063 and must provide all information required by Probate Code section 1064 in the petition for approval of their account or the report accompanying their account. (Adopted, eff. Jan. 1, 2008.)

Chapter 14

PRELIMINARY AND FINAL DISTRIBUTIONS

Cross References

Final distribution of estate, see Probate Code § 11640 et seq.
Preliminary distribution of estate, see Probate Code § 11620 et seq.

Rule 7.650.   Decree of distribution establishing testamentary trusts

(a) Determining the trust

Upon distribution, the court must:

(1) Determine whether or not a valid trust has been created by the will;

(2) Determine the terms of the trust; and

(3) Order distribution of the trust property to the trustee.

(b) Terms of the trust

The order for distribution must incorporate the terms of the trust so as to give effect to the conditions existing at the time distribution is ordered. The pertinent provisions must be stated in the present tense and in the third person instead of quoting the will verbatim. (Adopted, eff. Jan. 1, 2000. As amended, eff. Jan. 1, 2002.)

Rule 7.651.   Description of property in petition for distribution

(a) Property description

A petition for distribution must list and describe in detail the property to be distributed, in the body of the petition or in an attachment that is incorporated in the petition by reference. If an account is filed with the petition, the description must be included in a schedule in the account.

(b) Specific description requirements

The description under (a) must:

(1) Include the amount of cash on hand;

(2) Indicate whether promissory notes are secured or unsecured, and describe in detail the security interest of any secured notes;

(3) Include the complete legal description, street address (if any), and assessor's parcel number (if any) of real property; and

(4) Include the complete description of each individual security held in "street name" in security brokers' accounts. *(Adopted, eff. Jan. 1, 2004.)*

Cross References

Distribution of property in estate, see Probate Code § 11750 et seq.

Rule 7.652. Allegations in petition for distribution concerning character of property

(a) Required allegations

If the character of property to be distributed may affect the distribution, a petition for distribution must allege:

(1) The character of the property to be distributed, whether separate, community, or quasi-community; and

(2) That the community or quasi-community property to be distributed is either the decedent's one-half interest only, or the entire interest of the decedent and the decedent's spouse.

(b) Compliance with Probate Code section 13502

If any property is to be distributed outright to the surviving spouse, a written election by the surviving spouse that complies with Probate Code section 13502 must have been filed, and the petition must show the filing date of the election. *(Adopted, eff. Jan. 1, 2004.)*

Cross References

Distribution of property in estate, see Probate Code § 11750 et seq.

Chapter 15

COMPENSATION OF PERSONAL REPRESENTATIVES AND ATTORNEYS

Cross References

Compensation of personal representative and attorney for personal representative, see Probate Code § 10800 et seq.

Rule 7.700. Compensation paid in advance

(a) No compensation in advance of court order

The personal representative must neither pay nor receive, and the attorney for the personal representative must not receive, statutory commissions or fees or fees for extraordinary services in advance of an order of the court authorizing their payment.

(b) Surcharge for payment or receipt of advance compensation

In addition to removing the personal representative and imposing any other sanctions authorized by law against the personal representative or the attorney for the personal representative, the court may surcharge the personal representative for payment or receipt of statutory commissions or fees or fees for extraordinary services in advance of an order of the court authorizing their payment. The surcharge may include interest at the legal rate from the date of payment. *(Adopted, eff. Jan. 1, 2003.)*

Rule 7.701. Allowance on account of statutory compensation

The court may authorize an allowance of statutory fees or commissions on account before approval of the final account and the decree of final distribution. Any allowance made before settlement of the final account must be low enough to avoid the possibility of overpayment. The allowance:

(1) Must be based on the estimated amount of statutory compensation payable on the estate determined as of the date of the petition for allowance;

(2) Must be in proportion to the work actually performed; and

(3) Must be based upon a detailed description of the ordinary services performed and remaining to be performed. *(Adopted, eff. Jan. 1, 2003.)*

Rule 7.702. Petition for extraordinary compensation

A petition for extraordinary compensation must include, or be accompanied by, a statement of the facts upon which the petition is based. The statement of facts must:

(1) Show the nature and difficulty of the tasks performed;

(2) Show the results achieved;

(3) Show the benefit of the services to the estate;

(4) Specify the amount requested for each category of service performed;

(5) State the hourly rate of each person who performed services and the hours spent by each of them;

(6) Describe the services rendered in sufficient detail to demonstrate the productivity of the time spent; and

(7) State the estimated amount of statutory compensation to be paid by the estate, if the petition is not part of a final account or report. *(Adopted, eff. Jan. 1, 2003.)*

Additional compensation for extraordinary services, see Probate Code § 10811.

Rule 7.703. Extraordinary compensation

(a) Discretion of the court

An award of extraordinary compensation to the personal representative or to the attorney for the personal representative is within the discretion of the court. The court may consider the amount of statutory compensation when determining compensation for extraordinary services.

(b) Examples of extraordinary services by personal representative

The following is a nonexclusive list of activities for which extraordinary compensation may be awarded to the personal representative:

(1) Selling, leasing, exchanging, financing, or foreclosing real or personal property;

(2) Carrying on decedent's business if necessary to preserve the estate or under court order;

(3) Preparing tax returns; and

(4) Handling audits or litigation connected with tax liabilities of the decedent or of the estate.

(c) Examples of extraordinary services by attorney

The following is a nonexclusive list of activities for which extraordinary compensation may be awarded to the attorney for the personal representative:

(1) Legal services in connection with the sale of property held in the estate;

(2) Services to secure a loan to pay estate debts;

(3) Litigation undertaken to benefit the estate or to protect its interests;

(4) Defense of the personal representative's account;

(5) Defense of a will contested after its admission to probate;

(6) Successful defense of a will contested before its admission to probate;

(7) Successful defense of a personal representative in a removal proceeding;

(8) Extraordinary efforts to locate estate assets;

(9) Litigation in support of attorney's request for extraordinary compensation, where prior compensation awards are not adequate compensation under all the circumstances;

(10) Coordination of ancillary administration; and

(11) Accounting for a deceased, incapacitated, or absconded personal representative under Probate Code section 10953.

(d) Contingency fee agreement for extraordinary legal services

An attorney may agree to perform extraordinary services for a personal representative on a contingent-fee basis on the following conditions:

(1) The agreement must be in writing and must comply with section 6147 of the Business and Professions Code;

(2) The court must approve the agreement in the manner provided in Probate Code section 10811(c), based on findings that the compensation under the agreement is just and reasonable, that the agreement is to the advantage of the estate, and that the agreement is in the best interest of the persons interested in the estate; and

(3) In the absence of an emergency or other unusual circumstances, the personal representative must obtain the court's approval of the contingency fee agreement before services are performed under it.

(e) Use of paralegals in the performance of extraordinary services

Extraordinary legal services may include the services of a paralegal as defined in Business and Professions Code section 6450(a) only if the request for extraordinary legal fees for the paralegal's services:

(1) Describes the qualifications of the paralegal (including education, certification, continuing education, and experience). The description must state that the paralegal:

(A) Acted under the direction and supervision of an attorney;

(B) Satisfies one or more of the minimum qualifications specified in Business and Professions Code section 6450(c); and

(C) Has completed mandatory continuing education required by Business and Professions Code section 6450(d) for the last two-year certification period ending before the year during which any part of the paralegal's services were performed.

(2) States the hours spent by the paralegal and the hourly rate requested for the paralegal's services;

(3) Describes the services performed by the paralegal;

(4) States why it was appropriate to use the paralegal's services in the particular case; and

(5) Demonstrates that the total amount requested for the extraordinary services of the attorney and the paralegal does not exceed the amount appropriate if the attorney had performed the services without the paralegal's assistance. *(Adopted, eff. Jan. 1, 2003. As amended, eff. Jan. 1, 2007; July 1, 2010.)*

Additional compensation for extraordinary services, see Probate Code § 10811.

Rule 7.704. Apportionment of statutory compensation

(a) One statutory commission and fee

There is one statutory commission for ordinary services by the personal representative of the estate and one statutory attorney fee for ordinary legal services to the personal representative, regardless of the number of personal representatives or attorneys performing the services. The court may apportion statutory commissions and fees among multiple, successive, and concurrent personal representatives or attorneys. The apportionment must be based on the agreement of the multiple personal representatives or attorneys or, if there is no agreement, according to the services actually rendered by each of them.

(b) Notice of hearing

If there has been a change of personal representative or a substitution of attorneys for the personal representative, notice of hearing of any interim or final petition seeking or waiving an award of statutory compensation must be given to all prior personal representatives or attorneys unless:

(1) A waiver of notice executed by all prior personal representatives or attorneys is on file or is filed with the petition;

(2) A written, signed agreement on the allocation of statutory commissions or fees between the present personal representative or attorney and all prior personal representatives or attorneys is on file or is included in or filed with the petition; or

(3) The court's file and the petition demonstrate that the commissions or fees of the prior personal representatives or attorneys have been previously provided for and allowed by the court. *(Adopted, eff. Jan. 1, 2003.)*

Cross References

Apportionment of compensation, see Probate Code § 10814.

Rule 7.705. Calculation of statutory compensation

(a) Account filed

A petition for statutory commissions or attorney fees must state the amount of statutory compensation payable and set forth the estate accounted for and the calculation of statutory compensation. The calculation must be stated in the petition in substantially the following form:

COMMISSION OR FEE BASE

Inventory and Appraisal	$ _____
Receipts, Excluding Principal	$ _____
Gains on Sales	$ _____
Losses on Sales	$ (_____)
TOTAL COMMISSION OR FEE BASE	$ _____

COMMISSION OR FEE COMPUTATION

4% on first $100,000	($_____)[1]	$_____[2]
3% on next $100,000	($_____)	$_____
2% on next $800,000	($_____)	$_____
1% on next $9,000,000	($_____)	$_____
½ of 1% on next $15,000,000	($_____)	$_____
Amount requested from the court for estates above $25,000,000	($_____)	$_____
TOTAL COMMISSION OR FEE		$_____[3]

   1 Enter in this column the amount of the estate accounted for in each category. The sum of the entries in this column would equal the total commission or fee base.

   2 Enter in this column the product of the amount of the estate accounted for in each category multiplied by the percentage for that category.

   3 Enter here the sum of the products entered in this column.

(b) Account waived

When an account has been waived, the report must contain the information required by rule 7.550. If the report is accompanied by a request for statutory commissions or fees, the basis for their computation must be included in the petition substantially in the form provided in (a). Notwithstanding the waiver of account, if the petition and report requests statutory commissions or fees based on any amount other than the amount of the Inventory and Appraisal, detailed schedules of receipts and gains and losses on sales must be included. *(Adopted, eff. Jan. 1, 2003.)*

Rule 7.706. Compensation when personal representative is an attorney

(a) Personal representative's compensation only

Notwithstanding the provisions of the decedent's will, a personal representative who is an attorney may receive the personal representative's compensation but may not receive compensation for legal services as the attorney for the personal representative unless the court approves the right to compensation for legal services in advance and finds the arrangement is to the advantage, benefit, and best interest of the decedent's estate.

(b) Agreement not to participate in compensation

A law firm of which the personal representative is a partner or shareholder may request compensation for legal services in addition to the personal representative's compensation if a written agreement not to participate in each other's compensation, signed by the personal representative and by authorized representatives of the law firm, has been filed in the estate proceeding. *(Adopted, eff. Jan. 1, 2003.)*

Cross References

Compensation of personal representative who is an attorney, see Probate Code § 10804.

Rule 7.707. Application of compensation provisions

For proceedings commenced after June 30, 1991, the law in effect on the date of the court's order awarding statutory compensation determines the amount of such compensation. *(Adopted, eff. Jan. 1, 2003.)*

Chapter 16

COMPENSATION IN ALL MATTERS OTHER THAN DECEDENTS' ESTATES

Rule 7.750. Application of rules to guardianships and conservatorships

The rules in this chapter apply to guardianships and conservatorships under division 4 of the Probate Code (Prob. Code, § 1400 et seq.) and to conservatorships under the Lanterman–Petris–Short Act (Welf. & Inst. Code, §§ 5350–5371). They do not apply to guardianships under chapter 2 of division 2 of the Welfare and Institutions Code (Welf. & Inst. Code, § 200 et seq.). Under Probate Code section 2646, the rules in this chapter applicable to guardianships and conservatorships apply only to compensation payable from the estate of the ward or conservatee or from money or property recovered or collected for the estate of the ward or conservatee. *(Adopted, eff. Jan. 1, 2003.)*

Rule 7.751. Petitions for orders allowing compensation for guardians or conservators and their attorneys

(a) Petition for allowance of compensation for services performed before appointment of guardian or conservator

A petition for allowance of compensation to a guardian or conservator or to the attorney for a guardian or conservator may include a request for compensation for services rendered before an order appointing a guardian or conservator. The petition must show facts demonstrating the necessity for preappointment services.

(b) Required showing in petition for allowance of compensation

All petitions for orders fixing and allowing compensation must comply with the requirements of rule 7.702 concerning petitions for extraordinary compensation in decedents' estates, to the extent applicable to guardianships and conservatorships, except that the best interest of the ward or conservatee is to be considered instead of the interest of beneficiaries of the estate. *(Adopted, eff. Jan. 1, 2003. As amended, eff. Jan. 1, 2007.)*

Cross References

Allowance on compensation, see Probate Code § 10830.

Rule 7.752. Court may order accounting before allowing compensation

Notwithstanding the time period after which a petition may be filed for an allowance of compensation to a guardian, conservator, or an attorney for a guardian or conservator, the court may order the guardian or conservator to file an accounting before or at the time a petition for an allowance of compensation is filed or heard. *(Adopted, eff. Jan. 1, 2003.)*

Rule 7.753. Contingency fee agreements in guardianships and conservatorships

A guardian or conservator of the estate may contract with an attorney for a contingency fee for the attorney's services on behalf of the ward or conservatee, or the estate, in connection with a matter that is of a type customarily the subject of a contingency fee agreement, if the court has authorized the guardian or conservator to do so, or if the agreement has been approved by the court under Probate Code section 2644. The agreement must also satisfy the requirements of rule 7.703(d)(1). *(Adopted, eff. Jan. 1, 2003.)*

Rule 7.754. Use of paralegals in the performance of legal services for the guardian or conservator

An attorney for a guardian or conservator may use the services of a paralegal acting under the direction and supervision of the attorney. A request for an allowance of compensation for the services of a paralegal must satisfy the requirements of rule 7.703(e). *(Adopted, eff. Jan. 1, 2003.)*

Rule 7.755. Advance payments and periodic payments to guardians, conservators, and to their attorneys on account for future services

(a) No advance payments

A guardian or conservator must neither pay nor receive, and the attorney for a guardian or conservator must not receive, any payment from the estate of the ward or conservatee for services rendered in advance of an order of the court authorizing the payment. If an advance payment is made or received, the court may surcharge the guardian or conservator in the manner provided in rule 7.700(b), in addition to removing the guardian or conservator or imposing any other sanction authorized by law on the guardian or conservator or on the attorney.

(b) Periodic payments to attorneys on account

A guardian or conservator may request the court to authorize periodic payment of attorney fees on account of future services under Probate Code section 2643 on a showing of an ongoing need for legal services. *(Adopted, eff. Jan. 1, 2003.)*

Rule 7.756. Compensation of conservators and guardians

(a) Standards for determining just and reasonable compensation

The court may consider the following nonexclusive factors in determining just and reasonable compensation for a conservator from the estate of the conservatee or a guardian from the estate of the ward:

(1) The size and nature of the conservatee's or ward's estate;

(2) The benefit to the conservatee or ward, or his or her estate, of the conservator's or guardian's services;

(3) The necessity for the services performed;

(4) The conservatee's or ward's anticipated future needs and income;

(5) The time spent by the conservator or guardian in the performance of services;

(6) Whether the services performed were routine or required more than ordinary skill or judgment;

(7) Any unusual skill, expertise, or experience brought to the performance of services;

(8) The conservator's or guardian's estimate of the value of the services performed; and

(9) The compensation customarily allowed by the court in the community where the court is located for the management of conservatorships or guardianships of similar size and complexity.

(b) No single factor determinative

No single factor listed in (a) should be the exclusive basis for the court's determination of just and reasonable compensation.

(c) No inflexible maximum or minimum compensation or maximum approved hourly rate

This rule is not authority for a court to set an inflexible maximum or minimum compensation or a maximum approved hourly rate for compensation. *(Adopted, eff. Jan. 1, 2008.)*

Rule 7.776. Compensation of trustees

In determining or approving compensation of a trustee, the court may consider, among other factors, the following:

(1) The gross income of the trust estate;

(2) The success or failure of the trustee's administration;

(3) Any unusual skill, expertise, or experience brought to the trustee's work;

(4) The fidelity or disloyalty shown by the trustee;

(5) The amount of risk and responsibility assumed by the trustee;

(6) The time spent in the performance of the trustee's duties;

(7) The custom in the community where the court is located regarding compensation authorized by settlors, compensation allowed by the court, or charges of corporate trustees for trusts of similar size and complexity; and

(8) Whether the work performed was routine, or required more than ordinary skill or judgment. *(Formerly Rule 7.756, adopted, eff. Jan. 1, 2003. As amended, eff. Jan. 1, 2007. Renumbered Rule 7.776, eff. Jan. 1, 2008.)*

Chapter 17

CONTESTED HEARINGS AND TRIALS

Rule
7.801. Objections and responses.
7.802. Electronic filing and service in contested probate proceedings.

Rule 7.801. Objections and responses

If the court continues a matter to allow a written objection or response to be made, and the responding or objecting party fails to serve and file a timely objection or response, the court may deem the objections or responses waived. *(Adopted, eff. Jan. 1, 2000.)*

Rule 7.802. Electronic filing and service in contested probate proceedings

The provisions of Code of Civil Procedure section 1010.6 and rules 2.250–2.261 of the California Rules of Court concerning filing and service by electronic means apply to contested proceedings under the Probate Code and the Probate Rules to the same extent as they apply to other contested civil proceedings in each superior court in this state. *(Adopted, eff. Jan. 1, 2016.)*

Chapter 19

TRUSTS

Rule
7.901. Trustee's accounts.
7.902. Beneficiaries to be listed in petitions and accounts.
7.903. Trusts funded by court order.

Cross References

Trust law, generally, see Probate Code § 15000 et seq.

Rule 7.901. Trustee's accounts

(a) Period covered

A trustee's account must state the period covered by the account.

(b) First account

The first account in a testamentary trust must reconcile the initial assets on hand with the decree of distribution of the estate.

(c) Principal and income

All trustee's accounts in a trust that distributes income to a beneficiary must allocate receipts and disbursements between (1) principal receipts and disbursements, and (2) income receipts and disbursements. *(Adopted, eff. Jan. 1, 2001. As amended, eff. Jan. 1, 2002.)*

Rule 7.902. Beneficiaries to be listed in petitions and accounts

A petition and account involving a trust must state the names and last known addresses of all vested or contingent beneficiaries, including all persons in being who may or will receive income or corpus of the trust, provided, however, that (1) during the time that the trust is revocable and the person holding the power to revoke the trust is competent, the names and last known addresses of beneficiaries who do not hold the power to revoke do not need to be stated, and (2) the petition or account does not need to state the name and last known address of any beneficiary who need not be given notice under Probate Code section 15804. *(Adopted, eff. Jan. 1, 2002. As amended, eff. Jan. 1, 2007.)*

Rule 7.903. Trusts funded by court order

(a) Definitions

(1) "Trust funded by court order" under this rule means and refers to a trust that will receive funds under Probate Code section 2580 et seq. (substituted judgment); section 3100 et seq. (proceedings for particular transactions involving disabled spouses or registered domestic partners); or section 3600 et seq. (settlement of claims or actions or disposition of judgments involving minors or persons with disabilities).

(2) "Continuing jurisdiction of the court" under (b) means and refers to the court's continuing subject matter jurisdiction over trust proceedings under division 9 of the Probate Code (Prob. Code, § 15000 et seq.).

(3) "Court supervision under the Probate Code" under (b) means and refers to the court's authority to require prior court approval or subsequent confirmation of the actions of the trustee as for the actions of a guardian or conservator of

the estate under division 4 of the Probate Code (Prob. Code, § 1400 et seq.).

(b) Continuing jurisdiction and court supervision

The order creating or approving the funding of a trust funded by court order must provide that the trust is subject to the continuing jurisdiction of the court and may provide that the trust is to be subject to court supervision under the Probate Code.

(c) Required provisions in trust instruments

Except as provided in (d), unless the court otherwise orders for good cause shown, trust instruments for trusts funded by court order must:

(1) Not contain "no-contest" provisions;

(2) Prohibit modification or revocation without court approval;

(3) Clearly identify the trustee and any other person with authority to direct the trustee to make disbursements;

(4) Prohibit investments by the trustee other than those permitted under Probate Code section 2574;

(5) Require persons identified in (3) to post bond in the amount required under Probate Code section 2320 et seq.;

(6) Require the trustee to file accounts and reports for court approval in the manner and frequency required by Probate Code sections 1060 et seq. and 2620 et seq.;

(7) Require court approval of changes in trustees and a court order appointing any successor trustee; and

(8) Require compensation of the trustee, the members of any advisory committee, or the attorney for the trustee, to be in just and reasonable amounts that must be fixed and allowed by the court. The instrument may provide for periodic payments of compensation on account, subject to the requirements of Probate Code section 2643 and rule 7.755.

(d) Trust instruments for smaller trusts

Unless the court otherwise orders for good cause shown, the requirements of (c)(5)–(8) of this rule do not apply to trust instruments for trusts that will have total assets of $20,000 or less after receipt of the property ordered by the court. *(Adopted, eff. Jan. 1, 2005. As amended, eff. July 1, 2005; Jan. 1, 2007.)*

Chapter 20

CLAIMS OF MINORS AND PERSONS WITH DISABILITIES

Cross References

Money or property paid or delivered pursuant to compromise or judgment for minor or incompetent person, see Probate Code § 3600 et seq.

Rule 7.950. Petition for court approval of the compromise of, or a covenant on, a disputed claim; a compromise or settlement of a pending action; or the disposition of the proceeds of a judgment

A petition for court approval of a compromise of or a covenant not to sue or enforce judgment on a minor's disputed claim; a compromise or settlement of a pending action or proceeding to which a minor or person with a disability is a party; or disposition of the proceeds of a judgment for a minor or person with a disability under chapter 4 of part 8 of division 4 of the Probate Code (commencing with section 3600) or Code of Civil Procedure section 372 must be verified by the petitioner and must contain a full disclosure of all information that has any bearing upon the reasonableness of the compromise, covenant, settlement, or disposition. Except as provided in rule 7.950.5, the petition must be prepared on a fully completed *Petition to Approve Compromise of Disputed Claim or Pending Action or Disposition of Proceeds of Judgment for Minor or Person With a Disability* (form MC–350). *(Adopted, eff. Jan. 1, 2002. As amended, eff. Jan. 1, 2007; Jan. 1, 2010.)*

Rule 7.950.5. Expedited petition for court approval of the compromise of, or a covenant on, a disputed claim; a compromise or settlement of a pending action; or the disposition of the proceeds of a judgment

(a) Authorized use of expedited petition

Notwithstanding the provisions of rule 7.950, a petitioner for court approval of a compromise of or a covenant not to sue or enforce judgment on a minor's disputed claim; a compromise or settlement of a pending action or proceeding to which a minor or person with a disability is a party; or disposition of the proceeds of a judgment for a minor or person with a disability under chapter 4 of part 8 of division 4 of the Probate Code (commencing with section 3600) or Code of Civil Procedure section 372 may, in the following circumstances, satisfy the information requirements of that rule by fully completing the *Expedited Petition to Approve Compromise of Disputed Claim or Pending Action or Disposition of Proceeds of Judgment for Minor or Person With a Disability* (form MC–350EX):

(1) The petitioner is represented by an attorney authorized to practice in the courts of this state;

(2) The claim is not for damages for the wrongful death of a person;

(3) No portion of the net proceeds of the compromise, settlement, or judgment in favor of the minor or disabled claimant is to be placed in a trust;

(4) There are no unresolved disputes concerning liens to be satisfied from the proceeds of the compromise, settlement, or judgment;

(5) The petitioner's attorney did not become involved in the matter at the direct or indirect request of a person against whom the claim is asserted or an insurance carrier for that person;

(6) The petitioner's attorney is neither employed by nor associated with a defendant or insurance carrier in connection with the petition;

(7) If an action has been filed on the claim:

(A) All defendants that have appeared in the action are participating in the compromise; or

(B) The court has finally determined that the settling parties entered into the settlement in good faith;

(8) The judgment for the minor or disabled claimant (exclusive of interest and costs) or the total amount payable to the minor or disabled claimant and all other parties under the proposed compromise or settlement is $50,000 or less or, if greater:

(A) The total amount payable to the minor or disabled claimant represents payment of the individual-person policy limits of all liability insurance policies covering all proposed contributing parties; and

(B) All proposed contributing parties would be substantially unable to discharge an adverse judgment on the minor's or disabled person's claim from assets other than the proceeds of their liability insurance policies; and

(9) The court does not otherwise order.

(b) Determination of expedited petition

An expedited petition must be determined by the court not more than 35 days after it is filed, unless a hearing is requested, required, or scheduled under (c) or the time for determination is extended for good cause by order of the court.

(c) Hearing on expedited petition

(1) The expedited petition must be determined by the court without a hearing unless a hearing is requested by the petitioner at the time the expedited petition is filed, an objection or other opposition to the petition is filed by an interested party, or a hearing is scheduled by the court under (2) or (3).

(2) The court may on its own motion elect to schedule and conduct a hearing on an expedited petition. The court must make its election to schedule the hearing and must give notice of its election and the date, time, and place of the hearing to the petitioner and all other interested parties not more than 25 days after the date the expedited petition is filed.

(3) If the court decides not to grant an expedited petition in full as requested, it must schedule a hearing and give notice of its intended ruling and the date, time, and place of the hearing to the petitioner and all other interested parties within the time provided in (2). *(Adopted, eff. Jan. 1, 2010.)*

Rule 7.951. Disclosure of the attorney's interest in a petition to compromise a claim

If the petitioner has been represented or assisted by an attorney in preparing the petition to compromise the claim or in any other respect with regard to the claim, the petition must disclose the following information:

(1) The name, state bar number, law firm, if any, and business address of the attorney;

(2) Whether the attorney became involved with the petition, directly or indirectly, at the instance of any party against whom the claim is asserted or of any party's insurance carrier;

(3) Whether the attorney represents or is employed by any other party or any insurance carrier involved in the matter;

(4) Whether the attorney has received any attorney's fees or other compensation for services provided in connection with the claim giving rise to the petition or with the preparation of the petition, and, if so, the amounts and the identity of the person who paid the fees or other compensation;

(5) If the attorney has not received any attorney's fees or other compensation for services provided in connection with the claim giving rise to the petition or with the preparation of the petition, whether the attorney expects to receive any fees or other compensation for these services, and, if so, the amounts and the identity of the person who is expected to pay the fees or other compensation; and

(6) The terms of any agreement between the petitioner and the attorney. *(Adopted, eff. Jan. 1, 2002.)*

Rule 7.952. Attendance at hearing on the petition to compromise a claim

(a) Attendance of the petitioner and claimant

The person compromising the claim on behalf of the minor or person with a disability and the minor or person with a disability must attend the hearing on the compromise of the claim unless the court for good cause dispenses with their personal appearance.

(b) Attendance of the physician and other witnesses

At the hearing, the court may require the presence and testimony of witnesses, including the attending or examining physician. *(Adopted, eff. Jan. 1, 2002. As amended, eff. Jan. 1, 2007.)*

Rule 7.953. Order for the deposit of funds of a minor or a person with a disability

(a) Acknowledgment of receipt by financial institution

In any case in which the court orders that funds to be received by a minor or a person with a disability must be deposited in a financial institution and not disbursed without further order of the court, the order must include a provision that a certified or filed endorsed copy of the order must be delivered to a manager at the financial institution where the funds are to be deposited, and that a receipt from the financial institution must be promptly filed with the court, acknowledging receipt of both the funds deposited and the order for deposit of funds.

(b) Order permitting the withdrawal of funds by a former minor

If, in the order approving the compromise of a minor's claim, there is a finding that the minor will attain the age of majority on a definite date, the order for deposit may require that the depository permit the withdrawal of funds by the former minor after that date, without further order of the court. *(Adopted, eff. Jan. 1, 2002. As amended, eff. Jan. 1, 2007.)*

Rule 7.954. Petition for the withdrawal of funds deposited for a minor or a person with a disability

(a) Verified petition required

A petition for the withdrawal of funds deposited for a minor or a person with a disability must be verified and must include the identity of the depository, a showing of the amounts previously withdrawn, a statement of the balance on deposit at the time of the filing of the petition, and a justification for the withdrawal.

(b) Ex parte or noticed hearing

A petition for the withdrawal of funds may be considered ex parte or set for a hearing at the discretion of the court. *(Adopted, eff. Jan. 1, 2002. As amended, eff. Jan. 1, 2007.)*

Rule 7.955. Attorney's fees for services to a minor or a person with a disability

(a) Reasonable attorney's fees

(1) In all cases under Code of Civil Procedure section 372 or Probate Code sections 3600–3601, unless the court has approved the fee agreement in advance, the court must use a reasonable fee standard when approving and allowing the amount of attorney's fees payable from money or property paid or to be paid for the benefit of a minor or a person with a disability.

(2) The court must give consideration to the terms of any representation agreement made between the attorney and the representative of the minor or person with a disability and must evaluate the agreement based on the facts and circumstances existing at the time the agreement was made, except where the attorney and the representative of the minor or person with a disability contemplated that the attorney's fee would be affected by later events.

(b) Factors the court may consider in determining a reasonable attorney's fee

In determining a reasonable attorney's fee, the court may consider the following nonexclusive factors:

(1) The fact that a minor or person with a disability is involved and the circumstances of that minor or person with a disability.

(2) The amount of the fee in proportion to the value of the services performed.

(3) The novelty and difficulty of the questions involved and the skill required to perform the legal services properly.

(4) The amount involved and the results obtained.

(5) The time limitations or constraints imposed by the representative of the minor or person with a disability or by the circumstances.

(6) The nature and length of the professional relationship between the attorney and the representative of the minor or person with a disability.

(7) The experience, reputation, and ability of the attorney or attorneys performing the legal services.

(8) The time and labor required.

(9) The informed consent of the representative of the minor or person with a disability to the fee.

(10) The relative sophistication of the attorney and the representative of the minor or person with a disability.

(11) The likelihood, if apparent to the representative of the minor or person with a disability when the representation agreement was made, that the attorney's acceptance of the particular employment would preclude other employment.

(12) Whether the fee is fixed, hourly, or contingent.

(13) If the fee is contingent:

(A) The risk of loss borne by the attorney;

(B) The amount of costs advanced by the attorney; and

(C) The delay in payment of fees and reimbursement of costs paid by the attorney.

(14) Statutory requirements for representation agreements applicable to particular cases or claims.

(c) Attorney's declaration

A petition requesting court approval and allowance of an attorney's fee under (a) must include a declaration from the attorney that addresses the factors listed in (b) that are applicable to the matter before the court.

(d) Preemption

The Judicial Council has preempted all local rules relating to the determination of reasonable attorney's fees to be awarded from the proceeds of a compromise, settlement, or judgment under Probate Code sections 3600–3601. No trial court, or any division or branch of a trial court, may enact or enforce any local rule concerning this field, except a rule pertaining to the assignment or scheduling of a hearing on a petition or application for court approval or allowance of attorney's fees under sections 3600–3601. All local rules concerning this field are null and void unless otherwise permitted by a statute or a rule in the California Rules of Court. *(Adopted, eff. Jan. 1, 2003. As amended, eff. Jan. 1, 2007; Jan. 1, 2010.)*

Chapter 21

GUARDIANSHIPS

Cross References

Guardianship, generally, see Probate Code § 1500 et seq.

Rule 7.1001. Guardian screening form

(a) Screening form to be submitted with petition

Each proposed probate guardian, except a public guardian, or a bank or other entity entitled to conduct the business of a trust company, must submit to the court with the petition for appointment of guardian a completed *Confidential Guardian Screening Form* (form GC–212).

(b) Use of form

The information on the *Confidential Guardian Screening Form* is used by the court and by persons or agencies designated by the court to assist the court in determining whether a proposed guardian should be appointed.

(c) Form to be confidential

The *Confidential Guardian Screening Form* and the information contained on the form are confidential. The clerk must maintain these forms in a manner that will protect and preserve their confidentiality. *(Adopted, eff. Jan. 1, 2001. As amended, eff. Jan. 1, 2002; Jan. 1, 2007.)*

Rule 7.1002. Acknowledgment of receipt of *Duties of Guardian*

Before the court issues letters, each guardian must execute and file an acknowledgment of receipt of the *Duties of Guardian* (form GC–248). *(Adopted, eff. Jan. 1, 2001. As amended, eff. Jan. 1, 2002; Jan. 1, 2007; July 1, 2016.)*

Rule 7.1002.5. Guardianship of ward 18 to 20 years of age

(a) Authority

The court may extend an existing guardianship of the person past a ward's 18th birthday or appoint a new guardian of the person for a ward who is at least 18 but not yet 21 years of age if the ward is the petitioner or has given consent as provided in section 1510.1 of the Probate Code and this rule.

(b) Consent to appointment of guardian of the person

The court may appoint a new guardian of the person under this rule only if the ward has given consent, both to the appointment and to the guardian's performance of the duties of a guardian, by signing the petition.

(c) Consent to extension of guardianship of the person

The court may extend a guardianship of the person under this rule only if the ward has given consent, both to the extension and to the guardian's continued performance of the duties of a guardian, by signing the *Petition to Extend Guardianship of the Person* (form GC–210(PE)).

(d) Dispute

In the event of a dispute over the guardian's intended action, the guardian may not act against the ward's desires without the ward's express consent unless failure to act as intended would breach the guardian's fiduciary duties to the ward.

(e) Modification of consent

(1) A ward may withdraw his or her consent to the establishment or extension of a guardianship under this rule by filing a petition to terminate the guardianship under rule 7.1004(b)(2)(B).

(2) In addition to any other petition authorized by section 2359(a), the ward may file a petition at any time during a guardianship established or extended under this rule to withdraw or modify his or her consent to the guardian's performance of a specific duty or duties. *(Adopted, eff. July 1, 2016.)*

Rule 7.1003. Confidential guardianship status report form

(a) Due date of status report

Each guardian required by the court to complete, sign, and file the status report authorized by Probate Code section 1513.2 must file the completed and signed report no later than one month after the anniversary of the date of the order appointing him or her as guardian. Co–guardians may sign and file their reports jointly.

(b) Court clerk's duties

The clerk of each court that requires guardians to file the status report authorized by Probate Code section 1513.2 must:

(1) Determine the annual due date for the completed report from each appointed guardian required to file the report;

(2) Fill in the due date for the completed report, in the space provided in the form for that purpose, on each blank copy of the form that must be mailed to appointed guardians under (3); and

(3) Mail by first class mail to each appointed guardian no later than one month prior to the date the status report is due under (a) a blank copy of *Confidential Guardianship Status Report* (form GC–251) for each child under guardianship under the same case number. *(Adopted, eff. Jan. 1, 2004. As amended, eff. Jan. 1, 2007.)*

Rule 7.1004. Termination of guardianship

(a) Operation of law or court order

A guardianship of the person or estate of a minor may terminate by operation of law or may be terminated by court order where the court determines that it would be in the ward's best interest to terminate the guardianship.

(b) Guardian of the person

(1) Under Probate Code section 1600 a guardianship of the person terminates by operation of law, and the guardian

of the person need not file a petition for its termination, when the ward attains majority <u>except as provided in (2)</u>, dies, is adopted, or is emancipated.

<u>(2) If the court has appointed a guardian of the person for a ward 18 years of age or older or extended a guardianship of the person past the ward's 18th birthday, the guardianship terminates:</u>

<u>(A) By operation of law when the ward attains 21 years of age, marries, or dies; or</u>

<u>(B) By order of the court when the ward files a petition under Probate Code section 1601.</u>

(c) Duty of guardian of estate on termination

A guardian of the estate whose administration is terminated by operation of law or court order must file and obtain the court's approval of a final account or report of the administration. *(Adopted, eff. Jan. 1, 2004. As amended, eff. July 1, 2016.)*

Rule 7.1005. Service of copy of final account or report after resignation or removal of guardian

A resigned or removed guardian of the estate must serve a copy of the guardian's final account or report and the petition for its settlement, with the notice of hearing that must be served on the successor guardian of the estate under Probate Code section 1460(b)(1), unless the court dispenses with such service. *(Adopted, eff. Jan. 1, 2004.)*

Rule 7.1006. Service of copy of final account on termination of guardianship

(a) Minor living

In addition to service of notices of hearing required under Probate Code section 1460(b), on termination of the guardianship the guardian of the estate must serve a copy of the guardian's final account and petition for its settlement on the minor, unless the court dispenses with such service.

(b) Personal representative of deceased minor

If the minor is deceased, in addition to service of notices of hearing required under Probate Code section 1460(b), on termination of the guardianship the guardian of the estate must serve a notice of hearing and a copy of the guardian's final account and petition for its settlement on the personal representative of the deceased minor's estate, unless the court dispenses with such service.

(c) Successors in interest to deceased minor

If the minor is deceased and no personal representative of the minor's estate has been appointed or qualified or if the personal representative of the minor's estate is also the guardian, on termination of the guardianship, in addition to the notices of hearing required under Probate Code section 1460(b), the guardian of the estate must serve a notice of hearing and a copy of the guardian's final account and petition for its settlement on the persons entitled to succeed to the deceased minor's estate, unless the court dispenses with such service. *(Adopted, eff. Jan. 1, 2004.)*

Rule 7.1007. Settlement of accounts and release by former minor

(a) Release of guardian of estate by ward after majority

A ward who has attained majority may settle accounts with his or her guardian of the estate and may give a valid release to the guardian if the court determines, at the time of the hearing on the final account, or on the final report and petition for termination on waiver of account, that the release has been obtained fairly and without undue influence. The release is not effective to discharge the guardian until one year after the ward has attained majority.

(b) Appearance of ward

The court may require the personal appearance of the ward at the hearing on the final account or report of the guardian of the estate after termination of the guardianship. *(Adopted, eff. Jan. 1, 2004.)*

Rule 7.1008. Visitation by former guardian after termination of guardianship

(a) Visitation order at time of termination of guardianship

Subject to the provisions of Welfare and Institutions Code section 304, a guardian may request the court to order visitation with the child under guardianship at the time of termination of the guardianship either in the guardian's petition for termination or in the guardian's objections or other pleading filed in response to the petition of another party for termination. The court may then order visitation if it is in the best interest of the child.

(b) Request for visitation after termination of guardianship

If no order was entered under (a) concerning visitation between the former guardian and the former ward at termination of the guardianship and no dependency proceedings for the child are pending, the former guardian may request the court to order visitation with the former ward after termination of the guardianship as provided in Family Code section 3105, Probate Code section 1602, rule 5.475, and this rule, as follows:

(1) If either parent of the former ward is living, in an independent action for visitation under the Family Code; or

(2) If neither parent of the former ward is living, in a guardianship proceeding under the Probate Code, including a proceeding commenced for that purpose.

(c) Declaration under UCCJEA

A guardian or former guardian requesting visitation under this rule must file a *Declaration Under Uniform Child Custody Jurisdiction and Enforcement Act (UCCJEA)* (form FL–105/GC–120) with his or her request for visitation.

(d) Transmission of visitation order

Following the termination of the guardianship the clerk of the superior court issuing the visitation order concerning the guardian or former guardian and the ward or former ward must promptly transmit an endorsed filed copy of the order to the superior court of the county where a custody proceeding under the Family Code is pending or, if none, to the superior court of the county in which the custodial parent resides. An order transmitted to the court in the county where the custodial parent resides may be sent to the receiving court's Court Operations Manager, Family Division, or similar senior manager or clerk responsible for the operations of the family law departments of the court. If the receiving court has more than one location, the order may be sent to the main or central district of the court. *(Adopted, eff. Jan. 1, 2006. As amended, eff. Jan. 1, 2007.)*

Rule 7.1009. Standards of conduct for the guardian of the estate

Except as otherwise required by statute, in the exercise of ordinary care and diligence in managing and controlling the estates of the ward, the guardian of the estate is to be guided by the following principles:

(a) Avoidance of actual and apparent conflicts of interest with the ward

The guardian must avoid actual conflicts of interest and, consistent with his or her fiduciary duty to the ward, the appearance of conflicts of interest. The guardian must avoid any personal, business, or professional interest or relationship that is or reasonably could be perceived as being self-serving or adverse to the best interest of the ward. In particular:

(1) Except as appropriate for guardians who are not professional fiduciaries with full disclosure to the court, the guardian should not personally provide medical or legal services to the ward;

(2) The guardian must be independent from all service providers, except when (a) no other guardian or service providers are reasonably available, (b) the exception is in the best interest of the ward, (c) the circumstances are fully disclosed to the court, and (d) prior court approval has been obtained;

(3) The guardian must neither solicit nor accept incentives from service providers; and

(4) The guardian must not engage his or her family members to provide services to the ward for a profit or fee when other alternatives are reasonably available. Where family members do provide such services, their relationship to the guardian must be fully disclosed to the court, the terms of engagement must be in the best interest of the ward compared to the terms available from independent service providers, the services must be competently performed, and the guardian must be able to exercise appropriate control and supervision.

A guardian's employees, including family members, are not service providers and are not providing services to the ward for a profit or fee within the meaning of this rule if their compensation is paid by the guardian and their services are either included in the guardian's petition for allowance of the guardian's compensation or are not paid from the ward's estate.

(b) Guardianship estate management

In addition to complying with applicable standards of estate management specified in rule 7.1059(b), the guardian of the estate must:

(1) Manage the estate primarily for the ward's long-term benefit if the ward has a parent available who can provide sufficient support;

(2) If it would be in the best interest of the ward and the estate, consider requesting court authority to support the ward from the estate if the ward does not have a parent

available who can provide sufficient support. *(Adopted, eff. Jan. 1, 2008.)*

Rule 7.1011. Taking possession of an asset of the ward at an institution or opening or changing ownership of an account or safe-deposit box in a financial institution

(a) Definitions

As used in this rule, the following terms have the meanings stated below:

(1) An "institution" is an insurance company, insurance broker, insurance agent, investment company, investment bank, securities broker-dealer, investment advisor, financial planner, financial advisor, or any other person who takes, holds, or controls an asset subject to a guardianship that is not a "financial institution" within the meaning of this rule;

(2) A "financial institution" is a bank, trust (except as provided in (d)), savings and loan association, savings bank, industrial bank, or credit union; and

(3) "Taking possession" or "taking control" of an asset held or controlled by an institution includes changing title to the asset, withdrawing all or any portion of the asset, or transferring all or any portion of the asset from the institution.

(b) Responsibilities of the guardian when taking possession or control of an asset of the ward at an institution

When taking possession or control of an asset held by an institution in the name of the ward, the temporary or general guardian of the estate must provide the following to the institution:

(1) A certified copy of the guardian's *Letters of Temporary Guardianship or Conservatorship* (form GC–150) or *Letters of Guardianship* (form GC–250) containing the Notice to Institutions and Financial Institutions on the second page; and

(2) A blank copy of a *Notice of Taking Possession or Control of an Asset of Minor or Conservatee* (form GC–050).

(c) Responsibilities of the guardian when opening or changing the name on an account or a safe-deposit box in a financial institution

When opening or changing the name on an account or a safe-deposit box in a financial institution, the temporary or general guardian of the estate must provide the following to the financial institution:

(1) A certified copy of the guardian's *Letters of Temporary Guardianship or Conservatorship* (form GC–150) or *Letters of Guardianship* (form GC–250) containing the Notice to Institutions and Financial Institutions on the second page; and

(2) A blank copy of a *Notice of Opening or Changing a Guardianship or Conservatorship Account or Safe–Deposit Box* (form GC–051).

(d) Application of this rule to trust arrangements

This rule applies to Totten trust accounts but does not apply to any other trust arrangement described in Probate Code section 82(b). *(Adopted, eff. Jan. 1, 2009.)*

Rule 7.1012. The good cause exception to notice of the hearing on a petition for appointment of a temporary guardian

(a) Purpose

The purpose of this rule is to establish uniform standards for the good cause exception to the notice of the hearing required on a petition for appointment of a temporary guardian under Probate Code section 2250(e).

(b) Good cause for exceptions to notice limited

Good cause for an exception to the notice required by section 2250(e) must be based on a showing that the exception is necessary to protect the proposed ward or his or her estate from immediate and substantial harm.

(c) Court may waive or change the time or manner of giving notice

An exception to the notice requirement of section 2250(e) may include one or any combination of the following:

(1) Waiving notice to one, more than one, or all persons entitled to notice;

(2) Requiring a different period of notice; and

(3) Changing the required manner of giving notice, including requiring notice by telephone, fax, e-mail, or a combination of these methods, instead of notice by personal delivery to the proposed ward's parents or to a person with a visitation order.

(d) Good cause exceptions to notice

Good cause for an exception to the notice requirement of section 2250(e) may include a showing of:

(1) Harm caused by the passage of time. The showing must demonstrate the immediate and substantial harm to the ward or the ward's estate that could occur during the notice period.

(2) Harm that one or more persons entitled to notice might do to the proposed ward, including abduction; or harm to the proposed ward's estate if notice to those persons is given. Such a showing would not support an exception to the requirement to give notice to any other person entitled to notice unless it also demonstrates that notice cannot reasonably be given to the other person without also giving notice to the persons who might cause harm.

(3) The death or incapacity of the proposed ward's custodial parent and the petitioner's status as the custodial parent's nominee.

(4) Medical emergency. The emergency must be immediate and substantial and treatment (1) must be reasonably unavailable unless a temporary guardian is appointed and (2) cannot be deferred for the notice period because of the proposed ward's pain or extreme discomfort or a significant risk of harm.

(5) Financial emergency. The emergency must be immediate and substantial and other means shown likely to be ineffective to prevent loss or further loss to the proposed ward's estate or loss of support for the proposed ward during the notice period.

(e) Contents of request for good cause exception to notice

(1) When the temporary guardianship petition is prepared on the *Petition for Appointment of Temporary Guardian* (form GC–110), a request for a good cause exception to the notice requirement of section 2250(e) must be in writing, separate from the petition for appointment of a temporary guardian, and must include:

(A) An application containing the case caption and stating the relief requested;

(B) An affirmative factual showing in support of the application in a declaration under penalty of perjury containing competent testimony based on personal knowledge;

(C) A declaration under penalty of perjury based on personal knowledge containing the information required for an ex parte application under rule 3.1204(b); and

(D) A proposed order.

(2) When the temporary guardianship petition is prepared on the *Petition for Appointment of Temporary Guardian of the Person* (form GC–110(P)), a request for a good cause exception to the notice requirement of section 2250(e) may be included in the petition. *(Adopted, eff. Jan. 1, 2008. As amended, eff. Jan. 1, 2009.)*

Rule 7.1013. Change of ward's residence

(a) Pre–move notice of change of personal residence required

Unless an emergency requires a shorter period of notice, the guardian of the person must mail copies of a notice of an intended change of the ward's personal residence to the persons listed below at least 15 days before the date of the proposed change, and file the original notice with proof of mailing with the court. Copies of the notice must be mailed to:

(1) The ward if he or she is 12 years of age or older;

(2) The attorney of record for the ward;

(3) The ward's parents;

(4) Any person who had legal custody of the ward when the first petition for appointment of a guardian was filed in the proceeding;

(5) A guardian of the ward's estate; and

(6) Any person who was nominated as guardian of the ward under Probate Code sections 1500 or 1501 but was not appointed guardian in the proceeding.

(b) Ward's personal residence

The "ward's personal residence" under (a) is the ward's residence when the first petition for appointment of a guardian was filed in the proceeding.

(c) Post–move notice of a change of residence required

The guardian of the person of a minor must file a notice of a change of the ward's residence with the court within 30 days of the date of any change. Unless waived by the court for good cause to prevent harm to the ward, the guardian, the guardian's attorney, or an employee of the guardian's attorney must also mail a copy of the notice to the persons listed below and file a proof of mailing with the original notice. Unless waived, copies of the notice must be mailed to:

(1) The ward's attorney of record;

(2) The ward's parents;

(3) Any person who had legal custody of the ward when the first petition for appointment of a guardian was filed in the proceeding;

(4) A guardian of the ward's estate; and

(5) Any person who was nominated as guardian of the ward under Probate Code sections 1500 or 1501 but was not appointed guardian in the proceeding.

(d) Ward's residence

The "ward's residence" under (c) is the ward's residence at any time after appointment of a guardian.

(e) Use of Judicial Council forms GC–079 and GC–080

(1) The *Pre–Move Notice of Proposed Change of Personal Residence of Conservatee or Ward* (form GC–079) must be used for the pre-move notice required under (a) and Probate Code section 2352(e)(3). The guardian, the guardian's attorney, or an employee of the attorney may complete the mailing and sign the proof of mailing on page 2 of the form. If the notice is mailed less than 15 days before the date of the move because an emergency requires a shorter period of notice, the basis for the emergency must be stated in the notice.

(2) The *Post–Move Notice of Change of Residence of Conservatee or Ward* (form GC–080) must be used for the post-move notice required under (c) and Probate Code section 2352(e)(1) and (2). The guardian, the guardian's attorney, or an employee of the attorney may complete the mailing and sign the proof of mailing on page 2 of the form.

(f) Prior court approval required to establish ward's residence outside California

Notwithstanding any other provision of this rule, prior court approval is required before a ward's residence may be established outside the state of California.

(g) Wards 18 to 20 years of age

For a ward who is at least 18 but not yet 21 years of age, a copy of any notice under this rule must be mailed only to the ward and the ward's attorney of record. *(Adopted, eff. Jan. 1, 2008. As amended, eff. July 1, 2016.)*

Rule 7.1014. Communications between courts in different California counties concerning guardianship venue

(a) Purpose of rule

This rule addresses the communications between courts concerning guardianship venue required by Probate Code section 2204(b). These communications are between the superior court in one California county where a guardianship proceeding has been filed (referred to in this rule as the guardianship court) and one or more superior courts in one or more other California counties where custody or visitation proceedings under the Family Code involving the ward or proposed ward were previously filed (referred to in this rule as the family court or courts, or the other court or courts).

(b) Substantive communications between judicial officers

Before making a venue decision on a petition for appointment of a general guardian in a guardianship proceeding described in (a), or a decision on a petition to transfer under Probate Code section 2212 filed in the proceeding before the appointment of a guardian or temporary guardian, the judicial officer responsible for the proceeding in the guardianship court must communicate with the judicial officer or officers responsible for the custody proceeding or proceedings in the family court or courts concerning which county provides the venue for the guardianship proceeding that is in the best interests of the ward or the proposed ward.

(1) If the currently responsible judicial officer in the family court or courts cannot be identified, communication must be made with the managing or supervising judicial officer of the family departments of the other court or courts, if any, or his or her designee, or with the presiding judge of the other court or courts or his or her designee.

(2) If courts in more than two counties are involved, simultaneous communications among judicial officers of all of the courts are recommended, if reasonably practicable. If communications occur between some but not all involved courts, the record of these communications must be made available to those judicial officers of the courts who were not included at or before the time the judicial officer of the guardianship court communicates with them.

(3) A record must be made of all communications between judicial officers under this subdivision.

(4) The parties to the guardianship proceeding, including a petitioner for transfer; all persons entitled to notice of the hearing on the petition for appointment of a guardian; and any additional persons ordered by the guardianship court must promptly be informed of the communications and given access to the record of the communications.

(5) The provisions of Family Code section 3410(b) apply to communications between judicial officers under this subdivision, except that the term "jurisdiction" in that section corresponds to "venue" in this context, and the term "parties" in that section identifies the persons listed in (4).

(c) Preliminary communications

To assist the judicial officer in making the communication required in (b), the guardianship court may have preliminary communications with each family court to collect information about the proceeding in that court or for other routine matters, including calendar management, and scheduling.

(1) The guardianship court should attempt to collect, and each family court is encouraged to provide, as much of the following information about the proceeding in the family court as is reasonable under the circumstances:

(A) The case number or numbers and the nature of each family court proceeding;

(B) The names of the parties to each family court proceeding, including contact information for self-represented parties; their relationship or other connection to the ward or proposed ward in the guardianship proceeding, and the names and contact information of counsel for any parties represented by counsel;

(C) The current status (active or inactive) of each family court proceeding, whether any future hearings are set in each proceeding, and if so, their dates and times, locations, and nature;

(D) The contents and dates filed of orders in the each family court proceeding that decide or resolve custody or visitation issues concerning the ward or proposed ward in the guardianship proceeding;

(E) Whether any orders of each family court are final, were appealed from, or were the subject of extraordinary writ proceedings, and the current status of any such appeal or proceeding;

(F) The court branch and department where each family court proceeding was assigned and where the proceeding is currently assigned or pending;

(G) The identity of the judicial officer currently assigned to or otherwise responsible for each family court proceeding; and

(H) Other information about each family court proceeding requested by the judicial officer of the guardianship court.

(2) In the discretion of the judicial officer of the guardianship court, preliminary communications under this rule may be between judicial officers of the courts involved or between staff of the guardianship court and judicial officers or court staff of each other court.

(3) Family Code section 3410(c) applies to preliminary communications under this rule.

(d) Applicability of this rule to petitions to transfer filed after the appointment of a guardian or temporary guardian

Subdivisions (b) and (c) of this rule may, in the discretion of the guardianship court, apply to petitions for transfer described in Probate Code section 2204(b)(2).

(e) "Record" under this rule

"Record" under this rule has the meaning provided in Family Code section 3410(e). *(Adopted, eff. Jan. 1, 2013.)*

Rule 7.1015. Indian Child Welfare Act in guardianship and certain conservatorship proceedings

(a) Definitions

As used in this rule, unless the context or subject matter otherwise requires:

(1) "Act" means the Indian Child Welfare Act (25 United States Code sections 1901–1963).

(2) "Petitioner" means and refers to a petitioner for the appointment of a guardian of the person of a child or a petitioner for the appointment of a conservator of the person of a formerly married minor child.

(b) Applicability of this rule and rules 5.480 through 5.487

(1) This rule applies to the following proceedings under division 4 of the Probate Code when the proposed ward or conservatee is an Indian child, within the meaning of the act:

(A) A guardianship of the person or the person and estate in which the proposed guardian of the person is not the proposed ward's natural parent or Indian custodian within the meaning of the act;

(B) A conservatorship of the person or the person and estate of a formerly married minor in which the proposed conservator is not a natural parent or Indian custodian of the minor and is seeking physical custody of the proposed conservatee.

(2) Unless the context otherwise requires, rules 5.480 through 5.487 apply to the proceedings listed in (1).

(3) When applied to the proceedings listed in (1), references in rules 5.480 through 5.487 to social workers, probation officers, county probation departments, or county social welfare departments are references to the petitioner or petitioners for the appointment of a guardian or conservator of the person of an Indian child and to an Indian child's appointed temporary or general guardian or conservator of the person.

(4) If the court appoints a temporary or general guardian or conservator of the person of the child involved in a proceeding listed in (1), the duties and responsibilities of a petitioner under this rule are transferred to and become the duties and responsibilities of the appointed guardian or conservator. The petitioner must cooperate with and provide any information the petitioner has concerning the child to the appointed guardian or conservator.

(c) Notice

If, at any time after the filing of a petition for appointment of a guardian or conservator for a minor child, the court or petitioner knows or has reason to know, within the meaning of Probate Code sections 1449 and 1459.5 and Welfare and Institutions Code section 224.3(b), that an Indian child is involved, the petitioner and the court must notify the child's parents or legal guardian and Indian custodian, and the Indian child's tribe, of the pending proceeding and the right of the tribe to intervene, as follows:

(1) Notice to the Indian child's parents, Indian custodian, and Indian tribe of the commencement of a guardianship or conservatorship must be given by serving copies of the completed *Notice of Child Custody Proceeding for Indian Child* (form ICWA–030), the petition for appointment of a guardian or conservator, and all attachments, by certified or registered mail, fully prepaid with return receipt requested.

(2) The petitioner and his or her attorney, if any, must complete the *Notice* and the petitioner must date and sign the declaration. If there is more than one petitioner, the statements about the child's ancestors and background provided in the *Notice of Child Custody Proceeding for Indian Child* (form ICWA–030) must be based on all information known to each petitioner, and all petitioners must sign the declaration.

(3) When the petitioner is represented by an attorney in the proceeding, the attorney must serve copies of the *Notice of Child Custody Proceeding for Indian Child* (form ICWA–030) in the manner described in (1) and sign the declaration of mailing on the *Notice*.

(4) When the guardianship or conservatorship petitioner or petitioners are not represented by an attorney in the proceeding, the clerk of the court must serve the *Notice* in the manner described in (1) and sign the certificate of mailing on the *Notice*.

(5) The original of all *Notices of Child Custody Proceeding for Indian Child* (form ICWA–030) served under the act, and all return receipts and responses received, must be filed with the court before the hearing.

(6) Notice to an Indian child's tribe must be sent to the tribal chairperson unless the tribe has designated another agent for service.

(7) Notice must be served on all tribes of which the child may be a member or eligible for membership. If there are more tribes or bands to be served than can be listed on the last page of the *Notice*, the additional tribes or bands may be listed on an *Attachment to Notice of Child Custody Proceeding for Indian Child* (form ICWA–030(A)).

(8) Notice under the act must be served whenever there is any reason to know that the child is or may be an Indian child and for every hearing after the first hearing unless and until it is determined that the act does not apply to the proceeding.

(9) If, after a reasonable time following the service of notice under the act—but in no event less than 60 days—no determinative response to the *Notice of Child Custody Proceeding for Indian Child* (form ICWA–030) is received, the court may determine that the act does not apply to the proceeding unless further evidence of its applicability is later received.

(10) If an Indian child's tribe intervenes in the proceeding, service of the *Notice of Child Custody Proceeding for Indian Child* (form ICWA–030) is no longer required and subsequent notices to the tribe may be sent to all parties in the form and in the manner required under the Probate Code and these rules. All other provisions of the act, this rule, and rules 5.480 through 5.487 continue to apply.

(11) Notice under the act must be served in addition to all notices otherwise required for the particular proceeding under the provisions of the Probate Code.

(d) Duty of inquiry

(1) The court, a court investigator or county officer appointed to conduct an investigation under Probate Code section 1513 or 1826, a petitioner, and an appointed temporary or general guardian or conservator of the person of a minor child each have an affirmative and continuing duty to inquire whether the child involved in the matters identified in (b)(1) is or may be an Indian child.

(2) Before filing his or her petition, the petitioner must ask the child involved in the proceeding, if the child is old enough, and the parents, any other legal guardian, and any Indian custodian, whether the child is or may be an Indian child, and must complete items 1c and 8 of the *Guardianship Petition—Child Information Attachment* (form GC–210(CA)) and attach it to his or her petition.

(3) At the first personal appearance by a parent or previously appointed legal guardian at a hearing in a guardianship or conservatorship, the court must if requested by petitioner, or may on its own motion, order the parent or legal guardian to complete a *Parental Notification of Indian Status* (form ICWA–020) and deliver the completed form to the petitioner.

(4) If the parent, Indian custodian, or guardian does not personally appear at a hearing in a proceeding identified in (b)(1), the court may order the petitioner to use reasonable diligence to find and ask the parent, Indian custodian, or legal guardian to complete and deliver to petitioner a *Parental Notification of Indian Status* (form ICWA–020).

(5) If the court or county investigator, petitioner, appointed guardian or conservator, or the attorney for a petitioner or appointed guardian or conservator, knows or has reason to

know that an Indian child is involved in the proceeding, he or she must make further inquiry as soon as practicable by:

(A) Interviewing the parents, Indian custodian, and "extended family members" as defined in 25 United States Code section 1903(2), to gather the information listed in Probate Code section 1460.2(b)(5) that is required to complete the *Notice of Child Custody Proceeding for Indian Child* (form ICWA–030);

(B) Contacting the U.S. Department of the Interior, Bureau of Indian Affairs and the California Department of Social Services for assistance in identifying the names and contact information of the tribes of which the child may be a member or eligible for membership; and

(C) Contacting the tribes and any other person who reasonably can be expected to have information regarding the child's tribal membership status or eligibility for membership.

(6) If the court knows or has reason to know that an Indian child is involved in the proceeding, the court may direct any of the persons named in (5) to conduct the inquiry described in that paragraph.

(7) The circumstances that may provide reason to know the child is an Indian child include the following:

(A) The child or person having an interest in the child, including an Indian tribe, an Indian organization, an officer of the court, a public or private agency, or a member of the child's extended family, informs or otherwise provides information suggesting that the child is an Indian child to the court or to any person listed in (5);

(B) The residence or domicile of the child, the child's parents, or an Indian custodian is in a predominantly Indian community; or

(C) The child or the child's family has received services or benefits from a tribe or services that are available to Indians from tribes or the federal government, such as the U.S. Department of Health and Human Services, Indian Health Service, or Tribal Temporary Assistance to Needy Families benefits.

(Adopted, eff. Jan. 1, 2008. As amended, eff. July 1, 2012.)

Rule 7.1016. Participation and testimony of wards in guardianship proceedings

(a) Definitions

As used in this rule, the following terms have the meanings specified:

(1) "Ward" includes "proposed ward."

(2) A "proceeding" is a matter before the court for decision in a probate guardianship of the person that concerns appointment or removal of a guardian, visitation, determination of the ward's place of residence, or termination of the guardianship by court order.

(3) "Party," as used in this rule to refer to the ward, means a ward who has filed a petition or opposition to a petition concerning a proceeding or other matter subject to this rule.

(b) Purpose and scope of rule

(1) This rule applies Family Code section 3042 to the participation and testimony of the ward in a proceeding in a probate guardianship of the person. The testimony of other

minors in a guardianship case is governed by Evidence Code sections 765(b) and 767(b).

(2) The court in its discretion may apply this rule, in whole or in part, to the participation and testimony of a ward in a guardianship of the estate or in a matter before the court in a guardianship of the person that is not a proceeding within the meaning of this rule. The phrase "or other matter subject to this is rule" following the term "proceeding" is a reference to the matters described in this paragraph.

(3) No statutory mandate, rule, or practice requires a ward who is not a party to the proceeding or other matter subject to this rule to participate in court or prohibits him or her from doing so. When a ward desires to participate but is not a party to the proceeding or other matter subject to this rule, the court must balance the protection of the ward, the statutory duty to consider the wishes of and input from the ward, and the probative value of the ward's input while ensuring all parties' due process rights to challenge evidence relied on by the court in making decisions affecting the ward in matters covered by the rule.

(4) This rule rather than rule 5.250, on children's participation and testimony in family court proceedings, applies in probate guardianship proceedings.

(c) Determining whether the nonparty ward wishes to address the court

(1) The following persons must inform the court if they have information indicating that a ward who is not a party wishes to address the court in a proceeding or other matter subject to this rule:

(A) The ward's counsel;

(B) A court or county guardianship investigator;

(C) A child custody recommending counselor who provides recommendations to the judicial officer under Family Code section 3183;

(D) An expert appointed by the court under Evidence Code section 730 to assist the court in the matter; or

(E) The ward's guardian ad litem.

(2) The following persons may inform the court if they have information indicating that a ward who is not a party wishes to address the court in a proceeding or other matter subject to this rule:

(A) A party in the guardianship case; and

(B) An attorney for a party in the guardianship case.

(3) In the absence of information indicating that a ward who is not a party wishes to address the court in a proceeding or other matter subject to this rule, the judicial officer may inquire whether the ward wishes to do so.

(d) Guidelines for determining whether addressing the court is in the nonparty ward's best interest

(1) When a ward who is not a party indicates that he or she wishes to address the court, the judicial officer must consider whether involving the ward in the proceeding or other matter subject to this rule is in the ward's best interest.

(2) If the ward is 12 years old or older, the judicial officer must hear from the ward unless the court makes a finding that addressing the court is not in the ward's best interest and states the reasons on the record.

(3) In determining whether addressing the court is in the ward's best interest, the judicial officer should consider the following:

(A) Whether the ward is of sufficient age and capacity to form an intelligent preference as to the matter to be decided;

(B) Whether the ward is of sufficient age and capacity to understand the nature of testimony;

(C) Whether information has been presented indicating that the ward may be at risk emotionally if he or she is permitted or denied the opportunity to address the court or that the ward may benefit from addressing the court;

(D) Whether the subject areas about which the ward is anticipated to address the court are relevant to the decision the court must make;

(E) Whether the appointment of counsel under Probate Code section 1470 or a guardian ad litem for the ward would be helpful to the determination or would be necessary to protect the ward's interests; and

(F) Whether any other factors weigh in favor of or against having the ward address the court, taking into consideration the ward's desire to do so.

(e) Guidelines for receiving testimony and other input from the nonparty ward

(1) No testimony of a ward may y be received without such testimony being heard on the record or in the presence of the parties. This requirement may not be waived.

(2) On deciding to take the testimony of a ward who is not a party in a proceeding or other matter subject to this rule, the judicial officer should balance the necessity of taking the ward's testimony in the courtroom with parents, the guardian or proposed guardian, other parties, and attorneys present with the need to create an environment in which the ward can be open and honest. In each case in which a ward's testimony will be taken, the judicial officer should consider:

(A) Where the testimony will be taken;

(B) Who should be present when the testimony is taken;

(C) How the ward will be questioned; and

(D) Whether a court reporter is available in all instances, but especially when the ward's testimony may be taken outside the presence of the parties and their attorneys. If the court reporter will not be available, whether there are other means to collect, preserve, transcribe, and make the ward's testimony available to parties and their attorneys.

(3) In taking testimony from a ward who is not a party to the proceeding or other matter subject to this rule, the court must take the special care required by Evidence Code section 765(b). If the ward is not represented by an attorney, the court must inform the ward in an age-appropriate manner about the limitations on confidentiality of testimony and that the information provided to the court will be on the record and provided to the parties in the case.

(4) In the process of listening to and inviting the ward's input, the court must allow but not require the ward to state a preference regarding the matter to be decided in the proceeding or other matter subject to this rule and should provide information in an age-appropriate manner about the process by which the court will make a decision.

(5) In any case in which a ward who is not a party to the proceeding or other matter subject to this rule will be called to testify, the court must consider the appointment of counsel for the ward under Probate Code section 1470 and may consider the appointment of a guardian ad litem for the ward. In addition to satisfying the requirements for minor's counsel under rule 7. 1101, minor's counsel must:

(A) Provide information to the ward in an age-appropriate manner about the limitations on the confidentiality of testimony and indicate to the ward the possibility that information provided to the court will be on the record and provided to the parties in the case;

(B) Allow but not require the ward to state a preference regarding the issues to be decided in the proceeding or other matter subject to this rule, and provide information in an age-appropriate manner about the process by which the court will make a decision;

(C) If appropriate, provide the ward with an orientation to the courtroom or other place where the ward will testify; and

(D) Inform the parties and the court about the ward's desire to provide input.

(6) If the court precludes the calling of a ward who is not a party as a witness in a proceeding or other matter subject to this rule, alternatives for the court to obtain information or other input from the ward may include:

(A) A court or county guardianship investigator participating in the case under Probate Code section 1513 or 1513.2;

(B) Appointment of a child custody evaluator or investigator under Evidence Code section 730;

(C) Appointment of counsel or a guardian ad litem for the ward;

(D) Admissible evidence provided by the ward's parents, parties, or witnesses in the proceeding or other matter subject to this rule;

(E) Information provided by a child custody recommending counselor authorized under Family Code section 3183 to make a recommendation to the court; and

(F) Information provided from a child interview center or professional to avoid unnecessary multiple interviews.

(7) If the court precludes the calling of a ward who is not a party as a witness in a proceeding or other matter subject to this rule and specifies one of the other alternatives, the court must require that the information or evidence obtained by alternative means and provided by a professional (other than counsel for the ward or counsel for any party) or a nonparty:

(A) Be in writing and fully document the ward's views on the matters on which he or she wished to express an opinion;

(B) Describe the ward's input in sufficient detail to assist the court in making its decision;

(C) Be provided to the court and to the parties by a person who will be available for testimony and cross-examination; and

(D) Be filed in the confidential portion of the case file.

(f) Responsibilities of court-connected or appointed professionals—all wards

A child custody evaluator, an expert witness appointed under Evidence Code section 730, an investigator, a child custody recommending counselor or other custody mediator appointed or assigned to meet with a ward must:

(1) Provide information to the ward in an age-appropriate manner about the limitations on confidentiality of testimony and the possibility that information provided to the professional may be shared with the court on the record and provided to the parties in the case;

(2) Allow but not require the ward to state a preference regarding the issues to be decided in the proceeding or other matter subject to this rule, and provide information in an age-appropriate manner about the process by which the court will make a decision; and

(3) Provide to the other parties in the case information about how best to support the interest of the ward during the court process.

(g) Methods of providing information to parties and supporting nonparty wards

Courts should provide information to the parties and the ward who is not a party to the proceeding or other matter subject to this rule when the ward wants to participate or testify. Methods of providing information may include:

(1) Having court or county guardianship investigators and experts appointed under Evidence Code section 730 meet jointly or separately with the parties and their attorneys to discuss alternatives to having the ward provide direct testimony;

(2) Providing an orientation for the ward about the court process and the role of the judicial officer in making decisions, how the courtroom or chambers will be set up, and what participating or testifying will entail;

(3) Providing information to parties before the ward participates or testifies so that they can consider the possible effect on the ward of participating or not participating in the proceeding or other matter subject to this rule;

(4) Appointing counsel under Probate Code section 1470 or a guardian ad litem for the ward to assist in the provision of information to the ward concerning his or her decision to participate in the proceeding or testify;

(5) Including information in guardianship orientation presentations and publications about the options available to a ward who is not a party to the proceeding or other matter subject to this rule to participate or testify or not to do so, and the consequences of a ward's decision whether to become a party to the proceeding or other matter subject to this rule; and

(6) Providing an interpreter for the ward.

(h) If the ward is a party to the proceeding

(1) A ward who is a party to the proceeding or other matter subject to this rule is subject to the law of discovery applied to parties in civil actions and may be called as a witness by any other party unless the court makes a finding that providing information in response to discovery requests or testifying as a witness is not in the ward's best interest and states the reasons on the record.

(2) The court must consider appointing counsel under Probate Code section 1470 or a guardian ad litem for a ward

who is a party to the proceeding or other matter subject to this rule if the ward is not represented by counsel.

(3) In determining whether providing information in response to discovery requests or testifying as a witness is in the ward's best interest, the judicial officer should consider the following:

(A) Whether information has been presented indicating that the ward may be at risk emotionally if he or she is permitted or denied the opportunity to provide information in response to discovery requests or by testimony;

(B) Whether the subject areas about which the ward is anticipated to provide information in response to discovery requests or by testimony are relevant to the decision the court must make; and

(C) Whether any other factors weigh in favor of or against having the ward provide information in response to discovery requests or by testimony.

(4) In taking testimony from a ward who is a party to the proceeding or other matter subject to this rule, the court must take the special care required by Evidence Code section 765(b). If the ward is not represented by an attorney, the court must inform the ward in an age-appropriate manner about the limitations on confidentiality of testimony and that the information provided to the court will be on the record and provided to the parties in the case.

(i) Education and training of judicial officers and court staff

Education and training content for court staff and judicial officers should include information on wards' participation in proceedings or other matters subject to this rule, methods other than direct testimony for receiving input from a ward, procedures for taking a ward's testimony, and differences in the application of this rule to wards who are and are not parties to the proceeding or other matters subject to this rule. *(Adopted, eff. Jan. 1, 2013.)*

Rule 7.1020. Special Immigrant Juvenile findings in guardianship proceedings

(a) Application

This rule applies to a request by or on behalf of a minor who is a ward or a proposed ward in a probate guardianship proceeding for judicial findings needed as a basis for filing a petition for classification as a Special Immigrant Juvenile (SIJ) under federal immigration law. The term "request under this rule" as used in this rule refers exclusively to such a request. This rule also applies to any opposition to a request under this rule, any hearing on such a request and opposition, and any findings of the court in response to such a request.

(b) Request for findings

(1) *Who may file request*

Any person or entity authorized under Probate Code section 1510 or 1510.1 to petition for the appointment of a guardian of the person of a minor, including the ward or proposed ward if 12 years of age or older, may file a request for findings regarding the minor under this rule.

(A) If there is more than one ward or proposed ward in the proceeding, a minor eligible to file a request for

findings under this rule may do so only for himself or herself.

(B) The court may appoint an attorney under Probate Code section 1470 or a guardian ad litem under Probate Code sections 1003 and 1003.5 to file and present a request for findings under this rule for a minor or to represent the interests of a minor in a proceeding to decide a request filed on the minor's behalf by another.

(2) *Form of request*

(A) A request for findings under this rule must be made by verified petition. A separate request must be filed for each minor seeking SIJ findings.

(B) A request for findings under this rule by or on behalf of a minor filed concurrently with a petition for the appointment of a guardian of the person or for extension of a guardianship of the person past the 18th birthday of the minor must be prepared and filed as a separate petition, not as an attachment to the petition for appointment.

(c) Notice of hearing

Notice of a hearing of a request for findings under this rule, and a copy of the request, must be sent to the minor's parents and the persons listed in section 1460(b) of the Probate Code, in the manner and within the time provided in that section, subject to the provisions of subdivision (e) of that section and sections 1202 and 1460.1 of that code.

(d) Opposition to request

Any of the persons who must be given notice of hearing of a request for findings under this rule may file an objection or other opposition to the request.

(e) Hearing on request

(1) If filed concurrently, a request for findings under this rule by or on behalf of a minor and a petition for appointment of a guardian of the person or extension of a guardianship of the person past the 18th birthday of that minor may be heard and determined together.

(2) Hearings on separate requests for findings under this rule by or on behalf of more than one ward or proposed ward in the same guardianship proceeding may be consolidated on the motion of any party or on the court's own motion.

(3) Hearings on requests for findings under this rule by or on behalf of minors who are siblings or half-siblings and are wards or proposed wards in separate guardianship proceedings may be consolidated on the motion of any party in either proceeding or on the motion of the court in either proceeding. If multiple departments of a single court or courts in more than one county are involved, they may communicate with each other on consolidation issues in the manner provided for inter-court communications on venue issues in guardianship and family law matters under section 2204 of the Probate Code and rule 7.1014.

(4) Hearings on contested requests for findings under this rule must be conducted in the same manner as hearings on other contested petitions under the Probate Code.

(5) Probate Code section 1022 applies to uncontested requests for findings under this rule.

(f) Separate findings in multi-ward cases under this rule

The court must issue separate findings for each minor in a guardianship proceeding in which more than one minor is the subject of a request under this rule. *(Adopted, eff. Jan. 1, 2016. As amended, eff. July 1, 2016.)*

Chapter 22

CONSERVATORSHIPS

Cross References

Conservatorship, generally, see Probate Code § 1800 et seq.

Rule 7.1050.   Conservator forms

(a) Forms to be submitted with petition

Each petitioner, unless the petitioner is a bank or other entity entitled to conduct the business of a trust company, must submit to the court with the petition for appointment of conservator a completed *Confidential Supplemental Information* statement (form GC–312). In addition, each proposed conservator, except a bank or other entity entitled to conduct the business of a trust company, or a public guardian, must submit a completed *Confidential Conservator Screening Form* (form GC–314).

(b) Use of form

The information on the *Confidential Conservator Screening Form* is used by the court and by persons or agencies designated by the court to assist the court in determining whether a proposed conservator should be appointed.

(c) Forms to be confidential

The *Confidential Conservator Screening Form*, the *Confidential Supplemental Information* statement, and the information contained on these forms are confidential. The clerk must maintain these forms in a manner that will protect and preserve their confidentiality. *(Adopted, eff. Jan. 1, 2001. As amended, eff. Jan. 1, 2002; Jan. 1, 2007.)*

Rule 7.1051.   Acknowledgment of receipt of Duties of Conservator

Before the court issues letters, each conservator must execute and file an acknowledgment of receipt of the *Duties of Conservator and Acknowledgment of Receipt of Handbook*

(form GC–348). *(Adopted, eff. Jan. 1, 2001. As amended, eff. Jan. 1, 2002.)*

Rule 7.1052.   Termination of conservatorship

(a) Operation of law or court order

A conservatorship of the person or estate may terminate by operation of law or may be terminated by court order if the court determines that it is no longer required.

(b) Conservator of the person

Under Probate Code section 1860(a), a conservatorship of the person terminates by operation of law when the conservatee dies, and the conservator of the person need not file a petition for its termination.

(c) Duty of conservator of estate on termination

A conservator of the estate whose administration is terminated by operation of law or by court order must file and obtain the court's approval of a final account of the administration. *(Adopted, eff. Jan. 1, 2004.)*

Rule 7.1053.   Service of final account of removed or resigned conservator

A resigned or removed conservator of the estate must serve a copy of the conservator's final account and the petition for its settlement with the notice of hearing that must be served on the successor conservator of the estate under Probate Code section 1460(b)(1), unless the court dispenses with such service. *(Adopted, eff. Jan. 1, 2004.)*

Rule 7.1054.   Service of final account after termination of conservatorship

After termination of the conservatorship, the conservator of the estate must serve copies of the conservator's final account and the petition for its settlement with the notices of hearing that must be served on the former conservatee and on the spouse or domestic partner of the former conservatee under Probate Code sections 1460(b)(2) and (3), unless the court dispenses with such service. *(Adopted, eff. Jan. 1, 2004.)*

Rule 7.1059.   Standards of conduct for the conservator of the estate

Except as otherwise required by statute, in the exercise of ordinary care and diligence in managing and controlling the estate of the conservatee, the conservator of the estate is to be guided by the following principles:

(a) Avoidance of actual and apparent conflicts of interest with the conservatee

The conservator must avoid actual conflicts of interest and, consistent with his or her fiduciary duty to the conservatee, the appearance of conflicts of interest. The conservator must avoid any personal, business, or professional interest or relationship that is or reasonably could be perceived as being self-serving or adverse to the best interest of the conservatee. In particular:

(1) Except as appropriate for conservators who are not professional fiduciaries with full disclosure to the court, the conservator should not personally provide housing, medical, or legal services to the conservatee;

(2) The conservator must be independent from all service providers, except when (a) no other conservator or service providers are reasonably available, (b) the exception is in the best interest of the conservatee, (c) the circumstances are fully disclosed to the court, and (d) prior court approval has been obtained;

(3) The conservator must neither solicit nor accept incentives from service providers; and

(4) The conservator must not engage his or her family members to provide services to the conservatee for a profit or fee when other alternatives are reasonably available. Where family members do provide such services, their relationship to the conservator must be fully disclosed to the court, the terms of engagement must be in the best interest of the conservatee compared to the terms available from independent service providers, the services must be competently performed, and the conservator must be able to exercise appropriate control and supervision.

A conservator's employees, including family members, are not service providers and are not providing services to the conservatee for a profit or fee within the meaning of this rule if their compensation is paid by the conservator and their services are either included in the conservator's petition for allowance of the conservator's compensation or are not paid from the conservatee's estate.

(b) Conservatorship estate management

The conservator of the estate must:

(1) Provide competent management of the conservatee's property, with the care of a prudent person dealing with someone else's property;

(2) Refrain from unreasonably risky investments;

(3) Refrain from making loans or gifts of estate property, except as authorized by the court after full disclosure;

(4) Manage the estate for the benefit of the conservatee;

(5) Subject to the duty of full disclosure to the court and persons entitled under law to receive it, closely guard against unnecessary or inappropriate disclosure of the conservatee's financial information;

(6) Keep the money and property of the estate separate from the conservator's or any other person's money or property, except as may be permitted under statutes authorizing public guardians or public conservators and certain regulated private fiduciaries to maintain common trust funds or similar common investments;

(7) Hold title reflecting the conservatorship in individual securities, mutual funds, securities broker accounts, and accounts with financial institutions;

(8) Keep accurate records of all transactions. Professional fiduciaries must maintain prudent accounting systems and procedures designed to protect against embezzlement and other cash-asset mismanagement;

(9) Undertake as soon as possible after appointment and qualification to locate and safeguard the conservatee's estate planning documents, including wills, living trusts, powers of attorney for health care and finances, life insurance policies, and pension records;

(10) Undertake as soon as possible after appointment and qualification to secure the real and personal property of the estate, insuring it at appropriate levels, and protecting it against damage, destruction, or loss;

(11) Make reasonable efforts to preserve property identified in the conservatee's estate planning documents;

(12) Communicate as necessary and appropriate with the conservator of the person of the conservatee, if any, and with the trustee of any trust of which the conservatee is a beneficiary;

(13) Pursue claims against others on behalf of the estate when it would be in the best interest of the conservatee or the estate to do so. Consider requesting prior court authority to pursue or compromise large or complex claims, particularly those that might require litigation and the assistance of counsel and those that might result in an award of attorneys' fees for the other party against the estate if unsuccessful, and request such approval before entering into a contingent fee agreement with counsel;

(14) Defend against actions or claims against the estate when it would be in the best interest of the conservatee or the estate to do so. Consider requesting court approval or instructions concerning the defense or compromise of litigation against the estate;

(15) Collect all public and insurance benefits for which the conservatee is eligible;

(16) Evaluate the conservatee's ability to manage cash or other assets and take appropriate action, including obtaining prior court approval when necessary or appropriate, to enable the conservatee to do so to the level of his or her ability;

(17) When disposing of the conservatee's tangible personal property, inform the conservatee's family members in advance and give them an opportunity to acquire the property, with approval or confirmation of the court; and

(18) In deciding whether it is in the best interest of the conservatee to dispose of property of the estate, consider the following factors, among others, as appropriate in the circumstances:

(A) The likely benefit or improvement of the conservatee's life that disposing of the property would bring;

(B) The likelihood that the conservatee would need or benefit from the property in the future;

(C) Subject to the factors specified in Probate Code section 2113, the previously expressed or current desires of the conservatee concerning the property;

(D) The provisions of the conservatee's estate plan concerning the property;

(E) The tax consequences of the disposition transaction;

(F) The impact of the disposition transaction on the conservatee's entitlement to public benefits;

(G) The condition of the entire estate;

(H) Alternatives to disposition of the property;

(I) The likelihood that the property will deteriorate or be subject to waste if retained in the estate; and

(J) The benefit versus the cost or liability of maintaining the property in the estate.

(Adopted, eff. Jan. 1, 2008.)

Rule 7.1060. Investigations and reports by court investigators

(a) *Order Appointing Court Investigator* (form GC–330)

Order Appointing Court Investigator (form GC–330) is an optional form within the meaning of rule 1.35 of these rules, except as follows:

(1) A court may, by local rule, require that form GC–330 be used for orders appointing court investigators and directing them to conduct all or any of the investigations described in the form and to prepare, file, and serve copies of reports concerning those investigations. The local rule may also prescribe the form's preparation, service, and delivery to the court for execution and filing.

(2) A court may, by local rule, require that a general order, a court-prepared order, or a local form order instead of form GC–330 be used to appoint and direct the actions of court investigators concerning all or any of the investigations and reports described in form GC–330.

(b) *Order Appointing Court Investigator (Review and Successor Conservator Investigations)* (form GC–331)

Order Appointing Court Investigator (Review and Successor Conservator Investigations) (form GC–331) is an optional form within the meaning of rule 1.35 of these rules, except as follows:

(1) A court may, by local rule, require that form GC–331 be used for orders appointing court investigators and directing them to conduct all or any of the review investigations under Probate Code sections 1850 and 1851 or investigations concerning the appointment of successor conservators under Probate Code sections 2684 and 2686 described in the form and to prepare, file, and serve copies of reports concerning those investigations. Form GC–331 is to be prepared by the court only.

(2) A court may, by local rule, require that a general order, a court-prepared order, or a local form order instead of form GC–331 be used to appoint and direct the actions of court investigators concerning all or any of the investigations and reports described in form GC–331.

(c) *Order Setting Biennial Review Investigation and Directing Status Report Before Review* (form GC–332)

Order Setting Biennial Review Investigation and Directing Status Report Before Review (form GC–332) is an optional form within the meaning of rule 1.35 of these rules, except as follows:

(1) A court may, by local rule, require that form GC–332 be used for orders setting biennial review investigations and directing status reports under Probate Code section 1850(a)(2). Form GC–332 is to be prepared by the court only.

(2) A court may, by local rule, require that a general order, a court-prepared order, or a local form order instead of form GC–332 be used concerning the matters described in form GC–332. *(Adopted, eff. Jan. 1, 2011.)*

Rule 7.1061. Taking possession of an asset of the conservatee at an institution or opening or changing ownership of an account or safe-deposit box in a financial institution

(a) Definitions

As used in this rule, the following terms have the meanings stated below:

(1) An "institution" is an insurance company, insurance broker, insurance agent, investment company, investment bank, securities broker-dealer, investment advisor, financial planner, financial advisor, or any other person who takes, holds, or controls an asset subject to a guardianship that is not a "financial institution" within the meaning of this rule;

(2) A "financial institution" is a bank, trust (except as provided in (d)), savings and loan association, savings bank, industrial bank, or credit union; and

(3) "Taking possession" or "taking control" of an asset held or controlled by an institution includes changing title to the asset, withdrawing all or any portion of the asset, or transferring all or any portion of the asset from the institution.

(b) Responsibilities of the conservator when taking possession or control of an asset of the conservatee at an institution

When taking possession or control of an asset held by an institution in the name of the conservatee, the temporary, general, or limited conservator of the estate must provide the following to the institution:

(1) A certified copy of the conservator's *Letters of Temporary Guardianship or Conservatorship* (form GC–150) or *Letters of Conservatorship* (form GC–350) containing the Notice to Institutions and Financial Institutions on the second page; and

(2) A blank copy of a *Notice of Taking Possession or Control of an Asset of Minor or Conservatee* (form GC–050).

(c) Responsibilities of the conservator when opening or changing the name on an account or a safe-deposit box at a financial institution

When opening or changing the name on an account or a safe-deposit box in a financial institution, the temporary, general, or limited conservator of the estate must provide the following to the financial institution:

(1) A certified copy of the guardian's *Letters of Temporary Guardianship or Conservatorship* (form GC–150) or *Letters of Conservatorship* (form GC–350) containing the Notice to Institutions and Financial Institutions on the second page; and

(2) A blank copy of a *Notice of Opening or Changing a Guardianship or Conservatorship Account or Safe–Deposit Box* (form GC–051).

(d) Application of this rule to Totten trust accounts

This rule applies to Totten trust accounts but does not apply to any other trust arrangement described in Probate Code section 82(b). *(Adopted, eff. Jan. 1, 2009.)*

Rule 7.1062. The good cause exception to notice of the hearing on a petition for appointment of a temporary conservator

(a) Purpose

The purpose of this rule is to establish uniform standards for the good cause exception to the notice of the hearing required on a petition for appointment of a temporary conservator under Probate Code section 2250(e).

(b) Good cause for exceptions to notice limited

Good cause for an exception to the notice required by section 2250(e) must be based on a showing that the exception is necessary to protect the proposed conservatee or his or her estate from immediate and substantial harm.

(c) Court may change the time or manner of giving notice

An exception to the notice requirement of section 2250(e) may include one or any combination of the following:

(1) Waiving notice to one, more than one, or all persons entitled to notice;

(2) Requiring a different period of notice; and

(3) Changing the required manner of giving notice, including requiring notice by telephone, fax, e-mail, or personal delivery, or a combination of these methods, instead of or in addition to notice by mail to the proposed conservatee's spouse or registered domestic partner and relatives.

(d) Good cause exceptions to notice

Good cause for an exception to the notice requirement of section 2250(e) may include a showing of:

(1) Harm caused by the passage of time. The showing must demonstrate the immediate and substantial harm to the conservatee or the conservatee's estate that could occur during the notice period.

(2) Harm that one or more persons entitled to notice might do to the proposed conservatee or the proposed conservatee's estate if notice is given. Such a showing would not support an exception to the requirement to give notice to any other person entitled to notice unless it also demonstrates that notice cannot reasonably be given to the other person without also giving notice to the persons who might cause harm.

(3) Medical emergency. The emergency must be immediate and substantial and treatment (1) must be reasonably unavailable unless a temporary conservator is appointed and (2) cannot be deferred for the notice period because of the proposed conservatee's pain or extreme discomfort or a significant risk of harm.

(4) Financial emergency. The emergency must be immediate and substantial and other means shown likely to be ineffective to prevent loss or further loss to the proposed conservatee's estate during the notice period.

(e) Contents of request for good cause exception to notice

A request for a good cause exception to the notice requirement of section 2250(e) must be in writing, separate from the petition for appointment of a temporary conservator, and must include:

(1) An application containing the case caption and stating the relief requested;

(2) An affirmative factual showing in support of the application in a declaration under penalty of perjury containing competent testimony based on personal knowledge;

(3) A declaration under penalty of perjury based on personal knowledge containing the information required for an ex parte application under rule 3. 1204(b); and

(4) A proposed order. *(Adopted, eff. Jan. 1, 2008. As amended, eff. July 1, 2008; Jan. 1, 2009.)*

Rule 7.1063. Change of conservatee's residence

(a) Pre–move notice of change of personal residence required

Unless an emergency requires a shorter period of notice, the conservator of the person must mail copies of a notice of an intended change of the conservatee's personal residence to the persons listed below at least 15 days before the date of the proposed change, and file the original notice with proof of mailing with the court. Copies of the notice must be mailed to:

(1) The conservatee;

(2) The conservatee's attorney of record;

(3) The conservatee's spouse or registered domestic partner; and

(4) The conservatee's relatives named in the *Petition for Appointment of Probate Conservator* (form GC–310), including the conservatee's "deemed relatives" under Probate Code section 1821(b)(1)–(4) if the conservatee has no spouse or registered domestic partner and no second-degree relatives.

(b) Conservatee's personal residence

(1) The "conservatee's personal residence" under (a) is the residence the conservatee understands or believes, or reasonably appears to understand or believe, to be his or her permanent residence on the date the first petition for appointment of a conservator was filed in the proceeding, whether or not the conservatee was living in that residence on that date. A residential care facility, including a board and care, intermediate care, skilled nursing, or secured perimeter facility, may be the conservatee's personal residence under this rule.

(2) If the conservatee cannot form or communicate an understanding or belief concerning his or her permanent residence on the date the first petition for appointment of a conservator was filed in the proceeding, his or her personal residence under this rule is the residence he or she last previously understood or believed, or appeared to understand or believe, to be his or her permanent residence.

(3) For purposes of this rule, the following changes of residence are or are not changes of the conservatee's personal residence, as indicated:

(A) A move from the conservatee's personal residence under this rule to a residential care facility or other residence is a change of the conservatee's personal residence under (a).

(B) A move from a residential care facility or other residence to another residence that is not the conservatee's personal residence under this rule is a change of the conservatee's personal residence under (a).

(C) A move from a residential care facility or other residence to the conservatee's personal residence under this rule is not a change of the conservatee's personal residence under (a).

(c) Post–move notice of a change of residence required

The conservator of the person must file a notice of a change of the conservatee's residence with the court within 30 days of the date of the change. Unless waived by the court for good cause to prevent harm to the conservatee, the conservator must mail a copy of the notice to the persons named below and file a proof of mailing with the original notice filed with the court. Unless waived, the notice must be mailed to:

(1) The conservatee's attorney of record;

(2) The conservatee's spouse or registered domestic partner; and

(3) The conservatee's relatives named in the *Petition for Appointment of Probate Conservator* (form GC–310), including the conservatee's "deemed relatives" under Probate Code section 1821(b)(1)–(4) if the conservatee has no spouse or registered domestic partner and no second-degree relatives.

(d) Conservatee's residence

The "conservatee's residence" under (c) is the conservatee's residence at any time after appointment of a conservator.

(e) Use of Judicial Council forms GC–079 and GC–080

(1) The *Pre–Move Notice of Proposed Change of Personal Residence of Conservatee or Ward* (form GC–079) must be used for the pre-move notice required under (a) and Probate Code section 2352(e)(3). The conservator, the conservator's attorney, or an employee of the attorney may complete the mailing and sign the Proof of Mailing on page 2 of the form. If the notice is mailed less than 15 days before the date of the move because an emergency requires a shorter period of notice, the basis for the emergency must be stated in the notice.

(2) The *Post–Move Notice of Change of Residence of Conservatee or Ward* (form GC–080) must be used for the post-move notice required under (c) and Probate Code section 2352(e)(1) and (2). The conservator, the conservator's attorney, or an employee of the attorney may complete the mailing and sign the Proof of Mailing on page 2 of the form.

(f) Prior court approval required to establish conservatee's residence outside California

Notwithstanding any other provision of this rule, prior court approval is required before a conservatee's residence may be established outside the state of California. *(Adopted, eff. Jan. 1, 2008.)*

Chapter 23

COURT–APPOINTED COUNSEL IN PROBATE PROCEEDINGS

Rule 7.1101. Qualifications and continuing education required of counsel appointed by the court in guardianships and conservatorships

(a) Definitions

As used in this rule, the following terms have the meanings stated below:

(1) "Appointed counsel" or "counsel appointed by the court" are legal counsel appointed by the court under Probate Code sections 1470 or 1471, including counsel in private practice and deputy public defenders directly responsible for the performance of legal services under the court's appointment of a county's public defender.

(2) A "probate guardianship" or "probate conservatorship" is a guardianship or conservatorship proceeding under division 4 of the Probate Code.

(3) "LPS" and "LPS Act" refer to the Lanterman–Petris–Short Act, Welfare and Institutions Code section 5000 et seq.

(4) An "LPS conservatorship" is a conservatorship proceeding for a gravely disabled person under chapter 3 of the LPS Act, Welfare and Institutions Code sections 5350–5371.

(5) A "contested matter" in a probate or LPS conservatorship proceeding is a matter that requires a noticed hearing and in which written objections are filed by any party or made by the conservatee or proposed conservatee orally in open court.

(6) "Counsel in private practice" includes attorneys employed by or performing services under contracts with nonprofit organizations.

(b) Qualifications of appointed counsel in private practice

Except as provided in this rule, each counsel in private practice appointed by the court on or after January 1, 2008, must be an active member of the State Bar of California for at least three years immediately before the date of appointment, with no discipline imposed within the 12 months immediately preceding any date of availability for appointment after January 1, 2008; and

(1) *Appointments to represent minors in guardianships*

For an appointment to represent a minor in a guardianship:

(A) Within the five years immediately before the date of first availability for appointment after January 1, 2008, must have represented at least three wards or proposed wards in probate guardianships, three children in juvenile court dependency or delinquency proceedings, or three children in custody proceedings under the Family Code; or

(B) At the time of appointment, must be qualified:

(i) For appointments to represent children in juvenile dependency proceedings under rule 5.660 and the court's local rules governing court-appointed juvenile court dependency counsel; or

(ii) For appointments to represent children in custody proceedings under the Family Code under rule 5.242, including the alternative experience requirements of rule 5.242(g).

(C) Except as provided in (f)(2), counsel qualified for appointments in guardianships under (B) must satisfy the continuing education requirements of this rule in addition to the education or training requirements of the rules mentioned in (B).

(2) *Appointments to represent conservatees or proposed conservatees*

For an appointment to represent a conservatee or a proposed conservatee, within the five years immediately before the date of first availability for appointment after January 1, 2008, counsel in private practice must have:

(A) Represented at least three conservatees or proposed conservatees in either probate or LPS conservatorships; or

(B) Completed any three of the following five tasks:

(i) Represented petitioners for the appointment of a conservator at commencement of three probate conservatorship proceedings, from initial contact with the petitioner through the hearing and issuance of Letters of Conservatorship;

(ii) Represented a petitioner, a conservatee or a proposed conservatee, or an interested third party in two contested probate or LPS conservatorship matters. A contested matter that qualifies under this item and also qualifies under (i) may be applied toward satisfaction of both items;

(iii) Represented a party for whom the court could appoint legal counsel in a total of three matters described in Probate Code sections 1470, 1471, 1954, 2356.5, 2357, 2620.2, 3140, or 3205;

(iv) Represented fiduciaries in three separate cases for settlement of a court-filed account and report, through filing, hearing, and settlement, in any combination of probate conservatorships or guardianships, decedent's estates, or trust proceedings under division 9 of the Probate Code; or

(v) Prepared five wills or trusts, five durable powers of attorney for health care, and five durable powers of attorney for asset management.

(3) Except as provided in (e)(2), private counsel qualified under (1) or (2) must also be covered by professional liability insurance satisfactory to the court in the amount of at least $100,000 per claim and $300,000 per year.

(c) Qualifications of deputy public defenders performing legal services on court appointments of the public defender

(1) Except as provided in this rule, beginning on January 1, 2008, each county deputy public defender with direct responsibility for the performance of legal services in a particular case on the appointment of the county public defender under Probate Code sections 1470 or 1471 must be an active member of the State Bar of California for at least three years immediately before the date of appointment; and either

(A) Satisfy the experience requirements for private counsel in (b)(1) for appointments in guardianships or (b)(2) for appointments in conservatorships; or

(B) Have a minimum of three years' experience representing minors in juvenile dependency or delinquency proceedings or patients in postcertification judicial proceedings or conservatorships under the LPS Act.

(2) A deputy public defender qualified under (1) must also be covered by professional liability insurance satisfactory to the court in the amount of at least $100,000 per claim and $300,000 per year, or be covered for professional liability at an equivalent level by a self-insurance program for the professional employees of his or her county.

(3) A deputy public defender who is not qualified under this rule may periodically substitute for a qualified deputy public defender with direct responsibility for the performance of legal services in a particular case. In that event, the county public defender or his or her designee, who may be the qualified supervisor, must certify to the court that the substitute deputy is working under the direct supervision of a deputy public defender who is qualified under this rule.

(d) Transitional provisions on qualifications

(1) Counsel appointed before January 1, 2008, may continue to represent their clients through March 2008, whether or not they are qualified under (b) or (c). After March 2008, through conclusion of these matters, the court may retain or replace appointed counsel who are not qualified under (b) or (c) or may appoint qualified co-counsel to assist them.

(2) In January, February, and March 2008, the court may appoint counsel in new matters who have not filed the certification of qualifications required under (h) at the time of appointment but must replace counsel appointed under this paragraph who have not filed the certificate before April 1, 2008.

(e) Exemption for small courts

(1) Except as provided in (2) and (3), the qualifications required under (b) or (c) may be waived by a court with four or fewer authorized judges if it cannot find qualified counsel or for other grounds of hardship.

(2) A court described in (1) may, without a waiver, appoint counsel in private practice who do not satisfy the insurance requirements of (b)(3) if counsel demonstrate to the court that they are adequately self-insured.

(3) A court may not waive or disregard the self-insurance requirements of (c)(2) applicable to deputy public defenders.

(4) A court waiving the qualifications required under (b) or (c) must make express written findings showing the circumstances supporting the waiver and disclosing all alternatives considered, including appointment of qualified counsel from adjacent counties and other alternatives not selected.

(f) Continuing education of appointed counsel

(1) Except as provided in (2), beginning on January 1, 2008, counsel appointed by the court must complete three hours of education each calendar year that qualifies for Minimum Continuing Legal Education credit for State Bar-certified specialists in estate planning, trust, and probate law.

(2) Counsel qualified to represent minors in guardianships under (b)(1)(B) and who are appointed to represent minors in guardianships of the person only may satisfy the continuing education requirements of this rule by satisfying the annual education and training required under rule 5.242(d) or the continuing education required under rule 5.660(d)(3).

(g) Additional court-imposed qualifications, education, and other requirements

The qualifications in (b) and (c) and the continuing education requirement in (f) are minimums. A court may establish higher qualification or continuing education requirements, including insurance requirements; require initial education or training; and impose other requirements, including an application by private counsel.

(h) Initial certification of qualifications; annual post-qualification reports and certifications

(1) Each counsel appointed or eligible for appointment by the court before January 1, 2008, including deputy public defenders, must certify to the court in writing before April 1, 2008, that he or she satisfies the qualifications under (b) or (c) to be eligible for a new appointment on or after that date.

(2) After March 2008, each counsel must certify to the court that he or she is qualified under (b) or (c) before becoming eligible for an appointment under this rule.

(3) Each counsel appointed or eligible for appointment by the court under this rule must immediately advise the court of the imposition of any State Bar discipline.

(4) Beginning in 2009, each appointed counsel must certify to the court before the end of March of each year that:

(A) His or her history of State Bar discipline and professional liability insurance coverage or, if appointed by

a court with four or fewer authorized judges under (e)(2), the adequacy of his or her self-insurance, either has or has not changed since the date of his or her qualification certification or last annual certification; and

(B) He or she has completed the continuing education required for the preceding calendar year.

(5) Annual certifications required under this subdivision showing changes in State Bar disciplinary history, professional liability insurance coverage, or adequacy of self-insurance must include descriptions of the changes.

(6) Certifications required under this subdivision must be submitted to the court but are not to be filed or lodged in a case file.

(i) Reporting

The Judicial Council may require courts to report appointed counsel's qualifications and completion of continuing education required by this rule to ensure compliance with Probate Code section 1456. *(Adopted, eff. Jan. 1, 2008. As amended, eff. Jan. 1, 2009; Jan. 1, 2011; Jan. 1, 2016.)*

Title 10

JUDICIAL ADMINISTRATION RULES

Division 4

TRIAL COURT ADMINISTRATION

Chapter 7

QUALIFICATIONS OF COURT INVESTIGATORS, PROBATE ATTORNEYS, AND PROBATE EXAMINERS

Rule
10.776.   Definitions.
10.777.   Qualifications of court investigators, probate attorneys, and probate examiners.

Rule 10.776.   Definitions

As used in the rules in this chapter, the following terms have the meanings stated below:

(1) A "court investigator" is a person described in Probate Code section 1454(a) employed by or under contract with a court to provide the investigative services for the court required or authorized by law in guardianships, conservatorships, and other protective proceedings under division 4 of the Probate Code;

(2) A "probate examiner" is a person employed by a court to review filings in probate proceedings in order to assist the court and the parties to get the filed matters ready for consideration by the court in accordance with the requirements of the Probate Code, title 7 of the California Rules of Court, and the court's local rules;

(3) A "probate attorney" is an active member of the State Bar of California who is employed by a court to perform the functions of a probate examiner and also to provide legal

analysis, recommendations, advice, and other services to the court pertaining to probate proceedings;

(4) "Probate proceedings" are decedents' estates, guardianships and conservatorships under division 4 of the Probate Code, trust proceedings under division 9 of the Probate Code, and other matters governed by provisions of that code and the rules in title 7 of the California Rules of Court;

(5) An "accredited educational institution" is a college or university, including a community or junior college, accredited by a regional accrediting organization recognized by the Council for Higher Education Accreditation; and.

(6) "AOC" is the Administrative Office of the Courts. *(Adopted, eff. Jan. 1, 2008. As amended, eff. Jan. 1, 2016.)*

Rule 10.777.   Qualifications of court investigators, probate attorneys, and probate examiners

(a) Qualifications of court investigators

Except as otherwise provided in this rule, a person who begins employment with a court or enters into a contract to perform services with a court as a court investigator on or after January 1, 2008, must:

(1) Have a bachelor of arts or bachelor of science degree in a science, a social science, a behavioral science, liberal arts, or nursing from an accredited educational institution; and

(2) Have a minimum of two years' employment experience performing casework or investigations in a legal, financial, law enforcement, or social services setting.

(b) Qualifications of probate attorneys

Except as otherwise provided in this rule, a person who begins employment with a court as a probate attorney on or after January 1, 2008, must:

(1) Be an active member of the State Bar of California for:

(A) A minimum of five years; or

(B) A minimum of two years, plus a minimum of five years' current or former active membership in the equivalent organization of another state or eligibility to practice in the highest court of another state or in a court of the United States; and

(2) Have a minimum of two years' total experience, before or after admission as an active member of the State Bar of California, in one or more of the following positions:

(A) Court–employed staff attorney;

(B) Intern, court probate department (minimum six-month period);

(C) Court–employed probate examiner or court-employed or court-contracted court investigator;

(D) Attorney in a probate-related public or private legal practice;

(E) Deputy public guardian or conservator;

(F) Child protective services or adult protective services worker or juvenile probation officer; or

(G) Private professional fiduciary appointed by a court or employee of a private professional fiduciary or bank or trust company appointed by a court, with significant fiduciary responsibilities, including responsibility for court accountings.

(c) Qualifications of probate examiners

Except as otherwise provided in this rule, a person who begins employment with a court as a probate examiner on or after January 1, 2008, must have:

(1) A bachelor of arts or bachelor of science degree from an accredited educational institution and a minimum of two years' employment experience with one or more of the following employers:

(A) A court;

(B) A public or private law office; or

(C) A public administrator, public guardian, public conservator, or private professional fiduciary; or

(2) A paralegal certificate or an Associate of Arts degree from an accredited educational institution and a minimum of a total of four years' employment experience with one or more of the employers listed in (1); or

(3) A juris doctor degree from an educational institution approved by the American Bar Association or accredited by the Committee of Bar Examiners of the State Bar of California and a minimum of six months' employment experience with an employer listed in (1).

(d) Additional court-imposed qualifications and requirements

The qualifications in (a), (b), and (c) are minimums. A court may establish higher qualification standards for any position covered by this rule and may require applicants to comply with its customary hiring or personal-service contracting practices, including written applications, personal references, personal interviews, or entrance examinations.

(e) Exemption for smaller courts

The qualifications required under this rule may be waived by a court with eight or fewer authorized judges if it cannot find suitable qualified candidates for the positions covered by this rule or for other grounds of hardship. A court electing to waive a qualification under this subdivision must make express written findings showing the circumstances supporting the waiver and disclosing all alternatives considered, including those not selected.

(f) Record keeping and reporting

The ~~AOC~~ Judicial Council may require courts to report on the qualifications of the court investigators, probate attorneys, or probate examiners hired or under contract under this rule, and on waivers made under (e), as necessary to ensure compliance with Probate Code section 1456. *(Adopted, eff. Jan. 1, 2008. As amended, eff. Jan. 1, 2016.)*

STANDARDS OF JUDICIAL ADMINISTRATION

Title 7

STANDARDS FOR PROBATE PROCEEDINGS

Standard
7.10. Settlements or judgments in certain civil cases involving minors or persons with disabilities.

Standard 7.10. Settlements or judgments in certain civil cases involving minors or persons with disabilities

In matters assigned to or pending in civil departments of the court where court approval of trusts that will receive proceeds of settlements or judgments is required under Probate Code section 3600, each court should develop practices and procedures that:

(1) Provide for determination of the trust issues by the probate department of the court or, in a court that does not have a probate department, a judicial officer who regularly hears proceedings under the Probate Code; or

(2) Ensure that judicial officers who hear these matters are experienced or have received training in substantive and technical issues involving trusts (including special needs trusts). *(Formerly § 40, adopted, eff. Jan. 1, 2005. Renumbered Standard 7.10, eff. Jan. 1, 2007.)*

CALIFORNIA CODE OF REGULATIONS

TABLE OF CONTENTS

TITLE 18. PUBLIC REVENUES

Division 3. Franchise Tax Board

Chapter 2.5. Personal Income Tax
(Taxable Years Beginning After 12–31–54)

Subchapter 9. Estates, Trusts, Beneficiaries and Decedents

Article 1. General Rules for Taxation of Estates and Trusts

§ 17742. Taxability of Estates.

(a) In the case of an estate, if the decedent and noncontingent beneficiaries are all nonresidents of this State, and, in the case of a trust, if the fiduciaries and noncontingent beneficiaries are all nonresidents of this State, only income from real or personal property located in this State (see Reg. 17951–3), business carried on within this State (see Reg. 17951–4), and intangible personal property having a business or taxable situs in this State (see Section 17952) is taxable.

In computing the taxable income from these sources, only the gross income from these sources is considered. From such gross income, the deductions allowed by the law are subtracted. See Sections 17301–17303 and Section 17734. The amount remaining is taxable income of the estate or trust to which the rates of tax specified in Section 17041 apply.

EXAMPLE. B is the executor of the estate of A, who was a nonresident of this State at the time of death. All the beneficiaries are likewise nonresidents. During the year 1980, the gross income of the estate from all sources amounted to $100,000, $50,000 of which was derived from real and personal property located, and from business transacted, in this State. The losses, depreciation, and depletion sustained with respect to the property in California, and the taxes, licenses, expenses, bad debts, etc., properly deductible from the California income amounted to $40,000. Thus, the income from California sources, prior to deducting amounts distributed to beneficiaries, amounted to $10,000. Of this amount, $6,000 was distributed to beneficiaries during the year pursuant to a partial distribution of the estate. The remaining $4,000 is the net income of the estate, as defined in Section 18411.

(b) A noncontingent beneficiary is one whose interest is not subject to a condition precedent.

(c) On the death of a married person, the deceased spouse's share of the community property is, in some circumstances, subject to administration in the hands of his or her estate (California Probate Code Sections 201–206). The estate of the deceased spouse is taxable on the income from that part of his or her one–half of the community property that is properly subject to administration. Income received by the estate, but derived from the surviving spouse's share of the community property (acquired after July 28, 1927) is taxable to the surviving spouse.

§ 17743. Taxability of Trust Dependent upon Residence of Fiduciary.

If there are two or more fiduciaries of a trust, and one or more are residents and one or more are nonresidents, and all the beneficiaries are nonresidents, the trust is taxable upon (a) all net income (less the deductions allowed under Article 1 of Chapter 9 (Section 17731 and following)) from business carried on within this State, from real or tangible personal property located in this State, and from intangible personal property having a business or taxable situs in this State (see Reg. 17952); and (b) that proportion of the net income (less the deductions allowed under Article 1 of Chapter 9 (Section 17731 and following)) from all other sources which the number of fiduciaries who are residents of this State bears to the total number of fiduciaries.

EXAMPLE (1). B, a resident, and C, a nonresident of this State, are the trustees of a trust created by A. All the beneficiaries are nonresidents. During the year 1980, the trust received $60,000 as rent from real and tangible personal property located in, and from business carried on in this State, from which expenses of $10,000 were deducted, $60,000 from real and personal property located, and business carried on, outside this State from which expenses of $10,000 were deducted, and $50,200 income from stocks and bonds, none of which had a business or taxable situs in this State. None of the income was paid or credited to the beneficiaries during the year. The $50,000 income from real and personal property located in, and business transacted in this State is taxable. Since there are two fiduciaries, one of which is a resident of this State, one–half of the balance of the income of the trust is likewise taxable to the trust. Thus, the taxable income amounts to $100,100 ($50,000 from property located in this State, plus one–half of $100,200 which is the remainder of the trust's income).

EXAMPLE (2). E, a resident, and F and G, nonresidents of this State, are the trustees of a trust created by D. All of the beneficiaries are nonresidents. The corpus of the trust consists entirely of stocks and bonds and property located outside this State. One–third of the income taxable under Section 17742 (i.e., net income less the deductions allowed under Article 1 of Chapter 9), which is the proportion of total income taxable which the number of fiduciaries who are residents of this State bears to the total number of fiduciaries, is taxable to the trust.

§ 17744. Taxability of Trust Dependent upon Residence of Beneficiary.

If one or more of the noncontingent beneficiaries of a trust are residents and one or more are nonresidents, and the fiduciaries are nonresidents, the trust is taxable upon (a) all income (less the deduction allowed under Article 1 of Chapter 9 (Section 17731 and following) from real and tangible personal property located in this State, and from business carried on within this State and from intangible personal property having a business or taxable situs in this State (see Reg. 17952); and (b) that proportion of all net income (less the deduction allowed under Article 1 of Chapter 9 (Section 17731 and following)) from all other sources which eventually is to be distributed to the noncontingent beneficiaries who are residents of this State.

EXAMPLE (1). A transferred property located outside this State in trust to pay equal shares of the income to B, a resident, and C, a nonresident of this State. The beneficiaries have noncontingent interests. The fiduciaries of the trust are nonresidents. During the year 1980, the trust realized $50,000 from real and tangible personal property located, and business carried on, within this State, $50,000 from real and tangible personal property located, and business carried on, outside this State, and $50,000 from stocks and bonds, none of which had a business or taxable situs in this State. None of the income was paid or credited to the beneficiaries during the year. The trust is taxable upon the $50,000 realized from real and tangible personal property located, and business carried on, within this State. The trust is also taxable upon one–half of the balance of the income since one–half of such income will eventually be distributed to B, a resident of this State.

EXAMPLE (2). A transferred stocks and bonds and real and personal property located outside this State in trust to B, a nonresident of this State. Under the terms of the trust, the income from the intangible personal property is to be accumulated for a number of years and then distributed to C, a resident of this State with a noncontingent interest. The balance of the income is to be distributed to certain named beneficiaries who are nonresidents of this State. The trust is taxable upon all the income from the intangible personal property, i.e., the stocks and bonds, but is not taxable upon any of the income from the remainder of the trust property.

INDEX TO PROBATE CODE

Abbreviations

COMMUNITY

CONSERVATORS

CONSERVATORS AND CONSERVATORSHIPS—Cont'd

Conservators of person—Cont'd

Experimental drugs, prescribing or administering, **Prob 2356**

Foreign states, **Prob 1980 et seq.**

Jurisdiction, **Prob 1980 et seq.**

Limitation of powers, **Prob 2351**

Medical treatment,
Consent, **Prob 2354, 2355**
Order of court, **Prob 2357**

Mental health treatment facilities, involuntary placement, **Prob 2356**

Nonresidents, **Prob 2107**

Petitions, unsuccessful opposition, compensation and salaries, **Prob 2641**

Powers and duties, **Prob 2350 et seq.**

Public Guardian, generally, this index

Residence of conservatee, **Prob 2352**

Sterilization, **Prob 2356**

Conservatorship estate, definitions, **Prob 3006**

Conservatorship proceedings, definitions, **Prob 3008**

Conspiracy, finality of judgment, order or decree, **Prob 2103**

Enforcement of support orders, **Prob 3090**

Contempt,
Accounts and accounting, failure to file, **Prob 2620.2**
Enforcement of support orders, **Prob 3090**
Examination concerning assets, **Prob 2619**
Removal from office, **Prob 2655**

Contingent fees, attorneys, **Prob 2644**

Continuance,
Spouse lacking legal capacity, enforcement of support, **Prob 3086**
Transfers, property, hearings, **Prob 852**

Continuation of conservatorship, court orders, **Prob 1873**

Contracts,
Conservators of estate, **Prob 2451.5**
Contingent fee contracts, attorneys, **Prob 2644**
Legal capacity of conservatee, **Prob 1870 et seq.**
Limited conservatorship, **Prob 2351.5**
Personal liability, **Prob 2110**
Powers independently exercisable, **Prob 2591**

Control by court, **Prob 2102**

Control of conservatee, conservator of person, power, **Prob 2351**

Control of estate, **Prob 2401**
Breach of fiduciary duty, liability, **Prob 2401.3 et seq.**

Copies, notices, **Prob 1461.7**

Corporations,
Disabled persons, **Welf & I 5355**
Gravely disabled persons, **Welf & I 5355**

Costs,
Accounting, objections, **Prob 2622.5**
Bonds (officers and fiduciaries), **Prob 2320**
Examination concerning assets, **Prob 2618**
Investigations and investigators, **Prob 1851.5**
Jurisdiction, unjustifiable conduct, **Prob 1997**
Removal of conservator, **Prob 2653**
Sterilization proceedings, **Prob 1963**
Transfers, property, **Prob 859**
Unsuccessful petitions, **Prob 2640.1**

Court investigators,
Accounts and accounting, **Prob 1851.2**
Appointment, **Prob 1454**
Confidential or privileged information, reports, **Prob 1851**
Definitions, guardianship or conservatorship, **Prob 1419**
Jurisdiction, transfers, **Prob 1851.1**

CONSERVATORS AND CONSERVATORSHIPS—Cont'd

Court investigators—Cont'd

Medical records, disclosure, **Prob 1826**

Powers and duties, **Prob 1826**
Medical treatment, capacity to give informed consent, **Prob 1894**
Successor conservator appointment hearings, **Prob 2684**

Qualifications, **Prob 1456**

Reports, **Prob 1826, 1851**
Medical treatment, capacity of conservatee to give informed consent, **Prob 1894**
Temporary conservatorships, appointments, **Prob 2250.6**

Review of conservatorship, **Prob 1851**
Costs, **Prob 1851.5**

Successor conservator, **Prob 2684**
Appointment, **Prob 2686**

Courts,
Compromise and settlement, approval, **Prob 2501 et seq.**
Definitions, **Prob 1418**
Orders of court, generally, post
Supervision, **Prob 2450**

Crimes and offenses,
Adverse or pecuniary interest, **Prob 2111.5**
Property, disclosure, **Prob 2359, 2403**
Investigations and investigators, reports, **Welf & I 5354**
Removal, **Prob 2650**
Sterilization, **Prob 1967**

Custodial parent, terminal condition, joint conservators, **Prob 2105**

Custody of conservatee, **Prob 2351; Welf & I 5358.5**

Damages,
Failure to file inventory, **Prob 2615**
Inventories, failure to file, **Prob 2615**
Transfers, property, **Prob 859**

Death,
Accounts and accounting, **Prob 2620, 2632**
Care of estate pending delivery to personal representative, **Prob 2467**
Expenses, last illness and funeral, **Prob 2631**
Legal capacity of conservatee, **Prob 1870 et seq.**
Limited conservatorship termination, **Prob 1860.5**
Notice, **Prob 2361**
Spouse, conservatorship estate, termination of consent, **Prob 3055**
Termination of conservatorship, **Prob 1860**

Debtors and creditors,
Collection, **Prob 2451**
Payment, **Prob 2430**

Declarations, legal capacity, spouse, orders of court, **Prob 3143**

Dedication of real estate, **Prob 2556**

Deeds and conveyances, **Prob 850 et seq., 2556, 2591**
Acceptance in lieu of foreclosure or trustees sale, **Prob 2464**
Good faith purchaser or incumbrancer for value, community or homestead property, spouse lacking legal capacity, **Prob 3074**
Legal capacity of conservatee, **Prob 1870 et seq.**
Spouse lacking legal capacity, community property, proceeding for particular transaction, **Prob 3100 et seq.**

Deeds of trust, personal liability, **Prob 2110**

Deferred payments, sales terms, **Prob 2542**

Definitions, **Prob 30, 1400 et seq., 2600**
Change of venue, **Prob 2210**
Community or homestead property, **Prob 3004 et seq.**

CONSERVATORS AND CONSERVATORSHIPS—Cont'd

Definitions—Cont'd

Conservatee, **Prob 29**

Conservator of estate, **Prob 2400**

Conservator of person, **Prob 2350**

Domicile and residence, **Prob 2352**

Health care decisions, **Prob 4613**

Jurisdiction, **Prob 1982**

Limited conservator, **Prob 30**

Medical treatment, **Prob 2357**

Secretary concerned, **Prob 1440**

Uniform Transfers to Minors Act, **Prob 3901**

Delegation of powers, wartime substitutions, **Prob 380 et seq.**

Delivery, tangible personal property of decedent, **Prob 330**

Deposits,
Bonds (officers and fiduciaries), **Prob 2328**
Checks, warrants or drafts, authorization, **Prob 2452**
Commercial paper and warrants for payment of money, authorization, **Prob 2452**
Notice, orders, **Prob 2456**
Orders, copies, **Prob 2456**
Personal property with trust company, **Prob 2454**
Securities, **Prob 2455**
Withdrawal, **Prob 2456**

Designated payee, public assistance payments, **Prob 2452**

Developmental disability, definitions, **Prob 1420**

Developmentally disabled persons. Mentally Retarded and Developmentally Disabled Persons, this index

Diligence, ordinary diligence, conservator of estate, **Prob 2401**

Director, notice, **Prob 1461**

Disability insurance, **Prob 2459**

Discharge of conservator, **Prob 1853**
Temporary conservator, **Prob 2258**

Disclaimer of testamentary and other interests, filing, **Prob 276 et seq.**

Disclosure,
Absence and absentees, husband and wife, appointment, **Prob 1813**
Adverse or pecuniary interest,
Conservators of estates, **Prob 2401, 2403**
Conservators of persons, **Prob 2351, 2359**
Ex parte communications, **Prob 1051**

Discretion of court, selection of conservator, **Prob 1812**

Dismissal or nonsuit, jurisdiction, **Prob 1994, 1999**

Dispensing with notices, **Prob 1460**

Disposal, valueless property, **Prob 2465**

Disposition, community or homestead property, spouse lacking legal capacity, **Prob 3000 et seq.**

Disqualification of electors, powers of conservator, **Welf & I 5357**

Dissolution of marriage, absence and absentees, husband and wife, appointment, **Prob 1813**

Domestic partnership, **Prob 1813.1, 1900, 1901**
Limited conservatorships, **Prob 2351.5**
Nominations, **Prob 1811**
Petitions,
Appointments, **Prob 1820 et seq.**
Successor conservator, **Prob 2681 et seq.**

Domicile and residence,
Change of residence of conservatee, change of venue, **Prob 2113**
Conservator of person, residence of conservatee, **Prob 2352**
Emergencies, temporary conservatees, removal from residence, **Prob 2254**

CONSERVATORS

CONSERVATORS

CONSERVATORS

COUNTIES—Cont'd

Firefighters and Fire Departments, generally, this index

Funds, treasurers. County Treasurers, generally, this index

Health Facilities, generally, this index

Industrial Farms and Road Camps, generally, this index

Jails, generally, this index

Liens and incumbrances, trusts and trustees, special needs trusts, priority, **Prob 3604, 3605**

Limitation of actions, probate proceedings, claims against decedents estates, **Prob 9200 et seq.**

Local criminal justice facilities. Jails, generally, this index

Local sales and use taxes. Sales and Use Taxes, this index

Mentally Ill Persons, this index

Mentally Retarded and Developmentally Disabled Persons, this index

National defense. War and Civil Defense, generally, this index

Prisoners. Jails, generally, this index

Probate Proceedings, this index

Public assistance. Social Services, generally, this index

Public Guardian, generally, this index

Resolutions, mentally ill persons, attorneys, appointments, **Welf & I 5370.1**

Taxation, generally, this index

Treasurers. County Treasurers, generally, this index

War and Civil Defense, generally, this index

COUNTY FUNDS

County Treasurers, generally, this index

COUNTY HEALTH FACILITIES

Health Facilities, generally, this index

COUNTY JAILS

Jails, generally, this index

COUNTY OFFICERS AND EMPLOYEES

Public administrators. Probate Proceedings, this index

Public Guardian, generally, this index

Treasurers. County Treasurers, generally, this index

COUNTY TREASURERS

Children and minors, special needs trusts, protective proceedings, deposits, **Prob 3611**

Escheat, unclaimed funds,
  Coroner, **CCP 1444.5**
  Public administrator, **CCP 1444.5**

Guardian and ward,
  Money, children and minors, deposits, **Prob 3413**
  Termination of guardianship, money, children and minors, deposits, **Prob 3412**

Handicapped persons, special needs trusts, protective proceedings, deposits, **Prob 3611**

Mentally ill persons, special needs trusts, protective proceedings, deposits, **Prob 3611**

Mentally retarded and developmentally disabled persons, special needs trusts, protective proceedings, deposits, **Prob 3611**

Public administrators, deposits, **Prob 7640 et seq.**

COUNTY WARRANTS

Social Services, generally, this index

COURT INVESTIGATORS

Conservators and Conservatorships, this index

Guardian and Ward, this index

COURT OFFICERS AND EMPLOYEES

Adverse or pecuniary interest, guardian and ward, conservators and conservatorships, **Prob 2111.5**

COURT ORDERS

Orders of Court, generally, this index

COURT SUPERVISION

Definitions, independent administration of estates, **Prob 10401**

COURTS

Conservators and Conservatorships, this index

Costs, generally, this index

Definitions,
  Fiduciaries, digital assets, access, **Prob 871**
  Guardianships and conservatorships, **Prob 1418, 2644**
  Uniform Transfers to Minors Act, **Prob 3901**

Guardian and Ward, generally, this index

Judgments and Decrees, generally, this index

Orders of Court, generally, this index

Superior Courts, generally, this index

Venue, generally, this index

Witnesses, generally, this index

COWS

Animals, generally, this index

CREATING INSTRUMENT

Definitions, power of appointment, **Prob 610**

CREATOR OF INTEREST

Definitions, testamentary and other interests, **Prob 263**

CREDIT

Estate Taxes, this index

Personal representatives, credit sales, personal property, **Prob 10257, 10258**

Probate proceedings, securing sale of personal property, **Prob 10257, 10258**

CREDIT UNIONS

Account in an insured credit union defined, Probate Code, **Prob 22**

Accounts and accounting,
  Conservators and conservatorships, notice, **Prob 2892, 2893**
  Guardian and ward, notice, **Prob 2892, 2893**
  Homicide, joint tenants, severance of interest, **Prob 251**
  Multiple Party Account, generally, this index

Certificates of deposit. Multiple Party Account, generally, this index

Conservators and conservatorships, accounts and accounting, notice, **Prob 2892, 2893**

Death, homicide, joint tenants, severance of interest, **Prob 251**

Guardian and ward, accounts and accounting, notice, **Prob 2892, 2893**

Joint accounts. Multiple Party Account, generally, this index

Joint tenants, homicide, severance of interests, **Prob 251**

Multiple Party Account, generally, this index

Nonprobate transfers. Multiple Party Account, generally, this index

Probate proceedings, share accounts, certificates, sales, **Prob 10201**

Savings accounts. Multiple Party Account, generally, this index

Share accounts. Multiple Party Account, generally, this index

CREDITORS

Debtors and Creditors, generally, this index

CREDITS

Credit, generally, this index

CRIMES AND OFFENSES

Conservators and Conservatorships, this index

Correctional Institutions, generally, this index

Developmentally disabled persons. Mentally Retarded and Developmentally Disabled Persons, this index

Estate taxes, confidential or privileged information, disclosure, **Rev & T 14251**

False representation. Fraud, generally, this index

Fraud, generally, this index

CRIMES AND OFFENSES—Cont'd

Generation skipping transfer tax, **Rev & T 16910**

Guardian and Ward, this index

Homicide, generally, this index

Jails, generally, this index

Juvenile Delinquents and Dependents, generally, this index

Juvenile Institutions and Schools, generally, this index

Local detention facilities. Jails, generally, this index

Mandatory supervision. Parole and Probation, generally, this index

Mentally Retarded and Developmentally Disabled Persons, this index

Murder. Homicide, generally, this index

Parole and Probation, generally, this index

Perjury, generally, this index

Prisoners. Jails, generally, this index

Probation. Parole and Probation, generally, this index

Restitution, generally, this index

Suicide, generally, this index

Venue, generally, this index

Victims of crime,
  Compensation and salaries. Restitution, generally, this index
  Restitution, generally, this index

Witnesses, generally, this index

CRIPPLED PERSONS

Handicapped Persons, generally, this index

CRUDE OIL

Oil and Gas, generally, this index

CURTESY

Succession, nonrecognition, **Prob 6412**

CUSTODIAL PARENT

Definitions, guardians and conservators, **Prob 1419.5**

CUSTODIAL PROPERTY

Definitions, Uniform Transfers to Minors Act, **Prob 3901**

Uniform Transfers to Minors Act, **Prob 3900 et seq.**

CUSTODIANS

Children and minors, Uniform Transfers to Minors Act, **Prob 3900 et seq.**
  Devise subject to Uniform Transfers to Minors Act, **Prob 6341 et seq.**

Definitions,
  Fiduciaries, digital assets, access, **Prob 871**
  Statutory wills, **Prob 6206**
  Uniform Transfers to Minors Act, **Prob 3901**

Gifts, Uniform Transfers to Minors Act, **Prob 3900 et seq.**
  Devises subject to Uniform Transfers to Minors Act, **Prob 6341 et seq.**

Jurisdiction, Uniform Transfers to Minors Act, **Prob 3902**

Small estate collection or transfer without administration, **Prob 13051**

Transfers, Uniform Transfers to Minors Act, **Prob 3900 et seq.**
  Devise subject to Uniform Transfers to Minors Act, **Prob 6341 et seq.**

Uniform Transfers to Minors Act, **Prob 3900 et seq.**

DAMAGES

Cause of action against decedent, **CCP 377.42**

Conservators and Conservatorships, this index

Decedents cause of action, commencement or continuance by personal representative or successor in interest, **CCP 377.34**

Exemplary damages,
  Conservators and conservatorships, adverse or pecuniary interest, **Prob 2111.5, 2359, 2403**
  Guardian and ward, adverse or pecuniary interest, **Prob 2111.5, 2359, 2403**

ESTATE

FUTURE

FUTURE ESTATES OR INTERESTS —Cont'd
Uniform Transfers to Minors Act, **Prob 3900 et seq.**

FUTURE PAYMENTS
Uniform Transfers to Minors Act, **Prob 3900 et seq.**

GARNISHMENT
Executions, generally, this index

GAS
Oil and Gas, generally, this index

GAS COMPANIES
Oil and Gas, generally, this index

GASOLINE
Motor Vehicle Fuel Tax, generally, this index
Taxation. Motor Vehicle Fuel Tax, generally, this index
Use Fuel Tax, generally, this index

GENERAL ACUTE CARE HOSPITALS
Advance health care directives, emergency services, **Prob 4717**
Disasters, surrogates, notice, **Prob 4717**
Emergency services,
Advance health care directives, **Prob 4717**
Notice, surrogates, **Prob 4717**
Surrogates, notice, **Prob 4717**
Exemptions, surrogates, notice, **Prob 4717**
Medical records, surrogates, **Prob 4717**
Notice, surrogates, **Prob 4717**
Surrogates, notice, **Prob 4717**

GENERAL CORPORATION LAW
Corporations, generally, this index

GENERAL LAWS
Statutes, generally, this index

GENERAL OBLIGATION BONDS
Bonds, generally, this index
State Bonds, generally, this index

GENERAL PERSONAL REPRESENTATIVE
Definitions, Probate Code, **Prob 42, 58**

GENERAL POWER OF APPOINTMENT
Definitions, **Prob 611**

GENERAL SALES TAX
Sales and Use Taxes, generally, this index

GENERATION SKIPPING TRANSFER TAX
Generally, **Rev & T 16700 et seq.**
Actions and proceedings,
Collection, **Rev & T 16800**
Court jurisdiction and procedure, **Rev & T 16880, 16881**
Erroneous deficiencies, **Rev & T 16734**
Refunds, **Rev & T 16860 et seq.**
Rules of court, **Rev & T 16890**
Administration of Act, **Rev & T 16900 et seq.**
Amending returns, **Rev & T 16722**
Appearance, **Rev & T 16905**
Civil Procedure Code, application of law, **Rev & T 16890**
Claims, erroneous deficiency determination, **Rev & T 16734**
Confidential or privileged information, **Rev & T 16910**
Correcting erroneous deficiency determinations, **Rev & T 16732**
Court jurisdiction and procedure, **Rev & T 16880, 16881**
Crimes and offenses, **Rev & T 16910**
Deeds and conveyances, transfer on death deeds, **Prob 5680**
Deficiencies, payment, **Rev & T 16730 et seq.**
Definitions, **Rev & T 16700 et seq.**
Estate taxes, generation skipping transfers, **Prob 20200**
Delinquencies, time, **Rev & T 16752**
Disclosure, confidential information, **Rev & T 16910**
Disposition of proceeds, **Rev & T 16950**

GENERATION SKIPPING TRANSFER TAX—Cont'd
Due date determination, **Rev & T 16751**
Enforcement of tax liens, **Rev & T 16800**
Equalization board, cooperation, **Rev & T 16904**
Erroneous deficiency determinations, correcting or setting aside, **Rev & T 16732**
Execution, collection, **Rev & T 16820, 16821**
Fines and penalties, **Rev & T 16760, 16761**
Notice, **Rev & T 16733**
Forms, returns, **Rev & T 16721**
Franchise tax board, cooperation, **Rev & T 16903**
Fraud, **Rev & T 16730 et seq.**
Funds, deposits, **Rev & T 16950**
Hearings, judgments, **Rev & T 16862**
Imposition, **Rev & T 16710**
Inspection of records, **Rev & T 16910, 16911**
Interest, **Rev & T 16760, 16761**
Refunds, **Rev & T 16870**
Judgments and decrees,
Civil procedure, application of law, **Rev & T 16890**
Hearings, **Rev & T 16862**
Jurisdiction of court, **Rev & T 16880, 16881**
Deficiencies, erroneous claims, **Rev & T 16734**
Labor and employment, assistants, **Rev & T 16901**
Liens and incumbrances, **Rev & T 16810**
Enforcement, **Rev & T 16800**
Limitation of actions, **Rev & T 16830**
Refunds, **Rev & T 16860**
Nonresidents, jurisdiction, **Rev & T 16881**
Notice, deficiency and penalties, **Rev & T 16733**
Overpayments, refunds, **Rev & T 16850**
Payment, **Rev & T 16750 et seq.**
Process, refund actions, **Rev & T 16861**
Proration, **Prob 20200 et seq.**
Rates and charges, interest, **Rev & T 16760**
Records and recordation, **Rev & T 16910, 16911**
Refunds, **Rev & T 16850 et seq.**
Returns,
Filing, **Rev & T 16720 et seq.**
Fraud, **Rev & T 16730, 16731**
Rules and regulations, **Rev & T 16902**
Service of process, refund actions, **Rev & T 16861**
Setting aside erroneous deficiency determinations, **Rev & T 16732**
Time,
Action, refunds, **Rev & T 16860**
Delinquency, **Rev & T 16752**
Due date determination, **Rev & T 16751**
Refund, **Rev & T 16851**
Tax lien duration, **Rev & T 16810**
Transfer on death deeds, **Prob 5680**

GEOLOGY
Mines and Minerals, generally, this index

GEOTHERMAL ENERGY
Geothermal Resources, generally, this index

GEOTHERMAL RESOURCES
Leases,
Decedents estates, probate court authorization, **Prob 9946**
Probate proceedings, sales, **Prob 10203**
Probate proceedings, leases, authorization, **Prob 9946**

GIFT TAX
Prohibition, **Rev & T 13301 et seq.**

GIFTS, DEVISES AND BEQUESTS
Aged persons, fraud, presumptions, **Prob 21360 et seq.**
Annuities, classification, **Prob 21117**
Application of law, transfers to minors, **Prob 3923**
Protective proceedings, **Prob 3303**

GIFTS, DEVISES AND BEQUESTS—Cont'd
Attorney fees, fraud, presumptions, **Prob 21380**
Attorneys, fraud, presumptions, **Prob 21360 et seq.**
Care custodians, dependent adults, fraud, presumptions, **Prob 21360 et seq.**
Causa mortis, action for recovery, **Prob 9653**
Certificates and certification, fraud, presumptions, attorneys, **Prob 21384**
Charities, generally, this index
Cohabitation, fraud, presumptions, **Prob 21360 et seq.**
Conservators and Conservatorships, this index
Death, gifts in contemplation of death, recovery, **Prob 9653**
Definitions, impending death, **Prob 5700**
Demonstrative devises, classification, **Prob 21117**
Dependent adults, fraud, presumptions, **Prob 21360 et seq.**
Drafters, fraud, presumptions, **Prob 21360 et seq.**
Eminent domain, specific gifts, **Prob 21133, 21134**
Exoneration, **Prob 21131**
Specific devises, **Prob 21131**
Fiduciaries, fraud, presumptions, **Prob 21360 et seq.**
Fraud, presumptions, **Prob 21360 et seq.**
General devises, classification, **Prob 21117**
General pecuniary devises, classification, **Prob 21117**
Generation skipping transfer tax, **Rev & T 16700 et seq.**
Institutional funds, managers and management, **Prob 18501 et seq.**
Insurance, this index
Law firms, fraud, presumptions, **Prob 21360 et seq.**
Liability, fraud, presumptions, **Prob 21388**
Lifetime gifts, **Prob 21135**
Mentally retarded and developmentally disabled persons, fraud, presumptions, **Prob 21360 et seq.**
Nonprobate transfers,
Holders of property, duties and protection, **Prob 5002, 5003**
Validity, **Prob 5000**
Notice, fraud, presumptions, **Prob 21388**
Officers and employees, fraud, presumptions, **Prob 21360 et seq.**
Presumptions, fraud, **Prob 21360 et seq.**
Probate Proceedings, generally, this index
Process, service of process, fraud, presumptions, **Prob 21388**
Real estate, Uniform Transfers to Minors Act, **Prob 3900 et seq.**
Relatives, fraud, presumptions, **Prob 21360 et seq.**
Residuary devises, classification, **Prob 21117**
Satisfaction, lifetime gifts, **Prob 21135**
Securities, **Prob 21132**
Service of process, fraud, presumptions, **Prob 21388**
Specific devises, **Prob 21131 et seq.**
Classification, **Prob 21117**
Exoneration, **Prob 21131**
Securities, **Prob 21132**
Trusts and trustees,
Abatement, **Prob 21400 et seq.**
Income earned during probate, distribution, property subject to trust, **Prob 15410**
Undue influence, presumptions, **Prob 21360 et seq.**
Uniform Transfers to Minors Act, **Prob 3900 et seq.**
Value, lifetime gifts, **Prob 21135**
Wills, generally, this index

GUARDIAN

GUARDIAN

GUARDIAN

GUARDIAN AND WARD—Cont'd
Wills, powers of guardian,
Mandatory clauses, statutory wills, **Prob 6241**
Nominated by will, **Prob 2108**
Withdrawal,
Deposits, **Prob 2456**
Guardian powers, **Prob 2593**
Request for special notice, **Prob 2701**
Witnesses,
Examination concerning assets, **Prob 2618**
Sterilization proceedings, **Prob 1963**
Wrongful death, compromise and settlement, **Prob 2504**

GUARDIANS OF ESTATES
Guardian and Ward, this index

GUARDIANS OF PERSONS
Guardian and Ward, this index

GUARDIANSHIP CONSERVATORSHIP LAW
Generally, **Prob 1400 et seq.**

HABIT FORMING DRUGS
Drugs and Medicine, generally, this index

HALF BLOODS
Wills, construction, **Prob 21115**

HANDICAPPED PERSONS
Conservators and conservatorship, treatment, powers of conservator, **Welf & I 5357, 5358**
County treasurers, special needs trusts, protective proceedings, deposits, **Prob 3611**
Custodians, Uniform Transfers to Minors Act, successor, **Prob 3918**
Guardian and Ward, generally, this index
Jurisdiction, special needs trusts, protective proceedings, continuing jurisdiction, **Prob 3612**
Notice, gravely disabled conservatees, placement, **Welf & I 5358**
Special needs trusts, protective proceedings, **Prob 3604, 3605**
Trusts and trustees, special needs trust, protection proceedings, **Prob 3604, 3605**
Uniform Transfers to Minors Act, custodians, successors, **Prob 3918**

HANDWRITING
Proof of will, **Prob 8221**
Wills, proof, **Prob 8221**

HARASSMENT
Conservators and conservatorships, vexatious litigants, **Prob 1970**

HARRISON NARCOTIC ACT
Drugs and Medicine, generally, this index

HAWKERS AND PEDDLERS
Sales and Use Taxes, generally, this index

HEALTH AND SANITATION
Cemeteries and Dead Bodies, generally, this index
Dead bodies. Cemeteries and Dead Bodies, generally, this index
Drugs and Medicine, generally, this index
Hospitals, generally, this index
Medicine. Drugs and Medicine, generally, this index

HEALTH AND WELFARE BENEFITS
Social Services, generally, this index

HEALTH CARE DECISIONS LAW
Generally, **Prob 4600 et seq.**

HEALTH CARE FACILITIES
Health Facilities, generally, this index

HEALTH CARE PROVIDERS
Advance health care directives, **Prob 4730 et seq.**
Attorney fees, advance health care directives, **Prob 4742**
Confidential or privileged information, POLST eRegistry, **Prob 4788**

HEALTH CARE PROVIDERS—Cont'd
Crimes and offenses,
Advance health care directives, **Prob 4740 et seq.**
Request to forgo resuscitative measures, **Prob 4782**
Damages,
Advance health care directives, **Prob 4740 et seq.**
Request to forgo resuscitative measures, **Prob 4782**
Definitions,
Health care decisions, **Prob 4621**
Request to forego resuscitative measures, medical care and treatment, **Prob 4781**
Discipline,
Advance health care directives, **Prob 4740, 4741**
Request to forgo resuscitative measures, **Prob 4782**
Do not resuscitate orders, **Prob 4780 et seq.**
Emergencies, POLST eRegistry, **Prob 4788**
Orders for life sustaining treatment forms, **Prob 4780 et seq.**
Physician orders for life sustaining treatment, POLST eRegistry, **Prob 4788**
Physicians and Surgeons, generally, this index
POLST eRegistry, physician orders for life sustaining treatment, **Prob 4788**
Power of attorney, **Prob 4730 et seq.**
Privileges and immunities,
Advance health care directives, **Prob 4740 et seq.**
POLST eRegistry, **Prob 4788**
Request to forgo resuscitative measures, **Prob 4782**
Registers and registries, physician orders for life sustaining treatment, **Prob 4788**
Request to forgo resuscitative measures, **Prob 4780 et seq.**
Resuscitative measures, request to forgo, **Prob 4780 et seq.**

HEALTH CARE SERVICES DEPARTMENT
Social Services, generally, this index

HEALTH CARE SURROGATES
Medical Care and Treatment, this index

HEALTH FACILITIES
Advance health care directives, **Prob 4730 et seq.**
Attorney fees, advance health care directives, **Prob 4742**
Crimes and offenses,
Advance health care directives, **Prob 4740 et seq.**
Request to forgo resuscitative measures, **Prob 4782**
Damages,
Advance health care directives, **Prob 4740 et seq.**
Request to forgo resuscitative measures, **Prob 4782**
Discipline,
Advance health care directives, **Prob 4740, 4741**
Request to forgo resuscitative measures, **Prob 4782**
Do not resuscitate orders, **Prob 4780 et seq.**
General Acute Care Hospitals, generally, this index
Hospitals, generally, this index
Medical Records, generally, this index
Nursing Homes, generally, this index
Orders for life sustaining treatment forms, **Prob 4780 et seq.**
Physicians and surgeons, orders for life sustaining treatment forms, **Prob 4780 et seq.**
Power of attorney, **Prob 4730 et seq.**
Privileges and immunities,
Advance health care directives, **Prob 4740 et seq.**

HEALTH FACILITIES—Cont'd
Privileges and immunities—Cont'd
Request to forgo resuscitative measures, **Prob 4782**
Records and recordation. Medical Records, generally, this index
Request to forgo resuscitative measures, **Prob 4780 et seq.**
Sterilization of persons. Birth Control, this index

HEIRS
Application of law, cloning, posthumous conception, **Prob 249.5**
Artificial insemination, posthumous conception, **Prob 249.5 et seq.**
Correctional institutions, victim compensation board, notice, **Prob 216, 9202**
Definitions, probate proceedings, **Prob 44**
Identity and identification, **Prob 248 et seq.**
Industrial farms and road camps, victim compensation board, notice, **Prob 216, 9202**
Jails, victim compensation board, notice, **Prob 216, 9202**
Juvenile institutions and schools, victim compensation board, notice, **Prob 216, 9202**
Notice,
Probate proceedings, hearings, **Prob 8110**
Survivorship status, determination hearings, **Prob 233**
Road camps, victim compensation board, notice, **Prob 216, 9202**
Signatures, posthumous conception, **Prob 249.5**
Succession, generally, this index
Wills, generally, this index
Witnesses, posthumous conception, **Prob 249.5**

HIGHWAYS AND ROADS
County highways. Industrial Farms and Road Camps, generally, this index
Industrial Farms and Road Camps, generally, this index

HIRING PROPERTY
Leases, generally, this index

HOLDER
Definitions, probate without administration, **Prob 13002**

HOLOGRAPHIC WILLS
Generally, **Prob 6111**
Wills, this index

HOME STATE
Definitions, conservators and conservatorships, jurisdiction, appointments, **Prob 1991**

HOMELAND SECURITY
War and Civil Defense, generally, this index

HOMESTEADS
Conservators and Conservatorships, this index
Guardian and Ward, this index
Probate Proceedings, this index

HOMICIDE
Administration of estates, effect of homicide, **Prob 250**
Advance health care directives, **Prob 4656**
Medical care and treatment, withholding or withdrawing health care, **Prob 4656**
Power of attorney, medical care and treatment, **Prob 4656**
Suicide, generally, this index
Surrogates, medical care and treatment, **Prob 4656**
Trusts and trustees, killer of decedent benefiting from trust, **Prob 250**
Wills, killer taking under will, **Prob 250 et seq.**
Wrongful death, actions and proceedings, **Prob 258**

HOSPITALS
See, also, Health Facilities, generally, this index

I-36

MENTALLY RETARDED AND DEVELOPMENTALLY DISABLED PERSONS—Cont'd

Gifts, devises and bequests, fraud, presumptions, **Prob 21360 et seq.**
Gravely disabled,
  Conservatorship, **Welf & I 5350 et seq.**
    Individualized treatment plans, **Welf & I 5350.1**
  Temporary conservatorship, **Welf & I 5352**
Grievance procedure, advocacy services, **Welf & I 5370.2**
Guardian and Ward, generally, this index
Hearings,
  Limited conservators, appointments, **Prob 1828.5**
  Sterilization proceedings, attendance of proposed conservatees, **Prob 1956**
Hysterectomy, sterilization procedure option, **Prob 1961**
Indigent persons, attorneys, appointments, conservatorship, **Welf & I 5370.1**
Individual program plans, conservatorship, **Welf & I 5352.6**
Investigations and investigators, sterilization proceedings, **Prob 1955**
Judgments and decrees,
  Conservatorship,
    Gravely disabled persons, ratification acts beyond term, **Welf & I 5363**
    Termination, **Welf & I 5362**
  Money or property paid or delivered, **Prob 3600 et seq.**
  Sterilization proceedings, **Prob 1955**
Jurisdiction, special needs trusts, protective proceedings, continuing jurisdiction, **Prob 3612**
Jury, conservatorship, **Welf & I 5350**
  Temporary conservatorship, **Welf & I 5352.1**
Liens and incumbrances, state or political subdivision claims, priority, special needs trust, **Prob 3604, 3605**
Limited conservatorship, **Prob 1801 et seq.**
Marriage, capacity, **Prob 810 et seq.**
Motor vehicles,
  Conservatorship, investigation, recommendation, **Welf & I 5357**
  License, **Welf & I 5357**
Notice,
  Conservators and conservatorships, **Welf & I 5350.2**
  Acceptance, **Welf & I 5354.5**
  Termination, **Welf & I 5362**
  Gravely disabled conservatees, placement, **Welf & I 5358**
  Hearing, guardian or conservator appointment, **Prob 1461.4**
Orders of court,
  Conservatorship, **Prob 1830**
  Payment of expenses, costs and fees, money or property paid or delivered pursuant to compromise or judgment, **Prob 3601**
  Right to consent to sterilization without court order, **Prob 1969**
  Sterilization proceedings, **Prob 1962**
Outpatients, gravely disabled persons, **Welf & I 5358.6**
Patients rights advocates,
  Conservatorship, **Welf & I 5351 et seq.**
  Contracts, **Welf & I 5370.2**
Peace officers, personal liability, actions of conservatee, **Welf & I 5358.1**
Personal property, temporary conservator selling or relinquishing, **Welf & I 5353**
Petitions, sterilization proceedings, subsequent petitions, **Prob 1966**
Placement, hospital or other facility, conservatee, **Welf & I 5358**
  Alternative placement, **Welf & I 5359**

MENTALLY RETARDED AND DEVELOPMENTALLY DISABLED PERSONS—Cont'd

Plans and specifications, patients rights advocacy services, contracts, **Welf & I 5370.2**
Privileges and immunities, sterilization, **Prob 1967**
Probate Proceedings, this index
Psychologists and psychology, sterilization, examination, **Prob 1955**
Public defenders,
  Conservatorship petitions, **Welf & I 5365**
  Fees, sterilization proceedings, **Prob 1963**
    Expiration, **Prob 1964**
Public Guardian, generally, this index
Ratification, conservatorship, acts beyond term, **Welf & I 5363**
Recommendations, conservatorship, **Welf & I 5352 et seq.**
Regional centers, sterilization, examinations, **Prob 1955**
Rehearing, conservatorship, **Welf & I 5364**
Reports,
  Conservators and conservatorships, investigations and investigators, **Welf & I 5352.1 et seq.**
  Outpatient treatment, gravely disabled persons, **Welf & I 5358.6**
  Sterilization, **Prob 1955**
Sales, estate or interests in real or personal property, conservatees, temporary conservator powers, **Welf & I 5353**
Sex, sterilization, **Prob 1955, 1959**
Shelters, temporary conservator, arrangements, **Welf & I 5353**
Social Services, generally, this index
Special needs trusts, protective proceedings, **Prob 3604, 3605**
State Institutions, generally, this index
Status quo, conservatee residence, temporary conservator, maintaining, **Welf & I 5353**
Stay, sterilization proceedings, **Prob 1965**
Sterilization, **Prob 1950 et seq.**
Stipulations, conservatorship for gravely disabled persons, documents and records of professional person who recommended conservatorship, **Welf & I 5365.1**
Temporary conservatorship, **Welf & I 5352, 5352.1**
  Civil and criminal liability for actions of conservatee, **Welf & I 5358.1**
Termination, conservatorship, **Welf & I 5361, 5362**
Time,
  Conservatorship,
    Petitions, **Welf & I 5365**
    Termination, **Welf & I 5361**
  Detention duration period, **Welf & I 5366.1**
Torts, conservator, public guardian or peace officer, actions of conservatee, **Welf & I 5358.1**
Transfer of patients, conservatorship proceedings, **Welf & I 5352.5**
Trial,
  Conservatorship, **Welf & I 5350**
  Gravely disabled persons, right to demand court or jury trial, **Welf & I 5350**
  Temporary conservatorship, **Welf & I 5352.1**
Trusts and trustees,
  Capacity, **Prob 810 et seq.**
  Special needs trust, protective proceedings, **Prob 3604, 3605**
Veterans, Veterans Administration facility, duration of detention, **Welf & I 5366.1**
Vulnerability to unlawful sexual conduct, sterilization proceedings consideration, **Prob 1959**

MENTALLY RETARDED AND DEVELOPMENTALLY DISABLED PERSONS—Cont'd

Waiver, conservatorship for gravely disabled persons, presence of professional person recommending conservatorship, **Welf & I 5365.1**
Weapons, conservatee, possession, **Welf & I 5357**
Wills, capacity, **Prob 810 et seq.**
Witnesses, sterilization proceedings, **Prob 1963**
MESSAGES
Telecommunications, generally, this index
MILITARY DEPARTMENT
Military Forces, generally, this index
MILITARY FORCES
Fiduciaries, wartime substitution, **Prob 350 et seq.**
Missing persons. Probate Proceedings, this index
Personal property, absentees, protective proceedings, **Prob 3700 et seq.**
Power of attorney, uniform statutory form power of attorney, benefits, **Prob 4461**
Trusts and trustees, wartime substitution, **Prob 350 et seq.**
MINES AND MINERALS
Geothermal Resources, generally, this index
Oil and Gas, generally, this index
Principal and Income Act, **Prob 16320 et seq.**
Probate Proceedings, this index
Royalties, generally, this index
Trusts and trustees, principal and income, allocation, **Prob 16363**
Uniform Principal and Income Act, **Prob 16320 et seq.**
MINORS
Children and Minors, generally, this index
MISCREANT CHILDREN
Juvenile Delinquents and Dependents, generally, this index
MISREPRESENTATION
Fraud, generally, this index
MISSING PERSONS
Definitions, probate proceedings, **Prob 12400**
Probate Proceedings, this index
MODIFICATION OR CHANGE
Charities, funds, managers and management, restrictions, **Prob 18506**
Probate Proceedings, this index
Trusts and Trustees, this index
MONEY
Children and minors, accounting for money or property belonging to minors, **Prob 3300, 3400 et seq.**
Probate proceedings, distribution of decedents estates, advances and advancements, assignments, **Prob 11604.5**
Warrants for Payment of Money, generally, this index
MONEY MARKET FUNDS
Conservators and conservatorships, **Prob 2574**
Guardian and ward, **Prob 2574**
Probate proceedings, **Prob 9730**
  Appraisal and appraisers, **Prob 8901**
MORTGAGES
Conservators and Conservatorships, this index
Guardian and Ward, this index
Nonprobate transfers,
  Holders of property, duties and protection, **Prob 5002, 5003**
  Validity, **Prob 5000**
Probate Proceedings, this index
Trust Deeds, generally, this index
Trusts and Trustees, this index
Wills, specific gifts, **Prob 21134**
MOTHER AND CHILD
Children and Minors, generally, this index

MOTIONS

MOTIONS
Guardian and ward, vexatious litigants, **Prob 1610, 1611**
New trial, guardianships, conservatorships and protective proceedings, **Prob 1453**
Probate Proceedings, this index
Vexatious litigants, guardian and ward, **Prob 1610, 1611**

MOTOR CARRIERS
Use Fuel Tax, generally, this index

MOTOR VEHICLE FUEL
Motor Vehicle Fuel Tax, generally, this index
Retail sales. Motor Vehicle Fuel Tax, generally, this index
Sales and use taxes. Motor Vehicle Fuel Tax, generally, this index
Taxation. Motor Vehicle Fuel Tax, generally, this index
Use Fuel Tax, generally, this index

MOTOR VEHICLE FUEL LICENSE TAX
Motor Vehicle Fuel Tax, generally, this index

MOTOR VEHICLE FUEL TAX
Actions and proceedings, probate proceedings, claims against estates, **Prob 9200 et seq.**
Decedents estates, claims, **Prob 9200 et seq.**
Estates of decedents, claims, **Prob 9200 et seq.**
Fines and penalties, **Prob 9200 et seq.**
Limitation of actions, probate proceedings, claims against decedents estates, **Prob 9200 et seq.**
Probate proceedings, claims against estates, **Prob 9200 et seq.**
Refunds, claims, decedents estates, **Prob 9200 et seq.**

MOTOR VEHICLES
Conservators and conservatorships, investigation, license retention, **Welf & I 5357**
Use Fuel Tax, generally, this index

MULTIPLE PARTY ACCOUNT
Generally, **Prob 5000, 5100 et seq.**
Application of law, **Prob 5201, 5205**
Beneficial ownership, application of law, **Prob 5201**
Beneficiaries, relative ownership, **Prob 5301 et seq.**
Burden of proof, presumptions, husband and wife, **Prob 5305**
Children and minors, payments, **Prob 5407**
Community property, **Prob 5305, 5307**
Contributions, relative ownership, **Prob 5301 et seq.**
Creation, designated accounts, **Prob 5203**
Creditors,
    Application of law, **Prob 5201**
    Fraudulent transfers, application of law, **Prob 5202**
Debtors and creditors,
    Application of law, **Prob 5201**
    Fraud, transfers, **Prob 5202**
Definitions, **Prob 5120 et seq.**
    Multiple party accounts, **Prob 5140**
    Probate proceedings, **Prob 55, 5132**
    Small estates, **Prob 6600**
Deposits remaining at death, ownership, **Prob 5302**
Designated account types, **Prob 5203**
Evidence, proof of death, payments, **Prob 5403**
Excess withdrawals, **Prob 5301**
Financial institutions,
    Liability, application of law, **Prob 5201**
    Protection, **Prob 5401 et seq.**
Forms, modification, **Prob 5303**
Fraud, creditors, **Prob 5202**
Heirs, payments, **Prob 5402 et seq.**
Holders of property, duties and protection, **Prob 5002, 5003**
Husband and wife, contributions, presumptions, **Prob 5305**

MULTIPLE PARTY ACCOUNT—Cont'd
Injunctions, payments, restraining orders, **Prob 5405**
Language, account creation, **Prob 5203**
Lifetime ownership, **Prob 5301**
Modification agreements, terms, **Prob 5303**
Notice, protection of financial institutions, payments, **Prob 5405**
Orders of court, payments, restraining orders, **Prob 5405**
Ownership between parties, **Prob 5301 et seq.**
Parties, relative ownership, **Prob 5301 et seq.**
Payments, **Prob 5401 et seq.**
    Proof of death, **Prob 5403**
Personal representatives, payments, **Prob 5402 et seq.**
Presumptions, husband and wife, contributions, **Prob 5305**
Protection, financial institutions, **Prob 5401 et seq.**
Restraining orders, payments, **Prob 5405**
Shares, survivors, relative ownership, **Prob 5301 et seq.**
Signatures, payments, **Prob 5401 et seq.**
Small estates,
    Collection without administration, **Prob 13050**
    Setaside proceedings, **Prob 6600**
Special power of attorney, **Prob 5204**
Survivorship rights, **Prob 5301 et seq.**
Tenancy in common accounts, survivorship rights, **Prob 5306**
Terms, modification, **Prob 5303**
Wills, right of survivorship, **Prob 5301**
Withdrawals,
    Excess withdrawals, **Prob 5301**
    Modification, **Prob 5303**
Writing, necessity, **Prob 5304**

MULTIPLE PARTY ACCOUNTS LAW
Generally, **Prob 5100 et seq.**

MUNICIPAL CORPORATIONS
Municipalities, generally, this index

MUNICIPAL OFFICERS AND EMPLOYEES
Firefighters and Fire Departments, generally, this index
Police, generally, this index

MUNICIPALITIES
Actions and proceedings,
    Claims against decedents estates, **Prob 9200 et seq.**
    Probate proceedings, claims against estates, **Prob 9200 et seq.**
Alleys. Streets and Alleys, generally, this index
Cemeteries and Dead Bodies, generally, this index
Civil defense. War and Civil Defense, generally, this index
Claims, decedents estates, **Prob 9200 et seq.**
Decedents estates, claims against, **Prob 9200 et seq.**
Estates of decedents, claims against, **Prob 9200 et seq.**
Firefighters and Fire Departments, generally, this index
Health Facilities, generally, this index
Industrial Farms and Road Camps, generally, this index
Jails, generally, this index
Liens and incumbrances, trusts and trustees, special needs trust, priority, **Prob 3604, 3605**
Limitation of actions,
    Claims against decedents estates, **Prob 9200 et seq.**
    Probate proceedings, claims against estate, **Prob 9200 et seq.**
Local sales and use taxes. Sales and Use Taxes, this index

MUNICIPALITIES—Cont'd
National defense. War and Civil Defense, generally, this index
Peace Officers, generally, this index
Police, generally, this index
Probate proceedings,
    Claims against estates, **Prob 9200 et seq.**
    Real property, dedication, conveyance, **Prob 9900, 9901**
Social Services, generally, this index
Streets and Alleys, generally, this index
Taxation, generally, this index
War and Civil Defense, generally, this index

MURDER
Homicide, generally, this index

MUSIC AND MUSICIANS
Royalties, generally, this index

MUTUAL CAPITAL CERTIFICATES
Definitions, probate proceedings, **Prob 23, 10201**

MUTUAL FUNDS
Conservators and conservatorship, **Prob 2459**
Guardian and ward, **Prob 2459**
Money Market Funds, generally, this index

NAMES
Power of attorney, attorney in fact, **Prob 4233**
Signatures, generally, this index

NARCOTICS
Drugs and Medicine, generally, this index

NATIONAL BANKS
Trust Companies, generally, this index

NATIONAL DEFENSE
War and Civil Defense, generally, this index

NATIVE AMERICANS
Indians, generally, this index

NATURAL GAS
Oil and Gas, generally, this index
Use Fuel Tax, generally, this index

NATURAL PARENTS
Definitions, succession, **Prob 6453**

NATURAL PERSONS
Power of attorney, **Prob 4120**

NATURAL RESOURCES
Geothermal Resources, generally, this index
Trusts and trustees, principal and income, allocation, **Prob 16363**

NAVY
Military Forces, generally, this index

NEEDY CHILDREN
Social Services, generally, this index

NEGLECTED CHILDREN
Juvenile Delinquents and Dependents, generally, this index

NEGLIGENCE
Children and minors, Uniform Transfers to Minors Act, **Prob 3912**
Death. Wrongful Death, generally, this index
Gifts, Uniform Transfers to Minors Act, **Prob 3912**
Transfers, Uniform Transfers to Minors Act, **Prob 3912**
Trusts and trustees,
    Cotrustees, **Prob 16402**
    Degree of care required by trustees, **Prob 16041 et seq.**
Uniform Transfers to Minors Act, custodians, **Prob 3912**
Wrongful Death, generally, this index

NEGOTIABLE INSTRUMENTS
Checks,
    Conservators, powers, **Prob 2452**
    Guardians, powers, **Prob 2452**
    Multiple Party Account, generally, this index
Compensation and salaries, nonprobate transfer provisions and compensation plans, holders of property, duties and protection, **Prob 5002, 5003**

NEGOTIABLE INSTRUMENTS—Cont'd
Conservators and conservatorships,
Endorsing, cashing or depositing, **Prob 2452**
Personal liability, **Prob 2110**
Powers of conservators, **Prob 2452**
Guardian and ward,
Endorsing, cashing or depositing, **Prob 2452**
Personal liability, **Prob 2110**
Powers of guardians, **Prob 2452**
Indorsements,
Conservators, powers, **Prob 2452**
Guardians, powers, **Prob 2452**
Investment Securities, generally, this index
Multiple Party Account, generally, this index
Nonprobate transfers,
Holders of property, duties and protection, **Prob 5002, 5003**
Validity, **Prob 5000**
Probate proceedings,
Acceptance on credit sale of personal property, **Prob 10257, 10258**
Appraisals, **Prob 8901**
Borrowing money, authority, **Prob 9800 et seq.**
Checks, administrative funds, **Prob 9705**
Credit sale, real estate, **Prob 10315**
Execution, borrowing money, **Prob 9805**
Personal representative, personal liability, **Prob 9606**
Sale, **Prob 10200 et seq.**
Securing sale of personal property, **Prob 10257, 10258**

NET CONTRIBUTION
Definitions, multiple party accounts, **Prob 5134**

NET INCOME
Definitions, Uniform Principal and Income Act, **Prob 16328**

NETWORKS
Telecommunications, generally, this index

NEW TRIAL
Probate proceedings, **Prob 7220**

NEWBORN CHILDREN
Children and Minors, generally, this index

NEWSPAPERS
Notice, generally, this index

NEXT OF KIN
Relatives, generally, this index

NOMINATIONS
Attorneys, practice administrators, **Prob 2468, 9764**
Conservators and Conservatorships, this index
Guardian and Ward, this index
Probate proceedings, attorneys, practice administrators, **Prob 2468, 9764**
Uniform Transfers to Minors Act, custodians, **Prob 3903**

NONCITIZENS
Aliens, generally, this index

NONPROBATE TRANSFERS
Generally, **Prob 5000 et seq., 5100 et seq.**
Community Property, this index
Definitions, marriage, death, **Prob 5040**
Holders of property, duties and protection, **Prob 5002, 5003**
Labor and employment, holders of property, duties and protection, **Prob 5002, 5003**
Multiple Party Account, generally, this index
Negotiable Instruments, this index

NONPROFIT CHARITABLE ORGANIZATIONS
Charities, generally, this index

NONPROFIT CORPORATIONS
Charities, generally, this index
Conservators and Conservatorships, this index
Credit Unions, generally, this index
Guardian and Ward, this index

NONPROFIT ORGANIZATIONS
Charities, generally, this index

NONPROFIT ORGANIZATIONS—Cont'd
Taxation, trusts, distribution of income, self dealing, **Prob 16102**

NONRESIDENT DECEDENT
Definitions, estate tax, **Rev & T 13408**

NONRESIDENT PERSONAL REPRESENTATIVE
Definitions, **Prob 8570**

NONRESIDENTS
Conservators and Conservatorships, this index
Definitions, estate tax, **Rev & T 13408**
Estate Taxes, this index
Guardian and ward, removal of property, **Prob 3800 et seq.**
Removal of property, guardianship or conservatorship, **Prob 3800 et seq.**

NONSUPPORT
Support, generally, this index

NOT DUE
Definitions, probate proceedings, debts, **Prob 11460**

NOTARIES PUBLIC
Advance health care directives, **Prob 4673**
Certified copies, power of attorney, **Prob 4307**

NOTES
Negotiable Instruments, generally, this index

NOTICE
Absentees, personal property, protective proceedings, **Prob 3704**
Alcoholics and Alcoholism, this index
Attorneys, this index
Conservators and Conservatorships, this index
Definitions, trusts and trustees, adverse or pecuniary interest, **Prob 15804**
Estate Taxes, this index
Gifts, devises and bequests, fraud, presumptions, **Prob 21388**
Guardian and Ward, this index
Indians, this index
Mentally Retarded and Developmentally Disabled Persons, this index
Multiple party accounts, protection of financial institutions, payments, **Prob 5405**
Nonprobate transfers, **Prob 5003**
Power of Attorney, this index
Probate Proceedings, this index
Public guardian, prefiling investigations, hearings, **Prob 2910**
Special needs trust, protector proceedings, beneficiary death notice, **Prob 3605**
Trusts and Trustees, this index
Unitrusts,
Conversion, **Prob 16336.4, 16336.5**
Reconversion, **Prob 16336.6**

NOTIFICATION
Notice, generally, this index

NURSING HOMES
See, also, Health Facilities, generally, this index
Notice, public administrators, existence of decedents estate, **Prob 7600.5**
Public administrators, notice, existence of decedents estate, **Prob 7600.5**
Skilled nursing facilities,
Advance health care directives, witnesses, **Prob 4675**
Definitions, health care decisions, **Prob 4639**

OATHS AND AFFIRMATIONS
Affidavits, generally, this index
Conservators and Conservatorships, this index
Estate Taxes, this index
Perjury, generally, this index

OFFICERS AND EMPLOYEES
Power of attorney, third person conducting activities through, **Prob 4308**

OFFICIAL BONDS
Bonds (Officers and Fiduciaries), generally, this index

OIL AND GAS
Cancellation, death, customers, **Prob 217**
Death, customers, cancellation, **Prob 217**
Principal and Income Act, **Prob 16320 et seq.**
Uniform Principal and Income Act, **Prob 16320 et seq.**
Use Fuel Tax, generally, this index

OIL AND GAS LEASES
Probate Proceedings, this index
Trusts and trustees, powers, **Prob 16232**

OLD AGE
Aged Persons, generally, this index

OLD PERSONS
Aged Persons, generally, this index

OMITTED SPOUSES AND CHILDREN LAW
Wills and trusts, **Prob 21600 et seq.**

OPTIONS
Estate real property, purchase, **Prob 9734, 9960 et seq.**
Personal representatives, exercise of right, **Prob 9734**
Probate Proceedings, this index

ORDERS
Definitions, probate proceedings, **Prob 7250**
Estate Taxes, this index

ORDERS FOR PAYMENT OF MONEY
Warrants for Payment of Money, generally, this index

ORDERS OF COURT
Absentees, personal property, protective proceedings, **Prob 3705**
Conservators and Conservatorships, this index
Consultants, failure to delegate powers, wartime substitutions, **Prob 386**
Decedents cause of action, commencement or continuance by successor in interest, **CCP 377.33**
Definitions, guardianships and conservatorships, **Prob 2103**
Estate tax, fees, filing, recording or certifying, **Rev & T 14013**
Fiduciaries, digital assets, access, **Prob 881**
Disclosure, **Prob 875**
Guardian and Ward, this index
Injunction, generally, this index
Mentally Retarded and Developmentally Disabled Persons, this index
Motions, generally, this index
Multiple party accounts, payments, restraining orders, **Prob 5405**
Power of appointment, releases, minors, **Prob 662**
Probate Proceedings, this index
Protective orders, probate proceedings, reference and referees, **Prob 453**
Public guardian,
Appointments, **Prob 2920**
Prefiling investigations, **Prob 2911**
Service of process. Process, this index
Trusts and Trustees, this index
Unitrusts,
Conversion, **Prob 16336.5**
Reconversion, **Prob 16336.6**
Wills, this index

ORDINANCES
Counties, mentally ill persons, attorneys, appointments, **Welf & I 5370.1**
Mentally ill persons, attorneys, appointments, **Welf & I 5370.1**

ORPHANS AND ORPHANAGES
Foster homes. Social Services, this index

OSTEOPATHS
Advance health care directives, **Prob 4730 et seq.**
Attorney fees, advance health care directives, **Prob 4742**
Crimes and offenses,
Advance health care directives, **Prob 4740 et seq.**

OSTEOPATHS

OSTEOPATHS—Cont'd
Crimes and offenses—Cont'd
Request to forgo resuscitative measures, **Prob 4782**
Damages,
Advance health care directives, **Prob 4740 et seq.**
Request to forgo resuscitative measures, **Prob 4782**
Discipline,
Advance health care directives, **Prob 4740, 4741**
Request to forgo resuscitative measures, **Prob 4782**
Do not resuscitate orders, **Prob 4780 et seq.**
Orders for life sustaining treatment forms, **Prob 4780 et seq.**
Physician orders for life sustaining treatment forms, **Prob 4780 et seq.**
Power of attorney, **Prob 4730 et seq.**
Privileges and immunities,
Advance health care directives, **Prob 4740 et seq.**
Request to forgo resuscitative measures, **Prob 4782**
Request to forgo resuscitative measures, **Prob 4780 et seq.**

OTHER STATES
Foreign States, generally, this index

OVERPAYMENTS
Estate taxes, refunds, **Rev & T 13560**

OWNERS AND OWNERSHIP
Deeds and conveyances, transfer on death deeds, **Prob 5650**
Transfer on death deeds, **Prob 5650**

P.O.D. ACCOUNTS
Multiple Party Account, generally, this index

PAPERS
Negotiable Instruments, generally, this index
Production of Books and Papers, generally, this index

PARAGRAPH
Definitions, Probate Code, statutory construction, **Prob 8**

PARAMEDICS
Emergency Medical Technicians, generally, this index

PARAPLEGICS
Handicapped Persons, generally, this index

PARENT AND CHILD RELATIONSHIP
Children and Minors, generally, this index

PARENTS
Children and Minors, generally, this index
Definitions, probate proceedings, **Prob 54**

PAROLE AND PROBATION
Conservators and conservatorships, investigations and investigators, reports, **Welf & I 5354**
Probation officers, conservatorship, investigation, **Welf & I 5351 et seq.**
Records and recordation, guardianship proposal, access to records, **Prob 1513**

PARTIES
Absence and absentees, petition to set aside personal property of absentee, **Prob 3702**
Death, effect on actions, **CCP 377.10 et seq.**
Definitions,
Conservators and conservatorships, jurisdiction, **Prob 1982**
Multiple party accounts, **Prob 5136**
Joinder of parties,
Personal representatives, heirs or devisees in action for possession or quieting title to real property, **Prob 9654**
Probate proceedings, liability of decedent covered by insurance, **Prob 550**
Probate Proceedings, this index
Third Parties, generally, this index

PARTIES—Cont'd
Witnesses, generally, this index

PARTITION
Distribution, decedents estates, **Prob 11950 et seq.**
Personal representatives, **Prob 9823**
Probate proceedings, distribution of decedents estates, **Prob 11950 et seq.**

PARTNERSHIP
Domestic Partnership, generally, this index
Limited partnership, decedents estates, continuation of business, **Prob 9762, 9763**
Probate Proceedings, this index

PARTY
Parties, generally, this index

PASSING OFF
Fraud, generally, this index

PASTURE ASSOCIATIONS
Real estate purchases, decedents estates, **Prob 10207**

PATROLMEN
Police, generally, this index

PAY
Compensation and Salaries, generally, this index

PAY ON DEATH ACCOUNTS
Multiple Party Account, generally, this index

PAYMENT
Advances and Advancements, generally, this index
Definitions,
Multiple party accounts, **Prob 5138**
Uniform Principal and Income Act, **Prob 16361**
Estate Taxes, this index
Multiple party accounts, **Prob 5401 et seq.**
Probate Proceedings, this index
Receipts, generally, this index
Royalties, generally, this index
Trusts and Trustees, this index
Unitrusts, **Prob 16336.4, 16336.5**
Warrants for Payment of Money, generally, this index

PAYROLL DEDUCTIONS
Compensation and Salaries, generally, this index

PEACE OFFICERS
Alcoholics and intoxicated persons, personal liability, actions of conservatee, **Welf & I 5358.1**
Civil liability, actions of conservatee, **Welf & I 5358.1**
Crimes and offenses,
Liability, actions of conservatee, **Welf & I 5358.1**
Request to forgo resuscitative measures, **Prob 4782**
Damages, request to forgo resuscitative measures, **Prob 4782**
Definitions, aged persons, financial abuse, **Prob 2951**
Discipline, request to forgo resuscitative measures, **Prob 4782**
Do not resuscitate orders, **Prob 4780 et seq.**
Liability, actions of conservatee, **Welf & I 5358.1**
Medical care and treatment, request to forgo resuscitative measures, **Prob 4780 et seq.**
Orders for life sustaining treatment forms, **Prob 4780 et seq.**
Physicians and surgeons, orders for life sustaining treatment forms, **Prob 4780 et seq.**
Police, generally, this index
Privileges and immunities, request to forgo resuscitative measures, **Prob 4782**
Request to forgo resuscitative measures, **Prob 4780 et seq.**

PEACE OFFICERS—Cont'd
Resuscitative measures, request to forgo, **Prob 4780 et seq.**

PECUNIARY INTEREST
Adverse or Pecuniary Interest, generally, this index

PENAL INSTITUTIONS
Correctional Institutions, generally, this index

PENDING ACTIONS
Death, abatement of actions, **CCP 377.21**
Decedents cause of action, continuation against personal representative or successor in interest, **CCP 377.31, 377.41**
Lis Pendens, generally, this index

PENITENTIARIES
Correctional Institutions, generally, this index

PENSIONS
Retirement and Pensions, generally, this index

PERFORMANCE BONDS
Bonds (Officers and Fiduciaries), generally, this index

PERISHABLE PROPERTY
Personal representatives, sales without notice, **Prob 10252**
Probate proceedings, sales, confirmation, title passing without, **Prob 10259**

PERJURY
Conservators and conservatorships, interrogatory answers, assets examination, **Prob 2617**
Fiduciaries, digital assets, access, disclosure, **Prob 879**
Power of attorney, **Prob 878**
Guardian and ward, interrogatory answers, assets examination, **Prob 2617**
Interrogatories, discovery of decedents property, **Prob 8871**

PERPETUITIES
Rule Against Perpetuities, generally, this index

PERSONAL INCOME TAX
Income Tax—State, generally, this index

PERSONAL INJURIES
Conservators and conservatorships, compromise and settlement, **Prob 2504**
Damages, generally, this index
Guardian and ward, compromise and settlement, **Prob 2504**
Negligence, generally, this index

PERSONAL LIABILITY
Conservators and conservatorships, public guardian or police officer, actions of conservatee, **Welf & I 5358.1**
Executors and administrators. Probate Proceedings, this index
Probate Proceedings, this index

PERSONAL PROPERTY
Abandoned or Unclaimed Property, generally, this index
Absentees, protective proceedings, **Prob 3700 et seq.**
Affidavit procedure, small estates, transfer or collection without administration, **Prob 13100 et seq.**
Aged persons, financial abuse, peace officers, declarations, **Prob 2950 et seq.**
Attachment, generally, this index
Auctions and Auctioneers, generally, this index
Children and minors, Uniform Transfers to Minors Act, **Prob 3900 et seq.**
Collection or transfer, affidavit procedure, **Prob 13100 et seq.**
Community Property, generally, this index
Conservators and Conservatorships, this index
Decedents, tangible personal property, delivery, **Prob 330**
Delivery, decedents property, **Prob 330**
Elections, community property, passage to surviving spouse without administration, **Prob 13502, 13503**

POPULAR

PROBATE

PROBATE

PROBATE

PROBATE

PROBATE

PROBATE PROCEEDINGS—Cont'd

Forms—Cont'd

Nondomiciliary decedent will probate petition, **Prob 12521**

Notice, publication, **Prob 8123**

Notice of hearings, opening of administration, **Prob 8100**

Orders of court, **Prob 1047**

Partition petitions, **Prob 11951**

Personal property sale notice, **Prob 10253**

Real estate sale notice, **Prob 10304**

Revocation of probate petition, **Prob 8270**

Signatures, **Prob 1020**

Small estates,

Set aside proceedings petition, **Prob 6604**

Succession determination petition, **Prob 13152**

Status of administration report, **Prob 12201**

Foster children,

Construction of law, **Prob 21115**

Notice, **Prob 1207**

Fractional interest, surviving spouse, administration, **Prob 13502.5**

Franchise tax board, personal representatives, notice, **Prob 9202**

Fraud,

Collateral attack of order admitting will to probate, grounds, **Prob 8007**

Compensation and salaries, deceased, collection by affidavit, **Prob 13605**

Disclaimers, testamentary and other interests, **Prob 283**

Distribution of decedents estates, posthumous conception, liabilities, **Prob 249.6**

Double liability, sale of real property, **Prob 10381**

Executors and administrators, **Prob 7250**

Limitation of actions,

Recovery of real property, **Prob 10382**

Sales, recovery of property, **Prob 10382**

Personal property, affidavits to collect, **Prob 13110, 13111**

Personal representatives, removal or suspension, **Prob 8502**

Posthumous conception, distribution of decedents estates, liabilities, **Prob 249.6**

Sale of realty, action to recovery, limitation of actions, **Prob 10382**

Fraudulent conveyances, action for recovery of property, **Prob 9653**

Funeral expenses, **Prob 11420, 11421**

Allocation between trusts and estate, **Prob 19326**

Community share of surviving spouse, **Prob 11446**

Executors and administrators, payment, **Prob 8400**

Order of payment, **Prob 11420, 11421**

Small estates, setaside proceedings, **Prob 6609**

Time, payment, **Prob 11421**

Furniture, exempt property, **Prob 6500 et seq.**

Future estates, disclaimer of interests, **Prob 282**

Gains and losses, accounting for, **Prob 10005**

General debts, payment priorities, **Prob 11420**

General gifts, classification, **Prob 21117**

General pecuniary devises,

Classification, **Prob 21117**

Income and interest accruing during administration of estate, **Prob 12003**

General personal representative, definitions, **Prob 42, 58**

Generation skipping transfer tax, **Rev & T 16700 et seq.**

Geothermal energy, leases, **Prob 9946**

Independent administration of estates, **Prob 10536**

PROBATE PROCEEDINGS—Cont'd

Geothermal energy, leases—Cont'd

Sales, **Prob 10203**

Gifts in contemplation of death, action for recovery, **Prob 9653**

Postponement, notice, **Prob 1205**

Gifts in view of impending death, **Prob 5700 et seq.**

Application of law, **Prob 5701, 5705**

Definitions, **Prob 5700**

Intent, **Prob 5702**

Presumptions, **Prob 5703**

Revocation, **Prob 5704**

Gifts to minors, jurisdiction, **Prob 6348**

Good faith purchasers, property distribution validity, **Prob 11750**

Grounds,

Disqualification of judges, **Prob 7060**

Personal representative,

Appointment, contesting, **Prob 8004**

Removal, **Prob 8502**

Guardian ad litem,

Appointments, **Prob 1003**

Disclaimers, petitions, filing, hearings, **Prob 277**

Guardian and Ward, generally, this index

Half blood relatives, construction of law, **Prob 21115**

Handwriting, proof of wills, **Prob 8221**

Headings, Probate Code, effect, **Prob 4**

Hearings, **Prob 1040 et seq.**

Accounts and accounting, settlement, **Prob 11002**

Admission of wills to probate, **Prob 8003 et seq.**

Appearances, interested persons, **Prob 1043**

Closing estate administration,

Orders of court, **Prob 12202**

Status reports, **Prob 12201**

Continuances, **Prob 1045**

Notice, **Prob 1205**

Defendants, **Prob 1044**

Disclaimer petition, **Prob 277**

Evidence, **Prob 1046**

Exempt property, **Prob 6501**

Family allowances, modification, **Prob 6541**

Filing, papers, **Prob 1041**

Forms, notice, **Prob 1211**

Independent administration, **Prob 10451 et seq.**

Revoking authority, **Prob 10454**

Issues, **Prob 1046**

Judgment roll, **Prob 1050**

Leases, estate property, **Prob 9945**

Notice, post

Options to purchase, real property of estate, **Prob 9734**

Partition, distribution of decedents estates, **Prob 11952**

Plaintiffs, **Prob 1044**

Postponement, **Prob 1045**

Notice, **Prob 1205**

Reference and referees, removal or suspension, **Prob 8924**

Setting petition for, **Prob 10001**

Simultaneous death, survivorship status, petitions, **Prob 233 et seq.**

Small estate succession determination hearings, **Prob 13153**

Small estates, setaside proceedings, **Prob 6607**

Sterilization, developmentally disabled persons, **Prob 1953**

Attendance of proposed conservatees, **Prob 1956**

Summary dispute determination, **Prob 9620**

Wartime substitution, **Prob 365, 366**

Heirs of the body, identification of particular parties, **Prob 248 et seq.**

PROBATE PROCEEDINGS—Cont'd

Holographic wills,

Extrinsic evidence, admissibility, **Prob 6111.5**

Proof, **Prob 8222**

Homesteads,

Children and minors, selection, **Prob 6521 et seq.**

Contracts, waiver of rights, **Prob 141**

Definitions, **Prob 60**

Liens and incumbrances, **Prob 6526**

Modification of rights, **Prob 6527**

Notice, petitions, **Prob 6525**

Petitions, parties, **Prob 6525**

Setting apart property, **Prob 6520 et seq.**

Selection of property, **Prob 6522, 6523**

Surviving spouse, selection, **Prob 6521 et seq.**

Time, limitations, **Prob 6524**

Homicide,

Effect, **Prob 250 et seq.**

Sales to innocent purchasers, **Prob 255**

Household furniture and furnishings, preliminary distributions, independent administration of estates, **Prob 10520**

Husband and wife,

Marital deduction gifts, Internal Revenue Code compliance, **Prob 21520 et seq.**

Simultaneous death, **Prob 220 et seq.**

Surviving spouse, generally, post

Hydrocarbon substances, leases, **Prob 9946**

Independent administration of estates, **Prob 10536**

Sales, **Prob 10203**

Identity and identification,

Heirs, **Prob 248 et seq.**

Persons to whom tangible personal property of decedent is delivered, **Prob 330**

Surviving spouse, deceased spouse compensation collection purposes, **Prob 13601**

Improvements,

Borrowing money for, **Prob 9800 et seq.**

Estate property, independent administration of estates, **Prob 10562**

Incapacitated persons, guardian ad litem, appointment, **Prob 1003**

Income,

Distribution of decedents estates,

Accruing during administration, **Prob 12000 et seq.**

Independent administration, **Prob 10520**

Principal and Income Act, **Prob 16320 et seq.**

Special administrators, powers, **Prob 8544**

Uniform Principal and Income Act, **Prob 16320 et seq.**

Indebtedness,

Claims against estate, generally, ante

Compromise, **Prob 9830 et seq.**

Discharge of debtor, **Prob 9830 et seq.**

Independent administration of estates,

Court supervision, **Prob 10501**

Powers, **Prob 10554**

Personal representative accountable, **Prob 9650**

Indemnity and indemnification, collection or transfer of property, affidavit procedures, **Prob 13102**

Independent administration of estates, **Prob 10400 et seq., 10588**

Abandonment of property, notice of proposed action, **Prob 10513**

Acceptance of deed to property subject to in lieu of foreclosure, trustee sale, **Prob 10563**

Actions and proceedings,

Compromise or settlement, court supervision, **Prob 10501**

PROBATE

PROBATE

PROBATE

PROBATE

PROBATE

PROBATE PROCEEDINGS—Cont'd
Withdrawal—Cont'd
  Personal representatives, withdrawing money or personal property from financial institutions, **Prob 9700 et seq.**
  Request for special notice, **Prob 1251**
Withdrawal of notice, **Prob 1251**
Witnesses,
  Absentees estates, **Prob 12406**
  Discovery of property of decedent, **Prob 8870 et seq.**
  Fees, sterilization proceedings, **Prob 1963**
  Opening of administration, hearings, **Prob 8005**
  Subscribing witnesses, **Prob 8220, 8221**
  Will contests, production of witnesses, **Prob 8253**
  Wills,
    Judge acting as witness, disqualification grounds, **Prob 7060**
    Proof, **Prob 8220**
    Testimony in writing, evidence, **Prob 8224**
Worthier Title Law, application, **Prob 21108**
Writing,
  Disclaimer, **Prob 278**
  Document constituting a will, evidence, **Prob 6111.5**
  Waiver, surviving spouses, **Prob 142**
Wrongful death, **CCP 377.60 et seq.; Prob 1251**
  Compromise and settlement, **Prob 9835**
PROBATE REFEREES
Reference and referees. Probate Proceedings, this index
PROBATE RULES
See text immediately preceding index
PROBATION
Parole and Probation, generally, this index
PROCEEDINGS
Actions and Proceedings, generally, this index
PROCESS
Attachment, generally, this index
Conservators and Conservatorships, this index
Generation skipping transfer tax, refund actions, **Rev & T 16861**
Guardian and Ward, this index
Injunction, generally, this index
Probate Proceedings, this index
Service of process,
  Conservators and Conservatorships, this index
  Generation skipping transfer tax, refund actions, **Rev & T 16861**
  Gifts, devises and bequests, fraud, presumptions, **Prob 21388**
  Probate proceedings, attachment lien conversion to judgment lien, **Prob 9304**
  Public guardian, prefiling investigations, **Prob 2910**
  Trusts and Trustees, this index
PRODUCTION OF BOOKS AND PAPERS
Conservators and conservatorships, accounts and accounting, **Prob 2620**
Estate Taxes, this index
Guardian and ward, accounts and accounting, **Prob 2620**
Probate referees, powers, **Prob 452**
PROFESSIONS AND OCCUPATIONS
Attorneys, generally, this index
Emergency Medical Technicians, generally, this index
Osteopaths, generally, this index
Physicians and Surgeons, generally, this index
Psychiatrists and Psychiatry, generally, this index
Psychologists and Psychology, generally, this index
Social Workers, generally, this index
PROFIT SHARING PLANS
Conservators and conservatorship, **Prob 2459**

PROFIT SHARING PLANS—Cont'd
Guardian and ward, **Prob 2459**
Testamentary trusts, **Prob 6320 et seq.**
Trusts and trustees, testamentary trusts, **Prob 6320 et seq.**
PROFITS
Spendthrift trusts, creditors claims, **Prob 15307**
Trusts and trustees,
  Accounting, **Prob 16440**
  Spendthrift trust, creditors claims, **Prob 15307**
PROMISSORY NOTES
Negotiable Instruments, generally, this index
PROOF
Evidence, generally, this index
PROPERTY
Agreements, nonprobate transfers, holders of property, duties and protection, **Prob 5002, 5003**
Children and Minors, this index
Community Property, generally, this index
Conservators and Conservatorships, this index
Deeds and Conveyances, generally, this index
Definitions,
  Aged persons, financial abuse, **Prob 2951**
  Estate tax, **Rev & T 13402**
    Generation skipping transfers, **Prob 20200**
    Proration, **Prob 20100**
  Probate proceedings, **Prob 62**
Escheat, generally, this index
Future Estates or Interests, generally, this index
Gifts, Uniform Transfers to Minors Act, **Prob 3900 et seq.**
Guardian and Ward, this index
Income, generally, this index
Joint Tenants, generally, this index
Leases, generally, this index
Partition, generally, this index
Perpetuities, statutory ruling against, **Prob 21200 et seq.**
Personal Property, generally, this index
Power of appointment, **Prob 675**
  Takers in default of appointment, **Prob 676**
Real Estate, generally, this index
Rule Against Perpetuities, **Prob 21200 et seq.**
Statutory Rule Against Perpetuities, **Prob 21200 et seq.**
Trusts and Trustees, this index
Uniform Statutory Rule Against Perpetuities, **Prob 21200 et seq.**
Uniform Transfers to Minors Act, **Prob 3900 et seq.**
PROPERTY DAMAGE
Damages, generally, this index
PROPERTY TAXES
Taxation, generally, this index
PRORATION
Estate Taxes, this index
PROXIES
Personal representatives, vote shares, powers, **Prob 9655**
PRUDENT INVESTOR ACT
Generally, **Prob 16045 et seq.**
PRUDENT MAN ACT
Generally, **Prob 16040**
PRUDENT MANAGEMENT OF INSTITUTIONAL FUNDS ACT
Generally, **Prob 18501 et seq.**
PSYCHIATRISTS AND PSYCHIATRY
Examinations and examiners, guardianship proposal, access to records, **Prob 1513**
Guardian and ward, proposed guardianship, access to records, **Prob 1513**
Records, proposed guardianship, access, **Prob 1513**

PSYCHOLOGISTS AND PSYCHOLOGY
Examinations and examiners, guardian and ward, records and recordation, access, **Prob 1513**
Guardian and ward, proposed guardianship, access to records, **Prob 1513**
Records and recordation, guardianship proposal, access to records, **Prob 1513**
Sterilization, developmentally disabled persons, examination, **Prob 1955**
PUBLIC ADMINISTRATORS
Probate Proceedings, this index
PUBLIC AGENCIES
Actions and proceedings, probate proceedings, claims against estate, **Prob 9200 et seq.**
Claims, decedents estates, **Prob 9200 et seq.**
Decedents estates, claims against, **Prob 9200 et seq.**
Estates of decedents, claims against, **Prob 9200 et seq.**
Limitation of actions, probate proceedings, claims against estate, **Prob 9200 et seq.**
Local Agencies, generally, this index
Probate proceedings, claims against estates, **Prob 9200 et seq.**
State Agencies, generally, this index
PUBLIC ASSISTANCE
Social Services, generally, this index
PUBLIC AUCTIONS
Auctions and Auctioneers, generally, this index
PUBLIC AUTHORITIES
Authorities, generally, this index
PUBLIC BODIES
Political Subdivisions, generally, this index
Public Agencies, generally, this index
PUBLIC CONSERVATORS
Continuing education, **Prob 1456.2**
Removal of occupants, temporary possession or control of property, **Prob 2900**
Temporary possession or control of property, **Prob 2900 et seq.**
PUBLIC CORPORATIONS
Actions and proceedings, probate proceedings, claims against estate, **Prob 9200 et seq.**
Claims, decedents estates, **Prob 9200 et seq.**
Decedents estates, claims against, **Prob 9200 et seq.**
Estates of decedents, claims against, **Prob 9200 et seq.**
Limitation of actions, probate proceedings, claims against estate, **Prob 9200 et seq.**
Probate proceedings, claims against estates, **Prob 9200 et seq.**
PUBLIC DEFENDERS
Conservators and Conservatorships, this index
Guardian and Ward, this index
Mentally Retarded and Developmentally Disabled Persons, this index
Sterilization, developmentally disabled persons, appointment, **Prob 1954**
PUBLIC EMPLOYEES RETIREMENT SYSTEM
Simultaneous death, survivorship status, determination, **Prob 230**
PUBLIC ENTITIES
Definitions,
  Claims against trusts, **Prob 19200**
  Probate proceedings, claims, **Prob 9200**
PUBLIC GUARDIAN
Generally, **Prob 2900 et seq.; Welf & I 5350 et seq.**
Accounts and accounting, death, **Prob 2620**
Administration of property, **Prob 2940 et seq.**
Aged persons, financial abuse, peace officers, declarations, **Prob 2950 et seq.**
Application of law, temporary possession or control of property, **Prob 2903**
Appointment, **Prob 2920 et seq.**
  Trusts and trustees, **Prob 15660.5**

I-80

TRIAL

TRIAL—Cont'd
Witnesses, generally, this index
TRIAL COURTS
Courts, generally, this index
TRUST COMPANIES
See, also, Banks and Banking, generally, this index
Appointments, successor trustees, testamentary trusts, **Prob 17353**
Bonds (officers and fiduciaries), **Prob 15602**
Service in fiduciary capacity, **Prob 301**
Children and minors, Uniform Transfers to Minors Act, **Prob 3900 et seq.**
Conservators and conservatorships,
Appointment, **Prob 300**
Bonds (officers and fiduciaries), **Prob 301**
Deposits,
Personal property, **Prob 2454**
Securities, **Prob 2455**
Interest, **Prob 2453.5**
Investments, **Prob 2401**
Securities, deposits, **Prob 2455**
Continuing court jurisdiction, removal of trust from, **Prob 17351**
Definitions, **Prob 83**
Executors and administrators, **Prob 300, 301**
Successor in interest, **Prob 8423**
Fiduciaries,
Appointments, **Prob 300**
Bonds (officers and fiduciaries), **Prob 301**
Gifts, devises and bequests, Uniform Transfers to Minors Act, **Prob 3900 et seq.**
Guardian and ward,
Appointments, **Prob 300**
Bonds (officers and fiduciaries), **Prob 301**
Deposits, **Prob 2454**
Personal property, **Prob 2454**
Securities, **Prob 2455**
Interest, **Prob 2453.5**
Investments, **Prob 2401**
Securities, deposits, **Prob 2455**
Oaths and affirmations, serving in fiduciary capacity, **Prob 301**
Personal representatives,
Appointments, **Prob 300**
Bonds (officers and fiduciaries), **Prob 301**
Deposits, securities, **Prob 9702**
Direct distribution of property, **Prob 9704**
Interest, chargeable rate, **Prob 9705**
Principal and Income Act, **Prob 16320 et seq.**
Probate Proceedings, this index
Removal of trust from continuing jurisdiction, **Prob 17351**
Safe Deposit Boxes, generally, this index
Transfers, Uniform Transfers to Minors Act, **Prob 3900 et seq.**
Uniform Principal and Income Act, **Prob 16320 et seq.**
TRUST DEEDS
See, also, Mortgages, generally, this index
Conservators and conservatorships, personal liability, **Prob 2110**
Guardian and ward, personal liability, **Prob 2110**
Probate Proceedings, this index
Trusts and trustees, exoneration of gift, abatement, **Prob 21404**
Wills, specific gifts, **Prob 21134**
TRUSTEE SALES
Conservators or guardians, acceptance of deeds in lieu of sale, **Prob 2464**
TRUSTEES FEE
Definitions, **Prob 15686**
TRUSTS AND TRUSTEES
Generally, **Prob 15000 et seq.**
Abatement of actions or proceedings, **Prob 21400 et seq.**
Claims, property, hearings, **Prob 854**
Absence and absentees, cotrustees, other cotrustees acting for trusts, **Prob 15622**

TRUSTS AND TRUSTEES—Cont'd
Abuse, aged persons, dependent adults, **Prob 259**
Acceptance,
Transfer of trusts from another jurisdiction, court order, **Prob 17451, 17455**
Trustees, **Prob 15600**
Accounts and accounting, **Prob 16062, 16069**
Animals, care trusts, **Prob 15212**
Conservators and conservatorships, notice, **Prob 2892, 2893**
Form, **Prob 16063**
Guardian and ward, notice, **Prob 2892, 2893**
Objections and exceptions, **Prob 16461**
Principal and Income Act, **Prob 16320 et seq.**
Profits, **Prob 16440**
Settling actions, **Prob 17200**
Uniform Principal and Income Act, **Prob 16320 et seq.**
Accumulations,
Rents and profits, creditor claims, **Prob 15307**
Spendthrift, creditors claims, **Prob 15307**
Acquisitions, trustee powers, **Prob 16226**
Actions and proceedings, **Prob 17000 et seq.**
Accounts and accounting, settling, **Prob 17200**
Appointment, trustees, **Prob 17200**
Beneficiaries,
Determination, **Prob 17200**
Notice, **Prob 16500 et seq.**
Breach of trust, remedies, **Prob 16420, 16421**
Commencement of actions, filing of petitions, **Prob 17201**
Construction of trust instruments, **Prob 17200**
Creditors,
Jurisdiction, **Prob 17000**
Rejected claims, **Prob 19255**
Dismissal, **Prob 17202**
Duties of trustees, **Prob 16010, 16011**
To beneficiaries, **Prob 16060 et seq.**
Existence of trust, jurisdiction, **Prob 17000**
Federal Tax Reform Act of 1969 proceedings, parties, **Prob 16105**
Internal affairs of trusts, **Prob 17200**
Modification or termination of trust, **Prob 17200**
Notice, generally, post
Orders, petitions, **Prob 17206**
Powers of trustees, **Prob 16249**
Principal and income, notice, **Prob 16337, 16500 et seq.**
Rejected creditors claims, **Prob 19255**
Removal, **Prob 17200**
Reports, compelling trustee to make, **Prob 17200**
Resignation, **Prob 17200**
Revocable or irrevocable trusts, changes, notice, **Prob 16061.7, 16061.8**
Right to jury trial, **Prob 17006**
Third party claims, **Prob 18004**
Determination, **Prob 18005**
Undisclosed beneficiaries, innocent purchasers, presumptions, **Prob 18104**
Validity of trust provision, **Prob 17200**
Actual notice to creditors of revocable trust, **Prob 19050 et seq.**
Additions to trust property, trustee powers, **Prob 16221**
Administration of trust, **Prob 16000 et seq.**
Expenses, equitable lien, trustee, **Prob 15685**
Judicial intervention, minimizing, **Prob 17209**
Principal place of administration, jurisdiction, actions, **Prob 17002**

TRUSTS AND TRUSTEES—Cont'd
Administration of trust—Cont'd
Standard of care, **Prob 16040 et seq.**
Testamentary trust, continuing court jurisdiction, **Prob 17300 et seq.**
Torts by trustee, liability to third parties, **Prob 18002**
Transfer to another jurisdiction, **Prob 17401 et seq.**
Trusts transferred from another jurisdiction, **Prob 17457**
Adopted persons, class gifts, **Prob 21115**
Adverse or pecuniary interest, **Prob 16082**
Duties of trustees, **Prob 16004, 16005**
Notice to beneficiaries, **Prob 15804**
Obtain advantage from beneficiary, **Prob 16002**
Removal, **Prob 15642**
Affidavits,
Change of trustees, records and recordation, **Prob 18105 et seq.**
Claims against trust, supporting filing, **Prob 19151**
Publication of notice, claims against revocable trusts, **Prob 19040**
Qualifications and powers, third parties, **Prob 18100.5**
Agents,
Authority to act as general agent, **Prob 16200**
Breach of trust, liability to trustees, **Prob 16401**
Liability of trustees to beneficiaries for agents actions, **Prob 16401**
Powers of trustees to hire, **Prob 16247**
Allocation,
Claims against revocable trust, multiple trust, **Prob 19020 et seq.**
Debt, trust and surviving spouse, **Prob 19320 et seq.**
Disbursements, principal and income, **Prob 16370 et seq.**
Distributees of trusts, creditors claims, **Prob 19402**
Receipts, principal and income, **Prob 16350 et seq., 16355 et seq., 16360 et seq.**
Allowance,
Claims, **Prob 19250 et seq.**
Revocable trust, petition, **Prob 19020 et seq.**
Forms, creditors claims, **Prob 19011**
Alterations in trust properties, trustee powers, **Prob 16229**
Amendments, creditors claims, time, **Prob 19104**
Animals, care trusts, **Prob 15212**
Annuities,
Abatement, **Prob 21403**
Testamentary trusts, **Prob 6320 et seq.**
Appeal and review, **Prob 1300 et seq.**
Adverse or pecuniary interest, removal of trustee, **Prob 15642**
Discretionary powers, **Prob 16081**
Application of law, **Prob 15001**
Abatement, **Prob 21401**
Administration of trust, minimum judicial intervention, **Prob 17209**
Attorney general powers, **Prob 15805**
Charitable trusts, **Prob 15004**
Claims of homicide perpetrators, **Prob 257**
Common law, **Prob 15002**
Constructive or resulting trusts, **Prob 15003**
Continuing jurisdiction,
Administration of testamentary trusts, **Prob 17302**
Trust administration, **Prob 17300**
Effective date, new law, **Prob 3**
Illegally acquired amounts, public entity claims, restitution liability, **Prob 19205**

TRUSTS

TRUSTS AND TRUSTEES—Cont'd

Death,

Cotrustees, survivorship, **Prob 15621**

Donee of power, exercise by surviving donees, **Prob 15643**

Homicide, killer nominated as trustee, **Prob 250**

Simultaneous death, **Prob 220 et seq.**

Vacation of office, **Prob 15643**

Debtors and creditors. Creditors, generally, ante

Declaration by owner, creation of trusts, **Prob 15200**

Declaration of trust, obedience by trustee, **Prob 16000**

Dedication of real estate to public use, trustee powers, **Prob 16230**

Deeds and conveyances, **Prob 15410**

Omission of trust from grant to trustee, innocent purchasers, **Prob 18103**

Deeds of trust, claims based on, filing conditions, **Prob 19152**

Defenses, distributees liability for creditors claims, **Prob 19402**

Definitions, **Prob 82**

Estate taxes, generation skipping transfers, **Prob 20200**

Fiduciaries, digital assets, access, **Prob 871**

Principal and income, **Prob 16321 et seq.**

Probate proceedings, **Prob 82, 84**

Revocable trust, **Prob 19000**

Statutory wills, **Prob 6204**

Trustees fee, **Prob 15686**

Delegation of powers and duties,

Restrictions, **Prob 16012**

Wartime, **Prob 380 et seq.**

Delivery of instruments, trustee powers, **Prob 16248**

Delivery of property to trustee, third person obligations, **Prob 18101**

Demand,

Certification of trusts, **Prob 18100.5**

Payment, creditors, treatment by trustee, **Prob 19154**

Depositories, use of securities depositories, **Prob 16239**

Deposits, **Prob 16225**

Estate planning documents, attorneys, **Prob 700 et seq.**

Public guardian, **Prob 16042**

Depreciation,

Breach of trust, liability, **Prob 16440**

Principal and income, **Prob 16372**

Destroyed instrument, copy, filing with creditors claims, **Prob 19152**

Development of real estate, trustee powers, **Prob 16230**

Devises and devisees, **Prob 15410**

Disbursements, Principal and Income Act, **Prob 16320 et seq.**

Discharge of trustee, **Prob 15640**

Transfer of trusts to another jurisdiction, **Prob 17405**

Disclosure,

Adverse interest, **Prob 15642**

Trust existence or provisions to creditors or beneficiaries, **Prob 19009**

Discretionary powers,

Control by court, **Prob 16080**

Duties of trustees, **Prob 16080, 16081**

Dismissal, claims against revocable trust, petition, **Prob 19026**

Dismissal of petitions, **Prob 17202**

Disposal of interest, spendthrift trusts, restraint, **Prob 15300**

Disposition, termination, **Prob 15410**

Dissenting cotrustees, personal liability, actions taken by other trustees, **Prob 18003**

TRUSTS AND TRUSTEES—Cont'd

Distributee liability, creditors claims, **Prob 19400 et seq.**

Distribution of funds, **Prob 16081**

Beneficiaries, powers, **Prob 16245, 16246**

Late creditors claims, effect of prior distribution, **Prob 19103**

Liabilities, waiver, **Prob 16004.5**

Principal and income, beneficiaries, **Prob 16374.5**

Public entity claims, reclaiming distributions, **Prob 19203**

Termination of trust for low market value of principal, **Prob 15408**

Division,

Petition for good cause, **Prob 15412**

Shares, representation, **Prob 245 et seq.**

Doctrine of merger, exception, **Prob 15209**

Dual compensation, **Prob 15687**

Petition to allow, **Prob 17200**

Duration,

Animals, care trusts, **Prob 15212**

Creation of trusts, **Prob 15204**

Noncharitable corporation trust, **Prob 15211**

Unincorporated society trust, **Prob 15211**

Duties. Powers and duties, generally, post

Easements, powers of trustees, **Prob 16230**

Economic considerations in continuing trust, **Prob 15408**

Effective date, new law, **Prob 3**

Emergencies, wartime substitution, **Prob 350 et seq.**

Employee benefits, testamentary trusts, **Prob 6320 et seq.**

Endowment funds, assets, limited appropriations, **Prob 18502.5**

Endowments, testamentary trusts, **Prob 6320 et seq.**

Equitable lien, advances made by trustee for protection of trusts, **Prob 15685**

Equity, beneficiaries, remedy for breach of trust, **Prob 16421**

Escheat, application of law, **Prob 6806**

Essentials to validity, **Prob 15206**

Estate taxes,

Generation skipping transfers, **Prob 20213 et seq.**

Proration, **Prob 20113**

Estates for years, estate tax proration, **Prob 20113**

Evidence,

Change of trustees, affidavits, records and recordation, **Prob 18107**

Final money judgments, claim validity, establishment, **Prob 19301**

Title to property, presumptions, **Prob 18104**

Transactions between trustee and beneficiary, presumptions, **Prob 16004**

Exchanges between trusts, trustee disclosures to beneficiaries, **Prob 16002**

Execution of instruments, trustee powers, **Prob 16248**

Executions, liens and incumbrances, enforcement against trusts, **Prob 19303**

Exemptions,

Attachment or execution, deceased settlors family, **Prob 19304**

Settlors, creditors rights, **Prob 18201**

Exercise of trustee powers, **Prob 16202**

Acceptance by trustee, **Prob 15600**

Existence of trust,

Action to determine, petitions, **Prob 17200**

Certification, **Prob 18100.5**

Expenses and expenditures,

Abatement, **Prob 21400 et seq.**

Indemnification of trustee, **Prob 15684**

Payment, trustee powers, **Prob 16243**

Principal and Income Act, **Prob 16320 et seq.**

TRUSTS AND TRUSTEES—Cont'd

Expenses and expenditures—Cont'd

Revocable trust, payment from, **Prob 19000 et seq.**

Uniform Principal and Income Act, **Prob 16320 et seq.**

Expiration of trust, **Prob 15407**

Failure of transfer, **Prob 21111**

Failure of trustee to perform duties, removal of trustee, **Prob 15642**

Failure or termination, transfer or devise upon, **Prob 15410**

Fair market value,

Low in relationship to class of administration, termination, **Prob 15408**

Unitrusts, assets, **Prob 16336.4**

Federal Tax Reform Act of 1969 proceedings, parties, **Prob 16105**

Fees, trustee fee, **Prob 15686**

Fiduciary relationships, **Prob 15003, 16081**

Powers of trustees, **Prob 16202**

Filing claims, creditors, **Prob 19150 et seq.**

Final money judgments, **Prob 19301**

Financial institutions,

Deposit of funds, powers of trustees, **Prob 16225**

Provision of services, duties of trustees, **Prob 16015**

Foreign states,

Transfer of trusts from another jurisdiction, **Prob 17450 et seq.**

Transfer of trusts to another jurisdiction, **Prob 17400 et seq.**

Forgery, public entity claims, **Prob 19205**

Form of business, change, consent, trustee powers, **Prob 16237**

Former trustees, third person contracts with, liability, **Prob 18102**

Forms,

Accounts, **Prob 16063**

Allowance, creditor claims, **Prob 19251**

Forms, **Prob 19011**

Certification of trusts, **Prob 18100.5**

Creditors claims,

Forms, **Prob 19153**

Petitions, **Prob 19022**

Debt allocation order, petition, **Prob 19321**

Notice of claim, **Prob 19011**

Creditors, revocable trusts, **Prob 19052**

Notice to creditors, **Prob 19040**

Rejection of claim, **Prob 19251**

Creditors claims, **Prob 19011**

Transfer of trusts from another jurisdiction petitions, **Prob 17453**

Transfer of trusts to another jurisdiction petitions, **Prob 17402**

Foster children, class gifts, **Prob 21115**

Fraud, **Prob 15642, 16400**

Public entity claims, **Prob 19205**

Frauds, statute of, application of law, **Prob 15206**

Fulfillment of purpose of trust, termination, **Prob 15407**

Funeral expenses, **Prob 19326; Rev & T 17760.5**

Good cause, removal of trustees, **Prob 15642**

Good faith,

Purchasers from distributees, liability for creditors claims, **Prob 19403**

Revocable or irrevocable trusts, changes, notice, **Prob 16061.7**

Third parties, contracts as trustees, **Prob 18102**

Third persons, dealings with trustees, protection, **Prob 18100**

Gross negligence, relief from liability, trust instrument, **Prob 16461**

Grounds, removal of trustees, **Prob 15642**

Group legal insurance, **Prob 15642**

TRUSTS

TRUSTS

WILLS

WORDS

WORDS